# THE COMPACT BEDFORD INTRODUCTION TO LITERATURE

Reading · Thinking · Writing

THIRTEENTH EDITION

# THE COMPACT BEDFORD INTRODUCTION TO LITERATURE

## Reading · Thinking · Writing

### Michael Meyer

*University of Connecticut*

### D. Quentin Miller

*Suffolk University*

bedford/st.martin's
Macmillan Learning
Boston | New York

*Program Director:* Laura Arcari
*Senior Program Manager:* Nancy Tran
*Director of Content Development:* Jane Knetzger
*Development Editor:* Cari Goldfine
*Assistant Editor:* Juliana Verrelli
*Director of Media Editorial:* Adam Whitehurst
*Media Editor:* Daniel Johnson
*Marketing Manager:* Vivian Garcia
*Senior Director, Content Management Enhancement:* Tracey Kuehn
*Executive Managing Editor:* Michael Granger
*Manager of Publishing Services:* Edward Dionne
*Senior Content Project Managers:* Kendra LeFleur and Lidia MacDonald-Carr
*Senior Workflow Project Manager:* Lisa McDowell
*Production Supervisor:* Jose Olivera
*Director of Design, Content Management:* Diana Blume
*Cover Design:* William Boardman
*Senior Director, Rights and Permissions:* Hilary Newman
*Permissions Editor:* Allison Ziebka-Viering
*Text Permissions Researcher:* Elaine Kosta, Lumina Datamatics, Inc.
*Senior Executive Permissions Editor:* Cecilia Varas
*Photo Researcher:* Cheryl DuBois, Lumina Datamatics, Inc.
*Senior Director of Digital Production:* Keri deManigold
*Media Project Manager:* Sarah O'Connor Kepes
*Project Management:* Lumina Datamatics, Inc.
*Project Manager:* Murugesh Rajkumar, Lumina Datamatics, Inc.
*Editorial Services:* Lumina Datamatics, Inc.
*Copyeditor:* Nancy Benjamin, Lumina Datamatics, Inc.
*Composition:* Lumina Datamatics, Inc.
*Printing and Binding:* Lakeside Book Company

ISBN    978-1-319-33182-5

Library of Congress Control Number: 2022952269

Printed in the United States of America.

1    2    3    4    5    6        28   27   26   25   24   23

## Acknowledgments

*Text acknowledgments and copyrights appear at the back of the book on pages 1509–1516, which constitute an extension of the copyright page. Art acknowledgments and copyrights appear on the same page as the art selections they cover.*

*For information, write: Bedford/St. Martin's, 75 Arlington Street, Boston, MA 02116*

For My Wife
Regina Barreca
—M.M.

For Michael:
Mentor, Guide, Friend.
—D.Q.M.

## About Michael Meyer

Michael Meyer, Emeritus Professor of English, taught writing and literature courses for more than thirty years — since 1981 at the University of Connecticut and before that at the University of North Carolina at Charlotte and the College of William and Mary. In addition to being an experienced teacher, Meyer is a highly regarded literary scholar. His scholarly articles have appeared in distinguished journals such as *American Literature, Studies in the American Renaissance*, and *Virginia Quarterly Review*. An internationally recognized authority on Henry David Thoreau, Meyer is a former president of the Thoreau Society and coauthor (with Walter Harding) of *The New Thoreau Handbook*, a standard reference source. His first book, *Several More Lives to Live: Thoreau's Political Reputation in America*, was awarded the Ralph Henry Gabriel Prize by the American Studies Association. He is also the editor of *Frederick Douglass: The Narrative and Selected Writings*. He has lectured on a variety of American literary topics from Cambridge University to Peking University. His other books for Bedford/St. Martin's include *The Bedford Introduction to Literature, Literature to Go, Thinking and Writing about Poetry, Poetry: An Introduction*, and *Thinking and Writing about Literature*.

## About D. Quentin Miller

D. Quentin Miller, Professor of English, has taught literature and writing at Suffolk University in Boston since 2000. Prior to that he taught at Gustavus Adolphus College in Minnesota, at the University of Connecticut (where he wrote his dissertation under the direction of Michael Meyer), and in a variety of other settings, including prisons. Miller is the author, editor, or coeditor of more than a dozen books and over two dozen critical essays in collections and in scholarly journals such as *American Literature, African American Review*, and *The James Baldwin Review*. He is an internationally renowned scholar on the works of James Baldwin and has also published original fiction and reviews in publications such as *TLS*. His most recent books are *The Routledge Introduction to the American Novel* (2024), *African American Literature in Transition 1980-1990* (2023), *James Baldwin in Context* (2019), *Understanding John Edgar Wideman* (2018), *American Literature in Transition: 1980-1990* (2018), and *The Routledge Introduction to African American Literature* (2016).

# Preface for Instructors

Like its predecessors, the thirteenth edition of *The Compact Bedford Introduction to Literature* assumes that reading and understanding literature offers a valuable means of apprehending life in its richness and diversity. This book also reflects the hope that its selections will inspire students to become lifelong readers of imaginative literature, as well as more thoughtful and skillful writers.

As before, the text is flexibly organized into four parts focusing on fiction, poetry, drama, and critical thinking and writing. The first three parts explain the literary elements of each genre. These three parts also explore several additional approaches to reading literature and conclude with an anthology of literary works. The fourth part provides detailed instruction on thinking, reading, and writing about literature that can be assigned selectively throughout the course. Sample student papers and hundreds of assignments appear in the text, offering students the support they need to read and write about literature.

*The Compact Bedford Introduction to Literature* accommodates many different teaching styles. New to the thirteenth edition are seventy-five carefully chosen stories, poems, and plays — as well as an in-depth author case study on Alice Munro, case studies on poetry and protest and the poetry of solitude, a cultural case study on Quiara Alegría Hudes's Pulitzer-winning play *Water by the Spoonful* and a collection of very short plays by acclaimed playwright Suzan-Lori Parks in the drama section, and up-to-date support for critical thinking, reading, and writing.

## FEATURES OF *THE COMPACT BEDFORD INTRODUCTION TO LITERATURE*, THIRTEENTH EDITION

### *A wide and well-balanced selection of literature*

54 stories, 308 poems, and 18 plays represent a variety of periods, nationalities, cultures, styles, and voices — from the serious to the humorous, and from the traditional to the contemporary. Each selection has been chosen for its appeal to students and for its effectiveness in demonstrating the elements, significance, and pleasures of literature. As in previous editions, canonical works by Ernest Hemingway, John Keats, Susan Glaspell, and many others are generously represented. In addition, there are many contemporary selections from well-regarded writers including Joy Harjo, Zadie Smith, Adrian Tomine,

and Suzan-Lori Parks. This edition also includes an updated selection of song lyrics as poetry, a topic that should generate considerable interest for both instructors and students.

## Many options for teaching and learning about literature

In an effort to make literature come to life for students and the course a pleasure to teach for instructors, *The Compact Bedford Introduction to Literature* offers these innovative features:

PERSPECTIVES ON LITERATURE    Intriguing documents — including letters, critical essays, interviews, and contextual images — appear throughout the book to stimulate class discussion and writing.

CONNECTIONS BETWEEN "POPULAR" AND "LITERARY" CULTURE    The fiction, poetry, and drama introductions incorporate examples from popular culture, effectively introducing students to the literary elements of a given genre through what they already know, such as song lyrics as a close relative of poetry, or a case study on the genre of speculative fiction.

CASE STUDIES THAT TREAT AUTHORS IN DEPTH    Each genre section includes chapters that focus closely on major figures. There are three stories each by Flannery O'Connor and Alice Munro; an extensive selection of poems by Emily Dickinson and Robert Frost; and a play each by Sophocles and Shakespeare with background information to help students engage with these master works. Complementing the literature in these chapters are biographical introductions (with author photographs); critical perspectives (including complementary critical readings where writers argue for different interpretations of the same texts); cultural documents (such as letters and draft manuscript pages); and a generous collection of images that serve to contextualize the works. A variety of critical thinking and writing questions follow the selections to stimulate student responses. All these supplementary materials engage students more fully with the writers and their works. In addition, three case studies created in collaboration with contemporary authors Dagoberto Gilb, Billy Collins, and Julia Alvarez present the authors' own works alongside rare photographs, manuscript pages, and their insights (written specifically for this book) into each work, giving students a unique opportunity to have a major writer speak directly to them.

CULTURAL, CRITICAL, AND THEMATIC CASE STUDIES    The *Cultural Case Study* for Drama presents Quiara Alegría Hudes's play *Water by the Spoonful* together with documents to help students understand the work in its cultural context, such as an excerpt from an Iraq War veteran's memoir. The Poetry section provides a *Cultural Case Study* on the Harlem Renaissance: a beautifully illustrated and thoughtfully curated presentation of the work of four canonical poets — Langston Hughes, Countee Cullen, Georgia Douglas Johnson, and Claude McKay — who helped shape the movement. Each *Thematic Case Study* invites students to explore literature through a particular topic, such as "Poetry and Protest." The fiction *Genre Case Study* invites students to delve deeply into different aspects of a single genre, in this case, speculative fiction.

**ACCESSIBLE COVERAGE OF LITERARY THEORY** For instructors who wish to incorporate literary theory into their courses, Chapter 42, "Critical Strategies for Reading," introduces students to a variety of critical strategies, ranging from formalism to cultural criticism with a new section on Affect Theory. In brief examples, the approaches are applied in analyzing Kate Chopin's "The Story of an Hour" as well as other works, so that students will develop a sense of how to use these strategies in their own reading and writing.

## Plenty of help with reading, writing, and research

**CRITICAL READING**[1] Advice on how to read literature appears at the beginning of each genre section. Sample Close Readings of selections including Kate Chopin's "The Story of an Hour" (Fiction), Gregory Corso's "I am 25" (Poetry), and Susan Glaspell's *Trifles* (Drama) provide analyses of the language, images, and other literary elements at work in these selections. Interpretive annotations in the Chopin and Glaspell selections clearly show students the process of close reading and provide examples of the kind of critical thinking that leads to strong academic writing.

Later in the book, Chapter 43, "Writing about Literature," provides more instruction on how to read a work closely, annotate a text, take notes, keep a reading journal, and develop a topic into a thesis, with a section on arguing persuasively about literature. An Index of Terms appears at the back of the book, and a glossary provides thorough explanations of more than two hundred terms central to the study of literature.

**THE WRITING AND RESEARCH PROCESS** The fourth part of the anthology, "Strategies for Reading and Writing," covers every step of the writing process — from generating topics to documenting sources — while sample student papers model the results.

Chapter 43, "Writing about Literature," offers models of the types of papers most frequently assigned in the introductory course and contains sections on the particular demands of writing about fiction, poetry, and drama.

Sample student papers — all in up-to-date MLA style — model how to analyze and argue about literature and how to support ideas by citing examples. The papers are integrated throughout the book, as are "Questions for Writing"

---

[1] A reference chart on the book's inside front cover outlines all of the book's help for reading and writing about literature.

units that guide students through particular writing tasks: reading and writing responsively; developing a topic into a revised thesis; incorporating secondary sources; applying a critical approach to a work; and writing about multiple works by an author.

Chapter 44, "The Literary Research Paper," offers detailed advice for finding, evaluating, and incorporating sources in a paper and includes current, detailed MLA documentation guidelines.

QUESTIONS FOR CRITICAL READING AND WRITING    More than two thousand questions and assignments — "Considerations for Critical Thinking and Writing," "Connections to Other Selections," "First Response" prompts, "Critical Strategies" questions, and "Creative Response" assignments — spark students' interest, sharpen their thinking, and improve their reading, discussion, and writing skills.

## NEW TO THIS EDITION

### *75 new classic and contemporary selections*

15 stories, 50 poems, and 11 plays representing canonical, multicultural, contemporary, and popular literature are new to this edition. Complementing the addition of several classic literary works are numerous stories, poems, and plays not frequently anthologized. These include stories by Zadie Smith, Carmen Maria Machado, N. K. Jemisin, Jennifer Nansubuga Makumbi, and Adrian Tomine; poems by José Angel Araguz, Kamau Brathwaite, Claudia Rankine, and Amanda Gorman; and plays by Suzan-Lori Parks and Quiara Alegría Hudes. The stories, poems, and plays new to this edition are a rich collection of traditional, contemporary, and multicultural literature — works that will make classroom discussion come alive.

### *New guidance on approaching sensitive topics in literature*

To aid teachers and students in navigating an increasingly polarized response to what should be read and why, a new section in the Introduction explores how to engage with challenging literature — literature with explicit themes, disturbing depictions of reality, or offensive language — that may elicit strong emotions in readers. Students are encouraged to respond to these literary texts cautiously and responsibly while considering historical, cultural, and societal contexts that may alter the meaning of these works.

### *A genre case study on speculative fiction*

An all-new Chapter 11 samples the broad category of what might be considered speculative fiction — magical realism, fantasy, science fiction, and the paranormal, providing students with the opportunity to think deeply about the functions of genre in fiction.

### An author case study on Alice Munro

A new in-depth author case study on the only Nobel Laureate in literature from Canada and the only one known primarily for her accomplishments in the short story, Chapter 12 highlights the subtle power of Alice Munro's writing, offering stories and secondary criticism that encourage students to reflect more deeply on her body of work and on their own experiences as readers and as people.

### A thematic case study on poetry and protest

A timely new Chapter 24 illuminates the power of poetry to affect public debates about divisive issues — racial injustice, the #sayhername movement, class, war, and more — through art, detailing for students the powerful relationship between the power of words and the work of effecting change.

### A reimagined thematic case study on our fragile planet

No subject is more urgent than the way humans are affecting the natural world we inhabit. Nature has long been a primary subject of poetry, but the poems in Chapter 25 concentrate specifically on what's at stake.

### A thematic case study on solitude

The recent pandemic shutdown caused a widespread reevaluation of what it means to be separated from others. At the same time, technologies such as smart phones have made humans feel more connected than ever before, and true solitude is often hard to achieve. The poems in Chapter 27 elicit a deeper engagement with these two contradictory developments.

### A cultural case study on Water by the Spoonful

Quiara Alegría Hudes's Pulitzer Prize–winning play, accompanied by relevant secondary sources, provides rich, unique opportunities for exploring topics of interest to contemporary students, including addiction, PTSD, and identity in a mediated world.

### Three new sample student essays

Three new student essays — a student's exploration of theme in Adrian Tomine's graphic narrative "Intruders," a research paper on Quiara Alegría

Hudes's *Water by the Spoonful*, and a comparison paper on Alice Munro's "Silence" and David Auburn's *Proof*—provide students with updated models of analysis, argument, and proper citation.

## ACKNOWLEDGMENTS

This book has benefited from the ideas, suggestions, and corrections of scores of careful readers who helped transform various stages of an evolving manuscript into a finished book and into subsequent editions. We remain grateful to those we have thanked in previous prefaces, particularly the late Robert Wallace of Case Western Reserve University. In addition, many instructors who have used these anthologies responded to a questionnaire. For their valuable comments and advice, we are grateful to Krysten Anderson, Roane State Community College; Erika L. Bass, University of Northern Iowa; Edison Cassadore, Tohono O'Odham Community College; N. Bradley Christie, Erskine College and Seminary; Ann-Marie Dunbar, Winona State University; Ann Dyer Stuart, Bloomsburg University of Pennsylvania; Jeffrey Eagan, Bakersfield College; Holly Fling, Georgia Military College Milledgeville Campus; Terri Hilgendorf, Professor Emerita, Lewis and Clark Community College; Dr. Ying Kong, University College of the North; Christine Schott, Erskine College and Seminary; Heather Shea Fitch, Kilgore College; Pamela Stone, North Arkansas College; and Kara Wilson, Indian Hills Community College.

We would also like to give special thanks to the following instructors who contributed teaching tips to *Resources for Teaching The Compact Bedford Introduction to Literature*: Sandra Adickes, Helen J. Aling, Sr. Anne Denise Brenann, Robin Calitri, James H. Clemmer, Robert Croft, Thomas Edwards, Elizabeth Kleinfeld, Olga Lyles, Timothy Peters, Catherine Rusco, Robert M. St. John, Richard Stoner, Nancy Veiga, Karla Walters, and Joseph Zeppetello.

We are also indebted to those who cheerfully answered questions and generously provided miscellaneous bits of information. What might have seemed to them like inconsequential conversations turned out to be important leads. Among these friends and colleagues are Raymond Anselment, Barbara Campbell, Ann Charters, Karen Chow, John Christie, Eleni Coundouriotis, Irving Cummings, William Curtin, Patrick Hogan, Hannah Hudson, Lee Jacobus, Thomas Jambeck, Bonnie Januszewski-Ytuarte, Greta Little, Brennan Miller, Amy Monticello, George Monteiro, Brenda Murphy, Joel Myerson, Julie Nash, Rose Quiello, Thomas Recchio, William Sheidley, Stephanie Smith, Milton Stern, Kenneth Wilson, and the dedicated reference librarians at the Homer Babbidge Library, University of Connecticut. We are particularly happy to acknowledge the tactful help of Roxanne Cody, owner of R. J. Julia Booksellers in Madison, Connecticut, whose passion for books authorizes her as the consummate matchmaker for writers, readers, and titles.

We continue to be grateful for what we have learned from teaching our students and for the many student papers we have received over the years that have served as good and accessible models of student writing.

At Bedford/St. Martin's, our debts require more time to acknowledge than the deadline allows. As our development editor, Cari Goldfine expertly kept the book on track and made the journey a pleasure to the end; her valuable contributions richly remind us of how fortunate we are to be Bedford/St. Martin's authors. Juliana Verrelli, assistant editor, gracefully handled a variety of important editorial tasks. Permissions were deftly arranged by Hilary Newman, Allison Ziekba-Vering, Elaine Kosta, Cecilia Varas, and Cheryl DuBois. The difficult tasks of production were skillfully managed by Kendra LeFleur, Lidia MacDonald-Carr, and Murugesh Rajkumar, whose attention to details and deadlines was essential to the completion of this project. We thank all of the people at Bedford/St. Martin's — including senior program manager Nancy Tran, William Boardman, who designed the cover, and Vivian Garcia, the marketing manager — who helped to make this formidable project a manageable one. And we thank Bedford/St. Martin's founders Charles H. Christensen and Joan E. Feinberg for initiating the first edition and launching it with their intelligence, energy, and sound advice.

Finally, we are grateful for our families: Michael for his sons, Timothy and Matthew, for all kinds of help, but mostly he's just grateful they're his sons. And for making all the difference, Michael thanks his wife, Regina Barreca. Quentin is grateful for his sons, Brennan and Owen, for helping him rediscover the pleasures of reading and teaching all over again, and for his wife, Julie Nash, his first and best reader.

— Michael Meyer
— D. Quentin Miller

# BEDFORD/ST. MARTIN'S PUTS YOU FIRST

From day one, our goal has been simple: to provide inspiring resources that are grounded in best practices for teaching reading and writing. For over forty years, Bedford/St. Martin's has partnered with the field, listening to teachers, scholars, and students about the support writers need. No matter the moment or teaching context, we are committed to helping every writing instructor make the most of our resources designed to inspire what's possible for every learner.

## How can we help you?

- Our editors can align our resources to your outcomes through correlation and transition guides for your syllabus. Just ask us.
- Our sales representatives specialize in helping you find the right materials to support your course goals.
- Our digital solutions and implementation and engagement specialists help you make the most of the resources you choose for your course.
- Our *Bits* blog on the Bedford/St. Martin's English Community (**community .macmillan.com**) publishes fresh teaching ideas regularly. You'll also find easily downloadable professional resources and links to author webinars on our community site.

Contact your Bedford/St. Martin's sales representative or visit **macmillanlearning .com** to learn more.

## Digital and Print Options for The Compact Bedford Introduction to Literature

Choose the format that works best for your course, and ask about our packaging options that offer savings for students.

### Digital

- *Achieve with The Compact Bedford Introduction to Literature.* Macmillan Learning's Achieve for selected Bedford/St. Martin's Literature titles offers a dedicated composition space that guides students through draft, review, plagiarism checks, reflection, and revision. It provides trusted content with a robust e-book, as well as interactive close reading models, skill-building close reading activities, LearningCurve for Literature, reading comprehension quizzes, and videos of professional writers and students discussing literary works. Macmillan Learning's Achieve can be seamlessly integrated into your school's LMS and supports students with a single point of access. To order *Achieve with The Compact Bedford Introduction to Literature*, use ISBN 978-1-319-33184-9. For details, visit **macmillanlearning.com/achieve/english**.
- *Popular e-book formats.* For details about our e-book partners, visit **macmillanlearning.com/ebooks**.

- *Inclusive Access.* Enable every student to receive their course materials through your LMS on the first day of class. Macmillan Learning's Inclusive Access program is the easiest, most affordable way to ensure all students have access to quality educational resources. Find out more at **macmillanlearning.com/inclusiveaccess**.

### Print

- *Paperback.* To order the paperback edition, use ISBN 978-1-319-33182-5. To order the paperback packaged with Macmillan Learning's Achieve for additional savings, use ISBN 978-1-319-54372-3.
- *Literature to Go.* To order the paperback brief edition — a streamlined, portable version, with the coverage of the elements of literature you love — use ISBN 978-1-319-33214-3.

## Your Course, Your Way

No two writing programs or classrooms are exactly alike. Our Curriculum Solutions team works with you to design custom digital (e-book and Achieve) and print options that provide the resources your students need. (Options below require enrollment minimums.)

- *ForeWords for English.* Customize your text to fit the focus of your course or program by choosing from a range of prepared topics, such as Sentence Guides for Academic Writers.
- *Macmillan Author Program (MAP).* Add excerpts or package acclaimed works from Macmillan's trade imprints to connect students with prominent authors and timely public conversations. A list of popular examples or academic themes is available upon request.
- *Add your own original course- or program-specific materials.* Add original material to your text and return money to your department for professional development or scholarships.

## Instructor Resources

You have a lot to do in your course. We want to make it easy for you to find the support you need — and to get it quickly.

*Resources for Teaching with The Compact Bedford Introduction to Literature* is available as a PDF that can be downloaded from **macmillanlearning .com** and is also available in Achieve. In addition to chapter overviews and teaching tips, the instructor's manual includes sample syllabi, classroom activities, and other helpful resources.

# Brief Contents

# DRAMA 969

## THE STUDY OF DRAMA 971

## STRATEGIES FOR READING AND WRITING 1379

# Contents

## 8. Style, Tone, and Irony 229

Style 229

Tone 231

Irony 232

## APPROACHES TO FICTION 249

### THEMATIC APPROACHES

## 9. A Thematic Case Study: War and Its Aftermath 251

## 10. A Thematic Case Study: Privacy 276

### GENRE STUDIES

## 11. A Genre Case Study: Speculative Fiction 314

AUTHORS IN DEPTH

# POETRY   519

## THE ELEMENTS OF POETRY   521

## Poetry and the Visual Arts   A

### Tone   561

### Diction and Tone in Four Love Poems   565

### Poems for Further Study   568

## 20. Symbol, Allegory, and Irony   611

## APPROACHES TO POETRY   717

### CASE STUDIES

## 26. A Case Study: Song Lyrics as Poetry  758

## 27. A Thematic Case Study: The Poetry of Solitude  774

FOUR POETS IN DEPTH

## 30. A Study of Robert Frost 857

A Brief Biography 858

An Introduction to His Work 862

**Robert Frost**

*The Road Not Taken* 863

*The Pasture* 865

*Mowing* 865

*Mending Wall* 866

*Birches* 867

*"Out, Out—"* 869

*Fire and Ice* 870

*The Need of Being Versed in Country Things* 870

*Nothing Gold Can Stay* 871

*Neither Out Far nor In Deep* 872

*Design* 874

*Desert Places* 874

*The Gift Outright* 875

PERSPECTIVES

Robert Frost • *On the Living Part of a Poem* 876

Amy Lowell • *On Frost's Realistic Technique* 877

Herbert R. Coursen Jr. • *A Parodic Interpretation of "Stopping by Woods on a Snowy Evening"* 877

SUGGESTED TOPICS FOR LONGER PAPERS 878

## 31. A Study of Julia Alvarez: The Author Reflects on Five Poems 879

A Brief Biography 880

An Introduction to Her Work 881

**Julia Alvarez** • *Queens, 1963* (POEM) 883

**Julia Alvarez** • *On Writing "Queens, 1963"* (ESSAY) 885

*Queens Civil Rights Demonstration* (PHOTO) 886

**Julia Alvarez** • *Housekeeping Cages* (ESSAY) 887

**Julia Alvarez** • *On Writing "Housekeeping Cages" and Her Housekeeping Poems* (ESSAY) 888

**Julia Alvarez** • *Dusting* (POEM) 890

**Julia Alvarez** • *On Writing "Dusting"* (ESSAY) 891

**Julia Alvarez** • *Ironing Their Clothes* (POEM) 891

**Julia Alvarez** • *On Writing "Ironing Their Clothes"* (ESSAY) 892

## 32. A Study of Billy Collins: The Author Reflects on Five Poems  900

## AN ANTHOLOGY OF POEMS  927

## 33. An Anthology of Classic Poems  929

# DRAMA 969

## THE STUDY OF DRAMA 971

## STRATEGIES FOR READING AND WRITING

# THE COMPACT
# BEDFORD
# INTRODUCTION
# TO LITERATURE

Reading · Thinking · Writing

# INTRODUCTION

# Reading
# Imaginative Literature

To seek the source, the impulse of a
story is like tearing a flower to pieces
for wantonness.
— KATE CHOPIN

Missouri Historical Society,
St. Louis.

## THE NATURE OF LITERATURE

Literature does not lend itself to a single tidy definition because the making of
it over the centuries has been as complex, unwieldy, and natural as life itself.
Is literature everything that has been written, from ancient prayers to graffiti?
Does it include songs and stories that were not written down until many years
after they were recited? Does literature include the television scripts from
*The Simpsons* as well as Shakespeare's *King Lear*? Is literature only writing
that has permanent value and continues to move people? Must literature be
true or beautiful or moral? Should it be socially useful?

Although these kinds of questions are not conclusively answered in this book,
they are implicitly raised by the stories, poems, and plays included here. No definition of literature, particularly a brief one, is likely to satisfy everyone because

definitions tend to weaken and require qualification when confronted by the uniqueness of individual works. In this context it is worth recalling Herman Melville's humorous use of a definition of a whale in *Moby-Dick* (1851). In the course of the novel Melville presents his imaginative and symbolic whale as inscrutable, but he begins with a quotation from Georges Cuvier, a French naturalist who defines a whale in his nineteenth-century study *The Animal Kingdom* this way: "The whale is a mammiferous animal without hind feet." Cuvier's description is technically correct, of course, but there is little wisdom in it. Melville understood that the reality of the whale (which he describes as the "ungraspable phantom of life") cannot be caught by isolated facts. If the full meaning of the whale is to be understood, it must be sought on the open sea of experience, where the whale itself is, rather than in exclusionary definitions. Facts and definitions are helpful; however, they do not always reveal the whole truth.

Despite Melville's reminder that a definition can be too limiting and even comical, it is useful for our purposes to describe literature as a fiction consisting of carefully arranged words designed to stir the imagination. Stories, poems, and plays are fictional. They are made up — imagined — even when based on actual historic events. Such imaginative writing differs from other kinds of writing because its purpose is not primarily to transmit facts or ideas. Imaginative literature is a source more of pleasure than of information, and we read it for basically the same reasons we listen to music or view a dance: enjoyment, delight, and satisfaction. Like other art forms, imaginative literature offers pleasure and usually attempts to convey a perspective, mood, feeling, or experience. Writers transform the facts the world provides — people, places, and objects — into experiences that suggest meanings.

One of the ways literature transforms facts is by playing with language's slipperiness. We rely on language for meaning, but the meanings of words change every time we rearrange them or place them in new contexts. We are delighted by imaginative literature because of its capacity to surprise. Consider the following poem by Danusha Laméris:

## DANUSHA LAMÉRIS (B. 1971)

### *Feeding the Worms*  2020

Ever since I found out that earth worms have taste buds
all over the delicate pink strings of their bodies,
I pause dropping apple peels into the compost bin, imagine
the dark, writhing ecstasy, the sweetness of apples
permeating their pores. I offer beets and parsley,     5
avocado, and melon, the feathery tops of carrots.

I'd always thought theirs a menial life, eyeless and hidden,
almost vulgar — though now, it seems, they bear a pleasure
so sublime, so decadent, I want to contribute however I can,
forgetting, a moment, my place on the menu.     10

The title of the poem immediately sets us up for something unusual. Humans tend to feed animals, whether we open a can of food for a cat, toss a stale loaf of bread to ducks in a pond, or sprinkle grain on the ground for egg-laying chickens. It's highly unusual to feed worms, who are lowly animals that do not inspire human affection. The speaker begins with an interesting, obscure fact: earthworms have taste buds covering their bodies. This is new knowledge for the speaker as well as the reader, and the speaker reacts to it.

But first, the speaker transforms worms in her mind's eye. Their bodies are "delicate pink strings." That initially makes them seem inanimate, like human-made things rather than animals, but the speaker surprises us again by turning them into animals that can experience "pleasure," or even "dark, writhing ecstasy," which are experiences associated more with humans than with other animals. Rather than just throwing scraps of fruits and vegetables in the compost, the speaker sees this action as significant, an "offering," which is something humans give to one another, or even to their gods.

So are worms in this poem things, animals, humans, or gods? The magic of literature is that they can be all of the above, or can change over the course of the poem. The speaker admits, "I'd always thought theirs a menial life, eyeless and hidden / almost vulgar." The speaker's mind also changes over the course of the poem, or perhaps that change of mind is what caused the poet to want to explore her newfound understanding. She starts by saying, "Ever since I found out . . ." meaning that she's been pondering the situation for some time. The art of poetry involves contemplation and revision.

There's yet another transformation, another surprise at the end of the poem. The speaker almost seems to want to dedicate her life to the marvelous fact she's discovered about worms. They are "sublime" and "decadent," and she wants to "contribute however I can." The menial existence of worms has become something wonderful. At this moment the big transformation happens: the speaker recognizes mortality. The term "feeding the worms" is a gloomy euphemism for death: when we're buried in the ground, it is said, we become food for worms. The speaker is "on the menu" and it may be possible to forget that fact, but only for "a moment." Feeding the worms while you're alive is a way to avoid the grim fact that you will feed the worms when you're dead. There is pleasure and a sense of purpose in one, and a despair of the meaning of human existence in the other. The single phrase of the title captures both.

The poem goes well beyond the trivia fact that occasions it. To learn that earthworms are covered in taste buds is interesting, but to transform that fact into a meditation on life's pleasures and horrors — and to do so by playing with the double meaning of a single phrase — is to engage in literary thinking. Imaginative literature gives us not so much the full, factual proportions of the world as some of its experiences and meanings. Instead of defining the world, literature encourages us to try it out in our imaginations.

## THE VALUE OF LITERATURE

Mark Twain once shrewdly observed that a person who chooses not to read has no advantage over a person who is unable to read. In industrialized societies today, however, the question is not who reads, because nearly everyone can and does, but what is read. Why should anyone spend precious time with literature when there is so much informational reading material available on our smart phones? Why should a literary artist's imagination compete for attention that could be spent on the firm realities that constitute everyday life? In fact, national best-seller lists much less often include collections of stories, poems, or plays than they do cookbooks and, not surprisingly, diet books. Although such fare may be filling, it doesn't stay with you. Most people have other appetites too.

Certainly one of the most important values of literature is that it nourishes our emotional lives. An effective literary work may seem to speak directly to us, especially if we are ripe for it. The inner life that good writers reveal in their characters often gives us glimpses of some portion of ourselves. We can be moved to laugh, cry, tremble, dream, ponder, shriek, or rage with a character by simply turning a page instead of turning our lives upside down. Although the experience itself is imagined, the emotion is real. That's why the final chapters of a good adventure novel can make a reader's heart race as much as a 100-yard dash or why we can fret and become physically anxious when we immerse ourselves in impossible decision between murdering one's infant daughter or allowing her to be returned to slavery in Toni Morrison's *Beloved* (1987) is painful to a sympathetic reader. Human emotions speak a universal language regardless of when or where a work was written.

In addition to appealing to our emotions, literature broadens our perspectives on the world. Most of the people we meet tend to be like ourselves, and what we can see of the world even over the course of a lifetime is astonishingly limited. Literature allows us to move beyond the inevitable boundaries of our own lives and culture because it introduces us to people different from ourselves, places remote from our neighborhoods, and times other than our own. Reading makes us more aware of life's possibilities as well as its subtleties and ambiguities. Put simply, people who read literature experience more life and have a keener sense of a common human identity than those who do not. It is true, of course, that many people go through life without reading imaginative literature, but they are missing out on an essential human experience. They may find themselves troubled by the same kinds of questions that reveal Daisy Buchanan's restless, vague discontentment in F. Scott Fitzgerald's *The Great Gatsby* (1925): "What'll we do with ourselves this afternoon?" cried Daisy, "and the day after that, and the next thirty years?"

Sometimes students mistakenly associate literature more with school than with life. Accustomed to reading it in order to write a paper or pass an examination, students may perceive such reading as a chore instead of a pleasurable opportunity, something considerably less important than studying for the "practical" courses that prepare them in obvious ways for a career. The study of literature, however, is also practical because it engages readers in the kinds of problem solving important in a variety of fields, from philosophy to medicine and computer programming. The interpretation of literary texts demands an engagement with ambiguity, morality, and emotional volatility, all of which are unavoidable aspects of life.

Because it pushes the boundaries of language, literature embraces the complexity of human experience. People who make the most significant contributions to their professions — whether in business, engineering, teaching, or some other area — tend to become excited about the existence of multiple possibilities. Instead of retreating to the way things have always been done, they bring freshness and creativity to their work. F. Scott Fitzgerald once astutely described the "test of a first-rate intelligence" as "the ability to hold two opposed ideas in the mind at the same time, and still retain the ability to function." People with such intelligence know how to read situations, shape questions, interpret details, and evaluate competing points of view. Equipped with a healthy respect for facts, they also understand the value of pursuing hunches and exercising their imaginations. They are interested as much in "problem finding" as "problem solving." Reading literature encourages a suppleness of mind that is helpful in any discipline or work.

Once the requirements for your degree are completed, what ultimately matters are not the courses listed on your transcript but the sensibilities and habits of mind that you bring to your work, friends, family, and every other dimension of your life. A healthy economy changes and grows with the times; people do too, but only if they are prepared for more than simply filling a job description, or solving a problem that someone else has identified. The range and variety of life that literature affords can help you to interpret your own experiences and the world in which you live.

To discover the insights that literature reveals requires careful reading and sensitivity. One of the purposes of a college introduction to literature class is to cultivate the analytic skills necessary for reading well. Class discussions often help establish an understanding of a work that might not be available if you were reading in solitude. You can also develop interpretive skills by writing about what you read. Writing is an effective means of clarifying and deepening your responses and ideas because it requires you to account for the author's use of language as well as your own. This book is based on two premises: that reading literature is pleasurable and that reading and understanding a work sensitively by thinking, talking, or writing about it increases the pleasure of the experience of it.

Understanding literature's basic elements — such as point of view, symbol, theme, tone, irony, and so on — is a prerequisite to an informed appreciation of it. This kind of understanding allows you to perceive more in a literary work in much the same way that a spectator at a tennis match sees more if he or she understands the rules and conventions of the game. But rules and conventions are just the beginning. It might take many years of watching tennis to understand the unique gifts of Rafael Nadal or Serena Williams even if you see them dominate (or even lose) an individual match. The more literature you read, the richer the experience becomes as you understand how every poem, play, or story is a unique contribution to the ever-growing literary landscape even though all of them are basically rearrangements of the same twenty-six letters of the alphabet. The analytic skills that open up literature also have their uses when you listen to music, or watch a television program or film and, more important, when you attempt to sort out the significance of the people, places, and events that constitute your own life. Literature enhances and sharpens your perceptions. What could be more lastingly practical as well as satisfying?

## THE CHANGING LITERARY CANON

Perhaps the best reading creates some kind of change in us: we see more clearly; we're alert to nuances; we ask questions that previously didn't occur to us. Henry David Thoreau had that sort of reading in mind when he remarked in *Walden* (1854) that the books he valued most were those that caused him to date "a new era in his life from the reading." Readers are sometimes changed by literature, but it is also worth noting that the life of a literary work can also be affected by the ways books are distributed, reviewed, and recommended (as well as assigned in courses like the one you are taking). Fitzgerald's *The Great Gatsby*, for instance, really achieved the status of an accepted classic not when it was first published, but a quarter-century later during World War II, when the American military distributed tens of thousands of copies of the book to G.I.s who needed to pass the time. This is not to take away from the book's greatness, worth, or appeal, but rather to suggest that a huge number of readers help a book's reputation. Around the turn of the twenty-first century Oprah Winfrey's televised book club could instantly turn an obscure writer into a household name. Today book reviews on Amazon or on social media sites such as Goodreads have weakened the power of traditional professional literary reviewers in venues like the *New York Times Book Review* or the *Times Literary Supplement.*

Such changes have steadily accelerated as the literary ***canon*** — those works considered by scholars, critics, and teachers to be the most important to read and study — has undergone a significant series of shifts. The importance of certain canonical writers such as William Shakespeare or Charles Dickens has rarely been questioned, but other writers that your great-grandparents might have heard of such as Anthony Trollope or Sherwood Anderson are probably not in your field of reference. There has also been a widespread effort to scrutinize whether the establishment of an agreed-upon list of "great books" excludes writers whose voices, perspectives, and backgrounds have historically been marginal to society's mainstream. In the nineteenth and twentieth centuries, the people who established the canon were almost uniformly wealthy, educated, white, and male, and the authors they canonized were as well. Writers who previously were overlooked, undervalued, neglected, or studiously ignored have been brought into focus in an effort to create a more diverse literary canon, one that recognizes the contributions of many cultures and a wide range of individual perspectives. In the 1980s, for example, the famous novelist Alice Walker argued convincingly that American readers had been neglecting the work of Zora Neale Hurston, a folklorist and fiction writer who died in poverty and obscurity in 1960 after achieving some fame during the Harlem Renaissance in the 1920s. Walker argued that Hurston was neglected partially because of her race, gender, and refusal to conform to standard literary tastes. Walker's argument was convincing: at least for a time, Hurston's novel *Their Eyes Were Watching God* (1937) was widely taught in high schools and colleges alongside established canonical works like J. D. Salinger's *The Catcher in the Rye* (1951). This kind of enlargement of the canon resulted from reform movements of the 1960s and 1970s. The civil rights, feminist, and gay pride movements of that era sensitized literary critics to the political, moral, and esthetic necessity of reevaluating women writers and Black American literature. More recently, LGBTQ+, Native American, Asian, and Latino/a writers have been making their way into the American literary canon. Moreover, on a broader scale, the canon is being revised and enlarged to include the works of writers from parts of the world other than the West, a development that reflects the changing values, concerns, and complexities of recent decades, when literary landscapes have shifted as dramatically as the political boundaries of much of the world.

No semester's reading list — or anthology — can adequately or accurately echo all the new voices competing to be heard as part of the mainstream literary canon, but recent efforts to open up the canon attempt to introduce readers to a plurality of writers from all over the world. This development has not occurred without its urgent advocates or passionate dissenters. It's no surprise that issues about race, gender, and class often get people off the fence and on their feet. (These controversies are discussed further in Chapter 42, "Critical Strategies for Reading.") Although what we regard as literature — whether it's called great, classic, essential, or canonical — continues to generate debate, there is no question that such controversy will continue to reflect readers' values as well as the writers they admire.

## APPROACHING SENSITIVE SUBJECTS

Literature reflects life, or, to quote Shakespeare's Hamlet giving instruction to a group of actors, it "hold[s] as 'twere the mirror up to nature." Life is not always wonderful, as we all know, and sometimes we don't like what we see in a mirror, or through a window, or on the various screens we stare at daily. A good deal of what we see reflected in literature is, in fact, disturbing. The book some consider to be the very first novel in English — Samuel Richardson's *Pamela* (1740) — is on the surface an 800-page account of persistent sexual harassment. Vladimir Nabokov's *Lolita* (1955) traffics in pedophilia. Toni Morrison's *Beloved* — or any other novel that responsibly takes on the era of slavery in the United States — contains graphic descriptions of racial violence.

Works that take place in times of war frequently describe mutilated bodies, often in stomach-turning detail.

This list of examples could be endless, and there is no way of anticipating everything that might trigger a strong emotional response in readers because individuals don't always find the same things disturbing. Television shows, news broadcasts, and Internet sites are sometimes flagged for their content and preface the airing with the phrase "viewer discretion is advised," but literature rarely if ever comes with such warnings. The power to "surprise" we spoke of when interpreting Danusha Laméris's poem above is part of what makes literature appealing, but it can also be a shock to the reader's senses. A suicide, rape, instance of racial violence, or physical violence of any kind in a work of fiction can seem real if the reader is deeply immersed in the act of sensitive reading, so real that it can catalyze psychological trauma, and even re-incur it on survivors of these acts. Language, too, has special power in this regard. While reading literature you may come across a racial slur, or vulgarly sexist, homophobic, or otherwise harmful language. It helps to be aware of this general fact so you can navigate the border between surprise and unpleasant shock — not necessarily in order to only seek the former while avoiding the latter, but just to be prepared that both are possible.

Literature can be perceived as threatening or damaging to those who consider themselves protectors of culture or decorum. There is a long history of literary works now considered classics that were put on trial during their times as obscene with the goal of forbidding their publication: James Joyce's *Ulysses* (1922), Henry Miller's *Tropic of Cancer* (1934), and Allen Ginsberg's *Howl* (1955) are just a few examples. Even in our time there are renewed attempts to ban books from school curricula and public libraries due to their content. It is clear that literature has the power to influence and that many cultural watchdogs over time have thought that its primary power was to corrupt. Certain religious leaders in the early days of the British and American novel thought reading *any* fiction was immoral because it took time away from Bible reading. It might seem silly to one reader that anyone would take offense to a word, idea, or character represented in literature, but history shows that other readers are dead serious about their opposition to it. Censorship and free artistic expression are at odds with one another. The only way readers can trust their own judgment is, of course, through direct encounter. It may be challenging to be receptive to the nuances of a work if you have a strong ideology, or if you have experiences with topics that might be harmful or troubling to you or your various communities. The more aware you are of the potential for such reactions, the stronger you will be as a reader.

In short, though it is a work of the imagination, literature will not protect us from reality. Far from it, in many cases: certain writers hold nature's mirror right up in our face. If we close our eyes, those writers will still be there when we open them, insisting on getting us to confront something we would rather not see. Indeed, one of literature's greatest powers is its ability to force us to empathize with other perspectives and to engage with challenging realities.

Though we emphasize the pleasure of encountering literature, we also understand that reading it can be a profoundly troubling experience.

There is no easy way around the fact that literature can touch on raw nerves, and that your own raw nerves aren't necessarily the same as someone else's. We don't believe that the topics raised by literature or the language used to address these ideas should be avoided just because they could cause discomfort. We do not have control over literature once it has been published. As editors of this volume we do not feel it is our right to play the role of censor. This is literature, and its range of possible effects is boundless. We acknowledge that premise, and we fully realize that the language, description, and ideas contained in these pages have disruptive power. We also want readers to develop their capacity to evaluate it, though, and the way to become a more powerful reader is through facing writing directly. We do, however, have some control over the way we frame our responses, and we can offer the following guidelines:

First, be ever mindful of context. What might have been considered obscene in the nineteenth century might be perfectly benign or common today, and the opposite is also possibly true. Tastes change over time, and even the meaning of individual words can evolve: studying those changes is a branch of linguistic study known as etymology. Beyond historical changes, there are personal and cultural contexts that are worth considering, too. We are all shaped by our life experiences. If an author you read was raised in very different circumstances from yours, you would do well to learn more about those circumstances. Identity and group membership are important to consider: the same word that can be considered insulting if used by someone outside a group can be used as a bonding word within that group. For some of the more upsetting works in this anthology, we have attempted to provide you with some of this important context in the headnotes and surrounding content. The more we understand about the circumstances that surround a text's production, the better chance we have of grasping it.

Second, it's unwise to assume that the author of a work automatically endorses what is represented in that work. We know that Stephen King writes horrifying tales that often reveal gruesomely mutilated bodies, but we don't assume he's a murderer or that he expects us to admire murderers. (Those fans lucky enough to have met King are surprised by how down-to-earth and funny he is.) If a writer presents something disturbing in a text, be it racism, torture, or suicide, there is probably a specific reason for doing so. That reason is rarely mere indulgence or indifferent approval. Writers tend to choose language carefully and to have a broad understanding of its effects. That said, writers are imperfect humans like all of us, and there have been multiple instances in recent years when their pronouncements in interviews or behavior in public life have caused readers to scrutinize the content of their work. If a writer makes pronouncements that are sexist, transphobic, or harmful in any other way, they should not be surprised when readers reevaluate their work.

Finally, be honest about your reactions to a text and aware that other readers might react differently to it. If you feel neutrally about a text and your classmates all had a strong reaction, that does not necessarily mean you are "right" and they are "wrong" (or vice versa). It means that readers are varied and literary texts are powerful. That power can be a difficult topic to deal with as we are not always prepared for what we will encounter, as discussed above. Sensitive topics call on us to be especially careful readers and to articulate our written and verbal responses with equal sensitivity to the responses of all other readers we encounter. Interpreters of literature are not in the business of telling other readers that they have no right to react to a text as they have done, provided they have not misrepresented its content. Rather, in the spirit of both civility and intellectual discourse, our responsibility is to explore and explain the world of the text — which is also our world — in terms that are respectful and responsible. This principle is a key both to critical thinking and to persuasive communication. The overall goal of reading literature is to elevate our humanity. It can come as a surprise to discover that sometimes the path to that elevation is not only to showcase the best humanity has to offer. Hamlet's mirror up to nature begs us to tell what we see, and what we think about it.

# FICTION

*Credits, clockwise from top left:* Everett Collection/Newscom; Everett Collection Inc/Alamy; Apic/Getty Images; Carlo Allegri/Getty Images; David Levenson/Getty Images; Neville Elder/Getty Images.

# The Elements
# of Fiction

# 1

# Reading Fiction

Everett Collection Inc/Alamy.

When you're writing, you're trying to find out something which you don't know. The whole language of writing for me is finding out what you don't want to know, what you don't want to find out. But something forces you to anyway.

— JAMES BALDWIN

## READING FICTION RESPONSIVELY

Reading a literary work responsively can be an intensely demanding activity. Henry David Thoreau — about as intense and demanding a reader and writer as they come — insists that "books must be read as deliberately and reservedly as they were written." Thoreau is right about the necessity for a conscious, sustained involvement with a literary work. Imaginative literature does demand more from us than, say, browsing through *People* magazine in a dentist's waiting room, but Thoreau makes the process sound a little more daunting than it really is. For when we respond to the demands of responsive reading, our efforts are usually rewarded with pleasure as well as understanding. Careful, deliberate reading — the kind that engages a reader's imagination as it calls forth the writer's — is a means of exploration that can take a reader outside whatever circumstance or experience previously defined their world. Just as we respond moment by moment to people and situations in our lives, we also respond to literary works as we read them, though we may not be fully aware of how we are affected at each point along the way. The more conscious we are of how and why we respond to works in particular ways, the more likely we are to be imaginatively engaged in our reading.

In a very real sense both the reader and the author create the literary work. How a reader responds to a story, poem, or play will help to determine its meaning. Authors arrange the various elements that constitute their craft — elements such as plot, character, setting, point of view, symbolism, theme, and style, which you will be examining in subsequent chapters and which are defined in the Glossary of Literary Terms (p. 1483) — but an author cannot completely control a reader's response any more than a person can absolutely predict how a remark or action will be received by a stranger, a friend, or even a family member. Few authors *tell* readers how to respond. Our sympathy, anger, confusion, delight, sadness, or whatever the feeling might be is left up to us to experience. Writers may have the talent to evoke such feelings, but they don't have the power and authority to enforce them. Because of the range of possible responses produced by imaginative literature, there is no single, correct, definitive response or interpretation. There can be readings that are wrongheaded or foolish, and some readings are better than others — that is, more responsive to a work's details and more persuasive — but that doesn't mean there is only one possible reading of a work (see Chapter 43, "Writing about Literature").

Experience tells us that different people respond differently to the same work. Consider, for example, how often you've heard Melville's *Moby-Dick* described as one of the greatest American novels. This, however, is how a reviewer in *New Monthly Magazine* described the book when it was published in 1851: it is "a huge dose of hyperbolical slang, maudlin sentimentalism and tragic-comic bubble and squeak." Melville surely did not intend or desire this response; but there it is, and it was not a singular, isolated reaction. This reading — like any other reading — was influenced by the values, assumptions, and expectations that some readers brought to the novel from both previous readings and life experiences. The reviewer's refusal to take the book seriously may have caused him to miss the boat from the perspective of many other readers of *Moby-Dick*, but it indicates that even "classics" (perhaps especially those kinds of works) can generate disparate readings.

Consider the following brief story by Kate Chopin, a writer whose fiction (like Melville's) sometimes met with indifference or hostility in her own time. As you read, keep track of your responses to the central character, Mrs. Mallard. Write down your feelings about her in a substantial paragraph when you finish the story. Think, for example, about how you respond to the emotions she expresses concerning news of her husband's death. What do you think of her feelings about marriage? Do you think you would react the way she does under similar circumstances?

KATE CHOPIN (1851–1904)

## *The Story of an Hour*   1894

Knowing that Mrs. Mallard was afflicted with a heart trouble, great care was taken to break to her as gently as possible the news of her husband's death.

It was her sister Josephine who told her, in broken sentences; veiled hints that revealed in half concealing. Her husband's friend Richards was there, too, near her. It was he who had been in the newspaper office when intelligence of the rail-

Missouri Historical Society, St. Louis.

road disaster was received, with Brently Mallard's name leading the list of "killed." He had only taken the time to assure himself of its truth by a second telegram, and had hastened to forestall any less careful, less tender friend in bearing the sad message.

She did not hear the story as many women have heard the same, with a para-lyzed inability to accept its significance. She wept at once, with sudden, wild aban-donment, in her sister's arms. When the storm of grief had spent itself she went away to her room alone. She would have no one follow her.

There stood, facing the open window, a comfortable, roomy armchair. Into this she sank, pressed down by a physical exhaustion that haunted her body and seemed to reach into her soul.

She could see in the open square before her house the tops of trees that were   5 all aquiver with the new spring life. The delicious breath of rain was in the air. In the street below a peddler was crying his wares. The notes of a distant song which some one was singing reached her faintly, and countless sparrows were twittering in the eaves.

There were patches of blue sky showing here and there through the clouds that had met and piled one above the other in the west facing her window.

She sat with her head thrown back upon the cushion of the chair, quite motionless, except when a sob came up into her throat and shook her, as a child who has cried itself to sleep continues to sob in its dreams.

She was young, with a fair, calm face, whose lines bespoke repression and even a certain strength. But now there was a dull stare in her eyes, whose gaze was fixed away off yonder on one of those patches of blue sky. It was not a glance of reflec-tion, but rather indicated a suspension of intelligent thought.

There was something coming to her and she was waiting for it, fearfully. What was it? She did not know; it was too subtle and elusive to name. But she felt it, creeping out of the sky, reaching toward her through the sounds, the scents, the color that filled the air.

Now her bosom rose and fell tumultuously. She was beginning to recognize   10 this thing that was approaching to possess her, and she was striving to beat it back with her will — as powerless as her two white slender hands would have been.

When she abandoned herself a little whispered word escaped her slightly parted lips. She said it over and over under her breath: "free, free, free!" The vacant stare and the look of terror that had followed it went from her eyes. They stayed keen and bright. Her pulses beat fast, and the coursing blood warmed and relaxed every inch of her body.

She did not stop to ask if it were or were not a monstrous joy that held her. A clear and exalted perception enabled her to dismiss the suggestion as trivial.

She knew that she would weep again when she saw the kind, tender hands folded in death; the face that had never looked save with love upon her, fixed and gray and dead. But she saw beyond that bitter moment a long procession of years to come that would belong to her absolutely. And she opened and spread her arms out to them in welcome.

There would be no one to live for her during those coming years; she would live for herself. There would be no powerful will bending hers in that blind persistence with which men and women believe they have a right to impose a private will upon a fellow-creature. A kind intention or a cruel intention made the act seem no less a crime as she looked upon it in that brief moment of illumination.

And yet she had loved him — sometimes. Often she had not. What did it 15 matter! What could love, the unsolved mystery, count for in face of this possession of self-assertion which she suddenly recognized as the strongest impulse of her being!

"Free! Body and soul free!" she kept whispering.

Josephine was kneeling before the closed door with her lips to the keyhole, imploring for admission. "Louise, open the door! I beg; open the door — you will make yourself ill. What are you doing, Louise? For heaven's sake open the door."

"Go away. I am not making myself ill." No; she was drinking in a very elixir of life through that open window.

Her fancy was running riot along those days ahead of her. Spring days, and summer days, and all sorts of days that would be her own. She breathed a quick prayer that life might be long. It was only yesterday she had thought with a shudder that life might be long.

She arose at length and opened the door to her sister's importunities. There 20 was a feverish triumph in her eyes, and she carried herself unwittingly like a goddess of Victory. She clasped her sister's waist, and together they descended the stairs. Richards stood waiting for them at the bottom.

Some one was opening the front door with a latchkey. It was Brently Mallard who entered, a little travel-stained, composedly carrying his gripsack and umbrella. He had been far from the scene of accident, and did not even know there had been one. He stood amazed at Josephine's piercing cry; at Richards' quick motion to screen him from the view of his wife.

But Richards was too late.

When the doctors came they said she had died of heart disease — of joy that kills.

## A SAMPLE CLOSE READING

### *An Annotated Section of "The Story of an Hour"*

Even as you read a story for the first time, you can highlight passages, circle or underline words, and write responses in the margins. Subsequent readings will yield more insights once you begin to understand how various elements such as plot, characterization, and word choice build toward the conclusion and what you perceive to be the story's central ideas. The following annotations for the first eleven paragraphs of "The Story of an Hour" provide a perspective written by someone who had read the work several times. Your own approach might, of course, be quite different — as the sample paper that follows the annotated passage amply demonstrates.

## KATE CHOPIN (1851–1904)

### *The Story of an Hour*   1894

Knowing that |Mrs. Mallard| was |afflicted with a heart trouble|, great care was taken to break to her as gently as possible the news of her husband's death.

It was her sister |Josephine| who told her, in broken sentences; |veiled hints| that revealed in half concealing. Her husband's friend Richards was there, too, near her. It was he who had been in the newspaper office when intelligence of the railroad disaster was received, with Brently Mallard's name leading the list of "killed." He had only taken the time to assure himself of its truth by a second telegram, and had hastened to forestall any less careful, less tender friend in bearing the sad message.

She did not hear the story as many women have heard the same, with a paralyzed inability to accept its significance. |She wept at once|, with sudden, |wild abandonment|, in her sister's arms. When the storm of grief had spent itself she went away to her room alone. She would have no one follow her.

There stood, facing the |open window|, a comfortable, roomy armchair. Into this she sank, pressed down by a physical exhaustion that haunted her body and seemed to reach into her soul.

She could see in the |open square| before her house the tops of trees that were all |aquiver| with the |new spring life|. The |delicious breath| of rain was in the air. In the street below a peddler was crying his wares. The notes of a distant song which some one was singing reached her faintly, and countless |sparrows were twittering| in the eaves.

There were |patches of blue sky| showing here and there through the clouds that had met and piled one above the other in the west facing her window.

She sat with her head thrown back upon the cushion of the chair, quite motionless, except when a sob came up into her throat and shook her, as a child who has cried itself to sleep continues to sob in its dreams.

She was young, with a fair, calm face, whose lines bespoke repression and even a certain strength. |But now there was a dull stare in her eyes|, whose gaze was fixed away off yonder on one of those patches of blue sky. It was not a glance of reflection, but rather indicated a suspension of intelligent thought.

There was |something coming to her| and she was |waiting for it, fearfully|. What was it? She did not know; it was |too subtle and elusive to name|. But she felt it, creeping out of the sky,

**Marginal annotations:**

The title could point to the brevity of the story — only 23 short paragraphs — or to the decisive nature of what happens in a very short period of time. Or both.

Mrs. Mallard's first name (Louise) is not given until paragraph 17, yet her sister Josephine is named immediately. This emphasizes Mrs. Mallard's married identity.

Given the nature of the cause of Mrs. Mallard's death at the story's end, it's worth noting the ambiguous description that she "was afflicted with a heart trouble." Is this one of Chopin's (rather than Josephine's) "veiled hints"?

When Mrs. Mallard weeps with "wild abandonment," the reader is again confronted with an ambiguous phrase: she grieves in an overwhelming manner yet seems to express relief at being abandoned by Brently's death.

These 3 paragraphs create an increasingly "open" atmosphere that leads to the "delicious" outside where there are inviting sounds and "patches of blue sky." There's a definite tension between the inside and outside worlds.

Though still stunned by grief, Mrs. Mallard begins to feel a change come over her owing to her growing awareness of a world outside her room. What that change is remains "too subtle and elusive to name."

Mrs. Mallard's conflicted struggle is described in passionate, physical terms as if she is "possess[ed]" by a lover she is "power-less" to resist.

Once she has "aban-doned" herself (see the "abandonment" in paragraph 3), the reader realizes that her love is to be "free, free, free." Her recognition is evi-dent in the "coursing blood [that] warmed and relaxed every inch of her body."

reaching toward her through the sounds, the scents, the color that filled the air.

Now her bosom rose and fell tumultuously. She was begin-ning to recognize this thing that was approaching to possess her, and she was striving to beat it back with her will — as powerless as her two white slender hands would have been.

When she abandoned herself a little whispered word escaped her slightly parted lips. She said it over and over under her breath: "free, free, free!" The vacant stare and the look of terror that had followed it went from her eyes. They stayed keen and bright. Her pulses beat fast, and the coursing blood warmed and relaxed every inch of her body . . . .

10

Do you find Mrs. Mallard a sympathetic character? Some readers think that she is callous, selfish, and unnatural — even monstrous — because she ecstat-ically revels in her newly discovered sense of freedom so soon after learn-ing of her husband's presumed death. Others read her as a victim of her inability to control her own life in a repressive, male-dominated society. Is it possible to hold both views simultaneously, or are they mutually exclu-sive? Are your views in any way influenced by your gender? Does your age affect your perception? What about your social and economic background? Does your nationality, race, or religion in any way shape your attitudes? Do you have particular views about the institution of marriage that inform your assessment of Mrs. Mallard's character? Have other reading experiences — perhaps a familiarity with some of Chopin's other stories — predisposed you one way or another to Mrs. Mallard?

Understanding potential influences might be useful in determining whether a particular response to Mrs. Mallard is based primarily on the story's details and their arrangement or on an overt or a subtle bias that is brought to the story. If you unconsciously project your beliefs and assumptions onto a literary work, you run the risk of distorting it to accommodate your predispo-sitions. Your feelings can be a reliable guide to interpretation, but you should be aware of what those feelings are based on.

Often specific questions about literary works cannot be answered defini-tively. For example, Chopin does not explain why Mrs. Mallard suffers a heart attack at the end of this story. Is the shock of seeing her "dead" husband simply too much for this woman "afflicted with a heart trouble"? Does she die of what the doctors call a "joy that kills" because she is so glad to see her husband? Is she so profoundly guilty about feeling "free" at her husband's expense that she has a heart attack? Is her death a kind of willed suicide in reaction to her loss of freedom? Your answers to these questions will depend on which details you emphasize in your interpretation of the story and the kinds of perspectives and values you bring to it. If, for example, you read the story from a feminist perspective, you would be likely to pay close attention to Chopin's comments about marriage in paragraph 14. Or if you read the story as an oblique attack on the insensitivity of physicians of the period, you might want to find out whether Chopin wrote elsewhere about doctors (she did) and compare her comments with historic sources. (A number of critical strategies for reading, including feminist and historical approaches, appear in Chapter 42.)

Reading responsively makes you an active participant in the process of creating meaning in a literary work. The experience that you and the author create will most likely not be identical to another reader's encounter with the same work, but then that's true of nearly any experience you'll have, and it is part of the pleasure of reading. Indeed, talking and writing about literature is a way of sharing responses so that they can be enriched and deepened.

## A SAMPLE PAPER

### *Differences in Responses to Kate Chopin's "The Story of an Hour"*

The following paper was written in response to an assignment that called for a three- to four-page discussion of how different readers might interpret Mrs. Mallard's character. The paper is based on the story as well as on the discussion of reader-response criticism in Chapter 42, "Critical Strategies for Reading." As that discussion indicates, reader-response criticism is a critical approach that focuses on the reader rather than on the work itself in order to describe how the reader creates meaning from the text.

Villa 1

Wally Villa

Professor Brian

English 210

12 January 2023

Differences in Responses to

Kate Chopin's "The Story of an Hour"

Kate Chopin's "The Story of an Hour" appears merely to explore a woman's unpredictable reaction to her husband's assumed death and reappearance, but actually Chopin offers Mrs. Mallard's bizarre story to reveal problems that are inherent in the institution of marriage. By offering this depiction of a marriage that stifles the woman to the point that she celebrates the death of her kind and loving husband, Chopin challenges her

Thesis providing writer's interpretation of story's purpose

readers to examine their own views of marriage and relationships between men and women. Each reader's judgment of Mrs. Mallard and her behavior inevitably stems from their own personal feelings about marriage and the influences of societal expectations. Readers of differing genders, ages, and marital experiences are, therefore, likely to react differently to Chopin's startling portrayal of the Mallards' marriage, and that certainly is true of my response to the story compared to my father's and grandmother's responses.

Introduction setting up other reader responses discussed later in paper

Marriage often establishes boundaries between people that make them unable to communicate with each other. The Mallards' marriage was evidently crippled by both their inability to talk to one another and Mrs. Mallard's conviction that her marriage was defined by a "powerful will bending hers in that blind persistence with which men and women believe they have a right to impose a private will upon a fellow-creature" (18). Yet she does not recognize that it is not just men who impose their will upon women and that the problems inherent in marriage affect men and women equally. To me, Mrs. Mallard is a somewhat sympathetic character, and I appreciate her longing to live out the "years to come that would belong to her absolutely" (18). However, I also believe that she could have tried to improve her own situation somehow, either by reaching out to her husband or by abandoning the marriage altogether. Chopin uses Mrs. Mallard's tragedy to illuminate aspects of marriage that are harmful and, in this case, even deadly. Perhaps the Mallards' relationship should be taken as a warning to others: sacrificing one's own happiness in order to satisfy societal expectations can poison one's life and even destroy entire families.

Analysis of story's portrayal of marriage, with textual evidence

Analysis of character and plot, connecting with story's purpose

When my father read "The Story of an Hour," his reaction to Mrs. Mallard was more antagonistic than my own. He sees Chopin's story as a timeless "battle of the sexes," serving as further proof that men will never really be able to understand what it is that women want. Mrs. Mallard endures an obviously unsatisfying marriage without ever explaining to her husband that she feels trapped and unfulfilled. Mrs. Mallard dismisses the question of whether or not she is experiencing a "monstrous joy" (17) as trivial, but my father does not think that this is a trivial question. He believes Mrs. Mallard is guilty of a monstrous joy because she selfishly celebrates the death of her husband without ever having allowed him the opportunity to understand her feelings. He believes that, above all, Brently Mallard should be seen as the

Contrasting summary and analysis of another reader's response most victimized character in the story. Mr. Mallard is a good, kind man, with friends who care about him and a marriage that he thinks he can depend on. He "never looked save with love" (18) upon his wife, his only "crime" (18) was his presence in the house, and yet he is the one who is bereaved at the end of the story, for reasons he will never understand. Mrs. Mallard's passion for her newly discovered freedom is perhaps understandable, but according to my father, Mr. Mallard is the character most deserving of sympathy.

Maybe not surprisingly, my grandmother's interpretation of "The Story of an Hour" was radically different from both mine and my father's. My grandmother was married in 1936 and widowed in 1959 and therefore can identify with Chopin's characters, who live at the turn of the twentieth century. Her first reaction, aside from her unwavering support for Mrs. Mallard and her predicament, was that this story demonstrates the differences between the ways men and women related to each other a century ago and the way they relate today. Unlike my father, who thinks Mrs. Mallard is too passive, my grandmother believes that Mrs. Mallard doesn't even know that she is feeling repressed until after she is told that Brently is dead. In 1894, divorce was so scandalous and stigmatized that it simply wouldn't have been an option for Mrs. Mallard, and so her only way out of the marriage would have been one of their deaths. Being relatively young, Mrs. Mallard probably considered herself doomed to a long life in an unhappy marriage. My grandmother also feels that, in spite of all we know of Mrs. Mallard's feelings about her husband and her marriage, she still manages to live up to everyone's expectations of her as a woman both in life and in death. She is a dutiful wife to Brently, as she is expected to be. She weeps "with sudden, wild abandonment" (17) when she hears the news of his death; she locks herself in her room to cope with her new situation, and she has a fatal heart attack upon seeing her husband arrive home. Naturally the male doctors would think that she died of the "joy that kills" (18)—nobody could have guessed that she was unhappy with her life, and she would never have wanted them to know.

Interpretations of "The Story of an Hour" seem to vary according to the gender, age, and experience of the reader. While both male and female readers can certainly sympathize with Mrs. Mallard's plight, female

---

Contrasting summary and analysis of another reader's response

Cultural and historical background providing context for response and story itself

Analysis supported with textual evidence

Villa 4

readers—as was evident in our class discussions—seem to relate more easily to her predicament and more quickly exonerate her of any responsibility for her unhappy situation. Conversely, male readers are more likely to feel compassion for Mr. Mallard, who loses his wife for reasons that will always remain entirely unknown to him. Older readers probably understand more readily the strength of social forces and the difficulty of trying to deny societal expectations concerning gender roles in general and marriage in particular. Younger readers seem to feel that Mrs. Mallard is too passive and that she could have improved her domestic life immeasurably if she had taken the initiative to either improve or end her relationship with her husband. Ultimately, how each individual reader responds to Mrs. Mallard's story reveals their own ideas about marriage, society, and how men and women communicate with each other.

Conclusion summarizing reader responses explored in the paper

Villa 5

Work Cited

Chopin, Kate. "The Story of an Hour." *The Compact Bedford Introduction to Literature*, edited by Michael Meyer and D. Quentin Miller, 13th ed., Bedford/St. Martin's, 2024, pp. 17–18.

Before beginning your own writing assignment on fiction, you should review Chapter 43, "Writing about Literature," which provides a step-by-step explanation of how to choose a topic, develop a thesis, and organize various types of writing assignments. If you use outside sources, you should also be familiar with the conventional documentation procedures described in Chapter 44, "The Literary Research Paper."

# EXPLORATIONS AND FORMULAS

Each time we pick up a work of fiction, go to the theater, or turn on the television, we have a trace of the same magical expectation that can be heard in the voice of a child who begs, "Tell me a story." Human beings have enjoyed stories ever since they learned to speak. Whatever the motive for creating stories — even if simply to delight or instruct — the basic human impulse to tell and hear stories existed long before the development of written language. Myths about the origins of the world and legends about the heroic exploits of demigods were among the earliest forms of storytelling to develop into oral traditions, which were eventually written down. These narratives are the ancestors of the stories we read on the printed page today. Unlike the early listeners to ancient myths and legends, we tend to read our stories silently, but the pleasure derived from the mysterious power of someone else's artfully arranged words remains largely the same. Every one of us likes a good story.

The stories that appear in anthologies for college students are generally chosen for their high literary quality. Such stories can affect us at the deepest emotional level, reveal new insights into ourselves or the world, and stretch us to exercise our imaginations. They warrant careful reading and close study to appreciate the art that has gone into creating them. The following chapters on plot, character, setting, and the other elements of literature are designed to provide the terms and concepts that can help you understand how a work of fiction achieves its effects and meanings. It is worth acknowledging, however, that many people buy and read fiction that is quite different from the stories usually anthologized in college texts. What about all those paperbacks with exciting, colorful covers near the cash registers in shopping malls and airports?

These books, known as ***formula fiction***, are the adventure, western, mystery, science fiction, horror, and romance novels that entertain millions of readers annually. What makes them so popular? What do their characters, plots, and themes offer readers that accounts for the tremendous sales of stories with titles like *Caves of Doom, My Knight, My Lover, Range Riders,* and *Slay Ride*? Many of the writers included in this book have enjoyed wide popularity and written best-sellers, but there are more readers of formula fiction than there are readers of Virginia Woolf, William Faulkner, or Joyce Carol Oates, to name only a few. Formula novels do provide entertainment, of course, but that makes them no different from serious stories, if entertainment means pleasure. Any of the stories in this or any other anthology can be read for pleasure even as we scrutinize them carefully in the service of interpretation.

Formula fiction, though, is usually characterized as escape literature. There are sensible reasons for this description. Readers who enjoy adventure stories about soldiers of fortune live pretty average lives doing ordinary jobs. Readers who gravitate toward romance novels featuring torrid love affairs can dream themselves out of their humdrum existences. The excitement, violence, and passion that such stories provide are a kind of reprieve from everyday experience.

And yet readers of serious fiction may also use it as a refuge, a liberation from monotony and boredom. Mark Twain's (p. 239) humorous stories have, for example, given countless hours of pleasurable relief to readers who would rather spend time in Twain's light and funny world than in their own. Others might prefer the terror of Edgar Allan Poe's fiction (p. 498) or the poignant rendering of family relationships in Alice Munro's short stories (p. 350).

Thus, to get at some of the differences between formula fiction and serious literature, it is necessary to go beyond the motives of the reader to the motives of the writer and the qualities of the work itself.

Unlike serious fiction, the books displayed next to the cash registers (and their short story equivalents between the covers of magazines) are written with essentially one goal: to be sold. They are aimed at specific consumer markets that can be counted on to buy them. This does not mean that all serious writers must live in cold garrets writing for audiences who have not yet discovered their work. Virtually all writers want readers, and they ought to get paid for their efforts. It does mean, however, that if a writer's primary purpose is to anticipate readers' generic expectations about when the next steamy love scene, bloody gunfight, or thrilling chase is due, there is little room to be original or to have something significant to say. There is little if any chance to explore seriously a character, idea, or incident if the major focus is not on the integrity of the work itself.

Although the specific elements of formula fiction differ depending on the type of story, some basic ingredients go into all westerns, mysteries, adventures, and romances. From the very start, a reader can anticipate a happy ending for the central character, with whom they will identify. There may be suspense, but no matter what or how many the obstacles, complications, or near defeats, the hero or heroine succeeds and reaffirms the values and attitudes the reader brings to the story. Virtue triumphs, love conquers all, honesty is the best policy, and hard work guarantees success. Hence, the villains are corralled, the wedding vows are exchanged, the butler confesses, and gold is discovered at the last moment. The visual equivalents of such formula stories are readily available at movie theaters and in television series. Some are better than others, but all are relatively limited by the writer's goal of giving an audience what will sell.

While formula fiction may not offer many surprises, it provides pleasure to a wide variety of readers. College professors, for example, are just as likely to be charmed by formula stories as anyone else. Readers of serious fiction who revel in exploring unpredictable imaginative worlds can also enjoy formulaic stories, which offer little more than an image of the world as a simple place in which our assumptions and desires are confirmed. The familiarity of a given formula is emotionally satisfying because we are secure in our expectations of it. We know at the start of a Sherlock Holmes story that the mystery will be solved by that famous detective's relentless scientific analysis of the clues, but we enjoy seeing how Holmes unravels the mystery before us. Similarly, we know that James Bond's wit, grace, charm, courage, and skill will ultimately prevail over the diabolic schemes of eccentric villains, but we volunteer for the mission anyway.

Although it is useful to recognize the conventions of genre fiction and to know that they are in place for a certain kind of reader's expectations, there are limitations to any classification system. A novel doesn't have to have dragons and trolls to be considered "high fantasy," for example. The emphasis on plot in adventure novels doesn't mean that they can't also have compelling characters. Also, literary fiction (as we've been calling it) is not necessarily free from conventions, although it might be said that the best literary fiction is comprised of the works that are willing to push those conventions to their limits, or to break them, or at least to reveal a keen awareness of how they provide the framework for a story that is distinctive and important. Literary fiction is an art as well as a craft, and its practitioners experience the freedom that excites artists even if they are somewhat aware of the marketplace that will provide them with readers — and a living.

As you read the following story, "Janus" by Ann Beattie, consider the way it is both like and unlike other stories you have read, perhaps beginning with a comparison to Chopin's "The Story of an Hour" earlier in this chapter.

## ANN BEATTIE (B. 1947)

Ann Beattie published her first novel and first story collection the same year, 1976, to great acclaim. Since then she has produced a steady stream of novels and stories; like other authors in this book (John Cheever and John Updike, for example), many of her stories were published in the *New Yorker*, one of the premier literary magazines. Beattie has been recognized with the Rea Award, which recognizes authors for their significant achievements in the short story genre. She is often associated with a literary movement that flourished in the 1970s and 1980s known as minimalism, a style that portrays the emotionally stark lives of its characters in prose that is straightforward and stripped down, and that maintains a certain narrative distance.

## *Janus*   1986

The bowl was perfect. Perhaps it was not what you'd select if you faced a shelf of bowls, and not the sort of thing that would inevitably attract a lot of attention at a crafts fair, yet it had real presence. It was as predictably admired as a mutt who has no reason to suspect he might be funny. Just such a dog, in fact, was often brought out (and in) along with the bowl.

Andrea was a real estate agent, and when she thought that some prospective buyers might be dog lovers, she would drop off her dog at the same time she placed the bowl in the house that was up for sale. She would put a dish of water in the kitchen for Mondo, take his squeaking plastic frog out of her purse and drop it on the floor. He would pounce delightedly, just as he did every day at home, batting around his favorite toy. The bowl usually sat on a coffee table, though recently she had displayed it on top of a pine blanket chest and on a lacquered table. It was once placed on a cherry table beneath a Bonnard° still life, where it held its own.

Everyone who has purchased a house or who has wanted to sell a house must be familiar with some of the tricks used to convince a buyer that the house is quite special: a fire in the fireplace in early evening; jonquils in a pitcher on the kitchen counter, where no one ordinarily has space to put flowers; perhaps the slight aroma of spring, made by a single drop of scent vaporizing from a lamp bulb.

The wonderful thing about the bowl, Andrea thought, was that it was both subtle and noticeable — a paradox of a bowl. Its glaze was the color of cream and seemed to glow no matter what light it was placed in. There were a few bits of color in it — tiny geometric flashes — and some of these were tinged with flecks of silver. They were as mysterious as cells seen under a microscope; it was difficult not to study them, because they shimmered, flashing for a split second, and then resumed their shape. Something about the colors and their random placement suggested motion. People who liked country furniture always commented on the bowl, but then it turned out that people who felt comfortable with Biedermeier° loved it just as much. But the bowl was not at all ostentatious, or even so noticeable that any-one would suspect that it had been put in place deliberately. They might notice the height of the ceiling on first entering a room, and only when their eye moved down from that, or away from the refraction of sunlight on a pale wall, would they see the bowl. Then they would go immediately to it and comment. Yet they always faltered when they tried to say something. Perhaps it was because they were in the house for a serious reason, not to notice some object.

Once, Andrea got a call from a woman who had not put in an offer on a house ⁵ she had shown her. That bowl, she said — would it be possible to find out where the owners had bought that beautiful bowl? Andrea pretended that she did not know what the woman was referring to. A bowl, somewhere in the house? Oh, on a table under the window. Yes, she would ask, of course. She let a couple of days pass, then called back to say that the bowl had been a present and the people did not know where it had been purchased.

When the bowl was not being taken from house to house, it sat on Andrea's coffee table at home. She didn't keep it carefully wrapped (although she trans-ported it that way, in a box); she kept it on the table, because she liked to see it. It was large enough so that it didn't seem fragile, or particularly vulnerable if anyone sideswiped the table or Mondo blundered into it at play. She had asked her hus-band to please not drop his house key in it. It was meant to be empty.

When her husband first noticed the bowl, he had peered into it and smiled briefly. He always urged her to buy things she liked. In recent years, both of them had acquired many things to make up for all the lean years when they were graduate students, but now that they had been comfortable for quite a while, the pleasure of new possessions dwindled. Her husband had pronounced the bowl "pretty," and he had turned away without picking it up to examine it. He had no more interest in the bowl than she had in his new Leica.°

She was sure that the bowl brought her luck. Bids were often put in on houses where she had displayed the bowl. Sometimes the owners, who were

---

*Bonnard*: Pierre Bonnard, a French painter active in the early to mid-twentieth century.
*Biedermeier*: A style of German furniture design from the mid-nineteenth century; elegant but simple.
*Leica*: An expensive camera.

always asked to be away or to step outside when the house was being shown, didn't even know that the bowl had been in their house. Once — she could not imagine how — she left it behind, and then she was so afraid that something might have happened to it that she rushed back to the house and sighed with relief when the woman owner opened the door. The bowl, Andrea explained — she had purchased a bowl and set it on the chest for safekeeping while she toured the house with the prospective buyers, and she . . . She felt like rushing past the frowning woman and seizing her bowl. The owner stepped aside, and it was only when Andrea ran to the chest that the lady glanced at her a little strangely. In the few seconds before Andrea picked up the bowl, she realized that the owner must have just seen that it had been perfectly placed, that the sunlight struck the bluer part of it. Her pitcher had been moved to the far side of the chest, and the bowl predominated. All the way home, Andrea wondered how she could have left the bowl behind. It was like leaving a friend at an outing — just walking off. Sometimes there were stories in the paper about families forgetting a child somewhere and driving to the next city. Andrea had only gone a mile down the road before she remembered.

In time, she dreamed of the bowl. Twice, in a waking dream — early in the morning, between sleep and a last nap before rising — she had a clear vision of it. It came into sharp focus and startled her for a moment — the same bowl she looked at every day.

She had a very profitable year selling real estate. Word spread, and she had more clients than she felt comfortable with. She had the foolish thought that if only the bowl were an animate object she could thank it. There were times when she wanted to talk to her husband about the bowl. He was a stockbroker, and sometimes told people that he was fortunate to be married to a woman who had such a fine aesthetic sense and yet could also function in the real world. They were a lot alike, really — they had agreed on that. They were both quiet people — reflective, slow to make value judgments, but almost intractable once they had come to a conclusion. They both liked details, but while ironies attracted her, he was more impatient and dismissive when matters became many sided or unclear. But they both knew this; it was the kind of thing they could talk about when they were alone in the car together, coming home from a party or after a weekend with friends. But she never talked to him about the bowl. When they were at dinner, exchanging their news of the day, or while they lay in bed at night listening to the stereo and murmuring sleepy disconnections, she was often tempted to come right out and say that she thought that the bowl in the living room, the cream-colored bowl, was responsible for her success. But she didn't say it. She couldn't begin to explain it. Sometimes in the morning, she would look at him and feel guilty that she had such a constant secret.

Could it be that she had some deeper connection with the bowl — a relationship of some kind? She corrected her thinking: how could she imagine such a thing, when she was a human being and it was a bowl? It was ridiculous. Just think of how people lived together and loved each other . . . But was that always so clear, always a relationship? She was confused by these thoughts, but they remained in her mind. There was something within her now, something real, that she never talked about.

The bowl was a mystery, even to her. It was frustrating, because her involvement with the bowl contained a steady sense of unrequited good fortune; it would have been easier to respond if some sort of demand were made in return. But that only happened in fairy tales. The bowl was just a bowl. She did not believe that for one second. What she believed was that it was something she loved.

In the past, she had sometimes talked to her husband about a new property she was about to buy or sell — confiding some clever strategy she had devised to persuade owners who seemed ready to sell. Now she stopped doing that, for all her strategies involved the bowl. She became more deliberate with the bowl, and more possessive. She put it in houses only when no one was there, and removed it when she left the house. Instead of just moving a pitcher or a dish, she would remove all the other objects from a table. She had to force herself to handle them carefully, because she didn't really care about them. She just wanted them out of sight.

She wondered how the situation would end. As with a lover, there was no exact scenario of how matters would come to a close. Anxiety became the operative force. It would be irrelevant if the lover rushed into someone else's arms, or wrote her a note and departed to another city. The horror was the possibility of the disappearance. That was what mattered.

She would get up at night and look at the bowl. It never occurred to her that 15 she might break it. She washed and dried it without anxiety, and she moved it often, from coffee table to mahogany corner table or wherever, without fearing an accident. It was clear that she would not be the one who would do anything to the bowl. The bowl was only handled by her, set safely on one surface or another; it was not very likely that anyone would break it. A bowl was a poor conductor of electricity: it would not be hit by lightning. Yet the idea of damage persisted. She did not think beyond that — to what her life would be without the bowl. She only continued to fear that some accident would happen. Why not, in a world where people set plants where they did not belong, so that visitors touring a house would be fooled into thinking that dark corners got sunlight — a world full of tricks?

She had first seen the bowl several years earlier, at a crafts fair she had visited half in secret, with her lover. He had urged her to buy the bowl. She didn't *need* any more things, she told him. But she had been drawn to the bowl, and they had lingered near it. Then she went on to the next booth, and he came up behind her, tapping the rim against her shoulder as she ran her fingers over a wood carving. "You're still insisting that I buy that?" she said. "No," he said. "I bought it for you." He had bought her other things before this — things she liked more, at first — the child's ebony-and-turquoise ring that fitted her little finger; the wooden box, long and thin, beautifully dovetailed, that she used to hold paper clips; the soft gray sweater with a pouch pocket. It was his idea that when he could not be there to hold her hand she could hold her own — clasp her hands inside the lone pocket that stretched across the front. But in time she became more attached to the bowl than to any of his other presents. She tried to talk herself out of it. She owned other things that were more striking or valuable. It wasn't an object whose beauty jumped out at you; a lot of people must have passed it by before the two of them saw it that day.

Her lover had said that she was always too slow to know what she really loved. Why continue with her life the way it was? Why be two-faced, he asked her. He had made the first move toward her. When she would not decide in his favor, would not change her life and come to him, he asked her what made her think she could have it both ways. And then he made the last move and left. It was a decision meant to break her will, to shatter her intransigent ideas about honoring previous commitments.

Time passed. Alone in the living room at night, she often looked at the bowl sitting on the table, still and safe, unilluminated. In its way, it was perfect: the world cut in half, deep and smoothly empty. Near the rim, even in dim light, the eye moved toward one small flash of blue, a vanishing point on the horizon.

## CONSIDERATIONS FOR CRITICAL THINKING AND WRITING

1. FIRST RESPONSE. This story is about Andrea, but it spends much of its energy describing the bowl rather than her. Why?

2. In paragraph 11 Andrea begins to wonder about her attachment to the bowl: "Could it be that she had some deeper connection with the bowl — a relationship of some kind?" If you were to describe her connection to it as a human relationship, how would you characterize the relationship? For starters, is it healthy?

3. What are the important characteristics of Andrea's husband (who is never named)?

4. Why is Andrea's profession particularly suitable to her character?

5. The story's title refers to a Roman god who has two faces. Conduct some Internet research to understand how the allusion to Janus might enhance your understanding of the story.

6. How would your reading of the story be different if the title were "The Bowl" rather than "Janus"?

7. In paragraph 6 there is a striking line regarding the bowl: "It was meant to be empty." The very purpose of a bowl is to be filled. How do you understand this line in conjunction with what you take to be the story's theme, or main unstated idea?

8. In a few words, what is your response to Andrea as a person? Point to a sentence or two in the text that explains why you reacted as you did.

## CONNECTIONS TO OTHER SELECTIONS

1. How do this story and Kate Chopin's "The Story of an Hour" (p. 17) both let us into a character's inner life and keep us somewhat distant from it? How is this balance between a character's interior world and exterior world roughly similar in the two stories? Is the effect the same in both?

2. Consider the relationship between people and objects in this story and in Louise Erdrich's story "The Red Convertible" (p. 170). Do the stories have similar attitudes toward the interaction between humans and the things they value?

# 2

# Plot

Ermeni Studio, Milan.
Courtesy of the Ernest
Hemingway Photographic
Collection, John Fitzgerald
Kennedy Library, Boston.

Never mistake motion for action.
— ERNEST HEMINGWAY

Created by a writer's imagination, a work of fiction need not be factual or historically accurate. Although actual people, places, and events may be included in fiction, facts are not as important as is the writer's use of them. We can learn much about Russian life in the early part of the nineteenth century from Leo Tolstoy's *War and Peace* (1867), but that historical information is secondary to Tolstoy's exploration of human nature. Tolstoy, like most successful writers, makes us accept as real the world in his novel no matter how foreign it may be to our own reality. One of the ways a writer achieves this acceptance and engagement — and one of a writer's few obligations — is to interest us in what is happening in the story. We are carried into the writer's fictional world by the plot.

    ***Plot*** is the author's arrangement of incidents in a story. It is the organizing principle that controls the order of events. This structure is, in a sense, what remains after a writer edits out what is irrelevant to the story being told. We don't need to know, for example, what Sonny had for breakfast on the morning of the opening action of James Baldwin's powerful story "Sonny's Blues"

32

(p. 91). Instead, what is told takes on meaning as it is brought into focus by a skillful writer who selects and orders the events that constitute the story's plot.

Events can be presented in a variety of orders. A chronological arrangement begins with what happens first, then second, and so on, until the last incident is related. That is how Shirley Jackson's "The Lottery" (p. 233), is told. The events in William Faulkner's "A Rose for Emily" (p. 47), however, are not arranged in chronological order because that would give away the story's surprise ending; instead, Faulkner moves back and forth between the past and present to provide information that leads up to the final startling moment (which won't be given away here either).

Some stories begin at the end and then lead up to why or how events worked out as they did. Stories can also begin in the middle of things (the Latin term for this common plot strategy is *in medias res*). In this kind of plot we enter the story on the verge of some important moment. John Updike's "A & P" (p. 145) begins with the narrator, a teenager working at a checkout counter in a supermarket, telling us: "In walks these three girls in nothing but bathing suits." Right away we are brought into the middle of a situation that will ultimately create the conflict in the story, though the true conflict had been simmering before the girls walk in.

Another common strategy is the *flashback*, a device that informs us about events that happened before the opening scene of a work. Baldwin's "Sonny's Blues" (p. 91) begins with news of the character Sonny's arrest, but much of the rest of the story returns to incidents earlier in his life that might have changed the way the narrator (and the reader) respond to that arrest. Whatever the plot arrangement, you should be aware of how the writer's conscious ordering of events affects your responses to the action.

A great many stories share a standard plot pattern that might best be described as cause and effect. Even stories that rely heavily on very detailed plots leave out as much as they include. Incidents or episodes in stories are significant because the author has chosen to include them and thus emphasize their potential meaning, but plot does not mean "everything that happened." Authors tend to write in episodes, or scenes (similar to plays), and the reader must either mentally fill in the details of what happens between the scenes, or assume that they don't matter to the plot. The following short story, "The Hit Man," is a darkly humorous attempt to tell the story of a character's entire life through a series of incidents, complete with section titles for those incidents. In one sense, this story is all about character, but he is a character type whose only function, as the title suggests, is to assassinate people.

## T. C. Boyle (b. 1948)

### *The Hit Man*    1977

**Early Years**

The Hit Man's early years are complicated by the black bag that he wears over his head. Teachers correct his pronunciation, the coach criticizes his attitude, the principal dresses him down for branding preschoolers with a lit cigarette. He is a poor student. At lunch he sits alone, feeding bell peppers and salami into the dark slot of his mouth. In the hallways, wiry young athletes snatch at the black hood and slap the back of his head. When he is thirteen he is approached by the captain of the football team, who pins him down and attempts to remove the hood. The Hit Man wastes him. Five years, says the judge.

### Back on the Street

The Hit Man is back on the street in two months.

### First Date

The girl's name is Cynthia. The Hit Man pulls up in front of her apartment in his father's hearse. (The Hit Man's father, whom he loathes and abominates, is a mortician. At breakfast the Hit Man's father had slapped the cornflakes from his son's bowl. The son threatened to waste his father. He did not, restrained no doubt by considerations of filial loyalty and the deep-seated taboos against patricide that permeate the universal unconscious.)

Cynthia's father has silver sideburns and plays tennis. He responds to the Hit Man's knock, expresses surprise at the Hit Man's appearance. The Hit Man takes Cynthia by the elbow, presses a twenty into her father's palm, and disappears into the night.

### Father's Death

At breakfast the Hit Man slaps the cornflakes from his father's bowl. Then 5 wastes him.

### Mother's Death

The Hit Man is in his early twenties. He shoots pool, lifts weights, and drinks milk from the carton. His mother is in the hospital, dying of cancer or heart disease. The priest wears black. So does the Hit Man.

### First Job

Porfirio Buñoz, a Cuban financier, invites the Hit Man to lunch. I hear you're looking for work, says Buñoz.

That's right, says the Hit Man.

### Peas

The Hit Man does not like peas. They are too difficult to balance on the fork.

### Talk Show

The Hit Man waits in the wings, the white slash of a cigarette scarring the mid- 10 night black of his head and upper torso. The makeup girl has done his mouth and eyes, brushed the nap of his hood. He has been briefed. The guest who precedes him is a pediatrician. A planetary glow washes the stage where the host and the pediatrician, separated by a potted palm, cross their legs and discuss the little disturbances of infants and toddlers.

After the station break the Hit Man finds himself squeezed into a director's chair, white lights in his eyes. The talk-show host is a baby-faced man in his early forties. He smiles like God and all His Angels. Well, he says. So you're a hit man. Tell me — I've always wanted to know — what does it feel like to hit someone?

## Death of Mateo María Buñoz

The body of Mateo María Buñoz, the cousin and business associate of a prominent financier, is discovered down by the docks on a hot summer morning. Mist rises from the water like steam, there is the smell of fish. A large black bird perches on the dead man's forehead.

## Marriage

Cynthia and the Hit Man stand at the altar, side by side. She is wearing a white satin gown and lace veil. The Hit Man has rented a tuxedo, extra-large, and a silk-lined black-velvet hood.

. . . Till death do you part, says the priest.

## Moods

The Hit Man is moody, unpredictable. Once, in a luncheonette, the waitress     15
brought him the meatloaf special but forgot to eliminate the peas. There was a spot of gravy on the Hit Man's hood, about where his chin should be. He looked up at the waitress, his eyes like pins behind the triangular slots, and wasted her.

Another time he went to the track with $25, came back with $1,800. He stopped at a cigar shop. As he stepped out of the shop a wino tugged at his sleeve and solicited a quarter. The Hit Man reached into his pocket, extracted the $1,800 and handed it to the wino. Then wasted him.

## First Child

A boy. The Hit Man is delighted. He leans over the edge of the playpen and molds the tiny fingers around the grip of a nickel-plated derringer. The gun is loaded with blanks — the Hit Man wants the boy to get used to the noise. By the time he is four the boy has mastered the rudiments of Tae Kwon Do, can stick a knife in the wall from a distance of ten feet and shoot a moving target with either hand. The Hit Man rests his broad palm on the boy's head. You're going to make the Big Leagues, Tiger, he says.

## Work

He flies to Cincinnati. To L.A. To Boston. To London. The stewardesses get to know him.

## Half an Acre and a Garage

The Hit Man is raking leaves, amassing great brittle piles of them. He is wearing a black T-shirt, cut off at the shoulders, and a cotton work hood, also black. Cynthia is edging the flower bed, his son playing in the grass. The Hit Man waves to his neighbors as they drive by. The neighbors wave back.

When he has scoured the lawn to his satisfaction, the Hit Man draws the 20 smaller leaf-hummocks together in a single mound the size of a pickup truck. Then he bends to ignite it with his lighter. Immediately, flames leap back from the leaves, cut channels through the pile, engulf it in a ball of fire. The Hit Man stands back, hands folded beneath the great meaty biceps. At his side is the three-headed dog. He bends to pat each of the heads, smoke and sparks raging against the sky.

## Stalking the Streets of the City

He is stalking the streets of the city, collar up, brim down. It is late at night. He stalks past department stores, small businesses, parks, and gas stations. Past apartments, picket fences, picture windows. Dogs growl in the shadows, then slink away. He could hit any of us.

## Retirement

A group of businessman-types — sixtyish, seventyish, portly, diamond rings, cigars, liver spots — throws him a party. Porfirio Buñoz, now in his eighties, makes a speech and presents the Hit Man with a gilded scythe. The Hit Man thanks him, then retires to the lake, where he can be seen in his speedboat, skating out over the blue, hood rippling in the breeze.

## Death

He is stricken, shrunken, half his former self. He lies propped against the pillows at Mercy Hospital, a bank of gentians drooping round the bed. Tubes run into the hood at the nostril openings, his eyes are clouded and red, sunk deep behind the triangular slots. The priest wears black. So does the Hit Man.

On the other side of town the Hit Man's son is standing before the mirror of a shop that specializes in Hit Man attire. Trying on his first hood.

This story begins with **exposition**, the background information the reader needs to make sense of the situation in which the characters are placed. Like everything in the story, the intent is parody: we learn that the Hit Man had a "complicated" childhood because, like an executioner, he wore a black hood on his head, but Boyle thwarts our desire to know *why* he wore the hood. The fact of the hood is the salient detail that separates the main character from everyone else, and it may even be read as a **symbol** of that difference and alienation, but the point is that the reader has to accept that detail in order to move on. The poet Samuel Taylor Coleridge in 1817 spoke of the "willing suspension of disbelief": a reader has to be somewhat willing to go along with what a writer posits even if the writer pushes the boundaries of plausibility. Other details in the first paragraph seem less important than the black hood: why are we told that the Hit Man's lunch consisted of bell peppers and salami? If we dismiss that detail as insignificant, we are also likely to dismiss the detail later in the story that he doesn't like peas . . . but the story forces us to reconsider that dismissal a few paragraphs later when he murders a waitress for bringing him peas.

Once this exposition supplies a context for the main character's difference, the plot gains momentum with the **rising action**, a complication that intensifies the situation: the Hit Man, having more or less gotten away with murder in high school, determines that there are no consequences for his actions, so he continues to kill at will. We might assume that the main plot points of the rest of the story occur every time he "wastes" someone, but these moments gradually vanish. We are told that he flies to various cities for work, but we don't actually see him doing his work in those places: he might as well be a travelling salesman by that point in the story. In fact, many of what we might consider to be the details we most want to hear — like *how* does he "waste" people? — are omitted. Even his first lunch meeting to arrange his first professional "hit" is far from complete: his future boss says, "I hear you're looking for work," and he replies, "That's right." That's it.

All stories must have a **conflict**, or a problem that must be addressed if not solved. This story makes us work a bit to identify the conflict. Since the murders are described in a matter-of-fact way, it could be said that the conflict is not in the episodes when the Hit Man kills someone, but in the difference between those and the episodes when he courts his future wife, or gets married, or is delighted by the birth of his child, or rakes leaves in his yard. These sound like the details of a very common, boring middle-class life, difficult to reconcile with the fact that our **protagonist** or **hero** is a cold-blooded killer. (*Protagonist* is often a better term for the central character of a story than *hero* or **heroine** because heroism is also associated with positive moral behavior: Can a man who mows down his father, a waitress who serves him peas, and a wino be considered heroic?)

Related to the *conflict*, then, is often an **antagonist**, a character who represents a force that opposes the protagonist. Just as we are not told why the Hit Man wears a black hood, we are not told why he "loathes and abominates" his father, but we should also notice that he doesn't seem to have any emotions whatsoever toward his other victims. We know little about his father except that he is a mortician who drives a hearse, and that he behaves violently toward his son. The conflict between fathers and sons is a familiar one, and in this case it is briefly complicated by the protagonist's sense of morality: he doesn't want to kill his father because of "filial loyalty and the deep-seated taboos against patricide that permeate the universal unconscious." A writer who was not trafficking in dark humor would perhaps use the tension between a murderous urge and moral restraint to create **suspense**: over time there might be a series of episodes that make the Hit Man feel ever more conflicted about what to do with his negative feelings. In this story, though, Boyle deprives us of the pleasures of suspense: impulsively, the Hit Man "wastes" his father. The author gives us all of the elements of plot in a very short space: the *conflict* between the Hit Man and his father reaches an immediate **climax** when he slaps the cornflakes out of his father's bowl just as his father had done to him, and it reaches a seeming **resolution** when he then sends his father to the great beyond.

Is that true, though? Generally, the arc of a story builds to a *resolution* that occurs toward the story's end. The *resolution* is a dramatic moment that addresses if not fully resolves the conflict. In most stories, the resolution is followed by a *dénouement* (a French word meaning the "untying of the knot"), which is sometimes referred to as the *falling action* or, in tragedy, catastrophe. The *dénouement* promises to clear up all the mysteries of the story, but that doesn't happen here, not if we are only looking at plot. If we look at it another way, the Hit Man's father's sudden and unremarkable death can be seen as a suggestion of what's to come, also known as *foreshadowing*, in this case of the protagonist's sudden and unremarkable death at the story's conclusion.

In a story this playful in terms of *plot* — meaning the selection, development, and arrangement of significant episodes — we might have to reframe what the conflict actually is. We know that the protagonist is the Hit Man — there aren't any other candidates — and that the antagonist must be his father, the only person toward whom he shows any emotion. There is the mystery about why he wears a black hood that seems to simply be a fact we must accept, but consider that his father was a mortician who drove a hearse. The Hit Man's executioner's hood and executioner's behavior suggests that he is, on some level, just like his father. This connection is reinforced when he slaps his father's cereal bowl just like his father had done to him. It could be said that the story is about the way sons have no choice but to repeat their fathers' behaviors, even if they hate their fathers. Looking at the story this way, the true *conflict* is not what we do with negative emotions, but whether or not we have control over our destiny. When the Hit Man's son is born, he is "delighted" and does what every good father would do: he hands his infant boy a gun and wraps his tiny fingers around its grip. That moment could properly be identified as the *climax*. When the boy tries on his first Hit Man hood at the end of the story, we should not be surprised. The story tells us that we can't control our destiny, that we are doomed to repeat the sins of our parents. The absurd plot is merely a structure for that *theme*. The story is funny, but its intent is dead serious.

Although the classic pattern of exposition, rising action, conflict, suspense, climax, and resolution provides a useful outline of many plots that emphasize physical action, a greater value of this pattern is that it helps us to see how innovative artists move beyond formula fiction by manipulating and changing the pattern for their own purposes. At the furthest extreme are those modern storytellers like Boyle who reject or manipulate traditional plotting techniques in favor of experimental approaches. Instead of including fully developed characters who wrestle with conflicts, experimental fiction frequently may remove traditional identity markers: note that "the Hit Man" doesn't have a name. Rather than ordering experience, such writers disrupt it by insisting that meanings in fiction are as elusive — or nonexistent — as meanings in life; they are likely to question both traditional values and traditional forms of writing. More traditional writers, however, use conflicts in their plots to reveal characters and convey meanings. The nature of those conflicts can help determine how important physical action is to the plot.

The primary conflict the Hit Man experiences in his interactions with society is external. External conflicts may place the protagonist in opposition to another individual, nature, or society. The Hit Man's battle with societal values begins the moment he wears his executioner's hood to school and faces pressure to conform. He will learn that an individual's conflict with society can be as frustrating as it is complex, which is why so many plots in serious fiction focus on this conflict. It can be seen, to cite only two examples, in a repressive society's insistence on absolute control in Ursula K. Le Guin's "The Ones Who Walk Away from Omelas" (p. 121) and in the need for a young man to play jazz music despite his brother's demands for a more stable career path in James Baldwin's "Sonny's Blues" (p. 91).

Conflict may also be internal; in such a case, some moral or psychological issue must be resolved within the protagonist. Inner conflicts frequently accompany external ones, as in Manuel Muñoz's "Zigzagger" (p. 152). The conflict, though puzzling, is more significant in "Zigzagger" because that story subtly explores some troubling issues that cannot be resolved simply through action. The protagonist struggles with both internal and external forces. His parents and friends know he is sick and try to cure him with typical remedies, but they are unaware of (as is the reader, initially) what caused the sickness. It is only through telling the story through multiple points of view with significant flashbacks that the internal and external conflicts can be resolved. Muñoz creates questions for the reader rather than suspense. We are compelled to keep asking why the protagonist in his story is ill instead of what is going to happen next. The meaning of the action is not self-evident as it would be in a conventionally arranged story in which plot follows chronology. Instead, meaning must be drawn from a careful reading of the interrelated details and dialogues that constitute this story's action.

"The Hit Man" plays with plot conventions partly to amuse the reader who might be expecting something different, but partly to lull us into thinking that the story is only meant to delight; then it offers the possibility that it has an important instructional function as well. This kind of reading is more demanding, but ultimately more satisfying, because as we confront conflicts in serious fiction we read not only absorbing stories but also ourselves. We are invited not to escape life but to look long and hard at it. Although serious fiction can be as diverting and pleasurable as most standard action-packed plots, serious fiction offers an additional important element: a perspective on experience that reflects rather than deflects life.

The following three stories — Joy Harjo's "The Reckoning," William Faulkner's "A Rose for Emily," and Andre Dubus's "Killings" — are remarkable for the different kinds of tension produced in each by a subtle use of plot.

# JOY HARJO (B. 1951)

Joy Harjo is the first Native American to hold the title of U.S. Poet Laureate. Although she is known primarily as a poet — and her poems are represented later in this volume — she has never been tied to any one literary genre. In addition to fiction like the story included here, she has authored children's literature, nonfiction, and drama in addition to her many prize-winning volumes of poetry. She has also

Carlo Allegri/Getty Images.

recorded a significant amount of music. After earning her undergraduate degree from the University of New Mexico and her Masters of Fine Arts from the University of Iowa, she has had a long and varied academic career. She is also a political activist for Native American causes as well as for the rights of all oppressed people.

## The Reckoning   2002

Everyone has their own version of the world I tell myself as I wait on the Central Avenue sidewalk while Larry disappears behind the Starlight Motel to take a piss. The vacancy sign flashes on and off. Closing hour traffic jams the street. I imagine everyone taking off for the forty-nine,° squeezed into cars and pickups with cases of beer under their legs heading in a caravan to the all-night sing on West Mesa. Each direction is a world and each world has its own set of rules, its own hierarchy of gods and demigods, its own particular color. I am painting a series based on the four directions, but I am stalled. It has been months since I've painted.

When I was five my mother began standing me on a chair to wash dishes after dinner because I couldn't otherwise reach. The front of my dress was usually soaked when I finished. "Don't get your dress wet like that; it means you'll marry a drunk." Yet night after night after dinner she would drag a chair to the sink and my dress would soak no matter my efforts otherwise. Every morning I wake up with a hangover after trying to keep up with Larry I remember the wet stomach of my dress. I then promise I will let him go. I know I cannot save him, but to let him go feels unbearable.

This morning Larry mentioned that his cousin was coming into town from California and wanted to have dinner before heading out to the pueblo. Would I like to go to Alonzo's for pizza with them? A wedge of tension cut the air between us. I tried to ignore it. Last night he said he was going to quit drinking again and Alonzo's is one of his favorite bars. I watched as he fried the bacon and stirred the eggs, as he placed them in a perfect arrangement on our plates. He cooked as deftly as he honed out an argument or turned a piece of silver into the wind. I poured Joe Junior a glass of milk and wrapped a sandwich for his lunch. He fidgeted, running his Hot Wheels cars up and down his chair, across the table, faster and faster in response to the tension. "Stop it!" I yelled, surprised at the vehemence in my voice. He put his head down on the table and began slowly kicking the table leg. I told myself then that I could use a break.

That night after cleaning the house and walking guiltily by my easel I took Joe Junior to the babysitter. He liked going to Larry's sister's house because she had twin boys his age so I didn't mind leaving him for the night. When I handed him over with his pack of clothes, toys and snacks I hugged him close, savoring his freshly shampooed hair. I felt bad for yelling at him this morning. He saw the twins peeking around the corner and wriggled free. Larry's sister was roasting chile and had just pulled out of the oven a fresh batch of those little fruit pies her people make. She offered me some.

"And take some for Larry, too," she said. When she said her brother's name 5 worry flickered across her forehead. I was worried too, but to entertain all the

*Forty-nine:* A Native social dance.

reasons would cause an avalanche. I would prefer to stay here with Joe Junior in Larry's sister's warm house, to wash dishes and set the table and visit, but the zig-zag of anxiety went way back, over tortuous territory. If I followed the source it would slam me back into childhood, to my father staggering in drunk, beating my mother, the shame and hate in him burning, burning. Then he'd hit my brothers. And then me whom it was said he loved most. He'd save me for last, when his anger was ashes, when the fire was hottest. And then he'd hold me, "Sugar, Sugar" he'd croon, the tears so thick they made a lake on the linoleum floor.

There is a world of mist in which my father now lives. It is beyond the Milky Way, but it is also as close as my voice to your ear. I have often seen my father in the middle of the night when I am painting. Or when I have tucked his grandson in after he has fallen asleep. He is just the other side of the spin, the same fre-quency as moonlight. He's held here by disappointment, by the need to speak. He tells me he loves me and asks if I will forgive him. I do not say anything. "You're a dreamer," my mother says when I tell her, "just like your father. And you won't ever get it together until you decide to deal with the real world." She is an elected tribal official and she teaches Sunday school every week. She has a mission in her small world. She wants to make sure there are rules and that they are enforced.

The first time Larry hit me was on a Saturday night like this one. We hadn't been together long. We were still amazed we had found each other. We were partying away not at Alonzo's, but at the Feathered Dancer on the other side of town. He was talking politics with his buddies while I played pool with my best friend Jolene and some other students in the backroom. I kept feeding the jukebox with quarters, playing the Rolling Stones, "wild horses couldn't drag me away" over and over again. He was down about the anniversary of the death of his best friend a few years ago. That should have been a warning to me. This man had been his idol. He had been the only man from his pueblo° to finish law school and he fought the U.S. legal system by any means possible, including his fists. But he couldn't fight alcohol. He was taken down by drink, his body found in a field weeks after his death. His grieving brothers were honoring him by drinking to oblivion and they were getting rowdy. I tried to ignore them and kept shooting the solids into the pockets, just as I had ignored my father when he and his friends partied, argued and played. I knew the routine. There was a high and then there was a low.

Every small hair on my neck was on alert. "Fuck you," I heard Larry yell. We ran in from the pool tables to see what was the matter. Larry aimed a pitcher of beer at his cousin Leno's head. It missed and smashed into the bar mirror. There was a terrible crash. We all scattered as the bartender called the police. Larry refused to go; instead, he decided to climb the fence to the roof of the bar. Leno and I tried to stop him. He punched me and I went down. He climbed to the roof and jumped, then stood up like a defiant child, without a scratch, and walked away, the sound of approaching sirens growing loud and shrill.

I should have left him then, instead I caught a ride back with Jolene who tried to convince me to stay at her place. "No, I want to get the sad good-bye over with," I told her. The next morning he apologized profusely. This will never happen again, he promised as he made us breakfast of his specialty: chorizo and eggs. He came back from the 7-Eleven with a newspaper and a bouquet of wilted flowers. I told him to pack his bags, to get out.

*Pueblo:* A Native American village in the Southwest United States.

"No," he said. "How can we make a better world for the people if we cannot ₁₀ hold it together in our own house?"

I convinced myself that we owed it to ourselves to keep trying. I found excuses. He was taken over by grief for his buddy, I told myself. And most of the time he wasn't like that, I reasoned. I took him back.

The next few weeks were tender and raw. Carefully he planted a garden in the small yard behind the apartment with my son. He worked obsessively. He held fire in his hands and he crafted a bracelet to bridge the hole in our universe. I believed he didn't mean to lose control. I believed that he loved me.

"So did your father," Jolene reminded me. "You've gone and married your father."

"I haven't married him yet. I will never get married again," I laughed.

I didn't want to hear her and after that I talked to Jolene only when I had to, ₁₅ at rallies, at Indian center meetings. She was a distant reminder of prickly truth, a predictor of trouble. I watched her disappear on the horizon as I turned to tend to my shaky world. When he asked me to marry him, I said yes.

We were nervous the day we headed up to Santa Fe in a borrowed car to get married. I had never planned to marry anyone and this would be my second. The first had been to Joe Junior's father. Larry had gotten grief from his parents for shacking up with a girl who wasn't from his tribe. Marriage would make me one step closer to acceptable.

It was a perfect spring day as we headed north. Joe Junior stayed at Larry's sister's place and was excited about getting to help make the wedding cake. A small reception was planned for the next day. We'd just passed the city limits when the Ranchero Bar came into view, poised on the reservation line. All the windows were painted and broken glass mixed with gravel in the parking lot. Larry pulled the car over and parked. "Let's go in, just for a beer," he said. "To celebrate." It had been a few months since he had stopped drinking, after the punching incident. He already had enough jewelry for a show and had attracted a dealer who talked New York and Europe markets. We had been happy.

"No. You can't drink."

"One drink will not hurt me, or you either," he said as he opened his door. "We have a lot to celebrate."

"Okay, you promised," I reminded him. ₂₀

"I promise," he said.

One beer turned into a pitcher because these were his brothers, he announced eloquently to the bar. The pueblo farm workers sitting around him smiled at me and nodded their heads. "It's time to go," I urged him under my breath, all the while smiling at his new friends.

"I can't turn down a drink because I would offend them," he whispered to me, looking at me sharply because I should know better. Obviously he wasn't afraid of offending me.

I sipped my beer and felt my heart sag in disbelief. This was my wedding day. If I had another drink I wouldn't hear the voice telling me to get out, to get out now. I poured myself another beer from the pitcher, matching Larry drink for drink to the delight of Larry's new friends. The day stumbled into oblivion. I have a faint memory of dancing a ranchera in front of the jukebox with a cowboy, and of a hippie girl coming into the bar and sitting on Larry's lap. "It's part of my job," he told me once after I had yanked a blonde girl off him and demanded he come home with me. He had pocketed the girl's phone number as he slid off the stool and followed me. He had a reason for everything.

We didn't make it to Santa Fe to get married. I tore up the marriage license     25
and tossed it like confetti over him and his drinking partners, confirming that I
wasn't the kind of girl his pueblo parents wanted for his wife. His mother would
never embarrass his father in that manner no matter what he did to her. I left
him with the borrowed car and hitchhiked back. I called Larry's sister and told
her the wedding was off and I'd pick up Joe Junior tomorrow when I could pull
myself together. I could not think; I could not paint. I looked up the Women's
Center in the student directory. What would I say to them? Do you have a crisis
center for idiots? I missed Jolene and my friends, but I had too much pride to
call them now. I dialed my mother's number and hung up. She would just say,
"I told you so."

It is now two thirty in the morning and the avenue is quiet. Larry should have
been back by now. The small desk light in the motel office makes me feel lonely.
I feel far away from everything. There's that ache under my ribs that's like radar. It
tells me that I am miles away from the world I intended to make for my son and
me. I imagine my easel set up in the corner of the living room in our apartment,
next to Joe Junior's box of toys. I imagine my little boy asleep in my arms. I imagine
having the money to walk up to the motel office to rent a room of my own. I know
what I would do.

First I would sleep until I could sleep no more. Then I would dream. I fly to
the first world of my mother and father, locate them as a young married couple
just after the war, living with my father's mother, in her small house in Sapulpa.
I am a baby in my mother's arms, cooing and kicking my legs. Then I am a girl on
my father's shoulders as he spins and dances me through the house drunk on beer
stolen from the bootlegger. I hold on tight. I hear my mother tell him to be careful,
let me down. We are all laughing. He spins until I am in high school and I have
won the art award. Then I am a teenage mother. "A new little Sugar," he says as he
holds his grandson and sings to him. Then I am standing with my mother at my
grandmother's funeral; singing those sad Creek hymns that lead her spirit to the
Milky Way. My father can't be found in time for the funeral. Then he's next. The
centrifugal force of memory keeps moving through the sky, slowly sifting lies from
the shining truth.

My mother told me that if you go to sleep laughing you will wake up to tears.
My father's mother told me that to predict the shape of the end of something take a
hard look at the beginning.

"I'm not interested in marriage or finding yet another man to break my heart,"
I remember telling my friend Jolene as we stood in the heat in front of the student
union the day I met Larry. The tech people were making racket while they set up
the microphones and tables for the press conference. I had just gotten over Joe
Junior's father. He left me before the baby was born, even took the junk car, drove
off dragging it behind his cousin's truck to his mother's house in Talihina.

"Well, there are always women," she said nodding toward a table that had     30
been set up by the Women's Resource Center. They were passing out information on their services. I walked by the Women's Center every day on my way to
work at the Indian Center after classes. Once I stopped to visit on my way to an
organizational meeting. I had heard a speaker from their center address students on the mall about women's rights and it occurred to me that our centers
could link up in an action. But the day I walked in with my son in hand I got
the distinct feeling that Indian women with children weren't too welcome. I had
never gone back.

"Women would certainly open up our options," I agreed with Jolene and we laughed. We thought it was funny, but we agreed that as women we spent most of our time with each other, took classes together and cried on each others' shoulders in the shifting dance of creation and destruction.

It was a fine-looking contingent from the National Council on Indian Rights who made their way to the makeshift stage. They were modern-age warriors dressed with the intent of justice in their sunglasses and long black hair. "There is my future," I said lightly and nodded to the Pueblo man whose hair was pulled back in a sleek ponytail. I watched as he balanced his coffee and unclasped his shoulder bag of papers. He felt familiar at the level of blood cells and bones though I didn't know him. I had heard him holding forth before at meetings and had seen him in passing on campus.

"Who is he?" Jolene knew everyone because her father was a name in local Indian politics.

"His name is Larry. He's an artist," she said, "a fine artist. He makes jewelry. Be careful. Women love him and are always chasing him." I could see why and I could not stop watching him as he read the press release demanding justice and detailing how it could occur. He was as beautifully drawn as he was smart.

As we stood in the hot sun listening to the prepared statements I was suddenly 35 aware of the fragility of life, how immensely precious was each breath. We all mattered — even our small core fighting for justice despite all odds. And then the press conference was over. That day would become one of those memories that surfaced at major transitional points like giving birth and dying. I would feel the sun on my shoulders, hear the scratch of the cheap sound system and feel emotional. I would recall a small Navajo girl in diapers learning how to walk, her arms outstretched to her father. I would remember picking up my son at the daycare across campus, his bright yellow lunchbox shaped like a school bus.

That night at the impromptu party after the strategy meeting I watched from the doorway of the kitchen of Jolene's cousin's apartment as Larry easily rolled a cigarette with his hands. His hands were warm sienna and snapped with the energy of his quick mind, his ability to shape metal. He lit a cigarette and blew smoke with his perfect lips in my direction. The lazy lasso hung in the air between us. I passed him a beer as I was the end of a brigade passing out beer from the cooler in the kitchen.

"So who are you, Skinny Girl?" I kept passing and throwing beer to the rest of the party as he talked, pretending to ignore him.

"You must be one of those Oklahoma Indians," he said. I had been warned that he was used to getting what he wanted when it came to women.

"Come on over here and sit next to me, next to an Indian who is still the real thing." I considered hitting him with a beer for that remark. These local Indians could be short-sighted in their world.

"Why would I want to?" I retorted. "Besides, you look Mexican to me." His 40 eyebrows flew up. His identity had never been challenged, especially by a woman he was interested in.

"We're full-bloods. We haven't lost our ways."

"And what does that mean? That my people have?" I questioned. "Then why do you have a Spanish last name?" Of course I knew the history but he had pissed me off, still I couldn't help but notice his long eyelashes that cast shadows on his cheeks. I caught the last beer and opened it, stood close enough for his smell to alert my heart.

"All tribes traveled, took captives and were taken captive." I emphasized "captive" and leaned in to take a puff on the cigarette he offered me. Jolene waltzed over and grabbed my arm, dancing me to the living room in time to the music in order to save me. I didn't talk to him again until I headed out the door with my ride, two other first-year students. We were buzzed on smoke and flying sweetly.

"Hey girl," he shouted from the corner as I reluctantly made my escape. "I'm going to get you yet."

It happened quickly. When I got home that night there was a message that my father had died. Joe Junior and I left for a week. When we returned Larry met us at the bus station with flowers and toys. He took us for breakfast at the Chuck-wagon and then we went home together. It wasn't long after my father's death that I dreamed a daughter who wanted to be born. I had been painting all night when she appeared to me. She was a baby with fat cheeks and then she was a grown woman, with a presence as familiar as my father's mother. She asked me to give birth to her. I was in the middle of finals and planning for a protest of the killing of Navajo street drunks by white high school students on weekends for fun. They had just been questioned and set free with no punishment. 45

"This is not a good time," I said. "And why come into this kind of world?" Funny, I don't remember her answer but her intent was a fine unwavering line that connected my heart to hers.

I walk behind the motel to look for Larry. He isn't anywhere, but I find his shoes under a tree where he has taken them off. And ahead of them, like two dark salamanders, are his socks. A little farther beyond is his belt, and then a trail of pants, shirt and underwear until I am standing in the courtyard of the motel. My stomach turns and twists as I consider, all the scenarios a naked and drunk Indian man might get into in a motel on the main street of the city.

I hear a splash in the pool. He's a Pueblo; he can't swim. I consider leaving him there to his fate. It would be his own foolish fault, as well as the fault of a society that builds its cities over our holy places. At this moment his disappearance would be a sudden relief. Strange that it is now that I first feel our daughter moving within me. She awakens me with a flutter, a kick. I don't know whether to laugh or cry. I never told Larry about the night she showed up to announce her intention, or how I saw her spirit when she was conceived wavering above us on a fine sheen of light. Behind her my father was waving good-bye. The weave pulled tighter and tighter, it opened and then he was gone.

## CONSIDERATIONS FOR CRITICAL THINKING AND WRITING

1. FIRST RESPONSE. The story begins in the middle of things (*in medias res*), but it also ends in the middle of things. What happens immediately after? Does the narrator help Larry (who cannot swim) or not? What informs your answer?

2. The story moves back and forth across time, causing the reader to work hard to reconstruct the plot chronologically. If you were to reduce the story to five key episodes in chronological order, what would they be? What about eight key episodes?

3. The narrator's paternal grandmother tells her, "to predict the shape of the end of something take a hard look at the beginning" (par. 28). How might this wisdom provide a key to reading the story?

4. What is the relationship between the narrator's ill-fated love affair with Larry and their connected roles as activists and artists?

5. The narrator reveals an important detail in the final paragraph. How would the story's effect have been different if she had revealed it in the opening paragraph?

### CONNECTIONS TO OTHER SELECTIONS

1. Another objectively bad relationship is detailed in Zora Neale Hurston's "Sweat" (p. 475). How does it compare to this one?

2. Write an essay comparing the ending of Harjo's story with that of Alice Walker's "The Flowers" (p. 507). What is the effect of the ending on your reading of each story?

## WILLIAM FAULKNER (1897–1962)

Born into an old Mississippi family that had lost its influence and wealth during the Civil War, William Faulkner lived nearly all his life in the South writing about Yoknapatawpha County, an imagined Mississippi county similar to his home in Oxford. Among his novels based on this fictional location are *The Sound and the Fury* (1929), *As I Lay Dying* (1930), *Light in August* (1932), and *Absalom, Absalom!* (1936). Although his writings are regional in their emphasis on local social history, his concerns are broader. In his 1950 acceptance speech for the Nobel Prize for Literature, he insisted that the "problems

Cofield Collection, Archives and Special Collections, University of Mississippi Libraries.

of the human heart in conflict with itself . . . alone can make good writing because only that is worth writing about, worth the agony and the sweat." This commitment is evident in his novels and in *The Collected Stories of William Faulkner* (1950). "A Rose for Emily," about the mysterious life of Emily Grierson, presents a personal conflict rooted in her southern identity. It also contains a grim surprise.

**A Note on the Text:** This story contains a harmful and offensive racial epithet. As discussed in "Approaching Sensitive Subjects" (p. 7), it is important to be aware of context when encountering difficult content. As you read, consider that Faulkner lived in and wrote about the South, an area of the United States that has a long history of fraught race relationships. This story is set in a period of time when the Jim Crow laws were in effect, the South was racially segregated, and racism was often explicit. Additionally, it was written prior to the civil rights movement. While this does not excuse Faulkner's use of the word, it may help you as you encounter it in this story.

## A Rose for Emily    1931

### I

When Miss Emily Grierson died, our whole town went to her funeral: the men through a sort of respectful affection for a fallen monument, the women mostly out of curiosity to see the inside of her house, which no one save an old manservant — a combined gardener and cook — had seen in at least ten years.

It was a big, squarish frame house that had once been white, decorated with cupolas and spires and scrolled balconies in the heavily lightsome style of the seventies, set on what had once been our most select street. But garages and cotton gins had encroached and obliterated even the august names of that neighborhood; only Miss Emily's house was left, lifting its stubborn and coquettish decay above the cotton wagons and the gasoline pumps — an eyesore among eyesores. And now Miss Emily had gone to join the representatives of those august names where they lay in the cedar-bemused cemetery among the ranked and anonymous graves of Union and Confederate soldiers who fell at the battle of Jefferson.

Alive, Miss Emily had been a tradition, a duty, and a care; a sort of hereditary obligation upon the town, dating from that day in 1894 when Colonel Sartoris, the mayor — he who fathered the edict that no Negro woman should appear on the streets without an apron — remitted her taxes, the dispensation dating from the death of her father on into perpetuity. Not that Miss Emily would have accepted charity. Colonel Sartoris invented an involved tale to the effect that Miss Emily's father had loaned money to the town, which the town, as a matter of business, preferred this way of repaying. Only a man of Colonel Sartoris' generation and thought could have invented it, and only a woman could have believed it.

When the next generation, with its more modern ideas, became mayors and aldermen, this arrangement created some little dissatisfaction. On the first of the year they mailed her a tax notice. February came, and there was no reply. They wrote her a formal letter, asking her to call at the sheriff's office at her convenience. A week later the mayor wrote her himself, offering to call or to send his car for her, and received in reply a note on paper of an archaic shape, in a thin, flowing calligraphy in faded ink, to the effect that she no longer went out at all. The tax notice was also enclosed, without comment.

They called a special meeting of the Board of Aldermen. A deputation waited 5 upon her, knocked at the door through which no visitor had passed since she ceased giving china-painting lessons eight or ten years earlier. They were admitted by the old Negro into a dim hall from which a stairway mounted into still more shadow. It smelled of dust and disuse — a close, dank smell. The Negro led them into the parlor. It was furnished in heavy, leather-covered furniture. When the Negro opened the blinds of one window, they could see that the leather was cracked; and when they sat down, a faint dust rose sluggishly about their thighs, spinning with slow motes in the single sun-ray. On a tarnished gilt easel before the fireplace stood a crayon portrait of Miss Emily's father.

They rose when she entered — a small, fat woman in black, with a thin gold chain descending to her waist and vanishing into her belt, leaning on an ebony cane with a tarnished gold head. Her skeleton was small and spare; perhaps that was why what would have been merely plumpness in another was obesity in her. She looked bloated, like a body long submerged in motionless water, and of that pallid hue. Her eyes, lost in the fatty ridges of her face, looked like two small pieces of coal pressed into a lump of dough as they moved from one face to another while the visitors stated their errand.

She did not ask them to sit. She just stood in the door and listened quietly until the spokesman came to a stumbling halt. Then they could hear the invisible watch ticking at the end of the gold chain.

Her voice was dry and cold. "I have no taxes in Jefferson. Colonel Sartoris explained it to me. Perhaps one of you can gain access to the city records and satisfy yourselves."

"But we have. We are the city authorities, Miss Emily. Didn't you get a notice from the sheriff, signed by him?"

"I received a paper, yes," Miss Emily said. "Perhaps he considers himself the   10 sheriff . . . I have no taxes in Jefferson."

"But there is nothing on the books to show that, you see. We must go by the—"

"See Colonel Sartoris. I have no taxes in Jefferson."

"But, Miss Emily—"

"See Colonel Sartoris." (Colonel Sartoris had been dead almost ten years.) "I have no taxes in Jefferson. Tobe!" The Negro appeared. "Show these gentlemen out."

## II

So she vanquished them, horse and foot, just as she had vanquished their fathers   15 thirty years before about the smell. That was two years after her father's death and a short time after her sweetheart—the one we believed would marry her—had deserted her. After her father's death she went out very little; after her sweetheart went away, people hardly saw her at all. A few of the ladies had the temerity to call, but were not received, and the only sign of life about the place was the Negro man—a young man then—going in and out with a market basket.

"Just as if a man—any man—could keep a kitchen properly," the ladies said; so they were not surprised when the smell developed. It was another link between the gross, teeming world and the high and mighty Griersons.

A neighbor, a woman, complained to the mayor, Judge Stevens, eighty years old.

"But what will you have me do about it, madam?" he said.

"Why, send her word to stop it," the woman said. "Isn't there a law?"

"I'm sure that won't be necessary," Judge Stevens said. "It's probably just a   20 snake or a rat that nigger of hers killed in the yard. I'll speak to him about it."

The next day he received two more complaints, one from a man who came in diffident deprecation. "We really must do something about it, Judge. I'd be the last one in the world to bother Miss Emily, but we've got to do something." That night the Board of Aldermen met—three graybeards and one younger man, a member of the rising generation.

"It's simple enough," he said. "Send her word to have her place cleaned up. Give her a certain time to do it in, and if she don't . . ."

"Dammit, sir," Judge Stevens said, "will you accuse a lady to her face of smelling bad?"

So the next night, after midnight, four men crossed Miss Emily's lawn and slunk about the house like burglars, sniffing along the base of the brickwork and at the cellar openings while one of them performed a regular sowing motion with his hand out of a sack slung from his shoulder. They broke open the cellar door and sprinkled lime there, and in all the outbuildings. As they recrossed the lawn, a window that had been dark was lighted and Miss Emily sat in it, the light behind her, and her upright torso motionless as that of an idol. They crept quietly across the lawn and into the shadow of the locusts that lined the street. After a week or two the smell went away.

That was when people had begun to feel really sorry for her. People in our 25 town, remembering how old lady Wyatt, her great-aunt, had gone completely crazy at last, believed that the Griersons held themselves a little too high for what they really were. None of the young men were quite good enough for Miss Emily and such. We had long thought of them as a tableau, Miss Emily a slender figure in white in the background, her father a spraddled silhouette in the foreground, his back to her and clutching a horsewhip, the two of them framed by the back-flung front door. So when she got to be thirty and was still single, we were not pleased exactly, but vindicated; even with insanity in the family she wouldn't have turned down all of her chances if they had really materialized.

When her father died, it got about that the house was all that was left to her; and in a way, people were glad. At last they could pity Miss Emily. Being left alone, and a pauper, she had become humanized. Now she too would know the old thrill and the old despair of a penny more or less.

The day after his death all the ladies prepared to call at the house and offer condolence and aid, as is our custom. Miss Emily met them at the door, dressed as usual and with no trace of grief on her face. She told them that her father was not dead. She did that for three days, with the ministers calling on her, and the doctors, trying to persuade her to let them dispose of the body. Just as they were about to resort to law and force, she broke down, and they buried her father quickly.

We did not say she was crazy then. We believed she had to do that. We remembered all the young men her father had driven away, and we knew that with nothing left, she would have to cling to that which had robbed her, as people will.

### III

She was sick for a long time. When we saw her again, her hair was cut short, making her look like a girl, with a vague resemblance to those angels in colored church windows — sort of tragic and serene.

The town had just let the contracts for paving the sidewalks, and in the sum- 30 mer after her father's death they began the work. The construction company came with niggers and mules and machinery, and a foreman named Homer Barron, a Yankee — a big, dark, ready man, with a big voice and eyes lighter than his face. The little boys would follow in groups to hear him cuss the niggers, and the niggers singing in time to the rise and fall of picks. Pretty soon he knew everybody in town. Whenever you heard a lot of laughing anywhere about the square, Homer Barron would be in the center of the group. Presently we began to see him and Miss Emily on Sunday afternoons driving in the yellow-wheeled buggy and the matched team of bays from the livery stable.

At first we were glad that Miss Emily would have an interest, because the ladies all said, "Of course a Grierson would not think seriously of a Northerner, a day laborer." But there were still others, older people, who said that even grief could not cause a real lady to forget *noblesse oblige°* — without calling it *noblesse*

---

*noblesse oblige:* The obligation of people of high social position.

*oblige.* They just said, "Poor Emily. Her kinsfolk should come to her." She had some kin in Alabama; but years ago her father had fallen out with them over the estate of old lady Wyatt, the crazy woman, and there was no communication between the two families. They had not even been represented at the funeral.

And as soon as the old people said, "Poor Emily," the whispering began. "Do you suppose it's really so?" they said to one another. "Of course it is. What else could . . ." This behind their hands; rustling of craned silk and satin behind jalousies closed upon the sun of Sunday afternoon as the thin, swift clop-clop-clop of the matched team passed: "Poor Emily."

She carried her head high enough — even when we believed that she was fallen. It was as if she demanded more than ever the recognition of her dignity as the last Grierson; as if it had wanted that touch of earthiness to reaffirm her imperviousness. Like when she bought the rat poison, the arsenic. That was over a year after they had begun to say "Poor Emily," and while the two female cousins were visiting her.

"I want some poison," she said to the druggist. She was over thirty then, still a slight woman, though thinner than usual, with cold, haughty black eyes in a face the flesh of which was strained across the temples and about the eye-sockets as you imagine a lighthouse-keeper's face ought to look. "I want some poison," she said.

"Yes, Miss Emily. What kind? For rats and such? I'd recom — "                                    35

"I want the best you have. I don't care what kind."

The druggist named several. "They'll kill anything up to an elephant. But what you want is — "

"Arsenic," Miss Emily said. "Is that a good one?"

"Is . . . arsenic? Yes, ma'am. But what you want — "

"I want arsenic."                                                                                  40

The druggist looked down at her. She looked back at him, erect, her face like a strained flag. "Why, of course," the druggist said. "If that's what you want. But the law requires you to tell what you are going to use it for."

Miss Emily just stared at him, her head tilted back in order to look him eye for eye, until he looked away and went and got the arsenic and wrapped it up. The Negro delivery boy brought her the package; the druggist didn't come back. When she opened the package at home there was written on the box, under the skull and bones: "For rats."

## IV

So the next day we all said, "She will kill herself"; and we said it would be the best thing. When she had first begun to be seen with Homer Barron, we had said, "She will marry him." Then we said, "She will persuade him yet," because Homer himself had remarked — he liked men, and it was known that he drank with the younger men in the Elks' Club — that he was not a marrying man. Later we said, "Poor Emily" behind the jalousies as they passed on Sunday afternoon in the glittering buggy, Miss Emily with her head high and Homer Barron with his hat cocked and a cigar in his teeth, reins and whip in a yellow glove.

Then some of the ladies began to say that it was a disgrace to the town and a bad example to the young people. The men did not want to interfere, but at last the ladies forced the Baptist minister — Miss Emily's people were Episcopal — to call upon her. He would never divulge what happened during that interview, but he refused to go back again. The next Sunday they again drove about the streets, and the following day the minister's wife wrote to Miss Emily's relations in Alabama.

So she had blood-kin under her roof again and we sat back to watch develop- 45
ments. At first nothing happened. Then we were sure that they were to be married.
We learned that Miss Emily had been to the jeweler's and ordered a man's toilet
set in silver, with the letters H. B. on each piece. Two days later we learned that
she had bought a complete outfit of men's clothing, including a nightshirt, and we
said, "They are married." We were really glad. We were glad because the two female
cousins were even more Grierson than Miss Emily had ever been.

So we were not surprised when Homer Barron — the streets had been finished some time since — was gone. We were a little disappointed that there was
not a public blowing-off, but we believed that he had gone on to prepare for Miss
Emily's coming, or to give her a chance to get rid of the cousins. (By that time it
was a cabal, and we were all Miss Emily's allies to help circumvent the cousins.)
Sure enough, after another week they departed. And, as we had expected all along,
within three days Homer Barron was back in town. A neighbor saw the Negro man
admit him at the kitchen door at dusk one evening.

And that was the last we saw of Homer Barron. And of Miss Emily for some
time. The Negro man went in and out with the market basket, but the front door
remained closed. Now and then we would see her at a window for a moment, as
the men did that night when they sprinkled the lime, but for almost six months she
did not appear on the streets. Then we knew that this was to be expected too; as if
that quality of her father which had thwarted her woman's life so many times had
been too virulent and too furious to die.

When we next saw Miss Emily, she had grown fat and her hair was turning
gray. During the next few years it grew grayer and grayer until it attained an even
pepper-and-salt iron-gray, when it ceased turning. Up to the day of her death at
seventy-four it was still that vigorous iron-gray, like the hair of an active man.

From that time on her front door remained closed, save for a period of six
or seven years, when she was about forty, during which she gave lessons in
china-painting. She fitted up a studio in one of the downstairs rooms, where the
daughters and granddaughters of Colonel Sartoris' contemporaries were sent to
her with the same regularity and in the same spirit that they were sent to church on
Sundays with a twenty-five-cent piece for the collection plate. Meanwhile her taxes
had been remitted.

Then the newer generation became the backbone and the spirit of the town, 50
and the painting pupils grew up and fell away and did not send their children to
her with boxes of color and tedious brushes and pictures cut from the ladies' magazines. The front door closed upon the last one and remained closed for good.
When the town got free postal delivery, Miss Emily alone refused to let them fasten
the metal numbers above her door and attach a mailbox to it. She would not listen
to them.

Daily, monthly, yearly we watched the Negro grow grayer and more stooped,
going in and out with the market basket. Each December we sent her a tax notice,
which would be returned by the post office a week later, unclaimed. Now and then
we would see her in one of the downstairs windows — she had evidently shut up
the top floor of the house — like the carven torso of an idol in a niche, looking or
not looking at us, we could never tell which. Thus she passed from generation to
generation — dear, inescapable, impervious, tranquil, and perverse.

And so she died. Fell ill in the house filled with dust and shadows, with only a
doddering Negro man to wait on her. We did not even know she was sick; we had
long since given up trying to get information from the Negro. He talked to no one,
probably not even to her, for his voice had grown harsh and rusty, as if from disuse.

She died in one of the downstairs rooms, in a heavy walnut bed with a curtain, her gray head propped on a pillow yellow and moldy with age and lack of sunlight.

## V

The Negro met the first of the ladies at the front door and let them in, with their hushed, sibilant voices and their quick, curious glances, and then he disappeared. He walked right through the house and out the back and was not seen again.

The two female cousins came at once. They held the funeral on the second 55 day, with the town coming to look at Miss Emily beneath a mass of bought flowers, with the crayon face of her father musing profoundly above the bier and the ladies sibilant and macabre; and the very old men — some in their brushed Confederate uniforms — on the porch and the lawn, talking of Miss Emily as if she had been a contemporary of theirs, believing that they had danced with her and courted her perhaps, confusing time with its mathematical progression, as the old do, to whom all the past is not a diminishing road but, instead, a huge meadow which no winter ever quite touches, divided from them now by the narrow bottle-neck of the most recent decade of years.

Already we knew that there was one room in that region above stairs which no one had seen in forty years, and which would have to be forced. They waited until Miss Emily was decently in the ground before they opened it.

The violence of breaking down the door seemed to fill this room with pervading dust. A thin, acrid pall as of the tomb seemed to lie everywhere upon this room decked and furnished as for a bridal: upon the valance curtains of faded rose color, upon the rose-shaded lights, upon the dressing table, upon the delicate array of crystal and the man's toilet things backed with tarnished silver, silver so tarnished that the monogram was obscured. Among them lay a collar and tie, as if they had just been removed, which, lifted, left upon the surface a pale crescent in the dust. Upon a chair hung the suit, carefully folded; beneath it the two mute shoes and the discarded socks.

The man himself lay in the bed.

For a long while we just stood there, looking down at the profound and flesh-less grin. The body had apparently once lain in the attitude of an embrace, but now the long sleep that outlasts love, that conquers even the grimace of love, had cuck-olded him. What was left of him, rotted beneath what was left of the nightshirt, had become inextricable from the bed in which he lay; and upon him and upon the pillow beside him lay that even coating of the patient and biding dust.

Then we noticed that in the second pillow was the indentation of a head. One 60 of us lifted something from it, and leaning forward, that faint and invisible dust dry and acrid in the nostrils, we saw a long strand of iron-gray hair.

### Considerations for Critical Thinking and Writing

1. **FIRST RESPONSE.** The story has five numbered sections. If you were to give them titles as in T. C. Boyle's story "The Hit Man" (p. 33), what would those titles be? What effect would each have on the reader?

2. What is the effect of the final paragraph of the story? How does it contribute to your understanding of Emily? Why is it important that we get this information last rather than at the beginning of the story?

3. What details foreshadow the conclusion of the story? Did you anticipate the ending?

4. Contrast the order of events as they happen in the story with the order in which they are told. How does this plotting create interest and suspense?

5. Faulkner uses a number of gothic elements in this plot: the imposing decrepit house, the decayed corpse, and the mysterious secret horrors connected with Emily's life. How do these elements forward the plot and establish the atmosphere?

6. How does the information provided by the exposition indicate the nature of the conflict in the story? What does Emily's southern heritage contribute to the story?

7. Who or what is the antagonist of the story? Why is it significant that Homer Barron is a construction foreman and a northerner?

8. In what sense does the narrator's telling of the story serve as "A Rose for Emily"? Why does the narrator uses *we* rather than *I*?

9. Explain how Emily's reasons for murdering Homer are related to her personal history and to the ways she handled previous conflicts.

10. Discuss how Faulkner's treatment of the North and the South contributes to the meaning of the story.

11. Provide an alternative title and explain how the emphasis in your title is reflected in the story.

### CONNECTIONS TO OTHER SELECTIONS

1. Contrast Faulkner's ordering of events with Tim O'Brien's "How to Tell a True War Story" (p. 253). How does each writer's arrangement of incidents create different effects on the reader?

2. To what extent do concepts of honor and tradition influence the action in "A Rose for Emily" and "How to Tell a True War Story" (p. 253)?

---

## Perspective

### WILLIAM FAULKNER (1897–1962)

## *On "A Rose for Emily"*  1959

Q. What is the meaning of the title "A Rose for Emily"?

A. Oh, it's simply the poor woman had had no life at all. Her father had kept her more or less locked up and then she had a lover who was about to quit her, she had to murder him. It was just "A Rose for Emily" — that's all.

Q. ... What ever inspired you to write this story?

A. That to me was another sad and tragic manifestation of man's condition in which he dreams and hopes, in which he is in conflict with himself or with his environment or with others. In this case there was the young girl with a young girl's normal aspirations to find love and then a husband and a family, who was brow-beaten and kept down by her father, a selfish man who didn't want her to leave home because he wanted a housekeeper, and it was a natural instinct of — repressed which — you can't repress it — you can mash it down but it comes up somewhere else and very likely in a tragic form, and that was simply another manifestation of man's injustice to man, of the poor tragic human being struggling with its own heart, with others, with its environment, for the simple things which all human beings want. In that case it was a young girl that just wanted to be loved and to love and to have a husband and a family.

Q. And that purely came from your imagination?

A. Well, the story did but the condition is there. It exists. I didn't invent that condition, I didn't invent the fact that young girls dream of someone to love and children and a home, but the story of what her own particular tragedy was invented, yes. . . .

Q. Sir, it has been argued that "A Rose for Emily" is a criticism of the North, and others have argued saying that it is a criticism of the South. Now, could this story, shall we say, be more properly classified as a criticism of the times?

A. Now that I don't know, because I was simply trying to write about people. The writer uses environment — what he knows — and if there's a symbolism in which the lover represented the North and the woman who murdered him represents the South, I don't say that's not valid and not there, but it was no intention of the writer to say, Now let's see, I'm going to write a piece in which I will use a symbolism for the North and another symbol for the South, that he was simply writing about people, a story which he thought was tragic and true, because it came out of the human heart, the human aspiration, the human — the conflict of conscience with glands, with the Old Adam. It was a conflict not between North and the South so much as between, well you might say, God and Satan.

Q. Sir, just a little more on that thing. You say it's a conflict between God and Satan. Well, I don't quite understand what you mean. Who is — did one represent the —

A. The conflict was in Miss Emily, that she knew that you do not murder people. She had been trained that you do not take a lover. You marry, you don't take a lover. She had broken all the laws of her tradition, her background, and she had finally broken the law of God too, which says you do not take human life. And she knew she was doing wrong, and that's why her own life was wrecked. Instead of murdering one lover, and then to go and take another and when she used him up to murder him, she was expiating her crime.

Q. Was the "Rose for Emily" an idea or a character? Just how did you go about it?

A. That came from a picture of the strand of hair on the pillow. It was a ghost story. Simply a picture of a strand of hair on the pillow in the abandoned house.

From *Faulkner in the University*, edited by
Frederick Gwynn and Joseph Blotner

## CONSIDERATIONS FOR CRITICAL THINKING AND WRITING

1. Discuss whether Faulkner's explanation of the conflict between "God and Satan" limits or expands the meaning of the story for you.

2. In what sense is "A Rose for Emily" a ghost story?

# A SAMPLE CLOSE READING

## *An Annotated Section of "A Rose for Emily"*

Even as you read a story for the first time, you can highlight passages, circle or underline words, and write responses in the margins. Subsequent readings will yield more insights once you begin to understand how various elements such as plot, character, and wording build toward the conclusion and what you perceive to be the story's central ideas. The following annotations for the first five paragraphs of "A Rose for Emily" provide a perspective written by someone who had read the work several times.

The title suggests that the story is an expression of affection and mourning, as well as a tribute, for Emily — despite her bizarre behavior.

WILLIAM FAULKNER (1897–1962)

## From *A Rose for Emily*    1931

I

The story begins (and ends) with death, and the "fallen monument" signals Emily's special meaning to the narrator and the community.

When Miss Emily Grierson died, our whole town went to her funeral: the men through a sort of respectful affection for a fallen monument, the women mostly out of curiosity to see the inside of her house, which no one save an old manservant — a combined gardener and cook — had seen in at least ten years.

The importance of the decayed old South setting is emphasized by being detailed even before Emily is described. The Civil War between the North and South is implicitly linked to the garages and gas pumps (the modern) that overtake the old southern neighborhood and hint at a lingering conflict.

It was a big, squarish frame house that had once been white, decorated with cupolas and spires and scrolled balconies in the heavily lightsome style of the seventies, set on what had once been our most select street. But garages and cotton gins had encroached and obliterated even the august names of that neighborhood; only Miss Emily's house was left, lifting its stubborn and coquettish decay above the cotton wagons and the gasoline pumps — an eyesore among eyesores. And now Miss Emily had gone to join the representatives of those august names where they lay in the cedar-bemused cemetery among the ranked and anonymous graves of Union and Confederate soldiers who fell at the battle of Jefferson.

Emily is associated with southern tradition, duty, and privilege that require protection. This helps explain why the townspeople attend her funeral.

Alive, Miss Emily had been a tradition, a duty, and a care; a sort of hereditary obligation upon the town, dating from that day in 1894 when Colonel Sartoris, the mayor — he who fathered the edict that no Negro woman should appear on the streets without an apron — remitted her taxes, the dispensation dating from the death of her father on into perpetuity. Not that Miss Emily would have accepted charity. Colonel Sartoris invented an involved tale to the effect that Miss Emily's father had loaned money to the town, which the town, as a matter of business, preferred this way of repaying. Only a man of Colonel Sartoris' generation and thought could have invented it, and only a woman could have believed it.

When the next generation, with its more |modern ideas,| became mayors and aldermen, this arrangement created some little dissatisfaction. On the first of the year they mailed her a tax notice. February came, and there was no reply. They wrote her a formal letter, asking her to call at the sheriff's office at her convenience. A week later the mayor wrote her himself, offering to call or to send his car for her, and received in reply |a note on paper of an archaic shape, in a thin, flowing calligraphy in faded ink, to the effect that she no longer went out at all.| The tax notice was also enclosed, without comment.

Like Emily, her "archaic," "thin," and "faded" note resists change and "modern ideas." She dismisses any attempts by the town to assess her for taxes or for anything else. She won't even leave the house.

They called a special meeting of the Board of Aldermen. 5 A deputation waited upon her, knocked at the door through which no visitor had passed since she ceased giving china-painting lessons |eight or ten years earlier.| They were admitted by the old Negro into a dim hall from which a stairway mounted into still more shadow. |It smelled of dust and disuse — a close, dank smell.| The Negro led them into the parlor. It was furnished in heavy, leather-covered furniture. When the Negro opened the blinds of one window, they could see that the leather was cracked; and when they sat down, a |faint dust rose| sluggishly about their thighs, spinning with slow motes in the single sun-ray. On a |tarnished gilt| easel before the fireplace stood a crayon portrait of Miss Emily's father.

The description of the "dank" house smelling of "dust and disuse" reinforces Emily's connection with the past and her refusal to let go of it. As the men sat down, "a faint dust rose" around them. The passage of time is alluded to in each of these paragraphs and ultimately emerges as a kind of antagonist.

# A SAMPLE STUDENT RESPONSE

Josiah Parker

Professor Altschuler

English 200-A

14 December 2023

Conflict in the Plot of William Faulkner's "A Rose for Emily"

The conflict of William Faulkner's "A Rose for Emily" is the driving force of the story's plot. However, the conflict is not the act of murder, nor is it Miss Emily's bizarre, reclusive lifestyle. The conflict is located instead in Miss Emily's background, her history. She is portrayed as a hardened, bitter old woman, but we soon realize she herself is a victim. She has been oppressed

Parker 2

her entire life by her domineering father, unable to take a suitor and marry, which is what she desires most. This lifelong oppression becomes the central conflict, and is what drives Miss Emily, causing her "to cling to that which had robbed her" (Faulkner, "Rose" 49).

After her father's death, Miss Emily immediately takes a lover, then poisons him when he tries to leave her. Both actions are what Faulkner himself claims "had broken all the laws of her tradition" (Faulkner, "On 'A Rose'" 54). She has been taught her whole life not to take a lover, certainly not to take a life. Her willingness to go against what she has always known to be moral and right creates dramatic tension and advances the story. In this way, the act of murder is nothing more than a portion of the plot, "the author's arrangement of incidents in a story," rather than the conflict itself (Meyer and Miller 32). . . .

Parker 5

Works Cited

Faulkner, William. "A Rose for Emily." Meyer and Miller, pp. 47–52.

- - -. "On 'A Rose for Emily.'" Meyer and Miller, pp. 53–54.

Meyer, Michael, and D. Quentin Miller, editors. *The Compact Bedford Introduction to Literature*. 13th ed., Bedford/St. Martin's, 2024.

# ANDRE DUBUS (1936–1999)

Though a native of Louisiana, where he attended the Christian Brothers School and McNeese State College, Andre Dubus lived much of his life in Massachusetts; many of his stories are set in the Merrimack Valley north of Boston. After college Dubus served as an officer for five years in the Marine Corps. He then earned an M.F.A. at the University of Iowa in 1966 and began teaching at Bradford College in Massachusetts. His fiction garnered numerous awards, and Dubus was both a Guggenheim and a MacArthur Fellow. Among his collections of fiction are *Separate Flights* (1975); *Adultery and Other Choices* (1977); *Finding a Girl in America* (1980), from which "Killings" is taken; *The Last Worthless Evening* (1986); *Collected Stories* (1988); and *Dancing after Hours* (1996). In 1991 he published *Broken Vessels,* a collection of autobiographical essays. His stories are often tense with violence, anger, tenderness, and guilt; they are populated by characters who struggle to understand and survive their experiences, painful with failure and the weight of imperfect relationships. In "Killings," the basis for a 2001 film titled *In the Bedroom,* Dubus offers a powerful blend of intimate domestic life and shocking violence.

## *Killings*   1979

On the August morning when Matt Fowler buried his youngest son, Frank, who had lived for twenty-one years, eight months, and four days, Matt's older son, Steve, turned to him as the family left the grave and walked between their friends, and said: "I should kill him." He was twenty-eight, his brown hair starting to thin in front where he used to have a cowlick. He bit his lower lip, wiped his eyes, then said it again. Ruth's arm, linked with Matt's, tightened; he looked at her. Beneath her eyes there was swelling from the three days she had suffered. At the limousine Matt stopped and looked back at the grave, the casket, and the Congregationalist minister who he thought had probably had a difficult job with the eulogy though he hadn't seemed to, and the old funeral director who was saying something to the six young pallbearers. The grave was on a hill and overlooked the Merrimack, which he could not see from where he stood; he looked at the opposite bank, at the apple orchard with its symmetrically planted trees going up a hill.

Next day Steve drove with his wife back to Baltimore where he managed the branch office of a bank, and Cathleen, the middle child, drove with her husband back to Syracuse. They had left the grandchildren with friends. A month after the funeral Matt played poker at Willis Trottier's because Ruth, who knew this was the second time he had been invited, told him to go, he couldn't sit home with her for the rest of her life, she was all right. After the game Willis went outside to tell everyone good night and, when the others had driven away, he walked with Matt to his car. Willis was a short, silver-haired man who had opened a diner after World War II, his trade then mostly very early breakfast, which he cooked, and then lunch for the men who worked at the leather and shoe factories. He now owned a large restaurant.

"He walks the Goddamn streets," Matt said.

"I know. He was in my place last night, at the bar. With a girl."

"I don't see him. I'm in the store all the time. Ruth sees him. She sees him too   5 much. She was at Sunnyhurst today getting cigarettes and aspirin, and there he was. She can't even go out for cigarettes and aspirin. It's killing her."

"Come back in for a drink."

Matt looked at his watch. Ruth would be asleep. He walked with Willis back into the house, pausing at the steps to look at the starlit sky. It was a cool summer night; he thought vaguely of the Red Sox, did not even know if they were at home tonight; since it happened he had not been able to think about any of the small pleasures he believed he had earned, as he had earned also what was shattered now forever: the quietly harried and quietly pleasurable days of fatherhood. They went inside. Willis's wife, Martha, had gone to bed hours ago, in the rear of the large house which was rigged with burglar and fire alarms. They went downstairs to the game room: the television set suspended from the ceiling, the pool table, the poker table with beer cans, cards, chips, filled ashtrays, and the six chairs where Matt and his friends had sat, the friends picking up the old banter as though he had only been away on vacation; but he could see the affection and courtesy in their eyes. Willis went behind the bar and mixed them each a Scotch and soda; he stayed behind the bar and looked at Matt sitting on the stool.

"How often have you thought about it?" Willis said.

"Every day since he got out. I didn't think about bail. I thought I wouldn't have to worry about him for years. She sees him all the time. It makes her cry."

"He was in my place a long time last night. He'll be back." 10

"Maybe he won't."

"The band. He likes the band."

"What's he doing now?"

"He's tending bar up to Hampton Beach. For a friend. Ever notice even the worst bastard always has friends? He couldn't get work in town. It's just tourists and kids up to Hampton. Nobody knows him. If they do, they don't care. They drink what he mixes."

"Nobody tells me about him." 15

"I hate him, Matt. My boys went to school with him. He was the same then. Know what he'll do? Five at the most. Remember that woman about seven years ago? Shot her husband and dropped him off the bridge in the Merrimack with a hundred-pound sack of cement and said all the way through it that nobody helped her. Know where she is now? She's in Lawrence now, a secretary. And whoever helped her, where the hell is he?"

"I've got a .38 I've had for years, I take it to the store now. I tell Ruth it's for the night deposits. I tell her things have changed: we got junkies here now too. Lots of people without jobs. She knows though."

"What does she know?"

"She knows I started carrying it after the first time she saw him in town. She knows it's in case I see him, and there's some kind of a situation —"

He stopped, looked at Willis, and finished his drink. Willis mixed him 20 another.

"What kind of situation?"

"Where he did something to me. Where I could get away with it."

"How does Ruth feel about that?"

"She doesn't know."

"You said she does, she's got it figured out." 25

He thought of her that afternoon: when she went into Sunnyhurst, Strout was waiting at the counter while the clerk bagged the things he had bought; she turned down an aisle and looked at soup cans until he left.

"Ruth would shoot him herself, if she thought she could hit him."

"You got a permit?"

"No."

"I do. You could get a year for that." 30

"Maybe I'll get one. Or maybe I won't. Maybe I'll just stop bringing it to the store."

Richard Strout was twenty-six years old, a high school athlete, football scholarship to the University of Massachusetts where he lasted for almost two semesters before quitting in advance of the final grades that would have forced him not to return. People then said: Dickie can do the work; he just doesn't want to. He came home and did construction work for his father but refused his father's offer to learn the business; his two older brothers had learned it, so that Strout and Sons trucks going about town, and signs on construction sites, now slashed wounds into Matt Fowler's life. Then Richard married a young girl and became a bartender, his salary and tips augmented and perhaps sometimes matched by his father, who also posted his bond. So his friends, his enemies (he had those: fist fights or, more often, boys and then young men who had not fought him when they thought they should have), and those who simply knew him by face and name, had a series of images of him which they recalled when they heard of the killing: the high school running back, the young drunk in bars, the oblivious hard-hatted young man eating lunch at a counter, the bartender who could perhaps be called courteous but not more than that: as he tended bar, his dark eyes and dark, wide-jawed face appeared less sullen, near blank.

One night he beat Frank. Frank was living at home and waiting for September, for graduate school in economics, and working as a lifeguard at Salisbury Beach, where he met Mary Ann Strout, in her first month of separation. She spent most days at the beach with her two sons. Before ten o'clock one night Frank came home; he had driven to the hospital first, and he walked into the living room with stitches over his right eye and both lips bright and swollen.

"I'm all right," he said, when Matt and Ruth stood up, and Matt turned off the television, letting Ruth get to him first: the tall, muscled but slender suntanned boy. Frank tried to smile at them but couldn't because of his lips.

"It was her husband, wasn't it?" Ruth said.     35

"Ex," Frank said. "He dropped in."

Matt gently held Frank's jaw and turned his face to the light, looked at the stitches, the blood under the white of the eye, the bruised flesh.

"Press charges," Matt said.

"No."

"What's to stop him from doing it again? Did you hit him at all? Enough so he   40 won't want to next time?"

"I don't think I touched him."

"So what are you going to do?"

"Take karate," Frank said, and tried again to smile.

"That's not the problem," Ruth said.

"You know you like her," Frank said.     45

"I like a lot of people. What about the boys? Did they see it?"

"They were asleep."

"Did you leave her alone with him?"

"He left first. She was yelling at him. I believe she had a skillet in her hand."

"Oh for God's sake," Ruth said.     50

Matt had been dealing with that too: at the dinner table on evenings when Frank wasn't home, was eating with Mary Ann; or, on the other nights — and Frank was with her every night — he talked with Ruth while they watched television, or lay in bed with the windows open and he smelled the night air and imagined, with both pride and muted sorrow, Frank in Mary Ann's arms. Ruth didn't like it because Mary Ann was in the process of divorce, because she had two children, because she was four years older than Frank, and finally — she told this in bed, where she had during all of their marriage told him of her deepest feelings: of love, of passion, of fears about one of the children, of pain Matt had caused her or she had caused him — she was against it because of what she had heard: that the marriage had gone bad early, and for most of it Richard and Mary Ann had both played around.

"That can't be true," Matt said. "Strout wouldn't have stood for it."

"Maybe he loves her."

"He's too hot-tempered. He couldn't have taken that."

But Matt knew Strout had taken it, for he had heard the stories too. He won- 55 dered who had told them to Ruth; and he felt vaguely annoyed and isolated: living with her for thirty-one years and still not knowing what she talked about with her friends. On these summer nights he did not so much argue with her as try to comfort her, but finally there was no difference between the two: she had concrete objections, which he tried to overcome. And in his attempt to do this, he neglected his own objections, which were the same as hers, so that as he spoke to her he felt as disembodied as he sometimes did in the store when he helped a man choose a blouse or dress or piece of costume jewelry for his wife.

"The divorce doesn't mean anything," he said. "She was young and maybe she liked his looks and then after a while she realized she was living with a bastard. I see it as a positive thing."

"She's not divorced yet."

"It's the same thing. Massachusetts has crazy laws, that's all. Her age is no problem. What's it matter when she was born? And that other business: even if it's true, which it probably isn't, it's got nothing to do with Frank, and it's in the past. And the kids are no problem. She's been married six years; she ought to have kids. Frank likes them. He plays with them. And he's not going to marry her anyway, so it's not a problem of money."

"Then what's he doing with her?"

"She probably loves him, Ruth. Girls always have. Why can't we just leave it at 60 that?"

"He got home at six o'clock Tuesday morning."

"I didn't know you knew. I've already talked to him about it."

Which he had: since he believed almost nothing he told Ruth, he went to Frank with what he believed. The night before, he had followed Frank to the car after dinner.

"You wouldn't make much of a burglar," he said.

"How's that?" 65

Matt was looking up at him; Frank was six feet tall, an inch and a half taller than Matt, who had been proud when Frank at seventeen outgrew him; he had only felt uncomfortable when he had to reprimand or caution him. He touched Frank's bicep, thought of the young taut passionate body, believed he could sense the desire, and again he felt the pride and sorrow and envy too, not knowing whether he was envious of Frank or Mary Ann.

"When you came in yesterday morning, I woke up. One of these mornings your mother will. And I'm the one who'll have to talk to her. She won't interfere with you. Okay? I know it means — " But he stopped, thinking: I know it means getting up and leaving that suntanned girl and going sleepy to the car, I know —

"Okay," Frank said, and touched Matt's shoulder and got into the car.

There had been other talks, but the only long one was their first one: a night driving to Fenway Park, Matt having ordered the tickets so they could talk, and knowing when Frank said yes, he would go, that he knew the talk was coming too. It took them forty minutes to get to Boston, and they talked about Mary Ann until they joined the city traffic along the Charles River, blue in the late sun. Frank told him all the things that Matt would later pretend to believe when he told them to Ruth.

"It seems like a lot for a young guy to take on," Matt finally said.　　　　70

"Sometimes it is. But she's worth it."

"Are you thinking about getting married?"

"We haven't talked about it. She can't for over a year. I've got school."

"I *do* like her," Matt said.

He did. Some evenings, when the long summer sun was still low in the sky,　75 Frank brought her home; they came into the house smelling of suntan lotion and the sea, and Matt gave them gin and tonics and started the charcoal in the back-yard, and looked at Mary Ann in the lawn chair: long and very light brown hair (Matt thinking that twenty years ago she would have dyed it blonde), and the long brown legs he loved to look at; her face was pretty; she had probably never in her adult life gone unnoticed into a public place. It was in her wide brown eyes that she looked older than Frank; after a few drinks Matt thought what he saw in her eyes was something erotic, testament to the rumors about her; but he knew it wasn't that, or all that: she had, very young, been through a sort of pain that his children, and he and Ruth, had been spared. In the moments of his recognizing that pain, he wanted to tenderly touch her hair, wanted with some gesture to give her solace and hope. And he would glance at Frank, and hope they would love each other, hope Frank would soothe that pain in her heart, take it from her eyes; and her divorce, her age, and her children did not matter at all. On the first two evenings she did not bring her boys, and then Ruth asked her to bring them the next time. In bed that night Ruth said, "She hasn't brought them because she's embarrassed. She shouldn't feel embarrassed."

---

Richard Strout shot Frank in front of the boys. They were sitting on the living room floor watching television, Frank sitting on the couch, and Mary Ann just return-ing from the kitchen with a tray of sandwiches. Strout came in the front door and shot Frank twice in the chest and once in the face with a 9 mm automatic. Then he looked at the boys and Mary Ann, and went home to wait for the police.

It seemed to Matt that from the time Mary Ann called weeping to tell him until now, a Saturday night in September, sitting in the car with Willis, parked beside Strout's car, waiting for the bar to close, that he had not so much moved through his life as wandered through it, his spirit like a dazed body bumping into furniture and corners. He had always been a fearful father: when his children were young, at the start of each summer he thought of them drowning in a pond or the sea, and he was relieved when he came home in the evenings and they were there; usually that relief was his only acknowledgment of his fear, which he never spoke of, and which he controlled within his heart. As he had when they were very young and all of them in turn, Cathleen too, were drawn to the high oak in the backyard, and had to climb it. Smiling, he watched them, imagining the fall: and he was poised to catch the small body before it hit the earth. Or his legs were poised; his hands were in his pockets or his arms were folded and, for the child looking down, he appeared relaxed and confident while his heart beat with the two words he wanted to call out but did not: *Don't fall.* In winter he was less afraid: he made sure the ice would hold him before they skated, and he brought or sent them to places where they could sled without ending in the street. So he and his children had survived their childhood, and he only worried about them when he knew they were driving a long distance, and then he lost Frank in a way no father expected to lose his son, and he felt that all the fears he had borne while they were growing up, and all the grief he had been afraid of, had backed up like a huge wave and struck him on the beach and swept him out to sea. Each day he felt the same and when he was able to forget how he felt, when he was able to force himself not to feel that way, the eyes of his clerks and customers defeated him. He wished those eyes were oblivious, even cold; he felt he was withering in their tenderness. And beneath his listless wandering, every day in his soul he shot Richard Strout in the face; while Ruth, going about town on errands, kept seeing him. And at nights in bed she would hold Matt and cry, or sometimes she was silent and Matt would touch her tightening arm, her clenched fist.

As his own right fist was now, squeezing the butt of the revolver, the last of the drinkers having left the bar, talking to each other, going to their separate cars which were in the lot in front of the bar, out of Matt's vision. He heard their voices, their cars, and then the ocean again, across the street. The tide was in and sometimes it smacked the sea wall. Through the windshield he looked at the dark red side wall of the bar, and then to his left, past Willis, at Strout's car, and through its windows he could see the now-emptied parking lot, the road, the sea wall. He could smell the sea.

The front door of the bar opened and closed again and Willis looked at Matt then at the corner of the building; when Strout came around it alone Matt got out of the car, giving up the hope he had kept all night (and for the past week) that Strout would come out with friends, and Willis would simply drive away; thinking: *All right then. All right;* and he went around the front of Willis's car, and at Strout's he stopped and aimed over the hood at Strout's blue shirt ten feet away. Willis was aiming too, crouched on Matt's left, his elbow resting on the hood.

"Mr. Fowler," Strout said. He looked at each of them, and at the guns. 80 "Mr. Trottier."

Then Matt, watching the parking lot and the road, walked quickly between the car and the building and stood behind Strout. He took one leather glove from his pocket and put it on his left hand.

"Don't talk. Unlock the front and back and get in."

Strout unlocked the front door, reached in and unlocked the back, then got in, and Matt slid into the back seat, closed the door with his gloved hand, and touched Strout's head once with the muzzle.

"It's cocked. Drive to your house."

When Strout looked over his shoulder to back the car, Matt aimed at his tem- 85 ple and did not look at his eyes.

"Drive slowly," he said. "Don't try to get stopped."

They drove across the empty front lot and onto the road, Willis's headlights shining into the car; then back through town, the sea wall on the left hiding the beach, though far out Matt could see the ocean; he uncocked the revolver; on the right were the places, most with their neon signs off, that did so much business in summer: the lounges and cafés and pizza houses, the street itself empty of traffic, the way he and Willis had known it would be when they decided to take Strout at the bar rather than knock on his door at two o'clock one morning and risk that one insomniac neighbor. Matt had not told Willis he was afraid he could not be alone with Strout for very long, smell his smells, feel the presence of his flesh, hear his voice, and then shoot him. They left the beach town and then were on the high bridge over the channel: to the left the smacking curling white at the breakwater and beyond that the dark sea and the full moon, and down to his right the small fishing boats bobbing at anchor in the cove. When they left the bridge, the sea was blocked by abandoned beach cottages, and Matt's left hand was sweating in the glove. Out here in the dark in the car he believed Ruth knew. Willis had come to his house at eleven and asked if he wanted a nightcap; Matt went to the bedroom for his wallet, put the gloves in one trouser pocket and the .38 in the other and went back to the living room, his hand in his pocket covering the bulge of the cool cylinder pressed against his fingers, the butt against his palm. When Ruth said good night she looked at his face, and he felt she could see in his eyes the gun, and the night he was going to. But he knew he couldn't trust what he saw. Willis's wife had taken her sleeping pill, which gave her eight hours — the reason, Willis had told Matt, he had the alarms installed, for nights when he was late at the restaurant — and when it was all done and Willis got home he would leave ice and a trace of Scotch and soda in two glasses in the game room and tell Martha in the morning that he had left the restaurant early and brought Matt home for a drink.

"He was making it with my wife." Strout's voice was careful, not pleading.

Matt pressed the muzzle against Strout's head, pressed it harder than he wanted to, feeling through the gun Strout's head flinching and moving forward; then he lowered the gun to his lap.

"Don't talk," he said.

Strout did not speak again. They turned west, drove past the Dairy Queen closed until spring, and the two lobster restaurants that faced each other and were crowded all summer and were now also closed, onto the short bridge crossing the tidal stream, and over the engine Matt could hear through his open window the water rushing inland under the bridge; looking to his left he saw its swift moon-lit current going back into the marsh which, leaving the bridge, they entered: the salt marsh stretching out on both sides, the grass tall in patches but mostly low and leaning earthward as though windblown, a large dark rock sitting as though it rested on nothing but itself, and shallow pools reflecting the bright moon.

Beyond the marsh they drove through woods, Matt thinking now of the hole he and Willis had dug last Sunday afternoon after telling their wives they were going to Fenway Park. They listened to the game on a transistor radio, but heard none of it as they dug into the soft earth on the knoll they had chosen because elms and maples sheltered it. Already some leaves had fallen. When the hole was deep enough they covered it and the piled earth with dead branches, then cleaned their shoes and pants and went to a restaurant farther up in New Hampshire where they ate sandwiches and drank beer and watched the rest of the game on television. Looking at the back of Strout's head he thought of Frank's grave; he had not been back to it; but he would go before winter, and its second burial of snow.

He thought of Frank sitting on the couch and perhaps talking to the children as they watched television, imagined him feeling young and strong, still warmed from the sun at the beach, and feeling loved, hearing Mary Ann moving about in the kitchen, hearing her walking into the living room; maybe he looked up at her and maybe she said something, looking at him over the tray of sandwiches, smiling at him, saying something the way women do when they offer food as a gift, then

90

the front door opening and this son of a bitch coming in and Frank seeing that he meant the gun in his hand, this son of a bitch and his gun the last person and thing Frank saw on earth.

When they drove into town the streets were nearly empty: a few slow cars, a policeman walking his beat past the darkened fronts of stores. Strout and Matt both glanced at him as they drove by. They were on the main street, and all the stoplights were blinking yellow. Willis and Matt had talked about that too: the lights changed at midnight, so there would be no place Strout had to stop and where he might try to run. Strout turned down the block where he lived and Willis's headlights were no longer with Matt in the back seat. They had planned that too, had decided it was best for just the one car to go to the house, and again Matt had said nothing about his fear of being alone with Strout, especially in his house: a duplex, dark as all the houses on the street were, the street itself lit at the corner of each block. As Strout turned into the driveway Matt thought of the one insomniac neighbor, thought of some man or woman sitting alone in the dark living room, watching the all-night channel from Boston. When Strout stopped the car near the front of the house, Matt said: "Drive it to the back."

He touched Strout's head with the muzzle. 95

"You wouldn't have it cocked, would you? For when I put on the brakes."

Matt cocked it, and said: "It is now."

Strout waited a moment; then he eased the car forward, the engine doing little more than idling, and as they approached the garage he gently braked. Matt opened the door, then took off the glove and put it in his pocket. He stepped out and shut the door with his hip and said: "All right."

Strout looked at the gun, then got out, and Matt followed him across the grass, and as Strout unlocked the door Matt looked quickly at the row of small backyards on either side, and scattered tall trees, some evergreens, others not, and he thought of the red and yellow leaves on the trees over the hole, saw them falling soon, probably in two weeks, dropping slowly, covering. Strout stepped into the kitchen.

"Turn on the light." 100

Strout reached to the wall switch, and in the light Matt looked at his wide back, the dark blue shirt, the white belt, the red plaid pants.

"Where's your suitcase?"

"My suitcase?"

"Where is it?"

"In the bedroom closet." 105

"That's where we're going then. When we get to a door you stop and turn on the light."

They crossed the kitchen, Matt glancing at the sink and stove and refrigerator: no dishes in the sink or even the dish rack beside it, no grease splashings on the stove, the refrigerator door clean and white. He did not want to look at any more but he looked quickly at all he could see: in the living room magazines and newspapers in a wicker basket, clean ashtrays, a record player, the records shelved next to it, then down the hall where, near the bedroom door, hung a color photograph of Mary Ann and the two boys sitting on a lawn — there was no house in the picture — Mary Ann smiling at the camera or Strout or whoever held the camera, smiling as she had on Matt's lawn this summer while he waited for the charcoal and they all talked and he looked at her brown legs and at Frank touching her arm, her shoulder, her hair; he moved down the hall with her smile in his mind, wondering: was that when they were both playing around and she was smiling like that at him and they were happy, even sometimes, making it worth it? He recalled her eyes, the pain in them, and he was conscious of the circles of love he was touching with the hand that held the revolver so tightly now as Strout stopped at the door at the end of the hall.

"There's no wall switch."

"Where's the light?"

"By the bed."                                                                                                        110

"Let's go."

Matt stayed a pace behind, then Strout leaned over and the room was lighted: the bed, a double one, was neatly made; the ashtray on the bedside table clean, the bureau top dustless, and no photographs; probably so the girl — who *was* she? — would not have to see Mary Ann in the bedroom she believed was theirs. But because Matt was a father and a husband, though never an ex-husband, he knew (and did not want to know) that this bedroom had never been theirs alone. Strout turned around; Matt looked at his lips, his wide jaw, and thought of Frank's doomed and fearful eyes looking up from the couch.

"Where's Mr. Trottier?"

"He's waiting. Pack clothes for warm weather."

"What's going on?"                                                                                                 115

"You're jumping bail."

"Mr. Fowler —"

He pointed the cocked revolver at Strout's face. The barrel trembled but not much, not as much as he had expected. Strout went to the closet and got the suitcase from the floor and opened it on the bed. As he went to the bureau, he said: "He was making it with my wife. I'd go pick up my kids and he'd be there. Sometimes he spent the night. My boys told me."

He did not look at Matt as he spoke. He opened the top drawer and Matt stepped closer so he could see Strout's hands: underwear and socks, the socks rolled, the underwear folded and stacked. He took them back to the bed, arranged them neatly in the suitcase, then from the closet he was taking shirts and trousers and a jacket; he laid them on the bed and Matt followed him to the bathroom and watched from the door while he packed those things a person accumulated and that became part of him so that at times in the store Matt felt he was selling more than clothes.

"I wanted to try to get together with her again." He was bent over the suitcase.   120
"I couldn't even talk to her. He was always with her. I'm going to jail for it; if I ever get out I'll be an old man. Isn't that enough?"

"You're not going to jail."

Strout closed the suitcase and faced Matt, looking at the gun. Matt went to his rear, so Strout was between him and the lighted hall; then using his handkerchief he turned off the lamp and said: "Let's go."

They went down the hall, Matt looking again at the photograph, and through the living room and kitchen, Matt turning off the lights and talking, frightened that he was talking, that he was telling this lie he had not planned: "It's the trial. We can't go through that, my wife and me. So you're leaving. We've got you a ticket, and a job. A friend of Mr. Trottier's. Out west. My wife keeps seeing you. We can't have that anymore."

Matt turned out the kitchen light and put the handkerchief in his pocket, and they went down the two brick steps and across the lawn. Strout put the suitcase on the floor of the back seat, then got into the front seat and Matt got in the back and put on his glove and shut the door.

"They'll catch me. They'll check passenger lists." 125

"We didn't use your name."

"They'll figure that out too. You think I wouldn't have done it myself if it was that easy?"

He backed into the street, Matt looking down the gun barrel but not at the profiled face beyond it.

"You were alone," Matt said. "We've got it worked out."

"There's no planes this time of night, Mr. Fowler." 130

"Go back through town. Then north on 125."

They came to the corner and turned, and now Willis's headlights were in the car with Matt.

"Why north, Mr. Fowler?"

"Somebody's going to keep you for a while. They'll take you to the airport." He uncocked the hammer and lowered the revolver to his lap and said wearily: "No more talking."

As they drove back through town, Matt's body sagged, going limp with his 135 spirit and its new and false bond with Strout, the hope his lie had given Strout. He had grown up in this town whose streets had become places of apprehension and pain for Ruth as she drove and walked, doing what she had to do; and for him too, if only in his mind as he worked and chatted six days a week in his store; he wondered now if his lie would have worked, if sending Strout away would have been enough; but then he knew that just thinking of Strout in Montana or whatever place lay at the end of the lie he had told, thinking of him walking the streets there, loving a girl there (who *was* she?) would be enough to slowly rot the rest of his days. And Ruth's. Again he was certain that she knew, that she was waiting for him.

They were in New Hampshire now, on the narrow highway, passing the shopping center at the state line, and then houses and small stores and sandwich shops. There were few cars on the road. After ten minutes he raised his trembling hand, touched Strout's neck with the gun, and said: "Turn in up here. At the dirt road."

Strout flicked on the indicator and slowed.

"Mr. Fowler?"

"They're waiting here."

Strout turned very slowly, easing his neck away from the gun. In the moon- 140 light the road was light brown, lighter and yellowed where the headlights shone; weeds and a few trees grew on either side of it, and ahead of them were the woods.

"There's nothing back here, Mr. Fowler."

"It's for your car. You don't think we'd leave it at the airport, do you?"

He watched Strout's large, big-knuckled hands tighten on the wheel, saw Frank's face that night: not the stitches and bruised eye and swollen lips, but his own hand gently touching Frank's jaw, turning his wounds to the light. They rounded a bend in the road and were out of sight of the highway: tall trees all around them now, hiding the moon. When they reached the abandoned gravel pit on the left, the bare flat earth and steep pale embankment behind it, and the black crowns of trees at its top, Matt said: "Stop here."

Strout stopped but did not turn off the engine. Matt pressed the gun hard against his neck, and he straightened in the seat and looked in the rearview mirror, Matt's eyes meeting his in the glass for an instant before looking at the hair at the end of the gun barrel.

"Turn it off."    145

Strout did, then held the wheel with two hands, and looked in the mirror.

"I'll do twenty years, Mr. Fowler; at least. I'll be forty-six years old."

"That's nine years younger than I am," Matt said, and got out and took off the glove and kicked the door shut. He aimed at Strout's ear and pulled back the hammer. Willis's headlights were off and Matt heard him walking on the soft thin layer of dust, the hard earth beneath it. Strout opened the door, sat for a moment in the interior light, then stepped out onto the road. Now his face was pleading. Matt did not look at his eyes, but he could see it in the lips.

"Just get the suitcase. They're right up the road."

Willis was beside him now, to his left. Strout looked at both guns. Then he    150
opened the back door, leaned in, and with a jerk brought the suitcase out. He was turning to face them when Matt said: "Just walk up the road. Just ahead."

Strout turned to walk, the suitcase in his right hand, and Matt and Willis followed; as Strout cleared the front of his car he dropped the suitcase and, ducking, took one step that was the beginning of a sprint to his right. The gun kicked in Matt's hand, and the explosion of the shot surrounded him, isolated him in a nimbus of sound that cut him off from all his time, all his history, isolated him standing absolutely still on the dirt road with the gun in his hand, looking down at Richard Strout squirming on his belly, kicking one leg behind him, pushing himself forward, toward the woods. Then Matt went to him and shot him once in the back of the head.

---

Driving south to Boston, wearing both gloves now, staying in the middle lane and looking often in the rearview mirror at Willis's headlights, he relived the suitcase dropping, the quick dip and turn of Strout's back, and the kick of the gun, the sound of the shot. When he walked to Strout, he still existed within the first shot, still trembled and breathed with it. The second shot and the burial seemed to be happening to someone else, someone he was watching. He and Willis each held an arm and pulled Strout face-down off the road and into the woods, his bouncing sliding belt white under the trees where it was so dark that when they stopped at the top of the knoll, panting and sweating, Matt could not see where Strout's blue shirt ended and the earth began. They pulled off the branches then dragged Strout to the edge of the hole and went behind him and lifted his legs and pushed him in. They stood still for a moment. The woods were quiet save for their breathing, and Matt remembered hearing the movements of birds and small animals after the first shot. Or maybe he had not heard them. Willis went down to the road. Matt could see him clearly out on the tan dirt, could see the glint of Strout's car and, beyond the road, the gravel pit. Willis came back up the knoll with the suitcase. He dropped it in the hole and took off his gloves and they went down to his car for the spades. They worked quietly. Sometimes they paused to listen to the woods. When they were finished Willis turned on his flashlight and they covered the earth with leaves and branches and then went down to the spot in front of the car, and while Matt held the light Willis crouched and sprinkled dust on the blood, backing up till he reached the grass and leaves, then he used leaves until they had worked up to the grave again. They did not stop. They walked around the grave and through the woods, using the light on the ground, looking up through the trees to where they ended at the lake. Neither of them spoke above the sounds of their heavy and clumsy strides through low brush and over fallen branches. Then they reached it: wide and dark, lapping softly at the bank, pine needles smooth under Matt's feet, moonlight on the lake, a small island near its middle, with black, tall evergreens. He took out the gun and threw for the island: taking two steps back on the pine needles, striding with the throw and going to one knee as he followed through, looking up to see the dark shapeless object arcing downward, splashing.

They left Strout's car in Boston, in front of an apartment building on Commonwealth Avenue. When they got back to town Willis drove slowly over the bridge and Matt threw the keys into the Merrimack. The sky was turning light. Willis let him out a block from his house, and walking home he listened for sounds from the houses he passed. They were quiet. A light was on in his living room. He turned it off and undressed in there, and went softly toward the bedroom; in the hall he smelled the smoke, and he stood in the bedroom doorway and looked at the orange of her cigarette in the dark. The curtains were closed. He went to the closet and put his shoes on the floor and felt for a hanger.

"Did you do it?" she said.

He went down the hall to the bathroom and in the dark he washed his hands 155 and face. Then he went to her, lay on his back, and pulled the sheet up to his throat.

"Are you all right?" she said.

"I think so."

Now she touched him, lying on her side, her hand on his belly, his thigh.

"Tell me," she said.

He started from the beginning, in the parking lot at the bar; but soon with his 160 eyes closed and Ruth petting him, he spoke of Strout's house: the order, the woman presence, the picture on the wall.

"The way she was smiling," he said.

"What about it?"

"I don't know. Did you ever see Strout's girl? When you saw him in town?"

"No."

"I wonder who she was." 165

Then he thought: *not was: is. Sleeping now she is his girl.* He opened his eyes, then closed them again. There was more light beyond the curtains. With Ruth now he left Strout's house and told again his lie to Strout, gave him again that hope that Strout must have for a while believed, else he would have to believe only the gun pointed at him for the last two hours of his life. And with Ruth he saw again the dropping suitcase, the darting move to the right: and he told of the first shot, feeling her hand on him but his heart isolated still, beating on the road still in that explosion like thunder. He told her the rest, but the words had no images for him, he did not see himself doing what the words said he had done; he only saw himself on that road.

"We can't tell the other kids," she said. "It'll hurt them, thinking he got away. But we mustn't."

"No."

She was holding him, wanting him, and he wished he could make love with her but he could not. He saw Frank and Mary Ann making love in her bed, their eyes closed, their bodies brown and smelling of the sea; the other girl was faceless, bodiless, but he felt her sleeping now; and he saw Frank and Strout, their faces alive; he saw red and yellow leaves falling on the earth, then snow: falling and freezing and falling; and holding Ruth, his cheek touching her breast, he shuddered with a sob that he kept silent in his heart.

## Considerations for Critical Thinking and Writing

1. **FIRST RESPONSE.** How do you feel about Matt's act of revenge? Trace the emotions his character produces in you as the plot unfolds.

2. Discuss the significance of the title. Why is "Killings" a more appropriate title than "Killers"?

3. What are the effects of Dubus's ordering of events in the story? How would the effects be different if the story were told in a chronological order?

4. Describe the Fowler family before Frank's murder. How does the murder affect Matt?

5. What is learned about Richard from the flashback in paragraphs 32 through 75? How does this information affect your attitude toward him?

6. What is the effect of the description of Richard shooting Frank in paragraph 76?

7. How well planned is Matt's revenge? Why does he lie to Richard about sending him out west?

8. Describe Matt at the end of the story when he tells his wife about the killing. How do you think this revenge killing will affect the Fowler family?

9. How might "Killings" be considered a love story as well as a murder story?

10. **CRITICAL STRATEGIES.** Read the section on psychological criticism in Chapter 42, "Critical Strategies for Reading." How do the details of the killing and the disposal of Richard's body reveal Matt's emotions? What is he thinking and feeling as he performs these actions? How did you feel as you read about them?

## Connections to Other Selections

1. Compare and contrast Matt's motivation for murder with Emily's in "A Rose for Emily" (p. 47). Which character made you feel more empathy and sympathy for their actions? Why?

2. Consider the topic of revenge in this story and in Jennifer Nansubuga Makumbi's "Let's Tell This Story Properly" (p. 487). How does the way each story is plotted change your comparison between them?

# 3

# Character

When I find a well-drawn character in fiction or biography, I generally take a warm personal interest in him, for the reason that I have known him before — met him on the river.
— MARK TWAIN

Bettmann/Getty Images.

Character is essential to plot. Without characters, Ann Beattie's "Janus" (p. 27) would be a story about a decorative bowl and Faulkner's "A Rose for Emily" (p. 47) little more than a faded history of a sleepy town in the South. If stories were depopulated, the plots would disappear because characters and plots are interrelated. A well-made bowl is important only because we care what effect it has on a character. Characters are influenced by events just as events are shaped by characters. The protagonist of Beattie's story is someone who is guarded and protective of her private self. The fact that she carries a bowl around during her work, places it carefully to help sell houses, and panics when she forgets it in a house are some of the basic plot points of "Janus," but they are also strong indications of the type of person she is.

The methods by which a writer creates people in a story so that they seem actually to exist are called **characterization**. Huck Finn never lived, yet those who have read Mark Twain's novel about Huck's adventures along the

Mississippi River feel as if they know him. A good writer gives us the illusion that a character is real, but we should also remember that a character is not an actual person but instead has been created by the author. Though we might walk out of a room in which Huck Finn's Pap talks racist nonsense, we would not throw away the book in a similar fit of anger. This illusion of reality is the magic that allows us to move beyond the circumstances of our own lives into a writer's fictional world, where we can encounter everyone from royalty to paupers, murderers, lovers, cheaters, martyrs, artists, destroyers, and, nearly always, some part of ourselves. The life that a writer breathes into a character adds to our own experiences and enlarges our view of the world.

A character is usually but not always a person. In Jack London's *Call of the Wild*, the protagonist is a devoted sled dog; in Ernest Hemingway's "The Short, Happy Life of Francis Macomber," the story's point of view occasionally enters the mind of a wounded lion. Perhaps the only possible qualification to be placed on character is that whatever it is — whether an animal or even an inanimate object, such as a robot — it must have some recognizable human qualities. The action of the plot interests us primarily because we care about what happens to people and what they do. We may identify with characters' desires and aspirations, or we may be disgusted by their viciousness and selfishness. To understand our response to a story, we should be able to recognize the methods of characterization the author uses.

## TOBIAS WOLFF (B. 1945)

Known as much for his memoirs (*This Boy's Life* in 1989 and *In Pharaoh's Army* in 1994) as his award-winning fiction, Tobias Wolff writes prose that is clean and honest. He deals with the gritty realities of experience, sometimes relying on his own years as a soldier and sometimes on his upbringing, including the often strained relationships among family members, as in the following story, "Powder," about a boy and his father navigating a hazardous winter road.

## *Powder*  1996

Just before Christmas my father took me skiing at Mount Baker. He'd had to fight for the privilege of my company, because my mother was still angry with him for sneaking me into a nightclub during his last visit, to see Thelonious Monk.

He wouldn't give up. He promised, hand on heart, to take good care of me and have me home for dinner on Christmas Eve, and she relented. But as we were checking out of the lodge that morning it began to snow, and in this snow he observed some rare quality that made it necessary for us to get in one last run. We got in several last runs. He was indifferent to my fretting. Snow whirled around us in bitter, blinding squalls, hissing like sand, and still we skied. As the lift bore us to the peak yet again, my father looked at his watch and said, "Criminy. This'll have to be a fast one."

By now I couldn't see the trail. There was no point in trying. I stuck to him like white on rice and did what he did and somehow made it to the bottom without sailing off a cliff. We returned our skis and my father put chains on the Austin-Healey while I swayed from foot to foot, clapping my mittens and wishing I was home. I could see everything. The green tablecloth, the plates with the holly pattern, the red candles waiting to be lit.

We passed a diner on our way out. "You want some soup?" my father asked. I shook my head. "Buck up," he said. "I'll get you there. Right, doctor?"

I was supposed to say, "Right, doctor," but I didn't say anything.      5

A state trooper waved us down outside the resort. A pair of sawhorses were blocking the road. The trooper came up to our car and bent down to my father's window. His face was bleached by the cold. Snowflakes clung to his eyebrows and to the fur trim of his jacket and cap.

"Don't tell me," my father said.

The trooper told him. The road was closed. It might get cleared, it might not. Storm took everyone by surprise. So much, so fast. Hard to get people moving. Christmas Eve. What can you do.

My father said, "Look. We're talking about five, six inches. I've taken this car through worse than that."

The trooper straightened up. His face was out of sight but I could hear him.      10 "The road is closed."

My father sat with both hands on the wheel, rubbing the wood with his thumbs. He looked at the barricade for a long time. He seemed to be trying to master the idea of it. Then he thanked the trooper, and with a weird, old-maidy show of caution turned the car around. "Your mother will never forgive me for this," he said.

"We should have left before," I said. "Doctor."

He didn't speak to me again until we were in a booth at the diner, waiting for our burgers. "She won't forgive me," he said. "Do you understand? Never."

"I guess," I said, but no guesswork was required; she wouldn't forgive him.

"I can't let that happen." He bent toward me. "I'll tell you what I want. I want      15 us all to be together again. Is that what you want?"

"Yes, sir."

He bumped my chin with his knuckles. "That's all I needed to hear."

When we finished eating he went to the pay phone in the back of the diner, then joined me in the booth again. I figured he'd called my mother, but he didn't give a report. He sipped at his coffee and stared out the window at the empty road. "Come on, come on," he said, though not to me. A little while later he said it again. When the trooper's car went past, lights flashing, he got up and dropped some money on the check. "Okay. Vamanos."

The wind had died. The snow was falling straight down, less of it now and lighter. We drove away from the resort, right up to the barricade. "Move it," my father told me. When I looked at him he said, "What are you waiting for?" I got out and dragged one of the sawhorses aside, then put it back after he drove through. He pushed the door open for me. "Now you're an accomplice," he said. "We go down together." He put the car into gear and gave me a look. "Joke, son."

Down the first long stretch I watched the road behind us, to see if the      20 trooper was on our tail. The barricade vanished. Then there was nothing but snow: snow on the road, snow kicking up from the chains, snow on the trees, snow in the sky; and our trail in the snow. Then I faced forward and had a shock.

The lay of the road behind us had been marked by our own tracks, but there were no tracks ahead of us. My father was breaking virgin snow between a line of tall trees. He was humming "Stars Fell on Alabama." I felt snow brush along the floorboards under my feet. To keep my hands from shaking I clamped them between my knees.

My father grunted in a thoughtful way and said, "Don't ever try this yourself."

"I won't."

"That's what you say now, but someday you'll get your license and then you'll think you can do anything. Only you won't be able to do this. You need, I don't know — a certain instinct."

"Maybe I have it."

"You don't. You have your strong points, but not this. I only mention it because  25 I don't want you to get the idea this is something just anybody can do. I'm a great driver. That's not a virtue, okay? It's just a fact, and one you should be aware of. Of course you have to give the old heap some credit, too. There aren't many cars I'd try this with. Listen!"

I did listen. I heard the slap of the chains, the stiff, jerky rasp of the wipers, the purr of the engine. It really did purr. The old heap was almost new. My father couldn't afford it, and kept promising to sell it, but here it was.

I said, "Where do you think that policeman went to?"

"Are you warm enough?" He reached over and cranked up the blower. Then he turned off the wipers. We didn't need them. The clouds had brightened. A few sparse, feathery flakes drifted into our slipstream and were swept away. We left the trees and entered a broad field of snow that ran level for a while and then tilted sharply downward. Orange stakes had been planted at intervals in two parallel lines and my father steered a course between them, though they were far enough apart to leave considerable doubt in my mind as to exactly where the road lay. He was humming again, doing little scat riffs around the melody.

"Okay then. What are my strong points?"

"Don't get me started," he said. "It'd take all day."  30

"Oh, right. Name one."

"Easy. You always think ahead."

True. I always thought ahead. I was a boy who kept his clothes on numbered hangers to insure proper rotation. I bothered my teachers for homework assignments far ahead of their due dates so I could draw up schedules. I thought ahead, and that was why I knew that there would be other troopers waiting for us at the end of our ride, if we even got there. What I did not know was that my father would wheedle and plead his way past them — he didn't sing "O Tannenbaum," but just about — and get me home for dinner, buying a little more time before my mother decided to make the split final. I knew we'd get caught; I was resigned to it. And maybe for this reason I stopped moping and began to enjoy myself.

Why not? This was one for the books. Like being in a speedboat, only better. You can't go downhill in a boat. And it was all ours. And it kept coming, the laden trees, the unbroken surface of snow, the sudden white vistas. Here and there I saw hints of the road, ditches, fences, stakes, but not so many that I could have found my way. But then I didn't have to. My father was driving. My father in his forty-eighth year, rumpled, kind, bankrupt of honor, flushed with certainty. He was a great driver. All persuasion, no coercion. Such subtlety at the wheel, such tactful pedalwork. I actually trusted him. And the best was yet to come — switchbacks and hairpins impossible to describe. Except maybe to say this: if you haven't driven fresh powder, you haven't driven.

If this story were included in the chapter that explains *plot*, you might scratch your head a bit. The plot? A man and his son get caught in a snowstorm, drive down a harrowing road in defiance of the police, and survive, maybe even enjoy the ride. In a plot-heavy story, we would expect a car crash, perhaps followed by a full-throated argument between father and son, maybe even an arrest for driving on a forbidden road. The restrained plot in "Powder" gives the author ample room to develop rich and full characters in a relatively small space. There are a total of four characters in this story: the narrator, his father, his mother (who is not technically in the story, but whose invisible presence is significant), and the trooper. The mother and the trooper are minor characters who both represent the same oppositional force: they set the rules and parameters that the narrator's father breaks. The story wouldn't be the same without them: it might not even exist. They are minor, but significant in that the guidelines they set highlight the salient points of contact between the two main characters.

We evaluate fictional characters in much the same way we understand people in our own lives. By piecing together bits of information, we create a context that allows us to interpret their behavior. We can predict, for instance, that an acquaintance who is a chronic complainer is not likely to get along terrifically with a roommate. Complaints can be verbal or nonverbal: a rant and an eye-roll can convey similar gripes. One of the most crucial techniques to pay attention to in determining character is to observe the balance between **dialogue** and description. *Dialogue* simply refers to the words people speak in a story. Plays, as we discuss in Chapter 35 and beyond, are composed almost entirely of dialogue, and yet an actor's job on stage is rarely to stand stock still and recite dialogue: actors also wring their hands, run, slap each other, or stab each other while reciting their lines. When a character speaks in a short story, it is generally as part of a conversation, in reaction to something someone else has said. We can't always control what we say in such situations: emotions, fatigue, drunkenness, or being caught off guard are all circumstances that might alter our expected words. In "Powder" the narrator and his father have some sort of in-joke: the narrator is supposed to respond, "Right, doctor" when his father says, "Right, doctor?" When he does not fill in this formula, we can assume that his father understands that his silence indicates extreme displeasure. Later on, he chides his father by adding "Doctor" to the stern sentence, "We should have left earlier," probably after a measured pause. His choice to omit "doctor" from their conversation and then to include it when it isn't called for are important clues to their relationship at this particular moment. We interpret words and actions in light of what we already know about someone, and that is why keeping track of what characters say (and how they say it) along with what they do (and don't do) is important. Characters have histories, habits, quirks, and psychological responses to their environments, all of which combine to tell us who they are.

In addition to dialogue, authors reveal characters by a wide variety of means. It should be noted that some stories are all description and some are all dialogue, but these cases are rare: most authors blend them, and in a very particular way. Try highlighting all the dialogue in two or three stories: do you notice any patterns about where it tends to be most prevalent?

Physical descriptions can indicate important inner qualities; disheveled appearance, a crafty smile, or a blush might communicate as much as or more than what a character says. Even clothing matters: in the parodic story "The Hit Man" by T. C. Boyle (p. 33), the protagonist is always wearing black, notably his trademark executioner's hood: he wouldn't be "the Hit Man" without this costume. Sometimes clothing can be an obvious indicator of character: in classic Western movies the good guys wore white hats and the bad guys wore black hats. More often, we are encouraged to attend to subtler traits based on context. If a character wears a bright, flowery outfit to a somber funeral where everyone else is dressed in traditional black, are they clueless? Do they care little for convention? Are they ecstatic at the death of the deceased because they always hated them? Are they the type of person who believes we should celebrate someone's life rather than mourn their passing? We would have to learn a little more about the character and the context of the funeral to decide. Characters can also be revealed by the words and actions of others who respond to them. In literature, moreover, we have one great advantage that life cannot offer: a work of fiction can give us access to a person's thoughts, which may come in the form of fully formed sentences that look like dialogue or in incoherent partial sentences or word jumbles known as **stream of consciousness**. Although in Ralph Ellison's "King of the Bingo Game" (p. 178) we learn about the protagonist primarily through descriptive details, words, actions, and his relationships with the other characters, Ellison allows us to enter the man's consciousness. Jamaica Kincaid's "Girl" (p. 150) is all dialogue, but it's actually snippets of many conversations that have occurred over a period of time, and it's certainly one-sided as dialogues go.

Authors have two major methods of presenting characters: **showing** and **telling**. Characters shown in dramatic situations reveal themselves indirectly by what they say and do. The general preference in modern fiction is to choose showing over telling when there is a choice. The art of fiction involves exercising the imagination, so fiction writers (like poets) gravitate toward images, or mental pictures. The narrator of Wolff's story has the option of telling you the type of person his father is; he might say, "My father was a jazz enthusiast who loved me and my mom, but who was bad at fulfilling his duties to the point of reckless irresponsibility." Instead, the author *shows* the father's love of jazz: he once got in trouble for sneaking his son into a club to see the legendary Thelonious Monk, he hums "Stars Fell on Alabama" as they barrel through the virgin snow, he does "little scat riffs around the melody" as the drive continues. There are many illustrations of his love for his wife and son, but also of his irresponsibility. We detect a little clownishness in the story's second paragraph when the father "promised, hand on heart, to take good care" of his son: the hand on heart is an insincere gesture, and we can almost picture his mother scowling in response, knowing how hollow the promise is after a lifetime of such behavior. In that same paragraph the father consults his watch after they take "several last runs" and is surprised by the time. The narrator isn't. He's been aware of the time all day, and worried about it.

By showing us the father's character rather than telling it, the author is able to reveal a character patiently and subtly, and to offer some ambiguity as a result. If the narrator merely proclaimed his father "reckless and irresponsible," we might be less likely to see his charms: his obvious joy in life, his confidence, his willingness to take risks. When he hums jazz tunes at a time that might seem stressful, we understand that he is a man bursting with positive energy: if the narrator just told us his father liked jazz, we might not intuit that trait. There are times, though, when telling is the most efficient or only possible way to communicate. The first sentence of the story — "Just before Christmas my father took me skiing at Mount Baker" — is all telling, and it's necessary information for us to have. It doesn't require interpretation: it's simply a fact that the narrator must establish before the story can continue. In a ***first-person narrative*** like this one, we should always be wary of perspective, though, because the storyteller is also a character whose perspective might be limited or distorted by their involvement in the story. For example, late in the story the narrator asks his father to list the narrator's "strong points." If we were evaluating the narrator's character at that moment, we might assume he's a little insecure. His father initially deflects the question, saying, "Don't get me started. . . . It'd take all day," and the narrator responds, "Oh, right. Name one." This response indicates either that possible insecurity or a skepticism that his father really values what he considers his strong points: their values are different. They seem to agree that one of the narrator's strong points is that he "always think[s] ahead," but the illustrations of this thinking ahead border on obsession or anxiety: do you know anyone who keeps their "clothes on numbered hangers to insure proper rotation"? That's a fairly extreme version of "thinking ahead," to be generous. The narrator and his father tell us one thing but show us something slightly different. In this way, telling and showing complement each other.

Characters can be convincing whether they are presented by telling or showing, provided their actions are ***motivated***. There must be reasons for how they behave and what they say. If adequate motivation is offered, we can understand and find ***plausible*** their actions no matter how bizarre. In "A Rose for Emily" (p. 47), Faulkner makes Emily Grierson's intimacy with a corpse credible by preparing us with information about her father's death along with her inability to leave the past and live in the present. Emily turns out to be consistent. Although we are surprised by the ending of the story, the behavior it reveals is compatible with her temperament. Sometimes a character is motivated but unsure how best to achieve their goals and desires. The father in "Powder" says plainly, "I'll tell you what I want. I want us all to be together again." We are likely to believe him, but we also must question if he's going about that goal the right way. He seems less concerned with considering his wife's and son's desires for a punctual Christmas Eve dinner than he is with his own need for adventure.

Some kinds of fiction consciously break away from our expectations of traditional realistic stories. Consistency, plausibility, and motivation are not very useful concepts for understanding and evaluating characterizations in modern absurdist literature, for instance, in which characters are often alienated from themselves and their environment in an irrational world. In this world there is no possibility for traditional heroic action; instead we find an ***antihero*** who has little control over events. T. C. Boyle's protagonist in "The Hit Man" (p. 33) is petting a three-headed dog toward the story's end.

Gregor Samsa, the protagonist of Franz Kafka's "The Metamorphosis" (1915), wakes up as a bug one morning and has to deal with the human world as an insect would. The narrator of John Barth's story "Night-Sea Journey" (1968) is a sperm swimming toward an egg among millions of sperm just like him. These works force us to consider the notion of character in terms that derive less from our experience than from our capacity for imaginative understanding.

In most realistic stories we expect characters to act plausibly and in ways consistent with their personalities, but that does not mean that characters cannot develop and change. A *dynamic* character undergoes some kind of change because of the action of the plot. Huck Finn's view of Jim, the runaway enslaved person in Mark Twain's novel, develops during their experiences on the raft. Huck discovers Jim's humanity and, therefore, cannot betray him because Huck no longer sees his companion as merely the property of a white slave holder. On the other hand, Huck's friend Tom Sawyer is a *static* character because he does not change. He remains interested only in high adventure, even at the risk of Jim's life. As static characters often do, Tom serves as a foil to Huck; his frivolous concerns are contrasted with Huck's serious development. A *foil* helps to reveal by contrast the distinctive qualities of another character. We can see a similar dynamic in "Powder." The narrator's father is *static* in the sense that he cannot or is not willing to change. It would seem that the narrator is also static in that it appears as if he is doomed to worry, perhaps as a way of compensating for his father's tendency to break rules, but for a brief, important moment in the crucial final two paragraphs of the story he relaxes: "I stopped moping and began to enjoy myself." Even if it's a temporary change, we have to be a little relieved by this response. The easygoing, joyful final sentence of the story sounds more like his father than like him.

The protagonist in a story is usually a dynamic character who experiences some conflict that makes an impact on their life. Less commonly, static characters can also be protagonists. The title character in Boyle's "The Hit Man" (p. 33) doesn't change in any meaningful way over the course of his life, growing up, living, and dying a masked hit man. The protagonist in Faulkner's "A Rose for Emily" (p. 47) is also a static character; indeed, she rejects all change. The reader understands her changes, but she does not. Ordinarily, however, a plot contains one or two dynamic characters with any number of static characters in supporting roles. This is especially true of short stories, in which brevity limits the possibilities of character development.

The extent to which a character is developed is another means by which character can be analyzed. The novelist E. M. Forster coined the terms *flat* and *round* to distinguish degrees of character development. A *flat character* embodies one or two qualities, ideas, or traits that can be readily described in a brief summary. For instance, the trooper in "Powder" might be a fascinating guy at home with an extensive collection of rare artwork and the ability to juggle running chainsaws, but in this story his role is to say, "The road is closed," and to haunt the narrator's worried mind thereafter. He's just a cop, doing his job. Flat characters tend to be one-dimensional. They are readily accessible because their characteristics are few and simple; they are not created to be psychologically complex.

Some flat characters are immediately recognizable as **stock characters**. These stereotypes are particularly popular in formula fiction, television programs, and action movies. Stock characters are types rather than individuals. The poor but dedicated writer falls in love with a hard-working understudy, who gets nowhere because the corrupt producer favors their boozy, pampered lover for the leading role. Characters such as these — the loyal servant, the mean stepparent, the henpecked spouse, the dumb blonde, the sadistic army officer, the dotty grandparent — are prepackaged; they lack individuality because their authors have, in a sense, not imaginatively created them but simply summoned them from a warehouse of clichés and social prejudices. Stock characters can become fresh if a good writer makes them vivid, interesting, or memorable, but too often a writer's use of these stereotypes is simply weak characterization.

**Round characters** are more complex than flat or stock characters. Round characters have more depth and require more attention. They may surprise us or puzzle us. Although they are more fully developed, round characters are also more difficult to summarize because we are aware of competing ideas, values, and possibilities in their lives. As a flat character, Huck Finn's alcoholic, bigoted father is clear to us; we know that Pap is the embodiment of racism and irrationality. But Huck is considerably less predictable because he struggles with what Twain calls a "sound heart and a deformed conscience."

An author's use of a flat character — even as a protagonist — does not necessarily represent an artistic flaw. It might be a conscious choice so that we pay even closer attention to the dynamic, round characters in the story, particularly as they interact with flat characters. Moreover, both flat and round characters can be either dynamic or static. Each plot can be made most effective by its own special kind of characterization. Terms such as *round* and *flat* are helpful tools to use to determine what we know about a character, but they are not an infallible measurement of the quality of a story.

The next two stories — Zadie Smith's "Martha, Martha" and James Baldwin's "Sonny's Blues" — offer character studies worthy of close analysis. As you read them, notice the methods of characterization used to bring each to life.

## ZADIE SMITH (B. 1975)

David Levenson/Getty Images.

Zadie Smith, the daughter of a Jamaican mother and an English father, was born and raised in a borough just northwest of London. She has been a literary star since the publication of her debut novel, *White Teeth*, in 2000. Her fame brought her to Cambridge, Massachusetts, where she was a Fellow at the Radcliffe Institute for Advanced Study at Harvard University in 2003. Her time in the Boston area provided the setting for her highly praised third novel, *On Beauty* (2005), and for the following story, "Martha, Martha." In addition to London and Boston, she has lived in New York City and Rome. As you read, consider the way global perspectives and regional or provincial perspectives help to develop character.

## Martha, Martha    2003

Though the telephone is a perfectly useless indicator of most human qualities, it's pretty percise about age. From her tiny office on the third floor, Pam Roberts looked through a window and correctly identified the Martha Penk she was waiting for, a shrimpish girl pushing twenty-two, lost down there. She had on a red overcoat and cream snow boots, putting her weight on their edges like an ice skater; she seemed to waver between two doorways. Pam opened her mouth to call out "Miss Penk!" but never got to make the curious sound — abruptly the girl turned the corner and headed back down Apple towards the river. Pam went to her own door, opened it, worried her chapped lips with a finger, closed it again. The cold was just too extreme; today the first snows were due, opening performance of a show that would last a dreary, relentless four months. Besides, she had her slippers on. Miss Martha Penk, who appeared to believe that two bedrooms and a garden could be had for a thousand dollars a month, would figure out her second mistake soon enough, come back, discover the bell. The confusion was common; it arose from the higgledy-piggledy arrangement of the ground floor — a busy bookshop and a swing-doored optician obscured the sign that told you of the dentist, the insurers, the accountant and Pam's own dinky realty business at the top of the building; also the antique elevator that would take you to them. Pam tapped her door with a knuckle, warning it she would return, and crossed the room to the filing cabinet. On tiptoes she slid open the top drawer and began flicking through files, her Mozart swelling behind her. She sang along with that section of the *Requiem* that sounds so very like "OH I SEE YOU WILL GO DOWN! AND I SEE YOU WILL GO ALSO!," although it could not be this for the words are Latin. As she sang she ground one of her Chinese slippers rhythmically into the carpet and pressed herself into the metal drawer to reach for something at the very back: "OH I SEE YOU WILL GO DOWN, OH! I SEE YOU WILL GO DOWN! ALSO! ALSO!"

Pam found what she wanted, closed the cabinet suddenly with an elbow and sat down in a fat armchair opposite a lithograph of Venice. She put a foot in her hand and said "Phee-yoo! Now, *there* you go," pressing relief into a sore instep. She started picking out every third sheet or so from the listings and laying them on the floor before her in a small pile. At the opening of the "Lacrimosa"° she removed her slipper entirely, but then hearing someone gallop up the stairs, replaced it and quickly rose to greet a large, dark, bearded man in a sheepskin overcoat, who stood bent at the knees like a shortstop, trying to recover his breath in the hallway. He took a step towards her, looked up and frowned. He paused where he was, supporting himself with a hand on the door frame. Pam knew exactly why he had come and the two spoke at the same time.

"This temping agency?" he asked, a heavy accent, quickly identified by Pam as Middle-Easterny. A Middle-Easterny scarf, too, and a hat.

"No dear, *no*," said Pam, and let her glasses fall to her chest from their chain, "It's above the *other* Milliner's Books, right? There's two Milliner's Books — you need the one on the corner of Apple and Wallace — this is the wrong Milliner's, this is above the *children's* Milliner's — I don't know why they just don't say that to people —"

*The Lacrimosa:* One of the movements of Mozart's *Requiem Mass* that Pam is humming; the word connotes sorrow, sadness, or tears.

The man groaned pleasantly and hit his temple with the hub of his palm.    5
"I make mistake. Sorry, please."

"No, they just didn't say, they never *do*. It's not *you,* dear, it's them — people always come here by mistake, it's not *you*. It's two minutes from here. Now, you go back down, turn left, then immediately right, you can see it from there. I've got somebody who just did the *exact* same, but *exactly* — only vice versa — she's gone to . . ."

A further thundering on the stairs and three more men, younger, also bearded. They stood bent like their friend, panting, one man crying the involuntary tears of a Massachusetts winter. They stared at Pam who stared frankly back at them, with her hands on her makeshift hips, up there where her black linen trousers began, high under the breasts. A black T-shirt and cardigan finished the thing off. Pam was a recognized doodlenut when it came to clothes, buying the same things over and over, black and loose, like a fat Zen monk. She didn't mind. Her moustache was moist and visible — oh, so let 'em *stare* was how Pam felt about it. Young men did not register with Pam any more.

"My friends," explained the man, and with his friends began the descent, emptying out a demotic° mystery language into the stairwell. Miss Penk must have passed them on the bend. A moment later she was in the room apologizing for her lateness.

"Sorry I'm late, I'm sorry," she said, but did not look sorry. Her face, very black,    10
could not blush, and her accent, to Pam's ears very English, could not apologize. She stood in the centre of the room, clumsily divesting herself of the loud red coat. She was short, but more muscular, more solid than she had appeared from three floors up. A cheap-looking grey trouser suit and some fake pearls were conspiring to make her older than she was. The buttons on the jacket looked like rusty spare change.

"No, I saw *you,* you see," began Pam warmly, coming forward to catch what was falling, a scarf, a woolly hat, "There's *two* Milliner's — did you see those men? On the stairs? They did the exact same thing — and I saw you down — "

"The lift's broken, it don't work," said Martha, and now lifted her head and reached out a hand. Pam felt faintly interrupted, but took the hand and gave it a double-handed shake.

"Pam Roberts, we spoke on the phone. It's so good to *meet* you!"

"I'm Martha," she replied and quickly freed herself. She passed a smoothing hand over her own short ironed hair, cut in a flapper's style, a helmet brilliant with some kind of polish. A concrete kiss curl had been plastered on to her left cheek. Pam had never seen anything quite like it in her office before.

"Well. Now, did you come from far? Are you nearby?" Pam asked, a question    15
that had a little business in it.

"Near, yeah," said the girl, firmly. She stood oddly, hands by her sides, feet together, "A hotel, it's called The Charles? It's just like by the river — it's just if you go down by — "

"Oh, I know where it is — it's *very* nice."

"It costs too much, man," said Martha, tutting loudly, removing a pair of childish mittens, "But I came right from London and I didn't have any place arranged — I just arksed the taxi to take me to the nearest hotel — I been there a week, but I can't afford it for much longer, you know?"

---

*Demotic:* Ordinary or colloquial speech.

Usually Pam would use these minutes in the office to ascertain something about likely wealth, class, all very gently — what kind of house, what kind of taste, what kind of price — but she had been wrong about English accents before, not knowing which were high class, which not. Or whether high class meant money at *all* — if you watched PBS as Pam did you soon found out that in England it could, often did, mean the exact opposite.

"It *is* such a nice place, The Charles. They really do things properly there, don't     20 they? They really make the best of that location, I think. I stayed there once for a realty conference, and I really appreciated the standard of the breakfasts. People talk about pool this, steamroom that, but in actual fact it's the little things, like a *breakfast*. A good hot *breakfast*. But my *God* the price isn't any fun — Martha, we'll have you out of there in no time, I promise, especially if we find something empty —"

"Yes," said Martha, but rather too quick, too desperate, "How long would it be before I could move in somewhere?"

Pam felt herself immediately on surer ground and slipped down a gear into patter, "Well, as I'm saying, dear, it depends on whether the place has people in it at the *moment* — but even then, we can turn it around very *very* quickly. It just needs to happen so that everybody wants to make it work, that's all. Don't worry, we'll find something that works. And if it doesn't work, we'll cut it loose and go on to the next," she said loudly, clapping her hands and glancing at a clock on the wall, "Now, I've got about two hours free — it's really very dry at the moment so there's *plenty* to show." She bent down to scoop the remembered listings from the floor, "I think I understand what you're looking for, Martha, I received your letter, I have it right here — Wait — " Pam reached over to her stereo like a woman with one foot each in two drifting boats; she punched at a couple of buttons to no avail, "Sometimes it gets a little loud. Funny little machine. It's completely wireless! It's like a single unit stereo for single people, very liberating. You can't really adjust it without the remote, though, which is a little frustrating. And I find it gets louder sometimes, do you know? Sort of when you don't expect it?"

"Classical," said Martha, and looked at Pam and the surrounding office with determined reverence, "I want to listen to more classical music. I want to know more about it. It's on my list."

And this she said in such a way that Pam had no doubt that there was such a list, and that renting an apartment *today* was somewhere on it. The girl had a manner that was all itinerary, charmless and determined, and Pam, a Midwesterner by birth, had the shameful idea that she might go far, this Martha Penk, here on the East Coast.

"Oh! Well, I don't know what there is to *know,* really. I mean; I don't know any-     25 thing at *all*. It's the violins that do it for me, I guess, the way they sound like some-body's crying? The 'Lacrimosa' means crying, I'm pretty sure. Lachrymose — that's from the eye, isn't it? But are you at the university?"

"No!" said Martha but her face at last released a flood of undisguised plea-sure, as when a girl is told she could be a model or an actress or do whatever she does amateurishly, professionally, "I wish! Maybe one day. I'm looking for that next level — qualifications, getting forward, raising myself, my consciousness. But that's like a dream, yeah, for me at this stage?"

She looked serious again, began enlisting her hands in her speech, drawing out these "levels" in the air, "It's about stepping a bit further, I mean, for me, I really want to improve myself while I'm here, go up a bit, like listening to different music, like that."

"*Well,*" said Pam brightly, and sounded her desk with her hand, "We'll just have to find you the right place where you can do that. Hmm?" But Miss Penk had returned her attention to the CD case, and Pam found herself nodding into the silence, and talking to fill it, "Oh, I just like all kinds of music, really. I am just the *biggest* fan of music. Cuban, classical, hillbilly — or whatever you call that sort of close harmony singing? A lot of jazz . . . don't know a thing about it, though! Oh *my*. Maybe I can't be improved. Too old to be any better than I am," said Pam in a saccharine sing-song, as if it were a proverb.

"Yeah," said Martha, the sort of absent yes that a silly proverb probably deserves. She took the sleeve notes out of the case and opened them up.

"Now," said Pam, struggling a little, "From your letter I understood you were   30 thinking around the thousand mark — but that's really a little *low* — I mean, I'll *show* you those places, Martha, but I can't guarantee you're going to *like* them. I mean, they're not there to be *liked,*" Pam said patiently, and gathered up her car keys from her desk, "But we'll find something that works — we just need to get a handle on it. I'd like to show you a big place that's going for two thousand, maybe — maybe lower — it's negotiable with the present owner. In more vibrant times, it's worth at least three. It'll give us some idea anyway. I'm here to make it work for you, so, I'm going to be led by you . . ."

Outside a plane roared low like some prehistoric bird, Pam shuddered; Martha did not move. Pam tried jostling her keys expectantly in her hand; Martha put down the CD case leaving the notes unfolded and walked over to the window. From behind she was an even more neatly made girl than from the front, everything tight and defined, fighting slightly against the banal restraint of polyester.

"We'll take my car; if that's all right," tried Pam, anxious that Martha should not open a window but unwilling to ask her not to. It *was* hot in the room, but it was that time of year: you either fried or you froze. But Martha had already tugged on the sash, in a second her head was out there in the open air. Pam winced. She hated to see people lean all the way out of a window like that.

"Do you get a lot of university people? Students?"

"Oh, *yes*. At the beginning of a semester, certainly. Students around here have some money to spare, if you know what I mean."

Martha took her plastic pearls in her hand and twisted them.   35

"They must be amazing. Focused people."

"Oh! Well, yes, I suppose. Certainly, they're *bright*. There's just no denying that. But I'm afraid," said Pam in her own, overused, comic whisper, "They can be pretty *obnoxious* as well."

"There aren't any black students," Martha said in a tone somewhere between statement and question. Pam, who was in the middle of forcing her arm though a recalcitrant coat sleeve, stopped in her position like a scarecrow, "Well, of *course* there are students of colour, dear! I see them all the time — I mean, even before the affirmative action and all of that — I mean, there's *always* been the basketball scholarships and the rest — though it's much, much better now of course. They're *completely* here on their own steam *now*. Lots of Chinese young people too, and Indian, many. Many! Oh, there's plenty, *plenty* of people of colour here, you'll see," said Pam and switched off her desk lamp. "But have you been to America before?"

"Only Florida when I was twelve. I didn't like it — it's quite vulgar?" said Martha, and the word was most definitely borrowed in her mouth. Pam, who also occasionally borrowed words, recognized the habit and tried to look kindly upon it.

"Florida and Nigeria are the only places I've been, really, out of England," con- 40
tinued Martha, leaning yet further out, gazing across the square, "And now here."

"Oh, are you Nigerian?" Pam asked, kicked off her slippers and began to
replace them with treasured walking boots. When people remarked that Pam had
become "so *hard*" recently or suggested that she'd turned into a doodlenut since
her divorce, they often meant these boots and nothing more than these boots.

"My parents."

"Penk, it's very unusual, isn't it?" said Pam to Martha's back, "Is that a Nigerian
name?"

"No."

Nothing further came. Discovering her remote control behind a coffee cup, 45
Pam stopped the CD and then approached, reaching briskly around Martha to
close the window. Clearly, the girl blew hot and cold; in the end Pam just needed
her name on a contract, nothing more. Even that was not essential — plenty of people take up your whole afternoon and never call again; Pam called them her one-
day stands.

"Look at that sky. It's gonna snow any minute. You know, we should try to get
going before it really starts to come down . . ."

With a simple, businesslike nod Pam indicated the coat that Martha had left
draped over the photocopier.

About a half-hour later the two of them were completing their tour of Professor
Herrin's house, climbing back down the stairs into his open-plan ground-floor
lounge. The place was big, but in some disrepair. The carpets felt springy, damp.
Mould was the overarching theme. Martha was stepping over an empty cat-food
can, and Pam's voice was taking on the fluidity of a woman who feels she is moving down the home straight of her anecdote, "He's just a very, very impressive
man. Not only is he a Professor of Chinese, he holds a law degree — can you
imagine — he's on all *kinds* of boards, I'm sure he plays that piano — When the
*President of the United States* wants advice on China, the *President,* mind you,
he calls up Professor Herrin. It's such a pleasure talking with that man about
*Taoism* or, I don't know, *science* or health matters . . . So many men, they just don't
achieve anything at *all* — they don't *expect* to — beyond *business* or a little bit of
*golf,* maybe. But there's no attention to the spiritual side, not at all. I mean, his
wife, well, actually his wife's a little peculiar — but the mind just boggles to think
about living with a man like Professor Herrin, I mean, the attempt to satisfy him,
*mentally* . . . and it's *such* a beautiful house, a little fusty; but — have you seen this?
He carved it, he really did. He's a Zen Buddhist, death for him is just an *idea.* He
*made* the bookshelf — and of course that would all stay here — he would just want
to know from you how many of his books he'll have to store, I mean how much
shelving you would need, and so on. He's already in New York, and he's intending to be there until at *least* next February. He's a sort of an *expert* on relations
between the races," whispered Pam, "so he feels it's important to be in New York
right now. In its hour of *need,* you know."°

"I don't have any books," said Martha, opening the screen door and stepping
into a small walled garden, "I'm going to get books, though, prob'ly, I'll — Oh, it's
snowing — it must've started when we were in there. It's on the ground, look."

*New York. . . in its hour of need:* A reference to the terror attacks on the World Trade Center on
September 11, 2001.

Pam turned to look and already the ebony sheen of Martha's hair was speckled  50
white, like dusting on a chocolate cake.

"This house feels sad, man," said Martha, and lifted one foot off the ground.
She reached behind herself and grabbed the ankle, pressing the foot into her buttocks. First one leg, then the other.

"Does it?" asked Pam, as if the idea had never occurred to her, but her passion for gossip was stronger then her instinct for business, "Well, actually his wife
is very peculiar, a terrible thing happened to her. Terrible. It's partly why they're
moving again — she can't stand to be in one place, she *broods.* Now, aren't you *cold*
out there?"

Martha shrugged, crouched, and tried sweeping a half-inch of snow into her
hands, began packing it. Pam sat on the piano stool and stretched her legs out in
front of her.

"His wife, Professor Herrin's wife — it's such an awful story — she was in
*China,* about twenty-five years ago, and this young man stole her bag. Well, *naturally* she reported it — and what do you think? Two months later when she got
back to America, she heard he'd been executed, can you imagine? What that would
*do* to a person, it's just terrible. It's a terrible weight to bear."

"She shouldn't have said nothing," said Martha, and appeared to think no  55
more about it.

"Well," considered Pam, pushing her glasses up her nose, "I think it's quite a
difficult marriage — I think he's quite eager to leave this place, so I imagine he'd be
flexible vis-à-vis the rent, Martha. Martha?"

"Yeah? Sorry, what?"

"Now, Martha, let's talk now. What are you thinking — are you at all . . . ?"

Martha took her half-packed snowball and threw it limply at the wall.

"I can't afford it. It's too much. Loads too much. Why does it smell weird  60
out here?"

"*Okay.* . . . well, now I wanted to ask about money," said Pam slowly, coming
to the opening and hugging herself against the chill, "I mean, are we talking about
savings? You're very young. Or will you be working? Just so I have some *idea* of
how much space we have to manoeuvre."

Martha stayed where she was in the garden but put both hands out in front of
her, awaiting whatever came. The flakes were massive, consistent and quick, as if
the snow was not merely falling but being delivered, like manna, because people
needed it.

"I've been left some," said Martha quietly, "In a will. My uncle passed. Basically,
it's enough for a year. A thousand a month, two bedrooms and a garden, yeah?
Maybe a bit more, maybe. I need space for people. To come." She paused. "If they
want." Suddenly she seemed agitated, even panicked; she attacked her bottom lip
with her teeth and looked up and over into the next garden, "People who might
visit, you get me? But this is too too big, I can't afford it. I can't. Don't you have
anything I can *afford?*"

It looked for a moment that the girl was about to cry — out of instinct Pam
hurried towards her — but by the time she stepped outside Martha had already
recovered herself, turning to peer now over the back wall towards the piercing towers and stark white crosses of the university. She seemed calmly framed by them
and remote, a figure in a plastic snowstorm.

"Something a bit further out, maybe," offered Pam a minute later as they  65
climbed back into the car.

"If I had all that education," said Martha, fastening her seat belt, "Believe me, I wouldn't live somewhere like *that*."

"Oh no?"

"I'd live somewhere *new*."

"I see," said Pam tersely, starting the car and welcoming the automatic resuscitation of the stereo, Mozart and his death song as background filler. "Well, each to their own, I suppose, Martha, that's what this business is about, of course. Actually, I used to live on this street, at the top end, at this end, in the more modern architecture, and I must say I found it very pleasant for a long time. Though I also enjoy — I have a sort of apartment now, downtown, and that's also very nice, in a different way."

"You used to live in one of these big houses?" Martha asked, with unseemly 70 incredulity, and as she spoke they drove past the very house. For the first time in months Pam resisted the urge to inspect the curtains, the lawn, the little things he'd changed for somebody else.

"Why'd you go?"

"Circumstances. My circumstances changed. I guess you could say that."

"How?"

"My *gosh,* you *are* a nosy parker. I'll guess I'll have to tell you my dress size next."

"I'm just arksing, you don't have to answer." 75

"You should be a lawyer or something, it's like being cross-*examined*."

"So why'd you go?"

Pam sighed, but in fact she had, some time ago, designed a speech to answer the question, whoever it came from, "Well, I suppose at my age, Martha, and especially in the light of the events of last September, I just think you have to make things work for you, work for you *personally,* because life is really too short, arid if they don't work, you just have to go ahead and cut them loose, and that's basically — "

"I'd love to be a lawyer," interrupted Martha, "My friend is a lawyer. She has a house like that. Big-up house. We used to get the bus together to school. Now she's a big lawyer. That's like the best thing you can be."

"You know what?" said Pam, drumming the steering wheel and preparing to 80 lie, "I like what I do. I don't think I'd change it to be a lawyer for all the tea in China. I really don't. I guess that's just me."

Martha pulled down the passenger mirror, licked her finger and began to reshape her kiss curl.

"She's my role model, Kara — she definitely took it to the next level — as a young black woman, you know? She didn't get caught up in a lot of the things you can get caught up in — kids and that. She took it forward. That's where I'm aiming for — if you don't aim high, there's no point, really."

Martha wound down the window that Pam had just closed and Pam felt she might just scream if the girl kept letting the outside in everywhere they went.

"Now, *good* for her! And good for you, too. God knows, when I was your age, all I did was have children, oh *my*. I've *three* girls. But it's such a different world. I wouldn't even want to bring up children in this world now. My *gosh,* it's really snowing. That's a couple of inches since we left the office."

They drove twenty minutes and then parked a street from the one they wanted so 85 Martha would have an opportunity to see a bit of this new neighbourhood by foot. It was cold beyond cold. Everything laid out like a promise, delayed for summer;

bleached porches, dead gardens, naked trees, a sky-blue clapboard house, its rose-pink neighbour. Part of the East Coast realtor's skill is to explain what places will look like when the sun finally comes.

"And this just goes the most *incredible* orange when the fall comes. It's like the whole city is on fire. Just life, life, life *everywhere*. Now, the couple we're about to see," said Pam, walking briskly ahead, "They are just darling. Yousef and Amelia. He's Moroccan and *so* handsome and she's American, just American, and they have such a beautiful daughter, Lily."

"Where they going to go, then, if I move in?"

"They're moving to Morocco. It's just what we were saying, they don't really want to bring up children in this country, I'm afraid. And frankly, I can understand that. They're *artists* too, so, they're a little bit flaky. But *very* sophisticated. So witty, and they make you feel comfortable right away, you know? Now, Martha, I've shown so many people this house, but it's a little too small for a family and a little too big for a single person, so it's awkward — but it's *perfect* for you — now, what *is* that — "

There had been a babbling noise the past minute or so, excited foreign voices, and as they turned the corner Martha saw some snow come flying and guessed at children, but the next second revealed the depth of the voices — these were bearded men, with dark, ashen skins — and the argument was over design, a snowman. It was incompetently begun, a tall upturned cone upon which a future head would never sit. And now work had stopped entirely; at the sight of the two women, the men froze and looked at their gloved hands and seemed to find themselves ridiculous.

"But those are the men!" cried Pam when they were not five yards out of hear-   90
ing range, "From my office. They just came just before you. But isn't that *weird*? They're making a snowman!"

"Is what they were doing?" asked Martha, and dug into her pocket for a mint she had quietly lifted from the bowl of same in Pam's office.

"Well what *else* were they doing. You know, Martha, they've probably never seen snow. Isn't that amazing — what a thing to see!"

"Grown men playing in the snow," said Martha, but Pam could not be dissuaded from the romance of it, and it was the first anecdote she told as they walked through the door of 28 Linnaean, a canary-yellow first-floor apartment with two porches, front and back, nestled behind a nineteenth-century police station. Yousef was handsome as promised, curly-haired and with eyes many shades lighter brown than his skin; he was frying something with a great deal of chilli in it and offered his elbow for Martha to shake. Amelia was very skinny and freckled, with an angular hip and a toddler perched on it. She had the kindly, detached air of a young mother, the world outside the screen door having grown distant and surreal, brought to her only in tiresome reports from other people. But she good-humouredly let Pam hustle her to a window at the front of the house and followed the direction of her finger.

"Over there, can you see? They're making a *snow*man! Egyptian or Iranian or *something*. They were so *sheepish* about it. They were so embarrassed. I don't think they've ever seen snow before! And I saw these men, an *hour* ago in my *office*. It's the same men. But the *exact* same. Martha doesn't think anything of it, but I think it's darling."

"That is sweet," conceded Amelia, and hitched Lily up over her shoulder.   95

"Amelia — " said Pam, suddenly, taking a step back from her and appraising a small bulge around her middle, "Now, are you pregnant again?"

"NO," called Yousef from the other room, laughing, "She's just a fat girl now! I feed her too much!"

"Four months," said Amelia, shaking her head, "And I'm going to have it in Morocco, God help me. Hey there, Martha. Do you think you'll take this place off our hands? *Please* won't you, please? We're totally desperate!"

"I don't know yet, do I?" said Martha very fiercely and made the odd, contemptuous noise with her teeth again. Lily reached out a doughy pink hand for Martha's face; she flinched from it.

"Oh," said Amelia, reddening, and battling Lily's tiny kicking legs, "I didn't    100 mean to—"

Pam almost blew up right there—she just *could not* understand what kind of a girl this was, where she came from, what kind of conversation was normal for her. She drummed her fingers on the patch of wall behind her—as close an expression of suppressed fury as Pam ever managed.

"Martha, I'm sure Amelia only meant—"

"I was really joking, I didn't—" said Amelia, putting an incautious hand on Martha's shoulder, feeling a taut, inflexible muscle. She soon retracted it, but Martha continued to look and speak to the spot where the hand had been, "I didn't mean that, I mean I meant I think I want to be nearer the university, nearer all of that, yeah? It's very alone up here, if you're alone, isn't it?"

"Well, you know, there's a very convenient bus—" said Amelia, looking over Martha to Pam who was performing a minimal mime with her thumbs to the effect that she did not know the girl well nor could she explain her.

"I'll look around," said Martha, and walked away from them both, down    105 the hall.

"Look everywhere," said Amelia feelingly. She let Lily loose from her struggle, laying her on the floor. "Please, feel absolutely at liberty."

"Oh, she will," said Pam rather tartly, but Amelia did not smile and Pam was mortified to see that she had thought the comment cruel. Without any skill, Pam turned the conversation to the problem of noisy plumbing.

At the other end of the apartment, Martha's walk changed; she was alone. She moved through the two big bedrooms, loose and alert, examining the strange foreign things in them: Arabic writing, meaningless paintings, and all those touches that rich people seem to use to look poor: wood floors, threadbare rugs, no duvets, all blankets, nothing matching. Old leather instead of new, fireplaces instead of central heating, everything wrong. Only the bathroom was impressive; very clean, white tiled. It had a mirror with a movie star's bald light bulbs circling it. Martha locked herself in here, ran both of the taps full blast, and sat on the closed toilet seat. She took a worn-looking, folded photograph from her coat pocket and wept. She was crying even before she had unfolded it, but flattening it out now against her knee made it almost impossible for her to breathe. In the picture a grinning, long-lashed boy, about eighteen months old, with a head like a polished ackee nut, sat on the lap of a handsome black man. Neither the picture nor their mutual beauty was in any way marred by the fact that both of them had sellotaped their noses to their foreheads to give the impression of pigs' snouts. Martha turned over the photograph and read what was written there.

> Martha, Martha, I love U
> And I'm trying 2 tell U true
> For this New Year 2002
> I am going to be there for U

I know that U have many dreams
And life is not always how it seems
But I want U 2 put me 2 the test
And I will do all the rest
Together we will get so much higher
Through my love and our desire
Don't give up on what we've got
Cos Ben and Jamal love U a lot!

It took another five minutes to recover herself. She rinsed her face in the sink and flushed the toilet. She came close up to the mirror and gave thanks to God for her secretive skin that told nobody anything; no flush, no puffiness. She could hear a great deal of laughter the other side of the door and wondered what they were saying about her; especially *him,* who was probably the worst, because he'd married like that and those ones that marry white always feel even more superior. She hadn't expected this. She didn't know what she'd expected.

"Martha!" cried Pam as she appeared again in the kitchen-lounge, "I thought  110
you'd been eaten by something. Eaten by a bear."

"Just looking around. It's nice."

Pam sat on a high kitchen stool beaming at Yousef, but he was busy pulling a giggling Lily out from under the sofa by her ankles.

"So you've had a good look around — she's had a good look around, Yousef, so that's something. Now," said Pam, reaching down to the floor to get her bag, "I don't want to hurry anybody. It always helps to get to know each other a little bit, I think. How can we make this work, for everybody?"

"But I don't know if I — I can't — "

"Martha, *dear,*" said Pam, returning a pen and pad she was holding back to  115
her bag, "There's no hurry whatsoever, that's not the way this works at all."

"You know what?" replied Martha. With trembling fingers, she undid and then retied the waistband of her coat, "I've got to go."

"Well — " said Pam, completely astonished, and shook her head, "But — if you'll give me — just wait a *minute,* I'll — "

"I'll walk. I want to walk — I need some air."

Pam put down her coffee cup, and smiled awkwardly between Yousef and Amelia on the one hand and Martha on the other, increasing, as only Pam knew how, the awkwardness on both sides.

"I think I want a one bedroom thing," mumbled Martha, her hand already on  120
the doorknob, "One bedroom would be more . . . " she said but could not finish. "I'm sorry," she said, and again Pam could not tell if she meant it. You can't tell anything about a one-day stand. They aren't there to be known. Pam shunted herself off the stool and put her hands out as if for something falling but Martha had already backed on to the porch. She struggled down the snowy steps, felt the same panic that rightly belongs to a fire escape. She could hear the clamour of snowman builders, speaking in tongues, laughing about something.

### CONSIDERATIONS FOR CRITICAL THINKING AND WRITING

1. **FIRST RESPONSE.** The initial encounter between Pam and Martha in Pam's office is awkward. Which of them is more responsible for the awkwardness?

2. Look carefully at the descriptions of the ways Pam and Martha are dressed early in the story. What do their clothes say about them?

3. Martha's initial speech is striking for its British inflections. What does Pam assume about her based on the way she talks?

4. We learn that Pam is originally from the Midwest and that she has "the shameful idea" (par. 24) that Martha will do well here on the East Coast. What does Pam mean by that? And how does her regional origin help to define her character?

5. Note that Pam tends to talk at length while Martha is often silent or speaks in short sentences. What do these tendencies say about their characters?

6. Martha is constantly rolling down windows and stepping outside, a trait that drives Pam crazy. Why does this bother her so much?

7. Pam becomes increasingly furious and frustrated with Martha, thinking at one point, "she just *could not* understand what kind of a girl this was" (par. 101). What behavior or characteristics is this response based on?

8. A key scene for understanding Martha is when she is alone in the bathroom, crying and reading the back of the photograph she carries with her (par. 108). How does your understanding of her change at that point? Does your understanding of the story also change?

9. Pam refers to her visits with real estate clients as "one-day stands" and concludes, "You can't tell anything about a one-day stand" (par. 120). Is that true? Do we understand more about Martha or about Pam by the end of the story?

## CONNECTIONS TO OTHER SELECTIONS

1. Pam in this story and Andrea in Ann Beattie's "Janus" (p. 27) are both realtors. How are they similar and different? To what degree does this particular profession help you to understand this character type?

2. Discuss the limitations of the way characters know or understand each other in this story and in the following story, "Sonny's Blues" by James Baldwin (p. 91). What inhibits understanding? What could aid it?

## JAMES BALDWIN (1924–1987)

The most prominent African American writer of the civil rights era of the 1950s and 1960s, James Baldwin wrote prolifically and passionately in many styles and genres. His book-length essay *The Fire Next Time* (1963) was a groundbreaking meditation on race relations and religion that ended on a note of fiery prophecy about America's possible future. His novels *Go Tell It on the Mountain* (1953) and *Giovanni's Room* (1956) demonstrated early in his career the range of his topics and interests, anticipating topics that writers would deal with in even more depth after his premature death in 1987 — topics such as racial mythology, bisexuality, and gender identity. As an expatriate who lived

Everett Collection Inc/Alamy.

for extended periods in Paris, the south of France, and Turkey, Baldwin gained a global perspective that is only now being fully appreciated. His works have recently been made into acclaimed films: *I Am Not Your Negro* (2016) and *If Beale Street Could Talk* (2018). The following short story, "Sonny's Blues," is one of the finest in the English language.

## Sonny's Blues   1957

I read about it in the paper, in the subway, on my way to work. I read it, and I couldn't believe it, and I read it again. Then perhaps I just stared at it, at the news-print spelling out his name, spelling out the story. I stared at it in the swinging lights of the subway car, and in the faces and bodies of the people, and in my own face, trapped in the darkness which roared outside.

It was not to be believed and I kept telling myself that, as I walked from the subway station to the high school. And at the same time I couldn't doubt it. I was scared, scared for Sonny. He became real to me again. A great block of ice got settled in my belly and kept melting there slowly all day long, while I taught my classes algebra. It was a special kind of ice. It kept melting, sending trickles of ice water all up and down my veins, but it never got less. Sometimes it hardened and seemed to expand until I felt my guts were going to come spilling out or that I was going to choke or scream. This would always be at a moment when I was remembering some specific thing Sonny had once said or done.

When he was about as old as the boys in my classes his face had been bright and open, there was a lot of copper in it; and he'd had wonderfully direct brown eyes, and great gentleness and privacy. I wondered what he looked like now. He had been picked up, the evening before, in a raid on an apartment downtown, for peddling and using heroin.

I couldn't believe it: but what I mean by that is that I couldn't find any room for it anywhere inside me. I had kept it outside me for a long time. I hadn't wanted to know. I had had suspicions, but I didn't name them, I kept putting them away. I told myself that Sonny was wild, but he wasn't crazy. And he'd always been a good boy, he hadn't ever turned hard or evil or disrespectful, the way kids can, so quick, so quick, especially in Harlem. I didn't want to believe that I'd ever see my brother going down, coming to nothing, all that light in his face gone out, in the condition I'd already seen so many others. Yet it had happened and here I was, talking about algebra to a lot of boys who might, every one of them for all I knew, be popping off needles every time they went to the head. Maybe it did more for them than algebra could.

I was sure that the first time Sonny had ever had horse, he couldn't have been 5 much older than these boys were now. These boys, now, were living as we'd been living then, they were growing up with a rush and their heads bumped abruptly against the low ceiling of their actual possibilities. They were filled with rage. All they really knew were two darknesses, the darkness of their lives, which was now closing in on them, and the darkness of the movies, which had blinded them to that other darkness, and in which they now, vindictively, dreamed, at once more together than they were at any other time, and more alone.

When the last bell rang, the last class ended, I let out my breath. It seemed I'd been holding it for all that time. My clothes were wet — I may have looked as though I'd been sitting in a steam bath, all dressed up, all afternoon. I sat alone in the classroom a long time. I listened to the boys outside, downstairs, shouting and cursing and laughing. Their laughter struck me for perhaps the first time. It was not the joyous laughter which — God knows why — one associates with children. It was mocking and insular, its intent was to denigrate. It was disenchanted, and in this, also, lay the authority of their curses. Perhaps I was listening to them because I was thinking about my brother and in them I heard my brother. And myself.

One boy was whistling a tune, at once very complicated and very simple, it seemed to be pouring out of him as though he were a bird, and it sounded very cool and moving through all that harsh, bright air, only just holding its own through all those other sounds.

I stood up and walked over to the window and looked down into the court-yard. It was the beginning of the spring and the sap was rising in the boys. A teacher passed through them every now and again, quickly, as though he or she couldn't wait to get out of that courtyard, to get those boys out of their sight and off their minds. I started collecting my stuff. I thought I'd better get home and talk to Isabel.

The courtyard was almost deserted by the time I got downstairs. I saw this boy standing in the shadow of a doorway, looking just like Sonny. I almost called his name. Then I saw that it wasn't Sonny, but somebody we used to know, a boy from around our block. He'd been Sonny's friend. He'd never been mine, having been too young for me, and, anyway, I'd never liked him. And now, even though he was a grown-up man, he still hung around that block, still spent hours on the street corners, was always high and raggy. I used to run into him from time to time and he'd often work around to asking me for a quarter or fifty cents. He always had some real good excuse, too, and I always gave it to him, I don't know why.

But now, abruptly, I hated him. I couldn't stand the way he looked at me,   10 partly like a dog, partly like a cunning child. I wanted to ask him what the hell he was doing in the school courtyard.

He sort of shuffled over to me, and he said, "I see you got the papers. So you already know about it."

"You mean about Sonny? Yes, I already know about it. How come they didn't get you?"

He grinned. It made him repulsive and it also brought to mind what he'd looked like as a kid. "I wasn't there. I stay away from them people."

"Good for you." I offered him a cigarette and I watched him through the smoke. "You come all the way down here just to tell me about Sonny?"

"That's right." He was sort of shaking his head and his eyes looked strange, as   15 though they were about to cross. The bright sun deadened his damp dark brown skin and it made his eyes look yellow and showed up the dirt in his kinked hair. He smelled funky. I moved a little away from him and I said, "Well, thanks. But I already know about it and I got to get home."

"I'll walk you a little ways," he said. We started walking. There were a couple of kids still loitering in the courtyard and one of them said goodnight to me and looked strangely at the boy beside me.

"What're you going to do?" he asked me. "I mean, about Sonny?"

"Look. I haven't seen Sonny for over a year, I'm not sure I'm going to do any-thing. Anyway, what the hell *can* I do?"

"That's right," he said quickly, "ain't nothing you can do. Can't much help old Sonny no more, I guess."

It was what I was thinking and so it seemed to me he had no right to say it.   20

"I'm surprised at Sonny, though," he went on — he had a funny way of talking, he looked straight ahead as though he were talking to himself — "I thought Sonny was a smart boy, I thought he was too smart to get hung."

"I guess he thought so too," I said sharply, "and that's how he got hung. And how about you? You're pretty goddamn smart, I bet."

Then he looked directly at me, just for a minute. "I ain't smart," he said. "If I smart, I'd have reached for a pistol a long time ago."

"Look. Don't tell *me* your sad story, if it was up to me, I'd give you one." Then I felt guilty — guilty, probably, for never having supposed that the poor bastard *had* a story of his own, much less a sad one, and I asked, quickly, "What's going to happen to him now?"

He didn't answer this. He was off by himself some place. "Funny thing," he  25 said, and from his tone we might have been discussing the quickest way to get to Brooklyn, "when I saw the papers this morning, the first thing I asked myself was if I had anything to do with it. I felt sort of responsible."

I began to listen more carefully. The subway station was on the corner, just before us, and I stopped. He stopped, too. We were in front of a bar and he ducked slightly, peering in, but whoever he was looking for didn't seem to be there. The juke box was blasting away with something black and bouncy and I half watched the barmaid as she danced her way from the juke box to her place behind the bar. And I watched her face as she laughingly responded to something someone said to her, still keeping time to the music. When she smiled one saw the little girl, one sensed the doomed, still-struggling woman beneath the battered face of the semi-whore.

"I never *give* Sonny nothing," the boy said finally, "but a long time ago I come to school high and Sonny asked me how it felt." He paused, I couldn't bear to watch him, I watched the barmaid, and I listened to the music which seemed to be causing the pavement to shake. "I told him it felt great." The music stopped, the barmaid paused and watched the juke box until the music began again. "It did."

All this was carrying me some place I didn't want to go. I certainly didn't want to know how it felt. It filled everything, the people, the houses, the music, the dark, quicksilver barmaid, with menace; and this menace was their reality.

"What's going to happen to him now?" I asked again.

"They'll send him away some place and they'll try to cure him." He shook his  30 head. "Maybe he'll even think he's kicked the habit. Then they'll let him loose" — he gestured, throwing his cigarette into the gutter. "That's all."

"What do you mean, that's *all*?"

But I knew what he meant.

"I *mean*, that's *all*." He turned his head and looked at me, pulling down the corners of his mouth. "Don't you know what I mean?" he asked, softly.

"How the hell *would* I know what you mean?" I almost whispered it, I don't know why.

"That's right," he said to the air, "how would *he* know what I mean?" He turned  35 toward me again, patient and calm, and yet I somehow felt him shaking, shaking as though he were going to fall apart. I felt that ice in my guts again, the dread I'd felt all afternoon; and again I watched the barmaid, moving about the bar, washing glasses, and singing. "Listen. They'll let him out and then it'll just start all over again. That's what I mean."

"You mean — they'll let him out. And then he'll just start working his way back in again. You mean he'll never kick the habit. Is that what you mean?"

"That's right," he said, cheerfully. "*You* see what I mean."

"Tell me," I said at last, "why does he want to die? He must want to die, he's killing himself, why does he want to die?"

He looked at me in surprise. He licked his lips. "He don't want to die. He wants to live. Don't nobody want to die, ever."

Then I wanted to ask him — too many things. He could not have answered, or 40 if he had, I could not have borne the answers. I started walking. "Well, I guess it's none of my business."

"It's going to be rough on old Sonny," he said. We reached the subway station. "This is your station?" he asked. I nodded. I took one step down. "Damn!" he said, suddenly. I looked up at him. He grinned again. "Damn it if I didn't leave all my money home. You ain't got a dollar on you, have you? Just for a couple of days, is all."

All at once something inside gave and threatened to come pouring out of me. I didn't hate him any more. I felt that in another moment I'd start crying like a child.

"Sure," I said. "Don't sweat." I looked in my wallet and didn't have a dollar, I only had a five. "Here," I said. "That hold you?"

He didn't look at it — he didn't want to look at it. A terrible, closed look came over his face, as though he were keeping the number on the bill a secret from him and me. "Thanks," he said, and now he was dying to see me go. "Don't worry about Sonny. Maybe I'll write him or something."

"Sure," I said. "You do that. So long."                                          45

"Be seeing you," he said. I went on down the steps.


And I didn't write Sonny or send him anything for a long time. When I finally did, it was just after my little girl died, he wrote me back a letter which made me feel like a bastard.

Here's what he said:

> Dear brother,
> You don't know how much I needed to hear from you. I wanted to write you many a time but I dug how much I must have hurt you and so I didn't write. But now I feel like a man who's been trying to climb up out of some deep, real deep and funky hole and just saw the sun up there, outside. I got to get outside.
> I can't tell you much about how I got here. I mean I don't know how to tell you. I guess I was afraid of something or I was trying to escape from something and you know I have never been very strong in the head (smile). I'm glad Mama and Daddy are dead and can't see what's happened to their son and I swear if I'd known what I was doing I would never have hurt you so, you and a lot of other fine people who were nice to me and who believed in me.
> I don't want you to think it had anything to do with me being a musician. It's more than that. Or maybe less than that. I can't get anything straight in my head down here and I try not to think about what's going to happen to me when I get outside again. Sometime I think I'm going to flip and *never* get outside and sometime I think I'll come straight back. I tell you one thing, though, I'd rather blow my brains out than go through this again. But that's what they all say, so they tell me. If I tell you when I'm coming to New York and if you could meet me, I sure would appreciate it. Give my love to Isabel and the kids and I was sure sorry to hear about little Gracie. I wish I could be like Mama and say the Lord's will be done, but I don't know it seems to me that trouble is the one thing that never does get stopped and I don't know what good it does to blame it on the Lord. But maybe it does some good if you believe it.
>
> Your brother,
> Sonny

Then I kept in constant touch with him and I sent him whatever I could and I went to meet him when he came back to New York. When I saw him many things I thought I had forgotten came flooding back to me. This was because I had begun, finally, to wonder about Sonny, about the life that Sonny lived inside. This life, whatever it was, had made him older and thinner and it had deepened the distant stillness in which he had always moved. He looked very unlike my baby brother. Yet, when he smiled, when we shook hands, the baby brother I'd never known looked out from the depths of his private life, like an animal waiting to be coaxed into the light.

"How you been keeping?" he asked me.                                                50

"All right. And you?"

"Just fine." He was smiling all over his face. "It's good to see you again."

"It's good to see you."

The seven years' difference in our ages lay between us like a chasm: I wondered if these years would ever operate between us as a bridge. I was remembering, and it made it hard to catch my breath, that I had been there when he was born; and I had heard the first words he had ever spoken. When he started to walk, he walked from our mother straight to me. I caught him just before he fell when he took the first steps he ever took in this world.

"How's Isabel?"                                                                     55

"Just fine. She's dying to see you."

"And the boys?"

"They're fine, too. They're anxious to see their uncle."

"Oh, come on. You know they don't remember me."

"Are you kidding? Of course they remember you."                                     60

He grinned again. We got into a taxi. We had a lot to say to each other, far too much to know how to begin.

As the taxi began to move, I asked, "You still want to go to India?"

He laughed. "You still remember that. Hell, no. This place is Indian enough for me."

"It used to belong to them," I said.

And he laughed again. "They damn sure knew what they were doing when  65 they got rid of it."

Years ago, when he was around fourteen, he'd been all hipped on the idea of going to India. He read books about people sitting on rocks, naked, in all kinds of weather, but mostly bad, naturally, and walking barefoot through hot coals and arriving at wisdom. I used to say that it sounded to me as though they were getting away from wisdom as fast as they could. I think he sort of looked down on me for that.

"Do you mind," he asked, "if we have the driver drive alongside the park? On the west side — I haven't seen the city in so long."

"Of course not," I said. I was afraid that I might sound as though I were humoring him, but I hoped he wouldn't take it that way.

So we drove along, between the green of the park and the stony, lifeless elegance of hotels and apartment buildings, toward the vivid, killing streets of our childhood. These streets hadn't changed, though housing projects jutted up out of them now like rocks in the middle of a boiling sea. Most of the houses in which we had grown up had vanished, as had the stores from which we had stolen, the basements in which we had first tried sex, the rooftops from which we had hurled tin cans and bricks. But houses exactly like the houses of our past yet dominated the landscape, boys exactly like the boys we once had been found themselves smothering in these houses, came down into the streets for light and air and found themselves encircled by disaster. Some escaped the trap, most didn't. Those who got out always left something of themselves behind, as some animals amputate a leg and leave it in the trap. It might be said, perhaps, that I had escaped, after all, I was a school teacher; or that Sonny had, he hadn't lived in Harlem for years. Yet, as the cab moved uptown through streets which seemed, with a rush, to darken with dark people, and as I covertly studied Sonny's face, it came to me that what we both were seeking through our separate cab windows was that part of ourselves which had been left behind. It's always at the hour of trouble and confrontation that the missing member aches.

We hit 110th Street and started rolling up Lenox Avenue. And I'd known this 70 avenue all my life, but it seemed to me again, as it had seemed on the day I'd first heard about Sonny's trouble, filled with a hidden menace which was its very breath of life.

"We almost there," said Sonny.

"Almost." We were both too nervous to say anything more.

We live in a housing project. It hasn't been up long. A few days after it was up it seemed uninhabitably new, now, of course, it's already rundown. It looks like a parody of the good, clean, faceless life — God knows the people who live in it do their best to make it a parody. The beat-looking grass lying around isn't enough to make their lives green, the hedges will never hold out the streets, and they know it. The big windows fool no one, they aren't big enough to make space out of no space. They don't bother with the windows, they watch the TV screen instead. The playground is most popular with the children who don't play at jacks, or skip rope, or roller skate, or swing, and they can be found in it after dark. We moved in partly because it's not too far from where I teach, and partly for the kids; but it's really just like the houses in which Sonny and I grew up. The same things happen, they'll have the same things to remember. The moment Sonny and I started into the house I had the feeling that I was simply bringing him back into the danger he had almost died trying to escape.

Sonny has never been talkative. So I don't know why I was sure he'd be dying to talk to me when supper was over the first night. Everything went fine, the oldest boy remembered him, and the youngest boy liked him, and Sonny had remembered to bring something for each of them; and Isabel, who is really much nicer than I am, more open and giving, had gone to a lot of trouble about dinner and was genuinely glad to see him. And she's always been able to tease Sonny in a way that I haven't. It was nice to see her face so vivid again and to hear her laugh and watch her make Sonny laugh. She wasn't, or, anyway, she didn't seem to be, at all uneasy or embarrassed. She chatted as though there were no subject which had to be avoided and she got Sonny past his first, faint stiffness. And thank God she was there, for I was filled with that icy dread again. Everything I did seemed awkward to me, and everything I said sounded freighted with hidden meaning. I was trying to remember everything I'd heard about dope addiction and I couldn't help watching Sonny for signs. I wasn't doing it out of malice. I was trying to find out something about my brother. I was dying to hear him tell me he was safe.

"Safe!" my father grunted, whenever Mama suggested trying to move to a 75 neighborhood which might be safer for children. "Safe, hell! Ain't no place safe for kids, nor nobody."

He always went on like this, but he wasn't, ever, really as bad as he sounded, not even on weekends, when he got drunk. As a matter of fact, he was always on the lookout for "something a little better," but he died before he found it. He died suddenly, during a drunken weekend in the middle of the war, when Sonny was fifteen. He and Sonny hadn't ever got on too well. And this was partly because Sonny was the apple of his father's eye. It was because he loved Sonny so much and was frightened for him, that he was always fighting with him. It doesn't do any good to fight with Sonny. Sonny just moves back, inside himself, where he can't be reached. But the principal reason that they never hit it off is that they were so much alike. Daddy was big and rough and loud-talking, just the opposite of Sonny, but they both had — that same privacy.

Mama tried to tell me something about this, just after Daddy died. I was home on leave from the army.

This was the last time I ever saw my mother alive. Just the same, this picture gets all mixed up in my mind with pictures I had of her when she was younger. The way I always see her is the way she used to be on a Sunday afternoon, say, when the old folks were talking after the big Sunday dinner. I always see her wearing pale blue. She'd be sitting on the sofa. And my father would be sitting in the easy chair, not far from her. And the living room would be full of church folks and relatives. There they sit, in chairs all around the living room, and the night is creeping up outside, but nobody knows it yet. You can see the darkness growing against the windowpanes and you hear the street noises every now and again, or maybe the jangling beat of a tambourine from one of the churches close by, but it's real quiet in the room. For a moment nobody's talking, but every face looks darkening, like the sky outside. And my mother rocks a little from the waist, and my father's eyes are closed. Everyone is looking at something a child can't see. For a minute they've forgotten the children. Maybe a kid is lying on the rug, half asleep. Maybe somebody's got a kid in his lap and is absent-mindedly stroking the kid's head. Maybe there's a kid, quiet and big-eyed, curled up in a big chair in the corner. The silence, the darkness coming, and the darkness in the faces frightens the child obscurely. He hopes that the hand which strokes his forehead will never stop — will never die. He hopes that there will never come a time when the old folks won't be sitting around the living room, talking about where they've come from, and what they've seen, and what's happened to them and their kinfolk.

But something deep and watchful in the child knows that this is bound to end, is already ending. In a moment someone will get up and turn on the light. Then the old folks will remember the children and they won't talk any more that day. And when light fills the room, the child is filled with darkness. He knows that every time this happens he's moved just a little closer to that darkness outside. The darkness outside is what the old folks have been talking about. It's what they've come from. It's what they endure. The child knows that they won't talk any more because if he knows too much about what's happened to *them*, he'll know too much too soon, about what's going to happen to *him*.

The last time I talked to my mother, I remember I was restless. I wanted to 80 get out and see Isabel. We weren't married then and we had a lot to straighten out between us.

There Mama sat, in black, by the window. She was humming an old church song. *Lord, you brought me from a long ways off.* Sonny was out somewhere. Mama kept watching the streets.

"I don't know," she said, "if I'll ever see you again, after you go off from here. But I hope you'll remember the things I tried to teach you."

"Don't talk like that," I said, and smiled. "You'll be here a long time yet."

She smiled, too, but she said nothing. She was quiet for a long time. And I said, "Mama, don't you worry about nothing. I'll be writing all the time, and you be getting the checks. . . ."

"I want to talk to you about your brother," she said, suddenly. "If anything hap- 85
pens to me he ain't going to have nobody to look out for him."

"Mama," I said, "ain't nothing going to happen to you *or* Sonny. Sonny's all
right. He's a good boy and he's got good sense."

"It ain't a question of his being a good boy," Mama said, "nor of his having good
sense. It ain't only the bad ones, nor yet the dumb ones that gets sucked under." She
stopped, looking at me. "Your Daddy once had a brother," she said, and she smiled
in a way that made me feel she was in pain. "You didn't never know that, did you?"

"No," I said, "I never knew that," and I watched her face.

"Oh, yes," she said, "your Daddy had a brother." She looked out of the window
again. "I know you never saw your Daddy cry. But *I* did — many a time, through
all these years."

I asked her, "What happened to his brother? How come nobody's ever talked 90
about him?"

This was the first time I ever saw my mother look old.

"His brother got killed," she said, "when he was just a little younger than you
are now. I knew him. He was a fine boy. He was maybe a little full of the devil, but
he didn't mean nobody no harm."

Then she stopped and the room was silent, exactly as it had sometimes been
on those Sunday afternoons. Mama kept looking out into the streets.

"He used to have a job in the mill," she said, "and, like all young folks, he just
liked to perform on Saturday nights. Saturday nights, him and your father would
drift around to different place, go to dances and things like that, or just sit around
with people they knew, and your father's brother would sing, he had a fine voice,
and play along with himself on his guitar. Well, this particular Saturday night, him
and your father was coming home from some place, and they were both a little
drunk and there was a moon that night, it was bright like day. Your father's brother
was feeling kind of good, and he was whistling to himself, and he had his guitar
slung over his shoulder. They was coming down a hill and beneath them was a
road that turned off from the highway. Well, your father's brother, being always
kind of frisky, decided to run down this hill, and he did, with that guitar banging
and clanging behind him, and he ran across the road, and he was making water
behind a tree. And your father was sort of amused at him and he was still coming down the hill, kind of slow. Then he heard a car motor and that same minute
his brother stepped from behind the tree, into the road, in the moonlight. And he
started to cross the road. And your father started to run down the hill, he says he
don't know why. This car was full of white men. They was all drunk, and when they
seen your father's brother they let out a great whoop and holler and they aimed
the car straight at him. They was having fun, they just wanted to scare him, the
way they do sometimes, you know. But they was drunk. And I guess the boy, being
drunk, too, and scared, kind of lost his head. By the time he jumped it was too late.
Your father says he heard his brother scream when the car rolled over him, and he
heard the wood of that guitar when it give, and he heard them strings go flying,
and he heard them white men shouting, and the car kept on a-going and it ain't
stopped till this day. And, time your father got down the hill, his brother weren't
nothing but blood and pulp."

Tears were gleaming on my mother's face. There wasn't anything I could say. 95

"He never mentioned it," she said, "because I never let him mention it before
you children. Your Daddy was like a crazy man that night and for many a night
thereafter. He says he never in his life seen anything as dark as that road after the

lights of that car had gone away. Weren't nothing, weren't nobody on that road, just your Daddy and his brother and that busted guitar. Oh, yes. Your Daddy never did really get right again. Till the day he died he weren't sure but that every white man he saw was the man that killed his brother."

She stopped and took out her handkerchief and dried her eyes and looked at me.

"I ain't telling you all this," she said, "to make you scared or bitter or to make you hate nobody. I'm telling you this because you got a brother. And the world ain't changed."

I guess I didn't want to believe this. I guess she saw this in my face. She turned away from me, toward the window again, searching those streets.

"But I praise my Redeemer," she said at last, "that He called your Daddy home 100 before me. I ain't saying it to throw no flowers at myself, but, I declare, it keeps me from feeling too cast down to know I helped your father get safely through this world. Your father always acted like he was the roughest, strongest man on earth. And everybody took him to be like that. But if he hadn't had *me* there — to see his tears!"

She was crying again. Still, I couldn't move. I said, "Lord, Lord, Mama, I didn't know it was like that."

"Oh, honey," she said, "there's a lot that you don't know. But you are going to find it out." She stood up from the window and came over to me. "You got to hold on to your brother," she said, "and don't let him fall, no matter what it looks like is happening to him and no matter how evil you gets with him. You going to be evil with him many a time. But don't you forget what I told you, you hear?"

"I won't forget," I said. "Don't you worry, I won't forget. I won't let nothing happen to Sonny."

My mother smiled as though she were amused at something she saw in my face. Then, "You may not be able to stop nothing from happening. But you got to let him know you's *there*."

Two days later I was married, and then I was gone. And I had a lot of things on 105 my mind and I pretty well forgot my promise to Mama until I got shipped home on a special furlough for her funeral.

And, after the funeral, with just Sonny and me alone in the empty kitchen, I tried to find out something about him.

"What do you want to do?" I asked him.

"I'm going to be a musician," he said.

For he had graduated, in the time I had been away, from dancing to the juke box to finding out who was playing what, and what they were doing with it, and he had bought himself a set of drums.

"You mean, you want to be a drummer?" I somehow had the feeling that being 110 a drummer might be all right for other people but not for my brother Sonny.

"I don't think," he said, looking at me very gravely, "that I'll ever be a good drummer. But I think I can play a piano."

I frowned. I'd never played the role of the older brother quite so seriously before, had scarcely ever, in fact, *asked* Sonny a damn thing. I sensed myself in the presence of something I didn't really know how to handle, didn't understand. So I made my frown a little deeper as I asked: "What kind of musician do you want to be?"

He grinned. "How many kinds do you think there are?"

"Be *serious*," I said.

He laughed, throwing his head back, and then looked at me. "I *am* serious." 115

"Well, then, for Christ's sake, stop kidding around and answer a serious question. I mean, do you want to be a concert pianist, you want to play classical music and all that, or — or what?" Long before I finished he was laughing again. "For Christ's *sake*, Sonny!"

He sobered, but with difficulty. "I'm sorry. But you sound so — *scared*!" and he was off again.

"Well, you may think it's funny now, baby, but it's not going to be so funny when you have to make your living at it, let me tell you *that*." I was furious because I knew he was laughing at me and I didn't know why.

"No," he said, very sober now, and afraid, perhaps, that he'd hurt me, "I don't want to be a classical pianist. That isn't what interests me. I mean" — he paused, looking hard at me, as though his eyes would help me to understand, and then gestured helplessly, as though perhaps his hand would help — "I mean, I'll have a lot of studying to do, and I'll have to study *everything*, but, I mean, I want to play *with* — jazz musicians." He stopped. "I want to play jazz," he said.

Well, the word had never before sounded as heavy, as real, as it sounded that 120 afternoon in Sonny's mouth. I just looked at him and I was probably frowning a real frown by this time. I simply couldn't see why on earth he'd want to spend his time hanging around nightclubs, clowning around on bandstands, while people pushed each other around a dance floor. It seemed — beneath him, somehow. I had never thought about it before, had never been forced to, but I suppose I had always put jazz musicians in a class with what Daddy called "good-time people."

"Are you *serious*?"

"Hell, *yes*, I'm serious."

He looked more helpless than ever, and annoyed, and deeply hurt.

I suggested, helpfully: "You mean — like Louis Armstrong?"

His face closed as though I'd struck him. "No. I'm not talking about none of 125 that old-time, down home crap."

"Well, look, Sonny, I'm sorry, don't get mad. I just don't altogether get it, that's all. Name somebody — you know, a jazz musician you admire."

"Bird."

"Who?"

"Bird! Charlie Parker! Don't they teach you nothing in the goddamn army?"

I lit a cigarette. I was surprised and then a little amused to discover that I was 130 trembling. "I've been out of touch," I said, "You'll have to be patient with me. Now. Who's this Parker character?"

"He's just one of the greatest jazz musicians alive," said Sonny, sullenly, his hands in his pockets, his back to me. "Maybe *the* greatest," he added, bitterly, "that's probably why *you* never heard of him."

"All right," I said, "I'm ignorant. I'm sorry. I'll go out and buy all the cat's records right away, all right?"

"It don't," said Sonny, with dignity, "make any difference to me. I don't care what you listen to. Don't do me no favors."

I was beginning to realize that I'd never seen him so upset before. With another part of my mind I was thinking that this would probably turn out to be one of those things kids go through and that I shouldn't make it seem important by pushing it too hard. Still, I didn't think it would do any harm to ask: "Doesn't all this take a lot of time? Can you make a living at it?"

He turned back to me and half leaned, half sat, on the kitchen table. 135
"Everything takes time," he said, "and — well, yes, sure, I can make a living at it.
But what I don't seem to be able to make you understand is that it's the only thing
I want to do."

"Well, Sonny," I said, gently, "you know people can't always do exactly what
they *want* to do — "

"*No*, I don't know that," said Sonny, surprising me. "I think people *ought* to do
what they want to do, what else are they alive for?"

"You getting to be a big boy," I said desperately, "it's time you started thinking
about your future."

"I'm thinking about my future," said Sonny, grimly. "I think about it all the
time."

I gave up. I decided, if he didn't change his mind, that we could always talk 140
about it later. "In the meantime," I said, "you got to finish school." We had already
decided that he'd have to move in with Isabel and her folks. I knew this wasn't the
ideal arrangement because Isabel's folks are inclined to be dicty and they hadn't
especially wanted Isabel to marry me. But I didn't know what else to do. "And we
have to get you fixed up at Isabel's."

There was a long silence. He moved from the kitchen table to the window.
"That's a terrible idea. You know it yourself."

"Do you have a *better* idea?"

He just walked up and down the kitchen for a minute. He was as tall as I was.
He had started to shave. I suddenly had the feeling that I didn't know him at all.

He stopped at the kitchen table and picked up my cigarettes. Looking
at me with a kind of mocking, amused defiance, he put one between his lips.
"You mind?"

"You smoking already?"                                                          145

He lit the cigarette and nodded, watching me through the smoke. "I just
wanted to see if I'd have the courage to smoke in front of you." He grinned and
blew a great cloud of smoke to the ceiling. "It was easy." He looked at my face.
"Come on, now. I bet you was smoking at my age, tell the truth."

I didn't say anything but the truth was on my face, and he laughed. But now
there was something very strained in his laugh. "Sure. And I bet that ain't all you
was doing."

He was frightening me a little. "Cut the crap," I said. "We already decided that
you was going to go and live at Isabel's. Now what's got into you all of a sudden?"

"*You* decided it," he pointed out. "*I* didn't decide nothing." He stopped in front
of me, leaning against the stove, arms loosely folded. "Look, brother. I don't want to
stay in Harlem no more, I really don't." He was very earnest. He looked at me, then
over toward the kitchen window. There was something in his eyes I'd never seen
before, some thoughtfulness, some worry all his own. He rubbed the muscle of one
arm. "It's time I was getting out of here."

"Where do you want to *go*, Sonny?"                                              150

"I want to join the army. Or the navy, I don't care. If I say I'm old enough,
they'll believe me."

Then I got mad. It was because I was so scared. "You must be crazy. You goddamn fool, what the hell do you want to go and join the *army* for?"

"I just told you. To get out of Harlem."

"Sonny, you haven't even finished *school*. And if you really want to be a musician, how do you expect to study if you're in the *army*?"

He looked at me, trapped, and in anguish. "There's ways. I might be able to 155
work out some kind of deal. Anyway, I'll have the G.I. Bill when I come out."

"*If* you come out." We stared at each other. "Sonny, please. Be reasonable. I
know the setup is far from perfect. But we got to do the best we can."

"I ain't learning nothing in school," he said. "Even when I go." He turned away
from me and opened the window and threw his cigarette out into the narrow alley.
I watched his back. "At least, I ain't learning nothing you'd want me to learn." He
slammed the window so hard I thought the glass would fly out, and turned back to
me. "And I'm sick of the stink of these garbage cans!"

"Sonny," I said, "I know how you feel. But if you don't finish school now, you're
going to be sorry later that you didn't." I grabbed him by the shoulders. "And you
only got another year. It ain't so bad. And I'll come back and I swear I'll help you do
*whatever* you want to do. Just try to put up with it till I come back. Will you please
do that? For me?"

He didn't answer and he wouldn't look at me.

"Sonny. You hear me?" 160

He pulled away. "I hear you. But you never hear anything *I* say."

I didn't know what to say to that. He looked out of the window and then back
at me. "OK," he said, and sighed. "I'll try."

Then I said, trying to cheer him up a little, "They got a piano at Isabel's. You
can practice on it."

And as a matter of fact, it did cheer him up for a minute. "That's right," he said
to himself. "I forgot that." His face relaxed a little. But the worry, the thoughtfulness, played on it still, the way shadows play on a face which is staring into the fire.

But I thought I'd never hear the end of that piano. At first, Isabel would write 165
me, saying how nice it was that Sonny was so serious about his music and how, as
soon as he came in from school, or wherever he had been when he was supposed
to be at school, he went straight to that piano and stayed there until suppertime.
And, after supper, he went back to that piano and stayed there until everybody
went to bed. He was at the piano all day Saturday and all day Sunday. Then he
bought a record player and started playing records. He'd play one record over and
over again, all day long sometimes, and he'd improvise along with it on the piano.
Or he'd play one section of the record, one chord, one change, one progression,
then he'd do it on the piano. Then back to the record. Then back to the piano.

Well, I really don't know how they stood it. Isabel finally confessed that it
wasn't like living with a person at all, it was like living with sound. And the sound
didn't make any sense to her, didn't make any sense to any of them — naturally.
They began, in a way, to be afflicted by this presence that was living in their home.
It was as though Sonny were some sort of god, or monster. He moved in an atmosphere which wasn't like theirs at all. They fed him and he ate, he washed himself, he walked in and out of their door; he certainly wasn't nasty or unpleasant
or rude, Sonny isn't any of those things; but it was as though he were all wrapped
up in some cloud, some fire, some vision all his own; and there wasn't any way to
reach him.

At the same time, he wasn't really a man yet, he was still a child, and they had
to watch out for him in all kinds of ways. They certainly couldn't throw him out.
Neither did they dare to make a great scene about that piano because even they
dimly sensed, as I sensed, from so many thousands of miles away, that Sonny was
at that piano playing for his life.

But he hadn't been going to school. One day a letter came from the school board and Isabel's mother got it — there had, apparently, been other letters but Sonny had torn them up. This day, when Sonny came in, Isabel's mother showed him the letter and asked where he'd been spending his time. And she finally got it out of him that he'd been down in Greenwich Village, with musicians and other characters, in a white girl's apartment. And this scared her and she started to scream at him and what came up, once she began — though she denies it to this day — was what sacrifices they were making to give Sonny a decent home and how little he appreciated it.

Sonny didn't play the piano that day. By evening, Isabel's mother had calmed down but then there was the old man to deal with, and Isabel herself. Isabel says she did her best to be calm but she broke down and started crying. She says she just watched Sonny's face. She could tell, by watching him, what was happening with him. And what was happening was that they penetrated his cloud, they had reached him. Even if their fingers had been a thousand times more gentle than human fingers ever are, he could hardly help feeling that they had stripped him naked and were spitting on that nakedness. For he also had to see that his presence, that music, which was life or death to him, had been torture for them and that they had endured it, not at all for his sake, but only for mine. And Sonny couldn't take that. He can take it a little better today than he could then but he's still not very good at it and, frankly, I don't know anybody who is.

The silence of the next few days must have been louder than the sound of all the music ever played since time began. One morning, before she went to work, Isabel was in his room for something and she suddenly realized that all of his records were gone. And she knew for certain that he was gone. And he was. He went as far as the navy would carry him. He finally sent me a postcard from some place in Greece and that was the first I knew that Sonny was still alive. I didn't see him any more until we were both back in New York and the war had long been over.

He was a man by then, of course, but I wasn't willing to see it. He came by the house from time to time, but we fought almost every time we met. I didn't like the way he carried himself, loose and dreamlike all the time, and I didn't like his friends, and his music seemed to be merely an excuse for the life he led. It sounded just that weird and disordered.

Then we had a fight, a pretty awful fight, and I didn't see him for months. By and by I looked him up, where he was living, in a furnished room in the Village, and I tried to make it up. But there were lots of other people in the room and Sonny just lay on his bed, and he wouldn't come downstairs with me, and he treated these other people as though they were his family and I weren't. So I got mad and then he got mad, and then I told him that he might just as well be dead as live the way he was living. Then he stood up and he told me not to worry about him any more in life, that he *was* dead as far as I was concerned. Then he pushed me to the door and the other people looked on as though nothing were happening, and he slammed the door behind me. I stood in the hallway, staring at the door. I heard somebody laugh in the room and then the tears came to my eyes. I started down the steps, whistling to keep from crying, I kept whistling to myself, *You going to need me, baby, one of these cold, rainy days.*

I read about Sonny's trouble in the spring. Little Grace died in the fall. She was a beautiful little girl. But she only lived a little over two years. She died of polio and she suffered. She had a slight fever for a couple of days, but it didn't seem like any-thing and we just kept her in bed. And we would certainly have called the doctor, but the fever dropped, she seemed to be all right. So we thought it had just been a cold. Then, one day, she was up, playing, Isabel was in the kitchen fixing lunch for the two boys when they'd come in from school, and she heard Grace fall down in the living room. When you have a lot of children you don't always start running when one of them falls, unless they start screaming or something. And, this time, Grace was quiet. Yet, Isabel says that when she heard that *thump* and then that silence, something happened in her to make her afraid. And she ran to the living room and there was little Grace on the floor, all twisted up, and the reason she hadn't screamed was that she couldn't get her breath. And when she did scream, it was the worst sound, Isabel says, that she'd ever heard in all her life, and she still hears it sometimes in her dreams. Isabel will sometimes wake me up with a low, moaning, strangled sound and I have to be quick to awaken her and hold her to me and where Isabel is weeping against me seems a mortal wound.

I think I may have written Sonny the very day that little Grace was buried. I was sitting in the living room in the dark, by myself, and I suddenly thought of Sonny. My trouble made his real.

One Saturday afternoon, when Sonny had been living with us, or, anyway, 175 been in our house, for nearly two weeks, I found myself wandering aimlessly about the living room, drinking from a can of beer, and trying to work up the courage to search Sonny's room. He was out, he was usually out whenever I was home, and Isabel had taken the children to see their grandparents. Suddenly I was standing still in front of the living room window, watching Seventh Avenue. The idea of searching Sonny's room made me still. I scarcely dared to admit to myself what I'd be searching for. I didn't know what I'd do if I found it. Or if I didn't.

On the sidewalk across from me, near the entrance to a barbecue joint, some people were holding an old-fashioned revival meeting. The barbecue cook, wearing a dirty white apron, his conked hair reddish and metallic in the pale sun, and a cig-arette between his lips, stood in the doorway, watching them. Kids and older people paused in their errands and stood there, along with some older men and a couple of very tough-looking women who watched everything that happened on the ave-nue, as though they owned it, or were maybe owned by it. Well, they were watching this, too. The revival was being carried on by three sisters in black, and a brother. All they had were their voices and their Bibles and a tambourine. The brother was testifying and while he testified two of the sisters stood together, seeming to say, amen, and the third sister walked around with the tambourine outstretched and a couple of people dropped coins into it. Then the brother's testimony ended and the sister who had been taking up the collection dumped the coins into her palm and transferred them to the pocket of her long black robe. Then she raised both hands, striking the tambourine against the air, and then against one hand, and she started to sing. And the two other sisters and the brother joined in.

It was strange, suddenly, to watch, though I had been seeing these street meet-ings all my life. So, of course, had everybody else down there. Yet, they paused and watched and listened and I stood still at the window. "*Tis the old ship of Zion,*" they sang, and the sister with the tambourine kept a steady, jangling beat, "*it has rescued many a thousand!*" Not a soul under the sound of their voices was hearing this song for the first time, not one of them had been rescued. Nor had they seen much in the way of rescue work being done around them. Neither did they especially believe in the holiness of the three sisters and the brother, they knew too much about them, knew where they lived, and how. The woman with the tambourine, whose voice dominated the air, whose face was bright with joy, was divided by very little from the woman who stood watching her, a cigarette between her heavy, chapped lips, her hair a cuckoo's nest, her face scarred and swollen from many beatings, and her black eyes glittering like coal. Perhaps they both knew this, which was why, when, as rarely, they addressed each other, they addressed each other as Sister. As the singing filled the air the watching, listening faces underwent a change, the eyes focusing on something within; the music seemed to soothe a poison out of them; and time seemed, nearly, to fall away from the sullen, belligerent, battered faces, as though they were fleeing back to their first condition, while dreaming of their last. The barbecue cook half shook his head and smiled, and dropped his cigarette and disappeared into his joint. A man fumbled in his pockets for change and stood holding it in his hand impatiently, as though he had just remembered a pressing appointment further up the avenue. He looked furious. Then I saw Sonny, standing on the edge of the crowd. He was carrying a wide, flat notebook with a green cover, and it made him look, from where I was standing, almost like a schoolboy. The coppery sun brought out the copper in his skin, he was very faintly smiling, stand ing very still. Then the singing stopped, the tambourine turned into a collection plate again. The furious man dropped in his coins and vanished, so did a couple of the women, and Sonny dropped some change in the plate, looking directly at the woman with a little smile. He started across the avenue, toward the house. He has a slow, loping walk, something like the way Harlem hipsters walk, only he's imposed on this his own half-beat. I had never really noticed it before.

I stayed at the window, both relieved and apprehensive. As Sonny disappeared from my sight, they began singing again. And they were still singing when his key turned in the lock.

"Hey," he said.

"Hey, yourself. You want some beer?"                                                    180

"No. Well, maybe." But he came up to the window and stood beside me, looking out. "What a warm voice," he said.

They were singing *If I could only hear my mother pray again!*

"Yes," I said, "and she can sure beat that tambourine."

"But what a terrible song," he said, and laughed. He dropped his notebook on the sofa and disappeared into the kitchen. "Where's Isabel and the kids?"

"I think they went to see their grandparents. You hungry?"                              185

"No." He came back into the living room with his can of beer. "You want to come some place with me tonight?"

I sensed, I don't know how, that I couldn't possibly say no. "Sure. Where?"

He sat down on the sofa and picked up his notebook and started leafing through it. "I'm going to sit in with some fellows in a joint in the Village."

"You mean, you're going to play, tonight?"

"That's right." He took a swallow of his beer and moved back to the window. 190 He gave me a sidelong look. "If you can stand it."

"I'll try," I said.

He smiled to himself and we both watched as the meeting across the way broke up. The three sisters and the brother, heads bowed, were singing *God be with you till we meet again.* The faces around them were very quiet. Then the song ended. The small crowd dispersed. We watched the three women and the lone man walk slowly up the avenue.

"When she was singing before," said Sonny, abruptly, "her voice reminded me for a minute of what heroin feels like sometimes — when it's in your veins. It makes you feel sort of warm and cool at the same time. And distant. And — and sure." He sipped his beer, very deliberately not looking at me. I watched his face. "It makes you feel — in control. Sometimes you've got to have that feeling."

"Do you?" I sat down slowly in the easy chair.

"Sometimes." He went to the sofa and picked up his notebook again. "Some  195 people do."

"In order," I asked, "to play?" And my voice was very ugly, full of contempt and anger.

"Well" — he looked at me with great, troubled eyes, as though, in fact, he hoped his eyes would tell me things he could never otherwise say — "they *think* so. And *if* they think so — !"

"And what do *you* think?" I asked.

He sat on the sofa and put his can of beer on the floor. "I don't know," he said, and I couldn't be sure if he were answering my question or pursuing his thoughts. His face didn't tell me. "It's not so much to *play*. It's to *stand* it, to be able to make it at all. On any level." He frowned and smiled: "In order to keep from shaking to pieces."

"But these friends of yours," I said, "they seem to shake themselves to pieces  200 pretty goddamn fast."

"Maybe." He played with the notebook. And something told me that I should curb my tongue, that Sonny was doing his best to talk, that I should listen. "But of course you only know the ones that've gone to pieces. Some don't — or at least they haven't *yet* and that's just about all *any* of us can say." He paused. "And then there are some who just live, really, in hell, and they know it and they see what's happening and they go right on. I don't know." He sighed, dropped the notebook, folded his arms. "Some guys, you can tell from the way they play, they on something *all* the time. And you can see that, well, it makes something real for them. But of course," he picked up his beer from the floor and sipped it and put the can down again, "they *want* to, too, you've got to see that. Even some of them that say they don't — *some*, not all."

"And what about you?" I asked — I couldn't help it. "What about you? Do *you* want to?"

He stood up and walked to the window and remained silent for a long time. Then he sighed. "Me," he said. Then: "While I was downstairs before, on my way here, listening to that woman sing, it struck me all of a sudden how much suffering she must have had to go through — to sing like that. It's *repulsive* to think you have to suffer that much."

I said: "But there's no way not to suffer — is there, Sonny?"

"I believe not," he said and smiled, "but that's never stopped anyone from  205 trying." He looked at me. "Has it?" I realized, with this mocking look, that there stood between us, forever, beyond the power of time or forgiveness, the fact that I had held silence — so long! — when he had needed human speech to help him. He turned back to the window. "No, there's no way not to suffer. But you try all kinds of ways to keep from drowning in it, to keep on top of it, and to make it seem — well, like *you*. Like you did something, all right, and now you're suffering for it. You know?" I said nothing. "Well you know," he said, impatiently, "why *do* people suffer? Maybe it's better to do something to give it a reason, *any* reason."

"But we just agreed," I said, "that there's no way not to suffer. Isn't it better, then, just to — take it?"

"But nobody just takes it," Sonny cried, "that's what I'm telling you! *Everybody* tries not to. You're just hung up on the *way* some people try — it's not *your* way!"

The hair on my face began to itch, my face felt wet. "That's not true," I said, "that's not true. I don't give a damn what other people do, I don't even care how they suffer. I just care how *you* suffer." And he looked at me. "Please believe me," I said, "I don't want to see you — die — trying not to suffer."

"I won't," he said, flatly, "die trying not to suffer. At least, not any faster than anybody else."

"But there's no need," I said, trying to laugh, "is there? in killing yourself."     210

I wanted to say more, but I couldn't. I wanted to talk about will power and how life could be — well, beautiful. I wanted to say that it was all within; but was it? or, rather, wasn't that exactly the trouble? And I wanted to promise that I would never fail him again. But it would all have sounded — empty words and lies.

So I made the promise to myself and prayed that I would keep it.

"It's terrible sometimes, inside," he said, "that's what's the trouble. You walk these streets, black and funky and cold, and there's not really a living ass to talk to, and there's nothing shaking, and there's no way of getting it out — that storm inside. You can't talk it and you can't make love with it, and when you finally try to get with it and play it, you realize *nobody's* listening. So *you've* got to listen. You got to find a way to listen."

And then he walked away from the window and sat on the sofa again, as though all the wind had suddenly been knocked out of him. "Sometimes you'll do *anything* to play, even cut your mother's throat." He laughed and looked at me. "Or your brother's." Then he sobered, "Or your own." Then: "Don't worry. I'm all right now and I think I'll *be* all right. But I can't forget — where I've been. I don't mean just the physical place I've been, I mean where I've *been*. And *what* I've been."

"What have you been, Sonny?" I asked.     215

He smiled — but sat sideways on the sofa, his elbow resting on the back, his fingers playing with his mouth and chin, not looking at me. "I've been something I didn't recognize, didn't know I could be. Didn't know anybody could be." He stopped, looking inward, looking helplessly young, looking old. "I'm not talking about it now because I feel *guilty* or anything like that — maybe it would be better if I did, I don't know. Anyway, I can't really talk about it. Not to you, not to anybody," and now he turned and faced me. "Sometimes, you know, and it was actually when I was most *out* of the world, I felt that I was in it, that I was *with* it, really, and I could play or I didn't really have to *play*, it just came out of me, it was there. And I don't know how I played, thinking about it now, but I know I did awful things, those times, sometimes, to people. Or it wasn't that I *did* anything to them — it was that they weren't real." He picked up the beer can; it was empty; he rolled it between his palms: "And other times — well, I needed a fix, I needed to find a place to lean, I needed to clear a space to *listen* — and I couldn't find it, and I — went crazy, I did terrible things to *me*, I was terrible *for* me." He began pressing the beer can between his hands, I watched the metal begin to give. It glittered, as he played with it, like a knife, and I was afraid he would cut himself, but I said nothing. "Oh well. I can never tell you. I was all by myself at the bottom of something, stinking and sweating and crying and shaking, and I smelled it, you know? *my* stink, and I thought I'd die if I couldn't get away from it and yet, all the same, I knew that everything I was doing was just locking me in with it. And I didn't know," he paused, still flattening the beer can, "I didn't know, I still *don't* know, something kept telling me that maybe it was good to smell your own stink, but I didn't think that *that* was what I'd been trying to do — and — who can stand it?" and he abruptly dropped the ruined beer can, looking at me with a small, still smile, and then rose, walking to the window as though it were the lodestone rock. I watched his face, he watched the avenue. "I couldn't tell you when Mama died — but the reason I wanted to leave Harlem so bad was to get away from drugs. And then, when I ran away, that's what I was running from — really. When I came back, nothing had changed, *I* hadn't changed, I was just — older." And he stopped, drumming with his fingers on the windowpane. The sun had vanished, soon darkness would fall. I watched his face. "It can come again," he said, almost as though speaking to himself. Then he turned to me. "It can come again," he repeated. "I just want you to know that."

"All right," I said, at last. "So it can come again. All right."

He smiled, but the smile was sorrowful. "I had to try to tell you," he said.

"Yes," I said. "I understand that."

"You're my brother," he said, looking straight at me, and not smiling at all.       220

"Yes," I repeated, "yes. I understand that."

He turned back to the window, looking out. "All that hatred down there," he said, "all that hatred and misery and love. It's a wonder it doesn't blow the avenue apart."

We went to the only nightclub on a short, dark street, downtown. We squeezed through the narrow, chattering, jam-packed bar to the entrance of the big room, where the bandstand was. And we stood there for a moment, for the lights were very dim in this room and we couldn't see. Then, "Hello, boy," said a voice and an enormous black man, much older than Sonny or myself, erupted out of all that atmospheric lighting and put an arm around Sonny's shoulder. "I been sitting right here," he said, "waiting for you."

He had a big voice, too, and heads in the darkness turned toward us.

Sonny grinned and pulled a little away, and said, "Creole, this is my brother. I   225 told you about him."

Creole shook my hand. "I'm glad to meet you, son," he said, and it was clear that he was glad to meet me *there*, for Sonny's sake. And he smiled, "You got a real musician in *your* family," and he took his arm from Sonny's shoulder and slapped him, lightly, affectionately, with the back of his hand.

"Well. Now I've heard it all," said a voice behind us. This was another musician, and a friend of Sonny's, a coal-black, cheerful-looking man, built close to the ground. He immediately began confiding to me, at the top of his lungs, the most terrible things about Sonny, his teeth gleaming like a lighthouse and his laugh coming up out of him like the beginning of an earthquake. And it turned out that everyone at the bar knew Sonny, or almost everyone; some were musicians, working there, or nearby, or not working, some were simply hangers-on, and some were there to hear Sonny play. I was introduced to all of them and they were all very polite to me. Yet, it was clear that, for them, I was only Sonny's brother. Here, I was in Sonny's world. Or, rather: his kingdom. Here, it was not even a question that his veins bore royal blood.

They were going to play soon and Creole installed me, by myself, at a table in a dark corner. Then I watched them, Creole, and the little black man, and Sonny, and the others, while they horsed around, standing just below the bandstand. The light from the bandstand spilled just a little short of them and, watching them laughing and gesturing and moving about, I had the feeling that they, nevertheless, were being most careful not to step into that circle of light too suddenly: that if they moved into the light too suddenly, without thinking, they would perish in flame. Then, while I watched, one of them, the small, black man, moved into the light and crossed the bandstand and started fooling around with his drums. Then — being funny and being, also, extremely ceremonious — Creole took Sonny by the arm and led him to the piano. A woman's voice called Sonny's name and a few hands started clapping. And Sonny, also being funny and being ceremonious, and so touched, I think, that he could have cried, but neither hiding it nor showing it, riding it like a man, grinned, and put both hands to his heart and bowed from the waist.

Creole then went to the bass fiddle and a lean, very bright-skinned brown man jumped up on the bandstand and picked up his horn. So there they were, and the atmosphere on the bandstand and in the room began to change and tighten. Someone stepped up to the microphone and announced them. Then there were all kinds of murmurs. Some people at the bar shushed others. The waitress ran around, frantically getting in the last orders, guys and chicks got closer to each other, and the lights on the bandstand, on the quartet, turned to a kind of indigo. Then they all looked different there. Creole looked about him for the last time, as though he were making certain that all his chickens were in the coop, and then he — jumped and struck the fiddle. And there they were.

All I know about music is that not many people ever really hear it. And even then, on the rare occasions when something opens within, and the music enters, what we mainly hear, or hear corroborated, are personal, private, vanishing evocations. But the man who creates the music is hearing something else, is dealing with the roar rising from the void and imposing order on it as it hits the air. What is evoked in him, then, is of another order, more terrible because it has no words, and triumphant, too, for that same reason. And his triumph, when he triumphs, is ours. I just watched Sonny's face. His face was troubled, he was working hard, but he wasn't with it. And I had the feeling that, in a way, everyone on the bandstand was waiting for him, both waiting for him and pushing him along. But as I began to watch Creole, I realized that it was Creole who held them all back. He had them on a short rein. Up there, keeping the beat with his whole body, wailing on the fiddle, with his eyes half closed, he was listening to everything, but he was listening to Sonny. He was having a dialogue with Sonny. He wanted Sonny to leave the shoreline and strike out for the deep water. He was Sonny's witness that deep water and drowning were not the same thing — he had been there, and he knew. And he wanted Sonny to know. He was waiting for Sonny to do the things on the keys which would let Creole know that Sonny was in the water.

And, while Creole listened, Sonny moved, deep within, exactly like someone in torment. I had never before thought of how awful the relationship must be between the musician and his instrument. He has to fill it, this instrument, with the breath of life, his own. He has to make it do what he wants it to do. And a piano is just a piano. It's made out of so much wood and wires and little hammers and big ones, and ivory. While there's only so much you can do with it, the only way to find this out is to try; to try and make it do everything.

And Sonny hadn't been near a piano for over a year. And he wasn't on much better terms with his life, not the life that stretched before him now. He and the piano stammered, started one way, got scared, stopped; started another way, panicked, marked time, started again; then seemed to have found a direction, panicked again, got stuck. And the face I saw on Sonny I'd never seen before. Everything had

230

been burned out of it, and, at the same time, things usually hidden were being burned in, by the fire and fury of the battle which was occurring in him up there.

Yet, watching Creole's face as they neared the end of the first set, I had the feeling that something had happened, something I hadn't heard. Then they finished, there was scattered applause, and then, without an instant's warning, Creole started into something else, it was almost sardonic, it was *Am I Blue.* And, as though he commanded, Sonny began to play. Something began to happen. And Creole let out the reins. The dry, low, black man said something awful on the drums, Creole answered, and the drums talked back. Then the horn insisted, sweet and high, slightly detached perhaps, and Creole listened, commenting now and then, dry, and driving, beautiful and calm and old. Then they all came together again, and Sonny was part of the family again. I could tell this from his face. He seemed to have found, right there beneath his fingers, a damn brand-new piano. It seemed that he couldn't get over it. Then, for awhile, just being happy with Sonny, they seemed to be agreeing with him that brand-new pianos certainly were a gas.

Then Creole stepped forward to remind them that what they were playing was the blues. He hit something in all of them, he hit something in me, myself, and the music tightened and deepened, apprehension began to beat the air. Creole began to tell us what the blues were all about. They were not about anything very new. He and his boys up there were keeping it new, at the risk of ruin, destruction, madness, and death, in order to find new ways to make us listen. For, while the tale of how we suffer, and how we are delighted, and how we may triumph is never new, it always must be heard. There isn't any other tale to tell, it's the only light we've got in all this darkness.

And this tale, according to that face, that body, those strong hands on those    235
strings, has another aspect in every country, and a new depth in every generation. Listen, Creole seemed to be saying, listen. Now these are Sonny's blues. He made the little black man on the drums know it, and the bright, brown man on the horn. Creole wasn't trying any longer to get Sonny in the water. He was wishing him Godspeed. Then he stepped back, very slowly, filling the air with the immense suggestion that Sonny speak for himself.

Then they all gathered around Sonny and Sonny played. Every now and again one of them seemed to say, amen. Sonny's fingers filled the air with life, his life. But that life contained so many others. And Sonny went all the way back, he really began with the spare, flat statement of the opening phrase of the song. Then he began to make it his. It was very beautiful because it wasn't hurried and it was no longer a lament. I seemed to hear with what burning he had made it his, with what burning we had yet to make it ours, how we could cease lamenting. Freedom lurked around us and I understood, at last, that he could help us to be free if we would listen, that he would never be free until we did. Yet, there was no battle in his face now. I heard what he had gone through, and would continue to go through until he came to rest in earth. He had made it his: that long line, of which we knew only Mama and Daddy. And he was giving it back, as everything must be given back, so that, passing through death, it can live forever. I saw my mother's face again, and felt, for the first time, how the stones of the road she had walked on must have bruised her feet. I saw the moonlit road where my father's brother died. And it brought something else back to me, and carried me past it, I saw my little girl again and felt Isabel's tears again, and I felt my own tears begin to rise. And I was yet aware that this was only a moment, that the world waited outside, as hungry as a tiger, and that trouble stretched above us, longer than the sky.

Then it was over. Creole and Sonny let out their breath, both soaking wet, and grinning. There was a lot of applause and some of it was real. In the dark, the girl came by and I asked her to take drinks to the bandstand. There was a long pause, while they talked up there in the indigo light and after awhile I saw the girl put a Scotch and milk on top of the piano for Sonny. He didn't seem to notice it, but just before they started playing again, he sipped from it and looked toward me, and nodded. Then he put it back on top of the piano. For me, then, as they began to play again, it glowed and shook above my brother's head like the very cup of trembling.

## Considerations for Critical Thinking and Writing

1. FIRST RESPONSE. Do you share the narrator's fear for his brother's life? Does your response change over the course of the story?

2. Why is it significant that the narrator encounters the news of what happened to Sonny first in a newspaper and then through one of Sonny's friends?

3. One important factor in gaining an insight into a character is their chosen profession. Compare the professions of math teacher and jazz musician. To what degree do those careers outline other important features of the narrator's and Sonny's characters?

4. The narrator is an educator, and yet he seems to be the one who has something to learn in the story. What does he learn, when does he learn it, and what are the significant steps that lead to his learning it?

5. Sonny claims that the main difference between him and his brother is the way they try to avoid suffering. How do their two methods of avoiding suffering compare?

6. The story is titled after Sonny, but is he the protagonist?

7. The primary relationship examined in the story is obviously between the narrator and Sonny. How many other significant characters populate the story? (These might include characters who are not technically in the story.) How does each of them affect the way the relationship between Sonny and his brother unfolds?

8. What motivates the narrator?

9. If there is growth in either of the main characters, is it emotional, intellectual, or spiritual?

10. From the title onward, the story is largely about music. What are the various ways music helps to define these two characters?

11. The narrator has always wanted to change Sonny, but Sonny is resistant to those efforts. Does that make Sonny a static character as defined earlier in this chapter?

12. Is the narrator's character revealed more in his conversations with Sonny or in his "private" admissions to the reader?

13. How is the story framed in terms of the tension between private and public selves?

## Connections to Other Selections

1. Compare the way "Sonny's Blues" and Charlotte Perkins Gilman's story "The Yellow Wallpaper" (p. 126) examine relationships and the will to control the behavior of a loved one, sometimes as a result of societal conventions.

2. John Edgar Wideman's "All Stories Are True" (p. 509) is also about two brothers, one of whom is incarcerated. Are the sibling dynamics in the two stories essentially similar or different?

# 4

# Setting

One of the troubles with our culture is we do not respect and train the imagination. It needs exercise. It needs practice. You can't tell a story unless you've listened to a lot of stories and then learned how to do it.
— URSULA K. LE GUIN

Beth Gwinn/Michael Ochs
Archives/Getty Images.

*Setting* is the context in which the action of a story occurs. The major elements of setting are time, place, and the social environment that frames the characters. These elements establish the world in which the characters act. In most stories they also serve as more than backgrounds and furnishings. If we are sensitive to the contexts provided by setting, we are better able to understand the behavior of the characters and the significance of their actions. It may be tempting to read quickly through a writer's descriptions and ignore the details of the setting once a geographic location and a historic period are established. But if you read a story so impatiently, the significance of the setting may slip by you. That kind of reading is similar to traveling on interstate highways: a lot of ground gets covered, but very little is seen along the way.

Settings can be used to evoke a mood or atmosphere that will prepare the reader for what is to come. In Zadie Smith's "Martha, Martha" (p. 80) the story begins with Pam Roberts looking out the window of her real estate office at her potential client Martha Penk who is trying to figure out how to get into the office, and Pam knows that Martha will have trouble getting in:

> The confusion was common; it arose from the higgledy-piggledy arrangement of the ground floor — a busy bookshop and a swing-doored optician obscured the sign that told you of the dentist, the insurers, the accountant and Pam's own dinky realty business at the top of the building; also the antique elevator that would take you to them. Pam tapped her door with a knuckle, warning it she would return, and crossed the room to the filing cabinet.

We learn a great deal about Pam and the story's situation from this rich description. There is a tension between confusion and order. The ground floor of the building is so chaotic that Pam and her business are difficult to find. She tries to compensate by keeping her space in order, represented by the filing cabinet she approaches at the end of this description. We also get a sense of her feelings about her importance: her "dinky realty business" and the "antique elevator" that brings clients to her are not as vibrant as the "busy bookshop" downstairs. She is someone who likes control and likes to figure things out, but her space indicates that these desires face challenges.

If we ask why a writer chooses to include certain details in a work, then we are likely to make connections that relate the details to some larger purpose, such as the story's meaning. John Updike's story "A & P" (p. 145) takes place, as the title indicates, in the grocery store where the protagonist works. The story confronts the opposing forces of conformity and rebellion, so it is fitting that it takes place in a supermarket chain where every store is the same, from the Atlantic to the Pacific (which is what A & P stands for). There is usually a reason for placing a story in a particular time or location. N. K. Jemisin's story "Sinners, Saints, Dragons, and Haints in the City Beneath the Still Waters" (p. 320) takes place in a very specific city (New Orleans) at a very specific moment in its history (after Hurricane Katrina devastated the Gulf of Mexico in 2005). The story's very existence depends on that setting, with both plot and characterizations dependent on its specificity.

Time, location, and the physical features of a setting can all be relevant to the overall purpose of a story. So too is the social environment in which the characters are developed. In Faulkner's "A Rose for Emily" (p. 47) the changes in Emily's southern town serve as a foil for her tenacious hold on a lost past. She is regarded as a "fallen monument," as old-fashioned and peculiar as the "stubborn and coquettish decay" of her house. Neither she nor her house fits into the modern changes that are paving and transforming the town. Without the social context, this story would be mostly an account of a bizarre murder rather than an exploration of the conflicts Faulkner associated with the changing South. Setting enlarges the meaning of Emily's actions.

Some settings have traditional associations that are closely related to the action of a story. In a story that takes place in the first months of college, like ZZ Packer's "Drinking Coffee Elsewhere" (p. 292), we expect that characters will be open to growth, change, and exploring new identities, which is exactly what happens to the two main characters, but to differing degrees.

Sometimes writers reverse traditional expectations. When a tranquil garden is the scene for a horrendously bloody murder, we are as much taken by surprise as the victim is. In Updike's "A & P" (p. 145) there seems to be little possibility for heroic action in so mundane a place as a supermarket, but the setting turns out to be appropriate for the important, unexpected decision the protagonist makes about life. Traditional associations are also disrupted in Tobias Wolff's "Powder" (p. 72) by making a blizzard a place of excitement and father-son bonding rather than a site of danger and peril. By drawing on traditional associations, a writer can fulfill or disrupt a reader's expectations about a setting in order to complement the elements of the story.

Not every story uses setting as a means of revealing mood, idea, meaning, or characters' actions. Some stories have no particularly significant setting. It is entirely possible to envision a story in which two characters speak to each other about a conflict between them and little or no mention is made of the time or place they inhabit. If, however, a shift in setting would make a serious difference to our understanding of a story, then the setting is probably an important element in the work.

The following three stories — Ernest Hemingway's "Soldier's Home," Ursula K. Le Guin's "The Ones Who Walk Away from Omelas," and Charlotte Perkins Gilman's "The Yellow Wallpaper" — include settings that serve to shape their meanings.

## ERNEST HEMINGWAY (1899–1961)

Because of his writing's stylistic innovations, Ernest Hemingway was considered one of the most influential writers of his time and was awarded the Nobel Prize in Literature in 1954, one of only eleven Americans in history to earn that honor. In 1918, a year after graduating from high school in Oak Park, Illinois, Hemingway volunteered as an ambulance driver in World War I. At the Italian front, he was seriously wounded. This experience haunted him and many of the characters in his short stories and novels. *In Our Time* (1925) is a collection of short stories, including "Soldier's Home," that reflect some of Hemingway's own attempts to readjust to life back home after the war. *The Sun Also Rises* (1926), *A Farewell to Arms* (1929), and *For Whom the Bell Tolls* (1940) are also

Ermeni Studio, Milan. Courtesy of the Ernest Hemingway Photographic Collection, John Fitzgerald Kennedy Library, Boston.

about war and its impact on people's lives. Hemingway courted violence all his life in war, the bullring, the boxing ring, and big game hunting. When he was sixty-two years old and terminally ill with cancer, he died by suicide, shooting himself with a shotgun. "Soldier's Home" takes place in a small town in Oklahoma; the war, however, is never distant from the protagonist's mind as he struggles to come home again.

## Soldier's Home    1925

Krebs went to the war from a Methodist college in Kansas. There is a picture which shows him among his fraternity brothers, all of them wearing exactly the same height and style collar. He enlisted in the Marines in 1917 and did not return to the United States until the second division returned from the Rhine in the summer of 1919.

There is a picture which shows him on the Rhine with two German girls and another corporal. Krebs and the corporal look too big for their uniforms. The German girls are not beautiful. The Rhine does not show in the picture.

By the time Krebs returned to his home town in Oklahoma the greeting of heroes was over. He came back much too late. The men from the town who had been drafted had all been welcomed elaborately on their return. There had been a great deal of hysteria. Now the reaction had set in. People seemed to think it was rather ridiculous for Krebs to be getting back so late, years after the war was over.

At first Krebs, who had been at Belleau Wood, Soissons, the Champagne, St. Mihiel, and in the Argonne° did not want to talk about the war at all. Later he felt the need to talk but no one wanted to hear about it. His town had heard too many atrocity stories to be thrilled by actualities. Krebs found that to be listened to at all he had to lie, and after he had done this twice he, too, had a reaction against the war and against talking about it. A distaste for everything that had happened to him in the war set in because of the lies he had told. All of the times that had been able to make him feel cool and clear inside himself when he thought of them; the times so long back when he had done the one thing, the only thing for a man to do, easily and naturally, when he might have done something else, now lost their cool, valuable quality and then were lost themselves.

His lies were quite unimportant lies and consisted in attributing to himself  5
things other men had seen, done, or heard of, and stating as facts certain apocryphal incidents familiar to all soldiers. Even his lies were not sensational at the pool room. His acquaintances, who had heard detailed accounts of German women found chained to machine guns in the Argonne forest and who could not comprehend, or were barred by their patriotism from interest in, any German machine gunners who were not chained, were not thrilled by his stories.

Krebs acquired the nausea in regard to experience that is the result of untruth or exaggeration, and when he occasionally met another man who had really been a soldier and they talked a few minutes in the dressing room at a dance he fell into the easy pose of the old soldier among other soldiers: that he had been badly, sickeningly frightened all the time. In this way he lost everything.

---

*Belleau Wood . . . Argonne:* Sites of battles in World War I in which American troops were instrumental in pushing back the Germans.

During this time, it was late summer, he was sleeping late in bed, getting up to walk down town to the library to get a book, eating lunch at home, reading on the front porch until he became bored, and then walking down through the town to spend the hottest hours of the day in the cool dark of the pool room. He loved to play pool.

In the evening he practiced on his clarinet, strolled down town, read, and went to bed. He was still a hero to his two young sisters. His mother would have given him breakfast in bed if he had wanted it. She often came in when he was in bed and asked him to tell her about the war, but her attention always wandered. His father was noncommittal.

Before Krebs went away to the war he had never been allowed to drive the family motor car. His father was in the real estate business and always wanted the car to be at his command when he required it to take clients out into the country to show them a piece of farm property. The car always stood outside the First National Bank building where his father had an office on the second floor. Now, after the war, it was still the same car.

Nothing was changed in the town except that the young girls had grown up. 10 But they lived in such a complicated world of already defined alliances and shifting feuds that Krebs did not feel the energy or the courage to break into it. He liked to look at them, though. There were so many good-looking young girls. Most of them had their hair cut short. When he went away only little girls wore their hair like that or girls that were fast. They all wore sweaters and shirt waists with round Dutch collars. It was a pattern. He liked to look at them from the front porch as they walked on the other side of the street. He liked to watch them walking under the shade of the trees. He liked the round Dutch collars above their sweaters. He liked their silk stockings and flat shoes. He liked their bobbed hair and the way they walked.

When he was in town their appeal to him was not very strong. He did not like them when he saw them in the Greek's ice cream parlor. He did not want them themselves really. They were too complicated. There was something else. Vaguely he wanted a girl but he did not want to have to work to get her. He would have liked to have a girl but he did not want to have to spend a long time getting her. He did not want to get into the intrigue and the politics. He did not want to have to do any courting. He did not want to tell any more lies. It wasn't worth it.

He did not want any consequences. He did not want any consequences ever again. He wanted to live alone without consequences. Besides he did not really need a girl. The army had taught him that. It was all right to pose as though you had to have a girl. Nearly everybody did that. But it wasn't true. You did not need a girl. That was the funny thing. First a fellow boasted how girls mean nothing to him, that he never thought of them, that they could not touch him. Then a fellow boasted that he could not get along without girls, that he had to have them all the time, that he could not go to sleep without them.

That was all a lie. It was all a lie both ways. You did not need a girl unless you thought about them. He learned that in the army. Then sooner or later you always got one. When you were really ripe for a girl you always got one. You did not have to think about it. Sooner or later it would come. He had learned that in the army.

Now he would have liked a girl if she had come to him and not wanted to talk. But here at home it was all too complicated. He knew he could never get through it all again. It was not worth the trouble. That was the thing about French girls and German girls. There was not all this talking. You couldn't talk much and you did not need to talk. It was simple and you were friends. He thought about France and then he began to think about Germany. On the whole he had liked Germany better. He did not want to leave Germany. He did not want to come home. Still, he had come home. He sat on the front porch.

He liked the girls that were walking along the other side of the street. He liked 15 the look of them much better than the French girls or the German girls. But the world they were in was not the world he was in. He would like to have one of them. But it was not worth it. They were such a nice pattern. He liked the pattern. It was exciting. But he would not go through all the talking. He did not want one badly enough. He liked to look at them all, though. It was not worth it. Not now when things were getting good again.

He sat there on the porch reading a book on the war. It was a history and he was reading about all the engagements he had been in. It was the most interesting reading he had ever done. He wished there were more maps. He looked forward with a good feeling to reading all the really good histories when they would come out with good detail maps. Now he was really learning about the war. He had been a good soldier. That made a difference.

One morning after he had been home about a month his mother came into his bedroom and sat on the bed. She smoothed her apron.

"I had a talk with your father last night, Harold," she said, "and he is willing for you to take the car out in the evenings."

"Yeah?" said Krebs, who was not fully awake. "Take the car out? Yeah?"

"Yes. Your father has felt for some time that you should be able to take the car 20 out in the evenings whenever you wished but we only talked it over last night."

"I'll bet you made him," Krebs said.

"No. It was your father's suggestion that we talk the matter over."

"Yeah. I'll bet you made him," Krebs sat up in bed.

"Will you come down to breakfast, Harold?" his mother said.

"As soon as I get my clothes on," Krebs said.                                    25

His mother went out of the room and he could hear her frying something downstairs while he washed, shaved, and dressed to go down into the dining-room for breakfast. While he was eating breakfast his sister brought in the mail.

"Well, Hare," she said. "You old sleepyhead. What do you ever get up for?"

Krebs looked at her. He liked her. She was his best sister.

"Have you got the paper?" he asked.

She handed him the Kansas City *Star* and he shucked off its brown wrapper 30 and opened it to the sporting page. He folded the *Star* open and propped it against the water pitcher with his cereal dish to steady it, so he could read while he ate.

"Harold," his mother stood in the kitchen doorway, "Harold, please don't muss up the paper. Your father can't read his *Star* if it's been mussed."

"I won't muss it," Krebs said.

His sister sat down at the table and watched him while he read.

"We're playing indoor over at school this afternoon," she said. "I'm going to pitch."

"Good," said Krebs. "How's the old wing?"                                        35

"I can pitch better than lots of the boys. I tell them all you taught me. The other girls aren't much good."

"Yeah?" said Krebs.

"I tell them all you're my beau. Aren't you my beau, Hare?"

"You bet."

"Couldn't your brother really be your beau just because he's your brother?"     40

"I don't know."

"Sure you know. Couldn't you be my beau, Hare, if I was old enough and if you wanted to?"

"Sure. You're my girl now."

"Am I really your girl?"

"Sure." 45

"Do you love me?"

"Uh, huh."

"Will you love me always?"

"Sure."

"Will you come over and watch me play indoor?" 50

"Maybe."

"Aw, Hare, you don't love me. If you loved me, you'd want to come over and watch me play indoor."

Krebs's mother came into the dining-room from the kitchen. She carried a plate with two fried eggs and some crisp bacon on it and a plate of buckwheat cakes.

"You run along, Helen," she said. "I want to talk to Harold."

She put the eggs and bacon down in front of him and brought in a jug of maple 55 syrup for the buckwheat cakes. Then she sat down across the table from Krebs.

"I wish you'd put down the paper a minute, Harold," she said.

Krebs took down the paper and folded it.

"Have you decided what you are going to do yet, Harold?" his mother said, taking off her glasses.

"No," said Krebs.

"Don't you think it's about time?" His mother did not say this in a mean way. 60 She seemed worried.

"I hadn't thought about it," Krebs said.

"God has some work for everyone to do," his mother said. "There can be no idle hands in His Kingdom."

"I'm not in His Kingdom," Krebs said.

"We are all of us in His Kingdom."

Krebs felt embarrassed and resentful as always. 65

"I've worried about you so much, Harold," his mother went on. "I know the temptations you must have been exposed to. I know how weak men are. I know what your own dear grandfather, my own father, told us about the Civil War and I have prayed for you. I pray for you all day long, Harold."

Krebs looked at the bacon fat hardening on his plate.

"Your father is worried, too," his mother went on. "He thinks you have lost your ambition, that you haven't got a definite aim in life. Charley Simmons, who is just your age, has a good job and is going to be married. The boys are all settling down; they're all determined to get somewhere; you can see that boys like Charley Simmons are on their way to being really a credit to the community."

Krebs said nothing.

"Don't look that way, Harold," his mother said. "You know we love you and I 70 want to tell you for your own good how matters stand. Your father does not want to hamper your freedom. He thinks you should be allowed to drive the car. If you want to take some of the nice girls out riding with you, we are only too pleased. We want you to enjoy yourself. But you are going to have to settle down to work, Harold. Your father doesn't care what you start in at. All work is honorable as he says. But you've got to make a start at something. He asked me to speak to you this morning and then you can stop in and see him at his office."

"Is that all?" Krebs said.

"Yes. Don't you love your mother, dear boy?"

"No," Krebs said.

His mother looked at him across the table. Her eyes were shiny. She started crying.

"I don't love anybody," Krebs said.                                            75

It wasn't any good. He couldn't tell her, he couldn't make her see it. It was silly to have said it. He had only hurt her. He went over and took hold of her arm. She was crying with her head in her hands.

"I didn't mean it," he said. "I was just angry at something. I didn't mean I didn't love you."

His mother went on crying. Krebs put his arm on her shoulder.

"Can't you believe me, mother?"

His mother shook her head.                                                     80

"Please, please, mother. Please believe me."

"All right," his mother said chokily. She looked up at him. "I believe you, Harold."

Krebs kissed her hair. She put her face up to him.

"I'm your mother," she said. "I held you next to my heart when you were a tiny baby."

Krebs felt sick and vaguely nauseated.                                         85

"I know, Mummy," he said. "I'll try and be a good boy for you."

"Would you kneel and pray with me, Harold?" his mother asked.

They knelt down beside the dining-room table and Krebs's mother prayed.

"Now, you pray, Harold," she said.

"I can't," Krebs said.                                                         90

"Try, Harold."

"I can't."

"Do you want me to pray for you?"

"Yes."

So his mother prayed for him and then they stood up and Krebs kissed his 95 mother and went out of the house. He had tried so to keep his life from being complicated. Still, none of it had touched him. He had felt sorry for his mother and she had made him lie. He would go to Kansas City and get a job and she would feel all right about it. There would be one more scene maybe before he got away. He would not go down to his father's office. He would miss that one. He wanted his life to go smoothly. It had just gotten going that way. Well, that was all over now, anyway. He would go over to the schoolyard and watch Helen play indoor baseball.

## CONSIDERATIONS FOR CRITICAL THINKING AND WRITING

1. FIRST RESPONSE. The title, "Soldier's Home," focuses on the setting. Do you have a clear picture of Krebs's home? Describe it, filling in missing details from your associations of home, Krebs's routine, or anything else you can use.

2. What does the photograph of Krebs, the corporal, and the German girls reveal?

3. Belleau Wood, Soissons, the Champagne, St. Mihiel, and the Argonne were the sites of fierce and bloody fighting. What effect have these battles had on Krebs? Why won't he talk about them to the people at home?

4. Why does Krebs avoid complications and consequences? How has the war changed his attitudes toward work and women? How is his hometown different from Germany and France? What is the conflict in the story?

5. Why does Hemingway refer to the protagonist as Krebs rather than Harold? What is the significance of his sister calling him "Hare"?

6. How does Krebs's mother embody the community's values? What does Krebs think of those values?

7. Why can't Krebs pray with his mother?

8. What is the resolution to Krebs's conflict?

9. Comment on the appropriateness of the story's title.

10. Explain how Krebs's war experiences are present throughout the story even though we get no details about them.

11. CRITICAL STRATEGIES. Read the section on reader-response criticism in Chapter 42, "Critical Strategies for Reading," and consider the following: Perhaps, after having been away from home for a time, you have returned to find yourself alienated from your family or friends. Describe your experience. What caused the change? How does this experience affect your understanding of Krebs? Alternately, if alienation hasn't been your experience, how does that difference affect your reading of Krebs?

## CONNECTIONS TO OTHER SELECTIONS

1. Contrast the attitudes toward patriotism implicit in this story with those in Tim O'Brien's "How to Tell a True War Story" (p. 253). How do the stories' settings help to account for the differences between them?

2. Explain how the violent details that O'Brien uses to establish the setting in "How to Tell a True War Story" (p. 253) can be considered representative of the kinds of horrors that haunt Krebs after he returns home.

3. How might Krebs's rejection of his community's values relate to Sammy's relationship to his supermarket job in John Updike's "A & P" (p. 145)? What details does Updike use to make the setting in "A & P" a comic, though nonetheless serious, version of Krebs's hometown?

## URSULA K. LE GUIN (1929–2018)

Ursula K. Le Guin is most strongly associated with the genres of fantasy and science fiction, though she resisted such labels. The daughter of an anthropologist and a writer, Le Guin combined those sensibilities in her work, which constructs fabulous landscapes to address social interactions familiar to late twentieth- and early twenty-first-century Americans, such as the challenges of cultural contact, environmental destruction, and feminist activism. A prolific writer, she is perhaps best remembered for her Earthsea fantasy novels (1968–2001) and for her Hainish series of science fiction works (1966–2000). The

Beth Gwinn/Michael Ochs Archives/ Getty Images.

following story, "The Ones Who Walk Away from Omelas," is a good starting point into the rest of Le Guin's work in terms of her themes and style.

# The Ones Who Walk Away from Omelas    1973

*(Variations on a theme by William James)°*

With a clamor of bells that set the swallows soaring, the Festival of Summer came to the city Omelas, bright-towered by the sea. The rigging of the boats in harbor sparkled with flags. In the streets between houses with red roofs and painted walls, between old moss-grown gardens and under avenues of trees, past great parks and public buildings, processions moved. Some were decorous: old people in long stiff robes of mauve and grey, grave master workmen, quiet, merry women carrying their babies and chatting as they walked. In other streets the music beat faster, a shimmering of gong and tambourine, and the people went dancing, the procession was a dance. Children dodged in and out, their high calls rising like the swallows' crossing flights over the music and the singing. All the processions wound towards the north side of the city, where on the great water-meadow called the Green Fields boys and girls, naked in the bright air, with mud-stained feet and ankles and long, lithe arms, exercised their restive horses before the race. The horses wore no gear at all but a halter without bit. Their manes were braided with streamers of silver, gold, and green. They flared their nostrils and pranced and boasted to one another; they were vastly excited, the horse being the only animal who has adopted our ceremonies as his own. Far off to the north and west the mountains stood up half encircling Omelas on her bay. The air of morning was so clear that the snow still crowning the Eighteen Peaks burned with white-gold fire across the miles of sunlit air, under the dark blue of the sky. There was just enough wind to make the banners that marked the racecourse snap and flutter now and then. In the silence of the broad green meadows one could hear the music winding through the city streets, farther and nearer and ever approaching, a cheerful faint sweetness of the air that from time to time trembled and gathered together and broke out into the great joyous clanging of the bells.

Joyous! How is one to tell about joy? How describe the citizens of Omelas?

They were not simple folk, you see, though they were happy. But we do not say the words of cheer much any more. All smiles have become archaic. Given a description such as this one tends to make certain assumptions. Given a description such as this one tends to look next for the King, mounted on a splendid stallion and surrounded by his noble knights, or perhaps in a golden litter borne by a great-muscled slave. But there was no king. They did not use swords, or keep slaves. They were not barbarians. I do not know the rules and laws of their society, but I suspect that they were singularly few. As they did without monarchy and slavery, so they also got on without the stock exchange, the advertisement, the secret police, and the bomb. Yet I repeat that these were not simple folk, not dulcet shepherds, noble savages, bland utopians. They were not less complex than us. The trouble is that we have a bad habit, encouraged by pedants and sophisticates, of considering happiness as something rather stupid. Only pain is intellectual, only evil interesting. This is the treason of the artist: a refusal to admit the banality of evil and the terrible boredom of pain. If you can't lick 'em, join 'em. If it hurts, repeat it. But to praise despair is to condemn delight, to embrace violence is to

---

*William James:* James (1842–1910) was an influential philosopher who is considered to be one of the founders of modern psychology. He was also the brother of the renowned American writer Henry James.

lose hold of everything else. We have almost lost hold; we can no longer describe a happy man, nor make any celebration of joy. How can I tell you about the people of Omelas? They were not naïve and happy children — though their children were, in fact, happy. They were mature, intelligent, passionate adults whose lives were not wretched. O miracle! but I wish I could describe it better. I wish I could convince you. Omelas sounds in my words like a city in a fairy tale, long ago and far away, once upon a time. Perhaps it would be best if you imagined it as your own fancy bids, assuming it will rise to the occasion, for certainly I cannot suit you all. For instance, how about technology? I think that there would be no cars or helicopters in and above the streets; this follows from the fact that the people of Omelas are happy people. Happiness is based on a just discrimination of what is necessary, what is neither necessary nor destructive, and what is destructive. In the middle category, however — that of the unnecessary but undestructive, that of comfort, luxury, exuberance, etc. — they could perfectly well have central heating, subway trains, washing machines, and all kinds of marvelous devices not yet invented here, floating light-sources, fuelless power, a cure for the common cold. Or they could have none of that: it doesn't matter. As you like it. I incline to think that people from towns up and down the coast have been coming in to Omelas during the last days before the Festival on very fast little trains and double-decked trams, and that the train station of Omelas is actually the handsomest building in town, though plainer than the magnificent Farmers' Market. But even granted trains, I fear that Omelas so far strikes some of you as goody-goody. Smiles, bells, parades, horses, bleh. If so, please add an orgy. If an orgy would help, don't hesitate. Let us not, however, have temples from which issue beautiful nude priests and priest-esses already half in ecstasy and ready to copulate with any man or woman, lover or stranger, who desires union with the deep godhead of the blood, although that was my first idea. But really it would be better not to have temples in Omelas — at least, not manned temples. Religion yes, clergy no. Surely the beautiful nudes can just wander about, offering themselves like divine soufflés to the hunger of the needy and the rapture of the flesh. Let them join the processions. Let tambourines be struck above the copulations, and the glory of desire be proclaimed upon the gongs, and (a not unimportant point) let the offspring of these delightful rituals be beloved and looked after by all. One thing I know there is none of in Omelas is guilt. But what else should there be? I thought at first there were no drugs, but that is puritanical. For those who like it, the faint insistent sweetness of *drooz* may per-fume the ways of the city, *drooz* which first brings a great lightness and brilliance to the mind and limbs, and then after some hours a dreamy langour, and wonder-ful visions at last of the very arcana and inmost secrets of the Universe, as well as exciting the pleasure of sex beyond all belief; and it is not habit-forming. For more modest tastes I think there ought to be beer. What else, what else belongs in the joyous city? The sense of victory, surely, the celebration of courage. But as we did without clergy, let us do without soldiers. The joy built upon successful slaughter is not the right kind of joy; it will not do; it is fearful and it is trivial. A boundless and generous contentment, a magnanimous triumph felt not against some outer enemy but in communion with the finest and fairest in the souls of all men everywhere and the splendor of the world's summer: this is what swells the hearts of the people of Omelas, and the victory they celebrate is that of life. I really don't think many of them need to take *drooz*.

Most of the processions have reached the Green Fields by now. A marvelous smell of cooking goes forth from the red and blue tents of the provisioners. The faces of small children are amiably sticky; in the benign grey beard of a man a couple of crumbs of rich pastry are entangled. The youths and girls have mounted their horses and are beginning to group around the starting line of the course. An old woman, small, fat, and laughing, is passing out flowers from a basket, and tall young men wear her flowers in their shining hair. A child of nine or ten sits at the edge of the crowd, alone, playing on a wooden flute. People pause to listen, and they smile, but they do not speak to him, for he never ceases playing and never sees them, his dark eyes wholly rapt in the sweet, thin magic of the tune.

He finishes, and slowly lowers his hands holding the wooden flute.                          5

As if that little private silence were the signal, all at once a trumpet sounds from the pavilion near the starting line: imperious, melancholy, piercing. The horses rear on their slender legs, and some of them neigh in answer. Sober-faced, the young riders stroke the horses' necks and soothe them, whispering, "Quiet, quiet, there my beauty, my hope. . . ." They begin to form in rank along the starting line. The crowds along the racecourse are like a field of grass and flowers in the wind. The Festival of Summer has begun.

Do you believe? Do you accept the festival, the city, the joy? No? Then let me describe one more thing.

In a basement under one of the beautiful public buildings of Omelas, or perhaps in the cellar of one of its spacious private homes, there is a room. It has one locked door, and no window. A little light seeps in dustily between cracks in the boards, secondhand from a cobwebbed window somewhere across the cellar. In one corner of the little room a couple of mops, with stiff, clotted, foul-smelling heads, stand near a rusty bucket. The floor is dirt, a little damp to the touch, as cellar dirt usually is. The room is about three paces long and two wide: a mere broom closet or disused tool room. In the room a child is sitting. It could be a boy or a girl. It looks about six, but actually is nearly ten. It is feebleminded. Perhaps it was born defective, or perhaps it has become imbecile through fear, malnutrition, and neglect. It picks its nose and occasionally fumbles vaguely with its toes or genitals, as it sits hunched in the corner farthest from the bucket and the two mops. It is afraid of the mops. It finds them horrible. It shuts its eyes, but it knows the mops are still standing there; and the door is locked; and nobody will come. The door is always locked; and nobody ever comes, except that sometimes — the child has no understanding of time or interval — sometimes the door rattles terribly and opens, and a person, or several people, are there. One of them may come in and kick the child to make it stand up. The others never come close, but peer in at it with frightened, disgusted eyes. The food bowl and the water jug are hastily filled, the door is locked, the eyes disappear. The people at the door never say anything, but the child, who has not always lived in the tool room, and can remember sunlight and its mother's voice, sometimes speaks. "I will be good," it says. "Please let me out. I will be good!" They never answer. The child used to scream for help at night, and cry a good deal, but now it only makes a kind of whining, "eh-haa, eh-haa," and it speaks less and less often: It is so thin there are no calves to its legs; its belly protrudes; it lives on a half-bowl of corn meal and grease a day. It is naked. Its buttocks and thighs are a mass of festered sores, as it sits in its own excrement continually.

They all know it is there, all the people of Omelas. Some of them have come to see it, others are content merely to know it is there. They all know that it has to be there. Some of them understand why, and some do not, but they all understand that their happiness, the beauty of their city, the tenderness of their friendships, the health of their children, the wisdom of their scholars, the skill of their makers, even the abundance of their harvest and the kindly weathers of their skies, depend wholly on this child's abominable misery.

This is usually explained to children when they are between eight and twelve, 10 whenever they seem capable of understanding; and most of those who come to see the child are young people, though often enough an adult comes, or comes back, to see the child. No matter how well the matter has been explained to them, these young spectators are always shocked and sickened at the sight. They feel disgust, which they had thought themselves superior to. They feel anger, outrage, impotence, despite all the explanations. They would like to do something for the child. But there is nothing they can do. If the child were brought up into the sunlight out of that vile place, if it were cleaned and fed and comforted, that would be a good thing, indeed; but if it were done, in that day and hour all the prosperity and beauty and delight of Omelas would wither and be destroyed. Those are the terms. To exchange all the goodness and grace of every life in Omelas for that single, small improvement: to throw away the happiness of thousands for the chance of the happiness of one: that would be to let guilt within the walls indeed.

The terms are strict and absolute; there may not even be a kind word spoken to the child.

Often the young people go home in tears, or in a tearless rage, when they have seen the child and faced this terrible paradox. They may brood over it for weeks or years. But as time goes on they begin to realize that even if the child could be released, it would not get much good of its freedom: a little vague pleasure of warmth and food, no doubt, but little more. It is too degraded and imbecile to know any real joy. It has been afraid too long ever to be free of fear. Its habits are too uncouth for it to respond to humane treatment. Indeed, after so long it would probably be wretched without walls about it to protect it, and darkness for its eyes, and its own excrement to sit in. Their tears at the bitter injustice dry when they begin to perceive the terrible justice of reality, and to accept it. Yet it is their tears and anger, the trying of their generosity and the acceptance of their helplessness, which are perhaps the true source of the splendor of their lives. Theirs is no vapid, irresponsible happiness. They know that they, like the child, are not free. They know compassion. It is the existence of the child, and their knowledge of its existence, that makes possible the nobility of their architecture, the poignancy of their music, the profundity of their science. It is because of the child that they are so gentle with children. They know that if the wretched one were not there snivelling in the dark, the other one, the flute-player, could make no joyful music as the young riders line up in their beauty for the race in the sunlight of the first morning of summer.

Now do you believe in them? Are they not more credible? But there is one more thing to tell, and this is quite incredible.

At times one of the adolescent girls or boys who go to see the child does not go home to weep or rage, does not, in fact, go home at all. Sometimes also a man or woman much older falls silent for a day or two, and then leaves home. These people go out into the street, and walk down the street alone. They keep walking, and walk straight out of the city of Omelas, through the beautiful gates. They keep walking across the farmlands of Omelas. Each one goes alone, youth or girl, man or woman. Night falls; the traveler must pass down village streets, between the houses with yellow-lit windows, and on out into the darkness of the fields. Each alone, they go west or north, towards the mountains. They go on. They leave Omelas, they walk ahead into the darkness, and they do not come back. The place they go towards is a place even less imaginable to most of us than the city of happiness. I cannot describe it at all. It is possible that it does not exist. But they seem to know where they are going, the ones who walk away from Omelas.

## CONSIDERATIONS FOR CRITICAL THINKING AND WRITING

1. FIRST RESPONSE. In paragraph 1 the narrator describes Omelas in very familiar, fairy tale-like terms, but in the third paragraph she alters her description to counter some of our expectations, and even criticizes her own powers of description: "Omelas sounds in my words like a city in a fairy tale, long ago and far away, once upon a time." What is the effect of the initial description followed by the later correction?

2. Note all of the adjectives in the story's first paragraph. Which are the most significant, and what is their overall effect in terms of enabling you to "see" Omelas?

3. Toward the end of paragraph 3 the narrator invites the reader to help create the world. Orgies and drugs are permissible, but clergy and soldiers are not. Do these qualifications to the initial description — which is quite vivid and definite — make the picture of Omelas clearer or fuzzier?

4. The story discusses joy and happiness at length. How are those concepts related to Omelas as a setting?

5. The setting is not only the city of Omelas in general, but the Festival of Summer in particular. How does a momentous occasion associated with a particular place affect your sense of setting? (Consider, for instance, Mardi Gras in New Orleans or New Year's Eve in New York's Times Square.)

6. What is the effect on you as a reader when the narrator asks you if you believe her description, and even voices your scepticism for you? ("Do you believe? . . . No?")

7. Compare the details of the description of the cellar room where the child is locked to the descriptions of the public spaces in Omelas. Are they parallel? Is one easier to picture than the other? Why?

8. How would the story be changed if Le Guin had described the cellar room with the abused child first and the descriptions of the Festival of Summer second?

9. The narrator abandons the description of the Festival of Summer at a crucial moment, just as it is about to begin, with horses lining up and crowds gathering around them. Why does the narrator not return to this scene after introducing the miserable child in the cellar?

10. The descriptions of both Omelas and the cellar room are fairly detailed, and they appeal to multiple senses. Given the narrator's powers of description, why is it significant when her powers of description abandon her with regard to the place where the exiles are going: "I cannot describe it at all"?

## CONNECTIONS TO OTHER SELECTIONS

1. Consider the importance of ritual and the relationship between an individual and a community in this story and in Shirley Jackson's "The Lottery" (p. 233).

2. Discuss attitudes toward privilege and its opposite in this story and in ZZ Packer's "Drinking Coffee Elsewhere" (p. 292).

## CHARLOTTE PERKINS GILMAN (1860–1935)

At the intersection of a number of reform movements in the late nineteenth century, Charlotte Perkins Gilman was an activist and lecturer as well as a professional writer of poems, essays, and fiction. Suffering from what we now understand to be postpartum depression after the birth of her daughter, Gilman was prescribed a "rest cure" by one Dr. Silas Weir Mitchell. It involved nearly complete isolation and a severe reduction in intellectual and creative activities, and, of course, it worsened her symptoms rather than curing them. This misguided "treatment" provided the basis for what is by far Gilman's most renowned work, "The Yellow Wallpaper."

## *The Yellow Wallpaper*    1892

It is very seldom that mere ordinary people like John and myself secure ancestral halls for the summer.

A colonial mansion, a hereditary estate, I would say a haunted house, and reach the height of romantic felicity — but that would be asking too much of fate!

Still I will proudly declare that there is something queer about it.

Else, why should it be let so cheaply? And why have stood so long untenanted?

John laughs at me, of course, but one expects that in marriage.                              5

John is practical in the extreme. He has no patience with faith, an intense horror of superstition, and he scoffs openly at any talk of things not to be felt and seen and put down in figures.

John is a physician, and *perhaps* — (I would not say it to a living soul, of course, but this is dead paper and a great relief to my mind) — *perhaps* that is one reason I do not get well faster.

You see he does not believe I am sick!

And what can one do?

If a physician of high standing, and one's own husband, assures friends and   10 relatives that there is really nothing the matter with one but temporary nervous depression — a slight hysterical tendency° — what is one to do?

My brother is also a physician, and also of high standing, and he says the same thing.

So I take phosphates or phosphites° — whichever it is, and tonics, and journeys, and air, and exercise, and am absolutely forbidden to "work" until I am well again.

Personally, I disagree with their ideas.

Personally, I believe that congenial work, with excitement and change, would do me good.

---

*hysterical tendency:* In the nineteenth century, women's illnesses of all sorts were generally characterized as "hysteria," although the symptoms might range from pain to anxiety, fatigue to depression. These symptoms were presumed to have a somatic origin.
*phosphates or phosphites:* Any salt or ester of phosphoric acid, used during the nineteenth century to cure exhaustion of the nerve centers, neuralgia, mania, melancholia, and often sexual exhaustion.

But what is one to do? 15

I did write for a while in spite of them; but it *does* exhaust me a good deal — having to be so sly about it, or else meet with heavy opposition.

I sometimes fancy that in my condition if I had less opposition and more society and stimulus — but John says the very worst thing I can do is to think about my condition, and I confess it always makes me feel bad.

So I will let it alone and talk about the house.

The most beautiful place! It is quite alone, standing well back from the road, quite three miles from the village. It makes me think of English places that you read about, for there are hedges and walls and gates that lock, and lots of separate little houses for the gardeners and people.

There is a *delicious* garden! I never saw such a garden — large and shady, full 20 of box-bordered paths, and lined with long grape-covered arbors with seats under them.

There were greenhouses, too, but they are all broken now.

There was some legal trouble, I believe, something about the heirs and co-heirs; anyhow, the place has been empty for years.

That spoils my ghostliness, I am afraid, but I don't care — there is something strange about the house — I can feel it.

I even said so to John one moonlight evening, but he said what I felt was a *draught,* and shut the window.

I get unreasonably angry with John sometimes. I'm sure I never used to be so 25 sensitive. I think it is due to this nervous condition.

But John says if I feel so, I shall neglect proper self-control; so I take pains to control myself — before him, at least, and that makes me very tired.

I don't like our room a bit. I wanted one downstairs that opened on the piazza and had roses all over the window, and such pretty old-fashioned chintz hangings! but John would not hear of it.

He said there was only one window and not room for two beds, and no near room for him if he took another.

He is very careful and loving, and hardly lets me stir without special direction.

I have a schedule prescription for each hour in the day; he takes all care from 30 me, and so I feel basely ungrateful not to value it more.

He said we came here solely on my account, that I was to have perfect rest and all the air I could get. "Your exercise depends on your strength, my dear," said he, "and your food somewhat on your appetite; but air you can absorb all the time." So we took the nursery at the top of the house.

It is a big, airy room, the whole floor nearly, with windows that look all ways, and air and sunshine galore. It was nursery first and then playroom and gymnasium, I should judge; for the windows are barred for little children, and there are rings and things in the walls.

The paint and paper look as if a boys' school had used it. It is stripped off — the paper — in great patches all around the head of my bed, about as far as I can reach, and in a great place on the other side of the room low down. I never saw a worse paper in my life.

One of those sprawling flamboyant patterns committing every artistic sin.

It is dull enough to confuse the eye in following, pronounced enough to con- 35 stantly irritate and provoke study, and when you follow the lame uncertain curves for a little distance they suddenly commit suicide — plunge off at outrageous angles, destroy themselves in unheard of contradictions.

The color is repellant, almost revolting; a smouldering unclean yellow, strangely faded by the slow-turning sunlight.

It is a dull yet lurid orange in some places, a sickly sulphur tint in others.

No wonder the children hated it! I should hate it myself if I had to live in this room long.

There comes John, and I must put this away, — he hates to have me write a word.

----

We have been here two weeks, and I haven't felt like writing before, since that 40 first day.

I am sitting by the window now, up in this atrocious nursery, and there is nothing to hinder my writing as much as I please, save lack of strength.

John is away all day, and even some nights when his cases are serious.

I am glad my case is not serious!

But these nervous troubles are dreadfully depressing.

John does not know how much I really suffer. He knows there is no *reason* to 45 suffer, and that satisfies him.

Of course it is only nervousness. It does weigh on me so not to do my duty in any way!

I meant to be such a help to John, such a real rest and comfort, and here I am a comparative burden already!

Nobody would believe what an effort it is to do what little I am able, — to dress and entertain, and order things.

It is fortunate Mary is so good with the baby. Such a dear baby!

And yet I *cannot* be with him, it makes me so nervous. 50

I suppose John never was nervous in his life. He laughs at me so about this wall-paper!

At first he meant to repaper the room, but afterwards he said that I was letting it get the better of me, and that nothing was worse for a nervous patient than to give way to such fancies.

He said that after the wall-paper was changed it would be the heavy bedstead, and then the barred windows, and then that gate at the head of the stairs, and so on.

"You know the place is doing you good," he said, "and really, dear, I don't care to renovate the house just for a three months' rental."

"Then do let us go downstairs," I said, "there are such pretty rooms there." 55

Then he took me in his arms and called me a blessed little goose, and said he would go down cellar, if I wished, and have it whitewashed into the bargain.

But he is right enough about the beds and windows and things.

It is an airy and comfortable room as any one need wish, and, of course, I would not be so silly as to make him uncomfortable just for a whim.

I'm really getting quite fond of the big room, all but that horrid paper.

Out of one window I can see the garden, those mysterious deep-shaded 60 arbors, the riotous old-fashioned flowers, and bushes and gnarly trees.

Out of another I get a lovely view of the bay and a little private wharf belonging to the estate. There is a beautiful shaded lane that runs down there from the house. I always fancy I see people walking in these numerous paths and arbors, but

John has cautioned me not to give way to fancy in the least. He says that with my imaginative power and habit of story-making, a nervous weakness like mine is sure to lead to all manner of excited fancies, and that I ought to use my will and good sense to check the tendency. So I try.

I think sometimes that if I were only well enough to write a little it would relieve the press of ideas and rest me.

But I find I get pretty tired when I try.

It is so discouraging not to have any advice and companionship about my work. When I get really well, John says we will ask Cousin Henry and Julia down for a long visit; but he says he would as soon put fireworks in my pillow-case as to let me have those stimulating people about now.

I wish I could get well faster. 65

But I must not think about that. This paper looks to me as if it *knew* what a vicious influence it had!

There is a recurrent spot where the pattern lolls like a broken neck and two bulbous eyes stare at you upside down.

I get positively angry with the impertinence of it and the everlastingness. Up and down and sideways they crawl, and those absurd, unblinking eyes are everywhere. There is one place where two breadths didn't match, and the eyes go all up and down the line, one a little higher than the other.

I never saw so much expression in an inanimate thing before, and we all know how much expression they have! I used to lie awake as a child and get more entertainment and terror out of blank walls and plain furniture than most children could find in a toy-store.

I remember what a kindly wink the knobs of our big, old bureau used to have, 70 and there was one chair that always seemed like a strong friend.

I used to feel that if any of the other things looked too fierce I could always hop into that chair and be safe.

The furniture in this room is no worse than inharmonious, however, for we had to bring it all from downstairs. I suppose when this was used as a playroom they had to take the nursery things out, and no wonder! I never saw such ravages as the children have made here.

The wall-paper, as I said before, is torn off in spots, and it sticketh closer than a brother—they must have had perseverance as well as hatred.

Then the floor is scratched and gouged and splintered, the plaster itself is dug out here and there, and this great heavy bed which is all we found in the room, looks as if it had been through the wars.

But I don't mind it a bit—only the paper. 75

There comes John's sister. Such a dear girl as she is, and so careful of me! I must not let her find me writing.

She is a perfect and enthusiastic housekeeper, and hopes for no better profession. I verily believe she thinks it is the writing which made me sick!

But I can write when she is out, and see her a long way off from these windows.

There is one that commands the road, a lovely shaded winding road, and one that just looks off over the country. A lovely country, too, full of great elms and velvet meadows.

This wallpaper has a kind of sub-pattern in a different shade, a particularly 80 irritating one, for you can only see it in certain lights, and not clearly then.

But in the places where it isn't faded and where the sun is just so — I can see a strange, provoking, formless sort of figure, that seems to skulk about behind that silly and conspicuous front design.

There's sister on the stairs!

--------

Well, the Fourth of July is over! The people are all gone and I am tired out. John thought it might do me good to see a little company, so we just had mother and Nellie and the children down for a week.

Of course I didn't do a thing. Jennie sees to everything now.

But it tired me all the same.                                                    85

John says if I don't pick up faster he shall send me to Weir Mitchell° in the fall.

But I don't want to go there at all. I had a friend who was in his hands once, and she says he is just like John and my brother, only more so!

Besides, it is such an undertaking to go so far.

I don't feel as if it was worth while to turn my hand over for anything, and I'm getting dreadfully fretful and querulous.

I cry at nothing, and cry most of the time.                                      90

Of course I don't when John is here, or anybody else, but when I am alone.

And I am alone a good deal just now. John is kept in town very often by serious cases, and Jennie is good and lets me alone when I want her to.

So I walk a little in the garden or down that lovely lane, sit on the porch under the roses, and lie down up here a good deal.

I'm getting really fond of the room in spite of the wallpaper. Perhaps *because* of the wallpaper.

It dwells in my mind so!                                                          95

I lie here on this great immovable bed — it is nailed down, I believe — and follow that pattern about by the hour. It is as good as gymnastics, I assure you. I start, we'll say, at the bottom, down in the corner over there where it has not been touched, and I determine for the thousandth time that I *will* follow that pointless pattern to some sort of a conclusion.

I know a little of the principle of design, and I know this thing was not arranged on any laws of radiation, or alternation, or repetition, or symmetry, or anything else that I ever heard of.

It is repeated, of course, by the breadths, but not otherwise.

Looked at in one way each breadth stands alone, the bloated curves and flourishes — a kind of "debased Romanesque"° with *delirium tremens* — go waddling up and down in isolated columns of fatuity.

But, on the other hand, they connect diagonally, and the sprawling outlines  100
run off in great slanting waves of optic horror, like a lot of wallowing seaweeds in full chase.

The whole thing goes horizontally, too, at least it seems so, and I exhaust myself in trying to distinguish the order of its going in that direction.

--------

*S. Weir Mitchell:* Mitchell (1829–1914) was a famous Civil War doctor and later novelist, who treated shell shock during and after the Civil War. Later, he developed a "rest cure" for women and men suffering from neurasthenia.

*debased Romanesque:* European architectural style with elaborate ornamentation and complexity, as well as repeated motifs.

They have used a horizontal breadth for a frieze,° and that adds wonderfully to the confusion.

There is one end of the room where it is almost intact, and there, when the crosslights fade and the low sun shines directly upon it, I can almost fancy radiation after all, — the interminable grotesques seem to form around a common centre and rush off in headlong plunges of equal distraction.

It makes me tired to follow it. I will take a nap I guess.

---

I don't know why I should write this.                                                   105

I don't want to.

I don't feel able.

And I know John would think it absurd. But I *must* say what I feel and think in some way — it is such a relief!

But the effort is getting to be greater than the relief.

Half the time now I am awfully lazy, and lie down ever so much.                         110

John says I mustn't lose my strength, and has me take cod liver oil and lots of tonics and things, to say nothing of ale and wine and rare meat.

Dear John! He loves me very dearly, and hates to have me sick. I tried to have a real earnest reasonable talk with him the other day, and tell him how I wish he would let me go and make a visit to Cousin Henry and Julia.

But he said I wasn't able to go, nor able to stand it after I got there; and I did not make out a very good case for myself, for I was crying before I had finished.

It is getting to be a great effort for me to think straight. Just this nervous weakness I suppose.

And dear John gathered me up in his arms, and just carried me upstairs and          115
laid me on the bed, and sat by me and read to me till it tired my head.

He said I was his darling and his comfort and all he had, and that I must take care of myself for his sake, and keep well.

He says no one but myself can help me out of it, that I must use my will and self-control and not let any silly fancies run away with me.

There's one comfort, the baby is well and happy, and does not have to occupy this nursery with the horrid wallpaper.

If we had not used it, that blessed child would have! What a fortunate escape! Why, I wouldn't have a child of mine, an impressionable little thing, live in such a room for worlds.

I never thought of it before, but it is lucky that John kept me here after all, I    120
can stand it so much easier than a baby, you see.

Of course I never mention it to them any more — I am too wise, — but I keep watch of it all the same.

There are things in that paper that nobody knows but me, or ever will.

Behind that outside pattern the dim shapes get clearer every day.

It is always the same shape, only very numerous.

And it is like a woman stooping down and creeping about behind that pattern.    125
I don't like it a bit. I wonder — I begin to think — I wish John would take me away from here!

---

*frieze:* A decorative band used as a border around a room or mantle.

It is so hard to talk to John about my case, because he is so wise, and because he loves me so.

But I tried it last night.

It was moonlight. The moon shines in all around just as the sun does.

I hate to see it sometimes, it creeps so slowly, and always comes in by one window or another.

John was asleep and I hated to waken him, so I kept still and watched the moonlight on that undulating wallpaper till I felt creepy.                      130

The faint figure behind seemed to shake the pattern, just as if she wanted to get out.

I got up softly and went to feel and see if the paper *did* move, and when I came back John was awake.

"What is it, little girl?" he said. "Don't go walking about like that — you'll get cold."

I thought it was a good time to talk, so I told him that I really was not gaining here, and that I wished he would take me away.

"Why, darling!" said he, "our lease will be up in three weeks, and I can't see   135
how to leave before.

"The repairs are not done at home, and I cannot possibly leave town just now. Of course if you were in any danger, I could and would, but you really are better, dear, whether you can see it or not. I am a doctor, dear, and I know. You are gaining flesh and color, your appetite is better, I feel really much easier about you."

"I don't weigh a bit more," said I, "nor as much; and my appetite may be better in the evening when you are here, but it is worse in the morning when you are away!"

"Bless her little heart!" said he with a big hug, "she shall be as sick as she pleases! But now let's improve the shining hours° by going to sleep, and talk about it in the morning!"

"And you won't go away?" I asked gloomily.

"Why, how can I, dear? It is only three weeks more and then we will take a nice   140
little trip of a few days while Jennie is getting the house ready. Really dear you are better!"

"Better in body perhaps —" I began, and stopped short, for he sat up straight and looked at me with such a stern, reproachful look that I could not say another word.

"My darling," said he, "I beg of you, for my sake and for our child's sake, as well as for your own, that you will never for one instant let that idea enter your mind! There is nothing so dangerous, so fascinating, to a temperament like yours. It is a false and foolish fancy. Can you not trust me as a physician when I tell you so?"

So of course I said no more on that score, and we went to sleep before long. He thought I was asleep first, but I wasn't, and lay there for hours trying to decide whether that front pattern and the back pattern really did move together or separately.

———————

On a pattern like this, by daylight, there is a lack of sequence, a defiance of law, that is a constant irritant to a normal mind.

*improve the shining hours:* These lines are adapted from "Song XX" by English hymnist Isaac Watts (1674–1748): "How doth the little busy bee / Improve each shining hour, / And gather honey all the day / From every opening flower!"

The color is hideous enough, and unreliable enough, and infuriating enough, 145
but the pattern is torturing.

You think you have mastered it, but just as you get well underway in following,
it turns a back-somersault and there you are. It slaps you in the face, knocks you
down, and tramples upon you. It is like a bad dream.

The outside pattern is a florid arabesque, reminding one of a fungus. If you
can imagine a toadstool in joints, an interminable string of toadstools, budding
and sprouting in endless convolutions — why, that is something like it.

That is, sometimes!

There is one marked peculiarity about this paper, a thing nobody seems to
notice but myself, and that is that it changes as the light changes.

When the sun shoots in through the east window — I always watch for that 150
first long, straight ray — it changes so quickly that I never can quite believe it.

That is why I watch it always.

By moonlight — the moon shines in all night when there is a moon — I
wouldn't know it was the same paper.

At night in any kind of light, in twilight, candlelight, lamplight, and worst of
all by moonlight, it becomes bars! The outside pattern I mean, and the woman
behind it is as plain as can be.

I didn't realize for a long time what the thing was that showed behind, that
dim sub-pattern, but now I am quite sure it is a woman.

By daylight she is subdued, quiet. I fancy it is the pattern that keeps her so still. 155
It is so puzzling. It keeps me quiet by the hour.

I lie down ever so much now. John says it is good for me, and to sleep all I can.

Indeed he started the habit by making me lie down for an hour after each meal.

It is a very bad habit I am convinced, for you see I don't sleep.

And that cultivates deceit, for I don't tell them I'm awake — O no!

The fact is I am getting a little afraid of John. 160

He seems very queer sometimes, and even Jennie has an inexplicable look.

It strikes me occasionally, just as a scientific hypothesis, — that perhaps it is
the paper!

I have watched John when he did not know I was looking, and come into the
room suddenly on the most innocent excuses, and I've caught him several times
*looking at the paper*! And Jennie too. I caught Jennie with her hand on it once.

She didn't know I was in the room, and when I asked her in a quiet, a very
quiet voice, with the most restrained manner possible, what she was doing with
the paper — she turned around as if she had been caught stealing, and looked quite
angry — asked me why I should frighten her so!

Then she said that the paper stained everything it touched, that she had found 165
yellow smooches on all my clothes and John's, and she wished we would be more
careful!

Did not that sound innocent? But I know she was studying that pattern, and I
am determined that nobody shall find it out but myself!

———

Life is very much more exciting now than it used to be. You see I have something more to expect, to look forward to, to watch. I really do eat better, and am
more quiet than I was.

John is so pleased to see me improve! He laughed a little the other day, and
said I seemed to be flourishing in spite of my wall-paper.

I turned it off with a laugh. I had no intention of telling him it was *because* of the wall-paper—he would make fun of me. He might even want to take me away.

I don't want to leave now until I have found it out. There is a week more, and  170 I think that will be enough.

_____

I'm feeling ever so much better! I don't sleep much at night, for it is so interesting to watch developments; but I sleep a good deal in the daytime.

In the daytime it is tiresome and perplexing.

There are always new shoots on the fungus, and new shades of yellow all over it. I cannot keep count of them, though I have tried conscientiously.

It is the strangest yellow, that wall-paper! It makes me think of all the yellow things I ever saw—not beautiful ones like buttercups, but old foul, bad yellow things.

But there is something else about that paper—the smell! I noticed it the  175 moment we came into the room, but with so much air and sun it was not bad. Now we have had a week of fog and rain, and whether the windows are open or not, the smell is here.

It creeps all over the house.

I find it hovering in the dining-room, skulking in the parlor, hiding in the hall, lying in wait for me on the stairs.

It gets into my hair.

Even when I go to ride, if I turn my head suddenly and surprise it—there is that smell!

Such a peculiar odor, too! I have spent hours in trying to analyze it, to find  180 what it smelled like.

It is not bad—at first, and very gentle, but quite the subtlest, most enduring odor I ever met.

In this damp weather it is awful, I wake up in the night and find it hanging over me.

It used to disturb me at first. I thought seriously of burning the house—to reach the smell.

But now I am used to it. The only thing I can think of that it is like is the *color* of the paper! A yellow smell.

There is a very funny mark on this wall, low down, near the mop-board. A  185 streak that runs round the room. It goes behind every piece of furniture, except the bed, a long, straight, even *smooch*, as if it had been rubbed over and over.

I wonder how it was done and who did it, and what they did it for. Round and round and round—round and round and round—it makes me dizzy!

_____

I really have discovered something at last.

Through watching so much at night, when it changes so, I have finally found out.

The front pattern *does* move—and no wonder! The woman behind shakes it!

Sometimes I think there are a great many women behind, and sometimes only  190 one, and she crawls around fast, and her crawling shakes it all over.

Then in the very bright spots she keeps still, and in the very shady spots she just takes hold of the bars and shakes them hard.

And she is all the time trying to climb through. But nobody could climb through that pattern — it strangles so; I think that is why it has so many heads.

They get through, and then the pattern strangles them off and turns them upside down, and makes their eyes white!

If those heads were covered or taken off it would not be half so bad.

---

I think that woman gets out in the daytime! 195

And I'll tell you why — privately — I've seen her!

I can see her out of every one of my windows!

It is the same woman, I know, for she is always creeping, and most women do not creep by daylight.

I see her in that long shaded lane, creeping up and down. I see her in those dark grape arbors, creeping all around the garden.

I see her on that long road under the trees, creeping along, and when a car- 200 riage comes she hides under the blackberry vines.

I don't blame her a bit. It must be very humiliating to be caught creeping by daylight!

I always lock the door when I creep by daylight. I can't do it at night, for I know John would suspect something at once.

And John is so queer now, that I don't want to irritate him. I wish he would take another room! Besides, I don't want anybody to get that woman out at night but myself.

I often wonder if I could see her out of all the windows at once.

But, turn as fast as I can, I can only see out of one at one time. 205

And though I always see her, she *may* be able to creep faster than I can turn!

I have watched her sometimes away off in the open country, creeping as fast as a cloud shadow in a high wind.

---

If only that top pattern could be gotten off from the under one! I mean to try it, little by little.

I have found out another funny thing, but I shan't tell it this time! It does not do to trust people too much.

There are only two more days to get this paper off, and I believe John is begin- 210 ning to notice. I don't like the look in his eyes.

And I heard him ask Jennie a lot of professional questions about me. She had a very good report to give.

She said I slept a good deal in the daytime.

John knows I don't sleep very well at night, for all I'm so quiet!

He asked me all sorts of questions, too, and pretended to be very loving and kind.

As if I couldn't see through him! 215

Still, I don't wonder he acts so, sleeping under this paper for three months.

It only interests me, but I feel sure John and Jennie are secretly affected by it.

---

Hurrah! This is the last day, but it is enough. John to stay in town over night, and won't be out until this evening.

Jennie wanted to sleep with me — the sly thing! But I told her I should undoubtedly rest better for a night all alone.

That was clever, for really I wasn't alone a bit! As soon as it was moonlight and that poor thing began to crawl and shake the pattern, I got up and ran to help her.

I pulled and she shook, I shook and she pulled, and before morning we had peeled off yards of that paper.

A strip about as high as my head and half around the room.

And then when the sun came and that awful pattern began to laugh at me, I declared I would finish it to-day!

We go away to-morrow, and they are moving all my furniture down again to leave things as they were before.

Jennie looked at the wall in amazement, but I told her merrily that I did it out of pure spite at the vicious thing.

She laughed and said she wouldn't mind doing it herself, but I must not get tired.

How she betrayed herself that time!

But I am here, and no person touches this paper but me, — not *alive!*

She tried to get me out of the room — it was too patent! But I said it was so quiet and empty and clean now that I believed I would lie down again and sleep all I could; and not to wake me even for dinner — I would call when I woke.

So now she is gone, and the servants are gone, and the things are gone, and there is nothing left but that great bedstead nailed down, with the canvas mattress we found on it.

We shall sleep downstairs to-night, and take the boat home tomorrow.

I quite enjoy the room, now it is bare again.

How those children did tear about here!

This bedstead is fairly gnawed!

But I must get to work.

I have locked the door and thrown the key down into the front path.

I don't want to go out, and I don't want to have anybody come in, till John comes.

I want to astonish him.

I've got a rope up here that even Jennie did not find. If that woman does get out, and tries to get away, I can tie her!

But I forgot I could not reach far without anything to stand on!

This bed will *not* move!

I tried to lift and push it until I was lame, and then I got so angry I bit off a little piece at one corner — but it hurt my teeth.

Then I peeled off all the paper I could reach standing on the floor. It sticks horribly and the pattern just enjoys it! All those strangled heads and bulbous eyes and waddling fungus growths just shriek with derision!

I am getting angry enough to do something desperate. To jump out of the window would be admirable exercise, but the bars are too strong even to try.

Besides I wouldn't do it. Of course not. I know well enough that a step like that is improper and might be misconstrued.

I don't like to *look* out of the windows even — there are so many of those creeping women, and they creep so fast.

I wonder if they all come out of that wall-paper as I did?

But I am securely fastened now by my well-hidden rope — you don't get *me* out in the road there!

I suppose I shall have to get back behind the pattern when it comes night, and that is hard!

It is so pleasant to be out in this great room and creep around as I please! 250

I don't want to go outside. I won't, even if Jennie asks me to.

For outside you have to creep on the ground, and everything is green instead of yellow.

But here I can creep smoothly on the floor, and my shoulder just fits in that long smooch around the wall, so I cannot lose my way.

Why there's John at the door!

It is no use, young man, you can't open it! 255

How he does call and pound!

Now he's crying for an axe.

It would be a shame to break down that beautiful door!

"John dear!" said I in the gentlest voice, "the key is down by the front steps, under a plaintain leaf!"

That silenced him for a few moments. 260

Then he said — very quietly indeed, "Open the door, my darling!"

"I can't," said I. "The key is down by the front door under a plantain leaf!"

And then I said it again, several times, very gently and slowly, and said it so often that he had to go and see, and he got it of course, and came in. He stopped short by the door.

"What is the matter?" he cried. "For God's sake, what are you doing!"

I kept on creeping just the same, but I looked at him over my shoulder. 265

"I've got out at last," said I, "in spite of you and Jane. And I've pulled off most of the paper, so you can't put me back!"

Now why should that man have fainted? But he did, and right across my path by the wall, so that I had to creep over him every time!

## Considerations for Critical Thinking and Writing

1. FIRST RESPONSE. How would you describe the narrator based on her voice? Do the paragraphs — which are often notably short — contribute to your impression?

2. The narrator describes the house she inhabits as "the most beautiful place!" Are there elements of the description that initially cause you to question its beauty or do we take her words at face value at that point in the story?

3. Look again at the initial description of the yellow wallpaper (pars. 33–37). How does the description take on new significance after you have completed the story?

4. Aside from the wallpaper, what details does the narrator share about her room that help us to picture it, and what do these details collectively tell us?

5. How is John's character developed through his words and/or through summaries of his words? Would your impression be different, do you imagine, if you encountered him directly rather than through the narrator's writing?

6. The narrator's descriptions of the wallpaper become increasingly fanciful as the story continues. She is clearly equipped to describe it in terms of the principles of design (frieze, arabesque, etc.), but are you ever really able to visualize it? If so, which details are the most vivid?

7. Whether or not the yellow wallpaper is visible to you, what feelings do the narrator's descriptions of it evoke?

8. How does John attempt to assert and reinforce his control over the narrator? What words or phrases would you use to describe their relationship?

9. Discuss attitudes toward the imagination in "The Yellow Wallpaper." Is imagination dangerous or liberating? Regardless of your answer, what factors make it so?

10. Jennie is a less central figure in the story than either the narrator or John, but she is mentioned frequently. What makes Jennie important to the story overall?

11. The wallpaper is personified repeatedly. Could it be considered a character in the story or are its human characteristics just the narrator's projections?

12. CRITICAL STRATEGIES. Read the section on feminist criticism in Chapter 42, "Critical Strategies for Reading." How might a feminist critic interpret the gender dynamics in "The Yellow Wallpaper"?

## CONNECTIONS TO OTHER SELECTIONS

1. Compare the way the narrator of "Sonny's Blues" (p. 91) attempts to control his brother to the way John attempts to control the narrator in this story. Are the narrator of "Sonny's Blues" and John similarly motivated? Are their methods of control similar in significant ways?

2. The narrator of ZZ Packer's "Drinking Coffee Elsewhere" (p. 292) and the narrator of this story are both skeptical of the "treatments" they are subjected to. Describe their resistance to these treatments, and discuss the way their resistance helps shape their characterization.

# 5

# Point of View

Joanne Rathe/Boston Globe/
Getty Images.

... though words are spoken things,
to write and read we must see.
— JOHN UPDIKE

Because one of the pleasures of reading fiction consists of seeing the world through someone else's eyes, it is easy to overlook the eyes that control our view of the plot, characters, and setting. ***Point of view*** refers to who tells us the story and how it is told. What we know and how we feel about the events in a story are shaped by the author's choice of a point of view. The teller of a story, the ***narrator***, inevitably affects our understanding of the characters' actions by filtering what is told through their own perspective. The narrator should not be confused with the author who has created the narrative voice because the two are usually distinct (more on this point later).

If the narrative voice is changed, the story will change. Consider, for example, how different "The Yellow Wallpaper" (p. 126) would be if Gilman had chosen to tell the story from John's point of view. Your opinion of his wife would undoubtedly change. You would see her, to some degree, as John sees her: as a mentally ill woman who will only get better if she sticks to the "rest cure" he has prescribed. Your sympathy for her wretched situation would likely be diminished, and you would probably see John more as a frustrated, dutiful husband than as a condescending oppressor.

The possible ways of telling a story are many, and the point of view can shift within a single story (as you will see in Manuel Muñoz's "Zigzagger" later in this chapter). However, the various points of view that storytellers draw on can be conveniently grouped into two broad categories: (1) the third-person narrator and (2) the first-person narrator. The third-person narrator uses *he, she,* or *they* to tell the story and does not participate in the action. The first-person narrator uses *I* and is a major or minor participant in the action. A second-person narrator, *you,* is possible but is seldom used because of the unnatural way the reader is thrust into the story, as in "You are minding your own business on a park bench when a drunk steps out of the bushes and demands your lunch bag." Lorrie Moore's "How to Become a Writer" (p. 161) is a good example of how a writer can use the second-person point of view to great advantage, but the other two modes are much more common. A first-person narrator will sometimes "break the fourth wall" and address the reader directly, but that's not the same as a second-person narrator in which "you" becomes a character in the story. A famous example of a first-person narrator directly addressing a reader comes from Charlotte Brontë's *Jane Eyre* (1847) when Jane states, simply, "Reader, I married him." In "The Ones Who Walk Away from Omelas" (p. 121), Le Guin's narrator also addresses the reader directly, asking if we find her description of Omelas plausible. To reiterate: these examples of addressing the reader are not the same thing as a second-person narrative: in the second person, "you" is a character, not just a reader.

The distinction between first-, second-, and third-person points of view is just the beginning of the range of possibilities that authors explore when framing a story from a certain perspective. Let's look now at the most important and most often used variations within first- and third-person narrations.

## THIRD-PERSON NARRATOR (Nonparticipant)

1. Omniscient (the narrator takes us inside multiple characters' minds)
2. Limited omniscient (the narrator takes us inside one or two characters' minds)
3. Objective (the narrator is outside the consciousness of all the characters)

No type of third-person narrator appears as a character in a story. The **omniscient narrator** is all-knowing. From this point of view, the narrator can move from place to place and pass back and forth through time, slipping into and out of characters' consciousnesses as no human being possibly could in real life. This narrator can report the characters' thoughts and feelings as well as what they say and do. In Nathaniel Hawthorne's "The Minister's Black Veil" (p. 209), the narrator can move deftly into the minds of the minister (Mr. Hooper), his wife, and all the members of his church. When Hooper dies, the narrator proclaims, "[A]wful is still the thought that [his face] moldered beneath the Black Veil!" This kind of intrusion is called **editorial omniscience**.

In contrast, narration that allows characters' actions and thoughts to speak for themselves is known as **neutral omniscience.** Most modern writers use neutral omniscience so that readers can reach their own conclusions.

The **limited omniscient narrator** is much more restricted than the omniscient narrator. With limited omniscience the author very often limits the narrator to the single perspective of either a major or a minor character. Sometimes a narrator can see into more than one character, particularly in a longer work that focuses, for example, on two characters alternately from one chapter to the next. Short stories, however, frequently limit themselves to a single character's point of view. The way people, places, and events appear to that character is the way they appear to the reader. The reader has access to the thoughts and feelings of the characters revealed by the narrator, but neither the reader nor the character has access to the inner lives of any of the other characters in the story. The events in Ann Beattie's "Janus" (p. 27) arc viewed entirely through the protagonist's eyes; we see her days at work, her interactions with her husband, and especially her unusual attachment to a decorative bowl through her consciousness. She unifies the story by being present through all the action. We are not told of anything that happens away from the character because the narration is based on her perception of things.

In Hemingway's "Soldier's Home" (p. 115) a limited omniscient narrator is the predominant point of view. Krebs's thoughts and reaction to being home from the war are made available to the reader by the narrator, who tells us that Krebs "felt embarrassed and resentful" or "sick and vaguely nauseated" by the small-town life he has reentered. (Phrases like "He thought," "She felt," "She remembered," and so forth should clue you in to the fact that this narrative is filtered through a character's consciousness.) Occasionally, Hemingway uses an objective point of view when he dramatizes particularly tense moments between Krebs and his mother. In this excerpt, Hemingway's narrator shows us Krebs's feelings instead of telling us what they are. Krebs's response to his mother's concerns is presented without comment. The external details of the scene reveal his inner feelings.

> "I've worried about you so much, Harold," his mother went on. "I know the temptations you must have been exposed to. I know how weak men are. I know what your own dear grandfather, my own father, told us about the Civil War and I have prayed for you. I pray for you all day long, Harold."
>
> Krebs looked at the bacon fat hardening on his plate.
>
> "Your father is worried, too," his mother went on. "He thinks you have lost your ambition, that you haven't got a definite aim in life. Charley Simmons, who is just your age, has a good job and is going to be married. The boys are all settling down; they're all determined to get somewhere; you can see that boys like Charley Simmons are on their way to being really a credit to the community."
>
> Krebs said nothing.
>
> "Don't look that way, Harold. . . ."

When Krebs looks at the bacon fat, we can see him cooling and hardening too. Hemingway does not describe the expression on Krebs's face, yet we know it is a look that disturbs his mother as she goes on about what she thinks she knows. Krebs and his mother are clearly tense and upset; the details, action, and dialogue reveal that tension without the narrator telling the reader how each character feels.

The most intense use of a central consciousness in narration can be seen in the stream-of-consciousness technique developed by modern writers such as James Joyce, Virginia Woolf, and William Faulkner. This technique takes a reader inside a character's mind to reveal perceptions, thoughts, and feelings that are not fully formed and that record impressions more than organized ideas. A stream of consciousness suggests the flow of thought as well as its content; hence complete sentences may give way to fragments as the character's mind makes rapid associations free of conventional logic or transitions.

The following passage is from Joyce's *Ulysses* (1922), a novel famous for its extended use of this technique. In this paragraph Joyce takes us inside the mind of a character who is describing a funeral:

> Coffin now. Got here before us, dead as he is. Horse looking round at it with his plume skeowways [askew]. Dull eye: collar tight on his neck, pressing on a blood-vessel or something. Do they know what they cart out of here every day? Must be twenty or thirty funerals every day. Then Mount Jerome for the protestants. Funerals all over the world everywhere every minute. Shovelling them under by the cartload doublequick. Thousands every hour. Too many in the world.

The character's thoughts range from specific observations to speculations about death. Joyce creates the illusion that we are reading the character's thoughts as they occur. The stream-of-consciousness technique provides an intimate perspective on a character's thoughts.

In contrast, the **objective point of view** employs a narrator who does not see into the mind of any character. From this detached and impersonal perspective, the narrator reports action and dialogue without telling us directly what the character feels and thinks. We observe the characters in much the same way we would perceive events in a film or play: we supply the meanings; no analysis or interpretation is provided by the narrator. This point of view places a heavy premium on dialogue, actions, and details to reveal character. Shirley Jackson's "The Lottery" (p. 233) is a good example of this type of narration. Note how the narrator of that story is factual, like a reporter. Instead of telling us "Mrs. Delacroix felt dread as she anticipated what would happen next," the objective narrator says, "She held her breath while her husband went forward." We feel more removed from the characters in this story than we might in another story in which we are permitted to enter their minds.

## FIRST-PERSON NARRATOR (Participant)

1. Major character
2. Minor character

With a first-person narrator, the *I* presents the point of view of only one character's consciousness. The reader is restricted to the perceptions, thoughts, and feelings of that single character. This is Baldwin's technique with the narrator of "Sonny's Blues" (p. 91). Everything learned about the characters, action, and plot comes from the unnamed teacher. He knows Sonny well — he is his brother, after all — but the story is largely about the limits of his knowledge. He first reads about Sonny's arrest in the newspaper, a fact that indicates right away that they do not communicate well. There are huge swaths of Sonny's life that are unavailable to the narrator, as the two men lead separate lives. The story reveals how our understanding of another person is always limited, yet communication — sometimes through nonverbal means such as music — is essential to our humanity.

The narrator of "Sonny's Blues" is a major character; indeed, many readers may consider him the ***protagonist***, or the character most poised to change. A first-person narrator can, however, also be a minor character (imagine how different the story would be if it were told by, say, the bandleader named Creole or by an observer who had little or nothing to do with the action). Faulkner uses an observer in "A Rose for Emily" (p. 47). His *we*, though plural and representative of the town's view of Emily, is nonetheless a first-person narrator.

One of the primary reasons for identifying the point of view in a story is to determine where the author stands in relation to the story. Behind the narrative voice of any story is the author, manipulating events and providing or withholding information. It is a mistake to assume that the narrative voice of a story is the author. The narrator, whether a first-person participant or a third-person nonparticipant, is a creation of the writer. To return to "Sonny's Blues," James Baldwin was the oldest brother in his family, but the similarities between him and the narrator end there: he was not a math teacher, was never married, did not have a child who died of polio, and loved jazz music: these biographical facts distance the author from his fictional narrator. A narrator's perceptions may be accepted, rejected, or modified by an author, depending on how the narrative voice is articulated, but we should be wary, always, of equating them.

The narrator of Charlotte Perkins Gilman's "The Yellow Wallpaper" (p. 126) is an ***unreliable narrator***, whose interpretation of events is dependent on a subjective perspective that perhaps does not coincide with objective reality. As her mental illness intensifies over the course of the story, we become more skeptical of her version of events. At the story's beginning we are likely to accept her assessment of the wallpaper as ugly, but later we are not likely to go along with her account of a woman crawling around behind it. She interprets bars on the window, a bed nailed to the floor, metal rings on the wall, and scratch marks all around the room as evidence that children had played there with excitement and vigor, but we begin to understand that the room had been more prison than playroom, and it still is.

Narrators can be unreliable for a variety of reasons: they might lack self-knowledge, like Sonny's brother, or they might be innocent and inexperienced, like John Updike's narrator in "A & P" (p. 145). Youthful innocence frequently characterizes a ***naive narrator*** such as Mark Twain's Huck Finn or Holden Caulfield, J. D. Salinger's twentieth-century version of Huck in *The Catcher in the Rye* (1951). These narrators lack the sophistication to interpret accurately what they see; they are unreliable because the reader must go beyond their understanding of events to comprehend the situations described. Huck and Holden describe their respective social environments, but the reader, with more experience, supplies the critical perspective that each boy lacks. In "A & P" the narrator is actually in the process of maturing during the course of the story, leading him to question the consequences of his actions by the end of the story rather than to view them as pure heroism.

Few generalizations can be made about the advantages or disadvantages of using a specific point of view. What can be said with confidence, however, is that writers choose a point of view to achieve particular effects because point of view determines what we know about the characters and events in a story. We should, therefore, be aware of who is telling the story and whether the narrator sees things clearly and reliably.

The next four works warrant a careful examination of their points of view. In John Updike's "A & P," the youthful narrator makes a crucial decision that will change his sensibilities. In Jamaica Kincaid's "Girl" the protagonist's mother attempts to fully control her daughter by defining her world and overwhelming her with commands. In Manuel Muñoz's "Zigzagger," a boy falls ill after a sexual encounter at a local dance. And in Lorrie Moore's "How to Become a Writer" the career aspirations of a second-person character ("you") is told using the familiar conventions of self-help books that tell the reader how to succeed.

## JOHN UPDIKE  (1932–2009)

John Updike grew up in the small town of Shillington, Pennsylvania, and on a family farm nearby. Academic success in school earned him a scholarship to Harvard, where he studied English and graduated in 1954. He soon sold his first story and poem to the *New Yorker,* to which he contributed regularly through his career. Updike's second novel, *Rabbit, Run* (1960), about a discontented young father who struggles to find meaning after peaking in high school, solidified his reputation as one of the most important American writers of his time. It

Joanne Rathe/Boston Globe/Getty Images.

was to be the first of a series of novels he published at roughly ten-year intervals which together constitute a chronicle of American history in the latter twentieth century. The prolific Updike — he published more than sixty books — lived in Massachusetts the rest of his life and continued to publish essays, poems, a novel, or a book of stories nearly every year, including *The Centaur* (1963), winner of the National Book Award; *Rabbit Is Rich* (1981) and *Rabbit at Rest* (1990), both Pulitzer Prize winners; and *The Witches of Eastwick* (1984), which was made into a major motion picture (Warner Bros., 1987). He was also a prolific book reviewer, and his astonishing number of essay collections reveal only a fraction of what he managed to read when he was not writing. Updike's fiction is noted for its exemplary use of storytelling conventions, its unique prose style, and its engaging picture of middle-class American life, although he also ranged considerably into other landscapes (like Brazil, eastern Europe, and sub-Saharan Africa) and other time periods (as in the time-traveling novel *Toward the End of Time* [1997] and *Gertrude and Claudius* [2000], a rewritten version of Shakespeare's *Hamlet*).

## *A & P*    1961

In walks these three girls in nothing but bathing suits. I'm in the third checkout slot, with my back to the door, so I don't see them until they're over by the bread. The one that caught my eye first was the one in the plaid green two-piece. She was a chunky kid, with a good tan and a sweet broad soft-looking can with those two crescents of white just under it, where the sun never seems to hit, at the top of the backs of her legs. I stood there with my hand on a box of HiHo crackers trying to remember if I rang it up or not. I ring it up again and the customer starts giving me hell. She's one of these cash-register-watchers, a witch about fifty with rouge on her cheekbones and no eyebrows, and I know it made her day to trip me up. She'd been watching cash registers for fifty years and probably never seen a mistake before.

By the time I got her feathers smoothed and her goodies into a bag — she gives me a little snort in passing, if she'd been born at the right time they would have burned her over in Salem — by the time I get her on her way the girls had circled around the bread and were coming back, without a pushcart, back my way along the counters, in the aisle between the checkouts and the Special bins. They didn't even have shoes on. There was this chunky one, with the two-piece — it was bright green and the seams on the bra were still sharp and her belly was still pretty pale so I guessed she just got it (the suit) — there was this one, with one of those chubby berry-faces, the lips all bunched together under her nose, this one, and a tall one, with black hair that hadn't quite frizzed right, and one of these sunburns right across under the eyes, and a chin that was too long — you know, the kind of girl other girls think is very "striking" and "attractive" but never quite makes it, as they very well know, which is why they like her so much — and then the third one, that wasn't quite so tall. She was the queen. She kind of led them, the other two peeking around and making their shoulders round. She didn't look around, not this queen, she just walked straight on slowly, on these long white prima-donna legs. She came down a little hard on her heels, as if she didn't walk in her bare feet that much, putting down her heels and then letting the weight move along to her toes as if she was testing the floor with every step, putting a little deliberate extra action into it. You never know for sure how girls' minds work (do you really think it's a mind in there or just a little buzz like a bee in a glass jar?) but you got the idea she had talked the other two into coming in here with her, and now she was showing them how to do it, walk slow and hold yourself straight.

She had on a kind of dirty-pink — beige maybe, I don't know — bathing suit with a little nubble all over it and, what got me, the straps were down. They were off her shoulders looped loose around the cool tops of her arms, and I guess as a result the suit had slipped a little on her, so all around the top of the cloth there was this shining rim. If it hadn't been there you wouldn't have known there could have been anything whiter than those shoulders. With the straps pushed off, there was nothing between the top of the suit and the top of her head except just *her*, this clean bare plane of the top of her chest down from the shoulder bones like a dented sheet of metal tilted in the light. I mean, it was more than pretty.

She had sort of oaky hair that the sun and salt had bleached, done up in a bun that was unraveling, and a kind of prim face. Walking into the A & P with your straps down, I suppose it's the only kind of face you *can* have. She held her head so high her neck, coming up out of those white shoulders, looked kind of stretched, but I didn't mind. The longer her neck was, the more of her there was.

She must have felt in the corner of her eye me and over my shoulder Stokesie 5 in the second slot watching, but she didn't tip. Not this queen. She kept her eyes moving across the racks, and stopped, and turned so slow it made my stomach rub the inside of my apron, and buzzed to the other two, who kind of huddled against her for relief, and then they all three of them went up the cat-and-dogfood-breakfast-cereal-macaroni-rice-raisins-seasonings-spreads-spaghetti-soft-drinks-crackers-and-cookies aisle. From the third slot I look straight up this aisle to the meat counter, and I watched them all the way. The fat one with the tan sort of fumbled with the cookies, but on second thought she put the package back. The sheep pushing their carts down the aisle — the girls were walking against the usual traffic (not that we have one-way signs or anything) — were pretty hilarious. You could see them, when Queenie's white shoulders dawned on them, kind of jerk, or hop, or hiccup, but their eyes snapped back to their own baskets and on they pushed. I bet you could set off dynamite in an A & P and the people would by and large keep reaching and checking oatmeal off their lists and muttering "Let me see, there was a third thing, began with A, asparagus, no, ah, yes, applesauce!" or whatever it is they do mutter. But there was no doubt, this jiggled them. A few houseslaves in pin curlers even looked around after pushing their carts past to make sure what they had seen was correct.

You know, it's one thing to have a girl in a bathing suit down on the beach, where what with the glare nobody can look at each other much anyway, and another thing in the cool of the A & P, under the fluorescent lights, against all those stacked packages, with her feet paddling along naked over our checker-board green-and-cream rubber-tile floor.

"Oh Daddy," Stokesie said beside me. "I feel so faint."

"Darling," I said. "Hold me tight." Stokesie's married, with two babies chalked up on his fuselage already, but as far as I can tell that's the only difference. He's twenty-two, and I was nineteen this April.

"Is it done?" he asks, the responsible married man finding his voice. I forgot to say he thinks he's going to be manager some sunny day, maybe in 1990 when it's called the Great Alexandrov and Petrooshki Tea Company or something.

What he meant was, our town is five miles from a beach, with a big summer 10
colony out on the Point, but we're right in the middle of town, and the women
generally put on a shirt or shorts or something before they get out of the car into
the street. And anyway these are usually women with six children and varicose
veins mapping their legs and nobody, including them, could care less. As I say,
we're right in the middle of town, and if you stand at our front doors you can see
two banks and the Congregational church and the newspaper store and three
real-estate offices and about twenty-seven old freeloaders tearing up Central Street
because the sewer broke again. It's not as if we're on the Cape, we're north of Boston and there's people in this town haven't seen the ocean for twenty years.

The girls had reached the meat counter and were asking McMahon something. He pointed, they pointed, and they shuffled out of sight behind a pyramid of
Diet Delight peaches. All that was left for us to see was old McMahon patting his
mouth and looking after them sizing up their joints. Poor kids, I began to feel sorry
for them, they couldn't help it.

Now here comes the sad part of the story, at least my family says it's sad, but
I don't think it's so sad myself. The store's pretty empty, it being Thursday afternoon, so there was nothing much to do except lean on the register and wait for
the girls to show up again. The whole store was like a pinball machine and I didn't
know which tunnel they'd come out of. After a while they come around out of the
far aisle, around the light bulbs, records at discount of the Caribbean Six or Tony
Martin Sings or some such gunk you wonder they waste the wax on, sixpacks of
candy bars, and plastic toys done up in cellophane that fall apart when a kid looks
at them anyway. Around they come, Queenie still leading the way, and holding a
little gray jar in her hands. Slots Three through Seven are unmanned and I could
see her wondering between Stokes and me, but Stokesie with his usual luck draws
an old party in baggy gray pants who stumbles up with four giant cans of pineapple
juice (what do these bums *do* with all that pineapple juice? I've often asked myself).
So the girls come to me. Queenie puts down the jar and I take it into my fingers icy
cold. Kingfish Fancy Herring Snacks in Pure Sour Cream: 49¢. Now her hands are
empty, not a ring or a bracelet, bare as God made them, and I wonder where the
money's coming from. Still with that prim look she lifts a folded dollar bill out of
the hollow at the center of her nubbled pink top. The jar went heavy in my hand.
Really, I thought that was so cute.

Then everybody's luck begins to run out. Lengel comes in from haggling with
a truck full of cabbages on the lot and is about to scuttle into that door marked
MANAGER behind which he hides all day when the girls touch his eye. Lengel's
pretty dreary, teaches Sunday school and the rest, but he doesn't miss that much.
He comes over and says, "Girls, this isn't the beach."

Queenie blushes, though maybe it's just a brush of sunburn I was noticing for
the first time, now that she was so close. "My mother asked me to pick up a jar of
herring snacks." Her voice kind of startled me, the way voices do when you see the
people first, coming out so flat and dumb yet kind of tony, too, the way it ticked
over "pick up" and "snacks." All of a sudden I slid right down her voice into the living room. Her father and the other men were standing around in ice-cream coats
and bow ties and the women were in sandals picking up herring snacks on tooth-
picks off a big glass plate and they were all holding drinks the color of water with
olives and sprigs of mint in them. When my parents have somebody over they get
lemonade and if it's a real racy affair Schlitz in tall glasses with "They'll Do It Every
Time" cartoons stenciled on.

"That's all right," Lengel said. "But this isn't the beach." His repeating this 15
struck me as funny, as if it had just occurred to him, and he had been thinking all
these years the A & P was a great big dune and he was the head lifeguard. He didn't
like my smiling — as I say he doesn't miss much — but he concentrates on giving
the girls that sad Sunday-school-superintendent stare.

Queenie's blush is no sunburn now, and the plump one in plaid, that I liked
better from the back — a really sweet can — pipes up, "We weren't doing any shopping. We just came in for the one thing."

"That makes no difference," Lengel tells her, and I could see from the way his
eyes went that he hadn't noticed she was wearing a two-piece before. "We want you
decently dressed when you come in here."

"We *are* decent," Queenie says suddenly, her lower lip pushing, getting sore
now that she remembers her place, a place from which the crowd that runs
the A & P must look pretty crummy. Fancy Herring Snacks flashed in her very
blue eyes.

"Girls, I don't want to argue with you. After this come in here with your shoulders covered. It's our policy." He turns his back. That's policy for you. Policy is what
the kingpins want. What the others want is juvenile delinquency.

All this while, the customers had been showing up with their carts but, you 20
know, sheep, seeing a scene, they had all bunched up on Stokesie, who shook open
a paper bag as gently as peeling a peach, not wanting to miss a word. I could feel in
the silence everybody getting nervous, most of all Lengel, who asks me, "Sammy,
have you rung up their purchase?"

I thought and said "No" but it wasn't about that I was thinking. I go through
the punches, 4, 9, GROC. TOT — it's more complicated than you think, and
after you do it often enough, it begins to make a little song, that you hear words
to, in my case "Hello *(bing)* there, you *(gung)* hap-py *pee*-pul *(splat)!*" — the
*splat* being the drawer flying out. I uncrease the bill, tenderly as you may imagine, it just having come from between the two smoothest scoops of vanilla I had
ever known were there, and pass a half and a penny into her narrow pink palm,
and nestle the herrings in a bag and twist its neck and hand it over, all the time
thinking.

The girls, and who'd blame them, are in a hurry to get out, so I say "I quit"
to Lengel quick enough for them to hear, hoping they'll stop and watch me, their
unsuspected hero. They keep right on going, into the electric eye; the door flies
open and they flicker across the lot to their car, Queenie and Plaid and Big Tall
Goony-Goony (not that as raw material she was so bad), leaving me with Lengel
and a kink in his eyebrow.

"Did you say something, Sammy?"

"I said I quit."

"I thought you did." 25

"You didn't have to embarrass them."

"It was they who were embarrassing us."

I started to say something that came out "Fiddle-de-doo." It's a saying of my
grandmother's, and I know she would have been pleased.

"I don't think you know what you're saying," Lengel said.

"I know you don't," I said. "But I do." I pull the bow at the back of my apron 30
and start shrugging it off my shoulders. A couple customers that had been heading
for my slot begin to knock against each other, like scared pigs in a chute.

Lengel sighs and begins to look very patient and old and gray. He's been a friend of my parents for years. "Sammy, you don't want to do this to your Mom and Dad," he tells me. It's true, I don't. But it seems to me that once you begin a gesture it's fatal not to go through with it. I fold the apron, "Sammy" stitched in red on the pocket, and put it on the counter, and drop the bow tie on top of it. The bow tie is theirs, if you've ever wondered. "You'll feel this for the rest of your life," Lengel says, and I know that's true, too, but remembering how he made the pretty girl blush makes me so scrunchy inside I punch the No Sale tab and the machine whirs "pee-pul" and the drawer splats out. One advantage to this scene taking place in summer, I can follow this up with a clean exit, there's no fumbling around getting your coat and galoshes, I just saunter into the electric eye in my white shirt that my mother ironed the night before, and the door heaves itself open, and outside the sunshine is skating around on the asphalt.

I look around for my girls, but they're gone, of course. There wasn't anybody but some young married screaming with her children about some candy they didn't get by the door of a powder-blue Falcon station wagon. Looking back in the big windows, over the bags of peat moss and aluminum lawn furniture stacked on the pavement, I could see Lengel in my place in the slot, checking the sheep through. His face was dark gray and his back stiff, as if he'd just had an injection of iron, and my stomach kind of fell as I felt how hard the world was going to be to me hereafter.

### CONSIDERATIONS FOR CRITICAL THINKING AND WRITING

1. FIRST RESPONSE. Describe the setting. How accurate do you think Updike's treatment of the A & P is?

2. What kind of person is Sammy? How do his actions and speech constitute his own individual style?

3. Analyze the style of the first paragraph. How does it set the tone for the rest of the story?

4. What is the story's central conflict? Does it seem to be a serious or trivial conflict to you?

5. With what kind of values is Lengel associated? Do you feel any sympathy for him?

6. What is Stokesie's function in the story?

7. Consider Sammy's treatment of the three girls. Is his account of them is sexist? Explain why or why not.

8. Locate the climax of the story. How does the climax affect your attitude toward Sammy?

9. How would the story be different if it were told from another character's point of view instead of Sammy's?

10. Discuss the thematic significance of the story's final paragraph. Would you read the story differently if this last paragraph were eliminated?

### CONNECTION TO ANOTHER SELECTION

1. Compare the reliability of the narrator in this story and in another famous work, Edgar Allen Poe's "The Cask of Amontillado" (p. 499).

# JAMAICA KINCAID (B. 1949)

Jamaica Kincaid was born Elaine Potter Richardson on the Caribbean island of Antigua. She moved to New York in 1965 to work as an au pair, studied photography at both the New School for Social Research and Franconia College, and changed her name to Jamaica Kincaid in 1973 with her first publication, "When I Was 17," a series of interviews. Over the next few years, she wrote for the *New Yorker* magazine, first as a freelancer and then as a staff writer. In 1978, Kincaid wrote her first piece of fiction, "Girl," published in the *New Yorker* and included in her debut short story collection, *At the Bottom of the River* (1983), which won an award from the Academy and

Photo © Effigie / Bridgeman Images.

Institute of Arts and Letters and was nominated for the PEN/Faulkner Award. Her other work includes *Annie John* (1985), *Lucy* (1990), *Autobiography of My Mother* (1994), *Mr. Potter* (2002), *See Now Then* (2013), and three nonfiction books, *A Small Place* (1988), *My Brother* (1997), and *Among Flowers: A Walk in the Himalaya* (2005). Whether autobiographical fiction or nonfiction, her work usually focuses on the perils of postcolonial society, paralleled by an examination of rifts in mother-daughter relationships.

## *Girl* 1978

Wash the white clothes on Monday and put them on the stone heap; wash the color clothes on Tuesday and put them on the clothesline to dry; don't walk bare-head in the hot sun; cook pumpkin fritters in very hot sweet oil; soak your little cloths right after you take them off; when buying cotton to make yourself a nice blouse, be sure that it doesn't have gum on it, because that way it won't hold up well after a wash; soak salt fish overnight before you cook it; is it true that you sing benna° in Sunday school?; always eat your food in such a way that it won't turn someone else's stomach; on Sundays try to walk like a lady and not like the slut you are so bent on becoming; don't sing benna in Sunday school; you mustn't speak to wharf-rat boys, not even to give directions; don't eat fruits on the street — flies will follow you; *but I don't sing benna on Sundays at all and never in Sunday school*; this is how to sew on a button; this is how to make a buttonhole for the button you have just sewed on; this is how to hem a dress when you see the hem coming down and so to prevent yourself from looking like the slut I know you are so bent on becoming; this is how you iron your father's khaki shirt so that it doesn't have a crease; this is how you iron your father's khaki pants so that they don't have a crease; this is how you grow okra — far from the house, because okra

*benna:* Calypso music.

tree harbors red ants; when you are growing dasheen,° make sure it gets plenty of water or else it makes your throat itch when you are eating it; this is how you sweep a corner; this is how you sweep a whole house; this is how you sweep a yard; this is how you smile to someone you don't like too much; this is how you smile to someone you don't like at all; this is how you smile to someone you like completely; this is how you set a table for tea; this is how you set a table for dinner; this is how you set a table for dinner with an important guest; this is how you set a table for lunch; this is how you set a table for breakfast; this is how to behave in the presence of men who don't know you very well, and this way they won't recognize immediately the slut I have warned you against becoming; be sure to wash every day, even if it is with your own spit; don't squat down to play marbles — you are not a boy, you know; don't pick people's flowers — you might catch something; don't throw stones at blackbirds, because it might not be a blackbird at all; this is how to make a bread pudding; this is how to make doukona;° this is how to make pepper pot;° this is how to make a good medicine for a cold; this is how to make a good medicine to throw away a child before it even becomes a child; this is how to catch a fish; this is how to throw back a fish you don't like, and that way something bad won't fall on you; this is how to bully a man; this is how a man bullies you; this is how to love a man, and if this doesn't work there are other ways, and if they don't work don't feel too bad about giving up; this is how to spit up in the air if you feel like it, and this is how to move quick so that it doesn't fall on you; this is how to make ends meet; always squeeze bread to make sure it's fresh; *but what if the baker won't let me feel the bread?*; you mean to say that after all you are really going to be the kind of woman who the baker won't let near the bread?

*dasheen:* The edible rootstock of taro, a tropical plant.
*doukona:* A spicy plantain pudding.
*pepper pot:* A stew.

### Considerations for Critical Thinking and Writing

1. **FIRST RESPONSE.** Explain whether the "Girl" is the protagonist or antagonist in this story.

2. The story is entirely dialogue even though it is one continuous sentence. To what degree can we understand the characters without access to their thoughts?

3. It's hard as a reader to warm up to the mother because she is so demanding and judgmental. Is it easy, though, to sympathize with the daughter given how few lines she has?

4. How might your interpretation of the story change if it were titled "Mother" rather than "Girl"?

5. **CREATIVE RESPONSE.** Write a one-paragraph response to the mother from the daughter's perspective. If possible, try to make it one continuous sentence as is the style in Kincaid's story.

### Connections to Other Selections

1. Compare the teenager's relationship to authority in Kincaid's story and in John Updike's "A & P" (p. 145).

2. Discuss the mother-daughter relationship in "Girl" and in Julia Alvarez's poem "Dusting" (p. 890).

## MANUEL MUÑOZ (B. 1972)

Born and raised in a small farming town in central California, Manuel Muñoz was educated at Harvard and Cornell universities and now teaches at the University of Arizona. He is the author of two collections of short fiction set in the Central Valley of his upbringing and of one novel, *What You See in the Dark* (2011). This novel begins in the second person to draw the reader in, though much of it is narrated in the more conventional third person. Note the way the point of view shifts in the following story, "Zigzagger," the title story of Muñoz's first collection.

## *Zigzagger*   2003

By six in the morning, the boy's convulsions have stopped. The light is graying in the window, allowing the boy's bedroom a shadowy calm — they can see without the lamp; and the father rises to turn it out. The boy's mother moves to stop him and the father realizes that she is still afraid, so he leaves it on. The sun seems slow to rise, and the room cannot brighten as quickly as they would like — it will be cloudy today.

The father is a bold man, but even he could not touch his teenage son several hours ago, when his jerking body was at its worst. The father makes the doorways in their house look narrow and small, his shoulders threatening to brush the jambs, yet even he had trouble controlling the boy and his violent sleep. And it was the father who first noticed how the room had become strangely cold to them, and they put on sweaters in the middle of July — the boy's body glistening, his legs kicking away the blankets as he moaned. The mother had been afraid to touch him at all and, even as the sun began rising, still made no move toward the boy.

In the morning light, the boy seems to have returned to health. He is sleeping peacefully now; he has not pushed away the quilts. His face has come back to a dark brown, the swelling around the eyes gone.

"I'll check his temperature," the father tells the mother, and she does not shake her head at the suggestion. She watches her husband closely as he moves to the bed and reaches for the edge of the quilt. She holds her breath. He pulls the quilt back slowly and reveals their son's brown legs, his bare feet. He puts out his hand to touch the boy's calf but doesn't pull away his fingers once he makes contact with the skin. The father turns to the mother, his fingers moving to the boy's hands and face. "I think he's okay now."

The mother sighs and, for the first time in hours, looks away from the bed. 5 She remembers that today is Sunday and, with the encouragement of the coming morning, she rises from her chair to see for herself.

Saturdays in this town are for dancing. The churchgoers think it is a vile day, and when they drive by the fields on their way to morning services, they sometimes claim to see workers swaying their hips as they pick tomatoes or grapes. They say that nothing gets done on Saturday afternoons because the workers go home too early in order to prepare for a long night of dancing. It is not just evenings, but the stretch of day — a whole cycle of temptation — and the churchgoers feel thwarted in their pleadings to bring back the ones who have strayed. They see them in town at the dry cleaners or waxing their cars. They see them buying food that isn't necessary.

The churchgoers have war veterans among them, some of whom serve as administrators for the town's Veterans Hall. They argue with each other about the moral questions of renting out their hall for Saturday's recklessness. The war veterans tell them that theirs is a public building and that the banquet room, the ballroom, and the wing of tidy classrooms are for all sorts of uses. Sometimes the veterans toss out angry stories about Korea, and the more civil of the lot mention how they converted villagers while fighting. But others claim freedom, including their hall, and to mortify the churchgoers, they tell tales of Korean girls spreading their legs for soldiers and the relief it brought. The churchgoers end the conversation there.

By Saturday afternoon, there is always a bus from Texas or Arizona parked in back of the Veterans Hall, and sometimes workers on their way home will catch a glimpse of the musicians descending from the vehicle with accordions and sequined suits and sombreros in tow. Some days it is simply a chartered bus. But other times, it is a bus with the band's name painted along the side — CONJUNTO ALVAREZ, BENNIE JIMÉNEZ Y FUEGO — and the rumor of a more popular group coming through town will start the weekend much earlier than usual. It means people from towns on the other side of the Valley will make the trek. It means new and eager faces.

The churchgoers smart at the sight of young girls walking downtown toward the hall, their arms crossed in front of their breasts and holding themselves, as if the July evening breeze were capable of giving them a chill. For some of them, these young girls with arm-crossed breasts remind them of their own daughters who no longer live in town. They have moved away with babies to live alone in Los Angeles. All over town, the churchgoers know, young girls sneak from their homes to visit the friends their parents already dislike. There, they know, the girls put on skirts that twirl and makeup that might glisten against the dull lights of the makeshift dance floor. These girls practice walking on high heels, dance with each other in their bedrooms to get the feel in case a man asks them to do a *cumbia.*° The churchgoers remember when they were parents and listening to the closed doors and the girls too silent. Or their teenage boys, just as quiet, then leaving with their pockets full of things hidden craftily in their rooms.

And much of this starts early in the day: the general movement of the town, the activity in the streets and shops — women buying panty hose at the last minute, twisting lipsticks at the pharmacy in search of a plum color. Men carry cases of beer home to drink in their front yards. Pumpkin seeds and beef jerky. Taking showers only minutes before it is time to go.

Saturdays in this town are for dancing, have always been. This town is only slightly bigger than the ones around it, but it is the only one with a Veterans Hall, big enough to hold hundreds. By evening, those other little towns are left with bare streets, their lone gas stations shutting down for the night, a stream of cars heading away to the bigger town. They leave only the churchgoers and the old people

10

*cumbia:* A Latin American style of dance.

already in their beds. They leave parents awake, listening for the slide of a window or too many footsteps. They leave the slow blink atop the height of the water tower, a red glow that dulls and then brightens again as if it were any other day of the week.

For a moment, the mother does not know whether to go to the kitchen herself or to send her husband. She does not want to take her eyes away from her son and yet at the same time is afraid to be alone with him. She says to her husband, "*Una crema*"° but doesn't move toward getting the items she needs to make a lotion for the boy. She needs crushed mint leaves from the kitchen. She needs oil and water, rose petals from the yard.

"Do you want me to go?" her husband asks her. On the bed, the boy is sound asleep, and the sight of him in such a peaceful state almost makes her say yes. But she resists.

"No," she tells her husband. "I'll go."

She is sore from so much sitting, and the tension of having stayed awake makes movement all the worse. The rest of the house seems strangely pleasant: the living room bright because it faces east, the large clock ticking contentedly. She wishes she could tell her husband what to do, but she knows they cannot call a doctor and have him witness this. She has considered a priest, but her husband does not go to church. In the face of this indecision, the calm rooms in the rest of the house frustrate her. She wants to make noise, even from simple activity. From the kitchen, she takes a large bowl and searches her windowsill for a few sprigs of mint. She sets out a bottle of olive oil and a cup of cold water from the faucet.

In the front yard, where the roses line the skinny walkway to their door, the day is brighter than it appeared through the windows. It is overcast, but not a ceiling of low clouds, only large ones with spaces in between, and she can see how the sun will be able to shine through them. They appear to be fast-racing clouds, and, once the sun is high enough, they will plummet the town into gray before giving way to light again. Though slight, the day erases the fear in her.

She notices the skinny walkway and the open gate where their son stumbled home, the place where he vomited into the grass. She had watched from the living room window, his friends behind him at a far distance, dark forms in the street, and she had waited for them to go away as her son entered the house, cursing terribly. From her rosebushes, she notices a gathering of flies buzzing around the mess, some of it on the gray stone of their walkway. There's a streak of red in it, she can see. She quickens her pace with the rose petals when the breeze comes up and the smell of the vomit in the grass lifts, reminding her of how ill her son was only hours ago. Dropping the petals into the bowl, she hurries back into the house, trying to get away from that smell.

She is crying in the kitchen, mixing the mint and the oil and the water, and to make it froth, she adds a bit of milk and egg. The concoction doesn't seem right to her anymore, doesn't match what she recalls as a young girl, her grandmother taking down everyday bottles from the cabinets and blessing their cuts and coughs. The mother does it without any knowledge, only guessing, but it makes her feel better despite feeling lost in her inability to remember. She takes the bowl into the bathroom and dumps half a bottle of hand lotion into the bowl, and the mix turns softer and creamy.

*Una crema:* A cream.

Back in the bedroom, her husband is still at their son's bedside, but the boy has not moved. The stale odor of the room reminds her again of outside and the earlier hours and her son's vile language and her husband's frantic struggle to keep the boy in bed, wild as he was. The boy tore off his own clothes, his thin hands ripping through his shirt and even his pants, shredding them, and he stalked into his bedroom naked and growling and strong. Her husband came to tower over him, beat him for coming home this way. The fear crept into her when the boy fought back and challenged and then, only by exhaustion, collapsed on the bed. He was quiet. And then the odor came. The smell was of liquor at first, but then a heavy urine. Then of something rotting. Her husband had yelled at her to open the windows. Even now, the smell lingers in the air.

"He's still sleeping," her husband whispers. "What do you have there?"   20

"A cure my grandmother used to give us," she says, half expecting her husband to ignore her and the bowl.

"You want to put it on him?" he offers, and she knows that her husband is asking whether or not she is still afraid.

She does not answer him but moves to the bed, setting the bowl on the floor. With her fingertips, she dips into the concoction and then, resisting an impulse to hold her breath, rubs it on her son's bare legs. They are remarkably smooth, and she looks at her husband as if to have him reassure her that what she had seen last night had not been an illusion. Her son's legs are hairless and cool to the touch. There are no raised veins. They are not reddened with welts. They are not laced with deep scratches made with terrible fingers.

The boy spent the early part of Saturday evening with a group of friends, all of them drinking in the backyard at the house of a girl whose parents were visiting relatives in another town. Even before the sun had set, most of the boy's friends had already had enough to drink, and they tried to convince some of the older boys to go back out and buy beer. But by then, the girls put a stop to all of it, saying the hall wouldn't let them in if they smelled beer on them.

The boy liked being with these friends because he did not have to do much.   25 He laughed at other people when the joke was on them, and it made him feel more comfortable about himself. He smoked cigarettes and watched the orange tips get brighter and brighter as the sun went down. He looked at the girls coming in and out of the back door as they got ready for the dance. He did not drink, because he did not like the acrid taste of beer, yet he liked being here with them, knowing that every sip was what their own parents had done at their age. He did not mind seeing the others drunk — after a certain point, he knew that the drunker boys would sit next to him and talk. He would not respond except to smile, because he didn't know what else to do, what to make of their joking, their arms heavy around his shoulders.

They gathered themselves after the girls were ready and they walked to the hall, twos and threes along the sidewalk, some of them chewing big wads of hard pink gum and then spitting them into the grass. He was not as crass as the other boys, who waited to spit until they saw the dark figures of the churchgoers scowling from their porches. They divided mints between them when the hall came into view: the taillights of cars easing into the parking lot, women sitting in passenger seats waiting for their doors to be opened.

The boy got in line with the rest of them, watching as a pair of older women at the ticket table looked disapprovingly at the girls and motioned with their fingers for each of them to extend their arms. They fastened pink plastic bracelets around their wrists, ignoring the odor of alcohol. When the boy made it to them, he tried to move as close as possible, to show he was not like the rest of them, but one of the women only said, "No beer," strapping the pink bracelet tightly and taking his dollar bills.

Inside, his friends had already fractured. A flurry of kids their age milled around the edge of the dance floor while the older couples swayed gently to the band's ballad of horns and *bandeneón*.° All he saw were bodies pressed together, light coming through in the spaces cleared for the dance steps of other couples, hips and fake jewelry catching. He saw the smoke blue in the air around the hanging lights; the cigarettes, which he felt contributed to the heat; the men with unbuttoned shirt collars, their hands around the backs of laughing women.

When the song ended, with a long and mournful note on a single horn, the couples separated to applaud, and some of the women went back to their own tables. He saw that people of every situation were there — older, single women sitting at the circular tables, men his father's age with shiny belt buckles and boots. Of his own age, the boys were pestering some of the older men to buy them beer, hiding the telltale pink bands that showed their age, sneaking sips in the darker shadows of the hall's great room.

As the next song began — a wild, brash *ranchera* complete with accordion at   30
full expansion — the milling began again, people alone, people together. He put his hands in his pockets while men removed their hats and cornered women for a dance. Couples with joined hands pushed their way to the floor that had only just settled its dust. Some alone, some together. The music roared its way through the hall, and the boy reasoned that everyone felt the way he did at the moment — lost and unnoticed, standing in place as he was.

The boy's mother spreads the concoction more vigorously, her son's legs giving way where the flesh is soft, reminding her that he is not fully grown, not a man yet. She believes her rubbing will wake him, and when he doesn't respond, she looks at her husband, who does nothing but look back.

She speaks to her son. "Are you awake?" she asks him, her hands grasping his legs quickly to shake him, but he only stirs, his head moving to one side and then stopping. "Are you in pain?"

Her husband stands up to look closely at their son's face and says to her, "His eyes are open." He waves his hand slowly in front of the boy, but still he will not speak. "I don't think he sees me."

"Are you awake?" she says again, rising to see for herself. His eyes are open, just as her husband said, but they don't seem to stare back at her. She thinks for a moment that his open eyes will begin to water and she waits for him to blink, but he only closes his eyes once more.

"It's early still," the father says. "Don't worry."                                          35

The boy felt as if he had been the only person to notice the man with the plain silver buckle, a belt that shimmered against the glow of the yellow bulbs strung across the hall's high rafters. A plain silver buckle that gleamed like a cold eye, open and watching. Even from a distance, the boy knew it was plain, that it had no etchings, no tarnish, no scratches. He watched it tilt at the waist as the man put

*bandeneón*: A musical instrument.

his boot up on the leg of a stool, leaning down to one of the girls who had come with the boy, whispering to her.

He felt as if he were the only one watching how the girl flicked her hair deliberately with her left wrist, as if to show the pink bracelet in a polite gesture to move on: she was too young.

The boy pictured himself with the same kind of arrogance, the posture that cocked the man's hips, the offering he suggested to this girl, and he wondered if he would ever grow into that kind of superiority, being capable of seducing and tempting. He watched the silver buckle blink at him, as if it watched back, as if it knew where the boy was looking.

The man finally left the girl alone, but the boy watched him, circling the dance floor, sometimes losing him between songs as the hall dimmed the lighting to invite a slow dance. Or losing him when one of the other boys distracted him with a stolen beer. But he would quickly find him again, the belt buckle gleaming and catching—a circle of silver light moving through the dark tables.

The girl from before came up to the boy and said, "That man kept bugging 40 me," as if she expected the boy to do something about it. He turned to look at her—she was one of the girls who regularly went to church, didn't know how to behave at a dance, put up her hair because her girlfriends told her to. And now, with that strange man, she wanted trouble for its own sake, he thought. He could hear in her voice that she wanted the attention in some form—his defense, or that man's proposal—so no one would look at her as the girl with the straight dark hair, a Sunday girl.

So the boy moved, without looking at the girl, keeping his eye on the silver buckle and followed the man, catching up to him toward the back of the hall, where only the couples who could not wait to get home were kissing, leaning against each other, backing into the wall. The man stood next to a woman, facing her and talking among all the bodies rubbing against each other, his silver buckle the only still thing, and the boy noticed that the man wore nothing but black, down to his boots. The man's teeth gleamed as he smiled, watching the boy approach. He smiled as if he expected him and ignored the woman, who disappeared into the dark bodies.

Before the boy could say anything about the girl, the man extended his hand, offering a beer. "My apologies," he said to the boy, his voice clear and strong, and the boy noticed his face—what a handsome man he was, his skin as dark as anyone's in town—but his voice not anchored by the heaviness of accent. He was not like them, the boy knew instantly.

The mother opens all the doors in the house, though the sky doesn't look as if it will break one way or the other. She draws more curtains, all the rooms filled with the muted daylight. Even the closet doors are open, flush against the walls, and she pushes the clothes apart to allow the light in the tight spaces. She thinks of the kitchen cabinets and the drawers, the small knobs that pull out of tables and nightstands, the blankets hiding the dust motes under the beds. The husband lets her do this and then says nothing as she sits in the living room all by herself with her head in her hands.

Because the front door is wide open, she hears the footsteps on the sidewalk long before they approach the house, and she looks to the porch to see a group of her son's friends coming. They walk so close together; they seem afraid and apologetic at the same time. All of them have their heads bowed, the girls and the boys in fresh Sunday church clothes, and she knows they see the mess her son made on the front lawn.

It is odd for her to be sitting on her living room couch and seeing not the tele- 45 vision but her own front yard, and she can do nothing but watch as the boys and girls stop at the porch, almost startled that they do not have to knock.

"What do you want?" she hears her husband say, and she turns to see him in the archway to the kitchen, where he must have heard them coming. "What did you give him last night?"

Her husband's voice is filled with rage, but she can see that her son's friends have come out of concern. And she knows they will tell her that her son had not been drinking, that they will deny that he took any drugs, and she will believe them. But she knots her fingers and her hands, trying to build up a false anger, because she is too ashamed and afraid to let them know what she and her husband saw on her boy's body, the things he said in a voice that was not his, how the house seemed to swell and breathe as if it were living itself, the whole space filling out in the same terrible way that her chest wanted to burst forth.

"We didn't give him anything," one of the boys says. "He wouldn't even take one beer."

"He's sick now!" her husband yells at them. "You understand that? *¿Entienden?*"

"Let them go home," the mother says. "They don't need to know anything." 50

The boys and girls still stand on the porch, because they see she has been talking to her husband and not them, waiting for him to order them away. But the husband does not say anything, and then one of the boys speaks up and says, "I brought him home because we found him sick. Outside the hall. He was just sick. We don't know how."

No one responds, no one asks questions. Not the husband, not the mother. And just when the mother is about to rise from the couch to point her finger to the street, to show them away from the porch, they all know to look in the hall archway leading to the bedroom. There, clad only in his underwear, his skin pale and the dampness of the day swimming through the house, stands the boy.

He is aware of himself in a way that is unsettling, as if he has escaped his body once and for all and yet, exhausted as he feels, knows that his body is his own again. He is aware that the window to his bedroom is open and the day is overcast; the curtains move in a breeze that is chilly and has made the sheets underneath him cold. He shivers.

He hears the voices in the front of the house, the sound of his father's anger, the way only his father can sound, and his mother's hesitations. He hears the sounds of his friends but can't tell how many.

He feels the cold on his legs and he rises from the bed slowly, putting his feet 55 on the floor, and the act of moving — like water, like the leaves outside his bedroom window today — startles him, the ease of it. Looking at his thin legs, the hollow of his own chest, he does not feel ashamed of himself as he once did.

The boy knows what he has done, what has happened, and yet, deep inside, he believes it could not have been. He thinks back to the man in the black clothes and the silver buckle, the offered beer, and the few words they spoke. The man had asked him if he spoke Spanish and when he had said no, the man had looked almost pleased. He does not remember what else they might have spoken of, only that the hall seemed to tilt and sway, the *ranchera* amplified to ten times as loud as he has ever heard, so that the man's voice came from within him. It came from the darkness when he closed his eyes to the hall's dipping and sinking, and when he opened them, it was still dark and he felt the nip of the outside air, the summer night cool compared to the pushed-together bodies of the dance inside. The cool of the sheets beneath him this morning makes him recall that outside air, how he had felt it not against his face but the bare skin of his chest, then his belly, and the metallic touch of the silver belt buckle pressing close. The music was distant — they were away from the hall, away from the cars in the parking lot, where couples were leaving, the engines starting. He recalls now the rough edges of a tree against his back, the bark and the summer sap, the branches a canopy that hid the stars, because he looked up and saw nothing but the spaces between leaves, small stars peeking through to see him.

He had said nothing to this man, remembers how he allowed the man's hands to grab his waist, his entire arm wrapped around, lifting the boy's feet from the ground, the feeling of rising, almost levitating. He felt as if the man rose with him because he felt the hot press of the man's belly, the rough texture of hair, and now he remembers how he had let his hands run down the man's back, the knots on his spine, the fine-worked furrow, their feet on air. He kept looking up, searching for the stars between the branches.

The man, his back broad, grunted heavily. The sound frightens the boy now as he recalls it in broad daylight. The man's sound made him grow, pushing the boy up higher and higher, to where the boy could see himself in the arms of the man who glowed in the darkness of the canopy of branches, his skin a dull red, the pants and boots gone. And though he felt he was in air, he saw a flash of the man's feet entrenched fast in the ground — long, hard hooves digging into the soil, the height of horses when they charge — it was then that the boy remembers seeing and feeling at the same time — the hooves, then a piercing in the depth of his belly that made his eyes flash a whole battalion of stars, shooting and brilliant, more and more of them, until he had no choice but to scream out.

And now, at midmorning, his father and mother in the front of the house, his skin smelling of mint and roses, he knows enough to go forward and send his friends away. He wonders if he will sound different; he wonders if they will see how he carries himself now; he remembers how feeling the furrow of the man's back reminded him of the hard work of picking grapes in the summer months — his father will punish him with it. The hard work and the rattlers under the vines, their forked tongues brushing the air, and the boy remembers that the man's tongue pushed into his with the same vigor, searching him with the same kind of terrible flick.

He rises from the bed and steps, with an unfamiliar grace, to the wide-open 60 door of his bedroom and down the hall.

The mother sees him, the look in his eye, and she wants to say nothing at all. She believes, as she always has, that talking aloud brings moments to light, and she has refused to speak of her mother's death, of her husband's cheating, of the hatred of her brothers and sisters. She sees her son at the doorway and wants to tell him not to speak.

They all stand and wait for the boy to talk, the doors and windows open as wide as possible and every last secret of their home ready to make an easy break to the outside. The curtains swell with a passing breeze.

"You're awake," the father says, and walks toward the boy, and the mother hopes that he will not speak and reveal his voice. She wonders if her husband knows now, if he can tell how the side-to-side swivel of the dancers at the hall and the zigzag of their steps have invited an ancient trouble, if her husband knows the countless stories of midnight goings-on, of women with broken blood vessels streaming underneath their skin from the touch of every strange man.

She keeps wondering, even when her husband turns to the boy's friends and tells them, "See? He's fine. Now go home," and motions them away from the porch and they leave without asking her son anything at all. She wonders now if her husband has ever awakened at night, dreaming of dances where bags of church-blessed rattlesnakes have been opened in the darkness of the place, the mad slithering between feet and the screams, the rightness of that punishment, the snakes that spoke in human voices, the rushed side-to-side movement of the snakes before they coiled underneath tables to strike at ankles.

When her husband turns his back to walk to the porch, watching the boy's 65 friends walk off warily, she takes her chance and rushes to her underwear-clad son in the archway and grabs him by his arms — his flesh cold — and says, under her breath, "I know, I know," and then bravely, without waiting to hear what his voice might sound like, tries to pry open his mouth and check for herself.

## Considerations for Critical Thinking and Writing

1. FIRST RESPONSE. No one in this story is named. How does that choice affect your emotional response to the story? Would you feel differently about the story if at least the protagonist ("the boy") had a name?

2. There are two basic groups of people in town: the field workers and the churchgoers. How does this division frame the story's main conflict? What is that conflict?

3. The point of view in the story shifts not only from the mother to the son, but from the present to the preceding night. How does the author control this movement without confusing the reader?

4. The boy is fascinated by the man with the silver buckle because he can tell he is somehow different from everyone else in the dance hall. What are some of the factors that indicate the boy's own difference from his friend group?

5. In question 1 we identify the boy as the story's protagonist, but the story's shifting point of view essentially begins and ends with his mother. Is she actually the story's protagonist? If so, does the meaning of the story shift?

6. Leaving aside for a moment the boy's sexual encounter with the man at the dance, discuss the opposition between his group of friends and his family as a way of articulating his central conflict.

7. How do you interpret the story's title?

8. Discuss the passages in the story that are most abstract, or least realistic. How do these passages interact with the more straightforward or realistic passages?

9. Consider the way gender roles are reinforced in this town. What is the boy's reaction to these roles? How does he both uphold and resist them?

## Connections to Other Selections

1. Discuss the treatment of parental expectations in this story and in Jamaica Kincaid's "Girl" (p. 150). What important similarities and differences do you see?

2. Consider the relationship between home towns and individual transformations in this story and in Ernest Hemingway's "Soldier's Home" (p. 115).

## LORRIE MOORE (B. 1957)

Although she has published novels, essays, and children's literature, Lorrie Moore is especially praised for her gifts as a short story writer. Like many contemporary writers, she has also had a career as a professor of creative writing, notably at the University of Wisconsin-Madison where she taught for three decades. Educated at St. Lawrence University and Cornell University, she published her master's thesis as her debut story collection, *Self-Help*, in 1985, which plays with the conventions of popular advice books, that is, the "self-help" books that tell readers how to improve their lives. The following story is from that collection.

## *How to Become a Writer*    1985

First, try to be something, anything, else. A movie star/astronaut. A movie star/missionary. A movie star/kindergarten teacher. President of the World. Fail miserably. It is best if you fail at an early age — say, fourteen. Early, critical disillusionment is necessary so that at fifteen you can write long haiku sequences about thwarted desire. It is a pond, a cherry blossom, a wind brushing against sparrow wing leaving for mountain. Count the syllables. Show it to your mom. She is tough and practical. She has a son in Vietnam and a husband who may be having an affair. She believes in wearing brown because it hides spots. She'll look briefly at your writing, then back up at you with a face blank as a donut. She'll say: "How about emptying the dishwasher?" Look away. Shove the forks in the fork drawer. Accidentally break one of the freebie gas station glasses. This is the required pain and suffering. This is only for starters.

In your high school English class look only at Mr. Killian's face. Decide faces are important. Write a villanelle° about pores. Struggle. Write a sonnet. Count the syllables: nine, ten, eleven, thirteen. Decide to experiment with fiction. Here you don't have to count syllables. Write a short story about an elderly man and woman who accidentally shoot each other in the head, the result of an inexplicable malfunction of a shotgun which appears mysteriously in their living room one night. Give it to Mr. Killian as your final project. When you get it back, he has written on it: "Some of your images are quite nice, but you have no sense of plot." When you are home, in the privacy of your own room, faintly scrawl in pencil beneath his black-inked comments: "Plots are for dead people, pore-face."

Take all the babysitting jobs you can get. You are great with kids. They love you. You tell them stories about old people who die idiot deaths. You sing them songs like "Blue Bells of Scotland," which is their favorite. And when they are in their pajamas and have finally stopped pinching each other, when they are fast asleep, you read every sex manual in the house, and wonder how on earth anyone could ever do those things with someone they truly loved. Fall asleep in a chair reading Mr. McMurphy's *Playboy*. When the McMurphys come home, they will tap you on the shoulder, look at the magazine in your lap, and grin. You will

*villanelle:* A poetic form, like the more familiar sonnet and haiku also alluded to here. See Chapter 23.

want to die. They will ask you if Tracey took her medicine all right. Explain, yes, she did, that you promised her a story if she would take it like a big girl and that seemed to work out just fine. "Oh, marvelous," they will exclaim.

Try to smile proudly.

Apply to college as a child psychology major.                                                    5

As a child psychology major, you have some electives. You've always liked birds. Sign up for something called "The Ornithological Field Trip." It meets Tuesdays and Thursdays at two. When you arrive at Room 134 on the first day of class, everyone is sitting around a seminar table talking about metaphors. You've heard of these. After a short, excruciating while, raise your hand and say diffidently, "Excuse me, isn't this Bird-watching One-oh-one?" The class stops and turns to look at you. They seem to all have one face — giant and blank as a vandalized clock. Someone with a beard booms out, "No, this is Creative Writing." Say: "Oh — right," as if perhaps you knew all along. Look down at your schedule. Wonder how the hell you ended up here. The computer, apparently, has made an error. You start to get up to leave and then don't. The lines at the registrar this week are huge. Perhaps you should stick with this mistake. Perhaps your creative writing isn't all that bad. Perhaps it is fate. Perhaps this is what your dad meant when he said, "It's the age of computers, Francie, it's the age of computers."

Decide that you like college life. In your dorm you meet many nice people. Some are smarter than you. And some, you notice, are dumber than you. You will continue, unfortunately, to view the world in exactly these terms for the rest of your life.

The assignment this week in creative writing is to narrate a violent happening. Turn in a story about driving with your Uncle Gordon and another one about two old people who are accidentally electrocuted when they go to turn on a badly wired desk lamp. The teacher will hand them back to you with comments: "Much of your writing is smooth and energetic. You have, however, a ludicrous notion of plot." Write another story about a man and a woman who, in the very first paragraph, have their lower torsos accidentally blitzed away by dynamite. In the second paragraph, with the insurance money, they buy a frozen yogurt stand together. There are six more paragraphs. You read the whole thing out loud in class. No one likes it. They say your sense of plot is outrageous and incompetent. After class someone asks you if you are crazy.

Decide that perhaps you should stick to comedies. Start dating someone who is funny, someone who has what in high school you called a "really great sense of humor" and what now your creative writing class calls "self-contempt giving rise to comic form." Write down all of his jokes, but don't tell him you are doing this. Make up anagrams of his old girlfriend's name and name all of your socially handicapped characters with them. Tell him his old girlfriend is in all of your stories and then watch how funny he can be, see what a really great sense of humor he can have.

Your child psychology advisor tells you you are neglecting courses in your   10 major. What you spend the most time on should be what you're majoring in. Say yes, you understand.

In creative writing seminars over the next two years, everyone continues to smoke cigarettes and ask the same things: "But does it work?" "Why should we care about this character?" "Have you earned this cliché?" These seem like important questions.

On days when it is your turn, you look at the class hopefully as they scour your mimeographs° for a plot. They look back up at you, drag deeply, and then smile in a sweet sort of way.

You spend too much time slouched and demoralized. Your boyfriend suggests bicycling. Your roommate suggests a new boyfriend. You are said to be self-mutilating and losing weight, but you continue writing. The only happiness you have is writing something new, in the middle of the night, armpits damp, heart pounding, something no one has yet seen. You have only those brief, fragile, untested moments of exhilaration when you know: you are a genius. Understand what you must do. Switch majors. The kids in your nursery project will be disappointed, but you have a calling, an urge, a delusion, an unfortunate habit. You have, as your mother would say, fallen in with a bad crowd.

Why write? Where does writing come from? These are questions to ask yourself. They are like: Where does dust come from? Or: Why is there war? Or: If there's a God, then why is my brother now a cripple?

These are questions that you keep in your wallet, like calling cards. These are   15 questions, your creative writing teacher says, that are good to address in your journals but rarely in your fiction.

The writing professor this fall is stressing the Power of the Imagination. Which means he doesn't want long descriptive stories about your camping trip last July. He wants you to start in a realistic context but then to alter it. Like recombinant DNA. He wants you to let your imagination sail, to let it grow big-bellied in the wind. This is a quote from Shakespeare.

Tell your roommate your great idea, your great exercise of imaginative power: a transformation of Melville to contemporary life. It will be about monomania° and the fish-eat-fish world of life insurance in Rochester, New York. The first line will be "Call me Fishmeal," and it will feature a menopausal suburban husband named Richard, who because he is so depressed all the time is called "Mopey Dick" by his witty wife Elaine. Say to your roommate: "Mopey Dick, get it?" Your roommate looks at you, her face blank as a large Kleenex. She comes up to you, like a buddy, and puts an arm around your burdened shoulders. "Listen, Francie," she says, slow as speech therapy. "Let's go out and get a big beer."

The seminar doesn't like this one either. You suspect they are beginning to feel sorry for you. They say: "You have to think about what is happening. Where is the story here?"

The next semester the writing professor is obsessed with writing from personal experience. You must write from what you know, from what has happened

---

*mimeographs:* Photocopies.
*monomania:* Single-minded obsession.

to you. He wants deaths, he wants camping trips. Think about what has happened to you. In three years there have been three things: you lost your virginity; your parents got divorced; and your brother came home from a forest ten miles from the Cambodian border with only half a thigh, a permanent smirk nestled into one corner of his mouth.

About the first you write: "It created a new space, which hurt and cried in a   20 voice that wasn't mine, I'm not the same anymore, but I'll be okay." "

About the second you write an elaborate story of an old married couple who stumble upon an unknown land mine in their kitchen and accidentally blow themselves up. You call it: "For Better or for Liverwurst."

About the last you write nothing. There are no words for this. Your typewriter hums. You can find no words.

At undergraduate cocktail parties, people say, "Oh, you write? What do you write about?" Your roommate, who has consumed too much wine, too little cheese, and no crackers at all, blurts: "Oh, my god, she always writes about her dumb boyfriend."

Later on in life you will learn that writers are merely open, helpless texts with no real understanding of what they have written and therefore must half-believe anything and everything that is said of them. You, however, have not yet reached this stage of literary criticism. You stiffen and say, "I do not," the same way you said it when someone in the fourth grade accused you of really liking oboe lessons and your parents really weren't just making you take them.

Insist you are not very interested in any one subject at all, that you are inter-  25 ested in the music of language, that you are interested in — in — syllables, because they are the atoms of poetry, the cells of the mind, the breath of the soul. Begin to feel woozy. Stare into your plastic wine cup.

"Syllables?" you will hear someone ask, voice trailing off, as they glide slowly toward the reassuring white of the dip.

Begin to wonder what you do write about. Or if you have anything to say. Or if there even is such a thing as a thing to say. Limit these thoughts to no more than ten minutes a day; like sit-ups, they can make you thin.

You will read somewhere that all writing has to do with one's genitals. Don't dwell on this. It will make you nervous.

Your mother will come visit you. She will look at the circles under your eyes and hand you a brown book with a brown briefcase on the cover. It is entitled: *How to Become a Business Executive*. She has also brought the *Names for Baby* encyclopedia you asked for; one of your characters, the aging clown–school teacher, needs a new name. Your mother will shake her head and say: "Francie, Francie, remember when you were going to be a child psychology major?"

Say: "Mom, I like to write."                                                              30

She'll say: "Sure you like to write. Of course. Sure you like to write."

Write a story about a confused music student and title it: "Schubert Was the One with the Glasses, Right?" It's not a big hit, although your roommate likes the part where the two violinists accidentally blow themselves up in a recital room. "I went out with a violinist once," she says, snapping her gum.

Thank god you are taking other courses. You can find sanctuary in nineteenth-century ontological snags and invertebrate courting rituals. Certain globular mollusks have what is called "Sex by the Arm." The male octopus, for instance, loses the end of one arm when placing it inside the female body during intercourse. Marine biologists call it "Seven Heaven." Be glad you know these things. Be glad you are not just a writer. Apply to law school.

From here on in, many things can happen. But the main one will be this: you decide not to go to law school after all, and, instead, you spend a good, big chunk of your adult life telling people how you decided not to go to law school after all. Somehow you end up writing again. Perhaps you go to graduate school. Perhaps you work odd jobs and take writing courses at night. Perhaps you are working on a novel and writing down all the clever remarks and intimate personal confessions you hear during the day. Perhaps you are losing your pals, your acquaintances, your balance.

You have broken up with your boyfriend. You now go out with men who, 35 instead of whispering "I love you," shout: "Do it to me, baby." This is good for your writing.

Sooner or later you have a finished manuscript more or less. People look at it in a vaguely troubled sort of way and say, "I'll bet becoming a writer was always a fantasy of yours, wasn't it?" Your lips dry to salt. Say that of all the fantasies possible in the world, you can't imagine being a writer even making the top twenty. Tell them you were going to be a child psychology major. "I bet," they always sigh, "you'd be great with kids." Scowl fiercely. Tell them you're a walking blade.

Quit classes. Quit jobs. Cash in old savings bonds. Now you have time like warts on your hands. Slowly copy all of your friends' addresses into a new address book.

Vacuum. Chew cough drops. Keep a folder full of fragments.

*An eyelid darkening sideways.*

*World as conspiracy.*

*Possible plot? A woman gets on a bus.*

*Suppose you threw a love affair and nobody came.*

At home drink a lot of coffee. At Howard Johnson's order the cole slaw. Consider how it looks like the soggy confetti of a map: where you've been, where you're going — "You Are Here," says the red star on the back of the menu.

Occasionally a date with a face blank as a sheet of paper asks you whether 40 writers often become discouraged. Say that sometimes they do and sometimes they do. Say it's a lot like having polio.

"Interesting," smiles your date, and then he looks down at his arm hairs and starts to smooth them, all, always, in the same direction.

### CONSIDERATIONS FOR CRITICAL THINKING AND WRITING

1. **FIRST RESPONSE.** Have you ever received discouraging advice about a career path? If so, did this story make you wince with recognition, laugh at the degree to which the story develops this idea, or some other more complex reaction?

Alternately, do you think discouraging career advice opens up opportunities for young people or closes them off?

2. The character is a very specific person ("Francie") with specific experiences. What is the effect of turning that character into a second-person generic "you"? What are the advantages and disadvantages of this approach?

3. How does the story use humor to develop its main concerns? What lines did you find particularly funny?

4. What are a few adjectives you would use to describe the protagonist? If the story were written in first person, how might the author have communicated those same qualities? How about third person?

5. The characters surrounding the protagonist include her mother, father, roommate, boyfriend, and teachers/professors. Do they all fulfill roughly the same role in her narrative or do some seem more significant than others?

6. The story of Francie's brother who lost a leg during the Vietnam War is a particularly serious incident in a story that tends toward humor. Is there a possible connection between the pain of this story and the choice to write the story in the second person?

7. How does this story play with the familiar process of choosing a major? What does it have to say about that process?

8. The end of the story seems to give up on the advice to become a writer. How do you interpret the conclusion?

## Connections to Other Selections

1. Compare the college experience of this protagonist to Deena's experience in ZZ Packer's "Drinking Coffee Elsewhere" (p. 292). Although the circumstances and events of the two stories are different, do they have the same attitude toward higher education? If so, what is it?

2. Consider how advice is given and received in this story and in Carmen Maria Machado's "Eight Bites" (p. 218).

# 6

# Symbolism

Everett Collection/Newscom.

Symbols serve a dual function: they allow the artist to speak of complex experiences and to annihilate time.
— RALPH ELLISON

A *symbol* is a person, object, or event that suggests more than its literal meaning. This basic definition is simple enough, but the use of symbol in literature makes some students slightly nervous because they tend to regard it as a booby trap, a hidden device that can go off during a seemingly harmless class discussion. "I didn't see that when I was reading the story" is a frequently heard comment. This sort of surprise and recognition is both natural and common. Most readers go through a story for the first time getting their bearings, figuring out what is happening to whom and so on. Patterns and significant details often require a second or third reading before they become evident — before a symbol sheds light on a story. Then the details of a work may suddenly fit together, and its meaning may be reinforced, clarified, or enlarged by the symbol. Symbolic meanings are usually embedded in the texture of a story, but they are not "hidden"; instead, they are carefully placed. Reading between the lines (where there is only space) is unnecessary. What is needed is a careful consideration of the elements of the story, a sensitivity to its language, and some common sense.

Common sense is a good place to begin. Symbols appear all around us; anything can be given symbolic significance. Without symbols our lives would be stark and vacant. Awareness of a writer's use of symbols is not all that different from the kinds of perceptions and interpretations that allow us to make sense of our daily lives. We know, for example, that a ring exchanged in a wedding is more than just a piece of jewelry because it suggests the unity and intimacy of a closed circle, with no beginning or end. The bride's gown may be white because we tend to associate innocence and purity with that color. Or consider the emojis you use on a daily basis: a heart means you love something, a thumbs-up means you approve, a four-leaf clover represents good luck. The ring, the white gown, and these emojis are symbolic because each has meanings that go beyond its specific qualities and functions.

Symbols such as these that are widely recognized by a society or culture are called **conventional symbols**. The U.S. flag, for instance, has specific meanings and associations: each star represents a state, each stripe one of the thirteen original colonies, and the colors are even meaningful (red symbolizing valor, white purity, and blue perseverance and justice). Certain kinds of experiences also have traditional meanings in Western cultures. Winter, the setting sun, and the color black suggest death, while spring, the rising sun, and the color green evoke images of youth and new beginnings. (It is worth noting, however, that individual cultures sometimes have their own conventions; some Eastern cultures associate white rather than black with death and mourning.) These broadly shared symbolic meanings are second nature to us.

Writers use conventional symbols to reinforce meanings. Kate Chopin, for example, emphasizes the spring setting in "The Story of an Hour" (p. 17) as a way of suggesting the renewed sense of life that Mrs. Mallard feels when she thinks herself free from her husband.

A *literary symbol* can include traditional, conventional, or public meanings, but it may also be established internally by the total context of the work in which it appears. In "Soldier's Home" (p. 115), Hemingway does not use Krebs's family home as a conventional symbol of safety, comfort, and refuge from the war. Instead, Krebs's home becomes symbolic of small-town biases compounded by blind innocence, sentimentality, and smug middle-class respectability. The symbolic meaning of his home reveals that Krebs no longer shares his family's and town's view of the world. Their notions of love, the value of a respectable job, and belief in God seem to him petty, complicated, and meaningless. The significance of Krebs's home is determined by the events within the story, which reverse and subvert the traditional associations readers might bring to it. Krebs's interactions with his family and the people in town reveal what home has come to mean to him.

A literary symbol can be a setting, character, action, object, name, or anything else in a work that maintains its literal significance while suggesting other meanings. Symbols cannot be restricted to a single meaning; they are suggestive rather than definitive. Their evocation of multiple meanings allows a writer to say more with less. Symbols are economical devices for evoking complex ideas without having to resort to painstaking explanations that would make a story more like an essay than an experience. In Gilman's "The Yellow Wallpaper" (p. 126), the symbol is named in the title, and it suggests multiple meanings that unify the story. Wallpaper covers up a wall, hiding its imperfections with a decorative surface. This story is about revealing the truth, though, so the narrator finds the wallpaper not pleasing, but menacing. Like the rest cure her husband enforces, the wallpaper suffocates her. She not only rejects its hideous color and chaotic patterns, but she sees it as a living thing that oppresses a woman hiding behind it. Her action of tearing it off the wall represents much more than just a desire to redecorate.

When a character, object, or incident indicates a single, fixed meaning, the writer is using ***allegory*** rather than symbol. Whereas symbols have literal functions as well as multiple meanings, the primary focus in allegory is on the abstract idea called forth by the concrete object. John Bunyan's *Pilgrim's Progress*, published during the seventeenth century, is a classic example of allegory because the characters, action, and setting have no existence beyond their abstract meanings. Bunyan's purpose is to teach his readers the exemplary way to salvation and heaven. The protagonist, named Christian, flees the City of Destruction in search of the Celestial City. Along the way he encounters characters who either help or hinder his spiritual journey. Among them are Mr. Worldly Wiseman, Faithful, Prudence, Piety, and a host of others named after the virtues or vices they display. These characters, places, and actions exist solely to illustrate religious doctrine. Allegory tends to be definitive rather than suggestive. It drives meaning into a corner and keeps it there. Most modern writers prefer the exploratory nature of symbol to the reductive nature of pure allegory.

Stories often include symbols that you may or may not perceive on a first reading. Their subtle use is a sign of a writer's skill in weaving symbols into the fabric of the characters' lives. Symbols may sometimes escape you, but that is probably better than finding symbols where only literal meanings are intended. Allow the text to help you determine whether a symbolic reading is appropriate. Once you are clear about what literally happens, read carefully and notice the placement of details that are emphasized. The pervasive references to time in Faulkner's "A Rose for Emily" (p. 47) and the glass of scotch whiskey and milk that the narrator sends to his brother at the conclusion of Baldwin's "Sonny's Blues" (p. 91) call attention to themselves and warrant symbolic readings. A symbol, however, need not be repeated to have an important purpose in a story. The drink that Sonny accepts is only mentioned at the end of the story and is accompanied by an ***allusion*** to the Bible, the "cup of trembling." The unpleasant-sounding cocktail also represents a blend of the dangerous or self-destructive — whiskey, representing Sonny's experiences — and his need for nurturing (milk). It was also the preferred drink of Charlie Parker, the jazz musician who is Sonny's hero, and who died at a very young age from drug addiction, which is exactly what the narrator fears will happen to Sonny.

By keeping track of the multiple contexts of the story, you should be able to decide whether your reading is reasonable and consistent with the other facts; plenty of lemons in literature yield no symbolic meaning even if they are squeezed. Be sensitive to the meanings that the author associates with people, places, objects, and actions. You may not associate home with provincial innocence as Hemingway does in "Soldier's Home," but a close reading of the story will permit you to see how and why he constructs that symbolic meaning. If you treat stories like people — with tact and care — they ordinarily are accessible and enjoyable.

The next three stories — Louise Erdrich's "The Red Convertible," Ralph Ellison's "King of the Bingo Game," and Cynthia Ozick's "The Shawl" — rely on symbols to convey meanings that go far beyond the specific incidents described in their plots.

## LOUISE ERDRICH (B. 1954)

Louise Erdrich's poetry and fiction deal mainly with the experiences of Native Americans of the Great Plains and upper Midwest. Born in Minnesota to a father of German heritage and a Chippewa mother, Erdrich is best known for a series of novels begun in 1984 with *Love Medicine*. This novel, which some would argue is more a story sequence, traces the intertwined stories of a number of families who connect and clash over a long period of history on an Ojibwe res-

Agence Opale/Alamy.

ervation in North Dakota. Subsequent books such as *The Beet Queen* (1986) and *Tracks* (1988) continue and deepen this saga. The following story, "The Red Convertible," is taken from *Love Medicine*. It takes place in 1974 toward the end of the U.S. war in Vietnam.

## *The Red Convertible*   1984

I was the first one to drive a convertible on my reservation. And of course it was red, a red Olds. I owned that car along with my brother Henry Junior. We owned it together until his boots filled with water on a windy night and he bought out my share. Now Henry owns the whole car, and his younger brother Lyman (that's myself), Lyman walks everywhere he goes.

How did I earn enough money to buy my share in the first place? My one talent was I could always make money. I had a touch for it, unusual in a Chippewa. From the first I was different that way, and everyone recognized it. I was the only kid they let in the American Legion Hall to shine shoes, for example, and one Christmas I sold spiritual bouquets for the mission door to door. The nuns let me keep a percentage. Once I started, it seemed the more money I made the easier the money came. Everyone encouraged it. When I was fifteen I got a job washing dishes at the Joliet Café, and that was where my first big break happened.

It wasn't long before I was promoted to busing tables, and then the short-order cook quit and I was hired to take her place. No sooner than you know it I was managing the Joliet. The rest is history. I went on managing. I soon became part owner, and of course there was no stopping me then. It wasn't long before the whole thing was mine.

After I'd owned the Joliet for one year, it blew over in the worst tornado ever seen around here. The whole operation was smashed to bits. A total loss. The fryalator was up in a tree, the grill torn in half like it was paper. I was only sixteen. I had it all in my mother's name, and I lost it quick, but before I lost it I had every one of my relatives, and their relatives, to dinner, and I also bought that red Olds I mentioned, along with Henry.

The first time we saw it! I'll tell you when we first saw it. We had gotten a ride up 5 to Winnipeg, and both of us had money. Don't ask me why, because we never mentioned a car or anything, we just had all our money. Mine was cash, a big bankroll from the Joliet's insurance. Henry had two checks — a week's extra pay for being laid off, and his regular check from the Jewel Bearing Plant.

We were walking down Portage anyway, seeing the sights, when we saw it. There it was, parked, large as life. Really as *if* it was alive. I thought of the word *repose,* because the car wasn't simply stopped, parked, or whatever. That car reposed, calm and gleaming, a FOR SALE sign in its left front window. Then, before we had thought it over at all, the car belonged to us and our pockets were empty. We had just enough money for gas back home.

We went places in that car, me and Henry. We took off driving all one whole summer. We started off toward the Little Knife River and Mandaree in Fort Berthold and then we found ourselves down in Wakpala somehow, and then suddenly we were over in Montana on the Rocky Boy, and yet the summer was not even half over. Some people hang on to details when they travel, but we didn't let them bother us and just lived our everyday lives here to there.

I do remember this one place with willows. I remember I laid under those trees and it was comfortable. So comfortable. The branches bent down all around me like a tent or a stable. And quiet, it was quiet, even though there was a powwow close enough so I could see it going on. The air was not too still, not too windy either. When the dust rises up and hangs in the air around the dancers like that, I feel good. Henry was asleep with his arms thrown wide. Later on, he woke up and we started driving again. We were somewhere in Montana, or maybe on the Blood Reserve — it could have been anywhere. Anyway it was where we met the girl.

All her hair was in buns around her ears, that's the first thing I noticed about her. She was posed alongside the road with her arm out, so we stopped. That girl was short, so short her lumber shirt looked comical on her, like a nightgown. She had jeans on and fancy moccasins and she carried a little suitcase.

"Hop on in," says Henry. So she climbs in between us.                                    10

"We'll take you home," I says. "Where do you live?"

"Chicken," she says.

"Where the hell's that?" I ask her.

"Alaska."

"Okay," says Henry, and we drive.                                                        15

We got up there and never wanted to leave. The sun doesn't truly set there in summer, and the night is more a soft dusk. You might doze off, sometimes, but before you know it you're up again, like an animal in nature. You never feel like you have to sleep hard or put away the world. And things would grow up there. One day just dirt or moss, the next day flowers and long grass. The girl's name was Susy. Her family really took to us. They fed us and put us up. We had our own tent to live in by their house, and the kids would be in and out of there all day and night. They couldn't get over me and Henry being brothers, we looked so different. We told them we knew we had the same mother, anyway.

One night Susy came in to visit us. We sat around in the tent talking of this and that. The season was changing. It was getting darker by that time, and the cold was even getting just a little mean. I told her it was time for us to go. She stood up on a chair.

"You never seen my hair," Susy said.

That was true. She was standing on a chair, but still, when she unclipped her buns the hair reached all the way to the ground. Our eyes opened. You couldn't tell how much hair she had when it was rolled up so neatly. Then my brother Henry did something funny. He went up to the chair and said, "Jump on my shoulders." So she did that, and her hair reached down past his waist, and he started twirling, this way and that, so her hair was flung out from side to side.

"I always wondered what it was like to have long pretty hair," Henry says. Well we laughed. It was a funny sight, the way he did it. The next morning we got up and took leave of those people. 20

On to greener pastures, as they say. It was down through Spokane and across Idaho then Montana and very soon we were racing the weather right along under the Canadian border through Columbus, Des Lacs, and then we were in Bottineau County and soon home. We'd made most of the trip, that summer, without putting up the car hood at all. We got home just in time, it turned out, for the army to remember Henry had signed up to join it.

I don't wonder that the army was so glad to get my brother that they turned him into a Marine. He was built like a brick outhouse anyway. We liked to tease him that they really wanted him for his Indian nose. He had a nose big and sharp as a hatchet, like the nose on Red Tomahawk, the Indian who killed Sitting Bull, whose profile is on signs all along the North Dakota highways. Henry went off to training camp, came home once during Christmas, then the next thing you know we got an overseas letter from him. It was 1970, and he said he was stationed up in the northern hill country. Whereabouts I did not know. He wasn't such a hot letter writer, and only got off two before the enemy caught him. I could never keep it straight, which direction those good Vietnam soldiers were from.

I wrote him back several times, even though I didn't know if those letters would get through. I kept him informed all about the car. Most of the time I had it up on blocks in the yard or half taken apart, because that long trip did a hard job on it under the hood.

I always had good luck with numbers, and never worried about the draft myself. I never even had to think about what my number was. But Henry was never lucky in the same way as me. It was at least three years before Henry came home. By then I guess the whole war was solved in the government's mind, but for him it would keep on going. In those years I'd put his car into almost perfect shape.

I always thought of it as his car while he was gone, even though when he left he said, "Now it's yours," and threw me his key.

"Thanks for the extra key," I'd said. "I'll put it up in your drawer just in case 25 I need it." He laughed.

When he came home, though, Henry was very different, and I'll say this: the change was no good. You could hardly expect him to change for the better, I know. But he was quiet, so quiet, and never comfortable sitting still anywhere but always up and moving around. I thought back to times we'd sat still for whole afternoons, never moving a muscle, just shifting our weight along the ground, talking to whoever sat with us, watching things. He'd always had a joke, then, too, and now you couldn't get him to laugh, or when he did it was more the sound of a man choking, a sound that stopped up the throats of other people around him. They got to leaving him alone most of the time, and I didn't blame them. It was a fact: Henry was jumpy and mean.

I'd bought a color TV set for my mom and the rest of us while Henry was away. Money still came very easy. I was sorry I'd ever bought it though, because of Henry. I was also sorry I'd bought color, because with black-and-white the pictures seem older and farther away. But what are you going to do? He sat in front of it, watching it, and that was the only time he was completely still. But it was the kind of stillness that you see in a rabbit when it freezes and before it will bolt. He was not easy. He sat in his chair gripping the armrests with all his might, as if the chair itself was moving at a high speed and if he let go at all he would rocket forward and maybe crash right through the set.

Once I was in the room watching TV with Henry and I heard his teeth click at something. I looked over, and he'd bitten through his lip. Blood was going down his chin. I tell you right then I wanted to smash that tube to pieces. I went over to it but Henry must have known what I was up to. He rushed from his chair and shoved me out of the way, against the wall. I told myself he didn't know what he was doing.

My mom came in, turned the set off real quiet, and told us she had made something for supper. So we went and sat down. There was still blood going down Henry's chin, but he didn't notice it and no one said anything, even though every time he took a bite of his bread his blood fell onto it until he was eating his own blood mixed in with the food.

While Henry was not around we talked about what was going to happen to him. 30 There were no Indian doctors on the reservation, and my mom couldn't come around to trusting the old man, Moses Pillager, because he courted her long ago and was jealous of her husbands. He might take revenge through her son. We were afraid that if we brought Henry to a regular hospital they would keep him.

"They don't fix them in those places," Mom said; "they just give them drugs."

"We wouldn't get him there in the first place," I agreed, "so let's just forget about it."

Then I thought about the car.

Henry had not even looked at the car since he'd gotten home, though like I said, it was in tip-top condition and ready to drive. I thought the car might bring the old Henry back somehow. So I bided my time and waited for my chance to interest him in the vehicle.

One night Henry was off somewhere. I took myself a hammer. I went out to that 35 car and I did a number on its underside. Whacked it up. Bent the tail pipe double.

Ripped the muffler loose. By the time I was done with the car it looked worse than any typical Indian car that has been driven all its life on reservation roads, which they always say are like government promises — full of holes. It just about hurt me, I'll tell you that! I threw dirt in the carburetor and I ripped all the electric tape off the seats. I made it look just as beat up as I could. Then I sat back and waited for Henry to find it.

Still, it took him over a month. That was all right, because it was just getting warm enough, not melting, but warm enough to work outside.

"Lyman," he says, walking in one day, "that red car looks like shit."

"Well it's old," I says. "You got to expect that."

"No way!" says Henry. "That car's a classic! But you went and ran the piss right out of it, Lyman, and you know it don't deserve that. I kept that car in A-one shape. You don't remember. You're too young. But when I left, that car was running like a watch. Now I don't even know if I can get it to start again, let alone get it anywhere near its old condition."

"Well you try," I said, like I was getting mad, "but I say it's a piece of junk."      40

Then I walked out before he could realize I knew he'd strung together more than six words at once.

After that I thought he'd freeze himself to death working on that car. He was out there all day, and at night he rigged up a little lamp, ran a cord out the window, and had himself some light to see by while he worked. He was better than he had been before, but that's still not saying much. It was easier for him to do the things the rest of us did. He ate more slowly and didn't jump up and down during the meal to get this or that or look out the window. I put my hand in the back of the TV set, I admit, and fiddled around with it good, so that it was almost impossible now to get a clear picture. He didn't look at it very often anyway. He was always out with that car or going off to get parts for it. By the time it was really melting outside, he had it fixed.

I had been feeling down in the dumps about Henry around this time. We had always been together before. Henry and Lyman. But he was such a loner now that I didn't know how to take it. So I jumped at the chance one day when Henry seemed friendly. It's not that he smiled or anything. He just said, "Let's take that old shitbox for a spin." Just the way he said it made me think he could be coming around.

We went out to the car. It was spring. The sun was shining very bright. My only sister, Bonita, who was just eleven years old, came out and made us stand together for a picture. Henry leaned his elbow on the red car's windshield, and he took his other arm and put it over my shoulder, very carefully, as though it was heavy for him to lift and he didn't want to bring the weight down all at once.

"Smile," Bonita said, and he did.      45

That picture. I never look at it anymore. A few months ago, I don't know why, I got his picture out and tacked it on the wall. I felt good about Henry at the time, close to him. I felt good having his picture on the wall, until one night when I was looking at television. I was a little drunk and stoned. I looked up at the wall and Henry was staring at me. I don't know what it was, but his smile had changed, or maybe it was gone. All I know is I couldn't stay in the same room with that picture. I was shaking. I got up, closed the door, and went into the kitchen. A little later my friend Ray came over and we both went back into that room. We put the picture in a brown bag, folded the bag over and over tightly, then put it way back in a closet.

I still see that picture now, as if it tugs at me, whenever I pass that closet door. The picture is very clear in my mind. It was so sunny that day Henry had to squint against the glare. Or maybe the camera Bonita held flashed like a mirror, blinding him, before she snapped the picture. My face is right out in the sun, big and round. But he might have drawn back, because the shadows on his face are deep as holes. There are two shadows curved like little hooks around the ends of his smile, as if to frame it and try to keep it there — that one, first smile that looked like it might have hurt his face. He has his field jacket on and the worn-in clothes he'd come back in and kept wearing ever since. After Bonita took the picture, she went into the house and we got into the car. There was a full cooler in the trunk. We started off, east, toward Pembina and the Red River because Henry said he wanted to see the high water.

The trip over there was beautiful. When everything starts changing, drying up, clearing off, you feel like your whole life is starting. Henry felt it, too. The top was down and the car hummed like a top. He'd really put it back in shape, even the tape on the seats was very carefully put down and glued back in layers. It's not that he smiled again or even joked, but his face looked to me as if it was clear, more peaceful. It looked as though he wasn't thinking of anything in particular except the bare fields and windbreaks and houses we were passing.

The river was high and full of winter trash when we got there. The sun was still out, but it was colder by the river. There were still little clumps of dirty snow here and there on the banks. The water hadn't gone over the banks yet, but it would, you could tell. It was just at its limit, hard swollen, glossy like an old gray scar. We made ourselves a fire, and we sat down and watched the current go. As I watched it I felt something squeezing inside me and tightening and trying to let go all at the same time. I knew I was not just feeling it myself; I knew I was feeling what Henry was going through at that moment. Except that I couldn't stand it, the closing and opening. I jumped to my feet. I took Henry by the shoulders and I started shaking him. "Wake up," I says, "wake up, wake up, wake up!" I didn't know what had come over me. I sat down beside him again.

His face was totally white and hard. Then it broke, like stones break all of a 50 sudden when water boils up inside them.

"I know it," he says. "I know it. I can't help it. It's no use."

We start talking. He said he knew what I'd done with the car. It was obvious it had been whacked out of shape and not just neglected. He said he wanted to give the car to me for good now, it was no use. He said he'd fixed it just to give it back and I should take it.

"No way," I says. "I don't want it."

"That's okay," he says, "you take it."

"I don't want it, though," I says back to him, and then to emphasize, just to 55 emphasize, you understand, I touch his shoulder. He slaps my hand off.

"Take that car," he says.

"No," I say. "Make me," I say, and then he grabs my jacket and rips the arm loose. That jacket is a class act, suede with tags and zippers. I push Henry backwards, off the log. He jumps up and bowls me over. We go down in a clinch and come up swinging hard, for all we're worth, with our fists. He socks my jaw so hard I feel like it swings loose. Then I'm at his rib cage and land a good one under his chin so his head snaps back. He's dazzled. He looks at me and I look at him and then his eyes are full of tears and blood and at first I think he's crying. But no, he's laughing. "Ha! Ha!" he says. "Ha! Ha! Take good care of it."

"Okay," I says. "Okay, no problem. Ha! Ha!"

I can't help it, and I start laughing, too. My face feels fat and strange, and after a while I get a beer from the cooler in the trunk, and when I hand it to Henry he takes his shirt and wipes my germs off. "Hoof-and-mouth disease," he says. For some reason this cracks me up, and so we're really laughing for a while, and then we drink all the rest of the beers one by one and throw them in the river and see how far, how fast, the current takes them before they fill up and sink.

"You want to go on back?" I ask after a while. "Maybe we could snag a couple  60 nice Kashpaw girls."

He says nothing. But I can tell his mood is turning again.

"They're all crazy, the girls up here, every damn one of them."

"You're crazy too," I say, to jolly him up. "Crazy Lamartine boys!"

He looks as though he will take this wrong at first. His face twists, then clears, and he jumps up on his feet. "That's right!" he says. "Crazier 'n hell. Crazy Indians!"

I think it's the old Henry again. He throws off his jacket and starts springing  65 his legs up from the knees like a fancy dancer. He's down doing something between a grass dance and a bunny hop, no kind of dance I ever saw before, but neither has anyone else on all this green growing earth. He's wild. He wants to pitch whoopee! He's up and at me and all over. All this time I'm laughing so hard, so hard my belly is getting tied up in a knot.

"Got to cool me off!" he shouts all of a sudden. Then he runs over to the river and jumps in.

There's boards and other things in the current. It's so high. No sound comes from the river after the splash he makes, so I run right over. I look around. It's getting dark. I see he's halfway across the water already, and I know he didn't swim there but the current took him. It's far. I hear his voice, though, very clearly across it.

"My boots are filling," he says.

He says this in a normal voice, like he just noticed and he doesn't know what to think of it. Then he's gone. A branch comes by. Another branch. And I go in.

By the time I get out of the river, off the snag I pulled myself onto, the sun is down.  70 I walk back to the car, turn on the high beams, and drive it up the bank. I put it in first gear and then I take my foot off the clutch. I get out, close the door, and watch it plow softly into the water. The headlights reach in as they go down, searching, still lighted even after the water swirls over the back end. I wait. The wires short out. It is all finally dark. And then there is only the water, the sound of it going and running and going and running and running.

### Considerations for Critical Thinking and Writing

1. FIRST RESPONSE. The way Lyman describes his brother's death and the fate of the car in the first paragraph is abstract: the reader would have no way of knowing what he means by "his boots filled with water" or "Now Henry owns the whole car." What is the effect of this indirect description at the beginning of the story?

2. Why does Lyman emphasize money? What is his attitude toward it?

3. Based on Lyman's initial description of the car, what is its importance? What can you tell about Lyman's and Henry's lives that makes sense of their attraction to the car?

4. Compare the scenes when Lyman describes lying under willow trees and when the Alaskan girl they temporarily live with lets her hair down all the way to the ground. Can you make sense of these two parallel scenes within the context of the story as a whole?

5. Discuss the tension between motion and stillness in the story.

6. If Henry needs to be healed after his war experience, why does Lyman damage the red convertible (which is strongly associated with Henry)?

7. From the moment Lyman describes a fryolator in a tree after a tornado, we are aware that nature and mechanical objects have a strange relationship in this story. Locate descriptions of both and discuss their relationship to one another as a way of sharpening your sense of the story's theme.

8. Look again at the section of the story where Lyman discusses the last photograph taken of his brother, and of his reaction to having that photo in his house. What is the significance of this section to the story overall?

9. The red convertible is obviously meaningful to the story: it is the title, after all. As a symbol, how do you interpret it? Bear in mind its color as you respond, since its redness is emphasized.

### CONNECTION TO ANOTHER SELECTION

1. Discuss the relationship between brothers in James Baldwin's "Sonny's Blues" (p. 91) and in this story. How do the narrators of each story both reveal and conceal their own motivation for telling stories about their brothers?

## RALPH ELLISON (1913–1994)

Everett Collection/Newscom.

Born in Oklahoma and educated at the Tuskegee Institute in Alabama, Ralph Waldo Ellison won the National Book Award in 1953 for his magisterial novel *Invisible Man* (1952), considered by many critics to be one of the most important American novels ever published. His winning the National Book Award was a momentous occasion, for it was the first time the award was given to an African American. Although Ellison lived for another four decades, *Invisible Man* was the only novel he published in his lifetime. He published essays and short stories and was a sought-after public speaker, but his highly anticipated second novel never arrived, although two posthumous versions of it have been published. The following story, "King of the Bingo Game," was published in 1944, and Ellison rehearses many of the themes and techniques in this piece that undergird *Invisible Man*.

## King of the Bingo Game    1944

The woman in front of him was eating roasted peanuts that smelled so good that he could barely contain his hunger. He could not even sleep and wished they'd hurry and begin the bingo game. There, on his right, two fellows were drinking wine out of a bottle wrapped in a paper bag, and he could hear soft gurgling in the dark. His stomach gave a low, gnawing growl. If this was down South, he thought, all I'd have to do is lean over and say, "Lady, gimme a few of those peanuts, please, ma'm," and she'd pass me the bag and never think nothing of it. Or he could ask the fellows for a drink in the same way. Folks down South stuck together that way; they didn't even have to know you. But up here it was different. Ask some-body for something, and they'd think you were crazy. Well, I ain't crazy. I'm just broke, 'cause I got no birth certificate to get a job, and Laura 'bout to die 'cause we got no money for a doctor. But I ain't crazy. And yet a pinpoint of doubt was focused in his mind as he glanced toward the screen and saw the hero stealthily entering a dark room and sending the beam of a flashlight along a wall of book-cases. This is where he finds the trapdoor, he remembered. The man would pass abruptly through the wall and find the girl tied to a bed, her legs and arms spread wide, and her clothing torn to rags. He laughed softly to himself. He had seen the picture three times, and this was one of the best scenes.

On his right the fellow whispered wide-eyed to his companion, "Man, look a-yonder!"

"Damn!"

"Wouldn't I like to have her tied up like that. . ."

"Hey! That fool's letting her loose!"                                                    5

"Aw, man, he loves her."

"Love or no love!"

The man moved impatiently beside him, and he tried to involve himself in the scene. But Laura was on his mind. Tiring quickly of watching the picture, he looked back to where the white beam filtered from the projection room above the balcony. It started small and grew large, specks of dust dancing in its whiteness as it reached the screen. It was strange how the beam always landed right on the screen and didn't mess up and fall somewhere else. But they had it all fixed. Everything was fixed. Now suppose when they showed that girl with her dress torn the girl started taking off the rest of her clothes, and when the guy came in he didn't untie her but kept her there and went to taking off his own clothes? *That* would be something to see. If a picture got out of hand like that those guys up there would go nuts. Yeah, and there'd be so many folks in here you couldn't find a seat for nine months! A strange sensation played over his skin. He shuddered. Yesterday he'd seen a bed-bug on a woman's neck as they walked out into the bright street. But exploring his thigh through a hole in his pocket he found only goose pimples and old scars.

The bottle gurgled again. He closed his eyes. Now a dreamy music was accom-panying the film and train whistles were sounding in the distance, and he was a boy again walking along a railroad trestle down South, and seeing the train com-ing, and running back as fast as he could go, and hearing the whistle blowing, and getting off the trestle to solid ground just in time, with the earth trembling beneath his feet, and feeling relieved as he ran down the cinder-strewn embankment onto the highway, and looking back and seeing with terror that the train had left the track and was following him right down the middle of the street, and all the white people laughing as he ran screaming . . .

"Wake up there, buddy! What the hell do you mean hollering like that? Can't you see we trying to enjoy this here picture?"

He stared at the man with gratitude.

"I'm sorry, old man," he said. "I musta been dreaming."

"Well, here, have a drink. And don't be making no noise like that, damn!"

His hands trembled as he tilted his head. It was not wine but whiskey. Cold rye whiskey. He took a deep swoller, decided it was better not to take another, and handed the bottle back to its owner.

"Thanks, old man," he said.

Now he felt the cold whiskey breaking a warm path straight through the middle of him, growing hotter and sharper as it moved. He had not eaten all day, and it made him light-headed. The smell of the peanuts stabbed him like a knife, and he got up and found a seat in the middle aisle. But no sooner did he sit than he saw a row of intense-faced young girls, and got up again, thinking, You chicks musta been Lindy-hopping° somewhere. He found a seat several rows ahead as the lights came on, and he saw the screen disappear behind a heavy red-and-gold curtain; then the curtain rising, and the man with the microphone and a uniformed attendant coming on the stage.

He felt for his bingo cards, smiling. The guy at the door wouldn't like it if he knew about his having *five* cards. Well, not everyone played the bingo game; and even with five cards he didn't have much of a chance. For Laura, though, he had to have faith. He studied the cards, each with its different numerals, punching the free center hole in each and spreading them neatly across his lap; and when the lights faded, he sat slouched in his seat so that he could look from his cards to the bingo wheel with but a quick shifting of his eyes.

Ahead, at the end of the darkness, the man with the microphone was pressing a button attached to a long cord and spinning the bingo wheel and calling out the number each time the wheel came to rest. And each time the voice rang out, his finger raced over the cards for the number. With five cards he had to move fast. He became nervous; there were too many cards, and the man went too fast with his grating voice. Perhaps he should just select one and throw the others away. But he was afraid. He became warm. Wonder how much Laura's doctor would cost? Damn that, watch the cards! And with despair he heard the man call three in a row which he missed on all five cards. This way he'd never win. . .

When he saw the row of holes punched across the third card, he sat paralyzed and heard the man call three more numbers before he stumbled forward, screaming, "Bingo! Bingo!"

"Let that fool up there," someone called.

"Get up there, man!"

He stumbled down the aisle and up the steps to the stage into a light so sharp and bright that for a moment it blinded him, and he felt that he had moved into the spell of some strange, mysterious power. Yet it was as familiar as the sun, and he knew it was the perfectly familiar bingo.

The man with the microphone was saying something to the audience as he held out his card. A cold light flashed from the man's finger as the card left his hand. His knees trembled. The man stepped closer, checking the card against the numbers chalked on the board. Suppose he had made a mistake?

---

*Lindy-hopping:* The Lindy-hop was a spirited popular dance.

The pomade on the man's hair made him feel faint, and he backed away. But the man was checking the card over the microphone now, and he had to stay. He stood tense, listening.

"Under the *O*, forty-four," the man chanted. "Under the *I*, seven. Under the *G*, three. Under the *B*, ninety-six. Under the *N*, thirteen!"

His breath came easier as the man smiled at the audience.  25

"Yessir, ladies and gentlemen, he's one of the chosen people!"

The audience rippled with laughter and applause.

"Step right up to the front of the stage."

He moved slowly forward, wishing that the light was not so bright.

"To win tonight's jackpot of $36.90 the wheel must stop between the double  30
zero, understand?"

He nodded, knowing the ritual from the many days and nights he had watched the winners march across the stage to press the button that controlled the spinning wheel and receive the prizes. And now he followed the instructions as though he'd crossed the slippery stage a million prize-winning times.

The man was making some kind of a joke, and he nodded vacantly. So tense had he become that he felt a sudden desire to cry, and shook it away. He felt vaguely that his whole life was determined by the bingo wheel; not only that which would happen now that he was at last before it, but all that had gone before, since his birth and his mother's birth and the birth of his father. It had always been there, even though he had not been aware of it, handing out the unlucky cards and numbers of his days. The feeling persisted, and he started quickly away. I better get down from here before I make a fool of myself, he thought.

"Here, boy," the man called. "You haven't started yet."

Someone laughed as he went hesitantly back.

"Are you all reet?"  35

He grinned at the man's jive talk, but no words would come, and he knew it was not a convincing grin. For suddenly he knew that he stood on the slippery brink of some terrible embarrassment.

"Where are you from, boy?" the man asked.

"Down South."

"He's from down South, ladies and gentlemen," the man said. "Where from? Speak right into the mike."

"Rocky Mont," he said. "Rock' Mont, North Car'lina."  40

"So you decided to come down off that mountain to the U.S.," the man laughed. He felt that the man was making a fool of him, but then something cold was placed in his hand, and the lights were no longer behind him.

Standing before the wheel he felt alone, but that was somehow right, and he remembered his plan. He would give the wheel a short quick twirl. Just a touch of the button. He had watched it many times, and always it came close to double zero when it was short and quick. He steeled himself; the fear had left, and he felt a profound sense of promise, as though he were about to be repaid for all the things he'd suffered all his life. Trembling, he pressed the button. There was a whirl of lights, and in a second he realized with finality that though he wanted to, he could not stop. It was as though he held a high-powered line in his naked hand. His nerves tightened. As the wheel increased its speed it seemed to draw him more and more into his power, as though it held his fate; and with it came a deep need to submit, to whirl, to lose himself in its swirl of color. He could not stop it now, he knew. So let it be.

The button rested snugly in his palm where the man had placed it. And now he became aware of the man beside him, advising him through the microphone while, behind, the shadowy audience hummed with noisy voices. He shifted his feet. There was still that feeling of helplessness within him, making part of him desire to turn back, even now that the jackpot was right in his hand. He squeezed the button until his fist ached. Then, like the sudden shriek of a subway whistle, a doubt tore through his head. Suppose he did not spin the wheel long enough? What could he do, and how could he tell? And then he knew, even as he wondered, that as long as he pressed the button, he could control the jackpot. He and only he could determine whether or not it was to be his. Not even the man with the microphone could do anything about it now. He felt drunk. Then, as though he had come down from a high hill into a valley of people, he heard the audience yelling.

"Come down from there, you jerk!"

"Let somebody else have a chance . . ." 45

"Ole Jack thinks he done found the end of the rainbow . . ."

The last voice was not unfriendly, and he turned and smiled dreamily into the yelling mouths. Then he turned his back squarely on them.

"Don't take too long, boy," a voice said.

He nodded. They were yelling behind him. Those folks did not understand what had happened to him. They had been playing the bingo game day in and night out for years, trying to win rent money or hamburger change. But not one of those wise guys had discovered this wonderful thing. He watched the wheel whirling past the numbers and experienced a burst of exaltation: This is God! This is the really truly God! He said it aloud: "This is God!"

He said it with such absolute conviction that he feared he would fall fainting 50 into the footlights. But the crowd yelled so loud that they could not hear. Those fools, he thought. I'm here trying to tell them the most wonderful secret in the world, and they're yelling like they gone crazy. A hand fell upon his shoulder.

"You'll have to make a choice now, boy. You've taken too long."

He brushed the hand violently away.

"Leave me alone, man. I know what I'm doing!"

The man looked surprised and held on to the microphone for support. And because he did not wish to hurt the man's feelings he smiled, realizing with a sudden pang that there was no way of explaining to the man just why he had to stand there pressing the button forever.

"Come here," he called tiredly. 55

The man approached, rolling the heavy microphone across the stage.

"Anybody can play this bingo game, right?" he said.

"Sure, but. . ."

He smiled, feeling inclined to be patient with this slick-looking white man with his blue sport shirt and his sharp gabardine suit.

"That's what I thought," he said. "Anybody can win the jackpot as long as they 60 get the lucky number, right?"

"That's the rule, but after all. . ."

"That's what I thought," he said. "And the big prize goes to the man who knows how to win it?"

The man nodded speechlessly.

"Well then, go on over there and watch me win like I want to. I ain't going to hurt nobody," he said, "and I'll show you how to win. I mean to show the whole world how it's got to be done."

And because he understood, he smiled again to let the man know that he 65
held nothing against him for being white and impatient. Then he refused to
see the man any longer and stood pressing the button, the voices of the crowd
reaching him like sounds in distant streets. Let them yell. All the Negroes down
there were just ashamed because he was black like them. He smiled inwardly,
knowing how it was. Most of the time he was ashamed of what Negroes did
himself. Well, let them be ashamed for something this time. Like him. He
was like a long thin black wire that was being stretched and wound upon the
bingo wheel; wound until he wanted to scream; wound, but this time himself
controlling the winding and the sadness and the shame, and because he did,
Laura would be all right. Suddenly the lights flickered. He staggered backward.
Had something gone wrong? All this noise. Didn't they know that although he
controlled the wheel, it also controlled him, and unless he pressed the button
forever and forever and ever it would stop, leaving him high and dry, dry and
high on this hard high slippery hill and Laura dead? There was only one chance;
he had to do whatever the wheel demanded. And gripping the button in despair,
he discovered with surprise that it imparted a nervous energy. His spine tingled.
He felt a certain power.

Now he faced the raging crowd with defiance, its screams penetrating his
eardrums like trumpets shrieking from a jukebox. The vague faces glowing in the
bingo lights gave him a sense of himself that he had never known before. He was
running the show, by God! They had to react to him, for he was their luck. This is
*me*, he thought. Let the bastards yell. Then someone was laughing inside him, and
he realized that somehow he had forgotten his own name. It was a sad, lost feeling
to lose your name, and a crazy thing to do. That name had been given him by the
white man who had owned his grandfather a long lost time ago down South. But
maybe those wise guys knew his name.

"Who am I?" he screamed.

"Hurry up and bingo, you jerk!"

They didn't know either, he thought sadly. They didn't even know their own
names, they were all poor nameless bastards. Well, he didn't need that old name;
he was reborn. For as long as he pressed the button he was The-man-who-pressed-
the-button-who-held-the-prize-who-was-the-King-of-Bingo. That was the way it
was, and he'd have to press the button even if nobody understood, even though
Laura did not understand.

"Live!" he shouted. 70

The audience quieted like the dying of a huge fan.

"Live, Laura, baby. I got holt of it now, sugar. Live!"

He screamed it, tears streaming down his face. "I got nobody but YOU!"

The screams tore from his very guts. He felt as though the rush of blood
to his head would burst out in baseball seams of small red droplets, like a head
beaten by police clubs. Bending over he saw a trickle of blood splashing the toe
of his shoe. With his free hand he searched his head. It was his nose. God, suppose something has gone wrong? He felt that the whole audience had somehow
entered him and was stamping its feet in his stomach and he was unable to throw
them out. They wanted the prize, that was it. They wanted the secret for themselves. But they'd never get it; he would keep the bingo wheel whirling forever,
and Laura would be safe in the wheel. But would she? It had to be, because if she
were not safe the wheel would cease to turn; it could not go on. He had to get

away, *vomit* all, and his mind formed an image of himself running with Laura in his arms down the tracks of the subway just ahead of an A train, running desperately *vomit* with people screaming for him to come out but knowing no way of leaving the tracks because to stop would bring the train crushing down upon him and to attempt to leave across the other tracks would mean to run into a hot third rail as high as his waist which threw blue sparks that blinded his eyes until he could hardly see.

He heard singing, and the audience was clapping its hands.   75

> *"Shoot the liquor to him, Jim, boy!*
> *Clap-clap-clap*
> *Well a-calla the cop*
> *He's blowing his top!*
> *Shoot the liquor to him, Jim, boy!"*

Bitter anger grew within him at the singing. They think I'm crazy. Well let 'em laugh. I'll do what I got to do.

He was standing in an attitude of intense listening when he saw that they were watching something on the stage behind him. He felt weak. But when he turned he saw no one. If only his thumb did not ache so. Now they were applauding. And for a moment he thought that the wheel had stopped. But that was impossible, his thumb still pressed the button. Then he saw them. Two men in uniform beckoned from the end of the stage. They were coming toward him, walking in step, slowly, like a tap-dance team returning for a third encore. But their shoulders shot forward, and he backed away, looking wildly about. There was nothing to fight them with. He had only the long black cord which led to a plug somewhere backstage, and he couldn't use that because it operated the bingo wheel. He backed slowly, fixing the men with his eyes as his lips stretched over his teeth in a tight, fixed grin; moved toward the end of the stage and realizing that he couldn't go much further, for suddenly the cord became taut and he couldn't afford to break the cord. But he had to do something. The audience was howling. Suddenly he stopped dead, seeing the men halt, their legs lifted as in an interrupted step of a slow-motion dance. There was nothing to do but run in the other direction and he dashed forward, slipping and sliding. The men fell back, surprised. He struck out violently going past.

"Grab him!"

He ran, but all too quickly the cord tightened, resistingly, and he turned and ran back again. This time he slipped them, and discovered by running in a circle before the wheel he could keep the cord from tightening. But this way he had to flail his arms to keep the men away. Why couldn't they leave a man alone? He ran, circling.

"Ring down the curtain," someone yelled. But they couldn't do that. If they  80 did, the wheel flashing from the projection room would be cut off. But they had him before he could tell them so, trying to pry open his fist, and he was wrestling and trying to bring his knees into the fight and holding on to the button, for it was his life. And now he was down, seeing a foot coming down, crushing his wrist cruelly, down, as he saw the wheel whirling serenely above.

"I can't give it up," he screamed. Then quietly, in a confidential tone, "Boys, I really can't give it up."

It landed hard against his head. And in the blank moment they had it away from him, completely now. He fought them trying to pull him up from the stage as he watched the wheel spin slowly to a stop. Without surprise he saw it rest at double zero.

"You see." He pointed bitterly.

"Sure, boy, sure, it's okay," one of the men said, smiling.

And seeing the man bow his head to someone he could not see, he felt very, very happy; he would receive what all the winners received.   85

But as he warmed in the justice of the man's tight smile he did not see the man's slow wink, nor see the bowlegged man behind him step clear of the swiftly descending curtain and set himself for a blow. He only felt the dull pain exploding in his skull, and he knew even as it slipped out of him that his luck had run out on the stage.

## CONSIDERATIONS FOR CRITICAL THINKING AND WRITING

1. FIRST RESPONSE. Why is it significant that the man is watching a movie before the bingo game begins? How might a movie be interpreted symbolically?

2. The protagonist cries out briefly during the movie and thinks he must have been dreaming. How do dreaming and rational thought work against each other in this story? Where does it seem like the story pushes against the boundaries of realism?

3. Note the interplay between light and darkness in the story. How does it point toward the story's main human concerns, or toward its theme?

4. What is the story's point with regard to fate and free will?

5. How does the bingo wheel operate as a complex symbol?

6. The story repeatedly calls attention to the differences between the southern and northern United States. Why is this distinction important in the context of the story? What other social divisions are evident?

7. List all of the machines in the story and make some notes about their properties. Together, what do they symbolize?

8. What is the protagonist's relationship to the crowd watching him play the bingo game? Does it change?

9. Can you make sense of the protagonist's equation of the bingo wheel with "God"?

10. How does race become significant as the story nears its conclusion?

11. Why is the protagonist's wife Laura crucial to the story even though she only enters it in his consciousness?

12. At one point the protagonist likens his experience to being reborn. Is there other birth imagery in the story? How does it function?

13. How do you interpret the story's ending?

## CONNECTION TO ANOTHER SELECTION

1. Discuss the relationship between fate and individual destiny in this story and in T. C. Boyle's "The Hit Man" (p. 33).

# Cynthia Ozick (b. 1928)

Born in New York City, Cynthia Ozick was raised by parents who had emigrated from Russia. She was educated at New York University and the Ohio State University. Ozick's work has garnered many prestigious awards, including the National Book Award, the PEN/Nabokov Award, and the PEN/Malamud Award. Most of her two dozen books are novels and story collections, though she has also published eight essay collections and a play. Her work engages deeply with Jewish identity, particularly with the trauma in the aftermath of the Holocaust. Such is the case in the following short story, "The Shawl," first published in 1980 and widely studied since.

Ulf Andersen/Getty Images Entertainment/Getty Images.

## The Shawl    1980

Stella, cold, cold, the coldness of hell. How they walked on the roads together, Rosa with Magda curled up between sore breasts, Magda wound up in the shawl. Sometimes Stella carried Magda. But she was jealous of Magda. A thin girl of fourteen, too small, with thin breasts of her own, Stella wanted to be wrapped in a shawl, hidden away, asleep, rocked by the march, a baby, a round infant in arms. Magda took Rosa's nipple, and Rosa never stopped walking, a walking cradle. There was not enough milk; sometimes Magda sucked air; then she screamed. Stella was ravenous. Her knees were tumors on sticks, her elbows chicken bones.

Rosa did not feel hunger; she felt light, not like someone walking but like someone in a faint, in trance, arrested in a fit, someone who is already a floating angel, alert and seeing everything, but in the air, not there, not touching the road. As if teetering on the tips of her fingernails. She looked into Magda's face through a gap in the shawl: a squirrel in a nest, safe, no one could reach her inside the little house of the shawl's windings. The face, very round, a pocket mirror of a face: but it was not Rosa's bleak complexion, dark like cholera, it was another kind of face altogether, eyes blue as air, smooth feathers of hair nearly as yellow as the Star sewn into Rosa's coat. You could think she was one of *their* babies.

Rosa, floating, dreamed of giving Magda away in one of the villages. She could leave the line for a minute and push Magda into the hands of any woman on the side of the road. But if she moved out of line they might shoot. And even if she fled the line for half a second and pushed the shawl-bundle at a stranger, would the woman take it? She might be surprised, or afraid; she might drop the shawl, and Magda would fall out and strike her head and die. The little round head. Such a good child, she gave up screaming, and sucked now only for the taste of the drying nipple itself. The neat grip of the tiny gums. One mite of a tooth tip sticking up in the bottom gum, how shining, an elfin tombstone of white marble gleaming there.

Without complaining, Magda relinquished Rosa's teats, first the left, then the right; both were cracked, not a sniff of milk. The duct-crevice extinct, a dead volcano, blind eye, chill hole, so Magda took the corner of the shawl and milked it instead. She sucked and sucked, flooding the threads with wetness. The shawl's good flavor, milk of linen.

It was a magic shawl, it could nourish an infant for three days and three nights. Magda did not die, she stayed alive, although very quiet. A peculiar smell, of cinnamon and almonds, lifted out of her mouth. She held her eyes open every moment, forgetting how to blink or nap, and Rosa and sometimes Stella studied their blueness. On the road they raised one burden of a leg after another and studied Magda's face. "Aryan," Stella said, in a voice grown as thin as a string; and Rosa thought how Stella gazed at Magda like a young cannibal. And the time that Stella said "Aryan," it sounded to Rosa as if Stella had really said "Let us devour her."

But Magda lived to walk. She lived that long, but she did not walk very well, 5 partly because she was only fifteen months old, and partly because the spindles of her legs could not hold up her fat belly. It was fat with air, full and round. Rosa gave almost all her food to Magda, Stella gave nothing; Stella was ravenous, a growing child herself, but not growing much. Stella did not menstruate. Rosa did not menstruate. Rosa was ravenous, but also not; she learned from Magda how to drink the taste of a finger in one's mouth. They were in a place without pity, all pity was annihilated in Rosa, she looked at Stella's bones without pity. She was sure that Stella was waiting for Magda to die so she could put her teeth into the little thighs.

Rosa knew Magda was going to die very soon; she should have been dead already, but she had been buried away deep inside the magic shawl, mistaken there for the shivering mound of Rosa's breasts; Rosa clung to the shawl as if it covered only herself. No one took it away from her. Magda was mute. She never cried. Rosa hid her in the barracks, under the shawl, but she knew that one day someone would inform; or one day someone, not even Stella, would steal Magda to eat her. When Magda began to walk, Rosa knew that Magda was going to die very soon, something would happen. She was afraid to fall asleep; she slept with the weight of her thigh on Magda's body; she was afraid she would smother Magda under her thigh. The weight of Rosa was becoming less and less; Rosa and Stella were slowly turning into air.

Magda was quiet, but her eyes were horribly alive, like blue tigers. She watched. Sometimes she laughed — it seemed a laugh, but how could it be? Magda had never seen anyone laugh. Still, Magda laughed at her shawl when the wind blew its corners, the bad wind with pieces of black in it, that made Stella's and Rosa's eyes tear. Magda's eyes were always clear and tearless. She watched like a tiger. She guarded her shawl. No one could touch it; only Rosa could touch it. Stella was not allowed. The shawl was Magda's own baby, her pet, her little sister. She tangled herself up in it and sucked on one of the corners when she wanted to be very still.

Then Stella took the shawl away and made Magda die.

Afterward Stella said: "I was cold."

And afterward she was always cold, always. The cold went into her heart: Rosa 10 saw that Stella's heart was cold. Magda flopped onward with her little pencil legs scribbling this way and that, in search of the shawl; the pencils faltered at the barracks opening, where the light began. Rosa saw and pursued. But already Magda was in the square outside the barracks, in the jolly light. It was the roll-call arena. Every morning Rosa had to conceal Magda under the shawl against a wall of the barracks and go out and stand in the arena with Stella and hundreds of others, sometimes for hours, and Magda, deserted, was quiet under the shawl, sucking on her corner. Every day Magda was silent, and so she did not die. Rosa saw that today Magda was going to die, and at the same time a fearful joy ran in Rosa's two palms, her fingers were on fire, she was astonished, febrile:° Magda, in the sunlight, swaying on her pencil legs, was howling. Ever since the drying up of Rosa's nipples, ever since Magda's last scream on the road, Magda had been devoid of any syllable; Magda was a mute. Rosa believed that something had gone wrong with her vocal cords, with her windpipe, with the cave of her larynx; Magda was defective, without a voice; perhaps she was deaf; there might be something amiss with her intelligence; Magda was dumb. Even the laugh that came when the ash-stippled wind made a clown out of Magda's shawl was only the air-blown showing of her teeth. Even when the lice, head lice and body lice, crazed her so that she became as wild as one of the big rats that plundered the barracks at daybreak looking for carrion, she rubbed and scratched and kicked and bit and rolled without a whimper. But now Magda's mouth was spilling a long viscous rope of clamor.

"Maaaa — "

It was the first noise Magda had ever sent out from her throat since the drying up of Rosa's nipples.

"Maaaa . . . aaa!"

Again! Magda was wavering in the perilous sunlight of the arena, scribbling on such pitiful little bent shins. Rosa saw. She saw that Magda was grieving for the loss of her shawl, she saw that Magda was going to die. A tide of commands hammered in Rosa's nipples: Fetch, get, bring! But she did not know which to go after first, Magda or the shawl. If she jumped out into the arena to snatch Magda up, the howling would not stop, because Magda would still not have the shawl; but if she ran back into the barracks to find the shawl, and if she found it, and if she came after Magda holding it and shaking it, then she would get Magda back, Magda would put the shawl in her mouth and turn dumb again.

Rosa entered the dark. It was easy to discover the shawl. Stella was heaped 15 under it, asleep in her thin bones. Rosa tore the shawl free and flew — she could fly, she was only air — into the arena. The sunheat murmured of another life, of butterflies in summer. The light was placid, mellow. On the other side of the steel fence, far away, there were green meadows speckled with dandelions and deep-colored violets; beyond them, even farther, innocent tiger lilies, tall, lifting their orange bonnets. In the barracks they spoke of "flowers," of "rain": excrement, thick turd-braids, and the slow stinking maroon waterfall that slunk down from the upper bunks, the stink mixed with a bitter fatty floating smoke that greased Rosa's skin. She stood for an instant at the margin of the arena. Sometimes the electricity inside the fence would seem to hum; even Stella said it was only an imagining, but Rosa heard real sounds in the wire: grainy sad voices. The farther she was from the fence, the more clearly the voices crowded at her. The lamenting voices strummed so convincingly, so passionately, it was impossible to suspect them of being phantoms. The voices told her to hold up the shawl, high; the voices told her to shake it, to whip with it, to unfurl it like a flag. Rosa lifted, shook, whipped, unfurled. Far off, very far, Magda leaned across her air-fed belly, reaching out with the rods of her arms. She was high up, elevated, riding someone's shoulder. But the shoulder that carried Magda was not coming toward Rosa and

*febrile:* Feverish, excited.

the shawl, it was drifting away, the speck of Magda was moving more and more into the smoky distance. Above the shoulder a helmet glinted. The light tapped the helmet and sparkled it into a goblet. Below the helmet a black body like a domino and a pair of black boots hurled themselves in the direction of the electrified fence. The electric voices began to chatter wildly. "Maamaa, maaamaaa," they all hummed together. How far Magda was from Rosa now, across the whole square, past a dozen barracks, all the way on the other side! She was no bigger than a moth.

All at once Magda was swimming through the air. The whole of Magda traveled through loftiness. She looked like a butterfly touching a silver vine. And the moment Magda's feathered round head and her pencil legs and balloonish belly and zigzag arms splashed against the fence, the steel voices went mad in their growling, urging Rosa to run and run to the spot where Magda had fallen from her flight against the electrified fence; but of course Rosa did not obey them. She only stood, because if she ran they would shoot, and if she tried to pick up the sticks of Magda's body they would shoot, and if she let the wolf's screech ascending now through the ladder of her skeleton break out, they would shoot; so she took Magda's shawl and filled her own mouth with it, stuffed it in and stuffed it in, until she was swallowing up the wolf's screech and tasting the cinnamon and almond depth of Magda's saliva; and Rosa drank Magda's shawl until it dried.

### CONSIDERATIONS FOR CRITICAL THINKING AND WRITING

1. FIRST RESPONSE. The shawl is twice described as "a magic shawl." Which other elements in the story are in the realm of the unrealistic, otherworldly, or abstract? What is the effect of a story about one of the harshest events in history employing imagery of this nature?

2. The shawl is a complex symbol. What are its primary associations? What are its less obvious associations? Ultimately, what does it symbolize?

3. In addition to symbolism, the story relies on the figurative language common in poetry (metaphor and simile, see pp. 599–602). For example, in the first paragraph, Stella's body is described this way: "Her knees were tumors on sticks, her elbows chicken bones." List other examples of figurative language in the story and consider how they contribute to its overall effect on the reader.

4. Discuss the motifs of hunger and eating throughout the story.

5. In the arresting eighth paragraph, the baby Magda's death is blamed on the fact that Stella took the shawl away from her. It is clear that her death and her miserable existence are the fault of the Nazis who created the concentration camps. What is the effect of blaming Stella, who is also a victim?

6. What images of predators and prey do you see in the story? What is their significance in terms of its theme?

7. Why does Ozick chose to refer to the three characters in the story by their first names instead of by their relationships (mother, daughter, sister, etc.)?

8. How do you interpret the voices Rosa hears toward the end of the story?

9. Although the story's setting is clearly a Nazi concentration camp, the story does not name that setting explicitly. How does Ozick evoke that setting without naming it?

10. How would you characterize the story's point of view (see Chapter 5)? Is it consistent throughout?

11. The story presents its characters' bodies in an unusual way: How does it present them and why is this presentation effective in terms of the story's broader aims?

12. Appropriate to its subject matter, the story is gruesome and horrifying. Is there anything to balance its horrifying imagery? Is the shawl, in fact, that balancing force or does it ultimately become part of the horror?

### CONNECTION TO ANOTHER SELECTION

1. Compare human suffering in "The Shawl" and in Ursula K. Le Guin's "The Ones Who Walk Away from Omelas" (p. 121). Does the fact that one story is rooted in grim reality and the other in fantasy affect your comparison?

## A SAMPLE STUDENT RESPONSE

Aria Sergany

Professor Curtis

English 101

19 January 2023

Layers of Symbol in Cynthia Ozick's "The Shawl"

Although it is a profound and unsettling depiction of life in the barracks during the Holocaust, "The Shawl" never directly states the nature of the conflict, the surrounding events, or anything substantial about the characters. The story introduces Rosa and her two daughters: Magda, a baby wrapped in a shawl, and Stella, a fourteen-year-old who is "jealous of Magda" and the special treatment the shawl provides her (Ozick 185). The shawl immediately becomes representative of a one-sided conflict in the daughters' relationship: "Stella [is] not allowed" to even touch the shawl (186). The sparse information given about character, setting, and time period forces the reader to focus all of their attention on this symbol. The weight given to the shawl makes it a magical object to the reader, as it is for the family in the story. The careful unpacking of this symbol reveals a contradiction: the shawl is representative of not only what the reader expects it to be (like safety, life, and food), but also of the failure to speak out for people who have had these rights taken away. By so successfully utilizing the symbol of the shawl, Cynthia Ozick captures the core of the

Holocaust and the struggle of each individual in it through the story of one family and their personal tragedy. The shawl comes to represent not only comfort in life, but the phenomenon in which humanity looks the other way in times of tragedy and the cost of that silence.

The shawl, at first, seems an uncomplicated symbol to analyze. Ozick says outright that it is "a magic shawl, it [can] nourish an infant for three days and three nights" (186). Without the shawl "Stella [is] ravenous" the story repeats (185; 186). The imaginary world of the shawl works in contrast with the horrors of reality outside of it; "Stella want[s] to be wrapped in a shawl, hidden away, asleep, rocked by the march, a baby, a round infant in arms" (185). On this march where Rosa and Stella cannot attain simple means of survival, the physical object of the shawl comes to represent a much larger, metaphorical, magical meaning. Rosa considers giving Magda away because "[y]ou could think [Magda is] one of *their* babies" (185). Part of the magic is that the shawl makes one passably Aryan: the one thing they cannot be, and the only thing that could save them. This chance at survival, along with the façade of Magda's present health and safety, is what drives Stella's jealousy: when Stella says "'Aryan,' it sound[s] to Rosa as if Stella had really said 'Let us devour [Magda]'" (186). Rosa is driven by saving Magda, which leaves Stella to fend for herself. Stella makes a choice; she takes "the shawl away and [makes] Magda die" (186). It is easy to blame Stella for this choice, but Ozick reminds the reader that this family is "in a place without pity" (186).

Stella has lost her compassion for Magda. From the very start, Stella is "cold, cold, the coldness of hell" (185). Stella sees Magda living in relative bliss and not sharing any of it with her sister. Stella looks "into Magda's face through a gap in the shawl: a squirrel in a nest, safe, no one could reach her inside the little house of the shawl's windings" (185). When Stella takes the shawl, the symbol expands to include the tendency that humans have to be unwilling to help others when their own lives are comfortable, or because they are afraid of what will happen to them. This aspect of the symbol is what makes the story universal. People can relate to the fear or reality of being ignored in times of distress, as well as the desire not to get involved in what are considered other's problems. The shawl is not only representative of comfort, but of the psychological effect that having or not having that comfort can have on an individual. Stella, with no comfort of her own in a horrible situation, starts to look at Magda "like a young cannibal" (186). Rosa is sure that Stella is "waiting for Magda to die so she [can] put her teeth into the little thighs" (186). Stella's decision to take the shawl away from Magda only makes Stella even colder. After, Stella is "always cold, always. The cold went into her heart" (186). Rosa is old enough to understand the consequences of taking the shawl from Magda: Rosa sees "that Magda [is] grieving for the loss of her shawl, she [sees] that Magda [is] going to die" (187). Stella fails to comprehend that without the shawl Magda's fate is set. She does not realize this until it is too late.

Stella's ignorance allows her to become apathetic toward Magda. Apathy, in many ways, exacerbated the Holocaust. While the average person did not start the Holocaust, by doing and saying nothing to stop it they allowed it to continue. It is easy to choose the wellbeing of oneself over someone else, as in the case of Stella and Magda. However, there is another issue at play here: silence. No one in this story speaks out against the many atrocities that are happening: the exception being Magda's cries right at the end. In fact, there is little sound in the story at all. Stella says "I was cold" as her reasoning for taking the shawl (186). The sound of Magda's laughter: "Sometimes she laughed — it seemed a laugh, but how could it be? Magda had never seen anyone laugh" (186). But mostly, it is just Magda's silence; it is brought up over and over again. "Every day Magda was silent, and so she did not die" (187). "Magda was quiet" (186). "Magda had been devoid of any syllable: Magda was a mute" (187). Magda's silence when in the shawl is emphasized to dramatize her screams at the end. Without the comfort of the shawl, Magda's "mouth [is] spilling a long viscous rope of clamor"; she is pushed to speak out, to yell, and eventually to be seen by a guard and taken to her death (187). Fear keeps Rosa and Stella from speaking even without the shawl, but Magda is too young to have developed that fear. Magda still has a chance to speak out, and she briefly gets to have her voice heard.

Ozick uses symbol so effectively that the reader is pulled into the story and forced to live through the impossible choices that the characters have to make. Rosa makes a very difficult decision in the final moments of the story: she can either snatch up Magda and try to get her to safety although she will be noticed, or she can go get the shawl to quiet Magda. She chooses the shawl. Returning to Magda with the shawl, Rosa realizes it is already too late. Rosa hears "real sounds in the wire: grainy sad voices" coming from the electric fence (187). These voices represent the victims of the past and all of Rosa's personal history telling her that she needs to do something. To speak. To stop this from ever happening again. To act in Magda's memory despite that she would certainly die as well. "[T]he steel voices went mad in their growling, urging Rosa to run and run to the spot where Magda had fallen" (188). Rosa stays quiet in her fear; she shoves the shawl into her mouth to keep from screaming. With the loss of Magda (and the silence of her family in the face of her loss) the potential for change dies and the fear lives on. Then "Rosa [drinks] Magda's shawl until it drie[s]" in an attempt to mitigate her pain (188). The last bit of the shawl's magic is used up, and Rosa and Stella are left with nothing. Without the shawl and without Magda there is nothing to look forward to, there is no hope for any sort of future. There is not even anything for Stella to be jealous of anymore. In Stella's selfishness and Rosa's silence, they lose themselves to the war. The shawl now symbolizes what the constant fear and oppression can do to a person. In the same way the shawl shifts from seemingly comforting to horrifying, Stella shifts from her expected role as a loving sister to a selfish person able to commit indirect murder. Stella's heart turns cold like the rest of her, and the last of her humanity is lost. The shawl can give us a blissful life, but it is up to us to use that privilege to speak out for those who cannot speak for themselves.

## Work Cited

Ozick, Cynthia. "The Shawl." *The Compact Bedford Introduction to Literature*, edited by Michael Meyer and D. Quentin Miller, 13th ed., Bedford/ St. Martin's, 2024, pp. 185–88.

# 7

# Theme

GL Archive/Alamy.

Nothing ever really ends. That's the horrible part of being in the short-story business — you have to be a real expert on ends. Nothing in real life ends. "Millicent at last understands." Nobody ever understands.

— KURT VONNEGUT

**Theme** is the central idea or meaning of a story. It provides a unifying point around which the plot, characters, setting, point of view, symbols, and other elements of a story are organized. In some works the theme is explicitly stated. Nathaniel Hawthorne's "Wakefield," for example, begins with the author telling the reader that the point of his story is "done up neatly, and condensed into the final sentence." Most modern writers, however, present their themes implicitly (as Hawthorne does in the majority of his stories), so determining the underlying meaning of a work often requires more effort than it does from the reader of "Wakefield." One reason for the difficulty is that the theme is fused into the elements of the story, and these must be carefully examined in relation to one another as well as to the work as a whole. But then that's the value of determining the theme, for it requires a close analysis of all the elements of a work. Such a close reading often results in sharper insights into this overlooked character

193

or that seemingly unrelated incident. Accounting for the details and seeing how they fit together result in greater understanding of the story. Such familiarity creates pleasure in much the same way that a musical piece heard more than once becomes a rich experience rather than simply a repetitive one.

Themes are not always easy to express, but some principles can aid you in articulating the central meaning of a work. First distinguish between the theme of a story and its subject. They are not equivalents. Many stories share identical subjects, such as fate, death, innocence, youth, loneliness, racial prejudice, and disillusionment. T. C. Boyle's "The Hit Man" (p. 33) and John Updike's "A & P" (p. 145) both focus on the connection between the main character and his job. Yet each story usually makes its own statement about the subject and expresses a different view of life.

People have different responses to life, and so it is hardly surprising that responses to literature are not identical. When theme is considered, the possibilities for meaning are usually expanded and not reduced to categories such as "right" or "wrong." Although readers may differ in their interpretations of a story, that does not mean that *any* interpretation is valid. If we were to assert that the soldier's dissatisfactions in Ernest Hemingway's "Soldier's Home" (p. 115) could be readily eliminated by his settling down to marriage and a decent job (his mother's solution), we would have missed Hemingway's purposes in writing the story; we would have failed to see how Krebs's war experiences have caused him to reexamine the assumptions and beliefs that previously nurtured him but now seem unreal to him. We would have to ignore much in the story in order to arrive at such a reading. To be valid, the statement of the theme should be responsive to the details of the story. It must be based on evidence within the story rather than solely on experiences, attitudes, or values the reader brings to the work — such as personally knowing a war veteran who successfully adjusted to civilian life after getting a good job and marrying. Familiarity with the subject matter of a story can certainly be an aid to interpretation, but it should not get in the way of seeing the author's perspective.

Sometimes readers too hastily conclude that a story's theme always consists of a moral, some kind of lesson that is dramatized by the various elements of the work. There are stories that do this — Hawthorne's "Wakefield," for example. Here are the final sentences in his story about a middle-aged man who drops out of life for twenty years:

> He has left us much food for thought, a portion of which shall lend its wisdom to a moral, and be shaped into a figure. Amid the seeming confusion of our mysterious world, individuals are so nicely adjusted to a system, and systems to one another and to a whole, that, by stepping aside for a moment, a man exposes himself to a fearful risk of losing his place forever. Like Wakefield, he may become, as it were, the Outcast of the Universe.

Most stories, however, do not include such direct caveats about the conduct of life. A tendency to look for a lesson in a story can produce a reductive and inaccurate formulation of its theme. Consider the damage done to Ursula K. Le Guin's "The Ones Who Walk Away from Omelas" (p. 121) if its theme is described this way: "People who imprison and torment children are bad and should not be allowed to enjoy their lives if they do so." Note that even the title focuses not on the people of Omelas who sanction the suffering of a child, but rather on the ones who walk away from a society who would do that. We don't know much about those people — who they are, where they go, whether they live or die — but their reaction to the situation is significant in determining the story's theme. In fact, a good many stories go beyond traditional social values to explore human behavior instead of condemning or endorsing it.

Determining the theme of a story can be a difficult task because the theme isn't buried treasure hidden within a single element. Articulating the theme involves active interpretation and a keen understanding of how multiple elements work together. Indeed, you may discover that finding the theme is more challenging than coming to grips with the writer's values as they are revealed in the story. There is no precise formula that can take you to the center of a story's meaning and help you to articulate it. However, several strategies are practical and useful once you have read the story. Apply these pointers during a second or third reading:

1. Pay attention to the title of the story. It often provides a lead to a major symbol (Ernest Hemingway's "Soldier's Home," p. 115) or to the subject around which the theme develops (Alice Munro's "Silence," p. 376).

2. Look for details in the story that have potential for symbolic meanings. Careful consideration of names, places, objects, minor characters, and incidents can lead you to the central meaning — for example, think of the narrator's daughter Grace in Baldwin's "Sonny's Blues" (p. 91). Be especially attentive to elements you did not understand on the first reading.

3. Decide whether the protagonist changes or develops some important insight as a result of the action. Carefully examine any generalizations the protagonist or narrator makes about the events in the story.

4. When you formulate the theme of the story in your own words, write it down in one or two complete sentences that make some point about the subject matter. Revenge may be the subject of a story, but its theme should make a statement about revenge: "Instead of providing satisfaction, revenge often defeats the best in one's self" is one possibility.

5. Be certain that your expression of the theme is a generalized statement rather than a specific description of particular people, places, and incidents in the story. Contrast the preceding statement of a theme on revenge with this too-specific one: "In Nathaniel Hawthorne's *The Scarlet Letter*, Roger Chillingworth loses his humanity owing to his single-minded attempts to punish Arthur Dimmesdale for fathering a child with Chillingworth's wife, Hester." Hawthorne's theme is not restricted to a single fictional character named Chillingworth but to anyone whose life is ruined by revenge. Be certain that your statement of theme does not focus on only part of the story. The theme just cited for *The Scarlet Letter*, for example, relegates Hester to the status of a minor character. What it says about Chillingworth is true, but the statement is incomplete as a generalization about the novel.

6. Be wary of using clichés as a way of stating theme. They tend to short-circuit ideas instead of generating them. It may be tempting to resort to something like "the love of money is the root of all evil" as a statement of the theme of Ralph Ellison's story "King of the Bingo Game" (p. 178); however, even the shortest reflection reveals how much more nuanced and ambiguous that story is.

7. Be aware that some stories emphasize theme less than others. Stories that have as their major purpose adventure, humor, mystery, or terror may have little or no theme. In Edgar Allan Poe's "The Pit and the Pendulum," for example, the protagonist is not used to condemn torture; instead, he becomes a sensitive gauge to measure the pain and horror he endures at the hands of his captors.

What is most valuable about articulating the theme of a work is the process by which the theme is determined. Ultimately, the theme is expressed by the story itself and is inseparable from the experience of reading the story. Tim O'Brien's explanation of "How to Tell a True War Story" (p. 253) is probably true of most kinds of stories: "In a true war story, if there's a moral [or theme] at all, it's like the thread that makes the cloth. You can't tease it out. You can't extract the meaning without unraveling the deeper meaning." Describing the theme should not be a way to consume a story, to be done with it. It is a means of clarifying our thinking about what we've read and probably felt intuitively.

Adrian Tomine's "Intruders," Nathaniel Hawthorne's "The Minister's Black Veil," and Carmen Maria Machado's "Eight Bites" are three stories whose respective themes emerge from the authors' skillful use of plot, character, setting, and symbol.

## Adrian Tomine (b. 1974)

Born in California to Japanese American parents who spent part of their early years in Japanese American internment camps during World War II, Adrian Tomine has lived all over the world and currently calls New York City home. Along with writers like Art Spiegelman, Alison Bechdel, and Daniel Clowes, he has gained recognition for his innovative contributions to the expanding field of graphic narrative, also known as comics, comix, or (colloquially) cartoons. His illustrations have been featured in the *New Yorker*, and he is well-known for his comic book series *Optic Nerve*. Although the following story is illustrated, you can approach it the same way you would a traditional print story, paying attention to plot, character, and the other elements we discuss that lead to an articulation of theme. One key to enhance the experience is to consider how the author uses visual art to enhance the words on the page: how do the images you see complement the words that accompany them?

Neville Elder/Getty Images.

## Intruders    2015

BETWEEN MY SECOND AND THIRD TOURS, I CAME BACK TO A BUNCH OF BULLSHIT AND NOT MUCH ELSE.

I HAD A COUSIN WHO LET ME CRASH IN HER BASEMENT. SHE WAS MARRIED WITH THREE KIDS.

ONE NIGHT I HEARD THEM ALL TALKING ABOUT ME THROUGH THE CEILING, AND SOME OF THE THINGS THEY SAID JUST ABOUT KILLED ME.

I ENDED UP AT A PLACE CALLED EXTENDED STAY AMERICA, OUT BY THE CAR DEALERSHIPS AND STRIP MALLS.

RIGHT ACROSS THE FREEWAY WAS AN IN-N-OUT, A KRISPY KREME, AND A PANDA EXPRESS.

I FIGURED WORSE CAME TO WORSE, I COULD ALWAYS EAT MYSELF TO DEATH AND THE AUTOPSY WOULD STILL COME BACK CLEAN.

ONE OF THOSE PLACES, THAT'S WHERE I RAN INTO THE GIRL, WHATEVER HER NAME WAS.

OH MY GOD!

I BLUFFED MY WAY THROUGH ABOUT TEN MINUTES OF SMALL TALK BEFORE IT FINALLY CLICKED.

I WAS TOTALLY JUST THINKING ABOUT YOU GUYS!

SHE WAS SOMEONE'S KID OR NIECE OR SOMETHING. SHE HOUSESAT FOR ME AND MARIA THAT TIME WE WENT TO CATALINA.

I WAS CLEANING OUT MY CAR, AND GUESS WHAT I FOUND!

I DIDN'T LIKE THE IDEA OF SOMEONE STAYING THERE, BUT MARIA HAD A THING ABOUT LEAVING THE APARTMENT EMPTY.

COME ON! I'M RIGHT OUTSIDE!

I WAS SUPPOSED TO GO PICK UP THE KEYS FROM THE GIRL WHEN WE GOT BACK, BUT I KEPT PUTTING IT OFF.

SO HOW IS MARIA?

GREAT! YEAH...

THEN SHE OFFERED TO DROP THEM BY SOMETIME, AND THEN MARIA WAS GONNA GET THEM, BUT EVENTUALLY WE ALL JUST FORGOT ABOUT IT.

I JUST THINK THIS IS SO CRAZY, RUNNING INTO YOU HERE!

THEY WERE JUST COPIES, ANYWAY, MADE AT THE HARDWARE STORE FOR A BUCK A PIECE.

AMA-A-A-A-ZING!

TNK TNK

STANDING THERE IN THE PARKING LOT, I SHOULD'VE JUST BACKTRACKED AND EXPLAINED EVERYTHING, BUT THE RIGHT MOMENT NEVER CAME.

HA HA... FUCKIN' UNBELIEVABLE!

I GUESS I GOT SWEPT UP IN HER EXCITEMENT AND DIDN'T WANT TO MAKE THINGS AWKWARD.

OH!

I'M ACTUALLY SUPPOSED TO BE MEETING UP WITH MY BOYFRIEND, SO...

YEAH, I WASN'T--

NO, I JUST MEANT--

YOU DIDN'T HAVE TO SAY THAT.

BACK AT THE HOTEL, I STARED AT THE KEYS FOR AWHILE, THREW THEM IN THE TRASH, AND WENT TO SLEEP.

NEXT MORNING, I WOKE UP, DUG THE KEYS OUT OF THE TRASH, AND CAUGHT A BUS INTO TOWN.

THE CAFE ACROSS FROM OUR APARTMENT DIDN'T SELL COFFEE ANYMORE, THANKS TO THE NEW PEET'S UP THE BLOCK.

NOW THEY SPECIALIZED IN CREPES, SMOOTHIES, AND SOME SHIT CALLED BUBBLE TEA.

I WAS DYING FOR A COFFEE, BUT THE TRUTH IS, I WAS JUST THERE FOR THE VIEW.

IT WAS DEPRESSING TO SEE EVERYONE TRAPPED ON THE SAME HAMSTER WHEEL. GO TO WORK, COME HOME, REPEAT.

I TRACKED THE GUY IN OUR OLD PLACE FOR A WEEK, AND THE ONLY THING THAT CHANGED WAS THE COLOR OF HIS SUIT.

NO ONE REALLY GIVES A SHIT ABOUT RENTERS, BUT A DECENT LANDLORD WILL RE-KEY THE LOCKS AS A BASIC SECURITY MEASURE WHEN A PLACE TURNS OVER.

THE OLD CHINESE GUY WOULD'VE DONE IT. EVERYTHING WENT DOWNHILL WHEN HE CROAKED AND HIS SCUMBAG KIDS TOOK OVER.

WE HAD TO MAIL OUR KEYS TO THE DAUGHTER TO GET OUR DEPOSIT BACK WHEN WE LEFT, BUT SO WHAT?

IT SMELLED DIFFER-
ENT. THAT'S WHAT I
NOTICED BEFORE
ANYTHING ELSE.

ONCE I MADE SURE
THE PLACE WAS
EMPTY, I OPENED A
FEW WINDOWS TO
AIR IT OUT.

EVERYTHING WAS UP-
GRADED, REPAIRED,
RE-DONE. MARIA
WOULD'VE LOVED IT.

THINGS THAT WE
LEARNED TO LIVE
WITH, LIKE THE
PEELING PAINT IN
THE BATHROOM AND
THE BROKEN LIGHT
IN THE FRIDGE, HAD
ALL BEEN TAKEN
CARE OF.

BUT THERE WAS
ENOUGH THAT HADN'T
CHANGED: SAME FIX-
TURES, SAME APPLI-
ANCES, SAME SHIT-
BROWN CARPET IN
THE BEDROOM.

I FOUND THE HOLE
IN THE WALL THAT
I'D PUNCHED AND
THEN PUTTIED OVER.
THE BATHROOM
SHELF I PUT UP WAS
STILL THERE.

THE GUY EVEN KEPT
THE COBWEBBY
PIECE OF 2X4 I
USED TO PROP THE
KITCHEN WINDOW
OPEN.

I COULD'VE SNOOPED
AROUND, TURNED ON
THE COMPUTER,
RIFLED THROUGH
THE DRAWERS, BUT
THAT'S A LINE I
WOULDN'T CROSS.

THERE'S A MILLION
THINGS I COULD'VE
DONE, BUT I'D SATIS-
FIED MY CURIOSITY
AND THAT WAS THAT.

I COULDN'T SLEEP THAT NIGHT, AND THE SAME STUPID THOUGHT KEPT RATTLING AROUND IN MY HEAD: THAT THE GUY WOULD COME HOME AND NOTICE THE MISSING EGG.

OF COURSE THE PROBABILITY OF THAT WAS SLIM, AND PLUS, WHAT WAS HE GONNA DO? CALL THE COPS TO REPORT IT?

BUT I'D BEEN CARELESS AND IT NAGGED AT ME. I COULDN'T DO ANYTHING ABOUT IT UNTIL MORNING, AND THAT MADE IT EVEN WORSE.

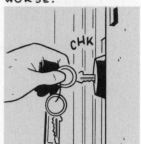

THE KID AT SAFEWAY WOULDN'T JUST SELL ME AN EGG, SO I BOUGHT A DOZEN.

I PUT ONE IN MY POCKET, TOSSED THE REST, AND -- WHEN THE COAST WAS CLEAR-- WENT BACK TO THE APARTMENT.

IT FELT GOOD TO SOLVE A PROBLEM, TO MAKE SOMETHING RIGHT, NO MATTER HOW SMALL.

AFTER THAT, I GUESS I FELL INTO A ROUTINE JUST LIKE EVERYONE ELSE.

THE GUY AT THE BUBBLE TEA PLACE STARTED MAKING COFFEE AGAIN, JUST FOR ME.

SOME DAYS I'D BRING A LUNCH WITH ME, ALWAYS MAKING SURE TO CLEAN UP AND REMOVE ANY TRASH.

I SET THE ALARM ON MY WATCH TO AVOID ANY OVERLAP.

I SKETCHED A FLOOR-PLAN AND WORKED OUT SOME EXIT STRATEGIES, JUST IN CASE.

BUT FOR THE MOST PART, IT'S HARD TO SAY HOW I PASSED THOSE HOURS, TO BE HONEST.

THAT ONE DAY, I'D ACTUALLY FALLEN ASLEEP WHEN IT ALL STARTED.

I ALMOST ANSWERED THE DOOR OUT OF HABIT.

IT WAS A KID, PROB-ABLY HIGH SCHOOL AGE. I FIGURED HE WAS LOOKING FOR A DONATION OR A SIGNATURE ON A PETITION.

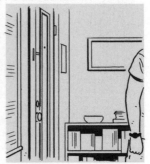

HE RANG THE DOOR-BELL A FEW TIMES, THEN KNOCKED AGAIN BEFORE GIVING UP.

A FEW MINUTES LATER, I HEARD THE SCREEN FROM THE BATHROOM WINDOW CLATTERING INTO THE BATHTUB.

BY THE TIME I GOT THERE, THE KID WAS HALFWAY THROUGH THE WINDOW.

I REACTED ON PURE INSTINCT, LIKE IT WAS STILL MY HOME TO PROTECT.

IT FELT LIKE THE POWER COMING BACK ON AFTER A BLACKOUT.

I WAS A HUNDRED PERCENT IN THE RIGHT. WHATEVER HAPPENED, THE KID HAD IT COMING.

HE WAS SLOPPY AND SCARED, BUT HE MANAGED TO THINK ON HIS FEET.

IT WAS A GIFT-- LIKE HE'D JUST GIVEN ME PERMISSION TO TURN IT UP A NOTCH.

STILL, I HELD BACK. THE LAST THING I NEEDED WAS AN AMBULANCE SHOWING UP THERE.

THE KID HAD ME OVER A BARREL AND HE DIDN'T EVEN KNOW IT.

HE TRIED TO MAKE A BREAK FOR THE WINDOW, BUT BY THAT POINT HE WAS STRUGGLING.

I WALKED DOWN THE HALL AND OPENED THE BACK DOOR. COOL AIR BLEW IN FROM THE ALLEY.

GO AHEAD.

I DON'T KNOW WHAT I WAS EXPECTING, EXACTLY. DID HE UNDERSTAND HOW LUCKY HE WAS?

FUCK YOU, BITCH!

AFTER THAT IT WAS A RACE AGAINST THE CLOCK TO GET EVERYTHING BACK IN ORDER.

KLAK

IT TOOK LONGER THAN I EXPECTED, AND ALL I WANTED TO DO WAS GET OUT.

I WAS JUST ABOUT DONE WHEN I REALIZED I'D DEPLETED THE GUY'S CLEANING SUPPLIES.

IT WAS A LONG AFTERNOON.

BEEP
BEEP
BEEP

THE LAST DAY, I WAS LATER THAN USUAL.

I CAN'T REMEMBER HOW IT STARTED, BUT I GOT INTO A LITTLE SQUABBLE WITH THE GUY AT THE CAFE.

NO, NO, SIR... I AM BEING FRIENDLY!

HE MADE A COMMENT-- A LITTLE PASSIVE-AGRESSIVE DIG-- AND AFTER ALL THE MONEY I'D PUT IN HIS COFFERS, IT BOTHERED ME.

MOST BUSINESSES **VALUE** A REGULAR CUSTOMER.

THE LIGHTS WERE ON IN THE APARTMENT WHEN I GOT THERE. THAT SHOULD'VE TIPPED ME OFF.

AS I MOVED TOWARD THE KITCHEN, I HEARD A SERIES OF SOUNDS: A THUD, SOMETHING CLATTERING ACROSS THE FLOOR, A MOAN.

SHE MUST'VE BEEN AT LEAST EIGHTY, MAYBE OLDER. WAS SHE THE GUY'S MOTHER? HIS GRANDMOTHER?

SHE STARTED SCREAMING IN SOME LANGUAGE I DIDN'T KNOW, AND SHE WOULDN'T STOP.

I TRIED TO HELP HER UP AND MAKE SURE SHE WASN'T HURT, BUT SHE KICKED AND SPAT AT ME AND SHRIEKED EVEN LOUDER.

I WANTED TO APOLOGIZE AND EXPLAIN EVERYTHING, BUT MOST OF ALL I WANTED TO DISAPPEAR.

KRAK

I LOCKED THE DOOR BEHIND ME WHEN I LEFT. I LISTENED FOR SIRENS, ALMOST HOPING THAT I'D HEAR THEM.

I WALKED UP THE BLOCK, INTO THE STREAM OF OBLIVIOUS, HAPPY PEOPLE WITH THEIR FAMILIES, THEIR SHOPPING, THEIR CHATTER.

TNK

AND STARTING RIGHT THERE, I TRIED MY BEST TO BECOME ONE OF THEM.

## CONSIDERATIONS FOR CRITICAL THINKING AND WRITING

1. FIRST RESPONSE. What significant adjustments did you have to make as a reader in order to approach this work as a piece of literature? Did you find the experience easier or harder? Less or more enjoyable? Why?

2. Point to three specific panels where your opinion of the narrator changes, even slightly. What is your final response to him? What complicates it?

3. Even though the narrator is telling his own story, we often see him rather than see what he's seeing. What is the effect of this movement between the inside and the outside of a protagonist? How is this kind of point of view unique to graphic narratives?

4. Keys and key cards are recurrent images in this story. What might they symbolize?

5. What do we know about the narrator's past? How much does it explain his somewhat unpredictable present actions?

6. After returning the egg to the apartment the narrator muses, "It felt good to solve a problem, to make something right, no matter how small." How does this observation help to contextualize the narrator's actions?

7. What is the relationship between public and private spaces in this story?

8. How do you interpret the title, particularly the fact that it's plural?

9. Why does the narrator resist the lifestyle of most other people he sees? What is his view of routine?

10. The narrator clearly has some mental health issues, especially when it comes to controlling his rage. Does he have any positive qualities or resources that might be harnessed to address them? What would have to happen to facilitate that change?

11. To the best of your ability, state the story's theme.


## CONNECTIONS TO OTHER SELECTIONS

1. The first panel indicates that the narrator is in the military. Compare this story to Tim O'Brien's "How to Tell a True War Story" (p. 253). Does this story also address the trauma of someone who has been trained for combat?

2. Ernest Hemingway's "Soldier's Home" (p. 115) is, like "Intruders," about an uncomfortable return to one's home after serving in the military. Are the protagonists of the two stories affected in the same way? To the same degree?

# A SAMPLE STUDENT RESPONSE

Kimberly Pike

Professor Verrelli

English 102

February 2023

Danger among Us: Distilling the Theme in "Intruders"

The fear of danger lurking among us, blended and hidden in society at large, is a major cultural fear that has influenced American culture for decades. Historically, we can trace this anxiety through such periods as in the McCarthy era, the Salem Witch Trials, and so on. This worry pervades in a culture that is fixated on concerns about illegal immigration and potential terrorist attacks. Adrian Tomine synthesizes this central theme of fear and presents it at the micro level in his short comic *Intruders*. In the story, the apartment is symbolic of society at large, Tomine's main character represents the presence of danger lurking within, and the tenant is a stand-in for unknowing civilians.

Established in the first page of panels is the main character of this story: a man who is, at the start of this narrative, already ostracized from normative society. He has been put out because of the sour relations with his family and is currently subject to unstable living conditions, staying for an extended period at a hotel (panel 4). Given general disdain society has for those experiencing homelessness, readers are primed to view the protagonist as an outcast. Tomine's artwork even highlights his menace: frequently, readers see him from behind (panels 4, 6, 18, 20, 24), and shadowed (2, 4, 6, 18). When he is in frame with other figures, readers see how he towers over them (15-17). However, this view is complicated by the main characters' veteran status (1). Soldiers, after all, are traditionally seen as individuals who serve their country; as protectors and defenders of their nations. Instead, the protector is subverted into the threat. This subversion amplifies the theme of danger lurking within, highlighting the reality that threats can come from anywhere and anyone, even those we would normally deem to be safe. As readers, we follow the Intruder as he gains a set of keys to his old apartment and begins an unsettling journey. He finds that a new tenant has taken up residence; from the café across the street, our main character watches the man, learning his routines so that he can enter the house and emulate living in it himself. When inside, he cooks for himself, hangs out in the living room, and washes dishes (30-35). These actions of almost "playing house" while in a stranger's home are eerie, a deep and conscious invasion of privacy. In a matter of pages, the unnamed veteran has acquired new labels — he is a voyeur, an intruder, a criminal, which only the readers are able to see.

Tomine doubles this voyeurism, inviting readers to violate the Intruder's privacy in the same way he does the apartment's tenant. Stepped back viewpoints throughout (such as panels 6, 7, 11, 12, 18, 19, 24, 37, 43, and more) place the reader in a state of surveillance, watching the Intruder from a distance. Truly, danger lurks everywhere — anyone can be a threat, even readers. The consequences of this microcosm of danger can be seen in its larger implications at the very end of the comic. The last panel (panel 81) shows the Intruder slipping into a crowd. Above this panel and the one before it are captions that read: "I walked up the block, into the stream of oblivious, happy people with their families, their shopping, their chatter. And starting right there, I tried my best to become one of them" (80-81). This off-putting combination of text and image forms the viewers' impression that the danger represented by the main character has escaped the confines of his activities and is now free to impact more of the population than just the tenant. He reverts back to a faceless member of the crowd — a crowd that, given the viewpoint, readers are a part of. As a result, Tomine leaves readers with the disturbing knowledge that danger lurks among and within us, ever-present, and we are helpless to sniff it out.

## Work Cited

Tomine, Adrian. "Intruders." *The Compact Bedford Introduction to Literature*, edited by Michael Meyer and D. Quentin Miller, 13th ed., Bedford/ St. Martin's, 2024, pp. 197–205.

## NATHANIEL HAWTHORNE (1804–1864)

Nathaniel Hawthorne is widely considered one of the most important and influential American writers of the period known as the American Renaissance of the mid-nineteenth century along with Ralph Waldo Emerson, Henry David Thoreau, Herman Melville, Emily Dickinson, and Walt Whitman. His 1850 novel *The Scarlet Letter*, set in the early years of Puritan New England, is one of the most celebrated works of that

Universal Art Archive/Alamy.

period. He wrote about individuals who suffer from inner conflicts caused by sin, pride, untested innocence, hidden guilt, perverse secrecy, cold intellectuality, and isolation. His characters are often consumed by their own passions, whether those passions are motivated by an obsession with goodness or evil.

## *The Minister's Black Veil*    1836

### A Parable[1]

The sexton stood in the porch of Milford meeting-house, pulling lustily at the bell-rope. The old people of the village came stooping along the street. Children, with bright faces, tript merrily beside their parents, or mimicked a graver gait, in the conscious dignity of their Sunday clothes. Spruce bachelors looked sidelong at the pretty maidens, and fancied that the Sabbath sunshine made them prettier than on weekdays. When the throng had mostly streamed into the porch, the sexton began to toll the bell, keeping his eye on the Reverend Mr. Hooper's door. The first glimpse of the clergyman's figure was the signal for the bell to cease its summons.

"But what has good Parson Hooper got upon his face?" cried the sexton in astonishment.

All within hearing immediately turned about, and beheld the semblance of Mr. Hooper, pacing slowly his meditative way towards the meeting-house. With one accord they started, expressing more wonder than if some strange minister were coming to dust the cushions of Mr. Hooper's pulpit.

"Are you sure it is our parson?" inquired Goodman Gray of the sexton.

"Of a certainty it is good Mr. Hooper," replied the sexton. "He was to have 5 exchanged pulpits with Parson Shute of Westbury; but Parson Shute sent to excuse himself yesterday, being to preach a funeral sermon."

The cause of so much amazement may appear sufficiently slight. Mr. Hooper, a gentlemanly person of about thirty, though still a bachelor, was dressed with due

---

[1] Another clergyman in New England, Mr. Joseph Moody, of York, Maine, who died about eighty years since, made himself remarkable by the same eccentricity that is here related of the Reverend Mr. Hooper. In his case, however, the symbol had a different import. In early life he had accidentally killed a beloved friend; and from that day till the hour of his own death, he hid his face from men. [Author's note.]

clerical neatness, as if a careful wife had starched his band, and brushed the weekly dust from his Sunday's garb. There was but one thing remarkable in his appearance. Swathed about his forehead, and hanging down over his face, so low as to be shaken by his breath, Mr. Hooper had on a black veil. On a nearer view, it seemed to consist of two folds of crape, which entirely concealed his features, except the mouth and chin, but probably did not intercept his sight, farther than to give a darkened aspect to all living and inanimate things. With this gloomy shade before him, good Mr. Hooper walked onward, at a slow and quiet pace, stooping somewhat and looking on the ground, as is customary with abstracted men, yet nodding kindly to those of his parishioners who still waited on the meeting-house steps. But so wonder-struck were they, that his greeting hardly met with a return.

"I can't really feel as if good Mr. Hooper's face was behind that piece of crape," said the sexton.

"I don't like it," muttered an old woman, as she hobbled into the meeting-house. "He has changed himself into something awful, only by hiding his face."

"Our parson has gone mad!" cried Goodman Gray, following him across the threshold.

A rumor of some unaccountable phenomenon had preceded Mr. Hooper  10 into the meeting-house, and set all the congregation astir. Few could refrain from twisting their heads towards the door; many stood upright, and turned directly about; while several little boys clambered upon the seats, and came down again with a terrible racket. There was a general bustle, a rustling of the women's gowns and shuffling of the men's feet, greatly at variance with that hushed repose which should attend the entrance of the minister. But Mr. Hooper appeared not to notice the perturbation of his people. He entered with an almost noiseless step, bent his head mildly to the pews on each side, and bowed as he passed his oldest parishioner, a white-haired great-grandsire, who occupied an arm-chair in the center of the aisle. It was strange to observe, how slowly this venerable man became conscious of something singular in the appearance of his pastor. He seemed not fully to partake of the prevailing wonder, till Mr. Hooper had ascended the stairs, and showed himself in the pulpit, face to face with his congregation, except for the black veil. That mysterious emblem was never once withdrawn. It shook with his measured breath as he gave out the psalm; it threw its obscurity between him and the holy page, as he read the Scriptures; and while he prayed, the veil lay heavily on his uplifted countenance. Did he seek to hide it from the dread Being whom he was addressing?

Such was the effect of this simple piece of crape, that more than one woman of delicate nerves was forced to leave the meeting-house. Yet perhaps the pale-faced congregation was almost as fearful a sight to the minister, as his black veil to them.

Mr. Hooper had the reputation of a good preacher, but not an energetic one: he strove to win his people heavenward, by mild persuasive influences, rather than to drive them thither, by the thunders of the Word. The sermon which he now delivered, was marked by the same characteristics of style and manner, as the general series of his pulpit oratory. But there was something, either in the sentiment of the discourse itself, or in the imagination of the auditors, which made it greatly the most powerful effort that they had ever heard from their pastor's lips. It was tinged, rather more darkly than usual, with the gentle gloom of Mr. Hooper's temperament. The subject had reference to secret sin, and those sad mysteries which we hide from our nearest and dearest, and would fain conceal from our own consciousness, even forgetting that the Omniscient can detect them. A subtle power was breathed into his words. Each member of the congregation, the most innocent girl, and the man of hardened breast, felt as if the preacher had crept upon them, behind his awful veil, and discovered their hoarded iniquity of deed or thought. Many spread their clasped hands on their bosoms. There was nothing terrible in what Mr. Hooper said; at least, no violence; and yet, with every tremor of his melancholy voice, the hearers quaked. An unsought pathos came hand in hand with awe. So sensible were the audience of some unwonted attribute in their minister, that they longed for a breath of wind to blow aside the veil, almost believing that a stranger's visage would be discovered, though the form, gesture, and voice were those of Mr. Hooper.

At the close of the services, the people hurried out with indecorous confusion, eager to communicate their pent-up amazement, and conscious of lighter spirits, the moment they lost sight of the black veil. Some gathered in little circles, huddled closely together, with their mouths all whispering in the center; some went homeward alone, wrapt in silent meditation; some talked loudly, and profaned the Sabbath-day with ostentatious laughter. A few shook their sagacious heads, intimating that they could penetrate the mystery; while one or two affirmed that there was no mystery at all, but only that Mr. Hooper's eyes were so weakened by the midnight lamp, as to require a shade. After a brief interval, forth came good Mr. Hooper also, in the rear of his flock. Turning his veiled face from one group to another, he paid due reverence to the hoary heads, saluted the middle-aged with kind dignity, as their friend and spiritual guide, greeted the young with mingled authority and love, and laid his hands on the little children's heads to bless them. Such was always his custom on the Sabbath-day. Strange and bewildered looks repaid him for his courtesy. None, as on former occasions, aspired to the honor of walking by their pastor's side. Old Squire Saunders, doubtless by an accidental lapse of memory, neglected to invite Mr. Hooper to his table, where the good clergyman had been wont to bless the food, almost every Sunday since his settlement. He returned, therefore, to the parsonage, and, at the moment of closing the door, was observed to look back upon the people, all of whom had their eyes fixed upon the minister. A sad smile gleamed faintly from beneath the black veil, and flickered about his mouth, glimmering as he disappeared.

"How strange," said a lady, "that a simple black veil, such as any woman might wear on her bonnet, should become such a terrible thing on Mr. Hooper's face!"

"Something must surely be amiss with Mr. Hooper's intellects," observed 15 her husband, the physician of the village. "But the strangest part of the affair is the effect of this vagary, even on a sober-minded man like myself. The black veil, though it covers only our pastor's face, throws its influence over his whole person, and makes him ghost-like from head to foot. Do you not feel it so?"

"Truly do I," replied the lady; "and I would not be alone with him for the world. I wonder he is not afraid to be alone with himself!"

"Men sometimes are so," said her husband.

That afternoon service was attended with similar circumstances. At its conclusion, the bell tolled for the funeral of a young lady. The relatives and friends were assembled in the house, and the more distant acquaintances stood about the door, speaking of the good qualities of the deceased, when their talk was interrupted by the appearance of Mr. Hooper, still covered with his black veil. It was now an appropriate emblem. The clergyman stepped into the room where the corpse was laid, and bent over the coffin, to take a last farewell of his deceased parishioner. As he stooped, the veil hung straight down from his forehead, so that, if her eye-lids had not been closed for ever, the dead maiden might have seen his face. Could Mr. Hooper be fearful of her glance, that he so hastily caught back the black veil? A person, who watched the interview between the dead and living, scrupled not to affirm, that, at the instant when the clergyman's features were disclosed, the corpse had slightly shuddered, rustling the shroud and muslin cap, though the countenance retained the composure of death. A superstitious old woman was the only witness of this prodigy. From the coffin, Mr. Hooper passed into the chamber of the mourners, and thence to the head of the staircase, to make the funeral prayer. It was a tender and heart-dissolving prayer, full of sorrow, yet so imbued with celestial hopes, that the music of a heavenly harp, swept by the fingers of the dead, seemed faintly to be heard among the saddest accents of the minister. The people trembled, though they but darkly understood him, when he prayed that they, and himself, and all of mortal race, might be ready, as he trusted this young maiden had been, for the dreadful hour that should snatch the veil from their faces. The bearers went heavily forth, and the mourners followed, saddening all the street, with the dead before them, and Mr. Hooper in his black veil behind.

"Why do you look back?" said one in the procession to his partner.

"I had a fancy," replied she, "that the minister and the maiden's spirit were 20 walking hand in hand."

"And so had I, at the same moment," said the other.

That night, the handsomest couple in Milford village were to be joined in wedlock. Though reckoned a melancholy man, Mr. Hooper had a placid cheerfulness for such occasions, which often excited a sympathetic smile, where livelier merriment would have been thrown away. There was no quality of his disposition which made him more beloved than this. The company at the wedding awaited his arrival with impatience, trusting that the strange awe, which had gathered over him throughout the day, would now be dispelled. But such was not the result. When Mr. Hooper came, the first thing that their eyes rested on was the same horrible black veil, which had added deeper gloom to the funeral, and could portend nothing but evil to the wedding. Such was its immediate effect on the guests, that a cloud seemed to have rolled duskily from beneath the black crape, and dimmed the light of the candles. The bridal pair stood up before the minister. But the bride's cold fingers quivered in the tremulous hand of the bridegroom, and her death-like paleness caused a whisper, that the maiden who had been buried a few hours before, was come from her grave to be married. If ever another wedding were so dismal, it was that famous one, where they tolled the wedding-knell. After performing the ceremony, Mr. Hooper raised a glass of wine to his lips, wishing happiness to the new-married couple, in a strain of mild pleasantry that ought to have brightened the features of the guests, like a cheerful gleam from the hearth. At that instant, catching a glimpse of his figure in the looking-glass, the black veil involved his own spirit in the horror with which it overwhelmed all others. His frame shuddered — his lips grew white — he spilt the untasted wine upon the carpet — and rushed forth into the darkness. For the Earth, too, had on her Black Veil.

The next day, the whole village of Milford talked of little else than Parson Hooper's black veil. That, and the mystery concealed behind it, supplied a topic for discussion between acquaintances meeting in the street, and good women gossiping at their open windows. It was the first item of news that the tavernkeeper told to his guests. The children babbled of it on their way to school. One imitative little imp covered his face with an old black handkerchief, thereby so affrighting his playmates, that the panic seized himself, and he well nigh lost his wits by his own waggery.

It was remarkable, that, of all the busy-bodies and impertinent people in the parish, not one ventured to put the plain question to Mr. Hooper, wherefore he did this thing. Hitherto, whenever there appeared the slightest call for such interference, he had never lacked advisers, nor shown himself averse to be guided by their judgment. If he erred at all, it was by so painful a degree of self-distrust, that even the mildest censure would lead him to consider an indifferent action as a crime. Yet, though so well acquainted with this amiable weakness, no individual among his parishioners chose to make the black veil a subject of friendly remonstrance. There was a feeling of dread, neither plainly confessed nor carefully concealed, which caused each to shift the responsibility upon another, till at length it was found expedient to send a deputation of the church, in order to deal with Mr. Hooper about the mystery, before it should grow into a scandal. Never did an embassy so ill discharge its duties. The minister received them with friendly courtesy, but became silent, after they were seated, leaving to his visitors the whole burthen of introducing their important business. The topic, it might be supposed, was obvious enough. There was the black veil, swathed round Mr. Hooper's forehead, and concealing every feature above his placid mouth, on which, at times, they could perceive the glimmering of a melancholy smile. But that piece of crape, to their imagination, seemed to hang down before his heart, the symbol of a fearful secret between him and them. Were the veil but cast aside, they might speak freely of it, but not till then. Thus they sat a considerable time, speechless, confused, and shrinking uneasily from Mr. Hooper's eye, which they felt to be fixed upon them with an invisible glance. Finally, the deputies returned abashed to their constituents, pronouncing the matter too weighty to be handled, except by a council of the churches, if, indeed, it might not require a general synod.

But there was one person in the village, unappalled by the awe with which the 25 black veil had impressed all beside herself. When the deputies returned without an explanation, or even venturing to demand one, she, with the calm energy of her character, determined to chase away the strange cloud that appeared to be settling round Mr. Hooper, every moment more darkly than before. As his plighted wife, it should be her privilege to know what the black veil concealed. At the minister's first visit, therefore, she entered upon the subject, with a direct simplicity, which made the task easier both for him and her. After he had seated himself, she fixed her eyes steadfastly upon the veil, but could discern nothing of the dreadful gloom that had so overawed the multitude: it was but a double fold of crape, hanging down from his forehead to his mouth, and slightly stirring with his breath.

"No," said she aloud, and smiling, "there is nothing terrible in this piece of crape, except that it hides a face which I am always glad to look upon. Come, good sir, let the sun shine from behind the cloud. First lay aside your black veil: then tell me why you put it on."

Mr. Hooper's smile glimmered faintly.

"There is an hour to come," said he, "when all of us shall cast aside our veils. Take it not amiss, beloved friend, if I wear this piece of crape till then."

"Your words are a mystery too," returned the young lady. "Take away the veil for them, at least."

"Elizabeth, I will," said he, "so far as my vow may suffer me. Know, then, this 30 veil is a type and a symbol, and I am bound to wear it ever, both in light and darkness, in solitude and before the gaze of multitudes, and as with strangers, so with my familiar friends. No mortal eye will see it withdrawn. This dismal shade must separate me from the world: even you, Elizabeth, can never come behind it!"

"What grievous affliction hath befallen you," she earnestly inquired, "that you should thus darken your eyes for ever?"

"If it be a sign of mourning," replied Mr. Hooper, "I, perhaps, like most other mortals, have sorrows dark enough to be typified by a black veil."

"But what if the world will not believe that it is the type of an innocent sorrow?" urged Elizabeth. "Beloved and respected as you are, there may be whispers, that you hide your face under the consciousness of secret sin. For the sake of your holy office, do away this scandal!"

The color rose into her cheeks, as she intimated the nature of the rumors that were already abroad in the village. But Mr. Hooper's mildness did not forsake him. He even smiled again — that same sad smile, which always appeared like a faint glimmering of light, proceeding from the obscurity beneath the veil.

"If I hide my face for sorrow, there is cause enough," he merely replied; "and if 35 I cover it for secret sin, what mortal might not do the same?"

And with this gentle, but unconquerable obstinacy, did he resist all her entreaties. At length Elizabeth sat silent. For a few moments she appeared lost in thought, considering, probably, what new methods might be tried, to withdraw her lover from so dark a fantasy, which, if it had no other meaning, was perhaps a symptom of mental disease. Though of a firmer character than his own, the tears rolled down her cheeks. But, in an instant, as it were, a new feeling took the place of sorrow: her eyes were fixed insensibly on the black veil, when, like a sudden twilight in the air, its terrors fell around her. She arose, and stood trembling before him.

"And do you feel it then at last?" said he mournfully.

She made no reply, but covered her eyes with her hand, and turned to leave the room. He rushed forward and caught her arm.

"Have patience with me, Elizabeth!" cried he passionately. "Do not desert me, though this veil must be between us here on earth. Be mine, and hereafter there shall be no veil over my face, no darkness between our souls! It is but a mortal veil — it is not for eternity! Oh! you know not how lonely I am, and how frightened to be alone behind my black veil. Do not leave me in this miserable obscurity for ever!"

"Lift the veil but once, and look me in the face," said she.                    40

"Never! It cannot be!" replied Mr. Hooper.

"Then, farewell!" said Elizabeth.

She withdrew her arm from his grasp, and slowly departed, pausing at the door, to give one long, shuddering gaze, that seemed almost to penetrate the mystery of the black veil. But, even amid his grief, Mr. Hooper smiled to think that only a material emblem had separated him from happiness, though the horrors which it shadowed forth, must be drawn darkly between the fondest of lovers.

From that time no attempts were made to remove Mr. Hooper's black veil, or, by a direct appeal, to discover the secret which it was supposed to hide. By persons who claimed a superiority to popular prejudice, it was reckoned merely an eccentric whim, such as often mingles with the sober actions of men otherwise rational, and tinges them all with its own semblance of insanity. But with the multitude, good Mr. Hooper was irreparably a bugbear. He could not walk the streets with any peace of mind, so conscious was he that the gentle and timid would turn aside to avoid him, and that others would make it a point of hardihood to throw themselves in his way. The impertinence of the latter class compelled him to give up his customary walk, at sunset, to the burial ground, for when he leaned pensively over the gate, there would always be faces behind the grave-stones, peeping at his black veil. A fable went the rounds that the stare of the dead people drove him thence. It grieved him, to the very depth of his kind heart, to observe how the children fled from his approach, breaking up their merriest sports, while his melancholy figure was yet afar off. Their instinctive dread caused him to feel, more strongly than aught else, that a preternatural horror was interwoven with the threads of the black crape. In truth, his own antipathy to the veil was known to be so great, that he never willingly passed before a mirror, nor stooped to drink at a still fountain, lest, in its peaceful bosom, he should be affrighted by himself. This was what gave plausibility to the whispers, that Mr. Hooper's conscience tortured him for some great crime, too horrible to be entirely concealed, or otherwise than so obscurely intimated. Thus, from beneath the black veil, there rolled a cloud into the sunshine, an ambiguity of sin or sorrow, which enveloped the poor minister, so that love or sympathy could never reach him. It was said, that ghost and fiend consorted with him there. With self-shudderings and outward terrors, he walked continually in its shadow, groping darkly within his own soul, or gazing through a medium that saddened the whole world. Even the lawless wind, it was believed, respected his dreadful secret, and never blew aside the veil. But still good Mr. Hooper sadly smiled, at the pale visages of the worldly throng as he passed by.

Among all its bad influences, the black veil had the one desirable effect, 45 of making its wearer a very efficient clergyman. By the aid of his mysterious emblem — for there was no other apparent cause — he became a man of awful power, over souls that were in agony for sin. His converts always regarded him with a dread peculiar to themselves, affirming, though but figuratively, that, before he brought them to celestial light, they had been with him behind the black veil. Its gloom, indeed, enabled him to sympathize with all dark affections. Dying sinners cried aloud for Mr. Hooper, and would not yield their breath till he appeared; though ever, as he stooped to whisper consolation, they shuddered at the veiled face so near their own. Such were the terrors of the black veil, even when Death had bared his visage! Strangers came long distances to attend service at his church, with the mere idle purpose of gazing at his figure, because it was forbidden them to behold his face. But many were made to quake ere they departed! Once, during Governor Belcher's administration, Mr. Hooper was appointed to preach the election sermon. Covered with his black veil, he stood before the chief magistrate, the council, and the representatives, and wrought so deep an impression, that the legislative measures of that year were characterized by all the gloom and piety of our earliest ancestral sway.

In this manner Mr. Hooper spent a long life, irreproachable in outward act, yet shrouded in dismal suspicions; kind and loving, though unloved, and dimly feared; a man apart from men, shunned in their health and joy, but ever summoned to their aid in mortal anguish. As years wore on, shedding their snows above his sable veil, he acquired a name throughout the New-England churches, and they called him Father Hooper. Nearly all his parishioners, who were of mature age when he was settled, had been borne away by many a funeral: he had one congregation in the church, and a more crowded one in the churchyard; and having wrought so late into the evening, and done his work so well, it was now good Father Hooper's turn to rest.

Several persons were visible by the shaded candlelight, in the death-chamber of the old clergyman. Natural connections he had none. But there was the decorously grave, though unmoved physician, seeking only to mitigate the last pangs of the patient whom he could not save. There were the deacons, and other eminently pious members of his church. There, also, was the Reverend Mr. Clark, of Westbury, a young and zealous divine, who had ridden in haste to pray by the bedside of the expiring minister. There was the nurse, no hired handmaiden of death, but one whose calm affection had endured thus long, in secrecy, in solitude, amid the chill of age, and would not perish, even at the dying hour. Who, but Elizabeth! And there lay the hoary head of good Father Hooper upon the death-pillow, with the black veil still swathed about his brow and reaching down over his face, so that each more difficult gasp of his faint breath caused it to stir. All through life that piece of crape had hung between him and the world: it had separated him from cheerful brotherhood and woman's love, and kept him in that saddest of all prisons, his own heart; and still it lay upon his face, as if to deepen the gloom of his darksome chamber, and shade him from the sunshine of eternity.

For some time previous, his mind had been confused, wavering doubtfully between the past and the present, and hovering forward, as it were, at intervals, into the indistinctness of the world to come. There had been feverish turns, which tossed him from side to side, and wore away what little strength he had. But in his most convulsive struggles, and in the wildest vagaries of his intellect, when no other thought retained its sober influence, he still showed an awful solicitude lest the black veil should slip aside. Even if his bewildered soul could have forgotten, there was a faithful woman at his pillow, who, with averted eyes, would have covered that aged face, which she had last beheld in the comeliness of manhood. At length the death-stricken old man lay quietly in the torpor of mental and bodily exhaustion, with an imperceptible pulse, and breath that grew fainter and fainter, except when a long, deep, and irregular inspiration seemed to prelude the flight of his spirit.

The minister of Westbury approached the bedside.

"Venerable Father Hooper," said he, "the moment of your release is at hand.  50
Are you ready for the lifting of the veil, that shuts in time from eternity?"

Father Hooper at first replied merely by a feeble motion of his head; then, apprehensive, perhaps, that his meaning might be doubtful, he exerted himself to speak.

"Yea," said he, in faint accents, "my soul hath a patient weariness until that veil be lifted."

"And is it fitting," resumed the Reverend Mr. Clark, "that a man so given to prayer, of such a blameless example, holy in deed and thought, so far as mortal judgment may pronounce; is it fitting that a father in the church should leave a shadow on his memory, that may seem to blacken a life so pure? I pray you, my venerable brother, let not this thing be! Suffer us to be gladdened by your triumphant aspect, as you go to your reward. Before the veil of eternity be lifted, let me cast aside this black veil from your face!"

And thus speaking, the Reverend Mr. Clark bent forward to reveal the mystery of so many years. But, exerting a sudden energy, that made all the beholders stand aghast, Father Hooper snatched both his hands from beneath the bedclothes, and pressed them strongly on the black veil, resolute to struggle, if the minister of Westbury would contend with a dying man.

"Never!" cried the veiled clergyman. "On earth, never!"  55

"Dark old man!" exclaimed the affrighted minister, "with what horrible crime upon your soul are you now passing to the judgment?"

Father Hooper's breath heaved; it rattled in his throat; but, with a mighty effort, grasping forward with his hands, he caught hold of life, and held it back till he should speak. He even raised himself in bed; and there he sat, shivering with the arms of death around him, while the black veil hung down, awful, at that last moment, in the gathered terrors of a life-time. And yet the faint, sad smile, so often there, now seemed to glimmer from its obscurity, and linger on Father Hooper's lips.

"Why do you tremble at me alone?" cried he, turning his veiled face round the circle of pale spectators. "Tremble also at each other! Have men avoided me, and women shown no pity, and children screamed and fled, only for my black veil? What, but the mystery which it obscurely typifies, has made this piece of crape so awful? When the friend shows his inmost heart to his friend; the lover to his best-beloved; when man does not vainly shrink from the eye of his Creator, loathsomely treasuring up the secret of his sin; then deem me a monster, for the symbol beneath which I have lived, and die! I look around me, and, lo! on every visage a Black Veil!"

While his auditors shrank from one another, in mutual affright, Father Hooper fell back upon his pillow, a veiled corpse, with a faint smile lingering on the lips. Still veiled, they laid him in his coffin, and a veiled corpse they bore him to the grave. The grass of many years has sprung up and withered on that grave, the burial-stone is moss-grown, and good Mr. Hooper's face is dust; but awful is still the thought, that it moldered beneath the Black Veil!

## CONSIDERATIONS FOR CRITICAL THINKING AND WRITING

1. FIRST RESPONSE. Why do you think Hooper wears the veil? Explain whether you think Hooper is right or wrong to wear it.

2. Describe the veil Hooper wears. How does it affect his vision?

3. Characterize the townspeople. How does the community react to the veil?

4. What is Hooper's explanation for why he wears the veil? Is he more or less effective as a minister because he wears it?

5. What is the one feature of Hooper's face that we see? What does that feature reveal about him?

6. Describe what happens at the funeral and wedding ceremonies at which Hooper officiates. How are the incidents at these events organized around the veil?

7. Why does Elizabeth think "it should be her privilege to know what the black veil concealed" (par. 25)? Why doesn't Hooper remove it at her request?

8. How does Elizabeth react to Hooper's refusal to take off the veil? Why is her response especially significant?

9. How do others in town explain why Hooper wears the veil? Do these explanations seem adequate to you? Why or why not?

10. Why is Hooper buried with the veil? Of what significance is it that grass "withered" on his grave (par. 59)?

11. Describe the story's point of view. How would a first-person narrative change the story dramatically?

## CONNECTIONS TO ANOTHER SELECTION

1. Compare the subject of private and public selves in this story and in David Long's "Morphine" (p. 282). Do the stories share a common theme?

## CARMEN MARIA MACHADO (B. 1986)

Randy Shropshire/Getty Images.

Born in Allentown, Pennsylvania, Carmen Maria Machado is a celebrated young author who has published essays, a memoir, and a graphic novel in addition to short stories. She earned her undergraduate degree from American University and her M.F.A. in creative writing from the prestigious Iowa Writers' Workshop at the University of Iowa. Her work has been widely recognized with prestigious awards and honors, including a Guggenheim Fellowship. Her collection *Her Body and Other Parties* (2017), in which the following story appears, was a finalist for the National Book Award. Her work, difficult to categorize, borrows from many traditions, including feminism, horror, speculative fiction, lesbian literature, and fantasy.

## *Eight Bites*  2017

As they put me to sleep, my mouth fills with the dust of the moon. I expect to choke on the silt but instead it slides in and out, and in and out, and I am, impossibly, breathing.

I have dreamt of inhaling underneath water and this is what it feels like: panic, and then acceptance, and then elation. I am going to die, I am not dying, I am doing a thing I never thought I could do.

Back on earth, Dr. U is inside me. Her hands are in my torso, her fingers searching for something. She is loosening flesh from its casing, slipping around where she's been welcomed, talking to a nurse about her vacation to Chile. "We were going to fly to Antarctica," she says, "but it was too expensive."

"But the penguins," the nurse says.

"Next time," Dr. U responds.                                                                  5

Before this, it was January, a new year. I waded through two feet of snow on a silent street, and came to a shop where wind chimes hung silently on the other side of the glass, mermaid-shaped baubles and bits of driftwood and too-shiny seashells strung through with fishing line and unruffled by any wind.

The town was deep dead, a great distance from the late-season smattering of open shops that serve the day-trippers and the money savers. Owners had fled to Boston or New York, or, if they were lucky, farther south. Businesses had shuttered for the season, leaving their wares in the windows like a tease. Underneath, a second town had opened up, familiar and alien at the same time. It's the same every year. Bars and restaurants made secret hours for locals, the rock-solid Cape Codders who've lived through dozens of winters. On any given night you could look up from your plate to see round bundles stomp through the doorway; only when they peeled their outsides away could you see who was beneath. Even the ones you knew from the summer were more or less strangers in this perfunctory daylight; all of them were alone, even when they were with each other.

On this street, though, I might as well have been on another planet. The beach bunnies and art dealers would never see the town like this, I thought, when the streets are dark and a liquid chill roils through the gaps and alleys. Silence and sound bumped up against each other but never intermingled; the jolly chaos of warm summer nights was as far away as it could be. It was hard to stop moving between doorways in this weather, but if you did you could hear life pricking the stillness: a rumble of voices from a local tavern, wind livening the buildings, sometimes even a muffled animal encounter in an alley: pleasure or fear, it was all the same noise.

Foxes wove through the streets at night. There was a white one among them, sleek and fast, and she looked like the ghost of the others.

I was not the first in my family to go through with it. My three sisters had gotten  10 the procedure over the years, though they didn't say anything before showing up for a visit. Seeing them suddenly svelte after years of watching them grow organically, as I have, was like a palm to the nose, more painful than you'd expect. My first sister, well, I thought she was dying. Being sisters, I thought we all were dying, noosed by genetics. When confronted by my anxiety — "What disease is sawing off this branch of the family tree?" I asked, my voice crabwalking up an octave — my first sister confessed: a surgery.

Then, all of them, my sisters, a chorus of believers. Surgery. A surgery. As easy as when you broke your arm as a kid and had to get the pins in — maybe even easier. A band, a sleeve, a gut rerouted. *Rerouted*? But their stories — *it melts away, it's just gone* — were spring-morning warm, when the sun makes the difference between happiness and shivering in a shadow.

When we went out, they ordered large meals and then said, "I couldn't possibly." They always said this, always, that decorous insistence that they *couldn't possibly*, but for once, they actually meant it — that bashful lie had been converted into truth vis-à-vis a medical procedure. They angled their forks and cut impossibly tiny portions of food — doll-sized cubes of watermelon, a slender stalk of pea shoot, a corner of a sandwich as if they needed to feed a crowd loaves-and-fishes-style with that single serving of chicken salad — and swallowed them like a great decadence.

"I feel so good," they all said. Whenever I talked to them, that was what always came out of their mouths, or really, it was a mouth, a single mouth that once ate and now just says, "I feel really, really good."

Who knows where we got it from, though — the bodies that needed the surgery. It didn't come from our mother, who always looked normal, not hearty or curvy or Rubenesque° or Midwestern or voluptuous, just normal. She always said eight bites are all you need to get the sense of what you are eating. Even though she never counted out loud, I could hear the eight bites as clearly as if a game show audience were counting backward, raucous and triumphant, and after *one* she would set her fork down, even if there was food left on her plate. She didn't mess around, my mother. No pushing food in circles or pretending. Iron will, slender waistline. Eight bites let her compliment the hostess. Eight bites lined her

*Rubenesque:* Peter Paul Rubens (1577–1640) was an influential Dutch painter whose work frequently featured full-figured nude women.

stomach like insulation rolled into the walls of houses. I wished she was still alive, to see the women her daughters had become.

And then, one day, not too soon after my third sister sashayed out of my house with more spring in her step than I'd ever seen, I ate eight bites and then stopped. I set the fork down next to the plate, more roughly than I'd intended, and took a chip of ceramic off the rim in the process. I pressed my finger into the shard and carried it to the trash can. I turned and looked back at my plate, which had been so full before and was full still, barely a dent in the raucous mass of pasta and greens. 15

I sat down again, picked up my fork, and had eight more bites. Not much more, still barely a dent, but now twice as much as necessary. But the salad leaves were dripping vinegar and oil and the noodles had lemon and cracked pepper and everything was just so beautiful, and I was still hungry, and so I had eight more. After, I finished what was in the pot on the stove and I was so angry I began to cry.

I don't remember getting fat. I wasn't a fat child or teenager; photos of those young selves are not embarrassing, or if they are, they're embarrassing in the right ways. Look how young I am! Look at my weird fashion! Saddle shoes—who thought of those? Stirrup pants—are you joking? Squirrel barrettes? Look at those glasses, look at that face: mugging for the camera. Look at that expression, mugging for a future self who is holding those photos, sick with nostalgia. Even when I thought I was fat, I wasn't; the teenager in those photos is very beautiful, in a wistful kind of way.

But then I had a baby. Then I had Cal—difficult, sharp-eyed Cal, who has never gotten me half as much as I have never gotten her—and suddenly everything was wrecked, like she was a heavy-metal rocker trashing a hotel room before departing. My stomach was the television set through the window. She was now a grown woman and so far away from me in every sense, but the evidence still clung to my body. It would never look right again.

As I stood over the empty pot, I was tired. I was tired of the skinny-minny women from church who cooed and touched each other's arms and told me I had beautiful skin, and having to rotate my hips sideways to move through rooms like crawling over someone at the movie theater. I was tired of flat, unforgiving dressing room lights; I was tired of looking into the mirror and grabbing the things that I hated and lifting them, clawing deep, and then letting them drop and everything aching. My sisters had gone somewhere else and left me behind, and as I always have, I wanted nothing more than to follow.

I could not make eight bites work for my body and so I would make my body work for eight bites. 20

Dr. U did twice-a-week consultations in an office a half-hour drive south on the Cape. I took a slow, circuitous route getting there. It had been snowing on and off for days, and the sleepy snowdrifts caught on every tree trunk and fencepost like blown-away laundry. I knew the way because I'd driven past her office before—usually after a sister's departure—and so as I drove this time I daydreamt about buying clothes in the local boutiques, spending too much for a sundress taken off a mannequin, pulling it against my body in the afternoon sun as the mannequin stood, less lucky than I.

Then I was in her office, on her neutral carpet, and a receptionist was pushing open a door. The doctor was not what I expected. I suppose I had imagined that because of the depth of her convictions, as illustrated by her choice of profession, she should have been a slender woman: either someone with excessive self-control or a sympathetic soul whose insides had also been rearranged to suit her vision of herself. But she was sweetly plump — why had I skipped over the phase where I was round and unthreatening as a panda, but still lovely? She smiled with all her teeth. What was she doing, sending me on this journey she herself had never taken?

She gestured, and I sat.

There were two Pomeranians running around her office. When they were separated — when one was curled up at Dr. U's feet and the other was decorously taking a shit in the hallway — they appeared identical but innocuous, but when one came near the other they were spooky, their heads twitching in sync, as if they were two halves of a whole. The doctor noticed the pile outside of the door and called for the receptionist. The door closed.

"I know what you're here for," she said, before I could open my mouth. "Have  25 you researched bariatric surgery before?"

"Yes," I said. "I want the kind you can't reverse."

"I admire a woman of conviction," she said. She began pulling binders out of a drawer. "There are some procedures you'll have to go through. Visiting a psychiatrist, seeing another doctor, support groups — administrative nonsense, taking up a lot of time. But everything is going to change for you," she promised, shaking a finger at me with an accusing, loving smile. "It will hurt. It won't be easy. But when it's over, you're going to be the happiest woman alive."

My sisters arrived a few days before the surgery. They set themselves up in the house's many empty bedrooms, making up their side tables with lotions and crossword puzzles. I could hear them upstairs and they sounded like birds, distinct and luminously choral at the same time.

I told them I was going out for a final meal.

"We'll come with you," said my first sister.  30

"Keep you company," said my second sister.

"Be supportive," said my third sister.

"No," I said, "I'll go alone. I need to be alone."

I walked to my favorite restaurant, Salt. It hadn't always been Salt, though, in name or spirit. It was Linda's, for a while, and then Family Diner, then The Table. The building remains the same, but it is always new and always better than before.

I thought about people on death row and their final meals, as I sat at a corner  35 table, and for the third time that week I worried about my moral compass, or lack thereof. They aren't the same, I reminded myself as I unfolded the napkin over my lap. Those things are not comparable. Their last meal comes before death; mine comes before not just life, but a new life. *You are horrible,* I thought, as I lifted the menu to my face, higher than it needed to be.

I ordered a cavalcade of oysters. Most of them had been cut the way they were supposed to be, and they slipped down as easily as water, like the ocean, like nothing at all, but one fought me: anchored to its shell, a stubborn hinge of flesh. It resisted. It was resistance incarnate. Oysters are alive, I realized. They are nothing but muscle; they have no brains or insides, strictly speaking, but they are alive nonetheless. If there were any justice in the world, this oyster would grab hold of my tongue and choke me dead.

I almost gagged, but then I swallowed.

My third sister sat down across the table from me. Her dark hair reminded me of my mother's: almost too shiny and homogenous to be real, though it was. She smiled kindly at me, as if she were about to give me some bad news.

"Why are you here?" I asked her.

"You look troubled," she said. She held her hands in a way that showed off her 40 red nails, which were so lacquered they had horizontal depth, like a rose trapped in glass. She tapped them against her cheekbones, scraping them down her face with the very lightest touch. I shuddered. Then she picked up my water and drank deeply of it, until the water had filtered through the ice and the ice was nothing more than a fragile lattice and then the whole construction slid against her face as she tipped the glass higher and she chewed the slivers that landed in her mouth.

"Don't waste that stomach space on water," she said, *crunch-crunch-crunch*ing. "Come on now. What are you eating?"

"Oysters," I said, even though she could see the precarious pile of shells before me.

She nodded. "Are they good?" she asked.

"They are."

"Tell me about them." 45

"They are the sum of all healthy things: seawater and muscle and bone," I said. "Mindless protein. They feel no pain, have no verifiable thoughts. Very few calories. An indulgence without being an indulgence. Do you want one?"

I didn't want her to be there — I wanted to tell her to leave — but her eyes were glittering as if she had a fever. She ran her fingernail lovingly along an oyster shell. The whole pile shifted, doubling down on its own mass.

"No," she said. Then, "Have you told Cal? About the procedure?"

I bit my lip. "No," I said. "Did you tell your daughter, before you got it?"

"I did. She was so excited for me. She sent me flowers." 50

"Cal will not be excited," I said. "There are many daughter duties Cal does not perform, and this will be one, too."

"Do you think she needs the surgery, too? Is that why?"

"I don't know," I said. "I have never understood Cal's needs."

"Do you think it's because she will think badly of you?"

"I've also never understood her opinions," I said. 55

My sister nodded.

"She will not send me flowers," I concluded, even though this was probably not necessary.

I ordered a pile of hot truffle fries, which burned the roof of my mouth. It was only after the burn that I thought about how much I'd miss it all. I started to cry, and my sister put her hand over mine. I was jealous of the oysters. They never had to think about themselves.

At home, I called Cal to tell her. My jaw was so tightly clenched, it popped when she answered the phone. On the other end I could hear another woman's voice, stopped short by a finger to the lips unseen; then a dog whined.

"Surgery?" she repeated. 60

"Yes," I said.

"Jesus Christ," she said.

"Don't swear," I told her, even though I am not a religious woman.

"What? That's not even a fucking swear," she yelled. "*That* was a fucking swear. And this. *Jesus Christ* is not a swear. It's a proper name. And if there's ever a time to swear, it's when your mom tells you she's getting half of one of her most important organs cut away for no reason —"

She was still talking, but it was growing into a yell. I shooed the words away 65 like bees.

"— occur to you that you're never going to be able to eat like a normal human —"

"What is wrong with you?" I finally asked her.

"Mom, I just don't understand why you can't be happy with yourself. You've never been —"

She kept talking. I stared at the receiver. When did my child sour? I didn't remember the process, the top-down tumble from sweetness to curdled anger. She was furious constantly, she was all accusation. She had taken the moral high ground from me by force, time and time again. I had committed any number of sins: Why didn't I teach her about feminism? Why did I persist in not understanding anything? And *this,* this takes the cake, no, *don't* forgive the pun; language is infused with food like everything else, or at least like everything else should be. She was so angry, I was glad I couldn't read her mind. I knew her thoughts would break my heart.

The line went dead. She'd hung up on me. I set the phone on the receiver and 70 realized my sisters were watching me from the doorway, two looking sympathetic, the other smug.

I turned away. Why didn't Cal understand? Her body was imperfect but it was also fresh, pliable. She could sidestep my mistakes. She could have the release of a new start. I had no self-control, but tomorrow I would relinquish control and everything would be right again.

The phone rang. Cal, calling back? But it was my niece. She was selling knife sets so she could go back to school and become a — well, I missed that part, but she would get paid just for telling me about the knives, so I let her walk me through, step-by-step, and I bought a cheese knife with a special cut-out center — "So the cheese doesn't stick to the blade, see?" she said.

In the operating room, I was open to the world. Not that kind of open, not yet, everything was still sealed up inside, but I was naked except for a faintly patterned cloth gown that didn't quite wrap around my body.

"Wait," I said. I laid my hand upon my hip and squeezed a little. I trembled, though I didn't know why. There was an IV, and the IV would relax me; soon I would be very far away.

Dr. U stared at me over her mask. Gone was the sweetness from her office; her 75 eyes looked transformed. Icy.

"Did you ever read that picture book about Ping the duck?" I asked her.

"No," she said.

"Ping the duck was always punished for being the last duck home. He'd get whacked across the back with a switch. He hated that. So he ran away. After he ran away he met some black fishing birds with metal bands around their necks. They caught fish for their masters but could not swallow the fish whole, because of the bands. When they brought fish back, they were rewarded with tiny pieces they could swallow. They were obedient, because they had to be. Ping, with no band, was always last and now was lost. I don't remember how it ends. It seems like a book you should read."

She adjusted her mask a little. "Don't make me cut out your tongue," she said.

"I'm ready," I told her. 80

The mask slipped over me and I was on the moon.

Afterward, I sleep and sleep. It's been a long time since I've been so still. I stay on the couch because stairs, stairs are impossible. In the watery light of morning, dust motes drift through the air like plankton. I have never seen the living room so early. A new world.

I drink shaking sips of clear broth, brought to me by my first sister, who, silhouetted against the window, looks like a branch stripped bare by the wind. My second sister checks in on me every so often, opening the windows a crack despite the cold — to let some air in, she says softly. She does not say the house smells stale and like death but I can see it in her eyes as she fans the door open and shut and open and shut as patiently as a mother whose child has vomited. I can see her cheekbones, high and tight as cherries, and I smile at her as best I can.

My third sister observes me at night, sitting on a chair near the sofa, where she glances at me from above her book, her brows tightening and loosening with concern. She talks to her daughter — who loves her without judgment, I am sure — in the kitchen, so softly I can barely hear her, but then forgets herself and laughs loudly at some joke shared between them. I wonder if my niece has sold any more knives.

I am transformed but not yet, exactly. The transformation has begun — this 85 pain, this excruciating pain, it is part of the process — and will not end until — well, I suppose I don't know when. Will I ever be done, transformed in the past tense, or will I always be transforming, better and better until I die?

Cal does not call. When she does I will remind her of my favorite memory of her: when I caught her with a chemical depilatory in the bathroom in the wee hours of morning, creaming her little tan arms and legs and upper lip so the hair dissolved like snow in sunlight. I will tell her, when she calls.

The shift, at first, is imperceptible, so small as to be a trick of the imagination. But then one day I button a pair of pants and they fall to my feet. I marvel at what is beneath. A pre-Cal body. A pre-me body. It is emerging, like the lie of snow withdrawing from the truth of the landscape. My sisters finally go home. They kiss me and tell me that I look beautiful.

I am finally well enough to walk along the beach. The weather has been so cold that the water is thick with ice and the waves churn creamily, like soft serve. I take a photo and send it to Cal, but I know she won't respond.

At home, I cook a very small chicken breast and cut it into white cubes. I count the bites and when I reach eight I throw the rest of the food in the garbage. I stand over the can for a long while, breathing in the salt-and-pepper smell of chicken mixed in with coffee grounds and something older and closer to decay. I spray window cleaner into the garbage can so the food cannot be retrieved. I feel a little light but good; righteous, even. Before, I would have been growling, climbing up the walls from want. Now I feel only slightly empty, and fully content.

That night, I wake up because something is standing over me, something 90 small, and before I slide into being awake I think it's my daughter, up from a nightmare, or perhaps it's morning and I've overslept, except even as my hands exchange blanket warmth for chilled air and it is so dark, I remember that my daughter is in her late twenties and lives in Portland with a roommate who is not really her roommate and she will not tell me and I don't know why.

But something is there, darkness blotting out darkness, a person-shaped out-line. It sits on the bed, and I feel the weight, the mattress springs creaking and pinging. Is it looking at me? Away from me? Does it look, at all?

And then there is nothing, and I sit up alone.

As I learn my new diet — my forever diet, the one that will end only when I do — something is moving in the house. At first I think it is mice, but it is larger, more autonomous. Mice in walls scurry and drop through unexpected holes, and you can hear them scrabbling in terror as they plummet behind your family portraits. But this thing occupies the hidden parts of the house with purpose, and if I drop my ear to the wallpaper it breathes audibly.

After a week of this, I try to talk to it.

"Whatever you are," I say, "please come out. I want to see you."  95

Nothing. I am not sure whether I am feeling afraid or curious or both.

I call my sisters. "It might be my imagination," I explain, "but did you also hear something, after? In the house? A presence?"

"Yes," says my first sister. "My joy danced around my house, like a child, and I danced with her. We almost broke two vases that way!"

"Yes," says my second sister. "My inner beauty was set free and lay around in patches of sunlight like a cat, preening itself."

"Yes," says my third sister. "My former shame slunk from shadow to shadow,  100 as it should have. It will go away, after a while. You won't even notice and then one day it'll be gone."

After I hang up with her, I try to take a grapefruit apart with my hands, but it's an impossible task. The skin clings to the fruit, and between them is an intermediary skin, thick and impossible to separate from the meat. Eventually I take a knife and lop off domes of rinds and cut the grapefruit into a cube before ripping it open with my fingers. It feels like I am dismantling a human heart. The fruit is delicious, slick. I swallow eight times, and when the ninth bite touches my lips I pull it back and squish it in my hand as if I am crumpling an old receipt. I put the remaining half of the grapefruit in a Tupperware. I close the fridge. Even now I can hear it. Behind me. Above me. Too large to perceive. Too small to see.

When I was in my twenties, I lived in a place with bugs and had the same sense of knowing invisible things moved, coordinated, in the darkness. Even if I flipped on the kitchen light in the wee hours and saw nothing, I would just wait, Then my eyes would adjust and I would see it: a cockroach who, instead of scuttling two-dimensionally across the yawn of a white wall, was instead perched at the lip of a cupboard, probing the air endlessly with his antennae. He desired and feared in three dimensions. He was less vulnerable there, and yet somehow more, I realized as I wiped his guts across the plywood.

In the same way, now, the house is filled with something else. It moves, restless. It does not say words but it breathes. I want to know it, and I don't know why.

"I've done research," Cal says. The line crackles as if she is somewhere with a bad signal, so she is not calling from her house. I listen for the voice of the other woman who is always in the background whose name I have never learned.

"Oh, you're back?" I say. I am in control, for once.  105

Her voice is clipped, but then softens. I can practically hear the therapist cooing to her. She is probably going through a list that she and the therapist created together. I feel a spasm of anger.

"I am worried because," she says, and then pauses.

"Because?"

"Sometimes there can be all of these complications —"

"It's done, Cal. It's been done for months. There's no point to this."          110

"Do you hate my body, Mom?" she says. Her voice splinters in pain, as if she were about to cry. "You hated yours, clearly, but mine looks just like yours used to, so —"

"Stop it."

"You think you're going to be happy but this is not going to make you happy," she says.

"I love you," I say.

"Do you love every part of me?"          115

It's my turn to hang up and then, after a moment's thought, disconnect the phone. Cal is probably calling back right now, but she won't be able to get through. I'll let her, when I'm ready.

I wake up because I can hear a sound like a vase breaking in reverse: thousands of shards of ceramic whispering along hardwood toward a reassembling form. From my bedroom, it sounds like it's coming from the hallway. From the hallway, it sounds like it's coming from the stairs. Down, down, foyer, dining room, living room, down deeper, and then I am standing at the top of the basement steps.

From below, from the dark, something shuffles. I wrap my fingers around the ball chain hanging from the naked light bulb and I pull.

The thing is down there. In the light, it crumples to the cement floor, curls away from me.

It looks like my daughter, as a girl. That's my first thought. It's body-shaped.          120
Prepubescent, boneless. It is one hundred pounds, dripping wet.

And it does. Drip.

I descend to the bottom and up close it smells warm, like toast. It looks like the clothes stuffed with straw on someone's porch at Halloween — the vague person-shaped lump made from pillows to aid a midnight escape plan. I am afraid to step over it. I walk around it, admiring my unfamiliar face in the reflection of the water heater even as I hear its sounds: a gasping, arrested sob.

I kneel down next to it. It is a body with nothing it needs: no stomach or bones or mouth. Just soft indents. I crouch down and stroke its shoulder, or what I think is its shoulder.

It turns and looks at me. It has no eyes, but still, it looks at me. *She* looks at me. She is awful but honest. She is grotesque but she is real.

I shake my head. "I don't know why I wanted to meet you," I say. "I should          125
have known."

She curls a little tighter. I lean down and whisper where an ear might be.

"You are unwanted," I say. A tremor ripples her mass.

I do not know I am kicking her until I am kicking her. She has nothing and I feel nothing except she seems to solidify before my foot meets her, and so every kick is more satisfying than the last. I reach for a broom and I pull a muscle swinging back and in and back and in, and the handle breaks off in her and I kneel down and pull soft handfuls of her body out of herself, and I throw them against the wall, and I do not know I am screaming until I stop, finally.

I find myself wishing she would fight back, but she doesn't. Instead, she sounds like she is being deflated. A hissing, defeated wheeze.

I stand up and walk away. I shut the basement door. I leave her there until I can't 130
hear her anymore.

———————

Spring has come, marking the end of winter's long contraction.

Everyone is waking up. The first warm day, when light cardigans are enough, the streets begin to hum. Bodies move around. Not fast, but still: smiles. Neighbors suddenly recognizable after a season of watching their lumpy outlines walk past in the darkness.

"You look wonderful," says one.

"Have you lost weight?" asks another.

I smile. I get a manicure and tap my new nails along my face, to show them 135 off. I go to Salt, which is now called The Peppercorn, and eat three oysters.

I am a new woman. A new woman becomes best friends with her daughter. A new woman laughs with all of her teeth. A new woman does not just slough off her old self; she tosses it aside with force.

Summer will come next. Summer will come and the waves will be huge, the kind of waves that feel like a challenge. If you're brave, you'll step out of the bright-hot day and into the foaming roil of the water, moving toward where the waves break and might break you. If you're brave, you'll turn your body over to this water that is practically an animal, and so much larger than yourself.

Sometimes, if I sit very still, I can hear her gurgling underneath the floorboards. She sleeps in my bed when I'm at the grocery store, and when I come back and slam the door, loudly, there are padded footsteps above my head. I know she is around, but she never crosses my path. She leaves offerings on the coffee table: safety pins, champagne bottle corks, hard candies twisted in strawberry-patterned cellophane. She shuffles through my dirty laundry and leaves a trail of socks and bras all the way to the open window. The drawers and air are rifled through. She turns all the soup can labels forward and wipes up the constellations of dried coffee spatter on the kitchen tile. The perfume of her is caught on the linens. She is around, even when she is not around.

I will see her only one more time, after this.

I will die the day I turn seventy-nine. I will wake up early because outside a neigh- 140
bor is talking loudly to another neighbor about her roses, and because Cal is coming today with her daughter for our annual visit, and because I am a little hungry, and because a great pressure is on my chest. Even as it tightens and compresses I will perceive what is beyond my window: a cyclist bumping over concrete, a white fox loping through underbrush, the far roll of the ocean. I will think, *it is as my sisters prophesied.* I will think, *I miss them, still.* I will think, *here is where I learn if it's all been worth it.* The pain will be unbearable until it isn't anymore; until it loosens and I will feel better than I have in a long time.

There will be such a stillness, then, broken only by a honeybee's soft-winged stumble against the screen, and a floorboard's creak.

Arms will lift me from my bed — her arms. They will be mother-soft, like dough and moss. I will recognize the smell. I will flood with grief and shame.

I will look where her eyes would be. I will open my mouth to ask but then realize the question has answered itself: by loving me when I did not love her, by being abandoned by me, she has become immortal. She will outlive me by a hundred million years; more, even. She will outlive my daughter, and my daughter's daughter, and the earth will teem with her and her kind, their inscrutable forms and unknowable destinies.

She will touch my cheek like I once did Cal's, so long ago, and there will be no accusation in it. I will cry as she shuffles me away from myself, toward a door propped open into the salty morning. I will curl into her body, which was my body once, but I was a poor caretaker and she was removed from my charge.

"I'm sorry," I will whisper into her as she walks me toward the front door.      145
"I'm sorry," I will repeat. "I didn't know."

## CONSIDERATIONS FOR CRITICAL THINKING AND WRITING

1. FIRST RESPONSE. When Dr. U makes the absurd promise, "when it's over, you're going to be the happiest woman alive" (par. 27), why does the narrator buy it?

2. The narrator's three sisters are arguably the most influential people in her life. What is the effect of her withholding their names?

3. How does the animal imagery throughout the story (foxes, dogs, oysters) help to frame the theme?

4. How does the scene of the narrator's last indulgent supper before surgery deepen the conflict?

5. Are you able to easily summarize the narrator's relationship with her daughter, Cal? Does it mirror her relationship with her own mother or is it different?

6. What does the concept of *control* have to do with the story's theme? Begin by listing examples of control (or its opposite) and try to discern a pattern from there.

7. Much of the story's power has to do with "the presence" in the narrator's house after her surgery. How do you interpret it?

8. The story has a great deal to do with our bodies and the way we treat them. What's the relationship between the body and the mind, especially considering the story's final line?

## CONNECTIONS TO OTHER SELECTIONS

1. What parallels can you draw between this story and Ursula K. Le Guin's "The Ones Who Walk Away from Omelas" (p. 121)? Consider drawing an analogy between the narrator's relationship to "the presence" and the town's relationship with the child in the basement.

2. Compare this narrator to the narrator of Charlotte Perkins Gilman's "The Yellow Wallpaper" (p. 126). Do the stories have similar themes?

# 8

# Style, Tone, and Irony

We writers may see, observe, care and feel, but language is the medium by which that all comes across. Language is the transom of thought and feeling.
— ZZ PACKER

Rose Lincoln/Harvard Staff Photographer.

## STYLE

Style is a concept that everyone understands on some level because in its broadest sense it refers to the particular way in which anything is made or done. Style is everywhere around us. The world is saturated with styles in cars, clothing, buildings, teaching, dancing, music, politics — in anything that reflects a distinctive manner of expression or design. Consider, for example, how a tune sung by the Beatles differs from the same tune performed by a string orchestra. There's no way to confuse those two styles.

Authors also have different characteristic styles. **Style** refers to the distinctive manner in which a writer arranges words to achieve particular effects. That arrangement includes individual word choices and matters such as the length of sentences, their structure and tone, and the use of irony.

**Diction** refers to a writer's choice of words. Because different words evoke different associations in a reader's mind, the writer's choice of words is crucial in controlling a reader's response. The diction must be appropriate for the characters and the situations in which the author places them. In T. C. Boyle's story "The Hit Man" (p. 33), the protagonist repeatedly "wastes" people around him, from his classmate, to his father, to a waitress who serves him peas. The word *wastes* is slang for "murders," and it is a particular type of slang. To understand it, we probably have to have some familiarity with the popular culture lore of a hired assassin, and we would probably have access to it through movies or TV shows. Although it refers to murder, the word is humorous in the context of the story, especially since it is repeated so often, and so factually. If Boyle had chosen the flatter word *murders* or a specific description of how the murder took place (*shoots, strangles*, etc.), the effect would be different.

Sentence structure is another element of a writer's style. Ernest Hemingway's terse, economical sentences are frequently noted and readily perceived. Here are the concluding sentences of Hemingway's "Soldier's Home" (p. 115), in which Krebs decides to leave home:

> He had tried so to keep his life from being complicated. Still, none of it had touched him. He had felt sorry for his mother and she had made him lie. He would go to Kansas City and get a job and she would feel all right about it. There would be one more scene maybe before he got away. He would not go down to his father's office. He would miss that one. He wanted his life to go smoothly. It had just gotten going that way. Well, that was all over now, anyway. He would go over to the schoolyard and watch Helen play indoor baseball.

Hemingway expresses Krebs's thought the way Krebs thinks. The style avoids any "complicated" sentence structures. Seven of the eleven sentences begin with the word *He*. There are no abstractions or qualifications. We feel as if we are listening not only to *what* Krebs thinks but also to *how* he thinks. The style reflects his firm determination to make, one step at a time, a clean, unobstructed break from his family and the entangling complications they would impose on him.

Contrast this straightforward style with the first paragraph of James Baldwin's story "Sonny's Blues" (p. 91):

> I read about it in the paper, in the subway, on my way to work. I read it, and I couldn't believe it, and I read it again. Then perhaps I just stared at it, at the newsprint spelling out his name, spelling out the story. I stared at it in the swinging lights of the subway car, and in the faces and bodies of the people, and in my own face, trapped in the darkness which roared outside.

The cadence of Baldwin's sentences, the rhythmic repetitions, are striking here. It is like a relay race with each sentence passing a baton to the next one: "I read it" joins the first two sentences and is repeated within the second. That phrase slides into "I stared at it" in the third sentence, which is urged ahead by the repetition of the word *spelling* within that sentence. The final sentence begins again with "I stared at it" and leads us to the final image: the narrator looks outward at the subway window and it becomes a mirror, leading him back to his own face and a feeling of being trapped. This image sets up contrasts that recur throughout the story: of darkness and light, interiors and exteriors, others and selves. We are lulled by these repetitions, drawn into the mystery of the narrator's words, which flow without giving us the same factual details that typify Hemingway's work. The word *it* is in each of these four initial sentences, but we haven't yet been told what it is. We trust that the flowing river of Baldwin's sentences will eventually carry us there.

Hemingway's and Baldwin's uses of language are very different, yet each style successfully fuses what is said with how it is said. We could write summaries of both passages, but our summaries, owing to their styles, would not have the same effect as the originals. And that makes all the difference.


## TONE

Style reveals *tone*, the author's implicit attitude toward the people, places, and events in a story. When we speak, tone is conveyed by our voice inflections, our wink of an eye, or some other gesture. A professor who says "You're going to fail the next exam" may be indicating concern, frustration, sympathy, alarm, humor, or indifference, depending on the tone of voice. In a literary work that spoken voice is unavailable; instead we must rely on the context surrounding a statement in order to interpret it correctly.

In Kate Chopin's "The Story of an Hour" (p. 17), for example, we can determine that the author sympathizes with Mrs. Mallard despite the fact that her grief over her husband's assumed death is mixed with joy. Though Mrs. Mallard thinks she's lost her husband, she experiences relief because she feels liberated from an oppressive male-dominated life. That's why she collapses when she sees her husband alive at the end of the story. Chopin makes clear by the tone of the final line ("When the doctors came they said she had died of heart disease — of joy that kills") that the men misinterpret both her grief and joy, for in the larger context of Mrs. Mallard's emotions we see, unlike the doctors, that her death may well have been caused not by a shock of joy but by an overwhelming recognition of her lost freedom.

If we are sensitive to tone, we can get behind characters and see them from their own perspective. In John Updike's "A & P" (p. 145), the narrator clues us into his perspective right away: "In walks these three girls," he begins. This sounds like the beginning of an anecdote someone might tell at a party, maybe even a joke. Sammy, we learn, is a teenaged worker in a grocery store. His casual tone is meant to lull us into the false sense that this story is not monumental, just something that happened at work. Yet the story builds subtly in intensity to the point that Sammy's dramatic, almost impulsive decision to quit takes on the weight of self-definition. A teen quits a dead-end job: no big deal, happens all the time. But the story's final line reveals that this decision has profound consequences in terms of his life's trajectory. He may not realize that, but his author — a Harvard-educated professional writer with a tremendous command of the English language and a boundless vocabulary, as the reader of his other works will quickly see — is well aware of the difference between his character's voice and his own. An insensitivity to tone can lead a reader astray in determining the theme of a work. Regardless of who is speaking in a story, it is wise to listen for subtle indications of the author's voice too.

# IRONY

One of the enduring themes in literature is that things are not always what they seem to be. What we see — or think we see — is not always what we get. The unexpected complexity that often surprises us in life — what Herman Melville in *Moby-Dick* called the "universal thump" — is fertile ground for writers of imaginative literature. They cultivate that ground through the use of *irony*, a device that reveals a reality different from what appears to be true.

**Verbal irony** consists of a person saying one thing but meaning the opposite. If a student driver smashes into a parked car and the angry instructor turns to say "Great job," the statement is an example of verbal irony. What is meant is not what is said. Verbal irony that is calculated to hurt someone by false praise is commonly known as **sarcasm**. In literature, however, verbal irony is usually not openly aggressive; instead, it is more subtle and restrained though no less intense.

In Charlotte Perkins Gilman's "The Yellow Wallpaper" (p. 126), the narrator says, "John laughs at me, of course, but one expects that in a marriage." Does "one"? If there were no irony intended in the statement, the reader would chuckle and say, "One sure does! That's marriage for you! Lots of mockery makes everyone happy." We know immediately that we're not supposed to agree. We scowl at John and wonder to what degree the narrator believes her own statement. Is she conditioned to believe she should be laughed at or is she burying feelings of resentment and even anger that might come out as the story progresses?

**Situational irony** exists when there is an incongruity between what is expected to happen and what actually happens. For instance, at the end of Chopin's "The Story of an Hour" (p. 17), we expect Mrs. Mallard to hug her husband and shed tears of joy when he returns, not to die. In Ralph Ellison's "King of the Bingo Game" (p. 178), we expect that the protagonist will be handed a check when the bingo wheel lands on double zero, the only number that signifies a win, but he is instead clubbed and hauled off stage. In each of these instances the ironic situation creates a distinction between appearances and realities and brings the reader closer to the central meaning of the story.

Another form of irony occurs when a writer allows the reader to know more about a situation than a character knows. **Dramatic irony** creates a discrepancy between what a character believes or says and what the reader understands to be true. In Flannery O'Connor's "A Good Man Is Hard to Find" (p. 405), the grandmother insists that the Misfit is a good man, but the reader knows him to be a heartless psychopath who does not have a conscience, much less a heaven-bound soul. The grandmother's attempts to placate the Misfit are futile. Dramatic irony can be an effective way for a writer to have a character unwittingly reveal himself or herself.

As you read Shirley Jackson's "The Lottery," Mark Twain's "The Story of the Good Little Boy," and Virginia Woolf's "The Man Who Loved His Kind," pay attention to the authors' artful use of style, tone, and irony to convey meanings.

## SHIRLEY JACKSON (1916–1965)

Although she published more than two hundred stories in her relatively short lifetime, Shirley Jackson is undoubtedly best remembered for the following story, "The Lottery," published in the *New Yorker* in 1948. A native of San Francisco, Jackson relocated with her family to upstate New York when she was a senior in high school. She graduated from Syracuse University, where she published her first short story and where she met her future husband, Stanley Edgar Hyman, a prominent literary critic. They moved to Vermont, where they raised four children, although biographers have described their domestic situation as far from the mid-twentieth-century stereotype of pros-

Pictorial Press Ltd/Alamy.

perity and harmony. Jackson earned a good living through publishing her stories and six novels, including the challenging, inventive horror novel *The Haunting of Hill House* (1959), but she became increasingly reclusive and her health declined precipitously, leading to her death of heart failure at the age of forty-eight. Her works are known for their explorations of psychological horror and what might be termed the dark side of human experience, as you will clearly see in "The Lottery."

## *The Lottery*   1948

The morning of June 27th was clear and sunny, with the fresh warmth of a full-summer day; the flowers were blossoming profusely and the grass was richly green. The people of the village began to gather in the square, between the post office and the bank, around ten o'clock; in some towns there were so many people that the lottery took two days and had to be started on June 26th, but in this village, where there were only about three hundred people, the whole lottery took less than two hours, so it could begin at ten o'clock in the morning and still be through in time to allow the villagers to get home for noon dinner.

The children assembled first, of course. School was recently over for the summer, and the feeling of liberty sat uneasily on most of them; they tended to gather together quietly for a while before they broke into boisterous play, and their talk was still of the classroom and the teacher, of books and reprimands. Bobby Martin had already stuffed his pockets full of stones, and the other boys soon followed his example, selecting the smoothest and roundest stones; Bobby and Harry Jones and Dickie Delacroix — the villagers pronounced this name "Dellacroy" — eventually made a great pile of stones in one corner of the square and guarded it against the raids of the other boys. The girls stood aside, talking among themselves, looking over their shoulders at the boys, and the very small children rolled in the dust or clung to the hands of their older brothers or sisters.

Soon the men began to gather, surveying their own children, speaking of planting and rain, tractors and taxes. They stood together, away from the pile of stones in the corner, and their jokes were quiet and they smiled rather than laughed. The women, wearing faded house dresses and sweaters, came shortly after their menfolk. They greeted one another and exchanged bits of gossip as they went to join their husbands. Soon the women, standing by their husbands, began to call to their children, and the children came reluctantly, having to be called four or five times. Bobby Martin ducked under his mother's grasping hand and ran, laughing, back to the pile of stones. His father spoke up sharply, and Bobby came quickly and took his place between his father and his oldest brother.

The lottery was conducted — as were the square dances, the teenage club, the Halloween program — by Mr. Summers, who had time and energy to devote to civic activities. He was a roundfaced, jovial man and he ran the coal business, and people were sorry for him, because he had no children and his wife was a scold. When he arrived in the square, carrying the black wooden box, there was a murmur of conversation among the villagers and he waved and called, "Little late today, folks." The postmaster, Mr. Graves, followed him, carrying a three-legged stool, and the stool was put in the center of the square and Mr. Summers set the black box down on it. The villagers kept their distance, leaving a space between themselves and the stool, and when Mr. Summers said, "Some of you fellows want to give me a hand?" there was a hesitation before two men, Mr. Martin and his oldest son, Baxter, came forward to hold the box steady on the stool while Mr. Summers stirred up the papers inside it.

The original paraphernalia for the lottery had been lost long ago, and the black    5 box now resting on the stool had been put into use even before Old Man Warner, the oldest man in town, was born. Mr. Summers spoke frequently to the villagers about making a new box, but no one liked to upset even as much tradition as was represented by the black box. There was a story that the present box had been made with some pieces of the box that had preceded it, the one that had been constructed when the first people settled down to make a village here. Every year, after the lottery, Mr. Summers began talking again about a new box, but every year the subject was allowed to fade off without anything's being done. The black box grew shabbier each year; by now it was no longer completely black but splintered badly along one side to show the original wood color, and in some places faded or stained.

Mr. Martin and his oldest son, Baxter, held the black box securely on the stool until Mr. Summers had stirred the papers thoroughly with his hand. Because so much of the ritual had been forgotten or discarded, Mr. Summers had been successful in having slips of paper substituted for the chips of wood that had been used for generations. Chips of wood, Mr. Summers had argued, had been all very well when the village was tiny, but now that the population was more than three hundred and likely to keep on growing, it was necessary to use something that would fit more easily into the black box. The night before the lottery, Mr. Summers and Mr. Graves made up the slips of paper and put them in the box, and it was then taken to the safe of Mr. Summers's coal company and locked up until Mr. Summers was ready to take it to the square next morning. The rest of the year, the box was put away, sometimes one place, sometimes another; it had spent one year in Mr. Graves's barn and another year underfoot in the post office, and sometimes it was set on a shelf in the Martin grocery and left there.

There was a great deal of fussing to be done before Mr. Summers declared the lottery open. There were lists to make up — of heads of families, heads of households in each family, members of each household in each family. There was the proper swearing-in of Mr. Summers by the postmaster, as the official of the lottery; at one time, some people remembered, there had been a recital of some sort, performed by the official of the lottery, a perfunctory, tuneless chant that had been rattled off duly each year; some people believed that the official of the lottery used to stand just so when he said or sang it, others believed that he was supposed to walk among the people, but years and years ago this part of the ritual had been allowed to lapse. There had been, also, a ritual salute, which the official of the lottery had had to use in addressing each person who came up to draw from the *box,* but this also had changed with time, until now it was felt necessary only for the official to speak to each person approaching. Mr. Summers was very good at all this; in his clean white shirt and blue jeans, with one hand resting carelessly on the black box, he seemed very proper and important as he talked interminably to Mr. Graves and the Martins.

Just as Mr. Summers finally left off talking and turned to the assembled villagers, Mrs. Hutchinson came hurriedly along the path to the square, her sweater thrown over her shoulders, and slid into place in the back of the crowd. "Clean forgot what day it was," she said to Mrs. Delacroix, who stood next to her, and they both laughed softly. "Thought my old man was out back stacking wood," Mrs. Hutchinson went on, "and then I looked out the window and the kids were gone, and then I remembered it was the twenty-seventh and came a-running." She dried her hands on her apron, and Mrs. Delacroix said, "You're in time, though. They're still talking away up there."

Mrs. Hutchinson craned her neck to see through the crowd and found her husband and children standing near the front. She tapped Mrs. Delacroix on the arm as a farewell and began to make her way through the crowd. The people separated good-humoredly to let her through; two or three people said, in voices just loud enough to be heard across the crowd, "Here comes your Missus, Hutchinson," and "Bill, she made it after all." Mrs. Hutchinson reached her husband, and Mr. Summers, who had been waiting, said cheerfully, "Thought we were going to have to get on without you, Tessie." Mrs. Hutchinson said, grinning, "Wouldn't have me leave m'dishes in the sink, now would you, Joe?" and soft laughter ran through the crowd as the people stirred back into position after Mrs. Hutchinson's arrival.

"Well, now," Mr. Summers said soberly, "guess we better get started, get this over with, so's we can go back to work. Anybody ain't here?"  10

"Dunbar," several people said. "Dunbar, Dunbar."

Mr. Summers consulted his list. "Clyde Dunbar," he said. "That's right. He's broke his leg, hasn't he? Who's drawing for him?"

"Me, I guess," a woman said, and Mr. Summers turned to look at her. "Wife draws for her husband," Mr. Summers said. "Don't you have a grown boy to do it for you, Janey?" Although Mr. Summers and everyone else in the village knew the answer perfectly well, it was the business of the official of the lottery to ask such questions formally. Mr. Summers waited with an expression of polite interest while Mrs. Dunbar answered.

"Horace's not but sixteen yet," Mrs. Dunbar said regretfully. "Guess I gotta fill in for the old man this year."

"Right," Mr. Summers said. He made a note on the list he was holding. Then  15 he asked, "Watson boy drawing this year?"

A tall boy in the crowd raised his hand. "Here," he said. "I'm drawing for m'mother and me." He blinked his eyes nervously and ducked his head as several voices in the crowd said things like "Good fellow, Jack," and "Glad to see your mother's got a man to do it."

"Well," Mr. Summers said, "guess that's everyone. Old Man Warner make it?"

"Here," a voice said, and Mr. Summers nodded.

A sudden hush fell on the crowd as Mr. Summers cleared his throat and looked at the list. "All ready?" he called. "Now, I'll read the names — heads of families first — and the men come up and take a paper out of the box. Keep the paper folded in your hand without looking at it until everyone has had a turn. Everything clear?"

The people had done it so many times that they only half listened to the directions; most of them were quiet, wetting their lips, not looking around. Then Mr. Summers raised one hand high and said, "Adams." A man disengaged himself from the crowd and came forward. "Hi, Steve," Mr. Summers said, and Mr. Adams said, "Hi, Joe." They grinned at one another humorlessly and nervously. Then Mr. Adams reached into the black box and took out a folded paper. He held it firmly by one corner as he turned and went hastily back to his place in the crowd, where he stood a little apart from his family, not looking down at his hand.

"Allen," Mr. Summers said. "Anderson. . . . Bentham."

"Seems like there's no time at all between lotteries any more," Mrs. Delacroix said to Mrs. Graves in the back row. "Seems like we got through with the last one only last week."

"Time sure goes fast," Mrs. Graves said.

"Clark. . . . Delacroix."

"There goes my old man," Mrs. Delacroix said. She held her breath while her husband went forward.

"Dunbar," Mr. Summers said, and Mrs. Dunbar went steadily to the box while one of the women said, "Go on, Janey," and another said, "There she goes."

"We're next," Mrs. Graves said. She watched while Mr. Graves came around from the side of the box, greeted Mr. Summers gravely, and selected a slip of paper from the box. By now, all through the crowd there were men holding the small folded papers in their large hands, turning them over and over nervously. Mrs. Dunbar and her two sons stood together, Mrs. Dunbar holding the slip of paper.

"Harburt. . . . Hutchinson."

"Get up there, Bill," Mrs. Hutchinson said, and the people near her laughed.

"Jones."

"They do say," Mr. Adams said to Old Man Warner, who stood next to him, "that over in the north village they're talking of giving up the lottery."

Old Man Warner snorted. "Pack of crazy fools," he said. "Listening to the young folks, nothing's good enough for *them*. Next thing you know, they'll be wanting to go back to living in caves, nobody work any more, live *that* way for a while. Used to be a saying about 'Lottery in June, corn be heavy soon.' First thing you know, we'd all be eating stewed chickweed and acorns. There's *always* been a lottery," he added petulantly. "Bad enough to see young Joe Summers up there joking with everybody."

"Some places have already quit lotteries," Mrs. Adams said.

"Nothing but trouble in *that*," Old Man Warner said stoutly. "Pack of young fools."

"Martin." And Bobby Martin watched his father go forward. "Overdyke. . . . Percy."

"I wish they'd hurry," Mrs. Dunbar said to her older son. "I wish they'd hurry."

"They're almost through," her son said.

"You get ready to run tell Dad," Mrs. Dunbar said.

Mr. Summers called his own name and then stepped forward precisely and selected a slip from the box. Then he called, "Warner."

"Seventy-seventh year I been in the lottery," Old Man Warner said as he went 40 through the crowd. "Seventy-seventh time."

"Watson." The tall boy came awkwardly through the crowd. Someone said, "Don't be nervous, Jack," and Mr. Summers said, "Take your time, son."

"Zanini."

————

After that, there was a long pause, a breathless pause, until Mr. Summers, holding his slip of paper in the air, said, "All right, fellows." For a minute, no one moved, and then all the slips of paper were opened. Suddenly, all women began to speak at once, saying, "Who is it?" "Who's got it?" "Is it the Dunbars?" "Is it the Watsons?" Then the voices began to say, "It's Hutchinson. It's Bill." "Bill Hutchinson's got it."

"Go tell your father," Mrs. Dunbar said to her older son.

People began to look around to see the Hutchinsons. Bill Hutchinson was 45 standing quiet, staring down at the paper in his hand. Suddenly, Tessie Hutchinson shouted to Mr. Summers, "You didn't give him time enough to take any paper he wanted. I saw you. It wasn't fair!"

"Be a good sport, Tessie," Mrs. Delacroix called, and Mrs. Graves said, "All of us took the same chance."

"Shut up, Tessie," Bill Hutchinson said.

"Well, everyone," Mr. Summers said, "that was done pretty fast, and now we've got to be hurrying a little more to get done in time." He consulted his next list. "Bill," he said, "you draw for the Hutchinson family. You got any other households in the Hutchinsons?"

"There's Don and Eva," Mrs. Hutchinson yelled. "Make *them* take their chance!"

"Daughters draw with their husbands' families, Tessie," Mr. Summers said 50 gently. "You know that as well as anyone else."

"It wasn't fair," Tessie said.

"I guess not, Joe," Bill Hutchinson said regretfully. "My daughter draws with her husband's family, that's only fair. And I've got no other family except the kids."

"Then, as far as drawing for families is concerned, it's you," Mr. Summers said in explanation, "and as far as drawing for households is concerned, that's you, too. Right?"

"Right," Bill Hutchinson said.

"How many kids, Bill?" Mr. Summers asked formally. 55

"Three," Bill Hutchinson said. "There's Bill, Jr., and Nancy, and little Dave. And Tessie and me."

"All right, then," Mr. Summers said. "Harry, you got their tickets back?"

Mr. Graves nodded and held up the slips of paper. "Put them in the box, then," Mr. Summers directed. "Take Bill's and put it in."

"I think we ought to start over," Mrs. Hutchinson said, as quietly as she could. "I tell you it wasn't *fair*. You didn't give him time enough to choose. *Everybody* saw that."

Mr. Graves had selected the five slips and put them in the box, and he dropped 60 all the papers but those onto the ground, where the breeze caught them and lifted them off.

"Listen, everybody," Mrs. Hutchinson was saying to the people around her.

"Ready, Bill?" Mr. Summers asked, and Bill Hutchinson, with one quick glance around at his wife and children, nodded.

"Remember," Mr. Summers said, "take the slips and keep them folded until each person has taken one. Harry, you help little Dave." Mr. Graves took the hand of the little boy, who came willingly with him up to the box. "Take a paper out of the box, Davy," Mr. Summers said. Davy put his hand into the box and laughed. "Take just *one* paper," Mr. Summers said. "Harry, you hold it for him." Mr. Graves took the child's hand and removed the folded paper from the tight fist and held it while little Dave stood next to him and looked up at him wonderingly.

"Nancy next," Mr. Summers said. Nancy was twelve, and her school friends breathed heavily as she went forward, switching her skirt, and took a slip daintily from the box. "Bill, Jr.," Mr. Summers said, and Billy, his face red and his feet over-large, nearly knocked the box over as he got a paper out. "Tessie," Mr. Summers said. She hesitated for a minute, looking around defiantly, and then set her lips and went up to the box. She snatched a paper out and held it behind her.

"Bill," Mr. Summers said, and Bill Hutchinson reached into the box and felt   65 around, bringing his hand out at last with the slip of paper in it.

The crowd was quiet. A girl whispered, "I hope it's not Nancy," and the sound of the whisper reached the edges of the crowd.

"It's not the way it used to be," Old Man Warner said clearly. "People ain't the way they used to be."

"All right," Mr. Summers said. "Open the papers. Harry, you open little Dave's."

Mr. Graves opened the slip of paper and there was a general sigh through the crowd as he held it up and everyone could see that it was blank. Nancy and Bill, Jr., opened theirs at the same time, and both beamed and laughed, turning around to the crowd and holding their slips of paper above their heads.

"Tessie," Mr. Summers said. There was a pause, and then Mr. Summers looked   70 at Bill Hutchinson, and Bill unfolded his paper and showed it. It was blank.

"It's Tessie," Mr. Summers said, and his voice was hushed. "Show us her paper, Bill."

Bill Hutchinson went over to his wife and forced the slip of paper out of her hand. It had a black spot on it, the black spot Mr. Summers had made the night before with the heavy pencil in the coal-company office. Bill Hutchinson held it up, and there was a stir in the crowd.

"All right, folks," Mr. Summers said, "let's finish quickly."

Although the villagers had forgotten the ritual and lost the original black box, they still remembered to use stones. The pile of stones the boys had made earlier was ready; there were stones on the ground with the blowing scraps of paper that had come out of the box. Mrs. Delacroix selected a stone so large she had to pick it up with both hands and turned to Mrs. Dunbar. "Come on," she said. "Hurry up."

Mrs. Dunbar had small stones in both hands, and she said, gasping for breath,   75 "I can't run at all. You'll have to go ahead and I'll catch up with you."

The children had stones already, and someone gave little Davy Hutchinson a few pebbles.

Tessie Hutchinson was in the center of a cleared space by now, and she held her hands out desperately as the villagers moved in on her. "It isn't fair," she said. A stone hit her on the side of the head.

Old Man Warner was saying, "Come on, come on, everyone." Steve Adams was in the front of the crowd of villagers, with Mrs. Graves beside him.

"It isn't fair, it isn't right," Mrs. Hutchinson screamed, and then they were upon her.

## CONSIDERATIONS FOR CRITICAL THINKING AND WRITING

1. FIRST RESPONSE. Would you have a different emotional response to the story if the character selected in the lottery was someone other than Tessie Hutchinson? Put differently, do individual characters matter in this story?

2. The village in which the story takes place is contrasted with other towns in the first paragraph, and they are brought up again later in the narrative. Why is it important to know about these other towns if they are not part of the story?

3. Is it ironic that the story takes place in summer (and, further, that the man who oversees the lottery is Mr. Summers)? Why does the narrator emphasize the behavior of the out-of-school children in the second paragraph?

4. What is the effect of the objective narrative point of view on the story's tone? Put differently, if the narrator chose to occupy Tessie's mind (or any other character's) and to narrate from that perspective, how would the story change?

5. The lottery is obviously a ritual that the author has imagined as opposed to something that happened historically, but how is it connected to actual rituals? Do these connections help you to articulate the story's theme?

6. The narrator emphasizes that certain aspects of the ritual have changed over time. Why is that fact important?

7. Husbands and wives seem to have what we would now call traditional roles in this story. How is that observation significant to your understanding of its theme?

8. How does the story frame a conflict between younger and older generations?

9. Why is it significant that children as well as adults take part in the ritual?

10. The story does not indicate why the ritual sacrifice takes place, or why it began in the first place. Would your understanding of the story's style change if you were given this information?

### CONNECTIONS TO OTHER SELECTIONS

1. Discuss the ways ritual is a major component of this story and of Ursula K. Le Guin's "The Ones Who Walk Away from Omelas" (p. 121).

2. Discuss the relationship between fate and choice in this story and in Ralph Ellison's "King of the Bingo Game" (p. 178). Do the stories express exactly the same theme?

## MARK TWAIN (1835–1910)

Mark Twain is the pen name of Samuel Clemens, born in Missouri in 1835. Twain spent most of his childhood in Hannibal, Missouri, on the Mississippi River, and after the death of his father when he was eleven, he worked at a series of jobs to help support his family. A newspaper job prepared him to wander east working for papers and exploring St. Louis, New York, and Philadelphia. Later he trained as a steamboat pilot on the Mississippi and piloted boats professionally until the onset of the Civil War. Clemens

Bettmann/Getty Images.

had used a couple of different pseudonyms for minor publications before this point, but in 1863 he signed a travel narrative "Mark Twain," from a boating term that means "two fathoms deep," and the name for the great American humorist was created. Twain gained fame in 1865 with his story "The Celebrated Jumping Frog of Calaveras County," which appeared in the New York–based *Saturday Press*. He then became a traveling correspondent, writing pieces on his travels to Europe and the Middle East, and returned to the United States in 1870, when he married and moved to Connecticut. Twain produced *Roughing It* (1872) and *The Gilded Age* (1873) while he toured the country lecturing, and in 1876 published *The Adventures of Tom Sawyer*, an instant hit. His subsequent publications include *A Tramp Abroad* (1880), *The Prince and the Pauper* (1881), and the masterpiece *Adventures of Huckleberry Finn* (1884). Often traveling and lecturing, Twain wrote several more books, including story collections, *The Tragedy of Pudd'nhead Wilson* (1894), and *Tom Sawyer, Detective* (1896), before he died in Italy in 1910. His work is noted for the combination of rough humor and vernacular language it often uses to convey keen social insights.

## *The Story of the Good Little Boy*  1870

Once there was a good little boy by the name of Jacob Blivens. He always obeyed his parents, no matter how absurd and unreasonable their demands were; and he always learned his book, and never was late at Sabbath-school. He would not play hookey, even when his sober judgment told him it was the most profitable thing he could do. None of the other boys could ever make that boy out, he acted so strangely. He wouldn't lie, no matter how convenient it was. He just said it was wrong to lie, and that was sufficient for him. And he was so honest that he was simply ridiculous. The curious ways that that Jacob had, surpassed everything. He wouldn't play marbles on Sunday, he wouldn't rob birds' nests, he wouldn't give hot pennies to organ-grinders' monkeys; he didn't seem to take any interest in any kind of rational amusement. So the other boys used to try to reason it out and come to an understanding of him, but they couldn't arrive at any satisfactory conclusion. As I said before, they could only figure out a sort of vague idea that he was "afflicted," and so they took him under their protection, and never allowed any harm to come to him.

This good little boy read all the Sunday-school books; they were his greatest delight. This was the whole secret of it. He believed in the good little boys they put in the Sunday-school books; he had every confidence in them. He longed to come across one of them alive once; but he never did. They all died before his time, maybe. Whenever he read about a particularly good one he turned over quickly to the end to see what became of him, because he wanted to travel thousands of miles and gaze on him; but it wasn't any use; that good little boy always died in the last chapter, and there was a picture of the funeral, with all his relations and the Sunday-school children standing around the grave in pantaloons that were too short, and bonnets that were too large, and everybody crying into handkerchiefs that had as much as a yard and a half of stuff in them. He was always headed off in this way. He never could see one of those good little boys on account of his always dying in the last chapter.

Jacob had a noble ambition to be put in a Sunday-school book. He wanted to be put in, with pictures representing him gloriously declining to lie to his mother, and her weeping for joy about it; and pictures representing him standing on the doorstep giving a penny to a poor beggar-woman with six children, and telling her to spend it freely, but not to be extravagant, because extravagance is a sin; and pictures of him magnanimously refusing to tell on the bad boy who always lay in wait for him around the corner as he came from school, and welted him over the head with a lath, and then chased him home, saying, "Hi! hi!" as he proceeded. That was the ambition of young Jacob Blivens. He wished to be put in a Sunday-school book. It made him feel a little uncomfortable sometimes when he reflected that the good little boys always died. He loved to live, you know, and this was the most unpleasant feature about being a Sunday-school-book boy. He knew it was not healthy to be good. He knew it was more fatal than consumption to be so supernaturally good as the boys in the books were; he knew that none of them had ever been able to stand it long, and it pained him to think that if they put him in a book he wouldn't ever see it, or even if they did get the book out before he died it wouldn't be popular without any picture of his funeral in the back part of it. It couldn't be much of a Sunday-school book that couldn't tell about the advice he gave to the community when he was dying. So at last, of course, he had to make up his mind to do the best he could under the circumstances — to live right, and hang on as long as he could, and have his dying speech all ready when his time came.

But somehow nothing ever went right with this good little boy; nothing ever turned out with him the way it turned out with the good little boys in the books. They always had a good time, and the bad boys had the broken legs; but in his case there was a screw loose somewhere, and it all happened just the other way. When he found Jim Blake stealing apples, and went under the tree to read to him about the bad little boy who fell out of a neighbor's apple tree and broke his arm, Jim fell out of the tree, too, but he fell on *him* and broke *his* arm, and Jim wasn't hurt at all. Jacob couldn't understand that. There wasn't anything in the books like it.

And once, when some bad boys pushed a blind man over in the mud, and 5 Jacob ran to help him up and receive his blessing, the blind man did not give him any blessing at all, but whacked him over the head with his stick and said he would like to catch him shoving *him* again, and then pretending to help him up. This was not in accordance with any of the books. Jacob looked them all over to see.

One thing that Jacob wanted to do was to find a lame dog that hadn't any place to stay, and was hungry and persecuted, and bring him home and pet him and have that dog's imperishable gratitude. And at last he found one and was happy; and he brought him home and fed him, but when he was going to pet him the dog flew at him and tore all the clothes off him except those that were in front, and made a spectacle of him that was astonishing. He examined authorities, but he could not understand the matter. It was of the same breed of dogs that was in the books, but it acted very differently. Whatever this boy did he got into trouble. The very things the boys in the books got rewarded for turned out to be about the most unprofitable things he could invest in.

Once, when he was on his way to Sunday-school, he saw some bad boys starting off pleasuring in a sailboat. He was filled with consternation, because he knew from his reading that boys who went sailing on Sunday invariably got drowned. So he ran out on a raft to warn them, but a log turned with him and slid him into the river. A man got him out pretty soon, and the doctor pumped the water out of him, and gave him a fresh start with his bellows, but he caught cold and lay sick abed nine weeks. But the most unaccountable thing about it was that the bad boys in the boat had a good time all day, and then reached home alive and well in the most surprising manner. Jacob Blivens said there was nothing like these things in the books. He was perfectly dumbfounded.

When he got well he was a little discouraged, but he resolved to keep on trying anyhow. He knew that so far his experiences wouldn't do to go in a book, but he hadn't yet reached the allotted term of life for good little boys, and he hoped to be able to make a record yet if he could hold on till his time was fully up. If everything else failed he had his dying speech to fall back on.

He examined his authorities, and found that it was now time for him to go to sea as a cabin-boy. He called on a ship-captain and made his application, and when the captain asked for his recommendations he proudly drew out a tract and pointed to the word, "To Jacob Blivens, from his affectionate teacher." But the captain was a coarse, vulgar man, and he said, "Oh, that be blowed! *that* wasn't any proof that he knew how to wash dishes or handle a slush-bucket, and he guessed he didn't want him." This was altogether the most extraordinary thing that ever happened to Jacob in all his life. A compliment from a teacher, on a tract, had never failed to move the tenderest emotions of ship-captains, and open the way to all offices of honor and profit in their gift — it never had in any book that ever *he* had read. He could hardly believe his senses.

This boy always had a hard time of it. Nothing ever came out according to the authorities with him. At last, one day, when he was around hunting up bad little boys to admonish, he found a lot of them in the old iron-foundry fixing up a little joke on fourteen or fifteen dogs, which they had tied together in long procession, and were going to ornament with empty nitroglycerin cans made fast to their tails. Jacob's heart was touched. He sat down on one of those cans (for he never minded grease when duty was before him), and he took hold of the foremost dog by the collar, and turned his reproving eye upon wicked Tom Jones. But just at that moment Alderman McWelter, full of wrath, stepped in. All the bad boys ran away, but Jacob Blivens rose in conscious innocence and began one of those stately little Sunday-school-book speeches which always commence with "Oh, sir!" in dead opposition to the fact that no boy, good or bad, ever starts a remark with "Oh, sir." But the alderman never waited to hear the rest. He took Jacob Blivens by the ear and turned him around, and hit him a whack in the rear with the flat of his hand; and in an instant that good little boy shot out through the roof and soared away toward the sun, with the fragments of those fifteen dogs stringing after him like the tail of a kite. And there wasn't a sign of that alderman or that old iron-foundry left on the face of the earth; and, as for young Jacob Blivens, he never got a chance to make his last dying speech after all his trouble fixing it up, unless he made it to the birds; because, although the bulk of him came down all right in a tree-top in an adjoining county, the rest of him was apportioned around among four townships, and so they had to hold five inquests on him to find out whether he was dead or not, and how it occurred. You never saw a boy scattered so.[1]

10

---

[1] This glycerin catastrophe is borrowed from a floating newspaper item, whose author's name I would give if I knew it. M.T.

Thus perished the good little boy who did the best he could, but didn't come out according to the books. Every boy who ever did as he did prospered except him. His case is truly remarkable. It will probably never be accounted for.

### CONSIDERATIONS FOR CRITICAL THINKING AND WRITING

1. FIRST RESPONSE. Twain is well known as a humorist. This story is about the death of a child. How does he manage to make that tragic circumstance funny (if you agree that it is)?

2. What is the story's central irony?

3. Which sentences are particularly effective in imitating the style of Sunday-school books? Which sentences are clearly Twain's own style? What is the effect of having both styles side by side?

4. How does the story's irony reveal Twain's attitude toward Jacob? Find specific passages to support your points.

5. What sort of lesson does Twain's version of Sunday-school instruction teach?

6. Is there a serious point to the humor here that allows you to identify the theme of the story?

7. It might be tempting to sum up this story with a cliché like "Nice guys finish last." Why would such a statement be inadequate as a statement of theme?

8. Characterize the tone of voice that tells the story. Is it indignant, amused, cynical, bitter, disinterested, or some other adjective of your choosing?

### CONNECTIONS TO OTHER SELECTIONS

1. Jamaica Kincaid's short story "Girl" (p. 150) also grapples with the subject of proper behavior for children. Contrast the styles of the two stories as a way of probing the nuances of their effects on the reader.

2. Write an essay comparing notions of goodness and obedience in this story and in John Updike's "A & P" (p. 145).

## VIRGINIA WOOLF (1882–1941)

One of the most important novelists of the twentieth century, Virginia Woolf is responsible — along with her Irish peer James Joyce and her American peers William Faulkner and Gertrude Stein — for introducing the stream-of-consciousness technique into fiction. Born into a wealthy London family, Woolf became a prominent writer affiliated with a cohort called the Bloomsbury Group and founded the Hogarth Press, a publishing house that helped to showcase the works of avant-garde writers ushering in the new aesthetic known as Modernism. Her best-known works, including the novels *Mrs. Dalloway* (1925) and *To the Lighthouse* (1927) and the lengthy essay *A Room of One's Own* (1929), remain classics that have fascinated and challenged readers for nearly a century. Many contemporary readers note the way her work anticipated currents of feminist thought that developed after her lifetime. All of her work, including the following story, rewards careful reading with an understanding of her characters' complex psychological makeup.

## The Man Who Loved His Kind

Trotting through Deans Yard that afternoon, Prickett Ellis ran straight into Richard Dalloway, or rather, just as they were passing, the covert side glance which each was casting on the other, under his hat, over his shoulder, broadened and burst into recognition; they had not met for twenty years. They had been at school together. And what was Ellis doing? The Bar?° Of course, of course — he had followed the case in the papers. But it was impossible to talk here. Wouldn't he drop in that evening. (They lived in the same old place — just round the corner.) One or two people were coming. Joynson perhaps. "An awful swell now," said Richard.

"Good — till this evening then," said Richard, and went his way, "jolly glad" (that was quite true) to have met that queer chap, who hadn't changed one bit since he had been at school — just the same knobbly, chubby little boy then, with prejudices sticking out all over him, but uncommonly brilliant — won the Newcastle°. Well-off he went.

Prickett Ellis, however, as he turned and looked at Dalloway disappearing, wished now he had not met him or, at least, for he had always liked him personally, hadn't promised to come to this party. Dalloway was married, gave parties; wasn't his sort at all. He would have to dress. However, as the evening drew on, he supposed, as he had said that, and didn't want to be rude, he must go there.

But what an appalling entertainment! There was Joynson; they had nothing to say to each other. He had been a pompous little boy; he had grown rather more self-important — that was all; there wasn't a single other soul in the room that Prickett Ellis knew. Not one. So, as he could not go at once, without saying a word to Dalloway, who seemed altogether taken up with his duties, bustling about in a white waistcoat, there he had to stand. It was the sort of thing that made his gorge rise. Think of grown up, responsible men and women doing this every night of their lives! The lines deepened on his blue and red shaven cheeks as he leant against the wall in complete silence, for though he worked like a horse, he kept himself fit by exercise; and he looked hard and fierce, as if his moustaches were dipped in frost. He bristled; he grated. His meagre dress clothes made him look unkempt, insignificant, angular.

Idle, chattering, overdressed, without an idea in their heads, these fine ladies  5
and gentlemen went on talking and laughing; and Prickett Ellis watched them and compared them with the Brunners who, when they won their case against Fenners' Brewery and got two hundred pounds' compensation (it was not half what they should have got) went and spent five of it on a clock for him. That was a decent sort of thing to do; that was the sort of thing that moved one, and he glared more severely than ever at these people, overdressed, cynical, prosperous, and compared what he felt now with what he felt at eleven o'clock that morning when old Brunner and Mrs. Brunner, in their best clothes, awfully respectable and clean looking old people, had called in to give him that small token, as the old man put it, standing perfectly upright to make his speech, of gratitude and respect for the very able way in which you conducted our case, and Mrs. Brunner piped up, how it was all due to him they felt. And they deeply appreciated his generosity — because, of course, he hadn't taken a fee.

*The Bar:* Ellis works in the legal profession; lawyers in England are called barristers.
*The Newcastle:* A prize for superior writing given annually to a student at the elite Eton College.

And as he took the clock and put it on the middle of his mantelpiece, he had felt that he wished nobody to see his face. That was what he worked for — that was his reward; and he looked at the people who were actually before his eyes as if they danced over that scene in his chambers and were exposed by it, and as it faded — the Brunners faded — there remained as if left of that scene, himself, confronting this hostile population, a perfectly plain, unsophisticated man, a man of the people (he straightened himself), very badly dressed, glaring, with not an air or a grace about him, a man who was an ill hand at concealing his feelings, a plain man, an ordinary human being, pitted against the evil, the corruption, the heartlessness of society. But he would not go on staring. Now he put on his spectacles and examined the pictures. He read the titles on a line of books; for the most part poetry. He would have liked well enough to read some of his old favourites again — Shakespeare, Dickens — he wished he ever had time to turn into the National Gallery, but he couldn't — no, one could not. Really one could not — with the world in the state it was in. Not when people all day long wanted your help, fairly clamoured for help. This wasn't an age for luxuries. And he looked at the arm chairs and the paper knives and the well bound books, and shook his head, knowing that he would never have the time, never he was glad to think have the heart, to afford himself such luxuries. The people here would be shocked if they knew what he paid for his tobacco; how he had borrowed his clothes. His one and only extravagance was his little yacht on the Norfolk Broads. And that he did allow himself. He did like once a year to get right away from everybody and lie on his back in a field. He thought how shocked they would be — these fine folk — if they realized the amount of pleasure he got from what he was old fashioned enough to call the love of nature; trees and fields he had known ever since he was a boy.

These fine people would be shocked. Indeed, standing there, putting his spectacles away in his pocket, he felt himself grow more and more shocking every instant. And it was a very disagreeable feeling. He did not feel this — that he loved humanity, that he paid only fivepence an ounce for tobacco and loved nature — naturally and quietly. Each of these pleasures had been turned into a protest. He felt that these people whom he despised made him stand and deliver and justify himself. "I am an ordinary man," he kept saying. And what he said next he was really ashamed of saying, but he said it. "I have done more for my kind in one day than the rest of you in all your lives." Indeed, he could not help himself; he kept recalling scene after scene, like that when the Brunners gave him the clock — he kept reminding himself of the nice things people had said of his humanity, of his generosity, how he had helped them. He kept seeing himself as the wise and tolerant servant of humanity. And he wished he could repeat his praises aloud. It was unpleasant that the sense of his goodness should boil within him. It was still more unpleasant that he could tell no one what people had said about him. Thank the Lord, he kept saying, I shall be back at work tomorrow; and yet he was no longer satisfied simply to slip through the door and go home. He must stay, he must stay until he had justified himself. But how could he? In all that room full of people, he did not know a soul to speak to.

At last Richard Dalloway came up.

"I want to introduce Miss O'Keefe," he said. Miss O'Keefe looked him full in the eyes. She was a rather arrogant, abrupt mannered woman in the thirties.

Miss O'Keefe wanted an ice or something to drink. And the reason why she asked Prickett Ellis to give it her in what he felt a haughty, unjustifiable manner, was that she had seen a woman and two children, very poor, very tired, pressing against the railings of a square, peering in, that hot afternoon. Can't they be let in? she had thought, her pity rising like a wave; her indignation boiling. No; she rebuked herself the next moment, roughly, as if she boxed her own ears. The whole force of the world can't do it. So she picked up the tennis ball and hurled it back. The whole force of the world can't do it, she said in a fury, and that was why she said so commandingly, to the unknown man:

"Give me an ice."

Long before she had eaten it, Prickett Ellis, standing beside her without taking anything, told her that he had not been to a party for fifteen years; told her that his dress suit was lent him by his brother-in-law; told her that he did not like this sort of thing, and it would have eased him greatly to go on to say that he was a plain man, who happened to have a liking for ordinary people, and then would have told her (and been ashamed of it afterwards) about the Brunners and the clock, but she said: "Have you seen *The Tempest?*°" then (for he had not seen *The Tempest*), had he read some book? Again no, and then, putting her ice down, did he never read poetry?

And Prickett Ellis feeling something rise within him which would decapitate this young woman, make a victim of her, massacre her, made her sit down there, where they would not be interrupted, on two chairs, in the empty garden, for everyone was upstairs, only you could hear a buzz and a hum and a chatter and a jingle, like the mad accompaniment of some phantom orchestra to a cat or two slinking across the grass, and the wavering of leaves, and the yellow and red fruit like Chinese lanterns wobbling this way and that — the talk seemed like a frantic skeleton dance music set to something very real, and full of suffering.

"How beautiful!" said Miss O'Keefe.

Oh, it was beautiful, this little patch of grass, with the towers of Westminster 15 massed round it black, high in the air, after the drawing-room; it was silent, after that noise. After all, they had that — the tired woman, the children.

Prickett Ellis lit a pipe. That would shock her; he filled it with shag tobacco — fivepence halfpenny an ounce. He thought how he would lie in his boat smoking, he could see himself, alone, at night, smoking under the stars. For always tonight he kept thinking how he would look if these people here were to see him. He said to Miss O'Keefe, striking a match on the sole of his boot, that he couldn't see anything particularly beautiful out here.

"Perhaps," said Miss O'Keefe, "you don't care for beauty." (He had told her that he had not seen *The Tempest;* that he had not read a book; he looked ill-kempt, all moustache, chin, and silver watch chain.) She thought nobody need pay a penny for this; the Museums are free and the National Gallery; and the country. Of course she knew the objections — the washing, cooking, children; but the root of things, what they were all afraid of saying, was that happiness is dirt cheap. You can have it for nothing. Beauty.

Then Prickett Ellis let her have it — this pale, abrupt, arrogant woman. He told her, puffing his shag tobacco, what he had done that day. Up at six; interviews; smelling a drain in a filthy slum; then to court.

Here he hesitated, wishing to tell her something of his own doings. Suppressing that, he was all the more caustic. He said it made him sick to hear well-fed,

---

*The Tempest:* A play by William Shakespeare, presumably being produced in London at the time of the story.

well-dressed women (she twitched her lips, for she was thin, and her dress not up to standard) talk of beauty.

"Beauty!" he said. He was afraid he did not understand beauty apart from 20 human beings.

So they glared into the empty garden where the lights were swaying, and one cat hesitating in the middle, its paw lifted.

Beauty apart from human beings? What did he mean by that? she demanded suddenly.

Well, this: getting more and more wrought up, he told her the story of the Brunners and the clock, not concealing his pride in it. That was beautiful, he said.

She had no words to specify the horror his story roused in her. First his conceit; then his indecency in talking about human feelings; it was a blasphemy; no one in the whole world ought to tell a story to prove that they had loved their kind. Yet as he told it — how the old man had stood up and made his speech — tears came into her eyes; ah, if anyone had ever said that to her! but then again, she felt how it was just this that condemned humanity for ever; never would they reach beyond affecting scenes with clocks; Brunners making speeches to Prickett Ellises, and the Prickett Ellises would always say how they had loved their kind; they would always be lazy, compromising, and afraid of beauty. Hence sprang revolutions; from laziness and fear and this love of affecting scenes. Still this man got pleasure from his Brunners; and she was condemned to suffer for ever and ever from her poor poor women shut out from squares. So they sat silent. Both were very unhappy. For Prickett Ellis was not in the least solaced by what he had said; instead of picking her thorn out he had rubbed it in; his happiness of the morning had been ruined. Miss O'Keefe was muddled and annoyed; she was muddy instead of clear.

"I am afraid I am one of those very ordinary people," he said, getting up, "who 25 love their kind."

Upon which Miss O'Keefe almost shouted: "So do I."

Hating each other, hating the whole houseful of people who had given them this painful, this disillusioning evening, these two lovers of their kind got up, and without a word, parted for ever.

## CONSIDERATIONS FOR CRITICAL THINKING AND WRITING

1. FIRST RESPONSE. Based on the thoughts that run through Prickett Ellis's mind before he speaks to anyone at Dalloway's party, what exactly would you say is responsible for his contempt for the people there?

2. Would you use the term "introvert" or "misanthrope" (or another term) to characterize Ellis? Cite textual evidence.

3. How does Woolf's style enable us to see Ellis from the inside and the outside simultaneously?

4. Part of Woolf's style involves sentences that run on longer than usual. Locate a few such sentences and explore their effect.

5. The story changes markedly when Ellis meets Miss O'Keefe: how does her introduction alter the story's trajectory? What might have happened to Ellis if she was not part of the story?

6. How does Ellis interpret the story of the Brunners giving him a clock?

7. Miss O'Keefe reflects on an anecdote from that same morning, the story of the poor women and her children who are kept out of a square by railings. Contrast her reaction to this story to Ellis's reaction to the Brunners giving him a clock.

8. Why is it significant that the two characters disagree violently about the definition of beauty?

9. The story's title echoes a thought Miss O'Keefe has: "no one in the whole world ought to tell a story to prove that they had loved their kind" (par. 24). Look carefully at that line in its context: what does it do to your understanding of the story's title? Is the title ironic?

10. Both characters declare that they "love their kind." Are they both right? Is neither right? If they are alike in this regard, why do they seem to take an instant dislike to one another?

11. Much of the story leads us deep into the feelings of these two characters. What is the effect of ending the story so distant from both of them?

## CONNECTIONS TO OTHER SELECTIONS

1. The narrative styles of this story and Shirley Jackson's "The Lottery" (p. 233) are markedly different. Are the themes similar?

2. Compare depictions of public and private selves in this story and in Oscar Wilde's "The Sphinx Without a Secret" (p. 278).

---

## Perspective

---

### VIRGINIA WOOLF (1882–1941)

## *On Conventions in Writing* 1924

A convention in writing is not much different from a convention in manners. Both in life and in literature it is necessary to have some means of bridging the gulf between the hostess and her unknown guest on the one hand, the writer and his unknown reader on the other. The hostess bethinks her of the weather, for generations of hostesses have established the fact that this is a subject of universal interest in which we all believe. She begins by saying that we are having a wretched May, and, having thus got into touch with her unknown guest, proceeds to matters of greater interest. So it is in literature. The writer must get into touch with his reader by putting before him something which he recognizes, which therefore stimulates his imagination, and makes him willing to cooperate in the far more difficult business of intimacy. And it is of the highest importance that this common meeting-place should be reached easily, almost instinctively, in the dark, with one's eyes shut.

From *Mr. Bennet and Mrs. Brown*, 1924

### CONSIDERATIONS FOR CRITICAL THINKING AND WRITING

1. Woolf uses the relationship between a hostess and a guest as an analogy, but in "The Man Who Loved His Kind" there is an actual guest-host relationship. Use it to illustrate and further explain Woolf's point in this essay.

2. How do you interpret Woolf's final sentence in this passage?

3. What is meant by "intimacy" in this context, and how is it crucial to Woolf's ideas about the art of fiction?

# Approaches
# to Fiction

# 9

## A THEMATIC CASE STUDY
# War and Its Aftermath

Agence Opale/Alamy.

There is a hunger in people like me to know everything from the story tellers, the story carriers in my life, because I absolutely need those stories. . . . I especially need them for the next generation of my family. . . . I need them to know how we lived before they knew us. I need them to know who we were before we came here. I need them to know how we managed to survive, how we managed not to die. I need them to have these stories as tools for their future.

— EDWIDGE DANTICAT

The literature of war is, lamentably, a major and persistent topic for writers and readers because human history has marched to a steady drumbeat of violent conflict. In *What Every Person Should Know about War* (2003), Chris Hedges, a best-selling author and a former foreign correspondent for the *New York Times*, reports that for the past 3,400 years complete peace has been established in only 268 years. This means that in 92 percent of recorded history, some portion of the world has been at war. Since the beginning of the twenty-first century, when this estimate was made, the percentage of peacetime has not increased. Peace may briefly break out, but every news source imprints upon us the dominating fact of life that war is a permanent course of human action. It is not surprising, then, that writers choose to explore war and its aftermath.

This chapter offers three short stories about war and postwar settings written within the last half century. Such a limited selection cannot be representative of the thematic and stylistic range of such narratives, but these stories do suggest some perennial concerns as well as contemporary responses to war. They maneuver around the profound and lasting impact of war on people, both combatants and civilians, who confront its meaning and its meaninglessness. What emerges from the fog is a series of complicated contradictions that map its confusion, brutality, horror, boredom, and futility. Unlike history books, these stories don't seek to explain the causes of war; instead, they explore its effects. What Tim O'Brien describes in "How to Tell a True War Story" (p. 253) as "the awful majesty of combat" is the discovery of the intensity of life amid the possibility, indeed the likelihood, of death. This extraordinary tension italicizes immediate experience even though the broader context of political abstractions and historical justifications might raise fatal questions about the efficacy of war. Ernest Hemingway suggests as much in a little-read introduction he wrote for *Men at War*, an anthology he put together in 1942, one year into World War II: "The editor of this anthology, who took part and was wounded in [World War I], hates war and hates all the politicians whose mismanagement, gullibility, cupidity, selfishness and ambition brought this present war and made it inevitable. But once we have a war there is only one thing to do." The stories that follow explore some of the things one might do.

In addition to O'Brien's work about Vietnam, the chapter includes two recent stories about the lasting effects of war. Kurt Vonnegut's posthumously published "Happy Birthday, 1951" (p. 263) explores the psychology of a boy who was abandoned during World War II and raised by an old man after its conclusion, and Edwidge Danticat's "The Missing Peace" (p. 267) examines the life of a young woman during the military occupation of Port-au-Prince, Haiti, following a revolution there in the 1980s. Another classic war story elsewhere in this anthology is Hemingway's "Soldier's Home" (p. 115), about returning from World War I. Louise Erdrich's "The Red Convertible" (p. 170) considers the effects of the Vietnam War on a soldier who returns from it obviously damaged, but also unwilling to talk about his experiences, and the same could be said of the narrator of Adrian Tomine's graphic short story "Intruders" (p. 197), although it's unclear whether he has seen combat. Each of these six stories offers a fresh and original approach to understanding the lasting effects of war that goes beyond the sort of assessments that reduce it to clichés. Collectively, these stories might enable you to understand only one thing about war: its unfathomable complexity.

## TIM O'BRIEN (B. 1946)

Born in Austin, Minnesota, Tim O'Brien was educated at Macalester College and Harvard University. He was drafted to serve in the Vietnam War and received a Purple Heart. His work is heavily influenced by his service in the war. His first book, *If I Die in a Combat Zone, Box Me Up and Ship Me Home* (1973), is a blend of fiction and actual experiences during his tour of duty. *Going after Cacciato*, judged by many critics to be the best work of American fiction about the Vietnam War, won the National Book Award in 1978.

He has also published five other novels, *Northern Lights* (1974), *The Nuclear Age* (1985), *In the Lake of the Woods* (1994), *Tomcat in Love* (1998), and *July, July* (2002). "How to Tell a True War Story" is from a collection of interrelated stories titled *The Things They Carried* (1990). Originally published in *Esquire*, this story is at once grotesque and beautiful in its attempt to be true to experience.

## How to Tell a True War Story    1987

This is true.

I had a buddy in Vietnam. His name was Bob Kiley, but everybody called him Rat.

A friend of his gets killed, so about a week later Rat sits down and writes a letter to the guy's sister. Rat tells her what a great brother she had, how strack° the guy was, a number one pal and comrade. A real soldier's soldier, Rat says. Then he tells a few stories to make the point, how her brother would always volunteer for stuff nobody else would volunteer for in a million years, dangerous stuff, like doing recon° or going out on these really badass night patrols. Stainless steel balls, Rat tells her. The guy was a little crazy, for sure, but crazy in a good way, a real daredevil, because he liked the challenge of it, he liked testing himself, just man against gook. A great, great guy, Rat says.

Anyway, it's a terrific letter, very personal and touching. Rat almost bawls writing it. He gets all teary telling about the good times they had together, how her brother made the war seem almost fun, always raising hell and lighting up villes° and bringing smoke to bear every which way. A great sense of humor, too. Like the time at this river when he went fishing with a whole damn crate of hand grenades. Probably the funniest thing in world history, Rat says, all that gore, about twenty zillion dead gook fish. Her brother, he had the right attitude. He knew how to have a good time. On Halloween, this real hot spooky night, the dude paints up his body all different colors and puts on this weird mask and goes out on ambush almost stark naked, just boots and balls and an M-16. A tremendous human being, Rat says. Pretty nutso sometimes, but you could trust him with your life.

And then the letter gets very sad and serious. Rat pours his heart out. He says    5
he loved the guy. He says the guy was his best friend in the world. They were like soul mates, he says, like twins or something, they had a whole lot in common. He tells the guy's sister he'll look her up when the war's over.

So what happens?

Rat mails the letter. He waits two months. The dumb cooze never writes back.

A true war story is never moral. It does not instruct, nor encourage virtue, nor suggest models of proper human behavior, nor restrain men from doing the things they have always done. If a story seems moral, do not believe it. If at the end of a war story you feel uplifted, or if you feel that some small bit of rectitude has been salvaged from the larger waste, then you have been made the victim of a very old

---

*strack:* A strict military appearance.
*doing recon:* Reconnaissance, or exploratory survey of enemy territory.
*villes:* Villages.

and terrible lie. There is no rectitude whatsoever. There is no virtue. As a first rule of thumb, therefore, you can tell a true war story by its absolute and uncompromising allegiance to obscenity and evil. Listen to Rat Kiley. *Cooze*, he says. He does not say *bitch*. He certainly does not say *woman*, or *girl*. He says *cooze*. Then he spits and stares. He's nineteen years old — it's too much for him — so he looks at you with those big gentle killer eyes and says *cooze*, because his friend is dead, and because it's so incredibly sad and true: she never wrote back.

You can tell a true war story if it embarrasses you. If you don't care for obscenity, you don't care for the truth; if you don't care for the truth, watch how you vote. Send guys to war, they come home talking dirty.

Listen to Rat: "Jesus Christ, man, I write this beautiful fucking letter, I slave  10
over it, and what happens? The dumb cooze never writes back."

The dead guy's name was Curt Lemon. What happened was, we crossed a muddy river and marched west into the mountains, and on the third day we took a break along a trail junction in deep jungle. Right away, Lemon and Rat Kiley started goofing off. They didn't understand about the spookiness. They were kids; they just didn't know. A nature hike, they thought, not even a war, so they went off into the shade of some giant trees — quadruple canopy, no sunlight at all — and they were giggling and calling each other motherfucker and playing a silly game they'd invented. The game involved smoke grenades, which were harmless unless you did stupid things, and what they did was pull out the pin and stand a few feet apart and play catch under the shade of those huge trees. Whoever chickened out was a motherfucker. And if nobody chickened out, the grenade would make a light popping sound and they'd be covered with smoke and they'd laugh and dance around and then do it again.

It's all exactly true.

It happened nearly twenty years ago, but I still remember that trail junction and the giant trees and a soft dripping sound somewhere beyond the trees. I remember the smell of moss. Up in the canopy there were tiny white blossoms, but no sunlight at all, and I remember the shadows spreading out under the trees where Lemon and Rat Kiley were playing catch with smoke grenades. Mitchell Sanders sat flipping his yo-yo. Norman Bowker and Kiowa and Dave Jensen were dozing, or half-dozing, and all around us were those ragged green mountains.

Except for the laughter things were quiet.

At one point, I remember, Mitchell Sanders turned and looked at me, not  15
quite nodding, then after a while he rolled up his yo-yo and moved away.

It's hard to tell what happened next.

They were just goofing. There was a noise, I suppose, which must've been the detonator, so I glanced behind me and watched Lemon step from the shade into bright sunlight. His face was suddenly brown and shining. A handsome kid, really. Sharp gray eyes, lean and narrow-waisted, and when he died it was almost beautiful, the way the sunlight came around him and lifted him up and sucked him high into a tree full of moss and vines and white blossoms.

In any war story, but especially a true one, it's difficult to separate what happened from what seemed to happen. What seems to happen becomes its own happening and has to be told that way. The angles of vision are skewed. When a booby trap explodes, you close your eyes and duck and float outside yourself. When a guy dies, like Lemon, you look away and then look back for a moment and then look away again. The pictures get jumbled; you tend to miss a lot. And then afterward, when you go to tell about it, there is always that surreal seemingness, which makes the story seem untrue, but which in fact represents the hard and exact truth as it seemed.

In many cases a true war story cannot be believed. If you believe it, be skeptical. It's a question of credibility. Often the crazy stuff is true and the normal stuff isn't because the normal stuff is necessary to make you believe the truly incredible craziness.

In other cases you can't even tell a true war story. Sometimes it's just beyond    20
telling.

I heard this one, for example, from Mitchell Sanders. It was near dusk and we were sitting at my foxhole along a wide, muddy river north of Quang Ngai. I remember how peaceful the twilight was. A deep pinkish red spilled out on the river, which moved without sound, and in the morning we would cross the river and march west into the mountains. The occasion was right for a good story.

"God's truth," Mitchell Sanders said. "A six-man patrol goes up into the mountains on a basic listening-post operation. The idea's to spend a week up there, just lie low and listen for enemy movement. They've got a radio along, so if they hear anything suspicious — anything — they're supposed to call in artillery or gunships, whatever it takes. Otherwise they keep strict field discipline. Absolute silence. They just listen."

He glanced at me to make sure I had the scenario. He was playing with his yo-yo, making it dance with short, tight little strokes of the wrist.

His face was blank in the dusk.

"We're talking hardass LP.° These six guys, they don't say boo for a solid week.    25
They don't got tongues. *All* ears."

"Right," I said.

"Understand me?"

"Invisible."

Sanders nodded.

"Affirm," he said. "Invisible. So what happens is, these guys get themselves    30
deep in the bush, all camouflaged up, and they lie down and wait and that's all they do, nothing else, they lie there for seven straight days and just listen. And man, I'll tell you — it's spooky. This is mountains. You don't *know* spooky till you been there. Jungle, sort of, except it's way up in the clouds and there's always this fog — like rain, except it's not raining — everything's all wet and swirly and tangled up and you can't see jack, you can't find your own pecker to piss with. Like you don't even have a body. Serious spooky. You just go with the vapors — the fog sort of takes you in. . . . And the sounds, man. The sounds carry forever. You hear shit nobody should *ever* hear."

Sanders was quiet for a second, just working the yo-yo, then he smiled at me. "So, after a couple days the guys start hearing this real soft, kind of wacked-out music. Weird echoes and stuff. Like a radio or something, but it's not a radio, it's this strange gook music that comes right out of the rocks. Faraway, sort of, but right up close, too. They try to ignore it. But it's a listening post, right? So they listen. And every night they keep hearing this crazyass gook concert. All kinds of chimes and xylophones. I mean, this is wilderness — no way, it can't be real — but

*LP:* Listening post.

there it *is,* like the mountains are tuned in to Radio Fucking Hanoi. Naturally they get nervous. One guy sticks Juicy Fruit in his ears. Another guy almost flips. Thing is, though, they can't report music. They can't get on the horn and call back to base and say, 'Hey, listen, we need some firepower, we got to blow away this weirdo gook rock band.' They can't do that. It wouldn't go down. So they lie there in the fog and keep their mouths shut. And what makes it extra bad, see, is the poor dudes can't horse around like normal. Can't joke it away. Can't even talk to each other except maybe in whispers, all hush-hush, and that just revs up the willies. All they do is listen."

Again there was some silence as Mitchell Sanders looked out on the river. The dark was coming on hard now, and off to the west I could see the mountains rising in silhouette, all the mysteries and unknowns.

"This next part," Sanders said quietly, "you won't believe."

"Probably not," I said.

"You won't. And you know why?"                                   35

"Why?"

He gave me a tired smile. "Because it happened. Because every word is absolutely dead-on true."

Sanders made a little sound in his throat, like a sigh, as if to say he didn't care if I believed it or not. But he did care. He wanted me to believe, I could tell. He seemed sad, in a way.

"These six guys, they're pretty fried out by now, and one night they start hearing voices. Like at a cocktail party. That's what it sounds like, this big swank gook cocktail party somewhere out there in the fog. Music and chitchat and stuff. It's crazy, I know, but they hear the champagne corks. They hear the actual martini glasses. Real hoity-toity, all very civilized, except this isn't civilization. This is Nam.

"Anyway, the guys try to be cool. They just lie there and groove, but after a   40
while they start hearing — you won't believe this — they hear chamber music. They hear violins and shit. They hear this terrific mama-san soprano. Then after a while they hear gook opera and a glee club and the Haiphong Boys Choir and a barbershop quartet and all kinds of weird chanting and Buddha-Buddha stuff. The whole time, in the background, there's still that cocktail party going on. All these different voices. Not human voices, though. Because it's the mountains. Follow me? The rock — it's *talking.* And the fog, too, and the grass and the goddamn mongooses. Everything talks. The trees talk politics, the monkeys talk religion. The whole country. Vietnam, the place talks.

"The guys can't cope. They lose it. They get on the radio and report enemy movement — a whole army, they say — and they order up the firepower. They get arty° and gunships. They call in air strikes. And I'll tell you, they fuckin' crash that cocktail party. All night long, they just smoke those mountains. They make jungle juice. They blow away trees and glee clubs and whatever else there is to blow away. Scorch time. They walk napalm up and down the ridges. They bring in the Cobras and F-4s, they use Willie Peter and HE° and incendiaries. It's all fire. They make those mountains burn.

"Around dawn things finally get quiet. Like you never even *heard* quiet before. One of those real thick, real misty days — just clouds and fog, they're off in this special zone — and the mountains are absolutely dead-flat silent.

---

*arty:* Artillery.
*Willie Peter and HE:* White phosphorus, an incendiary substance, and high explosives.

Like Brigadoon° — pure vapor, you know? Everything's all sucked up inside the fog. Not a single sound, except they still *hear* it.

"So they pack up and start humping. They head down the mountain, back to base camp, and when they get there they don't say diddly. They don't talk. Not a word, like they're deaf and dumb. Later on this fat bird colonel comes up and asks what the hell happened out there. What'd they hear? Why all the ordnance? The man's ragged out, he gets down tight on their case. I mean, they spent six trillion dollars on firepower, and this fatass colonel wants answers, he wants to know what the fuckin' story is.

"But the guys don't say zip. They just look at him for a while, sort of funny-like, sort of amazed, and the whole war is right there in that stare. It says everything you can't ever say. It says, man, you got *wax* in your ears. It says, poor bastard, you'll never know — wrong frequency — you don't *even* want to hear this. Then they salute the fucker and walk away, because certain stories you don't ever tell."

You can tell a true war story by the way it never seems to end. Not then, not ever. 45
Not when Mitchell Sanders stood up and moved off into the dark.

It all happened.

Even now I remember that yo-yo. In a way, I suppose, you had to be there, you had to hear it, but I could tell how desperately Sanders wanted me to believe him, his frustration at not quite getting the details right, not quite pinning down the final and definitive truth.

And I remember sitting at my foxhole that night, watching the shadows of Quang Ngai, thinking about the coming day and how we would cross the river and march west into the mountains, all the ways I might die, all the things I did not understand.

Late in the night Mitchell Sanders touched my shoulder.

"Just came to me," he whispered. "The moral, I mean. Nobody listens. Nobody 50
hears nothing. Like that fatass colonel. The politicians, all the civilian types, what they need is to go out on LP. The vapors, man. Trees and rocks — you got to *listen* to your enemy."

And then again, in the morning, Sanders came up to me. The platoon was preparing to move out, checking weapons, going through all the little rituals that preceded a day's march. Already the lead squad had crossed the river and was filing off toward the west.

"I got a confession to make," Sanders said. "Last night, man, I had to make up a few things."

"I know that."

"The glee club. There wasn't any glee club."

"Right." 55

"No opera."

"Forget it, I understand."

"Yeah, but listen, it's still true. Those six guys, they heard wicked sound out there. They heard sound you just plain won't believe."

Sanders pulled on his rucksack, closed his eyes for a moment, then almost smiled at me.

I knew what was coming but I beat him to it. 60

---

*Brigadoon:* A fictional village in Scotland that appears only once every one hundred years; subject of a popular American musical (1947).

"All right," I said, "what's the moral?"

"Forget it."

"No, go ahead."

For a long while he was quiet, looking away, and the silence kept stretching out until it was almost embarrassing. Then he shrugged and gave me a stare that lasted all day.

"Hear that quiet, man?" he said. "There's your moral."                                    65

In a true war story, if there's a moral at all, it's like the thread that makes the cloth. You can't tease it out. You can't extract the meaning without unraveling the deeper meaning. And in the end, really, there's nothing much to say about a true war story, except maybe "Oh."

True war stories do not generalize. They do not indulge in abstraction or analysis.

For example: War is hell. As a moral declaration the old truism seems perfectly true, and yet because it abstracts, because it generalizes, I can't believe it with my stomach. Nothing turns inside.

It comes down to gut instinct. A true war story, if truly told, makes the stomach believe.

This one does it for me. I've told it before — many times, many versions — but    70
here's what actually happened.

We crossed the river and marched west into the mountains. On the third day, Curt Lemon stepped on a booby-trapped 105 round. He was playing catch with Rat Kiley, laughing, and then he was dead. The trees were thick; it took nearly an hour to cut an LZ for the dustoff.°

Later, higher in the mountains, we came across a baby VC° water buffalo. What it was doing there I don't know — no farms or paddies — but we chased it down and got a rope around it and led it along to a deserted village where we set for the night. After supper Rat Kiley went over and stroked its nose.

He opened up a can of C rations, pork and beans, but the baby buffalo wasn't interested.

Rat shrugged.

He stepped back and shot it through the right front knee. The animal did not    75
make a sound. It went down hard, then got up again, and Rat took careful aim and shot off an ear. He shot it in the hindquarters and in the little hump at its back. He shot it twice in the flanks. It wasn't to kill; it was just to hurt. He put the rifle muzzle up against the mouth and shot the mouth away. Nobody said much. The whole platoon stood there watching, feeling all kinds of things, but there wasn't a great deal of pity for the baby water buffalo. Lemon was dead. Rat Kiley had lost his best friend in the world. Later in the week he would write a long personal letter to the guy's sister, who would not write back, but for now it was a question of pain. He shot off the tail. He shot away chunks of meat below the ribs. All around us there was the smell of smoke and filth, and deep greenery, and the evening was humid and very hot. Rat went to automatic. He shot randomly, almost casually, quick little spurts in the belly and butt. Then he reloaded, squatted down, and shot it in

---

*LZ for the dustoff*: Landing zone for a helicopter evacuation of a casualty.
*VC*: Vietcong (North Vietnamese).

the left front knee. Again the animal fell hard and tried to get up, but this time it couldn't quite make it. It wobbled and went down sideways. Rat shot it in the nose. He bent forward and whispered something, as if talking to a pet, then he shot it in the throat. All the while the baby buffalo was silent, or almost silent, just a light bubbling sound where the nose had been. It lay very still. Nothing moved except the eyes, which were enormous, the pupils shiny black and dumb.

Rat Kiley was crying. He tried to say something, but then cradled his rifle and went off by himself.

The rest of us stood in a ragged circle around the baby buffalo. For a time no one spoke. We had witnessed something essential, something brand-new and profound, a piece of the world so startling there was not yet a name for it.

Somebody kicked the baby buffalo.

It was still alive, though just barely, just in the eyes.

"Amazing," Dave Jensen said. "My whole life, I never seen anything like it."    80

"Never?"

"Not hardly. Not once."

Kiowa and Mitchell Sanders picked up the baby buffalo. They hauled it across the open square, hoisted it up, and dumped it in the village well.

Afterward, we sat waiting for Rat to get himself together.

"Amazing," Dave Jensen kept saying.    85

"For sure."

"A new wrinkle. I never seen it before."

Mitchell Sanders took out his yo-yo.

"Well, that's Nam," he said. "Garden of Evil. Over here, man, every sin's real fresh and original."

How do you generalize?    90

War is hell, but that's not the half of it, because war is also mystery and terror and adventure and courage and discovery and holiness and pity and despair and longing and love. War is nasty; war is fun. War is thrilling; war is drudgery. War makes you a man; war makes you dead.

The truths are contradictory. It can be argued, for instance, that war is grotesque. But in truth war is also beauty. For all its horror, you can't help but gape at the awful majesty of combat. You stare out at tracer rounds unwinding through the dark like brilliant red ribbons. You crouch in ambush as a cool, impassive moon rises over the nighttime paddies. You admire the fluid symmetries of troops on the move, the harmonies of sound and shape and proportion, the great sheets of metal-fire streaming down from a gunship, the illumination rounds, the white phosphorous, the purply black glow of napalm, the rocket's red glare. It's not pretty, exactly. It's astonishing. It fills the eye. It commands you. You hate it, yes, but your eyes do not. Like a killer forest fire, like cancer under a microscope, any battle or bombing raid or artillery barrage has the aesthetic purity of absolute moral indifference — a powerful, implacable beauty — and a true war story will tell the truth about this, though the truth is ugly.

To generalize about war is like generalizing about peace. Almost everything is true. Almost nothing is true. At its core, perhaps, war is just another name for death, and yet any soldier will tell you, if he tells the truth, that proximity to death brings with it a corresponding proximity to life. After a fire fight, there is always the immense pleasure of aliveness. The trees are alive. The grass, the soil — everything. All around you things are purely living, and you among them, and the aliveness makes you tremble. You feel an intense, out-of-the-skin awareness of your living self—your truest self, the human being you want to be and then become by the force of wanting it. In the midst of evil you want to be a good man. You want decency. You want justice and courtesy and human concord, things you never knew you wanted. There is a kind of largeness to it; a kind of godliness. Though it's odd, you're never more alive than when you're almost dead. You recognize what's valuable. Freshly, as if for the first time, you love what's best in yourself and in the world, all that might be lost. At the hour of dusk you sit at your foxhole and look out on a wide river turning pinkish red, and at the mountains beyond, and although in the morning you must cross the river and go into the mountains and do terrible things and maybe die, even so, you find yourself studying the fine colors on the river, you feel wonder and awe at the setting of the sun, and you are filled with a hard, aching love for how the world could be and always should be, but now is not.

Mitchell Sanders was right. For the common soldier, at least, war has the feel—the spiritual texture—of a great ghostly fog, thick and permanent. There is no clarity. Everything swirls. The old rules are no longer binding, the old truths no longer true. Right spills over into wrong. Order blends into chaos, love into hate, ugliness into beauty, law into anarchy, civility into savagery. The vapors suck you in. You can't tell where you are, or why you're there, and the only certainty is absolute ambiguity.

In war you lose your sense of the definite, hence your sense of truth itself, and 95 therefore it's safe to say that in a true war story nothing much is ever very true.

Often in a true war story there is not even a point, or else the point doesn't hit you until twenty years later, in your sleep, and you wake up and shake your wife and start telling the story to her, except when you get to the end you've forgotten the point again. And then for a long time you lie there watching the story happen in your head. You listen to your wife's breathing. The war's over. You close your eyes. You smile and think, Christ, what's the *point*?

This one wakes me up.

In the mountains that day, I watched Lemon turn sideways. He laughed and said something to Rat Kiley. Then he took a peculiar half step, moving from shade into bright sunlight, and the booby-trapped 105 round blew him into a tree. The parts were just hanging there, so Norman Bowker and I were ordered to shinny up and peel him off. I remember the white bone of an arm. I remember pieces of skin and something wet and yellow that must've been the intestines. The gore was horrible, and stays with me, but what wakes me up twenty years later is Norman Bowker singing "Lemon Tree" as we threw down the parts.

You can tell a true war story by the questions you ask. Somebody tells a story, let's say, and afterward you ask, "Is it true?" and if the answer matters, you've got your answer.

For example, we've all heard this one. Four guys go down a trail. A grenade 100 sails out. One guy jumps on it and takes the blast and saves his three buddies.

Is it true?

The answer matters.

You'd feel cheated if it never happened. Without the grounding reality, it's just a trite bit of puffery, pure Hollywood, untrue in the way all such stories are untrue. Yet even if it did happen—and maybe it did, anything's possible—even then you know it can't be true, because a true war story does not depend upon that kind of truth. Happeningness is irrelevant. A thing may happen and be a total lie; another thing may not happen and be truer than the truth. For example: four guys go down a trail. A grenade sails out. One guy jumps on it and takes the blast, but it's a killer grenade and everybody dies anyway. Before they die, though, one of the dead guys says, "The fuck you do *that* for?" and the jumper says, "Story of my life, man," and the other guy starts to smile but he's dead.

That's a true story that never happened.

Twenty years later, I can still see the sunlight on Lemon's face. I can see him turn- 105 ing, looking back at Rat Kiley, then he laughed and took that curious half step from shade into sunlight, his face suddenly brown and shining, and when his foot touched down, in that instant, he must've thought it was the sunlight that was kill- ing him. It was not the sunlight. It was a rigged 105 round. But if I could ever get the story right, how the sun seemed to gather around him and pick him up and lift him into a tree, if I could somehow recreate the fatal whiteness of that light, the quick glare, the obvious cause and effect, then you would believe the last thing Lemon believed, which for him must've been the final truth.

Now and then, when I tell this story, someone will come up to me afterward and say she liked it. It's always a woman. Usually it's an older woman of kindly temper- ament and humane politics. She'll explain that as a rule she hates war stories, she can't understand why people want to wallow in blood and gore. But this one she liked. Sometimes, even, there are little tears. What I should do, she'll say, is put it all behind me. Find new stories to tell.

I won't say it but I'll think it.

I'll picture Rat Kiley's face, his grief, and I'll think, *You dumb cooze.*

Because she wasn't listening.

It wasn't a war story. It was a love story. It was a ghost story. 110

But you can't say that. All you can do is tell it one more time, patiently, adding and subtracting, making up a few things to get at the real truth. No Mitchell Sanders, you tell her. No Lemon, no Rat Kiley. And it didn't happen in the mountains, it happened in this little village on the Batangan Peninsula, and it was raining like crazy, and one night a guy named Stink Harris woke up screaming with a leech on his tongue. You can tell a true war story if you just keep on telling it.

In the end, of course, a true war story is never about war. It's about the special way that dawn spreads out on a river when you know you must cross the river and march into the mountains and do things you are afraid to do. It's about love and memory. It's about sorrow. It's about sisters who never write back and people who never listen.

## Considerations for Critical Thinking and Writing

1. **FIRST RESPONSE.** What implicit problem is created about the story by its first line, "This is true"? How is the notion of "truth" problematized throughout the story and subjected to irony?

2. Why is Rat Kiley so upset over Curt Lemon's sister's not writing back?

3. How are you affected by the descriptions of Curt Lemon being blown up in paragraphs 17, 98, and 105?

4. Analyze the story told about the six-man patrol in paragraphs 19–65. How is this story relevant to the rest of the plot?

5. What emotions did you feel as you read about the shooting of the water buffalo? How does paragraph 75 achieve these effects?

6. Explain what O'Brien means when he writes "After a fire fight, there is always the immense pleasure of aliveness" (par. 93).

7. Trace the narrator's comments about what constitutes a true war story. What do these competing and contradictory ideas finally add up to?

8. Characterize the narrator. Why must he repeatedly "keep on telling" his war story?

9. Consider O'Brien's use of profanity and violence in this story. Are they essential or merely sensational?

10. CRITICAL STRATEGIES. Read the discussion concerning historical criticism in Chapter 42, "Critical Strategies for Reading," and research American protests and reactions to the war in Vietnam. How are these responses relevant to O'Brien's story, particularly paragraphs 1–10 and 106–111?

### CONNECTIONS TO OTHER SELECTIONS

1. Imagine Krebs from Ernest Hemingway's "Soldier's Home" (p. 115) writing a letter home recommending "How to Tell a True War Story" to his parents. Write that letter from Krebs's point of view.

2. How does the treatment of violence in O'Brien's story compare with that in Andre Dubus's "Killings" (p. 58)? Write an essay that points to specific descriptions and explains the function of the violence in each story.

3. O'Brien's narrator says, "Often in a true war story there is not even a point, or else the point doesn't hit you until twenty years later" (par. 96). Discuss how time and reflection change the meaning of war in O'Brien's story and either of the stories that follow, Kurt Vonnegut's "Happy Birthday, 1951" (p. 263) or Edwidge Danticat's "The Missing Peace" (p. 267).

## KURT VONNEGUT JR. (1922–2007)

The author of fourteen novels and nearly two hundred short stories as well as several volumes of nonfiction, Kurt Vonnegut Jr. remains as popular among college-aged readers today as he was during his heyday in the 1960s. Vonnegut left college to enlist in the army in 1943, during the second World War. He was captured by the German army and witnessed the Allied forces' attack on the city of Dresden. He survived by taking shelter in a slaughterhouse. This experience became the basis for his most enduring novel, *Slaughterhouse Five* (1969). The mode of his most popular novels is absurd satire, but his collected stories, many of which were

GL Archive/Alamy.

written before his novels (though some were published posthumously, including the following story), tend to be closer to a traditional realist mode.

## Happy Birthday, 1951    2008

"Summer is a fine time for a birthday," said the old man. "And, as long as you have a choice, why not choose a summer day?" He wet his thumb on his tongue, and leafed through the sheaf of documents the soldiers had ordered him to fill out. No document could be complete without a birthdate, and, for the boy, one had to be chosen.

"Today can be your birthday, if you like it," said the old man.

"It rained in the morning," said the boy.

"All right, then — tomorrow. The clouds are blowing off to the south. The sun should shine all day tomorrow."

Looking for shelter from the morning rainstorm, the soldiers had found the 5 hiding place where, miracle of miracles, the old man and the boy had lived in the ruins for seven years without documents — without, as it were, official permission to be alive. They said no person could get food or shelter or clothing without documents. But the old man and the boy had found all three for the digging in the catacombs of cellars beneath the shattered city, for the filching at night.

"Why are you shaking?" said the boy.

"Because I'm old. Because soldiers frighten old men."

"They don't frighten me," said the boy. He was excited by the sudden intrusion into their underground world. He held something shiny, golden in the narrow shaft of light from the cellar window. "See? One of them gave me a brass button."

There had been nothing frightening about the soldiers. Since the man was so old and the child so young, the military took a playful view of the pair — who, of all the people in the city, alone had recorded their presence nowhere, had been inoculated against nothing, had sworn allegiance to nothing, renounced or apologized for nothing, voted or marched for nothing, since the war.

"I meant no harm," the old man had told the soldiers with a pretense of senil- 10 ity. "I didn't know." He told them how, on the day the war ended, a refugee woman had left a baby in his arms and never returned. That was how he got the boy. The child's nationality? Name? Birthdate? He didn't know.

The old man rolled potatoes from the stove's wood fire with a stick, knocked the embers from their blackened skins. "I haven't been a very good father, letting you go without birthdays this long," he said. "You're entitled to one every year, you know, and I've let six years go by without a birthday. And presents, too. You're supposed to get presents." He picked up a potato gingerly, and tossed it to the boy, who caught it and laughed. "So you've decided tomorrow's the day, eh?"

"Yes, I think so."

"All right. That doesn't give me much time to get you a present, but there'll be something."

"What?"

"Birthday presents are better if they're a surprise." He thought of the wheels he 15 had seen on a pile of rubble down the street. When the boy fell asleep, he would make some sort of cart.

"Listen!" said the boy.

As at every sunset, over the ruins from a distant street came the sound of marching.

"Don't listen," said the old man. He held up a finger for attention. "And you know what we'll do on your birthday?"

"Steal cakes from the bakery?"

"Maybe — but that isn't what I was thinking of. You know what I'd like to do   20 tomorrow? I'd like to take you where you've never been in all your life — where I haven't been for years." The thought made the old man excited and happy. This would be *the* gift. The cart would be nothing. "Tomorrow I'll take you away from war."

He didn't see that the boy looked puzzled, and a little disappointed.

———

It was the birthday the boy had chosen for himself, and the sky, as the old man had promised, was clear. They ate breakfast in the twilight of their cellar. The cart the old man had made late at night sat on the table. The boy ate with one hand, his other hand resting on the cart. Occasionally, he paused in eating to move the cart back and forth a few inches, and to imitate the sound of a motor.

"That's a nice truck you've got there, Mister," said the old man. "Bringing animals to the market, are you?"

"Brummmaaaa, brummmaaaa. Out of my way! Brummmaaaa. Out of the way of my tank."

"Sorry," sighed the old man, "thought you were a truck. You like it anyway, and   25 that's what counts." He dropped his tin plate into the bucket of water simmering on the stove. "And this is only the beginning, only the beginning," he said expansively. "The best is yet to come."

"Another present?"

"In a way. Remember what I promised? We'll get away from war today. We'll go to the woods."

"Brummmaaaa, brummmaaaa. Can I take my tank?"

"If you'll let it be a truck, just for today."

The boy shrugged. "I'll leave it, and play with it when I get back."   30

Blinking in the bright morning, the two walked down their deserted street, turned into a busy boulevard lined with brave new façades. It was as though the world had suddenly become fresh and clean and whole again. The people didn't seem to know that desolation began a block on either side of the fine boulevard, and stretched for miles. The two, with lunches under their arms, walked toward the pine-covered hills to the south, toward which the boulevard lifted in a gentle grade.

Four young soldiers came down the sidewalk abreast. The old man stepped into the street, out of their way. The boy saluted, and held his ground. The soldiers smiled, returned his salute, and parted their ranks to let him pass.

"Armored infantry," said the boy to the old man.

"Hmmmm?" said the old man absently, his eyes on the green hills. "Really? How did you know that?"

"Didn't you see the green braid?"   35

"Yes, but those things change. I can remember when armored infantry was black and red, and green was — " He cut the sentence short, "It's all nonsense," he said, almost sharply. "It's all meaningless, and today we're going to forget all about it. Of all days, on your birthday, you shouldn't be thinking about — "

"Black and red is the engineers," interrupted the boy seriously. "Plain black is the military police, and red is the artillery, and blue and red is the medical corps, and black and orange is . . ."

The pine forest was very still. The centuries-old carpet of needles and green roof deadened the sounds floating up from the city. Infinite colonnades of thick brown trunks surrounded the old man and the boy. The sun, directly overhead, showed itself to them only as a cluster of bright pinpoints through the fat, dense blanket of needles and boughs above.

"Here?" said the boy.

The old man looked about himself. "No — just a little farther." He pointed. 40 "There — see through there? We can see the church from here." The black skeleton of a burned steeple was framed against a square of sky between two trunks on the edge of the forest. "But listen — hear that? Water. There's a brook up above, and we can get down in its little valley and see nothing but treetops and sky."

"All right," said the boy. "I like this place, but all right." He looked at the steeple, then at the old man, and raised his eyebrows questioningly.

"You'll see — you'll see how much better," said the old man.

As they reached the top of the ridge, he gestured happily at the brook below. "There! And what do you think of this? Eden! As it was in the beginning — trees, sky, and water. This is the world you should have had, and today, at least, you can have it."

"And look!" said the boy, pointing to the ridge on the other side.

A huge tank, rusted to the color of the fallen pine needles, squatted on shat- 45 tered treads on the ridge, with scabs of corrosion about the black hole where its gun had once been.

"How can we cross the water to get to it?" said the boy.

"We don't want to get to it," said the old man irritably. He held the boy's hand tightly. "Not today. Some other day we can come out here, maybe. But not today."

The boy was crestfallen. His small hand grew limp in the old man's.

"Here's a bend up ahead, and around that we'll find exactly what we want."

The boy said nothing. He snatched up a rock, and threw it at the tank. As 50 the little missile fell toward the target, he tensed, as though the whole world were about to explode. A faint click came from the turret, and he relaxed, somehow satisfied. Docilely, he followed the old man.

Around the bend, they found what the old man had been looking for: a smooth, dry table of rock, out by the stream, walled in by high banks. The old man stretched out on the moss, affectionately patted the spot beside him, where he wanted the boy to sit. He unwrapped his lunch.

After lunch, the boy fidgeted. "It's very quiet," he said at last.

"It's as it should be," said the old man. "One corner of the world — as it should be."

"It's lonely."

"That's its beauty." 55

"I like it better in the city, with the soldiers and — "

The old man seized his arm roughly, squeezed it hard. "No you don't. You just don't know. You're too young, too young to know what this is, what I'm trying to give you. But, when you're older, you'll remember, and want to come back here — long after your little cart is broken."

"I don't want my cart to be broken," said the boy.

"It won't, it won't. But just lie here, close your eyes and listen, and forget about everything. This much I can give you — a few hours away from war." He closed his eyes.

The boy lay down beside him, and dutifully closed his eyes, too. 60

The sun was low in the sky when the old man awakened. He ached and felt damp from his long nap by the brook. He yawned and stretched. "Time to go," he said, his eyes still closed. "Our day of peace is over." And then he saw that the boy was gone. He called the boy's name unconcernedly at first; and then, getting no answer but the wind's, he stood and shouted.

Panic welled up in him. The boy had never been in the woods before, could easily get lost if he were to wander north, deeper into the hills and forest. He climbed onto higher ground and shouted again. No answer.

Perhaps the boy had gone down to the tank again, and tried to cross the stream. He couldn't swim. The old man hurried downstream, around the bend to where he could see the tank. The ugly relic gaped at him balefully from across the cut. Nothing moved, and there was only the sound of wind and the water.

"Bang!" cried a small voice.

The boy raised his head from the turret triumphantly. "Gotcha!" he said.       65

## Considerations for Critical Thinking and Writing

1. **FIRST RESPONSE.** Parents sometimes forbid their children to play with violent toys such as fake swords or guns, or even toy soldiers, and will also later in life restrict their children's use of violent video games. How does this story comment indirectly on those parenting choices?

2. Everyone has a birthday, but the boy gets to choose his own. Why is that fact significant in terms of the story's broader thematic concerns?

3. The fact that the man and the boy lived in the ruins of war for seven years is extraordinary. What is your response to the soldier's implied reaction, that the two of them "had lived [without] official permission to be alive" (par. 5)?

4. How do you interpret the repetition of the word "nothing" in paragraph 9?

5. Explain the different reactions the boy and the old man have toward soldiers.

6. The man is dedicated to protecting the boy from everything associated with the war. How does the boy seem to know so much about, for instance, the meaning of insignia on soldiers' uniforms?

7. The old man takes the boy into nature and declares it "Eden" (par. 43). How does this allusion to the biblical place of innocence and tranquility function in the story?

8. Why is the boy so uncomfortable in nature?

9. The old man tells the boy that he will someday appreciate nature: Do you think he's right?

10. The boy gets to choose his birthday. What other choices does he make throughout the story? How do they collectively form his identity?

11. Why do you suppose Vonnegut chose not to name these characters?

## Connections to Other Selections

1. Compare this story to Tobias Wolff's "Powder" (p. 72) in terms of significant moments in the maturity of young men.

2. Apply Tim O'Brien's definitions of truth in "How to Tell a True War Story" (p. 253) to "Happy Birthday, 1951." What is the story's ultimate "truth," and is it a "moral"?

## EDWIDGE DANTICAT (B. 1969)

Born in Port-au-Prince, Haiti, Edwidge Danticat immigrated to the United States when she was twelve. She was influenced by Haitian storytelling as a youth and showed an interest in writing from a young age. She published her first work in English while still a teenager and went on to study writing as an undergraduate at Barnard College and to earn her M.F.A. at Brown University. Danticat is the author of over a dozen books, including story collections, young adult novels, novels, a memoir, and travel writing, and she has won many prestigious literary awards including the National Book Critics Circle Award. The following story is from her first collection, *Krik? Krak!* (1996), the title of which refers to the call a Haitian storyteller uses to get the audience's attention ("Krik?") and the audience's attentive response ("Krak!").

Agence Opale/Alamy.

## *The Missing Peace*   1996

We were playing with leaves shaped like butterflies. Raymond limped from the ashes of the old schoolhouse and threw himself on top of a high pile of dirt. The dust rose in clouds around him, clinging to the lapels of his khaki uniform.

"You should see the sunset from here." He grabbed my legs and pulled me down on top of him. The rusty grass brushed against my chin as I slipped out of his grasp.

I got up and tried to run to the other side of the field, but he caught both my legs and yanked me down again.

"Don't you feel like a woman when you are with me?" He tickled my neck. "Don't you feel beautiful?"

He let go of my waist as I turned over and laid flat on my back. The sun was    5 sliding behind the hills, and the glare made the rocks shimmer like chunks of gold.

"I know I can make you feel like a woman," he said, "so why don't you let me?"

"My grandmother says I can have babies."

"Forget your grandmother."

"Would you tell me again how you got your limp?" I asked to distract him.

It was a question he liked to answer, a chance for him to show his bravery.    10

"If I tell you, will you let me touch your breasts?"

"It is an insult that you are even asking."

"Will you let me do it?"

"You will never know unless you tell me the story."

He closed his eyes as though the details were never any farther than a stage    15 behind his eyelids.

I already knew the story very well.

"I was on guard one night," he said, taking a deep theatrical breath. "No one told me that there had been a coup in Port-au-Prince. I was still wearing my old régime uniform. My friend Toto from the youth corps says he didn't know if I was old régime or new régime. So he shot a warning at the uniform. Not at me, but at the uniform.

"The shots were coming fast. I was afraid. I forgot the password. Then one of Toto's bullets hit me on my leg and I remembered. I yelled out the password and he stopped shooting."

"Why didn't you take off your uniform?" I asked, laughing.

He ignored the question, letting his hand wander between the buttons of my 20 blouse.

"Do you remember the password?" he asked.

"Yes."

"I don't tell it to just anyone. Lean closer and whisper it in my ear."

I leaned real close and whispered the word in his ear.

"Don't ever forget it if you're in trouble. It could save your life," he said. 25

"I will remember."

"Tell me again what it is."

I swallowed a gulp of dusty air and said, "Peace."

A round of gunshots rang through the air, signaling that curfew was about to begin.

"I should go back now," I said. 30

He made no effort to get up, but raised his hand to his lips and blew me a kiss.

"Look after yourself tonight," I said.

"Peace."

On the way home, I cut through a line of skeletal houses that had been torched the night of the coup. A lot of the old régime followers died that night. Others fled to the hills or took boats to Miami.

I rushed past a churchyard, where the security officers sometimes buried the 35 bodies of old régime people. The yard was bordered with a chain link fence. But every once in a while, if you looked very closely, you could see a bushy head of hair poking through the ground.

There was a bed of red hibiscus on the footpath behind the yard. Covering my nose, I pulled up a few stems and ran all the way home with them.

My grandmother was sitting in the rocking chair in front of our house, making knots in the sisal rope around her waist. She grabbed the hibiscus from my hand and threw them on the ground.

"How many times must I tell you?" she said. "Those things grow with blood on them." Pulling a leaf from my hair, she slapped me on the shoulder and shoved me inside the house.

"Somebody rented the two rooms in the yellow house," she said, saliva flying out from between her front teeth. "I want you to bring the lady some needles and thread."

My grandmother had fixed up the yellow house very nicely so that many 40 visitors who passed through Ville Rose came to stay in it. Sometimes our boarders were French and American journalists who wanted to take pictures of the churchyard where you could see the bodies.

I rushed out to my grandmother's garden, hoping to catch a glimpse of our new guest. Then I went over to the basin of rainwater in the yard and took off my clothes. My grandmother scrubbed a handful of mint leaves up and down my back as she ran a comb through my hair.

"It's a lady," said my grandmother. "Don't give her a headful of things to worry about. Things you say, thoughts you have, will decide how people treat you."

"Is the lady alone?"

"She is like all those foreign women. She feels she can be alone. And she smokes too." My grandmother giggled. "She smokes just like an old woman when life gets hard."

"She smokes a pipe?" 45

"Ladies her age don't smoke pipes."

"Cigarettes, then?"

"I don't want you to ask her to let you smoke any."

"Is she a journalist?" I asked.

"That is no concern of mine," my grandmother said. 50

"Is she intelligent?"

"Intelligence is not only in reading and writing."

"Is she old régime or new régime?"

"She is like us. The only régime she believe in is God's régime. She says she wants to write things down for posterity."

"What did you tell her when she said that?" 55

"That I already have posterity. I was once a baby and now I am an old woman. That is posterity."

"If she asks me questions, I am going to answer them," I said.

"One day you will stick your hand in a stew that will burn your fingers. I told her to watch her mouth as to how she talks to people. I told her to watch out for vagabonds like Toto and Raymond."

"Never look them in the eye."

"I told her that too," my grandmother said as she discarded the mint leaves. 60

My whole body felt taut and taint-free. My grandmother's face softened as she noticed the sheen of cleanliness.

"See, you can be a pretty girl," she said, handing me her precious pouch of needles, thimbles, and thread. "You can be a very pretty girl. Just like your mother used to be."

A burst of evening air chilled my face as I walked across to the yellow house. I was wearing my only Sunday outfit, a white lace dress that I had worn to my confirmation two years before.

The lady poked her head through the door after my first knock.

"Mademoiselle Gallant?" 65

"How do you know my name?"

"My grandmother sent me."

She was wearing a pair of *abakos*, American blue jeans.

"It looks as though your grandmother has put you to some inconvenience," she said. Then she led me into the front room, with its oversized mahogany chairs and a desk that my grandmother had bought especially for the journalists to use when they were working there.

"My name is really Emilie," she said in Creole, with a very heavy American 70 accent. "What do people call you?"

"Lamort."

"How did your name come to be 'death'?"

"My mother died while I was being born," I explained. "My grandmother was really mad at me for that."

"They should have given you your mother's name," she said, taking the pouch of needles, thread, and thimbles from me. "That is the way it should have been done."

She walked over to the table in the corner and picked up a pitcher of lemonade 75 that my grandmother made for all her guests when they first arrived.

"Would you like some?" she said, already pouring the lemonade.

"*Oui*, Madame. Please."

She held a small carton box of butter cookies in front of me. I took one, only one, just as my grandmother would have done.

"Are you a journalist?" I asked her.

"Why do you ask that?" 80

"The people who stay here in this house usually are, journalists."

She lit a cigarette. The smoke breezed in and out of her mouth, just like her own breath.

"I am not a journalist," she said. "I have come here to pay a little visit."

"Who are you visiting?"

"Just people." 85

"Why don't you stay with the people you are visiting?"

"I didn't want to bother them."

"Are they old régime or new régime?"

"Who?"

"Your people?" 90

"Why do you ask?"

"Because things you say, thoughts you have, will decide how people treat you."

"It seems to me, *you* are the journalist," she said.

"What do you believe in? Old régime or new régime?"

"Your grandmother told me to say to anyone who is interested, 'The only 95 régime I believe in is God's régime.' I would wager that you are a very good source for the journalists. Do you have any schooling?"

"A little."

Once again, she held the box of cookies in front of me. I took another cookie, but she kept the box there, in the same place. I took yet another cookie, and another, until the whole box was empty.

"Can you read what it says there?" she asked, pointing at a line of red letters.

"I cannot read American," I said. Though many of the journalists who came to stay at the yellow house had tried to teach me, I had not learned.

"It is not American," she said. "They are French cookies. That says *Le Petit* 100 *Ecolier*."

I stuffed my mouth in shame.

"Intelligence is not only in reading and writing," I said.

"I did not mean to make you feel ashamed," she said, dropping her cigarette into the half glass of lemonade in her hand. "I want to ask you a question."

"I will answer if I can."

"My mother was old régime," she said. "*She* was a journalist. For a newspaper 105 called *Libèté* in Port-au-Prince."

"She came to Ville Rose?"

"Maybe. Or some other town. I don't know. The people who worked with her in Port-au-Prince think she might be in this region. Do you remember any shootings the night of the coup?"

"There were many shootings," I said.

"Did you see any of the bodies?"

"My grandmother and me, we stayed inside." 110

"Did a woman come to your door? Did anyone ever say that a woman in a purple dress came to their door?"

"No."

"I hear there is a mass burial site," she said. "Do you know it?"

"Yes. I have taken journalists there."

"I would like to go there. Can you take me?" 115

"Now?"

"Yes."

She pulled some coins from her purse and placed them on the table.

"I have more," she said.

From the back pocket of her jeans, she took out an envelope full of pictures. 120 I ran my fingers over the glossy paper that froze her mother into all kinds of smiling poses: a skinny brown woman with shiny black hair in short spiral curls.

"I have never seen her," I admitted.

"It is possible that she arrived in the evening, and then the coup took place in the middle of the night. Do you know if they found any dead women the day after the coup?"

"There were no bodies," I said, "That is to say no funerals."

I heard my grandmother's footsteps even before she reached the door to the yellow house.

"If you tell her that I'm here, I can't go with you," I said. 125

"Go into the next room and stay there until I come for you."

My grandmother knocked once and then a second time. I rushed to the next room and crouched in a corner.

The plain white sheets that we usually covered the bed with had been replaced by a large piece of purple cloth. On the cement floor were many small pieces of cloth lined up in squares, one next to the other.

"Thank you for sending me the needles," I heard Emilie say to my grandmother. "I thought I had packed some in my suitcase, but I must have forgotten them."

"My old eyes are not what they used to be," my grandmother said, in the shy 130 humble voice she reserved for prayers and for total strangers. "But if you need some mending, I can do it for you."

"Thank you," said Emilie, "but I can do the mending myself."

"Very well then. Is my granddaughter here?"

"She had to run off," Emilie said.

"Do you know where she went?"

"I don't know. She was dressed for a very fancy affair." 135

My grandmother was silent for a minute as her knuckles tapped the wood on the front door.

"I will let you rest now," said my grandmother.

"Thank you for the needles," said Emilie.

Emilie bolted the door after my grandmother had left.

"Is there a way we can leave without her seeing you?" She came into the room 140 with a flashlight and her American passport. "You might get a little beating when you go home."

"What are all these small pieces of cloth for?" I asked.

"I am going to sew them onto that purple blanket," she said. "All her life, my mother's wanted to sew some old things together onto that piece of purple cloth."

She raised a piece of white lace above her head. "That's from my mother's wedding dress."

Grabbing a piece of pink terry cloth, she said, "That's an old baby bib."

Tears were beginning to cloud her eyes. She fought them away fast by pushing her head back. 145

"Purple," she said, "was Mama's favorite color."

"I can ask my grandmother if she saw your mother," I said.

"When I first came, this afternoon," she said, "I showed her the pictures and, like you, she said no."

"We would tell you if we had seen her."

"I want to go to the churchyard," she said. "You say you have already taken other people there." 150

"I walk by it every day."

"Let's go then."

"Sometimes the yard's guarded at night," I warned her.

"I have an American passport. Maybe that will help."

"The soldiers don't know the difference. Most of them are like me. They would not be able to identify your cookies either." 155

"How old are you?" she asked.

"Fourteen."

"At your age, you already have a wide reputation. I have a journalist friend who has stayed in this house. He told me you are the only person who would take me to the yard."

I could not think which particular journalist would have given me such a high recommendation, there had been so many.

"Better to be known for good than bad," I said to her. 160

"I am ready to go," she announced.

"If she is there, will you take her away?"

"Who?"

"Your mother?"

"I have not thought that far." 165

"And if you see them carrying her, what will you do? She will belong to them and not you."

"They say a girl becomes a woman when she loses her mother," she said. "You, child, were born a woman."

We walked through the footpath in my grandmother's garden, toward the main road.

"I have been having these awful dreams," Emilie whispered as she plucked some leaves off my grandmother's pumpkin vines. "I see my mother sinking into a river, and she keeps calling my name."

A round of gunshots echoed in the distance, signals from the night guards who had no other ways of speaking to one another. 170

We stopped on the side of the road and waited for a while and then continued on our way.

The night air blew the smell of rotting flesh to my nose. We circled the churchyard carefully before finding an entrance route. There was a rustle in the yard, like pieces of tin scraping the moist dirt.

"Who is there?"

I thought she stopped breathing when the voice echoed in the night air.

"I am an American journalist," Emilie said in breathless Creole.              175

She pulled out her passport and raised it toward a blinding flashlight beam. The guard moved the light away from our faces.

It was Raymond's friend, Toto, the one who had shot at him. He was tall and skinny and looked barely sixteen. He was staring at me as though he was possessed by a spirit. In the night, he did not know me.

He took Emilie's passport and flipped through it quickly.

"What are you doing here?" he asked, handing the passport back to her. "It is after curfew."

"The lady was not feeling well," I said. "So she asked me to take her for a walk."   180

"Didn't you hear the signals?" asked Toto. "The curfew has already started. You would not want to have blood on your nice communion dress."

Two other soldiers passed us on their way to the field. They were dragging the blood-soaked body of a bearded man with an old election slogan written on a T-shirt across his chest: ALONE WE ARE WEAK. TOGETHER WE ARE A FLOOD. The guards were carrying him, feet first, like a breech birth.

Emilie moved toward the body as though she wanted to see it better.

"You see nothing," Toto said, reaching up to turn Emilie's face. Her eyes twitched from Toto's touch on her cheek.

"Under God's sky, you do this to people!" she hollered in a brazen Creole.      185

Toto laughed loudly.

"We are doing that poor indigent a favor burying him," he said.

Emilie moved forward, trying to follow the guards taking the body into the yard.

"You see nothing," Toto said again, grabbing her face. She raised her arm as if to strike him. He seized her wrist in midair and whisked her hand behind her back.

"You see nothing," he said, his voice hissing between his teeth. "Repeat after    190 me. You see nothing."

"I see nothing," I said in her place. "The lady does not understand."

"I see you," she said in Creole. "How can that be nothing?"

"Peace, let her go," I said.

"You are a coward," she told him.

He lowered his head so he was staring directly into her eyes. He twisted her    195 arm like a wet rag.

"Peace, have mercy on her," I said.

"Let her ask for herself," he said.

She stamped her feet on his boots. He let go of her hand and tapped his rifle on her shoulder. Emilie looked up at him, angry and stunned. He moved back, aiming his rifle at her head, squinting as though he was going to shoot.

"Peace!" I hollered.

My eyes fell on Raymond's as he walked out of the field. I mouthed the word,   200 pleading for help. *Peace. Peace. Peace.*

"They'll go," Raymond said to Toto.

"Then go!" Toto shouted. "Let me watch you go."

"Let's go," I said to Emilie. "My grandmother will be mad at me if I get killed."

Raymond walked behind us as we went back to the road.

"The password has changed," he said. "Stop saying 'peace.'"              205

By the time I turned around to look at his face, he was already gone.

Emilie and I said nothing to each other on the way back. The sound of bullets continued to ring through the night.

"You never look them in the eye," I told her when we got to the yellow house doorstep.

"Is that how you do it?"

I helped her up the steps and into the house. 210

"I am going to sew these old pieces of cloth onto my mother's blanket tonight," she said.

She took a needle from my grandmother's bundle and began sewing. Her fingers moved quickly as she stitched the pieces together.

"I should go," I said, eyeing the money still on the table.

"Please, stay. I will pay you more if you stay with me until the morning."

"My grandmother will worry." 215

"What was your mother's name?" she asked.

"Marie Magdalène," I said.

"They should have given you that name instead of the one you got. Was your mother pretty?"

"I don't know. She never took portraits like the ones you have of yours."

"Did you know those men who were in the yard tonight?" 220

"Yes."

"I didn't fight them because I didn't want to make trouble for you later," she said. "We should write down their names. For posterity."

"We have already had posterity," I said.

"When?"

"We were babies and we grew old." 225

"You're still young," she said. "You're not old."

"My grandmother is old for me."

"If she is old for you, then doesn't it matter if you get old? You can't say that. You can't just say what she wants for you to say. I didn't get in a fight with them because I did not want them to hurt you," she said.

"I will stay with you," I said, "because I know you are afraid."

I curled my body on the floor next to her and went to sleep. 230

She had the patches sewn together on the purple blanket when I woke up that morning. On the floor, scattered around her, were the pictures of her mother.

"I became a woman last night," she said. "I lost my mother and all my other dreams."

Her voice was weighed down with pain and fatigue. She picked up the coins from the table, added a dollar from her purse, and pressed the money into my palm.

"Will you whisper their names in my ear?" she asked. "I will write them down."

"There is Toto," I said. "He is the one that hit you." 235

"And the one who followed us?"

"That is Raymond who loves leaves shaped like butterflies."

She jotted their names on the back of one of her mother's pictures and gave it to me.

"My mother's name was Isabelle," she said, "keep this for posterity."

Outside, the morning sun was coming out to meet the day. Emilie sat on the porch 240
and watched me go to my grandmother's house. Loosely sewn, the pieces on the
purple blanket around her shoulders were coming apart.

My grandmother was sitting in front of the house waiting for me. She did not
move when she saw me. Nor did she make a sound.

"Today, I want you to call me by another name," I said.

"Haughty girls don't get far," she said, rising from the chair.

"I want you to call me by her name," I said.

She looked pained as she watched me moving closer to her. 245

"Marie Magdalène?"

"Yes, Marie Magdalène," I said. "I want you to call me Marie Magdalène."
I liked the sound of that.

## CONSIDERATIONS FOR CRITICAL THINKING AND WRITING

1. FIRST RESPONSE. Explore Danticat's use of the word *peace* both in the title
   and throughout the story.

2. Lamort has Raymond tell his war story even though she has heard it before.
   Why?

3. Characterize the relationship between Raymond and Lamort.

4. Describe the relationship between nature and the war-torn landscape in this
   story.

5. Lamort's grandmother speaks in proverbs. How do you understand the fact
   that Lamort repeats some of them?

6. Lamort's name means "death" in French, as Emilie points out, and yet it can
   also sound like *l'amour*, which means "love." How does this paradox complicate her character?

7. What do gunshots signify at different points in the story?

8. Why is it significant that Lamort compares the blood-soaked body of a dead
   man being dragged by soldiers to a "breach birth"?

9. What are the various definitions of womanhood in the story? Is it possible to
   reconcile them?

10. Lamort concludes the story by asking to be renamed. What is the signifi-
    cance of names and naming throughout the story?

11. Emilie claims that she has lost her dreams after her confrontation with the
    soldier Toto. Is she defeated or does the phrase mean something else in the
    context of the story?

## CONNECTIONS TO OTHER SELECTIONS

1. Compare depictions of soldiers in this story and in Adrian Tomine's "Intruders"
   (p. 197). Do we know enough about them to judge whether the two stories
   approach the topic of the effect of military training the same way?

2. Discuss growth and maturity in the context of war in this story and in Kurt
   Vonnegut's "Happy Birthday, 1951" (p. 263).

# 10

## A THEMATIC CASE STUDY

# Privacy

Ulf Andersen/Hulton Archive/Getty Images.

All human beings have three lives: public, private, and secret.

— GABRIEL GARCIA MARQUEZ

Whether or not you support Marquez's sentiment in the above quotation, one undeniable fact underlies it: our private and secret lives have become compromised or even overtly threatened by modern technology. Some of us seem all too willing to relinquish our privacy: social media can turn even the most mundane moments of our days into a public event. In other cases, we are unaware that our private lives are being invaded. We frequently read news stories about how social media platforms sell untold amounts of personal data to corporations. The cameras on your smart phone or your computer can work to spy on you. Touch ID (which uses your fingerprints to unlock your phone, for instance) is potentially a way for government agencies to have records of your fingerprints even if you've never committed a crime. Customers wanting to know about their genealogy voluntarily send their saliva to a lab for testing, but that lab can then share the resulting data and the DNA that produced it. Ever heard of Bluetooth beacons? They track your movement around stores to see what you're buying, and companies can then send you coupons, ads, or information about the products you pause to look at. How many security cameras do you believe you've passed by today?

Is privacy a right, or is it an ideal that is constantly in negotiation with the fact that we are social animals? Individuals do seem to need or crave privacy, some more than others. We value "down time," or express fatigue when we've had to be "on" all day. We set aside our phones to get away from the tweets, texts, and notifications that steal our concentration and make tranquility an impossibility. If you're like most of your peers, you spent a good deal of your adolescence in your room with the door closed. This tension between the need for privacy and our connection to other people is nothing new, even though our current technological moment may have made us more conscious of it. Our selves are a complex combination of who we are when we're alone and who we are in public. As the speaker of T. S. Eliot's poem "The Love Song of J. Alfred Prufrock" (p. 936) acknowledges, we periodically withdraw into ourselves, but sometimes it is just "time to prepare a face to meet the faces that you meet."

And then, according to Marquez's quotation, there is secrecy. If privacy is something we feel we have a right to, secrecy does not necessarily hold that same status. Secrets have negative connotations. We often append the adjective "dirty" to them. They whisper of crimes, of unacceptable behavior, of the darkest parts of our experience. Secrets are intensely personal, yet they want to be shared. When a friend says, "You can't tell anyone what I'm about to tell you," you immediately want to, and, let's face it, you probably do. Yet isn't secrecy just an intense form of privacy? Shouldn't we all be allowed to keep a diary without worrying that someone will read it? Don't we have the right to keep experiences or thoughts entirely to ourselves, even if those experiences aren't shameful, or criminal, or in any way untoward?

These questions — not easy ones to answer in the abstract — should be on your mind as you read the following stories. Oscar Wilde's "The Sphinx without a Secret" (p. 278) asks questions about how we react to mysterious behavior. David Long's "Morphine" (p. 282) brings us ever deeper into the life of a country doctor with some dark secrets. ZZ Packer's "Drinking Coffee Elsewhere" (p. 292) traces the experience of a college student feeling isolated because of her race, class, and sexuality, and also because of her aggressive personality, which may or may not be related to that isolation. Finally, in John Cheever's "The Enormous Radio" (p. 306), a couple in an apartment building find themselves privy to the personal conversations of others in the building and confronted with the ethics of listening in. Conflict, as discussed in Chapter 2, is essential to fiction. In these stories, and perhaps in your life, the conflict between our secret, private, and public lives is familiar and vexing.

## OSCAR WILDE (1854–1900)

Although he may be remembered primarily as a playwright (see *The Importance of Being Earnest* in Chapter 38), Irish-born Oscar Wilde published in many genres, including poetry, essays, and short fiction. (He also wrote one novel, *The Picture of Dorian Gray* [1890], which has endured mainly for its interesting premises about aging, but which also has interesting psychological and social implications.) Part of an "art for art's sake" movement around the end of the nineteenth century, Wilde had sophisticated ideas about the nature of art, and yet he is remembered as much

Photo 12/Universal Images Group/Getty Images.

for his startling wit and pithy sayings as for the weight of his ideas. Despite being one of the most successful playwrights in late Victorian London, Wilde's life ended early and tragically after he was put on trial twice for "gross indecency" — a euphemism for homosexuality, which was a crime at that time in London — and the second trial led to a conviction resulting in nearly two years of incarceration. Wilde did not recover, either financially or in terms of his health, and he died impoverished. In *De Profundis*, an account of his jail time published posthumously, Wilde wrote, "To deny one's own experiences is to put a lie into the lips of one's own life. It is no less than a denial of the soul." His great theme was identity, and he looked at lying and the performance of one's identity in original ways, as is evident in the following story.

## *The Sphinx without a Secret: An Etching*   1893

One afternoon I was sitting outside the Café de la Paix, watching the splendour and shabbiness of Parisian life, and wondering over my vermouth at the strange panorama of pride and poverty that was passing before me, when I heard some one call my name. I turned round and saw Lord Murchison. We had not met since we had been at college together, nearly ten years before, so I was delighted to come across him again, and we shook hands warmly. At Oxford we had been great friends. I had liked him immensely, he was so handsome, so high-spirited, and so honourable. We used to say of him that he would be the best of fellows, if he did not always speak the truth, but I think we really admired him all the more for his frankness. I found him a good deal changed. He looked anxious and puzzled, and seemed to be in doubt about something. I felt it could not be modern scepticism, for Murchison was the stoutest of Tories, and believed in the Pentateuch° as firmly

*Pentateuch:* The first five books of the Hebrew Bible.

as he believed in the House of Peers; so I concluded that it was a woman, and asked him if he was married yet.

"I don't understand women well enough," he answered.

"My dear Gerald," I said, "women are meant to be loved, not to be understood."

"I cannot love where I cannot trust," he replied.

"I believe you have a mystery in your life, Gerald," I exclaimed; "tell me about it." 5

"Let us go for a drive," he answered, "it is too crowded here. No, not a yellow carriage, any other colour — there, that dark green one will do"; and in a few moments we were trotting down the boulevard in the direction of the Madeleine.°

"Where shall we go to?" I said.

"Oh, anywhere you like!" he answered — "to the restaurant in the Bois;° we will dine there, and you shall tell me all about yourself."

"I want to hear about you first," I said. "Tell me your mystery."

He took from his pocket a little silver-clasped morocco case, and handed it 10 to me. I opened it. Inside there was the photograph of a woman. She was tall and slight, and strangely picturesque with her large vague eyes and loosened hair. She looked like a *clairvoyante*, and was wrapped in rich furs.

"What do you think of that face?" he said; "is it truthful?"

I examined it carefully. It seemed to me the face of some one who had a secret, but whether that secret was good or evil I could not say. Its beauty was a beauty moulded out of many mysteries — the beauty, in fact, which is psychological, not plastic — and the faint smile that just played across the lips was far too subtle to be really sweet.

"Well," he cried impatiently, "what do you say?"

"She is the Gioconda° in sables," I answered. "Let me know all about her."

"Not now," he said; "after dinner," and began to talk of other things. 15

When the waiter brought us our coffee and cigarettes I reminded Gerald of his promise. He rose from his seat, walked two or three times up and down the room, and, sinking into an arm-chair, told me the following story: —

"One evening," he said, "I was walking down Bond Street about five o'clock. There was a terrific crush of carriages, and the traffic was almost stopped. Close to the pavement was standing a little yellow brougham, which, for some reason or other, attracted my attention. As I passed by there looked out from it the face I showed you this afternoon. It fascinated me immediately. All that night I kept thinking of it, and all the next day. I wandered up and down that wretched Row, peering into every carriage, and waiting for the yellow brougham; but I could not find *ma belle inconnue*,° and at last I began to think she was merely a dream. About a week afterwards I was dining with Madame de Rastail. Dinner was for eight o'clock; but at half-past eight we were still waiting in the drawing-room. Finally the servant threw open the door, and announced Lady Alroy. It was the woman I had been looking for. She came in very slowly, looking like a moonbeam in grey lace, and, to my intense delight, I was asked to take her in to dinner. After we had sat down, I remarked quite innocently, 'I think I caught sight of you in Bond Street some time ago, Lady Alroy.' She grew very pale, and said to me in a low voice, 'Pray do not talk so loud;

*Madeleine:* A church in Paris.
*Bois:* French for "forest": probably the Bois de Boulogne, a large park.
*Gioconda:* Refers to the subject of da Vinci's famous painting known as the "Mona Lisa," known for her mysterious smile.
*ma belle inconnue:* My lovely stranger.

you may be overheard.' I felt miserable at having made such a bad beginning, and plunged recklessly into the subject of the French plays. She spoke very little, always in the same low musical voice, and seemed as if she was afraid of some one listening. I fell passionately, stupidly in love, and the indefinable atmosphere of mystery that surrounded her excited my most ardent curiosity. When she was going away, which she did very soon after dinner, I asked her if I might call and see her. She hesitated for a moment, glanced round to see if any one was near us, and then said, 'Yes; to-morrow at a quarter to five.' I begged Madame de Rastail to tell me about her; but all that I could learn was that she was a widow with a beautiful house in Park Lane, and as some scientific bore began a dissertation on widows, as exemplifying the survival of the matrimonially fittest, I left and went home.

"The next day I arrived at Park Lane punctual to the moment, but was told by the butler that Lady Alroy had just gone out. I went down to the club quite unhappy and very much puzzled, and after long consideration wrote her a letter, asking if I might be allowed to try my chance some other afternoon. I had no answer for several days, but at last I got a little note saying she would be at home on Sunday at four and with this extraordinary postscript: 'Please do not write to me here again; I will explain when I see you.' On Sunday she received me, and was perfectly charming; but when I was going away she begged of me, if I ever had occasion to write to her again, to address my letter to 'Mrs. Knox, care of Whittaker's Library, Green Street.' 'There are reasons,' she said, 'why I cannot receive letters in my own house.'

"All through the season I saw a great deal of her, and the atmosphere of mystery never left her. Sometimes I thought she was in the power of some man, but she looked so unapproachable that I could not believe it. It was really very difficult for me to come to any conclusion, for she was like one of those strange crystals that one sees in museums, which are at one moment clear, and at another clouded. At last I determined to ask her to be my wife: I was sick and tired of the incessant secrecy that she imposed on all my visits, and on the few letters I sent her. I wrote to her at the library to ask her if she could see me the following Monday at six. She answered yes, and I was in the seventh heaven of delight. I was infatuated with her: in spite of the mystery, I thought then — in consequence of it, I see now. No; it was the woman herself I loved. The mystery troubled me, maddened me. Why did chance put me in its track?"

"You discovered it, then?" I cried.

"I fear so," he answered. "You can judge for yourself."

20

"When Monday came round I went to lunch with my uncle, and about four o'clock found myself in the Marylebone Road. My uncle, you know, lives in Regent's Park. I wanted to get to Piccadilly, and took a short cut through a lot of shabby little streets. Suddenly I saw in front of me Lady Alroy, deeply veiled and walking very fast. On coming to the last house in the street, she went up the steps, took out a latch-key, and let herself in. 'Here is the mystery,' I said to myself; and I hurried on and examined the house. It seemed a sort of place for letting lodgings. On the doorstep lay her handkerchief, which she had dropped. I picked it up and put it in my pocket. Then I began to consider what I should do. I came to the conclusion that I had no right to spy on her, and I drove down to the club. At six I called to see her. She was lying on a sofa, in a tea-gown of silver tissue looped up by some strange moonstones that she always wore. She was looking quite lovely. 'I am so glad to see you,' she said; 'I have not been out all day.' I stared at her in amazement, and pulling the handkerchief out of my pocket, handed it to her. 'You dropped this in Cumnor Street this afternoon, Lady Alroy,' I said very calmly. She looked at me in terror, but made no attempt to take the handkerchief. 'What were you doing there?' I asked. 'What right have you to question me?' she answered. 'The right of a man who loves you,' I replied; 'I came here to ask you to be my wife.' She hid her face in her hands, and burst into floods of tears. 'You must tell me,' I continued. She stood up, and, looking me straight in the face, said, 'Lord Murchison, there is noth-ing to tell you.' — 'You went to meet some one,' I cried; 'this is your mystery.' She grew dreadfully white, and said, 'I went to meet no one.' — 'Can't you tell the truth?' I exclaimed. 'I have told it,' she replied. I was mad, frantic; I don't know what I said, but I said terrible things to her. Finally I rushed out of the house. She wrote me a letter the next day; I sent it back unopened, and started for Norway with Alan Colville. After a month I came back, and the first thing I saw in the *Morning Post* was the death of Lady Alroy. She had caught a chill at the Opera, and had died in five days of congestion of the lungs. I shut myself up and saw no one. I had loved her so much, I had loved her so madly. Good God! how I had loved that woman!"

"You went to the street, to the house in it?" I said.

"Yes," he answered.

"One day I went to Cumnor Street. I could not help it; I was tortured with 25 doubt. I knocked at the door, and a respectable-looking woman opened it to me. I asked her if she had any rooms to let. 'Well, sir,' she replied, 'the drawing-rooms are supposed to be let; but I have not seen the lady for three months, and as rent is owing on them, you can have them.' — 'Is this the lady?' I said, showing the photograph. 'That's her, sure enough,' she exclaimed; 'and when is she com-ing back, sir?' — 'The lady is dead,' I replied. 'Oh, sir, I hope not!' said the woman; 'she was my best lodger. She paid me three guineas a week merely to sit in my drawing-rooms now and then.' — 'She met some one here?' I said; but the woman assured me that it was not so, that she always came alone, and saw no one. 'What on earth did she do here?' I cried. 'She simply sat in the drawing-room, sir, reading books, and sometimes had tea,' the woman answered. I did not know what to say, so I gave her a sovereign and went away. Now, what do you think it all meant? You don't believe the woman was telling the truth?"

"I do."

"Then why did Lady Alroy go there?"

"My dear Gerald," I answered, "Lady Alroy was simply a woman with a mania for mystery. She took these rooms for the pleasure of going there with her veil down, and imagining she was a heroine. She had a passion for secrecy, but she herself was merely a Sphinx without a secret."

"Do you really think so?"

"I am sure of it," I replied.                                                          30

He took out the morocco case, opened it, and looked at the photograph. "I wonder?" he said at last.

## CONSIDERATIONS FOR CRITICAL THINKING AND WRITING

1. FIRST RESPONSE. When the narrator first sees a picture of Lady Alroy he writes, "It seemed to me the face of some one who had a secret, but whether that secret was good or evil I could not say" (par. 12). By the end of the story we know of her secret, but is there any clarity about whether it is "good or evil"?

2. Why is the subtitle of this story "An Etching"?

3. The narrator writes of Lord Murchison, "We used to say of him that he would be the best of fellows, if he did not always speak the truth" (par. 1). Is this just an attempt at wit or does it have thematic implications for the story?

4. Before he tells his story, Murchison says, "I cannot love where I cannot trust" (par. 4). What is the relationship between love and trust? Try to go beyond platitudes in your response, and use examples from this story to illustrate your beliefs.

5. What is the purpose of the frame tale — that is, the discussion of their first meeting, their taxi ride, and their dinner — prior to the main action, which is Murchison's telling of the story of him and Lady Alroy?

6. Is there evidence that Murchison falls in love with Lady Alroy *because of* her mysterious nature? If so, how can it also be true that mystery is the aspect of her he cannot tolerate?

7. Why does Murchison believe that marrying Lady Alroy will abolish the secrecy that stands between them?

8. How is Lady Alroy described throughout the story? How does her appearance contribute to her other qualities as Murchison describes them?

9. Lord Murchison is presented to us as a character who is honest and trustworthy to a fault. Do any details of his story strike you as possibly untrue? Do you trust him as a narrator?

10. The narrator sums up Lady Alroy's character as someone who had "a mania for mystery" and "a passion for secrecy," and concludes that she was "a Sphinx without a secret." Lord Murchison is still troubled at the story's conclusion. Are you? As Murchison asks his companion, "[W]hat do you think it all meant?"

### CONNECTION TO ANOTHER SELECTION

1. Compare the importance of having a private world separate from one's partner in this story and in Charlotte Perkins Gilman's "The Yellow Wallpaper" (p. 126).

## DAVID LONG (B. 1948)

The author of three collections of short fiction and four novels, David Long focuses on everyday characters living ordinary lives who sometimes experience concentrated moments of intense emotion. Speaking of the difference between writing in the two genres, he said in a 2011 interview, "Novels are hard . . . but they're less trouble than a book of stories. Novels are mostly middle; stories are all beginnings and endings." Consider what you have learned about plot as you read the following story, set in Montana in 1959, and also consider point of view. How does the narrator's cautious distance from the protagonist contribute to the story's effect?

## *Morphine*   1998

He's a handsome man, lanky, with black sleepy eyes and soft skillful hands: Gerald Wilcox, a doctor in Sperry, Montana, specializing in the ear, nose, and throat. He no longer drinks much now — champagne at a wedding, wine at the table if guests are present. A glass, maybe two. He's not graced with a huge reservoir of will power. You do what you can, and what he's been able to do is rein in the drinking. Not give it dominion.

"It makes you morose, don't you see that? Not to mention the driving around, not to mention people's trust in you. It's too small a town. Why do I have to say these things?"

This is Charlotte talking, his wife of twenty-two years. Born Charlotte Timmins — calls to mind "timid," that's the joke of it — she is a tall, forthright woman, brassy-haired. "Gerald," she tells him, "I am forty-four years old. I never intended to be a woman who wears a girdle, a woman with chins." She pinches the excess flesh, creates a wattle, and exhales with showy contempt. Of their marriage, she has lately said, "This is not a business arrangement, Gerald. This is something else. Do I make myself clear?"

He pretends bafflement. "Darling," he says, "my feelings have not changed one iota — in fact they've grown deeper, more complex."

But, yes, he knows what she's talking about. Blessedly, these complaints are 5 intermittent. Life proceeds, slips from one state to the next; at odd moments, passions reawaken.

Their only child, Jeanette, is plain-faced, secretive, bookish, as lanky as Gerald. She has recently asked that he knock off calling her his Little Bean.

"And what might you prefer," he inquired, "Jeanette, Queen of the Euphrates?"°

"Don't be mean," Charlotte told him.

He said he wasn't. "You don't think I'm being mean, do you, honey?" he asked his daughter.

She cut her eyes at him, made them slits. "No, Daddy."                               10

Last year she was reading *Little Women*,° this year — it's 1959 — John O'Hara.° Wilcox came upon the book among her things while foraging for the stapler. "Well, we don't censor what a person chooses to read in this house," Charlotte said when he showed one passage to her.

Wilcox read aloud: "'He kissed her and put his hand on her breast. Without taking her mouth away from his she unbuttoned the jacket of her suit and he discovered that she was wearing a dickey, not a blouse, and then put his hand down into her brassiere until he was able to cup her breast in the curving palm of his hand.'"

A great arching of Charlotte's brows. She brought her face near his. "Oh *my*," she said. "Would you put your hand down into my brassiere, Gerald? Would you cup my breast?"

He has decided that each of them has a talent for secretiveness. Three secret hearts under one roof.

Nearly every night, he inscribes a few lines in his journal. He notes the ebb 15 and flow of infectious disease. If he and Charlotte have been to a movie, a synopsis appears, a terse critique. He makes reference to the weather, if noteworthy: *Cheated of summer this year. Such gloom.* Or: *Woke last evening to a lightning storm. Jeanette came into our bed, fearing wildfires . . . explained how remote the possibility.* Or: *Walked uptown over the noon hour. Green fuzz on the trees all along First.*

---

*Euphrates:* A river that begins in Turkey, flows through Syria, and in Iraq merges with the Tigris River to empty into the Persian Gulf. One of the four possible sites for what is called the cradle of civilization.
*Little Women:* A nineteenth-century American novel for young adults written by Louisa May Alcott.
*John O'Hara:* A twentieth-century American fiction writer (1905–1970).

Now and then, something like: *Saw Mrs. D—— this forenoon, had the very disagreeable task of telling her that the tumor has begun to encroach on the esophagus. Where some people get their stoicism is more than I can fathom.*

Flipping back a few years — 1952, 1949 — he finds the occasional entry he can make no sense of: *That business with the Bagnolds continues to nettle me.*

Not a clue.

Strangely, he seldom rereads what he's written. He's not addicted to it. If pressed, he couldn't say why he goes to the trouble, except it pleases him to keep this accounting. Giving up the journal falls outside the realm of what he can do.

In any case, the daily drinking is history, done with two years now and not much missed. But one night perhaps every six weeks, he takes to his office — it occupies the spacious front parlor of the house at 118 Plympton Street, a house of high ceilings spidered with hairline cracks, endowed with several rooms the Wilcoxes barely use — and injects himself with an ampule of morphine. Then he composes longer entries in his journal.

For instance: *I do not feel invincible. Indeed, I feel so near the great powers that it is no trouble to imagine being crushed by them, ground into powder, yet I do feel very much alive, there is no doubt of that. A pity one cannot feel this way more of the Goddamned time.* Having written this, he pauses. *No, disastrous,* he writes, lets the fountain pen dawdle in his hand.

The journal books, black and soft-sided, are kept in the top-right drawer of his desk. It's a locking desk, but the key has long ago vanished, so it's conceivable that Charlotte has inspected them at length. Perhaps even his daughter as well. Once, he went to the trouble of plucking a long hair from his head, licking it, and pasting it unobtrusively across the opening of the drawer, a trick he'd acquired from a mystery story. Then he thought better of it, and had a laugh at himself.

And, too, some incidents fail to appear in the journals. The night, for instance, when he drove his car onto the ice of McCafferty's Slough. A luscious, ludicrous evening. This slough had the shape of an oxbow, nearly a full circle segregated from the river's main channel by a narrow, birch-lined dike. A thin crust of snow lay atop the ice, but in places the wind had blown it clear. He drove from one end to the other, spinning gloriously, dodging the occasional squat black icehouse. It was late winter, the air mild and seductive. How had he come to be there, out on the ice? Drinking, yes, he'd been to a roadhouse called Sammy's, but he wasn't very drunk, only softened, estranged from care.

Driving, he had been telling one of his oldest, lamest jokes — *Hey, you in the field there, I been going up this hill close to two hours, don't it ever end? Oh hell, stranger, there ain't no hill here, you just lost your two hind wheels* — when the hind wheels of his own car cracked through the ice. McCafferty's Slough wasn't deep, seven or eight feet at most. It harbored perch and whitefish. Muskrats burrowed in the mud along its bank. Walking the ice, you'd see them squiggle out and follow beneath your boots, elongated, trailing bubbles. But there were — he *did* know this — springs feeding the slough, which left the ice untrustworthy in spots. And so as he finessed a lovely skidding spin, telling his lame joke, the back end of the Buick dropped through, stopping them short. It was quickly apparent that no amount of clever rocking back and forth would help.

"For shit's sake, Gerry," his companion said.

She was Glenny Parker, a slender girl with a ferocious hook nose, and a belly that was literally concave. A shallow white basin. At work, sometimes, he thought of his hand idling there, making quarter-size circles, which seemed to please her. She hadn't believed him at first, that he was a doctor, thought he was teasing her.

They set out across the ice, she gripping his arm, with his topcoat around her shoulders, her shoes red kidskin with straps like fine red wire. The night's hilarity had leached away. They hiked back up the gravel ramp they'd barrelled down a half hour before. The air seemed less mild now. Wind poured off the foothills, jangling the snowberries and the brittle remains of the cottonwood leaves. Up the way, not far, was a farmhouse with a light burning. As they drew closer, the light went out.

Wilcox squinted at the mailbox, saw the name, "Maki." Old Finn, he thought, starring up the drive. A dog emerged from the blackest patch of shadow and ratcheted off a few congested barks, but made no serious effort to charge him.

A cowled light came on above the door. Glenny Parker didn't know whether to follow or stand back out of sight. She elected to do a little of both.

After a moment, a man in pants and nightshirt came onto the canted slab of  30 concrete that served as a back stoop. Unshaven at this hour, he had a big, fair boy's face gone to thickness.

"Who's there?" he said. "Is someone there?" Then, shielding his eyes, "Dr. Wilcox? Is that you?"

All along, the doctor knew, there'd been the chance he'd be recognized, though, naturally, he'd hoped otherwise. But who was this man? A patient? Husband or son of a patient?

Maki looked beyond him. "Somebody out there with you?"

The doctor hesitated, then, hearing Glenny's feet on the gravel, found himself in the position of saying yes, actually, he did have a friend along.

Maki nodded. "That wouldn'ta been you out on the ice?" he asked.                35

Wilcox wiped his face, chuckled uneasily. "To be honest with you," he said, "I'm in kind of a jam here."

Maki acknowledged that he was. The girl's hands were plunged up to her elbows in the deep pockets of his coat; she looked tiny, brutally out of place. Maki eyed her without comment.

"Let me get the tractor," he said to the doctor.

Wilcox began to protest. All he really wanted was the use of the telephone, though just who he'd had in mind to call at one in the morning wasn't at all clear.

Maki turned back to the girl. "You better wait inside," he said. Head down, she  40 slipped away from Wilcox, went up the stoop, and passed through the mudroom into the bright-lit kitchen.

Maki secured the door, then the two men made their way back to the slough, Maki a stolid unhurried presence at the wheel of the tractor, and the doctor standing on the back, grasping the back rim of the seat, authentically chilled now. Yet thinking, This could turn out all right.

Maki insisted on doing the work himself, crouching on the ice with his tow chain, grunting out a few words that were lost to the Buick's undercarriage. He hoisted himself back up to the seat of the tractor. A short blast of diesel smoke, a slippage of the tire cleats before they grabbed, and the car bumped from its hole.

Wilcox stood by, rubbing his hands.

Maki got down again to uncouple the chain, dropped it with a clank into the box on the side of the tractor, and climbed back to the seat.

A week later, undressing in their bedroom, Charlotte asked, "You remember  45 Arlette Bledsoe? She said her brother gave you a hand the other day."

Arlette Bledsoe's brother?

"Helped with the car, fixed a flat or some such thing?"

"Oh, that," he said. "Yes."

"You didn't mention it."

"I guess I didn't, no." 50

"They've had a rotten time of it," Charlotte said. She reminded him that Walter Maki had lost his wife, and that she, Charlotte, had attended the service. At Immanuel Lutheran? In the pouring rain? She was deploying the voice she used for reminding him of things an ordinary person would remember.

He dropped his cufflinks into the wooden tray on his dresser, studying his wife a moment. Nothing accusatory there.

Briefly, he let himself recall the trip back to town with Glenny Parker. Reaching a pint bottle from the glove box, asking if she wanted a little warmup. "Sure, why not?" she said. She took a small mouthful, swished it between her teeth, then bounced the bottle down on the seat between them. She rode with her head against the far window, eyes shut. He drove her into town, back to her apartment on Lancaster Street, but did not go in.

And so tonight, three winters later, Gerald Wilcox is sequestered in his front room, stocking feet on desk, savoring the distant murmur of the furnace, the first swirls of wind brushing the waters of his thoughts. *Morphine, alkaloid derivative of opium . . . from the Greek "morph," the curious shapes seen in dreams.* He can't hear the word in his mind's ear without hearing as well his orotund, long-deceased Grandfather Vail. Each evening, one hand on newel post, the old man would announce he was headed up into the arms of Morpheus, if the seedy bastard would have him. It's an association Wilcox can't shake to this day: morphia and sleep, forgetting. Yet unless he overdoes it, unless the day has drained him, he can bypass the sludgy, soporific effect, and achieve a state he thinks of as *attentiveness*.

Or that's his aim. 55

His wife is upstairs in bed. She's been soldiering through a life of Michelangelo, so bloated a tome she has to brace it with a pillow. She reads bits aloud, saying, "What that man endured, up on that scaffolding?" She says, "Oh, that Pope, that Julius, what a *monster*."

He hears her neck crack as she turns to see if he's listening, before she chides him. He says he hasn't missed a word. Secretly, it pleases him that Charlotte still gives a good God damn about matters beyond the Sperry Golf Club, the hospital auxiliary, the preparation of sauces, and that she cares that the life they'd set out to lead together is not entirely extinguished. And, beyond that, isn't there a deep, atavistic pleasure in being read to? She has a whiskey voice, as a mystery writer would put it, though in fact the scratchy timbre results from tiny polyps on her vocal cords. Sometimes she lets the book fall, and asks about his patients: the McVicar sisters, Valen and Isabel, six-footers, retired nurses; the Lomasny girl, whose larynx was crushed by a strand of barbed wire; and so on, the human parade, morning and afternoon. He should keep their infirmities to himself, but instead he tells Charlotte these true stories, and none of it goes beyond her. If she knows of his wandering, there's no sign of it. If she knows it's in the past now, there's no sign of that, either.

But tonight he's downstairs, with the latest journal book in his lap. Charlotte will have doused the light and gone to sleep.

The telephone sounds.

The upstairs phone rests on the bedside table. By the third ring, Charlotte will 60 have reached for it; her free hand will be sweeping the empty sheets in search of him. He fetches the thing quickly into his lap, and says, "Yes?"

"Walter Maki," the caller says.

"What's the trouble, Mr. Maki?"

"I was counting on having you," Maki says. Already there's a note of intransigence. It's Maki's boy, Leonard. Ear problem.

"He's in a certain amount of pain then?"                                         65

"I told him to go back to sleep, there wasn't anything we could do till morning, but he was past that."

Infected mastoid, Wilcox imagines. He asks how old the boy is. He wonders, hearing his words go out, if he sounds drugged. No, certainly not.

Maki says the boy is thirteen.

"All right," the doctor says. "Bring him in to the office."

That pushiness in Maki's voice: "I was thinking of you coming out here."         70

So Wilcox agrees to a house call. Driving out Lower Valley Road, he thinks, isn't it a wonder he's never before been summoned out on a night he's injected himself. He feels robust — *in the pocket*, as the horn players used to say. He lifts his hands from the wheel and the car careers along, hugging the blacktop's soft-edged runnels, bending neither right nor left. Taking hold again, he drives past the old community hall at Aaberg's Landing, past the low spot choked with cattails that floods each spring. A burst of aspen leaves blows through the splay of headlights, the words "gold leaf" appear in his head, and he thinks then about angels. Imagine the ceiling of the world ruptured, spewing forth angels. He's not a believer — not remotely — but this is how his mind works on these nights. Another few miles and he draws alongside the slough. The water is black, still.

Maki admits him, leads him through the mudroom into the kitchen. The boy is on the sofa in the front room. Maki has the stove cranked. There's a smell, a scent added to the water kettle atop it. Mentholatum. The boy's cheeks are fiery, and the skin of his neck clammy. He lacks Maki's square features. His eyes are tipped and melancholy, his face long and weak-chinned.

The swelling is greater than Wilcox had supposed. He palpates the space behind the ear with a light touch. It's too late in the game for medication alone.

"This has been hurting for a few days, hasn't it, Leonard?" he asks.

The boy offers a constricted nod.                                                75

"You can lie back down."

To his son, Maki says, fiercely, "Whyn't you say anything before now?"

"You thought it would take care of itself," the doctor says, "Isn't that right?"

Leonard stares at the two men, blinking, his mouth open in a shallow pant.

"Just human nature," Wilcox says. He goes back to the brightness of the          80
kitchen and Maki follows.

"We should get him into town," Wilcox says.

Again Maki balks. He looks intractable, almost menacing.

"We're not going to tussle over this are we?" Wilcox asks, but immediately he undergoes a change of heart, rises to the challenge. "Never mind," he says. "We can do it here."

Leonard is brought into the kitchen and seated at the enamel-topped table, with his head on a folded towel covered by a sheet. The doctor numbs the skin behind the ear, though this will work only minimally.

"I have a girl," he says to the boy. "She's a little older than you. Jeanette, Queen  85
of the Tigris and Euphrates, I call her."

With one hand he holds the head still, and with the other makes a cut. The boy flinches, but his reaction is remarkably controlled. The incision produces perhaps three tablespoons of pus, viscous green, vile-smelling. "That's it," Wilcox says.

"Good." He irrigates the area with antiseptic, bandages it, administers a hefty dose of sulfa, and Leonard is put to bed again in the front room.

"You'll sleep now," Wilcox tells him. The boy stares back, disbelieving, but his eyes already have a glassy, listing look.

"Give you a drink?" Maki says.

"Thanks, no."

"No drink for you?"                                                                                      90

"No."

"Can I give you some tea?"

"That's all right," Wilcox says. He has entered the stage where his thoughts wither, when if he were home he might consider a second dose, a touch-up. It's never the right idea. He need only recall the night he lost track and went to his knees, retching in the downstairs lavatory, his heart thready and arrhythmic, his rubbery blue-phantomed skin the skin of a corpse. He was mortified that Charlotte might discover him, horrified that she wouldn't. Nearly three months elapsed before he picked up the needle again. He thought maybe he'd cured himself, but no.

Maki has taken a seat at the table. His palms are turned down upon it, as if to keep it from levitating.

"The boy will be fine," Wilcox says. He's still on his feet, bag in hand.          95

"Sit down," Maki says.

Wilcox smiles and sits down. "I could stay a minute," he says.

"This evens us out," Maki says.

"Well, now, I wouldn't look at it that way."

"That night on the ice," Maki says. "You were a sorry-looking thing."          100

Wilcox looks at him, waiting.

"You and that girl."

"Yes, sir."

"So let me ask you," Maki says. "Do you think I ever stepped out on my wife?"

"Mr. Maki, I wouldn't hazard the first thought on that subject," Wilcox says.     105

So this is a chastising. There are worse things.

"You're sure he's O.K.," Maki says. "He won't lose his hearing?"

"His hearing will be fine," Wilcox says. "Trust me."

"He plays the trumpet."

"Is that so?"                                                                                           110

"His mother was musical," Maki says. "She wanted him to have the lessons."

"This shouldn't hurt a thing."

Maki shakes his head. He says, "You're hopped up on something, aren't you?"

"I'm going to have to be going now," Wilcox says, standing again. "I'll leave you this prescription. Be sure he takes all of it." He pulls out the blank and writes, watching the extravagant looping that is his signature. "Let me see him in a few days," he says.

Maki leaves the paper where it lies. "You and that silly girl," he says.          115

Wilcox's headlights judder on the washboard, the Buick's hindquarters drift as he corners at the section lines. Then, abruptly, he's on blacktop again. He pictures Leonard Maki off in a back room with his trumpet, his embouchure, hopes to Christ the boy possesses a little natural aptitude. The idea of him bleating away in his mother's memory is more than Wilcox can take just now.

He lets himself in the rear door of the house on Plympton Street, hangs his coat on the ivory knob in the hall, listens for symptoms of unrest. He pours himself a short inch of bourbon and carries it to his office. Ten past three. No, that's unfair, he thinks. She was not a silly girl, Glenny — just in the wrong company. She had her talents. For a moment, he recalls her lips creeping into the hollow beneath his ear as he drove, keeping to the back roads, her voice tiny but remorseless, *I know what you'd like, Gerry. Stop the car, can't you?* Yet he only saw her one more time after that night on the frozen slough, and it had not gone well.

He sits for a time. Eventually, he takes up the journal, and writes: *Why do you never get used to the stink of pus? If you could smell that exact hue of green, that's how it would be , , , and yet it's just a broth of white cells, the body's defenses. What purpose is served? Why not the rusty smell of blood, the sweetness of breast milk instead? Was I ever taught this?*

Again he finds himself picturing the ceiling of the world, with white cells clustering like a mob of angels.

He writes: *Why this clamoring for purpose?*                                        120

There's a footfall outside his door. He slaps the journal shut and braces himself.

But it proves to be his daughter. "What are you writing?" she asks.

"Oh, you know, these notebooks of mine," he says. "You don't mean you've never poked around in them?"

"I wouldn't do *that*," Jeanette says, aggrieved.

Getting to be quite a capable liar, Wilcox thinks, not unhappily.                   125

"What are you doing up?"

Jeanette shrugs, approaches the desk.

"Not sleeping again?" he asks. "Would you like me to give you something?"

"No."

"I could."                                                                           130

"I know," Jeanette says. "Anyway, it's too *late*."

Wilcox checks the filagreed clock hands again and somehow it's gotten to be five past five. "So it is," he says.

Jeanette is barefoot, wearing a long flannel gown with a tiny satin bow at the collar. Her hair is profuse, like Charlotte's, but not nearly so radiant a yellow, and at the moment it looks sea-wracked. She has a long neck and still no bust to speak of, though she's been menstruating for a good two years. Were it not for her gaze — watchful, not in the least dreamy — she might have been painted by Maxfield Parrish.°

"Aren't your feet cold?" he says.

"I suppose."                                                                         135

Wilcox asks if she knows a boy named Leonard Maki.

Jeanette shakes her head.

"He plays the trumpet."

"Don't know him," she says.

"I thought you might. From school."                                                  140

She stands, arms crossed, shifting her weight, her lungs filling and emptying.

After a moment, he asks, "Anything troubling your soul, dear heart?"

"No."

"You can tell me."

But of course she can't.                                                             145

*Maxfield Parrish* (1870-1966): A famous American illustrator known for idealized forms and bold colors.

"Something's always troubling the soul," Wilcox says. "It's an irritable organ."

He offers a smile, which is not returned.

"I'm all right," she says. "I'm not *disconsolate*."

Wilcox smiles inwardly at this word she's plucked from the ether. "Well, it is the way it is," he says. Then it's her turn to nod, and he supposes they understand one another.

"You hungry?" he asks, standing, putting the journal aside. He touches her on 150 the head, works his fingers into the tumbling snarls, which, briefly, she allows.

She follows him down the dim hallway into the kitchen. He opens the refrigerator and stares in at the lighted shelves and closes the door again.

"Do you know how to make that coffee cake?" he asks his daughter. "With the crumbles?"

"In the brown book," Jeanette says, pointing with her chin. "Fannie Farmer."

Wilcox reaches it down, locates the page, which is grease-spattered to transparency in places, with notations in his wife's dishevelled, back-slanting hand: "Gerald likes."

"No yeast in this one?" he asks.                                         155

"No, Daddy."

He gets out what he needs, also the coffee tin. An easy recipe. In a matter of minutes, he slides the baking pan onto the oven rack.

"Better set the timer," Jeanette says, and so he sets the timer.

He collects the bowl and the utensils and runs water on them in the sink. Over his shoulder, he says, "Why don't you go wake your mother?"

"She won't want to get up this early."                                    160

"Oh, I know," he says. "But go anyway. Tell her she won't want to miss this." He shakes his hands, dries them under his armpits, looks his daughter in the eye. "Use those exact words. Say, 'He says you won't want to miss this.'"

No further objection from Jeanette. In fact, he detects a twitch of conspiracy about the lips as she leaves the room. After a moment, he notes her tread along the squeaky boards of the upstairs hall.

He goes and stands at the back door, looking out where a thin silver light is falling through the empty chestnut branches. He doesn't feel too damn awful, considering. Has the makings of a headache, where the neck cords meet the skull, but it will pass. Food will help, and caffeine. Later, in the afternoon, the fatigue will hit, the fuzziness he detests. If there's no one in the office, maybe he can sneak upstairs and lie down and shut his eyes. If not, the tiredness, too, will pass. He pictures himself beginning a new page: *18 November. Made Charlotte a coffee cake.* Maybe he'll record what she has to say about this unusual occurrence. Maybe she'll notice him climbing the stairs, and follow, launching salacious suggestions at him in a stage whisper. Maybe later he'll get to write: *C. and I napped before supper.* He watches a black dog cut through the yard, tail switching. After a while, the timer dings; his whole upper body startles, as if he's been seized from behind. Then he remembers to breathe again.

He slides the baking pan from the oven, sniffs the sugary cinnamon, pokes a toothpick into the center the way Charlotte would. It comes out clean and dry. He sets the pan on a wire rack, runs water into the percolator, taps in coffee, sets the flame. He listens for his wife. He pictures her getting to her feet and pulling on her robe, the slippery blue nylon, yanking the sash, then tousling some life into her night-heavy hair. Waiting, alone here in the kitchen, he suddenly wonders what will become of the journals after his death. He's barely given this a thought before. He's not fifty yet — how many more will have accumulated in the drawer by then, the pebbled-leather volumes swollen with his daily commentary, his nagging queries of himself? And how soon will it be before he relaxes his guard and lets the rest come forth — that chill along his inner arm before the needle slips in. The warming flood of ruminations. He pictures the heap of journals pulled into a lap, flopped open and read, one after another. How can it feel like comfort to him that they will be? And then what? Strange to admit, it's not a thought that troubles him.

## CONSIDERATIONS FOR CRITICAL THINKING AND WRITING

1. FIRST RESPONSE. Paragraph 14 reads, "[Gerald] has decided that each of them has a talent for secretiveness. Three secret hearts under one roof." Are they all equally secretive, or is this assessment something Gerald wishes were true so he can accept his own secrecy?

2. Describe Gerald and Charlotte's marriage: What makes it "typical" and what makes it unique?

3. Gerald, Charlotte, and their daughter Jeanette are all introduced with a series of descriptive adjectives. Look again at these descriptions. What do they tell us about their characters and what do they *not* tell us?

4. How is Gerald's journal a key aspect of the story?

5. Discuss the way key details are revealed in the story and consider the relationship between the reader and Gerald in terms of privacy.

6. If Gerald is the protagonist, would you describe the farmer Maki as the antagonist? How does their relationship frame the story's theme?

7. Is Gerald honest about his triumph over alcohol? What evidence do you have to support your response?

8. Morpheus was the Greek god of dreams whose name is the basis for morphine, the opiate that Gerald periodically injects. The dream world of Morpheus also contains the River of Forgetfulness. Discuss this concept in terms of Gerald's occasional lapses in memory.

9. Before he makes the house call to Maki's home, Gerald assures himself that no one could detect that he had taken morphine, yet Maki knows. How?

10. What is the relationship between art and science in the story? How does this opposition comment on the story's concerns with the soul, with the meaning of human existence, and with death?

## CONNECTIONS TO OTHER SELECTIONS

1. Compare the way marriage is depicted in this story and in Ann Beattie's "Janus" (p. 27). How do both marriages allow for privacy or secrecy (depending on which word you find more appropriate)?

2. Gerald in this story is like the narrator of Adrian Tomine's graphic story "Intruders" (p. 197) in that they both try to cover up their secret activities. Who is more successful at doing so?

## ZZ PACKER (B. 1973)

Rose Lincoln/Harvard Staff Photographer.

Born in Chicago and raised in Georgia and Kentucky, ZZ Packer earned her undergraduate degree from Yale, a master's degree from Johns Hopkins, and an M.F.A. in creative writing from the University of Iowa. She has taught creative writing at a variety of prestigious American universities. Her collection *Drinking Coffee Elsewhere*, the title story of which is included below, was one of the most celebrated publications of 2003.

## *Drinking Coffee Elsewhere*   2000

Orientation games began the day I arrived at Yale from Baltimore. In my group we played heady, frustrating games for smart people. One game appeared to be charades reinterpreted by existentialists; another involved listening to rocks. Then a freshman counselor made everyone play Trust. The idea was that if you had the faith to fall backward and wait for four scrawny former high school geniuses to catch you, just before your head cracked on the slate sidewalk, then you might learn to trust your fellow students. Russian roulette sounded like a better way to go.

"No way," I said. The white boys were waiting for me to fall, holding their arms out for me, sincerely, gallantly. "No fucking way."

"It's all cool, it's all cool," the counselor said. Her hair was a shade of blond I'd seen only on *Playboy* covers, and she raised her hands as though backing away from a growling dog. "Sister," she said, in an I'm-down-with-the-struggle voice, "you don't have to play this game. As a person of color, you shouldn't have to fit into any white, patriarchal system."

I said, "It's a bit too late for that."

In the next game, all I had to do was wait in a circle until it was my turn to say 5
what inanimate object I wanted to be. One guy said he'd like to be a gadfly, like Socrates. "Stop me if I wax Platonic," he said. I didn't bother mentioning that gadflies weren't inanimate — it didn't seem to make a difference. The girl next to him was eating a rice cake. She wanted to be the Earth, she said. Earth with a capital E.

There was one other black person in the circle. He wore an Exeter T-shirt and his overly elastic expressions resembled a series of facial exercises. At the end of each person's turn, he smiled and bobbed his head with unfettered enthusiasm. "Oh, that was good," he said, as if the game were an experiment he'd set up and the results were turning out better than he'd expected. "Good, good, good!"

When it was my turn I said, "My name is Dina, and if I had to be any object, I guess I'd be a revolver." The sunlight dulled as if on cue. Clouds passed rapidly overhead, presaging rain. I don't know why I said it. Until that moment I'd been good in all the ways that were meant to matter. I was an honor roll student — though I'd learned long ago not to mention it in the part of Baltimore where I lived. Suddenly

I was hard-bitten and recalcitrant, the kind of kid who took pleasure in sticking pins into cats; the kind who chased down smart kids to spray them with Mace.

"A revolver," a counselor said, stroking his chin, as if it had grown a rabbinical beard. "Could you please elaborate?"

The black guy cocked his head and frowned, as if the beakers and Erlenmeyer flasks of his experiment had grown legs and scurried off.

"You were just kidding," the dean said, "about wiping out all of mankind. 10 That, I suppose, was a joke." She squinted at me. One of her hands curved atop the other to form a pink, freckled molehill on her desk.

"Well," I said, "maybe I meant it at the time." I quickly saw that this was not the answer she wanted. "I don't know. I think it's the architecture."

Through the dimming light of the dean's office window, I could see the fortress of the old campus. On my ride from the bus station to the campus, I'd barely glimpsed New Haven — a flash of crumpled building here, a trio of straggly kids there. A lot like Baltimore. But everything had changed when we reached those streets hooded by gothic buildings. I imagined how the college must have looked when it was founded, when most of the students owned slaves. I pictured men wearing tights and knickers, smoking pipes.

"The architecture," the dean repeated. She bit her lip and seemed to be making a calculation of some sort. I noticed that she blinked less often than most people. I sat there, intrigued, waiting to see how long it would be before she blinked again.

My revolver comment won me a year's worth of psychiatric counseling, weekly meetings with Dean Guest, and — since the parents of the roommate I'd never met weren't too hip on the idea of their Amy sharing a bunk bed with a budding homicidal loony — my very own room.

Shortly after getting my first C ever, I also received the first knock on my 15 door. The female counselors never knocked. The dean had spoken to them; I was a priority. Every other day, right before dinnertime, they'd look in on me, unannounced. "Just checking up," a counselor would say. It was the voice of a suburban mother in training. By the second week, I had made a point of sitting in a chair in front of the door, just when I expected a counselor to pop her head around. This was intended to startle them. I also made a point of being naked. The unannounced visits ended.

The knocking persisted. Through the peephole I saw a white face, distorted and balloonish.

"Let me in." The person looked like a boy but it sounded like a girl. "Let me in," the voice repeated.

"Not a chance," I said. I had a suicide single, and I wanted to keep it that way. No roommates, no visitors.

Then the person began to sob, and I heard a back slump against the door. If I hadn't known the person was white from the peephole, I'd have known it from a display like this. Black people didn't knock on strangers' doors, crying. Not that I understood the black people at Yale. Most of them were from New York and tried hard to pretend that they hadn't gone to prep schools. And there was something pitiful in how cool they were. Occasionally one would reach out to me with missionary zeal, but I'd rebuff the person with haughty silence.

"I don't have anyone to talk to!" the person on the other side of the door cried. 20

"That is correct."

"When I was a child," the person said, "I played by myself in a corner of the schoolyard all alone. I hated dolls and I hated games, animals were not friendly and birds flew away. If anyone was looking for me I hid behind a tree and cried out 'I am an orphan—'"

I opened the door. It was a she.

"Plagiarist!" I yelled. She had just recited a Frank O'Hara poem as though she'd thought it up herself. I knew the poem because it was one of the few things I'd been forced to read that I wished I'd written myself.

The girl turned to face me, smiling weakly, as though her triumph was not in 25 getting me to open the door but in the fact that she was able to smile at all when she was so accustomed to crying. She was large but not obese, and crying had turned her face the color of raw chicken. She blew her nose into the waist end of her T-shirt, revealing a pale belly.

"How do you know that poem?"

She sniffed. "I'm in your Contemporary Poetry class."

She said she was Canadian and her name was Heidi, although she said she wanted people to call her Henrik. "That's a guy's name," I said. "What do you want? A sex change?"

She looked at me with so little surprise that I suspected she hadn't discounted this as an option. Then her story came out in teary, hiccup-like bursts. She had sucked some "cute guy's dick" and he'd told everybody and now people thought she was "a slut."

"Why'd you suck his dick? Aren't you a lesbian?" 30

She fit the bill. Short hair, hard, roach-stomping shoes. Dressed like an aspiring plumber. And then there was the name Henrik. The lesbians I'd seen on TV were wiry, thin strips of muscle, but Heidi was round and soft and had a moonlike face. Drab henna-colored hair. And lesbians had cats. "Do you have a cat?" I asked.

Her eyes turned glossy with new tears. "No," she said, her voice quavering, "and I'm not a lesbian. Are you?"

"Do I look like one?" I said.

She didn't answer.

"O.K.," I said. "I could suck a guy's dick, too, if I wanted. But I don't. The 35 human penis is one of the most germ-ridden objects there is." Heidi looked at me, unconvinced. "What I meant to say," I began again, "is that I don't like anybody. Period. Guys or girls. I'm a misanthrope."

"I am, too."

"No," I said, guiding her back through my door and out into the hallway. "You're not."

"Have you had dinner?" she asked. "Let's go to Commons."

I pointed to a pyramid of ramen noodle packages on my windowsill. "See that? That means I never have to go to Commons. Aside from class, I have contact with no one."

"I hate it here, too," she said. "I should have gone to McGill, eh." 40

"The way to feel better," I said, "is to get some ramen and lock yourself in your room. Everyone will forget about you and that guy's dick and you won't have to see anyone ever again. If anyone looks for you —"

"I'll hide behind a tree."

"A revolver?" Dr. Raeburn said, flipping through a manila folder. He looked up at me as if to ask another question, but he didn't.

Dr. Raeburn was the psychiatrist. He had the gray hair and whiskers of a Civil War general. He was also a chain smoker with beige teeth and a navy wool jacket smeared with ash. He asked about the revolver at the beginning of my first visit. When I was unable to explain myself, he smiled, as if this were perfectly reasonable.

"Tell me about your parents." 45

I wondered what he already had on file. The folder was thick, though I hadn't said a thing of significance since Day One.

"My father was a dick and my mother seemed to like him."

He patted his pockets for his cigarettes. "That's some heavy stuff," he said. "How do you feel about Dad?" The man couldn't say the word "father." "Is Dad someone you see often?"

"I hate my father almost as much as I hate the word 'Dad.'"

He started tapping his cigarette. 50

"You can't smoke in here."

"That's right," he said, and slipped the cigarette back into the packet. He smiled, widening his eyes brightly. "Don't ever start."

I thought that that first encounter would be the last of Heidi or Henrik, or whatever, but then her head appeared in a window of Linsly-Chit during my Chaucer class. A few days later, she swooped down a flight of stairs in Harkness, following me. She hailed me from across Elm Street and found me in the Sterling Library stacks. After one of my meetings with Dr. Raeburn, she was waiting for me outside Health Services, legs crossed, cleaning her fingernails.

"You know," she said, as we walked through Old Campus, "you've got to stop eating ramen. Not only does it lack a single nutrient but it's full of MSG."

I wondered why she even bothered, and was vaguely flattered she cared, but 55 I said, "I like eating chemicals. It keeps the skin radiant."

"There's also hepatitis." She knew how to get my attention — mention a disease.

"You get hepatitis from unwashed lettuce," I said. "If there's anything safe from the perils of the food chain, it's ramen."

"But do you refrigerate what you don't eat? Each time you reheat it, you're killing good bacteria, which then can't keep the bad bacteria in check. A guy got sick from reheating Chinese noodles, and his son died from it. I read it in the *Times*." With this, she put a jovial arm around my neck. I continued walking, a little stunned. Then, just as quickly, she dropped her arm and stopped walking. I stopped, too.

"Did you notice that I put my arm around you?"

"Yes," I said. "Next time, I'll have to chop it off." 60

"I don't want you to get sick," she said. "Let's eat at Commons."

In the cold air, her arm had felt good.

The problem with Commons was that it was too big; its ceiling was as high as a cathedral's, but below it there were no awestruck worshippers, only eighteen-year-olds at heavy wooden tables, chatting over veal patties and Jell-O.

We got our food, tacos stuffed with meat substitute, and made our way through the maze of tables. The Koreans had a table. Each singing group had a table. The crew team sat at a long table of its own. We passed the black table. Heidi was so plump and moonfaced that the sheer quantity of her flesh accentuated just how white she was. The black students gave me a long, hard stare.

"How you doing, sista?" a guy asked, his voice full of accusation, eyeballing 65
me as though I were clad in a Klansman's sheet and hood. "I guess we won't see you
till graduation."

"If," I said, "you graduate."

The remark was not well received. As I walked past, I heard protests, angry
and loud as if they'd discovered a cheat at their poker game. Heidi and I found an
unoccupied table along the periphery, which was isolated and dark. We sat down.
Heidi prayed over her tacos.

"I thought you didn't believe in God," I said.

"Not in the God depicted in the Judeo-Christian Bible, but I do believe that
nature's essence is a spirit that —"

"All right," I said. I had begun to eat, and cubes of diced tomato fell from my 70
mouth when I spoke. "Stop right there. Tacos and spirits don't mix."

"You've always got to be so flip," she said. "I'm going to apply for another
friend."

"There's always Mr. Dick," I said. "Slurp, slurp."

"You are so lame. So unbelievably lame. I'm going out with Mr. Dick. Thursday night at Atticus. His name is Keith."

Heidi hadn't mentioned Mr. Dick since the day I'd met her. That was more
than a month ago and we'd spent a lot of that time together. I checked for signs that
she was lying; her habit of smiling too much, her eyes bright and cheeks full so that
she looked like a chipmunk. But she looked normal. Pleased, even, to see me so
flustered.

"You're insane! What are you going to do this time?" I asked. "Sleep with him? 75
Then when he makes fun of you, what? Come pound your head on my door reciting the collected poems of Sylvia Plath?"

"He's going to apologize for before. And don't call me insane. You're the one
going to the psychiatrist."

"Well, I'm not going to suck his dick, that's for sure."

She put her arm around me in mock comfort, but I pushed it off, and ignored
her. She touched my shoulder again, and I turned, annoyed, but it wasn't Heidi
after all; a sepia-toned boy dressed in khakis and a crisp plaid shirt was standing
behind me. He thrust a hot-pink square of paper toward me without a word, then
briskly made his way toward the other end of Commons, where the crowds blossomed. Heidi leaned over and read it: "Wear Black Leather — the Less, the Better."

"It's a gay party," I said, crumpling the card. "He thinks we're fucking gay."

Heidi and I signed on to work at the Saybrook dining hall as dishwashers. The 80
job consisted of dumping food from plates and trays into a vat of rushing water.
It seemed straightforward, but then I learned better. You wouldn't believe what
people could do with food until you worked in a dish room. Lettuce and crackers
and soup would be bullied into a pulp in the bowl of some bored anorexic; ziti
would be mixed with honey and granola; trays would appear heaped with mashed
potato snow women with melted chocolate ice cream for hair. Frat boys arrived
at the dish-room window, en masse. They liked to fill glasses with food, then seal
them, airtight, onto their trays. If you tried to prize them off, milk, Worcestershire
sauce, peas, chunks of bread vomited onto your dish-room uniform.

When this happened one day in the middle of the lunch rush, for what seemed
like the hundredth time, I tipped the tray toward one of the frat boys as he turned to
walk away, popping the glasses off so that the mess spurted onto his Shetland sweater.

He looked down at his sweater. "Lesbo bitch!"

"No," I said, "that would be your mother."

Heidi, next to me, clenched my arm in support, but I remained motionless, waiting to see what the frat boy would do. He glared at me for a minute, then walked away.

"Let's take a smoke break," Heidi said.

I didn't smoke, but Heidi had begun to, because she thought it would help her lose weight. As I hefted a stack of glasses through the steamer, she lit up.

"Soft packs remind me of you," she said. "Just when you've smoked them all and you think there's none left, there's always one more, hiding in that little crushed corner." Before I could respond she said, "Oh, God. Not another mouse. You know whose job that is."

By the end of the rush, the floor mats got full and slippery with food. This was when mice tended to appear, scurrying over our shoes; more often than not, a mouse got caught in the grating that covered the drains in the floor. Sometimes the mouse was already dead by the time we noticed it. This one was alive.

"No way," I said. "This time you're going to help. Get some gloves and a trash bag."

"That's all I'm getting. I'm not getting that mouse out of there."

"Put on the gloves," I ordered. She winced, but put them on. "Reach down," I said. "At an angle, so you get at its middle. Otherwise, if you try to get it by its tail, the tail will break off."

"This is filthy, eh."

"That's why we're here," I said. "To clean up filth. Eh."

She reached down, but would not touch the mouse. I put my hand around her arm and pushed it till her hand made contact. The cries from the mouse were soft, songlike. "Oh, my God," she said. "Oh, my God, ohmigod." She wrestled it out of the grating and turned her head away.

"Don't you let it go," I said.

"Where's the food bag? It'll smother itself if I drop it in the food bag. Quick," she said, her head still turned away, her eyes closed. "Lead me to it."

"No. We are not going to smother this mouse. We've got to break its neck."

"You're one heartless bitch."

I wondered how to explain that if death is unavoidable it should be quick and painless. My mother had died slowly. At the hospital, they'd said it was kidney failure, but I knew, in the end, it was my father. He made her so scared to live in her own home that she was finally driven away from it in an ambulance.

"Breaking its neck will save it the pain of smothering," I said. "Breaking its neck is more humane. Take the trash bag and cover it so you won't get any blood on you, then crush."

The loud jets of the steamer had shut off automatically and the dish room grew quiet. Heidi breathed in deeply, then crushed the mouse. She shuddered, disgusted. "Now what?"

"What do you mean, 'now what?' Throw the little bastard in the trash."

At our third session, I told Dr. Raeburn I didn't mind if he smoked. He sat on the sill of his open window, smoking behind a jungle screen of office plants.

We spent the first ten minutes discussing the Iliad, and whether or not the text actually states that Achilles had been dipped in the River Styx. He said it did, and I said it didn't. After we'd finished with the Iliad, and with my new job in what he called "the scullery," he asked questions about my parents. I told him nothing. It was none of his business. Instead, I talked about Heidi. I told him about that day in Commons, Heidi's plan to go on a date with Mr. Dick, and the invitation we'd been given to the gay party.

"You seem preoccupied by this soirée." He arched his eyebrows at the word 105 "soirée."

"Wouldn't you be?"

"Dina," he said slowly, in a way that made my name seem like a song title, "have you ever had a romantic interest?"

"You want to know if I've ever had a boyfriend?" I said. "Just go ahead and ask if I've ever fucked anybody."

This appeared to surprise him. "I think that you are having a crisis of identity," he said.

"Oh, is that what this is?" 110

His profession had taught him not to roll his eyes. Instead, his exasperation revealed itself in a tiny pursing of his lips, as though he'd just tasted something awful and was trying very hard not to offend the cook.

"It doesn't have to be, as you say, someone you've fucked, it doesn't have to be a boyfriend," he said.

"Well, what are you trying to say? If it's not a boy, then you're saying it's a girl —"

"Calm down. It could be a crush, Dina." He lit one cigarette off another. "A crush on a male teacher, a crush on a dog, for heaven's sake. An interest. Not necessarily a relationship."

It was sacrifice time. If I could spend the next half hour talking about some 115 boy, then I'd have given him what he wanted.

So I told him about the boy with the nice shoes.

I was sixteen and had spent the last few coins in my pocket on bus fare to buy groceries. I didn't like going to the Super Fresh two blocks away from my house, plunking government food stamps into the hands of the cashiers.

"There she go reading," one of them once said, even though I was only carrying a book. "Don't your eyes get tired?"

On Greenmount Avenue you could read schoolbooks — that was understandable. The government and your teachers forced you to read them. But anything else was antisocial. It meant you'd rather submit to the words of some white dude than shoot the breeze with your neighbors.

I hated those cashiers, and I hated them seeing me with food stamps, so I took 120 the bus and shopped elsewhere. That day, I got off the bus at Govans, and though the neighborhood was black like my own — hair salon after hair salon of airbrushed signs promising arabesque hair styles and inch-long fingernails — the houses were neat and orderly, nothing at all like Greenmount, where every other house had at least one shattered window. The store was well swept, and people quietly checked long grocery lists — no screaming kids, no loud cashier-customer altercations. I got the groceries and left the store.

I decided to walk back. It was a fall day, and I walked for blocks. Then I sensed someone following me. I walked more quickly, my arms around the sack, the leafy lettuce tickling my nose. I didn't want to hold the sack so close that it would break the eggs or squash the hamburger buns, but it was slipping, and as I looked behind me a boy my age, maybe older, rushed toward me.

"Let me help you," he said.

"That's all right." I set the bag on the sidewalk. Maybe I saw his face, maybe it was handsome enough, but what I noticed first, splayed on either side of the bag, were his shoes. They were nice shoes, real leather, a stitched design like a widow's peak on each one, or like birds' wings, and for the first time in my life I understood what people meant when they said "wing-tip shoes."

"I watched you carry them groceries out that store, then you look around, like you're lost, but like you liked being lost, then you walk down the sidewalk for blocks and blocks. Rearranging that bag, it almost gone to slip, then hefting it back up again."

"Uh-huh," I said.                                                                                    125

"And then I passed my own house and was still following you. And then your bag really look like it was gone crash and everything. So I just thought I'd help." He sucked in his bottom lip, as if to keep it from making a smile. "What's your name?" When I told him, he said, "Dina, my name is Cecil." Then he said, "D comes right after C."

"Yes," I said, "it does, doesn't it."

Then, half question, half statement, he said, "I could carry your groceries for you? And walk you home?"

I stopped the story there. Dr. Raeburn kept looking at me. "Then what happened?"

I couldn't tell him the rest: that I had not wanted the boy to walk me home,   130 that I didn't want someone with such nice shoes to see where I lived.

Dr. Raeburn would only have pitied me if I'd told him that I ran down the sidewalk after I told the boy no, that I fell, the bag slipped, and the eggs cracked, their yolks running all over the lettuce. Clear amniotic fluid coated the can of cinnamon rolls. I left the bag there on the sidewalk, the groceries spilled out randomly like cards loosed from a deck. When I returned home, I told my mother that I'd lost the food stamps.

"Lost?" she said. I'd expected her to get angry, I'd wanted her to get angry, but she hadn't. "Lost?" she repeated. Why had I been so clumsy and nervous around a harmless boy? I could have brought the groceries home and washed off the egg yolk, but instead I'd just left them there. "Come on," Mama said, snuffing her tears, pulling my arm, trying to get me to join her and start yanking cushions off the couch. "We'll find enough change here. We got to get something for dinner before your father gets back."

We'd already searched the couch for money the previous week, and I knew there'd be nothing now, but I began to push my fingers into the couch's boniest corners, pretending that it was only a matter of time before I'd find some change or a lost watch or an earring. Something pawnable, perhaps.

"What happened next?" Dr. Raeburn asked again. "Did you let the boy walk you home?"

"My house was far, so we went to his house instead." Though I was sure   135 Dr. Raeburn knew that I was making this part up, I continued. "We made out on his sofa. He kissed me."

Dr. Raeburn lit his next cigarette like a detective. Cool, suspicious. "How did it feel?"

"You know," I said. "Like a kiss feels. It felt nice. The kiss felt very, very nice."

Raeburn smiled gently, though he seemed unconvinced. When he called time on our session, his cigarette had become one long pole of ash. I left his office, walking quickly down the corridor, afraid to look back. It would be like him to trot after me, his navy blazer flapping, just to get the truth out of me. *You never kissed anyone.* The words slid from my brain, and knotted in my stomach.

When I reached my dorm, I found an old record player blocking my door and a Charles Mingus LP propped beside it. I carried them inside and then, lying on the floor, I played the Mingus over and over again until I fell asleep. I slept feeling as though Dr. Raeburn had attached electrodes to my head, willing into my mind a dream about my mother. I saw the lemon meringue of her skin, the long bone of her arm as she reached down to clip her toenails. I'd come home from a school trip to an aquarium, and I was explaining the differences between baleen and sperm whales according to the size of their heads, the range of their habitats, their feeding patterns.

I awoke remembering the expression on her face after I'd finished my dizzying 140 whale lecture. She looked like a tourist who'd asked for directions to a place she thought was simple enough to get to only to hear a series of hypothetical turns, alleys, one-way streets. Her response was to nod politely at the perilous elaborateness of it all; to nod and save herself from the knowledge that she would never be able to get where she wanted to go.

The dishwashers always closed down the dining hall. One night, after everyone else had punched out, Heidi and I took a break, and though I wasn't a smoker, we set two milk crates upside down on the floor and smoked cigarettes.

The dishwashing machines were off, but steam still rose from them like a jungle mist. Outside in the winter air, students were singing carols in their groomed and tailored singing-group voices. The Whiffenpoofs° were back in New Haven after a tour around the world, and I guess their return was a huge deal. Heidi and I craned our necks to watch the year's first snow through an open window.

"What are you going to do when you're finished?" Heidi asked. Sexy question marks of smoke drifted up to the windows before vanishing.

"Take a bath."

She swatted me with her free hand. "No, silly. Three years from now. When 145 you leave Yale."

"I don't know. Open up a library. Somewhere where no one comes in for books. A library in a desert."

She looked at me as though she'd expected this sort of answer and didn't know why she'd asked in the first place.

"What are you going to do?" I asked her.

"Open up a psych clinic. In a desert. And my only patient will be some wacko who runs a library."

"Ha," I said. "Whatever you do, don't work in a dish room ever again. You're 150 no good." I got up from the crate. "C'mon. Let's hose the place down."

We put out our cigarettes on the floor, since it was our job to clean it anyway. We held squirt guns in one hand and used the other to douse the floors with the standard-issue, eye-burning cleaning solution. We hosed the dish room, the kitchen, the serving line, sending the water and crud and suds into the drains. Then we hosed them again so the solution wouldn't eat holes in our shoes as we left. Then I had an idea. I unbuckled my belt.

"What the hell are you doing?" Heidi said.

---

*Whiffenpoofs:* Yale's a capella group.

"Listen, it's too cold to go outside with our uniforms all wet. We could just take a shower right here. There's nobody but us."

"What the fuck, eh?"

I let my pants drop, then took off my shirt and panties. I didn't wear a bra, since I didn't have much to fill one. I took off my shoes and hung my clothes on the stepladder.                                                                                     155

"You've flipped," Heidi said. "I mean, really, psych-ward flipped."

I soaped up with the liquid hand soap until I felt as glazed as a ham. "Stand back and spray me."

"Oh, my God," she said. I didn't know whether she was confused or delighted, but she picked up the squirt gun and sprayed me. She was laughing. Then she got too close and the water started to sting.

"God damn it!" I said. "That hurt!"

"I was wondering what it would take to make you say that."                           160

When all the soap had been rinsed off, I put on my regular clothes and said, "O.K. You're up next."

"No way," she said.

"Yes way."

She started to take off her uniform shirt, then stopped.

"What?"                                                                               165

"I'm too fat."

"You goddam right." She always said she was fat. One time I'd told her that she should shut up about it, that large black women wore their fat like mink coats. "You're big as a house," I said now. "Frozen yogurt may be low in calories, but not if you eat five tubs of it. Take your clothes off. I want to get out of here."

She began taking off her uniform, then stood there, hands cupped over her breasts, crouching at the pubic bone.

"Open up," I said, "or we'll never get done."

Her hands remained where they were. I threw the bottle of liquid soap at her, and she had to catch it, revealing herself as she did.                                     170

I turned on the squirt gun, and she stood there, stiff, arms at her side, eyes closed, as though awaiting mummification. I began with the water on low, and she turned around in a full circle, hesitantly, letting the droplets from the spray fall on her as if she were submitting to a death by stoning.

When I increased the water pressure, she slipped and fell on the sudsy floor. She stood up and then slipped again. This time she laughed and remained on the floor, rolling around on it as I sprayed.

I think I began to love Heidi that night in the dish room, but who is to say that I hadn't begun to love her the first time I met her? I sprayed her and sprayed her, and she turned over and over like a large beautiful dolphin, lolling about in the sun.

Heidi started sleeping at my place. Sometimes she slept on the floor; sometimes we slept sardinelike, my feet at her head, until she complained that my feet were "taunting" her. When we finally slept head to head, she said, "Much better." She was so close I could smell her toothpaste. "I like your hair," she told me, touching it through the darkness. "You should wear it out more often."

"White people always say that about black people's hair. The worse it looks, the     175
more they say they like it."

I'd expected her to disagree, but she kept touching my hair, her hands passing through it till my scalp tingled. When she began to touch the hair around the edge of my face, I felt myself quake. Her fingertips stopped for a moment, as if checking my pulse, then resumed.

"I like how it feels right here. See, mine just starts with the same old texture as the rest of my hair." She found my hand under the blanket and brought it to her hairline. "See," she said.

It was dark. As I touched her hair, it seemed as though I could smell it, too. Not a shampoo smell. Something richer, murkier. A bit dead, but sweet, like the decaying wood of a ship. She guided my hand.

"I see," I said. The record she'd given me was playing in my mind, and I kept trying to shut it off. I could also hear my mother saying that this is what happens when you've been around white people: things get weird. So weird I could hear the stylus etching its way into the flat vinyl of the record. "Listen," I said finally, when the bass and saxes started up. I heard Heidi breathe deeply, but she said nothing.

We spent the winter and some of the spring in my room — never hers — missing 180 tests, listening to music, looking out my window to comment on people who wouldn't have given us a second thought. We read books related to none of our classes. I got riled up by *The Autobiography of Malcolm X* and *The Chomsky Reader*; Heidi read aloud passages from *The Anxiety of Influence*. We guiltily read mysteries and *Clan of the Cave Bear*, then immediately threw them away. Once we looked up from our books at exactly the same moment, as though trapped at a dinner table with nothing to say. A pleasant trap of silence.

Then one weekend I went back to Baltimore and stayed with my father. He asked me how school was going, but besides that, we didn't talk much. He knew what I thought of him. I stopped by the Enoch Pratt Library, where my favorite librarian, Mrs. Ardelia, cornered me into giving a little talk to the after-school kids, telling them to stay in school. They just looked at me like I was crazy; they were only nine or ten, and it hadn't even occurred to them to bail.

When I returned to Yale — to a sleepy, tree-scented spring — a group of students were holding what was called "Coming Out Day." I watched it from my room.

The emcee was the sepia boy who'd given us the invitation months back. His speech was strident but still smooth and peppered with jokes. There was a speech about AIDS, with lots of statistics: nothing that seemed to make "coming out" worth it. Then the women spoke. One girl pronounced herself "out" as casually as if she'd announced the time. Another said nothing at all: she came to the microphone with a woman who began cutting off her waist-length, bleached-blond hair. The woman doing the cutting tossed the shorn hair in every direction as she cut. People were clapping and cheering and catching the locks of hair.

And then there was Heidi. She was proud that she liked girls, she said when she reached the microphone. She loved them, wanted to sleep with them. She was a dyke, she said repeatedly, stabbing her finger to her chest in case anyone was unsure to whom she was referring. She could not have seen me. I was across the street, three stories up. And yet, when everyone clapped for her, she seemed to be looking straight at me.

Heidi knocked. "Let me in."    185

It was like the first time I met her. The tears, the raw pink of her face.

We hadn't spoken in weeks. Outside, pink-and-white blossoms hung from the Old Campus trees. Students played Hacky Sack in T-shirts and shorts. Though I was the one who'd broken away after she went up to that podium, I still half expected her to poke her head out a window in Linsly-Chit, or tap on my back in Harkness, or even join me in the Commons dining hall, where I'd asked for my dish-room shift to be transferred. She did none of these.

"Well," I said, "what is it?"

She looked at me. "My mother," she said.

She continued to cry, but seemed to have grown so silent in my room I won- 190
dered if I could hear the numbers change on my digital clock.

"When my parents were getting divorced," she said, "my mother bought a car. A used one. An El Dorado. It was filthy. It looked like a huge crushed can coming up the street. She kept trying to clean it out. I mean — "

I nodded and tried to think what to say in the pause she left behind. Finally I said, "We had one of those," though I was sure ours was an Impala.

She looked at me, eyes steely from trying not to cry. "Anyway, she'd drive me around in it and although she didn't like me to eat in it, I always did. One day I was eating cantaloupe slices, spitting the seeds on the floor. Maybe a month later, I saw this little sprout, growing right up from the car floor. I just started laughing and she kept saying what, what? I was laughing and then I saw she was so — "

She didn't finish. So what? So sad? So awful? Heidi looked at me with what seemed to be a renewed vigor. "We could have gotten a better car, eh?"

"It's all right. It's not a big deal," I said.                                                    195

Of course, that was the wrong thing to say. And I really didn't mean it to sound the way it had come out.

I told Dr. Raeburn about Heidi's mother having cancer and how I'd said it wasn't a big deal, though I'd wanted to say the opposite. I told Dr. Raeburn how I meant to tell Heidi that my mother had died, that I knew how one eventually accustoms oneself to the physical world's lack of sympathy: the buses that are still running late, the kids who still play in the street, the clocks that won't stop ticking for the person who's gone.

"You're pretending," Dr. Raeburn said, not sage or professional, but a little shocked by the discovery, as if I'd been trying to hide a pack of his cigarettes behind my back.

"I'm pretending?" I shook my head. "All those years of psych grad," I said. "And to tell me *that*?"

"What I mean is that you construct stories about yourself and dish them 200
out — one for you, one for you — " Here he reenacted this process, showing me handing out lies as if they were apples.

"Pretending. I believe the professional name for it might be denial," I said. "Are you calling me gay?"

He pursed his lips noncommittally, then finally said, "No, Dina. I don't think you're gay."

I checked his eyes. I couldn't read them.

"No. Not at all," he said, sounding as if he were telling a subtle joke. "But maybe you'll finally understand."

"Understand what?"                                                                              205

"Oh, just that constantly saying what one doesn't mean accustoms the mouth to meaningless phrases." His eyes narrowed. "Maybe you'll understand that when you finally need to express something truly significant your mouth will revert to the insignificant nonsense it knows so well." He looked at me, his hands sputtering in the air in a gesture of defeat. "Who knows?" he asked with a glib, psychiatric smile I'd never seen before. "Maybe it's your survival mechanism. Black living in a white world."

I heard him, but only vaguely. I'd hooked on to that one word, pretending. Dr. Raeburn would never realize that "pretending" was what had got me this far. I remembered the morning of my mother's funeral. I'd been given milk to settle my stomach; I'd pretended it was coffee. I imagined I was drinking coffee elsewhere. Some Arabic-speaking country where the thick coffee served in little cups was so strong it could keep you awake for days.

Heidi wanted me to go with her to the funeral. She'd sent this message through the dean. "We'll pay for your ticket to Vancouver," the dean said.

These people wanted you to owe them for everything. "What about my return ticket?" I asked the dean. "Maybe the shrink will chip in for that."

The dean looked at me as though I were an insect she'd like to squash. "We'll pay for the whole thing. We might even pay for some lessons in manners." <sub>210</sub>

So I packed my suitcase and walked from my suicide single dorm to Heidi's room. A thin wispy girl in ragged cutoffs and a shirt that read "LSBN!" answered the door. A group of short-haired girls in thick black leather jackets, bundled up despite the summer heat, encircled Heidi in a protective fairy ring. They looked at me critically, clearly wondering if Heidi was too fragile for my company.

"You've got our numbers," one said, holding on to Heidi's shoulder. "And Vancouver's got a great gay community."

"Oh, God," I said. "She's going to a funeral, not a Save the Dykes rally."

One of the girls stepped in front of me.

"It's O.K., Cynthia," Heidi said. Then she ushered me into her bedroom and closed the door. A suitcase was on her bed, half packed. <sub>215</sub>

"I could just uninvite you," Heidi said. "How about that? You want that?" She folded a polka-dotted T-shirt that was wrong for any occasion and put it in her suitcase. "Why haven't you talked to me?" she said, looking at the shirt instead of me. "Why haven't you talked to me in two months?"

"I don't know," I said.

"*You don't know*," she said, each syllable steeped in sarcasm. "You don't know. Well, I know. You thought I was going to try to sleep with you."

"Try to? We slept together all winter!"

"If you call smelling your feet sleeping together, you've got a lot to learn." She <sub>220</sub> seemed thinner and meaner; every line of her body held me at bay.

"So tell me," I said. "What can you show me that I need to learn?" But as soon as I said it I somehow knew she still hadn't slept with anyone. "Am I supposed to come over there and sweep your enraged self into my arms?" I said. "Like in the movies? Is this the part where we're both so mad we kiss each other?"

She shook her head and smiled weakly. "You don't get it," she said. "My mother is dead." She closed her suitcase, clicking shut the old-fashioned locks. "My mother is dead," she said again, this time reminding herself. She set her suitcase upright on the floor and sat on it. She looked like someone waiting for a train.

"Fine," I said. "And she's going to be dead for a long time." Though it sounded stupid, I felt good saying it. As though I had my own locks to click shut.

Heidi went to Vancouver for her mother's funeral. I didn't go with her. Instead, I went back to Baltimore and moved in with an aunt I barely knew. Every day was the same: I read and smoked outside my aunt's apartment, studying the row of hair salons across the street, where girls in denim cutoffs and tank tops would troop in and come out hours later, a flash of neon nails, coifs the color and sheen of patent leather. And every day I imagined Heidi's house in Vancouver. Her place would not be large, but it would be clean. Flowery shrubs would line the walks. The Canadian wind would whip us about like pennants. I'd be visiting her in some vague time in the future, deliberately vague, for people like me, who realign past events to suit themselves. In that future time, you always have a chance to catch the groceries before they fall; your words can always be rewound and erased, rewritten and revised.

Then I'd imagine Heidi visiting me. There are no psychiatrists or deans, no  225
boys with nice shoes or flip cashiers. Just me in my single room. She knocks on the door and says, "Open up."

### CONSIDERATIONS FOR CRITICAL THINKING AND WRITING

1. FIRST RESPONSE. Dina is obviously plagued by a lack of trust. Does she trust us, her readers? Why or why not?

2. How does Dina's response to the initial orientation exercises at Yale set up key aspects of her character that develop throughout the story?

3. Dina is in the minority at Yale for multiple reasons: she is Black, she comes from a poor background, and she has same-sex yearnings. Do any of these factors seem to explain her feelings of alienation more than the others or do they all operate equally together? Are there other factors as well?

4. Dina is often the smartest person in the room. Does her intelligence contribute to her difficult relationships or is it the one attribute that connects her to other people who are like her?

5. What is the narrative function of Dina's school-assigned therapist, Dr. Raeburn? Does he help her in any way?

6. When Dina encourages Heidi to crush a mouse, Heidi calls her "heartless," but Dina claims she is being "humane." Who is right?

7. Why is the anecdote about "the boy with the nice shoes" crucial to understanding Dina's mind-set?

8. Find examples of Dina rejecting identity labels. Can you speculate about why she rejects them?

9. How does Dina's room function as a symbol within the story?

10. Explain the title, at first only using Dina's association and then building on that to offer your own assessment of her character.

11. Analyze the final line of the story. Where else is that line repeated?

### CONNECTIONS TO OTHER SELECTIONS

1. Compare this story to John Updike's "A & P" (p. 145) in terms of maturity. Who makes more progress toward growing up: Sammy or Dina?

2. Contrast attitudes toward same-sex desire in this story and in Manuel Muñoz's "Zigzagger" (p. 152).

## JOHN CHEEVER (1912–1982)

Though John Cheever was a native of Quincy, Massachusetts, his work is mostly associated with New York City and its suburbs, where he lived after a stint in the army during World War II. During the 1940s and 1950s his short stories were frequently published in the *New Yorker*. Dissatisfied with being too closely associated with that magazine, Cheever began to publish novels in the late 1950s and continued to write short fiction, which began to take some experimental risks. His novel, *Falconer* (1977), which takes place mostly in prison, was a noted departure and enjoyed both critical and popular acclaim, yet Cheever is remembered more as a master of the short story form than as a novelist. His collection *The Stories of John Cheever*, published in 1979, won the Pulitzer Prize that year. The following is the title story from his first collection.

## *The Enormous Radio*    1947

Jim and Irene Westcott were the kind of people who seem to strike that satisfactory average of income, endeavor, and respectability that is reached by the statistical reports in college alumni bulletins. They were the parents of two young children, they had been married nine years, they lived on the twelfth floor of an apartment house near Sutton Place, they went to the theatre on an average of 10.3 times a year, and they hoped someday to live in Westchester. Irene Westcott was a pleasant, rather plain girl with soft brown hair and a wide, fine forehead upon which nothing at all had been written, and in the cold weather she wore a coat of fitch skins dyed to resemble mink. You could not say that Jim Westcott looked younger than he was, but you could at least say of him that he seemed to feel younger. He wore his graying hair cut very short, he dressed in the kind of clothes his class had worn at Andover, and his manner was earnest, vehement, and intentionally naïve. The Westcotts differed from their friends, their classmates, and their neighbors only in an interest they shared in serious music. They went to a great many concerts — although they seldom mentioned this to anyone — and they spent a good deal of time listening to music on the radio.

Their radio was an old instrument, sensitive, unpredictable, and beyond repair. Neither of them understood the mechanics of radio — or of any of the other appliances that surrounded them — and when the instrument faltered, Jim would strike the side of the cabinet with his hand. This sometimes helped. One Sunday afternoon, in the middle of a Schubert quartet, the music faded away altogether. Jim struck the cabinet repeatedly, but there was no response; the Schubert was lost to them forever. He promised to buy Irene a new radio, and on Monday when he came home from work he told her that he had got one. He refused to describe it, and said it would be a surprise for her when it came.

The radio was delivered at the kitchen door the following afternoon, and with the assistance of her maid and the handyman Irene uncrated it and brought it into the living room. She was struck at once with the physical ugliness of the large gum-wood cabinet. Irene was proud of her living room, she had chosen its furnishings and colors as carefully as she chose her clothes, and now it seemed to her that the new radio stood among her intimate possessions like an aggressive intruder.

She was confounded by the number of dials and switches on the instrument panel, and she studied them thoroughly before she put the plug into a wall socket and turned the radio on. The dials flooded with a malevolent green light, and in the distance she heard the music of a piano quintet. The quintet was in the distance for only an instant; it bore down upon her with a speed greater than light and filled the apartment with the noise of music amplified so mightily that it knocked a china ornament from a table to the floor. She rushed to the instrument and reduced the volume. The violent forces that were snared in the ugly gumwood cabinet made her uneasy. Her children came home from school then, and she took them to the park. It was not until later in the afternoon that she was able to return to the radio.

The maid had given the children their suppers and was supervising their baths when Irene turned on the radio, reduced the volume, and sat down to listen to a Mozart quintet that she knew and enjoyed. The music came through clearly. The new instrument had a much purer tone, she thought, than the old one. She decided that tone was most important and that she could conceal the cabinet behind a sofa. But as soon as she had made her peace with the radio, the interference began. A crackling sound like the noise of a burning powder fuse began to accompany the singing of the strings. Beyond the music, there was a rustling that reminded Irene unpleasantly of the sea, and as the quintet progressed, these noises were joined by many others. She tried all the dials and switches but nothing dimmed the interference, and she sat down, disappointed and bewildered, and tried to trace the flight of the melody. The elevator shaft in her building ran beside the living-room wall, and it was the noise of the elevator that gave her a clue to the character of the static. The rattling of the elevator cables and the opening and closing of the elevator doors were reproduced in her loudspeaker, and, realizing that the radio was sensitive to electrical currents of all sorts, she began to discern through the Mozart the ringing of telephone bells, the dialing of phones, and the lamentation of a vacuum cleaner. By listening more carefully, she was able to distinguish doorbells, elevator bells, electric razors, and Waring mixers, whose sounds had been picked up from the apartments that surrounded hers and transmitted through her loudspeaker. The powerful and ugly instrument, with its mistaken sensitivity to discord, was more than she could hope to master, so she turned the thing off and went into the nursery to see her children.

When Jim Westcott came home that night, he went to the radio confidently 5 and worked the controls. He had the same sort of experience Irene had had. A man was speaking on the station Jim had chosen, and his voice swung instantly from the distance into a force so powerful that it shook the apartment. Jim turned the volume control and reduced the voice. Then, a minute or two later, the interference began. The ringing of telephones and doorbells set in, joined by the rasp of the elevator doors and the whir of cooking appliances. The character of the noise had changed since Irene had tried the radio earlier; the last of the electric razors was being unplugged, the vacuum cleaners had all been returned to their closets, and the static reflected that change in pace that overtakes the city after the sun goes down. He fiddled with the knobs but couldn't get rid of the noises, so he turned the radio off and told Irene that in the morning he'd call the people who had sold it to him and give them hell.

The following afternoon, when Irene returned to the apartment from a luncheon date, the maid told her that a man had come and fixed the radio. Irene went into the living room before she took off her hat or her furs and tried the instrument. From the loudspeaker came a recording of the "Missouri Waltz." It reminded her of the thin, scratchy music from an old-fashioned phonograph that she some-times heard across the lake where she spent her summers. She waited until the waltz had finished, expecting an explanation of the recording, but there was none. The music was followed by silence, and then the plaintive and scratchy record was repeated. She turned the dial and got a satisfactory burst of Caucasian° music — the thump of bare feet in the dust and the rattle of coin jewelry — but in the background she could hear the ringing of bells and a confusion of voices. Her children came home from school then, and she turned off the radio and went to the nursery.

When Jim came home that night, he was tired, and he took a bath and changed his clothes. Then he joined Irene in the living room. He had just turned on the radio when the maid announced dinner, so he left it on, and he and Irene went to the table.

Jim was too tired to make even a pretense of sociability, and there was nothing about the dinner to hold Irene's interest, so her attention wandered from the food to the deposits of silver polish on the candlesticks and from there to the music in the other room. She listened for a few minutes to a Chopin prelude and then was surprised to hear a man's voice break in. "For Christ's sake, Kathy," he said, "do you always have to play the piano when I get home?" The music stopped abruptly. "It's the only chance I have," a woman said. "I'm at the office all day." "So am I," the man said. He added something obscene about an upright piano, and slammed a door. The passionate and melancholy music began again.

"Did you hear that?" Irene asked.

"What?" Jim was eating his dessert.                                                          10

"The radio. A man said something while the music was still going on — something dirty."

"It's probably a play."

"I don't think it *is* a play," Irene said.

They left the table and took their coffee into the living room. Irene asked Jim to try another station. He turned the knob. "Have you seen my garters?" a man asked. "Button me up," a woman said. "Have you seen my garters?" the man said again. "Just button me up and I'll find your garters," the woman said. Jim shifted to another station. "I wish you wouldn't leave apple cores in the ashtrays," a man said. "I hate the smell."

"This is strange," Jim said.                                                                 15

"Isn't it?" Irene said.

Jim turned the knob again. "'On the coast of Coromandel where the early pumpkins blow,'" a woman with a pronounced English accent said, "'in the middle of the woods lived the Yonghy-Bonghy-Bò. Two old chairs, and half a candle, one old jug without a handle. . .'"

"My God!" Irene cried. "That's the Sweeneys' nurse."

"'These were all his worldly goods,'" the British voice continued.

"Turn that thing off," Irene said. "Maybe they can hear *us*." Jim switched the   20
radio off. "That was Miss Armstrong, the Sweeneys' nurse," Irene said. "She must be reading to the little girl. They live in 17-B. I've talked with Miss Armstrong in the Park. I know her voice very well. We must be getting other people's apartments."

"That's impossible," Jim said.

*Caucasian:* Refers to the Caucasus region, the border of Europe and Asia between the Caspian and Black Seas.

"Well, that was the Sweeneys' nurse," Irene said hotly. "I know her voice. I know it very well. I'm wondering if they can hear us."

Jim turned the switch. First from a distance and then nearer, nearer, as if borne on the wind, came the pure accents of the Sweeneys' nurse again: "'*Lady Jingly! Lady Jingly!*'" she said, "'*sitting where the pumpkins blow, will you come and be my wife? said the Yonghy-Bonghy-Bò. . .'*"

Jim went over to the radio and said "Hello" loudly into the speaker.

"'*I am tired of living singly,*'" the nurse went on, "'*on this coast so wild and shingly,* 25 *I'm a-weary of my life; if you'll come and be my wife, quite serene would be my life. . .'*"

"I guess she can't hear us," Irene said. "Try something else."

Jim turned to another station, and the living room was filled with the uproar of a cocktail party that had overshot its mark. Someone was playing the piano and singing the "Whiffenpoof Song," and the voices that surrounded the piano were vehement and happy. "Eat some more sandwiches," a woman shrieked. There were screams of laughter and a dish of some sort crashed to the floor.

"Those must be the Fullers, in 11-E," Irene said. "I knew they were giving a party this afternoon. I saw her in the liquor store. Isn't this too divine? Try something else. See if you can get those people in 18-C."

The Westcotts overheard that evening a monologue on salmon fishing in Canada, a bridge game, running comments on home movies of what had apparently been a fortnight at Sea Island, and a bitter family quarrel about an overdraft at the bank. They turned off their radio at midnight and went to bed, weak with laughter. Sometime in the night, their son began to call for a glass of water and Irene got one and took it to his room. It was very early. All the lights in the neighborhood were extinguished, and from the boy's window she could see the empty street. She went into the living room and tried the radio. There was some faint coughing, a moan, and then a man spoke. "Are you all right, darling?" he asked. "Yes," a woman said wearily. "Yes, I'm all right, I guess," and then she added with great feeling, "But, you know, Charlie, I don't feel like myself any more. Sometimes there are about fifteen or twenty minutes in the week when I feel like myself. I don't like to go to another doctor, because the doctor's bills are so awful already, but I just don't feel like myself, Charlie. I just never feel like myself." They were not young, Irene thought. She guessed from the timbre of their voices that they were middle-aged. The restrained melancholy of the dialogue and the draft from the bedroom window made her shiver, and she went back to bed.

The following morning, Irene cooked breakfast for the family — the maid didn't 30 come up from her room in the basement until ten — braided her daughter's hair, and waited at the door until her children and her husband had been carried away in the elevator. Then she went into the living room and tried the radio. "I don't want to go to school," a child screamed. "I hate school. I won't go to school. I hate school." "You will go to school," an enraged woman said. "We paid eight hundred dollars to get you into that school and you'll go if it kills you." The next number on the dial produced the worn record of the "Missouri Waltz." Irene shifted the control and invaded the privacy of several breakfast tables. She overheard demonstrations of indigestion, carnal love, abysmal vanity, faith, and despair. Irene's life was nearly as simple and sheltered as it appeared to be, and the forthright and sometimes brutal language that came from the loudspeaker that morning astonished and troubled her. She continued to listen until her maid came in. Then she turned off the radio quickly, since this insight, she realized, was a furtive one.

Irene had a luncheon date with a friend that day, and she left her apartment at a little after twelve. There were a number of women in the elevator when it stopped at her floor. She stared at their handsome and impassive faces, their furs, and the cloth flowers in their hats. Which one of them had been to Sea Island? she wondered. Which one had overdrawn her bank account? The elevator stopped at the tenth floor and a woman with a pair of Skye terriers joined them. Her hair was rigged high on her head and she wore a mink cape. She was humming the "Missouri Waltz."

Irene had two Martinis at lunch, and she looked searchingly at her friend and wondered what her secrets were. They had intended to go shopping after lunch, but Irene excused herself and went home. She told the maid that she was not to be disturbed; then she went into the living room, closed the doors, and switched on the radio. She heard, in the course of the afternoon, the halting conversation of a woman entertaining her aunt, the hysterical conclusion of a luncheon party, and a hostess briefing her maid about some cocktail guests. "Don't give the best Scotch to anyone who hasn't white hair," the hostess said. "See if you can get rid of that liver paste before you pass those hot things, and could you lend me five dollars? I want to tip the elevator man."

As the afternoon waned, the conversations increased in intensity. From where Irene sat, she could see the open sky above the East River. There were hundreds of clouds in the sky, as though the south wind had broken the winter into pieces and were blowing it north, and on her radio she could hear the arrival of cocktail guests and the return of children and businessmen from their schools and offices. "I found a good-sized diamond on the bathroom floor this morning," a woman said. "It must have fallen out of that bracelet Mrs. Dunston was wearing last night." "We'll sell it," a man said. "Take it down to the jeweler on Madison Avenue and sell it. Mrs. Dunston won't know the difference, and we could use a couple of hundred bucks. . ." "'Oranges and lemons, say the bells of St. Clement's,'" the Sweeneys' nurse sang. "'Halfpence and farthings, say the bells of St. Martin's. When will you pay me? say the bells at old Bailey. . .'" "It's not a hat," a woman cried, and at her back roared a cocktail party. "It's not a hat, it's a love affair. That's what Walter Florell said. He said it's not a hat, it's a love affair," and then, in a lower voice, the same woman added, "Talk to somebody, for Christ's sake, honey, talk to somebody. If she catches you standing here not talking to anybody, she'll take us off her invitation list, and I love these parties."

The Westcotts were going out for dinner that night, and when Jim came home, Irene was dressing. She seemed sad and vague, and he brought her a drink. They were dining with friends in the neighborhood, and they walked to where they were going. The sky was broad and filled with light. It was one of those splendid spring evenings that excite memory and desire, and the air that touched their hands and faces felt very soft. A Salvation Army band was on the corner playing "Jesus Is Sweeter." Irene drew on her husband's arm and held him there for a minute, to hear the music. "They're really such nice people, aren't they?" she said. "They have such nice faces. Actually, they're so much nicer than a lot of the people we know." She took a bill from her purse and walked over and dropped it into the tambourine. There was in her face, when she returned to her husband, a look of radiant melancholy that he was not familiar with. And her conduct at the dinner party that night seemed strange to him, too. She interrupted her hostess rudely and stared at the people across the table from her with an intensity for which she would have punished her children.

It was still mild when they walked home from the party, and Irene looked up  35
at the spring stars. " 'How far that little candle throws its beams,' " she exclaimed.
" 'So shines a good deed in a naughty world.' " She waited that night until Jim had
fallen asleep, and then went into the living room and turned on the radio.

Jim came home at about six the next night. Emma, the maid, let him in, and he
had taken off his hat and was taking off his coat when Irene ran into the hall. Her
face was shining with tears and her hair was disordered. "Go up to 16-C, Jim!" she
screamed. "Don't take off your coat. Go up to 16-C. Mr. Osborn's beating his wife.
They've been quarreling since four o'clock, and now he's hitting her. Go up there
and stop him."

From the radio in the living room, Jim heard screams, obscenities, and
thuds. "You know you don't have to listen to this sort of thing," he said. He strode
into the living room and turned the switch. "It's indecent," he said. "It's like looking in windows. You know you don't have to listen to this sort of thing. You can
turn it off."

"Oh, it's so horrible, it's so dreadful," Irene was sobbing. "I've been listening all
day, and it's so depressing."

"Well, if it's so depressing, why do you listen to it? I bought this damned radio
to give you some pleasure," he said. "I paid a great deal of money for it. I thought it
might make you happy. I wanted to make you happy."

"Don't, don't, don't, don't quarrel with me," she moaned, and laid her head on  40
his shoulder. "All the others have been quarreling all day. Everybody's been quarreling. They're all worried about money. Mrs. Hutchinson's mother is dying of cancer
in Florida and they don't have enough money to send her to the Mayo Clinic. At
least, Mr. Hutchinson says they don't have enough money. And some woman in
this building is having an affair with the handyman — with that hideous handyman. It's too disgusting. And Mrs. Melville has heart trouble and Mr. Hendricks is
going to lose his job in April and Mrs. Hendricks is horrid about the whole thing
and that girl who plays the 'Missouri Waltz' is a whore, a common whore, and the
elevator man has tuberculosis and Mr. Osborn has been beating Mrs. Osborn." She
wailed, she trembled with grief and checked the stream of tears down her face with
the heel of her palm.

"Well, why do you have to listen?" Jim asked again. "Why do you have to listen
to this stuff if it makes you so miserable?"

"Oh, don't, don't, don't," she cried. "Life is too terrible, too sordid and awful.
But we've never been like that, have we, darling? Have we? I mean, we've always
been good and decent and loving to one another, haven't we? And we have two
children, two beautiful children. Our lives aren't sordid, are they, darling? Are
they?" She flung her arms around his neck and drew his face down to hers. "We're
happy, aren't we, darling? We are happy, aren't we?"

"Of course we're happy," he said tiredly. He began to surrender his resentment.
"Of course we're happy. I'll have that damned radio fixed or taken away tomorrow."
He stroked her soft hair. "My poor girl," he said.

"You love me, don't you?" she asked. "And we're not hypercritical or worried
about money or dishonest, are we?"

"No, darling," he said.                                                          45

A man came in the morning and fixed the radio. Irene turned it on cautiously and
was happy to hear a California-wine commercial and a recording of Beethoven's

Ninth Symphony, including Schiller's "Ode to Joy." She kept the radio on all day and nothing untoward came from the speaker.

A Spanish suite was being played when Jim came home. "Is everything all right?" he asked. His face was pale, she thought. They had some cocktails and went in to dinner to the "Anvil Chorus" from *Il Trovatore*. This was followed by Debussy's "La Mer."

"I paid the bill for the radio today," Jim said. "It cost four hundred dollars. I hope you'll get some enjoyment out of it."

"Oh, I'm sure I will," Irene said.

"Four hundred dollars is a good deal more than I can afford," he went on.    50
"I wanted to get something that you'd enjoy. It's the last extravagance we'll be able to indulge in this year. I see that you haven't paid your clothing bills yet. I saw them on your dressing table." He looked directly at her. "Why did you tell me you'd paid them? Why did you lie to me?"

"I just didn't want you to worry, Jim," she said. She drank some water. "I'll be able to pay my bills out of this month's allowance. There were the slipcovers last month, and that party."

"You've got to learn to handle the money I give you a little more intelligently, Irene," he said. "You've got to understand that we won't have as much money this year as we had last. I had a very sobering talk with Mitchell today. No one is buying anything. We're spending all our time promoting new issues, and you know how long that takes. I'm not getting any younger, you know. I'm thirty-seven. My hair will be gray next year. I haven't done as well as I'd hoped to do. And I don't suppose things will get any better."

"Yes, dear," she said.

"We've got to start cutting down," Jim said. "We've got to think of the children. To be perfectly frank with you, I worry about money a great deal. I'm not at all sure of the future. No one is. If anything should happen to me, there's the insurance, but that wouldn't go very far today. I've worked awfully hard to give you and the children a comfortable life," he said bitterly. "I don't like to see all of my energies, all of my youth, wasted in fur coats and radios and slipcovers and — "

"Please, Jim," she said. "Please. They'll hear us."    55

"*Who'll hear us*? Emma can't hear us."

"The radio."

"Oh, I'm sick!" he shouted. "I'm sick to death of your apprehensiveness. The radio can't hear us. Nobody can hear us. And what if they can hear us? Who cares?"

Irene got up from the table and went into the living room. Jim went to the door and shouted at her from there. "Why are you so Christly all of a sudden? What's turned you overnight into a convent girl? You stole your mother's jewelry before they probated her will. You never gave your sister a cent of that money that was intended for her — not even when she needed it. You made Grace Howland's life miserable, and where was all your piety and your virtue when you went to that abortionist? I'll never forget how cool you were. You packed your bag and went off to have that child murdered as if you were going to Nassau. If you'd had any reasons, if you'd had any good reasons — "

Irene stood for a minute before the hideous cabinet, disgraced and sickened,    60
but she held her hand on the switch before she extinguished the music and the voices, hoping that the instrument might speak to her kindly, that she might hear the Sweeneys' nurse. Jim continued to shout at her from the door. The voice on the radio was suave and noncommittal. "An early-morning railroad disaster in Tokyo,"

the loudspeaker said, "killed twenty-nine people. A fire in a Catholic hospital near Buffalo for the care of blind children was extinguished early this morning by nuns. The temperature is forty-seven. The humidity is eighty-nine."

## Considerations for Critical Thinking and Writing

1. FIRST RESPONSE. The story was published in 1947, long before the Internet was invented. What parallels can you see between the enormous radio and contemporary technology (and average Americans' responses to it)?

2. The Westcotts are initially described in terms of their averageness. Why is that detail important to the story?

3. How is the radio described physically? What are the connotations of this description?

4. Examine the differences between the way Irene and Jim react to the radio as a way of scrutinizing 1940s gender roles and expectations.

5. When the Westcotts first figure out that they can hear the conversations of their neighbors through the radio, they are wary of it and Irene wants to turn it off. What causes them to change?

6. The maid (Emma) never speaks. Why is she integral to the story?

7. If the sordid stories of her neighbors' private lives depress Irene, why does she continue to listen to them?

8. What would you describe as the story's climax? Does it resolve the conflict? How?

## Connection to Another Selection

1. Compare the difference between the outward appearances of characters and their hidden lives in this story and in "The Man Who Loved His Kind" (p. 244) by Virginia Woolf. Do the stories have the same theme?

## Suggestion for Critical Analysis

1. Read the section on cultural criticism in Chapter 42, Critical Strategies for Reading. The immediate aftermath of World War II is often considered a time of tranquility and domestic harmony in the United States, the era when our understanding of the term "American Dream" was cemented. Research the cultural history of the decade following the end of the war. How might the story be read as a critique of that era?

# 11

## A GENRE CASE STUDY
# Speculative Fiction

Let's start with the end of the world, why don't we? Get it over with and move on to more interesting things.
— N. K. JEMISIN

Matt Winkelmeyer/ Getty Images.

As we discuss in the Introduction, Shakespeare's Hamlet famously told a group of actors "to hold as 'twere the mirror up to nature," and many readers have seen the aim of literature in these terms. Like other forms of imaginative literature, fiction reflects our world, in other words, but note that the word "imaginative" invites dimensions of our experience beyond those we see in reality. What if literature could do more than reflect the world we experience through our senses? Rather than a mirror capturing nature, what if we had a camera that could follow the mind wherever it ventures to travel, into nightmares, distant planets, or parallel universes?

Welcome to the world of speculative fiction, an expansive category that brings the reader outside of normal experience. Many subgenres make up this category, and you are no doubt familiar with some of them. From a young age you read tales about animals that can talk, or gods and goddesses who play with humans as though they were chess pieces, or men who can fly and leap tall buildings at a single bound. You have no doubt watched movies or TV shows that take place in the future (*Star Trek*) or that feature paranormal events that invade normal lives (*Stranger Things*). Stories get interesting when you add the capacity for magic (*Harry Potter*) or allow dragons, zombies, and other fanciful creatures to play a part (*Game of Thrones* or *The Walking Dead*). You've probably encountered fictional explorations about human obsession with science and technology getting out of control (*Jurassic Park* or *Westworld*). Even if they're not to your taste, you certainly know about horror films, and it's very likely that you've heard the name Stephen King, one of the most popular contemporary authors, who deals in horror and the paranormal. As the epigraph from N. K. Jemisin above indicates, writers are sometimes drawn not to our origins, but to our ends: apocalyptic fiction is not uncommon. A writer like Jemisin sees the end of the world not as an end, but as a beginning — that is, the beginning of fiction.

We call this fiction "speculative" because it invites author and reader alike to speculate about a world that has its roots in the familiar one we observe, but that is willing to explore a detour from it. Witches? Aliens? Malevolent or benevolent forces? Reincarnated dinosaurs? The annihilation of virtually everything we know? These and many more possibilities are all fair play in this category.

And yet, what's so interesting about speculative fiction within the context of literary inquiry is that it's still very much grounded in the elements explored in the first eight chapters of this book. Authors of speculative fiction let their minds wander past the boundaries of our world, but they're drawn to the questions and conflicts that have always provided the basis for fiction. Often, these stories are opportunities to examine the basic premises of human nature. Within the alternative worlds they create, speculative authors scrutinize concepts like good and evil, selfishness and caring, belonging and exclusion. More, they employ the same strategies as realistic fiction writers do. There's still a *plot* with a conflict that needs to be resolved. *Characters* are at the center of it all, even if they aren't always human. The principles of *point of view* still obtain.

One element that tends to take on more importance in speculative fiction is *setting*. Readers of speculative fiction often talk about *world building*, which is an especially conscious approach to setting with even greater demands than just the basic one of enabling the reader to experience with one's senses the world depicted in a story. Sometimes world building involves genealogy or geography: we might need to know that our main character was descended from kings and queens even if she doesn't know that at first. We might need to visualize where one planet is in relation to its rival planet. Many works in the genre known as high fantasy include a map at the beginning that readers can consult as they get to know the invented place names within the work. Others include family trees or timelines of the invented history that precedes the story. Basic information of that type can be a solid reference point, but much of this invented world prefers to be revealed within the context of narrative. If a character possesses some kind of magical power, or if we're in a world where new forms of technology frame a character's experience, authors work to find subtle ways to communicate those details. They don't often begin by simply telling you how this world is different from ours. If a novel began, "Ruth, who could shoot laser beams from her eyes to kill her enemies like everyone could on the planet Zong, was shopping for glurg, which is like yogurt, but made of feathers," a reader would likely feel more insulted than intrigued. Usually, world building must be patient to be effective, and readers must trust that they will eventually figure out what is special about the world they've entered, even if it isn't immediately clear.

There is nothing new about speculative fiction. As alluded to above, the mythologies of ancient civilizations were very much under this umbrella term. Medieval stories from England and other European countries were filled with fantastical elements: perhaps you've encountered "Sir Gawain and the Green Knight" from the late fourteenth century, a tale that features a knight who is not only green, but who is capable of picking up his own head and walking away after someone cuts it off. Some of Edgar Allan Poe's stories in the mid-nineteenth century could be considered horror tales shaded by the uncanny, the supernatural, or the inexplicable. Also in the nineteenth century, the French author Jules Verne was laying the groundwork for speculative science fiction about the future, a genre that became extremely popular in the mid-twentieth century. American writers in the late twentieth century became aware of a genre that had become well established in South and Central America known as magical realism that freely sprinkled supernatural events into realistic stories. The global reach of the speculative in fiction allows traditions to combine and reform. A mode known as Afrofuturism attempts to reimagine the trajectory of the African diaspora through combining the shameful history of Western oppression and exploitation of Africans with the possibilities afforded by fantasy and science fiction. The work of the American author Octavia Butler was pioneering in this field. Perhaps the most popular example of Afrofuturism is the 2018 Marvel movie *Black Panther*, based on the comic of the same name.

Movements such as Afrofuturism point to the possibility of replacing *what happened* with *what could have happened*. One branch of speculative fiction plays with history, creating what might be called a counterfactual account of the past. A recent example is Philip Roth's novel *The Plot Against America* (2004), which posits that the aviator Charles Lindbergh became president in 1940 and revealed that he was a Nazi sympathizer. The lives of the Jewish American characters in the book, including the narrator who has the same name as the author, are menaced by the rise of Nazism in America as opposed to the heroic narrative of America entering World War II to stop its spread.

Authors from minoritized groups have increasingly turned to the possibilities of speculative fiction to respond, critically and imaginatively, to a world that has historically oppressed them or considered them marginal. The speculative merges in interesting and expansive ways with authors who are from minoritized racial and ethnic groups, who are queer, or who hold radical political views. Although this is certainly not true of all authors who write under the broad umbrella of the term "speculative," the ability of speculative fiction to accommodate multiple viewpoints demonstrates how flexible and expansive it can be.

Even though we've included four works of speculative fiction from distinct traditions here, a chapter is inadequate to cover anything like the full range of speculative fiction. This mode is ubiquitous in our literary history and in our culture more generally. Even some stories in other chapters of this textbook such as Ursula K. Le Guin's "The Ones Who Walk Away from Omelas" (p. 121) and Carmen Maria Machado's "Eight Bites" (p. 218) could have been placed in this one.

The following four stories are thus not meant to be fully representative of this category, but rather to open your mind to some of the possibilities it presents. Peter Ho Davies's very short fiction "Minotaur" gives a creature from Greek mythology the opportunity to explain the world from his viewpoint. N. K. Jemisin's story "Sinners, Saints, Dragons and Haints, in the City Beneath the Still Waters" allows dragons to do battle with malevolent forces called "haints" in the aftermath of Hurricane Katrina, a natural disaster that devastated New Orleans in 2005. Mariana Enriquez's "Back When We Talked to the Dead" takes seriously the possibility of necromancy, or communication with the dead. Philip K. Dick, whose stories inspired blockbuster futuristic movies like *Bladerunner* and *Minority Report*, rounds out the collection with "To Serve the Master," a future fiction piece that plays on his favorite subject, a paranoid protagonist whose instincts about what to believe are challenged by a difficult-to-interpret world. Note how your reading muscles are strengthened and stretched by the experience of entering these unfamiliar spaces.

## PETER HO DAVIES (B. 1966)

Peter Ho Davies was born and raised in Coventry, a city in the west midlands of England, to parents from Wales and China. He studied at Manchester University and Cambridge University in the United Kingdom before moving to the United States in 1992 to pursue a graduate degree in creative writing from Boston University. He is the author of three novels and two short story collections as well as a volume of nonfiction about writing revision. In an interview Davies said of his novel *Equal Love*, "Like all my work, it's about identity, I suppose, and that comes a little bit out of my mixed race background." This perspective should help frame the following story.

## *Minotaur*   1998

Half man, half bull, that's me. Half myth; half monster. And you thought you had it bad. *My* mother fell for a white *bull*. Not that he ever loved her back. She had to have a false cow constructed, climb inside, and have it rolled into his field, before he'd give her a second look. Try explaining that next time someone asks, "And how did your parents meet?" Even the most liberal have difficulty understanding a woman degrading herself like that. Half-pathetic; half contemptible. I just tell them: "Don't have a cow!"

Not that I get out much, not since I entered my teens. My stepfather's ashamed of me, won't be seen dead with me. Oh, it was cute enough when I was a kid — people liked to pet my muzzle, watch me flare my silky nostrils — and I was always a hit at Halloween. But now I'm an adolescent — half-child, half adult — now it's clear I'm not growing out of it, that it isn't just 'a phase', he's lost patience.

"What?" he asks my mother. "I suppose you'd like to take him to a china shop?" It was his idea to confine me to this basement labyrinth. "Not confined," I can hear him telling her, overhead. "He can come out anytime he wants. I'm a man, not a beast. Maybe you've forgotten the difference?" Which always shuts her up. I feel sorry for her, in truth. Anyone can make a mistake. The heart is the heart. And now she's gone from bull to bully. She visits me every day — I'm home-schooled — and even slips down in the night sometimes to cradle my head in her lap, stroke my velvety head. I lie very still so as not to gore her. *Your father,* she whispers, *was a god; Zeus in disguise.* She means it as a consolation, but I fear I inherited only the disguise, none of the godliness.

*My demi-god,* she calls me. 'Demi' being the polite word for a half of something worth having, the cup half full, the *demi-tasse.*

Technically, of course, he's correct, my stepfather: I'm not confined. There are 5 no locks, no gates, no chains, no bars. I'm just here at the center of the labyrinth. The room's pretty comfortable — cable, microwave, internet, even a cramped little bathroom (it's hard to maneouver in a shower stall with horns). All the usual amenities you'd expect in a finished basement. Bow-flex°, knotty pine, futon. And I can call out, order in — half pepperoni, half field-greens (the pizza guy used to bring his own thread, but now he's got the route down). But it's *hard* to leave, you know. Agoraphobia, is what I tell people if they ask (they often do in chatrooms). Sometimes, I say, I don't have the use of my legs.

But really, it's this — at the door of my room, there are two choices: left or right. I stand there for hours at a time, looking down one passage, then the other, staring into the darkness. What would it be like to charge down there? Or there? But I can't choose. If I think of going right, start to imagine it, pretty soon I start to feel half-hearted, regret not turning left. Then again, if I'm of half-a-mind to go left, I soon feel the same thing about the right. And the worst of it is, as I understand from the pizza guy, these choices just keep recurring, every few steps — left or right? Right or left? Of course, even if they didn't, even if the labyrinth is a lie, an invention of my stepfather's — he pays for the pizza, after all, probably tips the guy well — it wouldn't matter. Why ten choices, or a hundred, when two are enough to stop me in my tracks, snorting and pawing a bald spot in the shag?

The horns of a dilemma? My horns *are* my dilemma.

Sometimes I hear my stepfather up there — he drinks, no surprise — when my mother is out. He likes to stamp around, sometimes it sounds like he's doing a jig, sometimes a rain dance. And when he has my attention, he calls down, in a mocking sing-song: *Pick me! No, pick me!*

---

*Bow-flex:* A brand of exercise machine.

I toss my head and snort hotly.

"Half-breed? Half-wit!" he taunts. "Half-man? Half bullshit!"  10

"Half-*father*?" I bellow back. "Half cuckold! These are *your* horns, old man! I got them from *you*!"

"Want to give them back? Come on then!" He pounds the floor. "What are you waiting for? A red rag?"

He wants to make me angry enough to choose, but I can't. *I can't!* For a long time, I thought it was fear, indecisiveness. Half-coward; half-Hamlet. But why does it have to be left or right? Why settle for half-measures? Given those choices, I refuse to choose. And why just those two? Why not up, or down, or straight ahead. Why not a third choice? So I've been trying to make a new way for myself, charging and running my head against the wall, ripping through the pine and particle board with my horns. Beyond them, as I guessed, are dirt walls, hard packed, but dry and crumbling. It's hard work — I have awful migraines that flash like sparks from horn tip to horn tip — but the sight of my own blood on the earth only urges me on. What's a bull's head good for, after all, if not butting and battering, gouging and goring.

And all the while, over the ringing in my ears, I tell myself, *This is my choice,* and lower my head once more.

## CONSIDERATIONS FOR CRITICAL THINKING AND WRITING

1. FIRST RESPONSE. What adjustments to your expectations, if any, did you have to make as a reader once you'd read the title and first line?

2. Look up the myth of the Minotaur: even if you were familiar with it before, did you learn anything new that helps to interpret or reinterpret the story?

3. How does the story use humor to achieve its effect? What kind of humor is it?

4. How does the story mix elements of contemporary culture with ancient stories? To what effect?

5. How do you interpret the line, "I fear I inherited only the disguise, none of the godliness" (par. 3)?

6. The word "half" (or its prefix "demi") dominate the story. What does this concept suggest about its theme?

7. The story indicates a familiar tension in fiction: fate vs. choice. How does it play out here?

8. When you read the story, how do you picture the narrator? Are you picturing an actual Minotaur — a creature who is half-man, half-bull — or do you "translate" the character in your mind so that he seems fully human? What effect does your mental image have on your interpretation of the story?

## CONNECTION TO ANOTHER SELECTION

1. Compare the confinement of this narrator to the narrator of Charlotte Perkins Gilman's "The Yellow Wallpaper" (p. 126). How do the identities of each narrator (their humanity — or lack thereof — their gender, etc.) affect your response to their confinement?

# N. K. JEMISIN (B. 1972)

N. K. Jemisin had a career as a counselor before turning to writing. She has published prolifically ever since, producing nearly a novel every year since 2010 (including the acclaimed *Broken Earth* trilogy) as well as dozens of short stories. She is the recipient of many awards in the field of speculative fiction including the prestigious Hugo and Nebula awards, and she was recently awarded the MacArthur Fellow grant (commonly known as the "Genius Grant.") The fact that she has lived in multiple locations — Iowa, New

Matt Winkelmeyer/Getty Images.

York, Massachusetts, Alabama, and Louisiana — perhaps accounts for her ability to create and inhabit new or newly imagined worlds in her fiction.

> **A Note on the Text:** Readers should note that this story contains a harmful racial slur. As discussed in "Approaching Sensitive Subjects" (p. 7), it is important to be aware of context when encountering difficult content. As you read, consider in- vs. out-group usage: Jemisin, the author of this story, is a Black American, as are both the protagonist and one of the speakers of the slur. Further, this story deals broadly and intentionally with racial inequity, reflecting the author's original intent in depicting a specific character, incident, time period, place, and culture. Be mindful of this context as you read this story.

## *Sinners, Saints, Dragons, and Haints, in the City Beneath the Still Waters*   2015

The days which bracketed hurricanes were painful in their clarity. Sharp-edged clouds, blue sky hard as a cop's eyes, air so clear that every sound ground at the ear. If a person held still enough, he would feel the slow, unreal descent as all the air for miles around scrape-slip-slid downhill into the whirlpool maw of the approaching storm. If the streets were silent enough, he would hear his own heartbeat, and the crunch of rocks beneath his feet, and the utter stillness of the earth as it held its breath for the dunking to come.

Tookie listened for a while longer, then hefted the plastic bag a little higher on his shoulder and resumed walking home. A ways behind him, a hulking shadow stayed put.

Tookie sat on the porch of his shotgun house, watching the rain fall sideways. A lizard strolled by on the worn dirt strip that passed for a sidewalk, easy as you please, as if there wasn't an inch of water already collected around its paws. It noticed him and stopped.

"Hey," it said, inclining its head to him in a neighborly fashion.

" 'Sup," Tookie replied, jerking his chin up in return.                                    5

"You gon' stay put?" it asked. "Storm comin'."

"Yeah," said Tookie. "I got food from the grocery."

"Ain gon' need no food if you drown, man."

Tookie shrugged.

The lizard sat down on the sidewalk, oblivious to the driving wind, and joined    10
Tookie in watching the rain fall. Tookie idly reflected that the lizard might be
an alligator, in which case he should maybe go get his gun. He decided against
it, though, because the creature had wide batlike wings and he was fairly certain
gators didn't have those. These wings were the color of rusty, jaundiced clouds, like
those he'd seen approaching from the southeast just before the rain began.

"Levee gon' break," said the lizard after a while. "You shoulda got out, man."

"No car, man." It occurred to Tookie only after this that "man" was
inappropriate.

The lizard snorted. "Big strong buck like you oughtta get off your ass, buy a
hooptie."

"The fuck I need a car for? The bus and streetcar go everywhere I want to go."

"Except out of the city, with a hurricane on your ass."                                    15

Tookie shrugged again. "My mama had a car. She and my sister and her kids
was all that could fit." He had sent them along with the last of his cash, though he
had not told them this. "We called the rental folks, too, but they was out of cars.
They want a credit card anyway. Don't nobody give you a card without a job, unless
you a college student, and I ain' even got a GED."

"Why not?" asked the lizard. "You don' look stupid."

"Teachers thought I did." Stupid and good for nothing, waste of time to educate, waste of space on this earth. Maybe, Tookie thought, the hurricane would
take care of that. "I got tired of hearin' that shit after a while."

The lizard considered this. Then it came over to the steps of Tookie's house
and climbed up on the first step, its tail — as long as its body — dangling into the
water.

"How you get a house, then, with no job?"                                                  20

Tookie couldn't help smiling. "You the nosiest damn lizard I ever saw."

The creature grinned at him, flashing tiny needlelike teeth. "Ain' I? They don'
let me out much."

"So I see." Perhaps Tookie was feeling lonely; he decided to answer. "I sell a
little weed," he said. "Get some Adam from over the bridge, sell it to the white kids
over by Tulane. Don't take much to make the rent."

"Adam?"

"Ex. MDMA°. Little pills, make you happy."                                                 25

"Oh." The lizard settled itself more comfortably on the doorstep, then abruptly
raised itself again. "Hey, you ain't got no pit bulls, do you? I been smellin' somethin'
big and mean now and again. I hate dogs."

Tookie chuckled. "Nah. I'm just a foot soldier, man."

The lizard relaxed. "Me, too."

"You ain't a foot soldier, you a fuckin' lizard."

"Shut the fuck up, man." The lizard followed this amused statement with a       30
yawn. "Mind if I crash here for a minute? I'm tired as hell."

---

*Ex. MDMA:* Refers to illegal drugs known as Ecstasy or Molly.

"Come up on the porch," Tookie said. The polite thing would've been to invite the creature inside, but he'd never been one for letting animals in the house. "I got some Vienna sausages."

"I ain' hungry, and the step is fine, thank you." The lizard rolled onto its side like a cat sunning itself, except it wasn't a cat and the pelting rain wasn't sun.

"Suit yourself." Tookie got to his feet, mopping warm rain from his own face; the porch overhang wasn't stopping it at all now. The wind had gotten bad enough that the stop sign on the corner was bent at a sharp angle, its four letters so blurred with driving water that they seemed ready to wash off. Across the street, three shingles blew off Miss Mary's roof in rapid succession, the sound of destruction muted by the rising freight train wind.

The lizard turned to follow Tookie's gaze. "She shoulda got out, too."

"Yeah," Tookie said. He sighed. "She should've."    35

He went inside, and the lizard went to sleep on his porch steps.

The next day, watching through the attic door as his secondhand furniture floated, Tookie wondered about the lizard. His food bags were secure between two half-rotted wooden slats — his gun was in one of them — and the water didn't look too bad, so carefully he lowered himself through the attic door into the drink.

On the porch, he paused for a moment to marvel at the sight of Dourgenois Street° transformed into a river. Driven by the still-powerful wind, the water was up to his waist; down on the street it would probably be chest-deep. Only the topmost edge of the bent-over stop sign was visible. All the houses had been strangely truncated, like mushrooms only half-emerged from rippling gray soil.

"Hey," said a voice, and Tookie looked up to see the lizard clinging to his porch ceiling, upside down. It yawned, blinking sleepily. "I tol' you the levee'd go."

"I guess you did," Tookie said, a note of grudging wonder entering his voice.    40 Most of the other denizens of his street had gone to the convention center if they couldn't get out of town. There was only him and Miss Mary —

And Miss Mary's door was stove in, a little rapids frothing on her porch as water flowed in.

"Damn shame," said the lizard.

Tookie stepped off the porch. For an instant his feet floated, and a fleeting panic set in. The voice of a long-dead uncle barked in his head: *Niggas don't float, fool, sank like stones inna water, waste of money teachin' you how to swim.* But then his feet touched solid ground and he found that when he stood, the current wasn't as swift or strong as it appeared. Simple enough to walk perpendicular to it. So he did, navigating around a neighbor's derelict car (now submerged) and pausing as a shapeless spiderwebbed lump (basketball net?) floated past.

The top of Miss Mary's hollow door had broken in, but the bottom was still in place and locked. Tookie pulled himself over it and looked around the old lady's living room. "Miss Mary?" he called. "It's Tookie from 'cross the street. Where you at?"

"In here 'bout to drown, goddamn, what you think?" returned the old woman's    45 voice, and he followed it into her kitchen, where she sat on a chair that was probably resting atop her dining table. He couldn't tell for sure because the table was under water. He pushed his way through floating jars of spices and wooden spoons.

*Dorgenois Street:* Dorgenois Street (no *u*) in New Orleans is the first indication of the story's real-world location; Hurricane Katrina devastated that city in 2005.

"Come on here, Miss Mary," he said. "Ain' no point in you stayin'."

"It's my house," she said. "It's all I got." She had said the same thing a few days before when he'd invited her to pass the storm with him, in his house, which was higher off the ground and newer, or at least not as old.

"I ain gon' let you stay up in here." In a flash of inspiration, he added, "Lord don't mean for nobody to just sit and wait to die."

Miss Mary, eighty-four years old and about as many pounds, threw him a glare from her waterlogged throne. "Lord don't like bullshit neither."

He grinned. "No, I guess He don't. So come on, then, 'fore I drown in your 50 kitchen and stank up the place."

So she gingerly eased herself off the chair and Tookie helped her into the water. He had her wrap her skinny arms around his neck. Then with her on his back, he waded out of her house and back across the street to his own personal bayou. There, with much huffing and cursing, he managed to hoist her up into the attic without breaking any of her old bones.

Once that was done, he headed out onto the porch again to see to the lizard. But it was gone.

After a sigh, Tookie went back inside and climbed to the attic himself.

Outside, unseen, something large and dark moved under the water. It did not surface — though for an instant it came near to doing so, and the water rose in a swell half-obscured by surging wavelets from the broken levee two blocks away. But then it moved away from Tookie's steps, and the water flowed free again.

The water kept rising even after the wind fell, all through the skin-stingingly beau- 55 tiful day that arrived in the storm's wake. Helicopters began thwapping past, lots of them, but none of them ever slowed over or landed in the Ninth Ward, so Tookie paid them no attention. He made sure Miss Mary ate some Vienna sausages and drank half a Sunny Delight, then he went out again in search of something that would float.

A few feet beyond his door he encountered a family of nutrias, the giant-rat denizens of the city's boggiest places. The first three nutrias, two dog-sized adults and a smaller one, dogpaddled past with a quick by-your-leave glance in Tookie's direction. The fourth came along some ways later, swimming slowly, its eyes dull, mouth open and panting. As its right foreleg came near the surface, Tookie saw that it had a bad break, white bone flashing under the brown water. Flies already crawled around its sleek wet back.

Tookie reached out and caught the creature, lifting it and giving its neck a quick wring. It went limp in his hands without a squeak. As Tookie tossed the small body up onto a nearby rooftop — the water was already foul, but he couldn't abide adding to the mess — he noticed that the two adult nutrias had stopped. They did not look angry, though they watched him for a long moment. Then they resumed their trek, and Tookie did, too.

Two streets over he ran into Dre Amistad, who was pushing an inflatable kiddie pool that contained a scrawny teenaged girl and a naked baby nearly as thin. The girl threw Tookie a hostile, defensive look as he approached, but Dre seemed relieved. "I'm so glad to see you, man. Can you push for a while?" He looked exhausted.

"I can't," Tookie said, nodding apologetically to the girl. "I got to find something to carry this old lady who's stayin' at my house. My neighbor."

Dre frowned. "Old lady?" He glanced up at the young girl and baby pointedly. 60 But the girl frowned at Tookie, some of her hostility fading.

Heartened by this, Tookie added, "She ain't got nobody, man. Her daughter over in Texas — " Tookie cut himself off then, annoyed at his urge to justify his actions. Above their heads, another helicopter flitted past, going to rescue someone else. "Look, where you headed?"

Dre shook his head. "We was gonna go to Chalmette, but we heard the cops was shootin' people there. They even shootin' white folks — anybody comin' out of New Orleans. Guess they think the flood's catchin', like the flu or somethin'.."

"*Gretna,* not Chalmette," said the girl, in a tone that suggested she had said it before. Dre shrugged. He looked too tired to care.

"Where you goin' now?" Tookie asked, trying to restrain his impatience.

"We heard people was goin' to the navy base," said the girl. "The government  65 was gon' close it 'cause all the soldiers is off in Iraq. Maybe they got beds and medicine." She looked down at her child, her small face tightening.

Tookie frowned but decided not to say anything. If they wanted to trust a bunch of soldiers, that was their business.

"See if you can get everybody up on a roof, rest for a bit," Tookie said to Dre, turning to splash away from them. "I got food and stuff. Let me fetch the old lady and then I can help you push."

"I ain' waitin, Tookie."

Tookie stopped and turned back to him, incredulous. Any fool could see they had a better chance together than alone.

"I just got to get somewhere dry," Dre said softly, a plea. "Tookie, man. I just . . ."  70 Dre faltered silent, then looked away. After a moment, during which Tookie just stared at him, Dre blinked quickly and then resumed his dogged pushing of the kiddie pool. The girl watched Tookie until they were out of sight.

Turning away, Tookie stopped as he saw the lizard, this time crouched atop a crazily leaning traffic light pole. It was looking in the direction Dre had gone.

"Them soldiers ain' gon' let nobody in," it said scornfully. "Buncha poor-ass folks like that? Soldiers gon' shoot 'em and get a medal for it. Mus' be out they damn minds."

"You ain't dead," Tookie said, surprised at how glad he felt.

"Nope. Hey. It's a little rowboat 'round back of that house." It nodded toward a house on the corner that had been washed off its foundations. It leaned at a drunken angle, surrounded by its own vomited debris. "And it's a barge a couple of streets over, all dry and high"

"A *barge?*"  75

The lizard shrugged. "I ain' lyin'. Big as three or four houses, sittin' in the middle of the street. Guess they didn't tie it up, put down anchor, whatever. You can hole up there for a little while. Safer than these houses." It tilted its head up to peer at another passing helicopter. "They gon' have to start actually helpin' people soon."

Tookie nodded slowly, too polite to say he'd believe it when he saw it. "It's a dead nutria over on Reynes," he said. "On a rooftop, maybe three houses from the neutral ground." Which was underwater. Tookie grimaced. "The corner, I mean. Its leg is broke, but the rest is all right. I just killed it."

The lizard grinned its needle grin again. "What, I look skinny?"

Tookie shrugged, smiling in spite of himself. "Yeah, you right, you the most fucked-up-lookin' lizard I ever saw. Skinny ain't half."

The lizard laughed. Its laugh was a strange, high-pitched trilling sound, and  80 with each exhalation, the water around Tookie reacted, tiny pointillations dancing on the murky surface. When it stopped laughing, the water became still once more.

"Nutria's good eating," it said thoughtfully, and bobbed its head at him in a gesture that might've been thanks. "Might call some folks to come share."

Tookie stepped quickly aside as a ball of fire ants floated past. "What, it's more of you?"

"Mmm-hmm. My whole family all over town right now."

"That right?"

"Yeah right." It drew itself up proudly. "My people been here generations. New  85 Orleans born an' bred."

Tookie nodded. His people were the same.

"Hey," said the lizard, its grin fading. "Listen. You be careful. It's some kind of big thing around here. A *mean* thing."

"Like what?"

The lizard shook its head. This movement was not remotely humanlike; its neck wove like a snake's. "I ain' seen it, but I *smelled* it. Saw a dead dog over by the playground, looked like somethin' had been at it."

"'Nother dog, maybe." Tookie had seen several in the past few hours, roaming  90 or swimming, looking lean and forlorn.

"Musta been hungry. Dog was bit in half." The lizard shuddered, wings making a papery rattle. It looked away down the long street of listing houses, car-roof islands, and still dark water.

"Might be anything," Tookie said, though he was aware that this was not reassuring. "That storm was bad. Worst I ever saw, even if the levees hadn't broke. Feel like it ain' done yet, somehow."

Another helicopter passed, this one low enough that Tookie could see a person inside with a big TV camera aimed at him. He put his hands on his hips and regarded the helicopter coldly. If it wasn't going to help, he wished it would just go away.

"It ain't," the lizard said softly, its eyes distant and burnished with worry. "Done, I mean. Somethin' ain' right. Somethin' keepin' this storm goin'."

They both watched as the helicopter circled once, filming the whole area,  95 and then flew on. Gradually the silence returned, peaceful and liquid, and Tookie relaxed, absorbing it.

"I got to go get that rowboat," he said at last. "Thanks."

The lizard made a dismissive sound. "I'm'a go eat my thanks right now." Turning, the lizard spread its rustcloud wings and flicked its tail at him. Tookie waved farewell as it took off and flew away.

Tookie fetched the rowboat, used it to collect the old lady and what remained of the food from his attic, then headed over to the big barge on Jourdan Avenue.

The barge was jammed on a schoolbus and a couple of houses, causing it to list at a nearly 45-degree angle. Because of this, most of the deck was dry, the rainwater having pooled on the downside. The pilot house or bridge or whatever it was called — where they drove the barge — was even better, dry and enclosed with only one broken glass window. Tookie used his T-shirt to stuff the hole so they could sleep the night without feeding a million mosquitoes.

Then, as dusk fell, they ate the last of Tookie's food. He hadn't gotten much  100 from the store to begin with, since he'd had to wait until it was closed; by the time he'd arrived with his crowbar, others had already pried the door open and gotten the best goods. He had collected enough to see himself through three or four days without electricity, since that was the worst any storm had done in his lifetime.

Standing at the pilot's window, gazing out at the ocean that had been his neighborhood, Tookie reflected that he had, perhaps, underplanned.

"We got to put somethin' on the roof," said Miss Mary. She was half asleep already, curled up with her head pillowed on an over-turned leatherbacked chair. "Tell the rescue people to come get us."

Tookie nodded, chewing absently on an oily sardine. "I'll go out tomorrow, find some paint."

"You be careful," the old woman said. Tookie turned to her, surprised to hear this echo of his lizard friend. Miss Mary yawned. "Haints° be out, after a storm like this."

At first Tookie heard *hates,* not haints. Then he realized what she was saying. "Ain' no haints, Miss Mary."

"How the hell you know? This the first *real* hurricane you been through." She 105 waved a hand contemptuously. "I was aroun' for Camille. Lived in Mississippi then. Me an' my man come here after, 'cause when that storm was through, we ain' had nothin' left. No house, no town, no people. All my family died." She lifted her head to glare at him. The fading light fell along the smooth planes of her face just so; he saw that she must have been beautiful in those days. "Even after that storm, the killin' kept on. It was somethin' else around, *keepin'* it goin'. Turnin' people ugly."

"My mama said haints was just ghosts," Tookie said. "Scare you, but can't kill nobody."

"Demons, then. Spirits, monsters, don't matter what you call 'em. They come with the storm, some bringin' it, some seein' it through, some sendin' it on. And some keepin' it on, so it can kill some more. So you watch yo' ass." She spoke the last three words leaning forward, precisely enunciating her vehemence.

"A'ight, a'ight, Miss Mary." Tookie came over and sat down beside her, making himself comfortable as best he could against the hard metal of a bulkhead. "You get some sleep now. I'll keep a eye out."

She sighed, weary, and lay down again. A long silence fell.

"I'm too old to start over again," she said softly. 110

He fanned himself with one hand; it was stuffy in the little chamber with the windows closed. "We gon' both do what we got to do, Miss Mary." She said nothing in reply, so he added, "Good night."

After a while, she slept. And despite his intention to keep watch, Tookie did, too.

Deep in the night, when the city was still but for frogs and drifting water, they were jolted awake by the low groan of metal crunching and grinding against itself. Something made the barge jump, rocking alarmingly toward wobbly straightness before it settled back into its leaning stability.

Years of nights spent crouched low in his house, wondering whether the people outside his window were assassins or just ordinary robbers, kept Tookie silent beyond an initial startled curse. Years of whatever life Miss Mary had lived kept her silent as well. She stayed put while he crept to the window and peered out.

With no streetlights, the dark was all-encompassing. A sliver of moon was up, 115 illuminating the water and fog curling off its surface, but everything else was just shapes.

The water was rippling, though, in the wake of some movement. Something *big,* to judge by the ripples.

---

*Haints:* Ghosts or related supernatural creatures, derived from the word "haunt." This usage is most common in the American South and in Appalachia.

Tookie waited. When the water was still again, he turned back to see that Miss Mary had pulled a crooked steak knife from one of her many pockets. His heart leapt in irrational alarm, though he should've laughed; the little knife would be no use against whatever had jolted the barge.

"What you see?" she stage-whispered.

"Nothin'," he replied. "Just water."

She scowled. "You lyin'."                                                                                                        120

Anger blazed away days of waterlogged weariness in Tookie. She sounded like those old teachers of his, years gone; and for a moment he hated her as he'd hated them. "How you gon' say I'm lyin'? You can't half see, crazy ol' biddy."

"I can see *you* just fine." There was no mistaking the menace in the old woman's tone. Belatedly two things occurred to Tookie: First, that her knife wasn't too small to hurt *him,* and second that his gun was tucked away safe and useless inside the bag that had held their food.

*Don' need no damn gun,* he thought, his hands clenching into fists — they both froze as, somewhere on the next street over a house collapsed. They had heard this happen several times over the past few days, cheap wood splintering and plaster crumbling like so much sand, but never had the sound been so violent or sudden. It was as if something had *knocked* the house down, or perhaps stomped on it. Either way, the demolition hadn't taken much effort.

Tookie met Miss Mary's eye, and she gave him an I-told-you-so nod. She had put the knife away, he saw, so he decided to say nothing more about it. His own anger was gone, shattered like a ruined house's walls, leaving him feeling foolish and ashamed. What the hell was he doing, getting so worked up over a little old lady anyhow? They had bigger problems.

In the morning they rose and went out on deck.                                                                              125

By the clear light of dawn, the city's devastation somehow seemed more stark: the reeking water, the melting houses, the silence. Tookie stood transfixed by it, for the first time realizing that the city would never be the same no matter how well they fixed it. Yet he could not bring himself to mourn, because despite the evidence of his eyes, he could feel that nothing was dead. The city had withstood storms before, been destroyed and rebuilt and destroyed again. Indeed, as he stood there, he could almost feel the land somewhere below, still holding its breath, waiting and untroubled. Calm, like the eye of a storm.

Miss Mary was the first to spot something odd: a long flap of something that looked like stiff cloth near the barge's prow. It had not been there the day before.

Tookie poked at the cloth with his toe, trying to figure out what it was and troubled by a nagging sense of familiarity, as Miss Mary muttered about haints and a plague of devilry. Finally Tookie picked up the thing to toss it overboard. As he did, he noticed blood on one corner of it. Only then did he realize that the stiff thing was not cloth. It felt of leather and thin bone under his fingers, and the underside was patterned with clouds, the deep gray color of when they were right overhead and about to drop a bucket.

He caught himself before he gasped, which would've gotten the sharp-eared Miss Mary's attention. Instead he simply went to the deck wall and peered overboard, dreading what he might see.

There was no lizard corpse, but he noticed something else: the schoolbus that     130
had been lodged under the barge's stern? keel? The front underside. The bus had been almost comically jammed in place the day before, its hood invisible beneath

the water and its rear end jutting undignified into the air. Now the bus's butt was crumpled as if something huge had stepped on it in an effort to climb aboard the barge. The weight of whatever it was had pushed the bus down, and levered the barge upright; that was what had caused the shift the night before.

"What you see?" Miss Mary asked, not as belligerently as the night before.

"Nothin' but water," Tookie said again, and he dropped the wing back onto the deck bloody-side down, so it looked like a rag again.

When the waters receded, he vowed privately, he would find a place to bury it proper.

The water seemed lower when Tookie dropped into it from the ladder. It had been up to his neck the day before; now it was only up to his chest. Progress. There was no current, so the rowboat hadn't drifted far. Tookie climbed into it and, using the nail-studded plank of wood that he'd appropriated for an oar, set off.

After an hour of fruitlessly searching the handful of corner stores dotting the    135
neighborhood, he began searching houses instead. This went better, though on several occasions there were unpleasant surprises. In one house he found a bloated old man still seated in an armchair, with the TV remote in his floating gray hand. The water hadn't risen *that* fast. Tookie figured the old fellow had just wanted to go his own way.

He was coming out of that house with his hands full of white paint cans, when movement in the rowboat made him start and drop the cans and grab for a gun he did not possess. He cursed himself for forgetting it again.

"Hey," said the lizard, lifting its head over the boat's rim. "Thought I smelled you 'roun' here."

Tookie stared at it. "You all right?"

The lizard looked puzzled. "Why wouldn' I be?"

"Somethin' came after the barge last night. I found — " He hesitated, suddenly    140
recalling what the lizard had said about its family. "A wing. Like yours, but gray."

The lizard stiffened, then closed its eyes. "My cousin," it said finally. "We was lookin' for him."

Tookie lowered his head respectfully. "I still got the wing, you want it."

"Yeah. Later."

"It's that thing, ain' it?" Tookie asked. "The ugly thing you been smellin'." Miss Mary's words came back to him. "The Hate."

The lizard nodded grimly. "I aksed my daddy about it. Come around some-    145
times, this thing, after a real big storm. Killin' is what draws it. Like *mean* got a shape and gone walkin' around, spreadin' more mean everywhere it go."

Tookie frowned, recalling their near-brush with the thing the night before. *It was somethin' else around,* Miss Mary had said, of the time after Hurricane Camille. *Turnin' people ugly.* Was this the same kind of thing? If it had gotten onto the barge, would it have eaten them as it had the lizard's cousin? Or — he shivered as he remembered Miss Mary looking so mean with that knife. He probably hadn't looked all that friendly himself, with the urge to beat the old woman to death running hot in his blood.

"Last time it come 'roun'," said the lizard, "it kill a whole lot of us 'fore we finally got it. It like us even more'n you folks."

Tookie scowled. "Then you oughtta be inside somewhere, not out here talkin' shit with me."

The lizard scowled back and slapped a paw on the boat's metal rim. "Ain' gon' let no damn monster run me out of town. They killed it before, my daddy said. Took a lot, but they did, so we gon' have to do it again."

Tookie nodded, then picked up the paint cans and began to load them onto the boat. "Come on back to the barge," he said. "Let me get my gun." 150

But the lizard came up to him and put its paw on his hand. Its skin was cool despite the heat, dry despite the humidity, and up close it smelled of ozone and soupy dawn fog. "Ain' your fight," it said.

"I still be up in my attic but for you. Maybe dead."

"Might'a been rescued by now but for me," it said stubbornly. "This thing make people so ugly they don' even want to help each other. You know they ain' give no food or water to all those people at the Superdome? Just lef' 'em there." It shook its head, as Tookie gaped at it in disbelief. "This storm three days gone and still killin' people. That ain' right."

Tookie set his mouth in a grim line. "Man, people don' need no monster to make 'em do evil-hearted shit. All it take is a brown face, or somebody wearin' old tore-up clothes."

"This thing make it *worse*." The lizard hopped out of Tookie's boat, dogpad- 155 dling easily in the water. "I told you, man, I'm a foot soldier. Y'know — " It hesitated. "Y'know, right? I brought the storm? Me and mine?"

Tookie nodded slowly. He had suspected that from their first meeting. "Storms gotta come," he said. "Everybody in this city know that."

The lizard looked relieved. "Yeah, but storms gotta go, too. That's my job, and I been fuckin' around." It nodded to him, then turned and began to paddle away. Abruptly it stopped and turned, glancing back at him over its wing. It gazed at him for a long while. "I'll holla at you later, man," it said at last.

Tookie nodded, raising a hand to wave. The lizard flickered up out of the water and away.

Tookie lowered his hand. He knew that when the waters receded, even if the lizard survived its battle, he would never see it again.

The day grew hot. With water everywhere, evaporating as best it could into the 160 already-saturated air, the city became a place of sunshine and steam. It took the rest of the afternoon to get back on the barge (Tookie had to climb up by way of the schoolbus, standing in the footsteps of the Hate, which gave him the heebie-jecbies) and paint the word HELP in five-foot letters on the barge's long flat roof.

The heat and humidity devoured Tookie's strength. He fell asleep on a pile of dry sheets he'd salvaged from a two-story house whose upstairs hadn't been damaged at all. There had been three other survivors inhabiting that house, he'd found; children, the oldest barely twelve. It wasn't their house either, so they hadn't protested his scavenging. He'd given them some of his food and invited them back to the barge, but leery of strangers, they'd politely declined.

Miss Mary called herself keeping watch, walking around on deck. Tookie suspected she just didn't want to smell him, after four days of funky water and no showers. (To his annoyance, she smelled the same as usual — like old lady.)

He was deep in a dream of being at a house party over on Elysian Fields, with a pretty red-boned girl checking him out across papers full of crawfish and corn and potatoes, when Miss Mary shook him awake. He sat up, snarfling drool, and looked around. Sundown; long golden colors arced over the sky.

"I hear somethin'," Miss Mary said. Her steak knife was out again, and he felt a sleepy species of worry.

"Hear what?" he asked, but on the heels of the question he heard it, too. A 165 sharp, echoing cough, loud and deep, like from the chest of some beast. A big beast, the size of an elephant maybe, somewhere on one of the streets toward the river. And then, before the echoes faded, he heard a harmony of other sounds: high-pitched trills. Over where he heard it, a small cloud hovered in the otherwise clear sky, growing thicker.

Tookie scrambled to his feet, searching among the plastic bags.

"Miss Mary, you stay in here," he said as he rummaged. "Don' go out less you hear a helicopter, or people in a boat. I got to go."

She did not ask where. "You got any people you want me to find once I get out the city?"

"My mama'll be in Baton Rouge, with my sister." There, it was there. Tookie pulled the gun out and checked it. It was fully loaded, but it needed cleaning. He had never liked handling the thing. Maybe it would jam. Maybe it would backfire, leave him blind and handless at the feet of the Hate. He thrust the gun into the waist of his pants.

"That ain' no haint," Miss Mary said. "You was right. It's somethin' else." 170

"I hope so," Tookie said. "Can't kill no haint. Bye, Miss Mary."

"Bye, fool." But she stayed on deck, watching him, as he swung himself over the ladder and climbed down.

The noise had gotten worse by the time Tookie paddled near, keeping low in the rowboat and moving the nail plank as little as possible to avoid telegraphing his approach. It wouldn't've mattered if he'd showed up with a secondline band, though; between the roars of the thing, the trills of the lizards, splashing water, and the crash of cars or houses being destroyed, Tookie didn't have to worry about being heard. And as he paddled, a deeper sound made him look up. The cloud that had gathered overhead was turning darker, thicker. He thought he saw flickers of lightning in its depths.

When he saw that the porches of the houses nearby were above water — they had chosen high ground for their battle — Tookie parked the boat, jumped onto a dry porch, and began running. His gun was in his hand. He ran low and leapt almost soundlessly across the gaps between houses. One porch. Another half-buckled by water damage. Another that overlapped the third because its house had collapsed sideways . . . and here Tookie stopped, because the thing was there, it was *there* and it was huge, its smell was like sulfured asphalt or the thick fermented funk of an algae bog, and instead of coughing, this time it roared like a barge horn gone mad with rage. It was hard to see in the fading light, and for that blessing Tookie thanked a god that he suddenly believed in, because what little of it he could see came near to shattering his mind. Or perhaps that was his own fault, because the thoughts that flowed into his head were so swift and twisted, so *wrong* yet powerful, that they had to come from somewhere inside him, didn't they? Some festering boil deep within, tucked under years of apathy, bursting now and spreading poison all through. *Got to go kill me some niggers* was one of the thoughts, even though he had never thought that way in his life and the cadence of the thought was all wrong; New Orleanians spoke with more rhythm. He tried to think his own thought: *Soun' like some 'Bama mothafucka in my head, what the,* but before he could complete it, there was an oily flipover, and then he thought *all these people in my city, ain' done shit to save it,* and also *gon' find me some bitches and fuck 'em* and then *shoot up them white mothafuckas over in Chalmette-maybe-Gretna give 'em somethin' to be scared of* and *of course that ol' lady slowin' me down, get rid of her.* And more, more, so much more. So much that Tookie cried out and fell to his knees on the crumbling porch, the gun clattering on the old wood as he clutched his head and wondered if one could die of pure evil.

But then a sharp squeal penetrated the hate, and Tookie looked up. The 175 monster had paid him no heed despite his shout, preoccupied as it was with the enemy before it: a sextet of tiny creatures that dipped and wheeled in aerobatic circles around its misshapen head as it turned to follow them. In profile it was even uglier, lumpen and raw, its lower jaw trailing spittle as it worked around a mouthful of something that wriggled and shrieked and beat at it with wings like rusted, ocher clouds — "*No, goddamn it!*" Tookie shouted. Suddenly his head was clear, the hate shattered by horror. He raised the gun, and something else rose in him: a great, huge feeling, as big as the monster and just as overwhelming, but cleaner. Familiar. It was the city beneath his feet, below the water, still patiently holding its breath. He felt the tension in his own lungs. He had played no music, faked no voodoo, paid no taxes and no court to the chattering throngs who came and spent themselves and left the city bruised and weary in their wake. But the city was *his,* low creature that he was, and it was his duty to defend it. It had spent years training him, honing him, making him ready to serve for its hour of need. He was a foot soldier, too, and in that breath of forever he heard the battle call of his home.

So Tookie planted his feet on the rotting wood, and aimed for one bulbous eye with his dirty gun, and screamed with the pent breath of ten thousand waterlogged streets as he blew it away.

The creature shrieked, whipping about in agony as its eye dissolved into a bloody mist. As it cried out, something mangled and small fell from its teeth, landing in the water with a near-silent plop.

"Now!" cried a trilling voice, and the darting batwinged shadows arranged themselves into a strange configuration, and the cloud overhead erupted with light. The thunderbolt caught the beast square in its thrashing head; when Tookie blinked, its body just stood there, headless.

But then the body lurched forward, lifting a far too human hand out of the water to reach for the hovering lizards. Tookie fired again. He saw the doorway of a sagging house through the hole his bullet opened in the thing's hand. It flinched, probably nerves since it no longer had a brain, and that gave the lizards another opening. Overhead, the cloud rumbled once more, and this time three lightning bolts came, *sizzle sizzle sizzle* on Tookie's vision, the air smelled of burning dog and seared rage, and by the time the afterimages faded and his eyes stopped watering, it was all over.

Still half-blind, Tookie stumbled off the porch and through the water, groping 180 with hands and gun toward the place where his friend had fallen. The other lizards converged around it, some hovering and some dropping into the water themselves to support a small, bloody body. Tookie reached them — the hovering ones parted to let him through, though they looked at him suspiciously — and then stopped, knowing at a glance there was nothing he could do.

"Hey," croaked his lizard. Two of its companions held it up in the water. It tilted its head to peer at him with its one remaining eye, and sighed. "Get that damn look off your face. I ain' dead."

"You look like you halfway," said Tookie.

It laughed softly, then grimaced as that caused it pain. "Maybe three-quarters, but I still ain' there." It looked past Tookie at the spot where the great hulking thing had been. There was nothing left; the lightning had evaporated it into mist. "That was the way to do it, but god*damn*, I hurt."

Tookie reached for the lizard, then drew his hand back as one of its companions — another cousin, maybe — hissed at him. He contented himself with a smile instead, though he hardly felt it past the surface of his face. "Hurts worse if you complain." He had been shot once.

"Shut the fuck up." The lizard laid its head across the back of the one who had    185 hissed at Tookie. "That shit ain' in your head, is it?"

Tookie knew what the lizard meant. And the truth was, the Hate *was* still in his head, its ugly thoughts gabbling amid Tookie's own, maybe because they'd been all his own thoughts to begin with. He'd had plenty of practice with hating himself and others. But the city was in his head, too, all that strength and breath and patience, and it occurred to Tookie that this would not have happened if he had not shaken off the Hate on his own. So he smiled again. "Just three-quarters," he said, "but it ain't got me."

The lizard narrowed its eye at him, but finally nodded. "You gon' leave when they rescue you? Run off to Texas or somewhere, settle down there?"

"I'll go, but I'm cornin' back." Tookie lifted his arms, encompassing the foul water, the ruined houses, the stars on the horizon. "This is me."

The lizard flashed its toothy grin, though its eye began to drift shut. "Yeah you right." It sighed heavily. "Got to go."

Tookie nodded. "I'll listen for you in the next big storm." He took a step back,    190 giving the lizards room. They lifted off, two of them carefully holding their injured companion between them. Tookie kept his gaze on his friend's eye, and not the ravaged wings or mangled limbs. Perhaps the lizard would live, but like the city, and like Tookie, it would never be the same. The thought filled him with a defiant ferocity. "An' that son of a bitch come back, you just holla."

It grinned. "I will. Next time, man."

In a soft thunder of wings, the lizards flew away, leaving Tookie alone in the wet dark.

The waters receded.

There was rescue then, and travel to Houston, and a long lonely time of shelters and strangers' homes. Miss Mary found her daughter, and they brought Tookie to live with them. He made contact with his mother and sister, and let them know he was all right. He did odd jobs, under-the-table construction work and the like, and made enough money to get by. His FEMA check took a whole year to come, but it wasn't completely useless. With it, he had enough.

So one evening, when the air was hazy and the sky soft, and something about    195 the arc of sunset reminded him of long days and thick, humid nights, Tookie packed his bags. The next morning he caught a ride to the depot and bought a ticket on the early bus. He let out a long-held, heavy breath as the bus hit the inter-state east, toward home.

## Considerations for Critical Thinking and Writing

1. FIRST RESPONSE. As you began to read the story, did you question the fact that the lizard/dragon could talk? Why or why not?

2. The flooding from the storm is apparently the biggest threat to Tookie's well-being: list the others. What, if anything, do they have in common?

3. How does the story imbue Tookie, a drug dealer, with heroic qualities that might challenge a reader's inherent bias?

4. Tookie is the protagonist, but what is the role of Miss Mary in the story?

5. Why is it significant that Tookie doesn't question the talking lizard/dragon at the beginning of the story but is skeptical when Miss Mary brings up the "haints" that come with the storm?

6. The lizard defines the haint this way: "Like *mean* got a shape and gone walkin' around, spreadin' more mean everywhere it go" (par. 145). Does this definition help or hinder your interpretation of what the haint is, or your ability to visualize it?

7. Tookie indicates that prejudice toward poor people or people of color is a social ill that is firmly in place in this world; if that is the case, what function does the haint serve in the story?

8. Why does it make a difference that Tookie joins forces with the dragons rather than fighting the haint by himself?

9. Would the story's meaning have been different if Tookie had stayed with Miss Mary and her daughter in Houston?

10. The "dragons" and "haints" of the title are clear enough, but how do you interpret the words "sinners and saints"?

11. Discuss the many ways setting is crucial to the story. Jemisin is clearly a writer with a vivid imagination: Would the story have had a different effect if she set it in an invented world?

## Connections to Other Selections

1. Discuss the concepts of good and evil in this story and in Flannery O'Connor's "A Good Man Is Hard to Find" (p. 405).

2. Sonny in James Baldwin's "Sonny's Blues" (p. 91) is, like Tookie, in danger of being a character that readers might dismiss because of their association with the world of illegal drugs. How do Baldwin and Jemisin redeem Sonny and Tookie? Do they use the same methods? Would it be possible for readers to continue to harbor prejudice against either character despite these attempts to depict them as "saints" rather than "sinners"?

## MARIANA ENRIQUEZ (B. 1973)

Mariana Enriquez was born and raised near Buenos Aires, the capital of Argentina. She has published a great deal of fiction and journalism in Spanish which has recently begun to be translated into English, allowing her work to be appreciated by a global audience. From the

Awakening/Getty Images.

mid-1970s until the mid-1980s, Enriquez's country was ruled by a military dictatorship responsible for abducting pregnant women, keeping them captive until they gave birth, then murdering the mothers and giving the babies to families closely tied to the military. This period was known as Argentina's "Dirty War," and the murdered mothers (as well as others who might have spoken out against the government) are known as "*desaparecidos*," or "the disappeared." In a recent interview, speaking of the way she mixes the horror genre with realism, Enriquez said, "It's very difficult to write about Argentina using only realism. . . .[For] people like me who grew up in the 80s and 90s . . . slasher movies, Stephen King, and *Twin Peaks* all got mixed with our reality which was already full of the language of horror, the disappeared, the children of the dead, children of the lost generation."

## Back When We Talked to the Dead     2017

At that age there's music playing in your head all the time, as if a radio were transmitting from the nape of your neck, inside your skull. Then one day that music starts to grow softer, or it just stops. When that happens, you're no longer a teenager. But we weren't there yet, not even close, back when we talked to the dead. Back then, the music was at full blast and it sounded like Slayer, *Reign in Blood*°.

We started with the Ouija board at the Polack's house, locked in her room. We had to do it in secret because Mara, the Polack's sister, was afraid of ghosts and spirits. She was afraid of everything — man, she was a stupid little kid. And we had to do it during the day, because of the sister in question and because the Polack had a big family and they all went to bed early, and the whole Ouija board thing didn't go over well with any of them because they were crazy Catholic, the kind who went to mass and prayed the rosary°. The only cool one in that family was the Polack, and she had gotten her hands on a tremendous Ouija board° that came as a special offer with this magazine on magic, witchcraft, and inexplicable events that was part of a series called *The World of the Occult*; they sold them at newspaper kiosks and you could collect and bind them. Several issues had already had promotions for Ouija boards, but they always ran out before any of us could save the money to buy one. Until the Polack started to take the thing seriously and really tightened her belt, and then there we were with our lovely board, with its numbers and letters in gray, a red background, and some very satanic and mystical drawings all around the central circle.

It was always the five of us who met: me, Julita, Pinocchia (we called her that because she was thick as wood, the slowest in the whole school, not because she had a big nose), the Polack, and Nadia. All five of us smoked, so the planchette°

*Slayer, Reign in Blood:* Slayer was a thrash metal band who became popular in the 1980s; *Reign in Blood* was their third album.

*Rosary:* A set of strung beads used for a Catholic prayer ritual: each bead represents a prayer to recite.

*Ouija board:* A board embossed with letters, numbers, and drawings used in seances to communicate with the dead.

*Planchette:* The device at the center of a Ouija board. Participants place fingertips on the planchette which moves around the board to point to letters, numbers, and symbols.

seemed to be floating on fog as we played, and we left a terrible stench in the room the Polack shared with her sister. Plus, it was winter when we started with the Ouija board, and we couldn't even open the windows because we'd freeze our asses off.

And that was how the Polack's mother found us: shut in with all the smoke and the planchette going all kinds of crazy. She kicked us all out. I managed to salvage the board — it stayed with me after that — and Julita kept the planchette from breaking, which would have been a disaster for the poor Polack and her family, because the dead guy we were talking to right then seemed really evil. He'd even said he wasn't a dead spirit, but a fallen angel. Still, by that point we knew that spirits are some crafty liars and we didn't get scared anymore by their cheap tricks, like guessing birthdays or grandparents' middle names. All five of us pricked our fingers with a needle and swore with blood that we didn't move the planchette, and I believed it was true. I know I didn't. I never moved it, and I really believe my friends didn't either. It was always hard for the planchette to start moving at first, but once it got going it seemed like there was a magnet connecting it to our fingers. We barely even had to touch it, we never pushed it, not even a nudge; it slid over the mystical drawings and the letters so fast that sometimes we didn't even have time to jot down the answers to the questions (one of us always took notes) in the special notebook we kept for just that purpose.

When the Polack's crazy mom caught us (and accused us of being satanists 5 and whores, and called all our parents: it was a clusterfuck), we had to stop the game for a while, because it was hard to find another place where we could keep going. At my house, impossible: my mom was sick in those days and she didn't want anyone in the house. She could barely stand my grandmother and me, and she would straight up kill me if I brought friends home. Julita's was no good because the apartment where she lived with her grandparents and her little brother had only one room, which they divided with a wardrobe to make two rooms, kind of. But it was just that space, no privacy at all, otherwise just the kitchen and bathroom, plus a little balcony full of aloe vera and crown-of-thorns plants — impossible any way you looked at it. Nadia's place was also impossible because it was in the slum: the other four of us didn't exactly live in fancy neighborhoods, but no chance in hell would our parents let us spend the night in a slum, they would never go for that. We could have snuck around and done it without telling them, but the truth is we were also a little scared to go. Plus, Nadia didn't bullshit us: she told us it was really rough where she lived, and she wanted to get the hell out of there as soon as she could, because she'd had it with hearing the gunshots at night and the shouts of the drunk gauchos, and with people being too scared to come visit her.

So we were left with Pinocchia's place. The only problem with her house was that it was really far away, we'd have to take two buses, plus convince our parents to let us go all the way out to East Bumfuck. But we managed it. Pinocchia's parents pretty much left her alone, so at her house there was no risk of getting kicked out with a lecture on God. And Pinocchia had her own room, because her siblings had already left home.

So finally, one summer night, all four of us got permission and went to Pinocchia's house. It was really far, her house was on a street that wasn't even paved, with a ditch running alongside it. It took us like two hours to get there. But when we did, we realized right away that it was the best idea in the world to make the trek all the way out there. Pinocchia's room was really big, with a double bed plus bunk beds: all five of us could sleep there, easy. It was an ugly house because it was still under construction: unpainted, plaster, lightbulbs hanging from ugly black cords, no lamps, and a bare cement floor, no tile or wood or anything. But it was really big, with a terrace and a barbecue pit, and it was much better than any of our houses. It sucked to live so far away, sure, but if it meant having a house like that — even an unfinished one — it was worth it. Out there, far from the center of Buenos Aires, the night sky looked navy blue, there were fireflies, and the smell was different, like a mixture of burnt grass and river. Pinocchia's house had bars on all the windows, it's true, and it also had a giant black dog guarding it. I think it was a rottweiler, and you couldn't play with it because it was so mean. It seemed that living far away had its dangers too, but Pinocchia never complained.

Maybe it was because the place was so different — because that night in Pinocchia's house we did feel different, with her parents listening to Los Redondos and drinking beer while the dog barked at shadows — that Julita got up the nerve to tell us exactly which dead people she wanted to talk to.

Julita wanted to talk to her mom and dad.

It was really good that Julita finally spoke up about her folks, because we could  10 never bring ourselves to ask. At school people talked about it a lot, but no one ever said a thing to her face, and we jumped to her defense if anyone came out with any bullshit. The thing was that everyone knew Julita's parents hadn't died in any accident: Julita's folks had disappeared. They were disappeared. They'd been disappeared. We didn't really know the right way to say it. Julita said they'd been taken away, because that's how, her grandparents talked. They'd been taken away, and luckily the kids had been left in the bedroom (no one had checked the bedroom, maybe: anyway, Julita and her brother didn't remember anything, not of that night or of their parents either).

Julita wanted to find them with the board, or ask some other spirit if they'd seen them. She wanted to talk to them, and she also wanted to know where their bodies were. Because that question drove her grandparents crazy, she said; her grandma cried every day because she had nowhere to bring flowers to. Plus, Julita was really something else: she said that if we found the bodies, if the dead told us where they were and it turned out to be really real, we'd have to go on TV or to the newspapers, and we'd be famous and everyone in the world would love us.

To me, at least, Julita's cold-bloodedness seemed really harsh, but I thought, Whatever, let Julita do her thing. What we for sure had to start doing, she told us, was coming up with other disappeared people we knew, so they could help us. In a book on how to use the board, we'd read that it helped to concentrate on a dead person you knew, to recall their smell, their clothes, their mannerisms, their hair color, construct a mental image, and then it would be easier for the dead person to really come. Because sometimes a lot of false spirits would turn up and lie to you and go around and around in circles. It was hard to tell the difference.

The Polack said that her aunt's boyfriend was disappeared, that he'd been taken during the World Cup°. We were all surprised because the Polack's family was really uppity. She explained that they almost never talked about the subject, but her aunt had told her once in confidence, when she was a little drunk after a

---

*World Cup:* The largest international soccer tournament, the World Cup was both hosted and won by Argentina in 1978.

barbecue at her house. The men were getting all nostalgic about Kempes° and the World Cup, and the aunt got pissed off, downed her red wine, and told the Polack all about her boyfriend and how scared she'd been. Nadia contributed a friend of her dad's who used to come for dinner on Sundays when she was little, and one day had just stopped coming. She hadn't really noticed that friend's absence, mostly because he used to go to the field a lot with her dad and brothers, and they didn't take her to games. But her brothers noticed it more when he didn't come around, and they asked their old man, and the old man couldn't bring himself to lie to them and say they'd had a fight or something. He told the boys that the friend had been taken away, same thing Julita's grandparents said. Later, Nadia's brothers told her. At the time, neither the boys nor Nadia had any idea where he'd been taken, or if being taken away was common, or if it was good or bad. But now we all knew about those things, after we saw the movie *Night of the Pencils* (which made us bawl our eyes out; we rented it about once a month) and after the *Nunca Más* report on the disappeared — which Pinocchia had brought to school, because in her house they let her read it. Plus there was all the stuff we read in magazines and saw on TV. I contributed with our neighbor in back, a guy who'd lived there only a short time, less than a year. He didn't go out much but we could see him moving around out the back windows, in his little backyard. I didn't remember him much, it was kind of like a dream, and it wasn't like he spent a lot of time in the yard. But one night they came for him, and my mom told everyone about it, and she said that thanks to that son of a bitch they could have easily taken us too. Maybe because she repeated it so much, the thing with the neighbor stuck with me, and I couldn't relax until another family moved into that house and I knew he wasn't ever going to come back.

Pinocchia didn't have anyone to contribute, but we decided we had enough disappeared dead for our purposes. That night we played until four in the morning, and by then we were starting to yawn and our throats were getting scratchy from so much smoking, and the most fantastic thing of all was that Pinocchia's parents didn't even come knock on the door to send us to bed. I think — I'm not sure, because the Ouija consumed my full attention — that they were watching TV or listening to music until dawn, too.

After that first night, we got permission to go to Pinocchia's house two more   15 times that same month. It was incredible, but all our parents or guardians had talked on the phone with Pinocchia's parents, and for some reason the conversation left them totally reassured. But we had a different problem: we were having trouble talking to the particular dead people we wanted — that is, Julita's parents. We talked to some spirits, but they gave us the runaround, they couldn't make up their minds yes or no, and they always stopped at the same place: they'd tell us where they'd been captured, but then they wouldn't go any further, they couldn't tell us if they'd been killed there or if they'd been taken somewhere else. They'd talk in circles, and then they'd leave. It was frustrating. I think we talked to my neighbor, and he got as far as naming the detention center Pozo de Arana, but then he left. It was him, for sure: he told us his name, we looked him up in

---

*Kempes:* Mario Kempes (b. 1954) was the hero of Argentina's national soccer team in 1978, scoring two goals in the World Cup final.

*Nunca Más,* and there he was, on the list. We were scared shitless: it was the first certified for-real dead guy we'd talked to. But as for Julita's parents, nothing.

It was our fourth time at Pinocchia's when what happened happened. We'd managed to communicate with someone who knew the Polack's aunt's boyfriend; they'd gone to school together, he said. The dead guy we were talking to was named Andrés, and his story was that he hadn't been taken away and he hadn't disappeared: he'd escaped on his own to Mexico, and he died there later in a car accident, totally unrelated. Well, this Andrés guy was cool, and we asked him why all the dead people took off as soon as we asked them where their bodies were. He told us that some of them left because they didn't know where they were, and they got nervous, uncomfortable. But others didn't answer because someone bothered them. One of us. We wanted to know why, and he told us he didn't know the reason, but that was the deal, one of us didn't belong.

Then the spirit left.

We sat for a beat thinking about what he'd said, but we decided not to give it too much importance. At first, when we'd started playing with the board, we always asked the spirit that came if any of us bothered it. But then we stopped doing that because the spirits loved to run with the question, and they'd play with us. First they'd say Nadia, then they'd say no, everything was cool with Nadia, the one who bothered them was Julita, and they could keep us going all night, telling one of us to put our fingers on the planchette or take them off, or even to leave the room, because those fuckers would ask us for all kinds of things.

The episode with Andrés left enough of an impression, anyway, that we decided to go over the conversation in the notebook while we cracked open a beer. Then there was a knock at the door. It startled us a little, because Pinocchia's parents never bugged us.

"Who is it?" asked Pinocchia, and her voice came out a bit shaky. We were all  20
shitting ourselves a little, to tell the truth.

"It's Leo. Can I come in?"

"Hell yeah!" Pinocchia jumped up and opened the door. Leo was her older brother who lived downtown and only visited their parents on weekends, because he worked every weekday. And he didn't even come every weekend, because sometimes he was too tired. We knew him because before, when we were little, first and second grade, sometimes he came to pick up Pinocchia at school when their parents couldn't make it. Then, when we were big enough, we started to take the bus. A shame, because then we stopped seeing Leo, who was really fine, a big dark guy with green eyes and a murderous face, to die for. And that night, at Pinocchia's house, he was hot as ever. We all sighed a little and tried to hide the board, just so he wouldn't think we were weird. But he didn't care.

"Playing Ouija? That thing's fucked up, I'm scared of it," he said. "You girls have some balls." And then he looked at his sister: "Hey, kiddo, can you help me unload some stuff from the truck? It's for the folks, but Mom already went to bed and Dad's back is hurting . . ."

"Aw, don't be a pain in the ass, it's really late!"

"Well, I could only make it out here just now, what can I say, the time got away  25
from me. Come on, if I leave the stuff in the truck it could get lifted."

Pinocchia gave a grudging okay and asked us to wait for her. We stayed sitting on the floor around the board, talking in low voices about how cute Leo was, how he must be around twenty-three by now — he was a lot older than us.

Pinocchia was gone a long time, and we thought it was strange, so after half an hour Julita offered to go see what was going on. Then everything happened really fast, almost at the same time. The planchette moved on its own. We'd never seen anything like it. All by itself, really, none of us had a finger on it, not even close. It moved and wrote really quickly, "Ready." Ready? Ready for what? Just then we heard a scream from the street, or from the front door — it was Pinocchia's voice. We went running out to see what was going on, and we found her in her mother's arms, crying, the two of them sitting on the sofa next to the phone table. Just then we didn't understand a thing, but later, when things calmed down a little — just a little — we more or less put it together.

Pinocchia had followed her brother down to the corner. She didn't understand why he'd left the truck there when there was plenty of room by the house, but he didn't answer any of her questions. He'd changed as soon as they left the house, he'd turned mean and wouldn't talk to her. When they got to the corner he told her to wait, and, according to Pinocchia, he disappeared. It was dark, so it could be that he walked a few steps away and she lost sight of him, but according to her he'd disappeared. She waited a while to see if he would come back, but since the truck wasn't there either, she got scared. She went back to the house and found her parents awake, in bed. She told them Leo had been there, that he'd been acting really weird, and that he'd asked her to help unload things from his truck. Her parents looked at her like she was crazy. "Leo wasn't here, sweetie, what are you talking about? He has to work early tomorrow." Pinocchia started trembling with fear and saying, "It was Leo, it was Leo," and then her dad got all worked up, and shouted at her and asked if she was high or what. Her mom was calmer, and she said, "Listen, let's call Leo at home. He's probably asleep, but we'll wake him up." She was doubting a little now too, because she could tell that Pinocchia was really positive and really upset. She called, and after a long time Leo answered, cursing, because he'd been fast asleep. Their mom told him, "I'll explain later," or something like that, and she started to soothe Pinocchia, who was having a terrible meltdown.

They even called an ambulance, because Pinocchia couldn't stop screaming that "the thing" had touched her (an arm around the shoulders, in a sort of hug that had made her feel more cold than warm), and that it had come for her because she was "the one who bothered them."

Julita whispered into my ear, "It's because she didn't have anyone disappear." 30 I told her to shut her mouth — poor Pinocchia. I was really scared, too. If it wasn't Leo, who was it? Because that person who'd come to get Pinocchia looked exactly like her brother, he was like an identical twin, and she hadn't doubted for a second either. Who was it? I didn't want to remember his eyes. And I didn't want to play with the Ouija board ever again, let me tell you, or even go back to Pinocchia's house at all.

Our little group never got together again. Pinocchia was hit really hard, and her parents blamed us — poor things, they had to blame someone. They said we'd played a mean prank on her, and it was our fault she went a little crazy after that. But we all knew they were wrong; we knew the spirits had come to get her because, as the dead guy Andrés told us, one of us bothered them, and it was her. And just like that, the time when we talked to the dead came to an end.

## CONSIDERATIONS FOR CRITICAL THINKING AND WRITING

1. FIRST RESPONSE. From the title of the story on we're aware of the adult narrator reflecting on experiences of adolescence. Why are teenagers more receptive to the occult than adults are?

2. The narrator takes pains to defend the practice of the Ouija board, insisting that she and the other girls did not move the planchette. "I believed it was true," she says (par. 4). Does it matter whether you, the reader, also believe it is true?

3. The narrator talks at length about where she and her friends could and could not carry out their secret activities. Young teens are always trying to hide their secret activities from their parents: Why does the search for this location matter especially in this story?

4. The narrator makes a point about the difference between communicating with dead people in general and with a specific dead person one once knew. Why is this distinction important?

5. How does the suppression of official information about "the disappeared" relate to the girls' interest in the Ouija board? How else would they get information?

6. Why are the girls especially scared when they identify a "certified for-real dead guy" who has spoken to them through the Ouija board as opposed to the "spirits" who give them incomplete information?

7. How does the idea that one girl from the group "bothers" the spirit world change the story's trajectory, or tone?

8. In addition to communicating with the dead, the girls engage in fairly typical young teen behavior, like smoking cigarettes and drinking beer in secret. Are these activities related to their seances or are they just for atmosphere? How do these activities affect your interpretation of the girls, and their seances?

9. Are there any rational explanations for what happened on the final night of the story (either the appearance of the presence who looks just like Leo or the movement of the planchette without anyone touching it)?

10. How do you interpret the word that the Ouija board spells out on its own ("ready")?

11. Why do the girls stop trying to communicate with the dead?

## CONNECTIONS TO OTHER SELECTIONS

1. In which story is the border between reality and the supernatural easier to discern: this story or Charlotte Perkins Gilman's "The Yellow Wallpaper" (p. 126)? Why?

2. Discuss the way the urge to discover the truth about the dead is treated in this story and in Jennifer Nansubuga Makumbi's "Let's Tell This Story Properly" (p. 487).

3. How is the search for information treated in this story and in Philip K. Dick's "To Serve the Master" (p. 341)? What does each story have to say about the relationship between authority figures and information?

## PHILIP K. DICK (1928–1982)

Philip K. Dick was a prolific author of science fiction who published over forty novels and more than one hundred short stories in his abbreviated lifetime. Unlike many of the contemporary writers included in this textbook, Dick did not benefit from formal training in an educational setting: his higher education did not even last a semester at the University of California, Berkeley. His life was marked by challenging circumstances, including the death of his twin sister as an infant, his parents' divorce, five failed marriages, and years of drug addiction and episodes of mental instability. Dick channeled this personal darkness into one of the most impressive and recognizable bodies of speculative fiction in the twentieth century. His stories and novels have achieved an afterlife in the form of blockbuster Hollywood movies and television shows, including *Total Recall, Minority Report, A Scanner Darkly, Man in the High Castle*, and above all, *Blade Runner*, widely regarded as one of the top science fiction films of all time.

## *To Serve the Master*  1956

Applequist was cutting across a deserted field, up a narrow path beside the yawning crack of a ravine, when he heard the voice.

He stopped frozen, hand on his S-pistol. For a long time he listened, but there was only the distant lap of the wind among the broken trees along the ridge, a hollow murmuring that mixed with the rustle of the dry grass beside him. The sound had come from the ravine. Its bottom was snarled and debris-filled. He crouched down at the lip and tried to locate the voice.

There was no motion. Nothing to give away the place. His legs began to ache. Flies buzzed at him, settled on his sweating forehead. The sun made his head ache; the dust clouds had been thin the last few months.

His radiation-proof watch told him it was three o'clock. Finally he shrugged and got stiffly to his feet. The hell with it. Let them send out an armed team. It wasn't his business; he was a letter carrier grade four, and a civilian.

As he climbed the hill toward the road, the sound came again. And this time, 5 standing high above the ravine, he caught a flash of motion. Fear and puzzled disbelief touched him. It couldn't be — but he had seen it with his own eyes. It wasn't a newscircular rumor.

What was a robot doing down in the deserted ravine? All robots had been destroyed years ago. But there it lay, among the debris and weeds. A rusted, half-corroded wreck. Calling feebly up at him as he passed along the trail.

The Company defense ring admitted him through the three-stage lock into the tunnel area. He descended slowly, deep in thought all the way down to the organizational level. As he slid off his letter pack Assistant Supervisor Jenkins hurried over.

"Where the hell have you been? It's almost four."

"Sorry." Applequist turned his S-pistol over to a nearby guard. "What are the chances of a five hour pass? There's something I want to look into."

"Not a chance. You know they're scrapping the whole right wing setup. They <sup>10</sup> need everybody on strict twenty-four hour alert."

Applequist began sorting letters. Most were personals between big-shot supervisors of the North American Companies. Letters to entertainment women beyond the Company peripheries. Letters to families and petitions from minor officials. "In that case," he said thoughtfully, "I'll have to go anyhow."

Jenkins eyed the young man suspiciously. "What's going on? Maybe you found some undamaged equipment left over from the war. An intact cache, buried someplace? Is that it?"

Applequist almost told him, at that point. But he didn't. "Maybe," he answered indifferently. "It's possible."

Jenkins shot him a grimace of hate and stalked off to roll aside the doors of the observation chamber. At the big wall map officials were examining the day's activities. Half a dozen middle-aged men, most of them bald, collars dirty and stained, lounged around in chairs. In the corner Supervisor Rudde was sound asleep, fat legs stuck out in front of him, hairy chest visible under his open shirt. These were the men who ran the Detroit Company. Ten thousand families, the whole subsurface living-shelter, depended on them.

"What's on your mind?" a voice rumbled in Applequist's ear. Director Laws <sup>15</sup> had come into the chamber and, as usual, taken him unawares.

"Nothing, sir," Applequist answered. But the keen eyes, blue as china, bored through and beneath. "The usual fatigue. My tension index is up. I've been meaning to take some of my leave, but with all the work. . . "

"Don't try to fool me. A fourth-class letter carrier isn't needed. What are you really getting at?"

"Sir," Applequist said bluntly, "why were the robots destroyed?"

There was silence. Laws' heavy face registered surprise, then hostility. Before he could speak Applequist hurried on: "I know my class is forbidden to make theoretical inquiries. But it's very important I find out."

"The subject is closed," Laws rumbled ominously. "Even to top-level <sup>20</sup> personnel."

"What did the robots have to do with the war? Why was the war fought? What was life like before the war?"

"The subject," Laws repeated, "is closed." He moved slowly toward the wall map and Applequist was left standing alone, in the middle of the clicking machines, among the murmuring officials and bureaucrats.

Automatically, he resumed sorting letters. There had been the war, and robots were involved in it. That much he knew. A few had survived; when he was a child his father had taken him to an industrial center and he had seen them at their machines. Once, there had been more complex types. Those were all gone; even the simple ones would soon be scrapped. Absolutely no more were manufactured.

"*What happened?*" he had asked, as his father dragged him away. "Where did all the robots go?"

No answer then either. That was sixteen years ago, and now the last had been <sup>25</sup> scrapped. Even the memory of robots was disappearing; in a few years the word itself would cease. *Robots.* What had happened?

He finished with the letters and moved out of the chamber. None of the supervisors noticed; they were arguing some erudite point of strategy. Maneuvering and countermaneuvering among the Companies. Tension and exchanged insults. He found a crushed cigarette in his pocket and inexpertly lit up.

"Dinner call," the passage speaker announced tinnily. "One hour break for top class personnel."

A few supervisors filed noisily past him. Applequist crushed out his cigarette and moved toward his station. He worked until six. Then his dinner hour came up. No other break until Saturday. But if he went without dinner . . .

The robot was probably a low-order type, scrapped with the final group. The inferior kind he had seen as a child. It couldn't be one of the elaborate war-time robots. To have survived in the ravine, rusting and rotting through the years since the war . . .

His mind skirted the hope. Heart pounding, he entered a lift and touched the stud. By nightfall he'd know. 30

The robot lay among heaps of metal slag and weeds. Jagged, rusted fragments barred Applequist's way as he move cautiously down the side of the ravine, S-gun in one hand, radiation mask pulled tight over his face.

His counter clicked loudly: the floor of the ravine was hot. Pools of contamination, over the reddish metal fragments, the piles and masses of fused steel and plastic and gutted equipment. He kicked webs of blackened wiring aside and gingerly stepped past the yawning fuel-tank of some ancient machine, now overgrown with vines. A rat scuttled off. It was almost sunset. Dark shadows lay over everything.

The robot was watching him silently. Half of it was gone; only the head, arms, and upper trunk remained. The lower waist ended in shapeless struts, abruptly sliced off. It was clearly immobile. Its whole surface was pitted and corroded. One eye-lens was missing. Some of its metal fingers were bent grotesquely. It lay on its back facing the sky.

It was a war-time robot, all right. In the one remaining eye glinted archaic consciousness. This was not the simple worker he had glimpsed as a child. Applequist's breath hammered in his throat. This was the real thing. It was following his movements intently. It was alive.

*All this time,* Applequist thought. *All these years.* The hackles of his neck rose. 35 Everything was silent, the hills and trees and masses of ruin. Nothing stirred; he and the ancient robot were the only living things. *Down here in this crack waiting for somebody to come along.*

A cold wind rustled at him and he automatically pulled his overcoat together. Some leaves blew over the inert face of the robot. Vines had crept along its trunk, twisted into its works. It had been rained on; the sun had shone on it. In winter the snow had covered it. Rats and animals had sniffed at it. Insects had crawled through it. And it was still alive.

"I heard you," Applequist muttered. "I was walking along the path."

Presently the robot said, "I know. I saw you stop." Its voice was faint and dry. Like, ashes rubbing together. Without quality or pitch. "Would you make the date known to me? I suffered a power failure for an indefinite period. Wiring terminals shorted temporarily."

"It's June 11," Applequist said. "2136," he added.

The robot was obviously hoarding its meager strength. It moved one arm slightly, then let it fall back. Its one good eye blurred over, and deep within, gears whirred rustily. Realization came to Applequist: the robot might expire any moment. It was a miracle it had survived this long. Snails clung to its body. It was criss-crossed with slimy trails. A century . . . 40

"How long have you been here?" he demanded. "Since the war?"

"Yes."

Applequist grinned nervously. "That's a long time. Over a hundred years."

"That's so."

It was getting dark fast. Automatically, Applequist fumbled for his flashlight. 45 He could hardly make out the sides of the ravine. Someplace a long way off a bird croaked dismally in the darkness. The bushes rustled.

"I need help," the robot said. "Most of my motor equipment was destroyed. I can't move from here."

"In what condition is the rest of you? Your energy supply. How long can — "

"There's been considerable cell destruction. Only a limited number of relay circuits still function. And those are overloaded." The robot's one good eye was on him again. "What is the technological situation? I have seen airborne ships fly overhead. You still manufacture and maintain electronic equipment?"

"We operate an industrial unit near Pittsburgh."

"If I describe basic electronic units will you understand?" the robot asked. 50

"I'm not trained in mechanical work. I'm classed as a fourth grade letter carrier. But I have contacts in the repair department. We keep our own machines functioning." He licked his lips tensely. "It's risky, of course. There are laws."

"Laws?"

"All robots were destroyed. You are the only one left. The rest were liquidated years ago."

No expression showed in the robot's eye. "Why did you come down here?" it demanded. Its eye moved to the S-gun in Applequist's hand. "You are a minor official in some hierarchy. Acting on orders from above. A mechanically-operating integer in a larger system."

Applequist laughed. "I suppose so." Then he stopped laughing. "Why was the 55 war fought? What was life like before?"

"Don't you know?"

"Of course not. No theoretical knowledge is permitted, except to top-level personnel. And even the Supervisors don't know about the war." Applequist squatted down and shone the beam of his flashlight into the darkening face of the robot. "Things were different before, weren't they? We didn't always live in subsurface shelters. The world wasn't always a scrap heap. People didn't always slave for their Companies."

"Before the war there were no Companies."

Applequist grunted with triumph. "I knew it."

"Men lived in cities, which were demolished in the war. Companies, which 60 were protected, survived. Officials of these Companies became the government. The war lasted a long time. Everything of value was destroyed. What you have left is a burned-out shell." The robot was silent a moment and then continued, "The first robot was built in 1979. By 2000 all routine work was done by robots. Human beings were free to do what they wanted. Art, science, entertainment, whatever they liked."

"What is art?" Applequist asked.

"Creative work, directed toward realization of an internal standard. The whole population of the earth was free to expand culturally. Robots maintained the world; man enjoyed it."

"What were cities like?"

"Robots rebuilt and reconstructed new cities according to plans drawn up by human artists. Clean, sanitary, attractive. They were the cities of gods."

"Why was the war fought?" 65

The robot's single eye flickered. "I've already talked too much. My power supply is dangerously low."

Applequist trembled. "What do you need? I'll get it."

"Immediately, I need an atomic A pack. Capable of putting out ten thousand f-units."

"Yes."

"After that, I'll need tools and aluminum sections. Low resistance wiring. 70 Bring pen and paper — I'll give you a list. You won't understand it, but someone in electronic maintenance will. A power supply is the first need."

"And you'll tell me about the war?"

"Of course." The robot's dry rasp faded into silence. Shadows flickered around it; cold evening air stirred the dark weeds and bushes. "Kindly hurry. Tomorrow, if possible."

"I ought to turn you in," Assistant Supervisor Jenkins snapped. "Half an hour late, and now this business. What are you doing? You want to get fired out of the Company?'

Applequist pushed close to the man. "I have to get this stuff. The — cache is below surface. I have to construct a secure passage. Otherwise the whole thing will be buried by falling debris."

"How large a cache is it?" Greed edged suspicion off Jenkins' gnarled face. He 75 was already spending the Company reward. "Have you been able to see in? Are there unknown machines?"

"I didn't recognize any," Applequist said impatiently. "Don't waste time. The whole mass of debris is apt to collapse. I have to work fast."

"Where is it? I want to see it!"

"I'm doing this alone. You supply the material and cover for my absence. That's your part."

Jenkins twisted uncertainly. "If you're lying to me, Applequist —"

"I'm not lying," Applequist answered angrily. "When can I expect the power 80 unit?"

"Tomorrow morning. I'll have to fill out a bushel of forms. Are you sure you can operate it? I better send a repair team along with you. To be sure —"

"I can handle it." Applequist interrupted. "Just get me the stuff. I'll take care of the rest."

Morning sunlight filtered over the rubble and trash. Applequist nervously fitted the new power pack in place, screwed the leads tight, clamped the corroded shield over it, and then got shakily to his feet. He tossed away the old pack and waited.

The robot stirred. Its eye gained life and awareness. Presently it moved its arm in exploratory motions, over its damaged trunk and shoulders.

"All right?" Applequist demanded huskily. 85

"Apparently." The robot's voice was stronger; full and more confident. "The old power pack was virtually exhausted. It was fortunate you came along when you did."

"You say men lived in cities," Applequist plunged in eagerly. "Robots did the work?"

"Robots did the routine labor needed to maintain the industrial system. Humans had leisure to enjoy whatever they wanted. We were glad to do their work for them. It was our job."

"What happened? What went wrong?'

The robot accepted the pencil and paper; as it talked it carefully, wrote 90 down figures. "There was a fanatic group of humans. A religious organization. They claimed that God intended man to work by the sweat of his brow. They wanted robots scrapped and men put back in the factories to slave away at routine tasks."

"But why?"

"They claimed work was spiritually ennobling." The robot tossed the paper back. "Here's the list of what I want. I'll need those materials and tools to restore my damaged system."

Applequist fingered the paper. "This religious group—"

"Men separated in two factions. The Moralists and the Leisurists. They fought each other for years, while we stood on the sidelines waiting to know our fate. I couldn't believe the Moralists would win out over reason and common sense. But they did."

"Do you think—" Applequist began, and then broke off. He could hardly give 95 voice to the thought that was struggling inside him. "Is there a chance robots might be brought back?"

"Your meaning is obscure." The robot abruptly snapped the pencil in half and threw it away. "What are you driving at?"

"Life isn't pleasant in the Companies. Death and hard work. Forms and shifts and work periods and orders."

"It's your system. I'm not responsible."

"How much do you recall about robot construction? What were you, before the war?"

"I was a unit controller. I was on my way to an emergency unit-factory, when 100 my ship was shot down." The robot indicated the debris around it. "That was my ship and cargo."

"What is a unit controller?"

"I was in charge of robot manufacture. I designed and put into production. basic robot types."

Applequist's head spun dizzily. "Then you do know robot construction."

"Yes." The robot gestured urgently at the paper in Applequist's hand. "Kindly get those tools and materials as soon as possible. I'm completely helpless this way. I want my mobility back. If a rocketship should fly overhead . . ."

"Communication between Companies is bad. I deliver my letters on foot. 105 Most of the country is in ruins. You could work undetected. What about your emergency unit-factory? Maybe it wasn't destroyed."

The robot nodded slowly. "It was carefully concealed. There is the bare possibility. It was small, but completely outfitted. Self-sufficient."

"If I get repair parts, can you—"

"We'll discuss this later." The robot sank back down. "When you return, we'll talk further."

He got the material from Jenkins, and a twenty-four hour pass, Fascinated, he crouched against the wall of the ravine as the robot systematically pulled apart its own body and replaced the damaged elements. In a few hours a new motor system had been installed. Basic leg cells were welded into position. By noon the robot was experimenting with its pedal extremities.

"During the night," the robot said, "I was able to make weak radio contact 110 with the emergency unit-factory. It exists intact, according to the robot monitor."

"Robot? You mean —"

"An automatic machine for relaying transmission. Not alive, as I am. Strictly speaking, I'm not a robot." Its voice swelled. "I'm an android."

The fine distinction was lost on Applequist. His mind was racing excitedly over the possibilities. "Then we can go ahead. With your knowledge, and the materials available at the —"

"You didn't see the terror and destruction. The Moralists systematically demolished us. Each town they seized was cleared of androids. Those of my race were brutally wiped out, as the Leisurists retreated. We were torn from our machines and destroyed."

"But that was a century ago! Nobody wants to destroy robots anymore. We need 115 robots to rebuild the world. The Moralists won the war and left the world in ruins."

The robot adjusted its motor system until its legs were coordinated. "Their victory was a tragedy, but I understand the situation better than you. We must advance cautiously. If we are wiped out this time, it maybe for good."

Applequist followed after the robot as it moved hesitantly through the debris toward the wall of the ravine. "We're crushed by work. Slaves in underground shelters. We can't go on this way. People will welcome robots. We need you. When I think how it must have been in the Golden Age, the fountains and flowers, the beautiful cities above ground . . . Now there's nothing but ruin and misery. The Moralists won, but nobody's happy. We'd gladly —"

"Where are we? What is the location here?"

"Slightly west of the Mississippi, a few miles or so. We must have freedom. We can't live this way, toiling underground. If we had free time we could investigate the mysteries of the whole universe. I found some old scientific tapes. Theoretical work in biology. Those men spent years working on abstract topics. They had the time. They were free. While robots maintained the economic system those men could go out and —"

"During the war," the robot said thoughtfully, "the Moralists rigged up detec- 120 tion screens over hundreds of square miles. Are those screens still functioning?"

"I don't know. I doubt it. Nothing outside of the immediate Company shelters still works."

The robot was deep in thought. It had replaced its ruined eye with a new cell; both eyes flickered with concentration. "Tonight we'll make plans concerning your Company. I'll let you know my decision then. Meanwhile, don't bring this situation up with anyone. You understand? Right now I'm concerned with the road system."

"Most roads are in ruins." Applequist tried hard to hold back his excitement. "I'm convinced most in my Company are — Leisurists. Maybe a few at the top are Moralists. Some of the supervisors, perhaps. But the lower classes and families —"

"All right," the robot interrupted. "We'll see about that later." It glanced around. "I can use some of that damaged equipment. Part of it will function. For the moment, at least."

Applequist managed to avoid Jenkins, as he hurriedly made his way across 125 the organizational level to his work station. His mind was in a turmoil. Everything around him seemed vague and unconvincing. The quarreling supervisors.

The clattering, humming machines. Clerks and minor bureaucrats hurrying back and forth with messages and memoranda. He grabbed a mass of letters and mechanically began sorting them into their slots.

"You've been outside," Director Laws observed sourly. "What is it, a girl? If you marry outside the Company you lose the little rating you have."

Applequist pushed aside his letters. "Director, I want to talk to you."

Director Laws shook his head. "Be careful. You know the ordinances governing fourth-class personnel. Better not ask any more questions. Keep your mind on your work and leave the theoretical issues to us."

"Director," Applequist asked, "which side was our Company, Moralist or Leisurist?"

Laws didn't seem to understand the question. "What do you mean?" He shook  130
his head. "I don't know those words."

"In the war. Which side of the war were we on?"

"Good God," Law said. "The human side, of course." An expression like a curtain dropped over his heavy face. "What do you mean, *Moralist*? What are you talking about?"

Suddenly Applequist was sweating. His voice would hardly come. "Director, something's wrong. The war was between the two groups of humans. The Moralists destroyed the robots because they disapproved of humans living in leisure."

"The war was fought between men and robots," Laws said harshly. "We won. We destroyed the robots."

"But they worked for us!"  135

"They were built as workers, but they revolted. They had a philosophy. Superior beings — androids. They considered us nothing but cattle."

Applequist was shaking all over. "But it told me — "

"They slaughtered us. Millions of humans died, before we got the upper hand. They murdered, lied, hid, stole, did everything to survive. It was them or us — no quarter." Laws grabbed Applequist by the collar. "You damn fool! What the hell have you done? Answer me! What have you done?"

The sun was setting, as the armored twin-track roared up to the edge of the ravine. Troops leaped out and poured down the sides, S-rifles clattering. Laws emerged quickly, Applequist beside him.

"This is the place?" Laws demanded.  140

"Yes." Applequist sagged. "But it's gone."

"Naturally. It was fully repaired. There was nothing to keep it here." Laws signalled his men. "No use looking. Plant a tactical A-bomb and let's get out of here. The air fleet may be able to catch it. We'll spray this area with radioactive gas."

Applequist wandered numbly to the edge of the ravine. Below, in the darkening shadows, were the weeds and tumbled debris. There was no sign of the robot, of course. A place where it had been, bits of wire and discarded body sections. The old power pack where he had thrown it. A few tools. Nothing else.

"Come on," Laws ordered his men. "Let's get moving. We have a lot to do. Get the general alarm system going."

The troops began climbing the sides of the ravine. Applequist started after  145
them, toward the twin-track.

"No," Laws said quickly. "You're not coming with us."

Applequist saw the look on their faces. The pent-up fear, the frantic terror and hate. He tried to run, but they were on him almost at once. They worked grimly and silently. When they were through they kicked aside his still-living remains and climbed into the twin-track. They slammed the locks and the motor thundered up. The track rumbled down the trail to the road. In a few moments it dwindled and was gone.

He was alone, with the half-buried bomb and the settling shadows. And the vast empty darkness that was collecting everywhere.

### CONSIDERATIONS FOR CRITICAL THINKING AND WRITING

1. FIRST RESPONSE. This story was written in 1956, before the rise of personal computers, mobile devices, or the Internet. What does it predict about the current relationship between humans and their machines? Does it help you understand that relationship differently?

2. We wrote about world building in the introduction to this chapter (p. 315). Describe how the author builds the story's world in paragraphs 1–6 (before the first break): What details are important? What do they immediately indicate about the world you are entering?

3. Applequist's job connects to recognizable structures in both the military and the corporate world. Which is a more important context for helping you understand the story's theme?

4. How do you interpret Applequist's name?

5. In what ways is Applequist like and unlike a robot at the beginning of the story?

6. When Applequist sees the robot (or, technically, android) up close for the first time he declares, "It was alive" (par. 34). How do you think he understands that word? What constitutes the line between being "alive" and being something else in this context?

7. When Applequist interrogates the robot about life before the war, what do his questions tell us about the story's critique of contemporary society?

8. Applequist's coworker Jenkins wants to join him to see what he's found, but Applequist insists on completing his work alone. Why is this insistence important? What does it reveal about Applequist as a character?

9. For what reasons is Applequist especially interested in the robot? For information about the past? For trusted companionship? For a way to get out of his routine? Justify your answer with evidence from the story.

10. How does the story comment on the relative value of work and leisure in human lives?

11. Applequist gets two versions of the story of the war: one from the robot and one from Director Laws. Should anything about the way they speak clue him in to which one is true?

12. How do you interpret the title of this story?

### CONNECTIONS TO OTHER SELECTIONS

1. Although they did not know each other, Philip K. Dick and Ursula K. Le Guin attended Berkeley High School at the same time. This fact might seem a mere coincidence, but do you see common themes in this story and in Le Guin's "The Ones Who Walk Away from Omelas" (p. 121)?

2. Discuss the theme of fate and free will in this story and in Ralph Ellison's "King of the Bingo Game" (p. 178).

# 12

# A Study of Alice Munro

PETER MUHKY/Getty Images.

For years and years I thought that stories were just practice, till I got time to write a novel. Then I found that they were all I could do, and so I faced that. I suppose that my trying to get so much into stories has been a compensation.
— ALICE MUNRO

## AN INTRODUCTION

The Nobel Prize in Literature is the most prestigious international award an author can receive. It is given not for a single work, but for a lifetime of achievement and it must be awarded to an author who is still living when the prizewinner is selected. Since it was first awarded in 1901, the Nobel Prize has been awarded to writers in twenty-five different languages who, according to the original guidelines, "confer the greatest benefit to mankind" in their work. Alice Munro, the author we are showcasing here, won the Nobel Prize in Literature in 2013 and is unique on the list of winners for

Munro's daughter, Jenny Munro, accepts the Nobel Prize in Literature on behalf of her mother on December 10, 2013.

Pascal Le Segretain/Getty Images.

two reasons: (1) she is the only Canadian to have won the prize, and (2) she is the only recipient known primarily — and actually exclusively — as a short story writer. Since her first collection in 1968 Munro has published fourteen collections of short stories as well as a number of compilations of selected stories. She is widely considered one of the most influential and most praised practitioners of the art of short fiction alive today.

Why, then, have you not heard of her before now? We may be presumptuous by asking that question — for all we know you read Munro's stories all the time — but we're fairly confident we're right. Margaret Atwood, a Canadian writer you're more likely to be familiar with for her work *The Handmaid's Tale*, acknowledges Munro's odd obscurity outside her native country: "Alice Munro has been among those writers subject to periodic rediscovery, at least outside Canada. It's as if she jumps out of a cake — *Surprise!* — and then has to jump out of it again, and then again. Readers don't see her name in lights on every billboard." Part of the reason, Atwood argues, is that Munro does not write novels, and those are the works that gain fiction writers the most fame, but the notion that Canada is often in the shadow of the United States is also at play. There is some truth to the sense that many famous Canadians are unknown even within the neighboring United States, with a few exceptions like Sidney Crosby, Drake, and Justin Bieber. Even Canadian geography baffles Americans who look at a map and marvel that such a vast landmass — the second largest country in the world — contains so few people, fewer than live in California. Munro, who writes mostly about a specific swath of land near Lake Huron in the province of Ontario, might in fact be better known if her native country were better understood.

## A BRIEF BIOGRAPHY

Alice Munro was born Alice Laidlaw in 1931 in the small town of Wingham, Ontario, a town over an hour west of Toronto, and nearly the same distance from the U.S. border near Detroit. Her mother, Anne Chamney, grew up on a farm and left that life to become a schoolteacher before marrying Robert Laidlaw. Laidlaw established himself as a farmer during the Great Depression, raising and selling

Alice Munro in 1979.
Fairfax Media Archives/Getty Images.

foxes for their fur. Munro, the oldest of three children, began elementary school at the Lower Town school, but starting in fourth grade she attended the Wingham schools. Her mother preferred that she attend the Wingham schools, partly to get a better education away from the poverty of her immediate neighborhood. Attendance at the new school involved a lengthy walk to and from school each day, and these walks exposed Munro to the class structure of her town. The Laidlaws were not wealthy; she describes her upbringing as working class.

When Munro turned twelve her family life began to deteriorate. Her mother was diagnosed with Parkinson's disease and her father's fox farm was no longer prosperous, forcing him to find other work as it became clear he would have to shut down the farm. As the eldest child, Munro's domestic duties increased due to her parents' troubles. Her social life in high school suffered as a result, but she dedicated herself to her studies. She graduated valedictorian of her class and was given a two-year scholarship to the University of Western Ontario, where she studied journalism before switching to English. She published her first story, "The Dimensions of a Shadow," in *Folio*, the undergraduate student journal, in 1950 at the age of nineteen. Writing quickly became at least as important as her general studies. She started dating Jim Munro that same year and by the end of 1951 they married. She was twenty years old.

When Munro turned twenty-one the next July her husband gave her a typewriter as a gift. This became a pivotal moment in her life's arc. Her scholarship money only lasted two years, and her decision to devote herself to her writing was perhaps at odds with the pressure to return to her hometown where she had spent her adolescence in a caretaking role. In her marriage she developed a domestic world based on but separate from the one of her youth. The couple moved to Vancouver, and Jim worked in an office while Munro stayed home and kept house, but also cultivated her interests in reading and writing. Between 1953 and 1957 she gave birth to three daughters.

Entrance and window display of Munro's Books in Victoria, British Columbia.
Gregory Perkins/Alamy.

Unfortunately, due to birth defects, her middle daughter did not survive beyond her first day. During this period, Munro sold a number of stories to the Canadian Broadcasting Company. Her mother died in 1959.

In the early 1960s Munro and her family moved to Victoria, the capital of British Columbia, and opened an independent bookstore called Munro's Books (which continues to flourish today, though it has moved twice from its original location). The initial years when Alice and Jim owned and operated the store were reportedly happy ones, but the marriage started to fray in the mid-1960s. Another daughter arrived in 1966 just after the Munros moved into a house that Munro didn't like, and it was becoming clear that the couple were leaning in opposite directions. Her first story collection, *Dance of the Happy Shades*, was published in 1968 and literary fame ensued. The marriage dissolved in the early 1970s and in 1973 she left British Columbia to return to her native Ontario where she dedicated herself to her craft.

The return to her home was significant for Munro, both personally and artistically. She reconnected with her father, and as the first two of the stories included here indicate, father-daughter relationships are important motifs in her work. She also reconnected with a man she had known at university, Gerald Fremlin, who became her second husband in 1976 (the same year her father died). Most significantly to her craft, she reconnected with the people and culture associated with Huron County. Although some of her stories take place outside this geographical location, the vast majority take place within it. Some writers are associated with a particular place so strongly that it is almost impossible to imagine one without the other: James Joyce and Dublin, William Faulkner and his fictional Yoknapatawpha County (based on his native Lafayette County, Mississippi), the Brontë sisters and West Yorkshire. Huron County would not be the same without Alice Munro, and she would not be the same without Huron County.

A collection of Munro's works on display.
JONATHAN NACKSTRAND/Getty Images.

Having settled into her new life, Munro dedicated herself to her craft, and the rest is literary history. As her reputation grew, she was given increased exposure through publishing venues, notably *The New Yorker*, the most visible venue for mainstream fiction writers over the past century. Yet even as her career took off, Munro remained relatively private, a tireless worker rather than a showboat. Perhaps another factor in explaining why she does not have the superstar status one might expect for someone who won as many literary awards as she has is that she doesn't seek the spotlight. She has only accepted one honorary degree (from the University of Western Ontario, where she got her start), and she also tends to refuse the visiting writer positions that often contribute to contemporary writers' reputations while also demanding that they give public readings and lectures. Munro has sought and achieved her notoriety fairly quietly, completing her work steadily and patiently.

In the excerpt that appears later in this chapter, from the interview she gave as a substitute for the traditional speech accepting the Nobel Prize, Munro claims she is "not political." This phrase can be widely interpreted and, depending on one's perspective of what fiction is for, criticized, but it is her honest understanding of that term. For years prior to Munro's award, the widespread opinion held that the Nobel foundation tended to prefer writers whose works were overtly political in nature. She might have been acknowledging that her motivation was to record, faithfully and artistically, the lives she both observed and lived, not to use those observations to make broader statements about human interaction. There may also be an implied acknowledgment that her work is quite different from that of her Canadian contemporary Margaret Atwood, whose fictional works take definite political stances against misogyny, environmental destruction, and capitalist greed, to name a few. Although Munro is still alive at the time of this writing, the consensus is that she has stopped writing stories for publication: her 2012 collection *Dear Life* is considered to be her final one.

## Walker Brothers Cowboy   1968

After supper my father says, "Want to go down and see if the Lake's still there?" We leave my mother sewing under the dining-room light, making clothes for me against the opening of school. She has ripped up for this purpose an old suit and an old plaid wool dress of hers, and she has to cut and match very cleverly and also make me stand and turn for endless fittings, sweaty, itching from the hot wool, ungrateful. We leave my brother in bed in the little screened porch at the end of the front veranda, and sometimes he kneels on his bed and presses his face against the screen and calls mournfully, "Bring me an ice-cream cone!" but I call back, "You will be asleep," and do not even turn my head.

Then my father and I walk gradually down a long, shabby sort of street, with Silverwoods Ice Cream signs standing on the sidewalk, outside tiny, lighted stores. This is in Tuppertown, an old town on Lake Huron, an old grain port. The street is shaded, in some places, by maple trees whose roots have cracked and heaved the sidewalk and spread out like crocodiles into the bare yards. People are sitting out, men in shirtsleeves and undershirts and women in aprons — not people we know but if anybody looks ready to nod and say, "Warm night," my father will nod too and say something the same. Children are still playing. I don't know them either because my mother keeps my brother and me in our own yard, saying he is too young to leave it and I have to mind him. I am not so sad to watch their evening games because the games themselves are ragged, dissolving. Children, of their own will, draw apart, separate into islands of two or one under the heavy trees, occupying themselves in such solitary ways as I do all day, planting pebbles in the dirt or writing in it with a stick.

Presently we leave these yards and houses behind; we pass a factory with boarded-up windows, a lumberyard whose high wooden gates are locked for the night. Then the town falls away in a defeated jumble of sheds and small junkyards, the sidewalk gives up and we are walking on a sandy path with burdocks, plantains, humble nameless weeds all around. We enter a vacant lot, a kind of park really, for it is kept clear of junk and there is one bench with a slat missing on the back, a place to sit and look at the water. Which is generally gray in the evening, under a lightly overcast sky, no sunsets, the horizon dim. A very quiet, washing noise on the stones of the beach. Further along, towards the main part of town, there is a stretch of sand, a water slide, floats bobbing around the safe swimming area, a lifeguard's rickety throne. Also a long dark-green building, like a roofed veranda, called the Pavilion, full of farmers and their wives, in stiff good clothes, on Sundays. That is the part of the town we used to know when we lived at Dungannon and came here three or four times a summer, to the Lake. That, and the docks where we would go and look at the grain boats, ancient, rusty, wallowing, making us wonder how they got past the breakwater let alone to Fort William.

Tramps hang around the docks and occasionally on these evenings wander up the dwindling beach and climb the shifting, precarious path boys have made, hanging on to dry bushes, and say something to my father which, being frightened of tramps, I am too alarmed to catch. My father says he is a bit hard up himself. "I'll roll you a cigarette if it's any use to you," he says, and he shakes tobacco out carefully on one of the thin butterfly papers, flicks it with his tongue, seals it and hands it to the tramp, who takes it and walks away. My father also rolls and lights and smokes one cigarette of his own.

He tells me how the Great Lakes came to be. All where Lake Huron is now, he says, used to be flat land, a wide flat plain. Then came the ice, creeping down from the North, pushing deep into the low places. Like *that* — and he shows me his hand with his spread fingers pressing the rock-hard ground where we are sitting. His fingers make hardly any impression at all and he says, "Well, the old ice cap had a lot more power behind it than this hand has." And then the ice went back, shrank back, towards the North Pole where it came from, and left its fingers of ice in the deep places it had gouged, and ice turned to lakes and there they were today. They were *new,* as time went. I try to see that plain before me, dinosaurs walking on it, but I am not able even to imagine the shore of the Lake when the Indians were there, before Tuppertown. The tiny share we have of time appalls me, though my father seems to regard it with tranquillity. Even my father, who sometimes seems to me to have been at home in the world as long as it has lasted, has really lived on this earth only a little longer than I have, in terms of all the time there has been to live in. He has not known a time, any more than I, when automobiles and electric lights did not at least exist. He was not alive when this century started. I will be barely alive — old, old — when it ends. I do not like to think of it. I wish the Lake to be always just a lake, with the safe-swimming floats marking it, and the breakwater and the lights of Tuppertown.

My father has a job, selling for Walker Brothers. This is a firm that sells almost entirely in the country, the back country. Sunshine, Boylesbridge, Turnaround — that is all his territory. Not Dungannon where we used to live, Dungannon is too near town and my mother is grateful for that. He sells cough medicine, iron tonic, corn plasters, laxatives, pills for female disorders, mouthwash, shampoo, liniment, salves, lemon and orange and raspberry concentrate for making refreshing drinks, vanilla, food coloring, black and green tea, ginger, cloves, and other spices, rat poison. He has a song about it, with these two lines:

> And have all liniments and oils,
> For everything from corns to boils. . . .

Not a very funny song, in my mother's opinion. A peddler's song, and that is what he is, a peddler knocking at backwoods kitchens. Up until last winter we had our own business, a fox farm. My father raised silver foxes and sold their pelts to the people who make them into capes and coats and muffs. Prices fell, my father hung on hoping they would get better next year, and they fell again, and he hung on one more year and one more and finally it was not possible to hang on anymore, we owed everything to the feed company. I have heard my mother explain this, several times, to Mrs. Oliphant, who is the only neighbor she talks to. (Mrs. Oliphant also has come down in the world, being a schoolteacher who married the janitor.) We poured all we had into it, my mother says, and we came out with nothing. Many people could say the same thing, these days, but my mother has no time for the national calamity°, only ours. Fate has flung us onto a street

---

*The national calamity:* This story takes place in the 1930s, during the Great Depression.

of poor people (it does not matter that we were poor before; that was a different sort of poverty), and the only way to take this, as she sees it, is with dignity, with bitterness, with no reconciliation. No bathroom with a claw-footed tub and a flush toilet is going to comfort her, nor water on tap and sidewalks past the house and milk in bottles, not even the two movie theatres and the Venus Restaurant and Woolworth's so marvellous it has live birds singing in its fan-cooled corners and fish as tiny as fingernails, as bright as moons, swimming in its green tanks. My mother does not care.

In the afternoons she often walks to Simon's Grocery and takes me with her to help carry things. She wears a good dress, navy blue with little flowers, sheer, worn over a navy-blue slip. Also a summer hat of white straw, pushed down on the side of the head, and white shoes I have just whitened on a newspaper on the back steps. I have my hair freshly done in long damp curls which the dry air will fortunately soon loosen, a stiff large hair ribbon on top of my head. This is entirely different from going out after supper with my father. We have not walked past two houses before I feel we have become objects of universal ridicule. Even the dirty words chalked on the sidewalk are laughing at us. My mother does not seem to notice. She walks serenely like a lady shopping, like a *lady* shopping, past the housewives in loose beltless dresses torn under the arms. With me her creation, wretched curls and flaunting hair bow, scrubbed knees and white socks — all I do not want to be. I loathe even my name when she says it in public, in a voice so high, proud, and ringing, deliberately different from the voice of any other mother on the street.

My mother will sometimes carry home, for a treat, a brick of ice cream — pale Neapolitan; and because we have no refrigerator in our house we wake my brother and eat it at once in the dining room, always darkened by the wall of the house next door. I spoon it up tenderly, leaving the chocolate till last, hoping to have some still to eat when my brother's dish is empty. My mother tries then to imitate the conversations we used to have at Dungannon, going back to our earliest, most leisurely days before my brother was born, when she would give me a little tea and a lot of milk in a cup like hers and we would sit out on the step facing the pump, the lilac tree, the fox pens beyond. She is not able to keep from mentioning those days. "Do you remember when we put you in your sled and Major pulled you?" (Major our dog, that we had to leave with neighbors when we moved.) "Do you remember your sandbox outside the kitchen window?" I pretend to remember far less than I do, wary of being trapped into sympathy or any unwanted emotion.

My mother has headaches. She often has to lie down. She lies on my brother's    10 narrow bed in the little screened porch, shaded by heavy branches. "I look up at that tree and I think I am at home," she says.

"What you need," my father tells her, "is some fresh air and a drive in the country." He means for her to go with him, on his Walker Brothers route.

That is not my mother's idea of a drive in the country.

"Can I come?"

"Your mother might want you for trying on clothes."

"I'm beyond sewing this afternoon," my mother says.    15

"I'll take her then. Take both of them, give you a rest."

What is there about us that people need to be given a rest from? Never mind. I am glad enough to find my brother and make him go to the toilet and get us both into the car, our knees unscrubbed, my hair unringleted. My father brings from the house his two heavy brown suitcases, full of bottles, and sets them on the back seat. He wears a white shirt, brilliant in the sunlight, a tie, light trousers belonging to his summer suit (his other suit is black, for funerals, and belonged to my uncle before he died), and a creamy straw hat. His salesman's outfit, with pencils clipped in the shirt pocket. He goes back once again, probably to say goodbye to my mother, to ask her if she is sure she doesn't want to come, and hear her say, "No. No thanks, I'm better just to lie here with my eyes closed." Then we are backing out of the driveway with the rising hope of adventure, just the little hope that takes you over the bump into the street, the hot air starting to move, turning into a breeze, the houses growing less and less familiar as we follow the shortcut my father knows, the quick way out of town. Yet what is there waiting for us all afternoon but hot hours in stricken farmyards, perhaps a stop at a country store and three ice-cream cones or bottles of pop, and my father singing? The one he made up about himself has a title — "The Walker Brothers Cowboy" — and it starts out like this:

> Old Ned Fields, he now is dead,
> So I am ridin' the route instead....

Who is Ned Fields? The man he has replaced, surely, and if so he really is dead; yet my father's voice is mournful-jolly, making his death some kind of nonsense, a comic calamity. "Wisht I was back on the Rio Grande, plungin' through the dusky sand." My father sings most of the time while driving the car. Even now, heading out of town, crossing the bridge and taking the sharp turn onto the highway, he is humming something, mumbling a bit of a song to himself, just tuning up, really, getting ready to improvise, for out along the highway we pass the Baptist Camp, the Vacation Bible Camp, and he lets loose:

> "Where are the Baptists, where are the Baptists,
> where are all the Baptists today?
> They're down in the water, in Lake Huron water,
> with their sins all a-gittin' washed away."

My brother takes this for straight truth and gets up on his knees trying to see down to the Lake. "I don't see any Baptists," he says accusingly. "Neither do I, son," says my father. "I told you, they're down in the Lake."

No roads paved when we left the highway. We have to roll up the windows 20 because of dust. The land is flat, scorched, empty. Bush lots at the back of the farms hold shade, black pine-shade like pools nobody can ever get to. We bump up a long lane and at the end of it what could look more unwelcoming, more deserted than the tall unpainted farmhouse with grass growing uncut right up to the front door, green blinds down, and a door upstairs opening on nothing but air? Many houses have this door, and I have never yet been able to find out why. I ask my father and he says they are for walking in your sleep. *What?* Well, if you happen to be walking in your sleep and you want to step outside. I am offended, seeing too late that he is joking, as usual, but my brother says sturdily, "If they did that they would break their necks."

The 1930s. How much this kind of farmhouse, this kind of afternoon seem to me to belong to that one decade in time, just as my father's hat does, his bright flared tie, our car with its wide running board (an Essex, and long past its prime). Cars somewhat like it, many older, none dustier, sit in the farmyards. Some are past running and have their doors pulled off, their seats removed for use on porches. No living things to be seen, chickens or cattle. Except dogs. There are dogs lying in any kind of shade they can find, dreaming, their lean sides rising and sinking rapidly. They get up when my father opens the car door, he has to speak to them. "Nice boy, there's a boy, nice old boy." They quiet down, go back to their shade.

He should know how to quiet animals, he has held desperate foxes with tongs around their necks. One gentling voice for the dogs and another, rousing, cheerful, for calling at doors. "Hello there, missus, it's the Walker Brothers man and what are you out of today?" A door opens, he disappears. Forbidden to follow, forbidden even to leave the car, we can just wait and wonder what he says. Sometimes trying to make my mother laugh, he pretends to be himself in a farm kitchen, spreading out his sample case. "Now then, missus, are you troubled with parasitic life? Your children's scalps, I mean. All those crawly little things we're too polite to mention that show up on the heads of the best of families? Soap alone is useless, kerosene is not too nice a perfume, but I have here — " Or else, "Believe me, sitting and driving all day the way I do I *know* the value of these fine pills. Natural relief. A problem common to old folks too, once their days of activity are over — How about you, Grandma?" He would wave the imaginary box of pills under my mother's nose and she would laugh finally, unwillingly. "He doesn't say that really, does he?" I said, and she said no of course not, he was too much of a gentleman.

One yard after another, then, the old cars, the pumps, dogs, views of gray barns and falling-down sheds and unturning windmills. The men, if they are working in the fields, are not in any fields that we can see. The children are far away, following dry creek beds or looking for blackberries, or else they are hidden in the house, spying at us through cracks in the blinds. The car seat has grown slick with our sweat. I dare my brother to sound the horn, wanting to do it myself but not wanting to get the blame. He knows better. We play I Spy, but it is hard to find many colors. Gray for the barns and sheds and toilets and houses, brown for the yard and fields, black or brown for the dogs. The rusting cars show rainbow patches, in which I strain to pick out purple or green; likewise I peer at doors for shreds of old peeling paint, maroon or yellow. We can't play with letters, which would be better, because my brother is too young to spell. The game disintegrates anyway. He claims my colors are not fair, and wants extra turns.

In one house no door opens, though the car is in the yard. My father knocks and whistles, calls, "Hullo there! Walker Brothers man!" but there is not a stir of reply anywhere. This house has no porch, just a bare, slanting slab of cement on which my father stands. He turns around, searching the barnyard, the barn whose mow must be empty because you can see the sky through it, and finally he bends to pick up his suitcases. Just then a window is opened upstairs, a white pot appears on the sill, is tilted over and its contents splash down the outside wall. The window is not directly above my father's head, so only a stray splash would catch him. He picks up his suitcases with no particular hurry and walks, no longer whistling, to the car. "Do you know what that was?" I say to my brother. "*Pee.*" He laughs and laughs.

My father rolls and lights a cigarette before he starts the car. The window has been slammed down, the blind drawn, we never did see a hand or face. "Pee, pee," sings my brother ecstatically. "Somebody dumped down pee!" "Just don't tell your mother that" my father says. "She isn't liable to see the joke." "Is it in your song?" my brother wants to know. My father says no but he will see what he can do to work it in.

I notice in a little while that we are not turning in any more lanes, though it does not seem to me that we are headed home. "Is this the way to Sunshine?" I ask my father, and he answers, "No, ma'am, it's not." "Are we still in your territory?" He shakes his head. "We're going *fast*," my brother says approvingly, and in fact we are bouncing along through dry puddle-holes so that all the bottles in the suitcases clink together and gurgle promisingly.

Another lane, a house, also unpainted, dried to silver in the sun.

"I thought we were out of your territory."

"We are."

"Then what are we going in here for?"

"You'll see."                                                                                                                     30

In front of the house a short, sturdy woman is picking up washing, which had been spread on the grass to bleach and dry. When the car stops she stares at it hard for a moment, bends to pick up a couple more towels to add to the bundle under her arm, comes across to us and says in a flat voice, neither welcoming nor unfriendly, "Have you lost your way?"

My father takes his time getting out of the car. "I don't think so," he says. "I'm the Walker Brothers man."

"George Golley is our Walker Brothers man," the woman says, "and he was out here no more than a week ago. Oh, my Lord God," she says harshly, "it's you."

"It was, the last time I looked in the mirror," my father says.

The woman gathers all the towels in front of her and holds on to them tightly,   35 pushing them against her stomach as if it hurt. "Of all the people I never thought to see. And telling me you were the Walker Brothers man."

"I'm sorry if you were looking forward to George Golley," my father says humbly.

"And look at me, I was prepared to clean the henhouse. You'll think that's just an excuse but it's true. I don't go round looking like this every day." She is wearing a farmer's straw hat, through which pricks of sunlight penetrate and float on her face, a loose, dirty print smock, and canvas shoes. "Who are those in the car, Ben? They're not yours?"

"Well, I hope and believe they are," my father says, and tells our names and ages. "Come on, you can get out. This is Nora, Miss Cronin. Nora, you better tell me, is it still Miss, or have you got a husband hiding in the woodshed?"

"If I had a husband that's not where I'd keep him, Ben," she says, and they both laugh, her laugh abrupt and somewhat angry. "You'll think I got no manners, as well as being dressed like a tramp," she says. "Come on in out of the sun. It's cool in the house."

We go across the yard ("Excuse me taking you in this way but I don't think the   40 front door has been opened since Papa's funeral, I'm afraid the hinges might drop off"), up the porch steps, into the kitchen, which really is cool, high-ceilinged, the blinds of course down, a simple, clean, threadbare room with waxed worn lino-leum, potted geraniums, drinking-pail and dipper, a round table with scrubbed oilcloth. In spite of the cleanness, the wiped and swept surfaces, there is a faint sour smell — maybe of the dishrag or the tin dipper or the oilcloth, or the old lady, because there is one, sitting in an easy chair under the clock shelf. She turns her head slightly in our direction and says, "Nora? Is that company?" '

"Blind," says Nora in a quick explaining voice to my father. Then, "You won't guess who it is, Momma. Hear his voice."

My father goes to the front of her chair and bends and says hopefully, "After-noon, Mrs. Cronin."

"Ben Jordan," says the old lady with no surprise. "You haven't been to see us in the longest time. Have you been out of the country?"

My father and Nora look at each other.

"He's married, Momma," says Nora cheerfully and aggressively. "Married and 45 got two children and here they are." She pulls us forward, makes each of us touch the old lady's dry, cool hand while she says our names in turn. Blind! This is the first blind person I have ever seen close up. Her eyes are closed, the eyelids sunk away down, showing no shape of the eyeball, just hollows. From one hollow comes a drop of silver liquid, a medicine, or a miraculous tear.

"Let me get into a decent dress," Nora says. "Talk to Momma. It's a treat for her. We hardly ever see company, do we, Momma?"

"Not many makes it out this road," says the old lady placidly. "And the ones that used to be around here, our old neighbors, some of them have pulled out."

"True everywhere," my father says.

"Where's your wife then?"

"Home. She's not too fond of the hot weather, makes her feel poorly." 50

"Well." This is a habit of country people, old people, to say "well," meaning, "Is that so?" with a little extra politeness and concern.

Nora's dress, when she appears again — stepping heavily on Cuban heels down the stairs in the hall — is flowered more lavishly than anything my mother owns, green and yellow on brown, some sort of floating sheer crêpe, leaving her arms bare. Her arms are heavy, and every bit of her skin you can see is covered with little dark freckles like measles. Her hair is short, black, coarse and curly, her teeth very white and strong. "It's the first time I knew there was such a thing as green poppies," my father says, looking at her dress.

"You would be surprised all the things you never knew," says Nora, sending a smell of cologne far and wide when she moves and displaying a change of voice to go with the dress, something more sociable and youthful. "They're not poppies anyway, they're just flowers. You go and pump me some good cold water and I'll make these children a drink." She gets down from the cupboard a bottle of Walker Brothers Orange syrup.

"You telling me you were the Walker Brothers man!"

"It's the truth, Nora. You go and look at my sample cases in the car if you don't 55 believe me. I got the territory directly south of here."

"Walker Brothers? Is that a fact? You selling for Walker Brothers?" "Yes, ma'am."

"We always heard you were raising foxes over Dungannon way."

"That's what I was doing, but I kind of run out of luck in that business."

"So where're you living? How long've you been out selling?"

"We moved into Tuppertown. I been at it, oh, two, three months. It keeps the 60 wolf from the door. Keeps him as far away as the back fence."

Nora laughs. "Well, I guess you count yourself lucky to have the work. Isabel's husband in Brantford, he was out of work the longest time. I thought if he didn't find something soon I was going to have them all land in here to feed, and I tell you I was hardly looking forward to it. It's all I can manage with me and Momma."

"Isabel married," my father says. "Muriel married too?"

"No, she's teaching school out West. She hasn't been home for five years. I guess she finds something better to do with her holidays. I would if I was her." She gets some snapshots out of the table drawer and starts showing him. "That's Isabel's oldest boy, starting school. That's the baby sitting in her carriage. Isabel and her husband. Muriel. That's her roommate with her. That's a fellow she used to go around with, and his car. He was working in a bank out there. That's her school, it has eight rooms. She teaches Grade Five." My father shakes his head. "I can't think of her any way but when she was going to school, so shy I used to pick her up on the road — I'd be on my way to see you — and she would not say one word, not even to agree it was a nice day."

"She's got over that."

"Who are you talking about?" says the old lady. 65

"Muriel. I said she's got over being shy."

"She was here last summer."

"No, Momma, that was Isabel. Isabel and her family were here last summer. Muriel's out West."

"I meant Isabel."

Shortly after this the old lady falls asleep, her head on the side, her mouth 70 open. "Excuse her manners," Nora says. "It's old age." She fixes an afghan over her mother and says we can all go into the front room where our talking won't disturb her.

"You two," my father says. "Do you want to go outside and amuse yourselves?"

Amuse ourselves how? Anyway, I want to stay. The front room is more interesting than the kitchen, though barer. There is a gramophone and a pump organ and a picture on the wall of Mary, Jesus' mother — I know that much — in shades of bright blue and pink with a spiked band of light around her head. I know that such pictures are found only in the homes of Roman Catholics and so Nora must be one. We have never known any Roman Catholics at all well, never well enough to visit in their houses. I think of what my grandmother and my Aunt Tena, over in Dungannon, used to always say to indicate that somebody was a Catholic. *So-and-so digs with the wrong foot,* they would say. *She digs with the wrong foot.* That was what they would say about Nora.

Nora takes a bottle, half full, out of the top of the organ and pours some of what is in it into the two glasses that she and my father have emptied of the orange drink.

"Keep it in case of sickness?" my father says.

"Not on your life," says Nora. "I'm never sick. I just keep it because I keep it. 75 One bottle does me a fair time, though, because I don't care for drinking alone. Here's luck!" She and my father drink and I know what it is. Whisky. One of the things my mother has told me in our talks together is that my father never drinks whisky. But I see he does. He drinks whisky and he talks of people whose names I have never heard before. But after a while he turns to a familiar incident. He tells about the chamberpot that was emptied out the window. "Picture me there," he says, "hollering my heartiest. *Oh, lady, it's your Walker Brothers man, anybody home?*" He does himself hollering, grinning absurdly, waiting, looking up in pleased expectation, and then — oh, ducking, covering his head with his arms, looking as if he begged for mercy (when he never did anything like that, I was watching), and Nora laughs, almost as hard as my brother did at the time.

"That isn't true! That's not a word true!"

"Oh, indeed it is, ma'am. We have our heroes in the ranks of Walker Brothers. I'm glad you think it's funny," he says sombrely.

I ask him shyly, "Sing the song."

"What song? Have you turned into a singer on top of everything else?"

Embarrassed, my father says, "Oh, just this song I made up while I was driving 80 around, it gives me something to do, making up rhymes."

But after some urging he does sing it, looking at Nora with a droll, apologetic expression, and she laughs so much that in places he has to stop and wait for her to get over laughing so he can go on, because she makes him laugh too. Then he does various parts of his salesman's spiel. Nora when she laughs squeezes her large bosom under her folded arms. "You're crazy," she says. "That's all you are." She sees my brother peering into the gramophone and she jumps up and goes over to him. "Here's us sitting enjoying ourselves and not giving you a thought, isn't it terrible?" she says. "You want me to put a record on, don't you? You want to hear a nice record? Can you dance? I bet your sister can, can't she?"

I say no. "A big girl like you and so good-looking and can't dance!" says Nora. "It's high time you learned. I bet you'd make a lovely dancer. Here, I'm going to put on a piece I used to dance to and even your daddy did, in his dancing days. You didn't know your daddy was a dancer, did you? Well, he is a talented man, your daddy!"

She puts down the lid and takes hold of me unexpectedly around the waist, picks up my other hand, and starts making me go backwards. "This is the way, now, this is how they dance. Follow me. This foot, see. One and one-two. One and one-two. That's fine, that's lovely, don't look at your feet! Follow me, that's right, see how easy? You're going to be a lovely dancer! One and one-two. One and one-two. Ben, see your daughter dancing!" *Whispering while you cuddle near me, Whispering so no one can hear me....*

Round and round the linoleum, me proud, intent, Nora laughing and moving with great buoyancy, wrapping me in her strange gaiety, her smell of whisky, cologne, and sweat. Under the arms her dress is damp, and little drops form along her upper lip, hang in the soft black hairs at the corners of her mouth. She whirls me around in front of my father — causing me to stumble, for I am by no means so swift a pupil as she pretends — and lets me go, breathless.

"Dance with me, Ben."                                                                                                          85

"I'm the world's worst dancer, Nora, and you know it."

"I certainly never thought so."

"You would now."

She stands in front of him, arms hanging loose and hopeful, her breasts, which a moment ago embarrassed me with their warmth and bulk, rising and falling under her loose flowered dress, her face shining with the exercise, and delight.

"Ben."                                                                                                                         90

My father drops his head and says quietly, "Not me, Nora."

So she can only go and take the record off. "I can drink alone but I can't dance alone," she says. "Unless I am a whole lot crazier than I think I am."

"Nora," says my father, smiling. "You're not crazy."

"Stay for supper."

"Oh, no. We couldn't put you to the trouble."                                                                                95

"It's no trouble. I'd be glad of it."

"And their mother would worry. She'd think I'd turned us over in a ditch."

"Oh, well. Yes."

"We've taken a lot of your time now."

"Time," says Nora bitterly. "Will you come by ever again?"                                                                   100

"I will if I can," says my father.

"Bring the children. Bring your wife."

"Yes, I will," says my father. "I will if I can."

When she follows us to the car he says, "You come to see us too, Nora. We're right on Grove Street, left-hand side going in, that's north, and two doors this side — east — of Baker Street."

Nora does not repeat these directions. She stands close to the car in her 105 soft, brilliant dress. She touches the fender, making an unintelligible mark in the dust there.

On the way home my father does not buy any ice cream or pop, but he does go into a country store and get a package of licorice, which he shares with us. She digs with the wrong foot, I think, and the words seem sad to me as never before, dark, perverse. My father does not say anything to me about not mentioning things at home, but I know, just from the thoughtfulness, the pause when he passes the licorice, that there are things not to be mentioned. The whisky, maybe the dancing. No worry about my brother, he does not notice enough. At most he might remember the blind lady, the picture of Mary.

"Sing," my brother commands my father, but my father says gravely, "I don't know, I seem to be fresh out of songs. You watch the road and let me know if you see any rabbits."

So my father drives and my brother watches the road for rabbits and I feel my father's life flowing back from our car in the last of the afternoon, darkening and turning strange, like a landscape that has an enchantment on it, making it kindly, ordinary and familiar while you are looking at it, but changing it, once your back is turned, into something you will never know, with all kinds of weathers, and distances you cannot imagine.

When we get closer to Tuppertown the sky becomes gently overcast, as always, nearly always, on summer evenings by the Lake.

## CONSIDERATIONS FOR CRITICAL THINKING AND WRITING

1. FIRST RESPONSE. After finishing the story, look back at the first five paragraphs, where a great deal of attention is paid to establishing setting: Does anything about it prepare you for the story's important shifts?

2. "Walker Brothers Cowboy" takes place in the 1930s, when roles available to men and women were scripted. The parents in this story take on traditional work roles: the father is a traveling salesman and the mother sews clothes at home. How does the story comment on the way those roles shape the behavior and personalities of the narrator's parents?

3. Are the narrator and her brother fated to follow the pattern established by their mother and father, respectively? Use evidence from the text to substantiate your response.

4. What is the narrator's attitude toward the past and the future? Do they help her understand her present more clearly or do they cloud her perception of it?

5. The story's title is also the title of the song the narrator's father improvises when he is out selling goods. What role do the song lyrics play in the story?

6. What is the relationship between the narrator's family and the rest of their community? What are some key details that lead to your interpretation?

7. Ben, the narrator's father, is a clown: we can tell that from the story's beginning. It also becomes clear as the story goes on that he is a liar. Does your opinion of him change? If so, at what point in the story?

8. The narrator and her brother are mostly silent during the encounter between their father and Nora. How are they feeling as the scene takes place? What clues or details help you determine their emotions?

9. How does the narrator feel about Nora, especially in contrast to her mother?

10. The narrator senses that she shouldn't speak of this day ever again: "there are things not to be mentioned" (par. 106). How do you interpret this silence? Is it an alliance with her father, compliance with a code of repression, a growing knowledge of the world of adulthood that contains necessary secrets, or something else entirely?

11. The narrator has a revelation in the story's penultimate paragraph as she sees her father's life story "darkening and turning strange" (par. 108). Interpret this revelation: Does she feel sorry for him? Does she feel closer or more distant from him?

## CONNECTIONS TO OTHER SELECTIONS

1. Compare the depiction of fathers in this story and in Tobias Woolf's "Powder" (p. 72). Define what it means to be a good father, and then determine (if you're able) which of these characters is a better father, according to your definition.

2. Discuss the notion of secrets within families in this story and in David Long's "Morphine" (p. 282).

## *The Moons of Jupiter*   1977

I found my father in the heart wing, on the eighth floor of Toronto General Hospital. He was in a semi-private room. The other bed was empty. He said that his hospital insurance covered only a bed in the ward, and he was worried that he might be charged extra.

"I never asked for a semi-private," he said.

I said the wards were probably full.

"No. I saw some empty beds when they were wheeling me by."

"Then it was because you had to be hooked up to that thing," I said. "Don't 5 worry. If they're going to charge you extra, they tell you about it."

"That's likely it," he said. "They wouldn't want those doohickeys set up in the wards. I guess I'm covered for that kind of thing."

I said I was sure he was.

He had wires taped to his chest. A small screen hung over his head. On the screen a bright jagged line was continually being written. The writing was accompanied by a nervous electronic beeping. The behavior of his heart was on display. I tried to ignore it. It seemed to me that paying such close attention — in fact, dramatizing what ought to be a most secret activity — was asking for trouble. Anything exposed that way was apt to flare up and go crazy.

My father did not seem to mind. He said they had him on tranquillizers. You know, he said, the happy pills. He did seem calm and optimistic.

It had been a different story the night before. When I brought him into the 10 hospital, to the emergency room, he had been pale and closemouthed. He had opened the car door and stood up and said quietly, "Maybe you better get me one of those wheelchairs." He used the voice he always used in a crisis. Once, our chimney caught on fire; it was on a Sunday afternoon and I was in the dining room pinning together a dress I was making. He came in and said in that same matter-of-fact, warning voice, "Janet. Do you know where there's some baking powder?" He wanted it to throw on the fire. Afterwards he said, "I guess it was your fault — sewing on Sunday."

I had to wait for over an hour in the emergency waiting room. They summoned a heart specialist who was in the hospital, a young man. He called me out into the hall and explained to me that one of the valves of my father's heart had deteriorated so badly that there ought to be an immediate operation.

I asked him what would happen otherwise.

"He'd have to stay in bed," the doctor said.

"How long?"

"Maybe three months."                                                           15

"I meant, how long would he live?"

"That's what I meant too," the doctor said.

I went to see my father. He was sitting up in bed in a curtained-off corner. "It's bad, isn't it?" he said. "Did he tell you about the valve?"

"It's not as bad as it could be," I said. Then I repeated, even exaggerated, anything hopeful the doctor had said. "You're not in any immediate danger. Your physical condition is good, otherwise."

"Otherwise," said my father gloomily.                                           20

I was tired from the drive — all the way up to Dalgleish, to get him, and back to Toronto since noon — and worried about getting the rented car back on time, and irritated by an article I had been reading in a magazine in the waiting room. It was about another writer, a woman younger, better-looking, probably more talented than I am. I had been in England for two months and so I had not seen this article before, but it crossed my mind while I was reading that my father would have. I could hear him saying, Well, I didn't see anything about you in *Maclean's*. And if he had read something about me he would say, Well, I didn't think too much of that write-up. His tone would be humorous and indulgent but would produce in me a familiar dreariness of spirit. The message I got from him was simple: Fame must be striven for, then apologized for. Getting or not getting it, you will be to blame.

I was not surprised by the doctor's news. I was prepared to hear something of the sort and was pleased with myself for taking it calmly, just as I would be pleased with myself for dressing a wound or looking down from the frail balcony of a high building. I thought, Yes, it's time; there has to be something, here it is. I did not feel any of the protest I would have felt twenty, even ten, years before. When I saw from my father's face that he felt it — that refusal leapt up in him as readily as if he had been thirty or forty years younger — my heart hardened, and I spoke with a kind of badgering cheerfulness. "Otherwise is plenty," I said.

The next day he was himself again.

That was how I would have put it. He said it appeared to him now that the young fellow, the doctor, might have been a bit too eager to operate. "A bit knife-happy," he said. He was both mocking and showing off the hospital slang. He said that another doctor had examined him, an older man, and had given it as his opinion that rest and medication might do the trick.

I didn't ask what trick.                                                        25

"He says I've got a defective valve, all right. There's certainly some damage. They wanted to know if I had rheumatic fever when I was a kid. I said I didn't think so. But half the time then you weren't diagnosed what you had. My father was not one for getting the doctor."

The thought of my father's childhood, which I always pictured as bleak and dangerous — the poor farm, the scared sisters, the harsh father — made me less resigned to his dying. I thought of him running away to work on the lake boats, running along the railway tracks, toward Goderich, in the evening light. He used to tell about that trip. Somewhere along the track he found a quince tree. Quince trees are rare in our part of the country; in fact, I have never seen one. Not even the one my father found, though he once took us on an expedition to look for it. He thought he knew the crossroad it was near, but we could not find it. He had not been able to eat the fruit, of course, but he had been impressed by its existence. It made him think he had got into a new part of the world.

The escaped child, the survivor, an old man trapped here by his leaky heart. I didn't pursue these thoughts. I didn't care to think of his younger selves. Even his bare torso, thick and white — he had the body of a working-man of his generation, seldom exposed to the sun — was a danger to me; it looked so strong and young. The wrinkled neck, the age-freckled hands and arms, the narrow, courteous head, with its thin gray hair and mustache, were more what I was used to.

"Now, why would I want to get myself operated on?" said my father reasonably. "Think of the risk at my age, and what for? A few years at the outside. I think the best thing for me to do is go home and take it easy. Give in gracefully. That's all you can do, at my age. Your attitude changes, you know. You go through some mental changes. It seems more natural."

"What does?" I said. 30

"Well, death does. You can't get more natural than that. No, what I mean, specifically, is not having the operation."

"That seems more natural?"

"Yes."

"It's up to you," I said, but I did approve. This was what I would have expected of him. Whenever I told people about my father I stressed his independence, his self-sufficiency, his forbearance. He worked in a factory, he worked in his garden, he read history books. He could tell you about the Roman emperors or the Balkan wars. He never made a fuss.

Judith, my younger daughter, had come to meet me at Toronto Airport two days 35 before. She had brought the boy she was living with, whose name was Don. They were driving to Mexico in the morning, and while I was in Toronto I was to stay in their apartment. For the time being, I live in Vancouver. I sometimes say I have my headquarters in Vancouver.

"Where's Nichola?" I said, thinking at once of an accident or an overdose. Nichola is my older daughter. She used to be a student at the Conservatory, then she became a cocktail waitress, then she was out of work. If she had been at the airport, I would probably have said something wrong. I would have asked her what her plans were, and she would have gracefully brushed back her hair and said, "Plans?" — as if that was a word I had invented,

"I knew the first thing you'd say would be about Nichola," Judith said.

"It wasn't. I said hello and I — "

"We'll get your bag," Don said neutrally.

"Is she all right?" 40

"I'm sure she is," said Judith, with a fabricated air of amusement. "You wouldn't look like that if I was the one who wasn't here."

"Of course I would."

"You wouldn't. Nichola is the baby of the family. You know, she's four years older than I am."

"I ought to know."

Judith said she did not know where Nichola was exactly. She said Nichola had 45 moved out of her apartment (that dump!) and had actually telephoned (which is quite a deal, you might say, Nichola phoning) to say she wanted to be incommunicado for a while but she was fine.

"I told her you would worry," said Judith more kindly on the way to their van. Don walked ahead carrying my suitcase. "But don't. She's all right, believe me."

Don's presence made me uncomfortable. I did not like him to hear these things. I thought of the conversations they must have had, Don and Judith. Or Don and Judith and Nichola, for Nichola and Judith were sometimes on good terms. Or Don and Judith and Nichola and others whose names I did not even know. They would have talked about me. Judith and Nichola comparing notes, relating anecdotes; analyzing, regretting, blaming, forgiving. I wished I'd had a boy and a girl. Or two boys. They wouldn't have done that. Boys couldn't possibly know so much about you.

I did the same thing at that age. When I was the age Judith is now I talked with my friends in the college cafeteria or, late at night, over coffee in our cheap rooms. When I was the age Nichola is now I had Nichola herself in a carry-cot or squirming in my lap, and I was drinking coffee again all the rainy Vancouver afternoons with my one neighborhood friend, Ruth Boudreau, who read a lot and was bewildered by her situation, as I was. We talked about our parents, our childhoods, though for some time we kept clear of our marriages. How thoroughly we dealt with our fathers and mothers, deplored their marriages, their mistaken ambitions or fear of ambition, how competently we filed them away, defined them beyond any possibility of change. What presumption.

I looked at Don walking ahead. A tall ascetic-looking boy, with a St. Francis cap of black hair, a precise fringe of beard. What right did he have to hear about me, to know things I myself had probably forgotten? I decided that his beard and hairstyle were affected.

Once, when my children were little, my father said to me, "You know those 50 years you were growing up — well, that's all just a kind of a blur to me. I can't sort out one year from another." I was offended. I remembered each separate year with pain and clarity. I could have told how old I was when I went to look at the evening dresses in the window of Benbow's Ladies' Wear. Every week through the winter a new dress, spotlit — the sequins and tulle, the rose and lilac, sapphire, daffodil — and me a cold worshipper on the slushy sidewalk. I could have told how old I was when I forged my mother's signature on a bad report card, when I had measles, when we papered the front room. But the years when Judith and Nichola were little, when I lived with their father — yes, *blur* is the word for it. I remember hanging out diapers, bringing in and folding diapers; I can recall the kitchen counters of two houses and where the clothesbasket sat. I remember the television programs — *Popeye the Sailor, The Three Stooges, Funorama.* When *Funorama* came on it was time to turn on the lights and cook supper. But I couldn't tell the years apart. We lived outside Vancouver in a dormitory suburb: Dormir, Dormer, Dormouse — something like that. I was sleepy all the time then; pregnancy made me sleepy, and the night feedings, and the west coast rain falling. Dark dripping cedars, shiny dripping laurel; wives yawning, napping, visiting, drinking coffee, and folding diapers; husbands coming home at night from the city across the water. Every night I kissed my homecoming husband in his wet Burberry and hoped he might wake me up; I served up meat and potatoes and one of the four vegetables he permitted. He ate with a violent appetite, then fell asleep on the living-room sofa. We had become a cartoon couple, more middle-aged in our twenties than we would be in middle age.

Those bumbling years are the years our children will remember all their lives. Corners of the yards I never visited will stay in their heads.

"Did Nichola not want to see me?" I said to Judith.

"She doesn't want to see anybody, half the time;" she said. Judith moved ahead and touched Don's arm. I knew that touch — an apology, an anxious reassurance. You touch a man that way to remind him that you are grateful, that you realize he is doing for your sake something that bores him or slightly endangers his dignity. It made me feel older than grandchildren would to see my daughter touch a man — a boy — this way. I felt her sad jitters, could predict her supple attentions. My blunt and stocky, blond and candid child. Why should I think she wouldn't be suscepti-ble, that she would always be straight forward, heavy-footed, self-reliant? Just as I go around saying that Nichola is sly and solitary, cold, seductive. Many people must know things that would contradict what I say.

In the morning Don and Judith left for Mexico. I decided I wanted to see somebody who wasn't related to me, and who didn't expect anything in particular from me. I called an old lover of mine, but his phone was answered by a machine: "This is Tom Shepherd speaking. I will be out of town for the month of September. Please record your message, name, and phone number."

Tom's voice sounded so pleasant and familiar that I opened my mouth to ask   55 him the meaning of this foolishness. Then I hung up. I felt as if he had deliberately let me down, as if we had planned to meet in a public place and then he hadn't shown up. Once, he had done that, I remembered.

I got myself a glass of vermouth, though it was not yet noon, and I phoned my father.

"Well, of all things," he said. "Fifteen more minutes and you would have missed me."

"Were you going downtown?"

"Downtown Toronto."

He explained that he was going to the hospital. His doctor in Dalgleish wanted   60 the doctors in Toronto to take a look at him, and had given him a letter to show them in the emergency room.

"Emergency room?" I said.

"It's not an emergency. He just seems to think this is the best way to handle it. He knows the name of a fellow there. If he was to make me an appointment, it might take weeks."

"Does your doctor know you're driving to Toronto?" I said.

"Well, he didn't say I couldn't."

The upshot of this was that I rented a car, drove to Dalgleish, brought my   65 father back to Toronto, and had him in the emergency room by seven o'clock that evening.

Before Judith left I said to her, "You're sure Nichola knows I'm staying here?"

"Well, I told her," she said.

Sometimes the phone rang, but it was always a friend of Judith's.

"Well, it looks like I'm going to have it," my father said. This was on the fourth day. He had done a complete turnaround overnight. "It looks like I might as well."

I didn't know what he wanted me to say. I thought perhaps he looked to me for 70
a protest, an attempt to dissuade him.

"When will they do it?" I said.

"Day after tomorrow."

I said I was going to the washroom. I went to the nurses' station and found a woman there who I thought was the head nurse. At any rate, she was gray-haired, kind, and serious-looking.

"My father's having an operation the day after tomorrow?" I said.

"Oh, yes." 75

"I just wanted to talk to somebody about it. I thought there'd been a sort of decision reached that he'd be better not to. I thought because of his age."

"Well, it's his decision and the doctor's." She smiled at me without condescension. "It's hard to make these decisions."

"How were his tests?"

"Well, I haven't seen them all."

I was sure she had. After a moment she said, "We have to be realistic. But the 80 doctors here are very good."

When I went back into the room my father said, in a surprised voice, "*Shore*-less seas."

"What?" I said. I wondered if he had found out how much, or how little, time he could hope for. I wondered if the pills had brought on an untrustworthy euphoria. Or if he had wanted to gamble. Once, when he was talking to me about his life, he said, "The trouble was I was always afraid to take chances."

I used to tell people that he never spoke regretfully about his life, but that was not true. It was just that I didn't listen to it. He said that he should have gone into the Army as a tradesman — he would have been better off. He said he should have gone on his own, as a carpenter, after the war. He should have got out of Dalgleish. Once, he said, "A wasted life, eh?" But he was making fun of himself, saying that, because it was such a dramatic thing to say. When he quoted poetry too, he always had a scoffing note in his voice, to excuse the showing-off and the pleasure.

"Shoreless seas," he said again. " 'Behind him lay the gray Azores, / Behind the Gates of Hercules; / Before him not the ghost of shores, / Before him only shoreless seas°.' That's what was going through my head last night. But do you think I could remember what kind of seas? I could not. Lonely seas? Empty seas? I was on the right track but I couldn't get it. But there now when you came into the room and I wasn't thinking about it at all, the word popped into my head. That's always the way, isn't it? It's not all that surprising. I ask my mind a question. The answer's there, but I can't see all the connections my mind's making to get it. Like a computer. Nothing out of the way. You know, in my situation the thing is, if there's anything you can't explain right away, there's a great temptation to — well, to make a mystery out of it. There's a great temptation to believe in — You know."

"The soul?" I said, speaking lightly, feeling an appalling rush of love and 85 recognition.

"Oh, I guess you could call it that. You know, when I first came into this room there was a pile of papers here by the bed. Somebody had left them here — one of those tabloid sort of things I never looked at. I started reading them. I'll read anything handy. There was a series running in them on personal experiences of people

*Behind him lay the gray Azores...*: A quotation from the 1900 poem "Columbus" by the American poet Joaquin Miller (1837–1913).

who had died, medically speaking — heart arrest, mostly — and had been brought back to life. It was what they remembered of the time when they were dead. Their experiences."

"Pleasant or un-?" I said.

"Oh, pleasant. Oh, yes. They'd float up to the ceiling and look down on themselves and see the doctors working on them, on their bodies. Then float on further and recognize some people they knew who had died before them. Not see them exactly but sort of sense them. Sometimes there would be a humming and sometimes a sort of — what's that light that there is or color around a person?"

"Aura?"

"Yes. But without the person. That's about all they'd get time for; then 90 they found themselves back in the body and feeling all the mortal pain and so on — brought back to life."

"Did it seem — convincing?"

"Oh, I don't know. It's all in whether you want to believe that kind of thing or not. And if you are going to believe it, take it seriously, I figure you've got to take everything else seriously that they print in those papers."

"What else do they?"

"Rubbish — cancer cures, baldness cures, bellyaching about the younger generation and the welfare bums. Tripe about movie stars."

"Oh, yes. I know."                                                               95

"In my situation you have to keep a watch," he said, "or you'll start playing tricks on yourself." Then he said, "There's a few practical details we ought to get straight on," and he told me about his will, the house, the cemetery plot. Everything was simple.

"Do you want me to phone Peggy?" I said. Peggy is my sister. She is married to an astronomer and lives in Victoria.

He thought about it. "I guess we ought to tell them," he said finally. "But tell them not to get alarmed."

"All right."

"No, wait a minute. Sam is supposed to be going to a conference the end of 100 this week, and Peggy was planning to go along with him. I don't want them wondering about changing their plans."

"Where is the conference?"

"Amsterdam," he said proudly. He did take pride in Sam, and kept track of his books and articles. He would pick one up and say, "Look at that, will you? And I can't understand a word of it!" in a marvelling voice that managed nevertheless to have a trace of ridicule.

"Professor Sam," he would say. "And the three little Sams." This is what he called his grandsons, who did resemble their father in braininess and in an almost endearing pushiness — an innocent energetic showing-off. They went to a private school that favored old-fashioned discipline and started calculus in Grade 5. "And the dogs," he might enumerate further, "who have been to obedience school. And Peggy . . ."

But if I said, "Do you suppose she has been to obedience school too?" he would play the game no further. I imagine that when he was with Sam and Peggy he spoke of me in the same way — hinted at my flightiness just as he hinted at their stodginess, made mild jokes at my expense, did not quite conceal his amazement (or pretended not to conceal his amazement) that people paid money for things I had written. He had to do this so that he might never seem to brag, but he would put up the gates when the joking got too rough. And of course I found later, in the house, things of mine he had kept — a few magazines, clippings, things I had never bothered about.

Now his thoughts travelled from Peggy's family to mine. "Have you heard   105
from Judith?" he said.

"Not yet."

"Well, it's pretty soon. Were they going to sleep in the van?"

"Yes."

"I guess it's safe enough, if they stop in the right places."

I knew he would have to say something more and I knew it would come as   110
a joke.

"I guess they put a board down the middle, like the pioneers?"

I smiled but did not answer.

"I take it you have no objections?"

"No," I said.

"Well, I always believed that too. Keep out of your children's business. I tried   115
not to say anything. I never said anything when you left Richard."

"What do you mean, 'said anything'? Criticize?"

"It wasn't any of my business."

"No."

"But that doesn't mean I was pleased."

I was surprised — not just at what he said but at his feeling that he had any   120
right, even now, to say it. I had to look out the window and down at the traffic to control myself.

"I just wanted you to know," he added.

A long time ago, he said to me in his mild way, "It's funny. Richard when I first saw him reminded me of what my father used to say. He'd say if that fellow was half as smart as he thinks he is, he'd be twice as smart as he really is."

I turned to remind him of this, but found myself looking at the line his heart was writing. Not that there seemed to be anything wrong, any difference in the beeps and points. But it was there.

He saw where I was looking. "Unfair advantage," he said.

"It is," I said. "I'm going to have to get hooked up too."                125

We laughed, we kissed formally; I left. At least he hadn't asked me about Nichola, I thought.

The next afternoon I didn't go to the hospital, because my father was having some more tests done, to prepare for the operation. I was to see him in the evening instead. I found myself wandering through the Bloor Street dress shops, trying on clothes. A preoccupation with fashion and my own appearance had descended on me like a raging headache. I looked at the women in the street, at the clothes in the shops, trying to discover how a transformation might be made, what I would have to buy. I recognized this obsession for what it was but had trouble shaking it. I've had people tell me that waiting for life-or-death news they've stood in front of an open refrigerator eating anything in sight — cold boiled potatoes, chili sauce, bowls of whipped cream. Or have been unable to stop doing crossword puzzles. Attention narrows in on something — some distraction — grabs on, becomes fanatically serious. I shuffled clothes on the racks, pulled them on in hot little changing rooms in front of cruel mirrors. I was sweating; once or twice I thought

I might faint. Out on the street again, I thought I must remove myself from Bloor Street, and decided to go to the museum.

I remembered another time, in Vancouver. It was when Nichola was going to kindergarten and Judith was a baby. Nichola had been to the doctor about a cold, or maybe for a routine examination, and the blood test revealed something about her white blood cells — either that there were too many of them or that they were enlarged. The doctor ordered further tests, and I took Nichola to the hospital for them. Nobody mentioned leukemia but I knew, of course, what they were looking for. When I took Nichola home I asked the babysitter who had been with Judith to stay for the afternoon and I went shopping. I bought the most daring dress I ever owned, a black silk sheath with some laced-up arrangement in front. I remembered that bright spring afternoon, the spike-heeled shoes in the department store, the underwear printed with leopard spots.

I also remembered going home from St. Paul's Hospital over the Lions Gate Bridge on the crowded bus and holding Nichola on my knee. She suddenly recalled her baby name for *bridge* and whispered to me, "Whee — over the whee." I did not avoid touching my child — Nichola was slender and graceful even then, with a pretty back and fine dark hair — but realized I was touching her with a difference, though I did not think it could ever be detected. There was a care — not a withdrawal exactly but a care — not to feel anything much. I saw how the forms of love might be maintained with a condemned person but with the love in fact measured and disciplined, because you have to survive. It could be done so discreetly that the object of such care would not suspect, any more than she would suspect the sentence of death itself. Nichola did not know, would not know. Toys and kisses and jokes would come tumbling over her; she would never know, though I worried that she would feel the wind between the cracks of the manufactured holidays, the manufactured normal days. But all was well. Nichola did not have leukemia. She grew up — was still alive, and possibly happy. Incommunicado.

I could not think of anything in the museum I really wanted to see, so I walked past it to the planetarium. I had never been to a planetarium. The show was due to start in ten minutes. I went inside, bought a ticket, got in line. There was a whole class of schoolchildren, maybe a couple of classes, with teachers and volunteer mothers riding herd on them. I looked around to see if there were any other unattached adults. Only one — a man with a red face and puffy eyes, who looked as if he might be here to keep himself from going to a bar.

Inside, we sat on wonderfully comfortable seats that were tilted back so that you lay in a sort of hammock, attention directed to the bowl of the ceiling, which soon turned dark blue, with a faint rim of light all around the edge. There was some splendid, commanding music. The adults all around were shushing the children, trying to make them stop crackling their potato-chip bags. Then a man's voice, an eloquent professional voice, began to speak slowly, out of the walls. The voice reminded me a little of the way radio announcers used to introduce a piece of classical music or describe the progress of the Royal Family to Westminster Abbey on one of their royal occasions. There was a faint echo-chamber effect.

The dark ceiling was filling with stars. They came out not all at once but one after another, the way the stars really do come out at night, though more quickly. The Milky Way appeared, was moving closer; stars swam into brilliance and kept on going, disappearing beyond the edges of the sky-screen or behind my head. While the flow of light continued, the voice presented the stunning facts. A few light-years away, it announced, the sun appears as a bright star, and the planets are not visible. A few dozen light-years away, the sun is not visible, either, to the naked eye. And that distance—a few dozen light-years—is only about a thousandth part of the distance from the sun to the center of our galaxy, one galaxy, which itself contains about two hundred billion suns. And is, in turn, one of millions, perhaps billions, of galaxies. Innumerable repetitions, innumerable variations. All this rolled past my head too, like balls of lightning.

Now realism was abandoned, for familiar artifice. A model of the solar system was spinning away in its elegant style. A bright bug took off from the earth, heading for Jupiter. I set my dodging and shrinking mind sternly to recording facts. The mass of Jupiter two and a half times that of all the other planets put together. The Great Red Spot. The thirteen moons. Past Jupiter, a glance at the eccentric orbit of Pluto, the icy rings of Saturn. Back to Earth and moving in to hot and dazzling Venus. Atmospheric pressure ninety times ours. Moonless Mercury rotating three times while circling the sun twice; an odd arrangement, not as satisfying as what they used to tell us—that it rotated once as it circled the sun. No perpetual darkness after all. Why did they give out such confident information, only to announce later that it was quite wrong? Finally, the picture already familiar from magazines: the red soil of Mars, the blooming pink sky.

When the show was over I sat in my seat while the children clambered across me, making no comments on anything they had just seen or heard. They were pestering their keepers for eatables and further entertainments. An effort had been made to get their attention, to take it away from canned pop and potato chips and fix it on various knowns and unknowns and horrible immensities, and it seemed to have failed. A good thing too, I thought. Children have a natural immunity, most of them, and it shouldn't be tampered with. As for the adults who would deplore it, the ones who promoted this show, weren't they immune themselves to the extent that they could put in the echo-chamber effects, the music, the churchlike solemnity, simulating the awe that they supposed they ought to feel? Awe—what was that supposed to be? A fit of the shivers when you looked out the window? Once you know what it was, you wouldn't be courting it.

Two men came with brooms to sweep up the debris the audience had left 135 behind. They told me that the next show would start in forty minutes. In the meantime, I had to get out.

"I went to the show at the planetarium," I said to my father. "It was very exciting—about the solar system." I thought what a silly word I had used: *exciting.* "It's like a slightly phony temple," I added.

He was already talking. "I remember when they found Pluto. Right where they thought it had to be. Mercury, Venus, Earth, Mars," he recited. "Jupiter, Saturn, Nept—no, Uranus, Neptune, Pluto. Is that right?"

"Yes," I said. I was just as glad he hadn't heard what I said about the phony temple. I had meant that to be truthful, but it sounded slick and superior. "Tell me the moons of Jupiter."

"Well, I don't know the new ones. There's a bunch of new ones, isn't there?"

"Two. But they're not new." 140

"New to us," said my father. "You've turned pretty cheeky now I'm going under the knife."

" 'Under the knife.' What an expression."

He was not in bed tonight, his last night. He had been detached from his apparatus, and was sitting in a chair by the window. He was bare-legged, wearing a hospital dressing gown, but he did not look self-conscious or out of place. He looked thoughtful but good-humored, an affable host.

"You haven't even named the old ones," I said.

"Give me time. Galileo named them. Io." 145

"That's a start."

"The moons of Jupiter were the first heavenly bodies discovered with the telescope." He said this gravely, as if he could see the sentence in an old book. "It wasn't Galileo named them, either; it was some German. Io, Europa, Ganymede, Callisto. There you are."

"Yes."

"Io and Europa, they were girlfriends of Jupiter's, weren't they? Ganymede was a boy. A shepherd? I don't know who Callisto was."

"I think she was a girlfriend too," I said. "Jupiter's wife — Jove's wife — changed 150 her into a bear and stuck her up in the sky. Great Bear and Little Bear. Little Bear was her baby."

The loudspeaker said that it was time for visitors to go.

"I'll see you when you come out of the anesthetic," I said.

"Yes."

When I was at the door, he called to me, "Ganymede wasn't any shepherd. He was Jove's cupbearer."

When I left the planetarium that afternoon, I had walked through the museum 155 to the Chinese garden. I saw the stone camels again, the warriors, the tomb. I sat on a bench looking toward Bloor Street. Through the evergreen bushes and the high grilled iron fence I watched people going by in the late-afternoon sunlight. The planetarium show had done what I wanted it to after all — calmed me down, drained me. I saw a girl who reminded me of Nichola. She wore a trenchcoat and carried a bag of groceries. She was shorter than Nichola — not really much like her at all — but I thought that I might see Nichola. She would be walking along some street maybe not far from here — burdened, preoccupied, alone. She was one of the grown-up people in the world now, one of the shoppers going home.

If I did see her, I might just sit and watch, I decided. I felt like one of those people who have floated up to the ceiling, enjoying a brief death. A relief, while it lasts. My father had chosen and Nichola had chosen. Someday, probably soon, I would hear from her, but it came to the same thing.

I meant to get up and go over to the tomb, to look at the relief carvings, the stone pictures, that go all the way around it. I always mean to look at them and I never do. Not this time, either. It was getting cold out, so I went inside to have coffee and something to eat before I went back to the hospital.

## Considerations for Critical Thinking and Writing

1. **FIRST RESPONSE.** Consider some of the common symbolic values of the heart, such as love, or the will to live. How does the heart operate symbolically in this story?

2. What does Janet's description of her father's heart monitor in paragraph 8 tell you about her character? How is that character trait developed elsewhere?

3. Though Janet obviously didn't know her father when he was a child, how does her understanding of his childhood affect her relationship with him now that he is elderly and facing his mortality?

4. Janet is the mother of two daughters, but in frustration she says, "I wished I'd had a boy and a girl. Or two boys" (par. 47). How do you understand this confession, and what does it say about her character?

5. How does Janet's attitude toward Judith's boyfriend, Don, further complicate her character?

6. How might the topic of memory in this story lead to a statement of theme?

7. The story is not told in chronological order. What is the effect of its movement back and forward across the time of its present action?

8. Both Janet and her father have a particular response to what they read: What is it? Do they feel the same way about the value and importance of published writing?

9. Compare the scene in which Janet's father contemplates the afterlife to Janet's experience in the planetarium. How do the premises about belief and understanding in these scenes form a kind of dialogue?

10. Janet talks with her father about the moons of Jupiter, which leads to a discussion about the figures from Roman mythology they're named after. How does ancient myth figure into the story's themes?

11. How does the disappearance of Nichola from Janet's life affect her?

12. Is the story more about Janet or her father? What affects your answer?

13. Janet's father alludes to a poem about the explorer Christopher Columbus. How does exploration or discovery figure into the story's theme?

## Connections to Other Selections

1. Discuss mortality and human significance in this story and in Nathaniel Hawthorne's "The Minister's Black Veil" (p. 209).

2. Consider the depiction of motherhood in this story and in Cynthia Ozick's "The Shawl" (p. 185).

## *Silence*   2004

On the short ferry ride from Buckley Bay to Denman Island°, Juliet got out of her car and stood at the front of the boat, in the summer breeze. A woman standing there recognized her, and they began to talk. It is not unusual for people to take a second look at Juliet and wonder where they've seen her before, and, sometimes, to remember. She appears regularly on the Provincial Television channel, interviewing people who are leading singular or notable lives, and deftly directing panel discussions, on a program called *Issues of the Day*. Her hair is cut short now, as short as possible, and has taken on a very dark auburn color, matching the frames of her glasses. She often wears black pants — as she does today — and an ivory silk shirt, and sometimes a black jacket. She is what her mother would have called a striking-looking woman.

"Forgive me. People must be always bothering you."

"It's okay," Juliet says. "Except when I've just been to the dentist or something."

---

*Denman Island:* An island near Vancouver in British Columbia on Canada's west coast.

The woman is about Juliet's age. Long black hair streaked with gray, no makeup, long denim skirt. She lives on Denman, so Juliet asks her what she knows about the Spiritual Balance Centre.

"Because my daughter is there," Juliet says. "She's been on a retreat there or taking a course, I don't know what they call it. For six months. This is the first time I've got to see her, in six months."

"There are a couple of places like that," the woman says. "They sort of come and go. I don't mean there's anything suspect about them. Just that they're generally off in the woods, you know, and don't have much to do with the community. Well, what would be the point of a retreat if they did?"

She says that Juliet must be looking forward to seeing her daughter again, and Juliet says yes, very much.

"I'm spoiled," she says. "She's twenty years old, my daughter — she'll be twenty-one this month, actually — and we haven't been apart much."

The woman says that she has a son of twenty and a daughter of eighteen and another of fifteen, and there are days when she'd *pay* them to go on a retreat, singly or all together.

Juliet laughs. "Well. I've only the one. Of course, I won't guarantee that I won't be all for shipping her back, given a few weeks."

This is the kind of fond but exasperated mother-talk she finds it easy to slip into (Juliet is an expert at reassuring responses), but the truth is that Penelope has scarcely ever given her cause for complaint, and if she wanted to be totally honest, at this point she would say that one day without some contact with her daughter is hard to bear, let alone six months. Penelope has worked at Banff°, as a summer chambermaid, and she has gone on bus trips to Mexico, a hitchhiking trip to Newfoundland. But she has always lived with Juliet, and there has never been a six-month break.

*She gives me delight, Juliet could have said. Not that she is one of those song-and-dance purveyors of sunshine and cheer and looking-on-the-bright-side. I hope I've brought her up better than that. She has grace and compassion and she is as wise as if she'd been on this earth for eighty years. Her nature is reflective, not all over the map like mine. Somewhat reticent, like her father's. She is also angelically pretty, she's like my mother, blond like my mother but not so frail. Strong and noble. Molded, I should say, like a caryatid. And contrary to popular notions I am not even faintly jealous. All this time without her — and with no word from her, because Spiritual Balance does not allow letters or phone calls — all this time I've been in a sort of desert, and when her message came I was like an old patch of cracked earth getting a full drink of rain.*

*Hope to see you Sunday afternoon. It's time.*

Time to go home, was what Juliet hoped this meant, but of course she would leave that up to Penelope.

Penelope had drawn a rudimentary map, and Juliet shortly found herself parked in front of an old church — that is, a church building seventy-five or eighty years old, covered with stucco, not as old or anything like as impressive as churches usually were in the part of Canada where Juliet had grown up. Behind it was a more recent building, with a slanting roof and windows all across its front, also

---

*Banff:* A resort in the Canadian province of Alberta within a national park of the same name.

a simple stage and some seating benches and what looked like a volleyball court with a sagging net. Everything was shabby, and the once-cleared patch of land was being reclaimed by juniper and poplars.

A couple of people — she could not tell whether men or women — were doing some carpentry work on the stage, and others sat on the benches in separate small groups. All wore ordinary clothes, not yellow robes or anything of that sort. For a few minutes no notice was taken of Juliet's car. Then one of the people on the benches rose and walked unhurriedly towards her. A short, middle-aged man wearing glasses.

She got out of the car and greeted him and asked for Penelope. He did not speak — perhaps there was a rule of silence — but nodded and turned away and went into the church. From which there shortly appeared, not Penelope, but a heavy, slow-moving woman with white hair, wearing jeans and a baggy sweater.

"What an honor to meet you," she said. "Do come inside. I've asked Donny to make us some tea."

She had a broad fresh face, a smile both roguish and tender, and what Juliet supposed must be called twinkling eyes. "My name is Joan," she said. Juliet had been expecting an assumed name like Serenity, or something with an Eastern flavor, nothing so plain and familiar as Joan. Later, of course, she thought of Pope Joan°.

"I've got the right place, have I? I'm a stranger on Denman," she said disarm-  20
ingly. "You know I've come to see Penelope?"

"Of course. Penelope." Joan prolonged the name, with a certain tone of celebration.

The inside of the church was darkened with purple cloth hung over the high windows. The pews and other church furnishings had been removed, and plain white curtains had been strung up to form private cubicles, as in a hospital ward. The cubicle into which Juliet was directed had, however, no bed, just a small table and a couple of plastic chairs, and some open shelves piled untidily with loose papers.

"I'm afraid we're still in the process of getting things fixed up in here," Joan said. "Juliet. May I call you Juliet?"

"Yes, of course."

"I'm not used to talking to a celebrity." Joan held her hands together in a prayer  25
pose beneath her chin. "I don't know whether to be informal or not."

"I'm not much of a celebrity."

"Oh, you are. Now don't say things like that. And I'll just get it off my chest right away, how I admire you for the work you do. It's a beam in the darkness. The only television worth watching."

"Thank you," said Juliet. "I had a note from Penelope —"

"I know. But I'm sorry to have to tell you, Juliet, I'm very sorry and I don't want you to be too disappointed — Penelope is not here."

The woman says those words — *Penelope is not here* — as lightly as possible.  30
You would think that Penelope's absence could be turned into a matter for amused contemplation, even for their mutual delight.

Juliet has to take a deep breath. For a moment she cannot speak. Dread pours through her. Foreknowledge. Then she pulls herself back to reasonable consider-ation of this fact. She fishes around in her bag.

*Pope Joan:* A legend suggests that a woman named Pope Joan reigned as supreme head of the Catholic Church during the Middle Ages.

"She said she hoped —"

"I know. I know," says Joan. "She did intend to be here, but the fact was, she could not —"

"Where is she? Where did she go?"

"I cannot tell you that."                                                          35

"You mean you can't or you won't?"

"I can't. I don't know. But I can tell you one thing that may put your mind at rest. Wherever she has gone, whatever she has decided, it will be the right thing for her. It will be the *right* thing for her spirituality and her growth."

Juliet decides to let this pass. She gags on the word *spirituality,* which seems to take in — as she often says — everything from prayer wheels to High Mass. She never expected that Penelope, with her intelligence, would be mixed up in anything like this.

"I just thought I should know," she says, "in case she wanted me to send on any of her things."

"Her possessions?" Joan seems unable to suppress a wide smile, though she   40 modifies it at once with an expression of tenderness. "Penelope is not very concerned right now about her *possessions."*

Sometimes Juliet has felt, in the middle of an interview, that the person she faces has reserves of hostility that were not apparent before the cameras started rolling. A person whom Juliet has underestimated, whom she has thought rather stupid, may have strength of that sort. Playful but deadly hostility. The thing then is never to show that you are taken aback, never to display any hint of hostility in return.

"What I mean by growth is our inward growth, of course," Joan says.

"I understand," says Juliet, looking her in the eye.

"Penelope has had such a wonderful opportunity in her life to meet interesting people — goodness, she hasn't needed to meet interesting people, she's *grown up* with an interesting person, you're her *mother* — but you know, sometimes there's a dimension that is missing, grown-up children feel that they've *missed out* on something —"

"Oh yes," says Juliet. "I know that grown-up children can have all sorts of   45 complaints."

Joan has decided to come down hard.

"The spiritual dimension — I have to say this — was it not altogether lacking in Penelope's life? I take it she did not grow up in a faith-based home."

"Religion was not a banned subject. We could talk about it."

"But perhaps it was the way you talked about it. Your intellectual way? If you know what I mean. You are so clever," she adds, kindly.

"So you say."                                                                       50

Juliet is aware that any control of the interview, and of herself, is faltering, and may be lost.

"Not so *I* say, Juliet. So *Penelope* says. Penelope is a dear fine girl, but she has come to us here in great hunger. Hunger for the things that were not available to her in her home. There you were, with your wonderful busy successful life — but Juliet, I must tell you that your daughter has known loneliness. She has known unhappiness."

"Don't most people feel that, one time or another? Loneliness and unhappiness?"

"It's not for me to say. Oh, Juliet. You are a woman of marvellous insights. I've often watched you on television and I've thought, how does she get right to the heart of things like that, and all the time being so nice and polite to people? I never thought I'd be sitting talking to you face-to-face. And what's more, that I'd be in a position to *help* you —"

"I think that maybe you're mistaken about that." 55

"You feel hurt. It's natural that you should feel hurt."

"It's also my own business."

"Ah well. Perhaps she'll get in touch with you. After all."

Penelope did get in touch with Juliet, a couple of weeks later. A birthday card arrived on her own — Penelope's — birthday, the 19th of June. Her twenty-first birthday. It was the sort of card you send to an acquaintance whose tastes you cannot guess. Not a crude jokey card or a truly witty card or a sentimental card. On the front of it was a small bouquet of pansies tied by a thin purple ribbon whose tail spelled out the words *Happy Birthday.* These words were repeated inside, with the words *Wishing you a very* added in gold letters above them.

And there was no signature. Juliet thought at first that someone had sent 60 this card to Penelope, and forgotten to sign it, and that she, Juliet, had opened it by mistake. Someone who had Penelope's name and the date of her birth on file. Her dentist, maybe, or her driving teacher. But when she checked the writing on the envelope she saw that there had been no mistake — there was her own name, indeed, written in Penelope's own handwriting.

Postmarks gave you no clue anymore. They all said *Canada Post.* Juliet had some idea that there were ways of telling at least which province a letter came from, but for that you would have to consult the Post Office, go there with the letter and very likely be called upon to prove your case, your right to the information. And somebody would be sure to recognize her.

She went to see her old friend Christa, who had lived in Whale Bay when she herself lived there, even before Penelope was born. Christa was in Kitsilano, in an assisted-living facility. She had multiple sclerosis. Her room was on the ground floor, with a small private patio, and Juliet sat with her there, looking out at a sunny bit of lawn, and the wisteria all in bloom along the fence that concealed the garbage bins.

Juliet told Christa the whole story of the trip to Denman Island. She had told nobody else, and had hoped perhaps not to have to tell anybody. Every day when she was on her way home from work she had wondered if perhaps Penelope would be waiting in the apartment. Or at least that there would be a letter. And then there had been — that unkind card — and she had torn it open with her hands shaking.

"It means something," Christa said. "It lets you know she's okay. Something will follow. It will. Be patient."

Juliet talked bitterly for a while about Mother Shipton. That was what she 65 finally decided to call her, having toyed with and become dissatisfied with Pope Joan. What bloody chicanery, she said. What creepiness, nastiness, behind the second-rate, sweetly religious facade. It was impossible to imagine Penelope's having been taken in by her.

Christa suggested that perhaps Penelope had visited the place because she had considered writing something about it. Some sort of investigative journalism. Fieldwork. The personal angle — the long-winded personal stuff that was so popular nowadays.

Investigating for six months? said Juliet. Penelope could have figured out Mother Shipton in ten minutes.

"It's weird," admitted Christa.

"You don't know more than you're letting on, do you?" said Juliet. "I hate to even ask that. I feel so at sea. I feel stupid. That woman intended me to feel stupid, of course. Like the character who blurts out something in a play and everybody turns away because they all know something she doesn't know —"

"They don't do that kind of play anymore," Christa said. "Now nobody knows  70
anything. No — Penelope didn't take me into her confidence any more than she did you. Why should she? She'd know I'd end up telling you."

Juliet was quiet for a moment, then she muttered sulkily, "There have been things you didn't tell me."

"Oh, for God's sake," said Christa, but without any animosity. "Not that again."

"Not that again," Juliet agreed. "I'm in a lousy mood, that's all."

"Just hold on. One of the trials of parenthood. She hasn't given you many, after all. In a year this will all be ancient history."

Juliet didn't tell her that in the end she had not been able to walk away with  75
dignity. She had turned and cried out beseechingly, furiously.

"What did she tell you?"

And Mother Shipton was standing there watching her, as if she had expected this. A fat pitying smile had stretched her closed lips as she shook her head.

During the next year Juliet would get phone calls, now and then, from people who had been friendly with Penelope. Her reply to their inquiries was always the same. Penelope had decided to take a year off. She was travelling. Her travelling agenda was by no means fixed, and Juliet had no way of contacting her, nor any address she could supply.

She did not hear from anybody who had been a close friend. This might mean that people who had been close to Penelope knew quite well where she was. Or it might be that they too were off on trips to foreign countries, had found jobs in other provinces, were embarked on new lives, too crowded or chancy at present to allow them to wonder about old friends.

(Old friends, at that stage in life, meaning somebody you had not seen for half  80
a year.)

Whenever she came in, the first thing Juliet did was to look for the light flashing on her answering machine — the very thing she used to avoid, thinking there would be someone pestering her about her public utterances. She tried various silly tricks, to do with how many steps she took to the phone, how she picked it up, how she breathed. *Let it be her.*

Nothing worked. After a while the world seemed emptied of the people Penelope had known, the boyfriends she had dropped and the ones who had dropped her, the girls she had gossiped with and probably confided in. She had gone to a private girls' boarding school — Torrance House — rather than to a public high school, and this meant that most of her longtime friends — even those who were still her friends at college — had come from places out of town. Some from Alaska or Prince George or Peru.

There was no message at Christmas. But in June, another card, very much in the style of the first, not a word written inside. Juliet had a drink of wine before she opened it, then threw it away at once. She had spurts of weeping, once in a while of uncontrollable shaking, but she came out of these in quick fits of fury, walking around the house and slapping one fist into her palm. The fury was directed at Mother Shipton, but the image of that woman had faded, and finally Juliet had to recognize that she was really only a convenience.

All pictures of Penelope were banished to her bedroom, with sheaves of drawings and crayonings she had done before they left Whale Bay, her books, and the European one-cup coffeemaker with the plunger that she had bought as a present for Juliet with the first money she had made in her summer job at McDonald's. Also such whimsical gifts for the apartment as a tiny plastic fan to stick on the refrigerator, a wind-up toy tractor, a curtain of glass beads to hang in the bathroom window. The door of that bedroom was shut and in time could be passed without disturbance.

Juliet gave a great deal of thought to getting out of this apartment, giving herself 85 the benefit of new surroundings. But she said to Christa that she could not do that, because that was the address Penelope had, and mail could be forwarded for only three months, so there would be no place then where her daughter could find her.

"She could always get to you at work," said Christa.

"Who knows how long I'll be there?" Juliet said. "She's probably in some commune where they're not allowed to communicate. With some guru who sleeps with all the women and sends them out to beg on the streets. If I'd sent her to Sunday school and taught her to say her prayers this probably wouldn't have happened. I should have. I should have. It would have been like an inoculation. I neglected her *spirituality*. Mother Shipton said so."

When Penelope was barely thirteen years old, she had gone away on a camping trip to the Kootenay Mountains of British Columbia, with a friend from Torrance House, and the friend's family. Juliet was in favor of this. Penelope had been at Torrance House for only one year (accepted on favorable financial terms because of her mother's once having taught there), and it pleased Juliet that she had already made so firm a friend and been accepted readily by the friend's family. Also that she was going camping — something that regular children did and that Juliet, as a child, had never had the chance to do. Not that she would have wanted to, being already buried in books — but she welcomed signs that Penelope was turning out to be a more normal sort of girl than she herself had been.

Eric was apprehensive about the whole idea. He thought Penelope was too young. He didn't like her going on a holiday with people he knew so little about. And now that she went to boarding school they saw too little of her as it was — so why should that time be shortened?

Juliet had another reason — she simply wanted Penelope out of the way for the 90 first couple of weeks of the summer holidays, because the air was not clear between herself and Eric. She wanted things resolved, and they were not resolved. She did not want to have to pretend that all was well, for the sake of the child.

Eric, on the other hand, would have liked nothing better than to see their trouble smoothed over, hidden out of the way. To Eric's way of thinking, civility would restore good feeling, the semblance of love would be enough to get by on until love itself might be rediscovered. And if there was never anything more than a semblance — well, that would have to do. Eric could manage with that.

Indeed he could, thought Juliet, despondently.

Having Penelope at home, a reason for them to behave well — for Juliet to behave well, since she was the one, in his opinion, who stirred up all the rancor — that would suit Eric very well.

So Juliet told him, and created a new source of bitterness and blame, because he missed Penelope badly.

The reason for their quarrel was an old and ordinary one. In the spring, 95 through some trivial disclosure — and the frankness or possibly the malice of their longtime neighbor Ailo, who had a certain loyalty to Eric's dead wife and some reservations about Juliet — Juliet had discovered that Eric had slept with Christa. Christa had been for a long time her close friend, but she had been, before that, Eric's girlfriend, his *mistress* (though nobody said that anymore). He had given her up when he asked Juliet to live with him. She had known all about Christa then and she could not reasonably object to what had happened in the time before she and Eric were together. She did not. What she did object to — what she claimed had broken her heart — had happened after that. (But still a long time ago, said Eric.) It had happened when Penelope was a year old, and Juliet had taken her back to Ontario. When Juliet had gone home to visit her parents. To visit — as she always pointed out now — to visit her dying mother. When she was away, and loving and missing Eric with every shred of her being (she now believed this), Eric had simply returned to his old habits.

At first he confessed to once (drunk), but with further prodding, and some drinking in the here-and-now, he said that possibly it had been more often.

Possibly? He could not remember? So many times he could not remember?

He could remember.

Christa came to see Juliet, to assure her that it had been nothing serious. (This was Eric's refrain, as well.) Juliet told her to go away and never come back. Christa decided that now would be a good time to go to see her brother in California.

Juliet's outrage at Christa was actually something of a formality. She did under- 100 stand that a few rolls in the hay with an old girlfriend (Eric's disastrous description, his ill-judged attempt to minimize things) were nowhere near as threatening as a hot embrace with some woman newly met. Also, her outrage at Eric was so fierce and irrepressible as to leave little room for blame of anybody else.

Her contentions were that he did not love her, had never loved her, had mocked her, with Christa, behind her back. He had made her a laughingstock in front of people like Ailo (who had always hated her). That he had treated her with contempt, he regarded the love she felt (or had felt) for him with contempt, he had lived a lie with her. Sex meant nothing to him, or at any rate it did not mean what it meant (had meant) to her, he would have it off with whoever was handy.

Only the last of these contentions had the least germ of truth in it, and in her quieter states she knew that. But even that little truth was enough to pull every-thing down around her. It shouldn't do that, but it did. And Eric was not able — in all honesty he was not able — to see why that should be so. He was not surprised that she should object, make a fuss, even weep (though a woman like Christa would never have done that), but that she should really be damaged, that she should con-sider herself bereft of all that had sustained her — and for something that had hap-pened *twelve years ago* — this he could not understand.

Sometimes he believed that she was shamming, making the most of it, and at other times he was full of real grief, that he had made her suffer. Their grief aroused them, and they made love magnificently. And each time he thought that would be the end of it, their miseries were over. Each time he was mistaken.

In bed, Juliet laughed and told him about Pepys and Mrs. Pepys°, inflamed with passion under similar circumstances. (Since more or less giving up on her classical studies, she was reading widely, and nowadays everything she read seemed to have to do with adultery.) Never so often and never so hot, Pepys had said, though he recorded as well that his wife had also thought of murdering him in his sleep. Juliet laughed about this, but half an hour later, when he came to say good-bye before going out in the boat to check his prawn traps, she showed a stony face and gave him a kiss of resignation, as if he'd been going to meet a woman out in the middle of the bay and under a rainy sky.

There was more than rain. The water was hardly choppy when Eric went out,   105 but later in the afternoon a wind came up suddenly, from the southeast, and tore up the waters of Desolation Sound and Malaspina Strait. It continued almost till dark — which did not really close down until around eleven o'clock in this last week of June. By then a sailboat from Campbell River was missing, with three adults and two children aboard. Also two fish boats — one with two men aboard and the other with only one man — Eric.

The next morning was calm and sunny — the mountains, the waters, the shores, all sleek and sparkling.

It was possible, of course, that none of these people were lost, that they had found shelter and spent the night in any of the multitude of little bays. That was more likely to be true of the fishermen than of the family in the sailboat, who were not local people but vacationers from Seattle. Boats went out at once, that morning, to search the mainland and island shores and the water.

The drowned children were found first, in their life jackets, and by the end of the day the bodies of their parents were located as well. A grandfather who had accompanied them was not found until the day after. The bodies of the men who had been fishing together never showed up, though the remnants of their boat washed up near Refuge Cove.

Eric's body was recovered on the third day. Juliet was not allowed to see it. Something had got at him, it was said (meaning some animal), after the body was washed ashore.

It was perhaps because of this — because there was no question of viewing the   110 body and no need for an undertaker — that the idea caught hold amongst Eric's old friends and fellow fishermen of burning Eric on the beach. Juliet did not object to this. A death certificate had to be made out, so the doctor who came to Whale Bay once a week was telephoned at his office in Powell River, and he gave Ailo, who was his weekly assistant and a registered nurse, the authority to do this.

There was plenty of driftwood around, plenty of the sea-salted bark which makes a superior fire. In a couple of hours all was ready. News had spread — somehow, even at such short notice, women began arriving with food. It was Ailo who took charge — her Scandinavian blood, her upright carriage and flowing white hair, seeming to fit her naturally for the role of Widow of the Sea. Children ran about on the logs, and were shooed away from the growing pyre, the shrouded, surprisingly meager bundle that was Eric. A coffee urn was supplied to

*Pepys and Mrs. Pepys:* Samuel Pepys (1633–1703) was a British naval administrator who is remembered for his sexually explicit diary, begun in 1660 and published after his death.

this half-pagan ceremony by the women from one of the churches, and cartons of beer, bottles of drink of all sorts, were left discreetly, for the time being, in the trunks of cars and cabs of trucks.

The question arose of who would speak, and who would light the pyre. They asked Juliet, would she do it? And Juliet — brittle and busy, handing out mugs of coffee — said that they had it wrong, as the widow she was supposed to throw herself into the flames. She actually laughed as she said this, and those who had asked her backed off, afraid that she was getting hysterical. The man who had partnered Eric most often in the boat agreed to do the lighting, but said he was no speaker. It occurred to some that he would not have been a good choice anyway, since his wife was an Evangelical Anglican, and he might have felt obliged to say things which would have distressed Eric if he had been able to hear them. Then Ailo's husband offered — he was a little man disfigured by a fire on a boat, years ago, a grumbling socialist and atheist, and in his talk he rather lost track of Eric, except to claim him as a Brother in the Battle. He went or at surprising length, and this was ascribed, afterwards, to the suppressed life he led under the rule of Ailo. There might have been some restlessness in the crowd before his recital of grievances got stopped, some feeling that the event was turning out to be not so splendid, or solemn, or heartrending, as might have been expected. But when the fire began to burn this feeling vanished, and there was great concentration, even, or especially among the children, until the moment when one of the men cried, "Get the kids out of here." This was when the flame had reached the body, bringing the realization, coming rather late, that consumption of fat, of heart and kidneys and liver, might produce explosive or sizzling noises disconcerting to hear. So a good many of the children were hauled away by their mothers — some willingly, some to their own dismay. So the final act of the fire became a mostly male ceremony, and slightly scandalous, even if not, in this case, illegal.

Juliet stayed, wide-eyed, rocking on her haunches, face pressed against the heat. She was not quite there. She thought of whoever it was — Trelawny? — snatching Shelley's heart° out of the flames. The heart, with its long history of significance. Strange to think how even at that time, not so long ago, one fleshly organ should be thought so precious, the site of courage and love. It was just flesh, burning. Nothing connected with Eric.

Penelope knew nothing of what was going on. There was a short item in the Vancouver paper — not about the burning on the beach, of course, just about the drowning — but no newspapers or radio reports reached her, deep in the Kootenay Mountains. When she got back to Vancouver she phoned home, from her friend Heather's house. Christa answered — she had got back too late for the ceremony, but was staying with Juliet, and helping as she could. Christa said that Juliet was not there — it was a lie — and asked to speak to Heather's mother. She explained what had happened, and said that she was driving Juliet to Vancouver, they would leave at once, and Juliet would tell Penelope herself when they got there.

Christa dropped Juliet at the house where Penelope was, and Juliet went inside 115 alone. Heather's mother left her in the sunroom, where Penelope was waiting. Penelope received the news with an expression of fright, then — when Juliet rather

---

*Shelley's heart:* Percy Bysshe Shelley (1792–1822) was one of the principal British Romantic poets. Shelley died in a boating accident and his body was cremated; his friend Edward Trelawny is said to have taken his heart and preserved it in wine.

formally put her arms around her — of something like embarrassment. Perhaps in Heather's house, in the white and green and orange sunroom, with Heather's brothers shooting baskets in the backyard, news so dire could hardly penetrate. The burning was not mentioned — in this house and neighborhood it would surely have seemed uncivilized, grotesque. In this house, also, Juliet's manner was sprightly beyond anything intended — her behavior close to that of *a good sport*.

Heather's mother entered after a tiny knock — with glasses of iced tea. Penelope gulped hers down and went to join Heather, who had been lurking in the hall.

Heather's mother then had a talk with Juliet. She apologized for intruding with practical matters but said that time was short. She and Heather's father were driving east in a few days' time to see relatives. They would be gone for a month, and had planned to take Heather with them. (The boys were going to camp.) But now Heather had decided she did not want to go, she had begged to stay here in the house, with Penelope. A fourteen-year-old and a thirteen-year-old could not really be left alone, and it had occurred to her that Juliet might like some time away, a respite, after what she had been through. After her loss and tragedy.

So Juliet shortly found herself living in a different world, in a large spotless house brightly and thoughtfully decorated, with what are called conveniences — but to her were luxuries — on every hand. This on a curving street lined with similar houses, behind trimmed bushes and showy flower beds. Even the weather, for that month, was flawless — warm, breezy, bright. Heather and Penelope went swimming, played badminton in the backyard, went to the movies, baked cookies, gorged, dieted, worked on their tans, filled the house with music whose lyrics seemed to Juliet sappy and irritating, sometimes invited girlfriends over, did not exactly invite boys but held long, taunting, aimless conversations with some who passed the house or had collected next door. By chance, Juliet heard Penelope say to one of the visiting girls, "Well, I hardly knew him, really."

She was speaking about her father.

How strange.                                                                                      120

She had never been afraid to go out in the boat, as Juliet was, when there was a chop on the water. She had pestered him to be taken and was often successful. When following after Eric, in her businesslike orange life jacket, carrying what gear she could manage, she always wore an expression of particular seriousness and dedication. She took note of the setting of the traps and became skilful, quick, and ruthless at the deheading and bagging of the catch. At a certain stage of her childhood — say from eight to eleven — she had always said that she was going to go out fishing when she grew up, and Eric had told her there were girls doing that nowadays. Juliet had thought it was possible, since Penelope was bright but not bookish, and exuberantly physical, and brave. But Eric, out of Penelope's hearing, said that he hoped the idea would wear off, he wouldn't wish the life on anybody. He always spoke this way, about the hardship and uncertainty of the work he had chosen, but took pride, so Juliet thought, in those very things.

And now he was dismissed. By Penelope, who had recently painted her toenails purple and was sporting a false tattoo on her midriff. He who had filled her life. She dismissed him.

But Juliet felt as if she was doing the same. Of course, she was busy looking for a job and a place to live. She had already put the house in Whale Bay up for sale — she could not imagine remaining there. She had sold the truck and given away Eric's tools, and such traps as had been recovered, and the dinghy. Eric's grown son from Saskatchewan had come and taken the dog.

She had applied for a job in the reference department of the college library, and a job in the public library, and she had a feeling she would get one or the other. She looked at apartments in the Kitsilano or Dunbar or Point Grey areas. The cleanness, tidiness, and manageability of city life kept surprising her. This was how people lived where the man's work did not take place out of doors, and where various operations connected with it did not end up indoors. And where the weather might be a factor in your mood but never in your life, where such dire matters as the changing habits and availability of prawns and salmon were merely interesting, or not remarked upon at all. The life she had been leading at Whale Bay, such a short time ago, seemed haphazard, cluttered, exhausting, by comparison. And she herself was cleansed of the moods of the last months — she was brisk and competent, and better-looking.

Eric should see her now.                                                                              125

She thought about Eric in this way all the time. It was not that she failed to realize that Eric was dead — that did not happen for a moment. But nevertheless she kept constantly referring to him, in her mind, as if he was still the person to whom her existence mattered more than it could to anyone else. As if he was still the person in whose eyes she hoped to shine. Also the person to whom she presented arguments, information, surprises. This was such a habit with her, and took place so automatically, that the fact of his death did not seem to interfere with it.

Nor was their last quarrel entirely resolved. She held him to account, still, for his betrayal. When she flaunted herself a little now, it was against that.

The storm, the recovery of the body, the burning on the beach — that was all like a pageant she had been compelled to watch and compelled to believe in, which still had nothing to do with Eric and herself.

She got the job in the reference library, she found a two-bedroom apartment that she could just afford, Penelope went back to Torrance House as a day student. Their affairs at Whale Bay were wound up, their life there finished. Even Christa was moving out, coming to Vancouver in the spring.

On a day before that, a day in February, Juliet stood in the shelter at the cam-   130
pus bus stop when her afternoon's work was over. The day's rain had stopped, there was a band of clear sky in the west, red where the sun had gone down, out over the Strait of Georgia. This sign of the lengthening days, the promise of the change of season, had an effect on her that was unexpected and crushing.

She realized that Eric was dead.

As if all this time, while she was in Vancouver, he had been waiting somewhere, waiting to see if she would resume her life with him. As if being with him was an option that had stayed open. Her life since she came here had still been lived against a backdrop of Eric, without her ever quite understanding that Eric did not exist. Nothing of him existed. The memory of him in the daily and ordinary world was in retreat.

So this is grief. She feels as if a sack of cement has been poured into her and quickly hardened. She can barely move. Getting onto the bus, getting off the bus, walking half a block to her building (why is she living here?), is like climbing a cliff. And now she must hide this from Penelope.

At the supper table she began to shake, but could not loosen her fingers to drop the knife and fork. Penelope came around the table and pried her hands open. She said, "It's Dad, isn't it?"

Juliet afterwards told a few people — such as Christa — that these seemed the   135
most utterly absolving, the most tender words, that anybody had ever said to her.

Penelope ran her cool hands up and down the insides of Juliet's arms. She phoned the library the next day to say that her mother was sick, and she took care of her for a couple of days, staying home from school until Juliet recovered. Or until, at least, the worst was over.

During those days Juliet told Penelope everything. Christa, the fight, the burning on the beach (which she had so far managed, almost miraculously, to conceal from her). Everything.

"I shouldn't burden you with all this."

Penelope said, "Yeah, well, maybe not." But added staunchly, "I forgive you. I guess I'm not a baby."

Juliet went back into the world. The sort of fit she had had in the bus stop 140 recurred, but never so powerfully.

Through her research work in the library, she met some people from the Provincial Television channel, and took a job they offered. She had worked there for about a year when she began to do interviews. All the indiscriminate reading she'd done for years (and that Ailo had so disapproved of, in the days at Whale Bay), all the bits and pieces of information she'd picked up, her random appetite and quick assimilation, were now to come in handy. And she cultivated a self-deprecating, faintly teasing manner that usually seemed to go over well. On camera, few things fazed her. Though in fact she would go home and march back and forth, letting out whimpers or curses as she recalled some perceived glitch or fluster or, worse still, a mispronunciation.

After five years the birthday cards stopped coming.

"It doesn't mean anything," Christa said. "All they were for was to tell you she's alive somewhere. Now she figures you've got the message. She trusts you not to send some tracker after her. That's all."

"Did I put too much on her?"

"Oh, Jul."                                                                     145

"I don't mean just with Eric dying. Other men, later. I let her see too much misery. My stupid misery."

For Juliet had had two affairs during the years that Penelope was between fourteen and twenty-one, and during both of these she had managed to fall hectically in love, though she was ashamed afterwards. One of the men was much older than she, and solidly married. The other was a good deal younger, and was alarmed by her ready emotions. Later she wondered at these herself. She really had cared nothing for him, she said.

"I wouldn't think you did," said Christa, who was tired. "I don't know."

"Oh Christ. I was such a fool. I don't get like that about men anymore. Do I?"

Christa did not mention that this might be because of a lack of candidates.   150

"No, Jul. No."

"Actually I didn't do anything so terrible," Juliet said then, brightening up. "Why do I keep lamenting that it's my fault? She's a conundrum, that's all. I need to face that.

"A conundrum and a cold fish," she said, in a parody of resolution.

"No," said Christa.

"No," said Juliet. "No — that's not true."                                     155

After the second June had passed without any word, Juliet decided to move. For the first five years, she told Christa, she had waited for June, wondering what might come. The way things were now, she had to wonder every day. And be disappointed every day.

She moved to a high-rise building in the West End. She meant to throw away the contents of Penelope's room, but in the end she stuffed it all into garbage bags and carried it with her. She had only one bedroom now but there was storage space in the basement.

She took up jogging in Stanley Park. Now she seldom mentioned Penelope, even to Christa. She had a boyfriend — that was what you called them now — who had never heard anything about her daughter.

Christa grew thinner and moodier. Quite suddenly, one January, she died.

You don't go on forever, appearing on television. However agreeable the viewers  160
have found your face, there comes a time when they'd prefer somebody different. Juliet was offered other jobs — researching, writing voice-over for nature shows — but she refused them cheerfully, describing herself as in need of a total change. She went back to Classical Studies — an even smaller department than it used to be — she meant to resume writing her thesis for her Ph.D. She moved out of the high-rise apartment and into a bachelor flat, to save money.

Her boyfriend had got a teaching job in China.

Her flat was in the basement of a house, but the sliding doors at the back opened out at ground level. And there she had a little brick-paved patio, a trellis with sweet peas and clematis, herbs and flowers in pots. For the first time in her life, and in a very small way, she was a gardener, as her father had been.

Sometimes people said to her — in stores, or on the campus bus — "Excuse me, but your face is so familiar," or, "Aren't you the lady that used to be on television?" But after a year or so this passed. She spent a lot of time sitting and reading, drinking coffee at sidewalk tables, and nobody noticed her. She let her hair grow out. During the years that it had been dyed red it had lost the vigor of its natural brown — it was a silvery brown now, fine and wavy. She was reminded of her mother, Sara. Sara's soft, fair, flyaway hair, going gray and then white.

She did not have room to have people to dinner anymore, and she had lost interest in recipes. She ate meals that were nourishing enough, but monotonous. Without exactly meaning to, she lost contact with most of her friends.

It was no wonder. She lived now a life as different as possible from the life  165
of the public, vivacious, concerned, endlessly well-informed woman that she had been. She lived amongst books, reading through most of her waking hours and being compelled to deepen, to alter, whatever premise she had started with. She often missed the world news for a week at a time.

She had given up on her thesis and become interested in some writers referred to as the Greek novelists, whose work came rather late in the history of Greek literature (starting in the first century B.C.E., as she had now learned to call it, and continuing into the early Middle Ages). Aristeides, Longus, Heliodorus, Achilles Tatius. Much of their work is lost or fragmentary and is also reported to be indecent. But there is a romance written by Heliodorus, and called the *Aethiopica* (originally in a private library, retrieved at the siege of Buda), that has been known in Europe since it was printed at Basle in 1534.

In this story the queen of Ethiopia gives birth to a white baby, and is afraid she will be accused of adultery. So she gives the child — a daughter — into the care of the gymnosophists — that is, the naked philosophers, who are hermits and mystics. The girl, who is called Charicleia, is finally taken to Delphi, where she becomes one of the priestesses of Artemis. There she meets a noble Thessalian named Theagenes, who falls in love with her and, with the help of a clever Egyptian, carries her off. The Ethiopian queen, as it turns out, has never ceased to long for her daughter and has hired this very Egyptian to search for her. Mischance and adventures continue until all the main characters meet at Meroe, and Charicleia is rescued — again — just as she is about to be sacrificed by her own father.

Interesting themes were thick as flies here, and the tale had a natural continuing fascination for Juliet. Particularly the part about the gymnosophists. She tried to find out as much as she could about these people, who were usually referred to as Hindu philosophers. Was India, in this case, presumed to be adjacent to Ethiopia? No — Heliodorus came late enough to know his geography better than that. The gymnosophists would be wanderers, far spread, attracting and repelling those they lived amongst with their ironclad devotion to purity of life and thought, their contempt for possessions, even for clothing and food. A beautiful maiden reared amongst them might well be left with some perverse hankering for a bare, ecstatic life.

Juliet had made a new friend named Larry. He taught Greek, and he had let Juliet store the garbage bags in the basement of his house. He liked to imagine how they might make the *Aethiopica* into a musical. Juliet collaborated in this fantasy, even to making up the marvellously silly songs and the preposterous stage effects. But she was secretly drawn to devising a different ending, one that would involve renunciation, and a backward search, in which the girl would be sure to meet fakes and charlatans, impostors, shabby imitations of what she was really looking for. Which was reconciliation, at last, with the erring, repentant, essentially great-hearted queen of Ethiopia.

Juliet was almost certain that she had seen Mother Shipton here in Vancouver. 170 She had taken some clothes that she would never wear again (her wardrobe had grown increasingly utilitarian) to a Salvation Army Thrift Store, and as she set the bag down in the receiving room she saw a fat old woman in a muumuu fixing tags onto trousers. The woman was chatting with the other workers. She had the air of a supervisor, a cheerful but vigilant overseer — or perhaps the air of a woman who would assume that role whether she had any official superiority or not.

If she was in fact Mother Shipton, she had come down in the world. But not by very much. For if she was Mother Shipton, would she not have reserves of buoyancy and self-approbation, such as to make real downfall impossible?

Reserves of advice, pernicious advice, as well.

*She has come to us here in great hunger.*

Juliet had told Larry about Penelope. She had to have one person who knew. "Should I have talked to her about a noble life?" she said. "Sacrifice? Opening your life to the needs of strangers? I never thought of it. I must have acted as if it would have been good enough if she turned out like me. Would that sicken her?"

Larry was not a man who wanted anything from Juliet but her friendship and 175 good humor. He was what used to be called an old-fashioned bachelor, asexual as far as she could tell (but probably she could not tell far enough), squeamish about any personal revelations, endlessly entertaining.

Two other men had appeared who wanted her as a partner. One of them she had met when he sat down at her sidewalk table. He was a recent widower. She liked him, but his loneliness was so raw and his pursuit of her so desperate that she became alarmed.

The other man was Christa's brother, whom she had met several times during Christa's life. His company suited her — in many ways he was like Christa. His marriage had ended long ago, he was not desperate — she knew, from Christa, that there had been women ready to marry him whom he had avoided. But he was too rational, his choice of her verged on being cold-blooded, there was something humiliating about it.

But why humiliating? It was not as if she loved him.

It was while she was still seeing Christa's brother — his name was Gary Lamb — that she ran into Heather, on a downtown street in Vancouver. Juliet and Gary had just come out of a theater where they had seen an early-evening movie, and they were talking about where to go for dinner. It was a warm night in summer, the light still not gone from the sky.

A woman detached herself from a group on the sidewalk. She came straight at   180 Juliet. A thin woman, perhaps in her late thirties. Fashionable, with taffy streaks in her dark hair.

"Mrs. Porteous. Mrs. Porteous."

Juliet knew the voice, though she would never have known the face. Heather.

"This is incredible," Heather said. "I'm here for three days and I'm leaving tomorrow. My husband's at a conference. I was thinking that I don't know anybody here anymore and then I turn around and see you."

Juliet asked her where she was living now and she said Connecticut.

"And just about three weeks ago I was visiting Josh — you remember my   185 brother Josh? — I was visiting my brother Josh and his family in Edmonton and I ran into Penelope. Just like this, on the street. No — actually it was in the mall, that humongous mall they have. She had a couple of her kids with her, she'd brought them down to get uniforms for that school they go to. The boys. We were both flabbergasted. I didn't know her right away but she recognized me. She'd flown down, of course. From that place way up north. But she says it's quite civilized, really. And she said you were still living here. But I'm with these people — they're my husband's friends — and I really haven't had time to ring you up —"

Juliet made some gesture to say that of course there would not be time and she had not expected to be rung up.

She asked how many children Heather had.

"Three. They're all monsters. I hope they grow up in a hurry. But my life's a picnic compared with Penelope's. *Five*."

"Yes."

"I have to run now, we're going to see a movie. I don't even know anything   190 about it, I don't even like French movies. But it was altogether great meeting you like this. My mother and dad moved to White Rock. They used to see you all the time on TV. They used to brag to their friends that you'd lived in our house. They say you're not on anymore, did you get sick of it?"

"Something like that."

"I'm coming, I'm coming." She hugged and kissed Juliet, the way everybody did now, and ran to join her companions.

So. Penelope did not live in Edmonton — she had *come down* to Edmonton. Flown down. That meant she must live in Whitehorse or in Yellowknife°. Where else was there that she could describe as *quite civilized?* Maybe she was being ironical, mocking Heather a bit, when she said that.

*Whitehorse or Yellowknife:* The capitals of the Yukon Territory and Northwest Territory, Canada's vastest and least populated provinces.

She had five children and two at least were boys. They were being outfitted with school uniforms. That meant a private school. That meant money.

Heather had not known her at first. Did that mean she had aged? That she was out of shape after five pregnancies, that she had not *taken care of herself*? As Heather had. As Juliet had, to a certain extent. That she was one of those women to whom the whole idea of such a struggle seemed ridiculous, a confession of insecurity? Or just something she had no time for — far outside of her consideration.

Juliet had thought of Penelope being involved with transcendentalists, of her having become a mystic, spending her life in contemplation. Or else — rather the opposite but still radically simple and spartan — earning her living in a rough and risky way, fishing, perhaps with a husband, perhaps also with some husky little children, in the cold waters of the Inside Passage off the British Columbia coast.

Not at all. She was living the life of a prosperous, practical matron. Married to a doctor, maybe, or to one of those civil servants managing the northern parts of the country during the time when their control is being gradually, cautiously, but with some fanfare, relinquished to the native people. If she ever met Penelope again they might laugh about how wrong Juliet had been. When they told about their separate meetings with Heather, how weird that was, they would laugh.

No. No. The fact was surely that she had already laughed too much around Penelope. Too many things had been jokes. Just as too many things — personal things, loves that were maybe just gratification — had been tragedies. She had been lacking in motherly inhibitions and propriety and self-control.

Penelope had said that she, Juliet, was still living in Vancouver. She had not told Heather anything about the breach. Surely not. If she had been told, Heather would not have spoken so easily.

How did Penelope know that she was still here, unless she checked in the phone directory? And if she did, what did that mean?

Nothing. Don't make it mean anything.

She walked to the curb to join Gary, who had tactfully moved away from the scene of the reunion.

Whitehorse, Yellowknife. It was painful indeed to know the names of those places — places she could fly to. Places where she could loiter in the streets, devise plans for catching glimpses.

But she was not so mad. She must not be so mad.

At dinner, she thought that the news she had just absorbed put her into a better situation for marrying Gary, or living with him — whatever it was he wanted. There was nothing to worry about, or hold herself in wait for, concerning Penelope. Penelope was not a phantom, she was safe, as far as anybody is safe, and she was probably as happy as anybody is happy. She had detached herself from Juliet and very likely from the memory of Juliet, and Juliet could not do better than to detach herself in turn.

But she had told Heather that Juliet was living in Vancouver. Did she say *Juliet*? Or *Mother. My mother.*

Juliet told Gary that Heather was the child of old friends. She had never spoken to him about Penelope, and he had never given any sign of knowing about Penelope's existence. It was possible that Christa had told him, and he had remained silent out of a consideration that it was none of his business. Or that Christa had told him, and he had forgotten. Or that Christa had never mentioned anything about Penelope, not even her name.

If Juliet lived with him the fact of Penelope would never surface, Penelope would not exist.

Nor did Penelope exist. The Penelope Juliet sought was gone. The woman Heather had spotted in Edmonton, the mother who had brought her sons to Edmonton to get their school uniforms, who had changed in face and body so that Heather did not recognize her, was nobody Juliet knew.

Does Juliet believe this?                                                                               210

If Gary saw that she was agitated he pretended not to notice. But it was probably on this evening that they both understood they would never be together. If it had been possible for them to be together she might have said to him, *My daughter went away without telling me good-bye and in fact she probably did not know then that she was going. She did not know it was for good. Then gradually, I believe, it dawned on her how much she wanted to stay away. It is just a way that she has found to manage her life.*

*"It's maybe the explaining to me that she can't face. Or has not time for, really. You know, we always have the idea that there is this reason or that reason and we keep trying to find out reasons. And I could tell you plenty about what I've done wrong. But I think the reason may be something not so easily dug out. Something like purity in her nature. Yes. Some fineness and strictness and purity, some rock-hard honesty in her. My father used to say of someone he disliked, that he had no use for that person. Couldn't those words mean simply what they say? Penelope does not have a use for me.*

*Maybe she can't stand me. It's possible.*

Juliet has friends. Not so many now — but friends. Larry continues to visit, and to make jokes. She keeps on with her studies. The word *studies* does not seem to describe very well what she does — *investigations* would be better.

And being short of money, she works some hours a week at the coffee place   215 where she used to spend so much time at the sidewalk tables. She finds this work a good balance for her involvement with the old Greeks — so much so that she believes she wouldn't quit even if she could afford to.

She keeps on hoping for a word from Penelope, but not in any strenuous way. She hopes as people who know better hope for undeserved blessings, spontaneous remissions, things of that sort.

### CONSIDERATIONS FOR CRITICAL THINKING AND WRITING

1. **FIRST RESPONSE.** Is the dominant emotion of the story guilt or grief? Why, and what difference does it make to your reading of it?

2. At the end of the paragraph 12 Juliet expresses a thought about her daughter in great detail: What does it say about her that she doesn't express anything like it to the stranger who approaches her on the ferry?

3. Why is Juliet's profession significant to the story?

4. Why does Juliet find her conversation with Joan (a.k.a. Mother Shipton) about Penelope's odd absence disarming?

5. Juliet is self-conscious about what other people think of her. How does this character trait figure into the story?

6. Penelope sends two greeting cards to her mother with nothing written in them. What is Juliet's reaction? Is it understandable? How would you react in this situation?

7. In addition to the blank greeting cards, how else might you interpret the "silence" of the title?

8. How does the story of Eric's infidelity and his tragic death affect your response to Juliet's character?

9. Penelope's father dies at a time when she is especially vulnerable (when she is thirteen). Does it make sense that she tells her friend that she barely knew her father? Does the fact that she was away when he died and that she didn't experience his funeral explain her behavior as an adult?

10. Once Juliet's career as a television interviewer ends, she turns to the study of classical literature. Is this a surprising move or not? What does it tell you?

11. When Mother Shipton first suggests to Juliet that Penelope had come to the spiritual center "in great hunger," Juliet scoffs (par. 52). Why does the comment haunt her? Is it because she suspects it's true or because she feels remorse for having failed to see it before?

12. Does Juliet change over the course of the story? If so, in what way? Is it a positive change?

### CONNECTIONS TO OTHER SELECTIONS

1. Compare the mother-daughter relationship depicted in this story to the multiple versions of that relationship depicted in Carmen Maria Machado's "Eight Bites" (p. 218).

2. How does Juliet's attempt to cope with grief compare to that of the narrator of James Baldwin's "Sonny's Blues" (p. 91), who loses his daughter to polio?

---

## Perspectives

---

### ALICE MUNRO (B. 1931)

## From *In Her Own Words* 2013

I got interested in reading very early, because a story was read to me, by Hans Christian Andersen, which was *The Little Mermaid*, and I don't know if you remember *The Little Mermaid*, but it's dreadfully sad. The little mermaid falls in love with this prince, but she cannot marry him, because she is a mermaid. And it's so sad I can't tell you the details. But anyway, as soon as I had finished this story I got outside and walked around and around the house where we lived, at the brick house, and I made up a story with a happy ending, because I thought that was due to the little mermaid, and it sort of slipped my mind that it was only made up to be a different story for me, it wasn't going to go all around the world, but I felt I had done my best, and from now on the little mermaid would marry the prince and live happily ever after, which was certainly her desert, because she had done awful things to win the prince's power, his ease. She had had to change her limbs. She had had to get limbs that ordinary people have and walk, but every step she took, agonizing pain! This is what she was willing to go through, to get the prince. So I thought she deserved more than death on the water. And I didn't worry about the fact that maybe the rest of the world wouldn't know the new story, because I felt it had been published once I thought about it. So, there you are. That was an early start, on writing . . .

I made stories up all the time, I had a long walk to school, and during that walk I would generally make up stories. As I got older the stories would be more and more about myself, as a heroine in some situation or other, and it didn't bother me that the stories were not going to be published to the world immediately, and I don't know if I even thought about other people knowing them or reading them. It was about the story itself, generally a very satisfying story from my point of view, with the general idea of the little mermaid's bravery, that she was clever, that she was in general able to make a better world, because she would jump in there, and have magic powers and things like that . . .

Well, obviously, in those early days the important thing was the happy ending, I did not tolerate unhappy endings, for my heroines anyway. And later on I began to read things like *Wuthering Heights*, and very very unhappy endings would take place, so I changed my ideas completely and went in for the tragic, which I enjoyed . . .

. . . I want my stories to move people, I don't care if they are men or women or children. I want my stories to be something about life that causes people to say, not, oh, isn't that the truth, but to feel some kind of reward from the writing, and that doesn't mean that it has to be a happy ending or anything, but just that everything the story tells moves the reader in such a way that you feel you are a different person when you finish . . .

I don't care what they feel as long as they enjoy reading the book. I want peo- 5 ple to find not so much inspiration as great enjoyment. That's what I want; I want people to enjoy my books, to think of them as related to their own lives in ways. But that isn't the major thing. I am trying to say that I am not, I guess I am not a political person.

From "Nobel Lecture in absentia"

## CONSIDERATIONS FOR CRITICAL THINKING AND WRITING

1. What's wrong with a happy ending? Why is it significant that Munro changed her opinion on that topic?

2. Munro claims she wants fiction to "move" people. How do you understand that term? Does it describe all fiction or just a certain type?

## MARGARET ATWOOD (B. 1939)

## *Alice Munro: An Appreciation* 2008

. . . Alice Munro has been among those writers subject to periodic rediscovery, at least outside Canada. It's as if she jumps out of a cake — *Surprise!* — and then has to jump out of it again, and then again. Readers don't see her name in lights on every billboard. . . .

Alice Munro did not spring from nowhere. She sprang — though it's a verb her characters would find overly sprightly, and indeed pretentious — from Huron County, in southwestern Ontario.

Ontario is the large province of Canada that stretches from the Ottawa River to the western end of Lake Superior. This is a huge and varied space, but southwestern Ontario is a distinct part of it. It was named Sowesto by the painter Greg Curnoe, a name that has stuck. Curnoe's view was that Sowesto was an area of considerable interest, but also of considerable psychic darkness and oddity, a view shared by many. Robertson Davies, also from Sowesto, used to say, "I know the dark folkways of my people," and Alice Munro knows them too. You are likely to run into quite a few signs in Sowesto wheat fields telling you to be prepared to meet your God, or else your doom — felt to be much the same thing.

Lake Huron lies at the western edge of Sowesto, Lake Erie to the south. The country is mostly flat farmland, cut by several wide, winding rivers prone to flooding, and on the rivers — because of the available boat transport, and the power provided by water-driven mills — a number of smaller and larger towns grew up in the nineteenth century. Each has its red-brick town hall (usually with a tower), each its post office building and its handful of churches of various denominations, each its main street and its residential section of gracious homes, and its other residential section on the wrong side of the tracks. Each has its families with long memories and stashes of bones in the closets.

Sowesto contains the site of the famous Donnelly Massacre of the nine- 5 teenth century, when a large family was slaughtered and their home burnt as a result of political resentments carried over from Ireland. Lush nature, repressed emotions, respectable fronts, hidden sexual excesses, outbreaks of violence, lurid crimes, long-held grudges, strange rumours — none are ever far away in Munro's Sowesto, partly because all have been provided by the real life of the region itself.

Oddly enough, a number of writers have come from Sowesto. Oddly because when Alice Munro was growing up in the 1930s and 1940s, the idea of a person from Canada — but especially one from small-town southwestern Ontario — thinking they could be a writer to be taken seriously in the world at large was laughable. Even by the 1950s and 1960s, there were very few publishers in Canada, and even they were mostly textbook publishers who imported whatever so-called literature was to be had from England and the United States. There might be some amateur theatre — high-school performances, Little Theatre groups. There was, however, the radio, and in the 1960s Alice Munro got her start through a CBC program called *Anthology,* produced by Robert Weaver.

But very few Canadian writers of any sort were known to an international readership, and it was taken for granted that if you had hankerings of that kind — hankerings about which you would of course feel defensive and ashamed, because art was not something a grown-up morally credible person would fool around with — it would be best for you if you left the country. Everyone knew that writing was not a thing you could ever expect to make your living at.

### CONSIDERATIONS FOR CRITICAL THINKING AND WRITING

1. What does Atwood mean by "psychic darkness and oddity"? How do you see those traits reflected in one or more of Munro's stories?

2. Atwood, like Munro, is a Canadian writer who is internationally famous. Why does she emphasize the rarity of that situation? How does it help us contextualize Munro's work?

BEVERLY RASPORICH (B. 1941)

## Alice: The Woman Behind the Art    1990

By now, Virginia Woolf's argument that the female author has the uphill battle of resisting the conventional female role, which is obviously historically and
socially determined, is a familiar one.[1] Munro has not taken the route of the
single-minded artist in bohemian protest against what society expected her to be
as a woman. She did not give up the conventional responsibilities of daughter,
mother, wife. In some basic ways, her lived experiences have conformed to the
social-sexual history of upwardly mobile females of her Canadian generation: she
moved from rural roots through education to middle class marriage, to motherhood, divorce, economic displacement and remarriage. Her solution to the
problem of artist-as-female was quite naturally and bravely to become the female-
as-artist, and as an interpreter and puzzling critic of the roles of women and codes
of sexual conduct she knew and witnessed, a quiet revolutionary.

Munro has travelled beyond Woolf who consciously fought the constraints of
Victorian respectability and domestic duty, a specter that Woolf named the Angel
in the House. Despite her revolt, as Elaine Showalter has argued, Woolf capitu-
lated mightily.

> Virginia Woolf developed a literary theory which had the effect of neutralizing
> her own conflict between the desire to present a woman's whole experience, and
> the fear of such revelation. It is a theory of the androgynous mind and spirit; a
> fusion of masculine and feminine elements, calm, stable, subtle, unimpeded by
> consciousness of sex or individuality. . . . Whatever else one may say of androg-
> yny, it represents an escape from the confrontation with femininity.[2]

If, as Showalter observes, Woolf was pressed to neutralize her femininity, to
consciously refrain from writing about her own sexuality and to renounce female
passion, Munro works closely to the core of her own feminine consciousness and
through the authority of her own fragmented and transformational experience.
In a letter to Joyce Johnson of McGraw-Hill Book Co., dated 8 February 1973,
Showalter praises Munro's effort:

> Thank you for sending me Alice Munro's *Lives of Girls and Women;* I had seen
> some enthusiastic reviews. Reading such a strong novel of the female conscious-
> ness makes me feel rather like an astronomer who had predicted the existence
> of a comet, and then watching it appear — it's very exciting to read beyond
> androgyny.[3]

Munro's life has been that of meeting the challenge of shifting roles for herself, and her fiction has been, and continues to be, that of a cathartic feminism,
moving beyond androgyny. Unlike a Mary Wollstonecraft, a Virginia Woolf or a
Sylvia Plath, she is, as a female author of feminine persuasion, a survivor.

From *Dance of the Sexes: Art and Gender in the Fiction of Alice Munro*

---

[1] See Virginia Woolf: *Women and Writing*, ed. Michele Barrett (New York: Harcourt Brace
Jovanovich, 1980), p. 17.
[2] Elaine Showalter, "Killing the Angel in the House: The Autonomy of Women Writers," *The
Antioch Review* 32, no. 3, (June 1973), p. 341.
[3] Showalter, letter to Joyce Johnson, McGraw-Hill Book Company, New York, 8 February 1973,
Correspondence Series, *The Alice Munro Papers: First Accession,* (Calgary: University of Calgary
Press, 1986), p. 15.

CONSIDERATIONS FOR CRITICAL THINKING AND WRITING

1. What distinctions do you make between "artist-as-female" and "female-as-artist"? How are they contrasted in this excerpt?
2. How do Munro's stories illustrate the term "quiet revolutionary"? Is this a perfect term to contextualize her work or can you think of a better one?

## W.R. MARTIN (1920–2015) AND WARREN U. OBER (B. 1925)

# Alice Munro as Small-Town Historian: "Spaceships Have Landed"    1998

In an interview with Eleanor Wachtel a few years before the appearance of *Open Secrets* (1994), Alice Munro said, "One of the things that interest me so much in writing, and in observing people, is that things keep changing. Cherished beliefs change. Ways of dealing with life change. The importance of certain things in life changes. All this seems to me endlessly interesting. I think that is the thing that doesn't change" ("Interview" 292). Her observation is worth pondering.

In "Society and Culture in Rural and Small-Town Ontario: Alice Munro's Testimony on the Last Forty Years," John Weaver shows how Munro's work has been a comprehensive record of the enduring conditions and details of small town. At first glance, then, it might seem strange for Munro to put such emphasis on change, and indeed much of her work is a record of seemingly unchanging life that she knew as a child and young adult. But the strangeness of her statement is only superficial. In *Lives of Girls and Women,* Del, the protagonist, tries to cram into what she writes the sorts of objective detail that Uncle Craig, the diligent amateur historian, has collected, but she comes to realize that "no list could hold what I wanted, for what I wanted was every last thing, every layer of speech and thought, stroke of light on bark or walls, every smell, pothole, pain, crack, delusion held still and held together — radiant, everlasting" (210). In the end Munro not only uses a much finer mesh than Uncle Craig but also, by capturing the "emotional" dimensions and intensities of that life through the magic of art, far transcends what he strives for.

As early as *Lives of Girls and Women,* then, as Weaver has shown, Munro identifies "two poles of historical inquiry" (381). At one pole is "the historian as a collector," who, like Uncle Craig, "reifies facts and artifacts without ordering their meaning"; at the other is "the creative soul," such as Del, who strives to "record the concrete but also the passions." The "artist's vision" possessed by this kind of historian involves "an aspiration to total history" (382). The passion and insight conveyed by what Weaver calls total history must go together with, and in part derive from, an awareness of the unique and delicate balance, as well as the transience, of the world of experience that the artist is driven to record and preserve, as it were, in amber. It is the artist-historian's way of arresting change, of preserving what is loved.

### Works Cited

Munro, Alice. "An Interview with Alice Munro." With Eleanor Wachtel. *The Brick Reader.* Ed. Linda Spalding and Michael Ondaatje. Toronto: Coach House, 1991. 288–94.

Munro, Alice. *Lives of Girls and Women.* 1971. New York: New American Library, 1983

Weaver, John. "Society and Culture in Rural and Small-Town Ontario: Alice Munro's Testimony on the Last Forty Years." *Patterns of the Past: Interpreting Ontario's History.* Ed. Roger Hall, William Westfall, and Laurel Sefton MacDowell. Toronto: Dundurn, 1988. 381–403.

From *The Rest of the Story: Critical Essays on Alice Munro*,
edited by Robert Thacker

## CONSIDERATIONS FOR CRITICAL THINKING AND WRITING

1. How does Munro's analysis of "change" in the opening quotation apply to her fiction?

2. What is the relationship between the role of the artist and the role of the historian as it is outlined here? How might you apply that insight to Munro's fiction?

## SUGGESTED TOPICS FOR LONGER PAPERS: ALICE MUNRO

1. The three stories included here are arranged in chronological order. Even though these are not the same characters, do you see connections between the three protagonists who go from young girl, to middle-aged woman, to a slightly older woman?

2. All of these stories deal with parent-child relationships. Does Munro provide a consistent idea about this particular relationship, or is it significantly different in every story?

3. How do these stories regard the past? What is its chief power over people's lives, and is it a positive or a negative force?

4. Munro has said that one of her motivations to become a writer involved a growing distrust of happy endings. (See "Alice Munro: In Her Own Words," p. 394). If you had to select one of these stories as one with a happier ending than the other two, which would you select and why?

5. All of Munro's characters seem to be on a quest for understanding. Which of these three protagonists seems to understand the most by the end of the story?

6. Reading these stories in order of their publication, do you see stylistic changes over the course of Munro's career? What are they?

7. The first two stories in the collection are written in the first person and the third is in third person. Does the change in point of view matter in terms of your responses to the stories?

8. Develop an idea from Margaret Atwood's appreciation of Munro (p. 395) by engaging with two or all three of the stories included here.

# 13

# A Study of
# Flannery O'Connor

Apic/Getty Images.

In most English classes the short story has
become a kind of literary specimen to be
dissected. Every time a story of mine appears in a
Freshman anthology, I have a vision of it, with its
little organs laid open, like a frog in a bottle.
— FLANNERY O'CONNOR

I am always having it pointed out to me that
life in Georgia is not at all the way I picture it,
that escaped criminals do not roam the roads
exterminating families, nor Bible salesmen prowl
about looking for girls with wooden legs.
— FLANNERY O'CONNOR

When Flannery O'Connor (1925–1964) died of lupus before her fortieth
birthday, her work was cruelly cut short. Nevertheless, she had completed two
novels, *Wise Blood* (1952) and *The Violent Bear It Away* (1960), as well as
thirty-one short stories. Despite her brief life and relatively modest output,
her work is regarded as among the most distinguished American fiction of
the mid-twentieth century. Her two collections of short stories, *A Good Man
Is Hard to Find* (1955) and *Everything That Rises Must Converge* (1965), were
included in *The Complete Stories of Flannery O'Connor* (1971), which won
the National Book Award. The stories included in this chapter offer a glimpse
into the work of this important twentieth-century writer.

*Cheers,*
*Flannery*

# A BRIEF BIOGRAPHY AND INTRODUCTION

O'Connor's fiction grapples with living a spiritual life in a secular world. Although this major concern is worked into each of her stories, she takes a broad approach to spiritual issues by providing moral, social, and psychological contexts that offer a wealth of insights and passion that her readers have found both startling and absorbing. Her stories are challenging because her characters, who initially seem radically different from people we know, turn out to be, by the end of each story, somehow familiar — somehow connected to us.

O'Connor inhabited simultaneously two radically different worlds. The world she created in her stories is populated with bratty children, malcontents, incompetents, pious frauds, bewildered intellectuals, deformed cynics, rednecks, hucksters, racists, perverts, and murderers who experience dramatically intense moments that surprise and shock readers. Her personal life, however, was largely uneventful. She humorously acknowledged its quiet nature in 1958 when she claimed that "there won't be any biographies of me because, for only one reason, lives spent between the house and the chicken yard do not make exciting copy."

A broad outline of O'Connor's life may not offer very much "exciting copy," but it does provide clues about why she wrote such powerful fiction. The only child of Catholic parents, O'Connor was born in Savannah, Georgia, where she attended a parochial grammar school and high school. When she was thirteen, her father became ill with disseminated lupus, a rare, incurable blood disease, and had to abandon his real-estate business. The family moved to Milledgeville in central Georgia, where her mother's family had lived for generations. Because there were no Catholic schools in Milledgeville, O'Connor attended a public high school. In 1942, the year after her father died of lupus, O'Connor graduated from high school and enrolled in Georgia State College for Women. There she wrote for the literary magazine until receiving her diploma in 1945. Her stories earned her a fellowship to the Writers' Workshop at the University of Iowa, and for two years she learned to write steadily and seriously. She sold her first story to *Accent* in 1946 and earned her Master of Fine Arts degree in 1947. She wrote stories about life in the rural South, and this subject matter, along with her devout Catholic perspective, became central to her fiction.

With her formal education behind her, O'Connor was ready to begin her professional career at the age of twenty-two. Equipped with determination ("No one can convince me that I shouldn't rewrite as much as I do") and offered the opportunity to be around other practicing writers, she moved to New York, where she worked on her first novel, *Wise Blood*. In 1950, however, she was diagnosed as having lupus, and, returning to Georgia for treatment, she took up permanent residence on her mother's farm in Milledgeville. There she lived a severely restricted but productive life, writing stories and raising peacocks.

**Flannery O'Connor** (above left) as a child and (above right) in her teens (age sixteen or seventeen). O'Connor, whose youth was marked by the declining health and death of her father, once wrote, "[A]nybody who has survived childhood has enough information about life to last him the rest of the days."

*Both images*: © Flannery O'Connor, © renewed by Regina Cline O'Connor. Permission granted by Harold Matson Co., Inc on behalf of The Mary Flannery O'Connor Charitable Trust. All rights reserved.

**Flannery O'Connor poses with her book *Wise Blood* in 1952.**

Apic/Getty Images.

**The *Corinthian* Staff.** Flannery O'Connor (seated, center) as editor of the *Corinthian*, the literary magazine at Georgia State College for Women (now Georgia College and State University). O'Connor attended the college from 1942 through 1945 and earned a B.A. in social science.

Courtesy of Ina Dillard Russell Library Special Collections, Georgia College and State University.

With the exception of O'Connor's early years in Iowa and New York and some short lecture trips to other states, she traveled little. Although she made a pilgrimage to Lourdes (apparently more for her mother's sake than for her own) and then to Rome for an audience with the pope, her life was centered in the South. Like those of William Faulkner and many other southern writers, O'Connor's stories evoke the rhythms of rural southern speech and manners in insulated settings where widely diverse characters mingle. Also like Faulkner, she created works whose meanings go beyond their settings. She did not want her fiction to be seen in the context of narrowly defined regionalism: she complained that "in almost every hamlet you'll find at least one old lady writing epics in Negro dialect and probably two or three old gentlemen who have impossible historical novels on the way." Refusing to be caricatured, she knew that "the woods are full of regional writers, and it is the great horror of every serious Southern writer that he will become one of them." O'Connor's stories are rooted in rural southern culture, but in a larger sense they are set within the psychological and spiritual landscapes of the human soul. This interior setting universalizes local materials in much the same way that Nathaniel Hawthorne's New England stories do. Indeed, O'Connor once described herself as "one of his descendants": "I feel more of a kinship with him than any other American."

O'Connor's deep spiritual convictions coincide with the traditional emphasis on religion in the South, where, she said, there is still the belief "that man has fallen and that he is only perfectible by God's grace, not by his own unaided efforts." Although O'Connor's Catholicism differs from the prevailing

Protestant fundamentalism of the South, the religious ethos so pervasive even in rural southern areas provided fertile ground for the spiritual crises her characters experience. In a posthumous collection of her articles, essays, and reviews aptly titled *Mystery and Manners* (1969), she summarized her basic religious convictions:

> I am no disbeliever in spiritual purpose and no vague believer. I see from the standpoint of Christian orthodoxy. This means that for me the meaning of life is centered in our Redemption by Christ and what I see in the world I see in its relation to that. I don't think that this is a position that can be taken halfway or one that is particularly easy in these times to make transparent in fiction.

O'Connor realized that she was writing against the grain of the readers who discovered her stories in the *Partisan Review, Sewanee Review, Mademoiselle,* or *Harper's Bazaar.* Many readers thought that Christian dogma would make her writing doctrinaire, but she insisted that the perspective of Christianity allowed her to interpret the details of life and guaranteed her "respect for [life's] mystery." O'Connor's stories contain no prepackaged prescriptions for living, no catechisms that lay out all the answers. Instead, her characters struggle with spiritual questions in bizarre, incongruous situations. Their lives are grotesque — even comic — precisely because they do not understand their own spiritual natures. Their actions are extreme and abnormal. O'Connor explains the reasons for this in *Mystery and Manners*; she says she sought to expose the "distortions" of "modern life" that appear "normal" to her audience. Hence, she used "violent means" to convey her vision to a "hostile audience." "When you can assume that your audience holds the same beliefs you do, you can relax a little and use more normal means of talking to it." But when the audience holds different values, "you have to make your vision apparent by shock — to the hard of hearing you shout, and for the almost-blind you draw large and startling figures." O'Connor's characters lose or find their soul-saving grace in painful, chaotic circumstances that bear little or no resemblance to the slow but sure progress to the Celestial City of repentant pilgrims in traditional religious stories.

Because her characters are powerful creations who live convincing, even if ugly, lives, O'Connor's religious beliefs never supersede her storytelling. One need not be either Christian or Catholic to appreciate her concerns about human failure and degradation and her artistic ability to render fictional lives that are alternately absurdly comic and tragic. The ironies that abound in her work leave plenty of room for readers of all persuasions. O'Connor's work is narrow in the sense that her concerns are emphatically spiritual, but her compassion and her belief in human possibilities — even among the most unlikely characters — afford her fictions a capacity for wonder that is exhilarating. Her precise, deft use of language always reveals more than it seems to tell.

O'Connor's stories present complex experiences that cannot be tidily summarized; it takes the entire story to suggest the meanings. Read the following three stories for the pleasure of entering the remarkable world O'Connor creates. You're in for some surprises.

**A Note on the Text:** The first of these three stories contains the repeated use of harmful and offensive racial slurs. As you read, remember that O'Connor was writing in the segregated South just prior to the civil rights movement — a period of time when the Jim Crow laws were in effect, the South was racially segregated, and racism was often explicit. The author was well aware of the power of words to divide societies and to expose racial prejudice, and the appearance of the slurs reflects her original intent in depicting a specific character (here, the grandmother), time period, place, and culture. Be mindful of this context as you read and think critically about the story.

## A Good Man Is Hard to Find    1953

The grandmother didn't want to go to Florida. She wanted to visit some of her connections in east Tennessee and she was seizing at every chance to change Bailey's mind. Bailey was the son she lived with, her only boy. He was sitting on the edge of his chair at the table, bent over the orange sports section of the *Journal*. "Now look here, Bailey," she said, "see here, read this," and she stood with one hand on her thin hip and the other rattling the newspaper at his bald head. "Here this fellow that calls himself The Misfit is aloose from the Federal Pen and headed toward Florida and you read here what it says he did to these people. Just you read it. I wouldn't take my children in any direction with a criminal like that aloose in it. I couldn't answer to my conscience if I did."

Bailey didn't look up from his reading so she wheeled around then and faced the children's mother, a young woman in slacks, whose face was as broad and innocent as a cabbage and was tied around with a green headkerchief that had two points on the top like a rabbit's ears. She was sitting on the sofa, feeding the baby his apricots out of a jar. "The children have been to Florida before," the old lady said. "You all ought to take them somewhere else for a change so they would see different parts of the world and be broad. They never have been to east Tennessee."

The children's mother didn't seem to hear her but the eight-year-old boy, John Wesley, a stocky child with glasses, said, "If you don't want to go to Florida, why dontcha stay at home?" He and the little girl, June Star, were reading the funny papers on the floor.

"She wouldn't stay at home to be queen for a day," June Star said without raising her yellow head.

"Yes and what would you do if this fellow, The Misfit, caught you?" the grand-  5
mother asked.

"I'd smack his face," John Wesley said.

"She wouldn't stay at home for a million bucks," June Star said. "Afraid she'd miss something. She has to go everywhere we go."

"All right, Miss," the grandmother said. "Just remember that the next time you want me to curl your hair."

June Star said her hair was naturally curly.

The next morning the grandmother was the first one in the car, ready to go.  10
She had her big black valise that looked like the head of a hippopotamus in one corner, and underneath it she was hiding a basket with Pitty Sing, the cat, in it. She didn't intend for the cat to be left alone in the house for three days because he

would miss her too much and she was afraid he might brush against one of the gas burners and accidentally asphyxiate himself. Her son, Bailey, didn't like to arrive at a motel with a cat.

She sat in the middle of the back seat with John Wesley and June Star on either side of her. Bailey and the children's mother and the baby sat in front and they left Atlanta at eight forty-five with the mileage on the car at 55890. The grandmother wrote this down because she thought it would be interesting to say how many miles they had been when they got back. It took them twenty minutes to reach the outskirts of the city.

The old lady settled herself comfortably, removing her white cotton gloves and putting them up with her purse on the shelf in front of the back window. The children's mother still had on slacks and still had her head tied up in a green kerchief, but the grandmother had on a navy blue straw sailor hat with a bunch of white violets on the brim and a navy blue dress with a small white dot in the print. Her collars and cuffs were white organdy trimmed with lace and at her neckline she had pinned a purple spray of cloth violets containing a sachet. In case of an accident, anyone seeing her dead on the highway would know at once that she was a lady.

She said she thought it was going to be a good day for driving, neither too hot nor too cold, and she cautioned Bailey that the speed limit was fifty-five miles an hour and that the patrolmen hid themselves behind billboards and small clumps of trees and sped out after you before you had a chance to slow down. She pointed out interesting details of the scenery: Stone Mountain; the blue granite that in some places came up to both sides of the highway; the brilliant red clay banks slightly streaked with purple; and the various crops that made rows of green lace-work on the ground. The trees were full of silver-white sunlight and the meanest of them sparkled. The children were reading comic magazines and their mother had gone back to sleep.

"Let's go through Georgia fast so we won't have to look at it much," John Wesley said.

"If I were a little boy," said the grandmother, "I wouldn't talk about my native 15 state that way. Tennessee has the mountains and Georgia has the hills."

"Tennessee is just a hillbilly dumping ground," John Wesley said, "and Georgia is a lousy state too."

"You said it," June Star said.

"In my time," said the grandmother, folding her thin veined fingers, "children were more respectful of their native states and their parents and everything else. People did right then. Oh look at the cute little pickaninny!" she said and pointed to a Negro child standing in the door of a shack. "Wouldn't that make a picture, now?" she asked and they all turned and looked at the little Negro out of the back window. He waved.

"He didn't have any britches on," June Star said.

"He probably didn't have any," the grandmother explained. "Little niggers in 20 the country don't have things like we do. If I could paint, I'd paint that picture," she said.

The children exchanged comic books.

The grandmother offered to hold the baby and the children's mother passed him over the front seat to her. She set him on her knee and bounced him and told him about the things they were passing. She rolled her eyes and screwed up her mouth and stuck her leathery thin face into his smooth bland one. Occasionally he gave her a faraway smile. They passed a large cotton field with five or six graves fenced in the middle of it, like a small island. "Look at the graveyard!" the grandmother said, pointing it out. "That was the old family burying ground. That belonged to the plantation."

"Where's the plantation?" John Wesley asked.

"Gone With the Wind," said the grandmother. "Ha. Ha."

When the children finished all the comic books they had brought, they 25 opened the lunch and ate it. The grandmother ate a peanut butter sandwich and an olive and would not let the children throw the box and the paper napkins out the window. When there was nothing else to do they played a game by choosing a cloud and making the other two guess what shape it suggested. John Wesley took one the shape of a cow and June Star guessed a cow and John Wesley said, no, an automobile, and June Star said he didn't play fair, and they began to slap each other over the grandmother.

The grandmother said she would tell them a story if they would keep quiet. When she told a story, she rolled her eyes and waved her head and was very dramatic. She said once when she was a maiden lady she had been courted by a Mr. Edgar Atkins Teagarden from Jasper, Georgia. She said he was a very good-looking man and a gentleman and that he brought her a watermelon every Saturday afternoon with his initials cut in it, E.A.T. Well, one Saturday, she said, Mr. Teagarden brought the watermelon and there was nobody at home and he left it on the front porch and returned in his buggy to Jasper, but she never got the water-melon, she said, because a nigger boy ate it when he saw the initials, E.A.T.! This story tickled John Wesley's funny bone and he giggled and giggled but June Star didn't think it was any good. She said she wouldn't marry a man that just brought her a watermelon on Saturday. The grandmother said she would have done well to marry Mr. Teagarden because he was a gentleman and had bought Coca-Cola stock when it first came out and that he had died only a few years ago, a very wealthy man.

They stopped at The Tower for barbecued sandwiches. The Tower was a part stucco and part wood filling station and dance hall set in a clearing outside of Timothy. A fat man named Red Sammy Butts ran it and there were signs stuck here and there on the building and for miles up and down the highway saying, TRY RED SAMMY'S FAMOUS BARBECUE. NONE LIKE FAMOUS RED SAMMY'S! RED SAM! THE FAT BOY WITH THE HAPPY LAUGH. A VETERAN! RED SAMMY'S YOUR MAN!

Red Sammy was lying on the bare ground outside The Tower with his head under a truck while a gray monkey about a foot high, chained to a small chinaberry tree, chattered nearby. The monkey sprang back into the tree and got on the highest limb as soon as he saw the children jump out of the car and run toward him.

Inside, The Tower was a long dark room with a counter at one end and tables at the other and dancing space in the middle. They all sat down at a board table next to the nickelodeon and Red Sam's wife, a tall burnt-brown woman with hair and eyes lighter than her skin, came and took their order. The children's mother put a dime in the machine and played "The Tennessee Waltz," and the grand-mother said that tune always made her want to dance. She asked Bailey if he would like to dance but he only glared at her. He didn't have a naturally sunny disposition like she did and trips made him nervous. The grandmother's brown eyes were very bright. She swayed her head from side to side and pretended she was dancing in her chair. June Star said play something she could tap to so the children's mother put in another dime and played a fast number and June Star stepped out onto the dance floor and did her tap routine.

"Ain't she cute?" Red Sam's wife said, leaning over the counter. "Would you 30 like to come be my little girl?"

"No I certainly wouldn't," June Star said. "I wouldn't live in a broken-down place like this for a million bucks!" and she ran back to the table.

"Ain't she cute?" the woman repeated, stretching her mouth politely.

"Aren't you ashamed?" hissed the grandmother.

Red Sam came in and told his wife to quit lounging on the counter and hurry up with these people's order. His khaki trousers reached just to his hip bones and his stomach hung over them like a sack of meal swaying under his shirt. He came over and sat down at a table nearby and let out a combination sigh and yodel. "You can't win," he said. "You can't win," and he wiped his sweating red face off with a gray handkerchief. "These days you don't know who to trust," he said. "Ain't that the truth?"

"People are certainly not nice like they used to be," said the grandmother. 35

"Two fellers come in here last week," Red Sammy said, "driving a Chrysler. It was a old beat-up car but it was a good one and these boys looked all right to me. Said they worked at the mill and you know I let them fellers charge the gas they bought? Now why did I do that?"

"Because you're a good man!" the grandmother said at once.

"Yes'm, I suppose so," Red Sam said as if he were struck with this answer.

His wife brought the orders, carrying the five plates all at once without a tray, two in each hand and one balanced on her arm. "It isn't a soul in this green world of God's that you can trust," she said. "And I don't count nobody out of that, not nobody," she repeated, looking at Red Sammy.

"Did you read about that criminal, The Misfit, that's escaped?" asked the 40 grandmother.

"I wouldn't be a bit surprised if he didn't attack this place right here," said the woman. "If he hears about it being here, I wouldn't be none surprised to see him. If he hears it's two cent in the cash register, I wouldn't be a tall surprised if he. . . ."

"That'll do," Red Sam said. "Go bring these people their Co'-Colas," and the woman went off to get the rest of the order.

"A good man is hard to find," Red Sammy said. "Everything is getting terrible. I remember the day you could go off and leave your screen door unlatched. Not no more."

He and the grandmother discussed better times. The old lady said that in her opinion Europe was entirely to blame for the way things were now. She said the way Europe acted you would think we were made of money and Red Sam said it was no use talking about it, she was exactly right. The children ran outside into the white sunlight and looked at the monkey in the lacy chinaberry tree. He was busy catching fleas on himself and biting each one carefully between his teeth as if it were a delicacy.

They drove off again into the hot afternoon. The grandmother took cat naps 45 and woke up every few minutes with her own snoring. Outside of Toombsboro she woke up and recalled an old plantation that she had visited in this neighborhood once when she was a young lady. She said the house had six white columns across the front and that there was an avenue of oaks leading up to it and two little wooden trellis arbors on either side in front where you sat down with your suitor after a stroll in the garden. She recalled exactly which road to turn off to get to it. She knew that Bailey would not be willing to lose any time looking at an old house, but the more she talked about it, the more she wanted to see it once again and find out if the little twin arbors were still standing. "There was a secret panel in this house," she said craftily, not telling the truth but wishing that she were, "and the story went that all the family silver was hidden in it when Sherman° came through but it was never found. . . ."

"Hey!" John Wesley said. "Let's go see it! We'll find it! We'll poke all the wood-work and find it! Who lives there? Where do you turn off at? Hey Pop, can't we turn off there?"

"We never have seen a house with a secret panel!" June Star shrieked. "Let's go to the house with the secret panel! Hey Pop, can't we go see the house with the secret panel!"

"It's not far from here, I know," the grandmother said. "It won't take over twenty minutes."

Bailey was looking straight ahead. His jaw was as rigid as a horseshoe. "No," he said.

The children began to yell and scream that they wanted to see the house with  50
the secret panel. John Wesley kicked the back of the front seat and June Star hung over her mother's shoulder and whined desperately into her ear that they never had any fun even on their vacation, that they could never do what THEY wanted to do. The baby began to scream and John Wesley kicked the back of the seat so hard that his father could feel the blows in his kidney.

"All right!" he shouted and drew the car to a stop at the side of the road. "Will you all shut up? Will you all just shut up for one second? If you don't shut up, we won't go anywhere."

"It would be very educational for them," the grandmother murmured.

"All right," Bailey said, "but get this: this is the only time we're going to stop for anything like this. This is the one and only time."

"The dirt road that you have to turn down is about a mile back," the grand-mother directed. "I marked it when we passed."

"A dirt road," Bailey groaned.                                    55

After they had turned around and were headed toward the dirt road, the grandmother recalled other points about the house, the beautiful glass over the front doorway and the candle-lamp in the hall. John Wesley said that the secret panel was probably in the fireplace.

"You can't go inside this house," Bailey said. "You don't know who lives there."

"While you all talk to the people in front, I'll run around behind and get in a window," John Wesley suggested.

"We'll all stay in the car," his mother said.

They turned onto the dirt road and the car raced roughly along in a swirl of  60
pink dust. The grandmother recalled the times when there were no paved roads and thirty miles was a day's journey. The dirt road was hilly and there were sudden washes in it and sharp curves on dangerous embankments. All at once they would be on a hill, looking down over the blue tops of trees for miles around, then the next minute, they would be in a red depression with the dust-coated trees looking down on them.

"This place had better turn up in a minute," Bailey said, "or I'm going to turn around."

*Sherman:* William Tecumseh Sherman (1820–91), Union Army commander who led infamous marches through the South during the Civil War.

The road looked as if no one had traveled on it for months.

"It's not much farther," the grandmother said and just as she said it, a horrible thought came to her. The thought was so embarrassing that she turned red in the face and her eyes dilated and her feet jumped up, upsetting her valise in the corner. The instant the valise moved, the newspaper top she had over the basket under it rose with a snarl and Pitty Sing, the cat, sprang onto Bailey's shoulder.

The children were thrown to the floor and their mother, clutching the baby, was thrown out the door onto the ground; the old lady was thrown into the front seat. The car turned over once and landed right-side-up in a gulch off the side of the road. Bailey remained in the driver's seat with the cat — gray-striped with a broad white face and an orange nose — clinging to his neck like a caterpillar.

As soon as the children saw they could move their arms and legs, they scram- 65 bled out of the car, shouting, "We've had an ACCIDENT!" The grandmother was curled up under the dashboard, hoping she was injured so that Bailey's wrath would not come down on her all at once. The horrible thought she had before the accident was that the house she had remembered so vividly was not in Georgia but in Tennessee.

Bailey removed the cat from his neck with both hands and flung it out the window against the side of a pine tree. Then he got out of the car and started looking for the children's mother. She was sitting against the side of the red gutted ditch, holding the screaming baby, but she only had a cut down her face and a broken shoulder. "We've had an ACCIDENT!" the children screamed in a frenzy of delight.

"But nobody's killed," June Star said with disappointment as the grandmother limped out of the car, her hat still pinned to her head but the broken front brim standing up at a jaunty angle and the violet spray hanging off the side. They all sat down in the ditch, except the children, to recover from the shock. They were all shaking.

"Maybe a car will come along," said the children's mother hoarsely.

"I believe I have injured an organ," said the grandmother, pressing her side, but no one answered her. Bailey's teeth were clattering. He had on a yellow sport shirt with bright blue parrots designed in it and his face was as yellow as the shirt. The grandmother decided that she would not mention that the house was in Tennessee.

The road was about ten feet above and they could see only the tops of the 70 trees on the other side of it. Behind the ditch they were sitting in there were more woods, tall and dark and deep. In a few minutes they saw a car some distance away on top of a hill, coming slowly as if the occupants were watching them. The grandmother stood up and waved both arms dramatically to attract their attention. The car continued to come on slowly, disappeared around a bend and appeared again, moving even slower, on top of the hill they had gone over. It was a big black battered hearse-like automobile. There were three men in it.

It came to a stop just over them and for some minutes, the driver looked down with a steady expressionless gaze to where they were sitting, and didn't speak. Then he turned his head and muttered something to the other two and they got out. One was a fat boy in black trousers and a red sweat shirt with a silver stallion embossed on the front of it. He moved around on the right side of them and stood staring, his mouth partly open in a kind of loose grin. The other had on khaki pants and a blue striped coat and a gray hat pulled down very low, hiding most of his face. He came around slowly on the left side. Neither spoke.

The driver got out of the car and stood by the side of it, looking down at them. He was an older man than the other two. His hair was just beginning to gray and he wore silver-rimmed spectacles that gave him a scholarly look. He had a long creased face and didn't have on any shirt or undershirt. He had on blue jeans that were too tight for him and was holding a black hat and a gun. The two boys also had guns.

"We've had an ACCIDENT!" the children screamed.

The grandmother had the peculiar feeling that the bespectacled man was someone she knew. His face was as familiar to her as if she had known him all her life but she could not recall who he was. He moved away from the car and began to come down the embankment, placing his feet carefully so that he wouldn't slip. He had on tan and white shoes and no socks, and his ankles were red and thin. "Good afternoon," he said. "I see you all had you a little spill."

"We turned over twice!" said the grandmother. 75

"Oncet," he corrected. "We seen it happen. Try their car and see will it run, Hiram," he said quietly to the boy with the gray hat.

"What you got that gun for?" John Wesley asked. "Whatcha gonna do with that gun?"

"Lady," the man said to the children's mother, "would you mind calling them children to sit down by you? Children make me nervous. I want all you all to sit down right together there where you're at."

"What are you telling US what to do for?" June Star asked.

Behind them the line of woods gaped like a dark open mouth. "Come here," 80 said their mother.

"Look here now," Bailey said suddenly, "we're in a predicament! We're in. . . ."

The grandmother shrieked. She scrambled to her feet and stood staring. "You're The Misfit!" she said. "I recognized you at once!"

"Yes'm," the man said, smiling slightly as if he were pleased in spite of himself to be known, "but it would have been better for all of you, lady, if you hadn't of reckernized me."

Bailey turned his head sharply and said something to his mother that shocked even the children. The old lady began to cry and The Misfit reddened.

"Lady," he said, "don't you get upset. Sometimes a man says things he don't 85 mean. I don't reckon he meant to talk to you thataway."

"You wouldn't shoot a lady, would you?" the grandmother said and removed a clean handkerchief from her cuff and began to slap at her eyes with it.

The Misfit pointed the toe of his shoe into the ground and made a little hole and then covered it up again. "I would hate to have to," he said.

"Listen," the grandmother almost screamed, "I know you're a good man. You don't look a bit like you have common blood. I know you must come from nice people!"

"Yes mam," he said, "finest people in the world." When he smiled he showed a row of strong white teeth. "God never made a finer woman than my mother and my daddy's heart was pure gold," he said. The boy with the red sweat shirt had come around behind them and was standing with his gun at his hip. The Misfit squatted down on the ground. "Watch them children, Bobby Lee," he said. "You know they make me nervous." He looked at the six of them huddled together in front of him and he seemed to be embarrassed as if he couldn't think of anything to say. "Ain't a cloud in the sky," he remarked, looking up at it. "Don't see no sun but don't see no cloud neither."

"Yes, it's a beautiful day," said the grandmother. "Listen," she said, "you 90 shouldn't call yourself The Misfit because I know you're a good man at heart. I can just look at you and tell."

"Hush!" Bailey yelled. "Hush! Everybody shut up and let me handle this!" He was squatting in the position of a runner about to sprint forward but he didn't move.

"I pre-chate that, lady," The Misfit said and drew a little circle in the ground with the butt of his gun.

"It'll take a half a hour to fix this here car," Hiram called, looking over the raised hood of it.

"Well, first you and Bobby Lee get him and that little boy to step over yonder with you," The Misfit said, pointing to Bailey and John Wesley. "The boys want to ast you something," he said to Bailey. "Would you mind stepping back in them woods there with them?"

"Listen," Bailey began, "we're in a terrible predicament! Nobody realizes what 95 this is," and his voice cracked. His eyes were as blue and intense as the parrots in his shirt and he remained perfectly still.

The grandmother reached up to adjust her hat brim as if she were going to the woods with him but it came off in her hand. She stood staring at it and after a second she let it fall to the ground. Hiram pulled Bailey up by the arm as if he were assisting an old man. John Wesley caught hold of his father's hand and Bobby Lee followed. They went off toward the woods and just as they reached the dark edge, Bailey turned and supporting himself against a gray naked pine trunk, he shouted, "I'll be back in a minute, Mamma, wait on me!"

"Come back this instant!" his mother shrilled but they all disappeared into the woods.

"Bailey Boy!" the grandmother called in a tragic voice but she found she was looking at The Misfit squatting on the ground in front of her. "I just know you're a good man," she said desperately. "You're not a bit common!"

"Nome, I ain't a good man," The Misfit said after a second as if he had considered her statement carefully, "but I ain't the worst in the world neither. My daddy said I was a different breed of dog from my brothers and sisters. 'You know,' Daddy said, 'it's some that can live their whole life out without asking about it and it's others has to know why it is, and this boy is one of the latters. He's going to be into everything!'" He put on his black hat and looked up suddenly and then away deep into the woods as if he were embarrassed again. "I'm sorry I don't have on a shirt before you ladies," he said, hunching his shoulders slightly. "We buried our clothes that we had on when we escaped and we're just making do until we can get better. We borrowed these from some folks we met," he explained.

"That's perfectly all right," the grandmother said. "Maybe Bailey has an extra 100 shirt in his suitcase."

"I'll look and see terrectly," The Misfit said.

"Where are they taking him?" the children's mother screamed.

"Daddy was a card himself," The Misfit said. "You couldn't put anything over on him. He never got in trouble with the Authorities though. Just had the knack of handling them."

"You could be honest too if you'd only try," said the grandmother. "Think how wonderful it would be to settle down and live a comfortable life and not have to think about somebody chasing you all the time."

The Misfit kept scratching in the ground with the butt of his gun as if he were 105
thinking about it. "Yes'm, somebody is always after you," he murmured.

The grandmother noticed how thin his shoulder blades were just behind his hat
because she was standing up looking down on him. "Do you ever pray?" she asked.

He shook his head. All she saw was the black hat wiggle between his shoulder
blades. "Nome," he said.

There was a pistol shot from the woods, followed closely by another. Then
silence. The old lady's head jerked around. She could hear the wind move through
the tree tops like a long satisfied insuck of breath. "Bailey Boy!" she called.

"I was a gospel singer for a while," The Misfit said. "I been most everything.
Been in the arm service, both land and sea, at home and abroad, been twict
married, been an undertaker, been with the railroads, plowed Mother Earth, been
in a tornado, seen a man burnt alive oncet," and he looked up at the children's
mother and the little girl who were sitting close together, their faces white and their
eyes glassy; "I even seen a woman flogged," he said.

"Pray, pray," the grandmother began, "pray, pray. . . ."                                110

"I never was a bad boy that I remember of," The Misfit said in an almost
dreamy voice, "but somewheres along the line I done something wrong and got
sent to the penitentiary. I was buried alive," and he looked up and held her attention to him by a steady stare.

"That's when you should have started to pray," she said. "What did you do to
get sent to the penitentiary that first time?"

"Turn to the right, it was a wall," The Misfit said, looking up again at the
cloudless sky. "Turn to the left, it was a wall. Look up it was a ceiling, look down it
was a floor. I forget what I done, lady. I set there and set there, trying to remember
what it was I done and I ain't recalled it to this day. Oncet in a while, I would think
it was coming to me, but it never come."

"Maybe they put you in by mistake," the old lady said vaguely.

"Nome," he said. "It wasn't no mistake. They had the papers on me."          115

"You must have stolen something," she said.

The Misfit sneered slightly. "Nobody had nothing I wanted," he said. "It was a
head-doctor at the penitentiary said what I had done was kill my daddy but I known
that for a lie. My daddy died in nineteen ought nineteen of the epidemic flu and
I never had a thing to do with it. He was buried in the Mount Hopewell Baptist
churchyard and you can see for yourself."

"If you would pray," the old lady said, "Jesus would help you."

"That's right," The Misfit said.

"Well then, why don't you pray?" she asked trembling with delight suddenly.   120

"I don't want no hep," he said. "I'm doing all right by myself."

Bobby Lee and Hiram came ambling back from the woods. Bobby Lee was
dragging a yellow shirt with bright blue parrots in it.

"Throw me that shirt, Bobby Lee," The Misfit said. The shirt came flying at
him and landed on his shoulder and he put it on. The grandmother couldn't name
what the shirt reminded her of. "No, lady," The Misfit said while he was buttoning
it up, "I found out the crime don't matter. You can do one thing or you can do
another, kill a man or take a tire off his car, because sooner or later you're going to
forget what it was you done and just be punished for it."

The children's mother had begun to make heaving noises as if she couldn't get
her breath. "Lady," he asked, "would you and that little girl like to step off yonder
with Bobby Lee and Hiram and join your husband?"

"Yes, thank you," the mother said faintly. Her left arm dangled helplessly and 125 she was holding the baby, who had gone to sleep, in the other. "Hep that lady up, Hiram," The Misfit said as she struggled to climb out of the ditch, "and Bobby Lee, you hold onto that little girl's hand."

"I don't want to hold hands with him," June Star said. "He reminds me of a pig."

The fat boy blushed and laughed and caught her by the arm and pulled her off into the woods after Hiram and her mother.

Alone with The Misfit, the grandmother found that she had lost her voice. There was not a cloud in the sky nor any sun. There was nothing around her but woods. She wanted to tell him that he must pray. She opened and closed her mouth several times before anything came out. Finally she found herself saying, "Jesus, Jesus," meaning Jesus will help you, but the way she was saying it, it sounded as if she might be cursing.

"Yes'm," The Misfit said as if he agreed. "Jesus thown everything off balance. It was the same case with Him as with me except He hadn't committed any crime and they could prove I had committed one because they had the papers on me. Of course," he said, "they never shown me my papers. That's why I sign myself now. I said long ago, you get your signature and sign everything you do and keep a copy of it. Then you'll know what you done and you can hold up the crime to the punishment and see do they match and in the end you'll have something to prove you ain't been treated right. I call myself The Misfit," he said, "because I can't make what all I done wrong fit what all I gone through in punishment."

There was a piercing scream from the woods, followed closely by a pistol 130 report. "Does it seem right to you, lady, that one is punished a heap and another ain't punished at all?"

"Jesus!" the old lady cried. "You've got good blood! I know you wouldn't shoot a lady! I know you come from nice people! Pray! Jesus, you ought not to shoot a lady. I'll give you all the money I've got!"

"Lady," The Misfit said, looking beyond her far into the woods, "there never was a body that give the undertaker a tip."

There were two more pistol reports and the grandmother raised her head like a parched old turkey hen crying for water and called, "Bailey Boy, Bailey Boy!" as if her heart would break.

"Jesus was the only One that ever raised the dead," The Misfit continued, "and He shouldn't have done it. He thown everything off balance. If He did what He said, then it's nothing for you to do but thow away everything and follow Him, and if He didn't, then it's nothing for you to do but enjoy the few minutes you got left the best way you can — by killing somebody or burning down his house or doing some other meanness to him. No pleasure but meanness," he said and his voice had become almost a snarl.

"Maybe He didn't raise the dead," the old lady mumbled, not knowing what 135 she was saying and feeling so dizzy that she sank down in the ditch with her legs twisted under her.

"I wasn't there so I can't say He didn't," The Misfit said. "I wisht I had of been there," he said, hitting the ground with his fist. "It ain't right I wasn't there because if I had of been there I would of known. Listen lady," he said in a high voice, "if I had of been there I would of known and I wouldn't be like I am now." His voice seemed about to crack and the grandmother's head cleared for an instant.

She saw the man's face twisted close to her own as if he were going to cry and she murmured, "Why you're one of my babies. You're one of my own children!" She reached out and touched him on the shoulder. The Misfit sprang back as if a snake had bitten him and shot her three times through the chest. Then he put his gun down on the ground and took off his glasses and began to clean them.

Hiram and Bobby Lee returned from the woods and stood over the ditch, looking down at the grandmother who half sat and half lay in a puddle of blood with her legs crossed under her like a child's and her face smiling up at the cloudless sky.

Without his glasses, The Misfit's eyes were red-rimmed and pale and defenseless-looking. "Take her off and thow her where you thown the others," he said, picking up the cat that was rubbing itself against his leg.

"She was a talker, wasn't she?" Bobby Lee said, sliding down the ditch with a yodel.

"She would of been a good woman," The Misfit said, "if it had been somebody    140 there to shoot her every minute of her life."

"Some fun!" Bobby Lee said.

"Shut up, Bobby Lee," The Misfit said. "It's no real pleasure in life."

## CONSIDERATIONS FOR CRITICAL THINKING AND WRITING

1. FIRST RESPONSE. How does O'Connor portray the family? What is comic about them? What qualities about them are we meant to take seriously? Are you shocked by what happens to them? Does your attitude toward them remain constant during the course of the story?

2. How do the grandmother's concerns about the trip to Florida foreshadow events in the story?

3. Describe the grandmother. How does O'Connor make her the central character?

4. What is Red Sammy's purpose in the story? Relate his view of life to the story's conflicts.

5. Characterize The Misfit. What makes him so? Can he be written off as simply insane? How does the grandmother respond to him?

6. Why does The Misfit say that "Jesus thown everything off balance" (par. 129)? What does religion have to do with the brutal action of this story?

7. What does The Misfit mean at the end when he says about the grandmother, "She would of been a good woman . . . if it had been somebody there to shoot her every minute of her life" (par. 140)?

8. Describe the story's tone. Is it consistent? What is the effect of O'Connor's use of tone?

9. How is coincidence used to advance the plot? How do coincidences lead to ironies in the story?

10. Explain how the title points to the story's theme.

## CONNECTION TO ANOTHER SELECTION

1. What makes "A Good Man Is Hard to Find" so difficult to interpret in contrast, say, to Charlotte Perkins Gilman's "The Yellow Wallpaper" (p. 126)?

## Good Country People 1955

Besides the neutral expression that she wore when she was alone, Mrs. Freeman had two others, forward and reverse, that she used for all her human dealings. Her forward expression was steady and driving like the advance of a heavy truck. Her eyes never swerved to left or right but turned as the story turned as if they followed a yellow line down the center of it. She seldom used the other expression because it was not often necessary for her to retract a statement, but when she did, her face came to a complete stop, there was an almost imperceptible movement of her black eyes, during which they seemed to be receding, and then the observer would see that Mrs. Freeman, though she might stand there as real as several grain sacks thrown on top of each other, was no longer there in spirit. As for getting anything across to her when this was the case, Mrs. Hopewell had given it up. She might talk her head off. Mrs. Freeman could never be brought to admit herself wrong on any point. She would stand there and if she could be brought to say anything, it was something like, "Well, I wouldn't of said it was and I wouldn't of said it wasn't," or letting her gaze range over the top kitchen shelf where there was an assortment of dusty bottles, she might remark, "I see you ain't ate many of them figs you put up last summer."

They carried on their most important business in the kitchen at breakfast. Every morning Mrs. Hopewell got up at seven o'clock and lit her gas heater and Joy's. Joy was her daughter, a large blonde girl who had an artificial leg. Mrs. Hopewell thought of her as a child though she was thirty-two years old and highly educated. Joy would get up while her mother was eating and lumber into the bathroom and slam the door, and before long, Mrs. Freeman would arrive at the back door. Joy would hear her mother call, "Come on in," and then they would talk for a while in low voices that were indistinguishable in the bathroom. By the time Joy came in, they had usually finished the weather report and were on one or the other of Mrs. Freeman's daughters, Glynese or Carramae, Joy called them Glycerin and Caramel. Glynese, a redhead, was eighteen and had many admirers; Carramae, a blonde, was only fifteen but already married and pregnant. She could not keep anything in her stomach. Every morning Mrs. Freeman told Mrs. Hopewell how many times she had vomited since the last report.

Mrs. Hopewell liked to tell people that Glynese and Carramae were two of the finest girls she knew and that Mrs. Freeman was a *lady* and that she was never ashamed to take her anywhere or introduce her to anybody they might meet. Then she would tell how she had happened to hire the Freemans in the first place and how they were a godsend to her and how she had had them four years. The reason for her keeping them so long was that they were not trash. They were good country people. She had telephoned the man whose name they had given as a reference and he had told her that Mr. Freeman was a good farmer but that his wife was the nosiest woman ever to walk the earth. "She's got to be into everything," the man said. "If she don't get there before the dust settles, you can bet she's dead, that's all. She'll want to know all your business. I can stand him real good," he had said, "but me nor my wife neither could have stood that woman one more minute on this place." That had put Mrs. Hopewell off for a few days.

She had hired them in the end because there were no other applicants but she had made up her mind beforehand exactly how she would handle the woman. Since she was the type who had to be into everything, then, Mrs. Hopewell decided, she would not only let her be into everything, she would *see to it* that she was into everything — she would give her the responsibility of everything, she would put her in charge. Mrs. Hopewell had no bad qualities of her own but she was able to use other people's in such a constructive way that she never felt the lack. She had hired the Freemans and she had kept them four years.

Nothing is perfect. This was one of Mrs. Hopewell's favorite sayings. Another 5 was: that is life! And still another, the most important, was: well, other people have their opinions too. She would make these statements, usually at the table, in a tone of gentle insistence as if no one held them but her, and the large hulking Joy, whose constant outrage had obliterated every expression from her face, would stare just a little to the side of her, her eyes icy blue, with the look of someone who has achieved blindness by an act of will and means to keep it.

When Mrs. Hopewell said to Mrs. Freeman that life was like that, Mrs. Freeman would say, "I always said so myself." Nothing had been arrived at by anyone that had not first been arrived at by her. She was quicker than Mr. Freeman. When Mrs. Hopewell said to her after they had been on the place a while, "You know, you're the wheel behind the wheel," and winked, Mrs. Freeman had said, "I know it. I've always been quick. It's some that are quicker than others."

"Everybody is different," Mrs. Hopewell said.

"Yes, most people is," Mrs. Freeman said.

"It takes all kinds to make the world."

"I always said it did myself."                                                    10

The girl was used to this kind of dialogue for breakfast and more of it for dinner; sometimes they had it for supper too. When they had no guest they ate in the kitchen because that was easier. Mrs. Freeman always managed to arrive at some point during the meal and to watch them finish it. She would stand in the doorway if it were summer but in the winter she would stand with one elbow on top of the refrigerator and look down on them, or she would stand by the gas heater, lifting the back of her skirt slightly. Occasionally she would stand against the wall and roll her head from side to side. At no time was she in any hurry to leave. All this was very trying on Mrs. Hopewell but she was a woman of great patience. She realized that nothing is perfect and that in the Freemans she had good country people and that if, in this day and age, you get good country people, you had better hang onto them.

She had had plenty of experience with trash. Before the Freemans she had averaged one tenant family a year. The wives of these farmers were not the kind you would want to be around you for very long. Mrs. Hopewell, who had divorced her husband long ago, needed someone to walk over the fields with her; and when Joy had to be impressed for these services, her remarks were usually so ugly and her face so glum that Mrs. Hopewell would say, "If you can't come pleasantly, I don't want you at all," to which the girl, standing square and rigid-shouldered with her neck thrust slightly forward, would reply, "If you want me, here I am — LIKE I AM."

Mrs. Hopewell excused this attitude because of the leg (which had been shot off in a hunting accident when Joy was ten). It was hard for Mrs. Hopewell to real-ize that her child was thirty-two now and that for more than twenty years she had had only one leg. She thought of her still as a child because it tore her heart to think instead of the poor stout girl in her thirties who had never danced a step or had any *normal* good times. Her name was really Joy but as soon as she was twenty-one and away from home, she had had it legally changed. Mrs. Hopewell was certain that she had thought and thought until she had hit upon the ugliest name in any language. Then she had gone and had the beautiful name, Joy, changed without telling her mother until after she had done it. Her legal name was Hulga.

When Mrs. Hopewell thought the name, Hulga, she thought of the broad blank hull of a battleship. She would not use it. She continued to call her Joy to which the girl responded but in a purely mechanical way.

Hulga had learned to tolerate Mrs. Freeman who saved her from taking walks 15 with her mother. Even Glynese and Carramae were useful when they occupied attention that might otherwise have been directed at her. At first she had thought she could not stand Mrs. Freeman for she had found that it was not possible to be rude to her. Mrs. Freeman would take on strange resentments and for days together she would be sullen but the source of her displeasure was always obscure; a direct attack, a positive leer, blatant ugliness to her face — these never touched her. And without warning one day, she began calling her Hulga.

She did not call her that in front of Mrs. Hopewell who would have been incensed but when she and the girl happened to be out of the house together, she would say something and add the name Hulga to the end of it, and the big spectacled Joy-Hulga would scowl and redden as if her privacy had been intruded upon. She considered the name her personal affair. She had arrived at it first purely on the basis of its ugly sound and then the full genius of its fitness had struck her. She had a vision of the name working like the ugly sweating Vulcan° who stayed in the furnace and to whom, presumably, the goddess had to come when called. She saw it as the name of her highest creative act. One of her major triumphs was that her mother had not been able to turn her dust into Joy, but the greater one was that she had been able to turn it herself into Hulga. However, Mrs. Freeman's relish for using the name only irritated her. It was as if Mrs. Freeman's beady steel-pointed eyes had penetrated far enough behind her face to reach some secret fact. Something about her seemed to fascinate Mrs. Freeman and then one day Hulga realized that it was the artificial leg. Mrs. Freeman had a special fondness for the details of secret infections, hidden deformities, assaults upon children. Of diseases, she preferred the lingering or incurable. Hulga had heard Mrs. Hopewell give her the details of the hunting accident, how the leg had been literally blasted off, how she had never lost consciousness. Mrs. Freeman could listen to it any time as if it had happened an hour ago.

When Hulga stumped into the kitchen in the morning (she could walk without making the awful noise but she made it — Mrs. Hopewell was certain — because it was ugly-sounding), she glanced at them and did not speak. Mrs. Hopewell would be in her red kimono with her hair tied around her head in rags. She would be sitting at the table, finishing her breakfast and Mrs. Freeman would be hanging by her elbow outward from the refrigerator, looking down at the table. Hulga always put her eggs on the stove to boil and then stood over them with her arms folded, and Mrs. Hopewell would look at her — a kind of indirect gaze divided between her and Mrs. Freeman — and would think that if she would only keep herself up a little, she wouldn't be so bad looking. There was nothing wrong with her face that a pleasant expression wouldn't help. Mrs. Hopewell said that people who looked on the bright side of things would be beautiful even if they were not.

Whenever she looked at Joy this way, she could not help but feel that it would have been better if the child had not taken the Ph.D. It had certainly not brought her out any and now that she had it, there was no more excuse for her to go to

*Vulcan:* Roman god of fire.

school again. Mrs. Hopewell thought it was nice for girls to go to school to have a good time but Joy had "gone through." Anyhow, she would not have been strong enough to go again. The doctors had told Mrs. Hopewell that with the best of care, Joy might see forty-five. She had a weak heart. Joy had made it plain that if it had not been for this condition, she would be far from these red hills and good country people. She would be in a university lecturing to people who knew what she was talking about. And Mrs. Hopewell could very well picture her there, looking like a scarecrow and lecturing to more of the same. Here she went about all day in a six-year-old skirt and a yellow sweat shirt with a faded cowboy on a horse embossed on it. She thought this was funny; Mrs. Hopewell thought it was idiotic and showed simply that she was still a child. She was brilliant but she didn't have a grain of sense. It seemed to Mrs. Hopewell that every year she grew less like other people and more like herself—bloated, rude, and squint-eyed. And she said such strange things! To her own mother she had said—without warning, without excuse, standing up in the middle of a meal with her face purple and her mouth half full—"Woman! do you ever look inside? Do you ever look inside and see what you are *not*? God!" she had cried sinking down again and staring at her plate, "Malebranche° was right: we are not our own light. We are not our own light!" Mrs. Hopewell had no idea to this day what brought that on. She had only made the remark, hoping Joy would take it in, that a smile never hurt anyone.

The girl had taken the Ph.D. in philosophy and this left Mrs. Hopewell at a complete loss. You could say, "My daughter is a nurse," or "My daughter is a schoolteacher," or even, "My daughter is a chemical engineer." You could not say, "My daughter is a philosopher." That was something that had ended with the Greeks and Romans. All day Joy sat on her neck in a deep chair, reading. Sometimes she went for walks but she didn't like dogs or cats or birds or flowers or nature or nice young men. She looked at nice young men as if she could smell their stupidity.

One day Mrs. Hopewell had picked up one of the books the girl had just put 20 down and opening it at random, she read, "Science, on the other hand, has to assert its soberness and seriousness afresh and declare that it is concerned solely with what-is. Nothing—how can it be for science anything but a horror and a phantasm? If science is right, then one thing stands firm: science wishes to know nothing of nothing. Such is after all the strictly scientific approach to Nothing. We know it by wishing to know nothing of Nothing." These words had been underlined with a blue pencil and they worked on Mrs. Hopewell like some evil incantation in gibberish. She shut the book quickly and went out of the room as if she were having a chill.

This morning when the girl came in, Mrs. Freeman was on Carramae. "She thrown up four times after supper," she said, "and was up twict in the night after three o'clock. Yesterday she didn't do nothing but ramble in the bureau drawer. All she did. Stand up there and see what she could run up on."

"She's got to eat," Mrs. Hopewell muttered, sipping her coffee, while she watched Joy's back at the stove. She was wondering what the child had said to the Bible salesman. She could not imagine what kind of a conversation she could possibly have had with him.

He was a tall gaunt hatless youth who had called yesterday to sell them a Bible. He had appeared at the door, carrying a large black suitcase that weighted him so heavily on one side that he had to brace himself against the door facing. He

---

*Malebranche:* Nicolas Malebranche (1638–1715), a French philosopher.

seemed on the point of collapse but he said in a cheerful voice, "Good morning, Mrs. Cedars!" and set the suitcase down on the mat. He was not a bad-looking young man though he had on a bright blue suit and yellow socks that were not pulled up far enough. He had prominent face bones and a streak of sticky-looking brown hair falling across his forehead.

"I'm Mrs. Hopewell," she said.

"Oh!" he said, pretending to look puzzled but with his eyes sparkling, "I saw 25 it said 'The Cedars' on the mailbox so I thought you was Mrs. Cedars!" and he burst out in a pleasant laugh. He picked up the satchel and under cover of a pant, he fell forward into her hall. It was rather as if the suitcase had moved first, jerking him after it. "Mrs. Hopewell!" he said and grabbed her hand. "I hope you are well!" and he laughed again and then all at once his face sobered completely. He paused and gave her a straight earnest look and said, "Lady, I've come to speak of serious things."

"Well, come in," she muttered, none too pleased because her dinner was almost ready. He came into the parlor and sat down on the edge of a straight chair and put the suitcase between his feet and glanced around the room as if he were sizing her up by it. Her silver gleamed on the two sideboards; she decided he had never been in a room as elegant as this.

"Mrs. Hopewell," he began, using her name in a way that sounded almost intimate, "I know you believe in Chrustian service."

"Well yes," she murmured.

"I know," he said and paused, looking very wise with his head cocked on one side, "that you're a good woman. Friends have told me."

Mrs. Hopewell never liked to be taken for a fool. "What are you selling?" she 30 asked.

"Bibles," the young man said and his eye raced around the room before he added, "I see you have no family Bible in your parlor, I see that is the one lack you got!"

Mrs. Hopewell could not say, "My daughter is an atheist and won't let me keep the Bible in the parlor." She said, stiffening slightly, "I keep my Bible by my bedside." This was not the truth. It was in the attic somewhere.

"Lady," he said, "the word of God ought to be in the parlor."

"Well, I think that's a matter of taste," she began. "I think . . ."

"Lady," he said, "for a Chrustian, the word of God ought to be in every room 35 in the house besides in his heart. I know you're a Chrustian because I can see it in every line of your face."

She stood up and said, "Well, young man, I don't want to buy a Bible and I smell my dinner burning."

He didn't get up. He began to twist his hands and looking down at them, he said softly, "Well lady, I'll tell you the truth — not many people want to buy one nowadays and besides, I know I'm real simple. I don't know how to say a thing but to say it. I'm just a country boy." He glanced up into her unfriendly face. "People like you don't like to fool with country people like me!"

"Why!" she cried, "good country people are the salt of the earth! Besides, we all have different ways of doing, it takes all kinds to make the world go 'round. That's life!"

"You said a mouthful," he said.

"Why, I think there aren't enough good people in the world!" she said, stirred. 40 "I think that's what's wrong with it!"

His face had brightened. "I didn't introduce myself," he said. "I'm Manley Pointer from out in the country around Willohobie, not even from a place, just from near a place."

"You wait a minute," she said. "I have to see about my dinner." She went out to the kitchen and found Joy standing near the door where she had been listening.

"Get rid of the salt of the earth," she said, "and let's eat."

Mrs. Hopewell gave her a pained look and turned the heat down under the vegetables. "I can't be rude to anybody," she murmured and went back into the parlor.

He had opened the suitcase and was sitting with a Bible on each knee.                45

"You might as well put those up," she told him. "I don't want one."

"I appreciate your honesty," he said. "You don't see any more real honest people unless you go way out in the country."

"I know," she said, "real genuine folks!" Through the crack in the door she heard a groan.

"I guess a lot of boys come telling you they're working their way through college," he said, "but I'm not going to tell you that. Somehow," he said, "I don't want to go to college. I want to devote my life to Chrustian service. See," he said, lowering his voice, "I got this heart condition. I may not live long. When you know it's something wrong with you and you may not live long, well then, lady. . . ." He paused, with his mouth open, and stared at her.

He and Joy had the same condition! She knew that her eyes were filling with   50
tears but she collected herself quickly and murmured, "Won't you stay for dinner? We'd love to have you!" and was sorry the instant she heard herself say it.

"Yes mam," he said in an abashed voice, "I would sher love to do that!"

Joy had given him one look on being introduced to him and then throughout the meal had not glanced at him again. He had addressed several remarks to her, which she had pretended not to hear. Mrs. Hopewell could not understand deliberate rudeness, although she lived with it, and she felt she had always to overflow with hospitality to make up for Joy's lack of courtesy. She urged him to talk about himself and he did. He said he was the seventh child of twelve and that his father had been crushed under a tree when he himself was eight years old. He had been crushed very badly, in fact, almost cut in two and was practically not recognizable. His mother had got along the best she could by hard working and she had always seen that her children went to Sunday School and that they read the Bible every evening. He was now nineteen years old and he had been selling Bibles for four months. In that time he had sold seventy-seven Bibles and had the promise of two more sales. He wanted to become a missionary because he thought that was the way you could do most for people. "He who losest his life shall find it," he said simply and he was so sincere, so genuine and earnest that Mrs. Hopewell would not for the world have smiled. He prevented his peas from sliding onto the table by blocking them with a piece of bread which he later cleaned his plate with. She could see Joy observing sidewise how he handled his knife and fork and she saw too that every few minutes, the boy would dart a keen appraising glance at the girl as if he were trying to attract her attention.

After dinner Joy cleared the dishes off the table and disappeared and Mrs. Hopewell was left to talk with him. He told her again about his childhood and his father's accident and about various things that had happened to him. Every five minutes or so she would stifle a yawn. He sat for two hours until finally she told him she must go because she had an appointment in town.

He packed his Bibles and thanked her and prepared to leave, but in the doorway he stopped and wrung her hand and said that not on any of his trips had he met a lady as nice as her and he asked if he could come again. She had said she would always be happy to see him.

Joy had been standing in the road, apparently looking at something in the distance, when he came down the steps toward her, bent to the side with his heavy valise. He stopped where she was standing and confronted her directly. Mrs. Hopewell could not hear what he said but she trembled to think what Joy would say to him. She could see that after a minute Joy said something and that then the boy began to speak again, making an excited gesture with his free hand. After a minute Joy said something else at which the boy began to speak once more. Then to her amazement, Mrs. Hopewell saw the two of them walk off together, toward the gate. Joy had walked all the way to the gate with him and Mrs. Hopewell could not imagine what they had said to each other, and she had not yet dared to ask.

Mrs. Freeman was insisting upon her attention. She had moved from the 55 refrigerator to the heater so that Mrs. Hopewell had to turn and face her in order to seem to be listening. "Glynese gone out with Harvey Hill again last night," she said. "She had this sty."

"Hill," Mrs. Hopewell said absently, "is the one who works in the garage?"

"Nome, he's the one that goes to chiropractor school," Mrs. Freeman said. "She had this sty. Been had it two days. So she says when he brought her in the other night he says, 'Lemme get rid of that sty for you,' and she says, 'How?' and he says, 'You just lay yourself down acrost the seat of that car and I'll show you.' So she done it and he popped her neck. Kept on a-popping it several times until she made him quit. This morning," Mrs. Freeman said, "she ain't got no sty. She ain't got no traces of a sty."

"I never heard of that before," Mrs. Hopewell said.

"He ast her to marry him before the Ordinary,"° Mrs. Freeman went on, "and she told him she wasn't going to be married in no *office*."

"Well, Glynese is a fine girl," Mrs. Hopewell said. "Glynese and Carramae are 60 both fine girls."

"Carramae said when her and Lyman was married Lyman said it sure felt sacred to him. She said he said he wouldn't take five hundred dollars for being married by a preacher."

"How much would he take?" the girl asked from the stove.

"He said he wouldn't take five hundred dollars," Mrs. Freeman repeated.

"Well we all have work to do," Mrs. Hopewell said.

"Lyman said it just felt more sacred to him," Mrs. Freeman said. "The doctor 65 wants Carramae to eat prunes. Says instead of medicine. Says them cramps is coming from pressure. You know where I think it is?"

"She'll be better in a few weeks," Mrs. Hopewell said.

"In the tube," Mrs. Freeman said. "Else she wouldn't be as sick as she is."

Hulga had cracked her two eggs into a saucer and was bringing them to the table along with a cup of coffee that she had filled too full. She sat down carefully and began to eat, meaning to keep Mrs. Freeman there by questions if for any reason she showed an inclination to leave. She could perceive her mother's eye on her. The first round-about question would be about the Bible salesman and she did not wish to bring it on. "How did he pop her neck?" she asked.

*Ordinary:* Justice of the peace.

Mrs. Freeman went into a description of how he had popped her neck. She said he owned a '55 Mercury but that Glynese said she would rather marry a man with only a '36 Plymouth who would be married by a preacher. The girl asked what if he had a '32 Plymouth and Mrs. Freeman said what Glynese had said was a '36 Plymouth.

Mrs. Hopewell said there were not many girls with Glynese's common sense. 70 She said what she admired in those girls was their common sense. She said that reminded her that they had had a nice visitor yesterday, a young man selling Bibles. "Lord," she said, "he bored me to death but he was so sincere and genuine I couldn't be rude to him. He was just good country people, you know," she said, "— just the salt of the earth."

"I seen him walk up," Mrs. Freeman said, "and then later — I seen him walk off," and Hulga could feel the slight shift in her voice, the slight insinuation, that he had not walked off alone, had he? Her face remained expressionless but the color rose into her neck and she seemed to swallow it down with the next spoonful of egg. Mrs. Freeman was looking at her as if they had a secret together.

"Well, it takes all kinds of people to make the world go 'round," Mrs. Hopewell said. "It's very good we aren't all alike."

"Some people are more alike than others," Mrs. Freeman said.

Hulga got up and stumped, with about twice the noise that was necessary, into her room and locked the door. She was to meet the Bible salesman at ten o'clock at the gate. She had thought about it half the night. She had started thinking of it as a great joke and then she had begun to see profound implications in it. She had lain in bed imagining dialogues for them that were insane on the surface but that reached below to depths that no Bible salesman would be aware of. Their conversation yesterday had been of this kind.

He had stopped in front of her and had simply stood there. His face was bony 75 and sweaty and bright, with a little pointed nose in the center of it, and his look was different from what it had been at the dinner table. He was gazing at her with open curiosity, with fascination, like a child watching a new fantastic animal at the zoo, and he was breathing as if he had run a great distance to reach her. His gaze seemed somehow familiar but she could not think where she had been regarded with it before. For almost a minute he didn't say anything. Then on what seemed an insuck of breath, he whispered, "You ever ate a chicken that was two days old?"

The girl looked at him stonily. He might have just put this question up for consideration at the meeting of a philosophical association. "Yes," she presently replied as if she had considered it from all angles.

"It must have been mighty small!" he said triumphantly and shook all over with little nervous giggles, getting very red in the face, and subsiding finally into his gaze of complete admiration, while the girl's expression remained exactly the same.

"How old are you?" he asked softly.

She waited some time before she answered. Then in a flat voice she said, "Seventeen."

His smiles came in succession like waves breaking on the surface of a little 80 lake. "I see you got a wooden leg," he said. "I think you're brave. I think you're real sweet."

The girl stood blank and solid and silent.

"Walk to the gate with me," he said. "You're a brave sweet little thing and I liked you the minute I seen you walk in the door."

Hulga began to move forward.

"What's your name?" he asked, smiling down on the top of her head.

"Hulga," she said.                                                                                    85

"Hulga," he murmured, "Hulga. Hulga. I never heard of anybody name Hulga before. You're shy, aren't you, Hulga?" he asked.

She nodded, watching his large red hand on the handle of the giant valise.

"I like girls that wear glasses," he said. "I think a lot. I'm not like these people that a serious thought don't ever enter their heads. It's because I may die."

"I may die too," she said suddenly and looked up at him. His eyes were very small and brown, glittering feverishly.

"Listen," he said, "don't you think some people was meant to meet on account  90 of what all they got in common and all? Like they both think serious thoughts and all?" He shifted the valise to his other hand so that the hand nearest her was free. He caught hold of her elbow and shook it a little. "I don't work on Saturday," he said. "I like to walk in the woods and see what Mother Nature is wearing. O'er the hills and far away. Picnics and things. Couldn't we go on a picnic tomorrow? Say yes, Hulga," he said and gave her a dying look as if he felt his insides about to drop out of him. He had even seemed to sway slightly toward her.

During the night she had imagined that she seduced him. She imagined that the two of them walked on the place until they came to the storage barn beyond the two back fields and there, she imagined, that things came to such a pass that she very easily seduced him and that then, of course, she had to reckon with his remorse. True genius can get an idea across even to an inferior mind. She imagined that she took his remorse in hand and changed it into a deeper understanding of life. She took all his shame away and turned it into something useful.

She set off for the gate at exactly ten o'clock, escaping without drawing Mrs. Hopewell's attention. She didn't take anything to eat, forgetting that food is usually taken on a picnic. She wore a pair of slacks and a dirty white shirt, and as an afterthought, she had put some Vapex° on the collar of it since she did not own any perfume. When she reached the gate no one was there.

She looked up and down the empty highway and had the furious feeling that she had been tricked, that he had only meant to make her walk to the gate after the idea of him. Then suddenly he stood up, very tall, from behind a bush on the opposite embankment. Smiling, he lifted his hat which was new and wide-brimmed. He had not worn it yesterday and she wondered if he had bought it for the occasion. It was toast-colored with a red and white band around it and was slightly too large for him. He stepped from behind the bush still carrying the black valise. He had on the same suit and the same yellow socks sucked down in his shoes from walking. He crossed the highway and said, "I knew you'd come!"

The girl wondered acidly how he had known this. She pointed to the valise and asked, "Why did you bring your Bibles?"

He took her elbow, smiling down on her as if he could not stop. "You can  95 never tell when you'll need the word of God, Hulga," he said. She had a moment in which she doubted that this was actually happening and then they began to climb the embankment. They went down into the pasture toward the woods. The boy walked lightly by her side, bouncing on his toes. The valise did not seem to be heavy today; he even swung it. They crossed half the pasture without saying

*Vapex:* Trade name for a nasal spray.

anything and then, putting his hand easily on the small of her back, he asked softly, "Where does your wooden leg join on?"

She turned an ugly red and glared at him and for an instant the boy looked abashed. "I didn't mean you no harm," he said. "I only meant you're so brave and all. I guess God takes care of you."

"No," she said, looking forward and walking fast, "I don't even believe in God."

At this he stopped and whistled. "No!" he exclaimed as if he were too astonished to say anything else.

She walked on and in a second he was bouncing at her side, fanning with his hat. "That's very unusual for a girl," he remarked, watching her out of the corner of his eye. When they reached the edge of the wood, he put his hand on her back again and drew her against him without a word and kissed her heavily.

The kiss, which had more pressure than feeling behind it, produced that extra 100 surge of adrenaline in the girl that enables one to carry a packed trunk out of a burning house, but in her, the power went at once to the brain. Even before he released her, her mind, clear and detached and ironic anyway, was regarding him from a great distance, with amusement but with pity. She had never been kissed before and she was pleased to discover that it was an unexceptional experience and all a matter of the mind's control. Some people might enjoy drain water if they were told it was vodka. When the boy, looking expectant but uncertain, pushed her gently away, she turned and walked on, saying nothing as if such business, for her, were common enough.

He came along panting at her side, trying to help her when he saw a root that she might trip over. He caught and held back the long swaying blades of thorn vine until she had passed beyond them. She led the way and he came breathing heavily behind her. Then they came out on a sunlit hillside, sloping softly into another one a little smaller. Beyond, they could see the rusted top of the old barn where the extra hay was stored.

The hill was sprinkled with small pink weeds. "Then you ain't saved?" he asked suddenly, stopping.

The girl smiled. It was the first time she had smiled at him at all. "In my economy," she said, "I'm saved and you are damned but I told you I didn't believe in God."

Nothing seemed to destroy the boy's look of admiration. He gazed at her now as if the fantastic animal at the zoo had put its paw through the bars and given him a loving poke. She thought he looked as if he wanted to kiss her again and she walked on before he had the chance.

"Ain't there somewheres we can sit down sometime?" he murmured, his voice 105 softening toward the end of the sentence.

"In that barn," she said.

They made for it rapidly as if it might slide away like a train. It was a large two-story barn, cool and dark inside. The boy pointed up the ladder that led into the loft and said, "It's too bad we can't go up there."

"Why can't we?" she asked.

"Yer leg," he said reverently.

The girl gave him a contemptuous look and putting both hands on the lad- 110 der, she climbed it while he stood below, apparently awestruck. She pulled herself expertly through the opening and then looked down at him and said, "Well, come on if you're coming," and he began to climb the ladder, awkwardly bringing the suitcase with him.

"We won't need the Bible," she observed.

"You never can tell," he said, panting. After he had got into the loft, he was a few seconds catching his breath. She had sat down in a pile of straw. A wide sheath of sunlight, filled with dust particles, slanted over her. She lay back against a bale, her face turned away, looking out the front opening of the barn where hay was thrown from a wagon into the loft. The two pink-speckled hillsides lay back against a dark ridge of woods. The sky was cloudless and cold blue. The boy dropped down by her side and put one arm under her and the other over her and began methodically kissing her face, making little noises like a fish. He did not remove his hat but it was pushed far enough back not to interfere. When her glasses got in his way, he took them off of her and slipped them into his pocket.

The girl at first did not return any of the kisses but presently she began to and after she had put several on his cheek, she reached his lips and remained there, kissing him again and again as if she were trying to draw all the breath out of him. His breath was clear and sweet like a child's and the kisses were sticky like a child's. He mumbled about loving her and about knowing when he first seen her that he loved her, but the mumbling was like the sleepy fretting of a child being put to sleep by his mother. Her mind, throughout this, never stopped or lost itself for a second to her feelings. "You ain't said you loved me none," he whispered finally, pulling back from her. "You got to say that."

She looked away from him off into the hollow sky and then down at a black ridge and then down farther into what appeared to be two green swelling lakes. She didn't realize he had taken her glasses but this landscape could not seem exceptional to her for she seldom paid any close attention to her surroundings.

"You got to say it," he repeated. "You got to say you love me."          115

She was always careful how she committed herself. "In a sense," she began, "if you use the word loosely, you might say that. But it's not a word I use. I don't have illusions. I'm one of those people who see *through* to nothing."

The boy was frowning. "You got to say it. I said it and you got to say it," he said.

The girl looked at him almost tenderly. "You poor baby," she murmured. "It's just as well you don't understand," and she pulled him by the neck, face-down, against her. "We are all damned," she said, "but some of us have taken off our blindfolds and see that there's nothing to see. It's a kind of salvation."

The boy's astonished eyes looked blankly through the ends of her hair. "Okay," he almost whined, "but do you love me or don'tcher?"

"Yes," she said and added, "in a sense. But I must tell you something. There    120
mustn't be anything dishonest between us." She lifted his head and looked him in the eye. "I am thirty years old," she said. "I have a number of degrees."

The boy's look was irritated but dogged. "I don't care," he said. "I don't care a thing about what all you done. I just want to know if you love me or don'tcher?" and he caught her to him and wildly planted her face with kisses until she said, "Yes, yes."

"Okay then," he said, letting her go. "Prove it."

She smiled, looking dreamily out on the shifty landscape. She had seduced him without even making up her mind to try. "How?" she asked, feeling that he should be delayed a little.

He leaned over and put his lips to her ear. "Show me where your wooden leg joins on," he whispered.

The girl uttered a sharp little cry and her face instantly drained of color.    125
The obscenity of the suggestion was not what shocked her. As a child she had

sometimes been subject to feelings of shame but education had removed the last traces of that as a good surgeon scrapes for cancer; she would no more have felt it over what he was asking than she would have believed in his Bible. But she was as sensitive about the artificial leg as a peacock about his tail. No one ever touched it but her. She took care of it as someone else would his soul, in private and almost with her own eyes turned away. "No," she said.

"I known it," he muttered, sitting up. "You're just playing me for a sucker."

"Oh no no!" she cried. "It joins on at the knee. Only at the knee. Why do you want to see it?"

The boy gave her a long penetrating look. "Because," he said, "it's what makes you different. You ain't like anybody else."

She sat staring at him. There was nothing about her face or her round freezing-blue eyes to indicate that this had moved her; but she felt as if her heart had stopped and left her mind to pump her blood. She decided that for the first time in her life she was face to face with real innocence. This boy, with an instinct that came from beyond wisdom, had touched the truth about her. When after a minute, she said in a hoarse high voice, "All right," it was like surrendering to him completely. It was like losing her own life and finding it again, miraculously, in his.

Very gently he began to roll the slack leg up. The artificial limb, in a white 130 sock and brown flat shoe, was bound in a heavy material like canvas and ended in an ugly jointure where it was attached to the stump. The boy's face and his voice were entirely reverent as he uncovered it and said, "Now show me how to take it off and on."

She took it off for him and put it back on again and then he took it off himself, handling it as tenderly as if it were a real one. "See!" he said with a delighted child's face. "Now I can do it myself!"

"Put it back on," she said. She was thinking that she would run away with him and that every night he would take the leg off and every morning put it back on again. "Put it back on," she said.

"Not yet," he murmured, setting it on its foot out of her reach. "Leave it off for a while. You got me instead."

She gave a little cry of alarm but he pushed her down and began to kiss her again. Without the leg she felt entirely dependent on him. Her brain seemed to have stopped thinking altogether and to be about some other function that it was not very good at. Different expressions raced back and forth over her face. Every now and then the boy, his eyes like two steel spikes, would glance behind him where the leg stood. Finally she pushed him off and said, "Put it back on me now."

"Wait," he said. He leaned the other way and pulled the valise toward him and 135 opened it. It had a pale blue spotted lining and there were only two Bibles in it. He took one of these out and opened the cover of it. It was hollow and contained a pocket flask of whiskey, a pack of cards, and a small blue box with printing on it. He laid these out in front of her one at a time in an evenly-spaced row, like one presenting offerings at the shrine of a goddess. He put the blue box in her hand. THIS PRODUCT TO BE USED ONLY FOR THE PREVENTION OF DISEASE, she read, and dropped it. The boy was unscrewing the top of the flask. He stopped and pointed, with a smile, to the deck of cards. It was not an ordinary deck but one with an obscene picture on the back of each card. "Take a swig," he said, offering her the bottle first. He held it in front of her, but like one mesmerized, she did not move.

Her voice when she spoke had an almost pleading sound. "Aren't you," she murmured, "aren't you just good country people?"

The boy cocked his head. He looked as if he were just beginning to understand that she might be trying to insult him. "Yeah," he said, curling his lip slightly, "but it ain't held me back none. I'm as good as you any day in the week."

"Give me my leg," she said.

He pushed it farther away with his foot. "Come on now, let's begin to have us a good time," he said coaxingly. "We ain't got to know one another good yet."

"Give me my leg!" she screamed and tried to lunge for it but he pushed her    140 down easily.

"What's the matter with you all of a sudden?" he asked, frowning as he screwed the top on the flask and put it quickly back inside the Bible. "You just a while ago said you didn't believe in nothing. I thought you was some girl!"

Her face was almost purple. "You're a Christian!" she hissed. "You're a fine Christian! You're just like them all — say one thing and do another. You're a perfect Christian, you're . . ."

The boy's mouth was set angrily. "I hope you don't think," he said in a lofty indignant tone, "that I believe in that crap! I may sell Bibles but I know which end is up and I wasn't born yesterday and I know where I'm going!"

"Give me my leg!" she screeched. He jumped up so quickly that she barely saw him sweep the cards and the blue box into the Bible and throw the Bible into his valise. She saw him grab the leg and then she saw it for an instant slanted forlornly across the inside of the suitcase with a Bible at either side of its opposite ends. He slammed the lid shut and snatched up the valise and swung it down the hole and then stepped through himself.

When all of him had passed but his head, he turned and regarded her with a    145 look that no longer had any admiration in it. "I've gotten a lot of interesting things," he said. "One time I got a woman's glass eye this way. And you needn't to think you'll catch me because Pointer ain't really my name. I use a different name at every house I call at and don't stay nowhere long. And I'll tell you another thing, Hulga," he said, using the name as if he didn't think much of it, "you ain't so smart. I been believing in nothing ever since I was born!" and then the toast-colored hat disappeared down the hole and the girl was left, sitting on the straw in the dusty sunlight. When she turned her churning face toward the opening, she saw his blue figure struggling successfully over the green speckled lake.

Mrs. Hopewell and Mrs. Freeman, who were in the back pasture, digging up onions, saw him emerge a little later from the woods and head across the meadow toward the highway. "Why, that looks like that nice dull young man that tried to sell me a Bible yesterday," Mrs. Hopewell said, squinting. "He must have been selling them to the Negroes back in there. He was so simple," she said, "but I guess the world would be better off if we were all that simple."

Mrs. Freeman's gaze drove forward and just touched him before he disappeared under the hill. Then she returned her attention to the evil-smelling onion shoot she was lifting from the ground. "Some can't be that simple," she said. "I know I never could."

## Considerations for Critical Thinking and Writing

1. **FIRST RESPONSE.** What do you think of Hulga's conviction that intelligence and education are incompatible with religious faith?

2. Why is it significant that Mrs. Hopewell's daughter has two names? How do the other characters' names serve to characterize them?

3. Why do you think Mrs. Freeman and Mrs. Hopewell are introduced before Hulga? What do they contribute to Hulga's story?

4. Identify the conflict in this story. How is it resolved?

5. Hulga and the Bible salesman play a series of jokes on each other. How are these deceptions related to the theme?

6. What is the effect of O'Connor's use of the phrase "good country people" throughout the story? Why is it an appropriate title?

7. The Bible salesman's final words to Hulga are "[y]ou ain't so smart. I been believing in nothing ever since I was born!" (par. 145). What religious values are expressed in the story?

8. After the Bible salesman leaves Hulga at the end of the story, O'Connor adds two more paragraphs concerning Mrs. Hopewell and Mrs. Freeman. What is the purpose of these final paragraphs?

9. Hulga's perspective on life is ironic, but she is also the subject of O'Connor's irony. Explain how O'Connor uses irony to reveal Hulga's character.

10. This story would be different if told from Hulga's point of view. Describe how the use of a limited omniscient narrator contributes to the story's effects.

### CONNECTIONS TO OTHER SELECTIONS

1. How do Mrs. Hopewell's assumptions about life compare with those of Krebs's mother in Ernest Hemingway's "Soldier's Home" (p. 115)? Explain how the conflict in each story is related to what the mothers come to represent in the eyes of the central characters.

2. Discuss the treatment of faith and belief in this story and in N. K. Jemisin's "Sinners, Saints, Dragons, and Haints in the City Beneath the Still Waters" (p. 320).

## The Life You Save May Be Your Own   1955

The old woman and her daughter were sitting on their porch when Mr. Shiftlet came up their road for the first time. The old woman slid to the edge of her chair and leaned forward, shading her eyes from the piercing sunset with her hand. The daughter could not see far in front of her and continued to play with her fingers. Although the old woman lived in this desolate spot with only her daughter and she had never seen Mr. Shiftlet before, she could tell, even from a distance, that he was a tramp and no one to be afraid of. His left coat sleeve was folded up to show there was only half an arm in it and his gaunt figure listed slightly to the side as if the breeze were pushing him. He had on a black town suit and a brown felt hat that was turned up in the front and down in the back and he carried a tin tool box by a handle. He came on, at an amble, up her road, his face turned toward the sun which appeared to be balancing itself on the peak of a small mountain.

The old woman didn't change her position until he was almost into her yard; then she rose with one hand fisted on her hip. The daughter, a large girl in a short blue organdy dress, saw him all at once and jumped up and began to stamp and point and make excited speechless sounds.

Mr. Shiftlet stopped just inside the yard and set his box on the ground and tipped his hat at her as if she were not in the least afflicted; then he turned toward the old woman and swung the hat all the way off. He had long black slick hair that hung flat from a part in the middle to beyond the tips of his ears on either side. His face descended in forehead for more than half its length and ended suddenly with his features just balanced over a jutting steel-trap jaw. He seemed to be a young man but he had a look of composed dissatisfaction as if he understood life thoroughly.

"Good evening," the old woman said. She was about the size of a cedar fence post and she had a man's gray hat pulled down low over her head.

The tramp stood looking at her and didn't answer. He turned his back and 5 faced the sunset. He swung both his whole and his short arm up slowly so that they indicated an expanse of sky and his figure formed a crooked cross. The old woman watched him with her arms folded across her chest as if she were the owner of the sun, and the daughter watched, her head thrust forward and her fat helpless hands hanging at the wrists. She had long pink-gold hair and eyes as blue as a peacock's neck.

He held the pose for almost fifty seconds and then he picked up his box and came on to the porch and dropped down on the bottom step. "Lady," he said in a firm nasal voice, "I'd give a fortune to live where I could see me a sun do that every evening."

"Does it every evening," the old woman said and sat back down. The daughter sat down too and watched him with a cautious sly look as if he were a bird that had come up very close. He leaned to one side, rooting in his pants pocket, and in a second he brought out a package of chewing gum and offered her a piece. She took it and unpeeled it and began to chew without taking her eyes off him. He offered the old woman a piece but she only raised her upper lip to indicate she had no teeth.

Mr. Shiftlet's pale sharp glance had already passed over everything in the yard—the pump near the corner of the house and the big fig tree that three or four chickens were preparing to roost in—and had moved to a shed where he saw the square rusted back of an automobile. "You ladies drive?" he asked.

"That car ain't run in fifteen year," the old woman said. "The day my husband died, it quit running."

"Nothing is like it used to be, lady," he said. "The world is almost rotten." 10

"That's right," the old woman said. "You from around here?"

"Name Tom T. Shiftlet," he murmured, looking at the tires.

"I'm pleased to meet you," the old woman said. "Name Lucynell Crater and daughter Lucynell Crater. What you doing around here, Mr. Shiftlet?"

He judged the car to be about a 1928 or '29 Ford. "Lady," he said, and turned and gave her his full attention, "lemme tell you something. There's one of these doctors in Atlanta that's taken a knife and cut the human heart—the human heart," he repeated, leaning forward, "out of a man's chest and held it in his hand," and he held his hand out, palm up, as if it were slightly weighted with the human heart, "and studied it like it was a day-old chicken, and lady," he said, allowing a long significant pause in which his head slid forward and his clay-colored eyes brightened, "he don't know no more about it than you or me."

"That's right," the old woman said. 15

"Why, if he was to take that knife and cut into every corner of it, he still wouldn't know no more than you or me. What you want to bet?"

"Nothing," the old woman said wisely. "Where you come from, Mr. Shiftlet?"

He didn't answer. He reached into his pocket and brought out a sack of tobacco and a package of cigarette papers and rolled himself a cigarette, expertly with one hand, and attached it in a hanging position to his upper lip. Then he took a box of wooden matches from his pocket and struck one on his shoe. He held the burning match as if he were studying the mystery of flame while it traveled dangerously toward his skin. The daughter began to make loud noises and to point to his hand and shake her finger at him, but when the flame was just before touching him, he leaned down with his hand cupped over it as if he were going to set fire to his nose and fit the cigarette.

He flipped away the dead match and blew a stream of gray into the evening. A sly look came over his face. "Lady," he said, "nowadays, people'll do anything anyways. I can tell you my name is Tom T. Shiftlet and I come from Tarwater, Tennessee, but you never have seen me before: how you know I ain't lying? How you know my name ain't Aaron Sparks, lady, and I come from Singleberry, Georgia, or how you know it's not George Speeds and I come from Lucy, Alabama, or how you know I ain't Thompson Bright from Toolafalls, Mississippi?"

"I don't know nothing about you," the old woman muttered, irked.                  20

"Lady," he said, "people don't care how they lie. Maybe the best I can tell you is, I'm a man; but listen lady," he said and paused and made his tone more ominous still, "what is a man?"

The old woman began to gum a seed. "What you carry in that tin box, Mr. Shiftlet?" she asked.

"Tools," he said, put back. "I'm a carpenter."

"Well, if you come out here to work, I'll be able to feed you and give you a place to sleep but I can't pay. I'll tell you that before you begin," she said.

There was no answer at once and no particular expression on his face. He     25 leaned back against the two-by-four that helped support the porch roof. "Lady," he said slowly, "there's some men that some things mean more to them than money." The old woman rocked without comment and the daughter watched the trigger that moved up and down in his neck. He told the old woman then that all most people were interested in was money, but he asked what a man was made for. He asked her if a man was made for money, or what. He asked her what she thought she was made for but she didn't answer, she only sat rocking and wondered if a one-armed man could put a new roof on her garden house. He asked a lot of questions that she didn't answer. He told her that he was twenty-eight years old and had lived a varied life. He had been a gospel singer, a foreman on the railroad, an assistant in an undertaking parlor, and he had come over the radio for three months with Uncle Roy and his Red Creek Wranglers. He said he had fought and bled in the Arm Service of his country and visited every foreign land and that everywhere he had seen people that didn't care if they did a thing one way or another. He said he hadn't been raised thataway.

A fat yellow moon appeared in the branches of the fig tree as if it were going to roost there with the chickens. He said that a man had to escape to the country to see the world whole and that he wished he lived in a desolate place like this where he could see the sun go down every evening like God made it to do.

"Are you married or are you single?" the old woman asked.

There was a long silence. "Lady," he asked finally, "where would you find you an innocent woman today? I wouldn't have any of this trash I could just pick up."

The daughter was leaning very far down, hanging her head almost between her knees, watching him through a triangular door she had made in her overturned hair; and she suddenly fell in a heap on the floor and began to whimper. Mr. Shiftlet straightened her out and helped her get back in the chair.

"Is she your baby girl?" he asked.                                30

"My only," the old woman said, "and she's the sweetest girl in the world. I wouldn't give her up for nothing on earth. She's smart too. She can sweep the floor, cook, wash, feed the chickens, and hoe. I wouldn't give her up for a casket of jewels."

"No," he said kindly, "don't ever let any man take her away from you."

"Any man come after her," the old woman said, " 'll have to stay around the place."

Mr. Shiftlet's eye in the darkness was focused on a part of the automobile bumper that glittered in the distance. "Lady," he said, jerking his short arm up as if he could point with it to her house and yard and pump, "there ain't a broken thing on this plantation that I couldn't fix for you, one-arm jackleg or not. I'm a man," he said with a sullen dignity, "even if I ain't a whole one. I got," he said, tapping his knuckles on the floor to emphasize the immensity of what he was going to say, "a moral intelligence!" and his face pierced out of the darkness into a shaft of doorlight and he stared at her as if he were astonished himself at this impossible truth.

The old woman was not impressed with the phrase. "I told you you could   35 hang around and work for food," she said, "if you don't mind sleeping in that car yonder."

"Why listen, Lady," he said with a grin of delight, "the monks of old slept in their coffins!"

"They wasn't as advanced as we are," the old woman said.

The next morning he began on the roof of the garden house while Lucynell, the daughter, sat on a rock and watched him work. He had not been around a week before the change he had made in the place was apparent. He had patched the front and back steps, built a new hog pen, restored a fence, and taught Lucynell, who was completely deaf and had never said a word in her life, to say the word "bird."

The big rosy-faced girl followed him everywhere, saying "Burrttddt ddbirr-rttdt," and clapping her hands. The old woman watched from a distance, secretly pleased. She was ravenous for a son-in-law.

Mr. Shiftlet slept on the hard narrow back seat of the car with his feet out the   40 side window. He had his razor and a can of water on a crate that served him as a bedside table and he put up a piece of mirror against the back glass and kept his coat neatly on a hanger that he hung over one of the windows.

In the evenings he sat on the steps and talked while the old woman and Lucynell rocked violently in their chairs on either side of him. The old woman's three mountains were black against the dark blue sky and were visited off and on by various planets and by the moon after it had left the chickens. Mr. Shiftlet pointed out that the reason he had improved this plantation was because he had taken a personal interest in it. He said he was even going to make the automobile run.

He had raised the hood and studied the mechanism and he said he could tell that the car had been built in the days when cars were really built. You take now, he said, one man puts in one bolt and another man puts in another bolt and another man puts in another bolt so that it's a man for a bolt. That's why you have to pay so much for a car: you're paying all those men. Now if you didn't have to pay but one man, you could get you a cheaper car and one that had had a personal interest taken in it, and it would be a better car. The old woman agreed with him that this was so.

Mr. Shiftlet said that the trouble with the world was that nobody cared, or stopped and took any trouble. He said he never would have been able to teach Lucynell to say a word if he hadn't cared and stopped long enough.

"Teach her to say something else," the old woman said.

"What you want her to say next?" Mr. Shiftlet asked. 45

The old woman's smile was broad and toothless and suggestive. "Teach her to say 'sugarpie,' " she said.

Mr. Shiftlet already knew what was on her mind.

The next day he began to tinker with the automobile and that evening he told her that if she would buy a fan belt, he would be able to make the car run.

The old woman said she would give him the money. "You see that girl yonder?" she asked, pointing to Lucynell who was sitting on the floor a foot away, watching him, her eyes blue even in the dark. "If it was ever a man wanted to take her away, I would say, 'No man on earth is going to take that sweet girl of mine away from me!' but if he was to say, 'Lady, I don't want to take her away, I want her right here,' I would say, 'Mister, I don't blame you none. I wouldn't pass up a chance to live in a permanent place and get the sweetest girl in the world myself. You ain't no fool,' I would say."

"How old is she?" Mr. Shiftlet asked casually. 50

"Fifteen, sixteen," the old woman said. The girl was nearly thirty but because of her innocence it was impossible to guess.

"It would be a good idea to paint it too," Mr. Shiftlet remarked. "You don't want it to rust out."

"We'll see about that later," the old woman said.

The next day he walked into town and returned with the parts he needed and a can of gasoline. Late in the afternoon, terrible noises issued from the shed and the old woman rushed out of the house, thinking Lucynell was somewhere having a fit. Lucynell was sitting on a chicken crate, stamping her feet and screaming, "Burrddttt! bddurrddtttt!" but her fuss was drowned out by the car. With a volley of blasts it emerged from the shed, moving in a fierce and stately way. Mr. Shiftlet was in the driver's seat, sitting very erect. He had an expression of serious modesty on his face as if he had just raised the dead.

That night, rocking on the porch, the old woman began her business at once. 55 "You want you an innocent woman, don't you?" she asked sympathetically. "You don't want none of this trash."

"No'm, I don't," Mr. Shiftlet said.

"One that can't talk," she continued, "can't sass you back or use foul language. That's the kind for you to have. Right there," and she pointed to Lucynell sitting cross-legged in her chair, holding both feet in her hands.

"That's right," he admitted. "She wouldn't give me any trouble."

"Saturday," the old woman said, "you and her and me can drive into town and get married."

Mr. Shiftlet eased his position on the steps. 60

"I can't get married right now," he said. "Everything you want to do takes money and I ain't got any."

"What you need with money?" she asked.

"It takes money," he said. "Some people'll do anything anyhow these days, but the way I think, I wouldn't marry no woman that I couldn't take on a trip like she was somebody. I mean take her to a hotel and treat her. I wouldn't marry the Duchesser Windsor," he said firmly, "unless I could take her to a hotel and give her something good to eat.

"I was raised thataway and there ain't a thing I can do about it. My old mother taught me how to do."

"Lucynell don't even know what a hotel is," the old woman muttered. "Listen 65 here, Mr. Shiftlet," she said, sliding forward in her chair, "you'd be getting a permanent house and a deep well and the most innocent girl in the world. You don't need no money. Lemme tell you something: there ain't any place in the world for a poor disabled friendless drifting man."

The ugly words settled in Mr. Shiftlet's head like a group of buzzards in the top of a tree. He didn't answer at once. He rolled himself a cigarette and lit it and then he said in an, even voice, "Lady, a man is divided into two parts, body and spirit."

The old woman clamped her gums together.

"A body and a spirit," he repeated. "The body, lady, is like a house: it don't go anywhere; but the spirit, lady, is like a automobile: always on the move, always . . ."

"Listen, Mr. Shiftlet," she said, "my well never goes dry and my house is always warm in the winter and there's no mortgage on a thing about this place. You can go to the courthouse and see for yourself. And yonder under that shed is a fine automobile." She laid the bait carefully. "You can have it painted by Saturday. I'll pay for the paint."

In the darkness, Mr. Shiftlet's smile stretched like a weary snake waking up 70 by a fire. After a second he recalled himself and said, "I'm only saying a man's spirit means more to him than anything else. I would have to take my wife off for the week end without no regards at all for cost. I got to follow where my spirit says to go."

"I'll give you fifteen dollars for a week-end trip," the old woman said in a crabbed voice. "That's the best I can do."

"That wouldn't hardly pay for more than the gas and the hotel," he said. "It wouldn't feed her."

"Seventeen-fifty," the old woman said. "That's all I got so it isn't any use you trying to milk me. You can take a lunch."

Mr. Shiftlet was deeply hurt by the word "milk." He didn't doubt that she had more money sewed up in her mattress but he had already told her he was not interested in her money. "I'll make that do," he said and rose and walked off without treating with her further.

On Saturday the three of them drove into town in the car that the paint had 75 barely dried on and Mr. Shiftlet and Lucynell were married in the Ordinary's office while the old woman witnessed. As they came out of the courthouse, Mr. Shiftlet began twisting his neck in his collar. He looked morose and bitter as if he had been insulted while someone held him. "That didn't satisfy me none," he said. "That was just something a woman in an office did, nothing but paper work and blood tests. What do they know about my blood? If they was to take my heart and cut it out," he said, "they wouldn't know a thing about me. It didn't satisfy me at all."

"It satisfied the law," the old woman said sharply.

"The law," Mr. Shiftlet said and spit. "It's the law that don't satisfy me."

He had painted the car dark green with a yellow band around it just under the windows. The three of them climbed in the front seat and the old woman said,

"Don't Lucynell look pretty? Looks like a baby doll." Lucynell was dressed up in a white dress that her mother had uprooted from a trunk and there was a Panama hat on her head with a bunch of red wooden cherries on the brim. Every now and then her placid expression was changed by a sly isolated little thought like a shoot of green in the desert. "You got a prize!" the old woman said.

Mr. Shiftlet didn't even look at her.

They drove back to the house to let the old woman off and pick up the lunch. When they were ready to leave, she stood staring in the window of the car, with her fingers clenched around the glass. Tears began to seep sideways out of her eye and run along the dirty creases in her face. "I ain't ever been parted with her for two days before," she said.

Mr. Shiftlet started the motor.

"And I wouldn't let no man have her but you because I seen you would do right. Good-by, Sugarbaby," she said, clutching at the sleeve of the white dress. Lucynell looked straight at her and didn't seem to see her there at all. Mr. Shiftlet eased the car forward so that she had to move her hands.

The early afternoon was clear and open and surrounded by pale blue sky. Although the car would go only thirty miles an hour, Mr. Shiftlet imagined a terrific climb and dip and swerve that went entirely to his head so that he forgot his morning bitterness. He had always wanted an automobile but he had never been able to afford one before. He drove very fast because he wanted to make Mobile by nightfall.

Occasionally he stopped his thoughts long enough to look at Lucynell in the seat beside him. She had eaten the lunch as soon as they were out of the yard and now she was pulling the cherries off the hat one by one and throwing them out the window. He became depressed in spite of the car. He had driven about a hundred miles when he decided that she must be hungry again and at the next small town they came to, he stopped in front of an aluminum-painted eating place called The Hot Spot and took her in and ordered her a plate of ham and grits. The ride had made her sleepy and as soon as she got up on the stool, she rested her head on the counter and shut her eyes. There was no one in The Hot Spot but Mr. Shiftlet and the boy behind the counter, a pale youth with a greasy rag hung over his shoulder. Before he could dish up the food, she was snoring gently.

"Give it to her when she wakes up," Mr. Shiftlet said. "I'll pay for it now." 85

The boy bent over her and stared at the long pink-gold hair and the half-shut sleeping eyes. Then he looked up and stared at Mr. Shiftlet. "She looks like an angel of Gawd," he murmured.

"Hitch-hiker," Mr. Shiftlet explained. "I can't wait. I got to make Tuscaloosa."

The boy bent over again and very carefully touched his finger to a strand of the golden hair and Mr. Shiftlet left.

He was more depressed than ever as he drove on by himself. The late afternoon had grown hot and sultry and the country had flattened out. Deep in the sky a storm was preparing very slowly and without thunder as if it meant to drain every drop of air from the earth before it broke. There were times when Mr. Shiftlet preferred not to be alone. He felt too that a man with a car had a responsibility to others and he kept his eye out for a hitch-hiker. Occasionally he saw a sign that warned: "Drive carefully. The life you save may be you own."

The narrow road dropped off on either side into dry fields and here and there 90 a shack or a filling station stood in a clearing. The sun began to set directly in front of the automobile. It was a reddening ball that through his windshield was slightly flat on the bottom and top. He saw a boy in overalls and a gray hat standing on the edge of the road and he slowed the car down and stopped in front of him. The boy didn't have his hand raised to thumb the ride, he only standing there, but he had a small cardboard suitcase and his hat was set on his head in a way to indicate that he had left somewhere for good. "Son," Mr. Shiftlet said, "I see you want a ride."

The boy didn't say he did or he didn't but he opened the door of the car and got in, and Mr. Shiftlet started driving again. The child held the suitcase on his lap and folded his arms on top of it. He turned his head and looked out the window away from Mr. Shiftlet. Mr. Shiftlet felt oppressed. "Son," he said after a minute, "I got the best old mother in the world so I reckon you only got the second best."

The boy gave him a quick dark glance and then turned his face back out the window.

"It's nothing so sweet," Mr. Shiftlet continued, "as a boy's mother. She taught him his first prayers at her knee, she give him love when no other would, she told him what was right and what wasn't, and she seen that he done the right thing. Son," he said, "I never rued a day in my life like the one I rued when I left that old mother of mine."

The boy shifted in his seat but he didn't look at Mr. Shiftlet. He unfolded his arms and put one hand on the door handle.

"My mother was a angel of Gawd," Mr. Shiftlet said in very strained voice.   95 "He took her from heaven and giver to me and I left her." His eyes were instantly clouded over, with a mist of tears. The car was barely moving.

The boy turned angrily in the seat. "You go to the devil!" he cried. "My old woman is a flea bag and yours is a stinking pole cat!" and with that he flung the door open and jumped out with his suitcase into the ditch.

Mr. Shiftlet was so shocked that for about a hundred feet he drove along slowly with the door still open. A cloud, the exact color of the boy's hat and shaped like a turnip, had descended over the sun, and another, worse looking, crouched behind the car. Mr. Shiftlet felt that the rottenness of the world was about to engulf him. He raised his arm and let it fall again to his breast. "Oh Lord!" he prayed. "Break forth and wash the slime from this earth!"

The turnip continued slowly to descend. After a few minutes there was a guffawing peal of thunder from behind and fantastic raindrops, like tin-can tops, crashed over the rear of Mr. Shiftlet's car. Very quickly he stepped on the gas and with his stump sticking out the window he raced the galloping shower into Mobile.

## CONSIDERATIONS FOR CRITICAL THINKING AND WRITING

1. **FIRST RESPONSE.** The two evident candidates for the story's protagonist are Tom Shiftlet and the elder Lucynell Crater. Which do you see as the protagonist and why?

2. Sun imagery dominates the story. List the various passages in which the sun is mentioned; then, advance a theory about how O'Connor uses this imagery.

3. How does Shiftlet's recurrent repetition about heart surgery point toward the story's theme?

4. Another recurrent phrase is "Angel of Gawd," applied both to the younger Lucynell and to Shiftlet's mother. Why is the repetition of this phrase significant?

5. Each of the three main characters is characterized by a physical defect. Is this just a coincidence or are their defects as integral to the story's concerns?

6. There are a few associations between Shiftlet and Jesus: he poses in the shape of a crooked cross for almost a minute (par. 5), he is a carpenter (par. 23), and he professes to care about others in a way most people don't (par. 44). How do these associations affect your interpretation of the story?

7. Discuss the contrast between settled life and adventure, symbolized by the house and the car.

8. Shiftlet talks at length about how he could lie to the old woman about anything, including his name and place of origin. We later learn that she lies automatically about her daughter's age and he lies to the restaurant worker about the younger Lucynell, saying she's a hitchhiker. How does the story comment on the human tendency to deceive?

9. Lucynell the younger cannot speak except to say "bird." The boy Shiftlet picks up can speak, and he says something that shocks Shiftlet. How are the two characters related despite this basic difference?

10. How do you interpret the title?

### CONNECTIONS TO OTHER SELECTIONS

1. Compare the symbolic value of cars in this story and in Louise Erdrich's "The Red Convertible" (p. 170).

2. The silence of the younger Lucynell in this story connects to the silence of the daughter in Alice Munro's "Silence" (p. 376). Do the stories have broader thematic connections or is this motif a coincidence?

## Perspectives

### FLANNERY O'CONNOR (1925–1964)

## *On the Use of Exaggeration and Distortion*  1969

When I write a novel in which the central action is a baptism, I am very well aware that for a majority of my readers, baptism is a meaningless rite, and so in my novel I have to see that this baptism carries enough awe and mystery to jar the reader into some kind of emotional recognition of its significance. To this end I have to bend the whole novel — its language, its structure, its action. I have to make the reader feel, in his bones if nowhere else, that something is going on here that counts. Distortion in this case is an instrument; exaggeration has a purpose, and the whole structure of the story or novel has been made what it is because of belief. This is not the kind of distortion that destroys; it is the kind that reveals, or should reveal.

From "Novelist and Believer" in *Mystery and Manners*

### CONSIDERATIONS FOR CRITICAL THINKING AND WRITING

1. It has been observed that in many of O'Connor's works the central action takes the form of some kind of "baptism" that initiates, tests, or purifies a character. Select an O'Connor story that illustrates this generalization, and explain how the conflict results in a kind of baptism.

2. O'Connor says that exaggeration and distortion reveal something in her stories. What is the effect of such exaggeration and distortion? Typically, what is revealed? Focus your comments on a single story to illustrate your points.

3. Do you think that O'Connor's stories have anything to offer a reader who has no religious faith? Explain why or why not.

## JOSEPHINE HENDIN (B. 1946)

### On O'Connor's Refusal to "Do Pretty"    1970

There is, in the memory of one Milledgeville matron, the image of O'Connor at nineteen or twenty who, when invited to a wedding shower for an old family friend, remained standing, her back pressed against the wall, scowling at the group of women who had sat down to lunch. Neither the devil nor her mother could make her say yes to this fiercely gracious female society, but Flannery O'Connor could not say no even in a whisper. She could not refuse the invitation but she would not accept it either. She did not exactly "fuss" but neither did she "do pretty."

From *The World of Flannery O'Connor*

### CONSIDERATIONS FOR CRITICAL THINKING AND WRITING

1. How is O'Connor's personality revealed in this anecdote about her ambivalent response to society? Allow the description to be suggestive for you, and flesh out a brief portrait of her.

2. Consider how this personality makes itself apparent in any one of O'Connor's stories you have read. How does the anecdote help to characterize the narrator's voice in the story?

3. To what extent do you think biographical details such as this — assuming the Milledgeville matron's memory to be accurate — can shed light on a writer's works?

## CLAIRE KATZ (B. 1935)

### The Function of Violence in O'Connor's Fiction    1974

From the moment the reader enters O'Connor's backwoods, he is poised on the edge of a pervasive violence. Characters barely contain their rage; images reflect a hostile nature; and even the Christ to whom the characters are ultimately driven is a threatening figure . . . full of the apocalyptic wrath of the Old Testament.

O'Connor's conscious purpose is evident enough . . . : to reveal the need for grace in a world grotesque without a transcendent context. "I have found that my subject in fiction is the action of grace in territory largely held by the devil," she wrote [in *Mystery and Manners*], and she was not vague about what the devil is: "an evil intelligence determined on its own supremacy." It would seem that for O'Connor, given the fact of original Sin, any intelligence determined on its own supremacy was intrinsically evil. For in each work, it is the impulse toward secular autonomy, the smug confidence that human nature is perfectible by its own efforts, that she sets out to destroy, through an act of violence so intense that the character is rendered helpless, a passive victim of a superior power. Again and again she creates a fiction in which a character attempts to live autonomously, to define himself and his values, only to be jarred back to what she calls "reality" — the recognition of helplessness in the face of contingency, and the need for absolute submission to the power of Christ.

From "Flannery O'Connor's Rage of Vision" in *American Literature*

### CONSIDERATIONS FOR CRITICAL THINKING AND WRITING

1. Choose an O'Connor story, and explain how grace — the divine influence from God that redeems a person — is used in it to transform a character.

2. Which O'Connor characters can be accurately described as having an "evil intelligence determined on its own supremacy" (par. 2)? Choose one character, and write an essay explaining how this description is central to the conflict of the story.

3. Compare an O'Connor story with Nathanial Hawthorne's "The Minister's Black Veil" (p. 209) "in which a character attempts to live autonomously, to define himself and his values, only to be jarred back to . . . 'reality' — the recognition of helplessness in the face of contingency . . ." (par. 2).

## EDWARD KESSLER (B. 1927)

## *On O'Connor's Use of History* 1986

In company with other Southern writers . . . who aspire to embrace a lost tradition and look on history as a repository of value, Flannery O'Connor seems a curious anomaly. She wrote of herself: "I am a Catholic peculiarly possessed of the modern consciousness . . . unhistorical, solitary, and guilty." Likewise her characters comprise a gallery of misfits isolated in a present and sentenced to a lifetime of exile from the human community. In O'Connor's fiction, the past neither justifies nor even explains what is happening. If she believed, for example, in the importance of the past accident that maimed Joy in "Good Country People," she could have demonstrated how the event predetermined her present rejection of both human and external nature; but Joy's past is parenthetical: "Mrs. Hopewell excused this attitude because of the leg (which had been shot off in a hunting accident when Joy was ten)." Believing that humankind is fundamentally flawed, O'Connor spends very little time constructing a past for her characters. The cure is neither behind us nor before us but within us; therefore, the past — even historical time itself — supplies only a limited base for self-discovery.

From *Flannery O'Connor and the Language of Apocalypse*

### CONSIDERATIONS FOR CRITICAL THINKING AND WRITING

1. Consider how O'Connor uses history in any one of her stories in this anthology and compare that "unhistorical" vision with the imagined society that Ursula K. Le Guin creates in "The Ones Who Walk Away from Omelas" (p. 121).

2. Write an essay in which you discuss Kessler's assertion that for O'Connor the "past is parenthetical," in contrast to most southern writers, who "embrace a lost tradition and look on history as a repository of value." For your point of comparison use William Faulkner's "A Rose for Emily" (p. 47).

# Time *Magazine,* On *A Good Man Is Hard to Find and Other Stories*   1962

Highly unladylike . . . a brutal irony, a slam-bang humor, and a style of writing as balefully direct as a death sentence.

> From a *Time* magazine blurb quoted on the cover of the second American edition of *A Good Man Is Hard to Find and Other Stories*

### CONSIDERATIONS FOR CRITICAL THINKING AND WRITING

1. How accurate do you think this blurb is in characterizing the three O'Connor stories in this chapter?

2. CREATIVE RESPONSE. Write your own blurb for the three stories and be prepared to justify your pithy description.

# A Study of
# Dagoberto Gilb: The Author
# Reflects on Three Stories

Courtesy of Dagoberto Gilb.

For me, fiction is life transformed and fueled by imagination.
— DAGOBERTO GILB

## AN INTRODUCTION

Dagoberto Gilb chose the three short stories in this chapter and provides commentary on each of them. Along with his personal observations on the stories are relevant images and documents that offer perspectives for interpreting and appreciating his fiction. Gilb's candid comments on the stories are written specifically for readers who are interested in why and how the stories were composed. He reveals some of the biographical contexts and circumstances that led him to become an avid reader and then a successful writer (despite the dismal grade he received for his first college English paper) and how he managed to build a fictional world while working full time on construction sites.

Courtesy of Dagoberto Gilb.

In addition to the stories and commentaries, this chapter also offers contexts for the stories, including photographs of his family and his life as a construction carpenter in Los Angeles, California, and El Paso, Texas. Also included are a draft manuscript page from an essay collection, an edited galley from the short story "Uncle Rock" originally published in the *New Yorker*, Gilb's comments on physical labor and popular perceptions of Mexican American culture, and an interview with Michael Meyer that ranges from issues of political correctness to how "advocacy" is embedded in Gilb's literary art. You'll find this ex-carpenter to be a straightforward storyteller who makes a point of being on the level.

## A BRIEF BIOGRAPHY

Born in Los Angeles in 1950, Dagoberto Gilb worked as a construction worker and a journeyman high-rise carpenter with the United Brotherhood of Carpenters for some sixteen years as he began hammering out his fiction. Though born and raised in California, he considers both Los Angeles and El Paso to be home. His Anglo father was a laconic, hardened World War II Marine Corps veteran who worked for nearly fifty years in a Los Angeles industrial laundry, his mother was an undocumented Mexican immigrant, and their marriage ended early. Gilb's life, like his fiction, is grounded by working-class circumstances in which laborers sweat to pay bills and put food on the table. He does not list any unpaid internships on his résumé.

As Gilb acknowledges in *Gritos*, a collection of essays, he was not in his youth "precocious in matters of literature, even to the end of my teenage years when I still thought of 'book' more as a verb." He did, however, read on the job and make his way to junior college and then to the University of California, Santa Barbara, where he earned a B.A. and an M.A. in philosophy and religious studies. In college, he devoured canonical American and European writers and then discovered Chicano literature, works that ultimately inspired him to write about his own experiences. After graduate school, he followed construction jobs between Los Angeles and El Paso, making a living and finding the material for framing much of his writing.

Following some success in publishing a number of short stories in literary journals, a chapbook-size collection of stories, *Winners on the Pass Line*, appeared in 1985. His first full collection, the critically acclaimed book *The Magic of Blood* (1993), won the PEN/Ernest Hemingway Award as well as the Jesse Jones Award from the Texas Institute of Letters and was a finalist for the PEN/Faulkner Award. On the heels of a National Endowment for the Arts Fellowship, he published a novel, *The Last Known Residence of Mickey Acuna* (1994), which was followed by a Guggenheim Foundation Fellowship. *Gritos* (2003), consisting of essays previously published in such venues as the *New Yorker*, the *New York Times*, the *Los Angeles Times*, and *The Nation*, along with commentaries written for National Public Radio's "Fresh Air," offers a perspective on how a Mexican American working man became a nationally recognized working writer. Another novel, *The Flowers* (2008), and two more collections of stories, *Woodcuts of Women* (2001) and *Before the End,*

(*Top*) Dagoberto Gilb's mother. Los Angeles, California, late 1940s.
Courtesy of Dagoberto Gilb.

(*Right*) Dagoberto Gilb with his older son, Antonio. El Paso, Texas, 1978.
Courtesy of Dagoberto Gilb.

The author with his son, Antonio. Los Angeles, California, 1981.
The '62 Chevy pictured here is the very one mentioned in "On
Writing 'Love in L.A.'"
Courtesy of Dagoberto Gilb.

*After the Beginning* (2011), have solidified his reputation as a highly regarded fiction writer. His works have been translated into Spanish, French, German, Italian, Japanese, Chinese, and Turkish, and he has been invited to be a visiting writer at a number of schools, including the University of Texas at Austin, the University of Wyoming, the University of Arizona, and Vassar College.

Previously a tenured professor in the Creative Writing Program at Texas State University in San Marcos, Gilb is currently writer-in-residence and executive director of Centro Victoria, a center for Mexican American literature and culture at the University of Houston in Victoria, Texas, where the undergraduate student body is primarily Latino, a school he describes as "the smallest, most just barely at its beginning university in the country." Located equidistant from Houston, Austin, San Antonio, and Corpus Christi, in a state that in several years will be 50 percent Latino, Centro Victoria was founded, in part, to educate Texans of all ethnicities and educational levels — and others outside the state — about the history and culture of Mexican Americans, who make up two-thirds of the Latino population in the United States.

Dagoberto Gilb at work. Los Angeles, California, 1986.
Courtesy of Dagoberto Gilb.

The purpose of the center is to foster an understanding and appreciation of Mexican American literature and art in Texas and beyond.

One of Centro Victoria's major projects is to provide Texas students and teachers with lesson plans based on *Hecho en Tejas: An Anthology of Texas Mexican Literature* (2006), edited by Gilb, which ranges from sixteenth-century exploration narratives to twenty-first-century poetry and prose. By integrating Mexican American arts into the curriculum, the program elevates the vicissitudes of Latinos' lives — satisfactions as well as challenges — to an art and helps to validate the very existence and presence of Latinos in the United States who never before had the opportunity to read about their own unique experiences. Gilb makes clear in his introduction to *Hecho en Tejas* that the predominant popular attitude toward people of Mexican descent in the United States, whether toward legitimate citizens or undocumented migrants, what some in the media call "illegals," is shaped by cultural distortions:

> The kindest attitude portrays the culture as an homage in a children's museum, or as in a folklorico dance show, and the prevailing images, framed and shelved in the state's unconscious, are of men in sombreros and serapes walking burros, women patting tortillas or stuffing tamales in color-frilled white housedresses, while the stories of Mexican adventures are of border whorehouses and tequila drunks — not meant as harmful, only fascinating, and wild.

Gilb insists on moving beyond such patronizing images and passionately announces as the anthology's major theme: "We have been here, we are still here." (For a brief provocative comparison of Mexican American and African American cultural experiences in the West and South, see Gilb's "On Distortions of Mexican American Culture," p. 465.)

(*Left*) The author in 2002, on the Brownsville, Texas–Matamoros, Mexico, borderline.
Courtesy of Dagoberto Gilb.

(*Below*) Dagoberto Gilb with his younger son, Ricardo. Uruapan, Mexico, 2005.
Courtesy of Dagoberto Gilb.

(*Top*) The author at the Pirámedes del Sol y Luna, Mexico, 2008.

Courtesy of Dagoberto Gilb.

(*Left*) Dagoberto Gilb at the PEN/ Faulkner Reading at the Folger Shakespeare Library. Washington, D.C., 2012.

Courtesy of Dagoberto Gilb.

Furthering his goal of making Mexican Americans apparent in American culture, in 2011 Gilb founded *Huizache: The Magazine of Latino Literature*, published by Centro Victoria at the University of Houston–Victoria. Featuring literary works from mostly Latino writers who are largely neglected or ignored, the magazine also opens its pages to all fiction, poetry, and essays that challenge ethnic, gender, or social stereotyping. "A huizache," as explained on the title page, "is an acacia tree that is native to Mexico but also grows wild in South and East Texas. It irritates the regional farmers because, no matter what they do, it keeps growing and populating." The editor, Diana López, asks readers to "think of this journal as the nursery that fosters this tree and any species considered 'invasive.'" *Huizache* is founded on the energy, ambition, and neglected talent of Latino and Latina writers in Texas and the Southwest.

Gilb's own writing offers a broad landscape of Mexican American experience in a direct, straightforward style that is energized by his unapologetically hearty and robust take on ordinary life. His characters work pretty hard in the face of ugly inequities, make money but not enough of it, get fired, find work, fall in love, desire marriage, settle on divorce, suffer loss, maintain dignity, strive to succeed, frequently fail, raise kids, embody fear, and stubbornly persevere — all of them serially engaged in the disorderly conduct of being human.

## DAGOBERTO GILB

### *How Books Bounce*   2012

Many have asked me, how did you become a writer? This is one of those ordinary questions that comes at Q&A's, but at mine I sometimes catch a snarky or world-weary, all-caps emphasis on the *you*. I could snap off a couple of words in defense, but the truth is that I, too, find me a curious representative of literature. Real writers are bred like champion racehorses, the offspring of Seabiscuit and Secretariat. When real writers discuss their careers, they refer back (modestly, of course) to what they published before their double-digit birthdays. They had books at home (that's all I need to say there). The very classiest universities begged them to be undergrads, and while there they briefly thought they might become a molecular chemist or an avant-garde sculptor. Now, modestly, these real writers will say they were probably better at one of those. Whereas, in contrast, I read my first book when I was seventeen because, in a less than advanced English class for we special few (I worked a full-time, graveyard shift job as a janitor), one day the teacher mentioned a novel hippies were reading. I wanted to know what hippies read because they seemed to have all kinds of easy goings-on that weren't like mine. And nothing in mine included any books. My pre-janitor years I can't say were busy with any poetic forms other than chrome spokes on wheels and girls who didn't read poetry either. Where I came up, balls were as close to books as I got. I bounced them, hit them, threw them, caught them, guarded them, blocked them, kicked them, jump-shot them. They weren't books. Nobody expected me to read them. I didn't. Neither was it suggested that maybe I try an actual volume with unrounded corners, though if anyone had, I would have made it bounce too.

I was not, in other words, born a writer. And then I went to a junior college. Much of that incentive was not so much improving my brains as not losing them, or my legs, walking point in Vietnam (older friends, drafted, came back not doing great). My first freshman comp paper I got a D. The teacher told me she was being generous. When I failed the class, I was smart enough to know who took night classes — on the curve with the most tired day job students (mine was full-time too, a department store stock boy), this time, at a lesser community college, I got a B. I did not consider a major in chemistry. The only sculpture I knew of came from Mexico, which, cool-looking and deep, I couldn't say I understood any better than what was taught in art history (nothing Mexican, indigenous, colonial, or modern). I tried a business law class. I liked math but too much homework. Sociology, political science, geography, history, philosophy — each offered original news to me. I was learning. Excited, I began eating it all up. Though I still feared English. That second semester requirement, when you study literature, I remember having to look up a word in virtually every sentence of Melville's *Billy Budd*. Supposedly American, I thought it had to be from a foreign language, and I wasn't sure if I understood what exactly happened to Mr. Budd. I took the teacher at his word for the explanation of it. Great story!

Oh, how I then fell in love. In the beginning it was any books I called on or which called on me. Books stacked and piled and neatly lined up in rows, new or used or checked out (I even stole them, yes, I here confess!). There were the small ones forgotten in quirky, cramped bottom corners, and ones that took tall ladders to touch, and ones that saw so little light their covers seemed to have recast inward — I loved them the most, these difficult ones, hard to get to know, to understand, odd, too quiet and bashful, secret. When suddenly I became furtive: though I would never take a lit class again, I was reading novels and poetry.

How did I become a writer? Something happened, that's pretty clear. Did lightning strike and skip the ears hearing, override the memory but alter the brain? Am I the product of some secret government experiment that maybe went wrong? How did a boy who cared only about sports — what little reading I would do young was from a newspaper sports page — become a man who would idealize books like classic teams and then become one of its professional "athletes"?

I've always been obsessed with story. Whether it's nature or nurture, or what   5
I like to call my family mess, I cannot recall a time when I wasn't listening to a story being told. Maybe because I have only a single blurry memory of my father leaving my childhood home, it opens with ones about him and my mother. Of German descent, he was born in Kentucky but came to Los Angeles young. She was baptized in Mexico City at the Basilica de Guadalupe. He joined the Marines to fight the Japanese at Pearl Harbor. She kept the rising sun flag he'd captured as an advanced scout. Older, he watched her growing up next door to the industrial laundry where he started working when he was thirteen, where she eventually did too as a teenager (not for long). She grew up in that house next door with her mother, who was my grandmother, who was the mistress of the owner of the laundry who owned the house (what in Spanish is known as *la casa chica*). My grandmother came to the United States after her husband, my grandfather, was killed. By knife, went the story, and in the back. My grandmother came to the United States following her sister, my great-aunt, whose mother — this story! — had been married at fourteen to a man in his sixties and she had . . . not sure how many but a number of children by him. When my great-aunt turned eighteen, her mother traveled from Xalapa

and in the capital rented the finest limousine for a visit to the presidential palace. And thus, my great-aunt represented Mexico on a tour to Europe and the United States as an opera singer. She wound up in Hollywood, married to a minor French director. My grandmother died young, making my mother closer to my great-aunt. By the time I am old enough to first see her — old, a widow for years, hard for a young person to imagine any glamorous youth attaching to her — she is nothing but a seamstress who needed money, a job, one of fifty at the industrial laundry where my father had become the floor supervisor. She repaired the elastic on bras, my father, bitter by divorce and who knows, enjoyed pointing out. He gave me a job there when I too turned thirteen. And this was when I begin to have stories.

When I think about being a writer now, I can't help but think of the improbable travel that my genes have made to get here. This journey. And to think we *each* have one, no matter to what breeding or privilege we were born. Why we perk up to listen, why we are driven to, I have no idea. It's so fun to bounce books on your ride — it's a necessary skill. But go, get out there, and what I know is you'll meet people, you'll see places, you'll hear stories that only you will be able to tell.

— D.G.

# Dagoberto Gilb

## *Love in L.A.*   1993

Jake slouched in a clot of near motionless traffic, in the peculiar gray of concrete, smog, and early morning beneath the overpass of the Hollywood Freeway on Alvarado Street. He didn't really mind because he knew how much worse it could be trying to make a left onto the onramp. He certainly didn't do that every day of his life, and he'd assure anyone who'd ask that he never would either. A steady occupation had its advantages and he couldn't deny thinking about that too. He needed an FM radio in something better than this '58 Buick he drove. It would have crushed velvet interior with electric controls for the L.A. summer, a nice warm heater and defroster for the winter drives at the beach, a cruise control for those longer trips, mellow speakers front and rear of course, windows that hum closed, snuffing out that nasty exterior noise of freeways. The fact was that he'd probably have to change his whole style. Exotic colognes, plush, dark nightclubs, maitais and daiquiris, necklaced ladies in satin gowns, misty and sexy like in a tequila ad. Jake could imagine lots of possibilities when he let himself, but none that ended up with him pressed onto a stalled freeway.

Jake was thinking about this freedom of his so much that when he glimpsed its green light he just went ahead and stared bye bye to the steadily employed. When he turned his head the same direction his windshield faced, it was maybe one second too late. He pounced the brake pedal and steered the front wheels away from the tiny brakelights but the smack was unavoidable. Just one second sooner and it would only have been close. One second more and he'd be crawling up the Toyota's trunk. As it was, it seemed like only a harmless smack, much less solid than the one against his back bumper.

Jake considered driving past the Toyota but was afraid the traffic ahead would make it too difficult. As he pulled up against the curb a few carlengths ahead, it occurred to him that the traffic might have helped him get away too. He slammed the car door twice to make sure it was closed fully and to give himself another second more, then toured front and rear of his Buick for damage on or near the bumpers. Not an impressionable scratch even in the chrome. He perked up. Though the car's beauty was secondary to its ability to start and move, the body and paint were clean except for a few minor dings. This stood out as one of his few clearcut accomplishments over the years.

Before he spoke to the driver of the Toyota, whose looks he could see might present him with an added complication, he signaled to the driver of the car that hit him, still in his car and stopped behind the Toyota, and waved his hands and shook his head to let the man know there was no problem as far as he was concerned. The driver waved back and started his engine.

"It didn't even scratch my paint," Jake told her in that way of his. "So how you 5 doin? Any damage to the car? I'm kinda hoping so, just so it takes a little more time and we can talk some. Or else you can give me your phone number now and I won't have to lay my regular b.s. on you to get it later."

He took her smile as a good sign and relaxed. He inhaled her scent like it was clean air and straightened out his less than new but not unhip clothes.

"You've got Florida plates. You look like you must be Cuban."

"My parents are from Venezuela."

"My name's Jake." He held out his hand.

"Mariana."    10

They shook hands like she'd never done it before in her life.

"I really am sorry about hitting you like that." He sounded genuine. He fondled the wide dimple near the cracked taillight. "It's amazing how easy it is to put a dent in these new cars. They're so soft they might replace waterbeds soon." Jake was confused about how to proceed with this. So much seemed so unlikely, but there was always possibility. "So maybe we should go out to breakfast somewhere and talk it over."

"I don't eat breakfast."

"Some coffee then."

"Thanks, but I really can't."    15

"You're not married, are you? Not that that would matter that much to me. I'm an openminded kinda guy."

She was smiling. "I have to get to work."

"That sounds boring."

"I better get your driver's license," she said.

Jake nodded, disappointed. "One little problem," he said. "I didn't bring it. 20 I just forgot it this morning. I'm a musician," he exaggerated greatly, "and, well, I dunno, I left my wallet in the pants I was wearing last night. If you have some paper and a pen I'll give you my address and all that."

He followed her to the glove compartment side of her car.

"What if we don't report it to the insurance companies? I'll just get it fixed for you."

"I don't think my dad would let me do that."

"Your dad? It's not your car?"

"He bought it for me. And I live at home."    25

"Right." She was slipping away from him. He went back around to the back of her new Toyota and looked over the damage again. There was the trunk lid, the bumper, a rear panel, a taillight.

"You do have insurance?" she asked, suspicious, as she came around the back of the car.

"Oh yeah," he lied.

"I guess you better write the name of that down too."

He made up a last name and address and wrote down the name of an insur-  30
ance company an old girlfriend once belonged to. He considered giving a real
phone number but went against that idea and made one up.

"I act too," he lied to enhance the effect more. "Been in a couple of movies."

She smiled like a fan.

"So how about your phone number?" He was rebounding maturely.

She gave it to him.

"Mariana, you are beautiful," he said in his most sincere voice.  35

"Call me," she said timidly.

Jake beamed. "We'll see you, Mariana," he said holding out his hand. Her hand
felt so warm and soft he felt like he'd been kissed.

Back in his car he took a moment or two to feel both proud and sad about his
performance. Then he watched the rear view mirror as Mariana pulled up behind
him. She was writing down the license plate numbers on his Buick, ones that he'd
taken off a junk because the ones that belonged to his had expired so long ago.
He turned the ignition key and revved the big engine and clicked into drive. His
sense of freedom swelled as he drove into the now moving street traffic, though he
couldn't stop the thought about that FM stereo radio and crushed velvet interior
and the new car smell that would even make it better.

### CONSIDERATIONS FOR CRITICAL THINKING AND WRITING

1. **FIRST RESPONSE.** Readers sometimes root for main characters to get away with
   something even if it is unethical, immoral, or illegal. Did you feel anything
   like that when you read this story? Why or why not?

2. Jake is clearly not heroic. Does he possess any positive qualities that could be
   turned into heroism in a longer narrative?

3. The narrator often indicates when Jake is lying or exaggerating. What is the
   effect of that choice? Put differently, would we respond differently if we didn't
   know immediately and with certainty that Jake is untrustworthy?

4. The story's title indicates that setting is of primary importance. How, exactly,
   is this a particularly Los Angeles story?

## DAGOBERTO GILB

## *On Writing "Love in L.A."*  2012

I was unemployed when I wrote "Love in L.A." I wasn't happy about that. I had
two young sons and a wife and a landlord and utility companies I supported and
I drove an older car that needed, at the very least, springs and shocks and often
gas. When I'd come back to L.A. in the early '80s after many years here and there
but mostly El Paso, I did so with dreams of good money as a construction worker
with high-rise skills. I'd joined the carpenters' union, and I was a journeyman,
and there were cranes in the skyline everywhere. I was good at it. And work was
great when I was working, but a job ended, and it always ended too fast. . . . As
I was saying, I drove an old car, a 1962 Chevy II wagon. I used to joke around that
it was a vintage classic. It came with a red vinyl interior its previous owner had

done pretty in Juárez, and I kept the rest up. It roared with a rebuilt six-cylinder, and I did the tune-ups myself. I'd gotten it super cheap and the best you could say about it, years later, was that it still ran. I had no money for anything else. And I was, again, unemployed, close to broke.

I'd been going like this for years by then, surviving. Only surviving. Should I be trying to find some better line of work? Not to say that I hadn't tried before. Physically able, I could do this if there were regular paychecks. The last time there were no checks for too long, we lost our apartment. Could be this is nothing but the way life is. Lots of my friends didn't do much better. But with me there was also this: was it really that I was trying to be a writer? If I stopped wanting that, maybe even construction work would get easier for me to find because I would give in to it only. They were parallel dream worlds, one where I made a good living as a carpenter, another where I made a living as a writer. Most thought the writer one was fantasy. I didn't, but then I didn't know any better. I did know that I was having a hard time.

Were mine dreams that you have to push forward to reach, or were they fantasies that you get over?

Writing is like having a fever: your brain can't shy away, won't stop. It's a few lines of a lyric or melody that you can't shut down, a word or lover's name that follows you, whether you're talking to who you know or overhearing strangers, an image that has superimposed itself so equally on the familiar and not, that it can't be "out there," only in you. It won't quit you until you write it.

Her: I do not remember where I was driving from one day when I was inching 5 along in some ridiculous street traffic caused by a minor accident. Except nothing in this part of Los Angeles, on Melrose Avenue, is minor, right? And it wasn't really so minor, as car-only damage goes. It was an elderly man, nondescript, whose little car had been rear-ended. He was standing there. A tall, leggy, too curvy woman in the bigger car (her hood wouldn't shut) was pacing and going on, upset as though it weren't her fault. She wore the highest heels and the slinkiest dress. It wasn't three in the morning, it was three in the afternoon. Like everyone else crawling by, it didn't seem like the man knew how to respond other than to stare at her.

Him: many years earlier, I knew a creepy guy who pretended his occupation was connected to Hollywood movies and that he had money. Since he was dark, he saw himself in an ethnic category of an Anthony Quinn or even a Charles Bronson, though more leading man — he would say that people thought he looked like Omar Sharif. Really only he saw Dr. Zhivago in his mirror. He combed his hair with a quality mousse once he began to share an apartment with an older dude who had done some TV show westerns, who knows what else, and drove a red Corvette convertible. Only slightly dangerous (low-level Tony Montana), he scored his women with props — he might lay out a black book to a certain page, incidentally, where no one could miss the famous names he had fake numbers for.

I worried I was as messed up as him, worse in a way, because I had a family. No I wasn't. Yes I was. No. Yes. Was I a construction worker pretending to be a writer? Writing was this full of it dude who was getting me. Or was I this man looking in a mirror, not seeing the screws tightening or falling out under my hardhat? Was I doing the right thing? Did I know what the right thing was? I worried that writing was that woman in the accident — excessive, spoiled, flashy, gaudy, not responsible for the wreck. Writing was beautiful, and sexy, and dramatic. Writing was fun even when there was a minor accident. Writing was L.A., cruising Melrose, a neighborhood where rich people lived lives unlike mine, drove Mercedes.

Then I wrote this story. I'd lived alone for a bit over by 3rd and Alvarado, an older *mexicano* part of town. I made her Venezuelan because I wanted her to be the fairy tale Latina beauty. I wanted her to be driving an economical Toyota. I wanted her to smile. I wanted her to have a family and be getting an education. I didn't want her to be a fool. Him, surviving, I wanted in an old luxury car with dreams, or fantasies, of a better one without dings, a little lost, a little scared, not in the system. I wanted them both in a brief moment together. The writer, I didn't know which of the two characters I was. The carpenter, I got another job out of the union hall soon after.

## DAGOBERTO GILB

### *Shout*   2001

He beat on the screen door. "Will somebody open this?!" Unlike most men, he didn't leave his hard hat in his truck, he took it inside his home, and he had it in his hand. His body was dry now, at least wasn't like it was two hours ago at work, when he wrung his T-shirt of sweat, made it drool between the fingers of his fist, he and his partner making as much of a joke out of it as they could. That's how hot it was, how humid, and it'd been like this, in the nineties and hundreds, for two weeks, and it'd been hot enough before that. All he could think about was unlacing his dirty boots, then peeling off those stinky socks, then the rest. He'd take a cold one into the shower. The second one. He'd down the first one right at the refrigerator. "Come on!" Three and four were to be appreciated, five was mellow, and six let him nap before bed.

"I didn't hear you," his wife said.

"Didn't *hear* me? How *couldn't* you hear me? And why's it locked anyways? When I get here I don't feel like waiting to come in. Why can't you leave the thing unlocked?"

"Why do you think?"

"Well don't let the baby open it. I want this door open when I get home." He   5 carried on in Spanish, *hijos de* and *putas* and *madres* and *chingadas*. This was the only Spanish he used at home. He tossed the hard hat near the door, relieved to be inside, even though it was probably hotter than outside, even though she was acting mad. He took it that she'd been that way all day already.

Their children, three boys, were seven, four, and almost two, and they were, as should be expected, battling over something.

"Everybody shut up and be quiet!" he yelled. Of course that worsened the situation, because when he got mad he scared the baby, who immediately started crying.

"I'm so tired," he muttered.

She glared at him, the baby in her arms.

"You know sometimes I wish you were a man cuz I wouldn't let you get away   10 with looks like that. I wouldn't take half the shit I take from you." He fell back into the wooden chair nobody sat in except him when he laced the high-top boots on, or off, as he already had. "You know how hot it was today? A hundred and five. It's unbelievable." He looked at her closely, deeply, which he didn't often do, especially this month. She was trying to settle down the baby and turned the TV on to distract the other two.

"It's too hard to breathe," he said to her. He walked bare-footed for the beer and took out two. They were in the door tray of the freezer and almost frozen.

"So nothing happened today?" she asked. Already she wasn't mad at him. It was how she was, why they could get along.

"Nothing else was said. Maybe nothing's gonna happen. God knows this heat's making everybody act unnatural. But tomorrow's check day. If he's gonna get me most likely it'll be tomorrow." He finished a beer leaning against the tile near the kitchen sink, enjoying a peace that had settled into the apartment. The baby was content, the TV was on, the Armenians living an arm's reach away were chattering steadily, there was a radio on from an apartment in a building across from them, Mexican TV upstairs, pigeons, a dog, traffic noise, the huge city out there groaning its sound — all this silence in the apartment.

"There's other jobs," he said. "All of 'em end no matter what anyways."

It was a job neither of them wanted to end too soon. This year he'd been 15 laid up for months after he fell and messed up his shoulder and back. He'd been drunk — a happy one that started after work — but he did it right there at his own front door, playing around. At the same time the duplex apartment they'd been living in for years had been sold and they had to move here. It was all they could get, all they were offered, since so few landlords wanted three children, boys no less, at a monthly rent they could afford. They were lucky to find it and it wasn't bad as places went, but they didn't like it much. They felt like they were starting out again, and that did not seem right. They'd talked this over since they'd moved in until it degenerated into talk about separation. And otherwise, in other details, it also wasn't the best year of their lives.

He showered in warm water, gradually turning the hot water down until it came out as cold as the summer allowed, letting the iced beer do the rest.

She was struggling getting dinner together, the boys were loud and complaining about being hungry, and well into the fifth beer, as he sat near the bright color and ever-happy tingle of the TV set, his back stiffening up, he snapped.

"Everybody has to shut up! I can't stand this today! I gotta relax some!"

She came back at him screaming too. "I can't stand *you!*"

He leaped. "You don't talk to me like that!" 20

She came right up to him. "You gonna hit me?!" she dared him.

The seven-year-old ran to his bed but the other two froze up, waiting for the tension to ease enough before their tears squeezed out.

"Get away from me," he said trying to contain himself. "You better get away from me right now. You know, just go home, go to your mother's, just go."

"*You* go! *You* get out! We're gonna stay!"

He looked through her, then slapped a wall, rocking what seemed like the 25 whole building. "You don't know how close you are."

He wouldn't leave. He walked into the bedroom, then walked out, sweating. He went into the empty kitchen — they were all in the children's room, where there was much crying — and he took a plate and filled it with what she'd made and went in front of the tube and he clicked on a ball game, told himself to calm himself and let it all pass at least tonight, at least while the weather was like it was and while these other things were still bothering both of them, and then he popped the sixth beer. He wasn't going to fall asleep on the couch tonight.

Eventually his family came out, one by one peeking around a corner to see what he looked like. Then they ate in a whisper, even cutting loose here and there with a little giggle or gripe. Eventually the sun did set, though that did nothing to wash off the glue of heat.

And eventually the older boys felt comfortable enough to complain about bedtime. Only the baby cried — he was tired and wanted to sleep but couldn't because a cold had clogged his nose. Still, they were all trying to maintain the truce when from outside, a new voice came in: SHUT THAT FUCKING KID UP YOU FUCKING PEOPLE! HEY! SHUT THAT FUCKING KID UP OVER THERE!

It was like an explosion except that he flew toward it. He shook the window screen with his voice. "You fuck yourself, asshole! You stupid asshole, you shut your mouth!" He ran out the other way, out the screen door and around and under the heated stars. "Come on out here, mouth! Come out and say that to my face!" He squinted at all the windows around him, no idea where it came from. "So come on! Say it right now!" There was no taker, and he turned away, his blood still bright red.

When he came back inside, the children had gone to bed and she was lying down with the baby, who'd fallen asleep. He went back to the chair. The game ended, she came out, half-closing the door behind her, and went straight to their bed. He followed.

"I dunno," he said after some time. He'd been wearing shorts and nothing else since his shower, and it shouldn't have taken him so long, yet he just sat there on the bed. Finally he turned on the fan and it whirred, ticking as it pivoted left and right. "It doesn't do any good, but it's worse without it." He looked at her like he did earlier. "I'm kinda glad nobody came out. Afterwards I imagined some nut just shooting me, or a few guys coming. I'm getting too old for that shit."

She wasn't talking.

"So what did they say?" he asked her. "At the clinic?"

"Yes."

"Yes what?"

"That I am."

They both listened to the fan and to the mix of music from the Armenians and that TV upstairs.

"I would've never thought it could happen," he said. "That one time, and it wasn't even good."

"Maybe for you. I knew it then."

"You did?"

She rolled on her side.

"I'm sorry about all the yelling," he said.

"I was happy you went after that man. I always wanna do stuff like that."

He rolled to her.

"I'm too sticky. It's too hot."

"I have to. We do. It's been too long, and now it doesn't matter."

"It does matter," she said. "I love you."

"I'm sorry," he said, reaching over to touch her breast. "You know I'm sorry."

He took another shower afterward. A cold shower. His breath sputtered and noises hopped from his throat. He crawled into the bed naked, onto the sheet that seemed as hot as ever, and listened to outside, to that mournful Armenian music mixing with Spanish, and to the fan, and it had stilled him. It was joy, and it was so strange. She'd fallen asleep and so he resisted kissing her, telling her. He thought he should hold on to this as long as he could, until he heard the pitch of the freeway climb, telling him that dawn was near and it was almost time to go back to work.

## CONSIDERATIONS FOR CRITICAL THINKING AND WRITING

1. FIRST RESPONSE. The story contains a great deal of rage and ends with calm. Are these forces balanced? Are they codependent?

2. List the many details the writer could have included but rather chose to render in nonspecific terms. What is the cumulative effect of this style choice?

3. The protagonist seems to be seeking relief through most of the story. Where does he find it, even temporarily? What happens to his failed attempts to find it?

4. What is the story's theme?

## DAGOBERTO GILB

# *On Writing "Shout"*    2012

I suspect that younger readers — though older ones too — believe that a writer would enjoy going back and reading his earlier work. Probably a few do. I do not. It's like going back and looking at old photographs. I see a younger me, and I think of all the decisions I made, or didn't, because I didn't know what I didn't know. Worse, I read these stories and see what I would cut over there and add right here. And who am I to do that now to these full-grown stories? I think about where I was in my head when I wrote them . . . but let me give you this easier where: when I wrote "Shout," we were living in an East Hollywood apartment building beneath an elderly Armenian couple who grew parsley in the cracks of the cement pathways, who were miserable whenever my two baby boys rode their noisy Big Wheels. If the horrible thing about construction work was those times I didn't have a job, one of the great things was those times when I didn't have a job — not banging nails meant, instead, me getting to stay home at my wooden desk. (I still had the one I bought used in college. Beside me then was a Mexican calavera who oversaw whatever was on it, which it does to this day, on a newer wood desk.) That was when I allowed myself to write "officially" these pages I wanted published, the ones crafted, the ones you read. Not to say I was not always writing. Even working eleven hours, six days a week for as many months as a job would hold me, I wrote every day, but it would be in a notebook, recording conversations, incidents, descriptions, deep philosophical insights, and dear diary type boo-hoos or longings. Thousands of pages accumulated. My best writing hours were when my sons were asleep, and there was quiet, though once I got onto something, I could work anytime, in any noise.

It's surely obvious that much of my fiction comes from my own life and experiences. "Shout," for instance, could be said to have come out of the same period of my life as "Love in L.A." Hard to avoid what lasted over a decade. It used to be that most writers wrote out of their lived experience. Herman Melville, of *Moby-Dick* (and *Billy Budd*), was a whaler. Nowadays people expect fiction to be nothing but mental creation and research, drawn on the page. Art is the imagination, goes this view, is the writer's desk alone, and the discipline there. That's not untrue, and it alone works well for very many. Gustave Flaubert, imagining a life as a woman, is said to have written one of the greatest novels of a woman, *Madame Bovary*. For me, fiction is life transformed and fueled by imagination. Experience often teaches by surprise — what cannot be predicted by the best reader in the library. My own favorite writers are out there, feeling the wind, on an adventure. Fiction I admire the most captures what, like life, smacks you when and where you're not looking, and the blow can seem so small, and it's so big.

Which brings up the subject of the small and the big, the short story and the novel. In many respects, a novel is simply a short story that is made larger, fuller, with more characters, more involved situations, a longer and more casual read. Thus, many short stories can be expanded into novels, or become segments of one. But I want to say that the best short fiction has more kinship with poetry: the goal is to reduce words and condense, and it is driven more by image than plot, both contrary to the novel. War can be described in a hundred pages of a battle scene, but might be more lastingly understood in an image of a tear falling, red itself or what is seen through it. There are never enough pages for love, but isn't it only the neighbor's *gallo* waking you up angry until you see, sound asleep next to you. . . .

The small. If novels are often about epic sweeps of history and issues, the big ideas of big egos, characters who are larger than whole nations and journeys that are bold, short fiction goes for what's left off-screen, following characters who would be minor against the headliners in those novels, but whose conclusions, The Ends, if less grandiose and more subtle, are anything shy of large.

And so, my own stories are about the small things and the people who aren't  5 seen much in literature. There was a time when characters like those who populate my fiction were written about more, just not very much in recent decades. By that I mean common Americans, what many call working people, be they employed or looking to be. There are not a lot of stories about men like the main character in "Shout." I have found over the years that many know them as fathers and uncles, brothers and husbands, but they are not in the books they read. What you see in "Shout" as well is this man in a Mexican American family, yet another huge segment of American culture seldom read about. What I hoped to offer was not a simple portrayal of a construction worker coming home from work exhausted from a long day in the heat, not just a domestic squabble he causes with a patient wife, the mother of their three children. Left there, it would be a working-class cliché, the macho stereotype not only of that kind of man but also of a Mexican male. What I wanted seen was the same bullish rage he had in his home being used to defend his family when a stranger screams at them. And then the intimacy, what is hidden in the broad, usual expectation, what is forgotten when you don't know characters as living people, that the man and woman are lovers.

## DAGOBERTO GILB

### *Uncle Rock*    2011

In the morning, at his favorite restaurant, Erick got to order his favorite American food, sausage and eggs and hash-brown *papitas*° fried crunchy on top. He'd be sitting there, eating with his mother, not bothering anybody, and life was good, when a man started changing it all. Lots of times it was just a man staring too much — but then one would come over. Friendly, he'd put his thick hands on the table as if he were touching water, and squat low, so that he was at sitting level, as though he were so polite, and he'd smile, with coffee-and-tobacco-stained teeth. He might wear a

---

*papitas:* Potatoes.

bolo tie and speak in a drawl. Or he might have on a tan uniform, a company logo on the back, an oval name patch on the front. Or he'd be in a nothing-special work shirt, white or striped, with a couple of pens clipped onto the left side pocket, tucked into a pair of jeans or chinos that were morning-clean still, with a pair of scuffed work boots that laced up higher than regular shoes. He'd say something about her earrings, or her bracelet, or her hair, or her eyes, and if she had on her white uniform how nice it looked on her. Or he'd come right out with it and tell her how pretty she was, how he couldn't keep himself from walking up, speaking to her directly, and could they talk again? Then he'd wink at Erick. Such a fine-looking boy! How old is he, eight or nine? Erick wasn't even small for an eleven-year-old. He tightened his jaw then, slanted his eyes up from his plate at his mom and not the man, definitely not this man he did not care for. Erick drove a fork into a goopy American egg yolk and bled it into his American potatoes. She wouldn't offer the man Erick's correct age either, saying only that he was growing too fast.

She almost always gave the man her number if he was wearing a suit. Not a sports coat but a buttoned suit with a starched white shirt and a pinned tie meant something to her. Once in a while, Erick saw one of these men again at the front door of the apartment in Silverlake. The man winked at Erick as if they were buddies. Grabbed his shoulder or arm, squeezed the muscle against the bone. What did Erick want to be when he grew up? A cop, a jet-airplane mechanic, a travel agent, a court reporter? A dog groomer? Erick stood there, because his mom said that he shouldn't be impolite. His mom's date said he wanted to take Erick along with them sometime. The three of them. What kind of places did Erick think were fun? Erick said nothing. He never said anything when the men were around, and not because of his English, even if that was what his mother implied to explain his silence. He didn't talk to any of the men and he didn't talk much to his mom either. Finally they took off, and Erick's night was his alone. He raced to the grocery store and bought half a gallon of chocolate ice cream. When he got back, he turned on the TV, scooted up real close, as close as he could, and ate his dinner with a soup spoon. He was away from all the men. Even though a man had given the TV to them. He was a salesman in an appliance store who'd bragged that a rich customer had given it to him and so why shouldn't he give it to Erick's mom, who couldn't afford such a good TV otherwise?

When his mom was working as a restaurant hostess, and was going to marry the owner, Erick ate hot-fudge sundaes and drank chocolate shakes. When she worked at a trucking company, the owner of all the trucks told her he was getting a divorce. Erick climbed into the rigs, with their rooms full of dials and levers in the sky. Then she started working in an engineer's office. There was no food or fun there, but even he could see the money. He was not supposed to touch anything, but what was there to touch — the tubes full of paper? He and his mom were invited to the engineer's house, where he had two horses and a stable, a swimming pool, and two convertible sports cars. The engineer's family was there: his grown children, his gray-haired parents. They all sat down for dinner in a dining room that seemed bigger than Erick's apartment, with three candelabras on the table, and a tablecloth and cloth napkins. Erick's mom took him aside to tell him to be well mannered at the table and polite to everyone. Erick hadn't said anything. He never spoke anyway, so how could he have said anything wrong? She leaned into his ear and said that she wanted them to know that he spoke English. That whole dinner he was silent, chewing quietly, taking the smallest bites, because he didn't want them to think he liked their food.

When she got upset about days like that, she told Erick that she wished they could just go back home. She was tired of worrying. "Back," for Erick, meant mostly the stories he'd heard from her, which never sounded so good to him: she'd had to share a room with her brothers and sisters. They didn't have toilets. They didn't have electricity. Sometimes they didn't have enough food. He saw this Mexico as if it were the backdrop of a movie on afternoon TV, where children walked around barefoot in the dirt or on broken sidewalks and small men wore wide-brimmed straw hats and baggy white shirts and pants. The women went to church all the time and prayed to alcoved saints and, heads down, fearful, counted rosary beads. There were rocks everywhere, and scorpions and tarantulas and rattlesnakes, and vultures and no trees and not much water, and skinny dogs and donkeys, and ugly bad guys with guns and bullet vests who rode laughing into town to drink and shoot off their pistols and rifles, driving their horses all over like dirt bikes on desert dunes. When they spoke English, they had stupid accents — his mom didn't have an accent like theirs. It didn't make sense to him that Mexico would only be like that, but what if it was close? He lived on paved, lighted city streets, and a bicycle ride away were the Asian drugstore and the Armenian grocery store and the corner where black Cubans drank coffee and talked Dodgers baseball.

When he was in bed, where he sometimes prayed, he thanked God for his 5 mom, who he loved, and he apologized for not talking to her, or to anyone, really, except his friend Albert, and he apologized for her never going to church and for his never taking Holy Communion, as Albert did — though only to God would he admit that he wanted to only because Albert did. He prayed for good to come, for his mom and for him, since God was like magic, and happiness might come the way of early morning, in the trees and bushes full of sparrows next to his open window, louder and louder when he listened hard, eyes closed.

---

The engineer wouldn't have mattered if Erick hadn't told Albert that he was his dad. Albert had just moved into the apartment next door and lived with both his mother and his father, and since Albert's mother already didn't like Erick's mom, Erick told him that his new dad was an engineer. Erick actually believed it, too, and thought that he might even get his own horse. When that didn't happen, and his mom was lying on her bed in the middle of the day, blowing her nose, because she didn't have the job anymore, that was when Roque came around again. Roque was nobody — or he was anybody. He wasn't special, he wasn't not. He tried to speak English to Erick, thinking that was the reason Erick didn't say anything when he was there. And Erick had to tell Albert that Roque was his uncle, because the engineer was supposed to be his new dad any minute. Uncle Rock, Erick said. His mom's brother, he told Albert. Roque worked at night and was around during the day, and one day he offered Erick and Albert a ride. When his mom got in the car, she scooted all the way over to Roque on the bench seat. Who was supposed to be her brother, Erick's Uncle Rock. Albert didn't say anything, but he saw what had happened, and that was it for Erick. Albert had parents, grandparents, and a brother and a sister, and he'd hang out only when one of his cousins wasn't coming by. Erick didn't need a friend like him.

What if she married Roque, his mom asked him one day soon afterward. She told Erick that they would move away from the apartment in Silverlake to a better neighborhood. He did want to move, but he wished that it weren't because of Uncle Rock. It wasn't just because Roque didn't have a swimming pool or horses or a big ranch house. There wasn't much to criticize except that he was always too willing and nice, too considerate, too generous. He wore nothing flashy or expensive, just ordinary clothes that were clean and ironed, and shoes he kept shined. He combed and parted his hair neatly. He didn't have a buzzcut like the men who didn't like kids. He moved slow, he talked slow, as quiet as night. He only ever said yes to Erick's mom. How could she not like him for that? He loved her so much — anybody could see his pride when he was with her. He signed checks and gave her cash. He knocked on their door carrying cans and fruit and meat. He was there when she asked, gone when she asked, back whenever, grateful. He took her out to restaurants on Sunset, to the movies in Hollywood, or on drives to the beach in rich Santa Monica.

---

Roque knew that Erick loved baseball. Did Roque like baseball? It was doubtful that he cared even a little bit — he didn't listen to games on the radio or TV, and he never looked at a newspaper. He loved boxing though. He knew the names of all the Mexican fighters as if they lived here, as if they were Dodgers players like Steve Yeager, Dusty Baker, Kenny Landreaux or Mike Marshall, or Pedro Guerrero. Roque did know about Fernando Valenzuela, everyone did, even his mom, which is why she agreed to let Roque take them to a game. What Mexican didn't love Fernando? Dodger Stadium was close to their apartment. He'd been there once with Albert and his family — well, outside it, on a nearby hill, to see the fireworks for Fourth of July. His mom decided that all three of them would go on a Saturday afternoon, since Saturday night, Erick thought, she might want to go somewhere else, even with somebody else.

Roque, of course, didn't know who the Phillies were. He knew nothing about the strikeouts by Steve Carlton or the homeruns by Mike Schmidt. He'd never heard of Pete Rose. It wasn't that Erick knew very much either, but there was nothing that Roque could talk to him about, if they were to talk.

If Erick showed his excitement when they drove up to Dodger Stadium and 10 parked, his mom and Roque didn't really notice it. They sat in the bleachers, and for him the green of the field was a magic light; the stadium decks surrounding them seemed as far away as Rome. His body was somewhere it had never been before. The fifth inning? That's how late they were. Or were they right on time, because they weren't even sure they were sitting in the right seats yet when he heard the crack of the bat, saw the crowd around them rising as it came at them. Erick saw the ball. He had to stand and move and stretch his arms and want that ball until it hit his bare hands and stayed there. Everybody saw him catch it with no bobble. He felt all the eyes and voices around him as if they were every set of eyes and every voice in the stadium. His mom was saying something, and Roque, too, and then, finally, it was just him and that ball and his stinging hands. He wasn't even sure if it had been hit by Pete Guerrero. He thought for sure it had been, but he didn't ask. He didn't watch the game then — he couldn't. He didn't care who won. He stared at his official National League ball, reimagining what had happened. He ate a hot dog and drank a soda and he sucked the salted peanuts and the wooden spoon from his chocolate-malt ice cream. He rubbed the bumpy seams of his homerun ball.

Game over, they were the last to leave. People were hanging around, not going straight to their cars. Roque didn't want to leave. He didn't want to end it so quickly, Erick thought, while he still had her with him. Then one of the Phillies came out of the stadium door and people swarmed — boys mostly, but also men and some women and girls — and they got autographs before the player climbed onto the team's bus. Joe Morgan, they said. Then Garry Maddox appeared. Erick clutched the ball but he didn't have a pen. He just watched, his back to the gray bus the Phillies were getting into.

Then a window slid open. *Hey, big man*, a voice said. Erick really wasn't sure. *Gimme the ball, la pelota,°* the face in the bus said. *I'll have it signed, comprendes?° Échalo,° just toss it to me.* Erick obeyed. He tossed it up to the hand that was reaching out. The window closed. The ball was gone a while, so long that his mom came up to him, worried that he'd lost it. The window slid open again and the voice spoke to her. *We got the ball, Mom. It's not lost, just a few more.* When the window opened once more, this time the ball was there. *Catch.* There were all kinds of signatures on it, though none that he could really recognize except for Joe Morgan and Pete Rose.

Then the voice offered more, and the hand threw something at him. *For your mom, okay? Comprendes?* Erick stared at the asphalt lot where the object lay, as if he'd never seen a folded-up piece of paper before. *Para tu mamá, bueno?* He picked it up, and he started to walk over to his mom and Roque, who were so busy talking they hadn't noticed anything. Then he stopped. He opened the note himself. No one had said he couldn't read it. It said, *I'd like to get to know you. You are muy linda. Very beautiful and sexy. I don't speak Spanish very good, may be you speak better English, pero No Importa.° Would you come by tonite and let me buy you a drink?* There was a phone number and a hotel room number. A name, too. A name that came at him the way that the homerun had.

Erick couldn't hear. He could see only his mom ahead of him. She was talking to Roque, Roque was talking to her. Roque was the proudest man, full of joy because he was with her. It wasn't his fault he wasn't an engineer. Now Erick could hear again. Like sparrows hunting seed, boys gathered round the bus, calling out, while the voice in the bus was yelling at him, *Hey, big guy! Give it to her!* Erick had the ball in one hand and the note in the other. By the time he reached his mom and Roque, the note was already somewhere on the asphalt parking lot. *Look*, he said in a full voice. *They all signed my ball.*

*la pelota:* The ball.
*comprendes?:* Understand?
*Échalo:* Throw it.
*pero No Importa:* It doesn't matter.

## Considerations for Critical Thinking and Writing

1. **FIRST RESPONSE.** What does Erick want? Does it change over the course of the story?

2. The beginning of the story emphasizes the word "American." How does the depiction of the United States, especially in contrast to Erick's vision of Mexico, frame the story's concerns?

3. How do the baseball and the piece of paper handed to Erick from the baseball team's tour bus function as symbols?

4. The story's title is about a lie Erick tells his neighbor Albert, a lie that is connected to a moment of embarrassment. How does the decision to title the story "Uncle Rock" as opposed to, say, "The Catch" alter your understanding of the story's theme?

# Dagoberto Gilb

## *On Writing "Uncle Rock"*   2012

Mostly I don't like talking about my work. What can I say without implying a boast that it is fine writing you will want to know at least as well as me, if not better? (Of course it is!) Not only tasteless, it's a little questionable. Because, of course, this is somebody else's occupation, not my mirror's. Do you go to a restaurant telling you that it has "The Best Mexican Food in Texas!" (Of course it does, right?) All this aside, "Uncle Rock" might be one of my easiest stories to disassemble to see how it was put together.

As a craft, what I do isn't that much different than what a tile setter does. My fictional tiles, however, are broken, chipped, cracked, and come in different sizes and proportions and colors, and what I do is make a mosaic. There are sentences based on experience of my own years ago, and there are graphs which are what I remember doing with my sons when they were children; there are objects much like I owned, and a character who is memories of two people on the body of a third I worked with. Even within a single sentence, the imaginary is beside the Googled. The drama is invention. "Uncle Rock" appears to be a story of an eleven-year-old boy's life in the '80s, when really it is a set of disconnected images from several decades flipped through so quickly that it gives the illusion of movement (yes, like a "movie"), a story of a single experience. People read this story and assume it must be autobiographical. A compliment to my craft. You now know it was written willfully, by design.

Where the shards of tiles come from is what distinguishes what's mine from another writer's. And no doubt there are all sorts of piles to go through. I studied religion in college. That wasn't because I made a mistake and picked a degree plan that I thought I would cash in on. It's that I learned we live on a circling planet and noticed that I am alive and conscious. My curiosity about this has driven me to where I am. What I write is called literary fiction. The purpose of commercial fiction is, besides making money, to pass the time pleasantly, to get some relief from the grind — to entertain. Though this used to be more the function of reading in the past, now that is primarily handled by television and film. Literary fiction intends to entertain as well (and I say it does, more and especially so when it's great), and wishes to make money, but its goal — as is mine — is to reach out from the ordinary to realize the extraordinary. To point to the mystery that is being alive, in a strange place, in a time — a reader's, a writer's — that is not only in time. Is Erick's story about the '60s, '80s, these teens? Is his mom or Roque only a product of a class or culture? Is this story about males and single women, about the boundaries of love between a fatherless boy and a mother?

Don't think I'm denying that my fiction has autobiography in it. But this is true of most works of art, no more mine than many. Still, "Uncle Rock" could be used to do a clinical, psychological take on me through my work, digging out the root troubles haunting me. Most likely not wrong. It could be pointed out that, for instance, how the too wild single mother theme and character comes up here as it does in other pieces by me. That I have a *mami* issue. Probably true. But in my defense, my mom really did create some stories. Say you were the littlest broke, or even felt like splurging, treating yourself, or just felt like making life easy for yourself, and you knew where there was a chest of gold coins. Wouldn't you go there and grab one? It's only one here, and another couple in the past, not like I got greedy and grabbed the whole suitcase.

It's easiest for me to talk about my work when it has to do with advo- 5 cacy. I would argue that all art advocates, like it or not, and that a writer represents a group of people and their interests. My fiction is very much about the common people in America, those who work and support families with their hands and bodies for hourly wages, who go about their lives hidden from media and celebrity links. Characters with "careers" like Erick's mother or Roque are not read about. Which brings up the American West — it is still unusual to read literary work set in and written by those who live west of the Mississippi. But it is more than rare to read stories set in the American Southwest, and more so still when they are about Mexican American people in their historical homeland — why the mountains and rivers and cities have names in Spanish. And I do that. My stories represent the Chicano story. It could be said that this is unavoidable for me, and that's not wrong, but my advocacy began only vaguely when I was young. In college I was lucky enough to see Luis Valdez's plays performed by his Teatro Campesino. I went to events supporting, and featuring, Cesar Chavez. Both were synonymous with the farm workers' movement. Broccoli, to me, only came from a Safeway grocery store, and other people ate that kind of food. But the urban Mexican American was, obviously, always there too. There was simply little to no publicly documented evidence of it. Many call this an "invisibility" of the culture and history in the United States. I don't see it that way, not when what's loved about the Mexican American West, from cowboys to adobes, from margaritas to enchiladas, tacos, and burritos, are now as American as an iPod and a hamburger. I say Mexican Americans are being ignored willfully, an ignorance that has gotten worse in the past decade as a seismic demographic shift is altering the region's, and nation's, political landscape.

Which finally brings me back to "Uncle Rock." Take it apart, and you find a description of the Mexican American situation: Roque, a working man who struggles with English, an anybody, nobody special, who only works hard and is steady, is the only one who treats Erick's mother well. He adores her. But, despite the humiliation she endures, she wants more than what he is able to offer. She is beautiful and attracts all kinds of attention, so how can she not want more than what everyone else accepts? Her American dream. Erick is as embarrassed by his mom as he is attached to her. He is bothered so much that he has gone mute — he does not want to talk to anyone but God and his friend Albert. From the outside, it would appear that his is a struggle with the English language. One day he realizes a dream. In the days of Fernandomania, Roque takes him and his mom to a Dodgers game. Not only does he get to go to his first professional baseball game, not only does he catch a homerun ball, but a famous baseball player wants to meet his mother. At first thrilled, as young as he is Erick knows the offer is disrespectful and crude. And when he walks back to the two of them, who are unaware of what happened, he speaks to them. I want Erick's voice to get louder, smarter, and more confident.

## Perspectives

### DAGOBERTO GILB

## *On Physical Labor*   2003

Not everybody wants to sit at a desk for a living. So many of us come from cultures where it is expected that we will move our bodies in the wind and sun, at dawn and into dusk. Many of us have been taught by family that physical work feels good and is good — when the day is over, we know what we did because we see it, we feel the efforts in our feet and hands and bones, and when we go home, when the wife puts food on the table and the family sits down and eats, there is unmistakable pride that all of it is because we have done our job.

It is human to work, to bend and grip, to lift and pull. It's never about getting tired or dirty. There is nothing wrong with sweat and toil. It is only about conditions and decent wages that there can come complaint. This is what so many people don't understand, especially those who sit in chairs in offices. They see us tired, they see us worried. They say, Well, if you don't like your situation, why don't you get a better job? Because it isn't the job, the kind of work. The job is good. Being a carpenter, an electrician, a plumber, an ironworker, a laborer, those are all good. What isn't good is to be earning a living that can't bring in enough money to raise a healthy family, buy a home, go to a dentist and doctor, and be around comfortably for grandchildren.

A writer from Detroit who worked years for the Fisher Body Plant in Flint, Michigan, has recently been profiled in the newspapers because he won a prize for his writing. In the exultation of winning, he has been quoted often about those years he worked on the assembly line, saying, "I can't stress to you enough how much I hated it." This writer, he is certainly a good man, but like so many, he simply forgot what a joy employment is, what a job means to people and their families. There is only good in work, and the very best people are those who work hard.

From "Work Union," in *Gritos*

### DAGOBERTO GILB

## *On Distortions of Mexican American Culture*   2011

When Americans think of the South, some might think of its white society, Antebellum and post, its white literature, its wealth, yet the black culture is undeniably ever there, present. Others might discuss the history of the South in terms of black people, their history of slavery, their struggle with poverty, as the homeland of African Americans. This binary is a permanent overlay on the topography of the Southeast region, that quadrangle of the U.S. It is a black-white that has come to define much of America's internal history. Now consider a comparable Southwest quadrangle, one whose historical binary could be called — should be called — brown and white. We are all taught passionately about the American expansion into the West, cattle drives, cowboys and Indians, John Wayne movies, but if someone were to say it is the homeland of Mexican Americans, would anyone associate that with populations in Los Angeles, the state of New Mexico, El Paso, San Antonio, the state of New Mexico, El Paso, San Antonio, the Rio Grande Valley? Visitors thrill at oversized enchilada plates and the bountiful bowls of tortilla chips (Americanisms, both), visits to seventeenth- and early eighteenth-century missions, and they see and hear the vast numbers of "Mexican" people who speak to them in homegrown English at shops, stores, and stations — and yet somehow, relaxing in adobe-themed motels or new Spanish Villa homes, the binary here is not brown and white but *blank* and white, the dominant Mexican culture as if from an uninhabited ghost town. Meanwhile, what brown people they encounter — what articles appear in the media — are recent immigrants, invaders from the border. Part of American history? Curiously, if we were to assert that we are part of Mexico's history — which nobody here or there ever has or does — that would be far more of an outrage than lament that, unless photographed in folklorico costume, we have no images in our nation's history other than as foreigners.

From "La Próxima Parada Is Next," *American Book Review*

## Michael Meyer Interviews Dagoberto Gilb   2012

**Meyer:** Here is a potentially annoying but sincere usage question concerning a simple matter of terms that has caused me and my students to sometimes stumble: Do we (do you) use Chicano or Latino, Hispanic or Mexican American or Tex Mex to describe your writings? Should I even bring up feminine endings and hyphens as well? Do the terms define important distinctions? Is there a single umbrella term? Can you help sort this out for us?

**Gilb:** Aww, the rage of the nomenclature. All these words are better than the ones when I was young — *beaner* and *wetback* are the hit oldies, but just the word *Mexican*, with but a soft decibel of racist tone, could clear the bench. The Chicano period was the beginning of the alternative. The problem with that became the masculine "o" at the end. Since the linguistic rules of Spanish reflected a macho boys' club mentality that did rule beyond usage, Chicanas rightfully fought for the equal status of the feminine "a," which has since created the slash usage, Chicana/o. It was the Nixon administration which came in with the word *Hispanic* as a *non-political* term (Chicanos and Chicanas, college-educated, did not vote Republican). It is a word now predominantly used in Republican circles. Latino, Latina, and Latina/o are the alternative to that. For me the problem with this is its application in the West. While Mexican Americans are close to 70 percent of the national demographic, Latinas and Latinos in the West are 95 percent Mexican American. One may note that neither do I love the hyphen that can be used in *Mexican American* (as in, the diminutive, hyphenated American). Me being me, I don't love the exhausting bureaucracy of slash world, and me being as American as the rest of us, I want nicknames of one or at most two syllables, so I've been going with the gender-neutral *MexAm* when it fits in easily. Sorry for the extra cap. And so it goes.

**Meyer:** It's not likely that any of your characters subscribe to the *American Book Review*, because they are mostly working-class, hard-working individuals struggling to earn a living. Do you think your work reaches an audience that includes the kind of characters that you write about? Do you worry about making the connection?

**Gilb:** Sadly, yes, improbable that an under-educated community would read or receive suggestions to read any of my writing, fiction or nonfiction. Is that because reading has become a luxury item? Is education a luxury item? Historically this has been true in most countries, in Europe, in Mexico, in Latin America. It was just less true in ours. At least as ideals went. Today, it would seem that's our direction. But putting that aside, my writing does reach a segment of the population that does care. And it touches enough even in my own community of people who recognize family members in the stories, who recognize their own voices through hearing mine. And I was invited into a literary world that has rewarded me. Not only have my books been published by Grove Press (the house whose books I was most infatuated with as a young reader), but my work has been in the most honored pages of the literary establishment — the *New Yorker* and *Harper's* magazines — and has been granted their finer awards. That doesn't mean that the mainstream public cares about what I do enough to make me a rich author, but it does mean that there is a respect in our country's literary marketplace for the ideas that pass through me and the people those ideas intend to honor. I am proud that this is true.

*Meyer:* In your comments about "Uncle Rock" you write that "It's easiest for 5 me to talk about my work when it has to do with advocacy." Which of the three stories that you've chosen to include in this anthology do you think most fully seems to be an "advocacy story"?

*Gilb:* All art advocates. The one who says his doesn't, he's someone who's advocating for the way things are, someone who's comfortable. I'm not saying that's right or wrong (though I'm sure I would pick a better or worse), only that it is a stance. For those who are less than comfortable, that status of ghosts, in situations that are less romantic or sitcom popular. I myself have gone through stages of understanding about the role of advocacy. I used to think that, like Dostoevsky, it — the politics, the spirituality — was contained in the art of the fiction alone, not in tracts or marches. A writer writes quietly alone, no option. It's in the finished work, and readers who are ready to find it, will. But I have changed. Maybe because I became a parent. Maybe because, as a journeyman, I worked with an apprentice often. Maybe because I was a coach for nine years and both yelled at and encouraged boys and girls who needed the coaching and got better. Once I became a teacher, a professor even, I found that, being in front of a class, students knowing that it was real and could be earned and I'd come from where they did, their learning altered their views, broke down their clichés and stereotypes. How many Chicano professors of English have you had? Why should it be surprising, even, that Mexican Americans have as many professional and personal complexities as others? As to the stories in this anthology, I don't really think of any one of them having more or less advocacy than another. Choose any of mine anywhere. A different emphasis in that one as opposed to this one, that's it. As to me, I am simply more aware of saying aloud, maybe saying louder, HEY! LOOK! Not sure if that's me, or survival in noisy times.

*Meyer:* In interviews and essays you have described the disadvantages of not being a northeastern writer snugly situated in the New York literary scene. Are there any encouraging advantages to being a southwestern writer in today's literary market?

*Gilb:* If you're from San Francisco, you're a Bay Area writer. From Oregon or Washington, a writer from the Pacific Northwest. Colorado, Utah, Wyoming, Montana, a western writer. If you're from the Southeast, a southern writer. If you live in New York, even Boston, you're a national writer. Hard to argue with the economic demographics and the number of readers who live in those cities and the history of colleges and universities there, as well as magazines and publishers. Traditions groove permanent paths. Hard for anyone to not follow the money,

*Hecho en Tejas: An Anthology of Texas Mexican Literature* was edited by Gilb and published in 2006 by the University of New Mexico Press.

From Hecho en Tejas: An Anthology of TexasMexican Literature by Dagoberto Gilb. Copyright © 2006. University of New Mexico Press, 2006.

An event celebrating the anthology at the historic Cine El Rey Theatre. McAllen, Texas, 2007.
Courtesy of Dagoberto Gilb.

and that's where the money is, too. Also hard not to be born where you're born. The Southwest has always had an exoticized legacy. D. H. Lawrence and Georgia O'Keeffe are New Mexico. Meanwhile, the MexAm Southwest has barely registered on an art stat, but no doubt that too has to change. The Apaches came to learn the force of America's westward expansion onto their land. Mexican Americans — though probably less, are no more immigrant than those from European descent, despite the demagoguery — will be 50 percent of the American Southwest soon, and its beautiful culture and epic history is unavoidably blending into the American mainstream.

**Meyer:** You suffered a debilitating stroke in 2009 from which you have since remarkably recovered, but if you were to write a short story about that experience,

Dagoberto Gilb's desk — and the Mexican *calavera* that oversees it, mentioned in his essay "On Writing 'Shout'" (p. 457).
Courtesy of Dagoberto Gilb.

the fact that it is your writing hand that remains impaired seems to conjure all kinds of symbolic meanings. What has that stroke meant to you as a writer?

*Gilb:* A story titled "please, thank you," first published in *Harper's* and then 10 collected in *Before the End, After the Beginning*, does deal with a character, Mr. Sanchez, who suffered a stroke similar to the one I did. He and I have had to learn how to type only, first one-handed, then slowly with one finger on the other hand, instead of using a pen to write. I can't say I like it a lot, so I do not recommend anyone use the technique to gain insights or to seek material. Yes, it's hard not to consider the metaphor: a writer losing the use of his writing hand. Add to that it happening the night he is celebrating the beginning of a new future as a full-time writer. But that metaphor is only one. Another is the obstacle it is for many of us to be writers. To be artists. To do what we dream, not what is expected, not what we accept. What we have to work hard for. That has always been me, and so adding this new element is not really new. When I wrote the stories for my last collection (mentioned above), for me it was an act of calm defiance — no, I am not done yet — but also gratitude for the generous gifts still given. I'm lucky I can do what I always wanted to do, that I am a writer, and I only need a keyboard. That's not so bad.

# DAGOBERTO GILB
## *Two Draft Manuscript Pages*

gilb / story
8

I don't want that, but then again, yes, that'd probaby be better, because, then again, I don't believe
that's the explanation. *a third Mexican American* This is a campus where my work can be taught in a Chicano lit course only. I
wonder when, if ever, we would *will* be considered gourmet enough, talented enough, important enough.

I am guilty too because I don't think I'm smart enough. Flawed in a couple of personal areas,

I wish I could claim to be better here, I wish instead of wanting to collapse and watch HBO (even, I

admit, those cheap TV judge shows), I read *could* another book. I know those kind of writers. My God,

they are so brilliant and articulate. I even know a couple who are genuises. But what I can only hope

might be seen is what gets undervalued: Not only has writing saved my life, projected it into New *and Washington, D.C.,*

York and European fantasylands I'd never know otherwise, but has offered me joy and fun. In this,

there are limits to how much that might be seen in these essays. I assure you, everyone of them has

given me such pleasure and satisfaction, the same kind I have had when I used to cut wood with my

skilsaw and drive nails and build, watch a building rise high, *a huge* a fun of the kind that trowels the back

of a tile with adhesive and sets it in, the pattern mounting. Each word is rock I've placed personally

into a wall—five go in and *then* I pick through a pile and find another, shift them around until I like it,

I've chipped and knicked at most so that they look to me like good sentences, good paragraphs. If I

don't think of myself as the smartest, I do feel a strength in my working the craft, so that everytime I *of*

finish something I'm impressed, proud of myself, can hardly believe I did it, that I could. Because it's *maybe too*
almost as though it came from another consciousness, beyond my own physical self or nature, *The words are*

because I don't think I was *not* born to be a writer, I've just done it anyway. Often this work is outright

fun, almost as fun as it would be at a good construction job where we were all muscles sweating and

laughing and building shit and getting paid all at the same time—living and working—except writing

work is alone, only an imaginary crew. Sometimes you see that laughter in these essays, but even

4G

A draft manuscript page for the introduction to Gilb's essay collection, *Gritos*, published in 2003 by Grove Press.
Courtesy of Dagoberto Gilb.

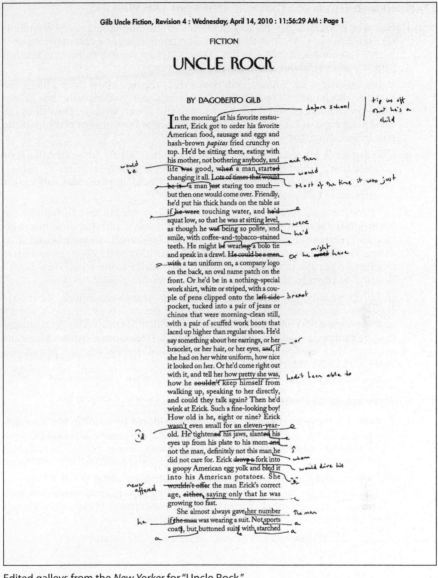

Edited galleys from the *New Yorker* for "Uncle Rock."
Courtesy of Dagoberto Gilb.

## CONSIDERATIONS FOR CRITICAL THINKING AND WRITING

1. Gilb describes two "parallel dream worlds" in his autobiographical commentary on "Love in L.A.": "one where I made a good living as a carpenter, another where I made a living as a writer" (par. 2). How do you think this tension informs Jake's behavior and character in the story?

2. In his reflections on "Shout," Gilb posits that "the best short fiction has more kinship with poetry: the goal is to reduce words and condense, and it is driven more by image than plot, both contrary to the novel" (par. 3). How does the final paragraph of "Shout" serve as an example of how images can supersede plot in this short story?

3. Gilb argues in his discussion of "Uncle Rock" that "all art advocates, like it or not, and that a writer represents a group of people and their interests" (par. 5). Explain to what extent you think that "Uncle Rock," in particular, fulfills this description of Gilb's writing.

4. In "How Books Bounce" and in the three Gilb stories in this anthology, the life exhibited is often fraught with volatile economic and domestic instabilities, and yet these challenges are typically met by shrewd strength, sound sturdiness, and determination. Do you think this ultimately adds up to a grim or positive perspective on life? Discuss two stories along with "How Books Bounce" to consider this question.

5. In his comments "On Distortions of Mexican American Culture," Gilb contrasts how Black culture in the South has had deep roots in America's history and consciousness compared to the ways in which Mexican American culture in the Southwest is largely overlooked or distorted. Consider how Mexicans are portrayed in popular American culture and discuss whether or not you agree with Gilb's observations.

## CONNECTIONS TO OTHER SELECTIONS

1. How might "Love in L.A." or "Shout" be considered love stories but very different from John Updike's "A & P" (p. 145) or ZZ Packer's "Drinking Coffee Elsewhere" (p. 292)? Choose one of Gilb's stories and one of these other stories to compare the social setting, conflicts, protagonists, and tone.

2. Do Gilb's insights into his identity as a southwestern writer of color help you to approach either Joy Harjo's "The Reckoning" (p. 40) or Manuel Muñoz's "Zigzagger" (p. 152), or do the themes and concerns in those stories depart from Gilb's?

# 15

## Stories for Further Reading

Marka/Getty Images.

The demand that I make of the reader is that he should devote his whole life to reading my works.
— JAMES JOYCE

### JUDITH ORTIZ COFER (1952–2016)

Judith Ortiz Cofer was born in Puerto Rico and immigrated to New Jersey with her family at the age of four. Her early years were characterized by frequent trips between the New York metropolitan area and her native Puerto Rico, a dynamic that can be seen in the following story "Volar." When Cofer was fifteen the family relocated to Georgia, where she remained the rest of her life. Fluent in Spanish and English, she became a teacher initially before pursuing a decorated career in creative writing. She wrote in many genres, including creative nonfiction, poetry, fiction, and works that are not easily classified. She has the distinction of being the first Hispanic author to win the O. Henry short story prize.

## *Volar°*   1993

At twelve I was an avid consumer of comic books — *Supergirl* being my favorite. I spent my allowance of a quarter a day on two twelve-cent comic books or a double issue for twenty-five. I had a stack of *Legion of Super Heroes* and *Supergirl* comic books in my bedroom closet that was as tall as I am. I had a recurring dream in those days: that I had long blond hair and could fly. In my dream I climbed the stairs to the top of our apartment building as myself, but as I went up each flight, changes would be taking place. Step by step I would fill out: My legs would grow long, my arms harden into steel, and my hair would magically go straight and turn a golden color. Of course I would add the bonus of breasts, but not too large; Supergirl had to be aerodynamic. Sleek and hard as a super-sonic missile. Once on the roof, my parents safely asleep in their beds, I would get on tiptoe, arms outstretched in the position for flight, and jump out my fifty-story-high window into the black lake of the sky. From up there, over the rooftops, I could see everything, even beyond the few blocks of our barrio;° with my X-ray vision I could look inside the homes of people who interested me. Once I saw our landlord, whom I knew my parents feared, sitting in a treasure-room dressed in an ermine coat and a large gold crown. He sat on the floor counting his dollar bills. I played a trick on him. Going up to his building's chimney, I blew a little puff of my superbreath into his fire-place, scattering his stacks of money so that he had to start counting all over again. I could more or less program my Supergirl dreams in those days by focusing on the object of my current obsession. This way I "saw" into the private lives of my neighbors, my teachers, and in the last days of my childish fantasy and the beginning of adolescence, into the secret room of the boys I liked. In the mornings I'd wake up in my tiny bedroom with the incongruous — at least in our tiny apartment — white "princess" furniture my mother had chosen for me, and find myself back in my body: my tight curls still clinging to my head, skinny arms and legs and flat chest unchanged.

In the kitchen my mother and father would be talking softly over a café con leche.° She would come "wake me" exactly forty-five minutes after they had gotten up. It was their time together at the beginning of each day and even at an early age I could feel their disappointment if I interrupted them by getting up too early. So I would stay in my bed recalling my dreams of flight, perhaps planning my next flight. In the kitchen they would be discussing events in the barrio. Actually, he would be carrying that part of the conversation; when it was her turn to speak she would, more often than not, try shifting the topic toward her desire to see her *familia* on the Island: *How about a vacation in Puerto Rico together this year, Querido?°* We could rent a car, go to the beach. We could ... And he would answer patiently, gently, *Mi amor,°* do you know how much it would cost for all of us to fly there? It is not possible for me to take the time off ... Mi vida,° please understand. ... And I knew that soon she would rise from the table. Not abruptly. She would light a cigarette and look out the kitchen window. The view was of a dismal alley that was littered with refuse thrown from windows. The space was too narrow for anyone larger than a skinny child to enter safely, so it was never cleaned. My mother would check the time on the clock over her sink, the one with a prayer for patience and

*Volar:* To fly (Spanish).
*barrio:* Spanish-speaking neighborhood.
*café con leche:* Coffee with milk.
*Querido:* Beloved, dear.
*Mi amor:* My love.
*Mi vida:* My life.

grace written in Spanish. A birthday gift. She would see that it was time to wake me. She'd sigh deeply and say the same thing the view from her kitchen window always inspired her to say: *Ay, si yo pudiera volar.°*

*Ay, si . . . volar:* Oh, if only I could fly.

## ZORA NEALE HURSTON (1891–1960)

Zora Neale Hurston was one of the central figures of the Harlem Renaissance (see Chapter 28). Born in Alabama and raised in the incorporated all-Black town of Eatonville, Florida, she eventually moved to New York City to attend Barnard College and Columbia University, where she was trained as an anthropologist, a field that would greatly influence her fiction. Hurston also published books of nonfiction based on her anthropological field studies in the American South and the Caribbean (especially Haiti), but most readers today know her as the author of *Their Eyes Were Watching God*, a 1937 novel. Although she was one of the most celebrated writers of the Harlem Renaissance through the end of the 1930s, the end of Hurston's life was marked by financial and medical difficulties. She died in relative obscurity and was buried in an unmarked grave, but novelist Alice Walker (see "The Flowers," p. 507) led a campaign to reconsider the importance of her life and legacy, and she is now widely read, studied, and appreciated. The following story, "Sweat," demonstrates two hallmarks of Hurston's writing: sensitivity to the powerless and an emphasis on beauty and hope in a world that can be cruel.

> **A Note on the Text:** Readers should note that this story contains a harmful racial slur. As discussed in "Approaching Sensitive Subjects" (p. 7), it is important to be aware of context when encountering difficult content. Hurston, the author of this story, was a Black American writing during the Harlem Renaissance, a movement that centered Black authors, voices, and stories. This story reflects Hurston's original intent in depicting a specific character, incident, time period, place, and culture.

## *Sweat*    1926

It was eleven o'clock of a Spring night in Florida. It was Sunday. Any other night, Delia Jones would have been in bed for two hours by this time. But she was a washwoman, and Monday morning meant a great deal to her. So she collected the soiled clothes on Saturday when she returned the clean things. Sunday night after church, she sorted them and put the white things to soak. It saved her almost a half day's start. A great hamper in the bedroom held the clothes that she brought home. It was so much neater than a number of bundles lying around.

She squatted in the kitchen floor beside the great pile of clothes, sorting them into small heaps according to color, and humming a song in a mournful key, but wondering through it all where Sykes, her husband, had gone with her horse and buckboard.

Just then something long, round, limp and black fell upon her shoulders and slithered to the floor beside her. A great terror took hold of her. It softened her knees and dried her mouth so that it was a full minute before she could cry out or move. Then she saw that it was the big bull whip her husband liked to carry when he drove.

She lifted her eyes to the door and saw him standing there bent over with laughter at her fright. She screamed at him.

"Sykes, what you throw dat whip on me like dat? You know it would skeer 5 me — looks just like a snake, an' you knows how skeered Ah is of snakes."

"Course Ah knowed it! That's how come Ah done it." He slapped his leg with his hand and almost rolled on the ground in his mirth. "If you such a big fool dat you got to have a fit over a earth worm or a string, Ah don't keer how bad Ah skeer you."

"You aint got no business doing it. Gawd knows it's a sin. Some day Ah'm gointuh drop dead from some of yo' foolishness. 'Nother thing, where you been wid mah rig? Ah feeds dat pony. He aint fuh you to be drivin' wid no bull whip."

"You sho is one aggravatin' nigger woman!" he declared and stepped into the room. She resumed her work and did not answer him at once. "Ah done tole you time and again to keep them white folks' clothes outa dis house."

He picked up the whip and glared down at her. Delia went on with her work. She went out into the yard and returned with a galvanized tub and set it on the washbench. She saw that Sykes had kicked all of the clothes together again, and now stood in her way truculently, his whole manner hoping, *praying*, for an argument. But she walked calmly around him and commenced to re-sort the things.

"Next time, Ah'm gointer kick 'em outdoors," he threatened as he struck a 10 match along the leg of his corduroy breeches.

Delia never looked up from her work, and her thin, stooped shoulders sagged further.

"Ah aint for no fuss t'night Sykes. Ah just come from taking sacrament at the church house."

He snorted scornfully. "Yeah, you just come from de church house on a Sunday night, but heah you is gone to work on them clothes. You ain't nothing but a hypocrite. One of them amen-corner Christians — sing, whoop, and shout; then come home and wash white folks clothes on the Sabbath."

He stepped roughly upon the whitest pile of things, kicking them helter-skelter as he crossed the room. His wife gave a little scream of dismay, and quickly gathered them together again.

"Sykes, you quit grindin' dirt into these clothes! How can Ah git through by 15 Sat'day if Ah don't start on Sunday?"

"Ah don't keer if you never git through. Anyhow, Ah done promised Gawd and a couple of other men, Ah aint gointer have it in mah house. Don't gimme no lip neither, else Ah'll throw 'em out and put mah fist up side yo' head to boot."

Delia's habitual meekness seemed to slip from her shoulders like a blown scarf. She was on her feet; her poor little body, her bare knuckly hands bravely defying the strapping hulk before her.

"Looka heah, Sykes, you done gone too fur. Ah been married to you fur fifteen years, and Ah been takin' in washin' fur fifteen years. Sweat, sweat, sweat! Work and sweat, cry and sweat, pray and sweat!"

"What's that got to do with me?" he asked brutally.

"What's it got to do with you, Sykes? Mah tub of suds is filled yo' belly with 20 vittles more times than yo' hands is filled it. Mah sweat is done paid for this house and Ah reckon Ah kin keep on sweatin' in it."

She seized the iron skillet from the stove and struck a defensive pose, which act surprised him greatly, coming from her. It cowed him and he did not strike her as he usually did.

"Naw you won't," she panted, "that ole snaggle-toothed black woman you runnin' with aint comin' heah to pile up on *mah* sweat and blood. You aint paid for nothin' on this place, and Ah'm gointer stay right heah till Ah'm toted out foot foremost."

"Well, you better quit gittin' me riled up, else they'll be totin' you out sooner than you expect. Ah'm so tired of you Ah don't know whut to do. Gawd! how Ah hates skinny wimmen!"

A little awed by this new Delia, he sidled out of the door and slammed the back gate after him. He did not say where he had gone, but she knew too well. She knew very well that he would not return until nearly daybreak also. Her work over, she went on to bed but not to sleep at once. Things had come to a pretty pass!

She lay awake, gazing upon the debris that cluttered their matrimonial trail. 25 Not an image left standing along the way. Anything like flowers had long ago been drowned in the salty stream that had been pressed from her heart. Her tears, her sweat, her blood. She had brought love to the union and he had brought a longing after the flesh. Two months after the wedding, he had given her the first brutal beating. She had the memory of his numerous trips to Orlando with all of his wages when he had returned to her penniless, even before the first year had passed. She was young and soft then, but now she thought of her knotty, muscled limbs, her harsh knuckly hands, and drew herself up into an unhappy little ball in the middle of the big feather bed. Too late now to hope for love, even if it were not Bertha it would be someone else. This case differed from the others only in that she was bolder than the others. Too late for everything except her little home. She had built it for her old days, and planted one by one the trees and flowers there. It was lovely to her, lovely.

Somehow, before sleep came, she found herself saying aloud: "Oh well, whatever goes over the Devil's back, is got to come under his belly. Sometime or ruther, Sykes, like everybody else, is gointer reap his sowing." After that she was able to build a spiritual earthworks against her husband. His shells could no longer reach her. *Amen.* She went to sleep and slept until he announced his presence in bed by kicking her feet and rudely snatching the covers away.

"Gimme some kivah heah, an' git yo' damn foots over on yo' own side! Ah oughter mash you in yo' mouf fuh drawing dat skillet on me."

Delia went clear to the rail without answering him. A triumphant indifference to all that he was or did.

The week was as full of work for Delia as all other weeks, and Saturday found her behind her little pony, collecting and delivering clothes.

It was a hot, hot day near the end of July. The village men on Joe Clarke's porch 30 even chewed cane listlessly. They did not hurl the cane-knots° as usual. They let them dribble over the edge of the porch. Even conversation had collapsed under the heat.

"Heah come Delia Jones," Jim Merchant said, as the shaggy pony came 'round the bend of the road toward them. The rusty buckboard was heaped with baskets of crisp, clean laundry.

*cane-knots:* Leftover stubs after chewing on sugar cane.

"Yep," Joe Lindsay agreed. "Hot or col', rain or shine, jes ez reg'lar ez de weeks roll roun' Delia carries 'em an' fetches 'em on Sat'day."

"She better if she wanter eat," said Moss. "Syke Jones aint wuth de shot an' powder hit would tek tuh kill 'em. Not to *huh* he aint."

"He sho' aint," Walter Thomas chimed in. "It's too bad, too, cause she wuz a right pritty lil trick when he got huh. Ah'd uh mah'ied huh mahseff if he hadnter beat me to it."

Delia nodded briefly at the men as she drove past.                                35

"Too much knockin' will ruin *any* 'oman. He done beat huh 'nough tuh kill three women, let 'lone change they looks," said Elijah Moseley. "How Syke kin stommuck dat big black greasy Mogul he's layin' roun' wid, gits me. Ah swear dat eight-rock° couldn't kiss a sardine can Ah done thowed out de back do' 'way las' yeah."

"Aw, she's fat, thass how come. He's allus been crazy 'bout fat women," put in Merchant. "He'd a' been tied up wid one long time ago if he could a' found one tuh have him. Did Ah tell yuh 'bout him come sidlin' roun' *mah* wife — bringin' her a basket uh peecans outa his yard fuh a present? Yeah, mah wife! She tol' him tuh take 'em right straight back home, cause Delia works so hard ovah dat washtub she reckon everything on de place taste lak sweat an' soapsuds. Ah jus' wisht Ah'd a' caught 'im 'roun' dere! Ah'd a' made his hips ketch on fiah down dat shell road."

"Ah know he done it, too. Ah sees 'im grinnin' at every 'oman dat passes," Walter Thomas said. "But even so, he useter eat some mighty big hunks uh humble pie tuh git dat lil' 'oman he got. She wuz ez pritty ez a speckled pup! Dat wuz fifteen yeahs ago. He useter be so skeered uh losin' huh, she could make him do some parts of a husband's duty. Dey never wuz de same in de mind."

"There oughter be a law about him," said Lindsay. "He aint fit tuh carry guts tuh a bear."

Clarke spoke for the first time. "Taint no law on earth dat kin make a man   40 be decent if it aint in 'im. There's plenty men dat takes a wife lak dey do a joint uh sugar-cane. It's round, juicy an' sweet when dey gits it. But dey squeeze an' grind, squeeze an' grind an' wring tell dey wring every drop uh pleasure dat's in 'em out. When dey's satisfied dat dey is wrung dry, dey treats 'em jes lak dey do a cane-chew. Dey thows 'em away. Dey knows whut dey is doin' while dey is at it, an' hates theirselves fuh it but they keeps on hangin' after huh tell she's empty. Den dey hates huh fuh bein' a cane-chew an' in de way."

"We oughter take Syke an' dat stray 'oman uh his'n down in Lake Howell swamp an' lay on de rawhide till they cain't say Lawd a' mussy. He allus wuz uh ovahbearin' niggah, but since dat white 'oman from up north done teached 'im how to run a automobile, he done got too biggety to live — an' we oughter kill 'im," Old Man Anderson advised.

A grunt of approval went around the porch. But the heat was melting their civic virtue and Elijah Moseley began to bait Joe Clarke.

"Come on, Joe, git a melon outa dere an' slice it up for yo' customers. We'se all sufferin' wid de heat. De bear's done got *me!*"

"Thass right, Joe, a watermelon is jes' whut Ah needs tuh cure de eppizu-dicks,"° Walter Thomas joined forces with Moseley. "Come on dere, Joe. We all is steady customers an' you aint set us up in a long time. Ah chooses dat long, bow-legged Floridy favorite."

---

*eight-rock:* Person with very dark skin.
*eppizudicks:* Form of disease or illness, related to "epidemic," but in a playful colloquial way.

"A god, an' be dough. You all gimme twenty cents and slice way," Clarke   45
retorted. "Ah needs a col' slice m'self. Heah, everybody chip in. Ah'll lend y'll mah
meat knife."

The money was quickly subscribed and the huge melon brought forth. At that
moment, Sykes and Bertha arrived. A determined silence fell on the porch and the
melon was put away again.

Merchant snapped down the blade of his jackknife and moved toward the
store door.

"Come on in, Joe, an' gimme a slab uh sow belly an' uh pound uh coffee —
almost fuhgot 'twas Sat'day. Got to git on home." Most of the men left also.

Just then Delia drove past on her way home, as Sykes was ordering magnificently for Bertha. It pleased him for Delia to see.

"Git whutsoever yo' heart desires, Honey. Wait a minute, Joe. Give huh two   50
botles uh strawberry soda-water, uh quart uh parched ground-peas, an' a block uh
chewin' gum."

With all this they left the store, with Sykes reminding Bertha that this was his
town and she could have it if she wanted it.

The men returned soon after they left, and held their watermelon feast.

"Where did Syke Jones git da 'oman from nohow?" Lindsay asked.

"Ovah Apopka. Guess dey musta been cleanin' out de town when she lef'. She
don't look lak a thing but a hunk uh liver wid hair on it."

"Well, she sho' kin squall," Dave Carter contributed. "When she gits ready tuh   55
laff, she jes' opens huh mouf an' latches it back tuh de las' notch. No ole grandpa
alligator down in Lake Bell ain't got nothin' on huh."

Bertha had been in town three months now. Sykes was still paying her room rent
at Della Lewis' — the only house in town that would have taken her in. Sykes took
her frequently to Winter Park to "stomps."° He still assured her that he was the
swellest man in the state.

"Sho' you kin have dat lil' ole house soon's Ah kin git dat 'oman outa dere.
Everything b'longs tuh me an' you sho' kin have it. Ah sho' 'bominates uh skinny
'oman. Lawdy, you sho' is got one portly shape on you! You kin git *anything* you
wants. Dis is *mah* town an' you sho' kin have it."

Delia's work-worn knees crawled over the earth in Gethsemane° and up the
rocks of Calvary many, many times during these months. She avoided the villagers
and meeting places in her efforts to be blind and deaf. But Bertha nullified this to a
degree, by coming to Delia's house to call Sykes out to her at the gate.

Delia and Sykes fought all the time now with no peaceful interludes. They
slept and ate in silence. Two or three times Delia had attempted a timid friendliness, but she was repulsed each time. It was plain that the breaches must remain
agape.

The sun had burned July to August. The heat streamed down like a million hot   60
arrows, smiting all things living upon the earth. Grass withered, leaves browned,
snakes went blind in shedding and men and dogs went mad. Dog days!

Delia came home one day and found Sykes there before her. She wondered,
but started to go on into the house without speaking, even though he was standing

---

*stomps:* Dance parties.
*Gethsemane:* The garden outside Jerusalem where Jesus was arrested the night before his
crucifixion.

in the kitchen door and she must either stoop under his arm or ask him to move. He made no room for her. She noticed a soap box beside the steps, but paid no particular attention to it, knowing that he must have brought it there. As she was stooping to pass under his outstretched arm, he suddenly pushed her backward, laughingly.

"Look in de box dere Delia, Ah done brung yuh somethin'!"

She nearly fell upon the box in her stumbling, and when she saw what it held, she all but fainted outright.

"Syke! Syke, mah Gawd! You take dat rattlesnake 'way from heah! You *gottuh*. Oh, Jesus, have mussy!"

"Ah aint gut tuh do nuthin' uh de kin' — fact is Ah aint got tuh do nothin'  65 but die. Taint no use uh you puttin' on airs makin' out lak you skeered uh dat snake — he's gointer stay right heah tell he die. He wouldn't bite me cause Ah knows how tuh handle 'im. Nohow he wouldn't risk breakin' out his fangs 'gin *yo'* skinny laigs."

"Naw, now Syke, don't keep dat thing 'roun' heah tuh skeer me tuh death. You knows Ah'm even feared uh earth worms. Thass de biggest snake Ah evah did see. Kill 'im Syke, please."

"Doan ast me tuh do nothin' fuh yuh. Goin' 'roun' tryin' tuh be so damn asterperious.° Naw, Ah aint gonna kill it. Ah think uh damn sight mo' uh him dan you! Dat's a nice snake an' anybody doan lak 'im kin jes' hit de grit."

The village soon heard that Sykes had the snake, and came to see and ask questions.

"How de hen-fire did you ketch dat six-foot rattler, Syke?" Thomas asked.

"He's full uh frogs so he caint hardly move, thass how Ah eased up on 'm. But  70 Ah'm a snake charmer an' knows how tuh handle 'em. Shux, dat aint nothin'. Ah could ketch one eve'y day if Ah so wanted tuh."

"Whut he needs is a heavy hick'ry club leaned real heavy on his head. Dat's de bes' way tuh charm a rattlesnake."

"Naw, Walt, y'll jes' don't understand dese diamon' backs lak Ah do," said Sykes in a superior tone of voice.

The village agreed with Walter, but the snake stayed on. His box remained by the kitchen door with its screen wire covering. Two or three days later it had digested its meal of frogs and literally came to life. It rattled at every movement in the kitchen or the yard. One day as Delia came down the kitchen steps she saw his chalky-white fangs curved like scimitars hung in the wire meshes. This time she did not run away with averted eyes as usual. She stood for a long time in the doorway in a red fury that grew bloodier for every second that she regarded the creature that was her torment.

That night she broached the subject as soon as Sykes sat down to the table.

"Syke, Ah wants you tuh take dat snake 'way fum heah. You done starved me  75 an' Ah put up widcher, you done beat me an Ah took dat, but you done kilt all mah insides bringin' dat varmint heah."

Sykes poured out a saucer full of coffee and drank it deliberately before he answered her.

"A whole lot Ah keer 'bout how you feels inside uh out. Dat snake aint goin' no damn wheah till Ah gits ready fuh 'im tuh go. So fur as beatin' is concerned, yuh aint took near all dat you gointer take ef yuh stay' roun' *me*."

*asterperious:* Uppity.

Delia pushed back her plate and got up from the table. "Ah hates you, Sykes," she said calmly. "Ah hates you tuh de same degree dat Ah useter love yuh. Ah done took an' took till mah belly is full up tuh mah neck. Dat's de reason Ah got mah letter fum de church an' moved mah membership tuh Woodbridge — so Ah don't haftuh take no sacrament wid yuh. Ah don't wantuh see yuh 'roun' me atall. Lay 'roun' wid dat 'oman all yuh wants tuh, but gwan 'way fum me an' mah house. Ah hates yuh lak uh suck-egg dog."

Sykes almost let the huge wad of corn bread and collard greens he was chewing fall out of his mouth in amazement. He had a hard time whipping himself up to the proper fury to try to answer Delia.

"Well, Ah'm glad you does hate me. Ah'm sho' tiahed uh you hangin' ontuh 80 me. Ah don't want yuh. Look at yuh stringey ole neck! Yo' rawbony laigs an' arms is enough tuh cut uh man tuh death. You looks jes' lak de devvul's doll-baby tuh *me*. You cain't hate me no worse dan Ah hates you. Ah been hatin' *you* fuh years."

"Yo' ole black hide don't look lak nothin' tuh me, but uh passle uh wrinkled up rubber, wid yo' big ole yeahs flappin' on each side lak uh paih uh buzzard wings. Don't think Ah'm gointuh be run 'way fum mah house neither. Ah'm goin' tuh de white folks about *you*, mah young man, de very nex' time you lay yo' han's on me. Mah cup is done run ovah." Delia said this with no signs of fear and Sykes departed from the house, threatening her, but made not the slightest move to carry out any of them.

That night he did not return at all, and the next day being Sunday, Delia was glad she did not have to quarrel before she hitched up her pony and drove the four miles to Woodbridge.

She stayed to the night service — "love feast" — which was very warm and full of spirit. In the emotional winds her domestic trials were borne far and wide so that she sang as she drove homeward,

> "Jurden° water, black an' col'
> Chills de body, not de soul
> An' Ah wantah cross Jurden in uh calm time."

She came from the barn to the kitchen door and stopped.

"Whut's de mattah, ol' satan, you aint kickin' up yo' racket?" She addressed the 85 snake's box. Complete silence. She went on into the house with a new hope in its birth struggles. Perhaps her threat to go to the white folks had frightened Sykes! Perhaps he was sorry! Fifteen years of misery and suppression had brought Delia to the place where she would hope *anything* that looked towards a way over or through her wall of inhibitions.

She felt in the match safe behind the stove at once for a match. There was only one there.

"Dat niggah wouldn't fetch nothin' heah tuh save his rotten neck, but he kin run thew whut Ah brings quick enough. Now he done toted off nigh on tuh haff uh box uh matches. He done had dat 'oman heah in mah house, too."

Nobody but a woman could tell how she knew this even before she struck the match. But she did and it put her into a new fury.

Presently she brought in the tubs to put the white things to soak. This time she decided she need not bring the hamper out of the bedroom; she would go in there and do the sorting. She picked up the pot-bellied lamp and went in. The room was

*Jurden:* The biblical River Jordan, site of Jesus' baptism.

small and the hamper stood hard by the foot of the white iron bed. She could sit and reach through the bedposts — resting as she worked.

"Ah wantah cross Jurden in uh calm time." She was singing again. The mood of the "love feast" had returned. She threw back the lid of the basket almost gaily. Then, moved by both horror and terror, she sprang back toward the door. *There lay the snake in the basket!* He moved sluggishly at first, but even as she turned round and round, jumped up and down in an insanity of fear, he began to stir vigorously. She saw him pouring his awful beauty from the basket upon the bed, then she seized the lamp and ran as fast as she could to the kitchen. The wind from the open door blew out the light and the darkness added to her terror. She sped to the darkness of the yard, slamming the door after her before she thought to set down the lamp. She did not feel safe even on the ground, so she climbed up in the hay barn.

There for an hour or more she lay sprawled upon the hay a gibbering wreck.

Finally she grew quiet, and after that, coherent thought. With this, stalked through her a cold, bloody rage. Hours of this. A period of introspection, a space of retrospection, then a mixture of both. Out of this an awful calm.

"Well, Ah done de bes' Ah could. If things aint right, Gawd knows taint mah fault."

She went to sleep — a twitch sleep — and woke up to a faint gray sky. There was a loud hollow sound below. She peered out. Sykes was at the wood-pile, demolishing a wire-covered box.

He hurried to the kitchen door, but hung outside there some minutes before he entered, and stood some minutes more inside before he closed it after him.

The gray in the sky was spreading. Delia descended without fear now, and crouched beneath the low bedroom window. The drawn shade shut out the dawn, shut in the night. But the thin walls held back no sound.

"Dat ol' scratch° is woke up now!" She mused at the tremendous whirr inside, which every woodsman knows, is one of the sound illusions. The rattler is a ventriloquist. His whirr sounds to the right, to the left, straight ahead, behind, close under foot — everywhere but where it is. Woe to him who guesses wrong unless he is prepared to hold up his end of the argument! Sometimes he strikes without rattling at all.

Inside, Sykes heard nothing until he knocked a pot lid off the stove while trying to reach the match safe in the dark. He had emptied his pockets at Bertha's.

The snake seemed to wake up under the stove and Sykes made a quick leap into the bedroom. In spite of the gin he had had, his head was clearing now.

"Mah Gawd!" he chattered, "ef Ah could on'y strack uh light!"

The rattling ceased for a moment as he stood paralyzed. He waited. It seemed that the snake waited also.

"Oh, fuh de light! Ah thought he'd be too sick" — Sykes was muttering to himself when the whirr began again, closer, right underfoot this time. Long before this, Sykes' ability to think had been flattened down to primitive instinct and he leaped — onto the bed.

Outside Delia heard a cry that might have come from a maddened chimpanzee, a stricken gorilla. All the terror, all the horror, all the rage that man possibly could express, without a recognizable human sound.

A tremendous stir inside there, another series of animal screams, the intermittent whirr of the reptile. The shade torn violently down from the window, letting

*scratch:* Another name for the devil.

in the red dawn, a huge brown hand seizing the window stick, great dull blows upon the wooden floor punctuating the gibberish of sound long after the rattle of the snake had abruptly subsided. All this Delia could see and hear from her place beneath the window, and it made her ill. She crept over to the four-o'clocks and stretched herself on the cool earth to recover.

She lay there. "Delia, Delia!" She could hear Sykes calling in a most despairing 105 tone as one who expected no answer. The sun crept on up, and he called. Delia could not move — her legs were gone flabby. She never moved, he called, and the sun kept rising.

"Mah Gawd!" She heard him moan, "Mah Gawd fum Heben!" She heard him stumbling about and got up from her flower-bed. The sun was growing warm. As she approached the door she heard him call out hopefully, "Delia, is dat you Ah heah?"

She saw him on his hands and knees as soon as she reached the door. He crept an inch or two toward her — all that he was able, and she saw his horribly swollen neck and his one open eye shining with hope. A surge of pity too strong to support bore her away from that eye that must, could not, fail to see the tubs. He would see the lamp. Orlando with its doctors was too far. She could scarcely reach the Chinaberry tree, where she waited in the growing heat while inside she knew the cold river was creeping up and up to extinguish that eye which must know by now that she knew.

## JAMES JOYCE (1882–1941)

Born in Dublin, Ireland at a precarious time in that country's history, James Joyce is considered one of the most enduring and influential fiction writers of the twentieth century. Raised in a large, working-class Catholic family, Joyce received his higher education at University College, Dublin before leaving for Paris for a short-lived dream to study medicine. The rest of his life was spent in self-imposed exile in multiple countries on the European continent, and exile is a recurrent theme in his work, especially in his short story collection *Dubliners* (1914), where the following story appeared. His later work, notably his masterpiece *Ulysses* (1922), experimented exuberantly with language, style, and layers of meaning. Although the same cannot be said for "Eveline," you will still find that it is a carefully wrought story, intense and precise in its emotional effect.

## *Eveline*   1914

She sat at the window watching the evening invade the avenue. Her head was leaned against the window curtains and in her nostrils was the odor of dusty cretonne. She was tired.

Few people passed. The man out of the last house passed on his way home; she heard his footsteps clacking along the concrete pavement and afterwards crunching on the cinder path before the new red houses. One time there used to be a field there in which they used to play every evening with other people's children. Then a man from Belfast bought the field and built houses in it — not like their little brown houses but bright brick houses with shining roofs. The children of the avenue used to play together in that field — the Devines, the Waters, the Dunns, little Keogh the cripple, she and her brothers and sisters. Ernest, however, never played: he was too grown up. Her father used often to hunt them in out of the field with his blackthorn stick; but usually little Keogh used to keep *nix* and call out when he saw her father coming. Still they seemed to have been rather happy then. Her father was not so bad then; and besides, her mother was alive. That was a long time ago; she and her brothers and sisters were all grown up; her mother was dead. Tizzie Dunn was dead, too, and the Waters had gone back to England. Everything changes. Now she was going to go away like the others, to leave her home.

Home! She looked round the room, reviewing all its familiar objects which she had dusted once a week for so many years, wondering where on earth all the dust came from. Perhaps she would never see again those familiar objects from which she had never dreamed of being divided. And yet during all those years she had never found out the name of the priest whose yellowing photograph hung on the wall above the broken harmonium beside the colored print of the promises made to Blessed Margaret Mary Alacoque. He had been a school friend of her father. Whenever he showed the photograph to a visitor her father used to pass it with a casual word:

— He is in Melbourne now.

She had consented to go away, to leave her home. Was that wise? She tried to   5
weigh each side of the question. In her home anyway she had shelter and food; she had those whom she had known all her life about her. Of course she had to work hard both in the house and at business. What would they say of her in the Stores when they found out that she had run away with a fellow? Say she was a fool, perhaps; and her place would be filled up by advertisement. Miss Gavan would be glad. She had always had an edge on her, especially whenever there were people listening.

— Miss Hill, don't you see these ladies are waiting?

— Look lively, Miss Hill, please.

She would not cry many tears at leaving the Stores.

But in her new home, in a distant unknown country, it would not be like that. Then she would be married — she, Eveline. People would treat her with respect then. She would not be treated as her mother had been. Even now, though she was over nineteen, she sometimes felt herself in danger of her father's violence. She knew it was that that had given her the palpitations. When they were growing up he had never gone for her, like he used to go for Harry and Ernest, because she was a girl; but latterly he had begun to threaten her and say what he would do to her only for her dead mother's sake. And now she had nobody to protect her. Ernest was dead and Harry, who was in the church decorating business, was nearly always down somewhere in the country. Besides, the invariable squabble for money on Saturday nights had begun to weary her unspeakably. She always gave her entire wages — seven shillings — and Harry always sent up what he could but the trouble was to get any money from her father. He said she used to squander the money, that she had no head, that he wasn't going to give her his hard-earned money to throw about the streets, and much more, for he was usually fairly bad of a Saturday night. In the end he would give her the money and ask her had she any intention of buying Sunday's dinner. Then she had to rush out as quickly as she could and do her marketing, holding her black leather purse tightly in her hand as she elbowed her way through the crowds and returning home late under her load of provisions. She had hard work to keep the house together and to see that the two young children who had been left to her charge went to school regularly and got their meals regularly. It was hard work — a hard life — but now that she was about to leave it she did not find it a wholly undesirable life.

She was about to explore another life with Frank. Frank was very kind, manly, 10 open-hearted. She was to go away with him by the night-boat to be his wife and to live with him in Buenos Aires where he had a home waiting for her. How well she remembered the first time she had seen him; he was lodging in a house on the main road where she used to visit. It seemed a few weeks ago. He was standing at the gate, his peaked cap pushed back on his head and his hair tumbled forward over a face of bronze. Then they had come to know each other. He used to meet her outside the Stores every evening and see her home. He took her to see *The Bohemian Girl* and she felt elated as she sat in an unaccustomed part of the theater with him. He was awfully fond of music and sang a little. People knew that they were courting and, when he sang about the lass that loves a sailor, she always felt pleasantly confused. He used to call her Poppens out of fun. First of all it had been an excitement for her to have a fellow and then she had begun to like him. He had tales of distant countries. He had started as a deck boy at a pound a month on a ship of the Allan Line going out to Canada. He told her the names of the ships he had been on and the names of the different services. He had sailed through the Straits of Magellan and he told her stories of the terrible Patagonians. He had fallen on his feet in Buenos Aires, he said, and had come over to the old country just for a holiday. Of course, her father had found out the affair and had forbidden her to have anything to say to him.

— I know these sailor chaps, he said.

One day he had quarreled with Frank and after that she had to meet her lover secretly.

The evening deepened in the avenue. The white of two letters in her lap grew indistinct. One was to Harry; the other was to her father. Ernest had been her favorite but she liked Harry too. Her father was becoming old lately, she noticed; he would miss her. Sometimes he could be very nice. Not long before, when she had been laid up for a day, he had read her out a ghost story and made toast for her at the fire. Another day, when their mother was alive, they had all gone for a picnic to the Hill of Howth. She remembered her father putting on her mother's bonnet to make the children laugh.

Her time was running out but she continued to sit by the window, leaning her head against the window curtain, inhaling the odor of dusty cretonne. Down far in the avenue she could hear a street organ playing. She knew the air. Strange that it should come that very night to remind her of the promise to her mother, her promise to keep the home together as long as she could. She remembered the last night of her mother's illness; she was again in the close dark room at the other side of the hall and outside she heard a melancholy air of Italy. The organ-player had been ordered to go away and given sixpence. She remembered her father strutting back into the sickroom saying:

— Damned Italians! coming over here!   15

As she mused the pitiful vision of her mother's life laid its spell on the very quick of her being — that life of commonplace sacrifices closing in final craziness. She trembled as she heard again her mother's voice saying constantly with foolish insistence:

— Derevaun Seraun! Derevaun Seraun!°

She stood up in a sudden impulse of terror. Escape! She must escape! Frank would save her. He would give her life, perhaps love, too. But she wanted to live. Why should she be unhappy? She had a right to happiness. Frank would take her in his arms, fold her in his arms. He would save her.

She stood among the swaying crowd in the station at the North Wall. He held her hand and she knew that he was speaking to her, saying something about the passage over and over again. The station was full of soldiers with brown baggages. Through the wide doors of the sheds she caught a glimpse of the black mass of the boat, lying in beside the quay wall, with illumined portholes. She answered nothing. She felt her cheek pale and cold and, out of a maze of distress, she prayed to God to direct her, to show her what was her duty. The boat blew a long mournful whistle into the mist. If she went, tomorrow she would be on the sea with Frank, steaming toward Buenos Aires. Their passage had been booked. Could she still draw back after all he had done for her? Her distress awoke a nausea in her body and she kept moving her lips in silent fervent prayer.

A bell clanged upon her heart. She felt him seize her hand:                    20

— Come!

All the seas of the world tumbled about her heart. He was drawing her into them: he would drown her. She gripped with both hands at the iron railing.

— Come!

No! No! No! It was impossible. Her hands clutched the iron in frenzy. Amid the seas she sent a cry of anguish!

— Eveline! Evvy!                                                            25

He rushed beyond the barrier and called to her to follow. He was shouted at to go on but he still called to her. She set her white face to him, passive, like a helpless animal. Her eyes gave him no sign of love or farewell or recognition.

*Derevaun Seraun!:* "The end of pleasure is pain!" (Gaelic).

# JENNIFER NANSUBUGA MAKUMBI (B. 1960s)

Born in Uganda in eastern Africa, Jennifer Makumbi grew up during the reign of Idi Amin, a dictator responsible for brutal military rule and the genocide of an untold number of Ugandans. She immigrated to England in 2001 where she earned advanced graduate degrees in creative writing. She currently teaches at Lancaster University; in 2021 her novel *The First Woman* won the Jhalak Prize, an award given to the best book of the year in England written by a writer of color.

## Let's Tell This Story Properly    2014

If you go inside Nnam's house right now the smell of paint will choke you but she enjoys it. She enjoys it the way her mother loved the smell of the outside toilet, a pit latrine, when she was pregnant. Her mother would sit a little distance away from the toilet doing her chores, or eating, and disgusting everyone until the baby was born. But Nnam is not pregnant. She enjoys the smell of paint because her husband Kayita died a year ago, but his scent lingered, his image stayed on objects and his voice was absorbed in the bedroom walls: every time Nnam lay down to sleep, the walls played back his voice like a record. This past week, the paint has drowned Kayita's odour and the bedroom walls have been quiet. Today, Nnam plans to wipe his image off the objects.

A week ago Nnam took a month off work and sent her sons, Lumumba and Sankara, to her parents in Uganda for Kayita's last funeral rites. That is why she is naked. Being naked, alone with silence in the house, is therapy. Now Nnam understands why when people lose their minds the first impulse is to strip naked. Clothes are constricting but you don't realize until you have walked naked in your house all day, every day for a week.

Kayita died in the bathroom with his pants down. He was forty-five years old and should have pulled up his pants before he collapsed. The more shame because it was Easter. Who dies naked on Easter?

That morning, he got up and swung his legs out of bed. He stood up but then sat down as if he had been pulled back. Then he put his hand on his chest and listened.

Nnam, lying next to the wall, propped her head on her elbow and said,   5
"What?"

"I guess I've not woken up yet," he yawned.

"Then come back to bed."

But Kayita stood up and wrapped a towel around his waist. At the door he turned to Nnam and said, "Go back to sleep: I'll give the children their breakfast."

Lumumba woke her up. He needed the bathroom but "Dad won't come out." Nnam got out of bed cursing the builders who put the bathroom and the toilet in the same room. She knocked and opened the bathroom door saying, "It's only me."

Kayita lay on the floor with his head near the heater, his stomach on the bath-   10
room mat, one end of the towel inside the toilet bowl, the other on the floor, him totally naked save for the briefs around the ankles.

Nnam did not scream. Perhaps she feared that Lumumba would come in and see his father naked. Perhaps it was because Kayita's eyes were closed like he had only fainted. She closed the door and calling his name, pulled his briefs up. She took the towel out of the toilet bowl and threw it in the bath tub. Then she shouted, "Get me the phone, Lum."

She held the door closed when Lumumba gave it to her.

"Get me your father's gown too," she said, dialling.

She closed the door and covered Kayita with his grey gown.

On the phone, the nurse told her what to do while she waited for the ambu-   15
lance to arrive.

"Put him in recovery position . . . keep him warm . . . you need to talk to him . . . make sure he can hear you . . ."

When the paramedics arrived, Nnam explained that the only thing she had noticed was Kayita falling back in bed that morning. Tears gathered a bit when she explained to the boys, "Daddy is unwell but he'll be fine." She got dressed and rang a friend to come and pick up the boys. When the paramedics emerged from the bathroom, they had put an oxygen mask on Kayita which reassured her. Because the friend had not arrived to take the boys, Nnam did not go with the ambulance. The paramedics would ring to let her know which hospital had admitted Kayita.

When she arrived in Casualty, a receptionist told her to sit and wait. Then a young nurse came and asked, "Did you come with someone?"

Nnam shook her head and the nurse disappeared. After a few moments, the same nurse returned and asked, "Are you driving?"

She was and the nurse went away again.                                            20

"Mrs Kayita?"

Nnam looked up.

"Come with me." It was an African nurse. "The doctor working on your husband is ready."

She led Nnam to a consultation room and told her to sit down.

"The doctor will be with you shortly," and closed the door behind her.           25

Presently, a youngish doctor wearing blue scrubs came in and introduced himself.

"Mrs Kayita, I am sorry we could not save your husband; he was dead on arrival." His voice was velvety. "There was nothing we could do. I am sorry for your loss." His hands crossed each other and settled on the chest. Then one hand pinched his lips. "Is there anything we can do?"

In Britain grief is private — you know how women throw themselves about howling this, screaming that back home? None of that. You can't force your grief on other people. When Nnam was overcome she ran to the toilet and held onto the sink. As she washed her face to walk out, she realised that she did not have her handbag. She went back to the consultation room. The African nurse was holding it.

Her name was Lesego. Was there something she could do? Nnam shook her head. "Is there someone you need me to call? You cannot drive in this state." Before Nnam said no Lesego said, "Give me your phone."

Nnam passed it to her.                                                           30

She scrolled down the contacts calling out the names. When Nnam nodded at a name, Lesego rang the number and said, "I am calling from Manchester Royal infirmary . . . I am sorry to inform you that . . . Mrs Kayita is still here . . . yes of course . . . I'll stay with her until you arrive."

Leaving the hospital was the hardest. You know when you get those two *namasasana* bananas joined together by the skin and you rip them apart and eat one? That is how Nnam felt.

Nnam starts cleaning in the bathroom. The floor has been replaced by blue mini mosaic vinyl. Rather than the wash basket, she puts the toilet mats in the bin. She goes to the cupboard to get clean ones. Instead she picks up all the toilet mats there are and stuffs them in the bin too: Kayita's stomach died on one of them. Then she bleaches the bathtub, the sink and the toilet bowl. She unhooks the shower curtain and stuffs it into the bin too. When she opens the cabinet, she finds Kayita's anti-beard-bumps powder, a shaver and cologne. They go into the bin. Mould has collected on the shelves inside the cabinet. She unhooks the cabinet off the wall and takes it to the front door. She will throw it outside later. When she returns, the bathroom is more spacious and breezy. She ties the bin-liner up and takes that to the front door as well.

Kayita had had two children before he met Nnam. He had left them in Uganda with their mother but his relationship with their mother had ended long before he met Nnam. On several occasions Nnam asked him to bring the children to Britain but he said, "*Kdt,* you don't know their mother; the children are her cash cow."

Still Nnam was uneasy about his children being deprived of their father. She  35 insisted that he rang them every weekend: she even bought the phone cards. When he visited, she sent them clothes.

Kayita had adapted well to the changing environment of a Western marriage unlike other Ugandan men, married to women who emigrated before they did. Many such marriages strained when a groom, fresh from home, was "culture-shocked" and began to feel emasculated by a Britain-savvy wife. Kayita had no qualms about assuming a domestic role when he was not working. They could only afford a small wedding, they could only afford two children. At the end of the month they pooled their salaries together: Kayita worked for G4S° so his money was considerably smaller but he tried to offset this by doing a lot of overtime. After paying the bills and other households, they deducted monies to send home to his children and sometimes for issues in either family — someone has died, someone is sick, someone is getting married.

Nnam had bought a nine-acre tract of land in rural Kalule before she met Kayita. After decades in Manchester, she dreamt of retiring in rural Uganda. But when Kayita came along, he suggested that they buy land in Kampala and build a city house first.

"Why build a house we are not going to live in for the next two decades in rural Kalule where no one will rent it? The rent from the city house will be saved to build the house in Kalule."

It made sense.

They bought a piece of land at Nsangi. But Nnam's father, who purchased it for  40 them, knew that most of the money came from his daughter. He put the title deed in her name. When Kayita protested that he was being sidelined, Nnam told her father to put everything in Kayita's name.

Because they could not afford the fare for the whole family to visit, Kayita was the one who few to Uganda regularly to check on the house. However it was largely built by Nnam's father, the only person she could trust with their money and who was an engineer. When the house was finished, Kayita found the tenants to rent it. That was in 1990, six years before his death. They had had the same tenants all that time. Nnam had been to see the house and had met the tenants.

Nnam is cleaning the bedroom now. The windowsill is stained. Kayita used to put his wallet, car keys, spectacles and G4S-pass on the windowsill at night. Once he put a form near the window while it was open. It rained and the paper got soaked. The ink melted and the colour spread on the windowsill discolouring it. Nnam sprays *Muscle* cleaner on the stains but the ink will not budge. She goes for the bleach.

*G4S:* A security company headquartered in London.

She clears out the old handbags and shoes from the wardrobe's floor. She had sent Kayita's clothes to a charity shop soon after the burial, but she finds a belt and a pair of his underwear behind the bags. Perhaps they are the reason his scent has persisted. After cleaning, she drops a scented tablet on the wardrobe floor

Ugandans rallied around her during that first week of Kayita's death. The men took over the mortuary issues, the women took care of the home, while Nnam floated between weeping and sleeping. They arranged the funeral service in Manchester and masterminded the fundraising drive saying, "We are not burying one of us in snow."

Throughout that week, women who worked shifts slept at Nnam's house look-  45
ing after the children then going to work. People brought food and money in the evening and prayed and sang. Two of her friends took leave and bought tickets to fly back to Uganda with her.

It was when she was buying the tickets that she wondered where the funeral would be held in Uganda as their house had tenants. She rang and asked her father. He said that Kayita's family was not forthcoming about the arrangements.

"Not forthcoming?"

"Evasive."

"But why?"

"They are peasants, Nnameya; you knew that when you married him."  50

Nnam kept quiet. Her father was like that. He never liked Kayita. Kayita had neither the degrees nor the right background.

"Bring Kayita home; we'll see when you get here," he said finally.

As soon as she saw Kayita's family at Entebbe Airport, Nnam knew that something was wrong. They were not the brothers she had met before and they were unfriendly. When she asked her family where Kayita's real family was they said, "That's the *real* family."

Nnam scratched her chin for a long time. There were echoes in her ears.

When the coffin was released from customs, Kayita's family took it, loaded it  55
on a van they had brought and drove off.

Nnam was mouth-open shocked.

"Do they think I killed him? I have the post-mortem documents."

"Post-mortem, who cares?"

"Perhaps he was ashamed of his family." Nnam was beginning to blame her father's snobbery. "Perhaps they think we're snobs."

She got into one of her family's cars to drive after Kayita's brothers.  60

"No, not snobbery," Meya, Nnam's oldest brother said quietly. Then he turned to Nnam who sat in the back seat and said, "I think you need to be strong Nnameya."

Instead of asking *what do you mean,* Nnam twisted her mouth and clenched her teeth as if anticipating a blow.

"Kayita is . . . *was* married. He has the two older children he told you about, but in the few times he returned, he has had two other children with his wife."

Nnam did not react. Something stringy was stuck between her lower front teeth. Her tongue, irritated, kept poking at it. Now she picked at it with her thumbnail.

"We only found out when he died but father said we wait to tell you until you  65
are home with family."

In the car were three of her brothers, all older than her. Her sisters were in another car behind. Her father and the boys were in another; uncles and aunts were yet in another. Nnam was silent.

"We need to stop them and ask how far we are going in case we need to fill the tank," another brother pointed at the van with the coffin.

Still Nnam remained silent. She was a *kiwuduwudu*, a dismembered torso — no feelings.

They came to Ndeeba roundabout and the coffin van veered into Masaka Road. In Ndeeba town, near the timber shacks, they overtook the van and flagged it down. Nnam's brothers jumped out of the car and went to Kayita's family. Nnam still picked at the irritating something in her teeth. Ndeeba was recognisable by its mouldy smell of half-dry timber and sawdust.

Heavy planks fell on each other and rumbled. Planks being cut sounded like 70 a lawnmower. She looked across the road at the petrol station with a carwash and smiled, *You need to be strong Nnameya* as if she had an alternative.

"How far we are going?" Meya asked Kayita's brothers. "We might need to fill the tank."

"Only to Nsangi," one of them replied.

"Don't try to lose us: we shall call the police."

The van drove off rudely. The three brothers went back to the car.

"They are taking him to Nsangi, Nnam; I thought your house in Nsangi is 75 rented out?"

Like a dog pricking up its ears, Nnam sat up. Her eyes moved from one brother to another to another, as if the answer was written on their faces.

"Get me father on the phone," she said.

Meya set the phone on speaker. When their father's voice came Nnam asked, "Father, do you have the title deeds for the house in Nsangi?"

"They are in the safe deposit." 80

"Are they in his name?"

"Am I stupid?"

Nnam closed her eyes. "Thanks Father thanks Father thanks thank you."

He did not reply.

"When was rent last paid?" 85

"Three weeks ago. Where are you?"

"Don't touch it, father," she said. "We're in Ndeeba. We're not spending any more money on this funeral. His family will bury him: I don't care whether they stuff him into a hole. They are taking him to Nsangi."

"Nsangi? It does not make sense."

"Neither to us."

When Nnam switched off the phone she said to her brothers, "The house is 90 safe," as if they had not heard. "Now they can hold the vigil in a cave if they please."

The brothers did not respond.

"When we get there," there was life in Nnam's voice now, "you shall find out what is going on; I'll be in the car. Then you shall take me back to town: I need to go to a good salon and pamper myself. Then I'll get a good busuuti and dress up. I am not a widow anymore."

"There is no need . . ." Meya began.

"I said I am going to a salon to do my hair, my nails and my face. But first I'll have a bath and a good meal. We'll see about the vigil later."

Then she laughed as if she was demented. 95

"I've just remembered," she coughed and hit her chest to ease it. "When we were young," she swallowed hard, "remember how people used to say that we Ganda women are property-minded? Apparently, when a husband dies unexpectedly, the first thing you do is to look for the titles of ownership, contracts, car logbook and keys and all such things. You wrap them tight in a cloth and wear them as a sanitary towel. When they are safe between your legs, you let off a rending cry, *Bazze wange!*"°

Her brothers laughed nervously.

"As soon as I realised that my house was threatened —*pshooo!*" She made a gesture of wind whizzing over her head. "Grief, pain, shock — gone."

As the red brick double-storeyed house in Nsangi came into view, Nnam noted with trepidation that the hedge and compound were taken good care of. When the coffin van drove in Kayita's people, excitable, surrounded it. The women cried their part with clout. Kayita's wife's wail stood out: a lament for a husband who had died alone in the cold. The crying was like a soundtrack to Kayita's coffin being offloaded and carried into the house. But then the noise receded. Nnam had just confirmed that Kayita's wife had been the tenant all along. She had met her. Kayita had been paying his wife's rent with Nnam's money. Nnam held her mouth in disbelief.

"Kayita was not a thief; he was a murderer." She twisted her mouth again.        100

Even then, the heart is a coward — Nnam's confidence crumbled as her brothers stepped out of the car. Travelling was over. The reality of her situation stared straight in her face. Her sisters too arrived. They came and sat in the car with her. Her father, the boys, her uncles and aunts parked outside the compound. They were advised not to get out of their cars. The situation stared in Nnam's face without blinking.

People walked in and out of the her house while she was frightened of stepping out of the car. She did not even see an old man come over. He had bent low and was peering inside the car when she noticed him. He introduced himself as Kayita's father. He addressed Nnam, "I understand you are the woman who has been living with my son in London."

"Manchester," one of Nnam's sisters corrected rudely.

"Manchester, London, New York, they are like flies to me: I can't tell male from female." The old man turned back to Nnam. "You realise Kayita had a wife." Before Nnam answered he carried on, "Can you allow her to have this last moment with her husband with dignity. We do not expect you to advertise your presence. The boys however, we accept. We'll need to show them to the clan when you're ready."

The sisters were speechless. Nnam watched the man walk back to her house.        105

The two friends from Manchester arrived and came to the car where Nnam sat. At that point, Nnam decided to confront her humiliation. She looked in to the eyes of her friends and explained the details of Kayita's deception the way a doctor explains the extent of infection to a patient. There was dignity in her explaining it to them herself.

There is nothing much to clean in the kitchen but she pulls out all the movable appliances to clean out the accumulated grime and rubbish. Under the sink, hidden behind the shopping bags, is Kayita's mug. Nnam bought it on their fifth wedding anniversary — WORLD'S BEST HUSBAND. She takes it to the front door

*Bazze wange:* Translated from Luganda, "They have come to me."

and puts it into a bin. On top of the upper cabinets are empty tins of Quality Street° that Kayita treated himself to at Christmas. Kayita had a sweet tooth: he loved muffins, ice-cream, ginger nuts and éclairs. He hoarded the tins saying that one day they would need them. Nnam smiles as she takes the tins to the front door — Kayita's tendency to hoard things now makes sense.

Nnam, her friends and family returned to the funeral at around 11 p.m. Where she sat, she was able to observe Kayita's wife. The woman looked old enough to be her mother. That observation, rather than give her satisfaction, stung. Neither the pampering nor the expensive busuuti and expensive jewellery and British airs could keep away the pain that Kayita had remained loyal to such a woman. It dented her well choreographed air of indifference. Every time she looked at his wife, it was not jealousy that wrung her heart: it was the whisper *of you were not good enough*.

Just then, her aunt, the one who prepared her for marriage, came to whisper tradition. She leaned close and said,

"When a husband dies you must wear a sanitary towel immediately. As he is wrapped for burial, it is placed on his genitals so that he does not return for . . ." 110

"Fuck that shit!"

"I was only . . ."

"Fuck it," Nnam did not bother with Luganda.

The aunt melted away.

As more of Nnam's relations arrived so did a gang of middle-aged women. Nnam did not know who invited them. One thing was clear, though: they were angry. Apparently, Nnam's story was common. They had heard about her plight and had come to her aid. The women looked like former *nkuba kyeyo* — the broom swinging economic immigrants to the West. They were dressed expensively. They mixed Luganda and English as if the languages were sisters. They wore weaves or wigs. Their makeup was defiant as if someone had dared to tell them off. Some were bleached. They unloaded crates of beer and cartons of Uganda Waragi°. They brought them to the tent where Nnam sat with her family and started sharing out. One of them came to her and asked, "You are the Nnameya from Manchester?" She had a raspy voice like she loved her Waragi. 115

Nnam nodded and the woman leaned closer.

"If you want to do crying widow thing, go ahead, but leave the rest to us."

"Do I look like I am crying?"

The woman laughed triumphantly. It was as if she had been given permission to do whatever she wanted to do. Nnam decided that the gang were business women, perhaps single mothers, wealthy and bored.

Just then a cousin of Nnam arrived. It was clear she carried burning news. She sat next to Nnam and whispered, "Yours are the only sons." She rubbed her hands as though Nnam had just won the lottery. She turned her head and pointed with her mouth towards Kayita's widow. "Hers are daughters only." 120

*Quality Street*: A brand of chocolates in England manufactured by Cadbury.
*Waragi*: A distilled spirit

Nnam smiled. She turned and whispered to her family, "Lumumba is the heir. Our friend has no sons," and a current of joy rippled through the tent as her family passed on the news.

At first the gang of women mourned quietly, drinking their beer and enquiring about Britain as if they had come to the vigil out of goodness towards Kayita. At around two o'clock, when the choir got tired, one of the women stood up.

"Fellow mourners," she started in a gentle voice as if she was bringing the good tidings of resurrection.

A reverent hush fell over the mourners.

"Let's tell this story properly." She paused. "There is another woman in this story." 125

Stunned silence.

"There are also two innocent children in the story."

"*Amiina mwattu.*°" The amens from the gang could have been coming from evangelists.

"But I'll start with the woman's story."

According to her, the story started when Nnam's parents sent her to Britain 130 to study and better herself. She had worked hard and studied and saved but along came a liar and a thief.

"She was lied to," the woman with a raspy voice interrupted impatiently. She stood up as if the storyteller was ineffectual. "He married her — we have the pictures, we have the video. He even lied to her parents — look at that shame!"

"Come on," the interrupted woman protested gently. "I was unwrapping the story properly: you are tearing into it."

"Sit down: we don't have all night," the raspy woman said.

The gentle woman sat down. The other mourners were still dumbfounded by the women's audacity.

"A clever person asks," the raspy woman carried on. "Where did Kayita get the 135 money to build such a house when he is just broom swinging in Britain? Then you realise that ooooh, he's married a rich woman, *a proper lawyer in Manchester.*"

"How does she know all that?" Nnam whispered to her cousin.

"Hmmm, words have legs."

"He told her that he was not married but this wife here knew what was going on," the woman was saying. "Does anyone here know the shock this woman is going through? No, why, because she is one of those women who emigrated? For those who do not know, this is her house built with her money. I am finished."

There was clapping as she sat down and grabbed her beer. The mourning ambiance of the funeral had now turned to the excitement of a political rally.

"Death came like a thief," a woman with a squeaky voice stood up. "It did not 140 knock to alert Kayita. The curtain blew away and what filth!"

"If this woman had not fought hard to bring Kayita home, the British would have burnt him. They don't joke. They have no space to waste on unclaimed bodies. But has anyone had the grace to thank her? No. Instead, Kayita's father tells her to shut up. What a peasant!"

The gang had started throwing words about haphazardly. It could turn into throwing insults. An elder came to calm them down.

"You have made your point, mothers of the nation, and I add it is a valid point because let's face it, he lied to her and as you say, there are two innocent children involved."

*Amiina mwattu:* Amen.

"But first let us see the British wife," a woman interrupted him. "Her name is Nnameya. Let the world see the woman this peasant family has used like arse wipes."

Nnam did not want to stand up but she did not want to seem ungrateful to the women's effort. She stood up head held high. 145

"Come." A drunk woman grabbed her hand and led her through the mourners into the living room. "Look at her," she said to Kayita's family.

The mourners, even those who had been at the back of the house, had come to stare at Nnam. She looked away from the coffin because tears were letting down her *hold your head high* stance.

"Stealing from me I can live with, but what about my children?"

At that moment the gang's confrontational attitude fell away and they shook their heads and wiped their eye and sucked their teeth,

"The children indeed . . . *Abaana maama . . yiyi* but men also . . . this lack of choice to whom you're born to . . . who said men are human . . ." 150

The vigil had turned in favour of Nnam.

It was then that Nnam's eyes betrayed her. She glanced at the open coffin. There is no sight more revolting than a corpse caught telling lies.

Nnam is in the lounge. She has finished cleaning. She has taken all the photographs that had been on the walls — wedding, birthdays, school portraits, Christmases — and all the pictures taken before Kayita's death, whether he is in the picture or not, are separated from the others. She throws them in the bin-bag and ties it. She takes the others to the bedroom. She gets her nightgown and covers her nakedness. Then she takes the bin with the pictures to the front door. She opens the door and the freshness of the air outside hits her. She ferries all the bin-bags, one by one, and places them below the chute's mouth. She throws down the smaller bin-bags first. They drop as if in a new long drop latrine — the echo is delayed. She breaks the cabinet and drops the bits down. Finally, she stuffs the largest bin-bag, the one with the pictures, down the chute's throat. The chute chokes. Nnam goes back to the house and brings back a mop. In her mind her father's recent words are still ringing:

"We can't throw them out of the house just like that. There are four innocent children in that house and Lumumba, being Kayita's eldest son, has inherited all of them. Let's not heap that guilt on his shoulders."

She uses the handle to dig at the bag. After a while of breaking glass and the bin-bag falls through. When she comes back to the house, the smell of paint is overwhelming. She takes the mop to the kitchen and washes her hands. Then she opens all the windows and the wind blows the curtains wildly. She takes off the gown and the cool wind blows on her bare skin. She closes her eyes and raises her arms. The sensation of wind on her skin, of being naked, of the silence in a clean house is so overwhelming, but she does not cry. 155

# JOYCE CAROL OATES (B. 1938)

The sheer volume of Joyce Carol Oates's writing is almost hard to fathom. Since the publication of her first story collection in 1963, she has published fifty-eight novels, thirteen novellas, and forty-six collections of short stories, and those numbers don't include an almost equal number of works in other genres: essay collections, memoirs, poetry, young adult fiction, and children's fiction. She has received dozens of awards, including the Rea Award for Short Fiction and the National Book Award, and she has been a finalist for the Pulitzer Prize for Fiction on five occasions. Although it is impossible to generalize about a body of work as varied and as wide-ranging as hers, the passionate emotional and psychological intensity evident in the following story, "Tick," is one hallmark of her work.

## *Tick*   1988

She said, I can't live with you under these conditions, and her husband said, But these *are* the conditions. And moved out. And did not telephone her for several days. And when he did call she told him quickly, I'm happy here alone — I've gotten through the worst of it. Don't spoil my happiness again.

Since then the telephone rings at odd hours and she never answers. She will never answer — it's that simple. She does her work in the apartment spreading her books and papers out on the dining room table and she is working well, better than she has in years but it's all precarious, she knows it's precarious, not the temptation to kill herself — she understands this is an adolescent fantasy and would never act upon it — but the temptation to succumb to thoughts of despair, self-hatred. Easier, she thinks, to hate yourself than to respect yourself: it involves less imagination.

Tonight, contemplating these matters, she runs her fingers through her hair and comes upon a small bump on her head, the very crown of her head. A pimple, except it isn't a pimple. A mysterious hardness, shell-like. Could it be a tiny pebble embedded in her scalp? But how? She tries gently to dislodge it with her fingernails but it is stuck fast. What can it be? — she's fastidious about grooming, shampooing her hair every morning when she showers.

She tries to comb the thing out of her hair first with a plastic comb and then with a fine-toothed steel comb her husband left behind. It won't budge. Perhaps it is a tiny wound, a tiny scab, she thinks, and then she thinks, It's alive, it has its jaws in me. And she realizes it must be a tick.

Since her husband moved out and it is possible for her to go for days without  5 seeing anyone she has made a conscientious effort to be better groomed than she has ever been in her life. Shaves her underarms before the harsh stubble appears, keeps her legs smooth and hairless. Always dresses no matter the black rain falling against the windows in the early morning and the faint odors of garbage and wet ashes pervading the apartment building. Puts on lipstick, sometimes even a touch of cologne on her wrist, behind her ear. Pride! she thinks, winking in the mirror. Self-reliance! There you go!

She's in the bathroom trying desperately to inspect the top of her head in the medicine cabinet mirror. Roughly parting her hair, stooping, her eyes rolling up in their sockets. But she can't see — it's impossible. She runs for a hand mirror and holds it at such an angle that she can see into the cabinet mirror where she parts her hair clumsily with the fingers of one hand and she gives a little scream and nearly drops the mirror: it *is* a tick, bloated and purplish-black, stuck fast in her scalp.

She instructs herself to be calm. Not to panic. Not to give in to nausea, gagging. It's only an insect after all, one of those tiny black spiderlike things, parasites that suck animal and human blood, it's said the woods and fields are filled with them because of the rain this spring, and the heat, or is it because of the dryness and the heat, they're remarkably quick, darting and leaping and flying, raining from the trees onto unknowing human heads which is how she must have picked this one up — walking through the park the other morning, forcing herself to look and to really *see* the beauty of the natural world which she'd lost these past several months or has it been these past several years, embarked upon the precarious enterprise of adulthood, wifehood, loneliness.

She recalls that ticks secrete an anesthetic when they bite so you can't feel the bite. She recalls they're so hardy they can't be killed by ordinary methods, can't be squashed — the most practical method is to flush them down the toilet.

She is digging furiously at her scalp with her nails and the sink is flecked with blood, her blood, and a number of hairs. No reason to panic but she can't stop the frantic digging, she's bent low over the sink, panting, cursing, blood beating in her eyeballs and rivulets of sweat running down her back. She feels a sensation of nausea, a taste of something hot and acid at the back of her mouth but she manages to swallow it down. She thinks of the book she'd been planning to read this evening and the piano pieces by a contemporary composer whose work she admires she'd planned to study and work out though she hasn't a piano in the apartment yet (she intends to buy one, or rent one, soon, now that she'll have more time for it, and more energy) and these activities strike her suddenly as remote, preposterous.

Her husband once had a medical handbook, she goes to look for it in the bed- 10
room in a pile of books he left behind but can't find it, she tries the bookshelves in the living room then the stack of books in the kitchen beside the refrigerator, mostly paperbacks and shamelessly dusty, and when she's about to give up she discovers it, *The Family Medical Companion*, thank God her husband was so angry and hurt, so eager to get away from her, he'd left it behind. With trembling fingers she opens it to the section "Insects" that begins, "Insects are both friends and enemies of man. Some simply annoy by their bites and stings, but a few carry disease-bearing microbes."

The paragraph on ticks is disappointingly brief. She reads that she should not try to yank the tick out of her skin since ticks embed themselves so snugly, part of its body will very likely remain and there's the chance of infection. She has her choice of several procedures: she can hold a lighted match or cigarette against the tick's back until it wriggles free; she can coat it with Vaseline, gasoline, kerosene, or turpentine; she can pick the tick off gently with a tweezers.

She tries the tweezers. Tries repeatedly, a dozen times or more, at the bathroom sink, until the tweezers slips from her numbed fingers. She's crying. Her face is flushed as if with sunstroke, her eyes in the mirror are those of a deranged woman. To her horror she feels, or believes she feels, the tick stirring in her scalp — enlivened, enraged, burrowing more deeply into her flesh. She wonders if it has the power to pierce the bone, to embed itself in her very brain.

She jams her knuckles into her mouth to muffle her screaming.

She's close to hysteria so she leaves the bathroom and paces about the apartment, from one room to another, one room to another, in an effort to calm herself. Minutes pass: she has no idea how many. She beats her hands softly together, the fleshy parts of the palms, she tries to breathe deeply and rhythmically, after all this is such a minor problem, hardly a matter of life and death, if worse comes to worst she can take a taxi to a hospital to an emergency room but what if they laugh at her there? — what if they're furious with her there? — her with her face like death, trembling and panting as if she'd been physically assaulted, *a mere tick embedded in her scalp*. More plausibly, she might go next door and ask for help from her neighbor — but when she envisions knocking at the door, handing the astonished young woman the tweezers and begging her to extricate the thing in her head, she knows she can't do it. She isn't acquainted with the woman even casually — she's a shy cold girl very like herself. When they meet in the foyer or in the elevator each smiles faintly and pointedly looks away thinking, *Don't talk to me. Please. Not right now*.

Perhaps she should kill herself after all — it would be the easiest solution to all    15 her problems.

By this time she's walking fast, on the verge of breaking into a run, can't stop! can't sit down! her heart beating wildly and her breath audible. At the crown of her head there's a hot piercing throbbing pain. Her fingernails are edged with blood. She's rushing from room to room, pacing, turning in tight corners like a trapped animal, hardly seeing where she's careening, her eyes filled with tears of hurt, rage, frustration, shame — this is what it comes to, she's thinking, this is all it comes to, and she's leaning in a doorway trying to get her breath trying to stave off an attack of faintness when she hears the telephone ring and understands it has been ringing for some time.

She heads for it like a sleepwalker, propelled by a rough shove. She foresees a reconciliation, lovemaking both anguished and tender. She foresees starting a child. It's time.

## Edgar Allan Poe (1809–1849)

Edgar Allan Poe grew up in the home of John Allan, in Richmond, Virginia, after his mother died in 1811, and he was educated in Scotland and England for five years before completing his classical education in Richmond. After a short stint at the University of Virginia, Poe went to Boston, where he began publishing his poetry. His foster father sent him to West Point Military Academy, but Poe was expelled and moved on to New York City, where he published a book of poems inspired by the Romantic movement. Moving among editorial jobs in Baltimore, Richmond, and New York, Poe married his thirteen-year-old cousin Virginia Clemm. Early in his story-writing career, Poe published his only novel-length piece, *The Narrative of Arthur Gordon Pym* (1838), and the following year, he began to work in the genre of the supernatural and horrible, with the stories "William Wilson" and "The Fall of the House of Usher." He gained publicity with the detective story "The Murders in the Rue Morgue," became nationally famous with the publication of his poem "The Raven" in 1845, and died four years later in Baltimore after a drinking binge. Poe theorized that the short story writer should plan every word toward the achievement of a certain effect, and that stories should be read in a single sitting. Morbidity and dreamlike flights of fancy, for which Poe is often recognized, do not detract from his lucid crafting of suspense and his erudite control of language and symbol.

# The Cask of Amontillado    1846

The thousand injuries of Fortunato I had borne as I best could; but when he ventured upon insult, I vowed revenge. You, who so well know the nature of my soul, will not suppose, however, that I gave utterance to a threat. *At length* I would be avenged; this was a point definitely settled — but the very definitiveness with which it was resolved precluded the idea of risk. I must not only punish, but punish with impunity. A wrong is unredressed when retribution overtakes its redresser. It is equally unredressed when the avenger fails to make himself felt as such to him who has done the wrong.

It must be understood, that neither by word nor deed had I given Fortunato cause to doubt my good-will. I continued, as was my wont, to smile in his face, and he did not perceive that my smile *now* was at the thought of his immolation.

He had a weak point — this Fortunato — although in other regards he was a man to be respected and even feared. He prided himself on his connoisseurship in wine. Few Italians have the true virtuoso spirit. For the most part their enthusiasm is adopted to suit the time and opportunity — to practice imposture upon the British and Austrian *millionaires*. In painting and gemmary Fortunato, like his countrymen, was a quack — but in the matter of old wines he was sincere. In this respect I did not differ from him materially: I was skilful in the Italian vintages myself, and bought largely whenever I could.

It was about dusk, one evening during the supreme madness of the carnival season, that I encountered my friend. He accosted me with excessive warmth, for he had been drinking much. The man wore motley. He had on a tight-fitting parti-striped dress, and his head was surmounted by the conical cap and bells. I was so pleased to see him, that I thought I should never have done wringing his hand.

I said to him: "My dear Fortunato, you are luckily met. How remarkably well 5 you are looking to-day! But I have received a pipe° of what passes for Amontillado, and I have my doubts."

"How?" said he. "Amontillado? A pipe? Impossible! And in the middle of the carnival!"

"I have my doubts," I replied; "and I was silly enough to pay the full Amontillado price without consulting you in the matter. You were not to be found, and I was fearful of losing a bargain."

"Amontillado!"

"I have my doubts."

"Amontillado!"    10

"And I must satisfy them."

"Amontillado!"

"As you are engaged, I am on my way to Luchesi. If any one has a critical turn, it is he. He will tell me — — "

"Luchesi cannot tell Amontillado from Sherry."

"And yet some fools will have it that his taste is a match for your own."    15

"Come, let us go."

"Whither?"

"To your vaults."

"My friend, no; I will not impose upon your good nature. I perceive you have an engagement. Luchesi — — "

"I have no engagement; — come."    20

*pipe:* A large keg.

"My friend, no. It is not the engagement, but the severe cold with which I perceive you are afflicted. The vaults are insufferably damp. They are encrusted with nitre."

"Let us go, nevertheless. The cold is merely nothing. Amontillado! You have been imposed upon. And as for Luchesi, he cannot distinguish Sherry from Amontillado."

Thus speaking, Fortunato possessed himself of my arm. Putting on a mask of black silk, and drawing a *roquelaire*° closely about my person, I suffered him to hurry me to my palazzo.

There were no attendants at home; they had absconded to make merry in honor of the time. I had told them that I should not return until the morning, and had given them explicit orders not to stir from the house. These orders were suffi- cient, I well knew, to insure their immediate disappearance, one and all, as soon as my back was turned.

I took from their sconces two flambeaux, and giving one to Fortunato, bowed   25 him through several suites of rooms to the archway that led into the vaults. I passed down a long and winding staircase, requesting him to be cautious as he followed. We came at length to the foot of the descent, and stood together on the damp ground of the catacombs of the Montresors.

The gait of my friend was unsteady, and the bells upon his cap jingled as he strode.

"The pipe?" said he.

"It is farther on," said I; "but observe the white web-work which gleams from these cavern walls."

He turned toward me, and looked into my eyes with two filmy orbs that dis- tilled the rheum of intoxication.

"Nitre?" he asked, at length.   30

"Nitre," I replied. "How long have you had that cough?"

"Ugh! ugh! ugh! — ugh! ugh! ugh! — ugh! ugh! ugh! — ugh! ugh! ugh! — ugh! ugh! ugh!"

My poor friend found it impossible to reply for many minutes.

"It is nothing," he said, at last.

"Come," I said, with decision, "we will go back; your health is precious. You   35 are rich, respected, admired, beloved; you are happy, as once I was. You are a man to be missed. For me it is no matter. We will go back; you will be ill, and I cannot be responsible. Besides, there is Luchesi —"

"Enough," he said; "the cough is a mere nothing; it will not kill me. I shall not die of a cough."

"True — true," I replied; "and, indeed, I had no intention of alarming you unnecessarily; but you should use all proper caution. A draught of this Medoc will defend us from the damps."

Here I knocked off the neck of a bottle which I drew from a long row of its fellows that lay upon the mould.

"Drink," I said, presenting him the wine.

He raised it to his lips with a leer. He paused and nodded to me familiarly,   40 while his bells jingled.

"I drink," he said, "to the buried that repose around us."

"And I to your long life."

He again took my arm, and we proceeded.

---

*roquelaire:* A short cloak.

"These vaults," he said, "are extensive."

"The Montresors," I replied, "were a great and numerous family."    45

"I forget your arms."

"A huge human foot d'or,° in a field azure; the foot crushes a serpent rampant whose fangs are imbedded in the heel."

"And the motto?"

"*Nemo me impune lacessit.*"°

"Good!" he said.    50

The wine sparkled in his eyes and the bells jingled. My own fancy grew warm with the Medoc. We had passed through walls of piled bones, with casks and puncheons intermingling into the inmost recesses of the catacombs. I paused again, and this time I made bold to seize Fortunato by an arm above the elbow.

"The nitre!" I said; "see, it increases. It hangs like moss upon the vaults. We are below the river's bed. The drops of moisture trickle among the bones. Come, we will go back ere it is too late. Your cough — "

"It is nothing," he said; "let us go on. But first, another draught of the Medoc."

I broke and reached him a flagon of De Grâve. He emptied it at a breath. His eyes flashed with a fierce light. He laughed and threw the bottle upward with a gesticulation I did not understand.

I looked at him in surprise. He repeated the movement — a grotesque one.    55

"You do not comprehend?" he said.

"Not I," I replied.

"Then you are not of the brotherhood."

"How?"

"You are not of the masons."    60

"Yes, yes," I said; "yes, yes."

"You? Impossible! A mason?"

"A mason," I replied.

"A sign," he said.

"It is this," I answered, producing a trowel from beneath the folds of my    65
*roquelaire.*

"You jest," he exclaimed, recoiling a few paces. "But let us proceed to the Amontillado."

"Be it so," I said, replacing the tool beneath the cloak, and again offering him my arm. He leaned upon it heavily. We continued our route in search of the Amontillado. We passed through a range of low arches, descended, passed on, and descending again, arrived at a deep crypt, in which the foulness of the air caused our flambeaux rather to glow than flame.

At the most remote end of the crypt there appeared another less spacious. Its walls had been lined with human remains, piled to the vault overhead, in the fashion of the great catacombs of Paris. Three sides of this interior crypt were still ornamented in this manner. From the fourth the bones had been thrown down, and lay promiscuously upon the earth, forming at one point a mound of some size. Within the wall thus exposed by the displacing of the bones, we perceived a still interior recess, in depth about four feet, in width three, in height six or seven. It seemed to have been constructed for no especial use within itself, but formed merely the interval between two of the colossal supports of the roof of the catacombs, and was backed by one of their circumscribing walls of solid granite.

---

*d'or:* Of gold.
*Nemo . . . lacessit* (Latin): No one wounds me with impunity.

It was in vain that Fortunato, uplifting his dull torch, endeavored to pry into the depth of the recess. Its termination the feeble light did not enable us to see.

"Proceed," I said; "herein is the Amontillado. As for Luchesi — " 70

"He is an ignoramus," interrupted my friend, as he stepped unsteadily forward, while I followed immediately at his heels. In an instant he had reached the extremity of the niche, and finding his progress arrested by the rock, stood stupidly bewildered. A moment more and I had fettered him to the granite. In its surface were two iron staples, distant from each other about two feet, horizontally. From one of these depended a short chain, from the other a padlock. Throwing the links about his waist, it was but the work of a few seconds to secure it. He was too much astounded to resist. Withdrawing the key I stepped back from the recess.

"Pass your hand," I said, "over the wall; you cannot help feeling the nitre. Indeed it is *very* damp. Once more let me *implore* you to return. No? Then I must positively leave you. But I must first render you all the little attentions in my power."

"The Amontillado!" ejaculated my friend, not yet recovered from his astonishment.

"True," I replied; "the Amontillado."

As I said these words I busied myself among the pile of bones of which I have 75 before spoken. Throwing them aside, I soon uncovered a quantity of building stone and mortar. With these materials and with the aid of my trowel, I began vigorously to wall up the entrance of the niche.

I had scarcely laid the first tier of the masonry when I discovered that the intoxication of Fortunato had in a great measure worn off. The earliest indication I had of this was a low moaning cry from the depth of the recess. It was *not* the cry of a drunken man. There was then a long and obstinate silence. I laid the second tier, and the third, and the fourth; and then I heard the furious vibrations of the chain. The noise lasted for several minutes, during which, that I might hearken to it with the more satisfaction, I ceased my labors and sat down upon the bones. When at last the clanking subsided, I resumed the trowel, and finished without interruption the fifth, the sixth, and the seventh tier. The wall was now nearly upon a level with my breast. I again paused, and holding the flambeaux over the masonwork, threw a few feeble rays upon the figure within.

A succession of loud and shrill screams, bursting suddenly from the throat of the chained form, seemed to thrust me violently back. For a brief moment I hesitated — I trembled. Unsheathing my rapier, I began to grope with it about the recess; but the thought of an instant reassured me. I placed my hand upon the solid fabric of the catacombs, and felt satisfied. I reapproached the wall. I replied to the yells of him who clamored. I reechoed — I aided — I surpassed them in volume and in strength. I did this, and the clamorer grew still.

It was now midnight, and my task was drawing to a close. I had completed the eighth, the ninth, and the tenth tier. I had finished a portion of the last and the eleventh; there remained but a single stone to be fitted and plastered in. I struggled with its weight; I placed it partially in its destined position. But now there came from out the niche a low laugh that erected the hairs upon my head. It was succeeded by a sad voice, which I had difficulty in recognizing as that of the noble Fortunato. The voice said —

"Ha! ha! ha! — he! he! — a very good joke indeed — an excellent jest. We will have many a rich laugh about it at the palazzo — he! he! he! — over our wine — he! he! he!"

"The Amontillado!" I said. 80

"He! he! he! — he! he! he! — yes, the Amontillado. But is it not getting late? Will not they be awaiting us at the palazzo, the Lady Fortunato and the rest? Let us be gone."

"Yes," I said, "let us be gone."

*"For the love of God, Montresor!"*

"Yes," I said, "for the love of God!"

But to these words I hearkened in vain for a reply. I grew impatient. I called  85 aloud:

"Fortunato!"

No answer. I called again:

"Fortunato!"

No answer still, I thrust a torch through the remaining aperture and let it fall within. There came forth in return only a jingling of the bells. My heart grew sick — on account of the dampness of the catacombs. I hastened to make an end of my labor. I forced the last stone into its position; I plastered it up. Against the new masonry I re-erected the old rampart of bones. For the half of a century no mortal has disturbed them. *In pace requiescat!*°

*In pace requiescat!* (Latin): In peace may he rest!

## George Saunders (b. 1958)

A native of Amarillo, Texas, George Saunders earned his bachelor's degree at the Colorado School of Mines and his master's degree at Syracuse University, where he has taught since 1997. Most of his publications have been short stories, often with absurdist or comic overtones. He has won many prestigious awards, including the National Magazine Award for Fiction four times, and he is the recipient of both a Guggenheim Fellowship and a MacArthur "genius" grant. Breaking the pattern of many fiction writers, Saunders published his only novel, *Lincoln in the Bardo* (2017), after many years as a short story writer. That novel was published to great critical acclaim, including Britain's prestigious Man Booker Prize. He is only the second American author to win that prize. He cites as influences many short story writers included in this anthology — Ernest Hemingway, Mark Twain, and Tobias Wolff, and critics have compared him to another — Kurt Vonnegut Jr. All of their selections would make interesting stylistic and thematic comparisons to the following story.

## *I Can Speak*™   1999

Mrs. Ruth Faniglia
210 Lester Street
Rochester, N.Y. 14623

Dear Mrs. Faniglia,

We were very sorry to receive your letter of 23 Feb., which accompanied the I CAN SPEAK!™ you returned, much to our disappointment. We here at KidLuv believe that the I CAN SPEAK!™ is an innovative and essential educational tool that, used with proper parental guidance, offers a rare early-development opportunity for babies and toddlers alike. And so I thought I would take some of my personal time (I am on lunch) and try to address the questions you raised in your letter, which is here in front of me on my (cluttered!) desk.

First, may I be so bold as to suggest that your disappointment may stem from your own, perhaps unreasonable, expectations? Because in your letter, what you indicated, when I read it, was that you think and/or thought that somehow the product can read your baby's mind? Our product cannot read your baby's mind, Mrs. Faniglia. No one can read a baby's mind, at least not yet. Although believe me, we are probably working on it! All the I CAN SPEAK!™ can do, however, is respond to aural patterns in a way that makes baby seem older. Say baby sees a peach. If you or Mr. Faniglia (I hope I do not presume) were to loudly say something like "What a delicious peach!" the I CAN SPEAK!™, hearing this, through that little slotted hole near the neck, would respond by saying something like "I LIKE PEACH." Or "I WANT PEACH." Or, if you had chosen the ICS2000 (you chose the ICS1900, which is fine, perfectly good for most babies), the I CAN SPEAK!™ might even respond by saying something like "FRUIT, ISN'T THAT ONE OF THE MAJOR FOOD GROUPS?" Which would be pretty good, for a six-month-old like Derek, your son, don't you think?

But here I must reiterate: That would not in reality be Derek speaking. Derek would not in reality know that a peach is fruit, or that fruit is a major food group. The I CAN SPEAK!™ knows, however, and, from its position on Derek's face, it will give the illusion that Derek knows, by giving the illusion that Derek is speaking out of the twin moving SimuLips. But that is it. That is all we claim.

Furthermore, in your letter, Mrs. Faniglia, you state that the I CAN SPEAK!™ 5 "mask" (your terminology) takes on a "stressed-out look when talking that is not what a real baby's talking face appears like but is more like some nervous middle-aged woman." Well, maybe that is so, but, with all due respect, you try it! You try making a latex face look and talk and move like the real face of an actual live baby! Inside are over 5000 separate circuits and 390 moving parts. And as far as looking like a middle-aged woman, we beg to differ: we do not feel that a middle-aged stressed-out woman has (1) no hair on head and (2) chubby cheeks and (3) fine downy facial hair. The ICS1900 unit is definitely the face of a baby, Mrs. Faniglia. We took over twenty-five hundred photos of different babies and using a computer combined them to make this face, this face we call Male Composite 37 or, affectionately, Little Roger. But what you possibly seem to be unhappy about is that Little Roger's face is not Derek's face? To be frank, Mrs. Faniglia, many of you, our customers, have found it disconcerting that their baby looks different with the I CAN SPEAK!™ on. Which we find so surprising. Did you, we often wonder, not look at the cover of the box? On that cover the ICS1900 is very plainly shown, situated on a sort of rack, looking facewise like Little Roger, albeit Little Roger is a bit crumpled and has a forehead furrow of sorts.

But this is why we came up with the ICS2100. With the ICS2100, your baby looks just like your baby. And, because we do not want anyone to be unhappy with us, we would like to give you a complimentary ICS2100 upgrade! We would like to come to your house on Lester Street and make a personalized plaster cast of Derek's real, actual face! And soon, via FedEx, here will come Derek's face in a box, and when you slip that ICS2100 over Derek's head and Velcro the Velcro, he will look so very much like himself! Plus we have another free surprise, which is that, while at your house, we will tape his actual voice and use it to make our phrases, the phrases Derek will subsequently say. So not only will he look like himself, he will sound like himself, as he crawls around your house appearing to speak!

Plus we will throw in several other personalizing options. Say you call Derek "Lovemeister." (I am using this example from my own personal home, as my wife, Ann, and I call our son Billy "Lovemeister," because he is so sweet.) With the ICS2100, you might choose to have Derek say, upon crawling into a room, "HERE COMES THE LOVEMEISTER!" or "STOP TALKING DIRTY, THE LOVEMEISTER HAS ARRIVED!" How we do this is, laser beams coming out of the earlobes, which sense the doorframe. So the I CAN SPEAK!™ knows it has just entered a room, from its position on Derek's head! And also you will have over one hundred Discretionary Phrases to more highly personalize Derek. For instance, you might choose to have him say, on his birthday, "MOMMY AND DADDY, REMEMBER THAT TIME YOU CONCEIVED ME IN ARUBA?" Although probably you did not in fact conceive Derek in Aruba. That we do not know. (Our research is not that extensive!) Or say your dog comes up and gives Derek a lick. You could make Derek say (if your dog's name is Queenie), "QUEENIE, GIVE IT A REST!" Which, you know what? It makes you love him more. Because suddenly he is articulate. Suddenly he is not just sitting there going glub glub glub while examining a piece of his own feces on his own thumb, which is something we recently found Billy doing! Sometimes we have felt that our childless friends think badly of us for having a kid who just goes glub glub glub in the corner while looking at his feces on his thumb. But now when childless friends are over, what we have found, my wife, Ann, and I, is that it's great to have your kid say something witty and self-possessed years before he or she would actually in reality be able to say something witty or self-possessed. The bottom line is that it's just *fun* when you and your childless friends are playing cards, and your baby suddenly blurts out (in his *very own probable future voice*), "IT IS LIKELY THAT WE STILL DON'T FULLY UNDERSTAND THE IMPORT OF ALL OF EINSTEIN'S FINDINGS!"

Here I must admit that we have several times seen a sort of softening in the eyes of our resolute childless friends, as if they, too, would suddenly like to have a baby.

And as far as Derek flinching whenever that voice issues forth from him? When that speaker near his mouth sort of buzzes his lips? May I say this is not unusual? What I suggest? Try putting the ICS on Derek for a short time at first, maybe ten minutes a day, then gradually building up his Wearing Time. That is what we did. And it worked super. Now Billy wears his even while sleeping. In fact, if we forget to put it back on after his bath, he pitches a fit. Kind of begs for it! He starts to say, you know, "Mak! Mak!" Which we think is his word for mask. And when we put the mask on and Velcro the Velcro, he says, or rather it says, "GUTEN MORGEN, PAPA!" because we are trying to teach him German, and have installed the German Learning module in our ICS2100. Or for example, if his pants are not yet on, he'll say, "HOW ABOUT SLAPPING ON MY ROMPERS SO I CAN GET ON WITH MY DAY!" (I wrote that one.)

My point is, with the ICS2100 Billy is much, much cleverer than he ever was 10 with the ICS1900. He has recently learned, for example, that if he spills a little milk on his chin, his SimuLips will issue a MOO sound. Which he really seems to get a kick out of! I'll be in the living room doing a little evening paperwork and from the kitchen I'll hear, you know, "MOO! MOO! MOO!" And I'll rush in, and there'll be this sort of lake of milk on the floor. And there'll be Billy, pouring milk on his chin until I yank the milk away, at which point he bellows, "DON'T FENCE ME IN." (Ann's contribution — she was raised in Wyoming!)

I, for one, Mrs. Faniglia, do not believe that any baby wants to sit around all day going glub glub glub. My feeling is that a baby, sitting in its diaper, looking around at the world, thinks to itself, albeit in some crude nonverbal way, What the heck is wrong with me, why am I the only one going glub glub glub while all these other folks are talking in whole complete sentences? And hence, possibly, lifelong psychological damage may result. Now, am I saying that your Derek runs the risk of feeling bad about himself as a grownup because as a baby he felt he didn't know how to talk right? No, it is not for me to say that, Mrs. Faniglia, I am only in Sales. But I will say that I am certainly not taking any chances with our Billy. My belief is that when Billy hears a competent, intelligent voice issuing from the area near his mouth, he feels excellent about himself. And I feel excellent about him. Not that I didn't feel excellent about him before. But now we can actually have a sort of conversation! And also — and most importantly — when that voice issues from his SimuLips he learns something invaluable; namely, that when he finally does begin speaking, he will be speaking via using his mouth.

Now, Mrs. Faniglia, you may be thinking, Hold on a sec, of course this guy loves his I CAN SPEAK!™ He probably gets his for free! But not so, Mrs. Faniglia, I get mine for two grand, just like you. We get no discounts, so much in demand is the I CAN SPEAK!™, and in addition we are strongly encouraged by our management to purchase and use the I CAN SPEAK!™ at home, on our own kids. (Or even, in one case, on an elderly senile mom! Suffice it to say that, though she looks sort of funny with the Little Roger head on her somewhat frail frame, the family takes great comfort in hearing all the witty things she has to say. Just like her old self!) Not that I wouldn't use it otherwise. Believe me, I would. Since we upgraded to the ICS2100, things have been great, Billy looks almost identical to himself; and is not nearly so, you know, boring as before, when we had the ICS1900, which (frankly) says some rather predictable things, which I expect is partly why you were so unhappy with it, Mrs. Faniglia, you seem like a very intelligent woman. When people come over now, sometimes we just gather around Billy and wait for his next howler, and last weekend my supervisor, Mr. Ted Ames, stopped by (a super guy, he has really given me support, please let him know if you've found this letter at all helpful) and boy did we all crack up laughing when Billy began rubbing his face very rapidly across the carpet in order to make his ICS2100 shout, "FRICTION IS A COMMON AND USEFUL SOURCE OF HEAT!"

Mrs. Faniglia, it is nearing the end of my lunch, and so I must wrap this up, but I hope I have been of service. On a personal note, I did not have the greatest of pasts when I came here, having been in a few scrapes and even rehab situations, but now, wow, the commissions roll in, and I have made a nice life for me and Ann and Billy. Not that the possible loss of my commission is the reason for my concern. Please do not think so. While it is true that, if you decline my upgrade offer and persist in your desire to return your ICS1900, my commission must be refunded, by me, to Mr. Ames, it is no big deal, I have certainly refunded commissions to Mr. Ames before, especially lately. I don't quite know what I'm doing wrong. But that is not your concern, Mrs. Faniglia. Your concern is Derek. My real reason for writing this letter, on my lunch break, is that, hard as we all work at KidLuv to provide innovative and essential development tools for families like yours, Mrs. Faniglia, it is always sort of a heartbreak when our products are misapprehended. Please do accept our offer of a free ICS2100 upgrade. We at KidLuv really love what kids are, Mrs. Faniglia, which is why we want them to become something better as soon as possible! Baby's early years are so precious, and must not be wasted, as we are finding out, as our Billy grows and grows, learning new skills every day.

Sincerely yours,
Rick Sminks
Product Service Representative
KidLuv, Inc.

## ALICE WALKER (B. 1944)

Alice Walker was born in 1944 to Minnie Tallulah Grant Walker and Willie Lee Walker, sharecroppers in Eatonton, Georgia. Walker started her collegiate career at Spelman College in Atlanta, but graduated from Sarah Lawrence College in New York in 1965. After teaching history in Mississippi, she won a fellowship from the Radcliffe Institute and went on to teach at Wellesley College, where she pioneered one of the first women's studies courses in the country. Walker has published several volumes of poetry, including *Once* (1968), *Revolutionary Petunias and Other Poems* (1973), *Horses Make a Land-scape Look More Beautiful* (1984), *Collected Poems* (2005), *Hard Times Require Furious Dancing* (2000), and a book of essays, *Living by the Word* (1988). Her numerous works of fiction include *In Love and Trouble: Stories of Black Women* (1973), *The Temple of My Familiar* (1989), *Possessing the Secret of Joy* (1992), *The Complete Stories* (1994), *By the Light of My Father's Smile* (1998), *Now Is the Time to Open Your Heart* (2004), and the Pulitzer Prize–winning *The Color Purple* (1982). The acclaim for her novel *Meridian* (1976) won her a Guggenheim Fellowship and led her to San Francisco, where she still lives.

## *The Flowers*    1973

It seemed to Myop as she skipped lightly from hen house to pigpen to smoke-house that the days had never been as beautiful as these. The air held a keenness that made her nose twitch. The harvesting of the corn and cotton, peanuts and squash, made each day a golden surprise that caused excited little tremors to run up her jaws.

Myop carried a short, knobby stick. She struck out at random at chickens she liked, and worked out the beat of a song on the fence around the pigpen. She felt light and good in the warm sun. She was ten, and nothing existed for her but her song, the stick clutched in her dark brown hand, and the tat-de-ta-ta-ta of accompaniment.

Turning her back on the rusty boards of her family's sharecropper cabin, Myop walked along the fence till it ran into the stream made by the spring. Around the spring, where the family got drinking water, silver ferns and wild-flowers grew.

Along the shallow banks pigs rooted. Myop watched the tiny white bubbles disrupt the thin black scale of soil and the water that silently rose and slid away down the stream.

She had explored the woods behind the house many times. Often, in late autumn, her mother took her to gather nuts among the fallen leaves. Today she made her own path, bouncing this way and that way, vaguely keeping an eye out for snakes. She found, in addition to various common but pretty ferns and leaves, an armful of strange blue flowers with velvety ridges and a sweet-suds bush full of the brown, fragrant buds.

By twelve o'clock, her arms laden with sprigs of her findings, she was a mile or  5 more from home. She had often been as far before, but the strangeness of the land made it not as pleasant as her usual haunts. It seemed gloomy in the little cove in which she found herself. The air was damp, the silence close and deep.

Myop began to circle back to the house, back to the peacefulness of the morning. It was then she stepped smack into his eyes. Her heel became lodged in the broken ridge between brow and nose, and she reached down quickly, unafraid, to free herself. It was only when she saw his naked grin that she gave a little yelp of surprise.

He had been a tall man. From feet to neck covered a long space. His head lay beside him. When she pushed back the leaves and layers of earth and debris Myop saw that he'd had large white teeth, all of them cracked or broken, long fingers, and very big bones. All his clothes had rotted away except some threads of blue denim from his overalls. The buckles of the overalls had turned green.

Myop gazed around the spot with interest. Very near where she'd stepped into the head was a wild pink rose. As she picked it to add to her bundle she noticed a raised mound, a ring, around the rose's root. It was the rotted remains of a noose, a bit of shredding plowline, now blending benignly into the soil. Around an overhanging limb of a great spreading oak clung another piece. Frayed, rotted, bleached, and frazzled — barely there — but spinning restlessly in the breeze. Myop laid down her flowers.

And the summer was over.

# JOHN EDGAR WIDEMAN (B. 1941)

John Edgar Wideman is the author of ten novels, six short story collections, and five works of nonfiction, but as his readers well know, the boundaries between his fiction and nonfiction are sometimes difficult to discern. Much (though certainly not all) of his fiction has its roots in stories from his own upbringing in the impoverished neighborhood of Pittsburgh known as Homewood. Wideman earned a scholarship to the University of Pennsylvania and later a prestigious Rhodes Scholarship to Oxford, and he returned to teach at Penn while developing his craft as a novelist. He then took a position at the University of Wyoming, and he was there when his brother Robby arrived in 1975, on the lam after being involved in a botched robbery that resulted in a murder charge. Robby was sentenced to life in prison, and Wideman wrote movingly about the difference in their trajectories in his 1984 memoir *Brothers and Keepers*. (After forty-four years in prison and numerous appeals,

Robby's sentence was commuted in 2019). Wideman has also reimagined Robby's story in fictional contexts as he does in the following story, "All Stories Are True." That phrase is an Igbo proverb that Wideman repeats throughout his career: at one point he writes, "All stories are true, as [novelist Chinua] Achebe tells us the Igbo say. Reliable and unverifiable as dreams." How does that second phrase complicate the meaning of this story's title?

> **A Note on the Text:** Readers should note that this story contains a harmful racial slur. As discussed in "Approaching Sensitive Subjects" (p. 7), it is important to be aware of context when encountering difficult content. As you read, consider in- vs. out-group usage: Wideman, the author of this story, is a Black American, as is the narrator of this story. Further, this story deals broadly and intentionally with racial inequity, reflecting the author's original intent in depicting a specific character, incident, time period, place, and culture. Be mindful of this context as you read this story.

## All Stories Are True   1992

> *And for fear of him the guards trembled*
> *and became like dead men.*
> Matthew 28:4

My mother is standing on her porch. May 10, 1991. Early morning and the street is quiet now, as peaceful as it gets here, as peaceful as it always stays in other neighborhoods, invisible, not a half mile away behind the tree-topped ridge that separates Tokay, Susquehanna, Dunfermline, Seagirt from their neighbors to the west. The litany of streets always sweet on my tongue. I think I murmur their names, a silence unless you are inside my skull, sing them as a kind of background music that doesn't break the quiet of morning. If I'm not reciting them to myself, I hear the names anyway coming from somewhere else, a place that also knows what lies within the sound of these streets said to oneself again and again. Footsteps, voices, a skein of life dragged bead by bead through a soft needle's eye. And knows the names of streets can open like the gates of a great city, everyone who's ever inhabited the city, walked its streets, suddenly, like a shimmer, like the first notes of a Monk° solo, breathing, moving, a world quickens as the gates swing apart. And knows my mother is not alone on her porch this May morning. Knows she hears beneath the stillness enveloping her the sound of street names, what is animated when they are recalled. The presence of other souls as palpable as light playing in the edges of her robe. Her mother and father and children. Her brother and sisters. Grands and great-grands. The man I have become and those whom I've lost becoming him. The song of street names a medium in which we all float, suspended, as if each of us is someone's precious, precious child who must never be allowed to slip from the arms cradling, rocking. And knows my mother is listening to time, time voiced in no manmade measurements of days or minutes or

---

*Monk:* Refers to the jazz pianist Thelonious Monk.

years, time playing as it always must, background or foreground or taking up all the space we have, a tape of the street names chanted that releases every Homewood footstep she's ever heard or dreamed.

I'm afraid for her. Experience one of those moments of missing her intensely, her gone, final good-byes said, though she is here, just ten feet away, through the front door screen, framed by two of the rusty wrought iron columns supporting the roof. A moment where fear of losing her overwhelms me to such an extent that I am bereft, helpless, unconsoled even by her presence, one price I pay for other moments when she's thousands of miles away and I've needed her and she is there, *there* beside me. After nine months of chemo her hair has grown in again, softer, curlier. Many shades of bushy gray and a crown of lighter hair, nearly white, nearly spun to invisibility by morning. I'm aware as I seldom am of her dimensions, how tall, how wide, how much this woman on the porch with her newborn's hair weighs. I need what is tangible, no matter how small she turns out to be, to offset words like frail and vulnerable I can't help saying to myself, words popping up though I try not to think them. I hate words with the power to take her away. *Frail. Old.* The effort of denying them makes her disappear anyway. My eyes cross Tokay, counting cobblestones as they go, remarking the incredible steepness of the street slanting out of my field of vision, the broken curbs and littered gutters, settling on the gigantic tree islanded in the delta where Seagirt and Tokay converge and Bricelyn begins. If the downtown wedge of skyscrapers where three rivers meet is the city's Golden Triangle, this could be its Green Triangle. A massive tree centuries old holds out against the odds here across from my mother's house, one of the biggest trees in Pittsburgh, anchored in a green tangle of weeds and bushes, trunk thick as a Buick, black as night after rain soaks its striated hide. Huge spread of its branches canopies the foot of the hill where the streets come together. Certain times of day in summer it shades my mother's front porch. If it ever tore loose from its moorings, it would crush her house like a sledgehammer. As big as it is, its roots must run under her cellar. The sound of it drinking, lapping nourishment deep underground is part of the quiet when her house is empty. How the tree survived a city growing around it is a mystery. For years no more than a twig, a sapling, a switch someone could have snapped off to beat a balky animal, swat a child's behind. I see a dark fist exploding through the asphalt, thrusting to the sky, the fingers opening, multiplying, fanning outward to form a vast umbrella of foliage. The arm behind it petrifies, other thick limbs burst from knots of hardened flesh, each one duplicating the fan of leaves, the delicate network of branches, thinning, twisting as they climb higher and farther from the source. Full-blown in a matter of seconds, ready to stand here across from my mother's house forever, till its time to be undone in the twinkling of an eye, just the way it arrived.

I didn't say any of this to my mother as I pushed through the screen door with my cup of coffee to join her on the porch. Then it was just one quiet thing after the other, a matter of seconds, the sight of her standing still, her back to me, me thinking thoughts that flashed at warp speed but would take forever to unpack, the door creaking, her turning slowly towards the noise, *You up, Baby,* a quick welcoming smile before she turns back to whatever it was, wherever she was gazing when I saw her first, small, bathed in the soft, remorseless light of morning, when I heard the sound of Homewood street names playing, transforming a commonplace scene into something else, restoring the invisible omnipresence of time, the enabling medium, what brought you to this moment and will carry you away, how things begin and end, always, you about to step out onto your mother's porch, catching her staring off at something, somewhere, home again, morning again, steamy coffee mug in one hand, sure of what you will do next, your fingers press the doorframe, pushing, absolutely unsure, fearing what will happen next, wondering what's in her eyes, behind them this morning in May, and which ghosts crowd the porch, regretting her privacy you are invading with yours. Who will the two of you together summon if you steal her attention, if you are ready and willing to offer yours, if you can break away from the tune playing over and over in your head and maybe in hers of the street names, sorrow and loss in every syllable when you say them to yourself the way you must to locate yourself here, back home in Pittsburgh this morning, Tioga Susquehanna Seagirt Cassina, praying your mother won't move, won't be gone before you reach her.

You hug each other. Not hard, not soft. Briefly. Long enough to remember everything.

I love my flowers. 5

A guy was selling them in the gas station. At Braddock and Penn. You know. The two big stations across from one another. A white guy in Mickey Mouse bermudas. He said these hadn't been out in the sun. Too much direct sun's not good for them, he said. These were shoved under a folding table he had set up. Pansies or some other kind, I forget. They just looked pretty to me and I thought you'd like something pretty and growing.

Impatiens. They're beautiful.

And you already have a hook by the door to hang them.

I used to keep a few little plants out here. Then one night just before Easter the flowers grew feet. Woke up one morning and everybody's flowers were gone. I only had a couple nice little plants. Nothing special. But they were gone just like everybody else's up and down both blocks. Flowers grew feet that night and walked away.

You mean somebody ripped off people's flowers. 10

Should have heard Eva. See the house with the green and white aluminum awning. That's Eva's. You know who I mean, don't you. Small brown-skinned woman always dressed nice. Used to ride the bus to town with me to work. Eva had big-time flowers on her porch. Gone that morning like everybody else's and Eva's fit to be tied. She said she was marching down to the corner and beat the black off him with her own two hands if she caught him with one of her flowers. Said she'd know her flowers if she saw them, pot or no pot or new pot she'd know her own flowers and strangle him with her bare hands if she caught him with her flowers.

Somebody selling flowers on the corner.

Right there on Bennett. Day after the night the flowers walked.

No. You got to be kidding.

Huh uh. Some guy down there big as life selling flowers. Had his stand right 15 on Bennett and Bricelyn. No pots. Dog probably sold people's pots somewhere else. He wasn't completely crazy. A flower sale day after everybody's flowers disappeared off their porches.

He's lucky he didn't get shot.

Eva said she was going down there and look for her flowers. Tear him up if she found any. But how could you know for sure. I kinds looked for mine when I passed by that way, but he had everything tied up in plastic bags of dirt so how you supposed to tell. Flowers are flowers. Eva swore she'd know hers, but I didn't notice any commotion down there. Did his business all day. Gone next morning.

Walked away like the flowers walked. Never saw the guy before. Don't care if I ever see him again.

A brazen brother.

That's how they do us. Steal anything and everything. Stained-glass windows out the church. I worry about one of them getting into the house.

Sorry-assed junkies.                                                                                                  20

Dope turns them crazy. Knock you down as soon as look at you. Kids you've watched grow up around here. I don't believe they intend to hurt anybody, but when that sickness is down on them, my, my, my, they'll do anything. I shudder when I think of your brother crazy that way. Him hurting someone or someone hurting him. Those so-called friends of his he'd bring home. Yes ma'am and no ma'am me and all the time I know their dope eyes counting up what they could come back and steal. Tommy knew it, too. God have mercy on me for saying this about my own son, but I believe now that's why he brought some of them around. To steal from me.

Coffee's not hot. Not cold. I try the porch railing with my hand. It feels solid enough. I remember helping Wade from next door mix concrete for the porch. The good feel of doing hard work with my brothers, the three of us, Dave, Ote and me, Wade's crew sweating into the wet cement, the moment during one cold Iron City break we all felt the presence of the brother missing who should be with us building this porch for our mother. I sit on the rail anchored in our concrete. Ask about Wade.

Poor man had a tough year. Dog died, wife died, he hit that paperboy. Old Wade was way down. Said he wouldn't have made it if it hadn't been for the boy's parents. They didn't blame him. People who witnessed the accident said Wade never had a chance. Going normal speed. The boy rode his bike straight into Wade's car. And thank goodness Wade was on his way to work. So he hadn't been drinking. Wade said if the parents had blamed him for the boy's death, he wouldn't have pulled through.

Dog died. Wife died. That's a rather strange order to put things in, Mother Dear.

You know what I mean. Didn't mean one thing worse than the other or first   25 things first. You know I didn't mean anything like that.

I'm just teasing.

Teasing your fuddle-brained old mother. I know. I know most the time nobody understands what I'm talking about. Half the time don't know my own self. Pay me no mind. I didn't intend any disrespect. Wade loved Nadine dearly and misses her terribly. Loved that raggedy, stump-tailed dog, too. It was just one terrible thing after another falling on the poor man. I don't know how he survived. Thought for awhile he was going to drink himself to death. But he'd clean up every morning and drive off to work. Wade's a strong man. A good man, too, in his way.

Sounds like he was Job last year.

I prayed for him. All alone in his house. I know how that feels, rattling around in a house all by yourself.

The porch is holding up fine, isn't it. A little crack by the glider and one where   30 the steps come up but this porch will be here awhile.

Youall did quite a job.

Wade the only one who knew what he was doing. Me and Dave and Ote supplied the muscle.

It was one hot day. I was worried about youall. None of you used to working out in the broiling sun that way.

Little sweat mixed in the cement makes it stronger, last longer. Why you think the Pyramids been standing all these centuries. Good African blood gluing the stones.

What do you think about this idea going around that Egyptians were black.   35

Better late than never, Mom. I guess. Most of them a mixture of black Africans and brown Asiatics. Look at what part of the world we're talking about. Look at them today. Not exactly a matter of color, though. More about culture. People migrating and invading and mixing since the dawn of time. Everybody's a mongrel. The wonder is it's taken this long for the obvious to be said out loud. Wonder is it's 1991 and the obvious still resisted in some quarters.

I try to change the faces of the people in the Bible. I can't do it. They still look like the faces I saw in Sunday school, in the little picture books we had to study from. No black faces, except for that one dark wise man with Jesus in the manger. When I close my eyes, I still can't put black faces on the Bible people.

Well, we must of had the same books when I was in Sunday school. Maybe that's one of the reasons you had to drag me. Child abuse every Sunday morning.

Bit more child abuse might not have been a bad idea. I felt terrible knowing I was raising a bunch of little heathens.

Anyway, what I started to say is we used those same jive comic books, but the   40
Bible people never were white to me. They never had a color, really. The funny-looking robes and beards and turbans stuck in my mind. But as far as color, well it's Reverend Felder I think of when I think of Bible days and Bible stories. Him up on the pulpit of A.M.E. Zion shouting and strutting and banging his big fist. Old Frank Felder black as coal and that's the color of everything he preached. Like his voice tar-brushed the Bible. If the faces in the books weren't black it didn't matter cause black was in charge, telling the story.

I did think of Job more than once when I prayed for Wade. And I guess Job surely did have Wade's face and Wade's face, God bless him, surely isn't white. Poor man bent down under all his burdens. I needed the story of Job to understand how Wade could handle it. Strength to bear up to the worst, no matter what, has to come from somewhere. I needed God and Job. Needed them both to understand how Wade survived what he did.

You know, Mom, people look at you and what you've had to deal with and you're just as much a miracle to them as you say Wade is to you.

God doesn't give you more than you can handle.

Not everybody has that kind of god.

I worry about your brother. Where will he turn now. He's still a Muslim, isn't   45
he. He still goes by his Muslim name.

Told me not long ago he's not as active in the group as he once was. But he does pray. Not as regular as he once did, he says, but he keeps the faith.

I hope he has something. Because this last blow. The pardons board turning him down again without a hearing. He believed they'd almost have to let him go. Didn't see how they could say no.

They say whatever they want to say.

Other times he held something back. In his heart he hoped they'd give him a chance, believed he'd earned a chance, but like you say. He knows they don't have to answer to anybody. Do what they want to do. Every time but this he'd held something back to fight the no.

He's in danger now. Like when he was first locked up and wild and determined   50
to tear the prison apart with his bare hands. Worse now because he's on his own. No crew of young wild ones like him fighting back. All he has is us. And we're out

here. All he has really is the chance anybody has. To keep pushing on and try to make something of a life, whatever.

Don't think I can go with you today. I'm too shaky today to face that evil prison. Tell him I'll come next week with Denise and Chance.

Don't want to leave you if you're feeling badly.

I'll be all right here. You go talk to your brother. It's just one of those days. I'll take my pills and sit myself down awhile. I'll get it together, Babe.

Is something specific hurting.

Just one of those not so good days. I'm shaky. I have bad days every now and    55
then. Hug him for me. Tell him I love him. I'll be fine here.

I rise with her. The porch one of those quiet, extrawide, featureless elevators in the hospital where she goes Tuesdays for treatments. Below us the map of streets, veins, arteries. We wait on this floor, at this height. The porch rocks like a Ferris wheel car stopped at the apex of the ride. Perhaps the huge motor's broken. Cable snapped. Gears stripped. We wait and listen for music to drift up from the streets.

---

My brother's arms are prison arms. The kind you see in the street that clue you where a young brother's been spending his time. Bulging biceps, the rippled look of ropy sinews and cords of muscle snaking around the bones. Skinned. Excess flesh boiled away in this cauldron. Must be noisy as a construction site where the weightlifters hang out in the prison yard. Metal clanking. Grunts and groans. Iron pumped till shoulders and chests swell to the bursting point. Men fashioning arms thick enough to wrestle fate, hold off the pressure of walls and bars always bearing down. Large. Big. Nothing else to do all day. Size one measure of time served. Serious time. Bodies honed to stop-time perfection, beyond vulnerability and pain. I see them in their sun-scoured playground sprawled like dazed children.

Hot today in the visiting area, fiery heat like the day we paddled round in Wade's cement. Row row row your concrete boat. It ain't heavy, it's your brother.

Hey, bro, I'd be the last one to deny I'm fucked up. We both know good and well I've had problems all my life doing what I been supposed to do. Here I sit in this godforsaken hole if anybody needs proof I couldn't handle. Something's wrong wit me, man, but the people who runs this joint, something's real wrong wit them, too.

Pressure in my face muscles from the permanent squint I'm wearing to keep    60
sun out of my eyes. A mask of age. Forehead furrowed, cheeks tensed and hollow, eyes narrow, tiny creases incised at their corners, vision dimmed by the hazy porch of lashes and brow pouting to shade the eyes. Sun cooks my right side. I look past my brother to avoid the direct glare, beyond him to the bricks of the visiting room wall, the glass doors opening to this roofless enclosure where we sit. I listen closely but he's a blur in the center of the space across the round table where my eyes would naturally focus if I wasn't hiding from the sun. I don't need to see him. He will be wearing the same face I am. Pinched and sweaty. Older than it should be. Glazed eyes seeking something other than me to fix on, so what I say is a voice-over, as his is to me, listening while I tour the stones stacked forty feet high that surround us, the glass doors black as water, reflecting scraps of the yard.

Motherfuckers don't say shit for three months. Know I'm on pins and needles every minute of every day since I filed my commutation papers, but don't nobody say one god-blessed single solitary word good or bad for three months. I'm going crazy wit the waiting. And too scared to ask anybody what's happening cause you know how that works. Ask a question and they say *no* just to spite you, just to get you out their face. Limbo, man, for three months. Then last week I'm by the desk in the visiting room waiting for Denise and Chance and the guard at the desk hands me the phone, call for you. Lieutenant's on the line and he says to me Board turned you down. Tells me I can cancel my visit and speak to him now or check by his office later. That's it. Boom. Turned down.

Like getting hit in the chest wit a hammer. Couldn't breathe, man. Couldn't catch my breath for three days. Still can't breathe right. Felt like somebody had taken a hammer and whammed me in the heart.

No warning. No explanation. I'm standing in the visiting room trying to catch my breath and Denise and the baby be in here in a minute. Dying, man, and ready to die. My life was over soon's the lieutenant said Board turned you down.

Weird thing is the night before I had a dream. Woke me up. Couldn't go back to sleep. Dreamed I was in one the offices around here and my papers was on the desk. My papers. What I'd been waiting for all these months and finally there they sat. On top the desk and nobody else around. All I had to do was peep at the last sheet, right. There it'd be in black and white. Yes or no. Couldn't believe it be this easy. So much waiting and praying and begging and cursing boneheads out cause they wouldn't give me a clue. Wouldn't tell me nothing, nothing, and now alls I had to do was turn to the last page and I'd know.

Awful thing was I already knew the answer. Couldn't peep at the bottom sheet 65 cause I already knew. Knew in my heart so I kept standing, staring, too scared to read what I knew I'd find.

Right when the dream ended I did look. Couldn't hold out. Looked and saw *denied* stamped on the last page. Whole dream came back to me soon as I put down that phone in the visiting room. Been *denied* all along. And all along I guess I knowed.

Nothing for three months then I'm waiting for a visit from my old lady and son and I get a phone call. Turned you down. Bam. Take that. Like a hammer in my chest. Tell me that ain't evil, man. Saying no is bad enough. They don't have to treat people like dirt saying it.

My own fault I'm in here. I know I done some bad things. I'm in here, man, doing my time. Uh huh. Hard time. Lots of time for doing wrong. But they treat us like dog shit in here and that's wrong too. Guys get killed in here. Go crazy. But nobody cares. Long as they keep us locked up they can do us anyway they want. Figure we in here, so they don't owe us nothing. But wrong is wrong, ain't it. Just cause we down, is it right to keep on kicking us. Guys get meaner and crazier in here. Every day you see the ones can't take it slipping further and further off. Distance in their eyes, bro. Ain't nobody home in them eyes. They shuffle around here like ghosts. Stop speaking to people. Stop keeping theyselves clean. Gone, man. If you been around here any length of time you seen it happen to a lot of guys. You understand how easy it is to tune out and drop off the edge into your own little world. Another planet. You see why guys go off. Why they so cold and mean if they ever hit the street again.

Now our eyes are meeting. The sun's part of the meeting. A sting, a rawness you try to blink away but only make worse as sweat drips and irritates. Only one other table occupied when you sat down at yours. Now no free ones. The visiting room wall forms one end of the outdoor enclosure. Its other three walls rise forty feet at least, smooth blocks of stone topped by razor wire, a walkway, a guard tower in the far corner. At the base of the sheer stone walls fresh plantings, shrubbery dense and spiky bordering the concrete pavement. A few trees, also recently planted, have been spaced along the inside of the walls, each in a square collar of earth the size of a missing section of paving. You register these details for later. You think it will be crucial at some point to remember this yard exactly. You are uncertain why. Then, still listening to what he's saying, you realize how little of your brother's life you can share. This yard, detail by detail, is part of what you do share. You would be compromised if you come away with only a vague recollection. To fight this place, to force it to disappear, you must not miss anything. The map of it in your head makes its horror real, but also is what you must depend upon to plan an escape.

I think I'm finally beginning to understand why they so evil to us. They're 70 scared of the black man. Really scared. More scared than I ever knew. More scared than they know themselves. When I first come in the joint I knew something about the fear. Knew we had something on them. Wild as we was we didn't give them no chance to run game on us. We had learned the hard way coming up running the streets what they thought of us. Crazy killers. Animals. Dope fiends. Niggers you got to lock up or kill before they kill you. That was the deal. So we played the hand dealed us. We was stone outlaws. Fuck wit us you better be prepared to take us down cause if you don't we coming down on you. I was young and hot-blooded and that cowboy and indian gangster shit okay wit me. Bring it on. Let's git down and dirty. Rock and roll. We saw fear in their eyes. We fucked with them to keep it there. But they didn't kill me and, all praises to Allah, I didn't kill a guard. I changed. Wasn't really me in the first place. I was just playing the outlaw role I thought I needed to play to survive the joint. I changed but they stayed scared of me. And they hate me for keeping them scared. My buddy Rick. You remember Ricky from up the hill on Tokay. Took him dying to make me really understand what I'm telling you now. You know he got sick in here. Come in when I did, one of our wild bunch. Take no shit from nobody, none of us. But Rick changed, too. Wised up. Then he got sick, real sick, like I said. They wouldn't treat him. Wouldn't try to find out what was wrong. Why should they. If you scared of somebody, why you gon try and help them, fix them up, make them well so they can jump in your chest again. Huh uh. Ricky just rotted. Chased him away from the clinic. Or handed him a aspirin. You know the story. He shrunk down to nothing. Ninety-three goddamn pounds. Finally they had to stick him in the clinic. Let him rot in the clinic till his mother got to somebody and they transferred Ricky out of here and chained him to a bed in a locked ward in a real hospital and diagnosed stomach cancer. By that time Ricky too far gone to help. Drugged him up so he just nodded away. Didn't know people when they came to see him his mother said. Said he was so weak they unchained him. A cop in the room when she visited, but Ricky just laying there. A pitiful sight, plugged up to machines, not even recognizing his own mama. She was in a chair beside his bed on a Sunday she said it must have been Sunday cause she'd been there a couple hours that afternoon and she works six days a week so it must of been Sunday and Rick been sleeping like he always did the whole time so she was just sitting half sleep herself when Ricky's hand reached over and patted hers where she'd laid it on the blanket. She couldn't believe it she said. Tears started rolling down her cheeks she told me because what his touching her meant she thought was that he was ready to die. Too far gone to get better so she just knew Rick using his last strength to say good-bye.

The cop in the room had a different idea. See, he was still scared of Ricky so Ricky moving that hand meant Ricky was dangerous again. Cop jumped up and started refastening the chains.

None of it makes any goddamn sense. Who they keep. Who they let go. Never give you any reasons. They don't have to give reasons for what they do. They just do it. Denied. They stamp your papers *denied* and that's all the reason they got to give. Denied.

One the dudes they didn't deny, a white boy, he busted out of here not too long ago. Busted out and stayed out till he got tired of running and turned hisself in. Escaped the joint, man, and now they granted him a hearing with the full parole board. What kind of sense do it make.

Maybe you ought to arrange a little vacation for yourself before you apply next time.

Don't think I ain't thought about it. Been keeping my eye on that tree over there. Shimmy up, leap over to the wall. Gone. 75

Not much of a tree yet.

Yeah, well, it's still pretty scraggly. But I been watching it.

Long time before those branches grow as high as the wall. And you'd still have a pretty good leap.

Guys in here would try. Plenty of them. Scoot up that tree in a minute. Do a super monkey jump.

Branches awful skinny at the top. Even for a monkey. 80

Right. Right. Skinny enough so you get up there it'll bend to the wall. Ride it like a surfboard.

You got it all figured out, bro.

Told you I've been keeping my eye on that little tree.

This is where you and Denise were when the leaf got out.

At the table closest to the wall. In the shade. Uh huh. We was sitting there but 85 by the time that leaf blew up near the top of the wall both of us on our feet cheering. Other people had got into it, too. Saw what we was watching and that leaf had a whole lot of fans when it sailed over the wall. Would have thought people cheering for the Steelers or somebody's lottery number hit. Wasn't nothing but a leaf me and Denise noticed that had started blowing higher and higher. Each time the wind would grab it, it would circle up higher. Over in that corner like it was riding a draft or a whirlwind or some damn something keeping it up. You know how something dumb catch your attention and you can't let it go. Leaf kept spinning round and round and rising each time it spinned. Like on a yo-yo. After watching it a while you know that leaf has flying out of here on its mind. Every little whip and twist and bounce starts to matter. Before you know it you're blowing with your breath to help it over the wall and you know something inside you will be hurt if that silly leaf can't finish what it started. Whole visiting yard whooping and hollering when it finally blew over the wall.

Denise cried. And damn. It was everything I could do to keep the tears out of my eyes. Everybody in here needed that leaf to go free.

Kind of magic, man, if you was here in the yard and seen it. Know I sound dumb trying to tell you how it was. But that's how it was. Specially for Denise and me cause earlier in the visit she told me she was carrying my baby. We'd already picked names: Jazz Melody for a girl, Chance Mandela if it was a boy. Couldn't help taking the leaf as a sign.

Chance because the odds were stacked against him ever being conceived, let alone born.

Million to one, bro. And Mandela° cause Mandela's my man. You know. In the joint like me but still taking care of business.

Chance Mandela. When Mom called and told me he was born the day after 90 Mandela walked out of prison, I couldn't believe it.

Little day late rascal. But my little guy was close. Real close. Bust out right behind Nelson.

The leaf, the day, the name. Pretty amazing, little brother. Has to be a sign. Gives you something special to fight for. A son, a family. You've come too far to let this denial turn you around.

I think a lot about it. Everything I mean. When I'm alone at night in my cell. Ain't never really alone no more since they double-bunking everybody, but you know what I mean. When I think about giving up, truth is, nothing but me can pull me back from the edge. I got to do it for me. No matter how much I love Chance and Denise and Mom and youall, nothing, not all the love in the world can fill the hole that opens up when I get down, really down. Only way to save myself is to do it for me. I got to be the reason. I got to be worth saving. Can't live a life for nobody else. Nobody can live one for me. You understand what I'm saying.

I'm trying.

The leaf. I told you how it finally blowed free overtop the wall. Couldn't see it 95 no more. Denise grabbed my hand. She was crying and we was bouncing up and down. People shouting. Some even clapped. But you know something. I'm gonna tell you something I don't tell nobody when I tell about the leaf. The dumb thing blew back in here again.

---

*Mandela:* Nelson Mandela (1918–2013) was a political activist in South Africa who served twenty-seven years in prison for opposing the racially segregated form of government known as apartheid. After his release he became president of South Africa from 1994 to 1999.

# POETRY

# The Elements
of Poetry

# 16

# Reading Poetry

Chris Felver/Getty Images.

Ink runs from the corners of my mouth.
There is no happiness like mine.
I have been eating poetry.
— MARK STRAND

## READING POETRY RESPONSIVELY

Perhaps the best way to begin reading poetry responsively is not to allow yourself to be intimidated by it. Come to it, initially at least, the way you might listen to a song on the radio. You probably listen to a song several times before you hear it all, before you have a sense of how it works, where it's going, and how it gets there. You don't worry about analyzing a song when you listen to it, even though after repeated experiences with it you know and anticipate a favorite part and know, on some level, why it works for you. Give yourself a chance to respond to poetry the same way. The hardest work has already been done by the poet, so all you need to do at the start is listen for the pleasure produced by the poet's arrangement of words.

Try reading the following poem aloud. Read it aloud before you read it silently. You may stumble once or twice, but you'll make sense of it if you pay attention to its punctuation and don't stop at the end of every line where there is no punctuation. The title gives you an initial sense of what the poem is about.

Lisa Parker (b. 1972)

## Snapping Beans    1998

*For Fay Whitt*

I snapped beans into the silver bowl
that sat on the splintering slats
of the porchswing between my grandma and me.
I was home for the weekend,
from school, from the North,                                                5
Grandma hummed "What A Friend We Have In Jesus"
as the sun rose, pushing its pink spikes
through the slant of cornstalks,
through the fly-eyed mesh of the screen.
We didn't speak until the sun overcame                                     10
the feathered tips of the cornfield
and Grandma stopped humming. I could feel
the soft gray of her stare
against the side of my face
when she asked, *How's school a-goin'?*                                     15
I wanted to tell her about my classes,
the revelations by book and lecture,
as real as any shout of faith
and potent as a swig of strychnine.
She reached the leather of her hand                                         20
over the bowl and cupped
my quivering chin; the slick smooth of her palm
held my face the way she held tomatoes
under the spigot, careful not to drop them,
and I wanted to tell her                                                    25
about the nights I cried into the familiar
heartsick panels of the quilt she made me,
wishing myself home on the evening star.
I wanted to tell her
the evening star was a planet,                                             30
that my friends wore noserings and wrote poetry
about sex, about alcoholism, about Buddha.
I wanted to tell her how my stomach burned
acidic holes at the thought of speaking in class,
speaking in an accent, speaking out of turn,                              35
how I was tearing, splitting myself apart
with the slow-simmering guilt of being happy
despite it all.
I said, *School's fine.*
We snapped beans into the silver bowl between us                          40
and when a hickory leaf, still summer green,
skidded onto the porchfront,
Grandma said,
*It's funny how things blow loose like that.*

**CONSIDERATIONS FOR CRITICAL THINKING AND WRITING**

1. FIRST RESPONSE. Describe the speaker's feelings about starting a life at college. How do those feelings compare with your own experiences?

2. How does the grandmother's world differ from the speaker's at school? What details especially reveal those differences?

3. Discuss the significance of the grandmother's response to the hickory leaf in line 44. How do you read the last line?

The next poem creates a different kind of mood. The title refers to something you might have seen or experienced when a car battery dies: a mechanic or someone resourceful enough to keep jumper cables in his or her car "jump starts" the car with the dead battery.

## LINDA PASTAN (B. 1932)

### *Jump Cabling*  1984

| | | |
|---|---|---|
| When our cars | touched | |
| When you lifted the hood | of mine | |
| To see the intimate workings | underneath, | |
| When we were bound | together | |
| By a pulse of pure | energy, | 5 |
| When my car like the | princess | |
| In the tale woke with a | start, | |
| I thought why not ride the rest of the way together? | | |

The poem's most striking feature is the layout of the lines. Try reading it out loud. Did you automatically pause in the first line when you saw the long, blank space between "cars" and "touched"? Did you pause again after "touched" before going on to the next line? The poem forces the reader into an unusual sense of rhythm, for starters. There are hesitations in it, just as cars that are being jump-started sometimes take a few revs of the engine before they catch. The poem is only about cars on the surface level, though. We are encouraged to think of a relationship right away. You might do well to ask some questions about the relationship: what characterizes it, primarily? What is the "pulse of pure energy" (l. 5) that binds them? Do you see the relationship as positive and equal since it builds to the word "together"? Are you troubled by the connection to a fairy-tale princess who wakes up with a start because those stories tend to give men all the power? Does the question mark at the end unsettle the poem's conclusion, or make it seem more casual than it would be if it were a declarative statement?

What is most important about your initial readings of a poem is that you ask questions. If you read responsively, you'll find yourself asking all kinds of questions about the words, descriptions, sounds, and structure of a poem. The specifics of those questions will be generated by the particular poem. We don't, for example, ask why "Jump Cabling" is such a depressing poem because it is not, but it is worth asking what kind of tone is established by the gaps in lines 1–7: is the speaker at first hesitant? The "intimate workings underneath" her hood sounds somewhat sexual, and it could be read that way, but what about the intimate workings of her mind? Do we glimpse the speaker's complex psychology? The remaining chapters in this part of the book will help you formulate and answer questions about a variety of specific elements in poetry, such as speaker, image, metaphor, symbol, rhyme, and rhythm. For the moment, however, read the following poem several times and note your response at different points in the poem. Then write down a half-dozen or so questions about what produces your response to the poem. To answer questions, it's best to know first what the questions are, and that's what the rest of this chapter is about.

## JOHN UPDIKE  (1932–2009)

### *Dog's Death*   1969

She must have been kicked unseen or brushed by a car.
Too young to know much, she was beginning to learn
To use the newspapers spread on the kitchen floor
And to win, wetting there, the words, "Good dog! Good dog!"

We thought her shy malaise was a shot reaction.                                    5
The autopsy disclosed a rupture in her liver.
As we teased her with play, blood was filling her skin
And her heart was learning to lie down forever.

Monday morning, as the children were noisily fed
And sent to school, she crawled beneath the youngest's bed.        10
We found her twisted and limp but still alive.
In the car to the vet's, on my lap, she tried

To bite my hand and died. I stroked her warm fur
And my wife called in a voice imperious with tears.
Though surrounded by love that would have upheld her,               15
Nevertheless she sank and, stiffening, disappeared.

Back home, we found that in the night her frame,
Drawing near to dissolution, had endured the shame
Of diarrhoea and had dragged across the floor
To a newspaper carelessly left there. *Good dog.*                            20

   Here's a simple question to get started with your own questions: What would the poem's effect have been if Updike had titled it "Good Dog" instead of "Dog's Death"?

# THE PLEASURE OF WORDS

The impulse to create and appreciate poetry is as basic to human experience as language itself. Although no one can point to the precise origins of poetry, it is one of the most ancient of the arts, because it has existed ever since human beings discovered pleasure in language. The ceremonies of peoples without written languages suggest that the earliest cultures incorporated rhythmic patterns of words into their rituals. These chants, very likely accompanied by the music of a simple beat and the dance of a measured step, expressed what people regarded as significant and memorable in their lives. They echoed the concerns of the chanters and the listeners by chronicling acts of bravery, fearsome foes, natural disasters, mysterious events, births, deaths, and whatever else brought people pain or joy, bewilderment or revelation. Later cultures, such as the ancient Greeks, made poetry an integral part of religion.

Thus, from its very beginnings, poetry has been associated with what has mattered most to people. These concerns — whether natural or supernatural — can, of course, be expressed without vivid images, rhythmic patterns, and pleasing sounds, but human beings have always sensed a magic in words that goes beyond rational, logical understanding. Poetry is not simply a method of communication; it is a unique experience in itself.

What is special about poetry? What makes it valuable? Why should we read it? How is reading it different from reading prose? To begin with, poetry pervades our world in a variety of forms, ranging from advertising jingles to song lyrics. These may seem to be a long way from the chants heard around a primitive campfire, but they serve some of the same purposes. Like poems printed in a magazine or book, ancient chants, catchy jingles, and popular songs attempt to stir the imagination through the carefully measured use of words.

Although reading poetry usually makes more demands than reading a magazine or newspaper, the appreciation of poetry comes naturally enough to anyone who enjoys playing with words. Play is an important element of poetry. Consider, for example, how the following words appeal to the children who gleefully chant them in playgrounds:

> I scream, you scream
> We all scream
> For ice cream.

These lines are an exuberant evocation of the joy of ice cream. Indeed, chanting the words turns out to be as pleasurable as eating ice cream. In poetry, the expression of the idea is as important as the idea expressed.

But is "I scream . . ." poetry? Some poets and literary critics would say that it certainly is one kind of poem because the children who chant it experience some of the pleasures of poetry in its measured beat, repeated sounds, and the pun that connects the first two and last two words. However, other poets and critics would define poetry more narrowly and insist, for a variety of reasons, that this isn't true poetry but merely ***doggerel***, a term used for lines whose subject matter is trite and whose rhythm and sounds are monotonously heavy-handed.

Although probably no one would argue that "I scream . . ." is a great poem, it does contain some poetic elements that appeal, at the very least, to children. Does that make it poetry? The answer depends on one's definition, but poetry has a way of breaking loose from definitions. Because there are nearly as many definitions of poetry as there are poets, Edwin Arlington Robinson's succinct observations are useful: "[P]oetry has two outstanding characteristics. One is that it is undefinable. The other is that it is eventually unmistakable."

This comment places more emphasis on how a poem affects a reader than on how a poem is defined. By characterizing poetry as "undefinable," Robinson acknowledges that it can include many different purposes, subjects, emotions, styles, and forms. What effect does the following poem have on you?

## Gregory Corso (1930–2001)

### *I am 25*  1955

With a love a madness for Shelley
Chatterton      Rimbaud
and the needy-yap of my youth
          has gone from ear to ear:
     I HATE OLD POETMEN!                                              5
Especially old poetmen who retract
who consult other old poetmen
who speak their youth in whispers,
saying:—I did those then
          but that was then                                          10
          that was then—
O I would quiet old men
say to them:—I am your friend
          what you once were, thru me
          you'll be again—                                           15
then at night in the confidence of their homes
rip out their apology-tongues
          and steal their poems.

## A SAMPLE CLOSE READING

### *An Explication of "I am 25"*

After you've read a poem two or three times, a deeper, closer reading — line by line, word by word, syllable by syllable — will help you discover even more about the poem. Ask yourself: What happens (or does not happen) in the poem? What are the poem's central ideas? How do the poem's words, images, and sounds, for example, contribute to its meaning? What is the poem's overall tone? How is the poem put together?

Before you dive into the poem, take a moment to appreciate the way it looks. Your eyes are probably drawn to the capitalized line "I HATE OLD POETMEN!" This shouted line, complete with an exclamation point, probably gives you an immediate sense of the poem's tone: it's either anger or humor. We often associate poetry with love — the opposite emotion of hatred. This poem derives its power from its antagonism, from its opposition, to some sort of poetry. How seriously are we to take this line, though? "Poetmen" — is that even a word? The speaker could have said "poets." Poetmen — an invented word, or *neologism*, he repeats twice in the next two lines — makes those poets sound silly. There is undoubtedly a violent undercurrent to the poem, but when deciding on the poem's tone, humor might be a better bet than anger initially. It could, of course, be both.

Other visual effects of the poem might strike you as well. There is a gap in the middle of the second line, creating white space on the page. There are also a few gaps on the left-hand side of the poem: some lines are indented, and not in a way that forms a pattern. There are also dashes surrounding some of the lines, and capital letters at the beginning of lines are irregularly used. It is not a tidy poem: it looks ragged; it refuses to be contained. You might begin to think that it is a poem about rebelliousness even before you really look into its content.

So let's dive in. The prominent line we lifted out is one about hatred, but the poem leads with love, then corrects itself: "With a love a madness for Shelley. . . ." Before we get to the identity of Shelley, consider what the **speaker** has done. (Note that we refer to the speaker of the poem just as we refer to the narrator of a story: it's misguided to automatically associate these voices with the author.) The speaker corrects himself: "With a love for Shelley . . . no, that's not right: with a *madness* for Shelley. . . ." Madness is stronger than love, in a way: to love Shelley is perhaps to admire him, to appreciate him from a distance. "Madness" connotes obsession: "I cannot get enough of Shelley. I am crazy for Shelley. Love is too mild a word for what I feel for Shelley." But since the speaker started with love, he feels the need to hang onto it: he's someone who wants to get the words right, but who is also aware he makes mistakes and does not erase them. The making of poetry is a messy process, he seems to say: here's my mess.

Alright, so who are Shelley, Chatterton, and Rimbaud? Poets, of course, but more particularly poets who died young (at the ages of 29, 17, and 37, respectively). Age is on the speaker's mind: the title states his age overtly and it is a declaration of the most salient feature of his identity: I am a young poetman, he declares. Here are other young poetmen from the past, and I am mad for them, meaning I admire their vision, their work, their spirit. If we are willing to do even a little reading into the lives of Percy Shelley, Thomas Chatterton, and Arthur Rimbaud, we will learn that they all lived passionately, that they were interested in the extreme emotions associated with what might be called the life force. They were also so passionate that art was their only vehicle to express it, and like many musicians you may be familiar with, they lived fast and burned out young. Chatterton died by suicide. Rimbaud had a torrid affair with another poet, Paul Verlaine, who shot him in the wrist during a drunken lovers' quarrel. Shelley drowned under suspicious circumstances after leading a chaotic life, including the apparently suicidal drowning of his first wife who had been pregnant at the time. In summary, these models represent the kind of "madness" that the speaker feels for them. If we were to read their work, we would perhaps understand even more why the speaker of Corso's poem was "mad" for them. (See Shelley's "Ozymandias," p. 945.)

The tension in the poem is not what we might expect, that a young poet has no respect for the poetic tradition and wants to do his own thing. Quite the contrary: the poets he loves are from the eighteenth and nineteenth centuries; Corso is writing in 1955. He hates a certain type of old poetman, though he doesn't name them:

Especially old poetmen who retract
who consult other old poetmen
who speak their youth in whispers,
saying: — I did those then
    but that was then
    that was then —

These old poetmen can be understood through their actions: they retract, they consult others, they speak in whispers. They sound, in short, like librarians or cautious lawyers more than what the speaker wants a poet to be: risky, dangerous, passionate, and unapologetic about the power of youth. Why apologize for what you did when you were younger? These old poetmen pretend they are wise and no longer capable of handling the wild energies of their youth. What they really are, the speaker implies, is boring.

This 25-year-old speaker must do something then. It is a sneaky response: he seems to repress the line that he wants to shout — I HATE OLD POETMEN! — in favor of an approach that will allow him to conquer these old poetmen without directly battling them. He begins his next sentence with an antiquated poetic word: "O." This is known as the "vocative O": it indicates that the speaker is addressing someone or something directly. The reader is thus involved: we are drawn in as we would be during an anthem ("O say can you see . . ."). The speaker is letting us in on his plan and implicating us. He writes a little poem that is parallel to the ones the old poetmen whisper. Note the similarities between what they say and what he says:

  — I did those then
  but that was then
  that was then —

and
  — I am your friend
  what you once were, thru me
  you'll be again —

They're both surrounded by dashes; they use simple, almost monosyllabic language; and they even rhyme! This is how the speaker will get the old poetmen to take him into their confidence: by imitating them. He knows they are vain: he promises that their spirit will be reborn in him, a young poet, and they will thus be comforted and "quieted."

And here is where the speaker asserts himself: "[T]hen at night in the confidence of their homes / rip out their apology-tongues / and steal their poems." This is violent, criminal behavior! Ripping out tongues? Stealing poems? Our young poet sounds like a burglar and a torturer rather than someone who likes to mess around with words. We must understand, though, the degree to which poetry relies on *figurative language*. Essentially, figurative language is not literal. We do not think the speaker actually wants to do bodily harm to these older poets, but rather that he wants to take away their power — their voice — and replace it with his own. "Steal" is a little more ambiguous: does he want to plagiarize their poems? Or does he want to take them away and destroy them or maybe even just hide them? He seems capable of writing poetry like theirs as he demonstrates in his short three-line *parody*, but he has no respect for them. He also seems to be having a wonderful time writing his own original poems, even inventing words like "poetmen" and "needy-yap" or spelling "thru" in an inventive way. It's a poem about rebelliousness, as we originally said: if we've been following the speaker's logic and his tone, this stealing probably doesn't involve taking someone else's work and claiming it for his own. This stealing is another enactment of power: everything in the poem suggests that's what he wants. He steals their poems not to claim them for his own, but to show that he can. He is 25; he believes that his youth implies strength, confidence, brashness, and freedom from doubt or regret. Yes, I'm stealing your poem, old poetman: what are you going to do about it?

All of this careful unpacking is what the poem demands. You could accurately say, "Gregory Corso's 'I am 25' is about a young poet who struggles to assert his voice in a world dominated by old poets." As you can see, reading a description of what happens in a poem is not the same as experiencing a poem. The exuberance of "I scream (for ice cream)" and the somewhat sinister promise of violence in "I am 25" are in the hearing or reading rather than in the retelling. A *paraphrase* is a prose restatement of the central ideas of a poem in your own language. Consider the difference between the following poem and the paraphrase that follows it. What is missing from the paraphrase?

## ROBERT FRANCIS (1901–1987)

### *Catch*   1950

Two boys uncoached are tossing a poem together,
Overhand, underhand, backhand, sleight of hand, every hand,
Teasing with attitudes, latitudes, interludes, altitudes,
High, make him fly off the ground for it, low, make him stoop,
Make him scoop it up, make him as-almost-as-possible miss it,
Fast, let him sting from it, now, now fool him slowly,
Anything, everything tricky, risky, nonchalant,
Anything under the sun to outwit the prosy,

5

Over the tree and the long sweet cadence down,
Over his head, make him scramble to pick up the meaning,                    10
And now, like a posy, a pretty one plump in his hands.

Paraphrase: A poet's relationship to a reader is similar to a game of catch. The poem, like a ball, should be pitched in a variety of ways to challenge and create interest. Boredom and predictability must be avoided if the game is to be engaging and satisfying.

A paraphrase can help us achieve a clearer understanding of a poem, but, unlike a poem, it misses all the sport and fun. It is the poem that "outwit[s] the prosy" because the poem serves as an example of what it suggests poetry should be. Moreover, the two players — the poet and the reader — are "uncoached." They know how the game is played, but their expectations do not preclude spontaneity and creativity or their ability to surprise and be surprised. The solid pleasure of the workout — of reading poetry — is the satisfaction derived from exercising your imagination and intellect.

That pleasure is worth emphasizing. Poetry uses language to move and delight even when it threatens to rip out the tongues of old men. The pleasure is in having the poem work its spell on us. For that to happen, it is best to relax and enjoy poetry rather than worry about definitions of it. Pay attention to what the poet throws you. We read poems for emotional and intellectual discovery — to feel and to experience something about the world and ourselves. The ideas in poetry — what can be paraphrased in prose — are important, but the real value of a poem consists in the words that work their magic by allowing us to feel, see, and be more than we were before. Perhaps the best way to approach a poem is similar to what Francis's "Catch" implies: expect to be surprised, stay on your toes, and concentrate on the delivery.

## A SAMPLE STUDENT ANALYSIS

### *Tossing Metaphors Together in Robert Francis's "Catch"*

The following sample paper on Robert Francis's "Catch" was written in response to an assignment that asked students to discuss the use of metaphor in the poem. Notice that Chris Leggett's paper is clearly focused and well organized. His discussion of the use of metaphor in the poem stays on track from beginning to end without any detours concerning unrelated topics (for a definition of *metaphor*, see p. 598). His title draws on the central metaphor of the poem, and he organizes the paper around four key words used in the poem: "attitudes, latitudes, interludes, altitudes." These constitute the heart of the paper's four substantive paragraphs, and they are effectively framed by introductory and concluding paragraphs. Moreover, the transitions between paragraphs clearly indicate that the student writer was not merely tossing a paper together.

Chris Leggett

Professor Lyles

English 203-1

9 November 2023

Tossing Metaphors Together in Robert Francis's "Catch"

The word *catch* is an attention getter. It usually means something
is about to be hurled at someone and that he or she is expected to
catch it. *Catch* can also signal a challenge to another player if the toss
is purposefully difficult. Robert Francis, in his poem "Catch," uses the
extended metaphor of two boys playing catch to explore the considerations
a poet makes when "tossing a poem together" (line 1). Line 3 of "Catch"
enumerates these considerations metaphorically as "attitudes, latitudes,
interludes, [and] altitudes." While regular prose is typically straightforward
and easily understood, poetry usually takes great effort to understand
and appreciate. To exemplify this, Francis presents the reader not with a
normal game of catch with the ball flying back and forth in a repetitive and
predictable fashion, but with a physically challenging game in which one
must concentrate, scramble, and exert oneself to catch the ball, as one must
stretch the intellect to truly grasp a poem.

The first consideration mentioned by Francis is attitude. Attitude,
when applied to the game of catch, indicates the ball's pitch in flight—
upward, downward, or straight. It could also describe the players' attitudes
toward each other or toward the game in general. Below this literal level lies
*attitude*'s meaning in relation to poetry. Attitude in this case represents a
poem's tone. A poet may "Teas[e] with attitudes" (3) by experimenting with
different tones to achieve the desired mood. The underlying tone of "Catch"
is a playful one, set and reinforced by the use of a game. This playfulness
is further reinforced by such words and phrases as "[t]easing" (3), "outwit"
(8), and "fool him" (6).

Considered also in the metaphorical game of catch is latitude, which,
when applied to the game, suggests the range the object may be thrown—
how high, how low, or how far. Poetic latitude, along similar lines, concerns
a poem's breadth, or the scope of topic. Taken one level further, latitude
suggests freedom from normal restraints or limitations, indicating the ability

---

Exploration of the meaning of the word *catch*.

Thesis statement identifying purpose of poem's metaphors.

Reference to specific language in poem, around which the paper is organized.

Introductory analysis of the poem's purpose.

Analysis of the meaning of *attitude* in the poem.

Discussion of how the attitude metaphor contributes to poem's tone.

Analysis of the meaning of *latitude* in the poem.

to go outside the norm to find originality of expression. The entire game of catch described in Francis's poem reaches outside the normal expectations of something being merely tossed back and forth in a predictable manner. The ball is thrown in almost every conceivable fashion, "Overhand, underhand . . . every hand" (2). Other terms describing the throws—such as "tricky," "risky," "Fast," "slowly," and "Anything under the sun" (6-8)—express endless latitude for avoiding predictability in Francis's game of catch and metaphorically in writing poetry.

> **Discussion of how the latitude metaphor contributes to the poem's scope and message.**

During a game of catch the ball may be thrown at different intervals, establishing a steady rhythm or a broken, irregular one. Other intervening features, such as the field being played on or the weather, could also affect the game. These features of the game are alluded to in the poem by the use of the word *interludes*. *Interlude* in the poetic sense represents the poem's form, which can similarly establish or diminish rhythm or enhance meaning. Lines 6 and 9, respectively, show a broken and a flowing rhythm. Line 6 begins rapidly as a hard toss that stings the catcher's hand is described. The rhythm of the line is immediately slowed, however, by the word "now" followed by a comma, followed by the rest of the line. In contrast, line 9 flows smoothly as the reader visualizes the ball flying over the tree and sailing downward. The words chosen for this line function perfectly. The phrase "the long sweet cadence down" establishes a sweet rhythm that reads smoothly and rolls off the tongue easily. The choice of diction not only affects the poem's rhythmic flow but also establishes through connotative language the various levels at which the poem can be understood, represented in "Catch" as altitude.

> **Analysis of the meaning of *interlude* in the poem.**

> **Discussion of how the interlude metaphor contributes to the poem's form and rhythm.**

While *altitudes* when referring to the game of catch means how high an object is thrown, in poetry it could refer to the level of diction, lofty or down-to-earth, formal or informal. It suggests also the levels at which a poem can be comprehended, the literal as well as the interpretive. In Francis's game of catch, the ball is thrown high to make the player reach, low to "make him stoop" (4), or "Over his head [to] make him scramble" (10), implying that the player should have to exert himself to catch it. So too, then, should the reader of poetry put great effort into understanding the full meaning of a poem. Francis exemplifies this consideration in writing poetry by giving "Catch" not only an enjoyable literal meaning concerning the

> **Analysis of the meaning of *altitudes* in the poem.**

Leggett 3

game of catch, but also a rich metaphorical meaning—reflecting the process of writing poetry. Francis uses several phrases and words with multiple meanings. The phrase "tossing a poem together" (1) can be understood as tossing something back and forth or the process of constructing a poem. While "prosy" (8) suggests prose itself, it also means the mundane or the ordinary. In the poem's final line the word *posy* of course represents a flower, while it is also a variant of the word *poesy*, meaning poetry, or the practice of composing poetry.

> Discussion of how the altitude metaphor contributes to the poem's literal and symbolic meanings, with references to specific language.

Francis effectively describes several considerations to be taken in writing poetry in order to "outwit the prosy" (8). His use of the extended metaphor in "Catch" shows that a poem must be unique, able to be comprehended on multiple levels, and a challenge to the reader. The various rhythms in the lines of "Catch" exemplify the ideas they express. While achieving an enjoyable poem on the literal level, Francis has also achieved a rich metaphorical meaning. The poem offers a good workout both physically and intellectually.

> Conclusion summarizing ideas explored in paper.

Leggett 4

Work Cited

Francis, Robert. "Catch." *The Compact Bedford Introduction to Literature,*
      edited by Michael Meyer and D. Quentin Miller, 13th ed., Bedford/
      St. Martin's, 2024, pp. 531–32.

Before beginning your own writing assignment on poetry, you should review Chapter 43, "Writing about Literature," which provides a step-by-step overview of how to choose a topic, develop a thesis, and organize various types of writing assignments. If you are using outside sources in your essay, you should make sure that you are familiar with the conventional documentation procedures described in Chapter 44, "The Literary Research Paper."

How does the speaker's description in Francis's "Catch" of what readers might expect from reading poetry compare with the speaker's expectations concerning fiction in the next poem by Jane Hirshfield?

## JANE HIRSHFIELD (B. 1953)

### *This Morning, I Wanted Four Legs*   2017

Nothing on two legs weighs much,
or can.
An elephant, a donkey, even a cookstove—
those legs, a person could stand on.
Two legs pitch you forward.                                          5
Two legs tire.
They look for another two legs to be with,
to move one set forward to music
while letting the other move back.
They want to carve into a tree trunk:                               10
*2gether 4ever.*
Nothing on two legs can bark,
can whinny or chuff.
Tonight, though, everything's different.
Tonight I want wheels.                                              15

Desire is at the heart of much of literature. One could argue that desires are what make us human, and learning how to become fully human involves a choice: we either reach for that which we desire or accept that we can't have it. The title of this poem sounds like a child's fantasy: I wanted four legs. I wanted to be able to fly. I wanted to go through my day without worrying. All of these traits are, of course, characteristics of certain animals.

Humans *are* animals, though. We're animals who walk on two legs. We're animals who desire things and can articulate that desire in language. That is to say, we're animals capable of writing poetry, poetry that expresses our animal needs in complex human ways. At first this speaker wants four legs like "An elephant, a donkey" but then we're spun around as to the speaker's intent: "a cookstove." Yes, those have legs, too.

We might think we get it: the speaker wants stability. She goes into what's wrong with having only two legs: "Two legs pitch you forward. / Two legs tire." These certainly make it sound easier to have four legs, but she seems to be aware that we can't become elephants, donkeys, or cookstoves just by wishing it so. Maybe that's not it, either, or all of it. Two legs want to dance with another two legs. We want companionship and partnership. The speaker puns on the graffiti we see carved into a tree trunk: "*2gether 4ever.*" Here two unstable twos become a solid four, one that is eternal. That's a little bit of a fantasy, too. Humans are the animals who know that we're not immortal, even if we believe love is.

So maybe it's better to be a two-legged human who knows love than to be a lower animal. So what if we can't "bark . . . whinny or chuff"? We have love. We have language.

But we also have desire, and that is something that doesn't go away easily. This morning the speaker wanted four legs. She seems to have resolved that, but tonight she wants wheels. It's possible that humans are animals that are destined never to be satisfied.

What is "unmistakable" in poetry (to use Robinson's term again) is its intense, concentrated use of language — its emphasis on individual words to convey meanings, experiences, emotions, and effects. Poets never simply process words; they savor them. Words in poems frequently create their own tastes, textures, scents, sounds, and shapes. They often seem more sensuous than ordinary language, and readers usually sense that a word has been hefted before making its way into a poem. Although poems are crafted differently from the ways a painting, sculpture, or musical composition is created, in each form of art the creator delights in the medium. Poetry is carefully orchestrated so that the words work together as elements in a structure to sustain close, repeated readings. The words are chosen to interact with one another to create the maximum desired effect, whether the purpose is to capture a mood or feeling, create a vivid experience, express a point of view, narrate a story, or portray a character. Some poems may also have a carefully constructed *volta*, or turn. The turn in a poem is a discernible shift or movement when the tone or rhetoric shifts. In fact, the word *verse*, a term used for lines composed in a measured rhythmical pattern, which are often, but not necessarily, rhymed, is related to the Italian term *volta*. Verse implies a turn, as in the word "reverse."

Here is a poem that looks quite different from most verse.

ROBERT MORGAN (B. 1944)

## *Mountain Graveyard*   1979

*for the author of "Slow Owls"*

*Spore Prose*

| | |
|---|---|
| stone | notes |
| slate | tales |
| sacred | cedars |
| heart | earth |
| asleep | please |
| hated | death |

Though unconventional in its appearance, this is unmistakably poetry because of its concentrated use of language. The poem demonstrates how serious play with words can lead to some remarkable discoveries. At first glance "Mountain Graveyard" may seem intimidating. What, after all, does this list of words add up to? How is it in any sense a poetic use of language? But if the words are examined closely, it is not difficult to see how they work. The wordplay here is literally in the form of a game. Morgan uses a series of *anagrams* (words made from the letters of other words, such as *read* and *dare*) to evoke feelings about death. "Mountain Graveyard" is one of several poems that Morgan has called "Spore Prose" (another anagram) because he finds in individual words the seeds of poetry. He wrote the poem in honor of the fiftieth birthday of another poet, Jonathan Williams, the author of "Slow Owls," whose title is also an anagram.

The title, "Mountain Graveyard," indicates the poem's setting, which is also the context in which the individual words in the poem interact to provide a larger meaning. Morgan's discovery of the words on the stones of a grave-yard is more than just clever. The observations he makes among the silent graves go beyond the curious pleasure a reader experiences in finding that the words *sacred cedars*, referring to evergreens common in cemeteries, consist of the same letters. The surprise and delight of realizing the connection between *heart* and *earth* are tempered by the more sober recognition that everyone's story ultimately ends in the ground. The hope that the dead are merely asleep is expressed with a plea that is answered grimly by a hatred of death's finality.

Little is told in this poem. There is no way of knowing who is buried or who is looking at the graves, but the emotions of sadness, hope, and pain are unmistakable — and are conveyed in fewer than half the words of this sentence. Morgan takes words that initially appear to be a dead, prosaic list and energizes their meanings through imaginative juxtapositions.

The following poem also involves a startling discovery about words. With the peculiar title "l(a," the poem cannot be read aloud, so there is no sound, but is there sense, a ***theme*** — a central idea or meaning — in the poem?

## E. E. CUMMINGS (1894–1962)

### *l(a*   1958

l(a

le
af
fa
ll
s)
one
l
iness

Bettmann/Getty Images.

### CONSIDERATIONS FOR CRITICAL THINKING AND WRITING

1. FIRST RESPONSE. Discuss the connection between what appears inside and outside the parentheses in this poem.

2. What does Cummings draw attention to by breaking up the words? How do this strategy and the poem's overall shape contribute to its theme?

3. Which seems more important in this poem — what is expressed or the way it is expressed?

Although "Mountain Graveyard" and "l(a" do not resemble the kind of verse that readers might recognize immediately as poetry on a page, both are actually a very common type of poem, called the **lyric**, usually a brief poem that expresses the personal emotions and thoughts of a single speaker. Lyrics are often written in the first person, but sometimes — as in "Mountain Graveyard" and "l(a" — no speaker is specified. Lyrics present a subjective mood, emotion, or idea. Very often they are about love or death, but almost any subject or experience that evokes some intense emotional response can be found in lyrics. In addition to brevity and emotional intensity, lyrics are also frequently characterized by their musical qualities. The word *lyric* derives from the Greek word *lyre*, meaning a musical instrument that originally accompanied the singing of a lyric. Lyric poems can be organized in a variety of ways, such as the sonnet, elegy, and ode (see Chapter 23), but it is enough to point out here that lyrics are an extremely popular kind of poetry with writers and readers.

The following anonymous lyric was found in a sixteenth-century manuscript.

## Anonymous

### *Western Wind*   ca. 1500

Western wind, when wilt thou blow,
The small rain down can rain?
Christ, if my love were in my arms,
And I in my bed again!

This speaker's intense longing for their lover is characteristic of lyric poetry. They impatiently address the western wind that brings spring to England and could make it possible for them to be reunited with the person they love. We do not know the details of these lovers' lives because this poem focuses on the speaker's emotion. We do not learn why the lovers are apart or if they will be together again. We don't even know the speaker's gender. But those issues are not really important. The poem gives us a feeling rather than a story.

A poem that tells a story is called a **narrative poem**. Narrative poetry may be short or very long. An **epic**, for example, is a long narrative poem on a serious subject chronicling heroic deeds and important events. Among the most famous epics are Homer's *Iliad* and *Odyssey*, the Old English *Beowulf*, Dante's *Divine Comedy*, and John Milton's *Paradise Lost*. More typically, however, narrative poems are considerably shorter, as is the case with the following poem, which tells the story of a child's memory of her father.

**WHEN I WRITE** "There are lots of things that are going on . . . that could set you on fire if you gave them a chance. Poetry isn't only about what you feel, it's about what you think, and about capturing the way the world exists in one particular moment." — REGINA BARRECA

Regina Barreca (b. 1957)

## *Nighttime Fires*   1986

Nicolette Theriault.

When I was five in Louisville
we drove to see nighttime fires. Piled seven of us,
all pajamas and running noses, into the Olds,
drove fast toward smoke. It was after my father
lost his job, so not getting up in the morning          5
gave him time: awake past midnight, he read old
        newspapers
with no news, tried crosswords until he split the pencil
between his teeth, mad. When he heard
the wolf whine of the siren, he woke my mother,
and she pushed and shoved                                10
us all into waking. Once roused we longed for burnt wood
and a smell of flames high into the pines. My old man liked
driving to rich neighborhoods best, swearing in a good mood
as he followed fire engines that snaked like dragons
and split the silent streets. It was festival, carnival.    15

If there were a Cadillac or any car
in a curved driveway, my father smiled a smile
from a secret, brittle heart.
His face lit up in the heat given off by destruction
like something was being made, or was being set right.    20
I bent my head back to see where sparks
ate up the sky. My father who never held us
would take my hand and point to falling cinders that
covered the ground like snow, or, excited, show us
the swollen collapse of a staircase. My mother               25
watched my father, not the house. She was happy
only when we were ready to go, when it was finally over
and nothing else could burn.
Driving home, she would sleep in the front seat
as we huddled behind. I could see his quiet face in the      30
rearview mirror, eyes like hallways filled with smoke.

This narrative poem could have been a short story if the poet had wanted to say more about the "brittle heart" of this unemployed man whose daughter so vividly remembers the desperate pleasure he took in watching fire consume other people's property. Indeed, a reading of William Faulkner's famous short story "Barn Burning" suggests how such a character can be further developed and how his child responds to him. The similarities between Faulkner's angry character and the poem's father, whose "eyes [are] like hallways filled with smoke," are coincidental, but the characters' sense of "something . . . being set right" by flames is worth comparing. Although we do not know everything about this man and his family, we have a much firmer sense of their story than we do of the story of the couple in "Western Wind."

Although narrative poetry is still written, short stories and novels have largely replaced the long narrative poem. Lyric poems tend to be the predominant type of poetry today. Regardless of whether a poem is a narrative or a lyric, however, the strategies for reading it are somewhat different from those for reading prose. Try these suggestions for approaching poetry.

---

### Suggestions for Approaching Poetry

1. Assume that it will be necessary to read a poem more than once. Give yourself a chance to become familiar with what the poem has to offer. Like a piece of music, a poem becomes more pleasurable with each encounter.

2. Pay attention to the title; it will often provide a helpful context for the poem and serve as an introduction to it. Robert Frost's "Design" (p. 874) announces its subject; the poem explores examples.

3. As you read the poem for the first time, avoid becoming entangled in words or lines that you don't understand. Instead, give yourself a chance to take in the entire poem before attempting to resolve problems encountered along the way.

4. On a second reading, identify any words or passages that you don't understand. Look up words you don't know; these might include names, places, historical and mythical references, or anything else that is unfamiliar to you.

5. Read the poem aloud (or perhaps have a friend read it to you). You'll probably discover that some puzzling passages suddenly fall into place when you hear them. You'll find that nothing helps, though, if the poem is read in an artificial, exaggerated manner. Read in as natural a voice as possible, with slight pauses at line breaks. Silent reading is preferable to imposing a te-tumpty-te-tum reading on a good poem.

6. Attend to the punctuation. Poems use punctuation marks — in addition to the space on the page — as signals for readers. Be especially careful not to assume that the end of a line marks the end of a sentence, unless it is concluded by punctuation.

7. Paraphrase the poem to determine whether you understand what happens in it. As you work through each line of the poem, a paraphrase will help you to see which words or passages need further attention.

8. Try to get a sense of who is speaking and what the setting or situation is. Don't assume that the speaker is the author; often it is a created character.

9. Assume that each element in the poem has a purpose. Try to explain how the elements of the poem work together.

10. Be generous. Be willing to entertain perspectives, values, experiences, and subjects that you might not agree with or approve of. Even if baseball bores you, you should be able to comprehend its imaginative use in Francis's "Catch."

11. Try developing a coherent approach to the poem that helps you to shape a discussion of the text. See Chapter 42, "Critical Strategies for Reading," to review formalist, biographical, historical, psychological, feminist, and other possible critical approaches.

12. Don't expect to produce a definitive reading. Many poems do not resolve all the ideas, issues, or tensions in them, and so it is not always possible to drive their meaning into an absolute corner. Your reading will explore rather than define the poem. Poems are not trophies to be stuffed and mounted. They're usually more elusive. And don't be afraid that a close reading will damage the poem. Poems aren't hurt when we analyze them; instead, they come alive as we experience them and put into words what we discover through them.

A list of more specific questions using the literary terms and concepts discussed in the following chapters, "Questions for Responsive Reading and Writing about Poetry," begins on page 1445. That list, like the suggestions just made, raises issues and questions that can help you read just about any poem closely. These strategies should be a useful means for getting inside poems to understand how they work. Furthermore, because reading poetry inevitably increases sensitivity to language, you're likely to find yourself a better reader of words in any form — whether in a novel, a blog post, an advertisement, a political speech, or a conversation — after having studied poetry. In short, many of the reading skills that make poetry accessible also open up the world you inhabit.

You'll probably find some poems amusing or sad, some fierce or tender, and some fascinating or dull. You may find, too, some poems that will get inside you. Their kinds of insights — the poet's and yours — are what Emily Dickinson had in mind when she defined poetry this way: "If I read a book and it makes my whole body so cold no fire can ever warm me, I know that it is poetry. If I feel physically as if the top of my head were taken off, I know that it is poetry." Dickinson's response may be more intense than most — poetry was, after all, at the center of her life — but you, too, might find yourself moved by poems in unexpected ways. In any case, as Edwin Arlington Robinson knew, poetry is, to an alert and sensitive reader, "eventually unmistakable."

## POETIC DEFINITIONS OF POETRY

It is quite common for poets to try to articulate what they are doing while they are doing it — to write poetry about poetry, in other words. The term for this phenomenon is *ars poetica*, a Latin term meaning "the art of poetry." There are hundreds of examples, dating back to antiquity: Horace's "Ars Poetica" is generally considered the earliest. These poems reflect the perspective of a particular poet at a particular time: definitions of poetry, its meaning, its intent, and its ideal form change over time, and even within a time period, poets are not likely to agree. As a reader of poetry, you might concentrate on what types of poems reach you in a particularly exciting way. Do you prefer poems with vivid imagery, poems with an inventive use of language, poems with a regular meter and rhyme scheme, or poems that disregard poetical conventions?

Are you more attuned to a loud voice in a poem or to a subtle metaphor? Should poetry change the world, describe the world, or just exist in the world? The following five poems are variations on the *ars poetica* genre: spend a little time appreciating them and comparing them.

## MARIANNE MOORE  (1887–1972)

### *Poetry*   1919

I, too, dislike it: there are things that are important beyond all
    this fiddle.
Reading it, however, with a perfect contempt for it, one
    discovers in
it after all, a place for the genuine.
  Hands that can grasp, eyes
    that can dilate, hair that can rise                  5
      if it must, these things are important not because a

high-sounding interpretation can be put upon them but because
    they are
useful. When they become so derivative as to become
    unintelligible,
the same thing may be said for all of us, that we
  do not admire what                             10
    we cannot understand: the bat
      holding on upside down or in quest of something to

eat, elephants pushing, a wild horse taking a roll, a tireless wolf
    under
a tree, the immovable critic twitching his skin like a horse
    that feels a flea, the base-
ball fan, the statistician—                           15
    nor is it valid
      to discriminate against "business documents and

school-books"; all these phenomena are important. One must
    make a distinction
however: when dragged into prominence by half poets, the
    result is not poetry,
nor till the poets among us can be                    20
    "literalists of
    the imagination"—above
      insolence and triviality and can present

for inspection, "imaginary gardens with real toads in them," shall
    we have
it. In the meantime, if you demand on the one hand,        25
  the raw material of poetry in
    all its rawness and
    that which is on the other hand
genuine, then you are interested in poetry.

## Billy Collins (b. 1941)

### *Introduction to Poetry*    1988

I ask them to take a poem
and hold it up to the light
like a color slide

or press an ear against its hive.

I say drop a mouse into a poem                                    5
and watch him probe his way out,

or walk inside the poem's room
and feel the walls for a light switch.

I want them to water-ski
across the surface of a poem                                      10
waving at the author's name on the shore.

But all they want to do
is tie the poem to a chair with rope
and torture a confession out of it.

They begin beating it with a hose                                 15
to find out what it really means.

## Ruth Forman (b. 1968)

### *Poetry Should Ride the Bus*    1993

poetry should hopscotch in a polka dot dress
wheel cartwheels
n hold your hand
when you walk past the yellow crackhouse

poetry should wear bright red lipstick          5
n practice kisses in the mirror
for all the fine young men with fades
shootin craps around the corner

Christine Bennett, http://www
.naturalbalancedliving.com/

poetry should dress in fine plum linen suits
n not be so educated that it don't stop in                       10
every now n then to sit on the porch
and talk about the comins and goins of the world

poetry should ride the bus
in a fat woman's Safeway bag
between the greens n chicken wings                                15
to be served with tuesday's dinner

poetry should drop by a sweet potato pie
ask about the grandchildren
n sit through a whole photo album
on a orange plastic covered lazy boy with no place to go         20

poetry should sing red revolution love songs
that massage your scalp
and bring hope to your blood
when you think you're too old to fight

yeah                                                              25
poetry should whisper electric blue magic
all the years of your life
never forgettin to look you in the soul
every once in a while
n smile                                                          30

## Charles Bukowski (1920–1994)

### *a poem is a city*   1962

a poem is a city filled with streets and sewers
filled with saints, heroes, beggars, madmen,
filled with banality and booze,
filled with rain and thunder and periods of
drought, a poem is a city at war,                                5
a poem is a city asking a clock why,
a poem is a city burning,
a poem is a city under guns
its barbershops filled with cynical drunks,
a poem is a city where God rides naked                           10
through the streets like Lady Godiva,
where dogs bark at night, and chase away
the flag; a poem is a city of poets,
most of them quite similar
and envious and bitter . . .                                     15
a poem is this city now,
50 miles from nowhere,
9:09 in the morning,
the taste of liquor and cigarettes,
no police, no lovers, walking the streets,                       20
this poem, this city, closing its doors,
barricaded, almost empty,
mournful without tears, aging without pity,
the hardrock mountains,
the ocean like a lavender flame,                                 25
a moon destitute of greatness,
a small music from broken windows . . .

a poem is a city, a poem is a nation,
a poem is the world . . .
and now I stick this under glass                                 30
for the mad editor's scrutiny,
and night is elsewhere
and faint gray ladies stand in line,

dog follows dog to estuary,
the trumpets bring on gallows                                          35
as small men rant at things
they cannot do.

ADA LIMÓN (B. 1976)

## The End of Poetry   2020

Enough of osseous and chickadee and sunflower
and snowshoes, maple and seeds, samara and shoot,
enough chiaroscuro, enough of thus and prophecy
and the stoic farmer and faith and our father and tis
of thee, enough of bosom and bud, skin and god                        5
not forgetting and star bodies and frozen birds,
enough of the will to go on and not go on or how
a certain light does a certain thing, enough
of the kneeling and the rising and the looking
inward and the looking up, enough of the gun,                         10
the drama, and the acquaintance's suicide, the long-lost
letter on the dresser, enough of the longing and
the ego and the obliteration of ego, enough
of the mother and the child and the father and the child
and enough of the pointing to the world, weary                        15
and desperate, enough of the brutal and the border,
enough of can you see me, can you hear me, enough
I am human, enough I am alone and I am desperate,
enough of the animal saving me, enough of the high
water, enough sorrow, enough of the air and its ease,                 20
I am asking you to touch me.

### CONSIDERATIONS FOR CRITICAL THINKING AND WRITING

1. FIRST RESPONSE. Which of the five poems most intrigues you? Why?

2. There is a recurrent idea within these poems that poetry should be treated a
   certain way by its readers: How would you summarize that idea? Do you agree
   with the poets who express it?

3. These poems rely heavily on metaphor to make their argument. Find a metaphor in each poem and discuss in detail how it works.

## RECURRENT POETIC FIGURES:
## FIVE WAYS OF LOOKING AT ROSES

One of poetry's charms is the way it encourages us to look at something from
a new perspective. Wallace Stevens's poem "Thirteen Ways of Looking at a
Blackbird" (p. 946) does just that: he places the image of a blackbird in each of

thirteen numbered stanzas. We may initially scrutinize the blackbird — what does it mean? — but we will probably come around to the idea that the poem is not about the blackbird: it is about the looking.

Roses have been a favored image in poetry for many centuries. They are beautiful; they are associated with a tribute of love; their beauty is ephemeral; they have thorns on their stems that make them difficult to grab; they require special care and knowledge to reach their perfect bloom, and so forth. Dandelions have not received the same poetic attention. Maybe the American experimental writer Gertrude Stein was just tired of reading about roses when she famously (and cryptically) wrote, "A rose is a rose is a rose is a rose." Read the following five short poems to consider how much can be done with roses.

## ROBERT BURNS (1759–1796)

### *A Red, Red Rose*   1799

O my luve's like a red, red rose
That's newly sprung in June;
O my luve's like the melodie
That's sweetly played in tune.

As fair art thou, my bonny lass,                                   5
So deep in luve am I;
And I will luve thee still my dear,
Till a' the seas gang° dry —                                      *go*

Till a' the seas gang dry, my dear,
And the rocks melt wi' the sun:                                  10
O I will luve thee still, my dear,
While the sands o' life shall run.

And fare thee weel, my only luve,
And fare thee weel awhile!
And I will come again, my luve,                                  15
Though it were a thousand mile.

## EDMUND WALLER (1606–1687)

### *Go, Lovely Rose*   1645

Go, lovely rose,
Tell her that wastes her time and me
    That now she knows,
When I resemble° her to thee,                                 *compare*
How sweet and fair she seems to be,                                5

    Tell her that's young
And shuns to have her graces spied,

That hadst thou sprung
In deserts where no men abide,
Thou must have uncommended died.                    10

    Small is the worth
Of beauty from the light retired:
    Bid her come forth,
Suffer herself to be desired,
And not blush so to be admired.                      15

    Then die, that she
The common fate of all things rare
    May read in thee,
How small a part of time they share
That are so wondrous sweet and fair.                 20


## WILLIAM BLAKE (1757–1827)

### *The Sick Rose*    1794

O Rose, thou art sick;
The invisible worm
That flies in the night,
In the howling storm,

Hath found out thy bed                                5
Of crimson joy,
And her dark secret love
Does thy life destroy.


## DOROTHY PARKER (1893–1967)

### *One Perfect Rose*    1926

A single flow'r he sent me, since we met.
   All tenderly his messenger he chose;
Deep-hearted, pure, with scented dew still wet—
   One perfect rose.

I knew the language of the floweret;                  5
   "My fragile leaves," it said, "his heart enclose."
Love long has taken for his amulet
   One perfect rose.

Why is it no one ever sent me yet
   One perfect limousine, do you suppose?          10
Ah no, it's always just my luck to get
   One perfect rose.

## H. D. (HILDA DOOLITTLE) (1886–1961)

### *Sea Rose*   1916

Rose, harsh rose,
marred and with stint of petals,
meagre flower, thin,
sparse of leaf,

more precious                                                    5
than a wet rose
single on a stem—
you are caught in the drift.

Stunted, with small leaf,
you are flung on the sand,                                       10
you are lifted
in the crisp sand
that drives in the wind.

Can the spice-rose
drip such acrid fragrance                                        15
hardened in a leaf?

#### CONSIDERATIONS FOR CRITICAL THINKING AND WRITING

1. FIRST RESPONSE. Which treatment of roses is the most conventional and which one is the most surprising? What factors explain your choices?
2. What precise emotion is expressed in each poem?
3. Is there a meaningful difference between poems in which the rose is the subject and poems in which it is a tool for comparison? How would you express that difference?

## POEMS FOR FURTHER STUDY

### MARY OLIVER (1935–2019)

### *The Poet with His Face in His Hands*   2005

You want to cry aloud for your
mistakes. But to tell the truth the world
doesn't need any more of that sound.

So if you're going to do it and can't
stop yourself, if your pretty mouth can't                        5
hold it in, at least go by yourself across

the forty fields and the forty dark inclines
of rocks and water to the place where
the falls are flinging out their white sheets

like crazy, and there is a cave behind all that 10
jubilation and water fun and you can
stand there, under it, and roar all you

want and nothing will be disturbed; you can
drip with despair all afternoon and still,
on a green branch, its wings just lightly touched 15

by the passing foil of the water, the thrush,
puffing out its spotted breast, will sing
of the perfect, stone-hard beauty of everything.

### CONSIDERATIONS FOR CRITICAL THINKING AND WRITING

1. FIRST RESPONSE. Describe the kind of poet the speaker characterizes. What is the speaker's attitude toward that sort of poet?

2. Explain which single phrase used by the speaker to describe the poet most reveals for you the speaker's attitude toward the poet.

3. How is nature contrasted with the poet?

### CONNECTION TO ANOTHER SELECTION

1. Compare the thematic use of nature in Oliver's poem and in Robert Frost's "Design" (p. 874).

---

WHEN I WRITE "When I'm creating a story, I try to keep writing until I finish a draft — same for a poem, but I don't set aside a specific block of time. When the inkling of a poem is there, I write. When it's not, I go for a walk until it arrives." — JIM TILLEY

---

## JIM TILLEY (B. 1950)

### *The Big Questions*    2011

The big questions are big only
because they have never been answered.
Some questions, big as they seem,
are big only in the moment,
like when you're hiking a trail alone 5

and you encounter a mammoth
grizzly who hasn't had lunch
in a fortnight, and he eyes you
as the answer to his only big question.
Life turns existential, and you can't 10

help questioning why you are here —
in this place on this planet
within this universe —
at this precise time,
or why he is, and you know he's not, 15

even for a moment, wondering
the same thing, because he's already
figured it out. And you, too,
know exactly what to do.
So, this can be a defining moment,                                20

but not a big question,
because no one ever figures those out.
Still, one day when someone does,
might it not be a person like you
staring down a bear looking for lunch?                            25

### Considerations for Critical Thinking and Writing

1. **FIRST RESPONSE.** What are the "big questions" raised in this poem?
2. Explain whether you think the bear and his "lunch" have much in common.
3. How does Tilley's use of language create a poem that is philosophically serious as well as genuinely funny?

### Connection to Another Selection

1. To what extent does Mary Oliver's "The Poet with His Face in His Hands" (p. 549) also raise the existential question of "why are you here"?

## Alberto Ríos (b. 1952)

### *Seniors*   1985

William cut a hole in his Levi's pocket
so he could flop himself out in class
behind the girls so the other guys
could see and shit what guts we all said.
All Konga wanted to do over and over                              5
was the rubber band trick, but he showed
everyone how, so nobody wanted to see
anymore and one day he cried, just cried
until his parents took him away forever.
Maya had a Hotpoint refrigerator standing                         10
in his living room, just for his family to show
anybody who came that they could afford it.

Me, I got a French kiss, finally, in the catholic
darkness, my tongue's farthest half vacationing
loudly in another mouth like a man in Bermudas,                   15
and my body jumped against a flagstone wall,
I could feel it through her thin, almost
nonexistent body: I had, at that moment, that moment,
a hot girl on a summer night, the best of all
the things we tried to do. Well, she                              20
let me kiss her, anyway, all over.

Alberto Rios.

Or it was just a flagstone wall
with a flaw in the stone, an understanding cavity
for burning young men with smooth dreams —
the true circumstance is gone, the true                                    25
circumstances about us all then
are gone. But when I kissed her, all water,
she would close her eyes, and they into somewhere
would disappear. Whether she was there
or not, I remember her, clearly, and she moves                             30
around the room, sometimes, until I sleep.

I have lain on the desert in watch
low in the back of a pick-up truck
for nothing in particular, for stars, for
the things behind stars, and nothing comes                                 35
more than the moment: always now, here in a truck,
the moment again to dream of making love and sweat,
this time to a woman, or even to all of them
in some allowable way, to those boys, then,
who couldn't cry, to the girls before they were                            40
women, to friends, me on my back, the sky over me
pressing its simple weight into her body
on me, into the bodies of them all, on me.

### CONSIDERATIONS FOR CRITICAL THINKING AND WRITING

1. FIRST RESPONSE. Comment on the use of slang in the poem. Does it surprise
   you? How does it characterize the speaker?

2. How does the language of the final stanza differ from that of the first stanza?
   To what purpose?

3. Write an essay that discusses the speaker's attitudes toward sex and life. How
   are they related?

### CONNECTION TO ANOTHER SELECTION

1. Think about "Seniors" as a kind of love poem and compare the speaker's
   voice here with the one in T. S. Eliot's "The Love Song of J. Alfred Prufrock"
   (p. 936). How are these two voices used to evoke different cultures? Of what
   value is love in these cultures?

## ALFRED, LORD TENNYSON (1809–1892)

### *The Eagle* 1851

*Fragment*

He clasps the crag with crooked hands;
Close to the sun in lonely lands,
Ringed with the azure world, he stands.

The wrinkled sea beneath him crawls:
He watches from his mountain walls,                                          5
And like a thunderbolt he falls.

### CONSIDERATIONS FOR CRITICAL THINKING AND WRITING

1. **FIRST RESPONSE.** How does the speaker distinguish between the eagle's movements in the second stanza and those in the first stanza?

2. Although this poem is considered to be a fragment by Tennyson, how might it also be considered as a kind of complete portrait of an eagle?

### CONNECTION TO ANOTHER SELECTION

1. Why can "The Eagle" and the anonymously written "Western Wind" (p. 539) be accurately described as lyric poems?

## EDGAR ALLAN POE (1809–1849)

### *Sonnet — To Science*   1845

Science! true daughter of Old Time thou art!
   Who alterest all things with thy peering eyes.
Why preyest thou thus upon the poet's heart,
   Vulture, whose wings are dull realities?
How should he love thee? or how deem thee wise,                              5
   Who wouldst not leave him in his wandering
To seek for treasure in the jewelled skies,
   Albeit he soared with an undaunted wing?
Hast thou not dragged Diana° from her car?   *goddess of hunting and the moon*
     And driven the Hamadryad° from the wood   *tree nymph*  10
To seek a shelter in some happier star?
     Hast thou not torn the Naiad° from her flood,   *water nymph*
The Elfin from the green grass, and from me
     The summer dream beneath the tamarind tree?°   *exotic Asian tree*

### CONSIDERATIONS FOR CRITICAL THINKING AND WRITING

1. **FIRST RESPONSE.** How is science characterized in lines 1–4? Which words are particularly revealing?

2. Given the references to Diana, the Hamadryad, the Naiad, the Elfin, and the tamarind tree, how would you describe the poet's world compared to the scientist's?

3. How do you think a scientist might respond to this poem?

### CONNECTION TO ANOTHER SELECTION

1. Compare the speaker's attitudes toward what Poe calls in this poem "peering eyes" with the speaker's attitude toward the readers in Billy Collins's "Introduction to Poetry" (p. 544).

## CORNELIUS EADY (B. 1954)

### *The Supremes*   1991

We were born to be gray. We went to school,
Sat in rows, ate white bread,
Looked at the floor a lot. In the back
Of our small heads

A long scream. We did what we could,                                    5
And all we could do was
Turn on each other. How the fat kids suffered!
Not even being jolly could save them.

And then there were the anal retentives,
The terrified brown-noses, the desperately                              10
Athletic or popular. This, of course,
Was training. At home

Our parents shook their heads and waited.
We learned of the industrial revolution,
The sectioning of the clock into pie slices.                           15
We drank cokes and twiddled our thumbs. In the
Back of our minds
A long scream. We snapped butts in the showers,
Froze out shy girls on the dance floor,
Pin-pointed flaws like radar.                                          20
Slowly we understood: this was to be the world.

We were born insurance salesmen and secretaries,
Housewives and short order cooks,
Stock room boys and repairmen,
And it wouldn't be a bad life, they promised,                          25
In a tone of voice that would force some of us
To reach in self-defense for wigs,
Lipstick,

Sequins.

### CONSIDERATIONS FOR CRITICAL THINKING AND WRITING

1. FIRST RESPONSE. Who were the Supremes? Why is the title so crucial for this poem?

2. Explain how the meanings and mood of this poem would change if it ended with line 25.

3. How does the speaker's recollection of school experiences compare with your own?

### CONNECTION TO ANOTHER SELECTION

1. Discuss the speakers' memories of school in "The Supremes" and in Judy Page Heitzman's "The Schoolroom on the Second Floor of the Knitting Mill" (p. 606).

# 17

# Word Choice, Word Order, and Tone

I still feel that a poet has a duty to words, and that words can do wonderful things. And it's too bad to just let them lie there without doing anything with and for them.

— GWENDOLYN BROOKS

GRANGER — Historical Picture Archive.

## WORD CHOICE

### Diction

Like all good writers, poets are keenly aware of **diction**, their choice of words. Poets, however, choose words especially carefully because the words in poems call attention to themselves. Characters, actions, settings, and symbols may appear in a poem, but in the foreground, before all else, is the poem's language. Also, poems are usually briefer than other forms of writing. A few poorly considered words in a 200-page novel (which would have about 100,000 words) create fewer problems than they would in a 100-word poem. Functioning in a compressed atmosphere, the words in a poem must convey meanings gracefully and economically. Readers therefore have to be alert to the ways in which those meanings are released.

Although poetic language is often more intensely charged than ordinary speech, the words used in poetry are not necessarily different from everyday speech. Inexperienced readers may sometimes assume that language must be high-flown and out-of-date to be included in a poem: instead of reading about a boy "enjoying a swim," they expect to read about a boy "disporting with pliant arm o'er a glassy wave." During the eighteenth century this kind of **poetic diction** — the use of elevated language rather than ordinary language — was highly valued in English poetry, but since the nineteenth century poets have generally overridden the distinctions that were once made between words used in everyday speech and those used in poetry. Today all levels of diction can be found in poetry.

A poet, like any writer, has several levels of diction from which to choose; they range from formal to middle to informal. **Formal diction** consists of a dignified, impersonal, and elevated use of language. Notice, for example, the formality of Andrew Marvell's "To His Coy Mistress" (the entire poem appears on p. 941):

> Thou by the Indian Ganges' side
> Shouldst rubies find; I by the tide
> Of Humber would complain. . . .

There is nothing casual or relaxed about these lines. Marvell's use of "Thou" and "Shouldst" clearly signals a formal speaker, and the structure of the lines is also stilted, with the verbs at the end of the lines instead of following their subjects directly as they would in more relaxed or spoken English.

The language used in Sharon Olds's "Last Night" represents a less formal level of diction; the speaker uses a **middle diction** spoken by most educated people. Consider how Olds's speaker struggles the next day to comprehend her passion:

> Love? It was more like dragonflies
> in the sun, 100 degrees at noon,
> [...], I
> close my eyes when I remember.

The words used to describe this encounter are common enough, yet it is precisely Olds's use of precise though not unfamiliar language that evokes the extraordinary nature of this couple's connection.

**Informal diction** is evident in Langston Hughes's "Ballad of the Landlord" (p. 814). The speaker's imagined conversation with his landlord is presented **colloquially**, in a conversational manner that in this instance includes widely recognized misspellings:

> What? You gonna get eviction orders?
> You gonna cut off my heat?
> You gonna take my furniture and
> Throw it in the street?

This level of diction is clearly not that of Marvell's or Olds's speakers, but we certainly hear the speaker's voice.

Poets may also draw on another form of informal diction, called **dialect**. Dialects are spoken by definable groups of people from a particular geographic region, economic group, or social class. New England dialects are often heard in Robert Frost's poems, for example. Gwendolyn Brooks uses a Black dialect in "We Real Cool" (p. 706) to characterize a group of pool players. Another form of diction related to particular groups is *jargon*, a category of language defined by a trade or profession. Sociologists, photographers, carpenters, baseball players, and dentists, for example, all use words that are specific to their fields. Sally Croft offers an appetizing dish of cookbook jargon in "Home-Baked Bread" (p. 592).

Many levels of diction are available to poets. The variety of diction to be found in poetry is enormous, and that is how it should be. No language is foreign to poetry because it is possible to imagine any human voice as the speaker of a poem. When we say a poem is formal, informal, or somewhere in between, we are making a descriptive statement rather than an evaluative one. What matters in a poem is not only which words are used but how they are used.

## Denotations and Connotations

One important way that the meaning of a word is communicated in a poem is through sound: snakes *hiss*, saws *buzz*. This and other matters related to sound are discussed in Chapter 21. Individual words also convey meanings through denotations and connotations. **Denotations** are the literal, dictionary meanings of a word. For example, *bird* denotes a feathered animal with wings (other denotations for the same word include a middle finger used as an insulting gesture, an airplane, a derogatory term for a woman in Britain, or an odd person), but in addition to its denotative meanings, *bird* also carries **connotations** — associations and implications that go beyond a word's literal meanings. Connotations derive from how the word has been used and the associations people make with it. Therefore, the connotations of *bird* might include fragility, vulnerability, altitude, the sky, or freedom, depending on the context in which the word is used. Consider also how different the connotations are for the following types of birds: hawk, dove, penguin, pigeon, chicken, peacock, duck, crow, turkey, gull, owl, goose, coot, and vulture. These words have long been used to refer to types of people as well as birds. They are rich in connotative meanings.

Connotations derive their resonance from a person's experiences with a word. Those experiences may not always be the same, especially when they are uttered or written in different times and places. *Theater*, for instance, was once associated with depravity, disease, and sin, whereas today the word usually evokes some sense of high culture and perhaps visions of elegant opulence. Many people find *squid* appetizing, but for others the very word might produce negative connotations not only from a revulsion to this particular seafood but from the sound of the word. (Most restaurants use the much more pleasant-sounding Italian word, *calamari*.) Readers must recognize, then, that words written in other times and places may have unexpected connotations.

Annotations such as footnotes or margin notes usually help in these matters, which is why it makes sense to pay attention to them when they are available.

Ordinarily, though, the language of poetry is accessible, even when the circumstances of the reader and the poet are different. Although connotative language may be used subtly, it mostly draws on associations experienced by many people. Poets rely on widely shared associations rather than on the idiosyncratic response that an individual might have to a word. Someone who has received a severe burn from a fireplace accident may associate the word *hearth* with intense pain instead of home and family life, but that reader must not allow a personal experience to undermine the response the poem evokes for most. Connotative meanings are usually public meanings.

Perhaps this can be seen most clearly in advertising, where language is also used primarily to convey moods and feelings rather than information. For instance, three decades of increasing interest in nutrition and general fitness have created a collective consciousness that advertisers have capitalized on successfully. Knowing that we want to be slender or lean or slim (not *spare* or *scrawny* and certainly not *gaunt*), advertisers have created a new word to describe beers, wines, sodas, cheeses, canned fruits, and other products that tend to overload what used to be called sweatclothes and sneakers. The word is *lite*. The assumed denotative meaning of *lite* is "low in calories," but as close readers of ingredient labels know, some *lites* are heavier than regularly prepared products. There can be no doubt about the connotative meaning of *lite*, however. Whatever is *lite* cannot hurt you; less is more. Even the word is lighter than *light*; there is no unnecessary droopy *g* or plump *h*. *Lite* is a brilliantly manufactured use of connotation.

Connotative meanings are valuable because they allow poets to be economical and suggestive simultaneously. In this way emotions and attitudes are carefully woven into the texture of the poem's language. Read the following poem and pay close attention to the connotative meanings of its words.

RANDALL JARRELL (1914–1965)

## *The Death of the Ball Turret Gunner*    1945

From my mother's sleep I fell into the State
And I hunched in its belly till my wet fur froze.
Six miles from earth, loosed from its dream of life,
I woke to black flak and the nightmare fighters.
When I died they washed me out of the turret with a hose.                    5

The title of this poem establishes the setting and the speaker's situation. Like the setting of a short story, the setting of a poem is important when the time and place influence what happens. "The Death of the Ball Turret Gunner" is set in the midst of a war and, more specifically, in a ball turret — a Plexiglas sphere housing machine guns on the underside of a bomber. The speaker's situation obviously places him in extreme danger; indeed, his fate is announced in the title.

Although the poem is written in the first-person singular, its speaker is clearly not the poet. Jarrell uses a **persona**, a speaker created by the poet. In this poem the persona is a disembodied voice that makes the gunner's story all the more powerful. What is his story? A paraphrase might read something like this:

> After I was born, I grew up to find myself at war, cramped into a bomber's turret some 31,000 feet above the ground. Below me were exploding shells from anti-aircraft guns and attacking fighter planes. I was killed, but the bomber returned to base, where my remains were cleaned out of the turret so the next man could take my place.

This paraphrase is accurate, but its language is much less suggestive than the poem's. The first line of the poem has the speaker emerge from his "mother's sleep," the anesthetized sleep of her giving birth. The phrase also suggests the comfort, warmth, and security he knew as a child and has a grotesque transformation when he finds himself in the bomber's "belly." This safety was left behind when he "fell," a verb that evokes the danger and involuntary movement associated with his subsequent "State" (*fell* also echoes, perhaps, the fall from innocence to experience related in the Bible).

Several dictionary definitions appear for the noun *state*; it can denote a territorial unit, the power and authority of a government, a person's social status, or a person's emotional or physical condition. The context provided by the rest of the poem makes clear that "State" has several denotative meanings here: because it is capitalized, it certainly refers to the violent world of a government at war, but it also refers to the gunner's vulnerable status as well as his physical and emotional condition. By having "State" carry more than one meaning, Jarrell has created an intentional ambiguity. **Ambiguity** allows for two or more simultaneous interpretations of a word, a phrase, an action, or a situation, all of which can be supported by the context of a work. Through his ambiguous use of "State," Jarrell connects the horrors of war not just to bombers and gunners but to the governments that control them.

Related to this ambiguity is the connotative meaning of "State" in the poem. The context demands that the word be read with a negative charge. The word is used not to indicate patriotic pride but to suggest an anonymous, impersonal "State" that kills rather than nurtures the life in its "belly." The state's "belly" is a bomber, and the gunner is "hunched" like a fetus in the cramped turret, where, in contrast to the warmth of his mother's womb, everything is frozen, even the "wet fur" of his flight jacket (newborn infants have wet fur too). The gunner is not just 31,000 feet from the ground but "Six miles from earth." *Six miles* has roughly the same denotative meaning as 31,000 feet, but Jarrell knew that the connotative meaning of *six miles* makes the speaker's position seem even more remote and frightening.

When the gunner is born into the violent world of war, he finds himself waking up to a "nightmare" that is all too real. The poem's final line is grimly understated, but it hits the reader with the force of an exploding shell: what the State-bomber-turret gives birth to is a gruesome death that is merely one of an endless series. It may be tempting to reduce the theme of this poem to the idea that "war is hell," but Jarrell's target is more specific. He implicates the "State," which routinely executes such violence, and he does so without preaching or hysterical denunciations. Instead, his use of language conveys his theme subtly and powerfully.

## ALLUSION

An *allusion* is a brief cultural reference to a person, a place, a thing, an event, or an idea in history or literature. Allusive words, like connotative words, are both suggestive and economical; poets use allusions to conjure up biblical authority, scenes from Shakespeare's plays, historic figures, wars, great love stories, and anything else that might serve to deepen and enrich their own work. Rap lyrics are full of allusions; in "Encore," Jay-Z raps, "And I need you to remember one thing / I came, I saw, I conquered / From record sales to sold-out concerts." The second of these three lines is an allusion to Julius Caesar's signature saying, known to most of the world through Shakespeare's play *Julius Caesar*. The speaker invites an automatic comparison (and maybe a cautious warning against the tradition of excessive bragging in rap, as things didn't end peacefully for Caesar). Allusions imply cultural experiences shared by the poet and the reader. Literate audiences once had more in common than they do today because more people had similar economic, social, and educational backgrounds. But a judicious use of specialized dictionaries, encyclopedias, and online reference tools such as Google Search can help you decipher allusions that grow out of this body of experience. As you read more, you'll be able to make connections based on your own experiences with literature. In a sense, allusions make available what other human beings have deemed worth remembering, and that is certainly an economical way of supplementing and enhancing your own experience.

## WORD ORDER

Meanings in poems are conveyed not only by denotations, connotations, and allusions, but also by the poet's arrangement of words into phrases, clauses, and sentences to achieve particular effects. The ordering of words into meaningful verbal patterns is called *syntax*. A poet can manipulate the syntax of a line to place emphasis on a word; this is especially apparent when a poet varies normal word order. In Emily Dickinson's "A narrow Fellow in the Grass," for example, the speaker says about the snake that "His notice sudden is." Ordinarily, that would be expressed as "his notice is sudden." By placing the verb *is* unexpectedly at the end of the line, Dickinson creates the sense of surprise we feel when we suddenly come upon a snake. Dickinson's inversion of the standard word order also makes the final sound of the line a hissing *is*.

# Poetry and the Visual Arts

In the "Reading" chapter of *Walden* (1854), Henry David Thoreau confidently asserts: "A written word is the choicest of relics. It is something at once more intimate with us and more universal than any other work of art. It is the work of art nearest to life itself." This proclivity was true for Thoreau, but it may not be true for you and may register simply as the bias of a committed writer. No doubt a good many writers and avid readers would readily agree with Thoreau's preference for literature, but his contention would likely be qualified or even refuted by painters, musicians, sculptors, architects, filmmakers, and anyone else who creates or deeply connects to an art medium that relies on materials other than the written word. Our own experiences and preferences — whether we are producers or audiences or both — determine what kinds of works of art are "nearest to life itself." Moreover, these various media aren't mutually exclusive, as is demonstrated by eclectic audiences who enjoy the arts without making sweeping claims about the intimate and universal. Literature needn't compete with the visual arts; indeed, over time it has allied itself with other arts, as the six poems in this section will demonstrate.

The poems included here are examples of ekphrasis, from the Greek term *ekphrasis* (*ek*, "out of," and *phrasis*, "expression" or "speech"), which is often translated simply as "description." Ekphrastic literature consists of works that attempt to capture some quality or essential feature of another work of art. Such attempts are common in other types of art as well: a sculpture, for example, might evoke a heroic figure from a painting depicting a famous battle while a musical score might capture the explosive violence of the same painting. In literature, to cite an example from this anthology that you might have already read, John Keats's "Ode on a Grecian Urn" (p. 572) explores the possible meanings to be discovered concerning the lovers portrayed on a now-celebrated piece of pottery. One of the intriguing features of ekphrasis is the opportunity to contemplate an inspired artist in one medium prompted by another artist's work in a different medium.

A

This section offers six ekphrastic poems that reflect on the visual arts represented by a range of styles in four paintings, a woodblock print, and a memorial sculpture.

## Questions for Responsive Reading and Writing

The following questions can help you respond to important elements in the visual arts. The questions may not apply to every work nor are they exhaustive, but they should help you organize your thoughts, discussions, and writing about each piece in this section. These questions will encourage you to see what's going on in a painting or some other media rather than to merely look at it. An analysis of particular elements will allow you to understand how various parts of a work contribute to its entire effect (to review Questions for Responsive Reading and Writing about Poetry, see Chapter 43).

1. What does the title reveal? How does it lead you into the work?
2. What is the subject matter? Is there a definable setting of time and place that makes the historical context important?
3. What details seem particularly significant? How does the artist relate them to one another and achieve a mood or tone in terms of proportion, lights and darks, colors, lines, and perspective?
4. How do the foreground, middleground, and background create a focus in the work?
5. Is it possible to describe the overall style as realistic, impressionistic, or abstract?
6. Do any of the details have symbolic significance or do they allude to other works, historical moments, contemporary events, people, or myths?
7. Does the artist offer a particular point of view or set of values associated with the subject matter?
8. Is there any humor, satire, or irony in the work?
9. How do the artist's choices of what is included in the work also suggest what has been purposely omitted from it?
10. After examining the work closely, have you confirmed, expanded, or qualified your first impression? Would you want to have a copy of this art in your room? Why or why not?

## AMERICAN GOTHIC

Grant Wood (1891–1942) was born in Anamosa, Iowa. After studying at the School of the Art Institute of Chicago, he continued his studies for a number of years in Europe, but unlike a number of Americans traveling abroad in the 1920s, he returned home declaring that "all the really good ideas I'd ever had came to me while I was milking a cow. So I went back to Iowa." One of his early self-portraits has him in overalls similar to those worn by the farmer in *American Gothic* (1930), a work that made him an extraordinarily popular painter during the Depression of the 1930s when midwestern security and solidity offered simple American perseverance as an antidote to economic chaos. Curiously, many commentators regarded the painting as a satire of small-town parochialism and provincialism. Some viewers interpreted the painting as a negative critique of rural life rather than a celebration of it. John Stone's treatment of *American Gothic* doesn't resolve that issue, but it clearly appreciates the humanity of the couple depicted in the painting. Stone, born in Jackson, Mississippi, was both a poet and a cardiologist. After earning a medical degree at Washington University School of Medicine in St. Louis, he served on the medical faculty at Emory University School of Medicine, where he had a strong reputation for dealing with patients, students, and ultimately readers with directness and humor. Among his collections are *Where Water Begins* (1998) and *Music from Apartment 8: New and Selected Poems* (2004). In his "American Gothic," he makes a cordial and good-natured house call.

**American Gothic** Painted with oil on beaver board in 1930, *American Gothic* was created in a precise, realistic style reminiscent of fifteenth-century northern European artists. It earned a bronze medal at the Art Institute of Chicago's annual painting competition. The museum purchased it soon after, and it has been housed there ever since.

American Gothic, 1930 by Grant Wood © 2023 Figge Art Museum, successors to the Estate of Nan Wood Graham/ Licensed by VAGA at Artists Rights Society (ARS), NY. Photo: The Art Institute of Chicago/Art Resource, NY.

## JOHN STONE (1936–2008)
### *American Gothic*   1998

*after the painting by Grant Wood, 1930*

Just outside the frame
there has to be a dog
chickens, cows and hay

and a smokehouse
where a ham in hickory                                        5
is also being preserved

Here for all time
the borders of the Gothic window
anticipate the ribs

of the house                                                         10
the tines of the pitchfork
repeat the triumph

of his overalls
and front and center
the long faces, the sober lips                               15

above the upright spines
of this couple
arrested in the name of art

These two
by now                                                                 20
the sun this high

ought to be
in mortal time
about their businesses

Instead they linger here                                      25
within the patient fabric
of the lives they wove

he asking the artist silently
*how much longer*
and worrying about the crops                            30

she no less concerned about the crops
but more to the point just now
whether she remembered

to turn off the stove.

## CONSIDERATIONS FOR CRITICAL THINKING AND WRITING

1. FIRST RESPONSE. In what sense can Stone's poem be regarded as an analysis of Grant's painting? Explain whether you think he sees Grant's depiction of the two figures more as a satire or a celebration. How do you read them?

2. What symbolic elements can you describe in the painting?

3. Discuss the humor in the poem. Explain whether you find any humor in the painting.

## CONNECTION TO ANOTHER SELECTION

1. Compare the depiction of rural life and work in this poem and in Robert Frost's "Mowing" (p. 865).

## GIRL POWDERING HER NECK

Little is known about the details of Kitagawa Utamaro's life (1753–1806). An eighteenth-century Japanese painter and printmaker especially appreciated for his woodblock prints called *ukiyo-e,* Utamaro focuses on the intimate world of cultivated courtesans and geishas who entertained male clients. His work includes nature scenes and martial themes, but he is best known for his mysterious delicate portraits of beautiful sensuous women whose inner lives are subtly revealed, as in *Girl Powdering Her Neck* (ca. 1795). Cathy Song, of Chinese and Korean descent, was born in Honolulu, Hawaii, and was educated at Wellesley College and Boston University. Her poetry frequently explores the world of family and ancestry. Among her collections of poetry are *Frameless Windows, Squares of Light* (1988) and *Cloud Moving Hands* (2007). In "Girl Powdering Her Neck," Song responds to Utamaro's print with a series of vivid images that add imaginative details to the woodblock while simultaneously scrutinizing the female's life depicted in Utamaro's image.

## CATHY SONG  (B. 1955)
### *Girl Powdering Her Neck*   1983

*from a ukiyo-e print by Utamaro*

The light is the inside
sheen of an oyster shell,
sponged with talc and vapor,
moisture from a bath.

A pair of slippers                                                5
are placed outside

the rice-paper doors.
She kneels at a low table
in the room,
her legs folded beneath her                                          10
as she sits on a buckwheat pillow.

Her hair is black
with hints of red,
the color of seaweed
spread over rocks.                                                   15

Morning begins the ritual
wheel of the body,
the application of translucent skins.
She practices pleasure:
the pressure of three fingertips                                    20
applying powder.
Fingerprints of pollen
some other hand will trace.

The peach-dyed kimono
patterned with maple leaves                                          25
drifting across the silk,
falls from right to left
in a diagonal, revealing
the nape of her neck
and the curve of a shoulder                                          30
like the slope of a hill
set deep in snow in a country
of huge white solemn birds.
Her face appears in the mirror,
a reflection in a winter pond,                                       35
rising to meet itself.

She dips a corner of her sleeve
like a brush into water
to wipe the mirror;
she is about to paint herself.                                       40
The eyes narrow
in a moment of self-scrutiny.
The mouth parts
as if desiring to disturb
the placid plum face;                                                45
break the symmetry of silence.
But the berry-stained lips,

stenciled into the mask of beauty,
do not speak.

Two chrysanthemums                                                    50
touch in the middle of the lake
and drift apart.

**Girl Powdering Her Neck** This
woodblock print is one of many of
Utamaro's masterfully composed
studies of women, a genre known
as *bijin-ga*.
© RMN-Grand Palais/Art Resource, NY.

### CONSIDERATIONS FOR CRITICAL THINKING AND WRITING

1. FIRST RESPONSE. What does Song's poem add to the visual information provided in Utamaro's woodcut?

2. Explain whether you think Song's treatment of the girl is sympathetic or
   something else.

3. Discuss the relationship of the final three lines to the rest of the poem. What
   effect do they have on you?

### CONNECTION TO ANOTHER SELECTION

1. Contrast the conception of beauty in this poem to J. Estanislao Lopez's "Meditation on Beauty" (p. 750).

## THE VIETNAM VETERANS MEMORIAL WALL

The Vietnam Veterans Memorial Wall was designed by Maya Lin to honor U.S. troops who fought and died in the Vietnam War. Installed on the National Mall in Washington, D.C., the memorial wall is made up of two intersecting pieces set into the ground, ranging in depth from 8 inches at their outside edges, to 10 feet in the center, where the two sections of the wall meet. More than 58,000 names of the dead and missing are etched into the polished black granite in the chronological order in which they died or disappeared. At first, the wall generated controversy because, though it made no statement about the divisive war, its stark design was created by a twenty-one-year-old Asian student at Yale University and was perceived by some as an insensitive memorial to those who had died. Yusef Komunyakaa's "Facing It" is based on his service as a correspondent in the war for which he was awarded a Bronze Star. His reflections on the wall offer a different take from the way it was initially received. Among his dozen poetry collections is *Dien Cai* (1988), often cited as one of the best poetry collections about the war.

### Yusef Komunyakaa (b. 1947)

### *Facing It*   *1988*

My black face fades,
hiding inside the black granite.
I said I wouldn't,
dammit: No tears.
I'm stone. I'm flesh.                                                5
My clouded reflection eyes me
like a bird of prey, the profile of night
slanted against morning. I turn
this way — the stone lets me go.
I turn that way — I'm inside                                        10
the Vietnam Veterans Memorial
again, depending on the light
to make a difference.
I go down the 58,022 names,
half-expecting to find                                             15
my own in letters like smoke.
I touch the name Andrew Johnson;
I see the booby trap's white flash.
Names shimmer on a woman's blouse
but when she walks away                                            20
the names stay on the wall.
Brushstrokes flash, a red bird's

wings cutting across my stare.
The sky. A plane in the sky.
A white vet's image floats                                  25
closer to me, then his pale eyes
look through mine. I'm a window.
He's lost his right arm
inside the stone. In the black mirror
a woman's trying to erase names:                            30
No, she's brushing a boy's hair.

**Vietnam Veterans Memorial Wall**   The wall is the best-known part of the larger
Vietnam Veterans Memorial. Here, one can see the haunting effect the black
granite creates with a visitor's reflection. Millions of people visit the wall each year.
Library of Congress, Prints & Photographs Division, Reproduction number HABS DC, WASH, 643–45.

## CONSIDERATIONS FOR CRITICAL THINKING AND WRITING

1. FIRST RESPONSE. Explain the significance of the title. How are the speaker's war experiences reflected in the war memorial?

2. Discuss the possible meanings of the poem's final lines: "In the black mirror / a woman's trying to erase names: / No, she's brushing a boy's hair."

3. Explain why you think the speaker's response to the memorial indicates that its conception and composition are successful or unsuccessful as a public memorial.

## CONNECTION TO ANOTHER SELECTION

1. Discuss the speaker's tone and attitudes toward war in "Facing It" and in E. E. Cummings's "next to of course god america i" (p. 619).

## TWO MONKEYS

Though it is not clear when or where Pieter Bruegel the Elder (ca. 1525–1569) was born, he eventually settled in Brussels and is considered to be a major northern European painter of the mid-sixteenth century, particularly of peasant life (Bruegel dropped the *h* in his name, originally Brueghel, but his sons later restored it). In *Two Monkeys,* Bruegel moves away from depicting peasant life directly, but he seems to imply that the two primates nonetheless evoke a common human condition since they are in chains. Beyond them, in contrast, a sky is populated with soaring birds and a waterfront bay filled with sailboats. This subject matter appealed to Wisława Szymborska, who was born in Kraków, Poland, where she studied literature and sociology and where her education and sensibilities were shaped by living under Nazi occupation during World War II (1939–1945). The year before she published "Bruegel's Two Monkeys," Poland was threatened by Soviet Russian armies under the orders of Joseph Stalin. Szymborska was no stranger to her country's history of violence, oppression, and death. Among her translated volumes are *Poems: New and Collected, 1957–1997* (1998) and *Here: New Poems* (2010). In 1996, she was awarded the Nobel Prize for Literature.

## WISŁAWA SZYMBORSKA (1923–2012)

### Bruegel's Two Monkeys   *1957*

TRANSLATED FROM THE POLISH BY STANISLAW BARAŃCZAK AND CLARE CAVANAGH

This is what I see in my dreams about final exams:
two monkeys, chained to the floor, sit on the windowsill,
the sky behind them flutters,
the sea is taking its bath.

The exam is History of Mankind.                                                   5
I stammer and hedge.

One monkey stares and listens with mocking disdain,
the other seems to be dreaming away —
but when it's clear I don't know what to say
he prompts me with a gentle                                                      10
clinking of his chain.

***Two Monkeys*** This oil on wood painting is housed in Germany's Gemäldegalerie in Berlin. Bruegel is believed to have completed the work in 1562.
The Print Collector/Alamy.

## CONSIDERATIONS FOR CRITICAL THINKING AND WRITING

1. **FIRST RESPONSE.** Why do you suppose Bruegel chooses monkeys as his subject? What does that have to do with taking an exam on the "History of Mankind"?

2. What kind of answer do you think the "gentle / clinking of his chain" prompts in the speaker? What does it mean to you?

3. Consider the shape of the space created by the arch and the monkey's tails. What does that suggest about their situation?

## CONNECTION TO ANOTHER SELECTION

1. Discuss the way education is treated in this poem and in Kwame Dawes's "History Lesson at Eight a.m." (p. 569)

## HOUSE BY THE RAILROAD

Edward Hopper (1882–1967) became an influential realist painter during his long painting career in the twentieth century. His seemingly simple rural and urban scenes sparsely populated with figures that appear vaguely anxious and uncomfortable produce a complexity that is often mysterious in its capacity to evoke a pervading sense of loneliness and alienation. In *House by the Railroad* (1925), Hopper brings together a solitary old Victorian house looming beside a railroad track that slices across the bottom of the painting. The house is clearly the dominant image, but the angle of vision creates a problematic perspective that makes the train tracks a powerful presence. Edward Hirsch explores the effects of that presence in "Edward Hopper and the House by the Railroad (1925)." Born in Chicago and educated at the University of Pennsylvania, where he earned a Ph.D. in folklore, Hirsch has published poetry collections that include *Wild Gratitude* (1986), *Earthly Measures* (1989), *Special Orders* (2003), and *The Living Fire* (2010). Hirsch's poem ruminates on the relationship between what the culture of the house represents and what the culture of the railroad implies about the pending nature of American life.

### EDWARD HIRSCH (B. 1950)

### *Edward Hopper and the House by the Railroad (1925)*   1982

Out here in the exact middle of the day,
This strange, gawky house has the expression
Of someone being stared at, someone holding
His breath underwater, hushed and expectant;

This house is ashamed of itself, ashamed                                    5
Of its fantastic mansard rooftop
And its pseudo-Gothic porch, ashamed
of its shoulders and large, awkward hands.

But the man behind the easel is relentless.
He is as brutal as sunlight, and believes                                    10
The house must have done something horrible
To the people who once lived here

Because now it is so desperately empty,
It must have done something to the sky
Because the sky, too, is utterly vacant                                      15
And devoid of meaning. There are no

Trees or shrubs anywhere — the house
Must have done something against the earth.
All that is present is a single pair of tracks
Straightening into the distance. No trains pass.                             20

Now the stranger returns to this place daily
Until the house begins to suspect
That the man, too, is desolate, desolate
And even ashamed. Soon the house starts

To stare frankly at the man. And somehow                                    25
The empty white canvas slowly takes on
The expression of someone who is unnerved,
Someone holding his breath underwater.

And then one day the man simply disappears.
He is a last afternoon shadow moving                                        30
Across the tracks, making its way
Through the vast, darkening fields.

This man will paint other abandoned mansions,
And faded cafeteria windows, and poorly lettered
Storefronts on the edges of small towns.                                    35
Always they will have this same expression,

The utterly naked look of someone
Being stared at, someone American and gawky.
Someone who is about to be left alone
Again, and can no longer stand it.                                          40

**House by the Railroad**  Art patron Stephen Clark donated this oil on canvas painting to the Museum of Modern Art in New York City in 1930. It was the first oil painting the museum acquired for its collection.

Digital Image © The Museum of Modern Art/Licensed by SCALA/Art Resource, NY. © 2023 Heirs of Josephine Hopper / Licensed by Artists Rights Society (ARS), NY.

## CONSIDERATIONS FOR CRITICAL THINKING AND WRITING

1. FIRST RESPONSE. Why do you think Hopper places railroad tracks rather than a paved road directly in front of the house?

2. The title of this poem and the poem itself include both the painting and the painter. What do you think is the effect of incorporating Hopper into the poem?

3. Try to match particular images in the poem with the physical details in the painting. How do both create the tone and potential themes?

## CONNECTION TO ANOTHER SELECTION

1. Compare the portrayal of artists in this poem and in Lawrence Ferlinghetti's "Constantly Risking Absurdity" (p. 955).

## THE MILKMAID

Johannes Vermeer (1632–1675), born in Delft, the Netherlands, had no formal training as a painter. Although he enjoyed only a modest reputation in his lifetime based upon some thirty paintings, he was rediscovered in the nineteenth century and is now widely regarded as a major artist of the golden age of Dutch painting. *The Milkmaid* (ca. 1660), housed in Amsterdam's Rijksmuseum, is considered a national treasure. Vermeer is celebrated for his detailed, almost photographic, representations of middle-class life, particularly his depictions of women performing simple domestic tasks that reveal the subjects' quiet strength and ordinary beauty. During the mid-seventeenth century, however, the world outside his paintings was daubed with the tumult produced by war, plague, and economic crisis. In "Vermeer," Wisława Szymborska reflects upon the significance of the painting's serenity in contrast to her own historical moment more than 350 years later. Born in Poland, Szymborska lived in Kraków most of her life. Although she steadfastly refused to reveal autobiographical details, insisting that her poems, essays, and translations should speak for themselves, the fact that she survived the genocidal Nazi occupation of Poland during World War II clearly affected her response to twentieth-century history, as well as her calm appreciation of everyday human concerns. In an interview, she once said, "[M]y poems are strictly not political. They are more about people and life." Among the collections of her poems that have been translated into English are *Poems, New and Collected, 1957–1997* (1998) and *Here: New Poems* (2010). Her reading of *The Milkmaid* in "Vermeer" helps explain the painting's enduring appeal, and, fittingly, her international reputation was made secure in 1996 when she was awarded the Nobel Prize for Literature.

# Wisława Szymborska (1923–2012)

## *Vermeer*   2010

*Translated by Clare Cavanagh and Stanisław Barańczak*

So long as that woman from the Rijksmuseum
in painted quiet and concentration
keeps pouring milk day after day
from the pitcher to the bowl
the World hasn't earned
the world's end.

**The Milkmaid**  This small, oil-on-canvas painting is housed in the Netherlands' Rijksmuseum in Amsterdam. Vermeer is believed to have completed the work around 1660.
Erich Lessing/Art Resource, NY.

### CONSIDERATIONS FOR CRITICAL THINKING AND WRITING

1. FIRST RESPONSE. Why do you suppose Szymborska capitalizes "World" in line 5 but not in line 6?

2. Describe the ways in which the line length and shape of the poem relate to its content.

3. How does the poem's treatment of time and motion invest significance in the simple act of pouring milk into a bowl?

### CONNECTION TO ANOTHER SELECTION

1. Compare the tone and theme of "Vermeer" with those of John Stone's "American Gothic" (Poetry and the Visual Arts insert, p. D).

# TONE

**Tone** is the writer's attitude toward the subject, the mood created by all the elements in the poem. Writing, like speech, can be characterized as serious or light, sad or happy, private or public, angry or affectionate, bitter or nostalgic, or by any other attitudes and feelings that human beings experience. In Jarrell's "The Death of the Ball Turret Gunner," the tone is clearly serious; the voice in the poem even sounds dead. Listen again to the persona's final words: "When I died they washed me out of the turret with a hose." The brutal, restrained matter-of-factness of this line is effective because the reader is called on to supply the appropriate anger and despair — a strategy that makes those emotions all the more convincing.

Consider how tone is used to convey meaning in the next poem, inspired by the poet's recognition of the power of words.

**A Note on the Text:** This poem contains offensive racial language. Its use here reflects the author's original intent in depicting a specific incident, time period, place, and culture, as well as underscoring the power of language. Be mindful of this context as you read.

## Marilyn Nelson (b. 1946)

### *How I Discovered Poetry*    1997

> When I Write "Although I usually [show] poems to my best friend, sometimes I ask other people to be first-readers because I don't want to ask too much of my friend! I recently joined a poetry group. Their suggestions are useful, mostly in helping me see what I'm really trying to get at."
> — MARILYN NELSON

It was like soul-kissing, the way the words
filled my mouth as Mrs. Purdy read from her desk.
All the other kids zoned an hour ahead to 3:15,
but Mrs. Purdy and I wandered lonely as clouds borne
by a breeze off Mount Parnassus. She must have seen          5
the darkest eyes in the room brim: The next day
she gave me a poem she'd chosen especially for me
to read to the all except for me white class.
She smiled when she told me to read it, smiled harder,
said oh yes I could. She smiled harder and harder          10
until I stood and opened my mouth to banjo playing
darkies, pickaninnies, disses and dats. When I finished
my classmates stared at the floor. We walked silent
to the buses, awed by the power of words.

### Considerations for Critical Thinking and Writing

1. **FIRST RESPONSE.** Trace your response to Mrs. Purdy from the beginning to the end of the poem.
2. How do you interpret the tone of the final two lines?

The next work is a ***dramatic monologue***, a type of poem in which a character — the speaker — addresses a silent audience in such a way as to reveal unintentionally some aspect of his or her temperament or personality. What tone is created by Machan's use of a persona?

## KATHARYN HOWD MACHAN (B. 1952)

### *Hazel Tells LaVerne*   1976

last night
im cleanin out my
howard johnsons ladies room
when all of a sudden
up pops this frog                                                5
musta come from the sewer
swimmin aroun an tryin ta
climb up the sida the bowl
so i goes ta flushm down
but sohelpmegod he starts talkin                                10
bout a golden ball
an how i can be a princess
me a princess
well my mouth drops
all the way to the floor                                        15
an he says
kiss me just kiss me
once on the nose
well i screams
ya little green pervert                                         20
an i hitsm with my mop
an has ta flush
the toilet down three times
me
a princess                                                      25

> **WHEN I WRITE** "When a poem begins to find its shape and form and voice inside you, let your heart and your head join to give it the best life you can: passion! imagery! music! And if it will let you, humor: ah, the world needs all it can get."
> —KATHARYN HOWD MACHAN

### CONSIDERATIONS FOR CRITICAL THINKING AND WRITING

1. FIRST RESPONSE. What do you imagine the situation and setting are for this poem? Do you like this revision of the fairy tale "The Frog Prince"?

2. What creates the poem's humor? How does Hazel's use of language reveal her personality? Is her treatment of the frog consistent with her character?

3. Although it has no punctuation, this poem is easy to follow. How does the arrangement of the lines organize Hazel's speech for clarity and emphasis?

4. What is the theme? Is it conveyed through denotative or connotative language?

5. CREATIVE RESPONSE. Write what you think might be LaVerne's reply to Hazel. First, write LaVerne's response as a series of ordinary sentences, and then try editing and organizing them into poetic lines.

### CONNECTION TO ANOTHER SELECTION

1. Although Robert Browning's "My Last Duchess" (p. 636) is a more complex poem than Machan's, both use dramatic monologues to reveal character. How are the strategies in each poem similar?

# A SAMPLE STUDENT RESPONSE

Alex Georges

Professor Myerov

English 200

2 October 2023

Tone in Katharyn Howd Machan's "Hazel Tells LaVerne"

"Tone," Meyer and Miller write, "is the writer's attitude toward the subject, the mood created by all the elements in the poem" (561) and is used to convey meaning and character. In her dramatic monologue, "Hazel Tells LaVerne," the poet Katharyn Howd Machan reveals through the persona of Hazel—a funny, tough-talking, no-nonsense cleaning lady—a satirical revision of "The Frog Prince" fairy tale. Hazel's attitude toward the possibility of a fairy-tale romance is evident in her response to the frog prince. She has no use for him or his offers "bout a golden ball / an how i can be a princess" (lines 11-12). If Hazel is viewed by the reader as a princess, it is clear from her words and tone that she is far from a traditional one.

Machan's word choice and humorous tone also reveal much about Hazel's personality and circumstances. Through the use of slang, alternate spellings, and the omission of punctuation, we learn a great deal about the character:

well i screams

ya little green pervert

an i hitsm with my mop

an has ta flush

the toilet down three times

me

a princess (19-25)

Listening to her speak, the reader understands that Hazel, a cleaner at Howard Johnson's, does not have an extensive education. She speaks in the colloquial, running words into one another and using phrases like "ya little green pervert" (20) and "i screams" (19). The lack of complete sentences, capital letters, and punctuation adds to her informal tone. Hazel's

Georges 2

speech defines her social status, brings out details of her personality, and gives the reader her view of herself. She is accustomed to the thankless daily grind of work and will not allow herself even a moment's fantasy of becoming a princess. It is a notion that she has to flush away—literally, has "ta flush . . . down three times." She tells LaVerne that the very idea of such fantasy is absurd to her, as she states in the final lines: "me / a princess" (24-25).

Georges 3

Works Cited

Machan, Katharyn Howd. "Hazel Tells LaVerne." Meyer and Miller, p. 562.

Meyer, Michael, and D. Quentin Miller, editors. *The Compact Bedford Introduction to Literature*, 13th ed., Bedford/St. Martin's, 2024.

## MARTÍN ESPADA (B. 1957)
### *Latin Night at the Pawnshop*    1987

*Chelsea, Massachusetts*
*Christmas, 1987*

The apparition of a salsa band
gleaming in the Liberty Loan
pawnshop window:

Golden trumpet,
silver trombone,
congas, maracas, tambourine,

all with price tags dangling
like the city morgue ticket
on a dead man's toe.

> **WHEN I WRITE** "As a poet and a reader, I am most interested in the theme of justice. I am interested in poems that address justice vividly, concretely, specifically. Poets are, as Shelley put it, the 'unacknowledged legislators of the world.' We shouldn't leave justice to the lawyers and the politicians."
> —MARTÍN ESPADA

5

### CONSIDERATIONS FOR CRITICAL THINKING AND WRITING

1. **FIRST RESPONSE.** What is "Latin" about this night at the pawnshop?
2. What kind of tone is created by the poet's word choice and by the poem's rhythm?

3. Does it matter that this apparition occurs on Christmas night? Why or why not?

4. What do you think is the central point of this poem? How do the speaker's attitude and tone change during the course of the poem?

## JOY HARJO (B. 1951)

### *Granddaughters*   2019

Carlo Allegri/Getty Images.

I was a thought, a dream, a fish, a wing
And then a human being
When I emerged from my mother's river
On my father's boat of potent fever
I carried a sack of dreams from a starlit dwelling          5
To be opened when I begin bleeding
There's a red dress, deerskin moccasins
The taste of berries made of promises
While the memories shift in their skins
At every moon, to do their ripening                          10

### CONSIDERATIONS FOR CRITICAL THINKING AND WRITING

1. FIRST RESPONSE. How does the title of the poem challenge its meaning?

2. The poem is intent on carefully ordering the way it is presented. How does the order of the words contribute to the poem's effect?

3. What's the relationship between humanity and nature in this poem?

## DICTION AND TONE IN FOUR LOVE POEMS

Love is one of the most common subjects of poetry. Why? Possibly because love is different for everyone, and poets are in the business of exploring rather than defining. Possibly because love is mysterious and difficult to comprehend, no matter how wise and experienced we become. Poetry is drawn to mystery, to experiences or to ideas that can't be easily explained scientifically or rationally. Pay attention to how the diction used by each poet creates a unique tone and contributes to the variety of approaches to love in these poems.

## SHAMIM AZAD (B. 1952)

### *First Love*   2008

In Jamalpur, behind the Public Library,
in the house near the steps down to the river
I first met you.
The sky was filled with fragrance, and
youth, your song                                             5
              was my first love—

Perhaps because you were so young
                you'd swim away so easily—
before I could turn you into a verse
you eluded me again and again.             10
All day it was like this—all night, all day
I looked for you through that curtain of smoke.

After a while, profoundly weary, I lay down—
suddenly a sound broke through my sleep:
        even with my eyes closed I could feel        15
                the red moonlight outside,
                        the sound of water in the wind,
                              in the room.
I got up to look for the source, and you
were right next to my heart.             20

### CONSIDERATIONS FOR CRITICAL THINKING AND WRITING

1. FIRST RESPONSE. In what ways is "first love" different from later love? Does the poem reinforce your response or offer new ideas?

2. This is obviously an emotional poem. What emotions other than love characterize it? How do those emotions contribute to the tone of the poem?

3. The speaker's senses seem confused (feeling moonlight and hearing water in the wind, for instance). How does that confusion operate within the poem?

## ELIZABETH BARRETT BROWNING (1806-1861)

### *Sonnet XLIII*   1886

How do I love thee? Let me count the ways.
I love thee to the depth and breadth and height
My soul can reach, when feeling out of sight
For the ends of Being and ideal Grace.
I love thee to the level of every day's        5
Most quiet need, by sun and candlelight.
I love thee freely, as men strive for Right;
I love thee purely, as they turn from Praise.
I love thee with the passion put to use
In my old griefs, and with my childhood's faith.        10
I love thee with a love I seemed to lose
With my lost saints, – I love thee with the breath,
Smiles, tears, of all my life! – and, if God choose,
I shall but love thee better after death.

### CONSIDERATIONS FOR CRITICAL THINKING AND WRITING

1. FIRST RESPONSE. If you were the person addressed in this poem, how would you respond? Would you feel flattered, humbled, overwhelmed, nervous, or something else? Why?

2. This poem is a Petrarchan or Italian sonnet (see p. 683). What is the effect of containing such expansive emotion in such a precise short form?

3. There are some abstract ideas in this poem that bring it outside the realm of the strictly personal (such as "Being" (l. 4), "Grace" (l. 4), "Right" (l. 7), and a nod to the afterlife in the final line). What is the effect of this abstraction? Does it make the poem more or less moving than it would if the examples the speaker gave were more down to earth?

## JOHN FREDERICK NIMS (1913–1999)

### *Love Poem*  1947

My clumsiest dear, whose hands shipwreck vases,
At whose quick touch all glasses chip and ring,
Whose palms are bulls in china, burs in linen,
And have no cunning with any soft thing

Except all ill-at-ease fidgeting people:                                    5
The refugee uncertain at the door
You make at home; deftly you steady
The drunk clambering on his undulant floor.

Unpredictable dear, the taxi drivers' terror,
Shrinking from far headlights pale as a dime                      10
Yet leaping before red apoplectic streetcars: —
Misfit in any space. And never on time.

A wrench in clocks and the solar system. Only
With words and people and love you move at ease.
In traffic of wit expertly manoeuvre                                    15
And keep us, all devotion, at your knees.

Forgetting your coffee spreading on our flannel,
Your lipstick grinning on our coat,
So gayly in love's unbreakable heaven
Our souls on glory of spilt bourbon float.                            20

Be with me, darling, early and late. Smash glasses —
I will study wry music for your sake.
For should your hands drop white and empty
All the toys of the world would break.

### CONSIDERATIONS FOR CRITICAL THINKING AND WRITING

1. FIRST RESPONSE. What's the relationship between praise or flattery and love?

2. The tone of the last two lines is sorrowful and maudlin, yet most of the poem is light and humorous. Where, exactly, does the tone turn? What is the effect of this contrast?

3. While the speaker seems to admire the addressee, are all of their qualities equally charming to the speaker, or are some more irksome or delighting?

4. Discuss the imagery of breaking and/or of disruption in the poem as it relates to the theme.

5. CREATIVE RESPONSE. Write an imitation of the poem from the addressee to the speaker, imagining their contrasted personalities while still trying to express the same type of love we see expressed here.

## PABLO NERUDA (1904–1973)

### *Drunk as drunk on turpentine*   1969

TRANSLATED BY CHRISTOPHER LOGUE

STF/Getty Images.

Drunk as drunk on turpentine
From your open kisses,
Your wet body wedged
Between my wet body and the strake°
Of our boat that is made out of flowers,                    5
Feasted, we guide it — our fingers
Like tallows adorned with yellow metal —
Over the sky's hot rim,
The day's last breath in our sails.

Pinned by the sun between solstice                          10
And equinox, drowzy and tangled together
We drifted for months and woke
With the bitter taste of land on our lips,
Eyelids all sticky, and we longed for lime
And the sound of a rope                                     15
Lowering a bucket down its well. Then,
We came by night to the Fortunate Isles,°
And lay like fish
Under the net of our kisses.

4 *strake:* A ridge or line of planks that runs the length of a boat.
17 *Fortunate Isles:* Legendary islands considered an earthly paradise in Greek mythology, free from strife or foul weather.

### CONSIDERATIONS FOR CRITICAL THINKING AND WRITING

1. FIRST RESPONSE.  Does this pair of lovers seem more like two individuals or a single being? How does your response help focus the understanding of love advanced here?

2. What are the various ways the poem appeals to the senses? What is the effect of this emphasis?

3. The recurrent imagery here involves the ocean. How does the poet exploit the potential of the ocean as a setting to explore love?

## POEMS FOR FURTHER STUDY

### WALT WHITMAN (1819–1892)

### *The Dalliance of the Eagles*   1880

Skirting the river road, (my forenoon walk, my rest,)
Skyward in air a sudden muffled sound, the dalliance of the eagles,
The rushing amorous contact high in space together,
The clinching interlocking claws, a living, fierce, gyrating wheel,

Four beating wings, two beaks, a swirling mass tight grappling,                    5
In tumbling turning clustering loops, straight downward falling,
Till o'er the river pois'd, the twain yet one, a moment's lull,
A motionless still balance in the air, then parting, talons loosing,
Upward again on slow-firm pinions slanting, their separate diverse flight,
She hers, he his, pursuing.                                                        10

### CONSIDERATIONS FOR CRITICAL THINKING AND WRITING

1. FIRST RESPONSE. Why do you think Whitman chose the word *dalliance* rather than, perhaps, *mating*?

2. List the verbs in the poem and comment on their effects in evoking the scene.

### CONNECTION TO ANOTHER SELECTION

1. Compare Whitman's treatment of the eagles with Alfred, Lord Tennyson's description of "The Eagle" (p. 552). Which do you find more powerful? Why?

## KWAME DAWES (B. 1962)

## *History Lesson at Eight a.m.*   1993

History class at eight a.m.
Who discover Jamaica, class?
*Christopher Columbus*
Tell me when?
*Fourteen ninety-two*                                                             5
And where?

*Discovery Bay*
*Discovery Bay*

Twisting through Mount Diablo
Where Juan de Bolas was hiding                                                     10
Musket, fife, and powder
Guerrilla, revolutionary
I am traveling to Discovery Bay
Traveling to Discovery Bay

How many ships?                                                                   15
*Three ships*
What them name?
*Niña*
One
*Pinta*                                                                           20
Two
*Santa Maria*
Tell me where?

*Discovery Bay*
*Discovery Bay*                                                        25

Twisting through Fern Gully
Arawak blood was shed here
Crack their brains with musket shot
History is buried here
I am traveling to Discovery Bay                                        30
Traveling to Discovery Bay

Who lived here first?
*Arawak and Carib*
What were the Arawak?
*Peaceful flat-head people*                                            35
What were the Caribs?
*Cannibals*
Cannibals?
*Yes, cannibals!*
Now tell me where?                                                     40

*Discovery Bay*
*Discovery Bay*

Rush past Saint Ann's Bay
Marcus was preaching from the altar
See the slave auction inna Falmouth                                    45
Cane field wild with fire
I am traveling to Discovery Bay
Traveling to Discovery Bay

You teach me all kind of madness
From Hawkins to Drake to Pizarro                                       50
From Cortés to Penn to Venables
At eight a.m. each blessed day

No wonder I can't find Discovery Bay
Was looking for the gold
And all I see is blood                                                 55
All I see is blood
All I see is blood

## CONSIDERATIONS FOR CRITICAL THINKING AND WRITING

1. FIRST RESPONSE. How does the poem function as a history lesson for the reader as well as for the children speaking in the poem?

2. How can you tell the difference between speakers in the poem?

3. What effect does repetition have throughout the poem? Does its effect change?

4. How does the blending of informal diction and dialect contribute to the poem's overall effect?

CATHY SONG (B. 1955)

## *The Youngest Daughter*   1983

The sky has been dark
for many years.
My skin has become as damp
and pale as rice paper
and feels the way                                                    5
mother's used to before the drying sun
parched it out there in the fields.

  Lately, when I touch myself,
my hands react as if
I had just touched something                                         10
hot enough to burn.
My skin, aspirin-colored,
tingles with migraine. Mother
has been massaging the left side of my face
especially in the evenings                                           15
when it flares up.

This morning
her breathing was graveled,
her voice gruff with affection
when I took her into the bath.                                       20
She was in good humor,
making jokes about her great breasts,
floating in the milky water
like two walruses,
flaccid and whiskered around the nipples.                            25
I scrubbed them with a sour taste
in my mouth, thinking:
six children and an old man
have sucked from these brown nipples.

I was almost tender                                                  30
when I came to the blue bruises
that freckle her body,
places where she has been injecting insulin
for thirty years, ever since
I can remember. I soaped her slowly,                                 35
she sighed deeply, her eyes closed.

In the afternoons
when she has rested,
she prepares our ritual of tea and rice,
garnished with a shred of gingered fish,                             40
a slice of pickled turnip
a token for my white body.
We eat in the familiar silence.

She knows I am not to be trusted,
even now planning my escape.                                    45
As I toast to her health
with the tea she has poured,
a thousand cranes curtain the window,
fly up in a sudden breeze.

### CONSIDERATIONS FOR CRITICAL THINKING AND WRITING

1. FIRST RESPONSE. Though the speaker is the youngest daughter in the family, how old do you think she is based on the description of her in the poem? What, specifically, makes you think so?

2. How would you characterize the relationship between mother and daughter? How are lines 44–45 ("She knows I am not to be trusted, / even now planning my escape") particularly revealing of the nature of the relationship?

3. Interpret the final four lines of the poem. Why do you think it ends with this image?

## JOHN KEATS (1795–1821)

### *Ode on a Grecian Urn*    1819

### I

Thou still unravished bride of quietness,
   Thou foster-child of silence and slow time,
Sylvan° historian, who canst thus express
   A flowery tale more sweetly than our rhyme:
What leaf-fringed legend haunts about thy shape                5
    Of deities or mortals, or of both,
      In Tempe or the dales of Arcady?°
What men or gods are these? What maidens loath?
    What mad pursuit? What struggle to escape?
      What pipes and timbrels? What wild ecstasy?      10

### II

Heard melodies are sweet, but those unheard
   Are sweeter; therefore, ye soft pipes, play on;
Not to the sensual ear, but, more endeared,
   Pipe to the spirit ditties of no tone:
Fair youth, beneath the trees, thou canst not leave           15
    Thy song, nor ever can those trees be bare;

3 *Sylvan*: Rustic. The urn is decorated with a forest scene.
7 *Tempe, Arcady*: Beautiful rural valleys in Greece.

Bold Lover, never, never canst thou kiss,
Though winning near the goal — yet, do not grieve;
  She cannot fade, though thou hast not thy bliss,
    For ever wilt thou love, and she be fair!                    20

### III

Ah, happy, happy boughs! that cannot shed
  Your leaves, nor ever bid the Spring adieu;
And, happy melodist, unwearièd,
  For ever piping songs for ever new;
More happy love! more happy, happy love!                         25
  For ever warm and still to be enjoyed,
    For ever panting, and for ever young;
All breathing human passion far above,
  That leaves a heart high-sorrowful and cloyed,
    A burning forehead, and a parching tongue.                   30

### IV

Who are these coming to the sacrifice?
  To what green altar, O mysterious priest,
Lead'st thou that heifer lowing at the skies,
  And all her silken flanks with garlands drest?
What little town by river or sea shore,                          35
  Or mountain-built with peaceful citadel,
    Is emptied of this folk, this pious morn?
And, little town, thy streets for evermore
  Will silent be; and not a soul to tell
    Why thou art desolate, can e'er return.                      40

### V

O Attic° shape! Fair attitude! with brede°
  Of marble men and maidens overwrought,
With forest branches and the trodden weed;
  Thou, silent form, dost tease us out of thought
As doth eternity: Cold Pastoral!                                 45
  When old age shall this generation waste,
    Thou shalt remain, in midst of other woe
Than ours, a friend to man, to whom thou say'st,
  Beauty is truth, truth beauty — that is all
    Ye know on earth, and all ye need to know.                   50

41 *Attic*: Possessing classic Athenian simplicity.    *brede*: Design.

## CONSIDERATIONS FOR CRITICAL THINKING AND WRITING

1. FIRST RESPONSE. What does the speaker's diction reveal about their attitude toward the urn in this ode? Does this view develop or change?
2. How is the happiness in stanza 3 related to the assertion in lines 11–12 that "Heard melodies are sweet, but those unheard / Are sweeter"?
3. What is the difference between the world depicted on the urn and the speaker's world?
4. What do lines 49 and 50 suggest about the relation of art to life? Why is the urn described as a "Cold Pastoral" (line 45)?
5. Which world does the speaker seem to prefer, the urn's or their own?
6. Describe the overall tone of the poem.

## CONNECTIONS TO OTHER SELECTIONS

1. Write an essay comparing the view of time in this ode with that in Marvell's "To His Coy Mistress" (p. 941). Pay particular attention to the connotative language in each poem.
2. Compare the tone and attitude toward life in this ode with those in John Keats's "When I have fears that I may cease to be" (p. 940).

## ALICE JONES (B. 1949)

### *The Lungs*   1997

WHEN I WRITE "The process of becoming a writer involves recognizing the desire to write, allowing ourselves to take the desire seriously, and then learning to recognize the obstacles we put in our own way."
— ALICE JONES

In the tidal flux, the lobed pair avidly
   grasp the invisible.

Along oblique fissures, gnarled vascular roots
   anchor the puffed cushions,

soot-mottled froth, the pink segmented sponges                                5
   that soak up the atmosphere,

then squeezed by the rising dome of the diaphragm's
   muscular bellows, exhale.

Braids of vessels and cartilage descend
   in vanishing smallness,                                10

to grape clusters of alveoli, the sheerest
   of membranes, where oxygen

crosses the infinite cellular web, where air turns
   to blood, spirit to flesh,

in a molecular transubstantiation, to bring rich                                15
   food to that red engine,

the heart, which like an equitable mother, pumps
   to each organ and appendage

according to need, so even the cells in the darkest
   corners can breathe.                                20

### CONSIDERATIONS FOR CRITICAL THINKING AND WRITING

1. FIRST RESPONSE. Why are the lines in this poem arranged in pairs? How does the length of the sentences contribute to the poem's meaning?

2. Make a list of words and phrases from the poem that strike you as scientific, and compare those with a list of words that seem poetic. How do they compete or complement each other in terms of how they affect your reading?

3. Comment on the use of personification (see the Glossary, p. 1483) in the poem.

### CONNECTION TO ANOTHER SELECTION

1. Compare the diction and the ending in "The Lungs" with those of "The Foot" (p. 574), another poem by Jones.

## LOUIS SIMPSON (1923–2012)

### *In the Suburbs*  1963

There's no way out.
You were born to waste your life.
You were born to this middleclass life

As others before you
Were born to walk in procession                                      5
To the temple, singing.

### CONSIDERATIONS FOR CRITICAL THINKING AND WRITING

1. FIRST RESPONSE. Is the title of this poem especially significant? What images does it conjure up for you?

2. What does the repetition in lines 2–3 suggest?

3. Discuss the possible connotative meanings of lines 5 and 6. Who are the "others before you"?

### CONNECTION TO ANOTHER SELECTION

1. Write an essay on suburban life based on this poem and Gregory Corso's "Marriage" (p. 952).

## A NOTE ON READING TRANSLATIONS

Sometimes translation can inadvertently be a comic business. Consider, for example, the discovery made by John Steinbeck's wife, Elaine, when in a Yokohama bookstore she asked for a copy of her husband's famous novel *The Grapes of Wrath* and learned that it had been translated into Japanese as *Angry Raisins.* Close but no cigar (perhaps translated as: nearby, yet no smoke). As amusing as that *Angry Raisins* title is, it teaches an important lesson about the significance of a poet's or a translator's choices when crafting a poem: a powerful piece moves us through diction and tone, both built word by careful word. Translations are frequently regarded as merely vehicular, a way to arrive at the original work. It is, of course, the original work — its spirit, style, and meaning — that most readers expect to find in a translation. Even so, it is important to understand that a translation is *by nature* different from the original — and that despite that difference, a fine translation can be an important part of the journey and become part of the literary landscape itself. Reading a translation of a poem is not the same as reading the original, but neither is watching two different performances of *Hamlet.* The translator provides a reading of the poem in much the same way that a director shapes the play. Each interprets the text from a unique perspective.

Basically, there are two distinct approaches to translation: literal translations and adaptations. A literal translation sets out to create a word-for-word equivalent that is absolutely faithful to the original. As simple and direct as this method may sound, literal translations are nearly impossible over extended passages because of the structural differences between languages. Moreover, the meaning of a single word in one language may not exist in another language, or it may require a phrase, clause, or entire sentence to capture its implications. Adaptations of works offer broader, more open-ended approaches to translation. Unlike a literal translation, an adaptation moves beyond denotative meanings in an attempt to capture the spirit of a work so that its idioms, dialects, slang, and other conventions are recreated in the language of the translation.

The question we ask of an adaptation should not be "Is this exactly how the original reads?" Instead, we ask, "Is this an insightful, graceful rendering worth reading?" To translate poetry it is not enough to know the language of the original; it is also necessary that the translator be a poet. A translated poem is more than a collation of decisions based on dictionaries and grammars; it must also be poetry. However undefinable poetry may be, it is unmistakable in its intense use of language. Poems are not merely translated; they are savored.

## Three Translations of a Poem by Sappho

Sappho, born about 630 B.C.E. and a native of the Greek island of Lesbos, is the author of a hymn to Aphrodite, the goddess of love and beauty in Greek myth. The three translations that follow suggest how widely translations can differ from one another. Each represents the translator's unique approach and values.

# SAPPHO (CA. 630 B.C.E.–CA. 570 B.C.E.)

## *Immortal Aphrodite of the broidered throne*  date unknown

TRANSLATED BY HENRY T. WHARTON (1885)

Immortal Aphrodite of the broidered throne, daughter of Zeus, weaver of wiles, I pray thee break not my spirit with anguish and distress, O Queen. But come hither, if ever before thou didst hear my voice afar, and listen, and leaving thy father's golden house camest with chariot yoked, and fair fleet sparrows drew thee, flapping fast their wings around the dark earth, from heaven

Bettmann/Getty Images.

through mid sky. Quickly arrived they; and thou, blessed one, smiling with immortal countenance, didst ask What now is befallen me, and Why now I call, and What I in my mad heart most desire to see. "What Beauty now wouldst thou draw to love thee? Who wrongs thee, Sappho? For even if she flies she shall soon follow, and if she rejects gifts shall yet give, and if she loves not shall soon love, however loth." Come, I pray thee, now too, and release me from cruel cares; and all that my heart desires to accomplish, accomplish thou, and be thyself my ally.

## *Beautiful-throned, immortal Aphrodite*

TRANSLATED BY THOMAS WENTWORTH HIGGINSON (1871)

Beautiful-throned, immortal Aphrodite,
Daughter of Zeus, beguiler, I implore thee,
Weigh me not down with weariness and anguish
    O Thou most holy!

Come to me now, if ever thou in kindness      5
Hearkenedst my words, — and often hast thou hearkened —
Heeding, and coming from the mansions golden
    Of thy great Father,

Yoking thy chariot, borne by the most lovely
Consecrated birds, with dusky-tinted pinions,      10
Waving swift wings from utmost heights of heaven
    Through the mid-ether;

Swiftly they vanished, leaving thee, O goddess,
Smiling, with face immortal in its beauty,
Asking why I grieved, and why in utter longing      15
    I had dared call thee;

Asking what I sought, thus hopeless in desiring,
Wildered in brain, and spreading nets of passion —
Alas, for whom? and saidst thou, "Who has harmed thee?
      "O my poor Sappho! 20

"Though now he flies, ere long he shall pursue thee;
"Fearing thy gifts, he too in turn shall bring them;
"Loveless to-day, to-morrow he shall woo thee,
      "Though thou shouldst spurn him."

Thus seek me now, O holy Aphrodite! 25
Save me from anguish; give me all I ask for,
Gifts at thy hand; and thine shall be the glory,
      Sacred protector!

## *Prayer to my lady of Paphos*

TRANSLATED BY MARY BARNARD (1958)

Dapple-throned Aphrodite,
eternal daughter of God,
snare-knitter! Don't, I beg you,

cow my heart with grief! Come,
as once when you heard my far- 5
off cry and, listening, stepped

from your father's house to your
gold car, to yoke the pair whose
beautiful thick-feathered wings

oaring down mid-air from heaven 10
carried you to light swiftly
on dark earth; then, blissful one,

smiling your immortal smile
you asked, What ailed me now that
made me call you again? What 15

was it that my distracted
heart most wanted? "Whom has
Persuasion to bring round now

"to your love? Who, Sappho, is
unfair to you? For, let her 20
run, she will soon run after;

"if she won't accept gifts, she
will one day give them; and if
she won't love you — she soon will

"love, although unwillingly . . ."                                          25
If ever — come now! Relieve
this intolerable pain!

What my heart most hopes will
happen, make happen; you your-
self join forces on my side!                                                30

### CONSIDERATIONS FOR CRITICAL THINKING AND WRITING

1. FIRST RESPONSE. You've probably encountered multiple versions of songs you
   like, such as a live version versus a studio version, or acoustic versus electric,
   or a remix, or a cover by another artist. What's your general reaction toward
   the existence of multiple versions of the same work? Would you prefer to have
   a single version that you can depend on, or do you like the variety experienced
   through multiple artists' interpretations?

2. Discuss the images and metaphors in the three versions. Which version is
   most appealing to you? Explain why.

3. What are the key differences between the translations? How does each translator's use of diction create a unique effect? Does an examination of these differences bring you closer to an appreciation of the poem?

# 18

# Images

AP Photo/Rogelio V. Solis.

> I think poetry is always a kind of faith. It is the kind that I have.
>
> — NATASHA TRETHEWEY

## POETRY'S APPEAL TO THE SENSES

A poet, to borrow a phrase that Henry James used to describe fiction writers, is one on whom nothing is lost. Poets take in the world and give us impressions of what they experience through images. An *image* is language that addresses the senses. The most common images in poetry are visual; they provide verbal pictures of the poet's encounters — real or imagined — with the world. But poets also create images that appeal to our other senses. Li Ho arouses several senses in this excerpt from "A Beautiful Girl Combs Her Hair":

> Awake at dawn
> she's dreaming
> by cool silk curtains
>
> fragrance of spilling hair
> half sandalwood, half aloes
>
> windlass creaking at the well
> singing jade

5

These vivid images deftly blend textures, fragrances, and sounds that tease out the sensuousness of the moment. Images give us the physical world to experience in our imaginations. Some poems, like the following one, are written to do just that; they make no comment about what they describe.

## WILLIAM CARLOS WILLIAMS (1883–1963)

### *Poem*   1934

As the cat
climbed over
the top of

the jamcloset
first the right                                                                5
forefoot

carefully
then the hind
stepped down

into the pit of                                                               10
the empty
flowerpot

This poem defies paraphrase because it is all an image of agile movement. No statement is made about the movement; the title, "Poem" — really no title — signals Williams's refusal to comment on the movements. To impose a meaning on the poem, we'd probably have to knock over the flowerpot.

We experience the image in Williams's "Poem" more clearly because of how the sentence is organized into lines and groups of lines, or stanzas. Consider how differently the sentence is read if it is arranged as prose:

> As the cat climbed over the top of the jamcloset, first the right forefoot carefully then the hind stepped down into the pit of the empty flowerpot.

The poem's line and stanza division transforms what is essentially an awkward prose sentence into a rhythmic verbal picture. Especially when the poem is read aloud, this line and stanza division allows us to feel the image we see. Even the lack of a period at the end suggests that the cat is only pausing.

Images frequently do more than offer only sensory impressions, however. They also convey emotions and moods, as in the following poem's view of Civil War troops moving across a river.

## WALT WHITMAN (1819–1892)

### *Cavalry Crossing a Ford*  1865

A line in long array where they wind betwixt green islands,
They take a serpentine course, their arms flash in the sun — hark to the
    musical clank,
Behold the silvery river, in it the splashing horses loitering stop to drink,
Behold the brown-faced men, each group, each person, a picture, the
    negligent rest on the saddles,
Some emerge on the opposite bank, others are just entering the ford — while,    5
Scarlet and blue and snowy white,
The guidon flags flutter gaily in the wind.

### CONSIDERATIONS FOR CRITICAL THINKING AND WRITING

1. **FIRST RESPONSE.** Do the colors and sounds establish the mood of this poem? What is the mood?

2. How would the poem's mood have been changed if Whitman had used "look" or "see" instead of "behold" (lines 3–4)?

3. From where is the speaker observing this troop movement?

4. Does "serpentine" in line 2 have an evil connotation in this poem? Explain your answer.

Whitman seems to capture momentarily all of the troop's actions, and through carefully chosen, suggestive details — really very few — he succeeds in making "each group, each person, a picture." Specific details, even when few are provided, give us the impression that we see the entire picture; it is as if those are the details we would remember if we had viewed the scene ourselves. Notice, too, that the movement of the "line in long array" is emphasized by the continuous winding syntax of the poem's lengthy lines.

The following poem is rich with images and dense with the specialized language of horticulture, or gardening. On your first read-through, focus on the picture that is painted rather than the terms you are unfamiliar with: you can research those and come back to them on subsequent readings to enhance the experience.

## SUJI KWOCK KIM (B. 1968)

### *The Korean Community Garden in Queens*  1994

In the vacant lot nobody else wanted to rebuild,
dirt scumbled for years with syringes and dead
weed-husks, tire-shreds and smashed beer bottles,
the first green shoots of spring spike through—

Photo by Jill D'Alessandro.

bullbrier, redroot, pokeweed, sowthistle,                                    5
an uprising of grasses whose only weapons are themselves.
Blades slit through scurf. Spear-tips spit dust
as if thrust from the other side. They spar and glint.

How far will they climb, grappling for light?
Inside I see coils of fern-bracken called *kosari*,                         10
bellflower cuts named *toraji* in the old country.
Knuckles of ginger and mugwort dig upward,

shoving through mulched soil until they break
the surface. Planted by immigrants they survive,
like their gardeners, ripped from their native                              15
plot. What is it that they want, driving and driving

toward a foreign sky? How not to mind the end
we'll come to. I imagine the garden underground,
where gingko and ailanthus grub cement rubble.
They tunnel slag for foothold. Wring crumbs of rot                          20

for water. Of shadows, seeds foresung as *Tree
of Heaven* and *Silver Apricot* in ancient Mandarin,
their roots tangle now with plum or weeping willow,
their branches mingling with tamarack or oak.

I love how nothing in these furrows grows unsnarled,                        25
nothing stays unscathed. How last year's fallen stalks,
withered to pith, cleave to this year's crocus bulbs,
each infant knot burred with bits of garbage or tar.

Fist to fist with tulips, iris, selving and unselving
glads, they work their metamorphoses in loam                                30
pocked with rust-flints, splinters of rodent-skull—
a ground so mixed, so various that everything

seems born of what it's not. Who wouldn't want
to flower like this? How strangely they become
themselves, this gnarl of azaleas and roses-of-Sharon,                      35
native to both countries, blooming as if drunk

with blossoming. Green buds suck and bulge.
Stem-nubs thicken. Sepals swell and crack their cauls.
Lately every time I walk down this street to look
through the fence, I'm surprised by something new.                          40

Yesterday hydrangea and chrysanthemums burst
their calyxes, corolla-skins blistering into welts.
Today jonquils slit blue shoots from their sheaths.
Tomorrow day lilies and asters will flame petals,

each incandescent color unlike: sulfur, blood, ice,                         45
coral, fire-gold, violet the hue of shaman robes—
every flower with its unique glint or slant, faithful
to each particular. All things lit by what they neighbor

but are not, each tint flaring without a human soul,
without human rage at its passing. In the summer        50
there will be scallions, mung beans, black sesame,
muskmelons, to be harvested into buckets and sold

at market. How do they live without wanting to live
forever? May I, and their gardeners in the old world,
who kill for warring dreams and warring heavens,        55
who stop at nothing, see life and paradise as one.

## CONSIDERATIONS FOR CRITICAL THINKING AND WRITING

1. FIRST RESPONSE. Pretend you're "weeding" the garden that is this poem: what
   do you harvest, or lift out as potentially precious?

2. Other than the technical language of horticulture, what are some of the notable words in the poem? What effect do they have?

3. From the title on, this is a poem about transplanting culture. How does the
   difference between the old world and the new inform the poem?

4. What's the essential relationship between humanity and nature in this
   poem?

## CONNECTION TO ANOTHER SELECTION

1. Compare the feeling of nature bursting from the earth in this poem and in
   Ruth Fainlight's "Crocuses" (p. 586). What is the effect of nature in each? The
   theme?

Movement is central to the next poem, in which action and motion are
created through carefully chosen verbs.

## DAVID SOLWAY (B. 1941)

### *Windsurfing*   1993

> WHEN I READ "The good poet always generates a sense of lexical surprise, an openness toward the unexpected, a feeling of novelty and delight."
> — DAVID SOLWAY

It rides upon the wrinkled hide
of water, like the upturned hull
of a small canoe or kayak
waiting to be righted — yet its law
is opposite to that of boats,                           5
it floats upon its breastbone and
brings whatever spine there is to light.
A thin shaft is slotted into place.
Then a puffed right-angle of wind
pushes it forward, out into the bay,                    10
where suddenly it glitters into speed,
tilts, knifes up, and for the moment's
nothing but a slim projectile
of cambered fiberglass,
peeling the crests.                                     15

The man's
clamped to the mast, taut as a guywire.
Part of the sleek apparatus
he controls, immaculate nerve
of balance, plunge and curvet,                                      20
he clinches all component movements
into single motion.
It bucks, stalls, shudders, yaws, and dips
its hissing sides beneath the surface
that sustains it, tensing                                           25
into muscle that nude ellipse
of lunging appetite and power.

And now the mechanism's wholly
dolphin, springing toward its prey
of spume and beaded sunlight,                                       30
tossing spray, and hits the vertex
of the wide, salt glare of distance,
and reverses.

              Back it comes through
a screen of particles,                                             35
scalloped out of water, shimmer
and reflection, the wind snapping
and lashing it homeward,
shearing the curve of the wave,
breaking the spell of the caught breath                            40
and articulate play of sinew, to enter
the haven of the breakwater
and settle in a rush of silence.

Now the crossing drifts
in the husk of its wake                                             45
and nothing's the same again
as, gliding elegantly on a film of water,
the man guides
his brash, obedient legend
into shore.                                                        50

### CONSIDERATIONS FOR CRITICAL THINKING AND WRITING

1. FIRST RESPONSE. Highlight the verbs that seem especially effective in convey-
   ing a strong sense of motion, and explain why they are effective.
2. How is the man made to seem to be one with his board and sail?
3. How does the rhythm of the poem change beginning with line 44?

### CONNECTION TO ANOTHER SELECTION

1. Consider the effects of the images in "Windsurfing" and Robert Frost's
   "Birches" (p. 867). In an essay, explain how these images elicit the emotional
   responses they do.

"Windsurfing" is awash with images of speed, fluidity, and power. Even the calming aftermath of the breakwater is described as a "rush of silence," adding to the sense of motion that is detailed and expanded throughout the poem.

## POEMS FOR FURTHER STUDY

### Adelaide Crapsey (1878–1914)

## *November Night*    1913

Listen . . .
With faint dry sound,
Like steps of passing ghosts,
The leaves, frost-crisp'd, break from the trees
And fall.                                                                                    5

#### Considerations for Critical Thinking and Writing

1. **First response.** Which senses are evoked in the poem? What sort of tone do the words produce?
2. Explain whether or not "November Night" has a theme.

#### Connection to Another Selection

1. Compare the use of images and their effects in this poem and in E. E. Cummings's "l(a" (p. 538).

### Ruth Fainlight (b. 1931)

## *Crocuses*    2006

Pale, bare, tender stems rising
from the muddy winter-faded grass,

shivering petals the almost luminous
blue and mauve of bruises on the naked

bodies of men, women, children                                                      5
herded into a forest clearing

before the shouted order, crack of gunfire,
final screams and prayers and moans.

#### Considerations for Critical Thinking and Writing

1. **First response.** Comment on Fainlight's choice of title. What effect does it have on your reading of the poem?
2. Trace your response to each image in the poem and describe the poem's tone as it moves from line to line.
3. **Creative response.** Try writing an eight-line poem that, similar to Fainlight's, is based on images that gradually but radically shift in tone.

MARY ROBINSON (1758–1800)

## London's Summer Morning    1806

Who has not wak'd to list° the busy sounds                                *listen to*
Of summer's morning, in the sultry smoke
Of noisy London? On the pavement hot
The sooty chimney-boy, with dingy face
And tatter'd covering, shrilly bawls his trade,                                5
Rousing the sleepy housemaid. At the door
The milk-pail rattles, and the tinkling bell
Proclaims the dustman's office; while the street
Is lost in clouds impervious. Now begins
The din of hackney-coaches, waggons, carts;                                10
While tinmen's shops, and noisy trunk-makers,
Knife-grinders, coopers, squeaking cork-cutters,
Fruit-barrows, and the hunger-giving cries
Of vegetable venders, fill the air.
Now ev'ry shop displays its varied trade,                                15
And the fresh-sprinkled pavement cools the feet
Of early walkers. At the private door
The ruddy housemaid twirls the busy mop,
Annoying the smart 'prentice, or neat girl,
Tripping with band-box° lightly. Now the sun                      *hatbox* 20
Darts burning splendour on the glitt'ring pane,
Save where the canvas awning throws a shade
On the gay merchandize. Now, spruce and trim,
In shops (where beauty smiles with industry),
Sits the smart damsel; while the passenger                                25
Peeps thro' the window, watching ev'ry charm.
Now pastry dainties catch the eye minute
Of humming insects, while the limy snare
Waits to enthral them. Now the lamp-lighter
Mounts the tall ladder, nimbly vent'rous,                                30
To trim the half-fill'd lamp; while at his feet
The pot-boy° yells discordant! All along                      *drink server*
The sultry pavement, the old-clothes-man cries
In tones monotonous, and side-long views
The area for his traffic: now the bag                                35
Is slily open'd, and the half-worn suit
(Sometimes the pilfer'd treasure of the base
Domestic spoiler), for one half its worth,
Sinks in the green abyss. The porter now
Bears his huge load along the burning way;                                40
And the poor poet wakes from busy dreams,
To paint the summer morning.

## CONSIDERATIONS FOR CRITICAL THINKING AND WRITING

1. **FIRST RESPONSE.** How effective is this picture of a London summer morning in 1806? Which images do you find particularly effective?

2. How does the end of the poem bring us full circle to its beginning? What effect does this structure have on your understanding of the poem?

3. CREATIVE RESPONSE. Try writing about the start of your own day — in the dormitory, at home, at the start of a class — using a series of images that provide a vivid sense of what happens and how you experience it.

## CONNECTION TO ANOTHER SELECTION

1. How does Robinson's description of London differ from William Blake's "London," the next poem? What would you say is the essential difference in purpose between the two poems?

## WILLIAM BLAKE (1757–1827)

### *London*  1794

| | |
|---|---|
| I wander through each chartered° street, | *defined by law* |
| Near where the chartered Thames does flow, | |
| And mark in every face I meet | |
| Marks of weakness, marks of woe. | |

In every cry of every man,                                         5
In every Infant's cry of fear,
In every voice, in every ban,
The mind-forged manacles I hear.

How the Chimney-sweeper's cry
Every black'ning Church appalls;                                  10
And the hapless Soldier's sigh
Runs in blood down Palace walls.

But most through midnight streets I hear
How the youthful Harlot's curse
Blasts the new-born Infant's tear,                                15
And blights with plagues the Marriage hearse.

## CONSIDERATIONS FOR CRITICAL THINKING AND WRITING

1. FIRST RESPONSE. What feelings do the visual images in this poem suggest?

2. What is the predominant sound heard in the poem?

3. What is the meaning of line 8? What is the cause of the problems that the speaker sees and hears in London? Does the speaker suggest additional causes?

4. The image in lines 11 and 12 cannot be read literally. Comment on its effectiveness.

5. How does Blake's use of denotative and connotative language enrich this poem's meaning?

6. An earlier version of Blake's last stanza appeared this way:

> But most the midnight harlot's curse
> From every dismal street I hear,
> Weaves around the marriage hearse
> And blasts the new-born infant's tear.

Examine carefully the differences between the two versions. How do Blake's revisions affect his picture of London life? Which version do you think is more effective? Why?

# A SAMPLE STUDENT RESPONSE

Anna Tamara

Professor Burton

English 211

30 September 2023

Imagery in William Blake's "London" and Mary Robinson's
"London's Summer Morning"

Both William Blake and Mary Robinson use strong imagery to examine and bring to life the city of London, yet each writer paints a very different picture. The images in both poems "[address] the senses," as Meyer and Miller write (580). But while Blake's images depict a city weighed down by oppression and poverty, Robinson's images are lighter, happier, and, arguably, idealized. Both poems use powerful imagery in very different ways to establish theme.

In Blake's poem, oppression and social discontent are defined by the speaker, who sees "weakness" and "woe" (line 4) in the faces he meets; he hears cries of men and children and "mind-forged manacles" (8). And, through imagery, the poem makes a political statement:

How the Chimney-sweeper's cry

Every black'ning Church appalls;

And the hapless Soldier's sigh

Runs in blood down Palace walls. (9-12)

These images indicate the speaker's dark view of the religious and governmental institutions that he believes cause the city's suffering. The "black'ning Church" and bloody "Palace walls" can be seen to represent misused power and corruption, while the "manacles" are the rules and physical and psychological burdens that lead to societal ills. In Blake's view of London, children are sold into servitude (as chimney sweeps) and soldiers pay in blood.

Robinson's poem, on the other hand, offers the reader a pleasant view of a sunny London morning through a different series of images. The reader hears "the tinkling bell" (7) and sees a bright moment in which "the sun / Darts burning splendour on the glitt'ring pane" (20-21). Even the chimney-boy is shown in a rosy glow. Though he is described as having

a "dingy face / And tatter'd covering," he wakes the "sleepy" house servant
when he "shrilly bawls his trade" (4-6). In contrast to the chimney-sweep
of Blake's "London," Robinson's boy is painted as a charming character
who announces the morning amid a backdrop of happy workers. Also unlike
Blake's London, Robinson's is a city of contentment in which a "ruddy
housemaid twirls the busy mop" (18) . . .

Works Cited

Blake, William. "London." Meyer and Miller, p. 588.

Meyer, Michael, and D. Quentin Miller, editors. *The Compact Bedford
Introduction to Literature,* 13th ed., Bedford/St. Martin's, 2024.

Robinson, Mary. "London's Summer Morning." Meyer and Miller, p. 587.

## KWAME DAWES (B. 1962)
### *The Habits of Love* 1998

Since his wife Loretta's death, Monty collects
the burn-stained clicking carcasses of bulbs,
storing them in cotton stuffed into plastic
pastel-colored party cups. He shelves

them in the tinderbox-shed in the backyard,    5
visiting them each week as a ritual
for the dead. He tries not to discard
the multiples, but relishes the collapsed oval

of one he found glowing in an open field,
the sun humming in the shattered filament,    10
as if the earth fed power to make light bleed
through, so a man would stare in wonderment.

Mike Coppola/Getty Images.

It is still the cherished one, despite the hundreds
he has gathered in the gloomy innards
of his shed. Esther has seen but not said                                    15
a thing; so grand his pain, so hard, so hard.

### CONSIDERATIONS FOR CRITICAL THINKING AND WRITING

1. FIRST RESPONSE. Look closely at the image Dawes creates in the first stanza. How does it evoke a stronger image than if he had said, "Monty collects used light bulbs"?

2. How does the image of the one glowing bulb Monty found in a field — an effect produced by a trick of sunlight — deepen the poem's visual appeal?

3. Identify all the adjectives in the poem. How does that list of words alone suggest the poem's dominant emotion?

## CHARLES SIMIC  (1938–2023)

### *House of Cards*    2006

I miss you winter evenings
With your dim lights.
The shut lips of my mother
And our held breaths
As we sat at a dining room table.                                            5

Her long, thin fingers
Stacking the cards,
Then waiting for them to fall.
The sound of boots in the street
Making us still for a moment.                                                10

There's no more to tell.
The door is locked,
And in one red-tinted window,
A single tree in the yard,
Leafless and misshapen.                                                      15

### CONSIDERATIONS FOR CRITICAL THINKING AND WRITING

1. FIRST RESPONSE. What is the tone of the poem and how is it achieved?

2. Who is being addressed in the first line? How clear is this?

3. How do you account for the silences within the poem? How do they relate to the final image of the tree viewed through the red-tinted window?

# SALLY CROFT (1935–2006)

## *Home-Baked Bread*  1981

*Nothing gives a household a greater sense of stability and common comfort than the aroma of cooling bread. Begin, if you like, with a loaf of whole wheat, which requires neither sifting nor kneading, and go on from there to more cunning triumphs.*

— The Joy of Cooking

What is it she is not saying?
*Cunning triumphs.* It rings
of insinuation. Step into my kitchen,
I have prepared a cunning triumph
for you. Spices and herbs                                                    5
sealed in this porcelain jar,

a treasure of my great-aunt
who sat up past midnight
in her Massachusetts bedroom
when the moon was dark. Come,                                        10
rest your feet. I'll make
you tea with honey and slices

of warm bread spread with peach butter.
I picked the fruit this morning
still fresh with dew. The fragrance                                    15
is seductive? I hoped you would say that.
See how the heat rises
when the bread opens. Come,

we'll eat together, the small flakes
have scarcely any flavor. What cunning                           20
triumphs we can discover in my upstairs room
where peach trees breathe their sweetness
beside the open window and
sun lies like honey on the floor.

### CONSIDERATIONS FOR CRITICAL THINKING AND WRITING

1. FIRST RESPONSE. Why does the speaker in this poem seize on the phrase "cunning triumphs" from the *Joy of Cooking* excerpt?

2. Distinguish between the voice we hear in lines 1–3 and the second voice in lines 3–24. Who is the "you" in the poem?

3. Why is the word "insinuation" an especially appropriate choice in line 3?

4. How do the images in lines 20–24 bring together all the senses evoked in the preceding lines?

5. CREATIVE RESPONSE. Write a paragraph — or stanza — that describes the sensuous (and perhaps sensual) qualities of a food you enjoy.

JOHN KEATS (1795–1821)

## *To Autumn*  1819

### I

Season of mists and mellow fruitfulness,
    Close bosom-friend of the maturing sun;
Conspiring with him how to load and bless
    With fruit the vines that round the thatch-eves run;
To bend with apples the mossed cottage-trees,         5
    And fill all fruit with ripeness to the core;
        To swell the gourd, and plump the hazel shells
    With a sweet kernel; to set budding more,
And still more, later flowers for the bees,
Until they think warm days will never cease,       10
        For summer has o'er-brimmed their clammy cells.

### II

Who hath not seen thee oft amid thy store?
    Sometimes whoever seeks abroad may find
Thee sitting careless on a granary floor,
    Thy hair soft-lifted by the winnowing wind;       15
Or on a half-reaped furrow sound asleep,
    Drowsed with the fume of poppies, while thy hook°      *scythe*
        Spares the next swath and all its twinèd flowers:
And sometimes like a gleaner thou dost keep
    Steady thy laden head across a brook;       20
    Or by a cider-press, with patient look,
        Thou watchest the last oozings hours by hours.

### III

Where are the songs of spring? Ay, where are they?
    Think not of them, thou hast thy music too —
While barred clouds bloom the soft-dying day,       25
    And touch the stubble-plains with rosy hue;
Then in a wailful choir the small gnats mourn
    Among the river swallows,° borne aloft      *willows*
        Or sinking as the light wind lives or dies;
And full-grown lambs loud bleat from hilly bourn;°   *territory*  30
    Hedge-crickets sing; and now with treble soft
    The redbreast whistles from a garden-croft,
        And gathering swallows twitter in the skies.

## CONSIDERATIONS FOR CRITICAL THINKING AND WRITING

1. **FIRST RESPONSE.** How is autumn made to seem like a person in each stanza of this ode?

2. Which senses are most emphasized in each stanza?

3. How is the progression of time expressed in the ode?

4. How does the imagery convey tone? Which words have especially strong connotative values?

5. What is the speaker's view of death?

## Perspective

## T. E. HULME (1883–1917)

### *On the Differences between Poetry and Prose*   1924

In prose as in algebra concrete things are embodied in signs or counters which are moved about according to rules, without being visualized at all in the process. There are in prose certain type situations and arrangements of words, which move as automatically into certain other arrangements as do functions in algebra. One only changes the $X$'s and the $Y$'s back into physical things at the end of the process. Poetry, in one aspect at any rate, may be considered as an effort to avoid this characteristic of prose. It is not a counter language, but a visual concrete one. It is a compromise for a language of intuition which would hand over sensations bodily. It always endeavors to arrest you, and to make you continuously see a physical thing, to prevent you gliding through an abstract process. It chooses fresh epithets and fresh metaphors, not so much because they are new, and we are tired of the old, but because the old cease to convey a physical thing and become abstract counters. A poet says a ship "coursed the seas" to get a physical image, instead of the counter word "sailed." Visual meanings can only be transferred by the new bowl of metaphor; prose is an old pot that lets them leak out. Images in verse are not mere decoration, but the very essence of an intuitive language. Verse is a pedestrian taking you over the ground, prose — a train which delivers you at a destination.

From "Romanticism and Classicism," in *Speculations*,
edited by Herbert Read

### CONSIDERATIONS FOR CRITICAL THINKING AND WRITING

1. What distinctions does Hulme make between poetry and prose? Which seems to be the most important difference?

2. Write an essay that discusses Hulme's claim that poetry "is a compromise for a language of intuition which would hand over sensations bodily."

# 19

# Figures of Speech

Bettmann/Getty Images.

Like a piece of ice on a hot stove the poem must ride on its own melting.
— ROBERT FROST

*Figures of speech* are broadly defined as a way of saying one thing in terms of something else. An overeager funeral director might, for example, be described as a vulture. Although figures of speech are indirect, they are designed to clarify, not obscure, our understanding of what they describe. Poets frequently use them because, as Emily Dickinson said, the poet's work is to "tell all the Truth but tell it slant" to capture the reader's interest and imagination. But figures of speech are not limited to poetry. Hearing them, reading them, or using them is as natural as using language itself.

Suppose that in the middle of a class discussion concerning the economic causes of World War II your history instructor introduces a series of statistics by saying, "Let's get down to brass tacks." Would anyone be likely to expect a display of brass tacks for students to examine? To interpret the statement literally would be to wholly misunderstand the instructor's point that the time has come for a close look at the economic circumstances leading to the war. A literal response transforms the statement into the sort of

595

hilariously bizarre material often found in screwball comedies like *What We Do in the Shadows.*

The class does not look for brass tacks because, in a nutshell, they understand that the instructor is speaking figuratively. They would understand, too, that in the preceding sentence "in a nutshell" refers to brevity and conciseness rather than to the covering of a kernel of a nut. Figurative language makes its way into our everyday speech and writing as well as into literature because it is a means of achieving color, vividness, and intensity.

Consider the difference, for example, between these two statements:

*Literal:* The diner strongly expressed anger at the waiter.
*Figurative:* The diner leaped from his table and roared at the waiter.

The second statement is more vivid because it creates a picture of ferocious anger by likening the diner to some kind of wild animal, such as a lion or tiger. By comparison, "strongly expressed anger" is neither especially strong nor especially expressive; it is flat. Not all figurative language avoids this kind of flatness, however. Figures of speech such as "getting down to brass tacks" and "in a nutshell" are **clichés** because they lack originality and freshness. Still, they suggest how these devices are commonly used to give language some color, even if that color is sometimes a bit faded.

There is nothing weak about William Shakespeare's use of figurative language in the following passage from *Macbeth*. Macbeth has just learned that his wife is dead, and he laments her loss as well as the course of his own life.

## WILLIAM SHAKESPEARE (1564–1616)

### *From* Macbeth *(Act V, Scene v)*    1605–1606

Tomorrow, and tomorrow, and tomorrow
Creeps in this petty pace from day to day
To the last syllable of recorded time;
And all our yesterdays have lighted fools
The way to dusty death. Out, out, brief candle!                    5
Life's but a walking shadow, a poor player,
That struts and frets his hour upon the stage,
And then is heard no more. It is a tale
Told by an idiot, full of sound and fury,
Signifying nothing.                                               10

This passage might be summarized as "life has no meaning," but such a brief paraphrase does not take into account the figurative language that reveals the depth of Macbeth's despair and his view of the absolute meaninglessness of life. By comparing life to a "brief candle," Macbeth emphasizes the darkness and death that surround human beings. The light of life is too brief and unpredictable to be of any comfort. Indeed, life for Macbeth is a "walking shadow," futilely playing a role that is more farcical than dramatic, because life is, ultimately, a desperate story filled with pain and devoid of significance. What the figurative language provides, then, is the emotional force of Macbeth's assertion; his comparisons are disturbing because they are so apt.

The remainder of this chapter discusses some of the most important figures of speech used in poetry. A familiarity with them will help you to understand how poetry achieves its effects.

## SIMILE AND METAPHOR

The two most common figures of speech are simile and metaphor. Both compare things that are ordinarily considered unlike each other. A ***simile*** makes an explicit comparison between two things by using words such as *like*, *as*, *than*, *appears*, or *seems*: "A sip of Mrs. Cook's coffee is like a punch in the stomach." The force of the simile is created by the differences between the two things compared. There would be no simile if the comparison were stated this way: "Mrs. Cook's coffee is as strong as the cafeteria's coffee." This is a literal comparison because Mrs. Cook's coffee is compared with something like it, another kind of coffee. Consider how simile is used in this poem.

### LANGSTON HUGHES (1902–1967)

### *Harlem*   1951

What happens to a dream deferred?

Does it dry up
like a raisin in the sun?
Or fester like a sore —
And then run?                                                      5
Does it stink like rotten meat?
Or crust and sugar over —
like a syrupy sweet?

Maybe it just sags
like a heavy load.                                                10

*Or does it explode?*

This famous poem is a series of somewhat elaborate similes. Their effect is cumulative: the poem asks a number of questions based on these similes and asks the reader to supply an answer. The similes are made even more complicated in that the subject is slippery: we are being asked to compare the Harlem of the title and the concept of a dream deferred to all of the images that follow. The Manhattan neighborhood known as Harlem was a mostly African American neighborhood that had fallen on hard times at the time the poem was written: despite its "renaissance" in the 1920s (see Chapter 28), Harlem experienced damaging riots in 1935 and 1943 based on the frustrations built on poverty and the limited opportunities available to Black Americans at that time. The American dream for Harlemites was deferred. What happens to that dream? Hughes asks us to consider a number of possibilities, each of which connotes something slightly different. Take a few minutes to trace through each of these and consider what makes them different. By the end of the poem, the dream, Harlem, and the poem are so heavy with the weight of these similes that they threaten to burst, to explode. We might come away from this vision covered in rotting meat or a runny sore. Also important in this list of similes are the verbs Hughes chooses: *dry up, fester, run, stink, crust and sugar over, sag, explode*. The images are not the only aspect of these similes we have to deal with: these actions are part of the comparison.

A *metaphor*, like a simile, makes a comparison between two unlike things, but it does so implicitly, without words such as *like or as*: "Mrs. Cook's coffee is a punch in the stomach." Metaphor asserts the identity of dissimilar things. Macbeth tells us that life *is* a "brief candle," life *is* "a walking shadow," life *is* "a poor player," life *is* "a tale / Told by an idiot." Metaphor transforms people, places, objects, and ideas into whatever the poet imagines them to be, and if metaphors are effective, the reader's experience, understanding, and appreciation of what is described are enhanced. Metaphors are frequently more demanding than similes because they are not signaled by particular words. They are both subtle and powerful. Both similes and metaphors expand the sense of a poem economically, by compelling our minds to connect two things that are not obviously connected.

## Jane Kenyon (1947–1995)

### The Socks   1978

While you were away
I matched your socks
and rolled them into balls.
Then I filled your drawer with
tight dark fists.                                                        5

Although it would be creepy and cool to imagine the speaker dumping dozens of severed hands into her husband's sock drawer, that would clearly be a misreading of the poem's intent. We immediately understand that the speaker is saying the rolled-up matched socks are *like* fists, but she goes straight to the comparison: no "like" necessary. We are left to marvel at the comparison: What's the deal with this relationship? Why such a combative metaphor? The speaker leaves it to us to speculate. We know that the speaker is quite active: "I matched . . . and rolled . . . Then I filled." The addressee hasn't done anything . . . except leave. At first the speaker's act sounds like a kindness, but the sentiment shifts at the end. The addressee might take it as a warning to expect a fight upon returning home.

Some metaphors are more subtle than others because their comparison of terms is less explicit. Notice the difference between the following two metaphors, both of which describe a belligerent customer refusing to leave the bar at the end of the night: "He was a mule standing his ground" is a quite explicit comparison. The man is a mule; X is Y. But this metaphor is much more covert: "He brayed his refusal to leave." This second version is an **implied metaphor** because it does not explicitly identify the man with a mule. Instead it hints at or alludes to the mule. Braying is associated with mules and is especially appropriate in this context because of the mule's reputation for stubbornness. Implied metaphors can slip by readers, but they offer the alert reader the energy and resonance of carefully chosen, highly concentrated language.

Some poets write extended comparisons in which part or all of the poem consists of a series of related metaphors or similes. Extended metaphors are more common than extended similes. In "Catch" (p. 531), Robert Francis creates an **extended metaphor** that compares poetry to a game of catch. The entire poem is organized around this comparison. Because these comparisons are at work throughout the entire poem, they are called **controlling metaphors.** Extended comparisons can serve as a poem's organizing principle; they are also a reminder that in good poems metaphor and simile are not merely decorative but inseparable from what is expressed.

Notice the controlling metaphor in this poem, published posthumously by a woman whose contemporaries identified her more as a wife and mother than as a poet. Anne Bradstreet's first volume of poetry, *The Tenth Muse*, was published by her brother-in-law in 1650 without her prior knowledge.

## ANNE BRADSTREET (CA. 1612–1672)

### *The Author to Her Book*   1678

Thou ill-formed offspring of my feeble brain,
Who after birth did'st by my side remain,
Till snatched from thence by friends, less wise than true,
Who thee abroad exposed to public view;
Made thee in rags, halting, to the press to trudge,                                5
Where errors were not lessened, all may judge.
At thy return my blushing was not small,
My rambling brat (in print) should mother call;
I cast thee by as one unfit for light,
Thy visage was so irksome in my sight;                                              10
Yet being mine own, at length affection would
Thy blemishes amend, if so I could:
I washed thy face, but more defects I saw,
And rubbing off a spot, still made a flaw.
I stretched thy joints to make thee even feet,                                      15
Yet still thou run'st more hobbling than is meet;
In better dress to trim thee was my mind,
But nought save homespun cloth in the house I find.
In this array, 'mongst vulgars may'st thou roam;

In critics' hands beware thou dost not come;                    20
And take thy way where yet thou are not known.
If for thy Father asked, say thou had'st none;
And for thy Mother, she alas is poor,
Which caused her thus to send thee out of door.

The extended metaphor likening her book to a child came naturally to Bradstreet and allowed her to regard her work both critically and affectionately. Her conception of the book as her child creates just the right tone of amusement, self-deprecation, and concern.

## OTHER FIGURES

Perhaps the humblest figure of speech — if not one of the most familiar — is the pun. A *pun* is a play on words that relies on a word having more than one meaning or sounding like another word. For example, "A fad is in one era and out the other" is the sort of pun that produces obligatory groans. But most of us find pleasant and interesting surprises in puns. Here's one that has a slight edge to its humor.

### EDMUND CONTI (B. 1929)

### *Pragmatist*    1985

Apocalypse soon
Coming our way
Ground zero at noon
Halve a nice day.

Grimly practical under the circumstances, the pragmatist divides the familiar cheerful cliché by half. As simple as this poem is, its tone is mixed because it makes us laugh and wince at the same time.

Puns can be used to achieve serious effects as well as humorous ones. Although we may have learned to underrate puns as figures of speech, it is a mistake to underestimate their power and the frequency with which they appear in poetry. A close examination, for example, of Robert Frost's "Design" (p. 874), or almost any lengthy passage from a Shakespeare play will confirm the value of puns.

*Synecdoche* is a figure of speech in which part of something is used to signify the whole: a neighbor is a "wagging tongue" (a gossip); a criminal is placed "behind bars" (in prison). Less typically, synecdoche refers to the whole used to signify the part: "Germany invaded Poland"; "Princeton won the fencing match." Clearly, certain individuals participated in these activities, not all of Germany or Princeton. Another related figure of speech is *metonymy*, in which something closely associated with a subject is substituted for it: a traditional businessman is a "suit"; a Hollywood movie is "the silver screen."

Synecdoche and metonymy may overlap and are therefore sometimes difficult to distinguish. Consider this description of a disapproving minister entering a noisy tavern: "As those pursed lips came through the swinging door, the atmosphere was suddenly soured." The pursed lips signal the presence of the minister and are therefore a synecdoche, but they additionally suggest an inhibiting sense of sin and guilt that makes the bar patrons feel uncomfortable. Hence the pursed lips are also a metonymy, as they are in this context so closely connected with religion. Although the distinction between synecdoche and metonymy can be useful, a figure of speech is usually labeled a metonymy when it overlaps categories.

Knowing the precise term for a figure of speech is, finally, less important than responding to its use in a poem. Consider how metonymy and synecdoche convey the tone and meaning of the following poem.

## Dylan Thomas (1914–1953)

### *The Hand That Signed the Paper* 1936

Hulton Deutsch/Getty Images.

The hand that signed the paper felled a city;
Five sovereign fingers taxed the breath,
Doubled the globe of dead and halved a country;
These five kings did a king to death.

The mighty hand leads to a sloping shoulder,     5
The finger joints are cramped with chalk;
A goose's quill has put an end to murder
That put an end to talk.

The hand that signed the treaty bred a fever,
And famine grew, and locusts came;     10
Great is the hand that holds dominion over
Man by a scribbled name.

The five kings count the dead but do not soften
The crusted wound nor stroke the brow;
A hand rules pity as a hand rules heaven;     15
Hands have no tears to flow.

The "hand" in this poem is a synecdoche for a powerful ruler because it is a part of someone used to signify the entire person. The "goose's quill" is a metonymy that also refers to the power associated with the ruler's hand. By using these figures of speech, Thomas depersonalizes and ultimately dehumanizes the ruler. The final synecdoche tells us that "Hands have no tears to flow." It makes us see the political power behind the hand as remote and inhuman. How is the meaning of the poem enlarged when the speaker says, "A hand rules pity as a hand rules heaven"?

One of the ways writers energize the abstractions, ideas, objects, and animals that constitute their created worlds is through **personification**, the attribution of human characteristics to nonhuman things: temptation pursues the innocent; trees scream in the raging wind; mice conspire in the cupboard. We are not explicitly told that these things are people; instead, we are invited to see that they behave like people. Perhaps it is human vanity that makes personification a frequently used figure of speech. Whatever the reason, personification, a form of metaphor that connects the nonhuman with the human, makes the world understandable in human terms. Consider this concise example from William Blake's *The Marriage of Heaven and Hell*, a long poem that takes delight in attacking conventional morality: "Prudence is a rich ugly old maid courted by Incapacity." By personifying prudence, Blake transforms what is usually considered a virtue into a comic figure hardly worth emulating.

Often related to personification is another rhetorical figure called **apostrophe**, an address either to someone who is absent and therefore cannot hear the speaker or to something nonhuman that cannot comprehend. Apostrophe provides an opportunity for the speaker of a poem to think aloud, and often the thoughts expressed are in a formal tone. John Keats, for example, begins "Ode on a Grecian Urn" (p. 572) this way: "Thou still unravished bride of quietness." Apostrophe is frequently accompanied by intense emotion that is signaled by phrasing such as "O Life." In the right hands — such as Keats's — apostrophe can provide an intense and immediate voice in a poem, but when it is overdone or extravagant it can be ludicrous. Modern poets are more wary of apostrophe than their predecessors because apostrophizing strikes many self-conscious twenty-first-century sensibilities as too theatrical. Thus modern poets tend to avoid exaggerated situations in favor of less charged though equally meditative moments, as in this next poem, with its amusing, half-serious cosmic twist.

## Janice Townley Moore (b. 1939)

### *To a Wasp*  1984

You must have chortled
finding that tiny hole
in the kitchen screen. Right
into my cheese cake batter
you dived,                                          5
no chance to swim ashore,
no saving spoon,
the mixer whirring
your legs, wings, stinger,
churning you into such                              10
delicious death.
Never mind the bright April day.

> **When I Write** "I began writing poetry as a freshman in college. I wrote using poetic diction and sometimes rhyme. Then I discovered 'modern poetry.' Seeing what was published in literary magazines quickly changed my style."
> — Janice Townley Moore

Did you not see
rising out of cumulus clouds
That fist aimed at both of us?                                          15

Moore's apostrophe "To a Wasp" is based on the simplest of domestic circumstances; there is almost nothing theatrical or exaggerated in the poem's tone until "That fist" in the last line, when exaggeration takes center stage. As a figure of speech, exaggeration is known as **overstatement** or **hyperbole** and adds emphasis without intending to be literally true: "The teenage boy ate everything in the house." Notice how the speaker of Andrew Marvell's "To His Coy Mistress" (The full poem appears on p. 941) exaggerates his devotion in the following overstatement:

> An hundred years should go to praise
> Thine eyes and on thy forehead gaze,
> Two hundred to adore each breast,
> But thirty thousand to the rest:

That comes to 30,500 years. What is expressed here is heightened emotion, not deception.

The speaker also uses the opposite figure of speech, **understatement**, which says less than is intended. In the next section he sums up why he cannot take 30,500 years to express his love:

> The grave's a fine and private place,
> But none, I think, do there embrace.

The speaker is correct, of course, but by deliberately understating — saying "I think" when he is actually certain — he makes his point, that death will overtake their love, all the more emphatic. Another powerful example of understatement appears in the final line of Randall Jarrell's "The Death of the Ball Turret Gunner" (p. 558), when the disembodied voice of the machine-gunner describes his death in a bomber: "When I died they washed me out of the turret with a hose."

**Paradox** is a statement that initially appears to be self-contradictory but that, on closer inspection, turns out to make sense: "The pen is mightier than the sword." In a fencing match, anyone would prefer the sword, but if the goal is to win the hearts and minds of people, the art of persuasion can be more compelling than swordplay. To resolve the paradox, it is necessary to discover the sense that underlies the statement. If we see that "pen" and "sword" are used as metonymies for writing and violence, then the paradox rings true. **Oxymoron** is a condensed form of paradox in which two contradictory words are used together. Combinations such as "sweet sorrow," "silent scream," "sad joy," and "cold fire" indicate the kinds of startling effects that oxymorons can produce. Paradox is useful in poetry because it arrests a reader's attention by its seemingly stubborn refusal to make sense, and once a reader has penetrated the paradox, it is difficult to resist a perception so well earned. Good paradoxes are knotty pleasures. Here is a simple but effective one.

## TAJANA KOVICS (B. 1985)

### *Text Message* 2011

Because I think you're nearly perfect,
I want to love you best:
And since absence makes the heart grow fonder,
We should see each other less.

As the title suggests, the medium is part of the implicit subtext in this quatrain. Consider how the very idea of romantic love is conveyed and built on separation rather than intimacy in this witty paradox.

The following poems are rich in figurative language. As you read and study them, notice how their figures of speech vivify situations, clarify ideas, intensify emotions, and engage your imagination. Although the terms for the various figures discussed in this chapter are useful for labeling the particular devices used in poetry, they should not be allowed to get in the way of your response to a poem. Don't worry about rounding up examples of figurative language. First relax and let the figures work their effects on you. Use the terms as a means of taking you further into poetry, and they will serve your reading well.

## POEMS FOR FURTHER STUDY

## WILLIAM CARLOS WILLIAMS (1883–1963)

### *To Waken an Old Lady* 1921

Old age is
a flight of small
cheeping birds
skimming
bare trees                                                    5
above a snow glaze.
Gaining and failing
they are buffeted
by a dark wind —
But what?                                                     10
On harsh weedstalks
the flock has rested,
the snow
is covered with broken
seedhusks                                                     15
and the wind tempered
by a shrill
piping of plenty.

### CONSIDERATIONS FOR CRITICAL THINKING AND WRITING

1. FIRST RESPONSE. Consider the images and figures of speech in this poem and explain why you think it is a positive or negative assessment of old age.

2. How does the title relate to the rest of the poem?

## ERNEST SLYMAN (B. 1946)

### *Lightning Bugs*   1988

In my backyard,
They burn peepholes in the night
And take snapshots of my house.

### CONSIDERATIONS FOR CRITICAL THINKING AND WRITING

1. FIRST RESPONSE. Explain why the title is essential to this poem.

2. What makes the description of the lightning bugs effective? How do the second and third lines complement each other?

3. CREATIVE RESPONSE. As Slyman has done, take a simple, common fact of nature and make it vivid by using a figure of speech to describe it.

## MARTÍN ESPADA (B. 1957)

### *The Mexican Cabdriver's Poem for His Wife, Who Has Left Him*   2000

We were sitting in traffic
on the Brooklyn Bridge,
so I asked the poets
in the backseat of my cab
to write a poem for you.          5

They asked
if you are like the moon
or the trees.

Lauren Marie Schmidt.

I said no,
she is like the bridge                    10
when there is so much traffic
I have time
to watch the boats
on the river.

### CONSIDERATIONS FOR CRITICAL THINKING AND WRITING

1. FIRST RESPONSE. What do you think is the speaker's attitude toward the passengers?

2. Explore the potential meanings of the similes concerning the moon, trees, and the bridge. How does the bridge differ from the other two?

WHEN I WRITE "Only [rarely] is a poem complete in a first draft. The first draft of a poem can sit for a long time waiting for its other half, or its meaning. Save everything you write, no matter how unhappy you are with it. You often won't see the beauty until later."
—JUDY PAGE HEITZMAN

## JUDY PAGE HEITZMAN (B. 1952)

### The Schoolroom on the Second Floor of the Knitting Mill    1991

While most of us copied letters out of books,
Mrs. Lawrence carved and cleaned her nails.
Now the red and buff cardinals at my back-room window
make me miss her, her room, her hallway,
even the chimney outside                                                5
that broke up the sky.
In my memory it is afternoon.
Sun streams in through the door
next to the fire escape where we are lined up
getting our coats on to go out to the playground,                      10
the tether ball, its towering height, the swings.
She tells me to make sure the line
does not move up over the threshold.
That would be dangerous.
So I stand guard at the door.                                          15
Somehow it happens
the way things seem to happen when we're not really looking,
or we are looking, just not the right way.
Kids crush up like cattle, pushing me over the line.

*Judy is not a good leader* is all Mrs. Lawrence says.                  20
She says it quietly. Still, everybody hears.
Her arms hang down like sausages.
I hear her every time I fail.

### CONSIDERATIONS FOR CRITICAL THINKING AND WRITING

1. **FIRST RESPONSE.** Does your impression of Mrs. Lawrence change from the beginning to the end of the poem? How so?

2. How can line 2 be read as an implied metaphor?

3. Discuss the use of similes in the poem. How do they contribute to the poem's meaning?

## ROBERT PINSKY (B. 1940)

### Icicles    1990

A brilliant beard of ice
Hangs from the edge of the roof
Harsh and heavy as glass.
The spikes a child breaks off

Taste of wool and the sun.                                          5
In the house, some straw for a bed,
Circled by a little train,
Is the tiny image of God.

The sky is a fiery blue,
And a fiery morning light                                          10
Burns on the fresh deep snow:
Not one track in the street.

Just as the carols tell
Everything is calm and bright:
The town lying still                                               15
Frozen silver and white.

Is only one child awake,
Breaking the crystal chimes? —
Knocking them down with a stick,
Leaving the broken stems.                                          20

### CONSIDERATIONS FOR CRITICAL THINKING AND WRITING

1. FIRST RESPONSE. What did the poem make you feel upon first reading it?

2. List the things icicles are compared to throughout the poem. Do these separate comparisons work together or against one another in terms of creating a coherent picture?

3. Is the poem's mood violent or calm? Can it be both?

## JIM STEVENS (1922–2000)

## *Schizophrenia*    1992

It was the house that suffered most.

It had begun with slamming doors, angry feet scuffing the carpets,
dishes slammed onto the table,
greasy stains spreading on the cloth.

Certain doors were locked at night,                                5
feet stood for hours outside them,
dishes were left unwashed, the cloth
disappeared under a hardened crust.
The house came to miss the shouting voices,
the threats, the half-apologies, noisy                             10
reconciliations, the sobbing that followed.

Then lines were drawn, borders established,
some rooms declared their loyalties,
keeping to themselves, keeping out the other.
The house divided against itself.                                  15

Seeing cracking paint, broken windows,
the front door banging in the wind,
the roof tiles flying off, one by one,
the neighbors said it was a madhouse.

It was the house that suffered most.                               20

### CONSIDERATIONS FOR CRITICAL THINKING AND WRITING

1. FIRST RESPONSE. What is the effect of personifying the house in this poem?

2. How are the people who live in the house characterized? What does their behavior reveal about them? How does the house respond to them?

3. Comment on the title. If the title were missing, what, if anything, would be missing from the poem? Explain your answer.

## KAY RYAN (B. 1945)

### Learning 1996

Whatever must be learned
is always on the bottom,
as with the law of drawers
and the necessary item.
It isn't pleasant,                                                          5
whatever they tell children,
to turn out on the floor
the folded things in them.

### CONSIDERATIONS FOR CRITICAL THINKING AND WRITING

1. FIRST RESPONSE. Why does the speaker consider learning to be unpleasant and difficult?

2. Why is unfolding what must be learned an especially apt metaphor?

## RONALD WALLACE (B. 1945)

### Building an Outhouse 1991

Is not unlike building a poem: the pure
mathematics of shape; the music of hammer
and tenpenny nail, of floor joist, stud wall,
and sill; the cut wood's sweet smell.
If the Skil saw rear up in your unpracticed hand,                           5
cussing, hawking its chaw of dust,
and you're lost in the pounding particulars
of fly rafters, siding, hypotenuse, and load,
until nothing seems level or true
but the scorn of the tape's clucked tongue,                                 10

let the nub of your plainspoken pencil prevail
and it's up! Functional. Tight as a sonnet.
It will last forever (or at least for awhile)
though the critics come sit on it, and sit on it.

WHEN I WRITE "I've always admired people who can make beautiful things — out of wood, or paint, or the movement of the human body, or the strings of a musical instrument. I have spent my life trying to make beautiful things out of words." — RONALD WALLACE

CONSIDERATIONS FOR CRITICAL THINKING AND WRITING

1. FIRST RESPONSE. Explain how the poem's diction contributes to the extended simile. Why is the language of building especially appropriate here?

2. What is the effect of the repetition and sounds in the final line? How does that affect the poem's tone?

3. Consult the Glossary of Literary Terms (p. 1483) for the definition of *sonnet*. To what extent does "Building an Outhouse" conform to a sonnet's structure?

ELAINE MAGARRELL (1928–2014)

## *The Joy of Cooking*   1988

I have prepared my sister's tongue,
scrubbed and skinned it,
trimmed the roots, small bones, and gristle.
Carved through the hump it slices thin and neat.
Best with horseradish                                                                          5
and economical — it probably will grow back.
Next time perhaps a creole sauce
or mold of aspic?

I will have my brother's heart,
which is firm and rather dry,                                                            10
slow cooked. It resembles muscle
more than organ meat
and needs an apple-onion stuffing
to make it interesting at all.
Although beef heart serves six                                                         15
my brother's heart barely feeds two.
I could also have it braised
and served in sour sauce.

CONSIDERATIONS FOR CRITICAL THINKING AND WRITING

1. FIRST RESPONSE. Describe the poem's tone. Do you find it amusing, bitter, or something else?

2. How are the tongue and heart used to characterize the sister and brother in this poem?

3. How is the speaker's personality revealed in the poem's language?

CONNECTION TO ANOTHER SELECTION

1. Write an essay that explains how cooking becomes a way of talking about something else in this poem and in Sally Croft's "Home-Baked Bread" (p. 592).

## Perspective

### JOHN R. SEARLE (B. 1932)
### *Figuring Out Metaphors* 1979

If you hear somebody say, "Sally is a block of ice," or, "Sam is a pig," you are likely to assume that the speaker does not mean what he says literally, but that he is speaking metaphorically. Furthermore, you are not likely to have very much trouble figuring out what he means. If he says, "Sally is a prime number between 17 and 23," or "Bill is a barn door," you might still assume he is speaking metaphorically, but it is much harder to figure out what he means. The existence of such utterances — utterances in which the speaker means metaphorically something different from what the sentence means literally — poses a series of questions for any theory of language and communication: What is metaphor, and how does it differ from both literal and other forms of figurative utterances? Why do we use expressions metaphorically instead of saying exactly and literally what we mean? How do metaphorical utterances work, that is, how is it possible for speakers to communicate to hearers when speaking metaphorically inasmuch as they do not say what they mean? And why do some metaphors work and others do not?

*From Expression and Meaning*

#### CONSIDERATIONS FOR CRITICAL THINKING AND WRITING

1. Searle poses a series of important questions. Write an essay that explores one of these questions, basing your discussion on the poems in this chapter.

2. CREATIVE RESPONSE. Try writing a brief poem that provides a context for the line "Sally is a prime number between 17 and 23" or the line "Bill is a barn door." Your task is to create a context so that either one of these metaphoric statements is as readily understandable as "Sally is a block of ice" or "Sam is a pig." Share your poem with your classmates and explain how the line generated the poem you built around it.

# 20

# Symbol, Allegory, and Irony

Poetry is serious business; literature is
the apparatus through which the world
tries to keep intact its important ideas
and feelings.

— MARY OLIVER

Angel Valentin/The New York
Times/Redux.

## SYMBOL

A *symbol* is something that represents something else. An object, a person,
a place, an event, or an action can suggest more than its literal meaning.
A handshake between two world leaders might be simply a greeting, but if it
is done ceremoniously before cameras, it could be a symbolic gesture signifying unity, issues resolved, and joint policies that will be followed. We live
surrounded by symbols. If your classmate sitting on your right has a laptop
sticker of a peace sign, you can assume that person is signaling hope for a
world free of conflict. If your classmate on your left carries a backpack fes-
tooned with Nike swooshes and mascots of sports teams, it's fair to assume
that person enjoys competitive sports. Neither classmate has to say a word.

The meanings suggested by a symbol are determined by the context in
which it appears. The familiar hood ornament on a Mercedes-Benz — like the
peace symbol with a missing line at the bottom — could symbolize very different
things depending on where it was parked. Would an American political candidate be likely to appear in a Detroit blue-collar neighborhood with such a car?

611

Probably not. Although a candidate might be able to afford the car, it would be an inappropriate symbol for someone seeking votes in that area. As a symbol, the German-built Mercedes would backfire if voters perceived it as representing an entity partially responsible for layoffs of automobile workers or, worse, as a sign of decadence and corruption. Parked near the entrance to a casino or fancy hotel, however, that same symbol signals someone who has achieved a certain level of financial success and the confidence that often comes with it. Because symbols depend on contexts for their meaning, literary artists provide those contexts so that the reader has enough information to determine the probable range of meanings suggested by a symbol.

In the following poem, the speaker describes walking at night. How is the night used symbolically?

ROBERT FROST (1874–1963)

## Acquainted with the Night    1928

I have been one acquainted with the night.
I have walked out in rain — and back in rain.
I have outwalked the furthest city light.

I have looked down the saddest city lane.
I have passed by the watchman on his beat                          5
And dropped my eyes, unwilling to explain.

I have stood still and stopped the sound of feet
When far away an interrupted cry
Came over houses from another street,

But not to call me back or say good-by;                            10
And further still at an unearthly height
One luminary clock against the sky

Proclaimed the time was neither wrong nor right.
I have been one acquainted with the night.

In approaching this or any poem, you should read for literal meanings first and then allow the elements of the poem to invite you to symbolic readings, if they make sense within the poem's context. Here the somber tone suggests that the lines have symbolic meaning, too. The flat matter-of-factness created by the repetition of "I have" (lines 1–5, 7, 14) understates the symbolic subject matter of the poem, which is, finally, more about the "night" located in the speaker's mind or soul than it is about walking away from a city and back again. The speaker is "acquainted with the night." The importance of this phrase is emphasized by Frost's title and by the fact that he begins and ends the poem with it. Poets frequently use this kind of repetition to alert readers to details that carry more than literal meanings.

The speaker in this poem has personal knowledge of the night but does not indicate specifically what the night means. To arrive at the potential meanings of the night in this context, it is necessary to look closely at its connotations, along with the images provided in the poem. The connotative meanings of *night* suggest, for example, mystery, darkness, death, and grief. By drawing on these connotations, Frost uses a ***conventional symbol*** — something that is recognized by many people to represent certain ideas. Roses conventionally symbolize love or beauty; laurels, fame; spring, growth or rebirth; the moon, romance. Poets often use conventional symbols to convey tone and meaning.

Frost uses the night as a conventional symbol, but he also develops it into a ***literary*** or ***contextual symbol*** that goes beyond traditional, public meanings. A literary symbol cannot be summarized in a word or two. It tends to be as elusive as experience itself. The night cannot be reduced to or equated with darkness or death or grief, but it evokes those associations and more. Frost took what perhaps initially appears to be an overworked, conventional symbol and prevented it from becoming a cliché by deepening and extending its meaning.

The images in "Acquainted with the Night" lead to the poem's symbolic meaning. Unwilling, and perhaps unable, to explain explicitly to the watchman (and to the reader) what the night means, the speaker nevertheless conveys feelings about it. The brief images of darkness, rain, sad city lanes, the necessity for guards, the eerie sound of a distressing cry coming over rooftops, and the "luminary clock against the sky" proclaiming "the time was neither wrong nor right" all help to create a sense of anxiety in this tight-lipped speaker. Although we cannot know what unnamed personal experiences have acquainted the speaker with the night, the images suggest that whatever the night means, it is somehow associated with insomnia, loneliness, isolation, coldness, darkness, death, fear, and a sense of alienation from humanity and even time. Daylight — ordinary daytime thoughts and life itself — seems remote and unavailable in this poem. The night is literally the period from sunset to sunrise, but, more important, it is an internal state of being felt by the speaker and revealed through the images.

Frost uses symbols rather than an expository essay that would explain the conditions that cause these feelings because most readers can provide their own list of sorrows and terrors that evoke similar emotions. Through symbol, the speaker's experience is compressed and simultaneously expanded by the personal darkness that each reader brings to the poem. The suggestive nature of symbols makes them valuable for poets and evocative for readers.

## ALLEGORY

Unlike expansive, suggestive symbols, ***allegory*** is a narration or description usually restricted to a single meaning because its events, actions, characters, settings, and objects represent specific abstractions or ideas. Although the elements in an allegory may be interesting in themselves, the emphasis tends to be on what they ultimately mean. Characters may be given names such as Hope, Pride, Youth, and Charity; they have few, if any, personal qualities beyond their abstract meanings. These personifications are a form of extended metaphor, but their meanings are severely restricted. They are not symbols because, for instance, the meaning of a character named Charity is precisely that virtue.

There is little or no room for broad speculation and exploration in allegories. If Frost had written "Acquainted with the Night" as an allegory, he might have named his speaker Loneliness and had them leave the City of Despair to walk the Streets of Emptiness, where Crime, Poverty, Fear, and other characters would define the nature of city life. The literal elements in an allegory tend to be deemphasized in favor of the message. Symbols, however, function both literally and symbolically, so that "Acquainted with the Night" is about both a walk and a sense that something is terribly wrong.

Allegory especially lends itself to *didactic poetry*, which is designed to teach an ethical, moral, or religious lesson. Many stories, poems, and plays are concerned with values, but didactic literature is specifically created to convey a message. "Acquainted with the Night" does not impart advice or offer guidance. If the poem argued that city life is self-destructive or sinful, it would be didactic; instead, it is a lyric poem that expresses the emotions and thoughts of a single speaker.

Although allegory is often enlisted in didactic causes because it can so readily communicate abstract ideas through physical representations, not all allegories teach a lesson. The following poem reveals a difficult human condition — the attempt to resolve the eternal tensions between guilt and desire in order to achieve love. Its author, James Baldwin, spent much of his career trying to redefine love; in his famous essay "Down at the Cross" he claimed he was speaking of love not in the sentimental, traditional sense of the word, but rather associating love with "quest and daring and growth."

## JAMES BALDWIN (1924–1987)

### *Guilt, Desire and Love*  1983

At the dark street corner
where Guilt and Desire
are attempting to stare
each other down
(presently, one of them                    5
will light a cigarette
and glance in the direction
of the abandoned warehouse)
Love came slouching along,
an exploded silence                         10
standing a little apart
but visible anyway
in the yellow, silent, steaming light,
while Guilt and Desire wrangled,
trying not to be overheard                  15
by this trespasser.

Each time Desire looked towards Love,
hoping to find a witness,
Guilt shouted louder
and shook them hips                         20

Everett Collection Inc/Alamy.

and the fire of the cigarette
threatened to burn the warehouse down.
Desire actually started across the street,
time after time,
to hear what Love might have to say,                                   25
but Guilt flagged down a truckload
of other people
and knelt down in the middle of the street
and, while the truckload of other people
looked away, and swore that they                                      30
didn't see nothing
and couldn't testify nohow,
and Love moved out of sight,
Guilt accomplished upon the standing body
of Desire                                                             35
the momentary, inflammatory soothing
which seals their union
(for ever?)
and creates a mighty traffic problem.

The setting is important in this poem. As in Frost's poem, night is evoked: the street corner where Guilt and Desire meet is dark, and the "yellow, silent, steaming light" (line 13) that accompanies Love's entrance is more streetlight than sunlight. The cityscape is not desolate and spooky like Frost's, but rather hot and seedy. The props (if you will) of the abandoned warehouse and the lit cigarette seem like something out of a sordid movie or television show about a sinful city. Guilt and Desire are locked in a battle here, and a traditional moralist would associate Desire with sin, but Desire's goal is actually to connect with Love, who is a trespasser to their quarrel. Guilt is the most powerful of these three entities, the loudest of them (and probably the only one who speaks at all). Guilt's eventual bodily encounter with Desire is sexual, but it is not fulfilling; or if it is, that fulfilment is only "momentary." Love slinks out of sight; Desire is nearly a victim; and Guilt conquers all. The poem does not mention sin at all; in fact, if there is a lesson here, it is that guilt (which makes us associate certain human behaviors and emotions with sin) is itself a kind of sin, one that creates "a mighty traffic problem."

Modern writers generally prefer symbol over allegory because they tend to be more interested in opening up the potential meanings of an experience instead of transforming it into a closed pattern of meaning. Perhaps the major difference is that while allegory may delight a reader's imagination, symbol challenges and enriches it.

## IRONY

Another important resource writers use to take readers beyond literal meanings is *irony*, a technique that reveals a discrepancy between what appears to be and what is actually true. The following poem is a classic example in which appearances give way to the underlying reality.

## EDWIN ARLINGTON ROBINSON (1869–1935)

### *Richard Cory*   1897

Whenever Richard Cory went down town,
We people on the pavement looked at him:
He was a gentleman from sole to crown,
Clean favored, and imperially slim.

And he was always quietly arrayed,                              5
And he was always human when he talked;
But still he fluttered pulses when he said,
"Good-morning," and he glittered when he walked.

And he was rich — yes, richer than a king —
And admirably schooled in every grace:                         10
In fine, we thought that he was everything
To make us wish that we were in his place.

So on we worked, and waited for the light,
And went without the meat, and cursed the bread;
And Richard Cory, one calm summer night,                       15
Went home and put a bullet through his head.

Richard Cory seems to have it all. Those less fortunate, the "people on the pavement," regard him as well-bred, handsome, tasteful, and richly endowed with both money and grace. Until the final line of the poem, the reader, like the speaker, is charmed by Cory's good fortune, so quietly expressed in his decent, easy manner. That final, shocking line, however, shatters the appearances of Cory's life and reveals him to have been a desperately unhappy man. While everyone else assumes that Cory represented "everything" to which they aspire, the reality is that he could escape his miserable life only through suicide. This discrepancy between what appears to be true and what actually exists is known as **situational irony**: what happens is entirely different from what is expected. We are not told why Cory shoots himself; instead, the irony in the poem shocks us into the recognition that appearances do not always reflect realities.

Words are also sometimes intended to be taken at other than face value. **Verbal irony** is saying something different from what is meant. If after reading "Richard Cory," you said, "That rich gentleman sure was happy," your statement would be ironic. Your tone of voice would indicate that just the opposite was meant; hence verbal irony is usually easy to detect in spoken language. In literature, however, a reader can sometimes take literally what a writer intends ironically. The remedy for this kind of misreading is to pay close attention to the poem's context. There is no formula that can detect verbal irony, but contradictory actions and statements as well as the use of understatement and overstatement can often be signals that verbal irony is present.

# A SAMPLE STUDENT RESPONSE

Cipriano Diaz

Professor Young

English 200

16 September 2023

Irony in Edwin Arlington Robinson's "Richard Cory"

In Edwin Arlington Robinson's poem "Richard Cory," appearances are not reality. The character Richard Cory, viewed by the townspeople as "richer than a king" (line 9) and "a gentleman from sole to crown" (3), is someone who inspires envy. The poem's speaker says, "we thought that he was everything / To make us wish that we were in his place" (11-12). However, the final shocking line of the poem creates a situational irony that emphasizes the difference between what seems—and what really is.

In lines 1 through 14, the speaker sets up a shining, princely image of Cory, associating him with such regal words as "imperially" (4), "crown" (3), and "king" (9). Cory is viewed by the townspeople from the "pavement" as if he is on a pedestal (2); far below him, those who must work and "[go] without the meat" (14) stand in stark contrast. Further, not only is Cory a gentleman, he is so good-looking that he "flutter[s] pulses" (7) of those around him when he speaks. He's a rich man who "glitter[s] when he walk[s]" (8). He is also a decent man who is "always human when he talk[s]" (6). However, this noble image of Cory is unexpectedly shattered "one calm summer night" (15) in the final couplet. What the speaker and townspeople believed Cory to be and aspired to imitate was merely an illusion. The irony is that what Cory seemed to be—a happy, satisfied man—is exactly what he was not. . . .

Work Cited

Robinson, Edwin Arlington. "Richard Cory." *The Compact Bedford Introduction to Literature*, edited by Michael Meyer and D. Quentin Miller, 13th ed., Bedford/St. Martin's, 2024, p. 616.

Consider how verbal irony is used in this poem.

## GWENDOLYN BROOKS (1917–2000)
### *Sadie and Maud*  1945

Maud went to college.
Sadie stayed at home.
Sadie scraped life
With a fine-tooth comb.

She didn't leave a tangle in.                                    5
Her comb found every strand.
Sadie was one of the livingest chits°       *Sassy young girls.*
In all the land.

Sadie bore two babies
Under her maiden name.                                          10
Maud and Ma and Papa
Nearly died of shame.

When Sadie said her last so-long
Her girls struck out from home.
(Sadie had left as heritage                                     15
Her fine-tooth comb.)

Maud, who went to college,
Is a thin brown mouse.
She is living all alone
In this old house.                                             20

This poem was written at a time when opportunities for young women were at a crossroads. There was an expectation that young women should accept a domestic role, so it would seem at first that Sadie's staying at home is about obedience and conformity, but another expectation was that young women would be morally respectable. When Sadie "bore two babies / Under her maiden name" it's clear that she's not married, and her family's "shame" is profound. Maud, it would seem, is better positioned to be respectable and to become her parents' favorite. What happens next might be considered dramatic irony, though: Sadie's spirit of adventure allows both her and her two girls to "[strike] out from home," to "[scrape] life / With a fine-tooth comb." Maud played it safe, and her existence in the final stanza appears meek and lonely. Moreover, she's back at home, or as it's now known, "this old house." Maybe the appetites and recklessness of youth — the things that get us into trouble — aren't as damaging as our elders would have us believe. Maybe obedience and earnestness don't get us anywhere.

**Dramatic irony** is used when a writer allows a reader to know more about a situation than a character does. This creates a discrepancy between what a character says or thinks and what the reader knows to be true. Dramatic irony is often used to reveal character. In the following poem the speaker delivers a public address that ironically tells us more about him than it does about the patriotic holiday he is commemorating.

## E. E. CUMMINGS (1894–1962)

### *next to of course god america i*    1926

"next to of course god america i
love you land of the pilgrims' and so forth oh
say can you see by the dawn's early my
country 'tis of centuries come and go
and are no more what of it we should worry        5
in every language even deafanddumb
thy sons acclaim your glorious name by gorry
by jingo by gee by gosh by gum
why talk of beauty what could be more beautiful than these heroic happy dead        10
who rushed like lions to the roaring slaughter
they did not stop to think they died instead
then shall the voice of liberty be mute?"

He spoke. And drank rapidly a glass of water

This verbal debauch of chauvinistic clichés (notice the run-on phrases and lines) reveals that the speaker's relationship to God and country is not, as he claims, one of love. His public address suggests a hearty mindlessness that leads to "roaring slaughter" rather than to reverence or patriotism. Cummings allows the reader to see through the speaker's words to their dangerous emptiness. What the speaker means and what Cummings means are entirely different. This poem is a ***satire***, an example of the literary art of ridiculing a folly or vice in an effort to expose or correct it. The object of satire is usually some human frailty; people, institutions, ideas, and things are all fair game for satirists. The satirical nature of this poem invites the reader's laughter and contempt in order to deflate the benighted attitudes expressed in it.

When a writer uses God, destiny, or fate to dash the hopes and expectations of a character or humankind in general, it is called ***cosmic irony***. In "Yet Do I Marvel" (p. 816), for example, Countee Cullen enumerates multiple ways in which God has tormented his human creations, and while he believes God could explain all of them, he will never understand why he was born a Black poet at a time when America paid attention only to white poets. The context for understanding why he is so baffled by his condition is not explicitly stated; it must be filled in through the reader's understanding of racial discrimination.

Here's a painfully terse version of cosmic irony.

STEPHEN CRANE (1871–1900)

## *A Man Said to the Universe*   1899

A man said to the universe:
"Sir, I exist!"
"However," replied the universe,
"The fact has not created in me
A sense of obligation."                                            5

Unlike in "Yet Do I Marvel," there is the slightest bit of humor in Crane's poem,
but the joke is on us.

   Irony is an important technique that allows a writer to distinguish
between appearances and realities. In situational irony a discrepancy exists
between what we expect to happen and what actually happens; in verbal
irony a discrepancy exists between what is said and what is meant; in dramatic irony a discrepancy exists between what a character believes and what
the reader knows to be true; and in cosmic irony a discrepancy exists between
what a character aspires to and what universal forces provide. With each form
of irony, we are invited to move beyond surface appearances and sentimental
assumptions to see the complexity of experience. Irony is often used in literature to reveal a writer's perspective on matters that previously seemed settled.

## POEMS FOR FURTHER STUDY

CHRISTINA ROSSETTI (1830–1894)

## *Goblin Market*   1862

Morning and evening
Maids heard the goblins cry:
"Come buy our orchard fruits,
Come buy, come buy:
Apples and quinces,                                                5
Lemons and oranges,
Plump unpecked cherries,
Melons and raspberries,
Bloom-down-cheeked peaches,
Swart-headed° mulberries,                                         10
Wild free-born cranberries,
Crabapples, dewberries,
Pineapples, blackberries,
Apricots, strawberries;—
All ripe together                                                 15
In summer weather,—
Morns that pass by,

10 *Swart-headed:* Black-headed.

Fair eyes that fly;
Come buy, come buy:
Our grapes fresh from the vine,                                    20
Pomegranates full and fine,
Dates and sharp bullaces,
Rare pears and greengages,
Damsons° and bilberries,
Taste them and try:                                               25
Currants and gooseberries,
Bright-fire-like barberries,
Figs to fill your mouth,
Citrons from the South,
Sweet to tongue and sound to eye;                                 30
Come buy, come buy."

Evening by evening
Among the brookside rushes,
Laura bowed her head to hear,
Lizzie veiled her blushes:                                        35
Crouching close together
In the cooling weather,
With clasping arms and cautioning lips,
With tingling cheeks and finger tips.
"Lie close," Laura said,                                          40
Pricking up her golden head:
"We must not look at goblin men,
We must not buy their fruits:
Who knows upon what soil they fed
Their hungry thirsty roots?"                                      45
"Come buy," call the goblins
Hobbling down the glen.

"Oh," cried Lizzie, "Laura, Laura,
You should not peep at goblin men."
Lizzie covered up her eyes,                                       50
Covered close lest they should look;
Laura reared her glossy head,
And whispered like the restless brook:
"Look, Lizzie, look, Lizzie,
Down the glen tramp little men.                                   55
One hauls a basket,
One bears a plate,
One lugs a golden dish
Of many pounds' weight.
How fair the vine must grow                                       60
Whose grapes are so luscious;
How warm the wind must blow
Through those fruit bushes."
"No," said Lizzie: "No, no, no;

22-24 *bullaces . . . damsons:* Bullaces, greengages, and damsons are plums.

Their offers should not charm us, 65
Their evil gifts would harm us."
She thrust a dimpled finger
In each ear, shut eyes and ran:
Curious Laura chose to linger
Wondering at each merchant man. 70
One had a cat's face,
One whisked a tail,
One tramped at a rat's pace,
One crawled like a snail,
One like a wombat prowled obtuse and furry, 75
One like a ratel° tumbled hurry skurry.
She heard a voice like voice of doves
Cooing all together:
They sounded kind and full of loves
In the pleasant weather. 80

Laura stretched her gleaming neck
Like a rush-imbedded swan,
Like a lily from the beck,°
Like a moonlit poplar branch
Like a vessel at the launch 85
When its last restraint is gone.

Backwards up the mossy glen
Turned and trooped the goblin men,
With their shrill repeated cry,
"Come buy, come buy." 90
When they reached where Laura was
They stood stock still upon the moss,
Leering at each other,
Brother with queer brother;
Signaling each other, 95
Brother with sly brother.
One set his basket down,
One reared his plate;
One began to weave a crown
Of tendrils, leaves, and rough nuts brown 100
(Men sell not such in any town);
One heaved the golden weight
Of dish and fruit to offer her:
"Come buy, come buy," was still their cry.
Laura stared but did not stir, 105
Longed but had no money.
The whisk-tailed merchant bade her taste
In tones as smooth as honey,
The cat-faced purr'd,
The rat-paced spoke a word 110
Of welcome, and the snail-paced even was heard;

76  *ratel:* A south African badgerlike creature.
83  *beck:* Small brook.

One parrot-voiced and jolly
Cried "Pretty Goblin" still for "Pretty Polly;" —
One whistled like a bird.

But sweet-tooth Laura spoke in haste:                                                    115
"Good Folk, I have no coin;
To take were to purloin:
I have no copper in my purse,
I have no silver either,
And all my gold is on the furze                                                          120
That shakes in windy weather
Above the rusty heather."
"You have much gold upon your head."
They answered all together:
"Buy from us with a golden curl."                                                        125
She clipped a precious golden lock,
She dropped a tear more rare than pearl,
Then sucked their fruit globes fair or red.
Sweeter than honey from the rock,
Stronger than man-rejoicing wine,                                                        130
Clearer than water flowed that juice;
She never tasted such before,
How should it cloy with length of use?
She sucked and sucked and sucked the more
Fruits which that unknown orchard bore,                                                  135
She sucked until her lips were sore;
Then flung the emptied rinds away
But gathered up one kernel stone,
And knew not was it night or day
As she turned home alone.                                                                140

Lizzie met her at the gate
Full of wise upbraidings:
"Dear, you should not stay so late,
Twilight is not good for maidens;
Should not loiter in the glen                                                            145
In the haunts of goblin men.
Do you not remember Jeanie,
How she met them in the moonlight,
Took their gifts both choice and many,
Ate their fruits and wore their flowers                                                  150
Plucked from bowers
Where summer ripens at all hours?
But ever in the noonlight
She pined and pined away;
Sought them by night and day,                                                            155
Found them no more, but dwindled and grew gray;
Then fell with the first snow,
While to this day no grass will grow
Where she lies low:
I planted daisies there a year ago                                                       160

That never blow.°                                                        *bloom*
You should not loiter so."
"Nay, hush," said Laura:
"Nay, hush, my sister:
I ate and ate my fill,                                                      165
Yet my mouth waters still:
Tomorrow night I will
Buy more"; and kissed her.
"Have done with sorrow;
I'll bring you plums tomorrow                                              170
Fresh on their mother twigs,
Cherries worth getting;
You cannot think what figs
My teeth have met in,
What melons icy-cold                                                       175
Piled on a dish of gold
Too huge for me to hold,
What peaches with a velvet nap,
Pellucid grapes without one seed:
Odorous indeed must be the mead                                           180
Whereon they grow, and pure the wave they drink
With lilies at the brink,
And sugar-sweet their sap."

Golden head by golden head,
Like two pigeons in one nest                                              185
Folded in each other's wings,
They lay down in their curtained bed:
Like two blossoms on one stem,
Like two flakes of new-fallen snow,
Like two wands of ivory                                                    190
Tipped with gold for awful kings.
Moon and stars gazed in at them,
Wind sang to them lullaby,
Lumbering owls forebore to fly,
Not a bat flapped to and fro                                              195
Round their nest:
Cheek to cheek and breast to breast
Locked together in one nest.

Early in the morning
When the first cock crowed his warning.                                   200
Neat like bees, as sweet and busy,
Laura rose with Lizzie:
Fetched in honey, milked the cows,
Aired and set to rights the house,
Kneaded cakes of whitest wheat,                                           205
Cakes for dainty mouths to eat,
Next churned butter, whipped up cream,
Fed their poultry, sat and sewed;

Talked as modest maidens should:
Lizzie with an open heart,
Laura in an absent dream,                               210
One content, one sick in part;
One warbling for the mere bright day's delight,
One longing for the night.

At length slow evening came:                            215
They went with pitchers to the reedy brook;
Lizzie most placid in her look,
Laura most like a leaping flame,
They drew the gurgling water from its deep.
Lizzie plucked purple and rich golden flags,           220
Then turning homeward said: "The sunset flushes
Those furthest loftiest crags;
Come, Laura, not another maiden lags.
No willful squirrel wags,
The beasts and birds are fast asleep."                  225
But Laura loitered still among the rushes.
And said the bank was steep.

And said the hour was early still,
The dew not fallen, the wind not chill;
Listening ever, but not catching                        230
The customary cry,
"Come buy, come buy,"
With its iterated jingle
Of sugar-baited words:
Not for all her watching                                235
Once discerning even one goblin
Racing, whisking, tumbling, hobbling —
Let alone the herds
That used to tramp along the glen,
In groups or single,                                    240
Of brisk fruit-merchant men.

Till Lizzie urged, "O Laura, come;
I hear the fruit-call, but I dare not look:
You should not loiter longer at this brook:
Come with me home.                                      245
The stars rise, the moon bends her arc,
Each glow-worm winks her spark,
Let us get home before the night grows dark:
For clouds may gather
Though this is summer weather,                          250
Put out the lights and drench us through;
Then if we lost our way what should we do?"

Laura turned cold as stone
To find her sister heard that cry alone,
That goblin cry,                                        255
"Come buy our fruits, come buy."

Must she then buy no more such dainty fruit?
Must she no more such succous pasture find,
Gone deaf and blind?
Her tree of life dropped from the root:                            260
She said not one word in her heart's sore ache:
But peering through the dimness, nought discerning,
Trudged home, her pitcher dripping all the way;
So crept to bed, and lay
Silent till Lizzie slept;                                          265
Then sat up in a passionate yearning.
And gnashed her teeth for balked desire, and wept
As if her heart would break.

Day after day, night after night,
Laura kept watch in vain                                           270
In sullen silence of exceeding pain.
She never caught again the goblin cry,
"Come buy, come buy"; —
She never spied the goblin men
Hawking their fruits along the glen:                               275
But when the noon waxed bright
Her hair grew thin and gray;
She dwindled, as the fair full moon doth turn
To swift decay and burn
Her fire away.                                                     280

One day remembering her kernelstone
She set it by a wall that faced the south:
Dewed it with tears, hoped for a root,
Watched for a waxing shoot,
But there came none.                                              285
It never saw the sun,
It never felt the trickling moisture run:
While with sunk eyes and faded mouth
She dreamed of melons, as a traveler sees
False waves in desert drouth                                      290
With shade of leaf-crowned trees,
And burns the thirstier in the sandful breeze.

She no more swept the house,
Tended the fowls or cows,
Fetched honey, kneaded cakes of wheat,                            295
Brought water from the brook:
But sat down listless in the chimneynook
And would not eat.

Tender Lizzie could not bear
To watch her sister's cankerous care,                             300
Yet not to share.
She night and morning
Caught the goblins' cry:
"Come buy our orchard fruits,

Come buy, come buy;" —                                       305
Beside the brook, along the glen,
She heard the tramp of goblin men,
The voice and stir
Poor Laura could not hear;
Longed to buy fruit to comfort her,                          310
But feared to pay too dear.
She thought of Jeanie in her grave,
Who should have been a bride;
But who for joys brides hope to have
Fell sick and died                                           315
In her gay prime,
In earliest winter time,
With the first glazing rime,
With the first snow-fall of crisp winter time.

Till Laura dwindling                                         320
Seemed knocking at Death's door.
Then Lizzie weighed no more
Better and worse;
But put a silver penny in her purse,
Kissed Laura, crossed the heath with clumps of furze         325
At twilight, halted by the brook:
And for the first time in her life
Began to listen and look.

Laughed every goblin
When they spied her peeping:                                 330
Came towards her hobbling,
Flying, running, leaping,
Puffing and blowing,
Chuckling, clapping, crowing,
Cluckling and gobbling,                                      335
Mopping and mowing,
Full of airs and graces,
Pulling wry faces,
Demure grimaces,
Cat-like and rat-like,                                       340
Ratel- and wombat-like,
Snail-paced in a hurry,
Parrot-voiced and whistler,
Helter skelter, hurry skurry,
Chattering like magpies,                                     345
Fluttering like pigeons,
Gliding like fishes, —
Hugged her and kissed her:
Squeezed and caressed her:
Stretched up their dishes,                                   350
Panniers, and plates:
"Look at our apples
Russet and dun,

Bob at our cherries,
Bite at our peaches,                                              355
Citrons and dates,
Grapes for the asking,
Pears red with basking
Out in the sun,
Plums on their twigs;                                            360
Pluck them and suck them,
Pomegranates, figs." —

"Good folk," said Lizzie,
Mindful of Jeanie:
"Give me much and many":                                         365
Held out her apron,
Tossed them her penny
"Nay, take a seat with us,
Honor and eat with us,"
They answered grinning:                                          370
"Our feast is but beginning.
Night yet is early,
Warm and dew-pearly,
Wakeful and starry:
Such fruits as these                                             375
No man can carry;
Half their bloom would fly,
Half their dew would dry,
Half their flavor would pass by.
Sit down and feast with us,                                      380
Be welcome guest with us,
Cheer you and rest with us." —
"Thank you," said Lizzie: "But one waits
At home alone for me:
So without further parleying,                                    385
If you will not sell me any
Of your fruits though much and many,
Give me back my silver penny
I tossed you for a fee." —
They began to scratch their pates,                               390
No longer wagging, purring,
But visibly demurring,
Grunting and snarling.
One called her proud,
Cross-grained, uncivil;                                          395
Their tones waxed loud,
Their looks were evil.
Lashing their tails
They trod and hustled her,
Elbowed and jostled her,                                         400
Clawed with their nails,
Barking, mewing, hissing, mocking,
Tore her gown and soiled her stocking,

Twitched her hair out by the roots,
Stamped upon her tender feet,                                   405
Held her hands and squeezed their fruits
Against her mouth to make her eat.

White and golden Lizzie stood,
Like a lily in a flood, —
Like a rock of blue-veined stone                               410
Lashed by tides obstreperously, —
Like a beacon left alone
In a hoary roaring sea,
Sending up a golden fire, —
Like a fruit-crowned orange-tree                               415
White with blossoms honey-sweet
Sore beset by wasp and bee, —
Like a royal virgin town
Topped with gilded dome and spire
Close beleaguered by a fleet                                    420
Mad to tug her standard° down.                     *a banner, or flag*

One may lead a horse to water,
Twenty cannot make him drink.
Though the goblins cuffed and caught her,
Coaxed and fought her,                                          425
Bullied and besought her,
Scratched her, pinched her black as ink,
Kicked and knocked her,
Mauled and mocked her,
Lizzie uttered not a word;                                     430
Would not open lip from lip
Lest they should cram a mouthful in:
But laughed in heart to feel the drip
Of juice that syruped all her face,
And lodged in dimples of her chin,                             435
And streaked her neck which quaked like curd.
At last the evil people,
Worn out by her resistance,
Flungback her penny, kicked their fruit
Along whichever road they took,                                440
Not leaving root or stone or shoot;
Some writhed into the ground,
Some dived into the brook
With ring and ripple,
Some scudded on the gale without a sound.                      445
Some vanished in the distance.

In a smart, ache, tingle,
Lizzie went her way;
Knew not was it night or day;
Sprang up the bank, tore through the furze,                    450
Threaded copse and dingle,
And heard her penny jingle

Bouncing in her purse, —
Its bounce was music to her ear.
She ran and ran                                             455
As if she feared some goblin man
Dogged her with gibe or curse
Or something worse:
But not one goblin skurried after,
Nor was she pricked by fear;                               460
The kind heart made her windy-paced
That urged her home quite out of breath with haste
And inward laughter.

She cried, "Laura," up the garden,
"Did you miss me?                                          465
Come and kiss me.
Never mind my bruises,
Hug me, kiss me, suck my juices
Squeezed from goblin fruits for you,
Goblin pulp and goblin dew.                                470
Eat me, drink me, love me;
Laura, make much of me;
For your sake I have braved the glen
And had to do with goblin merchant men."

Laura started from her chair,                              475
Flung her arms up in the air,
Clutched her hair:
"Lizzie, Lizzie, have you tasted
For my sake the fruit forbidden?
Must your light like mine be hidden,                       480
Your young life like mine be wasted,
Undone in mine undoing,
And ruined in my ruin,
Thirsty, cankered, goblin-ridden?" —
She clung about her sister,                                485
Kissed and kissed and kissed her:
Tears once again
Refreshed her shrunken eyes,
Dropping like rain
After long sultry drouth;                                  490
Shaking with anguish, fear, and pain,
She kissed and kissed her with a hungry mouth.

Her lips began to scorch,
That juice was wormwood to her tongue,
She loathed the feast:                                     495
Writhing as one possessed she leaped and sung,
Rent all her robe, and wrung
Her hands in lamentable haste,
And beat her breast,
Her locks streamed like the torch                          500
Borne by a racer at full speed,

Or like the mane of horses in their flight,
Or like an eagle when she stems the light
Straight toward the sun,
Or like a caged thing freed,                                    505
Or like a flying flag when armies run.

Swift fire spread through her veins, knocked at her heart,
Met the fire smoldering there.
And overbore its lesser flame;
She gorged on bitterness without a name:                        510
Ah fool, to choose such part
Of soul-consuming care!
Sense failed in the mortal strife:
Like the watch-tower of a town
Which an earthquake shatters down,                              515
Like a lightning-stricken mast,
Like a wind-uprooted tree
Spun about,
Like a foam-topped waterspout
Cast down headlong in the sea,                                  520
She fell at last;
Pleasure past and anguish past,
Is it death or is it life?

Life out of death.
That night long Lizzie watched by her,                          525
Counted her pulse's flagging stir,
Felt for her breath,
Held water to her lips, and cooled her face
With tears and fanning leaves.
But when the first birds chirped about their eaves,            530
And early reapers plodded to the place
Of golden sheaves,
And dew-wet grass
Bowed in the morning winds so brisk to pass,
And new buds with new day                                       535
Opened of cup-like lilies on the stream,
Laura awoke as from a dream,
Laughed in the innocent old way,
Hugged Lizzie but not twice or thrice;
Her gleaming locks showed not one thread of gray,              540
Her breath was sweet as May,
And light danced in her eyes.

Days, weeks, months, years
Afterwards, when both were wives
With children of their own;                                     545
Their mother-hearts beset with fears,
Their lives bound up in tender lives:
Laura would call the little ones
And tell them of her early prime,
Those pleasant days long gone                                   550

Of not-returning time:
Would talk about the haunted glen,
The wicked quaint fruit-merchant men,
Their fruits like honey to the throat
But poison in the blood                                                        555
(Men sell not such in any town):
Would tell them how her sister stood
In deadly peril to do her good,
And win the fiery antidote:
Then joining hands to little hands                                             560
Would bid them cling together, —
"For there is no friend like a sister
In calm or stormy weather;
To cheer one on the tedious way,
To fetch one if one goes astray,                                              565
To lift one if one totters down,
To strengthen whilst one stands."

### CONSIDERATIONS FOR CRITICAL THINKING AND WRITING

1. FIRST RESPONSE. This is a lengthy poem from a bygone century, and yet even readers who are not particularly fond of poetry tend to find it riveting. How does the poet sustain your interest?

2. Goblins aren't real, but Lizzie and Laura are human. How do you interpret "goblins" symbolically? What specifically in the poem guides your response?

3. Based on the definition and example above, would you classify this poem as allegory or not?

### CONNECTION TO ANOTHER SELECTION

1. Compare the treatment of desire in this poem and in James Baldwin's "Guilt, Desire and Love" (p. 614).

### JANE KENYON (1947–1995)

## *The Thimble*    1993

I found a silver thimble
on the humusy floor of the woodshed,
neither large nor small, the open end
bent oval by the wood's weight,
or because the woman who wore it                                               5
shaped it to fit her finger.

Its decorative border of leaves, graceful
and regular, like the edge of acanthus
on the tin ceiling at church . . .
repeating itself over our heads                                              10
while we speak in unison
words the wearer must have spoken.

CONSIDERATIONS FOR CRITICAL THINKING AND WRITING

1. FIRST RESPONSE. Do you think the sound connection between "thimble" and "symbol" is coincidental?

2. How does the thimble function as a complex symbol? How does the speaker unpack its layers?

3. When does the pronoun shift from "I" to "we"? Why is this shift significant?

## KEVIN PIERCE (B. 1958)

### *Proof of Origin*   2005

*NEWSWIRE — A U.S. judge ordered a Georgia school district to remove from textbooks stickers challenging the theory of evolution.*

Though close to their hearts is the version that starts
With Adam and Eve and no clothes,
What enables their grip as the stickers they strip
Is Darwinian thumbs that oppose.

CONSIDERATIONS FOR CRITICAL THINKING AND WRITING

1. FIRST RESPONSE. How do the rhymes contribute to the humorous tone?

2. Discuss the levels of irony in the poem.

3. How do you read the title? Can it be explained in more than one way?

## CARL SANDBURG (1878–1967)

### *A Fence*   1916

Now the stone house on the lake front is finished and the workmen
        are beginning the fence.
The palings are made of iron bars with steel points that can stab the
        life out of any man who falls on them.
As a fence, it is a masterpiece, and will shut off the rabble and all
            vagabonds and hungry men and all wandering children looking
            for a place to play.
Passing through the bars and over the steel points will go nothing
            except Death and the Rain and Tomorrow.

CONSIDERATIONS FOR CRITICAL THINKING AND WRITING

1. FIRST RESPONSE. What is the effect of the capital letters in the final line?

2. Discuss the symbolic meaning of the fence and whether the symbolism is too spelled out or not.

### CONNECTION TO ANOTHER SELECTION

1. Consider the themes in "A Fence" and Robert Frost's "Mending Wall" (p. 866). Which poem do you prefer? Why?

## JULIO MARZÁN (B. 1946)

### *Ethnic Poetry*   1994

WHEN I WRITE "Words you are sure convey your truest feelings or thoughts may record only sentiment, not a line of poetry, while another arrangement, different words in another tone or rhythm, unlock and reveal what you really wanted to say." —JULIO MARZÁN

The ethnic poet said: "The earth is maybe
a huge maraca / and the sun a trombone /
and life / is to move your ass / to slow beats."
The ethnic audience roasted a suckling pig.

The ethnic poet said: "Oh thank Goddy, Goddy /          5
I be me, my toenails curled downward /
deep, deep, deep into Mama earth."
The ethnic audience shook strands of sea shells.

The ethnic poet said: "The sun was created black /
so we should imagine light / and also dream /          10
a walrus emerging from the broken ice."
The ethnic audience beat on sealskin drums.

The ethnic poet said: "Reproductive organs /
Eagles nesting California redwoods /
Shut up and listen to my ancestors."          15
The ethnic audience ate fried bread and honey.

The ethnic poet said: "Something there is that
doesn't love a wall / That sends
the frozen-ground-swell under it."
The ethnic audience deeply understood humanity.          20

### CONSIDERATIONS FOR CRITICAL THINKING AND WRITING

1. FIRST RESPONSE. What is the implicit definition of *ethnic poetry* in this poem?
2. The final stanza quotes lines from Robert Frost's "Mending Wall" (p. 866). Read the entire poem. Why do you think Marzán chooses these lines and this particular poem as one kind of ethnic poetry?
3. What is the poem's central irony? Pay particular attention to the final line. What is being satirized here?

### CONNECTION TO ANOTHER SELECTION

1. Write an essay that discusses the speakers' ideas about what poetry should be in "Ethnic Poetry" and in Ruth Forman's "Poetry Should Ride the Bus" (p. 544).

MARK HALLIDAY (B. 1949)

## Graded Paper 1991

On the whole this is quite successful work:
your main argument about the poet's ambivalence —
how he loves the very things he attacks —
is mostly persuasive and always engaging.

At the same time,                                                                    5
           there are spots
where your thinking becomes, for me,
alarmingly opaque, and your syntax seems to jump
backwards through unnecessary hoops,
as on p. 2 where you speak of "precognitive awareness            10
not yet disestablished by the shell that encrusts
each thing that a person actually says"
or at the top of p. 5 where your discussion of
"subverbal undertow miming the subversion of self-belief
woven counter to desire's outreach"                                             15
leaves me groping for firmer footholds.
(I'd have said it differently,
or rather, said something else.)
And when you say that women "could not fulfill themselves" (p. 6)
"in that era" (only forty years ago, after all!)                             20
are you so sure that the situation is so different today?
Also, how does Whitman bluff his way into
your penultimate paragraph? He is the *last* poet
I would have quoted in this context!
What plausible way of behaving                                                   25
does the passage you quote represent? Don't you think
literature should ultimately reveal possibilities for *action*?

Please notice how I've repaired your use of semicolons.

And yet, despite what may seem my cranky response,
I do admire the freshness of                                                         30
your thinking and your style; there is
a vitality here; your sentences thrust themselves forward
with a confidence as impressive as it is cheeky. . . .
You are not
           me, finally,                                                 35
and though this is an awkward problem, involving
the inescapable fact that you are so young, so young
it is also a delightful provocation.

$\left(A\text{-}\right)$

### CONSIDERATIONS FOR CRITICAL THINKING AND WRITING

1. **FIRST RESPONSE.** Have you ever had a teacher whose paper comments were
   widely considered to be unfair or inconsistent? Were the reasons similar to
   those glimpsed in this poem?

2. How do you characterize the grader of this paper based on the comments about the paper?

3. Explain whether or not you think the teacher's comments on the paper are consistent with the grade awarded it. How do you account for the grade?

4. Is this a satire? If so, exactly who or what is its target?

### CONNECTION TO ANOTHER SELECTION

1. Compare the ways in which Halliday reveals the speaker's character in this poem with the strategies used by Robert Browning in the next poem, "My Last Duchess."

## ROBERT BROWNING (1812–1889)

### *My Last Duchess*  1842

*Ferrara°*

That's my last Duchess painted on the wall,
Looking as if she were alive. I call
That piece a wonder, now: Frà Pandolf's° hands
Worked busily a day, and there she stands.
Will't please you sit and look at her? I said                                  5
"Frà Pandolf" by design, for never read
Strangers like you that pictured countenance,
The depth and passion of its earnest glance,
But to myself they turned (since none puts by
The curtain I have drawn for you, but I)                                       10
And seemed as they would ask me, if they durst,
How such a glance came there; so, not the first
Are you to turn and ask thus. Sir, 'twas not
Her husband's presence only, called that spot
Of joy into the Duchess' cheek: perhaps                                        15
Frà Pandolf chanced to say "Her mantle laps
Over my lady's wrist too much," or "Paint
Must never hope to reproduce the faint
Half-flush that dies along her throat": such stuff
Was courtesy, she thought, and cause enough                                    20
For calling up that spot of joy. She had
A heart — how shall I say? — too soon made glad,
Too easily impressed; she liked whate'er
She looked on, and her looks went everywhere.
Sir, 'twas all one! My favor at her breast,                                    25
The dropping of the daylight in the West,

---

*Ferrara:* In the sixteenth century, the duke of this Italian city arranged to marry a second time after the mysterious death of his very young first wife.     3 *Frà Pandolf:* A fictitious artist.

The bough of cherries some officious fool
Broke in the orchard for her, the white mule
She rode with round the terrace — all and each
Would draw from her alike the approving speech,            30
Or blush, at least. She thanked men, — good! but thanked
Somehow — I know not how — as if she ranked
My gift of a nine-hundred-years-old name
With anybody's gift. Who'd stoop to blame
This sort of trifling? Even had you skill            35
In speech — which I have not — to make your will
Quite clear to such an one, and say, "Just this
Or that in you disgusts me; here you miss,
Or there exceed the mark" — and if she let
Herself be lessoned so, nor plainly set            40
Her wits to yours, forsooth, and made excuse,
— E'en then would be some stooping; and I choose
Never to stoop. Oh sir, she smiled, no doubt,
Whene'er I passed her; but who passed without
Much the same smile? This grew; I gave commands;            45
Then all smiles stopped together. There she stands
As if alive. Will't please you rise? We'll meet
The company below, then. I repeat,
The Count your master's known munificence
Is ample warrant that no just pretense            50
Of mine for dowry will be disallowed;
Though his fair daughter's self, as I avowed
At starting, is my object. Nay, we'll go
Together down, sir. Notice Neptune, though,
Taming a sea-horse, thought a rarity,            55
Which Claus of Innsbruck° cast in bronze for me!

56 *Claus of Innsbruck:* Also a fictitious artist.

## CONSIDERATIONS FOR CRITICAL THINKING AND WRITING°

1. **FIRST RESPONSE.** What do you think happened to the duchess?

2. To whom is the duke addressing his remarks about the duchess in this poem? What is ironic about the situation?

3. Why was the duke unhappy with his first wife? What does this reveal about him? What does the poem's title suggest about his attitude toward women in general?

4. What seems to be the visitor's response (lines 53–54) to the duke's account of his first wife?

## CONNECTION TO ANOTHER SELECTION

1. Write an essay describing the ways in which the speakers of "My Last Duchess" and Katharyn Howd Machan's "Hazel Tells LaVerne" (p. 562) inadvertently reveal themselves.

## WILLIAM BLAKE (1757–1827)

### *A Poison Tree*    1794

I was angry with my friend:
I told my wrath, my wrath did end.
I was angry with my foe:
I told it not, my wrath did grow.

And I water'd it in fears,                                              5
Night & morning with my tears;
And I sunned it with smiles,
And with soft deceitful wiles.

And it grew both day and night,
Till it bore an apple bright.                                          10
And my foe beheld it shine,
And he knew that it was mine,

And into my garden stole,
When the night had veild the pole;
In the morning glad I see                                             15
My foe outstretched beneath the tree.

### CONSIDERATIONS FOR CRITICAL THINKING AND WRITING

1. FIRST RESPONSE. Considering the "apple bright" allusion in the third stanza,
   how can "A Poison Tree" be read as more than a meditation on a personal relationship gone bad?
2. What is the speaker's attitude toward anger and revenge? What do you think
   the speaker wants the reader's attitude to be?

## Perspective

## EZRA POUND (1885–1972)

### *On Symbols*    1912

I believe that the proper and perfect symbol is the natural object, that if a man uses
"symbols" he must so use them that their symbolic function does not obtrude; so
that *a* sense, and the poetic quality of the passage, is not lost to those who do not
understand the symbol as such, to whom, for instance, a hawk is a hawk.

From "Prolegomena," *Poetry Review,* February 1912

### CONSIDERATIONS FOR CRITICAL THINKING AND WRITING

1. Discuss whether you agree with Pound that the "perfect symbol" is a "natural
   object" that does not insist on being read as a symbol.
2. Write an essay in which you discuss Carl Sandburg's "A Fence" (p. 633) as an
   example of the "perfect symbol" Pound proposes.

# 21

# Sounds

Bettmann/Getty Images.

In a poem the words should be as
pleasing to the ear as the meaning is to
the mind.
— MARIANNE MOORE

## LISTENING TO POETRY

Poems yearn to be read aloud. Much of their energy, charm, and beauty come
to life only when they are heard. Poets choose and arrange words for their
sounds as well as for their meanings. Most poetry is best read with your lips,
teeth, and tongue because they serve to articulate the effects that sound may
have in a poem. When a voice is breathed into a good poem, there is pleasure
in the reading, the saying, and the hearing.

The earliest poetry — before writing and painting — was chanted or
sung. The rhythmic quality of such oral performances served two purposes:
it helped the chanting bard remember the lines and it entertained audiences
with patterned sounds of language, which were sometimes accompanied by
musical instruments. Poetry has always been closely related to music. Indeed,
as the word suggests, lyric poetry evolved from songs. Had Robert Frost lived
in a nonliterate society, he probably would have sung some version — a very
different version to be sure — of "Acquainted with the Night" (p. 612) instead

of writing it down. Even though Frost creates a speaking rather than a singing voice, the speaker's anxious tone is distinctly heard in any careful reading of the poem.

Like lyrics, early narrative poems were originally part of an anonymous oral folk tradition. A ***ballad*** told a story that was sung from one generation to the next until it was finally transcribed. Since the eighteenth century, this narrative form has sometimes been imitated by poets who write ***literary ballads***. In considering poetry as sound, we should not forget that poetry traces its beginnings to song. See Chapter 26, "Song Lyrics as Poetry," for an in-depth examination of the relationship between these categories.

The following poem, "Ogun," takes its title from a spirit warrior present in multiple African religions and in belief systems popular in Caribbean nations. The poet, Kamau Brathwaite, lived in Barbados and is among the most prominent poets from that island. In this poem he links the African god who is associated with metalwork to his uncle who is a furniture maker/artist on the island. The poem appeals to multiple senses, but especially hearing. As you read it, note the way it evokes sounds.

## Kamau Brathwaite (1930–2020)

### *Ogun*   1969

My uncle made chairs, tables, balanced doors on, dug out
coffins, smoothing the white wood out

with plane and quick sandpaper until
it shone like his short-sighted glasses.

The knuckles of his hands were sil-                                                5
vered knobs of nails hit, hurt and flat-

tened out with blast of heavy hammer. He was knock-knee'd, flat-
footed and his clip clop sandals slapped across the concrete

flooring of his little shop where canefield mulemen and a fleet
of Bedford lorry drivers° dropped in to scratch themselves and talk.        10

There was no shock of wood, no beam
of light mahogany his saw teeth couldn't handle.

When shaping squares for locks, a key hole
care tapped rat tat tat upon the handle

of his humpbacked chisel. Cold                                                  15
world of wood caught fire as he whittled: rectangle

---

*10 lorry drivers:* Truck drivers

window frames, the intersecting x of folding chairs; triangle

trellises, the donkey
box-cart in its squeaking square.                                        20

But he was poor and most days he was hungry.
Imported cabinets with mirrors, formica table

tops, spine-curving chairs made up of tubes, with hollow
steel-like bird bones that sat on rubber ploughs,

thin beds, stretched not on boards, but blue high-tensioned cables,      25
were what the world preferred.

And yet he had a block of wood that would have baffled them.
With knife and gimlet care he worked away at this on Sundays,

explored its knotted hurts, cutting his way
along its yellow whorls until his hands could feel                       30

how it had swelled and shivered, breathing air,
its weathered green burning to rings of time,

its contoured grain still tuned to roots and water.
And as he cut, he heard the creak of forests:

green lizard faces gulped, grey memories with moth                       35
eyes watched him from their shadows, soft

liquid tendrils leaked among the flowers
and a black rigid thunder he had never heard within his hammer

came stomping up the trunks. And as he worked within his shattered
Sunday shop, the wood took shape: dry shuttered                          40

eyes, slack anciently everted lips, flat
ruined face, eaten by pox, ravaged by rat

and woodworm, dry cistern mouth, cracked
gullet crying for the desert, the heavy black

enduring jaw; lost pain, lost iron;                                      45
emerging woodwork image of his anger.

### Considerations for Critical Thinking and Writing

1. **first response.** The speaker's uncle fashions a god figure out of wood at the
   poem's conclusion. Is the uncle also a kind of god? What informs your response?
2. List examples where the poem's language is pure sound. What effect does it have?
3. Where does the poem put sounds alongside images? Does it juxtapose sound
   and image to overwhelm us, to deepen the sense of the meaning of the uncle
   and his workshop, or something else?

Listen to the sound of this poem as you read it aloud. How do the words
provide, in a sense, their own rhythmic accompaniment?

# John Updike (1932–2009)

## *Player Piano* 1958

My stick fingers click with a snicker
And, chuckling, they knuckle the keys;
Light-footed, my steel feelers flicker
And pluck from these keys melodies.

My paper can caper; abandon                    5
Is broadcast by dint of my din,
And no man or band has a hand in
The tones I turn on from within.

At times I'm a jumble of rumbles,
At others I'm light like the moon,             10
But never my numb plunker fumbles,
Misstrums me, or tries a new tune.

Joanne Rathe/Boston Globe/Getty Images.

The speaker in this poem is a piano that can play automatically by means of a mechanism that depresses keys in response to signals on a perforated roll. Notice how the speaker's voice approximates the sounds of a piano. In each stanza a predominant sound emerges from the carefully chosen words. How is the sound of each stanza tuned to its sense?

Like Updike's "Player Piano," this next poem also employs sounds to reinforce meanings.

# Emily Dickinson (1830–1886)

## *A Bird came down the Walk —* ca. 1862

A Bird came down the Walk —
He did not know I saw —
He bit an Angleworm in halves
And ate the fellow, raw,

And then he drank a Dew                        5
From a convenient Grass —
And then hopped sidewise to the Wall
To let a Beetle pass —

He glanced with rapid eyes
That hurried all around —                       10
They looked like frightened Beads, I thought —
He stirred his Velvet Head

Like one in danger, Cautious,
I offered him a Crumb
And he unrolled his feathers                     15
And rowed him softer home —

Than Oars divide the Ocean,
Too silver for a seam —
Or Butterflies, off Banks of Noon
Leap, plashless as they swim.                                    20

This description of a bird offers a close look at how differently a bird moves when it hops on the ground than when it flies in the air. On the ground the bird moves quickly, awkwardly, and irregularly as it plucks up a worm, washes it down with dew, and then hops aside to avoid a passing beetle. The speaker recounts the bird's rapid, abrupt actions from a somewhat superior, amused perspective. By describing the bird in human terms (as if, for exam- ple, it chose to eat the worm "raw"), the speaker is almost condescending. But when the attempt to offer a crumb fails and the frightened bird flies off, the speaker is left looking up instead of down at the bird.

With that shift in perspective the tone shifts from amusement to awe in response to the bird's graceful flight. The jerky movements of lines 1 to 13 give way to the smooth motion of lines 15 to 20. The pace of the first three stanzas is fast and discontinuous. We tend to pause at the end of each line, and this reinforces a sense of disconnected movements. In contrast, the final six lines are to be read as a single sentence in one flowing movement, lubricated by various sounds.

Read again the description of the bird flying away. Several *o*-sounds contribute to the image of the serene, expansive, confident flight, just as the *s*-sounds serve as smooth transitions from one line to the next. Notice how these sounds are grouped in the following vertical columns:

| unr*o*lled | s*o*fter | T*oo* | hi*s* | *O*cean | Bank*s* |
|---|---|---|---|---|---|
| r*o*wed | *O*ars | N*oo*n | feather*s* | *s*ilver | pla*s*hle*ss* |
| h*o*me | *O*r | | *s*ofter | *s*eam | a*s* |
| *O*cean | *o*ff | | *O*ars | Butterflie*s* | *s*wim |

This blending of sounds (notice how "Leap, plashless" brings together the *p*- and *l*-sounds without a ripple) helps convey the bird's smooth grace in the air. Like a feathered oar, the bird moves seamlessly in its element.

The repetition of sounds in poetry is similar to the function of the tones and melodies that are repeated, with variations, in music. Just as the patterned sounds in music unify a work, so do the words in poems, which have been carefully chosen for the combinations of sounds they create. These sounds are produced in a number of ways.

The most direct way in which the sound of a word suggests its meaning is through **onomatopoeia**, which is the use of a word that resembles the sound it denotes: *quack, buzz, rattle, bang, squeak, bowwow, burp, choo-choo, ding- a-ling, sizzle.* In Brathwaite's "Ogun" (p. 640) we hear "rat tat tat" and "clip clop." The sound and sense of these words are closely related, but such words represent a very small percentage of the words available to us. Poets usually employ more subtle means for echoing meanings.

Onomatopoeia can consist of more than just single words. In its broadest meaning the term refers to lines or passages in which sounds help to convey meanings, as in these lines from Updike's "Player Piano":

> My stick fingers click with a snicker
> And, chuckling, they knuckle the keys.

The sharp, crisp sounds of these two lines approximate the sounds of a piano; the syllables seem to "click" against one another. Contrast Updike's rendition with the following lines:

> My long fingers play with abandon
> And, laughing, they cover the keys.

The original version is more interesting and alive because the sounds of the words are pleasurable and reinforce the meaning through a careful blending of consonants and vowels.

*Alliteration* is the repetition of the same consonant sounds at the beginnings of nearby words: "*d*escending *d*ewdrops," "*l*uscious *l*emons." Sometimes the term is also used to describe the consonant sounds within words: "tres*p*asser's re*p*roach," "we*dd*ed la*d*y." Alliteration is based on sound rather than spelling. "*K*een" and "*c*ar" alliterate, but "*c*ar" does not alliterate with "*c*ite." Rarely is heavy-handed alliteration effective. Used too self-consciously, it can be distracting instead of strengthening meaning or emphasizing a relation between words. Consider the relentless *h*'s in this line: "Horrendous horrors haunted Helen's happiness." Those *h*'s certainly suggest that Helen is being pursued, but they have a more comic than serious effect because they are overdone.

*Assonance* is the repetition of the same vowel sound in nearby words: "asl*ee*p under a tr*ee*," "t*i*me and t*i*de," "h*au*nt" and "*aw*esome," "*ea*ch *e*vening." Both alliteration and assonance help to establish relations among words in a line or a series of lines. Whether the effect is *euphony* (lines that are musically pleasant to the ear and smooth, like the final lines of Dickinson's "A Bird came down the Walk—") or *cacophony* (lines that are discordant and difficult to pronounce, like the claim that "never my numb plunker fumbles" in Updike's "Player Piano"), the sounds of words in poetry can be as significant as the words' denotative or connotative meanings.

# A SAMPLE STUDENT RESPONSE

Ryan Lee

Professor McDonough

English 211

1 December 2023

Sound in Emily Dickinson's "A Bird came down the Walk—"

In her poem "A Bird came down the Walk—" Emily Dickinson uses the sound and rhythm of each line to reflect the motion of a bird walking awkwardly—and then flying gracefully. Particularly when read aloud, the staccato phrases and stilted breaks in lines 1 through 14 create a sense of the bird's movement on land, quick and off-balanced, which helps bring the scene to life.

The first three stanzas are structured to make the bird's movement consistent. The bird hops around, eating worms while keeping guard for any threats. Vulnerable on the ground, the bird is intensely aware of danger:

> He glanced with rapid eyes
>
> That hurried all around—
>
> They looked like frightened Beads, I thought—
>
> He stirred his Velvet Head (9-12)

In addition to choosing words that portray the bird as cautious—it "glanced with rapid eyes" (9) that resemble "frightened Beads" (11)—Dickinson chooses to end each line abruptly. This abrupt halting of sound allows the reader to experience the bird's fear more immediately, and the effect is similar to the missing of a beat or a breath.

These halting lines stand in contrast to the smoothness of the last six lines, during which the bird takes flight. The sounds in these lines are pleasingly soft, and rich in the "s" sound. The bird

> unrolled his feathers
>
> And rowed him softer home—
>
>
> Than Oars divide the Ocean,
>
> Too silver for a seam—(15-18). . . .

Lee 4

Work Cited

Dickinson, Emily. "A Bird came down the Walk —." *The Compact Bedford Introduction to Literature*, edited by Michael Meyer and D. Quentin Miller, 13th ed., Bedford/St. Martin's, 2024, p. 642.

## RHYME

Like alliteration and assonance, **rhyme** is a way of creating sound patterns. Rhyme, broadly defined, consists of two or more words or phrases that repeat the same sounds: *happy* and *snappy*. Rhyme words often have similar spellings, but that is not a requirement of rhyme; what matters is that the words sound alike: *vain* rhymes with *reign* as well as *rain*. Moreover, words may look alike but not rhyme at all. In **eye rhyme** the spellings are similar, but the pronunciations are not, as with *bough* and *cough,* or *brow* and *blow.*

Not all poems use rhyme. Many great poems have no rhymes, and many weak verses use rhyme as a substitute for poetry. These are especially apparent in commercial messages and greeting-card lines. At its worst, rhyme is merely a distracting decoration that can lead to dullness and predictability. But used skillfully, rhyme creates lines that are memorable and musical.

Here is a poem using rhyme that you might remember the next time you are in a restaurant.

Rɪᴄʜᴀʀᴅ Aʀᴍᴏᴜʀ  (1906–1989)

### *Going to Extremes*   1954

Shake and shake
   The catsup bottle
None'll come —
   And then a lot'll.

The experience recounted in Armour's poem is common enough, but the rhyme's humor is special. The final line clicks the poem shut — an effect that is often achieved by the use of rhyme. That click provides a sense of a satisfying and fulfilled form. Rhymes have a number of uses: they can emphasize words, direct a reader's attention to relations between words, and provide an overall structure for a poem.

Rhyme is used in the following poem to imitate the sound of cascading water.

ROBERT SOUTHEY (1774–1843)

## *From "The Cataract of Lodore"* 1820

"How does the water
Come down at Lodore?"

. . . . . . . . . .

From its sources which well
  In the tarn on the fell;
    From its fountains                                  5
    In the mountains,
    Its rills and its gills;
Through moss and through brake,
    It runs and it creeps
    For awhile, till it sleeps                          10
    In its own little lake.
  And thence at departing,
  Awakening and starting,
  It runs through the reeds
    And away it proceeds,                               15
Through meadow and glade,
    In sun and in shade,
And through the wood-shelter,
  Among crags in its flurry,
    Helter-skelter,                                     20
    Hurry-scurry.
  Here it comes sparkling,
And there it lies darkling;
Now smoking and frothing
  Its tumult and wrath in,                              25
    Till in this rapid race
      On which it is bent,
    It reaches the place
    Of its steep descent.

. . . . . . . . . . . . . . . . . .

Dividing and gliding and sliding,                            30
And falling and brawling and sprawling,
And driving and riving and striving,
And sprinkling and twinkling and wrinkling,
And sounding and bounding and rounding,
And bubbling and troubling and doubling,                     35
And grumbling and rumbling and tumbling,
And clattering and battering and shattering;
Retreating and beating and meeting and sheeting,
Delaying and straying and playing and spraying,
Advancing and prancing and glancing and dancing,            40
Recoiling, turmoiling and toiling and boiling,
And gleaming and streaming and steaming and beaming,

And rushing and flushing and brushing and gushing,
And flapping and rapping and clapping and slapping,
And curling and whirling and purling and twirling,                        45
And thumping and plumping and bumping and jumping,
And dashing and flashing and splashing and clashing;
And so never ending, but always descending,
Sounds and motions forever and ever are blending,
All at once and all o'er, with a mighty uproar;                           50
And this way the water comes down at Lodore.

This deluge of rhymes consists of "Sounds and motions forever and ever . . .
blending" (line 49). The pace quickens as the water creeps from its mountain
source and then descends in rushing cataracts. As the speed of the water increases,
so do the number of rhymes, until they run in fours: "dashing and flashing and
splashing and clashing" (line 47). Most rhymes meander through poems instead
of flooding them; nevertheless, Southey's use of rhyme suggests how sounds can
flow with meanings. "The Cataract of Lodore" has been criticized, however, for
overusing onomatopoeia. Some readers find the poem silly; others regard it as a
brilliant example of sound effects. What do you think?

A variety of types of rhyme is available to poets. The most common form,
**end rhyme**, comes at the ends of lines (lines 14–17).

> It runs through the reeds
>     And away it proceeds,
> Through meadow and glade,
>     In sun and in shade.

**Internal rhyme** places at least one of the rhymed words within the line, as in
"Dividing and gliding and sliding" (line 30) or, more subtly, in the fourth and
final words of "In mist or cloud, on mast or shroud."

The rhyming of single-syllable words such as *glade* and *shade* is known as
**masculine rhyme**, as we see in these lines from A. E. Housman:

> Loveliest of trees, the cherry now
> Is hung with bloom along the bough.

Rhymes using words of more than one syllable are also called masculine when
the same sound occurs in a final stressed syllable, as in *defend, contend*; *betray,
away*. A *feminine rhyme* consists of a rhymed stressed syllable followed by one
or more rhymed unstressed syllables, as in *butter, clutter*; *gratitude, attitude*;
*quivering, shivering*. This rhyme is evident in John Millington Synge's verse:

> Lord confound this surly sister,
> Blight her brow and blotch and blister.

All of the examples so far have been **exact rhymes** because they share the
same stressed vowel sounds as well as any sounds that follow the vowel. In
**near rhyme** (also called **off rhyme, slant rhyme**, and **approximate rhyme**),
the sounds are almost but not exactly alike. There are several kinds of near
rhyme. One of the most common is **consonance**, an identical consonant

sound preceded by a different vowel sound: *home, same; worth, breath; trophy, daffy.* Near rhyme can also be achieved by using different vowel sounds with identical consonant sounds: *sound, sand; kind, conned; fellow, fallow.* The dissonance of *blade* and *blood* in the following lines from Wilfred Owen helps to reinforce their grim tone:

> Let the boy try along this bayonet-blade
> How cold steel is, and keen with hunger of blood.

Near rhymes greatly broaden the possibility for musical effects in English, a language that, compared with Spanish or Italian, contains few exact rhymes. Do not assume, however, that a near rhyme represents a failed attempt at exact rhyme. Near rhymes allow a musical subtlety and variety and can avoid the sometimes overpowering jingling effects that exact rhymes may create.

These basic terms hardly exhaust the ways in which the sounds in poems can be labeled and discussed, but the terms can help you to describe how poets manipulate sounds for effect. Read Gerard Manley Hopkins's "God's Grandeur" (p. 650) aloud and try to determine how the sounds of the lines contribute to their sense.

## Perspective

### DAVID LENSON (B. 1945)

## *On the Contemporary Use of Rhyme*  1988

One impediment to a respectable return to rhyme is the popular survival of "functional" verse: greeting cards, pedagogical and mnemonic devices ("Thirty days hath September"), nursery rhymes, advertising jingles, and of course song lyrics. Pentameters, irregular rhymes, and free verse aren't much use in songwriting, where the meter has to be governed by the time signature of the music.

Far from universities, there has been a revival of rhymed couplets in rap music, in which, to the accompaniment of synthesizers, vocalists deliver lengthy first-person narratives in tetrameter. While most writing teachers would dismiss such lyrics as doggerel, the aim of the songs is really not so far from that of Alexander Pope: to use rhyme to sharpen social insight, in the hope that the world may be reordered.

From *The Chronicle of Higher Education,* February 24, 1988

#### CONSIDERATIONS FOR CRITICAL THINKING AND WRITING

1. Read some contemporary song lyrics from a wide range of groups or vocalists (you may want to start with the lyrics included in Chapter 26). Is Lenson correct in his assessment that irregular rhyme is not much use in songwriting?

2. Examine the rhymed couplets of some rap music. Discuss whether they are used "to sharpen social insight." What is the effect of using rhymes in rap music?

3. What is your own response to rhymed poetry? Do you like yours with or without? What do you think informs your preference?

## SOUND AND MEANING

### GERARD MANLEY HOPKINS (1844–1889)

## God's Grandeur 1877

The world is charged with the grandeur of God.
    It will flame out, like shining from shook foil;°             *shaken gold foil*
    It gathers to a greatness, like the ooze of oil
Crushed.° Why do men then now not reck his rod?°
Generations have trod, have trod, have trod;                                5
    And all is seared with trade; bleared, smeared with toil;
    And wears man's smudge and shares man's smell: the soil
Is bare now, nor can foot feel, being shod.
And for all this, nature is never spent;
    There lives the dearest freshness deep down things;                  10
And though the last lights off the black West went
    Oh, morning, at the brown brink eastward, springs —
Because the Holy Ghost over the bent
    World broods with warm breast and with ah! bright wings.

---

4 *Crushed:* Olives crushed in their oil;    *reck his rod:* Obey God.

    The subject of this poem is announced in the title and the first line: "The world is charged with the grandeur of God." The poem is a celebration of the power and greatness of God's presence in the world, but the speaker is also perplexed and dismayed by people who refuse to recognize God's authority and grandeur as they are manifested in the creation. Instead of glorifying God, "men" have degraded the earth through meaningless toil and cut themselves off from the spiritual renewal inherent in the beauty of nature. The relentless demands of commerce and industry have blinded people to the earth's natural and spiritual resources. Despite this abuse and insensitivity to God's grandeur, however, "nature is never spent"; the morning light that "springs" in the east redeems the "black West" of the night and is a sign that the spirit of the Holy Ghost is ever present in the world. This summary of the poem sketches some of the thematic significance of the lines, but it does not do justice to how they are organized around the use of sound. Hopkins's poem, unlike Southey's "The Cataract of Lodore" (p. 647), uses sounds in a subtle and complex way.

    In the opening line Hopkins uses alliteration — a device apparent in almost every line of the poem — to connect "*G*od" to the "*w*orl*d*," which is "char*g*e*d*" with his "*g*randeur." These consonants unify the line as well. The alliteration in lines 2 and 3 suggests a harmony in the creation: the *f*'s in "*f*lame" and "*f*oil," the *sh*'s in "*sh*ining" and "*sh*ook," the *g*'s in "*g*athers" and "*g*reatness," and the visual (not alliterative) similarities of "*ooze* of *oil*" emphasize a world that is held together by God's will.

    That harmony is abruptly interrupted by the speaker's angry question in line 4: "Why do men then now not reck his rod?" The question is as painful to the speaker as it is difficult to pronounce. The arrangement of the alliteration ("*now*," "*not*"; "*reck*," "*rod*"), the assonance ("n*o*t," "r*o*d"; "m*en*," "th*en*," "r*e*ck"), and the internal rhyme ("m*en*," "th*en*") contribute to the difficulty in saying the line — a difficulty associated with human behavior. That behavior is introduced in line 5 by the repetition of "have trod" to emphasize the repeated mistakes — sins — committed by human beings. The tone is dirgelike because humanity persists in its mistaken path rather than progressing. The speaker's horror at humanity is evident in the cacophonous sounds of lines 6 to 8. Here the alliteration of "*sm*eared," "*sm*udge," and "*sm*ell" along with the internal rhymes of "s*eared*," "bl*eared*," and "sm*eared*" echo the disgust with which the speaker views humanity's "toil" with the "soil," an end rhyme that calls attention to our mistaken equation of nature with production rather than with spirituality.

In contrast to this cacophony, the final six lines build toward the joyful recognition of the new possibilities that accompany the rising sun. This recognition leads to the euphonic description of the "H*o*ly Gh*o*st *o*ver" (notice the reassuring consistency of the assonance) the world. Traditionally represented as a dove, the Holy Ghost brings love and peace to the "*wor*ld," and "*br*oods *w*ith *w*arm *br*east and *w*ith ah! *br*ight *w*ings." The effect of this alliteration is mellifluous: the sound bespeaks the harmony that prevails at the end of the poem resulting from the speaker's recognition that "nature is never spent" because God loves and protects the world.

The sounds of "God's Grandeur" enhance the poem's theme; more can be said about its sounds, but it is enough to point out here that for this poem the sound strongly echoes the theme in nearly every line. Here are some more poems in which sound plays a significant role.

## POEMS FOR FURTHER STUDY

### LEWIS CARROLL (CHARLES LUTWIDGE DODGSON/1832–1898)

### *Jabberwocky*   1871

'Twas brillig, and the slithy toves
   Did gyre and gimble in the wabe:
All mimsy were the borogoves,
   And the mome raths outgrabe.

"Beware the Jabberwock, my son!                                                    5
   The jaws that bite, the claws that catch!
Beware the Jubjub bird, and shun
   The frumious Bandersnatch!"

He took his vorpal sword in hand;
   Long time the manxome foe he sought —                                  10
So rested he by the Tumtum tree,
   And stood awhile in thought.

And, as in uffish thought he stood,
    The Jabberwock, with eyes of flame,
Came whiffling through the tulgey wood,                           15
    And burbled as it came!

One, two! One, two! And through and through
    The vorpal blade went snicker-snack!
He left it dead, and with its head
    He went galumphing back.                                      20

"And hast thou slain the Jabberwock?
    Come to my arms, my beamish boy!
O frabjous day! Callooh, Callay!"
    He chortled in his joy.

'Twas brillig, and the slithy toves                               25
    Did gyre and gimble in the wabe:
All mimsy were the borogoves,
    And the mome raths outgrabe.

### CONSIDERATIONS FOR CRITICAL THINKING AND WRITING

1. FIRST RESPONSE. What happens in this poem? Does it have any meaning?

2. Not all of the words used in this poem appear in dictionaries. In *Through the Looking Glass*, Humpty Dumpty explains to Alice that " 'slithy' means 'lithe and slimy.' 'Lithe' is the same as 'active.' You see it's like a portmanteau — there are two meanings packed up into one word." Are there any other portmanteau words in the poem?

3. Which words in the poem sound especially meaningful, even if they are devoid of any denotative meanings?

### CONNECTION TO ANOTHER SELECTION

1. Compare Carroll's strategies for creating sound and meaning with those used by John Updike in "Player Piano" (p. 642).

## WILLIAM HEYEN (B. 1940)

### *The Trains* 1984

Signed by Franz Paul Stangl, Commandant,
there is in Berlin a document,
an order of transmittal from Treblinka:

248 freight cars of clothing,
400,000 gold watches,                                            5
25 freight cars of women's hair.

Some clothing was kept, some pulped for paper.
The finest watches were never melted down.
All the women's hair was used for mattresses, or dolls.

Would these words like to use some of that same paper?    10
One of those watches may pulse in your own wrist.
Does someone you know collect dolls, or sleep on human hair?

He is dead at last, Commandant Stangl of Treblinka,
but the camp's three syllables still sound like freight cars
straining around a curve, Treblinka,    15

Treblinka. Clothing, time in gold watches,
women's hair for mattresses and dolls' heads.
Treblinka. The trains from Treblinka.

### Considerations for Critical Thinking and Writing

1. FIRST RESPONSE. How does the sound of the word *Treblinka* inform your understanding of the poem?

2. Why does the place name of Treblinka continue to resonate over time? To learn more about Treblinka, search online, perhaps starting at ushmm.org, the site of the United States Holocaust Memorial Museum.

3. Why do you suppose Heyen uses the word *in* instead of *on* in line 11?

4. Why is sound so important for establishing the tone of this poem? In what sense do "the camp's three syllables still sound like freight cars" (line 14)?

5. CRITICAL STRATEGIES. Read the section on reader-response strategies (pp. 1396–1397) in Chapter 42, "Critical Strategies for Reading." How does this poem make you feel? Why?

### Alfred, Lord Tennyson (1809–1892)

## *Break, Break, Break*    1842

Break, break, break,
　On thy cold gray stones, O Sea!
And I would that my tongue could utter
　The thoughts that arise in me.

O, well for the fisherman's boy,    5
　That he shouts with his sister at play!
O, well for the sailor lad,
　That he sings in his boat on the bay!

And the stately ships go on
　To their haven under the hill;    10
But O for the touch of a vanish'd hand,
　And the sound of a voice that is still!

Break, break, break
　At the foot of thy crags, O Sea!
But the tender grace of a day that is dead    15
　Will never come back to me.

## CONSIDERATIONS FOR CRITICAL THINKING AND WRITING

1. FIRST RESPONSE. The poem was written as an ***elegy*** following the death of Tennyson's friend, the poet Arthur Henry Hallam. Based on this context, what feelings does the poem evoke?

2. Which of the sound qualities of poetic language we have described can you find here? What is their effect?

3. Are the end rhymes at the end of alternating lines masculine or feminine as we describe those terms above? How does this type of rhyme intensify the feelings you associate with the poem?

4. What sound qualities of an ocean are evident in the words and rhythm of this poem?

## JOHN DONNE (1572–1631)

## *Song*   1633

Go and catch a falling star,
 Get with child a mandrake root,°
Tell me where all past years are,
 Or who cleft the Devil's foot,
Teach me to hear mermaids singing,                                               5
 Or to keep off envy's stinging,
   And find
   What wind
Serves to advance an honest mind.

If thou be'st borne to strange sights,                                          10
 Things invisible to see,
Ride ten thousand days and nights,
 Till age snow white hairs on thee,
Thou, when thou return'st, wilt tell me
 All strange wonders that befell thee,                                         15
   And swear
   Nowhere
Lives a woman true, and fair.

If thou findst one, let me know,
 Such a pilgrimage were sweet —                                               20
Yet do not, I would not go,
 Though at next door we might meet;
Though she were true, when you met her,
 And last, till you write your letter,
   Yet she                                                                    25
   Will be
False, ere I come, to two or three.

2 *mandrake root:* This V-shaped root resembles the lower half of the human body.

CONSIDERATIONS FOR CRITICAL THINKING AND WRITING

1. FIRST RESPONSE. What is the speaker's tone in this poem? What is his view of a woman's love? What does the speaker's use of hyperbole reveal about his emotional state?

2. Do you think Donne wants the speaker's argument to be taken seriously? Is there any humor in the poem?

3. Most of these lines end with masculine rhymes. What other kinds of rhymes are used for end rhymes?

## KAY RYAN (B. 1945)

### *Dew* 1996

As neatly as peas
in their green canoe,
as discretely as beads
strung in a row,
sit drops of dew                                    5
along a blade of grass.
But unattached and
subject to their weight,
they slip if they accumulate.
Down the green tongue                              10
out of the morning sun
into the general damp,
they're gone.

Chris Felver/Getty Images.

CONSIDERATIONS FOR CRITICAL THINKING AND WRITING

1. FIRST RESPONSE. How does reading the poem aloud affect your understanding of Ryan's use of rhyme to create a particular tone?

2. Explain whether the images in the poem are simply descriptive or are presented as a means of producing a theme. What is the role of the title?

## ANDREW HUDGINS (B. 1951)

### *The Ice-Cream Truck* 2009

From blocks away the music floats
to my enchanted ears.
It builds. It's here! And then it fades —
and I explode in tears.

I kick the TV set, and scream,                      5
sobbing to extort her,
while Mom stares at *One Life to Live*,
and won't give me a quarter.

I pause, change tactics, snatch a coin
from the bottom of her purse,                                    10
then race to catch the ice-cream truck,
ignoring Mama's curse.

I stop the truck, I start to choose —
then see I won't be eating.
I stare down at a goddamn dime,                                  15
and trudge home to my beating.

### CONSIDERATIONS FOR CRITICAL THINKING AND WRITING

1. FIRST RESPONSE. Describe the tone of each stanza. How do the rhymes serve to establish the tone?

2. Characterize the speaker. How do you reconcile what is said in the first stanza with the description in the final stanza?

3. This poem appeared in a collection by Hudgins titled *Shut Up, You're Fine: Poems for Very, Very Bad Children*. How does that context affect your reading of it?

4. CREATIVE RESPONSE. Add a four-line stanza in Hudgins's style that rhymes and concludes back at home.

## ROBERT FRANCIS (1901–1987)

## *The Pitcher*   1953

His art is eccentricity, his aim
How not to hit the mark he seems to aim at,

His passion how to avoid the obvious,
His technique how to vary the avoidance.

The others throw to be comprehended. He                          5
Throws to be a moment misunderstood.

Yet not too much. Not errant, arrant, wild,
But every seeming aberration willed.

Not to, yet still, still to communicate
Making the batter understand too late.                           10

### CONSIDERATIONS FOR CRITICAL THINKING AND WRITING

1. FIRST RESPONSE. Explain how each pair of lines in this poem works together to describe the pitcher's art.

2. Consider how the poem itself works the way a good pitcher does. Which lines illustrate what they describe?

3. Comment on the effects of the poem's rhymes. How are the final two lines different in their rhyme from the previous lines? How does sound echo sense in lines 9–10?

4. Write an essay that examines "The Pitcher" as an extended metaphor for talking about poetry. How well does the poem characterize strategies for writing poetry as well as pitching?

5. Write an essay that develops an extended comparison between writing or reading poetry and playing or watching another sport.

CONNECTION TO ANOTHER SELECTION

1. Write an essay comparing "The Pitcher" with another work by Francis, "Catch" (p. 531). One poem defines poetry implicitly; the other defines it explicitly. Which poem do you prefer? Why?

## HELEN CHASIN (1938–2015)

### *The Word* Plum    1968

The word *plum* is delicious

pout and push, luxury of
self-love, and savoring murmur
full in the mouth and falling
like fruit                                                                                      5

taut skin
pierced, bitten, provoked into
juice, and tart flesh

question
and reply, lip and tongue                                                          10
of pleasure.

### CONSIDERATIONS FOR CRITICAL THINKING AND WRITING

1. FIRST RESPONSE. What is the effect of the repetitions of the alliteration and assonance throughout the poem? How does it contribute to the poem's meaning?

2. Which sounds in the poem are like the sounds one makes while eating a plum?

3. Discuss the title. Explain whether you think this poem is more about the word *plum* or about the plum itself. Can the two be separated in the poem?

## RICHARD WAKEFIELD (B. 1952)

### *The Bell Rope*    2005

WHEN I READ "I like poems that don't tell me how the writer feels; they tell me how the world looks to someone who feels that way. They make sense by engaging the senses, and so they become an experience. The reader is not merely an audience but a participant."
— RICHARD WAKEFIELD

In Sunday school the boy who learned a psalm
by heart would get to sound the steeple bell
and send its tolling through the sabbath calm
to call the saved and not-so-saved as well.
For lack of practice all the lines are lost —                                  5
something about how angels' hands would bear
me up to God — but on one Pentecost
they won me passage up the steeple stair.
I leapt and grabbed the rope up high to ride
it down, I touched the floor, the rope went slack,                        10
the bell was silent. Then, beatified,
I rose, uplifted as the rope pulled back.
I leapt and fell again; again it took

me up, but still the bell withheld its word —
until at last the church foundation shook                                    15
in bass approval, felt as much as heard,
and after I let go the bell tolled long
and loud as if repaying me for each
unanswered pull with heaven-rending song
a year of Sunday school could never teach                                    20
and that these forty years can not obscure.
Some nights when sleep won't come I think of how
just once there came an answer, clear and sure.
If I could find that rope I'd grasp it now.

### CONSIDERATIONS FOR CRITICAL THINKING AND WRITING

1. FIRST RESPONSE. Describe the rhyme scheme and then read the poem aloud. How does Wakefield manage to avoid making this heavily rhymed poem sound clichéd or sing-songy?

2. Comment on the appropriateness of Wakefield's choice of diction and how it relates to the poem's images.

3. Explain how sound becomes, in a sense, the theme of the poem.

### CONNECTION TO ANOTHER SELECTION

1. Compare the images and themes of "The Bell Rope" with those in Robert Frost's "Birches" (p. 867).

### JEAN TOOMER (1894–1967)

## *Unsuspecting*   ca. 1929

There is a natty kind of mind
That slicks its thoughts,
Culls its oughts,
Trims its views,
Prunes its trues,                                                            5
And never suspects it is a rind.

Bettmann/Getty Images.

### CONSIDERATIONS FOR CRITICAL THINKING AND WRITING

1. FIRST RESPONSE. What sort of person do you think is described by the speaker?

2. Comment on the poem's diction and use of rhyme. Which word (or words) do you think are the most crucial for determining the poem's central idea?

### CONNECTION TO ANOTHER SELECTION

1. Discuss the tone and themes in "Unsuspecting" and in Emily Dickinson's "The Soul selects her own Society" (p. 777).

**JOHN KEATS** (1795–1821)

## *Ode to a Nightingale*    1819

### I

My heart aches, and a drowsy numbness pains
　My sense, as though of hemlock° I had drunk,　　　　　　　*a poison*
Or emptied some dull opiate to the drains
　One minute past, and Lethe-wards° had sunk:
'Tis not through envy of thy happy lot,　　　　　　　　　　5
　But being too happy in thine happiness —
　　That thou, light-wingèd Dryad° of the trees,　　　*wood nymph*
　　　In some melodious plot
Of beechen green, and shadows numberless,
　　Singest of summer in full-throated ease.　　　　　　　　10

### II

O, for a draught of vintage! that hath been
　Cooled a long age in the deep-delved earth,
Tasting of Flora° and the country green,　　　　　*goddess of flowers*
　Dance, and Provençal song,° and sunburnt mirth!
O for a beaker full of the warm South,　　　　　　　　　15
　Full of the true, the blushful Hippocrene,°
　　With beaded bubbles winking at the brim,
　　　And purple-stainèd mouth;
That I might drink, and leave the world unseen,
　　And with thee fade away into the forest dim.　　　　　20

### III

Fade far away, dissolve, and quite forget
　What thou among the leaves hast never known,
The weariness, the fever, and the fret
　Here, where men sit and hear each other groan;
Where palsy shakes a few, sad, last gray hairs,　　　　　25
　Where youth grows pale, and specter-thin, and dies,
　　Where but to think is to be full of sorrow
　　　And leaden-eyed despairs,
　Where Beauty cannot keep her lustrous eyes;
　　Or new Love pine at them beyond tomorrow.　　　　　30

---

4 *Lethe-wards:* Toward Lethe, the river of forgetfulness in the Hades of Greek mythology.
14 *Provençal song:* The medieval troubadours of Provence, France, were known for their singing.
16 *Hippocrene:* The fountain of the Muses in Greek mythology.

## IV

Away! away! for I will fly to thee,
   Not charioted by Bacchus and his pards,°
But on the viewless wings of Poesy,
   Though the dull brain perplexes and retards:
Already with thee! tender is the night,                          35
   And haply the Queen-Moon is on her throne,
      Clustered around by all her starry Fays;
         But here there is no light,
   Save what from heaven is with the breezes blown
      Through verdurous glooms and winding mossy ways.      40

## V

I cannot see what flowers are at my feet,
   Nor what soft incense hangs upon the boughs,
But, in embalmèd° darkness, guess each sweet                 *perfumed*
   Wherewith the seasonable month endows
The grass, the thicket, and the fruit-tree wild;                45
   What hawthorn, and the pastoral eglantine;
      Fast fading violets covered up in leaves;
         And mid-May's eldest child,
   The coming musk-rose, full of dewy wine,
      The murmurous haunt of flies on summer eves.          50

## VI

Darkling° I listen; and for many a time                   *in the dark*
   I have been half in love with easeful Death,
Called him soft names in many a musèd rhyme,
   To take into the air my quiet breath;
Now more than ever seems it rich to die,                   55
   To cease upon the midnight with no pain,
      While thou art pouring forth thy soul abroad
         In such an ecstasy!
   Still wouldst thou sing, and I have ears in vain —
      To thy high requiem become a sod.                   60

## VII

Thou wast not born for death, immortal Bird!
   No hungry generations tread thee down;
The voice I hear this passing night was heard
   In ancient days by emperor and clown:
Perhaps the selfsame song that found a path               65

---

32 *Bacchus and his pards:* The Greek god of wine traveled in a chariot drawn by leopards.

Through the sad heart of Ruth,° when, sick for home,
   She stood in tears amid the alien corn:
     The same that oft-times hath
Charmed magic casements, opening on the foam
   Of perilous seas, in faery lands forlorn.         70

### VIII

Forlorn! the very word is like a bell
   To toll me back from thee to my sole self!
Adieu! the fancy cannot cheat so well
   As she is famed to do, deceiving elf.
Adieu! adieu! thy plaintive anthem fades         75
   Past the near meadows, over the still stream,
     Up the hill side; and now 'tis buried deep
       In the next valley-glades:
Was it a vision, or a waking dream?
   Fled is that music: — Do I wake or sleep?         80

66 *Ruth:* A young widow in the Bible (see the Book of Ruth).

#### Considerations for Critical Thinking and Writing

1. **FIRST RESPONSE.** Why does the speaker in this ode want to leave their world for the nightingale's? What might the nightingale symbolize?
2. How does the speaker attempt to escape their world? Are they successful?
3. What changes the speaker's view of death at the end of stanza VI?
4. What does the allusion to Ruth (line 66) contribute to the ode's meaning?
5. In which lines is the imagery especially sensuous? How does this effect add to the conflict presented?
6. What calls the speaker back to themselves at the end of stanza VII and the beginning of stanza VIII?
7. Choose a stanza and explain how sound is related to its meaning.
8. How regular is the stanza form of this ode?

## Howard Nemerov (1920–1991)

### *Because You Asked about the Line between Prose and Poetry*   1980

Sparrows were feeding in a freezing drizzle
That while you watched turned into pieces of snow
Riding a gradient invisible
From silver aslant to random, white, and slow.

There came a moment that you couldn't tell.         5
And then they clearly flew instead of fell.

## Considerations for Critical Thinking and Writing

1. **FIRST RESPONSE.** Describe the distinction that this poem makes between prose and poetry. How does the poem itself become an example of that distinction?

2. Identify the kinds of rhymes Nemerov employs. How do the rhymes in the first and second stanzas differ from each other?

3. Comment on the poem's punctuation. How is it related to theme?

## MAJOR JACKSON (B. 1968)

### *Autumn Landscape* 2010

Seeking what I could not name, my vespertine°
spirit loitered evenings down leaf-lined
streets. Stray dogs for company, curbs were empty.
Afar dim poles resembled women. The wind pushed me
like an open hand. Flesh frothed in my head.                                    5
I reached for stirred shadows in windows aimed for bed.
When did I not strain for touch? I've a mind
to eat as many stars and refract their dark expanse.
My sadness brings tears, so many victims.
Close your eyes. Here comes the nightmare.                                    10

1 *Vespertine:* Occurring in the evening

## Considerations for Critical Thinking and Writing

1. **FIRST RESPONSE.** What type of poem do you envision with a title like "Autumn Landscape"? In what ways does this poem depart from your expectations?

2. Which of the sound qualities described above are present in the poem? What effects do they have on your understanding of the poem's meaning or its concerns?

3. In addition to sound, what other dimensions of poetry you have studied thus far (such as diction or figurative language) are on display in this poem, and how do they function?

## Connection to Another Selection

1. Another poem with the word *autumn* in the title is John Keats's "To Autumn" (p. 593). Compare and contrast the poems: does the season allow you to link them closely, to link them loosely, or to conclude that they are two very different poetic visions with only that word in common?

# 22

# Patterns of Rhythm

I would define, in brief, the Poetry of words as the Rhythmical Creation of Beauty. Its sole arbiter is Taste.

— EDGAR ALLAN POE

Library of Congress, Prints and Photographs Division [LC-USZ62-104482].

The rhythms of everyday life surround us in regularly recurring movements and sounds. As you read these words, your heart pulsates while somewhere else a clock ticks, a cradle rocks, a drum beats, a dancer sways, a foghorn blasts, a wave recedes, or a child skips. We may tend to overlook rhythm because it is so tightly woven into the fabric of our experience, but it is there nonetheless, one of the conditions of life. Rhythm is also one of the conditions of speech because the voice alternately rises and falls as words are stressed or unstressed and as the pace quickens or slackens. In poetry *rhythm* refers to the recurrence of stressed and unstressed sounds. Depending on how the sounds are arranged, this can result in a pace that is fast or slow, choppy or smooth.

## SOME PRINCIPLES OF METER

Poets use rhythm to create pleasurable sound patterns and to reinforce meanings. "Rhythm," Edith Sitwell once observed, "might be described as, to the world of sound, what light is to the world of sight. It shapes and gives new meaning." Prose can use rhythm effectively too, but prose that does so tends to be an exception. The following exceptional lines are from a speech by Winston Churchill to the House of Commons after Allied forces lost a great battle to German forces at Dunkirk during World War II:

> We shall not flag or fail. We shall go on to the end. We shall fight in France, we shall fight on the seas and oceans, we shall fight with growing confidence and growing strength in the air, we shall defend our island, whatever the cost may be, we shall fight on the beaches, we shall fight on the landing grounds, we shall fight in the fields and in the streets, we shall fight in the hills; we shall never surrender.

The stressed repetition of "we shall" bespeaks the resolute singleness of purpose that Churchill had to convey to the British people if they were to win the war. Repetition is also one of the devices used in poetry to create rhythmic effects. In the following excerpt from "Song of the Open Road" (1856), Walt Whitman urges the pleasures of limitless freedom on his reader:

> Allons!° the road is before us!                                                          *Let's go!*
> It is safe — I have tried it — my own feet have tried it well — be
>        not detain'd!
> Let the paper remain on the desk unwritten, and the
>        book on the shelf unopen'd!
> Let the tools remain in the workshop! Let the money remain
>        unearn'd!
> Let the school stand! mind not the cry of the teacher!                          5
> Let the preacher preach in his pulpit! Let the lawyer plead in the
>        court, and the judge expound the law.
>
> Camerado,° I give you my hand!                                                         *friend*
> I give you my love more precious than money,
> I give you myself before preaching or law;
> Will you give me yourself? will you come travel with me?
> Shall we stick by each other as long as we live?                                   10

These rhythmic lines quickly move away from conventional values to the open road of shared experiences. Their recurring sounds are created not by rhyme or alliteration and assonance (see Chapter 21) but by the repetition of words and phrases.

Although the repetition of words and phrases can be an effective means of creating rhythm in poetry, the more typical method consists of patterns of accented or unaccented syllables. Words naturally contain syllables that are either stressed or unstressed. A **stress** (or **accent**) places more emphasis on one syllable than on another. We say "*syl*lable" not "syl*la*ble" or "sylla*ble*," "*em*phasis" not "em*pha*sis" or "empha*sis*." We routinely stress syllables when we speak: "*Is* she con*tent* with the *con*tents of the *yel*low *pack*age?" To distinguish between two people we might put special emphasis on a single-syllable word, saying "Is *she* con*tent* . . . ?" In this way stress can be used to emphasize a particular word in a sentence. Poets often arrange words so that the desired meaning is suggested by the rhythm; hence emphasis is controlled by the poet rather than left entirely to the reader.

When a rhythmic pattern of stresses recurs in a poem, the result is **meter**. Taken together, all the metrical elements in a poem make up what is called the poem's **prosody**. **Scansion** consists of measuring the stresses in a line to determine its metrical pattern. Several methods can be used to mark lines. One widely used system uses ´ for a stressed syllable and ˘ for an unstressed syllable. In a sense, the stress mark represents the equivalent of tapping one's foot to a beat:

> Híckŏrў, díckŏrў, dóck,
> Tȟe móuse răn úp tȟe clóck
> Tȟe clóck strŭck oȟe,
> Aȟd dowȟ hĕ ruȟ,
> Híckŏrў, díckŏrў, dóck.

In the first two lines and the final line of this familiar nursery rhyme we hear three stressed syllables. In lines 3 and 4, where the meter changes for variety, we hear just two stressed syllables. The combination of stresses provides the pleasure of the rhythm we hear.

To hear the rhythms of "Hickory, dickory, dock" does not require a formal study of meter. Nevertheless, an awareness of the basic kinds of meter that appear in English poetry can enhance your understanding of how a poem achieves its effects. Understanding the sound effects of a poem and having a vocabulary with which to discuss those effects can intensify your pleasure in poetry. Although the study of meter can be extremely technical, the terms used to describe the basic meters of English poetry are relatively easy to comprehend.

The **foot** is the metrical unit by which a line of poetry is measured. A foot usually consists of one stressed and one or two unstressed syllables. A vertical line is used to separate the feet: "Tȟe clóck | strŭck oȟe" consists of two feet. A foot of poetry can be arranged in a variety of patterns; here are five of the chief ones:

| Foot | Pattern | Example |
|------|---------|---------|
| iamb | ˘ ´ | ăwáy |
| trochee | ´ ˘ | Lóvĕly |
| anapest | ˘ ˘ ´ | uȟdĕrstánd |
| dactyl | ´ ˘ ˘ | déspĕraȟe |
| spondee | ´ ´ | déad sét |

The most common lines in English poetry contain meters based on iambic feet. However, even lines that are predominantly iambic will often include variations to create particular effects. Other important patterns include trochaic, anapestic, and dactylic feet. The spondee is not a sustained meter but occurs for variety or emphasis.

| | |
|---|---|
| *iambic* | Whăt képt \| hĭs eyés \| frŏm gív \| iȟg báck \| tȟe gáze |
| *trochaic* | Hé wăs \| loúdĕr \| thán tȟe \| preáchĕr |
| *anapestic* | Ĭ aȟ callĕd \| tŏ tȟe frónt \| ŏf tȟe roóm |
| *dactylic* | Siȟg it all \| mérrĭlў |

These meters have different rhythms and can create different effects. Iambic and anapestic are known as **rising meters** because they move from unstressed to stressed sounds, while trochaic and dactylic are known as **falling meters**. Anapests and dactyls tend to move more lightly and rapidly than iambs or trochees. Although no single kind of meter can be considered always better than another for a given subject, it is possible to determine whether the meter of a specific poem is appropriate for its subject. A serious poem about a tragic death would most likely not be well served by lilting rhythms. Keep in mind, too, that though one or another of these four basic meters might constitute the predominant rhythm of a poem, variations can occur within lines to change the pace or call attention to a particular word.

A **line** is measured by the number of feet it contains. Here, for example, is an iambic line with three feet: "If she | shŏuld wríte | ă nóte." That would be described as "iambic trimeter." These are the names for line lengths:

| | |
|---|---|
| monometer: one foot | pentameter: five feet |
| dimeter: two feet | hexameter: six feet |
| trimeter: three feet | heptameter: seven feet |
| tetrameter: four feet | octameter: eight feet |

By combining the name of a line length with the name of a foot, we can describe the metrical qualities of a line concisely. Consider, for example, the pattern of feet and length of this line:

I didn't want the boy to hit the dog.

The iambic rhythm of this line falls into five feet; hence it is called **iambic pentameter**. Iambic is the most common pattern in English poetry because its rhythm appears so naturally in English speech and writing. Unrhymed iambic pentameter is called **blank verse**; Shakespeare's plays are built on such lines.

Less common than the iamb, trochee, anapest, or dactyl is the **spondee**, a two-syllable foot in which both syllables are stressed (′ ′). Note the effect of the spondaic foot at the beginning of this line:

Déad sét | ăgaiṅst | the plan | hĕ wént | ăwáy.

Spondees can slow a rhythm and provide variety and emphasis, particularly in iambic and trochaic lines. Also less common is a *pyrrhic* foot, which consists of two unstressed syllables, as in Shakespeare's "A horse! A horse! My kingdom for a horse!" Pyrrhic feet are typically variants for iambic verse rather than predominant patterns in lines. A line that ends with a stressed syllable is said to have a *masculine ending*, whereas a line that ends with an extra unstressed syllable is said to have a *feminine ending*. Consider, for example, these two lines from Timothy Steele's "Waiting for the Storm" (the entire poem appears on p. 668):

feminine: Thĕ sánd | ăt mý feet | grŏw cóld | eř,
masculine: Thĕ daṁp | aír chíll | and spréad.

The speed of a line is also affected by the number of pauses in it. A natural but not necessarily punctuated pause within a line is called a **caesura** and is indicated by a double vertical line (||). A caesura — a word that connotes "cut," related etymologically to a caesarean section — can occur anywhere within a line and need not be indicated by punctuation:

> Camerado, || I give you my hand!
> I give you my love || more precious than money.

A slight pause occurs within each of these lines and at its end. Both kinds of pauses contribute to the lines' rhythm.

When a line has a pause at its end, it is called an **end-stopped line**. Such pauses reflect normal speech patterns and are often marked by punctuation. A line that ends without a pause and continues into the next line for its meaning is called a **run-on line**. Running over from one line to another is also called **enjambment**. The first and eighth lines of the following poem are run-on lines; the rest are end-stopped.

## WILLIAM WORDSWORTH (1770–1850)

### My Heart Leaps Up   1807

My heart leaps up when I behold
   A rainbow in the sky:
So was it when my life began;
So is it now I am a man;
So be it when I shall grow old,                                          5
   Or let me die!
The child is father of the Man;
And I could wish my days to be
Bound each to each by natural piety.

Run-on lines have a different rhythm from end-stopped lines. Lines 3 and 4 and lines 8 and 9 are iambic, but the effect of their two rhythms is very different when we read these lines aloud. The enjambment of lines 8 and 9 reinforces their meaning; just as the "days" are bound together, so are the lines.

The rhythm of a poem can be affected by several devices: the kind and number of stresses within lines, the length of lines, and the kinds of pauses that appear within lines or at their ends. In addition, as we saw in Chapter 21, the sound of a poem is affected by alliteration, assonance, rhyme, and consonance. These sounds help to create rhythms by controlling our pronunciations, as in the following lines excerpted from "An Essay on Criticism," a poem by Alexander Pope:

> Soft is the strain when Zephyr gently blows,
> And the smooth stream in smoother numbers flows;
> But when loud surges lash the sounding shore,
> The hoarse, rough verse should like the torrent roar.

These lines are effective because their rhythm and sound work with their meaning.

---

### Suggestions for Scanning a Poem

These suggestions should help you in talking about a poem's meter.

1. After reading the poem through, read it aloud and mark the stressed syllables in each line. Then mark the unstressed syllables.

2. From your markings, identify what kind of foot is dominant (iambic, trochaic, dactylic, or anapestic) and divide the lines into feet, keeping in mind that the vertical line marking a foot may come in the middle of a word as well as at its beginning or end.

3. Determine the number of feet in each line. Remember that there may be variations; some lines may be shorter or longer than the predominant meter. What is important is the overall pattern. Do not assume that variations represent the poet's inability to fulfill the overall pattern. Notice the effects of variations and whether they emphasize words and phrases or disrupt your expectation for some other purpose.

4. Listen for pauses within lines and mark the caesuras; often there will be no punctuation to indicate them.

5. Recognize that scansion does not always yield a definitive measurement of a line. Even experienced readers may differ over the scansion of a given line. What is important is not a precise description of the line but an awareness of how a poem's rhythms contribute to its effects.

6. If possible, attend a live poetry reading. (If not possible, find a video clip on YouTube of a poet reading their own poetry.) Compare the poem as it looks on the page to the way a poet interprets its meter and its rhythm.

---

The following poem demonstrates how you can use an understanding of meter and rhythm to gain a greater appreciation for what a poem is saying.

## TIMOTHY STEELE (B. 1948)

### *Waiting for the Storm*   1986

Bréeze sént | ă wrínk | lĭng dárk | nĕss

Ácróss | thĕ báy. || Ĭ knélt

Bĕnéath | ăn úp | turňed bóat,

Aňd, mó | mĕnt bў mó | mĕnt, félt

The sánd | ăt mў féet | grŏw cóld | ér,                              5

The damp | áir chíll | aňd spréad.

Thĕn thĕ | fírst ráin | drŏps sóund | ĕd

Oň thĕ húll | ăbóve | mў héad.

The predominant meter of this poem is iambic trimeter, but there is plenty of variation as the storm rapidly approaches and finally begins to pelt the sheltered speaker. The emphatic spondee ("Breeze sent") pushes the darkness quickly across the bay while the caesura at the end of the sentence in line 2 creates a pause that sets up a feeling of suspense and expectation that is measured in the ticking rhythm of line 4, a run-on line that brings us into the chilly sand and air of the second stanza. Perhaps the most impressive sound effect used in the poem appears in the second syllable of "sounded" in line 7. That "ed" precedes the sound of the poem's final word, "head," just as if it were the first drop of rain hitting the hull above the speaker. The visual, tactile, and auditory images make "Waiting for the Storm" an intense sensory experience.

## A SAMPLE STUDENT RESPONSE

Marco Pacini

Professor Fierstein

English 201

2 November 2023

The Rhythm of Anticipation in Timothy Steele's "Waiting for the Storm"

In his poem "Waiting for the Storm," Timothy Steele uses run-on lines, or enjambment, to create a feeling of anticipation. Every line ends unfinished or is a continuation of the previous line, so we must read on to gain completion. This open-ended rhythm mirrors the waiting experienced by the speaker of the poem.

Nearly every line of the poem leaves the reader in suspense:

> I knelt
> Beneath an upturned boat,
> And, moment by moment, felt
>
> The sand at my feet grow colder,
> The damp air chill and spread. (2-6)

Action is interrupted at every line break. We have to wait to find out where the speaker knelt and what was felt, since information is given in small increments. So, like the speaker, we must take in the details of the storm little by little, "moment by moment" (4). Even when the first drops of rain hit the hull, the poem ends before we can see or feel the storm's full force, and we are left waiting, in a continuous state of anticipation. . . .

Pacini 3

Work Cited

Steele, Timothy. "Waiting for the Storm." *The Compact Bedford Introduction
to Literature*, edited by Michael Meyer and D. Quentin Miller, 13th ed.,
Bedford/St. Martin's, 2024, p. 668.

This next poem also reinforces meanings through its use of meter and
rhythm.

## WILLIAM BUTLER YEATS (1865–1939)

### *That the Night Come*   1912

She lived | in storm | and strife,
Her soul | had such | desire
For what | proud death | may bring
That it | could not | endure
The com | mon good | of life,                                        5
But lived | as 'twere | a king
That packed | his mar | riage day
With ban | neret | and pen | non,
Trumpet | and ket | tledrum,
And the | outrag | eous can | non,                                 10
To bun | dle time | away
That the | night come.

Scansion reveals that the predominant meter here is iambic trimeter: each
line contains three stressed and unstressed syllables that form a regular, predictable rhythm through line 7. That rhythm is disrupted, however, when the speaker
compares the woman's longing for what death brings to a king's eager anticipation
of his wedding night. The king packs the day with noisy fanfares and celebrations
to fill up time and distract himself. Unable to accept "The common good of life,"
the woman fills her days with "storm and strife." In a determined effort "To bundle time away," she, like the king, impatiently awaits the night.

Lines 8–10 break the regular pattern established in the first seven lines.
The extra unstressed syllable in lines 8 and 10 along with the trochaic feet in
lines 9 ("Trúmpĕt") and 10 ("Ánd thĕ") interrupt the basic iambic trimeter and

parallel the woman's and the king's frenetic activity. These lines thus echo the inability of the woman and king to "endure" regular or normal time. The last line is the most irregular in the poem. The final two accented syllables sound like the deep resonant beats of a kettledrum or a cannon firing. The words "night come" dramatically remind us that what the woman anticipates is not a lover but the mysterious finality of death. The meter serves, then, in both its regularity and variations to reinforce the poem's meaning and tone.

The following poems are especially rich in their rhythms and sounds. As you read and study them, notice how patterns of rhythm and the sounds of words reinforce meanings and contribute to the poems' effects. And, perhaps most important, read the poems aloud so that you can hear them.

## POEMS FOR FURTHER STUDY

### SAMUEL TAYLOR COLERIDGE (1772–1834)

### *Mnemonic*   1803

Trochee trips from long to short;
From long to long in solemn sort
Slow Spondee stalks; strong foot yet ill able
Ever to come up with Dactylic trisyllable.
Iambics march from short to long —                                           5
With a leap and a bound the swift Anapests throng.

#### CONSIDERATIONS FOR CRITICAL THINKING AND WRITING

1. FIRST RESPONSE. Scan each of the lines and explain how this little handbook of a poem works.
2. Memorize this poem (Coleridge wrote it for his son). By doing so, you will have learned from a master.

### JOHN MALONEY (B. 1947)

### *Good!*   1999

The ball goes up off glass and rebounded
down the court, outlet flung to the quick guard
like clicking seconds: he dribbles, hounded
by hands, calls the play, stops short, looking hard
for a slant opening, fakes it twice, passes                                    5
into the center — he lobs to the small
forward, top of the key, a pick: asses
crash (the pick-and-roll), he cuts, bumps, the ball
reaches him as he turns, dribbles, sends it
back to the baseline, forward back to him,                                    10
jump — and in midair, twisting, he bends it

over a tangle of arms — SHOOTS, the rim
rattles as it jerks against the back joints,
and into the net, trippingly drop two points.

## CONSIDERATIONS FOR CRITICAL THINKING AND WRITING

1. **FIRST RESPONSE.** Comment on the effects of the lines' rhythms.
2. Notice the precise pattern of rhyme. How is that related to the action in the poem?

## CONNECTION TO ANOTHER SELECTION

1. Compare the diction and tone in "Good!" and in Jim Tilley's "The Big Questions" (p. 550).

## ALICE JONES (B. 1949)

### *The Foot*   1993

Our improbable support, erected
on the osseous architecture
of the calcaneus, talus, cuboid,
navicular, cuneiforms, metatarsals,
phalanges, a plethora of hinges,                                    5

all strung together by gliding
tendons, covered by the pearly
plantar fascia, then fat-padded
to form the sole, humble surface
of our contact with earth.                                         10

Here the body's broadest tendon
anchors the heel's fleshy base,
the finely wrinkled skin stretches
forward across the capillaried arch,
to the ball, a balance point.                                      15

A wide web of flexor tendons
and branched veins maps the dorsum,
fades into the stub-laden bone
splay, the stuffed sausage sacks
of toes, each with a tuft                                          20

of proximal hairs to introduce
the distal nail, whose useless
curve remembers an ancestor,
the vanished creature's wild
and necessary claw.                                                25

## CONSIDERATIONS FOR CRITICAL THINKING AND WRITING

1. **FIRST RESPONSE.** What is the effect of the diction? What sort of tone is established by the use of anatomical terms? How do the terms affect the rhythm?

2. Jones has described the form of "The Foot" as "five stubby stanzas." Explain why the lines of this poem may or may not warrant this description of the stanzas.

3. CRITICAL STRATEGIES. Read the section on formalist strategies (pp. 1383–1385) in Chapter 42, "Critical Strategies for Reading." Describe the effect of the final stanza. How would your reading be affected if the poem ended after the comma in the middle of line 22?

## A. E. HOUSMAN (1859–1936)

### *When I was one-and-twenty*  1896

When I was one-and-twenty
  I heard a wise man say,
"Give crowns and pounds and guineas
  But not your heart away;
Give pearls away and rubies 5
  But keep your fancy free."
But I was one-and-twenty,

  No use to talk to me.
When I was one-and-twenty
  I heard him say again, 10
"The heart out of the bosom
  Was never given in vain;
'Tis paid with sighs a plenty
  And sold for endless rue."
And I am two-and-twenty, 15
  And oh, 'tis true, 'tis true.

### CONSIDERATIONS FOR CRITICAL THINKING AND WRITING

1. FIRST RESPONSE. How does the basic metrical pattern affect your understanding of the speaker?

2. How do lines 1–8 parallel lines 9–16 in their use of rhyme and metaphor? What significant differences between the stanzas do you notice?

3. What do you think has happened to change the speaker's attitude toward love?

4. Explain why you agree or disagree with the advice given by the "wise man."

5. What is the effect of the repetition in line 16?

## ROBERT HERRICK (1591–1674)

### *Delight in Disorder*  1648

A sweet disorder in the dress
Kindles in clothes a wantonness.
A lawn° about the shoulders thrown       *linen scarf*
Into a fine distraction;
An erring lace, which here and there 5

Enthralls the crimson stomacher,
A cuff neglectful, and thereby
Ribbons to flow confusedly;
A winning wave, deserving note,
In the tempestuous petticoat;                                               10
A careless shoestring, in whose tie
I see a wild civility;
Do more bewitch me than when art
Is too precise in every part.

### Considerations for Critical Thinking and Writing

1. FIRST RESPONSE. Why does the speaker in this poem value "disorder" so highly? How do the poem's organization and rhythmic order relate to its theme? Are they "precise in every part" (line 14)?

2. Which words in the poem indicate disorder? Which words indicate the speaker's response to that disorder? What are the connotative meanings of each set of words? Why are they appropriate? What do they suggest about the woman and the speaker?

3. Write a short essay in which you agree or disagree with the speaker's views on dress.

## Ben Jonson (1573–1637)

### *Still to Be Neat*    1609

Still° to be neat, still to be dressed,                        *continually*
As you were going to a feast;
Still to be powdered, still perfumed;
Lady, it is to be presumed,
Though art's hid causes are not found,                                      5
All is not sweet, all is not sound.

Give me a look, give me a face
That makes simplicity a grace;
Robes loosely flowing, hair as free;
Such sweet neglect more taketh me                                          10
Then all th' adulteries of art.
They strike mine eyes, but not my heart.

### Considerations for Critical Thinking and Writing

1. FIRST RESPONSE. What are the speaker's reservations about the lady in the first stanza? What do you think "sweet" means in line 6?

2. What does the speaker want from the lady in the second stanza? How has the meaning of "sweet" shifted from line 6 to line 10? What other words in the poem are especially charged with connotative meanings?

3. How do the rhythms of Jonson's lines help to reinforce meanings? Pay particular attention to lines 6 and 12.

## Connections to Other Selections

1. Write an essay comparing the themes of "Still to Be Neat" and Robert Herrick's preceding poem, "Delight in Disorder." How do the speakers make similar points but from different perspectives?

2. How does the rhythm of "Still to Be Neat" compare with that of "Delight in Disorder"? Which do you find more effective? Explain why.

## E. E. Cummings (1894–1962)

### O sweet spontaneous    1920

O sweet spontaneous
earth how often have
the
doting
    fingers of                                         5
prurient philosophers pinched
and
poked

thee
, has the naughty thumb                                      10
of science prodded
thy

    beauty     .how
often have religions taken
thee upon their scraggy knees                                15
squeezing and

buffeting thee that thou mightest conceive
gods
    (but
true                                               20

to the incomparable
couch of death thy
rhythmic
lover

    thou answerest                                     25

them only with

    spring)

## Considerations for Critical Thinking and Writing

1. FIRST RESPONSE. What is the controlling metaphor that Cummings uses to characterize philosophers, scientists, and theologians? How is the earth portrayed?

2. In what sense is spring the answer to the issues raised in the poem?

3. To what extent does the arrangement of lines on the page serve to establish rhythm?

CONNECTION TO ANOTHER SELECTION

1. Discuss the treatment of science in "O sweet spontaneous" and in Edgar Allan Poe's "Sonnet — To Science" (p. 553).

## WILLIAM BLAKE (1757–1827)

### The Lamb   1789

Bettmann/Getty Images.

> Little Lamb, who made thee?
> Dost thou know who made thee?
> Gave thee life, and bid thee feed
> By the stream and o'er the mead;
> Gave thee clothing of delight,                                    5
> Softest clothing, wooly, bright;
> Gave thee such a tender voice,
> Making all the vales rejoice?
>    Little Lamb, who made thee?
>    Dost thou know who made thee?               10
>
>    Little Lamb, I'll tell thee,
>    Little Lamb, I'll tell thee:
> He is callèd by thy name,
> For he calls himself a Lamb.
> He is meek, and he is mild;                                       15
> He became a little child.
> I a child, and thou a lamb,
> We are callèd by his name.
>    Little Lamb, God bless thee!
>    Little Lamb, God bless thee!                  20

CONSIDERATIONS FOR CRITICAL THINKING AND WRITING

1. FIRST RESPONSE. This poem is from Blake's *Songs of Innocence*. Describe its tone. How do the meter, rhyme, and repetition help to characterize the speaker's voice?

2. Why is it significant that the animal addressed by the speaker is a lamb? What symbolic value would be lost if the animal were, for example, a doe?

3. How does the second stanza answer the question raised in the first? What is the speaker's view of the creation?

## WILLIAM BLAKE (1757–1827)

### The Tyger   1794

> Tyger! Tyger! burning bright
> In the forests of the night,
> What immortal hand or eye
> Could frame thy fearful symmetry?

In what distant deeps or skies      5
Burnt the fire of thine eyes?
On what wings dare he aspire?
What the hand dare seize the fire?

And what shoulder, and what art,
Could twist the sinews of thy heart?      10
And when thy heart began to beat,
What dread hand? and what dread feet?

What the hammer? what the chain?
In what furnace was thy brain?
What the anvil? what dread grasp      15
Dare its deadly terrors clasp?

When the stars threw down their spears,
And watered heaven with their tears,
Did he smile his work to see?
Did he who made the Lamb make thee?      20

Tyger! Tyger! burning bright
In the forests of the night,
What immortal hand or eye
Dare frame thy fearful symmetry?

### Considerations for Critical Thinking and Writing

1. **FIRST RESPONSE.** This poem from Blake's *Songs of Experience* is often paired with "The Lamb." Describe the poem's tone. Is the speaker's voice the same here as in "The Lamb"? Which words are repeated, and how do they contribute to the tone?

2. What is revealed about the nature of the tiger by the words used to describe its creation? What do you think the tiger symbolizes?

3. Unlike in "The Lamb," more than one question is raised in "The Tyger." What are these questions? Are they answered?

4. Compare the rhythms in "The Lamb" and "The Tyger." Each basically uses a seven-syllable line, but the effects are very different. Why?

5. Using these two poems as the basis of your discussion, describe what distinguishes innocence from experience.

## CARL SANDBURG (1878–1967)

### *Chicago* 1916

Hog Butcher for the World,
Tool Maker, Stacker of Wheat,
Player with Railroads and the Nation's Freight Handler;
Stormy, husky, brawling,
City of the Big Shoulders:      5

They tell me you are wicked and I believe them, for I have seen your painted
     women under the gas lamps luring the farm boys.

And they tell me you are crooked and I answer: Yes, it is true I have seen the
     gunman kill and go free to kill again.
And they tell me you are brutal and my reply is: On the faces of women and
     children I have seen the marks of wanton hunger.
And having answered so I turn once more to those who sneer at this my city, and
     I give them back the sneer and say to them:
Come and show me another city with lifted head singing so proud to be alive and
     coarse and strong and cunning.           10
Flinging magnetic curses amid the toil of piling job on job, here is a tall bold
     slugger set vivid against the little soft cities;
Fierce as a dog with tongue lapping for action, cunning as a savage pitted against
     the wilderness,
    Bareheaded,
    Shoveling,
    Wrecking,           15
    Planning,
    Building, breaking, rebuilding,
Under the smoke, dust all over his mouth, laughing with white teeth,
Under the terrible burden of destiny laughing as a young man laughs,
Laughing even as an ignorant fighter laughs who has never lost a battle,     20
Bragging and laughing that under his wrist is the pulse, and under his ribs the
     heart of the people,
    Laughing!
Laughing the stormy, husky, brawling laughter of Youth, half-naked, sweating,
     proud to be Hog Butcher, Tool Maker, Stacker of Wheat, Player with
     Railroads and Freight Handler to the Nation.

### Considerations for Critical Thinking and Writing

1. **FIRST RESPONSE.** Sandburg's personification of Chicago creates a strong identity for the city. Explain why you find the city attractive or not.

2. How do the length and rhythm of lines 1–5 compare with those of the final
lines?

3. **CREATIVE RESPONSE.** Using "Chicago" as a model for style, try writing a tribute
to or a condemnation of a place that you know well. Make an effort to use
vivid images and stylistic techniques that capture its rhythms.

### Connection to Another Selection

1. Compare "Chicago" with William Blake's "London" (p. 588) in style and
theme.

## Perspective

LOUISE BOGAN (1897–1970)

### *On Formal Poetry*  1953

What is formal poetry? It is poetry written in form. And what is *form*? The elements of form, so far as poetry is concerned, are meter and rhyme. Are these elements merely mold and ornaments that have been impressed upon poetry from without? Are they indeed restrictions which bind and fetter language and the thought and emotion behind, under, within language in a repressive way? Are they arbitrary rules which have lost all validity since they have been broken to good purpose by "experimental poets," ancient and modern? Does the breaking up of form, or its total elimination, always result in an increase of power and of effect; and is any return to form a sort of relinquishment of freedom, or retreat to old fogeyism?

From *A Poet's Alphabet*

#### CONSIDERATIONS FOR CRITICAL THINKING AND WRITING

1. Choose one of the questions Bogan raises and write an essay in response to it using two or three poems from this chapter to illustrate your answer.

2. CRITICAL RESPONSE. Try writing a poem in regular meter and rhyme. Does the experience make your writing feel limited or not?

# 23

# Poetic Forms

Jose Okolo/Alamy.

Poetry gives you permission to say any kind of language, using any kind of grammar.
— GARY SNYDER

Poems come in a variety of shapes. Although the best poems always have their own unique qualities, many of them also conform to traditional patterns. Frequently the *form* of a poem — its overall structure or shape — follows an already established design. A poem that can be categorized by the patterns of its lines, meter, rhymes, and stanzas is considered a *fixed form* because it follows a prescribed model such as a sonnet. However, poems written in a fixed form do not always fit models precisely; writers sometimes work variations on traditional forms to create innovative effects.

Not all poets are content with variations on traditional forms. Some prefer to create their own structures and shapes. Poems that do not conform to established patterns of meter, rhyme, and stanza are called *free verse* or *open form* poetry, covered at the end of this chapter. This kind of poetry creates its own ordering principles through the careful arrangement of words and phrases in line lengths that embody rhythms appropriate to the meaning. Modern and contemporary poets in particular have learned to use the blank space on the page as a significant functional element (for a vivid example, see E. E. Cummings's "l(a" (on p. 538). Good poetry of this kind is structured in ways that can be as demanding, interesting, and satisfying as fixed forms. Open and fixed forms represent different poetic styles, but they are identical in the sense that both use language in concentrated ways to convey meanings, experiences, emotions, and effects.

## SOME COMMON POETIC FORMS

A familiarity with some of the most common fixed forms of poetry is useful because it allows for a better understanding of how a poem works. By classifying patterns we can talk about the effects of established rhythm and rhyme and recognize how the pace and meaning of the lines can be affected by variations or deviations from the patterns. An awareness of form also allows us to anticipate how a poem is likely to proceed. As we shall see, a sonnet creates a different set of expectations in a reader from those of, say, a limerick. A reader isn't likely to find in limericks the kind of serious themes that often make their way into sonnets. The discussion that follows identifies some of the important poetic forms frequently encountered in poetry, especially (but not exclusively) poetry in the English tradition.

The shape of a fixed form poem is often determined by the way in which the lines are organized into stanzas. A *stanza* — the Italian word for "room" — consists of a grouping of lines, set off by a space, that usually has a set pattern of meter and rhyme. This pattern is ordinarily repeated in other stanzas throughout the poem. What is usual is not obligatory, however; some poems may use a different pattern for each stanza, somewhat like paragraphs in prose.

Traditionally, though, stanzas do share a common *rhyme scheme*, the pattern of end rhymes. We can map out rhyme schemes by noting patterns of rhyme with lowercase letters: the first rhyme sound is designated *a*, the second becomes *b*, the third *c*, and so on. Using this system, we can describe the rhyme scheme in the following three-stanza poem this way: *aabb, ccdd, eeff.*

## A. E. HOUSMAN (1859–1936)

### *Loveliest of trees, the cherry now*   1896

| | |
|---|---|
| Loveliest of trees, the cherry now | *a* |
| Is hung with bloom along the bough, | *a* |
| And stands about the woodland ride | *b* |
| Wearing white for Eastertide. | *b* |
| | |
| Now, of my threescore years and ten, | *c* |
| Twenty will not come again, | *c* |
| And take from seventy springs a score, | *d* |
| It only leaves me fifty more. | *d* |

5

And since to look at things in bloom    *e*
Fifty springs are little room,           *e*            10
About the woodlands I will go      *f*
To see the cherry hung with snow.    *f*

### CONSIDERATIONS FOR CRITICAL THINKING AND WRITING

1. **FIRST RESPONSE.** What is the speaker's attitude in this poem toward time and life?

2. Why is spring an appropriate season for the setting rather than, say, winter?

3. Paraphrase each stanza. How do the images in each reinforce the poem's themes?

4. Lines 1 and 12 are not intended to rhyme, but they are close. What is the effect of the near rhyme of "now" and "snow"? How does the rhyme enhance the theme?

Poets often create their own stanzaic patterns; hence there is an infinite number of kinds of stanzas. One way of talking about stanzaic forms is to describe a given stanza by how many lines it contains.

A *couplet* consists of two lines that usually rhyme and have the same meter; couplets are frequently not separated from each other by space on the page. A *heroic couplet* consists of rhymed iambic pentameter. Here is an example from Alexander Pope's "Essay on Criticism":

One science only will one genius fit;      *a*
So vast is art, so narrow human wit:      *a*
Not only bounded to peculiar arts,        *b*
But oft in those confined to single parts.    *b*

A *tercet* is a three-line stanza. When all three lines rhyme, they are called a *triplet*. Two triplets make up the next captivating poem.

## ROBERT HERRICK (1591–1674)

### *Upon Julia's Clothes*    1648

Whenas in silks my Julia goes,            *a*
Then, then, methinks, how sweetly flows    *a*
That liquefaction of her clothes.          *a*

Next, when I cast mine eyes, and see      *b*
That brave vibration, each way free,      *b*          5
O, how that glittering taketh me!        *b*

### CONSIDERATIONS FOR CRITICAL THINKING AND WRITING

1. **FIRST RESPONSE.** How does the rhyme scheme contribute to this short poem's effect?

2. Comment on the effect of the meter. How is it related to the speaker's description of Julia's clothes?

3. Look up the word *brave* in the *Oxford English Dictionary.* Which of its meanings is appropriate to describe Julia's movement? Some readers interpret lines 4–6 to mean that Julia has no clothes on. What do you think?

## CONNECTION TO ANOTHER SELECTION

1. Compare the tone of this poem with that of Alfred, Lord Tennyson's "The Eagle" (p. 552), a poem of similar length and rhyme scheme. Is there any significant difference in tone between these two poems? If so, what accounts for it?

*Terza rima* consists of an interlocking three-line rhyme scheme: *aba, bcb, cdc, ded,* and so on. Dante's *Divine Comedy* uses this pattern, as does Robert Frost's "Acquainted with the Night" (p. 612).

A *quatrain*, or four-line stanza, is the most common stanzaic form in the English language and can have various meters and rhyme schemes (if any). The most common rhyme schemes are *aabb, abba, aaba,* and *abcb.* This last pattern is especially characteristic of the popular *ballad stanza*, which consists of alternating eight- and six-syllable lines. Samuel Taylor Coleridge adopted this pattern in "The Rime of the Ancient Mariner"; here is one representative stanza from that poem:

All in a hot and copper sky
The bloody Sun, at noon,
Right up above the mast did stand,
No bigger than the Moon.

There are a number of longer stanzaic forms, and the list of types of stanzas could be extended considerably, but knowing these three most basic patterns should prove helpful to you in talking about the form of a great many poems. In addition to stanzaic forms, there are fixed forms that characterize entire poems. Lyric poems (see p. 539) can be, for example, sonnets, villanelles, sestinas, or epigrams.

## Sonnet

The **sonnet** has been a popular literary form in English since the sixteenth century, when it was adopted from the Italian *sonnetto*, meaning "little song." A sonnet consists of fourteen lines, usually written in iambic pentameter. Because the sonnet has been such a favorite form, writers have experimented with many variations on its essential structure. Nevertheless, there are two basic types of sonnets: the Italian and the English.

The **Italian sonnet** (also known as the **Petrarchan sonnet**, from the fourteenth-century Italian poet Petrarch) divides into two parts. The first eight lines (the **octave**) typically rhyme *abbaabba.* The final six lines (the **sestet**) may vary; common patterns are *cdecde, cdcdcd,* and *cdccdc.* Very often the octave presents a situation, an attitude, or a problem that the sestet comments upon or resolves, as in John Keats's "On First Looking into Chapman's Homer."

## JOHN KEATS (1795–1821)

### On First Looking into Chapman's Homer°    1816

Much have I traveled in the realms of gold,
 And many goodly states and kingdoms seen;
 Round many western islands have I been
Which bards in fealty to Apollo° hold.
Oft of one wide expanse had I been told        5
 That deep-browed Homer ruled as his demesne;
 Yet did I never breathe its pure serene°     *atmosphere*
Till I heard Chapman speak out loud and bold:
Then felt I like some watcher of the skies
 When a new planet swims into his ken;      10
Or like stout Cortez° when with eagle eyes
 He stared at the Pacific — and all his men
Looked at each other with a wild surmise —
 Silent, upon a peak in Darien.

*Chapman's Homer:* Before reading George Chapman's (ca. 1560–1634) poetic Elizabethan translations of Homer's *Iliad* and *Odyssey,* Keats had known only stilted and pedestrian eighteenth-century
translations. 4 *Apollo:* Greek god of poetry. 11 *Cortez:* Vasco Núñez de Balboa, not Hernán
Cortés, was the first European to sight the Pacific from Darién, a peak in Panama.

#### CONSIDERATIONS FOR CRITICAL THINKING AND WRITING

1. FIRST RESPONSE. How do the images shift from the octave to the sestet? How
   does the tone change? Does the meaning change as well?
2. What is the controlling metaphor of this poem?
3. What is it that the speaker discovers?
4. How does the rhythm of the lines change between the octave and the sestet?
   How does that change reflect the tones of both the octave and the sestet?
5. Does Keats's mistake concerning Cortés and Balboa affect your reading of the
   poem? Explain why or why not.

The Italian sonnet pattern is also used in the next sonnet, but notice
that the thematic break between octave and sestet comes within line 9 rather
than between lines 8 and 9. This unconventional break helps to reinforce the
speaker's impatience with the conventional attitudes he describes.

## WILLIAM WORDSWORTH (1770–1850)

### The World Is Too Much with Us    1807

The world is too much with us; late and soon,
Getting and spending, we lay waste our powers;
Little we see in Nature that is ours;
We have given our hearts away, a sordid boon!

This Sea that bares her bosom to the moon;                                          5
The winds that will be howling at all hours,
And are up-gathered now like sleeping flowers;
For this, for everything, we are out of tune;
It moves us not. — Great God! I'd rather be
A Pagan suckled in a creed outworn;                                                10
So might I, standing on this pleasant lea,
Have glimpses that would make me less forlorn;
Have sight of Proteus rising from the sea;
Or hear old Triton blow his wreathèd horn.

### CONSIDERATIONS FOR CRITICAL THINKING AND WRITING

1. FIRST RESPONSE. What is the speaker's complaint in this sonnet? How do the conditions described affect them?
2. Look up "Proteus" and "Triton." What do these mythological allusions contribute to the sonnet's tone?
3. What is the effect of the personification of the sea and wind in the octave?

### CONNECTION TO ANOTHER SELECTION

1. Compare the theme of this sonnet with that of Gerard Manley Hopkins's "God's Grandeur" (p. 650).

The **English sonnet**, more commonly known as the **Shakespearean sonnet**, is organized into three quatrains and a couplet, which typically rhyme *abab cdcd efef gg*. This rhyme scheme is more suited to English poetry because English has fewer rhyming words than Italian. English sonnets, because of their four-part organization, also have more flexibility about where thematic breaks can occur. Frequently, however, the most pronounced break or turn comes with the concluding couplet.

In the following Shakespearean sonnet, the three quatrains compare the speaker's loved one to a summer's day and explain why the loved one is even more lovely. The couplet bestows eternal beauty and love upon both the loved one and the sonnet.

## WILLIAM SHAKESPEARE (1564–1616)

### *Shall I compare thee to a summer's day?*   1609

Shall I compare thee to a summer's day?
Thou art more lovely and more temperate:
Rough winds do shake the darling buds of May,
And summer's lease hath all too short a date.
Sometime too hot the eye of heaven shines,                                          5
And often is his gold complexion dimmed;
And every fair from fair sometime declines,
By chance, or nature's changing course, untrimmed.
But thy eternal summer shall not fade,

Nor lose possession of that fair thou ow'st°                          *possess*   10
Nor shall death brag thou wand'rest in his shade,
When in eternal lines to time thou grow'st.
> So long as men can breathe or eyes can see,
> So long lives this, and this gives life to thee.

### CONSIDERATIONS FOR CRITICAL THINKING AND WRITING

1. FIRST RESPONSE. Describe the shift in tone and subject matter that begins in line 9.
2. Why is the speaker's loved one more lovely than a summer's day? What qualities does the speaker admire in the loved one?
3. What does the couplet say about the relation between art and love?
4. Which syllables are stressed in the final line? How do these syllables relate to the line's meaning?

Sonnets have been the vehicles for all kinds of subjects, including love, death, politics, and cosmic questions. Although most sonnets tend to treat their subjects seriously, this fixed form does not mean a fixed expression; humor is also possible in it. Compare this next Shakespearean sonnet with "Shall I compare thee to a summer's day?" They are, finally, both love poems, but their tones are markedly different.

## WILLIAM SHAKESPEARE (1564–1616)

### *My mistress' eyes are nothing like the sun*   1609

My mistress' eyes are nothing like the sun;
Coral is far more red than her lips' red;
If snow be white, why then her breasts are dun;
If hairs be wires, black wires grow on her head.
I have seen roses damasked red and white,                                    5
But no such roses see I in her cheeks;
And in some perfumes is there more delight
Than in the breath that from my mistress reeks.
I love to hear her speak, yet well I know
That music hath a far more pleasing sound;                                   10
I grant I never saw a goddess go:
My mistress, when she walks, treads on the ground.
> And yet, by heaven, I think my love as rare
> As any she,° belied with false compare.                          *woman*

### CONSIDERATIONS FOR CRITICAL THINKING AND WRITING

1. FIRST RESPONSE. Write a description of this particular mistress based on the images used in the sonnet.
2. What sort of person is the speaker? Do they truly love the woman being described?
3. In what sense are this sonnet and "Shall I compare thee to a summer's day?" about poetry as well as love?

1. Compare the way this speaker depicts the "mistress" to that of the speaker in Andrew Marvell's "To His Coy Mistress" (p. 941). Which speaker is more persuasive?

## EDNA ST. VINCENT MILLAY (1892–1950)

## *I will put Chaos into fourteen lines*    1954

I will put Chaos into fourteen lines
And keep him there; and let him thence escape
If he be lucky; let him twist, and ape
Flood, fire, and demon — his adroit designs
Will strain to nothing in the strict confines                       5
Of this sweet Order, where, in pious rape,
I hold his essence and amorphous shape,
Till he with Order mingles and combines.
Past are the hours, the years, of our duress,
His arrogance, our awful servitude:                                 10
I have him. He is nothing more nor less
Than something simple not yet understood;
I shall not even force him to confess;
Or answer. I will only make him good.

### CONSIDERATIONS FOR CRITICAL THINKING AND WRITING

1. FIRST RESPONSE. How do you understand "Chaos" as the subject of this poem? Why would a poet want to contain Chaos? What else could be done with it?

2. What type of sonnet is this?

3. Chaos is personified in the poem and is understood to be male. Does that mean that Order is necessarily female? Or is the speaker's voice assumed to be female? Does gender matter to the poem?

### CONNECTION TO ANOTHER SELECTION

1. Write an essay comparing the understanding of poetry's meaning or function in this poem and in one or more of the poems of the "Poetic Definitions of Poetry" section of Chapter 16.

## MARK JARMAN (B. 1952)

## *Unholy Sonnet*    1998

Breath like a house fly batters the shut mouth.
The dream begins, turns over, and goes flat.
The virus cleans the attic and heads south.
Somebody asks, "What did you mean by that?"
But nobody says, "Nothing," in response.                            5

The body turns a last cell into cancer.
The ghost abandons all of his old haunts.
Silence becomes the question and the answer.
And then — banal epiphany — and then,
Time kick starts and the deaf brain hears a voice.          10
The eyes like orphans find the world again.
Day washes down the city streets with noise.
And oxygen repaints the blood bright red.
How good it is to come back from the dead!

### CONSIDERATIONS FOR CRITICAL THINKING AND WRITING

1. FIRST RESPONSE. This poem is one of forty-eight sonnets Jarman published under the title "Unholy Sonnets," clearly an allusion to John Donne's *Holy Sonnets* from the seventeenth century. Do you see any traditional Judeo-Christian religious themes in this poem?

2. Does this Shakespearean sonnet build an argument the same way that other examples of that form do?

3. If you were asked to make a case that the underlying subject of this poem is either sleep or death, which would you choose? How different would these two interpretations be?

## R. S. GWYNN (B. 1948)

### *Shakespearean Sonnet*   2010

*With a first line taken from the tv listings*

A man is haunted by his father's ghost.
Boy meets girl while feuding families fight.
A Scottish king is murdered by his host.
Two couples get lost on a summer night.
A hunchback murders all who block his way.          5
A ruler's rivals plot against his life.
A fat man and a prince make rebels pay.
A noble Moor has doubts about his wife.
An English king decides to conquer France.
A duke learns that his best friend is a she.          10
A forest sets the scene for this romance.
An old man and his daughters disagree.
A Roman leader makes a big mistake.
A sexy queen is bitten by a snake.

### CONSIDERATIONS FOR CRITICAL THINKING AND WRITING

1. FIRST RESPONSE. How many Shakespearean plays can you identify from the fourteen encapsulated plots that make up this poem?

2. Discuss the significance of the title.

3. CREATIVE RESPONSE. Try your hand at creating a poem — a sonnet or another form — in whole or in part from summaries of TV shows.

## Villanelle

The **villanelle** is a fixed form consisting of nineteen lines of any length divided into six stanzas: five tercets and a concluding quatrain. The first and third lines of the initial tercet rhyme; these rhymes are repeated in each subsequent tercet (*aba*) and in the final two lines of the quatrain (*abaa*). Moreover, line 1 appears in its entirety as lines 6, 12, and 18, while line 3 appears as lines 9, 15, and 19. This form may seem to risk monotony, but in competent hands a villanelle can create haunting echoes, as in Dylan Thomas's "Do Not Go Gentle into That Good Night."

### DYLAN THOMAS (1914–1953)

### Do Not Go Gentle into That Good Night 1952

Hulton Deutsch/Getty Images.

Do not go gentle into that good night,
Old age should burn and rave at close of day;
Rage, rage against the dying of the light.

Though wise men at their end know dark is right,
Because their words had forked no lightning they          5
Do not go gentle into that good night.

Good men, the last wave by, crying how bright
Their frail deeds might have danced in a green bay,
Rage, rage against the dying of the light.

Wild men who caught and sang the sun in flight,          10
And learn, too late, they grieved it on its way,
Do not go gentle into that good night.

Grave men, near death, who see with blinding sight
Blind eyes could blaze like meteors and be gay,
Rage, rage against the dying of the light.          15

And you, my father, there on the sad height,
Curse, bless, me now with your fierce tears, I pray.
Do not go gentle into that good night.
Rage, rage against the dying of the light.

### CONSIDERATIONS FOR CRITICAL THINKING AND WRITING

1. **FIRST RESPONSE.** How does Thomas vary the meanings of the poem's two refrains: "Do not go gentle into that good night" and "Rage, rage against the dying of the light"?
2. Thomas's father was close to death when this poem was written. How does the tone contribute to the poem's theme?
3. How is "good" used in line 1?
4. Characterize the men who are "wise" (line 4), "Good" (7), "Wild" (10), and "Grave" (13).
5. What do figures of speech contribute to this poem?
6. Discuss this villanelle's sound effects.

## Denise Duhamel (b. 1961)

### *Please Don't Sit Like a Frog, Sit Like a Queen*   2006

*—graffiti inside the cubicle of a ladies' bathroom*
*in a university in the Philippines*

Remember to pamper, remember to preen.
The world doesn't reward a pimply girl.
Don't sit like a frog, sit like a queen.

Buy a shampoo that gives your locks sheen.
If your hair is straight, get it curled.                                  5
Remember to pamper, remember to preen.

Keep your breath minty and your teeth white and clean.
Paint your nails so they glisten, ten pearls.
Don't sit like a frog, sit like a queen.

Smile, especially when you're feeling mean.                               10
Keep your top down when you take your car for a whirl.
Remember to pamper, remember to preen.

Don't give in to cravings, you need to stay lean
so you can lift up your skirt as you prance and twirl.
Don't sit like a frog, sit like a queen.                                  15

Don't marry the professor, marry the dean.
Marry the king, don't marry the earl.
Remember to pamper, remember to preen.
Don't sit like a frog, sit like a queen.

### Considerations for Critical Thinking and Writing

1. **First Response.** The poem was inspired by graffiti in a women's bathroom. Do you think its intention was to enforce "ladylike" behavior or has the poet interpreted it for her own uses?

2. Characterize the tone of the poem. Sarcastic? Satirical? How can you tell?

### Connection to Another Selection

1. Compare this villanelle to Dylan Thomas's "Do Not Go Gentle into That Good Night," the poem that precedes it. The subject of Thomas's poem is much weightier: does the villanelle form accommodate both subjects equally well or is it better suited to one or the other?

## Sestina

Although the **sestina** usually does not rhyme, it is perhaps an even more demanding fixed form than the villanelle. A sestina consists of thirty-nine lines of any length divided into six six-line stanzas and a three-line concluding stanza called an **envoy**. The difficulty lies in repeating the six words at the ends of the first stanza's lines at the ends of the lines in the other five six-line stanzas as well, but in a very specific order that varies from stanza to stanza. Those words must also appear in the final three lines, where they often resonate important themes. The sestina originated in the Middle Ages, but contemporary poets continue to find it a fascinating and challenging form.

## ALGERNON CHARLES SWINBURNE  (1837–1909)

### *Sestina*    1872

I saw my soul at rest upon a day
As a bird sleeping in the nest of night,
Among soft leaves that give the starlight way
To touch its wings but not its eyes with light;
So that it knew as one in visions may,                              5
And knew not as men waking, of delight.

This was the measure of my soul's delight;
It had no power of joy to fly by day,
Nor part in the large lordship of the light;
But in a secret moon-beholden way                                 10
Had all its will of dreams and pleasant night,
And all the love and life that sleepers may.

But such life's triumph as men waking may
It might not have to feed its faint delight
Between the stars by night and sun by day,                        15
Shut up with green leaves and a little light;
Because its way was as a lost star's way,
A world's not wholly known of day or night.

All loves and dreams and sounds and gleams of night
Made it all music that such minstrels may,                        20
And all they had they gave it of delight;
But in the full face of the fire of day
What place shall be for any starry light,
What part of heaven in all the wide sun's way?

Yet the soul woke not, sleeping by the way,                       25
Watched as a nursling of the large-eyed night,
And sought no strength nor knowledge of the day,
Nor closer touch conclusive of delight,
Nor mightier joy nor truer than dreamers may,
Nor more of song than they, nor more of light.                    30

For who sleeps once and sees the secret light
Whereby sleep shows the soul a fairer way
Between the rise and rest of day and night,
Shall care no more to fare as all men may,
But be his place of pain or of delight,                           35
There shall he dwell, beholding night as day.

Song, have thy day and take thy fill of light
Before the night be fallen across thy way;
Sing while he may, man hath no long delight.

### CONSIDERATIONS FOR CRITICAL THINKING AND WRITING

1. FIRST RESPONSE. How are the six end words — "day," "night," "way," "light," "may," and "delight" — central to the sestina's meaning?

2. Number the end words of the first stanza 1, 2, 3, 4, 5, and 6, and then use those numbers for the corresponding end words in the remaining five stanzas to see how the pattern of the line-end words is worked out in this sestina. Also locate the six end words in the envoy.

3. Underline the images that seem especially vivid to you. What effects do they create? What is the tone of the sestina?

4. CRITICAL STRATEGIES. Read the section on psychological strategies (pp. 1386-1388) in Chapter 42, "Critical Strategies for Reading." Write a brief essay explaining why you think a poet might derive pleasure from writing in a fixed form such as a villanelle or sestina. Can you think of similar activities outside the field of writing in which discipline and restraint give pleasure? How might this reflect an author's personal psychology?

## FLORENCE CASSEN MAYERS (B. 1940)

### *All-American Sestina* 1996

One nation, indivisible
two-car garage
three strikes you're out
four-minute mile
five-cent cigar                                                         5
six-string guitar

six-pack Bud
one-day sale
five-year warranty
two-way street                                                         10
fourscore and seven years ago
three cheers

three-star restaurant
sixty-
four-dollar question                                                   15
one-night stand
two-pound lobster
five-star general

five-course meal
three sheets to the wind                                               20
two bits
six-shooter
one-armed bandit
four-poster

four-wheel drive                                    25
five-and-dime
hole in one
three-alarm fire
sweet sixteen

two-wheeler                                         30
two-tone Chevy
four rms, hi flr, w/vu
six-footer
high five
three-ring circus                                   35
one-room schoolhouse

two thumbs up, five-karat diamond
Fourth of July, three-piece suit
six feet under, one-horse town

## CONSIDERATIONS FOR CRITICAL THINKING AND WRITING

1. FIRST RESPONSE. Discuss the significance of the title. What is "All-American" about this sestina?

2. How is the structure of this poem different from that of a conventional sestina? (What structural requirement does Mayers add for this sestina?)

3. Do you think important themes are raised by this poem, as is traditional for a sestina? If so, what are they? If not, what is being played with by using this convention?

## CONNECTION TO ANOTHER SELECTION

1. Describe and compare the strategy used to create meaning in "All-American Sestina" with that used by E. E. Cummings in "next to of course god america i" (p. 619).

## JULIA ALVAREZ (B. 1950)

### *Bilingual Sestina*   1995

Some things I have to say aren't getting said
in this snowy, blond, blue-eyed, gum-chewing English:
dawn's early light sifting through *persianas* closed
the night before by dark-skinned girls whose words
evoke *cama, aposento, sueños* in *nombres*                    5
from that first world I can't translate from Spanish.

Gladys, Rosario, Altagracia — the sounds of Spanish
wash over me like warm island waters as I say
your soothing names: a child again learning the *nombres*
of things you point to in the world before English              10
turned *sol, tierra, cielo, luna* to vocabulary words —
*sun, earth, sky, moon.* Language closed

like the touch-sensitive *moriviví* whose leaves closed
when we kids poked them, astonished. Even Spanish
failed us back then when we saw how frail a word is                    15
when faced with the thing it names. How saying
its name won't always summon up in Spanish or English
the full blown genie from the bottled *nombre*.

Gladys, I summon you back by saying your *nombre*.
Open up again the house of slatted windows closed                      20
since childhood, where *palabras* left behind for English
stand dusty and awkward in neglected Spanish.
Rosario, muse of *el patio*, sing in me and through me say
that world again, begin first with those first words

you put in my mouth as you pointed to the world —                      25
not Adam, not God, but a country girl numbering
the stars, the blades of grass, warming the sun by saying,
*¡Qué calor!* as you opened up the morning closed
inside the night until you sang in Spanish,
*Estas son las mañanitas*, and listening in bed, no English            30

yet in my head to confuse me with translations, no English
doubling the world with synonyms, no dizzying array of words
— the world was simple and intact in Spanish —
*luna, so, casa, luz, flor*, as if the *nombres*
were the outer skin of things, as if words were so close               35
one left a mist of breath on things by saying

their names, an intimacy I now yearn for in English —
words so close to what I mean that I almost hear my Spanish
heart beating, beating inside what I say *en inglés*.

### CONSIDERATIONS FOR CRITICAL THINKING AND WRITING

1. FIRST RESPONSE. Of the forms we have introduced, why is a sestina a particularly appropriate form for the poet to choose to express the tension between her two languages?

2. Of the six sestina words — the ones that conclude each line — one is varied from stanza to stanza. Write a brief essay on why the poet might choose to vary that one particular word.

3. How would you describe the relationship between Spanish and English in this poem?

### CONNECTION TO ANOTHER SELECTION

1. Compare the dilemma expressed in this poem to one or more of the poems in Chapter 31, "A Study of Julia Alvarez." Are similar tensions evident there? If not, what other concerns come to the foreground?

## Epigram

An *epigram* is a brief, pointed, and witty poem. Although most rhyme and they are often written in couplets, epigrams take no prescribed form. Instead, they are typically polished bits of compressed irony, satire, or paradox. Here is an epigram that defines itself.

### SAMUEL TAYLOR COLERIDGE (1772–1834)
### What Is an Epigram?   1802

What is an epigram? A dwarfish whole;
Its body brevity, and wit its soul.

These additional examples by David McCord and Paul Laurence Dunbar satisfy Coleridge's definition.

### DAVID McCORD (1897–1997)
### Epitaph on a Waiter   1954

By and by
God caught his eye.

### PAUL LAURENCE DUNBAR (1872–1906)
### Theology   1896

There is a heaven, for ever, day by day,
The upward longing of my soul doth tell
        me so.
There is a hell, I'm quite as sure; for pray,
If there were not, where would my
        neighbors go?

Library of Congress/Getty Images.

### CONSIDERATIONS FOR CRITICAL THINKING AND WRITING

1. FIRST RESPONSE. In what sense is each of these three epigrams, as Coleridge puts it, a "dwarfish whole"?

2. Explain how all three epigrams, in addition to being witty, make a serious point.

3. CREATIVE RESPONSE. Try writing a few epigrams that say something memorable about whatever you choose to focus on.

## *Limerick*

The *limerick* is always light and humorous. Its usual form consists of five predominantly anapestic lines rhyming *aabba*; lines 1, 2, and 5 contain three feet, while lines 3 and 4 contain two. Limericks have delighted everyone from schoolchildren to sophisticated adults, and they range in subject matter from the simply innocent and silly to the satiric or obscene. The sexual humor helps to explain why so many limericks are written anonymously. Here is one that is more concerned with physics than physiology.

### ARTHUR HENRY REGINALD BULLER (1874–1944)
### *There was a young lady named Bright* 1923

There was a young lady named Bright,
Whose speed was far faster than light,
  She set out one day,
  In a relative way,
And returned home the previous night.                              5

This next one is a particularly clever definition of a limerick.

### LAURENCE PERRINE (1915–1995)
### *The limerick's never averse* 1982

The limerick's never averse
To expressing itself in a terse
  Economical style,
  And yet, all the while,
The limerick's *always* a verse.                                   5

### CONSIDERATIONS FOR CRITICAL THINKING AND WRITING

1. **FIRST RESPONSE.** How does Perrine's limerick differ from others you know? How is it similar?

2. Scan Perrine's limerick. How do the lines measure up to the traditional fixed metrical pattern?

3. **CREATIVE RESPONSE.** Try writing a limerick. Use the following basic pattern.

```
    ˘ ˘ ´    ˘ ˘ ´    ˘ ˘ ´
    ˘ ˘ ´    ˘ ˘ ´    ˘ ˘ ´
             ˘ ˘ ´    ˘ ˘ ´
             ˘ ˘ ´    ˘ ˘ ´
    ˘ ˘ ´    ˘ ˘ ´    ˘ ˘ ´
```

You might begin with a friend's name or the name of your school or town. Your instructor is, of course, fair game, too, provided your tact matches your wit.

## *Haiku*

Another brief fixed poetic form, borrowed from the Japanese, is the *haiku*. A haiku is usually described as consisting of seventeen syllables organized into three unrhymed lines of five, seven, and five syllables. Owing to language difference, however, English translations of haiku are often only approximated, because a Japanese haiku exists in time (Japanese syllables have duration). The number of syllables in our sense is not as significant as the duration in Japanese. These poems typically present an intense emotion or vivid image of nature, which, in the Japanese, is also designed to lead to a spiritual insight.

### Matsuo Bashō (1644–1694)
### *Under cherry trees*   date unknown

Under cherry trees
Soup, the salad, fish and all . . .
Seasoned with petals.

### Carolyn Kizer (1925–2014)
### *After Bashō*   1984

Tentatively, you
slip onstage this evening,
pallid, famous moon.

### Amy Lowell (1874–1925)
### *Last night it rained*   1921

Last night it rained.
Now, in the desolate dawn,
Crying of blue jays.

### Gary Snyder (b. 1930)
### *A Dent in a Bucket*   2004

Hammering a dent out of a bucket
   a woodpecker
      answers from the woods

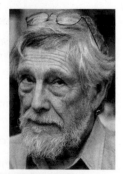

Jose Okolo/Alamy.

## CONSIDERATIONS FOR CRITICAL THINKING AND WRITING

1. FIRST RESPONSE. What different emotions do these four haiku evoke?

2. What differences and similarities are there between the effects of a haiku and those of an epigram?

3. CREATIVE RESPONSE. Compose a haiku. Try to make it as allusive and suggestive as possible.

## Ghazal

The ghazal form originated in Arabic poetry in the seventh and eighth centuries. Over the next thousand years its popularity spread from the Arabian Peninsula to Persia, India, and other parts of Asia, the Middle East, Africa, and Spain. Its theme, historically, deals with love: both the pain one feels upon separation and the beauty that love brings despite this pain. The form is slightly more flexible than some we have described, partly since the form evolved over centuries and was often accompanied by music, but it is always written in couplets, usually between five and fifteen in number.

## MIRZA ASADULLAH KHAN GHALIB (1797–1869)

## Ghazal 4    1864

Though beyond compare is the beauty of the full moon,
More beautiful is my beloved who shines like the sun at noon.

She will not let me kiss her but keeps her eyes on my heart to see:
She says to herself, "It is a good bargain if I get him for free."

As my face lights up when I set eyes upon her                                    5
She thinks my illness has passed, I must be better.

Let us see what lovers get from the gods they hold dear,
A soothsayer predicts this will be a lucky year.

We all know the truth about paradise, I fear,
But Ghalib, the illusion keeps the heart in good cheer.                         10

### CONSIDERATIONS FOR CRITICAL THINKING AND WRITING

1. FIRST RESPONSE. The poet addresses himself in the final line ("Ghalib" was his pen name). What is the effect of this self-address?

2. Who seems to be a stronger individual in the poem: the speaker or his lover? Why?

3. Discuss the emphasis on vision or the visual in this poem.

### CONNECTION TO ANOTHER SELECTION

1. Write an essay comparing the themes, relationships, and imagery of "Ghazal 4" and Shakespeare's "My mistress' eyes are nothing like the sun" (p. 686).

PATRICIA SMITH (B. 1955)

## *Hip-Hop Ghazal*   2007

Gotta love us brown girls, munching on fat, swinging blue hips,
decked out in shells and splashes, Lawdie, bringing them woo hips.

As the jukebox teases, watch my sistas throat the heartbreak,
inhaling bassline, cracking backbone and singing thru hips.

Like something boneless, we glide silent, seeping 'tween floorboards,          5
wrapping around the hims, and *ooh wee*, clinging like glue hips.

Engines grinding, rotating, smokin', gotta pull back some.
Natural minds are lost at the mere sight of ringing true hips.

Gotta love us girls, just struttin' down Manhattan streets
killing the menfolk with a dose of that stinging view. Hips.          10

Crying 'bout getting old — Patricia, you need to get up off
what God gave you. Say a prayer and start slinging. Cue hips.

### CONSIDERATIONS FOR CRITICAL THINKING AND WRITING

1. FIRST RESPONSE. This poem identifies itself as a ghazal in its title, but it also
   identifies the cultural context as hip-hop. Do the ghazal form and hip-hop
   sensibility cooperate or are they at odds with one another?
2. What effect does the repetition of "hips" at the end of more than half the lines
   have on the poem? How about the rhyming words that precede "hips" in each
   instance?
3. Is this a poem of seduction or of empowerment (or both)?

### CONNECTION TO ANOTHER SELECTION

1. As in Ghalib's "Ghazal 4," the poem that immediately precedes it, in "Hip-Hop
   Ghazal" the poet names and addresses herself in the final couplet. (This feature is not strictly a rule in the ghazal form, but it is not uncommon.) Write a
   brief essay about the effect of this convention on your understanding of individual identity in the ghazal.

## *Elegy*

An elegy in classical Greek and Roman literature was written in alternating
hexameter and pentameter lines. Since the seventeenth century, however, the
term **elegy** has been used to describe a lyric poem written to commemorate
someone who is dead. The word is also used to refer to a serious meditative
poem produced to express the speaker's melancholy thoughts. Elegies no longer conform to a fixed pattern of lines and stanzas, but their characteristic
subject is related to death and their tone is mournfully contemplative.

## Ben Jonson (1573–1637)

### *On My First Son*   1603

Farewell, thou child of my right hand,° and joy.
My sin was too much hope of thee, loved boy;
Seven years thou wert lent to me, and I thee pay,
Exacted by thy fate, on the just day. °                                *his birthday*
Oh, could I lose all father° now. For why                    *fatherhood*   5
Will man lament the state he should envy? —
To have so soon 'scaped world's and flesh's rage,
And, if no other misery, yet age.
Rest in soft peace, and asked, say, "Here doth lie
Ben Jonson his best piece of poetry,"                                       10
For whose sake henceforth all his vows be such
As what he loves may never like too much.

1 *child of my right hand:* This phrase translates the Hebrew name "Benjamin," Jonson's son.

### Considerations for Critical Thinking and Writing

1. FIRST RESPONSE. Describe the tone of this elegy. What makes it so emotionally convincing?

2. In what sense is Jonson's son "his best piece of poetry" (line 10)?

3. Interpret the final two lines. Do they seem consistent with the rest of the poem? Why or why not?

## Thomas Gray (1716–1771)

### *Elegy Written in a Country Churchyard*   1751

The curfew tolls the knell of parting day,
  The lowing herd wind slowly o'er the lea,
The plowman homeward plods his weary way,
  And leaves the world to darkness and to me.

Now fades the glimmering landscape on the sight,             5
  And all the air a solemn stillness holds,
Save where the beetle wheels his droning flight,
  And drowsy tinklings lull the distant folds;

Save that from yonder ivy-mantled tower
  The moping owl does to the moon complain             10
Of such, as wandering near her secret bower,
  Molest her ancient solitary reign.

Beneath those rugged elms, that yew tree's shade,
  Where heaves the turf in many a moldering heap,
Each in his narrow cell forever laid,                          15
  The rude forefathers of the hamlet sleep.

The breezy call of incense-breathing Morn,
　　The swallow twittering from the straw-built shed,
The cock's shrill clarion, or the echoing horn,
　　No more shall rouse them from their lowly bed.　　20

For them no more the blazing hearth shall burn,
　　Or busy housewife ply her evening care;
No children run to lisp their sire's return,
　　Or climb his knees the envied kiss to share.

Oft did the harvest to their sickle yield,　　25
　　Their furrow oft the stubborn glebe° has broke;　　cultivated land
How jocund did they drive their team afield!
　　How bowed the woods beneath their sturdy stroke!

Let not Ambition mock their useful toil,
　　Their homely joys, and destiny obscure;　　30
Nor Grandeur hear with a disdainful smile
　　The short and simple annals of the poor.

The boast of heraldry, the pomp of power,
　　And all that beauty, all that wealth e'er gave,
Awaits alike the inevitable hour.　　35
　　The paths of glory lead but to the grave.

Nor you, ye proud, impute to these the fault,
　　If Memory o'er their tomb no trophies raise,
Where through the long-drawn aisle and fretted vault
　　The pealing anthem swells the note of praise.　　40

Can storied urn or animated bust
　　Back to its mansion call the fleeting breath?
Can Honor's voice provoke the silent dust,
　　Or Flattery soothe the dull cold ear of Death?

Perhaps in this neglected spot is laid　　45
　　Some heart once pregnant with celestial fire;
Hands that the rod of empire might have swayed,
　　Or waked to ecstasy the living lyre.

But Knowledge to their eyes her ample page
　　Rich with the spoils of time did ne'er unroll;　　50
Chill Penury repressed their noble rage,
　　And froze the genial current of the soul.

Full many a gem of purest ray serene,
　　The dark unfathomed caves of ocean bear:
Full many a flower is born to blush unseen,　　55
　　And waste its sweetness on the desert air.

Some village Hampden, that with dauntless breast
　　The little tyrant of his fields withstood;
Some mute inglorious Milton here may rest,
　　Some Cromwell guiltless of his country's blood.　　60

The applause of listening senates to command,
    The threats of pain and ruin to despise,
To scatter plenty o'er a smiling land,
    And read their history in a nation's eyes,

Their lot forbade: nor circumscribed alone 65
    Their growing virtues, but their crimes confined;
Forbade to wade through slaughter to a throne,
    And shut the gates of mercy on mankind,

The struggling pangs of conscious truth to hide,
    To quench the blushes of ingenuous shame, 70
Or heap the shrine of Luxury and Pride
    With incense kindled at the Muse's flame.

Far from the madding crowd's ignoble strife,
    Their sober wishes never learned to stray;
Along the cool sequestered vale of life 75
    They kept the noiseless tenor of their way.

Yet even these bones from insult to protect
    Some frail memorial still erected nigh,
With uncouth rhymes and shapeless sculpture decked,
    Implores the passing tribute of a sigh. 80

Their name, their years, spelt by the unlettered Muse,
    The place of fame and elegy supply:
And many a holy text around she strews,
    That teach the rustic moralist to die.

For who to dumb Forgetfulness a prey, 85
    This pleasing anxious being e'er resigned,
Left the warm precincts of the cheerful day,
    Nor cast one longing lingering look behind?

On some fond breast the parting soul relies,
    Some pious drops the closing eye requires; 90
Even from the tomb the voice of Nature cries,
    Even in our ashes live their wonted fires.

For thee, who mindful of the unhonored dead
    Dost in these lines their artless tale relate;
If chance, by lonely contemplation led, 95
 Some kindred spirit shall inquire thy fate,

Haply some hoary-headed swain may say,
    "Oft have we seen him at the peep of dawn
Brushing with hasty steps the dews away
    To meet the sun upon the upland lawn. 100

"There at the foot of yonder nodding beech
    That wreathes its old fantastic roots so high,

His listless length at noontide would he stretch,
    And pore upon the brook that babbles by.

"Hard by yon wood, now smiling as in scorn, 105
    Muttering his wayward fancies he would rove,
Now drooping, woeful wan, like one forlorn,
    Or crazed with care, or crossed in hopeless love.

"One morn I missed him on the customed hill,
    Along the heath and near his favorite tree; 110
Another came; nor yet beside the rill,
    Nor up the lawn, nor at the wood was he;

"The next with dirges due in sad array
    Slow through the churchway path we saw him borne.
Approach and read (for thou canst read) the lay, 115
    Graved on the stone beneath yon aged thorn."

### The Epitaph

*Here rests his head upon the lap of Earth*
    *A youth to Fortune and to Fame unknown.*
*Fair Science frowned not on his humble birth,*
    *And Melancholy marked him for her own.* 120

*Large was his bounty, and his soul sincere,*
    *Heaven did a recompense as largely send:*
*He gave to Misery all he had, a tear,*
    *He gained from Heaven ('twas all he wished) a friend.*

*No farther seek his merits to disclose,* 125
    *Or draw his frailties from their dread abode*
*(There they alike in trembling hope repose),*
    *The bosom of his Father and his God.*

## CONSIDERATIONS FOR CRITICAL THINKING AND WRITING

1. **FIRST RESPONSE.** The poem presents a dichotomy between those who die unremembered and those whose names live on after their deaths. Does it resolve the differences between these two groups or does it just present them as a fact?

2. Do you understand the poem more as a commentary on life or on death?

3. What adjectives would you use to characterize the speaker? Gloomy? Morose? Philosophical? Passionate? Dispassionate? Choose other adjectives if none of these seems perfect.

## CONNECTION TO ANOTHER SELECTION

1. Discuss the theme of human insignificance in this poem and in Robert Frost's "Desert Places" (p. 874).

## KATE HANSON FOSTER (B. 1980)

### Elegy of Color    2018

Green shutters — white house.
Paper whites in the weak western light.
Brown mouse and its brown hush
across the stairs, four daughters
brushing long brown hair. Brown                                   5
beer in Black Label cans, black bible
on the nightstand. Baby Jesus
on the wall — incarnadine cheeks.
Shimmering red rosary beads. Red
garnet of my claddagh ring. A leak                              10
yellowing in the ceiling. The many
colors of my father singing. I was blessed
and I was blessed, like foreheads, like palm
wisps, like water my mother bought
from the church — colorless, colorless.                         15

### CONSIDERATIONS FOR CRITICAL THINKING AND WRITING

1. FIRST RESPONSE. If this poem did not have "elegy" in the title, would you classify it as an elegy? Why or why not?

2. The poem covers many topics. What would you identify as its central subject?

3. What is the effect of the speaker repeating the phrase "I was blessed" in lines 12 and 13?

## Ode

An **ode** is characterized by a serious topic and formal tone, but no prescribed formal pattern describes all odes. In some odes the pattern of each stanza is repeated throughout, while in others each stanza introduces a new pattern. Odes are lengthy lyrics that often include lofty emotions conveyed by a dignified style. Typical topics include truth, art, freedom, justice, and the meaning of life. Frequently such lyrics tend to be more public than private, and their speakers often use apostrophe.

## ALEXANDER POPE (1688–1744)

### Ode on Solitude    1700

Happy the man, whose wish and care
A few paternal acres bound,
Content to breathe his native air,
     In his own ground.

Whose herds with milk, whose fields with bread,                    5
Whose flocks supply him with attire,
Whose trees in summer yield him shade,
    In winter fire.

Blest, who can unconcernedly find
Hours, days, and years slide soft away,                             10
In health of body, peace of mind,
    Quiet by day,

Sound sleep by night; study and ease,
Together mixed; sweet recreation;
And innocence, which most does please,                             15
    With meditation.

Thus let me live, unseen, unknown;
Thus unlamented let me die;
Steal from the world, and not a stone
    Tell where I lie.                                               20

### CONSIDERATIONS FOR CRITICAL THINKING AND WRITING

1. FIRST RESPONSE. This poem is singularly populated. What distinction does the speaker make implicitly between solitude and loneliness?

2. Explain why "Ode on Solitude" can be accurately described as an ode.

3. How does the happy contentment expressed by the language in the first stanza anticipate the resolute wish expressed in the final stanza?

### CONNECTION TO ANOTHER SELECTION

1. Write an essay comparing the themes of "Ode on Solitude" and Thomas Gray's "Elegy Written in a Country Churchyard" (p. 700).

## Parody

A *parody* is a humorous imitation of another, usually serious, work. It can take any fixed or open form because parodists imitate the tone, language, and shape of the original. While a parody may be teasingly close to a work's style, it typically deflates the subject matter to make the original seem absurd. Parody can be used as a kind of literary criticism to expose the defects in a work, but it is also very often an affectionate acknowledgment that a well-known work has become both institutionalized in our culture and fair game for some fun. Read Gwendolyn Brooks' poem "We Real Cool," and then study Joan Murray's parody, "We Old Dudes."

## GWENDOLYN BROOKS (1917–2000)

### *We Real Cool* 1960

*The Pool Players.*
*Seven at the Golden Shovel.*

We real cool. We
Left school. We

Lurk late. We                                    5
Strike straight. We

Sing sin. We
Thin gin. We

Jazz June. We
Die soon.                                       10

GRANGER — Historical Picture
Archive.

### CONSIDERATIONS FOR CRITICAL THINKING AND WRITING

1. FIRST RESPONSE. How does the speech of the pool players in this poem help to characterize them? What is the effect of the pronouns coming at the ends of the lines? How would the poem sound if the pronouns came at the beginnings of lines?

2. What is the author's attitude toward the players? Is there a change in tone in the last line?

3. How is the pool hall's name related to the rest of the poem and its theme?

## JOAN MURRAY (B. 1945)

### *We Old Dudes* 2006

We old dudes. We
White shoes. We

Golf ball. We
Eat mall. We

Soak teeth. We                                   5
Palm Beach; We

Vote red. We
Soon dead.

> WHEN I READ "Reading stretches your mind and imagination. It lets you discover what you like and admire. Sometimes after I read a poem, I want to write one. It's as if someone's speaking my language, and I want to converse." — JOAN MURRAY

### CONSIDERATIONS FOR CRITICAL THINKING AND WRITING

1. FIRST RESPONSE. Consider the poem's humor. To what extent does it make a serious point?

2. What does the reference to Palm Beach tell you about these "old dudes"?

3. CREATIVE RESPONSE. Write a poem similar in style that characterizes your life as a student.

### CONNECTION TO ANOTHER SELECTION

1. Compare the themes of "We Old Dudes" and Brooks's "We Real Cool." How do the two poems speak to each other?

## Picture Poem

By arranging lines into particular shapes, poets can sometimes organize typography into *picture poems* of what they describe. Words have been arranged into all kinds of shapes, from apples to light bulbs. Notice how the shape of this next poem embodies its meaning.

> WHEN I WRITE "I've shared my poems with a friend . . . for decades now. He marks them up and gives them back; I do the same for him. You need a sympathetic critic who is not you, to help make your poetry as strong and clear as possible to readers who are not you." — MICHAEL MCFEE

## MICHAEL McFEE (B. 1954)

### *In Medias Res°* 1985

His waist
like the plot
thickens, wedding
pants now breathtaking,
belt no longer the cinch                                    5
it once was, belly's cambium
expanding to match each birthday,
his body a wad of anonymous tissue
swung in the same centrifuge of years
that separates a house from its foundation,               10
undermining sidewalks grim with joggers
and loose-filled graves and families
and stars collapsing on themselves,
no preservation society capable
of plugging entropy's dike,                               15
under his zipper's sneer
a belly hibernation-
soft, ready for
the kill.

*In Medias Res*: A Latin term for a story that begins "in the middle of things."

CONSIDERATIONS FOR CRITICAL THINKING AND WRITING

1. FIRST RESPONSE. Explain how the title is related to this poem's shape and meaning.
2. Identify the puns. How do they work in the poem?
3. What is "cambium" (line 6)? Why is the phrase "belly's cambium" especially appropriate?
4. What is the tone of this poem? Is it consistent throughout?

## Open Form

Many poems, especially those written in the past century, are composed of lines that cannot be scanned for a fixed or predominant meter. Moreover, very often these poems do not rhyme. Known as *free verse* (from the French, *vers libre*), such lines can derive their rhythmic qualities from the repetition of words, phrases, or grammatical structures; the arrangement of words on the printed page; or some other means. In recent years the term *open form* has been used in place of *free verse* to avoid the erroneous suggestion that this kind of poetry lacks all discipline and shape. Robert Frost (see Chapter 30), toward the end of his decorated career as a poet, archly dismissed free verse, saying, "I'd just as soon play tennis with the net down." This oft-quoted phrase indicates a shift in literary history in the 1950s, when Frost uttered it, but it's not as though all poets started open form verse in the mid-twentieth century. Contemporary poets have a wide range of choices, and poets from earlier times did too, although in some eras (like England in the eighteenth century) poets who did not adhere to strict conventions might not have found a publisher.

Although the following poem does not use measurable meters, it does have rhythm.

## WALT WHITMAN (1819–1892)

### *From "I Sing the Body Electric"* 1855

O my body! I dare not desert the likes of you in other men and women,
    nor the likes of the parts of you,
I believe the likes of you are to stand or fall with the likes of the soul,
    (and that they are the soul,)
I believe the likes of you shall stand or fall with my poems, and that
    they are my poems.
Man's, woman's, child's, youth's, wife's, husband's, mother's, father's,
    young man's, young woman's poems.
Head, neck, hair, ears, drop and tympan of the ears.          5
Eyes, eye-fringes, iris of the eye, eyebrows, and the waking or sleeping
    of the lids,
Mouth, tongue, lips, teeth, roof of the mouth, jaws, and the jaw-hinges,
Nose, nostrils of the nose, and the partition,
Cheeks, temples, forehead, chin, throat, back of the neck, neck-slue,
Strong shoulders, manly beard, scapula, hind-shoulders, and the
    ample side-round of the chest,          10

Upper-arm, armpit, elbow-socket, lower-arm, arm-sinews, arm-bones,
Wrist and wrist-joints, hand, palm, knuckles, thumb, forefinger, finger-joints,
    finger-nails,
Broad breast-front, curling hair of the breast, breast-bone, breast-side,
Ribs, belly, backbone, joints of the backbone,
Hips, hip-sockets, hip-strength, inward and outward round, man-balls,
    man-root,           15
Strong set of thighs, well carrying the trunk above,
Leg-fibers, knee, knee-pan, upper-leg, under-leg,
Ankles, instep, foot-ball, toes, toe-joints, the heel;
All attitudes, all the shapeliness, all the belongings of my or your body or of
    any one's body, male or female,
The lung-sponges, the stomach-sac, the bowels sweet and clean,     20
The brain in its folds inside the skull-frame,
Sympathies, heart-valves, palate-valves, sexuality, maternity,
Womanhood, and all that is a woman, and the man that comes from woman,
The womb, the teats, nipples, breast-milk, tears, laughter, weeping, love-looks,
    love-perturbations and risings,
The voice, articulation, language, whispering, shouting aloud,     25
Food, drink, pulse, digestion, sweat, sleep, walking, swimming,
Poise on the hips, leaping, reclining, embracing, arm-curving and tightening,
The continual changes of the flex of the mouth, and around the eyes,
The skin, the sunburnt shade, freckles, hair,
The curious sympathy one feels when feeling with the hand the naked
    meat of the body,           30
The circling rivers the breath, and breathing it in and out,
The beauty of the waist, and thence of the hips, and thence downward toward
    the knees,
The thin red jellies within you or within me, the bones and the marrow in the
    bones,
The exquisite realization of health;
O I say these are not the parts and poems of the body only, but of the soul,   35
O I say now these are the soul!

### CONSIDERATIONS FOR CRITICAL THINKING AND WRITING

1. FIRST RESPONSE. What informs this speaker's attitude toward the human body?

2. Read the poem aloud. Is it simply a tedious enumeration of body parts, or do the lines achieve some kind of rhythmic cadence?

---

Perspective

---

## WALT WHITMAN (1819–1892)

### *On Rhyme and Meter*   1855

The poetic quality is not marshaled in rhyme or uniformity or abstract addresses to things nor in melancholy complaints or good precepts, but is the life of these and much else and is in the soul. The profit of rhyme is that it drops seeds of a sweeter and more luxuriant rhyme, and of uniformity that it conveys itself into its own roots in the ground out of sight. The rhyme and uniformity of perfect poems show the free growth of metrical laws and bud from them as unerringly and loosely as lilacs or roses on a bush, and take shapes as compact as the shapes of chestnuts and oranges and melons and pears, and shed the perfume impalpable to form. The fluency and ornaments of the finest poems or music or orations or recitations are not independent but dependent. All beauty comes from beautiful blood and a beautiful brain. If the greatnesses are in conjunction in a man or woman it is enough . . . the fact will prevail through the universe . . . but the gaggery and gilt of a million years will not prevail. Who troubles himself about his ornaments or fluency is lost.

From the preface to the 1855 edition of Leaves of Grass

### Considerations for Critical Thinking and Writing

1. According to Whitman, what determines the shape of a poem?
2. Why does Whitman prefer open forms over fixed forms such as the sonnet?
3. Is Whitman's poetry devoid of any structure or shape? Choose one of his poems (listed in the index) to illustrate your answer.

---

# A SAMPLE STUDENT RESPONSE

Bloom 1

Avery Bloom

Professor Rios

English 212

7 October 2023

The Power of Walt Whitman's Open Form Poem

"I Sing the Body Electric"

Walt Whitman's "I Sing the Body Electric" is an ode to the human body. The poem is open form, without rhymes or consistent meter, and instead relies almost entirely on the use of language and the structure of lists to affect the reader. The result is a thorough inventory of parts of the body that illustrates the beauty of the human form and its intimate connection to the soul.

At times, Whitman lists the parts of the body with almost complete objectivity, making it difficult to understand the poem's purpose. The poem initially appears to do little more than recite the names of body parts: "Head, neck, hair, ears, drop and tympan of the ears" (line 5); "Mouth, tongue, lips, teeth, roof of the mouth, jaws, and the jaw-hinges" (7). There are no end rhymes, but the exhaustive and detailed list of body parts — from the brain to the "thin red jellies . . . , the bones and the marrow in the bones" (33) — offers language that has a certain rhythm. The language and rhythm of the list create a visual image full of energy and momentum that builds, emphasizing the body's functions and movements. As Michael Meyer and D. Quentin Miller write, open form poems "rely on an intense use of language to establish rhythms and relations between meaning and form. [They] use the arrangement of words and phrases . . . to create unique forms" (page 712). No doubt Whitman chose the open form for this work — relying on his "intense use of language" and the rhythm of the list — because it allowed a basic structure that held together but did not restrain, and a full freedom and range of motion to create a poem that is alive with movement and electricity. . . .

## Works Cited

Meyer, Michael, and D. Quentin Miller, editors. *The Compact Bedford Introduction to Literature*, 13th ed., Bedford/St. Martin's, 2024.

Whitman, Walt. "From 'I Sing the Body Electric.'" Meyer and Miller, pp. 708-09.

Open form poetry is sometimes regarded as formless because it is unlike the strict fixed forms of a sonnet, villanelle, or sestina. But even though open form poems may not employ traditional meters and rhymes, they still rely on an intense use of language to establish rhythms and relations between meaning and form. Open form poems use the arrangement of words and phrases on the printed page, pauses, line lengths, and other means to create unique forms that express their particular meaning and tone. The following poem challenges us with the length and structure of its lines:

## WILLIAM CARLOS WILLIAMS (1883–1963)

### The Red Wheelbarrow  1923

so much depends
upon

a red wheel
barrow

glazed with rain                                    5
water

beside the white
chickens

Oscar White/Getty Images.

### CONSIDERATIONS FOR CRITICAL THINKING AND WRITING

1. FIRST RESPONSE. What depends upon the red wheelbarrow? Explain your response with evidence from the poem.

2. Read the poem aloud several times, consciously emphasizing different words every time you do. Are there natural points of emphasis or does it all depend upon the reader?

## JULIO MARZÁN (B. 1946)

### The Translator at the Reception for Latin American Writers  1997

Air-conditioned introductions,
then breezy Spanish conversation
fan his curiosity to know
what country I come from.
"Puerto Rico and the Bronx."                        5

Spectacled downward eyes
translate disappointment
like a poison mushroom
puffed in his thoughts as if,
after investing a sizable                           10
intellectual budget, transporting

a huge cast and camera crew
to film on location
Mayan pyramid grandeur,
indigenes whose ancient gods                                              15
and comet-tail plumage
inspire a glorious epic
of revolution across a continent,
he received a lurid script
for a social documentary                                                  20
rife with dreary streets
and pathetic human interest,
meager in the profits of high culture.

Understandably he turns,
catches up with the hostess,                                              25
praising the uncommon quality
of her offerings of cheese.

### CONSIDERATIONS FOR CRITICAL THINKING AND WRITING

1. FIRST RESPONSE. What is the speaker's attitude toward the person they meet at the reception? What lines in particular lead you to that conclusion?

2. Why is that person so disappointed about the answer, "Puerto Rico and the Bronx" (line 5)?

3. Explain lines 6–23. How do they reveal both the speaker and the person encountered at the reception?

4. Why is the setting of this poem significant?

## MAJOR JACKSON (B. 1968)

### *The Chase*   2010

"What are you thinking?" she said. "Falling pheasants."
     He said. "Please look at me." she said.
"I've seen too much." he said. "You're like a wet cave."
     She said. "You're a feast of rhythms." he said.
"I want more than thunderbolts inside." she said.                         5
     "Wave after wave after wave." he said. "Your eyes
are stitching tighter." she said. "I am lost in a blizzard
     of feathers." he said. "You are lost." she said.

### CONSIDERATIONS FOR CRITICAL THINKING AND WRITING

1. FIRST RESPONSE. Look again at the poem's title. Who or what is being chased?

2. The repeated phrases "he said" and "she said" are punctuated as though they are complete sentences, but they don't always follow the convention of capitalizing the first letter. How difficult is it to tell who is saying what? How does that difficulty relate to the poem's theme?

3. Some phrases seem so personal to this couple's experience and/or so abstract that we cannot know their connotations. Despite their personal nature, are you able to discern the nature of their relationship?

## DAVID HERNANDEZ (B. 1971)

### *All-American* 2012

I'm this tiny, this statuesque, and everywhere
in between, and everywhere in between
bony and overweight, my shadow cannot hold
one shape in Omaha, in Tuscaloosa, in Aberdeen.
My skin is mocha brown, two shades darker 5
than taupe, your question is racist, nutmeg, beige,
I'm not offended by your question at all.
Penis or vagina? Yes and yes. Gay or straight?
Both boxes. Bi, not bi, who cares, stop
fixating on my sex life, Jesus never leveled 10
his eye to a bedroom's keyhole. I go to church
in Tempe, in Waco, the one with the exquisite
stained glass, the one with a white spire
like the tip of a Klansman's hood. Churches
creep me out, I never step inside one, 15
never utter hymns, Sundays I hide my flesh
with camouflage and hunt. I don't hunt
but wish every deer wore a bulletproof vest
and fired back. It's cinnamon, my skin,
it's more sandstone than any color I know. 20
I voted for Obama, McCain, Nader, I was too
apathetic to vote, too lazy to walk one block,
two blocks to the voting booth. For or against
a woman's right to choose? Yes, for and against.
For waterboarding, for strapping detainees 25
with snorkels and diving masks. Against burning
fossil fuels, let's punish all those smokestacks
for eating the ozone, bring the wrecking balls,
but build more smokestacks, we need jobs
here in Harrisburg, here in Kalamazoo. Against 30
gun control, for cotton bullets, for constructing
a better fence along the border, let's raise
concrete toward the sky, why does it need
all that space to begin with? For creating
holes in the fence, adding ladders, they're not 35
here to steal work from us, no one dreams
of crab walking for hours across a lettuce field
so someone could order the Caesar salad.
No one dreams of sliding a squeegee down
the cloud-mirrored windows of a high-rise, 40
but some of us do it. Some of us sell flowers.
Some of us cut hair. Some of us carefully
steer a mower around the cemetery grounds.
Some of us paint houses. Some of us monitor

the power grid. Some of us ring you up                                    45
while some of us crisscross a parking lot
to gather the shopping carts into one long,
rolling, clamorous and glittering backbone.

### CONSIDERATIONS FOR CRITICAL THINKING AND WRITING

1. FIRST RESPONSE. How does the arrangement of lines communicate a sense of energy and vitality?
2. How does the speaker characterize the United States?
3. Discuss the tone and thematic significance of the final image in lines 46–48.

### CONNECTION TO ANOTHER SELECTION

1. How does Hernandez's description of what is "All-American" compare with Julio Marzán's in "The Translator at the Reception for Latin American Writers" (p. 712)?

---

## Perspective

---

### ELAINE MITCHELL (1924–2012)

### *Form*   1994

Is it a corset
or primal wave?
Don't try to force it.

Even endorse it
to shape and deceive.                                                     5
Ouch, too tight a corset.

Take it off. No remorse. It
's an ace up your sleeve.
No need to force it.

Can you make a horse knit?                                                10
Who would believe?
Consider. Of course, it

might be a resource. Wit,
your grateful slave.
Form. Sometimes you force it,                                             15

sometimes divorce it
to make it behave.
So don't try to force it.
Respect a good corset.

## CONSIDERATIONS FOR CRITICAL THINKING AND WRITING

1. FIRST RESPONSE. What is the speaker's attitude toward form?
2. Explain why you think the form of this poem does or does not conform to the speaker's advice.
3. Why is the metaphor of a corset an especially apt image for this poem?

# Approaches
# to Poetry

# 24

## A THEMATIC CASE STUDY

# Poetry and Protest

"Protest poetry—could there be consensus poetry?"
—WILLIAM STAFFORD

ullsteinbild/TopFoto.

Newcomers to poetry often assume that it is only concerned with beauty and mystery. No doubt the poems you've encountered or will encounter in these pages will challenge that notion. Even if you've read plenty of poems that are concerned with beauty and mystery, you've read many others that simply aren't. Poetry exists to reaffirm us, to challenge us, and to free our minds, not just to awe us with what language can do. One of the ways it can challenge us is by taking a stance on an issue. William Stafford, whose poetry often spoke against war, asks the rhetorical question, "could there be consensus poetry?" From this, we can understand Stafford's definition of poetry as something that is bound to create controversy.

All writing is potentially a form of power. It is a misconception to think that poetry is any different just because it is also a form of art. Poets, like all writers, have something to say. To repeat the inherent definition Emily Dickinson uses to define it, poetry has the impetus to "tell all the truth, but tell it slant." Poetry tends to be subtler or less direct than something we might read on a sign at a street protest or in an opinion piece in a newspaper. Yet sometimes it has that same energy and the same urge to scream out against injustice, or to express frustration with one's society. One of the most famous poems of the twentieth century is Allen Ginsberg's *Howl*, which is just that: a deep, loud, sustained animal outcry of despair aimed at the society that willfully destroyed, as he said, "The best minds of my generation."

Poets aren't necessarily obligated to use their talents for protest, but they are certainly welcome to. There are as many reasons for poetry to exist as there are poets, and some are clearly enraged by the world they live in. Singer-songwriter Bob Dylan (p. 763), who was criticized by some of his fans in the mid-1960s when they said he no longer wrote protest songs, claimed that *all* his songs were protest songs. Maybe one of the things he was pointing out was that the subject of protest changed from song to song: it wasn't always about putting an end to war for Dylan, or calling out the hypocrisy of those in power. Often, he was challenging the way people thought, which meant he had to break into figurative language that evoked absurd dream-images. Langston Hughes spoke about the cry of protest one hears in the best art of the Harlem Renaissance, both in jazz music and in the poetry that imitates it, which showcases "revolt against weariness in a white world, a world of subway trains and work, work, work." Protest puts *the way things are* in conversation with *the way we want things to be.*

A poet's challenge is to channel that rage while still creating poems that utilize some of the many poetic features we discuss in previous chapters. It may seem unnatural to express outrage in a form like the sonnet, which has so many rules and conventions, but that's what some poets do.

Encountering protest poetry allows readers to expand their ideas of art and its social purpose. It allows readers to marvel at the control and facility of language that enables this odd marriage. Finally, it opens the possibility that readers might be persuaded to revise their opinions about an issue, even more than if they heard the same ideas expressed at a political debate or organized rally. It's important to continue to pay attention to the way poets express themselves, but we shouldn't overlook the fact that, whether they are protesting or not, poets are people who have something to say and who work hard to say it precisely and originally.

**A Note on the Chapter:** Given the often urgent and emotionally charged nature of protest (and, indeed, of poetry), you will find that the poems in this chapter address difficult topics, using imagery and language that may be harmful, offensive, or upsetting. Bear in mind the purpose of these poems — protest is a form of expression that desires change, and the creation of discomfort and strong emotional reactions is often a catalyst for this goal. As you respond to these poems, remember the suggestions we offer in "Approaching Sensitive Subjects" (p. 7). You may find that protest poetry, more than other topics, "holds a mirror" up to readers as individuals and members of society.

# FRANCES ELLEN WATKINS HARPER (1825–1911)

Frances Ellen Watkins Harper was born in Baltimore, Maryland. Her parents were free African Americans, and yet Harper was born at a time when the movement to abolish slavery affected all Americans. She began her career as a teacher but quickly turned to writing and activism. She wrote for antislavery newspapers such as *The Liberator* and also helped enslaved people escape to the North via the Underground Railroad. She was a prolific author in many genres in addition to poetry, notably her novel *Iola Leroy* (1892) and "The Two Offers" (1859), which is said to be the first short story published by an African American author. The following poem was based on an actual person, named in the title, who escaped slavery and fled across the Ohio River to Canada in 1838. Her story is also featured in the best-selling American novel of the nineteenth century, Harriet Beecher Stowe's *Uncle Tom's Cabin* (1852).

## *Eliza Harris*  1853

Like a fawn from the arrow, startled and wild,
A woman swept by us, bearing a child;
In her eye was the night of a settled despair,
And her brow was o'ershaded with anguish and care.

She was nearing the river—in reaching the brink,    5
She heeded no danger, she paused not to think!
For she is a mother—her child is a slave—
And she'll give him his freedom, or find him a grave!

'Twas a vision to haunt us, that innocent face—
So pale in its aspect, so fair in its grace;    10
As the tramp of the horse and the bay of the hound,
With the fetters that gall, were trailing the ground!

She was nerved by despair, and strengthen'd by woe,
As she leap'd o'er the chasms that yawn'd from below;
Death howl'd in the tempest, and rav'd in the blast,    15
But she heard not the sound till the danger was past.

Oh! how shall I speak of my proud country's shame?
Of the stains on her glory, how give them their name?
How say that her banner in mockery waves—
Her "star-spangled banner"—o'er millions of slaves?    20

How say that the lawless may torture and chase
A woman whose crime is the hue of her face?
How the depths of forest may echo around
With the shrieks of despair, and the bay of the hound?

With her step on the ice, and her arm on her child,                          25
The danger was fearful, the pathway was wild;
But, aided by Heaven, she gained a free shore,
Where the friends of humanity open'd their door.

So fragile and lovely, so fearfully pale,
Like a lily that bends to the breath of the gale,                          30
Save the heave of her breast, and the sway of her hair,
You'd have thought her a statue of fear and despair.

In agony close to her bosom she press'd
The life of her heart, the child of her breast:—
Oh! love from its tenderness gathering might,                          35
Had strengthen'd her soul for the dangers of flight.

But she's free!—yes, free from the land where the slave
From the hand of oppression must rest in the grave;
Where bondage and torture, where scourges and chains
Have plac'd on our banner indelible stains.                          40

The bloodhounds have miss'd the scent of her way;
The hunter is rifled and foil'd of his prey;
Fierce jargon and cursing, with clanking of chains,
Make sounds of strange discord on Liberty's plains.

With the rapture of love and fullness of bliss,                          45
She plac'd on his brow a mother's fond kiss:—
Oh! poverty, danger and death she can brave,
For the child of her love is no longer a slave!

## CONSIDERATIONS FOR CRITICAL THINKING AND WRITING

1. FIRST RESPONSE. Even though the poem was written more than 170 years ago, how does it manage to make the scene it describes vivid and immediate?

2. Where does the poem shift from concentrating on a single character to a broader consideration of the plight of all enslaved people? What is the effect of moving back and forth between individual and collective identity?

3. The speaker refers to "us" in lines 2 and 9. Who do you interpret "us" to be?

4. The speaker emphasizes Eliza's role as a mother. Why? Would the effect of the poem be different if the speaker focused on an enslaved person who escaped merely for their own liberty? Consider audience when you respond.

5. How does the rhyme scheme affect the way you receive the poem?

## CONNECTION TO ANOTHER SELECTION

1. Compare the relationship to history in this poem and in Kwame Dawes's "History Lesson at Eight a.m." (p. 569)

# CLAUDE MCKAY (1890–1948)

Jamaican-born Claude McKay was one of the central figures of the Harlem Renaissance (covered in depth in Chapter 28). Although this period of literature in the 1920s is frequently associated with an exuberant outpouring of African American art framing a celebration of Black identity, there was plenty of despair in and around the Renaissance. The reason behind the Great Migration from the South to the North in the early twentieth century — a period that saw the relocation of an estimated 1.5 million African Americans — was partly to seek economic opportunities in the industrialized North, but also to flee racism in the South. A sickening number of lynchings occurred in the South in the decades prior to the Harlem Renaissance. The year 1919 was a particularly awful one in this regard with major race riots in dozens of American cities and one horrific incident in Elaine, Arkansas, known as the "Elaine Massacre" that saw the murder of more than one hundred Black Americans — possibly more than twice that amount. The summer of 1919 was named the "Red Summer" by the poet and activist James Weldon Johnson for the amount of blood that was shed. This is the salient background for the following poem.

## *The Lynching* 1920

His Spirit in smoke ascended to high heaven.
His father, by the crudest way of pain,
Had bidden him to his bosom once again;
The awful sin remained still unforgiven.
All night a bright and solitary star                                    5
(Perchance the one that ever guided him,
Yet gave him up at last to Fate's wild whim)
Hung pitifully o'er the swinging char.
Day dawned, and soon the mixed crowds came to view
The ghastly body swaying in the sun                                    10
The women thronged to look, but never a one
Showed sorrow in her eyes of steely blue;
And little lads, lynchers that were to be,
Danced round the dreadful thing in fiendish glee.

### CONSIDERATIONS FOR CRITICAL THINKING AND WRITING

1. FIRST RESPONSE. The poem is emotionally powerful. What words or phrases make it so?

2. Lynch mobs are almost always composed entirely of men. How do you explain McKay's decision not to focus on men, but rather on women and children in the poem's final lines?

3. Trace the way the poem uses allusions to religion to make its point.

4. The poem is a variation on a Shakespearean (or Elizabethan, or English) sonnet (see Chapter 23). How does it depart from that form? Why might McKay have chosen to depart this way?

5. How do you explain the fact that the speaker refers to the murdered body as a "thing" in the final line?

### CONNECTION TO ANOTHER SELECTION

1. Compare the tone of this poem to another famous sonnet by the same author, "If We Must Die" (p. 801).

## TILLIE LERNER OLSEN  (1912–2007)

Tillie Olsen was raised in Nebraska, the daughter of Russian Jewish immigrants. She moved to California in the 1930s and became involved with union organizing, joining the American Communist party in a decade that saw a rise in socialist activism in the United States. Although she started writing in the 1930s, publishing both journalism and poetry, she did not publish her first book until 1961, the story collection *Tell Me a Riddle*, which gained critical notoriety and paved the way for a series of successes in multiple genres. Although Olsen was not prolific, she is considered an influential writer who consistently reflected on her own experiences in conversation with the experiences of women and other victims of societal oppression.

## *I Want You Women Up North to Know*   1934

(*Based on a Letter by Felipe Ibarro in* New Masses, *Jan. 9th, 1934.*)

I want you women up north to know
how those dainty children's dresses you buy.
   at macy's, wanamakers, gimbels, marshall fields,
are dyed in blood; are stitched in wasting flesh,
down in San Antonio, "where sunshine spends the winter."     5

I want you women up north to see
the obsequious smile, the salesladies trill
   "exquisite work, madame, exquisite pleats"
vanish into a bloated face, ordering more dresses,
   gouging the wages down,     10
dissolve into maria, ambrosa, catalina,
   stitching these dresses from dawn to night,
   In blood, in wasting flesh.

Catalina Rodriguez, 24,
   body shrivelled to a child's at twelve,     15
catalina rodriguez, last stages of consumption,
   works for three dollars a week from dawn to midnight.
A fog of pain thickens over her skull, the parching heat
   breaks over her body,

and the bright red blood embroiders the floor of her room. 20
    White rain stitching the night, the bourgeois poet would say,
    white gulls of hands, darting, veering,
    white lightning, threading the clouds,
this is the exquisite dance of her hands over the cloth,
and her cough, gay, quick, staccato, 25
    like skeleton's bones clattering,
is appropriate accompaniment for the esthetic dance
    of her fingers,
and the tremolo, tremolo when the hands tremble with pain.
Three dollars a week, 30
two fifty-five,
seventy cents a week,
no wonder two thousands eight hundred ladies of joy
are spending the winter with the sun after he goes down—
for five cents (who said this was a rich man's world?) you can 35
    get all the lovin you want
"clap and syph° aint much worse than sore fingers, blind eyes, and
      t.m.°"

Maria Vasquez, spinster,
    for fifteen cents a dozen stitches garments for children she has never 40
    had,
Catalina Torres, mother of four,
    to keep the starved body starving, embroiders from dawn to
    night.
Mother of four, what does she think of, 45
    as the needle pocked fingers shift over the silk—
    of the stubble-coarse rags that stretch on her own brood,
    and jut with the bony ridge that marks hunger's landscape
    of fat little prairie-roll bodies that will bulge in the
    silk she needles? 50
(Be not envious, Catalina Torres, look!
    on your own children's clothing, embroidery,
    more intricate than any a thousand hands could fashion,
    there where the cloth is ravelled, or darned,
    designs, multitudinous, complex and handmade by Poverty 55
    herself.)

Ambrosa Espinoza trusts in god,
    "Todos es de dios, everything is from god,"
    through the dwindling night, the waxing day, she bolsters herself up with
    it— 60
but the pennies to keep god incarnate, from ambrosa,
and the pennies to keep the priest in wine, from ambrosa,
ambrosa clothes god and priest with hand-made children's dresses.

Her brother lies on an iron cot, all day and watches,
on a mattress of rags he lies. 65

37 *clap and syph*: Sexually transmitted diseases
38 *t.m.*: A spinal disease

For twenty-five years he worked for the railroad, then they laid him off.
  (racked days, searching for work; rebuffs; suspicious eyes of policemen.)
  goodbye ambrosa, mebbe in dallas I find work; desperate swing for a
    freight,
  surprised hands, clutching air, and the wheel goes over a         70
  leg,
  the railroad cuts it off, as it cut off twenty-five years of his life.)
She says that he prays and dreams of another world, as he lies there, a
    heaven (which he does not know was brought to earth in 1917 in
    Russia,° by workers like him).                       75
Women up north, I want you to know
when you finger the exquisite hand made dresses
what it means, this working from dawn to midnight,
on what strange feet the feverish dawn must come
    to maria, catalina, ambrosa,                   80
how the malignant fingers twitching over the pallid faces jerk them to work,
and the sun and the fever mounts with the day—
  long plodding hours, the eyes burn like coals, heat jellies the flying fingers,
down comes the night like blindness.
  long hours more with the dim eye of the lamp, the breaking back,     85
  weariness crawls in the flesh like worms, gigantic like earth's in winter.
And for Catalina Rodriguez comes the night sweat and the blood
    embroidering the darkness.
  for Catalina Torres the pinched faces of four huddled
    children,                       90
  the naked bodies of four bony children,
  the chant of their chorale of hunger.
And for twenty eight hundred ladies of joy the grotesque act gone over—
  the wink—the grimace—the "feeling like it baby?"
And for Maria Vasquez, spinster, emptiness, emptiness       95
  flaming with dresses for children she can never fondle.
And for Ambrosa Espinoza—the skeleton body of her brother on his mattress
of rags, boring twin holes in the dark with his eyes to the image of christ
remembering a leg, and twenty-five years cut off from his life by the railroad.

Women up north, I want you to know,            100
I tell you this can't last forever.

I swear it won't.

75 *1917 in Russia:* The Russian Revolution of 1917 led to a socialist government and the formation of the Soviet Union. Social unrest and striking factory workers helped start the revolution.

### CONSIDERATIONS FOR CRITICAL THINKING AND WRITING

1. FIRST RESPONSE. What exactly is the target of the poet's protest here?
2. The poem was written almost a century ago, and it ends with a promise that
   the situation "can't last forever." Reflect on the rights of workers today. Has
   anything changed?
3. What is the effect of having multiple voices in the poem?
4. How does the poet play with conventions of capitalization? To what effect?
5. How are the length and open form of the poem essential to its intent?

1. Tato Laviera's poem "Latero Story" (p. 738) is also about invisible labor. Do these poems approach their topic similarly or differently? Is the effect similar or different?

## GENEVIEVE TAGGARD (1894–1948)

Genevieve Taggard published thirteen poetry collections during her lifetime as well as an influential biography of Emily Dickinson. She also founded the literary journal *Measure: A Journal of Poetry*. She lived in a great many locations in her relatively short life. Born in Washington, raised in Hawaii, educated in California, she moved to New York City in 1920, spent a year in France and Spain on a Guggenheim Fellowship, and later taught in Vermont and Massachusetts. Her poetry reflects a consistent engagement with social and political causes. The "crisis" in the title of the following poem refers to many possible crises: Taggard was affected by the Spanish Civil War (1936–39), the rise of Nazism and fascism in Europe, and anti-immigration xenophobia in the United States.

## *Ode in Time of Crisis*  1940

Now in the fright of change when bombed towns vanish
In fountains of debris
We say to the stranger coming across the sea
Not here, not here, go elsewhere!
Here we keep                                                                  5
Bars up. Wall out the danger, tightly seal
The ports, the intake from the alien world we fear.
It is a time of many errors now.
And this the error of children when they feel
But cannot say their terror. To shut off the stream             10
In which we moved and still move, if we move.
*The alien is the nation,* nothing more or less.
How set ourselves at variance to prove
The alien is not the nation. And so end the dream.
Forbid our deep resource from whence we came,               15
And the very seed of greatness.
                    This is to do
Something like suicide; to choose
Sterility—forget the secret of our past
Which like a magnet drew                                                 20
A wealth of men and women hopeward. And now to lose
In ignorant blindness what we might hold fast.
The fright of change, not readiness. Instead
Inside our wall we will today pursue

The man we call the alien, take his print,°          *fingerprint*  25
Give him a taste of the thing from which he fled,
Suspicion him. And again we fail.
How shall we release his virtue, his good-will
If by such pressure we hold his life in jail?
The alien is the nation. Nothing else.          30
And so we fail and so we jail ourselves.
Landlocked, the stagnant stream.
So ends the dream.

O country-men, are we working to undo
Our lusty strength, our once proud victory?          35
Yes, if by this fright we break our strength in two.
If we make of every man we jail the enemy.
If we make ourselves the jailer locked in jail.
Our laboring wills, our brave, too brave to fail
Remember this nation by millions believed to be          40
Great and of mighty forces born; and resolve to be free,
To continue and renew.

### CONSIDERATIONS FOR CRITICAL THINKING AND WRITING

1. **FIRST RESPONSE.** How would you describe the tone of this poem? Does it remind you of any other forms of writing you have encountered?
2. What phrases are repeated in the poem? What is the effect of this repetition?
3. How do you understand the speaker's use of "we" and "our"?
4. Discuss the imagery of imprisonment in the poem.

### CONNECTION TO ANOTHER SELECTION

1. Compare this poem's tone and intent to Danez Smith, "not an elegy for Mike Brown" (p. 742). How do the two poems augment your understanding of the two forms they allude to in their titles ("ode" and "elegy")?

## AUDRE LORDE (1934–1992)

Some poets would probably resist being primarily associated with protest, but Audre Lorde would not be one of those poets. She described herself as a "black, lesbian, mother, warrior, poet," and her work has the force and energy of all of those roles as they were understood in the 1960s when she came to prominence. Lorde was at the intersection of two movements that formed and gained strength in the late 1960s: the Black Arts Movement and second-wave feminism. The Black Arts Movement was the artistic counterpart of the 1960s cultural

Everett Collection Historical/Alamy.

uprising known as the Black Power movement and demanded that literature attempt to bring about social change. Second-wave feminism was a movement for gender equality that sought not only to raise awareness about the unfair treatment of women in contemporary America, but to pass laws to change it. Lorde's poetry is always fierce and uncompromising. She was also a powerful essay writer, and her memoir *The Cancer Journals* (1980) was an influential, unflinching account of her battle with breast cancer.

## *Power*   1978

The difference between poetry and rhetoric
is being ready to kill
yourself
instead of your children.

I am trapped on a desert of raw gunshot wounds                    5
and a dead child dragging his shattered black
face off the edge of my sleep
blood from his punctured cheeks and shoulders
is the only liquid for miles
and my stomach                                                   10
churns at the imagined taste while
my mouth splits into dry lips
without loyalty or reason
thirsting for the wetness of his blood
as it sinks into the whiteness                                   15
of the desert where I am lost
without imagery or magic
trying to make power out of hatred and destruction
trying to heal my dying son with kisses
only the sun will bleach his bones quicker.                      20

A policeman who shot down a ten year old in Queens
stood over the boy with his cop shoes in childish blood
and a voice said "Die you little motherfucker" and
there are tapes to prove it. At his trial
this policeman said in his own defense                           25
"I didn't notice the size nor nothing else
only the color." And
there are tapes to prove that, too.

Today that 37 year old white man
with 13 years of police forcing                                  30
was set free
by eleven white men who said they were satisfied
justice had been done
and one Black Woman who said
"They convinced me" meaning                                      35

they had dragged her 4'10" Black Woman's frame
over the hot coals
of four centuries of white male approval
until she let go
the first real power she ever had                                        40
and lined her own womb with cement
to make a graveyard for our children.

I have not been able to touch the destruction
within me.
But unless I learn to use                                                45
the difference between poetry and rhetoric
my power too will run corrupt as poisonous mold
or lie limp and useless as an unconnected wire
and one day I will take my teenaged plug
and connect it to the nearest socket                                     50
raping an 85 year old white woman
who is somebody's mother
and as I beat her senseless and set a torch to her bed
a greek chorus will be singing in 3/4 time
"Poor thing. She never hurt a soul. What beasts they are."               55

## CONSIDERATIONS FOR CRITICAL THINKING AND WRITING

1. FIRST RESPONSE. The poem was written in 1978, long before our current era
   in which the incident described here recurs with nauseating frequency. Were
   you surprised by the publication date?

2. Comment on the way the poem casts the relationship between adults and
   children in multiple ways.

3. Lorde said of the origin of this poem, after learning that the police officer had
   been acquitted, "A kind of fury rose up in me; the sky turned red. I felt so sick.
   I felt as if I would drive this car into a wall, into the next person I saw. So I
   pulled over. I took out my journal just to air some of my fury, to get it out of
   my fingertips." Discuss the way fury becomes poetry here: where is the poem
   pure fury and where is that feeling restrained or channeled?

4. How does the poem modulate between the abstract/impersonal and the spe-
   cific/personal? To what effect?

## CONNECTION TO ANOTHER SELECTION

1. Compare responses to racist violence in this poem and in Aja Monet's
   "#sayhername" (p. 744). Do they invoke similar emotional responses from
   you as the reader?

# JUNE JORDAN (1936–2002)

Born in Harlem to Jamaican immigrant parents, June Jordan was a prolific
poet and a major force of Black resistance in the turbulent late twentieth
century. She was also an educator who held teaching positions at City College

of New York, Yale University, SUNY-Stony Brook, and the University of
California, Berkeley. Her writings — twenty-seven books in total — were not
limited to poetry: she also wrote plays, a memoir, books for young readers,
and journalistic essays, mostly with a political/activist bent. Her poems, as
you will see, were marked by a use of vernacular diction and borrow some of
the conventions associated with the Black Arts Movement of the late 1960s,
such as an unconventional use of punctuation. The following poem contains
graphic language and imagery related to rape.

## Poem about My Rights    1978

Even tonight and I need to take a walk and clear
my head about this poem about why I can't
go out without changing my clothes my shoes
my body posture my gender identity my age
my status as a woman alone in the evening/                                    5
alone on the streets/alone not being the point/
the point being that I can't do what I want
to do with my own body because I am the wrong
sex the wrong age the wrong skin and
suppose it was not here in the city but down on the beach/          10
or far into the woods and I wanted to go
there by myself thinking about God/or thinking
about children or thinking about the world/all of it
disclosed by the stars and the silence:
I could not go and I could not think and I could not            15
stay there
alone
as I need to be
alone because I can't do what I want to do with my own
body and                                                              20
who in the hell set things up
like this
and in France they say if the guy penetrates
but does not ejaculate then he did not rape me
and if after stabbing him if after screams if                          25
after begging the bastard and if even after smashing
a hammer to his head if even after that if he
and his buddies fuck me after that
then I consented and there was
no rape because finally you understand finally              30
they fucked me over because I was wrong I was
wrong again to be me being me where I was/wrong
to be who I am
which is exactly like South Africa
penetrating into Namibia penetrating into                       35
Angola and does that mean I mean how do you know if

Pretoria ejaculates what will the evidence look like the
proof of the monster jackboot ejaculation on Blackland
and if
after Namibia and if after Angola and if after Zimbabwe          40
and if after all of my kinsmen and women resist even to
self-immolation of the villages and if after that
we lose nevertheless what will the big boys say will they
claim my consent:
Do You Follow Me: We are the wrong people of                     45
the wrong skin on the wrong continent and what
in the hell is everybody being reasonable about
and according to the *Times* this week
back in 1966 the C.I.A. decided that they had this problem
and the problem was a man named Nkrumah° so they               50
killed him and before that it was Patrice Lumumba°
and before that it was my father on the campus
of my Ivy League school and my father afraid
to walk into the cafeteria because he said he
was wrong the wrong age the wrong skin the wrong               55
gender identity and he was paying my tuition and
before that
it was my father saying I was wrong saying that
I should have been a boy because he wanted one/a
boy and that I should have been lighter skinned and            60
that I should have had straighter hair and that
I should not be so boy crazy but instead I should
just be one/a boy and before that
it was my mother pleading plastic surgery for
my nose and braces for my teeth and telling me                 65
to let the books loose to let them loose in other
words
I am very familiar with the problems of the C.I.A.
and the problems of South Africa and the problems
of Exxon Corporation and the problems of white                 70
America in general and the problems of the teachers
and the preachers and the F.B.I. and the social
workers and my particular Mom and Dad/I am very
familiar with the problems because the problems
turn out to be                                                 75
me
I am the history of rape
I am the history of the rejection of who I am
I am the history of the terrorized incarceration of
my self                                                        80

---

50 *Nkrumah:* Kwame Nkrumah (1909–1972) was the first Prime Minister and President of
Ghana following that country's drive for independence from Britain in 1957.
51 *Patrice Lumumba:* Lumumba (1925–1961) was the first Prime Minister of the Republic of
the Congo who helped that African nation in their fight for independence from Belgium. He
was executed shortly after independence was declared.

I am the history of battery assault and limitless
armies against whatever I want to do with my mind
and my body and my soul and
whether it's about walking out at night
or whether it's about the love that I feel or                                    85
whether it's about the sanctity of my vagina or
the sanctity of my national boundaries
or the sanctity of my leaders or the sanctity
of each and every desire
that I know from my personal and idiosyncratic                                   90
and indisputably single and singular heart
I have been raped
be-
cause I have been wrong the wrong sex the wrong age
the wrong skin the wrong nose the wrong hair the                                 95
wrong need the wrong dream the wrong geographic
the wrong sartorial I
I have been the meaning of rape
I have been the problem everyone seeks to
eliminate by forced                                                              100
penetration with or without the evidence of slime and/
but let this be unmistakable this poem
is not consent I do not consent
to my mother to my father to the teachers to
the F.B.I. to South Africa to Bedford-Stuy                                       105
to Park Avenue to American Airlines to the hardon
idlers on the corners to the sneaky creeps in
cars
*I am not wrong: Wrong is not my name*
My name is my own my own my own                                                  110
and I can't tell you who the hell set things up like this
but I can tell you that from now on my resistance
my simple and daily and nightly self-determination
may very well cost you your life

## Considerations for Critical Thinking and Writing

1. First response. Would you say the poem is more about the individual speaker or the multiple groups who help comprise her identity? What explains your response?

2. What is the poetic effect of interspersing very short (even single word) lines with much longer ones?

3. The word "wrong" recurs throughout the poem: how is the speaker using it?

4. The poem ends with a very different tone from that which characterizes most of it. Where is the crucial turn?

## Connection to Another Selection

1. Both Audre Lorde in the previous poem "Power" and Jordan in this one are coping with a great deal of rage. What are key differences in their delivery? Using your own definition of protest poetry, which one, in your reading, is more effective in achieving the ends of that category?

## DENISE LEVERTOV (1923–1997)

Denise Levertov was born and raised in Essex, United Kingdom, to a Welsh mother and a Jewish father who emigrated from Russia first to Germany and then to England. She regarded her mixed ancestry as something that benefited her rather than made her feel excluded. A product of home-schooling, she began writing poetry in her teens, served as a nurse during the Nazi siege of London (1940–43), and published her first book of poems in 1946 just after the end of World War II. She met and married an American and moved to the United States where she eventually became a naturalized citizen. Her poetry went through multiple phases, but in the politically turbulent 1960s and 1970s she was the poetry editor of the left-leaning journal *The Nation*, and her own poetry became political during this time, especially focused on opposition to the U.S. war in Vietnam, the subject of the following poem.

## *A Poem at Christmas, 1972, during the Terror-Bombing of North Vietnam*   1974

Now I have lain awake imagining murder.
At first my pockets were loaded with rocks, with knives,
wherever I ran windows smashed, but I was swift
        and unseen,
  I was saving the knives until I reached        5
certain men . . .
      Yes, Kissinger's° smile faded,
he clutched his belly, he reeled . . .
But as the night
wore on, what I held              10
hidden—under a napkin perhaps,
  I as a waitress at the inaugural dinner—
was a container of napalm:°
and as I threw it in Nixon's face
and his crowd leapt back from the flames with crude    15
           yells of horror,
and some came rushing to seize me:
  quick as thought I had ready

---

7 *Kissinger:* Henry Kissinger (b. 1923) served as Secretary of State and National Security advisor under Presidents Nixon and Ford in the late 1960s and early 1970s during the U.S. war in Vietnam. Although he received the Nobel Peace Prize in 1973 for negotiating a cease fire in Vietnam, he was associated with the war's escalation, and his recognition was one of the most controversial in the prize's long history.

13 *napalm:* A flammable chemical weapon deriving its name from its ingredients, naphthenic and palmitic acids. It was used by the United States during the Vietnam war and became especially controversial after the publication of widely published photographs of burned children in visible agony.

a round of those small bombs designed
to explode at the pressure of a small child's weight,                    20
and these instantly
dealt with the feet of Nixon's friends and henchmen,
who fell in their own blood
while the foul smoke of his body-oils
blackened the hellish room . . .                    25
It was of no interest
to imagine further. Instead,
the scene recommenced.
Each time around, fresh details,
variations of place and weapon.                    30
All night to imagining murder.
O, *to kill*
*the killers!*

It is
to this extremity                    35

the infection of their evil

thrusts us . . .

### CONSIDERATIONS FOR CRITICAL THINKING AND WRITING

1. FIRST RESPONSE. List a variety of attitudes toward revenge based on your prior experiences with stories, poems, or even television. How does this range help frame this poem?

2. Before line 34, how does the speaker feel about her own actions? What words or lines help you respond to this question?

3. How is the fact that the poem takes place on Christmas significant to its themes?

4. Comment on the way the poet structures the poem's lines and stanzas.

5. What is the relationship between the poem's last four lines and the rest of it? How do you explain the spaces in and around those lines?

### CONNECTION TO ANOTHER SELECTION

1. Contrast attitudes toward war and warfare in this poem and in Randall Jarrell's "The Death of the Ball Turret Gunner" (p. 558).

## KIMBERLY BLAESER (B. 1955)

Kimberly Blaeser is a Native American poet who was born in Montana and raised on the White Earth Chippewa reservation in northwest Minnesota. She teaches at the University of Wisconsin-Milwaukee and was named Poet Laureate of Wisconsin in 2015. In addition to her nine collections of poetry and fiction, she has published literary criticism including a book-length study on her prominent White Earth Ojibwe fellow writer Gerald Vizenor. Her work has been widely anthologized, and she has received multiple awards for her writing.

## *Apprenticed to Justice*   2002

The weight of ashes
from burned out camps.
Lodges smoulder in fire,
animal hides wither
their mythic images shrinking                                    5
pulling in on themselves,
all incinerated
fragments
of breath bone and basket
rest heavy                                                       10
sink deep
like wintering frogs.
And no dustbowl wind
can lift
this history                                                     15
of loss.

Now fertilized by generations—
ashes upon ashes,
this old earth erupts.
Medicine voices rise like mists                                  20
white buffalo memories
teeth marks on birch bark
forgotten forms
tremble into wholeness.

And the grey weathered stumps,                                   25
trees and treaties
cut down
trampled for wealth.
Flat potlatch plateaus
of ghost forests                                                 30
raked by bears
soften rot inward
until tiny arrows of green
sprout
rise erect                                                       35
rootfed
from each crumbling center.

Some will never laugh
as easily.
Will hide knives                                                 40
silver as fish in their boots,
hoard names
as if they could be stolen
as easily as land,
will paper their walls                                           45
with maps and broken promises,

scar their flesh
with this badge
heavy as ashes.

And this is a poem                                               50
for those
apprenticed
from birth.
In the womb
of your mother nation                                            55
heartbeats
sound like drums
drums like thunder
thunder like twelve thousand
walking                                                          60
then ten thousand
then eight
walking away
from stolen homes
from burned out camps                                            65
from relatives fallen
as they walked
then crawled
then fell.
This is the woodpecker sound                                     70
of an old retreat.
It becomes an echo,
an accounting
to be reconciled.
This is the sound                                                75
of trees falling in the woods
when they are heard,
of red nations falling
when they are remembered.
This is the sound                                                80
we hear
when fist meets flesh
when memories rattle hollow in stomachs.

And we turn this sound
over and over again                                              85
until it becomes
fertile ground
from which we will build
new nations
upon the ashes of our ancestors.                                 90
Until it becomes
the rattle of a new revolution
these fingers
drumming on keys.

### Considerations for Critical Thinking and Writing

1. FIRST RESPONSE. The poem evokes revolution in its last three lines. Is it a hopeful poem or a despairing one?

2. How do you interpret the title, "Apprenticed to Justice"?

3. How does the imagery of nature relate to the human conflict in the poem? Does the imagery act as a contrast, a counterpoint, or an element of support?

4. List images of destruction, death, and decay in the poem. Is there anything to balance this content?

5. Why does the poem emphasize sound in the second half?

### Connection to Another Selection

1. Discuss the role of art in this poem and in Audre Lorde's "Power" (p. 729).

## Tato Laviera (1950–2013)

Jesús Abraham "Tato" Laviera was born in Puerto Rico and migrated to New York City at the age of ten. He was associated with the storied Nuyorican Poets Cafe, a space in Manhattan's Lower East Side founded in 1973 that showcases the works of Latino/Latina poets to this day. Consistent with the Nuyorican movement's tenets, Laviera's art had an activist bent. In addition to a number of groundbreaking volumes of poetry, Laviera served as director of University of the Streets, a nonprofit organization that provided education to underprivileged groups. His interests often attached to characters who would ordinarily not be considered in poetry, as in the following poem about a "latero," someone who collects returnable cans and bottles for money.

## *Latero Story*  1988

i am a twentieth-century welfare recipient
moonlighting in the sun as a latero
a job invented by national state laws
designed to re-cycle aluminum cans
returned to consumer's acid laden                                 5
gastric inflammation pituitary glands
coca diet rites low cal godsons
of artificially flavored malignant
indigestions somewhere down the line
of a cancerous cell                                              10

i collect garbage cans in outdoor facilities
congested with putrid residues
my hands shelving themselves
opening plastic bags never knowing
what they'll encounter                                          15

several times a day i touch evil rituals
cut throats of chickens
tongues of poisoned rats
salivating my index finger
smells of month old rotten foods                                    20
next to pampers diarrhea
dry blood infectious diseases
hypodermic needles tissued with
heroin water drops pilfered in
slimy greases hazardous waste materials                            25
but i cannot use rubber gloves
they undermine my daily profits

i am a twentieth-century welfare recipient
moonlighting in the day as a latero
that is the only opportunity i have                                30
to make it big in america
some day i might become experienced enough
to offer technical assistance
to other lateros
i am thinking of publishing                                        35
my own guide to latero's collection
and founding a latero's union offering
medical dental benefits

i am a twentieth-century welfare recipient
moonlighting in the night as a latero                              40
i am considered some kind of expert
at collecting cans during fifth avenue parades
i can now hire workers at twenty
five cents an hour guaranteed salary
and fifty per cent of two and one half cents                       45
profit on each can collected

i am a twentieth-century welfare recipient
moonlighting in midnight as a latero
i am becoming an entrepreneur
an american success story                                          50
i have hired bag ladies to keep peddlers
from my territories
i have read in some guide to success
that in order to get rich
to make it big                                                     55
i have to sacrifice myself
moonlighting until dawn by digging
deeper into the extra can
margin of profit
i am on my way up the opportunistic                                60
ladder of success
in ten years i will quit welfare

to become a legitimate businessman
i'll soon become a latero executive
with corporate conglomerate intents                                    65
god bless america

### CONSIDERATIONS FOR CRITICAL THINKING AND WRITING

1. FIRST RESPONSE. What is the frequent social attitude toward people who collect cans and bottles for money, and how might anyone who espouses this
attitude receive this poem?

2. What is the poem's tone? When did you become aware of it, and does it change
over the course of the poem?

3. Why might the poet have chosen to eschew capitalization and punctuation in
the poem?

4. What connotations and values are embedded in the term "american success
story" (line 50)? How does the poem comment, directly or indirectly, on the
American definition of success?

5. Why might the poet have deliberately used imagery that is sometimes
disgusting?

### CONNECTION TO ANOTHER SELECTION

1. Do this poem and Allen Ginsberg's "Sunflower Sutra" (p. 752) regard human
garbage similarly? Do the poems have similar rhetorical aims?

## CLAUDIA RANKINE (B. 1963)

Jamaican-born American poet Claudia Rankine is the author of the first
volume of American poetry to make the *New York Times* best-seller list in
the nonfiction category. That book, *Citizen: An American Lyric* (2014), is one
of the most celebrated poetry volumes of the twenty-first century. "Stop-and-
Frisk," the poem included here, is from *Citizen*. A celebrated poet, essayist,
and playwright, Rankine was the recipient of the prestigious MacArthur Grant
in 2016, the funds from which she used to found the Racial Imaginary Institute, a think tank that invites participants to develop work that regards race as
a construct, one that has had detrimental effects throughout U.S. history.

## *Stop-and-Frisk*   2014

I knew whatever was in front of me was happening and then the police vehicle
came to a screeching halt in front of me like they were setting up a blockade.
Everywhere were flashes, a siren sounding and a stretched-out roar. Get on the
ground. Get on the ground now. Then I just knew.

And you are not the guy and still you fit the description because there is only one
guy who is always the guy fitting the description.

I left my client's house knowing I would be pulled over. I knew. I just knew. I opened my briefcase on the passenger seat, just so they could see. Yes officer rolled around on my tongue, which grew out of a bell that could never ring because its emergency was a tolling I was meant to swallow.

In a landscape drawn from an ocean bed, you can't drive yourself sane—so angry you are crying. You can't drive yourself sane. This motion wears a guy out. Our motion is wearing you out and still you are not that guy.

Then flashes, a siren, a stretched-out roar—and you are not the guy and still you   5
fit the description because there is only one guy who is always tire guy fitting the description.

Get on the ground. Get on the ground now. I must have been speeding. No, you weren't speeding. I wasn't speeding? You didn't do anything wrong. Then why are you pulling me over? Why am I pulled over? Put your hands where they can be seen. Put your hands in the air. Put your hands up.

Then you are stretched out on the hood. Then cuffed. Get on the ground now.

———

Each time it begins in the same way, it doesn't begin the same way, each time it begins it's the same. Flashes, a siren, the stretched-out roar—

Maybe because home was a hood the officer could not afford, not that a reason was needed, I was pulled out of my vehicle a block from my door, handcuffed and pushed into the police vehicle's backseat, the officer's knee pressing into my collarbone, the officer's warm breath vacating a face creased into the smile of its own private joke.

Each time it begins in the same way, it doesn't begin the same way, each time it   10
begins it's the same.

Go ahead hit me motherfucker fled my lips and the officer did not need to hit me, the officer did not need anything from me except the look on my face on the drive across town. You can't drive yourself sane. You are not insane. Our motion is wearing you out. You are not the guy.

This is what it looks like. You know this is wrong. This is not what it looks like. You need to be quiet. This is wrong. You need to close your mouth now. This is what it looks like. Why are you talking if you haven't done anything wrong?

And you are not the guy and still you fit the description because there is only one guy who is always the guy fitting the description.

———

In a landscape drawn from an ocean bed, you can't drive yourself sane — so angry you can't drive yourself sane.

The charge the officer decided on was exhibition of speed. I was told, after the   15
fingerprinting, to stand naked. I stood naked. It was only then I was instructed to dress, to leave, to walk all those miles back home.

And still you are not the guy and still you fit the description because there is only one guy who is always the guy fitting the description.

## Considerations for Critical Thinking and Writing

1. **first response.** You have obviously read about — or seen on TV or computer screens — instances of United States citizens, particularly those from the most vulnerable populations, being pulled over for no ostensible reason. How is it a different experience to encounter this situation in a poem?

2. Make a list of lines or phrases that are repeated throughout the poem. What is the effect of this repetition?

3. There are multiple voices in this poem. How do you sort them out without the benefit of quotation marks? Why do you think the poet made the choice not to include this punctuation?

4. Comment on the poem's structure as a way of getting closer to its theme. Would you categorize this as work as poetry or prose? Does it have lines and stanzas similar to other poems in this anthology? Why might Rankine have chosen this structure?

5. Rankine has made a number of "situation videos" to accompany her poems. Look up and view online the video that corresponds to this poem after you've read it. How does the video component enhance or expand your understanding of the poem?

## Connection to Another Selection

1. Both this poem and Audre Lorde's "Power" (p. 729) take on the topic of race-based police brutality. Are they "protest poems" in exactly the same way? What are their techniques and what are their aims?

## Danez Smith (b. 1990)

Justin Baker/Getty Images.

Danez Smith is a young poet whose three collections have already garnered many awards and recognition. A native of St. Paul, Minnesota, Smith, who identifies as queer and nonbinary, attended the University of Wisconsin-Madison and is one of the founding members of Dark Noise Collective. Their volume *Don't Call Us Dead* was a finalist for the National Book Award in poetry in 2017. The following poem addresses the fatal shooting of eighteen-year-old Michael Brown by a police officer in Ferguson, Missouri, in 2014. Brown's shooting was one of the catalysts of the Black Lives Matter movement, igniting widespread protests and discussions of race and police conduct. The final line of the poem alludes to the violent unrest in Ferguson following the shooting.

## *not an elegy for Mike Brown*    2014

I am sick of writing this poem
but bring the boy. his new name

his same old body. ordinary, black
dead thing. bring him & we will mourn
until we forget what we are mourning                                    5

& isn't that what being black is about?
not the joy of it, but the feeling

you get when you are looking
at your child, turn your head,
then, poof, no more child.                                            10

that feeling. that's black.

\\

think: once, a white girl

was kidnapped & that's the Trojan war°.

later, up the block, Troy got shot
& that was Tuesday. are we not worthy                                  15

of a city of ash? of 1000 ships
launched because we are missed?

always, something deserves to be burned.
it's never the right thing now a days.

I demand a war to bring the dead boy back                              20
no matter what his name is this time.

I at least demand a song. a song will do just fine.

\\

look at what the lord has made.
above Missouri, sweet smoke.

13 *Trojan War:* Legendary episode in Greek mythology, central to both Homer's epic works *The Iliad* and *The Odyssey*, this war waged over the kidnapping on Helen of Troy.

## Considerations for Critical Thinking and Writing

1. **FIRST RESPONSE.** How do you respond to the two demands of the speaker in response to the murder (a war or a song, lines 20–22)? How can a song do "just fine" as a substitute for war?

2. Comment on the structure of the poem, particularly the way the three sections diminish in length.

3. How do you imagine the speaker of the poem in relationship to the civil unrest following the murder? Is the speaker a witness, a participant, or would you use a different term?

## Connection to Another Selection

1. Write an essay comparing the treatment of the victim of racial violence in this poem and in Claude McKay's "The Lynching" (p. 723).

## AJA MONET (B. 1987)

Aja Monet was the youngest poet ever to win the Nuyorican Poets Cafe grand slam award at the age of nineteen. The Nuyorican Poets Cafe is an arts space founded in the Lower East Side of Manhattan in 1973 and has been a major showcase for the publication and recitation of poetry for half a century, championing poetry and other arts as a means of social empowerment, particularly for Latino/Latina artists. Monet, based in Brooklyn, is the author of four volumes of poetry and, like many of the authors in this chapter, dedicates her time not only to writing poetry, but also to cultural and community activism: she cofounded a political space for artists and activists called Smoke Signals Studio, and she facilitates a workshop called Voices: Poetry for the People.

## *#sayhername*   2015

i am a woman carrying other women in my mouth
behold a sister, a daughter, a mother, dear friend.
spirits demystified in a comrade's tone. they gather
to breathe and exhale, a dance with death we know
is not the end. all these nameless bodies haunted                    5

by pellet wounds in their chest. listen for us in
the saying of a name you cannot pronounce, *black*
and *woman*, is a sort of magic you cannot hashtag.
the mere weight of it, too vast to be held. we hold
ourselves, an inheritance felt between the hips                       10

woman of soft darkness. portal of light, watch them
envy the revolution of our movement. we break
open to give life flow. why the terror of our tears,
torment of our taste. my rage is righteous. my love
is righteous. my name is righteous. hear what i am                    15

not here to say, we, too, have died. we know we are
dying, *too*. i am not here to say, look at me, how i
died so brutal a death, i deserve a name to fit all
the horror in. i am here to tell you, how if they
mention me in their protests and their rallies,                       20

they would have to face their role in it, too, my
beauty, *too*. i died many times before the blow
to the body, i have bled many months before
bullet to the flesh. we know the body is not the
end. call it what you will but for all the hands,                     25

cuffed wrists of us, shackled ankles of us, the
bend over to make room for you of us, how dare
we speak anything less than *i love you*. we who
love just as loudly in the thunderous rain as when
the sun shines golden on our skin and the world                       30

kissed us unapologetically. we be so beautiful
when we be. how you gon be free without me?
your freedom tied up with mine at the nappy
edge of our soul singing with all our sisters, watch
them stretch their arms in my voice, how they                                    35
fly open-chested toward your ear, listen for

*Rekia Boyd*
                          *Tanisha Anderson*
          *Yvette Smith*
                          *Aiyana Jones*                                         40
*Kayla Moore*
                                *Shelly Frey*
*Miriam Carey*
                *Kendra James*
          *Alberta Spruill*                                                      45
                          *Tarika Wilson*
                *Shereese Francis*
                          *Shantel Davis*
          *Malissa Williams*
                                    *Darnisha Harris*                            50
*Michelle Cusseaux*
                *Pearlie Golden*
                                    *Kathryn Johnston*
                *Eleanor Bumpurs*
          *Natasha McKenna*                                                      55
                          *Sheneque Proctor*
                *Sandra Bland*

                                        we are each saying,

we do not vanish in the bated breath of
our brothers. show me, show me a man                                             60
willing to fight beside me, my hand in his,
the color of courage, there is no mountaintop
worth seeing without us. meet me

in the trenches, where we lay
our bodies down                                                                  65
in the valley
of a voice
              say it     say     her     name

## CONSIDERATIONS FOR CRITICAL THINKING AND WRITING

1. **FIRST RESPONSE.** You are probably acquainted with the #sayhername movement, a companion to the #BlackLivesMatter movement that has dominated
   public discourse for more than a decade. The #sayhername movement focuses
   specifically on the Black women who have experienced gender-specific
   forms of police violence. How does the list of names at the heart of this poem
   function within this movement? Can you make sense of the list's formatting?

2. Find instances of alliteration in the poem. What is the effect of using this device in this particular poem?

3. What is the relationship between individual and group identity in this poem?

4. How does the poem change toward the end, after the list of names? What is the effect of this change on the poem overall?

## CONNECTION TO ANOTHER SELECTION

1. Discuss the intersection of race and gender in this poem and in June Jordan's "Poem about My Rights" (p. 731).

## SUGGESTED TOPICS FOR LONGER PAPERS

1. How would you define "protest poem"? What elements make an effective protest poem? Which two or three poems in this chapter best illustrate your definition, and how do they achieve their ends?

2. The poems in this chapter span nearly two centuries. Do you see historical patterns repeating themselves, or is each one unique to its time?

3. Collectively, do these poems cause you to change your understanding of what poetry is for? If so, exactly how? If not, how do they compare to other poems in this book that are not explicitly protest-minded?

# 25

## A THEMATIC CASE STUDY

# Our Fragile Planet

"I find myself absolutely fulfilled when I have written a poem, when I'm writing one. Having written one, then you fall away very rapidly from having been a poet to becoming a sort of poet in rest, which isn't the same thing at all. But I think the actual experience of writing a poem is a magnificent one."

— SYLVIA PLATH

Everett Collection Historical/Alamy.

This chapter is a collection of poems thematically related to the natural environment we inhabit. Though poets may have a popular (and mistaken) reputation for being somewhat ethereal in their concerns, they still breathe the same air as the rest of us. Not surprisingly, because poets instinctively draw inspiration from nature, they are often as delighted to praise its vivid joys as they are compelled to warn us when it is abused. Having neither the technical knowledge of scientists nor the political means of legislators to defend the environment, poets nevertheless lend a voice to remind us of its pleasures, importance, and urgent fragility. The celebration of nature has always, of course, been a major poetic genre, but only fairly recently has poetry treated nature as a cause célèbre. Nature has forever inspired poets to write poems and so, given the contemporary environmental issues we face, it is only fitting that poetry is enlisted to champion nature.

The poems in this chapter provide some relatively recent or even contemporary reflections on our relationship to nature. Though they are not representative of all the kinds of environmental poetry being written today, these ten poems do offer a range of voices and issues that can serve as prompts for seeing and responding to your own natural environment through poetic language. You'll find among them detailed and vivid observations of nature, as well as meditations on climate change, the sustainability of the wild, and, indeed, the future of the planet. Some of the voices are quietly thoughtful, like Jennifer Franklin's "Memento Mori: Apple Orchard" (p. 756), while others directly question human behavior, especially our tendency toward violent destruction. In some ways, you might consider these poems similar to the protest poetry found in Chapter 24. Most of the poems in this chapter explore the natural world inhabited with human beings, though some concentrate primarily on nature itself. What is never absent, however, is the human perception that creates the poems.

## EILEEN CLEARY (B. 1963)

### *The Way We Fled*  2017

No branch
silhouettes the snow.

Tree limbs cut down by some bastard or buzz saw,
chipped remains scattered

afield around the stump                                        5
as if they'd tried to escape

the carnage, the way we fled
from my father after school.

Our legs gave out.
He'd gather our grains in a burlap sack,                       10

sprinkle us around the corners of the house,
soak his roots in whiskey.

If you ever find you are defenseless

it's best to compliment the buzz saw,
caress its teeth—                                             15

pour it a glass of Jack Daniels. Let it snarl.
Wait for the roars to become wheezes.

Then, walk from the field. Unhurried.

## Considerations for Critical Thinking and Writing

1. **FIRST RESPONSE.** Is the primary subject of this poem the field of sawed-down trees or the memory of the speaker's father, or are they equally balanced?

2. How does the poem use figurative language to connect humans to trees or other plants?

3. Discuss the use of personification in the poem.

## Connection to Another Selection

1. How do this poem and Robert Frost's "Out, Out" (p. 869) connect the act of cutting down trees to humanity more broadly? Are their intents or effects similar?

## Tess Gallagher (b. 1943)

### *Choices*   2006

*for Drago Štambuk*

I go to the mountain side
of the house to cut saplings,
and clear a view to snow
on the mountain. But when I look up
saw in hand, I see a nest clutched in                             5
the uppermost branches.
I don't cut that one.
I don't cut the others either.
Suddenly, in every tree,
an unseen nest                                                   10
where a mountain
would be.

## Considerations for Critical Thinking and Writing

1. **FIRST RESPONSE.** Why is the title of the poem plural?

2. Is the poem about realization, perception, or sacrifice? Explain your response with evidence from the poem.

3. What is the difference, thematically, between a snow-capped mountain and a bird's nest in this poem?

## Connection to Another Selection

1. Are the motivations to preserve nature in this poem and in Sylvia Plath's "Pheasant" (p. 754) similar? Identical?

## Joy Harjo (b. 1951)

### *Singing Everything*  2019

Carlo Allegri/Getty Images.

Once there were songs for everything,
Songs for planting, for growing, for harvesting,
For eating, getting drunk, falling asleep,
For sunrise, birth, mind-break, and war.
For death (those are the heaviest songs and they          5
Have to be pried from the earth with shovels of grief).
Now all we hear are falling-in-love songs and
Falling apart after falling in love songs.
The earth is leaning sideways
And a song is emerging from the floods                     10
And fires. Urgent tendrils lift toward the sun.
You must be friends with silence to hear.
The songs of the guardians of silence are the most powerful—
They are the most rare.

### Considerations for Critical Thinking and Writing

1. **First response.** Something changes between "Once" in line 1 and "Now" in line 7. Does the poem give any indication of what has changed, or does it leave it up to the reader to supply the answer? If the latter, what do you imagine it to be?

2. How do you interpret the crucial image, "The earth is leaning sideways," in line 9?

3. Who or what are the "friends with silence" / "guardians of silence" (lines 12–13) mentioned at the end of the poem?

4. Do the songs in this poem come from the earth or from people? Explain.

### Connection to Another Selection

1. Compare visions of the end of the world in this poem and in Robert Frost's "Fire and Ice" (p. 870).

## J. Estanislao Lopez (b. 1987)

### *Meditation on Beauty*  2018

There are days I think beauty has been exhausted
but then I read about the New York subway cars that,

dumped into the ocean, have become synthetic reefs.
Coral gilds the stanchions, feathered with dim Atlantic light.

Fish glisten, darting from a window into the sea grass          5
that bends around them like green flames —

this is human-enabled grace. So maybe there's room
in the margin of error for us to save ourselves

from the trends of self-destruction.
Or maybe such beauty is just another distraction,              10

stuffing our hearts with its currency, paraded for applause.
Here, in the South, you can hear applause

coming from the ground: even the buried are divided.
At the bottom of the Gulf, dark with Mississippi silt,

rests the broken derrick of an oil rig — and isn't oil          15
also beautiful? Ancient and opaque, like an allegory

that suggests we sacrifice our most beloved. Likely
ourselves. In one photograph, a sea turtle skims its belly

across a hull, unimpressed with what's restored,
barely aware of the ocean around it growing warm.              20

### CONSIDERATIONS FOR CRITICAL THINKING AND WRITING

1. FIRST RESPONSE. Where does the poem turn?
2. How does the meaning of "beauty" change throughout the poem? Is it competing with some more powerful force?
3. How would you describe the relationship between humanity and nature in this poem?

### CONNECTIONS TO OTHER SELECTIONS

1. Which is more optimistic about the planet's future: this poem or the one that precedes it, "Singing Everything" (p. 750) by Joy Harjo?
2. Compare the relationship between human garbage and natural life in this poem and in Allen Ginsberg's "Sunflower Sutra" (p. 752).

## GAIL WHITE (B. 1945)

### *Dead Armadillos*   2000

The smart armadillo stays
on the side of the road
where it was born. The dumb ones
get a sudden urge to check the pickings
across the asphalt, and nine                                    5
times out of ten, collide
with a ton of moving metal.
They're on my daily route — soft shells
of land crustacea, small blind knights
in armor. No one cares.                                         10
There is no Save the Armadillo
Society. The Sierra Club and Greenpeace
take no interest. There are too
damned many armadillos, and beauty,
like money, is worth more when it's scarce.                     15
Give us time. Let enough of them
try to cross the road.
When we're down to the last half dozen,
we'll see them with the eyes of God.

WHEN I WRITE "I'm a very secretive writer. Usually no one but me sees a poem before it's published. I don't especially recommend this. I probably miss a lot of helpful advice, but I also miss a lot of aggravation." —GAIL WHITE

## CONSIDERATIONS FOR CRITICAL THINKING AND WRITING

1. FIRST RESPONSE. Why do you think White chooses armadillos rather than, say, foxes to make her point?

2. What keeps this poem from becoming preachy?

3. How does the poem's language reveal the speaker's character?

## CONNECTION TO ANOTHER SELECTION

1. Discuss the similarities in theme in "Dead Armadillos" and Mary Oliver's "Wild Geese" (p. 753).

ALLEN GINSBERG (1926–1997)

## *Sunflower Sutra*  1955

I walked on the banks of the tincan banana dock and sat down under the huge
    shade of a Southern Pacific locomotive to look at the sunset over the box
    house hills and cry.
Jack Kerouac sat beside me on a busted rusty iron pole, companion, we thought
    the same thoughts of the soul, bleak and blue and sad-eyed, surrounded by   5
    the gnarled steel roots of trees of machinery.
The oily water on the river mirrored the red sky, sun sank on top of final Frisco
    peaks, no fish in that stream, no hermit in those mounts, just ourselves
    rheumy-eyed and hung-over like old bums on the riverbank, tired and wily.
Look at the Sunflower, he said, there was a dead gray shadow against the sky, big   10
    as a man, sitting dry on top of a pile of ancient sawdust —
— I rushed up enchanted — it was my first sunflower, memories of Blake — my
    visions — Harlem
and Hells of the Eastern rivers, bridges clanking Joes Greasy Sandwiches, dead
    baby carriages, black treadless tires forgotten and unretreaded, the poem   15
    of the riverbank, condoms & pots, steel knives, nothing stainless, only the
    dank muck and the razor-sharp artifacts passing into the past —
and the gray Sunflower poised against the sunset, crackly bleak and dusty with
    the smut and smog and smoke of olden locomotives in its eye —
corolla of bleary spikes pushed down and broken like a battered crown, seeds   20
    fallen out of its face, soon-to-be-toothless mouth of sunny air, sunrays
    obliterated on its hairy head like a dried wire spiderweb,
leaves stuck out like arms out of the stem, gestures from the sawdust root, broke
    pieces of plaster fallen out of the black twigs, a dead fly in its ear,
Unholy battered old thing you were, my sunflower O my soul, I loved you then!   25
The grime was no man's grime but death and human locomotives All that dress
    of dust, that veil of darkened railroad skin, that smog of cheek, that eyelid
    of black mis'ry, that sooty hand or phallus or protuberance of artificial
    worse-than-dirt — industrial — modern — all that civilization spotting your
    crazy golden crown —   30
and those blear thoughts of death and dusty loveless eyes and ends and withered
    roots below, in the home-pile of sand and sawdust, rubber dollar bills,
    skin of machinery, the guts and innards of the weeping coughing car, the
    empty lonely tin-cans with their rusty tongues alack, what more could I

name, the smoked ashes of some cock cigar, the cunts of wheel-barrows    35
    and the milky breasts of cars, wornout asses out of chairs & sphincters of
    dynamos — all these
entangled in your mummied roots — and you there standing before me in the
    sunset, all your glory in your form!
A perfect beauty of a sunflower! a perfect excellent lovely sunflower existence! a    40
    sweet natural eye to the new hip moon, woke up alive and excited grasping
    in the sunset shadow sunrise golden monthly breeze!
How many flies buzzed round you innocent of your grime, while you cursed the
    heavens of the railroad and your flower soul?
Poor dead flower? when did you forget you were a flower? when did you look at    45
    your skin and decide you were an impotent dirty old locomotive? the ghost
    of a locomotive? the specter and shade of a once powerful mad American
    locomotive?
You were never no locomotive, Sunflower, you were a sunflower!
And you Locomotive, you are a locomotive, forget me not!    50
So I grabbed up the skeleton thick sunflower and stuck it at my side like a scepter,
and deliver my sermon to my soul, and Jack's soul too, and anyone who'll listen,
— We're not our skin of grime, we're not our dread bleak dusty imageless loco-
    motive, we're all golden sunflowers inside, blessed by our own seed & hairy
    naked accomplishment-bodies growing into mad black formal sunflowers    55
    in the sunset, spied on by our eyes under the shadow of the mad locomo-
    tive riverbank sunset Frisco hilly tincan evening sit-down vision.

### CONSIDERATIONS FOR CRITICAL THINKING AND WRITING

1. FIRST RESPONSE. List the images of destruction, death, and/or decay in the
   poem. What is their cumulative effect?

2. A "sutra" (from Buddhism and Hinduism) is a series of bits of wisdom that
   together impart a kind of spiritual lesson. (The word *sutra* in Sanskrit means
   "string" or "thread.") Are you able to summarize the spiritual lesson here?

3. What initially prevents the speaker from recognizing the sunflower's beauty?
   What brings about his change in perspective?

4. When the speaker plucks the sunflower from the earth to give his sermon, he
   is essentially killing it. Is that action ironic or does it actually support what the
   speaker comes to understand about the nature of the sunflower?

### CONNECTION TO ANOTHER SELECTION

1. Discuss the importance of the mind, body, and soul in this poem and in Edna
   St. Vincent Millay's "Spring" (p. 942).

## MARY OLIVER (1935–2019)

## *Wild Geese*    1986

You do not have to be good.
You do not have to walk on your knees
for a hundred miles through the desert, repenting.
You only have to let the soft animal of your body
        love what it loves.

Tell me about despair, yours, and I will tell you mine.                    5
Meanwhile the world goes on.
Meanwhile the sun and the clear pebbles of the rain
are moving across the landscapes,
over the prairies and the deep trees,
the mountains and the rivers.                                             10
Meanwhile the wild geese, high in the clean blue air,
are heading home again.
Whoever you are, no matter how lonely,
the world offers itself to your imagination,
calls to you like the wild geese, harsh and exciting —                    15
over and over announcing your place
in the family of things.

### CONSIDERATIONS FOR CRITICAL THINKING AND WRITING

1. FIRST RESPONSE. Discuss the thematic significance of the wild geese. What do they offer that the poem's first three lines do not?

2. What phrases are repeated — and to what effect?

3. How would you describe the meaning of "the family of things" (last line)?

### CONNECTION TO ANOTHER SELECTION

1. Discuss the treatment of imagination in "Wild Geese" and in Emily Dickinson's "To make a prairie it takes a clover and one bee" (p. 834).

## SYLVIA PLATH (1932–1963)

## *Pheasant*   1962

You said you would kill it this morning.
Do not kill it. It startles me still,
The jut of that odd, dark head, pacing

Through the uncut grass on the elm's hill.
It is something to own a pheasant,                                        5
Or just to be visited at all.

I am not mystical: it isn't
As if I thought it had a spirit.
It is simply in its element.

Everett Collection Historical/Alamy.

That gives it a kingliness, a right.                                      10
The print of its big foot last winter,
The tail-track, on the snow in our court —

The wonder of it, in that pallor,
Through crosshatch of sparrow and starling.
Is it its rareness, then? It is rare.                                     15

But a dozen would be worth having,
A hundred, on that hill — green and red,
Crossing and recrossing: a fine thing!

It is such a good shape, so vivid.
It's a little cornucopia.                                                    20
It unclaps, brown as a leaf, and loud,

Settles in the elm, and is easy.
It was sunning in the narcissi.
I trespass stupidly. Let be, let be.

### CONSIDERATIONS FOR CRITICAL THINKING AND WRITING

1. FIRST RESPONSE. The speaker is trying to convince someone not to kill a pheasant. What is the most convincing aspect of the argument?

2. List examples of rhyme or near-rhyme in the poem and discuss their cumulative impact. Why do you think the poet chose not to adhere to a strict rhyme scheme?

3. What does the pheasant represent to the speaker? How does the speaker's diction and word choice help you understand the bird as a kind of symbol?

### CONNECTION TO ANOTHER SELECTION

1. Discuss the relationship between the speaker and nature in "Pheasant" and in "Sunflower Sutra" by Allen Ginsberg (p. 752).

## TERESA MEI CHUC (B. 1976)

### *Rainforest*   2014

I close my eyes so that I can see it.
What we freely eliminate. Who is

not guilty of it? We reek of paper.
Everywhere we go is paper. Our

hands are stained with paper.                                               5
Walls. What echoes from our walls.

The sweet whisper of rainforest—
even the name makes the sound of

rushing water or perhaps it's a ghost
that haunts us. They say the dead                                           10

that did not die a peaceful death are
doomed forever to wander the earth.

But perhaps this earth is for them
already a cemetery—stacks and

stacks of flesh on a desk. Which                                            15
one belongs to which tree?

Already, we've traded oxygen for
so much.

## CONSIDERATIONS FOR CRITICAL THINKING AND WRITING

1. FIRST RESPONSE. How do you respond to the use of the first-person plural pronouns (*we* and *our*) in the poem? Identify where the speaker uses the plural (*we*) and the singular (*I*). What is the effect of this switch?

2. How does the border between life and death frame the poem's theme?

3. Unpack the metaphor of the earth as a cemetery.

## CONNECTION TO ANOTHER SELECTION

1. Connect the motif of perception in this poem and in Tess Gallagher's "Choices" (p. 749).

## JENNIFER FRANKLIN (B. 1973)

### *Memento Mori: Apple Orchard* 2022

In the gold light of early October, we climb
the orchard hills searching empty trees
for apples. The boy at the gate tells us Ida Red,
Rome, Crispin, and Surprise are all ripe
and ready for our hands. We walk and walk.                    5
The dog investigates every fallen apple
with her frantic nose. Even as we savor
the autumnal sunlight of our beginning,
headlines remind us what is lost. Large families
have picked the trees clean, leaving plastic                   10
bottles and paper napkins blowing like white flags.
Instead of the fragrant apples on the ground
reminding me of my mother's baking,
I catch the smell of decay.

I catch the smell of decay                                     15
as we walk through so many rows
of stubby trees that we cannot find our way
back to the car. We do not say what we're thinking —
if we leave without a single apple, it might mean
what we have done to the earth cannot be undone.               20
The children who grow up on this imperiled planet
will not remember pulling the russet fruit
from the branches to bite into its sweet flesh. We see
boys throw bruised apples at each other. Still children,
they already know what is damaged becomes a weapon.            25
As we pull away, we watch them run the worn paths.
Their masks fall as they bend to collect
the blemished apples and fill their empty bags.

## CONSIDERATIONS FOR CRITICAL THINKING AND WRITING

1. FIRST RESPONSE. How do you read the line "what is damaged becomes a weapon" (line 25), beyond its meaning within the poem?

2. What is the effect of beginning the second stanza by repeating the same line that ends the first stanza? How does the meaning of the line change as the poem progresses?

3. The phrase "Memento Mori" in Latin means "remember that you will die." Philosophers and artists have long held the belief that a reminder of our death will protect us from the sin of excessive pride. How is it being used in the title based on the theme of the poem?

4. How do children figure into the poem's concerns?

## CONNECTION TO ANOTHER SELECTION

1. Consider the motif of garbage in this poem and in Allen Ginsberg's "Sunflower Sutra" (p. 752). Both poems are didactic; do they impart the same lesson?

## SUGGESTED TOPICS FOR LONGER PAPERS

1. Write an analysis of three or more poems in this chapter as commentaries on our civilization's problematic relationship to the environment. How does each poem add to and extend a consideration of the issue?

2. Selecting multiple poems from this chapter, would you characterize their main theme as irrevocable loss, tentative hope, desperation, or something else?

3. Using at least two poems from this chapter, and two poems from Chapter 24, "Poetry and Protest," write a paper in which you discuss whether poetry's traditional celebration of nature is an effective approach to challenging and changing our relationship with the planet.

# 26

## A CASE STUDY
# Song Lyrics as Poetry

Gijsbert Hanekroot/Getty Images.

> Anything I can sing, I
> call a song. Anything I
> can't sing, I call a poem.
> — BOB DYLAN

In 2016 the Nobel Prize committee shocked the world by awarding the Nobel Prize in Literature to a singer. No one was more shocked, perhaps, than the recipient, Bob Dylan, who mysteriously did not respond to the committee's announcement for more than a week. He eventually responded, but he didn't show up to accept the award, sending another rock musician (Patti Smith) in his place to sing one of his songs. The radical decision to award the prize to the folk-singer-turned-rock-star was surprising because literature has long been associated with written language rather than language meant to be performed live or recorded. Yet Dylan changed the direction of popular music by focusing on the artistic possibilities of lyrics, and his songs reveal a deep connection to literature proper. There are allusions in his work to countless books, from Edmund Spenser's *The Faerie Queen* to contemporary novelists such as Erica Jong. The recent study *Why Bob Dylan Matters* roots Dylan in the tradition of the ancient classics.

In 2018 Kendrick Lamar's album *Damn* was awarded the Pulitzer Prize in music, the first time the award was given to an artist outside of the classical and jazz traditions. "Rap," according to some legends, is an acronym for

Rhythm and Poetry. Whether or not that legend is factual, it is indisputable that rap lyrics are poetry (as Jay-Z argues convincingly in his book *Decoded*), and that they can be analyzed using techniques similar to the ones we introduce in this book. Like Dylan in the folk/rock world, some hip-hop artists are keen to expand the artistic boundaries of music while understanding that it can still function as entertainment. As they do so, they find new and exciting ways to manipulate language — exploiting its nuances, playing with its sound qualities, and creating metrical principles that are guided by the melodies that drive it.

Despite these relatively recent accolades for Bob Dylan and Kendrick Lamar, the connection between music and poetry is ancient. Note that the word "lyric" derives from "lyre," a stringed instrument that preceded guitars and that could be used to accompany songs. Ancient troubadours were storytellers responsible for transporting culture between lands before literature was able to be recorded, reproduced, and widely distributed in print. In this chapter we offer a sampling of song lyrics from a variety of traditions, but we are just scratching the surface of what could be included here. What we hope to communicate is that literature is already part of your daily life: think of how many song lyrics are permanently stored in your brain. To consider their poetic importance, all you have to do is to listen carefully and repeatedly, appreciating them not just for their catchy melodies, but for the way they do something special with language.

## FREDERIC WEATHERLY (1848–1929)

### *Danny Boy*   1910

Oh Danny boy, the pipes, the pipes are calling
From glen to glen, and down the mountain side
The summer's gone, and all the flowers are dying
'Tis you, 'tis you must go and I must bide.

But come ye back when summer's in the meadow          5
Or when the valley's hushed and white with snow
'Tis I'll be here in sunshine or in shadow
Oh Danny boy, oh Danny boy, I love you so.

And when you come, and all the flowers are dying
If I am dead, as dead I well may be          10
You'll come and find the place where I am lying
And kneel and say an "Ave" there for me.

And I shall hear, tho' soft you tread above me
And all my dreams will warm and sweeter be
If you'll not fail to tell me that you love me          15
I'll simply sleep in peace until you come to me.
I'll simply sleep in peace until you come to me.

## CONSIDERATIONS FOR CRITICAL THINKING AND WRITING

1. FIRST RESPONSE. Would you describe the poem as comforting or hopeless? Why?

2. What do you imagine the relationship between the speaker and Danny to be?

3. Do you have a sense of why Danny is leaving and the speaker must stay? Does it matter?

4. CREATIVE RESPONSE. Write a poem from the point of view of "Danny Boy" to the speaker of this poem, imitating its poetic form, rhyme scheme, and meter, but also considering what Danny's feelings are upon leaving.

### CONNECTION TO ANOTHER SELECTION

1. Compare the theme and context of this poem to the theme and context of Alfred, Lord Tennyson's "Break, Break, Break" (p. 653). Would you say the poems are *essentially* similar or opposite in terms of theme?

## BESSIE SMITH (1834–1937)

### *Careless Love Blues*   1925

Love, oh love, oh careless love
You fly through my head like wine
You wrecked the life of a many poor girl
And you nearly spoiled this life of mine

Love, oh love, oh careless love                                5
In your clutches of desire
You made me break a many true vow
Then you set my very soul on fire

Love, oh love, oh careless love
All my happiness I've left                                     10
You filled my heart with them weary old blues
Now I'm walkin', talkin' to myself

Love, oh love, oh careless love
Trusted you, now it's too late
You made me throw my old friend down                          15
That's why I sing this song of hate

Love, oh love, oh careless love
Night and day, I weep and moan
You brought the wrong man into this life of mine
For my sins, till judgment I'll atone                         20

Michael Ochs Archives/Getty Images

## CONSIDERATIONS FOR CRITICAL THINKING AND WRITING

1. FIRST RESPONSE. Why do we tend to blame love for problems? What kind of a force is it?

2. Is the speaker singing about love in general in this song or just a version of it called "careless love"? In other words, is all love "careless," or is this speaker just talking about a certain damaging version of love?

3. Is there anything positive about love in this song?

4. Where in the poem is love personified, and what is the effect of this literary device?

5. The first three stanzas address the effect of love on the speaker's head, soul, and heart, in that order. Does love have its most profound effect overall on the speaker's mind, spirit, or body?

6. In the final stanza the speaker seems to blame both love and herself. Does the final line represent a change of mind, a realization, or just a sense of shared guilt?

### CONNECTION TO ANOTHER SELECTION

1. Robert Lowell's "Skunk Hour" (p. 782) alludes directly to this poem. Compare the two in terms of theme.

## WOODY GUTHRIE (1912–1967)

### *Pretty Boy Floyd*    1944

If you'll gather 'round me, children,
A story I will tell
'Bout Pretty Boy Floyd, an outlaw,
Oklahoma knew him well.

It was in the town of Shawnee,                                                   5
A Saturday afternoon,
His wife beside him in his wagon
As into town they rode.

There a deputy sheriff approached him
In a manner rather rude,                                                          10
Vulgar words of anger,
An' his wife she overheard.

Pretty Boy grabbed a log chain,
And the deputy grabbed his gun;
In the fight that followed                                                       15
He laid that deputy down.

Then he took to the trees and timber
Along the river shore,
Hiding on the river bottom
And he never come back no more.                                                  20

Yes, he took to the trees and timber
To live a life of shame;
Every crime in Oklahoma
Was added to his name.

But a many a starvin' farmer                                                     25
The same old story told
How the outlaw paid their mortgage
And saved their little homes.

Others tell you 'bout a stranger
That come to beg a meal,                                    30
Underneath his napkin
Left a thousand-dollar bill.

It was in Oklahoma City,
It was on a Christmas Day,
There was a whole car load of groceries                    35
Come with a note to say:

"Well, you say that I'm an outlaw,
You say that I'm a thief.
Here's a Christmas dinner
For the families on relief."                                40

Yes, as through this world I've wandered
I've seen lots of funny men;
Some will rob you with a six-gun,
And some with a fountain pen.

And as through your life you travel,                        45
Yes, as through your life you roam,
You won't never see an outlaw
Drive a family from their home.

### Considerations for Critical Thinking and Writing

1.  FIRST RESPONSE. How do you feel about Floyd's crime, narrated in stanza 4?
    If you were on a jury trying him, what additional details would you need to
    know to make your determination?

2.  This motif is a familiar Robin Hood tale: can you provide other examples from
    folklore or popular culture? How does this version depart, even slightly, from the
    formula?

3.  In what ways does this poem conform, or not, to the ballad tradition (see
    Chapter 21)?

4.  How does the poem attempt to redefine the term "outlaw"?

5.  One of the famous lines, alluded to in a song by Bob Dylan, is "some [men]
    will rob you with a fountain pen" (lines 43–44). How do you interpret it?

### Connection to Another Selection

1.  Consider inherent definitions of respectability in this song and in Edward
    Arlington Robinson's "Richard Cory" (p. 616).

## Hank Williams (1923–1953)

### *I'm So Lonesome I Could Cry*   1949

Hear that lonesome whippoorwill
He sounds too blue to fly
The midnight train is whining low
I'm so lonesome I could cry

I've never seen a night so long                                                              5
When time goes crawling by
The moon just went behind the clouds
To hide its face and cry

Did you ever see a robin weep
When leaves began to die?                                                                   10
Like me, he's lost the will to live
I'm so lonesome I could cry

The silence of a falling star
Lights up a purple sky
And as I wonder where you are                                                               15
I'm so lonesome I could cry

### CONSIDERATIONS FOR CRITICAL THINKING AND WRITING

1. FIRST RESPONSE. Why does the speaker describe nature and a train rather than themselves when expressing loneliness?

2. Discuss the use of personification in the poem.

3. Is the speaker addressing the same person in the first three stanzas of the poem as the one addressed directly in the last? Would the poem have a different effect if the pronoun in the last stanza were "he" or "she" rather than "you"?

### CONNECTION TO ANOTHER SELECTION

1. Compare the way emotion is expressed in this poem and in Kwame Dawes's "The Habits of Love" (p. 590).

## BOB DYLAN (B. 1941)

### *It's Alright, Ma (I'm Only Bleeding)*   1965

Darkness at the break of noon
Shadows even the silver spoon
The handmade blade, the child's balloon
Eclipses both the sun and moon
To understand you know too soon                                                            5
There is no sense in trying

Pointed threats, they bluff with scorn
Suicide remarks are torn
From the fool's gold mouthpiece the hollow horn
Plays wasted words, proves to warn                                                          10
That he not busy being born is busy dying

Temptation's page flies out the door
You follow, find yourself at war
Watch waterfalls of pity roar

Gijsbert Hanekroot/Getty Images.

You feel to moan but unlike before 15
You discover that you'd just be one more
Person crying

So don't fear if you hear
A foreign sound to your ear
It's alright, Ma, I'm only sighing 20

As some warn victory some downfall
Private reasons great or small
Can be seen in the eyes of those that call
To make all that should be killed to crawl
While others say don't hate nothing at all 25
Except hatred

Disillusioned words like bullets bark
As human gods aim for their mark
Make everything from toy guns that spark
To flesh-colored Christs that glow in the dark 30
It's easy to see without looking too far
That not much is really sacred

While preachers preach of evil fates
Teachers teach that knowledge waits
Can lead to hundred-dollar plates 35
Goodness hides behind the gates
But even the president of the United States
Sometimes must have to stand naked

An' though the rules of the road have been lodged
It's only people's games that you got to dodge 40
And it's alright, Ma, I can make it

Advertising signs they con
You into thinking you're the one
That can do what's never been done
That can win what's never been won 45
Meantime life outside goes on
All around you

You lose yourself, you reappear
You suddenly find you got nothing to fear
Alone you stand with nobody near 50
When a trembling distant voice, unclear
Startles your sleeping ears to hear
That somebody thinks they really found you

A question in your nerves is lit
Yet you know there is no answer fit 55
To satisfy, insure you not to quit
To keep it in your mind and not forget
That it is not he or she or them or it
That you belong to

Although the masters make the rules
For the wise men and the fools
I got nothing, Ma, to live up to                    60

For them that must obey authority
That they do not respect in any degree
Who despise their jobs, their destinies              65
Speak jealously of them that are free
Cultivate their flowers to be
Nothing more than something they invest in

While some on principles baptized
To strict party platform ties                        70
Social clubs in drag disguise
Outsiders they can freely criticize
Tell nothing except who to idolize
And then say God bless him

While one who sings with his tongue on fire          75
Gargles in the rat race choir
Bent out of shape from society's pliers
Cares not to come up any higher
But rather get you down in the hole
That he's in                                         80

But I mean no harm nor put fault
On anyone that lives in a vault
But it's alright, Ma, if I can't please him

Old lady judges watch people in pairs
Limited in sex, they dare                            85
To push fake morals, insult and stare
While money doesn't talk, it swears
Obscenity, who really cares
Propaganda, all is phony

While them that defend what they cannot see          90
With a killer's pride, security
It blows the minds most bitterly
For them that think death's honesty
Won't fall upon them naturally
Life sometimes must get lonely                       95

My eyes collide head-on with stuffed
Graveyards, false gods, I scuff
At pettiness which plays so rough
Walk upside-down inside handcuffs
Kick my legs to crash it off                         100
Say okay, I have had enough, what else can you show me?

And if my thought-dreams could be seen
They'd probably put my head in a guillotine
But it's alright, Ma, it's life, and life only

CONSIDERATIONS FOR CRITICAL THINKING AND WRITING

1. FIRST RESPONSE. What is the poem's rhyme scheme and how does it contribute to its overall effect?

2. Identify all the individuals and groups of people in the poem. Is the speaker allied with any of them, or is the speaker completely isolated? If you believe the speaker is isolated, is everyone else basically in the same category? Is it the speaker against the world, in other words?

3. Besides end rhyme, what poetic devices does Dylan employ in this poem? To what effect?

CONNECTION TO ANOTHER SELECTION

1. Compare this poem to Genevieve Taggard's "Ode in Time of Crisis" (p. 727). Are both "protest poems" in the same way?

## JOHN LENNON (1940–1980) AND PAUL MCCARTNEY (B. 1942)

### *I Am the Walrus*　1967

PERFORMED BY THE BEATLES

I am he
As you are he
As you are me
And we are all together

See how they run                                            5
Like pigs from a gun
See how they fly
I'm crying

Sitting on a cornflake
Waiting for the van to come                                  10
Corporation tee shirt
Stupid bloody Tuesday
Man, you been a naughty boy
You let your face grow long

I am the eggman (Ooh)                                        15
They are the eggmen (Ooh)
I am the walrus
Goo goo g' joob

Mister city p'liceman sitting pretty
Little p'licemen in a row                                    20
See how they fly
Like Lucy in the sky
See how they run
I'm crying
I'm crying, I'm crying, I'm crying                           25

Yellow matter custard
Dripping from a dead dog's eye
Crabalocker fishwife pornographic priestess
Boy you been a naughty girl
You let your knickers down          30

I am the eggman (Ooh)
They are the eggmen (Ooh)
I am the walrus
Goo goo g' joob

Sitting in an English          35
Garden waiting for the sun
If the sun don't come
You get a tan from standing in the English rain

I am the eggman
They are the eggmen          40
I am the walrus
Goo goo g' joob g' goo goo g' joob

Expert texpert choking smokers
Don't you think the joker laughs at you?
See how they smile          45
Like pigs in a sty, see how they snied
I'm crying

Semolina pilchards
Climbing up the Eiffel Tower
Element'ry penguin singing Hare Krishna          50
Man, you should have seen them kicking Edgar Allan Poe

I am the eggman (Ooh)
They are the eggmen (Ooh)
I am the walrus
Goo goo g' job          55
Goo goo g' joob
G' goo goo g' joob
Goo goo g' joob, goo goo g' goo g' goo goo g' joob joob
Joob joob . . .

## CONSIDERATIONS FOR CRITICAL THINKING AND WRITING

1. FIRST RESPONSE. What sound qualities do the poets employ or exploit?

2. The poem juxtaposes a number of images that do not seem to belong together. What is the effect of this juxtaposition on the reader?

3. How does the poem employ allusion?

## CONNECTION TO ANOTHER SELECTION

1. Compare "I Am the Walrus" to Lewis Carroll's "Jabberwocky" (p. 651). Which one is more accessible? Why?

## PAUL SIMON (B. 1941)

### *Slip Slidin' Away*   1975

Slip slidin' away
Slip slidin' away
You know the nearer your destination
The more you're slip slidin' away

I know a man                                                           5
He came from my hometown
He wore his passion for his woman
Like a thorny crown
He said, "Delores, I live in fear
My love for you's so overpowering                                     10
I'm afraid that I will disappear"

Slip slidin' away
Slip slidin' away
You know the nearer your destination
The more you're slip slidin' away                                     15

And, I know a woman
Became a wife
These are the very words she uses to describe her life
She said, "A good day
Ain't got no rain"                                                    20
She said, "A bad day's when I lie in bed
And think of things that might have been"

Slip slidin' away
Slip slidin' away
You know the nearer your destination                                  25
The more you're slip slidin' away

And I know a father
Who had a son
He longed to tell him all the reasons
For the things he'd done                                              30
He came a long way
Just to explain
He kissed his boy as he lay sleeping
Then he turned around and headed home again

Slip slidin' away                                                     35
Slip slidin' away
You know the nearer your destination
The more you're slip slidin' away

God only knows
God makes his plan                                                    40
The information's unavailable
To the mortal man

We're working our jobs
Collect our pay
Believe we're gliding down the highway                                45
When in fact we're slip slidin' away

Slip slidin' away
Slip slidin' away
You know the nearer your destination
The more you're slip slidin' away                                     50

### CONSIDERATIONS FOR CRITICAL THINKING AND WRITING

1. FIRST RESPONSE. The speaker of the poem is someone who knows other people but does not reveal much personal information. Do we know anything
   about the speaker based on what they choose to report from the lives of
   others?

2. What does the wisdom from the chorus ("[t]he nearer your destination / The
   more you're slip slidin' away") have to do with each of the examples from the
   verses?

3. The author nicknamed himself "rhymin' Simon" around the time this song
   was released. How does he employ rhyme (not just end rhyme) in this poem?
   To what effect?

### CONNECTION TO ANOTHER SELECTION

1. Discuss the theme of impermanence in this poem and in Robert Frost's
   "Nothing Gold Can Stay" (p. 871).

## ANI DiFRANCO  (B. 1970)

### *Not a Pretty Girl*    1995

I am not a pretty girl
that is not what I do
I ain't no damsel in distress
and I don't need to be rescued
so put me down punk                                                   5
maybe you'd prefer a maiden fair
isn't there a kitten stuck up a tree somewhere

I am not an angry girl
but it seems like I've got everyone fooled
every time I say something they find hard to hear                     10
they chalk it up to my anger
and never to their own fear
and imagine you're a girl
just trying to finally come clean
knowing full well they'd prefer you                                   15

were dirty and smiling

and I am sorry
I am not a maiden fair
and I am not a kitten stuck up a tree somewhere

and generally my generation                                        20
wouldn't be caught dead working for the man
and generally I agree with them
trouble is you gotta have youself an alternate plan
and I have earned my disillusionment
I have been working all of my life                                 25
and I am a patriot
I have been fighting the good fight
and what if there are no damsels in distress
what if I knew that and I called your bluff?
don't you think every kitten figures out how to get down            30
whether or not you ever show up

I am not a pretty girl
I don't want to be a pretty girl
no I want to be more than a pretty girl

### CONSIDERATIONS FOR CRITICAL THINKING AND WRITING

1. FIRST RESPONSE. "Pretty" is historically a term of flattery. How is it used here?

2. When the speaker addresses someone as "punk" in the first stanza, to whom is she speaking? Is it the same person she addresses in the fourth stanza? How do you know?

3. The speaker defines herself by saying what she is not; does she also define who she is, directly or indirectly?

### CONNECTION TO ANOTHER SELECTION

1. Discuss attitudes toward clichés in this poem and in Dorothy Parker's "One Perfect Rose" (p. 548).

### TOM WAITS (B. 1949) AND KATHLEEN BRENNAN (B. 1955)

## *Alice*   2002

It is dreamy weather we're on
You waved your crooked wand
Along an icy pond
With a frozen moon
A murder of silhouette crows I saw                                  5
And the tears on my face
And the skates on the pond
They spell Alice.

I disappear in your name
But you must wait for me                                            10

David Corio/Getty Images

Somewhere across the sea
There's the wreck of a ship
Your hair is like meadow grass
On the tide
And the raindrops on my window                                              15
And the ice in my drink
Baby all I can think of
Is Alice.

Arithmetic arithmetock
Turn the hands back on the clock                                            20
How does the ocean rock the boat?
How did the razor find my throat?
The only strings that hold me here
Are tangled up around the pier.

And so a secret kiss                                                        25
Brings madness with the bliss
And I will think of this
When I'm dead in my grave
Set me adrift and I'm lost over there
And I must be insane                                                        30
To go skating on your name
And by tracing it twice
I fell through the ice
Of Alice.

And so a secret kiss                                                        35
Brings madness with the bliss
And I will think of this
When I'm dead in my grave
Set me adrift and I'm lost over there
And I must be insane                                                        40
To go skating on your name
And by tracing it twice
I fell through the ice
Of Alice.

There's only Alice.                                                         45

## CONSIDERATIONS FOR CRITICAL THINKING AND WRITING

1. FIRST RESPONSE. How would you characterize the relationship between the speaker and Alice?

2. Interpret all of the imagery having to do with ice and water as a way of articulating the poem's theme.

3. Love and death are two of the great subjects of literature. What is the relationship between them in this poem?

## CONNECTION TO ANOTHER SELECTION

1. Compare this poem to Edgar Allen Poe's "Annabel Lee" (p. 943) in terms of the motifs of obsession, naming, and death.

# ADRIANNE LENKER (B. 1991)

## *Not* 2019

PERFORMED BY BIG THIEF

Jana Legler/Getty Images.

It's not the energy reeling
Nor the lines in your face
Nor the clouds on the ceiling
Nor the clouds in space
It's not the phone on the table          5
Nor the bed in the earth
Nor the bed in the stable
Nor your stable words
It's not the formless being
Nor the cry in the air                   10
Nor the girl I'm seeing
With her long black hair
It's not the open weaving
Nor the furnace glow
Nor the blood of you bleeding            15
As you try to let go

It's not the room
Not beginning
Not the crowd
Not winning                              20
Not the planet
Not spinning
Not a ruse
Not heat
Not the fire lapping up the creek        25
Not food
Not to eat

Not the meat of your thigh
Nor your spine tattoo
Nor your shimmery eye                     30
Nor the wet of the dew
It's not the warm illusion
Nor the crack in the plate
Nor the breath of confusion
Nor the starkness of slate               35

It's not the room
Not beginning
Not the crowd
Not winning
Not the planet                           40
Not spinning
Not a ruse
Not heat

Not the fire lapping up the creek
Not food                                                            45
Not to eat

Not what you really wanted
Nor the mess in your purse
Nor the bed that is haunted
With the blanket of thirst                                          50
It's not the hunger revealing
Nor the ricochet in the cave
Nor the hand that is healing
Nor the nameless grave

It's not the room                                                   55
Not beginning
Not the crowd
Not winning
Not the planet
Not spinning                                                        60
Not a ruse
Not heat
Not the fire lapping up the creek
Not food
Not to eat                                                          65

Not to die
Not dying
Not to laugh
Not lying
Not the vacant wilderness vying                                     70

Not the room
Not beginning
Not the crowd
Not winning
Not the planet                                                      75
Not spinning

## CONSIDERATIONS FOR CRITICAL THINKING AND WRITING

1. FIRST RESPONSE. What is the "it" that the song is about? List three possibilities and choose the most compelling one.

2. Choose three images from the poem and discuss what connects them.

3. The poem *seems* chaotic. What does the rhyme scheme do to the chaos of the list?

## CONNECTION TO ANOTHER SELECTION

1. How do this poem and Ani DiFranco's "Not a Pretty Girl" (p. 769) define things by examining their opposites? Are their methods and intents essentially similar or significantly different?

# 27

## A THEMATIC CASE STUDY
# The Poetry of Solitude

Hulton Archive/Getty Images.

When from our better selves we have too long
Been parted by the hurrying world, and droop,
Sick of its business, of its pleasures tired,
How gracious, how benign, is Solitude.
— WILLIAM WORDSWORTH.

We all get "sick of [the world's] business" from time to time, but people tend to have different levels of tolerance. Social scientists divide people into two broad categories: introverts and extroverts. There are countless euphemisms for these terms. An extrovert may be referred to as a *people person*, or *outgoing*, or *always on*. An introvert is a *church mouse*, or a *shrinking violet*, or a *loner,* or a *wallflower*. A common assumption is that the extrovert is confident, and the introvert is shy. The reality, though, is more complex. Contemporary understandings of these terms regard introverts as people who derive their energy during periods of alone time but who are capable of using that energy to excellent effect in public settings. Extroverts recharge their batteries in those social settings, which might mean that alone time — which is a basic human need — could be a situation that those people avoid. The fact of the matter is that most of us move back and forth between these two modes, and blend or combine them within a week, a day, or even within an hour. Rarely is someone purely one way or the other. Our relationship to solitude is thus not entirely predictable.

In our contemporary world, solitude is rare. Even when we're alone, most of us are connected to human activity or to actual humans through the devices we carry in our pockets or unfold on our tables. In the twenty-first century we are surrounded by screens and bombarded by speakers. We put on noise-canceling headphones to listen to a podcast even while shutting out our family members who are trying to get our attention across the room. Even as solitude becomes rare, however, we continue to grapple with what it means to be alone. A number of sociologists and psychologists have fretted about the loss of genuine human contact in our mediated world even as we've found many ways to stay connected to people who aren't right in front of us or to the culture at large.

There are many seeming contradictions in this behavior, but it is an undeniable fact that true solitude is harder to come by than ever before. And yet, beginning in early 2020, the global COVID-19 pandemic forced virtually everyone into an unwelcome state of isolation. When the pandemic lockdown began in the United States in March 2020, the first rule to stop the virus's spread was "stay at home." We learned a new phrase — social distancing — that meant that if we absolutely had to be in public, we were encouraged to stay at least six feet away from others. It quickly became second nature to wear a mask, making communication and connection even more difficult. Our smart phones, it seemed, were suddenly a lifeline rather than a distraction from our ability to concentrate or to converse. Most would agree that while the amount required varies, solitude is a necessary state of being. No one would agree that a deadly pandemic that forces solitude is a desirable way to achieve that end.

The COVID-19 pandemic has caused a widespread reevaluation of social behavior. And yet, the balance between public and private life is an issue that has long been a human dilemma. A great number of human achievements depend on solitude, sometimes in massive doses. We hear a poet read her work in front of an audience, or see our favorite band in concert, or watch an expert from NASA explain a space mission on television, and we perhaps overlook the hours, days, or years they spent alone preparing for this moment, sometimes no doubt in a state of boredom waiting for inspiration, or practicing scales, or watching for a significant observation or data point.

Solitude is not necessarily the same as isolation, or alienation, or loneliness. You can feel lonely in a crowded room, after all. To seek solitude is, in some ways, to take a risk. Would you be willing to spend a week in a cabin by yourself, without a phone and without any human contact? If you're shaking your head emphatically *no*, you're not that unusual. It's scary to consider how much we depend on each other, not just for material support, but for companionship. The writer Henry David Thoreau famously spent a little over two years in a cabin by Walden Pond in Concord, Massachusetts, not exactly to get away from people, but "to live deliberately, to front only the essential facts of life, and see if I could not learn what it had to teach." There is wisdom in solitude, Thoreau believed, and his insights in *Walden* (1854) continue to inspire others to this day.

The poems that follow range from well before Thoreau's time to ours, and they embrace both the desire "to live deliberately" with the experience of solitude and the bleak realities of isolation and loneliness. Before reading, try to gauge your own relationship to solitude. Is it something you embrace or avoid? Something you would like more of or less of? Knowing your own inclinations about this topic will prepare you to understand the broad range of others that exist, and that have always existed.

## JIM MOORE (B. 1943)

### *How to Come Out of Lockdown*    2022

**1**

Someone will need to forgive me for being
who I am, for sneaking back to my blue chair

by the window, where for the last three hundred and seventy day
I have learned that to be alone is what is good for me. I am pretending

as if I really belong with those who want to return to this world      5
with open arms, even though it has done to us

what it has done. I wish I could love like that,
instead of wanting to turn my back on it all,

as if life in the world were a marriage
assumed too young and necessarily left behind.      10

Try as I might I will never become
one of the world's faithful ones.

My naked face and your naked face,
maskless. A cold March dawn,

harsh sunlight, impersonal and honest,      15
mindless like the light from a surgeon's lamp

worn on the forehead as you peer down
into the wound. Nothing in this new life

is asked of me except to remember how small I am.

**2**

Sometimes the world won't let itself      20
be sung. Can't become a poem. Sometimes

we are sane, but sanity alone is not enough.
Warm moonlight and wind. I am sitting here,

simply breathing because there is no other way
to be with those who no longer can.      25

I don't know what to say about it all,
but if you do please show me how to be you.

In the last play I saw, fourteen months ago,
before there were no more plays,

they had made a sea of the stage. Songs were chanted          30
on its shore. Lives lived. People pretended to die

and a ship sailed into the night. A moon. One star.
Afterward, applause. Then began that long silence

which it is now time for me to admit I have loved
beyond any reason or defense. Who among us          35

has not seen that star to the left
of the lockdown moon, shining

as the ship sets sail?

### Considerations for Critical Thinking and Writing

1. **First response.** What did you learn about yourself during the lockdown and how does it compare to what this speaker learns?

2. List the noticeable differences between parts 1 and 2 of the poem and consider what these differences mean to the poem's overall effect.

3. Each of the two parts contains exactly one stanza that is a complete sentence. Locate those two stanzas and consider how they are keys to interpreting the poem.

4. The final six stanzas of the poem develop an image that the speaker derives from watching a play. How does this image fit in with the themes developed prior to its introduction?

### Connection to Another Selection

1. Compare the tone and theme of this poem to Jennifer Franklin's "Memento Mori: Apple Orchard" (p. 756).

## Emily Dickinson (1830–1886)

### *The Soul selects her own Society —*   ca. 1862

The Soul selects her own Society —
Then — shuts the Door —
To her divine Majority —
Present no more —

Unmoved — she notes the Chariots — pausing —          5
At her low Gate —
Unmoved — an Emperor be kneeling
Upon her Mat —

I've known her — from an ample nation —
Choose One — 10
Then — close the Valves of her attention —
Like Stone —

## CONSIDERATIONS FOR CRITICAL THINKING AND WRITING

1. FIRST RESPONSE. How would the poem's meaning immediately change if the soul were still allowed to select her own society, but not to "shut the door" to others?

2. What is the tone of the poem and how does its imagery contribute to it?

3. What is the effect of repeating the word "Unmoved"? How does it help you understand the poem's theme?

4. How do you understand the introduction of an explicit speaker ("I") in line 9? What is that entity's relationship to "the Soul"?

## CONNECTION TO ANOTHER SELECTION

1. Compare the content and form of this poem to Alexander Pope's "Ode on Solitude" (p. 704). How much common ground exists between them?

## ROBERT FROST (1874–1963)

### *Stopping by Woods on a Snowy Evening*  1923

Whose woods these are I think I know.
His house is in the village, though;
He will not see me stopping here
To watch his woods fill up with snow.

My little horse must think it queer 5
To stop without a farmhouse near
Between the woods and frozen lake
The darkest evening of the year.

He gives his harness bells a shake
To ask if there is some mistake. 10
The only other sound's the sweep
Of easy wind and downy flake.

The woods are lovely, dark and deep,
But I have promises to keep,
And miles to go before I sleep, 15
And miles to go before I sleep.

## CONSIDERATIONS FOR CRITICAL THINKING AND WRITING

1. FIRST RESPONSE. The speaker claims he is stopping "to watch [the] woods fill up with snow" (line 4), and he acknowledges even his horse must consider it odd behavior. Do you understand why he stops?

2. What is the poem's rhyme scheme? What is the effect of repeating the final line?

3. If the speaker did not have "promises to keep" (line 14) and miles to travel, what would prevent him from staying in these woods indefinitely?

4. How is the horse personified, and why?

### CONNECTION TO ANOTHER SELECTION

1. Compare the relationship between humanity and nature in the context of solitude in this poem and in Robert Lowell's "Skunk Hour" (p. 782).

## JOHN KEATS (1795–1821)

### *To Solitude*   1816

O Solitude! if I must with thee dwell,
   Let it not be among the jumbled heap
   Of murky buildings: climb with me the steep, —
Nature's observatory — whence the dell,
Its flowery slopes, its river's crystal swell,             5
   May seem a span; let me thy vigils keep
   'Mongst boughs pavilion'd, where the deer's swift leap
Startles the wild bee from the foxglove bell.
But though I'll gladly trace these scenes with thee,
   Yet the sweet converse of an innocent mind,         10
   Whose words are images of thoughts refined,
Is my soul's pleasure; and it sure must be
   Almost the highest bliss of human-kind,
When to thy haunts two kindred spirits flee.

### CONSIDERATIONS FOR CRITICAL THINKING AND WRITING

1. FIRST RESPONSE. If you have to be alone, would you rather be in nature or tucked in a room somewhere in a populated place like a city or a campus? Why?

2. The poem is a Petrarchan sonnet (see Chapter 23): how does the poem's form help present its content?

3. Is the speaker lonely for a companion or just imagining that solitude in nature would be even better with one?

4. What's the effect of addressing the poem to solitude as opposed to talking about solitude as a concept?

### CONNECTION TO ANOTHER SELECTION

1. Compare the poem's exploration of human relationships to Emily Dickinson's "Some keep the Sabbath going to Church–" (p. 836).

## Elisa Gonzalez (b. 1989)

### In Quarantine, I Reflect on the Death of Ophelia  2020

Simon Bahçeli.

I wake early and angry, I eat oatmeal with
    thyme honey,
I call my sister, I call my mother, I call my other
    sisters, my brothers,
I worry about my feverish lover, I worry about
    my siblings, jobless now.
I send an ill-advised e-mail, I don't send an
    ill-advised tweet.

I'm alone so I'm lonely. That's what my sister says.     5

Time to stay indoors, the doctor says, all the doctors say,
but the open window betrays that not everyone's voice dies to solitude.
Shut up, shut up! the window slams.
Time to embrace the virtues of boredom, the price of happiness again, after.

The window shows men digging a place for survivors of the future,
    the rich ones.     10
It will be a condo tower, glass walls for better envy.
They've built the frames, I see, around the holes where doors will someday go.
Capitalism! So full of holes and hope.

If I try to remember what it was like, childhood, a period of kudzu
growth that *felt* like stasis in the white-glazed room where days
    upon days my father shut me—     15
if I try, I see the ceiling, that water stain trailing down
like brown Pre-Raphaelite° curls, hair of a drowning girl among reeds,
which later I recognized in a painting of a pale drowning Ophelia.

I love alone, I tell my sister. She says, You just want to.

I agree I want the past.     20
For a magnolia to bloom on a crowded street, all safe in beauty, for I
still love the world, though it drowns
and dies like that girl, avoidably.

A professor once asked, pleased we wouldn't know,
Who is really responsible for the death of Ophelia?     25
The answer, he said, ought to feel like we have arrived together
at a skyscraper's peak, where the inhuman
view reveals in windows and in streets
the small, sick or potentially sick bodies—each one a new array of questions.

The only possible epiphany is that the ending of a thought is never such.     30

---

17 *Pre-Raphaelite:* A group of artists and thinkers in mid-twentieth century England. Their paintings — including a famous one of a drowned Ophelia by John Everett Millais — are characterized by vivid colors and elaborate detail harkening back to the Italian Renaissance.

*Together.* I liked the word in the professor's mouth.
But if I am alone, and if I am lonely, and if I am not alone in loneliness,
    and if the everyone
together suffers, and if this everyone suffers and dies by the unguided
    motion of matter, and if
also by the motion of craven, murderous men, and if also by the motion
    of money, and if of course
you were always going to die, Ophelia, and if even so your death remains
    unforgivable,                                                                                      35
then what are the questions I should ask? All I have is sleeplessness and rage,
and that's no answer, it's not even a thought, though it might not end till
    my body does,
perhaps not even then, as I can imagine it going on past my ending, and really—
what more suitable ghost could I leave behind? Since I do love the world.

### CONSIDERATIONS FOR CRITICAL THINKING AND WRITING

1. **FIRST RESPONSE.** Do you read the poem more as a statement of the speaker's
   anxious mood or as a way to try to get beyond her anxiety by working through
   her feelings in verse?

2. The poem is built around an allusion to Hamlet's ill-fated lover Ophelia in
   Shakespeare's play. How does the allusion function in this poem?

3. How does the speaker's window operate as a symbol?

4. What is the speaker's reaction to what others say? Are everyone's pronouncements regarded as essentially the same or do some voices have added weight?

5. What is your response to the poem's final line? Does it contradict what precedes it or is it the key to understanding the poem?

### CONNECTION TO ANOTHER SELECTION

1. Compare responses to the pandemic lockdown in this poem and in Jim
   Moore's "How to Come Out of Lockdown" (p. 776).

## WILLIAM WORDSWORTH (1770–1850)
## *I Wandered Lonely as a Cloud*    1807

I wandered lonely as a cloud
That floats on high o'er vales and hills,
When all at once I saw a crowd,
A host, of golden daffodils;
Beside the lake, beneath the trees,                                    5
Fluttering and dancing in the breeze.

Continuous as the stars that shine
And twinkle on the milky way,
They stretched in never-ending line
Along the margin of a bay:                                             10
Ten thousand saw I at a glance,
Tossing their heads in sprightly dance.

Hulton Archive/Getty Images.

The waves beside them danced; but they
Out-did the sparkling waves in glee:
A poet could not but be gay,                    15
In such a jocund company:
I gazed — and gazed — but little thought
What wealth the show to me had brought:

For oft, when on my couch I lie
In vacant or in pensive mood,                   20
They flash upon that inward eye
Which is the bliss of solitude;
And then my heart with pleasure fills,
And dances with the daffodils.

### CONSIDERATIONS FOR CRITICAL THINKING AND WRITING

1. FIRST RESPONSE. What is the "bliss of solitude," both in the poem and in your own understanding of that term?

2. How does the simile comparing the speaker to a cloud work?

3. What's the difference between the outward eye and what the speaker calls "that inward eye" in the poem's final stanza? Why is the relationship between them crucial to the poem's theme?

4. What is important about the daffodils? What, symbolically, might they represent? Could anything else have provoked the same revelation in the speaker or did it have to be daffodils?

### CONNECTION TO ANOTHER SELECTION

1. Wordsworth was part of a group of poets known as the English Romantics, as was John Keats whose poem "To Solitude" (p. 779) is also in this chapter. In your reading of these two poems, is it clear why the two poets would be in the same category or not? What are the key connections or divergences that contribute to your response?

### ROBERT LOWELL (1917–1977)

## *Skunk Hour*   1960

*(For Elizabeth Bishop)*

Nautilus Island's° hermit
heiress still lives through winter in her Spartan cottage;
her sheep still graze above the sea.
Her son's a bishop. Her farmer
is first selectman in our village;                5
she's in her dotage.

Thirsting for
the hierarchic privacy

---

1 *Nautilus Island's:* In Maine.

of Queen Victoria's century,
she buys up all
the eyesores facing her shore,
and lets them fall.

The season's ill —
we've lost our summer millionaire,
who seemed to leap from an L.L. Bean°
catalogue. His nine-knot yawl
was auctioned off to lobstermen.
A red fox stain covers Blue Hill.

And now our fairy
decorator brightens his shop for fall;
his fishnet's filled with orange cork,
orange, his cobbler's bench and awl;
there is no money in his work,
he'd rather marry.

One dark night,
my Tudor Ford climbed the hill's skull;
I watched for love-cars. Lights turned down,
they lay together, hull to hull,
where the graveyard shelves on the town. . . .
My mind's not right.

A car radio bleats,
"Love, O careless Love. . . . " I hear
my ill-spirit sob in each blood cell,
as if my hand were at its throat. . . .
I myself am hell;
nobody's here —

only skunks, that search
in the moonlight for a bite to eat.
They march on their soles up Main Street:
white stripes, moonstruck eyes' red fire
under the chalk-dry and spar spire
of the Trinitarian Church.

I stand on top
of our back steps and breathe the rich air —
a mother skunk with her column of kittens swills the garbage pail.
She jabs her wedge-head in a cup
of sour cream, drops her ostrich tail,
and will not scare.

15 *L.L. Bean:* Freeport, Maine, mail-order house.

## CONSIDERATIONS FOR CRITICAL THINKING AND WRITING

1. **FIRST RESPONSE.** What is your opinion of skunks? Did you ever imagine one would be the heroic figure in a poem?

2. How does the rhyme scheme change over the course of the poem and why might this change be important?

3. When are you first aware of the speaker in the poem? Why might they wait so long to reveal themselves?

4. Carefully read stanza 6. How is it crucial to an understanding of the poem's theme?

5. How does the skunk act as inspiration for the speaker? What are its qualities?

## CONNECTION TO ANOTHER SELECTION

1. Contrast the speaker's views of nature's creatures in this poem and in Sylvia Plath's "The Pheasant" (p. 754).

## GALWAY KINNELL (1927–2014)

# *When One Has Lived a Long Time Alone*   1990

### 1

When one has lived a long time alone,
one refrains from swatting the fly
and lets him go, and one hesitates to strike
the mosquito, though more than willing to slap
the flesh under her, and one lifts the toad                                5
from the pit too deep for him to hop out of
and carries him to the grass, without minding
the toxic urine he slicks his body with,
and one envelops, in a towel, the swift
who fell down the chimney and knocks herself                              10
against window glass and releases her outside
and watches her fly free, a life line flung at reality,
when one has lived a long time alone.

### 2

When one has lived a long time alone,
one grabs the snake behind the head                                       15
and holds him until he stops trying to stick
the orange tongue, which splits at the end
into two black filaments and jumps out
like a fire-eater's belches and has little
in common with the pimpled pink lump that shapes                          20
sounds and sleeps inside the human mouth,
into one's flesh, and clamps it between his jaws,
letting the gaudy tips show, as children do
when concentrating, and as very likely
one does oneself, without knowing it,                                     25
when one has lived a long time alone.

## 3

When one has lived a long time alone,
among regrets so immense the past occupies
nearly all the room there is in consciousness,
one notices in the snake's eyes, which look back      30
without paying less attention to the future,
the first coating of the opaque milky-blue
leucoma snakes get when about to throw
their skins and become new—meanwhile continuing,
of course, to grow old—the exact *bleu passé,*°      35
that discolors the corneas of the blue-eyed
when they lie back at last and look for heaven,
a blurring one can see means they will never find it,
when one has lived a long time alone.

## 4

When one has lived a long time alone,            40
one holds the snake near a loudspeaker disgorging
gorgeous sound and watches him crook
his forepart into four right angles
as though trying to slow down the music
flowing through him, in order to absorb it        45
like milk of paradise into the flesh,
and now a glimmering appears at his mouth,
such a drop of intense fluid as, among humans,
could form after long exciting at the tip
of the penis, and as he straightens himself out   50
he has the pathos one finds in the penis,
when one has lived a long time alone.

## 5

When one has lived a long time alone,
one can fall to poring upon a creature,
contrasting its eternity's-face to one's own       55
full of hours, taking note of each difference,
exaggerating it, making it everything,
until the other is utterly other, and then,
with hard effort, possibly with tongue sticking out,
going back over each one once again                60
and cancelling it, seeing nothing now
but likeness, until . . . half an hour later
one starts awake, taken aback at how eagerly
one swoons into the happiness of kinship,
when one has lived a long time alone.              65

35 *bleu passé:* French for "past blue," a shade of faded blue.

**6**

When one has lived a long time alone
and listens at morning to mourning doves
sound their *kyrie eleison*,° or the small thing
spiritualizing onto one's shoulder cry "pewit-phoebe!"
or peabody-sparrows at midday send schoolboys'          70
whistlings across the field, or at dusk, undamped,
unforgiving clinks, as from stonemasons' chisels,
or on trees' backs tree frogs scratch the thighs'
needfire awake, or from the frog pond pond frogs
raise their *ave verum corpus*°— listens to those          75
who hop or fly call down upon us the mercy
of other tongues— one hears them as inner voices,
when one has lived a long time alone.

**7**

When one has lived a long time alone,
one knows only consciousness consummates,          80
and as the conscious one among these others
uttering compulsory cries of being here—
the least flycatcher witching up "che-bec,"
or redheaded woodpecker clanging out his
music from a metal drainpipe, or ruffed grouse          85
drumming "thrump thrump thrump thrump-thrump-
thrump-thrump-rup-rup-rup-rup-rup-r-r-r-r-r-r-"
through the trees, all of them in time's
unfolding trying to cry themselves into self-knowing—
one knows one is here to hear them into shining,          90
when one has lived a long time alone.

**8**

When one has lived a long time alone,
one likes alike the pig, who brooks no deferment
of gratification, and the porcupine, or thorned pig,
who enters the cellar but not the house itself          95
because of eating down the cellar stairs on the way up,
and one likes the worm, who by bunching herself together
and expanding rubs her way through the ground,
no less than the butterfly, who totters full of worry
among the day-lilies, as they darken,          100
and more and more one finds one likes
any other species better than one's own,
which has gone amok, making one self-estranged,
when one has lived a long time alone.

---

68  *kyrie eleison:* Greek, for "Lord, have mercy." This phrase is used in prayer and as a congregational response in several Christian churches.

75  *ave verum corpus:* A chant used in the Catholic Mass when the holy Eucharist is raised; it has also been set to music by many composers, including Mozart.

## 9

When one has lived a long time alone,                                    105
sour, misanthropic, one fits to one's defiance
the satanic boast— *It is better to reign*
*in hell than to submit on earth*—
and forgets one's kind, as does the snake,
who has stopped trying to escape and moves                               110
at ease across one's body, slumping into its contours,
adopting its temperature, and abandons hope
of the sweetness of friendship or love
—before long can barely remember what they are—
and covets the stillness in inorganic matter,                            115
in a self-dissolution one may not know how to halt,
when one has lived a long time alone.

## 10

When one has lived a long time alone,
and the hermit thrush calls and there is an answer,
and the bullfrog, head half out of water, remembers                      120
the exact sexual cantillations of his first spring,
and the snake slides over the threshold and disappears
among the stones, one sees they all live
to mate with their kind, and one knows,
after a long time of solitude, after the many steps taken                125
away from one's kind, toward the kingdom of strangers,
the hard prayer inside one's own singing
is to come back, if one can, to one's own,
a world almost lost, in the exile that deepens,
when one has lived a long time alone.                                    130

## 11

When one has lived a long time alone,
one wants to live again among men and women,
to return to that place where one's ties with the human
broke, where the disquiet of death and now
also of history glimmers its firelight on faces,                         135
where the gaze of the new baby looks past the gaze
of the great-granny, and where lovers speak,
on lips blowsy from kissing, that language
the same in each mouth, and like birds at daybreak
blether the song that is both earth's and heaven's,                      140
until the sun has risen, and they stand
in a halo of being united: kingdom come,
when one has lived a long time alone.

## Considerations for Critical Thinking and Writing

1. FIRST RESPONSE. The speaker uses the impersonal pronoun "one" in the repeated lines at the beginning and end of each stanza. What is the effect of "one" as opposed to "I" in this case?

2. List all the creatures from nature the speaker discusses. Is this just a random catalog or is there a pattern in it?

3. The first stanza shows the speaker's clear desire to preserve rather than harm or destroy other animals. Does that sentiment persist throughout the poem or is it replaced by something else?

4. The final stanza is clearly different from all the others. After you've read all of them, reread the poem with the final stanza in mind. Does its existence alter the way you read the rest of the poem?

5. Is this poem's tone joyful or sad, or would you use a different term altogether?

### Connection to Another Selection

1. Compare this poem to Robert Lowell's "Skunk Hour" (p. 782) in terms of the way the speakers approach their own crisis. Do they use similar methods? Do they arrive at similar conclusions?

## Robert Hayden (1913–1980)

### *Those Winter Sundays* 1962

Sundays too my father got up early
and put his clothes on in the blueblack cold,
then with cracked hands that ached
from labor in the weekday weather made
banked fires blaze. No one ever thanked him.           5

I'd wake and hear the cold splintering, breaking.
When the rooms were warm, he'd call,
and slowly I would rise and dress,
fearing the chronic angers of that house,

Speaking indifferently to him,                         10
who had driven out the cold
and polished my good shoes as well.
What did I know, what did I know
of love's austere and lonely offices?

## Considerations for Critical Thinking and Writing

1. FIRST RESPONSE. What emotion does the poem evoke with regard to the solitary father figure: Pity? Sorrow? Fear? Something else?

2. There is a bleak, spare tone to this poem. What words or phrases contribute to it? Does the "love" in the final line do anything to balance it?

3. The speaker notes that "No one ever thanked" his father for his labors (line 5). Is the poem an attempt to show gratitude or is it just an acknowledgment that it never came?

4. How does the phrase "chronic angers of that house" (line 9) function in relation to the rest of the poem?

### CONNECTION TO ANOTHER SELECTION

1. Compare understandings of love in this poem and in Kwame Dawes's "The Habits of Love" (p. 590).

## MATTHEW ARNOLD (1822–1888)

### *Dover Beach*    1867

The sea is calm tonight.
The tide is full, the moon lies fair
Upon the straits; — on the French coast the light
Gleams and is gone; the cliffs of England stand,
Glimmering and vast, out in the tranquil bay.                                  5
Come to the window, sweet is the night-air!
Only, from the long line of spray
Where the sea meets the moon-blanched land,
Listen! you hear the grating roar
Of pebbles which the waves draw back, and fling,                              10
At their return, up the high strand,
Begin, and cease, and then again begin,
With tremulous cadence slow, and bring
The eternal note of sadness in.

Sophocles long ago                                                           15
Heard it on the Aegean, and it brought
Into his mind the turbid ebb and flow
Of human misery;° we
Find also in the sound a thought,
Hearing it by this distant northern sea.                                     20

The Sea of Faith
Was once, too, at the full, and round earth's shore
Lay like the folds of a bright girdle furled.
But now I only hear
Its melancholy, long, withdrawing roar,                                      25
Retreating, to the breath
Of the night-wind, down the vast edges drear
And naked shingles° of the world.                              *pebble beaches*
Ah, love, let us be true
To one another! for the world, which seems                                   30
To lie before us like a land of dreams,

15–18 *Sophocles ... misery:* In Antigone (lines 656–677), Sophocles likens the disasters that beset the house of Oedipus to a "mounting tide."

So various, so beautiful, so new,
Hath really neither joy, nor love, nor light,
Nor certitude, nor peace, nor help for pain;
And we are here as on a darkling plain          35
Swept with confused alarms of struggle and flight,
Where ignorant armies clash by night.

### CONSIDERATIONS FOR CRITICAL THINKING AND WRITING

1. FIRST RESPONSE. Do you imagine that the speaker is speaking directly to his love or is this conversation in his head? Explain your response.

2. Contrast the images in lines 4–8 and 9–13. How do they reveal the speaker's mood?

3. What is the cause of the "sadness" in line 14? What is the speaker's response to the ebbing "Sea of Faith"? Is there anything to replace his sense of loss?

4. Describe the differences in tone between lines 1–8 and 35–37. What has caused the change?

### CONNECTION TO ANOTHER SELECTION

1. Compare ocean imagery in this poem to the imagery found in Alfred, Lord Tennyson's "Break, Break, Break" (p. 653)

## DIONISIO D. MARTÍNEZ (B. 1956)

### *Flood: Years of Solitude*   1995

To the one who sets a second place at the table anyway.
To the one at the back of the empty bus.
To the ones who name each piece of stained glass projected on a white wall.
To anyone convinced that a monologue is a conversation with the past.
To the one who loses with the deck he marked.          5
To those who are destined to inherit the meek.
To us.

### CONSIDERATIONS FOR CRITICAL THINKING AND WRITING

1. FIRST RESPONSE. Did the final line of the poem change your response to the rest of it?

2. Does each of the lines work separately or do they all depend on one another?

3. Line 6 contains an allusion to the Bible that states, "The meek shall inherit the earth." How does the poet invert its meaning?

4. How essential is the title to an understanding of the poem?

### CONNECTIONS TO OTHER SELECTIONS

1. Which poem best conforms to your definition or understanding of solitude: this one, Keats's "To Solitude" (p. 779), or Li Bai's "The Solitude of Night" (p. 791), all of which use the word in their titles?

## Li Bai (701–762)

## *The Solitude of Night*

TRANSLATED BY SHIGEYOSHI OBATA

It was at a wine party—
I lay in a drowse, knowing it not.
The blown flowers fell and filled my lap.
When I arose, still drunken,
The birds had all gone to their nests,                                    5
And there remained but few of my comrades.
I went along the river—alone in the moonlight.

### Considerations for Critical Thinking and Writing

1. FIRST RESPONSE. The speaker does not identify a feeling but rather describes a scene. What feeling is evoked in you as you read the poem?
2. How do the images of the birds and flowers connect to the speaker?
3. How crucial is it that the poem takes place at night? How is moonlight different from sunlight, symbolically?

### Connection to Another Selection

1. Compare the tone of this poem to that of Robert Frost's "Desert Places" (p. 874).

### Suggested Topics for Longer Papers

1. According to a selection of three to five poems from this chapter, what do poets see as the chief benefit of solitude?
2. Which speakers seek connection to end their solitude? Are they successful?
3. What element of poetry is the most crucial one when writing effectively about solitude? Cite examples from multiple poems in this chapter.

# 28

## A CULTURAL CASE STUDY

# Harlem Renaissance Poets
## Claude McKay, Georgia Douglas Johnson, Langston Hughes, and Countee Cullen

I believe that poetry should be direct, comprehensible, and the epitome of simplicity.
— LANGSTON HUGHES

Library of Congress/Getty Images.

The end of World War I coincided with a steady increase of Black Americans migrating from the rural South to major cities in the North, such as Chicago and New York, looking for work and for a more accepting racial environment. This period, known as the Great Migration, saw the movement of some 1.5 million African Americans from the rural southern United States to industrialized northern cities over the course of less than two decades. Along with the desire for a better life, they brought with them unique cultural expressions, notably the potent musical traditions that we have come to recognize as jazz and the blues. In the 1920s, Harlem, a neighborhood in uptown Manhattan, became the creative center of Black American literature, music, dance, painting, and sculpture. The artistic production that thrived during this period and in this section of New York City is known as the "Harlem Renaissance" (though Harlem was not its only location) and its ongoing influence on American cultural life is deep and broad. In addition to its status as a cultural

In this 1932 image taken by African American photographer James VanDerZee, a Harlem couple in fur coats poses with a gleaming Cadillac on West 127th Street. VanDerZee once commented, "I tried to pose each person in such a way as to tell a story." His work offered America a dazzling view of Black middle-class life in the 1920s and 1930s.

Couple in Raccoon Coats, Harlem, 1932 / Van Der Zee, James / Minneapolis Institute of Arts, MN, USA/Bridgeman Images.

center, Harlem was also a political center with access to a variety of publishing opportunities. Much of the energy driving the Harlem Renaissance was generated by the determination of civil rights organizations located in Harlem to improve the status and dignity of African Americans by exposing white audiences to Black artistic talent. The National Association for the Advancement of Colored People (NAACP), the National Urban League (NUL), and the Universal Negro Improvement Association (UNIA) all worked to further social progress by promoting, publishing, and reviewing Black writers and artists. Newspapers and journals by and for African Americans flourished during the Renaissance: journals and literary magazines such as *The Crisis, Survey Graphic, Opportunity, Fire!!*, and *The Messenger* provided a written record of the poems, essays, and stories that could be widely distributed in their day and are still studied in ours. A half century after the abolition of slavery, African Americans arrived at an extraordinary moment of creative and intellectual production.

In 1925, Alain Locke characterized this convergence of talent as a "Mecca" of creativity; in *The New Negro*, an influential anthology showcasing writers and artists, he announced that "[t]he pulse of the Negro world has begun to

The famous Lafayette Theatre, located near 132nd Street on 7th Avenue, known during the Harlem Renaissance as the "Boulevard of Dreams," was one of New York's first theaters to desegregate (ca. 1912). The theater (now a church) seated two thousand people and, beginning in 1916, employed its own Lafayette Players, who performed popular and classical plays for almost exclusively Black audiences. Known as the "House Beautiful" to many of its patrons, the Lafayette also showcased blues singer Bessie Smith (p. 760), jazz composer Duke Ellington, and other prominent African American performers. Shown here is the vibrant opening night of Shakespeare's *Macbeth*, staged by Orson Welles, with a musical score by James P. Johnson (1936). GRANGER — Historical Picture Archive.

beat in Harlem." Locke, a Rhodes scholar with a Ph.D. from Harvard, celebrated and encouraged the artistic and intellectual life in Harlem because he believed it was an enlargement of democratic opportunity for Black Americans. He described Harlem as "the first concentration in history of so many diverse elements of Negro life. It has attracted the African, the West Indian, the Negro American; has brought together the Negro of the North and the Negro of the South; the man from the city and the man from the town and the village; the peasant, the student, the businessman, the professional man, artist, poet, musician, adventurer and worker, preacher and criminal, exploiter and social outcast." Black expression and self-determination had found a home in Harlem, a neighborhood that offered not only an enticingly exotic nightlife but also some refuge and relief from the social oppression and racism routinely encountered elsewhere. Although the Prohibition nightclubs were mostly for "whites only" and Black workers and performers were required to enter through service doors, a good many Black Harlem residents exercised their freedom in the arts and in their own assertions of self-expression, even if the many white visitors who frequented the clubs for blues, jazz, and raucous fun ignored the hard realities of Black poverty as well as the achievements of Black artists.

In literature, the heart of that culture in the 1920s was primarily poetry — although fiction and drama also flourished — and Claude McKay, Langston Hughes, and Countee Cullen were three of its most significant poets. (Hughes — considered by most the central figure of the Renaissance — also wrote fiction, plays, memoirs, and journalism.) Georgia Douglas Johnson, another noteworthy poet, made important contributions to the Renaissance from her home in Washington, D.C., pointing to the fact that there was more to the Harlem Renaissance than the concentrated cultural explosion in Harlem. Her poetry, along with the meetings she orchestrated in her home for the socially and politically conscious literary elites who were at the intellectual center of the Harlem Renaissance, brought to center stage the value and importance of Black cultural awareness.

There were certainly tensions between the artists and unofficial architects of the Renaissance who strove to define what they were doing even as they were doing it. Not everyone agreed about the proper way to address the persistent effects of racism, for example. Zora Neale Hurston (see her story "Sweat" on p. 475) sought to distinguish herself from what she called "the sobbing school of Negrohood who hold that nature has somehow given them a lowdown dirty deal and whose feelings are all but about it." Her optimistic exuberance is in contrast with a more troubled writer like Countee Cullen: his poem "Incident" (p. 817) reveals a depth of psychological torment that will seemingly never be erased. These individual attitudes sometimes connected to attitudes toward race and the connection to an African past. Throughout his long career as a professional writer, Hughes remained true to the African American heritage he celebrated in his writings, which were frankly "racial in theme and treatment, derived from the life I know." In an influential essay, "The Negro Artist and the Racial Mountain" (1926), he insisted on the need for Black artists to draw on their heritage rather than "to run away spiritually from race":

> We younger Negro artists who create now intend to express our individual dark-skinned selves without fear or shame. If white people are pleased, we are glad. If they are not, it doesn't matter. We know we are beautiful. And ugly too. The tom-tom cries and the tom-tom laughs. If colored people are pleased we are glad. If they are not, their displeasure doesn't matter either. We build our temples for tomorrow, strong as we know how, and we stand on top of the mountain, free within ourselves.

The themes of racial pride and personal dignity work their way through some forty books that Hughes wrote, edited, or compiled during his forty-five years of writing.

Many Harlem Renaissance writers recognized the importance of reclaiming a neglected and discounted past damaged by slavery and bigotry as a means of forging a more promising future. In a famous 1925 essay, "The Negro Digs

Up His Past," Arthur A. Schomburg (best known as the creator and curator of what would eventually become the Schomburg Center for Research in Black Culture of the New York Public Library) argued that "African cultural origins and sources" had to be retrieved from obscurity: "The Negro has been a man without a history because he has been considered a man without a worthy culture." This understanding and appreciation of African art helped to generate an interest in the "primitive" and more experimental styles that broke through conventional forms.

Related to this reclamation is an important anthology edited by James Weldon Johnson that includes the work of a number of new poets, such as that of Claude McKay. In *The Book of American Negro Poetry* (1922), Johnson's introductory essay called for a new, uniquely African American aesthetic that acknowledged the past but was not confined by it. He recognized and applauded the necessity for Black poets to move beyond the sort of "subject-matter which went into the making of traditional dialect poetry, 'possums, watermelons, etc." and the limitations imposed by conventional "Negro dialect" expected by white people. The poet Paul Laurence Dunbar (1872–1906), for example, owed much of his literary reputation to the kind of poetry later denounced by Johnson, as illustrated by these lines from "Little Brown Baby" (1896):

> Little brown baby wif spa'klin' eyes
>    Who's pappy's darlin' an' who's pappy's chile?
> Who is it all de day nevah once tries
>    Fu' to be cross, er once loses dat smile?

Instead of writing this kind of stereotypical dialect, according to Johnson, what Black poets needed to do to make a genuine contribution to American literature was

> to find a form that will express the racial spirit by symbols from within rather than by symbols from without, such as the mere mutilation of English spelling and pronunciation. He needs a form that is freer and larger than dialect, but which will still hold the racial flavor; a form expressing the imagery, the idioms, the peculiar turns of thought, and the distinctive humor and pathos, too, of the Negro, but which will also be capable of voicing the deepest and highest emotions and aspirations, and allow of the widest scope of treatment.

Two of the major ingredients of that "racial flavor" were the everyday speech of Black people and the jazz rhythms produced by musicians like Louis Armstrong and Duke Ellington. By valuing the folk traditions of their people, many Black poets addressed the concerns of their fellow African Americans in poems that could be read with no formal training or extensive literary background, poems that were "direct, comprehensible, and the epitome of simplicity" as Hughes put it. Readers of James Weldon Johnson's *God's Trombones* (1927) did not require academic help to appreciate his free-verse arrangements adapted from the sermons of Black preachers. Hughes drew on an oral tradition of working-class folk poetry that embraced informal language at a time when some middle-class Black Americans felt that the use of the vernacular was an embarrassment and an impediment to social progress. Poets like Hughes, who were sometimes accompanied by jazz musicians or blues singers, nevertheless found appreciative audiences who reveled in the energy and freedom of the open, or free-verse, form and improvisations that incorporated suffering, yearning, and heartache, along with resilience and humor. Yet not all artists in the Renaissance agreed about how to strike a meaningful balance between the forging of a uniquely Black art and the demands of the white-dominated cultural marketplace. Poets like Countee Cullen and Claude McKay, for example, wrote sonnets while Hughes was attempting to imitate the blues in his poems.

Though extremely influential, the Harlem Renaissance was not long-lived. By the end of the 1920s, this energy could not sustain the level of artistic production and intensity that the decade had earlier promised. The ebullient optimism, patronage, and publishing opportunities that created attentive audiences in the Jazz Age twenties collapsed with the stock market crash of 1929 and the economic casualties produced by the Depression. In the 1930s and 1940s many African American intellectuals and artists turned toward communism as a way of sustaining the solidarity they had begun to discover during the Renaissance period. Even two of the primary figures of the Renaissance — Hughes and W. E. B. Du Bois — were drawn to that ideology, and the next generation of Black writers, especially Richard Wright, embraced it fully. Yet the undercurrents of the Renaissance — including the

The Renaissance Casino (or the "Renny," as it was often called) was an important center for the arts, sports, and more during the Harlem Renaissance.
Bridgeman Images.

intense examination of Black identity in the aftermath of slavery, the importance of Black popular cultural expression such as jazz and the blues, and the pursuit of racial pride in a country prone to racial hostility — have not gone away. It is productive to think of the Renaissance not as a distinct historical period, but as an opening that has produced cultural opportunities previously unavailable.

## CLAUDE McKAY (1889–1948)

Historical/Getty Images.

Claude McKay was born to peasant farmers on the island of Jamaica. His father, the son of enslaved people, descended from a West African tribe and familiarized him during his childhood with African folk stories. As a young man, McKay used money from the Jamaica Medal of the Institute for the Arts awarded for his two 1912 collections of dialect poetry, *Songs of Jamaica* and *Constab Ballads* (the latter about his experiences as a police constable) to immigrate to the United States. After studying at Tuskegee Institute and Kansas State College, he moved to New York City, where he placed poems in magazines such as the avant-garde *Seven Arts* and the leftist *Liberator*. In the early 1920s, he left the United States to live in Europe and North Africa for some dozen years, during which he became interested in socialism and communism and visited the Soviet Union.

Although McKay renounced Marxism and communism and converted to Catholicism in the 1940s, in the twenties he was considered radical when it came to taking on racial oppression. His reputation flourished among Black Americans in 1919 when he published the sonnet "If We Must Die" (p. 801) in the *Liberator*. Written after the 1919 "Red Summer" in Chicago, during which rioters threatened the livelihoods and lives of Black Americans, this poem was read as a strident voice of resistance for "fighting on!"

McKay's first volume of poems published in America, *Harlem Shadows*, appeared in 1922 and established his reputation as a gifted poet writing in traditional forms, particularly sonnets, that focused on two major themes: his lyric nostalgic memories of rural life in Jamaica and his experience with racism and economic injustice in New York. A curious tension exists between his conservative fixed forms and the politicized racial consciousness that challenged the status quo in his adopted country. Nevertheless, this paradoxical blend of orthodox prosody and radical themes made him a major Black poet in the twenties: it satisfied traditional expectations about how poetry should be written for popular audiences while it simultaneously empowered readers who admired its defiant message to refuse racism and to reject oppression.

McKay knew that his immediate audience consisted of Black readers, and he was not afraid of offending genteel readers, regardless of their race.

McKay's images of the underside of life in Harlem — the poverty, desperation, prostitution, and bleakness — appeared in his prose as well as in his poetry. His first novel, *Home to Harlem*, sold extremely well but was famously criticized by the highly respected W. E. B. Du Bois, one of the founders of the NAACP, as well as a historian, sociologist, teacher, writer, and editor. Writing in *The Crisis*, Du Bois acknowledged some success in the novel's prose style but strongly objected to the stark depiction of Black life: "[F]or the most part [it] nauseates me, and after the dirtier parts of its filth, I feel distinctly like taking a bath." McKay responded by making a case for his literary art and refused to write "propaganda" or merely uplifting literature. He went on to publish two more novels that aren't set in Harlem: *Banjo* (1929) and *Banana*

A 1925 edition of *Survey Graphic* magazine on the "Renaissance" in Harlem.
Schomburg Center, New York Public Library.

Harlem's famous Cotton Club in 1938, where legendary jazz musicians performed throughout the Harlem Renaissance.
Rue des Archives/GRANGER — Historical Picture Archive.

*Bottom* (1933); however, in *Gingertown*, a 1932 collection of short stories, some of the settings are located in Harlem. McKay's writing dropped off in the last decade of his life after he published his autobiography, *A Long Way from Home* (1937), and his *Complete Poems* were not published until 2003.

While McKay did not publish any volumes of poetry late in life, his poems remain the bedrock on which subsequent protest poetry depicting Harlem life was built.

### The Harlem Dancer   1917

Applauding youths laughed with young prostitutes
And watched her perfect, half-clothed body sway;
Her voice was like the sound of blended flutes
Blown by black players upon a picnic day.
She sang and danced on gracefully and calm,                    5
The light gauze hanging loose about her form;
To me she seemed a proudly-swaying palm
Grown lovelier for passing through a storm.
Upon her swarthy neck black shiny curls
Luxuriant fell; and tossing coins in praise,                    10

The wine-flushed, bold-eyed boys, and even the girls,
Devoured her shape with eager, passionate gaze;
But looking at her falsely-smiling face,
I knew her self was not in that strange place.

### CONSIDERATIONS FOR CRITICAL THINKING AND WRITING

1. FIRST RESPONSE. What does the speaker think of the dancer? Are they sympathetic? Why or why not?

2. How does the speaker's language characterize the audience?

3. What do you make of the dancer's "falsely-smiling face" (line 13)? What does
   it say about her relationship to herself and her work?

### CONNECTION TO ANOTHER SELECTION

1. Discuss the thematic significance of the respective crowds in "The Harlem
   Dancer" and in "The Lynching" (p. 723).

## *If We Must Die*  1919

If we must die, let it not be like hogs
Hunted and penned in an inglorious spot,
While round us bark the mad and hungry dogs,
Making their mock at our accurséd lot.
If we must die, O let us nobly die,                                         5
So that our precious blood may not be shed
In vain; then even the monsters we defy
Shall be constrained to honor us though dead!
O Kinsmen! we must meet the common foe!
Though far outnumbered let us show us brave,                                10
And for their thousand blows deal one deathblow!
What though before us lies the open grave?
Like men we'll face the murderous, cowardly pack,
Pressed to the wall, dying, but fighting back!

### CONSIDERATIONS FOR CRITICAL THINKING AND WRITING

1. FIRST RESPONSE. How do the poem's images influence its tone?

2. Notice that this sonnet does not specifically mention race. How does that
   affect your reading?

3. Describe the poem's sonnet form.

### CONNECTION TO ANOTHER SELECTION

1. Compare the themes in "If We Must Die" and in Langston Hughes's "Harlem"
   (p. 597).

## The Tropics in New York 1920

Bananas ripe and green, and ginger-root,
  Cocoa in pods and alligator pears,
And tangerines and mangoes and grape fruit,
  Fit for the highest prize at parish fairs,

Set in the window, bringing memories                          5
  Of fruit-trees laden by low-singing rills,
And dewy dawns, and mystical blue skies
  In benediction over nun-like hills.

My eyes grew dim, and I could no more gaze;
  A wave of longing through my body swept,                   10
And, hungry for the old, familiar ways,
  I turned aside and bowed my head and wept.

### CONSIDERATIONS FOR CRITICAL THINKING AND WRITING

1. FIRST RESPONSE. Explain how the title is an important element in the poem.
2. What do you think is the speaker's situation?
3. What does the fruit symbolize?

## America 1921

Although she feeds me bread of bitterness,
And sinks into my throat her tiger's tooth,
Stealing my breath of life, I will confess
I love this cultured hell that tests my youth.
Her vigor flows like tides into my blood,                    5
Giving me strength erect against her hate,
Her bigness sweeps my being like a flood.
Yet, as a rebel fronts a king in state,
I stand within her walls with not a shred
Of terror, malice, not a word of jeer.                       10
Darkly I gaze into the days ahead,
And see her might and granite wonders there,
Beneath the touch of Time's unerring hand,
Like priceless treasures sinking in the sand.

### CONSIDERATIONS FOR CRITICAL THINKING AND WRITING

1. FIRST RESPONSE. According to the speaker, what is there to love about "this cultured hell" in America?
2. Is the speaker a "rebel" or simply a patriotic citizen?
3. How do the tone, diction, and imagery reveal the speaker's sense of America's future?

**CONNECTION TO ANOTHER SELECTION**

1. Compare the themes of this poem with those in Tato Laviera's "Latero Story" (p. 738).

## The White City   1921

I will not toy with it nor bend an inch.
Deep in the secret chambers of my heart
I muse my life-long hate, and without flinch
I bear it nobly as I live my part.
My being would be a skeleton, a shell,                    5
If this dark Passion that fills my every mood,
And makes my heaven in the white world's hell,
Did not forever feed me vital blood.
I see the mighty city through a mist —
The strident trains that speed the goaded mass,            10
The poles and spires and towers vapor-kissed,
The fortressed port through which the great ships pass,
The tides, the wharves, the dens I contemplate,
Are sweet like wanton loves because I hate.

**CONSIDERATIONS FOR CRITICAL THINKING AND WRITING**

1. FIRST RESPONSE. In what sense do you think the speaker's hatred provides them with "vital blood"?

2. Discuss the poem's form. Why might a closed form be useful in the context of the speaker's "dark Passion"?

## The Barrier   1922

I must not gaze at them although
Your eyes are dawning day;
I must not watch you as you go
Your sun-illumined way;

I hear but I must never heed                               5
The fascinating note,
Which, fluting like a river reed,
Comes from your trembling throat;

I must not see upon your face
Love's softly glowing spark;                               10
For there's the barrier of race,
You're fair and I am dark.

CONSIDERATIONS FOR CRITICAL THINKING AND WRITING

1. FIRST RESPONSE. Describe the speaker's tone in each stanza.
2. Comment on the poem's sound effects.
3. How does the light imagery in the first stanza reinforce the theme?

## GEORGIA DOUGLAS JOHNSON
(1877–1966)

Schomburg Center, New York Public Library.

Born in Atlanta, Georgia, into an interracial family — an African American maternal grandfather, a Native American maternal grandmother, and an English paternal grandfather — Georgia Douglas Johnson is regarded as one of the first important African American women poets of the twentieth century. After her early education in Rome and Atlanta, Georgia, she graduated from Atlanta Normal School and then studied violin, piano, and voice at the Oberlin Conservatory and the Cleveland College of Music. She later taught in Marietta, Georgia, and became an assistant school principal in Atlanta, where in 1903 she married Henry Lincoln Johnson, a lawyer. Seven years later they moved to Washington, D.C., where her husband served in President William Howard Taft's administration and where they raised two children.

Although she lived in Washington, D.C., Johnson was one of the major women writers to play a central role in the Harlem Renaissance. She and her husband brought together a group of African American social and political elites by hosting meetings in their home, an illustrious group that included Langston Hughes, W. E. B. Du Bois, Alain Locke, Jean Toomer, as well as faculty from Howard University. These meetings, known as the Saturday Night's Club in the S Street Salon, consisted of lively discussions, debates, and plans for literary projects affecting Black Americans.

Johnson published *The Heart of Women* in 1918, the first of her four collections of poems. Written in traditional forms, these poems explored the pleasures and conflicts embedded in love relationships through a sensitive — and genteel — female voice. Her third volume of poetry, *An Autumn Love* (1928), offered similar subject matter and reflected the belief of some Black writers that poetry should reflect universal concerns rather than racially based topics. In between these two volumes, however, Johnson produced a more "racially conscious" collection in 1922 titled *Bronze* that focused on a Black woman's spiritual struggle in racial contexts. Some of these poems were originally published in *The Crisis* and *The Liberator*. The tone of W. E. B. Du Bois's one-page foreword to this collection suggests both the esteem and the difficulties associated with gender that attended Black female poets who lacked the patronage and fellow support enjoyed by their male counterparts:

> I hope Mrs. Johnson will have wide reading. Her word is simple, sometimes trite, but it is singularly sincere and true, and as a revelation of the soul struggle of the women of a race it is invaluable.

This mixed, tentative endorsement is a curious qualification that reflects the status of Black women poets during the 1920s.

After her husband died in 1925, Johnson eventually went to work at the Department of Labor to support her sons while simultaneously committing herself to writing even more than she had before. From 1926 to 1932, she wrote a weekly column titled "Homely Philosophy" offering inspirational advice and wisdom that was widely distributed to African American newspapers. Although she wrote more than thirty plays, only six were published, among them *Safe* (1925) and *Sunday Morning in the South* (1925), both about the horrific lynchings during the period. Her two best-known plays, *Blue Blood* (1926) and *Plumes* (1929), dealt with, respectively, the "mixing of races" and the importance of valuing African American heritage and culture. Johnson's final collection, *Share My World* (1962), includes poems and newspaper articles confirming the hopeful sensibilities that were also present at the beginning of her writing career in her author's note to *Bronze*:

> This book is the child of a bitter earth-wound. I sit on the earth and sing — sing out, and of, my sorrow. Yet, fully conscious of the potent agencies that silently work in their healing ministries, I know that God's sun shall one day shine upon a perfected and unhampered people.

Her faith in the possibilities of an "unhampered people" makes her writing an abiding contribution to the Harlem Renaissance.

## *Youth*   1918

The dew is on the grasses, dear,
  The blush is on the rose,
And swift across our dial-youth,°              *sundial*
  A shifting shadow goes,
The primrose moments, lush with bliss,             5
  Exhale and fade away,
Life may renew the Autumn time,
  But nevermore the May!

### CONSIDERATIONS FOR CRITICAL THINKING AND WRITING

1. FIRST RESPONSE. Describe the traditional fixed form of this poem.
2. How do the images contribute to the poem's theme?

CONNECTION TO ANOTHER SELECTION

1. Compare the theme and tone of this poem with those of Andrew Marvell's "To His Coy Mistress" (p. 941).

## Foredoom    1918

Her life was dwarfed, and wed to blight,
Her very days were shades of night,
Her every dream was born entombed,
Her soul, a bud, — that never bloomed.

### CONSIDERATIONS FOR CRITICAL THINKING AND WRITING

1. FIRST RESPONSE. How does this poem succeed in creating a kind of biography of the woman it describes?

2. What is the effect of repetition at the beginning of each line?

## Calling Dreams    1920

The right to make my dreams come true,
I ask, nay, I demand of life;
Nor shall fate's deadly contraband
Impede my steps, nor countermand;
Too long my heart against the ground                                    5
Has beat the dusty years around;
And now at length I rise! I wake!
And stride into the morning break!

### CONSIDERATIONS FOR CRITICAL THINKING AND WRITING

1. FIRST RESPONSE. Characterize the speaker's attitude toward life.

2. Comment on the poem's rhymes and their effects.

### CONNECTION TO ANOTHER SELECTION

1. Discuss the themes in "Calling Dreams" and in Langston Hughes's "Harlem" (p. 597).

## Lost Illusions    1922

Oh, for the veils of my far away youth,
Shielding my heart from the blaze of the truth,
Why did I stray from their shelter and grow

Into the sadness that follows — to know!
Impotent atom with desolate gaze                                                5
Threading the tumult of hazardous ways —
Oh, for the veils, for the veils of my youth
Veils that hung low o'er the blaze of the truth!

### CONSIDERATIONS FOR CRITICAL THINKING AND WRITING

1. FIRST RESPONSE. What kind of illusions do you imagine as the subject of this poem?
2. What is the speaker's attitude about knowledge? Do you think there is an acceptable alternative?

### CONNECTION TO ANOTHER SELECTION

1. Discuss the perils of youth that Johnson describes in this poem and in "Youth" (p. 805).

## *Fusion*   1922

How deftly does the gardener blend
This rose and that
To bud a new creation,
More gorgeous and more beautiful
Than any parent portion,                                                        5
And so,
I trace within my warring blood
The tributary sources,
They potently commingle
And sweep                                                                        10
With new-born forces!

### CONSIDERATIONS FOR CRITICAL THINKING AND WRITING

1. FIRST RESPONSE. Discuss the appropriateness of the poem's gardening metaphor.
2. In what sense is the speaker filled with "warring blood"?

### CONNECTION TO ANOTHER SELECTION

1. Discuss the source of pride that is found in "Fusion" and in "Calling Dreams" (p. 806).

## *Prejudice*    1922

These fell miasmic rings of mist with ghoulish menace bound,
Like noose-horizons tightening my little world around.
They still the soaring will to wing, to dance, to speed away,
And fling the soul insurgent back into its shell of clay.
Beneath incrusted silences, a seething Etna° lies,                    *Sicilian volcano*    5
The fire of whose furnaces may sleep, but never dies!

### CONSIDERATIONS FOR CRITICAL THINKING AND WRITING

1. FIRST RESPONSE. What are the emotional effects of prejudice on the speaker?
2. Discuss the tone produced by the images in each line. How does Johnson unify the images?

### CONNECTION TO ANOTHER SELECTION

1. Compare the speaker's sense of place in "Prejudice" and in Claude McKay's "The Tropics in New York" (p. 802).

## LANGSTON HUGHES (1902–1967)

Langston Hughes is the best-known writer of the Harlem Renaissance. His literary production includes volumes of poetry, novels, short stories, essays, plays, opera librettos, histories, documentaries, autobiographies, anthologies, children's books, and translations, as well as radio and television scripts. This impressive body of work makes him an important literary artist and a leading African American voice in the twentieth century. First and foremost, however, he considered himself a poet.

Born in Joplin, Missouri, Hughes grew up with his grandmother, although he did live from time to time with one or the other of his

Library of Congress/Getty Images.

parents, who had separated early in his life. After attending Columbia University in 1921, Hughes wrote and published poetry while he worked a series of odd jobs and then traveled as a merchant seaman to Europe and Africa from 1923 to 1924. He jumped ship to work for several months as a kitchen helper in a Paris nightclub. After his return to the United States in 1925, he published poems in two Black magazines, *The Crisis* and *Opportunity*, and met Carl Van Vechten, who sent his poems to the publisher Alfred A. Knopf. While working as a busboy in a Washington, D.C., hotel, he met the poet Vachel Lindsay, who was instrumental in advancing Hughes's reputation as a poet. In 1926, Hughes published his first volume of poems, *The Weary Blues*, and enrolled

(*Left*) The publication of *The Weary Blues* in 1926 established Hughes as an important figure in the Harlem Renaissance, a cultural movement characterized by an explosion of Black literature, theater, music, painting, and political and racial conscious-ness that began after the First World War. A stamp bearing the image at left, commemorating the centennial of Hughes's birth (2002), is but one example of his lasting impact on American poetry and culture.
Henri Cartier-Bresson/Magnum Photos.

(*Below*) Langston Hughes claimed that Walt Whitman, Carl Sandburg, and Paul Laurence Dunbar were his greatest influences as a poet. However, the experience of Black America from the 1920s through the 1960s, the life and language of Harlem, and a love of jazz and the blues clearly shaped the narra-tive and lyrical experimentation of his poetry. This image of a couple dancing in a Harlem nightclub is a snapshot of the life that influenced Hughes's work.
Bettmann/Getty Images.

at Lincoln University in Pennsylvania, his education funded by a generous patron. His second volume of verse, *Fine Clothes to the Jew*, appeared in 1927, and by the time he graduated from Lincoln University in 1929, he was reading his poems publicly on a book tour of the South. Hughes ended the decade as more than a promising poet; as Countee Cullen pronounced in a mixed review of *The Weary Blues* (mixed because Cullen believed that Black poets should embrace universal rather than racial themes), Hughes had "arrived."

Hughes wrote more prose than poetry in the 1930s, publishing his first novel, *Not without Laughter* (1930), and a collection of stories, *The Ways of White Folks* (1934). In addition to writing a variety of magazine articles, he also worked on a number of plays and screenplays. Many of his poems from this period reflect proletarian issues. During this decade, Hughes's travels took him to all points of the compass — Cuba, Haiti, the Soviet Union, China, Japan, Mexico, France, and Spain — but his general intellectual movement was decidedly left. Hughes was attracted to the American Communist Party, owing to its insistence on equality for all working-class people regardless of race. Like many other Americans in the thirties, he turned his attention away from the exotic twenties and focused on the economic and political issues attending the Great Depression that challenged the freedom and dignity of common humanity.

Over the course of his four-decade career writing fiction, nonfiction, and plays — many of them humorous — he continued to publish poems, among them the collections *Shakespeare in Harlem* (1942); *Lament for Dark Peoples, and Other Poems* (1944); *Montage of a Dream Deferred* (1951); and *Selected Poems by Langston Hughes* (1959). His work, regardless of genre, remained clearly centered on the Black experience in America, a focus that made him a powerful influence for subsequent writers who were encouraged by Hughes's writing to explore for themselves racial themes in literary art.

Despite the tremendous amount that Hughes published — including two autobiographies, *The Big Sea* (1940) and *I Wonder as I Wander* (1956) — he remains somewhat elusive. He never married or had friends who could lay claim to truly knowing him beyond what he wanted them to know (even though several biographies have been published). And yet Hughes is well known — not for his personal life but for his treatment of the possibilities of Black American experiences and identities.

## *The Negro Speaks of Rivers*   1921

I've known rivers:
I've known rivers ancient as the world and older than the
   flow of human blood in human veins.

My soul has grown deep like the rivers.

I bathed in the Euphrates when dawns were young.                        5
I built my hut near the Congo and it lulled me to sleep.
I looked upon the Nile and raised the pyramids above it.
I heard the singing of the Mississippi when Abe Lincoln
    went down to New Orleans, and I've seen its muddy
    bosom turn all golden in the sunset.                           10

I've known rivers:
Ancient, dusky rivers.

My soul has grown deep like the rivers.

### CONSIDERATIONS FOR CRITICAL THINKING AND WRITING

1. FIRST RESPONSE. What do you associate with images of rivers? What connotations run through them for you?
2. How does the speaker identify with the rivers?
3. Why do you think the poet chose to evoke the Euphrates, Congo, Nile, and Mississippi rivers in the poem?

### CONNECTION TO ANOTHER SELECTION

1. Compare the meaning of geography for this speaker with that for the speaker in Georgia Douglas Johnson's "Prejudice" (p. 808).

## *Jazzonia*   1923

Oh, silver tree!
Oh, shining rivers of the soul!

In a Harlem cabaret
Six long-headed jazzers play.
A dancing girl whose eyes are bold                                      5
Lifts high a dress of silken gold.

Oh, singing tree!
Oh, shining rivers of the soul!

Were Eve's eyes
In the first garden                                                     10
Just a bit too bold?
Was Cleopatra gorgeous
In a gown of gold?

Oh, shining tree!
Oh, silver rivers of the soul!                                          15

In a whirling cabaret
Six long-headed jazzers play.

### CONSIDERATIONS FOR CRITICAL THINKING AND WRITING

1. FIRST RESPONSE. Does "Jazzonia" capture what you imagine a Harlem cabaret to have been like? Discuss the importance of the setting.

2. What is the effect of the variations in lines 1–2, 7–8, and 14–15?

3. What do the allusions to Eve and Cleopatra add to the poem's meaning? Are the questions raised about them answered?

### CONNECTION TO ANOTHER SELECTION

1. Compare in an essay the rhythms of "Jazzonia" and of the poem "Lenox Avenue: Midnight" (p. 813).

## *The Weary Blues*  1925

Droning a drowsy syncopated tune,
Rocking back and forth to a mellow croon,
    I heard a Negro play.
Down on Lenox Avenue° the other night
By the pale dull pallor of an old gas light                                5
    He did a lazy sway. . . .
    He did a lazy sway. . . .
To the tune o' those Weary Blues.
With his ebony hands on each ivory key
He made that poor piano moan with melody.                                 10
    O Blues!
Swaying to and fro on his rickety stool
He played that sad raggy tune like a musical fool.
Sweet Blues!
Coming from a black man's soul.                                           15
    O Blues!
In a deep song voice with a melancholy tone
I heard that Negro sing, that old piano moan —
    "Ain't got nobody in all this world,
    Ain't got nobody but ma self.                                        20
    I's gwine to quit ma frownin'
    And put ma troubles on the shelf."
Thump, thump, thump, went his foot on the floor.
He played a few chords then he sang some more —
    "I got the Weary Blues                                               25
    And I can't be satisfied.
    Got the Weary Blues
    And can't be satisfied —
    I ain't happy no mo'
    And I wish that I had died."                                         30

*Lenox Avenue:* Major Harlem thoroughfare, now known as Malcolm X Boulevard.

And far into the night he crooned that tune.
The stars went out and so did the moon.
The singer stopped playing and went to bed
While the Weary Blues echoed through his head.
He slept like a rock or a man that's dead.                    35

### CONSIDERATIONS FOR CRITICAL THINKING AND WRITING

1. FIRST RESPONSE. In line 2, who is "[r]ocking back and forth": the blues player or the speaker? Why does it matter?

2. What is the effect of personifying the piano?

3. There are two sets of blues lyrics within the poem: How are they different? Would the poem's overall effect change if their order were reversed?

### CONNECTION TO ANOTHER SELECTION

1. Compare the way music is used poetically in this poem and in Hughes's "Jazzonia" (p. 811).

## *Lenox Avenue: Midnight*    1926

The rhythm of life
Is a jazz rhythm,
Honey.
The gods are laughing at us.

The broken heart of love,                                     5
The weary, weary heart of pain, —
    Overtones,
    Undertones,
To the rumble of street cars,
To the swish of rain.                                        10

Lenox Avenue,
Honey.
Midnight,
And the gods are laughing at us.

### CONSIDERATIONS FOR CRITICAL THINKING AND WRITING

1. FIRST RESPONSE. What, in your own experience, is the equivalent of what Lenox Avenue is for the speaker?

2. For so brief a poem there are many sounds in these fourteen lines. What are they? How do they reinforce the poem's meanings?

3. What do you think is the poem's theme?

### CONNECTION TO ANOTHER SELECTION

1. In an essay compare the theme of this poem with that of Emily Dickinson's "I know that He exists" (p. 852).

## *Ballad of the Landlord* 1940

Landlord, landlord,
My roof has sprung a leak.
Don't you 'member I told you about it
Way last week?

Landlord, landlord,                                                5
These steps is broken down.
When you come up yourself
It's a wonder you don't fall down.

Ten Bucks you say I owe you?
Ten Bucks you say is due?                                          10
Well, that's Ten Bucks more'n I'll pay you
Till you fix this house up new.

What? You gonna get eviction orders?
You gonna cut off my heat?
You gonna take my furniture and                                    15
Throw it in the street?

Um-huh! You talking high and mighty.
Talk on — till you get through.
You ain't gonna be able to say a word
If I land my fist on you.                                          20

*Police! Police!*
*Come and get this man!*
*He's trying to ruin the government*
*And overturn the land!*

Copper's whistle!                                                  25
Patrol bell!
Arrest.

Precinct Station.
Iron cell.
Headlines in press:                                                30

MAN THREATENS LANDLORD
TENANT HELD NO BAIL
JUDGE GIVES NEGRO 90 DAYS IN COUNTY JAIL

### CONSIDERATIONS FOR CRITICAL THINKING AND WRITING

1. FIRST RESPONSE. The poem incorporates both humor and serious social commentary. Which do you think is dominant? Explain.

2. Why is the literary ballad an especially appropriate form for the content of this poem?

3. How does the speaker's language simultaneously characterize him and the landlord?

## COUNTEE CULLEN (1903–1946)

MPI/Getty Images.

Little is known about Countee Cullen's early life. Although he claimed to have been born in New York City, various sources who were close to him have alternately indicated that he was born in Louisville, Kentucky, or Baltimore, Maryland. In any case, Cullen, always a private person, never definitively resolved the question. Raised by his paternal grandmother as Countee Porter, Cullen was apparently adopted by the Reverend Frederick A. Cullen after she died when he was around fifteen. Reverend Cullen was an activist pastor of the Salem Methodist Episcopal Church, which was home to a large congregation in Harlem. He eventually became head of the Harlem chapter of the National Association for the Advancement of Colored People, so Cullen found himself living at one of the focal points of the Black cultural and political movements near the very beginning of the Harlem Renaissance.

Cullen published his first book of poems, *Color*, in 1925, the year he graduated from New York University. This edition included a number of what were to become his major poems, some of which were simultaneously featured in Alain Locke's *The New Negro*. This remarkable success transformed an extraordinarily talented student into an important poet whose literary reputation was celebrated nationally as well as in Harlem. In 1926, he earned a master's degree in English and French from Harvard and subsequently began writing a column for *Opportunity*, the publication of the National Urban League, in which he articulated his ideas about literature and race. After publishing two more volumes of poetry in 1927, *Copper Sun* and *The Ballad of the Brown Girl*, he won a Guggenheim Fellowship to write poetry in France, one of many literary prizes he was awarded. His fourth collection of poetry, *The Black Christ and Other Poems*, appeared in 1929. Having achieved all of this, he was only twenty-six years old.

By the end of the decade, Cullen was considered a major poet of the Black experience in America. Owing to his early interest in Romantic writers — John Keats was a favorite inspiration — he was also read for his treatment of traditional themes concerning love, beauty, and mutability. As he made clear in his 1927 anthology of verse showcasing Black poets, he was more interested in being part of "an anthology of verse by Negro poets, rather than an anthology of Negro verse." In a poem titled "To John Keats, Poet, at Spring Time (1925)," he pledges his allegiance to a Romantic poetic tradition; consider this excerpt:

> "John Keats is dead," they say, but I
> Who hear your full insistent cry
> In bud and blossom, leaf and tree,
> Know John Keats still writes poetry.

Though Cullen habitually wrote about race consciousness and issues related to being Black in an often-hostile world, he insisted on being recognized for his credentials as a poet rather than for his race, and he did so writing in traditional English forms such as the sonnet and other closed forms that he had studied in college and graduate school. He was critical of the free verse that writers like Langston Hughes coupled with the blues and jazz rhythms, as they moved away from conventional rhyme and meter (see the Perspective "On Racial Poetry" by Cullen, p. 823). Refusing to be limited by racial themes, he believed that other Black Americans who allowed such limitations in their work did so to their artistic disadvantage. The result was that his poetry was popular among white as well as Black readers in the 1920s.

As meteoric and brilliant as Cullen's early writing career had been, it faded almost as quickly in the 1930s. Despite publication of a satiric novel, *One Way to Heaven* (1932); *The Media and Some Poems* (1935); two books for juveniles in the early 1940s; and several dramatic and musical adaptations, his reputation steadily declined as critics began to perceive him as written out, old-fashioned, and out of touch with contemporary racial issues and the realities of Black life in America. His conservative taste in conventional poetic forms was sometimes equated with staunch conservative politics. There can be no question, however, that his most successful poems are firmly based in an awareness of the social injustice produced by racism. Cullen was offered a number of opportunities teaching at the college level, but his overall influence waned as he chose in 1934 to teach French and creative writing at Frederick Douglass Junior High School in Harlem, where he worked until his poor health resulted in an early death in 1946.

## *Yet Do I Marvel*    1925

I doubt not God is good, well-meaning, kind,
And did He stoop to quibble could tell why
The little buried mole continues blind,
Why flesh that mirrors Him must some day die,
Make plain the reason tortured Tantalus                    5
Is baited by the fickle fruit, declare
If merely brute caprice dooms Sisyphus
To struggle up a never-ending stair.
Inscrutable His ways are, and immune
To catechism by a mind too strewn                          10
With petty cares to slightly understand
What awful brain compels His awful hand.
Yet do I marvel at this curious thing:
To make a poet black, and bid him sing!

### CONSIDERATIONS FOR CRITICAL THINKING AND WRITING

1. **FIRST RESPONSE.** How does the speaker envision the nature of God in lines 1–8?

2. Research the Tantalus and Sisyphus allusions. Why are these Greek myths particularly relevant in the context of the poem?

3. How do you interpret the meaning of *awful* in line 12?

### CONNECTION TO ANOTHER SELECTION

1. Compare the view of God in "Yet Do I Marvel" with the perspective offered by the speaker in Emily Dickinson's "I know that He exists" (p. 852).

**A Note on the Text:** The following poem contains a harmful and offensive racial epithet. As discussed in "Approaching Sensitive Subjects" (p. 7), it is important to be aware of context when encountering difficult content. As you read, consider in- vs. out-group usage: Cullen was a Black American, whose poetry dealt both directly and indirectly with the racial discrimination he and other people of color faced. This poem deals intentionally with racism, reflecting Cullen's original intent in depicting a specific incident, time period, place, and culture. Be mindful of this context as you read.

## *Incident*   1925

Once riding in old Baltimore,
   Heart-filled, head-filled with glee,
I saw a Baltimorean
   Keep looking straight at me.

Now I was eight and very small,                                         5
   And he was no whit bigger,
And so I smiled, but he poked out
   His tongue, and called me, "Nigger."

I saw the whole of Baltimore
   From May until December;                                    10
Of all the things that happened there
   That's all that I remember.

### CONSIDERATIONS FOR CRITICAL THINKING AND WRITING

1. FIRST RESPONSE.  What does the young narrator learn from this "incident"?

2. Why do you think Cullen chose to use the word *whit* in line 6?

3. Discuss the effects of the poem's rhymes.

### CONNECTION TO ANOTHER SELECTION

1. Compare the psychological effects of racism as expressed in this poem and in Georgia Douglas Johnson's "Prejudice" (p. 808).

## *Heritage* 1925

*(For Harold Jackman)*

What is Africa to me:
Copper sun or scarlet sea,
Jungle star or jungle track,
Strong bronzed men, or regal black
Women from whose loins I sprang                              5
When the birds of Eden sang?
*One three centuries removed*
*From the scenes his fathers loved,*
*Spicy grove, cinnamon tree,*
*What is Africa to me?*                                      10

So I lie, who all day long
Want no sound except the song
Sung by wild barbaric birds
Goading massive jungle herds,
Juggernauts of flesh that pass                              15
Trampling tall defiant grass
Where young forest lovers lie,
Plighting troth beneath the sky.

So I lie, who always hear,
Though I cram against my ear                                20
Both my thumbs, and keep them there,
Great drums throbbing through the air.
So I lie, whose fount of pride,
Dear distress, and joy allied,
Is my somber flesh and skin,                                25
With the dark blood dammed within
Like great pulsing tides of wine
That, I fear, must burst the fine
Channels of the chafing net
Where they surge and foam and fret.                         30

Africa? A book one thumbs
Listlessly, till slumber comes.
Unremembered are her bats
Circling through the night, her cats
Crouching in the river reeds,                               35
Stalking gentle flesh that feeds
By the river brink; no more
Does the bugle-throated roar
Cry that monarch° claws have leapt                    *lion*
From the scabbards where they slept.                        40
Silver snakes that once a year
Doff the lovely coats you wear,

Seek no covert in your fear
Lest a mortal eye should see;
What's your nakedness to me?                                    45
Here no leprous flowers rear
Fierce corollas° in the air;                          *crowns (of petals)*
Here no bodies sleek and wet,
Dripping mingled rain and sweat,
Tread the savage measures of                                   50
Jungle boys and girls in love.
What is last year's snow to me,
Last year's anything? The tree
Budding yearly must forget
How its past arose or set —                                    55
Bough and blossom, flower, fruit,
Even what shy bird with mute
Wonder at her travail there,
Meekly labored in its hair.
*One three centuries removed*                                  60
*From the scenes his fathers loved,*
*Spicy grove, cinnamon tree,*
*What is Africa to me?*

So I lie, who find no peace
Night or day, no slight release                                65
From the unremittant beat
Made by cruel padded feet
Walking through my body's street.
Up and down they go, and back,
Treading out a jungle track.                                   70
So I lie, who never quite
Safely sleep from rain at night —
I can never rest at all
When the rain begins to fall;
Like a soul gone mad with pain                                 75
I must match its weird refrain;
Ever must I twist and squirm,
Writhing like a baited worm,
While its primal measures drip
Through my body, crying, "Strip!                               80
Doff this new exuberance.
Come and dance the Lover's Dance!"
In an old remembered way
Rain works on me night and day.

Quaint, outlandish heathen gods                                85
Black men fashion out of rods,
Clay, and brittle bits of stone,
In a likeness like their own,
My conversion came high-priced;

I belong to Jesus Christ,                                                90
Preacher of humility;
Heathen gods are naught to me.

Father, Son, and Holy Ghost,
So I make an idle boast;
Jesus of the twice-turned cheek,                                         95
Lamb of God, although I speak
With my mouth thus, in my heart
Do I play a double part.
Ever at Thy glowing altar
Must my heart grow sick and falter,                                      100
Wishing He I served were black,
Thinking then it would not lack
Precedent of pain to guide it,
Let who would or might deride it;
Surely then this flesh would know                                        105
Yours had borne a kindred woe.
Lord, I fashion dark gods, too,

Daring even to give You
Dark despairing features where,
Crowned with dark rebellious hair,                                       110
Patience wavers just so much as
Mortal grief compels, while touches
Quick and hot, of anger, rise
To smitten cheek and weary eyes.
Lord, forgive me if my need                                              115
Sometimes shapes a human creed.
*All day long and all night through,*
*One thing only must I do:*
*Quench my pride and cool my blood,*
*Lest I perish in the flood.*                                            120
*Lest a hidden ember set*
*Timber that I thought was wet*
*Burning like the dryest flax,*
*Melting like the merest wax,*
*Lest the grave restore its dead.*                                       125
*Not yet has my heart or head*
*In the least way realized*
*They and I are civilized.*

## CONSIDERATIONS FOR CRITICAL THINKING AND WRITING

1. FIRST RESPONSE. The speaker repeats a question: "What is Africa to me?"
   Is there ever a coherent answer? If so, does it change over the course of the
   poem?

2. Discuss the use of italics in the poem.

3. Look for imagery that relates to the speaker's mind and imagery that relates to
   his body. How different are these? Are they ever reconciled?

CONNECTION TO ANOTHER SELECTION

1. Compare the attitude toward African culture in this poem and in Phillis Wheatley's "To S. M. a young *African* Painter, on seeing his Works" (p. 948).

## Perspectives

### KAREN JACKSON FORD (B. 1956)
### *Hughes's Aesthetics of Simplicity*  1992

The repression of the great bulk of Hughes's poems is the result of chronic critical scorn for their simplicity. Throughout his long career, but especially after his first two volumes of poetry (readers were at first willing to assume that a youthful poet might grow to be more complex), his books received their harshest reviews for a variety of "flaws" that all originate in an aesthetics of simplicity. From his first book, *The Weary Blues* (1926), to his last one, *The Panther and the Lash* (1967), the reviews invoke a litany of faults: the poems are superficial, infantile, silly, small, unpoetic, common, jejune, iterative, and, of course, simple.[1] Even his admirers reluctantly conclude that Hughes's poetics failed. Saunders Redding flatly opposes simplicity and artfulness. "While Hughes's rejection of his own growth shows an admirable loyalty to his self-commitment as the poet of the 'simple, Negro commonfolk' . . . it does a disservice to his art."[2] James Baldwin, who recognizes the potential of simplicity as an artistic principle, faults the poems for "tak[ing] refuge . . . in a fake simplicity in order to avoid the very difficult simplicity of the experience."[3]

Despite a lifetime of critical disappointments, then, Hughes remained loyal to the aesthetic program he had outlined in 1926 in his decisive poetic treatise, "The Negro Artist and the Racial Mountain." There he had predicted that the common people would "give to this world its truly great Negro artist, the one who is not afraid to be himself," a poet who would explore the "great field of unused [folk] material ready for his art" and recognize that this source would provide "sufficient matter to furnish a black artist with a lifetime of creative work."[4] This is clearly a portrait of the poet Hughes would become, and he maintained his fidelity to this ideal at great cost to his literary reputation.

From "Do Right to Write Right: Langston Hughes's Aesthetics of Simplicity,"
*Twentieth Century Literature* 38.4 (1992)

---

[1] Reviews in which these epithets appear are collected in Edward J. Mullen, *Critical Essays on Langston Hughes* (Boston: G. K. Hall, 1986). [Ford's note.]

[2] Redding's comments appear in Mullen 74. [Ford's note.]

[3] Baldwin's comments appear in Mullen 85. [Ford's note.]

[4] *The Nation* 122 (1926): 692. [Ford's note.]

CONSIDERATIONS FOR CRITICAL THINKING AND WRITING

1. What was Hughes's rationale for the value of simplicity in his poetry?

2. Explain whether or not you think there is any justification for regarding Hughes's poetry as "superficial" and too "simple."

DAVID CHINITZ (B. 1962)

## *The Romanticization of Africa in the 1920s* 1997

In Europe black culture was an exotic import; in America it was domestic and increasingly mass-produced. If postwar [World War I] disillusionment judged the majority culture mannered, neurotic, and repressive, Americans had an easily accessible alternative. The need for such an Other produced a discourse in which black Americans figured as barely civilized exiles from the jungle, with — so the clichés ran — tom-toms beating in their blood and dark laughter in their souls. The African American became a model of "natural" human behavior to contrast with the falsified, constrained, and impotent modes of the "civilized."

Far from being immune to the lure of this discourse, for the better part of the 1920s Hughes asserted an open pride in the supposed primitive qualities of his race, the atavistic legacy of the African motherland. Unlike most of those who romanticized Africa, Hughes had at least some firsthand experience of the continent; yet he processed what he saw there in images conditioned by European primitivism, rendering "[the land] wild and lovely, the people dark and beautiful, the palm trees tall, the sun bright, and the rivers deep."[1] His short story "Luani of the Jungle," in attempting to glorify aboriginal African vigor as against European anemia, shows how predictable and unextraordinary even Hughes's primitivism could be. To discover in the descendants of idealized Africans the same qualities of innate health, spontaneity, and naturalness requires no great leap; one has only to identify the African American as a displaced primitive, as Hughes does repeatedly in his first book, *The Weary Blues*:

> They drove me out of the forest.
> They took me away from the jungles.
> I lost my trees.
> I lost my silver moons.
> Now they've caged me
> In the circus of civilization.[2]

Hughes depicts black atavism vividly and often gracefully, yet in a way that is entirely consistent with the popular iconography of the time. His African Americans retain "among the skyscrapers" the primal fears and instincts of their ancestors "among the palms in Africa."[3] The scion of Africa is still more than half primitive: "All the tom-toms of the jungles beat in my blood, / And all the wild hot moons of the jungles shine in my soul."[4]

From "Rejuvenation through Joy: Langston Hughes, Primitivism and Jazz," in
*American Literary History*, Spring 1997

[1] *The Big Sea*. 1940. N.Y.: Thunder's Mouth, 1986, 11. [Chinitz's note.]
[2] *The Weary Blues*. N.Y.: Knopf, 1926, 100. [Chinitz's note.]
[3] Ibid. 101.
[4] Ibid. 102.

### CONSIDERATIONS FOR CRITICAL THINKING AND WRITING

1. According to Chinitz, why did Europeans and Americans romanticize African culture?

2. Consider McKay's "The Tropics in New York" (p. 802) and Hughes's "The Negro Speaks of Rivers" (p. 810) in the context of Chinitz's discussion of "primitivism," and discuss the similarities and differences you see in their approaches.

## ALAIN LOCKE (1886–1954)

### *Review of Georgia Douglas Johnson's* Bronze: A Book of Verse   1923

One of Mrs. Johnson's literary virtues is condensation. She often distills the trite and commonplace into an elixir. Following the old-fashioned lyric strain and the sentimentalist cult of the common emotions, she succeeds because by sincerity and condensation, her poetry escapes to a large extent its own limitations. Here in the subject of these verses, there is however a double pitfall; avoiding sentimentality is to come dangerously close to propaganda. This is also deftly avoided — more by instinct than by calculation. Mrs. Johnson's silences and periods are eloquent, she stops short of the preachy and prosaic and is always lyrical and human. Almost before one has shaped his life to "Oh! the pity of it," a certain fresh breeze of faith and courage blows over the heart, and the mind revives to a healthy, humanistic optimist. Mrs. Johnson seems to me to hear a message, a message that gains through being softly but intensely insinuated between the lines of her poems — "Let the traditional instincts of women heal the world that travails under the accumulated woes of the uncompensated instincts of men," or to speak more in her way, "May the saving grace of the mother-heart save humanity."

From *The Crisis*, February 1923

#### CONSIDERATIONS FOR CRITICAL THINKING AND WRITING

1. What does Locke admire about Johnson's poems? How positive do you think his assessment is of her poetry?
2. What do you think Locke means when he writes, "avoiding sentimentality is to come dangerously close to propaganda"?
3. Explain whether you think Johnson avoids sentimentality in the poems reprinted in this chapter.

## COUNTEE CULLEN (1903–1946)

### *On Racial Poetry*   1926

Here is a poet with whom to reckon, to experience, and here and there, with that apologetic feeling of presumption that should companion all criticism, to quarrel.

What has always struck me most forcibly in reading Mr. Hughes' poems has been their utter spontaneity and expression of a unique personality. . . . This poet represents a transcendently emancipated spirit among a class of young writers whose particular battle-cry is freedom. With the enthusiasm of a zealot, he pursues his way, scornful, in subject matter, in photography, and rhythmical treatment, of whatever obstructions time and tradition have placed before him. To him it is essential that he be himself. Essential and commendable surely; yet the thought persists that some of these poems would have been better had Mr. Hughes held himself a bit in check....

If I have the least powers of prediction, the first section of this book, *The Weary Blues*, will be most admired, even if less from intrinsic poetical worth than because of its dissociation from the traditionally poetic. Never having been one to think all subjects and forms proper for poetic consideration, I regard these jazz poems as interlopers in the company of the truly beautiful poems in other sections of the book. They move along with the frenzy and electric heat of a Methodist or Baptist revival meeting, and affect me in much the same manner. The revival meeting excites me, cooling and flushing me with alternate chills and fevers of emotion; so do these poems. But when the storm is over, I wonder if the quiet way of communing is not more spiritual for the God-seeking heart; and in the light of reflection I wonder if jazz poems really belong to that dignified company, that select and austere circle of high literary expression which we call poetry....

Taken as a group the selections in this book seem one-sided to me. They tend to hurl this poet into the gaping pit that lies before all Negro writers, in the confines of which they become racial artists instead of artists pure and simple. There is too much emphasis here on strictly Negro themes; and this is probably an added reason for my coldness toward the jazz poems — they seem to set a too definite limit upon an already limited field.

From *Opportunity: A Journal of Negro Life*

### Considerations for Critical Thinking and Writing

1. In Cullen's review of *The Weary Blues*, what is his "quarrel" (par. 1) with Hughes?

2. Given the tenor of Hughes's comments on racial pride in the excerpt from "The Negro Artist and the Racial Mountain" (p. 795), what do you think his response to Cullen would be?

3. Explain why you agree or disagree with Cullen's view that Hughes's poems are "one-sided" (par. 4).

4. Do you think Cullen's argument is dated, or is it relevant to today's social climate? Explain.

## Onwuchekwa Jemie (b. 1940)

## *On Universal Poetry* 1976

Hughes entertained no doubts as to the sufficiency and greatness of the molds provided by black music, nor of black life as subject matter. On the question of whether such black matter and manner could attain "universality," Hughes in his Spingarn Speech issued a definitive answer:

> There is so much richness in Negro humor, so much beauty in black dreams, so much dignity in our struggle, and so much universality in our problems, in us — in each living human being of color — that I do not understand the tendency today that some American Negro artists have of seeking to run away from themselves, of running away from us, of being afraid to sing our own songs, paint

our own pictures, write about ourselves — when it is our music that has given America its greatest music, our humor that has enriched its entertainment media, our rhythm that has guided its dancing feet from plantation days to the Charleston, the Lindy Hop, and currently the Madison. . . .

Could you possibly be afraid that the rest of the world will not accept it? Our spirituals are sung and loved in the great concert halls of the whole world. Our blues are played from Topeka to Tokyo. Harlem's jive talk delights Hong Kong. Those of our writers who have concerned themselves with our very special problems are translated and read around the world. The local, the regional can — and does — become universal. Sean O'Casey's Irishmen are an example. So I would say to young Negro writers, do not be afraid of yourselves. You are the world.[1]

Hughes's confidence in blackness is a major part of his legacy, for the questions he had to answer have had to be answered over again by subsequent generations of black artists. Black culture is still embattled; and Hughes provides a model for answering the questions and making the choices. Whether they say so or not, those who, like Cullen, . . . plead the need to be "universal" as an excuse for avoiding racial material, or for treating such material from perspectives rooted in alien sensibilities, invariably equate "white" or "Western" with "universal," and "black" or "non-Western" with its opposite, forgetting that the truly universal — that is, the foundation elements of human experience, the circumstances attending birth, growth, decline, and death, the emotions of joy and grief, love and hate, fear and guilt, anger and pain — are common to all humanity. The multiplicity of nations and cultures in the world makes it inevitable that the details and particulars of human experience will vary according to time, place, and circumstance, and it follows that the majority of writers will dramatize and interpret human life according to the usages of their particular nation and epoch. Indeed, the question whether a writer's work is universal or not rarely arises when that writer is European or white American. It arises so frequently in discussions of black writers for no other reason than that the long-standing myth of white superiority and black inferiority has led so many to believe that in literature, and in other areas of life as well, the black particular of universal human experience is less appropriate than the white particular.

From *Langston Hughes: An Introduction to Poetry*

[1] See Hughes, Letter to the Editor, *The Crisis*, 35:9 (September 1928), 302. [Jemie's note.]

## CONSIDERATIONS FOR CRITICAL THINKING AND WRITING

1. How does Jemie go beyond Hughes's own argument to make a case for the universality of poetry about the Black experience?

2. How might Jemie's argument be extended to other minoritized groups or to women?

3. Do you think that Jemie's or Cullen's argument is more persuasive? Explain your answer.

## SUGGESTED TOPICS FOR LONGER PAPERS

1. Discuss the four poets' use of rhyme, meter, and sounds in eight poems of your choice. How do these elements contribute to the poems' meanings?

2. Taken together, how do the four poets' poems provide a critique of race relations in America?

3. Do some exploratory reading, viewing, and listening to learn more about life in Harlem in the 1920s. Based on your research, how effectively do you think Hughes's poetry evokes Harlem life?

# 29

# A Study of Emily Dickinson

Todd-Bingham Picture Collection, 1837–1966 (inclusive). Manuscripts & Archives, Yale University.

My business is circumference.

— EMILY DICKINSON

In this chapter you'll find a variety of poems by Emily Dickinson so that you can study her work in some depth. While this collection is not wholly representative of her work, it does offer enough poems to suggest some of the techniques and concerns that characterize her writings. The poems speak not only to readers but also to one another. That's natural enough: the more familiar you are with a writer's work, the easier it is to perceive and enjoy the strategies and themes the poet uses. If you are asked to write about a number of poems by the same author, you may find useful the Questions for Writing about an Author in Depth (p. 850) and the sample paper on Dickinson's attitudes toward religious faith in four of her poems (p. 853).

*Emily E. Dickinson.*

Edward and Mary Judson Hitchcock Family Papers, Amherst College Archives & Special Collections.

This daguerreotype of Emily Dickinson, taken shortly after her sixteenth birthday, and the silhouette (see p. 829), created when she was fourteen years old, are the only authenticated mechanically produced images of the poet.

Todd-Bingham Picture Collection, 1837–1966 (inclusive). Manuscripts & Archives, Yale University.

## A BRIEF BIOGRAPHY

Emily Dickinson (1830–1886) grew up in a prominent and prosperous household in Amherst, Massachusetts. Along with her younger sister, Lavinia, and older brother, Austin, she experienced a quiet and reserved family life headed by her father, Edward Dickinson. In a letter to Austin at law school, she once described the atmosphere in her father's house as "pretty much all sobriety."

(*Right*) This silhouette shows Dickinson at age fourteen.
Archives and Special Collections, Amherst College.

(*Below*) This print of a mid-1850s daguerreotype
(unauthenticated), acquired by the scholar Philip F.
Gura in 2000, may represent the poet in her twenties,
though there is debate about its authenticity.
The History Collection/Alamy.

Her mother, Emily Norcross Dickinson, was not as powerful a presence in her life; she seems not to have been as emotionally accessible as Dickinson would have liked. Her daughter is said to have characterized her as not the sort of mother "to whom you hurry when you are troubled." Both parents raised Dickinson to be a cultured Christian woman who would one day be responsible for a family of her own. Her father attempted to protect her from reading books that might "joggle" her mind, particularly her religious faith, but Dickinson's individualistic instincts and irreverent sensibilities created conflicts that did not allow her to fall into step with the conventional piety, domesticity, and social duty prescribed by her father and the orthodox Congregationalism of Amherst.

The Dickinsons were well known in Massachusetts. Emily's father was a lawyer and served as the treasurer of Amherst College (a position Austin eventually took up as well), and her grandfather was one of the college's founders. Although nineteenth-century politics, economics, and social issues do not appear in the foreground of her poetry, Dickinson lived in a family environment that was steeped in them: her father was an active town official and served in the General Court of Massachusetts, the state senate, and the U.S. House of Representatives.

Dickinson, however, withdrew not only from her father's public world but also from almost all social life in Amherst. She refused to see most people, and aside from a single year at South Hadley Female Seminary (now Mount Holyoke College), one excursion to Philadelphia and Washington, and several brief trips to Boston to see a doctor about eye problems, she lived all her life in her father's house. She dressed only in white and developed a reputation as a reclusive eccentric. Dickinson selected her own society carefully and frugally. Like her poetry, her relationship to the world was intensely reticent. Indeed, during the last twenty years of her life she rarely left the house.

Though Dickinson never married, she had significant relationships with several men who were friends, confidants, and mentors. She also enjoyed an intimate relationship with her friend Susan Huntington Gilbert, who became her sister-in-law by marrying Austin. Susan and her husband lived next door and were extremely close with Dickinson. Biographers have attempted to find in a number of her relationships the source for the passion of some of her love poems and letters. Several possibilities have been put forward as the person she addressed in three letters as "Dear Master": Benjamin Newton, a clerk in her father's office who talked about books with her; Samuel Bowles, editor of the *Springfield Republican* and friend of the family; the Reverend Charles Wadsworth, a Presbyterian preacher with a reputation for powerful sermons; and an old friend and widower, Judge Otis P. Lord. Despite these speculations, no biographer has been able to identify definitively the object of Dickinson's love. What matters, of course, is not with whom she was in love — if, in fact, there was any single person — but that she wrote about such passions so intensely and convincingly in her poetry.

Choosing to live life internally within the confines of her home, Dickinson brought her life into sharp focus, for she also chose to live within the limitless expanses of her imagination — a choice she was keenly aware of and which she described in one of her poems this way: "I dwell in Possibility —" (p. 840). Her small circle of domestic life did not impinge on her creative sensibilities. Like Henry David Thoreau, she simplified her life so that doing without was a means of being within. In a sense, she redefined the meaning of deprivation because being denied something — whether faith, love, literary recognition, or some other desire — provided a sharper, more intense understanding than she would have experienced had she achieved what she wanted: "'Heaven,'" she wrote, "is what I cannot reach!" This poem (p. 837) — along with many others, such as "Water, is taught by thirst" (p. 835) and "Success is counted sweetest" (p. 835) — suggests just how persistently she saw deprivation as a way of sensitizing herself to the value of what she was missing. For Dickinson, hopeful expectation was always more satisfying than achieving a golden moment. Perhaps that's one reason she was so attracted to John Keats's poetry (see, for example, his "Ode on a Grecian Urn," p. 572).

Dickinson enjoyed reading Keats as well as other British writers from the nineteenth century: Charlotte and Emily Brontë (p. 933 for the latter); Robert and Elizabeth Barrett Browning (pp. 636 and 566, respectively); Alfred, Lord Tennyson (p. 552); and George Eliot. Even so, these writers had little or no effect on the style of her writing. In her own work she was original and innovative, but she did draw on her knowledge of the Bible, classical myths, and Shakespeare for allusions and references in her poetry. She also used contemporary popular church hymns, transforming their standard rhythms into free-form hymn meters. Among American writers she appreciated Ralph Waldo Emerson and Henry David Thoreau, but she apparently felt Walt Whitman was better left unread. She once mentioned to Thomas Wentworth Higginson, a leading critic with whom she corresponded about her poetry, that as for Whitman "I never read his Book — but was told that he was disgraceful" (for the kind of Whitman poetry she had been warned against, see his "I Sing the Body Electric," p. 708). Nathaniel Hawthorne, however, intrigued her with his faith in the imagination and his dark themes: "Hawthorne appals — entices," a remark that might be used to describe her own themes and techniques. (See Hawthorne's story "The Minister's Black Veil" on p. 209.)

## AN INTRODUCTION TO HER WORK

Today, Dickinson is regarded as one of America's greatest poets, but when she died at the age of fifty-six after devoting most of her life to writing poetry, her nearly two thousand poems — only a dozen of which were published, anonymously, during her lifetime — were unknown except to a small number of friends and relatives. Dickinson was not recognized as a major poet until the twentieth century, when modern readers ranked her as a major new voice whose literary innovations were unmatched by any other nineteenth-century poet in the United States.

Dickinson neither completed many poems nor prepared them for publication. She wrote her drafts on scraps of paper, grocery lists, and the backs of recipes and used envelopes. Early editors of her poems took the liberty of making them more accessible to nineteenth-century readers when several volumes of selected poems were published in the 1890s. The poems were made to appear like traditional nineteenth-century verse by assigning them titles, rearranging their syntax, normalizing their grammar, and regularizing their capitalizations. Instead of dashes, editors used standard punctuation; instead of the highly elliptical telegraphic lines so characteristic of her poems, editors added articles, conjunctions, and prepositions to make them more readable and in line with conventional expectations. In addition, the poems were made more predictable by organizing them into categories such as friendship, nature, love, and death. Not until 1955, when Thomas Johnson published Dickinson's complete works in a form that attempted to be true to her manuscript versions, did readers have the opportunity to see the full range of her style and themes.

Like that of Robert Frost (Chapter 30), Dickinson's popular reputation has sometimes relegated her to the role of a New England regionalist who writes quaint uplifting verses that touch the heart. In 1971 that image was mailed first class all over the country by the U.S. Postal Service. In addition to issuing a commemorative stamp featuring a portrait of Dickinson, the postal service affixed the stamp to a first-day-of-issue envelope that included an engraved rose and one of her poems. Here's the poem chosen from among the nearly two thousand she wrote:

## If I can stop one Heart from breaking    ca. 1864

If I can stop one Heart from breaking
I shall not live in vain
If I can ease one Life the Aching
or cool one Pain

Or help one fainting Robin                                                5
Unto his Nest again
I shall not live in Vain.

This is typical not only of many nineteenth-century popular poems but also of the kind of verse that can be found in contemporary greeting cards. The speaker tells us what we imagine we should think about and makes the point simply with a sentimental image of a "fainting Robin." To point out that robins don't faint or that altruism isn't necessarily the only rule of conduct by which one should live one's life is to make trouble for this poem. Moreover, its use of language is unexceptional; the metaphors used, like that robin, are a bit weary. If this poem were characteristic of Dickinson's poetry, the U.S. Postal Service probably would not have been urged to issue a stamp in her honor, nor would you be reading her poems in this anthology or many others. The next poem by Dickinson is more typical of her writing.

## If I shouldn't be alive  ca. 1860

If I shouldn't be alive
When the Robins come,
Give the one in Red Cravat,
A Memorial crumb.

If I couldn't thank you,                                              5
Being fast asleep,
You will know I'm trying
With my Granite lip!

This poem is more representative of Dickinson's sensibilities and techniques. Although the first stanza sets up a rather mild concern that the speaker might not survive the winter (a not uncommon fear for those who fell prey to pneumonia, for example, during Dickinson's time), the concern can't be taken too seriously — a gentle humor lightens the poem when we realize that all robins have red cravats and are therefore the speaker's favorite. Furthermore, the euphemism that describes the speaker "Being fast asleep" in line 6 makes death seem not so threatening after all. But the sentimental expectations of the first six lines — lines that could have been written by any number of popular nineteenth-century writers — are dashed by the penultimate word of the last line. *Granite* is the perfect word here because it forces us to reread the poem and to recognize that it's not about feeding robins or offering a cosmetic treatment of death; rather, it's a bone-chilling description of a corpse's lip that evokes the cold, hard texture and grayish color of tombstones. These lips will never say "thank you" or anything else.

Instead of the predictable rhymes and sentiments of "If I can stop one Heart from breaking," this poem is unnervingly precise in its use of language and tidily points out how much emphasis Dickinson places on an individual word. Her use of near rhyme with "asleep" and "lip" brilliantly mocks a euphemistic approach to death by its jarring dissonance. This is a better poem, not because it's grim or about death, but because it demonstrates Dickinson's skillful use of language to produce a shocking irony.

Dickinson found irony, ambiguity, and paradox lurking in the simplest and commonest experiences. The materials and subject matter of her poetry are quite conventional. Her poems are filled with robins, bees, winter light, household items, and domestic duties. These materials represent the range of what she experienced in and around her father's house. She used them because they constituted so much of her life and, more important, because she found meanings latent in them. Though her world was simple, it was also complex in its beauties and its terrors. Her lyric poems capture impressions of particular moments, scenes, or moods, and she characteristically focuses on topics such as nature, love, immortality, death, faith, doubt, pain, and the self.

Though her materials were conventional, her treatment of them was innovative because she was willing to break whatever poetic conventions stood in the way of the intensity of her thought and images. Her conciseness, brevity, and wit are tightly packed. Typically she offers her observations via one or two images that reveal her thought in a powerful manner. She once characterized her literary art by writing, "My business is circumference." Her method is to reveal the inadequacy of declarative statements by evoking qualifications and questions with images that complicate firm assertions and affirmations. In one of her poems she describes her strategies this way: "Tell all the Truth but tell it slant — / Success in Circuit lies" (p. 842). This might well stand as a working definition of Dickinson's aesthetics and is embodied in the following poem:

## The Thought beneath so slight a film — ca. 1860

The Thought beneath so slight a film —
Is more distinctly seen —
As laces just reveal the surge —
Or Mists — the Apennine°                               *Italian mountain range*

Paradoxically, "Thought" is more clearly understood precisely because a slight "film" — in this case language — covers it. Language, like lace, enhances what it covers and reveals it all the more — just as a mountain range is more engaging to the imagination if it is covered in mists rather than starkly presenting itself. Poetry for Dickinson intensifies, clarifies, and organizes experience.

Dickinson's poetry is challenging because it is radical and original in its rejection of most traditional nineteenth-century themes and techniques. Her poems require active engagement from the reader because she seems to leave out so much with her elliptical style and remarkable contracting metaphors. But these apparent gaps are filled with meaning if we are sensitive to her use of devices such as personification, allusion, symbolism, and startling syntax and grammar. Because her use of dashes is sometimes puzzling, it helps to read her poems aloud to hear how carefully the words are arranged. What might initially seem intimidating on a silent page can surprise the reader with meaning when heard. It's also worth keeping in mind that Dickinson was not always consistent in her views and that they can change from poem to poem, depending on how she felt at a given moment. For example, her definition of religious belief in "'Faith' is a fine invention" (p. 851) reflects an ironically detached wariness in contrast to the faith embraced in "I never saw a Moor —" (p. 852). Dickinson was less interested in absolute answers to questions than she was in examining and exploring their "circumference."

Because Dickinson's poems are all relatively brief (none is longer than fifty lines), they invite browsing and sampling, but perhaps a useful way into their highly metaphoric and witty world is this "how to" poem that reads almost like a recipe:

## To make a prairie it takes a clover and one bee   date unknown

To make a prairie it takes a clover and one bee,
One clover, and a bee,
And revery.
The revery alone will do,
If bees are few.                                                    5

This quiet but infinite claim for a writer's imagination brings together the range of ingredients in Dickinson's world of domestic and ordinary natural details. Not surprisingly, she deletes rather than adds to the recipe, because the one essential ingredient is the writer's creative imagination. *Bon appétit.*

## Success is counted sweetest    ca. 1859

Success is counted sweetest
By those who ne'er succeed.
To comprehend a nectar
Requires sorest need.

Not one of all the purple Host                                              5
Who took the Flag today
Can tell the definition
So clear of Victory

As he defeated — dying —
On whose forbidden ear                                                      10
The distant strains of triumph
Burst agonized and clear!

### Considerations for Critical Thinking and Writing

1. **First response.** How is *success* defined in this poem? To what extent does that definition agree with your own understanding of the word?
2. What do you think is meant by the use of *comprehend* in line 3? How can a nectar be comprehended?
3. Why do the defeated understand victory better than the victorious?
4. Discuss the effect of the poem's final line.

### Connection to Another Selection

1. In an essay compare the themes of this poem with those of John Keats's "Ode on a Grecian Urn" (p. 572).

## Water, is taught by thirst    ca. 1859

Water, is taught by thirst.
Land — by the Oceans passed.
Transport — by throe —
Peace — by its battles told —
Love, by Memorial Mold —                                                    5
Birds, by the Snow.

1. FIRST RESPONSE. Which image in the poem do you find most powerful? Explain why.

2. How is the paradox of each line of the poem resolved? How is the first word of each line "taught" by the phrase that follows it?

3. CREATIVE RESPONSE. Try your hand at writing similar lines in which something is "taught."

## CONNECTIONS TO OTHER SELECTIONS

1. What does this poem have in common with "Success is counted sweetest" (p. 835)? Which poem do you think is more effective? Explain why.

2. How is the crucial point of this poem related to "I like a look of Agony" (p. 838)?

## *Some keep the Sabbath going to Church* — ca. 1860

Some keep the Sabbath going to Church —
I keep it, staying at Home —
With a Bobolink for a Chorister —
And an Orchard, for a Dome —

Some keep the Sabbath in Surplice°                    *holy robes*    5
I just wear my Wings —
And instead of tolling the Bell, for Church,
Our little Sexton — sings.

God preaches, a noted Clergyman —
And the sermon is never long,                                           10
So instead of getting to Heaven, at last —
I'm going, all along.

### CONSIDERATIONS FOR CRITICAL THINKING AND WRITING

1. FIRST RESPONSE. What is the effect of referring to "Some" people (line 1)?

2. Characterize the speaker's tone.

3. How does the speaker distinguish themself from those who go to church?

4. How might "Surplice" (line 5) be read as a pun?

5. According to the speaker, how should the Sabbath be observed?

### CONNECTION TO ANOTHER SELECTION

1. Write an essay that discusses nature in this poem and in Walt Whitman's "When I Heard the Learn'd Astronomer" (p. 949).

## *I taste a liquor never brewed —*   1861

I taste a liquor never brewed —
From Tankards scooped in Pearl —
Not all the Vats upon the Rhine
Yield such an Alcohol!

Inebriate of Air — am I —                                                                     5
And Debauchee of Dew —
Reeling — thro endless summer days —
From inns of Molten Blue —

When "Landlords" turn the drunken Bee
Out of the Foxglove's door —                                                                 10
When Butterflies — renounce their "drams" —
I shall but drink the more!

Till Seraphs° swing their snowy Hats —                                           *angels*
And Saints — to windows run —
To see the little Tippler                                                                       15
Leaning against the — Sun —

### CONSIDERATIONS FOR CRITICAL THINKING AND WRITING

1. FIRST RESPONSE. What is the poem's central metaphor? How is it developed in each stanza?

2. Which images suggest the causes of the speaker's intoxication?

3. Characterize the speaker's relationship to nature.

### CONNECTION TO ANOTHER SELECTION

1. In an essay, compare this speaker's relationship with nature to that of "To make a prairie it takes a clover and one bee" (p. 834).

## *"Heaven" — is what I cannot reach!*   ca. 1861

"Heaven" — is what I cannot reach!
The Apple on the Tree —
Provided it do hopeless — hang —
That — "Heaven" is — to Me!

The Color, on the Cruising Cloud —                                                            5
The interdicted Land —
Behind the Hill — the House behind —
There — Paradise — is found!

Her teasing Purples — Afternoons —
The credulous — decoy —                                                                        10
Enamored — of the Conjuror —
That spurned us — Yesterday!

## Considerations for Critical Thinking and Writing

1. FIRST RESPONSE. How does the speaker define *heaven*? How does that definition compare with conventional views of heaven?

2. Look up the myth of Tantalus and explain the allusion in line 3.

3. Given the way *heaven* is defined in this poem, how do you think the speaker would describe hell?

## Connections to Other Selections

1. Write an essay that discusses desire in this poem and in "Water, is taught by thirst" (p. 835).

2. Discuss the speakers' attitudes toward pleasure and nature in this poem and in Edna St. Vincent Millay's "Spring" (p. 942).

## *I like a look of Agony*   ca. 1861

I like a look of Agony,
Because I know it's true —
Men do not sham Convulsion,
Nor simulate, a Throe —

The Eyes glaze once — and that is Death —                5
Impossible to feign
The Beads upon the Forehead
By homely Anguish strung.

## Considerations for Critical Thinking and Writing

1. FIRST RESPONSE. Why does the speaker "like a look of Agony"? How do you respond to her appreciation of "Convulsion" (line 3)?

2. Discuss the image of "The Eyes glaze once —" (line 5). Why is that a particularly effective metaphor for death?

3. Characterize the speaker. One critic described the voice in this poem as "almost a hysterical shriek." Explain why you agree or disagree.

## Connection to Another Selection

1. Write an essay on Dickinson's attitudes toward pain and deprivation, using this poem and " 'Heaven' — is what I cannot reach!" (p. 837).

## *Wild Nights — Wild Nights!*   ca. 1861

Wild Nights — Wild Nights!
Were I with thee
Wild Nights should be
Our luxury!

Futile — the Winds —                                                      5
To a Heart in port —
Done with the Compass —
Done with the Chart!

Rowing in Eden —
Ah, the Sea!                                                              10
Might I but moor — Tonight —
In Thee!

### CONSIDERATIONS FOR CRITICAL THINKING AND WRITING

1. FIRST RESPONSE. Thomas Wentworth Higginson, Dickinson's mentor, once said he was afraid that some "malignant" readers might "read into [a poem like this] more than that virgin recluse ever dreamed of putting there." What do you think?

2. Look up the meaning of *luxury* in a dictionary. Why does this word work especially well here?

3. Given the imagery of the final stanza, do you think the speaker is a man or a woman? Explain why.

4. CRITICAL STRATEGIES. Read the section on psychological strategies (pp. 1386–1388) in Chapter 42, "Critical Strategies for Reading." What do you think this poem reveals about the author's personal psychology?

### CONNECTION TO ANOTHER SELECTION

1. Write an essay that compares the voice, figures of speech, and theme of this poem with those of Kwame Dawes's "The Habits of Love" (p. 590).

## *Much Madness is divinest Sense* —   ca. 1862

Much Madness is divinest Sense —
To a discerning Eye —
Much Sense — the starkest Madness —
'Tis the Majority
In this, as All, prevail —                                               5
Assent — and you are sane —
Demur — you're straightway dangerous —
And handled with a Chain —

### CONSIDERATIONS FOR CRITICAL THINKING AND WRITING

1. FIRST RESPONSE. Thomas Wentworth Higginson's wife once referred to Dickinson as the "partially cracked poetess of Amherst." Assuming that Dickinson had some idea of how she was regarded by "the Majority" (line 4), how might this poem be seen as an insight into her life?

2. Discuss the conflict between the individual and society in this poem. Which images are used to describe each? How do these images affect your attitudes about them?

3. Comment on the effectiveness of the poem's final line.

### CONNECTION TO ANOTHER SELECTION

1. Discuss the theme of self-reliance in this poem and in "The Soul selects her own Society —" (p. 777).

## *I dwell in Possibility* —   ca. 1862

I dwell in Possibility —
A fairer House than Prose —
More numerous of Windows —
Superior — for Doors —

Of Chambers as the Cedars —                                                      5
Impregnable of Eye —
And for an Everlasting Roof
The Gambrels° of the Sky —                                    *angled roofs*

Of Visitors — the fairest —
For Occupation — This —                                                          10
The spreading wide my narrow Hands
To gather Paradise —

### CONSIDERATIONS FOR CRITICAL THINKING AND WRITING

1. FIRST RESPONSE. What distinction is made between poetry and prose in this poem? Explain why you agree or disagree with the speaker's distinctions.
2. What is the poem's central metaphor in the second and third stanzas?
3. How does the use of metaphor in this poem become a means for the speaker to envision and create a world beyond the circumstances of his or her actual life?

### CONNECTIONS TO OTHER SELECTIONS

1. Compare what this poem says about poetry and prose with T. E. Hulme's comments in "On the Differences between Poetry and Prose" (p. 594).
2. How can the speaker's sense of expansiveness in this poem be reconciled with the speaker's insistence on contraction in "The Soul selects her own Society —" (p. 777)? Are these poems contradictory? Explain why or why not.

## *I heard a Fly buzz — when I died* —   ca. 1862

I heard a Fly buzz — when I died —
The Stillness in the Room
Was like the Stillness in the Air —
Between the Heaves of Storm —

The Eyes around — had wrung them dry —                                                5
And Breaths were gathering firm
For that last Onset — when the King
Be witnessed — in the Room —

I willed my Keepsakes — Signed away
What portion of me be                                                                10
Assignable — and then it was
There interposed a Fly —

With Blue — uncertain stumbling Buzz —
Between the light — and me —
And then the Windows failed — and then                                               15
I could not see to see —

### CONSIDERATIONS FOR CRITICAL THINKING AND WRITING

1. **FIRST RESPONSE.** What was expected to happen "when the King" was "witnessed" (lines 7–8)? What happened instead?
2. Why do you think Dickinson chooses a fly rather than perhaps a bee or gnat?
3. What is the effect of the last line? Why not end the poem with "I could not see" instead of the additional "to see"?
4. Discuss the sounds in the poem. Are there any instances of onomatopoeia?

### CONNECTION TO ANOTHER SELECTION

1. Consider the meaning of *light* (line 14) in this poem and in "There's a certain Slant of light" (p. 1423).

## *Because I could not stop for Death —*     ca. 1863

Because I could not stop for Death —
He kindly stopped for me —
The Carriage held but just Ourselves —
And Immortality.

We slowly drove — He knew no haste                                                   5
And I had put away
My labor and my leisure too,
For His Civility —

We passed the School, where Children strove
At Recess — in the Ring —                                                            10
We passed the Fields of Gazing Grain —
We passed the Setting Sun —

Or rather — He passed Us —
The Dews drew quivering and chill —
For only Gossamer, my Gown —                                                         15
My Tippet° — only Tulle —                                                            *shawl*

We paused before a House that seemed
A Swelling of the Ground —
The Roof was scarcely visible —
The Cornice — in the Ground —                                          20

Since then — 'tis Centuries — and yet
Feels shorter than the Day
I first surmised the Horses' Heads
Were toward Eternity —

### CONSIDERATIONS FOR CRITICAL THINKING AND WRITING

1. FIRST RESPONSE. Why couldn't the speaker "stop for Death"?
2. How is death personified in this poem? How does the speaker respond to him? Why are they accompanied by Immortality?
3. What is the significance of the things they "passed" in the third stanza?
4. What is the "House" in lines 17–20?
5. Discuss the rhythm of the lines. How, for example, is the rhythm of line 14 related to its meaning?

### CONNECTIONS TO OTHER SELECTIONS

1. Compare the tone of this poem with that of Dickinson's "Apparently with no surprise" (p. 852).
2. Write an essay comparing Dickinson's view of death in this poem and in "If I shouldn't be alive" (p. 833). Which poem is more powerful for you? Explain why.

## Tell all the Truth but tell it slant —    ca. 1868

Tell all the Truth but tell it slant —
Success in Circuit lies
Too bright for our infirm Delight
The Truth's superb surprise

As Lightning to the Children eased                                     5
With explanation kind
The Truth must dazzle gradually
Or every man be blind —

### CONSIDERATIONS FOR CRITICAL THINKING AND WRITING

1. FIRST RESPONSE. What do you think the first line means? Why should truth be told "slant" and circuitously?
2. How does the second stanza explain the first?
3. How is this poem an example of its own theme?

CONNECTIONS TO OTHER SELECTIONS

1. How does the first stanza of "I know that He exists" (p. 852) suggest an idea similar to this poem's? Why do you think the last eight lines of the former aren't similar in theme to this poem?

2. Write an essay on Dickinson's attitudes about the purpose and strategies of poetry by considering this poem as well as "The Thought beneath so slight a film—" (p. 834).

## *Oh Sumptuous moment*     ca. 1868

Oh Sumptuous moment
Slower go
That I may gloat on thee —
'Twill never be the same to starve
Now I abundance see —                                             5

Which was to famish, then or now —
The difference of Day
Ask him unto the Gallows led —
With morning in the sky

CONSIDERATIONS FOR CRITICAL THINKING AND WRITING

1. FIRST RESPONSE. How do the sounds of the first stanza contribute to its meaning?

2. What kind of moment do you imagine the speaker is describing?

3. How do the final three lines shed light on the meaning of lines 1–6?

CONNECTIONS TO OTHER SELECTIONS

1. Compare and contrast the themes of this poem, "Water, is taught by thirst" (p. 835), and "'Heaven'—is what I cannot reach!" (p. 837).

## *A Route of Evanescence*     ca. 1879

A Route of Evanescence
With a revolving Wheel —
A Resonance of Emerald —
A Rush of Cochineal° —
And every Blossom on the Bush
Adjusts its tumbled Head —                                        5
The mail from Tunis, probably,
An easy Morning's Ride —

---

4 *Cochineal:* An insect whose pulverized body was used to produce a deep red dye.

## CONSIDERATIONS FOR CRITICAL THINKING AND WRITING

1. FIRST RESPONSE. What does this poem describe?
2. Discuss the effectiveness of the poem's images in capturing what is described.
3. Consider how the poem's sounds contribute to its meanings.
4. How do the last two lines affect the poem's tone?

### CONNECTION TO ANOTHER SELECTION

1. Discuss the style and theme of this poem and Dickinson's "A Bird came down the Walk —" (p. 642).

## *From all the Jails the Boys and Girls*   ca. 1881

From all the Jails the Boys and Girls
Ecstatically leap —
Beloved only Afternoon
That Prison doesn't keep

They storm the Earth and stun the Air,                                  5
A Mob of solid Bliss —
Alas — that Frowns should lie in wait
For such a Foe as this —

### CONSIDERATIONS FOR CRITICAL THINKING AND WRITING

1. FIRST RESPONSE. What are the "Jails"?
2. Comment on the effectiveness of the description in lines 5 and 6.
3. How might "Frowns" be read symbolically?

### CONNECTION TO ANOTHER SELECTION

1. In an essay, discuss the treatment of childhood in this poem and in Robert Frost's " 'Out, Out —'" (p. 869).

---

## Perspectives

---

### EMILY DICKINSON

## *A Description of Herself*   1862

Mr Higginson,
    Your kindness claimed earlier gratitude — but I was ill — and write today, from my pillow.
    Thank you for the surgery — it was not so painful as I supposed. I bring you others° — as you ask — though they might not differ —

---

*others:* Dickinson had sent poems to Higginson for his opinions and enclosed more with this letter.

While my thought is undressed — I can make the distinction, but when I put them in the Gown — they look alike, and numb.

You asked how old I was? I made no verse — but one or two° — until this winter — Sir —

I had a terror — since September — I could tell to none — and so I sing, as 5 the Boy does by the Burying Ground — because I am afraid — You inquire my Books — For Poets — I have Keats — and Mr and Mrs Browning. For Prose — Mr Ruskin — Sir Thomas Browne — and the Revelations. I went to school — but in your manner of the phrase — had no education. When a little Girl, I had a friend, who taught me Immortality — but venturing too near, himself — he never returned — Soon after, my Tutor, died — and for several years, my Lexicon — was my only companion — Then I found one more — but he was not contented I be his scholar — so he left the Land.

You ask of my Companions Hills — Sir — and the Sundown — and a Dog — large as myself, that my Father bought me — They are better than Beings — because they know — but do not tell — and the noise in the Pool, at Noon — excels my Piano. I have a Brother and Sister — My Mother does not care for thought — and Father, too busy with his Briefs — to notice what we do — He buys me many Books — but begs me not to read them — because he fears they joggle the Mind. They are religious — except me — and address an Eclipse, every morning — whom they call their "Father." But I fear my story fatigues you — I would like to learn — Could you tell me how to grow — or is it unconveyed — like Melody — or Witchcraft?

From a letter to Thomas Wentworth Higginson,
April 25, 1862

*one or two:* Actually she had written almost three hundred poems.

### Considerations for Critical Thinking and Writing

1. What impression does this letter give you of Dickinson?
2. What kinds of thoughts are there in the foreground of her thinking?
3. To what extent is the style of her letter writing like that of her poetry?

## Thomas Wentworth Higginson (1823–1911)

## *On Meeting Dickinson for the First Time*  1870

A large county lawyer's house, brown brick, with great trees & a garden — I sent up my card. A parlor dark & cool & stiffish, a few books & engravings & an open piano. . . .

A step like a pattering child's in entry & in glided a little plain woman with two smooth bands of reddish hair & a face a little like Belle Dove's; not plainer — with no good feature — in a very plain & exquisitely clean white pique & a blue net worsted shawl. She came to me with two day lilies which she put in a sort of childlike way into my hand & said "These are my introduction" in a soft frightened breathless childlike voice — & added under her breath Forgive me if I am frightened;

I never see strangers & hardly know what I say — but she talked soon & thenceforward continuously — & deferentially — sometimes stopping to ask me to talk instead of her — but readily recommencing . . . thoroughly ingenuous & simple . . . & saying many things which you would have thought foolish & I wise — & some things you wd. hv. liked. I add a few over the page. . . .

"Women talk; men are silent; that is why I dread women."

"My father only reads on Sunday — he reads *lonely* & *rigorous* books."

"If I read a book [and] it makes my whole body so cold no fire ever can warm  5
me I know *that* is poetry. If I feel physically as if the top of my head were taken off, I know *that* is poetry. These are the only ways I know it. Is there any other way."

"How do most people live without any thoughts. There are many people in the world (you must have noticed them in the street) How do they live. How do they get strength to put on their clothes in the morning"

"When I lost the use of my Eyes it was a comfort to think there were so few real *books* that I could easily find some one to read me all of them"

"Truth is such a *rare* thing it is delightful to tell it."

"I find ecstasy in living — the mere sense of living is joy enough"

I asked if she never felt want of employment, never going off the place & never  10
seeing any visitor "I never thought of conceiving that I could ever have the slightest approach to such a want in all future time" (& added) "I feel that I have not expressed myself strongly enough."

From a letter to his wife, August 16, 1870

### Considerations for Critical Thinking and Writing

1. How old is Dickinson when Higginson meets her? Does this description seem commensurate with her age? Explain why or why not.

2. Choose one of the quotations from Dickinson that Higginson includes and write an essay about what it reveals about her.

## Mabel Loomis Todd (1856–1932)

## *The* Character *of Amherst*    1881

I must tell you about the *character* of Amherst. It is a lady whom the people call the *Myth*. She is a sister of Mr. Dickinson, & seems to be the climax of all the family oddity. She has not been outside of her own house in fifteen years, except once to see a new church, when she crept out at night, & viewed it by moonlight. No one who calls upon her mother & sister ever see her, but she allows little children once in a great while, & one at a time, to come in, when she gives them cake or candy, or some nicety, for she is very fond of little ones. But more often she lets down the sweetmeat by a string, out of a window, to them. She dresses wholly in white, & her mind is said to be perfectly wonderful. She writes finely, but no one *ever* sees her. Her sister, who was at Mrs. Dickinson's party, invited me to come & sing to her mother sometime. . . . People tell me the *myth* will hear every note — she will be near, but unseen. . . . Isn't that like a book? So interesting.

From a letter to her parents, November 6, 1881

## Considerations for Critical Thinking and Writing

1. Todd, who in the 1890s would edit Dickinson's poems and letters, had known her for only two months when she wrote this letter. How does Todd characterize Dickinson?

2. Does this description seem positive or negative to you? Explain your answer.

3. A few of Dickinson's poems, such as "Much Madness is divinest Sense—" (p. 839), suggest that she was aware of this perception of her. Refer to her poems in discussing Dickinson's response to this perception.

## Sandra M. Gilbert (b. 1936) and Susan Gubar (b. 1944)

## On Dickinson's White Dress  1979

Today a dress that the Amherst Historical Society assures us is *the* white dress Dickinson wore — or at least one of her "Uniforms of Snow" — hangs in a drycleaner's plastic bag in the closet of the Dickinson homestead. Perfectly preserved, beautifully flounced and tucked, it is larger than most readers would have expected this self-consciously small poet's dress to be, and thus reminds visiting scholars of the enduring enigma of Dickinson's central metaphor, even while it draws gasps from more practical visitors, who reflect with awe upon the difficulties of maintaining such a costume. But what exactly did the literal and figurative whiteness of this costume represent? What rewards did it offer that would cause an intelligent woman to overlook those practical difficulties? Comparing Dickinson's obsession with whiteness to [Herman] Melville's, William R. Sherwood suggests that "it reflected in her case the Christian mystery and not a Christian enigma . . . a decision to announce . . . the assumption of a worldly death that paradoxically involved regeneration." This, he adds, her gown — "a typically slant demonstration of truth" — should have revealed "to anyone with the wit to catch on."[1]

We might reasonably wonder, however, if Dickinson herself consciously intended her wardrobe to convey any one message. The range of associations her white poems imply suggests, on the contrary, that for her, as for Melville, white is the ultimate symbol of enigma, paradox, and irony, "not so much a color as the visible absence of color, and at the same time the concrete of all colors." Melville's question [in *Moby-Dick*] might, therefore, also be hers: "is it for these reasons that there is such a dumb blankness, full of meaning, in a wide landscape of snows — a colorless, all-color of atheism from which we shrink?" And his concluding speculation might be hers too, his remark "that the mystical cosmetic which produces every one of [Nature's] hues, the great principle of light, for ever remains white or colorless in itself, and if operating without medium upon matter, would touch all objects . . . with its own blank tinge." For white, in Dickinson's poetry, frequently represents both the energy (the white heat) of Romantic creativity, and the loneliness (the polar cold) of the renunciation or tribulation Romantic creativity may demand, both the white radiance of eternity — or Revelation — and the white terror of a shroud.

> From *The Madwoman in the Attic: The Woman Writer*
> *and the Nineteenth-Century Literary Imagination*

---

[1] Sherwood, William R. *Circumference and Circumstance: Stages in the Mind and Art of Emily Dickinson* (New York: Columbia UP, 1968), 152, 231. [Gilbert and Gubar's note.]

1. What meanings do Gilbert and Gubar attribute to Dickinson's white dress?

2. What other reasons can you think of that might account for Dickinson's wearing only white?

## Paula Bennett (b. 1936)

### On "I heard a Fly buzz — when I died —"    1990

Dickinson's rage against death, a rage that led her at times to hate both life and death, might have been alleviated, had she been able to gather hard evidence about an afterlife. But, of course, she could not. "The *Bareheaded life* — under the grass —," she wrote to Samuel Bowles in c. 1860, "worries one like a Wasp." If death was the gate to a better life in "the childhood of the kingdom of Heaven," as the sentimentalists — and Christ — claimed, then, perhaps, there was compensation and healing for life's woes. . . . But how do we know? What can we know? In "I heard a Fly buzz — when I died," Dickinson concludes that we do not know much. . . .

Like many people in her period, Dickinson was fascinated by death-bed scenes. How, she asked various correspondents, did this or that person die? In particular, she wanted to know if their deaths revealed any information about the nature of the afterlife. In this poem, however, she imagines her own death-bed scene, and the answer she provides is grim, as grim (and, at the same time, as ironically mocking) as anything she ever wrote.

In the narrowing focus of death, the fly's insignificant buzz, magnified tenfold by the stillness in the room, is all that the speaker hears. This kind of distortion in scale is common. It is one of the "illusions" of perception. But here it is horrifying because it defeats every expectation we have. Death is supposed to be an experience of awe. It is the moment when the soul, departing the body, is taken up by God. Hence the watchers at the bedside wait for the moment when the "King" (whether God or death) "be witnessed" in the room. And hence the speaker assigns away everything but that which she expects God (her soul) or death (her body) to take.

What arrives instead, however, is neither God nor death but a fly, "[w]ith Blue — uncertain — stumbling Buzz," a fly, that is, no more secure, no more sure, than we are. Dickinson had associated flies with death once before in the exquisite lament, "How many times these low feet / staggered." In this poem, they buzz "on the / chamber window," and speckle it with dirt, reminding us that the housewife, who once protected us from such intrusions, will protect us no longer. Their presence is threatening but only in a minor way, "dull" like themselves. They are a background noise we do not have to deal with yet.

In "I heard a Fly buzz," on the other hand, there is only one fly and its buzz    5 is not only foregrounded. Before the poem is over, the buzz takes up the entire field of perception, coming between the speaker and the "light" (of day, of life, of knowledge). It is then that the "Windows" (the eyes that are the windows of the soul as well as, metonymically, the light that passes through the panes of glass) "fail" and the speaker is left in darkness — in death, in ignorance. She cannot "see" to "see" (understand).

Given that the only sure thing we know about "life after death" is that flies — in their adult form and more particularly, as maggots — devour us, the poem is at the very least a grim joke. In projecting her death-bed scene, Dickinson confronts her ignorance and gives back the only answer human knowledge can with any certainty give. While we may hope for an afterlife, no one, not even the dying, can prove it exists.

From *Emily Dickinson: Woman Poet*

### CONSIDERATIONS FOR CRITICAL THINKING AND WRITING

1. According to Bennett, what is the symbolic value of the fly?
2. Does Bennett leave out any significant elements of the poem in her analysis? Explain why you think she did or did not.
3. Choose a Dickinson poem and write a detailed analysis that attempts to account for all of its major elements.

## MARTHA NELL SMITH (B. 1953)

### On "Because I could not stop for Death —" 1993

That this poem begins and ends with humanity's ultimate dream of self-importance — Immortality and Eternity — could well be the joke central to its meaning, for Dickinson carefully surrounds the fantasy of living ever after with the dirty facts of life — dusty carriage rides, schoolyards, and farmers' fields. Many may contend that, like the Puritans and metaphysicals before her, Dickinson pulls the sublime down to the ridiculous but unavoidable facts of existence, thus imbues life on earth with its real import. On the other hand, Dickinson may have argued otherwise. Very late in her life, she wrote, "When Jesus tells us about his Father, we distrust him. When he shows us his Home, we turn away, but when he confides to us that he is 'acquainted with Grief,' we listen, for that is also an Acquaintance of our own." Instead of sharing their faith, Dickinson may be showing the community around her, most of whom were singing "When we all get to Heaven what a day of rejoicing that will be," how selfishly selective is their belief in a system that bolsters egocentrism by assuring believers not only that their individual identities will survive death, but also that they are one of the exclusive club of the saved. Waiting for the return of Eden or Paradise, which "is always eligible" and which she "never believed . . . to be a superhuman site," those believers may simply find themselves gathering dust. Surrounded by the faithful, Dickinson struggled with trust and doubt in Christian promises herself, but whether she believed in salvation or even in immortality is endlessly debatable. Readers can select poems and letters and construct compelling arguments to prove that she did or did not. But for every declaration evincing belief, there is one like that to Elizabeth Holland:

The Fiction of "Santa Claus" always reminds me of the reply to my early question of "Who made the Bible" — "Holy Men moved by the Holy Ghost," and though I have now ceased my investigations, the Solution is insufficient —

What "Because I could not stop for Death —" will not allow is any hard and fast conclusion to be drawn about the matter. Once again . . . by mixing tropes and tones Dickinson underscores the importance of refusing any single-minded response to a subject and implicitly attests to the power in continually opening possibilities by repeatedly posing questions.

From *Comic Power in Emily Dickinson*, by Suzanne Juhasz,
Cristanne Miller, and Martha Nell Smith

### Considerations for Critical Thinking and Writing

1. In what sense, according to Smith, could a joke be central to the meaning of "Because I could not stop for Death —" (p. 841)?

2. Compare the potential joke in this poem and in "I know that He exists" (p. 852). How is your reading of each poem influenced by considering them together?

3. Read the sample paper on "Religious Faith in Four Poems by Emily Dickinson" (p. 853) and write an analysis of "Because I could not stop for Death—" that supports or refutes the paper's thesis.

---

### Questions for Writing about an Author in Depth

As you read multiple works by the same author, you're likely to be struck by the similarities and differences in those selections. You'll begin to recognize situations, events, characters, issues, perspectives, styles, and strategies — even recurring words or phrases — that provide a kind of signature, making the poems in some way identifiable with that particular writer.

The following questions can help you respond to multiple works by the same author. They should help you listen to how a writer's works can speak to one another and to you. Additional useful questions can be found elsewhere in this book. See Chapter 43, "Reading and the Writing Process."

1. What topics reappear in the writer's work? What seem to be the major concerns of the author?

2. Does the author have a definable worldview that can be discerned from work to work? Is, for example, the writer liberal, conservative, apolitical, or religious?

3. What social values come through in the author's work? Do they seem to identify with a particular group or social class?

4. Is there a consistent voice or point of view from work to work? Is it a persona or the author's actual self?

5. How much of the author's own life experiences and historical moment make their way into the works?

6. Does the author experiment with style from work to work, or are the works mostly consistent with one another?

7. Can the author's work be identified with a literary tradition, such as *carpe diem* poetry, that aligns it with that of other writers?

8. What is distinctive about the author's writing? Is the language innovative? Are the themes challenging? Are the voices conventional? Is the tone characteristic?

9. Could you identify another work by the same author without a name being attached to it? What are the distinctive features that allow you to do so?

10. Do any of the writer's works seem *not* to be by that writer? Why?

11. What other writers are most like this author in style and content? Why?

12. Has the writer's work evolved over time? Are there significant changes or developments? Are there new ideas and styles, or do the works remain largely the same?

13. How would you characterize the author's writing habits? Is it possible to anticipate what goes on in different works, or are you surprised by their content or style?

14. Can difficult or ambiguous passages in a work be resolved by referring to a similar passage in another work?

15. What does the writer say about their own work? Do you trust the teller or the tale? Which do you think is more reliable?

## A SAMPLE IN-DEPTH STUDY

The following paper was written for an assignment that called for an analysis (about 750 words) on any topic that could be traced in three or four poems by Dickinson. The student, Michael Weitz, chose " 'Faith' is a fine invention," "I know that He exists," "I never saw a Moor —," and "Apparently with no surprise."

Previous knowledge of a writer's work can set up useful expectations in a reader. In the case of the four Dickinson poems included in this section, religion emerges as a central topic linked to a number of issues, including faith, immortality, skepticism, and the nature of God. The student selected these poems because he noticed Dickinson's intense interest in religious faith owing to the many poems that explore a variety of religious attitudes in her work. He chose these four because they were closely related, but he might have found equally useful clusters of poems about love, nature, domestic life, or writing. What especially intrigued him was some of the information he read about Dickinson's sternly religious father and the orthodox nature of the religious values of her hometown of Amherst, Massachusetts. Because this paper was not a research paper, he did not pursue these issues beyond the level of the general remarks provided in an introduction to her poetry (though he might have). He did, however, use this biographical and historical information as a means of framing his search for poems that were related to one another. In doing so he discovered consistent concerns along with contradictory themes that became the basis of his paper.

### *"Faith" is a fine invention*    ca. 1860

"Faith" is a fine invention
When Gentlemen can *see* —
But *Microscopes* are prudent
In an Emergency.

## I know that He exists    ca. 1862

I know that He exists.
Somewhere — in Silence —
He has hid his rare life
From our gross eyes.

'Tis an instant's play.                                                    5
'Tis a fond Ambush —
Just to make Bliss
Earn her own surprise!

But — should the play
Prove piercing earnest —                                                  10
Should the glee–glaze —
In Death's — stiff — stare —

Would not the fun
Look too expensive!
Would not the jest —                                                      15
Have crawled too far!

## I never saw a Moor —    ca. 1865

I never saw a Moor —
I never saw the Sea —
Yet know I how the Heather looks
And what a Billow be.

I never spoke with God                                                    5
Nor visited in Heaven —
Yet certain am I of the spot
As if the Checks were given —

## Apparently with no surprise    ca. 1884

Apparently with no surprise
To any happy Flower
The Frost beheads it at its play —
In accidental power —
The blond Assassin passes on —                                           5
The Sun proceeds unmoved
To measure off another Day
For an Approving God.

## A SAMPLE STUDENT PAPER

### *Religious Faith in Four Poems by Emily Dickinson*

Weitz 1

Michael Weitz

Professor Pearl

English 270

5 May 2023

Religious Faith in Four Poems by Emily Dickinson

Throughout much of her poetry, Emily Dickinson wrestles with complex notions of God, faith, and religious devotion. She adheres to no consistent view of religion; rather, her poetry reveals a vision of God and faith that is constantly evolving. Dickinson's gods range from the strict and powerful Old Testament father to a loving spiritual guide to an irrational and ridiculous imaginary figure. Through these varying images of God, Dickinson portrays contrasting images of the meaning and validity of religious faith. Her work reveals competing attitudes toward religious devotion as conventional religious piety struggles with a more cynical perception of God and religious worship.

Dickinson's "I never saw a Moor—" reveals a vision of traditional religious sensibilities. Although the speaker readily admits that "I never spoke with God / Nor visited in Heaven—" (lines 5-6), her devout faith in a supreme being does not waver. The poem appears to be a straightforward profession of true faith stemming from the argument that the proof of God's existence is the universe's existence. Dickinson's imagery therefore evolves from the natural to the supernatural, first establishing her convictions that moors and seas exist, in spite of her lack of personal contact with either. This leads to the foundation of her religious faith, again based not on physical experience but on intellectual convictions. The speaker professes that she believes in the existence of Heaven even without conclusive evidence: "Yet certain am I of the spot / As if the Checks were given—" (7-8). But the appearance of such idealistic views of God and faith in "I never saw a Moor—" are transformed in Dickinson's other poems into a much more skeptical vision of the validity of religious piety.

*Introduction providing overview of faith in Dickinson's work*

*Thesis analyzing poet's attitudes toward God and religion*

*Analysis of religious piety in "I never saw a Moor—" supported with textual evidence*

*Contrast between attitudes in "Moor" and other poems*

While faith is portrayed as an authentic and deeply important quality in "I never saw a Moor—," Dickinson's "'Faith' is a fine invention" portrays faith as much less essential. Faith is defined in the poem as "a fine invention" (1), suggesting that it is created by man for man and therefore is not a crucial aspect of the natural universe. Thus the strong idealistic faith of "I never saw a Moor—" becomes discredited in the face of scientific rationalism. The speaker compares religious faith with actual microscopes, both of which are meant to enhance one's vision in some way. But "Faith" is useful only "When Gentlemen can *see*—" already (2); "In an Emergency," when one ostensibly cannot see, "*Microscopes* are prudent" (4, 3). Dickinson pits religion against science, suggesting that science, with its tangible evidence and rational attitude, is a more reliable lens through which to view the world. Faith is irreverently reduced to a mere "invention" and one that is ultimately less useful than microscopes or other scientific instruments.

Rational, scientific observations are not the only contributing factor to the portrayal of religious skepticism in Dickinson's poems; nature itself is seen to be incompatible in some ways with conventional religious ideology. In "Apparently with no surprise," the speaker recognizes the inexorable cycle of natural life and death as a morning frost kills a flower. But the tension in this poem stems not from the "happy Flower" (2) struck down by the frost's "accidental power" (4) but from the apparent indifference of the "Approving God" (8) who condones this seemingly cruel and unnecessary death. God is seen as remote and uncompromising, and it is this perceived distance between the speaker and God that reveals the increasing absurdity of traditional religious faith. The speaker understands that praying to God or believing in religion cannot change the course of nature, and as a result feels so helplessly distanced from God that religious faith becomes virtually meaningless.

Dickinson's religious skepticism becomes even more explicit in "I know that He exists," in which the speaker attempts to understand the connection between seeing God and facing death. In this poem Dickinson characterizes God as a remote and mysterious figure; the speaker mockingly asserts, "I know that He exists" (1), even though "He has hid his rare life / From our gross eyes" (3-4). The skepticism toward religious faith revealed in this

**Analysis of scientific rationalism in "'Faith' is a fine invention" supported with textual evidence**

**Analysis of God and nature in "Apparently with no surprise" supported with textual evidence**

**Analysis of characterization of God in "I know that He exists" supported with textual evidence**

poem stems from the speaker's recognition of the paradoxical quest that people undertake to know and to see God. A successful attempt to see God, to win the game of hide-and-seek that He apparently is orchestrating, results inevitably in death. With this recognition the speaker comes to view religion as an absurd and reckless game in which the prize may be "Bliss" (7) but more likely is "Death's—stiff—stare—" (12). For, to see God and to meet one's death as a result certainly suggests that the game of trying to see God (the so-called "fun" of line 13) is much "too expensive" and that religion itself is a "jest" that, like the serpent in Genesis, has "crawled too far" (14-16).

Ultimately, the vision of religious faith that Dickinson describes in her poems is one of suspicion and cynicism. She cannot reconcile the physical world to the spiritual existence that Christian doctrine teaches, and as a result the traditional perception of God becomes ludicrous. "I never saw a Moor—" does attempt to sustain a conventional vision of religious devotion, but Dickinson's poems overall are far more likely to suggest that God is elusive, indifferent, and often cruel, thus undermining the traditional vision of God as a loving father worthy of devout worship. Thus, not only religious faith but also those who are religiously faithful become targets for Dickinson's irreverent criticism of conventional belief.

> Conclusion providing well-supported final analysis of poet's views on God and faith

## Works Cited

Dickinson, Emily. "Apparently with no surprise." Meyer and Miller, p. 852.

---. "'Faith' is a fine invention." Meyer and Miller, p. 851.

---. "I know that He exists." Meyer and Miller, p. 852.

---. "I never saw a Moor—." Meyer and Miller, p. 852.

Meyer, Michael, and D. Quentin Miller, editors. *The Compact Bedford Introduction to Literature,* 13th ed., Bedford/St. Martin's, 2024.

## Suggested Topics for Longer Papers

1. Irony is abundant in Dickinson's poetry. Choose five poems from this chapter that strike you as especially ironic and discuss her use of irony in each. Taken individually and collectively, what do these poems suggest to you about the poet's sensibilities and her ways of looking at the world?

2. Readers have sometimes noted that Dickinson's poetry does not reflect very much of the social, political, economic, religious, and historical events of her lifetime. Using the poems in this chapter as the basis of your discussion, what can you say about the contexts in which Dickinson wrote? What kind of world do you think she inhabited, and how did she respond to it?

# 30

## A Study of Robert Frost

Eric Schaal/The LIFE Picture Collection/
Shutterstock

A poem . . . begins as a lump in the throat,
a sense of wrong, a homesickness, a
love-sickness. . . . It finds the thought
and the thought finds the words.

— ROBERT FROST

Every poem is doubtlessly affected by the personal history of its composer, but Robert Frost's poems are especially known for their reflection of New England life. Although the poems included in this chapter evoke the landscapes of Frost's life and work, the depth and range of those landscapes are far more complicated than his popular reputation typically acknowledges. He was an enormously private man and a much more subtle poet than many of his readers have expected him to be. His poems warrant careful, close readings. As you explore his poetry, you may find useful the Questions for Writing

Art and History Collection/Alamy.

about an Author in Depth (p. 850) as a means of stimulating your thinking about his life and work.

## A BRIEF BIOGRAPHY

Few poets have enjoyed the popular success that Robert Frost (1874–1963) achieved during his lifetime, and no twentieth-century American poet has been as widely read and honored. Frost is as much associated with New England as the stone walls that help define its landscape; his reputation, however, transcends regional boundaries. Although he was named poet laureate of Vermont only two years before his death, he was for many years the nation's unofficial poet laureate. Frost collected honors the way some people pick up burrs on country walks. Among his awards were four Pulitzer Prizes, the Bollingen Prize, a Congressional Medal, and dozens of honorary degrees. Perhaps his most moving appearance was his recitation of "The Gift Outright" for millions of Americans at the inauguration of John F. Kennedy in 1961.

Robert Frost at age eighteen (1892), the year he graduated from high school. "Education," Frost once said, "is the ability to listen to almost anything without losing your temper or your self-confidence."
Dartmouth College Library.

Robert Frost with his wife Elinor Miriam White, and his children Lesley Frost Ballantine, Carol, Irma, and Marjorie. Both Carol and Marjorie would pass before Frost; Carol by suicide and Marjorie in childbirth.
Fotosearch/Getty Images

Robert Frost at age sixty-seven (1943). Frost wrote, "I would have written of me on my stone: I had a lover's quarrel with the world."
Eric Schaal/The LIFE Picture Collection/Shutterstock

Robert Frost at his writing desk in Franconia, New Hampshire, 1915. "I have never started a poem whose end I knew," Frost said. "Writing a poem is discovering."
History and Art Collection/Alamy

Frost's recognition as a poet is especially remarkable because his career as a writer did not attract any significant attention until he was nearly forty years old. He taught himself to write while he labored at odd jobs, taught school, or farmed.

Frost's early identity seems very remote from the New England soil. Although his parents were descended from generations of New Englanders, he was born in San Francisco and was named Robert Lee Frost after the Confederate general. After his father died in 1885, his mother moved the family back to Massachusetts to live with relatives. Frost graduated from high school sharing valedictorian honors with the classmate who would become his wife three years later. Between high school and marriage, he attended Dartmouth College for a few months and then taught. His teaching prompted him to enroll at Harvard in 1897, but after less than two years he withdrew without a degree (though Harvard would eventually award him an honorary doctorate in 1937, four years after Dartmouth conferred its honorary degree on him). For the next decade, Frost read and wrote poems when he was not chicken farming or teaching. In 1912, he sold his farm and moved his family to England, where he hoped to find the audience that his poetry did not have in America.

Three years in England made it possible for Frost to return home as a poet. His first two volumes of poetry, *A Boy's Will* (1913) and *North of Boston* (1914), were published in England. During the next twenty years, honors and awards were conferred on collections such as *Mountain Interval* (1916), *New Hampshire* (1923), *West-Running Brook* (1928), and *A Further Range* (1936). These are the volumes on which most of Frost's popular and critical reputation rests. Later collections include *A Witness Tree* (1942), *A Masque of Reason* (1945), *Steeple Bush* (1947), *A Masque of Mercy* (1947), *Complete Poems* (1949), and *In the Clearing* (1962). In addition to publishing his works, Frost endeared himself to audiences throughout the country by presenting his poetry almost as conversations. He also taught at a number of schools, including Amherst College, the University of Michigan, Harvard University, Dartmouth College, and Middlebury College.

Frost's countless poetry readings generated wide audiences eager to claim him as their poet. The image he cultivated resembled closely what the public likes to think a poet should be. Frost was seen as a lovable, wise old man; his simple wisdom and cracker-barrel sayings appeared comforting and homey. From this Yankee rustic, audiences learned that "There's a lot yet that isn't understood" or "We love the things we love for what they are" or "Good fences make good neighbors."

In a sense, Frost packaged himself for public consumption. "I am . . . my own salesman," he said. When asked direct questions about the meanings of his poems, he often winked or scratched his head to give the impression that the customer was always right. To be sure, there is a simplicity in Frost's language, but that simplicity does not fully reflect the depth of the man, the complexity of his themes, or the richness of his art.

The folksy optimist behind the public lectern did not reveal his private troubles to his audiences, although he did address those problems at his writing desk. Frost suffered from professional jealousies, anger, and depression. His family life was especially painful. Four of his six children died: a son at the age of four from cholera, a daughter three days after birth, another daughter in her late twenties from childbirth complications, and another son by suicide. His marriage was filled with tension. Although Frost's work is landscaped with sunlight, snow, birches, birds, blueberries, and squirrels, it is important to recognize that he was also intimately "acquainted with the night," a phrase that serves as the haunting title of one of his poems (see p. 612).

As a corrective to Frost's popular reputation, one critic, Lionel Trilling, described the world Frost creates in his poems as a "terrifying universe," characterized by loneliness, anguish, frustration, doubts, disappointment, and despair. To point this out is not to annihilate the pleasantness and even good-natured cheerfulness that can be enjoyed in Frost's poetry, but to say that Frost is not so one-dimensional as he is sometimes assumed to be. Frost's poetry requires readers who are alert and willing to penetrate the simplicity of its language to see the elusive and ambiguous meanings that lie below the surface.

## AN INTRODUCTION TO HIS WORK

Frost's treatment of nature helps explain the various levels of meaning in his poetry. The familiar natural world his poems evoke is sharply detailed. We hear icy branches clicking against themselves, we see the snow-white trunks of birches, we feel the smarting pain of a twig lashing across a face. The aspects of the natural world Frost describes are designated to give pleasure, but they are also frequently calculated to provoke thought. His use of nature tends to be symbolic. Complex meanings are derived from simple facts, such as a spider killing a moth or the difference between fire and ice (see "Design," p. 874, and "Fire and Ice," p. 870). Although Frost's strategy is to talk about particular events and individual experiences, his poems evoke universal issues.

Frost's poetry has strong regional roots and is "versed in country things," but it flourishes in any receptive imagination because, in the final analysis, it is concerned with human beings. Frost's New England landscapes are the occasion rather than the ultimate focus of his poems. Like the rural voices he creates in his poems, Frost typically approaches his themes indirectly. He explained the reason for this in a talk titled "Education by Poetry":

> Poetry provides the one permissible way of saying one thing and meaning another. People say, "Why don't you say what you mean?" We never do that, do we, being all of us too much poets. We like to talk in parables and in hints and in indirections — whether from diffidence or some other instinct.

The result is that the settings, characters, and situations that make up the subject matter of Frost's poems are vehicles for his perceptions about life.

In "Stopping by Woods on a Snowy Evening" (p. 778), for example, Frost uses the kind of familiar New England details that constitute his poetry for more than descriptive purposes. He shapes them into a meditation on the tension we sometimes feel between life's responsibilities and the "lovely, dark and deep" attraction that death offers. When the speaker's horse "gives his harness bells a shake," we are reminded that we are confronting a universal theme as well as a quiet moment of natural beauty.

Among the major concerns that appear in Frost's poetry are the fragility of life, the consequences of rejecting or accepting the conditions of one's life, the passion of inconsolable grief, the difficulty of sustaining intimacy, the fear of loneliness and isolation, the inevitability of change, the tensions between the individual and society, and the place of tradition and custom.

Whatever theme is encountered in a poem by Frost, a reader is likely to agree with him that "the initial delight is in the surprise of remembering something I didn't know." To achieve that fresh sense of discovery, Frost allowed himself to follow his instincts; his poetry

> inclines to the impulse, it assumes direction with the first line laid down, it runs a course of lucky events, and ends in a clarification of life — not necessarily a great clarification, such as sects and cults are founded on, but in a momentary stay against confusion.

This description from "On the Figure a Poem Makes," Frost's brief introduction to *Complete Poems*, may sound as if his poetry is formless and merely "lucky," but his poems tend to be more conventional than experimental: "The artist in me," as he put the matter in one of his poems, "cries out for design."

From Frost's perspective, "free verse is like playing tennis with the net down." He exercised his own freedom in meeting the challenges of rhyme and meter. His use of fixed forms such as couplets, tercets, quatrains, blank verse, and sonnets was not slavish because he enjoyed working them into the natural English speech patterns — especially the rhythms, idioms, and tones of speakers living north of Boston — that give voice to his themes. Frost often liked to use "Stopping by Woods on a Snowy Evening" as an example of his graceful way of making conventions appear natural and inevitable. He explored "the old ways to be new."

Frost's eye for strong, telling details was matched by his ear for natural speech rhythms. His flexible use of what he called "iambic and loose iambic" enabled him to create moving lyric poems that reveal the personal thoughts of a speaker and dramatic poems that convincingly characterize people caught in intense emotional situations. The language in his poems appears to be little more than a transcription of casual and even rambling speech, but it is in actuality Frost's poetic creation, carefully crafted to reveal the joys and sorrows that are woven into people's daily lives. What is missing from Frost's poems is artificiality, not art. Consider this poem.


## The Road Not Taken    1916

Two roads diverged in a yellow wood,
And sorry I could not travel both
And be one traveler, long I stood
And looked down one as far as I could
To where it bent in the undergrowth;                              5

Then took the other, as just as fair,
And having perhaps the better claim,
Because it was grassy and wanted wear;
Though as for that the passing there
Had worn them really about the same,                             10

And both that morning equally lay
In leaves no step had trodden black.
Oh, I kept the first for another day!
Yet knowing how way leads on to way,
I doubted if I should ever come back.                            15

I shall be telling this with a sigh
Somewhere ages and ages hence:
Two roads diverged in a wood, and I —
I took the one less traveled by,
And that has made all the difference.                            20

This poem intrigues readers because it is at once so simple and so deeply resonant. Recalling a walk in the woods, the speaker describes how he came to a fork in the road, which forced him to choose one path over another. Though "sorry" that he "could not travel both," he made a choice after carefully weighing his two options. This, essentially, is what happens in the poem; there is no other action. However, the incident is charged with symbolic significance by the speaker's reflections on the necessity and consequences of his decision.

The final stanza indicates that the choice concerns more than simply walking down a road, for the speaker says that choosing the "less traveled" path has affected his entire life — that "that has made all the difference." Frost draws on a familiar enough metaphor when he compares life to a journey, but he is also calling attention to a less commonly noted problem: despite our expectations, aspirations, appetites, hopes, and desires, we can't have it all. Making one choice precludes another. It is impossible to determine what particular decision the speaker refers to: perhaps he had to choose a college, a career, a spouse; perhaps he was confronted with mutually exclusive ideas, beliefs, or values. There is no way to know because Frost wisely creates a symbolic choice and implicitly invites us to supply our own circumstances.

The speaker's reflections about his choice are as central to an understanding of the poem as the choice itself; indeed, they may be more central. He describes the road taken as "having perhaps the better claim, / Because it was grassy and wanted wear"; he prefers the "less traveled" path. This seems to be an expression of individualism, which would account for "the difference" his choice made in his life. But Frost complicates matters by having the speaker also acknowledge that there was no significant difference between the two roads; one was "just as fair" as the other; each was "worn . . . really about the same"; and "both that morning equally lay / In leaves no step had trodden black."

The speaker imagines that in the future, "ages and ages hence," he will recount his choice with "a sigh" that will satisfactorily explain the course of his life, but Frost seems to be having a little fun here by showing us how the speaker will embellish his past decision to make it appear more dramatic. What we hear is someone trying to convince himself that the choice he made significantly changed his life. When he recalls what happened in the "yellow wood," a color that gives a glow to that irretrievable moment when his life seemed to be on the verge of a momentous change, he appears more concerned with the path he did not choose than with the one he took. Frost shrewdly titles the poem to suggest the speaker's sense of loss at not being able to "travel both" roads. When the speaker's reflections about his choice are examined, the poem reveals his nostalgia instead of affirming his decision to travel a self-reliant path in life.

The rhymed stanzas of "The Road Not Taken" follow a pattern established in the first five lines (*abaab*). This rhyme scheme reflects, perhaps, the speaker's efforts to shape his life into a pleasing and coherent form. The natural speech rhythms Frost uses allow him to integrate the rhymes unobtrusively, but there is a slight shift in lines 19 and 20, when the speaker asserts self-consciously that the "less traveled" road — which we already know to be basically the same as the other road — "made all the difference." Unlike all of the other rhymes in the poem, "difference" does not rhyme precisely with "hence." The emphasis that must be placed on "differ*ence*" to make it rhyme perfectly with "hence" may suggest that the speaker is trying just a little too hard to pattern his life on his earlier choice in the woods.

Perhaps the best way to begin reading Frost's poetry is to accept the invitation he placed at the beginning of many volumes of his poems. "The Pasture" means what it says, of course; it is about taking care of some farm chores, but it is also a means of "saying one thing in terms of another." "The Pasture" is a simple but irresistible songlike invitation to the pleasure of looking at the world through the eyes of a poet.

## The Pasture    1913

I'm going out to clean the pasture spring;
I'll only stop to rake the leaves away
(And wait to watch the water clear, I may):
I sha'n't be gone long. — You come too.

I'm going out to fetch the little calf                                                5
That's standing by the mother. It's so young
It totters when she licks it with her tongue.
I sha'n't be gone long. — You come too.

## Mowing    1913

There was never a sound beside the wood but one,
And that was my long scythe whispering to the ground.
What was it it whispered? I knew not well myself;
Perhaps it was something about the heat of the sun,
Something, perhaps, about the lack of sound —                                        5
And that was why it whispered and did not speak.
It was no dream of the gift of idle hours,
Or easy gold at the hand of fay or elf:
Anything more than the truth would have seemed too weak
To the earnest love that laid the swale in rows,                                     10
Not without feeble-pointed spikes of flowers
(Pale orchises), and scared a bright green snake.
The fact is the sweetest dream that labor knows.
My long scythe whispered and left the hay to make.

### CONSIDERATIONS FOR CRITICAL THINKING AND WRITING

1. **FIRST RESPONSE.** Describe the tone of "Mowing." How does reading the poem aloud affect your understanding of it?

2. Discuss the image of the scythe. Do you think it has any symbolic value? Explain why or why not.

3. Paraphrase the poem. What do you think its theme is?

4. Describe the type of sonnet Frost uses in "Mowing."

## *Mending Wall*   1914

Something there is that doesn't love a wall,
That sends the frozen-ground-swell under it,
And spills the upper boulders in the sun;
And makes gaps even two can pass abreast.
The work of hunters is another thing:                                    5
I have come after them and made repair
Where they have left not one stone on a stone,
But they would have the rabbit out of hiding,
To please the yelping dogs. The gaps I mean,
No one has seen them made or heard them made,                            10
But at spring mending-time we find them there.
I let my neighbor know beyond the hill;
And on a day we meet to walk the line
And set the wall between us once again.
We keep the wall between us as we go.                                     15
To each the boulders that have fallen to each.
And some are loaves and some so nearly balls
We have to use a spell to make them balance:
"Stay where you are until our backs are turned!"
We wear our fingers rough with handling them.                            20
Oh, just another kind of outdoor game,
One on a side. It comes to little more:
There where it is we do not need the wall:
He is all pine and I am apple orchard.
My apple trees will never get across                                     25
And eat the cones under his pines, I tell him.
He only says, "Good fences make good neighbors."
Spring is the mischief in me, and I wonder
If I could put a notion in his head:
"*Why* do they make good neighbors? Isn't it                             30
Where there are cows? But here there are no cows.
Before I built a wall I'd ask to know
What I was walling in or walling out,
And to whom I was like to give offense.
Something there is that doesn't love a wall,                             35
That wants it down." I could say "Elves" to him,
But it's not elves exactly, and I'd rather
He said it for himself. I see him there
Bringing a stone grasped firmly by the top
In each hand, like an old-stone savage armed.                            40
He moves in darkness as it seems to me,
Not of woods only and the shade of trees.
He will not go behind his father's saying,
And he likes having thought of it so well
He says again, "Good fences make good neighbors."                        45

## CONSIDERATIONS FOR CRITICAL THINKING AND WRITING

1. FIRST RESPONSE. What might the "Something" be that "doesn't love a wall" (line 1)? Why does the speaker remind his neighbor each spring that the wall needs to be repaired? Is it ironic that the *speaker* initiates the mending? Is there anything good about the wall?

2. How do the speaker and his neighbor differ in sensibilities? What is suggested about the neighbor in lines 41 and 42?

3. The neighbor likes the saying "Good fences make good neighbors" so well that he repeats it (lines 27, 45). Does the speaker also say something twice? What else suggests that the speaker's attitude toward the wall is not necessarily Frost's?

4. Although the speaker's language is colloquial, what is poetic about the sounds and rhythms he uses?

5. This poem was first published in 1914; Frost read it to an audience when he visited Russia in 1962. What do these facts suggest about the symbolic value of "Mending Wall"?

## CONNECTIONS TO OTHER SELECTIONS

1. How do you think the neighbor in this poem would respond to Emily Dickinson's idea of imagination in "To make a prairie it takes a clover and one bee" (p. 834)?

2. What similarities and differences does the neighbor have with the people Frost describes in "Neither Out Far nor In Deep" (p. 872)?

## *Birches*   1916

When I see birches bend to left and right
Across the lines of straighter darker trees,
I like to think some boy's been swinging them.
But swinging doesn't bend them down to stay
As ice-storms do. Often you must have seen them                           5
Loaded with ice a sunny winter morning
After a rain. They click upon themselves
As the breeze rises, and turn many-colored
As the stir cracks and crazes their enamel.
Soon the sun's warmth makes them shed crystal shells                       10
Shattering and avalanching on the snow-crust —
Such heaps of broken glass to sweep away
You'd think the inner dome of heaven had fallen.
They are dragged to the withered bracken by the load,
And they seem not to break; though once they are bowed                     15
So low for long, they never right themselves:
You may see their trunks arching in the woods
Years afterwards, trailing their leaves on the ground
Like girls on hands and knees that throw their hair
Before them over their heads to dry in the sun.                           20
But I was going to say when Truth broke in
With all her matter-of-fact about the ice-storm,
I should prefer to have some boy bend them

As he went out and in to fetch the cows —
Some boy too far from town to learn baseball,                    25
Whose only play was what he found himself,
Summer or winter, and could play alone.
One by one he subdued his father's trees
By riding them down over and over again
Until he took the stiffness out of them,                         30
And not one but hung limp, not one was left
For him to conquer. He learned all there was
To learn about not launching out too soon
And so not carrying the tree away
Clear to the ground. He always kept his poise                    35
To the top branches, climbing carefully
With the same pains you use to fill a cup
Up to the brim, and even above the brim.
Then he flung outward, feet first, with a swish,
Kicking his way down through the air to the ground.              40
So was I once myself a swinger of birches.
And so I dream of going back to be.
It's when I'm weary of considerations,
And life is too much like a pathless wood
Where your face burns and tickles with the cobwebs               45
Broken across it, and one eye is weeping
From a twig's having lashed across it open.
I'd like to get away from earth awhile
And then come back to it and begin over.
May no fate willfully misunderstand me                           50
And half grant what I wish and snatch me away
Not to return. Earth's the right place for love:
I don't know where it's likely to go better.
I'd like to go by climbing a birch tree,
And climb black branches up a snow-white trunk,                  55
*Toward* heaven, till the tree could bear no more,
But dipped its top and set me down again.
That would be good both going and coming back.
One could do worse than be a swinger of birches.

## CONSIDERATIONS FOR CRITICAL THINKING AND WRITING

1. FIRST RESPONSE. What do you think the swinging of birches symbolizes?

2. Why does the speaker in this poem prefer the birches to have been bent by boys instead of ice storms?

3. How is "Earth" (line 52) described in the poem? Why does the speaker choose it over "heaven" (line 56)?

4. How might the effect of this poem be changed if it were written in heroic couplets instead of blank verse?

5. CRITICAL STRATEGIES. Read the section on reader-response strategies (pp. 1396–1397) in Chapter 42, "Critical Strategies for Reading." Trace your response to this poem over three successive careful readings. How does your understanding of the poem change or develop?

## *"Out, Out—"*° 1916

The buzz-saw snarled and rattled in the yard
And made dust and dropped stove-length sticks of wood,
Sweet-scented stuff when the breeze drew across it.
And from there those that lifted eyes could count
Five mountain ranges one behind the other                                5
Under the sunset far into Vermont.
And the saw snarled and rattled, snarled and rattled,
As it ran light, or had to bear a load.
And nothing happened: day was all but done.
Call it a day, I wish they might have said                              10
To please the boy by giving him the half hour
That a boy counts so much when saved from work.
His sister stood beside them in her apron
To tell them "Supper." At the word, the saw,
As if to prove saws knew what supper meant,                            15
Leaped out at the boy's hand, or seemed to leap—
He must have given the hand. However it was,
Neither refused the meeting. But the hand!
The boy's first outcry was a rueful laugh,
As he swung toward them holding up the hand                            20
Half in appeal, but half as if to keep
The life from spilling. Then the boy saw all—
Since he was old enough to know, big boy
Doing a man's work, though a child at heart—
He saw all spoiled. "Don't let him cut my hand off—                    25
The doctor, when he comes. Don't let him, sister!"
So. But the hand was gone already.
The doctor put him in the dark of ether.
He lay and puffed his lips out with his breath.
And then—the watcher at his pulse took fright.                         30
No one believed. They listened at his heart.
Little—less—nothing!—and that ended it.
No more to build on there. And they, since they
Were not the one dead, turned to their affairs.

*"Out, Out—":* From Act V, Scene v, of Shakespeare's *Macbeth.*

### Considerations for Critical Thinking and Writing

1. **FIRST RESPONSE.** This narrative poem is about the accidental death of a Vermont boy. What is the purpose of the story? Some readers have argued that the final lines reveal the speaker's callousness and indifference. What do you think?

2. How does Frost's allusion to *Macbeth* contribute to the meaning of this poem? Does the speaker seem to agree with the view of life expressed in Macbeth's lines?

3. **CRITICAL STRATEGIES.** Read the section on Marxist criticism (p. 1389). How do you think a Marxist critic would interpret the family and events described in this poem?

### CONNECTIONS TO OTHER SELECTIONS

1. What are the similarities and differences in theme between this poem and Frost's "Nothing Gold Can Stay" (p. 871)?
2. Compare the tone and theme of "'Out, Out —'" with those of Edna St. Vincent Millay's "Spring" (p. 942).

## Fire and Ice    1923

Some say the world will end in fire,
Some say in ice.
From what I've tasted of desire
I hold with those who favor fire.
But if it had to perish twice,                                    5
I think I know enough of hate
To say that for destruction ice
Is also great
And would suffice.

### CONSIDERATIONS FOR CRITICAL THINKING AND WRITING

1. FIRST RESPONSE. What characteristics of human behavior does the speaker associate with fire and with ice?
2. What theories about the end of the world are alluded to in lines 1 and 2?
3. How does the speaker's use of understatement and rhyme affect the tone of this poem?

## The Need of Being Versed in Country Things    1923

The house had gone to bring again
To the midnight sky a sunset glow.
Now the chimney was all of the house that stood,
Like a pistil after the petals go.

The barn opposed across the way,                                  5
That would have joined the house in flame
Had it been the will of the wind, was left
To bear forsaken the place's name.

No more it opened with all one end
For teams that came by the stony road                             10
To drum on the floor with scurrying hoofs
And brush the mow with the summer load.

The birds that came to it through the air
At broken windows flew out and in,

Their murmur more like the sigh we sigh           15
From too much dwelling on what has been.

Yet for them the lilac renewed its leaf,
And the aged elm, though touched with fire;
And the dry pump flung up an awkward arm;
And the fence post carried a strand of wire.       20

For them there was really nothing sad.
But though they rejoiced in the nest they kept,
One had to be versed in country things
Not to believe the phoebes wept.

### CONSIDERATIONS FOR CRITICAL THINKING AND WRITING

1. FIRST RESPONSE. What kinds of moods are produced in the speaker by the house and the birds?
2. How is Frost's use of personification of thematic significance?
3. Why is it necessary for the speaker to be "versed in country things"?
4. Do you think this poem is sentimental? Why or why not?

### CONNECTION TO ANOTHER SELECTION

1. Compare what the speaker learns in this poem with the speaker's response to nature in "Design" (p. 874).

## *Nothing Gold Can Stay*    1923

Nature's first green is gold,
Her hardest hue to hold.
Her early leaf's a flower;
But only so an hour.
Then leaf subsides to leaf.                  5
So Eden sank to grief.
So dawn goes down to day.
Nothing gold can stay.

### CONSIDERATIONS FOR CRITICAL THINKING AND WRITING

1. FIRST RESPONSE. What is meant by "gold" in the poem? Why can't it "stay"?
2. What do the leaf, humanity, and a day have in common?

### CONNECTION TO ANOTHER SELECTION

1. Write an essay comparing the tone and theme of "Nothing Gold Can Stay" with those of Andrew Marvell's "To His Coy Mistress" (p. 941).

## *Neither Out Far nor In Deep*   1936

The people along the sand
All turn and look one way.
They turn their back on the land.
They look at the sea all day.

As long as it takes to pass                                    5
A ship keeps raising its hull;
The wetter ground like glass
Reflects a standing gull.

The land may vary more;
But wherever the truth may be —                               10
The water comes ashore,
And the people look at the sea.

They cannot look out far.
They cannot look in deep.
But when was that ever a bar                                   15
To any watch they keep?

### CONSIDERATIONS FOR CRITICAL THINKING AND WRITING

1. FIRST RESPONSE. Frost built this poem around a simple observation that raises
   some questions. Why do people at the beach almost always face the ocean?
   What feelings and thoughts are evoked by looking at the ocean?

2. Notice how the verb *look* takes on added meaning as the poem progresses.
   What are the people looking for?

3. How does the final stanza extend the poem's significance?

4. Does the speaker identify with the people described, or does he ironically distance himself from them?

Neither Out Far nor In Deep

The people along the sand
All turn and look one way.
They turn their backs on the land;
They look at the sea all day.

As long as it takes to pass
A ship keeps raising its hull.
The wetter ground like glass
Reflects a standing gull.

The land may vary more,
But wherever the truth may be —
The water comes ashore
And the people look at the sea.

They cannot look out far;
They cannot look in deep;
But when was that ever a bar
To any watch they keep.

Robert Frost

With the permission of The Yale Review.

Manuscript page for Robert Frost's "Neither Out Far nor In Deep" (see p. 872), which was first published in the *Yale Review* in 1934 and again in 1936, with a few punctuation changes, in *A Further Range*.

The Estate of Robert Frost.

## *Design*   1936

I found a dimpled spider, fat and white,
On a white heal-all,° holding up a moth
Like a white piece of rigid satin cloth —

Assorted characters of death and blight
Mixed ready to begin the morning right,                              5
Like the ingredients of a witches' broth —
A snow-drop spider, a flower like a froth,
And dead wings carried like a paper kite.

What had the flower to do with being white,
The wayside blue and innocent heal-all?                              10
What brought the kindred spider to that height,
Then steered the white moth thither in the night?
What but design of darkness to appall? —
If design govern in a thing so small.

2 *heal-all:* A common flower, usually blue, once used for medicinal purposes.

### CONSIDERATIONS FOR CRITICAL THINKING AND WRITING

1. FIRST RESPONSE. What kinds of speculations are raised in the poem's final two lines? Consider the meaning of the title. Is there more than one way to read it?

2. How does the division of the octave and sestet in this sonnet serve to organize the speaker's thoughts and feelings? What is the predominant rhyme? How does that rhyme relate to the poem's meaning?

3. Which words seem especially rich in connotative meanings? Explain how they function in the sonnet.

### CONNECTIONS TO OTHER SELECTIONS

1. Compare the ironic tone of "Design" with the tone of Countee Cullen's "Yet Do I Marvel" (p. 816). What would you have to change in Cullen's poem to make it more like Frost's?

2. In an essay discuss Frost's view of God in this poem and Emily Dickinson's perspective in "I know that He exists" (p. 852).

## *Desert Places*   1937

Snow falling and night falling fast, oh, fast
In a field I looked into going past,
And the ground almost covered smooth in snow,
But a few weeds and stubble showing last.

The woods around it have it — it is theirs.                          5
All animals are smothered in their lairs.

I am too absent-spirited to count;
The loneliness includes me unawares.

And lonely as it is that loneliness
Will be more lonely ere it will be less —                     10
A blanker whiteness of benighted snow
With no expression, nothing to express.

They cannot scare me with their empty spaces
Between stars—on stars where no human race is.
I have it in me so much nearer home                            15
To scare myself with my own desert places.

### CONSIDERATIONS FOR CRITICAL THINKING AND WRITING

1. FIRST RESPONSE. What poetic conventions (in addition to end rhyme) are evident in the poem? What effect do they contribute to?

2. In line 5, what does *it* refer to?

3. What is the speaker "scared" of in the final stanza?

4. *Desert* in the title and in the final line probably connotes "deserted" rather than a landscape that receives little to no annual rainfall. How is the landscape the speaker observes connected to the "desert places" within themself in the final stanza?

### CONNECTION TO ANOTHER SELECTION

1. Contrast the speaker's feelings of solitude in nature in this poem and in "Stopping by Woods on a Snowy Evening" (p. 778).

## *The Gift Outright*   1942

The land was ours before we were the land's.
She was our land more than a hundred years
Before we were her people. She was ours
In Massachusetts, in Virginia,
But we were England's, still colonials,                        5
Possessing what we still were unpossessed by,
Possessed by what we now no more possessed.
Something we were withholding made us weak
Until we found out that it was ourselves
We were withholding from our land of living,                   10
And forthwith found salvation in surrender.
Such as we were we gave ourselves outright
(The deed of gift was many deeds of war)
To the land vaguely realizing westward,
But still unstoried, artless, unenhanced,                      15
Such as she was, such as she would become.

**CONSIDERATIONS FOR CRITICAL THINKING AND WRITING**

1. FIRST RESPONSE. Frost once described this poem as "a history of the United States in sixteen lines." Is it? What events in American history does the poem focus on? What does it leave out?

2. This poem is built on several paradoxes. How are the paradoxes in lines 1, 6, 7, and 11 resolved?

**CONNECTION TO ANOTHER SELECTION**

1. Compare and contrast the theme and tone of this poem with those of E. E. Cummings's "next to of course god america i" (p. 619).

## Perspectives

### ROBERT FROST

## *On the Living Part of a Poem*   1914

The living part of a poem is the intonation entangled somehow in the syntax, idiom, and meaning of a sentence. It is only there for those who have heard it previously in conversation. . . . It is the most volatile and at the same time important part of poetry. It goes and the language becomes dead language, the poetry dead poetry. With it go the accents, the stresses, the delays that are not the property of vowels and syllables but that are shifted at will with the sense. Vowels have length there is no denying. But the accent of sense supersedes all other accent, overrides it and sweeps it away. I will find you the word *come* variously used in various passages, a whole, half, third, fourth, fifth, and sixth note. It is as long as the sense makes it. When men no longer know the intonations on which we string our words they will fall back on what I may call the absolute length of our syllables, which is the length we would give them in passages that meant nothing. . . . I say you can't read a single good sentence with the salt in it unless you have previously heard it spoken. Neither can you with the help of all the characters and diacritical marks pronounce a single word unless you have previously heard it actually pronounced. Words exist in the mouth not books.

From a letter to Sidney Cox in *A Swinger of Birches: A Portrait of Robert Frost*

**CONSIDERATIONS FOR CRITICAL THINKING AND WRITING**

1. FIRST RESPONSE. Why does Frost place so much emphasis on hearing poetry spoken?

2. Choose a passage from "Birches" (p. 867) and read it aloud. How does Frost's description of his emphasis on intonation help explain the effects he achieves in the passage you have selected?

3. Do you think it is true that all poetry must be heard? Do "[w]ords exist in the mouth not books"?

AMY LOWELL (1874–1925)

## On Frost's Realistic Technique  1915

I have said that Mr. Frost's work is almost photographic. The qualification was unnecessary, it is photographic. The pictures, the characters, are reproduced directly from life, they are burnt into his mind as though it were a sensitive plate. He gives out what has been put in unchanged by any personal mental process. His imagination is bounded by what he has seen, he is confined within the limits of his experience (or at least what might have been his experience) and bent all one way like the windblown trees of New England hillsides.

> From a review of *North of Boston, The New Republic*, February 20, 1915

### CONSIDERATIONS FOR CRITICAL THINKING AND WRITING

1. Consider the "photographic" qualities of Frost's poetry by discussing particular passages in poems from this chapter that strike you as having been "reproduced directly from life."

2. Write an essay that supports or refutes Lowell's assertion that "[Frost] gives out what has been put in unchanged by any personal mental process."

HERBERT R. COURSEN JR. (1932–2011)

## A Parodic Interpretation of "Stopping by Woods on a Snowy Evening"  1962

Much ink has spilled on many pages in exegesis of this little poem. Actually, critical jottings have only obscured what has lain beneath critical noses all these years. To say that the poem means merely that a man stops one night to observe a snowfall, or that the poem contrasts the mundane desire for creature comfort with the sweep of aesthetic appreciation, or that it renders worldly responsibilities paramount, or that it reveals the speaker's latent death-wish is to miss the point rather badly. Lacking has been that mind simple enough to see what is *really* there. . . .

The "darkest evening of the year" in New England is December 21st, a date near that on which the western world celebrates Christmas. It may be that December 21st *is* the date of the poem, or (and with poets this seems more likely) that this is the closest the poet can come to Christmas without giving it all away. Who has "promises to keep" at or near this date, and who must traverse much territory to fulfill these promises? Yes, and who but St. Nick would know the location of *each* home? Only he would know who had "just settled down for a long winter's nap" (the poem's third line — "He will not see me stopping here" — is clearly a veiled allusion) and would not be out inspecting his acreage this night. The unusual phrase "fill up with snow," in the poem's fourth line, is a transfer of Santa's occupational preoccupation to the countryside; he is mulling the filling of countless stockings hung above countless fireplaces by countless careful children. "Harness bells," of course, allude to "Sleighing Song," a popular Christmas tune of the time the poem was written in which the refrain "Jingle Bells! Jingle Bells!" appears; thus again are we put on the Christmas track. The "little horse," like the date, is another attempt at poetic obfuscation. Although the "rein-reindeer" ambiguity has been eliminated from the poem's final version,[1] probably because too obvious, we may speculate that the animal is really a reindeer disguised as a horse by the poet's desire for obscurity, a desire which we must concede has been fulfilled up to now.

The animal is clearly concerned, like the faithful Rudolph — another possible allusion (post facto, hence unconscious) — lest his master fail to complete his mission. Seeing no farmhouse in the second quatrain, but pulling a load of presents, no wonder the little beast wonders! It takes him a full two quatrains to rouse his driver to remember all the empty stockings which hang ahead. And Santa does so reluctantly at that, poor soul, as he ponders the myriad farmhouses and villages which spread between him and his own "winter's nap." The modern St. Nick, lonely and overworked, tosses no "Happy Christmas to all and to all a good night!" into the precipitation. He merely shrugs his shoulders and resignedly plods away.

> From "The Ghost of Christmas Past: 'Stopping by Woods
> on a Snowy Evening,'" *College English*, December 1962

[1]The original draft contained the following line: "That bid me give the reins a shake" (Stageberg-Anderson, *Poetry as Experience* [New York, 1952], p. 457). [Coursen's note.]

## Considerations for Critical Thinking and Writing

1. Is this critical spoof at all credible? Does the interpretation hold any water? Is the evidence reasonable? Why or why not? Which of the poem's details are accounted for, and which are ignored?

2. Choose a Frost poem and try writing a parodic interpretation of it.

3. What criteria do you use to distinguish between a sensible interpretation of a poem and an absurd one?

## Suggested Topics for Longer Papers

1. Research Frost's popular reputation and compare that with recent biographical accounts of his personal life. How does knowledge of his personal life affect your reading of his poetry?

2. Frost has been described as a cheerful poet of New England who creates pleasant images of the region as well as a poet who creates a troubling, frightening world bordered by anxiety, anguish, doubts, and darkness. How do the poems in this chapter support both of these readings of Frost's poetry?

# 31

# A Study of Julia Alvarez: The Author Reflects on Five Poems

AP Photo/Ramon Espinosa.

When I'm asked what made me into a writer, I point to the watershed experience of coming to this country. Not understanding the language, I had to pay close attention to each word — great training for a writer.

— JULIA ALVAREZ

This chapter offers five poems, chosen by Julia Alvarez for this anthology, with commentaries written by the poet herself. Alvarez's insights on each work, in addition to accompanying images and documents, provide a variety of contexts — personal, cultural, and historical — for understanding and appreciating her poems.

In her reflections on each of the poems, Alvarez shares her reasons for writing, what was on her mind when she wrote each work, and what she thinks now looking back at them, as well as providing a bird's-eye view into her writing process (see especially the drafts of the poem in progress on pp. 894–96). She also evokes the voices of those who have inspired her — muses that range from women talking and cooking in a kitchen to a character in *The Arabian Nights* to the poets Walt Whitman, Langston Hughes, and others. Alvarez writes, "A poem can be a resting place for the soul . . . a world teeming with discoveries and luminous little *ah-ha!* moments, a 'place for the genuine,' as Marianne Moore calls it."

In addition to Alvarez's inviting and richly detailed introductions, the chapter also presents a number of visual contexts, such as a photo of a 1963 civil rights demonstration in Queens, New York; the poet's passport photo taken at age ten, just before she moved back to the United States; and a collection of draft manuscript pages. Furthermore, a critical essay — which complements Alvarez's own perspectives throughout the chapter — by Kelli Lyon Johnson (p. 898) allows readers to consider Alvarez's work in a critical framework. (For a discussion on reading a work alongside critical theory, see Chapter 42, "Critical Strategies for Reading," p. 1381.)

## A BRIEF BIOGRAPHY

Although Julia Alvarez was born (1950) in New York City, she lived in the Dominican Republic until she was ten years old. She returned to New York after her father, a physician, was connected to a plot to overthrow the dictatorship of Rafael Trujillo, and the family had to flee. Growing up in Queens was radically different from the Latino Caribbean world she experienced during her early childhood. A new culture and new language sensitized Alvarez to her surroundings and her use of language so that emigration from the Dominican Republic to Queens was the beginning of her movement toward becoming a writer. Alvarez quotes the Polish poet Czeslaw Milosz's assertion that "language is the only homeland" to explain her own sense that what she really settled into was not so much the United States as the English language.

Her fascination with English continued into high school and took shape in college as she became a serious writer — first at Connecticut College from 1967 to 1969 and then at Middlebury College, where she earned her B.A. in 1971. At Syracuse University she was awarded the American Academy of Poetry Prize and, in 1975, earned an M.F.A. in creative writing.

Since then Alvarez has served as a writer-in-residence for the Kentucky Arts Commission, the Delaware Arts Council, and the Arts Council of Fayetteville, North Carolina. She has taught at California State College (Fresno), College of Sequoias, Phillips Andover Academy, the University of Vermont, George Washington University, the University of Illinois, and, since 1988, at Middlebury College, where she has been a professor of literature and creative writing and is currently a part-time writer-in-residence. Alvarez divides her time between Vermont and the Dominican Republic, where she and her husband have set up an organic coffee farm, Alta Gracia, that supports a literacy school for children and adults. *A Cafecito Story* (2001), which Alvarez considers a "green fable" or

Julia Alvarez with students from Middlebury College at her coffee farm, Alta Gracia, in the Dominican Republic.

"eco-parable," grew out of their experiences promoting fair trade and sustainability for coffee farmers in the Dominican Republic.

## AN INTRODUCTION TO HER WORK

Alvarez's poetry has been widely published in journals and magazines ranging from the *New Yorker* to *Mirabella* to the *Kenyon Review*. Her first book of poems, *Homecoming* (1984; a new expanded version, *Homecoming: New and Collected Poems*, was published in 1996 by Plume/Penguin), uses simple — yet incisive — language to explore issues related to love, domestic life, and work. Her second book of poetry, *The Other Side/El Otro Lado* (1995), is a collection of meditations on her childhood memories of immigrant life that shaped her adult identity and sensibilities. Some of these concerns are also manifested in her book of essays, titled *Something to Declare* (1998), a collection that describes her abiding concerns about how to respond to competing cultures. In her third poetry collection, *The Woman I Kept to Myself* (2004), Alvarez reflects on her personal life and development as a writer from the vantage point of her mid-fifties in seventy-five poems, each consisting of three ten-line stanzas.

    In addition to writing a number of books for children and young adults, Alvarez has also published six novels. The first, *How the García Girls Lost Their Accents* (1991), is a collection of fifteen separate but interrelated stories that cover thirty years of the lives of the García sisters from the late 1950s to the late 1980s. Drawing on her own experiences, Alvarez describes the sisters fleeing the Dominican Republic and growing up Latina in the United States. *In the Time of the Butterflies* (1994) is a fictional account of a true story concerning four sisters who opposed Trujillo's dictatorship. Three of the sisters were murdered in 1960 by the government, and the surviving fourth sister recounts the events of their personal and political lives that led to her sisters' deaths. Shaped by the history of Dominican freedom and tyranny, the novel also explores the sisters' relationships to each other and their country.

In *¡Yo!* (1997), Alvarez focuses on Yolanda, one of the García sisters from her first novel, who is now a writer. Written in the different voices of Yo's friends and family members, this fractured narrative constructs a complete picture of a woman who uses her relationships as fodder for fiction, a woman who is self-centered, aggravating, and finally lovable — who is deeply embedded in American culture while remaining aware of her Dominican roots. *¡Yo!*, which means "I" in English, is a meditation on points of view and narrative.

*In the Name of Salomé* (2000) is a fictional account of Salomé Ureña, who was born in the 1850s and considered to be "the Emily Dickinson of the Dominican Republic," and her daughter's efforts late in life to reconcile her relationship to her mother's reputation and her own response to Castro's revolution in Cuba. Alvarez published her sixth novel, *Saving the World*, in 2006, a story that also links two women's lives, one from the past and one from the present, around personal and political issues concerning humanitarian efforts to end smallpox in the nineteenth century and the global AIDS epidemic in the twenty-first century. Her most recent novel, *Afterlife* (2020), adds considerations of responsibility to others and moral decisions to her trademark themes of personal and cultural identity.

In "Queens, 1963," Alvarez remembers the neighborhood she lived in when she was a thirteen-year-old and how "Everyone seemed more American / than we, newly arrived." The tensions that arose when new immigrants and ethnic groups moved onto the block were mirrored in many American neighborhoods in 1963. Indeed, the entire nation was made keenly aware of such issues as integration when demonstrations were organized across the South and a massive march on Washington in support of civil rights for African Americans drew hundreds of thousands of demonstrators who listened to Martin Luther King Jr. deliver his electrifying "I Have a Dream" speech. But the issues were hardly resolved, as evidenced by 1963's two best-selling books: *Happiness Is a Warm Puppy* and *Security Is a Thumb and a Blanket*, both by Charles M. Schulz of *Peanuts* cartoon fame. The popularity of these books is, perhaps, understandable given the tensions that moved across the country and which seemed to culminate on November 22, 1963, when President Kennedy was assassinated in Dallas, Texas. These events are not mentioned in "Queens, 1963," but they are certainly part of the context that helps us understand Alvarez's particular neighborhood. In the following introductory essay, Alvarez reflects on the cultural moment of 1963 and her reasons for writing the poem.

Julia Alvarez

## *Queens, 1963*    1992

Everyone seemed more American
than we, newly arrived,
foreign dirt still on our soles.
By year's end, a sprinkler waving
like a flag on our mowed lawn,                                          5
we were blended into the block,
owned our own mock Tudor house.
Then the house across the street
sold to a black family.
Cop cars patrolled our block                                           10
from the Castellucci's at one end
to the Balakian's on the other.
We heard rumors of bomb threats,
a burning cross on their lawn.
(It turned out to be a sprinkler.)                                      15
Still the neighborhood buzzed.
The barber's family, Haralambides,
our left-side neighbors, didn't want trouble.
They'd come a long way to be free!
Mr. Scott, the retired plumber,                                        20
and his plump midwestern wife,
considered moving back home
where white and black got along
by staying where they belonged.
They had cultivated our street                                         25
like the garden she'd given up
on account of her ailing back,
bad knees, poor eyes, arthritic hands.
She went through her litany daily.
Politely, my mother listened —                                         30
*¡Ay, Mrs. Scott, qué pena!°*
— her Dominican good manners
still running on automatic.
The Jewish counselor next door,
had a practice in her house;                                           35
clients hurried up her walk
ashamed to be seen needing.
(I watched from my upstairs window,
gloomy with adolescence,
and guessed how they too must have                                     40
hypocritical old-world parents.)
Mrs. Bernstein said it was time
the neighborhood opened up.
As the first Jew on the block,
she remembered the snubbing she got                                    45
a few years back from Mrs. Scott.
But real estate worried her,

31 *qué pena:* What a shame!

our houses' plummeting value.
She shook her head as she might
at a client's grim disclosures.
*Too bad the world works this way.*                                    50
The German girl playing the piano
down the street abruptly stopped
in the middle of a note.
I completed the tune in my head                                       55
as I watched *their* front door open.
A dark man in a suit
with a girl about my age
walked quickly into a car.
My hand lifted but fell                                               60
before I made a welcoming gesture.
On her face I had seen a look
from the days before we had melted
into the United States of America.
It was hardness mixed with hurt.                                      65
It was knowing she never could be
the right kind of American.
A police car followed their car.
Down the street, curtains fell back.
Mrs. Scott swept her walk                                             70
as if it had just been dirtied.
Then the German piano commenced
downward scales as if tracking
the plummeting real estate.
One by one I imagined the houses                                      75
sinking into their lawns,
the grass grown wild and tall
in the past tense of this continent
before the first foreigners owned
any of this free country.                                             80

## Considerations for Critical Thinking and Writing

1. **FIRST RESPONSE.** What nationalities are the people in this neighborhood in the New York City borough of Queens? Are they neighborly to each other?

2. In line 3, why do you suppose Alvarez writes "foreign dirt still on our soles" rather than "foreign soil still on our shoes"? What does Alvarez's word choice suggest about her feelings for her native country?

3. Characterize the speaker. How old is she? How does she feel about having come from the Dominican Republic? About living in the United States?

4. Do you think this poem is optimistic or pessimistic about racial relations in the United States? Explain your answer by referring to specific details in the poem.

## Connections to Other Selections

1. Compare the use of irony in "Queens, 1963" with that in Gregory Corso's "Marriage" (p. 952). How does irony contribute to each poem?

2. Write an essay comparing and contrasting the tone and theme in "Queens, 1963" and in David Hernandez's "All-American" (p. 714).

## Julia Alvarez

# *On Writing "Queens, 1963"* 2006

I remember when we finally bought our very own house after three years of living in rentals. Back then, Queens, New York, was not the multicultural, multilingual place it is today. But the process was beginning. Our neighborhood was sprinkled with ethnicities, some who had been here longer than others. The Germans down the block — now we would call them German Americans — had been Americans for a couple of generations as had our Jewish neighbors, and most definitely, the Midwesterners across the street. Meanwhile, the Greek family next door were newcomers as were we, our accents still heavy, our cooking smells commingling

Julia Alvarez, age ten, in her 1960 passport photo.

across our backyard fences during mealtimes: their Greek lamb with rosemary, our Dominican habichuelas with sofrito.°

It seemed a peaceable enough kingdom until a black family moved in across the street. What a ruckus got started! Of course, it was the early 1960s: the civil rights movement was just getting under way in this country. Suddenly, our neighborhood was faced with discrimination, but coming from the very same people who themselves had felt discrimination from other, more mainstream Americans. It was my first lesson in hypocrisy and in realizing that America was still an experiment in process. The words on the Statue of Liberty [see "Sometimes the Words Are So Close," p. 893] were only a promise, not yet a practice in the deep South or in Queens, New York.

In writing this poem I wanted to suggest the many ethnic families in the neighborhood. Of course, I couldn't use their real names and risk being sued. (Though, come to think of it, I've never heard of a poem being sued, have you?) Plus, there is the matter of failing memory. (This was forty-two years ago!) So I chose names that suggested other languages, other places, and also — always the poet's ear at work — names that fit in with the rhythm and cadence of the lines.

*habichuelas with sofrito:* Kidney beans prepared with a sautéed mixture of spices, herbs, garlic, onion, pepper, and tomato.

### Queens Civil Rights Demonstration  1963

In this photograph police remove a Congress of Racial Equality (CORE) demonstrator from a Queens construction site. Demonstrators blocked the delivery entrance to the site because they wanted more African Americans and Puerto Ricans hired in the building-trade industry. AP Photo.

1. Discuss the role played by the police in this photograph and in "Queens, 1963." What attitudes toward the police do the photograph and the poem display?

2. How do you think the Scotts and Mrs. Bernstein would have responded to this photograph in 1963?

3. Compare the tensions in "Queens, 1963" to those depicted in this photo. How do the speaker's private reflections relate to this public protest?

## JULIA ALVAREZ

# *Housekeeping Cages*   1994

Sometimes people ask me why I wrote a series of poems about housekeeping if I'm a feminist. Don't I want women to be liberated from the oppressive roles they were condemned to live? I don't see housekeeping that way. They were the crafts we women had, sewing, embroidering, cooking, spinning, sweeping, even the lowly dusting. And like Dylan Thomas said, we sang in our chains like the sea. Isn't it already thinking from the point of view of the oppressor to say to ourselves, what we did was nothing?

You use what you have, you learn to work the structure to create what you need. I don't feel that writing in traditional forms is giving up power, going over to the enemy. The word belongs to no one, the houses built of words belong to no one. We have to take them back from those who think they own them.

Sometimes I get in a mood. I tell myself I am taken over. I am writing under somebody else's thumb and tongue. See, English was not my first language. It was, in fact, a colonizing language to my Spanish Caribbean. But then Spanish was also a colonizer's language; after all, Spain colonized Quisqueya.° There's no getting free. We are always writing in a form imposed on us. But then, I'm Scheherazade° in the Sultan's room. I use structures to survive and triumph! To say what's important to me as a woman and as a Latina.

I think of form as territory that has been colonized, but that you can free. See, I feel subversive in formal verse. A voice is going to inhabit that form that was barred from entering it before! That's what I tried in the "33" poems, to use my woman's voice in a sonnet as I would use it sitting in the kitchen with a close friend, talking womanstuff. In school, I was always trying to inhabit those forms as the male writers had. To pitch my voice to "Of man's first disobedience, and the fruit. . . ." If it didn't hit the key of "Sing in me, Muse, and through me tell the story," how could it be important poetry? The only kind.

While I was in graduate school some of the women in the program started   5 a Women's Writing Collective in Syracuse. We were musing each other into unknown writing territory. One woman advised me to listen to my own voice, deep inside, and put that down on paper. But what I heard when I listened were

---

*Quisqueya:* Another name for Hispaniola, the island comprised of Haiti and the Dominican Republic.
*Scheherazade:* The narrator of the Middle Eastern story cycle *One Thousand and One Nights.*

voices that said things like "Don't put so much salt on the lettuce, you'll wilt the salad!" I'd never heard that in a poem. So how could it be poetry? Then, with the "33" sonnet sequence, I said, I'm going to go in there and I'm going to sound like myself. I took on the whole kaboodle. I was going into form, sonnets no less. Wow.

What I wanted from the sonnet was the tradition that it offered as well as the structure. The sonnet tradition was one in which women were caged in golden cages of beloved, in perfumed gas chambers of stereotype. I wanted to go in that heavily mined and male labyrinth with the string of my own voice. I wanted to explore it and explode it too. I call my sonnets free verse sonnets. They have ten syllables per line, and the lines are in a loose iambic pentameter. But they are heavily enjambed and the rhymes are often slant-rhymes, and the rhyme scheme is peculiar to each sonnet. One friend read them and said, "I didn't know they were sonnets. They sounded like you talking!"

By learning to work the sonnet structure and yet remaining true to my own voice, I made myself at home in that form. When I was done with it, it was a totally different form from the one I learned in school. I have used other traditional forms. In my poem about sweeping, since you sweep with the broom and you dance — it's a coupling — I used rhyming couplets. I wrote a poem of advice mothers give to their daughters in a villanelle, because it's such a nagging form. But mostly the sonnet is the form I've worked with. It's the classic form in which we women were trapped, love objects, and I was trapped inside that voice and paradigm, and I wanted to work my way out of it.

My idea of traditional forms is that as women much of our heritage is trapped in them. But the cage can turn into a house if you housekeep it the right way. You housekeep it by working the words just so.

> From *A Formal Feeling Comes: Poems in Form by Contemporary Women,*
> edited by Annie Finch

### CONSIDERATIONS FOR CRITICAL THINKING AND WRITING

1. **FIRST RESPONSE.** How does Alvarez connect housekeeping to "writing in traditional forms"?

2. Compare "Sometimes the Words Are So Close" (p. 893) to Alvarez's description in her essay of how she writes sonnets. How closely does the poem's form follow her description?

3. Why does Alvarez consider "Dusting" (p. 890) and "Ironing Their Clothes" (p. 891) to be feminist poems? How can the poems be read as feminist in their sensibility?

## JULIA ALVAREZ

### *On Writing "Housekeeping Cages" and Her Housekeeping Poems*    1998

I can still remember the first time I heard my own voice on paper. It happened a few years after I graduated from a creative writing master's program. I had earned a short-term residency at Yaddo, the writer's colony, where I was assigned a studio in the big mansion — the tower room at the top of the stairs. The rules were clear: we artists and writers were to stick to our studios during the day and come out at night for supper and socializing. Nothing was to come between us and our work.

I sat up in my tower room, waiting for inspiration. All around me I could hear the typewriters going. Before me lay a blank sheet of paper, ready for the important work I had come there to write. That was the problem, you see. I was trying to do IMPORTANT work and so I couldn't hear myself think. I was trying to pitch my voice to "Turning and turning in the widening gyre," or "Of man's first disobedience, and the fruit of that forbidden tree," or "Sing in me, Muse, and through me tell the story." I was tuning my voice to these men's voices because I thought that was the way I had to sound if I wanted to be a writer. After all, the writers I read and admired sounded like that.

But the voice I heard when I listened to myself think was the voice of a woman, sitting in her kitchen, gossiping with a friend over a cup of coffee. It was the voice of Gladys singing her sad boleros, Belkis putting color on my face with tales of her escapades, Tití naming the orchids, Ada telling me love stories as we made the beds. I had, however, never seen voices like these in print. So, I didn't know poems could be written in those voices, *my* voice.

So there I was at Yaddo, trying to write something important and coming up with nothing. And then, hallelujah — I heard the vacuum going up and down the hall. I opened the door and introduced myself to the friendly, sweating woman, wielding her vacuum cleaner. She invited me down to the kitchen so we wouldn't disturb the other guests. There I met the cook, and as we all sat, drinking coffee, I paged through her old cookbook, *knead, poach, stew, whip, score, julienne, whisk, sauté, sift.* Hmm. I began hearing a music in these words. I jotted down the names of implements:

> Cup, spoon, ladle, pot, kettle,
> grater and peeler,
> colander, corer,
> waffle iron, small funnel.

"You working on a poem there?" the cook asked me.
I shook my head.

A little later, I went upstairs and wrote down in my journal this beauti-   5
ful vocabulary of my girlhood. As I wrote, I tapped my foot on the floor to the rhythm of the words. I could see Mami and the aunts with the cook in the kitchen bending their heads over a pot of habichuelas, arguing about what flavor was missing — what could it be they had missed putting in it? And then, the thought of Mami recalled Gladys, the maid who loved to sing, and that thought led me through the house, the mahogany furniture that needed dusting, the beds that needed making, the big bin of laundry that needed washing.

That day, I began working on a poem about dusting. Then another followed on sewing; then came a sweeping poem, an ironing poem. Later, I would collect these into a series I called "the housekeeping poems," poems using the metaphors, details, language of my first apprenticeship as a young girl. Even later, having found my woman's voice, I would gain confidence to explore my voice as a Latina and to write stories and poems using the metaphors, details, rhythms of that first world I had left behind in Spanish.

But it began, first, by discovering my woman's voice at Yaddo where I had found it as a child. Twenty years after learning to sing with Gladys, I was reminded of the lessons I had learned in childhood: that my voice would not be found up in a tower, in those upper reaches or important places, but down in the kitchen among the women who first taught me about service, about passion, about singing as if my life depended on it.

From *Something to Declare*

## JULIA ALVAREZ

### *Dusting*  1981

Each morning I wrote my name
on the dusty cabinet, then crossed
the dining table in script, scrawled
in capitals on the backs of chairs,
practicing signatures like scales                                5
while Mother followed, squirting
linseed from a burping can
into a crumpled-up flannel.

She erased my fingerprints
from the bookshelf and rocker,                                   10
polished mirrors on the desk
scribbled with my alphabets.
My name was swallowed in the towel
with which she jeweled the table tops.
The grain surfaced in the oak                                    15
and the pine grew luminous.
But I refused with every mark
to be like her, anonymous.

### CONSIDERATIONS FOR CRITICAL THINKING AND WRITING

1. FIRST RESPONSE. Describe the central conflict between the speaker and the mother.
2. Explain why the image of dusting is a particularly appropriate metaphor for evoking the central conflict.
3. Discuss the effect of the rhymes in lines 15–18.
4. Consider the tone of each stanza. Explain why you see the tones as identical or not.

### CONNECTION TO ANOTHER SELECTION

1. Discuss the mother-daughter relationships in "Dusting" and in Cathy Song's "The Youngest Daughter" (p. 571).

JULIA ALVAREZ

## *On Writing "Dusting"*  2006

Finally, I took the leap and began to write poems in my own voice and the voices of the women in my past, who inevitably were talking about their work, house-keeping. I had to trust that those voices, while not conventionally important, still had something to say. At school, I had been taught the formal canon of literature: epic poems with catalogues of ships, poems about wars and the rumors of wars. Why not write a poem in the voice of a mother cataloguing the fabrics, with names as beautiful as those of ships ("gabardine, organdy, wool, madras" from "Naming the Fabrics") or a poem about sweeping while watching a news report about the Vietnam War on TV ("How I Learned to Sweep")? Each time I delved into one of the housekeeping "arts," I discovered deeper, richer materials and metaphors than I had anticipated. This is wonderful news for a writer. As Robert Frost once said about rhymes in a poem, "No surprise for the writer, no surprise for the reader." The things we discover while writing what we write tingle with that special energy and delight of not just writing a poem, but enlarging our understanding.

Dusting is the lowliest of the housekeeping arts. Any little girl with a rag can dust. But rather than dust, the little girl in my poem is writing her name on the furniture, something her mother keeps correcting. What a perfect metaphor for the changing roles of women which I've experienced in my own life: the mother believing that a woman's place is in the home, not in the public sphere; the girl from a younger generation wanting to make a name for herself.

And in writing "Dusting," I also discovered a metaphor about writing. A complicated balancing act: like the mother, the artist has to disappear in her work; it's the poem that counts, not the name or celebrity of the writer. But the artist also needs the little girl's pluck and ambition to even imagine a public voice for herself. Otherwise, she'd be swallowed up in self-doubt, silenced by her mother's old-world way of viewing a woman's role.

JULIA ALVAREZ

## *Ironing Their Clothes*  1981

With a hot glide up, then down, his shirts,
I ironed out my father's back, cramped
and worried with work. I stroked the yoke,
the breast pocket, collar and cuffs,
until the rumpled heap relaxed into the shape                    5
of my father's broad chest, the shoulders shrugged off
the world, the collapsed arms spread for a hug.
And if there'd been a face above the buttondown neck,
I would have pressed the forehead out, I would
have made a boy again out of that tired man!                     10

If I clung to her skirt as she sorted the wash
or put out a line, my mother frowned,
a crease down each side of her mouth.

*This is no time for love!* But here
I could linger over her wrinkled bedjacket,                                    15
kiss at the damp puckers of her wrists
with the hot tip. Here I caressed
collars, scallops, ties, pleats which made
her outfits test of the patience of my passion.
Here I could lay my dreaming iron on her lap.                                   20

The smell of baked cotton rose from the board
and blew with a breeze out the window
to the family wardrobe drying on the clothesline,
all needing a touch of my iron. Here I could tickle
the underarms of my big sister's petticoat                                     25
or secretly pat the backside of her pajamas.
For she too would have warned me not to muss
her fresh blouses, starched jumpers, and smocks,
all that my careful hand had ironed out,
forced to express my excess love on cloth.                                     30

### Considerations for Critical Thinking and Writing

1. **FIRST RESPONSE.** Explain how the speaker expresses her love for her family in the extended metaphor of ironing.

2. How are ironing and the poem itself expressions of the speaker's "excess love" (line 30)? In what sense is her love excessive?

3. Explain how the speaker's relationship to her father differs from her relationship to her mother.

### Connection to Another Selection

1. **CREATIVE RESPONSE.** Compare the descriptions of mothers in this poem and in Alvarez's "Dusting" (p. 890). Write a one-paragraph character sketch that uses vivid details and metaphoric language to describe them.

## Julia Alvarez

## *On Writing "Ironing Their Clothes"*   2006

Maybe because ironing is my favorite of all the housekeeping chores, this is my favorite of the housekeeping poems. In the apprenticeship of household arts, ironing is for the advanced apprentice. After all, think about it, you're wielding an instrument that could cause some damage: You could burn yourself, you could burn the clothes. I was not allowed to iron clothes until I was older and could be trusted to iron all different kinds of fabrics ("gabardine, organdy, wool, madras") just right.

Again, think of how ironing someone's clothes can be a metaphor for all kinds of things. You have this power to take out the wrinkles and worries from someone's outer skin! You can touch and caress and love someone and not be told that you are making a nuisance of yourself!

In writing this poem I wanted the language to mirror the process. I wanted the lines to suggest all the fussy complications of trying to get your iron into hard corners and places ("I stroked the yoke, / the breast pocket, collar and cuffs, / until the rumpled heap relaxed . . .") and then the smooth sailing of a line that sails over the line break into the next line ("into the shape / of my father's broad chest . . ."). I wanted to get the hiss of the iron in those last four lines. I revised and revised this poem, especially the verbs, most especially the verbs that have to do the actual work of the iron. When I finally got that last line with its double rhymes ("express / excess"; "love / cloth"), I felt as if I'd done a whole laundry basket worth of ironing just right.

## Julia Alvarez

### *Sometimes the Words Are So Close*  1982
*From the "33" Sonnet Sequence*

Sometimes the words are so close I am
more who I am when I'm down on paper
than anywhere else as if my life were
practicing for the real me I become
unbuttoned from the anecdotal and                           5
unnecessary and undressed down
to the figure of the poem, line by line,
the real text a child could understand.
Why do I get confused living it through?
Those of you lost and yearning to be free,                   10
who hear these words, take heart from me.
I once was in as many drafts as you.
But briefly, essentially, here I am.
Who touches this poem touches a woman.

## Drafts of "Sometimes the Words Are So Close": A Poet's Writing Process

Sometimes the words are so close I am
more who I am when I'm down on paper
than anywhere else as if my life were
practising for the real me I become
unbuttoned f~~orm~~ the anecdotal and
unnecessary and undressed down
to the figure of the poem, line by line,
the real text a child could understand.
Why do I get confused living it through?
Those of you, lost and yearning to be free,
who hear these words, take heart from me.
I ~~was~~ once was in as many drafts as you.
But briefly, essentially, here I am...
Who touches this poem touches a woman.

Sometimes the words are so close I am
more who I am when I'm down on paper
than anywhere else as if my life were
practising for the real me I become
unbuttoned from the anecdotal and
unnecessary and undressed down
to the figure of the poem, line by line,
the real text a child could understand.
Why do I get confused living it through?
Those of you, lost and yearning to be free,
who hear these words, take heart from me.
I once was in as many drafts as you.
But briefly, essentially, here I am...
Who touches this poem touches a woman.

*pretentious*

### CONSIDERATIONS FOR CRITICAL THINKING AND WRITING

1. FIRST RESPONSE. Paraphrase lines 1–9. What produces the speaker's sense of frustration?

2. How do lines 10–14 resolve the question raised in line 9?

3. Explain how Alvarez's use of punctuation serves to reinforce the poem's meanings.

4. Discuss the elements of this poem that make it a sonnet.

5. Read carefully Alvarez's early drafts and discuss how they offer insights into your understanding and interpretation of the final version.

### CONNECTION TO ANOTHER SELECTION

1. The poem's final line echoes Walt Whitman's poem "So Long," in which he addresses the reader: "Camerado, this is no book, / Who touches this touches a man." Alvarez has said that Whitman is one of her favorite poets. Read the selections by Whitman in this anthology (check the index for titles) along with "So Long" (readily available online) and explain why you think she admires his poetry.

## JULIA ALVAREZ

# On Writing "Sometimes the Words Are So Close"    2006
### From the "33" Sonnet Sequence

I really believe that being a reader turns you into a writer. You connect with the voice in a poem at a deeper and more intimate level than you do with practically anyone in your everyday life. Seems like the years fall away, differences fall away, and when George Herbert asks in his poem, "The Flower,"

> Who would have thought my shrivel'd heart
> Could have recover'd greennesse?

you want to stroke the page and answer him, "I did, George." Instead you write a poem that responds to the feelings in his poem; you recover greenness for him and for yourself.

With the "33" sonnet sequence, I wanted the voice of the speaker to sound like a real woman speaking. A voice at once intimate and also somehow universal, essential. This sonnet #42 ["Sometimes the Words Are So Close"] is the last one in the sequence, a kind of final "testimony" about what writing is all about.

I mentioned that when you love something you read, you want to respond to it. You want to say it again, in fresh new language. Robert Frost speaks to this impulse in the poet when he says, "Don't borrow, steal!" Well, I borrowed / stole two favorite passages. One of them is from the poem on the Statue of Liberty, which was written by Emma Lazarus (1849–1887). These lines will sound familiar to you, I'm sure:

> "Give me your tired, your poor,
> Your huddled masses yearning to breathe free,
> The wretched refuse of your teeming shore.
> Send these, the homeless, tempest-tost to me,
> I lift my lamp beside the golden door!"

I think of these lines, not just as an invitation to the land of the brave and home of the free, but an invitation to poetry! A poem can be a resting place for the soul yearning to breathe free, a form that won't tolerate the misuses and abuses of language, a world teeming with discoveries and luminous little *ah-ha!* moments, a "place for the genuine," as Marianne Moore calls it in her poem, "Poetry." William Carlos Williams said that we can't get the news from poems, practical information, hard facts, but "men die daily for lack of what is found there."

I not only agreed with this idea, but I wanted to say so in my own words, and so I echoed those lines from the Statue of Liberty in my sonnet:

> Those of you lost and yearning to be free,
> who hear these words, take heart from me.

Another favorite line comes from Walt Whitman's book-length "Leaves of Grass": "Who touches this [book] touches a man." As a young, lonely immigrant girl reading Whitman, those words made me feel so accompanied, so connected. And so I borrowed / stole that line and made it my own at the end of this poem.

---

## Perspectives

---

### MARNY REQUA (B. 1971)

### *From an Interview with Julia Alvarez*    1997

**M.R.  What was it like when you came to the United States?**

J.A.  When we got to Queens, it was really a shock to go from a totally Latino, *familia* Caribbean world into this very cold and kind of forbidding one in which we didn't speak the language. I didn't grow up with a tradition of writing or reading books at all. People were always telling stories but it wasn't a tradition of literary . . . reading a book or doing something solitary like that. Coming to this country I discovered books, I discovered that it was a way to enter into a portable homeland that you could carry around in your head. You didn't have to suffer what was going on around you. I found in books a place to go. I became interested in language because I was learning a language intentionally at the age of ten. I was wondering, "Why is it that word and not another?" which any writer has to do with their language. I always say I came to English late but to the profession early. By high school I was pretty set: That's what I want to do, be a writer.

**M.R.  Did you have culture shock returning to the Dominican Republic as you were growing up?**

*J.A.*  The culture here had an effect on me — at the time this country was coming undone with protests and flower children and drugs. Here I was back in the Dominican Republic and I wouldn't keep my mouth shut. I had my own ideas and I had my own politics, and it, I just didn't gel anymore with the family. I didn't quite feel I ever belonged in this North American culture and I always had this nostalgia that when I went back I'd belong, and then I found out I didn't belong there either.

**M.R.  Was it a source of inspiration to have a foot in both cultures?**

*J.A.*  I only came to that later. [Then], it was a burden because I felt torn. I wanted to be part of one culture and then part of the other. It was a time when the model for the immigrant was that you came and you became an American and you cut off your ties and that was that. My parents had that frame of mind, because they were so afraid, and they were "Learn your English" and "Become one of them," and that left out so much. Now I see the richness. Part of what I want to do with my work is that complexity, that richness. I don't want it to be simplistic and either/or.

From "The Politics of Fiction," *Frontera* magazine 5 (1997)

### Considerations for Critical Thinking and Writing

1.  What do you think Alvarez means when she describes books as "a portable homeland that you could carry around in your head"?

2.  Why is it difficult for Alvarez to feel that she belongs in either the Dominican culture or the North American culture?

3.  Alvarez says that in the 1960s "the model for the immigrant was that you came and you became an American and you cut off your ties and that was that." Do you think this model has changed in the United States since then? Explain your response.

4.  How might this interview alter your understanding of "Queens, 1963"? What light is shed, for example, on the speaker's feeling that her family "blended into the block" in line 6?

## Kelli Lyon Johnson  (b. 1969)
### *Mapping an Identity*  2005

Alvarez poses the problem of how we are to understand and represent identity within the multiple migrations that characterize an increasingly global society. By "mapping a country that's not on the map," Alvarez, a Dominican immigrant forced into exile in the United States, is undertaking a journey that places her at the forefront of contemporary American letters.

The question of identity and agency is particularly acute for women, post-colonial peoples, and others upon whom an identity has traditionally been imposed. Given Alvarez's success, both commercial and artistic, a variety of groups have claimed her as a member of their communities: as woman, ethnic, exile, diaspora, Caribbean, Dominican, Latina, and American. In the keynote address at a conference for Caribbean Studies, Doña Aída Cartagena Portalatín, "the grand woman of letters in the Dominican Republic" (*Something*° 171) gently chides Alvarez for writing in English. "Come back to your country, to your language," she tells Alvarez. "You are a Dominican" (171). By conflating linguistic, national, and cultural identity, Portalatín underscores the importance of these factors for constructing a literary tradition that includes displaced writers like Alvarez, who quite consciously has not adopted for writing the language of her country of origin.

In response to such comments, Alvarez has asserted her own self-definition as both (and neither) Dominican and American by writing "a new place on the map" (*Something* 173). Placing herself among a multiethnic group of postcolonial authors who write in English — "Michael Ondaatje in Toronto, Maxine Hong Kingston in San Francisco, Seamus Heaney in Boston, Bharati Mukherjee in Berkeley, Marjorie Agosín in Wellesley, Edwidge Danticat in Brooklyn" (173) — Alvarez, like these authors, has altered contemporary American literature by stretching the literary cartography of the Americas. These authors have brought, through their writings, their own countries of origin into a body of work in which the word *American* expands across continents and seas and begins to recapture its original connotation.

Alvarez has also claimed membership among a *comunidad* of U.S. Latina writers — Sandra Cisneros, Ana Castillo, Judith Ortiz Cofer, Lorna Dee Cervantes, Cherríe Moraga, Helena María Viramontes, and Denise Chávez — despite her fears that "the cage of definition" will enclose her writing "with its 'Latino subject matter,' 'Latino style,' 'Latino concerns'" (169). Like these authors, Alvarez seeks to write women into a postcolonial tradition of literature that has historically excluded women, particularly in writings of exile. To counter imposed definitions and historical silences, Alvarez has found that "the best way to define myself is through stories and poems" (169). The space that Alvarez maps is thus a narrative space: the site of her emerging cartography of identity and exile.

From *Julia Alvarez: Writing a New Place on the Map*

*Something to Declare*, Alvarez's collection of essays published in 1998.

## CONSIDERATIONS FOR CRITICAL THINKING AND WRITING

1. Based on your reading of the poems in this chapter, which community identity — "woman, ethnic, exile, diaspora, Caribbean, Dominican, Latina, and American" — best describes Alvarez for you?

2. In what sense does Alvarez's poetry expand "the literary cartography of the Americas"?

# 32

## A Study of Billy Collins:
## The Author Reflects
## on Five Poems

More interesting to me than what a poem means is how it travels. In the classroom, I like to substitute for the question, "What is the meaning of the poem?" other questions: "How does this poem go?" or "How does this poem travel through itself in search of its own ending?"

— BILLY COLLINS

Billy Collins selected the five poems presented in this chapter and provided commentaries for each so that readers of this anthology might gain a sense of how he, a former U.S. poet laureate and teacher, writes and thinks about poetry. In his perspectives on these poems, Collins explores a variety of literary elements ranging from the poems' origins, allusions, images, metaphors, symbols, and tone to his strategies for maintaining his integrity and sensitivity to both language and the reader. Be advised, however, that these discussions do not constitute CliffsNotes to the poems; Collins does not interpret a single one of them for us. Instead of "beating it with a hose / to find out what it really means," as he writes in his poem "Introduction to Poetry" (p. 544), he "hold[s] it up to the light" so that we can see more clearly how each poem works. He explains that the purpose of his discussions is to have students "see how a poem gets written from the opening lines, through the shifts and maneuvers of the body to whatever closure the poem manages to achieve . . . to make the process of writing a poem less mysterious without taking away the mystery that is at the heart of every good poem."

Along with Collins's illuminating and friendly tutorial, the chapter also provides some additional contexts, such as photos from the poet's personal collection; screen shots that offer a look at his unique — and dynamic — Web presence, including a collection of short animated films set to his work; a collection of draft manuscript pages; and an interview with Michael Meyer.

## A BRIEF BIOGRAPHY AND AN INTRODUCTION TO HIS WORK

Born in New York City in 1941, Billy Collins grew up in Queens, the only child of a nurse and an electrician. His father had hoped that he might go to the Harvard Business School, but following his own lights, after graduating from The College of the Holy Cross, he earned a Ph.D. at the University of California, Riverside, in Romantic poetry, and then began a career in the English department at Lehman College, City University of New York, where he taught writing and literature for more than thirty years. He has also tutored writers at the National University of Ireland at Galway, Sarah Lawrence University, Arizona State University, Columbia University, and Rollins College. Along the way, he wrote poems that eventually earned him a reputation among many people as the most popular living poet in America.

Among his numerous collections of poetry are *Whale Day and Other Poems* (2020), *The Rain in Portugal* (2016), *Voyage* (2014), *Aimless Love* (2013), *Horoscopes for the Dead* (2011), *Ballistics* (2008), *The Trouble with Poetry* (2005), *Nine Horses* (2002), *Sailing Alone Around the Room* (2001), *Picnic, Lightning* (1998), *The Art of Drowning* (1995), *Questions About Angels* (1991), and *The Apple That Astonished Paris* (1988). Collins also edited two anthologies of contemporary poetry designed to entice high school students: *Poetry 180: A Turning Back to Poetry* (2003) and *180 More: Extraordinary Poems for Every Day* (2005). His many honors include fellowships from the New York Foundation for the Arts, the National Endowment for the Arts, and the Guggenheim Foundation. *Poetry* magazine has awarded him the Oscar Blumenthal Prize, the Bess Hokin Prize, the Frederick Bock Prize, and the Levinson Prize.

Collins characterizes himself as someone who was once a professor who wrote poems but who is now a poet who occasionally teaches. This transformation was hard earned because he didn't publish his first complete book of poems until he was in his early forties, with no expectation that twenty years later he would be named United States poet laureate (a gift of hope to writers everywhere). Just as writing poetry has been good for Billy Collins, he has

Billy Collins on his first day as a student at St. Joan of Arc School, Jackson Heights, New York, 1948.
Permission by Chris Calhoun Agency, © Billy Collins.

been good for poetry. Both their reputations have risen simultaneously owing to his appeal to audiences that pack high school auditoriums, college halls, and public theaters all over the country. His many popular readings — including broadcasts on National Public Radio — have helped to make him a best-selling poet, a phrase that is ordinarily an oxymoron in America.

Billy Collins on his first day at The College of the Holy Cross, 1959.
Permission by Chris Calhoun Agency, © Billy Collins.

Unlike many poetry readings, Collins's are attended by readers and fans who come to whoop, holler, and cheer after nearly every poem, as well as to laugh out loud. His audiences are clearly relieved to be in the presence of a poet who speaks to (not down to) them without a trace of pretension, superiority, or presumption. His work is welcoming and readable because he weaves

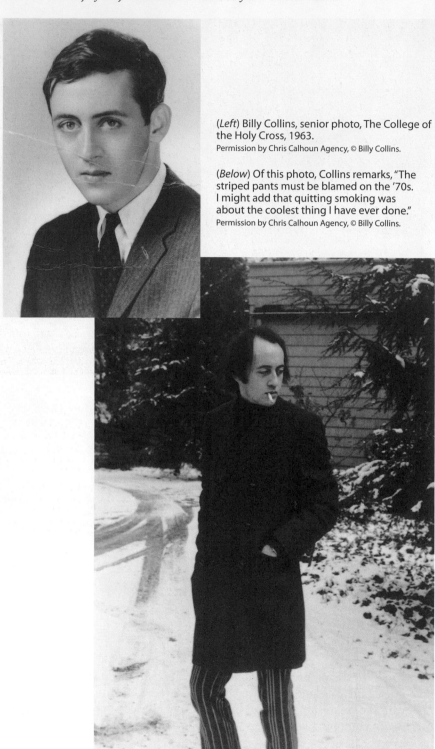

(*Left*) Billy Collins, senior photo, The College of the Holy Cross, 1963.
Permission by Chris Calhoun Agency, © Billy Collins.

(*Below*) Of this photo, Collins remarks, "The striped pants must be blamed on the '70s. I might add that quitting smoking was about the coolest thing I have ever done."
Permission by Chris Calhoun Agency, © Billy Collins.

(*Above*) The poet with his dog, Luke. Scarsdale, New York, 1970s.

Permission by Chris Calhoun Agency, © Billy Collins.

(*Left*) Billy Collins, in his office at Lehman College, 1984.

Permission by Chris Calhoun Agency, © Billy Collins.

observations about the commonplace materials of our lives — the notes we write in the margins of our books, the food we eat, the way we speak, even the way we think of death — into startling, evocative insights that open our eyes wider than they were before.

To understand Collins's attraction to audiences is to better understand his appeal on the page. He wins the affection of audiences with his warmth and genial charm, an affability that makes him appear unreserved and approachable but never intrusive or over-the-top. He is a quieter, suburban version of Walt Whitman — with a dash of Emily Dickinson's reserve. He gives just enough and lets the poems do the talking so that he remains as mysteriously appealing as his poems. His persona is well crafted and serves to engage readers in the world of his art rather than in his personal life. In a parallel manner, he has often described the openings of his poems as "hospitable" — an invitation to the reader to move further into the poem without having to worry about getting lost in the kind of self-referential obscurity and opacity that sometimes characterize modern poetry.

Perhaps not surprisingly, some critics and fellow poets have objected that Collins's poems may sometimes bear up to little more than the pleasures of one reading. Collins, however, believes immediate pleasure can be a primary motivation for reading poetry, and he argues that a poem using simple language should not be considered simpleminded. In his work the ordinary, the everyday, and the familiar often become curious, unusual, and surprising the more closely the poems are read. In interviews, he has compared a first reading of his poems to a reading of the large *E* at the top of an eye chart in an optometrist's office. What starts out clear and unambiguous gradually becomes more complicated and demanding as we squint to make our way to the end. That big *E* — it might be read as "enter" — welcomes us in and gives us the confidence to enjoy the experience, but it doesn't mean that there aren't challenges ahead. The casual, "easy" read frequently becomes a thought-provoking compound of humor, irony, and unconventional wisdom. Humor is such an essential part of Collins's work that in 2004 he was the first recipient of the Poetry Foundation's Mark Twain Award for Humor in Poetry. Given this remarkable trifecta of humor, popularity, and book sales, it is hardly to be unexpected that Collins gives some of his colleagues — as Mark Twain might have put it — the "fantods," but his audiences and readers eagerly anticipate whatever poetic pleasures he will offer them next. In any case, Whitman made the point more than 150 years ago in his preface to *Leaves of Grass:* "The proof of a poet is that his country absorbs him as affectionately as he has absorbed it."

BILLY COLLINS

## *"How Do Poems Travel?"* 2008

Asking a poet to examine his or her own work is a bit like trying to get a puppy interested in looking in a mirror. Parakeets take an interest in their own reflections but not puppies, who are too busy smelling everything and tumbling over themselves to have time for self-regard. Maybe the difficulty is that most imaginative poems issue largely from the intuitive right side of the brain, whereas literary criticism draws on the brain's more rational, analytic left side. So, writing about your own writing involves getting up, moving from one room of the brain to another, and taking all the furniture with you. When asked about the source of his work, one contemporary poet remarked that if he knew where his poems came from, he would go there and never come back. What he was implying is that much of what goes on in the creative moment takes place on a stealthy level beneath the writer's conscious awareness. If creative work did not offer access to this somewhat mysterious, less than rational region, we would all be writing annual reports or law briefs, not stories, plays, and poems.

Just because you don't know what you are doing doesn't mean you are not doing it; so let me say what I do know about the writing process. While writing a poem, I am also listening to it. As the poem gets underway, I am pushing it forward — after all, I am the one holding the pencil — but I am also ready to be pulled in the direction that the poem seems to want to go. I am willfully writing the poem, but I am also submitting to the poem's will. Emerson once compared writing poetry to ice-skating. I think he meant that both the skater on a frozen pond and the poet on the page might end up going places they didn't intend to go. And Mario Andretti, the Grand Prix driver, once remarked that "If you think everything is under control, you're just not driving fast enough."

Total control over any artistic material eliminates the possibility of surprise. I would not bother to start a poem if I already knew how it was going to end. I try to "maintain the benefits of my ignorance," as another poet put it, letting the poem work toward an understanding of itself (and of me) as I go along. In a student essay, the idea is to stick to the topic. In much imaginative poetry, the pleasure lies in finding a way to escape the initial topic, to transcend the subject and ride the poem into strange, unforeseen areas. As poet John Ashbery put it: "In the process of writing, all sorts of unexpected things happen that shift the poet away from his plan; these accidents are really what we mean whenever we talk about Poetry." Readers of poetry see only the finished product set confidently on the page; but the process of writing a poem involves uncertainty, ambiguity, improvisation, and surprise.

I think of poetry as the original travel literature in that a poem can take me to an imaginative place where I have never been. A good poem often progresses by a series of associative leaps, including sudden shifts in time and space, all of which results in a kind of mental journey. I never know the ending of the poem when I set out, but I am aware that I am moving the poem toward some destination, and when I find the ending, I recognize it right away. More interesting to me than what a poem means is how it travels. In the classroom, I like to substitute for the question, "What is the meaning of the poem?" other questions: "How does this poem go?" or "How does this poem travel through itself in search of its own ending?" Maybe a few of my poems that follow will serve as illustrations, and I hope what I have said so far will help you articulate how poems go and how they find their endings.

BILLY COLLINS

## *Osso Buco°*   1995

I love the sound of the bone against the plate
and the fortress-like look of it
lying before me in a moat of risotto,
the meat soft as the leg of an angel
who has lived a purely airborne existence.                         5
And best of all, the secret marrow,
the invaded privacy of the animal
prized out with a knife and swallowed down
with cold, exhilarating wine.

I am swaying now in the hour after dinner,                        10
a citizen tilted back on his chair,
a creature with a full stomach —
something you don't hear much about in poetry,
that sanctuary of hunger and deprivation.
You know: the driving rain, the boots by the door,               15
small birds searching for berries in winter.

But tonight, the lion of contentment
has placed a warm, heavy paw on my chest,
and I can only close my eyes and listen
to the drums of woe throbbing in the distance                    20
and the sound of my wife's laughter
on the telephone in the next room,
the woman who cooked the savory osso buco,
who pointed to show the butcher the ones she wanted.
She who talks to her faraway friend                              25
while I linger here at the table
with a hot, companionable cup of tea,
feeling like one of the friendly natives,
a reliable guide, maybe even the chief's favorite son.

Somewhere, a man is crawling up a rocky hillside                 30
on bleeding knees and palms, an Irish penitent
carrying the stone of the world in his stomach;
and elsewhere people of all nations stare
at one another across a long, empty table.
But here, the candles give off their warm glow,                  35
the same light that Shakespeare and Izaak Walton wrote by,
the light that lit and shadowed the faces of history.
Only now it plays on the blue plates,
the crumpled napkins, the crossed knife and fork.

In a while, one of us will go up to bed                          40
and the other one will follow.
Then we will slip below the surface of the night

*Osso Buco:* An Italian veal dish; translated as "hole [*buco*] bone [*osso*]."

into miles of water, drifting down and down
to the dark, soundless bottom
until the weight of dreams pulls us lower still,                    45
below the shale and layered rock,
beneath the strata of hunger and pleasure,
into the broken bones of the earth itself,
into the marrow of the only place we know.

### CONSIDERATIONS FOR CRITICAL THINKING AND WRITING

1. FIRST RESPONSE. The poem appeals to both the reader's senses and mind. Which is the lasting effect on you? In other words, reflecting on the poem, do you remember feelings or are you wrestling with ideas?

2. Collins talks about "associative leaps" in "How Do Poems Travel?" (p. 907). Where do those leaps occur in this poem, and how do they constitute a journey? A journey from what to what?

3. How does the poem use imagery to achieve its effect?

4. Locate figurative language throughout the poem and explore how it expands the sense of what you consider the poem's theme.

## BILLY COLLINS

### *On Writing "Osso Buco"*   2008

The critic Terry Eagleton pointed out that "writing is just language which can function perfectly well in the physical absence of its author." In other words, the author does not have to accompany his or her writing into the world to act as its interpreter or chaperone. One way for a poem to achieve that kind of independence is to exhibit a certain degree of clarity, at least in the opening lines. The ideal progression of a poem is from the clear to the mysterious. A poem that begins simply can engage the reader by establishing a common ground and then lead the reader into more challenging, less familiar territory. Robert Frost's poems are admirable models of this process of deepening. Of course, if the initial engagement is not made early, it's hard to see how the participation of a reader can be counted on.

"Osso Buco" opens with a gourmand's appreciation of a favorite dish, one commonly served up in Italian restaurants. The one thing I knew at the outset was that the poem was going to be a meditation on the subject of contentment. Misery, despondency, melancholy, and just plain human wretchedness are more likely to be the moods of poetry. Indeed, happiness in serious literature is often mistaken for a kind of cowlike stupidity. I thought I would address that imbalance by taking on the challenge of writing about the pleasures of a full stomach. Even the gloomiest of philosophers admits that there are occasional interruptions in the despondency that is the human lot; so why not pay those moments some poetic attention?

To me, the image of "the lion of contentment" suggested a larger set of metaphors connected to African exploration that might add glue to the poem. A metaphor can be deployed in one line of a poem and then dropped, but other times the poem develops an interest in its own language and a metaphor can be extended and explored. The result can bind together a number of disparate thoughts by giving them a common vocabulary. Thus, in this extended metaphor that begins with "the lion of contentment," "drums of woe" are heard "throbbing in the distance," and later the speaker feels like "one of the friendly natives" or "even the chief's favorite son."

In the fourth stanza, the camera pulls back from the domestic scene of the poem and its mood of contentment to survey examples of human suffering taking place elsewhere. The man with bleeding knees is a reference to the religious pilgrims who annually climb Croagh Patrick, a rocky mountain in the west of Ireland. The image of the "long, empty table" is meant to express the condition of world hunger and famine. But the poem offers those images only in contrast to its insistent theme: satisfaction. Back in the kitchen, there is the candle-lit scene of pleasures recently taken. The mention of Shakespeare and Izaak Walton, who wrote *The Compleat Angler,* a whimsical book on the pleasures of fly-fishing, adds some historic perspective and shows the speaker to be a person of some refinement, an appreciator of literature, history, and, of course, food.

The poem so far has made two noticeable maneuvers, shifting to a global then a historical perspective, but in the final stanza the poem takes its biggest turn when it hits upon the resolving metaphor of geology. The couple retires to bed — another pleasure — descends into sleep, then deeper into dreams, then deeper still through the layers of the earth and into its very center, a "marrow" which harkens back to the bone marrow of the eaten calf. Thus the poem travels from the domestic setting of a kitchen to the plains of Africa, a mountain in Ireland, then back to the kitchen before boring into the core of the earth itself — a fairly extensive journey for a poem of only fifty lines, but not untypical of the kind of ground a lyric poem can quickly cover.

### BILLY COLLINS

## *Nostalgia*   1991

Remember the 1340s? We were doing a dance called the Catapult.
You always wore brown, the color craze of the decade,
and I was draped in one of those capes that were popular,
the ones with unicorns and pomegranates in needlework.
Everyone would pause for beer and onions in the afternoon,                    5
and at night we would play a game called "Find the Cow."
Everything was hand-lettered then, not like today.

Where has the summer of 1572 gone? Brocade and sonnet
marathons were the rage. We used to dress up in the flags
of rival baronies and conquer one another in cold rooms of stone.          10
Out on the dance floor we were all doing the Struggle
while your sister practiced the Daphne all alone in her room.
We borrowed the jargon of farriers for our slang.
These days language seems transparent, a badly broken code.

The 1790s will never come again. Childhood was big.                            15
People would take walks to the very tops of hills
and write down what they saw in their journals without speaking.

Our collars were high and our hats were extremely soft.
We would surprise each other with alphabets made of twigs.
It was a wonderful time to be alive, or even dead.                    20

I am very fond of the period between 1815 and 1821.
Europe trembled while we sat still for our portraits.
And I would love to return to 1901 if only for a moment,
time enough to wind up a music box and do a few dance steps,
or shoot me back to 1922 or 1941, or at least let me                  25
recapture the serenity of last month when we picked
berries and glided through afternoons in a canoe.

Even this morning would be an improvement over the present.
I was in the garden then, surrounded by the hum of bees
and the Latin names of flowers, watching the early light              30
flash off the slanted windows of the greenhouse
and silver the limbs on the rows of dark hemlocks.

As usual, I was thinking about the moments of the past,
letting my memory rush over them like water
rushing over the stones on the bottom of a stream.                    35
I was even thinking a little about the future, that place
where people are doing a dance we cannot imagine,
a dance whose name we can only guess.

### CONSIDERATIONS FOR CRITICAL THINKING AND WRITING

1. FIRST RESPONSE. The speaker seems to be nostalgic for history rather than for a personal past. Would you describe this reminiscence as humorous, or do you see it as a more serious pursuit?

2. The poem is arranged chronologically. Is this the only possible structure to frame its theme, or could it be rearranged?

3. If the speaker had chosen to focus on events from personal history rather than our collective history, would the effect be different? If so, how?

BILLY COLLINS

## On Writing "Nostalgia"    2008

"Nostalgia" offers me the opportunity to say something about poetic form. Broadly speaking, *form* can mean any feature of a poem that keeps it together and gives it unity. Form is the nails and glue that hold the emotions and thoughts of a poem in place. Naturally, poets are in the business of self-expression, but paradoxically they are always looking for limits. Form can be inherited — the sonnet is an enduring example — or the poet may make up his own rules as he goes along. He might even decide at some point to break the very rules he just imposed upon himself. In either case, formal rules give the poet an enclosed space in which to work, and they keep the poem from descending into chaos or tantrum. As poet Stephen Dunn put it, "form is the pressure that an artist puts on his material in order to see what it will bear."

The Irish poet W. B. Yeats felt that "all that is personal will rot unless it is packed in ice and salt." For a formalist poet like Yeats, "ice and salt," which were common food preservatives of his day, probably meant rhyme and meter. After Walt Whitman showed in *Leaves of Grass* (1855) that poems could be written without those two traditional supporting pillars, poets still had many other formal devices at their disposal. Just because poets could now write poems without a design of rhyme words at the ends of lines or a regular meter such as iambic pentameter did not mean they had abandoned form. Some of these alternative formal strategies would include line length, stanza choice, repetition, rhetorical development (beginning–middle–end), and thematic recurrence as well as patterns of sound and imagery. Focusing on form allows us to see that poetry can combine a high level of imaginative freedom with the imposition of boundaries and rules of procedure. For the reader, the coexistence of these two contrary elements — liberty and restriction — may be said to create a pleasurable tension found to a higher degree in poetry than in any other literary genre.

An apparent formal element in "Nostalgia," besides its use of stanza breaks, is the chronological sequence it obediently follows. After the absurd opening question (to which the only answer is no), the poem moves forward from the Middle Ages (the 1340s would place us smack in the middle of the Black Death) to the Renaissance, to the beginnings of English Romanticism, that being 1798, when the first edition of *Lyrical Ballads,* a poetic collaboration between Wordsworth and Coleridge, was published. The poem then continues to travel forward in time, but now more whimsically with dates that seem plucked out of the air — 1901, 1922, 1941 — before arriving rather abruptly at "last month" and then "this morning." If nothing else, the poem demonstrates poetry's freedom from normal time constraints as it manages to travel more than 600 years from the Middle Ages to the present in only twenty-eight lines.

When the poem does arrive at the present, the speaker morphs from a kind of thousand-year-old man into an actual person, a sympathetic fellow who likes to garden and who appreciates the sounds and sights of the natural world. The imaginary historical journey of the poem ends amid the bees and flowers of the speaker's garden, where he continues to dwell nostalgically on the past until his attention turns to the future, really the only place left for him to go. Having relinquished his power as an eyewitness to centuries of human civilization, the speaker trails off in a dreamy speculation about the unknowable dance crazes of the future.

The poem takes a lot of imaginative liberties in the oddness of its premise and its free-ranging images, yet, formally speaking, it is held together by a strict chronological line drawn from the distant historical past right through the present moment and into the future.

I don't recall how a lot of my poems got started, but I do remember that this poem arose out of a kind of annoyance. Just as a grain of sand can irritate an oyster into producing a pearl by coating it with a smooth surface, so a poem may be irked into being. What was bugging me in this case was the popular twentieth-century habit of breaking the past into decades ("the fifties," "the sixties," and so forth), constructs which amounted to little more than a collage of stereotypes. What a gross simplification of this mysterious, invisible thing we call the past, I thought. Even worse, each decade was so sentimentalized as to make one feel that its passing was cause for feelings of melancholy and regret. "Nostalgia," then, is a poem with a motive, that is, to satirize that kind of enforced nostalgia.

Billy Collins

## Questions about Angels    1991

Of all the questions you might want to ask
about angels, the only one you ever hear
is how many can dance on the head of a pin.

No curiosity about how they pass the eternal time
besides circling the Throne chanting in Latin                                    5
or delivering a crust of bread to a hermit on earth
or guiding a boy and girl across a rickety wooden bridge.

Do they fly through God's body and come out singing?
Do they swing like children from the hinges
of the spirit world saying their names backwards and
          forwards?                                                              10
Do they sit alone in little gardens changing colors?

What about their sleeping habits, the fabric of their robes,
their diet of unfiltered divine light?
What goes on inside their luminous heads? Is there a wall
these tall presences can look over and see hell?                                 15

If an angel fell off a cloud, would he leave a hole
in a river and would the hole float along endlessly
filled with the silent letters of every angelic word?

If an angel delivered the mail, would he arrive
in a blinding rush of wings or would he just assume                             20
the appearance of the regular mailman and
whistle up the driveway reading the postcards?

No, the medieval theologians control the court.
The only question you ever hear is about
the little dance floor on the head of a pin                                     25
where halos are meant to converge and drift invisibly.

It is designed to make us think in millions,
billions, to make us run out of numbers and collapse
into infinity, but perhaps the answer is simply one:
one female angel dancing alone in her stocking feet,                            30
a small jazz combo working in the background.

She sways like a branch in the wind, her beautiful
eyes closed, and the tall thin bassist leans over
to glance at his watch because she has been dancing
forever, and now it is very late, even for musicians.                           35

### Considerations for Critical Thinking and Writing

1. **FIRST RESPONSE.** The title indicates that the speaker has questions, and there
   are many questions in the poem. What kind of answers are provided, if any?

2. How does the poem work with the cliché about angels dancing on the head of a pin? What does it do to that cliché?

3. Does any question in the poem seem more crucial than the others, or are they all random musings?

4. The bass player in the jazz combo at the poem's conclusion is a crucial figure, an image from the realm of humanity rather than divinity. What is his role in the poem?

## Billy Collins

### *On Writing "Questions about Angels"* 2008

I find that it doesn't take much to get a poem going. A poem can start casually with something trivial and then develop significance along the way. The first inkling may act as a keyhole that allows the poet to look into an imaginary room. When I started to write "Questions about Angels," I really had nothing on my mind except that odd, speculative question: How many angels can dance on the head of a pin? Seemingly unanswerable, the question originated as an attempt to mock certain medieval philosophers (notably Thomas Aquinas) who sought to solve arcane theological mysteries through the sheer application of reason. I had first heard the question when I was studying theology at a Jesuit college, but well before that, the phrase had made its way into the mainstream of modern parlance. It was typical of me to want to begin a poem with something everyone knows and then proceed from there. The poem found a direction to go in when it occurred to me to open up the discussion to include other questions. At that point, it was "Game on."

My investigation really begins in the second stanza, which draws on traditional images of angels in religious art, either worshipping God or paying helpful visits to earth, assisting the poor and protecting the innocent. Then the questions become more fanciful — off-the-wall, really: "Do they fly through God's body and come out singing?" No doubt you could come up with questions of your own about angel behavior; clearly, that has become the poem's game — an open inquiry into the spirit life of these creatures.

After the poem's most bizarre question, which involves a hole that a fallen angel has left in a river, the interrogation descends into the everyday with the image of an angel delivering mail, not gloriously "in a blinding rush of wings" but just like "the regular mailman." After a reminder of the monopoly "the medieval theologians" seem to have on questions about angels, the poem makes a sudden turn (one I did not see coming) by offering a simple, irreducible answer to that unanswerable question. On the little word "but" (line 29), the poem drops down abruptly from "billions" to "one," and the scene shrinks from heaven to a jazz club located in eternity.

In the process of composing a poem, the poet is mentally juggling many concerns, one of the most dominant and persistent being how the poem is going to find a place to end, a point where the journey of the poem was meant to stop, a point where the poet does not want to say any more, and the reader has heard just enough. In this case, the moment she appeared — rather miraculously, as I remember — I knew that this beautiful angel "dancing alone in her stocking feet" was how the poem would close. She was the hidden destination the poem was moving toward all along without my knowing it. I had only to add the detail of the bored bassist and the odd observation that even musicians playing in eternity cannot be expected to stay awake forever.

## BILLY COLLINS

### *Litany*  2002

*You are the bread and the knife,*
*The crystal goblet and the wine.*
        *— Jacques Crickillon*

You are the bread and the knife,
the crystal goblet and the wine.
You are the dew on the morning grass,
and the burning wheel of the sun.
You are the white apron of the baker,                    5
and the marsh birds suddenly in flight.

However, you are not the wind in the orchard,
the plums on the counter,
or the house of cards.
And you are certainly not the pine-scented air.          10

There is no way you are the pine-scented air.
It is possible that you are the fish under the bridge,
maybe even the pigeon on the general's head,
but you are not even close
to being the field of cornflowers at dusk.               15

And a quick look in the mirror will show
that you are neither the boots in the corner
nor the boat asleep in its boathouse.

It might interest you to know,
speaking of the plentiful imagery of the world,          20
that I am the sound of rain on the roof.

I also happen to be the shooting star,
the evening paper blowing down an alley,
and the basket of chestnuts on the kitchen table.

I am also the moon in the trees                          25
and the blind woman's teacup.
But don't worry, I am not the bread and the knife.
You are still the bread and the knife.
You will always be the bread and the knife,
not to mention the crystal goblet and — somehow — the wine.   30

### CONSIDERATIONS FOR CRITICAL THINKING AND WRITING

1. FIRST RESPONSE. The poem is bookended with the same comparisons: the addressee is bread, knife, goblet, and wine. How do the meanings of those comparisons change over the course of the poem?

2. Bread and wine are associated with the ritual of transubstantiation in the Catholic church: the bread and wine ritually eaten during Mass become the body and blood of Jesus Christ. How does this context frame this poem? How does the poet complicate it?

3. A "litany" is a form of prayer consisting of a recited list that sometimes involves a call and response element. How does the litany of this poem work as a back-and-forth study in metaphor? How do we understand the relationship between speaker and addressee based on the way these metaphors develop?

## BILLY COLLINS

## *On Writing "Litany"*    2008

As the epigraph to this poem indicates, "Litany" was written in reaction to another poem, a love poem I came across in a literary magazine by a poet I had not heard of. What struck me about his poem was its reliance on a strategy that had its heyday in the love sonnets of the Elizabethan age, namely, the convention of flattering the beloved by comparing her to various aspects of nature. Typically, her eyes were like twin suns, her lips red as coral or rubies, her skin pure as milk, and her breath as sweet as flowers or perfume. Such exaggerations were part of the overall tendency to idealize women who were featured in the courtly love poetry of the time, each of whom was as unattainable as she was beautiful and as cruel as she was fair. It took Shakespeare to point out the ridiculousness of these hyperboles, questioning in one of his sonnets the very legitimacy of comparisons ("Shall I compare thee to a summer's day?" [p. 685]), then drenching the whole process with the cold water of realism ("My mistress' eyes are nothing like the sun" [p. 686]). You might think that would have put an end to the practice, but the habit of appealing to women's vanity through comparisons persists even in the poetry of today. That poem in the magazine prompted me to respond.

Starting with the same first two lines, "Litany" seeks to rewrite the earlier poem by offering a corrective. It aims to point out the latent silliness in such comparisons and perhaps the potential absurdity at the heart of metaphor itself. The poem even wants us to think about the kind of romantic relationships that would permit such discourse.

The poem opens by adding some new metaphors (morning dew, baker's apron, marsh birds) to the pile, but in the second stanza, the poem reverses direction by trading in flattery for a mock-serious investigation of what this woman might be and what she is not. Instead of appealing to her sense of her own beauty, the speaker is perfectly willing to insult her by bringing up her metaphoric shortcomings. By the time he informs her that "There is no way you are the pine-scented air" and "you are not even close / to being the field of cornflowers at dusk," we know that this is a different kind of love poem altogether.

The second big turn comes in the fifth stanza when the speaker unexpectedly begins comparing himself to such things as "the sound of rain on the roof." Notice that the earlier comparisons were not all positive. The "pigeon on the general's head" should remind us of an equestrian statue in a park, and we all know what pigeons like to do to statues. But the speaker is not the least bit ashamed to flatter himself with a string of appealing images including a "shooting star," a "basket of chestnuts," and "the moon in the trees." Turning attention away from the "you" of the poem to the speaker is part of the poem's impertinence — the attentive lover turns into an egomaniac — but it echoes a strategy used by Shakespeare himself. Several of his sonnets begin by being about the beloved but end by being about the poet, specifically about his power to bestow immortality on the beloved through his art. Thus, what begins as a love poem ends as a self-love poem.

The last thing to notice is that "Litany" has a circular structure: It ends by swinging back to its beginning, to the imagery of the epigraph. True to the cheek-iness of the speaker, his last words are devoted to tossing the woman a bit of false reassurance that she is still and will always be "the bread and the knife." For what-ever that's worth.

## BILLY COLLINS

### *Building with Its Face Blown Off*   2005

How suddenly the private
is revealed in a bombed-out city,
how the blue and white striped wallpaper

of a second story bedroom is now
exposed to the lightly falling snow      5
as if the room had answered the explosion

wearing only its striped pajamas.
Some neighbors and soldiers
poke around in the rubble below

and stare up at the hanging staircase,      10
the portrait of a grandfather,
a door dangling from a single hinge.

And the bathroom looks almost embarrassed
by its uncovered ochre walls,
the twisted mess of its plumbing,      15

the sink sinking to its knees,
the ripped shower curtain,
the torn goldfish trailing bubbles.

It's like a dollhouse view
as if a child on its knees could reach in      20
and pick up the bureau, straighten a picture.

Or it might be a room on a stage
in a play with no characters,
no dialogue or audience,

no beginning, middle and end —                                          25
just the broken furniture in the street,
a shoe among the cinder blocks,

a light snow still falling
on a distant steeple, and people
crossing a bridge that still stands.                                     30

And beyond that — crows in a tree,
the statue of a leader on a horse,
and clouds that look like smoke,

and even farther on, in another country
on a blanket under a shade tree,                                         35
a man pouring wine into two glasses

and a woman sliding out
the wooden pegs of a wicker hamper
filled with bread, cheese, and several kinds of olives.

### CONSIDERATIONS FOR CRITICAL THINKING AND WRITING

1. FIRST RESPONSE. How is the title of the poem crucial to understanding its theme?

2. Discuss the way the poem uses personification, being sure to cite specific examples from the text.

3. The imagery of most of the poem explicitly involves war and destruction. How does the final imagery of a picnic operate in conjunction with the dominant mood?

## Perspectives

## On "Building with Its Face Blown Off": Michael Meyer Interviews Billy Collins    2009

**Meyer:** The subject matter of your poetry is well known for being typically about the patterns and rhythms of everyday life, along with its delights, humor, ironies, and inevitable pain. "Building with Its Face Blown Off," however, explicitly concerns war and is implicitly political. What prompted this minority report in your writing?

**Collins:** It's true that I usually steer away from big historical subjects in my poems. I don't want to assume a level of authority beyond what a reader might trust, nor do I want to appear ridiculous by taking a firm stand against some moral horror that any other humane person would naturally oppose. A few years back, I consciously avoided joining the movement called "Poets against the War" because I thought it was as self-obviating as "Generals for the War." A direct approach to subjects as enormous as war or slavery or genocide carries the risk that the poet will be smothered under the weight of the topic. Plus, readers are already morally wired to respond in a certain way to such things. As a writer, you want to *create* an emotion, not merely activate one that already exists in the reader. And who wants to preach to the choir? I have come across few readers of poetry who are all for war; and, besides, poets have enough work to do without trying to convert the lost. William Butler Yeats put it best in his "On Being Asked for a War Poem":

> I think it better that in times like these
> A poet's mouth be silent, for in truth
> We have no gift to set a statesman right;
> He has had enough of meddling who can please
> A young girl in the indolence of her youth,
> Or an old man upon a winter's night.

Before poetry can be political, it must be personal.

That's my dim view of poems that do little more than declare that the poet, walking the moral high road, is opposed to ethically reprehensible acts. But the world does press in on us, and I was stopped in my tracks one morning when I saw in a newspaper still another photograph of a bombed-out building, which echoed all the similar images I had seen for too many decades in too many conflicts around the world in Dresden, Sarajevo, or Baghdad, wherever shells happen to fall. That photograph revealed one personal aspect of the war: the apartment of a family blown wide open for all to see. "Building with Its Face Blown Off" was my response.

**Meyer:** The images in the poem have a photojournalistic quality, but they are snapped through the lens of personification rather than a camera. Isn't a picture better than a thousand words?

**Collins:** I wanted to avoid the moralistic antiwar rhetoric that the underlying subject invites, so I stuck to the visual. A photojournalist once observed that to capture the horrors of war, you don't have to go to the front lines and photograph actual armed conflict: just take a picture of a child's shoe lying on a road. That picture would be worth many words, but as a poet I must add, maybe not quite a thousand. In this poem, I wanted to downplay the horrible violence of the destruction by treating the event as a mere social embarrassment, an invasion of domestic privacy. As Chekhov put it, if you want to get the reader emotionally involved, write cold. For the same reason, I deployed nonviolent metaphors such as the dollhouse and the theater, where the fourth wall is absent. The poem finds a way to end by withdrawing from the scene like a camera pulling back to reveal a larger world. Finally, we are looking down as from a blimp on another country, one where the absence of war provides the tranquility that allows a man and a woman to have a picnic.

A reader once complimented me for ending this poem with olives, the olive branch being a traditional symbol of peace. Another reader heard an echo of Ernest Hemingway's short story "In Another Country," which concerns World War I. Just between you and me, neither of these references had ever occurred to me; but I am always glad to take credit for such happy accidents even if it is similar to drawing a target around a bullet hole. No writer can — or should want to — have absolute control over the reactions of his readers.

**Meyer:** In your essay on writing "Nostalgia," you point out that "formal rules give the poet an enclosed space in which to work, and they keep the poem from descending into chaos or tantrum" (p. 911). How does form in "Building with Its Face Blown Off" prevent its emotions and thoughts from being reduced to a prose bumper sticker such as "War is hell"?

**Collins:** I hope what keeps this poem from getting carried away with its traumatic subject is its concentration on the photograph so that the poem maintains a visual, even cinematic, focus throughout. You could think of the poem as a one-minute movie — a short subject about a big topic. Another sign of apparent form here is the division of the poem into three-line stanzas, or tercets, which slow down the reader's progress through the poem. Just as readers should pause slightly at the end of every poetic line (even an unpunctuated one — the equivalent of half a comma), they should also observe a little pause between stanzas. Poetry is famous for condensing large amounts of mental and emotional material into small packages, and it also encourages us to slow down from the speed at which we usually absorb information. The stanzas give the poem a look of regularity, and some of them make visible the grammatical structure of the poem's sentences. Regular stanzas suggest that the poem comes in sections, and they remind us that poetry is a spatial arrangement of words on the page. Think of such stanzas as stones in a stream; the reader steps from one to the next to get to the other side.

**Meyer:** In a classroom discussion of the final two stanzas, one of my students read the couple's picnic scene as "offering an image of hope and peace in contrast to the reckless destruction that precedes it," while another student countered that the scene appeared to be a depiction of "smug indifference and apathy to suffering." Care to comment?

**Collins:** I find it fascinating that such contrary views of the poem's ending could exist. Probably the most vexing question in poetry studies concerns interpretation. One thing to keep in mind is that readers of poetry, students especially, are much more preoccupied with "meaning" than poets are. While I am writing, I am not thinking about the poem's meaning; I am only trying to write a good poem, which involves securing the form of the poem and getting the poem to hold together so as to stay true to itself. Thinking about what my poem means would only distract me from the real work of poetry. Neurologically speaking, I am trying to inhabit the intuitive side of the brain, not the analytical side where critical thought and "study questions" come from. "Meaning," if I think of it at all, usually comes as an afterthought.

But the question remains: How do poets react to interpretations of their work? Generally speaking, once a poem is completed and then published, it is out of the writer's hands. I'm disposed to welcome interpretations that I did not consciously intend — that doesn't mean my unconscious didn't play a role — as long as those readings do not twist the poem out of shape. In "Building with Its Face Blown Off," I added the picnicking couple simply as a sharp contrast to the scene of destruction in the war-torn city. The man and woman are free to enjoy the luxury of each other's company, the countryside, wine, cheese, and even a choice of olives. Are they a sign of hope? Well, yes, insofar as they show us that the whole world is not at war. Smugness? Not so much to my mind, even though that strikes me as a sensible reaction. But if a reader claimed that the couple represented Adam and Eve, or more absurdly, Antony and Cleopatra, or Donny and Marie Osmond, then I would question the person's common sense or sanity. I might even ring for Security. Mainly, the couple is there simply to show us what is no longer available to the inhabitants of the beleaguered city and to give me a place to end the poem.

## *Draft Poems*

Billy Collins writes: "Poetry can and should be an important part of our daily lives. Poems can inspire and make us think about what it means to be a member of the human race. By just spending a few minutes reading a poem each day, new worlds can be revealed." As United States poet laureate, Collins instituted an ongoing student program through the Library of Congress called "Poetry 180: A Poem a Day for American High Schools." He chose 180 poems for the project — one for each day of the public school year — and offered some advice on reading poems aloud. (See loc.gov/poetry/180, where the poems can be read online.)

Library of Congress.

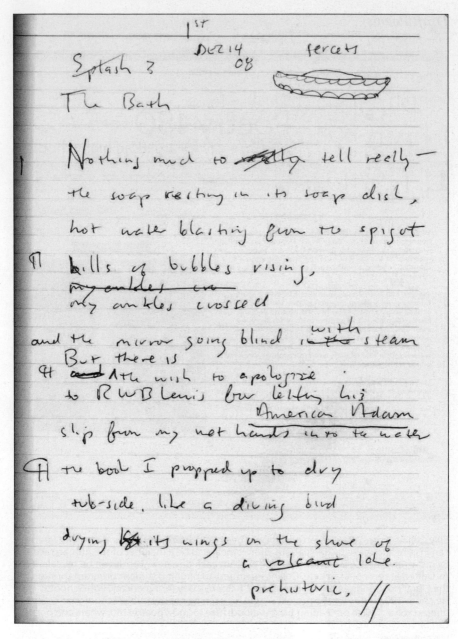

A draft of the unpublished poem "The Bath" from an entry in one of Collins's notebooks, dated December 14, 2008.

Permission by Chris Calhoun Agency, © Billy Collins.

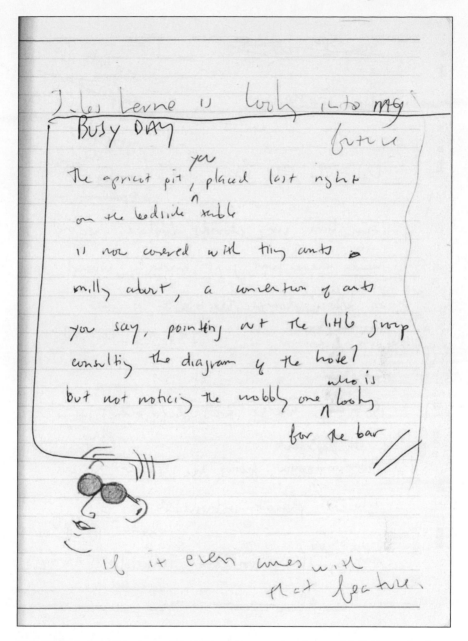

A draft of the unpublished poem "Busy Day" from an undated page of Collins's notebooks.
Permission by Chris Calhoun Agency, © Billy Collins.

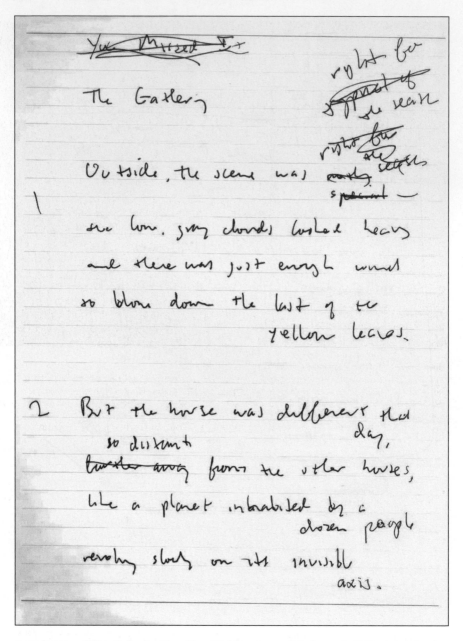

A draft page of "The Gathering" (working title) from an undated page in Collins's notebooks.
Published in 2006 in the *New York Times* as "For Your Digestion; The Gathering."
Permission by Chris Calhoun Agency, © Billy Collins.

**Billy Collins Action Poetry Website**
In a 2003 interview with the American Booksellers Association, Billy Collins explained that his goal as United States poet laureate was for poetry "to pop up in unexpected places, like the daily announcement in high schools and on airplanes." At the website for the Billy Collins Action Poetry film project (www.bcactionpoet.org), you can view artful new interpretations of the poet's work and hear them read aloud by Collins himself, in what makes for an imaginative and elegant combination of poetry and technology.
Library of Congress.

## SUGGESTED TOPICS FOR LONGER PAPERS

1. Analyze the humor in four of Collins's poems included in this anthology (see also "Introduction to Poetry," p. 544). What purpose does the humor serve? Does the humor appeal to you? Explain why or why not, giving examples.

2. View the poems available on the Billy Collins Action Poetry Website (see above and bcactionpoet.org), where you can find visual interpretations of individual poems and hear Collins read the poems aloud. Choose three of the poems and write an analysis of how the visual and auditory representations affect your response to the poems' language. Explain why you think this approach enhances or diminishes — or is simply different from — reading the poem on a page.

3. Collins has mentioned Robert Frost as an influence. Using two to three poems by each poet, trace the relationship between their work as you see it.

# An Anthology
## of Poems

# 33

## An Anthology of
## Classic Poems

Historical/Getty Images.

I find that I cannot exist without poetry.

— JOHN KEATS

**W. H. AUDEN** (1907–1973)

### *The Unknown Citizen*   1940

*(To JS/07/M/378*
*This Marble Monument*
*Is Erected by the State)*

He was found by the Bureau of Statistics to be
One against whom there was no official complaint,
And all the reports on his conduct agree
That, in the modern sense of an old-fashioned word, he was a saint,
For in everything he did he served the Greater Community.                5
Except for the War till the day he retired
He worked in a factory and never got fired,
But satisfied his employers, Fudge Motors Inc.
Yet he wasn't a scab or odd in his views,

929

For his Union reports that he paid his dues,　　　　　　　　　　　10
(Our report on his Union shows it was sound)
And our Social Psychology workers found
That he was popular with his mates and liked a drink.
The Press are convinced that he bought a paper every day
And that his reactions to advertisements were normal in every way.　　15
Policies taken out in his name prove that he was fully insured,
And his Health-card shows he was once in hospital but left it cured.
Both Producers Research and High-Grade Living declare
He was fully sensible to the advantages of the Installment Plan
And had everything necessary to the Modern Man,　　　　　　20
A phonograph, radio, car and a frigidaire.
Our researchers into Public Opinion are content
That he held the proper opinions for the time of year;
When there was peace, he was for peace; when there was war, he went.
He was married and added five children to the population,　　　25
Which our Eugenist says was the right number for a parent of his
　　　generation,
And our teachers report that he never interfered with their education.
Was he free? Was he happy? The question is absurd:
Had anything been wrong, we should certainly have heard.

## CHARLES BAUDELAIRE (1821–1867)

### *A Carrion*　1857

TRANSLATED FROM FRENCH BY ALLEN TATE

Remember now, my Love, what piteous thing
　　We saw on a summer's gracious day:
By the roadside a hideous carrion, quivering
　　On a clean bed of pebbly clay,

Her legs flexed in the air like a courtesan,　　　　　　　　5
　　Burning and sweating venomously,
Calmly exposed its belly, ironic and wan,
　　Clamorous with foul ecstasy.

The sun bore down upon this rottenness
　　As if to roast it with gold fire,　　　　　　　　　　　10
And render back to nature her own largess
　　A hundredfold of her desire.

Heaven observed the vaunting carcass there
　　Blooming with the richness of a flower;
And that almighty stink which corpses wear　　　　　　　15
　　Choked you with sleepy power!

The flies swarmed on the putrid vulva, then
　　A black tumbling rout would seethe
Of maggots, thick like a torrent in a glen,
　　Over those rags that lived and seemed to breathe.　　　20

They darted down and rose up like a wave
    Or buzzed impetuously as before;
One would have thought the corpse was held a slave
    To living by the life it bore!

This world had music, its own swift emotion        25
    Like water and the wind running,
Or corn that a winnower in rhythmic motion
    Fans with fiery cunning.

All forms receded, as in a dream were still,
    Where white visions vaguely start        30
From the sketch of a painter's long-neglected idyl
    Into a perfect art!

Behind the rocks a restless bitch looked on
    Regarding us with jealous eyes,
Waiting to tear from the livid skeleton        35
    Her loosed morsel quick with flies.

And even you will come to this foul shame,
    This ultimate infection,
Star of my eyes, my being's inner flame,
    My angel and my passion!        40

Yes: such shall you be, O queen of heavenly grace,
    Beyond the last sacrament,
When through your bones the flowers and sucking grass
    Weave their rank cerement.

Speak, then, my Beauty, to this dire putrescence,        45
    To the worm, that shall kiss your proud estate,
That I have kept the divine form and the essence
    Of my festered loves inviolate!

## Aphra Behn (1640–1689)

### *Song: Love Armed*    1684

Love in fantastic triumph sate,
    Whilst bleeding hearts around him flowed,
For whom fresh pains he did create,
    And strange tyrannic power he showed:
From thy bright eyes he took his fire,        5
    Which round about in sport he hurled;
But 'twas from mine he took desire,
    Enough to undo the amorous world.

From me he took his sighs and tears;
    From thee, his pride and cruelty;        10
From me, his languishments and fears;
    And every killing dart from thee.

Thus thou and I the god have armed
    And set him up a deity;
But my poor heart alone is harmed,                               15
    Whilst thine the victor is, and free.


## WILLIAM BLAKE (1757–1827)

### *Infant Sorrow*   1794

My mother groand! my father wept.
Into the dangerous world I leapt:
Helpless naked piping loud:
Like a fiend hid in a cloud.

Struggling in my father's hands:                                 5
Striving against my swaddling bands
Bound and weary I thought best
To sulk upon my mother's breast.


## ANNE BRADSTREET (CA. 1612–1672)

### *Before the Birth of One of Her Children*   1678

All things within this fading world hath end,
Adversity doth still our joys attend;
No ties so strong, no friends so dear and sweet,
But with death's parting blow is sure to meet.
The sentence past is most irrevocable,                           5
A common thing, yet oh, inevitable.
How soon, my Dear, death may my steps attend,
How soon't may be thy lot to lose thy friend,
We both are ignorant, yet love bids me
These farewell lines to recommend to thee,                       10
That when that knot's untied that made us one,
I may seem thine, who in effect am none.
And if I see not half my days that's due,
What nature would, God grant to yours and you;
The many faults that well you know I have                        15
Let be interred in my oblivious grave;
If any worth or virtue were in me,
Let that live freshly in thy memory
And when thou feel'st no grief, as I no harms,
Yet love thy dead, who long lay in thine arms,                   20
And when thy loss shall be repaid with gains
Look to my little babes, my dear remains.
And if thou love thyself, or loved'st me,
These O protect from stepdame's° injury.            *stepmother's*
And if chance to thine eyes shall bring this verse,              25

With some sad sighs honor my absent hearse;
And kiss this paper for thy love's dear sake,
Who with salt tears this last farewell did take.

## EMILY BRONTË (1818–1848)

### *Stars*    1845

Ah! why, because the dazzling sun
Restored my earth to joy
Have you departed, every one,
And left a desert sky?

All through the night, your glorious eyes                    5
Were gazing down in mine,
And with a full heart's thankful sighs
I blessed that watch divine!

I was at peace, and drank your beams
As they were life to me                                      10
And revelled in my changeful dreams
Like petrel on the sea.

Thought followed thought — star followed star
Through boundless regions on,
While one sweet influence, near and far,                     15
Thrilled through and proved us one.

Why did the morning rise to break
So great, so pure a spell,
And scorch with fire the tranquil cheek
Where your cool radiance fell?                               20

Blood-red he rose, and arrow-straight
His fierce beams struck my brow:
The soul of Nature sprang elate,
But mine sank sad and low!

My lids closed down — yet through their veil                 25
I saw him blazing still;
And bathe in gold the misty dale,
And flash upon the hill.

I turned me to the pillow then
To call back Night, and see                                  30
Your worlds of solemn light, again
Throb with my heart and me!

It would not do — the pillow glowed
And glowed both roof and floor,
And birds sang loudly in the wood,                           35
And fresh winds shook the door.

The curtains waved, the wakened flies
Were murmuring round my room,
Imprisoned there, till I should rise
And give them leave to roam.                                      40

O Stars and Dreams and Gentle Night;
O Night and Stars return!
And hide me from the hostile light
That does not warm, but burn —

That drains the blood of suffering men;                          45
Drinks tears, instead of dew:
Let me sleep through his blinding reign,
And only wake with you!

## SAMUEL TAYLOR COLERIDGE (1772–1834)

### *Kubla Khan: or, a Vision in a Dream°*    1798

In Xanadu did Kubla Khan°
    A stately pleasure-dome decree:
Where Alph, the sacred river, ran
Through caverns measureless to man
    Down to a sunless sea.                                    5

So twice five miles of fertile ground
With walls and towers were girdled round:
And here were gardens bright with sinuous rills
Where blossomed many an incense-bearing tree;
And there were forests ancient as the hills,                     10
Enfolding sunny spots of greenery.

But oh! that deep romantic chasm which slanted
Down the green hill athwart a cedarn cover!°
A savage place! as holy and enchanted
As e'er beneath a waning moon was haunted                        15
By woman wailing for her demon-lover!
And from this chasm, with ceaseless turmoil seething,
As if this earth in fast thick pants were breathing,
A mighty fountain momently was forced,
Amid whose swift half-intermitted burst                          20
Huge fragments vaulted like rebounding hail,
Of chaffy grain beneath the thresher's flail:
And 'mid these dancing rocks at once and ever

---

*Vision in a Dream:* This poem came to Coleridge in an opium-induced dream, but he was interrupted by a visitor while writing it down. He was later unable to remember the rest of the poem.
1 *Kubla Khan:* The historical Kublai Khan (1216–1294, grandson of Genghis Khan) was the founder of the Mongol dynasty in China.    13 *athwart . . . cover:* Spanning a grove of cedar trees.

It flung up momently the sacred river.
Five miles meandering with a mazy motion         25
Through wood and dale the sacred river ran,
Then reached the caverns measureless to man,
And sank in tumult to a lifeless ocean:
And 'mid this tumult Kubla heard from far
Ancestral voices prophesying war!               30

> The shadow of the dome of pleasure
> Floated midway on the waves;
> Where was heard the mingled measure
> From the fountain and the caves.

It was a miracle of rare device,                35
A sunny pleasure-dome with caves of ice!

> A damsel with a dulcimer
> In a vision once I saw:
> It was an Abyssinian maid,
> And on her dulcimer she played,              40
> Singing of Mount Abora.
> Could I revive within me
> Her symphony and song,
> To such a deep delight 'twould win me,

That with music loud and long,                  45
I would build that dome in air,
That sunny dome! those caves of ice!
And all who heard should see them there,
And all should cry, Beware! Beware!
His flashing eyes, his floating hair!           50
Weave a circle round him thrice,
And close your eyes with holy dread,
For he on honey-dew hath fed,
And drunk the milk of Paradise.

# JOHN DONNE (1572–1631)

## *The Flea*   1633

Mark but this flea, and mark in this,
How little that which thou deniest me is;
Me it sucked first, and now sucks thee,
And in this flea our two bloods mingled be;
Thou know'st that this cannot be said           5
A sin, or shame, or loss of maidenhead,
> Yet this enjoys before it woo,
> And pampered swells with one blood made of two,
> And this, alas, is more than we would do.°

8–9 *pampered...do:* I.e., we, alas, don't dare hope for this consummation of our love, which the
flea freely accepts. The idea of swelling suggests pregnancy.

Oh stay, three lives in one flea spare,       10
Where we almost, nay more than married are.
This flea is you and I, and this
Our marriage bed and marriage temple is;
Though parents grudge, and you, we are met,
And cloistered in these living walls of jet.       15
    Though use° make you apt to kill me,
    Let not to that, self-murder added be,
    And sacrilege, three sins in killing three.

Cruel and sudden, hast thou since
Purpled thy nail in blood of innocence?°       20
Wherein could this flea guilty be,
Except in that drop which it sucked from thee?
Yet thou triumph'st, and say'st that thou
Find'st not thy self nor me the weaker now;
    'Tis true; then learn how false fears be:       25
    Just so much honor, when thou yield'st to me,
    Will waste, as this flea's death took life from thee.

16 *use:* Habit.    20 *Purpled...innocence:* Like Herod, Donne's mistress has slaughtered the innocents and is now clothed in imperial purple.

## T. S. ELIOT (1888–1965)

### *The Love Song of J. Alfred Prufrock*    1917

*S'io credesse che mia risposta fosse*
*A persona che mai tornasse al mondo,*
*Questa fiamma staria senza più scosse.*
*Ma perciocchè giammai di questo fondo*
*Non tornò vivo alcun, s'i'odo il vero,*
*Senza tema d'infamia ti rispondo.°*

    Let us go then, you and I,
When the evening is spread out against the sky
Like a patient etherized upon a table;
Let us go, through certain half-deserted streets,
The muttering retreats       5
Of restless nights in one-night cheap hotels

*Epigraph: S'io credesse . . . rispondo:* Dante's *Inferno,* 27:58–63. In the Eighth Chasm of the Inferno, Dante and Virgil meet Guido da Montefeltro, one of the False Counselors, who is punished by being enveloped in an eternal flame. When Dante asks Guido to tell his life story, the spirit replies: "If I thought that my answer were to one who might ever return to the world, this flame would shake no more; but since from this depth none ever returned alive, if what I hear is true, I answer you without fear of infamy."

And sawdust restaurants with oyster-shells:
Streets that follow like a tedious argument
Of insidious intent
To lead you to an overwhelming question . . .          10

Oh, do not ask, "What is it?"
Let us go and make our visit.

In the room the women come and go
Talking of Michelangelo.

    The yellow fog that rubs its back upon the window panes,          15
The yellow smoke that rubs its muzzle on the window panes
Licked its tongue into the corners of the evening,
Lingered upon the pools that stand in drains,
Let fall upon its back the soot that falls from chimneys,
Slipped by the terrace, made a sudden leap,          20
And seeing that it was a soft October night,
Curled once about the house, and fell asleep.

    And indeed there will be time°
For the yellow smoke that slides along the street,
Rubbing its back upon the window panes;          25
There will be time, there will be time
To prepare a face to meet the faces that you meet;
There will be time to murder and create,
And time for all the works and days° of hands
That lift and drop a question on your plate:          30
Time for you and time for me,
And time yet for a hundred indecisions,
And for a hundred visions and revisions,
Before the taking of a toast and tea.

In the room the women come and go          35
Talking of Michelangelo.

    And indeed there will be time
To wonder, "Do I dare?" and, "Do I dare?" —
Time to turn back and descend the stair,
With a bald spot in the middle of my hair —          40
(They will say: "How his hair is growing thin!")
My morning coat, my collar mounting firmly to the chin,
My necktie rich and modest, but asserted by a simple pin —
(They will say: "But how his arms and legs are thin!")
Do I dare          45
Disturb the universe?
In a minute there is time
For decisions and revisions which a minute will reverse.

---

23 *there will be time:* An allusion to Ecclesiastes 3:1–8: "To everything there is a season, and
a time to every purpose under heaven. . . ."    29 *works and days:* Hesiod's eighth-century
B.C.E. poem *Works and Days* gives practical advice on how to conduct one's life in accordance
with the seasons.

For I have known them all already, known them all:
Have known the evenings, mornings, afternoons,       50
I have measured out my life with coffee spoons;
I know the voices dying with a dying fall
Beneath the music from a farther room.
     So how should I presume?

     And I have known the eyes already, known them all —       55
The eyes that fix you in a formulated phrase.
And when I am formulated, sprawling on a pin,
When I am pinned and wriggling on the wall,
Then how should I begin
To spit out all the butt-ends of my days and ways?       60
     And how should I presume?

     And I have known the arms already, known them all —
Arms that are braceleted and white and bare
(But in the lamplight, downed with light brown hair!)
     Is it perfume from a dress       65
     That makes me so digress?
Arms that lie along a table, or wrap about a shawl.
     And should I then presume?
     And how should I begin?

     Shall I say, I have gone at dusk through narrow streets,       70
And watched the smoke that rises from the pipes
Of lonely men in shirtsleeves, leaning out of windows? . . .

I should have been a pair of ragged claws
Scuttling across the floors of silent seas.

     And the afternoon, the evening, sleeps so peacefully!       75
Smoothed by long fingers,
Asleep . . . tired . . . or it malingers,
Stretched on the floor, here beside you and me.
Should I, after tea and cakes and ices,
Have the strength to force the moment to its crisis?       80
But though I have wept and fasted, wept and prayed,
Though I have seen my head (grown slightly bald) brought in upon a platter,°
I am no prophet — and here's no great matter;
I have seen the moment of my greatness flicker,
And I have seen the eternal Footman hold my coat, and snicker,       85
     And in short, I was afraid.

     And would it have been worth it, after all,
After the cups, the marmalade, the tea,
Among the porcelain, among some talk of you and me,
Would it have been worth while       90
To have bitten off the matter with a smile,

---

82 *head . . . upon a platter:* At Salome's request, Herod had John the Baptist decapitated and had
the severed head delivered to her on a platter (see Matt. 14:1–12 and Mark 6:17–29).

To have squeezed the universe into a ball°
To roll it toward some overwhelming question,
To say: "I am Lazarus,° come from the dead,
Come back to tell you all, I shall tell you all" —                   95
If one, settling a pillow by her head,
    Should say: "That is not what I meant at all;
        That is not it, at all."

    And would it have been worth it, after all,
Would it have been worth while,                             100
After the sunsets and the dooryards and the sprinkled streets,
After the novels, after the teacups, after the skirts that trail along the floor —
And this, and so much more? —
It is impossible to say just what I mean!
But as if a magic lantern threw the nerves in patterns on a screen:    105
Would it have been worth while
If one, settling a pillow or throwing off a shawl,
And turning toward the window, should say:
    "That is not it at all,
    That is not what I meant, at all."                      110

No! I am not Prince Hamlet, nor was meant to be;
Am an attendant lord,° one that will do
To swell a progress,° start a scene or two,                *state procession*
Advise the prince: withal, an easy tool,
Deferential, glad to be of use,                             115
Politic, cautious, and meticulous;
Full of high sentence, but a bit obtuse;
At times, indeed, almost ridiculous —
Almost, at times, the Fool.

I grow old . . . I grow old . . .                             120
I shall wear the bottoms of my trousers rolled.

    Shall I part my hair behind? Do I dare to eat a peach?
I shall wear white flannel trousers, and walk upon the beach.
I have heard the mermaids singing, each to each.

I do not think that they will sing to me.                      125

I have seen them riding seaward on the waves,
Combing the white hair of the waves blown back
When the wind blows the water white and black.

We have lingered in the chambers of the sea
By seagirls wreathed with seaweed red and brown,          130
Till human voices wake us, and we drown.

---

92 *squeezed the universe into a ball:* See Andrew Marvell's "To His Coy Mistress" (pp. 941–942), lines 41–42: "Let us roll all our strength and all / Our sweetness up into one ball."    94 *Lazarus:* The brother of Mary and Martha who was raised from the dead by Jesus (John 11:1–44). In Luke 16:19–31, a rich man asks that another Lazarus return from the dead to warn the living about their treatment of the poor.    112 *attendant lord:* Like Polonius in Shakespeare's *Hamlet.*

## GERARD MANLEY HOPKINS (1844–1889)

### *Pied° Beauty*  1918

Glory be to God for dappled things —
　　For skies of couple-colour as a brinded° cow;
　　　For rose-moles all in stipple upon trout that swim;
Fresh-firecoal chestnut-falls,° finches' wings;
　　Landscape plotted and pieced — fold, fallow, and plough;°　　　　5
　　　And áll trádes, their gear and tackle and trim.°　　　*equipment*

All things counter,° original, spare,° strange;　　　　*contrary, rare*
　　Whatever is fickle, freckled (who knows how?)
　　　With swift, slow; sweet, sour; adazzle, dim;
He fathers-forth whose beauty is past change:　　　　10
　　　　　Praise him.

*Pied:* Of two or more colors in blotches, variegated.　2 *brinded:* Brownish orange in color with streaks of gray.　4 *chestnut-falls:* I.e., freshly fallen chestnuts, bright as coals.　5 *fold... plough:* Divided into fields used as pastures ("fold"), lying fallow, or plowed for cultivation. The landscape thus appears like patches of different colors.

## JOHN KEATS (1795–1821)

### *When I have fears that I may cease to be*  1818

When I have fears that I may cease to be
　　Before my pen has gleaned my teeming brain,
Before high-piled books, in charactery,°　　　　*print*
　　Hold like rich garners the full ripened grain;
When I behold, upon the night's starred face,　　　　5
　　Huge cloudy symbols of a high romance,
And think that I may never live to trace
　　Their shadows, with the magic hand of chance;
And when I feel, fair creature of an hour,
　　That I shall never look upon thee more,　　　　10
Never have relish in the faery° power　　　　*magic*
　　Of unreflecting love; — then on the shore
Of the wide world I stand alone, and think
Till love and fame to nothingness do sink.

## EMMA LAZARUS (1849–1887)

### *The New Colossus*  1883

Not like the brazen giant of Greek fame,
With conquering limbs astride from land to land;
Here at our sea-washed, sunset gates shall stand
A mighty woman with a torch, whose flame
Is the imprisoned lightning, and her name　　　　5
Mother of Exiles. From her beacon-hand

Glows world-wide welcome; her mild eyes command
The air-bridged harbor that twin cities frame.
"Keep, ancient lands, your storied pomp!" cries she
With silent lips. "Give me your tired, your poor,                    10
Your huddled masses yearning to breathe free,
The wretched refuse of your teeming shore.
Send these, the homeless, tempest-tost to me,
I lift my lamp beside the golden door!"

## ANDREW MARVELL  (1621–1678)

### *To His Coy Mistress*    1681

Had we but world enough, and time,
This coyness, lady, were no crime.
We would sit down, and think which way
To walk, and pass our long love's day.
Thou by the Indian Ganges'° side                                     5
Shouldst rubies find; I by the tide
Of Humber° would complain.° I would
Love you ten years before the Flood,
And you should, if you please, refuse
Till the conversion of the Jews.                                     10
My vegetable love should grow°
Vaster than empires, and more slow;
An hundred years should go to praise
Thine eyes and on thy forehead gaze,
Two hundred to adore each breast,                                    15
But thirty thousand to the rest:
An age at least to every part,
And the last age should show your heart.
For, lady, you deserve this state,
Nor would I love at lower rate.                                      20
    But at my back I always hear
Time's wingèd chariot hurrying near;
And yonder all before us lie
Deserts of vast eternity.
Thy beauty shall no more be found,                                   25
Nor in thy marble vault shall sound
My echoing song; then worms shall try
That long preserved virginity,
And your quaint honor turn to dust,
And into ashes all my lust.                                          30
The grave's a fine and private place,
But none, I think, do there embrace.

---

5 *Ganges:* A river in India sacred to the Hindus.    7 *Humber:* A river that flows through
Marvell's native town, Hull. *complain:* write love songs.    11 *My vegetable love . . . grow:* A slow,
unconscious growth.

Now, therefore, while the youthful hue
Sits on thy skin like morning dew,
And while thy willing soul transpires°                    *breathes forth*    35
At every pore with instant fires,
Now let us sport us while we may,
And now, like amorous birds of prey,
Rather at once our time devour
Than languish in his slow-chapped° power.                *slow-jawed*    40
Let us roll all our strength and all
Our sweetness up into one ball,
And tear our pleasures with rough strife
Thorough° the iron gates of life.                          *through*
Thus, though we cannot make our sun                                      45
Stand still, yet we will make him run.

### EDNA ST. VINCENT MILLAY (1892–1950)

## *Spring*   1921

To what purpose, April, do you return again?
Beauty is not enough.
You can no longer quiet me with the redness
Of little leaves opening stickily.
I know what I know.                                                        5
The sun is hot on my neck as I observe
The spikes of the crocus.
The smell of the earth is good.
It is apparent that there is no death.
But what does that signify?                                              10
Not only under ground are the brains of men
Eaten by maggots.
Life in itself
Is nothing,
An empty cup, a flight of uncarpeted stairs.                            15
It is not enough that yearly, down this hill,
April
Comes like an idiot, babbling and strewing flowers.

### JOHN MILTON (1608–1674)

## *When I consider how my light is spent*   CA. 1655

When I consider how my light is spent,°
    Ere half my days in this dark world and wide,
    And that one talent° which is death to hide

---

1 *how my light is spent:* Milton had been totally blind since 1651.    3 *that one talent:* Refers to Jesus's parable of the talents (units of money), in which a servant entrusted with a talent buries it rather than invest it and is punished on his master's return (Matt. 25:14–30).

Lodged with me useless, though my soul more bent
To serve therewith my Maker, and present                                    5
    My true account, lest He returning chide;
    "Doth God exact day-labor, light denied?"
I fondly° ask. But Patience, to prevent                                *foolishly*
That murmur, soon replies, "God doth not need
    Either man's work or His own gifts. Who best                 10
    Bear His mild yoke, they serve Him best. His state
Is kingly: thousands at His bidding speed,
    And post o'er land and ocean without rest;
    They also serve who only stand and wait."

## EDGAR ALLAN POE (1809–1849)

### *Annabel Lee*  1849

It was many and many a year ago,
    In a kingdom by the sea,
That a maiden there lived whom you may know
    By the name of Annabel Lee;
And this maiden she lived with no other thought                             5
    Than to love and be loved by me.

*She* was a child and *I* was a child,
    In this kingdom by the sea,
But we loved with a love that was more than love —
    I and my Annabel Lee —                                           10
With a love that the wingéd seraphs° of Heaven      *angels of the highest order*
    Coveted her and me.

And this was the reason that, long ago,
    In this kingdom by the sea,
A wind blew out of a cloud by night                                         15
    Chilling my Annabel Lee;
So that her highborn kinsmen came
    And bore her away from me,
To shut her up in a sepulchre
    In this kingdom by the sea.                                      20

The angels, not half so happy in Heaven,
    Went envying her and me:
Yes! that was the reason (as all men know,
    In this kingdom by the sea)
That the wind came out of the cloud, chilling                               25
    And killing my Annabel Lee.

But our love it was stronger by far than the love
    Of those who were older than we —
    Of many far wiser than we —

And neither the angels in Heaven above 30
    Nor the demons down under the sea,
Can ever dissever my soul from the soul
    Of the beautiful Annabel Lee:

For the moon never beams without bringing me dreams
    Of the beautiful Annabel Lee; 35
And the stars never rise but I see the bright eyes
    Of the beautiful Annabel Lee;
And so, all the night-tide, I lie down by the side
Of my darling, my darling, my life and my bride,
    In her sepulchre there by the sea — 40
    In her tomb by the side of the sea.

## EDWIN ARLINGTON ROBINSON (1869–1935)

### *Miniver Cheevy*  1910

Miniver Cheevy, child of scorn,
    Grew lean while he assailed the seasons;
He wept that he was ever born,
    And he had reasons.

Miniver loved the days of old 5
    When swords were bright and steeds were prancing;
The vision of a warrior bold
    Would set him dancing.

Miniver sighed for what was not,
    And dreamed, and rested from his labors; 10
He dreamed of Thebes and Camelot,
    And Priam's neighbors.

Miniver mourned the ripe renown
    That made so many a name so fragrant;
He mourned Romance, now on the town, 15
    And Art, a vagrant.

Miniver loved the Medici,
    Albeit he had never seen one;
He would have sinned incessantly
    Could he have been one. 20

Miniver cursed the commonplace
    And eyed a khaki suit with loathing;
He missed the mediaeval grace
    Of iron clothing.

Miniver scorned the gold he sought, 25
    But sore annoyed was he without it;
Miniver thought, and thought, and thought,
    And thought about it.

Miniver Cheevy, born too late,
    Scratched his head and kept on thinking;         30
Miniver coughed, and called it fate,
    And kept on drinking.

## WILLIAM SHAKESPEARE (1564–1616)

### *When, in disgrace with Fortune and men's eyes*   1609

When, in disgrace with Fortune and men's eyes,
I all alone beweep my outcast state,
And trouble deaf heaven with my bootless cries,
And look upon myself and curse my fate,
Wishing me like to one more rich in hope,         5
Featured like him, like him with friends possessed,
Desiring this man's art, and that man's scope,
With what I most enjoy contented least,
Yet in these thoughts myself almost despising,
Haply I think on thee, and then my state,         10
Like to the lark at break of day arising
From sullen earth, sings hymns at heaven's gate;
    For thy sweet love remembered such wealth brings
    That then I scorn to change my state with kings.

## PERCY BYSSHE SHELLEY (1792–1822)

### *Ozymandias°*   1818

I met a traveler from an antique land
Who said: Two vast and trunkless legs of stone
Stand in the desert. . . . Near them, on the sand,
Half sunk, a shattered visage lies, whose frown,
And wrinkled lip, and sneer of cold command,         5
Tell that its sculptor well those passions read
Which yet survive, stamped on these lifeless things,
The hand that mocked them, and the heart that fed:
And on the pedestal these words appear:
"My name is Ozymandias, King of Kings:         10
Look on my works, ye Mighty, and despair!"
Nothing beside remains. Round the decay
Of that colossal wreck, boundless and bare
The lone and level sands stretch far away.

*Ozymandias:* Greek name for Ramses II, pharaoh of Egypt for sixty-seven years during the thirteenth century B.C.E. His colossal statue lies prostrate in the sands of Luxor. Napoleon's soldiers measured it (56 feet long, ear 3½ feet long, weight 1,000 tons). Its inscription, according to the Greek historian Diodorus Siculus, was "I am Ozymandias, King of Kings; if anyone wishes to know what I am and where I lie, let him surpass me in some of my exploits."

## STEVIE SMITH (1902–1971)

### *Not Waving but Drowning*    1957

Nobody heard him, the dead man,
But still he lay moaning:
I was much further out than you thought
And not waving but drowning.

Poor chap, he always loved larking                                   5
And now he's dead
It must have been too cold for him his heart gave way,
They said.

Oh, no no no, it was too cold always
(Still the dead one lay moaning)                                     10
I was much too far out all my life
And not waving but drowning.


## WALLACE STEVENS (1879–1955)

### *Thirteen Ways of Looking at a Blackbird*    1917

#### I

Among twenty snowy mountains,
The only moving thing
Was the eye of the blackbird.

#### II

I was of three minds,
Like a tree                                                          5
In which there are three blackbirds.

#### III

The blackbird whirled in the autumn winds.
It was a small part of the pantomime.

#### IV

A man and a woman
Are one.                                                             10
A man and a woman and a blackbird
Are one.

#### V

I do not know which to prefer,
The beauty of inflections

Or the beauty of innuendoes,                                    15
The blackbird whistling
Or just after.

## VI

Icicles filled the long window
With barbaric glass.
The shadow of the blackbird                                     20
Crossed it, to and fro.
The mood
Traced in the shadow
An indecipherable cause.

## VII

O thin men of Haddam,
Why do you imagine golden birds?                                25
Do you not see how the blackbird
Walks around the feet
Of the women about you?

## VIII

I know noble accents
And lucid, inescapable rhythms;
But I know, too,                                                30
That the blackbird is involved
In what I know.

## IX

When the blackbird flew out of sight,                           35
It marked the edge
Of one of many circles.

## X

At the sight of blackbirds
Flying in a green light,
Even the bawds of euphony                                       40
Would cry out sharply.

## XI

He rode over Connecticut
In a glass coach.
Once, a fear pierced him,
In that he mistook                                              45

The shadow of his equipage
For blackbirds.

### XII

The river is moving.
The blackbird must be flying.

### XIII

It was evening all afternoon.
It was snowing                                                                50
And it was going to snow.
The blackbird sat
In the cedar-limbs.

## PHILLIS WHEATLEY   (1753–1784)

### *To S. M.,° a young African Painter, on seeing his Works*   1773

TO show the lab'ring bosom's deep intent,
And thought in living characters to paint,
When first thy pencil did those beauties give,
And breathing figures learnt from thee to live,
How did those prospects give my soul delight,                    5
A new creation rushing on my sight?
Still, wond'rous youth! each noble path pursue,
On deathless glories fix thine ardent view:
Still may the painter's and the poet's fire
To aid thy pencil, and thy verse conspire!                          10
And may the charms of each seraphic theme
Conduct thy footsteps to immortal fame!
High to the blissful wonders of the skies
Elate thy soul, and raise thy wishful eyes.
Thrice happy, when exalted to survey                               15
That splendid city, crown'd with endless day,
Whose twice six gates on radiant hinges ring:
Celestial *Salem°* blooms in endless spring.

Calm and serene thy moments glide along,
And may the muse inspire each future song!                      20
Still, with the sweets of contemplation bless'd,
May peace with balmy wings your soul invest!
But when these shades of time are chas'd away,
And darkness ends in everlasting day,
On what seraphic pinions shall we move,                          25

---

*To S.M.:* Scipio Moorhead who, like Wheatley, was an enslaved person in colonial America.
18 *Salem:* The heavenly city of Jerusalem.

And view the landscapes in the realms above?
There shall thy tongue in heav'nly murmurs flow,
And there my muse with heav'nly transport glow:
No more to tell of *Damon's°* tender sighs,
Or rising radiance of *Aurora's°* eyes,                                30
For nobler themes demand a nobler strain,
And purer language on th' ethereal plain.
Cease, gentle muse! the solemn gloom of night
Now seals the fair creation from my sight.

29 *Damon:* A generic name for a shepherd in a pastoral poem.   30 *Aurora:* The Roman goddess of dawn.

## WALT WHITMAN (1819–1892)

### *When I Heard the Learn'd Astronomer*   1865

When I heard the learn'd astronomer,
When the proofs, the figures, were ranged in columns before me,
When I was shown the charts and diagrams, to add, divide, and measure them,
When I sitting heard the astronomer where he lectured with much applause in
      the lecture-room,
How soon unaccountable I became tired and sick,                      5
Till rising and gliding out I wandered off by myself,
In the mystical moist night-air, and from time to time,
Looked up in perfect silence at the stars.

## WILLIAM BUTLER YEATS (1865–1939)

### *The Lake Isle of Innisfree°*   1892

I will arise and go now, and go to Innisfree,
And a small cabin build there, of clay and wattles made:
Nine bean-rows will I have there, a hive for the honey-bee,
And live alone in the bee-loud glade.
And I shall have some peace there, for peace comes dropping slow,    5
Dropping from the veils of the morning to where the cricket sings;
There midnight's all a glimmer, and noon a purple glow,
And evening full of the linnet's wings.

I will arise and go now, for always night and day
I hear lake water lapping with low sounds by the shore:             10
While I stand on the roadway, or on the pavements grey,
I hear it in the deep heart's core.

*The Lake Isle of Innisfree:* An island in Lough (or Lake) Gill, in western Ireland.

# 34

## An Anthology of Recent Poems

Now the role of poetry is not simply to hold understanding in place but to help create and hold a realm of experience. Poetry has become a kind of tool for knowing the world in a particular way.
— JANE HIRSHFIELD

Chris Jackson/Getty Images.

### JOSÉ ANGEL ARAGUZ (B. 1982)

#### The Name   2017

*for Pedro Araguz Aldape*

Asked where the name comes from, I grow quiet,
and in another voice begin to tell
how those ending in *z* are from the Moors
who ruled Spain 800 years. Some agree,
read into my black hair and dark skin                                5
what they wish to. I let the disguise of story
take over, let it pass across the feeling
in my chest that tells me I've lied, even
when I haven't. A name is wind and ink,
a name is memory. What does it matter?                          10

What does it matter my mother didn't want
my father in my life, even in name,
and reached out to her father for his?
Who remembers that, and who can clearly
tell it, when Mexicans stack up last names                    15
like a trail of crumbs behind a person,
syllables broken off a whole to meet
and make another whole, a map of breath
drawn over so one can't get lost. Eventually,
everything gets lost. What does it matter?                    20

What does it matter letters and sounds hold,
become a space where the lost young man I am
can look and catch a part of the old man
my grandfather became? What does it matter,
except that I remain and have to face                         25
the name, have to explain it, give it meaning:
the name, the house at the edge of a landfill,
the hat held in his hands as we talked, the wind
leaving behind a faceless and fleeting sound.
Asked where the name comes from, I grow quiet.                30

## MICHELLE CLIFF (1946–2016)

### *The Land of Look Behind*    1985

*On the edge of each canefield or "piece" was a watch house, a tiny structure with
one entry. These were used for the babies of nursing slaves who worked in the
fields. An older woman was in charge of the infants and the mothers came there for
feeding time.*

— *tourist brochure of the Whim Great House*

A tiny structure with one entry
walls guttered with mortar
molasses    coral    sand
hold the whole thing fast.

One hundred years later                                        5
the cut limestone
sunned and salted
looks like new.

And feels like? And feels like?
I don't know.                                                  10
Describe it.
Sad? Lost? Angry?
Let me get my bearings.

Outside
A tamarind tree with a dead nest in the first crotch          15

Dense mud construction.
Immense. The inhabitants long gone.
Hard brown pods crack underfoot
The soursweet flesh is dried.
Inedible.                                                    20

Inside
One thin bench faces a blank wall.
No message from the watchwomen here.
No HELP ME carved in the mortar or the stone.
Try to capture the range —                                   25

What did their voices sound like?
What tongues? What words for day and night?
Hunger? Milk?
What songs devised to ease them?

Was there time to speak? To sing?                            30
To the riverain goddesses
The mermaids bringing secrets
To bring down Shàngó's° wrath.

No fatting-houses here.
Nowhere to learn the secrets                                 35
except through some new code
in spaces they will never own.

How many voices? How many drops of milk?
How many gums daubed with rum to soothe the teething
or bring on sleep?                                           40

How many breasts bore scars?
Not the sacred markings of the Carib —
but the mundane mark of the beast.

How many dropped in the field?
How many bare footfalls across the sand floor?              45
How many were buried?
I leave through the opening and take myself home.

33 *Shàngó:* The Yoruban god of thunder and lightning and vengeance.

# Gregory Corso (1930–2001)

## *Marriage*  1960

Should I get married? Should I be good?
Astound the girl next door with my velvet suit and faustus hood?
Don't take her to movies but to cemeteries
tell all about werewolf bathtubs and forked clarinets
then desire her and kiss her and all the preliminaries          5
and she going just so far and I understanding why

not getting angry saying You must feel! It's beautiful to feel!
Instead take her in my arms lean against an old crooked tombstone
and woo her the entire night the constellations in the sky—

When she introduces me to her parents                                          10
back straightened, hair finally combed, strangled by a tie,
should I sit knees together on their 3rd degree sofa
and not ask Where's the bathroom?
How else to feel other than I am,
often thinking Flash Gordon soap—                                              15
O how terrible it must be for a young man
seated before a family and the family thinking
We never saw him before! He wants our Mary Lou!
After tea and homemade cookies they ask What do you do for a living?

Should I tell them? Would they like me then?                                   20
Say All right get married, we're losing a daughter
but we're gaining a son—
And should I then ask Where's the bathroom?

O God, and the wedding! All her family and her friends
and only a handful of mine all scroungy and bearded                            25
just wait to get at the drinks and food—
And the priest! he looking at me as if I masturbated
asking me Do you take this woman for your lawful wedded wife?
And I trembling what to say say Pie Glue!
I kiss the bride all those corny men slapping me on the back                   30
She's all yours, boy! Ha-ha-ha!
And in their eyes you could see some obscene honeymoon going on—
Then all that absurd rice and clanky cans and shoes
Niagara Falls! Hordes of us! Husbands! Wives! Flowers! Chocolates!
All streaming into cozy hotels                                                  35
All going to do the same thing tonight
The indifferent clerk he knowing what was going to happen
The lobby zombies they knowing what
The whistling elevator man he knowing
The winking bellboy knowing                                                     40
Everybody knowing! I'd be almost inclined not to do anything!
Stay up all night! Stare that hotel clerk in the eye!
Screaming: I deny honeymoon! I deny honeymoon!
running rampant into those almost climactic suites
yelling Radio belly! Cat shovel!                                               45
O I'd live in Niagara forever! in a dark cave beneath the Falls
I'd sit there the Mad Honeymooner
devising ways to break marriages, a scourge of bigamy
a saint of divorce—

But I should get married I should be good                                       50
How nice it'd be to come home to her
and sit by the fireplace and she in the kitchen
aproned young and lovely wanting my baby
and so happy about me she burns the roast beef

and comes crying to me and I get up from my big papa chair                           55
saying Christmas teeth! Radiant brains! Apple deaf!
God what a husband I'd make! Yes, I should get married!
So much to do! like sneaking into Mr Jones' house late at night
and cover his golf clubs with 1920 Norwegian books
Like hanging a picture of Rimbaud on the lawnmower                                    60
like pasting Tannu Tuva postage stamps all over the picket fence
like when Mrs Kindhead comes to collect for the Community Chest
grab her and tell her There are unfavorable omens in the sky!
And when the mayor comes to get my vote tell him
When are you going to stop people killing whales!                                    65
And when the milkman comes leave him a note in the bottle
Penguin dust, bring me penguin dust, I want penguin dust —

Yet if I should get married and it's Connecticut and snow
and she gives birth to a child and I am sleepless, worn,
up for nights, head bowed against a quiet window, the past behind me,               70
finding myself in the most common of situations a trembling man
knowledged with responsibility not twig-smear nor Roman coin soup —
O what would that be like!
Surely I'd give it for a nipple a rubber Tacitus
For a rattle a bag of broken Bach records                                            75
Tack Della Francesca all over its crib
Sew the Greek alphabet on its bib
And build for its playpen a roofless Parthenon

No, I doubt I'd be that kind of father
not rural not snow no quiet window                                                   80
but hot smelly tight New York City
seven flights up, roaches and rats in the walls
a fat Reichian wife screeching over potatoes Get a job!
And five nose running brats in love with Batman
And the neighbors all toothless and dry haired                                       85
like those hag masses of the 18th century
all wanting to come in and watch TV
The landlord wants his rent
Grocery store Blue Cross Gas & Electric Knights of Columbus
Impossible to lie back and dream Telephone snow, ghost parking —                    90
No! I should not get married I should never get married!
But — imagine If I were married to a beautiful sophisticated woman
tall and pale wearing an elegant black dress and long black gloves
holding a cigarette holder in one hand and highball in the other
and we lived high up a penthouse with a huge window                                  95
from which we could see all of New York and even farther on clearer days
No, can't imagine myself married to that pleasant prison dream —

O but what about love? I forget love
not that I am incapable of love
it's just that I see love as odd as wearing shoes —                                 100
I never wanted to marry a girl who was like my mother
And Ingrid Bergman was always impossible
And there's maybe a girl now but she's already married

And I don't like men and —
but there's got to be somebody!                                        105
Because what if I'm 60 years old and not married,
all alone in a furnished room with pee stains on my underwear
and everybody else is married! All the universe married but me!
Ah, yet well I know that were a woman possible as I am possible
then marriage would be possible —                                      110
Like SHE in her lonely alien gaud waiting her Egyptian lover
so I wait — bereft of 2,000 years and the bath of life.

## RITA DOVE (B. 1952)

### *Daystar*    1986

She wanted a little room for thinking:
but she saw diapers steaming on the line,
a doll slumped behind the door.

So she lugged a chair behind the garage
to sit out the children's naps.                                          5

Sometimes there were things to watch —
the pinched armor of a vanished cricket,
a floating maple leaf. Other days
she stared until she was assured
when she closed her eyes                                                 10
she'd see only her own vivid blood.

She had an hour, at best, before Liza appeared
pouting from the top of the stairs.
And just *what* was mother doing
out back with the field mice? Why,                                       15

building a palace. Later
that night when Thomas rolled over and
lurched into her, she would open her eyes
and think of the place that was hers
for an hour — where                                                      20
she was nothing,
pure nothing, in the middle of the day.

## LAWRENCE FERLINGHETTI (B. 1919)

### *Constantly Risking Absurdity*    1960

Constantly risking absurdity
                                and death
               whenever he performs
                           above the heads
                                      of his audience                    5

                the poet like an acrobat
                            climbs on rime
                                        to a high wire of his own making
        and balancing on eyebeams
                            above a sea of faces                              10
            paces his way
                        to the other side of day
            performing entrechats
                            and sleight-of-foot tricks
        and other high theatrics                                             15
                            and all without mistaking
                any thing
                            for what it may not be
            For he's the super realist
                            who must perforce perceive                       20
                taut truth
                            before the taking of each stance or step
        in his supposed advance
                            toward that still higher perch
        where Beauty stands and waits                                        25
                            with gravity
                        to start her death-defying leap
        And he
                a little charleychaplin man
                            who may or may not catch                         30
                her fair eternal form
                            spreadeagled in the empty air
                    of existence

## Amanda Gorman (b. 1998)

### *In This Place (An American Lyric)*   2017

There's a poem in this place —
in the footfalls in the halls
in the quiet beat of the seats.
It is here, at the curtain of day,
where America writes a lyric                                                 5
you must whisper to say.

There's a poem in this place —
in the heavy grace,
the lined face of this noble building,
collections burned and reborn twice.                                        10

There's a poem in Boston's Copley Square
where protest chants
tear through the air
like sheets of rain,
where love of the many                                                      15
swallows hatred of the few.

There's a poem in Charlottesville°
where tiki torches string a ring of flame
tight round the wrist of night
where men so white they gleam blue —          20
seem like statues
where men heap that long wax burning
ever higher
where Heather Heyer°
blooms forever in a meadow of resistance.          25

There's a poem in the great sleeping giant
of Lake Michigan, defiantly raising
its big blue head to Milwaukee and Chicago—
a poem begun long ago, blazed into frozen soil,
strutting upward and aglow.          30

There's a poem in Florida, in East Texas
where streets swell into a nexus
of rivers, cows afloat like mottled buoys in the brown,
where courage is now so common
that 23-year-old Jesus Contreras rescues people from floodwaters.          35

There's a poem in Los Angeles
yawning wide as the Pacific tide
where a single mother swelters
in a windowless classroom, teaching
black and brown students in Watts          40
to spell out their thoughts
so her daughter might write
this poem for you.

There's a lyric in California
where thousands of students march for blocks,          45
undocumented and unafraid;
where my friend Rosa finds the power to blossom
in deadlock, her spirit the bedrock of her community.
She knows hope is like a stubborn
ship gripping a dock,          50
a truth: that you can't stop a dreamer
or knock down a dream.

How could this not be her city
su nación
our country          55
our America,
our American lyric to write —
a poem by the people, the poor,
the Protestant, the Muslim, the Jew,
the native, the immigrant,          60

17 *Charlottesville:* Charlottesville Virginia was the site of the so-called "Unite the Right" rally
from August 11–12, 2017 that included neo-Nazis and other hate groups.

24 *Heather Heyer:* Heather Heyer was killed by a white supremacist while peacefully protesting
the "Unite the Right" rally.

the black, the brown, the blind, the brave,
the undocumented and undeterred,
the woman, the man, the nonbinary,
the white, the trans,
the ally to all of the above                                          65
and more?

Tyrants fear the poet.
Now that we know it
we can't blow it.
We owe it                                                            70
to show it
not slow it
although it
hurts to sew it
when the world                                                       75
skirts below it.

Hope—
we must bestow it
like a wick in the poet
so it can grow, lit,                                                 80
bringing with it
stories to rewrite—
the story of a Texas city depleted but not defeated
a history written that need not be repeated
a nation composed but not yet completed.                            85

There's a poem in this place—
a poem in America
a poet in every American
who rewrites this nation, who tells
a story worthy of being told on this minnow of an earth             90
to breathe hope into a palimpsest of time—
a poet in every American
who sees that our poem penned
doesn't mean our poem's end.

There's a place where this poem dwells—                             95
it is *here*, it is *now*, in the yellow song of dawn's bell
where we write an American lyric
we are just beginning to tell.


# Seamus Heaney (1939–2013)

## *Digging*   1966

Between my finger and my thumb
The squat pen rests; snug as a gun.

Under my window, a clean rasping sound
When the spade sinks into gravelly ground;
My father, digging. I look down                                       5

Till his straining rump among the flowerbeds
Bends low, comes up twenty years away
Stooping in rhythm through potato drills
Where he was digging.

The coarse boot nestled on the lug, the shaft                    10
Against the inside knee was levered firmly.
He rooted out tall tops, buried the bright edge deep
To scatter new potatoes that we picked
Loving their cool hardness in our hands.

By God, the old man could handle a spade.                        15
Just like his old man.

My grandfather cut more turf in a day
Than any other man on Toner's bog.
Once I carried him milk in a bottle
Corked sloppily with paper. He straightened up                   20
To drink it, then fell to right away

Nicking and slicing neatly, heaving sods
Over his shoulder, going down and down
For the good turf. Digging.

The cold smell of potato mould, the squelch and slap             25
Of soggy peat, the curt cuts of an edge
Through living roots awaken in my head.
But I've no spade to follow men like them.

Between my finger and my thumb
The squat pen rests.                                             30
I'll dig with it.

## Brionne Janae (b. 1991)

### *Alternative Facts*    2018

*for Tamir Rice*

the officer stops    parks his car
at the frost chipped curb
the officer can see the boy
and spends a few more moments
in the heat of his patrol car    he studies the boy               5
his boy sized body and childish desire
to clutch power in the untried soft
of his palm    the officer remembers himself
at this age    how eager he was to matter
the officer can see how the toy gun                              10
makes the boy matter    the officer can see himself
in the boy    the officer can see the boy
his not yet manness
the memory of milk teeth

on his smooth cheeks                                    15
the officer can see how the boy
must've buried his face in his mother's flesh
when the world was too much
the world weary officer rubs his jaw and sighs
it reminds the officer of his own                       20
cherry cheeked mother
how he ought to call
when he has finished
sending this boy
home to his own momma                                   25
the thought of his mother
dimples the officer's cheeks

## PHILIP LARKIN (1922–1985)

### Sad Steps° 1968

Groping back to bed after a piss
I part thick curtains, and am startled by
The rapid clouds, the moon's cleanliness.

Four o'clock: wedge-shadowed gardens lie
Under a cavernous, a wind-picked sky.                    5
There's something laughable about this,

The way the moon dashes through clouds that blow
Loosely as cannon-smoke to stand apart
(Stone-coloured light sharpening the roofs below)

High and preposterous and separate —                    10
Lozenge of love! Medallion of art!
O wolves of memory! Immensements! No,

One shivers slightly, looking up there.
The hardness and the brightness and the plain
Far-reaching singleness of that wide stare              15

Is a reminder of the strength and pain
Of being young; that it can't come again,
But is for others undiminished somewhere.

*Sad Steps:* Cf. Sir Philip Sidney, *Astrophil and Stella* 31: "With how sad steps, O Moon, thou climb'st the skies."

## LUISA LOPEZ (B. 1957)

### Junior Year Abroad 2002

We were amateurs, that winter in Paris.

The summer before we agreed:
he would come over to keep me company at Christmas.

But the shelf life of my promise expired
before the date on his airline ticket.                                    5
So we ended up together under a French muslin sky.

Together alone.

Certainly I was alone, inside dark hair, inside foreign blankets,
against white sheets swirling like a cocoon,
covering my bare skin,                                                    10
keeping me apart.
The invited man snored beside me not knowing
I didn't love him anymore.

At first I tried,
perky as a circus pony waiting at the airport gate                       15
to be again as I once had been.
But even during the first night
betrayal, the snake under the evergreen,
threw me into nightmares
of floods and dying birds.                                               20

You see, a new boy just last month
had raised my shy hand to his warm mouth
and kissed the inside of my palm.
I thought "this is impossible,
too close to Christmas, too soon, too dangerous."                        25

In Paris I concede:
deceiving my old lover, the one now stirring in his sleep
is even more dangerous.
See him opening his eyes, looking at my face,
dropping his eyes to my breasts and smiling                              30
as if he were seeing two old friends? Dangerous.

When I move away and hold the sheet against
myself he,
sensing what this means,
refuses, adamant yet polite,
to traffic in the currency of my rejection.                             35

He made a journey. I offered a welcome.
Why should he give me up?

# AUDRE LORDE (1934–1992)

## *Learning to Write*    1986

Is the alphabet responsible
for the book
in which it is written
that makes me peevish and nasty
and wish I were dumb    again?                                            5

We practiced drawing our letters
digging into the top of the desk
and old Sister Eymard
rapped our knuckles
until they bled                                                        10
she was the meanest of all
and we knew she was crazy
but none of the grownups
would listen to us
until she died in a madhouse.                                          15

I am a bleak heroism of words
that refuse
to be buried alive
with the liars.


## Naomi Shihab Nye  (b. 1952)

### *To Manage*  2018

She writes to me —
    I can't sleep because I'm seventeen
Sometimes I lie awake thinking
    I didn't even clean my room yet
And soon I will be twenty-five                                          5
    And a failure
And when I am fifty — oh!
I write her back
    Slowly    slow
Clean one drawer                                                       10
    Arrange words on a page
Let them find one another
    Find you
Trust they might know something
    You aren't living    the whole thing                               15
        At once

That's what a minute        said to an hour
Without me        you are nothing


## Adelia Prado  (b. 1935)

### *Denouement*  1990

TRANSLATED FROM PORTUGUESE BY ELLEN WATSON

I have great admiration for ships
and for certain people's handwriting which I attempt to imitate.
Of my entire family, I'm the only one who has seen the ocean.

I describe it over and over, they say "hmm"
and continue circling the chicken-coop with wire.                              5
I tell about the spume, and the wearisome size of the waters,
they don't remember there's such a place as Kenya,
they'd never guess I'm thinking of Tanzania.
Eagerly they show me the lot: this is where the kitchen will be,
that's where we'll put in a garden.                                           10
So what do I do with the coast?
It was a pretty afternoon the day I planted myself in the window,
        between uncles,
and saw the man with his fly open,
the trellis angry with roses.
Hours and hours we talked unconsciously in Portuguese               15
as if it were the only language in the world.
Faith or no, I ask where are my people who are gone;
because I'm human, I zealously cover the pan of leftover sauce.
How could we know how to live a better life than this,
when even weeping it feels so good to be together?                  20
Suffering belongs to no language.
I suffered and I suffer both in Minas Gerais and at the edge of the ocean.
I stand in awe of being alive. Oh, moon over the backlands,
oh, forests I don't need to see to get lost in,
oh, great cities and states of Brazil that I love as if I had invented them.   25
Being Brazilian places me in a way I find moving
and this, which without sinning I can call fate,
gives my desire a rest.
Taken all at once, it's far too intelligible, I can't take it.
Night! Make yourself useful and cover me with sleep.               30
Me and the thought of death just can't get used to each other.
I'll tremble with fear until the end.
And meanwhile everything is so small.
Compared to my heart's desire
the sea is a drop.                                                  35


## Lois Red Elk (b. 1940)

### *All Thirst Quenched*    2013

   *for my granddaughter, Wahcawin*

I didn't want to scold the sky that year, but
Grandma's words taunted my senses. If there is
a thirst, then you need to pity the flowers

in a loud voice. Ask the frogs why they are
being punished, stomp on the ground and talk                        5
to the dried clay about cracking open the earth.

I know challenging the storm is risky. "Last
but not least, burn cedar and pray the lightning
doesn't strike your town." That night, the stars

disappeared, so did the birds. Perhaps it was                    10
the season for rain or the dance. In the western
distance, we thought we heard cannon blasts,

looking over we watched the horizon fill with
lightning strikes. Rain couldn't pour hard enough
over the thirsty plain. Accompanying clouds,                     15

called to thunder's voice in extreme decimals
requesting all the water heaven could send forth,
to come. Rain and more rain filled empty stream

bottoms. Rivers who had pulled their dry banks
farther and farther from their center begged for                 20
a drink to startle dusty beds with a flooding roar.

Lives in dormant places begin to stir and awaken.
The lives of water beings, those that swim, the
ones that hop, and the ones that fly, begin to stir.

That year all thirst was quenched.                               25

## PATRICIA SMITH    (B. 1955)

## What It's Like to Be a Black Girl
## (for those of you who aren't)    1991

First of all, it's being 9 years old and
feeling like you're not finished, like your
edges are wild, like there's something,
everything, wrong. it's dropping food
coloring in your eyes to make them blue and suffering            5
their burn in silence. it's popping a bleached
white mophead over the kinks of your hair and
primping in front of the mirrors that deny your
reflection. it's finding a space between your
legs, a disturbance in your chest, and not knowing               10
what to do with the whistles. it's jumping
double dutch until your legs pop, it's sweat
and vaseline and bullets, it's growing tall and
wearing a lot of white, it's smelling blood in
your breakfast, it's learning to say fuck with                   15
grace but learning to fuck without it, it's
flame and fists and life according to motown,
it's finally have a man reach out for you
then caving in
around his fingers.                                              20

# TRACY K. SMITH (B. 1972)

## *Self-Portrait as the Letter Y* 2003

**1.**

I waved a gun last night
In a city like some ancient Los Angeles.
It was dusk. There were two girls
I wanted to make apologize,
But the gun was useless.                                                    5
They looked sideways at each other
And tried to flatter me. I was angry.
I wanted to cry. I wanted to bury the pistol,
But I would've had to walk miles.
I would've had to learn to run.                                            10

**2.**

I have finally become that girl
In the photo you keep among your things,
Steadying myself at the prow of a small boat.
It is always summer here, and I am
Always staring into the lens of your camera,                               15
Which has not yet been stolen. Always
With this same expression. Meaning
I see your eye behind the camera's eye.
Meaning that in the time it takes
For the tiny guillotine                                                      20
To open and fall shut, I will have decided
I am just about ready to love you.

**3.**

Sun cuts sharp angles
Across the airshaft adjacent.

They kiss. They kiss again.                                                 25
Faint clouds pass, disband.

Someone left a mirror
At the foot of the fire escape.

They look down. They kiss.

She will never be free                                                      30
Because she is afraid. He

Will never be free
Because he has always

Been free.

**4.**

Was kind of a rebel then. 35
Took two cars. Took
Bad advice. Watched people's
Asses. Sniffed their heads.

Just left, so it looked
Like those half-sad cookouts, 40
Meats never meant to be
Flayed, meant nothing.

Made promises. Kept going.
Prayed for signs. Stooped
For coins. Needed them. 45
Had two definitions of family.

Had two families. Snooped.
Forgot easily. Well, didn't
Forget, but knew when it was safe
To remember. Woke some nights 50

Against a wet pillow, other nights
With the lights on, whispering
The truest things
Into the receiver.

**5.**

A dog scuttles past, like a wig 55
Drawn by an invisible cord. It is spring.
The pirates out selling fakes are finally
Able to draw a crowd. College girls
Show bare skin in good faith. They crouch
Over heaps of bright purses, smiling, 60
Willing to pay. Their arms
Swing forward as they walk away, balancing
That new weight on naked shoulders.
The pirates smile, too, watching
Pair after pair of thighs carved in shadow 65
As girl after girl glides into the sun.

**6.**

You are pure appetite. I am pure
Appetite. You are a phantom
In that far-off city where daylight
Climbs cathedral walls, stone by stolen stone. 70
I am invisible here, like I like it.
The language you taught me rolls
From your mouth into mine

The way kids will pass smoke
Between them. You feed it to me
Until my heart grows fat. I feed you                                              75
Tiny black eggs. I feed you
My very own soft truth. We believe.
We stay up talking all kinds of shit.

### Natasha Trethewey (B. 1966)

## *Graveyard Blues*    2006

It rained the whole time we were laying her down;
Rained from church to grave when we put her down.
The suck of mud at our feet was a hollow sound.

When the preacher called out I held up my hand;
When he called for a witness I raised my hand—                                   5
*Death stops the body's work, the soul's a journeyman.*

The sun came out when I turned to walk away,
Glared down on me as I turned and walked away—
My back to my mother, leaving her where she lay.

The road going home was pocked with holes,                                       10
That home-going road's always full of holes;
Though we slow down, time's wheel still rolls.

     I wander now among names of the dead:
     My mother's name, stone pillow for my head.

# DRAMA

# The Study
# of Drama

# 35

# Reading Drama

I know what stillness is.
— SUSAN GLASPELL

Provided courtesy of the Lear Center for Special Collections & Archives, Connecticut College.

## READING DRAMA RESPONSIVELY

The publication of a short story, novel, or poem represents for most writers the final step in a long creative process that might have begun with an idea, issue, emotion, or question that demanded expression. *Playwrights* — the *wright* refers to a craftsman, not to the word *write* — may begin a work in the same way as other writers, but rarely are they satisfied with only its publication because most *plays* are written to be performed by actors on a stage before an audience. Playwrights typically create a play keeping in mind not only readers but also actors, producers, directors, costumers, designers, technicians, and a theater full of other support staff who have a hand in presenting the play to a live audience.

Drama is literature equipped with arms, legs, tears, laughs, whispers, shouts, and gestures that are alive and immediate. Indeed, the word *drama* derives from the Greek word *dran*, meaning "to do" or "to perform." The text of many plays — the *script* — may fully come to life only when the written words are transformed into a performance. Although there are plays that do not invite production, they are relatively few. Such plays, written to be read rather than performed, are called **closet dramas**. In this kind of work (primarily associated with nineteenth-century English literature), literary art outweighs all other considerations. The majority of playwrights, however, view the written word as the beginning of a larger creation and hope that a producer will deem their scripts worthy of production.

Given that most playwrights intend their works to be performed, it might be argued that reading a play is a poor substitute for seeing it acted on a stage — perhaps something like reading a recipe without having access to the ingredients and a kitchen. This analogy is tempting, but it overlooks the literary dimensions of a script; the words we hear on a stage were written first. Read from a page, these words can feed an imagination in ways that a recipe cannot satisfy a hungry cook. We can fill in a play's missing faces, voices, actions, and settings in much the same way that we imagine these elements in a short story or novel. Like any play director, we are free to include as many ingredients as we have an appetite for.

This imaginative collaboration with the playwright creates a mental world that can be nearly as real and vivid as a live performance. Sometimes readers find that they prefer their own reading of a play to a director's interpretation. The title character of Shakespeare's *Hamlet,* for instance, has been presented as a whining son, but you may read him as a strong prince. Rich plays often accommodate a wide range of imaginative responses to their texts. Reading, then, is an excellent way to appreciate and evaluate a production of a play. Moreover, reading is valuable in its own right because it allows us to enter the playwright's created world even when a theatrical production is unavailable.

Reading a play, however, requires more creative imagining than sitting in an audience watching actors on a stage presenting lines and actions before you. As a reader you become the play's director; you construct an interpretation based on the playwright's use of language, development of character, arrangement of incidents, description of settings, and directions for staging. Keeping track of the playwright's handling of these elements will help you to organize your response to the play. You may experience suspense, fear, horror, sympathy, or humor, but whatever experience a play evokes, ask yourself why you respond to it as you do. You may discover that your assessment of Hamlet's character is different from someone else's, but whether you find him heroic, indecisive, neurotic, or a complex of competing qualities, you'll be better equipped to articulate your interpretation of him if you pay attention to your responses and ask yourself questions as you read. Consider, for example, how his reactions might be similar to or different from your own. How does his language reveal his character? Does his behavior seem justified? How would you play the role? What actor do you think might best play the Hamlet that you have created in your imagination? Why would they (actors of different genders have played Hamlet onstage) fill the role best?

These kinds of questions (see Questions for Responsive Reading and Writing about Drama, p. 1456) can help you to think and talk about your responses to a play. Happily, such questions needn't — and often can't — be fully answered as you read the play. Frequently you must experience the entire play before you can determine how its elements work together. That's why reading a play can be such a satisfying experience. You wouldn't think of asking a live actor onstage to repeat lines because you didn't quite comprehend their significance, but you can certainly reread a page in a book. Rereading allows you to replay language, characters, and incidents carefully and thoroughly to your own satisfaction.

## *Trifles*

In the following play, Susan Glaspell skillfully draws on many dramatic elements and creates an intense story that is as effective on the page as it is in the theater. Glaspell wrote *Trifles* in 1916 for the Provincetown Players on Cape Cod, in Massachusetts. Their performance of the work helped her develop a reputation as a writer sensitive to feminist issues. The year after *Trifles* was produced, Glaspell transformed the play into a short story titled "A Jury of Her Peers." (A passage from the story appears on p. 987 for comparison.)

Provided courtesy of the Lear Center for Special Collections & Archives, Connecticut College.

Glaspell's life in the Midwest provided her with the setting for *Trifles*. Born and raised in Davenport, Iowa, she graduated from Drake University in 1899 and then worked for a short time as a reporter on the *Des Moines News*, until her short stories were accepted in magazines such as *Harper's* and *Ladies' Home Journal*. Glaspell moved to the Northeast when she was in her early thirties to continue writing fiction and drama. She published novels, some twenty plays, and more than forty short stories. *Alison's House*, based on Emily Dickinson's life, earned her a Pulitzer Prize for drama in 1931. *Trifles* and "A Jury of Her Peers" remain, however, Glaspell's best-known works.

Glaspell wrote *Trifles* to complete a bill that was to feature several one-act plays by Eugene O'Neill. In *The Road to the Temple* (1926), she recalls how the play came to her as she sat in the theater looking at a bare stage. First, "the stage became a kitchen. . . . Then the door at the back opened, and people all bundled up came in — two or three men. I wasn't sure which, but sure enough about the two women, who hung back, reluctant to enter that kitchen. When I was a newspaper reporter out in Iowa, I was sent down-state to do a murder trial, and I never forgot going to the kitchen of a woman who had been locked up in town."

*Trifles* is about a murder committed in a midwestern farmhouse, but the play goes beyond the kinds of questions raised by most whodunit stories. The murder is the occasion instead of the focus. The play's major concerns are the moral, social, and psychological aspects of the assumptions and perceptions of the men and women who search for the murderer's motive. Glaspell is finally more interested in the meaning of Mrs. Wright's life than in the details of Mr. Wright's death.

As you read the play, keep track of your responses to the characters and note the moments when Glaspell reveals how men and women respond differently to the evidence before them. What do those moments suggest about the kinds of assumptions these men and women make about themselves and each other? How do their assumptions compare with your own?

## Susan Glaspell (1882–1948)

## *Trifles*  1916

CHARACTERS

*George Henderson,* county attorney
*Henry Peters,* sheriff
*Lewis Hale,* a neighboring farmer
*Mrs. Peters*
*Mrs. Hale*

SCENE: The kitchen in the now abandoned farmhouse of John Wright, a gloomy kitchen, and left without having been put in order — unwashed pans under the sink, a loaf of bread outside the breadbox, a dish towel on the table — other signs of incompleted work. At the rear the outer door opens and the Sheriff comes in followed by the County Attorney and Hale. The Sheriff and Hale are men in middle life, the County Attorney is a young man; all are much bundled up and go at once to the stove. They are followed by the two women — the Sheriff's wife first; she is a slight wiry woman, a thin nervous face. Mrs. Hale is larger and would ordinarily be called more comfortable looking, but she is disturbed now and looks fearfully about as she enters. The women have come in slowly, and stand close together near the door.

*County Attorney (rubbing his hands):*  This feels good. Come up to the fire, ladies.
*Mrs. Peters (after taking a step forward):*  I'm not — cold.
*Sheriff (unbuttoning his overcoat and stepping away from the stove as if to mark the beginning of official business):*  Now, Mr. Hale, before we move things about, you explain to Mr. Henderson just what you saw when you came here yesterday morning.
*County Attorney:*  By the way, has anything been moved? Are things just as you left them yesterday?
*Sheriff (looking about):*  It's just about the same. When it dropped below zero last night I thought I'd better send Frank out this morning to make a fire for us — no use getting pneumonia with a big case on, but I told him not to touch anything except the stove — and you know Frank.

**Trifles:** Brooke O'Harra directs this 2012 production of *Trifles* (p. 976) at the Theater of a Two-headed Calf.

Prudence Katze.

***Oedipus the King:*** At center stage is Jocasta (Ching Valdes-Aran) in a scene from the 1993 production of *Oedipus the King* (p. 1001) at Philadelphia's Wilma Theater, directed by Blanka Zizka and Jiri Zizka.

T. Charles Erickson.

**Othello:**   Chukwudi Iwuji as Othello and Corey Stoll as Iago in a scene from the 2018 production of *Othello* (p. 1055) at the Delacorte Theater in Central Park, New York City, directed by Ruben Santiago-Hudson and produced by New York's Public Theater.
Joan Marcus.

***The Importance of Being Earnest:*** Jane Ridley as Miss Prism, Rodney Gardiner as the Rev. Canon Chasuble, Matt Schwader as John Worthing, and Kate Abbruzzese as the Hon. Gwendolyn Fairfax in a 2018 production of *The Importance of Being Earnest* (p. 1148). Maria Aitken directed this production at San Diego's Old Globe Theatre.

***Water by the Spoonful:*** Luna Lauren Vélez plays Odessa in *Water by the Spoonful* (p. 1216), in this Center Theatre Group production in 2018, directed by Lileana Blain-Cruz and performed at the Mark Taper Forum in Los Angeles.

© Craig Schwartz Photography, "Mark Taper Forum."

***Proof:*** Johanna Day (left) and Mary-Louise Parker (right) in the 2000–2003 Broadway production of *Proof* (p. 1277), directed by Daniel Sullivan.

Joan Marcus/Photofest.

***Fences:*** Courtney B. Vance and James Earl Jones in the 46th Street Theater's 1987 production of *Fences* (p. 1329), directed by Lloyd Richards.

*County Attorney:* Somebody should have been left here yesterday.

*Sheriff:* Oh — yesterday. When I had to send Frank to Morris Center for that man who went crazy — I want you to know I had my hands full yesterday. I knew you could get back from Omaha by today and as long as I went over everything here myself —

*County Attorney:* Well, Mr. Hale, tell just what happened when you came here yesterday morning.

*Hale:* Harry and I had started to town with a load of potatoes. We came along the road from my place and as I got here I said, "I'm going to see if I can't get John Wright to go in with me on a party telephone." I spoke to Wright about it once before and he put me off, saying folks talked too much anyway, and all he asked was peace and quiet — I guess you know about how much he talked himself; but I thought maybe if I went to the house and talked about it before his wife, though I said to Harry that I didn't know as what his wife wanted made much difference to John —

*County Attorney:* Let's talk about that later, Mr. Hale. I do want to talk about that, but tell now just what happened when you got to the house.

*Hale:* I didn't hear or see anything; I knocked at the door, and still it was all quiet inside. I knew they must be up, it was past eight o'clock. So I knocked again, and I thought I heard somebody say, "Come in." I wasn't sure, I'm not sure yet, but I opened the door — this door *(indicating the door by which the two women are still standing)* and there in that rocker — *(pointing to it)* sat Mrs. Wright. *(They all look at the rocker.)*

*County Attorney:* What — was she doing?

*Hale:* She was rockin' back and forth. She had her apron in her hand and was kind of — pleating it.

*County Attorney:* And how did she — look?

*Hale:* Well, she looked queer.

*County Attorney:* How do you mean — queer?

*Hale:* Well, as if she didn't know what she was going to do next. And kind of done up.

*County Attorney:* How did she seem to feel about your coming?

*Hale:* Why, I don't think she minded — one way or other. She didn't pay much attention. I said, "How do, Mrs. Wright, it's cold, ain't it?" And she said, "Is it?" — and went on kind of pleating at her apron. Well, I was surprised; she didn't ask me to come up to the stove, or to set down, but just sat there, not even looking at me, so I said, "I want to see John." And then she — laughed. I guess you would call it a laugh. I thought of Harry and the team outside, so I said a little sharp: "Can't I see John?" "No," she says, kind o' dull like. "Ain't he home?" says I. "Yes," says she, "he's home." "Then why can't I see him?" I asked her, out of patience. " 'Cause he's dead," says she. "*Dead?*" says I. She just nodded her head, not getting a bit excited, but rockin' back and forth. "Why — where is he?" says I, not knowing what to say. She just pointed upstairs — like that *(himself pointing to the room above)*. I started for the stairs, with the idea of going up there. I walked from there to here — then I says, "Why, what did he die of?" "He died of a rope round his neck," says she, and just went on pleatin' at her apron. Well, I went out and called Harry. I thought I might — need help. We went upstairs and there he was lyin' —

*County Attorney:* I think I'd rather have you go into that upstairs, where you can point it all out. Just go on now with the rest of the story.

*Hale:* Well, my first thought was to get that rope off. It looked . . . (*stops; his face twitches*) . . . but Harry, he went up to him, and he said, "No, he's dead all right, and we'd better not touch anything." So we went back downstairs. She was still sitting that same way. "Has anybody been notified?" I asked. "No," says she, unconcerned. "Who did this, Mrs. Wright?" said Harry. He said it businesslike — and she stopped pleatin' of her apron. "I don't know," she says. "You don't *know*?" says Harry. "No," says she. "Weren't you sleepin' in the bed with him?" says Harry. "Yes," says she, "but I was on the inside." "Somebody slipped a rope round his neck and strangled him and you didn't wake up?" says Harry. "I didn't wake up," she said after him. We must 'a' looked as if we didn't see how that could be, for after a minute she said, "I sleep sound." Harry was going to ask her more questions but I said maybe we ought to let her tell her story first to the coroner, or the sheriff, so Harry went fast as he could to Rivers' place, where there's a telephone.

*County Attorney:* And what did Mrs. Wright do when she knew that you had gone for the coroner?

*Hale:* She moved from the rocker to that chair over there (*pointing to a small chair in the corner*) and just sat there with her hands held together and looking down. I got a feeling that I ought to make some conversation, so I said I had come in to see if John wanted to put in a telephone, and at that she started to laugh, and then she stopped and looked at me — scared. (*The County Attorney, who has had his notebook out, makes a note.*) I dunno, maybe it wasn't scared. I wouldn't like to say it was. Soon Harry got back, and then Dr. Lloyd came and you, Mr. Peters, and so I guess that's all I know that you don't.

*County Attorney (looking around):* I guess we'll go upstairs first — and then out to the barn and around there. (*To the Sheriff.*) You're convinced that there was nothing important here — nothing that would point to any motive?

*Sheriff:* Nothing here but kitchen things. (*The County Attorney, after again looking around the kitchen, opens the door of a cupboard closet. He gets up on a chair and looks on a shelf. Pulls his hand away, sticky.*)

*County Attorney:* Here's a nice mess. (*The women draw nearer.*)

*Mrs. Peters (to the other woman):* Oh, her fruit; it did freeze. (*To the Lawyer.*) She worried about that when it turned so cold. She said the fire'd go out and her jars would break.

*Sheriff (rises):* Well, can you beat the woman! Held for murder and worryin' about her preserves.

*County Attorney:* I guess before we're through she may have something more serious than preserves to worry about.

*Hale:* Well, women are used to worrying over trifles. (*The two women move a little closer together.*)

*County Attorney (with the gallantry of a young politician):* And yet, for all their worries, what would we do without the ladies? (*The women do not unbend. He goes to the sink, takes a dipperful of water from the pail, and pouring it into a basin, washes his hands. Starts to wipe them on the roller towel, turns it for a cleaner place.*) Dirty towels! (*Kicks his foot against the pans under the sink.*) Not much of a housekeeper, would you say, ladies?

*Mrs. Hale (stiffly):* There's a great deal of work to be done on a farm.

*County Attorney:* To be sure. And yet (*with a little bow to her*) I know there are some Dickson county farmhouses which do not have such roller towels. (*He gives it a pull to expose its full length again.*)

*Mrs. Hale:* Those towels get dirty awful quick. Men's hands aren't always as clean as they might be.

*County Attorney:* Ah, loyal to your sex, I see. But you and Mrs. Wright were neighbors. I suppose you were friends, too.

*Mrs. Hale (shaking her head):* I've not seen much of her of late years. I've not been in this house — it's more than a year.

*County Attorney:* And why was that? You didn't like her?

*Mrs. Hale:* I liked her all well enough. Farmers' wives have their hands full, Mr. Henderson. And then —

*County Attorney:* Yes — ?

*Mrs. Hale (looking about):* It never seemed a very cheerful place.

*County Attorney:* No — it's not cheerful. I shouldn't say she had the homemaking instinct.

*Mrs. Hale:* Well, I don't know as Wright had, either.

*County Attorney:* You mean that they didn't get on very well?

*Mrs. Hale:* No, I don't mean anything. But I don't think a place'd be any cheer-fuller for John Wright's being in it.

*County Attorney:* I'd like to talk more of that a little later. I want to get the lay of things upstairs now. *(He goes to the left where three steps lead to a stair door.)*

*Sheriff:* I suppose anything Mrs. Peters does'll be all right. She was to take in some clothes for her, you know, and a few little things. We left in such a hurry yesterday.

*County Attorney:* Yes, but I would like to see what you take, Mrs. Peters, and keep an eye out for anything that might be of use to us.

*Mrs. Peters:* Yes, Mr. Henderson. *(The women listen to the men's steps on the stairs, then look about the kitchen.)*

*Mrs. Hale:* I'd hate to have men coming into my kitchen, snooping around and criticizing. *(She arranges the pans under sink which the lawyer had shoved out of place.)*

*Mrs. Peters:* Of course it's no more than their duty.

*Mrs. Hale:* Duty's all right, but I guess that deputy sheriff that came out to make the fire might have got a little of this on. *(Gives the roller towel a pull.)* Wish I'd thought of that sooner. Seems mean to talk about her for not having things slicked up when she had to come away in such a hurry.

*Mrs. Peters (who has gone to a small table in the left rear corner of the room, and lifted one end of a towel that covers a pan):* She had bread set. *(Stands still.)*

*Mrs. Hale (eyes fixed on a loaf of bread beside the breadbox, which is on a low shelf at the other side of the room. Moves slowly toward it.):* She was going to put this in there. *(Picks up loaf, then abruptly drops it. In a manner of returning to familiar things.)* It's a shame about her fruit. I wonder if it's all gone. *(Gets up on the chair and looks.)* I think there's some here that's all right, Mrs. Peters. Yes — here; *(holding it toward the window)* this is cherries, too. *(Looking again.)* I declare I believe that's the only one. *(Gets down, bottle in her hand. Goes to the sink and wipes it off on the outside.)* She'll feel awful bad after all her hard work in the hot weather. I remember the afternoon I put up my cherries last summer. *(She puts the bottle on the big kitchen table, center of the room. With a sigh, is about to sit down in the rocking-chair. Before she is seated realizes what chair it is; with a slow look at it, steps back. The chair which she has touched rocks back and forth.)*

*Mrs. Peters:* Well, I must get those things from the front room closet. (*She goes to the door at the right, but after looking into the other room, steps back.*) You coming with me, Mrs. Hale? You could help me carry them. (*They go in the other room; reappear, Mrs. Peters carrying a dress and skirt, Mrs. Hale following with a pair of shoes.*) My, it's cold in there. (*She puts the clothes on the big table, and hurries to the stove.*)

*Mrs. Hale (examining the skirt):* Wright was close. I think maybe that's why she kept so much to herself. She didn't even belong to the Ladies' Aid. I suppose she felt she couldn't do her part, and then you don't enjoy things when you feel shabby. I heard she used to wear pretty clothes and be lively, when she was Minnie Foster, one of the town girls singing in the choir. But that — oh, that was thirty years ago. This all you want to take in?

*Mrs. Peters:* She said she wanted an apron. Funny thing to want, for there isn't much to get you dirty in jail, goodness knows. But I suppose just to make her feel more natural. She said they was in the top drawer in this cupboard. Yes, here. And then her little shawl that always hung behind the door. (*Opens stair door and looks.*) Yes, here it is. (*Quickly shuts door leading upstairs.*)

*Mrs. Hale (abruptly moving toward her):* Mrs. Peters?

*Mrs. Peters:* Yes, Mrs. Hale?

*Mrs. Hale:* Do you think she did it?

*Mrs. Peters (in a frightened voice):* Oh, I don't know.

*Mrs. Hale:* Well, I don't think she did. Asking for an apron and her little shawl. Worrying about her fruit.

*Mrs. Peters (starts to speak, glances up, where footsteps are heard in the room above. In a low voice):* Mr. Peters says it looks bad for her. Mr. Henderson is awful sarcastic in a speech and he'll make fun of her sayin' she didn't wake up.

*Mrs. Hale:* Well, I guess John Wright didn't wake when they was slipping that rope under his neck.

*Mrs. Peters:* No, it's strange. It must have been done awful crafty and still. They say it was such a — funny way to kill a man, rigging it all up like that.

*Mrs. Hale:* That's just what Mr. Hale said. There was a gun in the house. He says that's what he can't understand.

*Mrs. Peters:* Mr. Henderson said coming out that what was needed for the case was a motive; something to show anger, or — sudden feeling.

*Mrs. Hale (who is standing by the table):* Well, I don't see any signs of anger around here. (*She puts her hand on the dish towel which lies on the table, stands looking down at table, one-half of which is clean, the other half messy.*) It's wiped to here. (*Makes a move as if to finish work, then turns and looks at loaf of bread outside the breadbox. Drops towel. In that voice of coming back to familiar things.*) Wonder how they are finding things upstairs. I hope she had it a little more red-up up there. You know, it seems kind of *sneaking.* Locking her up in town and then coming out here and trying to get her own house to turn against her!

*Mrs. Peters:* But, Mrs. Hale, the law is the law.

*Mrs. Hale:* I s'pose 'tis. (*Unbuttoning her coat.*) Better loosen up your things, Mrs. Peters. You won't feel them when you go out. (*Mrs. Peters takes off her fur tippet, goes to hang it on hook at back of room, stands looking at the under part of the small corner table.*)

*Mrs. Peters:* She was piecing a quilt. (*She brings the large sewing basket and they look at the bright pieces.*)

*Mrs. Hale:* It's a log cabin pattern. Pretty, isn't it? I wonder if she was goin' to quilt it or just knot it? *(Footsteps have been heard coming down the stairs. The Sheriff enters followed by Hale and the County Attorney.)*

*Sheriff:* They wonder if she was going to quilt it or just knot it! *(The men laugh, the women look abashed.)*

*County Attorney (rubbing his hands over the stove):* Frank's fire didn't do much up there, did it? Well, let's go out to the barn and get that cleared up. *(The men go outside.)*

*Mrs. Hale (resentfully):* I don't know as there's anything so strange, our takin' up our time with little things while we're waiting for them to get the evidence. *(She sits down at the big table smoothing out a block with decision.)* I don't see as it's anything to laugh about.

*Mrs. Peters (apologetically):* Of course they've got awful important things on their minds. *(Pulls up a chair and joins Mrs. Hale at the table.)*

*Mrs. Hale (examining another block):* Mrs. Peters, look at this one. Here, this is the one she was working on, and look at the sewing! All the rest of it has been so nice and even. And look at this! It's all over the place! Why, it looks as if she didn't know what she was about! *(After she has said this they look at each other, then start to glance back at the door. After an instant Mrs. Hale has pulled at a knot and ripped the sewing.)*

*Mrs. Peters:* Oh, what are you doing, Mrs. Hale?

*Mrs. Hale (mildly):* Just pulling out a stitch or two that's not sewed very good. *(Threading a needle.)* Bad sewing always made me fidgety.

*Mrs. Peters (nervously):* I don't think we ought to touch things.

*Mrs. Hale:* I'll just finish up this end. *(Suddenly stopping and leaning forward.)* Mrs. Peters?

*Mrs. Peters:* Yes, Mrs. Hale?

*Mrs. Hale:* What do you suppose she was so nervous about?

*Mrs. Peters:* Oh — I don't know. I don't know as she was nervous. I sometimes sew awful queer when I'm just tired. *(Mrs. Hale starts to say something, looks at Mrs. Peters, then goes on sewing.)* Well, I must get these things wrapped up. They may be through sooner than we think. *(Putting apron and other things together.)* I wonder where I can find a piece of paper, and string. *(Rises.)*

*Mrs. Hale:* In that cupboard, maybe.

*Mrs. Peters (looking in cupboard):* Why, here's a bird-cage. *(Holds it up.)* Did she have a bird, Mrs. Hale?

*Mrs. Hale:* Why, I don't know whether she did or not — I've not been here for so long. There was a man around last year selling canaries cheap, but I don't know as she took one; maybe she did. She used to sing real pretty herself.

*Mrs. Peters (glancing around):* Seems funny to think of a bird here. But she must have had one, or why would she have a cage? I wonder what happened to it?

*Mrs. Hale:* I s'pose maybe the cat got it.

*Mrs. Peters:* No, she didn't have a cat. She's got that feeling some people have about cats — being afraid of them. My cat got in her room and she was real upset and asked me to take it out.

*Mrs. Hale:* My sister Bessie was like that. Queer, ain't it?

*Mrs. Peters (examining the cage):* Why, look at this door. It's broke. One hinge is pulled apart.

*Mrs. Hale (looking too):* Looks as if someone must have been rough with it.

*Mrs. Peters:* Why, yes. *(She brings the cage forward and puts it on the table.)*

*Mrs. Hale:* I wish if they're going to find any evidence they'd be about it. I don't like this place.

*Mrs. Peters:* But I'm awful glad you came with me, Mrs. Hale. It would be lonesome for me sitting here alone.

*Mrs. Hale:* It would, wouldn't it? *(Dropping her sewing.)* But I tell you what I do wish, Mrs. Peters. I wish I had come over sometimes when *she* was here. I — *(looking around the room)* — wish I had.

*Mrs. Peters:* But of course you were awful busy, Mrs. Hale — your house and your children.

*Mrs. Hale:* I could've come. I stayed away because it weren't cheerful — and that's why I ought to have come. I — I've never liked this place. Maybe because it's down in a hollow and you don't see the road. I dunno what it is, but it's a lonesome place and always was. I wish I had come over to see Minnie Foster sometimes. I can see now — *(Shakes her head.)*

*Mrs. Peters:* Well, you mustn't reproach yourself, Mrs. Hale. Somehow we just don't see how it is with other folks until — something turns up.

*Mrs. Hale:* Not having children makes less work — but it makes a quiet house, and Wright out to work all day, and no company when he did come in. Did you know John Wright, Mrs. Peters?

*Mrs. Peters:* Not to know him; I've seen him in town. They say he was a good man.

*Mrs. Hale:* Yes — good; he didn't drink, and kept his word as well as most, I guess, and paid his debts. But he was a hard man, Mrs. Peters. Just to pass the time of day with him — *(Shivers.)* Like a raw wind that gets to the bone. *(Pauses, her eye falling on the cage.)* I should think she would 'a' wanted a bird. But what do you suppose went with it?

*Mrs. Peters:* I don't know, unless it got sick and died. *(She reaches over and swings the broken door, swings it again, both women watch it.)*

*Mrs. Hale:* You weren't raised round here, were you? *(Mrs. Peters shakes her head.)* You didn't know — her?

*Mrs. Peters:* Not till they brought her yesterday.

*Mrs. Hale:* She — come to think of it, she was kind of like a bird herself — real sweet and pretty, but kind of timid and — fluttery. How — she — did — change. *(Silence: then as if struck by a happy thought and relieved to get back to everyday things.)* Tell you what, Mrs. Peters, why don't you take the quilt in with you? It might take up her mind.

*Mrs. Peters:* Why, I think that's a real nice idea, Mrs. Hale. There couldn't possibly be any objection to it could there? Now, just what would I take? I wonder if her patches are in here — and her things. *(They look in the sewing basket.)*

*Mrs. Hale:* Here's some red. I expect this has got sewing things in it. *(Brings out a fancy box.)* What a pretty box. Looks like something somebody would give you. Maybe her scissors are in here. *(Opens box. Suddenly puts her hand to her nose.)* Why — *(Mrs. Peters bends nearer, then turns her face away.)* There's something wrapped up in this piece of silk.

*Mrs. Peters:* Why, this isn't her scissors.

*Mrs. Hale (lifting the silk):* Oh, Mrs. Peters — it's — *(Mrs. Peters bends closer.)*

*Mrs. Peters:* It's the bird.

*Mrs. Hale (jumping up):* But, Mrs. Peters — look at it! Its neck! Look at its neck! It's all — other side *to.*

*Mrs. Peters:*  Somebody—wrung—its—neck. *(Their eyes meet. A look of growing comprehension, of horror. Steps are heard outside. Mrs. Hale slips box under quilt pieces, and sinks into her chair. Enter Sheriff and County Attorney. Mrs. Peters rises.)*

*County Attorney (as one turning from serious things to little pleasantries):*  Well, ladies, have you decided whether she was going to quilt it or knot it?

*Mrs. Peters:*  We think she was going to — knot it.

*County Attorney:*  Well, that's interesting, I'm sure. *(Seeing the bird-cage.)* Has the bird flown?

*Mrs. Hale (putting more quilt pieces over the box):*  We think the — cat got it.

*County Attorney (preoccupied):*  Is there a cat? *(Mrs. Hale glances in a quick covert way at Mrs. Peters.)*

*Mrs. Peters:*  Well, not *now.* They're superstitious, you know. They leave.

*County Attorney (to Sheriff Peters, continuing an interrupted conversation):*  No sign at all of anyone having come from the outside. Their own rope. Now let's go up again and go over it piece by piece. *(They start upstairs.)* It would have to have been someone who knew just the — *(Mrs. Peters sits down. The two women sit there not looking at one another, but as if peering into something and at the same time holding back. When they talk now it is in the manner of feeling their way over strange ground, as if afraid of what they are saying, but as if they cannot help saying it.)*

*Mrs. Hale:*  She liked the bird. She was going to bury it in that pretty box.

*Mrs. Peters (in a whisper):*  When I was a girl — my kitten — there was a boy took a hatchet, and before my eyes — and before I could get there — *(Covers her face an instant.)* If they hadn't held me back I would have — *(catches herself, looks upstairs where steps are heard, falters weakly) — hurt him.*

*Mrs. Hale (with a slow look around her):*  I wonder how it would seem never to have had any children around. *(Pause.)* No, Wright wouldn't like the bird — a thing that sang. She used to sing. He killed that, too.

*Mrs. Peters (moving uneasily):*  We don't know who killed the bird.

*Mrs. Hale:*  I knew John Wright.

*Mrs. Peters:*  It was an awful thing was done in this house that night, Mrs. Hale. Killing a man while he slept, slipping a rope around his neck that choked the life out of him.

*Mrs. Hale:*  His neck. Choked the life out of him. *(Her hand goes out and rests on the bird-cage.)*

*Mrs. Peters (with rising voice):*  We don't know who killed him. We don't *know.*

*Mrs. Hale (her own feeling not interrupted):*  If there'd been years and years of nothing, then a bird to sing to you, it would be awful — still, after the bird was still.

*Mrs. Peters (something within her speaking):*  I know what stillness is. When we homesteaded in Dakota, and my first baby died — after he was two years old, and me with no other then —

*Mrs. Hale (moving):*  How soon do you suppose they'll be through looking for the evidence?

*Mrs. Peters:*  I know what stillness is. *(Pulling herself back.)* The law has got to punish crime, Mrs. Hale.

*Mrs. Hale (not as if answering that):*  I wish you'd seen Minnie Foster when she wore a white dress with blue ribbons and stood up there in the choir and sang. *(A look around the room.)* Oh, I *wish* I'd come over here once in a while! That was a crime! That was a crime! Who's going to punish that?

*Mrs. Peters (looking upstairs):* We mustn't — take on.

*Mrs. Hale:* I might have known she needed help! I know how things can be — for women. I tell you, it's queer, Mrs. Peters. We live close together and we live far apart. We all go through the same things — it's all just a different kind of the same thing. *(Brushes her eyes, noticing the bottle of fruit, reaches out for it.)* If I was you I wouldn't tell her her fruit was gone. Tell her it *ain't*. Tell her it's all right. Take this in to prove it to her. She — she may never know whether it was broke or not.

*Mrs. Peters (takes the bottle, looks about for something to wrap it in; takes petticoat from the clothes brought from the other room, very nervously begins winding this around the bottle. In a false voice):* My, it's a good thing the men couldn't hear us. Wouldn't they just laugh! Getting all stirred up over a little thing like a — dead canary. As if that could have anything to do with — with — wouldn't they *laugh*! *(The men are heard coming down stairs.)*

*Mrs. Hale (under her breath):* Maybe they would — maybe they wouldn't.

*County Attorney:* No, Peters, it's all perfectly clear except a reason for doing it. But you know juries when it comes to women. If there was some definite thing. Something to show — something to make a story about — a thing that would connect up with this strange way of doing it — *(The women's eyes meet for an instant. Enter Hale from outer door.)*

*Hale:* Well, I've got the team around. Pretty cold out there.

*County Attorney:* I'm going to stay here a while by myself. *(To the Sheriff.)* You can send Frank out for me, can't you? I want to go over everything. I'm not satisfied that we can't do better.

*Sheriff:* Do you want to see what Mrs. Peters is going to take in? *(The Lawyer goes to the table, picks up the apron, laughs.)*

*County Attorney:* Oh, I guess they're not very dangerous things the ladies have picked out. *(Moves a few things about, disturbing the quilt pieces which cover the box. Steps back.)* No, Mrs. Peters doesn't need supervising. For that matter a sheriff's wife is married to the law. Ever think of it that way, Mrs. Peters?

*Mrs. Peters:* Not — just that way.

*Sheriff (chuckling):* Married to the law. *(Moves toward the other room.)* I just want you to come in here a minute, George. We ought to take a look at these windows.

*County Attorney (scoffingly):* Oh, windows!

*Sheriff:* We'll be right out, Mr. Hale. *(Hale goes outside. The Sheriff follows the County Attorney into the other room. Then Mrs. Hale rises, hands tight together, looking intensely at Mrs. Peters, whose eyes make a slow turn, finally meeting Mrs. Hale's. A moment Mrs. Hale holds her, then her own eyes point the way to where the box is concealed. Suddenly Mrs. Peters throws back quilt pieces and tries to put the box in the bag she is wearing. It is too big. She opens box, starts to take bird out, cannot touch it, goes to pieces, stands there helpless. Sound of a knob turning in the other room. Mrs. Hale snatches the box and puts it in the pocket of her big coat. Enter County Attorney and Sheriff.)*

*County Attorney (facetiously):* Well, Henry, at least we found out that she was not going to quilt it. She was going to — what is it you call it, ladies?

*Mrs. Hale (her hand against her pocket):* We call it — knot it, Mr. Henderson.

*Curtain*

## CONSIDERATIONS FOR CRITICAL THINKING AND WRITING

1. FIRST RESPONSE. Describe the setting of this play. What kind of atmosphere is established by the details in the opening scene? Does the atmosphere change through the course of the play?

2. Where are Mrs. Hale and Mrs. Peters while Mr. Hale explains to the county attorney how the murder was discovered? How does their location suggest the relationship between the men and the women in the play?

3. What kind of person was Minnie Foster before she married? How do you think her marriage affected her?

4. Characterize John Wright. Is it evident why his wife killed him?

5. Why do the men fail to see the clues that Mrs. Hale and Mrs. Peters discover?

6. What is the significance of the birdcage and the dead bird? Why do Mrs. Hale and Mrs. Peters respond so strongly to them? How do you respond?

7. Why don't Mrs. Hale and Mrs. Peters reveal the evidence they have uncovered? What would you have done?

8. How do the men's conversations and actions reveal their attitudes toward women?

9. Why does Glaspell allow us only to hear about Mr. and Mrs. Wright? What is the effect of their never appearing onstage?

10. Does your impression of Mrs. Wright change during the course of the play? If so, what changes it?

11. What is the significance of the play's last line, spoken by Mrs. Hale: "We call it — knot it, Mr. Henderson"? Explain what you think the tone of Mrs. Hale's voice is when she says this line. What is she feeling? What are you feeling?

12. Explain the significance of the play's title. Do you think *Trifles* or "A Jury of Her Peers," Glaspell's title for the short story version of the play, is more evocative? Can you think of other titles that would capture the play's central concerns?

13. Find a copy of "A Jury of Her Peers" online or in the library and write an essay that explores the differences between the play and the short story. (An alternative is to work with the excerpt on p. 987.)

14. CRITICAL STRATEGIES. Read the section on formalist criticism (p. 1383) in Chapter 42, "Critical Strategies for Reading." Several times the characters say things that they don't mean, and this creates a discrepancy between what appears to be and what is actually true. Point to instances of irony in the play and explain how they contribute to its effects and meanings. (For discussions of irony elsewhere in this book, see the Index of Terms, p. 1538.)

## CONNECTIONS TO OTHER SELECTIONS

1. Compare and contrast how Glaspell provides background information in *Trifles* with how Sophocles does so in *Oedipus the King* (p. 1001).

2. Write an essay comparing the views of marriage in *Trifles* and in Kate Chopin's short story "The Story of an Hour" (p. 17). What similarities do you find in the themes of these two works? Are there any significant differences between the works?

3. In an essay compare Mrs. Wright's motivation for committing murder with that of Matt Fowler, the central character from Andre Dubus's short story "Killings" (p. 58). To what extent do you think they are responsible for and guilty of these crimes?

# A SAMPLE CLOSE READING

## *An Annotated Section of Trifles*

As you read a play for the first time, highlight lines, circle or underline words, and record your responses in the margins. These responses will allow you to retrieve initial reactions and questions that in subsequent readings you can pursue and resolve. Just as the play is likely to have layered meanings, so too will your own readings as you gradually piece together a variety of elements such as exposition, plot, and character that will lead you toward their thematic significance. The following annotations for an excerpt from *Trifles* offer an interpretation that was produced by several readings of the play. Of course, your annotations could be quite different, depending upon your own approach to the play.

The following excerpt appears about two pages into this nine-page play and is preceded by a significant amount of exposition that establishes the bleak midwestern farm setting and some details about Mrs. Wright, who is the prime suspect in the murder of her husband. Prior to this dialogue, only the male characters speak as they try to discover a motive for the crime.

The Sheriff unknowingly announces a major conflict in the play that echoes the title: from a male point of view, there is nothing of any importance to be found in the kitchen—or in women's domestic lives. Mr. Hale confirms this by pronouncing such matters "trifles."

The County Attorney weighs in with his assessment of this "sticky" situation by calling it a "mess," from which he pulls away.

As the Attorney pulls away, the women move closer together (sides are slowly being drawn), and Mrs. Peters says more than she realizes when she observes, "Oh, her fruit; it did freeze." This antici-pates our understanding of the cold, fruitless life that drove Mrs. Wright to murder.

The Sheriff's exasperation about women worrying about "preserves" will ironically help preserve the secret of Mrs. Wright—a woman who was beaten down by her husband but who cannot be beaten by these male authorities.

**County Attorney** *(looking around):* I guess we'll go upstairs first — and then out to the barn and around there. *(To the Sheriff.)* You're convinced that there was nothing important here — nothing that would point to any motive?

**Sheriff:** Nothing here but kitchen things. *(The County Attorney, after again looking around the kitchen, opens the door of a cupboard closet. He gets up on a chair and looks on a shelf. Pulls his hand away, sticky.)*

**County Attorney:** Here's a nice mess. *(The women draw nearer.)*

**Mrs. Peters** *(to the other woman):* Oh, her fruit; it did freeze. *(To the Lawyer.)* She worried about that when it turned so cold. She said the fire'd go out and her jars would break.

**Sheriff** *(rises):* Well, can you beat the woman! Held for murder and worryin' about her preserves.

**County Attorney:** I guess before we're through she may have something more serious than preserves to worry about.

**Hale:** Well, women are used to worrying over trifles. *(The two women move a little closer together.)*

**County Attorney** *(with the gallantry of a young politician):* And yet, for all their worries, what would we do with-out the ladies? *(The women do not unbend. He goes to the sink, takes a dipperful of water from the pail, and pouring it into a basin, washes his hands. Starts to wipe them on the roller towel, turns it for a cleaner place.)*

|Dirty towels! |(*Kicks his foot against the pans under the sink.*) Not much of a housekeeper, would you say, ladies?

*Mrs. Hale (stiffly):* There's a great deal of work to be done on a farm.

*County Attorney:* To be sure. And yet (*with a little bow to her*) I know there are some Dickson county farmhouses which do not have such roller towels. (*He gives it a pull to expose its full length again.*)

*Mrs. Hale:* Those towels get dirty awful quick. |Men's hands aren't always as clean as they might be. |

*County Attorney:* Ah, loyal to your sex, I see. But you and Mrs. Wright were neighbors. I suppose you were friends, too.

*Mrs. Hale (shaking her head):* I've not seen much of her of late years. I've not been in this house — it's more than a year.

*County Attorney:* And why was that? You didn't like her?

*Mrs. Hale:* I liked her all well enough. |Farmers' wives have their hands full, |Mr. Henderson. And then —

*County Attorney:* Yes — ?

*Mrs. Hale (looking about):* It never seemed a very cheerful place.

*The Attorney has an eye for dirty towels but not for the real "dirt" embedded in the Wrights' domestic life.*

*The female characters are identified as "Mrs.," which emphasizes their roles as wives, while the men are autonomous and identified by their professions.*

*Mrs. Hale's comment begins a process of mitigating Mrs. Wright's murder of her husband. He — husbands, men — must share some of the guilt, too.*

*In contrast to men (a nice irony), farmers' wives' hands are full of responsibilities for which they receive little credit owing to the males' assumption that they fill their lives with trifles.*

## Perspective

### SUSAN GLASPELL (1882–1948)

### *From "A Jury of Her Peers," the Short Story Version of* Trifles  1917

When Martha Hale opened the storm-door and got a cut of the north wind, she ran back for her big woolen scarf. As she hurriedly wound that round her head her eye made a scandalized sweep of her kitchen. It was no ordinary thing that called her away — it was probably farther from ordinary than anything that had ever happened in Dickson County. But what her eye took in was that her kitchen was in no shape for leaving: her bread all ready for mixing, half the flour sifted and half unsifted.

She hated to see things half done; but she had been at that when the team from town stopped to get Mr. Hale, and then the sheriff came running in to say his wife wished Mrs. Hale would come too — adding, with a grin, that he guessed she was getting scarey and wanted another woman along. So she had dropped everything right where it was.

"Martha!" now came her husband's impatient voice. "Don't keep folks waiting out here in the cold."

She again opened the storm-door, and this time joined the three men and the one woman waiting for her in the big two-seated buggy.

After she had the robes tucked around her she took another look at the woman  5
who sat beside her on the back seat. She had met Mrs. Peters the year before at the
county fair, and the thing she remembered about her was that she didn't seem like
a sheriff's wife. She was small and thin and didn't have a strong voice. Mrs. Gorman,
sheriff's wife before Gorman went out and Peters came in, had a voice that somehow seemed to be backing up the law with every word. But if Mrs. Peters didn't
look like a sheriff's wife, Peters made it up in looking like a sheriff. He was to a
dot the kind of man who could get himself elected sheriff — a heavy man with a
big voice, who was particularly genial with the law-abiding, as if to make it plain
that he knew the difference between criminals and noncriminals. And right there
it came into Mrs. Hale's mind, with a stab, that this man who was so pleasant and
lively with all of them was going to the Wrights' now as a sheriff.

"The country's not very pleasant this time of year," Mrs. Peters at last ventured,
as if she felt they ought to be talking as well as the men.

Mrs. Hale scarcely finished her reply, for they had gone up a little hill and
could see the Wright place now, and seeing it did not make her feel like talking.
It looked very lonesome this cold March morning. It had always been a lonesome-looking place. It was down in a hollow, and the poplar trees around it were
lonesome-looking trees. The men were looking at it and talking about what had
happened. The county attorney was bending to one side of the buggy, and kept
looking steadily at the place as they drew up to it.

"I'm glad you came with me," Mrs. Peters said nervously, as the two women
were about to follow the men in through the kitchen door.

Even after she had her foot on the door-step, her hand on the knob, Martha
Hale had a moment of feeling she could not cross that threshold. And the reason it
seemed she couldn't cross it now was simply because she hadn't crossed it before.
Time and time again it had been in her mind, "I ought to go over and see Minnie
Foster" — she still thought of her as Minnie Foster, though for twenty years she had
been Mrs. Wright. And then there was always something to do and Minnie Foster
would go from her mind. But *now* she could come.

The men went over to the stove. The women stood close together by the door.  10
Young Henderson, the county attorney, turned around and said, "Come up to the
fire, ladies."

Mrs. Peters took a step forward, then stopped. "I'm not — cold," she said.

And so the two women stood by the door, at first not even so much as looking
around the kitchen.

The men talked for a minute about what a good thing it was the sheriff had sent
his deputy out that morning to make a fire for them, and then Sheriff Peters stepped
back from the stove, unbuttoned his outer coat, and leaned his hands on the kitchen
table in a way that seemed to mark the beginning of official business. "Now, Mr.
Hale," he said in a sort of semiofficial voice, "before we move things about, you tell
Mr. Henderson just what it was you saw when you came here yesterday morning."

The county attorney was looking around the kitchen.

"By the way," he said, "has anything been moved?" He turned to the sheriff.  15
"Are things just as you left them yesterday?"

Peters looked from cupboard to sink; from that to a small worn rocker a little
to one side of the kitchen table.

"It's just the same."

"Somebody should have been left here yesterday," said the county attorney.

"Oh — yesterday," returned the sheriff, with a little gesture as of yesterday
having been more than he could bear to think of. "When I had to send Frank to

Morris Center for that man who went crazy — let me tell you, I had my hands full *yesterday*. I knew you could get back from Omaha by to-day, George, and as long as I went over everything here myself —"

"Well, Mr. Hale," said the county attorney, in a way of letting what was past   20 and gone go, "tell just what happened when you came here yesterday morning."

Mrs. Hale, still leaning against the door, had that sinking feeling of the mother whose child is about to speak a piece. Lewis often wandered along and got things mixed up in a story. She hoped he would tell this straight and plain, and not say unnecessary things that would just make things harder for Minnie Foster. He didn't begin at once, and she noticed that he looked queer — as if standing in that kitchen and having to tell what he had seen there yesterday morning made him almost sick.

"Yes, Mr. Hale?" the county attorney reminded.

"Harry and I had started to town with a load of potatoes," Mrs. Hale's husband began.

Harry was Mrs. Hale's oldest boy. He wasn't with them now, for the very good reason that those potatoes never got to town yesterday and he was taking them this morning, so he hadn't been home when the sheriff stopped to say he wanted Mr. Hale to come over to the Wright place and tell the county attorney his story there, where he could point it all out. With all Mrs. Hale's other emotions came the fear that maybe Harry wasn't dressed warm enough — they hadn't any of them realized how that north wind did bite.

"We come along this road," Hale was going on, with a motion of his hand to   25 the road over which they had just come, "and as we got in sight of the house I says to Harry, 'I'm goin' to see if I can't get John Wright to take a telephone.' You see," he explained to Henderson, "unless I can get somebody to go in with me they won't come out this branch road except for a price *I* can't pay. I'd spoke to Wright about it once before; but he put me off, saying folks talked too much anyway, and all he asked was peace and quiet — guess you know about how much he talked himself. But I thought maybe if I went to the house and talked about it before his wife, and said all the women-folks liked the telephones, and that in this lonesome stretch of road it would be a good thing — well, I said to Harry that that was what I was going to say — though I said at the same time that I didn't know as what his wife wanted made much difference to John —"

Now, there he was! — saying things he didn't need to say. Mrs. Hale tried to catch her husband's eye, but fortunately the county attorney interrupted with:

"Let's talk about that a little later, Mr. Hale. I do want to talk about that, but I'm anxious now to get along to just what happened when you got here."

From "A Jury of Her Peers"

### CONSIDERATIONS FOR CRITICAL THINKING AND WRITING

1. In this opening scene from the story, how is the setting established differently from the way it is in the play (p. 976)?
2. What kind of information is provided in the opening paragraphs of the story that is missing from the play's initial scene? What is emphasized early in the story but not in the play?
3. Which version brings us into more intimate contact with the characters? How is that achieved?
4. Does the short story's title, "A Jury of Her Peers," suggest any shift in emphasis from the play's title, *Trifles*?
5. Explain why you prefer one version over the other.

# ELEMENTS OF DRAMA

*Trifles* is a **one-act play**; in other words, the entire play takes place in a single location and unfolds as one continuous action without a break. As in a short story, the characters in a one-act play are presented economically, and the action is sharply focused. In contrast, full-length plays can include many characters as well as different settings in place and time. The main divisions of a full-length play are typically **acts**; their ends are indicated by lowering a curtain, turning up the houselights, or turning down the stage lights while stagehands change the props. Playwrights frequently employ acts to accommodate changes in time, setting, characters on stage, or mood. In many full-length plays, such as Shakespeare's *Hamlet*, acts are further divided into **scenes**; according to tradition, a scene changes when the location of the action changes or when a new character enters. Acts and scenes are **conventions** that are understood and accepted by audiences because they have come, through usage and time, to be recognized as familiar structural techniques, akin to chapters in a novel or stanzas in a poem.

The major convention of a one-act play is that it typically consists of only a single scene; nevertheless, one-act plays contain many of the elements of drama that characterize their full-length counterparts. One-act plays create their effects through compression. They especially lend themselves to modestly budgeted productions with limited stage facilities. However, the potential of a one-act play to move audiences and readers is not related to its length. As *Trifles* shows, one-acts represent a powerful form of dramatic literature.

The single location that comprises the **setting** for *Trifles* is described at the very beginning of the play; it establishes an atmosphere that will later influence our judgment of Mrs. Wright. The "gloomy" kitchen is disordered, bare, and sparsely equipped with a stove, sink, rocker, cupboard, two tables, some chairs, three doors, and a window. These details are just enough to allow us to imagine the stark, uninviting place where Mrs. Wright spent most of her time. Moreover, "signs of incompleted work," coupled with the presence of the sheriff and county attorney, create an immediate tension by suggesting that something is terribly wrong. Before a single word is spoken, **suspense** is created as the characters enter. This suspenseful situation causes an anxious uncertainty about what will happen next.

The setting is further developed through the use of **exposition**, a device that provides the necessary background information about the characters and their circumstances. For example, we immediately learn through **dialogue** — the verbal exchanges between characters — that Mr. Henderson, the county attorney, is just back from Omaha. This detail establishes the setting as somewhere in the Midwest, where winters can be brutally cold and barren. We also find out that John Wright has been murdered and that his wife has been arrested for the crime.

Even more important, Glaspell deftly characterizes the Wrights through exposition alone. Mr. Hale's conversation with Mr. Henderson explains how Mr. Wright's body was discovered, but it also reveals that Wright was a non-communicative man, who refused to share a "party telephone" — that is, a telephone line shared by multiple customers — and who did not consider "what his wife wanted." Later Mrs. Hale adds to this characterization when she tells Mrs. Peters that though Mr. Wright was an honest, good man who paid his bills and did not drink, he was a "hard man" and "Like a raw wind that gets to the bone." Mr. Hale's description of Mrs. Wright sitting in the kitchen dazed and disoriented gives us a picture of a shattered, exhausted woman. But it is Mrs. Hale who again offers further insights when she describes how Minnie Foster, a sweet, pretty, timid young woman who sang in the choir, was changed by her marriage to Mr. Wright and by her childless, isolated life on the farm.

This information about Mr. and Mrs. Wright is worked into the dialogue throughout the play to suggest the nature of the *conflict* or struggle between them, a motive, and, ultimately, a justification for the murder. In the hands of a skillful playwright, exposition is not merely a mechanical device; it can provide important information while simultaneously developing characterizations and moving the action forward.

The action is shaped by the *plot*, the author's arrangement of incidents in the play that gives the story a particular focus and emphasis. Plot involves more than simply what happens; it involves how and why things happen. Glaspell begins with a discussion of the murder. Why? She could have begun with the murder itself: the distraught Mrs. Wright looping the rope around her husband's neck. The moment would be dramatic and horribly vivid. We neither see the body nor hear very much about it. When Mr. Hale describes finding Mr. Wright's body, Glaspell has the county attorney cut him off by saying, "I think I'd rather have you go into that upstairs, where you can point it all out. Just go on now with the rest of the story." It is precisely the "rest of the story" that interests Glaspell. Her arrangement of incidents prevents us from sympathizing with Mr. Wright. We are, finally, invited to see Mrs. Wright as a victim, perhaps at least as much as her husband is.

Mr. Henderson's efforts to discover a motive for the murder appear initially to be the play's focus, but the real conflicts are explored in what seems to be a *subplot*, a secondary action that reinforces or contrasts with the main plot. The discussions between Mrs. Hale and Mrs. Peters and the tensions between the men and the women turn out to be the main plot because they address the issues that Glaspell chooses to explore. Those issues are not about murder but about marriage and how men and women relate to each other.

The *protagonist* of *Trifles*, the central character with whom we tend to identify, is Mrs. Hale. The *antagonist*, the character who is in a position of direct opposition to the central character, is the county attorney, Mr. Henderson. These two characters embody the major conflicts presented in the play because each speaks for a different set of characters who represent disparate values. Mrs. Hale and Mr. Henderson are developed less individually than as representative types.

Mrs. Hale articulates a sensitivity to Mrs. Wright's miserable life as well as an awareness of how women are repressed in general by men; she also helps Mrs. Peters to arrive at a similar understanding. When Mrs. Hale defends Mrs. Wright's soiled towels from Mr. Henderson's criticism, Glaspell has her say more than the county attorney is capable of hearing. The **stage directions** — the playwright's instructions about how the actors are to move and behave — indicate that Mrs. Hale responds "stiffly" to Mr. Henderson's disparagements: "Men's hands aren't always as clean as they might be." Mrs. Hale eventually comes to see that the men are, in a sense, complicit because it was insensitivity like theirs that drove Mrs. Wright to murder.

Mr. Henderson, on the other hand, represents the law in a patriarchal, conventional society that blithely places a minimal value on the concerns of women. In his attempt to gather evidence against Mrs. Wright, he implicitly defends men's severe dominance over women. He also patronizes Mrs. Hale and Mrs. Peters. Like Sheriff Peters and Mr. Hale, he regards the women's world as nothing more than "kitchen things" and "trifles." Glaspell, however, patterns the plot so that the women see more about Mrs. Wright's motives than the men do and shows that the women have a deeper understanding of justice.

Many plays are plotted in what has come to be called a **pyramidal pattern**, because the plot is divided into three essential parts. Such plays begin with a **rising action**, in which complication creates conflict for the protagonist. The resulting tension builds to the second major division, known as the **climax**, when the action reaches a final **crisis**, a turning point that has a powerful effect on the protagonist. The third part consists of **falling action**; here the tensions are diminished in the **resolution** of the plot's conflicts and complications (the resolution is also referred to as the *conclusion* or **dénouement**, a French word meaning "unknotting"). These divisions may occur at different times. There are many variations to this pattern. The terms are helpful for identifying various moments and movements within a given plot, but they are less useful if seen as a means of reducing dramatic art to a formula.

Because *Trifles* is a one-act play, this pyramidal pattern is less elaborately worked out than it might be in a full-length play, but the basic elements of the pattern can still be discerned. The complication consists mostly of Mrs. Hale's refusal to assign moral or legal guilt to Mrs. Wright's murder of her husband. Mrs. Hale is able to discover the motive in the domestic details that are beneath the men's consideration. The men fail to see the significance of the fruit jars, messy kitchen, and badly sewn quilt.

At first Mrs. Peters seems to voice the attitudes associated with the men. Unlike Mrs. Hale, who is "more comfortable looking," Mrs. Peters is "a slight wiry woman" with "a thin nervous face" who sounds like her husband, the sheriff, when she insists, "the law is the law." She also defends the men's patronizing attitudes, because "they've got awful important things on their minds." But Mrs. Peters is a **foil** — a character whose behavior and values contrast with the protagonist's — only up to a point. When the most telling clue is discovered, Mrs. Peters suddenly understands, along with Mrs. Hale, the motive for the killing. Mrs. Wright's caged life was no longer tolerable to her after her husband had killed the bird (which was the one bright spot in her life and which represents her early life as the young Minnie Foster). This revelation brings about the climax, when the two women must decide whether to tell the men what they have discovered. Both women empathize with Mrs. Wright as they confront this crisis, and their sense of common experience leads them to withhold the evidence.

This resolution ends the play's immediate conflicts and complications. Presumably, without a motive the county attorney will have difficulty prosecuting Mrs. Wright — at least to the fullest extent of the law. However, the larger issues related to the *theme*, the central idea or meaning of the play, are left unresolved. The men have both missed the clues and failed to perceive the suffering that acquits Mrs. Wright in the minds of the two women. The play ends with Mrs. Hale's ironic answer to Mr. Henderson's question about quilting. When she says "knot it," she gives him part of the evidence he needs to connect Mrs. Wright's quilting with the knot used to strangle her husband. Mrs. Hale knows — and we know — that Mr. Henderson will miss the clue she offers because he is blinded by his own self-importance and assumptions.

Though brief, *Trifles* is a masterful representation of dramatic elements working together to keep both audiences and readers absorbed in its characters and situations.

# 36

# A Study of Sophocles

Bettmann/Getty Images.

I depict men as they ought to be . . .
— SOPHOCLES

Not all things are to be discovered;
many are better concealed.
— SOPHOCLES

Sophocles lived a long, productive life (496?–406 B.C.E.) in Athens. During his life Athens became a dominant political and cultural power after the Persian Wars, but before he died, Sophocles witnessed the decline of Athens as a result of the Peloponnesian Wars and the city's subsequent surrender to Sparta. He saw Athenian culture reach remarkable heights as well as collapse under enormous pressures.

Sophocles embodied much of the best of Athenian culture; he enjoyed success as a statesman, general, treasurer, priest, and, of course, prize-winning dramatist. Although surviving fragments indicate that he wrote over 120 plays, only a handful remain intact. Those that survive consist of the three plays he wrote about Oedipus and his children — *Oedipus the King, Oedipus at Colonus,* and *Antigone* — and four additional tragedies: *Philoctetes, Ajax, Maidens of Trachis,* and *Electra.*

His plays won numerous prizes at festival competitions because of his careful, subtle plotting and the sense of inevitability with which their action is charged. Moreover, his development of character is richly complex. Instead of relying on the extreme situations and exaggerated actions that earlier tragedians used, Sophocles created powerfully motivated characters who even today fascinate audiences with their psychological depth.

In addition to crafting sophisticated tragedies for the Greek theater, Sophocles introduced several important innovations to the stage. Most important, he broke the tradition of using only two actors; adding a third resulted in more complicated relationships and intricate dialogue among characters. As individual actors took center stage more often, Sophocles reduced the role of the chorus (discussed on p. 997). This shift placed even more emphasis on the actors, although the chorus remained important as a means of commenting on the action and establishing its tone. Sophocles was also the first dramatist to write plays with specific actors in mind, a development that many later playwrights, including Shakespeare, exploited usefully. But without question Sophocles' greatest contribution to drama was *Oedipus the King*, which, it has been argued, is the most influential drama ever written.

**Map of Ancient Greece.** During Sophocles' time, the city-state of Athens (roughly in the center of this map) was the leading cultural and intellectual center of Greece — until the Peloponnesian Wars (431–404 B.C.E.) and Athens's defeat in 404 B.C.E. by the city-state of Sparta (below Athens, to the left).
Steven Wright/Shutterstock.com.

## THEATRICAL CONVENTIONS OF GREEK DRAMA

More than twenty-four hundred years have passed since 430 B.C.E., when Sophocles' *Oedipus the King* was probably first produced on a Greek stage. We inhabit a vastly different planet than Sophocles' audience did, yet concerns about what it means to be human in a world that frequently runs counter to our desires and aspirations have remained relatively constant. The ancient Greeks continue to speak to us. But inexperienced readers or viewers may have some initial difficulty understanding the theatrical conventions used in classical Greek tragedies such as *Oedipus the King* and *Antigone*. If Sophocles were alive today, he would very likely need some sort of assistance with the conventions of an Arthur Miller play or a television production of *The Simpsons*.

Classical Greek drama developed from religious festivals that paid homage to Dionysus, the god of wine and fertility. Most of the details of these festivals have been lost, but we do know that they included dancing and singing that celebrated legends about Dionysus. From these choral songs developed stories of both Dionysus and mortal culture-heroes. These heroes became the subject of playwrights whose works were produced in contests at the festivals. The Dionysian festivals lasted more than five hundred years, but relatively few of their plays have survived. Among the works of the three great writers of tragedy, only seven plays each by Sophocles and Aeschylus (525?–456 B.C.E.) and nineteen plays by Euripides (480?–406 B.C.E.) survive.

Plays were such important events in Greek society that they were partially funded by the state. The Greeks associated drama with religious and community values as well as entertainment. In a sense, their plays celebrate their civilization; in approving the plays, audiences applauded their own culture. The enormous popularity of the plays is indicated by the size of surviving amphitheaters. Although information about these theaters is sketchy, we do know that most of them had a common form. They were built into hillsides with rising rows of seats accommodating more than fourteen thousand people. These seats partially encircled an *orchestra* or "dancing place," where the **chorus** of a dozen or so men chanted lines and danced.

Tradition credits the Greek poet Thespis with adding an actor who was separate from the choral singing and dancing of early performances. A second actor was subsequently included by Aeschylus and a third, as noted earlier, by Sophocles. These additions made possible the conflicts and complicated relationships that evolved into the dramatic art we know today. The two or three male actors who played all the roles appeared behind the orchestra in front of the *skene*, a stage building that served as dressing rooms. As Greek theater evolved, a wall of the skene came to be painted to suggest a palace or some

**Classical Greek Theater in Delphi, Greece.** This photo represents the features typical of a classical theater.
Lukiyanova Natalia frenta/Shutterstock.

other setting, and the roof was employed to indicate, for instance, a mountain location. Sometimes gods were lowered from the roof by mechanical devices to set matters right among the mortals below. This method of rescuing characters from complications beyond their abilities to resolve was known in Latin as *deus ex machina* ("god from the machine"), a term now used to describe any improbable means by which an author provides a too-easy resolution for a story.

Inevitably, the conventions of the Greek theaters affected how plays were presented. Few if any scene changes occurred because the amphitheater stage was set primarily for one location. If an important event happened somewhere else, it was reported by a minor character, such as a messenger. The chorus also provided necessary background information. In *Oedipus the King* and *Antigone*, the choruses, acting as townspeople, also assess the characters' strengths and weaknesses, praising them for their virtues, chiding them for their rashness, and giving them advice. The reactions of the chorus provide a connection between the actors and audience because the chorus is at once a participant in and an observer of the action. In addition, the chorus helps structure the action by indicating changes in scene or mood. Thus the chorus could be used in a variety of ways to shape the audience's response to the play's action and characters.

Actors in classical Greek amphitheaters faced considerable challenges. An intimate relationship with the audience was impossible because many spectators would have been too far away to see a facial expression or subtle gesture. Indeed, some in the audience would have had difficulty even hearing the voices of individual actors. To compensate for these disadvantages, actors wore large masks that extravagantly expressed the major characters' emotions or identified the roles of minor characters. The masks also allowed the two or three actors in a performance to play all the characters without confusing the audience. Each mask was fitted so that the mouthpiece amplified the actor's voice. The actors were further equipped with padded costumes and elevated shoes (*cothurni* or *buskins*) that made them appear larger than life.

As a result of these adaptive conventions, Greek plays tend to emphasize words — formal, impassioned speeches — more than physical action. We are invited to ponder actions and events rather than to see all of them enacted. Although the stark simplicity of Greek theater does not offer an audience realistic detail, the classical tragedies that have survived present characters in dramatic situations that transcend theatrical conventions. Tragedy, it seems, has always been compelling for human beings, regardless of the theatrical forms it has taken.

A Greek tragedy is typically divided into five parts: *prologue, parodos, episodia, stasimon,* and *exodus.* Understanding these terms provides a sense of the overall rhythm of a Greek play. The opening speech or dialogue is known as the **prologue** and usually gives the exposition necessary to follow the subsequent action. In the *parodos* the chorus makes its first entrance and gives its perspective on what the audience has learned in the prologue. Several *episodia,* or episodes, follow, in which characters engage in dialogue that frequently consists of heated debates dramatizing the play's conflicts. Following each episode is a choral ode or *stasimon,* in which the chorus responds to and interprets the preceding dialogue. The *exodus,* or last scene, follows the final episode and stasimon; in it the resolution occurs and the characters leave the stage.

The effect of alternating dialogues and choral odes has sometimes been likened to that of opera. Greek tragedies were written in verse, and the stasima were chanted or sung as the chorus moved rhythmically, so the plays have a strong musical element that is not always apparent on the printed page. If we remember their musical qualities, we are less likely to forget that no matter how terrifying or horrific the conflicts they describe, these plays are stately, measured, and dignified works that reflect a classical Greek sense of order and proportion.

## TRAGEDY

Newspapers are filled with daily reports of tragedies: a child is struck and injured by a car; an airplane plunges into a suburban neighborhood; a volcano erupts and kills thousands. These unexpected instances of suffering are commonly and accurately described as tragic, but they are not tragedies in the literary sense of the term. A literary ***tragedy*** presents courageous individuals who confront powerful forces within or outside themselves with a dignity that reveals the breadth and depth of the human spirit in the face of failure, defeat, and even death.

Aristotle (384–322 B.C.E.), in his *Poetics*, defined *tragedy* on the basis of the plays contemporary to him. His definition has generated countless variations, qualifications, and interpretations, but we still derive our literary understanding of this term from Aristotle.

The protagonist of a Greek tragedy is someone regarded as extraordinary rather than typical: a great man or woman brought from happiness to agony. The character's stature is important because it makes their fall all the more terrifying. The protagonist also carries mythic significance for the audience. Oedipus and Antigone, for example, are not only human beings but legendary figures from a distant, revered past. Although the gods do not appear onstage in either *Oedipus the King* or *Antigone*, their power is ever present as the characters invoke their help or attempt to defy them. In addition, Greek tragedy tends to be public rather than private. The fate of the community — the state — is often linked with that of the protagonist, as when Thebes suffers a plague as a result of Oedipus's mistaken actions.

The protagonists of classical Greek tragedies (and of those of Shakespeare) are often rulers of noble birth who represent the monarchical values of their periods, but in modern tragedies the protagonists are more likely to reflect democratic values that make it possible for anyone to be a suitable subject. What is finally important is not so much the protagonist's social stature as a greatness of character that steadfastly confronts suffering, whether it comes from supernatural, social, or psychological forces. Although Greek tragic heroes were aristocrats, the nobility of their characters was more significant than their inherited titles and privileges.

The protagonist's eminence and determination to complete some task or goal make them admirable in Greek tragedy, but that does not free the protagonist from what Aristotle described as "some error or frailty" that brings about their misfortune. The term Aristotle used for this weakness is ***hamartia***. This word has frequently been interpreted to mean that the protagonist's fall is the result of an internal ***tragic flaw***, such as an excess of pride, ambition, passion, or some other character trait that leads directly to disaster.

Sometimes, however, misfortunes are the result not of a character flaw but of misunderstood events that overtake and thwart the protagonist's best intentions. Thus, virtue can lead to tragedy too. *Hamartia* has also been interpreted to mean "wrong act" — a mistake based not on a personal failure but on circumstances outside the protagonist's personality and control. Many readers find that a combination of these two interpretations sheds the most light on the causes of the tragic protagonist's fall. Both internal and external forces can lead to downfall because the protagonist's personality may determine crucial judgments that result in mistaken actions.

However the idea of tragic flaw is understood, it is best not to use it as a means of reducing the qualities of a complex character to an adjective or two that labels Oedipus as guilty of "overweening pride" (the Greek term for which is **hubris** or **hybris**) or Antigone as "fated." The protagonists of tragedies require more careful characterization than a simplistic label can provide.

Whatever the causes of the tragic protagonist's downfall, they accept responsibility for it. Hence, even when encountering failure (and possibly death) the tragic protagonist displays greatness of character. Perhaps it is the witnessing of this greatness, which seems both to accept and to transcend human limitations, that makes audiences feel relief rather than hopelessness at the end of a tragedy. Aristotle described this response as a **catharsis**, or purgation of the emotions of "pity and fear." We are faced with the protagonist's misfortune, which often seems out of proportion to their actions, and so we are likely to feel compassionate pity. Simultaneously, we may experience fear because the failure of the protagonist, who is so great in stature and power, is a frightening reminder of our own vulnerabilities. Ultimately, however, both these negative emotions are purged because the tragic protagonist's suffering is an affirmation of human values — even if they are not always triumphant — rather than a despairing denial of them.

Nevertheless, tragedies are disturbing. Instead of coming away with the reassurance of a happy ending, we must take solace in the insight produced by the hero's suffering. And just as our expectations are changed, so are the protagonist's. Aristotle described the moment in the plot when this change occurs as a **reversal** (*peripeteia*), the point when the hero's fortunes turn in an unexpected direction. He more specifically defined this term as meaning an action performed by a character that has the opposite of its intended effect. An example cited by Aristotle is the messenger's attempts to relieve Oedipus's anxieties about his relationship to his father and mother. Instead, the messenger reveals previously unknown information that eventually results in a **recognition** (*anagnorisis*); Oedipus discovers the terrible truth that he has killed his father and married his mother.

Tragedy is typically filled with ironies because there are so many moments in the plot when what seems to be turns out to be radically different from what actually is. Because of this, a particular form of irony called **dramatic irony** is also known as **tragic irony**. In dramatic irony, the meaning of a character's words or actions is understood by the audience but not by the character. Audiences of Greek tragedy shared with the playwrights a knowledge of the stories on which many tragic plots were based. Consequently, they frequently were aware of what was going to happen before the characters were. When Oedipus declares that he will seek out the person responsible for the plague that ravishes his city, the audience already knows that the person Oedipus pursues is himself.

## Oedipus the King

A familiarity with the Oedipus legend allows modern readers to appreciate the series of ironies that unfolds in Sophocles' *Oedipus the King*. As an infant, Oedipus had been abandoned by his parents, Laius and Jocasta, the king and queen of Thebes, because a prophecy warned that their son would kill his father and marry his mother. They instructed a servant to leave him on a mountain to die. The infant's feet were pierced and pinned together, but he was not left on the mountain; instead the servant, out of pity, gave him to a shepherd, who in turn presented him to the king and queen of Corinth. They named him Oedipus (for "swollen foot") and raised him as their own son.

On reaching manhood, Oedipus learned from an oracle that he would kill his father and marry his mother; to avoid this horrendous fate, he left Corinth forever. In his travels, Oedipus found his way blocked by a chariot at a crossroads; in a fit of anger, he killed the servants and their passenger. That passenger, unknown to Oedipus, was his real father. In Thebes, Oedipus successfully answered the riddle of the Sphinx, a winged lion with a woman's head. The reward for defeating this dreaded monster was both the crown and the dead king's wife. Oedipus and Jocasta had four children and prospered. But when the play begins, Oedipus's rule is troubled by a plague that threatens to destroy Thebes, and he is determined to find the cause of the plague in order to save the city again.

*Oedipus the King* is widely recognized as the greatest of the surviving Greek tragedies. Numerous translations are available. We have selected the highly regarded translation of *Oedipus the King* by David Grene. The play has absorbed readers for centuries because Oedipus's character — his intelligence, confidence, rashness, and suffering — represents powers and limitations that are both exhilarating and chastening. Although no reader or viewer is likely to identify with Oedipus's extreme circumstances, anyone can appreciate his heroic efforts to find the truth about himself. In that sense, he is one of us — at our best.

SOPHOCLES (496?–406 B.C.E.)

## Oedipus the King    ca. 430 B.C.E.

TRANSLATED BY DAVID GRENE

CHARACTERS

*Oedipus*, King of Thebes
*Jocasta*, His Wife
*Creon*, His Brother-in-Law
*Teiresias*, an Old Blind Prophet

*A Priest*
*First Messenger*
*Second Messenger*
*A Herdsman*
*Chorus of Old Men of Thebes*

SCENE: In front of the palace of Oedipus at Thebes. To the right of the stage near the altar stands the Priest with a crowd of children. Oedipus emerges from the central door.

*Oedipus:* Children, young sons and daughters of old Cadmus,°
    why do you sit here with your suppliant crowns?
    The town is heavy with a mingled burden
    of sounds and smells, of groans and hymns and incense;
    I did not think it fit that I should hear            5
    of this from messengers but came myself, —
    I Oedipus whom all men call the Great.         *(He turns to the Priest.)*
    You're old and they are young; come, speak for them.
    What do you fear or want, that you sit here
    suppliant? Indeed I'm willing to give all           10
    that you may need; I would be very hard
    should I not pity suppliants like these.
*Priest:* O ruler of my country, Oedipus,
    you see our company around the altar;
    you see our ages; some of us, like these,           15
    who cannot yet fly far, and some of us
    heavy with age; these children are the chosen
    among the young, and I the priest of Zeus.
    Within the market place sit others crowned
    with suppliant garlands, at the double shrine     20
    of Pallas° and the temple where Ismenus
    gives oracles by fire. King, you yourself
    have seen our city reeling like a wreck
    already; it can scarcely lift its prow
    out of the depths, out of the bloody surf.        25
    A blight is on the fruitful plants of the earth,
    a blight is on the cattle in the fields,
    a blight is on our women that no children
    are born to them; a God that carries fire,
    a deadly pestilence, is on our town,          30
    strikes us and spares not, and the house of Cadmus
    is emptied of its people while black Death
    grows rich in groaning and in lamentation.
    We have not come as suppliants to this altar
    because we thought of you as of a God,       35
    but rather judging you the first of men

---

1 *Cadmus:* Founder and first king of Thebes.    21 *Pallas:* Pallas Athene, goddess of wisdom and daughter of Zeus.

in all the chances of this life and when
we mortals have to do with more than man.
You came and by your coming saved our city,
freed us from tribute which we paid of old            40
to the Sphinx,° cruel singer. This you did
in virtue of no knowledge we could give you,
in virtue of no teaching; it was God
that aided you, men say, and you are held
with God's assistance to have saved our lives.        45
Now Oedipus, Greatest in all men's eyes,
here falling at your feet we all entreat you,
find us some strength for rescue.
Perhaps you'll hear a wise word from some God,
perhaps you will learn something from a man          50
(for I have seen that for the skilled of practice
the outcome of their counsels live the most).
Noblest of men, go, and raise up our city,
go, — and give heed. For now this land of ours
calls you its savior since you saved it once.         55
So, let us never speak about your reign
as of a time when first our feet were set
secure on high, but later fell to ruin.
Raise up our city, save it and raise it up.
Once you have brought us luck with happy omen;       60
be no less now in fortune.
If you will rule this land, as now you rule it,
better to rule it full of men than empty.
For neither tower nor ship is anything
when empty, and none live in it together.            65
*Oedipus:* I pity you, children. You have come full of longing,
but I have known the story before you told it
only too well. I know you are all sick,
yet there is not one of you, sick though you are,
that is as sick as I myself.                         70
Your several sorrows each have single scope
and touch but one of you. My spirit groans
for city and myself and you at once.
You have not roused me like a man from sleep;
know that I have given many tears to this,           75
gone many ways wandering in thought,
but as I thought I found only one remedy
and that I took. I sent Menoeceus' son
Creon, Jocasta's brother, to Apollo,°
to his Pythian temple,                               80
that he might learn there by what act or word

---

41 *Sphinx:* A mythical creature with the body of a lion, wings of a bird, and the face of a woman. The Sphinx stumped Thebans with her riddle and killed those that could not answer it. Oedipus solved the riddle, the Sphinx killed herself, and Oedipus became king of Thebes.
79 *Apollo:* Oracular god of the sun, light, and truth, and son of Zeus.

I could save this city. As I count the days,
it vexes me what ails him; he is gone
far longer than he needed for the journey.
But when he comes, then, may I prove a villain,  85
if I shall not do all the God commands.

*Priest:* Thanks for your gracious words. Your servants here
 signal that Creon is this moment coming.

*Oedipus:* His face is bright. O holy Lord Apollo,
 grant that his news too may be bright for us  90
 and bring us safety.

*Priest:* It is happy news,
 I think, for else his head would not be crowned
 with sprigs of fruitful laurel.

*Oedipus:*                         We will know soon,
 he's within hail. Lord Creon, my good brother,  95
 what is the word you bring us from the God?        *(Creon enters.)*

*Creon:* A good word, — for things hard to bear themselves
 if in the final issue all is well
 I count complete good fortune.

*Oedipus:*                         What do you mean?
 What you have said so far  100
 leaves me uncertain whether to trust or fear.

*Creon:* If you will hear my news before these others
 I am ready to speak, or else to go within.

*Oedipus:* Speak it to all;
 the grief I bear, I bear it more for these  105
 than for my own heart.

*Creon:*                    I will tell you, then,
 what I heard from the God.
 King Phoebus° in plain words commanded us
 to drive out a pollution from our land,
 pollution grown ingrained within the land;  110
 drive it out, said the God, not cherish it,
 till it's past cure.

*Oedipus:*           What is the rite?
 of purification? How shall it be done?

*Creon:* By banishing a man, or expiation
 of blood by blood, since it is murder guilt  115
 which holds our city in this destroying storm.

*Oedipus:* Who is this man whose fate the God pronounces?

*Creon:* My Lord, before you piloted the state
 we had a king called Laius.°

*Oedipus:* I know of him by hearsay. I have not seen him.  120

*Creon:* The God commanded clearly: let some one
 punish with force this dead man's murderers.

*Oedipus:* Where are they in the world? Where would a trace
 of this old crime be found? It would be hard
 to guess where.

---

108 *King Phoebus:* Apollo.   119 *Laius:* Former king of Thebes.

Creon:                    The clue is in this land;                         125
    that which is sought is found;
    the unheeded thing escapes:
    so said the God.
Oedipus:                    Was it at home,
    or in the country that death came upon him,
    or in another country travelling?                         130
Creon:  He went, he said himself, upon an embassy,
    but never returned when he set out from home.
Oedipus:  Was there no messenger, no fellow traveller
    who knew what happened? Such a one might tell
    something of use.                         135
Creon:  They were all killed save one. He fled in terror
    and he could tell us nothing in clear terms
    of what he knew, nothing, but one thing only.
Oedipus:  What was it?
    If we could even find a slim beginning                         140
    in which to hope, we might discover much.
Creon:  This man said that the robbers they encountered
    were many and the hands that did the murder
    were many; it was no man's single power.
Oedipus:  How could a robber dare a deed like this                         145
    were he not helped with money from the city,
    money and treachery?
Creon:                    That indeed was thought.
    But Laius was dead and in our trouble
    there was none to help.
Oedipus:  What trouble was so great to hinder you                         150
    inquiring out the murder of your king?
Creon:  The riddling Sphinx induced us to neglect
    mysterious crimes and rather seek solution
    of troubles at our feet.
Oedipus:  I will bring this to light again. King Phoebus                         155
    fittingly took this care about the dead,
    and you too fittingly.
    And justly you will see in me an ally,
    a champion of my country and the God.
    For when I drive pollution from the land                         160
    I will not serve a distant friend's advantage,
    but act in my own interest. Whoever
    he was that killed the king may readily
    wish to dispatch me with his murderous hand;
    so helping the dead king I help myself.                         165
    Come, children, take your suppliant boughs and go;
    up from the altars now. Call the assembly
    and let it meet upon the understanding
    that I'll do everything. God will decide
    whether we prosper or remain in sorrow.                         170

*Priest:* Rise, children — it was this we came to seek,
  which of himself the king now offers us.
  May Phoebus who gave us the oracle
  come to our rescue and stay the plague.    *(Exeunt° all but the Chorus.)*

*Chorus (Strophe°):* What is the sweet spoken word of God from the shrine of
    Pytho° rich in gold                                              175
  that has come to glorious Thebes?
  I am stretched on the rack of doubt, and terror and trembling hold
  my heart, O Delian Healer,° and I worship full of fears
  for what doom you will bring to pass, new or renewed in the revolving years.
  Speak to me, immortal voice,                                      180
  child of golden Hope.

  *(Antistrophe°)* First I call on you, Athene, deathless daughter of Zeus,
    and Artemis, Earth Upholder,
  who sits in the midst of the market place in the throne which men
    call Fame,
  and Phoebus, the Far Shooter, three averters of Fate,             185
  come to us now, if ever before, when ruin rushed upon the state,
  you drove destruction's flame away
  out of our land.

  *(Strophe)* Our sorrows defy number;
  all the ship's timbers are rotten;                                190
  taking of thought is no spear for the driving away of the plague.
  There are no growing children in this famous land;
  there are no women bearing the pangs of childbirth.
  You may see them one with another, like birds swift on the wing,
  quicker than fire unmastered,                                     195
  speeding away to the coast of the Western God.

  *(Antistrophe)* In the unnumbered deaths
  of its people the city dies;
  those children that are born lie dead on the naked earth
  unpitied, spreading contagion of death; and grey haired mothers
    and wives                                                       200
  everywhere stand at the altar's edge, suppliant, moaning;
  the hymn to the healing God rings out but with it the wailing voices are
    blended.
  From these our sufferings grant us, O golden Daughter of Zeus,
  glad-faced deliverance.

  *(Strophe)* There is no clash of brazen shields but our fight is with
    the War God,                                                    205
  a War God ringed with the cries of men, a savage God who burns us;

---

*Exeunt:* Stage direction indicating that the characters have left the stage.   *Strophe:* The
song sung by the Chorus, dancing from stage right to stage left.   175 *shrine of Pytho:*
Delphi, site of the oracle and shrine dedicated to Apollo.   178 *Delian Healer:* Apollo.
*Antistrophe:* The song sung after the strophe by the Chorus, dancing back from stage left to
stage right.

grant that he turn in racing course backwards out of our country's bounds
to the great palace of Amphitrite° or where the waves of the Thracian sea
deny the stranger safe anchorage.
Whatsoever escapes the night                                               210
at last the light of day revisits;
so smite the War God, Father Zeus,
beneath your thunderbolt,
for you are the Lord of the lightning, the lightning that carries fire.

*(Antistrophe)* And your unconquered arrow shafts, winged by the golden
    corded bow,                                         215
Lycean King,° I beg to be at our side for help;
and the gleaming torches of Artemis with which she scours the Lycean hills,
and I call on the God with the turban of gold, who gave his name to this
    country of ours,
the Bacchic God° with the wind flushed face,
Evian One, who travel                                                      220
with the Maenad company,°
combat the God that burns us
with your torch of pine;
for the God that is our enemy is a God unhonoured among the Gods.
                                  *(Oedipus returns.)*

*Oedipus:* For what you ask me — if you will hear my words,                225
    and hearing welcome them and fight the plague,
    you will find strength and lightening of your load.

    Hark to me; what I say to you, I say
    as one that is a stranger to the story
    as stranger to the deed. For I would not                        230
    be far upon the track if I alone
    were tracing it without a clue. But now,
    since after all was finished, I became
    a citizen among you, citizens —
    now I proclaim to all the men of Thebes:                         235
    who so among you knows the murderer
    by whose hand Laius, son of Labdacus,
    died — I command him to tell everything
    to me, — yes, though he fears himself to take the blame
    on his own head; for bitter punishment                          240
    he shall have none, but leave this land unharmed.
    Or if he knows the murderer, another,
    a foreigner, still let him speak the truth.
    For I will pay him and be grateful, too.
    But if you shall keep silence, if perhaps                        245
    some one of you, to shield a guilty friend,
    or for his own sake shall reject my words —

---

208 *Amphitrite:* Sea goddess and wife of Poseidon.    216 *Lycean King:* Apollo.    219 *Bacchic God:* Bacchus, also known as Dionysus, god of wine and wild celebration.    221 *Maenad company:* Female followers of Bacchus.

hear what I shall do then:
I forbid that man, whoever he be, my land,
my land where I hold sovereignty and throne;                    250
and I forbid any to welcome him
or cry him greeting or make him a sharer
in sacrifice or offering to the Gods,
or give him water for his hands to wash.
I command all to drive him from their homes,                    255
since he is our pollution, as the oracle
of Pytho's God proclaimed him now to me.
So I stand forth a champion of the God
and of the man who died.
Upon the murderer I invoke this curse —                         260
whether he is one man and all unknown,
or one of many — may he wear out his life
in misery to miserable doom!
If with my knowledge he lives at my hearth
I pray that I myself may feel my curse.                          265
On you I lay my charge to fulfill all this
for me, for the God, and for this land of ours
destroyed and blighted, by the God forsaken.

Even were this no matter of God's ordinance
it would not fit you so to leave it lie,                        270
unpurified, since a good man is dead
and one that was a king. Search it out.
Since I am now the holder of his office,
and have his bed and wife that once was his,
and had his line not been unfortunate                          275
we would have common children — (fortune leaped
upon his head) — because of all these things,
I fight in his defence as for my father,
and I shall try all means to take the murderer
of Laius the son of Labdacus                                    280
the son of Polydorus and before him
of Cadmus and before him of Agenor.°
Those who do not obey me, may the Gods
grant no crops springing from the ground they plough
nor children to their women! May a fate                        285
like this, or one still worse than this consume them!
For you whom these words please, the other Thebans,
may Justice as your ally and all the Gods
live with you, blessing you now and for ever!
*Chorus:*  As you have held me to my oath, I speak:            290
I neither killed the king nor can declare
the killer; but since Phoebus set the quest
it is his part to tell who the man is.

280–282 *Labdacus, Polydorus, Cadmus, and Agenor:* Referring to the father, grandfather, great-grandfather, and great-great-grandfather of Laius.

*Oedipus:* Right; but to put compulsion on the Gods
    against their will — no man can do that.                 295
*Chorus:* May I then say what I think second best?
*Oedipus:* If there's a third best, too, spare not to tell it.
*Chorus:* I know that what the Lord Teiresias
    sees, is most often what the Lord Apollo
    sees. If you should inquire of this from him           300
    you might find out most clearly.
*Oedipus:* Even in this my actions have not been sluggard.
    On Creon's word I have sent two messengers
    and why the prophet is not here already
    I have been wondering.
*Chorus:*                His skill apart           305
    there is besides only an old faint story.
*Oedipus:* What is it?
    I look at every story.
*Chorus:*                It was said
    that he was killed by certain wayfarers.
*Oedipus:* I heard that, too, but no one saw the killer.           310
*Chorus:* Yet if he has a share of fear at all,
    his courage will not stand firm, hearing your curse.
*Oedipus:* The man who in the doing did not shrink
    will fear no word.
*Chorus:*              Here comes his prosecutor:
    led by your men the godly prophet comes           315
    in whom alone of mankind truth is native.

                    *(Enter Teiresias, led by a little boy.)*

*Oedipus:* Teiresias, you are versed in everything,
    things teachable and things not to be spoken,
    things of the heaven and earth-creeping things.
    You have no eyes but in your mind you know           320
    with what a plague our city is afflicted.
    My lord, in you alone we find a champion,
    in you alone one that can rescue us.
    Perhaps you have not heard the messengers,
    but Phoebus sent in answer to our sending           325
    an oracle declaring that our freedom
    from this disease would only come when we
    should learn the names of those who killed King Laius,
    and kill them or expel from our country.
    Do not begrudge us oracles from birds,°           330
    or any other way of prophecy
    within your skill; save yourself and the city,
    save me; redeem the debt of our pollution
    that lies on us because of this dead man.
    We are in your hands; pains are most nobly taken       335
    to help another when you have means and power.

---

330 *oracles from birds:* Bird flight, a method by which prophets predicted the future using the flight of birds.

*Teiresias:* Alas, how terrible is wisdom when
    it brings no profit to the man that's wise!
    This I knew well, but had forgotten it,
    else I would not have come here.
*Oedipus:*                               What is this?     340
    How sad you are now you have come!
*Teiresias:*                           Let me
    go home. It will be easiest for us both
    to bear our several destinies to the end
    if you will follow my advice.
*Oedipus:*                       You'd rob us
    of this your gift of prophecy? You talk     345
    as one who had no care for law nor love
    for Thebes who reared you.
*Teiresias:* Yes, but I see that even your own words
    miss the mark; therefore I must fear for mine.
*Oedipus:* For God's sake if you know of anything,     350
    do not turn from us; all of us kneel to you,
    all of us here, your suppliants.
*Teiresias:* All of you here know nothing. I will not
    bring to the light of day my troubles, mine —
    rather than call them yours.
*Oedipus:*                     What do you mean?     355
    You know of something but refuse to speak.
    Would you betray us and destroy the city?
*Teiresias:* I will not bring this pain upon us both,
    neither on you nor on myself. Why is it
    you question me and waste your labour? I     360
    will tell you nothing.
*Oedipus:* You would provoke a stone! Tell us, you villain,
    tell us, and do not stand there quietly
    unmoved and balking at the issue.
*Teiresias:* You blame my temper but you do not see     365
    your own that lives within you; it is me
    you chide.
*Oedipus:* Who would not feel his temper rise
    at words like these with which you shame our city?
*Teiresias:* Of themselves things will come, although I hide them     370
    and breathe no word of them.
*Oedipus:*                       Since they will come
    tell them to me.
*Teiresias:*              I will say nothing further.
    Against this answer let your temper rage
    as wildly as you will.
*Oedipus:*                Indeed I am
    so angry I shall not hold back a jot     375
    of what I think. For I would have you know
    I think you were complotter° of the deed

---

377 *complotter:* One who is part of a plot or conspiracy.

and doer of the deed save in so far
as for the actual killing. Had you had eyes
I would have said alone you murdered him.  380

*Teiresias:* Yes? Then I warn you faithfully to keep
    the letter of your proclamation and
    from this day forth to speak no word of greeting
    to these nor me; you are the land's pollution.

*Oedipus:* How shamelessly you started up this taunt!  385
    How do you think you will escape?

*Teiresias:*                      I have.
    I have escaped; the truth is what I cherish
    and that's my strength.

*Oedipus:*             And who has taught you the truth?
    Not your profession surely!

*Teiresias:*                You have taught me,
    for you have made me speak against my will.  390

*Oedipus:* Speak what? Tell me again that I may learn it better.

*Teiresias:* Did you not understand before or would you
    provoke me into speaking?

*Oedipus:*               I did not grasp it,
    not so to call it known. Say it again.

*Teiresias:* I say you are the murderer of the king  395
    whose murderer you seek.

*Oedipus:*              Not twice you shall
    say calumnies like this and stay unpunished.

*Teiresias:* Shall I say more to tempt your anger more?

*Oedipus:* As much as you desire; it will be said
    in vain.

*Teiresias:*    I say that with those you love best  400
    you live in foulest shame unconsciously
    and do not see where you are in calamity.

*Oedipus:* Do you imagine you can always talk
    like this, and live to laugh at it hereafter?

*Teiresias:* Yes, if the truth has anything of strength.  405

*Oedipus:* It has, but not for you; it has no strength
    for you because you are blind in mind and ears
    as well as in your eyes.

*Teiresias:*             You are a poor wretch
    to taunt me with the very insults which
    every one soon will heap upon yourself.  410

*Oedipus:* Your life is one long night so that you cannot
    hurt me or any other who sees the light.

*Teiresias:* It is not fate that I should be your ruin,
    Apollo is enough; it is his care
    to work this out.

*Oedipus:*          Was this your own design  415
    or Creon's?

*Teiresias:*    Creon is no hurt to you,
    but you are to yourself.

*Oedipus:*  Wealth, sovereignty and skill outmatching skill
      for the contrivance of an envied life!
      Great store of jealousy fill your treasury chests,       420
      if my friend Creon, friend from the first and loyal,
      thus secretly attacks me, secretly
      desires to drive me out and secretly
      suborns this juggling, trick devising quack,
      this wily beggar who has only eyes       425
      for his own gains, but blindness in his skill.
      For, tell me, where have you seen clear, Teiresias,
      with your prophetic eyes? When the dark singer,
      the sphinx, was in your country, did you speak
      word of deliverance to its citizens?       430
      And yet the riddle's answer was not the province
      of a chance comer. It was a prophet's task
      and plainly you had no such gift of prophecy
      from birds nor otherwise from any God
      to glean a word of knowledge. But I came,       435
      Oedipus, who knew nothing, and I stopped her.
      I solved the riddle by my wit alone.
      Mine was no knowledge got from birds. And now
      you would expel me,
      because you think that you will find a place       440
      by Creon's throne. I think you will be sorry,
      both you and your accomplice, for your plot
      to drive me out. And did I not regard you
      as an old man, some suffering would have taught you
      that what was in your heart was treason.       445
*Chorus:*  We look at this man's words and yours, my king,
      and we find both have spoken them in anger.
      We need no angry words but only thought
      how we may best hit the God's meaning for us.
*Teiresias:*  If you are king, at least I have the right       450
      no less to speak in my defence against you.
      Of that much I am master. I am no slave
      of yours, but Loxias', and so I shall not
      enroll myself with Creon for my patron.
      Since you have taunted me with being blind,       455
      here is my word for you.
      You have your eyes but see not where you are
      in sin, nor where you live, nor whom you live with.
      Do you know who your parents are? Unknowing
      you are an enemy to kith and kin       460
      in death, beneath the earth, and in this life.
      A deadly footed, double striking curse,
      from father and mother both, shall drive you forth
      out of this land, with darkness on your eyes,
      that now have such straight vision. Shall there be       465
      a place will not be harbour to your cries,

a corner of Cithaeron° will not ring
in echo to your cries, soon, soon, —
when you shall learn the secret of your marriage,
which steered you to a haven in this house, —                    470
haven no haven, after lucky voyage?
And of the multitude of other evils
establishing a grim equality
between you and your children, you know nothing.
So, muddy with contempt my words and Creon's!              475
Misery shall grind no man as it will you.

*Oedipus:* Is it endurable that I should hear
    such words from him? Go and a curse go with you!
    Quick, home with you! Out of my house at once!

*Teiresias:* I would not have come either had you not called me.    480

*Oedipus:* I did not know then you would talk like a fool —
    or it would have been long before I called you.

*Teiresias:* I am a fool then, as it seems to you —
    but to the parents who have bred you, wise.

*Oedipus:* What parents? Stop! Who are they of all the world?    485

*Teiresias:* This day will show your birth and will destroy you.

*Oedipus:* How needlessly your riddles darken everything.

*Teiresias:* But it's in riddle answering you are strongest.

*Oedipus:* Yes. Taunt me where you will find me great.

*Teiresias:* It is this very luck that has destroyed you.          490

*Oedipus:* I do not care, if it has saved this city.

*Teiresias:* Well, I will go. Come, boy, lead me away.

*Oedipus:* Yes, lead him off. So long as you are here,
    you'll be a stumbling block and a vexation;
    once gone, you will not trouble me again.

*Teiresias:*                                    I have said          495
    what I came here to say not fearing your
    countenance: there is no way you can hurt me.
    I tell you, king, this man, this murderer
    (whom you have long declared you are in search of,
    indicting him in threatening proclamation                      500
    as murderer of Laius) — he is here.
    In name he is a stranger among citizens
    but soon he will be shown to be a citizen
    true native Theban, and he'll have no joy
    of the discovery: blindness for sight                          505
    and beggary for riches his exchange,
    he shall go journeying to a foreign country
    tapping his way before him with a stick.
    He shall be proved father and brother both
    to his own children in his house; to her                       510
    that gave him birth, a son and husband both;
    a fellow sower in his father's bed

---

467 *Cithaeron:* Mountain in Greece and the location where Oedipus was abandoned as a baby.

with that same father that he murdered.
Go within, reckon that out, and if you find me
mistaken, say I have no skill in prophecy.                              515

*(Exeunt separately Teiresias and Oedipus.)*

Chorus *(Strophe):* Who is the man proclaimed
by Delphi's prophetic rock
as the bloody handed murderer,
the doer of deeds that none dare name?
Now is the time for him to run                                         520
with a stronger foot
than Pegasus
for the child of Zeus leaps in arms upon him
with fire and the lightning bolt,
and terribly close on his heels                                        525
are the Fates that never miss.

*(Antistrophe)* Lately from snowy Parnassus°
clearly the voice flashed forth,
bidding each Theban track him down,
the unknown murderer.                                                  530
In the savage forests he lurks and in
the caverns like
the mountain bull.
He is sad and lonely, and lonely his feet
that carry him far from the navel of earth;                            535
but its prophecies, ever living,
flutter around his head.

*(Strophe)* The augur has spread confusion,
terrible confusion;
I do not approve what was said                                         540
nor can I deny it.
I do not know what to say;
I am in a flutter of foreboding;
I never heard in the present
nor past of a quarrel between                                          545
the sons of Labdacus and Polybus,
that I might bring as proof
in attacking the popular fame
of Oedipus, seeking
to take vengeance for undiscovered                                     550
death in the line of Labdacus.

*(Antistrophe)* Truly Zeus and Apollo are wise
and in human things all knowing;
but amongst men there is no
distinct judgment, between the prophet                                 555
and me — which of us is right.
One man may pass another in wisdom

---

527 *Parnassus:* Mountain in Greece that was sacred to Apollo.

but I would never agree
with those that find fault with the king
till I should see the word                                    560
proved right beyond doubt. For once
in visible form the Sphinx
came on him and all of us
saw his wisdom and in that test
he saved the city. So he will not be condemned by my mind.    565

*(Enter Creon.)*

*Creon:* Citizens, I have come because I heard
deadly words spread about me, that the king
accuses me. I cannot take that from him.
If he believes that in these present troubles
he has been wronged by me in word or deed                     570
I do not want to live on with the burden
of such a scandal on me. The report
injures me doubly and most vitally —
for I'll be called a traitor to my city
and traitor also to my friends and you.                       575

*Chorus:* Perhaps it was a sudden gust of anger
that forced that insult from him, and no judgment.

*Creon:* But did he say that it was in compliance
with schemes of mine that the seer told him lies?

*Chorus:* Yes, he said that, but why, I do not know.           580

*Creon:* Were his eyes straight in his head? Was his mind right
when he accused me in this fashion?

*Chorus:* I do not know; I have no eyes to see
what princes do. Here comes the king himself.   *(Enter Oedipus.)*

*Oedipus:* You, sir, how is it you come here? Have you so much   585
brazen-faced daring that you venture in
my house although you are proved manifestly
the murderer of that man, and though you tried,
openly, highway robbery of my crown?
For God's sake, tell me what you saw in me,                    590
what cowardice or what stupidity,
that made you lay a plot like this against me?
Did you imagine I should not observe
the crafty scheme that stole upon me or
seeing it, take no means to counter it?                        595
Was it not stupid of you to make the attempt,
to try to hunt down royal power without
the people at your back or friends? For only
with the people at your back or money can
the hunt end in the capture of a crown.                        600

*Creon:* Do you know what you're doing? Will you listen
to words to answer yours, and then pass judgment?

*Oedipus:* You're quick to speak, but I am slow to grasp you,
for I have found you dangerous, — and my foe.

*Creon:* First of all hear what I shall say to that.            605

*Oedipus:* At least don't tell me that you are not guilty.

*Creon:* If you think obstinacy without wisdom
    a valuable possession, you are wrong.
*Oedipus:* And you are wrong if you believe that one,
    a criminal, will not be punished only         610
    because he is my kinsman.
*Creon:*                  This is but just —
    but tell me, then, of what offense I'm guilty?
*Oedipus:* Did you or did you not urge me to send
    to this prophetic mumbler?
*Creon:*                I did indeed,
    and I shall stand by what I told you.         615
*Oedipus:* How long ago is it since Laius. . . .
*Creon:* What about Laius? I don't understand.
*Oedipus:* Vanished — died — was murdered?
*Creon:*                     It is long,
    a long, long time to reckon.
*Oedipus:*              Was this prophet
    in the profession then?
*Creon:*              He was, and honoured     620
    as highly as he is today.
*Oedipus:* At that time did he say a word about me?
*Creon:* Never, at least when I was near him.
*Oedipus:* You never made a search for the dead man?
*Creon:* We searched, indeed, but never learned of anything.     625
*Oedipus:* Why did our wise old friend not say this then?
*Creon:* I don't know; and when I know nothing, I
    usually hold my tongue.
*Oedipus:*             You know this much,
    and can declare this much if you are loyal.
*Creon:* What is it? If I know, I'll not deny it.     630
*Oedipus:* That he would not have said that I killed Laius
    had he not met you first.
*Creon:*             You know yourself
    whether he said this, but I demand that I
    should hear as much from you as you from me.
*Oedipus:* Then hear, — I'll not be proved a murderer.     635
*Creon:* Well, then. You're married to my sister.
*Oedipus:*               Yes,
    that I am not disposed to deny.
*Creon:*           You rule
    this country giving her an equal share
    in the government?
*Oedipus:*         Yes, everything she wants
    she has from me.
*Creon:*         And I, as thirdsman to you,     640
    am rated as the equal of you two?
*Oedipus:* Yes, and it's there you've proved yourself false friend.
*Creon:* Not if you will reflect on it as I do.
    Consider, first, if you think any one
    would choose to rule and fear rather than rule     645

and sleep untroubled by a fear if power
were equal in both cases. I, at least,
I was not born with such a frantic yearning
to be a king — but to do what kings do.
And so it is with every one who has learned          650
wisdom and self-control. As it stands now,
the prizes are all mine — and without fear.
But if I were the king myself, I must
do much that went against the grain.
How should despotic rule seem sweeter to me          655
than painless power and an assured authority?
I am not so besotted yet that I
want other honours than those that come with profit.
Now every man's my pleasure; every man greets me;
now those who are your suitors fawn on me, —          660
success for them depends upon my favour.
Why should I let all this go to win that?
My mind would not be traitor if it's wise;
I am no treason lover, of my nature,
nor would I ever dare to join a plot.          665
Prove what I say. Go to the oracle
at Pytho and inquire about the answers,
if they are as I told you. For the rest,
if you discover I laid any plot
together with the seer, kill me, I say,          670
not only by your vote but by my own.
But do not charge me on obscure opinion
without some proof to back it. It's not just
lightly to count your knaves as honest men,
nor honest men as knaves. To throw away          675
an honest friend is, as it were, to throw
your life away, which a man loves the best.
In time you will know all with certainty;
time is the only test of honest men,
one day is space enough to know a rogue.          680
*Chorus:* His words are wise, king, if one fears to fall.
    Those who are quick of temper are not safe.
*Oedipus:* When he that plots against me secretly
    moves quickly, I must quickly counterplot.
    If I wait taking no decisive measure          685
    his business will be done, and mine be spoiled.
*Creon:* What do you want to do then? Banish me?
*Oedipus:* No, certainly; kill you, not banish you.
*Creon:* I do not think that you've your wits about you.
*Oedipus:* For my own interests, yes.
*Creon:*                                But for mine, too,          690
    you should think equally.
*Oedipus:*                                You are a rogue.
*Creon:* Suppose you do not understand?

*Oedipus:* But yet
　　I must be ruler.
*Creon:* Not if you rule badly.
*Oedipus:* O, city, city!
*Creon:* I too have some share
　　in the city; it is not yours alone. 695
*Chorus:* Stop, my lords! Here — and in the nick of time
　　I see Jocasta coming from the house;
　　with her help lay the quarrel that now stirs you. *(Enter Jocasta.)*
*Jocasta:* For shame! Why have you raised this foolish squabbling
　　brawl? Are you not ashamed to air your private 700
　　griefs when the country's sick? Go in, you, Oedipus,
　　and you, too, Creon, into the house. Don't magnify
　　your nothing troubles.
*Creon:* Sister, Oedipus,
　　your husband, thinks he has the right to do
　　terrible wrongs — he has but to choose between 705
　　two terrors: banishing or killing me.
*Oedipus:* He's right, Jocasta; for I find him plotting
　　with knavish tricks against my person.
*Creon:* That God may never bless me! May I die
　　accursed, if I have been guilty of 710
　　one tittle of the charge you bring against me!
*Jocasta:* I beg you, Oedipus, trust him in this,
　　spare him for the sake of this his oath to God,
　　for my sake, and the sake of those who stand here.
*Chorus:* Be gracious, be merciful, 715
　　we beg of you.
*Oedipus:* In what would you have me yield?
*Chorus:* He has been no silly child in the past.
　　He is strong in his oath now.
　　Spare him. 720
*Oedipus:* Do you know what you ask?
*Chorus:* Yes.
*Oedipus:* Tell me then.
*Chorus:* He has been your friend before all men's eyes; do not cast him
　　away dishonoured on an obscure conjecture. 725
*Oedipus:* I would have you know that this request of yours
　　really requests my death or banishment.
*Chorus:* May the Sun God, king of Gods, forbid! May I die without God's
　　blessing, without friends' help, if I had any such thought. But my
　　spirit is broken by my unhappiness for my wasting country; and 730
　　this would but add troubles amongst ourselves to the other troubles.
*Oedipus:* Well, let him go then — if I must die ten times for it,
　　or be sent out dishonoured into exile.
　　It is your lips that prayed for him I pitied,
　　not his; wherever he is, I shall hate him. 735
*Creon:* I see you sulk in yielding and you're dangerous
　　when you are out of temper; natures like yours
　　are justly heaviest for themselves to bear.

*Oedipus:* Leave me alone! Take yourself off, I tell you.
*Creon:* I'll go, you have not known me, but they have,     740
    and they have known my innocence.        *(Exit.)*
*Chorus:* Won't you take him inside, lady?
*Jocasta:* Yes, when I've found out what was the matter.
*Chorus:* There was some misconceived suspicion of a story, and on the
    other side the sting of injustice.     745
*Jocasta:* So, on both sides?
*Chorus:* Yes.
*Jocasta*: What was the story?
*Chorus:* I think it best, in the interests of the country, to leave it where
    it ended.     750
*Oedipus:* You see where you have ended, straight of judgment
    although you are, by softening my anger.
*Chorus*: Sir, I have said before and I say again — be sure that I would have
    been proved a madman, bankrupt in sane council, if I should put you
    away, you who steered the country I love safely when she was crazed     755
    with troubles. God grant that now, too, you may prove a fortunate guide
    for us.
*Jocasta:* Tell me, my lord, I beg of you, what was it
    that roused your anger so?
*Oedipus:*               Yes, I will tell you.
    I honour you more than I honour them.     760
    It was Creon and the plots he laid against me.
*Jocasta:* Tell me — if you can clearly tell the quarrel —
*Oedipus:*                            Creon says
    that I'm the murderer of Laius.
*Jocasta:* Of his own knowledge or on information?
*Oedipus:* He sent this rascal prophet to me, since     765
    he keeps his own mouth clean of any guilt.
*Jocasta:* Do not concern yourself about this matter;
    listen to me and learn that human beings
    have no part in the craft of prophecy.
    Of that I'll show you a short proof.     770
    There was an oracle once that came to Laius, —
    I will not say that it was Phoebus' own,
    but it was from his servants — and it told him
    that it was fate that he should die a victim
    at the hands of his own son, a son to be born     775
    of Laius and me. But, see now, he,
    the king, was killed by foreign highway robbers
    at a place where three roads meet — so goes the story;
    and for the son — before three days were out
    after his birth King Laius pierced his ankles     780
    and by the hands of others cast him forth
    upon a pathless hillside. So Apollo
    failed to fulfill his oracle to the son,
    that he should kill his father, and to Laius
    also proved false in that the thing he feared,     785
    death at his son's hands, never came to pass.

So clear in this case were the oracles,
so clear and false. Give them no heed, I say;
what God discovers need of, easily
he shows to us himself.

*Oedipus:*                    O dear Jocasta,                    790
as I hear this from you, there comes upon me
a wandering of the soul — I could run mad.

*Jocasta:* What trouble is it, that you turn again
and speak like this?

*Oedipus:*                    I thought I heard you say
that Laius was killed at a crossroads.                    795

*Jocasta:* Yes, that was how the story went and still
that word goes round.

*Oedipus:*                    Where is this place, Jocasta,
where he was murdered?

*Jocasta:*                    Phocis is the country
and the road splits there, one of two roads from Delphi,
another comes from Daulia.

*Oedipus:*                    How long ago is this?                    800

*Jocasta:* The news came to the city just before
you became king and all men's eyes looked to you.
What is it, Oedipus, that's in your mind?

*Oedipus:* What have you designed, O Zeus, to do with me?

*Jocasta:* What is the thought that troubles your heart?                    805

*Oedipus:* Don't ask me yet — tell me of Laius —
How did he look? How old or young was he?

*Jocasta:* He was a tall man and his hair was grizzled
already — nearly white — and in his form
not unlike you.

*Oedipus:*                    O God, I think I have                    810
called curses on myself in ignorance.

*Jocasta:* What do you mean? I am terrified
when I look at you.

*Oedipus:*                    I have a deadly fear
that the old seer had eyes. You'll show me more
if you can tell me one more thing.

*Jocasta:*                    I will.                    815
I'm frightened, — but if I can understand,
I'll tell you all you ask.

*Oedipus:*                    How was his company?
Had he few with him when he went this journey,
or many servants, as would suit a prince?

*Jocasta:* In all there were but five, and among them                    820
a herald; and one carriage for the king.

*Oedipus:* It's plain — it's plain — who was it told you this?

*Jocasta:* The only servant that escaped safe home.

*Oedipus:* Is he at home now?

*Jocasta:*                    No, when he came home again
and saw you king and Laius was dead,                    825
he came to me and touched my hand and begged

that I should send him to the fields to be
my shepherd and so he might see the city
as far off as he might. So I
sent him away. He was an honest man,                                    830
as slaves go, and was worthy of far more
than what he asked of me.

*Oedipus:*  O, how I wish that he could come back quickly!

*Jocasta:*  He can. Why is your heart so set on this?

*Oedipus:*  O dear Jocasta, I am full of fears                          835
that I have spoken far too much; and therefore
I wish to see this shepherd.

*Jocasta:*                          He will come;
but, Oedipus, I think I'm worthy too
to know what it is that disquiets you.

*Oedipus:*  It shall not be kept from you, since my mind                840
has gone so far with its forebodings. Whom
should I confide in rather than you, who is there
of more importance to me who have passed
through such a fortune?
Polybus was my father, king of Corinth,                                845
and Merope,° the Dorian, my mother.
I was held greatest of the citizens
in Corinth till a curious chance befell me
as I shall tell you — curious, indeed,
but hardly worth the store I set upon it.                               850
There was a dinner and at it a man,
a drunken man, accused me in his drink
of being bastard. I was furious
but held my temper under for that day.
Next day I went and taxed my parents with it;                          855
they took the insult very ill from him,
the drunken fellow who had uttered it.
So I was comforted for their part, but
still this thing rankled always, for the story
crept about widely. And I went at last                                 860
to Pytho, though my parents did not know.
But Phoebus sent me home again unhonoured
in what I came to learn, but he foretold
other and desperate horrors to befall me,
that I was fated to lie with my mother,                                865
and show to daylight an accursed breed
which men would not endure, and I was doomed
to be murderer of the father that begot me.
When I heard this I fled, and in the days
that followed I would measure from the stars                           870
the whereabouts of Corinth — yes, I fled
to somewhere where I should not see fulfilled
the infamies told in that dreadful oracle.

846 *Polybus and Merope:* King and queen that adopted and raised Oedipus.

And as I journeyed I came to the place
where, as you say, this king met with his death.                    875
Jocasta, I will tell you the whole truth.
When I was near the branching of the crossroads,
going on foot, I was encountered by
a herald and a carriage with a man in it,
just as you tell me. He that led the way                            880
and the old man himself wanted to thrust me
out of the road by force. I became angry
and struck the coachman who was pushing me.
When the old man saw this he watched his moment,
and as I passed he struck me from his carriage                      885
full on the head with his two pointed goad.
But he was paid in full and presently
my stick had struck him backwards from the car
and he rolled out of it. And then I killed them
all. If it happened there was any tie                               890
of kinship twixt this man and Laius,
who is then now more miserable than I,
what man on earth so hated by the Gods,
since neither citizen nor foreigner
may welcome me at home or even greet me,                            895
but drive me out of doors? And it is I,
I and no other have so cursed myself.
And I pollute the bed of him I killed
by the hands that killed him. Was I not born evil?
Am I not utterly unclean? I had to fly                              900
and in my banishment not even see
my kindred nor set foot in my own country,
or otherwise my fate was to be yoked
in marriage with my mother and kill my father,
Polybus who begot me and had reared me.                             905
Would not one rightly judge and say that on me
these things were sent by some malignant God?
O no, no, no — O holy majesty
of God on high, may I not see that day!
May I be gone out of men's sight before                             910
I see the deadly taint of this disaster
come upon me.
*Chorus:* Sir, we too fear these things. But until you see this man face to
        face and hear his story, hope.
*Oedipus:* Yes, I have just this much of hope — to wait until the herdsman comes.   915
*Jocasta:* And when he comes, what do you want with him?
*Oedipus:* I'll tell you; if I find that his story is the same as yours, I at least
        will be clear of this guilt.
*Jocasta:* Why what so particularly did you learn from my story?
*Oedipus:* You said that he spoke of highway *robbers* who killed Laius. Now    920
        if he uses the same number, it was not I who killed him. One man
        cannot be the same as many. But if he speaks of a man travelling
        alone, then clearly the burden of the guilt inclines towards me.

*Jocasta:* Be sure, at least, that this was how he told the story. He cannot unsay
　　it now, for everyone in the city heard it — not I alone. But, Oedipus, even　　925
　　if he diverges from what he said then, he shall never prove that the mur-
　　der of Laius squares rightly with the prophecy — for Loxias declared that
　　the king should be killed by his own son. And that poor creature did not
　　kill him surely, — for he died himself first. So as far as prophecy goes,
　　henceforward I shall not look to the right hand or the left.　　930
*Oedipus:* Right. But yet, send some one for the peasant to bring him here;
　　do not neglect it.
*Jocasta:* I will send quickly. Now let me go indoors. I will do nothing
　　except what pleases you.　　　　　　　　　　　　　　　*(Exeunt.)*
*Chorus (Strophe):* May destiny ever find me　　　　　　　　　935
　　pious in word and deed
　　prescribed by the laws that live on high:
　　laws begotten in the clear air of heaven,
　　whose only father is Olympus;
　　no mortal nature brought them to birth,　　　　　　　　940
　　no forgetfulness shall lull them to sleep;
　　for God is great in them and grows not old.

　　*(Antistrophe)* Insolence breeds the tyrant, insolence
　　if it is glutted with a surfeit, unseasonable, unprofitable,
　　climbs to the roof-top and plunges　　　　　　　　　945
　　sheer down to the ruin that must be,
　　and there its feet are no service.
　　But I pray that the God may never
　　abolish the eager ambition that profits the state.
　　For I shall never cease to hold the God as our protector.　　950

　　*(Strophe)* If a man walks with haughtiness
　　of hand or word and gives no heed
　　to Justice and the shrines of Gods
　　despises — may an evil doom
　　smite him for his ill-starred pride of heart!—　　　　　955
　　he reaps gains without justice
　　and will not hold from impiety
　　and his fingers itch for untouchable things.
　　When such things are done, what man shall contrive
　　to shield his soul from the shafts of the God?　　　　　960
　　When such deeds are held in honour,
　　why should I honour the Gods in the dance?

　　*(Antistrophe)* No longer to the holy place,
　　to the navel of earth I'll go
　　to worship, nor to Abae　　　　　　　　　　　　965
　　nor to Olympia,
　　unless the oracles are proved to fit,
　　for all men's hands to point at.
　　O Zeus, if you are rightly called
　　the sovereign lord, all-mastering,　　　　　　　　　970
　　let this not escape you nor your ever-living power!

The oracles concerning Laius
are old and dim and men regard them not.
Apollo is nowhere clear in honour; God's service perishes.

*(Enter Jocasta, carrying garlands.)*

*Jocasta:* Princes of the land, I have had the thought to go     975
to the Gods' temples, bringing in my hand
garlands and gifts of incense, as you see.
For Oedipus excites himself too much
at every sort of trouble, not conjecturing,
like a man of sense, what will be from what was,     980
but he is always at the speaker's mercy,
when he speaks terrors. I can do no good
by my advice, and so I came as suppliant
to you, Lycaean Apollo, who are nearest.
These are the symbols of my prayer and this     985
my prayer: grant us escape free of the curse.
Now when we look to him we are all afraid;
he's pilot of our ship and he is frightened.     *(Enter Messenger.)*

*Messenger:* Might I learn from you, sirs, where is the house of Oedipus? Or
best of all, if you know, where is the king himself?     990

*Chorus:* This is his house and he is within doors. This lady is his wife and
mother of his children.

*Messenger:* God bless you, lady, and God bless your household! God bless
Oedipus' noble wife!

*Jocasta:* God bless you, sir, for your kind greeting! What do you want     995
of us that you have come here? What have you to tell us?

*Messenger:* Good news, lady. Good for your house and for your husband.

*Jocasta:* What is your news? Who sent you to us?

*Messenger:* I come from Corinth and the news I bring will give you pleasure.
Perhaps a little pain too.     1000

*Jocasta:* What is this news of double meaning?

*Messenger:* The people of the Isthmus will choose Oedipus to be their king.
That is the rumour there.

*Jocasta:* But isn't their king still old Polybus?

*Messenger:* No. He is in his grave. Death has got him.     1005

*Jocasta:* Is that the truth? Is Oedipus' father dead?

*Messenger:* May I die myself if it be otherwise!

*Jocasta (to a servant):* Be quick and run to the King with the news! O oracles
of the Gods, where are you now? It was from this man Oedipus fled, lest
he should be his murderer! And now he is dead, in the course of     1010
nature, and not killed by Oedipus.     *(Enter Oedipus.)*

*Oedipus:* Dearest Jocasta, why have you sent for me?

*Jocasta:* Listen to this man and when you hear reflect what is the outcome
of the holy oracles of the Gods.

*Oedipus:* Who is he? What is his message for me?     1015

*Jocasta:* He is from Corinth and he tells us that your father Polybus is
dead and gone.

*Oedipus:* What's this you say, sir? Tell me yourself.

*Messenger:* Since this is the first matter you want clearly told: Polybus has
gone down to death. You may be sure of it.     1020

*Oedipus:* By treachery or sickness?
*Messenger:* A small thing will put old bodies asleep.
*Oedipus:* So he died of sickness, it seems, — poor old man!
*Messenger:* Yes, and of age — the long years he had measured.
*Oedipus:* Ha! Ha! O dear Jocasta, why should one                    1025
    look to the Pythian hearth?° Why should one look
    to the birds screaming overhead? They prophesied
    that I should kill my father! But he's dead,
    and hidden deep in earth, and I stand here
    who never laid a hand on spear against him, —                 1030
    unless perhaps he died of longing for me,
    and thus I am his murderer. But they,
    the oracles, as they stand — he's taken them
    away with him, they're dead as he himself is,
    and worthless.
*Jocasta:*            That I told you before now.                    1035
*Oedipus:* You did, but I was misled by my fear.
*Jocasta:* Then lay no more of them to heart, not one.
*Oedipus:* But surely I must fear my mother's bed?
*Jocasta:* Why should man fear since chance is all in all
    for him, and he can clearly foreknow nothing?                1040
    Best to live lightly, as one can, unthinkingly.
    As to your mother's marriage bed, — don't fear it.
    Before this, in dreams too, as well as oracles,
    many a man has lain with his own mother.
    But he to whom such things are nothing bears                  1045
    his life most easily.
*Oedipus:* All that you say would be said perfectly
    if she were dead; but since she lives I must
    still fear, although you talk so well, Jocasta.
*Jocasta:* Still in your father's death there's light of comfort?    1050
*Oedipus:* Great light of comfort; but I fear the living.
*Messenger:* Who is the woman that makes you afraid?
*Oedipus:* Merope, old man, Polybus' wife.
*Messenger:* What about her frightens the queen and you?
*Oedipus:* A terrible oracle, stranger, from the Gods.              1055
*Messenger:* Can it be told? Or does the sacred law
    forbid another to have knowledge of it?
*Oedipus:* O no! Once on a time Loxias said
    that I should lie with my own mother and
    take on my hands the blood of my own father.               1060
    And so for these long years I've lived away
    from Corinth; it has been to my great happiness;
    but yet it's sweet to see the face of parents.
*Messenger:* This was the fear which drove you out of Corinth?
*Oedipus:* Old man, I did not wish to kill my father.               1065

1026 *Pythian hearth:* Delphi.

*Messenger:* Why should I not free you from this fear, sir,
　　since I have come to you in all goodwill?
*Oedipus:* You would not find me thankless if you did.
*Messenger:* Why, it was just for this I brought the news, —
　　to earn your thanks when you had come safe home.　　　　　1070
*Oedipus:* No, I will never come near my parents.
*Messenger:*　　　　　　　　　　　　　　　Son,
　　it's very plain you don't know what you're doing.
*Oedipus:* What do you mean, old man? For God's sake, tell me.
*Messenger:* If your homecoming is checked by fears like these.
*Oedipus:* Yes, I'm afraid that Phoebus may prove right.　　　1075
*Messenger:* The murder and the incest?
*Oedipus:*　　　　　　　　　　　　　　Yes, old man;
　　that is my constant terror.
*Messenger:*　　　　　　　　Do you know
　　that all your fears are empty?
*Oedipus:*　　　　　　　　　　How is that,
　　if they are father and mother and I their son?
*Messenger:* Because Polybus was no kin to you in blood.　　　1080
*Oedipus:* What, was not Polybus my father?
*Messenger:* No more than I but just so much.
*Oedipus:*　　　　　　　　　　　　　　How can
　　my father be my father as much as one
　　that's nothing to me?
*Messenger:*　　　　　　　　Neither he nor I
　　begat you.
*Oedipus:*　　　Why then did he call me son?　　　　　　　1085
*Messenger:* A gift he took you from these hands of mine.
*Oedipus:* Did he love so much what he took from another's hand?
*Messenger:* His childlessness before persuaded him.
*Oedipus:* Was I a child you bought or found when I
　　was given to him?
*Messenger:*　　　　　　On Cithaeron's slopes　　　　　　1090
　　in the twisting thickets you were found.
*Oedipus:*　　　　　　　　　　　　　　　And why
　　were you a traveller in those parts?
*Messenger:*　　　　　　　　　　　　I was
　　in charge of mountain flocks.
*Oedipus:*　　　　　　　　　　You were a shepherd?
　　A hireling vagrant?
*Messenger:*　　　　　　　Yes, but at least at that time
　　the man that saved your life, son.
*Oedipus:* What ailed me when you took me in your arms?
*Messenger:* In that your ankles should be witnesses.
*Oedipus:* Why do you speak of that old pain?
*Messenger:*　　　　　　　　　　　　　　I loosed you;
　　the tendons of your feet were pierced and fettered, —
*Oedipus:* My swaddling clothes brought me a rare disgrace.　　1100

*Messenger:* So that from this you're called your present name.°
*Oedipus:* Was this my father's doing or my mother's?
    For God's sake, tell me.
*Messenger:*                    I don't know, but he
    who gave you to me has more knowledge than I.
*Oedipus:* You yourself did not find me then? You took me                    1105
    from someone else?
*Messenger:*                    Yes, from another shepherd.
*Oedipus:* Who was he? Do you know him well enough to tell?
*Messenger:* He was called Laius' man.
*Oedipus:* You mean the king who reigned here in the old days?
*Messenger:* Yes, he was that man's shepherd.
*Oedipus:*                              Is he alive                    1110
    still, so that I could see him?
*Messenger:*                              You who live here
    would know that best.
*Oedipus:*                         Do any of you here
    know of this shepherd whom he speaks about
    in town or in the fields? Tell me. It's time
    that this was found out once for all.                    1115
*Chorus:* I think he is none other than the peasant
    whom you have sought to see already; but
    Jocasta here can tell us best of that.
*Oedipus:* Jocasta, do you know about this man
    whom we have sent for? Is he the man he mentions?                    1120
*Jocasta:* Why ask of whom he spoke? Don't give it heed;
    nor try to keep in mind what has been said.
    It will be wasted labour.
*Oedipus:*                         With such clues
    I could not fail to bring my birth to light.
*Jocasta:* I beg you — do not hunt this out — I beg you,                    1125
    if you have any care for your own life.
    What I am suffering is enough.
*Oedipus:*                              Keep up
    your heart, Jocasta. Though I'm proved a slave,
    thrice slave, and though my mother is thrice slave,
    you'll not be shown to be of lowly lineage.                    1130
*Jocasta:* O be persuaded by me, I entreat you;
    do not do this.
*Oedipus:* I will not be persuaded to let be
    the chance of finding out the whole thing clearly.
*Jocasta:* It is because I wish you well that I                    1135
    give you this counsel — and it's the best counsel.
*Oedipus:* Then the best counsel vexes me, and has
    for some while since.
*Jocasta:*                    O Oedipus, God help you!
    God keep you from the knowledge of who you are!

---

1101 *name: Oedipus* literally translates to "swollen foot."

*Oedipus:* Here, some one, go and fetch the shepherd for me;                     1140
    and let her find her joy in her rich family!
*Jocasta:* O Oedipus, unhappy Oedipus!
    that is all I can call you, and the last thing
    that I shall ever call you.                                   *(Exit.)*
*Chorus:* Why has the queen gone, Oedipus, in wild                              1145
    grief rushing from us? I am afraid that trouble
    will break out of this silence.
*Oedipus:* Break out what will! I at least shall be
    willing to see my ancestry, though humble.
    Perhaps she is ashamed of my low birth,                       1150
    for she has all a woman's high-flown pride.
    But I account myself a child of Fortune,
    beneficent Fortune, and I shall not be
    dishonoured. She's the mother from whom I spring;
    the months, my brothers, marked me, now as small,             1155
    and now again as mighty. Such is my breeding,
    and I shall never prove so false to it,
    as not to find the secret of my birth.

*Chorus (Strophe):* If I am a prophet and wise of heart
    you shall not fail, Cithaeron,                                1160
    by the limitless sky, you shall not! —
    to know at tomorrow's full moon
    that Oedipus honours you,
    as native to him and mother and nurse at once;
    and that you are honoured in dancing by us, as finding favour in sight of     1165
      our king.
    Apollo, to whom we cry, find these things pleasing!

*(Antistrophe)* Who was it bore you, child? One of
    the long-lived nymphs who lay with Pan —
    the father who treads the hills?                              1170
    Or was she a bride of Loxias, your mother? The grassy slopes
    are all of them dear to him. Or perhaps Cyllene's king
    or the Bacchants' God that lives on the tops
    of the hills received you a gift from some
    one of the Helicon Nymphs, with whom he mostly plays?         1175
                *(Enter an old man, led by Oedipus' servants.)*
*Oedipus:* If some one like myself who never met him
    may make a guess, — I think this is the herdsman,
    whom we were seeking. His old age is consonant
    with the other. And besides, the men who bring him
    I recognize as my own servants. You                           1180
    perhaps may better me in knowledge since
    you've seen the man before.
*Chorus:*                 You can be sure
    I recognize him. For if Laius
    had ever an honest shepherd, this was he.
*Oedipus:* You, sir, from Corinth, I must ask you first,                        1185
    is this the man you spoke of?

*Messenger:*                              This is he
    before your eyes.
*Oedipus:*             Old man, look here at me
    and tell me what I ask you. Were you ever
    a servant of King Laius?
*Herdsman:*             I was, —
    no slave he bought but reared in his own house.                    1190
*Oedipus:*  What did you do as work? How did you live?
*Herdsman:*  Most of my life was spent among the flocks.
*Oedipus:*  In what part of the country did you live?
*Herdsman:*  Cithaeron and the places near to it.
*Oedipus:*  And somewhere there perhaps you knew this man?              1195
*Herdsman:*  What was his occupation? Who?
*Oedipus:*                              This man here,
    have you had any dealings with him?
*Herdsman:*                       No —
    not such that I can quickly call to mind.
*Messenger:*  That is no wonder, master. But I'll make him remember what
    he does not know. For I know, that he well knows the country of     1200
    Cithaeron, how he with two flocks, I with one kept company for
    three years — each year half a year — from spring till autumn time
    and then when winter came I drove my flocks to our fold home
    again and he to Laius' steadings. Well — am I right or not in what
    I said we did?                                                     1205
*Herdsman:*  You're right — although it's a long time ago.
*Messenger:*  Do you remember giving me a child
    to bring up as my foster child?
*Herdsman:*                       What's this?
    Why do you ask this question?
*Messenger:*                       Look old man,
    here he is — here's the man who was that child!                    1210
*Herdsman:* Death take you! Won't you hold your tongue?
*Oedipus:*                                        No, no,
    do not find fault with him, old man. Your words
    are more at fault than his.
*Herdsman:*                 O best of masters,
    how do I give offense?
*Oedipus:*                 When you refuse
    to speak about the child of whom he asks you.                      1215
*Herdsman:*  He speaks out of his ignorance, without meaning.
*Oedipus:*  If you'll not talk to gratify me, you
    will talk with pain to urge you.
*Herdsman:*                       O please, sir,
    don't hurt an old man, sir.
*Oedipus (to the servants):*     Here, one of you,
    twist his hands behind him.
*Herdsman:*                 Why, God help me, why?                       1220
    What do you want to know?
*Oedipus:*                 You gave a child
    to him, — the child he asked you of?

*Herdsman:*                                    I did.
    I wish I'd died the day I did.
*Oedipus:*                          You will
    unless you tell me truly.
*Herdsman:*                          And I'll die
    far worse if I should tell you.
*Oedipus:*                                This fellow                    1225
    is bent on more delays, as it would seem.
*Herdsman:* O no, no! I have told you that I gave it.
*Oedipus:* Where did you get this child from? Was it your own or did you
    get it from another?
*Herdsman:*                    Not
    my own at all; I had it from some one.                    1230
*Oedipus:* One of these citizens? or from what house?
*Herdsman:* O master, please — I beg you, master, please
    don't ask me more.
*Oedipus:*                    You're a dead man if I
    ask you again.
*Herdsman:*            It was one of the children
    of Laius.
*Oedipus:*      A slave? Or born in wedlock?                    1235
*Herdsman:* O God, I am on the brink of frightful speech.
*Oedipus:* And I of frightful hearing. But I must hear.
*Herdsman:* The child was called his child; but she within,
    your wife would tell you best how all this was.
*Oedipus: She* gave it to you?
*Herdsman:*                          Yes, she did, my lord.                    1240
*Oedipus:* To do what with it?
*Herdsman:*                          Make away with it.
*Oedipus:* She was so hard — its mother?
*Herdsman:*                                Aye, through fear
    of evil oracles.
*Oedipus:*            Which?
*Herdsman:*                      They said that he
    should kill his parents.
*Oedipus:*                          How was it that you
    gave it away to this old man?
*Herdsman:*                                O master,                    1245
    I pitied it, and thought that I could send it
    off to another country and this man
    was from another country. But he saved it
    for the most terrible troubles. If you are
    the man he says you are, you're bred to misery.                    1250
*Oedipus:* O, O, O, they will all come,
    all come out clearly! Light of the sun, let me
    look upon you no more after today!
    I who first saw the light bred of a match
    accursed, and accursed in my living                    1255
    with them I lived with, cursed in my killing.
                    *(Exeunt all but the Chorus.)*

**Chorus (Strophe):**  O generations of men, how I
    count you as equal with those who live
    not at all!
    What man, what man on earth wins more    1260
    of happiness than a seeming
    and after that turning away?
    Oedipus, you are my pattern of this,
    Oedipus, you and your fate!
    Luckless Oedipus, whom of all men    1265
    I envy not at all.

*(Antistrophe)* In as much as he shot his bolt
    beyond the others and won the prize
    of happiness complete —
    O Zeus — and killed and reduced to nought    1270
    the hooked taloned maid of the riddling speech,
    standing a tower against death for my land:
    hence he was called my king and hence
    was honoured the highest of all
    honours; and hence he ruled    1275
    in the great city of Thebes.

*(Strophe)* But now whose tale is more miserable?
    Who is there lives with a savager fate?
    Whose troubles so reverse his life as his?

    O Oedipus, the famous prince    1280
    for whom a great haven
    the same both as father and son
    sufficed for generation,
    how, O how, have the furrows ploughed
    by your father endured to bear you, poor wretch,    1285
    and hold their peace so long?

*(Antistrophe)* Time who sees all has found you out
    against your will; judges your marriage accursed,
    begetter and begot at one in it.

    O child of Laius,    1290
    would I had never seen you.
    I weep for you and cry
    a dirge of lamentation.

    To speak directly, I drew my breath
    from you at the first and so now I lull    1295
    my mouth to sleep with your name.    *(Enter a second messenger.)*
**Second Messenger:**  O Princes always honoured by our country,
    what deeds you'll hear of and what horrors see,
    what grief you'll feel, if you as true born Thebans
    care for the house of Labdacus's sons.    1300
    Phasis nor Ister cannot purge this house,

I think, with all their streams, such things
it hides, such evils shortly will bring forth
into the light, whether they will or not;
and troubles hurt the most                                    1305
when they prove self-inflicted.
*Chorus:* What we had known before did not fall short
of bitter groaning's worth; what's more to tell?
*Second Messenger:* Shortest to hear and tell — our glorious queen
Jocasta's dead.
*Chorus:*           Unhappy woman! How?                        1310
*Second Messenger:* By her own hand. The worst of what was done
you cannot know. You did not see the sight.
Yet in so far as I remember it
you'll hear the end of our unlucky queen.
When she came raging into the house she went                  1315
straight to her marriage bed, tearing her hair
with both her hands, and crying upon Laius
long dead — Do you remember, Laius,
that night long past which bred a child for us
to send you to your death and leave                           1320
a mother making children with her son?
And then she groaned and cursed the bed in which
she brought forth husband by her husband, children
by her own child, an infamous double bond.
How after that she died I do not know, —                      1325
for Oedipus distracted us from seeing.
He burst upon us shouting and we looked
to him as he paced frantically around,
begging us always: Give me a sword, I say,
to find this wife no wife, this mother's womb,                1330
this field of double sowing whence I sprang
and where I sowed my children! As he raved
some god showed him the way — none of us there.
Bellowing terribly and led by some
invisible guide he rushed on the two doors, —                1335
wrenching the hollow bolts out of their sockets,
he charged inside. There, there, we saw his wife
hanging, the twisted rope around her neck.
When he saw her, he cried out fearfully
and cut the dangling noose. Then, as she lay,                 1340
poor woman, on the ground, what happened after,
was terrible to see. He tore the brooches —
the gold chased brooches fastening her robe —
away from her and lifting them up high
dashed them on his own eyeballs, shrieking out               1345
such things as: they will never see the crime
I have committed or had done upon me!
Dark eyes, now in the days to come look on

forbidden faces, do not recognize
those whom you long for — with such imprecations          1350
he struck his eyes again and yet again
with the brooches. And the bleeding eyeballs gushed
and stained his beard — no sluggish oozing drops
but a black rain and bloody hail poured down.

So it has broken — and not on one head
but troubles mixed for husband and for wife.          1355
The fortune of the days gone by was true
good fortune — but today groans and destruction
and death and shame — of all ills can be named
not one is missing.          1360
*Chorus:*  Is he now in any ease from pain?
*Second Messenger:*                    He shouts
for some one to unbar the doors and show him
to all the men of Thebes, his father's killer,
his mother's — no I cannot say the word,
it is unholy — for he'll cast himself,          1365
out of the land, he says, and not remain
to bring a curse upon his house, the curse
he called upon it in his proclamation. But
he wants for strength, aye, and some one to guide him;
his sickness is too great to bear. You, too,          1370
will be shown that. The bolts are opening.
Soon you will see a sight to waken pity
even in the horror of it.                    *(Enter the blinded Oedipus.)*
*Chorus:*  This is a terrible sight for men to see!
I never found a worse!          1375
Poor wretch, what madness came upon you!
What evil spirit leaped upon your life
to your ill-luck — a leap beyond man's strength!
Indeed I pity you, but I cannot
look at you, though there's much I want to ask          1380
and much to learn and much to see.
I shudder at the sight of you.
*Oedipus:*  O, O,
where am I going? Where is my voice
borne on the wind to and fro?          1385
Spirit, how far have you sprung?
*Chorus:*  To a terrible place whereof men's ears
may not hear, nor their eyes behold it.
*Oedipus:*  Darkness!
Horror of darkness enfolding, resistless, unspeakable visitant sped by
an ill wind in haste!          1390
madness and stabbing pain and memory
of evil deeds I have done!
*Chorus:*  In such misfortunes it's no wonder
if double weighs the burden of your grief.

*Oedipus:*  My friend,                                                           1395
    you are the only one steadfast, the only one that attends on me;
    you still stay nursing the blind man.
    Your care is not unnoticed. I can know
    your voice, although this darkness is my world.
*Chorus:*  Doer of dreadful deeds, how did you dare                               1400
    so far to do despite to your own eyes?
    what spirit urged you to it?
*Oedipus:*  It was Apollo, friends, Apollo,
    that brought this bitter bitterness, my sorrows to completion.
    But the hand that struck me                                                1405
    was none but my own.
    Why should I see
    whose vision showed me nothing sweet to see?
*Chorus:*  These things are as you say.
*Oedipus:*  What can I see to love?                                               1410
    What greeting can touch my ears with joy?
    Take me away, and haste — to a place out of the way!
    Take me away, my friends, the greatly miserable,
    the most accursed, whom God too hates
    above all men on earth!                                                     1415
*Chorus:*  Unhappy in your mind and your misfortune,
    would I had never known you!
*Oedipus:*  Curse on the man who took
    the cruel bonds from off my legs, as I lay in the field.
    He stole me from death and saved me,                                        1420
    no kindly service.
    Had I died then
    I would not be so burdensome to friends.
*Chorus:*  I, too, could have wished it had been so.
*Oedipus:*  Then I would not have come                                           1425
    to kill my father and marry my mother infamously.
    Now I am godless and child of impurity,
    begetter in the same seed that created my wretched self.
    If there is any ill worse than ill,
    that is the lot of Oedipus.                                                 1430
*Chorus:*  I cannot say your remedy was good;
    you would be better dead than blind and living.
*Oedipus:*  What I have done here was best done — don't tell me
    otherwise, do not give me further counsel.
    I do not know with what eyes I could look                                   1435
    upon my father when I die and go
    under the earth, nor yet my wretched mother —
    those two to whom I have done things deserving
    worse punishment than hanging. Would the sight
    of children, bred as mine are, gladden me?                                  1440
    No, not these eyes, never. And my city,
    its towers and sacred places of the Gods,
    of these I robbed my miserable self

when I commanded all to drive *him* out,
the criminal since proved by God impure                                  1445
and of the race of Laius.
To this guilt I bore witness against myself —
with what eyes shall I look upon my people?
No. If there were a means to choke the fountain
of hearing I would not have stayed my hand                               1450
from locking up my miserable carcase,
seeing and hearing nothing; it is sweet
to keep our thoughts out of the range of hurt.

Cithaeron, why did you receive me? why
having received me did you not kill me straight?                         1455
And so I had not shown to men my birth.

O Polybus and Corinth and the house,
the old house that I used to call my father's —
what fairness you were nurse to, and what foulness
festered beneath! Now I am found to be                                   1460
a sinner and a son of sinners. Crossroads,
and hidden glade, oak and the narrow way
at the crossroads, that drank my father's blood
offered you by my hands, do you remember
still what I did as you looked on, and what                              1465
I did when I came here? O marriage, marriage!
you bred me and again when you had bred
bred children of your child and showed to men
brides, wives and mothers and the foulest deeds
that can be in this world of ours.                                       1470

Come — it's unfit to say what is unfit
to do. — I beg of you in God's name hide me
somewhere outside your country, yes, or kill me,
or throw me into the sea, to be forever
out of your sight. Approach and deign to touch me                        1475
for all my wretchedness, and do not fear.
No man but I can bear my evil doom.
Chorus:  Here Creon comes in fit time to perform
or give advice in what you ask of us.
Creon is left sole ruler in your stead.                                  1480
Oedipus:  Creon! Creon! What shall I say to him?
How can I justly hope that he will trust me?
In what is past I have been proved towards him
an utter liar.                                        (Enter Creon.)
Creon:     Oedipus, I've come
not so that I might laugh at you nor taunt you                           1485
with evil of the past. But if you still
are without shame before the face of men
reverence at least the flame that gives all life,
our Lord the Sun, and do not show unveiled

to him pollution such that neither land 1490
nor holy rain nor light of day can welcome. *(To a servant)*
Be quick and take him in. It is most decent
that only kin should see and hear the troubles
of kin.
*Oedipus:* I beg you, since you've torn me from 1495
my dreadful expectations and have come
in a most noble spirit to a man
that has used you vilely — do a thing for me.
I shall speak for your own good, not for my own.
*Creon:* What do you need that you would ask of me? 1500
*Oedipus:* Drive me from here with all the speed you can
to where I may not hear a human voice.
*Creon:* Be sure, I would have done this had not I
wished first of all to learn from the God the course
of action I should follow.
*Oedipus:* But his word 1505
has been quite clear to let the parricide,°
the sinner, die.
*Creon:* Yes, that indeed was said.
But in the present need we had best discover
what we should do.
*Oedipus:* And will you ask about
a man so wretched?
*Creon:* Now even you will trust 1510
the God.
*Oedipus:* So. I command you — and will beseech you —
to her that lies inside that house give burial
as you would have it; she is yours and rightly
you will perform the rites for her. For me —
never let this my father's city have me 1515
living a dweller in it. Leave me live
in the mountains where Cithaeron is, that's called
*my* mountain, which my mother and my father
while they were living would have made my tomb.
So I may die by their decree who sought 1520
indeed to kill me. Yet I know this much:
no sickness and no other thing will kill me.
I would not have been saved from death if not
for some strange evil fate. Well, let my fate
go where it will.
Creon, you need not care 1525
about my sons; they're men and so wherever
they are, they will not lack a livelihood.
But my two girls — so sad and pitiful —
whose table never stood apart from mine,
and everything I touched they always shared — 1530

---

1506 *parricide:* One who kills his parent or another close relative.

O Creon, have a thought for them! And most
I wish that you might suffer me to touch them
and sorrow with them.

> *(Enter Antigone and Ismene, Oedipus' two daughters.)*

O my lord! O true noble Creon! Can I
really be touching them, as when I saw?                                    1535
What shall I say?
Yes, I can hear them sobbing — my two darlings!
and Creon has had pity and has sent me
what I loved most?
Am I right?                                                               1540

*Creon:*  You're right: it was I gave you this
because I knew from old days how you loved them
as I see now.

*Oedipus:*          God bless you for it, Creon,
and may God guard you better on your road
than he did me!

                    O children,                                          1545
where are you? Come here, come to my hands,
a brother's hands which turned your father's eyes,
those bright eyes you knew once, to what you see,
a father seeing nothing, knowing nothing,
begetting you from his own source of life.                               1550
I weep for you — I cannot see your faces —
I weep when I think of the bitterness
there will be in your lives, how you must live
before the world. At what assemblages
of citizens will you make one? to what                                   1555
gay company will you go and not come home
in tears instead of sharing in the holiday?
And when you're ripe for marriage, who will he be,
the man who'll risk to take such infamy
as shall cling to my children, to bring hurt                             1560
on them and those that marry with them? What
curse is not there? "Your father killed his father
and sowed the seed where he had sprung himself
and begot you out of the womb that held him."
These insults you will hear. Then who will marry you?                    1565
No one, my children; clearly you are doomed
to waste away in barrenness unmarried.
Son of Menoeceus,° since you are all the father
left these two girls, and we, their parents, both
are dead to them — do not allow them wander                              1570
like beggars, poor and husbandless.
They are of your own blood.
And do not make them equal with myself
in wretchedness; for you can see them now

---

1568 *Son of Menoeceus:* Creon.

so young, so utterly alone, save for you only.                           1575
Touch my hand, noble Creon, and say yes.
If you were older, children, and were wiser,
there's much advice I'd give you. But as it is,
let this be what you pray: give me a life
wherever there is opportunity                                            1580
to live, and better life than was my father's.
*Creon:*  Your tears have had enough of scope; now go within the house.
*Oedipus:*  I must obey, though bitter of heart.
*Creon:*  In season, all is good.
*Oedipus:*  Do you know on what conditions I obey?
*Creon:*                                              You tell me them,     1585
     and I shall know them when I hear.
*Oedipus:*                                      That you shall send me out
     to live away from Thebes.
*Creon:*                            That gift you must ask of the God.
*Oedipus:*  But I'm now hated by the Gods.
*Creon:*                                       So quickly you'll obtain your prayer.
*Oedipus*:  You consent then?
*Creon:*                          What I do not mean, I do not use to say.
*Oedipus:*  Now lead me away from here.
*Creon:*                                    Let go the children, then, and come.   1590
*Oedipus:*  Do not take them from me.
*Creon:*                                  Do not seek to be master in everything,
     for the things you mastered did not follow you throughout your life.
                              *(As Creon and Oedipus go out.)*
*Chorus:*  You that live in my ancestral Thebes, behold this Oedipus, —
     him who knew the famous riddles and was a man most masterful;
     not a citizen who did not look with envy on his lot —                1595
     see him now and see the breakers of misfortune swallow him!
     Look upon that last day always. Count no mortal happy till
     he has passed the final limit of his life secure from pain.

## CONSIDERATIONS FOR CRITICAL THINKING AND WRITING

1. **FIRST RESPONSE.** How might a twenty-first-century reader identify with
   Oedipus's plight? What philosophic issues does Oedipus confront that remain
   relevant to humans today?

2. In the opening scene, what does the priest's speech reveal about how Oedipus
   has been regarded as a ruler of Thebes?

3. What do Oedipus's confrontations with Teiresias and Creon indicate about his
   character?

4. Aristotle defined a tragic flaw as consisting of "error and frailties." What errors
   does Oedipus make? What are his frailties?

5. What causes Oedipus's downfall? Is he simply a pawn in a predetermined
   game played by the gods? Can he be regarded as responsible for the suffering
   and death in the play?

6. Locate instances of dramatic irony in the play. How do they serve as foreshadowing?

7. Describe the function of the Chorus in this play. How does the Chorus's view of life and the gods differ from Jocasta's?

8. Trace the images of vision and blindness throughout the play. How are they related to the theme? Why does Oedipus blind himself instead of joining Jocasta in suicide?

9. What is your assessment of Oedipus at the end of the play? Was he foolish? Heroic? Fated? To what extent can your emotions concerning him be described as "pity and fear"?

10. CRITICAL STRATEGIES. Read the section on psychological criticism (p. 1386) in Chapter 42, "Critical Strategies for Reading," and Sigmund Freud's "On the Oedipus Complex" (p. 1041). Given that the Oedipus complex is a well-known term used in psychoanalysis, what does it mean? Does the concept offer any insights into the conflicts dramatized in the play?

### Connections to Other Selections

1. Consider the endings of *Oedipus the King* and William Shakespeare's *Othello* (p. 1055). What feelings do you have about these endings? Are they irredeemably unhappy? Is there anything that suggests hope for the future at the ends of these plays?

2. Sophocles does not include violence in his plays; any bloodshed occurs offstage. Compare and contrast the effects of this strategy with the use of violence in *Othello*.

3. Write an essay explaining why *Oedipus the King* cannot be considered a realistic play in the way that August Wilson's *Fences* (p. 1329) can be.

## Perspectives

### ARISTOTLE (384–322 B.C.E.)

## *On Tragic Character*   ca. 340 B.C.E.

Now since in the finest kind of tragedy the structure should be complex and not simple, and since it should also be a representation of terrible and piteous events (that being the special mark of this type of imitation), in the first place, it is evident that good men ought not to be shown passing from happiness to misfortune, for this does not inspire either pity or fear, but only revulsion; nor evil men rising from ill fortune to prosperity, for this is the most untragic plot of all — it lacks every requirement, in that it neither elicits human sympathy nor stirs pity or fear. And again, neither should an extremely wicked man be seen falling from prosperity into misfortune, for a plot so constructed might indeed call forth human sympathy, but would not excite pity or fear, since the first is felt for a person whose misfortune is undeserved and the second for someone like ourselves — pity for the man suffering undeservedly, fear for the man like ourselves — and hence neither pity nor fear would be aroused in this case. We are left with the man whose place is between these extremes. Such is the man who on the one hand is not preeminent in virtue and justice, and yet on the other hand does not fall into misfortune through vice or depravity, but falls because of some mistake; one among the number of the highly renowned and prosperous, such as Oedipus . . . and other famous men from families like [his].

It follows that the plot which achieves excellence will necessarily be single in outcome and not, as some say, double, and will consist in a change of fortune, not to prosperity from misfortune, but the opposite, from prosperity to misfortune, occasioned not by depravity, but by some great mistake on the part of one who is either such as I have described or better than this rather than worse. What actually has taken place has confirmed this; for though at first the poets accepted whatever myths came to hand, today the finest tragedies are founded upon the stories of only a few houses . . . and such . . . as have chanced to suffer terrible things or to do them. So then, tragedy having this construction is the finest kind of tragedy from an artistic point of view. And consequently those persons fall into the same error who bring it as a charge against Euripides° that this is what he does in his tragedies and that most of his plays have unhappy endings. For this is in fact the right procedure, as I have said; and the best proof is that on the stage and in the dramatic contests, plays of this kind seem the most tragic, provided they are successfully worked out, and Euripides, even if in everything else his management is faulty, seems at any rate to be the most tragic of the poets.

Second to this is the kind of plot that some persons place first, that which like the Odyssey° has a double structure and ends in opposite ways for the better characters and the worse. If it seems to be first, that is attributable to the weakness of the audience, since the poets only follow their lead and compose the kind of plays the spectators want. The pleasure it gives, however, is not that which comes from tragedy, but is rather the pleasure proper to comedy; for in comedy those who in the legend are the worst of enemies . . . end by leaving the scene as friends, and nobody is killed by anybody. . . .

With regard to the characters there are four things to aim at. First and foremost is that the characters be good. The personages will have character if, as aforesaid, they reveal in speech or in action what their moral choices are, and a good character will be one whose choices are good. It is possible to portray goodness in every class of persons; a woman may be good and a slave may be good, though perhaps as a class women are inferior and slaves utterly base. The second requisite is to make the character appropriate. Thus it is possible to portray any character as manly, but inappropriate for a female character to be manly or formidable in the way I mean. Third is to make the characters lifelike, which is something different from making them good and appropriate as described above. Fourth is to

---

*Euripides:* Fifth-century B.C.E. Greek playwright whose tragedies include *Electra, Medea,* and *Alcestis.* *Odyssey:* The epic by the ancient Greek poet Homer that chronicles the voyage home from the Trojan War of Odysseus (also known as Ulysses).

make them consistent. Even if the person being imitated is inconsistent and this is what the character is supposed to be, he should nevertheless be portrayed as consistently inconsistent. . . .

In the characters and in the plot-construction alike, one must strive for that which 5 is either necessary or probable, so that whatever a character of any kind says or does may be the sort of thing such a character will inevitably or probably say or do and the events of the plot may follow one after another either inevitably or with probability. (Obviously, then, the *dénouement* of the plot should arise from the plot itself and not be brought about "from the machine." . . . The machine is to be used for matters lying outside the drama, either antecedents of the action which a human being cannot know, or things subsequent to the action that have to be prophesied and announced; for we accept it that the gods see everything. Within the events of the plot itself, however, there should be nothing unreasonable, or if there is, it should be kept outside the play proper as is done in the *Oedipus* of Sophocles.)

Inasmuch as tragedy is an imitation of persons who are better than the average, the example of good portrait-painters should be followed. These, while reproducing the distinctive appearance of their subjects in a recognizable likeness, make them handsomer in the picture than they are in reality. Similarly the poet when he comes to imitate men who are irascible or easygoing or have other defects of character should depict them as such and yet as good men at the same time.

From *Poetics,* translated by James Hutton

### Considerations for Critical Thinking and Writing

1. Why does Aristotle insist that both virtuous and depraved characters are unsuitable as tragic figures? What kind of person constitutes a tragic character according to him?

2. Aristotle says that characters should be "lifelike" (par. 4), but he also points out that characters should be made "handsomer . . . than they are in reality" (par. 6). Is this a contradiction? Explain why or why not.

## Sigmund Freud (1856–1939)

## *On the Oedipus Complex*   1900

If *Oedipus Rex* moves a modern audience no less than it did the contemporary Greek one, the explanation can only be that its effect does not lie in the contrast between destiny and human will, but is to be looked for in the particular nature of the material on which that contrast is exemplified. There must be something which makes a voice within us ready to recognize the compelling force of destiny in the *Oedipus.* . . . His destiny moves us only because it might have been ours — because the oracle laid the same curse upon us before our birth as upon him. It is the fate of all of us, perhaps, to direct our first sexual impulse toward our mother and our first hatred and our first murderous wish against our father. Our dreams convince us that this is so. King Oedipus, who slew his father Laïus and married his mother

Jocasta, merely shows us the fulfillment of our own childhood wishes. But, more fortunate than he, we have meanwhile succeeded, in so far as we have not become psychoneurotics, in detaching our sexual impulses from our mothers and in forgetting our jealousy of our fathers. Here is one in whom these primeval wishes of our childhood have been fulfilled, and we shrink back from him with the whole force of the repression by which those wishes have since that time been held down within us. While the poet, as he unravels the past, brings to light the guilt of Oedipus, he is at the same time compelling us to recognize our own inner minds, in which those same impulses, though suppressed, are still to be found. The contrast with which the closing Chorus leaves us confronted —

> . . . Fix on Oedipus your eyes,
> Who resolved the dark enigma, noblest champion and most wise.
> Like a star his envied fortune mounted beaming far and wide:
> Now he sinks in seas of anguish, whelmed beneath a raging tide . . .[1]

— strikes as a warning at ourselves and our pride, at us who since our childhood have grown so wise and so mighty in our own eyes. Like Oedipus, we live in ignorance of these wishes, repugnant to morality, which have been forced upon us by Nature, and after their revelation we may all of us well seek to close our eyes to the scenes of our childhood.

There is an unmistakable indication in the text of Sophocles' tragedy itself that the legend of Oedipus sprang from some primeval dream material which had as its content the distressing disturbance of a child's relation to his parents owing to the first stirrings of sexuality. At a point when Oedipus, though he is not yet enlightened, has begun to feel troubled by his recollection of the oracle, Jocasta consoles him by referring to a dream which many people dream, though, as she thinks, it has no meaning:

> Many a man ere now in dreams hath lain
> With her who bare him. He hath least annoy
> Who with such omens troubleth not his mind.[2]

Today, just as then, many men dream of having sexual relations with their mothers, and speak of the fact with indignation and astonishment. It is clearly the key to the tragedy and the complement to the dream of the dreamer's father being dead. The story of Oedipus is the reaction of the imagination to these two typical dreams. And just as these dreams, when dreamt by adults, are accompanied by feelings of repulsion, so too the legend must include horror and self-punishment. Its further modification originates once again in a misconceived secondary revision of the material, which has sought to exploit it for theological purposes. . . . The attempt to harmonize divine omnipotence with human responsibility must naturally fail in connection with this subject matter just as with any other.

From Interpretation of Dreams, translated by James Strachey

---

[1] Lewis Campbell's translation, lines 1524ff. [in *The Compact Bedford Introduction to Literature,* lines 1593–1596].

[2] Lewis Campbell's translation, lines 982ff. [in *The Compact Bedford Introduction to Literature,* lines 1043–1046].

CONSIDERATIONS FOR CRITICAL THINKING AND WRITING

1. Read the section on psychological criticism in Chapter 42, "Critical Strate-gies for Reading" (p. 1386), for additional information about Freud's theory concerning the Oedipus complex. Explain whether you agree or disagree that Freud's approach offers the "key to the tragedy" of *Oedipus the King*.

2. How does Freud's view of tragic character differ from Aristotle's?

## MURIEL RUKEYSER (1913–1980)

### *On* Oedipus the King    1973

*Myth*

Long afterward, Oedipus, old and blinded, walked the
roads.       He smelled a familiar smell.       It was
the Sphinx.       Oedipus said, "I want to ask one question.
Why didn't I recognize my mother?"       "You gave the
wrong answer," said the Sphinx.       "But that was what          5
made everything possible," said Oedipus.       "No," she said.
"When I asked, What walks on four legs in the morning,
two at noon, and three in the evening, you answered,
Man.       You didn't say anything about woman."
"When you say Man," said Oedipus, "you include women          10
too. Everyone knows that."       She said, "That's what
you think."

CONSIDERATIONS FOR CRITICAL THINKING AND WRITING

1. What elements of the Oedipus story does Rukeyser allude to in the poem?

2. To what does the title of Rukeyser's poem, "Myth," refer? How does the word *myth* carry more than one meaning?

3. This poem is amusing, but its ironic ending points to a serious theme. What is it? Does Sophocles' play address any of the issues raised in the poem?

## DAVID WILES

### *On* Oedipus the King *as a Political Play*    2000

*Oedipus* becomes a political play when we focus on the interaction of actor and chorus, and see how the chorus form a democratic mass jury. Each sequence of dialogue takes the form of a contest for the chorus' sympathy, with Oedipus sliding from the role of prosecutor to that of defendant, and each choral dance offers a provisional verdict. After Oedipus' set-to with Teiresias the soothsayer, the chorus decide to trust Oedipus on the basis of his past record; after his argu-ment with his brother-in-law Creon, the chorus show their distress and urge com-promise. Once Oedipus has confessed to a killing and Jocasta has declared that oracles have no force, the chorus are forced to think about political tyranny, torn between respect for divine law and trust in their rulers. In the next dance they assume that the contradiction is resolved and Oedipus has turned out to be the son of a god. Finally a slave's evidence reveals that the man most honoured by society is in fact the least to be envied. The political implications are clear: there is no space in democratic society for such as Oedipus. Athenians, like the chorus of the play, must reject the temptation to believe one man can calculate the future.

From *Greek Theatre Performance: An Introduction*

### CONSIDERATIONS FOR CRITICAL THINKING AND WRITING

1. Consider one of the scenes mentioned by Wiles, and discuss in detail how "the chorus form a democratic mass jury" that judges Oedipus.

2. Discuss the "political implications" of the play that, according to Wiles, suggest "there is no space in democratic society for such as Oedipus."

# 37

# A Study of
# William Shakespeare

All the world's a stage,
And all the men and women
    merely players:
They have their exits and their
    entrances;
And one man in his time plays
    many parts . . .
— WILLIAM SHAKESPEARE

Universal History Archive/Getty
Images.

Bettmann/Getty Images.

Shakespeare — the nearest thing
in incarnation to the eye of God.
— SIR LAURENCE OLIVIER

Although relatively little is known about William Shakespeare's life, his writings reveal him to have been an extraordinary man. His vitality, compassion, and insights are evident in his broad range of characters, who have fascinated generations of audiences, and his powerful use of the English language, which has been celebrated since his death nearly four centuries ago. Ben Jonson, his contemporary, rightly claimed that "he was not of an age, but for all time!" Shakespeare's plays have been produced so often and his writings read so widely that quotations from them have woven their way into our everyday conversations. If you have ever experienced "fear and trembling" because there was "something in the wind" or discovered that it was "a foregone conclusion" that you would "make a virtue of necessity," then it wouldn't be quite accurate for you to say that Shakespeare "was Greek to me" because these phrases come, respectively, from his plays *Much Ado about Nothing, The Comedy of Errors, Othello, The Two Gentlemen of Verona,* and *Julius Caesar.* Many more examples could be cited, but it is enough to say that Shakespeare's art endures. His words may give us only an oblique glimpse of his life, but they continue to give us back the experience of our own lives.

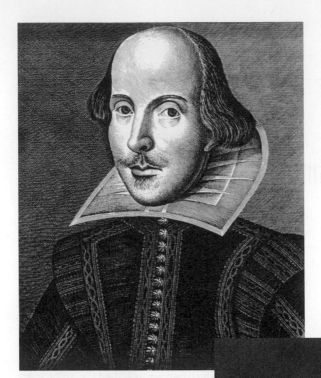

**"First Folio" portrait** (top). The image of William Shakespeare above is a portrait included in the *First Folio*, a collected edition of Shakespeare's plays published seven years after his death.

**"Chandos" portrait engraving** (middle). This engraving is of an image painted during Shakespeare's lifetime known as the "Chandos portrait," rumored to have been painted by Shakespeare's friend and fellow actor Richard Burbage.

**Shakespeare's signature** (bottom). The signature shown here is one of the bard's six authenticated signatures in existence and is from his last will and testament.

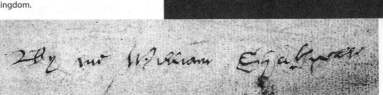

Shakespeare was born in Stratford-on-Avon on or about April 23, 1564. His father, an important citizen who held several town offices, married a woman from a prominent family; however, when their son was only a teenager, the family's financial situation became precarious. Shakespeare probably attended the Stratford grammar school, but no records of either his schooling or his early youth exist. As limited as his education was, it is clear that he was for his time a learned man. At the age of eighteen, he struck out on his own and married the twenty-six-year-old Anne Hathaway, who gave birth to a daughter in 1583 and twins, a boy and a girl, in 1585. Before he was twenty-one, Shakespeare had a wife and three children to support.

What his life was like for the next seven years is not known, but there is firm evidence that by 1592 he was in London enjoying some success as both an actor and a playwright. By 1594 he had also established himself as a poet with two lengthy poems, *Venus and Adonis* and *The Rape of Lucrece*. But it was in the theater that he made his living and his strongest reputation. He was well connected with a successful troupe first known as the Lord Chamberlain's Men; they built the famous Globe Theatre in 1599. Later this company, because of the patronage of King James, came to be known as the King's Men. Writing plays for the company throughout his career, Shakespeare also became one of its principal shareholders, an arrangement that allowed him to prosper in London as well as in his native Stratford, where in 1597 he bought a fine house called New Place. In about 1611 he retired there with his family, although he continued writing plays. He died on April 23, 1616, and was buried at Holy Trinity Church in Stratford.

The documented details of Shakespeare's life provide barely enough information for a newspaper obituary. But if his activities remain largely unknown, his writings — among them thirty-seven plays and 154 sonnets — more than compensate for that loss. Plenty of authors have produced more work, but no writer has created so much literature that has been so universally admired. Within twenty-five years Shakespeare's dramatic works included *Hamlet*, *Macbeth*, *King Lear*, *Othello*, *Julius Caesar*, *Richard III*, *Henry IV*, *Romeo and Juliet*, *Love's Labour's Lost*, *A Midsummer Night's Dream*, *The Tempest*, *Twelfth Night*, and *Measure for Measure*. These plays represent a broad range of characters and actions conveyed in poetic language that reveals human nature as well as the author's genius.

## SHAKESPEARE'S THEATER

Drama languished in Europe after the fall of Rome during the fifth and sixth centuries. From about 400 to 900 C.E. almost no record of dramatic productions exists except for those of minstrels and other entertainers, such as acrobats and jugglers, who traveled through the countryside. The Catholic church was instrumental in suppressing drama because the theater — represented by the excesses of Roman productions — was seen as subversive. No state-sponsored festivals brought people together in huge theaters the way they had in Greek and Roman times.

In the tenth century, however, the church helped revive theater by incorporating dialogues into the Mass as a means of dramatizing portions of the Gospels. These brief dialogues developed into more elaborate mystery plays, miracle plays, and morality plays, anonymous works that were created primarily to inculcate religious principles rather than to entertain. But these works also marked the reemergence of relatively large dramatic productions. *Mystery plays* dramatize stories from the Bible, such as the Creation, the Fall of Adam and Eve, or the Crucifixion. The most highly regarded surviving example is *The Second Shepherd's Play* (ca. 1400), which dramatizes Christ's nativity. *Miracle plays* are based on the lives of saints. An extant play of the late fifteenth century, for example, is titled *Saint Mary Magdalene*. *Morality plays* present allegorical stories in which virtues and vices are personified to teach humanity how to achieve salvation. *Everyman* (ca. 1500), the most famous example, has as its central conflict every person's struggle to avoid the sins that lead to hell and practice the virtues that are rewarded in heaven.

The clergy who performed these plays gave way to trade guilds that presented them outside the church on stages featuring scenery and costumed characters. The plays' didactic content was gradually abandoned in favor of broad humor and worldly concerns. Thus by the sixteenth century religious drama had been replaced largely by secular drama.

Because theatrical productions were no longer sponsored and financed by the church or trade guilds during Shakespeare's lifetime, playwrights had to figure out ways to draw audiences willing to pay for entertainment. This necessitated some simple but important changes. Somehow, people had to be prevented from seeing a production unless they paid. Hence an enclosed space with controlled access was created. In addition, the plays had to change frequently enough to keep audiences returning, and this resulted in more experienced actors and playwrights sensitive to their audiences' tastes and interests. Plays compelling enough to attract audiences had to employ powerful writing brought to life by convincing actors in entertaining productions. Shakespeare always wrote his dramas for the stage — for audiences who would see and hear the characters. The conventions of the theater for which he wrote are important, then, for appreciating and understanding his plays. Detailed information about Elizabethan theater (theater during the reign of Elizabeth I, from 1558 to 1603) is less than abundant, but historians have been able to piece together a good sense of what theaters were like from sources such as drawings, building contracts, and stage directions.

Early performances of various kinds took place in the courtyards of inns and taverns. These secular entertainments attracted people of all classes. To the dismay of London officials, such gatherings were also settings for the illegal activities of brawlers, thieves, and sex workers. To avoid licensing regulations, some theaters were constructed outside the city's limits. The Globe, for instance, built by the Lord Chamberlain's Company, with which Shakespeare was closely associated, was located on the south bank of the Thames River. Regardless of the play, an Elizabethan theatergoer was likely to have an exciting time. Playwrights understood the varied nature of their audiences, so the plays appealed to a broad range of sensibilities and tastes.

Philosophy and poetry rubbed shoulders with violence and sexual jokes, and somehow all were made compatible.

Physically, Elizabethan theaters resembled the courtyards where they originated, but the theaters could accommodate more people — perhaps as many as twenty-five hundred. The exterior of a theater building was many-sided or round and enclosed a yard that was only partially roofed over, to take advantage of natural light. The interior walls consisted of three galleries of seats looking onto a platform stage that extended from the rear wall. These seats were sheltered from the weather and more comfortable than the area in front of the stage, which was known as the *pit*. Here "groundlings" paid a penny to stand and watch the performance. Despite the large number of spectators, the theater created an intimate atmosphere because the audience closely surrounded the stage on three sides.

This arrangement produced two theatrical conventions: asides and soliloquies. An ***aside*** is a speech directed only to the audience. It makes the audience privy to a character's thoughts, allowing them to perceive ironies and intrigues that other characters know nothing about. In a large performing space, such as a Greek amphitheater, asides would be unconvincing because they would have to be declaimed loudly to be heard, but they were well suited to Elizabethan theaters. A ***soliloquy*** is a speech delivered while an actor is alone on the stage; like an aside, it reveals a character's state of mind. Hamlet's "To be or not to be" speech is the most famous example of a soliloquy.

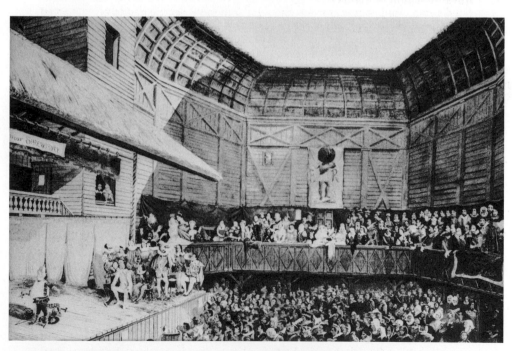

**A Conjectural Reconstruction of the Globe Theatre, 1599–1613.**
Bettmann/Getty Images.

The Elizabethan platform stage was large enough — approximately twenty-five feet deep and forty feet wide — to allow a wide variety of actions, ranging from festive banquets to bloody battles. Sections of the floor could be opened or removed to create, for instance, the gravediggers' scene in *Hamlet* or to allow characters to exit through trapdoors. At the rear of the platform an inner stage was covered by curtains that could be drawn to reveal an interior setting, such as a bedroom or tomb. The curtains were also a natural location for a character to hide in order to overhear conversations. On each side of the curtains were doors through which characters entered and exited. An upper stage could be used as a watchtower, a castle wall, or a balcony. Although most of the action occurred on the main platform stage, there were opportunities for fluid movements from one acting area to another, providing a variety of settings.

These settings were not, however, elaborately indicated by scenery or props. A scene might change when one group of characters left the stage and another entered. A table and some chairs could be carried on quickly to suggest a tavern. But the action was not interrupted for set changes. Instead, the characters' speeches often identify the location of a scene. (In modern editions of Shakespeare's plays, editors indicate in brackets the scene breaks, settings, and movements of actors not identified in the original manuscripts to help readers keep track of things.) Today's performances of the plays frequently use more elaborate settings and props. But Shakespeare's need to paint his scenery with words resulted in many poetic descriptions. Here is one of moonlight from *Merchant of Venice*:

> How sweet the moonlight sleeps upon this bank!
> Here will we sit and let the sounds of music
> Creep in our ears. Soft stillness and the night
> Become the touches of sweet harmony.

Although the settings were spare and the props mostly limited to what an actor carried onto the stage (a sword, a document, a shovel), Elizabethan costuming was an elaborate visual treat that identified the characters. Moreover, because women were not permitted to act in the theater, their roles were played by young boys dressed in female costumes. In addition, elaborate sound effects were used to create atmosphere. A flourish of trumpets might accompany the entrance of a king; small cannons might be heard during a battle; thunder might punctuate a storm. In short, Elizabethan theater was alive with sights and sounds, but at the center of the stage was the playwright's language; that's where the magic began.

## THE RANGE OF SHAKESPEARE'S DRAMA: HISTORY, COMEDY, AND TRAGEDY

Shakespeare's plays fall into three basic categories: histories, comedies, and tragedies. Broadly speaking, a history play is any drama based on historical materials. In this case, Shakespeare's *Antony and Cleopatra* and *Julius Caesar* would fit the definition, since they feature historical figures. More specifically, though, a *history play* is a British play based primarily on Raphael Holinshed's *Chronicles of England, Scotland, and Ireland* (1578). This account of British history was popular toward the end of the sixteenth century because of the patriotic pride that was produced by the British defeat of the Spanish Armada in 1588, and it was an important source for a series of plays Shakespeare wrote treating the reigns of British kings from Richard II to Henry VIII. The political subject matter of these plays both entertained audiences and instructed them in virtues and vices involved in England's past efforts to overcome civil war and disorder. Ambition, deception, and treason were of more than historical interest. Shakespeare's audiences saw these plays about the fifteenth century as ways of sorting through the meanings of both the calamities of the past and the uncertainties of the present.

Although Shakespeare used Holinshed's *Chronicles* as a source, he did not hesitate to make changes for dramatic purposes. In *1 Henry IV*, for example, he ages Henry IV to contrast him with the youthful Prince Hal, and he makes Hotspur younger than he actually was to have him serve as a foil to the prince. The serious theme of Hal's growth into the kind of man who would make an ideal king is counterweighted by Shakespeare's comic creation of Falstaff, that good-humored "huge hill of flesh" filled with delightful contradictions. Falstaff had historic antecedents, but the true source of his identity is the imagination of Shakespeare, a writer who was, after all, a dramatist first.

**Comedy** is a strong element in *1 Henry IV*, but the play's overall tone is serious. Falstaff's behavior ultimately gives way to the measured march of English history. While Shakespeare encourages us to laugh at some of the participants, we are not invited to laugh at the history of English monarchies. Comedy even appears in Shakespeare's tragedies, as in Hamlet's jests with the gravediggers or in Emilia's biting remarks in *Othello*. This use of comedy is called **comic relief**, a humorous scene or incident that alleviates tension in an otherwise serious work. In many instances these moments enhance the thematic significance of the story in addition to providing laughter. When Hamlet jokes with the gravediggers, we laugh, but something hauntingly serious about the humor also intensifies our more serious emotions.

A true comedy, however, lacks a tragedy's sense that some great disaster will finally descend on the protagonist. There are conflicts and obstacles that must be confronted, but in comedy the characters delight us by overcoming whatever initially thwarts them. We can laugh at their misfortunes because we are confident that everything will turn out fine in the end. Shakespearean comedy tends to follow this general principle; it begins with problems and ends with their resolution.

Shakespeare's comedies are called **romantic comedies** because they typically involve lovers whose hearts are set on each other but whose lives are complicated by disapproving parents, deceptions, jealousies, illusions, confused identities, disguises, or other misunderstandings. Conflicts are present, but they are more amusing than threatening. This lightness is apparent in some of the comedies' titles: the conflict in a play such as *A Midsummer Night's Dream* is, in a sense, *Much Ado about Nothing* — *As You Like It* in a comedy. Shakespeare orchestrates the problems and confusion that typify the initial plotting of a romantic comedy into harmonious wedding arrangements in the final scenes. In these comedies life is a celebration, a feast that always satisfies, because the generosity of the humor leaves us with a revived appetite for life's surprising possibilities. Discord and misunderstanding give way to concord and love. Marriage symbolizes a pledge that life itself is renewable, so we are left with a sense of new beginnings.

Although a celebration of life, comedy is also frequently used as a vehicle for criticizing human affairs. **Satire** casts a critical eye on vices and follies by holding them up to ridicule — usually to point out an absurdity so that it can be avoided or corrected. In *Twelfth Night* Malvolio is satirized for his priggishness and pomposity. He thinks himself better than almost everyone around him, but Shakespeare reveals him to be comic as well as pathetic. We come to understand what Malvolio will apparently never comprehend: that no one can take him as seriously as he takes himself. Polonius is subjected to a similar kind of scrutiny in *Hamlet*.

Malvolio's ambitious efforts to attract Olivia's affections are rendered absurd by Shakespeare's use of both high and low comedy. **High comedy** consists of verbal wit, while **low comedy** is generally associated with physical action and is less intellectual. Through puns and witty exchanges, Shakespeare's high comedy displays Malvolio's inconsistencies of character. His self-importance is deflated by low comedy. We are treated to a *farce*, a form of humor based on exaggerated, improbable incongruities, when the staid Malvolio is tricked into wearing bizarre clothing and behaving like a fool to win Olivia. Our laughter is Malvolio's pain, but though he has been "notoriously abus'd" and he vows in the final scene to be "reveng'd on the whole pack" of laughing conspirators who have tricked him, the play ends on a light note. Indeed, it concludes with a song, the last line of which reminds us of the predominant tone of the play as well as the nature of comedy: "And we'll strive to please you every day."

**Tragedy**, in contrast, does not promise peace and contentment. The basic characteristics of tragedy have already been outlined in the context of Greek drama (see Chapter 36). Like Greek tragic heroes, Shakespeare's protagonists are exceptional human beings whose stature makes their misfortune all the more dramatic. These characters pay a high price for their actions. Oedipus's search for the killer of Laios, Hamlet's agonized conviction that "The time is out of joint," and Othello's willingness to doubt his wife's fidelity all lead to irreversible results. Comic plots are largely free of this sense of inevitability. Instead of the festive mood that prevails once the characters in a comedy recognize their true connection to each other, tragedy gives us dark reflections that emanate from suffering. The laughter of comedy is a shared experience, a recognition of human likeness, but suffering estranges tragic heroes from the world around them.

Some of the wrenching differences between comedy and tragedy can be experienced in *Othello*. Although this play is a tragedy, Shakespeare includes in its plot many of the ingredients associated with comedy. For a time, it seems possible that Othello and Desdemona will overcome the complications of a disapproving father, along with the seemingly minor deceptions, awkward misperceptions, and tender illusions that hover around them. But in *Othello* marriage is not a sign of concord displacing discord; instead, love and marriage mark the beginning of the tragic action.

Another important difference between tragedy and comedy is the way characters are presented. The tragic protagonist is portrayed as a remarkable individual whose unique qualities compel us with their power and complexity. Macbeth is not simply a murderer, nor is Othello merely a jealous husband. But despite their extreme passions, behavior, and even crimes, we identify with tragic heroes in ways that we do not with comic characters. We can laugh at pretentious fools, smug hypocrites, clumsy oafs, and thwarted lovers because we see them from a distance. They are amusing precisely because their problems are not ours; we recognize them as types instead of as ourselves (or so we think). No reader of *Twelfth Night* worries about Sir Toby Belch's excessive drinking; he is a cheerful "sot" whose passion for ale is cause for celebration rather than concern. Shakespeare's comedy is sometimes disturbing — Malvolio's character certainly is — but it is never devastating. Tragic heroes do confront devastation; they command our respect and compassion because they act in spite of terrifying risks. Their triumph is measured not by the attainment of what they seek but by the wisdom that defeat imposes on them.

## A NOTE ON READING SHAKESPEARE

Readers who have had no previous experience with Shakespeare's language may find it initially daunting. They might well ask whether people ever talked the way, for example, Hamlet does in his most famous soliloquy:

> To be, or not to be: that is the question:
> Whether 'tis nobler in the mind to suffer
> The slings and arrows of outrageous fortune,
> Or to take arms against a sea of troubles,
> And by opposing end them?

People did not talk like this in Elizabethan times. Hamlet speaks poetry. Shakespeare might have had him say something like this: "The most important issue one must confront is whether the pain that life inevitably creates should be passively accepted or resisted." But Shakespeare chose poetry to reveal the depth and complexity of Hamlet's experience. This heightened language is used to clarify rather than obscure his characters' thoughts. Shakespeare has Hamlet, as well as many other characters, speak in prose too, but in general his plays are written in poetry. If you keep in mind that Shakespeare's dialogue is not typically intended to imitate everyday speech, it should be easier to understand that his language is more than simply a vehicle for expressing the action of the play.

Here are a few practical suggestions to enhance your understanding of and pleasure in reading Shakespeare's plays.

1. Keep track of the characters by referring to the *dramatis personae* (characters) listed and briefly described at the beginning of each play.
2. Remember that poetic language deserves to be read slowly and carefully. A difficult passage can sometimes be better understood if it's read aloud. Don't worry if every line isn't absolutely clear to you at first.
3. Pay attention to the annotations, which explain unfamiliar words, phrases, and allusions in the text. These can be distracting, but they are sometimes necessary to determine the basic meaning of a passage.
4. As you read each scene, try to imagine how it would be played on a stage.
5. If you find the reading especially difficult, try listening to a recording of the play. (Many college libraries have recordings of Shakespeare's plays, and the Internet might be useful for this purpose, too.) Allowing professional actors to do the reading aloud for you can enrich your imaginative reconstruction of the action and characters. Hearing a play can help you with subsequent readings of it.
6. After reading the play, view a recording of a performance. It is important to view the performance *after* your reading, though, so that your own mental re-creation of the play is not short-circuited by a director's production.

And finally, to quote Hamlet, "Be not too tame . . . let your own discretion be your tutor." Read Shakespeare's work as best you can; it warrants such careful attention not because the language and characters are difficult to understand but because they offer so much to enjoy.

## Othello, the Moor of Venice

*Othello* has compelled audiences since it was first produced in 1604. Its power is as simple and as complex as the elemental emotions it dramatizes; the play ebbs and flows with the emotional energy derived from the characters' struggles with love and hatred, good and evil, trust and jealousy, appearance and reality. These conflicts are played out on a domestic scale rather than on some metaphysical level. Anyone who has ever been in love will empathize with Othello and Desdemona. They embody a love story gone horribly — tragically — wrong.

Although the plot of *Othello* is filled with Iago's intrigues and a series of opaque mysteries for Othello, it moves swiftly and precisely to its catastrophic ending as the tragedy relentlessly claims its victims. On one level the plot is simple. As the Moorish general of the Venetian army, Othello chooses Cassio to serve as his lieutenant, a selection Iago resents and decides to subvert. To discredit Cassio, Iago poisons Othello's faith in his wife, Desdemona, by falsely insinuating that she and Cassio are having an affair. Through a series of cleverly demonic manipulations, Iago succeeds in convincing Othello of his wife's infidelity and his lieutenant's betrayal. Believing these lies, Othello insists on taking his revenge.

If the plot of *Othello* is relatively direct and simple in its focus on Iago's manipulation of events, the play's major characters are considerably more complex. Love and jealousy are central in *Othello*. Othello's virtues of openness and trust cause him to experience betrayal as intensely as he does love. He is distinguished by his nobility, bravery, strength, and deep sense of honor, but he is also vulnerable to the doubts Iago raises owing to his race ("I am black") and marginal status in Venetian society.

Iago, whose motivations are much deeper and more mysterious than his maneuvering for a coveted lieutenancy, personifies a nearly inexplicable evil in the play. Just as Desdemona's nature seems to be all goodness, Iago's is malignant destruction. His profound villainy both horrifies and fascinates us: How can he be what he is? He thrives on ambition, envy, deception, jealousy, and doubt. Although he commands absolutely no respect, he holds our attention because of his cunning duplicity.

The play is finally, however, Othello's story. As we watch him be seduced by Iago's veiled hints and seeming confidences, we see how his trusting nature is inextricably related to his propensity to suspect Desdemona. Iago plays on the complexity and paradox of Othello's character and manipulates those tensions to keep him off balance and blind to the truth of Desdemona's faithfulness. Ultimately, though, Othello must take responsibility for the destruction of his love, a responsibility that is both his tragedy and redemption.

## WILLIAM SHAKESPEARE (1564–1616)
### *Othello, the Moor of Venice*  1604

THE NAMES OF THE ACTORS

*Othello, the Moor*
*Brabantio,* [a Venetian senator,] father to Desdemona
*Cassio,* an honorable lieutenant [to Othello]
*Iago,* [Othello's ancient,] a villain
*Roderigo,* a gulled gentleman
*Duke of Venice*
*Senators* [of Venice]
*Montano,* governor of Cyprus
*Lodovico and Gratiano,* [kinsmen to Brabantio,] two noble Venetians
*Sailors*
*Clowns*
*Desdemona,* wife to Othello
*Emilia,* wife to Iago
*Bianca,* a courtesan
*[Messenger, Herald, Officers, Venetian Gentlemen, Musicians, Attendants*

SCENE: *Venice and Cyprus]*

# ACT I

SCENE I: *A street in Venice.*

*Enter Roderigo and Iago.*

*Roderigo:* Tush, never tell me! I take it much unkindly
    That thou, Iago, who hast had my purse
    As if the strings were thine, shouldst know of this.°
*Iago:* 'Sblood,° but you'll not hear me!
    If ever I did dream of such a matter,             5
    Abhor me.
*Roderigo:* Thou told'st me thou didst hold him in thy hate.
*Iago:* Despise me if I do not. Three great ones of the city,
    In personal suit to make me his lieutenant,
    Off-capped to him;° and, by the faith of man,       10
    I know my price; I am worth no worse a place.
    But he, as loving his own pride and
        purposes,
    Evades them with a bombast
        circumstance.°
    Horribly stuffed with epithets of war;
    [And, in conclusion,]                     15
    Nonsuits° my mediators; for, "Certes,"
        says he,
    "I have already chose my officer."
    And what was he?
    Forsooth, a great arithmetician,°
    One Michael Cassio, a Florentine           20
    (A fellow almost damned in a fair wife°)
    That never set a squadron in the field,
    Nor the division of a battle knows
    More than a spinster; unless the bookish
        theoric,
    Wherein the togèd consuls can propose       25
    As masterly as he. Mere prattle without
        practice
    Is all his soldiership. But he, sir, had th' election;
    And I (of whom his eyes had seen the proof
    At Rhodes, at Cyprus, and on other grounds
    Christian and heathen) must be belee'd and calmed°     30
    By debitor and creditor; this counter-caster,°
    He, in good time, must his lieutenant be,
    And I — God bless the mark! — his Moorship's ancient.°

---

**Act I, Scene I.**   3 *this:* i.e., Desdemona's elopement.   4 *'Sblood:* By God's blood.   10 *him:* i.e., Othello.   13 *a bombast circumstance:* Pompous circumlocutions.   16 *Nonsuits:* Rejects. 19 *arithmetician:* Theoretician.   21 *almost … wife:* (An obscure allusion; Cassio is unmarried, but see IV.i.114).   30 *belee'd and calmed:* Left in the lurch.   31 *counter-caster:* Bookkeeper. 33 *ancient:* Ensign.

*Roderigo:* By heaven, I rather would have been his hangman.
*Iago:* Why, there's no remedy; 'tis the curse of service.       35
    Preferment goes by letter and affection,°
    And not by old gradation, where each second
    Stood heir to th' first. Now, sir, be judge yourself,
    Whether I in any just term am affined°
    To love the Moor.
*Roderigo:*           I would not follow him then.       40
*Iago:* O, sir, content you;
    I follow him to serve my turn upon him.
    We cannot all be masters, nor all masters
    Cannot be truly followed. You shall mark
    Many a duteous and knee-crooking knave       45
    That, doting on his own obsequious bondage,
    Wears out his time, much like his master's ass,
    For naught but provender; and when he's old, cashiered.°
    Whip me such honest knaves! Others there are
    Who, trimmed° in forms and visages of duty,       50
    Keep yet their hearts attending on themselves;
    And, throwing but shows of service on their lords,
    Do well thrive by them, and when they have lined their coats,
    Do themselves homage. These fellows have some soul;
    And such a one do I profess myself. For, sir,       55
    It is as sure as you are Roderigo,
    Were I the Moor, I would not be Iago.
    In following him, I follow but myself;
    Heaven is my judge, not I for love and duty,
    But seeming so, for my peculiar end;       60
    For when my outward action doth demonstrate
    The native act and figure of my heart°
    In compliment extern,° 'tis not long after
    But I will wear my heart upon my sleeve
    For daws to peck at; I am not what I am.       65
*Roderigo:* What a full fortune does the thick-lips° owe°
    If he can carry't thus!
*Iago:*           Call up her father,
    Rouse him. Make after him, poison his delight,
    Proclaim him in the streets. Incense her kinsmen,
    And though he in a fertile climate dwell,       70
    Plague him with flies; though that his joy be joy,
    Yet throw such changes of vexation on't
    As it may lose some color.
*Roderigo:* Here is her father's house. I'll call aloud.
*Iago:* Do, with like timorous° accent and dire yell       75
    As when, by night and negligence, the fire
    Is spied in populous cities.

---

36 *affection:* Favoritism.   39 *affined:* Obliged.   48 *cashiered:* Turned off.   50 *trimmed:* Dressed up.   62 *The . . . heart:* What I really believe and intend.   63 *compliment extern:* Outward appearance.   66 *thick-lips:* An Elizabethan epithet for blacks, including Moors; *owe:* Own.   75 *timorous:* Terrifying.

*Roderigo:* What, ho, Brabantio! Signior Brabantio, ho!
*Iago:* Awake! What, ho, Brabantio! Thieves! thieves!
> Look to your house, your daughter, and your bags! 80
> Thieves! thieves!

*Brabantio at a window.°*

*Brabantio (above):* What is the reason of this terrible summons?
> What is the matter there?
*Roderigo:* Signior, is all your family within?
*Iago:* Are your doors locked?
*Brabantio:* Why, wherefore ask you this? 85
*Iago:* Zounds, sir, y' are robbed! For shame, put on your gown!
> Your heart is burst; you have lost half your soul.
> Even now, now, very now, an old black ram
> Is tupping your white ewe. Arise, arise!
> Awake the snorting° citizens with the bell. 90
> Or else the devil will make a grandsire of you.
> Arise, I say!
*Brabantio:* What, have you lost your wits?
*Roderigo:* Most reverend signior, do you know my voice?
*Brabantio:* Not I. What are you? 95
*Roderigo:* My name is Roderigo.
*Brabantio:* The worser welcome!
> I have charged thee not to haunt about my doors.
> In honest plainness thou hast heard me say
> My daughter is not for thee; and now, in madness,
> Being full of supper and distemp'ring draughts, 100
> Upon malicious knavery dost thou come
> To start my quiet.
*Roderigo:* Sir, sir, sir —
*Brabantio:* But thou must needs be sure
> My spirit and my place have in them power 105
> To make this bitter to thee.
*Roderigo:* Patience, good sir.
*Brabantio:* What tell'st thou me of robbing? This is Venice;
> My house is not a grange.°
*Roderigo:* Most grave Brabantio,
> In simple and pure soul I come to you.
*Iago:* Zounds, sir, you are one of those that will not serve God if the devil bid 110
> you. Because we come to do you service, and you think we are ruffians,
> you'll have your daughter covered with a Barbary horse; you'll have your
> nephews° neigh to you; you'll have coursers for cousins, and gennets for
> germans.°
*Brabantio:* What profane wretch art thou? 115
*Iago:* I am one, sir, that comes to tell you your daughter and the Moor are
> now making the beast with two backs.
*Brabantio:* Thou are a villain.

---

*Brabantio at a window:* (added from quarto). 90 *snorting:* Snoring. 108 *grange:* Isolated
farmhouse. 113 *nephews:* i.e., grandsons. 114 *gennets for germans:* Spanish horses for
near kinsmen.

*Iago:*                           You are — a senator.
*Brabantio:* This thou shalt answer. I know thee, Roderigo.
*Roderigo:* Sir, I will answer anything. But I beseech you,                     120
    If 't be your pleasure and most wise consent,
    As partly I find it is, that your fair daughter,
    At this odd-even° and dull watch o' th' night,
    Transported, with no worse nor better guard
    But with a knave of common hire, a gondolier,                     125
    To the gross clasps of a lascivious Moor —
    If this be known to you, and your allowance,°
    We then have done you bold and saucy wrongs;
    But if you know not this, my manners tell me
    We have your wrong rebuke. Do not believe                     130
    That, from the sense° of all civility,
    I thus would play and trifle with your reverence.
    Your daughter, if you have not given her leave,
    I say again, hath made a gross revolt,
    Tying her duty, beauty, wit, and fortunes                     135
    In an extravagant and wheeling° stranger
    Of here and everywhere. Straight satisfy yourself.
    If she be in her chamber, or your house,
    Let loose on me the justice of the state
    For thus deluding you.
*Brabantio:*                           Strike on the tinder, ho!                     140
    Give me a taper! Call up all my people!
    This accident° is not unlike my dream.
    Belief of it oppresses me already.
    Light, I say! light!                                        *Exit [above].*
*Iago:*                           Farewell, for I must leave you.
    It seems not meet, nor wholesome to my place,                     145
    To be produced — as, if I stay, I shall —
    Against the Moor. For I do know the state,
    However this may gall him with some check,°
    Cannot with safety cast° him; for he's embarked
    With such loud reason to the Cyprus wars,                     150
    Which even now stand in act,° that for their souls
    Another of his fathom° they have none
    To lead their business; in which regard,
    Though I do hate him as I do hell-pains,
    Yet, for necessity of present life,                     155
    I must show out a flag and sign of love,
    Which is indeed but sign. That you shall surely find him,
    Lead to the Sagittary° the raisèd search;
    And there will I be with him. So farewell.                     *Exit.*

123 *odd-even:* Between night and morning.     127 *allowance:* Approval.     131 *from the sense:* In violation.     136 *extravagant and wheeling:* Expatriate and roving.     142 *accident:* Occurrence.     148 *check:* Reprimand.     149 *cast:* Discharge.     151 *stand in act:* Are going on. 152 *fathom:* Capacity.     158 *Sagittary:* An inn.

*Enter [below] Brabantio in his nightgown,° and Servants with torches.*

*Brabantio:* It is too true an evil. Gone she is;                      160
    And what's to come of my despisèd time
    Is naught but bitterness. Now, Roderigo,
    Where didst thou see her? — O unhappy girl! —
    With the Moor, say'st thou? — Who would be a father? —
    How didst thou know 'twas she! — O, she deceives me       165
    Past thought! — What said she to you? — Get moe° tapers!
    Raise all my kindred! — Are they married, think you?
*Roderigo:* Truly I think they are.
*Brabantio:* O heaven! How got she out? O treason of the blood!
    Fathers, from hence trust not your daughters' minds       170
    By what you see them act. Is there not charms
    By which the property° of youth and maidhood
    May be abused? Have you not read, Roderigo,
    Of some such thing?
*Roderigo:*                Yes, sir, I have indeed.
*Brabantio:* Call up my brother. — O, would you had had her! —      175
    Some one way, some another. — Do you know
    Where we may apprehend her and the Moor?
*Roderigo:* I think I can discover him, if you please
    To get good guard and go along with me.
*Brabantio:* I pray you lead on. At every house I'll call;          180
    I may command at most. — Get weapons, ho!
    And raise some special officers of night. —
    On, good Roderigo; I'll deserve° your pains.        *Exeunt.*

SCENE II: *Before the lodgings of Othello.*

*Enter Othello, Iago, and Attendants with torches.*

*Iago:* Though in the trade of war I have slain men,
    Yet do I hold it very stuff o' th' conscience
    To do no contrived murder. I lack iniquity
    Sometimes to do me service. Nine or ten times
    I had thought t' have yerked° him here under the ribs.       5
*Othello:* 'Tis better as it is.
*Iago:*             Nay, but he prated,
    And spoke such scurvy and provoking terms
    Against your honor
    That with the little godliness I have
    I did full hard forbear him. But I pray you, sir,        10
    Are you fast° married? Be assured of this,
    That the magnifico° is much beloved,
    And hath in his effect a voice potential°
    As double° as the Duke's. He will divorce you,
    Or put upon you what restraint and grievance        15

---

*nightgown:* Dressing gown.   166 *moe:* More.   172 *property:* Nature.   183 *deserve:* Show gratitude for.   **Scene II.**   5 *yerked:* Stabbed.   11 *fast:* Securely.   12 *magnifico:* Grandee (Brabantio).   13 *potential:* Powerful.   14 *double:* Doubly influential.

The law, with all his might to enforce it on,
Will give him cable.

*Othello:*          Let him do his spite.
My services which I have done the signiory°
Shall out-tongue his complaints. 'Tis yet to know° —
Which, when I know that boasting is an honor,          20
I shall promulgate — I fetch my life and being
From men of royal siege;° and my demerits°
May speak unbonneted to as proud a fortune
As this that I have reached.° For know, Iago,
But that I love the gentle Desdemona,          25
I would not my unhousèd° free condition
Put into circumscription and confine
For the sea's worth. But look what lights come yond?

*Iago:* Those are the raisèd father and his friends.
You were best go in.

*Othello:*          Not I; I must be found.          30
My parts, my title, and my perfect soul°
Shall manifest me rightly. Is it they?

*Iago:* By Janus, I think no.

*Enter Cassio, with torches, Officers.*

*Othello:* The servants of the Duke, and my lieutenant.
The goodness of the night upon you, friends!          35
What is the news?

*Cassio:*          The Duke does greet you, general;
And he requires your haste-post-haste appearance
Even on the instant.

*Othello:*          What's the matter, think you?

*Cassio:* Something from Cyprus, as I may divine.
It is a business of some heat. The galleys          40
Have sent a dozen sequent° messengers
This very night at one another's heels,
And many of the consuls, raised and met,
Are at the Duke's already. You have been hotly called for;
When, being not at your lodging to be found,          45
The Senate hath sent about three several quests
To search you out.

*Othello:*          'Tis well I am found by you.
I will but spend a word here in the house,
And go with you.          *[Exit]*

*Cassio:*          Ancient, what makes he here?

*Iago:* Faith, he to-night hath boarded a land carack.°          50
If it prove lawful prize, he's made for ever.

*Cassio:* I do not understand.

---

18 *signiory:* Venetian government.   19 *yet to know:* Still not generally known.   22 *siege:* Rank; *demerits:* Deserts.   23–4 *May speak . . . reached:* Are equal, I modestly assert, to those of Desdemona's family.   26 *unhousèd:* Unrestrained.   31 *perfect soul:* Stainless conscience.   41 *sequent:* Consecutive.   50 *carack:* Treasure ship.

*Iago:*                                    He's married.
*Cassio:*                                                    To who?

   *[Enter Othello.]*

*Iago:* Marry, to — Come, captain, will you go?
*Othello:*                                                    Have with you.
*Cassio:* Here comes another troop to seek for you.

   *Enter Brabantio, Roderigo, and others with lights and weapons.*

*Iago:* It is Brabantio. General, be advised.                              55
   He comes to bad intent.
*Othello:*                              Holla! stand there!
*Roderigo:* Signior, it is the Moor.
*Brabantio:*                              Down with him, thief!

   *[They draw on both sides.]*

*Iago:* You, Roderigo! Come, sir, I am for you.
*Othello:* Keep up° your bright swords, for the dew will rust them.
   Good signior, you shall more command with years                        60
   Than with your weapons.
*Brabantio:* O thou foul thief, where hast thou stowed my daughter?
   Damned as thou art, thou hast enchanted her!
   For I'll refer me to all things of sense,
   If she in chains of magic were not bound,                              65
   Whether a maid so tender, fair, and happy,
   So opposite to marriage that she shunned
   The wealthy curlèd darlings of our nation,
   Would ever have, t' incur a general mock,
   Run from her guardage to the sooty bosom                              70
   Of such a thing as thou — to fear, not to delight.
   Judge me the world if 'tis not gross in sense°
   That thou hast practiced on her with foul charms,
   Abused her delicate youth with drugs or minerals
   That weaken motion.° I'll have't disputed on;                          75
   'Tis probable, and palpable to thinking.
   I therefore apprehend and do attach° thee
   For an abuser of the world, a practicer
   Of arts inhibited and out of warrant.
   Lay hold upon him. If he do resist,                                    80
   Subdue him at his peril.
*Othello:*                              Hold your hands,
   Both you of my inclining and the rest.
   Were it my cue to fight, I should have known it
   Without a prompter. Where will you that I go
   To answer this your charge?
*Brabantio:*                                    To prison, till fit time   85
   Of law and course of direct session°
   Call thee to answer.

─────────────

59 *Keep up:* i.e., sheath.   72 *gross in sense:* Obvious.   75 *motion:* Perception.   77 *attach:* Arrest.   86 *direct session:* Regular trial.

*Othello:*　　　　　　　　What if I do obey?
　　How may the Duke be therewith satisfied,
　　Whose messengers are here about my side
　　Upon some present business of the state　　　　　　　　　　90
　　To bring me to him?
*Officer:*　　　　　　　　'Tis true, most worthy signior.
　　The Duke's in council, and your noble self
　　I am sure is sent for.
*Brabantio:*　　　　　　　How? The Duke in council?
　　In this time of the night? Bring him away.
　　Mine's not an idle° cause. The Duke himself,　　　　　　　95
　　Or any of my brothers of the state,
　　Cannot but feel this wrong as 'twere their own;
　　For if such actions may have passage free,
　　Bondslaves and pagans shall our statesmen be.　　　　*Exeunt.*

**SCENE III:** *The Venetian Senate Chamber.*

*Enter Duke and Senators, set at a table, with lights and Attendants.*

*Duke:* There is no composition° in these news
　　That gives them credit.
*1. Senator:*　　　　　　　Indeed they are disproportioned.
　　My letters say a hundred and seven galleys.
*Duke:* And mine a hundred forty.
*2. Senator:*　　　　　　　　And mine two hundred.
　　But though they jump° not on a just account —　　　　　　5
　　As in these cases where the aim° reports
　　'Tis oft with difference — yet do they all confirm
　　A Turkish fleet, and bearing up to Cyprus.
*Duke:* Nay, it is possible enough to judgment.
　　I do not so secure me° in the error　　　　　　　　　　10
　　But the main article° I do approve°
　　In fearful sense.
*Sailor (within):*　　What, ho! what, ho! what, ho!
*Officer:* A messenger from the galleys.

　　*Enter Sailor.*

*Duke:*　　　　　　　　　　Now, what's the business?
*Sailor:* The Turkish preparation makes for Rhodes.
　　So was I bid report here to the state　　　　　　　　　15
　　By Signior Angelo.
*Duke:* How say you by this change?
*1. Senator:*　　　　　　　　This cannot be
　　By no assay° of reason. 'Tis a pageant
　　To keep us in false gaze.° When we consider
　　Th' importance of Cyprus to the Turk,　　　　　　　　20

---

95 *idle:* Trifling.　**Scene III.**　1 *composition:* Consistency.　5 *jump:* Agree.　6 *aim:* Conjecture.　10 *so secure me:* Take such comfort.　11 *article:* Substance; *approve:* Accept.　18 *assay:* Test.　19 *in false gaze:* Looking the wrong way.

And let ourselves again but understand
That, as it more concerns the Turk than Rhodes,
So may he with more facile question bear° it,
For that it stands not in such warlike brace,°
But altogether lacks th' abilities                                                25
That Rhodes is dressed in — if we make thought of this,
We must not think the Turk is so unskillful
To leave that latest which concerns him first,
Neglecting an attempt of ease and gain
To wake and wage° a danger profitless.                                          30
*Duke:*  Nay, in all confidence, he's not for Rhodes.
*Officer:*  Here is more news.

    *Enter a Messenger.*

*Messenger:*  The Ottomites, reverend and gracious,
    Steering with due course toward the isle of Rhodes,
    Have there injointed them with an after fleet.                              35
*1. Senator:*  Ay, so I thought. How many, as you guess?
*Messenger:*  Of thirty sail; and now they do restem°
    Their backward course, bearing with frank appearance
    Their purposes toward Cyprus, Signior Montano,
    Your trusty and most valiant servitor,                                      40
    With his free duty recommends you thus,
    And prays you to believe him.
*Duke:*  'Tis certain then for Cyprus.
    Marcus Luccicos,° is not he in town?
*1. Senator:*  He's now in Florence.                                            45
*Duke:*  Write from us to him; post, post-haste dispatch.
*1. Senator:*  Here comes Brabantio and the valiant Moor.

    *Enter Brabantio, Othello, Cassio, Iago, Roderigo, and Officers.*

*Duke:*  Valiant Othello, we must straight employ you
    Against the general enemy Ottoman.                    [*To Brabantio.*]
    I did not see you. Welcome, gentle signior.                                 50
    We lacked your counsel and your help to-night.
*Brabantio:*  So did I yours. Good your grace, pardon me.
    Neither my place, nor aught I heard of business,
    Hath raised me from my bed; nor doth the general care
    Take hold on me; for my particular grief                                    55
    Is of so floodgate° and o'erbearing nature
    That it engluts° and swallows other sorrows,
    And it is still itself.
*Duke:*                          Why, what's the matter?
*Brabantio:*  My daughter! O, my daughter!
*All:*                                      Dead?
*Brabantio:*                                        Ay, to me.

---

23 *with . . . bear:* More easily capture.    24 *brace:* Posture of defense.    30 *wake and wage:*
Rouse and risk.    37 *restem:* Steer again.    44 *Marcus Luccicos:* (Presumably a Venetian
envoy).    56 *floodgate:* Torrential.    57 *engluts:* Devours.

She is abused, stol'n from me, and corrupted                    60
By spells and medicines bought of mountebanks;
For nature so prepost'rously to err,
Being not deficient,° blind, or lame of sense,
Sans witchcraft could not.
*Duke:*  Whoe'er he be that in this foul proceeding             65
Hath thus beguiled your daughter of herself,
And you of her, the bloody book of law
You shall yourself read in the bitter letter
After your own sense; yea, though our proper° son
Stood in your action.°
*Brabantio:*                  Humbly I thank your grace.         70
Here is the man — this Moor, whom now, it seems,
Your special mandate for the state affairs
Hath hither brought.
*All:*                        We are very sorry for't.
*Duke [to Othello]:*  What, in your own part, can you say to this?
*Brabantio:*  Nothing, but this is so.                          75
*Othello:*  Most potent, grave, and reverend signiors,
My very noble, and approved° good masters,
That I have ta'en away this old man's daughter,
It is most true; true I have married her.
The very head and front of my offending                        80
Hath this extent, no more. Rude° am I in my speech,
And little blessed with the soft phrase of peace;
For since these arms of mine had seven years' pith°
Till now some nine moons wasted, they have used
Their dearest action in the tented field;                      85
And little of this great world can I speak
More than pertains to feats of broil and battle;
And therefore little shall I grace my cause
In speaking for myself. Yet, by your gracious patience,
I will a round° unvarnished tale deliver                       90
Of my whole course of love — what drugs, what charms,
What conjuration, and what mighty magic
(For such proceeding am I charged withal)
I won his daughter.
*Brabantio:*              A maiden never bold;
Of spirit so still and quiet that her motion                   95
Blushed° at herself; and she — in spite of nature,
Of years, of country, credit, everything —
To fall in love with what she feared to look on!
It is a judgment maimed and most imperfect
That will confess perfection so could err                      100
Against all rules of nature, and must be driven

---

63 *deficient:* Feeble-minded.  69 *our proper:* My own.  70 *Stood in your action:* Were accused by you.  77 *approved:* Tested by experience.  81 *Rude:* Unpolished.  83 *pith:* Strength.  90 *round:* Plain.  95–6 *her motion Blushed:* Her own emotions caused her to blush.

To find out practices° of cunning hell
Why this should be. I therefore vouch° again
That with some mixtures pow'rful o'er the blood,°
Or with some dram, conjured to this effect,                105
He wrought upon her.
*Duke:*                    To vouch this is no proof.
Without more certain and more overt test
Than these thin habits° and poor likelihoods
Of modern seeming° do prefer against him.
*1. Senator:* But, Othello, speak.                        110
Did you by indirect and forcèd° courses
Subdue and poison this young maid's affections?
Or came it by request, and such fair question°
As soul to soul affordeth?
*Othello:*                    I do beseech you,
Send for the lady to the Sagittary                        115
And let her speak of me before her father.
If you do find me foul in her report,
The trust, the office, I do hold of you
Not only take away, but let your sentence
Even fall upon my life.
*Duke:*                    Fetch Desdemona hither.          120
*Othello:* Ancient, conduct them; you best know the place.

*Exit [Iago, with] two or three [Attendants].*

And till she come, as truly as to heaven
I do confess the vices of my blood,
So justly to your grave ears I'll present
How I did thrive in this fair lady's love,                125
And she in mine.
*Duke:* Say it, Othello.
*Othello:* Her father loved me, oft invited me;
Still° questioned me the story of my life
From year to year — the battles, sieges, fortunes         130
That I have passed.
I ran it through, even from my boyish days
To th' very moment that he bade me tell it.
Wherein I spake of most disastrous chances,
Of moving accidents by flood and field;                   135
Of hairbreadth scapes i' th' imminent deadly breach;
Of being taken by the insolent foe
And sold to slavery; of my redemption thence
And portance° in my travels' history;
Wherein of anters° vast and deserts idle,                 140
Rough quarries, rocks, and hills whose heads touch heaven,
It was my hint° to speak — such was the process;
And of the Cannibals that each other eat,

102 *practices:* Plots.   103 *vouch:* Assert.   104 *blood:* Passions.   108 *thin habits:* Slight appearances.   109 *modern seeming:* Everyday supposition.   111 *forcèd:* Violent.   113 *question:* Conversation.   129 *Still:* Continually.   139 *portance:* Behavior.   140 *anters:* Caves.   142 *hint:* Occasion.

The Anthropophagi,° and men whose heads
Do grow beneath their shoulders. This to hear                                    145
Would Desdemona seriously incline;
But still the house affairs would draw her thence;
Which ever as she could with haste dispatch,
She'ld come again, and with a greedy ear
Devour up my discourse. Which I observing,                                       150
Took once a pliant° hour, and found good means
To draw from her a prayer of earnest heart
That I would all my pilgrimage dilate,°
Whereof by parcels° she had something heard,
But not intentively.° I did consent,                                             155
And often did beguile her of her tears
When I did speak of some distressful stroke
That my youth suffered. My story being done,
She gave me for my pains a world of sighs.
She swore, i' faith, 'twas strange, 'twas passing strange;                       160
'Twas pitiful, 'twas wondrous pitiful.
She wished she had not heard it; yet she wished
That heaven had made her such a man. She thanked me;
And bade me, if I had a friend that loved her,
I should but teach him how to tell my story,                                     165
And that would woo her. Upon this hint° I spake.
She loved me for the dangers I had passed,
And I loved her that she did pity them.
This only is the witchcraft I have used.
Here comes the lady. Let her witness it.                                         170

*Enter Desdemona, Iago, Attendants.*

*Duke:* I think this tale would win my daughter too.
Good Brabantio,
Take up this mangled matter at the best.
Men do their broken weapons rather use
Than their bare hands.
*Brabantio:*                           I pray you hear her speak.                 175
If she confess that she was half the wooer,
Destruction on my head if my bad blame
Light on the man! Come hither, gentle mistress.
Do you perceive in all this noble company
Where most you owe obedience?
*Desdemona:*                           My noble father,                          180
I do perceive here a divided duty.
To you I am bound for life and education;°
My life and education both do learn me
How to respect you: you are the lord of duty;
I am hitherto your daughter. But here's my husband;                              185
And so much duty as my mother showed
To you, preferring you before her father,

144 *Anthropophagi:* Man-eaters. 151 *pliant:* Propitious. 153 *dilate:* Recount in full.
154 *parcels:* Portions. 155 *intentively:* With full attention. 166 *hint:* Opportunity.
182 *education:* Upbringing.

So much I challenge° that I may profess
Due to the Moor my lord.
*Brabantio:*                    God be with you! I have done.
    Please it your grace, on to the state affairs.                    190
    I had rather to adopt a child than get° it.
    Come hither, Moor.
    I here do give thee that with all my heart
    Which, but thou hast already, with all my heart
    I would keep from thee. For your sake,° jewel,                    195
    I am glad at soul I have no other child;
    For thy escape° would teach me tyranny,
    To hang clogs on them. I have done, my lord.
*Duke:* Let me speak like yourself° and lay a sentence°
    Which, as a grise° or step, may help these lovers                    200
    [Into your favor.]
    When remedies are past, the griefs are ended
    By seeing the worst, which late on hopes depended.
    To mourn a mischief that is past and gone
    Is the next way to draw new mischief on.                    205
    What cannot be preserved when fortune takes,
    Patience her injury a mock'ry makes.
    The robbed that smiles steals something from the thief;
    He robs himself that spends a bootless grief.
*Brabantio:* So let the Turk of Cyprus us beguile:                    210
    We lose it not so long as we can smile.
    He bears the sentence well that nothing bears
    But the free comfort which from thence he hears;
    But he bears both the sentence and the sorrow
    That to pay grief must of poor patience borrow.                    215
    These sentences, to sugar, or to gall,
    Being strong on both sides, are equivocal.
    But words are words. I never yet did hear
    That the bruisèd heart was piercèd through the ear.
    Beseech you, now to the affairs of state.                    220
*Duke:* The Turk with a most mighty preparation makes for Cyprus.
    Othello, the fortitude° of the place is best known to you; and though
    we have there a substitute of most allowed° sufficiency, yet opinion,° a
    more sovereign mistress of effects, throws a more safer voice on you.
    You must therefore be content to slubber° the gloss of your new for-    225
    tunes with this more stubborn and boist'rous expedition.
*Othello:* The tyrant custom, most grave senators,
    Hath made the flinty and steel couch of war
    My thrice-driven bed of down. I do agnize
    A natural and prompt alacrity                    230
    I find in hardness;° and do undertake

---

*188 challenge:* Claim the right.    *191 get:* Beget.    *195 For your sake:* Because of you.
*197 escape:* Escapade.    *199 like yourself:* As you should; *sentence:* Maxim.    *200 grise:*
Step.    *222 fortitude:* Fortification.    *223 allowed:* Acknowledged; *opinion:* Public opinion.
*225 slubber:* Sully.    *229–31 agnize . . . hardness:* Recognize in myself a natural and easy
response to hardship.

These present wars against the Ottomites.
Most humbly, therefore, bending to your state,
I crave fit disposition for my wife,
Due reference of place, and exhibition,°                                            235
With such accommodation and besort°
As levels° with her breeding.
*Duke:*                               If you please,
Be't at her father's.
*Brabantio:*              I will not have it so.
*Othello:*  Nor I.
*Desdemona:*  Nor I. I would not there reside,
To put my father in impatient thoughts                                              240
By being in his eye. Most gracious Duke,
To my unfolding lend your prosperous° ear,
And let me find a charter in your voice,
T' assist my simpleness.°
*Duke:*  What would you, Desdemona?                                                 245
*Desdemona:*  That I did love the Moor to live with him,
My downright violence, and storm of fortunes,
May trumpet to the world. My heart's subdued
Even to the very quality of my lord.
I saw Othello's visage in his mind,                                                 250
And to his honors and his valiant parts
Did I my soul and fortunes consecrate.
So that, dear lords, if I be left behind,
A moth of peace, and he go to the war,
The rites for which I love him are bereft me,                                       255
And I a heavy interim shall support
By his dear absence. Let me go with him.
*Othello:*  Let her have your voice.
Vouch with me, heaven, I therefore beg it not
To please the palate of my appetite,                                               260
Not to comply with heat° — the young affects°
In me defunct — and proper satisfaction;
But to be free and bounteous to her mind;
And heaven defend your good souls that you think
I will your serious and great business scant                                       265
When she is with me. No, when light-winged toys
Of feathered Cupid seel° with wanton dullness
My speculative and officed instruments,°
That° my disports corrupt and taint my business,
Let housewives make a skillet of my helm,                                          270
And all indign° and base adversities
Make head against my estimation!°
*Duke:*  Be it as you shall privately determine,
Either for her stay or going. Th' affair cries haste,

---

235 *exhibition:* Allowance of money.   236 *besort:* Suitable company.   237 *levels:*
Corresponds.   242 *prosperous:* Favorable.   244 *simpleness:* Lack of skill.   261 *heat:* Passions;   *young affects:* Tendencies of youth.   267 *seel:* Blind.   268 *My . . . instruments:* My
perceptive and responsible faculties.   269 *That:* So that.   271 *indign:* Unworthy.
272 *estimation:* Reputation.

And speed must answer it.                                                       275
*1. Senator:* You must away to-night.
*Desdemona:* Tonight, my lord?
*Duke:*                    This night.
*Othello:*                              With all my heart.
*Duke:* At nine i' th' morning here we'll meet again.
    Othello, leave some officer behind,
    And he shall our commission bring to you,                                   280
    With such things else of quality and respect
    As doth import° you.
*Othello:*                   So please your grace, my ancient;
    A man he is of honesty and trust
    To his conveyance I assign my wife,
    With what else needful your good grace shall think                          285
    To be sent after me.
*Duke:*                   Let it be so.
    Good night to every one.
            *[To Brabantio.]*    And, noble signior,
    If virtue no delighted° beauty lack,
    Your son-in-law is far more fair than black.
*1. Senator:* Adieu, brave Moor. Use Desdemona well.                            290
*Brabantio:* Look to her, Moor, if thou hast eyes to see:
    She has deceived her father, and may thee.

                            *Exeunt [Duke, Senators, Officers, &c.].*

*Othello:* My life upon her faith! — Honest Iago,
    My Desdemona must I leave to thee.
    I prithee let thy wife attend on her,                                       295
    And bring them after in the best advantage.°
    Come, Desdemona. I have but an hour
    Of love, of worldly matters and direction,
    To spend with thee. We must obey the time.

                            *Exit Moor and Desdemona.*

*Roderigo:* Iago, —                                                            300
*Iago:* What say'st thou, noble heart?
*Roderigo:* What will I do, think'st thou?
*Iago:* Why, go to bed and sleep.
*Roderigo:* I will incontinently° drown myself.
*Iago:* If thou dost, I shall never love thee after. Why, thou silly           305
    gentleman!
*Roderigo:* It is silliness to live when to live is torment; and then have we a
    prescription to die when death is our physician.
*Iago:* O villainous! I have looked upon the world for four times seven years;
    and since I could distinguish betwixt a benefit and an injury, I never 310
    found man that knew how to love himself. Ere I would say I would drown
    myself for the love of a guinea hen, I would change my humanity with a
    baboon.

---

282 *import:* Concern.   288 *delighted:* Delightful.   296 *in the best advantage:* At the best
opportunity.   304 *incontinently:* Forthwith.

*Roderigo:* What should I do? I confess it is my shame to be so fond, but it is not in my virtue to amend it.                                                                          315

*Iago:* Virtue? a fig!° 'Tis in ourselves that we are thus or thus. Our bodies are our gardens, to which our wills are gardeners; so that if we will plant nettles or sow lettuce, set hyssop and weed up thyme, supply it with one gender° of herbs or distract it with many—either to have it sterile with idleness or manured with industry—why, the power and corrigible  320 authority° of this lies in our wills. If the balance of our lives had not one scale of reason to poise° another of sensuality, the blood and baseness° of our natures would conduct us to most preposterous conclusions. But we have reason to cool our raging motions,° our carnal strings, our unbitted° lusts; whereof I take this that you call love to be a sect or  325 scion.°

*Roderigo:* It cannot be.

*Iago:* It is merely a lust of the blood and a permission of the will. Come, be a man! Drown thyself? Drown cats and blind puppies! I have professed me thy friend, and I confess me knit to thy deserving with  330 cables of perdurable toughness. I could never better stead thee than now. Put money in thy purse. Follow thou the wars; defeat thy favor° with an usurped beard. I say, put money in thy purse. It cannot be that Desdemona should long continue her love to the Moor—put money in thy purse—nor he his to her. It was a violent commence-  335 ment in her, and thou shalt see an answerable sequestration°—put but money in thy purse. These Moors are changeable in their wills— fill thy purse with money. The food that to him now is as luscious as locusts shall be to him shortly as bitter as coloquintida.° She must change for youth: when she is sated with his body, she will find  340 the error of her choice. [She must have change, she must.] Therefore put money in thy purse. If thou wilt needs damn thyself, do it a more delicate way than drowning. Make° all the money thou canst. If sanctimony and a frail vow betwixt an erring° barbarian and a supersubtle Venetian be not too hard for my wits and all the tribe of hell, thou shalt  345 enjoy her. Therefore make money. A pox of drowning thyself! 'Tis clean out of the way. Seek thou rather to be hanged in compassing thy joy than to be drowned and go without her.

*Roderigo:* Wilt thou be fast to my hopes, if I depend on the issue?

*Iago:* Thou art sure of me. Go, make money. I have told thee often, and  350 I retell thee again and again, I hate the Moor. My cause is hearted;° thine hath no less reason. Let us be conjunctive in our revenge against him. If thou canst cuckold him, thou dost thyself a pleasure, me a sport. There are many events in the womb of time, which will be delivered. Traverse,° go, provide thy money! We will have more of  355 this to-morrow. Adieu.

*Roderigo:* Where shall we meet i' th' morning?

---

316 *fig:* Derogatory term, also referring to a vulgar gesture with the thumb between the first and second fingers.    319 *gender:* Species.    320–21 *corrigible authority:* Corrective power.    322 *poise:* Counterbalance; *blood and baseness:* Animal instincts.    324 *motions:* Appetites.    325 *unbitted:* Uncontrolled.    325–26 *sect or scion:* Offshoot, cutting.    332 *defeat thy favor:* Spoil thy appearance.    336 *sequestration:* Estrangement.    339 *coloquintida:* A medicine.    343 *Make:* Raise.    344 *erring:* Wandering.    351 *My cause is hearted:* My heart is in it.    355 *Traverse:* Forward march.

*Iago:* At my lodging.
*Roderigo:* I'll be with thee betimes.
*Iago:* Go to, farewell — Do you hear, Roderigo?                          360
*Roderigo:* What say you?
*Iago:* No more of drowning, do you hear?
*Roderigo:* I am changed.
*Iago:* Go to, farewell. Put money enough in your purse.
*Roderigo:* I'll sell all my land.                          *Exit.* 365
*Iago:* Thus do I ever make my fool my purse;
    For I mine own gained knowledge should profane
    If I would time expend with such a snipe°
    But for my sport and profit. I hate the Moor;
    And it is thought abroad that 'twixt my sheets                          370
    He's done my office. I know not if't be true;
    But I, for mere suspicion in that kind,
    Will do as if for surety. He holds me well;°
    The better shall my purpose work on him.
    Cassio's a proper man. Let me see now:                          375
    To get his place, and to plume up° my will
    In double knavery — How, how? — Let's see: —
    After some time, to abuse Othello's ears
    That he is too familiar with his wife.
    He hath a person and a smooth dispose°                          380
    To be suspected — framed to make women false.
    The Moor is of a free° and open nature
    That thinks men honest that but seem to be so;
    And will as tenderly be led by th' nose
    As asses are.                          385
    I have't! It is engend'red! Hell and night
    Must bring this monstrous birth to the world's light.                          *Exit.*

---

# ACT II

**Scene I:** *An open place in Cyprus, near the harbor.*

*Enter Montano and two Gentlemen.*

*Montano:* What from the cape can you discern at sea?
*1. Gentleman:* Nothing at all: it is a high-wrought flood.
    I cannot 'twixt the heaven and the main
    Descry a sail.
*Montano:* Methinks the wind hath spoke aloud at land;                          5
    A fuller blast ne'er shook our battlements.
    If it hath ruffianed so upon the sea,
    What ribs of oak, when mountains melt on them,
    Can hold the mortise?° What shall we hear of this?

---

368 *snipe:* Fool.   373 *well:* In high regard.   376 *plume up:* Gratify.   380 *dispose:* Manner.
382 *free:* Frank.   **Act II, Scene I.**   9 *hold the mortise:* Hold their joints together.

*2. Gentleman:* A segregation° of the Turkish fleet.                              10
　　For do but stand upon the foaming shore,
　　The chidden billow seems to pelt the clouds;
　　The wind-shaked surge, with high and monstrous mane,
　　Seems to cast water on the burning Bear
　　And quench the Guards° of th' ever-fixèd pole.°              15
　　I never did like molestation° view
　　On the enchafèd° flood.
*Montano:*　　　　　　　If that the Turkish fleet
　　Be not ensheltered and embayed, they are drowned;
　　It is impossible to bear it out.

　　*Enter a third Gentleman.*

*3. Gentleman:* News, lads! Our wars are done.                       20
　　The desperate tempest hath so banged the Turks
　　That their designment halts.° A noble ship of Venice
　　Hath seen a grievous wrack and sufferance°
　　On most part of their fleet.
*Montano:* How? Is this true?
*3. Gentleman:*　　　　　The ship is here put in,                25
　　A Veronesa;° Michael Cassio,
　　Lieutenant to the warlike Moor Othello,
　　Is come on shore; the Moor himself at sea,
　　And is in full commission here for Cyprus.
*Montano:* I am glad on't. 'Tis a worthy governor.              30
*3. Gentleman:* But this same Cassio, though he speak of comfort
　　Touching the Turkish loss, yet he looks sadly
　　And prays the Moor be safe, for they were parted
　　With foul and violent tempest.
*Montano:*　　　　　　　Pray heaven he be,
　　For I have served him, and the man commands           35
　　Like a full soldier. Let's to the seaside, ho!
　　As well to see the vessel that's come in
　　As to throw out our eyes for brave Othello,
　　Even till we make the main and th' aerial blue
　　An indistinct regard.°
*3. Gentleman:*　　　　　Come, let's do so;                       40
　　For every minute is expectancy
　　Of more arrivance.

　　*Enter Cassio.*

*Cassio:* Thanks, you the valiant of this warlike isle,
　　That so approve the Moor! O, let the heavens
　　Give him defense against the elements,                           45
　　For I have lost him on a dangerous sea!

---

10 *segregation:* Scattering.　15 *Guards:* Stars near the North Star;　*pole:* Polestar.
16 *molestation:* Tumult.　17 *enchafèd:* Angry.　22 *designment halts:* Plan is crippled.
23 *sufferance:* Disaster.　26 *Veronesa:* Ship furnished by Verona.　40 *An indistinct regard:* Indistinguishable.

*Montano:* Is he well shipped?
*Cassio:* His bark is stoutly timbered, and his pilot
    Of very expert and approved allowance;
    Therefore my hopes, not surfeited to death,°           50
    Stand in bold cure.°
            *(Within.)*     A sail, a sail, a sail!        *Enter a messenger.*
*Cassio:* What noise?
*Messenger:* The town is empty; on the brow o' th' sea
    Stand ranks of people, and they cry "A sail!"
*Cassio:* My hopes do shape him for the governor.           55

    *A shot.*

*2. Gentleman:* They do discharge their shot of courtesy:
    Our friends at least.
*Cassio:*             I pray you sir, go forth
    And give us truth who 'tis that is arrived.
*2. Gentleman:* I shall.                          *Exit.*
*Montano:* But, good lieutenant, is your general wived?     60
*Cassio:* Most fortunately. He hath achieved a maid
    That paragons° description and wild fame;
    One that excels the quirks° of blazoning° pens,
    And in th' essential vesture of creation
    Does tire the ingener.°

    *Enter Second Gentleman.*

                How now? Who has put in?         65
*2. Gentleman:* 'Tis one Iago, ancient to the general.
*Cassio:* H'as had most favorable and happy speed:
    Tempests themselves, high seas, and howling winds,
    The guttered° rocks and congregated sands,
    Traitors ensteeped° to clog the guiltless keel,       70
    As having sense of beauty, do omit
    Their mortal° natures, letting go safely by
    The divine Desdemona.
*Montano:*               What is she?
*Cassio:* She that I spake of, our great captain's captain,
    Left in the conduct of the bold Iago,            75
    Whose footing° here anticipates our thoughts
    A se'nnight's° speed. Great Jove, Othello guard,
    And swell his sail with thine own pow'rful breath,
    That he may bless this bay with his tall ship,
    Make love's quick pants in Desdemona's arms,     80
    Give renewed fire to our extincted spirits,
    [And bring all Cyprus comfort!]

    *Enter Desdemona, Iago, Roderigo, and Emilia [with Attendants].*

---

50 *surfeited to death:* Overindulged.   51 *in bold cure:* A good chance of fulfillment.   62 *paragons:* Surpasses.   63 *quirks:* Ingenuities; *blazoning:* Describing.   64–5 *And . . . ingener:* Merely to describe her as God made her exhausts her praiser.   69 *guttered:* Jagged. 70 *ensteeped:* Submerged.   72 *mortal:* Deadly.   76 *footing:* Landing.   77 *se'nnight's:* Week's.

O, behold!
The riches of the ship is come on shore!
You men of Cyprus, let her have your knees.°
Hail to thee, lady! and the grace of heaven,                                          85
Before, behind thee, and on every hand,
Enwheel thee round!
*Desdemona:*                    I thank you, valiant Cassio.
What tidings can you tell me of my lord?
*Cassio:* He is not yet arrived; nor know I aught
But that he's well and will be shortly here.                                          90
*Desdemona:* O but I fear! How lost you company?
*Cassio:* The great contention of the sea and skies
Parted our fellowship.
      *(Within.)*              A sail, a sail! *[A shot.]*
                                                        But hark. A sail!
*2. Gentleman:* They give their greeting to the citadel;
This likewise is a friend.
*Cassio:*                         See for the news.                                    95

                                                      *[Exit Gentleman.]*

Good ancient, you are welcome.
      *[To Emilia.]*                    Welcome, mistress. —
Let it not gall your patience, good Iago,
That I extend my manners. 'Tis my breeding
That gives me this bold show of courtesy.

      *[Kisses Emilia.°]*

*Iago:* Sir, would she give you so much of her lips                                   100
As of her tongue she oft bestows on me,
You would have enough.
*Desdemona:*                    Alas, she has no speech!
*Iago:* In faith, too much.
I find it still when I have list to sleep.
Marry, before your ladyship, I grant,                                                105
She puts her tongue a little in her heart
And chides with thinking.
*Emilia:* You have little cause to say so.
*Iago:* Come on, come on! You are pictures out of doors,
Bells in your parlors, wildcats in your kitchens,                                     110
Saints in your injuries, devils being offended,
Players in your housewifery,° and housewives° in your beds.
*Desdemona:* O, fie upon thee, slanderer!
*Iago:* Nay, it is true, or else I am a Turk:
You rise to play, and go to bed to work.                                             115
*Emilia:* You shall not write my praise.
*Iago:*                         No, let me not.
*Desdemona:* What wouldst thou write of me, if thou shouldst
praise me?

---

84 *knees:* i.e., kneeling.   *Kisses Emilia:* (Kissing was a common Elizabethan form of social courtesy).   112 *housewifery:* Housekeeping;   *housewives:* Hussies.

*Iago:* O gentle lady, do not put me to't,
  For I am nothing if not critical.
*Desdemona:* Come on, assay.° — There's one gone to the harbor? 120
*Iago:* Ay, madam.
*Desdemona:* I am not merry; but I do beguile
  The thing I am by seeming otherwise. —
  Come, how wouldst thou praise me?
*Iago:* I am about it; but indeed my invention 125
  Comes from my pate as birdlime° does from frieze° —
  It plucks out brains and all. But my Muse labors,
  And thus she is delivered:
  If she be fair and wise, fairness and wit —
  The one's for use, the other useth it. 130
*Desdemona:* Well praised! How if she be black° and witty?
*Iago:* If she be black, and thereto have a wit,
  She'll find a white that shall her blackness fit.
*Desdemona:* Worse and worse!
*Emilia:* How if fair and foolish? 135
*Iago:* She never yet was foolish that was fair,
  For even her folly° helped her to an heir.
*Desdemona:* These are old fond° paradoxes to make fools laugh i' th'
  alehouse. What miserable praise hast thou for her that's foul° and
  foolish? 140
*Iago:* There's none so foul, and foolish thereunto,
  But does foul pranks which fair and wise ones do.
*Desdemona:* O heavy ignorance! Thou praisest the worst best. But what
  praise couldst thou bestow on a deserving woman indeed — one that
  in the authority of her merit did justly put on the vouch° of very malice 145
  itself?
*Iago:* She that was ever fair, and never proud;
  Had tongue at will, and yet was never loud;
  Never lacked gold, and yet went never gay;
  Fled from her wish, and yet said "Now I may"; 150
  She that, being ang'red, her revenge being nigh,
  Bade her wrong stay, and her displeasure fly;
  She that in wisdom never was so frail
  To change the cod's head for the salmon's tail;°
  She that could think, and ne'er disclose her mind; 155
  See suitors following, and not look behind:
  She was a wight (if ever such wight were) —
*Desdemona:* To do what?
*Iago:* To suckle fools and chronicle small beer.°
*Desdemona:* O most lame and impotent conclusion! Do not learn of him, 160
  Emilia, though he be thy husband. How say you, Cassio? Is he not a most
  profane and liberal° counsellor?

---

120 *assay:* Try.  126 *birdlime:* A sticky paste;  *frieze:* Rough cloth.  131 *black:* Brunette.
137 *folly:* Wantonness.  138 *fond:* Foolish.  139 *foul:* Ugly.  145 *put on the vouch:* Compel
the approval.  154 *To . . . tail:* i.e., to exchange the good for the poor but expensive.
159 *chronicle small beer:* Keep petty household accounts.  162 *profane and liberal:* Worldly
and licentious.

*Cassio:* He speaks home,° madam. You may relish him more in the soldier
than in the scholar.

*Iago [aside]:* He takes her by the palm. Ay, well said, whisper! With as   165
little a web as this will I ensnare as great a fly as Cassio. Ay, smile
upon her, do! I will gyve thee in thine own courtship.° — You say true;
'tis so, indeed! — If such tricks as these strip you out of your lieu-
tenantry, it had been better you had not kissed your three fingers so
oft — which now again you are most apt to play the sir° in. Very good!   170
well kissed! an excellent courtesy! 'Tis so, indeed. Yet again
your fingers to your lips? Would they were clyster pipes° for your sake!
*(Trumpet within.)*
The Moor! I know his trumpet.

*Cassio:* 'Tis truly so.                                                                                    175

*Desdemona:* Let's meet him and receive him.

*Cassio:* Lo, where he comes.

> *Enter Othello and Attendants.*

*Othello:* O my fair warrior!

*Desdemona:*                                  My dear Othello!

*Othello:* It gives me wonder great as my content
To see you here before me. O my soul's joy!                               180
If after every tempest come such calms,
May the winds blow till they have wakened death!
And let the laboring bark climb hills of seas
Olympus-high, and duck again as low
As hell's from heaven! If it were now to die,                              185
'Twere now to be most happy;° for I fear
My soul hath her content so absolute
That not another comfort like to this
Succeeds in unknown fate.

*Desdemona:*                          The heavens forbid
But that our loves and comforts should increase                          190
Even as our days do grow.

*Othello:*                          Amen to that, sweet powers!
I cannot speak enough of this content;
It stops me here; it is too much of joy.
And this, and this, the greatest discords be

> *They kiss.*

That e'er our hearts shall make!

*Iago [aside]:*                          O, you are well tuned now!          195
But I'll set down° the pegs that make this music,
As honest as I am.

*Othello:*                          Come, let us to the castle.
News, friends! Our wars are done; the Turks are drowned.
How does my old acquaintance of this isle? —
Honey, you shall be well desired° in Cyprus;                              200

---

163 *home:* Bluntly.   167 *gyve . . . courtship:* Manacle you by means of your courtly
manners.   170 *sir:* Courtly gentleman.   172 *clyster pipes:* Syringes.   186 *happy:* Fortunate.   196 *set down:* Loosen.   200 *well desired:* Warmly welcomed.

I have found great love amongst them. O my sweet,
I prattle out of fashion, and I dote
In mine own comforts. I prithee, good Iago,
Go to the bay and disembark my coffers.
Bring thou the master° to the citadel;                                    205
He is a good one, and his worthiness
Does challenge° much respect. — Come, Desdemona,
Once more well met at Cyprus.

*Exit Othello [with all but Iago and Roderigo].*

*Iago [to an Attendant, who goes out]:* Do thou meet me presently at the
harbor. *[To Roderigo.]* Come hither. If thou be'st valiant (as they say 210
base men being in love have then a nobility in their natures more than
is native to them), list me. The lieutenant to-night watches on the court
of guard.° First, I must tell thee this: Desdemona is directly in love
with him.

*Roderigo:* With him? Why, 'tis not possible.                             215

*Iago:* Lay thy finger thus,° and let thy soul be instructed. Mark me with what
violence she first loved the Moor, but for bragging and telling
her fantastical lies; and will she love him still for prating? Let not thy
discreet heart think it. Her eye must be fed; and what delight shall
she have to look on the devil? When the blood is made dull with 220
the act of sport, there should be, again to inflame it and to give sati-
ety a fresh appetite, loveliness in favor, sympathy in years, manners,
and beauties; all which the Moor is defective in. Now for want of
these required conveniences,° her delicate tenderness will find itself
abused, begin to heave the gorge,° disrelish and abhor the Moor. Very 225
nature will instruct her in it and compel her to some second choice.
Now, sir, this granted — as it is a most pregnant° and unforced position — who stands so eminent in the degree of this fortune as Cassio
does? A knave very voluble; no further conscionable° than in putting on the mere form of civil and humane° seeming for the better 230
compassing of his salt° and most hidden loose affection? Why, none!
why, none! A slipper° and subtle knave; a finder-out of occasions;
that has an eye can stamp and counterfeit advantages, though true
advantage never present itself; a devilish knave! Besides, the knave is
handsome, young, and hath all those requisites in him that folly and 235
green minds look after. A pestilent complete knave! and the woman
hath found him already.

*Roderigo:* I cannot believe that in her; she's full of most blessed
condition.°

*Iago:* Blessed fig's-end! The wine she drinks is made of grapes. If she had 240
been blessed, she would never have loved the Moor. Blessed pudding!
Didst thou not see her paddle with the palm of his hand? Didst not
mark that?

*Roderigo:* Yes, that I did; but that was but courtesy.

---

205 *master:* Ship captain.   207 *challenge:* Deserve.   212–13 *court of guard:* Headquarters.
216 *thus:* i.e., on your lips.   224 *conveniences:* Compatibilities.   225 *heave the gorge:*
Be nauseated.   227 *pregnant:* Evident.   229 *conscionable:* Conscientious.   230 *humane:*
Polite.   231 *salt:* Lecherous.   232 *slipper:* Slippery.   239 *condition:* Character.

*Iago:* Lechery, by this hand! an index and obscure prologue to the history   245
of lust and foul thoughts. They met so near with their lips that their
breaths embraced together. Villainous thoughts, Roderigo! When these
mutualities° so marshal the way, hard at hand comes the master and
main exercise, th' incorporate° conclusion. Pish! But, sir, be you ruled
by me: I have brought you from Venice. Watch you to-night; for the   250
command, I'll lay't upon you. Cassio knows you not. I'll not be far from
you: do you find some occasion to anger Cassio, either by speaking too
loud, or tainting° his discipline, or from what other course you please
which the time shall more favorably minister.

*Roderigo:* Well.   255

*Iago:* Sir, he's rash and very sudden in choler,° and haply with his trun-
cheon may strike at you. Provoke him that he may; for even out of
that will I cause these of Cyprus to mutiny; whose qualification°
shall come into no true taste° again but by the displanting of Cassio. So shall you have a shorter journey to your desires by the means   260
I shall then have to prefer° them; and the impediment most profit-
ably removed without the which there were no expectation of our
prosperity.

*Roderigo:* I will do this if you can bring it to any opportunity.

*Iago:* I warrant thee. Meet me by and by at the citadel; I must fetch his neces-   265
saries ashore. Farewell.

*Roderigo:* Adieu.                                                    *Exit.*

*Iago:* That Cassio loves her, I do well believe't;
That she loves him, 'tis apt° and of great credit.
The Moor, howbeit that I endure him not,                              270
Is of a constant, loving, noble nature,
And I dare think he'll prove to Desdemona
A most dear husband. Now I do love her too;
Not out of absolute lust, though peradventure
I stand accountant° for as great a sin,                               275
But partly led to diet° my revenge,
For that I do suspect the lusty Moor
Hath leaped into my seat; the thought whereof
Doth, like a poisonous mineral, gnaw my inwards;
And nothing can or shall content my soul                             280
Till I am evened with him, wife for wife;
Or failing so, yet that I put the Moor
At least into a jealousy so strong
That judgment cannot cure. Which thing to do,
If this poor trash of Venice, whom I trash°                           285
For° his quick hunting, stand the putting on,°
I'll have our Michael Cassio on the hip,°

---

248 *mutualities:* Exchanges.   249 *incorporate:* Carnal.   253 *tainting:* Discrediting.
256 *sudden in choler:* Violent in anger.   258 *qualification:* Appeasement.   259 *true taste:*
Satisfactory state.   261 *prefer:* Advance.   269 *apt:* Probable.   275 *accountant:* Accountable.
276 *diet:* Feed.   285 *I trash:* I weight down (in order to keep under control).   286 *For:*
In order to develop; *stand the putting on:* Responds to my inciting.   287 *on the hip:* At my
mercy.

Abuse him to the Moor in the rank garb°
(For I fear Cassio with my nightcap too),
Make the Moor thank me, love me, and reward me                                  290
For making him egregiously an ass
And practicing upon° his peace and quiet
Even to madness. 'Tis here, but yet confused:
Knavery's plain face is never seen till used.                              *Exit.*

**Scene II:** *A street in Cyprus.*

*Enter Othello's Herald, with a proclamation.*

*Herald:* It is Othello's pleasure, our noble and valiant general, that, upon
certain tidings now arrived, importing the mere perdition° of the Turkish
fleet, every man put himself into triumph; some to dance, some to make
bonfires, each man to what sport and revels his addiction leads him. For,
besides these beneficial news, it is the celebration of his nuptial. So much          5
was his pleasure should be proclaimed. All offices° are open, and there is
full liberty of feasting from the present hour of five till the bell have told
eleven. Heaven bless the isle of Cyprus and our noble general Othello!    *Exit.*

**Scene III:** *The Cyprian Castle.*

*Enter Othello, Desdemona, Cassio, and Attendants.*

*Othello:* Good Michael, look you to the guard to-night.
Let's teach ourselves that honorable stop,
Not to outsport discretion.
*Cassio:* Iago hath direction what to do;
But not withstanding, with my personal eye                              5
Will I look to't.
*Othello:*               Iago is most honest.
Michael, good night. To-morrow with your earliest
Let me have speech with you.
        *[To Desdemona.]*        Come, my dear love.
The purchase made, the fruits are to ensue;
That profit 's yet to come 'tween me and you. —                              10
Good night.

*Exit [Othello with Desdemona and Attendants].*

*Enter Iago.*

*Cassio:* Welcome, Iago. We must to the watch.
*Iago:* Not this hour, lieutenant; 'tis not yet ten o' th' clock. Our general cast°
us thus early for the love of his Desdemona; who let us not therefore
blame. He hath not yet made wanton the night with her, and she is       15
sport for Jove.
*Cassio:* She's a most exquisite lady.

---

288 *rank garb:* Gross manner.   292 *practicing upon:* Plotting against.   **Scene II.**   2 *mere*
*perdition:* Complete destruction.   6 *offices:* Kitchens and storerooms.   **Scene III.**   13 *cast:*
Dismissed.

*Iago:* And, I'll warrant her, full of game.

*Cassio:* Indeed, she's a most fresh and delicate creature.

*Iago:* What an eye she has! Methinks it sounds a parley to provocation.          20

*Cassio:* An inviting eye; and yet methinks right modest.

*Iago:* And when she speaks, is it not an alarum to love?

*Cassio:* She is indeed perfection.

*Iago:* Well, happiness to their sheets! Come, lieutenant, I have a stoup° of wine, and here without are a brace of Cyprus gallants that would fain          25
have a measure to the health of black Othello.

*Cassio:* Not to-night, good Iago. I have very poor and unhappy brains for drinking; I could well wish courtesy would invent some other custom of entertainment.

*Iago:* O, they are our friends. But one cup! I'll drink for you.          30

*Cassio:* I have drunk but one cup to-night, and that was craftily quali-fied° too; and behold what innovation° it makes here. I am unfor-tunate in the infirmity and dare not task my weakness with any more.

*Iago:* What, man! 'Tis a night of revels: the gallants desire it.          35

*Cassio:* Where are they?

*Iago:* Here at the door; I pray you call them in.

*Cassio:* I'll do't, but it dislikes me.                                   *Exit.*

*Iago:* If I can fasten but one cup upon him
    With that which he hath drunk to-night already,          40
    He'll be as full of quarrel and offense
    As my young mistress' dog. Now my sick fool Roderigo,
    Whom love hath turned almost the wrong side out,
    To Desdemona hath to-night caroused
    Potations pottle-deep;° and he's to watch.          45
    Three lads of Cyprus — noble swelling spirits,
    That hold their honors in a wary distance,°
    The very elements° of this warlike isle —
    Have I to-night flustered with flowing cups,
    And they watch too. Now, 'mongst this flock of drunkards          50
    Am I to put our Cassio in some action
    That may offend the isle.

*Enter Cassio, Montano, and Gentlemen [; Servants following with wine].*

                  But here they come.
    If consequence do but approve my dream,
    My boat sails freely, both with wind and stream.

*Cassio:* 'Fore God, they have given me a rouse° already.          55

*Montano:* Good faith, a little one; not past a pint, as I am a soldier.

*Iago:* Some wine, ho!
    *[Sings.]*    And let me the cannikin clink, clink;
               And let me the cannikin clink
                  A soldier's a man;          60
                  O, man's life's but a span,
               Why then, let a soldier drink.

24 *stoup:* Two-quart tankard.   32 *qualified:* Diluted;   *innovation:* Disturbance.   45 *pottle-deep:* Bottoms up.   47 *That ... distance:* Very sensitive about their honor.   48 *very elements:* True representatives.   55 *rouse:* Bumper.

Some wine, boys!

*Cassio:* 'Fore God, an excellent song!

*Iago:* I learned it in England, where indeed they are most potent in    65
potting. Your Dane, your German, and your swag-bellied Hollander —
Drink, ho! — are nothing to your English.

*Cassio:* Is your Englishman so exquisite in his drinking?

*Iago:* Why, he drinks you with facility your Dane dead drunk; he sweats not
to overthrow your Almain; he gives your Hollander a vomit ere the next    70
pottle can be filled.

*Cassio:* To the health of our general!

*Montano:* I am for it, lieutenant, and I'll do you justice.

*Iago:* O sweet England!

> *[Sings.]*  King Stephen was and a worthy peer;    75
> His breeches cost him but a crown;
> He held 'em sixpence all too dear,
> With that he called the tailor lown.°
> He was a wight of high renown,
> And thou art but of low degree.    80
> 'Tis pride that pulls the country down;
> Then take thine auld cloak about thee.

Some wine, ho!

*Cassio:* 'Fore God, this is a more exquisite song than the other.

*Iago:* Will you hear't again?    85

*Cassio:* No, for I hold him to be unworthy of his place that does those things.°
Well, God's above all; and there be souls must be saved, and there be souls
must not be saved.

*Iago:* It's true, good lieutenant.

*Cassio:* For mine own part — no offense to the general, nor any man of    90
quality — I hope to be saved.

*Iago:* And so do I too, lieutenant.

*Cassio:* Ay, but, by your leave, not before me. The lieutenant is to be saved
before the ancient. Let's have no more of this; let's to our affairs. — God
forgive us our sins! — Gentlemen, let's look to our business. Do not think,    95
gentlemen, I am drunk. This is my ancient; this is my right hand, and this is
my left. I am not drunk now. I can stand well enough, and I speak well
enough.

*All:* Excellent well!

*Cassio:* Why, very well then. You must not think then that I am drunk.    *Exit.*    100

*Montano:* To th' platform, masters. Come, let's set the watch.

*Iago:* You see this fellow that is gone before.
He's a soldier fit to stand by Caesar
And give direction; and do but see his vice.    105
'Tis to his virtue a just equinox,°
The one as long as th' other. 'Tis pity of him.
I fear the trust Othello puts him in,
On some odd time of his infirmity,
Will shake this island.

---

78 *lown:* Rascal.    86 *does those things:* i.e., behaves in this fashion.    106 *just equinox:* Exact
equivalent.

*Montano:*                    But is he often thus?                                    110
*Iago:* 'Tis evermore his prologue to his sleep:
    He'll watch the horologe a double set°
    If drink rock not his cradle.
*Montano:*                    It were well
    The general were put in mind of it.
    Perhaps he sees it not, or his good nature                          115
    Prizes the virtue that appears in Cassio
    And looks not on his evils. Is not this true?

    *Enter Roderigo.*

*Iago [aside to him]:* How now, Roderigo?
    I pray you after the lieutenant, go!

                                *Exit Roderigo.*

*Montano:* And 'tis great pity that the noble Moor                          120
    Should hazard such a place as his own second
    With one of an ingraft° infirmity.
    It were an honest action to say
    So to the Moor.
*Iago:*                    Not I, for this fair island!
    I do love Cassio well and would do much                            125
    To cure him of this evil.

                      *(Within.) Help! help!*

    But hark! What noise?

    *Enter Cassio, driving in Roderigo.*

*Cassio:* Zounds, you rogue! you rascal!
*Montano:* What's the matter, lieutenant?
*Cassio:*                    A knave to teach me my duty?
    I'll beat the knave into a twiggen° bottle.                          130
*Roderigo:* Beat me?
*Cassio:*                    Dost thou prate, rogue? *[Strikes him.]*
*Montano:*                    Nay, good lieutenant!

                          *[Stays him.]*

    I pray you, sir, hold your hand.
*Cassio:*                    Let me go, sir,
    Or I'll knock you o'er the mazzard.°
*Montano:*                    Come, come, you're drunk!
*Cassio:* Drunk?

                              *They fight.*

*Iago [aside to Roderigo]:* Away, I say! Go out and cry a mutiny!          135

                          *Exit Roderigo.*

    Nay, good lieutenant. God's will, gentlemen!
    Help, ho! — lieutenant — sir — Montano — sir —
    Help, masters! — Here's a goodly watch indeed!

                          *A bell rung.*

    Who's that which rings the bell? Diablo, ho!

---

112 *watch . . . set:* Stay awake twice around the clock.   122 *ingraft:* i.e., ingrained.
130 *twiggen:* Wicker-covered.   133 *mazzard:* Head.

The town will rise.° God's will, lieutenant, hold!                    140
You'll be shamed for ever.

    *Enter Othello and Gentlemen with weapons.*

*Othello:*                  What is the matter here?
*Montano:* Zounds, I bleed still. I am hurt to th' death.
    He dies!
*Othello:* Hold for your lives!
*Iago:* Hold, ho! Lieutenant — sir — Montano — gentlemen!            145
    Have you forgot all sense of place and duty?
    Hold! The general speaks to you. Hold, for shame!
*Othello:* Why, how now ho? From whence ariseth this?
    Are we turned Turks, and to ourselves do that
    Which heaven hath forbid the Ottomites?                       150
    For Christian shame put by this barbarous brawl!
    He that stirs next to carve for° his own rage
    Holds his soul light; he dies upon his motion.
    Silence that dreadful bell! It frights the isle
    From her propriety.° What is the matter, masters?             155
    Honest Iago, that looks dead with grieving,
    Speak. Who began this? On thy love, I charge thee.
*Iago:* I do not know. Friends all, but now, even now,
    In quarter,° and in terms like bride and groom
    Devesting them for bed; and then, but now —                   160
    As if some planet had unwitted men —
    Swords out, and tilting one at other's breast
    In opposition bloody. I cannot speak
    Any beginning to this peevish odds,°
    And would in action glorious I had lost                       165
    Those legs that brought me to a part of it!
*Othello:* How comes it, Michael, you are thus forgot?
*Cassio:* I pray you pardon me; I cannot speak.
*Othello:* Worthy Montano, you were wont to be civil;
    The gravity and stillness of your youth                       170
    The world hath noted, and your name is great
    In mouths of wisest censure.° What's the matter
    That you unlace° your reputation thus
    And spend your rich opinion° for the name
    Of a night-brawler? Give me answer to it.                     175
*Montano:* Worthy Othello, I am hurt to danger.
    Your officer, Iago, can inform you,
    While I spare speech, which something now offends° me,
    Of all that I do know; nor know I aught
    By me that's said or done amiss this night,                   180
    Unless self-charity be sometimes a vice,
    And to defend ourselves it be a sin
    When violence assails us.

---

140 *rise:* Grow riotous.　152 *carve for:* Indulge.　155 *propriety:* Proper self.　159 *quarter:* Friendliness.　164 *peevish odds:* Childish quarrel.　172 *censure:* Judgment.　173 *unlace:* Undo.　174 *rich opinion:* High reputation.　178 *offends:* Pains.

*Othello:*                            Now, by heaven,
  My blood° begins my safer guides to rule,
  And passion, having my best judgment collied,°                    185
  Assays° to lead the way. Zounds, if I stir,
  Or do but lift this arm, the best of you
  Shall sink in my rebuke. Give me to know
  How this foul rout began, who set it on;
  And he that is approved in° this offense,                         190
  Though he had twinned with me, both at a birth,
  Shall lose me. What! in a town of war,
  Yet wild, the people's hearts brimful of fear,
  To manage° private and domestic quarrel?
  In night, and on the court and guard of safety?                  195
  'Tis monstrous. Iago, who began't?
*Montano:*  If partially affined, or leagued in office,°
  Thou dost deliver more or less than truth,
  Thou art no soldier.
*Iago:*                          Touch me not so near.
  I had rather have this tongue cut from my mouth                  200
  Than it should do offense to Michael Cassio;
  Yet I persuade myself, to speak the truth
  Shall nothing wrong him. This it is, general.
  Montano and myself being in speech,
  There comes a fellow crying out for help,                        205
  And Cassio following him with determined sword
  To execute° upon him. Sir, this gentleman
  Steps in to Cassio and entreats his pause.
  Myself the crying fellow did pursue,
  Lest by his clamor — as it so fell out —                         210
  The town might fall in fright. He, swift of foot,
  Outran my purpose; and I returned then rather
  For that I heard the clink and fall of swords,
  And Cassio high in oath;° which till to-night
  I ne'er might say before. When I came back —                     215
  For this was brief — I found them close together
  At blow and thrust, even as again they were
  When you yourself did part them.
  More of this matter cannot I report;
  But men are men; the best sometimes forget.                      220
  Though Cassio did some little wrong to him,
  As men in rage strike those that wish them best,
  Yet surely Cassio I believe received
  From him that fled some strange indignity,
  Which patience could not pass.°                                  225
*Othello:*                          I know, Iago,
  Thy honesty and love doth mince this matter,

---

184 *blood:* Passion.   185 *collied:* Darkened.   186 *Assays:* Tries.   190 *approved in:* Proved
guilty of.   194 *manage:* Carry on.   197 *partially . . . office:* Prejudiced by comradeship or
official relations.   207 *execute:* Work his will.   214 *high in oath:* Cursing.   225 *pass:* Pass
over, ignore.

Making it light to Cassio. Cassio, I love thee;
But never more be officer of mine.

*Enter Desdemona, attended.*

Look if my gentle love be not raised up!
I'll make thee an example.
*Desdemona:*                    What's the matter?                    230
*Othello:* All's well now, sweeting; come away to bed.
    *[To Montano.]*
Sir, for your hurts, myself will be your surgeon.
Lead him off.

*[Montano is led off.]*

Iago, look with care about the town
And silence those whom this vile brawl distracted.°                    235
Come, Desdemona; 'tis the soldiers' life
To have their balmy slumbers waked with strife.

*Exit [with all but Iago and Cassio].*

*Iago:* What, are you hurt, lieutenant?
*Cassio:* Ay, past all surgery.
*Iago:* Marry, God forbid!                    240
*Cassio:* Reputation, reputation, reputation! O, I have lost my reputation! I
    have lost the immortal part of myself, and what remains is bestial. My
    reputation, Iago, my reputation!
*Iago:* As I am an honest man, I thought you had received some bodily
    wound. There is more sense in that than in reputation. Reputa-                    245
    tion is an idle and most false imposition; oft got without merit and
    lost without deserving. You have lost no reputation at all unless you
    repute yourself such a loser. What, man! there are ways to recover°
    the general again. You are but now cast in his mood° — a punish-
    ment more in policy than in malice, even so as one would beat his                    250
    offenseless dog to affright an imperious lion. Sue to him again, and
    he's yours.
*Cassio:* I will rather sue to be despised than to deceive so good a
    commander with so slight, so drunken, and so indiscreet an
    officer. Drunk! and speak parrot!° and squabble! swagger! swear!                    255
    and discourse fustian° with one's own shadow! O thou invisible
    spirit of wine, if thou hast no name to be known by, let us call thee
    devil!
*Iago:* What was he that you followed with your sword? What had he done
    to you?                    260
*Cassio:* I know not.
*Iago:* Is't possible?
*Cassio:* I remember a mass of things, but nothing distinctly; a quarrel,
    but nothing wherefore. O God, that men should put an enemy
    in their mouths to steal away their brains! that we should with                    265
    joy, pleasance, revel, and applause° transform ourselves into
    beasts!

---

235 *distracted:* Excited.    248 *recover:* Regain favor with.    249 *in his mood:* Dismissed
because of his anger.    255 *parrot:* Meaningless phrases.    256 *fustian:* Bombastic nonsense.    266 *applause:* Desire to please.

*Iago:* Why, but you are now well enough. How came you thus
recovered?

*Cassio:* It hath pleased the devil drunkenness to give place to the devil   270
wrath. One unperfectness shows me another, to make me frankly despise myself.

*Iago:* Come, you are too severe a moraler. As the time, the place, and
the condition of this country stands, I could heartily wish this
had not so befall'n; but since it is as it is, mend it for your own   275
good.

*Cassio:* I will ask him for my place again: he shall tell me I am a drunk-
ard! Had I as many mouths as Hydra,° such an answer would stop
them all. To be now a sensible man, by and by a fool, and presently a
beast! O strange! Every inordinate cup is unblest, and the ingredient°   280
is a devil.

*Iago:* Come, come, good wine is a good familiar creature if it be well used.
Exclaim no more against it. And, good lieutenant, I think you think I
love you.

*Cassio:* I have well approved° it, sir. I drunk!   285

*Iago:* You or any man living may be drunk at some time, man. I'll tell you
what you shall do. Our general's wife is now the general. I may
say so in this respect, for that he hath devoted and given up himself to the contemplation, mark, and denotement of her parts and
graces. Confess yourself freely to her; importune her help to put you   290
in your place again. She is of so free,° so kind, so apt, so blessed a
disposition she holds it a vice in her goodness not to do more than
she is requested. This broken joint between you and her husband
entreat her to splinter;° and my fortunes against any lay° worth
naming, this crack of your love shall grow stronger than it was   295
before.

*Cassio:* You advise me well.

*Iago:* I protest, in the sincerity of love and honest kindness.

*Cassio:* I think it freely; and betimes in the morning will I beseech the virtuous Desdemona to undertake for me. I am desperate of my fortunes if   300
they check me here.

*Iago:* You are in the right. Good night, lieutenant; I must to the watch.

*Cassio:* Good night, honest Iago.                    *Exit Cassio.*

*Iago:* And what's he then that says I play the villain,
    When this advice is free I give and honest,   305
    Probal° to thinking, and indeed the course
    To win the Moor again? For 'tis most easy
    Th' inclining Desdemona to subdue°
    In an honest suit; she's framed as fruitful
    As the free elements. And then for her   310
    To win the Moor — were't to renounce his baptism,
    All seals and symbols of redeemèd sin —
    His soul is so enfettered to her love

---

278 *Hydra:* Monster with many heads.   280 *ingredient:* Contents.   285 *approved:* Proved.
291 *free:* Bounteous.   294 *splinter:* Bind up with splints; *lay:* Wager.   306 *Probal:*
Probable.   308 *subdue:* Persuade.

That she may make, unmake, do what she list,
Even as her appetite shall play the god                                    315
With his weak function. How am I then a villain
To counsel Cassio to this parallel° course,
Directly to his good? Divinity° of hell!
When devils will the blackest sins put on,°
They do suggest at first with heavenly shows,                               320
As I do now. For whiles this honest fool
Plies Desdemona to repair his fortunes,
And she for him pleads strongly to the Moor,
I'll pour this pestilence into his ear,
That she repeals him° for her body's lust;                                  325
And by how much she strives to do him good,
She shall undo her credit with the Moor.
So will I turn her virtue into pitch,
And out of her own goodness make the net
That shall enmesh them all.

*Enter Roderigo.*

                How, now, Roderigo?                                    330
*Roderigo:* I do follow here in the chase, not like a hound that hunts, but one
    that fills up the cry.° My money is almost spent; I have been to-night
    exceedingly well cudgelled; and I think the issue will be — I shall have
    so much experience for my pains; and so, with no money at all, and a
    little more wit, return again to Venice.                                 335
*Iago:* How poor are they that have not patience!
    What wound did ever heal but by degrees?
    Thou know'st we work by wit, and not by witchcraft;
    And wit depends on dilatory time.
    Does't not go well? Cassio hath beaten thee,                           340
    And thou by that small hurt hast cashiered Cassio.°
    Though other things grow fair against the sun,
    Yet fruits that blossom first will first be ripe.
    Content thyself awhile. By the mass, 'tis morning!
    Pleasure and action make the hours seem short.                        345
    Retire thee; go where thou art billeted.
    Away, I say! Thou shalt know more hereafter.
    Nay, get thee gone!                                    *Exit Roderigo.*
            Two things are to be done:
    My wife must move for Cassio to her mistress;
    I'll set her on;                                                       350
    Myself the while to draw the Moor apart
    And bring him jump° when he may Cassio find
    Soliciting his wife. Ay, that's the way!
    Dull no device by coldness and delay.                             *Exit.*

---

317 *parallel:* Corresponding.   318 *Divinity:* Theology.   319 *put on:* Incite.   325 *repeals him:* Seeks his recall.   332 *cry:* Pack.   341 *cashiered Cassio:* Maneuvered Cassio's discharge.
352 *jump:* At the exact moment.

## ACT III

SCENE I: *Before the chamber of Othello and Desdemona.*

*Enter Cassio, with Musicians and the Clown.*

*Cassio:* Masters, play here, I will content° your pains:
  Something that's brief; and bid "Good morrow, general."

*[They play.]*

*Clown:* Why, masters, ha' your instruments been in Naples,° that they speak
  i' th' nose thus?
*Musician:* How, sir, how?                                                5
*Clown:* Are these, I pray you, wind instruments?
*Musician:* Ay, marry, are they, sir.
*Clown:* O, thereby hangs a tail.
*Musician:* Whereby hangs a tale, sir?
*Clown:* Marry, sir, by many a wind instrument that I know. But, masters,   10
  here's money for you; and the general so likes your music that he desires
  you, for love's sake, to make no more noise with it.
*Musician:* Well, sir, we will not.
*Clown:* If you have any music that may not be heard, to't again: but, as they
  say, to hear music the general does not greatly care.                    15
*Musician:* We have none such, sir.
*Clown:* Then put up your pipes in your bag, for I'll away. Go, vanish into air,
  away!                                           *Exit Musician [with his fellows].*
*Cassio:* Dost thou hear, my honest friend?
*Clown:* No, I hear not your honest friend. I hear you.                    20
*Cassio:* Prithee keep up thy quillets.° There's a poor piece of gold for thee.
  If the gentlewoman that attends the general's wife be stirring, tell her
  there's one Cassio entreats her a little favor of speech. Wilt thou do
  this?
*Clown:* She is stirring sir. If she will stir hither, I shall seem to notify unto   25
  her.
*Cassio:* [Do, good my friend.]                              *Exit Clown.*

*Enter Iago.*

                    In happy time,° Iago.
*Iago:* You have not been abed then?
*Cassio:* Why, no; the day had broke
  Before we parted. I have made bold, Iago,                                30
  To send in to your wife: my suit to her
  Is that she will to virtuous Desdemona
  Procure me some access.
*Iago:*                     I'll send her to you presently;
  And I'll devise a mean to draw the Moor
  Out of the way, that your converse and business                          35
  May be more free.

Act III, Scene I.   1 *content*: Reward.   3 *Naples*: (Notorious for its association with venereal
disease).   21 *quillets*: Quips.   27 *In happy time*: Well met.

*Cassio:* I humbly thank you for't. Exit [Iago].
　　　　　　　　　　　　I never knew
　　A Florentine° more kind and honest.

*Enter Emilia.*

*Emilia:* Good morrow, good lieutenant. I am sorry
　　For your displeasure: but all will sure be well. 40
　　The general and his wife are talking of it,
　　And she speaks for you stoutly. The Moor replies
　　That he you hurt is of great fame in Cyprus
　　And great affinity,° and that in wholesome wisdom
　　He might not but refuse you; but he protests he loves you, 45
　　And needs no other suitor but his likings
　　[To take the safest occasion° by the front°]
　　To bring you in again.
*Cassio:*　　　　　　Yet I beseech you,
　　If you think fit, or that it may be done,
　　Give me advantage of some brief discourse 50
　　With Desdemona alone.
*Emilia:*　　　　　　Pray you come in.
　　I will bestow you where you shall have time
　　To speak your bosom° freely.
*Cassio:*　　　　　　I am much bound to you. *Exeunt.*

**SCENE II:** *The castle.*

*Enter Othello, Iago, and Gentlemen.*

*Othello:* These letters give, Iago, to the pilot
　　And by him do my duties to the Senate.
　　That done, I will be walking on the works;°
　　Repair there to me.
*Iago:*　　　　　　Well, my good lord, I'll do't.
*Othello:* This fortification, gentlemen, shall we see't? 5
*Gentlemen:* We'll wait upon your lordship. *Exeunt.*

**SCENE III:** *The castle grounds.*

*Enter Desdemona, Cassio, and Emilia.*

*Desdemona:* Be thou assured, good Cassio, I will do
　　All my abilities in thy behalf.
*Emilia:* Good madam, do. I warrant it grieves my husband
　　As if the cause were his.
*Desdemona:* O, that's an honest fellow. Do not doubt, Cassio, 5
　　But I will have my lord and you again
　　As friendly as you were.

---

38 *Florentine:* i.e., even a Florentine (like Cassio; Iago was a Venetian). 44 *affinity:* Family connections. 47 *occasion:* Opportunity; *front:* Forelock. 53 *your bosom:* Your inmost thoughts. **Scene II.** 3 *works:* Fortifications.

*Cassio:*                         Bounteous madam,
    Whatever shall become of Michael Cassio,
    He's never anything but your true servant.
*Desdemona:* I know't; I thank you. You do love my lord;          10
    You have known him long; and be you well assured
    He shall in strangeness° stand no farther off
    Than in a politic distance.°
*Cassio:*                         Ay, but, lady,
    That policy may either last so long,
    Or feed upon such nice and waterish diet,°          15
    Or breed itself so out of circumstance,
    That, I being absent, and my place supplied,
    My general will forget my love and service.
*Desdemona:* Do not doubt° that; before Emilia here
    I give thee warrant of thy place. Assure thee,          20
    If I do vow a friendship, I'll perform it
    To the last article. My lord shall never rest;
    I'll watch him tame° and talk him out of patience;
    His bed shall seem a school, his board a shrift;°
    I'll intermingle everything he does          25
    With Cassio's suit. Therefore be merry, Cassio,
    For thy solicitor shall rather die
    Than give thy cause away.

    *Enter Othello and Iago [at a distance].*

*Emilia:* Madam, here comes my lord.
*Cassio:* Madam, I'll take my leave.          30
*Desdemona:* Why, stay, and hear me speak.
*Cassio:* Madam, not now: I am very ill at ease,
    Unfit for mine own purposes.
*Desdemona:* Well, do your discretion.                         *Exit Cassio.*
*Iago:* Ha! I like not that.
*Othello:*                     What dost thou say?          35
*Iago:* Nothing, my lord; or if — I know not what.
*Othello:* Was not that Cassio parted from my wife?
*Iago:* Cassio, my lord? No, sure, I cannot think it,
    That he would steal away so guilty-like,
    Seeing your coming.
*Othello:*                     I do believe 'twas he.          40
*Desdemona:* How now, my lord?
    I have been talking with a suitor here,
    A man that languishes in your displeasure.
*Othello:* Who is't you mean?
*Desdemona:* Why, your lieutenant, Cassio. Good my lord,          45
    If I have any grace or power to move you,

**Scene III.**   12 *strangeness:* Aloofness.   13 *Than . . . distance:* Than wise policy requires.
15 *Or . . . diet:* Or be continued for such slight reasons.   19 *doubt:* Fear.   23 *watch him
tame:* Keep him awake until he gives in.   24 *shrift:* Confessional.

His present° reconciliation take;
For if he be not one that truly loves you,
That errs in ignorance, and not in cunning,
I have no judgment in an honest face,                                                    50
I prithee call him back.

*Othello:*                              Went he hence now?

*Desdemona:*  Ay, sooth; so humbled
That he hath left part of his grief with me
To suffer with him. Good love, call him back.

*Othello:*  Not now, sweet Desdemon; some other time.        55

*Desdemona:*  But shall't be shortly?

*Othello:*                                      The sooner, sweet, for you.

*Desdemona:*  Shall't be to-night at supper?

*Othello:*                                      No, not to-night.

*Desdemona:*  To-morrow dinner then?

*Othello:*                              I shall not dine at home;
I meet the captains at the citadel.

*Desdemona:*  Why then, to-morrow night, on Tuesday morn,     60
On Tuesday noon or night, on Wednesday morn.
I prithee name the time, but let it not
Exceed three days. I' faith, he's penitent;
And yet his trespass, in our common reason
(Save that, they say, the wars must make example             65
Out of her best), is not almost° a fault
T' incur a private check.° When shall he come?
Tell me, Othello. I wonder in my soul
What you would ask me that I should deny
Or stand so mamm'ring on.° What? Michael Cassio,             70
That came a-wooing with you, and so many a time,
When I have spoke of you dispraisingly,
Hath ta'en your part — to have so much to do
To bring him in? By'r Lady, I could do much —

*Othello:*  Prithee no more. Let him come when he will!      75
I will deny thee nothing.

*Desdemona:*                          Why, this is not a boon;
'Tis as I should entreat you wear your gloves,
Or feed on nourishing dishes, or keep you warm,
Or sue to you to do a peculiar profit
To your own person. Nay, when I have a suit                  80
Wherein I mean to touch your love indeed,
It shall be full of poise and difficult weight,
And fearful° to be granted.

*Othello:*                          I will deny thee nothing!
Whereon I do beseech thee grant me this,
To leave me but a little to myself.                          85

---

47 *present:* Immediate.   66 *not almost:* Hardly.   67 *a private check:* Even a private reprimand.   70 *mamm'ring on:* Hesitating about.   83 *fearful:* Dangerous.

*Desdemona:* Shall I deny you? No. Farewell, my lord.
*Othello:* Farewell, my Desdemona: I'll come to thee straight.
*Desdemona:* Emilia, come. — Be as your fancies teach you;
    Whate'er you be, I am obedient.        *Exit [with Emilia].*
*Othello:* Excellent wretch!° Perdition catch my soul        90
    But I do love thee! and when I love thee not,
    Chaos is come again.
*Iago:* My noble lord —
*Othello:*              What dost thou say, Iago?
*Iago:* Did Michael Cassio, when you wooed my lady,
    Know of your love?        95
*Othello:* He did, from first to last. Why dost thou ask?
*Iago:* But for a satisfaction of my thought;
    No further harm.
*Othello:*            Why of thy thought, Iago?
*Iago:* I did not think he had been acquainted with her.
*Othello:* O, yes, and went between us° very oft.        100
*Iago:* Indeed?
*Othello:* Indeed? Ay, indeed! Discern'st thou aught in that?
    Is he not honest?
*Iago:*          Honest, my lord?
*Othello:*                   Honest. Ay, honest.
*Iago:* My lord, for aught I know.
*Othello:* What dost thou think?
*Iago:*                Think, my lord?
*Othello:*                      Think, my lord?        105
    By heaven, thou echo'st me,
    As if there were some monster in thy thought
    Too hideous to be shown. Thou dost mean something:
    I heard thee say even now, thou lik'st not that,
    When Cassio left my wife. What didst not like?        110
    And when I told thee he was of my counsel
    In my whole course of wooing, thou cried'st "Indeed?"
    And didst contract and purse thy brow together,
    As if thou then hadst shut up in thy brain
    Some horrible conceit.° If thou dost love me,        115
    Show me thy thought
*Iago:* My lord, you know I love you.
*Othello:*                I think thou dost;
    And, for I know thou'rt full of love and honesty
    And weigh'st thy words before thou giv'st them breath,
    Therefore these stops of thine fright me the more;        120
    For such things in a false disloyal knave
    Are tricks of custom; but in a man that's just
    They're close dilations, working from the heart
    That passion cannot rule.°

---

90 *wretch:* (A term of endearment).   100 *went between us:* i.e., as messenger.   115 *conceit:* Fancy.   123–24 *close dilations . . . rule:* Secret emotions which well up in spite of restraint.

*Iago:*                                   For Michael Cassio,
    I dare be sworn I think that he is honest.         125
*Othello:* I think so too.
*Iago:*                             Men should be what they seem;
    Or those that be not, would they might seem none!°
*Othello:* Certain, men should be what they seem.
*Iago:* Why then, I think Cassio's an honest man.
*Othello:* Nay, yet there's more in this.         130
    I prithee speak to me as to thy thinkings,
    As thou dost ruminate, and give thy worst of thoughts
    The worst of words.
*Iago:*                             Good my lord, pardon me:
    Though I am bound to every act of duty,
    I am not bound to that all slaves are free to.°         135
    Utter my thoughts? Why, say they are vile and false,
    As where's that palace whereinto foul things
    Sometimes intrude not? Who has a breast so pure
    But some uncleanly apprehensions
    Keep leets and law days,° and in Sessions sit         140
    With meditations lawful?
*Othello:* Thou dost conspire against thy friend, Iago,
    If thou but think'st him wronged, and mak'st his ear
    A stranger to thy thoughts.
*Iago:*                             I do beseech you —
    Though I perchance am vicious in my guess         145
    (As I confess it is my nature's plague
    To spy into abuses, and oft my jealousy°
    Shapes faults that are not), that your wisdom yet
    From one that so imperfectly conjects°
    Would take no notice, nor build yourself a trouble       150
    Out of his scattering and unsure observance.
    It were not for your quiet nor your good,
    Nor for my manhood, honesty, and wisdom,
    To let you know my thoughts.
*Othello:*                             What dost thou mean?
*Iago:* Good name in man and woman, dear my lord,       155
    Is the immediate° jewel of their souls.
    Who steals my purse steals trash; 'tis something, nothing;
    'Twas mine, 'tis his, and has been slave to thousands;
    But he that filches from me my good name
    Robs me of that which not enriches him         160
    And makes me poor indeed.
*Othello:* By heaven, I'll know thy thoughts!
*Iago:* You cannot, if my heart were in your hand;
    Nor shall not whilst 'tis in my custody.

---

127 *seem none:* i.e., not pretend to be men when they are really monsters.   135 *bound...free to:* Bound to tell that which even slaves are allowed to keep to themselves.   140 *leets and law days:* Sittings of the courts.   147 *jealousy:* Suspicion.   149 *conjects:* Conjectures. 156 *immediate:* Nearest the heart.

*Othello:*  Ha!
*Iago:*          O, beware, my lord, of jealousy!                                            165
    It is the green-eyed monster, which doth mock°
    The meat it feeds on. That cuckold lives in bliss
    Who, certain of his fate, loves not his wronger;
    But O, what damnèd minutes tells he o'er
    Who dotes, yet doubts — suspects, yet fondly loves!                          170
*Othello:*  O misery!
*Iago:*  Poor and content is rich, and rich enough;
    But riches fineless° is as poor as winter
    To him that ever fears he shall be poor.
    Good God, the souls of all my tribe defend                                    175
    From jealousy!
*Othello:*          Why, why is this?
    Think'st thou I'd make a life of jealousy,
    To follow still the changes of the moon
    With fresh suspicions? No! To be once in doubt
    Is once to be resolved. Exchange me for a goat                               180
    When I shall turn the business of my soul
    To such exsufflicate and blown° surmises,
    Matching thy inference. 'Tis not to make me jealous
    To say my wife is fair, feeds well, loves company,
    Is free of speech, sings, plays, and dances well.                            185
    Where virtue is, these are more virtuous.
    Nor from mine own weak merits will I draw
    The smallest fear or doubt of her revolt,°
    For she had eyes, and chose me. No, Iago;
    I'll see before I doubt; when I doubt, prove;                                190
    And on the proof there is no more but this —
    Away at once with love or jealousy!
*Iago:*  I am glad of this; for now I shall have reason
    To show the love and duty that I bear you
    With franker spirit. Therefore, as I am bound,                               195
    Receive it from me. I speak not yet of proof.
    Look to your wife; observe her well with Cassio;
    Wear your eyes thus, not jealous nor secure:°
    I would not have your free and noble nature,
    Out of self-bounty,° be abused. Look to't.                                   200
    I know our country disposition well:
    In Venice they do let God see the pranks
    They dare not show their husbands; their best conscience
    Is not to leave't undone, but keep't unknown.
*Othello:*  Dost thou say so?                                                               205
*Iago:*  She did deceive her father, marrying you;
    And when she seemed to shake and fear your looks,
    She loved them most.

---

166 *mock:* Play with, like a cat with a mouse.   173 *fineless:* Unlimited.   182 *exsufflicate and blown:* Spat out and flyblown.   188 *revolt:* Unfaithfulness.   198 *secure:* Overconfident. 200 *self-bounty:* Natural goodness.

| | |
|---|---|
| *Othello:* | And so she did. |
| *Iago:* | Why, go to then! |

    She that, so young, could give out such a seeming
    To seel° her father's eyes up close as oak° —         210
    He thought 'twas witchcraft — but I am much to blame.
    I humbly do beseech you of your pardon
    For too much loving you.

*Othello:*                 I am bound to thee for ever.

*Iago:* I see this hath a little dashed your spirits.

*Othello:* Not a jot, not a jot.

*Iago:*                I' faith, I fear it has.         215
    I hope you will consider what is spoke
    Comes from my love. But I do see y' are moved.
    I am to pray you not to strain my speech
    To grosser issues° nor to larger reach
    Than to suspicion.               220

*Othello:* I will not.

*Iago:*            Should you do so, my lord,
    My speech should fall into such vile success°
    As my thoughts aim not at. Cassio's my worthy friend —
    My lord, I see y' are moved.

*Othello:*              No, not much moved:
    I do not think but Desdemona's honest.°      225

*Iago:* Long live she so! and long live you to think so!

*Othello:* And yet, how nature erring from itself —

*Iago:* Ay, there's the point! as (to be bold with you)
    Not to affect many proposèd matches
    Of her own clime, complexion, and degree,      230
    Whereto we see in all things nature tends —
    Foh! one may smell in such a will most rank,
    Foul disproportions, thoughts unnatural —
    But pardon me — I do not in position°
    Distinctly speak of her; though I may fear      235
    Her will, recoiling° to her better judgment,
    May fall to match° you with her country forms,
    And happily° repent.

*Othello:*             Farewell, farewell!
    If more thou dost perceive, let me know more.
    Set on thy wife to observe. Leave me, Iago.      240

*Iago:* My lord, I take my leave.              *[Going.]*

*Othello:* Why did I marry? This honest creature doubtless
    Sees and knows more, much more, than he unfolds.

*Iago [returns]:* My lord, I would I might entreat your honor
    To scan this thing no further: leave it to time.     245
    Although 'tis fit that Cassio have his place,

---

210 *seel:* Close; *oak:* Oak grain.   219 *To grosser issues:* To mean something more monstrous.   222 *vile success:* Evil outcome.   225 *honest:* Chaste.   234 *position:* Definite assertion.   236 *recoiling:* Reverting.   237 *fall to match:* Happen to compare.   238 *happily:* Haply, perhaps.

For sure he fills it up with great ability,
Yet, if you please to hold him off a while,
You shall by that perceive him and his means.
Note if your lady strain his entertainment°                              250
With any strong or vehement importunity;
Much will be seen in that. In the mean time
Let me be thought too busy° in my fears
(As worthy cause I have to fear I am)
And hold her free,° I do beseech your honor.                            255
*Othello:*  Fear not my government.°
*Iago:*  I once more take my leave.                          *Exit.*
*Othello:*  This fellow's of exceeding honesty,
And knows all qualities,° with a learned spirit
Of° human dealings. If I do prove her haggard,°                         260
Though that her jesses° were my dear heartstrings,
I'd whistle her off and let her down the wind
To prey at fortune.° Haply, for I am black
And have not those soft parts of conversation°
That chamberers° have, or for I am declined                             265
Into the vale of years — yet that's not much —
She's gone. I am abused, and my relief
Must be to loathe her. O curse of marriage,
That we can call these delicate creatures ours,
And not their appetites! I had rather be a toad                         270
And live upon the vapor of a dungeon
Than keep a corner in the thing I love
For others' uses. Yet 'tis the plague of great ones;°
Prerogatived° are they less than the base.
'Tis destiny unshunnable, like death.                                   275
Even then this forkèd plague° is fated to us
When we do quicken.° Look where she comes.

*Enter Desdemona and Emilia.*

If she be false, O, then heaven mocks itself!
I'll not believe't.
*Desdemona:*          How now, my dear Othello?
Your dinner, and the generous° islanders                                280
By you invited, do attend your presence.
*Othello:*  I am to blame.
*Desdemona:*          Why do you speak so faintly?
Are you not well?
*Othello:*  I have a pain upon my forehead, here.

---

250 *strain his entertainment:* Urge his recall.  253 *busy:* Meddlesome.  255 *hold her free:* Consider her guiltless.  256 *government:* Self-control.  259 *qualities:* Natures.  259–60 *learned spirit Of:* Mind informed about.  260 *haggard:* A wild hawk.  261 *jesses:* Thongs for controlling a hawk.  262–63 *whistle . . . fortune:* Turn her out and let her take care of herself.  264 *soft . . . conversation:* Ingratiating manners.  265 *chamberers:* Courtiers.  273 *great ones:* Prominent men.  274 *Prerogatived:* Privileged.  276 *forkèd plague:* i.e., horns of a cuckold.  277 *do quicken:* Are born.  280 *generous:* Noble.

*Desdemona:* Faith, that's with watching;° 'twill away again.    285
     Let me but bind it hard, within this hour
     It will be well.
*Othello:*          Your napkin° is too little;

*[He pushes the handkerchief from him, and it falls unnoticed.]*

     Let it° alone. Come, I'll go in with you.
*Desdemona:* I am very sorry that you are not well.      *Exit [with Othello].*
*Emilia:* I am glad I have found this napkin;    290
     This was her first remembrance from the Moor,
     My wayward husband hath a hundred times
     Wooed me to steal it; but she so loves the token
     (For he conjured her she should ever keep it)
     That she reserves it evermore about her    295
     To kiss and talk to. I'll have the work ta'en out°
     And give't Iago.
     What he will do with it heaven knows, not I;
     I nothing but to please his fantasy.°

*Enter Iago.*

*Iago:* How now? What do you here alone?    300
*Emilia:* Do not you chide; I have a thing for you.
*Iago:* A thing for me? It is a common thing —
*Emilia:* Ha?
*Iago:* To have a foolish wife.
*Emilia:* O, is that all? What will you give me now    305
     For that same handkerchief?
*Iago:*                 What handkerchief?
*Emilia:* What handkerchief!
     Why, that the Moor first gave to Desdemona;
     That which so often you did bid me steal.
*Iago:* Hast stol'n it from her?    310
*Emilia:* No, faith; she let it drop by negligence,
     And to th' advantage,° I, being here, took't up.
     Look, here 'tis.
*Iago:*         A good wench! Give it me.
*Emilia:* What will you do with't, that you have been so earnest
     To have me filch it?
*Iago:*          Why, what is that to you?    315

     *[Snatches it.]*

*Emilia:* If it be not for some purpose of import,°
     Give't me again. Poor lady, she'll run mad
     When she shall lack it.
*Iago:* Be not acknown on't;° I have use for it.
     Go, leave me.                 *Exit Emilia.*    320

---

285 *watching:* Working late.   287 *napkin:* Handkerchief.   288 *it:* i.e., his forehead.   296 *work ta'en out:* Pattern copied.   299 *fantasy:* Whim.   312 *to th' advantage:* Opportunely. 316 *import:* Importance.   319 *Be . . . on't:* Do not acknowledge it.

I will in Cassio's lodgings lose this napkin
And let him find it. Trifles light as air
Are to the jealous confirmations strong
As proofs of holy writ. This may do something.
The Moor already changes with my poison:                              325
Dangerous conceits° are in their natures poisons,
Which at the first are scarce found to distaste,
But with a little act upon the blood
Burn like the mines of sulphur.

*Enter Othello.*

                                     I did say so.
Look where he comes! Not poppy nor mandragora,°                      330
Nor all the drowsy syrups of the world,
Shall ever med'cine thee to that sweet sleep
Which thou owedst yesterday.
*Othello:*                        Ha! ha! false to me?
*Iago:* Why, how now, general? No more of that!
*Othello:* Avaunt! be gone! Thou hast set me on the rack.            335
I swear 'tis better to be much abused
Than but to know't a little.
*Iago:*                        How now, my lord?
*Othello:* What sense had I of her stol'n hours of lust?
I saw't not, thought it not, it harmed not me;
I slept the next night well, fed well, was free° and merry;          340
I found not Cassio's kisses on her lips.
He that is robbed, not wanting° what is stol'n,
Let him not know't, and he's not robbed at all.
*Iago:* I am sorry to hear this.
*Othello:* I had been happy if the general camp,                     345
Pioneers° and all, had tasted her sweet body,
So I had nothing known. O, now for ever
Farewell the tranquil mind! farewell content!
Farewell the plumèd troops, and the big° wars
That make ambition virtue! O, farewell!                             350
Farewell the neighing steed and the shrill trump,
The spirit-stirring drum, th' ear-piercing fife,
The royal banner, and all quality,
Pride, pomp, and circumstance° of glorious war!
And O you mortal engines° whose rude throats                         355
Th' immortal Jove's dread clamors counterfeit,°
Farewell! Othello's occupation's gone!
*Iago:* Is't possible, my lord?
*Othello:* Villain, be sure thou prove my love a whore!
Be sure of it; give me the ocular proof;                            360

---

326 *conceits:* Ideas.   330 *mandragora:* A narcotic.   340 *free:* Carefree.   342 *wanting:*
Missing.   346 *Pioneers:* Sappers, laborers.   349 *big:* Stately.   354 *circumstance:*
Pageantry.   355 *mortal engines:* Deadly artillery.   356 *counterfeit:* Imitate.

Or, by the worth of mine eternal soul,
Thou hadst been better have been born a dog
Than answer my waked wrath!
*Iago:*                               Is't come to this?
*Othello:*  Make me to see't; or at the least so prove it
That the probation° bear no hinge nor loop          365
To hang a doubt on — or woe upon thy life!
*Iago:*  My noble lord —
*Othello:*  If thou dost slander her and torture me,
Never pray more; abandon all remorse;
On horror's head horrors accumulate;                   370
Do deeds to make heaven weep, all earth amazed;
For nothing canst thou to damnation add
Greater than that.
*Iago:*                         O grace! O heaven forgive me!
Are you a man? Have you a soul or sense? —
God buy you! take mine office. O wretched fool,      375
That lov'st to make thine honesty a vice!
O monstrous world! Take note, take note, O world,
To be direct and honest is not safe.
I thank you for this profit;° and from hence
I'll love no friend, sith love breeds such offense.    380
*Othello:*  Nay, stay. Thou shouldst be honest.
*Iago:*  I should be wise; for honesty's a fool
And loses that it works for.
*Othello:*                         By the world,
I think my wife be honest, and think she is not;
I think that thou art just, and think thou art not.    385
I'll have some proof. Her name, that was as fresh
As Dian's visage, is now begrimed and black
As mine own face. If there be cords, or knives,
Poison, or fire, or suffocating streams,
I'll not endure it. Would I were satisfied!°            390
*Iago:*  I see, sir, you are eaten up with passion:
I do repent me that I put it to you.
You would be satisfied?
*Othello:*                     Would? Nay, and I will.
*Iago:*  And may; but how? how satisfied, my lord?
Would you, the supervisor,° grossly gape on?          395
Behold her topped?
*Othello:*                    Death and damnation! O!
*Iago:*  It were a tedious difficulty, I think,
To bring them to that prospect. Damn them then,
If ever mortal eyes do see them bolster°
More than their own! What then? How then?            400

365 *probation:* Proof.   379 *profit:* Profitable lesson.   390 *satisfied:* Completely informed.
395 *supervisor:* Spectator.   399 *bolster:* Lie together.

What shall I say? Where's satisfaction?
It is impossible you should see this,
Were they as prime° as goats, as hot as monkeys,
As salt° as wolves in pride,° and fools as gross
As ignorance made drunk. But yet, I say,                              405
If imputation and strong circumstances
Which lead directly to the door of truth
Will give you satisfaction, you might have't.
*Othello:*  Give me a living reason she's disloyal.
*Iago:*  I do not like the office.                                   410
    But sith I am ent'red in this cause so far,
    Pricked to't by foolish honesty and love,
    I will go on. I lay with Cassio lately,
    And being troubled with a raging tooth,
    I could not sleep.                                         415
    There are a kind of men so loose of soul
    That in their sleeps will mutter their affairs.
    One of this kind is Cassio.
    In sleep I heard him say, "Sweet Desdemona,
    Let us be wary, let us hide our loves!"                    420
    And then, sir, would he gripe and wring my hand,
    Cry "O sweet creature!" and then kiss me hard,
    As if he plucked up kisses by the roots
    That grew upon my lips; then laid his leg
    Over my thigh, and sighed, and kissed, and then            425
    Cried "Cursèd fate that gave thee to the Moor!"
*Othello:*  O monstrous! monstrous!
*Iago:*                                 Nay, this was but his dream.
*Othello:*  But this denoted a foregone conclusion;°
*Iago:*  'Tis a shrewd doubt,° though it be but a dream.
    And this may help to thicken other proofs                  430
    That do demonstrate thinly.
*Othello:*                          I'll tear her all to pieces!
*Iago:*  Nay, yet be wise. Yet we see nothing done;
    She may be honest yet. Tell me but this —
    Have you not sometimes seen a handkerchief
    Spotted with strawberries in your wife's hand?             435
*Othello:*  I gave her such a one; 'twas my first gift.
*Iago:*  I know not that; but such a handkerchief —
    I am sure it was your wife's — did I to-day
    See Cassio wipe his beard with.
*Othello:*  If it be that —
*Iago:*  If it be that, or any that was hers,                        440
    It speaks against her with the other proofs.

---

403 *prime:* Lustful.   404 *salt:* Lecherous; *pride:* Heat.   428 *foregone conclusion:* Previous
experience.   429 *a shrewd doubt:* Cursedly suspicious.

*Othello:* O, that the slave had forty thousand lives!
    One is too poor, too weak for my revenge.
    Now do I see 'tis true. Look here, Iago:
    All my fond love thus do I blow to heaven.         445
    'Tis gone.
    Arise, black vengeance, from thy hollow hell!
    Yield up, O love, thy crown and hearted throne
    To tyrannous hate! Swell, bosom, with thy fraught,°
    For 'tis of aspics'° tongues!
*Iago:*                   Yet be content.         450
*Othello:* O, blood, blood, blood!
*Iago:* Patience, I say. Your mind perhaps may change.
*Othello:* Never, Iago. Like to the Pontic sea,°
    Whose icy current and compulsive course
    Ne'er feels retiring ebb, but keeps due on         455
    To the Propontic and the Hellespont,
    Even so my bloody thoughts, with violent pace,
    Shall ne'er look back, ne'er ebb to humble love,
    Till that a capable° and wide revenge
    Swallow them up.
    *(He kneels.)*     Now, by yond marble heaven,     460
    In the due reverence of a sacred vow
    I here engage my words.
*Iago:*               Do not rise yet.
    *(Iago kneels.)*
    Witness, you ever-burning lights above,
    You elements that clip° us round about,
    Witness that here Iago doth give up         465
    The execution° of his wit,° hands, heart
    To wronged Othello's service! Let him command,
    And to obey shall be in me remorse,°
    What bloody business ever.

    *[They rise.]*

*Othello:*               I greet thy love,
    Not with vain thanks but with acceptance bounteous,     470
    And will upon the instant put thee to't.
    Within these three days let me hear thee say
    That Cassio's not alive.
*Iago:* My friend is dead; 'tis done at your request.
    But let her live.         475
*Othello:* Damn her, lewd minx! O, damn her! damn her!
    Come, go with me apart. I will withdraw
    To furnish me with some swift means of death
    For the fair devil. Now art thou my lieutenant.
*Iago:* I am your own forever.         *Exeunt.*   480

---

449 *fraught:* Burden.   450 *aspics:* Deadly poisonous snakes.   453 *Pontic sea:* Black Sea.
459 *capable:* All-embracing.   464 *clip:* Encompass.   466 *execution:* Activities; *wit:* Mind.
468 *remorse:* Pity.

**SCENE IV:** *The environs of the castle.*

    *Enter Desdemona, Emilia, and Clown.*

*Desdemona:* Do you know, sirrah, where Lieutenant Cassio lies?°
*Clown:* I dare not say he lies anywhere.
*Desdemona:* Why, man?
*Clown:* He's a soldier, and for me to say a soldier lies, 'tis stabbing.
*Desdemona:* Go to. Where lodges he?                       5
*Clown:* To tell you where he lodges is to tell you where I lie.
*Desdemona:* Can anything be made of this?
*Clown:* I know not where he lodges; and for me to devise a lodging, and say
    he lies here or he lies there, were to lie in mine own throat.
*Desdemona:* Can you enquire him out, and be edified by report?       10
*Clown:* I will catechize the world for him; that is, make questions, and by
    them answer.
*Desdemona:* Seek him, bid him come hither. Tell him I have moved° my lord
    on his behalf and hope all will be well.
*Clown:* To do this is within the compass of man's wit, and therefore I'll    15
    attempt the doing of it.                                *Exit.*
*Desdemona:* Where should I lose the handkerchief, Emilia?
*Emilia:* I know not, madam.
*Desdemona:* Believe me, I had rather have lost my purse
    Full of crusadoes;° and but my noble Moor                  20
    Is true of mind, and made of no such baseness
    As jealous creatures are, it were enough
    To put him to ill thinking.
*Emilia:*                Is he not jealous?
*Desdemona:* Who? he? I think the sun where he was born
    Drew all such humors° from him.

    *Enter Othello.*

*Emilia:*                Look where he comes.          25
*Desdemona:* I will not leave him now till Cassio
    Be called to him — How is't with you, my lord?
*Othello:* Well, my good lady. *[Aside.]* O, hardness to dissemble! —
    How do you, Desdemona?
*Desdemona:*              Well, my good lord.
*Othello:* Give me your hand. This hand is moist, my lady.       30
*Desdemona:* It yet hath felt no age nor known no sorrow.
*Othello:* This argues fruitfulness and liberal heart.
    Hot, hot, and moist. This hand of yours requires
    A sequester° from liberty, fasting and prayer,
    Much castigation, exercise devout;                  35
    For here's a young and sweating devil here
    That commonly rebels. 'Tis a good hand,
    A frank one.

---

**Scene IV.**  1 *lies:* Lives, lodges.  13 *moved:* Made proposals to.  20 *crusadoes:* Portuguese
gold coins.  25 *humors:* Inclinations.  34 *sequester:* Removal.

*Desdemona:* You may, indeed, say so;
    For 'twas that hand that gave away my heart.                    40
*Othello:* A liberal hand! The hearts of old gave hands;
    But our new heraldry° is hands, not hearts.
*Desdemona:* I cannot speak of this. Come now, your promise!
*Othello:* What promise, chuck?
*Desdemona:* I have sent to bid Cassio come speak with you.                    45
*Othello:* I have a salt and sorry rheum° offends me.
    Lend me thy handkerchief.
*Desdemona:*                Here, my lord.
*Othello:* That which I gave you.
*Desdemona:*                I have it not about me.
*Othello:* Not?
*Desdemona:* No, faith, my lord.
*Othello:*              That's a fault.
    That handkerchief                    50
    Did an Egyptian° to my mother give.
    She was a charmer,° and could almost read
    The thoughts of people. She told her, while she kept it,
    'Twould make her amiable° and subdue my father
    Entirely to her love; but if she lost it                    55
    Or made a gift of it, my father's eye
    Should hold her loathèd, and his spirits should hunt
    After new fancies. She, dying, gave it me,
    And bid me, when my fate would have me wived,
    To give it her. I did so; and take heed on't;                    60
    Make it a darling like your precious eye.
    To lose't or give't away were such perdition°
    As nothing else could match.
*Desdemona:*              Is't possible?
*Othello:* 'Tis true. There's magic in the web of it.
    A sibyl that had numb'red in the world                    65
    The sun to course two hundred compasses,°
    In her prophetic fury sewed the work;
    The worms were hallowed that did breed the silk;
    And it was dyed in mummy° which the skillful
    Conserved of maidens' hearts.
*Desdemona:*             I'faith? Is't true?                    70
*Othello:* Most veritable. Therefore look to't well.
*Desdemona:* Then would to God that I had never seen't!
*Othello:* Ha! Wherefore?
*Desdemona:* Why do you speak so startingly and rash?
*Othello:* Is't lost? Is't gone? Speak, is't out o' th' way?                    75
*Desdemona:* Heaven bless us!
*Othello:* Say you?

---

42 *heraldry:* Heraldic symbolism.   46 *salt . . . rheum:* Distressing head cold.   51 *Egyptian:* Gypsy.   52 *charmer:* Sorceress.   54 *amiable:* Lovable.   62 *perdition:* Disaster.   66 *compasses:* Annual rounds.   69 *mummy:* A drug made from mummies.

*Desdemona:* It is not lost. But what an if it were?
*Othello:* How?
*Desdemona:* I say it is not lost.
*Othello:*                          Fetch't, let me see't!          80
*Desdemona:* Why, so I can, sir; but I will not now.
     This is a trick to put° me from my suit:
     Pray you let Cassio be received again.
*Othello:* Fetch me the handkerchief! My mind misgives.
*Desdemona:* Come, come!          85
     You'll never meet a more sufficient man.
*Othello:* The handkerchief!
[*Desdemona:*                    I pray talk me of Cassio.
*Othello:* The handkerchief!]
*Desdemona:*                    A man that all his time °
     Hath founded his good fortunes on your love,
     Shared dangers with you —          90
*Othello:* The handkerchief!
*Desdemona:* I' faith, you are to blame.
*Othello:* Zounds!                                   *Exit Othello.*
*Emilia:* Is not this man jealous?
*Desdemona:* I ne'er saw this before.          95
     Sure there's some wonder in this handkerchief;
     I am most unhappy in the loss of it.
*Emilia:* 'Tis not a year or two shows us a man.
     They are all but stomachs, and we all but food;
     They eat us hungerly, and when they are full,          100
     They belch us.

     *Enter Iago and Cassio.*

                    Look you — Cassio and my husband!
*Iago:* There is no other way; 'tis she must do't.
     And lo the happiness!° Go and importune her.
*Desdemona:* How now, good Cassio? What's the news with you?
*Cassio:* Madam, my former suit. I do beseech you          105
     That by your virtuous means I may again
     Exist, and be a member of his love
     Whom I with all the office of my heart
     Entirely honor. I would not be delayed.
     If my offense be of such mortal kind          110
     That neither my service past, nor present sorrows,
     Nor purposed merit in futurity,
     Can ransom me into his love again,
     But to know so must be my benefit.
     So shall I clothe me in a forced content,          115
     And shut myself up in° some other course,
     To fortune's alms.

---

82 *put:* Divert.   88 *all his time:* During his whole career.   103 *happiness:* Good luck.   116 *shut myself up in:* Confine myself to.

*Desdemona:*              Alas, thrice-gentle Cassio!
   My advocation° is not now in tune.
   My lord is not my lord; nor should I know him,
   Were he in favor° as in humor altered.                     120
   So help me every spirit sanctified
   As I have spoken for you all my best
   And stood within the blank° of his displeasure
   For my free speech! You must a while be patient.
   What I can do I will; and more I will                        125
   Than for myself I dare. Let that suffice you.
*Iago:* Is my lord angry?
*Emilia:*                      He went hence but now,
   And certainly in strange unquietness.
*Iago:* Can he be angry? I have seen the cannon
   When it hath blown his ranks into the air                   130
   And, like the devil, from his very arm
   Puffed his own brother — and is he angry?
   Something of moment then. I will go meet him.
   There's matter in't indeed if he be angry.
*Desdemona:* I prithee do so.                          *Exit [Iago].*
             Something sure of state,°                 135
   Either from Venice or some unhatched practice°
   Made demonstrable here in Cyprus to him,
   Hath puddled° his clear spirit; and in such cases
   Men's natures wrangle with inferior things,
   Though great ones are their object. 'Tis even so;           140
   For let our finger ache, and it endues°
   Our other, healthful members even to a sense
   Of pain. Nay, we must think men are not gods,
   Nor of them look for such observancy
   As fits the bridal. Beshrew me much, Emilia,                145
   I was, unhandsome warrior° as I am,
   Arraigning his unkindness with my soul;°
   But now I find I had suborned the witness,
   And he's indicted falsely.
*Emilia:* Pray heaven it be state matters, as you think,         150
   And no conception nor no jealous toy°
   Concerning you.
*Desdemona:* Alas the day! I never gave him cause.
*Emilia:* But jealous souls will not be answered so;
   They are not ever jealous for the cause,                    155
   But jealous for they're jealous. It is a monster
   Begot upon itself,° born on itself.
*Desdemona:* Heaven keep that monster from Othello's mind!

---

118 *advocation:* Advocacy.  120 *favor:* Appearance.  123 *blank:* Bull's-eye of the target.
135 *state:* Public affairs.  136 *unhatched practice:* Budding plot.  138 *puddled:* Muddied.
141 *endues:* Brings.  146 *unhandsome warrior:* Inadequate soldier.  147 *Arraigning . . .
soul:* Indicting his unkindness before the bar of my soul.  151 *toy:* Fancy.  157 *Begot upon
itself:* Self-engendered.

*Emilia:*  Lady, amen.

*Desdemona:*  I will go seek him. Cassio, walk here about:          160
   If I do find him fit, I'll move your suit
   And seek to effect it to my uttermost.

*Cassio:*  I humbly thank your ladyship.

*Exeunt Desdemona and Emilia.*

   *Enter Bianca.*

*Bianca:*  Save you, friend Cassio!

*Cassio:*                              What make you from home?
   How is't with you, my most fair Bianca?          165
   I' faith, sweet love, I was coming to your house.

*Bianca:*  And I was going to your lodging, Cassio.
   What, keep a week away? seven days and nights?
   Eightscore eight hours? and lovers' absent hours,
   More tedious than the dial° eightscore times?          170
   O weary reck'ning!

*Cassio:*                    Pardon me, Bianca:
   I have this while with leaden thoughts been pressed;
   But I shall in a more continuate° time
   Strike off this score of absence. Sweet Bianca,

   *[Gives her Desdemona's handkerchief.]*

   Take me this work out.°

*Bianca:*                         O Cassio, whence came this?          175
   This is some token from a newer friend
   To the felt absence now I feel a cause.
   Is't come to this? Well, well.

*Cassio:*                          Go to, woman!
   Throw your vile guesses in the devil's teeth,
   From whence you have them. You are jealous now          180
   That this is from some mistress, some remembrance.
   No, by my faith, Bianca.

*Bianca:*                      Why, whose is it?

*Cassio:*  I know not, neither; I found it in my chamber.
   I like the work° well; ere it be demanded,
   As like enough it will, I'd have it copied.          185
   Take it and do't, and leave me for this time.

*Bianca:*  Leave you? Wherefore?

*Cassio:*  I do attend here on the general
   And think it no addition, nor my wish,
   To have him see me womaned.

*Bianca:*                          Why, I pray you?          190

*Cassio:*  Not that I love you not.

*Bianca:*                           But that you do not love me!
   I pray you bring me on the way a little,
   And say if I shall see you soon at night.

170 *dial:* Clock.   173 *continuate:* Uninterrupted.   175 *Take . . . out:* Copy this embroidery
for me.   184 *work:* Needlework.

*Cassio:* 'Tis but a little way that I can bring you,
 For I attend here; but I'll see you soon.     195
*Bianca:* 'Tis very good. I must be circumstanced.°   *Exeunt.*

---

# ACT IV

SCENE I: *The environs of the castle.*

 *Enter Othello and Iago.*

*Iago:* Will you think so?
*Othello:*      Think so, Iago?
*Iago:*           What,
 To kiss in private?
*Othello:*     An unauthorized kiss.
*Iago:* Or to be naked with her friend in bed
 An hour or more, not meaning any harm?
*Othello:* Naked in bed, Iago, and not mean harm?    5
 It is hypocrisy against the devil.°
 They that mean virtuously, and yet do so,
 The devil their virtue tempts, and they tempt heaven.
*Iago:* So they do nothing, 'tis a venial slip.
 But if I give my wife a handkerchief—     10
*Othello:* What then?
*Iago:* Why, then 'tis hers, my lord; and being hers,
 She may, I think, bestow't on any man.
*Othello:* She is protectress of her honor too;
 May she give that?          15
*Iago:* Her honor is an essence that's not seen;
 They have it very oft that have it not.
 But for the handkerchief—
*Othello:* By heaven, I would most gladly have forgot it!
 Thou said'st—O, it comes o'er my memory    20
 As doth the raven o'er the infected° house,
 Boding to all!—he had my handkerchief.
*Iago:* Ay, what of that?
*Othello:*     That's not so good now.
*Iago:*          What
 If I had said I had seen him do you wrong?
 Or heard him say—as knaves be such abroad    25
 Who having, by their own importunate suit,
 Or voluntary dotage of some mistress,
 Convincèd or supplied° them, cannot choose
 But they must blab—

---

196 *circumstanced:* Governed by circumstances. **Act IV, Scene I.** 6 *hypocrisy...devil:* i.e., feigned sin instead of feigned virtue. 21 *infected:* Plague-stricken. 28 *Convincèd or supplied:* Overcome or gratified.

*Othello:*                    Hath he said anything?
*Iago:* He hath, my lord; but be you well assured,                    30
    No more than he'll unswear.
*Othello:*                         What hath he said?
*Iago:* Faith, that he did — I know not what he did.
*Othello:* What? what?
*Iago:* Lie —
*Othello:* With her?
*Iago:*                    With her, on her; what you will.                    35
*Othello:* Lie with her? lie on her? — We say lie on her when they
    belie her. — Lie with her! Zounds, that's fulsome. — Handkerchief —
    confessions — handkerchief! — To confess, and be hanged for his
    labor — first to be hanged, and then to confess! I tremble at it.
    Nature would not invest herself in such shadowing passion without    40
    out some instruction.° It is not words that shakes me thus. — Pish!
    Noses, ears, and lips? Is't possible? — Confess? — Handkerchief? —
    O devil!

    *(Falls in a trance.)*

*Iago:* Work on,
    My med'cine, work! Thus credulous fools are caught,              45
    And many worthy and chaste dames even thus
    All guiltless, meet reproach. — What, ho! my lord!
    My lord, I say! Othello!
    *Enter Cassio.*          How now, Cassio?
*Cassio:* What's the matter?
*Iago:* My lord is fall'n into an epilepsy.                    50
    This is his second fit; he had one yesterday.
*Cassio:* Rub him about the temples.
*Iago:*                    No, forbear.
    The lethargy° must have his quiet course.
    If not, he foams at mouth, and by and by
    Breaks out to savage madness. Look, he stirs.                    55
    Do you withdraw yourself a little while.
    He will recover straight. When he is gone,
    I would on great occasion speak with you.          *[Exit Cassio.]*
    How is it, general? Have you not hurt your head?
*Othello:* Dost thou mock me?
*Iago:*                    I mock you? No, by heaven.                    60
    Would you would bear your fortune like a man!
*Othello:* A hornèd man's° a monster and a beast.
*Iago:* There's many a beast then in a populous city,
    And many a civil monster.
*Othello:* Did he confess it?
*Iago:*                    Good sir, be a man.                    65
    Think every bearded fellow that's but yoked

40–41 *Nature . . . instruction:* My natural faculties would not be so overcome by passion without reason.    53 *lethargy:* Coma.    62 *hornèd man:* Cuckold.

May draw with you. There's millions now alive
That nightly lie in those unproper° beds
Which they dare swear peculiar:° your case is better.
O, 'tis the spite of hell, the fiend's arch-mock,                              70
To lip a wanton in a secure° couch,
And to suppose her chaste! No, let me know;
And knowing what I am, I know what she shall be.
*Othello:* O, thou art wise! 'Tis certain.
*Iago:*                                        Stand you awhile apart;
Confine yourself but in a patient list.°                                        75
Whilst you were here, o'erwhelmèd with your grief —
A passion most unsuiting such a man —
Cassio came hither. I shifted him away
And laid good 'scuse upon your ecstasy;°
Bade him anon return, and here speak with me;                                    80
The which he promised. Do but encave° yourself
And mark the fleers, the gibes, and notable scorns
That dwell in every region of his face;
For I will make him tell the tale anew —
Where, how, how oft, how long ago, and when                                      85
He hath, and is again to cope° your wife.
I say, but mark his gesture. Marry, patience!
Or I shall say y'are all in all in spleen,°
And nothing of a man.
*Othello:*                          Dost thou hear, Iago?
I will be found most cunning in my patience;                                     90
But — dost thou hear? — most bloody.
*Iago:*                                        That's not amiss:
But yet keep time in all. Will you withdraw?

                                        *[Othello retires.]*

Now will I question Cassio of Bianca,
A huswife° that by selling her desires
Buys herself bread and clothes. It is a creature                                 95
That dotes on Cassio, as 'tis the strumpet's plague
To beguile many and be beguiled by one.
He, when he hears of her, cannot refrain
From the excess of laughter. Here he comes.

*Enter Cassio.*

As he shall smile, Othello shall go mad;                                         100
And his unbookish° jealousy must conster°
Poor Cassio's smiles, gestures, and light behavior
Quite in the wrong. How do you now, lieutenant?
*Cassio:* The worser that you give me the addition°
Whose want even kills me.                                                        105

---

68 *unproper:* Not exclusively their own.   69 *peculiar:* Exclusively their own.   71 *secure:*
Free from fear of rivalry.   75 *in a patient list:* Within the limits of self-control.   79 *ecstasy:*
Trance.   81 *encave:* Conceal.   86 *cope:* Meet.   88 *all in all in spleen:* Wholly overcome
by your passion.   94 *huswife:* Hussy.   101 *unbookish:* Uninstructed; *conster:* Construe,
interpret.   104 *addition:* Title.

*Iago:*  Ply Desdemona well, and you are sure on't.
　　　Now, if this suit lay in Bianca's power,
　　　How quickly should you speed!
*Cassio:*　　　　　　　　　　　　　Alas, poor caitiff!°
*Othello:*  Look how he laughs already!
*Iago:*  I never knew a woman love man so.                                110
*Cassio:*  Alas, poor rogue! I think, i' faith, she loves me.
*Othello:*  Now he denies it faintly, and laughs it out.
*Iago:*  Do you hear, Cassio?
*Othello:*　　　　　　　　　　Now he importunes him
　　　To tell it o'er. Go to! Well said, well said!
*Iago:*  She gives out that you marry her.                                115
　　　Do you intend it?
*Cassio:*  Ha, ha, ha!
*Othello:*  Do you triumph, Roman? Do you triumph?
*Cassio:*  I marry her? What, a customer?° Prithee bear some charity to my
　　　wit; do not think it so unwholesome. Ha, ha, ha!                    120
*Othello:*  So, so, so, so! They laugh that win!
*Iago:*  Faith, the cry goes that you marry her.
*Cassio:*  Prithee say true.
*Iago:*  I am a very villain else.
*Othello:*  Have you scored me?° Well.                                    125
*Cassio:*  This is the monkey's own giving out. She is persuaded I will marry her
　　　out of her own love and flattery, not out of my promise.
*Othello:*  Iago beckons° me; now he begins the story.
*Cassio:*  She was here even now; she haunts me in every place. I was t'
　　　other day talking on the sea bank with certain Venetians, and thither  130
　　　comes the bauble,° and, by this hand, she falls me thus about my
　　　neck—
*Othello:*  Crying "O dear Cassio!" as it were. His gesture imports it.
*Cassio:*  So hangs, and lolls, and weeps upon me; so shakes and pulls me! Ha,
　　　ha, ha!                                                             135
*Othello:*  Now he tells how she plucked him to my chamber. O, I see that
　　　nose of yours, but not that dog I shall throw it to.
*Cassio:*  Well, I must leave her company.

　　　*Enter Bianca.*

*Iago:*  Before me! Look where she comes.
*Cassio:*  'Tis such another fitchew!° marry, a perfumed one. What do you  140
　　　mean by this haunting of me?
*Bianca:*  Let the devil and his dam haunt you! What did you mean by
　　　that same handkerchief you gave me even now? I was a fine fool to
　　　take it. I must take out the work? A likely piece of work that
　　　you should find it in your chamber and know not who left it there!  145
　　　This is some minx's token, and I must take out the work? There!
　　　Give it your hobby-horse.° Wheresoever you had it, I'll take out
　　　no work on't.

---

108 *caitiff:* Wretch.   119 *customer:* Prostitute.   125 *scored me:* Settled my account (?).
128 *beckons:* Signals.   131 *bauble:* Plaything.   140 *fitchew:* Polecat (slang for *whore*).
147　*hobby-horse:* Harlot.

*Cassio:*  How now, my sweet Bianca? How now? how now?

*Othello:*  By heaven, that should be my handkerchief!  150

*Bianca:*  An you'll come to supper to-night, you may; an you will not,
   come when you are next prepared for.  *Exit.*

*Iago:*  After her, after her!

*Cassio:*  Faith, I must; she'll rail in the street else.

*Iago:*  Will you sup there?  155

*Cassio:*  Yes, I intend so.

*Iago:*  Well, I may chance to see you; for I would very fain speak with
   you.

*Cassio:*  Prithee come. Will you?

*Iago:*  Go to! say no more.  *Exit Cassio.*  160

*Othello [comes forward]:*  How shall I murder him, Iago?

*Iago:*  Did you perceive how he laughed at his vice?°

*Othello:*  O Iago!

*Iago:*  And did you see the handkerchief?

*Othello:*  Was that mine?  165

*Iago:*  Your, by this hand! And to see how he prizes° the foolish woman
   your wife! She gave it him, and he hath giv'n it his whore.

*Othello:*  I would have him nine years a-killing — A fine woman! a fair woman!
   a sweet woman!  170

*Iago:*  Nay, you must forget that.

*Othello:*  Ay, let her rot, and perish, and be damned to-night; for she shall not
   live. No, my heart is turned to stone; I strike it, and it hurts my hand. O,
   the world hath not a sweeter creature! She might lie by an emperor's side
   and command him tasks.  175

*Iago:*  Nay, that's not your way.

*Othello:*  Hang her! I do but say what she is. So delicate with her needle! an
   admirable musician! O, she will sing the savageness out of a bear! Of so
   high and plenteous wit and invention° —

*Iago:*  She's the worse for all this.  180

*Othello:*  O, a thousand thousand times! And then, of so gentle a
   condition!°

*Iago:*  Ay, too gentle.

*Othello:*  Nay, that's certain. But yet the pity of it, Iago! O Iago, the pity of it,
   Iago!  185

*Iago:*  If you are so fond over her iniquity, give her patent° to offend; for if it
   touch not you, it comes near nobody.

*Othello:*  I will chop her into messes! Cuckold me!

*Iago:*  O, 'tis foul in her.

*Othello:*  With mine officer!  190

*Iago:*  That's fouler.

*Othello:*  Get me some poison, Iago, this night. I'll not expostulate with
   her, lest her body and beauty unprovide° my mind again. This night,
   Iago!

---

162 *vice:* i.e., vicious conduct.   166 *prizes:* Values.   179 *invention:* Imagination.
182 *condition:* Disposition.   186 *patent:* License.   193 *unprovide:* Disarm.

*Iago:* Do it not with poison. Strangle her in her bed, even the bed she hath     195
    contaminated.
*Othello:* Good, good! The justice of it pleases. Very good!
*Iago:* And for Cassio, let me be his undertaker;° you shall hear more by
    midnight.
*Othello:* Excellent good!     200

    *A trumpet.*

                                      What trumpet is that same?
*Iago:* I warrant something from Venice.

    *Enter Lodovico, Desdemona, and Attendants.*

                                           'Tis Lodovico.
This comes from the Duke; and see, your wife is with him.
*Lodovico:* God save you, worthy general!
*Othello:*                                 With all my heart, sir.
*Lodovico:* The Duke and senators of Venice greet you.     205

    *[Gives him a letter.]*

*Othello:* I kiss the instrument of their pleasures.

    *[Opens the letter and reads.]*

*Desdemona:* And what's the news, good cousin Lodovico?
*Iago:* I am very glad to see you, signior.
    Welcome to Cyprus.
*Lodovico:* I thank you. How does Lieutenant Cassio?
*Iago:*                                    Lives, sir.     210
*Desdemona:* Cousin, there's fall'n between him and my lord
    An unkind breach; but you shall make all well.
*Othello:* Are you sure of that?
*Desdemona:* My lord?
*Othello [reads]:* "This fail you not to do, as you will —"     215
*Lodovico:* He did not call; he's busy in the paper.
    Is there division 'twixt my lord and Cassio?
*Desdemona:* A most unhappy one. I would do much
    T' atone° them, for the love I bear to Cassio.
*Othello:* Fire and brimstone!
*Desdemona:*                My lord?
*Othello:*                        Are you wise?     220
*Desdemona:* What, is he angry?
*Lodovico:*               May be the letter moved him;
    For, as I think, they do command him home,
    Deputing Cassio in his government.
*Desdemona:* By my troth, I am glad on't.
*Othello:*                     Indeed?
*Desdemona:*                        My lord?
*Othello:* I am glad to see you mad.°

---

198 *be his undertaker:* Undertake to deal with him.   219 *atone:* Reconcile.   224 *mad:* i.e.,
waggish.

*Desdemona:*                 Why, sweet Othello —      225
*Othello:* Devil!

     *[Strikes her.]*

*Desdemona:* I have not deserved this.
*Lodovico:* My lord, this would not be believed in Venice,
     Though I should swear I saw't. 'Tis very much.
     Make her amends; she weeps.
*Othello:*                O devil, devil!      230
     If that the earth could teem° with woman's tears,
     Each drop she falls would prove a crocodile.°
     Out of my sight!
*Desdemona:*          I will not stay to offend you.      *[Going.]*
*Lodovico:* Truly, an obedient lady.
     I do beseech your lordship call her back.      235
*Othello:* Mistress!
*Desdemona:* My lord?
*Othello:*            What would you with her, sir?
*Lodovico:* Who? I, my lord?
*Othello:* Ay! You did wish that I would make her turn.
     Sir, she can turn, and turn, and yet go on      240
     And turn again; and she can weep, sir, weep;
     And she's obedient; as you say, obedient,
     Very obedient. — Proceed you in your tears. —
     Concerning this, sir — O well-painted passion!° —
     I am commanded home. — Get you away;      245
     I'll send for you anon. — Sir, I obey the mandate
     And will return to Venice. — Hence, avaunt!

                     *[Exit Desdemona.]*

     Cassio shall have my place. And, sir, to-night
     I do entreat that we may sup together.
     You are welcome, sir, to Cyprus — Goats and monkeys!      *Exit.* 250
*Lodovico:* Is this the noble Moor whom our full Senate
     Call all in all sufficient? Is this the nature
     Whom passion could not shake? whose solid virtue
     The shot of accident nor dart of chance
     Could neither graze nor pierce?
*Iago:*                He is much changed.      255
*Lodovico:* Are his wits safe? Is he not light of brain?
*Iago:* He's that he is; I may not breathe my censure.
     What he might be — if what he might he is not —
     I would to heaven he were!
*Lodovico:*                What, strike his wife?
*Iago:* Faith, that was not so well; yet would I knew      260
     That stroke would prove the worst!
*Lodovico:*                  Is it his use?°

---

231 *teem:* Breed.    232 *crocodile:* (Crocodiles were supposed to shed hypocritical tears to lure men to destruction).    244 *passion:* Grief.    261 *use:* Custom.

> Or did the letters work upon his blood
> And new-create this fault?

*Iago:*                                       Alas, alas!
> It is not honesty in me to speak
> What I have seen and known. You shall observe him,                    265
> And his own courses will denote him so
> That I may save my speech. Do but go after
> And mark how he continues.

*Lodovico:*  I am sorry that I am deceived in him.                *Exeunt.*

---

SCENE II: *Within the castle.*

*Enter Othello and Emilia.*

*Othello:*  You have seen nothing then?
*Emilia:*  Nor ever heard, nor ever did suspect.
*Othello:*  Yes, you have seen Cassio and she together.
*Emilia:*  But then I saw no harm, and then I heard
> Each syllable that breath made up between them.                       5
*Othello:*  What, did they never whisper?
*Emilia:*                                   Never, my lord.
*Othello:*  Nor send you out o' th' way?
*Emilia:*  Never.
*Othello:*  To fetch her fan, her gloves, her mask, nor nothing?
*Emilia:*  Never, my lord.                                              10
*Othello:*  That's strange.
*Emilia:*  I durst, my lord, to wager she is honest,
> Lay down my soul at stake. If you think other,
> Remove your thought; it doth abuse your bosom.°
> If any wretch have put this in your head,                             15
> Let heaven requite it with the serpent's curse!°
> For if she be not honest, chaste, and true,
> There's no man happy; the purest of their wives
> Is foul as slander.
*Othello:*                 Bid her come hither. Go.          *Exit Emilia.*
> She says enough; yet she's a simple bawd                              20
> That cannot say as much. This is a subtle whore,
> A closet lock and key of villainous secrets;
> And yet she'll kneel and pray; I have seen her do't.

*Enter Desdemona and Emilia.*

*Desdemona:*  My lord, what is your will?
*Othello:*                               Pray you, chuck, come hither.
*Desdemona:*  What is your pleasure?
*Othello:*                            Let me see your eyes.             25
> Look in my face.
*Desdemona:*             What horrible fancy's this?

---

**Scene II.**  14 *abuse your bosom:* Deceive your heart.  16 *serpent's curse:* (cf. Genesis 3: 14).

*Othello [to Emilia]:*  Some of your function, mistress.
    Leave procreants° alone and shut the door;
    Cough or cry "hem" if anybody come.
    Your mystery, your mystery!° Nay, dispatch!                              30

                                      *Exit Emilia.*

*Desdemona:*  Upon my knees, what doth your speech import?
    I understand a fury in your words,
    [But not the words.]
*Othello:*  Why, what art thou?
*Desdemona:*                 Your wife, my lord; your true
    And loyal wife.
*Othello:*          Come, swear it, damn thyself;                       35
    Lest, being like one of heaven,° the devils themselves
    Should fear to seize thee. Therefore be double-damned —
    Swear thou art honest.°
*Desdemona:*             Heaven doth truly know it.
*Othello:*  Heaven truly knows that thou art false as hell.
*Desdemona:*  To whom, my lord? With whom? How am I false?        40
*Othello:*  Ah, Desdemona! away! away! away!
*Desdemona:*  Alas the heavy day! Why do you weep?
    Am I the motive of these tears, my lord?
    If haply you my father do suspect
    An instrument° of this your calling back,                              45
    Lay not your blame on me. If you have lost him,
    Why, I have lost him too.
*Othello:*                Had it pleased heaven
    To try me with affliction, had they rained
    All kinds of sores and shames on my bare head,
    Steeped me in poverty to the very lips,                                50
    Given to captivity me and my utmost hopes,
    I should have found in some place of my soul
    A drop of patience. But, alas, to make me
    The fixèd figure for the time of scorn°
    To point his slow unmoving finger at!                                  55
    Yet could I bear that too; well, very well.
    But there where I have garnered up my heart,
    Where either I must live or bear no life,
    The fountain from the which my current runs
    Or else dries up — to be discarded thence,                             60
    Or keep it as a cistern for foul toads
    To knot and gender in — turn thy complexion there,°
    Patience, thou young and rose-lipped cherubin!
    Ay, here look grim as hell!

---

28 *procreants:* Mating couples.  30 *mystery:* Trade, occupation.  36 *being . . . heaven:*
Looking like an angel.  38 *honest:* Chaste.  45 *An instrument:* To be the cause.  54 *time of
scorn:* Scornful world.  62 *turn thy complexion there:* Change thy color at that point.

*Desdemona:* I hope my noble lord esteems me honest.          65
*Othello:* O, ay; as summer flies are in the shambles,°
          That quicken° even with blowing. O thou weed,
          Who art so lovely fair, and smell'st so sweet,
          That the sense aches at thee, would thou hadst ne'er been born!
*Desdemona:* Alas, what ignorant sin have I committed?          70
*Othello:* Was this fair paper, this most goodly book,
          Made to write "whore" upon? What committed?
          Committed? O thou public commoner!°
          I should make very forges of my cheeks
          That would to cinders burn up modesty,          75
          Did I but speak thy deeds. What committed?
          Heaven stops the nose at it, and the moon winks;°
          The bawdy wind, that kisses all it meets,
          Is hushed within the hollow mine of earth
          And will not hear it. What committed?          80
          Impudent strumpet!
*Desdemona:*          By heaven, you do me wrong!
*Othello:* Are not you a strumpet?
*Desdemona:*          No, as I am a Christian!
          If to preserve this vessel for my lord
          From any other foul unlawful touch
          Be not to be a strumpet, I am none.          85
*Othello:* What, not a whore?
*Desdemona:*          No, as I shall be saved!
*Othello:* Is't possible?
*Desdemona:* O, heaven forgive us!
*Othello:*          I cry you mercy° then.
          I took you for that cunning whore of Venice
          That married with Othello. — *[Calling.]* You, mistress,          90
          That have the office opposite to Saint Peter
          And keep the gate of hell!

          *Enter Emilia.*

                    You, you, ay, you!
          We have done our course; there's money for your pains:
          I pray you turn the key, and keep our counsel.          *Exit.*
*Emilia:* Alas, what does this gentleman conceive?          95
          How do you, madam? How do you, my good lady?
*Desdemona:* Faith, half asleep.°
*Emilia:* Good madam, what's the matter with my lord?
*Desdemona:* With who?
*Emilia:* Why, with my lord, madam.          100
*Desdemona:* Who is thy lord?
*Emilia:*          He that is yours, sweet lady.

---

66 *shambles:* Slaughterhouse.   67 *quicken:* Come to life.   73 *commoner:* Harlot.
77 *winks:* Closes her eyes.   88 *cry you mercy:* Beg your pardon.   97 *half asleep:* i.e., stunned.

*Desdemona:* I have none. Do not talk to me, Emilia.
    I cannot weep; nor answer have I none
    But what should go by water. Prithee to-night
    Lay on my bed my wedding sheets, remember;    105
    And call thy husband hither.
*Emilia:*                   Here's a change indeed!     *Exit.*
*Desdemona:* 'Tis meet I should be used so, very meet.
    How have I been behaved, that he might stick
    The small'st opinion° on my least misuse?°

    *Enter Iago and Emilia.*

*Iago:* What is your pleasure, madam? How is't with you?     110
*Desdemona:* I cannot tell. Those that do teach young babes
    Do it with gentle means and easy tasks:
    He might have chid me so; for, in good faith,
    I am a child to chiding.
*Iago:*                What is the matter, lady?
*Emilia:* Alas, Iago, my lord hath so bewhored her,     115
    Thrown such despite and heavy terms upon her
    As true hearts cannot bear.
*Desdemona:* Am I that name, Iago?
*Iago:* What name, fair lady?
*Desdemona:* Such as she said my lord did say I was.     120
*Emilia:* He called her whore. A beggar in his drink
    Could not have laid such terms upon his callet.°
*Iago:* Why did he so?
*Desdemona:* I do not know; I am sure I am none such.
*Iago:* Do not weep, do not weep. Alas the day!
*Emilia:* Hath she forsook so many noble matches,     125
    Her father and her country, and her friends,
    To be called whore? Would it not make one weep?
*Desdemona:* It is my wretched fortune.
*Iago:*                  Beshrew him for't!
    How comes this trick° upon him?
*Desdemona:*              Nay, heaven doth know.
*Emilia:* I will be hanged if some eternal villain,     130
    Some busy and insinuating rogue,
    Some cogging, cozening° slave, to get some office,
    Have not devised this slander. I'll be hanged else.
*Iago:* Fie, there is no such man! It is impossible.
*Desdemona:* If any such there be, heaven pardon him!     135
*Emilia:* A halter pardon him! and hell gnaw his bones!
    Why should he call her whore? Who keeps her company?
    What place? what time? what form? what likelihood?
    The Moor 's abused by some most villainous knave,
    Some base notorious knave, some scurvy fellow.     140

---

109 *small'st opinion:* Least suspicion; *least misuse:* Slightest misconduct.   122 *callet:*
Whore.   129 *trick:* Freakish behavior.   132  *cogging, cozening:* Cheating, defrauding.

O heaven, that such companions° thou'dst unfold,°
And put in every honest hand a whip
To lash the rascals naked through the world
Even from the east to th' west!
*Iago:*                                Speak within door.°
*Emilia:* O, fie upon them! Some such squire he was          145
That turned your wit the seamy side without
And made you to suspect me with the Moor.
*Iago:* You are a fool. Go to.
*Desdemona:*                    O good Iago,
What shall I do to win my lord again?
Good friend, go to him; for, by this light of heaven,          150
I know not how I lost him. Here I kneel:
If e'er my will did trespass 'gainst his love
Either in discourse° of thought or actual deed,
Or that mine eyes, mine ears, or any sense
Delighted them in any other form,          155
Or that I do not yet, and ever did,
And ever will (though he do shake me off
To beggarly divorcement) love him dearly,
Comfort forswear° me! Unkindness may do much;
And his unkindness may defeat° my life,          160
But never taint my love. I cannot say "whore."
It does abhor me now I speak the word;
To do the act that might the addition earn
Not the world's mass of vanity could make me.
*Iago:* I pray you be content. 'Tis but his humor.          165
The business of the state does him offense,
[And he does chide with you.]
*Desdemona:* If 'twere no other —
*Iago:*                                'Tis but so, I warrant.

[*Trumpets within.*]

Hark how these instruments summon you to supper.
The messengers of Venice stay the meat:          170
Go in, and weep not. All things shall be well.
                    *Exeunt Desdemona and Emilia.*

*Enter Roderigo.*

How now, Roderigo?
*Roderigo:* I do not find that thou deal'st justly with me.
*Iago:* What in the contrary?
*Roderigo:* Every day thou daff'st me with some device,° Iago, and rather,   175
as it seems to me now, keep'st from me all conveniency° than suppliest
me with the least advantage of hope. I will indeed no longer endure it;

---

141 *companions:* Rogues;   *unfold:* Expose.   144 *within door:* With restraint.
153 *discourse:* Course.   159 *Comfort forswear:* Happiness forsake.   160 *defeat:*
Destroy.   175 *thou . . . device:* You put me off with some trick.   176 *conveniency:* Favorable
opportunities.

nor am I yet persuaded to put up in peace what already I have foolishly suffered.

*Iago:* Will you hear me, Roderigo?   180

*Roderigo:* Faith, I have heard too much; for your words and performances are no kin together.

*Iago:* You charge me most unjustly.

*Roderigo:* With naught but truth. I have wasted myself out of my means. The jewels you have had from me to deliver Desdemona would half 185 have corrupted a votarist.° You have told me she hath received them, and returned me expectations and comforts of sudden respect° and acquaintance; but I find none.

*Iago:* Well, go to; very well.

*Roderigo:* Very well! go to! I cannot go to, man; nor 'tis not very well. 190 By this hand, I say 'tis very scurvy, and begin to find myself fopped° in it.

*Iago:* Very well.

*Roderigo:* I tell you 'tis not very well. I will make myself known to Desdemona. If she will return me my jewels, I will give over my suit and repent 195 my unlawful solicitation; if not, assure yourself I will seek satisfaction of you.

*Iago:* You have said now.

*Roderigo:* Ay, and said nothing but what I protest intendment of doing.   200

*Iago:* Why, now I see there's mettle in thee; and even from this instant do build on thee a better opinion than ever before. Give me thy hand, Roderigo. Thou has taken against me a most just exception; but yet I protest I have dealt most directly° in thy affair.

*Roderigo:* It hath not appeared.   205

*Iago:* I grant indeed it hath not appeared, and your suspicion is not without wit and judgment. But, Roderigo, if thou hast that in thee indeed which I have greater reason to believe now than ever, I mean purpose, courage, and valor, this night show it. If thou the next night following enjoy not Desdemona, take me from this world with treachery and devise engines 210 for° my life.

*Roderigo:* Well, what is it? Is it within reason and compass?

*Iago:* Sir, there is especial commission come from Venice to depute Cassio in Othello's place.

*Roderigo:* Is that true? Why, then Othello and Desdemona return again to 215 Venice.

*Iago:* O, no; he goes into Mauritania and takes away with him the fair Desdemona, unless his abode be lingered here° by some accident; wherein none can be so determinate° as the removing of Cassio.   220

*Roderigo:* How do you mean removing of him?

*Iago:* Why, by making him uncapable of Othello's place — knocking out his brains.

---

186 *votarist:* Nun.   187 *sudden respect:* Immediate notice.   191 *fopped:* Duped.
204 *directly:* Straightforwardly.   210–11 *engines for:* Plots against.   218 *abode...here:* Stay
here be extended.   219 *determinate:* Effective.

*Roderigo:* And that you would have me to do?

*Iago:* Ay, if you dare do yourself a profit and a right. He sups to-night with  225
a harlotry, and thither will I go to him. He knows not yet of his honorable fortune. If you will watch his going thence, which I will fashion
to fall out between twelve and one, you may take him at your pleasure. I will be near to second your attempt, and he shall fall between
us. Come, stand not amazed at it, but go along with me. I will show  230
you such a necessity in his death that you shall think yourself bound
to put it on him. It is now high supper time, and the night grows to
waste. About it!

*Roderigo:* I will hear further reason for this.

*Iago:* And you shall be satisfied.                                    *Exeunt.*  235

**Scene III:** *Within the castle.*

*Enter Othello, Lodovico, Desdemona, Emilia, and Attendants.*

*Lodovico:* I do beseech you, sir, trouble yourself no further.

*Othello:* O, pardon me; 'twill do me good to walk.

*Lodovico:* Madam, good night. I humbly thank your ladyship.

*Desdemona:* Your honor is most welcome.

*Othello:*                                    Will you walk, sir?

   O, Desdemona —                                                        5

*Desdemona:* My lord?

*Othello:* Get you to bed on th' instant; I will be returned forthwith. Dismiss
   your attendant there. Look 't be done.

*Desdemona:* I will, my lord.

   *Exit [Othello, with Lodovico and Attendants].*

*Emilia:* How goes it now? He looks gentler than he did.                      10

*Desdemona:* He says he will return incontinent.°
   He hath commanded me to go to bed,
   And bade me to dismiss you.

*Emilia:*                                    Dismiss me?

*Desdemona:* It was his bidding; therefore, good Emilia,
   Give me my nightly wearing, and adieu.                                   15
   We must not now displease him.

*Emilia:* I would you had never seen him!

*Desdemona:* So would not I. My love doth so approve him
   That even his stubbornness,° his checks,° his frowns —
   Prithee unpin me — have grace and favor in them.                         20

*Emilia:* I have laid those sheets you bade me on the bed.

*Desdemona:* All's one. Good faith, how foolish are our minds!
   If I do die before thee, prithee shroud me
   In one of those same sheets.

*Emilia:*                                    Come, come! You talk.

*Desdemona:* My mother had a maid called Barbary.                            25
   She was in love; and he she loved proved mad°

**Scene III.**   11 *incontinent:* At once.   19 *stubbornness:* Roughness;   *checks:* Rebukes.
26 *mad:* Wild, faithless.

And did forsake her. She had a song of "Willow";
An old thing 'twas; but it expressed her fortune,
And she died singing it. That song to-night
Will not go from my mind; I have much to do          30
But to go hang my head all at one side
And sing it like poor Barbary. Prithee dispatch.
*Emilia:* Shall I go fetch your nightgown?°
*Desdemona:*                              No, unpin me here.
    This Lodovico is a proper man.
*Emilia:* A very handsome man.                       35
*Desdemona:* He speaks well.
*Emilia:* I know a lady in Venice would have walked barefoot to
    Palestine for a touch of his nether lip.
*Desdemona (sings):* "The poor soul sat sighing by a sycamore tree
        Sing all a green willow;                      40
    Her hand on her bosom, her head on her knee,
        Sing willow, willow, willow.
    The fresh streams ran by her and murmured her moans;
        Sing willow, willow, willow;
    Her salt tears fell from her, and soft'ned the stones" —   45
Lay by these.
    "Sing willow, willow, willow" —
Prithee hie thee;° he'll come anon.
    "Sing all a green willow must be my garland.
    Let nobody blame him; his scorn I approve" —      50
Nay, that's not next. Hark! who is't that knocks?
*Emilia:* It's the wind.
*Desdemona (sings):* "I call my love false love; but what said he then?
        Sing willow, willow, willow:
    If I court moe women, you'll couch with moe men."   55
So get thee gone; good night. Mine eyes do itch.
Doth that bode weeping?
*Emilia:*                            'Tis neither here nor there.
*Desdemona:* I have heard it said so. O, these men, these men!
    Dost thou in conscience think — tell me, Emilia —
    That there be women do abuse their husbands       60
    In such gross kind?
*Emilia:*                There be some such, no question.
*Desdemona:* Wouldst thou do such a deed for all the world?
*Emilia:* Why, would not you?
*Desdemona:*                    No, by this heavenly light!
*Emilia:* Nor I neither by this heavenly light.
    I might do't as well i' th' dark.                 65
*Desdemona:* Wouldst thou do such a deed for all the world?
*Emilia:* The world's a huge thing; it is a great price for a small vice.
*Desdemona:* In troth, I think thou wouldst not.
*Emilia:* In troth, I think I should; and undo't when I had done it. Marry, I
    would not do such a thing for a joint-ring,° nor for measures of lawn, nor   70

---

33 *nightgown:* Dressing gown.   48 *hie thee:* Hurry.   70 *joint-ring:* Ring made in separable halves.

for gowns, petticoats, nor caps, nor any petty exhibition;° but, for all the
   whole world — 'Ud's pity! who would not make her husband a cuckold to
   make him a monarch? I should venture purgatory for't.
*Desdemona:* Beshrew me if I would do such a wrong                              75
   For the whole world.
*Emilia:* Why, the wrong is but a wrong i' th' world; and having the world for
   your labor, 'tis a wrong in your own world, and you might quickly make
   it right.
*Desdemona:* I do not think there is any such woman.                           80
*Emilia:* Yes, a dozen; and as many to th' vantage° as
   would store° the world they played for.
   But I do think it is their husbands' faults
   If wives do fall. Say that they slack their duties
   And pour our treasures into foreign laps;                                   85
   Or else break out in peevish° jealousies,
   Throwing restraint upon us; or say they strike us,
   Or scant our former having° in despite —
   Why, we have galls;° and though we have some grace,
   Yet have we some revenge. Let husbands know                                 90
   Their wives have sense like them. They see, and smell,
   And have their palates both for sweet and sour,
   As husbands have. What is it that they do
   When they change us for others? Is it sport?
   I think it is. And doth affection breed it?                                 95
   I think it doth. Is't frailty that thus errs?
   It is so too. And have not we affections,
   Desires for sport, and frailty, as men have?
   Then let them use us well; else let them know,
   The ills we do, their ills instruct us so.                                 100
*Desdemona:* Good night, good night. God me such usage° send,
   Not to pick bad from bad, but by bad mend!               *Exeunt.*

---

## ACT V

**Scene I:** *A street in Cyprus.*

*Enter Iago and Roderigo.*

*Iago:* Here, stand behind this bulk;° straight will he come.
   Wear thy good rapier bare, and put it home.
   Quick, quick! Fear nothing; I'll be at thy elbow.
   It makes us, or it mars us — think on that,
   And fix most firm thy resolution.                                           5
*Roderigo:* Be near at hand; I may miscarry in't.

---

72 *exhibition:* Gift.  80 *toth'vantage:* Besides.  81 *store:* Populate.  85 *peevish:* Senseless.
87 *having:* Allowance.  88 *galls:* Spirits to resent.  100 *usage:* Habits.  **Act V, Scene I.**
1 *bulk:* Projecting shop-front.

*Iago:* Here, at thy hand. Be bold, and take thy stand.

　　*[Stands aside.]*

*Roderigo:* I have no great devotion to the deed,
　　And yet he hath given me satisfying reasons.
　　'Tis but a man gone. Forth my sword! He dies! 　　　　　　10
*Iago:* I have rubbed this young quat° almost to the sense,°
　　And he grows angry. Now whether he kill Cassio,
　　Or Cassio him, or each do kill the other,
　　Every way makes my gain. Live Roderigo,
　　He calls me to a restitution large 　　　　　　　　　　　15
　　Of gold and jewels that I bobbed° from him
　　As gifts to Desdemona.
　　It must not be. If Cassio do remain,
　　He hath a daily beauty in his life
　　That makes me ugly; and besides, the Moor 　　　　　　20
　　May unfold me to him; there stand I in much peril.
　　No, he must die. Be't so! I hear him coming.

　　*Enter Cassio.*

*Roderigo:* I know his gait. 'Tis he. Villain, thou diest!

　　*[Makes a pass at Cassio.]*

*Cassio:* That thrust had been mine enemy indeed
　　But that my coat° is better than thou know'st. 　　　　25
　　I will make proof of thine.

　　*[Draws, and wounds Roderigo.]*

*Roderigo:* 　　　　　　　　　　O, I am slain!

　　*[Iago darts from concealment behind Cassio, wounds him in the leg, and exit.]*

*Cassio:* I am maimed for ever. Help, ho! Murder! murder!

　　*[Falls.]*
　　*Enter Othello.*

*Othello:* The voice of Cassio. Iago keeps his word.
*Roderigo:* O, villain that I am!
*Othello:* 　　　　　　　　　It is even so.
*Cassio:* O, help, ho! light! a surgeon! 　　　　　　　　30
*Othello:* 'Tis he. O brave Iago, honest and just,
　　That hast such noble sense of thy friend's wrong!
　　Thou teachest me. Minion,° your dear lies dead,
　　And your unblest fate hies.° Strumpet, I come.
　　Forth of my heart those charms, thine eyes, are blotted. 　35
　　Thy bed, lust-stained, shall with lust's blood be spotted.

　　　　　　　　　　　　　　　*Exit Othello.*

---

11 *quat:* Pimple; *sense:* Quick.　16 *bobbed:* Swindled.　25 *coat:* Undershirt of mail.
33 *Minion:* Mistress.　34 *hies:* Hurries on.

*Enter Lodovico and Gratiano.*

*Cassio:* What, ho? No watch? No passage?° Murder! murder!
*Gratiano:* 'Tis some mischance. The voice is very direful.
*Cassio:* O, help!
*Lodovico:* Hark!                                                                              40
*Roderigo:* O wretched villain!
*Lodovico:* Two or three groan. 'Tis heavy° night.
     These may be counterfeits. Let's think't unsafe
     To come in to the cry without more help.
*Roderigo:* Nobody come? Then shall I bleed to death.                      45
*Lodovico:* Hark!

     *Enter Iago, with a light.*

*Gratiano:* Here's one comes in his shirt, with light and weapons.
*Iago:* Who's there? Whose noise is this that cries on° murder?
*Lodovico:* We do not know.
*Iago:*                              Did not you hear a cry?
*Cassio:* Here, here! For heaven's sake, help me!
*Iago:*                                                What's the matter?            50
*Gratiano:* This is Othello's ancient, as I take it.
*Lodovico:* The same indeed, a very valiant fellow.
*Iago:* What are you here that cry so grievously?
*Cassio:* Iago? O, I am spoiled, undone by villains!
     Give me some help.                                                                    55
*Iago:* O me, lieutenant! What villains have done this?
*Cassio:* I think that one of them is hereabout
     And cannot make° away.
*Iago:*                              O treacherous villains!

     *[To Lodovico and Gratiano.]*

     What are you there? Come in, and give some help.
*Roderigo:* O, help me here!                                                           60
*Cassio:* That's one of them.
*Iago:*                              O murd'rous slave! O villain!

     *[Stabs Roderigo.]*

*Roderigo:* O damned Iago! O inhuman dog!
*Iago:* Kill men i' th' dark? — Where be these bloody thieves? —
     How silent is this town! — Ho! murder! murder! —
     What may you be? Are you of good or evil?                                65
*Lodovico:* As you shall prove us, praise us.
*Iago:* Signior Lodovico?
*Lodovico:* He, sir.
*Iago:* I cry you mercy. Here's Cassio hurt by villains.
*Gratiano:* Cassio?                                                                         70
*Iago:* How is't, brother?
*Cassio:* My leg is cut in two.

---

37 *passage:* Passersby.   42 *heavy:* Cloudy, dark.   48 *cries on:* Raises the cry of.   58 *make:* Get.

*Iago:*                    Marry,° heaven forbid!
    Light, gentlemen. I'll bind it with my shirt.

    *Enter Bianca.*

*Bianca:* What is the matter, ho? Who is't that cried?                    75
*Iago:* Who is't that cried?
*Bianca:* O my dear Cassio! my sweet Cassio!
    O Cassio, Cassio, Cassio!
*Iago:* O notable strumpet! — Cassio, may you suspect
    Who they should be that have thus mangled you?
*Cassio:* No.                    80
*Gratiano:* I am sorry to find you thus. I have been to seek you.
*Iago:* Lend me a garter. So. O for a chair°
    To bear him easily hence!
*Bianca:* Alas, he faints! O Cassio, Cassio, Cassio!
*Iago:* Gentlemen all, I do suspect this trash                    85
    To be a party in this injury. —
    Patience a while, good Cassio. — Come, come!
    Lend me a light. Know we this face or no?
    Alas, my friend and my dear countryman
    Roderigo? No — Yes, sure. — O heaven, Roderigo!                    90
*Gratiano:* What, of Venice?
*Iago:* Even he, sir. Did you know him?
*Gratiano:*                    Know him? Ay.
*Iago:* Signior Gratiano? I cry your gentle pardon.
    These bloody accidents must excuse my manners
    That so neglected you.
*Gratiano:*                    I am glad to see you.                    95
*Iago:* How do you, Cassio? — O, a chair, a chair!
*Gratiano:* Roderigo?
*Iago:* He, he, 'tis he!

    *[A chair brought in.]*

    O, that's well said;° the chair.
    Some good man bear him carefully from hence.                    100
    I'll fetch the general's surgeon. *[To Bianca.]* For you, mistress,
    Save you your labor. — He that lies slain here, Cassio,
    Was my dear friend. What malice was between you?
*Cassio:* None in the world; nor do I know the man.
*Iago [to Bianca]:* What, look you pale? — O, bear him out o' th' air.                    105

    *[Cassio and Roderigo are borne off.]*

    Stay you, good gentlemen. — Look you pale, mistress? —
    Do you perceive the gastness° of her eye? —
    Nay, if you stare, we shall hear more anon.
    Behold her well; I pray you look upon her.
    Do you see, gentlemen? Nay, guiltiness will speak.                    110

73 *Marry:* (From "By Mary").   82 *chair:* Litter.   99 *well said:* Well done.   107 *gastness:* Terror.

Though tongues were out of use.

*Enter Emilia.*

*Emilia:* 'Las, what is the matter? What is the matter, husband?
*Iago:* Cassio hath here been set on in the dark
By Roderigo, and fellows that are scaped.
He's almost slain, and Roderigo dead.                                115
*Emilia:* Alas, good gentlemen! alas, good Cassio!
*Iago:* This is the fruits of whoring. Prithee, Emilia,
Go know of Cassio where he supped to-night.

*[To Bianca.]*

What, do you shake at that?
*Bianca:* He supped at my house; but I therefore shake not.          120
*Iago:* O, did he so? I charge you go with me.
*Emilia:* Fie, fie upon thee, strumpet!
*Bianca:* I am no strumpet, but of life as honest°
As you that thus abuse me.
*Emilia:*                           As I? Foh! fie upon thee!
*Iago:* Kind gentlemen, let's go see poor Cassio dressed.            125

*[To Bianca.]*

Come, mistress, you must tell's another tale.
Emilia, run you to the citadel
And tell my lord and lady what hath happed.
                                                    *[Exit Emilia.]*
Will you go on afore?                        *Exeunt [all but Iago].*
                This is the night
That either makes me or fordoes° me quite.          *[Exit.]* 130

SCENE II: *A bedchamber in the castle.*

*Desdemona [asleep] in her bed. Enter Othello with a light.*

*Othello:* It is the cause, it is the cause,° my soul.
Let me not name it to you, you chaste stars!
It is the cause. Yet I'll not shed her blood,
Nor scar that whiter skin of hers than snow,
And smooth as monumental alabaster.                                   5
Yet she must die, else she'll betray more men.
Put out the light, and then put out the light.
If I quench thee, thou flaming minister,°
I can again thy former light restore,
Should I repent me; but once put out thy light,                     10
Thou cunning'st pattern of excelling nature,
I know not where is that Promethean heat°
That can thy light relume.° When I have plucked thy rose,
I cannot give it vital growth again;
It needs must wither. I'll smell thee on the tree.                  15

123 *honest:* Chaste.   130 *fordoes:* Destroys.   **Scene II.**   1 *cause:* Cause of justice.
8 *minister:* Servant.   12 *Promethean heat:* Divine fire.   13 *relume:* Relight.

*(He kisses her.)*

O balmy breath, that dost almost persuade
Justice to break her sword! One more, one more!
Be thus when thou art dead, and I will kill thee,
And love thee after. One more, and that's the last!
So sweet was ne'er so fatal. I must weep,                             20
But they are cruel tears. This sorrow's heavenly;
It strikes where it doth love. She wakes.
*Desdemona:* Who's there? Othello?
*Othello:*                               Ay, Desdemona.
*Desdemona:* Will you come to bed, my lord?
*Othello:* Have you prayed to-night, Desdemon?
*Desdemona:*                               Ay, my lord.              25
*Othello:* If you bethink yourself of any crime°
   Unreconciled as yet to heaven and grace,
   Solicit for it straight.
*Desdemona:* Alack, my lord, what may you mean by that?
*Othello:* Well, do it, and be brief; I will walk by.              30
   I would not kill thy unpreparèd spirit.
   No, heaven forfend!° I would not kill thy soul.
*Desdemona:* Talk you of killing?
*Othello:*                               Ay, I do.
*Desdemona:*                               Then heaven
   Have mercy on me!
*Othello:*                       Amen, with all my heart!
*Desdemona:* If you say so, I hope you will not kill me.           35
*Othello:* Hum!
*Desdemona:* And yet I fear you; for you're fatal then
   When your eyes roll so. Why I should fear I know not,
   Since guiltiness I know not; but yet I feel I fear.
*Othello:* Think on thy sins.
*Desdemona:*                       They are loves I bear to you.    40
*Othello:* Ay, and for that thou diest.
*Desdemona:* That death 's unnatural that kills for loving.
   Alas, why gnaw you so your nether lip?
   Some bloody passion shakes your very frame.
   These are portents,° but yet I hope, I hope,               45
   They do not point on me.
*Othello:*                       Peace and be still!
*Desdemona:* I will so. What's the matter?
*Othello:* That handkerchief which I so loved and gave thee
   Thou gav'st to Cassio.
*Desdemona:*                       No, by my life and soul!
   Send for the man and ask him.
*Othello:*                               Sweet soul, take heed,       50
   Take heed of perjury; thou art on thy deathbed.

---

26 *crime:* Sin.   32 *forfend:* Forbid.   45 *portents:* Signs of impending violence.

*Desdemona:* Ay, but not yet to die.
*Othello:*                              Yes, presently.°
   Therefore confess thee freely of thy sin;
   For to deny each article with oath
   Cannot remove nor choke the strong conception°                55
   That I do groan withal. Thou art to die.
*Desdemona:* Then Lord have mercy on me!
*Othello:*                              I say amen.
*Desdemona:* And have you mercy too! I never did
   Offend° you in my life; never loved Cassio
   But with such general warranty of heaven                      60
   As I might love. I never gave him token.
*Othello:* By heaven, I saw my handkerchief in's hand!
   O perjured woman! thou dost stone my heart,°
   And mak'st me call what I intend to do
   A murder, which I thought a sacrifice.                        65
   I saw the handkerchief.
*Desdemona:*                    He found it then.
   I never gave it him. Send for him hither.
   Let him confess a truth.
*Othello:*                    He hath confessed.
*Desdemona:* What, my lord?
*Othello:* That he hath used thee.
*Desdemona:*                    How? Unlawfully?
*Othello:*                                        Ay.           70
*Desdemona:* He will not say so.
*Othello:*                    No, his mouth is stopped.
   Honest Iago hath ta'en order° for't.
*Desdemona:* O, my fear interprets. What, is he dead?
*Othello:* Had all his hairs been lives, my great revenge
   Had stomach for them all.                                     75
*Desdemona:* Alas, he is betrayed, and I undone!
*Othello:* Out, strumpet! Weep'st thou for him to my face?
*Desdemona:* O, banish me, my lord, but kill me not!
*Othello:* Down, strumpet!
*Desdemona:* Kill me to-morrow; let me live to-night!           80
*Othello:* Nay, if you strive —
*Desdemona:* But half an hour!
*Othello:*                    Being done, there is no pause.
*Desdemona:* But while I say one prayer!
*Othello:*                              It is too late.
[*Desdemona:* O Lord, Lord, Lord!]

   *(Smothers her.)*

   *Emilia at the door.*

---

52 *presently:* At once.   55 *conception:* Belief.   59 *Offend:* Wrong.   63 *stone my heart:*
Turn my heart to stone.   72 *ta'en order:* Taken measures.

*Emilia (calls within):*  My lord, my lord! What, ho! my lord, my lord!          85
*Othello:*  What noise is this? Not dead? not yet quite dead?
    I that am cruel am yet merciful;
    I would not have thee linger in thy pain.
    So, so.
*Emilia (within):*  What, ho! my lord, my lord!
*Othello:*                                            Who's there?          90
*Emilia (within):*  O, good my lord, I would speak a word with you!
*Othello:*  Yes, 'tis Emilia. — By and by.° — She's dead. —
    'Tis like she comes to speak of Cassio's death.
    The noise was high. Ha! no more moving?
    Still as the grave. — Shall she come in? Were't good! —          95
    I think she stirs again. No. — What's best to do?
    If she come in, she'll sure speak to my wife.
    My wife! my wife! what wife? I have no wife.
    O, insupportable! O heavy hour!
    Methinks it should be now a huge eclipse          100
    Of sun and moon, and that th' affrighted globe
    Should yawn° at alteration.
*Emilia (within):*                      I do beseech you
    That I may speak with you, O good my lord!
*Othello:*  I had forgot thee. O, come in, Emilia.
    Soft, by and by. — Let me the curtains draw. —          105

*[Closes the bed-curtains.]*

Where art thou?

*[Opens the door.]*
*Enter Emilia.*

               What's the matter with thee now?
*Emilia:*  O my good lord, yonder's foul murder done!
*Othello:*  What? Now?
*Emilia:*  But now, my lord.
*Othello:*  It is the very error° of the moon.          110
    She comes more nearer earth than she was wont
    And makes men mad.
*Emilia:*  Cassio, my lord, hath killed a young Venetian
    Called Roderigo.
*Othello:*                Roderigo killed?
    And Cassio killed?
*Emilia:*                      No, Cassio is not killed.          115
*Othello:*  Not Cassio killed? Then murder's out of tune,
    And sweet revenge grows harsh.
*Desdemona:*  O, falsely, falsely murdered!
*Emilia:*                                O, Lord! what cry is that?
*Othello:*  That? What?

92 *By and by:* Just a moment (addressed to Emilia).   102 *yawn:* Open, as in an earthquake.   110 *error:* Straying off course.

*Emilia:* Out and alas! that was my lady's voice.                                    120
    Help! help, ho! help! O lady, speak again!
    Sweet Desdemona! O sweet mistress, speak!
*Desdemona:* A guiltless death I die.
*Emilia:* O, who hath done this deed?
*Desdemona:* Nobody—I myself. Farewell.                                    125
    Commend° me to my kind lord. O, farewell!

    *(She dies.)*

*Othello:* Why, how should she be murd'red?
*Emilia:*                                                          Alas, who knows?
*Othello:* You heard her say herself, it was not I.
*Emilia:* She said so. I must needs report the truth.
*Othello:* She's like a liar gone to burning hell!                                    130
    'Twas I that killed her.
*Emilia:*                                        O, the more angel she,
    And you the blacker devil!
*Othello:* She turned to folly, and she was a whore.
*Emilia:* Thou dost belie her, and thou art a devil.
*Othello:* She was false as water.°
*Emilia:*                                        Thou art rash as fire to say                                    135
    That she was false. O, she was heavenly true!
*Othello:* Cassio did top her. Ask thy husband else.
    O, I were damned beneath all depth in hell
    But that I did proceed upon just grounds
    To this extremity. Thy husband knew it all.                                    140
*Emilia:* My husband?
*Othello:* Thy husband.
*Emilia:* That she was false to wedlock?
*Othello:* Ay, with Cassio. Nay, had she been true,
    If heaven would make me such another world                                    145
    Of one entire and perfect chrysolite,°
    I'd not have sold her for it.
*Emilia:* My husband?
*Othello:*                              Ay 'twas he that told me on her first.
    An honest man he is, and hates the slime
    That sticks on filthy deeds.
*Emilia:*                                        My husband?
*Othello:* What needs this iterance,° woman? I say thy husband.                                    150
*Emilia:* O mistress, villainy hath made mocks with love!
    My husband say that she was false?
*Othello:*                                        He, woman.
    I say, thy husband. Dost understand the word?
    My friend, thy husband; honest, honest Iago.                                    155
*Emilia:* If he say so, may his pernicious soul
    Rot half a grain a day! he lies to th' heart.
    She was too fond of her most filthy bargain.

---

126 *Commend:* Remember.   135 *water:* (Which is yielding).   146 *chrysolite:* (Precious topaz).   151 *iterance:* Repetition.

*Othello:* Ha!

*Emilia:* Do thy worst. 160
This deed of thine is no more worthy heaven
Than thou wast worthy her.

*Othello:* Peace, you were best.

*Emilia:* Thou hast not half the power to do me harm
As I have to be hurt.° O gull! O dolt!
As ignorant as dirt! thou hast done a deed — 165
I care not for thy sword; I'll make thee known,
Though I lost twenty lives. Help! help! Ho! help!
The Moor hath killed my mistress! Murder! murder!

*Enter Montano, Gratiano, Iago, and others.*

*Montano:* What is the matter? How now, general?

*Emilia:* O, are you come, Iago? You have done well, 170
That men must lay their murders on your neck.

*Gratiano:* What is the matter?

*Emilia:* Disprove this villain, if thou be'st a man.
He says thou told'st him that his wife was false.
I know thou didst not; thou'rt not such a villain. 175
Speak, for my heart is full.

*Iago:* I told him what I thought, and told no more
Than what he found himself was apt and true.

*Emilia:* But did you ever tell him she was false?

*Iago:* I did. 180

*Emilia:* You told a lie, an odious damnèd lie!
Upon my soul, a lie! a wicked lie!
She false with Cassio? Did you say with Cassio?

*Iago:* With Cassio, mistress. Go to, charm° your tongue.

*Emilia:* I will not charm my tongue; I am bound to speak: 185
My mistress here lies murdered in her bed —

*All:* O heavens forfend!

*Emilia:* And your reports have set the murder on.

*Othello:* Nay, stare not, masters. It is true indeed.

*Gratiano:* 'Tis a strange truth. 190

*Montano:* O monstrous act!

*Emilia:* Villainy, villainy, villainy!
I think upon't — I think I smell't! — O villainy!
I thought so then. — I'll kill myself for grief. —
O villainy, villainy!

*Iago:* What, are you mad? I charge you get you home. 195

*Emilia:* Good gentlemen, let me have leave to speak.
'Tis proper I obey him, but not now.
Perchance, Iago, I will ne'er go home.

*Othello:* O! O! O! *(Falls on the bed.)*

*Emilia:* Nay, lay thee down and roar!
For thou hast killed the sweetest innocent 200
That e'er did lift up eye.

164 *to be hurt:* To endure hurt.  184 *charm:* Cast a spell on.

*Othello:*                                   O, she was foul!

   *[Rises.]*

   I scarce did know you, uncle. There lies your niece,
   Whose breath, indeed, these hands have newly stopped.
   I know this act shows° horrible and grim.
*Gratiano:* Poor Desdemon! I am glad thy father's dead.                205
   Thy match was mortal to him, and pure grief
   Shore his old thread in twain. Did he live now,
   This sight would make him do a desperate turn;°
   Yea, curse his better angel from his side,
   And fall to reprobation.°                                         210
*Othello:* 'Tis pitiful; but yet Iago knows
   That she with Cassio hath the act of shame
   A thousand times committed. Cassio confessed it;
   And she did gratify° his amorous works
   With that recognizance° and pledge of love                        215
   Which I first gave her. I saw it in his hand.
   It was a handkerchief, an antique token
   My father gave my mother.
*Emilia:* O God! O heavenly God!
*Iago:* Zounds, hold your peace!
*Emilia:*                              'Twill out, 'twill out! I peace?     220
   No, I will speak as liberal as the north,°
   Let heaven and men and devils, let them all,
   All, all, cry shame against me, yet I'll speak.
*Iago:* Be wise, and get you home.
*Emilia:*                              I will not.

   *[Iago draws and threatens Emilia.]*

*Gratiano:*                                   Fie!
   Your sword upon a woman?                                          225
*Emilia:* O thou dull Moor, that handkerchief thou speak'st of
   I found by fortune, and did give my husband;
   For often with a solemn earnestness —
   More than indeed belonged to such a trifle —
   He begged of me to steal't.
*Iago:*                                   Villainous whore!               230
*Emilia:* She give it Cassio? No, alas, I found it,
   And I did give't my husband.
*Iago:*                                   Filth, thou liest!
*Emilia:* By heaven, I do not, I do not, gentlemen.
   O murd'rous coxcomb! what should such a fool
   Do with so good a wife?
*Othello:*                              Are there no stones° in heaven    235
   But what serves for the thunder? Precious villain!

---

204 *shows:* Appears.   208 *turn:* Act.   210 *reprobation:* Rejection by God, damnation.
214 *gratify:* Reward.   215 *recognizance:* Token.   221 *liberal as the north:* Unchecked as
the north wind blows.   235 *stones:* Bolts like those used for thunderbolts.

*The Moor runs at Iago [but is disarmed by Montano].*
*Iago kills his wife.*

**Gratiano:** The woman falls. Sure he hath killed his wife.
**Emilia:** Ay, ay. O, lay me by my mistress' side.        *Exit Iago.*
**Gratiano:** He's gone, but his wife's killed.
**Montano:** 'Tis a notorious° villain. Take you this weapon,        240
  Which I have here recovered from the Moor.
  Come, guard the door without. Let him not pass,
  But kill him rather. I'll after that same villain,
  For 'tis a damnèd slave.

  *Exit [Montano, with all but Othello and Emilia].*

**Othello:**                     I am not valiant neither;
  But every puny whipster° gets my sword.        245
  But why should honor outlive honesty?
  Let it go all.
**Emilia:**          What did thy song bode, lady?
  Hark, canst thou hear me? I will play the swan,
  And die in music. *[Sings.]* "Willow, willow, willow."
  Moor, she was chaste. She loved thee, cruel Moor:        250
  So come my soul to bliss as I speak true.
  So speaking as I think, I die, I die.

  *(She dies.)*

**Othello:** I have another weapon in this chamber;
  It is a sword of Spain, the ice brook's° temper.
  O, here it is. — Uncle, I must come forth.        255
**Gratiano (within):** If thou attempt it, it will cost thee dear.
  Thou hast no weapon, and perforce must suffer.
**Othello:** Look in upon me then and speak with me,
  Or, naked° as I am, I will assault thee.

  *[Enter Gratiano.]*

**Gratiano:** What is the matter?
**Othello:**                     Behold, I have a weapon;        260
  A better never did itself sustain
  Upon a soldier's thigh. I have seen the day
  That with this little arm and this good sword
  I have made my way through more impediments
  Than twenty times your stop.° But O vain boast!        265
  Who can control his fate? 'Tis not so now.
  Be not afraid, though you do see me weaponed.
  Here is my journey's end, here is my butt,°
  And very seamark° of my utmost sail:
  Do you go back dismayed? 'Tis a lost° fear.        270
  Man but a rush° against Othello's breast,
  And he retires. Where should Othello go?

---

240 *notorious:* Notable.   245 *puny whipster:* Whippersnapper.   254 *ice brook:* i.e., a Spanish blade, tempered in cold running water.   259 *naked:* Disarmed.   265 *stop:* Power to stop.   268 *butt:* Limit.   269 *seamark:* Beacon, destination.   270 *lost:* Wasted.   271 *Man but a rush:* Wield only a reed.

Now, how dost thou look now? O ill-starred wench!
Pale as thy smock! When we shall meet at compt,°
This look of thine will hurl my soul from heaven,                                   275
And fiends will snatch at it. Cold, cold, my girl?
Even like thy chastity.
O cursèd, cursèd slave! Whip me, ye devils,
From the possession of this heavenly sight!
Blow me about in winds! roast me in sulphur!                                        280
Wash me in steep-down gulfs of liquid fire!
Oh Desdemon! dead Desdemon! dead! Oh! Oh!

*Enter Lodovico, Montano, Iago [as prisoner], and Officers; Cassio in a chair.*

*Lodovico:*  Where is this rash and most unfortunate man?
*Othello:*  That's he that was Othello. Here I am.
*Lodovico:*  Where is that viper? Bring the villain forth.                          285
*Othello:*  I look down towards his feet° — but that's a fable.
If that thou be'st a devil, I cannot kill thee.

   *[Wounds Iago.]*

*Lodovico:*  Wrench his sword from him.

   *[Othello is disarmed.]*

*Iago:*                                I bleed, sir, but not killed.
*Othello:*  I am not sorry neither. I'd have thee live;
For in my sense, 'tis happiness to die.                                            290
*Lodovico:*  O thou Othello that wert once so good,
Fall'n in the practice° of a damnèd slave,
What shall be said to thee?
*Othello:*                                Why, anything;
An honorable murderer, if you will;
For naught did I in hate, but all in honor.                                        295
*Lodovico:*  This wretch hath part confessed his villainy.
Did you and he consent in° Cassio's death?
*Othello:*  Ay.
*Cassio:*  Dear general, I never gave you cause.
*Othello:*  I do believe it, and I ask your pardon.                                300
Will you, I pray, demand that demi-devil
Why he hath thus ensnared my soul and body?
*Iago:*  Demand me nothing. What you know, you know.
From this time forth I never will speak word.
*Lodovico:*  What, not to pray?
*Gratiano:*                                Torments will ope your lips.              305
*Othello:*  Well, thou dost best.
*Lodovico:*  Sir, you shall understand what hath befall'n,
Which, as I think, you know not. Here is a letter
Found in the pocket of the slain Roderigo;
And here another. The one of them imports                                          310
The death of Cassio to be undertook
By Roderigo.

---

274 *compt:* Final accounting, Last Judgment.    286 *I . . . feet:* i.e., to see if they are cloven, like
the Devil's.    292 *practice:* Plot.    297 *consent in:* Agree upon.

*Othello:* O villain!
*Cassio:*           Most heathenish and most gross!
*Lodovico:* Now here's another discontented paper
    Found in the pocket too; and this, it seems,             315
    Roderigo meant t' have sent this damnèd villain;
    But that, belike, Iago in the nick°
    Came in and satisfied him.
*Othello:*              O thou pernicious caitiff! —
    How came you, Cassio, by that handkerchief
    That was my wife's?
*Cassio:*            I found it in my chamber;       320
    And he himself confessed but even now
    That there he dropped it for a special purpose
    Which wrought to his desire.
*Othello:*             O fool! fool! fool!
*Cassio:* There is besides in Roderigo's letter,
    How he upbraids Iago that he made him          325
    Brave me upon the watch; whereon it came
    That I was cast;° and even but now he spake,
    After long seeming dead — Iago hurt him,
    Iago set him on.
*Lodovico:* You must forsake this room and go with us.     330
    Your power and your command is taken off,
    And Cassio rules in Cyprus. For this slave,
    If there be any cunning cruelty
    That can torment him much and hold him long,
    It shall be his. You shall close prisoner rest      335
    Till that the nature of your fault be known
    To the Venetian state. Come, bring away.
*Othello:* Soft you! a word or two before you go.
    I have done the state some service, and they know't.
    No more of that. I pray you, in your letters,       340
    When you shall these unlucky° deeds relate,
    Speak of me as I am. Nothing extenuate,
    Nor set down aught in malice. Then must you speak
    Of one that loved not wisely, but too well;
    Of one not easily jealous, but, being wrought,      345
    Perplexed° in the extreme; of one whose hand,
    Like the base Judean,° threw a pearl away
    Richer than all his tribe; of one whose subdued° eyes,
    Albeit unusèd to the melting mood,
    Drop tears as fast as the Arabian trees          350
    Their med'cinable gum. Set you down this.
    And say besides that in Aleppo once,
    Where a malignant and a turbaned Turk
    Beat a Venetian and traduced the state,
    I took by th' throat the circumcisèd dog         355
    And smote him — thus.

---

317 *nick:* Nick of time.    327 *cast:* Dismissed.    341 *unlucky:* Fatal.    346 *Perplexed:* Distracted.
347 *Judean:* Judas Iscariot (?) (quarto reads "Indian").    348 *subdued:* i.e., conquered by grief.

*(He stabs himself.)*
Lodovico:  O bloody period!°
Gratiano:                                   All that's spoke is marred.
Othello:  I kissed thee ere I killed thee. No way but this,
  Killing myself, to die upon a kiss.

*(He [falls upon the bed and] dies.)*

Cassio:  This did I fear, but thought he had no weapon;                          360
  For he was great of heart.
Lodovico [to Iago]:                        O Spartan dog,
  More fell° than anguish, hunger, or the sea!
  Look on the tragic loading of this bed.
  This is thy work. The object poisons sight;
  Let it be hid.° Gratiano, keep the house,                                    365
  And seize upon° the fortunes of the Moor,
  For they succeed on you. To you, lord governor,
  Remains the censure° of this hellish villain,
  The time, the place, the torture. O, enforce it!
  Myself will straight aboard, and to the state                                370
  This heavy act with heavy heart relate.

                                                          *Exeunt.*

357 *period:* Ending.   362 *fell:* Cruel.   365 *Let it be hid:* i.e., draw the bed curtains.
366 *seize upon:* Take legal possession of.   368 *censure:* Judicial sentence.

## CONSIDERATIONS FOR CRITICAL THINKING AND WRITING

1. FIRST RESPONSE. Characterize Othello. In what ways is he presented as having a jealous disposition as well as a noble one? Why is he so vulnerable to Iago's villainy?

2. Explain how Iago presents himself to the world. What is beneath the surface of his public identity? Why does he hate Othello so passionately? What makes Iago so effective at manipulating people? What do other characters, besides Othello, think of him?

3. Explain why you think Othello's racial identity does or doesn't affect events in the play.

4. How does Othello change during the course of the play? Do you feel the same about him from beginning to end? Trace your response to his character as it develops, paying particular attention to Othello's final speech.

5. Consider how women — Desdemona, Emilia, and Bianca — are presented in the play. What characteristics do they have in common? How do they relate to the men in their lives?

6. Despite its grinding emotional impact and bleak ending, Othello does have its humorous moments. Locate a scene that includes humor and describe its tone and function in the play.

## CONNECTIONS TO OTHER SELECTIONS

1. Do Othello and Sophocles' Oedipus fall from their places of high power for similar or different reasons? Put differently, do they have similar personalities and are they subject to the same character flaw despite the different circumstances of the two plays?

2. The historical contexts surrounding *Othello* and August Wilson's *Fences* (p. 1329) are obviously much different, and yet both plays are, on one level, about race relations. Compare Othello to Troy Maxson, the protagonist of *Fences*, as tragic heroes of these two plays with race as the context.

---

## Perspectives

---

### THE MAYOR OF LONDON (1597)
### *Objections to the Elizabethan Theater* 1597

The inconueniences that grow by Stage playes abowt the Citie of London.

1. They are a speaciall cause of corrupting their Youth, conteninge nothinge but vnchast matters, lascivious devices, shiftes of Coozenage,° & other lewd & vngodly practizes, being so as that they impresse the very qualitie & corruption of manners which they represent, Contrary to the rules & art prescribed for the makinge of Comedies eaven amonge the Heathen, who vsd them seldom & at certen sett tymes, and not all the year longe as our manner is. Whearby such as frequent them, beinge of the base & refuze sort of people or such young gentlemen as have small regard of credit or conscience, drawe the same into imitacion and not to the avoidinge the like vices which they represent.

2. They are the ordinary places for vagrant persons, Maisterles men, thieves, horse stealers, whoremongers, Coozeners, Conycatchers,° contrivers of treason, and other idele and daungerous persons to meet together & to make theire matches to the great displeasure of Almightie God & the hurt & annoyance of her Maiesties people, which cannot be prevented nor discovered by the Gouernours of the Citie for that they are owt of the Citiees iurisdiction.

3. They maintaine idlenes in such persons as haue no vocation & draw apprentices and other seruantes from theire ordinary workes and all sortes of people from the resort vnto sermons and other Christian exercises, to the great hinderance of traides & prophanation of religion established by her highnes within this Realm.

4. In the time of sickness it is fownd by experience, that many hauing sores and yet not hart sicke take occasion hearby to walk abroad & to recreat themselves by heareinge a play Whearby others are infected, and them selves also many things miscarry.

From Edmund K. Chambers, *The Elizabethan Stage*

*shiftes of Coozenage:* Perverse behavior.    *Conycatchers:* Tricksters.

#### CONSIDERATIONS FOR CRITICAL THINKING AND WRITING

1. Summarize the mayor's objections to the theater. Do any of his reasons for protesting theatrical productions seem reasonable to you? Why or why not?

2. Are any of these concerns reflected in attitudes about the theater today? Why or why not?

3. How would you defend *Othello* against charges that it draws some people into "imitacion and not to the avoidinge the like vices which they represent"?

## LISA JARDINE  (B. 1944)

### On Boy Actors in Female Roles    1989

Every schoolchild knows that there were no women actors on the Elizabethan stage; the female parts were taken by young male actors. But every schoolchild also learns that this fact is of little consequence for the twentieth-century reader of Shakespeare's plays. Because the taking of female parts by boys was universal and commonplace, we are told, it was accepted as "verisimilitude" by the Elizabethan audience, who simply disregarded it, as we would disregard the creaking of stage scenery and accept the backcloth forest as "real" for the duration of the play.

Conventional or not, the taking of female parts by boy players actually occasioned a good deal of contemporary comment and created considerable moral uneasiness, even amongst those who patronized and supported the theaters. Amongst those who opposed them, transvestism on stage was a main plank in the anti-stage polemic. "The appareil of wemen is a great provocation of men to lust and leacherie," wrote Dr. John Rainoldes, a leading Oxford divine (quoting the Bishop of Paris), in *Th' Overthrow of Stage-Playes* (Middleburgh, 1599). And he continues with an unhealthy interest which infuses the entire pamphlet: "A womans garment beeing put on a man doeth vehemently touch and moue him with the remembrance and imagination of a woman; and the imagination of a thing desirable doth stirr up the desire."

According to Rainoldes, and the authorities with whose independent testimony he lards his polemic, the wearing of female dress by boy players "is an occasion of wantonnes and lust." Sexuality, misdirected toward the boy masquerading in female dress, is "stirred" by attire and gesture; male prostitution and perverted sexual activity is the inevitable accompaniment of female impersonation.

From *Still Harping on Daughters*, Second Edition

#### CONSIDERATIONS FOR CRITICAL THINKING AND WRITING

1. How does Jardine complicate the Elizabethan convention of boy actors assuming female roles? To what extent does it add to the representation of Elizabethan theater put forward by the mayor of London?

2. What do you think your response would be to a male actor playing a female role? Consider, for example, Desdemona in *Othello*. You may also complicate your response by drawing on recent examples from film or television of roles being gender-swapped, something that has happened several ways in the other direction, with female actors taking on formerly male roles.

## SAMUEL JOHNSON  (1709–1784)

### On Shakespeare's Characters    1765

Shakespeare is above all writers, at least above all modern writers, the poet of nature: the poet that holds up to his readers a faithful mirror of manners and life. His characters are not modified by the customs of particular places, unpracticed by the rest of the world; by the peculiarities of studies or professions, which can operate but upon small numbers; or by the accidents of transient fashions or temporary opinions: they are the genuine progeny of common humanity, such as the world will always supply, and observation will always find. His persons act and speak by the influence of those general passions and principles by which all minds are agitated, and the whole system of life is continued in motion. In the writings of other poets a character is too often an individual; in those of Shakespeare it is commonly a species.

From the preface to Johnson's edition of Shakespeare's works

### CONSIDERATIONS FOR CRITICAL THINKING AND WRITING

1. Johnson made this famous assessment of Shakespeare's ability to portray "common humanity" in the eighteenth century. As a twenty-first-century reader, explain why you agree or disagree with Johnson's view that Shakespeare's characters have universal appeal.

2. Write an essay discussing whether you think it is desirable or necessary for characters to be "a faithful mirror of manners and life." Along the way consider whether you encountered any characters in *Othello* who do not provide what you consider to be an accurate mirror of human life.

## JANE ADAMSON

### *On Desdemona's Role in* Othello   1980

One of the oddest things about criticism of *Othello* is how little usually gets said about Desdemona. She is often considered as a necessary element in the drama only because she is a necessary element in its plot — the woman with whom Othello just happens to be in love — rather than a major dramatic figure conceived in relation to everyone else. There is a strong tendency in critics of all persuasions to take her as a helpless, hapless victim — like one of those ideal Victorian heroines in whose mouths not even margarine would melt. As Marvin Rosenberg points out [in *The Masks of Othello*], "Desdemona has been in grave danger of being canonized," with the result that the play is made to seem much simpler than it is. . . . As Rosenberg also points out, however, the same result follows from the (not uncommon) alternative view of Desdemona, which sees her not as an innocent victim but as the culpable agent of her fate, or as someone whose "flaws" or "indiscretions" are such that she partly "deserves" what happens because she "brings it upon herself."

It seems to me that Rosenberg is right: neither of these views of Desdemona will do. Not only is she a more interesting and complex character, but she also emerges as a crucial and complex element in the dramatic design. To miss or distort what she — and Emilia and Bianca, the play's other women in love — represent in the world of *Othello* is to miss an essential element in its tragic power. What [F. R.] Leavis, for instance, asserts [in "Diabolic Intellect and the Noble Hero"] but nowhere explains is true: "the tragedy is inherent in the Othello-Desdemona relation."

From Othello *as Tragedy: Some Problems of Judgment and Feeling*

### CONSIDERATIONS FOR CRITICAL THINKING AND WRITING

1. How might Desdemona be regarded as a "helpless, hapless victim"? What evidence is there in the play to support such a view?

2. Try to make a case for Desdemona as "the culpable agent of her fate."

3. Adamson agrees with Leavis that "the tragedy is inherent in the Othello-Desdemona relation." In an essay explore the possibilities of this provocative suggestion. What is there in these characters' relationship that could lead to their mutual suffering?

**DAVID BEVINGTON** (B. 1931)

## *On Othello's Heroic Struggle* 1992

As a tragic hero, Othello obtains self-knowledge at a terrible price. He knows finally that what he has destroyed was ineffably good. The discovery is too late for him to make amends, and he dies by his own hand as atonement. The deaths of Othello and Desdemona are, in their separate ways, equally devastating: He is in part the victim of racism, though he nobly refuses to deny his own culpability, and she is the victim of sexism, lapsing sadly into the stereotypical role of passive and silent sufferer that the Venetian world expects of women. Despite the loss, however, Othello's reaffirmation of faith in Desdemona's goodness undoes what the devil-like Iago had most hoped to achieve: the separation of Othello from his loving trust in one who is good. In this important sense, Othello's self-knowledge is cathartic and a compensation for the terrible price he has paid. The very existence of a person as good as Desdemona gives the lie to Iago's creed that everyone has his or her price. She is the sacrificial victim who must die for Othello's loss of faith and, by dying, rekindle that faith. ("My life upon her faith!" Othello prophetically affirms, in response to her father's warning that she may deceive [1.3.293].) She cannot restore him to himself, for self-hatred has done its ugly work, but she is the means by which he understands at last the chimerical and wantonly destructive nature of his jealousy. His greatness appears in his acknowledgment of this truth and in the heroic struggle with which he has confronted an inner darkness we all share.

From *The Complete Works of William Shakespeare*

### CONSIDERATIONS FOR CRITICAL THINKING AND WRITING

1. What kind of "self-knowledge" does Bevington attribute to Othello? Explain why you agree or disagree with this assessment of Othello.

2. Explain how Othello's "destructive . . . jealousy" has shaped the major events of the play.

3. Do you think Othello is engaged in a "heroic struggle," or is he merely the victim of a horrific plot against him? Refer to specific scenes to support your response.

**JAMES KINCAID** (B. 1937)

## *On the Value of Comedy in the Face of Tragedy* 1991

[O]ur current hierarchical arrangement (tragedy high — comedy low) betrays an acquiescence in the most smothering of political conservatisms. Put another way, by coupling tragedy with the sublime, the ineffable, the metaphysical and by aligning comedy with the mundane, the quotidian, and the material we manage to muffle, even to erase, the most powerful narratives of illumination and liberation we have. . . .

The point is comic relief, the *concept* of comic relief and who it relieves. Now we usually refer to comic relief in the same tone we use for academic deans, other people's children, Melanie Griffith, the new criticism, jogging, Big Macs, the *New York Times Book Review*, leisure suits, people who go on cruises, realtors, and the MLA: bemused contempt. (Which is what we think about comic relief.) Comedy is that which attends on, offers relaxation from, prepares us for more of — something else, something serious and demanding. Comedy is not demanding — it does not demand or take, it gives. And we know that any agency which gives cannot be worth much. Tragedy's seriousness is guaranteed by its bullying greed, its insistence on having things its own way and pulling from us not only our tears, which we value little, but our attention, which we hate to give. Comedy, on the other hand, doesn't care if we attend closely. Tragedy is sleek and single-minded, comedy rumpled and hospitable to any idea or agency. Tragedy stares us out of countenance; comedy winks and leers and drools. Tragedy is all dressed up; comedy is always taking things off, mooning us. We find it inevitable that we associate tragedy with the high, comedy with the low. What is at issue here is the nature of that inevitability, our willingness to conspire in a discourse which pays homage to tragic grandeur and reduces comedy to release, authorized license, periodic relief — like a sneeze or yawn or belch. By allowing such discourse to flow through us, we add our bit of cement to the cultural edifice that sits on top of comedy, mashes it down into a mere adjunct to tragedy, its reverse and inferior half, its silly little carnival. By cooperating in this move, we relieve orthodox and conservative power structures of any pressure that might be exercised against them. Comic relief relieves the status quo, in other words, contains the power of comedy. . . .

Let's put it this way, comedy is not a mode that stands in opposition to tragedy. Comedy is the *whole* story, the narrative which refuses to leave things out. Tragedy insists on a formal structure that is unified and coherent, formally balanced and elegantly tight. Only that which is coordinate is allowed to adorn the tragic body. With comedy, nothing is sacrificed, nothing lost; the discoordinate and the discontinuous are especially welcome. Tragedy protects itself by its linearity, its tight conclusiveness; comedy's generosity and ability never to end make it gloriously vulnerable. Pitting tragedy against comedy is running up algebra against recess. . . .

> From a paper read at the 1991 meeting of the Modern Language Association,
> "Who Is Relieved by the Idea of Comic Relief?"

### CONSIDERATIONS FOR CRITICAL THINKING AND WRITING

1. What distinctions does Kincaid make between comedy and tragedy? How does his description of tragedy compare with Aristotle's (see p. 1039)?

2. According to Kincaid, why is the denigration of comedy a conservative impulse? In an essay, explain why you agree or disagree with the argument.

### SUGGESTED TOPICS FOR LONGER PAPERS

1. Discuss Shakespeare's use of humor in *Othello*. Examine several humorous scenes as the basis of your discussion and characterize the tone of the humor. What generalizations can you make about the tone and purpose of the humor in the play?

2. Research how marriage was regarded in Elizabethan times and compare those attitudes and values with the treatment of marriage in *Othello*.

# 38

# Modern Drama

I love acting. It is so much more real than life.

— OSCAR WILDE

Photo 12/Universal Images Group/Getty Images.

## REALISM

*Realism* is a literary technique that attempts to create the appearance of life as it is actually experienced. Characters in modern realistic plays (written during and after the last quarter of the nineteenth century) speak dialogue that we might hear in our daily lives. These characters are not larger than life but representative of it; they seem to speak the way we do rather than in highly poetic language, formal declarations, asides, or soliloquies. It is impossible to imagine a heroic figure such as Oedipus inhabiting a comfortably furnished living room as characters do in so many plays of the late nineteenth and early twentieth century, including Oscar Wilde's *The Importance of Being Earnest* (p. 1148). Realism brings into focus commonplace, everyday life rather than the extraordinary kinds of events that make up Sophocles' *Oedipus the King* (p. 1001) or Shakespeare's *Othello* (p. 1055).

Realistic characters can certainly be heroic, but they find that their strength and courage are tested in the context of events ordinary people might experience. Work, love, marriage, children, and death are often the focus of realistic dramas. These subjects can also constitute much of the material in nonrealistic plays, but modern realistic dramas present such material in the realm of the probable. Conflicts in realistic plays are likely to reflect problems in our own lives. Making ends meet takes precedence over saving a kingdom; middle- and lower-class individuals take center stage as primary characters in main plots rather than being secondary characters in subplots. Thus, we can see why the nineteenth-century movement toward realism paralleled the rise of a middle class eagerly seeking representations of its concerns in the theater.

Before the end of the nineteenth century, however, few attempts were made in the theater to present life as it is actually lived. The chorus's role in Sophocles' *Oedipus the King*, the allegorical figures in morality plays, the remarkable mistaken identities in Shakespeare's comedies, or the rhymed couplets spoken in seventeenth-century plays such as Molière's *Tartuffe* represent theatrical conventions rather than life. Theatergoers have understood and appreciated these conventions for centuries — and still do — but in the nineteenth century in Europe and the United States social, political, and industrial revolutions helped create an atmosphere in which some playwrights found it necessary to create works that more directly reflected their audiences' lives.

Playwrights such as Henrik Ibsen and Anton Chekhov refused to join the ranks of their romantic contemporaries, who they felt falsely idealized life. The most popular plays immediately preceding the works of these realistic writers consisted primarily of love stories and action-packed plots. Such **melodramas** offer audiences thrills and chills as well as happy endings. They typically include a virtuous individual struggling under the tyranny of a wicked oppressor, who is defeated only at the last moment. Suspense is reinforced by a series of pursuits, captures, and escapes that move the plot quickly and de-emphasize character or theme. These representations of extreme conflicts enjoyed wide popularity in the nineteenth century because their formula was varied enough to be entertaining yet their outcomes were always comforting to the audience's sense of justice. From the realists' perspective, melodramas were merely escape fantasies that distorted life by refusing to examine the real world closely and objectively.

Realists attempted to open their audiences' eyes. To these playwrights' minds, the only genuine comfort was in knowing the truth. Many of their plays concern controversial issues of the day and focus on people who fall prey to indifferent societal institutions. English dramatist John Galsworthy (1867–1933) examined social values in *Strife* (1909) and *Justice* (1910), two plays whose titles broadly suggest the nature of his concerns. Irish-born playwright George Bernard Shaw (1856–1950) often used comedy and irony as a means of awakening his audiences to contemporary problems: *Arms and the Man* (1894) satirizes romantic attitudes toward war, and *Mrs. Warren's Profession* (1898) indicts a social and economic system that drives a woman to prostitution. Chekhov's major plays are populated by characters frustrated by their social situations and their own sensibilities; they are ordinary people who long for happiness but who become entangled in everyday circumstances that limit their lives. Ibsen also took a close look at his characters' daily lives. His plays attack social conventions and challenge popular attitudes toward marriage.

With these kinds of materials, Ibsen and his contemporaries popularized the *problem play*, a drama that represents a social issue in order to awaken the audience to it. These plays usually reject romantic plots in favor of holding up a mirror that reflects not simply what audiences want to see but what the playwright sees in them. Nineteenth-century realistic theater was no refuge from the social, economic, and psychological problems that melodrama ignored or sentimentalized.

## NATURALISM

Related to realism is another movement called *naturalism*. Essentially more of a philosophical attitude than a literary technique, naturalism derives its name from the idea that human beings are part of nature and subject to its laws. According to naturalists, heredity and environment shape and control people's lives; human behavior is determined as much by instinct as by reason. This deterministic view argues that human beings have no transcendent identity because there is no soul or spiritual world that ultimately distinguishes humanity from any other form of life. Characters in naturalistic plays are generally portrayed as victims overwhelmed by internal and external forces. Thus literary naturalism tends to include not only the commonplace but the sordid, destructive, and chaotic aspects of life. Naturalism, then, is an extreme form of realism that emphasizes fate rather than free will.

The earliest and most articulate voice of naturalism was that of French author Émile Zola (1840–1902), who urged artists to draw their characters from life and present their histories as faithfully as scientists report laboratory findings. Zola's best-known naturalistic play, *Thérèse Raquin* (1873), is a dramatization of an earlier novel involving a woman whose passion causes her to take a lover and plot with him to kill her husband. In his preface to the novel, Zola explains that his purpose is to take "a strong man and unsatisfied woman, . . . throw them into a violent drama and note scrupulously the sensations and acts of these creatures." The diction of Zola's statement reveals his nearly clinical approach, which becomes even more explicit when Zola likens his method of revealing character to that of an autopsy: "I have simply done on two living bodies the work which surgeons do on corpses."

Although some naturalistic plays have been successfully produced and admired, few important dramatists fully subscribed to naturalism's extreme methods and values. Nevertheless, the movement significantly influenced prominent playwrights, including Ireland's J. M. Synge (1871–1909) and Eugene O'Neill (1888–1953), who is considered one of the most important American playwrights. Because of its insistence on the necessity of closely observing characters' environment, playwrights placed a new emphasis on detailed settings and natural acting. This *verisimilitude* became a significant feature of realistic drama.

# THEATRICAL CONVENTIONS
# OF MODERN DRAMA

The picture-frame stage that is often used for realistic plays typically repro-
duces the setting of a room in some detail. (Brander Matthews, the first
American drama professor, pointed out that the invention of the light bulb
had much to do with other innovations in modern drama. Lighting is only
one of many technological innovations that forever changed the way theater
was conceived of in the modern age, which is an age defined largely by rapid
technological change.) Within the stage, framed by a proscenium arch — the
structure from which the curtain hangs — scenery and props are used to create an illusion of reality. Whether the "luxuriously and artistically furnished"
room of Algernon's Half Moon Street flat described in the opening setting
of Wilde's *The Importance of Being Earnest* is only painted scenery or an
actual furnished room, it will probably look real to the audience. Removing
the fourth wall of a room so that an audience can look in fosters the illusion
that the actions onstage are real events happening before unseen spectators.
The texture of Algernon's life is communicated by the set as well as by what
he says and does. That doesn't happen in a play like Sophocles' *Oedipus the
King*. Technical effects can make us believe there is wood burning in a fireplace or snow falling outside a window. Outdoor settings are made similarly
realistic by props and painted sets. In one of Chekhov's full-length plays, for
example, the second act opens in a meadow with the faint outline of a city on
the horizon.

In addition to lifelike sets, a particular method of acting is used to create
a realistic atmosphere. Actors address each other instead of directing formal
speeches toward the audience; they act within the setting, not merely before it.
At the beginning of the twentieth century Konstantin Stanislavsky (1863–1938),
a Russian director, teacher, and actor, developed a system of acting that was
an important influence in realistic theater. He trained actors to identify with
the inner emotions of the characters they played. They were encouraged to
recall from their own lives emotional responses similar to those they were
portraying. The goal was to present a role truthfully by first feeling and then
projecting the character's situation. Among Stanislavsky's early successes in
this method were the plays of Chekhov.

There are, however, degrees of realism on the stage. Tennessee Williams's
*The Glass Menagerie* (1945), for example, is a partially realistic portrayal of
characters whose fragile lives are founded on illusions. Williams's dialogue
rings true, and individual scenes resemble the kind of real-life action we
would imagine such vulnerable characters engaging in, but other elements of
the play are nonrealistic. For instance, Williams uses Tom as a major character in the play as well as narrator and stage manager. Here is part of Williams's
stage directions: "The narrator is an undisguised convention of the play.
He takes whatever license with dramatic convention as is convenient to his
purposes." Although this play can be accurately described as including realistic elements, Williams, like many other contemporary playwrights, does not
attempt an absolute fidelity to reality. He uses flashbacks to present incidents

that occurred before the opening scene because the past impinges so heavily on the present. Most playwrights don't attempt to duplicate reality, since that can now be done so well by movies and television.

Realism needn't lock a playwright into a futile attempt to make everything appear as it is in life. There is no way to avoid theatrical conventions: actors impersonate characters in a setting that is, after all, a stage. Indeed, even the dialogue in a realistic play is quite different from the pauses, sentence fragments, repetitions, silences, and incoherencies that characterize the way people usually speak. Realistic dialogue may seem like ordinary speech, but it, like Shakespeare's poetic language, is constructed. If we remember that realistic drama represents only the appearance of reality and that what we read on a page or see and hear onstage is the result of careful selecting, editing, and even distortion, then we are more likely to appreciate the playwright's art.

### The Importance of Being Earnest

Oscar Wilde (1854–1900) is most remembered as a playwright, but he was also a poet, an essayist, and a fiction writer. Born in Ireland, Wilde was educated at Trinity College in Dublin and moved to England on a scholarship to Oxford University. There he learned a great deal about aesthetics, becoming part of a movement that advocated "art for art's sake," the belief that art did not have to justify its existence, that it was inherently valuable. He remained in England for much of his life, becoming an integral part of the London theater scene. He was a notable public personality, known for his wit and eccentric sense of fashion nearly as much as for his writing. In 1884 he married Constance Mary Lloyd, and the couple had two children while enjoying his extreme success during the 1890s. Wilde was a complicated soul living in conservative times, though. The final five years of his life were plagued by scandal and tragedy after he was arrested and put on trial for "gross indecency" following an affair with a young man, Lord Alfred Douglas. Wilde was convicted and sentenced to two years hard labor. The final three years of his life were spent in obscurity. He died in Paris following complications from an ear infection.

The solitary tragedy of his final days is at odds with a body of work that is brilliant and effervescent. It is clear from even the first dialogue exchange in *The Importance of Being Earnest* — considered Wilde's masterwork — that he was delighted with language and that he found human society silly and yet not meaningless. He subtitled the play "A Trivial Comedy for Serious People." Wilde's play is the polar opposite of many of the moody plays that are considered classics of the modern era, and in fact it is the funniest play in this volume. (It may be the funniest play anywhere!) Tragedies are often regarded as the best plays, but that assessment may reveal a bias based on the essential gloominess of critics who tend to want literature to be heavy, anchored by the weight of dark ideas about humanity. Perhaps knowing this bias, Wilde advertises his play as "trivial." Yet what could be a more serious and mysterious subject than human identity? As you read *The Importance of Being Earnest*, try to ponder life's great questions with a smile on your face.

## OSCAR WILDE (1854–1900)

## *The Importance of Being Earnest*  1895

Photo 12/Universal Images Group/
Getty Images.

THE PERSONS OF THE PLAY

*John Worthing, J.P.*, of the Manor House, Woolton,
    Hertfordshire
*Algernon Moncrieff*, his friend
*Rev. Canon Chasuble, D.D.*, rector of Woolton
*Merriman*, butler to Mr. Worthing
*Lane*, Mr. Moncrieff's manservant
*Lady Bracknell*
*Hon. Gwendolen Fairfax*, her daughter
*Cecily Cardew*, John Worthing's ward
*Miss Prism*, her governess

THE SCENES OF THE PLAY

ACT I: *Algernon Moncrieff's Flat in Half Moon Street, W.*
ACT II: *The Garden at the Manor House, Woolton*
ACT III: *Morning Room at the Manor House, Woolton*

---

### ACT I

(*Scene: Morning room in Algernon's flat in Half Moon Street. The room is
luxuriously and artistically furnished. The sound of a piano is heard in the
adjoining room. Lane is arranging afternoon tea on the table, and after the
music has ceased, Algernon enters.*)

*Algernon:*  Did you hear what I was playing, Lane?
*Lane:*  I didn't think it polite to listen, sir.
*Algernon:*  I'm sorry for that, for your sake. I don't play accurately — anyone can
    play accurately — but I play with wonderful expression. As far as the piano is
    concerned, sentiment is my forte. I keep science for Life.
*Lane:*  Yes, sir.
*Algernon:*  And, speaking of the science of Life, have you got the cucumber sand-
    wiches cut for Lady Bracknell?
*Lane:*  Yes, sir.                                        (*Hands them on a salver.*)
*Algernon (inspects them, takes two, and sits down on the sofa):*  Oh! — by the
    way, Lane, I see from your book that on Thursday night, when Lord Shore-
    ham and Mr. Worthing were dining with me, eight bottles of champagne are
    entered as having been consumed.
*Lane:*  Yes, sir; eight bottles and a pint.
*Algernon:*  Why is it that at a bachelor's establishment the servants invariably
    drink the champagne? I ask merely for information.
*Lane:*  I attribute it to the superior quality of the wine, sir. I have often observed
    that in married households the champagne is rarely of a first-rate brand.
*Algernon:*  Good heavens! Is marriage so demoralizing as that?

*Lane:* I believe it *is* a very pleasant state, sir. I have had very little experience of it myself up to the present. I have only been married once. That was in consequence of a misunderstanding between myself and a young person.

*Algernon (languidly):* I don't know that I am much interested in your family life, Lane.

*Lane:* No, sir; it is not a very interesting subject. I never think of it myself.

*Algernon:* Very natural, I am sure. That will do, Lane, thank you.

*Lane:* Thank you, sir.                                        *(Lane goes out.)*

*Algernon:* Lane's views on marriage seem somewhat lax. Really, if the lower orders don't set us a good example, what on earth is the use of them? They seem, as a class, to have absolutely no sense of moral responsibility.

*(Enter Lane.)*

*Lane:* Mr. Ernest Worthing.

*(Enter Jack. Lane goes out.)*

*Algernon:* How are you, my dear Ernest? What brings you up to town?

*Jack:* Oh, pleasure, pleasure! What else should bring one anywhere? Eating as usual, I see, Algy!

*Algernon (stiffly):* I believe it is customary in good society to take some slight refreshment at five o'clock. Where have you been since last Thursday?

*Jack (sitting down on the sofa):* In the country.

*Algernon:* What on earth do you do there?

*Jack (pulling off his gloves):* When one is in town one amuses oneself. When one is in the country one amuses other people. It is excessively boring.

*Algernon:* And who are the people you amuse?

*Jack (airily):* Oh, neighbors, neighbors.

*Algernon:* Got nice neighbors in your part of Shropshire?

*Jack:* Perfectly horrid! Never speak to one of them.

*Algernon:* How immensely you must amuse them! (*Goes over and takes sandwich.*) By the way, Shropshire is your county, is it not?

*Jack:* Eh? Shropshire? Yes, of course. Hallo! Why all these cups? Why cucumber sandwiches? Why such reckless extravagance in one so young? Who is coming to tea?

*Algernon:* Oh! merely Aunt Augusta and Gwendolen.

*Jack:* How perfectly delightful!

*Algernon:* Yes, that is all very well; but I am afraid Aunt Augusta won't quite approve of your being here.

*Jack:* May I ask why?

*Algernon:* My dear fellow, the way you flirt with Gwendolen is perfectly disgraceful. It is almost as bad as the way Gwendolen flirts with you.

*Jack:* I am in love with Gwendolen. I have come up to town expressly to propose to her.

*Algernon:* I thought you had come up for pleasure? — I call that business.

*Jack:* How utterly unromantic you are!

*Algernon:* I really don't see anything romantic in proposing. It is very romantic to be in love. But there is nothing romantic about a definite proposal. Why, one may be accepted. One usually is, I believe. Then the excitement is all over. The very essence of romance is uncertainty. If ever I get married, I'll certainly try to forget the fact.

*Jack:* I have no doubt about that, dear Algy. The Divorce Court was specially invented for people whose memories are so curiously constituted.

*Algernon:* Oh! there is no use speculating on that subject. Divorces are made in heaven — (*Jack puts out his hand to take a sandwich. Algernon at once interferes.*) Please don't touch the cucumber sandwiches. They are ordered specially for Aunt Augusta. (*Takes one and eats it.*)

*Jack:* Well, you have been eating them all the time.

*Algernon:* That is quite a different matter. She is my aunt. (*Takes plate from below.*) Have some bread and butter. The bread and butter is for Gwendolen. Gwendolen is devoted to bread and butter.

*Jack (advancing to table and helping himself):* And very good bread and butter it is too.

*Algernon:* Well, my dear fellow, you need not eat as if you were going to eat it all. You behave as if you were married to her already. You are not married to her already, and I don't think you ever will be.

*Jack:* Why on earth do you say that?

*Algernon:* Well, in the first place, girls never marry the men they flirt with. Girls don't think it right.

*Jack:* Oh, that is nonsense!

*Algernon:* It isn't. It is a great truth. It accounts for the extraordinary number of bachelors that one sees all over the place. In the second place, I don't give my consent.

*Jack:* Your consent!

*Algernon:* My dear fellow, Gwendolen is my first cousin. And before I allow you to marry her, you will have to clear up the whole question of Cecily.

(*Rings bell.*)

*Jack:* Cecily! What on earth do you mean? What do you mean, Algy, by Cecily? I don't know anyone of the name of Cecily.

(*Enter Lane.*)

*Algernon:* Bring me that cigarette case Mr. Worthing left in the smoking room the last time he dined here.

*Lane:* Yes, sir. (*Lane goes out.*)

*Jack:* Do you mean to say you have had my cigarette case all this time? I wish to goodness you had let me know. I have been writing frantic letters to Scotland Yard about it. I was very nearly offering a large reward.

*Algernon:* Well, I wish you would offer one. I happen to be more than usually hard up.

*Jack:* There is no good offering a large reward now that the thing is found.

(*Enter Lane with the cigarette case on a salver. Algernon takes it at once. Lane goes out.*)

*Algernon:* I think that is rather mean of you, Ernest, I must say. (*Opens case and examines it.*) However, it makes no matter, for, now that I look at the inscription inside, I find that the thing isn't yours after all.

*Jack:* Of course it's mine. (*Moving to him.*) You have seen me with it a hundred times, and you have no right whatsoever to read what is written inside. It is a very ungentlemanly thing to read a private cigarette case.

*Algernon:* Oh! it is absurd to have a hard-and-fast rule about what one should read and what one shouldn't. More than half of modern culture depends on what one shouldn't read.

*Jack:* I am quite aware of the fact, and I don't propose to discuss modern culture. It isn't the sort of thing one should talk of in private. I simply want my cigarette case back.

*Algernon:* Yes; but this isn't your cigarette case. This cigarette case is a present from someone of the name of Cecily, and you said you didn't know anyone of that name.

*Jack:* Well, if you want to know, Cecily happens to be my aunt.

*Algernon:* Your aunt!

*Jack:* Yes. Charming old lady she is, too. Lives at Tunbridge Wells. Just give it back to me, Algy.

*Algernon (retreating to back of sofa):* But why does she call herself little Cecily if she is your aunt and lives at Tunbridge Wells? (*Reading.*) "From little Cecily with her fondest love."

*Jack (moving to sofa and kneeling upon it):* My dear fellow, what on earth is there in that? Some aunts are tall, some aunts are not tall. That is a matter that surely an aunt may be allowed to decide for herself. You seem to think that every aunt should be exactly like your aunt! That is absurd! For heaven's sake give me back my cigarette case.            (*Follows Algernon round the room.*)

*Algernon:* Yes. But why does your aunt call you her uncle? "From little Cecily, with her fondest love to her dear Uncle Jack." There is no objection, I admit, to an aunt being a small aunt, but why an aunt, no matter what her size may be, should call her own nephew her uncle, I can't quite make out. Besides, your name isn't Jack at all; it is Ernest.

*Jack:* It isn't Ernest; it's Jack.

*Algernon:* You have always told me it was Ernest. I have introduced you to everyone as Ernest. You answer to the name of Ernest. You look as if your name was Ernest. You are the most earnest looking person I ever saw in my life. It is perfectly absurd your saying that your name isn't Ernest. It's on your cards. Here is one of them (*taking it from case*) "Mr. Ernest Worthing, B.4, The Albany." I'll keep this as a proof that your name is Ernest if ever you attempt to deny it to me, or to Gwendolen, or to anyone else.

(*Puts the card in his pocket.*)

*Jack:* Well, my name is Ernest in town and Jack in the country, and the cigarette case was given to me in the country.

*Algernon:* Yes, but that does not account for the fact that your small Aunt Cecily, who lives at Tunbridge Wells, calls you her dear uncle. Come, old boy, you had much better have the thing out at once.

*Jack:* My dear Algy, you talk exactly as if you were a dentist. It is very vulgar to talk like a dentist when one isn't a dentist. It produces a false impression.

*Algernon:* Well, that is exactly what dentists always do. Now, go on! Tell me the whole thing. I may mention that I have always suspected you of being a confirmed and secret Bunburyist; and I am quite sure of it now.

*Jack:* Bunburyist? What on earth do you mean by a Bunburyist?

*Algernon:* I'll reveal to you the meaning of that incomparable expression as soon as you are kind enough to inform me why you are Ernest in town and Jack in the country.

*Jack:* Well, produce my cigarette case first.

*Algernon:* Here it is. (*Hands cigarette case.*) Now produce your explanation, and pray make it improbable.                    (*Sits on sofa.*)

*Jack:* My dear fellow, there is nothing improbable about my explanation at all. In fact it's perfectly ordinary. Old Mr. Thomas Cardew, who adopted me when I was a little boy, made me in his will guardian to his granddaughter, Miss Cecily Cardew. Cecily, who addresses me as her uncle from motives of respect that you could not possibly appreciate, lives at my place in the country under the charge of her admirable governess, Miss Prism.

*Algernon:* Where is that place in the country, by the way?

*Jack:* That is nothing to you, dear boy. You are not going to be invited — I may tell you candidly that the place is not in Shropshire.

*Algernon:* I suspected that, my dear fellow! I have Bunburyed all over Shropshire on two separate occasions. Now, go on. Why are you Ernest in town and Jack in the country?

*Jack:* My dear Algy, I don't know whether you will be able to understand my real motives. You are hardly serious enough. When one is placed in the position of guardian, one has to adopt a very high moral tone on all subjects. It's one's duty to do so. And as a high moral tone can hardly be said to conduce very much to either one's health or one's happiness, in order to get up to town I have always pretended to have a younger brother of the name of Ernest, who lives in the Albany, and gets into the most dreadful scrapes. That, my dear Algy, is the whole truth pure and simple.

*Algernon:* The truth is rarely pure and never simple. Modern life would be very tedious if it were either and modern literature a complete impossibility!

*Jack:* That wouldn't be at all a bad thing.

*Algernon:* Literary criticism is not your forte, my dear fellow. Don't try it. You should leave that to people who haven't been at a university. They do it so well in the daily papers. What you really are is a Bunburyist. I was quite right in saying you were a Bunburyist. You are one of the most advanced Bunburyists I know.

*Jack:* What on earth do you mean?

*Algernon:* You have invented a very useful younger brother called Ernest, in order that you may be able to come up to town as often as you like. I have invented an invaluable permanent invalid called Bunbury, in order that I may be able to go down into the country whenever I choose. Bunbury is perfectly invaluable. If it wasn't for Bunbury's extraordinary bad health, for instance, I wouldn't be able to dine with you at Willis's tonight, for I have been really engaged to Aunt Augusta for more than a week.

*Jack:* I haven't asked you to dine with me anywhere tonight.

*Algernon:* I know. You are absurdly careless about sending out invitations. It is very foolish of you. Nothing annoys people so much as not receiving invitations.

*Jack:* You had much better dine with your Aunt Augusta.

*Algernon:* I haven't the smallest intention of doing anything of the kind. To begin with, I dined there on Monday, and once a week is quite enough to dine with one's own relations. In the second place, whenever I do dine there I am always treated as a member of the family, and sent down with° either no woman at all, or two. In the third place, I know perfectly well whom she will place me next to, tonight. She will place me next Mary Farquhar, who always flirts with her own husband across the dinner table. That is not very pleasant. Indeed, it is not even decent — and that sort of thing is enormously on the increase. The amount of women in London who flirt with their own husbands is perfectly scandalous. It looks so bad. It is simply washing one's clean linen in public.

---

*sent down with:* Assigned a woman to escort into the dining room for dinner.

Besides, now that I know you to be a confirmed Bunburyist I naturally want to talk to you about Bunburying. I want to tell you the rules.

*Jack:* I'm not a Bunburyist at all. If Gwendolen accepts me, I am going to kill my brother, indeed I think I'll kill him in any case. Cecily is a little too much interested in him. It is rather a bore. So I am going to get rid of Ernest. And I strongly advise you to do the same with Mr. — with your invalid friend who has the absurd name.

*Algernon:* Nothing will induce me to part with Bunbury, and if you ever get married, which seems to me extremely problematic, you will be very glad to know Bunbury. A man who marries without knowing Bunbury has a very tedious time of it.

*Jack:* That is nonsense. If I marry a charming girl like Gwendolen, and she is the only girl I ever saw in my life that I would marry, I certainly won't want to know Bunbury.

*Algernon:* Then your wife will. You don't seem to realize, that in married life three is company and two is none.

*Jack (sententiously):* That, my dear young friend, is the theory that the corrupt French drama has been propounding for the last fifty years.

*Algernon:* Yes; and that the happy English home has proved in half the time.

*Jack:* For heaven's sake, don't try to be cynical. It's perfectly easy to be cynical.

*Algernon:* My dear fellow, it isn't easy to be anything nowadays. There's such a lot of beastly competition about. (*The sound of an electric bell is heard.*) Ah! that must be Aunt Augusta. Only relatives, or creditors, ever ring in that Wagnerian° manner. Now, if I get her out of the way for ten minutes, so that you can have an opportunity for proposing to Gwendolen, may I dine with you tonight at Willis's?

*Jack:* I suppose so, if you want to.

*Algernon:* Yes, but you must be serious about it. I hate people who are not serious about meals. It is so shallow of them.

(*Enter Lane.*)

*Lane:* Lady Bracknell and Miss Fairfax.

(*Algernon goes forward to meet them. Enter Lady Bracknell and Gwendolen.*)

*Lady Bracknell:* Good afternoon, dear Algernon, I hope you are behaving very well.

*Algernon:* I'm feeling very well, Aunt Augusta.

*Lady Bracknell:* That's not quite the same thing. In fact the two things rarely go together.

(*Sees Jack and bows to him with icy coldness.*)

*Algernon (to Gwendolen):* Dear me, you are smart!

*Gwendolen:* I am always smart! Aren't I, Mr. Worthing?

*Jack:* You're quite perfect, Miss Fairfax.

*Gwendolen:* Oh! I hope I am not that. It would leave no room for developments, and I intend to develop in many directions.

(*Gwendolen and Jack sit down together in the corner.*)

---

*Wagnerian:* Referring to the operas of Richard Wagner (1813–1883), whose music was popularly thought to be loud.

*Lady Bracknell:*  I'm sorry if we are a little late Algernon, but I was obliged to call on dear Lady Harbury. I hadn't been there since her poor husband's death. I never saw a woman so altered; she looks quite twenty years younger. And now I'll have a cup of tea, and one of those nice cucumber sandwiches you promised me.

*Algernon:*  Certainly, Aunt Augusta.                              (*Goes over to tea table.*)

*Lady Bracknell:*  Won't you come and sit here, Gwendolen?

*Gwendolen:*  Thanks, Mama, I'm quite comfortable where I am.

*Algernon (picking up empty plate in horror):*  Good heavens! Lane! Why are there no cucumber sandwiches? I ordered them specially.

*Lane (gravely):*  There were no cucumbers in the market this morning, sir. I went down twice.

*Algernon:*  No cucumbers?

*Lane:*  No, sir. Not even for ready money.

*Algernon:*  That will do, Lane, thank you.

*Lane:*  Thank you, sir.                                              (*Goes out.*)

*Algernon:*  I am greatly distressed, Aunt Augusta, about there being no cucumbers, not even for ready money.

*Lady Bracknell:*  It really makes no matter, Algernon. I had some crumpets with Lady Harbury, who seems to me to be living entirely for pleasure now.

*Algernon:*  I hear her hair has turned quite gold from grief.

*Lady Bracknell:*  It certainly has changed its color. From what cause I, of course, cannot say. (*Algernon crosses and hands tea.*) Thank you. I've quite a treat for you tonight, Algernon. I am going to send you down with Mary Farquhar. She is such a nice woman, and so attentive to her husband. It's delightful to watch them.

*Algernon:*  I am afraid, Aunt Augusta, I shall have to give up the pleasure of dining with you tonight after all.

*Lady Bracknell (frowning):*  I hope not, Algernon. It would put my table completely out. Your uncle would have to dine upstairs. Fortunately he is accustomed to that.

*Algernon:*  It is a great bore, and, I need hardly say, a terrible disappointment to me, but the fact is I have just had a telegram to say that my poor friend Bunbury is very ill again. (*Exchanges glances with Jack.*) They seem to think I should be with him.

*Lady Bracknell:*  It is very strange. This Mr. Bunbury seems to suffer from curiously bad health.

*Algernon:*  Yes; poor Bunbury is a dreadful invalid.

*Lady Bracknell:*  Well, I must say, Algernon, that I think it is high time that Mr. Bunbury made up his mind whether he was going to live or to die. This shilly-shallying with the question is absurd. Nor do I in any way approve of the modern sympathy with invalids. I consider it morbid. Illness of any kind is hardly a thing to be encouraged in others. Health is the primary duty of life. I am always telling that to your poor uncle, but he never seems to take much notice — as far as any improvement in his ailments goes. I should be much obliged if you would ask Mr. Bunbury, from me, to be kind enough not to have a relapse on Saturday, for I rely on you to arrange my music for me. It is my last reception, and one wants something that will encourage conversation, particularly at the end of the season when everyone has practically said whatever they had to say, which, in most cases, was probably not much.

*Algernon:* I'll speak to Bunbury, Aunt Augusta, if he is still conscious, and I think I can promise you he'll be all right by Saturday. Of course the music is a great difficulty. You see, if one plays good music, people don't listen, and if one plays bad music people don't talk. But I'll run over the program I've drawn out, if you will kindly come into the next room for a moment.

*Lady Bracknell:* Thank you, Algernon. It is very thoughtful of you. (*Rising, and following Algernon.*) I'm sure the program will be delightful, after a few expurgations. French songs I cannot possibly allow. People always seem to think that they are improper, and either look shocked, which is vulgar, or laugh, which is worse. But German sounds a thoroughly respectable language, and indeed, I believe is so. Gwendolen, you will accompany me.

*Gwendolen:* Certainly, Mama.

(*Lady Bracknell and Algernon go into the music room. Gwendolen remains behind.*)

*Jack:* Charming day it has been, Miss Fairfax.

*Gwendolen:* Pray don't talk to me about the weather, Mr. Worthing. Whenever people talk to me about the weather, I always feel quite certain that they mean something else. And that makes me so nervous.

*Jack:* I do mean something else.

*Gwendolen:* I thought so. In fact, I am never wrong.

*Jack:* And I would like to be allowed to take advantage of Lady Bracknell's temporary absence —

*Gwendolen:* I would certainly advise you to do so. Mama has a way of coming back suddenly into a room that I have often had to speak to her about.

*Jack (nervously):* Miss Fairfax, ever since I met you I have admired you more than any girl — I have ever met since — I met you.

*Gwendolen:* Yes, I am quite aware of the fact. And I often wish that in public, at any rate, you had been more demonstrative. For me you have always had an irresistible fascination. Even before I met you I was far from indifferent to you. (*Jack looks at her in amazement.*) We live, as I hope you know, Mr. Worthing, in an age of ideals. The fact is constantly mentioned in the more expensive monthly magazines, and has reached the provincial pulpits I am told: And my ideal has always been to love someone of the name of Ernest. There is something in that name that inspires absolute confidence. The moment Algernon first mentioned to me that he had a friend called Ernest, I knew I was destined to love you.

*Jack:* You really love me, Gwendolen?

*Gwendolen:* Passionately!

*Jack:* Darling! You don't know how happy you've made me.

*Gwendolen:* My own Ernest!

*Jack:* But you don't mean to say that you couldn't love me if my name wasn't Ernest?

*Gwendolen:* But your name is Ernest.

*Jack:* Yes, I know it is. But supposing it was something else? Do you mean to say you couldn't love me then?

*Gwendolen (glibly):* Ah! that is clearly a metaphysical speculation, and like most metaphysical speculations has very little reference at all to the actual facts of real life, as we know them.

*Jack:* Personally, darling, to speak quite candidly, I don't much care about the name of Ernest — I don't think the name suits me at all.

*Gwendolen:* It suits you perfectly. It is a divine name. It has a music of its own. It produces vibrations.

*Jack:* Well, really, Gwendolen, I must say that I think there are lots of other much nicer names. I think Jack, for instance, a charming name.

*Gwendolen:* Jack? — No, there is very little music in the name Jack, if any at all, indeed. It does not thrill. It produces absolutely no vibrations — I have known several Jacks, and they all, without exception, were more than usually plain. Besides, Jack is a notorious domesticity for John! And I pity any woman who is married to a man called John. She would probably never be allowed to know the entrancing pleasure of a single moment's solitude. The only really safe name is Ernest.

*Jack:* Gwendolen, I must get christened at once — I mean we must get married at once. There is no time to be lost.

*Gwendolen:* Married, Mr. Worthing?

*Jack (astounded):* Well — surely. You know that I love you, and you led me to believe, Miss Fairfax, that you were not absolutely indifferent to me.

*Gwendolen:* I adore you. But you haven't proposed to me yet. Nothing has been said at all about marriage. The subject has not even been touched on.

*Jack:* Well — may I propose to you now?

*Gwendolen:* I think it would be an admirable opportunity. And to spare you any possible disappointment, Mr. Worthing, I think it only fair to tell you quite frankly beforehand that I am fully determined to accept you.

*Jack:* Gwendolen!

*Gwendolen:* Yes, Mr. Worthing, what have you got to say to me?

*Jack:* You know what I have got to say to you.

*Gwendolen:* Yes, but you don't say it.

*Jack:* Gwendolen, will you marry me? (*Goes on his knees.*)

*Gwendolen:* Of course I will, darling. How long you have been about it! I am afraid you have had very little experience in how to propose.

*Jack:* My own one, I have never loved anyone in the world but you.

*Gwendolen:* Yes, but men often propose for practice. I know my brother Gerald does. All my girlfriends tell me so. What wonderfully blue eyes you have, Ernest! They are quite, quite blue. I hope you will always look at me just like that, especially when there are other people present.

(*Enter Lady Bracknell.*)

*Lady Bracknell:* Mr. Worthing! Rise, sir, from this semirecumbent posture. It is most indecorous.

*Gwendolen:* Mama! (*He tries to rise; she restrains him.*) I must beg you to retire. This is no place for you. Besides, Mr. Worthing has not quite finished yet.

*Lady Bracknell:* Finished what, may I ask?

*Gwendolen:* I am engaged to Mr. Worthing, Mama. (*They rise together.*)

*Lady Bracknell:* Pardon me, you are not engaged to anyone. When you do become engaged to someone, I, or your father, should his health permit him, will inform you of the fact. An engagement should come on a young girl as a surprise, pleasant or unpleasant, as the case may be. It is hardly a matter that she could be allowed to arrange for herself — And now I have a few questions to put to you, Mr. Worthing. While I am making these inquiries, you, Gwendolen, will wait for me below in the carriage.

*Gwendolen (reproachfully):* Mama!

*Lady Bracknell:* In the carriage, Gwendolen! (*Gwendolen goes to the door. She and Jack blow kisses to each other behind Lady Bracknell's back. Lady Bracknell looks vaguely about as if she could not understand what the noise was. Finally turns round.*) Gwendolen, the carriage!

*Gwendolen:* Yes, Mama.                    (*Goes out, looking back at Jack.*)

*Lady Bracknell (sitting down):* You can take a seat, Mr. Worthing.

(*Looks in her pocket for notebook and pencil.*)

*Jack:* Thank you, Lady Bracknell, I prefer standing.

*Lady Bracknell (pencil and notebook in hand):* I feel bound to tell you that you are not down on my list of eligible young men, although I have the same list as the dear Duchess of Bolton has. We work together, in fact. However, I am quite ready to enter your name, should your answers be what a really affectionate mother requires. Do you smoke?

*Jack:* Well, yes, I must admit I smoke.

*Lady Bracknell:* I am glad to hear it. A man should always have an occupation of some kind. There are far too many idle men in London as it is. How old are you?

*Jack:* Twenty-nine.

*Lady Bracknell:* A very good age to be married at. I have always been of opinion that a man who desires to get married should know either everything or nothing. Which do you know?

*Jack (after some hesitation):* I know nothing, Lady Bracknell.

*Lady Bracknell:* I am pleased to hear it. I do not approve of anything that tampers with natural ignorance. Ignorance is like a delicate exotic fruit; touch it and the bloom is gone. The whole theory of modern education is radically unsound. Fortunately in England, at any rate, education produces no effect whatsoever. If it did, it would prove a serious danger to the upper classes, and probably lead to acts of violence in Grosvenor Square. What is your income?

*Jack:* Between seven and eight thousand a year.

*Lady Bracknell (makes a note in her book):* In land, or in investments?

*Jack:* In investments, chiefly.

*Lady Bracknell:* That is satisfactory. What between the duties expected of one during one's lifetime, and the duties exacted from one after one's death, land has ceased to be either a profit or a pleasure. It gives one position, and prevents one from keeping it up. That's all that can be said about land.

*Jack:* I have a country house with some land, of course, attached to it, about fifteen hundred acres, I believe; but I don't depend on that for my real income. In fact, as far as I can make out, the poachers are the only people who make anything out of it.

*Lady Bracknell:* A country house! How many bedrooms? Well, that point can be cleared up afterwards. You have a town house, I hope? A girl with a simple, unspoiled nature, like Gwendolen, could hardly be expected to reside in the country.

*Jack:* Well, I own a house in Belgrave Square, but it is let by the year to Lady Bloxham. Of course, I can get it back whenever I like, at six months' notice.

*Lady Bracknell:* Lady Bloxham? I don't know her.

*Jack:* Oh, she goes about very little. She is a lady considerably advanced in years.

*Lady Bracknell:* Ah, nowadays that is no guarantee of respectability of character. What number in Belgrave Square?

*Jack:* 149.

*Lady Bracknell (shaking her head):* The unfashionable side. I thought there was something. However, that could easily be altered.

*Jack:* Do you mean the fashion, or the side?

*Lady Bracknell (sternly):* Both, if necessary, I presume. What are your politics?

*Jack:* Well, I am afraid I really have none. I am a Liberal Unionist.

*Lady Bracknell:* Oh, they count as Tories. They dine with us. Or come in the evening, at any rate. Now to minor matters. Are your parents living?

*Jack:* I have lost both my parents.

*Lady Bracknell:* Both? To lose one parent may be regarded as a misfortune — to lose *both* seems like carelessness. Who was your father? He was evidently a man of some wealth. Was he born in what the Radical papers call the purple of commerce, or did he rise from the ranks of the aristocracy?

*Jack:* I am afraid I really don't know. The fact is, Lady Bracknell, I said I had lost my parents. It would be nearer the truth to say that my parents seem to have lost me — I don't actually know who I am by birth. I was — well, I was found.

*Lady Bracknell:* Found!

*Jack:* The late Mr. Thomas Cardew, an old gentleman of a very charitable and kindly disposition, found me, and gave me the name of Worthing, because he happened to have a first-class ticket for Worthing in his pocket at the time. Worthing is a place in Sussex. It is a seaside resort.

*Lady Bracknell:* Where did the charitable gentleman who had a first-class ticket for this seaside resort find you?

*Jack (gravely):* In a handbag.

*Lady Bracknell:* A handbag?

*Jack (very seriously):* Yes, Lady Bracknell. I was in a handbag — a somewhat large, black leather handbag, with handles to it — an ordinary handbag in fact.

*Lady Bracknell:* In what locality did this Mr. James, or Thomas, Cardew come across this ordinary handbag?

*Jack:* In the cloakroom at Victoria Station. It was given to him in mistake for his own.

*Lady Bracknell:* The cloakroom at Victoria Station?

*Jack:* Yes. The Brighton line.

*Lady Bracknell:* The line is immaterial. Mr. Worthing, I confess I feel somewhat bewildered by what you have just told me. To be born, or at any rate bred, in a handbag, whether it had handles or not, seems to me to display a contempt for the ordinary decencies of family life that reminds one of the worst excesses of the French Revolution. And I presume you know what that unfortunate movement led to? As for the particular locality in which the handbag was found, a cloakroom at a railway station might serve to conceal a social indiscretion — has probably, indeed, been used for that purpose before now — but it could hardly be regarded as an assured basis for a recognized position in good society.

*Jack:* May I ask you then what you would advise me to do? I need hardly say I would do anything in the world to ensure Gwendolen's happiness.

*Lady Bracknell:* I would strongly advise you, Mr. Worthing, to try and acquire some relations as soon as possible, and to make a definite effort to produce at any rate one parent of either sex, before the season is quite over.

*Jack:* Well, I don't see how I could possibly manage to do that. I can produce the handbag at any moment. It is in my dressing room at home. I really think that should satisfy you, Lady Bracknell.

*Lady Bracknell:* Me, sir! What has it to do with me? You can hardly imagine that I and Lord Bracknell would dream of allowing our only daughter — a girl brought up with the utmost care — to marry into a cloakroom, and form an alliance with a parcel? Good morning, Mr. Worthing!

           (*Lady Bracknell sweeps out in majestic indignation.*)

*Jack:* Good morning! (*Algernon, from the other room, strikes up the Wedding March. Jack looks perfectly furious, and goes to the door.*) For goodness' sake don't play that ghastly tune, Algy! How idiotic you are!

(*The music stops, and Algernon enters cheerily.*)

*Algernon:* Didn't it go off all right, old boy? You don't mean to say Gwendolen refused you? I know it is a way she has. She is always refusing people. I think it is most ill-natured of her.

*Jack:* Oh, Gwendolen is as right as a trivet. As far as she is concerned, we are engaged. Her mother is perfectly unbearable. Never met such a Gorgon° — I don't really know what a Gorgon is like, but I am quite sure that Lady Bracknell is one. In any case, she is a monster, without being a myth, which is rather unfair. I beg your pardon, Algy, I suppose I shouldn't talk about your own aunt in that way before you.

*Algernon:* My dear boy, I love hearing my relations abused. It is the only thing that makes me put up with them at all. Relations are simply a tedious pack of people, who haven't got the remotest knowledge of how to live, nor the smallest instinct about when to die.

*Jack:* Oh, that is nonsense!

*Algernon:* It isn't!

*Jack:* Well, I won't argue about the matter. You always want to argue about things.

*Algernon:* That is exactly what things were originally made for.

*Jack:* Upon my word, if I thought that, I'd shoot myself — (*A pause.*) You don't think there is any chance of Gwendolen becoming like her mother in about a hundred and fifty years, do you, Algy?

*Algernon:* All women become like their mothers. That is their tragedy. No man does. That's his.

*Jack:* Is that clever?

*Algernon:* It is perfectly phrased! and quite as true as any observation in civilized life should be.

*Jack:* I am sick to death of cleverness. Everybody is clever nowadays. You can't go anywhere without meeting clever people. The thing has become an absolute public nuisance. I wish to goodness we had a few fools left.

*Algernon:* We have.

*Jack:* I should extremely like to meet them. What do they talk about?

*Algernon:* The fools? Oh! about the clever people, of course.

*Jack:* What fools!

*Algernon:* By the way, did you tell Gwendolen the truth about your being Ernest in town, and Jack in the country?

---

*Gorgon:* In Greek myth, one of three very ugly sisters who had, among other characteristics, serpents for hair.

*Jack (in a very patronizing manner):* My dear fellow, the truth isn't quite the sort of thing one tells to a nice sweet refined girl. What extraordinary ideas you have about the way to behave to a woman!

*Algernon:* The only way to behave to a woman is to make love to her if she is pretty, and to someone else if she is plain.

*Jack:* Oh, that is nonsense.

*Algernon:* What about your brother? What about the profligate Ernest?

*Jack:* Oh, before the end of the week I shall have got rid of him. I'll say he died in Paris of apoplexy. Lots of people die of apoplexy, quite suddenly, don't they?

*Algernon:* Yes, but it's hereditary, my dear fellow. It's a sort of thing that runs in families. You had much better say a severe chill.

*Jack:* You are sure a severe chill isn't hereditary, or anything of that kind?

*Algernon:* Of course it isn't!

*Jack:* Very well, then. My poor brother Ernest is carried off suddenly in Paris, by a severe chill. That gets rid of him.

*Algernon:* But I thought you said that — Miss Cardew was a little too much interested in your poor brother Ernest? Won't she feel his loss a good deal?

*Jack:* Oh, that is all right. Cecily is not a silly romantic girl, I am glad to say. She has got a capital appetite, goes on long walks, and pays no attention at all to her lessons.

*Algernon:* I would rather like to see Cecily.

*Jack:* I will take very good care you never do. She is excessively pretty, and she is only just eighteen.

*Algernon:* Have you told Gwendolen yet that you have an excessively pretty ward who is only just eighteen?

*Jack:* Oh! one doesn't blurt these things out to people. Cecily and Gwendolen are perfectly certain to be extremely great friends. I'll bet you anything you like that half an hour after they have met, they will be calling each other sister.

*Algernon:* Women only do that when they have called each other a lot of other things first. Now, my dear boy, if we want to get a good table at Willis's, we really must go and dress. Do you know it is nearly seven?

*Jack (irritably):* Oh! it always is nearly seven.

*Algernon:* Well, I'm hungry.

*Jack:* I never knew you when you weren't —

*Algernon:* What shall we do after dinner? Go to a theater?

*Jack:* Oh, no! I loathe listening.

*Algernon:* Well, let us go to the Club?

*Jack:* Oh, no! I hate talking.

*Algernon:* Well, we might trot round to the Empire° at ten?

*Jack:* Oh, no! I can't bear looking at things. It is so silly.

*Algernon:* Well, what shall we do?

*Jack:* Nothing!

*Algernon:* It is awfully hard work doing nothing. However, I don't mind hard work where there is no definite object of any kind.

(*Enter Lane.*)

*Lane:* Miss Fairfax.

(*Enter Gwendolen. Lane goes out.*)

---

*Empire:* Empire Theatre, a London music hall that was also a rendezvous for prostitutes.

*Algernon:*  Gwendolen, upon my word!

*Gwendolen:*  Algy, kindly turn your back. I have something very particular to say to Mr. Worthing.

*Algernon:*  Really, Gwendolen, I don't think I can allow this at all.

*Gwendolen:*  Algy, you always adopt a strictly immoral attitude towards life. You are not quite old enough to do that.　　　(*Algernon retires to the fireplace.*)

*Jack:*  My own darling!

*Gwendolen:*  Ernest, we may never be married. From the expression on Mama's face I fear we never shall. Few parents nowadays pay any regard to what their children say to them. The old-fashioned respect for the young is fast dying out. Whatever influence I ever had over Mama, I lost at the age of three. But although she may prevent us from becoming man and wife, and I may marry someone else, and marry often, nothing that she can possibly do can alter my eternal devotion to you.

*Jack:*  Dear Gwendolen!

*Gwendolen:*  The story of your romantic origin, as related to me by Mama, with unpleasing comments, has naturally stirred the deeper fibers of my nature. Your Christian name has an irresistible fascination. The simplicity of your character makes you exquisitely incomprehensible to me. Your town address at the Albany I have. What is your address in the country?

*Jack:*  The Manor House, Woolton, Hertfordshire.

(*Algernon, who has been carefully listening, smiles to himself, and writes the address on his shirt cuff. Then picks up the Railway Guide.*)

*Gwendolen:*  There is a good postal service, I suppose? It may be necessary to do something desperate. That of course will require serious consideration. I will communicate with you daily.

*Jack:*  My own one!

*Gwendolen:*  How long do you remain in town?

*Jack:*  Till Monday.

*Gwendolen:*  Good! Algy, you may turn round now.

*Algernon:*  Thanks, I've turned round already.

*Gwendolen:*  You may also ring the bell.

*Jack:*  You will let me see you to your carriage, my own darling?

*Gwendolen:*  Certainly.

*Jack (to Lane, who now enters):*  I will see Miss Fairfax out.

*Lane:*  Yes, sir.　　　　　　　　　　　　　　　(*Jack and Gwendolen go off.*)

(*Lane presents several letters on a salver to Algernon. It is to be surmised that they are bills, as Algernon, after looking at the envelopes, tears them up.*)

*Algernon:*  A glass of sherry, Lane.

*Lane:*  Yes, sir.

*Algernon:*  Tomorrow, Lane, I'm going Bunburying.

*Lane:*  Yes, sir.

*Algernon:*  I shall probably not be back till Monday. You can put up my dress clothes, my smoking jacket, and all the Bunbury suits —

*Lane:*  Yes, sir. (*Handing sherry.*)

*Algernon:*  I hope tomorrow will be a fine day, Lane.

*Lane:*  It never is, sir.

*Algernon:*  Lane, you're a perfect pessimist.

*Lane:* I do my best to give satisfaction, sir.

(*Enter Jack. Lane goes off.*)

*Jack:* There's a sensible, intellectual girl! the only girl I ever cared for in my life. (*Algernon is laughing immoderately.*) What on earth are you so amused at?

*Algernon:* Oh, I'm a little anxious about poor Bunbury, that is all.

*Jack:* If you don't take care, your friend Bunbury will get you into a serious scrape some day.

*Algernon:* I love scrapes. They are the only things that are never serious.

*Jack:* Oh, that's nonsense, Algy. You never talk anything but nonsense.

*Algernon:* Nobody ever does.

(*Jack looks indignantly at him, and leaves the room. Algernon lights a cigarette, reads his shirt cuff, and smiles.*)

## ACT II

(*Scene: Garden at the Manor House. A flight of gray stone steps leads up to the house. The garden, an old-fashioned one, full of roses. Time of year, July. Basket chairs, and a table covered with books, are set under a large yew tree. Miss Prism discovered seated at the table. Cecily is at the back watering flowers.*)

*Miss Prism (calling):* Cecily, Cecily! Surely such a utilitarian occupation as the watering of flowers is rather Moulton's duty than yours? Especially at a moment when intellectual pleasures await you. Your German grammar is on the table. Pray open it at page fifteen. We will repeat yesterday's lesson.

*Cecily (coming over very slowly):* But I don't like German. It isn't at all a becoming language. I know perfectly well that I look quite plain after my German lesson.

*Miss Prism:* Child, you know how anxious your guardian is that you should improve yourself in every way. He laid particular stress on your German, as he was leaving for town yesterday. Indeed, he always lays stress on your German when he is leaving for town.

*Cecily:* Dear Uncle Jack is so very serious! Sometimes he is so serious that I think he cannot be quite well.

*Miss Prism (drawing herself up):* Your guardian enjoys the best of health, and his gravity of demeanor is especially to be commended in one so comparatively young as he is. I know no one who has a higher sense of duty and responsibility.

*Cecily:* I suppose that is why he often looks a little bored when we three are together.

*Miss Prism:* Cecily! I am surprised at you. Mr. Worthing has many troubles in his life. Idle merriment and triviality would be out of place in his conversation. You must remember his constant anxiety about that unfortunate young man his brother.

*Cecily:* I wish Uncle Jack would allow that unfortunate young man, his brother, to come down here sometimes. We might have a good influence over him, Miss Prism. I am sure you certainly would. You know German, and geology, and things of that kind influence a man very much.

*(Cecily begins to write in her diary.)*

*Miss Prism (shaking her head):* I do not think that even I could produce any effect on a character that according to his own brother's admission is irretrievably weak and vacillating. Indeed I am not sure that I would desire to reclaim him. I am not in favor of this modern mania for turning bad people into good people at a moment's notice. As a man sows so let him reap. You must put away your diary, Cecily. I really don't see why you should keep a diary at all.

*Cecily:* I keep a diary in order to enter the wonderful secrets of my life. If I didn't write them down I should probably forget all about them.

*Miss Prism:* Memory, my dear Cecily, is the diary that we all carry about with us.

*Cecily:* Yes, but it usually chronicles the things that have never happened, and couldn't possibly have happened. I believe that Memory is responsible for nearly all the three-volume novels that Mudie sends us.

*Miss Prism:* Do not speak slightingly of the three-volume novel, Cecily. I wrote one myself in earlier days.

*Cecily:* Did you really, Miss Prism? How wonderfully clever you are! I hope it did not end happily? I don't like novels that end happily. They depress me so much.

*Miss Prism:* The good ended happily, and the bad unhappily. That is what Fiction means.

*Cecily:* I suppose so. But it seems very unfair. And was your novel ever published?

*Miss Prism:* Alas! no. The manuscript unfortunately was abandoned. I use the word in the sense of lost or mislaid. To your work, child, these speculations are profitless.

*Cecily (smiling):* But I see dear Dr. Chasuble coming up through the garden.

*Miss Prism (rising and advancing):* Dr. Chasuble! This is indeed a pleasure.

*(Enter Canon Chasuble.)*

*Chasuble:* And how are we this morning? Miss Prism, you are, I trust, well?

*Cecily:* Miss Prism has just been complaining of a slight headache. I think it would do her so much good to have a short stroll with you in the park, Dr. Chasuble.

*Miss Prism:* Cecily, I have not mentioned anything about a headache.

*Cecily:* No, dear Miss Prism, I know that, but I felt instinctively that you had a headache. Indeed I was thinking about that, and not about my German lesson, when the Rector came in.

*Chasuble:* I hope, Cecily, you are not inattentive.

*Cecily:* Oh, I am afraid I am.

*Chasuble:* That is strange. Were I fortunate enough to be Miss Prism's pupil, I would hang upon her lips. *(Miss Prism glares.)* I spoke metaphorically. — My metaphor was drawn from bees. Ahem! Mr. Worthing, I suppose, has not returned from town yet?

*Miss Prism:* We do not expect him till Monday afternoon.

*Chasuble:* Ah yes, he usually likes to spend his Sunday in London. He is not one of those whose sole aim is enjoyment, as, by all accounts, that unfortunate young man his brother seems to be. But I must not disturb Egeria° and her pupil any longer.

---

*Egeria:* Roman goddess of water.

*Miss Prism:* Egeria? My name is Laetitia, Doctor.

*Chasuble (bowing):* A classical allusion merely, drawn from the Pagan authors. I shall see you both no doubt at Evensong?

*Miss Prism:* I think, dear Doctor, I will have a stroll with you. I find I have a headache after all, and a walk might do it good.

*Chasuble:* With pleasure, Miss Prism, with pleasure. We might go as far as the schools and back.

*Miss Prism:* That would be delightful. Cecily, you will read your Political Economy in my absence. The chapter on the Fall of the Rupee° you may omit. It is somewhat too sensational. Even these metallic problems have their melodramatic side. (*Goes down the garden with Dr. Chasuble.*)

*Cecily (picks up books and throws them back on table):* Horrid Political Economy! Horrid Geography! Horrid, horrid German!

(*Enter Merriman with a card on a salver.*)

*Merriman:* Mr. Ernest Worthing has just driven over from the station. He has brought his luggage with him.

*Cecily (takes the card and reads it):* "Mr. Ernest Worthing, B.4, The Albany, W." Uncle Jack's brother! Did you tell him Mr. Worthing was in town?

*Merriman:* Yes, Miss. He seemed very much disappointed. I mentioned that you and Miss Prism were in the garden. He said he was anxious to speak to you privately for a moment.

*Cecily:* Ask Mr. Ernest Worthing to come here. I suppose you had better talk to the housekeeper about a room for him.

*Merriman:* Yes, Miss.                                    (*Merriman goes off.*)

*Cecily:* I have never met any really wicked person before. I feel rather frightened. I am so afraid he will look just like everyone else.

(*Enter Algernon, very gay and debonair.*)

He does!

*Algernon (raising his hat):* You are my little cousin Cecily, I'm sure.

*Cecily:* You are under some strange mistake. I am not little. In fact, I believe I am more than usually tall for my age. (*Algernon is rather taken aback.*) But I am your cousin Cecily. You, I see from your card, are Uncle Jack's brother, my cousin Ernest, my wicked cousin Ernest.

*Algernon:* Oh! I am not really wicked at all, Cousin Cecily. You mustn't think that I am wicked.

*Cecily:* If you are not, then you have certainly been deceiving us all in a very inexcusable manner. I hope you have not been leading a double life, pretending to be wicked and being really good all the time. That would be hypocrisy.

*Algernon (looks at her in amazement):* Oh! Of course I have been rather reckless.

*Cecily:* I am glad to hear it.

*Algernon:* In fact, now you mention the subject, I have been very bad in my own small way.

*Cecily:* I don't think you should be so proud of that, though I am sure it must have been very pleasant.

*Algernon:* It is much pleasanter being here with you.

---

*Fall of the Rupee:* Reference to the Indian rupee, whose steady deflation between 1873 and 1893 caused the Indian government finally to close the mints.

*Cecily:* I can't understand how you are here at all. Uncle Jack won't be back till Monday afternoon.

*Algernon:* That is a great disappointment. I am obliged to go up by the first train on Monday morning. I have a business appointment that I am anxious — to miss.

*Cecily:* Couldn't you miss it anywhere but in London?

*Algernon:* No: the appointment is in London.

*Cecily:* Well, I know, of course, how important it is not to keep a business engagement, if one wants to retain any sense of the beauty of life, but still I think you had better wait till Uncle Jack arrives. I know he wants to speak to you about your emigrating.

*Algernon:* About my what?

*Cecily:* Your emigrating. He has gone up to buy your outfit.

*Algernon:* I certainly wouldn't let Jack buy my outfit. He has no taste in neckties at all.

*Cecily:* I don't think you will require neckties. Uncle Jack is sending you to Australia.

*Algernon:* Australia! I'd sooner die.

*Cecily:* Well, he said at dinner on Wednesday night, that you would have to choose between this world, the next world, and Australia.

*Algernon:* Oh, well! The accounts I have received of Australia and the next world are not particularly encouraging. This world is good enough for me, Cousin Cecily.

*Cecily:* Yes, but are you good enough for it?

*Algernon:* I'm afraid I'm not that. That is why I want you to reform me. You might make that your mission, if you don't mind, Cousin Cecily.

*Cecily:* I'm afraid I've no time, this afternoon.

*Algernon:* Well, would you mind my reforming myself this afternoon?

*Cecily:* It is rather quixotic° of you. But I think you should try.

*Algernon:* I will. I feel better already.

*Cecily:* You are looking a little worse.

*Algernon:* That is because I am hungry.

*Cecily:* How thoughtless of me. I should have remembered that when one is going to lead an entirely new life, one requires regular and wholesome meals. Won't you come in?

*Algernon:* Thank you. Might I have a buttonhole° first? I never have any appetite unless I have a buttonhole first.

*Cecily:* A Maréchal Niel?°

*Algernon:* No, I'd sooner have a pink rose.

*Cecily:* Why?                                                    (*Cuts a flower.*)

*Algernon:* Because you are like a pink rose, Cousin Cecily.

*Cecily:* I don't think it can be right for you to talk to me like that. Miss Prism never says such things to me.

*Algernon:* Then Miss Prism is a shortsighted old lady. (*Cecily puts the rose in his buttonhole.*) You are the prettiest girl I ever saw.

*Cecily:* Miss Prism says that all good looks are a snare.

---

*quixotic:* Foolishly impractical, from the idealistic hero of Cervantes's *Don Quixote.*
*buttonhole:* Boutonniere.   *Maréchal Niel:* A yellow rose.

*Algernon:* They are a snare that every sensible man would like to be caught in.

*Cecily:* Oh! I don't think I would care to catch a sensible man. I shouldn't know what to talk to him about.

> (*They pass into the house. Miss Prism and Dr. Chasuble return.*)

*Miss Prism:* You are too much alone, dear Dr. Chasuble. You should get married. A misanthrope I can understand — a womanthrope, never!

*Chasuble (with a scholar's shudder):* Believe me, I do not deserve so neologistic a phrase. The precept as well as the practice of the Primitive Church was distinctly against matrimony.

*Miss Prism (sententiously):* That is obviously the reason why the Primitive Church has not lasted up to the present day. And you do not seem to realize, dear Doctor, that by persistently remaining single, a man converts himself into a permanent public temptation. Men should be more careful; this very celibacy leads weaker vessels astray.

*Chasuble:* But is a man not equally attractive when married?

*Miss Prism:* No married man is ever attractive except to his wife.

*Chasuble:* And often, I've been told, not even to her.

*Miss Prism:* That depends on the intellectual sympathies of the woman. Maturity can always be depended on. Ripeness can be trusted. Young women are green. (*Dr. Chasuble starts.*) I spoke horticulturally. My metaphor was drawn from fruits. But where is Cecily?

*Chasuble:* Perhaps she followed us to the schools.

(*Enter Jack slowly from the back of the garden. He is dressed in the deepest mourning, with crepe hatband and black gloves.*)

*Miss Prism:* Mr. Worthing!

*Chasuble:* Mr. Worthing?

*Miss Prism:* This is indeed a surprise. We did not look for you till Monday afternoon.

*Jack (shakes Miss Prism's hand in a tragic manner):* I have returned sooner than I expected. Dr. Chasuble, I hope you are well?

*Chasuble:* Dear Mr. Worthing, I trust this garb of woe does not betoken some terrible calamity?

*Jack:* My brother.

*Miss Prism:* More shameful debts and extravagance?

*Chasuble:* Still leading his life of pleasure?

*Jack (shaking his head):* Dead!

*Chasuble:* Your brother Ernest dead?

*Jack:* Quite dead.

*Miss Prism:* What a lesson for him! I trust he will profit by it.

*Chasuble:* Mr. Worthing, I offer you my sincere condolence. You have at least the consolation of knowing that you were always the most generous and forgiving of brothers.

*Jack:* Poor Ernest! He had many faults, but it is a sad, sad blow.

*Chasuble:* Very sad indeed. Were you with him at the end?

*Jack:* No. He died abroad, in Paris, in fact. I had a telegram last night from the manager of the Grand Hotel.

*Chasuble:* Was the cause of death mentioned?

*Jack:* A severe chill, it seems.

*Miss Prism:* As a man sows, so shall he reap.

*Chasuble (raising his hand):* Charity, dear Miss Prism, charity! None of us are perfect. I myself am peculiarly susceptible to drafts. Will the interment take place here?

*Jack:* No. He seemed to have expressed a desire to be buried in Paris.

*Chasuble:* In Paris! (*Shakes his head.*) I fear that hardly points to any very serious state of mind at the last. You would no doubt wish me to make some slight allusion to this tragic domestic affliction next Sunday. (*Jack presses his hand convulsively.*) My sermon on the meaning of the manna in the wilderness can be adapted to almost any occasion, joyful, or, as in the present case, distressing. (*All sigh.*) I have preached it at harvest celebrations, christenings, confirmations, on days of humiliation and festal days. The last time I delivered it was in the Cathedral, as a charity sermon on behalf of the Society for the Prevention of Discontent among the Upper Orders. The Bishop, who was present, was much struck by some of the analogies I drew.

*Jack:* Ah! that reminds me, you mentioned christenings I think, Dr. Chasuble? I suppose you know how to christen all right? (*Dr. Chasuble looks astounded.*) I mean, of course, you are continually christening, aren't you?

*Miss Prism:* It is, I regret to say, one of the Rector's most constant duties in this parish. I have often spoken to the poorer classes on the subject. But they don't seem to know what thrift is.

*Chasuble:* But is there any particular infant in whom you are interested, Mr. Worthing? Your brother was, I believe, unmarried, was he not?

*Jack:* Oh yes.

*Miss Prism (bitterly):* People who live entirely for pleasure usually are.

*Jack:* But it is not for any child, dear Doctor. I am very fond of children. No! the fact is, I would like to be christened myself, this afternoon, if you have nothing better to do.

*Chasuble:* But surely, Mr. Worthing, you have been christened already?

*Jack:* I don't remember anything about it.

*Chasuble:* But have you any grave doubts on the subject?

*Jack:* I certainly intend to have. Of course I don't know if the thing would bother you in any way, or if you think I am a little too old now.

*Chasuble:* Not at all. The sprinkling, and, indeed, the immersion of adults is a perfectly canonical practice.

*Jack:* Immersion!

*Chasuble:* You need have no apprehensions. Sprinkling is all that is necessary, or indeed I think advisable. Our weather is so changeable. At what hour would you wish the ceremony performed?

*Jack:* Oh, I might trot round about five if that would suit you.

*Chasuble:* Perfectly, perfectly! In fact I have two similar ceremonies to perform at that time. A case of twins that occurred recently in one of the outlying cottages on your own estate. Poor Jenkins the carter, a most hardworking man.

*Jack:* Oh! I don't see much fun in being christened along with other babies. It would be childish. Would half-past five do?

*Chasuble:* Admirably! Admirably! (*Takes out watch.*) And now, dear Mr. Worthing, I will not intrude any longer into a house of sorrow. I would merely beg you not to be too much bowed down by grief. What seem to us bitter trials are often blessings in disguise.

*Miss Prism:* This seems to me a blessing of an extremely obvious kind.

(*Enter Cecily from the house.*)

*Cecily:* Uncle Jack! Oh, I am pleased to see you back. But what horrid clothes you have got on! Do go and change them.

*Miss Prism:* Cecily!

*Chasuble:* My child! my child!

(*Cecily goes towards Jack; he kisses her brow in a melancholy manner.*)

*Cecily:* What is the matter, Uncle Jack? Do look happy! You look as if you had toothache, and I have got such a surprise for you. Who do you think is in the dining room? Your brother!

*Jack:* Who?

*Cecily:* Your brother Ernest. He arrived about half an hour ago.

*Jack:* What nonsense! I haven't got a brother.

*Cecily:* Oh, don't say that. However badly he may have behaved to you in the past he is still your brother. You couldn't be so heartless as to disown him. I'll tell him to come out. And you will shake hands with him, won't you, Uncle Jack?

(*Runs back into the house.*)

*Chasuble:* These are very joyful tidings.

*Miss Prism:* After we had all been resigned to his loss, his sudden return seems to me peculiarly distressing.

*Jack:* My brother is in the dining room? I don't know what it all means. I think it is perfectly absurd.

(*Enter Algernon and Cecily hand in hand. They come slowly up to Jack.*)

*Jack:* Good heavens!                                      (*Motions Algernon away.*)

*Algernon:* Brother John, I have come down from town to tell you that I am very sorry for all the trouble I have given you, and that I intend to lead a better life in the future.

(*Jack glares at him and does not take his hand.*)

*Cecily:* Uncle Jack, you are not going to refuse your own brother's hand?

*Jack:* Nothing will induce me to take his hand. I think his coming down here disgraceful. He knows perfectly well why.

*Cecily:* Uncle Jack, do be nice. There is some good in everyone. Ernest has just been telling me about his poor invalid friend Mr. Bunbury whom he goes to visit so often. And surely there must be much good in one who is kind to an invalid, and leaves the pleasures of London to sit by a bed of pain.

*Jack:* Oh! he has been talking about Bunbury has he?

*Cecily:* Yes, he has told me all about poor Mr. Bunbury, and his terrible state of health.

*Jack:* Bunbury! Well, I won't have him talk to you about Bunbury or about anything else. It is enough to drive one perfectly frantic.

*Algernon:* Of course I admit that the faults were all on my side. But I must say that I think that Brother John's coldness to me is peculiarly painful. I expected a more enthusiastic welcome, especially considering it is the first time I have come here.

*Cecily:* Uncle Jack, if you don't shake hands with Ernest I will never forgive you.

*Jack:* Never forgive me?

*Cecily:* Never, never, never!

*Jack:* Well, this is the last time I shall ever do it.

(*Shakes hands with Algernon and glares.*)

*Chasuble:* It's pleasant, is it not, to see so perfect a reconciliation? I think we might leave the two brothers together.

*Miss Prism:* Cecily, you will come with us.

*Cecily:* Certainly, Miss Prism. My little task of reconciliation is over.

*Chasuble:* You have done a beautiful action today, dear child.

*Miss Prism:* We must not be premature in our judgments.

*Cecily:* I feel very happy.                                   (*They all go off.*)

*Jack:* You young scoundrel, Algy, you must get out of this place as soon as possible. I don't allow any Bunburying here.

(*Enter Merriman.*)

*Merriman:* I have put Mr. Ernest's things in the room next to yours, sir. I suppose that is all right?

*Jack:* What?

*Merriman:* Mr. Ernest's luggage, sir. I have unpacked it and put it in the room next to your own.

*Jack:* His luggage?

*Merriman:* Yes, sir. Three portmanteaus, a dressing case, two hatboxes, and a large luncheon basket.

*Algernon:* I am afraid 1 can't stay more than a week this time.

*Jack:* Merriman, order the dog cart at once. Mr. Ernest has been suddenly called back to town.

*Merriman:* Yes, sir.                              (*Goes back into the house.*)

*Algernon:* What a fearful liar you are, Jack. I have not been called back to town at all.

*Jack:* Yes, you have.

*Algernon:* I haven't heard anyone call me.

*Jack:* Your duty as a gentleman calls you back.

*Algernon:* My duty as a gentleman has never interfered with my pleasures in the smallest degree.

*Jack:* I can quite understand that.

*Algernon:* Well, Cecily is a darling.

*Jack:* You are not to talk of Miss Cardew like that. I don't like it.

*Algernon:* Well, I don't like your clothes. You look perfectly ridiculous in them. Why on earth don't you go up and change? It is perfectly childish to be in deep mourning for a man who is actually staying for a whole week in your house as a guest. I call it grotesque.

*Jack:* You are certainly not staying with me for a whole week as a guest or anything else. You have got to leave — by the four-five train.

*Algernon:* I certainly won't leave you so long as you are in mourning. It would be most unfriendly. If I were in mourning you would stay with me, I suppose. I should think it very unkind if you didn't.

*Jack:* Well, will you go if I change my clothes?

*Algernon:* Yes, if you are not too long. I never saw anybody take so long to dress, and with such little result.

*Jack:* Well, at any rate, that is better than being always overdressed as you are.

*Algernon:* If I am occasionally a little overdressed, I make up for it by being always immensely overeducated.

*Jack:* Your vanity is ridiculous, your conduct an outrage, and your presence in my garden utterly absurd. However, you have got to catch the four-five, and

I hope you will have a pleasant journey back to town. This Bunburying, as you call it, has not been a great success for you. (*Goes into the house.*)

*Algernon:* I think it has been a great success. I'm in love with Cecily, and that is everything.

(*Enter Cecily at the back of the garden. She picks up the can and begins to water the flowers.*)

But I must see her before I go, and make arrangements for another Bunbury. Ah, there she is.

*Cecily:* Oh, I merely came back to water the roses. I thought you were with Uncle Jack.

*Algernon:* He's gone to order the dog cart for me.

*Cecily:* Oh, is he going to take you for a nice drive?

*Algernon:* He's going to send me away.

*Cecily:* Then have we got to part?

*Algernon:* I am afraid so. It's a very painful parting.

*Cecily:* It is always painful to part from people whom one has known for a very brief space of time. The absence of old friends one can endure with equanimity. But even a momentary separation from anyone to whom one has just been introduced is almost unbearable.

*Algernon:* Thank you.

(*Enter Merriman.*)

*Merriman:* The dog cart is at the door, sir.

(*Algernon looks appealingly at Cecily.*)

*Cecily:* It can wait, Merriman — for — five minutes.

*Merriman:* Yes, miss.                               (*Exit Merriman.*)

*Algernon:* I hope, Cecily, I shall not offend you if I state quite frankly and openly that you seem to me to be in every way the visible personification of absolute perfection.

*Cecily:* I think your frankness does you great credit, Ernest. If you will allow me I will copy your remarks into my diary.

                       (*Goes over to table and begins writing in diary.*)

*Algernon:* Do you really keep a diary? I'd give anything to look at it. May I?

*Cecily:* Oh no. (*Puts her hand over it.*) You see, it is simply a very young girl's record of her own thoughts and impressions, and consequently meant for publication. When it appears in volume form I hope you will order a copy. But pray, Ernest, don't stop. I delight in taking down from dictation. I have reached "absolute perfection." You can go on. I am quite ready for more.

*Algernon (somewhat taken aback):* Ahem! Ahem!

*Cecily:* Oh, don't cough, Ernest. When one is dictating one should speak fluently and not cough. Besides, I don't know how to spell a cough.

(*Writes as Algernon speaks.*)

*Algernon (speaking very rapidly):* Cecily, ever since I first looked upon your wonderful and incomparable beauty, I have dared to love you wildly, passionately, devotedly, hopelessly.

*Cecily:* I don't think that you should tell me that you love me wildly, passionately, devotedly, hopelessly. Hopelessly doesn't seem to make much sense, does it?

*Algernon:* Cecily!

(*Enter Merriman.*)

*Merriman:*  The dog cart is waiting, sir.

*Algernon:*  Tell it to come round next week, at the same hour.

*Merriman (looks at Cecily, who makes no sign):*  Yes, sir. (*Merriman retires.*)

*Cecily:*  Uncle Jack would be very much annoyed if he knew you were staying on till next week, at the same hour.

*Algernon:*  Oh, I don't care about Jack. I don't care for anybody in the whole world but you. I love you, Cecily. You will marry me, won't you?

*Cecily:*  You silly boy! Of course. Why, we have been engaged for the last three months.

*Algernon:*  For the last three months?

*Cecily:*  Yes, it will be exactly three months on Thursday.

*Algernon:*  But how did we become engaged?

*Cecily:*  Well, ever since dear Uncle Jack first confessed to us that he had a younger brother who was very wicked and bad, you of course have formed the chief topic of conversation between myself and Miss Prism. And of course a man who is much talked about is always very attractive. One feels there must be something in him after all. I daresay it was foolish of me, but I fell in love with you, Ernest.

*Algernon:*  Darling! And when was the engagement actually settled?

*Cecily:*  On the 14th of February last. Worn out by your entire ignorance of my existence, I determined to end the matter one way or the other, and after a long struggle with myself I accepted you under this dear old tree here. The next day I bought this little ring in your name, and this is the little bangle with the true lovers' knot I promised you always to wear.

*Algernon:*  Did I give you this? It's very pretty, isn't it?

*Cecily:*  Yes, you've wonderfully good taste, Ernest. It's the excuse I've always given for your leading such a bad life. And this is the box in which I keep all your dear letters.

(*Kneels at table, opens box, and produces letters tied up with blue ribbon.*)

*Algernon:*  My letters! But my own sweet Cecily, I have never written you any letters.

*Cecily:*  You need hardly remind me of that, Ernest. I remember only too well that I was forced to write your letters for you. I wrote always three times a week, and sometimes oftener.

*Algernon:*  Oh, do let me read them, Cecily!

*Cecily:*  Oh, I couldn't possibly. They would make you far too conceited. (*Replaces box.*) The three you wrote me after I had broken off the engagement are so beautiful, and so badly spelled, that even now I can hardly read them without crying a little.

*Algernon:*  But was our engagement ever broken off?

*Cecily:*  Of course it was. On the 22nd of last March. You can see the entry if you like. (*Shows diary.*) "Today I broke off my engagement with Ernest. I feel it is better to do so. The weather still continues charming."

*Algernon:*  But why on earth did you break it off? What had I done? I had done nothing at all. Cecily, I am very much hurt indeed to hear you broke it off. Particularly when the weather was so charming.

*Cecily:*  It would hardly have been a really serious engagement if it hadn't been broken off at least once. But I forgave you before the week was out.

*Algernon (crossing to her, and kneeling):*  What a perfect angel you are, Cecily.

*Cecily:* You dear romantic boy. (*He kisses her; she puts her fingers through his hair.*) I hope your hair curls naturally, does it?

*Algernon:* Yes, darling, with a little help from others.

*Cecily:* I am so glad.

*Algernon:* You'll never break off our engagement again, Cecily?

*Cecily:* I don't think I could break it off now that I have actually met you. Besides, of course, there is the question of your name.

*Algernon (nervously):* Yes, of course.

*Cecily:* You must not laugh at me, darling, but it had always been a girlish dream of mine to love someone whose name was Ernest. (*Algernon rises, Cecily also.*) There is something in that name that seems to inspire absolute confidence. I pity any poor married woman whose husband is not called Ernest.

*Algernon:* But, my dear child, do you mean to say you could not love me if I had some other name?

*Cecily:* But what name?

*Algernon:* Oh, any name you like — Algernon — for instance —

*Cecily:* But I don't like the name of Algernon.

*Algernon:* Well, my own dear, sweet, loving little darling, I really can't see why you should object to the name of Algernon. It is not at all a bad name. In fact, it is rather an aristocratic name. Half of the chaps who get into the Bankruptcy Court are called Algernon. But seriously, Cecily — (*moving to her*) — if my name was Algy, couldn't you love me?

*Cecily (rising):* I might respect you, Ernest, I might admire your character, but I fear that I should not be able to give you my undivided attention.

*Algernon:* Ahem! Cecily! (*Picking up hat.*) Your Rector here is, I suppose, thoroughly experienced in the practice of all the rites and ceremonials of the Church?

*Cecily:* Oh yes. Dr. Chasuble is a most learned man. He has never written a single book, so you can imagine how much he knows.

*Algernon:* I must see him at once on a most important christening — I mean on most important business.

*Cecily:* Oh!

*Algernon:* I shan't be away more than half an hour.

*Cecily:* Considering that we have been engaged since February the 14th, and that I only met you today for the first time, I think it is rather hard that you should leave me for so long a period as half an hour. Couldn't you make it twenty minutes?

*Algernon:* I'll be back in no time.

(*Kisses her and rushes down the garden.*)

*Cecily:* What an impetuous boy he is! I like his hair so much. I must enter his proposal in my diary.

(*Enter Merriman.*)

*Merriman:* A Miss Fairfax has just called to see Mr. Worthing. On very important business Miss Fairfax states.

*Cecily:* Isn't Mr. Worthing in his library?

*Merriman:* Mr. Worthing went over in the direction of the Rectory some time ago.

*Cecily:* Pray ask the lady to come out here; Mr. Worthing is sure to be back soon. And you can bring tea.

*Merriman:* Yes, miss.                                                                (*Goes out.*)

*Cecily:* Miss Fairfax! I suppose one of the many good elderly women who are
associated with Uncle Jack in some of his philanthropic work in London. I
don't quite like women who are interested in philanthropic work. I think it is
so forward of them.

(*Enter Merriman.*)

*Merriman:* Miss Fairfax.

(*Enter Gwendolen. Exit Merriman.*)

*Cecily (advancing to meet her):* Pray let me introduce myself to you. My name is
Cecily Cardew.

*Gwendolen:* Cecily Cardew? (*Moving to her and shaking hands.*) What a very
sweet name! Something tells me that we are going to be great friends. I like
you already more than I can say. My first impressions of people are never
wrong.

*Cecily:* How nice of you to like me so much after we have known each other such
a comparatively short time. Pray sit down.

*Gwendolen (still standing up):* I may call you Cecily, may I not?

*Cecily:* With pleasure!

*Gwendolen:* And you will always call me Gwendolen, won't you?

*Cecily:* If you wish.

*Gwendolen:* Then that is all quite settled, is it not?

*Cecily:* I hope so.

(*A pause. They both sit down together.*)

*Gwendolen:* Perhaps this might be a favorable opportunity for my mentioning who I am. My father is Lord Bracknell. You have never heard of Papa,
I suppose?

*Cecily:* I don't think so.

*Gwendolen:* Outside the family circle, Papa, I am glad to say, is entirely
unknown. I think that is quite as it should be. The home seems to me to
be the proper sphere for the man. And certainly once a man begins to
neglect his domestic duties he becomes painfully effeminate, does he
not? And I don't like that. It makes men so very attractive. Cecily, Mama,
whose views on education are remarkably strict, has brought me up to be
extremely shortsighted; it is part of her system, so do you mind my looking
at you through my glasses?

*Cecily:* Oh! not at all, Gwendolen. I am very fond of being looked at.

*Gwendolen (after examining Cecily carefully through a lorgnette):* You are here
on a short visit I suppose?

*Cecily:* Oh no! I live here.

*Gwendolen (severely):* Really? Your mother, no doubt, or some female relative of
advanced years, resides here also?

*Cecily:* Oh no! I have no mother, nor, in fact, any relations.

*Gwendolen:* Indeed?

*Cecily:* My dear guardian, with the assistance of Miss Prism, has the arduous task
of looking after me.

*Gwendolen:* Your guardian?

*Cecily:* Yes, I am Mr. Worthing's ward.

*Gwendolen:* Oh! It is strange he never mentioned to me that he had a ward. How secretive of him! He grows more interesting hourly. I am not sure, however, that the news inspires me with feelings of unmixed delight. (*Rising and going to her.*) I am very fond of you, Cecily; I have liked you ever since I met you! But I am bound to state that now that I know that you are Mr. Worthing's ward, I cannot help expressing a wish you were — well just a little older than you seem to be — and not quite so very alluring in appearance. In fact, if I may speak candidly —

*Cecily:* Pray do! I think that whenever one has anything unpleasant to say, one should always be quite candid.

*Gwendolen:* Well, to speak with perfect candor, Cecily, I wish that you were fully forty-two, and more than usually plain for your age. Ernest has a strong upright nature. He is the very soul of truth and honor. Disloyalty would be as impossible to him as deception. But even men of the noblest possible moral character are extremely susceptible to the influence of the physical charms of others. Modern, no less than Ancient History, supplies us with many most painful examples of what I refer to. If it were not so, indeed, History would be quite unreadable.

*Cecily:* I beg your pardon, Gwendolen, did you say Ernest?

*Gwendolen:* Yes.

*Cecily:* Oh, but it is not Mr. Ernest Worthing who is my guardian. It is his brother — his elder brother.

*Gwendolen (sitting down again):* Ernest never mentioned to me that he had a brother.

*Cecily:* I am sorry to say they have not been on good terms for a long time.

*Gwendolen:* Ah! that accounts for it. And now that I think of it I have never heard any man mention his brother. The subject seems distasteful to most men. Cecily, you have lifted a load from my mind. I was growing almost anxious. It would have been terrible if any cloud had come across a friendship like ours, would it not? Of course you are quite, quite sure that it is not Mr. Ernest Worthing who is your guardian?

*Cecily:* Quite sure. (*A pause.*) In fact, I am going to be his.

*Gwendolen (inquiringly):* I beg your pardon?

*Cecily (rather shy and confidingly):* Dearest Gwendolen, there is no reason why I should make a secret of it to you. Our little county newspaper is sure to chronicle the fact next week. Mr. Ernest Worthing and I are engaged to be married.

*Gwendolen (quite politely, rising):* My darling Cecily, I think there must be some slight error. Mr. Ernest Worthing is engaged to me. The announcement will appear in the Morning Post on Saturday at the latest.

*Cecily (very politely, rising):* I am afraid you must be under some misconception. Ernest proposed to me exactly ten minutes ago. (*Shows diary.*)

*Gwendolen (examines diary through her lorgnette carefully):* It is certainly very curious, for he asked me to be his wife yesterday afternoon at 5:30. If you would care to verify the incident, pray do so. (*Produces diary of her own.*) I never travel without my diary. One should always have something sensational to read in the train. I am so sorry, dear Cecily, if it is any disappointment to you, but I am afraid *I* have the prior claim.

*Cecily:* It would distress me more than I can tell you, dear Gwendolen, if it caused you any mental or physical anguish, but I feel bound to point out that since Ernest proposed to you he clearly has changed his mind.

*Gwendolen (meditatively):* If the poor fellow has been entrapped into any foolish promise I shall consider it my duty to rescue him at once, and with a firm hand.

*Cecily (thoughtfully and sadly):* Whatever unfortunate entanglement my dear boy may have got into, I will never reproach him with it after we are married.

*Gwendolen:* Do you allude to me, Miss Cardew, as an entanglement? You are presumptuous. On an occasion of this kind it becomes more than a moral duty to speak one's mind. It becomes a pleasure.

*Cecily:* Do you suggest, Miss Fairfax, that I entrapped Ernest into an engagement? How dare you? This is no time for wearing the shallow mask of manners. When I see a spade I call it a spade.

*Gwendolen (satirically):* I am glad to say that I have never seen a spade. It is obvious that our social spheres have been widely different.

*(Enter Merriman, followed by the Footman. He carries a salver, tablecloth, and plate stand. Cecily is about to retort. The presence of the servants exercises a restraining influence, under which both girls chafe.)*

*Merriman:* Shall I lay tea here as usual, miss?

*Cecily (sternly, in a calm voice):* Yes, as usual.

*(Merriman begins to clear table and lay cloth. A long pause. Cecily and Gwendolen glare at each other.)*

*Gwendolen:* Are there many interesting walks in the vicinity, Miss Cardew?

*Cecily:* Oh! Yes! a great many. From the top of one of the hills quite close one can see five counties.

*Gwendolen:* Five counties! I don't think I should like that. I hate crowds.

*Cecily (sweetly):* I suppose that is why you live in town?

*(Gwendolen bites her lip, and beats her foot nervously with her parasol.)*

*Gwendolen (looking round):* Quite a well-kept garden this is, Miss Cardew.

*Cecily:* So glad you like it, Miss Fairfax.

*Gwendolen:* I had no idea there were any flowers in the country.

*Cecily:* Oh, flowers are as common here, Miss Fairfax, as people are in London.

*Gwendolen:* Personally I cannot understand how anybody manages to exist in the country, if anybody who is anybody does. The country always bores me to death.

*Cecily:* Ah! This is what the newspapers call agricultural depression, is it not? I believe the aristocracy are suffering very much from it just at present. It is almost an epidemic amongst them, I have been told. May I offer you some tea, Miss Fairfax?

*Gwendolen (with elaborate politeness):* Thank you. (*Aside.*) Detestable girl! But I require tea!

*Cecily (sweetly):* Sugar?

*Gwendolen (superciliously):* No, thank you. Sugar is not fashionable anymore.

*(Cecily looks angrily at her, takes up the tongs, and puts four lumps of sugar into the cup.)*

*Cecily (severely):* Cake or bread and butter?

*Gwendolen (in a bored manner):* Bread and butter, please. Cake is rarely seen at the best houses nowadays.

*Cecily (cuts a very large slice of cake, and puts it on the tray):* Hand that to Miss Fairfax.

*(Merriman does so, and goes out with Footman. Gwendolen drinks the tea and makes a grimace. Puts down cup at once, reaches out her hand to the bread and butter, looks at it, and finds it is cake. Rises in indignation.)*

*Gwendolen:* You have filled my tea with lumps of sugar, and though I asked most distinctly for bread and butter, you have given me cake. I am known for the gentleness of my disposition, and the extraordinary sweetness of my nature, but I warn you, Miss Cardew, you may go too far.

*Cecily (rising):* To save my poor, innocent, trusting boy from the machinations of any other girl there are no lengths to which I would not go.

*Gwendolen:* From the moment I saw you I distrusted you. I felt that you were false and deceitful. I am never deceived in such matters. My first impressions of people are invariably right.

*Cecily:* It seems to me, Miss Fairfax, that I am trespassing on your valuable time. No doubt you have many other calls of a similar character to make in the neighborhood.

*(Enter Jack.)*

*Gwendolen (catching sight of him):* Ernest! My own Ernest!

*Jack:* Gwendolen! Darling!                                        *(Offers to kiss her.)*

*Gwendolen (drawing back):* A moment! May I ask if you are engaged to be married to this young lady? *(Points to Cecily.)*

*Jack (laughing):* To dear little Cecily! Of course not! What could have put such an idea into your pretty little head?

*Gwendolen:* Thank you. You may!                                        *(Offers her cheek.)*

*Cecily (very sweetly):* I knew there must be some misunderstanding, Miss Fairfax. The gentleman whose arm is at present round your waist is my dear guardian, Mr. John Worthing.

*Gwendolen:* I beg your pardon?

*Cecily:* This is Uncle Jack.

*Gwendolen (receding):* Jack! Oh!

*(Enter Algernon.)*

*Cecily:* Here is Ernest.

*Algernon (goes straight over to Cecily without noticing anyone else):* My own love!
                                        *(Offers to kiss her.)*

*Cecily (drawing back):* A moment, Ernest! May I ask you — are you engaged to be married to this young lady?

*Algernon (looking round):* To what young lady? Good heavens! Gwendolen!

*Cecily:* Yes! to good heavens, Gwendolen, I mean to Gwendolen.

*Algernon (laughing):* Of course not! What could have put such an idea into your pretty little head?

*Cecily:* Thank you. *(Presenting her cheek to be kissed.)* You may.
                                        *(Algernon kisses her.)*

*Gwendolen:* I felt there was some slight error, Miss Cardew. The gentleman who is now embracing you is my cousin, Mr. Algernon Moncrieff.

*Cecily (breaking away from Algernon):* Algernon Moncrieff! Oh!

(*The two girls move towards each other and put their arms round each other's waists as if for protection.*)

*Cecily:* Are you called Algernon?

*Algernon:* I cannot deny it.

*Cecily:* Oh!

*Gwendolen:* Is your name really John?

*Jack (standing rather proudly):* I could deny it if I liked. I could deny anything if I liked. But my name certainly is John. It has been John for years.

*Cecily (to Gwendolen):* A gross deception has been practiced on both of us.

*Gwendolen:* My poor wounded Cecily!

*Cecily:* My sweet wronged Gwendolen!

*Gwendolen (slowly and seriously):* You will call me sister, will you not?

(*They embrace. Jack and Algernon groan and walk up and down.*)

*Cecily (rather brightly):* There is just one question I would like to be allowed to ask my guardian.

*Gwendolen:* An admirable idea! Mr. Worthing, there is just one question I would like to be permitted to put to you. Where is your brother Ernest? We are both engaged to be married to your brother Ernest, so it is a matter of some importance to us to know where your brother Ernest is at present.

*Jack (slowly and hesitatingly):* Gwendolen — Cecily — it is very painful for me to be forced to speak the truth. It is the first time in my life that I have ever been reduced to such a painful position, and I am really quite inexperienced in doing anything of the kind. However I will tell you quite frankly that I have no brother Ernest. I have no brother at all. I never had a brother in my life, and I certainly have not the smallest intention of ever having one in the future.

*Cecily (surprised):* No brother at all?

*Jack (cheerily):* None!

*Gwendolen (severely):* Had you never a brother of any kind?

*Jack (pleasantly):* Never. Not even of any kind.

*Gwendolen:* I am afraid it is quite clear, Cecily, that neither of us is engaged to be married to anyone.

*Cecily:* It is not a very pleasant position for a young girl suddenly to find herself in. Is it?

*Gwendolen:* Let us go into the house. They will hardly venture to come after us there.

*Cecily:* No, men are so cowardly, aren't they?

(*They retire into the house with scornful looks.*)

*Jack:* This ghastly state of things is what you call Bunburying, I suppose?

*Algernon:* Yes, and a perfectly wonderful Bunbury it is. The most wonderful Bunbury I have ever had in my life.

*Jack:* Well, you've no right whatsoever to Bunbury here.

*Algernon:* That is absurd. One has a right to Bunbury anywhere one chooses. Every serious Bunburyist knows that.

*Jack:* Serious Bunburyist! Good heavens!

*Algernon:* Well, one must be serious about something, if one wants to have any amusement in life. I happen to be serious about Bunburying. What on earth you are serious about I haven't got the remotest idea. About everything, I should fancy. You have such an absolutely trivial nature.

*Jack:* Well, the only small satisfaction I have in the whole of this wretched business is that your friend Bunbury is quite exploded. You won't be able to run down to the country quite so often as you used to do, dear Algy. And a very good thing too.

*Algernon:* Your brother is a little off color, isn't he, dear Jack? You won't be able to disappear to London quite so frequently as your wicked custom was. And not a bad thing either.

*Jack:* As for your conduct towards Miss Cardew, I must say that your taking in a sweet, simple, innocent girl like that is quite inexcusable. To say nothing of the fact that she is my ward.

*Algernon:* I can see no possible defense at all for your deceiving a brilliant, clever, thoroughly experienced young lady like Miss Fairfax. To say nothing of the fact that she is my cousin.

*Jack:* I wanted to be engaged to Gwendolen, that is all. I love her.

*Algernon:* Well, I simply wanted to be engaged to Cecily. I adore her.

*Jack:* There is certainly no chance of your marrying Miss Cardew.

*Algernon:* I don't think there is much likelihood, Jack, of you and Miss Fairfax being united.

*Jack:* Well, that is no business of yours.

*Algernon:* If it was my business, I wouldn't talk about it. (*Begins to eat muffins.*) It is very vulgar to talk about one's business. Only people like stockbrokers do that, and then merely at dinner parties.

*Jack:* How you can sit there, calmly eating muffins when we are in this horrible trouble, I can't make out. You seem to me to be perfectly heartless.

*Algernon:* Well, I can't eat muffins in an agitated manner. The butter would probably get on my cuffs. One should always eat muffins quite calmly. It is the only way to eat them.

*Jack:* I say it's perfectly heartless your eating muffins at all, under the circumstances.

*Algernon:* When I am in trouble, eating is the only thing that consoles me. Indeed, when I am in really great trouble, as anyone who knows me intimately will tell you, I refuse everything except food and drink. At the present moment I am eating muffins because I am unhappy. Besides, I am particularly fond of muffins.                                                                      (*Rising.*)

*Jack (rising):* Well, that is no reason why you should eat them all in that greedy way.

(*Takes muffins from Algernon.*)

*Algernon (offering tea cake):* I wish you would have tea cake instead. I don't like tea cake.

*Jack:* Good heavens! I suppose a man may eat his own muffins in his own garden.

*Algernon:* But you have just said it was perfectly heartless to eat muffins.

*Jack:* I said it was perfectly heartless of you, under the circumstances. That is a very different thing.

*Algernon:* That may be, but the muffins are the same. (*He seizes the muffin dish from Jack.*)

*Jack:* Algy, I wish to goodness you would go.

*Algernon:* You can't possibly ask me to go without having some dinner. It's absurd. I never go without my dinner. No one ever does, except vegetarians and people like that. Besides I have just made arrangements with Dr. Chasuble to be christened at a quarter to six under the name of Ernest.

*Jack:* My dear fellow, the sooner you give up that nonsense the better. I made arrangements this morning with Dr. Chasuble to be christened myself at 5:30, and I naturally will take the name of Ernest. Gwendolen would wish it. We can't both be christened Ernest. It's absurd. Besides, I have a perfect right to be christened if I like. There is no evidence at all that I ever have been christened by anybody. I should think it extremely probable I never was, and so does Dr. Chasuble. It is entirely different in your case. You have been christened already.

*Algernon:* Yes, but I have not been christened for years.

*Jack:* Yes, but you have been christened. That is the important thing.

*Algernon:* Quite so. So I know my constitution can stand it. If you are not quite sure about your ever having been christened, I must say I think it rather dangerous your venturing on it now. It might make you very unwell. You can hardly have forgotten that someone very closely connected with you was very nearly carried off this week in Paris by a severe chill.

*Jack:* Yes, but you said yourself that a severe chill was not hereditary.

*Algernon:* It usen't to be, I know — but I daresay it is now. Science is always making wonderful improvements in things.

*Jack (picking up the muffin dish):* Oh, that is nonsense; you are always talking nonsense.

*Algernon:* Jack, you are at the muffins again! I wish you wouldn't. There are only two left. (*Takes them.*) I told you I was particularly fond of muffins.

*Jack:* But I hate tea cake.

*Algernon:* Why on earth then do you allow tea cake to be served up for your guests? What ideas you have of hospitality!

*Jack:* Algernon! I have already told you to go. I don't want you here. Why don't you go!

*Algernon:* I haven't quite finished my tea yet! and there is still one muffin left.

(*Jack groans, and sinks into a chair. Algernon still continues eating.*)

---

## ACT III

(*Scene: Morning room at the Manor House. Gwendolen and Cecily are at the window, looking out into the garden.*)

*Gwendolen:* The fact that they did not follow us at once into the house, as anyone else would have done, seems to me to show that they have some sense of shame left.

*Cecily:* They have been eating muffins. That looks like repentance.

*Gwendolen (after a pause):* They don't seem to notice us at all. Couldn't you cough?

*Cecily:* But I haven't got a cough.

*Gwendolen:* They're looking at us. What effrontery!

*Cecily:* They're approaching. That's very forward of them.

*Gwendolen:* Let us preserve a dignified silence.

*Cecily:* Certainly. It's the only thing to do now.

(*Enter Jack followed by Algernon. They whistle some dreadful popular air from a British opera.*)

*Gwendolen:* This dignified silence seems to produce an unpleasant effect.

*Cecily:* A most distasteful one.

*Gwendolen:* But we will not be the first to speak.

*Cecily:* Certainly not.

*Gwendolen:* Mr. Worthing, I have something very particular to ask you. Much depends on your reply.

*Cecily:* Gwendolen, your common sense is invaluable. Mr. Moncrieff, kindly answer me the following question. Why did you pretend to be my guardian's brother?

*Algernon:* In order that I might have an opportunity of meeting you.

*Cecily (to Gwendolen):* That certainly seems a satisfactory explanation, does it not?

*Gwendolen:* Yes, dear, if you can believe him.

*Cecily:* I don't. But that does not affect the wonderful beauty of his answer.

*Gwendolen:* True. In matters of grave importance, style, not sincerity is the vital thing. Mr. Worthing, what explanation can you offer to me for pretending to have a brother? Was it in order that you might have an opportunity of coming up to town to see me as often as possible?

*Jack:* Can you doubt it, Miss Fairfax?

*Gwendolen:* I have the gravest doubts upon the subject. But I intend to crush them. This is not the moment for German skepticism. (*Moving to Cecily.*) Their explanations appear to be quite satisfactory, especially Mr. Worthing's. That seems to me to have the stamp of truth upon it.

*Cecily:* I am more than content with what Mr. Moncrieff said. His voice alone inspires one with absolute credulity.

*Gwendolen:* Then you think we should forgive them?

*Cecily:* Yes. I mean no.

*Gwendolen:* True! I had forgotten. There are principles at stake that one cannot surrender. Which of us should tell them? The task is not a pleasant one.

*Cecily:* Could we not both speak at the same time?

*Gwendolen:* An excellent idea! I nearly always speak at the same time as other people. Will you take the time from me?

*Cecily:* Certainly.

(*Gwendolen beats time with uplifted finger.*)

*Gwendolen and Cecily (speaking together):* Your Christian names are still an insuperable barrier. That is all!

*Jack and Algernon (speaking together):* Our Christian names! Is that all? But we are going to be christened this afternoon.

*Gwendolen (to Jack):* For my sake you are prepared to do this terrible thing?

*Jack:* I am!

*Cecily (to Algernon):* To please me you are ready to face this fearful ordeal?

*Algernon:* I am!

*Gwendolen:* How absurd to talk of the equality of the sexes! Where questions of self-sacrifice are concerned, men are infinitely beyond us.

*Jack:* We are! (*Clasps hands with Algernon.*)

*Cecily:* They have moments of physical courage of which we women know absolutely nothing.

*Gwendolen (to Jack):* Darling!

*Algernon (to Cecily):* Darling!

(*They fall into each other's arms.*)

(*Enter Merriman. When he enters he coughs loudly, seeing the situation.*)

*Merriman:* Ahem! Ahem! Lady Bracknell!

*Jack:* Good heavens!

(*Enter Lady Bracknell. The couples separate, in alarm. Exit Merriman.*)

*Lady Bracknell:* Gwendolen! What does this mean?

*Gwendolen:* Merely that I am engaged to be married to Mr. Worthing, Mama.

*Lady Bracknell:* Come here. Sit down. Sit down immediately. Hesitation of any kind is a sign of mental decay in the young, of physical weakness in the old. (*Turns to Jack.*) Apprised, sir, of my daughter's sudden flight by her trusty maid, whose confidence I purchased by means of a small coin, I followed her at once by a luggage train. Her unhappy father is, I am glad to say, under the impression that she is attending a more than usually lengthy lecture by the University Extension Scheme on the influence of a permanent income on thought. I do not propose to undeceive him. Indeed I have never undeceived him on any question. I would consider it wrong. But of course, you will clearly understand that all communication between yourself and my daughter must cease immediately from this moment. On this point, as indeed on all points, I am firm.

*Jack:* I am engaged to be married to Gwendolen, Lady Bracknell!

*Lady Bracknell:* You are nothing of the kind, sir. And now, as regards Algernon! — Algernon!

*Algernon:* Yes, Aunt Augusta.

*Lady Bracknell:* May I ask if it is in this house that your invalid friend Mr. Bunbury resides?

*Algernon (stammering):* Oh! No! Bunbury doesn't live here. Bunbury is somewhere else at present. In fact, Bunbury is dead.

*Lady Bracknell:* Dead! When did Mr. Bunbury die? His death must have been extremely sudden.

*Algernon (airily):* Oh! I killed Bunbury this afternoon. I mean poor Bunbury died this afternoon.

*Lady Bracknell:* What did he die of?

*Algernon:* Bunbury? Oh, he was quite exploded.

*Lady Bracknell:* Exploded! Was he the victim of a revolutionary outrage? I was not aware that Mr. Bunbury was interested in social legislation. If so, he is well punished for his morbidity.

*Algernon:* My dear Aunt Augusta, I mean he was found out! The doctors found out that Bunbury could not live, that is what I mean — so Bunbury died.

*Lady Bracknell:* He seems to have had great confidence in the opinion of his physicians. I am glad, however, that he made up his mind at the last to some definite course of action, and acted under proper medical advice. And now that we have finally got rid of this Mr. Bunbury, may I ask, Mr. Worthing, who is that young person whose hand my nephew Algernon is now holding in what seems to me a peculiarly unnecessary manner?

*Jack:* That lady is Miss Cecily Cardew, my ward.

(*Lady Bracknell bows coldly to Cecily.*)

*Algernon:* I am engaged to be married to Cecily, Aunt Augusta.

*Lady Bracknell:* I beg your pardon?

*Cecily:* Mr. Moncrieff and I are engaged to be married, Lady Bracknell.

*Lady Bracknell (with a shiver, crossing to the sofa and sitting down):* I do not know whether there is anything peculiarly exciting in the air of this particular part of Hertfordshire, but the number of engagements that go on seems to me considerably above the proper average that statistics have laid down for our guidance. I think some preliminary inquiry on my part would not be out of place. Mr. Worthing, is Miss Cardew at all connected with any of the larger railway stations in London? I merely desire information. Until yesterday I had no idea that there were any families or persons whose origin was a Terminus.

*(Jack looks perfectly furious, but restrains himself.)*

*Jack (in a clear, cold voice):* Miss Cardew is the granddaughter of the late Mr. Thomas Cardew of 149, Belgrave Square, S.W.; Gervase Park, Dorking, Surrey; and the Sporran, Fifeshire, N.B.

*Lady Bracknell:* That sounds not unsatisfactory. Three addresses always inspire confidence, even in tradesmen. But what proof have I of their authenticity?

*Jack:* I have carefully preserved the Court Guides of the period. They are open to your inspection, Lady Bracknell.

*Lady Bracknell (grimly):* I have known strange errors in that publication.

*Jack:* Miss Cardew's family solicitors are Messrs. Markby, Markby, and Markby.

*Lady Bracknell:* Markby, Markby, and Markby? A firm of the very highest position in their profession. Indeed I am told that one of the Mr. Markbys is occasionally to be seen at dinner parties. So far I am satisfied.

*Jack (very irritably):* How extremely kind of you, Lady Bracknell! I have also in my possession, you will be pleased to hear, certificates of Miss Cardew's birth, baptism, whooping cough, registration, vaccination, confirmation, and the measles; both the German and the English variety.

*Lady Bracknell:* Ah! A life crowded with incident I see; though perhaps somewhat too exciting for a young girl. I am not myself in favor of premature experiences. (*Rises, looks at her watch.*) Gwendolen! the time approaches for our departure. We have not a moment to lose. As a matter of form, Mr. Worthing, I had better ask you if Miss Cardew has any little fortune?

*Jack:* Oh! about a hundred and thirty thousand pounds in the Funds. That is all. Good-bye, Lady Bracknell. So pleased to have seen you.

*Lady Bracknell (sitting down again):* A moment, Mr. Worthing. A hundred and thirty thousand pounds! And in the Funds! Miss Cardew seems to me a most attractive young lady, now that I look at her. Few girls of the present day have any really solid qualities, any of the qualities that last, and improve with time. We live, I regret to say, in an age of surfaces. (*To Cecily.*) Come over here, dear. (*Cecily goes across.*) Pretty child! your dress is sadly simple, and your hair seems almost as Nature might have left it. But we can soon alter all that. A thoroughly experienced French maid produces a really marvelous result in a very brief space of time: I remember recommending one to young Lady Lancing, and after three months her own husband did not know her.

*Jack (aside):* And after six months nobody knew her.

*Lady Bracknell (glares at Jack for a few moments. Then bends, with a practiced smile, to Cecily):* Kindly turn round, sweet child. (*Cecily turns completely round.*) No, the side view is what I want. (*Cecily presents her profile.*) Yes, quite as I expected. There are distinct social possibilities in your profile. The two weak points in our age are its want of principle and its want of profile. The chin a little higher, dear. Style largely depends on the way the chin is worn. They are worn very high, just at present. Algernon!

*Algernon:* Yes, Aunt Augusta!

*Lady Bracknell:* There are distinct social possibilities in Miss Cardew's profile.

*Algernon:* Cecily is the sweetest, dearest, prettiest girl in the whole world. And I don't care twopence about social possibilities.

*Lady Bracknell:* Never speak disrespectfully of Society, Algernon. Only people who can't get into it do that. (*To Cecily.*) Dear child, of course you know that Algernon has nothing but his debts to depend upon. But I do not approve of mercenary marriages. When I married Lord Bracknell I had no fortune of any kind. But I never dreamed for a moment of allowing that to stand in my way. Well, I suppose I must give my consent.

*Algernon:* Thank you, Aunt Augusta.

*Lady Bracknell:* Cecily, you may kiss me!

*Cecily (kisses her):* Thank you, Lady Bracknell.

*Lady Bracknell:* You may also address me as Aunt Augusta for the future.

*Cecily:* Thank you, Aunt Augusta.

*Lady Bracknell:* The marriage, I think, had better take place quite soon.

*Algernon:* Thank you, Aunt Augusta.

*Cecily:* Thank you, Aunt Augusta.

*Lady Bracknell:* To speak frankly, I am not in favor of long engagements. They give people the opportunity of finding out each other's character before marriage, which I think is never advisable.

*Jack:* I beg your pardon for interrupting you, Lady Bracknell, but this engagement is quite out of the question. I am Miss Cardew's guardian, and she cannot marry without my consent until she comes of age. That consent I absolutely decline to give.

*Lady Bracknell:* Upon what grounds may I ask? Algernon is an extremely, I may almost say an ostentatiously, eligible young man. He has nothing, but he looks everything. What more can one desire?

*Jack:* It pains me very much to have to speak frankly to you, Lady Bracknell, about your nephew, but the fact is that I do not approve at all of his moral character. I suspect him of being untruthful.

(*Algernon and Cecily look at him in indignant amazement.*)

*Lady Bracknell:* Untruthful! My nephew Algernon? Impossible! He is an Oxonian.°

*Jack:* I fear there can be no possible doubt about the matter. This afternoon, during my temporary absence in London on an important question of romance, he obtained admission to my house by means of the false pretense of being my brother. Under an assumed name he drank, I've just been informed by my butler, an entire pint bottle of my Perrier-Jouët, Brut, '89; a wine I was specially reserving for myself. Continuing his disgraceful deception, he

*Oxonian:* Educated at Oxford University.

succeeded in the course of the afternoon in alienating the affections of my only ward. He subsequently stayed to tea, and devoured every single muffin. And what makes his conduct all the more heartless is, that he was perfectly well aware from the first that I have no brother, that I never had a brother, and that I don't intend to have a brother, not even of any kind. I distinctly told him so myself yesterday afternoon.

*Lady Bracknell:* Ahem! Mr. Worthing, after careful consideration I have decided entirely to overlook my nephew's conduct to you.

*Jack:* That is very generous of you, Lady Bracknell. My own decision, however, is unalterable. I decline to give my consent.

*Lady Bracknell (to Cecily):* Come here, sweet child. (*Cecily goes over.*) How old are you, dear?

*Cecily:* Well, I am really only eighteen, but I always admit to twenty when I go to evening parties.

*Lady Bracknell:* You are perfectly right in making some slight alteration. Indeed, no woman should ever be quite accurate about her age. It looks so calculating — (*In a meditative manner.*) Eighteen but admitting to twenty at evening parties. Well, it will not be very long before you are of age and free from the restraints of tutelage. So I don't think your guardian's consent is, after all, a matter of any importance.

*Jack:* Pray excuse me, Lady Bracknell, for interrupting you again, but it is only fair to tell you that according to the terms of her grandfather's will Miss Cardew does not come legally of age till she is thirty-five.

*Lady Bracknell:* That does not seem to me to be a grave objection. Thirty-five is a very attractive age. London society is full of women of the very highest birth who have, of their own free choice, remained thirty-five for years. Lady Dumbleton is an instance in point. To my own knowledge she has been thirty-five ever since she arrived at the age of forty, which was many years ago now. I see no reason why our dear Cecily should not be even still more attractive at the age you mention than she is at present. There will be a large accumulation of property.

*Cecily:* Algy, could you wait for me till I was thirty-five?

*Algernon:* Of course I could, Cecily. You know I could.

*Cecily:* Yes, I felt it instinctively, but I couldn't wait all that time. I hate waiting even five minutes for anybody. It always makes me rather cross. I am not punctual myself, I know, but I do like punctuality in others, and waiting, even to be married, is quite out of the question.

*Algernon:* Then what is to be done, Cecily?

*Cecily:* I don't know, Mr. Moncrieff.

*Lady Bracknell:* My dear Mr. Worthing, as Miss Cardew states positively that she cannot wait till she is thirty-five — a remark which I am bound to say seems to me to show a somewhat impatient nature — I would beg of you to reconsider your decision.

*Jack:* But my dear Lady Bracknell, the matter is entirely in your own hands. The moment you consent to my marriage with Gwendolen, I will most gladly allow your nephew to form an alliance with my ward.

*Lady Bracknell (rising and drawing herself up):* You must be quite aware that what you propose is out of the question.

*Jack:* Then a passionate celibacy is all that any of us can look forward to.

*Lady Bracknell:* That is not the destiny I propose for Gwendolen. Algernon, of course, can choose for himself. (*Pulls out her watch.*) Come, dear; (*Gwendolen rises*) we have already missed five, if not six, trains. To miss any more might expose us to comment on the platform.

(*Enter Dr. Chasuble.*)

*Chasuble:* Everything is quite ready for the christenings.

*Lady Bracknell:* The christenings, sir! Is not that somewhat premature?

*Chasuble (looking rather puzzled, and pointing to Jack and Algernon):* Both these gentlemen have expressed a desire for immediate baptism.

*Lady Bracknell:* At their age? The idea is grotesque and irreligious! Algernon, I forbid you to be baptized. I will not hear of such excesses. Lord Bracknell would be highly displeased if he learned that that was the way in which you wasted your time and money.

*Chasuble:* Am I to understand then that there are to be no christenings at all this afternoon?

*Jack:* I don't think that, as things are now, it would be of much practical value to either of us, Dr. Chasuble.

*Chasuble:* I am grieved to hear such sentiments from you, Mr. Worthing. They savor of the heretical views of the Anabaptists,° views that I have completely refuted in four of my unpublished sermons. However, as your present mood seems to be one peculiarly secular, I will return to the church at once. Indeed, I have just been informed by the pew opener that for the last hour and a half Miss Prism has been waiting for me in the vestry.

*Lady Bracknell (starting):* Miss Prism! Did I hear you mention a Miss Prism?

*Chasuble:* Yes, Lady Bracknell. I am on my way to join her.

*Lady Bracknell:* Pray allow me to detain you for a moment. This matter may prove to be one of vital importance to Lord Bracknell and myself. Is this Miss Prism a female of repellent aspect, remotely connected with education?

*Chasuble (somewhat indignantly):* She is the most cultivated of ladies, and the very picture of respectability.

*Lady Bracknell:* It is obviously the same person. May I ask what position she holds in your household?

*Chasuble (severely):* I am a celibate, madam.

*Jack (interposing):* Miss Prism, Lady Bracknell, has been for the last three years Miss Cardew's esteemed governess and valued companion.

*Lady Bracknell:* In spite of what I hear of her, I must see her at once. Let her be sent for.

*Chasuble (looking off):* She approaches; she is nigh.

(*Enter Miss Prism hurriedly.*)

*Miss Prism:* I was told you expected me in the vestry, dear Canon. I have been waiting for you there for an hour and three-quarters.

(*Catches sight of Lady Bracknell who has fixed her with a stony glare. Miss Prism grows pale and quails. She looks anxiously round as if desirous to escape.*)

---

°*Anabaptists:* A religious sect founded in the sixteenth century and advocating adult baptism and church membership for adults only.

*Lady Bracknell (in a severe, judicial voice):*  Prism! (*Miss Prism bows her head in shame.*) Come here, Prism! (*Miss Prism approaches in a humble manner.*) Prism! Where is that baby? (*General consternation. The Canon starts back in horror. Algernon and Jack pretend to be anxious to shield Cecily and Gwendolen from hearing the details of a terrible public scandal.*) Twenty-eight years ago, Prism, you left Lord Bracknell's house, Number 104, Upper Grosvenor Street, in charge of a perambulator that contained a baby, of the male sex. You never returned. A few weeks later, through the elaborate investigations of the Metropolitan police, the perambulator was discovered at midnight, standing by itself in a remote corner of Bayswater. It contained the manuscript of a three-volume novel of more than usually revolting sentimentality. (*Miss Prism starts in involuntary indignation.*) But the baby was not there! (*Everyone looks at Miss Prism.*) Prism! Where is that baby?          (*A pause.*)

*Miss Prism:*  Lady Bracknell, I admit with shame that I do not know. I only wish I did. The plain facts of the case are these. On the morning of the day you mention, a day that is forever branded on my memory, I prepared as usual to take the baby out in its perambulator. I had also with me a somewhat old, but capacious handbag in which I had intended to place the manuscript of a work of fiction that I had written during my few unoccupied hours. In a moment of mental abstraction, for which I never can forgive myself, I deposited the manuscript in the bassinette, and placed the baby in the handbag.

*Jack (who has been listening attentively):*  But where did you deposit the handbag?

*Miss Prism:*  Do not ask me, Mr. Worthing.

*Jack:*  Miss Prism, this is a matter of no small importance to me. I insist on knowing where you deposited the handbag that contained that infant.

*Miss Prism:*  I left it in the cloakroom of one of the larger railway stations in London.

*Jack:*  What railway station?

*Miss Prism (quite crushed):*  Victoria. The Brighton line.          (*Sinks into a chair.*)

*Jack:*  I must retire to my room for a moment. Gwendolen, wait here for me.

*Gwendolen:*  If you are not too long, I will wait here for you all my life.

(*Exit Jack in great excitement.*)

*Chasuble:*  What do you think this means, Lady Bracknell?

*Lady Bracknell:*  I dare not even suspect, Dr. Chasuble. I need hardly tell you that in families of high position strange coincidences are not supposed to occur. They are hardly considered the thing.

(*Noises heard overhead as if someone was throwing trunks about. Everyone looks up.*)

*Cecily:*  Uncle Jack seems strangely agitated.

*Chasuble:*  Your guardian has a very emotional nature.

*Lady Bracknell:*  This noise is extremely unpleasant. It sounds as if he was having an argument. I dislike arguments of any kind. They are always vulgar, and often convincing.

*Chasuble (looking up):*  It has stopped now.          (*The noise is redoubled.*)

*Lady Bracknell:*  I wish he would arrive at some conclusion.

*Gwendolen:*  This suspense is terrible. I hope it will last.

(*Enter Jack with a handbag of black leather in his hand.*)

*Jack (rushing over to Miss Prism):* Is this the handbag, Miss Prism? Examine it carefully before you speak. The happiness of more than one life depends on your answer.

*Miss Prism (calmly):* It seems to be mine. Yes, here is the injury it received through the upsetting of a Gower Street omnibus in younger and happier days. Here is the stain on the lining caused by the explosion of a temperance beverage, an incident that occurred at Leamington. And here, on the lock, are my initials. I had forgotten that in an extravagant mood I had had them placed there. The bag is undoubtedly mine. I am delighted to have it so unexpectedly restored to me. It has been a great inconvenience being without it all these years.

*Jack (in a pathetic voice):* Miss Prism, more is restored to you than this handbag. I was the baby you placed in it.

*Miss Prism (amazed):* You?

*Jack (embracing her):* Yes — mother!

*Miss Prism (recoiling in indignant astonishment):* Mr. Worthing! I am unmarried!

*Jack:* Unmarried! I do not deny that is a serious blow. But after all, who has the right to cast a stone against one who has suffered? Cannot repentance wipe out an act of folly? Why should there be one law for men, and another for women? Mother, I forgive you. (*Tries to embrace her again.*)

*Miss Prism (still more indignant):* Mr. Worthing, there is some error. (*Pointing to Lady Bracknell.*) There is the lady who can tell you who you really are.

*Jack (after a pause):* Lady Bracknell, I hate to seem inquisitive, but would you kindly inform me who I am?

*Lady Bracknell:* I am afraid that the news I have to give you will not altogether please you. You are the son of my poor sister, Mrs. Moncrieff, and consequently Algernon's elder brother.

*Jack:* Algy's elder brother! Then I have a brother after all. I knew I had a brother! I always said I had a brother! Cecily, — how could you have ever doubted that I had a brother. (*Seizes hold of Algernon.*) Dr. Chasuble, my unfortunate brother. Miss Prism, my unfortunate brother. Gwendolen, my unfortunate brother. Algy, you young scoundrel, you will have to treat me with more respect in the future. You have never behaved to me like a brother in all your life.

*Algernon:* Well, not till today, old boy, I admit. I did my best, however, though I was out of practice.                                              (*Shakes hands.*)

*Gwendolen (to Jack):* My own! But what own are you? What is your Christian name, now that you have become someone else?

*Jack:* Good heavens! — I had quite forgotten that point. Your decision on the subject of my name is irrevocable, I suppose?

*Gwendolen:* I never change, except in my affections.

*Cecily:* What a noble nature you have, Gwendolen!

*Jack:* Then the question had better be cleared up at once. Aunt Augusta, a moment. At the time when Miss Prism left me in the handbag, had I been christened already?

*Lady Bracknell:* Every luxury that money could buy, including christening, had been lavished upon you by your fond and doting parents.

*Jack:* Then I was christened! That is settled. Now, what name was I given? Let me know the worst.

*Lady Bracknell:* Being the eldest son you were naturally christened after your father.

*Jack (irritably):* Yes, but what was my father's Christian name?

*Lady Bracknell (meditatively):* I cannot at the present moment recall what the General's Christian name was. But I have no doubt he had one. He was eccentric, I admit. But only in later years. And that was the result of the Indian climate, and marriage, and indigestion, and other things of that kind.

*Jack:* Algy! Can't you recollect what our father's Christian name was?

*Algernon:* My dear boy, we were never even on speaking terms. He died before I was a year old.

*Jack:* His name would appear in the Army Lists of the period, I suppose, Aunt Augusta?

*Lady Bracknell:* The General was essentially a man of peace, except in his domestic life. But I have no doubt his name would appear in any military directory.

*Jack:* The Army Lists of the last forty years are here. These delightful records should have been my constant study. (*Rushes to bookcase and tears the books out.*) M. Generals — Mallam, Maxbohm, Magley, what ghastly names they have — Markby, Migsby, Mobbs, Moncrieff! Lieutenant 1840, Captain, Lieutenant-Colonel, Colonel, General 1869, Christian names, Ernest John. (*Puts book very quietly down and speaks quite calmly.*) I always told you, Gwendolen, my name was Ernest, didn't I? Well, it is Ernest after all. I mean it naturally is Ernest.

*Lady Bracknell:* Yes, I remember now that the General was called Ernest. I knew I had some particular reason for disliking the name.

*Gwendolen:* Ernest! My own Ernest! I felt from the first that you could have no other name!

*Jack:* Gwendolen, it is a terrible thing for a man to find out suddenly that all his life he has been speaking nothing but the truth. Can you forgive me?

*Gwendolen:* I can. For I feel that you are sure to change.

*Jack:* My own one!

*Chasuble (to Miss Prism):* Laetitia! (*Embraces her.*)

*Miss Prism (enthusiastically):* Frederick! At last!

*Algernon:* Cecily! (*Embraces her.*) At last!

*Jack:* Gwendolen! (*Embraces her.*) At last!

*Lady Bracknell:* My nephew, you seem to be displaying signs of triviality.

*Jack:* On the contrary, Aunt Augusta, I've now realized for the first time in my life the vital Importance of Being Earnest.

## CONSIDERATIONS FOR CRITICAL THINKING AND WRITING

1. FIRST RESPONSE. Discuss the pun on the word *earnest*. Are these characters earnest about anything? If so, what?

2. One simplistic definition of a dramatic comedy is that it ends with the main characters getting married. How does Wilde play with that convention? What attitudes toward marriage are expressed in *The Importance of Being Earnest*, and which ones are we meant to take seriously? What sense do you make of the speed at which characters fall in and out of love?

3. Early in the play Jack suggests that an aunt's height is a characteristic she "may be allowed to decide for herself." Height is not a characteristic we can decide for ourselves. What does this play suggest about an individual's ability to make any decisions about identity?

4. What is "Bunburying," and how does it help frame the play's themes?

5. Algernon and Jack make a number of pronouncements about modern literature. List those pronouncements: Do they apply to this play as well? Are we meant to take them at face value?

6. What does the play suggest about the relationship between a romantic couple and society more generally? Is a romantic relationship entirely a private affair or does it depend largely on a social context?

7. What role does social class play in *The Importance of Being Earnest*? You might consider the role of the servants (Lane, Merriman, and Moulton) as well as Lady Bracknell's questions about Jack's suitability as a husband to Gwendolen.

8. The title contains a pun that is sustained throughout the play. List some other instances of puns or wordplay: What is their relationship to the play's broader concerns?

9. As it continues, the play pits men against women. How are the genders depicted? And how would you describe the relationship between them?

10. Jack and Algernon are both liars and scoundrels. Do you feel differently about each of them? If so, why?

## CONNECTIONS TO OTHER SELECTIONS

1. Compare the depiction of marriage and gender roles in this play and in Susan Glaspell's *Trifles* (p. 976).

2. Oscar Wilde's story "The Sphinx without a Secret" (p. 278) is much shorter and more serious than this play. Nonetheless, do they essentially share the same theme? If so, how would you articulate it?

# 39

# Contemporary Drama

John W. Ferguson/Getty Images.

> If you can hear the world singing, it's your job to write it down.
> — SUZAN-LORI PARKS

One of the most stunning American plays of the twenty-first century is Lin-Manuel Miranda's *Hamilton* (2016). It is stunning not only for its quality and its originality, but for the fact that countless audience members have shelled out an unconscionable amount of money for tickets. In June 2016, the *New York Times* reported that the top seats for the Broadway show cost $849, and many patrons paid much more than that to ticket reselling sites. In 2023, seven years later and without the original cast, prime tickets were still selling for over $500.

Not all theater is *that* expensive, of course — Broadway musicals are in their own stratosphere — but it has certainly become a less affordable experience than it once was. With the development of film in the early twentieth century, television in the mid-twentieth century, and streaming in recent years, one might expect that theater would have become dirt cheap as it strove to compete with these other forms. The fact that it has become a special event is testimony to the fact that people still value the experience of theatergoing, a tradition that stretches back to ancient times (see Chapter 36).

The high cost of Broadway musical theater is unfortunate in that it deprives access to this experience to anyone who is not financially comfortable, but it is only the most visible form of theater rather than the only form of theater left. Other cultures have developed a vibrant theater scene that is not limited to the wealthy. England has succeeded in holding onto its rich theatrical heritage while allowing the experience to be enjoyed by the full spectrum of social classes, just as it did in Shakespeare's day (see Chapter 37). Countries like Nigeria and Japan regard inexpensive access to theater as a vital means of preserving culture. And, of course, even within the United States, there are scores of community theaters that offer inexpensive theater experiences. A tradition of free theater in public urban spaces (think "Shakespeare in the Park") still exists. Many public schools in the United States include theater as part of their curriculum, from kindergarten through high school. The cost of blockbuster musicals like *Hamilton*, *Six*, *Wicked*, or *The Book of Mormon* should be seen as only one highly visible form of contemporary drama. Theater has certainly had to make room for its relatives — film, television, and the Internet — over the past hundred years, but it remains an important part of our culture and our literary heritage.

As modern drama (see Chapter 38) became established as an integral part of modern culture, it began to push against its own boundaries, as all literary traditions do. This is not surprising: the theme of many works of modern literature is the desire for escape or freedom. Early twentieth-century artists in many media were eager to see how far they could go. There was a reaction against what came to be called "the well-made play" — a conventional play, in short, that had become predictable and stale. Playwrights and audiences began to demand more of the form, and to ask questions: Could plays effect political change? Might they be a force for unsettling audiences rather than just entertaining them? Did they have to make sense?

## BEYOND REALISM

Realistic drama remained popular throughout the twentieth century, but from its beginnings it has been continually challenged by nonrealistic modes of theater. By the end of the nineteenth century, playwrights reacting against realism began to develop a variety of new approaches to setting, action, and character. Instead of creating a slice of life onstage, modern experimental playwrights drew on purely theatrical devices, ranging from stark sets and ritualistic actions to symbolic characterizations and audience participation. In general, such devices were designed to jar audiences' expectations and to heighten their awareness that what appeared before them was indeed a theatrical production. A glimpse of some of the nonrealistic movements in drama suggests how the possibilities for affecting audiences have been broadened by experimental theater.

**Symbolist drama** rejected the realists' assumption that life can be understood objectively and scientifically. The symbolists emphasized a subjective, emotional response to life because they believed that ultimate realities can be recognized only intuitively. Since absolute truth cannot be directly perceived, symbolists such as the Belgian playwright Maurice Maeterlinck sought to express spiritual truth through settings, characters, and actions that suggest a transcendent reality. Maeterlinck's most famous symbolist play, *Pelléas and Mélisande* (1892), is a story of love and vengeance that includes mysterious forebodings, symbolic objects, and unexplained powerful forces. The elements of the play make no attempt to create the texture of ordinary life, but rather project a parallel world that is more like imagined mythology than like reality.

Other early twentieth century playwrights — such as William Butler Yeats in Ireland, Paul Claudel in France, Leonid Andreyev in Russia, and Federico García Lorca in Spain — also used some of the techniques associated with symbolist plays, but the movement never enjoyed wide popularity because audiences often found the plays' action too vague and their language too cryptic. Nevertheless, symbolist drama had an important influence on the work of subsequent playwrights, such as Tennessee Williams's *The Glass Menagerie* (1944) and Arthur Miller's *Death of a Salesman* (1949). These dramatists effectively used symbols in plays that contain both realistic and nonrealistic qualities.

Another nonrealistic movement, known as **expressionism**, was popular from the end of World War I until the mid-1920s. Expressionist playwrights emphasized the internal lives of their characters and deliberately distorted reality by creating an outward manifestation of an inner state of being. The late plays of Swedish dramatist August Strindberg anticipate expressionistic techniques. Strindberg's preface to *A Dream Play* (1902) reflects the impact that Freudian psychology would eventually have on the theater:

> The author has tried to imitate the disconnected but seemingly logical form of the dream. Anything may happen; everything is possible and probable. Time and space do not exist. On an insignificant background of reality, imagination designs and embroiders novel patterns: a medley of memories, experiences, free fancies, absurdities, and improvisations.

In such nonrealistic drama the action does not have to proceed chronologically because the playwright dramatizes the emotional life of the characters, which blends the past with the present rather than moving in a fixed, linear way. This fluidity of development can be seen in the **flashbacks** of Williams's *The Glass Menagerie* and Miller's *Death of a Salesman*.

The **epic theater** of Bertolt Brecht is, like symbolism and expressionism, a long way from the realistic elements in realistic classics like Henrik Ibsen's *A Doll's House* (1879). Basing his methods on the political philosophy of Karl Marx, Brecht kept a distance between his characters and the audience. This strategy of alienation was designed to alert audiences to important social problems that might be overlooked if an individual's struggles became too emotionally absorbing (in other words, if the audience fell under the spell of realism). Brecht's drama, by casting new light on chronic human problems such as poverty, injustice, and war, was a means to convey hope and evidence that society could be changed for the better. Brecht called his drama "epic" to distinguish it from Aristotle's notion of drama. The episodic structure was designed to prevent the audience from being swept up in the action or losing themselves in an inevitable tragedy. Instead, Brecht wanted the audience to analyze the action and realize that certain consequences weren't inevitable but could be avoided. This distancing, the dramatization of societal issues, and the use of loosely connected scenes sometimes narrated by a kind of stage manager are the hallmarks of epic drama.

Epic theater revels in stylized theatricality. The major action in Brecht's *The Caucasian Chalk Circle* (1948), for example, consists of a play within a play. Brecht's dramas use suggestive rather than detailed settings, and their scenery and props are frequently changed as the audience watches. His actors make clear that they are pretending to be characters. They may speak or sing in verse, address the audience, or comment on issues with other characters who are not participants in the immediate action. In brief, Brecht's theater is keenly conscious of itself as theater.

In contrast to this didactic theater, the **theater of the absurd** was a response to the twentieth century's loss of faith in reason, religion, and life itself. These doubts produced an approach to drama that emphasizes chaotic, irrational forces and portrays human beings as more the victims than the makers of their world. This term was invented by drama critic Martin Esslin in 1961, reflecting an important trend that flourished in the 1950s.

Absurdists such as Samuel Beckett, French dramatist Eugène Ionesco, English playwright Harold Pinter, and American writer Edward Albee employ a variety of approaches to drama, but they share some assumptions about what subjects are important. Absurdism challenges the belief that life is ordered and meaningful, or that we can make sense of it rationally. Instead of positing traditional values that give human beings a sense of purpose in life, absurdists dramatize our inability to comprehend fully our identities and destinies. Unlike heroic characters such as Oedipus or Hamlet, who retain their dignity despite their defeats, the characters in absurdist dramas frequently seem pathetically comic as they drift from one destructive moment to the next. These **antiheroes** are often bewildered, ineffectual, deluded, and lost. If they learn anything, it is that the world isolates them in an existence devoid of God and absolute values.

The basic premise of absurdism — that life is meaningless — is often presented in a nonrealistic manner to disrupt our expectations. In a realistic play such as Wilde's *The Importance of Being Earnest*, characters act pretty much the way we believe people behave, though they may speak in a comically exaggerated way. The motivation of these characters and the plausibility of their actions are comprehensible, but in an absurdist drama we are confronted with characters who appear in a series of disconnected incidents that lead to deeper confusion. What would we make of Wilde's play if ten actors dressed in rhinoceros costumes appeared on stage in the final act (as they do in an absurdist play titled *Rhinoceros* (1959) by Eugène Ionesco)? This would be not only bizarre but unacceptable in a realistic play.

The appearance of ungulates on the stage of Wilde's play would, of course, be laughably inconsistent with what we judge to be real or reasonable. And yet it might serve to highlight the elements of the play that are not strictly realistic, like its extraordinary coincidences and implausible timing of events. The audience might be unsettled to the point of finding the characters' situations pathetic rather than amusing. This is the world of **tragicomedy**, where laughter and pain coexist and where there is neither the happy resolution that typifies comic plots nor the trans-formational suffering that brings clarification to the tragic hero. It is the world dramatized, for example, in the opening scene of Harold Pinter's *The Dumb Waiter* (1960) when Ben tells Gus about an item he's read in the paper.

*Ben:* A man of eighty-seven wanted to cross the road. But there was a lot of traf-fic, see? He couldn't see how he was going to squeeze through. So he crawled under a lorry [truck].

*Gus:* He what?

*Ben:* He crawled under a lorry. A stationary lorry.

*Gus:* No?

*Ben:* The lorry started and ran over him.

*Gus:* Go on!

*Ben:* That's what it says here.

*Gus:* Get away.

*Ben:* It's enough to make you want to puke, isn't it?

*Gus:* Who advised him to do a thing like that?

*Ben:* A man of eighty-seven crawling under a lorry!

*Gus:* It's unbelievable.

*Ben:* It's down here in black and white.

*Gus:* Incredible.

As much as Gus finds the story difficult to believe and Ben is sickened by it, it is a fact that the old man was crushed under ridiculous circumstances. His death is unexpected, accidental, incomprehensible, and meaningless — except that what happened to the old man is, from an absurdist's perspective, really no different from what life has in store for all of us one way or the other.

Absurdist playwrights may employ realistic settings and speech, but they go beyond realistic conventions to challenge the rational assumptions we make about our lives. Pinter insists that "a play is not an essay." Back-ground information, character motivation, action — nothing presented on an absurdist's stage is governed by the conventions of realism. The absurdists typically refuse to create the illusion of reality because there is, finally, no real-ity to imitate. If conversations in their plays are sometimes fragmented and seemingly inconsequential, the reason is that absurdists dramatize people's combined inability and unwillingness to communicate with one another. Indeed, Samuel Beckett's *Act without Words* contains no dialogue, and in his *Krapp's Last Tape* a single character addresses only his own tape-recorded voice. To some extent we must suspend common sense and logic if we are to appreciate the visions and voices in an absurdist play.

A related development in the mid- to late twentieth century is something French playwright Antonin Artaud defines as the ***theater of cruelty***. In this type of theater, the play isn't meant to represent life as realism did, but rather it emphasizes experience, including the experience of attending a play. The theater of cruelty was often based on primitive rituals and myths. "Cruelty," according to Artaud, was not necessarily bodily or emotional violence, but rather a kind of shock that audience members might feel, resulting in a changed outlook on the perception of their world. The theater of cruelty has not retained as much notoriety as the theater of the absurd, but the two are closely related. The theater of cruelty was embraced by later avant-garde playwrights such as Amiri Baraka who saw the political potential afforded by the techniques that Artaud and others initiated.

Although many other nonrealistic movements developed in the twentieth century, these four — symbolism, expressionism, epic theater, and the theater of the absurd/theater of cruelty —embrace the major differences between nonrealistic and realistic drama. Once realistic theater had been scrutinized as a middle-class fantasy, playwrights pushed theatrical conventions to extremes as a way of developing new political consciousness. In the 1960s and 1970s, for example, some acting companies in New York completely collapsed the usual distinctions between audience and actors. The Living Theater went even further by moving into the streets, where the actors and audiences engaged in dramatic political statements aimed at raising the social consciousness of people wherever they were. Some critics argued that this was not really theater but merely an exuberant kind of political rally. However, proponents of these productions — known as *guerrilla theater*— argued that protest drama is both politically and artistically valid. The Black Arts Movement of the late 1960s, led by a bohemian poet named LeRoi Jones, who changed his name to Amiri Baraka after undergoing a political awakening, wrote plays aimed at heightening the consciousness of Black Americans who had long been oppressed by white America and who had also been largely denied authentic representation on the American stage. Audience members of a play like Baraka's *Dutchman* (1964) or Ed Bullins's *Goin' a Buffalo* (1968) were likely to leave the theater agitated, angry, and inspired to change their society even though these plays did not have a clear or coherent message or moral. This effect is not as directly available through realism.

Although today's playwrights seem considerably less inclined to take to the streets, there is a tolerance for a wide range of possible relationships between actors and audiences. Audiences (and readers) can expect symbolic characters, expressionistic settings, poetic language, monologues, and extreme actions in productions that also contain realistic elements. In *Route 1 & 9* (1981), a piece created by an experimental theater company called the Wooster Group, for example, audiences found themselves confronted with passages from Thornton Wilder's idealized version of America in *Our Town* that were coupled with a pornographic film and a Black vaudeville act. This unlikely combination was used to comment on Wilder's conception of America in which issues of sex and race are largely ignored. Increasingly, experimental theater has cultivated an eclectic approach to drama, using a variety of media, cultures, playwrights, and even languages to enrich an audience's experience. Quiara Alegría Hudes's *Water by the Spoonful* (see Chapter 40), for instance, has characters interact in a virtual chat room rather than face-to-face. The stage directions give a range of creative license to the director in terms of these elements that would not have been available when modern realism was in vogue.

One important development of the experimental theater of the mid-twentieth century is ***metatheater***, a mode that calls attention to the conventions of theater itself, or to the fact that we are watching a performance rather than a representation of real life. Characters in these plays will reveal their understanding of their role, sometimes by addressing the audience directly (a practice commonly referred to as "breaking the fourth wall" — the invisible "wall" through which the audience watches the play) or by highlighting the fact that they are actors performing rather than actual people. This practice is not unique to contemporary theater: even Shakespeare's characters sometimes speak to the audience directly in ***asides***. Metatheater in modern and contemporary times takes the concept to a new level, though. Some contemporary metatheatrical plays, such as George C. Wolfe's *The Colored Museum* (1984), will actually involve the audience in the play, blurring the line between who is on stage and who is watching.

Experimental playwrights in the early twentieth century like Luigi Pirandello reveled in the possibilities of metatheater to question the audience's motivations for seeking truth in art: even the title of his best-known play, *Six Characters in Search of an Author* (1921), indicates Pirandello's inquiry into the nature of theater and the relationship between authors and their creations. Tom Stoppard's *Rosencrantz and Guildenstern Are Dead* (1966) takes two minor characters from Shakespeare's *Hamlet* and creates a drama around the absurdity of their existence, all the while reminding us that they never really existed in the first place: they're invented characters in a play. Metatheater is a technique closely related to the approaches taken in the theater of the absurd, but it allows the playwright more leeway since it does not have the obligation to reinforce the philosophical beliefs of the absurdists. It can be lighter and more playful (pardon the pun). The plays of Suzan-Lori Parks included in this chapter (p. 1198) are good examples of the range of possibilities afforded by metatheater.

## MUSICAL THEATER

Hudes's *Water by the Spoonful* (p. 1216) is not a musical, but it involves music as background, encouraging directors to play the music of jazz great John Coltrane as the curtain rises and including a college lecture on Coltrane later in the play. This is still a relatively mild introduction of music into the drama, though. Musical theater takes the relationship between acting and singing to the next level wherein characters will stop speaking and break into song, like opera. Since the early twentieth century, musical theater has been among the most popular versions of theater in the United States, and yet it is often dismissed by critics as light, tame, or formulaic. The essential difference between musical theater and its spoken counterpart is that the story is partly or entirely told in song in musical theater. Many of the songs of the so-called "great American songbook" have their origins in musical theater ("Old Man River" from *Showboat*, "I Got Rhythm" from *Girl Crazy*, "The Impossible Dream" from *Man of La Mancha*, "Hello, Dolly!" from *Hello, Dolly!*), but this popularity may be yet more ammunition for critics who find the form trite or flossy. Like any art form, though, we should be suspicious of the claims of critics who would denigrate a form just because it is popular. Rock and roll was considered trash entertainment for a time, too, until songwriters like the Beatles (p. 766) and Bob Dylan (p. 763) introduced musical and lyrical innovations that opened up a world of possibilities that have led to some of the most potent cultural expressions in the contemporary era. Composers in musical theater active in the 1950s through the 1970s — Leonard Bernstein, Stephen Sondheim, and Andrew Lloyd Webber — began to explore the possibilities of musical theater as a potentially serious form. (Sondheim won the Pulitzer Prize for Drama in 1985 for *Sunday in the Park with George*.) Their successes gave rise in the 1980s and 1990s to what might be called the mega-musical: theatrical productions such as *Miss Saigon*, *Cats* (one of Webber's works), and *Les Misérables* which became known for their spectacular stage effects and slick production as well as their catchy music.

These innovations might be seen as a way for theater to try to compete with the "special effects" readily available to filmmakers. The 1980s also gave rise to big-budget blockbusters on the silver screen in which special effects–heavy movies (think Steven Spielberg) were huge box office draws. In musical theater, as in film, these spectacles are garish and highly visible, but their popularity does not necessarily mean either medium has completely "sold out" or failed to take itself seriously as an art form. The critically acclaimed *Hamilton* mentioned in the opening paragraph of this chapter, for instance, reveals a form that is still evolving, and there are obviously excellent films being produced all the time with low budgets that do not rely on any special effects. As with any genre, we should attempt to understand the value of musical theater in terms of its artistic innovations, not just its commercial viability, although it is possible, of course, to have both qualities.

## DRAMA IN POPULAR FORMS

In addition to musical theater, drama has been adapted to accommodate the technologies available in the modern era, notably film and television. Audiences for live performances of plays have been thinned by high ticket prices but perhaps even more significantly by the impact of film and television. Movies, the original threat to live theater, have in turn been superseded by television (along with Netflix and other streaming services), now the most popular form of entertainment in America. Television audiences are measured in the millions. Probably more people have seen a single episode of a top-rated prime-time program in one evening than have viewed a live performance of *Hamlet* in nearly four hundred years.

Though most of us are seated more often before a television than before live actors, our limited experience with the theater presents relatively few obstacles to appreciation because many of the basic elements of drama are similar whether the performance is on a screen or on a stage. Television has undoubtedly seduced audiences that otherwise might have been attracted to the theater, but television obviously satisfies some aspects of our desire for drama and can be seen as a potential introduction to live theater rather than as its irresistible rival.

Significant differences do, of course, exist between television and theater productions. Most obviously, television's special camera effects can capture phenomena such as earthquakes, raging fires, car chases, and space travel that cannot be realistically rendered on a live stage. The presentation of characters and the plotting of action are also handled differently owing to both the possibilities and limitations of television and the theater. Television's multiple camera angles and close-ups provide a degree of intimacy that cannot be duplicated by actors onstage, yet this intimacy does not achieve the immediacy that live actors create. On commercial television the plot must accommodate itself to breaks in the action so that advertisements can be aired at regular intervals. Musical soundtracks are also common in films and television shows but rare in stage productions (other than musicals). Beyond these and many other differences, however, there are enough important similarities that the experience of watching television shows can enhance our understanding of a theater production.

## SUZAN-LORI PARKS: A COLLECTION OF TEN VERY SHORT PLAYS

### Suzan-Lori Parks (b. 1963)

The first African American woman to receive the Pulitzer Prize for drama (for *Topdog/Underdog* in 2002), Suzan-Lori Parks is one of the most acclaimed playwrights of our time. She was born in Kentucky, but as her father was in the military, she moved frequently around the United States and Germany, where she attended high school. She attended Mount Holyoke College in western Massachusetts when the author James Baldwin taught in the five colleges in and around Amherst, and she credits his encouragement

John W. Ferguson/Getty Images.

and mentorship as her main inspiration to write professionally. (Baldwin's story "Sonny's Blues" (p. 91) and his poem "Guilt, Desire and Love" (p. 614) are included earlier in this anthology).

Parks can be described as restlessly experimental, so it is difficult to characterize her work. There are some recurrent motifs, though. Abraham Lincoln is a frequent character on her stage, and characters who impersonate Lincoln for a living are featured in both *The America Play* (1995) and *Topdog/Underdog*. Her work reveals a deep engagement with the theatrical tradition and literature more generally: her nine-part play *Father Comes Home from the Wars* (begun in 2014), for instance, is a retelling of Homer's *Odyssey*. Her plays engage with the meaning of race in contemporary America on a deep level, revealing psychological realities that are explored both viscerally and intellectually.

Part of what makes Parks so intriguing is her willingness to take risks that other playwrights might avoid. The following very short plays were part of a project she titled *365 Days / 365 Plays* (2006). As the title indicates, she attempted to write a short play every day for a year while continuing to work on other projects. This creative challenge gave her the opportunity to explore her vast field of ideas while also committing to her craft in a way that obliterates the notion of "writer's block." As is clear from these selections, it also enables her and her audiences to see how fun theater can be while it encourages deep thinking. You'll likely be laughing and scratching your head at the same time as you read these pieces. Consider how each of them acts as drama in a very compressed space.

## From the Author's "Elements of Style"

I'm continuing the use of my slightly unconventional theatrical elements. Here's a road map.

▌ (*Rest*)

Take a little time, a pause, a breather; make a transition.

▌ A Spell

An elongated and heightened (*Rest*). Denoted by repetition of figures' names with no dialogue. Has sort of an architectural look:

**Krishna**
**Arjuna**
**Krishna**
**Arjuna**

This is a place where the figures experience their pure true simple state. While no action or stage business is necessary, directors should fill this moment as they best see fit.

▌ (Parentheses around dialogue indicate softly spoken passages (asides; sotto voce)).

▌ Some plays for two characters use no character names. The performers should alternate lines. Other plays for two or more characters use no character names, but each new speech is preceded by a dash. Each dash indicates when a new speaker begins. The lines below would be read by two different speakers:

–She dont talk.
–I do so talk.

## *Veuve Clicquot*   2006

*The Condemned:* Beef Bourguignonne, with the raspberry reduction, garlic mashed potatoes — and could they make them without milk?

*Waiter:* I'll ask.

*The Condemned:* Great. White poached asparagus, organic greens with a lemon vinaigrette.

*Waiter:* Dessert?

*The Condemned:* I get a dessert?

*Waiter:* Yep.

*The Condemned:* Death By Chocolate Soufflé.

*Waiter:* Thats funny.

*The Condemned:* I was a comedian. Once.

*Waiter:* Really.

*(Rest)*

What to drink?

*The Condemned:* Veuve Clicquot.

*Waiter:* Wassat?

*The Condemned:* Champagne.

*Waiter:* Why didnt you just say "champagne?"

*The Condemned:* Cause its called Veuve Clicquot.

*Waiter:* Thats yr whole entire problem, if you ask me.

*The Condemned:* Im not asking you.

*Waiter:* You think yr smarter than the rest of the general population, and *that* is yr whole entire problem.

*The Condemned:* Im just trying to enjoy myself is all.

*Waiter:* Veuve Clicquot.

*The Condemned:* Forget it.

*Waiter:* I'll see what I can do.

*The Condemned:* I dont want it anymore. I wanna change my order.

*Waiter:* I wrote everything down already.

*The Condemned*
*Waiter*

*(Rest)*

*Waiter:* I let you get away with —

*The Condemned:* With murder?

*Waiter:* Ima miss you. You make me laugh. But not in the way the others make me laugh. Yr jokes are — they always got like a twist to them.

*The Condemned:* Twisted jokes from a twisted mind.

*Waiter:* Yeah. I'll miss that.

*The Condemned:* Me too. I think. But I might not. Maybe missing is only something we do when we're alive. And when we're dead we are missed but dont miss.

*Waiter:* Yeah. Whatll it be?

*The Condemned:* Gimmie French fries, lotsa ketchup and hot sauce, double-decker burger with nice thick patties, root beer float and apple pie à la mode.

*Waiter:* Pie what?

*The Condemned:* "In the fashion."

*Waiter:* In the fashion of what?

*The Condemned:* For-get-it. Just bring me some apple pie with a scoop of
vanilla ice cream.

*Waiter:* You want the ice cream on top?

*The Condemned:* Yeah.

*Waiter:* You got it.

*The Condemned:* And make it a cheeseburger. With bacon. And a new battery
for the remote!

*Waiter:* Sure.

> *Waiter exits. A Chorus of Murdered Women comes in.*

*Murdered Women:*
On the last day of my life
I was minding my own bizness
I wasnt doing nothing special
I wasnt eating no
à la mode.
I was washing all the dishes
I was picking up the kids
on the last day of my life
when he did what he did.

> *They stand there staring at The Condemned.*
> *The Waiter comes back in with the food.*

*The Condemned:* Microwaved?

*Waiter:* Yeah.

*The Condemned:* Like I'll be in a minute.

*Waiter:* Hey. Enjoy yr meal.

*The Condemned:* Yeah.

> *He eats. The Waiter exits. The Chorus of Murdered Women*
> *stands there watching him eat. "Being a man is never*
> *having to say yr sorry," The Condemned says. Not out loud.*
> *Only to himself, in his head. He picks up the remote and eats*
> *with one hand and channel-surfs with the other,*
> *pretending theyre not staring at him but knowing that they are,*
> *and his guilt for his crimes comes moving toward him*
> *across the room like a shadow as the day grows longer,*
> *moving on toward him even as the tv goes full blast.*

### CONSIDERATIONS FOR CRITICAL THINKING AND WRITING

1. FIRST RESPONSE. What do you think about the convention of allowing prisoners on death row to choose their final meal? Why do you suppose it exists, even if only as a legend?

2. The play ends with a distinct emphasis on television watching. How do you read this content in the context of the overall play?

3. How might the guilt The Condemned silently experiences in the stage directions at the end of the play be communicated on stage?

## *Here Comes the Message*   2006

> *A Scout alone onstage,*
> *looking off into the distance with a telescope.*

*Scout:*  Hhhhh.

> *He looks and looks.*

*Scout:*  Ive been looking my whole life. Thats my lot, I guess. To look and look and never —

> *He looks. Becomes greatly agitated.*

*Scout:*  No. It cant be. HERE COMES THE MESSAGE! Good God! Here it comes! HERE COMES THE MESSAGE! HERE COMES THE MESSAGE! HERE COMES THE MESSAGE!

> *The stage quickly fills with Townspeople in various states.*
> *Some are in their nightclothes, some have napkins at their necks*
> *from breakfast or shaving, some are nursing children,*
> *some are milking cows, women flipping pancakes,*
> *men pitching hay — everybody is running*
> *from something very important to come have a look.*
> *They stand next to the Scout and look, as the Scout looks*
> *into the far distance.*

*Man:*  Gimmie yr telescope.

*Other Man:*  See anything?

*Man:*  A man. On his way. In our general direction.

*Scout:*  Its the Message.

*Townspeople:*  Here comes the message! Here comes the message! Here comes the message! Here comes the message!

> *A Messenger, nicely dressed, comes toward them,*
> *they have formed a tight knot and he pushes through them,*
> *working hard to get past.*

*Messenger:*  Let me pass! Let me pass!

*Scout:*  Hold on, man, yr the message.

*Man:*  Weve been waiting.

*Woman:*  Very patiently.

*Other Woman:*  Through thick and through thin.

*Other Man:*  For years.

*Messenger:*  Im the *messenger*. Im not the message. If youll excuse me. Im on official business.

> *The Messenger pushes through the crowd*
> *and continues on his way.*

Townspeople
Scout

*Scout:*  Good scouts dont grow on trees, now.

*Woman:*  Who says yr good? I for one says yr no good. Who seconds me?

*Townspeople:* I.

Townspeople
Scout

> *The Townspeople surround the Scout and stomp him to death.*
> *The Scout's telescope stands, like an eye,*
> *outside of the violent circle, looking at nothing.*

CONSIDERATIONS FOR CRITICAL THINKING AND WRITING

1. **FIRST RESPONSE.** Give an example of something people wait for their whole lives with great anticipation.
2. What does the townspeople's murder of the Scout say about human nature?

## Fine Animal    2006

> *A Princess and a Prince. The Prince's arms are clasped around the Princess's neck in an elongated hanging-on hug.*
> *Every so often, the Princess pulls a day off a large calendar.*

*Princess:* Bored?
*Prince:* Mmm.
*Princess:* Me too.
*Prince:* Much longer?
*Princess:* Not much.

> *The Princess rips more days off the calendar.*
> *At long last, she reaches the end.*

*Prince:* That it?
*Princess:* Looks that way.
*Prince:* Can I unclasp my hands?
*Princess:* What did she tell you?
*Prince:* She said after the time passed I could unclasp my hands.
*Princess:* The time's passed.
*Prince:* I'll unclasp then. Nervous?
*Princess:* A little. You?
*Prince:* Very. Being here, with my arms around yr neck all this time. There were several opportunities I missed out on. Several wars. And remember when my servant came by with news of that damsel in distress? And the dragons?
*Princess:* There will always be wars. There will always be damsels in distress. There will always be dragons.
*Prince:* One hopes.
*Princess:* Unclasp yr hands.

> *The Prince unclasps himself. He looks the Princess over.*

*Prince:* She lied.
*Princess:* Im sorry.
*Prince:* Its not yr fault. You didnt promise me anything. The witch did.
*Princess:* I thought you were doing this all on yr own.
*Prince:* I was, but, you know, at the witch's suggestion.
*Princess:* The witch with the funny hat?
*Prince:* Yeah.
*Princess:* Hhh.

> *The Princess whistles, like she's calling her dog. A Hag enters.*

*Hag:* Yes, maam.
*Prince:* Thats the witch. She doesnt have her hat on, though.
*Princess:* You a witch?

*Hag:* No, maam. Im not a witch, Im a hag.

*Prince:* A hag? You said you were a witch.

*Hag:* I was just trying to find somebody for my princess.

*Prince:* In my country, the punishment for impersonating a witch is death by dismemberment.

*Princess:* But yr not in yr country. Yr in my country.

*Hag:* I appreciate that.

*Princess:* Silence.

*Prince:* I wanted a good-looking wife. I dont mean any disrespect.

*Princess:* None taken.

*Hag:* I was only trying to help.

*Princess:* Silence.

*Prince:* And now Ive missed out on the tournaments. And the dragons. And the damsels. And the wars.

*Princess:* There will be more wars and tournaments and damsels and dragons too, wont there?

*Hag:* Im old and Ive seen plenty.

*Prince:* I dont trust you, Hag.

*Princess:* Silence. I mean —

*Prince:* No worries. We're all under stress here. I had a plan and its gone to shit. My plan was to have good-looking children. They would, when they got old enough of course, be featured in all the glossy magazines. Ive got good clear eyes and a strong enough chin. I was hoping to — well —

*Princess:* And here youve been tricked into spending all this time around my neck. You could go and find another.

*Prince:* I guess so.

*Hag:* I could help.

*Princess:* Silence.

*Hag:* Let me speak. Please.

*Princess*
*Prince*

*Princess:* Speak.

*Hag:* Take a look at this.

*Prince:* Its a glossy magazine.

*Hag:* With a 3-page picture in it.

> *The Prince opens the magazine and eyes the centerfold.*

*Prince:* Fine animal. Oh, yeah.

*Princess:* Yr not leaving then.

*Prince:* Fine animal.

*Hag:* He's staying. He's yrs.

*Princess:* You think?

*Hag:* Yep. I seen it before. Congratulations.

> *The Prince gives the Princess a kiss on the cheek.*

*Princess:* Hag, go fetch the prince, my husband, some slippers, a meatloaf, lots more magazines, and a pipe howbout.

> *The Hag curtsies and goes. They settle into domestic bliss.*

> *The Princess gazes at the Prince and*
> *the Prince gazes at the centerfold.*

1. FIRST RESPONSE. Why is such a premium put on beauty?
2. If this short play is a satire, who or what is its main target? What is its inherent statement about its subject?

## The Ends of the Earth    2006

> *A Throng chases a Man. They run pell-mell. They pass a small nondescript sign. They stop, run back, read the sign.*

*Throng:*  This is it.

*Man:*  What do you mean?

*Throng:*  Arent you beat?

*Man:*  I was just getting into it.

*Throng:*  This is as far as we go.

*Man:*  Have we crossed the county line or something? Dont be ridiculous! Where are you all headed? Dont turn back! You said youd hound me to the ends of the earth!

*Throng:*  And here we are. At the ends of the earth.

*Man:*  This isnt the ends of the earth.

*Throng:*  Read the sign.

*Man:*  Forget the sign. This isnt the ends of the earth.

*Throng:*  Ever been there?

*Man:*  No. But. Well, this is not the ends of the earth. Let-me-tell-you.

*Throng:*  Read the sign.

> *The Man reads the sign.*

*Throng:*  Whassit say?

*Man:*  "You Are Here."

*Throng:*  The fine print. Read the fine print.

*Man:*  "Welcome — to — the ends of the earth."

*Throng:*  Louder.

*Man:*  You heard me.

*Throng:*  So, ciao, K?

*Man:*  Youve been hounding me for years.

*Throng:*  We said we'd hound you to the ends of the earth.

*Man:*  Youve been — for so long — youve been —

*Throng:*  And here we are.

*Man:*  This isnt the ends of the earth. This is just a sign. The ends of the earth is — well — its a place of remarkable spirit and great beauty. And this place — well, it just looks like anyplace. No great chasm, no river not even a big red rock.

*Throng:*  We gotta go.

*Man:*  All those sleepless nights. Running. You hounding me. Because — . I forget why. Hhhh.

> *The Throng disappears into the distance. The Man sits and whistles something that sounds like the lonesome wind, or he bursts into tears. Real tears because he doesnt know what else to do.*

## CONSIDERATIONS FOR CRITICAL THINKING AND WRITING

1. FIRST RESPONSE. When are routines useful and when are they detrimental?

2. Assume one should read this play metaphorically. Does it make most sense as a metaphor for retirement, for death, or for a milestone like graduating from college? Explain how you might interpret the play following one of these possibilities or adding one of your own.

## *Beginning, Middle, End*   2006

*Traditionalist:*
Beginning, Middle, End
Beginning, Middle, End.
*Fresh One:*
End, Beginning
Beginning, Middle
Middle, End
Middle, Fiddle
Faddle, Paddle
yr own canoe.

> *They look at each other.*

*Traditionalist:* Yrs is better than mine.
*Fresh One:* No its not. Its just —
*Traditionalist:* Fresh. And fun. Im no fun. Im stuck in a rut.
    Everybody says so.

> *The Traditionalist bursts into tears.*

*Fresh One:* Forget what everybody says.
*Traditionalist:* I tried. I tried to be fresh. Once.
*Fresh One:* Howd it go?
*Traditionalist:* Felt lousy. Felt — fake.
*Fresh One:* Maybe you were trying too hard. I never try too hard.
*Traditionalist:* It just comes, right?
*Fresh One:* Kind of.

*(Rest)*

When I started out I looked to traditional forms. But the situations I wanted to
    explore, the characters I wanted to embrace didnt fit — you get the picture? —
*Traditionalist:* Sorta.
*Fresh One:* My stuff didnt fit traditional forms.
*Traditionalist:* But mine does. Most of it. Although, thinking back on it all, there
    have been things left out, discarded. But most things fit.
*Fresh One:* Then be traditional. Its not a CRIME.
*Traditionalist:* But being fresh is criminal.
*Fresh One:* In some circles.

> *The Traditionalist takes out a piece of chalk.*
> *He considers writing the following stage direction:*
> *"The Traditionalist draws a circle around the Fresh One."*

*Fresh One:* Whatcha doing?
*Traditionalist:* Whassit look like.
*Fresh One:* Yr drawing a circle around me.
*Traditionalist:* Mmm.
*Fresh One:* How come?
*Traditionalist:* Ha!
*Fresh One:* What?
*Traditionalist:* Nothing.
*Fresh One:* Wassup with the circle, pal?
*Traditionalist:* Im being experimental.
*Fresh One:* Good for you.
*Traditionalist:* We'll see. Heres a whistle.
*Fresh One:* Right.
*Traditionalist:* Blow it.

> *The Fresh One blows the whistle. They wait.*
> *A Group of Riot Police come in. They eye the circle.*
> *They stand at the circle and beat the Fresh One.*

*Traditionalist:*
Beginning, Middle, End.
*Riot Police Captain:* Says who?
*Traditionalist:* Says me. Says you. Says all of us. Its an accepted form.

Traditionalist
Riot Police

(Rest)

*Riot Police Captain:* Anybody watching?
*Riot Police Lieutenant:* Nope.
*Riot Police Captain:* Go for it.

> *The Police surround the Traditionalist and beat him.*
> *Then they exit.*

### CONSIDERATIONS FOR CRITICAL THINKING AND WRITING

1. FIRST RESPONSE. Who ultimately has more control over a play's meaning: artists or audiences?

2. According to the play's own definitions, is this play traditional or experimental?

### CONNECTION TO ANOTHER SELECTION

1. Compare this short play to Gregory Corso's poem "I am 25" (p. 528) to consider the relationship between traditional and experimental writers. Do these two works lead to the same conclusion?

## *What Do You See?*   2006

*Several speakers.*

—What do you see?
—Nothing.
—What else?
—What else is there?
—A blank page soon to be filled with water.
—No!
—A blank page soon to be filled with feelings.
—Tears of sadness?
—No, a murder by drowning.
—Oh.

*(Rest)*

—I would fill the blank page with body parts. And a list: of the people I'd like to raise from the dead.
—They'd stink.
—I dont smell. "Anosmia" its called.
—No smell at all?
—No.
—Never have?
—Never have.
—Never wanted to?
—Sometimes. Like roses.
—Roses.
—Yes roses. And less flowery things like piss on the subway.

*(Rest)*

—Whats she doing here?
—She was invited.
—Really? Does she belong?
—We're expanding our circle, dont be such a snob.
—Whats she doing over there?
—Jerking-off.
—No, she's not
—Yes she is too.
—God.
—She doesnt look like a heathen.
—Hard to say these days, everything's changed.
—Do me a favor.
—What?
—Talk to her.
—Why?
—She looks — lonesome.

*(Rest)*

—You should make that into the title of something. A play or something.
—You think?
—Do I think! It sounds like a money-maker.

–Not that title.

–Sure. I got a nose for money-makers.

–You dont know these days whats a money-maker and whats not. Take war for instance.

–Dont you get started talking about the war, we are sick of you talking about the war. Before we left the house you promised me you wouldnt talk about the war, in the goddamn fucking car for Christ's sake you promised me, you swore to me on everything that was sacred that you wouldnt talk about the war. Did I sell my house to get you out of the Service? Did I sell my fucking house?

–You sold yr house to yr mother.

–You wanna serve in the Service? Just say the word.

*(Rest)*

–Hush, both of you, people are looking.

–I want to start a family.

–Fuck you.

–I say I wanna start a family and you say fuck you.

–How else are families made, asshole.

–You dont want one. Admit it.

–All right. You wanna start a family, how about "over my dead body"?

> *The Assembled Speakers calmly make a circle.*
> *Then One lunges at Another. They struggle.*
> *Years of pent-up frustration, the mortgage on the mortgage,*
> *the 9-to-5, the hi honey Im home, and honey wishes you werent,*
> *the television showing you a life other than the life you or*
> *anybody you know will ever live, the discrepancy,*
> *the discrepancy within the discrepancy and the endless and*
> *therefore tragic distance between a guy and his own guts.*

### Considerations for Critical Thinking and Writing

1. **FIRST RESPONSE.** In one paragraph, answer the question posed by the title.

2. The stage directions call for "several speakers." How many would be the optimal amount, in your estimation? Once you've determined that number, attribute each line to one of the speakers (Speaker 1, Speaker 2, etc.). How do your decisions alter the play or clarify its concerns?

## *This Is Shit*  2006

> *An audience is gathered to watch a play. One person sleeps.*
> *Another constantly refers to his program, trying to "understand"*
> *the show. Another checks his watch. Another laughs.*
> *Another weeps. Another frowns a lot, cranking her head*
> *from side to side, trying to make heads or tails of the scenery.*
> *Another leaps up every chance she gets*
> *only to sit down again, embarrassed. Still another stands*
> *and throws her program at the stage.*

*Program Thrower:* This is shit!

> *Program Thrower exits. The rest give a standing ovation.*

### CONSIDERATIONS FOR CRITICAL THINKING AND WRITING

1. FIRST RESPONSE. What's the relationship between popular taste and a critical assessment? Give examples from your experience and use them to comment on this play.

2. The play does not indicate that anything is happening on the stage, nor even that there are actors on it. Is this play about audience reactions, or are the actions of the audience the play itself?

## *Barefoot and Pregnant in the Park* 2006

*Guard:* Just who do you think you are?

*Woman:* Im looking for my husband.

*Guard:* Likely story. Cant you read? Signs as big as Kansas, letters plain as the Plains: "No Barefoots on Grass." That means the likes of you. Guess you cant read.

*Woman:* I can read.

*Guard:* Get lost. Or I'll have to take you in. Lock you up in jail, then youll be having that baby in lockup.

*Woman:* My husband. He comes here. He's — he's got shoes. Harry! There he is! He left me because, well, long story and not important now is it? Ive been looking for him for 5 whole months! Im the laughingstock of our town. Harry! Harry! Its me! Harry! Harry!

> *The Guard blows a whistle. Harry comes in.*

*Guard:* You Harry?

*Harry:* Yeah.

*Guard:* You know her?

*Harry:* Never seen her in my life.

> *Harry goes on his way. The Guard blows his whistle and 2 other Guards come in and take the Woman away.*

### CONSIDERATIONS FOR CRITICAL THINKING AND WRITING

1. FIRST RESPONSE. Who is telling the truth: The Woman or Harry? How do you know?

2. What does the play say about power?

## *Orange* 2006

> *A Clown, with a strapped-on red nose and a colorful pointed hat, comes in. He/she juggles 3 oranges. A Man walks by in a hurry, talking on the phone, not a cell phone, but an old-style rotary-dial phone with a long extension cord.*

*Man:* So I told him, I said, if you think that is the way things are, youve got another thing coming, I said. I told him. Yeah, I told him. Over my dead body! I said. Oh, yeah, *I told him.* And do you know what he said to me? Not a goshdarn thing. Not one wor —

> *He sees the Clown juggling. The Clown juggles in a rhythmic,*
> *hypnotic, purposeful way, as if the movement of the 3 oranges*
> *were the very thing which keeps the world revolving. Or with the*
> *intensity of a mime who thinks the job of the mime is of great*
> *purpose. He sees himself at the bottom of the pile of man,*
> *but has made his peace with that, and works steadily on,*
> *knowing the meek and quiet will inherit.*
> *The Man, watching the Clown, begins to weep in*
> *an embarrassed way. Trying hard not to show it. Dabbing his*
> *eyes with his perfectly pressed handkerchief, and then replacing*
> *the handkerchief to make it look as if it never left his breast*
> *pocket. This is an impossible task, and it makes him cry*
> *all the more. He blubbers and wipes his face with his sleeve as*
> *a 5-year-old child would. Then he stops.*
> *The Clown continues juggling.*
> *The Man grabs 1 of the oranges, eating it like an apple, then*
> *stuffing the leftovers in his pocket.*
> *The Clown continues much as before,*
> *but with just the 2 oranges.*
> *The Man grabs the 2nd orange. Eats it. The Clown continues*
> *with 1 orange. The Man grabs and eats the last orange, then,*
> *as the lights fade, he makes sure no one is looking as he grabs*
> *off the Clown's red nose and pointed hat*
> *and puts them on himself.*
> *The Clown continues juggling even though*
> *he's got nothing to work with but air.*

### CONSIDERATIONS FOR CRITICAL THINKING AND WRITING

1. FIRST RESPONSE. What is this play about? Where in it do you look for meaning?
2. Why do you imagine the playwright specifies that the phone prop be "an old-style rotary-dial phone with a long extension cord" rather than a cell phone?
3. Would the play's meaning change if it were called "Phone" or "Clown" or "Air"? Explain your response.

## *(Again) Groundhog*   2006

> *Slow light fades up. The stage is bare. A Lady walks out*
> *onto the stage. She has on a winter coat and hat and mittens*
> *and scarf and galoshes, etc. She comes out not tentatively*
> *but not confidently either.*
> *She looks behind her. No shadow. She's relieved.*
> *As she speaks she removes her winterwear.*

*Lady:* Good thing thats over, right? I mean, almost over.
Groundhog Day today. Groundhog, or lady in groundhog play,
walks out, and should they see their shadow it means lots more winter is on
the way. No shadow, no winter. So its over. Winter. Most of it anyway.

*(Rest)*

Winter this year was hard. You know there was —

> *She makes a hand to clavicle gesture expressing extreme pain*
> *and sadness. Pain and sadness beyond measure.*

*Lady:* And if none of that got to you, or you know, even with bright spots theres
the —

> *She makes a gesture — arm sailing away from the body*
> *and returning slowly.*

*Lady:* So much of it is difficult and even more difficult to talk about. But its
over, winter is over, winter is on its way out — almost over — and so we can
finally, at last, we can finally — just be here — without our galoshes.

*(Rest)*

Every day I run to the window and see if my tulips are coming up. And soon
spring green will be here. Theres nothing better than that.

> *A man walks in, shrouded in black, the Shadow.*

*Lady*
*Shadow*
*Lady*
*Shadow*

*Lady:* Yr just "a" shadow, yr not "my" shadow, right?
*Shadow:* Sorry Im late. You were walking so fast and — I was out pretty late last
night and — I was drinking. Ok. I'll admit it. Even though my wife tells me that if
I keep drinking itll kill me. But — so I was out late and having a pretty good time.
And I went to bed, set my alarm. But, the alarm went off, and I was dead to the
world. Out cold. By the time I got myself together you were all the way down
the street.
*Lady:* I heard hollering —
*Shadow:* That was me. Yeah. Hollering for you to wait up.
*Lady:* Yr . . . *(Gesture)* I mean, last year I saw you and you were much . . .
*(Opposite gesture)* smaller.
*Shadow:* Ive been eating. Too much. Gaining weight. Its a little embarrassing.
*Lady:* I'll say.

> *She turns away, then steps away. He follows her.*
> *When she stops he stops.*

*Lady*
*Shadow*

*Shadow:* So you see me, right?
*Lady:* Yr a shadow, not my shadow.
*Shadow:* Come on —
*Lady:* Im not going back in.
*Shadow:* This is hard for me too.

*He takes out a pair of handcuffs, puts one around his wrist
then one around hers. He begins to lead her away.
She does not resist, then, dashes back to her pile of winter
clothes, collecting them as best she can before
he leads her offstage.*

## CONSIDERATIONS FOR CRITICAL THINKING AND WRITING

1. FIRST RESPONSE. What do you think the Lady's line "Yr a shadow, not my shadow" (p. 1212) means?

2. Does the play have a protagonist? Who is it?

3. If you had to label this play either a tragedy or a comedy, which would you choose and why?

## A COLLECTION OF TEN VERY SHORT PLAYS: CONSIDERATIONS FOR CRITICAL THINKING AND WRITING

1. FIRST RESPONSE. What specific elements of these plays would be a challenge to a director? How would you respond to that challenge if you were the director?

2. Examine the balance between talking and silent action in these plays. What can you say about the relationship between them? Using one or two plays to illustrate your idea, how does this balance help to frame a recurrent theme?

3. Which play is the funniest in your opinion, and how is humor being used?

4. Which play is the least funny, and what informs your response?

5. Use the ideas behind the play "Beginning, Middle, End" (p. 1206) to analyze Parks's methods in general: how is she commenting on her own work in that play?

6. Multiple plays comment on gender roles, specifically "Veuve Clicquot" (p. 1200), "Fine Animal" (p. 1203), and "Barefoot and Pregnant in the Park" (p. 1210). Do the three plays together formulate a coherent message about this topic or are they significantly different?

7. Many of the plays are philosophical in nature. What do the plays "Here Comes the Message" (p. 1202), "The Ends of the Earth" (p. 1205), and "Orange" (p. 1210) together say about human nature?

8. How do the plays "Beginning, Middle, End" (p. 1206), "This Is Shit" (p. 1209), and "(Again) Groundhog" (p. 1211) amplify your understanding of metatheater as it is described on p. 1196?

## CONNECTIONS TO OTHER SELECTIONS

1. Compare depictions of gender roles in one or more of the plays mentioned in question 6 of the above Considerations for Critical Thinking and Writing to Lynn Nottage's short play *POOF!* (p. 1322).

2. Contrast the conventions of drama Parks uses in these short plays to Sophocles' techniques in *Oedipus the King* (p. 1001). Rather than trying to judge which is better or worse, use your comparison to answer this question: what is the essential power of drama?

# 40

## A CULTURAL CASE STUDY
# Quiara Alegría Hudes's
# *Water by the Spoonful*

Writing is self-interrogation. Rigorous contemplation. That, in and of itself, is resistance in this capitalist amnesiac macho nation. No matter how clicky the banner ads, how triumphant the American history textbooks, and how magnitudinal the social media likes, the best writing exposes the loose screws in the scaffolding.
— QUIARA ALEGRÍA HUDES

John Lamparski/Getty Images.

Contemporary plays face a great deal of pressure. There is the pressure to entertain and captivate audiences in a form that might seem charmingly antiquated given the rise of movies, television, and Internet streaming. There is also the pressure to make a culturally relevant statement in an era of political turmoil. Very few contemporary American plays have nothing to say about the divided condition of our society, and no play considered important in the twenty-first century resembles a modern play like Oscar Wilde's *The Importance of Being Earnest* (p. 1148), which is primarily concerned with wit and social decorum. Additionally, there's pressure to acknowledge the history of drama from its origins through the present while still attempting something different. Finally, there's pressure to discover and present authentic stories, to get beneath the surface of what we experience and to expose the depths we might tend to avoid.

## *Water by the Spoonful*

Quiara Alegría Hudes (b. 1977) is a rising star of the contemporary theater who has turned this pressure into art. She is perhaps best known for her collaboration with Lin-Manuel Miranda (of *Hamilton* fame): he set her book *In the Heights* to music to create a highly moving musical drama that won multiple Tony Awards in 2008 (including best musical) and was adapted into a successful film in 2021. While *In the Heights* made Hudes a household name, the play included in this chapter, *Water by the Spoonful* (2012), garnered more attention in critical circles: it won the Pulitzer Prize for drama in 2012. It is the second part of a trilogy of plays: the first was *Elliot, a Soldier's Fugue*, which was nominated for the Pulitzer in 2007, and the third was *The Happiest Song Plays Last* (2014). Since her first play in 2003 (*Yemaya's Belly*), Hudes has written ten as well as the screenplay for the 2021 animated movie *Vivo* (also a collaboration with Miranda), and her acclaimed memoir, *My Broken Language* (2021), has also been adapted into a play.

Born in West Philadelphia to a Puerto Rican mother and a Jewish father, Hudes embraces her Puerto Rican heritage as her main source of identity, evident in her work and in multiple interviews. On her website she identifies her mother and aunt — Virginia Sanchez and Linda Hudes, respectively — as primary influences along with the playwright Paula Vogel, all of whom are listed in the acknowledgments of the published version of *Water by the Spoonful*. Vogel was her mentor at the M.F.A. playwriting program at Brown University where Hudes learned the craft, graduating in 2004, but Hudes's original field of study was music. She initially studied at the Settlement Music School in her native Philadelphia and went on to study music composition at Yale University, graduating in 1999 before embarking on a short-lived stint in a band. Although her musical background is most evident in the adaptability of *In the Heights* and *Vivo* to the musical theater form (and the fact that her memoir is divided into "movements" rather than chapters), her deep understanding and appreciation of it is clearly evident in *Water by the Spoonful*, which includes an extended treatise on the legendary jazz saxophonist John Coltrane.

As a way of inviting a deep engagement with this important playwright, we have included in this chapter some excerpts from other works that might contextualize the play's main concerns: with language, with the troubled legacy of the Iraq War (2003–2011), with music, and finally with the play's main topic, drug addiction. Like some other contemporary plays included in this volume (by Suzan-Lori Parks, p. 1198; Lynn Nottage, p. 1322; and David Auburn, p. 1276), this play is willing to experiment with dramatic conventions in order to get at essential truths of our contemporary world. In particular, Hudes plays with the way we communicate online in the Information Age. While concentrating on identity formation — one of the persistent concerns of contemporary writers, and in fact of playwrights from every era — she merges the conventions of a chat room and the stage. This innovation might initially challenge your reading practices, but you will quickly grow accustomed to the way the characters present themselves online and in person, which is a disparity the play examines. As with all plays, the stage directions and list of characters at the beginning are useful points of navigation if you temporarily get lost. The journey is worth it: *Water by the Spoonful* is engaging, relevant, innovative, and moving drama.

## Quiara Alegría Hudes (b. 1977)

### *Water by the Spoonful* 2012

John Lamparski/Getty Images.

CHARACTERS

*Elliot Ortiz,* an Iraq vet with a slight limp, works at Subway sandwich shop, scores an occasional job as a model or actor, Yazmin's cousin, Odessa's birth son, Puerto Rican, twenty-four.

*Yazmin Ortiz,* in her first year as an adjunct professor of music, Odessa's niece and Elliot's cousin, Puerto Rican, twenty-nine.

*Haikumom,* aka Odessa Ortiz, founder of *www.recover-together.com,* works odd janitorial jobs, lives one notch above squalor, Puerto Rican, thirty-nine.

*Fountainhead,* aka John, a computer programmer and entrepreneur, lives on Philadelphia's Main Line, white, forty-one.

*Chutes&Ladders,* lives in San Diego, has worked a low-level job at the IRS since the Reagan years, his real name is Clayton "Buddy" Wilkie, African American, fifty-six.

*Orangutan,* a recent community college graduate, her real name is Madeleine Mays and before that Yoshiko Sakai, Japanese by birth, thirty-one.

*A Ghost,* also plays Professor Aman, an Arabic professor at Swarthmore; also plays a Policeman in Japan.

SETTING

2009. Six years after Elliot left for Iraq. Philadelphia, San Diego, Japan and Puerto Rico.

The stage has two worlds. The "real world" is populated with chairs. The chairs are from many locations—living rooms, an office, a seminar room, a church, a diner, internet cafés, etc. They all have the worn-in feel of life. A duct-taped La-Z-Boy. Salvaged trash chairs. A busted-up metal folding chair from a rec center. An Aero chair. An Eames chair. A chair/desk from a college classroom. Diner chairs. A chair from an internet café in Japan. Living room chairs. Library chairs. A church pew. Facing in all different directions.

The "online world" is an empty space. A space that connects the chairs.

MUSIC

Jazz. John Coltrane.° The sublime stuff *(A Love Supreme).* And the noise *(Ascension).*

NOTE

Unless specifically noted, when characters are online, don't have actors typing on a keyboard. Treat it like regular conversation rather than the act of writing or typing. They can be doing things people do in the comfort of their home, like eating potato chips, walking around in jammies, cooking, doing dishes, clipping nails, etc.

---

*John Coltrane:* Coltrane (1926–1967) was one of the most important and influential jazz performers and composers of the twentieth century.

## Scene One

*Swarthmore College.° Elliot and Yaz eat breakfast. Elliot wears a Subway sandwich shop polo shirt.*

*Elliot:* This guy ain't coming. How do you know him?

*Yaz:* We're on a committee together.

*Elliot:* My shift starts in fifteen.

*Yaz:* All right, we'll go.

*Elliot:* Five more minutes. Tonight on the way home, we gotta stop by Whole Foods.

*Yaz:* Sure, I need toothpaste.

*Elliot:* You gotta help me with my mom, Yaz.

*Yaz:* You said she had a good morning.

*Elliot:* She cooked breakfast.

*Yaz:* Progress.

*Elliot:* No. The docs said she can't be eating all that junk, it'll mess with her chemo, so she crawls out of bed for the first time in days and cooks eggs for breakfast. In two inches of pork-chop fat. I'm like, Mom, recycle glass and plastic, not grease. She thinks putting the egg on top of a paper towel after you cook it makes it healthy. I told her, Mom, you gotta cook egg whites. In Pam spray. But it has to be her way. Like, "That's how we ate them in Puerto Rico and we turned out fine." You gotta talk to her. I'm trying to teach her about quinoa. Broccoli rabe. Healthy shit. So I get home the other day, she had made quinoa with bacon. She was like, "It's healthy!"

*Yaz:* That's Ginny. The more stubborn she's being, the better she's feeling.

*Elliot:* I gave those eggs to the dogs when she went to the bathroom.

*Yaz (Pulls some papers from her purse):* You wanna be my witness?

*Elliot:* To what?

*(Yaz signs the papers.)*

*Yaz:* My now-legal failure. I'm divorced.

*Elliot:* Yaz. I don't want to hear that.

*Yaz:* You've been saying that for months and I've been keeping my mouth closed. I just need a John Hancock.

*Elliot:* What happened to "trial separation"?

*Yaz:* There was a verdict. William fell out of love with me.

*Elliot:* I've never seen you two argue.

*Yaz:* We did, we just had smiles on our faces.

*Elliot:* That's bullshit. You don't divorce someone before you even have a fight with them. I'm calling him.

*Yaz:* Go ahead.

*Elliot:* He was just texting me about going to the Phillies game on Sunday.

*Yaz:* So, go. He didn't fall out of love with the family, just me.

*Elliot:* I'm going to ask him who he's been screwing behind your back.

*Yaz:* No one, Elliot.

*Elliot:* You were tappin' some extra on the side?

*Yaz:* He woke up one day and I was the same as any other person passing by on the street, and life is short, and you can only live in mediocrity so long.

---

*Swarthmore College:* A private, liberal arts college in Swarthmore, Pennsylvania (near Philadelphia).

*Elliot:* You two are the dog and the owner that look like each other. Ya'll are the *Cosby Show.* Conundrum, Yaz and William make a funny, end-of episode. You show all us cousins, maybe we can't ever do it ourselves, but it *is* possible.

*Yaz:* Did I ever say, "It's possible"?

*Elliot:* By example.

*Yaz:* Did I ever say those words?

*(Professor Aman enters.)*

*Aman:* Yazmin, forgive me. You must be . . .

*Elliot:* Elliot Ortiz. Nice to meet you, I appreciate it.

*Aman:* Professor Aman. *(They shake)* We'll have to make this short and sweet, my lecture begins . . . began . . . well, talk fast.

*Elliot:* Yaz, give us a second?

*Yaz:* I'll be in the car. *(Exits)*

*Elliot:* I'm late, too, so . . .

*Aman:* You need something translated.

*Elliot:* Just a phrase. Thanks, man.

*Aman:* Eh, your sister's cute.

*Elliot:* Cousin. I wrote it phonetically. You grow up speaking Arabic?

*Aman:* English. What's your native tongue?

*Elliot:* Spanglish. *(Hands Aman a piece of paper)*

*Aman:* Mom-ken men fad-luck ted-dini ga-waz saf-far-i. Mom-ken men-fadluck ted-dini gawaz saffari. Am I saying that right?

*Elliot (Spooked):* Spot on.

*Aman:* You must have some familiarity with Arabic to remember it so clearly.

*Elliot:* Maybe I heard it on TV or something.

*Aman:* An odd phrase.

*Elliot:* It's like a song I can't get out of my head.

*Aman:* Yazmin didn't tell me what this is for.

*Elliot:* It's not for anything.

*Aman:* Do you mind me asking, what's around your neck?

*Elliot:* Something my girl gave me.

*Aman:* Can I see? *(Elliot pulls dog tags from under his shirt)* Romantic gift. You were in the army.

*Elliot:* Marines.

*Aman:* Iraq?

*Elliot:* For a minute.

*Aman:* Were you reluctant to tell me that?

*Elliot:* No.

*Aman:* Still in the service?

*Elliot:* Honorable discharge. Leg injury.

*Aman:* When?

*Elliot:* A few years ago.

*Aman:* This is a long time to have a phrase stuck in your head.

*Elliot:* What is this, man?

*Aman:* You tell me.

*Elliot:* It's just a phrase. If you don't want to translate, just say so.

*Aman:* A college buddy is making a film about Marines in Iraq. Gritty, documentary-style. He's looking for some veterans to interview. Get an authentic point of view. Maybe I could pass your number onto him.

*Elliot:* Nope. No interviews for this guy.

*Aman:* You're asking me for a favor. *(Pause)* Yazmin told me you're an actor. Every actor needs a break, right?

*Elliot:* I did enough Q&As about the service. People manipulate you with the questions.

*Aman:* It's not just to interview. He needs a right-hand man, an expert to help him. How do Marines hold a gun? How do they kick in civilian doors, this sort of thing. How do they say "Ooh-rah" in a patriotic manner?

*Elliot:* Are you his headhunter or something?

*Aman:* I'm helping with the translations, I have a small stake and I want the movie to be accurate. And you seem not unintelligent. For a maker of sandwiches. *(Hands him a business card)* He's in L.A. In case you want a career change. I give you a cup of sugar, you give me a cup of sugar.

*Elliot:* If I have a minute, I'll dial the digits. *(Takes the business card)* So what's it mean?

*Aman:* Momken men-fadluck ted-dini gawaz saffari. Rough translation, "Can I please have my passport back?"

## Scene Two

*Odessa's living room and kitchen. She makes coffee. She goes over to her computer, clicks a button. On a screen we see:*

HAIKUMOM, SITEADMIN
STATUS: ONLINE

*Haikumom:* Rise and shine, kiddos, the rooster's a-crowin', it's a beautiful day to be sober. *(No response)* Your Thursday morning haiku:

> if you get restless
> buy a hydrangea or rose
> water it, wait, bloom

*(Odessa continues making coffee. A computer dings and on another screen we see:)*

ORANGUTAN
STATUS: ONLINE

*Orangutan:* Ninety-one days. Smiley face.

*Haikumom (Relieved):* Orangutan! Jesus, I thought my primate friend had disappeared back to the jungle.

*Orangutan:* Disappeared? Yes. Jungle? Happily, no.

*Haikumom:* I'm trying to put a high-five emoticon, but my computer is being a capital B. So, high-five!

*(They high-five in the air. Another computer screen lights up:)*

CHUTES&LADDERS
STATUS: ONLINE

*Chutes&Ladders:* Orangutan? I was about to send a search party after your rear end. Kid, *log on.* No news is bad news.

*Orangutan:* Chutes&Ladders, giving me a hard time as usual. I'd expect nothing less.

*Chutes&Ladders:* Your last post says: "Day One. Packing bags, gotta run," and then you don't log on for three months?

*Orangutan:* I was going to Japan, I had to figure out what shoes to bring.

*Haikumom:* The country?

*Chutes&Ladders:* What happened to Maine?

*Orangutan:* And I quote, "Get a hobby, find a new job, an exciting city, go teach English in a foreign country." Did you guys think I wouldn't take your seasoned advice? I was batting 0 for ten, and for the first time, guys, I feel fucking free.

*Haikumom (Nonjudgmental):* Censored.

*Orangutan:* I wake up and I think, What's the world got up its sleeve today? And I look forward to the answer. So, thank you.

*Chutes&Ladders:* We told you so.

*Orangutan (Playful):* Shut up.

*Haikumom:* You're welcome.

*Orangutan:* I gave my parents the URL. My username, my password. They logged on and read every post I've ever put on here and for once they said they understood. They had completely cut me off, but after reading this site they bought me the plane ticket. One way. I teach English in the mornings. I have a class of children, a class of teens, and a class of adults, most of whom are older than me. I am free in the afternoons. I have a paycheck which I use for legal things like ice cream, noodles and socks. I walk around feeling like maybe I *am* normal. Maybe, just possibly, I'm not that different. Or maybe it's just homeland delusions.

*Chutes&Ladders and Haikumom:* Homeland?

*Haikumom:* You're Japanese?

*Orangutan:* I *was,* for the first eight days of my life. Yoshiko Sakai. Then on day nine I was adopted and moved to Cape Lewiston, Maine, where I became Ma—M.M., and where in all my days I have witnessed *one* other Asian. In the Superfresh. Deli counter.

*Chutes&Ladders:* Japan . . . Wow, that little white rock° sure doesn't discriminate.

*Haikumom:* Amen.

*Orangutan:* Mango Internet Café. I'm sitting in an orange plastic chair, a little view of the Hokkaido waterfront.

*Haikumom:* Japan has a waterfront?

*Chutes&Ladders:* It's an island.

*Haikumom:* Really? Are there beaches? Can you go swimming?

*Orangutan:* The ocean reminds me of Maine. Cold water, very quiet, fisherman, boats, the breeze. I wouldn't try swimming. I'm just a looker. I was never one to actually have an experience.

*Chutes&Ladders:* Ah, the ocean . . . There's only one thing on this planet I'm more scared of than that big blue lady.

*Haikumom:* Let me guess: landing on a sliding board square?

*Chutes&Ladders:* Lol, truer words have never been spoken. You know I was born just a few miles from the Pacific. In the fresh salt air. Back in "those days" I'm at Coronado Beach with a few "friends" doing my "thing" and I get sucked up under this wave. I gasp, I breathe in and my lungs fill with water. I'm like, this is it, I'm going to meet my maker. I had never felt so heavy, not even during my two OD's. I was sinking to the bottom and my head hit the sand like a lead ball. My body just felt like an anvil. The next thing I know there's fingers digging in my ankles. This lifeguard pulls me out, I'm throwing up salt water. I say to him,

---

*little white rock:* An allusion to crack cocaine.

"Hey blondie, you don't know me from Adam but you are my witness: today's the day I start to *live*." And this lifeguard, I mean he was young with these muscles, this kid looks at me like, "Who is this big black dude who can't even doggy paddle?" When I stand up and brush the sand off me, people *applaud*. An old lady touches my cheek and says, "I thought you were done for." I get back to San Diego that night, make one phone call, the next day I'm in my first meeting, sitting in a folding chair, saying the serenity prayer.

*Orangutan:*  I hate to inflate your already swollen ego, but that was a lucid, touching story. By the way, did you get the lifeguard's name? He sounds hot.

*Haikumom:*  Hey Chutes&Ladders, it's never too late to learn. Most YMCAs offer adult swimming classes.

*Chutes&Ladders:*  I'll do the world a favor and stay out of a speedo.

*Orangutan:*  Sober air toast. To lifeguards.

*Chutes&Ladders and Haikumom:*  To lifeguards.

*Orangutan, Chutes&Ladders and Haikumom:*  Clink.

*Haikumom:*  Chutes&Ladders, I'm buying you a pair of water wings.

## Scene Three

*John Coltrane's* A Love Supreme *plays. A Subway sandwich shop on Philadelphia's Main Line. Elliot sits behind the counter. The phone rings. He gets up, hobbles to it—he walks with a limp.*

*Elliot:*  Subway Main Line. Lar! Laaar, what's it doing for you today? Staying in the shade? I got you, how many you need? Listen, the delivery guy's out and my little sports injury is giving me hell so can you pick up? Cool, sorry for the inconvenience. Let me grab a pen. A'ight, pick a hoagie, any hoagie!

*(Elliot begins writing the order.*
  *Lights rise to a seminar room at Swarthmore College. We find Yaz midclass. She hits a button on a stereo and the Coltrane stops playing.)*

*Yaz:*  Coltrane's *A Love Supreme*, 1964. Dissonance is still a gateway to resolution. A B-diminished chord is still resolving to? C-major. A tritone is still resolving up to? The major sixth. Diminished chords, tritones, still didn't have the right to be their own independent thought. In 1965 something changed. The ugliness bore no promise of a happy ending. The ugliness became an end in itself. Coltrane democratized the notes. He said, they're all equal. Freedom. It was called Free Jazz but freedom is a hard thing to express musically without spinning into noise. This is from *Ascension*, 1965.

*(She plays* Ascension. *It sounds uglier than the first sample. In the Subway, a figure comes into view. It is the Ghost.)*

*Ghost:*  Momken men-fadluck ted-dini gawaz saffari?

*(Elliot tries to ignore the Ghost, reading off the order.)*

*Elliot:*  That's three teriyaki onion with chicken. First with hots and onions. Second with everything. Third with extra bacon. Two spicy Italian with American cheese on whole grain. One BMT on flatbread. Good so far?

*Ghost:*  Momken men-fadluck ted-dini gawaz saffari?

*Elliot:*  Five chocolate chip cookies, one oatmeal raisin. Three Baked Lay's, three Doritos. Two Sprite Zeros, one Barq's, one Coke, two orange sodas. How'd I do?

*Ghost:* Momken men-fadluck ted-dini gawaz saffari?

*Elliot:* All right, that'll be ready in fifteen minutes. One sec for your total.

*(Elliot gets a text message. He reads it; his entire demeanor shifts.)*

Lar, I just got a text. There's a family emergency, I can't do this order right now.

*(Elliot hangs up. He exits, limping away.)*

*Yaz:* Oh come on, don't make that face. I know it feels academic. You're going to leave here and become R&B hit makers and Sondheim° clones and never think about this noise again. But this is Coltrane, people, this is not Schoenberg°! This is jazz, stuff people listen to *voluntarily*. Shopping period is still on — go sit in one session of "Germans and Noise" down the hall and you'll come running back begging for this muzak.

*(Yaz turns off the music.)*

In fact, change the syllabus. No listening report next week. Instead, I want you to pinpoint the first time you really noticed dissonance. The composer, the piece, the measures. Two pages analyzing the notes and two pages describing the experience personally. This is your creation myth. Before you leave this school you better figure out that story and cling to it for dear life or you'll be a stockbroker within a year.

I was thirteen, I worked in a corrugated box factory all summer, I saved up enough to find my first music teacher—up to that point I was self-taught, playing to the radio. I walked into Don Rappaport's room at Settlement Music School. He was old, he had jowls, he was sitting at the piano and he said, "What do you do?" I said, "I'm a composer, sir." Presumptuous, right? I sat down and played Mr. Rappaport a Yazmin original. He said, "It's pretty, everything goes together. It's like an outfit where your socks are blue and your pants, shirt, hat are all blue." Then he said, "Play an F-sharp major in your left hand." Then he said, "Play a C-major in your right hand." "Now play them together." He asked me, "Does it go together?" I told him, "No, sir." He said, "Now go home and write." My first music lesson was seven minutes long. I had never really heard dissonance before.

*(Yaz's phone vibrates. She sees the caller with concern.)*

Let's take five.

*(As students file out, Yaz makes a phone call. Lights up on Elliot outside the Subway.)*

What's the bad news? You called three times.

*Elliot:* She's still alive.

*Yaz:* Okay.

*Elliot:* Jefferson Hospital. They admitted her three hours ago. Pop had the courtesy to text me.

*Yaz:* Are you still at work?

---

*Sondheim:* Stephen Sondheim (1930–2021), the recipient of multiple Tony Awards, Grammy Awards, Academy Awards, and the Pulitzer Prize (among many others), was a composer and lyricist widely considered among the most important figures in the American musical theater.

*Schoenberg:* Arnold Schoenberg (1874–1951) was an influential Austrian-born American composer whose innovations changed the direction of classical music.

*Elliot:* Just smashed the bathroom mirror all over the floor. Boss sent me out to the parking lot.
*Yaz:* Wait there. I'm on my way.
*Elliot:* "Your mom is on breathing machine." Who texts that? Who texts that and then doesn't pick up the phone?
*Yaz:* I'll be there within twenty.
*Elliot:* Why did I come to work today?
*Yaz:* She had a good morning. You wanted your thing translated.
*Elliot:* She cooked and I wouldn't eat a bite off the fork. There's a Subway hoagies around the corner and I had to work half an hour away.
*Yaz:* You didn't want your buddies to see you working a normal job.
*Elliot:* Not normal job. Shit job. I'm a butler. A porter of sandwiches.
*Yaz:* Ginny's been to Hades and back, stronger each time.
*Elliot:* What is Hades?
*Yaz:* In Greek mythology, the river through the underworld—
*Elliot:* My mom's on a machine and you're dropping vocab words?!

   *(A ding.)*

*Yaz:* Text message, don't hang up. *(She looks at her phone. A moment, then)* You still there?
*Elliot:* It was my dad wasn't it? Yaz, spit it out.
*Yaz:* It was your dad.
*Elliot:* And? Yaz, I'm about to start walking down Lancaster Avenue for thirty miles till I get back to Philly and I don't care if I snap every wire out my leg and back—I need to get out of here. I need to see Mom, I need to talk to her!
*Yaz:* He said, "Waiting for Elliot till we turn off the machine."

**SCENE FOUR**

*The chat room. A screen lights up:*

FOUNTAINHEAD
STATUS: ONLINE

*Fountainhead:* I've uh, wow, hello there everyone. Delete, delete.
   Good afternoon. Evening. Delete.

   *(Deep breath.)*

   Things I am taking:

   —My life into my own hands.
   —My gorgeous, deserving wife out for our seventh anniversary.

Me: mildly athletic, but work twice as hard. Won state for javelin two years straight. Ran a half marathon last fall. Animated arguer. Two medals for undergrad debate. MBA from Wharton. Beautiful wife, two sons. Built a programming company from the ground up, featured in the *New York Times'* Circuits section, sold it at its peak, bought a yellow Porsche, got a day job to keep myself honest. Salary was 300K, company was run by morons, got laid off, handsome severance, which left me swimming in cash and free time.

Me and crack: long story short, I was at a conference with our CFO and two programmers and a not-unattractive lady in HR. They snorted, invited me to join. A few weeks later that little rock waltzed right into my hand. I've been using off and on since. One eight ball every Saturday, strict rations, portion control. Though the last three or four weeks, it's less like getting high and more like trying to build a time machine. Anything to get back the romance of that virgin smoke.

Last weekend I let myself buy more than my predetermined allotment — I buy in small quantity, because as with my food, I eat what's on my plate. Anyway, I ran over a curb, damaged the underside of my Porsche. Now it's in the shop and I'm driving a rental Mustang. So, not rock bottom but a rental Ford is as close to rock bottom as I'd like to get. Fast forward to tonight. I'm watching my wife's eyelids fall and telling myself, "You are on punishment, Poppa. Daddy's on time out. Do not get out of bed, do not tiptoe down those stairs, do not go down to that basement, do not sit beside that foosball table, do not smoke, and please do not crawl on the carpet looking for one last hit in the fibers."

*(Pause.)*

In kindergarten my son tested into G and T. Gifted and talented. You meet with the school, they tailor the program to the kid. Math, reading, art, whatever the parent chooses. I said, "Teach my son how to learn. How to use a library. How to find original source material, read a map, track down the experts so he becomes an expert." Which gets me to—

You: the experts. It's the first day of school and I'm knocking at your classroom door. I got my No. 2 pencils, I'll sit in the front row, pay attention, and do my homework. No lesson is too basic. Teach me every technique. Any tip so that Saturday doesn't become every day. Any actions that keep you in the driver seat. Healthy habits and rational thoughts to blot out that voice in the back of my head.

Today, I quit. My wife cannot know, she'd get suspicious if I were at meetings all the time. There can be no medical records, so therapy is out. At least it's not heroin, I'm not facing a physical war. It's a psychological battle and I'm armed with two weapons: willpower and the experts.

I'm taking my wife out tomorrow for our seventh anniversary and little does she know that when we clink glasses, I'll be toasting to Day One.

*(Odessa is emotional. Chutes&Ladders and Orangutan seem awestruck.)*

*Orangutan (Clapping):* That was brave.
*Chutes&Ladders:* What. The.
*Haikumom:* Careful.
*Chutes&Ladders:* Fuck.
*Haikumom:* Censored.
*Orangutan:* I'm making popcorn. Oh, this is gonna be fun!
*Chutes&Ladders:* Fountainhead, speaking of experts, I've been meaning to become an asshole. Can you teach me how?
*Haikumom:* Censored!
*Orangutan:* "Tips"? This isn't a cooking website. And what is a half marathon?
*Chutes&Ladders:* Maybe it's something like a half crack addict. Or a half husband.
*Orangutan:* Was that an addiction coming out or an online dating profile? "Married Male Dope Fiend. Smokin' hot."
*Chutes&Ladders:* Fountainhead, you sound like the kind of guy who's read *The 7 Habits of Highly Effective People* cover to cover. Was one of those habits crack? Give the essays a rest and type three words. "I'm. A. Crackhead."

*Orangutan:* You know, adderall is like totes cool. Us crack-heads, we're like yucky and stuff. We're like so nineties. Go try the adderall edge!

*Haikumom:* Hey.

*Orangutan:* The guy's a hoax. Twenty bucks says he's pranking. Let's start a new thread.

*Haikumom:* Hi, Fountainhead, welcome. As the site administrator, I want to honestly congratulate you for accomplishing what so many addicts only hope for: one clean day. Any time you feel like using, log on here instead. It's worked for me. When it comes to junkies, I dug lower than the dungeon. Once upon a time I had a beautiful family, too. Now all I have is six years clean. Don't lose what I lost, what Chutes&Ladders lost.

*Chutes&Ladders:* Excuse me.

*Haikumom:* Orangutan, I just checked and Fountainhead has no aliases and has never logged onto this site before under a different pseudonym, which are the usual markers of a scam.

*Orangutan:* I'm just saying. Who toasts to their first day of sobriety?

*Chutes&Ladders:* I hope it's seltzer in that there champagne glass.

*Orangutan:* Ginger ale, shirley temple.

*Chutes&Ladders:* "A toast, honey. I had that seven-year itch so I became a crackhead."

*Chutes&Ladders and Orangutan:* Clink.

*Haikumom:* Hey, kiddos. Your smiley administrator doesn't want to start purging messages. For rules of the forums click on this link. No personal attacks.

*Orangutan:* We don't come to this site for a pat on the back.

*Haikumom:* I'm just saying. R-e-s-p-e-c-t.

*Chutes&Ladders:* I will always give *crack* the respect it deserves. Some purebred poodle comes pissing on my tree trunk? Damn straight I'll chase his ass out my forest.

*Haikumom:* This here is my forest. You two think you were all humble pie when you started out? Check your original posts.

*Orangutan:* Oh, I know mine. "I-am-scared-I-will-kill-myself-talk-me-off-the-ledge."

*Haikumom:* So unless someone gets that desperate they don't deserve our noble company? "Suffer like me, or you ain't legit"?

*Orangutan:* Haikumom's growing claws.

*Haikumom:* Just don't act entitled because you got so low. *(To Fountainhead)* Sorry. Fountainhead, forgive us. We get very passionate because—

*Chutes&Ladders:* Fountainhead, your Porsche has a massive engine. You got bulging marathon muscles. I'm sure your penis is as big as that javelin you used to throw.

*Haikumom:* Censored.

*Chutes&Ladders:* But none of those things come close to the size of your ego. If you can put that aside, you may, *may* stand a chance. Otherwise, you're fucked, my friend.

*Haikumom:* Message purged.

*Orangutan:* OH MY GOD, WE'RE DYING HERE, DO WE HAVE TO BE SO POLITE ABOUT IT?

*Haikumom:* Censored.

*Orangutan:* Oh my G-zero-D. Democracy or dictatorship?

*Chutes&Ladders:* Hey Fountainhead, why the silence?

*(Fountainhead logs off.)*

*Haikumom:* Nice work, guys. Congratulations.

*Chutes&Ladders:* You don't suppose he's . . . crawling on the carpet looking for one last rock??

*Orangutan:* Lordy lord lord, I'm about to go over his house and start looking for one myself!

*Haikumom:* That's why you're in Japan, little monkey. For now, I'm closing this thread. Fountainhead, if you want to reopen it, email me directly.

## SCENE FIVE

*A flower shop in Center City Philadelphia. Yaz looks over some brochures. Elliot enters, his limp looking worse.*

*Yaz:* I was starting to get worried. How you holding?

*Elliot:* Joe's Gym, perfect remedy.

*Yaz:* You went boxing? Really?

*Elliot:* I had to blow off steam. Women don't get it.

*Yaz:* Don't be a pig. You've had four leg surgeries, no more boxing.

*Elliot:* Did Odessa call?

*Yaz:* You know how she is. Shutting herself out from the world.

*Elliot:* We need help this week.

*Yaz:* And I got your back.

*Elliot:* I'm just saying, pick up the phone and ask, "Do you need anything, Elliot?"

*Yaz:* I did speak to your dad. Everyone's gathering at the house. People start arriving from PR in a few hours. The next door neighbor brought over two trays of pigs feet.

*Elliot:* I just threw up in my mouth.

*Yaz:* Apparently a fight broke out over who gets your mom's pocketbooks.

*Elliot:* Those pleather things from the ten-dollar store?

*Yaz:* Thank you, it's not like she had Gucci purses!

*Elliot:* People just need to manufacture drama.

*Yaz:* He said they were tearing through Ginny's closets like it was a shopping spree. "I want this necklace!" "I want the photo album!" "Yo, those chancletas° are mine!" I'm like, damn, let the woman be buried first.

*Elliot:* Yo, let's spend the day here.

*Yaz (Handing him some papers):* Brochures. I was being indecisive so the florist went to work on a wedding bouquet. I ruled out seven, you make the final call. Celebration of Life, Blooming Garden, Eternity Wreath.

*Elliot:* All of those have carnations. I don't want a carnation within a block of the church.

*Yaz:* You told me to eliminate seven. I eliminated seven. Close your eyes and point.

*Elliot:* Am I a particularly demanding person?

*Yaz:* Yes. What's so wrong with a carnation?

*Elliot:* You know what a carnation says to the world? That they were out of roses at the 7-Eleven. It should look something like Mom's garden.

---

*chancletas:* Flip-flop sandals.

*Yaz (In agreement):* Graveside Remembrances? That looks something like it . . . I'm renominating Graveside Remembrances. Putting it back on the table.

*Elliot:* You couldn't find anything tropical? Yaz, you could find a needle in a damn haystack and you couldn't find a bird of paradise or something?

*Yaz:* He just shoved some brochures in my hand.

*Elliot (Stares her down):* You have an awful poker face.

*Yaz:* Now, look here.

*Elliot:* You did find something.

*Yaz:* No. Not exactly.

*Elliot:* How much does it cost? Yaz, this is my mom we're talking about.

*Yaz:* Five hundred more. Just for the casket piece.

*Elliot:* You can't lie for shit, you never could.

*Yaz:* Orchid Paradise.

*(Yaz hands him another brochure. They look at it together.)*

*Elliot:* Aw damn. Damn. That looks like her garden.

*Yaz:* Spitting image.

*Elliot (Pointing):* I think she grew those.

*Yaz:* Right next to the tomatoes.

*Elliot:* But hers were yellow. Fuck.

*Yaz:* It's very odd to order flowers when someone dies. Because the flowers are just gonna die, too. "Would you like some death with your death?"

*Elliot (A confession):* I didn't water them.

*Yaz (Getting it):* What, are you supposed to be a gardener all of a sudden?

*Elliot:* It doesn't rain for a month and do I grab the hose and water Mom's garden one time?

*Yaz:* You were feeding her. Giving her meds. Bathing her. I could've come over and watered a leaf. A single petal.

*Elliot:* The last four days, she'd wake me up in the middle of the night. "Did you water the flowers?" "Yeah, Mom, just like you told me to yesterday." "Carry me out back, I want to see." "Mom, you're too heavy, I can't carry you down those steps one more time today."

*Yaz:* Little white lies.

*Elliot:* Can you do the sermon?

*Yaz:* This is becoming a second career.

*Elliot:* Because you're the only one who doesn't cry.

*Yaz:* Unlike Julia.

*Elliot (Imitating):* "¡Ay dios mio! ¡Ay! ¡Ay!"

*Yaz:* I hate public speaking.

*Elliot:* You're a teacher.

*Yaz:* It's different when it's ideas. Talking about ideas isn't saying something, it's making syllables with your mouth.

*Elliot:* You love ideas. All you ever wanted to do was have ideas.

*Yaz:* It was an elaborate bait and switch. The ideas don't fill the void, they just help you articulate it.

*Elliot:* You've spoken at city hall. On the radio.

*Yaz:* You're the face of Main Line Chevrolet. *(Pause)* Can I do it in English?

*Elliot:* You could do it in Russian for all I care. I'll just be in the front row acting like my cheek is itchy so no one sees me crying.

*Yaz:* The elders want a good Spanish sermon.

*Elliot:* Mami Ginny was it. You're the elder now.

*Yaz:* I'm twenty-nine.

*Elliot:* But you don't look a day over fifty.

*Yaz:* You gotta do me a favor in return. I know this is your tragedy but . . . Call William. Ask him not to come to the funeral.

*Elliot:* Oh shit.

*Yaz:* He saw the obit in the *Daily News.*

*Elliot:* They were close. Mami Ginny loved that blond hair. She was the madrina of your wedding.

*Yaz:* William relinquished mourning privileges. You fall out of love with me, you lose certain rights. He calls talking about, "I want the condo." Fuck that. Fuck that. Coming from you it won't seem bitter. Wants the fucking condo all for hisself. That I decorated, that I painted. "Oh, and where's the funeral, by the way?" You know, he's been to four funerals in the Ortiz clan and I could feel it, there was a part of him, under it all, that was disgusted. The open casket. The prayers.

*Elliot:* It is disgusting.

*Yaz:* Sitting in the pew knowing what freaks we are.

*Elliot:* He's good people.

*Yaz:* I was probably at his side doing the same thing, thinking I'm removed, that I'm somehow different.

*Elliot:* Hey, hey, done.

*Yaz:* One more condition. I go to Puerto Rico with you. We scatter her ashes together.

*Elliot:* Mami Ginny couldn't be buried in Philly. She had to have her ashes thrown at a waterfall in El Yunque, just to be the most Puerto Rican motherfucker around.

*Yaz:* I saw your Colgate ad.

*Elliot:* Dang, cousin Yaz watches Spanish TV?

*Yaz:* Shut up.

*Elliot:* I walked into the casting office, flashed my pearly whites, showed them my military ID and I charmed them.

*Yaz:* Do it.

*Elliot:* Give me a dollar.

*Yaz:* For that big cheeseburger smile?

(*She gives him a dollar.*)

*Elliot (Smiling):* "Sonrisa, baby!"

(*Yaz cracks up laughing, which devolves into tears.*)

How we gonna pay for Orchid Paradise?

*Yaz:* They should have a frequent-flower card. They punch a hole. Buy nine funeral bouquets, get the tenth free. We'd be living in a house full of lilies. Look at that guy. Arranging his daisies like little treasures. What do you think it's like to be him? To be normal?

*Elliot:* Normal? A hundred bucks says that dude has a closet full of animal porno at home.

*Yaz:* I bet in his family, funerals are rare occasions. I bet he's never seen a cousin get arrested. Let alone one under the age of eighteen. I bet he never saw his eight-year-old cousin sipping rum through a twisty straw or . . . I just remembered this time cousin Maria was babysitting me . . .

*Elliot:* Fat Maria or Buck Tooth Maria?

*Yaz:* Pig.

*Elliot:* Ah, Fat Maria.

*Yaz:* I was dyeing her hair. I had never dyed hair before so I asked her to read me the next step and she handed me the box and said, "You read it." And I said, "My rubber gloves are covered in toxic goop, I can't really hold that right now." And so she held it in front of my eyes and said, "You gonna have to read it because I sure as hell can't."

*Elliot:* I been knowed that.

*Yaz:* I said, "But you graduated from high school." She said, "They just pass you, I just stood in the back." I was in fourth grade. *I* could read! *(Pause)* I have a degree written in Latin that I don't even understand. I paid seventeen thousand dollars for my piano.

*Elliot:* Oh shit.

*Yaz:* I have a mortgage on my piano. Drive two miles north? William told me every time I went to North Philly, I'd come back different. His family has Quaker Oats for DNA. They play Pictionary on New Year's. I'd sit there wishing I could scoop the blood out my veins like you scoop the seeds out a pumpkin and he'd be like, "Whatchu thinking about, honey?" And I'd be like, "Nothing. Let's play some Pictionary."

*Elliot:* Yo, being the scholarship case at an all-white prep school really fucked with your head, didn't it?

*Yaz:* I should've gone to Edison.

*Elliot:* Public school in el barrio. You wouldn't have survived there for a day.

*Yaz:* Half our cousins didn't survive there.

*Elliot:* True. But you would've pissed your pants. At least their pants was dry when they went down.

*Yaz:* You're sick.

*Elliot:* And the ladies love me.

*Yaz:* I thought abuela dying, that would be the end of us. But Ginny grabbed the torch. Christmas, Easter. Now what? Our family may be fucked-up but we had somewhere to go. A kitchen that connected us. Plastic-covered sofas where we could park our communal asses.

*Elliot:* Pop's selling the house. And the plastic-covered sofas. He's moving back to the Bronx, be with his sisters.

*Yaz:* You going with him? *(Elliot shrugs)* Wow. I mean, once that living room is gone, I may never step foot in North Philly again.

*Elliot:* Washed up at age twenty-four. Disabled vet. Motherless chil'. Working at Subway. Soon-to-be homeless.

*Yaz:* My couch is your couch.

*Elliot:* Until William takes your couch.

*Yaz:* My cardboard box is your cardboard box.

*Elliot:* I could go out to L.A. and be a movie star.

*Yaz:* You need a manager? Shoot I'm coming witchu. Forget Philly.

*Elliot:* Change of scene, baby. Dream team.

*Yaz:* Probably we should order some flowers first, though. Don'tcha think? *(Elliot nods. To the florist)* Sir?

SCENE SIX

*The chat room. Orangutan is online, seems upset.*

*Orangutan:* 2:38 A.M. Tuesday. The witching hour.

(*Chutes&Ladders logs on.*)

*Chutes&Ladders:* 1:38 P.M. Monday. The lunch hour.

*Orangutan:* I'm in a gay bar slash internet café in the city of Sapporo. Deafening dance music.

*Chutes&Ladders:* Sure you should be in a bar, little monkey?

*Orangutan (Disappointed):* I flew halfway around the world and guess what? It was still me who got off the plane. (*Taking comfort*) Sapporo is always open. The world turns upside down at night.

*Chutes&Ladders:* You're in a city named after a beer sitting in a bar. Go home.

*Orangutan:* Everything in this country makes sense but me. The noodles in soup make sense. The woodpecker outside my window every evening? Completely logical. The girls getting out of school in their miniskirts and shy smiles? Perfectly natural. I'm floating. I'm a cloud. My existence is one sustained out-of-body experience. It doesn't matter if I change my shoes, there's not a pair I've ever been able to fill. I'm a baby in a basket on an endless river. Wherever I go I don't make sense there.

*Chutes&Ladders:* Hey, little monkey. How many days you got?

*Orangutan:* I think day ninety-six is when the demons really come out to play.

*Chutes&Ladders:* Ninety-six? Girl, hang your hat on that.

*Orangutan:* I really really really want to smoke crack.

*Chutes&Ladders:* Yeah, well *don't*.

*Orangutan:* Distract me from myself. What do you really really really want, Chutes&Ladders?

*Chutes&Ladders:* I wouldn't say no to a new car—my Tercel is one sorry sight.

*Orangutan:* What else?

*Chutes&Ladders:* Tuesday's crossword. On Monday I'm done by the time I sit at my desk. I wish every day could be a Tuesday.

*Orangutan:* What about your son? Don't you really really really want to call him?

*Chutes&Ladders:* By all accounts, having me be a stranger these ten years has given him the best decade of his life.

*Orangutan:* I've known you for how long?

*Chutes&Ladders:* Three Christmas Eves. When you logged on you were a stone-cold user. We sang Christmas carols online all night. Now you've got ninety days.

*Orangutan:* Can I ask you a personal question? What's your day job?

*Chutes&Ladders:* IRS. GS4 paper pusher.

*Orangutan:* Got any vacation days?

*Chutes&Ladders:* A solid collection. I haven't taken a vacation in ten years.

*Orangutan:* Do you have money?

*Chutes&Ladders:* Enough to eat steak on Friday nights. Enough to buy pay-per-view boxing.

*Orangutan:* Yeah, I bet that's all the pay-per-view you buy. (*Pause*) Enough money to fly to Japan?

(*Pause.*)

*Chutes&Ladders:* You should know I'm fifty years old on a good day. I eat three and a half doughnuts for breakfast and save the remaining half for brunch. I have small hands, six toes on my left foot. And my face resembles a corgi.

*Orangutan:* If I was looking for a hot screw I wouldn't be logging on to this site.

*Chutes&Ladders:* Damn, was it something I said?

*Orangutan (With honest admiration):* I've been on this planet for thirty-one years and you're the only person I've ever met who's more sarcastic than I am yet still believes in God.

*Chutes&Ladders (Taking the compliment):* Says the agnostic.

*Orangutan:* The atheist. Who is very envious of believers. My brain is my biggest enemy—always arguing my soul into a corner. *(Pause)* I like you. Come to Japan. We can go get an ice cream. I can show you the countryside.

*Chutes&Ladders:* I don't have a passport. If my Tercel can't drive there, I generally don't go.

*Orangutan:* Come save me in Japan. Be my knight in shining armor.

*Chutes&Ladders:* I'll admit, I'm a dashing concept. If you saw my flesh and blood, you'd be disappointed.

*Orangutan:* I see my flesh and blood every day and I've learned to live with the disappointment.

*Chutes&Ladders:* I'm the squarest of the square. I live in a square house on a square block watching a square box eating square-cut fries.

*Orangutan:* I get it. You were the kid who colored inside the lines.

*Chutes&Ladders:* No, I was the kid who ate the crayons. *Was.* I went clean and all personality left my life. Flew right out the window. I had to take life on life's terms. Messy, disappointing, bad shit happens to good people, coffee stains on my necktie, boring life.

*Orangutan:* Maybe we could hang out and have a relationship that has very little to do with crack or addiction or history. We could watch DVDs and microwave popcorn and take walks on the waterfront while we gossip about celebrities. It could be the land of the living.

*Chutes&Ladders:* Stay in the box. Keep things in their place. It's a simple, effective recipe for ten clean years.

*Orangutan:* Forget simple. I want a goddamn challenge.

*Chutes&Ladders:* You're in recovery and work in a foreign country. That's a challenge.

*Orangutan:* No. No it's fucking not. Not if I just stay anonymous and alone. Like every day of my shit life so far. A friend, the kind that is nice to you and you are nice to in return. *That* would push the comfort zone. The invitation is open. Come tear my shyness open.

*Chutes&Ladders:* All right, now you're being weird. Can we change the subject?

*(Haikumom appears. She's reading the newspaper.)*

*Haikumom:* Orangutan, cover your ears.

*Orangutan:* Big Brother, always watching.

*Haikumom:* Cover your ears, kiddo.

*Orangutan:* That doesn't really work online.

*Haikumom:* Okay, Chutes and Ladders, can we g-chat? One on one?

*Orangutan:* Come on! No talking behind backs.

*Haikumom:* Fine. Chutes&Ladders, you listening?

*Chutes&Ladders:* Lord have mercy spit it out.

*Haikumom:* Orangutan may be immature . . .

*Orangutan:* Hey.

*Haikumom:* She may be annoying at times . . .

*Orangutan:* What the f ?

*Haikumom:* She may be overbearing and self-obsessed and a little bit of a concern troll and she can type faster than she can think which often leads to diarrhea of the keyboard—

*Chutes&Ladders:* Your point?

*Haikumom:* But she's telling you, "Be my friend." When's the last time someone opened your closet door, saw all them skeletons, and said, "Wassup?! Can I join the party?"

*Chutes&Ladders:* All right, my wrist is officially slapped. Thank you, oh nagging wives.

*Haikumom:* Internal Revenue Service, 300 North Los Angeles Street 90012? Is that you?

*Chutes&Ladders:* Need my name, too? It's Wilkie. I'll leave it at that.

*Haikumom:* I'm sending you a care package. Orangutan, you can uncover your ears now. I love you.

*Orangutan:* Middle finger.

*(Fountainhead's log-on appears.)*

*Fountainhead:* Hey all, thanks for the warm two-by-four to my head.

*Haikumom:* All right, look who's back.

*Fountainhead:* Knives sharpened? Last night we ran out of butter while my wife was cooking and she sent me to the store and it took every bit of strength I could summon not to make a "wrong turn" to that parking lot I know so well. I got the butter and on the car ride home, I couldn't help it, I drove by the lot, and there was my dealer in the shadows. My brain went on attack. "Use one more time just to prove you won't need another hit tomorrow." I managed to keep on driving and bring the butter home. Major victory. And my wife pulls it out of the plastic bag and says, "This is unsalted. I said salted." Then she feels guilty so she says never mind, never mind, she'll just add a little extra salt to the pie crust but I insist. "No, no, no, my wife deserves the right kind of butter and she's gonna get it!" I mean, I bark it, I'm already halfway out the door, my heart was racing all the way to the parking lot and raced even harder when I sat in the car and smoked. So, Michael Jordan is benched with a broken foot. But he'll come back in the finals.

*Haikumom:* Thanks for the update, Fountainhead. You may not believe this, but we were missing you and worried about you. Don't beat yourself up about the slip. You had three days clean. This time you'll make it to day four.

*Fountainhead:* Be ambitious. Why not reach for a whopping five?

*Orangutan:* Maybe you'll make it to day thirty if you tell your wife.

*Fountainhead:* I told you, I have my reasons, I cannot do that. My wife has some emotional issues.

*Orangutan (Sarcastic):* No!

*Fountainhead:* Listen? Please? Are you capable of that? She's in therapy twice a week. Depression, manic. I don't want to be the reason she goes down a tailspin. I actually have her best interest in mind.

*Chutes&Ladders:* Yawn.

*Fountainhead:* Ah, Chutes&Ladders. I could feel you circling like a vulture. Weigh in, by all means.

*Chutes&Ladders:* And I repeat. Yawn.

*Fountainhead:* Chutes&Ladders, why do I get the feeling you'd be the first in line for tickets to watch me smoke again? That you'd be in the bleachers cheering if I relapse?

*Chutes&Ladders:* How can you relapse when you don't even think you're addicted?

*Fountainhead:* If you read my original post clearly, I wrote that it's a psychological addiction, not like heroin.

*Chutes&Ladders:* Well see then, you're not a junkie after all.

*Fountainhead:* What is this, first-grade recess?

*Chutes&Ladders:* No, this is a site for crackheads trying not to be crackheads anymore. If you're not a crackhead, leave, we don't want you, you are irrelevant, get off my lawn, go.

*Haikumom:* Chutes&Ladders, please.

*Chutes&Ladders:* I got this.

*Orangutan:* He's still logged on.

*Chutes&Ladders:* Hey Fountainhead, why did you come to this website?

*Fountainhead:* Because I thoroughly enjoy getting shit on.

*Haikumom:* Censored.

*Chutes&Ladders:* Why do you want to be here?

*Fountainhead:* Want? The two times I've logged on here I've *wanted* to vomit.

*Chutes&Ladders:* Well? Did you receive some sort of invitation? Did one of us ask you here?

*Fountainhead:* Look, I'm the first to say it. I have a problem.

*Chutes&Ladders:* Adam had problems. Eve had problems. Why are *you here*?

*Fountainhead:* To get information.

*Chutes&Ladders:* Go to Wikipedia. Why are you *here*?

*Fountainhead:* Because I smoke crack.

*Chutes&Ladders:* Go to a dealer. Why are you here?

*Fountainhead:* Because I plan to stop smoking crack.

*Chutes&Ladders:* Fine, when your son has a tummy-ache in the middle of the night and walks in on you tweaking and geeking just tell him, "Don't worry, Junior, Daddy's sucking on a glass dick—"

*Haikumom (Overlaps):* Hey!

*Chutes&Ladders:* "—but Daddy makes 300K and this is all a part of Daddy's Plan!"

*Fountainhead:* I'M A FUCKING CRACKHEAD.

*Haikumom (Apologetic):* Censored.

*Fountainhead:* Fuck you, Chutes&Ladders.

*Haikumom:* Bleep.

*Fountainhead:* Fuck you . . . Don't talk about my sons. Don't fucking talk about my boys.

*Haikumom:* Bleep again.

*Fountainhead:* Are you happy, Chutes&Ladders?

*Chutes&Ladders:* Absolutely not, my friend. I'm a crackhead, too, and I wouldn't wish it on my worst enemy.

*Fountainhead:* And I *made* 300K, I'm currently unemployed. An unemployed crackhead. At least I still have all my teeth. *(They laugh)* Better than I can say for my dealer.

*Chutes&Ladders (Being a friend):* Ex-dealer, man.

*Fountainhead:* Ex-dealer. Thank you.

*Haikumom:* Fountainhead, welcome to the dinner party. Granted, it's a party we never wanted to be invited to, but pull up a chair and pass the salt. Some people here may pour it in your wounds. Just like you, we've all crawled on the floor with a flashlight. We've thrown out the brillo and bought some more. But guess what? You had three days. For three days straight, you didn't try to kill yourself on an hourly basis. Please. Talk to your wife about your addiction. You need every supporting resource. You are in for the fight of your life. You mentioned Wharton. I live in Philly. If you're still in the area and you have an emergency or even a craving, email me directly. Any time of night. Don't take it lightly when I say a sober day for you is a sober day for me. I know you can do this but I know you can't do it alone. So stop being a highly functioning isolator and start being a highly dysfunctional *person.* The only way out it is through it.

*Orangutan (Nostalgic):* Slogans . . .

*Haikumom:* Ya'll know I know 'em all.

*Chutes&Ladders:* They saved my life.

*Orangutan:* Your personal favorite. Go.

*Haikumom:* "Nothing changes if nothing changes."

*(Elliot appears at the boxing gym, punching a bag. The Ghost watches him.)*

*Ghost:* Momken men-fadluck ted-dini gawaz saffari?

*Orangutan:* "It came to pass, it didn't come to stay."

*Fountainhead:* "I obsessively pursue feeling good, no matter how bad it makes me feel."

*Chutes&Ladders:* Okay, now!

*Orangutan:* Nice!

*Haikumom:* Rookie don't play!

*Ghost:* Momken men-fadluck ted-dini gawaz saffari?

*Orangutan:* "One hit is too many, one thousand never enough."

*Haikumom:* "Have an at-ti-tude of gra-ti-tude."

*Chutes&Ladders:* "If you are eating a shit sandwich, chances are you ordered it."

*Orangutan:* Ding ding ding. We have a winner!

*Haikumom:* Censored. But good one.

*Ghost:* Momken men-fadluck ted-dini gawaz saffari?

*Haikumom (Turning a page in the paper):* Oh shit!

*Orangutan:* CENSORED!!!!!! YES!!!!!! Whoooooo!

*Haikumom:* You got me.

*Orangutan (Victorious):* You know how long I've been waiting to do that?!

*Haikumom:* My sister Ginny's in the *Daily News!* A nice big picture!

*Ghost:* Momken men-fadluck ted-dini gawaz saffari?

*Haikumom:* "Eugenia P. Ortiz, A Force For Good In Philadelphia!" Okay, now!

*(Elliot punches harder. His leg is starting to bother him.)*

*Elliot:* Your leg feels great. Your leg feels like a million bucks. No pain. No pain.

*Haikumom:* "In lieu of flowers contributions may be made to . . ."

*(Haikumom drops the newspaper.*
*The Ghost blows on Elliot, knocking him to the floor.)*

*Ghost:* Momken men-fadluck ted-dini gawaz saffari?

*(Intermission.)*

## Scene Seven

*A diner. Odessa and John, aka Fountainhead, sit in a booth.*

**Odessa:** To lapsed Catholics. *(They clink coffee mugs)* And you thought we had nothing in common.

**John:** When did you become interested in Buddhism?

**Odessa:** My older brother used to terrorize me during mass. He would point to a statue, tell me about the evil spirit hiding behind it. Fangs, claws. I thought Saint Lazarus was gonna come to life and suck my eyes out. Buddhism? Not scary. If there's spirits, they're hiding inside you.

**John:** Aren't those the scariest kind?

**Odessa:** So, how many days do you have? It should be two now.

**John:** I put my sons' picture on my cell phone so if I get the urge, I can just look at them instead.

**Odessa:** How many days?

**John (Small talk):** I love Puerto Rico. On my honeymoon we stayed at that hotel in Old San Juan, the old convent. *(Odessa shrugs)* And that Spanish fort at the top of the city? El Morro?

**Odessa:** I've always been meaning to make it there.

**John:** There are these keyholes where the cannons used to fit, and the view of the waves through them, you can practically see the Spanish armada approaching.

**Odessa:** I mean, one of these days I've gotta make it to PR.

**John:** Oh. I just figured . . .

**Odessa:** The Jersey Shore. Atlantic City. The Philadelphia airport. Oh, I've been places.

**John:** On an actual plane?

**Odessa:** I only fly first-class, and I'm still saving for that ticket.

*(Odessa's cell phone rings.)*

**John:** You're a popular lady.

**Odessa (Into her phone, her demeanor completely changing):** What? I told you, the diner on Spring Garden and Third. I'm busy, come in an hour. One hour. Now stop calling me and asking fucking directions. *(She hangs up)*

**John:** Says the one who censors.

**Odessa:** My sister died.

**John:** Right. You sure you're okay?

**Odessa:** She's dead, ain't nothing left to do. People act like the world is going to fall apart.

**John:** You write very Zen messages. And yet.

**Odessa:** My family knows every button to push.

**John:** My condolences. *(Pause)* You don't strike me as a computer nerd. I used to employ an entire floor of them.

**Odessa:** You should've seen me at first, pecking with two fingers. Now I'm like an octopus with ten little tentacles. In my neck of the woods staying clean is like trying to tap-dance on a minefield. The website fills the hours. So how are we gonna fill yours, huh? When was the last time you picked up a javelin?

**John:** Senior year of high school.

**Odessa (Hands him a sheet of paper):** There's a sober softball league. Fairmount Park, games on Sundays. Sober bowling on Thursdays.

*John:* I lied in my first post. I've been smoking crack for two years. I've tried quitting hundreds of times. Day two? Please, I'm in the seven-hundredth day of hell.

*Odessa:* You got it out of your system. Most people lie at one time or another on the site. The good news is, two years in, there's still time. *(Hands him another sheet of paper)* Talbott Recovery Center in Atlanta. It's designed for professionals with addictions. Paradise Recovery in Hawaii. They actually check your income before admitting you. Just for the wealthy. This place in Jersey, it's right over the bridge, they have an outpatient program for professionals like you.

*John:* I'm tenacious. I'm driven. I love my parents.

*Odessa:* Pitchforks against tanks.

*John:* I relish in paying my taxes.

*Odessa:* And you could be dead tomorrow. *(Pause)* Is your dealer male or female?

*John:* I had a few. Flushed their numbers down the toilet like you suggested.

*Odessa:* Your original connection. The one who got you hooked.

*John:* Female.

*Odessa:* Did you have sex with her?

*John:* You don't beat around the bush do you?

*Odessa:* I'll take that as a yes. *(No answer)* Do you prefer sex when you're high to sex when you're sober?

*John:* I've never really analyzed it.

*Odessa:* It can be a dangerous cocktail. Some men get off on smoking and fucking.

*John:* All men get off on fucking.

*Odessa:* Are you scared your wife will find out you're addicted to crack? Or are you scared she'll find out what came of your wedding vows?

*John:* I should go.

*Odessa:* We just ordered.

*John:* I promised my son. There's a science fair tomorrow. Something about dioramas and crazy glue.

*Odessa:* Don't talk about them. Get sober for them.

*John:* Fuck you.

*Odessa:* Leave me three bucks for your coffee cuz I ain't got it.

*(He stands, pulls out three dollars. She throws the money back at him.)*

You picked up the phone and called me.

*John (He sits down again):* I don't know how to do this. I've never done this before.

*Odessa:* I have and it usually doesn't end up so good. One in twenty, maybe, hang around. Most people just don't write one day and then thirty days and then you're wondering . . . And sometimes you get the answer. Cuz their wife looks on their computer and sees the website and logs on and writes, "I found him face down in the snow."

*John:* How many day ones did you have?

*Odessa:* Seven years' worth.

*John:* Do you still crave?

*Odessa:* On the good days, only every hour. Would you rather be honest with your wife, or would you rather end up like me? *(Pause)* That wasn't rhetorical.

*John:* You're not exactly what I wanted to be when I grew up.

*Odessa:* Truth. Now we're talking.

> *(Elliot and Yaz enter.)*

*Yaz:* There she is.

> *(Elliot and Yaz sit down in the booth.)*

*Elliot:* You were supposed to meet us at the flower place.

*Yaz:* The deposit was due at nine.

*Odessa:* My alarm clock didn't go off.

*Elliot:* Were you up on that chat room all night?

*Odessa (Ignoring him, to a waiter, off):* Can I get a refill, please?

*Elliot:* Where's the money?

*Odessa:* I told you I don't have any money.

*Elliot:* And you think I do? I been paying for Mami Ginny's meds for six months straight—

*Odessa:* Well get it from Yaz's mom.

*Yaz:* My mom put in for the headstone. She got an expensive one.

*Odessa:* Headstone? She's getting cremated.

*Yaz:* She still needs a proper Catholic piece of granite. Right beside abuela, right beside your dad and sister and brother.

*Elliot:* And daughter.

*Yaz:* Everyone agreed.

*Odessa:* No one asked my opinion.

*Elliot:* Everyone who showed up to the family meeting.

*Odessa:* I wasn't invited.

*Yaz:* I texted you twice.

*Odessa:* I was out of minutes.

*Elliot:* We just spoke on the phone.

*Odessa:* Whatchu want me to do, Elliot, if I say I ain't got no fucking money, I ain't got no money.

*John:* Hi, I'm John, nice to meet you.

*Yaz:* Yazmin.

*Elliot:* You one of Mom's rehab buddies?

*John:* We know each other from work.

*Elliot:* You scrub toilets?

*Odessa (To John):* I'm a practitioner of the custodial arts.

*Elliot:* Is she your sponsor?

*John (To Odessa):* I thought this was going to be a private meeting.

*Elliot:* I'm her son.

*John (To Odessa):* You must have been young.

*Elliot:* But I was raised by my Aunt Ginny and that particular aunt just died. *(To Odessa)* So now, you got three hours to find some money to pay for one basket of flowers in the funeral of the woman who changed my pampers.

*Yaz:* We're all supposed to be helping out.

*Odessa:* You both know I run out of minutes all the time. No one could be bothered to drive by and tell me face to face?

*Elliot:* Because you always bothered to drive by and say hello to Mami Ginny when you knew she was sick? Because you bothered to hit me up one time this week and say, "Elliot, I'm sorry your mom died."

*Odessa:* You still got one mom alive.

*Elliot:* Really? You want to go there?

*Yaz:* The flower place needs the money today.

*Odessa:* She was my sister and you are my son, too.

*Yaz:* Guys. Two hundred dollars by end of business day.

*Odessa:* That's my rent.

*Elliot:* Then fifty.

*Odessa:* I just spent fifty getting my phone back on.

*Elliot:* Ten dollars. For the woman who raised your son! Do we hear ten dollars? Going once!

*Odessa:* I spent my last ten at the post office.

*Elliot:* Going twice!

*(John goes into his wallet.)*

*John:* Here's fifty.

*(They all look at him like he's crazy. He pulls out some more money.)*

Two hundred?

*(Elliot pushes the money back to John with one pointer finger, as if the bills might be contaminated.)*

*Elliot:* No offense, I don't take money from users.

*John:* I'm not . . . I think that was my cue.

*Odessa:* Sit down. My son was just going.

*Elliot:* Did World's Best Mom here tell you about her daughter?

*Odessa:* I'm about to throw this coffee in your fucking face.

*Yaz:* Come on, Elliot, I'll pay for the flowers.

*(Elliot doesn't get up.)*

*Elliot:* I looked at that chat room once. The woman I saw there? She's literally not the same person I know. *(To John)* Did she tell you how she became such a saint?

*John:* We all have skeletons.

*Elliot:* Yeah well she's an archaeological dig. Did she tell you about her daughter?

*Odessa (Suddenly resigned):* Go ahead, I ain't got no secrets.

*Yaz (Getting up):* Excuse me.

*Elliot:* Sit here and listen, Yaz. You were born with a silver spoon and you need to know how it was for me.

*Yaz:* I said I'd pay for the goddamn flowers so LET'S GO. NOW!

*Elliot:* My sister and I had the stomach flu, right? For a whole day we couldn't keep nothing down.

*Odessa:* Three days . . . You were vomiting three days straight.

*Elliot:* Medicine, juice, anything we ate, it would come right back up. *(To John)* Your co-worker here took us to Children's Hospital.

*Odessa:* Jefferson.

*Elliot:* It was wall-to-wall packed. Every kid in Philly had this bug. ERs were turning kids away. They gave us a flier about stomach flu and sent us home. Bright blue paper. Little cartoon diagrams. It said give your kids a spoonful of water every five minutes.

*Odessa:* A teaspoon.

*Elliot:* A small enough amount that they can keep it down. Five minutes. Spoon. Five minutes. Spoon. I remember thinking, Wow, this is it. Family time. Quality time. Just the three of us. Because it was gentle, the way you said,

"Open up." I opened my mouth, you put that little spoon of water into my mouth. That little bit of relief. And then I watched you do the same thing with my little sister. And I remember being like, "Wow, I love you, Mom. My moms is all right." Five minutes. Spoon. Five minutes. Spoon. But you couldn't stick to something simple like that. You couldn't sit still like that. You had to have your thing. That's where I stop remembering.

*Odessa:*  I left.

*Elliot:*  A Department of Human Services report. That's my memory. Six hours later a neighbor kicks in the door. Me and my sister are lying in a pile of laundry. My shorts was all messed up. And what I really don't remember is my sister. Quote: "Female infant, approximately two years, pamper and tear ducts dry, likely cause of death, dehydration." Cuz when you dehydrate you can't form a single tear.

*John (To Elliot):*  I'm very sorry . . . *(He puts some money on the table)* For the coffee. *(Exits)*

*Elliot:*  That's some friend you got there.

*(Pause.)*

*Yaz:*  Mary Lou. We can at least say her name out loud. Mary Lou. Mary Lou. *(To Odessa)* One time you came to babysit me, you brought Elliot and Mary Lou — she was still in pampers — and Mary Lou had this soda from 7-Eleven. She didn't want to give me a sip. You yelled at her so bad, you totally cursed her out and I said, "You're not supposed to yell at people like that!" And you said, "No, Yaz, let her cry. She's gotta learn that ya'll are cousins, ya'll are flesh and blood, and we share everything. You hear me, Yaz? In this family we share *everything.*" You walked out of the room, came back from the kitchen with four straws in your hand, sat us down on the floor in a circle, pointed to me and said, "You first." I sipped. "Elliot's turn." He sipped. "Mary Lou's turn." She sipped. Then you sipped. You made us do like that, taking turns, going around the circle, till the cup was empty.

*(Odessa hands Elliot a key.)*

*Odessa:*  The pawn shop closes at five. Go into my house. Take my computer. Pawn it. However much you get, put towards a few flowers, okay?

*(Odessa exits.)*

### SCENE EIGHT

*Split scene:  Odessa's living room and the chat room.*
*Chutes&Ladders holds a phone.*

*Orangutan:*  Did you hit the call button yet?

*Chutes&Ladders:*  I'm working on it.

*Orangutan:*  Where are you? Are you at home?

*Chutes&Ladders:*  *Jeopardy!*'s on mute.

*Orangutan:*  Dude, turn off the tube. This is serious. Did you even dial?

*Chutes&Ladders:*  Yeah, yeah. *(He does)* All right, it's ringing. What am I going to say?

*Orangutan:*  "Hi, Son, it's Dad."

*Chutes&Ladders:* Wendell. That's his name. *(Hangs up)* No answer.

*Orangutan:* As in, you hung up?

*Chutes&Ladders:* Yes. I hung up.

*Orangutan:* Dude, way too quick!

*Chutes&Ladders:* What do you have, a stopwatch? Do you know the average time before someone answers a telephone?

*Orangutan:* 3.2 rings.

*Chutes&Ladders:* According to . . .

*Orangutan:* I don't reveal my sources.

*Chutes&Ladders:* Look, my son's a grown man with a good life.

*Orangutan:* Quit moping and dial Wendell's number.

*Chutes&Ladders:* This Japan thing is cramping my style. Different networks, different time zones. No concurrent *Jeopardy!* watching.

*Orangutan:* Deflection: nostalgia.

*Chutes&Ladders:* Humor me.

*Orangutan (Humoring him):* How's my little Trebeky° doing?

*Chutes&Ladders:* He's had work done. Man looks younger than he did twenty years ago.

*Orangutan:* Needle or knife?

*Chutes&Ladders:* Needle. His eyes are still in the right place.

*Orangutan:* Well, it's working. Meow. Purrrrr. Any good categories?

*Chutes&Ladders:* Before and After.

*Orangutan:* I love Before and After! But I'll go with . . . Quit Stalling for two hundred. *(She hums the* Jeopardy! *theme)*

*Chutes&Ladders:* It's ringing.

*Orangutan:* My stopwatch is running.

*Chutes&Ladders:* Still ringing.

*Orangutan:* You're going to be great.

*Chutes&Ladders:* It rang again.

*Orangutan:* You're a brave soul.

> *(We hear a man's voice at the other end of the line say, "Hello?"*
> *Chutes&Ladders hangs up.)*

*Chutes&Ladders:* He must not be around.

*Orangutan:* Leave a voice mail.

*Chutes&Ladders:* Maybe next time.

> *(Chutes&Ladders logs off.)*

*Orangutan:* Hey! Don't log off, come on. Chutes&Ladders. "Whatever happened to tough love? Log back on, we'll do a crossword. You can't fly before "Final Jeopardy!" Sigh. Anyone else online? Haikumom? I'm still waiting for that daily poem . . . Bueller? Bueller?°

> *(In Odessa's living room, Elliot and Yaz enter.)*

*Yaz:* Wow, look at that computer. Stone age.

*Elliot:* Fred Flinstone shit.

*Yaz:* Positively Dr. Who.

---

*Trebeky:* Alex Trebek (1940–2020) was the longtime host of the TV game show *Jeopardy!*

*Bueller:* Allusion to the popular 1986 movie *Ferris Bueller's Day Off,* this line is spoken by a teacher to a silent, unresponsive class.

*Elliot:* Dr. Who?

*Yaz:* That computer is actually worse than what they give the adjuncts at Swarthmore.

*Elliot:* What does "adjunct" even mean?

*Yaz:* Exactly. It's the nicest thing she owns.

*Elliot:* Let's not act like this is some heroic sacrifice. Like this makes her the world's martyr.

*Yaz:* We're not going to get more than fifteen bucks for it.

*Elliot:* Symbols matter, Yaz. This isn't about the money. This is shaking hands. This is tipping your hat. This is holding the door open. This is the bare minimum, the least effort possible to earn the label "person." *(Looks at the screen)* What do you think her password is? *(Types)* "Odessa." Nope. "Odessaortiz." Nope.

*Yaz:* It's probably Elliot.

*(He types. Haikumom's log-on appears.)*

*Elliot:* The irony.

*Yaz:* I think legally that might be like breaking and entering.

*Elliot (Typing):* Hello? Oh shit it posted.

*Orangutan:* Haikumom! Hit me with those seventeen syllables, baby!

*Yaz:* Haikumom? What the hell is that?

*Elliot:* Her username. She has the whole world thinking she's some Chinese prophet.

*Yaz:* Haiku are Japanese.

*Elliot:* "Haiku are Japanese." *(Typing)* Hello, Orangutan. How are you?

*Orangutan (Formal):* I am fine. How are you?

*Elliot (Typing):* So, I guess you like monkeys, huh?

*Orangutan:* An orangutan is a primate.

*Yaz:* Elliot.

*Elliot:* Chill.

*Orangutan:* And this primate has ninety-eight days. That deserves a poem, don't you think?

*Elliot (Typing):* I don't have a poem, but I have a question. What does crack feel like?

*Orangutan:* What?

*Yaz:* Elliot, cut it out.

*Elliot (Typing):* Sometimes I'm amazed I don't know first-hand.

*Orangutan:* Who is this?

*Elliot (Typing):* How does it make your brain feel?

*Orangutan:* Like it's flooded with dopamine. Listen, cyber-stalker, if you came here for shits and giggles, we are a sadly unfunny bunch.

*Elliot (Typing):* Are you just a smoker or do you inject it right into your eyeballs?

*Orangutan:* Who the fuck is this?

*Elliot (Typing):* Haikumom.

*Orangutan:* Bullshit, you didn't censor me. Quit screwing around, hacker, who are you?

*Yaz:* You think Ginny would want you acting this way?

*Elliot:* I think Mami Ginny would want Mami Odessa to pay for a single flower on her fucking casket.

*Yaz (Types):* This is not Haikumom. It's her son.

*Orangutan:* Well, if you're looking for the friends and family thread, you have to go to the home page and create a new log-on. This particular forum is for people actually in recovery. Wait, her son the actor? From the Crest ad?

*Elliot (Typing):* Colgate.

*Orangutan:* "Sonrisa baby!" I saw that on YouTube! Your teeth are insanely white. Ever worked in Hollywood?

*Elliot (Typing):* Psh. I just had this guy begging me to do a feature film. Gritty, documentary-style, about Marines in Iraq. I just don't want to do anything cheesy.

*Orangutan:* So you're the war hero . . .

*Elliot (Typing):* Haikumom brags.

*Orangutan:* How's your recovery going? *(No answer)* This is the crack forum, but there's a really good pain-meds forum on this site, too. Link here.

*Yaz:* What is she talking about?

*Orangutan:* There's a few war vets on that forum, just like you. You'd be in good company.

*Yaz:* Pain meds? Elliot? *(He doesn't respond. Yaz types)* What are you talking about?

*Orangutan:* Haikumom told us about your history.

*Yaz (Typing):* What history?

*Orangutan:* Sorry. Maybe she told us in confidence.

*Elliot:* Confidence? They call this shit "world wide" for a reason.

*Yaz (Typing):* I can search all the threads right now.

*Orangutan:* That you had a bunch of leg surgeries in Iraq. That if a soldier said they hurt, the docs practically threw pills at them. That you OD'd three times and were in the hospital for it. She was real messed up about it. I guess she had hoped the fruit would fall a little farther from the tree.

*Yaz (To Elliot):* Is this true?

*Elliot:* I wasn't a soldier. I was a Marine. Soldiers is the army.

*Yaz:* Oh my god.

*Elliot (Takes the keyboard, types):* What I am: sober. What I am not and never will be: a pathetic junkie like you.

*(He unplugs the computer. He throws the keyboard on the ground. He starts unplugging cables violently.)*

*Yaz:* Hold on. Just stop it, Elliot! Stop it!

*Elliot:* The one time I ever reached out to her for anything and she made me a story on a website.

*Yaz:* Why wouldn't you ask me for help? Why would you deal with that alone?

*Elliot:* The opposite of alone. I seen barracks that looked like dope houses. It was four months in my life, it's over. We've chopped up a lot of shit together, Yaz, but we ain't gonna chop this up. This shit stays in the vault. You got me?

*Yaz:* No!

*Elliot:* Yaz. *(He looks her straight in the eye)* Please. Please.

*Yaz:* I want to grab the sky and smash it into pieces. Are you clean?

*Elliot:* The only thing I got left from those days is the nightmares. That's when he came, and some days I swear he ain't never gonna leave.

*Yaz:* Who?

*(Elliot tries to walk away from the conversation, but the Ghost is there, blocking his path.)*

Who?!

*Elliot (Almost like a child):* Please, Yaz. Please end this conversation. Don't make me beg, Yaz.

*Yaz:* The pawn shop closes in fifteen minutes. I'll get the monitor, you grab the computer.

SCENE NINE

*Chutes&Ladders is at work, on his desk phone. A bundled pile of mail is on his desk. He takes off the rubber band, browses. Junk, mostly.*

*Chutes&Ladders (Into the work phone):* That's right. Three , Ws. Dot. Not the word, the punctuation mark. I-R-S. Not "F" like flamingo; "S" like Sam. Dot. Yup, another one. Gov. Grover orange victor.

*(Orangutan appears, online.)*

*Orangutan:* I'm doing it. I'm almost there. *And* I can chat! Japan is so advanced. Internet cafés are like parking meters here.

*Chutes&Ladders:* Where are you and what are you doing?

*Orangutan:* Sapporo train station. Just did some research. Get this: in the early eighties, they straightened all the rivers in Hokkaido.

*Chutes&Ladders:* Why?

*Orangutan:* To create jobs the government straightened the rivers! Huge bodies of water, manual laborers, scientists, engineers, bulldozers, and the rivers became straight! How nuts is that?

*Chutes&Ladders:* People can't leave good enough alone. Why are humans so damn restless?

*Orangutan:* It's not restlessness. It's ego. Massive, bizarre ego.

*Chutes&Ladders:* Can't let a river be a river. *(Into the phone)* The forms link is on the left.

*Orangutan:* Now it's the aughts, people keep being born, jobs still need creating, but there's no curves left to straighten, so, drum roll, the government is beginning a new program to put all the original turns back in the rivers!

*Chutes&Ladders:* Well good luck to them, but no amount of engineering can put a wrinkle back in Nicole Kidman's forehead.

*Orangutan:* Ever heard of Kushiro?

*Chutes&Ladders:* Is that your new boyfriend's name?

*Orangutan:* Ha. Ha ha ha. It's home of the hundred-mile-long Kushiro River, which is the pilot project, the first river they're trying to recurve.

*Chutes&Ladders:* Kushiro River. Got it. Burned in the brain. One day I'll win a Trivial Pursuit's wedge with that. *(Into the phone)* You, too, ma'am. *(He hangs up)*

*Orangutan:* My train to Kushiro leaves in twenty minutes. My heart is pounding.

*Chutes&Ladders:* I don't follow.

*Orangutan:* Kushiro is the town where I was born. I'm going. I'm doing it.

*Chutes&Ladders:* Hold on, now you're throwing curveballs.

*Orangutan:* In my hand is a sheet of paper. On the paper is the address of the house where my birth parents once lived. I'm going to knock on their door.

*(Chutes&Ladders' desk phone rings.)*

*Chutes&Ladders (Into the phone):* Help desk, please hold. *(To Orangutan)* How long have you had that address for?

*Orangutan:* It's been burning a hole in my pocket for two days. I hounded my mom before I left Maine. She finally wrote down the name of the adoption agency. The first clue, the first evidence of who I was I ever had. I made a vow to myself, if I could stay sober for three months, I would track my parents down. So a few days ago class ended early, I went to the agency, showed my passport, and thirty minutes later I had an address on a piece of paper. Ask me anything about Kushiro. All I've done the last two days is research it. I'm an expert. Population, 190,000. There's a tech school, there's an airport.

*Chutes&Ladders:* Why are you telling me this? To get my blessing?

*Orangutan:* I tell you about the things I do.

*Chutes&Ladders:* You don't want my opinion, you want my approval.

*Orangutan:* Hand it over.

*Chutes&Ladders:* No.

*Orangutan:* Don't get monosyllabic.

*Chutes&Ladders:* Take that piece of paper and use it as kindling for a warm winter fire.

*Orangutan:* Jeez, what did they slip into your Wheaties this morning?

*Chutes&Ladders:* Do a ritual burning and never look back. You have three months. Do you know the worth in gold of three months? Don't give yourself a reason to go back to the shadows.

*Orangutan:* I'm in recovery. I have no illusions about catharsis. I realize what will most likely happen is nothing. Maybe something tiny. A microscopic butterfly flapping her microscopic wings.

*Chutes&Ladders:* Live in the past, follow your ass.

*Orangutan:* Don't you have the slightest ambition?

*Chutes&Ladders:* Yes, and I achieve it every day: Don't use and don't hurt anyone. Two things I used to do on a daily basis. I don't do them anymore. Done. Dream realized. No more dreaming.

*(His phone rings again.)*

*(Into the phone)* Continue holding, please.

*Orangutan:* When was the last time you went out on a limb?

*Chutes&Ladders:* Three odd weeks ago.

*Orangutan:* Did you try hazelnut instead of french roast? Did you listen to *Soul Mornings* instead of NPR?

*Chutes&Ladders:* There's a new secretary down the hall, she's got a nice smile. I decided to go say hello. We had a little back and forth. I said, let's have lunch, she said maybe but meant no, I turned away, looked down and my tie was floating in my coffee cup.

*Orangutan:* I waited three months to tell you this, every step of the way, the train ride, what the river looks like. What their front door looks like. *(Pause)* I'm quitting this site. I hate this site. I fucking hate this site.

*Chutes&Ladders:* You're already losing it and you haven't even gotten on the train.

*Orangutan:* Three days ago I suggested you and I meet face to face and you blew a fucking gasket.

*Chutes&Ladders:* That's what this is about?

*Orangutan:* Don't flatter yourself. This is about me wanting relationships. With humans, not ones and zeroes. So we were once junkies. It's superficial. It's not real friendship.

*Chutes&Ladders:* I beg to differ.

*Orangutan:* Prove me wrong.

*Chutes&Ladders:* Search down that address and a hundred bucks says your heart comes back a shattered light bulb.

*Orangutan:* You mean, gasp, I'll actually FEEL something?

*Chutes&Ladders:* What are you going to do if the address is wrong? What if the building's been bulldozed? What if some new tenant lives there? What if the woman who gave you birth then gave you away answers the door?

*Orangutan:* I DON'T KNOW! A concept you clearly avoid at all costs. Learn how to live, that's all I'm goddamn trying to do!

*(His phone rings. He picks up the receiver and hangs it up.)*

*Chutes&Ladders:* I have three grandsons. You know how I know that? Because I rang my son's doorbell one day. Step 9, make amends. And his wife answered, and I don't blame her for hating me. But I saw three little boys in that living room and one of those boys said, "Daddy, who's that man at the door?" And my son said to *my grandson*, "I don't know. He must be lost." My son came outside, closed the door behind him, exchanged a few cordial words and then asked me to go.

*Orangutan:* So I shouldn't even try.

*Chutes&Ladders:* I had five years sober until that day.

*Orangutan:* You really believe in your heart of hearts I should not even try. *(Pause)* Coward.

*(His phone rings. He unplugs the phone line.)*

*Chutes&Ladders:* You think it's easy being your friend?

*Orangutan:* Sissy. You walk the goddamn earth scared of your own shadow, getting smaller and smaller, until you disappear.

*Chutes&Ladders:* You tease me. You insult me. It's like breathing to you.

*Orangutan:* You fucking idiot. Why do little girls tease little boys on the playground at recess? Why the fuck were cooties invented? You fucking imbecile!

*Chutes&Ladders:* You disappeared for three months. I couldn't sleep for three months!

*Orangutan:* I wanted to impress you. I wanted to log on and show you I could be better. And I was an idiot because you're just looking for cowards like you. I'm logging off. This is it. It's over.

*Chutes&Ladders:* Orangutan.

*Orangutan:* Into the abyss I climb, looking for a flesh-and-blood hand to grasp onto.

*Chutes&Ladders:* Little monkey, stop it.

*Orangutan:* I'm in the station. My train is in five minutes, you gave me all the motivational speech I need, I'm going to the platform, I'm getting on the train, I'm going to see the house where I was born.

*(She logs off. Chutes&Ladders grabs his phone and hurls it into his wastebasket He throws his calculator, his mail pile, his pen cup to the ground. Left on his desk is one padded envelope.)*

*Chutes&Ladders:* "To Chutes&Ladders Wilkie." "From Haikumom Ortiz."

*(He rips it open, pulls out a deflated orange water wing, puts it over his hand.)*

**SCENE TEN**

*Split scene. Lights rise on a church, Elliot and Yaz stand at the lectern.*

*Yaz:* It is time to honor a woman.[1]

*Elliot:* A woman who built her community with a hammer and nails.

*Yaz:* A woman who knew her nation's history. Its African roots. European roots. Indigenous roots. A woman who refused to be enslaved but lived to serve.

*Elliot:* A carpenter, a nurse, a comedian, a cook.

*Yaz:* Eugenia Ortiz.

*Elliot:* Mami Ginny.

> *(Lights rise on Odessa's house. She sits on her floor. She scoops a spoonful of water from a mug, pours it onto the floor in a slow ribbon.)*

*Yaz:* She grew vegetables in her garden lot and left the gate open so anyone could walk in and pick dinner off the vine.

*Elliot:* She drank beer and told dirty jokes and even the never-crack-a-smile church ladies would be rolling laughing.

*Yaz:* She told me every time I visited, "Yaz, you're going to Juilliard."

*Elliot:* Every morning when I left for school, "Elliot, nobody can make you invisible but you."

> *(Lights rise on the Sapporo train station. Orangutan is on the platform.)*

*Loudspeaker (An announcement in Japanese):* 3:00 express to Kushiro now boarding on track one. Please have tickets out and ready for inspection.

*Yaz:* Zero.

*Elliot:* Birth children.

*Yaz:* One.

*Elliot:* Adopted son.

> *(Odessa pours another spoonful of water on the floor. Again, it creates a slow ribbon.)*

*Yaz:* Three.

*Elliot:* Years in the army nurse corps.

*Yaz:* Three.

*Elliot:* Arrests for civil disobedience. I was in Iraq and she was demonstrating for peace.

*Yaz:* Forty-seven.

*Elliot:* Wheelchair ramps she installed in homes with disabled children or elderly.

> *(Odessa pours another spoonful of water on the floor. A small pool is forming.)*

*Yaz:* Twelve.

*Elliot:* Abandoned lots she turned into city-recognized public gardens.

> *(Another spoonful.)*

*Yaz:* Twenty-two.

*Elliot:* Godchildren recognized by this church.

> *(Another spoonful.)*

*Yaz:* One hundred and thirty.

---

[1]This eulogy is inspired by and owes much debt to Roger Zepernick's eulogy for Eugenia Burgos. [Hudes's note.]

*Elliot:* Abandoned homes she refurbished and sold to young families.

*Loudspeaker (Another announcement in Japanese):* Final boarding call, 3:00 express to Kushiro, track one.

*(Orangutan is still on the platform. She seems frozen, like she cannot move.)*

*Yaz:* All while having a fresh pot of rice and beans on the stove every night. For any hungry stranger. And the pilgrims stopped. And they planted roots, because she was here. We are the living, breathing proof.

*Elliot:* I am the . . . Excuse me.

*(He exits.)*

*Yaz:* Elliot is the standing, walking testimony to a life. She. Was. Here.

*(Odessa turns the cup upside down. It is empty.)*

## SCENE ELEVEN

*Chutes&Ladders at his desk. In front of him: an inflated orange water wing.*

*Chutes&Ladders (On the phone):* Yeah, it's a 1995 Tercel. Midnight blue. It's got a few miles. A hundred and twenty thousand. But like I said, I'll give it to you for three hundred below Kelley Blue Book. Yup, automatic. Just got new brake pads. Cassette deck, mint condition. I'll even throw in a few tapes. Tina Turner and Lionel Richie. Oh, hold on, call-waiting.

*(He presses mute. Sings to himself)*

> A tisket, a tasket.
> A green and yellow basket.
> I bought a basket for my mommy.
> On the way I dropped it.
> Was it red? No no no no!
> Was it brown? No no no no!

*(Back into the phone)* Sorry about that. I got someone else interested. No, it's all right, I have them on hold. You need to see this thing tonight if you're serious. I put this listing up thirty minutes ago, my phone is ringing off the hook. 6:30? Hey I didn't mention. Little lady has racing stripes.

## SCENE TWELVE

*Split scene. Lights rise on the Sapporo train station, same as before. Orangutan has laid down on the platform and fallen asleep, her backpack like a pillow.*
*Lights rise on Odessa's house, that night. Her phone rings. We hear loud knocking.*

*Elliot (Offstage):* Mami Odessa! Open the door!

*(More ringing.)*

*(Offstage)* Yo, Mom!

*Yaz (Offstage):* She's not there.

*Elliot (Offstage):* Can't you hear her phone ringing? Move out the way.

*Yaz (Offstage):* Be careful, your leg!

(*A few kicks and the door bursts open. Yaz and Elliot enter, switch on the lights. Odessa is in a heap, motionless, on the floor. Yaz runs and holds Odessa in her arms.*)

Oh shit. Odessa! Odessa! Wake up.

(*Yaz slaps Odessa's face a few times.*)

Her pulse is racing.

(*Yaz opens her cell phone, dials.*

Elliot finds a spoon on the floor.)

*Elliot:* Oh no. Oh no you fucking didn't! MOM!!! Get up!

*Yaz (Into the phone):* Hi, I need an ambulance. I have someone unconscious here. I think it's an overdose, crack cocaine. Yes, she has a pulse. 33 Ontario Street. No, no seizures, she's just a lump. Well what should we do while we wait? Okay. Yes. (*She hangs up*) They're on their way. Elevate her feet.

*Elliot:* Help me get her to the sofa. One, two, three.

(*Elliot lifts her with Yaz's help. They struggle under her weight. In fact they lift the air. Odessa stands up, lucid, and watches the action: Elliot and Yaz struggling under her invisible weight.*)

*Yaz:* Watch her head.

*Elliot:* Aw, fuck, my leg.

*Yaz:* Careful.

(*They set "Odessa" on the sofa, while Odessa watches, unseen, calm.*)

*Odessa:* I must be in the terminal. Between flights. The layover.

*Yaz:* Oh god, not two in one day, please.

*Elliot:* She's been through this shit a million times. She's a survivor! WAKE UP! Call your mom. She'll get here before the ambulance.

(*Yaz dials.*)

*Odessa:* I've been to the airport, one time. My dad flew here from Puerto Rico. First time I met him. We stood by the baggage claim, his flight was late, we waited forever. There was one single, lone suitcase, spinning around a carousel.

*Yaz (To Elliot):* Voice mail. (*Into the phone*) Mom? Call me back immediately, it's an emergency.

*Elliot:* Give me that. (*Grabs the phone*) Titi, Odessa fucking OD'd and she's dying on her living room floor and I can't take this anymore! COME GET US before I walk off and leave her on the sofa! (*He hangs up*)

*Yaz:* If you need to, go. No guilt. I got this.

*Elliot:* She's my *mom*. Can I be angry? Can you let me be angry?

*Yaz:* Why is this family plagued? (*Elliot moves to go*) Where are you going?

*Elliot:* To find something fragile.

(*He exits. We hear something shatter.*)

*Odessa:* Everyone had cleared away from the carousel. Everyone had their bags. But this one was unclaimed. It could still be there for all I know. Spiraling. Spinning. Looking for an owner. Abandoned.

*(In the Sapporo station, a Policeman enters with a bright, beaming flashlight and points it at Orangutan.*
*In Odessa's house, a radiant white light suddenly pours in from above. Odessa looks up, is overwhelmed. It is beautiful. Yaz sees it.)*

Yaz: Dear god, do you see that?

*(Elliot enters. Watching Yaz, he looks up.)*

Elliot *(Not seeing it):* What?

Yaz *(To Odessa):* It's okay, Odessa, go, go, we love you, I love you Titi, you are good, you *are* good. Oh my god, she's beautiful.

Elliot: What are you talking about?

Yaz: It's okay, it's okay. We love you Odessa.

Policeman *(In Japanese):* Miss, miss, are you okay?

Orangutan *(Waking):* English, please.

Policeman: No sleeping on the floor.

Orangutan *(Getting up slowly):* Sorry.

Policeman: Are you sick?

Orangutan: No.

Policeman: Are you intoxicated?

Orangutan: No. I'm very sorry. I just got tired. I'll go. I'm going.

Policeman: Please, can I give you a hand?

Orangutan: No. I got it.

*(Orangutan exits. The Policeman turns off his flashlight, exits.*
*The sound of an ambulance siren. Suddenly the white light disappears. Odessa crawls onto the couch and slips into Yaz's arms, where she's been all along.)*

Yaz: Holy shit. . .

Elliot: What's happening, Yaz? What the fuck was that?

Yaz: You've got to forgive her, Elliot. You have to.


## Scene Thirteen

*The chat room.*

Chutes&Ladders: Oh nagging wives? Orangutan? Hello? Earth to Orangutan. Come on, three days straight I been worrying about you. I have time-sensitive information. Ground control to Major Orangutan.

Orangutan: Ta-da.

Chutes&Ladders: Where you been?

Orangutan: Here. There. Morrissey and Nine Inch Nails° on loop.

Chutes&Ladders: Is that what the kids like these days?

Orangutan *(Rolls eyes):* That was me rolling my eyes.

Chutes&Ladders: Guess what I did.

Orangutan *(Shrugs):* That was me shrugging.

---

*Morrissey and Nine Inch Nails:* Morrissey is a singer/songwriter who was the lead singer of the moody British indie band The Smiths, popular in the 1980s and 1990s; Nine Inch Nails is an American industrial rock band who also reached their peak of popularity in the 1980s and 1990s.

*Chutes&Ladders:*  Guess.

*Orangutan:*  Guess what I didn't do?

*Chutes&Ladders:*  Meet your birth parents?

*Orangutan:*  Board the train.

*Chutes&Ladders:*  Sorry.

*Orangutan:*  Don't apologize. You had my number.

*Chutes&Ladders:*  Guess what I did.

*Orangutan:*  Told me so. Had my shit pegged.

*Chutes&Ladders:*  I sold my Tercel. My plane lands in Narita Airport a week from this Wednesday.

*Orangutan:*  What?

*Chutes&Ladders:*  American Airlines Flight 3312. Arriving 10:01 A.M.

*Orangutan:*  You're a dumbass. Tokyo? Do you have any idea how far that is from Hokkaido? And how much a ticket on the train costs? Oy, and how the hell am I going to get out of teaching that day? Oh, you dollface, you ducky!

*Chutes&Ladders:*  I'll be wearing a jean jacket and a Padres cap. That's how you'll know me.

*Orangutan:*  Oh Chutes&Ladders. You old bag of bones, you! You old so-and-so, you mensch, you human being! Why the hell didn't you tell me?

*Chutes&Ladders:*  I'm just hoping I have the guts to get on the plane.

*Orangutan:*  Of course you're getting on that damn plane! For me you did this?

*(Fountainhead logs on.)*

*Fountainhead:*  Hey everyone. I managed to find one computer here at the hospital that works. Odessa asked me to post a message on her behalf. She landed on: "Go." Hit reset on the timer. Back to day one.

*Orangutan:*  Who's Odessa?

*Fountainhead:*  Sorry. Haikumom.

*Orangutan:*  What? Do you log on here just to mock us?

*Chutes&Ladders:*  Hold on, is she okay?

*Fountainhead:*  Cardiac arrest. They said she was one hair from a coma. She hadn't used in six years and her system went nuts.

*Chutes&Ladders:*  So she's alive?

*Fountainhead:*  And just barely ticking. Tubes in and out of her nose. She's responsive, she mumbled a few words.

*Orangutan:*  You can't be serious.

*Chutes&Ladders:*  Why are you there? Were you using with her?

*Fountainhead:*  No.

*Chutes&Ladders:*  Did you sell her the stuff?

*Fountainhead:*  No, Jesus, of course not. She gave them my number, I'm her emergency contact. Why, I have no idea, we're practically strangers. Getting here to the hospital, seeing her like that . . . I don't mean this as an insult, but she looked not human. Bones with skin covering. Mummy-like.

*Orangutan:*  Fuck. You.

*Fountainhead:*  I'm being descriptive. I'm being honest. The thought of my boys walking in on me like that. My wife finding me . . .

*Orangutan:*  That woman is the reason I'm. Oh god, you get complacent for one second! One second! You get comfortable for one minute! Fountainhead, go to the stats page. You'll see. There's thousands of members on this site. People she has saved, people she may yet save some day. I am one of them. You are one of them.

*Chutes&Ladders:*  Fountainhead, does she have family there? Has anyone come through her room?

*Fountainhead:*  Apparently a son and a niece but they had to catch a flight to San Juan.

*Chutes&Ladders:*  No parents? No other children? A friend? A neighbor?

*Fountainhead:*  None showed up.

*Chutes&Ladders:*  Fountainhead. You have a family, I absolutely understand that, and I mean zero disrespect when I say, when I beg of you this:  your job on this earth has just changed. It is not to stay clean. It's not to be a husband or a father or a CEO. It's to stay by that woman's side. Make sure she gets home safe. Bathe her. Feed her. Get her checked into a rehab, inpatient. Do not leave her side for a second. Can you do this?

*Fountainhead:*  I have one day clean. I'm not meant to be a saint.

*Chutes&Ladders:*  Tell me now, swear on your mother's name, otherwise I'm on the first flight to Philadelphia.

*Fountainhead:*  I don't know.

*Chutes&Ladders:*  Look man, do you believe in God?

*Fountainhead:*  Sure, along with unicorns and the boogeyman.

*Chutes&Ladders:*  How about miracles?

*Fountainhead:*  When the Phils are winning.

*Chutes&Ladders:*  How about actions? I bet you believe in those.

*Fountainhead:*  Yeah.

*Chutes&Ladders:*  Your lifeboat has just arrived. Get on board or get out of the way.

*Fountainhead:*  I'll take care of Odessa. You have my word. My solemn word. *(Pause)* She did manage to say one thing: Someone has to take over site admin. She doesn't want the chat room full of curse words.

*(Yaz appears. A screen lights up:)*

FREEDOM&NOISE
STATUS: ONLINE

*Freedom&Noise:*  I'm good with computers. I'll throw my hat in the ring.

*Chutes&Ladders:*  Freedom&Noise, are you new here?

*Freedom&Noise:*  Yes. Very.

*(Fountainhead's phone rings.)*

*Fountainhead:*  Freedom&Noise, email me offline. Link attached. I gotta go.

*Chutes&Ladders:*  You gave us your word. Don't be a stranger.

*(Fountainhead logs off. Into the phone:)*

*Fountainhead:*  Hi, honey, sorry I haven't called sooner. Something came up. Listen, I'm not coming home tonight, just order in. I have a friend who got sick, she's having an emergency. No, it's not a romantic friend. I will tell you about it. When I get home. When I— Honey? Honey . . .

*(The call is over. He writes a text message.)*

Honey, under my bookmarks, click on "Fantasy Football" link. My username is "Fountainhead." My password is "Porsche71." Log on and read. Send.

SCENE FOURTEEN

*Puerto Rico. A hotel room. Yaz is online.*

*Freedom&Noise:* Hello, I am Freedom&Noise, your interim site manager, currently logging on from the Rainforest B&B in Puerto Rico. I am not a user, I've smoked pot twice, both times when I was thirteen, and am therefore unqualified for this position. There was a young woman I once knew. Let's call her "O." My crazy aunt, a fun babysitter, the baddest hide-and-seek player north of Girard Avenue. We played dress-up, built booby traps and forts, and when I was eight, she disappeared. No explanation, no acknowledgment she had ever existed, the grown-ups in the family had taken a vow of silence, and O. had been erased. My freshman year at college, I returned home for Thanksgiving, and thanks to a snow delay I walked into the middle of turkey dinner itself, and there was O., a plate full of food, chowing down. I hadn't seen her in ten years. After dinner she told me to congratulate her, it was her anniversary. I said, "Did you get married?" She pulled a necklace out from under her shirt and said, "You know what these gold letters mean? The 'N' is for narcotics, the 'A' is for anonymous and today is my two-year anniversary of being clean." *(Pause)* A few days ago I met a new woman: Haikumom. A woman who created a living, breathing ecosystem, and since I've never sown a single seed, let alone planted a garden, the least I can do is censor you, fix glitches — and one other thing . . . Formulating first line. Did Haikumom really do these on the fly? Five-seven-five, right? *(Counting the syllables on her fingers)* Box full of ashes . . .

*(Elliot enters from the bathroom, freshly showered, pulling on a shirt.)*

*Elliot:* Whatchu looking at, Willis?

*Yaz:* Sh. I'm counting syllables.

*(Elliot looks over Yaz's shoulder at the computer.)*

*Elliot:* Hold up. Don't read that shit, Yaz.

*Yaz:* You know how Odessa got into haiku in the first place?

*Elliot:* For real, close the computer.

*Yaz:* I went through this Japanese minimalist phase freshman year. Rock Gardens, Zen Buddhism, the works. I gave her a haiku collection for Christmas.

*Elliot:* Yeah, and you gave me a midget tree that died by New Year's.

*Yaz:* Bonsai. You didn't water it.

*Elliot (Closing Yaz's laptop):* For the two days I'm away from Philly, let me be away from Philly?

*Yaz:* You know where I was gonna be by thirty? Two kids. Equal-housework marriage. Tenure, no question. Waaaay tenured, like by the age of twenty-four. Carnegie Hall debuts: Yazmin Ortiz's "Oratorio for Electric Guitar and Children's Choir." I wrote a list on a piece of paper and dug a hole in Fairmount Park and put it in the ground and said, "When I turn thirty, I'll dig it up and cross it all off." And I promise you I'll never have the courage to go to that spot with a shovel and face my list full of crumbs, decoys and bandaids.

*Elliot:* Married with kids, what an awful goal.

*Yaz:* Odessa's done things.

*Elliot:* Well, when you throw her a parade, don't expect me to come.

*Yaz:*  You've done things.

*Elliot:*  I wouldn't come to my own parade, either.

*Yaz:*  Ginny did things. What have I done?

*Elliot:*  Second-grade Language Arts. You glued my book report.

*Yaz:*  I couldn't stop your leg from getting chewed up.

*Elliot:*  Fairmount little league basketball. You kept score, you brought our equipment.

*Yaz:*  I didn't hold your hand when you were in the desert popping pills trying to make yourself disappear. I didn't keep Odessa away from that needle. I didn't water a single plant in Ginny's garden. We're in PR and I'm gonna dig a new hole and I'm not putting a wish or a list in there, I'm putting a scream in there. And I'm gonna sow it like the ugliest foulest and most necessary seed in the world and it's going to bloom! This time it's going to fucking bloom!

*Elliot:*  My eyes just did this weird thing. For a second, it was Mom standing in front of me.

*Yaz:*  Odessa?

*Elliot:*  Ginny.

*Yaz:*  Elliot, your birth mother saved your life by giving you away. Tell me I'm wrong.

*(Elliot doesn't respond. Yaz begins gathering her stuff hastily.)*

Now we got some ashes to throw. El Yunque closes in an hour and a half.

*Elliot:*  Maybe we should do this tomorrow.

*Yaz:*  I gotta make a call. I'll be in the lobby!

*(She exits.)*

*Elliot:*  Yaz?

*(The Ghost appears. He's probably been there the whole time.)*

Yaz!

*Ghost:*  Momken men-fadluck ted-dini gawaz saffari?

*(The Ghost reaches out his hand to touch Elliot.)*

Momken men-fadluck ted-dini gawaz saffari?

*(The second they make contact, Elliot spins on his heels and grabs the Ghost. The Ghost defends himself, pulling away. They start pushing, grabbing, fighting. The Ghost is looking for something—is it Elliot's wallet?)*

Momken men-fadluck ted-dini gawaz saffari?

*(The Ghost finds Elliot's wallet and tears through it, hurling its contents onto the floor. Elliot attacks again, but this time the Ghost reaches out his hand and touches Elliot's face. Elliot freezes, unable to move, as the Ghost's hands glide across his features, considering each one with authority, taking inventory.)*

Momken men-fadluck ted-dini gawaz saffari?

*(The Ghost is gone. Elliot catches his breath, shaken. He reaches into his pocket and pulls out a bottle of pills. He puts one pill in his hand. Then he empties the entire bottle of pills into his hand. He stares at the pills, wanting to throw them away.)*

SCENE FIFTEEN

*Split scene. Odessa's bathroom. The bathtub is filled with water. John enters, carrying a very weak Odessa. Odessa is wearing shorts and a bra, a modest outfit for bathing. John lowers her gently into the bathtub.*

John:  Does that feel okay?

*(Odessa barely nods.)*

It's not too hot or cold?

*(Odessa shakes her head.)*

I don't know how to do this. These are things women do. Take care of sick people. Make the wounds go away.

*(He takes a sponge and starts to bathe her.)*

Is this okay?

*(He lifts her arms and washes her armpits. Embarrassed at first, but quickly gets the swing of it.)*

We check you in at 4:30 so we have plenty of time to clean you up and get you in good clothes, okay? You'll go in there looking like a decent woman.

*(Odessa whispers something inaudible.)*

What was that?

*(She gestures for him to lean in. She whispers into his ear.)*

One more time.

*(She whispers a little louder.)*

Did someone take swimming lessons?

*(She whispers again.)*

Did someone put on water wings?

*(She nods. He continues to bathe her, gently, in silence as:*
    *Lights rise on Tokyo. Narita Airport. Orangutan sits on the floor by the luggage carousel. At her feet is a sign that says Chutes&Ladders. She throws the sign like a frisbee across the floor and gets up to leave. Chutes&Ladders enters, rolling a suitcase behind him. He waves to Orangutan.)*

Chutes&Ladders:  Orangutan?

Orangutan:  What the holy hell?

Chutes&Ladders:  Sorry. Sorry. I tried calling but my cell doesn't work here. I told you I'm no good at this fancy kind of living.

Orangutan:  You were supposed to land yesterday, you were too scared to get on the plane. You rebook, you were supposed to land today, forty-five minutes ago. Everyone got their luggage already. The last person pulled the last suitcase from the carousel half an hour ago. I thought, Wow, this one sure knows how to play a joke on the ladies. I thought you had left me at the fucking altar.

Chutes&Ladders:  I got sick on the flight. Totally embarrassing. I had a panic attack as the plane landed and I started tossing into the doggy bag right next to this nice old lady. I've been sitting on the bathroom floor emptying my stomach. Then I had to find a toothbrush and toothpaste and mouthwash because I didn't want to greet you with bad breath and all.

(*She looks skeptical. She sniffs his mouth quickly.*)

*Orangutan:* Minty. (*Pause*) Oh, you dummy, you big old dummy. COME HERE, you San Diego Padre.

(*They hug. A warm and brief greeting.*)

What's your name?

*Chutes&Ladders:* Clay. Clayton "Buddy" Wilkie.

*Orangutan:* I'm Madeleine Mays.

*Chutes&Ladders:* It's weird, huh?

*Orangutan:* Totally weird. The land of the living.

(*They hug. They melt into each other's arms. A hug of basic survival and necessary friendship. Then, they exit, rolling Chutes&Ladders's suitcase off as lights rise in:*
    *Puerto Rico. A rock outcropping looking out over a waterfall. Elliot is there, looking down at the water.*)

*Elliot (Looking down):* Oh shit! Yaz, you gotta see this! Yaz? Fucking Johnny Appleseed of El Yunque.

(*Yaz enters holding a soil-covered flower bulb. She compares the root against a field book.*)

*Yaz:* I found my spiral ginger! This is going right next to the aloe by the kitchen door, baby!

*Elliot:* Yo, this science experiment ain't getting past security.

*Yaz:* Experiment my ass. I'm planting these in Ginny's garden.

*Elliot:* Customs gonna sniff that shit from a mile away.

*Yaz (Putting the bulb in a ziploc baggie full of dirt and bulbs):* China rose . . . Sea grape . . . Some kind of fern . . .

*Elliot:* When they cuff those wrists, I don't know you.

*Yaz:* I'll hide them in my tampon box.

*Elliot:* That don't work. My first trip to PR, Mami Ginny smuggled a coquí° back with her kotex and got arrested. Front page of the *Daily News*.

*Yaz:* Good shit. (*A dirty little secret*) You know what Grandma did?

*Elliot:* Do I want to?

*Yaz:* She used to smuggle stuff back, too. She'd tuck it below her boobs. She had storage space under there!

*Elliot:* Yeah after she was sixty and had nursed seven kids. Yo you think if I jumped off this rock right now and dove into that water, I'd survive?

*Yaz:* Just watch out for the huge boulders and the footbridge.

*Elliot:* It's tempting. That spray. (*His phone beeps*) Reception in the rainforest.

*Yaz:* Kind of ruins the romance.

*Elliot (Reads a text message):* Damn, that was fast.

*Yaz:* What?

*Elliot:* Pop sold the house. Did he even put out a listing?

*Yaz:* Not that I know of.

---

*coquí:* Common frog in Puerto Rico.

*Elliot:* That's like a VW bus going from zero to sixty in three seconds. Don't make no sense.

*Yaz:* Must have been an inside job.

*Elliot:* I guess so.

*Yaz:* A way way inside job . . .

*Elliot:* Yaz . . .

*Yaz (Conspiratorially):* Yeeeees?

*Elliot:* What did you do?

*Yaz (Very conspiratorially):* Nothing . . .

*Elliot:* Holy shit!

*Yaz:* Put my Steinway on craigslist. Got four responses before you made it down to the lobby. My eighty-eight keys are worth more than Ginny's whole house. Sadly. I'll buy an upright.

*Elliot:* You are one crazy motherfucking adjunct! Yo, I don't know if el barrio is ready for you. I don't know if they can handle you!

*Yaz:* Oh, they gonna handle me.

*Elliot:* Wait wait wait. You need a title.

*Yaz:* Yaz will do just fine.

*Elliot:* Hells no. Command respect. I step on those corners, I'm Big El. *(Pause)* "Professor."

*Yaz:* "Professor."

*Elliot:* You like that, huh?

*Yaz:* It'll be the Cousins House. We'll renovate the kitchen. You redo the plumbing, I'll hook up a little tile backsplash.

*Elliot:* I watched Bob Vila° with Pop, but I ain't no handyman.

*Yaz:* Just wait, Mr. Home Depot. You're gonna be like, "Fuacata, fuacata, fuacata,"° with your power drill and nail gun and vise grips.

*Elliot:* Something like that.

*Yaz:* Well? Get to it. Toss 'em.

*Elliot:* Me? Why the hell do you think I let you come along?
*(He hands Yaz the box.)*

*Yaz:* Well then say something. Pray.

*Elliot:* I'm all out of prayers.

*Yaz:* Me, too. Make a toast.

*Elliot:* To LAX.° I'm not flying back with you.

*Yaz:* What do you mean?

*Elliot:* I called from the hotel and changed my flight. One-way ticket. Watch out, Hollywood. *(Pause)* You know how you had to shake me awake last night?

*Yaz (Demeanor shifting):* You were literally sobbing in your sleep.

*Elliot:* This dream was different than usual. I'm fixing a Subway hoagie, I feel eyes on the back of my neck, I turn around and expect to see him, the first guy I shot down in Iraq. But instead it's Mami Ginny. Standing next to the bread oven, smiling. You know how her eyes smile?

*Yaz:* Best smile in the world.

*Elliot:* Looking at me, her son. Coming to say good-bye.

---

*Bob Vila:* Bob Vila (b. 1946) is best known as the host of the long-running home improvement television show *This Old House.*

*fuacata:* An onomatopoeic Spanish word best translated as "*Thwack, thwack, thwack.*"

*LAX:* The largest airport in the Los Angeles area.

*Yaz:* That's beautiful.

*Elliot:* She puts on her glasses to see my face even better. She squints and something changes. The moment I come into focus, her eyes widen. Her jaw drops, she starts trembling. Then she starts to cry. Something she's seeing scares her. Then she starts to scream. Loud, like, "Ahhh! Ahhh!" She won't stop looking at me, but she's terrified, horrified by what she sees. And I don't know if my lip is bleeding or there's a gash on my forehead or she's looking through my eyes and seeing straight into my fucking soul.

*Yaz:* Jesus.

*Elliot:* I wanted Mami Odessa to relapse, Yaz. I wanted her to pick up that needle. I knew precisely what to do, what buttons to push, I engineered that shit, I might as well have pushed the thing into her vein. Because I thought, Why would God take the good one? Yo, take the bad mom instead! I was like, Why wouldn't you take the bad fucking mom? If I stay in Philly, I'm gonna turn into it. I'm gonna become one of them. I'm already halfway there. You've got armor, you've got ideas, but I don't.

*Yaz:* Go. Go and don't you ever, ever look back.

*(She takes his hand.)*

But if you do, there will be a plastic-covered sofa waiting for you.

*(Below them, in Philadelphia, John is done bathing Odessa. He lifts her and holds her like an angel above the bathtub. She is dripping wet and seems almost radiant, and yet deeply, deeply sick.)*

I'm the elder now. I stay home. I hold down the fort.

*Elliot:* I'm walking.

*Yaz:* On three?

*Yaz and Elliot:* One.

    Two.

    Three.

*(They toss the ashes. Blackout.)*


## CONSIDERATIONS FOR CRITICAL THINKING AND WRITING

1. **FIRST RESPONSE.** Draw a line, one end labeled "Selfish" and the other "Selfless." Place all the characters in the play along this continuum, with the most selfish on the left and the most selfless on the right. Which characters were the easiest to place? Which were the hardest? Compare your line to a classmate's: is there significant disparity?

2. The play is largely about addiction. Does it contain a coherent message about this complicated topic? If so, how would you state that message concisely? Illustrate your statement with examples from the text.

3. It is clear from the title that water is an important symbol in the play. List the many times it appears, and then consider whether it always signifies the same thing.

4. Besides water, what other significant symbols do you see in the play?

5. What does the play suggest about the possibility for people to grow? Consider multiple characters in your response.

6. How does the play comment on identity formation and reformation in contemporary society?

7. There are many settings in this play, from Japan to Puerto Rico to Philadelphia to a virtual chat room. How might this observation contribute to your understanding of the play's theme?

8. Money is a recurrent topic in the play. Why is it significant?

9. The arts are also important in the form of acting, music, and poetry. What place do they have in the play's concerns overall?

10. The character John, whose chat name is Fountainhead, is initially scorned for his arrogance and insensitivity. Is he redeemed over the course of the play? Explain.

11. Is it possible to identify the play's protagonist? If so, who is it and why did you select that character? If not, what does the lack of a single protagonist do to your understanding of drama?

### CONNECTIONS TO OTHER SELECTIONS

1. Discuss the invention of names or aliases in this play and in Oscar Wilde's *The Importance of Being Earnest* (p. 1148) in terms of the broader subject of identity.

2. Odessa, a.k.a. Haikumom, is an evidently flawed character. Choose one of the major tragedies in this anthology — Sophocles' *Oedipus the King* (p. 1001), Shakespeare's *Othello* (p. 1055), or August Wilson's *Fences* (p. 1329) — and compare the flaws of the protagonist of that play to Odessa's Do you feel more sympathy for one character or the other? Why?

3. Compare family relationships in this play to David Auburn's *Proof* (p. 1277) in terms of the difficult balance between duty to family and the need to fulfill one's own needs.

## Perspectives

## QUIARA ALEGRÍA HUDES

### *Atonality*   2021

My naïveté surrounding college was a blessing. I saw no reason why Yale shouldn't be my oyster, and not knowing what to fear, I opted for boldness. First day of shopping period, when students tried out classes before formally registering, I went to Composers' Seminar, a 400-level course with extensive prerequisites. I had taken none of them.

"Wait, are you the girl who sent the tapes with her application? 'Three Piano Preludes'?"

"Yes."

"You have a memorable name. Those were great. But have you taken music theory?"

"No. But I learn by ear. I'm a quick study."

"Play the preludes, will you? Wait till the stragglers find a seat."

Yale seminars were capped at twelve but these professors accepted only half that. Judging by the greetings, here lay the inner sanctum. "How was that Boston Pops apprenticeship?" "Any headway on your thesis?" The students were boys, the

5

teachers men. No females in sight, and the room's whiteness rivaled Malvern's.° But its gleaming wealth added an unfamiliar edge, a new code for me to learn. Racks of digital music gear gleamed, supercomputers stood like installation art, sweaters and slacks looked costly though casual, and at the center stood a six-foot Yamaha digital hybrid.

I adjusted my stool at the piano, coaxed one deep breath into my trembling fingertips, and began. The dynamic range surprised me. Loud became majestic, soft became tender. It was the best instrument I'd ever played. On it, my preludes sounded magnificent. I had composed the first two a year earlier while avoiding piano homework. My teacher had assigned Scriabin;° while practicing, I'd made a note mistake, then gone down a rabbit hole chasing the cool sound. The third prelude had come a month later, as I grappled with some low-register Gershwin° stuff. Because of my composition's fungible meter, I hadn't figured out how to notate it in manuscript. Some measures were an obvious four-four, while others seemed to lack time altogether. But when played, they flowed like sentences. The chords crunched and resolved, journeying through dissonance to dreamier soundscapes. Ethereal legato traded with witty staccato, and you could hear the Scriabin and Gershwin all over it.

No applause came at the end. Brows were raised, legs crossed, arms folded. These were not the type to express affirmation, it seemed. And yet, I had a sense of having survived the hazing. To be the only girl around and yet hold center like that, it was ballsy. My hands had hardly trembled after the first few notes. I was twice as bold, I told myself, as any of these boys.

"Questions for our guest?" the longer-haired professor asked.                    10

A tall golden boy in cashmere leaned forward. "Most important influences?"

"Celina y Reutilio."° Until I said it, I hadn't realized mom's morning tape was especially meaningful. She had warped it after hundreds of plays, an ebullient Lukumí score by which to trim Pop's hairline. She would sing-yell above the clippers: "Que viva Changó!"° Celina's voice was twangy as the tres,° with the güiro° and bongo cutting right through. This was folkloric stuff, campesino to the core, but with chromatic solos that would've turned heads at the Blue Note. Their songs were rough joy, dirty praise. And their songs were influence. I had said it aloud for the first time.

Then we were diving into the syllabus, the professor introducing our semester's first two composers: Schoenberg and Ruggles. One was German Jewish, the other anti-Semitic American. One was a sought-out public intellectual, the other a cantankerous hermit. But both were pioneers of the atonality that had come to define Music Today. This was news to me. I jotted down *atonal* and *twelve-tone*

---

*Malvern:* A town in Pennsylvania, west of Philadelphia. Hudes lived in Malvern for part of her youth.

*Scriabin:* Alexander Scriabin (1872–1915) was a Russian pianist and composer whose work was challenging and avant-garde.

*Gershwin:* George Gershwin (1898–1937) was an American pianist and composer who became one of Broadway's most prominent songwriters.

*Celina y Reutilio:* The Cuban music duo Celina González and Reutilio Domínguez.

*Que viva Chango!:* The chorus to Celina y Reutilio's song ""A Santa Bárbara" (also known as "¡Qué Viva Chango!").

*tres:* A three-course stringed instrument; most commonly, the six-stringed Cuban tres.

*güiro:* A percussion instrument commonly used in Cuban, Puerto Rican, and other Latin American music.

*row*, vowing to look them up later. Then it was time to listen. Out of state-of-the-art speakers came the most inharmonious, nihilistic note combinations I'd ever heard. There was no rhythm at all, neither a pulse to steady nor a syncopation to pull. These were sonic inkblots, not songs. If my cousins had heard it, they'd have laughed the Cola Champagne out their noses. But I looked around at a dead-serious room: most brows furrowed in serious consideration.

I had already begun craving an uglier language, one that expressed the Perez resilience and maelstrom. North Philly's too-young death and mucky girlhood and gorgeous dance were eager to key their way out my cage. There was a poetics I longed to share with mom at home and the world at large, one messier than dainty Mozart, more syncopated than Chopin, more guttural than elegant Bach. But I hadn't yet found it. Schoenberg and Ruggles were too bleak. I needed a dissonance that spoke of love, too. A turbulent woman's tongue. Seated amidst all that spotless machinery, I worried that eight semesters of such exalted noise would sprinkle the wrong breadcrumbs on my path, that this laboratory would not lead me to my language. That, in fact, a four-year detour lay ahead and I would emerge off-course, lost. Having come here to study music, though, I resolved to proceed and learn all I could.

Then the listening was over and the boys analyzed it with mind-numbing 15 lingo and impressive facility. Taking notes was hopeless; I couldn't spell the dang vocab words. But dropping the course was off the table. Not after surviving the hazing.

*Girl*, I said, *you are in over your head.*

From *My Broken Language*

## CONSIDERATIONS FOR THINKING AND WRITING

1. The author is aware of her difference from the others, observing "a new code for me to learn." What "codes" are evident as she tries to navigate this classroom and the broader world?

2. What gender dynamics are at play in this scene, and how does the author respond?

3. Research the terms "atonal" and "dissonance," which recur in this excerpt. How do these concepts connect this memoir excerpt to *Water by the Spoonful*? Are you able to analyze the play in terms of them?

## JOHN COLTRANE (1926–1967) AND LEONARD FEATHER (1914–1994)

### Coltrane Shaping Musical Revolt: An Interview with John Coltrane  1964

John Coltrane is one of the handful of new wave performers who can claim artistic and commercial success. His quartet, formed soon after he left Miles Davis° in 1960, is widely accepted in nightclubs, recordings, and overseas tours.

*Miles Davis:* Miles Davis (1926–1991) was a jazz trumpeter, bandleader, and composer considered one of the most important figures in twentieth-century jazz; Coltrane played with his quintet beginning in the 1950s.

Though a real understanding of his music demands technical knowledge and intense attention, Coltrane's most devoted followers are young listeners, many of whom may be musically illiterate. Recently, at Shelly's Manne Hole in Hollywood, he discussed his audiences.

"I never even thought about whether or not they understand what I'm doing," he said. "The emotional reaction is all that matters; as long as there is some feeling of communication, it isn't necessary that it be understood. After all, I used to love music myself long before I could even identify a G Minor Seventh chord.

"Audiences haven't changed much. They say Dizzy and Bird° had to face a lot of hostility; but they had their good audiences too. Eventually, the listeners move right along with the musicians.

"Jazz is so much a music of individuality that every new artist with any orig-  5 inality effects a change in the overall scene. Lester Young represented as great a change, in his time, as some of the things that are happening now. So did Bird."

The ethos of Coltrane's music is a hypnotic quality, achieved through variations on a simple modal or harmonic basis. He has moved into areas that were once the exclusive preserve of Indian music. I asked him how he hoped to extend the audience for this process of acculturation:

"You've had no television exposure at all. How long do you think it will be before the layman is ready for what you're doing?"

"I don't know . . . do you think they ever will be? Anyhow, you can't really do what you want to do in television. You're restricted."

His meaning soon became clear: In the next set it took Coltrane an hour and 15 minutes to play two tunes. Both were framed by a 20-second theme; everything in between was improvised. The first tune ran 50 minutes, with Coltrane playing tenor sax mercurially and uninterruptedly, with unbelievably complex ideas and execution, for the first half-hour. The second tune, which included a 13-minute drum solo by the phenomenal Elvin Jones, featured Coltrane on soprano saxophone, an instrument he rescued from limbo almost single-handedly.

"It's a beautiful horn," he said later. "A friend of mine, a writer named Chip  10 Bayen, had one, and I tried it out one day in 1960."

Since that chance discovery, saxophonists from Paris to Tokyo have taken to doubling on soprano, in the Coltrane style. But the cult is modestly shrugged off by its leader:

"I don't think people are necessarily copying me. In any art, there may be certain things in the air at certain times. Another musician may come along with a concept independently, and a number of people reach the same end by making a similar discovery at the same, time."

Despite this disclaimer, Coltrane is shaping a musical revolution. For a while it will seem as unpalatable to the masses as was Goodman in 1934 or Gillespie in 1944, but Coltrane's time, as his already substantial audiences make abundantly clear, has just arrived.

From *Melody Maker*, December 19, 1964

---

*Dizzy and Bird:* Dizzy Gillespie (1917–1993) was one of the most influential jazz trumpeters of the twentieth century; Charlie Parker (1920–1955), nicknamed "Bird," was one of the most influential jazz saxophonists of the twentieth century.

## CONSIDERATIONS FOR CRITICAL THINKING AND WRITING

1. FIRST RESPONSE. What is the relationship between appreciating music and understanding its technical elements? Does this interview support or challenge your views on the subject?

2. According to the author, Coltrane took seventy-five minutes to play two tunes, each of which was mostly improvised. What does a lengthy, improvised solo do to the typical relationship between artist and audience?

3. *Water by the Spoonful* includes an analysis of Coltrane's music in the form of a lecture. How does this interview essay contribute to your understanding of this figure?

4. Is *Water by the Spoonful* influenced by the principles of free jazz as discussed in this essay? Explain your response.

ELLIOTT ACKERMAN (B. 1980)

## *A Summary of Action*   2019

Two years after the Battle of Fallujah, on a clear January day in Camp Lejeune, I was awarded a medal. My entire family came for the occasion. It was my last day in the battalion, which was standing in formation on the parade ground while the adjutant for the Second Marine Division read a citation. Most of the Marines I'd fought alongside weren't there — two years is a long time in the Corps, so they'd moved on, to civilian life, to other postings — but a few stood in formation. I searched for their faces, but I'd lost them in the ranks. After the award was presented, I was handed the citation and the more detailed "summary of action." Mine was written by my company commander. It is the story of what happened. Rereading it now, all these years later, I want to add some things — the kinds of things that don't make it into formal government documents, the personal reflections that fill the lines between them.

During this period of time, SNO (*. . . Said Named Officer . . .*) received imminent danger pay. (*. . . when we came back most of us didn't know what to do with all the imminent danger pay we'd saved up. We spent it on cars, on motorcycles, or partying. I spent some of mine on a weeklong trip running with the bulls in Pamplona . . .*)

———

Lieutenant Ackerman is enthusiastically recommended for the Silver Star for his heroic actions during OPERATION PHANTOM FURY in Fallujah, Iraq, between 10 November and 10 December 2004. (*. . . we wrote awards during the last days of the battle, when each officer—three of the remaining five lieutenants in my company— took turns working on a laptop fueled by a handheld diesel generator, while the next morning we'd once again be fighting . . .*) Lieutenant Ackerman's heroic actions during this period reflect a level of bravery, composure under fire, and combat leadership that is beyond expectations.

———

Lieutenant Ackerman served as a rifle platoon commander during OPERATION PHANTOM FURY. His platoon fought in more engagements than any other rifle platoon in the company. *(... two weeks into the battle, my company commander told me that I was both the luckiest and unluckiest lieutenant he'd ever met. The luckiest because right out the gate, I experienced the largest battle the Marine Corps had fought in decades, I was the unluckiest because everything I ever did after that would seem inconsequential...)* On numerous occasions he was tasked as the company's main effort during the company's attack south. During the course of the fighting in Fallujah, his platoon took casualties without the slightest degradation of motivation, professionalism, or effectiveness. *(... "I can't take it anymore," one of the Marines tells me. We're four days into the battle. His squad leader said he needed to talk to me. "I keep thinking about my daughter. Every time I go into a house I think about her." He is crying and the other Marines are watching and I know that fear is contagious. "Do you want me to get you out of here?" I ask. He keeps muttering that he can't take it. Twenty minutes later I'm loading him into an amtrack that will drive him out of Fallujah alongside wounded Marines. He and Pratt are married to a set of sisters. Pratt says he'll never speak to him again...)* Lieutenant Ackerman led his platoon with a level of disciplined violence that crushed the enemy and was critical to the company's success. *(... on the back of an M1 Abrams tank there is a little telephone in a box, tapped into the crew's intercom; It's called a "grunt phone." I've never been as scared as I was the times I had to run to that grunt phone, bullet impacts dancing on the tank's armor, their ricochets flashing like fistfuls of thrown pennies. I needed to get on the grunt phone to tell the tanks where to shoot. The tank crew would listen to music on their intercom, so if no one was talking you'd hear pop songs when you held the handset to your ear. The tankers I worked with liked Britney Spears. The squat crew chief, who looked like he was born to fit inside of a tank, told me that he played the music because it helped everyone in the tank stay "frosty"...)*

———

At 0400 on 10 November, the company crossed the line of departure on the north side of Fallujah and attacked to seize the government complex in the heart of the city. Lieutenant Ackerman was tasked with seizing the western side of the complex, *(... it was the Corps' birthday. As we loaded the tracks, the Marines swapped little pieces of MRE° cake and placed them gently in their mouths, like priests placing Communion wafers...)* As the company made the initial breach into the compound. Lieutenant Ackerman quickly established a foothold and seized the police station and high-rise building with little resistance. *(... Staff Sergeant Ricardo Sebastian, who we called Seabass, thought the insurgents might not fight, that they might withdraw. He was Dan's platoon sergeant. After my platoon sergeant was shot in the head, he became mine, but for less than two days, as he'd soon be shot through the arm and the leg. When we entered the mayor's complex and nobody was there, I thought maybe Seabass had been right...)* Using a combination of precise rocket shots and explosive breaches, he was able to quickly advance and clear his first two buildings prior to sunrise. *(... in the week before the battle, we'd rehearsed this dozens of times. We rehearsed and rehearsed and rehearsed as if rehearsing it enough meant we might never have to do it...)* As the sun came over the horizon, a heavy volume of enemy direct and indirect fire shattered the early-morning calm. It quickly became apparent that while there were no enemy personnel inside the compound, the buildings to the south, east, and west were teeming with insurgents. *(... Dan's up on the rooftop of the high-rise...)*

———

*MRE:* Meal, Ready-to-Eat. Individual military rations.

Lieutenant Ackerman quickly grasped the situation, and as the company began to respond to the enemy fire from all directions, he attacked and seized the southernmost buildings in the government complex. *(. . . we run as fast as we can to Mary-Kate and Ashley, kicking open locked doors, breaking windows; it is exciting, no one's been hurt, we are euphoric . . .)* From this position, he was able to provide timely and accurate reporting to the company commander on the enemy disposition that helped shape the company battle for the rest of the afternoon. From his position as the battalion's lead southern trace, Lieutenant Ackerman orchestrated both direct and indirect fires for six hours. *(. . . I am on my stomach, and each time I peek my head above the wall, I am convinced it's going to get shot. off. Second Platoon is in the building next to ours. A friendly air strike accidently hits them. We hear them screaming on the radio as they call in their wounded, and it mixes with the sounds of our jets overhead . . .)* During this time he acted as a forward observer for numerous mortar and artillery missions and is credited with destroying 20 enemy personnel. *(. . . the most difficult thing in a firefight is to find the people you are shooting at. Someone will manage a glimpse of a muzzle flash, or a silhouette in a window, and we will all shoot in that direction. Then another glimpse, and again we all shoot. I call in artillery, mortars. A sniper sets up in a minaret, his single shots inching closer to us. We are cleared to call in an air strike. The tip of the minaret explodes. The Marines film it, cheering. Later, one of them downloads the video clip to my computer. I still have it. I know I should delete it, but I don't . . .)*

———————

Under the cover of darkness in the early-morning hours of 11 November, Lieutenant Ackerman's platoon was tasked to attack to gain a foothold on the south side of MSR Michigan in order to open the MSR as an east-west line of communication, *(. . . no one has slept, and we won't really sleep for another two days. We are also running low on food and water. I catch the Marines stealing glances at me as I talk on the radio. They will do this constantly in the days and weeks to follow. They know that what is said over the radio—an order, a mission—can get them killed, but they have little control over these decisions. When we come home, one of the Marines in our platoon has to see the base psych, or "wizard," for PTSD symptoms. When I tell him I understand what he went through, he tells me that I don't. He says, "If you had to drive at a hundred fifty miles per hour down the freeway, what's scarier—driving the car or riding shotgun?" . . .)* He quickly seized a building with minimal resistance and once again became the forward southern trace for the battalion. *(. . . we shot a few rounds from a gunship—a cargo plane with a 120 mm cannon—into the first building we had wanted to fight from. It collapsed. So we had to go even deeper into the city, probably too deep. I've always wondered if we should have turned back . . .)* As the sun came up on 11 November, his platoon was in a position to engage multiple formations of enemy personnel moving into positions to attack the government complex. *(. . . we occupied a candy store. We ate Pringles and chugged soda. We reinforced our windows with bags of salt, using them like sandbags. When we saw the first insurgents we couldn't believe how casually they were walking around. They didn't expect us that far into the city. When we killed them it felt like murder . . .)* The enemy quickly realized that Lieutenant

Ackerman's position had to be destroyed in order for them to maneuver on the government complex. *(. . . the Marines are running room to room, shooting into the street. Above the window where one of our machine guns is peeking outside, there is a poster of a lake encircled by snowcapped mountains. I am looking at the poster when three men in black tracksuits bolt into the open. I don't see them until they are dead in front of us. One of them is lying on his side, with his head resting on the curb like it's a pillow. The machine gunner, a kid named Benji, looks back at me smiling . . .)* During the course of this firefight, his platoon took two casualties, to include his platoon sergeant, who was shot in the head but survived. *(. . . back in Lejeune, when he leaves our platoon, we give him his helmet as a gift. The other Marine, a nineteen-year-old named Brown, is shot through the femoral artery. We slip and fall on his blood. So we cut open a few bags of the salt and throw it on the ground. It takes a long time for the medevac to come. We're crawling across the room, trying to find the sniper who shot Brown, the salt and the blood crunching beneath our hands and knees . . .)* On two occasions, he exposed himself to enemy direct fire in order to pull the wounded Marines to safety. The first AAV that was sent for medical evacuation was hit with an RPG and engulfed in flames. *(. . . when I hear this on the radio, I don't tell anyone. Brown's pulse is fading . . .)* The second AAV had trouble finding the platoon casualty collection point due to the heavy enemy fire, smoke, and confusion. Lieutenant Ackerman, sensing the situation and recognizing the need to expedite the linkup, rushed into the street to flag down the AAV. *(. . . Banotai and I are out in the street. We're tossing smoke grenades everywhere, green smoke, purple smoke, yellow smoke, which marks our position, but we're also hidden in it. You can hear the bullet snaps from inside this cloud as they shoot at us, hoping for a lucky hit. I've often imagined what it looked like to them—just a huge burst of color that they're shooting at, hoping to kill whatever's inside. Then the Humvees show up. On the field hospital's operating table, Brown is given his last rites by the chaplain . . .)* He ran through a gauntlet of enemy fire to ensure his wounded Marines were evacuated. As soon as the linkup was complete, Lieutenant Ackerman bounded back to his building to resume the fight. *(. . . Brown survives. By this point, we're surrounded . . .)*

From *Places and Names: On War, Revolution, and Returning*

### Considerations for Critical Thinking and Writing

1. **FIRST RESPONSE.** What is gained from the author's impulse to "add some things" to the official account of his story presented at his award ceremony?

2. Which tells you more about the Iraq War: the official language used to present the reward to Lieutenant Ackerman or his italicized thoughts that he intersperses with that language? Do the two voices communicate completely different realities?

3. How does the account frame the traumatic dimensions of military combat? How does this insight connect to that theme as it is represented in *Water by the Spoonful*?

ANONYMOUS

## *Stepping Stones to Recovery from Cocaine/Crack Addiction*

### Cocaine—Basic Facts

#### What Is It?

We don't need to spend too much time on what cocaine is—as addicts, we know. The cocaine we have used comes to us as powder or rocks. It comes from the leaves of a plant which grows mostly in Central and South America. We didn't really care where it came from, because we knew where to get it locally. We usually didn't know how pure it was—how many times it had been stepped on. We knew it was illegal and we really didn't care.

#### What It Does

Cocaine does two things: it is a local anesthetic and a central nervous system stimulant. It numbs our skin where we put it and it gives our brain a rush. It's the only drug that does both.

#### How It Is Used

To get the effects of cocaine, one can shoot it, snort it, or smoke it.

#### Why We Used It

The reasons we used, as well as the way we were introduced to cocaine, are different for everyone. As recovering addicts, we won't tell you we never thought using cocaine was wonderful. At first we liked it, then we fell in love with it, then it tried to kill us. How did we go from the pleasure to the pain?

#### Addiction

We didn't start out to become addicts. During our early use, we thought the warn-  5
ings, "the big lie", etc., were funny. We didn't buy any of that. How could something be illegal and bad for you when it felt so good?

This was because nothing bad had happened to us "yet." As cocaine began to take control of our bodies, minds, and behavior, we denied more and more that it was harmful.

We really don't understand what it's like to be an occasional user of cocaine—someone who can take it and leave it alone. It was difficult for us to admit, finally, that we had a disease, that we were out of control. For those of us now in 12 Step recovery, we each have a different but similar story on how we became willing to live without mood-altering chemicals. We each have a different story about what got us the help we need.

We were not very happy when we looked at our addiction and thought of stopping. We were angry with the police, the courts, friends, family, doctors, or employers who made us face our addiction. We were the last ones to find out we were addicts. We were like the operator of a huge searchlight. We shone the spotlight on everything and everybody else before we put the beam on ourselves and took responsibility for finding a way out.

How did we finally discover we were addicts? That we had a disease which was doing everything to tell us we didn't have it? Many of us got the help and information at an in-patient or out-patient treatment facility through 12 Step members, counselors or therapists.

Many times, the information about addiction, chemical dependency, 10
alcoholism, or whatever name fits, came in the following ways.

Many of us took this "yes or no" test. The word "cocaine" can be replaced
with "drug" or "alcohol" or what fits for you.

### Am I an Addict?

| | Yes | No |
|---|---|---|
| 1. Do you lose time from work or school due to your cocaine use? | | |
| 2. Do you use cocaine alone? | | |
| 3. Is your cocaine use making your home life unhappy? | | |
| 4. Have your ever switched from one drug to another, thinking if you stop the drug that's giving you problems, you'll be O.K.? | | |
| 5. Do you use cocaine because you're shy with other people? | | |
| 6. Is your drug use affecting your reputation (have others lost respect for you)? | | |
| 7. Have you ever lied, conned, or manipulated a doctor to give you a prescription? | | |
| 8. Have your stolen drugs? | | |
| 9. Have you done anything illegal to get money for drugs? | | |
| 10. Have you felt guilty or ashamed after drug use? | | |
| 11. Has drug use caused financial difficulties? | | |
| 12. Have you mixed other drugs or alcohol with cocaine to get a better buzz? | | |
| 13. Have you used other drugs or alcohol to get over cocaine hangovers? | | |
| 14. Do you use cocaine to get you going in the morning? | | |
| 15. Do you hang out with people or go to places that could be dangerous? | | |
| 16. Do you sometimes think you're crazy? | | |
| 17. Has cocaine put you, your friends, or your loved ones in unhealthy situations? | | |
| 18. Do you crave cocaine at a certain time of the day? | | |
| 19. Has cocaine gotten you in trouble with the law? | | |
| 20. Has your ambition or efficiency decreased because or your cocaine use? | | |
| 21. Do you see or hear things that aren't real? | | |
| 22. Has cocaine affected your relationships or marriage? | | |
| 23. Have you ever minimized or denied your drug use when asked? | | |
| 24. Does cocaine interfere with eating or sleeping? | | |

*(table continued on next page)*

*(table continued from previous page)*

25. Have you experienced blackouts or loss of memory? ___ ___

26. Has cocaine affected your sex life negatively? ___ ___

27. Have you seen a doctor or been in a hospital or treatment center because of cocaine use? ___ ___

28. Do you keep using cocaine even though your life is going in the toilet? ___ ___

29. Do you use cocaine to escape from stress, worry, troubles, or responsibility? ___ ___

30. Have you ever tried to quit using cocaine and couldn't stop? ___ ___

31. Have you overdosed or gotten sick from using cocaine? ___ ___

32. Do you always think about getting and using cocaine? ___ ___

33. Does cocaine make you paranoid? ___ ___

34. Do you stay away from people and places that don't approve of your cocaine use? ___ ___

35. Do you believe you are a cocaine addict? ___ ___

We were told if we answered "yes" to too many of these questions, we were addicts. But we were the only ones who could make the choice of whether or not we believed it. These questions showed us we had a problem and our lives were out of control.

The *Diagnostic and Statistical Manual* (DSM-111-R) of the American Psy- 15 chiatric Association lists specific behaviors and signs of cocaine addiction. If a person shows three or more of the following, they have a problem:

1. Cocaine is often taken in large amounts or over a longer period of time than the user intended.

2. The user has a persistent desire, or has made one or more unsuccessful attempts to cut down or control his/her cocaine use.

3. The user spends a great deal of time in activities necessary to obtain cocaine, use cocaine, or recover from its effects.

4. The user is frequently intoxicated or experiencing post-drug reactions when expected to fulfill major role obligations at work, school, or home, or when cocaine use is physically hazardous (e.g., driving a car while high on cocaine).

5. The user foregoes important social, occupational, or recreational activities because of cocaine use.

6. The user continues to take cocaine despite the knowledge that persistent or recurrent social, psychological, or physical problems are being caused or exacerbated by the continued use.

7. The user shows marked tolerance to cocaine, evidenced by the need for substantially increased amounts of the drug in order to achieve intoxication or other desired effects, or shows a markedly diminished effect from continued use of the same amount.

We also learn about cocaine addiction by reviewing the definition of alcoholism from the American Society of Addiction Medicine, and the National Council on Alcoholism and Drug Dependence:

## Definition of Alcoholism

Alcoholism is a primary, chronic disease with genetic, psychosocial, and environmental factors influencing its development and manifestations. The disease is often progressive and fatal. It is characterized by continuous or periodic impaired control over drinking, preoccupation with the drug alcohol, use of alcohol despite adverse consequences, and distortions in thinking, most notably denial.

- **primary** refers to the nature of alcoholism as a disease entity in addition to and separate from other pathophysiologic states which may be associated with it. Primary suggests that alcoholism, as an addiction, is not a symptom of an underlying disease state.

- **disease** means an involuntary disability. It represents the sum of the abnormal phenomena displayed by a group of individuals. These phenomena are associated with a specified common set of characteristics by which these individuals differ from the norm, and which places them at a disadvantage.

- **often progressive and fatal** means that the disease persists over time and that physical, emotional, and social changes are often cumulative and may progress as drinking continues, Alcoholism causes premature death through overdose, organic complications involving the brain, liver, heart, and many other organs, and by contributing to suicide, homicide, motor vehicle crashes, and other traumatic events.

- **impaired control** means the inability to limit alcohol use or to consistently limit on any drinking occasion the duration of the episode, the quantity consumed, and/or the behavioral consequences of drinking.

- **preoccupation** in association with alcohol use indicates excessive, focused attention given to the drug alcohol, its effects, and/or its use. The relative value thus assigned to alcohol by the individual often leads to a diversion of energies away from important life concerns.

- **adverse consequences** are alcohol-related problems or impairments in such areas as physical health (e.g., alcohol withdrawal syndromes, liver disease, gastritis, anemia, neurological disorders); psychological function (e.g., impairments in cognition, changes in mood and behavior); interpersonal functioning (e.g., marital problems and child abuse, impaired social relationships); occupational functioning (e.g., scholastic or job problems); and legal, financial, or spiritual problems.

- **denial** is used here not only in the psychoanalytic sense of a single psychological defense mechanism disavowing the significance of events, but more broadly to include a range of psychological maneuvers designed to reduce awareness of the fact that alcohol use is the cause of an individual's problems rather than a solution to those problems. Denial becomes an integral part of the disease and a major obstacle to recovery.

(*This definition was prepared by the Joint Committee to Study the Definition and Criteria for the Diagnosis of Alcoholism of the National Council on Alcoholism and Drug Dependence and the American Society of Addiction Medicine. It was approved by the Board of Directors of NCADD on 3 February 1990 and the Board of Directors of ASAM on 25 February, 1990,* Prevention Pipeline 3(3), May/June 1990.)

Another way to understand what cocaine addiction is, is to list what it is not.

1. Cocaine addiction is a disease like diabetes, cancer, or AIDS. It is not an illness like a toothache, headache, or upset stomach.

2. Cocaine addiction creates problems; it is not caused by them. It is not caused by a job, financial difficulties, or family problems.

3. Cocaine addiction is not freedom; it controls those addicted to it.

4. Cocaine addiction is chronic and progressive (it keeps getting worse). It is not just about getting into fights, getting arrested, or the bad things it does to our minds and bodies.

5. Cocaine addiction is characterized by "loss of control" over how much and when we use it. It doesn't necessarily mean we use all the time. Even we stay away from cocaine for a while, when we start again we "lose control."

6. Cocaine addiction can be treated at any point. One does not have to lose everything to begin recovery.

7. Cocaine addiction is a disease. Why we have it is not as important as knowing it can be stopped and treated.

8. Cocaine addiction means not only staying abstinent from cocaine, but staying abstinent from all mood-altering drugs, including alcohol.

It is important to get the facts about addiction and admit that we are addicts. This is the starting point. Most of us knew we were addicts and in trouble with our drug use before the significant event which brought use to seek help. The help that we outline in this book is the 12 Step recovery program found in A.A. (Alcoholics Anonymous), N.A. (Narcotics Anonymous), D.A. (Drugs Anonymous), or C.A. (Cocaine Anonymous).

We, the authors, each came at our recovery from a different direction:       20

My name is Mark, and I'm an alcoholic. My recovery program is A.A. because alcohol was my drug of choice. All the other drugs I used were in addition to my alcohol use. I think of it as alcohol being the sun and the other drugs I used as the planets revolving around the sun. It wasn't until I got into cocaine that I really hit bottom. So my recovery has been in A.A. I don't talk about cocaine at meetings because I have put all other drugs into one—alcohol. I'm comfortable doing it this way, and I don't step on anyone's toes in A.A. talking about cocaine.

My name is Mary and I am an addict. I have found recovery in C.A. from my cocaine addiction. Cocaine was my drug of choice and C.A. meetings and friends have helped me the most. Both Mark and myself have found the 12 Step program that fits for us. Some go to N.A. or go to meetings of different fellowships, but remember to respect the boundaries of each fellowship.

## CONSIDERATIONS FOR CRITICAL THINKING AND WRITING

1. FIRST RESPONSE. How does the piece offer both an inside and an outside view into the experience of people struggling with substance use disorders?

2. Which points raised in this excerpt are directly reflected in *Water by the Spoonful*? How does this manual amplify the way characters are depicted in the play?

# A SAMPLE STUDENT PAPER

The following essay by Hayley Gervais responds to the way Hudes's play employs the Internet not only as an alternative setting, but as a tool for healing or self-improvement. The assignment called for two outside sources that would frame the play's concerns with technology. Note how the student author articulates those concerns and uses them to explore an issue in the play that is also topical and relevant to contemporary culture.

Hayley Gervais

Professor Miller

English 102

May 10, 2023

*Water by the Spoonful*: Exploring the Internet's Role

in Bettering the Self

An emotional play detailing the persistent ways in which past demons seem to infiltrate the present, Quiara Alegría Hudes' *Water by the Spoonful* explores its characters' never-ending battle of attempting to re-invent a better self while struggling with the weight of past mistakes. Set in the contemporary world of 2009, much of the play is not set in the physical world, but instead takes place in a virtual world created through online chat room communications. In the play, individuals recovering from cocaine addiction use online aliases to talk, sponsor, and support each other. Through these aliases, they preserve their past identities and the secrets they hold, a privilege which allows the users to instead project an identity of their choosing, one which is separated from the past traumas and mistakes. It is through this use of technology that Hudes explores the role of the Internet in shaping the modern person's identity, and how having the ability to re-establish oneself through electronic means allowing individuals to form an identity outside of past traumas and grow into a better and more well-rounded version of themselves.

> Thesis linking technology to identity and growth

One character in which the role of the Internet is explored is in Odessa, known virtually as Haikumom. In her real-world life, Odessa is viewed by her family as an addict, one whose identity is synonymous with the inability to properly care for children. In one confrontational meeting between Odessa and her son Elliot, he spends the entire encounter degrading his mother by bringing up her past charges of child neglect, her inability to afford funeral flowers, and by referring to her as a lowly "toilet scrubber" in front of her friend (Hudes 1237). Despite Odessa achieving six years sober, her son still views her as nothing more than an irresponsible junkie, an identity which, in response to his attitude, she appears to take on. Throughout her interaction with Elliot, Odessa becomes increasingly aggressive and tells Elliot she will "throw [her] coffee in [his] fucking face" (Hudes 1238). Such actions reaffirm Elliot's perception of Odessa's inability to properly parent and seemingly reaffirm the notion she is nothing more than a no-good junkie.

However, while Odessa behaves problematically in person, reinforcing the negative assumptions about her identity, she is known for much more in the virtual world. As Haikumom, Odessa functions as a maternal figure, who is known to have saved "thousands of members on [her web] site" (Hudes 1251). Additionally, Haikumom is known for her tranquility and daily meditation haikus and has a reputation as the chat room monitor since she will frequently censor any foul language used. Such actions are a stark contrast from Odessa, who uses profanity and violence when speaking with her biological son. In the article "Literature Review of Online Identity Reconstruction" by Jiao Huang et al., the authors discuss how such a difference in online versus physical identities can be possible, since the Internet is often used as a tool to "reconstruct [one's] identity to show off their true self" or "hoped-for self" when, due to societal pressure or social exclusion, that idealized identity is impossible to realize in the real-world. When certain social circles—like Odessa's family—refuse to accept a part of someone's identity, the Internet can be used instead as a way to creatively explore a part of the self that is locked away in the physical world, thus giving individuals in the virtual world the ability to function in roles they otherwise would be unable to fulfill.

This ability to function creatively in new roles is crucial in helping individuals achieve self-actualization and function in their highest capacity. For example, since Odessa's family refuses to accept any progress she has made since overcoming her addiction, she reverts to her past self when around her family. Odessa admits that her family "knows every button to

Summary and quotation from source #1

push" and constantly brings out the worst in her, since they only reaffirm her identity as a problematic individual (Hudes 1235). However, without the pressures and negative projections of her family, Odessa is able to explore, reclaim, and function in roles she is unable to accomplish in her personal life through her identity as Haikumom. Therefore, while Haikumom's maternal and relaxed nature may not completely align with the physical presentations of Odessa, she is nevertheless a valid and crucial form of Odessa's identity since she gives her the ability to explore and function as a healthier version of herself and escape her family's labels.

The role of the Internet and its aid in bettering users is even present after Odessa suffers a relapse and overdoses after her troublesome interaction with her son Elliot. Despite her inability to remain sober, Haikumom's identity as a role model and inspiring maternal figure does not waver; instead, her chat room friends are quick to show their support, and even offer to break the "virtual" wall and travel to see her despite never having physically met before. Such acceptance amongst the online community is discussed by Laurence J. Kirmayer et al. in "Cultures of the Internet: Identity, Community, and Mental Health," where the authors talk about how "the Internet reduces the richly embodied nature of interpersonal encounters and individuals' sensual engagement with the world to a few electronically mediated senses" and therefore the Internet creates an "epistemic reliance on sight (seeing is knowing)." So, while Haikumom suffered a relapse and proved herself imperfect, the chat users had only seen a portrayal of a woman dedicated to maintaining sobriety. For them, the Haikumom version of Odessa became part of their reality and true perception of who she is. Since the Internet allows individuals to take projections of themselves and make them part of other's perceptions of reality, Odessa was able to cement her reality as more than someone with a substance use disorder, proving again the ways in which the Internet can beneficially shape one's identity in the modern age.

While Kirmayer et al. talk about the ways the Internet can make favorable presentations of the self a part of reality, they also go on to talk about how the Internet has driven an increased need for acceptance and forgiveness of past mistakes. The authors discuss how in the modern age,

*Summary and quotation from source #2*

*Deeper engagement with source #2 as a way of developing argument*

people's "past indiscretions, childish mistakes, and other errancies can come back to haunt us endlessly" since the Internet can store years of information (Kirmayer et al.). After all, on the Internet, nothing is ever really gone. Because of this, online interactions "may ultimately demand a new level of caution and consistency (which few will be able to maintain)—or a new level of tolerance for human foibles [among Internet users]" (Kirmayer et al.). It is this "new level of tolerance" that Odessa finds amongst her fellow chat users, and it is this camaraderie that Odessa leans into in order to find the strength to recover. After her relapse, Odessa lists Fountainhead, a fellow recovering addict from the site, as her emergency contact instead of Elliot. Knowing her online community to be more accepting and understanding of her mistakes, Odessa responsibly calls upon this group to ensure she takes the necessary steps to regain her sobriety instead of succumbing to her addiction. In this way, the acceptance Haikumom finds amongst her online community gives Odessa the strength and knowledge that she is more than the negative projections her family thrusts upon her. Instead, she is capable of sobriety and so much more. It is through the support and forgiveness of her Internet community that Odessa finds the confidence to bravely restart her sobriety journey.

While neither Odessa nor Haikumom are portrayed as perfect figures, it is through the use of the Internet and the creation of her online identity as Haikumom that Odessa's journey towards self-actualization is realized. Through the Internet, Odessa is given a medium to express herself in a way her family prohibits and in roles she was unable to perform in person. While Haikumom's tranquility and maternal nature do not completely align with Odessa's real-world history, Haikumom is nevertheless a projection of who Odessa wants to be and gives her a medium to function in a space where she is accepted. It is this acceptance found among the Internet community that gives Odessa the confidence to begin acting like Haikumom and which gives her the strength to fight her addiction in the real world. Through Odessa's portrayal of strength and willingness to better herself, Hudes shows the importance of the Internet in shaping identities within the modern age, and how crucial exploring the self creatively through the Internet can be.

Conclusion paragraph reaffirms thesis and central claim of the paper

Gervais 5

## Works Cited

Huang, Jiao, et al. "A Literature Review of Online Identity Reconstruction."

 *Frontiers*, Frontiers Media, 23 Aug. 2021, https://www.frontiersin.org

 /articles/10.3389/fpsyg.2021.696552/full.

Hudes, Quiara Alegría. *Water by the Spoonful. The Compact Bedford Introduction*

 *to Literature,* edited by Michael Meyer and D. Quentin Miller, 13th ed.,

 Bedford/St. Martin's, 2024, pp. 1216-1257.

Kirmayer, Laurence J., et al. "Cultures of the Internet: Identity, Community

 and Mental Health." *Sage Journals*, SAGE Publishing, 5 June 2013,

 https://journals.sagepub.com/doi/10.1177/1363461513490626.

Works
Cited page
provides
sources in
MLA format

# 41

# A Collection of
# Contemporary Plays

My plays are about love, honor, duty, betrayal — things humans have written about since the beginning of time.
— AUGUST WILSON

Adger Cowans/Getty Images.

## DAVID AUBURN (B. 1969)

David Auburn was born in Chicago, the setting of the following play, *Proof*, which won the Pulitzer Prize for Drama in 2001. He was educated at the University of Chicago and at the Julliard School in New York City, where he now resides. He is the author of multiple plays and screenplays, with his latest play opening on Broadway in 2023, but *Proof* remains his most prominent work. It has had a long production history in many countries and was adapted as a 2005 film. *Proof* resembles realism on some levels: it is largely composed of conversations between recognizable characters in a single domestic setting. Yet as you will see, elements

PA Images/Alamy.

of imagination and memory, combined with the disruption of chronology, make it clear that the play departs from the type of realism encountered in plays like *The Importance of Being Earnest* (Chapter 38) or *Fences* (later in this chapter).

## *Proof*   2000

CHARACTERS

*Robert*, 50s
*Catherine*, 25
*Claire*, 29
*Hal*, 28

SETTING

The back porch of a house in Chicago.

---

## ACT I

### SCENE I

> *Night. Catherine sits in a chair. She is twenty-five, exhausted, haphazardly dressed. Eyes closed. Robert is standing behind her. He is Catherine's father. Rumpled academic look. Catherine does not know he is there. After a moment:*

*Robert:*  Can't sleep?
*Catherine:*  Jesus, you scared me.
*Robert:*  Sorry.
*Catherine:*  What are you doing here?
*Robert:*  I thought I'd check up on you. Why aren't you in bed?
*Catherine:*  Your student is still here. He's up in your study.
*Robert:*  He can let himself out.
*Catherine:*  I might as well wait up till he's done.
*Robert:*  He's not my student anymore. He's teaching now. Bright kid. *(Beat.)*
*Catherine:*  What time is it?
*Robert:*  It's almost one.
*Catherine:*  Huh.
*Robert:*  After midnight . . .
*Catherine:*  So?
*Robert:*  So: *(He indicates something on the table behind him: a bottle of champagne.)* Happy birthday.
*Catherine:*  Dad.
*Robert:*  Do I ever forget?
*Catherine:*  Thank you.
*Robert:*  Twenty-five. I can't believe it.
*Catherine:*  Neither can I. Should we have it now?
*Robert:*  It's up to you.
*Catherine:*  Yes.

*Robert:* You want me to open it?

*Catherine:* Let me. Last time you opened a bottle of champagne out here you broke a window.

*Robert:* That was a long time ago. I resent your bringing it up.

*Catherine:* You're lucky you didn't lose an eye. *(She opens the bottle.)*

*Robert:* Twenty-five!

*Catherine:* I feel old.

*Robert:* You're a kid.

*Catherine:* Glasses?

*Robert:* Goddamn it, I forgot the glasses. Do you want me to —

*Catherine:* Nah. *(She drinks from the bottle. A long pull. Robert watches her.)*

*Robert:* I hope you like it. I wasn't sure what to get you.

*Catherine:* This is the worst champagne I have ever tasted.

*Robert:* I am proud to say I don't know anything about wines. I hate those kind of people who are always talking about "vintages."

*Catherine:* It's not even champagne.

*Robert:* The bottle was the right shape.

*Catherine:* "Great Lakes Vineyards." I didn't know they made wine in Wisconsin.

*Robert:* A girl who's drinking from the bottle shouldn't complain. Don't guzzle it. It's an elegant beverage. Sip.

*Catherine:* *(Offering the bottle.)* Do you —

*Robert:* No, go ahead.

*Catherine:* You sure?

*Robert:* Yeah. It's your birthday.

*Catherine:* Happy birthday to me.

*Robert:* What are you going to do on your birthday?

*Catherine:* Drink this. Have some.

*Robert:* No. I hope you're not spending your birthday alone.

*Catherine:* I'm not alone.

*Robert:* I don't count.

*Catherine:* Why not?

*Robert:* I'm your old man. Go out with some friends.

*Catherine:* Right.

*Robert:* Your friends aren't taking you out?

*Catherine:* No.

*Robert:* Why not?

*Catherine:* Because in order for your friends to take you out you generally have to have friends.

*Robert:* *(Dismissive.)* Oh —

*Catherine:* It's funny how that works.

*Robert:* You have friends. What about that cute blonde, what was her name?

*Catherine:* What?

*Robert:* She lives over on Ellis Avenue — you used to spend every minute together.

*Catherine:* Cindy Jacobsen?

*Robert:* Cindy Jacobsen!

*Catherine:* That was in third grade, Dad. Her family moved to Florida in 1983.

*Robert:* What about Claire?

*Catherine:* She's not my friend, she's my sister. And she's in New York. And I don't like her.

*Robert:* I thought she was coming in.

*Catherine:* Not till tomorrow. *(Beat.)*

*Robert:* My advice, if you find yourself awake late at night, is to sit down and do some mathematics.

*Catherine:* Oh please.

*Robert:* We could do some together.

*Catherine:* No.

*Robert:* Why not?

*Catherine:* I can't think of anything worse. You sure you don't want any?

*Robert:* Yeah, thanks.

   You used to love it.

*Catherine:* Not anymore.

*Robert:* You knew what a prime number was before you could read.

*Catherine:* Well now I've forgotten.

*Robert:* *(Hard.)* Don't waste your talent, Catherine. *(Beat.)*

*Catherine:* I knew you'd say something like that.

*Robert:* I realize you've had a difficult time.

*Catherine:* Thanks.

*Robert:* That's not an excuse. Don't be lazy.

*Catherine:* I haven't been lazy, I've been taking care of you.

*Robert:* Kid, I've seen you. You sleep till noon, you eat junk, you don't work, the dishes pile up in the sink. If you go out it's to buy magazines. You come back with a stack of magazines this high — I don't know how you read that crap. And those are the good days. Some days you don't get up, you don't get out of bed.

*Catherine:* Those are the good days.

*Robert:* Bullshit. Those days are lost. You threw them away. And you'll never know what else you threw away with them — the work you lost, the ideas you didn't have, discoveries you never made because you were moping in your bed at four in the afternoon. *(Beat.)* You know I'm right. *(Beat.)*

*Catherine:* I've lost a few days.

*Robert:* How many?

*Catherine:* Oh, I don't know.

*Robert:* I bet you do.

*Catherine:* What?

*Robert:* I bet you count.

*Catherine:* Knock it off.

*Robert:* Well do you know or don't you?

*Catherine:* I don't.

*Robert:* Of course you do. How many days have you lost?

*Catherine:* A month. Around a month.

*Robert:* Exactly.

*Catherine:* Goddamn it, I don't —

*Robert:* HOW MANY?

*Catherine:* Thirty-three days.

*Robert:* Exactly?

*Catherine:* I don't know.

*Robert:* Be precise, for Chrissake.

*Catherine:* I slept till noon today.

*Robert:* Call it thirty-three and a quarter days.

*Catherine:* Yes, all right.

*Robert:* You're kidding!

*Catherine:* No.

*Robert:* Amazing number!

*Catherine:* It's a depressing fucking number.

*Robert:* Catherine, if every day you say you've lost were a year, it would be a very interesting fucking number.

*Catherine:* Thirty-three and a quarter years is not interesting.

*Robert:* Stop it. You know exactly what I mean.

*Catherine:* *(Conceding.)* 1,729 weeks.

*Robert:* 1,729. Great number. The smallest number expressible —

*Catherine:* — expressible as the sum of two cubes in two different ways.

*Robert:* Twelve cubed plus one cubed equals 1,729.

*Catherine:* And ten cubed plus nine cubed. Yes, we've got it, thank you.

*Robert:* You see? Even your depression is mathematical. Stop moping and get to work. The kind of potential you have —

*Catherine:* I haven't done anything good.

*Robert:* You're young. You've got time.

*Catherine:* I do?

*Robert:* Yes.

*Catherine:* By the time you were my age you were famous.

*Robert:* By the time I was your age I'd already done my best work. *(Beat.)*

*Catherine:* What about after?

*Robert:* After what?

*Catherine:* After you got sick.

*Robert:* What about it?

*Catherine:* You couldn't work then.

*Robert:* No, if anything I was sharper.

*Catherine:* *(She can't help it; she laughs.)* Dad.

*Robert:* I was. Hey, it's true. The clarity — that was the amazing thing. No doubts.

*Catherine:* You were happy?

*Robert:* Yeah, I was busy.

*Catherine:* Not the same thing.

*Robert:* I don't see the difference. I knew what I wanted to do and I did it.

If I wanted to work a problem all day long, I did it.

If I wanted to look for information — secrets, complex and tantalizing messages — I could find them all around me: in the air. In a pile of fallen leaves some neighbor raked together. In box scores in the paper, written in the steam coming up off a cup of coffee. The whole world was talking to me.

If I just wanted to close my eyes, sit quietly on the porch and listen for the messages, I did that.

It was wonderful. *(Beat.)*

*Catherine:* How old were you? When it started.

*Robert:* Mid-twenties. Twenty-three, four. *(Beat.)*

Is that what you're worried about?

*Catherine:* I've thought about it.

*Robert:* Just getting a year older means nothing, Catherine.

*Catherine:* It's not just getting older.

*Robert:* It's me. *(Beat.)*

*Catherine:* I've thought about it.

*Robert:* Really?

*Catherine:*  How could I not?

*Robert:*  Well if that's why you're worried you're not keeping up with the medical literature. There are all kinds of factors. It's not simply something you inherit. Just because I went bughouse doesn't mean you will.

*Catherine:*  Dad . . .

*Robert:*  Listen to me. Life changes fast in your early twenties and it shakes you up. You're feeling down. It's been a bad week. You've had a lousy couple years, no one knows that better than me. But you're gonna be okay.

*Catherine:*  Yeah?

*Robert:*  Yes. I promise you. Push yourself. Don't read so many magazines. Sit down and get the machinery going and I swear to God you'll feel fine. The simple fact that we can talk about this together is a good sign.

*Catherine:*  A good sign?

*Robert:*  Yes!

*Catherine:*  How could it be a good sign?

*Robert:*  Because! Crazy people don't sit around wondering if they're nuts.

*Catherine:*  They don't?

*Robert:*  Of course not. They've got better things to do. Take it from me. A very good sign that you're crazy is an inability to ask the question, "Am I crazy?"

*Catherine:*  Even if the answer is yes?

*Robert:*  Crazy people don't ask. You see?

*Catherine:*  Yes.

*Robert:*  So if you're asking . . .

*Catherine:*  I'm not.

*Robert:*  But if you were, it would be a very good sign.

*Catherine:*  A good sign . . .

*Robert:*  A good sign that you're fine.

*Catherine:*  Right.

*Robert:*  You see? You've just gotta think these things through.

Now come on, what do you say? Let's call it a night, you go up, get some sleep, and then in the morning you can —

*Catherine:*  Wait. No.

*Robert:*  What's the matter?

*Catherine:*  It doesn't work.

*Robert:*  Why not?

*Catherine:*  It doesn't make sense.

*Robert:*  Sure it does.

*Catherine:*  No.

*Robert:*  Where's the problem?

*Catherine:*  The problem is you are crazy!

*Robert:*  What difference does that make?

*Catherine:*  You admitted — You just told me that you are.

*Robert:*  So?

*Catherine:*  You said a crazy person would never admit that.

*Robert:*  Yeah, but it's . . . oh. I see.

*Catherine:*  So?

*Robert:*  It's a point.

*Catherine:*  So how can you admit it?

*Robert:*  Well. Because I'm also dead. *(Beat.)* Aren't I?

*Catherine:*  You died a week ago.

*Robert:* Heart failure. Quick. The funeral's tomorrow.
*Catherine:* That's why Claire's flying in from New York.
*Robert:* Yes.
*Catherine:* You're sitting here. You're giving me advice. You brought me champagne.
*Robert:* Yes. *(Beat.)*
*Catherine:* Which means . . .
*Robert:* For you?
*Catherine:* Yes.
*Robert:* For you, Catherine, my daughter, who I love very much . . . It could be a bad sign. *(They sit together for a moment. Noise off. Hal enters, twenty-eight, semi-hip clothes. He carries a backpack and a jacket, folded. He lets the door go and it bangs shut. Catherine sits up with a jolt.)*
*Catherine:* What?
*Hal:* Oh, God, sorry — Did I wake you?
*Catherine:* What?
*Hal:* Were you asleep? *(Beat. Robert is gone.)*
*Catherine:* You scared me, for Chrissake. What are you doing?
*Hal:* I'm sorry. I didn't realize it had gotten so late. I'm done for the night.
*Catherine:* Good.
*Hal:* Drinking alone? *(She realizes she is holding the champagne bottle. She puts it down quickly.)*
*Catherine:* Yes.
*Hal:* Champagne, huh?
*Catherine:* Yes.
*Hal:* Celebrating?
*Catherine:* No. I just like champagne.
*Hal:* It's festive.
*Catherine:* What?
*Hal:* Festive. *(He makes an awkward "party" gesture.)*
*Catherine:* Do you want some?
*Hal:* Sure.
*Catherine:* *(Gives him the bottle.)* I'm done. You can take the rest with you.
*Hal:* Oh. No thanks.
*Catherine:* Take it, I'm done.
*Hal:* No, I shouldn't. I'm driving. *(Beat.)*
     Well. I can let myself out.
*Catherine:* Good.
*Hal:* When should I come back?
*Catherine:* Come back?
*Hal:* Yeah. I'm nowhere near finished. Maybe tomorrow?
*Catherine:* We have a funeral tomorrow.
*Hal:* God, you're right, I'm sorry. I was going to attend, if that's all right.
*Catherine:* Yes.
*Hal:* What about Sunday? Will you be around?
*Catherine:* You've had three days.
*Hal:* I'd love to get in some more time up there.
*Catherine:* How much longer do you need?
*Hal:* Another week. At least.
*Catherine:* Are you joking?
*Hal:* No. Do you know how much stuff there is?

*Catherine:* A week?

*Hal:* I know you don't need anybody in your hair right now. Look, I spent the last couple days getting everything sorted out. It's mostly notebooks. He dated them all; now that I've got them in order I don't have to work here. I could take some stuff home, read it, bring it back.

*Catherine:* No.

*Hal:* I'll be careful.

*Catherine:* My father wouldn't want anything moved and I don't want anything to leave this house.

*Hal:* Then I should work here. I'll stay out of the way.

*Catherine:* You're wasting your time.

*Hal:* Someone needs to go through your dad's papers.

*Catherine:* There's nothing up there. It's garbage.

*Hal:* There are a hundred and three notebooks.

*Catherine:* I've looked at those. It's gibberish.

*Hal:* Someone should read them.

*Catherine:* He was crazy.

*Hal:* Yes, but he wrote them.

*Catherine:* He was a graphomaniac, Harold. Do you know what that is?

*Hal:* I know. He wrote compulsively. Call me Hal.

*Catherine:* There's no connection between the ideas. There's no ideas. It's like a monkey at a typewriter. One hundred and three notebooks full of bullshit.

*Hal:* Let's make sure they're bullshit.

*Catherine:* I'm sure.

*Hal:* I'm prepared to look at every page. Are you?

*Catherine:* No. I'M not crazy. *(Beat.)*

*Hal:* Well, I'm gonna be late . . . Some friends of mine are in this band. They're playing at a bar up on Diversey. Way down the bill, they're probably going on around two, two-thirty. I said I'd be there.

*Catherine:* Great.

*Hal:* They're all in the math department. They're really good. They have this great song, you'd like it, called "i" — lowercase I. They just stand there and don't play anything for three minutes.

*Catherine:* "Imaginary Number."

*Hal:* It's a math joke.

You see why they're way down the bill.

*Catherine:* Long drive to see some nerds in a band.

*Hal:* God I hate when people say that. It is not that long a drive.

*Catherine:* So they are nerds.

*Hal:* Oh they're raging geeks. But they're geeks who, you know, can dress them- selves . . . hold down a job at a major university . . . Some of them have switched from glasses to contacts. They play sports, they play in a band, they get laid surprisingly often, so in that sense they sort of make you question the whole set of terms — geek, nerd, wonk, dweeb, Dilbert, paste-eater.

*Catherine:* You're in this band, aren't you?

*Hal:* Okay, yes. I play drums. You want to come? I never sing, I swear to God.

*Catherine:* No thanks.

*Hal:* All right. Look, Catherine, Monday: What do you say?

*Catherine:* Don't you have a job?

*Hal:* Yeah, I have a full teaching load this quarter plus my own work.

*Catherine:* Plus band practice.

*Hal:* I don't have time to do this but I'm going to. If you'll let me. *(Beat.)* I loved your dad.

I don't believe a mind like his can just shut down. He had lucid moments. He had a lucid year, a whole year four years ago.

*Catherine:* It wasn't a year. It was more like nine months.

*Hal:* A school year. He was advising students . . . I was stalled on my Ph.D. I was this close to quitting. I met with your dad and he put me on the right track with my research. I owe him.

*Catherine:* Sorry.

*Hal:* Look. Let me — You're twenty-five, right?

*Catherine:* How old are you?

*Hal:* It doesn't matter. Listen.

*Catherine:* Fuck you, how old are you?

*Hal:* I'm twenty-eight, all right? When your dad was younger than both of us he made major contributions to three fields: game theory, algebraic geometry, and nonlinear operator theory. Most of us never get our heads around one. He basically invented the mathematical techniques for studying rational behavior, and he gave the astrophysicists plenty to work over too. Okay?

*Catherine:* Don't lecture me.

*Hal:* I'm not. I'm telling you if I came up with one-tenth of the shit your dad produced I could write my own ticket to any math department in the country. *(Beat.)*

*Catherine:* Give me your backpack.

*Hal:* What?

*Catherine:* Give me your backpack.

*Hal:* Why?

*Catherine:* I want to look inside it.

*Hal:* What?

*Catherine:* Open it and give it to me.

*Hal:* Oh come on.

*Catherine:* You're not taking anything out of this house.

*Hal:* I wouldn't do that.

*Catherine:* You're hoping to find something upstairs that you can publish.

*Hal:* Sure.

*Catherine:* Then you can write your own ticket.

*Hal:* What? No! It would be under your dad's name. It would be for your dad.

*Catherine:* I don't believe you. You have a notebook in that backpack.

*Hal:* What are you talking about?

*Catherine:* Give it to me.

*Hal:* You're being a little bit paranoid.

*Catherine:* PARANOID?

*Hal:* Maybe a little.

*Catherine:* Fuck you, HAL. I KNOW you have one of my notebooks.

*Hal:* I think you should calm down and think about what you're saying.

*Catherine:* I'm saying you're lying to me and stealing my family's property.

*Hal:* And I think that sounds paranoid.

*Catherine:* Just because I'm paranoid doesn't mean there isn't something in that backpack.

*Hal:* You just said yourself there's nothing up there. Didn't you?

*Catherine:* I—

*Hal:* Didn't you say that?

*Catherine:* Yes.

*Hal:* So what would I take?
    Right? *(Beat.)*

*Catherine:* You're right.

*Hal:* Thank you.

*Catherine:* So you don't need to come back.

*Hal:* *(Sighs.)* Please. Someone should know for sure whether—

*Catherine:* I LIVED WITH HIM.
    I spent my life with him. I fed him. Talked to him. Tried to listen when he talked. Talked to people who weren't there . . . Watched him shuffling around like a ghost. A very smelly ghost. He was filthy. I had to make sure he bathed. My own father.

*Hal:* I'm sorry. I shouldn't have . . .

*Catherine:* After my mother died it was just me here. I tried to keep him happy no matter what idiotic project he was doing. He used to read all day. He kept demanding more and more books. I took them out of the library by the carload. We had hundreds upstairs. Then I realized he wasn't reading: He believed aliens were sending him messages through the dewey decimal numbers on the library books. He was trying to work out the code.

*Hal:* What kind of messages?

*Catherine:* Beautiful mathematics. Answers to everything. The most elegant proofs, perfect proofs, proofs like music.

*Hal:* Sounds good.

*Catherine:* Plus fashion tips, knock-knock jokes—I mean it was NUTS, okay?

*Hal:* He was ill. It was a tragedy.

*Catherine:* Later the writing phase: scribbling, nineteen, twenty hours a day . . .
    I ordered him a case of notebooks and he used every one.
    I dropped out of school . . . I'm glad he's dead.

*Hal:* I understand why you'd feel that way.

*Catherine:* Fuck you.

*Hal:* You're right. I can't imagine dealing with that. It must have been awful.
    I know you—

*Catherine:* You don't know me. I want to be alone. I don't want him around.

*Hal:* *(Confused.)* Him? I don't—

*Catherine:* You. I don't want you here.

*Hal:* Why?

*Catherine:* He's dead.

*Hal:* But I'm not—

*Catherine:* HE's dead; I don't need any protégés around.

*Hal:* There will be others.

*Catherine:* What?

*Hal:* You think I'm the only one? People are already working over his stuff. Someone's gonna read those notebooks.

*Catherine:* I'll do it.

*Hal:* No, you—

*Catherine:* He's my father, I'll do it.

*Hal:* You can't.

*Catherine:* Why not?

*Hal:* You don't have the math. It's all just squiggles on a page. You wouldn't know the good stuff from the junk.

*Catherine:* It's all junk.

*Hal:* If it's not we can't afford to miss any through carelessness.

*Catherine:* I know mathematics.

*Hal:* If there were anything up there it would be pretty high-order. It would take a professional to recognize it.

*Catherine:* I think I could recognize it.

*Hal:* (*Patient.*) Cathy . . .

*Catherine:* WHAT?

*Hal:* I know your dad taught you some basic stuff, but come on.

*Catherine:* You don't think I could do it.

*Hal:* I'm sorry: I know that you couldn't. (*Beat. Catherine angrily snatches his backpack.*) Hey! Oh come on. Give me a break. (*She opens the backpack and rifles through it.*) This isn't an airport. (*Catherine removes items one by one. A water bottle. Some workout clothes. An orange. Drumsticks. Nothing else. She puts everything back in and gives it back. Beat.*)

*Catherine:* You can come tomorrow. (*Beat. They are both embarrassed.*)

*Hal:* The University health service is, uh, very good.

    My mom died a couple years ago and I was pretty broken up. Also my work wasn't going that well . . . I went over and talked to this doctor. I saw her for a couple months and it really helped.

*Catherine:* I'm fine. (*Beat.*)

*Hal:* Also exercise is great. I run along the lake a couple of mornings a week. It's not too cold yet. If you wanted to come sometime I could pick you up. We wouldn't have to talk . . .

*Catherine:* No thanks.

*Hal:* All right.

    I'm gonna be late for the show. I better go.

*Catherine:* Okay. (*Beat.*)

*Hal:* It's seriously like twenty minutes up to the club. We go on, we play, we're terrible but we buy everyone drinks afterward to make up for it. You're home by four, four-thirty, tops . . .

*Catherine:* Good night.

*Hal:* Good night. (*Hal starts to exit. He has forgotten his jacket.*)

*Catherine:* Wait, your coat.

*Hal:* No, you don't have to — (*She picks up his jacket. As she does a composition book that was folded up in the coat falls to the floor. Beat. Catherine picks it up, trembling with rage.*)

*Catherine:* I'm PARANOID?

*Hal:* Wait.

*Catherine:* You think I should go JOGGING?

*Hal:* Just hold on.

*Catherine:* Get out!

*Hal:* Can I please just —

*Catherine:* Get the fuck out of my house.

*Hal:* Listen to me for a minute.

*Catherine:* (*Waving the book.*) You stole this!

*Hal:* Let me explain!

*Catherine:* You stole it from ME, you stole it from my FATHER — (*Hal snatches the book.*)

*Hal:* I want to show you something, will you calm down?

*Catherine:* Give it back.

*Hal:* Just wait a minute.

*Catherine:* I'm calling the police. *(She picks up the phone and dials.)*

*Hal:* Don't. Look, I borrowed the book, all right? I'm sorry, I just picked it up before I came downstairs and thought I'd —

*Catherine: (On phone.)* Hello?

*Hal:* I did it for a reason.

*Catherine:* Hello, Police? I — Yes, I'd like to report a robbery in progress.

*Hal:* I noticed something — something your father wrote. All right? Not math, something he wrote. Here, let me show you.

*Catherine:* A ROBBERY.

*Hal:* Will you put the fucking phone down and listen to me?

*Catherine: (On phone.)* Yes, I'm at 5724 South —

*Hal:* It's about you. See? YOU. It was written about you. Here's your name: CATHY. See?

*Catherine:* South . . . *(She pauses. She seems to be listening.)*

*Hal: (Reads.)* "A good day. Some very good news from Catherine." I didn't know what that referred to, but I thought you might . . .

*Catherine.* When did he write this?

*Hal:* I think four years ago. The handwriting is steady. It must have been during his remission.

There's more. *(A moment. Catherine hangs up the phone.)* "Machinery not working yet but I am patient."

"The machinery" is what he called his mind, his ability to do mathematics.

*Catherine:* I know.

*Hal: (Reads.)* "I know I'll get there. I am an auto mechanic who after years of greasy work on a hopeless wreck turns the ignition and hears a faint cough. I am not driving yet but there's cause for optimism. Talking with students helps. So does being outside, eating meals in restaurants, riding busses, all the activities of 'normal' life.

"Most of all Cathy. The years she has lost caring for me. I almost wrote 'wasted.' Yet her refusal to let me be institutionalized — her keeping me at home, caring for me herself has certainly saved my life. Made writing this possible. Made it possible to imagine doing math again. Where does her strength come from? I can never repay her.

"Today is her birthday: She is twenty-one. I'm taking her to dinner."

Dated September fourth.

That's tomorrow.

*Catherine:* It's today.

*Hal:* You're right. *(She takes the book.)*

I thought you might want to see it. I shouldn't have tried to sneak it out. Tomorrow I was going to — it sounds stupid now. I was going to wrap it.

Happy birthday. *(Hal exits. Catherine is alone. She puts her head in her hands. She weeps. Eventually she stops, wipes her eyes. From off: a police siren, drawing closer.)*

*Catherine:* Shit.

**Fade**

SCENE II

*The next morning. Claire, stylish, attractive, drinks coffee from a mug. She has brought bagels and fruit out to the porch on a tray. She notices the champagne bottle lying on the floor. She picks it up and sets it on a table. Catherine enters. Her hair is wet from a shower.*

*Claire:* Better. Much.
*Catherine:* Thanks.
*Claire:* Feel better?
*Catherine:* Yeah.
*Claire:* You look a million times better. Have some coffee.
*Catherine:* Okay.
*Claire:* How do you take it?
*Catherine:* Black.
*Claire:* Have a little milk. *(She pours.)* Want a banana? It's a good thing I brought food: There was nothing in the house.
*Catherine:* I've been meaning to go shopping.
*Claire:* Have a bagel.
*Catherine:* No. I hate breakfast. *(Beat.)*
*Claire:* You didn't put on the dress.
*Catherine:* Didn't really feel like it.
*Claire:* Don't you want to try it on? See if it fits?
*Catherine:* I'll put it on later. *(Beat.)*
*Claire:* If you want to dry your hair I have a hair dryer.
*Catherine:* Nah.
*Claire:* Did you use that conditioner I brought you?
*Catherine:* No, shit, I forgot.
*Claire:* It's my favorite. You'll love it, Katie. I want you to try it.
*Catherine:* I'll use it next time.
*Claire:* You'll like it. It has jojoba.
*Catherine:* What is "jojoba"?
*Claire:* It's something they put in for healthy hair.
*Catherine:* Hair is dead.
*Claire:* What?
*Catherine:* It's dead tissue. You can't make it "healthy."
*Claire:* Whatever, it's something that's good for your hair.
*Catherine:* What, a chemical?
*Claire:* No, it's organic.
*Catherine:* Well it can be organic and still be a chemical.
*Claire:* I don't know what it is.
*Catherine:* Haven't you ever heard of organic chemistry?
*Claire:* It makes my hair feel, look, and smell good. That's the extent of my information about it. You might like it if you decide to use it.
*Catherine:* Thanks, I'll try it.
*Claire:* Good.
    If the dress doesn't fit we can go downtown and exchange it.
*Catherine:* Okay.
*Claire:* I'll take you to lunch.
*Catherine:* Great.

*Claire:*  Maybe Sunday before I go back. Do you need anything?

*Catherine:*  Like clothes?

*Claire:*  Or anything. While I'm here.

*Catherine:*  Nah, I'm cool. *(Beat.)*

*Claire:*  I thought we'd have some people over tonight. If you're feeling okay.

*Catherine:*  I'm feeling okay, Claire, stop saying that.

*Claire:*  You don't have any plans?

*Catherine:*  No.

*Claire:*  I ordered some food. Wine, beer.

*Catherine:*  We are burying Dad this afternoon.

*Claire:*  I think it will be all right. Anyone who's been to the funeral and wants to come over for something to eat, can. And it's the only time I can see any old Chicago friends. It'll be nice. It's a funeral but we don't have to be completely grim about it. If it's okay with you.

*Catherine:*  Yes, sure.

*Claire:*  It's been a stressful time. It would be good to relax in a low-key way.
   Mitch says hi.

*Catherine:*  Hi, Mitch.

*Claire:*  He's really sorry he couldn't come.

*Catherine:*  Yeah, he's gonna miss all the fun.

*Claire:*  He wanted to see you. He sends his love. I told him you'd see him soon enough.
   We're getting married.

*Catherine:*  No shit.

*Claire:*  Yes! We just decided.

*Catherine:*  Yikes.

*Claire:*  Yes!

*Catherine:*  When?

*Claire:*  January.

*Catherine:*  Huh.

*Claire:*  We're not going to do a huge thing. His folks are gone too. Just City Hall, then a big dinner at our favorite restaurant for all our friends. And you, of course, I hope you'll be in the wedding.

*Catherine:*  Yeah. Of course. Congratulations, Claire, I'm really happy for you.

*Claire:*  Thanks, me too. We just decided it was time. His job is great. I just got promoted . . .

*Catherine:*  Huh.

*Claire:*  You will come?

*Catherine:*  Yes, sure. January? I mean I don't have to check my calendar or anything. Sure.

*Claire:*  That makes me very happy. *(Beat.)* How are you?

*Catherine:*  Okay.

*Claire:*  How are you feeling about everything?

*Catherine:*  About "everything"?

*Claire:*  About Dad.

*Catherine:*  What about him?

*Claire:*  How are you feeling about his death? Are you all right?

*Catherine:*  Yes, I am.

*Claire:*  Honestly?

*Catherine:*  Yes.

*Claire:* I think in some ways it was the "right time." If there is ever a right time. Do you know what you want to do now?

*Catherine:* No.

*Claire:* Do you want to stay here?

*Catherine:* I don't know.

*Claire:* Do you want to go back to school?

*Catherine:* I haven't thought about it.

*Claire:* Well there's a lot to think about.
How do you feel?

*Catherine:* Physically? Great. Except my hair seems kind of unhealthy, I wish there were something I could do about that.

*Claire:* Come on, Catherine.

*Catherine:* What is the point of all these questions? *(Beat.)*

*Claire:* Katie, some policemen came by while you were in the shower.

*Catherine:* Yeah?

*Claire:* They said they were "checking up" on things here. Seeing how everything was this morning.

*Catherine:* *(Neutral.)* That was nice.

*Claire:* They told me they responded to a call last night and came to the house.

*Catherine:* Yeah?

*Claire:* Did you call the police last night?

*Catherine:* Yeah.

*Claire:* Why?

*Catherine:* I thought the house was being robbed.

*Claire:* But it wasn't.

*Catherine:* No. I changed my mind. *(Beat.)*

*Claire:* First you call 911 with an emergency and then you hang up on them —

*Catherine:* I didn't really want them to come.

*Claire:* So why did you call?

*Catherine:* I was trying to get this guy out of the house.

*Claire:* Who?

*Catherine:* One of Dad's students.

*Claire:* Dad hasn't had any students for years.

*Catherine:* No, he WAS Dad's student. Now he's — he's a mathematician.

*Claire:* Why was he in the house in the first place?

*Catherine:* Well he's been coming here to look at Dad's notebooks.

*Claire:* In the middle of the night?

*Catherine:* It was late. I was waiting for him to finish and last night I thought he might have been stealing them.

*Claire:* Stealing the notebooks.

*Catherine:* YES. So I told him to go.

*Claire:* Was he stealing them?

*Catherine:* Yes. That's why I called the police —

*Claire:* What is this man's name?

*Catherine:* Hal. Harold. Harold Dobbs.

*Claire:* The police said you were the only one here.

*Catherine:* He left before they got here.

*Claire:* With the notebooks?

*Catherine:* No, Claire, don't be stupid, there are over a hundred notebooks. He was only stealing ONE, but he was stealing it so he could give it BACK to me, so I let him go so he could play with his band on the North Side.

*Claire:* His band?

*Catherine:* He was late. He wanted me to come with him but I was like Yeah, right. *(Beat.)*

*Claire:* *(Gently.)* Is "Harold Dobbs" your boyfriend?

*Catherine:* No!

*Claire:* Are you sleeping with him?

*Catherine:* What? Euughh! No! He's a math geek!

*Claire:* And he's in a band? A rock band?

*Catherine:* No a marching band. He plays trombone. Yes a rock band!

*Claire:* What is the name of his band?

*Catherine:* How should I know?

*Claire:* "Harold Dobbs" didn't tell you the name of his rock band?

*Catherine:* No. I don't know. Look in the paper. They were playing last night. They do a song called "Imaginary Number" that doesn't exist. *(Beat.)*

*Claire:* I'm sorry, I'm just trying to understand: Is "Harold Dobbs" —

*Catherine:* Stop saying "Harold Dobbs."

*Claire:* Is this . . . person . . .

*Catherine:* HAROLD DOBBS EXISTS.

*Claire:* I'm sure he does.

*Catherine:* He's a mathematician at the University of Chicago. Call the fucking math department.

*Claire:* Don't get upset. I'm just trying to understand! I mean if you found out some creepy grad student was trying to take some of Dad's papers and you called the police I'd understand, and if you were out here partying, drinking with your boyfriend, I'd understand. But the two stories don't go together.

*Catherine:* Because you made up the "boyfriend" story. I was here ALONE —

*Claire:* Harold Dobbs wasn't here?

*Catherine:* No, he — YES, he was here, but we weren't "partying"!

*Claire:* You weren't drinking with him?

*Catherine:* No!

*Claire:* *(She holds up the champagne bottle.)* This was sitting right here. Who were you drinking champagne with? *(Catherine hesitates.)*

*Catherine:* With no one.

*Claire:* Are you sure?

*Catherine:* Yes. *(Beat.)*

*Claire:* The police said you were abusive. They said you're lucky they didn't haul you in.

*Catherine:* These guys were assholes, Claire. They wouldn't go away. They wanted me to fill out a report . . .

*Claire:* Were you abusive?

*Catherine:* This one cop kept spitting on me when he talked. It was disgusting.

*Claire:* Did you use the word "dickhead"?

*Catherine:* Oh I don't remember.

*Claire:* Did you tell one cop . . . to go fuck the other cop's mother?

*Catherine:* NO.

*Claire:* That's what they said.

*Catherine:* Not with that phrasing.

*Claire:* Did you strike one of them?

*Catherine:* They were trying to come in the house!

*Claire:* Oh my God.

*Catherine:* I might have pushed him a little.

*Claire:* They said you were either drunk or disturbed.

*Catherine:* They wanted to come in here and SEARCH MY HOUSE —

*Claire:* YOU called THEM.

*Catherine:* Yes but I didn't actually WANT them to come. But they did come and then they started acting like they owned the place — pushing me around, calling me "girly," smirking at me, laughing: They were assholes.

*Claire:* These guys seemed perfectly nice. They were off-duty and they took the trouble to come back here at the end of their shift to check up on you. They were very polite.

*Catherine:* Well people are nicer to you. *(Beat.)*

*Claire:* Katie. Would you like to come to New York?

*Catherine:* Yes, I told you, I'll come in January.

*Claire:* You could come sooner. We'd love to have you. You could stay with us. It'd be fun.

*Catherine:* I don't want to.

*Claire:* Mitch has become an excellent cook. It's like his hobby now. He buys all these gadgets. Garlic press, olive oil sprayer . . . Every night there's something new. Delicious, wonderful meals. The other day he made vegetarian chili!

*Catherine:* What the fuck are you talking about?

*Claire:* Stay with us for a while. We would have so much fun.

*Catherine:* Thanks, I'm okay here.

*Claire:* Chicago is dead. New York is so much more fun, you can't believe it.

*Catherine:* The "fun" thing is really not where my focus is at the moment.

*Claire:* I think New York would be a really fun and . . . safe . . . place for you to —

*Catherine:* I don't need a safe place and I don't want to have any fun! I'm perfectly fine here.

*Claire:* You look tired. I think you could use some downtime.

*Catherine:* Downtime?

*Claire:* Katie, please. You've had a very hard time.

*Catherine:* I'm PERFECTLY OKAY.

*Claire:* I think you're upset and exhausted.

*Catherine:* I was FINE till you got here.

*Claire:* Yes, but you —

*Hal:* *(From off.)* Catherine?

*Claire:* Who is that? *(A beat. Hal enters.)*

*Hal:* Hey, I — *(Catherine stands and points triumphantly at him.)*

*Catherine:* HAROLD DOBBS!

*Hal:* *(Confused.)* Hi.

*Catherine:* OKAY? I really don't need this, Claire. I'm fine, you know, I'm totally fine, and then you swoop in here with these questions, and "Are you okay?" and your soothing tone of voice and "Oh, the poor policemen" — I think the police can handle themselves! — and bagels and bananas and jojoba and "Come to New York" and vegetarian chili, I mean it really pisses me off so just save it. *(Beat.)*

*Claire:* *(Smoothly, to Hal.)* I'm Claire. Catherine's sister.

*Hal:* Oh, hi. Hal. Nice to meet you. *(Uncomfortable beat.)* I . . . hope it's not too early. I was just going to try to get some work done before the uh — if uh, if . . .

*Claire:* Yes!

*Catherine:* Sure, okay. *(Hal exits. A moment.)*

*Claire:* That's Harold Dobbs?
*Catherine:* Yes.
*Claire:* He's cute.
*Catherine:* *(Disgusted.)* Eugh.
*Claire:* He's a mathematician?
*Catherine:* I think you owe me an apology, Claire.
*Claire:* We need to make some decisions. But I shouldn't have tried to start first thing in the morning. I don't want an argument. *(Beat.)* Maybe Hal would like a bagel? *(Catherine doesn't take the hint. She exits.)*

**Fade**

## SCENE III

> *Night. Inside the house a party is in progress. Loud music from a not-very-good but enthusiastic band. Catherine is alone on the porch. She wears a flattering black dress. Inside, the band finishes a number. Cheers, applause. After a moment Hal comes out. He wears a dark suit. He has taken off his tie. He is sweaty and revved-up from playing. He holds two bottles of beer. Catherine regards him. A beat.*

*Catherine:* I feel that for a funeral reception this might have gotten a bit out of control.
*Hal:* Aw come on. It's great. Come on in.
*Catherine:* I'm okay.
*Hal:* We're done playing, I promise.
*Catherine:* No, thanks.
*Hal:* Do you want a beer?
*Catherine:* I'm okay.
*Hal:* I brought you one. *(Beat. She hesitates.)*
*Catherine:* Okay. *(She takes it, sips.)* How many people are in there?
*Hal:* It's down to about forty.
*Catherine:* Forty?
*Hal:* Just the hard-core partyers.
*Catherine:* My sister's friends.
*Hal:* No, mathematicians. Your sister's friends left hours ago.
    The guys were really pleased to be asked to participate. They worshiped your dad.
*Catherine:* It was Claire's idea.
*Hal:* It was good.
*Catherine:* *(Concedes.)* The performance of "Imaginary Number" was . . . sort of . . . moving.
*Hal:* Good funeral. I mean not "good," but —
*Catherine:* No. Yeah.
*Hal:* Can you believe how many people came?
*Catherine:* I was surprised.
*Hal:* I think he would have liked it. *(She looks at him.)* Sorry, it's not my place to —

*Catherine:* No, you're right. Everything was better than I thought. *(Beat.)*
*Hal:* You look great.
*Catherine:* *(Indicates the dress.)* Claire gave it to me.
*Hal:* I like it.
*Catherine:* It doesn't really fit.
*Hal:* No, Catherine, it's good. *(A moment. Noise from inside.)*
*Catherine:* When do you think they'll leave?
*Hal:* No way to know. Mathematicians are insane. I went to this conference in Toronto last fall. I'm young, right? I'm in shape, I thought I could hang with the big boys. Wrong. I've never been so exhausted in my life. Forty-eight straight hours of partying, drinking, drugs, papers, lectures . . .
*Catherine:* Drugs?
*Hal:* Yeah. Amphetamines, mostly. I mean I don't. Some of the older guys are really hooked.
*Catherine:* Really?
*Hal:* Yeah, they think they need it.
*Catherine:* Why?
*Hal:* They think math's a young man's game. Speed keeps them racing, makes them feel sharp. There's this fear that your creativity peaks around twenty-three and it's all downhill from there. Once you hit fifty it's over, you might as well teach high school.
*Catherine:* That's what my father thought.
*Hal:* I dunno. Some people stay prolific.
*Catherine:* Not many.
*Hal:* No, you're right. Really original work — it's all young guys.
*Catherine:* Young guys.
*Hal:* Young people.
*Catherine:* But it is men, mostly.
*Hal:* There are some women.
*Catherine:* Who?
*Hal:* There's a woman at Stanford, I can't remember her name.
*Catherine:* Sophie Germain.
*Hal:* Yeah? I've probably seen her at meetings, I just don't think I've met her.
*Catherine:* She was born in Paris in 1776. *(Beat.)*
*Hal:* So I've definitely never met her.
*Catherine:* She was trapped in her house.

    The French Revolution was going on, the Terror. She had to stay inside for safety and she passed the time reading in her father's study. The Greeks . . . Later she tried to get a real education but the schools didn't allow women. So she wrote letters. She wrote to Gauss. She used a man's name. Uh, "Antoine-August Le Blanc." She sent him some proofs involving a certain kind of prime number, important work. He was delighted to correspond with such a brilliant young man.

    Dad gave me a book about her.
*Hal:* I'm stupid. Sophie Germain, of course.
*Catherine:* You know her?
*Hal:* Germain Primes.
*Catherine:* Right.
*Hal:* They're famous. Double them and add one, and you get another prime. Like two. Two is prime, doubled plus one is five: also prime.

*Catherine:*  Right. Or 92,305 times $2^{16998}$ plus one.

*Hal:*  *(Startled.)* Right.

*Catherine:*  That's the biggest one. The biggest one known . . . *(Beat.)*

*Hal:*  Did he ever find out who she was? Gauss.

*Catherine:*  Yeah. Later a mutual friend told him the brilliant young man was a woman.

      He wrote to her: "A taste for the mysteries of numbers is excessively rare, but when a person of the sex which, according to our customs and prejudices, must encounter infinitely more difficulties than men to familiarize herself with these thorny researches, succeeds nevertheless in penetrating the most obscure parts of them, then without a doubt she must have the noblest courage, quite extraordinary talents and superior genius."

      *(Now self-conscious.)* I memorized it . . . *(Hal stares at her. He suddenly kisses her, then stops, embarrassed. He moves away.)*

*Hal:*  Sorry. I'm a little drunk.

*Catherine:*  It's okay. *(Uncomfortable beat.)* I'm sorry about yesterday. I wasn't helpful. About the work you're doing. Take as long as you need upstairs.

*Hal:*  You were fine. I was pushy.

*Catherine:*  I was awful.

*Hal:*  No. My timing was terrible. Anyway, you're probably right.

*Catherine:*  What?

*Hal:*  About it being junk.

*Catherine:*  *(Nods.)* Yes.

*Hal:*  I read through a lot of stuff today, just skimming. Except for the book I stole —

*Catherine:*  Oh, God, I'm sorry about that.

*Hal:*  No, you were right.

*Catherine:*  I shouldn't have called the police.

*Hal:*  It was my fault.

*Catherine:*  No.

*Hal:*  The point is, that book — I'm starting to think it's the only lucid one, really. And there's no math in it.

*Catherine:*  No.

*Hal:*  I mean, I'll keep reading, but if I don't find anything in a couple of days . . .

*Catherine:*  Back to the drums.

*Hal:*  Yeah.

*Catherine:*  And your own research.

*Hal:*  Such as it is.

*Catherine:*  What's wrong with it?

*Hal:*  It's not exactly setting the world on fire.

*Catherine:*  Oh come on.

*Hal:*  It sucks, basically.

*Catherine:*  Harold.

*Hal:*  My papers get turned down. For the right reasons — my stuff is trivial. The big ideas aren't there.

*Catherine:*  It's not about big ideas. It's work. You've got to chip away at a problem.

*Hal:*  That's not what your dad did.

*Catherine:*  I think it was, in a way. He'd attack a question from the side, from some weird angle, sneak up on it, grind away at it. He was slogging. He was just so much faster than anyone else that from the outside it looked magical.

*Hal:* I don't know.

*Catherine:* I'm just guessing.

*Hal:* Plus the work was beautiful. It's streamlined: no wasted moves, like a ninety-five-mile-an-hour fastball. It's just . . . elegant.

*Catherine:* Yeah.

*Hal:* And that's what you can never duplicate. At least I can't.
  It's okay. At a certain point you realize it's not going to happen, you read just your expectations. I enjoy teaching.

*Catherine:* You might come up with something.

*Hal:* I'm twenty-eight, remember? On the downhill slope.

*Catherine:* Have you tried speed? I've heard it helps.

*Hal:* (*Laughs.*) Yeah. (*Beat.*)

*Catherine:* So, Hal.

*Hal:* Yeah?

*Catherine:* What do you do for sex?

*Hal:* What?

*Catherine:* At your conferences.

*Hal:* Uh, I uh —

*Catherine:* Isn't that why people hold conferences? Travel. Room service. Tax-deductible sex in big hotel beds.

*Hal:* (*Laughs, nervous.*) Maybe. I don't know.

*Catherine:* So what do you do? All you guys. (*Beat. Is she flirting with him? Hal is not sure.*)

*Hal:* Well we are scientists.

*Catherine:* So?

*Hal:* So there's a lot of experimentation.

*Catherine:* (*Laughs.*) I see. (*Beat. Catherine goes to him. She kisses him. A longer kiss. It ends. Hal is surprised and pleased.*)

*Hal:* Huh.

*Catherine:* That was nice.

*Hal:* Really?

*Catherine:* Yes.

*Hal:* Again?

*Catherine:* Yes. (*Kiss.*)

*Hal:* I always liked you.

*Catherine:* You did?

*Hal:* Even before I knew you. I'd catch glimpses of you when you visited your dad's office at school. I wanted to talk to you but I thought, No, you do not flirt with your doctoral adviser's daughter.

*Catherine:* Especially when your adviser's crazy.

*Hal:* Especially then. (*Kiss.*)

*Catherine:* You came here once. Four years ago. Remember?

*Hal:* Sure. I can't believe you do. I was dropping off a draft of my thesis for your dad. Jesus I was nervous.

*Catherine:* You looked nervous.

*Hal:* I can't believe you remember that.

*Catherine:* I remember you. (*Kiss.*) I thought you seemed . . . not boring. (*They continue to kiss.*)

**Fade**

SCENE IV

>  *The next morning. Catherine alone on the porch, in a robe. Hal enters, half-*
>  *dressed. He walks up behind her quietly. She hears him and turns.*

*Hal:* How long have you been up?

*Catherine:* A while.

*Hal:* Did I oversleep?

*Catherine:* No. *(Beat. Morning-after awkwardness.)*

*Hal:* Is your sister up?

*Catherine:* No. She's flying home in a couple hours. I should probably wake her.

*Hal:* Let her sleep. She was doing some pretty serious drinking with the theoretical physicists last night.

*Catherine:* I'll make her some coffee when she gets up. *(Beat.)*

*Hal:* Sunday mornings I usually go out. Get the paper, have some breakfast.

*Catherine:* Okay. *(Beat.)*

*Hal:* Do you want to come?

*Catherine:* Oh. No. I ought to stick around until Claire leaves.

*Hal:* All right.
     Do you mind if I stay?

*Catherine:* No. You can work if you want.

*Hal:* *(Taken aback.)* Okay.

*Catherine:* Okay.

*Hal:* Should I?

*Catherine:* If you want to.

*Hal:* Do you want me to go?

*Catherine:* Do you want to go?

*Hal:* I want to stay here with you.

*Catherine:* Oh . . .

*Hal:* I want to spend the day with you if possible. I'd like to spend as much time
with you as I can unless of course I'm coming on way too strong right now
and scaring you in which case I'll begin back-pedaling immediately . . . *(She
laughs. Her relief is evident; so is his. They kiss.)*
     How embarrassing is it if I say last night was wonderful?

*Catherine:* It's only embarrassing if I don't agree.

*Hal:* Uh, so . . .

*Catherine:* Don't be embarrassed. *(They kiss. After a moment Catherine breaks
off. She hesitates, making a decision. Then she takes a chain from around her
neck. There is a key on the chain. She tosses it to Hal.)* Here.

*Hal:* What's this?

*Catherine:* It's a key.

*Hal:* Ah.

*Catherine:* Try it.

*Hal:* Where?

*Catherine:* Bottom drawer of the desk in my dad's office.

*Hal:* What's in there?

*Catherine:* There's one way to find out, Professor.

*Hal:* Now? *(Catherine shrugs. Hal laughs, unsure if this is a joke or not.)* Okay. *(He
kisses her quickly then goes inside. Catherine smiles to herself. She is happy, on
the edge of being giddy. Claire enters, hungover. She sits down, squinting.)*

*Catherine:*  Good morning.

*Claire:*  Please don't yell please.

*Catherine:*  Are you all right?

*Claire:*  No. *(Beat. She clutches her head.)* Those fucking physicists.

*Catherine:*  What happened?

*Claire:*  Thanks a lot for leaving me all alone with them.

*Catherine:*  Where were your friends?

*Claire:*  My stupid friends left — it was only eleven o'clock! — they all had to get home and pay their babysitters or bake bread or something. I'm left alone with these lunatics . . .

*Catherine:*  Why did you drink so much?

*Claire:*  I thought I could keep up with them. I thought they'd stop. They didn't. Oh God.

*Catherine:*  Do you want some coffee?

*Claire:*  In a minute.

That BAND.

*Catherine:*  Yeah.

*Claire:*  They were terrible.

*Catherine:*  They were okay. They had fun. I think.

*Claire:*  Well as long as everyone had fun.

Your dress turned out all right.

*Catherine:*  I love it.

*Claire:*  You do.

*Catherine:*  Yeah, it's wonderful.

*Claire:*  I was surprised you even wore it.

*Catherine:*  I love it, Claire. Thanks.

*Claire:*  *(Surprised.)* You're welcome. You're in a good mood.

*Catherine:*  Should I not be?

*Claire:*  Are you kidding? No. I'm thrilled.

I'm leaving in a few hours.

*Catherine:*  I know.

*Claire:*  The house is a wreck. Don't clean it up yourself. I'll hire someone to come in.

*Catherine:*  Thanks. You want your coffee?

*Claire:*  No, thanks.

*Catherine:*  *(Starting in.)* It's no trouble.

*Claire:*  Hold on a sec, Katie. I just . . . *(Claire takes a breath.)*

I'm leaving soon. I —

*Catherine:*  You said. I know. —

*Claire:*  I'd still like you to come to New York.

*Catherine:*  Yes: January.

*Claire:*  I'd like you to move to New York.

*Catherine:*  Move?

*Claire:*  Would you think about it? For me?

You could stay with me and Mitch at first. There's plenty of room. Then you could get your own place. I've already scouted some apartments for you, really cute places.

*Catherine:*  What would I do in New York?

*Claire:*  What are you doing here?

*Catherine:*  I live here.

*Claire:*  You could do whatever you want. You could work, you could go to school.

*Catherine:*  I don't know, Claire. This is pretty major.

*Claire:*  I realize that.

*Catherine:*  I know you mean well. I'm just not sure what I want to do. I mean to be honest you were right yesterday. I do feel a little confused. I'm tired. It's been a pretty weird couple of years. I think I'd like to take some time to figure things out.

*Claire:*  You could do that in New York.

*Catherine:*  And I could do it here.

*Claire:*  But it would be much easier for me to get you set up in an apartment in New York, and —

*Catherine:*  I don't need an apartment, I'll stay in the house.

*Claire:*  We're selling the house. *(Beat.)*

*Catherine:*  What?

*Claire:*  We — I'm selling it.

*Catherine:*  WHEN?

*Claire:*  I'm hoping to do the paperwork this week. I know it seems sudden.

*Catherine:*  No one was here looking at the place, who are you selling it to?

*Claire:*  The University. They've wanted the block for years.

*Catherine:*  I LIVE HERE.

*Claire:*  Honey, now that Dad's gone it doesn't make sense. It's in bad shape. It costs a fortune to heat. It's time to let it go. Mitch agrees, it's a very smart move. We're lucky, we have a great offer —

*Catherine:*  Where am I supposed to live?

*Claire:*  Come to New York.

*Catherine:*  I can't believe this.

*Claire:*  It'll be so good. You deserve a change. This would be a whole new adventure for you.

*Catherine:*  Why are you doing this?

*Claire:*  I want to help.

*Catherine:*  By kicking me out of my house?

*Claire:*  It was my house too.

*Catherine:*  You haven't lived here for years.

*Claire:*  I know that. You were on your own. I really regret that, Katie.

*Catherine:*  Don't.

*Claire:*  I know I let you down. I feel awful about it. Now I'm trying to help.

*Catherine:*  You want to help now?

*Claire:*  Yes.

*Catherine:*  Dad is dead.

*Claire:*  I know.

*Catherine:*  He's dead. Now that he's dead you fly in for the weekend and decide you want to help? YOU'RE LATE. Where have you been?

*Claire:*  I —

*Catherine:*  Where were you five years ago? You weren't helping then.

*Claire:*  I was working.

*Catherine:*  I was HERE. I lived with him ALONE.

*Claire:*  I was working fourteen-hour days. I paid every bill here. I paid off the mortgage on this three-bedroom house while I was living in a studio in Brooklyn.

*Catherine:*  You had your life. You got to finish school.

*Claire:* You could have stayed in school!

*Catherine:* How?

*Claire:* I would have done anything — I told you that. I told you a million times to do anything you wanted.

*Catherine:* What about Dad? Someone had to take care of him.

*Claire:* He was ill. He should have been in a full-time professional care situation.

*Catherine:* He didn't belong in the nuthouse.

*Claire:* He might have been better off.

*Catherine:* How can you say that?

*Claire:* This is where I'm meant to feel guilty, right?

*Catherine:* Sure, go for it.

*Claire:* I'm heartless. My own father.

*Catherine:* He needed to be here. In his own house, near the University, near his students, near everything that made him happy.

*Claire:* Maybe. Or maybe some real, professional care would have done him more good than rattling around in a filthy house with YOU looking after him.
   I'm sorry, Catherine, it's not your fault. It's my fault for letting you do it.

*Catherine:* I was right to keep him here.

*Claire:* No.

*Catherine:* What about his remission? Four years ago. He was healthy for almost a year.

*Claire:* And then he went right downhill again.

*Catherine:* He might have been worse in a hospital.

*Claire:* And he MIGHT have been BETTER. Did he ever do any work again?

*Catherine:* No.

*Claire:* NO.
   And you might have been better.

*Catherine:* *(Keeping her voice under control.)* Better than what?

*Claire:* Living here with him didn't do you any good. You said that yourself.
   You had so much talent . . .

*Catherine:* You think I'm like Dad.

*Claire:* I think you have some of his talent and some of his tendency toward . . . instability. *(Beat.)*

*Catherine:* Claire, in addition to the "cute apartments" that you've "scouted" for me in New York, would you by any chance also have devoted some of your considerable energies toward scouting out another type of —

*Claire:* NO.

*Catherine:* — living facility for your bughouse little sister?

*Claire:* NO! Absolutely not. That is not what this is about.

*Catherine:* Don't lie to me, Claire, I'm smarter than you. *(Beat.)*

*Claire:* The resources . . . I've investigated —

*Catherine:* Oh my GOD.

*Claire:* — if you WANTED to, all I'm saying is the doctors in New York and the people are the BEST, and they —

*Catherine:* FUCK YOU.

*Claire:* It would be entirely up to you. You wouldn't LIVE anywhere, you can —

*Catherine:* I hate you.

*Claire:* Don't yell, please, calm down.

*Catherine:* I HATE YOU. I — *(Hal enters, holding a notebook. Claire and Catherine stop suddenly. Beat.)*

*Claire:* What are you doing here? . . . *(She looks at Catherine. Hal is nearly speechless. He stares at Catherine.)*

*Hal:* How long have you known about this?

*Catherine:* A while.

*Hal:* Why didn't you tell me about it?

*Catherine:* I wasn't sure I wanted to. *(Beat.)*

*Hal:* Thank you.

*Catherine:* You're welcome.

*Claire:* What's going on?

*Hal:* God, Catherine, thank you.

*Catherine:* I thought you'd like to see it.

*Claire:* What is it?

*Hal:* It's incredible.

*Claire:* What IS it?

*Hal:* Oh, uh, it's a result. A proof.
      I mean it looks like one. I mean it is one, a very long one, I haven't read it all of course, or checked it, I don't even know if I could check it, but if it IS what I think it is a proof of, it's a very . . . important . . . proof.

*Claire:* What does it prove?

*Hal:* It looks like it proves a theorem . . . a mathematical theorem about prime numbers, something mathematicians have been trying to prove since . . . since there were mathematicians, basically. Most people thought it couldn't be done.

*Claire:* Where did you find it?

*Hal:* In your father's desk. Cathy told me about it.

*Claire:* You know what this is?

*Catherine:* Sure.

*Claire:* Is it good?

*Catherine:* Yes.

*Hal:* It's historic. If it checks out.

*Claire:* What does it say?

*Hal:* I don't know yet. I've just read the first few pages.

*Claire:* But what does it mean?

*Hal:* It means that during a time when everyone thought your dad was crazy . . . or barely functioning . . . he was doing some of the most important mathematics in the world. If it checks out it means you publish instantly. It means newspapers all over the world are going to want to talk to the person who found this notebook.

*Claire:* Cathy.

*Hal:* Cathy.

*Catherine:* I didn't find it.

*Hal:* Yes you did.

*Catherine:* No.

*Claire:* Well did you find it or did Hal find it?

*Hal:* I didn't find it.

*Catherine:* I didn't find it. I wrote it.

**Curtain**

## ACT II

### SCENE I

*Robert is alone on the porch. He sits quietly, enjoying the quiet, the September afternoon. A notebook nearby, unopened. He closes his eyes, apparently dozing. It is four years earlier than the events in Act One. Catherine enters quietly. She stands behind her father for a moment.*

*Robert:* Hello.
*Catherine:* How did you know I was here?
*Robert:* I heard you.
*Catherine:* I thought you were asleep.
*Robert:* On an afternoon like this? No.
*Catherine:* Do you need anything?
*Robert:* No.
*Catherine:* I'm going to the store.
*Robert:* What's for dinner?
*Catherine:* What do you want?
*Robert:* Not spaghetti.
*Catherine:* All right.
*Robert:* Disgusting stuff.
*Catherine:* That's what I was going to make.
*Robert:* I had a feeling. Good thing I spoke up. You make it too much.
*Catherine:* What do you want?
*Robert:* What do you have a taste for?
*Catherine:* Nothing.
*Robert:* Nothing at all?
*Catherine:* I don't care. I thought pasta would be easy.
*Robert:* Pasta, oh God don't even say the word "pasta." It sounds so hopeless, like surrender: "Pasta would be easy." Yes, yes it would. Pasta. It doesn't MEAN anything. It's just a euphemism people invented when they got sick of eating spaghetti.
*Catherine:* Dad, what do you want to eat?
*Robert:* I don't know.
*Catherine:* Well I don't know what to get.
*Robert:* I'll shop.
*Catherine:* No.
*Robert:* I'll do it.
*Catherine:* No, Dad, rest.
*Robert:* I wanted to take a walk anyway.
*Catherine:* Are you sure?
*Robert:* Yes. What about a walk to the lake? You and me.
*Catherine:* All right.
*Robert:* I would love to go to the lake. Then on the way home we'll stop at the store, see what jumps out at us.
*Catherine:* It's warm. It would be nice, if you're up for it.
*Robert:* You're damn right I'm up for it. We'll work up an appetite. Give me ten seconds, let me put this stuff away and we're out the door.
*Catherine:* I'm going to school. *(Beat.)*

*Robert:*  When?

*Catherine:*  I'm gonna start at Northwestern at the end of the month.

*Robert:*  Northwestern?

*Catherine:*  They were great about my credits. They're taking me in as a sophomore. I wasn't sure when to talk to you about it.

*Robert:*  Northwestern?

*Catherine:*  Yes.

*Robert:*  What's wrong with Chicago?

*Catherine:*  You still teach there. I'm sorry, it's too weird, taking classes in your department.

*Robert:*  It's a long drive.

*Catherine:*  Not that long, half an hour.

*Robert:*  Still, twice a day . . .

*Catherine:*  Dad, I'd live there. *(Beat.)*

*Robert:*  You'd actually want to live in Evanston?

*Catherine:*  Yes. I'll still be close. I can come home whenever you want. You've been well — really well — for almost seven months. I don't think you need me here every minute of the day. *(Beat.)*

*Robert:*  This is all a done deal? You're in.

*Catherine:*  Yes.

*Robert:*  You're sure.

*Catherine:*  Yes.

*Robert:*  Who pays for it?

*Catherine:*  They're giving me a free ride, Dad. They've been great.

*Robert:*  On tuition, sure. What about food, books, clothes, gas, meals out — do you plan to have a social life?

*Catherine:*  I don't know.

*Robert:*  You gotta pay your own way on dates, at least the early dates, say the first three, otherwise they expect something.

*Catherine:*  The money will be fine. Claire's gonna help out.

*Robert:*  When did you talk to Claire?

*Catherine:*  I don't know, a couple weeks ago.

*Robert:*  You talk to her before you talk to me?

*Catherine:*  There were a lot of details to work out. She was great, she offered to take care of all the expenses.

*Robert:*  This is a big step. A different city —

*Catherine:*  It's not even a long distance phone call.

*Robert:*  It's a huge place. They're serious up there. I mean serious. Yeah the football's a disaster but the math guys don't kid around. You haven't been in school. You sure you're ready? You can get buried up there.

*Catherine:*  I'll be all right.

*Robert:*  You're way behind.

*Catherine:*  I know.

*Robert:*  A year, at least.

*Catherine:*  Thank you, I KNOW. Look, I don't know if this is a good idea. I don't know if I can handle the work. I don't know if I can handle any of it.

*Robert:*  For Chrissake, Catherine, you should have talked to me.

*Catherine:*  Dad. Listen. If you ever . . . if for any reason it ever turned out that you needed me here full time again —

*Robert:*  I WON'T. That's not what I'm talking about —

*Catherine:* I can always take a semester off, or —

*Robert:* No. Stop it. I just — the end of the MONTH? Why didn't you say something before?

*Catherine:* Dad, come on. It took a while to set this up, and until recently, until very recently, you weren't —

*Robert:* You just said yourself I've been fine.

*Catherine:* Yes, but I didn't know — I hoped, but I didn't know, no one knew if this would last. I told myself to wait until I was sure about you. That you were feeling okay again. Consistently okay.

*Robert:* So I'm to take this conversation as a vote of confidence? I'm honored.

*Catherine:* Take it however you want. I believed you'd get better.

*Robert:* Well thank you very much.

*Catherine:* Don't thank me. I had to. I was living with you.

*Robert:* All right, that's enough, Catherine. Let's stay on the subject.

*Catherine:* This is the subject! There were LIBRARY BOOKS stacked up to the ceiling upstairs, do you remember that? You were trying to decode MESSAGES —

*Robert:* The fucking books are gone, I took them back myself. Why do you bring that garbage up? *(Knocking, off. Beat. Catherine goes inside to answer the door. She returns with Hal. He carries a manila envelope. He is nervous.)*
 Mr. Dobbs.

*Hal:* Hi. I hope it's not a bad time.

*Robert:* Yes it is, actually, you couldn't have picked worse.

*Hal:* Oh, I, uh —

*Robert:* You interrupted an argument.

*Hal:* I'm sorry. I can come back.

*Robert:* It's all right. We needed a break.

*Hal:* Are you sure?

*Robert:* Yes. The argument was about dinner. We don't know what to eat. What's your suggestion? *(A beat while Hal is on the spot.)*

*Hal:* Uh, there's a good pasta place not too far from here.

*Robert:* NO!

*Catherine:* *(With Robert.)* That is a BRILLIANT idea.

*Robert:* Oh dear Jesus God no.

*Catherine:* *(With Robert.)* What's it called? Give me the address.

*Robert:* No! Sorry. Wrong answer but thank you for trying. *(Hal stands there, looking at both of them.)*

*Hal:* I can come back.

*Robert:* Stay. *(To Catherine.)* Where are you going?

*Catherine:* Inside.

*Robert:* What about dinner?

*Catherine:* What about him?

*Robert:* What are you doing here, Dobbs?

*Hal:* My timing sucks. I am really sorry.

*Robert:* Don't be silly.

*Hal:* I'll come to your office.

*Robert:* Stop. Sit down. Glad you're here. Don't let the dinner thing throw you, you'll bounce back. *(To Catherine.)* This should be easier. Let's back off the problem, let it breathe, come at it again when it's not looking.

*Catherine:* Fine. *(Exiting.)* Excuse me.

*Robert:* Sorry, I'm rude. Hal, this is my daughter Catherine.
 *(To Catherine.)* Don't go, have a drink with us. Catherine, Harold Dobbs.

*Catherine:* Hi.

*Hal:* Hi.

*Robert:* Hal is a grad student. He's doing his Ph.D., very promising stuff. Unfortunately for him his work coincided with my return to the department and he got stuck with me.

*Hal:* No, no, it's been — I've been very lucky.

*Catherine:* How long have you been at U. of C.?

*Hal:* Well I've been working on my thesis for —

*Robert:* Hal's in our "Infinite" program. As he approaches completion of his dissertation, time approaches infinity. Would you like a drink, Hal?

*Hal:* Yes I would.

And uh, with all due respect . . . *(He hands Robert the envelope.)*

*Robert:* Really? *(He opens it and looks inside.)*

You must have had an interesting few months.

*Hal: (Cheerfully.)* Worst summer of my life.

*Robert:* Congratulations.

*Hal:* It's just a draft. Based on everything we talked about last spring. *(Robert pours a drink. Hal babbles.)*

I wasn't sure if I should wait till the quarter started, or if I should give it to you now, or hold off, do another draft, but I figured fuck it I, I mean I just . . . let's just get it over with, so I thought I'd just come over and see if you were home, and —

*Robert:* Drink this.

*Hal:* Thanks. *(He drinks.)*

I decided, I don't know, if it feels done, maybe it is.

*Robert:* Wrong. If it feels done there are major errors.

*Hal:* Uh, I —

*Robert:* That's okay, that's good, we'll find them and fix them.

Don't worry. You're on your way to a solid career, you'll be teaching younger, more irritating versions of yourself in no time.

*Hal:* Thank you.

*Robert:* Catherine's in the math department at Northwestern, Hal. *(Catherine looks up, startled.)*

*Hal:* Oh, who are you working with?

*Catherine:* I'm just starting this fall. Undergrad.

*Robert:* She's starting in . . . three weeks?

*Catherine:* A little more. *(Beat.)*

*Robert:* They have some good people at Northwestern. O'Donohue. Kaminsky.

*Catherine:* Yes.

*Robert:* They will work your ass off.

*Catherine:* I know.

*Robert:* You'll have to run pretty hard to catch up.

*Catherine:* I think I can do it.

*Robert:* Of course you can. *(Beat.)*

*Hal:* You must be excited.

*Catherine:* I am.

*Hal:* First year of school can be great.

*Catherine:* Yeah?

*Hal:* Sure, all the new people, new places, getting out of the house.

*Catherine: (Embarrassed.)* Yes.

*Hal: (Embarrassed.)* Or, no, I —

*Robert:* Absolutely, getting the hell out of here, thank God, it's about time. I'll be glad to see the back of her.

*Catherine:* You will?

*Robert:* Of course. Maybe I want to have the place to myself for a while, did that ever occur to you? *(To Hal.)* It's awful the way children sentimentalize their parents. *(To Catherine.)* We could use some quiet around here.

*Catherine:* Oh don't worry, I'll come back. I'll be here every Sunday cooking up big vats of spaghetti to last you through the week.

*Robert:* And I'll drive up, strut around Evanston, embarrass you in front of your classmates.

*Catherine:* Good. So we'll be in touch.

*Robert:* Sure. And if you get stuck with a problem, give me a call.

*Catherine:* Okay. Same to you.

*Robert:* Fine. Make sure to get me your number. *(To Hal.)* I'm actually looking forward to getting some work done.

*Hal:* Oh, what are you working on?

*Robert:* Nothing. *(Beat.)*

> Nothing at the moment.
>
> Which I'm glad of, really. This is the time of year when you don't want to be tied down to anything. You want to be outside. I love Chicago in September. Perfect skies. Sailboats on the water. Cubs losing. Warm, the sun still hot . . . with the occasional blast of Arctic wind to keep you on your toes, remind you of winter. Students coming back, bookstores full, everybody busy.
>
> I was in a bookstore yesterday. Completely full, students buying books . . . browsing . . . Students do a hell of a lot of browsing, don't they? Just browsing. You see them shuffling around with their backpacks, goofing off, taking up space. You'd call it loitering except every once in a while they pick up a book and flip the pages: "Browsing." I admire it. It's an honest way to kill an afternoon. In the back of a used bookstore, or going through a crate of somebody's old record albums — not looking for anything, just looking, what the hell, touching the old book jackets, seeing what somebody threw out, seeing what they underlined . . . maybe you find something great, like an old thriller with a painted cover from the forties, or a textbook one of your professors used when he was a student — his name is written in it very carefully . . . Yeah, I like it. I like watching the students. Wondering what they're gonna buy, what they're gonna read. What kind of ideas they'll come up with when they settle down and get to work . . .
>
> I'm not doing much right now. It does get harder. It's a stereotype that happens to be true, unfortunately for me — unfortunately for you, for all of us.

*Catherine:* Maybe you'll get lucky.

*Robert:* Maybe I will.

> Maybe you'll pick up where I left off.

*Catherine:* Don't hold your breath.

*Robert:* Don't underestimate yourself.

*Catherine:* Anyway. *(Beat.)*

*Robert:* Another drink? Cathy? Hal?

*Catherine:* No thanks.

*Hal:* Thanks, I really should get going.

*Robert:* Are you sure?

*Hal:* Yes.

*Robert:* I'll call you when I've looked at this. Don't think about it till then. Enjoy yourself, see some movies.

*Hal:* Okay.

*Robert:* You can come by my office in a week. Call it —

*Hal:* The eleventh?

*Robert:* Yes, we'll . . . *(Beat. He turns to Catherine. Grave:)*
I am sorry. I used to have a pretty good memory for numbers. Happy birthday.

*Catherine:* Thank you.

*Robert:* I am so sorry. I'm embarrassed.

*Catherine:* Dad, don't be stupid.

*Robert:* I didn't get you anything.

*Catherine:* Don't worry about it.

*Robert:* I'm taking you out.

*Catherine:* You don't have to.

*Robert:* We are going out. I didn't want to shop and cook. Let's go to dinner. Let's get the hell out of this neighborhood. What do you want to eat? Let's go to the North Side. Or Chinatown. Or Greektown. I don't know what's good anymore.

*Catherine:* Whatever you want.

*Robert:* Whatever you want goddamnit, Catherine, it's your birthday. *(Beat.)*

*Catherine:* Steak.

*Robert:* Steak. Yes.

*Catherine:* No, first beer, really cold beer. Really cheap beer.

*Robert:* Done.

*Catherine:* That Chicago beer that's watery with no flavor and you can just drink gallons of it.

*Robert:* They just pump the water out of Lake Michigan and bottle it.

*Catherine:* It's so awful.

*Robert:* I have a taste for it myself.

*Catherine:* Then the steak, grilled really black, and potatoes and creamed spinach.

*Robert:* I remember a place. If it's still there I think it will do the trick.

*Catherine:* And dessert.

*Robert:* That goes without saying. It's your birthday, hooray. And there's the solution to our dinner problem. Thank you for reminding me, Harold Dobbs.

*Catherine:* *(To Hal.)* We're being rude. Do you want to come?

*Hal:* Oh, no, I shouldn't.

*Robert:* Why not? Please, come.

*Catherine:* Come on. *(A tiny moment between Hal and Catherine. Hal wavers, then:)*

*Hal:* No, I can't, I have plans. Thank you though. Happy birthday.

*Catherine:* Thanks. Well. I'll let you out.

*Robert:* I'll see you on the eleventh, Hal.

*Hal:* Great.

*Catherine:* I'm gonna change my clothes, Dad. I'll be ready in a sec. *(Hal and Catherine exit. A moment. It's darker. Robert looks out at the evening. Eventually he picks up the notebook and a pen. He sits down. He opens to a blank page. He writes.)*

*Robert:* "September fourth.
A good day . . . " *(He continues to write.)*

**Fade**

SCENE II

*Morning. An instant after the end of Act One: Catherine, Claire, and Hal.*

*Hal:* You wrote this?
*Catherine:* Yes.
*Claire:* When?
*Catherine:* I started after I quit school. I finished a few months before Dad died.
*Claire:* Did he see it?
*Catherine:* No. He didn't know I was working on it. It wouldn't have mattered to him anyway, he was too sick.
*Hal:* I don't understand — you did this by yourself?
*Catherine:* Yes.
*Claire:* It's in Dad's notebook.
*Catherine:* I used one of his blank books. There were a bunch of them upstairs. *(Beat.)*
*Claire:* *(To Hal.)* Tell me exactly where you found this?
*Hal:* In his study.
*Catherine:* In his desk. I gave him the —
*Claire:* *(To Catherine.)* Hold on. *(To Hal.)* Where did you find it?
*Hal:* In the bottom drawer of the desk in the study, a locked drawer: Catherine gave me the key.
*Claire:* Why was the drawer locked?
*Catherine:* It's mine, it's the drawer I keep my private things in. I've used it for years.
*Claire:* *(To Hal.)* Was there anything else in the drawer?
*Hal:* No.
*Catherine:* No, that's the only —
*Claire:* Can I see it? *(Hal gives Claire the book. She pages through it. Beat.)* I'm sorry, I just . . . *(To Catherine.)* The book was in the . . . You told him where to find it . . . You gave him the key . . . You wrote this incredible thing and you didn't tell anyone?
*Catherine:* I'm telling you both now. After I dropped out of school I had nothing to do. I was depressed, really depressed, but at a certain point I decided Fuck it, I don't need them. It's just math, I can do it on my own. So I kept working here. I worked at night, after Dad had gone to sleep. It was hard but I did it. *(Beat.)*
*Claire:* Catherine, I'm sorry, but I just find this very hard to believe.
*Catherine:* Claire. I wrote. The proof.
*Claire:* I'm sorry, I —
*Catherine:* Claire . . .
*Claire:* This is Dad's handwriting.
*Catherine:* It's not.
*Claire:* It looks exactly like it.
*Catherine:* It's my writing.
*Claire:* I'm sorry —
*Catherine:* Ask Hal. He's been looking at Dad's writing for weeks. *(Claire gives Hal the book. He looks at it. Beat.)*
*Hal:* I don't know.
*Catherine:* Hal, come on.
*Claire:* What does it look like?

*Hal:* It looks . . . I don't know what Catherine's handwriting looks like.

*Catherine:* It LOOKS like THAT.

*Hal:* Okay. It . . . okay. *(Beat. He hands the book back.)*

*Claire:* I think — you know what? I think it's early, and people are tired, and not in the best state to make decisions about emotional things, so maybe we should all just take a breath . . .

*Catherine:* You don't believe me?

*Claire:* I don't know. I really don't know anything about this.

*Catherine:* Never mind. I don't know why I expected you to believe me about ANYTHING.

*Claire:* Could you tell us the proof? That would show it was yours.

*Catherine:* You wouldn't understand it.

*Claire:* Tell it to Hal.

*Catherine:* *(Taking the book.)* We could talk through it together. It might take a while.

*Claire:* *(Taking the book.)* You can't use the book.

*Catherine:* For God's sake, it's forty pages long. I didn't MEMORIZE it. It's not a muffin recipe. *(Beat.)* This is stupid. It's my book, my writing, my key, my drawer, my proof. Hal, tell her!

*Hal:* Tell her what?

*Catherine:* Whose book is that?

*Hal:* I don't know.

*Catherine:* What is the matter with you? You've been looking at his other stuff, you know there's nothing even remotely like this!

*Hal:* Look, Catherine —

*Catherine:* We'll go through the proof together. We'll sit down — if Claire will please let me have my book back —

*Claire:* *(Giving her the book.)* All right, talk him through it.

*Hal:* That might take days and it still wouldn't show that she wrote it.

*Catherine:* Why not?

*Hal:* Your dad might have written it and explained it to you later. I'm not saying he did, I'm just —

*Catherine:* Come on! He didn't do this, he couldn't have. He didn't do any mathematics at all for years. Even in the good year he couldn't work: You know that. You're supposed to be a scientist. *(Beat.)*

*Hal:* You're right. Okay. Here's my suggestion. I know three or four guys at the department, very sharp, disinterested people who knew your father, knew his work. Let me take this to them.

*Catherine:* WHAT?

*Hal:* I'll tell them we've found something, something potentially major, we're not sure about the authorship; I'll sit down with them. We'll go through the thing carefully —

*Claire:* Good.

*Hal:* — and figure out exactly what we've got. It would only take a couple of days, probably, and then we'd have a lot more information.

*Claire:* I think that's an excellent suggestion.

*Catherine:* You can't.

*Claire:* Catherine.

*Catherine:* No! You can't take it.

*Hal:* I'm not "taking" it.

*Catherine:* This is what you wanted.

*Hal:* Oh come on, Jesus.

*Catherine:* You don't waste any time, do you? No hesitation. You can't wait to show them your brilliant discovery.

*Hal:* I'm trying to determine what this is.

*Catherine:* I'm telling you what it is.

*Hal:* You don't know!

*Catherine:* I WROTE it.

*Hal:* IT'S YOUR FATHER'S HANDWRITING. *(Beat. Pained.)*

At least it looks an awful lot like the writing in the other books.

Maybe your writing looks exactly like his, I don't know.

*Catherine:* *(Softly.)* It does look like his.

I didn't show this to anyone else. I could have. I wanted you to be the first to see it. I didn't know I wanted that until last night. It's ME. I trusted you.

*Hal:* I know.

*Catherine:* Was I wrong?

*Hal:* No. I —

*Catherine:* I should have known she wouldn't believe me but why don't you?

*Hal:* This is one of his notebooks. The exact same kind he used.

*Catherine:* I told you. I just used one of his blank books. There were extras.

*Hal:* There aren't any extra books in the study.

*Catherine:* There were when I started writing the proof. I bought them for him. He used the rest up later.

*Hal:* And the writing.

*Catherine:* You want to test the handwriting?

*Hal:* No. It doesn't matter. He could have dictated it to you, for Chrissake. It still doesn't make sense.

*Catherine:* Why not?

*Hal:* I'm a mathematician.

*Catherine:* Yes.

*Hal:* I know how hard it would be to come up with something like this. I mean it's impossible. You'd have to be . . . you'd have to be your dad, basically. Your dad at the peak of his powers.

*Catherine:* I'm a mathematician too.

*Hal:* Not like your dad.

*Catherine:* Oh he's the only one who could have done this?

*Hal:* The only one I know.

*Catherine:* Are you sure?

*Hal:* Your father was the most —

*Catherine:* Just because you and the rest of the geeks worshiped him doesn't mean he wrote this proof, Hal!

*Hal:* He was the best. My generation hasn't produced anything like him. He revolutionized the field twice before he was twenty-two. I'm sorry, Catherine, but you took some classes at Northwestern for a few months.

*Catherine:* My education wasn't at Northwestern. It was living in this house for twenty-five years.

*Hal:* Even so, it doesn't matter. This is too advanced. I don't even understand most of it.

*Catherine:* You think it's too advanced.

*Hal:* Yes.

*Catherine:* It's too advanced for YOU.

*Hal:* You could not have done this work.

*Catherine:* But what if I did?

*Hal:* Well what if?

*Catherine:* It would be a real disaster for you, wouldn't it? And for the other geeks who barely finished their Ph.D.s, who are marking time doing lame research, bragging about the conferences they go to — WOW — playing in an awful band, and whining that they're intellectually past it at twenty-eight, BECAUSE THEY ARE. *(Beat. Hal hesitates, then abruptly exits. Beat. Catherine is furious and so upset she looks dazed.)*

*Claire:* Katie.

Let's go inside.

Katie? *(Catherine opens the book and tries to rip out the pages, destroy it. Claire goes to take it from her. They struggle. Catherine gets the book away. They stand apart, breathing hard. After a moment, Catherine throws the book to the floor. She exits.)*

## Fade

### SCENE III

*The next day. The porch is empty. Knocking, off. No one appears. After a moment Hal comes around the side of the porch and knocks on the back door.*

*Hal:* Catherine? *(Claire enters.)*

I thought you were leaving.

*Claire:* I had to delay my flight. *(Beat.)*

*Hal:* Is Catherine here?

*Claire:* I don't think this is a good time, Hal.

*Hal:* Could I see her?

*Claire:* Not now.

*Hal:* What's the matter?

*Claire:* She's sleeping.

*Hal:* Can I wait here until she gets up?

*Claire:* She's been sleeping since yesterday. She won't get up. She won't eat, won't talk to me. I couldn't go home. I'm going to wait until she seems okay to travel.

*Hal:* Jesus, I'm sorry.

*Claire:* Yes.

*Hal:* I'd like to talk to her.

*Claire:* I don't think that's a good idea.

*Hal:* Has she said anything?

*Claire:* About you? No.

*Hal:* Yesterday . . . I know I didn't do what she wanted.

*Claire:* Neither of us did.

*Hal:* I didn't know what to say. I feel awful.

*Claire:* Why did you sleep with her? *(Beat.)*

*Hal:* I'm sorry, that's none of your business.

*Claire:* Bullshit. I have to take care of her. It's a little bit harder with you jerking her around.

*Hal:* I wasn't jerking her around. It just happened.

*Claire:* Your timing was not great.

*Hal:* It wasn't my timing, it was both of our —

*Claire:* Why'd you do it? You know what she's like. She's fragile and you took advantage of her.

*Hal:* No. It's what we both wanted. I didn't mean to hurt her.

*Claire:* You did.

*Hal:* I'd like to talk to Catherine, please.

*Claire:* You can't.

*Hal:* Are you taking her away?

*Claire:* Yes.

*Hal:* To New York.

*Claire:* Yes.

*Hal:* Just going to drag her to New York.

*Claire:* If I have to.

*Hal:* Don't you think she should have some say in whether or not she goes?

*Claire:* If she's not going to speak, what else can I do?

*Hal:* Let me try. Let me talk to her.

*Claire:* Hal, give up. This has nothing to do with you.

*Hal:* I know her. She's tougher than you think, Claire.

*Claire:* What?

*Hal:* She can handle herself. She can handle talking to me — maybe it would help. Maybe she'd like it.

*Claire:* Maybe she'd LIKE it? Are you out of your MIND? You're the reason she's up there right now! You have NO IDEA what she needs. You don't know her! She's my sister. Jesus, you fucking mathematicians: You DON'T THINK. You don't know what you're doing. You stagger around creating these catastrophes and it's people like ME who end up flying in to clean them up. *(Beat.)*

    She needs to get out of Chicago, out of this house. I'll give you my number in New York. You can call her once she's settled there. That's it, that's the deal.

*Hal:* Okay. *(Beat. Hal doesn't move.)*

*Claire:* I don't mean to be rude but I have a lot to do.

*Hal:* There's one more thing. You're not going to like it.

*Claire:* Sure, take the notebook.

*Hal:* *(Startled.)* I —

*Claire:* Hold on a sec, I'll get it for you. *(She goes inside and returns with the notebook. She gives it to Hal.)*

*Hal:* I thought this would be harder.

*Claire:* Don't worry, I understand. It's very sweet you want to see Catherine but of course you'd like to see the notebook too.

*Hal:* *(Huffy.)* It's — No, it's my responsibility — as a professional I can't turn my back on the necessity of the —

*Claire:* Relax. I don't care. Take it. What would I do with it?

*Hal:* You sure?

*Claire:* Yes, of course.

*Hal:* You trust me with this?

*Claire:* Yes.

*Hal:* You just said I don't know what I'm doing.

*Claire:* I think you're a little bit of an idiot but you're not dishonest. Someone needs to figure out what's in there. I can't do it. It should be done here, at Chicago: my father would like that. When you decide what we've got let me know what the family should do.

*Hal:* Thanks.

*Claire:* Don't thank me, it's by far the most convenient option available. I put my card in there, call me whenever you want.

*Hal:* Okay. *(Hal starts to exit. Claire hesitates, then:)*

*Claire:* Hal.

*Hal:* Yeah?

*Claire:* Can you tell me about it? The proof. I'm just curious.

*Hal:* It would take some time. How much math have you got? *(Beat.)*

*Claire:* I'm a currency analyst. It helps to be very quick with numbers. I am. I probably inherited about one-one-thousandth of my father's ability. It's enough.

Catherine got more, I'm not sure how much.

## Fade

### Scene IV

*Winter. About three and a half years earlier. Robert is on the porch. He wears a T-shirt. He writes in a notebook. After a moment we hear Catherine's voice from off.*

*Catherine:* Dad? *(Catherine enters wearing a parka. She sees her father and stops.)* What are you doing out here?

*Robert:* Working.

*Catherine:* It's December. It's thirty degrees.

*Robert:* I know. *(Catherine stares at him, baffled.)*

*Catherine:* Don't you need a coat?

*Robert:* Don't you think I can make that assessment for myself?

*Catherine:* Aren't you cold?

*Robert:* Of course I am! I'm freezing my ass off!

*Catherine:* So what are you doing out here?

*Robert:* Thinking! Writing!

*Catherine:* You're gonna freeze.

*Robert:* It's too hot in the house. The radiators dry out the air. Also the clanking — I can't concentrate. If the house weren't so old we'd have central air heating but we don't so I have to come out here to get any work done.

*Catherine:* I'll turn off the radiators. They won't make any noise. Come inside, it isn't safe.

*Robert:* I'm okay.

*Catherine:* I've been calling. Didn't you hear the phone?

*Robert:* It's a distraction.

*Catherine:* I didn't know what was going on. I had to drive all the way down here.

*Robert:* I can see that.

*Catherine:* I had to skip class. *(She brings him a coat and he puts it on.)* Why don't you answer the phone?

*Robert:* Well I'm sorry, Catherine, but it's question of priorities and work takes priority, you know that.

*Catherine:* You're working?

*Robert:* Goddamnit I am working! I say "I" — the machinery. The machinery is working. Catherine, it's on full blast. All the cylinders are firing, I'm on fire. That's why I came out here, to cool off. I haven't felt like this for years.

*Catherine:* You're kidding.

*Robert:* No!

*Catherine:* I don't believe it.

*Robert:* I don't believe it either! But it's true. It started about a week ago. I woke up, came downstairs, made a cup of coffee and before I could pour in the milk it was like someone turned the LIGHT on in my head.

*Catherine:* Really?

*Robert:* Not the light, the whole POWER GRID. I LIT UP and it's like no time has passed since I was twenty-one.

*Catherine:* You're kidding!

*Robert:* No! I'm back! I'm back in touch with the source — the font, the — whatever the source of my creativity was all those years ago I'm in contact with it again. I'm SITTING on it. It's a geyser and I'm shooting right up into the air on top of it.

*Catherine:* My God.

*Robert:* I'm not talking about divine inspiration. It's not funneling down into my head and onto the page. It'll take work to shape these things; I'm not saying it won't be a tremendous amount of work. It will be a tremendous amount of work. It's not going to be easy. But the raw material is there. It's like I've been driving in traffic and now the lanes are opening up before me and I can accelerate. I see whole landscapes — places for the work to go, new techniques, revolutionary possibilities. I'm going to get whole branches of the profession talking to each other. I — I'm sorry, I'm being rude, how's school?

*Catherine:* *(Taken aback.)* Fine. —

*Robert:* You're working hard?

*Catherine:* Sure.

*Robert:* Faculty treating you all right?

*Catherine:* Yes. Dad —

*Robert:* Made any friends?

*Catherine:* Of course. I —

*Robert:* Dating?

*Catherine:* Dad, hold on.

*Robert:* No details necessary if you don't want to provide them. I'm just interested.

*Catherine:* School's great. I want to talk about what you're doing.

*Robert:* Great, let's talk.

*Catherine:* This work.

*Robert:* Yes.

*Catherine:* *(Indicating the notebook.)* Is it here?

*Robert:* Part of it, yes.

*Catherine:* Can I see it?

*Robert:* It's all at a very early stage.

*Catherine:* I don't mind.

*Robert:* Nothing's actually complete, to be honest. It's all in progress. I think we're talking years.

*Catherine:* That's okay. I don't care. Just let me see anything.

*Robert:* You really want to?

*Catherine:* Yes.

*Robert:* You're genuinely interested.

*Catherine:* Dad, of course!

*Robert:* Of course. It's your field.

*Catherine:* Yes.

*Robert:* You know how happy that makes me. *(Beat.)*

*Catherine:* Yes.

*Robert:* I think there's enough here to keep me working the rest of my life.

Not just me.

I was starting to imagine I was finished, Catherine. Really finished. Don't get me wrong, I was grateful I could go to my office, have a life, but secretly I was terrified I'd never work again. Did you know that?

*Catherine:* I wondered.

*Robert:* I was absolutely fucking terrified.

Then I remembered something and a part of the terror went away. I remembered you.

Your creative years were just beginning. You'd get your degree, do your own work. You were just getting started.

If you hadn't gone into math that would have been all right. Claire's done well for herself. I'm satisfied with her.

I'm proud of you.

I don't mean to embarrass you. It's part of the reason we have children. We hope they'll survive us, accomplish what we can't.

Now that I'm back in the game I admit I've got another idea, a better one.

*Catherine:* What?

*Robert:* I know you've got your own work. I don't want you to neglect that. You can't neglect it. But I could probably use some help. Work with me. If you want to, if you can work it out with your class schedule and everything else, I could help you with that, make some calls, talk to your teachers . . .

I'm getting ahead of myself.

Well, Jesus, look, enough bullshit, you asked to see something. Let's start with this. I've roughed something out. General outline for a proof. Major result. Important. It's not finished but you can see where it's going. Let's see: *(He selects a notebook.)* Here. *(He gives it to Catherine. She opens it and reads.)* It's very rough. *(After a long moment Catherine closes the notebook. A beat.)*

*Catherine:* Dad. Let's go inside.

*Robert:* The gaps might make it hard to follow. We can talk it through.

*Catherine:* You're cold. Let's go in.

*Robert:* Maybe we could work on this together. This might be a great place to start. What about it? What do you think? Let's talk it through.

*Catherine:* Not now. I'm cold too. It's really freezing out here. Let's go inside.

*Robert:* I'm telling you it's stifling in there, goddamn it. The radiators. Look, read out the first couple of lines. That's how we start: You read, and we go line by line, out loud, through the argument. See if there's a better way, a shorter way. Let's collaborate.

*Catherine:* No. Come on.

*Robert:* I've been waiting years for this. This is something I want to do. Come on, let's do some work together.

*Catherine:* We can't do it out here. It's freezing cold. I'm taking you in.

*Robert:* Not until we talk about the proof.

*Catherine:* No.

*Robert:* GODDAMNIT CATHERINE. Open the goddamn book and read me the lines. *(Beat. Catherine opens the book. She reads slowly, without inflection.)*

*Catherine:* "Let *x* equal the quantity of all quantities of *x*. Let *x* equal the cold. It is cold in December. The months of cold equal November through February. There are four months of cold, and four of heat, leaving four months of indeterminate temperature. In February it snows. In March the Lake is a lake of ice. In September the students come back and the bookstores are full. Let *x* equal the month of full bookstores. The number of books approaches infinity as the number of months of cold approaches four. I will never be as cold now as I will in the future. The future of cold is infinite. The future of heat is the future of cold. The bookstores are infinite and so are never full except in September . . . " *(She stops reading and slowly closes the book. Robert is shivering uncontrollably.)* It's all right. We'll go inside.

*Robert:* I'm cold.

*Catherine:* We'll warm you up. *(Catherine puts her arms around him and helps him to his feet.)*

*Robert:* Don't leave. Please.

*Catherine:* I won't.

Let's go inside.

## Fade

## SCENE V

*The present. A week after the events in Scene 3. Claire on the porch. Coffee in takeout cups. Claire takes a plane ticket out of her purse, checks the itinerary. A moment. Catherine enters with bags for travel. Claire gives her a cup of coffee. Catherine drinks in silence. Beat.*

*Catherine:* Good coffee.

*Claire:* It's all right, isn't it?

We have a place where we buy all our coffee. They roast it themselves, they have an old roaster down in the basement. You can smell it on the street. Some mornings you can smell it from our place, four stories up. It's wonderful. "Manhattan's Best": Some magazine wrote it up. Who knows. But it is very good.

*Catherine:* Sounds good.

*Claire:* You'll like it.

*Catherine:* Good. *(Beat.)*

*Claire:* You look nice.

*Catherine:* Thanks, so do you. *(Beat.)*

*Claire:* It's bright.

*Catherine:* Yes.

*Claire:* It's one of the things I do miss. All the space, the light. You could sit out here all morning.

*Catherine:* It's not that warm.
*Claire:* Are you cold?
*Catherine:* Not really. I just —
*Claire:* It has gotten chilly. I'm sorry. Do you want to go in?
*Catherine:* I'm okay.
*Claire:* I just thought it might be nice to have a quick cup of coffee out here.
*Catherine:* No, it is.
*Claire:* Plus the kitchen's all put away. If you're cold —
*Catherine:* I'm not. Not really.
*Claire:* Want your jacket?
*Catherine:* Yeah, okay. *(Claire gives it to her. Catherine puts it on.)* Thanks.
*Claire:* It's that time of year.
*Catherine:* Yes.
        You can feel it coming. *(Beat. Catherine stares out at the yard.)*
*Claire:* Honey, there's no hurry.
*Catherine:* I know.
*Claire:* If you want to hang out, be alone for a while —
*Catherine:* No. It's no big deal.
*Claire:* We don't have to leave for twenty minutes or so.
*Catherine:* I know. Thanks, Claire.
*Claire:* You're all packed.
*Catherine:* Yes.
*Claire:* If you missed anything it doesn't really matter. The movers will send us
     everything next month. *(Catherine doesn't move. Beat.)*
        I know this is hard.
*Catherine:* It's fine.
*Claire:* This is the right decision.
*Catherine:* I know.
*Claire:* I want to do everything I can to make this a smooth transition for you.
     So does Mitch.
*Catherine:* Good.
*Claire:* The actual departure is the hardest part. Once we get there we can relax.
     Enjoy ourselves.
*Catherine:* I know. *(Beat.)*
*Claire:* You'll love New York.
*Catherine:* I can't wait.
*Claire:* You'll love it. It's the most exciting city.
*Catherine:* I know.
*Claire:* It's not like Chicago, it's really alive.
*Catherine:* I've read about that.
*Claire:* I think you'll truly feel at home there.
*Catherine:* You know what I'm looking forward to?
*Claire:* What?
*Catherine:* Seeing Broadway musicals. *(Beat.)*
*Claire:* Mitch can get us tickets to whatever you'd like.
*Catherine:* And Rockefeller Center in winter — all the skaters.
*Claire:* Well, you —
*Catherine:* Also, the many fine museums! *(Beat.)*
*Claire:* I know how hard this is for you.
*Catherine:* Listening to you say how hard it is for me is what's hard for me.

*Claire:* Once you're there you'll see all the possibilities that are available.

*Catherine:* Restraints, lithium, electroshock.

*Claire:* SCHOOLS. In the New York area alone there's NYU, Columbia —

*Catherine:* Bright college days! Football games, road trips, necking on the "quad."

*Claire:* Or if that's not what you want we can help you find a job. Mitch has terrific contacts all over town.

*Catherine:* Does he know anyone in the phone sex industry?

*Claire:* I want to make this as easy a transition as I can.

*Catherine:* It's going to be easy, Claire, it's gonna be so fucking easy you won't believe it.

*Claire:* Thank you.

*Catherine:* I'm going to sit quietly on the plane to New York. And live quietly in a cute apartment. And answer Doctor Von Heimlich's questions very politely.

*Claire:* You can see any doctor you like, or you can see no doctor.

*Catherine:* I would like to see a doctor called Doctor Von Heimlich: Please find one. And I would like him to wear a monocle. And I'd like him to have a very soft, very well-upholstered couch, so that I'll be perfectly comfortable while I'm blaming everything on you. *(Claire's patience is exhausted.)*

*Claire:* Don't come.

*Catherine:* No, I'm coming.

*Claire:* Stay here, see how you do.

*Catherine:* I could.

*Claire:* You can't take care of yourself for five days.

*Catherine:* Bullshit!

*Claire:* You slept all week. I had to cancel my flight. I missed a week of work — I was this close to taking you to the hospital! I couldn't believe it when you finally dragged yourself up.

*Catherine:* I was tired!

*Claire:* You were completely out of it, Catherine, you weren't speaking!

*Catherine:* I didn't want to talk to you. *(Beat.)*

*Claire:* Stay here if you hate me so much.

*Catherine:* And do what?

*Claire:* You're the genius, figure it out. *(Claire is upset, near tears. She digs in her bag, pulls out a plane ticket, throws it on the table. She exits. Catherine is alone. She can't quite bring herself to leave the porch. A moment. Hal enters — not through the house, from the side. He is badly dressed and looks very tired. He is breathless from running.)*

*Hal:* You're still here. *(Catherine is surprised. She doesn't speak.)* I saw Claire leaving out front. I wasn't sure if you — *(He holds up the notebook.)* This fucking thing . . . checks out.

I have been over it, twice, with two different sets of guys, old geeks and young geeks. It is weird. I don't know where the techniques came from. Some of the moves are very hard to follow. But we can't find anything wrong with it! There might be something wrong with it but we can't find it. I have not slept. *(He catches his breath.)* It works. I thought you might want to know.

*Catherine:* I already knew. *(Beat.)*

*Hal:* I had to swear these guys to secrecy. They were jumping out of their skins. See, one email and it's all over. I threatened them. I think we're safe, they're physical cowards. *(Beat.)* I had to see you.

*Catherine:* I'm leaving.

*Hal:* I know. Just wait for a minute, please?

*Catherine:* What do you want? You have the book. She told me you came by for it and she gave it to you. You can do whatever you want with it. Publish it.

*Hal:* Catherine.

*Catherine:* Get Claire's permission and publish it. She doesn't care. She doesn't know anything about it anyway.

*Hal:* I don't want Claire's permission.

*Catherine:* You want mine? Publish. Go for it. Have a press conference. Tell the world what my father discovered.

*Hal:* I don't want to.

*Catherine:* Or fuck my father, pass it off as your own work. Who cares? Write your own ticket to any math department in the country.

*Hal:* I don't think your father wrote it. *(Beat.)*

*Catherine:* You thought so last week.

*Hal:* That was last week. I spent this week reading the proof.

   I think I understand it, more or less. It uses a lot of newer mathematical techniques, things that were developed in the last decade. Elliptic Curves. Modular Forms. I think I learned more mathematics this week than I did in four years of grad school.

*Catherine:* So?

*Hal:* So the proof is very . . . hip.

*Catherine:* Get some sleep, Hal.

*Hal:* What was your father doing the last ten years? He wasn't well, was he?

*Catherine:* Are you done?

*Hal:* I don't think he would have been able to master those new techniques.

*Catherine:* But he was a genius.

*Hal:* But he was nuts.

*Catherine:* So he read about them later.

*Hal:* Maybe. The books he would have needed are upstairs. *(Beat.)* Your dad dated everything. Even his most incoherent entries he dated. There are no dates in this.

*Catherine:* The handwriting—

*Hal:* —looks like your dad's. Parents and children sometimes have similar hand-writing, especially if they've spent a lot of time together. *(Beat.)*

*Catherine:* Interesting theory.

*Hal:* I like it.

*Catherine:* I like it too. It's what I told you last week.

*Hal:* I know.

*Catherine:* You blew it.

*Hal:* I—

*Catherine:* It's too bad, the rest of it was really good. All of it: "I loved your dad." "I always liked you." "I'd like to spend every minute with you . . . " It's killer stuff. You got laid AND you got the notebook! You're a genius!

*Hal:* I don't expect you to be happy with me. I just wanted . . . I don't know. I was hoping to discuss some of this with you before you left. Purely professional. I don't expect anything else.

*Catherine:* Forget it.

*Hal:* I mean we have questions. Working on this must have been amazing. I'd love just to hear you talk about some of this.

*Catherine:* No.

*Hal:* You'll have to deal with it eventually, you know. You can't ignore it, you'll have to get it published. You'll have to talk to someone.

    Take it, at least. Then I'll go. Here.

*Catherine:* I don't want it.

*Hal:* Come on, Catherine. I'm trying to correct things.

*Catherine:* You CAN'T. Do you hear me?

    You think you've figured something out? You run over here so pleased with yourself because you changed your mind. Now you're certain. You're so . . . sloppy. You don't know anything. The book, the math, the dates, the writing, all that stuff you decided with your buddies, it's just evidence. It doesn't finish the job. It doesn't prove anything.

*Hal:* Okay, what would?

*Catherine:* NOTHING.

    You should have trusted me. *(Beat.)*

*Hal:* I know. *(Beat. Catherine gathers her things.)*

    So Claire sold the house?

*Catherine:* Yes.

*Hal:* Stay in Chicago. You're an adult.

*Catherine:* She wants me in New York. She wants to look after me.

*Hal:* Do you need looking after?

*Catherine:* She thinks I do.

*Hal:* You looked after your dad for five years.

*Catherine:* So maybe it's my turn.

    I kick and scream but I don't know. Being taken care of, it doesn't sound so bad. I'm tired.

    And the house is a wreck, let's face it. It was my dad's house.

    I don't think I should spend another winter here.

*Hal:* There is nothing wrong with you.

*Catherine:* I think I'm like my dad.

*Hal:* I think you are too.

*Catherine:* I'm . . . afraid I'm like my dad.

*Hal:* You're not him.

*Catherine:* Maybe I will be.

*Hal:* Maybe. Maybe you'll be better. *(Pause. He offers her the book. This time she takes it. She looks down at the book, runs her fingers over the cover.)*

*Catherine:* It didn't feel "amazing" or — what word did you use?

*Hal:* Yeah, amazing.

*Catherine:* Yeah. It was just connecting the dots.

    Some nights I could connect three or four. Some nights they'd be really far apart, I'd have no idea how to get to the next one, if there was a next one.

*Hal:* He really never knew?

*Catherine:* No. I worked after midnight. He was usually in bed.

*Hal:* Every night?

*Catherine:* No. When I got stuck I watched TV. Sometimes if he couldn't sleep he'd come downstairs, sit with me. We'd talk. Not about math, he couldn't. About the movie we were watching. I'd explain the stories.

    Or about fixing the heat. Decide we didn't want to. We liked the radiators even though they clanked in the middle of the night, make the air dry.

    Or we'd plan breakfast, talk about what we were gonna eat together in the morning.

Those nights were usually pretty good.

I know . . . it works . . . But all I can see are the compromises, the approximations, places where it's stitched together. It's lumpy. Dad's stuff was way more elegant. When he was young. *(Beat.)*

*Hal:* Talk me through it? Whatever's bothering you. Maybe you'll improve it.

*Catherine:* I don't know . . .

*Hal:* Pick anything. Give it a shot? Maybe you'll discover something elegant. *(A moment. Hal sits next to her. Eventually she opens the book, turns the pages slowly, locates a section. She looks at him.)*

*Catherine:* Here: *(She begins to speak.)*

## Curtain

*Author's Note: For the Manhattan Theatre Club and Broadway productions, I wrote the following material for Catherine to speak during the final fade out, directly following her "Here:"*

*Catherine:* I've got Eberhart's Conjecture setting up this section, $qn$ as the $n$th prime, all that stuff, $b$'s a positive not divisible by $p$ . . . You know it. Pretty basic number theory. It just seems wrong to be using it to get to the Gauss. I'd like to go around, but when you eliminate it you get contradictions, or everything goes to zero. Unless . . .

### CONSIDERATIONS FOR CRITICAL THINKING AND WRITING

1. FIRST RESPONSE. How many ways can the title be read? How do the different meanings of the word *proof* help you articulate the play's theme?

2. The shock of the first scene, of course, is that Robert is actually dead and the Robert we see on the stage is a figment of Catherine's imagination. How does this revelation change the way you approach Catherine's character throughout the play?

3. What other important background information, or exposition, is provided in Act I, Scene I?

4. Both Claire and Hal are unsympathetic characters in some ways. Summarize their negative qualities as a way of responding to this question: Are they equally culpable in terms of worsening Catherine's plight?

5. How does Catherine's retelling of the story of Sophie Germain in Act I, Scene III advance the play's theme?

6. The characters in this play drink fairly constantly. Is alcohol just a prop or is its presence integral to the play?

7. Act II, Scene I abruptly shifts to a period four years before the action in Act I, and the next scene shifts back abruptly to the time of Act I. In what other ways does the play focus on the importance and meaning of time?

8. How does the play comment on the theme of responsibility to self versus responsibility to others?

9. Do you think Catherine's mental struggles are hereditary or the result of her circumstances? Try to find places where the play suggests one or the other.

### CONNECTIONS TO ANOTHER SELECTION

1. Compare this play to August Wilson's *Fences* (p. 1329) in terms of the way family expectations impact characters.

2. Discuss the way this play and Quiara Alegría Hudes's *Water by the Spoonful* (p. 1216) borrow from realism and depart from it.

## LYNN NOTTAGE (B. 1964)

Dimitrios Kambouris/Getty Images.

Lynn Nottage wrote her first play in high school and has contributed consistently and importantly to the American theater scene ever since. She has twice won the Pulitzer Prize for drama, in 2009 for *Ruined* and in 2017 for *Sweat* (which also won an Obie Award—an award given to an "off-Broadway" play that is not necessarily poised for commercial success). A native of New York City, Nottage earned her B.A. from Brown University and her Master of Fine Arts degree from Yale University and was recipient of the MacArthur "Genius Grant." She currently teaches at Columbia University. Nottage's work is varied in terms of setting and plot, but her characters tend to be from the margins of their society, such as the working class from beleaguered Reading, Pennsylvania, in *Sweat*, or women surviving a civil war in the Democratic Republic of Congo in *Ruined*. The following one-act play is considerably lighter and more humorous than much of her other work, but it addresses weighty subjects nonetheless.

## *POOF!*  2004

CHARACTERS

*Samuel,* Loureen's husband
*Loureen,* a demure housewife, early thirties
*Florence,* Loureen's best friend, early thirties

TIME

The present

PLACE

Kitchen

A NOTE

Nearly half the women on death row in the United States were convicted of killing abusive husbands. Spontaneous combustion is not recognized as a capital crime.

*Darkness.*

*Samuel (In the darkness):* WHEN I COUNT TO TEN I DON' WANT TO SEE
   YA! I DON' WANT TO HEAR YA! ONE, TWO, THREE, FOUR —
*Loureen (In the darkness):* DAMN YOU TO HELL, SAMUEL!
   *(A bright flash.*

   *Lights rise. A huge pile of smoking ashes rests in the middle of the kitchen.
   Loureen, a demure housewife in her early thirties, stares down at the ashes
   incredulously. She bends and lifts a pair of spectacles from the remains. She
   ever so slowly backs away.)*

   Samuel? Uh! *(Places the spectacles on the kitchen table)* Uh! . . . Samuel?
   *(Looks around)* Don't fool with me now. I'm not in the mood. *(Whispers)*
   Samuel? I didn't mean it really. I'll be good if you come back . . . Come
   on now, dinner's waiting. *(Chuckles, then stops abruptly)* Now stop your
   foolishness. . . . And let's sit down. *(Examines the spectacles)* Uh! *(Softly)*
   Don't be cross with me. Sure I forgot to pick up your shirt for tomorrow.
   I can wash another, I'll do it right now. Right now! Sam? . . . *(Cautiously)* You
   hear me! *(Awaits a response)* Maybe I didn't ever intend to wash your shirt.
   *(Pulls back as though about to receive a blow; a moment)* Uh! *(Sits down and
   dials the telephone)* Florence, honey, could you come on down for a moment.
   There's been a . . . little . . . accident. . . Quickly please. Uh!

   *Loureen hangs up the phone. She gets a broom and a dust pan. She hesitantly
   approaches the pile of ashes. She gets down on her hands and knees and takes
   a closer look. A fatuous grin spreads across her face. She is startled by a sudden
   knock on the door. She slowly walks across the room like a possessed child.
   Loureen lets in Florence, her best friend and upstairs neighbor. Florence, also
   a housewife in her early thirties, wears a floral housecoat and a pair of over
   sized slippers. Without acknowledgment Loureen proceeds to saunter back
   across the room.)*

*Florence:* HEY!
*Loureen (Pointing at the ashes):* Uh! . . . *(She struggles to formulate words, which
   press at the inside of her mouth, not quite realized)* Uh! . . .
*Florence:* You all right? What happened? *(Sniffs the air)* Smells like you burned
   something? *(Stares at the huge pile of ashes)* What the devil is that?
*Loureen (Hushed):* Samuel . . . It's Samuel, I think.
*Florence:* What's he done now?
*Loureen:* It's him. It's him. *(Nods her head repeatedly)*
*Florence:* Chile, what's wrong with you? Did he finally drive you out your mind?
   I knew something was going to happen sooner or later.
*Loureen:* Dial 911, Florence!
*Florence:* Why? You're scaring me!
*Loureen:* Dial 911!

   *(Florence picks up the telephone and quickly dials.)*

   I think I killed him.

   *(Florence hangs up the telephone.)*

*Florence:* What?
*Loureen (Whimpers):* I killed him! I killed Samuel!

*Florence:* Come again? . . . He's dead dead?

*(Loureen wrings her hands and nods her head twice, mouthing "dead dead." Florence backs away.)*

No, stop it, I don't have time for this. I'm going back upstairs. You know how Samuel hates to find me here when he gets home. You're not going to get me this time. *(Louder)* Y'all can have your little joke, I'm not part of it! *(A moment. She takes a hard look into Loureen's eyes; she squints)* Did you really do it this time?

*Loureen (Hushed):* I don't know how or why it happened, it just did.

*Florence:* Why are you whispering?

*Loureen:* I don't want to talk too loud — something else is liable to disappear.

*Florence:* Where's his body?

*Loureen (Points to the pile of ashes):* There! . . .

*Florence:* You burned him?

*Loureen:* I DON'T KNOW! *(Covers her mouth as if to muffle her words; hushed)* I think so.

*Florence:* Either you did or you didn't, what you mean you don't know? We're talking murder, Loureen, not oven settings.

*Loureen:* You think I'm playing?

*Florence:* How many times have I heard you talk about being rid of him. How many times have we sat at this very table and laughed about the many ways we could do it and how many times have you done it? None.

*Loureen (Lifting the spectacles):* A pair of cheap spectacles, that's all that's left. And you know how much I hate these. You ever seen him without them, no! . . . He counted to four and disappeared. I swear to God!

*Florence:* Don't bring the Lord into this just yet! Sit down now . . . What you got to sip on?

*Loureen:* I don't know whether to have a stiff shot of scotch or a glass of champagne.

*(Florence takes a bottle of sherry out of the cupboard and pours them each a glass. Loureen downs hers, then holds out her glass for more.)*

He was. . .

*Florence:* Take your time.

*Loureen:* Standing there.

*Florence:* And?

*Loureen:* He exploded.

*Florence:* Did that muthafucka hit you again?

*Loureen:* No . . . he exploded. Boom! Right in front of me. He was shouting like he does, being all colored, then he raised up that big crusty hand to hit me, and poof, he was gone . . . I barely got words out and I'm looking down at a pile of ash.

*(Florence belts back her sherry. She wipes her forehead and pours them both another.)*

*Florence:* Chile, I'll give you this, in terms of color you've matched my husband Edgar, the story king. He came in at six Sunday morning, talking about he'd hit someone with his car, and had spent all night trying to outrun the police. I felt sorry for him. It turns out he was playing poker with his paycheck no less. You don't want to know how I found out . . . But I did.

*Loureen:* You think I'm lying?

*Florence:* I certainly hope so, Loureen. For your sake and my heart's.

*Loureen:* Samuel always said if I raised my voice something horrible would happen. And it did. I'm a witch . . . the devil spawn!

*Florence:* You've been watching too much television.

*Loureen:* Never seen anything like this on television. Wish I had, then I'd know what to do ... There's no question, I'm a witch. *(Looks at her hands with disgust)*

*Florence:* Chile, don't tell me you've been messing with them mojo women again? What did I tell ya.

*(Loureen, agitated, stands and sits back down.)*

*Loureen:* He's not coming back. Oh no, how could he? It would be a miracle! Two in one day . . . I could be canonized. Worse yet, he could be . . . All that needs to happen now is for my palms to bleed and I'll be eternally remembered as Saint Loureen, the patron of battered wives. Women from across the country will make pilgrimages to me, laying pies and pot roast at my feet and asking the good saint to make their husbands turn to dust. How often does a man like Samuel get damned to hell, and go?

*(She breaks down. Florence moves to console her friend, then realizes that Loureen is actually laughing hysterically.)*

*Florence:* You smoking crack?

*Loureen:* Do I look like I am?

*Florence:* Hell, I've seen old biddies creeping out of crack houses, talking about they were doing church work.

*Loureen:* Florence, please be helpful, I'm very close to the edge! . . . I don't know what to do next! Do I sweep him up? Do I call the police? Do I . . .

*(The phone rings.)*

Oh God.

*Florence:* You gonna let it ring?

*(Loureen reaches for the telephone slowly.)*

*Loureen:* NO! *(Holds the receiver without picking it up, paralyzed)* What if it's his mother? . . . She knows!

*(The phone continues to ring. They sit until it stops. They both breathe a sigh of relief.)*

I should be mourning, I should be praying, I should be thinking of the burial, but all that keeps popping into my mind is what will I wear on television when I share my horrible and wonderful story with a studio audience . . . *(Whimpers)* He's made me a killer, Florence, and you remember what a gentle child I was. *(Whispers)* I'm a killer, I'm a killer, I'm a killer.

*Florence:* I wouldn't throw that word about too lightly even in jest. Talk like that gets around.

*Loureen:* You think they'll lock me up? A few misplaced words and I'll probably get the death penalty, isn't that what they do with women like me, murderesses?

*Florence:* Folks have done time for less.

*Loureen:* Thank you, just what I needed to hear!

*Florence:* What did you expect, that I was going to throw up my arms and congratulate you? Why'd you have to go and lose your mind at this time of day, while I got a pot of rice on the stove and Edgar's about to walk in the door and wonder where his goddamn food is. *(Losing her cool)* And he's going to start in on me about all the nothing I've been doing during the day and why I can't work and then he'll mention how clean you keep your home. And I don't know how I'm going to look him in the eye without . . .

*Loureen:* I'm sorry, Florence. Really. It's out of my hands now.

*(She takes Florence's hand and squeezes it.)*

*Florence (Regaining her composure):* You swear on your right tit?

*Loureen (Clutching both breasts):* I swear on both of them!

*Florence:* Both your breasts, Loureen! You know what will happen if you're lying. *(Loureen nods; hushed)* Both your breasts, Loureen?

*Loureen:* Yeah!

*Florence (Examines the pile of ashes, then shakes her head):* Oh sweet, sweet Jesus. He must have done something truly terrible.

*Loureen:* No more than usual. I just couldn't take being hit one more time.

*Florence:* You've taken a thousand blows from that man, couldn't you've turned the cheek and waited. I'd have helped you pack. Like we talked about.

*(A moment.)*

*Loureen:* Uh! . . . I could blow on him and he'd disappear across the linoleum. *(Snaps her fingers)* Just like that. Should I be feeling remorse or regret or some other "R" word? I'm strangely jubilant, like on prom night when Samuel and I first made love. That's the feeling! *(The women lock eyes)* Uh!

*Florence:* Is it . . .

*Loureen:* Like a ton of bricks been lifted from my shoulders, yeah.

*Florence:* Really?

*Loureen:* Yeah!

*(Florence walks to the other side of the room.)*

*Florence:* You bitch!

*Loureen:* What?

*Florence:* We made a pact.

*Loureen:* I know.

*Florence:* You've broken it . . . We agreed that when things got real bad for both of us we'd . . . you know . . . together . . . Do I have to go back upstairs to that? . . . What next?

*Loureen:* I thought you'd tell me! . . . I don't know!

*Florence:* I don't know!

*Loureen:* I don't know!

*(Florence begins to walk around the room, nervously touching objects. Loureen sits, wringing her hands and mumbling softly to herself.)*

*Florence:* Now you got me, Loureen, I'm truly at a loss for words.

*Loureen:* Everybody always told me, "Keep your place, Loureen." My place, the silent spot on the couch with a wine cooler in my hand and a pleasant smile that warmed the heart. All this time I didn't know why he was so afraid for me to say anything, to speak up. Poof! . . . I've never been by myself, except for them two weeks when he won the office pool and went to Reno with his cousin Mitchell. He wouldn't tell me where he was going until I got that post-card with the cowboy smoking a hundred cigarettes . . . Didn't Sonny Larkin look good last week at Caroline's? He looked good, didn't he . . .

*(Florence nods. She nervously picks up Samuel's jacket, which is hanging on the back of the chair. She clutches it unconsciously.)*

NO! No! Don't wrinkle that, that's his favorite jacket. He'll kill me. Put it back!

*(Florence returns the jacket to its perch. Loureen begins to quiver.)*

I'm sorry. *(She grabs the jacket and wrinkles it up)* There! *(She then digs into the coat pockets and pulls out his wallet and a movie stub)* Look at that, he said he didn't go to the movies last night. Working late. *(Frantically thumbs through his wallet)* Picture of his motorcycle, Social Security card, driver's license, and look at that from our wedding. *(Smiling)* I looked good, didn't I? *(She puts the pictures back in the wallet and holds the jacket up to her face)* There were some good things. *(She then sweeps her hand over the jacket to remove the wrinkles, and folds it ever so carefully, and finally throws it in the garbage)* And out of my mouth those words made him disappear. All these years and just words, Florence. That's all they were.

*Florence:* I'm afraid I won't ever get those words out. I'll start resenting you, honey. I'm afraid won't anything change for me.

*Loureen:* I been to that place.

*Florence:* Yeah? But now I wish I could relax these old lines *(Touches her forehead)* for a minute maybe. Edgar has never done me the way Samuel did you, but he sure did take the better part of my life.

*Loureen:* Not yet, Florence.

*Florence (Nods):* I have the children to think of . . . right?

*Loureen:* You can think up a hundred things before . . .

*Florence:* Then come upstairs with me . . . we'll wait together for Edgar and then you can spit out your words and . . .

*Loureen:* I can't do that.

*Florence:* Yes you can. Come on now.

*(Loureen shakes her head no.)*

Well, I guess my mornings are not going to be any different.

*Loureen:* If you can say for certain, then I guess they won't be. I couldn't say that.

*Florence:* But you got a broom and a dust pan, you don't need anything more than that . . . He was a bastard and nobody will care that he's gone.

*Loureen:* Phone's gonna start ringing soon, people are gonna start asking soon, and they'll care.

*Florence:* What's your crime? Speaking your mind?

*Loureen:* Maybe I should mail him to his mother. I owe her that. I feel bad for her, she didn't understand how it was. I can't just throw him away and pretend like it didn't happen. Can I?

*Florence:* I didn't see anything but a pile of ash. As far as I know you got a little careless and burned a chicken.

*Loureen:* He was always threatening not to come back.

*Florence:* I heard him.

*Loureen:* It would've been me eventually.

*Florence:* Yes.

*Loureen:* I should call the police, or someone.

*Florence:* Why? What are you gonna tell them? About all those times they refused to help, about all those nights you slept in my bed 'cause you were afraid to stay down here? About the time he nearly took out your eye 'cause you flipped the television channel?

*Loureen:* No.

*Florence:* You've got it, girl!

*Loureen:* Good-bye to the fatty meats and the salty food. Good-bye to the bourbon and the bologna sandwiches. Good-bye to the smell of his feet, his breath and his bowel movements . . . (*A moment. She closes her eyes and, reliving a horrible memory, she shudders*) Good-bye. (*Walks over to the pile of ashes*) Samuel? . . . Just checking.

*Florence:* Good-bye Samuel.

(*They both smile.*)

*Loureen:* I'll let the police know that he's missing tomorrow . . .

*Florence:* Why not the next day?

*Loureen:* Chicken's warming in the oven, you're welcome to stay.

*Florence:* Chile, I got a pot of rice on the stove, kids are probably acting out . . . and Edgar, well . . . Listen, I'll stop in tomorrow.

*Loureen:* For dinner?

*Florence:* Edgar wouldn't stand for that. Cards maybe.

*Loureen:* Cards.

(*The women hug for a long moment. Florence exits. Loureen stands over the ashes for a few moments contemplating what to do. She finally decides to sweep them under the carpet, and then proceeds to set the table and sit down to eat her dinner.*)

*End of play*

## Considerations for Critical Thinking and Writing

1. FIRST RESPONSE. The play centers around the death of one of its three characters. Is it somehow funny? Why?

2. Why do you think Nottage's stage directions specify what Florence is wearing? Why doesn't she specify what Loureen is wearing?

3. How does the playwright convey the exposition? What are the important details from the past that precede the play's present action?

4. We never see Samuel or Florence's husband Edgar on stage. How are they characterized?

5. Loureen occasionally describes her fantasies of what will happen to her in the future. How do those fantasies operate to help determine the play's theme?

6. How do witchcraft, superstition, personal oaths, and pacts function within the story? How about if you contrast them with traditional religion?

7. Why does Loureen refuse to do to Edgar what she did to Samuel?

8. Loureen is consumed by guilt for most of the play. Does she get over it? What details inform your answer?

9. How does Florence's relationship with her husband Edgar compare to Loureen's relationship with Samuel? Do you agree with Florence's prediction ("won't anything change for me")?

## Connections to Other Selections

1. Compare the plot, theme, and/or characters in *POOF!* with those of Susan Glaspell's *Trifles* (p. 976).

2. Discuss gender roles in this play and in two short plays by Suzan-Lori Parks: "Fine Animal" (p. 1203) and "Barefoot and Pregnant in the Park" (p. 1210).

## AUGUST WILSON (1945–2005)

August Wilson, who, as a young poet, "wanted to be Dylan Thomas," (see Thomas' poem on p. 689) went on to become a major force in the American theater. Between the 1980s and his death in 2005, Wilson wrote a sequence of ten plays that chronicled the Black experience in the United States in each decade of the twentieth century. *Ma Rainey's Black Bottom*, the first of these to be completed, premiered at the Yale Reper-tory Theatre in 1984, went to Broadway shortly there-

Adger Cowans/Getty Images.

after, and eventually won the New York Drama Critics' Circle Award. It was adapted into an award-winning film in 2020 that earned Chadwick Boseman a posthumous Golden Globe Award for his final role preceding his untimely death. Other plays in the sequence include *Joe Turner's Come and Gone* (1986), *The Piano Lesson* (1987), *Two Trains Running* (1989), and Wilson's last play, *Radio Golf* (2005).

    Born in Pittsburgh, Pennsylvania, Wilson grew up in the Hill, a Black neighborhood to which his mother had come from North Carolina. His white father never lived with the family. Wilson quit school at sixteen and worked in a variety of menial jobs, meanwhile submitting poetry to a number of local publications. He didn't begin to find his writing voice, however, until he moved to Minneapolis–St. Paul, where he founded the Black Horizons Theatre Company in 1968 and later started the Playwrights Center. He supported himself during part of this time by writing skits for the Science Museum of Minnesota.

> **A Note on the Text:** *Fences* offers a complex look at the internal and external pressures on a Black family living in a Pittsburgh tenement during the 1950s. Readers should be forewarned that the play makes frequent use of an offensive racial slur. In this case, the effect of the word is to intensify the racially charged society the characters live in. It is spoken by Black characters to Black characters: there are no white characters in the play.

## *Fences*  1985

CHARACTERS

*Troy Maxson*
*Jim Bono,* Troy's friend
*Rose,* Troy's wife
*Lyons,* Troy's oldest son by previous marriage
*Gabriel,* Troy's brother
*Cory,* Troy and Rose's son
*Raynell,* Troy's daughter

SETTING: The setting is the yard which fronts the only entrance to the Maxson household, an ancient two-story brick house set back off a small alley in a big-city neighborhood. The entrance to the house is gained by two or three steps leading to a wooden porch badly in need of paint.

A relatively recent addition to the house and running its full width, the porch lacks congruence. It is a sturdy porch with a flat roof. One or two chairs of dubious value sit at one end where the kitchen window opens onto the porch. An old-fashioned icebox stands silent guard at the opposite end.

The yard is a small dirt yard, partially fenced, except for the last scene, with a wooden sawhorse, a pile of lumber, and other fence-building equipment set off to the side. Opposite is a tree from which hangs a ball made of rags. A baseball bat leans against the tree. Two oil drums serve as garbage receptacles and sit near the house at right to complete the setting.

THE PLAY: Near the turn of the [twentieth] century, the destitute of Europe sprang on the city with tenacious claws and an honest and solid dream. The city devoured them. They swelled its belly until it burst into a thousand furnaces and sewing machines, a thousand butcher shops and bakers' ovens, a thousand churches and hospitals and funeral parlors, and money-lenders. The city grew. It nourished itself and offered each man a partnership limited only by his talent, his guile, and his willingness and capacity for hard work. For the immigrants of Europe, a dream dared and won true.

The descendants of African slaves were offered no such welcome or participation. They came from places called the Carolinas and the Virginias, Georgia, Alabama, Mississippi, and Tennessee. They came strong, eager, searching. The city rejected them and they fled and settled along the riverbanks and under bridges in shallow, ramshackle houses made of sticks and tarpaper. They collected rags and wood. They sold the use of their muscles and their bodies. They cleaned houses and washed clothes, they shined shoes, and in quiet desperation and vengeful pride, they stole, and lived in pursuit of their own dream. That they could breathe free, finally, and stand to meet life with the force of dignity and whatever eloquence the heart could call upon.

By 1957, the hard-won victories of the European immigrants had solidified the industrial might of America. War had been confronted and won with new energies that used loyalty and patriotism as its fuel. Life was rich, full, and flourishing. The Milwaukee Braves won the World Series, and the hot winds of change that would make the sixties a turbulent, racing, dangerous, and provocative decade had not yet begun to blow full.

---

# ACT I

## SCENE I

*It is 1957. Troy and Bono enter the yard, engaged in conversation. Troy is fifty-three years old, a large man with thick, heavy hands; it is this largeness that he strives to fill out and make an accommodation with. Together with his blackness, his largeness informs his sensibilities and the choices he has made in his life.*

> *Of the two men, Bono is obviously the follower. His commitment to their friendship of thirty-odd years is rooted in his admiration of Troy's honesty, capacity for hard work, and his strength, which Bono seeks to emulate.*
>
> *It is Friday night, payday, and the one night of the week the two men engage in a ritual of talk and drink. Troy is usually the most talkative and at times he can be crude and almost vulgar, though he is capable of rising to profound heights of expression. The men carry lunch buckets and wear or carry burlap aprons and are dressed in clothes suitable to their jobs as garbage collectors.*

*Bono:* Troy, you ought to stop that lying!

*Troy:* I ain't lying! The nigger had a watermelon this big. *(He indicates with his hands.)* Talking about . . . "What watermelon, Mr. Rand?" I liked to fell out! "What watermelon, Mr. Rand?" . . . And it sitting there big as life.

*Bono:* What did Mr. Rand say?

*Troy:* Ain't said nothing. Figure if the nigger too dumb to know he carrying a watermelon, he wasn't gonna get much sense out of him. Trying to hide that great big old watermelon under his coat. Afraid to let the white man see him carry it home.

*Bono:* I'm like you . . . I ain't got no time for them kind of people.

*Troy:* Now what he look like getting mad cause he see the man from the union talking to Mr. Rand?

*Bono:* He come to me talking about . . . "Maxson gonna get us fired." I told him to get away from me with that. He walked away from me calling you a trouble-maker. What Mr. Rand say?

*Troy:* Ain't said nothing. He told me to go down the Commissioner's office next Friday. They called me down there to see them.

*Bono:* Well, as long as you got your complaint filed, they can't fire you. That's what one of them white fellows tell me.

*Troy:* I ain't worried about them firing me. They gonna fire me cause I asked a question? That's all I did. I went to Mr. Rand and asked him, "Why? Why you got the white mens driving and the colored lifting?" Told him, "what's the matter, don't I count? You think only white fellows got sense enough to drive a truck. That ain't no paper job! Hell, anybody can drive a truck. How come you got all whites driving and the colored lifting?" He told me "take it to the union." Well, hell, that's what I done! Now they wanna come up with this pack of lies.

*Bono:* I told Brownie if the man come and ask him any questions . . . just tell the truth! It ain't nothing but something they done trumped up on you cause you filed a complaint on them.

*Troy:* Brownie don't understand nothing. All I want them to do is change the job description. Give everybody a chance to drive the truck. Brownie can't see that. He ain't got that much sense.

*Bono:* How you figure he be making out with that gal be up at Taylors' all the time . . . that Alberta gal?

*Troy:* Same as you and me. Getting just as much as we is. Which is to say nothing.

*Bono:* It is, huh? I figure you doing a little better than me . . . and I ain't saying what I'm doing.

*Troy:* Aw, nigger, look here . . . I know you. If you had got anywhere near that gal, twenty minutes later you be looking to tell somebody. And the first one you gonna tell . . . that you gonna want to brag to . . . is me.

*Bono:* I ain't saying that. I see where you be eyeing her.

*Troy:* I eye all the women. I don't miss nothing. Don't never let nobody tell you Troy Maxson don't eye the women.

*Bono:* You been doing more than eyeing her. You done bought her a drink or two.

*Troy:* Hell yeah, I bought her a drink! What that mean? I bought you one, too. What that mean cause I buy her a drink? I'm just being polite.

*Bono:* It's all right to buy her one drink. That's what you call being polite. But when you wanna be buying two or three . . . that's what you call eyeing her.

*Troy:* Look here, as long as you known me . . . you ever known me to chase after women?

*Bono:* Hell yeah! Long as I done known you. You forgetting I knew you when.

*Troy:* Naw, I'm talking about since I been married to Rose?

*Bono:* Oh, not since you been married to Rose. Now, that's the truth, there. I can say that.

*Troy:* All right then! Case closed.

*Bono:* I see you be walking up around Alberta's house. You supposed to be at Taylors' and you be walking up around there.

*Troy:* What you watching where I'm walking for? I ain't watching after you.

*Bono:* I seen you walking around there more than once.

*Troy:* Hell, you liable to see me walking anywhere! That don't mean nothing cause you see me walking around there.

*Bono:* Where she come from anyway? She just kinda showed up one day.

*Troy:* Tallahassee. You can look at her and tell she one of them Florida gals. They got some big healthy women down there. Grow them right up out the ground. Got a little bit of Indian in her. Most of them niggers down in Florida got some Indian in them.

*Bono:* I don't know about that Indian part. But she damn sure big and healthy. Woman wear some big stockings. Got them great big old legs and hips as wide as the Mississippi River.

*Troy:* Legs don't mean nothing. You don't do nothing but push them out of the way. But them hips cushion the ride!

*Bono:* Troy, you ain't got no sense.

*Troy:* It's the truth! Like you riding on Goodyears!

> *Rose enters from the house. She is ten years younger than Troy, her devotion to him stems from her recognition of the possibilities of her life without him: a succession of abusive men and their babies, a life of partying and running the streets, the Church, or aloneness with its attendant pain and frustration. She recognizes Troy's spirit as a fine and illuminating one and she either ignores or forgives his faults, only some of which she recognizes. Though she doesn't drink, her presence is an integral part of the Friday night rituals. She alternates between the porch and the kitchen, where supper preparations are under way.*

*Rose:* What you all out here getting into?

*Troy:* What you worried about what we getting into for? This is men talk, woman.

*Rose:* What I care what you all talking about? Bono, you gonna stay for supper?

*Bono:* No, I thank you, Rose. But Lucille say she cooking up a pot of pigfeet.

*Troy:* Pigfeet! Hell, I'm going home with you! Might even stay the night if you got some pigfeet. You got something in there to top them pigfeet, Rose?

*Rose:* I'm cooking up some chicken. I got some chicken and collard greens.

*Troy:* Well, go on back in the house and let me and Bono finish what we was talking about. This is men talk. I got some talk for you later. You know what kind of talk I mean. You go on and powder it up.

*Rose:* Troy Maxson, don't you start that now!

*Troy (puts his arm around her):* Aw, woman . . . come here. Look here, Bono . . . when I met this woman . . . I got out that place, say, "Hitch up my pony, saddle up my mare . . , there's a woman out there for me somewhere. I looked here. Looked there. Saw Rose and latched on to her." I latched on to her and told her — I'm gonna tell you the truth — I told her, "Baby, I don't wanna marry, I just wanna be your man." Rose told me . . . tell him what you told me, Rose.

*Rose:* I told him if he wasn't the marrying kind, then move out the way so the marrying kind could find me.

*Troy:* That's what she told me. "Nigger, you in my way. You blocking the view! Move out the way so I can find me a husband." I thought it over two or three days. Come back —

*Rose:* Ain't no two or three days nothing. You was back the same night.

*Troy:* Come back, told her . . . "Okay, baby . . . but I'm gonna buy me a banty rooster and put him out there in the backyard . . . and when he see a stranger come, he'll flap his wings and crow . . ." Look here, Bono, I could watch the front door by myself . . . it was that back door I was worried about.

*Rose:* Troy, you ought not talk like that. Troy ain't doing nothing but telling a lie.

*Troy:* Only thing is . . . when we first got married . . . forget the rooster . . . we ain't had no yard!

*Bono:* I hear you tell it. Me and Lucille was staying down there on Logan Street. Had two rooms with the outhouse in the back. I ain't mind the outhouse none. But when that goddamn wind blow through there in the winter . . . that's what I'm talking about! To this day I wonder why in the hell I ever stayed down there for six long years. But see, I didn't know I could do no better. I thought only white folks had inside toilets and things.

*Rose:* There's a lot of people don't know they can do no better than they doing now. That's just something you got to learn. A lot of folks still shop at Bella's.

*Troy:* Ain't nothing wrong with shopping at Bella's. She got fresh food.

*Rose:* I ain't said nothing about if she got fresh food. I'm talking about what she charge. She charge ten cents more than the A&P.

*Troy:* The A&P ain't never done nothing for me. I spends my money where I'm treated right. I go down to Bella, say, "I need a loaf of bread, I'll pay you Friday." She give it to me. What sense that make when I got money to go and spend it somewhere else and ignore the person who done right by me? That ain't in the Bible.

*Rose:* We ain't talking about what's in the Bible. What sense it make to shop there when she overcharge?

*Troy:* You shop where you want to. I'll do my shopping where the people been good to me.

*Rose:* Well, I don't think it's right for her to overcharge. That's all I was saying.

*Bono:* Look here . . . I got to get on. Lucille going be raising all kind of hell.

*Troy:* Where you going, nigger? We ain't finished this pint. Come here, finish this pint.

*Bono:* Well, hell, I am . . . if you ever turn the bottle loose.

*Troy (hands him the bottle):* The only thing I say about the A&P is I'm glad Cory got that job down there. Help him take care of his school clothes and things. Gabe done moved out and things getting tight around here. He got that job. . . . He can start to look out for himself.

*Rose:* Cory done went and got recruited by a college football team.

*Troy:* I told that boy about that football stuff. The white man ain't gonna let him get nowhere with that football. I told him when he first come to me with it. Now you come telling me he done went and got more tied up in it. He ought to go and get recruited in how to fix cars or something where he can make a living.

*Rose:* He ain't talking about making no living playing football. It's just something the boys in school do. They gonna send a recruiter by to talk to you. He'll tell you he ain't talking about making no living playing football. It's a honor to be recruited.

*Troy:* It ain't gonna get him nowhere. Bono'll tell you that.

*Bono:* If he be like you in the sports . . . he's gonna be all right. Ain't but two men ever played baseball as good as you. That's Babe Ruth° and Josh Gibson.° Them's the only two men ever hit more home runs than you.

*Troy:* What it ever get me? Ain't got a pot to piss in or a window to throw it out of.

*Rose:* Times have changed since you was playing baseball, Troy. That was before the war. Times have changed a lot since then.

*Troy:* How in hell they done changed?

*Rose:* They got lots of colored boys playing ball now. Baseball and football.

*Bono:* You right about that, Rose. Times have changed, Troy. You just come along too early.

*Troy:* There ought not never have been no time called too early! Now you take that fellow . . . what's that fellow they had playing right field for the Yankees back then? You know who I'm talking about, Bono. Used to play right field for the Yankees.

*Rose:* Selkirk?

*Troy:* Selkirk! That's it! Man batting .269, understand? .269. What kind of sense that make? I was hitting .432 with thirty-seven home runs! Man batting .269 and playing right field for the Yankees! I saw Josh Gibson's daughter yesterday. She walking around with raggedy shoes on her feet. Now I bet you Selkirk's daughter ain't walking around with raggedy shoes on her feet! I bet you that!

*Rose:* They got a lot of colored baseball players now. Jackie Robinson° was the first. Folks had to wait for Jackie Robinson.

*Troy:* I done seen a hundred niggers play baseball better than Jackie Robinson. Hell, I know some teams Jackie Robinson couldn't even make! What you talking about Jackie Robinson. Jackie Robinson wasn't nobody. I'm talking about if you could play ball then they ought to have let you play. Don't care what color you were. Come telling me I come along too early. If you could play . . . then they ought to have let you play.

*Troy takes a long drink from the bottle.*

---

*Babe Ruth* (1895–1948): One of the greatest American baseball players.  *Josh Gibson* (1911–1947): Powerful baseball player known in the 1930s as the Babe Ruth of the Negro leagues. *Jackie Robinson* (1919–1972): The first Black baseball player in the Major Leagues (1947).

*Rose:* You gonna drink yourself to death. You don't need to be drinking like that.

*Troy:* Death ain't nothing. I done seen him. Done wrassled with him. You can't tell me nothing about death. Death ain't nothing but a fastball on the outside corner. And you know what I'll do to that! Lookee here, Bono . . . am I lying? You get one of them fastballs, about waist high, over the outside corner of the plate where you can get the meat of the bat on it . . . and good god! You can kiss it goodbye. Now, am I lying?

*Bono:* Naw, you telling the truth there. I seen you do it.

*Troy:* If I'm lying . . . that 450 feet worth of lying! *(Pause.)* That's all death is to me. A fastball on the outside corner.

*Rose:* I don't know why you want to get on talking about death.

*Troy:* Ain't nothing wrong with talking about death. That's part of life. Everybody gonna die. You gonna die, I'm gonna die. Bono's gonna die. Hell, we all gonna die.

*Rose:* But you ain't got to talk about it. I don't like to talk about it.

*Troy:* You the one brought it up. Me and Bono was talking about baseball . . . you tell me I'm gonna drink myself to death. Ain't that right, Bono? You know I don't drink this but one night out of the week. That's Friday night. I'm gonna drink just enough to where I can handle it. Then I cuts it loose. I leave it alone. So don't you worry about me drinking myself to death. 'Cause I ain't worried about Death. I done seen him. I done wrestled with him.

Look here, Bono . . . I looked up one day and Death was marching straight at me. Like Soldiers on Parade! The Army of Death was marching straight at me. The middle of July, 1941. It got real cold just like it be winter. It seem like Death himself reached out and touched me on the shoulder. He touch me just like I touch you. I got cold as ice and Death standing there grinning at me.

*Rose:* Troy, why don't you hush that talk.

*Troy:* I say . . . what you want, Mr. Death? You be wanting me? You done brought your army to be getting me? I looked him dead in the eye. I wasn't fearing nothing. I was ready to tangle. Just like I'm ready to tangle now. The Bible say be ever vigilant. That's why I don't get but so drunk. I got to keep watch.

*Rose:* Troy was right down there in Mercy Hospital. You remember he had pneumonia? Laying there with a fever talking plumb out of his head.

*Troy:* Death standing there staring at me . . . carrying that sickle in his hand. Finally he say, "You want bound over for another year?" See, just like that . . . "You want bound over for another year?" I told him, "Bound over hell! Let's settle this now!"

It seem like he kinda fell back when I said that, and all the cold went out of me. I reached down and grabbed that sickle and threw it just as far as I could throw it . . . and me and him commenced to wrestling.

We wrestled for three days and three nights. I can't say where I found the strength from. Every time it seemed like he was gonna get the best of me, I'd reach way down deep inside myself and find the strength to do him one better.

*Rose:* Every time Troy tell that story he find different ways to tell it. Different things to make up about it.

*Troy:* I ain't making up nothing. I'm telling you the facts of what happened. I wrestled with Death for three days and three nights and I'm standing here to tell you about it. *(Pause.)* All right. At the end of the third night we done weakened each other to where we can't hardly move. Death stood up, throwed on his robe . . . had him a white robe with a hood on it. He throwed on that robe and went off to look for his sickle. Say, "I'll be back." Just like that. "I'll be back." I told him, say, "Yeah, but . . . you gonna have to find me!" I wasn't no fool. I wan't going looking for him. Death ain't nothing to play with. And I know he's gonna get me. I know I got to join his army . . . his camp followers. But as long as I keep my strength and see him coming . . . as long as I keep up my vigilance . . . he's gonna have to fight to get me. I ain't going easy.

Bono: Well, look here, since you got to keep up your vigilance . . . let me have the bottle.

Troy: Aw hell, I shouldn't have told you that part. I should have left out that part.

Rose: Troy be talking that stuff and half the time don't even know what he be talking about.

Troy: Bono know me better than that.

Bono: That's right. I know you. I know you got some Uncle Remus° in your blood. You got more stories than the devil got sinners.

Troy: Aw hell, I done seen him too! Done talked with the devil.

Rose: Troy, don't nobody wanna be hearing all that stuff.

> *Lyons enters the yard from the street. Thirty-four years old, Troy's son by a previous marriage, he sports a neatly trimmed goatee, sport coat, white shirt, tieless, and buttoned at the collar. Though he fancies himself a musician, he is more caught up in the rituals and "idea" of being a musician than in the actual practice of the music. He has come to borrow money from Troy, and while he knows he will be successful, he is uncertain as to what extent his lifestyle will be held up to scrutiny and ridicule.*

Lyons: Hey, Pop.

Troy: What you come "Hey, Popping" me for?

Lyons: How you doing, Rose? *(He kisses her.)* Mr. Bono. How you doing?

Bono: Hey, Lyons . . . how you been?

Troy: He must have been doing all right. I ain't seen him around here last week.

Rose: Troy, leave your boy alone. He come by to see you and you wanna start all that nonsense.

Troy: I ain't bothering Lyons. *(Offers him the bottle.)* Here . . . get you a drink. We got an understanding. I know why he come by to see me and he know I know.

Lyons: Come on, Pop . . . I just stopped by to say hi . . . see how you was doing.

Troy: You ain't stopped by yesterday.

Rose: You gonna stay for supper, Lyons? I got some chicken cooking in the oven.

Lyons: No, Rose . . . thanks. I was just in the neighborhood and thought I'd stop by for a minute.

Troy: You was in the neighborhood all right, nigger. You telling the truth there. You was in the neighborhood cause it's my payday.

Lyons: Well, hell, since you mentioned it . . . let me have ten dollars.

Troy: I'll be damned! I'll die and go to hell and play blackjack with the devil before I give you ten dollars.

Bono: That's what I wanna know about . . . that devil you done seen.

Lyons: What . . . Pop done seen the devil? You too much, Pops.

---

*Uncle Remus:* Black storyteller who recounts traditional Black tales in the book by Joel Chandler Harris.

*Troy:* Yeah, I done seen him. Talked to him too!

*Rose:* You ain't seen no devil. I done told you that man ain't had nothing to do with the devil. Anything you can't understand, you want to call it the devil.

*Troy:* Look here, Bono . . . I went down to see Hertzberger about some furniture. Got three rooms for two-ninety-eight. That what it say on the radio. "Three rooms . . . two-ninety-eight." Even made up a little song about it. Go down there . . . man tell me I can't get no credit. I'm working every day and can't get no credit. What to do? I got an empty house with some raggedy furniture in it. Cory ain't got no bed. He's sleeping on a pile of rags on the floor. Working every day and can't get no credit. Come back here — Rose'll tell you — madder than hell. Sit down . . . try to figure what I'm gonna do. Come a knock on the door. Ain't been living here but three days. Who know I'm here? Open the door . . . devil standing there bigger than life. White fellow . . . white fellow . . . got on good clothes and everything. Standing there with a clipboard in his hand. I ain't had to say nothing. First words come out of his mouth was . . . "I understand you need some furniture and can't get no credit." I liked to fell over. He say, "I'll give you all the credit you want, but you got to pay the interest on it." I told him, "Give me three rooms worth and charge whatever you want." Next day a truck pulled up here and two men unloaded them three rooms. Man what drove the truck give me a book. Say send ten dollars, first of every month to the address in the book and everything will be all right. Say if I miss a payment the devil was coming back and it'll be hell to pay. That was fifteen years ago. To this day . . . the first of the month I send my ten dollars, Rose'll tell you.

*Rose:* Troy lying.

*Troy:* I ain't never seen that man since. Now you tell me who else that could have been but the devil? I ain't sold my soul or nothing like that, you understand. Naw, I wouldn't have truck with the devil about nothing like that. I got my furniture and pays my ten dollars the first of the month just like clockwork.

*Bono:* How long you say you been paying this ten dollars a month?

*Troy:* Fifteen years!

*Bono:* Hell, ain't you finished paying for it yet? How much the man done charged you?

*Troy:* Ah hell, I done paid for it. I done paid for it ten times over! The fact is I'm scared to stop paying it.

*Rose:* Troy lying. We got that furniture from Mr. Glickman. He ain't paying no ten dollars a month to nobody.

*Troy:* Aw hell, woman. Bono know I ain't that big a fool.

*Lyons:* I was just getting ready to say . . . I know where there's a bridge for sale.

*Troy:* Look here, I'll tell you this . . . it don't matter to me if he was the devil. It don't matter if the devil give credit. Somebody has got to give it.

*Rose:* It ought to matter. You going around talking about having truck with the devil . . . God's the one you gonna have to answer to. He's the one gonna be at the Judgment.

*Lyons:* Yeah, well, look here, Pop . . . let me have that ten dollars. I'll give it back to you. Bonnie got a job working at the hospital.

*Troy:* What I tell you, Bono? The only time I see this nigger is when he wants something. That's the only time I see him.

*Lyons:* Come on, Pop, Mr. Bono don't want to hear all that. Let me have the ten dollars. I told you Bonnie working.

*Troy:* What that mean to me? "Bonnie working." I don't care if she working. Go ask her for the ten dollars if she working. Talking about "Bonnie working." Why ain't you working?

*Lyons:* Aw, Pop, you know I can't find no decent job. Where am I gonna get a job at? You know I can't get no job.

*Troy:* I told you I know some people down there. I can get you on the rubbish if you want to work. I told you that the last time you came by here asking me for something.

*Lyons:* Naw, Pop . . . thanks. That ain't for me. I don't wanna be carrying nobody's rubbish. I don't wanna be punching nobody's time clock.

*Troy:* What's the matter, you too good to carry people's rubbish? Where you think that ten dollars you talking about come from? I'm just supposed to haul people's rubbish and give my money to you cause you too lazy to work. You too lazy to work and wanna know why you ain't got what I got.

*Rose:* What hospital Bonnie working at? Mercy?

*Lyons:* She's down at Passavant working in the laundry.

*Troy:* I ain't got nothing as it is. I give you that ten dollars and I got to eat beans the rest of the week. Naw . . . you ain't getting no ten dollars here.

*Lyons:* You ain't got to be eating no beans. I don't know why you wanna say that.

*Troy:* I ain't got no extra money. Gabe done moved over to Miss Pearl's paying her the rent and things done got tight around here. I can't afford to be giving you every payday.

*Lyons:* I ain't asked you to give me nothing. I asked you to loan me ten dollars. I know you got ten dollars.

*Troy:* Yeah, I got it. You know why I got it? Cause I don't throw my money away out there in the streets. You living the fast life . . . wanna be a musician . . . running around in them clubs and things . . . then, you learn to take care of yourself. You ain't gonna find me going and asking nobody for nothing. I done spent too many years without.

*Lyons:* You and me is two different people, Pop.

*Troy:* I done learned my mistake and learned to do what's right by it. You still trying to get something for nothing. Life don't owe you nothing. You owe it to yourself. Ask Bono. He'll tell you I'm right.

*Lyons:* You got your way of dealing with the world . . . I got mine. The only thing that matters to me is the music.

*Troy:* Yeah, I can see that! It don't matter how you gonna eat . . . where your next dollar is coming from. You telling the truth there.

*Lyons:* I know I got to eat. But I got to live too. I need something that gonna help me to get out of the bed in the morning. Make me feel like I belong in the world. I don't bother nobody. I just stay with the music cause that's the only way I can find to live in the world. Otherwise there ain't no telling what I might do. Now I don't come criticizing you and how you live. I just come by to ask you for ten dollars. I don't wanna hear all that about how I live.

*Troy:* Boy, your mamma did a hell of a job raising you.

*Lyons:* You can't change me, Pop. I'm thirty-four years old. If you wanted to change me, you should have been there when I was growing up. I come by to see you . . . ask for ten dollars and you want to talk about how I was raised. You don't know nothing about how I was raised.

*Rose:* Let the boy have ten dollars, Troy.

*Troy (to Lyons):*  What the hell you looking at me for? I ain't got no ten dollars. You know what I do with my money. *(To Rose.)* Give him ten dollars if you want him to have it.

*Rose:*  I will. Just as soon as you turn it loose.

*Troy (handing Rose the money):*  There it is. Seventy-six dollars and forty-two cents. You see this, Bono? Now, I ain't gonna get but six of that back.

*Rose:*  You ought to stop telling that lie. Here, Lyons. *(She hands him the money.)*

*Lyons:*  Thanks, Rose. Look . . . I got to run . . . I'll see you later.

*Troy:*  Wait a minute. You gonna say, "thanks, Rose" and ain't gonna look to see where she got that ten dollars from? See how they do me, Bono?

*Lyons:*  I know she got it from you, Pop. Thanks. I'll give it back to you.

*Troy:*  There he go telling another lie. Time I see that ten dollars . . . he'll be owing me thirty more.

*Lyons:*  See you, Mr. Bono.

*Bono:*  Take care, Lyons!

*Lyons:*  Thanks, Pop. I'll see you again.

   *Lyons exits the yard.*

*Troy:*  I don't know why he don't go and get him a decent job and take care of that woman he got.

*Bono:*  He'll be all right, Troy. The boy is still young.

*Troy:*  The *boy* is thirty-four years old.

*Rose:*  Let's not get off into all that.

*Bono:*  Look here . . . I got to be going. I got to be getting on. Lucille gonna be waiting.

*Troy (puts his arm around Rose):*  See this woman, Bono? I love this woman. I love this woman so much it hurts. I love her so much . . . I done run out of ways of loving her. So I got to go back to basics. Don't you come by my house Monday morning talking about time to go to work . . . 'cause I'm still gonna be stroking!

*Rose:*  Troy! Stop it now!

*Bono:*  I ain't paying him no mind, Rose. That ain't nothing but gin-talk. Go on, Troy. I'll see you Monday.

*Troy:*  Don't you come by my house, nigger! I done told you what I'm gonna be doing.

   *The lights go down to black.*


## SCENE II

   *The lights come up on Rose hanging up clothes. She hums and sings softly to herself. It is the following morning.*

*Rose (sings):*  Jesus, be a fence all around me every day
   Jesus, I want you to protect me as I travel on my way.
   Jesus, be a fence all around me every day.

   *Troy enters from the house.*

   Jesus, I want you to protect me
   As I travel on my way.

*(To Troy.)* 'Morning. You ready for breakfast? I can fix it soon as I finish hanging up these clothes?

*Troy:* I got the coffee on. That'll be all right. I'll just drink some of that this morning.

*Rose:* That 651 hit yesterday. That's the second time this month. Miss Pearl hit for a dollar . . . seem like those that need the least always get lucky. Poor folks can't get nothing.

*Troy:* Them numbers don't know nobody. I don't know why you fool with them. You and Lyons both.

*Rose:* It's something to do.

*Troy:* You ain't doing nothing but throwing your money away.

*Rose:* Troy, you know I don't play foolishly. I just play a nickel here and a nickel there.

*Troy:* That's two nickels you done thrown away.

*Rose:* Now I hit sometimes . . . that makes up for it. It always comes in handy when I do hit. I don't hear you complaining then.

*Troy:* I ain't complaining now. I just say it's foolish. Trying to guess out of six hundred ways which way the number gonna come. If I had all the money niggers, these Negroes, throw away on numbers for one week — just one week — I'd be a rich man.

*Rose:* Well, you wishing and calling it foolish ain't gonna stop folks from playing numbers. That's one thing for sure. Besides . . . some good things come from playing numbers. Look where Pope done bought him that restaurant off of numbers.

*Troy:* I can't stand niggers like that. Man ain't had two dimes to rub together. He walking around with his shoes all run over bumming money for cigarettes. All right. Got lucky there and hit the numbers . . .

*Rose:* Troy, I know all about it.

*Troy:* Had good sense, I'll say that for him. He ain't throwed his money away. I seen niggers hit the numbers and go through two thousand dollars in four days. Man bought him that restaurant down there . . . fixed it up real nice . . . and then didn't want nobody to come in it! A Negro go in there and can't get no kind of service. I seen a white fellow come in there and order a bowl of stew. Pope picked all the meat out the pot for him. Man ain't had nothing but a bowl of meat! Negro come behind him and ain't got nothing but the potatoes and carrots. Talking about what numbers do for people, you picked a wrong example. Ain't done nothing but make a worser fool out of him than he was before.

*Rose:* Troy, you ought to stop worrying about what happened at work yesterday.

*Troy:* I ain't worried. Just told me to be down there at the Commissioner's office on Friday. Everybody think they gonna fire me. I ain't worried about them firing me. You ain't got to worry about that. *(Pause.)* Where's Cory? Cory in the house? *(Calls.)* Cory?

*Rose:* He gone out.

*Troy:* Out, huh? He gone out 'cause he know I want him to help me with this fence. I know how he is. That boy scared of work.

*Gabriel enters. He comes halfway down the alley and, hearing Troy's voice, stops.*

*Troy (continues):* He ain't done a lick of work in his life.

*Rose:* He had to go to football practice. Coach wanted them to get in a little extra
practice before the season start.

*Troy:* I got his practice . . . running out of here before he get his chores done.

*Rose:* Troy, what is wrong with you this morning? Don't nothing set right with
you. Go on back in there and go to bed . . . get up on the other side.

*Troy:* Why something got to be wrong with me? I ain't said nothing wrong
with me.

*Rose:* You got something to say about everything. First it's the numbers . . . then
it's the way the man runs his restaurant . . . then you done got on Cory. What's
it gonna be next? Take a look up there and see if the weather suits you . . . or
is it gonna be how you gonna put up the fence with the clothes hanging in
the yard.

*Troy:* You hit the nail on the head then.

*Rose:* I know you like I know the back of my hand. Go on in there and get you
some coffee . . . see if that straighten you up. 'Cause you ain't right this
morning.

*Troy starts into the house and sees Gabriel. Gabriel starts singing. Troy's
brother, he is seven years younger than Troy. Injured in World War II, he has
a metal plate in his head. He carries an old trumpet tied around his waist
and believes with every fiber of his being that he is the Archangel Gabriel.°
He carries a chipped basket with an assortment of discarded fruits and
vegetables he has picked up in the strip district and which he attempts to sell.*

*Gabriel (singing):* Yes, ma am, I got plums
    You ask me how I sell them
    Oh ten cents apiece
    Three for a quarter
    Come and buy now
    'Cause I'm here today
    And tomorrow I'll be gone

*Gabriel enters.*

Hey, Rose!

*Rose:* How you doing, Gabe?

*Gabriel:* There's Troy . . . Hey, Troy!

*Troy:* Hey, Gabe.

*Exit into kitchen.*

*Rose (to Gabriel):* What you got there?

*Gabriel:* You know what I got, Rose. I got fruits and vegetables.

*Rose (looking in basket):* Where's all these plums you talking about?

*Gabriel:* I ain't got no plums today, Rose. I was just singing that. Have some
tomorrow. Put me in a big order for plums. Have enough plums tomorrow
for St. Peter and everybody.

*Troy reenters from kitchen, crosses to steps.*

*(To Rose.)* Troy's mad at me.

---

*Archangel Gabriel:* Considered one of God's primary messengers in the Old and New
Testaments.

*Troy:* I ain't mad at you. What I got to be mad at you about? You ain't done nothing to me.

*Gabriel:* I just moved over to Miss Pearl's to keep out from in your way. I ain't mean no harm by it.

*Troy:* Who said anything about that? I ain't said anything about that.

*Gabriel:* You ain't mad at me, is you?

*Troy:* Naw . . . I ain't mad at you, Gabe. If I was mad at you I'd tell you about it.

*Gabriel:* Got me two rooms. In the basement. Got my own door too. Wanna see my key? *(He holds up a key.)* That's my own key! Ain't nobody else got a key like that. That's my key! My two rooms!

*Troy:* Well, that's good, Gabe. You got your own key . . . that's good.

*Rose:* You hungry, Gabe? I was just fixing to cook Troy his breakfast.

*Gabriel:* I'll take some biscuits. You got some biscuits? Did you know when I was in heaven . . . every morning me and St. Peter° would sit down by the gate and eat some big fat biscuits? Oh, yeah! We had us a good time. We'd sit there and eat us them biscuits and then St. Peter would go off to sleep and tell me to wake him up when it's time to open the gates for the judgment.

*Rose:* Well, come on . . . I'll make up a batch of biscuits.

*Rose exits into the house.*

*Gabriel:* Troy . . . St. Peter got your name in the book. I seen it. It say . . . Troy Maxson. I say . . . I know him! He got the same name like what I got. That's my brother!

*Troy:* How many times you gonna tell me that, Gabe?

*Gabriel:* Ain't got my name in the book. Don't have to have my name. I done died and went to heaven. He got your name though. One morning St. Peter was looking at his book . . . marking it up for the judgment . . . and he let me see your name. Got it in there under M. Got Rose's name . . . I ain't seen it like I seen yours . . . but I know it's in there. He got a great big book. Got everybody's name what was ever been born. That's what he told me. But I seen your name. Seen it with my own eyes.

*Troy:* Go on in the house there. Rose going to fix you something to eat.

*Gabriel:* Oh, I ain't hungry. I done had breakfast with Aunt Jemimah. She come by and cooked me up a whole mess of flapjacks. Remember how we used to eat them flapjacks?

*Troy:* Go on in the house and get you something to eat now.

*Gabriel:* I got to sell my plums. I done sold some tomatoes. Got me two quarters. Wanna see? *(He shows Troy his quarters.)* I'm gonna save them and buy me a new horn so St. Peter can hear me when it's time to open the gates. *(Gabriel stops suddenly. Listens.)* Hear that? That's the hellhounds. I got to chase them out of here. Go on get out of here! Get out!

*Gabriel exits singing.*

Better get ready for the judgment
Better get ready for the judgment
My Lord is coming down

*Rose enters from the house.*

*Troy:* He's gone off somewhere.

---

St. Peter:  One of Jesus's disciples, believed to be the keeper of the gates of Heaven.

*Gabriel (offstage):*  Better get ready for the judgment
           Better get ready for the judgment morning
           Better get ready for the judgment
           My God is coming down

*Rose:*  He ain't eating right. Miss Pearl say she can't get him to eat nothing.

*Troy:*  What you want me to do about it, Rose? I done did everything I can for the man. I can't make him get well. Man got half his head blown away . . . what you expect?

*Rose:*  Seem like something ought to be done to help him.

*Troy:*  Man don't bother nobody. He just mixed up from that metal plate he got in his head. Ain't no sense for him to go back into the hospital.

*Rose:*  Least he be eating right. They can help him take care of himself.

*Troy:*  Don't nobody wanna be locked up, Rose. What you wanna lock him up for? Man go over there and fight the war . . . messin' around with them Japs, get half his head blown off . . . and they give him a lousy three thousand dollars. And I had to swoop down on that.

*Rose:*  Is you fixing to go into that again?

*Troy:*  That's the only way I got a roof over my head . . . cause of that metal plate.

*Rose:*  Ain't no sense you blaming yourself for nothing. Gabe wasn't in no condition to manage that money. You done what was right by him. Can't nobody say you ain't done what was right by him. Look how long you took care of him . . . till he wanted to have his own place and moved over there with Miss Pearl.

*Troy:*  That ain't what I'm saying, woman! I'm just stating the facts. If my brother didn't have that metal plate in his head . . . I wouldn't have a pot to piss in or a window to throw it out of. And I'm fifty-three years old. Now see if you can understand that!

*Troy gets up from the porch and starts to exit the yard.*

*Rose:*  Where you going off to? You been running out of here every Saturday for weeks. I thought you was gonna work on this fence?

*Troy:*  I'm gonna walk down to Taylors'. Listen to the ball game. I'll be back in a bit. I'll work on it when I get back.

*He exits the yard. The lights go to black.*


## SCENE III

*The lights come up on the yard. It is four hours later. Rose is taking down the clothes from the line. Cory enters carrying his football equipment.*

*Rose:*  Your daddy like to had a fit with you running out of here this morning without doing your chores.

*Cory:*  I told you I had to go to practice.

*Rose:*  He say you were supposed to help him with this fence.

*Cory:*  He been saying that the last four or five Saturdays, and then he don't never do nothing, but go down to Taylors. Did you tell him about the recruiter?

*Rose:*  Yeah, I told him.

*Cory:*  What he say?

*Rose:*  He ain't said nothing too much. You get in there and get started on your chores before he gets back. Go on and scrub down them steps before he gets back here hollering and carrying on.

*Cory:* I'm hungry. What you got to eat, Mama?

*Rose:* Go on and get started on your chores. I got some meat loaf in there. Go on and make you a sandwich . . . and don't leave no mess in there.

> *Cory exits into the house. Rose continues to take down the clothes. Troy enters the yard and sneaks up and grabs her from behind.*

Troy! Go on, now. You liked to scared me to death. What was the score of the game? Lucille had me on the phone and I couldn't keep up with it.

*Troy:* What I care about the game? Come here, woman. *(He tries to kiss her.)*

*Rose:* I thought you went down Taylors' to listen to the game. Go on, Troy! You supposed to be putting up this fence.

*Troy (attempting to kiss her again):* I'll put it up when I finish with what is at hand.

*Rose:* Go on, Troy. I ain't studying you.

*Troy (chasing after her):* I'm studying you . . . fixing to do my homework!

*Rose:* Troy, you better leave me alone.

*Troy:* Where's Cory? That boy brought his butt home yet?

*Rose:* He's in the house doing his chores.

*Troy (calling):* Cory! Get your butt out here, boy!

> *Rose exits into the house with the laundry. Troy goes over to the pile of wood, picks up a board, and starts sawing. Cory enters from the house.*

*Troy:* You just now coming in here from leaving this morning?

*Cory:* Yeah, I had to go to football practice.

*Troy:* Yeah, what?

*Cory:* Yessir.

*Troy:* I ain't but two seconds off you noway. The garbage sitting in there over-flowing . . . you ain't done none of your chores . . . and you come in here talking about "Yeah."

*Cory:* I was just getting ready to do my chores now, Pop . . .

*Troy:* Your first chore is to help me with this fence on Saturday. Everything else come after that. Now get that saw and cut them boards.

> *Cory takes the saw and begins cutting the boards. Troy continues working. There is a long pause.*

*Cory:* Hey, Pop . . . why don't you buy a TV?

*Troy:* What I want with a TV? What I want one of them for?

*Cory:* Everybody got one. Earl, Ba Bra . . . Jesse!

*Troy:* I ain't asked you who had one. I say what I want with one?

*Cory:* So you can watch it. They got lots of things on TV. Baseball games and everything. We could watch the World Series.

*Troy:* Yeah . . . and how much this TV cost?

*Cory:* I don't know. They got them on sale for around two hundred dollars.

*Troy:* Two hundred dollars, huh?

*Cory:* That ain't that much, Pop.

*Troy:* Naw, it's just two hundred dollars. See that roof you got over your head at night? Let me tell you something about that roof. It's been over ten years since that roof was last tarred. See now . . . the snow come this winter and sit up there on that roof like it is . . . and it's gonna seep inside. It's just gonna be a little bit . . . ain't gonna hardly notice it. Then the next thing you know, it's gonna be leaking all over the house. Then the wood rot from all that water and you gonna need a whole new roof. Now, how much you think it cost to get that roof tarred?

*Cory:* I don't know.

*Troy:* Two hundred and sixty-four dollars . . . cash money. While you thinking about a TV, I got to be thinking about the roof . . . and whatever else go
wrong here. Now if you had two hundred dollars, what would you do . . . fix
the roof or buy a TV?

*Cory:* I'd buy a TV. Then when the roof started to leak . . . when it needed
fixing . . . I'd fix it.

*Troy:* Where you gonna get the money from? You done spent it for a TV. You
gonna sit up and watch the water run all over your brand new TV.

*Cory:* Aw, Pop. You got money. I know you do.

*Troy:* Where I got it at, huh?

*Cory:* You got it in the bank.

*Troy:* You wanna see my bankbook? You wanna see that seventy-three dollars
and twenty-two cents I got sitting up in there.

*Cory:* You ain't got to pay for it all at one time. You can put a down payment on it
and carry it on home with you.

*Troy:* Not me. I ain't gonna owe nobody nothing if I can help it. Miss a payment
and they come and snatch it right out your house. Then what you got? Now,
soon as I get two hundred dollars clear, then I'll buy a TV. Right now, as soon
as I get two hundred and sixty-four dollars, I'm gonna have this roof tarred.

*Cory:* Aw . . . Pop!

*Troy:* You go on and get you two hundred dollars and buy one if ya want it. I got
better things to do with my money.

*Cory:* I can't get no two hundred dollars. I ain't never seen two hundred dollars.

*Troy:* I'll tell you what . . . you get you a hundred dollars and I'll put the other
hundred with it.

*Cory:* All right, I'm gonna show you.

*Troy:* You gonna show me how you can cut them boards right now.

*Cory begins to cut the boards. There is a long pause.*

*Cory:* The Pirates won today. That makes five in a row.

*Troy:* I ain't thinking about the Pirates. Got an all-white team. Got that boy . . . that
Puerto Rican boy . . . Clemente.° Don't even half-play him. That boy could
be something if they give him a chance. Play him one day and sit him on the
bench the next.

*Cory:* He gets a lot of chances to play.

*Troy:* I'm talking about playing regular. Playing every day so you can get your
timing. That's what I'm talking about.

*Cory:* They got some white guys on the team that don't play every day. You can't
play everybody at the same time.

*Troy:* If they got a white fellow sitting on the bench . . . you can bet your last
dollar he can't play! The colored guy got to be twice as good before he get on
the team. That's why I don't want you to get all tied up in them sports. Man
on the team and what it get him? They got colored on the team and don't use
them. Same as not having them. All them teams the same.

---

*Clemente:* Roberto Clemente (1934–1972), a Puerto Rican right fielder for the Pittsburgh
Pirates, was the first Caribbean and first Latin American player to be inducted into the National
Baseball Hall of Fame.

*Cory:* The Braves got Hank Aaron° and Wes Covington.° Hank Aaron hit two home runs today. That makes forty-three.

*Troy:* Hank Aaron ain't nobody. That what you supposed to do. That's how you supposed to play the game. Ain't nothing to it. It's just a matter of timing . . . getting the right follow-through. Hell, I can hit forty-three home runs right now!

*Cory:* Not off no major-league pitching, you couldn't.

*Troy:* We had better pitching in the Negro leagues. I hit seven home runs off of Satchel Paige°. You can't get no better than that!

*Cory:* Sandy Koufax°. He's leading the league in strikeouts.

*Troy:* I ain't thinking of no Sandy Koufax.

*Cory:* You got Warren Spahn and Lew Burdette.° I bet you couldn't hit no home runs off of Warren Spahn.

*Troy:* I'm through with it now. You go on and cut them boards. *(Pause.)* Your mama tell me you done got recruited by a college football team? Is that right?

*Cory:* Yeah. Coach Zellman say the recruiter gonna be coming by to talk to you. Get you to sign the permission papers.

*Troy:* I thought you supposed to be working down there at the A&P. Ain't you suppose to be working down there after school?

*Cory:* Mr. Stawicki say he gonna hold my job for me until after the football season. Say starting next week I can work weekends.

*Troy:* I thought we had an understanding about this football stuff? You suppose to keep up with your chores and hold that job down at the A&P. Ain't been around here all day on a Saturday. Ain't none of your chores done . . . and now you telling me you done quit your job.

*Cory:* I'm going to be working weekends.

*Troy:* You damn right you are! And ain't no need for nobody coming around here to talk to me about signing nothing.

*Cory:* Hey, Pop . . . you can't do that. He's coming all the way from North Carolina.

*Troy:* I don't care where he coming from. The white man ain't gonna let you get nowhere with that football noway. You go on and get your book-learning so you can work yourself up in that A&P or learn how to fix cars or build houses or something, get you a trade. That way you have something can't nobody take away from you. You go on and learn how to put your hands to some good use. Besides hauling people's garbage.

*Cory:* I get good grades, Pop. That's why the recruiter wants to talk with you. You got to keep up your grades to get recruited. This way I'll be going to college. I'll get a chance . . .

*Troy:* First you gonna get your butt down there to the A&P and get your job back.

*Cory:* Mr. Stawicki done already hired somebody else 'cause I told him I was playing football.

*Troy:* You a bigger fool than I thought . . . to let somebody take away your job so you can play some football. Where you gonna get your money to take out your girlfriend and whatnot? What kind of foolishness is that to let somebody take away your job?

---

*Hank Aaron* (1934–2021): A Black right fielder, considered one of the greatest baseball players in history, Aaron played twenty-three seasons in Major League Baseball.  *Wes Covington* (1932–2011): Professional baseball left fielder.  *Satchel Paige* (1906–1982): Legendary Black pitcher in the Negro leagues.  *Sandy Koufax* (b. 1935), *Warren Spahn* (1921–2003), *Lew Burdette* (1926–2007): White Major League Baseball pitchers.

*Cory:* I'm still gonna be working weekends.

*Troy:* Naw . . . naw. You getting your butt out of here and finding you another job.

*Cory:* Come on, Pop! I got to practice. I can't work after school and play football too. The team needs me. That's what Coach Zellman say . . .

*Troy:* I don't care what nobody else say. I'm the boss . . . you understand? I'm the boss around here. I do the only saying what counts.

*Cory:* Come on, Pop!

*Troy:* I asked you . . . did you understand?

*Cory:* Yeah . . .

*Troy:* What?!

*Cory:* Yessir.

*Troy:* You go on down there to that A&P and see if you can get your job back. If you can't do both . . . then you quit the football team. You've got to take the crookeds with the straights.

*Cory:* Yessir. *(Pause.)* Can I ask you a question?

*Troy:* What the hell you wanna ask me? Mr. Stawicki the one you got the questions for.

*Cory:* How come you ain't never liked me?

*Troy:* Liked you? Who the hell say I got to like you? What law is there say I got to like you? Wanna stand up in my face and ask a damn fool-ass question like that. Talking about liking somebody. Come here, boy, when I talk to you.

*Cory comes over to where Troy is working. He stands slouched over and Troy shoves him on his shoulder.*

Straighten up, goddammit! I asked you a question . . . what law is there say I got to like you?

*Cory:* None.

*Troy:* Well, all right then! Don't you eat every day? *(Pause.)* Answer me when I talk to you! Don't you eat every day?

*Cory:* Yeah.

*Troy:* Nigger, as long as you in my house, you put that sir on the end of it when you talk to me!

*Cory:* Yes . . . sir.

*Troy:* You eat every day.

*Cory:* Yessir!

*Troy:* Got a roof over your head.

*Cory:* Yessir!

*Troy:* Got clothes on your back.

*Cory:* Yessir.

*Troy:* Why you think that is?

*Cory:* Cause of you.

*Troy:* Ah, hell I know it's cause of me . . . but why do you think that is?

*Cory (hesitant):* Cause you like me.

*Troy:* Like you? I go out of here every morning . . . bust my butt . . . putting up with them crackers° every day . . . cause I like you? You are the biggest fool I ever saw. *(Pause.)* It's my job. It's my responsibility! You understand that? A man got to take care of his family. You live in my house . . . sleep you behind on my bedclothes . . . fill you belly up with my food . . . cause you my son.

---

*crackers:* White people; often used to refer disparagingly to poor whites.

You my flesh and blood. Not cause I like you! Cause it's my duty to take care of you. I owe a responsibility to you! Let's get this straight right here . . . before it go along any further . . . I ain't got to like you. Mr. Rand don't give me my money come payday cause he likes me. He give me cause he owe me. I done give you everything I had to give you. I gave you your life! Me and your mama worked that out between us. And liking your black ass wasn't part of the bargain. Don't you try and go through life worrying about if somebody like you or not. You best be making sure they doing right by you. You understand what I'm saying, boy?

*Cory:* Yessir.

*Troy:* Then get the hell out of my face, and get on down to that A&P.

> *Rose has been standing behind the screen door for much of the scene.*
> *She enters as Cory exits.*

*Rose:* Why don't you let the boy go ahead and play football, Troy? Ain't no harm in that. He's just trying to be like you with the sports.

*Troy:* I don't want him to be like me! I want him to move as far away from my life as he can get. You the only decent thing that ever happened to me. I wish him that. But I don't wish him a thing else from my life. I decided seventeen years ago that boy wasn't getting involved in no sports. Not after what they did to me in the sports.

*Rose:* Troy, why don't you admit you was too old to play in the major leagues? For once . . . why don't you admit that?

*Troy:* What do you mean too old? Don't come telling me I was too old. I just wasn't the right color. Hell, I'm fifty-three years old and can do better than Selkirk's .269 right now!

*Rose:* How's was you gonna play ball when you were over forty? Sometimes I can't get no sense out of you.

*Troy:* I got good sense, woman. I got sense enough not to let my boy get hurt over playing no sports. You been mothering that boy too much. Worried about if people like him.

*Rose:* Everything that boy do . . . he do for you. He wants you to say "Good job, son." That's all.

*Troy:* Rose, I ain't got time for that. He's alive. He's healthy. He's got to make his own way. I made mine. Ain't nobody gonna hold his hand when he get out there in that world.

*Rose:* Times have changed from when you was young, Troy. People change. The world's changing around you and you can't even see it.

*Troy (slow, methodical):* Woman . . . I do the best I can do. I come in here every Friday. I carry a sack of potatoes and a bucket of lard. You all line up at the door with your hands out. I give you the lint from my pockets. I give you my sweat and my blood. I ain't got no tears. I done spent them. We go upstairs in that room at night . . . and I fall down on you and try to blast a hole into forever. I get up Monday morning . . . find my lunch on the table. I go out. Make my way. Find my strength to carry me through to the next Friday. (*Pause.*) That's all I got, Rose. That's all I got to give. I can't give nothing else.

> *Troy exits into the house. The lights go down to black.*

SCENE IV

> *It is Friday. Two weeks later. Cory starts out of the house with his football equipment. The phone rings.*

Cory *(calling):* I got it! *(He answers the phone and stands in the screen door talking.)* Hello? Hey, Jesse. Naw . . . I was just getting ready to leave now.

Rose *(calling):* Cory!

Cory: I told you, man, them spikes is all tore up. You can use them if you want, but they ain't no good. Earl got some spikes.

Rose *(calling):* Cory!

Cory *(calling to Rose):* Mam? I'm talking to Jesse. *(Into phone.)* When she say that? *(Pause.)* Aw, you lying, man. I'm gonna tell her you said that.

Rose *(calling):* Cory, don't you go nowhere!

Cory: I got to go to the game, Ma! *(Into the phone.)* Yeah, hey, look, I'll talk to you later. Yeah, I'll meet you over Earl's house. Later. Bye, Ma.

> *Cory exits the house and starts out the yard.*

Rose: Cory, where you going off to? You got that stuff all pulled out and thrown all over your room.

Cory *(in the yard):* I was looking for my spikes. Jesse wanted to borrow my spikes.

Rose: Get up there and get that cleaned up before your daddy get back in here.

Cory: I got to go to the game! I'll clean it up *when I get back.*

> *Cory exits.*

Rose: That's all he need to do is see that room all messed up.

> *Rose exits into the house. Troy and Bono enter the yard. Troy is dressed in clothes other than his work clothes.*

Bono: He told him the same thing he told you. Take it to the union.

Troy: Brownie ain't got that much sense. Man wasn't thinking about nothing. He wait until I confront them on it . . . then he wanna come crying seniority. *(Calls.)* Hey, Rose!

Bono: I wish I could have seen Mr. Rand's face when he told you.

Troy: He couldn't get it out of his mouth! Liked to bit his tongue! When they called me down there to the Commissioner's office . . . he thought they was gonna fire me. Like everybody else.

Bono: I didn't think they was gonna fire you. I thought they was gonna put you on the warning paper.

Troy: Hey, Rose! *(To Bono.)* Yeah, Mr. Rand like to bit his tongue.

> *Troy breaks the seal on the bottle, takes a drink, and hands it to Bono.*

Bono: I see you run right down to Taylors' and told that Alberta gal.

Troy *(calling):* Hey Rose! *(To Bono.)* I told everybody. Hey, Rose! I went down there to cash my check.

Rose *(entering from the house):* Hush all that hollering, man! I know you out here. What they say down there at the Commissioner's office?

Troy: You supposed to come when I call you, woman. Bono'll tell you that. *(To Bono.)* Don't Lucille come when you call her?

Rose: Man, hush your mouth. I ain't no dog . . . talk about "come when you call me."

*Troy (puts his arm around Rose):* You hear this, Bono? I had me an old dog used to get uppity like that. You say, "C'mere, Blue!" . . . and he just lay there and look at you. End up getting a stick and chasing him away trying to make him come.

*Rose:* I ain't studying you and your dog. I remember you used to sing that old song.

*Troy (he sings):* Hear it ring! Hear it ring! I had a dog his name was Blue.

*Rose:* Don't nobody wanna hear you sing that old song.

*Troy (sings):* You know Blue was mighty true.

*Rose:* Used to have Cory running around here singing that song.

*Bono:* Hell, I remember that song myself.

*Troy (sings):* You know Blue was a good old dog.
　　Blue treed a possum in a hollow log.
　　That was my daddy's song. My daddy made up that song.

*Rose:* I don't care who made it up. Don't nobody wanna hear you sing it.

*Troy (makes a song like calling a dog):* Come here, woman.

*Rose:* You come in here carrying on, I reckon they ain't fired you. What they say down there at the Commissioner's office?

*Troy:* Look here, Rose . . . Mr. Rand called me into his office today when I got back from talking to them people down there . . . it come from up top . . . he called me in and told me they was making me a driver.

*Rose:* Troy, you kidding!

*Troy:* No I ain't. Ask Bono.

*Rose:* Well, that's great, Troy. Now you don't have to hassle them people no more.

　　*Lyons enters from the street.*

*Troy:* Aw hell, I wasn't looking to see you today. I thought you was in jail. Got it all over the front page of the *Courier* about them raiding Sefus's place . . . where you be hanging out with all them thugs.

*Lyons:* Hey, Pop . . . that ain't got nothing to do with me. I don't go down there gambling. I go down there to sit in with the band. I ain't got nothing to do with the gambling part. They got some good music down there.

*Troy:* They got some rogues . . . is what they got.

*Lyons:* How you been, Mr. Bono? Hi, Rose.

*Bono:* I see where you playing down at the Crawford Grill tonight.

*Rose:* How come you ain't brought Bonnie like I told you? You should have brought Bonnie with you, she ain't been over in a month of Sundays.

*Lyons:* I was just in the neighborhood . . . thought I'd stop by.

*Troy:* Here he come . . .

*Bono:* Your daddy got a promotion on the rubbish. He's gonna be the first colored driver. Ain't got to do nothing but sit up there and read the paper like them white fellows.

*Lyons:* Hey, Pop . . . if you knew how to read you'd be all right.

*Bono:* Naw . . . naw . . . you mean if the nigger knew how to *drive* he'd be all right. Been fighting with them people about driving and ain't even got a license. Mr. Rand know you ain't got no driver's license?

*Troy:* Driving ain't nothing. All you do is point the truck where you want it to go. Driving ain't nothing.

*Bono:* Do Mr. Rand know you ain't got no driver's license? That's what I'm talking about. I ain't asked if driving was easy. I asked if Mr. Rand know you ain't got no driver's license.

*Troy:* He ain't got to know. The man ain't got to know my business. Time he find out, I have two or three driver's licenses.

*Lyons (going into his pocket):* Say, look here, Pop . . .

*Troy:* I knew it was coming. Didn't I tell you, Bono? I know what kind of "Look here, Pop" that was. The nigger fixing to ask me for some money. It's Friday night. It's my payday. All them rogues down there on the avenue . . . the ones that ain't in jail . . . and Lyons is hopping in his shoes to get down there with them.

*Lyons:* See, Pop . . . if you give somebody else a chance to talk sometimes, you'd see that I was fixing to pay you back your ten dollars like I told you. Here . . . I told you I'd pay you when Bonnie got paid.

*Troy:* Naw . . . you go ahead and keep that ten dollars. Put it in the bank. The next time you feel like you wanna come by here and ask me for something . . . you go on down there and get that.

*Lyons:* Here's your ten dollars, Pop. I told you I don't want you to give me nothing. I just wanted to borrow ten dollars.

*Troy:* Naw . . . you go on and keep that for the next time you want to ask me.

*Lyons:* Come on, Pop . . . here go your ten dollars.

*Rose:* Why don't you go on and let the boy pay you back, Troy?

*Lyons:* Here you go, Rose. If you don't take it I'm gonna have to hear about it for the next six months. *(He hands her the money.)*

*Rose:* You can hand yours over here too, Troy.

*Troy:* You see this, Bono. You see how they do me.

*Bono:* Yeah, Lucille do me the same way.

> *Gabriel is heard singing offstage. He enters.*

*Gabriel:* Better get ready for the Judgment! Better get ready for . . . Hey! . . . Hey! . . . There's Troy's boy!

*Lyons:* How are you doing, Uncle Gabe?

*Gabriel:* Lyons . . . The King of the Jungle! Rose . . . hey, Rose. Got a flower for you. *(He takes a rose from his pocket.)* Picked it myself. That's the same rose like you is!

*Rose:* That's right nice of you, Gabe.

*Lyons:* What you been doing, Uncle Gabe?

*Gabriel:* Oh, I been chasing hellhounds and waiting on the time to tell St. Peter to open the gates.

*Lyons:* You been chasing hellhounds, huh? Well . . . you doing the right thing, Uncle Gabe. Somebody got to chase them.

*Gabriel:* Oh, yeah . . . I know it. The devil's strong. The devil ain't no pushover. Hellhounds snipping at everybody's heels. But I got my trumpet waiting on the judgment time.

*Lyons:* Waiting on the Battle of Armageddon, huh?

*Gabriel:* Ain't gonna be too much of a battle when God get to waving that Judgment sword. But the people's gonna have a hell of a time trying to get into heaven if them gates ain't open.

*Lyons (putting his arm around Gabriel):* You hear this, Pop. Uncle Gabe, you all right!

*Gabriel (laughing with Lyons):* Lyons! King of the Jungle.

*Rose:* You gonna stay for supper, Gabe? Want me to fix you a plate?

*Gabriel:* I'll take a sandwich, Rose. Don't want no plate. Just wanna eat with my hands. I'll take a sandwich.

*Rose:* How about you, Lyons? You staying? Got some short ribs cooking.

*Lyons:* Naw, I won't eat nothing till after we finished playing. *(Pause.)* You ought to come down and listen to me play Pop.

*Troy:* I don't like that Chinese music. All that noise.

*Rose:* Go on in the house and wash up, Gabe . . . I'll fix you a sandwich.

*Gabriel (to Lyons, as he exits):* Troy's mad at me.

*Lyons:* What you mad at Uncle Gabe for, Pop?

*Rose:* He thinks Troy's mad at him cause he moved over to Miss Pearl's.

*Troy:* I ain't mad at the man. He can live where he want to live at.

*Lyons:* What he move over there for? Miss Pearl don't like nobody.

*Rose:* She don't mind him none. She treats him real nice. She just don't allow all that singing.

*Troy:* She don't mind that rent he be paying . . . that's what she don't mind.

*Rose:* Troy, I ain't going through that with you no more. He's over there cause he want to have his own place. He can come and go as he please.

*Troy:* Hell, he could come and go as he please here. I wasn't stopping him. I ain't put no rules on him.

*Rose:* It ain't the same thing, Troy. And you know it.

> *Gabriel comes to the door.*

Now, that's the last I wanna hear about that. I don't wanna hear nothing else about Gabe and Miss Pearl. And next week . . .

*Gabriel:* I'm ready for my sandwich, Rose.

*Rose:* And next week . . . when that recruiter come from that school . . . I want you to sign that paper and go on and let Cory play football. Then that'll be the last I have to hear about that.

*Troy (to Rose as she exits into the house):* I ain't thinking about Cory nothing.

*Lyons:* What . . . Cory got recruited? What school he going to?

*Troy:* That boy walking around here smelling his piss . . . thinking he's grown. Thinking he's gonna do what he want, irrespective of what I say. Look here, Bono . . . I left the Commissioner's office and went down to the A&P . . . that boy ain't working down there. He lying to me. Telling me he got his job back . . . telling me he working weekends . . . telling me he working after school . . . Mr. Stawicki tell me he ain't working down there at all!

*Lyons:* Cory just growing up. He's just busting at the seams trying to fill out your shoes.

*Troy:* I don't care what he's doing. When he get to the point where he wanna disobey me . . . then it's time for him to move on. Bono'll tell you that. I bet he ain't never disobeyed his daddy without paying the consequences.

*Bono:* I ain't never had a chance. My daddy came on through . . . but I ain't never knew him to see him . . . or what he had on his mind or where he went. Just moving on through. Searching out the New Land. That's what the old folks used to call it. See a fellow moving around from place to place . . . woman to woman . . . called it searching out the New Land. I can't say if he ever found it. I come along, didn't want no kids. Didn't know if I was gonna be in one place long enough to fix on them right as their daddy. I figured I was going searching too. As it turned out I been hooked up with Lucille near about as long as your daddy been with Rose. Going on sixteen years.

*Troy:* Sometimes I wish I hadn't known my daddy. He ain't cared nothing about no kids. A kid to him wasn't nothing. All he wanted was for you to learn how to walk so he could start you to working. When it come time for eating . . . he ate first. If there was anything left over, that's what you got. Man would sit down and eat two chickens and give you the wing.

*Lyons:* You ought to stop that, Pop. Everybody feed their kids. No matter how hard times is . . . everybody care about their kids. Make sure they have something to eat.

*Troy:* The only thing my daddy cared about was getting them bales of cotton in to Mr. Lubin. That's the only thing that mattered to him. Sometimes I used to wonder why he was living. Wonder why the devil hadn't come and got him. "Get them bales of cotton in to Mr. Lubin" and find out he owe him money . . .

*Lyons:* He should have just went on and left when he saw he couldn't get nowhere. That's what I would have done.

*Troy:* How he gonna leave with eleven kids? And where he gonna go? He ain't knew how to do nothing but farm. No, he was trapped and I think he knew it. But I'll say this for him . . . he felt a responsibility toward us. Maybe he ain't treated us the way I felt he should have . . . but without that responsibility he could have walked off and left us . . . made his own way.

*Bono:* A lot of them did. Back in those days what you talking about . . . they walk out their front door and just take on down one road or another and keep on walking.

*Lyons:* There you go! That's what I'm talking about.

*Bono:* Just keep on walking till you come to something else. Ain't you never heard of nobody having the walking blues? Well, that's what you call it when you just take off like that.

*Troy:* My daddy ain't had them walking blues! What you talking about? He stayed right there with his family. But he was just as evil as he could be. My mama couldn't stand him. Couldn't stand that evilness. She run off when I was about eight. She sneaked off one night after he had gone to sleep. Told me she was coming back for me. I ain't never seen her no more. All his women run off and left him. He wasn't good for nobody.

When my turn come to head out, I was fourteen and got to sniffing around Joe Canewell's daughter. Had us an old mule we called Greyboy. My daddy sent me out to do some plowing and I tied up Greyboy and went to fooling around with Joe Canewell's daughter. We done found us a nice little spot, got real cozy with each other. She about thirteen and we done figured we was grown anyway . . . so we down there enjoying ourselves . . . ain't thinking about nothing. We didn't know Greyboy had got loose and wandered back to the house and my daddy was looking for me. We down there by the creek enjoying ourselves when my daddy come up on us. Surprised us. He had them leather straps off the mule and commenced to whupping me like there was no tomorrow. I jumped up, mad and embarrassed. I was scared of my daddy. When he commenced to whupping on me . . . quite naturally I run to get out of the way. *(Pause.)* Now I thought he was mad cause I ain't done my work. But I see where he was chasing me off so he could have the gal for himself. When I see what the matter of it was, I lost all fear of my daddy. Right there is where I become a man . . . at fourteen years of age. *(Pause.)* Now it was my turn to run him off. I picked up them same reins that he had used on me. I picked up them reins and commenced to whupping on him. The gal jumped up and run off . . . and when my daddy turned to face me, I could see why the devil had never come to get him . . . cause he was the devil himself. I don't know what happened. When I woke up, I was laying right there by the creek, and Blue . . . this old dog we had . . . was licking my face. I thought I was blind. I couldn't see nothing. Both my eyes were swollen shut. I laid there and cried. I didn't know what I was gonna do. The only thing I knew was the time had come for me to leave my daddy's house. And right there the world suddenly got big. And it was a long time before I could cut it down to where I could handle it.

    Part of that cutting down was when I got to the place where I could feel him kicking in my blood and knew that the only thing that separated us was the matter of a few years.

*Gabriel enters from the house with a sandwich.*

*Lyons:*  What you got there, Uncle Gabe?
*Gabriel:*  Got me a ham sandwich. Rose gave me a ham sandwich.
*Troy:*  I don't know what happened to him. I done lost touch with everybody except Gabriel. But I hope he's dead. I hope he found some peace.
*Lyons:*  That's a heavy story, Pop. I didn't know you left home when you was fourteen.
*Troy:*  And didn't know nothing. The only part of the world I knew was the forty-two acres of Mr. Lubin's land. That's all I knew about life.
*Lyons:*  Fourteen's kinda young to be out on your own. *(Phone rings.)* I don't even think I was ready to be out on my own at fourteen. I don't know what I would have done.
*Troy:*  I got up from the creek and walked on down to Mobile. I was through with farming. Figured I could do better in the city. So I walked the two hundred miles to Mobile.
*Lyons:*  Wait a minute . . . you ain't walked no two hundred miles, Pop. Ain't nobody gonna walk no two hundred miles. You talking about some walking there.
*Bono:*  That's the only way you got anywhere back in them days.
*Lyons:*  Shhh. Damn if I wouldn't have hitched a ride with somebody!
*Troy:*  Who you gonna hitch it with? They ain't had no cars and things like they got now. We talking about 1918.
*Rose (entering):*  What you all out here getting into?
*Troy (to Rose):*  I'm telling Lyons how good he got it. He don't know nothing about this I'm talking.
*Rose:*  Lyons, that was Bonnie on the phone. She say you supposed to pick her up.
*Lyons:*  Yeah, okay, Rose.
*Troy:*  I walked on down to Mobile and hitched up with some of them fellows that was heading this way. Got up here and found out . . . not only couldn't you get a job . . . you couldn't find no place to live. I thought I was in freedom. Shhh. Colored folks living down there on the riverbanks in whatever kind of shelter they could find for themselves. Right down there under the Brady Street Bridge. Living in shacks made of sticks and tarpaper. Messed around there and went from bad to worse. Started stealing. First it was food. Then I figured, hell, if I steal money I can buy me some food. Buy me some shoes too! One thing led to another. Met your mama. I was young and anxious to

be a man. Met your mama and had you. What I do that for? Now I got to worry about feeding you and her. Got to steal three times as much. Went out one day looking for somebody to rob . . . that's what I was, a robber. I'll tell you the truth. I'm ashamed of it today. But it's the truth. Went to rob this fellow . . . pulled out my knife . . . and he pulled out a gun. Shot me in the chest. I felt just like somebody had taken a hot branding iron and laid it on me. When he shot me I jumped at him with my knife. They told me I killed him and they put me in the penitentiary and locked me up for fifteen years. That's where I met Bono. That's where I learned how to play baseball. Got out that place and your mama had taken you and went on to make life without me. Fifteen years was a long time for her to wait. But that fifteen years cured me of that robbing stuff. Rose'll tell you. She asked me when I met her if I had gotten all that foolishness out of my system. And I told her, "Baby, it's you and baseball all what count with me." You hear me, Bono? I meant it too. She say, "Which one comes first?" I told her, "Baby, ain't no doubt it's baseball . . . but you stick and get old with me and we'll both outlive this baseball." Am I right, Rose? And it's true.

*Rose:* Man, hush your mouth. You ain't said no such thing. Talking about, "Baby, you know you'll always be number one with me." That's what you was talking.

*Troy:* You hear that, Bono. That's why I love her.

*Bono:* Rose'll keep you straight. You get off the track, she'll straighten you up.

*Rose:* Lyons, you better get on up and get Bonnie. She waiting on you.

*Lyons (gets up to go):* Hey, Pop, why don't you come on down to the Grill and hear me play?

*Troy:* I ain't going down there. I'm too old to be sitting around in them clubs.

*Bono:* You got to be good to play down at the Grill.

*Lyons:* Come on, Pop . . .

*Troy:* I got to get up in the morning.

*Lyons:* You ain't got to stay long.

*Troy:* Naw, I'm gonna get my supper and go on to bed.

*Lyons:* Well, I got to go. I'll see you again.

*Troy:* Don't you come around my house on my payday.

*Rose:* Pick up the phone and let somebody know you coming. And bring Bonnie with you. You know I'm always glad to see her.

*Lyons:* Yeah, I'll do that, Rose. You take care now. See you, Pop. See you, Mr. Bono. See you, Uncle Gabe.

*Gabriel:* Lyons! King of the Jungle!

> *Lyons exits.*

*Troy:* Is supper ready, woman? Me and you got some business to take care of. I'm gonna tear it up too.

*Rose:* Troy, I done told you now!

*Troy (puts his arm around Bono):* Aw hell, woman . . . this is Bono. Bono like family. I done known this nigger since . . . how long I done know you?

*Bono:* It's been a long time.

*Troy:* I done know this nigger since Skippy was a pup. Me and him done been through some times.

*Bono:* You sure right about that.

*Troy:* Hell, I done know him longer than I known you. And we still standing shoulder to shoulder. Hey, look here, Bono . . . a man can't ask for no more than that. *(Drinks to him.)* I love you, nigger.

*Bono:* Hell, I love you too . . . I got to get home see my woman. You got yours in hand. I got to go get mine.

*Bono starts to exit as Cory enters the yard, dressed in his football uniform. He gives Troy a hard, uncompromising look.*

*Cory:* What you do that for, Pop?

*He throws his helmet down in the direction of Troy.*

*Rose:* What's the matter? Cory . . . what's the matter?

*Cory:* Papa done went up to the school and told Coach Zellman I can't play football no more. Wouldn't even let me play the game. Told him to tell the recruiter not to come.

*Rose:* Troy . . .

*Troy:* What you Troying me for. Yeah, I did it. And the boy know why I did it.

*Cory:* Why you wanna do that to me? That was the one chance I had.

*Rose:* Ain't nothing wrong with Cory playing football, Troy.

*Troy:* The boy lied to me. I told the nigger if he wanna play football . . . to keep up his chores and hold down that job at the A&P. That was the conditions. Stopped down there to see Mr. Stawicki . . .

*Cory:* I can't work after school during the football season, Pop! I tried to tell you that Mr. Stawicki's holding my job for me. You don't never want to listen to nobody. And then you wanna go and do this to me!

*Troy:* I ain't done nothing to you. You done it to yourself.

*Cory:* Just cause you didn't have a chance! You just scared I'm gonna be better than you, that's all.

*Troy:* Come here.

*Rose:* Troy . . .

*Cory reluctantly crosses over to Troy.*

*Troy:* All right! See. You done made a mistake.

*Cory:* I didn't even do nothing!

*Troy:* I'm gonna tell you what your mistake was. See . . . you swung at the ball and didn't hit it. That's strike one. See, you in the batter's box now. You swung and you missed. That's strike one. Don't you strike out!

*Lights fade to black.*

---

# ACT II

## SCENE I

*The following morning. Cory is at the tree hitting the ball with the bat. He tries to mimic Troy, but his swing is awkward, less sure. Rose enters from the house.*

*Rose:* Cory, I want you to help me with this cupboard.

*Cory:* I ain't quitting the team. I don't care what Poppa say.

*Rose:* I'll talk to him when he gets back. He had to go see about your Uncle Gabe. The police done arrested him. Say he was disturbing the peace. He'll be back directly. Come on in here and help me clean out the top of this cupboard.

*Cory exits into the house. Rose sees Troy and Bono coming down the alley.*

Troy . . . what they say down there?

*Troy:* Ain't said nothing. I give them fifty dollars and they let him go. I'll talk to you about it. Where's Cory?

*Rose:* He's in there helping me clean out these cupboards.

*Troy:* Tell him to get his butt out here.

*Troy and Bono go over to the pile of wood. Bono picks up the saw and begins sawing.*

*Troy (to Bono):* All they want is the money. That makes six or seven times I done went down there and got him. See me coming they stick out their hands.

*Bono:* Yeah. I know what you mean. That's all they care about . . . that money. They don't care about what's right. *(Pause.)* Nigger, why you got to go and get some hard wood? You ain't doing nothing but building a little old fence. Get you some soft pine wood. That's all you need.

*Troy:* I know what I'm doing. This is outside wood. You put pine wood inside the house. Pine wood is inside wood. This here is outside wood. Now you tell me where the fence is gonna be?

*Bono:* You don't need this wood. You can put it up with pine wood and it'll stand as long as you gonna be here looking at it.

*Troy:* How you know how long I'm gonna be here, nigger? Hell, I might just live forever. Live longer than old man Horsely.

*Bono:* That's what Magee used to say.

*Troy:* Magee's a damn fool. Now you tell me who you ever heard of gonna pull their own teeth with a pair of rusty pliers.

*Bono:* The old folks . . . my granddaddy used to pull his teeth with pliers. They ain't had no dentists for the colored folks back then.

*Troy:* Get clean pliers! You understand? Clean pliers! Sterilize them! Besides we ain't living back then. All Magee had to do was walk over to Doc Goldblum's.

*Bono:* I see where you and that Tallahassee gal . . . that Alberta . . . I see where you all done got tight.

*Troy:* What you mean "got tight"?

*Bono:* I see where you be laughing and joking with her all the time.

*Troy:* I laughs and jokes with all of them, Bono. You know me.

*Bono:* That ain't the kind of laughing and joking I'm talking about.

*Cory enters from the house.*

*Cory:* How you doing, Mr. Bono?

*Troy:* Cory? Get that saw from Bono and cut some wood. He talking about the wood's too hard to cut. Stand back there, Jim, and let that young boy show you how it's done.

*Bono:* He's sure welcome to it.

*Cory takes the saw and begins to cut the wood.*

Whew-e-e! Look at that. Big old strong boy. Look like Joe Louis.° Hell, must be getting old the way I'm watching that boy whip through that wood.

*Cory:* I don't see why Mama want a fence around the yard noways.

---

*Joe Louis* (1914–1981): Black American boxer who held the world heavyweight championship title.

*Troy:* Damn if I know either. What the hell she keeping out with it? She ain't got nothing nobody want.

*Bono:* Some people build fences to keep people out . . . and other people build fences to keep people in. Rose wants to hold on to you all. She loves you.

*Troy:* Hell, nigger, I don't need nobody to tell me my wife loves me. Cory . . . go on in the house and see if you can find that other saw.

*Cory:* Where's it at?

*Troy:* I said find it! Look for it till you find it!

*Cory exits into the house.*

What's that supposed to mean? Wanna keep us in?

*Bono:* Troy . . . I done known you seem like damn near my whole life. You and Rose both. I done know both of you all for a long time. I remember when you met Rose. When you was hitting them baseball out the park. A lot of them old gals was after you then. You had the pick of the litter. When you picked Rose, I was happy for you. That was the first time I knew you had any sense. I said . . . My man Troy knows what he's doing . . . I'm gonna follow this nigger . . . he might take me somewhere. I been following you too. I done learned a whole heap of things about life watching you. I done learned how to tell where the shit lies. How to tell it from the alfalfa. You done learned me a lot of things. You showed me how to not make the same mistakes . . . to take life as it comes along and keep putting one foot in front of the other. *(Pause.)* Rose a good woman, Troy.

*Troy:* Hell, nigger, I know she a good woman. I been married to her for eighteen years. What you got on your mind, Bono?

*Bono:* I just say she a good woman. Just like I say anything. I ain't got to have nothing on my mind.

*Troy:* You just gonna say she a good woman and leave it hanging out there like that? Why you telling me she a good woman?

*Bono:* She loves you, Troy. Rose loves you.

*Troy:* You saying I don't measure up. That's what you trying to say. I don't measure up cause I'm seeing this other gal. I know what you trying to say.

*Bono:* I know what Rose means to you, Troy. I'm just trying to say I don't want to see you mess up.

*Troy:* Yeah, I appreciate that, Bono. If you was messing around on Lucille I'd be telling you the same thing.

*Bono:* Well, that's all I got to say. I just say that because I love you both.

*Troy:* Hell, you know me . . . I wasn't out there looking for nothing. You can't find a better woman than Rose. I know that. But seems like this woman just stuck onto me where I can't shake her loose. I done wrestled with it, tried to throw her off me . . . but she just stuck on tighter. Now she's stuck on for good.

*Bono:* You's in control . . . that's what you tell me all the time. You responsible for what you do.

*Troy:* I ain't ducking the responsibility of it. As long as it sets right in my heart . . . then I'm okay. Cause that's all I listen to. It'll tell me right from wrong every time. And I ain't talking about doing Rose no bad turn. I love Rose. She done carried me a long ways and I love and respect her for that.

*Bono:* I know you do. That's why I don't want to see you hurt her. But what you gonna do when she find out? What you got then? If you try and juggle both of them . . . sooner or later you gonna drop one of them. That's common sense.

*Troy:* Yeah, I hear what you saying, Bono. I been trying to figure a way to work it out.

*Bono:* Work it out right, Troy. I don't want to be getting all up between you and Rose's business . . . but work it so it come out right.

*Troy:* Ah hell, I get all up between you and Lucille's business. When you gonna get that woman that refrigerator she been wanting? Don't tell me you ain't got no money now. I know who your banker is. Mellon don't need that money bad as Lucille want that refrigerator. I'll tell you that.

*Bono:* Tell you what I'll do . . . when you finish building this fence for Rose . . . I'll buy Lucille that refrigerator.

*Troy:* You done stuck your foot in your mouth now!

*Troy grabs up a board and begins to saw. Bono starts to walk out the yard.*

Hey, nigger . . . where you going?

*Bono:* I'm going home. I know you don't expect me to help you now. I'm protecting my money. I wanna see you put that fence up by yourself. That's what I want to see. You'll be here another six months without me.

*Troy:* Nigger, you ain't right.

*Bono:* When it comes to my money . . . I'm right as fireworks on the Fourth of July.

*Troy:* All right, we gonna see now. You better get out your bankbook.

*Bono exits, and Troy continues to work. Rose enters from the house.*

*Rose:* What they say down there? What's happening with Gabe?

*Troy:* I went down there and got him out. Cost me fifty dollars. Say he was disturbing the peace. Judge set up a hearing for him in three weeks. Say to show cause why he shouldn't be recommitted.

*Rose:* What was he doing that cause them to arrest him?

*Troy:* Some kids was teasing him and he run them off home. Say he was howling and carrying on. Some folks seen him and called the police. That's all it was.

*Rose:* Well, what's you say? What'd you tell the judge?

*Troy:* Told him I'd look after him. It didn't make no sense to recommit the man. He stuck out his big greasy palm and told me to give him fifty dollars and take him on home.

*Rose:* Where's he at now? Where'd he go off to?

*Troy:* He's gone about his business. He don't need nobody to hold his hand.

*Rose:* Well, I don't know. Seem like that would be the best place for him if they did put him into the hospital. I know what you're gonna say. But that's what I think would be best.

*Troy:* The man done had his life ruined fighting for what? And they wanna take and lock him up. Let him be free. He don't bother nobody.

*Rose:* Well, everybody got their own way of looking at it I guess. Come on and get your lunch. I got a bowl of lima beans and some cornbread in the oven. Come and get something to eat. Ain't no sense you fretting over Gabe.

*Rose turns to go into the house.*

*Troy:* Rose . . . got something to tell you.

*Rose:* Well, come on . . . wait till I get this food on the table.

*Troy:* Rose!

*She stops and turns around.*

I don't know how to say this. *(Pause.)* I can't explain it none. It just sort of grows on you till it gets out of hand. It starts out like a little bush . . . and the next thing you know it's a whole forest.

*Rose:*  Troy . . . what is you talking about?

*Troy:*  I'm talking, woman, let me talk. I'm trying to find a way to tell you . . . I'm gonna be a daddy. I'm gonna be somebody's daddy.

*Rose:*  Troy . . . you're not telling me this? You're gonna be . . . what?

*Troy:*  Rose . . . now . . . see . . .

*Rose:*  You telling me you gonna be somebody's daddy? You telling your *wife* this?

*Gabriel enters from the street. He carries a rose in his hand.*

*Gabriel:*  Hey, Troy! Hey, Rose!

*Rose:*  I have to wait eighteen years to hear something like this.

*Gabriel:*  Hey, Rose . . . I got a flower for you. *(He hands it to her.)* That's a rose. Same rose like you is.

*Rose:*  Thanks, Gabe.

*Gabriel:*  Troy, you ain't mad at me is you? Them bad mens come and put me away. You ain't mad at me is you?

*Troy:*  Naw, Gabe, I ain't mad at you.

*Rose:*  Eighteen years and you wanna come with this.

*Gabriel (takes a quarter out of his pocket):*  See what I got? Got a brand new quarter.

*Troy:*  Rose . . . it's just . . .

*Rose:*  Ain't nothing you can say, Troy. Ain't no way of explaining that.

*Gabriel:*  Fellow that give me this quarter had a whole mess of them. I'm gonna keep this quarter till it stop shining.

*Rose:*  Gabe, go on in the house there. I got some watermelon in the Frigidaire. Go on and get you a piece.

*Gabriel:*  Say, Rose . . . you know I was chasing hellhounds and them bad mens come and get me and take me away. Troy helped me. He come down there and told them they better let me go before he beat them up. Yeah, he did!

*Rose:*  You go on and get you a piece of watermelon, Gabe. Them bad mens is gone now.

*Gabriel:*  Okay, Rose . . . gonna get me some watermelon. The kind with the stripes on it.

*Gabriel exits into the house.*

*Rose:*  Why, Troy? Why? After all these years to come dragging this in to me now. It don't make no sense at your age. I could have expected this ten or fifteen years ago, but not now.

*Troy:*  Age ain't got nothing to do with it, Rose.

*Rose:*  I done tried to be everything a wife should be. Everything a wife could be. Been married eighteen years and I got to live to see the day you tell me you been seeing another woman and done fathered a child by her. And you know I ain't never wanted no half nothing in my family. My whole family is half. Everybody got different fathers and mothers . . . my two sisters and my brother. Can't hardly tell who's who. Can't never sit down and talk about Papa and Mama. It's your papa and your mama and my papa and my mama . . .

*Troy:*  Rose . . . stop it now.

*Rose:*  I ain't never wanted that for none of my children. And now you wanna drag your behind in here and tell me something like this.

*Troy:*  You ought to know. It's time for you to know.

*Rose:*  Well, I don't want to know, goddamn it!

*Troy:*  I can't just make it go away. It's done now. I can't wish the circumstance of the thing away.

*Rose:* And you don't want to either. Maybe you want to wish me and my boy away. Maybe that's what you want? Well, you can't wish us away. I've got eighteen years of my life invested in you. You ought to have stayed upstairs in my bed where you belong.

*Troy:* Rose . . . now listen to me . . . we can get a handle on this thing. We can talk this out . . . come to an understanding.

*Rose:* All of a sudden it's "we." Where was "we" at when you was down there rolling around with some godforsaken woman? "We" should have come to an understanding before you started making a damn fool of yourself. You're a day late and a dollar short when it comes to an understanding with me.

*Troy:* It's just . . . She gives me a different idea . . . a different understanding about myself. I can step out of this house and get away from the pressures and problems . . . be a different man. I ain't got to wonder how I'm gonna pay the bills or get the roof fixed. I can just be a part of myself that I ain't never been.

*Rose:* What I want to know . . . is do you plan to continue seeing her. That's all you can say to me.

*Troy:* I can sit up in her house and laugh. Do you understand what I'm saying. I can laugh out loud . . . and it feels good. It reaches all the way down to the bottom of my shoes. *(Pause.)* Rose, I can't give that up.

*Rose:* Maybe you ought to go on and stay down there with her . . . if she's a better woman than me.

*Troy:* It ain't about nobody being a better woman or nothing. Rose, you ain't the blame. A man couldn't ask for no woman to be a better wife than you've been. I'm responsible for it. I done locked myself into a pattern trying to take care of you all that I forgot about myself.

*Rose:* What the hell was I there for? That was my job, not somebody else's.

*Troy:* Rose, I done tried all my life to live decent . . . to live a clean . . . hard . . . useful life. I tried to be a good husband to you. In every way I knew how. Maybe I come into the world backwards, I don't know. But . . . you born with two strikes on you before you come to the plate. You got to guard it closely . . . always looking for the curve ball on the inside corner. You can't afford to let none get past you. You can't afford a call strike. If you going down . . . you going down swinging. Everything lined up against you. What you gonna do. I fooled them, Rose. I bunted. When I found you and Cory and a halfway decent job . . . I was safe. Couldn't nothing touch me. I wasn't gonna strike out no more. I wasn't going back to the penitentiary. I wasn't gonna lay in the streets with a bottle of wine. I was safe. I had me a family. A job. I wasn't gonna get that last strike. I was on first looking for one of them boys to knock me in. To get me home.

*Rose:* You should have stayed in my bed, Troy.

*Troy:* Then when I saw that gal . . . she firmed up my backbone. And I got to thinking that if I tried . . . I just might be able to steal second. Do you understand after eighteen years I wanted to steal second.

*Rose:* You should have held me tight. You should have grabbed me and held on.

*Troy:* I stood on first base for eighteen years and I thought . . . well, goddamn it . . . go on for it!

*Rose:* We're not talking about baseball! We're talking about you going off to lay in bed with another woman . . . and then bring it home to me. That's what we're talking about. We ain't talking about no baseball.

*Troy:* Rose, you're not listening to me. I'm trying the best I can to explain it to you. It's not easy for me to admit that I been standing in the same place for eighteen years.

*Rose:* I been standing with you! I been right here with you, Troy. I got a life too. I gave eighteen years of my life to stand in the same spot with you. Don't you think I ever wanted other things? Don't you think I had dreams and hopes? What about my life? What about me. Don't you think it ever crossed my mind to want to know other men? That I wanted to lay up somewhere and forget about my responsibilities? That I wanted someone to make me laugh so I could feel good? You not the only one who's got wants and needs. But I held on to you, Troy. I took all my feelings, my wants and needs, my dreams . . . and I buried them inside you. I planted a seed and watched and prayed over it. I planted myself inside you and waited to bloom. And it didn't take me no eighteen years to find out the soil was hard and rocky and it wasn't never gonna bloom.

But I held on to you, Troy. I held you tighter. You was my husband. I owed you everything I had. Every part of me I could find to give you. And upstairs in that room . . . with the darkness falling in on me . . . I gave everything I had to try and erase the doubt that you wasn't the finest man in the world. And wherever you was going . . . I wanted to be there with you. Cause you was my husband. Cause that's the only way I was gonna survive as your wife. You always talking about what you give . . . and what you don't have to give. But you take too. You take . . . and don't even know nobody's giving!

*Rose turns to exit into the house; Troy grabs her arm.*

*Troy:* You say I take and don't give!

*Rose:* Troy! You're hurting me!

*Troy:* You say I take and don't give!

*Rose:* Troy . . . you're hurting my arm! Let go!

*Troy:* I done give you everything I got. Don't you tell that lie on me.

*Rose:* Troy!

*Troy:* Don't you tell that lie on me!

*Cory enters from the house.*

*Cory:* Mama!

*Rose:* Troy. You're hurting me.

*Troy:* Don't you tell me about no taking and giving.

*Cory comes up behind Troy and grabs him. Troy, surprised, is thrown off balance just as Cory throws a glancing blow that catches him on the chest and knocks him down. Troy is stunned, as is Cory.*

*Rose:* Troy. Troy. No!

*Troy gets to his feet and starts at Cory.*

Troy . . . no. Please! Troy!

*Rose pulls on Troy to hold him back. Troy stops himself.*

*Troy (to Cory):* All right. That's strike two. You stay away from around me, boy. Don't you strike out. You living with a full count. Don't you strike out.

*Troy exits out the yard as the lights go down.*

### SCENE II

*It is six months later, early afternoon. Troy enters from the house and starts to exit the yard. Rose enters from the house.*

*Rose:* Troy, I want to talk to you.

*Troy:* All of a sudden, after all this time, you want to talk to me, huh? You ain't wanted to talk to me for months. You ain't wanted to talk to me last night. You ain't wanted no part of me then. What you wanna talk to me about now?

*Rose:* Tomorrow's Friday.

*Troy:* I know what day tomorrow is. You think I don't know tomorrow's Friday? My whole life I ain't done nothing but look to see Friday coming and you got to tell me it's Friday.

*Rose:* I want to know if you're coming home.

*Troy:* I always come home, Rose. You know that. There ain't never been a night I ain't come home.

*Rose:* That ain't what I mean . . . and you know it. I want to know if you're coming straight home after work.

*Troy:* I figure I'd cash my check . . . hang out at Taylors' with the boys . . . maybe play a game of checkers . . .

*Rose:* Troy, I can't live like this. I won't live like this. You livin' on borrowed time with me. It's been going on six months now you ain't been coming home.

*Troy:* I be here every night. Every night of the year. That's 365 days.

*Rose:* I want you to come home tomorrow after work.

*Troy:* Rose . . . I don't mess up my pay. You know that now. I take my pay and I give it to you. I don't have no money but what you give me back. I just want to have a little time to myself . . . a little time to enjoy life.

*Rose:* What about me? When's my time to enjoy life?

*Troy:* I don't know what to tell you, Rose. I'm doing the best I can.

*Rose:* You ain't been home from work but time enough to change your clothes and run out . . . and you wanna call that the best you can do?

*Troy:* I'm going over to the hospital to see Alberta. She went into the hospital this afternoon. Look like she might have the baby early. I won't be gone long.

*Rose:* Well, you ought to know. They went over to Miss Pearl's and got Gabe today. She said you told them to go ahead and lock him up.

*Troy:* I ain't said no such thing. Whoever told you that is telling a lie. Pearl ain't doing nothing but telling a big fat lie.

*Rose:* She ain't had to tell me. I read it on the papers.

*Troy:* I ain't told them nothing of the kind.

*Rose:* I saw it right there on the papers.

*Troy:* What it say, huh?

*Rose:* It said you told them to take him.

*Troy:* Then they screwed that up, just the way they screw up everything. I ain't worried about what they got on the paper.

*Rose:* Say the government send part of his check to the hospital and the other part to you.

*Troy:* I ain't got nothing to do with that if that's the way it works. I ain't made up the rules about how it work.

*Rose:* You did Gabe just like you did Cory. You wouldn't sign the paper for Cory . . . but you signed for Gabe. You signed that paper.

*The telephone is heard ringing inside the house.*

*Troy:* I told you I ain't signed nothing, woman! The only thing I signed was the release form. Hell, I can't read, I don't know what they had on that paper! I ain't signed nothing about sending Gabe away.

*Rose:* I said send him to the hospital . . . you said let him be free . . . now you done went down there and signed him to the hospital for half his money. You went back on yourself, Troy. You gonna have to answer for that.

*Troy:* See now . . . you been over there talking to Miss Pearl. She done got mad cause she ain't getting Gabe's rent money. That's all it is. She's liable to say anything.

*Rose:* Troy, I seen where you signed the paper.

*Troy:* You ain't seen nothing I signed. What she doing got papers on my brother anyway? Miss Pearl telling a big fat lie. And I'm gonna tell her about it too! You ain't seen nothing I signed. Say . . . you ain't seen nothing I signed.

*Rose exits into the house to answer the telephone. Presently she returns.*

*Rose:* Troy . . . that was the hospital. Alberta had the baby.

*Troy:* What she have? What is it?

*Rose:* It's a girl.

*Troy:* I better get on down to the hospital to see her.

*Rose:* Troy . . .

*Troy:* Rose . . . I got to go see her now. That's only right . . . what's the matter . . . the baby's all right, ain't it?

*Rose:* Alberta died having the baby.

*Troy:* Died . . . you say she's dead? Alberta's dead?

*Rose:* They said they done all they could. They couldn't do nothing for her.

*Troy:* The baby? How's the baby?

*Rose:* They say it's healthy. I wonder who's gonna bury her.

*Troy:* She had family, Rose. She wasn't living in the world by herself.

*Rose:* I know she wasn't living in the world by herself.

*Troy:* Next thing you gonna want to know if she had any insurance.

*Rose:* Troy, you ain't got to talk like that.

*Troy:* That's the first thing that jumped out your mouth. "Who's gonna bury her?" Like I'm fixing to take on that task for myself.

*Rose:* I am your wife. Don't push me away.

*Troy:* I ain't pushing nobody away. Just give me some space. That's all. Just give me some room to breathe.

*Rose exits into the house. Troy walks about the yard.*

*Troy (with a quiet rage that threatens to consume him):* All right . . . Mr. Death. See now . . . I'm gonna tell you what I'm gonna do. I'm gonna take and build me a fence around this yard. See? I'm gonna build me a fence around what belongs to me. And then I want you to stay on the other side. See? You stay over there until you're ready for me. Then you come on. Bring your army. Bring your sickle. Bring your wrestling clothes. I ain't gonna fall down on my vigilance this time. You ain't gonna sneak up on me no more. When you ready for me . . . when the top of your list say Troy Maxson . . . that's when you come around here. You come up and knock on the front door. Ain't nobody else got nothing to do with this. This is between you and me. Man to man. You stay on the other side of that fence until you ready for me. Then you come up and knock on the front door. Anytime you want. I'll be ready for you.

*The lights go down to black.*

## SCENE III

*The lights come up on the porch. It is late evening three days later. Rose sits listening to the ball game waiting for Troy. The final out of the game is made and Rose switches off the radio. Troy enters the yard carrying an infant wrapped in blankets. He stands back from the house and calls.*

*Rose enters and stands on the porch. There is a long, awkward silence, the weight of which grows heavier with each passing second.*

*Troy:*  Rose . . . I'm standing here with my daughter in my arms. She ain't but a wee bittie little old thing. She don't know nothing about grownups' business. She innocent . . . and she ain't got no mama.

*Rose:*  What you telling me for, Troy?

*She turns and exits into the house.*

*Troy:*  Well . . . I guess we'll just sit out here on the porch.

*He sits down on the porch. There is an awkward indelicateness about the way he handles the baby. His largeness engulfs and seems to swallow it. He speaks loud enough for Rose to hear.*

A man's got to do what's right for him. I ain't sorry for nothing I done. It felt right in my heart. *(To the baby.)* What you smiling at? Your daddy's a big man. Got these great big old hands. But sometimes he's scared. And right now your daddy's scared cause we sitting out here and ain't got no home. Oh, I been homeless before. I ain't had no little baby with me. But I been homeless. You just be out on the road by your lonesome and you see one of them trains coming and you just kinda go like this . . .

*He sings as a lullaby.*

Please, Mr. Engineer let a man ride the line
Please, Mr. Engineer let a man ride the line
I ain't got no ticket please let me ride the blinds

*Rose enters from the house. Troy, hearing her steps behind him, stands and faces her.*

She's my daughter, Rose. My own flesh and blood. I can't deny her no more than I can deny them boys. *(Pause.)* You and them boys is my family. You and them and this child is all I got in the world. So I guess what I'm saying is . . . I'd appreciate it if you'd help me take care of her.

*Rose:*  Okay, Troy . . . you're right. I'll take care of your baby for you . . . cause . . . like you say . . . she's innocent . . . and you can't visit the sins of the father upon the child. A motherless child has got a hard time. *(She takes the baby from him.)* From right now . . . this child got a mother. But you a womanless man.

*Rose turns and exits into the house with the baby. Lights go down to black.*

## SCENE IV

*It is two months later. Lyons enters from the street. He knocks on the door and calls.*

*Lyons:*  Hey, Rose! *(Pause.)* Rose!

*Rose (from inside the house):*  Stop that yelling. You gonna wake up Raynell. I just got her to sleep.

*Lyons:*  I just stopped by to pay Papa this twenty dollars I owe him. Where's Papa at?

*Rose:* He should be here in a minute. I'm getting ready to go down to the church. Sit down and wait on him.

*Lyons:* I got to go pick up Bonnie over her mother's house.

*Rose:* Well, sit it down there on the table. He'll get it.

*Lyons (enters the house and sets the money on the table):* Tell Papa I said thanks. I'll see you again.

*Rose:* All right, Lyons. We'll see you.

Lyons starts to exit as Cory enters.

*Cory:* Hey, Lyons.

*Lyons:* What's happening, Cory? Say man, I'm sorry I missed your graduation. You know I had a gig and couldn't get away. Otherwise, I would have been there, man. So what you doing?

*Cory:* I'm trying to find a job.

*Lyons:* Yeah I know how that go, man. It's rough out here. Jobs are scarce.

*Cory:* Yeah, I know.

*Lyons:* Look here, I got to run. Talk to Papa . . . he know some people. He'll be able to help get you a job. Talk to him . . . see what he say.

*Cory:* Yeah . . . all right, Lyons.

*Lyons:* You take care. I'll talk to you soon. We'll find some time to talk.

Lyons exits the yard. Cory wanders over to the tree, picks up the bat, and assumes a batting stance. He studies an imaginary pitcher and swings. Dissatisfied with the result, he tries again. Troy enters. They eye each other for a beat. Cory puts the bat down and exits the yard. Troy starts into the house as Rose exits with Raynell. She is carrying a cake.

*Troy:* I'm coming in and everybody's going out.

*Rose:* I'm taking this cake down to the church for the bake sale. Lyons was by to see you. He stopped by to pay you your twenty dollars. It's laying in there on the table.

*Troy (going into his pocket):* Well . . . here go this money.

*Rose:* Put it in there on the table, Troy. I'll get it.

*Troy:* What time you coming back?

*Rose:* Ain't no use in you studying me. It don't matter what time I come back.

*Troy:* I just asked you a question, woman. What's the matter . . . can't I ask you a question?

*Rose:* Troy, I don't want to go into it. Your dinner's in there on the stove. All you got to do is heat it up. And don't you be eating the rest of them cakes in there. I'm coming back for them. We having a bake sale at the church tomorrow.

Rose exits the yard. Troy sits down on the steps, takes a pint bottle from his pocket, opens it, and drinks. He begins to sing.

*Troy:* Hear it ring! Hear it ring!
Had an old dog his name was Blue
You know Blue was mighty true
You know Blue was a good old dog
Blue trees a possum in a hollow log
You know from that he was a good old dog

Bono enters the yard.

*Bono:* Hey, Troy.

*Troy:* Hey, what's happening, Bono?

*Bono:* I just thought I'd stop by to see you.

*Troy:* What you stop by and see me for? You ain't stopped by in a month of Sundays. Hell, I must owe you money or something.

*Bono:* Since you got your promotion I can't keep up with you. Used to see you every day. Now I don't even know what route you working.

*Troy:* They keep switching me around. Got me out in Greentree now . . . hauling white folks' garbage.

*Bono:* Greentree, huh? You lucky, at least you ain't got to be lifting them barrels. Damn if they ain't getting heavier. I'm gonna put in my two years and call it quits.

*Troy:* I'm thinking about retiring myself.

*Bono:* You got it easy. You can *drive* for another five years.

*Troy:* It ain't the same, Bono. It ain't like working the back of the truck. Ain't got nobody to talk to . . . feel like you working by yourself. Naw, I'm thinking about retiring. How's Lucille?

*Bono:* She all right. Her arthritis get to acting up on her sometime. Saw Rose on my way in. She going down to the church, huh?

*Troy:* Yeah, she took up going down there. All them preachers looking for some- body to fatten their pockets. *(Pause.)* Got some gin here.

*Bono:* Naw, thanks. I just stopped by to say hello.

*Troy:* Hell, nigger . . . you can take a drink. I ain't never known you to say no to a drink. You ain't got to work tomorrow.

*Bono:* I just stopped by. I'm fixing to go over to Skinner's. We got us a domino game going over his house every Friday.

*Troy:* Nigger, you can't play no dominoes. I used to whup you four games out of five.

*Bono:* Well, that learned me. I'm getting better.

*Troy:* Yeah? Well, that's all right.

*Bono:* Look here . . . I got to be getting on. Stop by sometime, huh?

*Troy:* Yeah, I'll do that, Bono. Lucille told Rose you bought her a new refrigerator.

*Bono:* Yeah, Rose told Lucille you had finally built your fence . . . so I figured we'd call it even.

*Troy:* I knew you would.

*Bono:* Yeah . . . okay. I'll be talking to you.

*Troy:* Yeah, take care, Bono. Good to see you. I'm gonna stop over.

*Bono:* Yeah. Okay, Troy.

> *Bono exits. Troy drinks from the bottle.*

*Troy:*  Old Blue died and I dig his grave
Let him down with a golden chain
Every night when I hear old Blue bark
I know Blue treed a possum in Noah's Ark.
Hear it ring! Hear it ring!

> *Cory enters the yard. They eye each other for a beat. Troy is sitting in the middle of the steps. Cory walks over.*

*Cory:* I got to get by.

*Troy:* Say what? What's you say?

*Cory:* You in my way. I got to get by.

*Troy:* You got to get by where? This is my house. Bought and paid for. In full. Took me fifteen years. And if you wanna go in my house and I'm sitting on the steps . . . you say excuse me. Like your mama taught you.

*Cory:* Come on, Pop . . . I got to get by.

> *Cory starts to maneuver his way past Troy. Troy grabs his leg and shoves him back.*

*Troy:* You just gonna walk over top of me?

*Cory:* I live here too!

*Troy (advancing toward him):* You just gonna walk over top of me in my own house?

*Cory:* I ain't scared of you.

*Troy:* I ain't asked if you was scared of me. I asked you if you was fixing to walk over top of me in my own house? That's the question. You ain't gonna say excuse me? You just gonna walk over top of me?

*Cory:* If you wanna put it like that.

*Troy:* How else am I gonna put it?

*Cory:* I was walking by you to go into the house cause you sitting on the steps drunk, singing to yourself. You can put it like that.

*Troy:* Without saying excuse me???

> *Cory doesn't respond.*

I asked you a question. Without saying excuse me???

*Cory:* I ain't got to say excuse me to you. You don't count around here no more.

*Troy:* Oh, I see . . . I don't count around here no more. You ain't got to say excuse me to your daddy. All of a sudden you done got so grown that your daddy don't count around here no more . . . Around here in his own house and yard that he done paid for with the sweat of his brow. You done got so grown to where you gonna take over. You gonna take over my house. Is that right? You gonna wear my pants. You gonna go in there and stretch out on my bed. You ain't got to say excuse me cause I don't count around here no more. Is that right?

*Cory:* That's right. You always talking this dumb stuff. Now, why don't you just get out my way?

*Troy:* I guess you got someplace to sleep and something to put in your belly. You got that, huh? You got that? That's what you need. You got that, huh?

*Cory:* You don't know what I got. You ain't got to worry about what I got.

*Troy:* You right! You one hundred percent right! I done spent the last seventeen years worrying about what you got. Now it's your turn, see? I'll tell you what to do. You grown . . . we done established that. You a man. Now, let's see you act like one. Turn your behind around and walk out this yard. And when you get out there in the alley . . . you can forget about this house. See? Cause this is my house. You go on and be a man and get your own house. You can forget about this. Cause this is mine. You go on and get yours cause I'm through with doing for you.

*Cory:* You talking about what you did for me . . . what'd you ever give me?

*Troy:* Them feet and bones! That pumping heart, nigger! I give you more than anybody else is ever gonna give you.

*Cory:* You ain't never gave me nothing! You ain't never done nothing but hold me back. Afraid I was gonna be better than you. All you ever did was try and make me scared of you. I used to tremble every time you called my name. Every time I heard your footsteps in the house. Wondering all the time . . . what's Papa gonna say if I do this? . . . What's he gonna say if I do that? . . . What's Papa gonna say if I turn on the radio? And Mama, too . . . she tries . . . but she's scared of you.

*Troy:* You leave your mama out of this. She ain't got nothing to do with this.

*Cory:* I don't know how she stand you . . . after what you did to her.

*Troy:* I told you to leave your mama out of this!

*He advances toward Cory.*

*Cory:* What you gonna do . . . give me a whupping? You can't whup me no more. You're too old. You just an old man.

*Troy (shoves him on his shoulder):* Nigger! That's what you are. You just another nigger on the street to me!

*Cory:* You crazy! You know that?

*Troy:* Go on now! You got the devil in you. Get on away from me!

*Cory:* You just a crazy old man . . . talking about I got the devil in me.

*Troy:* Yeah, I'm crazy! If you don't get on the other side of that yard . . . I'm gonna show you how crazy I am! Go on . . . get the hell out of my yard.

*Cory:* It ain't your yard. You took Uncle Gabe's money he got from the army to buy this house and then you put him out.

*Troy (advances on Cory):* Get your black ass out of my yard!

*Troy's advance backs Cory up against the tree. Cory grabs up the bat.*

*Cory:* I ain't going nowhere! Come on . . . put me out! I ain't scared of you.

*Troy:* That's my bat!

*Cory:* Come on!

*Troy:* Put my bat down!

*Cory:* Come on, put me out.

*Cory swings at Troy, who backs across the yard.*

What's the matter? You so bad . . . put me out!

*Troy advances toward Cory.*

*Cory (backing up):* Come on! Come on!

*Troy:* You're gonna have to use it! You wanna draw that bat back on me . . . you're gonna have to use it.

*Cory:* Come on! . . . Come on!

*Cory swings the bat at Troy a second time. He misses. Troy continues to advance toward him.*

*Troy:* You're gonna have to kill me! You wanna draw that bat back on me. You're gonna have to kill me.

*Cory, backed up against the tree, can go no farther. Troy taunts him. He sticks out his head and offers him a target.*

Come on! Come on!

*Cory is unable to swing the bat. Troy grabs it.*

*Troy:* Then I'll show you.

*Cory and Troy struggle over the bat. The struggle is fierce and fully engaged. Troy ultimately is the stronger and takes the bat from Cory and stands over him ready to swing. He stops himself.*

Go on and get away from around my house.

*Cory, stung by his defeat, picks himself up, walks slowly out of the yard and up the alley.*

*Cory:* Tell Mama I'll be back for my things.
*Troy:* They'll be on the other side of that fence.

> *Cory exits.*

*Troy:* I can't taste nothing. Helluljah! I can't taste nothing no more. *(Troy assumes a batting posture and begins to taunt Death, the fastball on the outside corner.)* Come on! It's between you and me now! Come on! Anytime you want! Come on! I be ready for you . . . but I ain't gonna be easy.

> *The lights go down on the scene.*

### Scene V

> *The time is 1965. The lights come up in the yard. It is the morning of Troy's funeral. A funeral plaque with a light hangs beside the door. There is a small garden plot off to the side. There is noise and activity in the house as Rose, Gabriel, and Bono have gathered. The door opens and Raynell, seven years old, enters dressed in a flannel nightgown. She crosses to the garden and pokes around with a stick. Rose calls from the house.*

*Rose:* Raynell!
*Raynell:* Mam?
*Rose:* What you doing out there?
*Raynell:* Nothing.

> *Rose comes to the door.*

*Rose:* Girl, get in here and get dressed. What you doing?
*Raynell:* Seeing if my garden growed.
*Rose:* I told you it ain't gonna grow overnight. You got to wait.
*Raynell:* It don't look like it never gonna grow. Dag!
*Rose:* I told you a watched pot never boils. Get in here and get dressed.
*Raynell:* This ain't even no pot, Mama.
*Rose:* You just have to give it a chance. It'll grow. Now you come on and do what I told you. We got to be getting ready. This ain't no morning to be playing around. You hear me?
*Raynell:* Yes, mam.

> *Rose exits into the house. Raynell continues to poke at her garden with a stick. Cory enters. He is dressed in a Marine corporal's uniform, and carries a duffel bag. His posture is that of a military man, and his speech has a clipped sternness.*

*Cory (to Raynell):* Hi. *(Pause.)* I bet your name is Raynell.
*Raynell:* Uh huh.
*Cory:* Is your mama home?

> *Raynell runs up on the porch and calls through the screen door.*

*Raynell:* Mama . . . there's some man out here. Mama?

> *Rose comes to the door.*

*Rose:* Cory? Lord have mercy! Look here, you all!

> *Rose and Cory embrace in a tearful reunion as Bono and Lyons enter from the house dressed in funeral clothes.*

*Bono:* Aw, looka here . . .

*Rose:* Done got all grown up!

*Cory:* Don't cry, Mama. What you crying about?

*Rose:* I'm just so glad you made it.

*Cory:* Hey Lyons. How you doing, Mr. Bono.

> *Lyons goes to embrace Cory.*

*Lyons:* Look at you, man. Look at you. Don't he look good, Rose. Got them Corporal stripes.

*Rose:* What took you so long?

*Cory:* You know how the Marines are, Mama. They got to get all their paperwork straight before they let you do anything.

*Rose:* Well, I'm sure glad you made it. They let Lyons come. Your Uncle Gabe's still in the hospital. They don't know if they gonna let him out or not. I just talked to them a little while ago.

*Lyons:* A Corporal in the United States Marines.

*Bono:* Your daddy knew you had it in you. He used to tell me all the time.

*Lyons:* Don't he look good, Mr. Bono?

*Bono:* Yeah, he remind me of Troy when I first met him. *(Pause.)* Say, Rose, Lucille's down at the church with the choir. I'm gonna go down and get the pallbearers lined up. I'll be back to get you all.

*Rose:* Thanks, Jim.

*Cory:* See you, Mr. Bono.

*Lyons (with his arm around Raynell):* Cory . . . look at Raynell. Ain't she precious? She gonna break a whole lot of hearts.

*Rose:* Raynell, come and say hello to your brother. This is your brother, Cory. You remember Cory.

*Raynell:* No, Mam.

*Cory:* She don't remember me, Mama.

*Rose:* Well, we talk about you. She heard us talk about you. *(To Raynell.)* This is your brother, Cory. Come on and say hello.

*Raynell:* Hi.

*Cory:* Hi. So you're Raynell. Mama told me a lot about you.

*Rose:* You all come on into the house and let me fix you some breakfast. Keep up your strength.

*Cory:* I ain't hungry, Mama.

*Lyons:* You can fix me something, Rose. I'll be in there in a minute.

*Rose:* Cory, you sure you don't want nothing? I know they ain't feeding you right.

*Cory:* No, Mama . . . thanks. I don't feel like eating. I'll get something later.

*Rose:* Raynell . . . get on upstairs and get that dress on like I told you.

> *Rose and Raynell exit into the house.*

*Lyons:* So . . . I hear you thinking about getting married.

*Cory:* Yeah, I done found the right one, Lyons. It's about time.

*Lyons:* Me and Bonnie been split up about four years now. About the time Papa retired. I guess she just got tired of all them changes I was putting her through. *(Pause.)* I always knew you was gonna make something out yourself. Your head was always in the right direction. So . . . you gonna stay in . . . make it a career . . . put in your twenty years?

*Cory:* I don't know. I got six already, I think that's enough.

*Lyons:* Stick with Uncle Sam and retire early. Ain't nothing out here. I guess Rose told you what happened with me. They got me down the workhouse. I thought I was being slick cashing other people's checks.

*Cory:* How much time you doing?

*Lyons:* They give me three years. I got that beat now. I ain't got but nine more months. It ain't so bad. You learn to deal with it like anything else. You got to take the crookeds with the straights. That's what Papa used to say. He used to say that when he struck out. I seen him strike out three times in a row . . . and the next time up he hit the ball over the grandstand. Right out there in Homestead Field. He wasn't satisfied hitting in the seats . . . he want to hit it over everything! After the game he had two hundred people standing around waiting to shake his hand. You got to take the crookeds with the straights. Yeah, Papa was something else.

*Cory:* You still playing?

*Lyons:* Cory . . . you know I'm gonna do that. There's some fellows down there we got us a band . . . we gonna try and stay together when we get out . . . but yeah, I'm still playing. It still helps me to get out of bed in the morning. As long as it do that I'm gonna be right there playing and trying to make some sense out of it.

*Rose (calling):* Lyons, I got these eggs in the pan.

*Lyons:* Let me go on and get these eggs, man. Get ready to go bury Papa. *(Pause.)* How you doing? You doing all right?

*Cory nods. Lyons touches him on the shoulder and they share a moment of silent grief. Lyons exits into the house. Cory wanders about the yard. Raynell enters.*

*Raynell:* Hi.

*Cory:* Hi.

*Raynell:* Did you used to sleep in my room?

*Cory:* Yeah . . . that used to be my room.

*Raynell:* That's what Papa call it. "Cory's room." It got your football in the closet.

*Rose comes to the door.*

*Rose:* Raynell, get in there and get them good shoes on.

*Raynell:* Mama, can't I wear these? Them other one hurt my feet.

*Rose:* Well, they just gonna have to hurt your feet for a while. You ain't said they hurt your feet when you went down to the store and got them.

*Raynell:* They didn't hurt then. My feet done got bigger.

*Rose:* Don't you give me no backtalk now. You get in there and get them shoes on.

*Raynell exits into the house.*

Ain't too much changed. He still got that piece of rag tied to that tree. He was out here swinging that bat. I was just ready to go back in the house. He swung that bat and then he just fell over. Seem like he swung it and stood there with this grin on his face . . . and then he just fell over. They carried him on down to the hospital, but I knew there wasn't no need . . . why don't you come on in the house?

*Cory:* Mama . . . I got something to tell you. I don't know how to tell you this . . . but I've got to tell you . . . I'm not going to Papa's funeral.

*Rose:* Boy, hush your mouth. That's your daddy you talking about. I don't want hear that kind of talk this morning. I done raised you to come to this? You standing there all healthy and grown talking about you ain't going to your daddy's funeral?

*Cory:* Mama . . . listen . . .

*Rose:* I don't want to hear it, Cory. You just get that thought out of your head.

*Cory:* I can't drag Papa with me everywhere I go. I've got to say no to him. One time in my life I've got to say no.

*Rose:* Don't nobody have to listen to nothing like that. I know you and your daddy ain't seen eye to eye, but I ain't got to listen to that kind of talk this morning. Whatever was between you and your daddy . . . the time has come to put it aside. Just take it and set it over there on the shelf and forget about it. Disrespecting your daddy ain't gonna make you a man, Cory. You got to find a way to come to that on your own. Not going to your daddy's funeral ain't gonna make you a man.

*Cory:* The whole time I was growing up . . . living in his house . . . Papa was like a shadow that followed you everywhere. It weighed on you and sunk into your flesh. It would wrap around you and lay there until you couldn't tell which one was you anymore. That shadow digging in your flesh. Trying to crawl in. Trying to live through you. Everywhere I looked, Troy Maxson was staring back at me . . . hiding under the bed . . . in the closet. I'm just saying I've got to find a way to get rid of that shadow, Mama.

*Rose:* You just like him. You got him in you good.

*Cory:* Don't tell me that, Mama.

*Rose:* You Troy Maxson all over again.

*Cory:* I don't want to be Troy Maxson. I want to be me.

*Rose:* You can't be nobody but who you are, Cory. That shadow wasn't nothing but you growing into yourself. You either got to grow into it or cut it down to fit you. But that's all you got to make life with. That's all you got to measure yourself against that world out there. Your daddy wanted you to be every-thing he wasn't . . . and at the same time he tried to make you into everything he was. I don't know if he was right or wrong . . . but I do know he meant to do more good than he meant to do harm. He wasn't always right. Sometimes when he touched he bruised. And sometimes when he took me in his arms he cut.

When I first met your daddy I thought . . . Here is a man I can lay down with and make a baby. That's the first thing I thought when I seen him. I was thirty years old and had done seen my share of men. But when he walked up to me and said, "I can dance a waltz that'll make you dizzy," I thought, Rose Lee, here is a man that you can open yourself up to and be filled to bursting. Here is a man that can fill all them empty spaces you been tipping around the edges of. One of them empty spaces was being somebody's mother.

I married your daddy and settled down to cooking his supper and keeping clean sheets on the bed. When your daddy walked through the house he was so big he filled it up. That was my first mistake. Not to make him leave some room for me. For my part in the matter. But at that time I wanted that. I wanted a house that I could sing in. And that's what your daddy gave me. I didn't know to keep up his strength I had to give up little pieces of mine. I did that. I took on his life as mine and mixed up the pieces so that you couldn't hardly tell which was which anymore. It was my choice. It was my life and I didn't have to live it like that. But that's what life offered me in the way of being a woman and I took it. I grabbed hold of it with both hands.

By the time Raynell came into the house, me and your daddy had done lost touch with one another. I didn't want to make my blessing off of nobody's misfortune . . . but I took on to Raynell like she was all them babies I had wanted and never had.

*The phone rings.*

Like I'd been blessed to relive a part of my life. And if the Lord see fit to keep up my strength . . . I'm gonna do her just like your daddy did you . . . I'm gonna give her the best of what's in me.

*Raynell (entering, still with her old shoes):* Mama . . . Reverend Tollivier on the phone.

*Rose exits into the house.*

*Raynell:* Hi.
*Cory:* Hi.
*Raynell:* You in the Army or the Marines?
*Cory:* Marines.
*Raynell:* Papa said it was the Army. Did you know Blue?
*Cory:* Blue? Who's Blue?
*Raynell:* Papa's dog what he sing about all the time.
*Cory (singing):* Hear it ring! Hear it ring!
   I had a dog his name was Blue
   You know Blue was mighty true
   You know Blue was a good old dog
   Blue treed a possum in a hollow log
   You know from that he was a good old dog.
   Hear it ring! Hear it ring!

*Raynell joins in singing.*

*Cory and Raynell:* Blue treed a possum out on a limb
   Blue looked at me and I looked at him
   Grabbed that possum and put him in a sack
   Blue stayed there till I came back
   Old Blue's feets was big and round
   Never allowed a possum to touch the ground.
   Old Blue died and I dug his grave
   I dug his grave with a silver spade
   Let him down with a golden chain
   And every night I call his name
   Go on Blue, you good dog you
   Go on Blue, you good dog you
*Raynell:* Blue laid down and died like a man
   Blue laid down and died . . .
*Both:* Blue laid down and died like a man
   Now he's treeing possums in the Promised Land
   I'm gonna tell you this to let you know
   Blue's gone where the good dogs go
   When I hear old Blue bark
   When I hear old Blue bark

Blue treed a possum in Noah's Ark
Blue treed a possum in Noah's Ark.

*Rose comes to the screen door.*

Rose:  Cory, we gonna be ready to go in a minute.
Cory *(to Raynell)*:  You go on in the house and change them shoes like Mama told you so we can go to Papa's funeral.
Raynell:  Okay, I'll be back.

*Raynell exits into the house. Cory gets up and crosses over to the tree. Rose stands in the screen door watching him. Gabriel enters from the alley.*

Gabriel *(calling)*:  Hey, Rose!
Rose:  Gabe?
Gabriel:  I'm here, Rose. Hey Rose, I'm here!

*Rose enters from the house.*

Rose:  Lord . . . Look here, Lyons!
Lyons:  See, I told you, Rose . . . I told you they'd let him come.
Cory:  How you doing, Uncle Gabe?
Lyons:  How you doing, Uncle Gabe?
Gabriel:  Hey, Rose. It's time. It's time to tell St. Peter to open the gates. Troy, you ready? You ready, Troy. I'm gonna tell St. Peter to open the gates. You get ready now.

*Gabriel, with great fanfare, braces himself to blow. The trumpet is without a mouthpiece. He puts the end of it into his mouth and blows with great force, like a man who has been waiting some twenty-odd years for this single moment. No sound comes out of the trumpet. He braces himself and blows again with the same result. A third time he blows. There is a weight of impossible description that falls away and leaves him bare and exposed to a frightful realization. It is a trauma that a sane and normal mind would be unable to withstand. He begins to dance. A slow, strange dance, eerie and life-giving. A dance of atavistic signature and ritual. Lyons attempts to embrace him. Gabriel pushes Lyons away. He begins to howl in what is an attempt at song, or perhaps a song turning back into itself in an attempt at speech. He finishes his dance and the gates of heaven stand open as wide as God's closet.*

That's the way that go!

## CONSIDERATIONS FOR CRITICAL THINKING AND WRITING

1. **FIRST RESPONSE.** Troy Maxson is clearly a flawed character. What would you describe as his most prominent flaw?

2. What is the general attitude toward forgiveness in the play?

3. What are some examples of true sacrifice in the play?

4. What are some examples of self-gratification in the play?

5. Why is death always described in terms of baseball metaphors?

6. Is Troy's struggle against death also a struggle against fate, or are they not the same struggle?

7. To what degree is the play about poverty or material constraints? Is money the true conflict or is it symbolic of larger concerns?

8. *Fences* is part of Wilson's "History Cycle." Note that the first African American baseball player in the major leagues, Jackie Robinson, crossed the line that segregated American society in 1947, and it wasn't until 1959 that all Major League teams included a Black player. How does this history, or the history of segregation more generally, help to contextualize the play, which is set in 1957?

9. More broadly, do the play's concerns with generations indicate that history is doomed to be repeated or that the course of history can be changed for the better? Explain your answer.

### CONNECTIONS TO OTHER SELECTIONS

1. Compare the father in David Auburn's *Proof* (p. 1277) to Troy Maxson in this play. Who is a stronger figure? Where does each character derive his strength from?

2. Discuss the concept of the tragic flaw (*hamartia*) in this play and either Sophocles' *Oedipus the King* (p. 1001) or Shakespeare's *Othello* (p. 1055). Despite the clear differences in time, place, and circumstances, are there significant similarities between Troy and the protagonist of the other play?

---

Perspective

---

## DAVID SAVRAN (B. 1950)

## *An Interview with August Wilson*  1987

*Savran:* In reading *Fences*, I came to view Troy more and more critically as the play progressed, sharing Rose's point of view. We see that Troy has been crippled by his father. That's being replayed in Troy's relationship with Cory. Do you think there's a way out of that cycle?

*Wilson:* Surely. First of all, we're all like our parents. The things we are taught early in life, how to respond to the world, our sense of morality — everything, we get from them. Now you can take that legacy and do with it anything you want to do. It's in your hands. Cory is Troy's son. How can he be Troy's son without sharing Troy's values? I was trying to get at why Troy made the choices he made, how they have influenced his values, and how he attempts to pass those along to his son. Each generation gives the succeeding generation what they think they need. One question in the play is "Are the tools we are given sufficient to compete in a world that is different from the one our parents knew?" I think they are — it's just that we have to do different things with the tools. That's all Troy has to give. Troy's flaw is that he does not recognize that the world was changing. That's because he spent fifteen years in a penitentiary.

As African-Americans, we should demand to participate in society as Africans. That's the way out of the vicious cycle of poverty and neglect that exists in 1987 in America, where you have a huge percentage of blacks living in the equivalent of South African townships, in housing projects. No one is inviting these people to participate in society. Look at the poverty levels — $8,500 for a family of four, if you have $8,501 you're not counted. Those statistics would go up enormously if we had an honest assessment of the cost of living in America. I don't know how anybody can support a family of four on $8,500. What I'm saying is that 85 or 90 percent of blacks in America are living in abject poverty and, for the most part, are crowded into what amount to concentration camps. The situation for blacks in America is worse than it was forty years ago. Some sociologists will tell you about the tremendous progress we've made. They didn't put me out when I walked in the door. And you can always point to someone who works on Wall Street, or is a doctor. But they don't count in the larger scheme of things.

*Savran:* Do you have any idea how these political changes could take place?

*Wilson:* I'm not sure. I know that blacks must be allowed their cultural dif- 5 ferences. I think the process of assimilation to white American society was a big mistake. We don't want to be like you. Blacks living in housing projects are isolated from the society, for the most part — living as they choose, as Africans. Only they don't realize the value in what they're doing because they have accepted their victimization. They've marked themselves as victims. Once they recognize that, they can begin to move through society in a different manner, from a stronger position, and claim what is theirs.

*Savran:* A project of yours is to point up what happens when oppression is internalized.

*Wilson:* Yes, transfer of aggression to the wrong target. I think it's interesting that the two roads open to blacks for "full participation" are entertainment and sports. *Ma Rainey* and *Fences,* and I didn't plan it that way. I don't think that they're the correct roads. I think Troy's right. Now with the benefit of historical perspective, I can say that the athletic scholarship was actually a way of exploiting. Now you've got two million kids who think they're going to play in the NBA. In the sixties, the universities made a lot of money off of athletics. You had kids playing for free who, by and large, were not getting educated, were taking courses in basketweaving. Some of them could barely read.

*Savran:* Troy may be right about that issue, but it seems that he has passed on certain destructive traits in spite of himself. Take the hostility between father and son.

*Wilson:* I think every generation says to the previous generation: you're in my way, I've got to get by. The father-son conflict is actually a normal generational conflict that happens all the time.

*Savran:* So it's a healthy and a good thing?  10

*Wilson:* Oh, sure. Troy is seeing this boy walk around, smelling his piss. Two men cannot live in the same household. Troy would have been tremendously disappointed if Cory had not challenged him. Troy knows that this boy has to go out and do battle with that world: "So I had best prepare him because I know that's a harsh, cruel place out there. But that's going to be easy compared to what he's getting here. Ain't nobody gonna whip your ass like I'm gonna whip it." He has a tremendous love for the kid. But he's not going to say, "I love you," he's going to demonstrate it. He's carrying garbage for seventeen years just for the kid. The only world Troy knows is the one that he made. Cory's going to go on to find another one, he's going to arrive at the same place as Troy. I think one of the most important lines in the play is when Troy is talking about his father: "I got to the place where I could feel him kicking in my blood and knew that the only thing that separated us was the matter of a few years."

Hopefully, Cory will do things a bit differently with his son. For Troy, sports was not the way to go, the white man wouldn't let him get away with that. "Get you a job, with your hands, something that nobody can take away from you." The idea of school — he doesn't know what that is. That's for white folks. Very few blacks had paperwork jobs. But if you knew how to fix cars, you could always make some money. That's what Troy wants for Cory. There aren't many people who ever jumped up in Troy's face. So he's proud of the kid at the same time that he expresses a hurt that all men feel. You got to cut your kid loose at some point. There's that sense of loss and separation. You find out how Troy left his father's house and you see how Cory leaves his house. I suspect with Cory it will repeat with some differences and maybe, after five or six generations, they'll find a different way to do it.

*Savran:* Where Cory ends up is very ambiguous, as a marine in 1965.

*Wilson:* Yes. For the average black kid on the street, that was an alternative. You went into the army because you could learn how to do something. I can remember my parents talking about the son of some friends: "He's in the navy. He *did* something" — as opposed to standing on the street corner, shooting drugs, drinking wine, and robbing stores. Lyons says to Cory, "I always knew you were going to make something out of yourself." It really wounds me. He's a corporal in the marines. For blacks, that is a sense of accomplishment. Therein lies one of the tragedies of blacks in America. Cory says, "I don't know. I put in six years. That's enough." Anyone who goes into the army and makes a career out of it is a loser. They sit there and are nurtured by the army and they don't have to confront life. Then they get out of the army and find there's nothing to do. They didn't learn any skills. And if they did, they can't find a job. Four months later, they're shooting dope. In the sixties, a whole bunch of blacks went over, fought, and died in the Vietnam War. The survivors came back to the same street corners and found out nothing had changed. They still couldn't get a job.

At the end of *Fences* every person, with the exception of Raynell, is institu- 15 tionalized. Rose is in a church. Lyons is in a penitentiary. Gabriel's in a mental hospital, and Cory's in the marines. The only free person is the girl, Troy's daughter, the hope for the future. That was conscious on my part because in '57 that's what I saw. Blacks have relied on institutions which are really foreign — except for the black church, which has been our saving grace. I have some problems with it but I recognize it as a central social organization and sometimes an economic organization for the black community. I would like to see blacks develop their own institutions that respond to their needs.

From *In Their Own Voices*

### CONSIDERATIONS FOR CRITICAL THINKING AND WRITING

1. Wilson describes Troy's "flaw" as an inability to "recognize that the world was changing" (p. 1376). Discuss how completely this assessment describes Troy.

2. Write an essay discussing how Wilson uses the hostility between father and son in *Fences* as a means of treating larger social issues for Black people in America.

3. Read the section on historical criticism (pp. 1390–1391) in Chapter 42, "Critical Strategies for Reading." Discuss how useful and accurate you think *Fences* is in depicting Black life in America for the past several decades.

# Strategies for Reading and Writing

*Credits, clockwise from top left*: Kathy deWitt/Alamy; Anthony Barboza/
Archive Photos/Getty Images; Library of Congress; Bettmann/Getty
Images.

# 42

# Critical Strategies
for Reading

© Kathy deWitt/Alamy.

The answers you get from literature
depend upon the questions you pose.
— MARGARET ATWOOD

## CRITICAL THINKING

Maybe this has happened to you: the assignment is to write an analysis of
some aspect of a work — let's say, James Baldwin's story "Sonny's Blues"
(p. 91) — that interests you and takes into account critical sources that comment on and interpret the work. You cheerfully begin research through
your library's website but quickly find yourself bewildered by several seemingly unrelated articles. The first traces the thematic significance of images
of light and darkness in the story; the second questions why the narrator's
wife has such a diminished role in the narrative; the third analyzes the narrator's speech and behavior as a form of anxiety; and the fourth scrutinizes the
narrator as an unquestioning supporter of capitalist values while his brother
Sonny subverts those values. These disparate treatments may seem random
and capricious — a confirmation of your worst suspicions that interpretations
of literature are hit-or-miss excursions into areas that you know little about
or didn't know even existed. But if you understand that the four articles are

written from four different perspectives — formalist, feminist, psychological, and Marxist — and that the purpose of each is to enhance your understanding of the story by discussing a particular element of it, then you can see that the articles' varying strategies represent potentially interesting ways of opening up the text that otherwise might not have occurred to you. There are many ways to approach a text, and a useful first step is to develop a sense of direction, an understanding of how a perspective — your own or a critic's — shapes a discussion of a text.

This chapter offers an introduction to critical approaches to literature by outlining a variety of strategies for reading fiction, poetry, or drama. These strategies include approaches that have long been practiced by readers who have used, for example, the insights gleaned from biography and history to illuminate literary works as well as more recent approaches, such as those used by critics who rely on theories related to specialized contextual categories like gender, reader-response, and deconstruction. Each of these perspectives is sensitive to point of view, symbol, tone, metaphor, and other literary elements that you have been studying, but each also casts those elements in a special light. The formalist approach emphasizes how the elements within a work achieve their effects, whereas biographical and psychological approaches lead outward from the work to consider the author's life and other writings. Even broader approaches, such as historical and cultural perspectives, connect the work to historic and social phenomena that frame literary production. Mythological readings represent the broadest approach because they link an individual work to narrative structures and tropes that have repeated across multiple cultures and time periods.

Any given strategy raises its own types of questions and issues while seeking particular kinds of evidence to illustrate its concerns. An awareness of the assumptions and methods that inform an approach can help you to understand better the validity and value of a given critic's strategy for making sense of a work. More important, such an understanding can widen and deepen the responses of your own reading.

The critical thinking that goes into understanding a professional critic's approach to a work is not foreign to you because you have already used essentially the same kind of thinking to understand the work itself. You have developed skills to produce a literary *analysis* that describes how a character, symbol, or rhyme scheme supports a theme. These same skills are also useful for reading literary criticism because they allow you to keep track of how the parts of a critical approach create a particular reading of a literary work. When you analyze a story, poem, or play by closely examining how its various elements relate to the whole, your *interpretation* — your articulation of what the work means to you as supported by an analysis of its elements — necessarily involves choosing what you focus on in the work. The same is true of professional critics.

The following overview of critical strategies for reading is neither exhaustive in the types of critical approaches covered nor complete in its presentation of the complexities inherent in them, but it should help you to develop an appreciation of the intriguing possibilities that attend literary inter-pretation. The emphasis in this chapter is on ways of thinking about literature rather than on daunting lists of terms, names, and movements. Although a working knowledge of critical schools — often referred to collectively as liter-ary theory — may be valuable and necessary for a fully informed use of a given critical approach, the aim here is more modest and practical. This chapter is no substitute for the shelves of literary criticism that can be found in your school's library or for the databases that can be accessed on its website, but it does suggest how different perspectives produce different readings of texts.

The summaries of critical approaches that follow are descriptive, not eval-uative. Each approach has its advantages and limitations. In practice, many critical approaches overlap and complement each other, but those matters are best left to further study. Like literary artists, critics have their personal val-ues, tastes, and styles. The appropriateness of a specific critical approach will depend, at least in part, on the nature of the literary work under discussion as well as on your own sensibilities and experience. However, any approach, if it is to enhance understanding, requires sensitivity, tact, and an awareness of the various literary elements of the text, including, of course, its use of language.

Successful critical approaches avoid eccentric decodings that reveal so-called hidden meanings that are not only hidden but totally absent from the text. For a parody of this sort of critical excess, see "A Parodic Interpretation of 'Stopping by Woods on a Snowy Evening'" (p. 877), in which Herbert R. Coursen Jr. has some fun with a Robert Frost poem and Santa Claus while making a serious point about the dangers of overly ingenious readings. Literary criticism attempts, like any valid hypothesis, to account for phenom-ena within a text without distorting or misrepresenting what it describes.

## FORMALIST STRATEGIES

*Formalist critics* focus on the formal elements of a work — its language, structure, tone, and the conventions of its genre. The word *form* at the root of formalism is key: each work of literature is a unique object, but one that helps us to understand the form it has taken, or the way it was formed. A formalist reads literature as an independent work of art rather than as a reflection of the author's state of mind or as a representation of a moment in history. Historic influences on a work, an author's intentions, or anything else outside the work are generally not the primary focus for formalists. (This is particularly true of the most famous modern formalists, known as the **New Critics**, who domi-nated American criticism from the 1940s through the 1960s.) Instead, formal-ists offer intense examinations of the relationship between form and meaning within a work, emphasizing the subtle complexity of how a work is arranged. This kind of close reading pays special attention to what are often described as *intrinsic* matters in a literary work, such as diction, irony, paradox, metaphor, and symbol, as well as larger elements, such as plot, characterization, and narrative technique. Formalists examine how these elements work together to give a coherent shape (or "unity") to a work while contributing to its meaning. The answers to the questions formalists raise about how the shape and effect of a work are related come from the work itself. Other kinds of information that go beyond the text — biography, history, politics, economics, and so on — are typically regarded by formalists as *extrinsic* matters, which are considerably less important than what goes on within the autonomous text.

For an example of a work in which the shape of the plot serves as the major organizing principle, let's examine Kate Chopin's "The Story of an Hour" (p. 17), a two-page short story that takes only a few minutes to read. A first reading probably results in surprise at the story's ending: a grieving wife "afflicted with a heart trouble" suddenly dies of a heart attack, not because she's learned that her kind and loving husband has been killed in a terrible train accident but because she discovers that he is alive, and thus still in her life. Clearly, we are witnessing an ironic situation since there is such a powerful incongruity between what is expected to happen and what actually happens. A likely formalist strategy for analyzing this story would be to raise questions about the ironic ending. Is this merely a trick ending, or is it a carefully wrought culmination of other elements in the story resulting in an interesting and challenging theme? Formalists value such complexities over simple surprise effects.

A second, closer reading indicates that Chopin's third-person narrator presents the story in a manner similar to Josephine's gentle attempts to break the news about Brently Mallard's death. The story is told in "veiled hints that [reveal] in half concealing." But unlike Josephine, who tries to protect her sister's fragile heart from stress, the narrator seeks to reveal Mrs. Mallard's complex heart. A formalist would look back over the story for signs of the ending in the imagery. Although Mrs. Mallard grieves immediately and unreservedly when she hears about the train disaster, she soon begins to feel a different emotion as she looks out the window at "the tops of trees . . . all aquiver with the new spring life." This symbolic evocation of renewal and rebirth — along with "the delicious breath of rain," the sounds of life in the street, and the birds singing — causes her to feel, in spite of her own efforts to repress her thoughts and emotions, "free, free, free!" She feels alive with a sense of possibility, with a "clear and exalted perception" that she "would live for herself" instead of for and through her husband.

It is ironic that this ecstatic "self-assertion" is interpreted by Josephine as grief, but the crowning irony for this "goddess of Victory" is the doctors' assumption that she dies of joy rather than of the shock of having to abandon her newly discovered self once she realizes her husband is still alive. In the course of an hour, Mrs. Mallard's life is irretrievably changed: her husband's assumed accidental death frees her, but the fact that he lives combined with all the expectations imposed on her by his continued life kill her. She does, indeed, die of a broken heart, but only Chopin's readers know the real ironic meaning of that explanation.

Although this brief discussion of some of the formal elements of Chopin's story does not describe all there is to say about how they produce an effect and create meaning, it does suggest the kinds of questions, issues, and evidence that a formalist strategy might raise in providing a close reading of the text itself.

## BIOGRAPHICAL STRATEGIES

A knowledge of an author's life can help readers understand a work more fully. Events in a work might follow actual events in a writer's life just as characters might be based on people known by the author. Relevant facts about an author's life can make clearer the source of their convictions and how their own experiences inform the major concerns showcased in a given work. Biographical details might also help to fill in some of the context for the author's motivation for writing about a certain subject, or for writing about it a certain way. The aim of a biographical critic would not be to equate the author and a character in a story, or voice in a poem. The *biographer* might want to solidify such connections between author and creation, but the *critic* would use those connections to frame an interpretive response.

Some formalist critics — some New Critics, for example — argue that interpretation should be based primarily on internal evidence rather than on any biographical information outside the work. They argue that it is not possible to determine an author's intention and that the work must stand by itself. Although this is a useful caveat for keeping the work in focus, a reader who finds biography relevant would argue that biography can at the very least serve to narrow the scope of possible interpretations.

However, it is also worth noting that biographical information can complicate a work. Chopin's "The Story of an Hour" presents a repressed wife's momentary discovery of what freedom from her husband might mean to her. She awakens to a new sense of herself when she learns of her husband's death, only to collapse of a heart attack when she sees that he is alive. Readers might be tempted to interpret this story as Chopin's fictionalized commentary about her own marriage because her husband died twelve years before she wrote the story and seven years before she began writing fiction seriously. Biographers seem to agree, however, that Chopin's marriage was evidently satisfying to her and that she was not oppressed by her husband and did not feel oppressed.

Moreover, consider this diary entry from only one month after Chopin wrote the story (quoted by Per Seyersted in *Kate Chopin: A Critical Biography*):

> If it were possible for my husband and my mother to come back to earth, I feel that I would unhesitatingly give up everything that has come into my life since they left it and join my existence again with theirs. To do that, I would have to forget the past ten years of my growth — my real growth. But I would take back a little wisdom with me; it would be the spirit of perfect acquiescence.

This passage raises provocative questions instead of resolving them. How does that "spirit of perfect acquiescence" relate to Mrs. Mallard's insistence that she "would live for herself"? Why would Chopin be willing to "forget the past ten years of . . . growth" given her protagonist's desire for "self-assertion"? Although these and other questions raised by the diary entry cannot be answered here, this kind of biographical perspective certainly adds to the possibilities of interpretation. Critics should always be cautious about assuming that a character is a stand-in for the author. The narrator of a short story, speaker of a poem, or protagonist of a play might in fact be a character far removed from the author's sensibility, even a character that the author has created in order to critique that character's thoughts, words, or behavior. There might be a literary reason for having created that character, such as to engage in a debate with another character in order to advance a work's theme. Unless you are thoroughly familiar with an author's biography, we would caution against taking the biographical details you know as the defining factors in an interpretation. These details are better thought of as signposts than treasure maps.

## PSYCHOLOGICAL STRATEGIES

Even if you haven't studied psychology formally, you are probably familiar with and intrigued by the basic premises of this field. If a friend tells you she dreamed about how she was climbing a mountain and kept falling back a few feet at a time, you might suggest the dream is really about an upcoming test she's worried about and that falling in the dream is akin to failing in reality. Given the enormous influence that Sigmund Freud's psychoanalytic theories had on twentieth-century interpretations of human behavior, it is nearly inevitable that most people have some familiarity with his ideas concerning dreams, unconscious desires, and sexual repression, as well as his terms for different aspects of the psyche — the id, ego, and superego. Certainly an enormous number of twentieth-century European and American authors knew Freud's theories, and that awareness is evident in many literary works, even if authors did not agree with Freud or with the other theorists he influenced. But a critic using Freud's theories would not even necessarily need to know how much an author engaged with those theories: the works themselves can be used to illustrate or dispute the validity of Freud's theories. Psychological approaches to literature often draw on Freud's theories or other psychoanalytic theories to understand more fully the text, the writer, and the reader. Critics use such approaches to explore the motivations of characters and the symbolic meanings of events, while biographers use them to speculate about a writer's own motivations — conscious or unconscious — in a literary work. Psychological approaches can also be used to describe and analyze a reader's responses to a text.

Although it is not feasible to explain psychoanalytic terms and concepts in so brief a space as this, it is possible to suggest the nature of a psychological approach. It is a strategy based heavily on the idea of the existence of a human unconscious — those impulses, desires, and feelings that a person is unaware of but that influence emotions and behavior. Freud is certainly not the only theorist whose ideas are employed to understand texts, and many other thinkers disagreed with him, instead focusing on such factors as stages of development or the circumstances of one's upbringing to explain human behavior. Yet Freud's theories are the foundation of modern psychoanalysis and are worth considering as a starting point even though the field has developed beyond them.

Central to a number of psychoanalytic critical readings is Freud's concept of what he called the **Oedipus complex**, a term derived from Sophocles' tragedy *Oedipus the King* (p. 1001). This complex is predicated on a boy's unconscious rivalry with his father for his mother's love and his desire to eliminate his father in order to take his father's place with his mother. The female version of the psychological conflict is known as the **Electra complex**, a term used to describe a daughter's unconscious rivalry with her mother for her father's affection. The name comes from a Greek legend about Electra, who avenged the death of her father, Agamemnon, by plotting the death of her mother. In *The Interpretation of Dreams*, Freud explains why *Oedipus the King* "moves a modern audience no less than it did the contemporary Greek one." What unites their powerful attraction to the play is an unconscious response:

> There must be something which makes a voice within us ready to recognize the compelling force of destiny in the *Oedipus*. . . . His destiny moves us only because it might have been ours — because the oracle laid the same curse upon us before our birth as upon him. It is the fate of all of us, perhaps, to direct our first sexual impulse towards our mother and our first hatred and our first murderous wish against our father. Our dreams convince us that this is so. King Oedipus, who slew his father Laios and married his mother Iokaste, merely shows us the fulfillment of our own childhood wishes . . . and we shrink back from him with the whole force of the repression by which those wishes have since that time been held down within us.

In this passage Freud interprets the unconscious motives of Sophocles in writing the play, Oedipus in acting within it, and the audience in responding to it. Although the Oedipus complex is, of course, not relevant to all psychological interpretations of literature, interpretations involving this complex do offer a useful example of how psychoanalytic critics might approach a text.

The situation in which Mrs. Mallard finds herself in Chopin's "The Story of an Hour" is not related to an Oedipus complex, but it is clear that news of her husband's death has released powerful unconscious desires for freedom that she had previously suppressed. As she grieved, "something" was "coming to her and she was waiting for it, fearfully." What comes to her is what she senses about the life outside her window; that's the stimulus, but the true source of what was to "possess her," which she strove to "beat . . . back with her [conscious] will," is her desperate desire for the autonomy and fulfillment she had been unable to admit did not exist in her marriage. A psychological approach to her story amounts to a case study in the destructive nature of self-repression. Moreover, the story might reflect Chopin's own views of her marriage despite her conscious statements about her loving husband, for to admit her true feelings to herself or to her public might not be possible.

One key motif to pay attention to if you are interested in psychological interpretations of literature is the presence of dreams or dream-imagery in literature. Although there has been a great deal of debate over the centuries about what dreams "mean" — ranging from prophecy, to random spasms of our brains, to the field of our unconscious desires — they are potent repositories of meaning in literary contexts. In Ralph Ellison's story "King of the Bingo Game" (p. 178), the protagonist initially dozes off during a movie, and much of the rest of the story depicts him in a kind of trance-like state in which the imagery doesn't make perfect sense — just as one might experience life in a dream. The speaker of John Keats's "Ode to a Nightingale" (p. 659) famously asks of his experience, "Was it a vision, or a waking dream? / Fled is that music: do I wake or sleep?" At the end of another famous poem, "The Love Song of J. Alfred Prufrock" (p. 936), T. S. Eliot's speaker concludes with surreal, dream-like, underwater imagery which will last "Till human voices wake us, and we drown." The juxtaposition of irrational images, whether or not framed as an actual dream, will alert the psychoanalytic critic to the possibility that we are witnessing the border between rational and irrational urges, or between the conscious and unconscious mind. Humans can't always articulate what they desire or fear; dreams can sometimes provide a key. Most broadly, though, psychology seeks to explain why people act as they do. The same urge to explain can be a fruitful lens through which to view a work of literature, especially when characters don't act as we (or they) expect them to.

## HISTORICAL STRATEGIES

Historians sometimes use literature as a window onto the past because literature frequently provides the nuances of a historic period that cannot be readily perceived through other sources. Another way of approaching the relationship between literature and history, however, is to use history as a means of understanding a literary work more clearly. The approach assumes that the writing contemporary to an author is an important element of the history that helps to shape a work. There are many ways to talk about the historical and cultural dimensions of a work. Some readings treat a literary text as a document reflecting, producing, or being produced by the social conditions of its time, giving equal focus to the social milieu and the work itself. Others treat history and literature both as texts to be "read," and the urge to explain the movements of history (such as cause and effect) parallels the inquiry into a work of literature (that is, this wouldn't have happened if that hadn't happened first). The general impulse to view literature through a historical lens provides context for meaning. There are more refined or more ideological versions of historical approaches, too, such as Marxist criticism, new historicist criticism, and cultural criticism.

A work of literature may transcend time to the extent that it addresses the concerns of readers over a span of decades or centuries, but it remains for the historical critic a part of the past in which it was composed, a past that can reveal more fully a work's language, ideas, and purposes. When using a historical approach, critics move beyond both the facts of an author's personal life and the text itself to the social and intellectual currents in which the author composed the work. They place the work in the context of its time, and sometimes they make connections with other literary or artistic works that may have influenced the author. The basic strategy of these critics is to illuminate the historical background in order to shed light on some aspect of the work itself.

To return to our recurrent example text: the repression expressed in the lines on Mrs. Mallard's face is more distinctly seen if Chopin's "The Story of an Hour" is placed in the context of "the Woman Question" as it continued to develop in the 1890s. Mrs. Mallard's impulse toward "self-assertion" runs parallel with a growing women's movement away from the role of long-suffering and unfulfilled housewife. This desire was widely regarded by traditionalists as a form of dangerous selfishness that was considered as unnatural as it was immoral. It is no wonder that Chopin raises the question of whether Mrs. Mallard's sense of freedom owing to her husband's death isn't a selfish, "monstrous joy." Mrs. Mallard, however, dismisses this question as "trivial" in the face of her new perception of life, a dismissal that Chopin endorses by way of the story's ironic ending. This is not to conclude simply that Mrs. Mallard was representative of all American women at the time of its publication, but rather that her internal struggle connected to a broader social context, one which would have been more immediately apparent to Chopin's readers in 1894 than it is to readers in the twenty-first century. That is why a historical reconstruction of the limitations placed on married women helps to explain the pressures, tensions, and momentary release that Mrs. Mallard experiences.

## MARXIST CRITICISM

Marxist readings developed from the heightened interest in radical reform during the 1930s, when many critics sought to understand literature in terms of proletarian social and economic goals, based largely on the writings of Karl Marx. **Marxist critics** focus on the ideological content of a work — its explicit and implicit assumptions and values about matters such as culture, race, class, and power. Marxist studies typically aim to reveal and clarify ideological issues and also to correct social injustices. Some Marxist critics have used literature to describe the competing socioeconomic interests that too often pit wealth and capitalist power against socialist morality and justice. They argue that criticism, like literature, is essentially political because it either challenges or supports economic inequality or oppression. Even if criticism attempts to ignore class conflicts, it is politicized, according to Marxists, because it accepts the status quo.

It is not surprising that Marxist critics pay more attention to the content and themes of literature than to its form. A Marxist reading of Chopin's

"The Story of an Hour" might draw on evidence made available in a book by Charlotte Perkins Gilman titled *Women and Economics: A Study of the Economic Relation between Men and Women as a Factor in Social Evolution* (1898) published only a few years after Chopin's story. An examination of this study could help explain how some of the "repression" Mrs. Mallard experiences was generated by the socioeconomic structure contemporary to her and how Chopin challenges the validity of that structure by having Mrs. Mallard resist it with her very life. A Marxist reading would see the protagonist's conflict as not only an individual issue but part of a larger class struggle. When Brently Mallard appears at the end of the story, "a little travel-stained, composedly carrying his gripsack and umbrella," a Marxist critic sees a bourgeois businessman oblivious to the human tragedy of the railroad accident. His triumphant survival depends on the suffering of the invisible masses. These are details that would be especially important to a Marxist reader.

## NEW HISTORICIST CRITICISM

Since the 1960s a development in historical approaches to literature known as **new historicism** has emphasized the interaction between the historic context of a work and a modern reader's understanding and interpretation of the work. In contrast to many traditional historical frameworks for reading literature, however, new historicists attempt to describe the culture of a period by reading many different kinds of texts that earlier critics might have previously left for economists, sociologists, and anthropologists. New historicists attempt to read a period in all its dimensions, including political, economic, social, and aesthetic concerns. These considerations could be used to explain the pressures that destroy Mrs. Mallard. A new historicist might examine the story and the public attitudes toward women contemporary to "The Story of an Hour" (p. 17) as well as documents such as suffragist tracts and medical diagnoses to explore how the same forces — expectations about how women are supposed to feel, think, and behave — shape different kinds of texts and how these texts influence each other. A new historicist might, for example, scrutinize medical records for evidence of "nervousness" and "hysteria" as common diagnoses for women who led lives regarded as too independent by their contemporaries.

Without an awareness of just how selfish and self-destructive Mrs. Mallard's impulses would have been in the eyes of some of her contemporaries, readers in the twenty-first century might miss the pervasive pressures embedded not only in her marriage but in the social fabric surrounding her. Her death is made more understandable by such an awareness. The doctors who diagnose her as suffering from the "joy that kills" are not merely insensitive or stupid; they represent a contrasting set of assumptions and values that are as historic and real as Mrs. Mallard's yearnings. Other important considerations might include the budding suffragist movement that sought to empower American women by granting them the right to vote, or the related temperance movement in the nineteenth century that sought to bring (sober) men back to their domestic commitments.

New historicist criticism acknowledges more fully than traditional historical approaches the competing nature of readings of the past and thereby tends to offer new emphases and perspectives. New historicism reminds us that there is not only one historic context for "The Story of an Hour." Those doctors reveal additional dimensions of late-nineteenth-century social attitudes that warrant our attention, whether we agree with them or not. By emphasizing that historical perceptions are governed, at least in part, by our own concerns and preoccupations, new historicists sensitize us to the fact that the history on which we choose to focus is reconstructed by concerns that have come to the foreground in our own present moment. This reconstructed history affects our reading of texts.

## CULTURAL CRITICISM

*Cultural critics*, like new historicists, focus on the historical contexts of a literary work, but they pay particular attention to popular manifestations of social, political, and economic contexts. Popular culture — mass-produced and consumed cultural artifacts, today ranging from advertising to popular fiction to television to rock music — and "high" culture are given equal emphasis. A cultural critic attempting to interpret Ellison's "King of the Bingo Game" (p. 178) might be less interested in the Great Depression as a global phenomenon than in the type of movie the protagonist watches before playing bingo. The critic might note that in 1934 Hollywood adopted a widespread set of guidelines that essentially amounted to censorship known as the "Hays Code." This code turned movies into escapist fantasies that upheld moral behavior: sex and violence were largely removed from the silver screen. The sexual desire the protagonist feels and the violence he experiences are thus in sharp contrast to the type of movie he would have been watching that day. Adding the "low" art of everyday life to "high" art opens up previously unexpected and unexplored areas of criticism. Cultural critics use widely eclectic strategies drawn from new historicism, psychology, gender studies, and deconstructionism (to name only a handful of approaches) to analyze not only literary texts but radio talk shows, comic strips, calendar art, commercials, travel guides, and baseball cards. Because all human activity falls within the ken of cultural criticism, nothing is too minor or major, obscure or pervasive, to escape the range of its analytic vision.

A cultural critic's approach to Chopin's "The Story of an Hour" might emphasize how the story reflects the potential dangers and horrors of train travel in the 1890s or it might examine how heart disease was often misdiagnosed by physicians or used as a metaphor in Mrs. Mallard's culture for a variety of emotional conditions. Each of these perspectives can serve to create a wider and more informed understanding of the story.

# GENDER STRATEGIES

*Gender critics* explore how ideas about how traditionally masculine and feminine behavior can be regarded as socially constructed by particular cultures. According to some critics, sex is determined by simple biological and anatomical categories of male or female, and gender is determined by a culture's values. Thus, ideas about gender and what constitutes masculine and feminine behavior are created by cultural institutions and conditioning. A gender critic might, for example, focus on Chopin's characterization of an emotionally sensitive Mrs. Mallard and a rational, composed husband in "The Story of an Hour" as a manifestation of socially constructed gender identity in the 1890s. *Gender criticism* expands categories and definitions of what is masculine or feminine and tends to regard sexuality as more complex than merely masculine or feminine, heterosexual or homosexual. Gender criticism, therefore, has come to include LGBTQ+ criticism as well as feminist criticism.

## Feminist Criticism

Like Marxist critics, *feminist critics* reading "The Story of an Hour" would also be interested in a text like Charlotte Perkins Gilman's *Women and Economics: A Study of the Economic Relation between Men and Women as a Factor in Social Evolution* (1898) because they seek to correct or supplement what they regard as a predominantly male-dominated critical perspective with a feminist consciousness. Like other forms of sociological criticism, feminist criticism places literature in a social context, and, like those of Marxist criticism, its analyses often have sociopolitical purposes — explaining, for example, how images of women in literature reflect the patriarchal social forces that have impeded women's efforts to achieve full equality with men. Consequently, feminist critics' approach to literature employs a broad range of disciplines, including history, sociology, psychology, and linguistics, to provide a perspective sensitive to feminist issues.

A feminist approach to Chopin's "The Story of an Hour" might explore the psychological stress created by the expectations that marriage imposes on Mrs. Mallard, expectations that literally and figuratively break her heart. Given that her husband is kind and loving, the issue is not her being married to Brently but her being married at all. Chopin presents marriage as an institution that creates in both men and women the assumed "right to impose a private will upon a fellow-creature." That "right," however, might be interpreted, especially from a feminist perspective, as primarily imposed on women by men. A feminist critic might note, for instance, that the protagonist is introduced as "Mrs. Mallard" (we learn that her first name is Louise only later); she is defined by her marital status and her husband's name, a name whose origin from the Old French is related to the word *masle*, which means "male." The appropriateness of her name points up the fact that her emotions and the cause of her death are interpreted in male terms by the doctors. The value of a feminist perspective on this work can be readily discerned if a reader imagines Mrs. Mallard's story being told from the point of view of one of the doctors who diagnoses the cause of her death as a weak heart rather than as a fierce struggle.

## LGBTQ+ Criticism

***LGBTQ+ critics*** focus on a variety of issues, including how individuals from across the gender and sexuality spectrums, including nonbinary and LGBTQ+ people, are represented in literature, how they read literature, and whether sexuality and gender are culturally constructed or innate. The emergence of "queer theory" in the 1990s served to destabilize the dominant ideology that normalizes heterosexuality and considers other sexualities deviant. These critics have produced new readings of works by established canonical writers in which underlying LGBTQ+ concerns, desires, motifs, or motivations are lifted out and examined as revealing components of these texts. A reading of "The Story of an Hour" for example, might consider whether Mrs. Mallard's ecstatic feeling of relief—produced by the belief that her marriage is over due to the presumed death of her husband—isn't also a rejection of her heterosexual identity. Perhaps her glimpse of future freedom, evoked by feminine images of a newly discovered nature "all aquiver with the new spring life," embraces a repressed new sexual identity that "was too subtle and elusive to name" but that was "approaching to possess her" no matter how much she "was striving to beat it back with her will."

A queer theorist would interrogate any simplistic assumptions about Mrs. Mallard's sexuality. A superficial reading of "The Story of an Hour" might point to the fact that Mrs. Mallard initially displays her grief by embracing a woman, her sister Josephine: "She wept at once, with sudden, wild abandonment, in her sister's arms." One might be tempted to read into this brief gesture a lifetime of latent homosexual longing, especially given the term "wild abandonment." But such a reading is potentially reductive and assumes that sexual desire must be placed in one of two categories (homosexual or heterosexual). Upon closer examination, the evidence for Mrs. Mallard's lesbian tendencies is thin given the fact that she is weeping here rather than experiencing sexual pleasure. Contemporary queer theorists tend to see sexuality and sexual desire as fluid, and sometimes difficult to label. A more nuanced reading might look at Mrs. Mallard's autoerotic identity. Focusing on her body, such a critic would concentrate on the scenes when Mrs. Mallard is alone. She anticipates "something coming to her . . . too subtle and elusive to name . . . creeping out of the sky." On the surface this feeling is merely relief, but a LGBTQ+ critic might focus on her body's reaction to it: "her bosom rose and fell tumultuously . . . a little whispered word escaped her slightly parted lips. . . . Her pulses beat fast, and the coursing blood warmed and relaxed every inch of her body." These descriptions sound unabashedly sexual, and Mrs. Mallard seems to gradually embrace the idea that she can achieve bodily ecstasy when alone: following the quotations above, she throws open her arms, comments on the freedom of her body (as well as her soul), and locks her bedroom door. Her sister desperately calls through the keyhole, alarmed by the clearly transgressive behavior going on inside: "open the door — you will make yourself ill. What are you doing, Louise?" What she is doing is private and clearly involves a feeling of bodily ecstasy. This critic might move in a number of directions from this initial observation — to discuss the effects of a repressive culture, for instance, or to examine the fact that Mrs. Mallard's feeling of freedom can only take place behind a locked door, which is nearly a closet, the central metaphor for the repression of one's natural sexual desires. Gender or sexuality focused readings have opened up provocative discussions of texts that might otherwise seem completely unconcerned with sexual desire.

## MYTHOLOGICAL STRATEGIES

Mythological approaches to literature attempt to identify the elements in a work that create deep universal responses in readers. Whereas psychological critics interpret the symbolic meanings of characters and actions in order to understand more fully the unconscious dimensions of an author's mind, a character's motivation, or a reader's response, *mythological critics* (also frequently referred to as *archetypal critics*) interpret the hopes, fears, and expectations of entire cultures based on the stories they tell and the symbols they employ repeatedly.

In this context myth is not to be understood simply as referring to stories about imaginary gods who perform astonishing feats in the causes of love, jealousy, or hatred. Nor are myths to be judged as merely erroneous, primitive accounts of how nature runs its course and humanity conducts its affairs. Instead, literary critics use myths or archetypes as a strategy for understanding how human beings try to account for their lives in symbolic narratives. Myths can be a window into a culture's deepest perceptions about itself because they attempt to explain what otherwise seems unexplainable: a people's origin, purpose, and destiny.

All human beings have a need to make sense of their lives, whether they are concerned about their natural surroundings, the seasons, sexuality, birth, death, or the very meaning of existence. Myths help people organize their experiences; these systems of belief (less formally held than religious or political tenets but no less important) embody a culture's assumptions and values. What is important to the mythological critic is not the validity or truth of those assumptions and values; what matters is that they reveal common human concerns.

It is not surprising that although the details of mythic stories vary enormously, the essential patterns are often similar because these myths attempt to explain universal experiences. There are, for example, numerous myths that redeem humanity from permanent death through a hero's resurrection or rebirth. The resurrection of Jesus symbolizes for Christians the ultimate defeat of death and coincides with the rebirth of nature's fertility in spring. Features of this rebirth parallel the Greek myths of Adonis and Hyacinth, who die but are subsequently transformed into living flowers; there are also similarities that connect these stories to the reincarnation of the Indian Buddha or the rebirth of the Egyptian Osiris. Important differences exist among these stories, but each reflects a basic human need to limit the power of death and to hope for eternal life.

Mythological critics look for underlying, recurrent patterns in literature that reveal universal meanings and basic human experiences for readers regardless of when or where they live. The characters, images, and themes that symbolically embody these meanings and experiences are called ***archetypes***. This term designates universal symbols that evoke deep and perhaps unconscious responses in a reader because archetypes bring with them hopes and fears that have always defined humanity. Surely one of the most powerfully compelling archetypes is the death and rebirth theme that relates the human life cycle to the cycle of the seasons. Many others could be cited and would be exhausted only after all human concerns were cataloged, but a few examples can suggest some of the range of plots, images, and characters addressed.

Among the most common literary archetypes are stories of quests, initiations, scapegoats, meditative withdrawals, descents to the underworld, and heavenly ascents. These stories are often filled with archetypal images — bodies of water that may symbolize the unconscious or eternity or baptismal rebirth; rising suns, suggesting reawakening and enlightenment; setting suns, pointing toward death; colors such as green, evocative of growth and fertility, or black, indicating chaos, evil, and death. Along the way are earth mothers, fatal women, wise old men, desert places, and paradisal gardens. No doubt your own reading has introduced you to any number of archetypal plots, images, and characters.

Mythological critics attempt to explain how archetypes are embodied in literary works. Employing various disciplines, these critics articulate the power a literary work has over us. Some critics are deeply grounded in classical literature, whereas others are more conversant with philology, anthropology, psychology, folklore, or cultural history. Whatever their emphases, however, mythological critics examine the elements of a work in order to make larger connections that explain the work's lasting appeal.

These kinds of archetypal patterns exist potentially in any literary period. Consider how in Chopin's "The Story of an Hour" Mrs. Mallard's life parallels the end of winter and the earth's renewal in spring. When she feels a surge of new life after grieving over her husband's death, her own sensibilities are closely aligned with the "new spring life" that is "all aquiver" outside her window. Although she initially tries to resist that renewal by "beat[ing] it back with her will," she cannot control the life force that surges within her and all around her. When she finally gives herself to the energy and life she experiences, she feels triumphant — like a "goddess of Victory." But this victory is short lived when she learns that her husband is still alive and with him all the obligations that made her marriage feel like a wasteland. Her death is an ironic version of a rebirth ritual. The coming of spring is an ironic contrast to her own discovery that she can no longer live a repressed, circumscribed life with her husband. Death turns out to be preferable to the living death that her marriage means to her. Although spring will go on, this "goddess of Victory" is defeated by a devastating social contract. The old, corrupt order continues, and that for Chopin is a cruel irony that mythological critics would see as an unnatural disruption of the nature of things.

## READER-RESPONSE STRATEGIES

*Reader-response criticism*, as its name implies, emphasizes the reader's experience more than the work itself. This approach to literature describes what goes on in the reader's mind during the process of reading a text and also the way communities of readers cooperate to advance an interpretation. In a sense, all critical approaches (especially psychological and mythological criticism) concern themselves with a reader's response to literature, but there is a stronger emphasis in reader-response criticism on the reader's active construction of the text's meaning. Although many critical theories inform reader-response criticism, all *reader-response critics* aim to describe the reader's experience of a work. In effect, rather than a reading of the text, we get a reading of the reader who comes to the work with certain expectations and assumptions which are either met or not met. Hence the consciousness of the reader — produced by reading the work — is the subject matter of reader-response critics. Just as writing is a creative act, reading is too, since it also leads to the production of a text (that is, an interpretation).

Reader-response critics do not assume that a literary work is a finished product with fixed formal properties, as, for example, formalist critics do. Instead, the literary work is seen as an evolving creation of readers who process characters, plots, images, and other elements while reading, and also how reading communities (such as your class) are vital in directing the trajectory of interpretation. Some reader-response critics argue that this act of creative reading is, to a degree, controlled by the text, but it can produce many interpretations of the same text by different readers. There is no single definitive reading of a work because the crucial assumption is that readers create rather than discover meanings in texts. Readers who have gone back to works they had read earlier in their lives often find that a later reading draws very different responses from them. What earlier seemed unimportant is now crucial; what at first seemed central is now barely worth noting. The reason, put simply, is that two different people have read the same text. Reader-response critics are not after the "correct" reading of the text or what the author presumably intended; instead they are interested in the reader's experience with the text.

Reader-response criticism calls attention to how we read and to what influences our readings. It does not attempt to define what a literary work means on the page but rather what it does to an informed reader, a reader who understands the language and conventions used in a given work. Reader-response criticism is not a rationale for mistaken or bizarre readings of works but an exploration of the possibilities for a plurality of readings shaped by readers' experiences with the text. This kind of strategy can help us understand how our responses are shaped by both the text and ourselves.

Chopin's "The Story of an Hour" illustrates how reader-response critical strategies read the reader. Chopin doesn't say that Mrs. Mallard's marriage is repressive; instead, that troubling fact dawns on the reader at the same time that the recognition forces its way into Mrs. Mallard's consciousness. Her surprise is also the reader's because although she remains in the midst of intense grief, she is on the threshold of a startling discovery about the new possibilities life offers. How the reader responds to that discovery, however, is not entirely controlled by Chopin. One reader, perhaps someone who has recently lost a spouse, might find Mrs. Mallard's "joy" indeed "monstrous" and selfish. Certainly that's how Mrs. Mallard's doctors — the seemingly authoritative diagnosticians in the story — would very likely read her. But for other readers Mrs. Mallard's feelings require no justification. Such readers might find Chopin's ending to the story more ironic than she seems to have intended because Mrs. Mallard's death could be read as Chopin's inability to envision a protagonist who has the strength of her convictions. In contrast, a reader in 1894 might have seen the ending as Mrs. Mallard's only escape from the repressive marriage her husband's assumed death suddenly allowed her to see. A reader in our times probably would argue that it was the marriage that should have died rather than Mrs. Mallard, that she had other alternatives, not just obligations (as the doctors would have insisted), to consider.

By imagining different readers, we can imagine a variety of responses to the story that are influenced by the readers' own impressions, memories, or experiences with marriage. Such imagining suggests the ways in which reader-response criticism opens up texts to a number of interpretations. A reader-response critic would be interested in the intersections and the divergences between the members of the reading community that is your class. If one of your classmates says something brilliant about a text in class, how might that change you as a reader? If you strongly disagree with another, how might that change you? For a sample reader-response student paper on "The Story of an Hour," see page 21.

## DECONSTRUCTIONIST STRATEGIES

**Deconstructionist critics** insist that literary works do not yield fixed, single, stable meanings. They argue that there can be no absolute knowledge about anything because language is unstable and thus can never establish fixed understandings. Anything we write conveys meanings that can be reframed through different contexts, so the deconstructionist argument goes. Language is not a precise instrument but a power domain whose meanings are caught in an endless web of possibilities that cannot be untangled. Accordingly, any idea or statement that insists on being understood separately can ultimately be "deconstructed" — literally taken apart — to reveal its relations and connections to contradictory and opposite meanings.

Unlike other forms of criticism, ***deconstructionism*** seeks to destabilize meanings instead of establishing them. In contrast to formalists such as the New Critics, who closely examine a work in order to call attention to how its various components interact to establish a unified whole, deconstructionists try to show how a close examination of the language in a text inevitably reveals conflicting, contradictory impulses that break down its apparent unity.

Although deconstructionists and New Critics both examine the language of a text closely, deconstructionists focus on the gaps and ambiguities that reveal a text's instability and indeterminacy, whereas New Critics and other formalists look for patterns that explain how the text's fixed meaning is structured. Deconstructionists painstakingly examine the competing meanings within the text rather than attempting to resolve them into a unified whole.

The questions deconstructionists ask are aimed at discovering and describing how a variety of possible readings are generated by the elements of a text. In contrast to a formalist's concerns about the ultimate meaning of a work, a deconstructionist is primarily interested in how the use of language — diction, tone, metaphor, symbol, and so on — yields only provisional, not definitive, meanings.

Deconstructionists look for ways to question and extend the meanings of a text. A deconstructionist might find, for example, the ironic ending of Chopin's "The Story of an Hour" less tidy and conclusive than would a New Critic, who might attribute Mrs. Mallard's death to her sense of lost personal freedom. A deconstructionist might use the story's ending to suggest that the narrative shares the doctors' inability to imagine a life for Mrs. Mallard apart from her husband. As difficult as it is controversial, deconstructionism is not easily summarized or paraphrased. The final sentence contains a number of phrases that are ambiguous: to whom are the doctors speaking? What does joy kill? Since language itself is unstable, its contradictions are of great interest to deconstructionists who like to examine its slippages and who like to show how the texts it produces are also unstable. Here's a thought that might delight a deconstructionist: how do we know that Mrs. Mallard is dead? Who says so? The story has already proven that Brently Mallard was presumed dead because of a story told by Josephine and Richards; who's to say that Mrs. Mallard is not also alive but only presumed dead because the doctors said so? Why trust them? The story does not end with a dead body, but with another story.

## AFFECT THEORY APPROACHES

One of the more recent schools of critical approaches is known as affect theory. Its concerns are more with emotions, feelings, and the general experiences of the body rather than just the mind. Works of representational art can clearly affect your feelings as you well know if you have ever laughed, cried, or screamed during a movie. ***Affect theorists*** not only examine the way literary works can move readers emotionally, but also consider how the forces within texts that reflect heightened emotional states can frame the way we understand them.

A critic using affect theory might pay attention to the moments in a text in which emotional intensity increases, and again to when it decreases, as though someone is turning the volume up and down while listening to music. One of the ways human beings conceive of themselves as different from other animals is that we have the ability to think, or to reason. But it is also true that we are aware of ourselves as creatures with bodies that are sometimes at odds with our thoughts. When we attend to the way our bodies respond to our environments, we may be challenged to explain our reactions. When we attend to the way bodies respond to environments in literary works, we are opening up the potential to explain something about literature that wouldn't be apparent if we were just concentrating on rational ideas like class struggle, gender identity, the instability of language, or the way metaphors and irony reveal a theme.

It might take a bit of retraining to allow yourself to respond to a work emotionally, or to attend to the way emotions are represented in it. When we're trained to understand and explain a work, we're engaging our rational selves, but emotions fall outside that realm. Emotions are sometimes hard to pin down, and they sometimes circulate unpredictably. By paying attention to feelings — both those represented in texts and those caused by texts — affect theorists hope to open up new spaces for understanding. If you consider fiction and drama in this light, you might begin to see how character is framed in terms of emotions: readers tend to respond — we almost *have to* respond — at a heightened level when a character is in a heightened emotional state. Plot is also governed by regulated emotion: what we call the climax of a story or a play is almost always at the point when emotions are most intense. Modern authors invented the **stream of consciousness** convention to approximate a character's deep, unformed, inner thoughts; however, authors have always rendered experience by concentrating on sensations rather than interior voices.

It might seem that emotions are universal, that they have not changed over time or that they are the same all over the globe. Affect theorists question that idea, sometimes tracing the history of emotions to complicate the notion that the way people feel has been determined by time period, or they might reveal how the expression of emotions differs across the globe. You may be aware that humor is culturally determined: what's funny to an American audience might be just the opposite somewhere else. If you were to read the earliest novels in English, written in the eighteenth century, you would notice a whole lot of swooning, fainting, sighing, and the like. You might conclude either that people expressed emotions more profoundly back then or that authors were especially concerned with highlighting those emotions for a certain effect. Many of these early works were labeled "sentimental" by their critics, but that was their aim: both to represent and to arouse passionately felt experiences. Affect theorists would suggest that all works participate in these strategies, just to varying degrees. On one level, it's how readers *connect to* or *relate to* the works they encounter.

On a different level, it involves an examination of the way the emotional lives of characters are represented in literary texts. This approach to literature pays particular attention to the way emotional sensations are always in flux. We often experience emotions based on our encounters with others, so there is a palpable tension between feelings that are deeply inside individuals and the expression of those feelings that develop in social settings. We often struggle to control our emotions in order to fit into social norms, and when we see characters blush, or laugh at an inappropriate moment, or ball their fists to keep from shouting, we are witnessing an important battle that reveals or complicates a character's identity. Similarly, the speaker of a poem strives to put into language intense and mysterious feelings like love, loneliness, or euphoria. Language is often deemed inadequate: the speaker of T. S. Eliot's "The Love Song of J. Alfred Prufrock" (p. 936) blurts out in frustration, "It is impossible to say just what I mean!" For critics paying attention to affect, this line would be much more important than all the speaker's allusions, similes, and images.

"The Story of an Hour" showcases a good deal of emotion in its short space. When Mrs. Mallard hears of her husband's death, "She wept at once, with sudden, wild abandonment." This so-called storm of grief lasts for an unspecified amount of time, but it's important to notice the phrases "at once" and "sudden," especially after the narrator has told us that Mrs. Mallard "did not hear the story as many women have heard the same, with a paralyzed inability to accept its significance." Her reaction, in short, is immediate, but afterward she calms down, only allowing an occasional sob to well up and shake her. The suddenness of her first reaction gives way to an extended moment of anticipation: "There was something coming to her and she was waiting for it, fearfully." As she waits, her body reacts: "her bosom rose and fell tumultuously." She goes from fear to something like ecstasy as she gives into this new feeling: "Her pulses beat fast, and the coursing blood warmed and relaxed every inch of her body." Her mind has trouble making sense of what she's feeling, and yet her body knows. The radical change she experiences is fascinating to the affect critic who realizes the importance of such varied emotions in determining the complexities of character. When her heart fails at the end, we are in a position to argue critically with the doctors who label her reaction "joy that kills." Given the turbulent roller coaster of emotions she's experienced (if not expressed to others), we know that "joy" is an inadequate word here.

The following lists of questions for the critical approaches covered in this chapter should be useful for discovering arguments you might make about a short story, poem, or play. As we stress above, we are only introducing these fields, and the questions that follow are designed to sharpen your sense of what these critical strategies entail, and also invite you to consider how the "meaning" of a text might look different based on the way you approach it, or the lens through which you view it.

**FORMALIST QUESTIONS**

1. How do various elements of the work — plot, character, point of view, setting, tone, diction, images, symbol, and so on — reinforce its meanings?

2. How are the elements related to the whole?

3. What is the work's major organizing principle? How is its structure unified?

4. What issues does the work raise? How does the work's structure resolve those issues?

**BIOGRAPHICAL QUESTIONS**

1. Are facts about the writer's life relevant to your understanding of the work?

2. Are characters and incidents in the work versions of the writer's own experiences? Are they treated factually or imaginatively?

3. How are the writer's values reflected in the work?

**PSYCHOLOGICAL QUESTIONS**

1. How does the work reflect the author's personal psychology?

2. What do the characters' emotions and behavior reveal about their psychological states? What types of personalities are they?

3. Are psychological matters such as repression, dreams, and desire presented consciously or unconsciously by the author?

**HISTORICAL QUESTIONS**

1. How does the work reflect the period in which it is written?

2. What literary or historical influences helped to shape the form and content of the work?

3. How important is the historical context to interpreting the work?

**MARXIST QUESTIONS**

1. How are class differences presented in the work? Are characters aware or unaware of the economic and social forces that affect their lives?

2. How do economic conditions determine the characters' lives?

3. What ideological values are explicit or implicit?

4. Does the work challenge or affirm the social order it describes?

**NEW HISTORICIST QUESTIONS**

1. What kinds of documents outside the work seem especially relevant for shedding light on the work?

2. How are social values contemporary to the work reflected or refuted in the work?

3. How does your own historical moment affect your reading of the work and its historical reconstruction?

## CULTURAL STUDIES QUESTIONS

1. What does the work reveal about the cultural behavior contemporary to it?
2. How does popular culture contemporary to the work reflect or challenge the values implicit or explicit in the work?
3. What kinds of cultural documents contemporary to the work add to your reading of it?
4. How do your own cultural assumptions affect your reading of the work and the culture contemporary to it?

## GENDER STUDIES QUESTIONS

1. How are the lives of men and women portrayed in the work? Do the men and women in the work accept or reject these roles?
2. Are the form and content of the work influenced by the author's gender?
3. What attitudes are explicit or implicit concerning sexual relationships? Are these relationships sources of conflict? Do they provide resolutions to conflicts?
4. Does the work challenge or affirm traditional ideas about men and women and same-sex relationships?
5. Are gender and/or sexuality presented as fixed or fluid?

## MYTHOLOGICAL QUESTIONS

1. How does the story resemble other stories in plot, character, setting, or use of symbols?
2. Are archetypes presented, such as quests, initiations, scapegoats, or withdrawals and returns?
3. Does the protagonist undergo any kind of transformation such as a movement from innocence to experience that seems archetypal?
4. Do any specific allusions to myths shed light on the text?

## READER-RESPONSE QUESTIONS

1. What is your initial reaction to the work?
2. How do your own experiences and expectations affect your reading and interpretation?
3. What is the work's original or intended audience? To what extent are you similar to or different from that audience?
4. Do you respond in the same way to the work after more than one reading?
5. What kind of interpretive community are you a part of? Is your reading of a text conditioned by the readings offered by your peers, by professional literary critics, by your instructor, and so on?

## DECONSTRUCTIONIST QUESTIONS

1. How are contradictory and opposing meanings expressed in the work?
2. How does meaning break down or deconstruct itself in the language of the text?

3. Would you say that ultimate definitive meanings are impossible to determine and establish in the text? Why? How does that affect your interpretation?

4. How are implicit ideological values revealed in the work?

### AFFECT THEORY QUESTIONS

1. What emotions are expressed overtly in a text, and how fully are they expressed?

2. What feelings are expressed only indirectly, and what is preventing their direct expression (such as social decorum, a speaker or character's fear of vulnerability, etc.)?

3. How does the text attempt to provoke an affective (or emotional) response on the part of the reader?

4. How does an examination of the way feelings are circulated within a text or between a text and a reader enable you to interpret it? What does this inquiry reveal?

These questions will not apply to all texts, and they are not mutually exclusive. They can be combined to explore a text from several critical perspectives or contexts simultaneously. A feminist approach to Kate Chopin's "The Story of an Hour" could also use Marxist concerns about class to make observations about the oppression of women's lives in the historical context of the nineteenth century. Your use of these questions should allow you to discover significant issues from which you can develop an argumentative essay that is organized around clearly defined terms, relevant evidence, and a persuasive analysis in response to your instructor's directions.

# 43

# Writing about Literature

Anthony Barboza/Archive
Photos/Getty Images.

Writing permits me to experience life as
any number of strange creations.
— ALICE WALKER

There's no question about it: writing about literature is a different experience
than reading it. Reading, as you no doubt realize by now, is not a passive activity, and yet when we pick up a book, it does feel that someone else has done the
hard labor and we're enjoying the fruits of it. Writing is, of course, work, but it
is also a pleasure when it goes well — when ideas feel solid and the writing is
fluid. You can experience that pleasure as well if you approach writing as an
intellectual and emotional opportunity rather than a chore. When Alice Walker
speaks of "strange creations," she's referring to possibilities. Writing allows her
to reframe reality, sensation, and perception. This idea does not apply only to
fiction, poetry, and drama. The writing you will complete in response to the
works in this book also has the capacity to liberate your mind and to demonstrate your intellectual power.

Just as reading literature requires an imaginative, conscious response,
so does writing about literature. Composing an essay is not just recording
your interpretive response to a work because the act of writing can change
your response as you explore, clarify, and discover relationships you hadn't

previously considered or recognized. Most writers discover new ideas and connections as they move through the process of rereading and annotating the text, taking notes, generating ideas, developing a thesis, and organizing an argumentative essay. (These activities are detailed later in this chapter.) To become more conscious of the writing process, first consider the ideas we articulate in the sections below, then study the following questions specifically aimed at sharpening your ability to interpret literature. Finally, examine the case studies of students' papers that take you through writing a first response to reading, brainstorming for a paper topic, writing a first draft, revising, and writing the final paper.

## WHY AM I BEING ASKED TO DO THIS?

The vast majority of college literature courses require that students write formal essays about the literature they study. You might be wondering why you are being asked to write about literature. You might be in awe of the writers you have read, and you think there is no point trying to write like they do because they are professionals with abundant gifts and talents. Why not allow stories, poems, and plays to speak for themselves? Isn't it presumptuous to interpret famous writers like Alice Munro, Emily Dickinson, or William Shakespeare? These writers do, of course, speak for themselves, but they do so indirectly. Literary criticism seeks not to replace the text by explaining it but to enhance our readings of works by calling attention to elements that we might have overlooked or only vaguely sensed.

Your instructor probably isn't asking you to write *like* the authors in this book (although an imitation exercise might be a valuable means to understanding an author's technique), but rather to write *about* them, or, put succinctly, to interpret their work. The questions that follow most of the selections in this anthology are designed to initiate this type of interpretation, and your class discussions extend and complicate such individual interpretations. A formal essay gives you the chance to develop a yet more sophisticated interpretation and to revise it so that it becomes full and persuasive. Through this process you will work toward mastery of a skill. You'll improve your ability to analyze works of literature and to develop a critical argument that showcases your analysis. But you will also increase your confidence as someone who can communicate clearly and think critically. Those broader competencies will invariably serve you well in social contexts, in your career, and in your quest to become a more impressive human. (Note that the study of literature is part of an academic branch called the *humanities*.)

Composition and rhetoric is a subfield of English that studies the type of writing you may be asked to complete in this course. It is a vast field, and since there have been so many people working in it for so long, there are bound to be disagreements about the best way to teach students to write. You have probably noticed that your teachers from an early age right up through your professors in college have laid down rules that might seem to contradict each other. If your eighth-grade teacher forbade you to use "I" in your formal essays and warned that he would take ten points off your grade if you did so, what do you do in college when your professor encourages you to use "I"? One of your teachers taught you how to perfect the five-paragraph essay, and the other asked you in a comment why your essay was only five paragraphs long when you clearly had more to say, especially in paragraph three which was three pages long and contained four paragraphs' worth of ideas. It might be tempting to throw up your hands and conclude that academic writing is arbitrary, but a critical thinker might instead conclude that writing is a situational activity, dependent on a series of codes that is always shifting. Your teacher who hammered home the virtues of a five-paragraph essay might have been preparing you to develop into a writer who would realize when five paragraphs were too few, or too many, for the task at hand. Think about the various conventions that shape the writing you already do on a daily basis. What if all of your text messages were as long and as stiff-sounding as the essay you wrote to get into college? (Conversely, where would you be if your college essay resembled any one of your texts?) Strong writers adapt to the various demands of their various audiences. There are a set of conventions for e-mails and office memos and another set of conventions for formal essays assigned in your literature class. This chapter will offer some broad outlines about those conventions, but it can only do so much. Your instructors will invariably want something specific from your writing that we can't anticipate here, and your instructors are your most important audience because they are poised to give you feedback designed to improve your writing.

That last point is crucial. Rhetoric and composition instructors may not agree on all methods instructors use to teach writing, but they all agree on this point: the only way to improve as a writer is to write, to receive feedback on that writing, and to write more, absorbing that feedback while accepting ever more challenging writing assignments. All writers receive feedback, even the ones represented in this book who you might consider to be literary geniuses. Their work is a form of art, but that doesn't mean they weren't subjected to a lengthy editorial process, or that they didn't show an early draft to a spouse or friend before going public with it. The same might be true for you if you end up in a business setting; you might hear from your boss, "Thanks for the info, Jones, but your e-mails are way too long: cut them in half or no one's going to read them." In this class the feedback you receive from your instructor might critique your writing on multiple levels, from comma usage to the organization of your entire essay. All of this feedback is designed not simply to "correct" your writing, but to help you develop your strength and flexibility as a writer. Writing about literature is a particularly good workout because you are responding to literature, the most sophisticated form of language. The acts of reading and interpreting literature encourage you to pay especially careful attention to the way language works, to its patterns, to its possibilities. Your own writing will invariably improve as you immerse yourself in it.

# FROM READING AND DISCUSSION TO WRITING

Introductory literature courses typically include three components — reading, discussion, and writing. Students usually find the readings a pleasure, the class discussions a revelation, and the writing assignments — at least initially — a little intimidating. Writing an analysis of the contrast between darkness and light in James Baldwin's "Sonny's Blues" (p. 91), for example, may seem considerably more daunting than making a case for animal rights or analyzing a campus newspaper editorial that debates the legalization of marijuana. Literary topics are not, however, all that different from the kinds of papers assigned in standard composition courses; many of the same skills are required for both. Regardless of the type of paper you're composing, you must eventually develop a structured argument with a clear thesis and support it with evidence in language that is clear and persuasive. Note the word *eventually*. Writing is a process, sometimes a long and messy one, and with practice you will develop effective strategies to produce drafts that will *eventually* lead to a polished, organized essay. More than anything, writing requires patience and faith in the process.

Whether the subject matter is a marketing survey, a political issue, or a literary work, writing is a method of communicating information and perceptions. Writing teaches. But before writing becomes an instrument for informing the reader, it serves as a means of learning for the writer. An essay is a process of discovery as well as a record of what has been discovered. One of the chief benefits of writing is that we frequently realize what we want to say only after trying out ideas on a page and seeing our thoughts take shape in language.

In terms of the assignments you will complete for this course, writing about a literary work encourages us to be better readers because it requires a close examination of the elements of a short story, poem, or play. To determine how plot, character, setting, point of view, metaphor, tone, irony, or any number of other literary elements function in a work, we must study them in relation to one another as well as separately. Speed-reading won't do. To read a text accurately and validly — neither ignoring nor distorting significant details — we must return to the work repeatedly to test our responses and interpretations. By paying attention to details and being sensitive to the author's use of language, we develop a clearer understanding of how the work conveys its effects and meanings, and we become literary critics.

Due to the connotations of the word *critical*, a common misunderstanding about the purpose of literary criticism is that it restricts itself to finding faults in a work. Although a critical essay may point out limitations and flaws, most criticism — and certainly the kind of essay usually written in an introductory literature course — is designed to explain, analyze, and reveal the complexities of a work. Such sensitive consideration increases our appreciation of the writer's achievement and significantly adds to our enjoyment of a short story, poem, or play. In short, the purpose and value of writing about literature are that doing so leads to greater understanding and pleasure.

# READING THE WORK CLOSELY

The more familiar you are with how the various elements of the text convey effects and meanings, the more confident you will be explaining your approach to it. Know the piece of literature you are writing about before you begin your essay. Think about how you respond to the work and how it is put together. Relax and enjoy yourself; you can be attentive and still allow the author's words to work their magic on you. With subsequent readings, go more slowly and analytically as you try to establish relations between characters, actions, images, or whatever else seems important. Ask yourself why you respond as you do. Think as you read and notice how the parts of a work contribute to its overall nature. Whether the work is a short story, poem, or play, you will read relevant portions of it over and over, and you will very likely find more to discuss with each rereading if the work is rich.

It's best to avoid reading other critical discussions of a work before you are thoroughly familiar with it. There are several good reasons for following this advice. By reading interpretations before you know a work, you deny yourself the pleasure of discovery. That would be like reading a review of a movie complete with spoilers before watching the movie. But perhaps even more important than protecting the surprise and delight that a work might offer is that a premature reading of a critical discussion will probably short-circuit your own responses. You will see the work through another critic's eyes and will have to struggle with someone else's perceptions and ideas before you can develop your own.

Reading criticism can be useful, but not until you have thought through your own impressions of the text. A guide should not be permitted to become a tyrant. This does not mean, however, that you should avoid background information about a work — for example, knowing that Charlie Parker was an extremely influential and highly regarded jazz musician who died young of a drug overdose is important contextual information for understanding Baldwin's story "Sonny's Blues" (p. 91). When you come across Parker's name in the story and realize that he was an actual person as opposed to a fictional character, you would be wise to Google it so that you grasp that context. Knowing something about the author as well as historic and literary contexts can help to create expectations that enhance your reading, and the headnotes that precede most of our selections help to provide a little of that information. That type of research is very different from looking up summaries on websites like Sparknotes or Shmoop. Those sites tend to do too much of the hard interpretive work for you, and there's no guarantee that their interpretations are better than yours would be, or that they are valid.

You will develop good writing habits over time, and/or you will improve on the good ones you have already developed. Regardless of your specific composition methods, there are three basic phases of the process to understand: *prewriting, writing,* and *revising.* There is not necessarily a clean break between these phases, though: you might find yourself revising even as you prewrite, for example, or writing more after you've revised your first draft. In general, though, there are distinct principles for these three stages that you should keep in mind as you approach your paper as a series of drafts. What we offer below are some tried-and-true methods: you may have developed others that work better for you, or your instructor might have more specific guidance, but these are also available.

## PREWRITING

### *Annotating the Text and Journal Note Taking*

We emphasize the value of critical reading above, and this type of reading is intertwined with prewriting. As you read, get in the habit of annotating your texts. Whether you write marginal notes, highlight, underline, or draw boxes and circles around important words and phrases, you'll eventually develop a system that allows you to retrieve significant ideas and elements from the text. Another way to record your impressions of a work — as with any other experience — is to keep a journal. By writing down your reactions to characters, images, language, actions, and other matters in a reading journal, you can often determine why you like or dislike a work or feel sympathetic or antagonistic to an author. You might also discover paths into a work that might have eluded you if you hadn't preserved your impressions. Your journal notes and annotations may take whatever form you find useful; full sentences and grammatical correctness are not essential (unless your instructor deems them important and requires that you hand them in), though fuller thoughts might allow you to make better sense of your own reflections than incomplete thoughts might. The point is simply to put in writing ideas that you can retrieve when you need them for class discussion or a writing assignment. Far from making extra work, this process saves you considerable time when you get to the writing phase.

Taking notes will preserve your initial reactions to the work. First impressions are often valid. Your response to a peculiar character in a story, a striking phrase in a poem, or a subtle bit of stage business in a play might lead to larger perceptions. The student paper on John Updike's "A & P" (p. 1443) later in this chapter, for example, began with the student writing "how come?" next to the story's title in her textbook. She thought it strange that the title didn't refer to a character or to the story's conflict. That brief annotated response eventually led her to examine the significance of the setting, which became the central focus of her paper.

Prewriting activities should not interfere with your initial encounter with a text, though. You would do well to keep your pen tucked behind your ear as you first read a text so that you can get a sense of its unique characteristics, its concerns, its possible meaning, or its pleasures and delights. You should take detailed notes only after you've read through the work. If you write too many notes during the first reading, you're likely to disrupt your response. Moreover, until you have a sense of the entire work, it will be difficult to determine how connections can be made among its various elements. In addition to recording your first impressions and noting significant passages, characters, actions, and so on, you should consult the Questions for Responsive Reading and Writing about Fiction (p. 1438), Poetry (p. 1445), and Drama (p. 1456). These questions can assist you in getting inside a work as well as organizing your notes.

Inevitably, you will take more notes than you finally use in the paper. Note taking is a form of thinking aloud, but because your ideas are on paper (or on a laptop, phone, or tablet), you don't have to worry about forgetting them. As you develop a better sense of a potential topic, your notes will become more focused and detailed.

## Choosing a Topic

If your instructor assigns a topic or list of approved topics, some of your work is already completed. Instead of being asked to come up with a topic about *Oedipus the King* (p. 1001), you may be asked to write a three-page essay that specifically discusses whether Oedipus's downfall is a result of fate or foolish pride. If that is the case, you also have the assurance that a specified topic will be manageable within the suggested number of pages. Unless you ask your instructor for permission to write on a different topic, be certain to address yourself to the assignment. There is room even in an assigned topic to develop your own approach. Assigned topics do not relieve you of thinking about an aspect of a work, but they do focus your thinking.

Other assignments might be left open so that you can engage your particular point of view more thoroughly. Before you start considering a topic, you should have a sense of how long the paper will be because the assigned length can help to determine the extent to which you should develop your topic. Ideally, the paper's length should be based on how much space you deem necessary to present your discussion clearly and convincingly, but if you have any doubts and no specific guidelines have been indicated, ask. The question is important; a topic that might be appropriate for a three-page paper could be too narrow for ten pages. Three pages would probably be adequate for a discussion of the role of the movies in Ralph Ellison's "King of the Bingo Game" (p. 178). Conversely, it would be futile to try to summarize Ellison's views on fate and choice throughout his fiction in even ten pages; this topic would have to be narrowed to focus on this specific story, for starters.

Once you have a firm sense of the scope of what you are expected to write, you can begin to decide on your topic. If you have a choice, it's generally best to write about a topic that you feel strongly about. If you're not fascinated by the rebellious act of tearing wallpaper off a wall in Gilman's "The Yellow Wallpaper" (p. 126), then perhaps you're more attuned to the murderous revenge that fuels Andre Dubus's "Killings" (p. 58), or maybe you can try to explain why the act of destroying a room's décor is so boring to you as an act of defiance. Choose a work that has moved you so that you have something to say about it. The student who wrote "John Updike's 'A & P' as a State of Mind" (p. 1443) was initially attracted to the story's title because she had once worked in a similar store. After reading the story, she became fascinated with its setting because Updike's descriptions seemed so accurate. Her paper then grew out of her curiosity about the setting's purpose. When a writer is engaged in a topic, the paper has a better chance of being interesting to a reader.

After you have settled on a particular work, your notes and annotations of the text should prove useful for generating a topic. The paper on "A & P" developed naturally from the notes the student jotted down about the setting and antagonist. You are likely to find when you review your notes that your thoughts have clustered into one or more topics. Perhaps there are patterns of imagery that seem to make a point about life. There may be scenes that are ironically paired or secondary characters who reveal certain qualities about the protagonist. Your notes and annotations on such aspects can lead you to a particular effect or impression. Having chuckled your way through "A & P," you may discover that your notations about the story's humor point to a serious satire of society's values.

### More Focused Prewriting

When you are satisfied that you have something interesting to say about a work and that your notes have led you to a focused topic, you are moving in the direction of formulating a **thesis statement**, the central idea of the paper. Whereas the topic indicates what the paper focuses on (the setting in "A & P"), the thesis explains what you have to say about the topic (because the intolerant setting of "A & P" is the antagonist in the story, it is crucial to our understanding of Sammy's decision to quit his job). The thesis is a statement that will fully emerge in the revision stage of your drafting process rather than during prewriting, but you should be aware during prewriting that you are eventually moving in the direction of an *argument*, which is the formal, structured analysis you are building; the thesis is the argument's distilled statement.

An intermediate step between deciding on a topic and formulating a thesis statement is to generate a *working thesis* that will direct your thinking. One simple first step to generate a working thesis about a literary work is to ask the question "why?" Why do these images appear in this particular order in the poem? Why do the main characters in Wilde's *The Importance of Being Earnest* (p. 1148) lie so much? Why does Hemingway choose the Midwest as the setting of "Soldier's Home" (p. 115)? Your responses to these kinds of questions can lead to a working thesis.

Writers sometimes use *freewriting* to help themselves explore possible answers to such questions. It can be an effective way of generating ideas. Freewriting is nonstop writing without concern for mechanics or editing of any kind. (The equivalent in fiction is *stream of consciousness*.) Freewriting for ten minutes or so on a question will result in fragments and repetitions, but it can also produce some ideas. A freewriting sentence that a student writer might generate in response to Updike's "A & P" could look like this: "Sammy's job like mine at the Cheesecake Factory both of us wear stupid uniforms and have to deal with obnoxious customers and incompetent bosses but he doesn't get to move around like I do." There's not much in that sentence that would end up in a final draft, especially the personal connection to the character in the story, but the writer is beginning to think about elements of the story that might be relevant: Sammy's uniform and lack of mobility could become important points for analysis.

## ARGUING ABOUT LITERATURE

Most writing assignments in a literature course require you to persuade readers that your thesis is reasonable and to support it with evidence. In developing a thesis, you are expected not merely to present information but to argue an interpretive point. An argumentative essay is your interpretation of a work arranged in a persuasive way. Arguing about literature doesn't mean that you're engaged in an angry, antagonistic dispute (though controversial topics do sometimes engender heated debates). Instead, argumentation requires that you present your interpretation of a work (or an aspect of it) by supporting your discussion with clearly defined terms, ample evidence, and a detailed analysis of relevant portions of the text.

If your essay is to be interesting and convincing, it is important that you write it from a strong point of view that persuasively argues your evaluation, analysis, and interpretation of a work. Although your response to a text might set you in motion, it is not enough to say that you like or dislike a work; instead, you must push beyond that response and give your reader some ideas and evidence that can be accepted or rejected based on the quality of the answers to the questions you raise.

One way to come up with persuasive answers is to generate good questions that will lead you further into the text and to critical issues related to it. Notice how the Perspectives and Cultural Case Studies in this anthology raise significant questions and issues about texts from a variety of points of view, or contexts. Moreover, the Critical Strategies for Reading summarized in Chapter 42 can be a resource for raising questions that can be shaped into an argument.

## WRITING

### *Writing a First Draft*

Writing is a process, as we have said, but it is not the same process for every writer. You may be the type of writer who needs a formal outline with headings and subheadings before you can begin a draft, or you may find such methods constraining. Whether you have started with freewriting, outlining, or some other prewriting method, you should have some sense of how your paper will be organized — or at least, what you need to cover — as you write your first draft. The working thesis you generate during prewriting, even if it is still somewhat tentative, should help you decide what information will need to be included and provide you with a sense of direction.

At this stage it is crucial to be flexible rather than to adhere too closely to whatever methods you used during the prewriting stage. By using the first draft as a means of thinking about what you want to say, you will very likely discover more than your notes originally suggested. Once again, writing is a process, and computers have made it easy to generate words without making a lifetime commitment to them. You do not need to get bogged down with sentence-level perfection at this early stage. Concentrate on what you are saying. Good writing most often occurs when you are in hot pursuit of an idea rather than in a nervous search for errors. You can improve on each draft paragraph by paragraph, sentence by sentence, and even word by word, but at this stage you should give yourself permission to generate the raw material you will eventually shape into something coherent and eloquent.

Once you have a first draft on your computer, you can delete material that is unrelated to your working thesis and add material necessary to illustrate your points and make your paper convincing. (Some writers find it useful to create a separate file of deleted items that they may want to resurrect at a later stage.) The student who wrote "John Updike's 'A & P' as a State of Mind" (p. 1443) wisely dropped a paragraph that questioned whether Sammy displays chauvinistic attitudes toward women. Although this is an interesting issue, it has nothing to do with her argument and eventual thesis, which explains how the setting influences Sammy's decision to quit his job. Instead of including that paragraph, she added one that described Lengel's crabbed response to the girls so that she could lead up to the A & P "policy" he enforces.

### Textual Evidence: Using Quotations, Summarizing, and Paraphrasing

We have been referring to your essay as an "argument," and we have tried to make it clear that you are not necessarily disagreeing with someone's interpretation. You might think of your role more as building a courtroom case. In order to do so, you have to stick to provable facts, or evidence. Each academic discipline approaches evidence slightly differently, but all of them require it. In your chemistry class, evidence might take the form of the results of lab work; in history, you might have to produce a primary document to argue, for instance, that a certain party was responsible for catalyzing a certain war. In the study of literature, the hardest evidence you have access to is a direct quotation from the text. Examining the language of a text is the best way to show that you are immersed in it, and that you are willing to look at it closely.

And yet, there are times when you might find it useful to broadly summarize a work of literature, or even to paraphrase segments of it. As an analogy, imagine a work of literature as a forest. Think of how different that forest would appear if you were (1) flying over it in a helicopter, or (2) strolling through it, or (3) kneeling down with a magnifying glass to examine an ant colony in a rotting stump. The third encounter with the forest provides the most substantial evidence, like the quotation from a work of literature, but you are not in a position to describe the entire forest from that vantage point. You want to develop a sense of when each perspective might be most useful.

As you introduce the primary text you are analyzing, you would do well to provide a bit of summary to orient the reader — the helicopter perspective in our analogy above. It might be jarring to provide direct evidence in the form of a quotation without any summary. Imagine a paper that starts like this: "Sammy says, 'She had sort of oaky hair that the sun and salt had bleached.' " That might be useful information to the author's argument, but the reader is likely to wonder, for starters, "Who is Sammy?" It might be more advantageous to think about an accurate summary of the story that also introduces your topic, like this sentence: "John Updike's 'A & P' is a story about Sammy, a teenaged grocery store clerk who is so upset by the way his boss treats three female customers that he quits his job." That's an accurate summary of the story's main plot, but it may or may not be detailed enough for your purposes. Do you need Sammy's boss's name in this summary? The age of the three female customers is not specified; should it be? Do we need to know that it is a story written from the first-person point of view? Does the fact that Sammy is keenly aware of class differences between himself and "Queenie" and the other girls matter enough to mention it in the summary?

These questions are a way of pointing out that summaries actually involve interpretation. If you and your classmates were all to summarize any work of literature you have read this semester, even if all of them are technically accurate and factual, what chance would there be that any two of them would be worded exactly the same way? Think of a summary, then, as a necessary way to frame your analysis, but also as an opportunity to begin to focus in on your perspective or context. Let's say you're writing about gender discrimination in "A & P." Your one-sentence summary might look like this: "John Updike's 'A & P' is the story of three teenaged girls who are shamed by a grocery store manager for dressing in a supposedly inappropriate manner." This is also an accurate summary of the story, and Sammy is nowhere in sight. He will probably become part of the author's argument, but this author's initial focus is clearly on the way the girls are treated rather than on Sammy's reaction to that treatment. When you summarize, you are making decisions, sometimes unconsciously, about how you have read and understood a text. You will gradually develop a sense of how much summary you need to make your point. We can distinguish between necessary and unnecessary summary in the abstract, but there is no firm rule dividing these categories. The examples above are one-sentence summaries. Depending on the length of your essay, the difficulty and length of the text under consideration, and a number of other factors, you might decide you need a fuller summary to situate the reader. Imagine that reader as someone who is familiar with the work you are writing about, but who needs a little reminder about it. That reader is not in your head, but he or she is also not someone who has never read a work of literature: you probably wouldn't need to say, "John Updike was an author (which is a name for someone who writes for a living) of a short story (which is a literary prose genre of imaginative writing that combines such elements as character, plot, theme, and imagery to form a certain effect on the reader) titled 'A & P' about Sammy (which is a nickname for Samuel . . .)." We're being a little facetious here, but hopefully you get the point: a summary can swell or shrink according to your needs. You are the author, and you are in control of its level of detail. Just make sure it is accurate: if you were to say, "John Updike's 'A & P' is a story set in Malaysia in the 1980s," you would be writing fiction rather than summarizing it.

Paraphrase is related to summary, but it tends to be more narrowly focused. The common understanding of paraphrasing is restatement, usually concise restatement. You'll want to make sure to paraphrase in a way that is both accurate and that does not risk triteness. Take Hamlet's famous "To be, or not to be" soliloquy. You could paraphrase it this way: "Hamlet is basically saying, 'You only live once, so go for it.' " To do so would be to significantly cheapen one of the more nuanced speeches in literature, though, and to reduce it to a pair of clichés. Like summary, paraphrase is an opportunity to interpret and frame a segment of the literary work you are analyzing. This segment might be important to your essay, but you might not need to spend as much time on it as you would spend on the passages, lines, or sentences that are really crucial to your argument. That's where the analysis of direct quotations comes in.

Quotations can be a valuable means of marshaling evidence to illustrate and support your ideas. A strategic use of quoted material will make your points clearer and more convincing. A key component to the use of direct quotation, though, is that you are charged with *working with* the language of the text. Some developing writers assume that placing a quotation in an essay is the final step, but it's really the first step. You can't expect these quotations to speak for themselves: again, you are in the business of interpreting them. You might even have to break down a quotation into smaller units, calling attention to individual words or phrases in order to look at them carefully. Imagine the essay we describe above in which the author is writing about gender discrimination in Updike's "A & P." The author might say, "A significant sentence is this one: 'Queenie's blush is no sunburn now, and the plump one in plaid, that I liked better from the back — a really sweet can — pipes up, 'We weren't doing any shopping.' " If the author moves on to the next point from there and leaves it at "significant," the reader is likely to ask, "What's significant about it?" Imagine the analysis that could and should follow this incorporated quotation, something like this: "It is important to note not only that Sammy is focused on the girls' bodies, from Queenie's blush to what he deems the most attractive features of the nameless 'plump one in plaid,' but also that he is as guilty as Lengel is of treating them like objects. The rear end of the 'plump one' becomes a commodity like anything else in the grocery store, a crassly described 'can.' In this way Sammy demonstrates how conditioned he has become by the materialistic sexist society he lives in." The quotation only becomes evidence when it is closely examined.

Here are some guidelines that should help you incorporate quotations effectively.

1. It is possible for you to include quotations at the beginning or the end of a paragraph, but we would recommend that you attempt to include them in the middle of a paragraph. The basic reason is that each paragraph is an idea-unit that helps you to further your argument; therefore, it's best to have your voice at the beginning and end of each paragraph. This method allows you to introduce the point you are making or claim you are stating, then to include the quotation in order to illustrate that point, and finally to interpret the language of the quotation as we demonstrate above.

2. Brief quotations (four lines or fewer of prose or three lines or fewer of poetry) should be carefully introduced and integrated into the text of your paper with quotation marks around them:

> According to the narrator, Bertha "had a reputation for strictness." He tells us that she always "wore dark clothes, dressed her hair simply, and expected contrition and obedience from her pupils."

For brief poetry quotations, use a slash to indicate a division between lines:

> The concluding lines of Blake's "The Tyger" pose a disturbing question: "What immortal hand or eye / Dare frame thy fearful symmetry?"

Lengthy quotations should be separated from the text of your paper. More than three lines of poetry or more than four lines of prose should be double spaced and indented one inch from the left margin, with the right margin the same as for the text. If you are quoting something of this length (called "block quotation format"), do not use quotation marks for the passage; the indentation indicates that the passage is a quotation. Lengthy quotations should not be used in place of your own writing. Use them only if an extended reproduction of the work's language is absolutely necessary.

3. If any words are added to a quotation, use brackets to distinguish your addition from the original source:

"He [Young Goodman Brown] is portrayed as self-righteous and disillusioned."

Any words inside quotation marks and not in brackets must be precisely those of the author.

Brackets can also be used to change the grammatical structure of a quotation so that it fits into your sentence:

Smith argues that Chekhov "present[s] the narrator in an ambivalent light."

If you drop any words from the source, use ellipses to indicate the omission:

"Early to bed . . . makes a man healthy, wealthy, and wise."

Use a single line of spaced periods to indicate the omission of a line or more of poetry or more than one paragraph of prose:

Nothing would sleep in that cellar, dank as a ditch,

Bulbs broke out of boxes hunting for chinks in the dark,

. . . . . . . . . . . . . . . . . . . . . . . .

Nothing would give up life:

Even the dirt kept breathing a small breath.

4. You will be able to punctuate quoted material accurately and confidently if you observe these conventions.

Place commas and periods inside quotation marks:

"Even the dirt," Roethke insists, "kept breathing a small breath."

Even though a comma does not appear after "dirt" in the original quotation, it is placed inside the quotation mark. The exception to this rule occurs when a parenthetical reference to a source follows the quotation:

"Even the dirt," Roethke insists, "kept breathing a small breath" (11).

Punctuation marks other than commas or periods go outside the quotation marks unless they are part of the material quoted:

What does Roethke mean when he writes that "the dirt kept breathing a small breath"?

Yeats asked, "How can we know the dancer from the dance?"

In the first quotation, there is no question mark in Roethke's original poem; in the second quotation, there is a question mark in Yeats's poem.

There is no formula about when to summarize, paraphrase, or analyze direct quotations as evidence. All three methods, though, are ways to demonstrate your engagement with the primary text. The body of your argument is based on this engagement. Consider these methods as different tools in your toolbox, each of which is designed for a different job. With practice, you'll develop a sense of proportion that will become almost instinctive, but as you start out it is good to be aware of everything you can use and to be conscious of your decisions. Feedback from readers is one of the best ways to fine-tune those decisions.

### Writing the Introduction and Conclusion

After you have clearly and adequately developed the body of your paper, pay particular attention to the introductory and concluding paragraphs. It's not a bad idea to write the introduction — at least the final version of it — last, after you know precisely what you are introducing, though some writers are not comfortable composing their argument until they have an introduction in place. Regardless of when you write your introductory paragraph during the writing progress, be aware of the special status of the introduction and the conclusion. Because the introductory paragraph is crucial for generating interest in the topic, it should engage the reader and provide a sense of what the paper is about. There is no formula for writing effective introductory paragraphs because each writing situation is different — depending on the audience, topic, and approach — but if you pay attention to the introductions of the essays you read (including the student examples throughout this book), you will notice the way introductions provide focus. The introductory paragraph to "John Updike's 'A & P' as a State of Mind" (p. 1443), for example, is a straightforward explanation of why the story's setting is important for understanding Updike's treatment of the antagonist. The rest of the paper then offers evidence to support this point.

The general expectation for an academic analytical essay is that the *thesis statement* will make its appearance at the end of the introductory paragraph. We mentioned the working thesis earlier when we discussed prewriting. Through the writing process it will evolve into the thesis statement, which is the aspect of your paper that will be scrutinized the most, and yet less experienced writers are often confused about what it is. As you move toward completing your first full draft, scrutinize your working thesis carefully and work patiently to make sure it covers the breadth of your argument. There are many burdens on the thesis: it should be a complete sentence (though sometimes it may require more than one sentence) that establishes your interpretation of a text in clear, unambiguous language. It is more than a statement of your topic: it also involves your approach to that topic, the interpretation that emerges from that approach, and the *conclusion* to your argument. We'll restate that point because it's crucial, and because it might seem paradoxical: *even though it appears in your introduction, the thesis is a kind of conclusion.* Many readers lose patience with a statement like this one in place of a true thesis: "In this paper I will examine Wilde's use of puns in *The Importance of Being Earnest.*" That is the promise of a thesis: stay tuned for my thesis, which will show up at some point over the next five pages! Your reader will invariably reply, "What did you learn when you examined that text?" The answer to that question is closer to your true thesis, which might look like this: "Puns in *The Importance of Being Earnest*, far more than a cheap form of humor, intensify the play's concerns with the instability of identity and the hypocritical nature of many revered social conventions." Now we know where we're going. The thesis may be revised as you get further into the topic and discover what you want to say about it, but once the thesis is established, it will serve as a guide for you and your reader.

Concluding paragraphs also demand special attention because they leave the reader with a final impression of the author's confidence, authority, and intellectual passion. The conclusion should provide a sense of closure instead of starting a new topic or ending abruptly. In the final paragraph about the significance of the setting in "A & P," the student brings together the reasons Sammy quit his job by referring to his refusal to accept Lengel's store policies. Simultaneously, she also explains the significance of Sammy ringing up the "No Sale" mentioned in her introductory paragraph. Thus, we are brought back to where we began, but we now have a greater understanding of why Sammy quits his job. Though they have something in common, the introduction and conclusion of a paper are not exactly the same: the conclusion reflects the journey that has taken place between them. Of course, the body of your paper is the substance of your presentation, but first and last impressions have a powerful impact on readers.

## REVISING AND EDITING

College students are sometimes known for procrastination and other, shall we say, emerging time management skills, but we urge you to be kind to yourself (and to your instructor) by following a drafting schedule that is not so hectic. Put some distance — a day or so if you can — between yourself and each draft of your paper. The phrase that seemed just right on Wednesday may appear all wrong on Friday. You'll have a better chance of detecting lumbering sentences and thin paragraphs if you plan ahead and give yourself the time to read your paper from a fresh perspective. Through the process of revision, you can transform a competent paper into an excellent one.

Begin by asking yourself if your approach to the topic requires any rethinking. One strategy is to identify the most interesting point in your essay. (If you can't find an interesting point, you have some work to do.) One of the most common issues for writers at your stage of development is not believing in your ability to generate a good, original idea. The consequence of this circumstance is usually that the writer begins to say something interesting, then immediately pulls back, like checking your swing in baseball. Readers would rather see you follow through with those ideas or develop them by delving deeper into the text. There is always room for development, and you would do well to create space for that development by deleting the parts of the argument that are not relevant to the thesis. This is often the most difficult aspect of writing, especially if you are overly focused on the number of words or pages specified in the assignment. You are likely to want to hold onto the words you have generated, but if they are not the best words to develop your thesis, they are not as valuable as you imagine them to be. Now that you have a draft in place, though, you have more freedom to concentrate on developing the important ideas and diminishing the parts of your paper that might be weighing it down.

If your thesis fails to capture what you've identified as the most interesting point in your paper, you should see an opportunity to revise. It is possible to revise your paper in order to conform to your uninteresting thesis, but it is preferable (and ultimately easier) to change your thesis to accommodate the paper's most important analysis. The thesis is meant to be malleable. Recall that we emphasized the word *eventually* when we introduced the idea of the thesis above. Your entire paper will change with each draft, and your thesis is especially susceptible to change.

The following checklist offers questions to ask about your paper as you revise and edit it. Most of these questions will be familiar to you; however, if you need help with any of them, ask your instructor for guidance.

---

### Questions for Writing: A Revision Checklist

1. Is the topic manageable? Is it too narrow or too broad?

2. Is the thesis clear? Is it based on a careful reading of the work and on your smartest, most passionate idea in response to that work?

3. Is the paper logically organized? Does it have a firm sense of direction?

4. Is your argument persuasive? Could anyone dispute it? (Note that if an argument is *completely* indisputable, that might mean that you aren't really saying anything interpretive.)

5. Should any material be deleted? Do any important points require further illustration or evidence?

6. Does the opening paragraph introduce the topic in an interesting manner indicating a context or critical framework that leads to your thesis?

7. Is each paragraph developed, unified, and coherent? Are any notably short or long? If so, do they truly represent a single idea-unit or should they be broken up and/or combined with the paragraphs around them?

8. Are there transitions linking the paragraphs? (This question is directly related to question #3 about organization.)

9. Does the concluding paragraph provide a sense of closure?

10. Is the tone appropriate for an academic essay? Is it, for example, flippant or pretentious?

11. Is the title engaging and suggestive?

12. Is every sentence clear, concise, and complete?

13. Are simple, complex, and compound sentences used for variety?

14. Have technical terms been used correctly? Are you certain of the meanings of all the words in the paper? Are they spelled correctly?

15. Have you documented any information borrowed from books, articles, or other sources? Have you achieved your desired balance between quoting, summarizing, and paraphrasing secondary material?

16. Have you used a standard format for citing sources (see p. 1470)?

17. Have you followed your instructor's guidelines for the format of the final draft?

18. Have you carefully proofread the final draft?

# TYPES OF WRITING ASSIGNMENTS

The term we've been using for your approach to literature — interpretation — is broad. Your instructor may be looking for different types of interpretive skills or rhetorical strategies in different assignments, so it's worthwhile to scrutinize each assignment for keywords that help you understand the intent.

Three types of papers frequently assigned in literature classes are explication, analysis, and comparison and contrast. Most writing about literature involves some combination of these skills. This section includes a sample explication, an analysis, and a comparison and contrast paper. For a sample research paper that demonstrates a variety of strategies for documenting outside sources, see Chapter 44. For genre-based assignments, see the sample papers for writing about fiction (p. 1443), poetry (p. 1453), and drama (p. 1459).

## Explication

The purpose of this approach to a literary work is to make the implicit explicit. *Explication* is a detailed explanation of a passage of poetry or prose. Because explication is an intensive examination of a text line by line, it is mostly used to interpret a short poem in its entirety or a brief passage from a long poem, short story, or play. Explication can be used in any kind of essay when you want to be specific about how a writer achieves a certain effect. An explication pays careful attention to language — the connotations of words, allusions, figurative language, irony, symbol, rhythm, sound, and so on. These elements are examined in relation to one another and to the overall effect of the work.

The simplest way to organize an explication is to move through the passage line by line, explaining whatever seems significant, but this approach can diminish your interpretation because it attributes equal significance to every word, line, or element of a poem. It is wise to avoid an assembly-line approach that begins each sentence with "In line one (two, three) . . ." Instead, organize your paper to best serve your thesis. You might find that the right place to start is with the final lines, working your way back to the beginning of the poem or passage while still paying careful attention to each line and to all components. The following sample explication on Dickinson's "There's a certain Slant of light" does just that. The student's opening paragraph refers to the final line of the poem in order to present her thesis. She explains that though the poem begins with an image of light, it is not a bright or cheery poem but one concerned with "the look of Death." Since the last line prompted her thesis, that is where she begins the explication.

You might also find it useful to structure a paper by discussing various elements of literature, so that you have a paragraph on connotative words followed by one on figurative language and so on. However your paper is organized, keep in mind that the aim of an explication is not simply to summarize the passage or work but to comment on the effects and meanings produced by the author's use of language in it. An effective explication (the Latin word *explicare* means "to unfold") displays a text to reveal how it works and what it signifies. Although writing an explication requires some patience and sensitivity, it is an excellent method for coming to understand and appreciate the elements and qualities that constitute literary art.

# A SAMPLE STUDENT EXPLICATION

## *A Reading of Emily Dickinson's "There's a certain Slant of light"*

The sample paper by student author Bonnie Katz is the result of an assignment calling for an explication of about 750 words on any poem by Emily Dickinson. Katz selected "There's a certain Slant of light."

### EMILY DICKINSON (1830–1886)

## *There's a certain Slant of light*   ca. 1861

There's a certain Slant of light,
Winter Afternoons —
That oppresses, like the Heft
Of Cathedral Tunes —

Heavenly Hurt, it gives us —                                        5
We can find no scar,
But internal difference,
Where the Meanings, are —

None may teach it — Any —
'Tis the Seal Despair —                                            10
An imperial affliction
Sent us of the Air —

When it comes, the Landscape listens —
Shadows — hold their breath —
When it goes, 'tis like the Distance                               15
On the look of Death —

This essay comments on every line of the poem and provides a coherent reading that relates each line to the speaker's intense awareness of death. Although the essay discusses each stanza in the order that it appears, the introductory paragraph provides a brief overview explaining how the poem's images contribute to its total meaning. In addition, the student does not hesitate to discuss a line out of sequence when it can be usefully connected to another phrase. This is especially apparent in the third paragraph, in her discussion of stanzas 2 and 3. The final paragraph describes some of the formal elements of the poem. It might be argued that this discussion could have been integrated into the previous paragraphs rather than placed at the end, but the author does make a connection in her concluding sentence between the pattern of language and its meaning.

Several other matters are worth noticing. The author works quotations into her own sentences to support her points. She quotes exactly as the words appear in the poem, even Dickinson's irregular use of capital letters. When something is added to a quotation to clarify it, it is enclosed in brackets so that the essayist's words will not be mistaken for the poet's: "Seal [of] Despair." A slash is used to indicate line divisions as in "imperial affliction / Sent us of the Air."

Bonnie Katz

Professor Quiello

English 109-2

26 February 2023

A Reading of Emily Dickinson's

"There's a certain Slant of light"

Because Emily Dickinson did not provide titles for her poetry, editors follow the customary practice of using the first line of a poem as its title. However, a more appropriate title for "There's a certain Slant of light," one that suggests what the speaker in the poem is most concerned about, can be drawn from the poem's last line, which ends with "the look of Death" (line 16). Although the first line begins with an image of light, nothing bright, carefree, or cheerful appears in the poem. Instead, the predominant mood and images are darkened by a sense of despair resulting from the speaker's awareness of death.

In the first stanza, the "certain Slant of light" is associated with "Winter Afternoons" (2), a phrase that connotes the end of a day, a season, and even life itself. Such light is hardly warm or comforting. Not a ray or beam, this slanting light suggests something unusual or distorted and creates in the speaker a certain slant on life that is consistent with the cold, dark mood that winter afternoons can produce. Like the speaker, most of us have seen and felt this sort of light: it "oppresses" (3) and pervades our sense of things when we encounter it. Dickinson uses the senses of hearing and touch as well as sight to describe the overwhelming oppressiveness that the speaker experiences. The light is transformed into sound by a simile that tells us it is "like the Heft / Of Cathedral Tunes" (3–4). Moreover, the "Heft" of that sound—the slow, solemn measures of tolling church bells and organ music—weighs heavily on our spirits. Through the use of shifting imagery, Dickinson evokes a kind of spiritual numbness that we keenly feel and perceive through our senses.

By associating the winter light with "Cathedral Tunes," Dickinson lets us know that the speaker is concerned about more than the weather. Whatever it is that "oppresses" is related by connotation to faith, mortality, and God. The second and third stanzas offer several suggestions about

---

**Thesis providing overview of explication**

**Line-by-line explication of first stanza, focusing on connotations of words and imagery, in relation to mood and meaning of poem as a whole; supported with references to the text**

this connection. The pain caused by the light is a "Heavenly Hurt" (5). This "imperial affliction / Sent us of the Air" (11–12) apparently comes from God above, and yet it seems to be part of the very nature of life. The oppressiveness we feel is in the air, and it can neither be specifically identified at this point in the poem nor be eliminated, for "None may teach it—Any" (9). All we know is that existence itself seems depressing under the weight of this "Seal [of] Despair" (10). The impression left by this "Seal" is stamped within the mind or soul rather than externally. "We can find no scar" (6), but once experienced this oppressiveness challenges our faith in life and its "Meanings" (8).

> Explication of second, third, and fourth stanzas, focusing on connotations of words and imagery in relation to mood and meaning of poem as a whole; supported with references to the text

    The final stanza does not explain what those "Meanings" are, but it does make clear that the speaker is acutely aware of death. As the winter daylight fades, Dickinson projects the speaker's anxiety onto the surrounding landscape and shadows, which will soon be engulfed by the darkness that follows this light: "the Landscape listens—/ Shadows—hold their breath—" (13–14). This image firmly aligns the winter light in the first stanza with darkness. Paradoxically, the light in this poem illuminates the nature of darkness. Tension is released when the light is completely gone, but what remains is the despair that the "imperial affliction" has imprinted on the speaker's sensibilities, for it is "like the Distance / On the look of Death—" (15–16). There can be no relief from what that "certain Slant of light" has revealed because what has been experienced is permanent—like the fixed stare in the eyes of someone who is dead.

    The speaker's awareness of death is conveyed in a thoughtful, hushed tone. The lines are filled with fluid *l* and smooth *s* sounds that are appropriate for the quiet, meditative voice in the poem. The voice sounds tentative and uncertain—perhaps a little frightened. This seems to be reflected in the slightly irregular meter of the lines. The stanzas are trochaic with the second and fourth lines of each stanza having five syllables, but no stanza is identical because each works a slight variation on the first stanza's seven syllables in the first and third lines. The rhymes also combine exact patterns with variations. The first and third lines of each stanza are not exact rhymes, but the second and fourth lines are exact so that the paired words are more closely related: Afternoons, Tunes; scar, are; Despair, Air; and

> Explication of the elements of rhythm and sound throughout poem

> Conclusion tying explication of rhythm and sound with explication of words and imagery in previous paragraphs

breath, Death. There is a pattern to the poem, but it is unobtrusively woven into the speaker's voice in much the same way that "the look of Death" (16) is subtly present in the images and language of the poem.

Work Cited

Dickinson, Emily. "There's a certain Slant of light." *The Compact Bedford Introduction to Literature,* edited by Michael Meyer and D. Quentin Miller, 13th ed., Bedford/St. Martin's, 2024, p. 1423.

## *Analysis*

The preceding sample essay shows how an explication examines in detail the important elements in a work and relates them to the whole. An analysis, however, usually examines only a single element — such as plot, character, point of view, symbol, tone, or irony — and relates it to the entire work. An analytic topic separates the work into parts and focuses on a specific one; you might consider "Point of View in 'A Rose for Emily,' " "Patterns of Rhythm in Browning's 'My Last Duchess,' " or "Ocean Imagery in *Water by the Spoonful.*" The specific element must be related to the work as a whole or it will appear irrelevant. It is not enough to point out that there are many death images in Andrew Marvell's "To His Coy Mistress" and to list them; the images must be shown to produce the poem's overall effect.

Whether an analytic paper is just a few pages or many, it cannot attempt to discuss everything about the work it is considering. Only those elements that are relevant to the topic should be treated. This kind of focusing makes the topic manageable; this is why most papers that you write will probably be some form of analysis. Explications are useful for a short passage, but a line-by-line commentary on a story, play, or long poem simply isn't practical. Because analysis allows you to consider a significant effect or meaning of an entire work by studying a single important element, it is a useful and common approach to longer works. The student author of the next essay focuses her analysis on a single literary element, theme, in the following poem by Elizabeth Bishop.

### ELIZABETH BISHOP (1911–1979)

## *Manners* 1965

Bettmann/Getty Images.

*for a Child of 1918*

My grandfather said to me
as we sat on the wagon seat,
"Be sure to remember to always
speak to everyone you meet."

We met a stranger on foot                              5
My grandfather's whip tapped his hat.
"Good day, sir. Good day. A fine day."
And I said it and bowed where I sat.

Then we overtook a boy we knew
with his big pet crow on his shoulder.                  10
"Always offer everyone a ride;
don't forget that when you get older,"

my grandfather said. So Willy
climbed up with us, but the crow
gave a "Caw!" and flew off. I was worried.              15
How would he know where to go?

But he flew a little way at a time
from fence post to fence post, ahead;
and when Willy whistled he answered.
"A fine bird," my grandfather said,                     20

"and he's well brought up. See, he answers
nicely when he's spoken to.
Man or beast, that's good manners.
Be sure that you both always do."

When automobiles went by,                               25
the dust hid the people's faces,
but we shouted "Good day! Good day!
Fine day!" at the top of our voices.

When we came to Hustler Hill,
he said that the mare was tired,                        30
so we all got down and walked,
as our good manners required.

# A SAMPLE CLOSE READING

## *An Annotated Version of "Manners"*

The following annotations represent insights about the relationship of various elements at work in the poem gleaned only after several close readings. Don't expect to be able to produce these kinds of interpretive notes on a first reading because such perceptions will not be apparent until you've read the poem and then gone back to the beginning to discover how each word, line, and stanza contributes to the overall effect. Writing your responses in the margins of the page can be a useful means of recording your impressions as well as discovering new insights as you read the text closely.

ELIZABETH BISHOP (1911–1979)

## *Manners* 1965

*for a Child of 1918*

My grandfather said to me
as we sat on the wagon seat,
"Be sure to remember to always
speak to everyone you meet."

We met a stranger on foot.                        5
My grandfather's whip tapped his hat.
"Good day, sir. Good day. A fine day."
And I said it and bowed where I sat.

Then we overtook a boy we knew
with his big pet crow on his shoulder.             10
"Always offer everyone a ride;
don't forget that when you get older,"

my grandfather said. So Willy
climbed up with us, but the crow
gave a "Caw!" and flew off. I was worried.         15
How would he know where to go?

**Margin annotations:**

Title refers to what is socially, correct, polite, and/or decent behavior.

WWI ended in 1918 and denotes a shift in values and manners that often follows rapid social changes brought about by war.

Wagon seat suggests a simpler past — as does simple language and informal diction of the child speaker.

Grandfather seems kind, but he also carries a whip that reinforces his authoritative voice.

Idea that values "always" transcend time is emphasized by the grandfather's urging: "don't forget."

"My grandfather," repeated four times in first five stanzas, reflects the child's affection and a sense of belonging in his world. The crow, however, worries the child and indicates an uncertain future.

But he flew a little way at a time

from fence post to fence post, ahead;

and when Willy whistled he answered.

"A fine bird," my grandfather said,          20

> Predictable quatrains and *abcb* rhyme scheme throughout the poem take the worry out of where they — and the crow — are headed.

"and he's well brought up. See, he answers

nicely when he's spoken to.

Man or beast, that's good manners.

Be sure that you both always do."

When automobiles went by,                     25

the dust hid the people's faces,

but we shouted "Good day! Good day!

Fine day!" at the top of our voices.

> The modern symbolic automobile races by, raising dust that obscures everyone's vision and forces them to shout. Rhymes in lines 26 and 28 are off (unlike all the other rhymes) just enough to suggest the dissonant future that will supersede the calm wagon ride.

> Third time the grandfather says "always." This and the inverted syntax of line 24 call attention, again, to idea that good manners are forever important.

When we came to Hustler Hill,

he said that the mare was tired,             30

so we all got down and walked,

as our good manners required.

> The horse, like the simple past it symbolizes, is weakened by the hustle of modern life, but even so, "our" good manners prevail, internalized from the grandfather's values.

## A SAMPLE STUDENT ANALYSIS

### *Memory in Elizabeth Bishop's "Manners"*

The following sample paper on Elizabeth Bishop's "Manners" was written in response to an assignment that called for a 750-word discussion of the ways in which at least five of the following elements work to develop and reinforce the poem's themes:

| | | |
|---|---|---|
| diction and tone | irony | form |
| images | sound and rhyme | speaker |
| figures of speech | rhythm and meter | setting and situation |
| symbols | | |

In her paper, Debra Epstein discusses the ways in which a number of these elements contribute to what she sees as a central theme of "Manners": the loss of a way of life that Bishop associates with the end of World War I. Not all the elements of poetry are covered equally in Epstein's paper because some, such as speaker and setting, are more important to her argument than others. Notice how rather than merely listing each of the elements, Epstein mentions them in her discussion as she needs to in order to develop the thesis that she clearly and succinctly expresses in her opening paragraph.

Epstein 1

Debra Epstein

Professor Brown

English 210

1 May 2023

Memory in Elizabeth Bishop's "Manners"

**Thesis providing interpretation of poem**

The subject of Elizabeth Bishop's "Manners" has to do with behaving well, but the theme of the poem has more to do with a way of life than with etiquette. The poem suggests that modern society has lost something important—a friendly openness, a generosity of spirit, a sense of decency and consideration—in its race toward progress. Although the narrative is simply told, Bishop enriches this poem about manners by developing an

**Statement of elements in poem to be discussed in paper**

implicit theme through her subtle use of such elements of poetry as speaker, setting, rhyme, meter, symbol, and images.

The dedication suggests that the speaker is "a Child of 1918" who

**Summary of poem's narrative and introduction to discussion of elements**

accompanies his or her grandfather on a wagon ride and who is urged to practice good manners by greeting people, offering everyone a ride, and speaking when spoken to by anyone. During the ride they say hello to a stranger, give a ride to a boy with a pet crow, shout greetings to a passing automobile, and get down from the wagon when they reach a hill because the horse is tired. They walk because "good manners required" (line 32) such consideration, even for a horse. This summary indicates what goes on in the poem but not its significance. That requires a closer look at some of the poem's elements.

**Analysis of speaker in poem**

Given the speaker's simple language (there are no metaphors or similes and only a few words out of thirty-two lines are longer than two syllables), it seems likely that he or she is a fairly young child rather than an adult reminiscing. (It is interesting to note that Bishop herself, though not identical with the speaker, would have been seven in 1918.) Because the speaker

Epstein 2

is a young child who uses simple diction, Bishop has to show us the ride's
significance indirectly rather than having the speaker explicitly state it.

The setting for the speaker's narrative is important because 1918
was the year World War I ended, and it marked the beginning of a new era
of technology that was the result of rapid industrialization during the war.
Horses and wagons would soon be put out to pasture. The grandfather's
manners emphasize a time gone by; the child must be told to "remember"
what the grandfather says because he or she will take that advice into a new
and very different world.

> Analysis
> of poem's
> setting

The grandfather's world of the horse and wagon is uncomplicated,
and this is reflected in both the simple quatrains that move predictably
along in an abcb rhyme scheme and the frequent anapestic meter (ăs wĕ sát
ŏn thĕ wágŏn [2]) that pulls the lines rapidly and lightly. The one moment
Bishop breaks the set rhyme scheme is in the seventh stanza when the
automobile (the single four-syllable word in the poem) rushes by in a cloud
of dust so that people cannot see or hear each other. The only off rhymes in
the poem—"faces" (26) and "voices" (28)—are also in this stanza, which
suggests that the automobile and the people in it are somehow off or out
of sync with what goes on in the other stanzas. The automobile is a symbol
of a way of life in which people—their faces hidden—and manners take a
backseat to speed and noise. The people in the car don't wave, don't offer a
ride, and don't speak when spoken to.

> Analysis
> of rhyme
> scheme and
> meter

> Analysis of
> symbols

Maybe the image of the crow's noisy cawing and flying from post to
post is a foreshadowing that should prepare readers for the automobile.
The speaker feels "worried" about the crow's apparent directionlessness:
"How would he know where to go?" (16). However, neither the child nor the
grandfather (nor the reader on a first reading) clearly sees the two worlds
that Bishop contrasts in the final stanza.

> Analysis of
> images

"Hustler Hill" is the perfect name for what finally tires out the mare.
There is no hurry for the grandfather and child, but there is for those people
in the car and the postwar hustle and bustle they represent. The fast-paced
future overtakes the tired symbol of the past in the poem. The pace slows as
the wagon passengers get down to walk, but the reader recognizes that the
grandfather's way has been lost to a world in which good manners are not
required.

> Conclusion
> supporting
> thesis on
> poem's
> theme

Epstein 3

Work Cited

Bishop, Elizabeth. "Manners." *The Compact Bedford Introduction to Literature*, edited by Michael Meyer and D. Quentin Miller, 13th ed., Bedford/St. Martin's, 2024, p. 1427.

## Comparison and Contrast

Another interpretive essay assignment in literature courses requires you to write about similarities and differences between or within works. You might be asked to discuss "How Sounds Express Meanings in John Updike's 'Player Piano' and Lewis Carroll's 'Jabberwocky,' " or "Sammy's and Stokesie's Attitudes about Conformity in Updike's 'A & P.' " A *comparison* of either topic would emphasize their similarities, while a *contrast* would stress their differences. It is possible, of course, to include both perspectives in a paper if you find significant likenesses and differences. A comparison of Robert Burns's "A Red, Red Rose" and Edmund Waller's "Go, Lovely Rose" (both p. 547) would, for example, yield similarities because each poem focuses on a familiar poetic symbol; however, important differences also exist in the tone and theme of each poem that would constitute a contrast. (You should, incidentally, be aware that the term *comparison* is often used inclusively to refer to both similarities and differences. If you are assigned a comparison of two works, be sure that you understand what your instructor's expectations are; the second word "contrast" is generally implied.) As we have stressed in other contexts, the desired outcome of this type of approach is not simply to point out similarities or differences, but to use them to advance an original interpretation.

When you choose your own topic, the paper will be more successful — more manageable — if you write on works that can be meaningfully related to each other. Although Robert Herrick's "To the Virgins, to Make Much of Time" and Shakespeare's *Hamlet* both have something to do with hesitation, the likelihood of anyone making a connection between the two that reveals something interesting and important is remote — though perhaps not impossible if the topic were conceived imaginatively and tactfully. That is not to say that comparisons of works from different genres should be avoided, but the relation between them should be strong, such as a treatment of African American masculine identity in Ralph Ellison's story "King of the Bingo Game" (p. 178) and August Wilson's play *Fences* (p. 1329). Choose a topic that encourages you to ask significant questions about each work; the purpose of a comparison or contrast is to understand the works more clearly for having examined them together. Despite the obvious differences between Quiara Alegría Hudes's *Water by the Spoonful* (p. 1216) and David Long's "Morphine" (p. 282), the two are closely related if we ask questions about the relationship between addiction and the creation of a persona.

Choose works to compare or contrast that intersect with each other in some significant way. They may, for example, be written by the same author, in the same genre, around the same time period, or about the same subject. Perhaps you can compare their use of some technique, such as irony or point of view. Regardless of the specific topic, your approach should allow you to organize your paper around a central idea that argues a point about the two works. Keep in the foreground of your thinking what the comparison or contrast reveals about the works.

There is no single way to organize comparative papers since each topic is likely to have its own particular issues to resolve, but it is useful to be aware of two basic patterns that can be helpful with a comparison, a contrast, or a combination of both. One method that can be effective for relatively short papers consists of dividing the paper in half, first discussing one work and then the other. Here, for example, is a partial informal outline for a discussion of Sophocles' *Oedipus the King* (p. 1001) and Shakespeare's *Othello* (p. 1055); the topic is a comparison and contrast: "Oedipus and *Othello* as Tragic Figures."

1. Oedipus
   a. The nature of the conflict
   b. Strengths and stature
   c. Weaknesses and mistakes
   d. What is learned
2. Othello
   a. The nature of the conflict
   b. Strengths and stature
   c. Weaknesses and mistakes
   d. What is learned

This organizational strategy can be effective provided that the second part of the paper combines the discussion of *Othello* with references to Oedipus so that the thesis is clear and the argument unified without being repetitive. If the two characters were treated entirely separately, then the discussion would be merely parallel rather than integrated. In a lengthy paper, this organization probably would not work well because readers would have difficulty remembering the points made in the first half as they read on.

Thus, for a longer paper it is usually better to create a more integrated structure that discusses both works as you take up each item in your outline. Here is the second basic pattern using the elements in the partial outline just cited:

1. The nature of the conflict
   a. Oedipus
   b. Othello
2. Strengths and stature
   a. Oedipus
   b. Othello
3. Weaknesses and mistakes
   a. Oedipus
   b. Othello
4. What is learned
   a. Oedipus
   b. Othello

This pattern allows you to discuss any number of topics without requiring that your reader recall what you first said about the conflict Oedipus confronts before you discuss Othello's conflicts fifteen pages later. However you structure your comparison or contrast paper, make certain that a reader can follow its elements and keep track of its thesis.

## A SAMPLE STUDENT COMPARISON

### *Coping with Loss in Alice Munro's "Silence" and David Auburn's* Proof

The following paper was written in response to an assignment that required a comparison and contrast — about 750 words — of two works of literature. The student chose to write an analysis of how the women in each text respond to the loss of family members.

Tess Seaver

Professor Stone

English 102

November 1, 2023

Coping with Loss in Alice Munro's "Silence" and David Auburn's *Proof*

In the short story "Silence" by Alice Munro and in the play *Proof* by David Auburn, loss is explored through the lens of parent-daughter relationships. In *Proof*, Catherine copes with the loss of her father after he dies. Similarly, in "Silence," Juliet copes with loss upon the realization that her daughter has chosen to not be a part of her life. However, the loss of Catherine's father is ultimately freeing, allowing her to finally live her own life, whereas Juliet's loss traps her and makes her continuously hope for the return for her daughter. These two divergent responses illustrate societally natural responses to loss: that of a parent versus that of a child.

Throughout "Silence," Juliet bases most of her decisions and thinking around her daughter's absence and therefore is unable to live her own life. For instance, when Juliet's daughter, Penelope, disappears into what Juliet thinks is a "cult," Juliet is unable to reach her. Because of this, Juliet stays in the same place with the hope that Penelope will be able to find her there: "Juliet gave a great deal of thought to getting out of this apartment. . . . But she said to Christa that she could not do that, because that was the address Penelope had, and mail could be forwarded for only three months, so there would be no place then where her daughter could find her" (Munro 382). Juliet does not have closure. Although she keeps expecting her daughter to return, she does not understand why her daughter has left, and thus cannot accept her absence.

Moreover, Penelope's rejection has caused Juliet to question everything about herself. Even when she learns that Penelope is not in a cult and is "living the life of a prosperous, practical matron" (Munro 392), Juliet is still unable to cope with this loss. She is trapped. As she says, "My daughter went away without telling me goodbye and in fact she probably did not know that she was going. She did not know it was for good. Then gradually, I believe, it dawned on her how much she wanted to stay away" (393). Juliet cannot move on or cope with this loss because she has not only lost her daughter, but her identity as a mother, too. She did, after all, spend twenty years raising Penelope and in all that time they "haven't been apart much" (377). Despite having a career, a large portion of Juliet's identity is tied to the raising and molding of her daughter. Penelope's rejection of her, then, is a rejection of her whole life.

In *Proof*, Catherine confronts the death of her father and, eventually, is able to live a life free of his influence and away from the pressure of his fame as a mathematician. At the start of the play, it is revealed that Catherine has been speaking to her father, Robert, who died only a week ago. Catherine, a mathematician like her father, quit university to care for him. She says, "I spent my life with him. I fed him. Talked to him. Tried to listen when he talked. Talked to people who weren't there . . ." (Auburn 1285). While her father is alive, Catherine is eclipsed—personally by his medical needs, and professionally by his genius. In many ways, she has taken on the role of the parent—putting Robert's needs before her own.

Catherine lives for him, instead of for herself, and hides her own abilities in order to cater to his needs. Nonetheless, the way she tries to escape the loss of her father is through starting anew and showing Hal and her sister, Claire, the mathematical proof she wrote years ago. However, she has spent so long downplaying her skills that when she informs Claire and Hal of her accomplishment, they do not believe her. Hal even says, "I'm sorry, Catherine, but you took some classes at Northwestern for a few months. . . . Even so, it doesn't matter. This is too advanced. I don't even understand most of it" (Auburn 1310). This further traps her in her sense of loss, as she is unable to escape her father's influence and reputation, even with his death. It is only once Hal returns to Catherine and concludes that she was right all along, and asks her to explain her proof to him, that Catherine is able to break free from her loss. Finally, she has the recognition she deserves and is able to exist separately from the shadow of her father as an independent, accomplished adult. With her proof acknowledged, Catherine is no longer trapped by her father's reputation and is now free.

Catherine in *Proof* and Juliet in "Silence" both struggle to cope with their respective losses. However, while Juliet is firmly trapped in grief and confusion, Catherine is able to break free from her loss and find herself. Although Juliet's and Catherine's lives are similar in that they both experience loss and struggle to cope with loss, the difference lies in who they have lost, and how that relates to their own identities. Catherine's father has died, but since the death of a parent—while tragic—is something that is eventually inevitable, she is able to develop her identity outside of her relationship with him. Juliet, however, finds herself unwillingly estranged from her daughter. The loss of a child is not something culturally expected, and further, Juliet's sense of identity is rooted in motherhood. Her loss, while not greater, is more destabilizing and she is unable to fully move on. The two different responses to loss indicate the type of relationship Juliet and Catherine are coping with and what that loss means for their sense of self.

### Works Cited

Auburn, David. *Proof*. Meyer and Miller, pp. 1277–1321.

Meyer, Michael, and D. Quentin Miller, editors. *The Compact Bedford Introduction to Literature*. 13th ed. Bedford/St. Martin's, 2024.

Munro, Alice. *Silence*. Meyer and Miller, pp. 376–93.

# WRITING ABOUT FICTION, POETRY, AND DRAMA

Writing about each of the genres of imaginative literature that comprise this book involves a series of closely related but significantly different sets of conventions. Even the way we refer to the different genres requires a slightly different vocabulary. For example, the person who tells the story in a work of short fiction is a narrator, but that voice in a poem is a speaker. In poetry we cite lines while in plays we often refer to acts and scenes. A character in a play or story might become a persona in a poem, and so forth. Although the three genres share certain elements — you can find metaphors in plays, stories, and poems — the emphasis is likely to be different. With these differences in mind, we have included sections below that apply the principles of writing about literature in general to each genre specifically.

## WRITING ABOUT FICTION

Writing about fiction is sometimes less intimidating to students than writing about poetry or drama, but it comes with a unique set of challenges. First and foremost, stories center around plots that tend to bewitch the reader and to obscure the story's other elements. You might find yourself recalling a story by saying, "Oh, that's the one about the guy who works in the grocery store," but as you know, plot is only one element. Most poems are only a page or two long, meaning you can see them all at once and visually compare their elements, whereas fiction tests your power of memory. Plays consist mostly of dialogue, whereas fiction tends to intersperse dialogue, description, and narration, sometimes demanding that your imagination make great leaps over time and space. In short, fiction often creates its own world, and its expansiveness is sometimes hard to gather in.

Given the fact that fiction tends to swell over time and space and focuses on the endlessly fascinating subject of human behavior, it is probably best to begin broadly and work toward narrowing down your topic. In writing about poetry, you might start with a single feature of language, like rhythm; in writing about fiction, you will probably be drawn initially toward a character. Fiction offers a wider variety of entry points. We'd suggest that you determine what you find unique, fascinating, noteworthy, or perhaps just recognizable within a given story as a way of figuring out where you want to begin.

---

### Questions for Responsive Reading and Writing about Fiction

The following questions can help you consider important elements of fiction that reveal your responses to a story's effects and meanings. The questions are general, so they will not always be relevant to a particular story. Many of them, however, should prove useful for thinking, talking, and writing about a work of fiction. Note that these are just initial approaches to a story as a way of generating ideas: you will probably end up combining elements or developing a context that will expand your sense of how to frame one or more of them. If you are uncertain about the meaning of a term used in a question, consult the Glossary of Literary Terms beginning on page 1483 of this book. You should also find useful the discussion of various critical approaches to literature and possible contexts in Chapter 42, "Critical Strategies for Reading."

## PLOT

1. Does the plot conform to a formula? Is it like those of any other stories you have read? Did you find it predictable?

2. What is the source and nature of the conflict for the protagonist? Was your major interest in the story based on what happens next or on some other concern? What does the title reveal now that you've finished the story?

3. Is the story told chronologically? If not, in what order are its events told, and what is the effect of that order on your response to the action?

4. What does the exposition reveal? Does the author employ flashbacks? Did you see any foreshadowing? Where is the climax?

5. Is the conflict resolved at the end? Would you characterize the ending as happy, unhappy, or somewhere in between?

6. Is the plot unified? How is each incident somehow related to some other element in the story?

## CHARACTER

1. Do you identify with the protagonist? Who (or what) is the antagonist?

2. Did your response to any characters change as you read? What caused the change? Do any characters change and develop over the course of the story? How?

3. Are round, flat, or stock characters used? Is their behavior motivated and plausible?

4. How does the author reveal characters? Are they directly described or indirectly presented through gestures, dialogue, interior monologue, etc.?

5. What is the purpose of the minor characters? Are they individualized, or do they primarily represent ideas or attitudes?

## SETTING

1. Is the setting important in shaping your response? If it were changed, would your response to the story's action and meaning be significantly different?

2. Is the setting used symbolically? Are the time, place, and atmosphere related to the theme?

3. Is the setting used as an antagonist?

*(continued)*

**POINT OF VIEW**

1. Who tells the story? Is it a first-person or third-person narrator? Is it a major or minor character or one who does not participate in the action at all? How much does the narrator know? Does the point of view change at all over the course of the story?

2. Is the narrator reliable and objective? Does the narrator appear too innocent, emotional, or self-deluded to be trusted?

3. Does the author directly comment on the action?

4. If it were told from a different point of view, how would your response to the story change? Would anything be lost?

**SYMBOLISM**

1. Did you notice any potentially significant symbols in the story? Are they actions, characters, settings, objects, or words?

2. How do the symbols contribute to your understanding of the story?

**THEME**

1. Did you identify a theme? If so, what is it?

2. Is the theme stated directly, or is it developed implicitly through the plot, characters, or some other element?

3. Is the theme a confirmation of conventional values, or does it challenge them?

**STYLE, TONE, AND IRONY**

1. Do you think the style is consistent and appropriate throughout the story? Do all the characters use the same kind of language, or did you hear different voices?

2. Would you describe the level of diction as formal or informal? Are the sentences short and simple, long and complex, or some combination?

3. How does the author's use of language contribute to the tone of the story? Did it seem, for example, intense, relaxed, sentimental, nostalgic, humorous, angry, sad, or remote?

4. Does the author's use of language bear close scrutiny so that you feel and experience more with each reading?

# A SAMPLE STUDENT ESSAY

## *John Updike's "A & P" as a State of Mind*

Nancy Lager's paper analyzes the setting in John Updike's "A & P" (the entire story appears on p. 145). The assignment simply asked for an essay of approximately 750 words on a short story written in the twentieth century. The approach was left to the student.

The idea for this essay began with Lager asking herself why Updike used "A & P" as the title. The initial answer to the question was that "the setting is important in this story." This answer was the rough beginning of a tentative thesis. What still had to be explained, though, was how the setting is important. To determine the significance of the setting, Lager jotted down some notes based on the passages she underlined and her marginal notations:

*A & P*

"usual traffic"

lights and tile

"electric eye"

shoppers like "sheep," "houseslaves," "pigs"

"Alexandrov and Petrooshki" — Russia

| *New England Town* | *Lengel* |
|---|---|
| typical: bank, church, etc. | "manager" |
| traditional | "doesn't miss that much" |
| conservative | (like lady shopper) |
| proper | Sunday school |
| near Salem — witch trials | "It's our policy" |
| puritanical | spokesman for A & P values |
| intolerant | |

From these notes Lager saw that Lengel serves as the voice of the A & P. He is, in a sense, a personification of the intolerant atmosphere of the setting. This insight led to another version of her thesis statement: "The setting of 'A & P' is the antagonist of the story." That explained at least some of the setting's importance. By seeing Lengel as a spokesman for A & P policies, Lager could view him as a voice that articulates the morally smug atmosphere created by the setting. Finally, she considered why it is significant that the setting is the antagonist, and this generated her last thesis: "Because the intolerant setting of 'A & P' is the antagonist in the story, it is crucial to our understanding of Sammy's decision to quit his job." This thesis sentence does not appear precisely in these words in the essay, but it is the backbone of the introductory paragraph.

The remaining paragraphs consist of details that describe the A & P in the second paragraph, the New England town in the third, Lengel in the fourth, and Sammy's reasons for quitting in the concluding paragraph. Paragraphs 2, 3, and 4 are largely based on Lager's notes, which she used as an outline once her thesis was established. The essay is sharply focused, well organized, and generally well written. In addition, it suggests a number of useful guidelines for analytic papers:

1. Only the points related to the thesis are included. In another type of essay the role of the girls in the bathing suits, for example, might have been considerably more prominent.

2. The analysis keeps the setting in focus while at the same time indicating how it is significant in the major incident in the story — Sammy's quitting.

3. The title is a useful lead-in to the essay; it provides a sense of what the topic is. In addition, the title is drawn from a sentence (the final one of the first paragraph) that clearly explains its meaning.

4. The introductory paragraph is direct and clearly indicates that the paper will argue that the setting serves as the antagonist of the story.

5. Brief quotations are deftly incorporated into the text of the essay to illustrate points. We are told what we need to know about the story as evidence is provided to support ideas. There is no unnecessary plot summary. Even though "A & P" is only a few pages in length and is an assigned topic, page numbers are included after quoted phrases. If the story were longer, page numbers would be especially helpful for the reader.

6. The paragraphs are well developed, unified, and coherent. They flow naturally from one to another. Notice, for example, the smooth transition worked into the final sentence of the third paragraph and the first sentence of the fourth paragraph.

7. Lager makes excellent use of her careful reading and notes by finding revealing connections among the details she has observed. The store's "electric eye," for instance, is related to the woman's and Lengel's watchfulness.

8. As Lager describes events, she uses the present tense. This decision (which is standard when writing about literature) avoids awkward tense shifts and lends an immediacy to the discussion.

9. The concluding paragraph establishes the significance of why the setting should be seen as the antagonist and provides a sense of closure by referring again to Sammy's "No Sale," which has been mentioned at the end of the first paragraph.

10. In short, Lager has demonstrated that she has read the work closely, has understood the relation of the setting to the major action, and has argued her thesis convincingly by using evidence from the story.

Nancy Lager

Professor Taylor

English 102-12

2 October 2023

John Updike's "A & P" as a State of Mind

The setting of John Updike's "A & P" is crucial to our understanding of Sammy's decision to quit his job. Although Sammy is the central character in the story and we learn that he is a principled, good-natured nineteen-year-old with a sense of humor, Updike seems to invest as much effort in describing the setting as he does in Sammy. The setting is the antagonist and plays a role that is as important as Sammy's. The title, after all, is not "Youthful Rebellion" or "Sammy Quits" but "A & P." Even though Sammy knows that his quitting will make life more difficult for him, he instinctively insists on rejecting what the A & P comes to represent in the story. When he rings up a "No Sale" and "saunter[s]" (149) out of the store, he leaves behind not only a job but the rigid state of mind associated with the A & P.

Sammy's descriptions of the A & P present a setting that is ugly, monotonous, and rigidly regulated. The fluorescent light is as blandly cool as the "checker-board green-and-cream rubber-tile floor" (146). We can see the uniformity Sammy describes because we have all been in chain stores. The "usual traffic" moves in one direction (except for the swimsuited girls, who move against it), and everything is neatly ordered and categorized in tidy aisles. The dehumanizing routine of this environment is suggested by Sammy's offhand references to the typical shoppers as "sheep" (146), "houseslaves" (146), and "pigs" (148). They seem to pace through the store in a stupor; as Sammy tells us, not even dynamite could move them.

The A & P is appropriately located "right in the middle" (147) of a proper, conservative, traditional New England town north of Boston. This location, coupled with the fact that the town is only five miles from Salem, the site of the famous seventeenth-century witch trials, suggests a narrow, intolerant social atmosphere in which there is no room for stepping beyond the boundaries of what is regarded as normal and proper. The importance of this setting can be appreciated even more if we imagine the action taking place in, say, a mellow suburb of southern California. In this prim New England setting, the girls in their bathing suits are bound to offend somebody's sense of propriety.

As soon as Lengel sees the girls, the inevitable conflict begins. He embodies the dull conformity represented by the A & P. As "manager" (147), he is both the guardian and enforcer of "policy" (148). When he gives the girls "that sad Sunday-school-superintendent stare" (148), we know we are in the presence of the A & P version of a dreary bureaucrat who "doesn't miss that much" (147). He is as unsympathetic and unpleasant as the woman "with rouge on her cheeks and no eyebrows" (145) who pounces on Sammy for ringing up her "HiHo crackers" twice. Like the "electric eye" (148) in the doorway, her vigilant eyes allow nothing to escape their notice. For Sammy the logical extension of Lengel's "policy" is the half-serious notion that one day the A & P might be known as the "Great Alexandrov and Petrooshki Tea Company" (146). Sammy's connection between what he regards as mindless "policy" (148) and Soviet oppression is obviously an exaggeration, but the reader is invited to entertain the similarities anyway.

The reason Sammy quits his job has less to do with defending the girls than with his own sense of what it means to be a decent human being. His decision is not an easy one. He doesn't want to make trouble or disappoint his parents, and he knows his independence and self-reliance (the other side of New England tradition) will make life more complex for him. In spite of his own hesitations, he finds himself blurting out "Fiddle-de-doo" (148) to Lengel's policies and in doing so knows that his grandmother "would have been pleased" (148). Sammy's "No Sale" rejects the crabbed perspective on life that Lengel represents as manager of the A & P. This gesture is more than just a negative, however, for as he punches in that last entry on the cash register, "the machine whirs 'pee-pul' " (149). His decision to quit his job at the A & P is an expression of his refusal to regard policies as more important than people.

## Work Cited

Updike, John. "A & P." *The Compact Bedford Introduction to Literature*, edited by Michael Meyer and D. Quentin Miller, 13th ed., Bedford/St. Martin's, 2024, pp. 145–49.

# WRITING ABOUT POETRY

Writing about poetry can be a rigorous means of developing and testing your initial response to a poem. Anyone who has been asked to write several pages about a fourteen-line poem knows how intellectually challenging this exercise is, because it means paying close attention to language. Such scrutiny of words, however, sensitizes you not only to the poet's use of language but also to your own use of language. At first you may feel intimidated by having to compose a paper that is longer than the poem you're writing about, but once you start writing — often the hardest part of the process — you will realize that you have plenty to say. Keep in mind that there is not a single hidden meaning to any poem: it is not like algebra where you are solving for *x*. Even Carl Sandburg once confessed, "I've written some poetry I don't understand myself." Because language is not stable, poems are not codes to be cracked. Don't worry about "the right answer": your role is to develop an interesting thesis and to support it clearly and persuasively in your argument.

An interesting thesis will come to you if you read and reread, take notes, annotate the text, and generate ideas. Although it requires energy to read closely and to write convincingly about the charged language found in poetry, there is nothing mysterious about such reading and writing. The set of Questions for Responsive Reading and Writing about Poetry below is designed to sharpen your reading and writing about poetry. After reading a poem, use the questions to help you think, talk, and write about any poem. Before you do, though, be sure that you have read the poem several times without worrying actively about interpretation. With poetry, as with all literature, it's important to allow yourself the pleasure of enjoying whatever catches your attention. On subsequent readings, use the questions to understand and appreciate how the poem works; remember to keep in mind that not all questions will necessarily be relevant to a particular poem.

Following these questions is a sample paper that offers a clear and well-developed thesis concerning John Donne's "Death Be Not Proud."

---

### Questions for Responsive Reading and Writing about Poetry

The following questions can help you respond to important elements that reveal a poem's effects and meanings. The questions are general, so not all of them will necessarily be relevant to a particular poem. Many, however, should prove useful for thinking, talking, and writing about each poem in this collection. If you are uncertain about the meaning of a term used in a question, consult the Glossary of Literary Terms beginning on page 1483.

Before addressing these questions, read the poem you are studying in its entirety. Don't worry about interpretation on a first reading; allow

*(continued)*

yourself the pleasure of discovery. Then on subsequent readings, use the questions to understand and appreciate how the poem works.

1. Who is the speaker? Is it possible to determine the speaker's age, gender, sensibilities, level of awareness, and values?

2. Is the speaker addressing anyone in particular?

3. How do you respond to the speaker? Favorably? Negatively? What is the situation? Are there any special circumstances that inform what the speaker says?

4. Is there a specific setting of time and place?

5. How does reading the poem aloud help you understand it?

6. Does a paraphrase reveal the basic purpose of the poem?

7. What does the title emphasize?

8. Is the theme presented directly or indirectly?

9. Do any allusions enrich the poem's meaning?

10. How does the diction reveal meaning? Are any words repeated? Do any carry evocative connotative meanings? Are there any puns or other forms of verbal wit?

11. Are figures of speech used? How does the figurative language contribute to the poem's vividness and meaning?

12. Do any objects, persons, places, events, or actions have allegorical or symbolic meanings? What other details in the poem support your interpretation?

13. Is irony used? Are there any examples of situational irony, verbal irony, or dramatic irony? Is understatement or paradox used?

14. What is the tone of the poem? Is the tone consistent?

15. Does the poem use onomatopoeia, assonance, consonance, or alliteration? How do these sounds affect you?

16. What sounds are repeated? If there are rhymes, what is their effect? Do they seem forced or natural? Is there a rhyme scheme? Do the rhymes contribute to the poem's meaning?

17. Do the lines have a regular meter? What is the predominant meter? Are there significant variations? Does the rhythm seem appropriate for the poem's tone?

18. Does the poem's form — its overall structure — follow an established pattern? Do you think the form is a suitable vehicle for the poem's meaning and effects?

19. Is the language of the poem intense and concentrated? Do you think it warrants more than one or two close readings?

20. Did you respond positively to the poem? What, specifically, pleased or displeased you about what was expressed and how it was expressed?

21. Is there a particular critical approach or context that seems especially appropriate for this poem? (See Chapter 42, "Critical Strategies for Reading".)

22. What kinds of evidence from the poem are you focusing on to support your interpretation? Does your interpretation leave out any important elements that might undercut or qualify your interpretation?

## THE ELEMENTS TOGETHER

The elements of poetry that you have studied in Chapters 16–23 of this book offer a vocabulary and a series of perspectives that open up avenues of inquiry into a poem. As you have learned, there are many potential routes that you can take. By asking questions about the speaker, diction, figurative language, sounds, rhythm, tone, or theme, you clarify your understanding while simultaneously sensitizing yourself to elements and issues especially relevant to the poem under consideration. This process of careful, informed reading allows you to see how the various elements of the poem reinforce its meanings.

A poem's elements do not exist in isolation, however. They work together to create a complete experience for the reader. Knowing how the elements combine helps you understand the poem's structure and appreciate it as a whole. Robert Herrick's "Delight in Disorder" (p. 673), for example, is more easily understood (and the humor of the poem is better appreciated) when meter and rhyme are considered together with the poem's meaning. Musing about how he is more charmed by a naturally disheveled appearance than by those that seem contrived, the speaker lists several attributes of dishevelment and concludes that they

Do more bewitch me than when art
Is too precise in every part.

Noticing how the couplet's precise and sing-songy rhythm combines with the solid, obvious, and final rhyme of *art / part* helps in understanding what the speaker means by "too precise," as the lines are a little too precise themselves. Noticing this, you may even want to chart how rhythm and rhyme work together throughout the early (more disheveled) lines of the poem. Finding a pattern in the ways the elements work together throughout the poem will help you understand how the poem works.

This section shows you how one student author, Rose Bostwick, moves through the stages of writing about how a poem's elements combine for a final effect. Included here are Rose's annotated version of the poem, her first response, her informal outline, and the final draft of an explication of John Donne's "Death Be Not Proud." (For more on explication, see page 1422.) After reviewing the elements of poetry covered in Chapters 16–23, Rose read the poem several times, paying careful attention to diction, figurative language, irony, symbol, rhythm, sound, and so on. Her final paper is more concerned with the overall effect of the combination of elements than with a line-by-line breakdown, and her annotated version of the poem details her attention to that task. As you read and reread "Death Be Not Proud," keep notes on how *you* think the elements of this poem work together and to what overall effect.

## JOHN DONNE  (1572–1631)

John Donne, now regarded as a major poet of the early seventeenth century, wrote love poems at the beginning of his career but shifted to religious themes after converting from Catholicism to Anglicanism in the early 1590s. Although trained in law, he was also ordained a priest and became dean of St. Paul's Cathedral in London in 1621. The following poem, from "Holy Sonnets," reflects both his religious faith and his ability to create elegant arguments in verse.

Michael Nicholson/Getty Images.

## *Death Be Not Proud*    1611

Death be not proud, though some have callèd thee
Mighty and dreadful, for thou art not so;
For those whom thou think'st thou dost overthrow
Die not, poor Death, nor yet canst thou kill me.
From rest and sleep, which but thy pictures° be,                    *images*    5
Much pleasure; then from thee much more must flow,
And soonest our best men with thee do go,
Rest of their bones, and soul's delivery.°                           *deliverance*
Thou art slave to Fate, Chance, kings, and desperate men,
And dost with Poison, War, and Sickness dwell;                       10
And poppy or charms can make us sleep as well,
And better than thy stroke; why swell'st° thou then?                 *swell with pride*
One short sleep past, we wake eternally
And death shall be no more; Death, thou shalt die.

## CONSIDERATIONS FOR CRITICAL THINKING AND WRITING

1. FIRST RESPONSE. Why doesn't the speaker fear death? Explain why you find the argument convincing or not.

2. How does the speaker compare death with rest and sleep in lines 5–8? What is the point of this comparison?

3. Discuss the poem's rhythm by examining the breaks and end-stopped lines. How does the poem's rhythm contribute to its meaning?

4. Why is this poem classified as a sonnet?

# A SAMPLE CLOSE READING

## *An Annotated Version of "Death Be Not Proud"*

As she read the poem closely several times, Rose annotated it with impressions and ideas that would lead to insights on which her analysis would be built. Her close examination of the poem's elements allowed her to understand how its parts contribute to its overall effect; her annotations provide a useful map of her thinking.

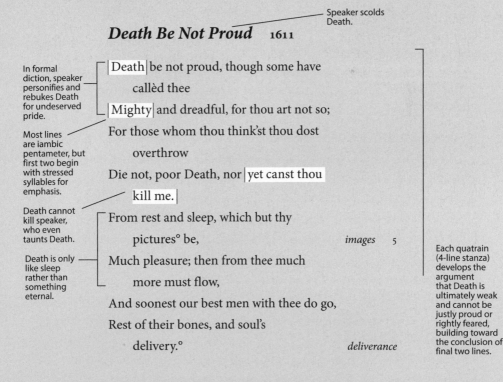

Speaker scolds Death.

### *Death Be Not Proud*   1611

In formal diction, speaker personifies and rebukes Death for undeserved pride.

|Death| be not proud, though some have
callèd thee

|Mighty| and dreadful, for thou art not so;

Most lines are iambic pentameter, but first two begin with stressed syllables for emphasis.

For those whom thou think'st thou dost
overthrow

Death cannot kill speaker, who even taunts Death.

Die not, poor Death, nor |yet canst thou
kill me.|

From rest and sleep, which but thy
pictures° be,                    *images*   5

Death is only like sleep rather than something eternal.

Much pleasure; then from thee much
more must flow,

And soonest our best men with thee do go,

Rest of their bones, and soul's
delivery.°                          *deliverance*

Each quatrain (4-line stanza) develops the argument that Death is ultimately weak and cannot be justly proud or rightly feared, building toward the conclusion of final two lines.

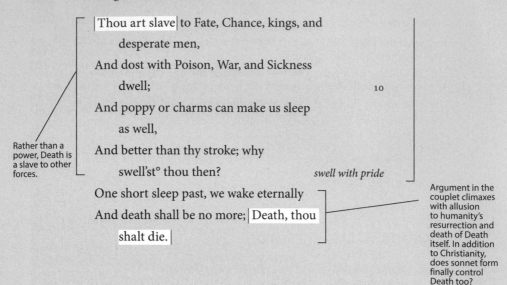

Rather than a power, Death is a slave to other forces.

> |Thou art slave| to Fate, Chance, kings, and
>
>     desperate men,
>
> And dost with Poison, War, and Sickness
>
>     dwell;                                   10
>
> And poppy or charms can make us sleep
>
>     as well,
>
> And better than thy stroke; why
>
>     swell'st° thou then?         *swell with pride*
>
> One short sleep past, we wake eternally
>
> And death shall be no more; |Death, thou
>
>     shalt die.|

Argument in the couplet climaxes with allusion to humanity's resurrection and death of Death itself. In addition to Christianity, does sonnet form finally control Death too?

## A SAMPLE FIRST RESPONSE

After Rose carefully read "Death Be Not Proud" and had a sense of how the elements work, she took the first step toward a formal explication by writing informally about the relevant elements and addressing the question *Why doesn't the speaker fear death? Explain why you find the argument convincing or not.* Note that at this point, she was not as concerned with textual evidence and detail as she would need to be in her final essay.

> I've read the poem "Death Be Not Proud" by John Donne a few times now, and I have
> a sense of how it works. The poem is a sonnet, and each of the three quatrains presents a
> piece of the argument that Death should not be proud, because it is not really all-powerful,
> and may even be a source of pleasure. As a reader, I resist this seeming paradox at first,
> but I know it must be a trick, a riddle of some sort that the poem will proceed to untangle.
> I think one of the reasons the poem comes off as such a powerful statement is that
> Donne at first seems to be playful and paradoxical in his characterizations of Death. He's
> almost teasing Death. But beneath the teasing tone you feel the strong foundation of the
> real reason Death should not be proud—Donne's faith in the immortality of the soul. The
> poem begins to feel more solemn as it progresses, as the hints at the idea of immortality
> become more clearly articulated.
>
> Donne utilizes two literary conventions to increase the effect of this poem: he
> uses the convention of personifying death, so that he can address it directly, and he uses

the metaphor of death as a kind of sleep. These two things determine the tone and the progression from playful to solemn in the poem.

The last clause of the poem (line 14) plays with the paradoxical-seeming character of what he's been declaring. Ironically, it seems the only thing susceptible to death is death itself. Or, when death becomes powerless is when it only has power over itself.

## ORGANIZING YOUR THOUGHTS

Showing in an essay how different elements of a particular poem work together is often quite challenging. While you may have a clear intuitive sense of what elements are important to the poem and how they complement one another, it is important to organize your thoughts in such a way as to make the relationships clear to your audience. The simplest way is to go line by line, but that can quickly become dull for writer and reader. Because you will want to organize your paper in the way that best serves your thesis, it may help to write an informal outline that charts how you think the argument moves. You may find, for example, that the argument is not persuasive if you start with the final lines and go back to the beginning of the poem or passage. However you decide to organize your argument, keep in mind that a unifying idea will run throughout the entire paper and that your thesis will express that idea concisely.

## A SAMPLE INFORMAL OUTLINE

In her informal outline (following), Rose discovers that her argument works best if she begins at the poem's beginning. Note that, though her later paper concerns itself with how several elements of poetry contribute to the poem's theme and message, her informal outline concerns itself much more with what that message is and how it develops as the poem progresses. She will fill in the details later.

*Working Thesis: From the very first word, addressing "Death" directly, Donne uses the literary conventions of personifying death and comparing it to sleep to begin an argument that Death should not be proud of its might or dreadfulness. But these two elements of his argument come to be seen as the superficial points when the true reason for death's powerlessness becomes clear. The Christian belief in the immortality of the soul is the reason for death's powerlessness and likeness to sleep.*

*Body of essay: Show how argument proceeds by quatrains from playful address to Death, and statement that Death is much like sleep, its "picture," to statement that Death is "slave" to other forces (and so should not be proud of being the mightiest), to the couplet, which articulates clearly the idea of immortality and gives the final paradox, "Death, thou shalt die."*

*Conclusion: Donne's faith in the immortality of the soul enables him to "prove" in this argument that Death is truly like its metaphorical representation, sleep. Faith allows him to derive a source for this conventional trope, and it allows him to state his truth in paradoxes. He relies on the conventional idea that death is an end, and a conqueror, and the only all-powerful force, to make the paradoxes that lend his argument the force of mystery — the mystery of faith.*

## THE ELEMENTS AND THEME

As you create an informal outline, your understanding of the poem will grow, change, and finally, solidify. You will develop a much clearer sense of what the poem's elements combine to create, and you will have chosen a scheme for organizing your argument. The next step before drafting is to generate a working thesis, which will not only keep your paper focused but will also help you center your thoughts. For papers that discuss how the elements of poetry come together, the thesis is a single and concise statement of what the elements combine to create — the idea around which all the elements revolve.

Once you understand how the elements of the poem fit together and have articulated your understanding in the thesis statement, the next step is to flesh out your argument. By including quotations from the poem to illustrate the points you will be making, you will better explain exactly how each element relates to the others and, more specifically, to your thesis.

## A SAMPLE EXPLICATION

### *The Use of Conventional Metaphors for Death in John Donne's "Death Be Not Proud"*

In Rose's final draft, she focuses on the use of metaphor in "Death Be Not Proud." Her essay provides a coherent reading that relates each line of the poem to the speaker's intense awareness of death. Although the essay discusses each stanza in order, the introductory paragraph provides a brief overview explaining how the poem's metaphor and arguments contribute to its total meaning. In addition, Rose does not hesitate to discuss a line out of sequence when it can be usefully connected to another phrase. She also works quotations into her sentences to support her points. When she adds something to a quotation to clarify it, she encloses her words in brackets so that they will not be mistaken for the poet's, and she uses a slash to indicate line divisions: "soonest . . . with thee do go, / [for] Rest of their bones, and soul's delivery." Finally, Rose is sure to cite the line numbers for any direct quotations from the poem. As you read through her final draft, remember that the word *explication* comes from the Latin *explicare*, "to unfold." How successful do you think Rose is at unfolding this poem to reveal how its elements — here ranging from metaphor, structure, meter, personification, paradox, and irony to theme — contribute to its meaning?

Rose Bostwick

English 101

Professor Hart

24 February 2023

The Use of Conventional Metaphors for Death

in John Donne's "Death Be Not Proud"

In the sonnet that begins "Death be not proud . . ." John Donne argues that death is not "mighty and dreadful" but is more like its metaphorical representation, sleep. Death, Donne puts forth, is even a source of pleasure and rest. The poet builds this argument on two foundations. One is made up of the metaphors and literary conventions for death: death is compared with sleep and is often personified so that it can be addressed directly. The poem is an address to death that at first seems paradoxical and somewhat playful, but which then rises in all the emotion of faith as it reveals the second foundation of the argument — the Christian belief in the immortality of the soul. Seen against the backdrop of this belief, death loses its powerful threat and is seen as only a metaphorical sleep, or rest.

> Thesis providing interpretation of the poem's use of metaphor and how it contributes to the poem's central argument

The poem is an ironic argument that proceeds according to the structure of the sonnet form. Each quatrain contains a new development or aspect of the argument, and the final couplet serves as a conclusion. The metrical scheme is mainly iambic pentameter, but in several places in the poem, the stress pattern is altered for emphasis. For example, the first foot of the poem is inverted, so that "Death," the first word, receives the stress. This announces to us right away that death is being personified and addressed. This inversion also serves to begin the poem energetically and forcefully. The second line behaves in the same way. The first syllable of "Mighty" receives the stress, emphasizing the meaning of the word and its assumed relation to death.

> Discussion of how form and meter contribute to the poem's central argument

This first quatrain offers the first paradox and sets up the argument that death has been conventionally personified with the wrong attributes, might and dreadfulness. The poet tells death not to be proud, "though some have callèd thee / Mighty and dreadful," because, he says, death is "not so" (lines 1-2). Donne will turn this conventional characterization of death on

> Discussion of how personification contributes to the poem's central argument

its head with the paradox of the third and fourth lines: he says the people overthrown by death (as if by a conqueror) "Die not, poor death, nor yet canst thou kill me." These lines establish the paradox of death not being able to cause death.

> Discussion of how metaphor of sleep and idea of immortality support the poem's central argument

The next quatrain will not begin to answer the question of why this paradox is so, but will posit another slight paradox—the idea of death as pleasurable. In lines 5-8, Donne uses the literary convention of describing death as a metaphorical sleep, or rest, to construct the argument that death must give pleasure: "From rest and sleep, which but thy pictures be, / Much pleasure; then from thee much more must flow" (5-6). At this point, the argument seems almost playful, but is carefully hinting at the solemnity of the deeper foundation of the belief in immortality. The metaphor of sleep for death includes the idea of waking; one doesn't sleep forever. The next two lines put forth the idea that death is pleasurable enough to be desired by "our best men" who "soonest . . . with thee do go, / [for] Rest of their bones, and soul's delivery" (7-8). This last line comes closer to announcing the true reason for death's powerlessness and pleasure: it is the way to the "soul's delivery" from the body and life on earth, and implicitly, into another, better realm.

A new reason for death's powerlessness arises in the next four lines. The poet says to death:

> Thou art slave to Fate, Chance, kings, and desperate men,
> And dost with Poison, War, and Sickness dwell;
> And poppy or charms can make us sleep as well,
> And better than thy stroke; why swell'st thou then? (9-12)

> Discussion of how language and tone contribute to the poem's central argument

Donne argues here that there are forces more powerful than death that actually control it. Fate and chance determine when death occurs, and to whom it comes. Kings, with the powers of law and war, can summon death and throw it on whom they wish. And desperate men, murderers or suicides, can also summon death with the strength of their emotions. In lines 11 and 12, Donne again uses the metaphor of death as a kind of sleep, but says that drugs or "charms" give one a better sleep than death. And he asks playfully why death should be so proud, after all these illustrations of its weakness have been given: "why swell'st thou then?" (12).

Bostwick 3

Finally, with the last couplet, Donne reveals the true, deeper reason behind his argument that death should not be proud of its power. These lines also offer an explanation of the metaphor for death of sleep, or rest: "One short sleep past, we wake eternally / And death shall be no more; Death, thou shalt die" (13-14). After death, the soul lives on, according to Christian theology and belief. In the Christian heaven, where the soul is immortal, death will no longer exist, and so this last paradox, "Death, thou shalt die," becomes true. Again in this line, a significant inversion of metrical stress occurs. "Death," in the second clause, receives the stress, recalling the first line, emphasizing that it is an address and giving the clause a forceful sense of finality. His belief in the immortality of the soul enables Donne to "prove" in this argument that death is in actuality like its metaphorical representation, sleep. His faith allows him to derive a source for this conventional metaphor and to "disprove" the metaphor of death as an all-powerful conqueror. His Christian beliefs also allow him to state his truth in paradoxes, the mysteries that are justified by the mystery of faith.

> Discussion of function of religious faith in the poem and how word order and meter create emphasis

> Conclusion supporting thesis in context of poet's beliefs

Bostwick 4

Work Cited

Donne, John. "Death Be Not Proud." *The Compact Bedford Introduction to Literature*, edited by Michael Meyer and D. Quentin Miller, 13th ed., Bedford/St. Martin's, 2024, p. 1448.

# WRITING ABOUT DRAMA

Because dramatic literature is written to be performed, writing about reading a play may seem twice removed from what playwrights intend the experience of drama to be: a live audience responding to live actors. Although reading a play creates distance between yourself and a performance of it, reading a play can actually bring you closer to understanding that the literary dimension of a script is what supports a stage production of any play. Writing about that script —examining carefully how the language of the stage directions, setting, exposition, dialogue, plot, and other dramatic elements serve to produce effects and meanings — can enhance an imaginative re-creation of a performance. In a sense, writing about a play gauges your own interpretative response as an audience member. The difference, of course, is that instead of applauding, you are typing.

Composing an essay about drama records more than your response to a play; writing also helps you explore, clarify, and discover dimensions of the play you may not have perceived by simply watching a performance of it. Writing is work, as we've suggested, but it's the kind of work that brings you closer to your own imagination as well as to the play. That process is more accessible if you read carefully, take notes, and annotate the text to generate ideas as we discuss earlier in this chapter. The following section offers a set of questions to help you read and write about drama and includes a sample paper that argues for a feminist reading of Susan Glaspell's *Trifles* (p. 1459).

---

### Questions for Responsive Reading and Writing about Drama

The questions in this section can help you consider important elements that reveal a play's effects and meanings. These questions are general and will not, therefore, always be relevant to a particular play. Many of them, however, should prove to be useful for thinking, talking, and writing about drama. If you are uncertain about the meaning of a term used in a question, consult the Glossary of Literary Terms beginning on page 1483.

1. Did you enjoy the play or did it agitate you? What, specifically, pleased or displeased you about what was expressed and how it was expressed?

2. What is the significance of the play's title? How does it suggest the author's overall emphasis?

3. What information do the stage directions provide about the characters, action, and setting? Are these directions primarily descriptive, or are they also keys to interpretation?

4. How is the exposition presented? What does it reveal? How does the playwright's choice *not* to dramatize certain events on stage help to determine what the focus of the play is?

5. In what ways is the setting important? Would the play be altered significantly if the setting were changed?

6. Are there instances of foreshadowing that suggest what is to come? Are flashbacks used to dramatize what has already happened?

7. What is the major conflict the protagonist faces? What complications constitute the rising action? Where is the climax? Is the conflict resolved?

8. Are one or more subplots used to qualify or complicate the main plot? Is the plot unified so that each incident somehow has a function that relates it to some other element in the play?

9. Does the author purposely avoid or employ a pyramidal plot structure of rising action, climax, and falling action? Is the plot experimental? Is the plot logically and chronologically organized, or is it fantastical or absurd? What effects are produced by the plot? How does it reflect the author's view of life?

10. Who is the protagonist? Who (or what) is the antagonist?

11. By what means does the playwright reveal character? What do the characters' names, physical qualities, actions, and words convey about them? What do the characters reveal about each other?

12. What is the purpose of the minor characters within the drama? Are they individualized, or do they primarily represent ideas or attitudes? Are any character foils used?

13. Do the characters all use the same kind of language, or is their speech differentiated? Is it formal or informal? How do the characters' diction and manner of speaking serve to characterize them?

14. Does your response to the characters change over the course of the play? What causes the change?

15. Are words and images repeated in the play so that they take on special meanings? Which speeches seem particularly important? Why?

16. How does the playwright's use of language contribute to the tone of the play? Is the dialogue, for example, predominantly light, humorous, relaxed, sentimental, sad, angry, intense, or violent?

*(continued)*

17. Are any symbols used in the play? Which actions, characters, settings, objects, or words convey more than their literal meanings?

18. Are any unfamiliar theatrical conventions used that present obstacles to understanding the play? How does knowing more about the nature of the theater from which the play originated help to resolve these problems?

19. Is the theme stated directly, or is it developed implicitly through the plot, characters, or some other element? Does the theme confirm or challenge most people's values?

20. How does the play reflect the values of the society in which it is set and in which it was written?

21. How does the play reflect or challenge your own values?

22. Is there a sound recording, film, or online source for the play available in your library or media center? How does this version compare with your own reading?

23. How would you produce the play on a stage? Consider scenery, costumes, casting, and characterizations. What would you emphasize most in your production?

24. Is there a particular critical approach or context that seems especially appropriate for this play? (See Chapter 42, "Critical Strategies for Reading.")

## A SAMPLE STUDENT PAPER

### *The Feminist Evidence in Susan Glaspell's* Trifles

The following paper was written in response to an assignment that required an analysis — about 750 words — of an assigned play. Chris Duffy's paper argues that although *Trifles* was written a century ago, it should be seen as a feminist play because its treatment of the tensions between men and women deliberately reveals the oppressiveness that women have had to cope with in their everyday lives. The paper discusses a number of the play's elements, but the discussion is unified through its focus on how the women characters are bound together by a set of common concerns. Notice that page numbers are provided to document quoted passages.

Duffy 1

Chris Duffy

Professor Barrina-Barrou

English 109-2

6 March 2023

The Feminist Evidence in Susan Glaspell's Trifles

Despite its early publication date, Susan Glaspell's *Trifles* (1916) can be regarded as a work of feminist literature. The play depicts the life of a woman who has been suppressed, oppressed, and subjugated by a patronizing, patriarchal husband. Mrs. Wright is eventually driven to kill her "hard" (982) husband who has stifled every last twitch of her identity. *Trifles* dramatizes the hypocrisy and ingrained discrimination of male-dominated society while simultaneously speaking to the dangers for women who succumb to such hierarchies. Because Mrs. Wright follows the role mapped by her husband and is directed by society's patriarchal expectations, her identity is lost somewhere along the way. However, Mrs. Hale and Mrs. Peters quietly insist on preserving their own identities by protecting Mrs. Wright from the men who seek to convict her of murder.

> General thesis statement

> More specific thesis offering analysis, with supporting evidence

Mrs. Wright is described as someone who used to have a flair for life. Her neighbor, Mrs. Hale, comments that the last time Mrs. Wright appeared happy and vivacious was before she was married or, more important, when she was Minnie Foster and not Mrs. Wright. Mrs. Hale laments, "I heard she used to wear pretty clothes and be lively, when she was Minnie Foster, one of the town girls singing in the choir" (980). But after thirty years of marriage, Mrs. Wright is now worried about her canned preserves freezing and being without an apron while she is in jail. This subservient image was so accepted in society that Mrs. Peters, the sheriff's wife, speculates that Mrs. Wright must want her apron in order to "feel more natural" (980). Any other roles would be considered uncharacteristic.

> Analysis of Mrs. Wright through perspectives of female characters

This wifely role is predicated on the supposition that women have no ability to make complicated decisions, to think critically, or to rely on themselves. As the title suggests, the men in this story think of homemaking as much less important than a husband's breadwinning role. Mr. Hale remarks, "Well, women are used to worrying over trifles" (978), and Sheriff Peters assumes the insignificance of "kitchen things" (978).

> Analysis of role of women through perspectives of male characters

Hence, women are forced into a domestic, secondary role, like it or not, and are not even respected for that. Mr. Hale, Sheriff Peters, and the county attorney all dismiss the dialogue between Mrs. Peters and Mrs. Hale as feminine chitchat. Further, the county attorney allows the women to leave the Wrights' house unsupervised because he sees Mrs. Peters as merely an extension of her husband.

Even so, the domestic system the men have set up for their wives and their disregard for them after the rules and boundaries have been laid down prove to be the men's downfall. The evidence that Mrs. Wright killed her husband is woven into Mrs. Hale's and Mrs. Peters's conversations about Mrs. Wright's sewing and her pet bird. The knots in her quilt match those in the rope used to strangle Mr. Wright, and the bird, the last symbol of Mrs. Wright's vitality to be taken by her husband, is found dead. Unable to play the role of subservient wife anymore, Mrs. Wright is foreign to herself and therefore lives a lie. As Mrs. Hale proclaims, "Why, it looks as if she didn't know what she was about!" (981).

Mrs. Hale, however, does ultimately understand what Mrs. Wright is about. She comprehends the desperation, loneliness, and pain that Mrs. Wright experienced, and she instinctively knows that the roles Mrs. Wright played — even that of murderer — are scripted by the male-dominated circumstances of her life. As Mrs. Hale shrewdly and covertly observes in the context of a discussion about housecleaning with the county attorney: "Men's hands aren't always as clean as they might be" (979). In fact, even Mrs. Hale feels some guilt for not having made an effort to visit Mrs. Wright over the years to help relieve the monotony of Mrs. Wright's life with her husband:

> I might have known she needed help! I know how things can be — for
> women. I tell you, it's queer, Mrs. Peters. We live close together and
> we live far apart. We all go through the same things — it's all just a
> different kind of the same thing. (984)

Mrs. Hale cannot help identifying with her neighbor.

In contrast, Mrs. Peters is initially reluctant to support Mrs. Wright. Not only is she married to the sheriff, but, as the county attorney puts it, "a sheriff's wife is married to the law" (984) as well. She reminds Mrs. Hale

*Marginal notes:*

Discussion of Mrs. Hale's identification with Mrs. Wright

Discussion of Mrs. Peters's identification with Mrs. Wright

Duffy 3

that "the law has got to punish crime" (983), even if it means revealing the existence of the dead bird and exposing the motive that could convict Mrs. Wright of murdering her husband. But finally Mrs. Peters also becomes complicit in keeping information from her husband and other men. She too—owing to the loss of her first child—understands what loss means and what Mrs. Hale means when she says that women "all go through the same things" (984).

The women in *Trifles* cannot, as the play reveals, be trifled with. Although Glaspell wrote the play more than one hundred years ago, it continues to be relevant to contemporary relationships between men and women. Its essentially feminist perspective provides a convincing case for the necessity of women to move beyond destructive stereotypes and oppressive assumptions in order to be true to their own significant—not trifling—experiences.

Conclusion summarizing analysis

Duffy 4

Work Cited

Glaspell, Susan. "Trifles." *The Compact Bedford Introduction to Literature*, edited by Michael Meyer and D. Quentin Miller, 13th ed., Bedford/St. Martin's, 2024, pp. 976–84.

# 44

## The Literary Research Paper

Library of Congress.

Research is formalized curiosity. It is poking and prying with a purpose.
— ZORA NEALE HURSTON

A close reading of a primary source such as a short story, poem, or play can give insights into a work's themes and effects, but sometimes you will want to know more. A published commentary by a critic who knows the work well and is familiar with the author's body of work or other contexts for interpretation can provide insights that otherwise may not be available. Such writings — known as *secondary sources* — are, of course, not a substitute for the work itself, but they often can explore interpretations that you might not have considered if you had not encountered them. The way to encounter these published commentaries is through research.

Students sometimes tense up when they are asked to write a research paper. It might seem like research just adds another demand to this challenging business of interpreting literature, but if you regard research as exploration, or as "poking and prying with a purpose" as Zora Neale Hurston says, it might become less daunting and more exciting. The literary criticism you will discover is really just an advanced version of what you've been learning to do in this course. These published essays are models as well as sources. They will allow you to ponder interpretations you had not considered, or they might provide a perspective that you resist as you become more convinced of the validity of your own interpretation. Another way to think about these sources is as a conversation, and you have the opportunity to raise your hand and offer your own opinion, just as you do during class discussion. A research paper is really just a more formal, more sophisticated version of these discussions. It's an even better version because you are more in control of the conversation: you can "call on" the critics who help articulate what you want to say.

There is no question that a research paper requires more time than a paper that only requires you to interpret a literary text. It is important to budget your time wisely so that you aren't spending too much of it on one stage of the process at the expense of another. For most writers at your level of development, the phase of locating and assessing the value of sources takes more time than anticipated. That's because it's an unfamiliar process. As you become more used to it, this phase of the process will go more quickly, but it's still important to reserve plenty of time so that you can experience the pleasures of discovery. You will get better results if you approach your research by wondering "What can I learn?" rather than focusing on the research simply as a requirement.

After you have adjusted to the challenges of locating and assessing the value of sources, perhaps the next most important requirement of a research paper is the ability to organize material. A bit of planning should help, just as prewriting strategies pave the way for smoother writing and revising. You already know the challenges of writing an interpretive essay. The research essay just adds four basic components to that process: locating secondary sources, evaluating their validity, positioning them comfortably within your essay, and documenting them.

The following list should give you a sense of what goes into creating a research paper. Although some steps on the list can be folded into one another, they offer an overview of the work that will involve you:

1. Choosing a topic
2. Finding sources
3. Evaluating sources
4. Taking notes
5. Developing a working thesis
6. Prewriting
7. Writing drafts
8. Revising
9. Documenting sources
10. Preparing the final draft and proofreading

Even if you have never written a research paper, you most likely have already had experience choosing a topic, developing a thesis, organizing an outline, and writing a draft that you then revised, proofread, and handed in. Those skills — detailed in Chapter 43 — represent six of the ten items on the list. This chapter briefly reviews some of these steps and focuses on the remaining tasks, unique to research paper assignments.

## CHOOSING A TOPIC

Chapter 43 discussed the importance of reading a work closely and taking careful notes as a means of generating topics for writing about literature. If you know a work well and record your understanding of it in notes, you'll have impressions and ideas to choose from for potential topics. You may find it useful to review the information on pages 1410–1411 before reading the advice about putting together a research paper in this chapter.

The student author of the sample research paper "How William Faulkner's Narrator Cultivates a Rose for Emily" (p. 1478) was asked to write a five-page paper that demonstrated some familiarity with published critical perspectives on a Faulkner story of his choice. Before looking into critical discussions of the story, he read "A Rose for Emily" several times, taking notes and making comments in the margin of his textbook on each reading.

What prompted his choice of "A Rose for Emily" was a class discussion in which many of his classmates found the story's title inappropriate or misleading because they could not understand how and why the story constituted a tribute (the "rose" of the title) to Emily given that she murdered a man and slept with his dead body over many years. Why did Faulkner use such a title? Only after having thoroughly examined the story did the student go to the library to see what professional critics had to say about this question.

## FINDING SOURCES

Whether your college library is large or small, its reference librarians can usually help you locate secondary sources about a particular work or author. Unless you choose a very recently published story, poem, play, or essay about which little or nothing has been written, you should be able to access sources, probably more than you would guess. Your college or university library is designed to give you access to excellent, useful information. The problem many students face is that too much information is available. If you were writing an essay on *Othello* and military history and you typed "William Shakespeare" into a search engine, you would come up with tens of thousands of sources and you would have countless hours of work ahead of you sifting through them to find a useful one. Part of the art of finding sources is knowing the right way to limit your search, just as the way to knowledge is through asking the right questions.

The image of a library as a cold, dusty space where severe-looking librarians shush you whenever you whisper is antiquated, and was never completely accurate. Libraries are some of the most exciting spaces that have adapted to and even helped to create our so-called Information Age. Just as students are sometimes intimidated by the very word *research*, they can also cower at the door of their college library, daunted by the sheer amount of wisdom it seems to contain or unsure where to start sifting through it. Your library, though, is a resource that was designed for you. Think of the offices on campus that exist to ensure your success: the registrar, financial aid, admissions, counseling . . . the list is long. All of these offices employ people whose job is to help you access their services, and you have no doubt learned the value of communicating with them. If you're feeling uncertain about how to go about your research, your reference librarians are there to help you to get started. They are trained professionals who tend to love the very challenge that you might find mysterious: locating sources.

In addition to being valuable human resources, librarians have also worked hard to design a website that helps you navigate their holdings, many of which are electronic as opposed to print sources. Libraries increasingly provide online databases that you can access remotely. This can be an efficient way to locate sources on your own schedule. There also might be a way to contact your reference librarians through that website with questions. As we suggest above, these employees of your college or university are funded through your tuition dollars: you should become comfortable asking them questions just as you would ask your professors to clarify something they said in class, or to guide you if you are having trouble with a writing assignment. Like your professors, research librarians are teachers who are eager to help you.

Some of the articles you locate through your library's databases are also available on the Internet, but know from the outset that the open Internet does not discriminate between a valid work of literary criticism and a blog post or tweet. In addition to the many electronic databases available, including your library's computerized holdings, the Internet also connects millions of sites with primary sources (the full texts of stories, poems, plays, and essays) and secondary sources (biography or criticism). If you have not had practice with online academic research, it is a good idea to get guidance from your instructor or a librarian, and by using your library's home page as a starting point. Browsing on the Internet can be absorbing as well as informative, and you are undoubtedly comfortable with the ease of Googling a term and finding what you were looking for on the first page of hits. Literary research isn't quite the same process, though. You're not simply looking for information; you're encountering a range of perspectives that might fall outside the algorithms used by Internet search engines. Your library's databases are adept at organizing these sources for your discovery. Some common databases useful for this type of research are the MLA International Bibliography, JSTOR, Project Muse, and Academic Search Premier. We cannot anticipate your library's holdings, though: an important early step for your research is to familiarize yourself with them. You should also note the difference between databases that link to a full-text article or e-book and those that do not. If there is a link to a full-text source, you automatically have access to it with a click of your mouse. If not, your library may or may not have access to that article or book. Part of the challenge is finding the sources that will be useful to you, but identifying them isn't always the same as being able to get your hands on them. We can't stress enough the value of familiarizing yourself with what your library offers and what its limitations are. The same can be said for the Internet: its powers and reach are not limitless, and it may not provide what you're looking for, or it may not present it when you approach it in customary ways.

## EVALUATING SOURCES AND TAKING NOTES

If your instructor specifies the minimum number of sources you need for your research paper, you might be focused on that number. But the number of sources you find is not as important as the usefulness of those sources for your purposes. If you were to locate seventeen articles and two books on your topic, would you just choose the first three you found to fulfill the requirement? What if one of those three was a Wikipedia entry and another was Shmoop or GradeSaver? Finding sources is only the first step: evaluating them is the second.

By "evaluate," we mean that you should assess the sources you find for reliability and the quality of their evidence. It is not always immediately clear, but there are some attributes that distinguish reliable sources from their counterparts. Shmoop and Wikipedia entries, for instance, generally are not attributed to an author, which is a sign that they are not the kind of source considered valid for a research paper. A popular magazine article, though it might be useful to your argument, will probably not be as suitable to the rhetorical purpose of your paper as an article in a scholarly journal will be. You should approach secondary sources just as you approach primary sources: as texts to be analyzed and interpreted. You should be able to summarize them, appreciate their rhetorical purpose, and quote from them, similar to the way you would position yourself in relation to one of your primary texts.

Just as you are being asked to document your sources in a Works Cited page or bibliography, the sources you find that cite other sources indicate their academic substance. Sources that are well documented with primary and secondary materials usually indicate that the author has done their homework. Books printed by university presses and established trade presses tend to be preferable to books privately printed (that is, self-published). As with articles in scholarly journals, books printed by university presses are subject to a lengthy process of peer review, meaning that experts in the field have attested to their value and importance. In some ways, these experts have done the work of evaluation for you. This is not to say that all scholarly articles or books published by university presses are equally valuable, or readable, or useful to your argument, but rather to suggest that they are substantial and that they are taken seriously as part of an established field of study.

Citations are another key. If you find six articles on a subject that all refer to a single article, it is probably important for you to locate that article. Its author is likely to be considered an expert or an important voice in that field. In academia this is referred to as an "impact factor," meaning that certain articles or critics have had a profound effect, or impact, on the way a work has been read, and other critics are compelled to contend in some way with that important source. If every article you read about your topic says something like, "According to Rowson . . . ," you would do well to find Rowson's text, and you can assume it is worth consulting.

Finally, think about when your source was published. This is not to suggest that the most recent articles or books are automatically the most valuable ones, but rather to consider their ongoing importance. A book published in 1957 isn't likely to be the most current work available on the text you are writing about, though it may have had a large impact on the way the source has been interpreted since 1957. A recently published source can help you locate important sources that preceded it. These sources can be helpful in both finding and evaluating sources that you can use. Also, if you are using one of the more recent critical strategies described in Chapter 42, a book published in 1957 would not be as useful. What we have come to understand as gender-based approaches to criticism, for example, probably would not have been employed by a 1957 critic.

As you prepare a list of reliable sources relevant to your topic, record the necessary bibliographic information so that it will be available when you make up the list of works cited for your paper. It is good practice to keep a record of all of the sources you consult initially. You may not know which sources you will ultimately use, so it is wise to play it safe and record all of them. You don't want to create an extra step for yourself later on in the process by forcing yourself to track down a source a second time. For a book, include the author, editor, and/or translator, complete title, publisher, and date of publication. For an article, include the author, complete title of the article, name of periodical, volume number, date of issue, and page numbers. For an Internet source, include the author, complete title, database title, periodical or site name, date of posting of the site (or last update), name of the institution or organization, date when you accessed the source, and its URL beginning with www (no need to include http://).

We will give specific information about how to organize these sources into a Works Cited on pages 1472–1478, but for now you can just have them as a list. Note that some online articles help you by linking to citation information. Once you have assembled a collection of sources that you may cite, you will need to take notes on your readings. Be sure to keep track of where the information comes from by writing the author's name and page number. If you use more than one work by the same author, include a brief title as well as the author's name.

## DEVELOPING A DRAFT, INTEGRATING SOURCES, AND ORGANIZING THE ESSAY

Chapter 43 describes the writing process for a standard literary analysis without research. The research paper adds the steps we describe above: locating, evaluating, and documenting sources. The next step is to integrate this work into your argument. There is no real formula for how much of the content of your research paper should be devoted to your analysis and how much to the sources you will incorporate. Your instructor's assignment may dictate this proportion, or you might consult directly with your instructor if you are unclear about this balance. In most cases, your essay will be constructed primarily of your ideas, and the sources you incorporate will help frame or support them. The key is to allow the secondary sources to contribute to rather than to inhibit the flow of your paper. It is generally evident when a writer has tacked on a quotation or two from outside sources just to fulfill the requirement of a research paper. You should think carefully about what benefits you gain by including the voice of another critic at a certain point in your paper. Are you using that source to give substance to what you are saying? Are you resisting or disagreeing with the critic? Is the source a stepping stone to help you advance a point that is key to your argument? All of these are valid reasons for bringing a secondary source into your paper, but you should be aware of how you are positioning the critical source within your argument.

Just as you might strategically summarize a story prior to quoting from it, you should consider whether it is necessary to do the same as you introduce a source. Chances are that the critical essay you've read is complex and lengthier than the essay you are writing. It is advantageous to give your reader a sense of the overall argument, not just to lift out a sentence from the essay that might not make sense without context. While taking notes on your sources, you would do well to summarize each article in a few sentences. (In fact, your instructor might require a formal version of such summaries, known as an annotated bibliography.) Even if this is not a requirement, you may be able to use your summary in the body of the paper, or it may serve as a reminder to you of the source's value to your argument.

It is an open question as to whether the location and evaluation of sources should be done during the prewriting, writing, or revision stage of your process. If you have already selected a topic and begun to gather ideas in writing, your search for valid sources will be more efficient because you will have a clearer idea of exactly what you want to say. If you wait until too late in the drafting process to conduct research, your argument may not be as flexible in terms of allowing these sources to work their way into your essay. It is best to think of the process as a fluid one in which your research and your writing cooperate instead of being two separate activities. You do not want your research to box you into a corner and limit what you want to say, nor do you want to write your paper completely and then go searching for sources that might be employed to chime in after your thesis is complete.

To return to our student example, as the notes on "A Rose for Emily" accumulated, the student sorted them into topics:

1. Publication history of the story
2. Faulkner on the title of "A Rose for Emily"
3. Is Emily simply insane?
4. The purpose of Emily's servant
5. The narrator
6. The townspeople's view of Emily
7. The surprise ending
8. Emily's admirable qualities
9. Homer's character

The student quickly saw that items 1, 4, and 9 were not directly related to his topic concerning the significance of the story's title. The remaining numbers (2, 3, 5, 6, 7, 8) are the topics taken up in the paper. The student had begun his reading of secondary sources with a working thesis that stemmed from his question about the appropriateness of the title. That "why" shaped itself into the expectation that his final thesis would look something like this: "The title justifies Emily's murder of Homer because . . ."

The author assumed that he would find information that indicated some specific reason. But the more he read, the more he discovered that it was possible to speak only about how the narrator prevents the reader from making a premature judgment about Emily rather than justifying her actions. Hence, he wisely changed his working thesis to this final thesis: "The narrator describes incidents and withholds information in such a way as to cause the reader to sympathize with Emily before her crime is revealed." This thesis helped the student explain why the title is accurate and useful rather than misleading.

After writing your first draft, you should review the advice and revision checklist on page 1420 so that you can read your paper with an objective eye. When writing a research paper, you should use this time to carefully scrutinize the sources you have brought into your essay (or the ones you still want to bring into it). Two days after writing his next-to-last draft, the writer of "How William Faulkner's Narrator Cultivates a Rose for Emily" realized that he had allotted too much space for critical discussions of the narrator that were not directly related to his approach. He wanted to demonstrate a familiarity with these studies, but it was not essential that he summarize or discuss them. He corrected this by consolidating parenthetical references: "Though a number of studies discuss the story's narrator (see, for example, Curry; Kempton; Sullivan; and Watkins). . . ." His earlier draft had included summaries of these studies that were tangential to his argument. He saw this need for revision after he took some time to approach the paper from a fresh perspective and to reconsider the relationship between his developing thesis and the sources he had located. If he had been rigid about the way he thought he was going to use his sources or if he had been completely unaware of what other critics had written at that point, his final draft would not have emerged the same way.

## DOCUMENTING SOURCES AND AVOIDING PLAGIARISM

You must acknowledge the use of a source when you (1) quote someone's exact words, (2) summarize or borrow someone's opinions or ideas, or (3) use information and facts that are not considered to be common knowledge. The purpose of this documentation is to acknowledge your sources, to demonstrate that you are familiar with what others have thought about the topic, and to provide your reader access to the same sources. If your paper is not adequately documented, it will be vulnerable to a charge of *plagiarism* — the presentation of someone else's work as your own. Academic plagiarism is a serious offense that your instructor and your college or university strongly discourages. It is a form of theft and it is antithetical to the hard work expected of you on the path to becoming a better writer and critical thinker. Conscious plagiarism is easy to avoid; honesty takes care of that for most people. However, there is an unconscious form of plagiarism that is often inadvertent yet just as problematic. To paraphrase a writer's ideas without attribution or to alter some of that author's language and claim it as your own is in the same category as including the author's language without citing it.

Let's look more closely at what constitutes plagiarism. Consider the following passage quoted from John Gassner's introduction to *Four Great Plays by Henrik Ibsen* (Bantam Books, 1959), p. viii:

Today it seems incredible that *A Doll's House* should have created the furor it did. In exploding Victorian ideals of feminine dependency the play seemed revolutionary in 1879. When its heroine Nora left her home in search of self-development it seemed as if the sanctity of marriage had been flouted by a playwright treading the stage with cloven-feet.

Now read this plagiarized version:

*A Doll's House* created a furor in 1879 by blowing up Victorian ideals about a woman's place in the world. Nora's search for self-fulfillment outside her home appeared to be an attack on the sanctity of marriage by a cloven-footed playwright.

Though the writer has shortened the passage and made some changes in the wording, this paragraph is basically the same as Gassner's. Indeed, several of his phrases are lifted almost intact. Even if a parenthetical reference had been included at the end of the passage and the source included in the Works Cited, the language of this passage would still be plagiarism because it is presented as the writer's own. Both language and ideas must be acknowledged.

Here is an adequately documented version of the passage:

John Gassner has observed how difficult it is for today's readers to comprehend the intense reaction against *A Doll's House* in 1879. When Victorian audiences watched Nora walk out of her stifling marriage, they assumed that Ibsen was expressing a devilish contempt for the "sanctity of marriage" (viii).

This passage makes absolutely clear that the observation is Gassner's, and it is written in the student's own language with the exception of one quoted phrase. Had Gassner not been named in the passage, the parenthetical reference would have included his name: (Gassner viii).

Some mention should be made of the notion of common knowledge before we turn to the standard format for documenting sources. Observations and facts that are widely known and routinely included in many of your sources do not require documentation. It is not necessary to cite a source for the fact that Alfred, Lord Tennyson was born in 1809 or that Ernest Hemingway lived for a time in Paris. Sometimes it will be difficult for you to determine what common knowledge is for a topic that you know little about. If you are in doubt, the best strategy is to supply a reference.

There are two basic ways to document sources. Traditionally, sources have been cited in footnotes at the bottom of each page or in endnotes grouped together at the end of the paper. Here is how a portion of the sample paper would look if footnotes were used instead of parenthetical documentation:

As Heller points out, before we learn of Emily's bizarre behavior we see her as a sympathetic—if antiquated—figure in a town whose life and concerns have passed her by; hence, "we are disposed to see Emily as victimized."[1]

[1]Terry Heller, "The Telltale Hair: A Critical Study of William Faulkner's 'A Rose for Emily,'" *Arizona Quarterly*, vol. 28, no. 4, 1972, p. 306.

Unlike endnotes, which are double spaced throughout under the title of "Notes" on separate pages at the end of the paper, footnotes appear four spaces below the text. They are single spaced with double spaces between notes.

No doubt you will have encountered these documentation methods in your reading. A different style is recommended, however, in the Modern Language Association's *MLA Handbook, Ninth Edition* (2021). This style employs parenthetical references within the text of the paper; these are keyed to an alphabetical list of Works Cited at the end of the paper. This method is designed to be less distracting for the reader. (An excellent website that describes the MLA style and other citation methods is the Online Writing Lab from Purdue University, commonly known as the Purdue OWL [www.owl.purdue.edu].) Unless you are instructed to follow the footnote or endnote style for documentation, use the parenthetical method explained in the next section.

## The List of Works Cited

Items in the list of works cited are arranged alphabetically according to the author's last name and indented a half inch after the first line. This practice allows the reader to locate quickly the complete bibliographic information for the author's name cited within the parenthetical reference in the text. The following are common entries for literature papers and should be used as models. The student essays throughout this book also follow this style and you can use them as models, though many of them are not research papers and only cite this anthology as their single source. If some of your sources are of a different nature (such as films or music), consult the *MLA Handbook, Ninth Edition* (MLA, 2021); or, for the latest updates, check MLA's website at style.mla.org.

When citing electronic sources, include as many of the following elements as apply and as are available:

- Author's name
- Title of work (if it's a book, italicized; if it's a short work, such as an article or poem, use quotation marks)
- Title of the site (or of the publication, if you're citing an online periodical, for example), italicized
- Sponsor or publisher of the site (if not named as the author)
- Date of publication or last update, or, if not available, date you accessed the source
- URL

### A BOOK BY ONE AUTHOR

Hendrickson, Robert. *The Literary Life and Other Curiosities*. Viking Press, 1981.

### AN ONLINE BOOK

Frost, Robert. *A Boy's Will*. Henry Holt, 1915. *Bartleby.com: Great Books Online*, 1999, www.bartleby.com/117/.

### PART OF AN ONLINE BOOK

Frost, Robert. "Into My Own." *A Boy's Will*. Henry Holt, 1915. *Bartleby.com: Great Books Online*, 1999, www.bartleby.com/117/1.html.

Notice that the author's name is in reverse order (last name first, separated by a comma). This information, along with the full title, publisher, and date, should be taken from the title and copyright pages of the book. The title is italicized and is also followed by a period. Use the publication date on the title page; if none appears there, use the copyright date (after ©) on the back of the title page.

**A BOOK BY TWO AUTHORS**

Horton, Rod W., and Herbert W. Edwards. *Backgrounds of American Literary Thought*.

    3rd ed., Prentice-Hall, 1974.

Only the first author's name is given in reverse order. The edition number appears after the title.

**A BOOK WITH MORE THAN TWO AUTHORS OR EDITORS**

Gates, Henry Louis, Jr., et al., editors. *The Norton Anthology of African American*

    *Literature*. 3rd ed., W. W. Norton, 2014.

(Note: The abbreviation *et al.* means "and others.")

**A WORK IN A COLLECTION BY THE SAME AUTHOR**

O'Connor, Flannery. "Greenleaf." *The Complete Stories*, by Flannery O'Connor, Farrar,

    Straus and Giroux, 1971, pp. 311–34.

Page numbers are given because the reference is to only a single story in the collection.

**A WORK IN A COLLECTION BY DIFFERENT AUTHORS**

Packer, ZZ. "Drinking Coffee Elsewhere." *The Compact Bedford Introduction to Literature*,

    edited by Michael Meyer and D. Quentin Miller, 13th ed., Bedford/St. Martin's,

    2024, pp. 292–305.

The titles of poems and short stories are enclosed in quotation marks; plays and novels are italicized.

**CROSS-REFERENCE TO A COLLECTION**

When citing more than one work from the same collection, use a cross-reference to avoid repeating the same bibliographic information that appears in the main entry for the collection.

Frost, Robert. "Design." Meyer and Miller, p. 874.

Meyer, Michael, and D. Quentin Miller, editors. *The Compact Bedford Introduction to Literature*, 13th ed., Bedford/St. Martin's, 2024.

O'Connor, Flannery. "A Good Man is Hard to Find." Meyer and Miller, pp. 405–15.

Packer, ZZ. "Drinking Coffee Elsewhere." Meyer and Miller, pp. 292–305.

### A TRANSLATED BOOK

Grass, Günter. *The Tin Drum*. Translated by Ralph Manheim, Pantheon Books, 1962.

### AN INTRODUCTION, PREFACE, FOREWORD, OR AFTERWORD

Johnson, Thomas H. Introduction. *Final Harvest: Emily Dickinson's Poems*, by Emily Dickinson, Little, Brown, 1961, pp. vii–xiv.

This cites the introduction by Johnson. Notice that a colon is used between the book's main title and subtitle. To cite a poem in this book, use this method:

Dickinson, Emily. "A Tooth upon Our Peace." *Final Harvest: Emily Dickinson's Poems*, edited by Thomas H. Johnson, Little, Brown, 1961, p. 110.

### AN ENTRY IN AN ENCYCLOPEDIA

Robinson, Lisa Clayton. "Harlem Writers Guild." *Africana: The Encyclopedia of the African and African American Experience*, edited by Kwame Anthony Appiah and Henry Louis Gates Jr., 2nd ed., Oxford UP, 2005, p. 163.

### AN ARTICLE IN A MAGAZINE

Morrow, Lance. "Scribble, Scribble, Eh, Mr. Toad?" *Time*, 24 Feb. 1986, p. 84.

### AN ARTICLE FROM AN ONLINE MAGAZINE

Wasserman, Elizabeth. "The Byron Complex." *TheAtlantic.com*, 1 Oct. 2002, www .theatlantic.com/entertainment/archive/2002/10/the-byron-complex/378504/.

The citation for an unsigned article would begin with the title and be alphabetized by the first word of the title other than "a," "an," or "the."

**AN ARTICLE IN A SCHOLARLY JOURNAL WITH CONTINUOUS
PAGINATION BEYOND A SINGLE ISSUE**

Fuqua, Amy. "'The Furrow of His Brow': Providence and Pragmatism in Toni Morrison's
Paradise." *Midwest Quarterly*, vol. 54, no. 1, autumn 2012, pp. 38-52.

Regardless of whether the journal uses continuous pagination or separate
pagination for each issue, it is necessary to include the volume number and
the issue number for every entry. If a journal does not offer an issue number,
use only the volume number, as in the next entry. If a journal uses *only* issue
numbers, use that in place of the volume number.

**AN ARTICLE IN A SCHOLARLY JOURNAL WITH SEPARATE
PAGINATION FOR EACH ISSUE**

Updike, John. "The Cultural Situation of the American Writer." *American Studies
International*, vol. 15, 1977, pp. 19-28.

In the following citation, noting the winter issue helps a reader find the correct article among all of the articles published by the online journal in 2004.

**AN ARTICLE FROM AN ONLINE SCHOLARLY JOURNAL**

Mamet, David. "Secret Names." *Threepenny Review*, vol. 96, winter 2004,
www .threepennyreview.com/samples/mamet_w04.html.

**AN ARTICLE IN A NEWSPAPER**

The following citation indicates that the article appears on page 1 and continues onto another page.

Ziegler, Philip. "The Lure of Gossip, the Rules of History." *The New York Times*, 23 Feb.
1986, pp. 1+.

**AN ARTICLE FROM AN ONLINE NEWSPAPER**

Brantley, Ben. "Souls Lost and Doomed Enliven London Stages." *The New York Times*,
4 Feb. 2004, www.nytimes.com/2004/02/04/theater/critic-s-notebook-souls-lost
-and-doomed-enliven-london-stages.html.

**A LECTURE**

Tilton, Robert. "The Beginnings of American Studies." English 270 class lecture, 12 Mar.
2023, University of Connecticut, Storrs.

## LETTER, E-MAIL, OR INTERVIEW

Vellenga, Carolyn. Letter to the author. 9 Oct. 2023. Typescript.

Harter, Stephen P. E-mail to the author. 28 Dec. 2022.

McConagha, Bill. Phone interview with the author. 9 May 2023.

Following are additional examples for citing electronic sources.

## WORK FROM A SUBSCRIPTION SERVICE

Libraries pay for access to databases such as *LexisNexis, ProQuest*, and *Expanded Academic Premier*. When you retrieve an article or other work from a subscription database, cite your source based on these models:

Coles, Kimberly Anne. "The Matter of Belief in John Donne's Holy Sonnets." *Renaissance Quarterly*, vol. 68, no. 3, Fall 2015, pp. 899-931. *JSTOR*, www.jstor.org/stable /10.1086/683855.

Harris, Ashleigh May, and Nicklas Hållén. "African Street Literature: A Method for an Emergent Form beyond World Literature." *Research in African Literatures*, vol. 51, no. 2, Summer 2020, pp. 1-26. *JSTOR*, https://doi.org/10.2979/reseafrilite.51.2.01.

## A DOCUMENT FROM A WEBSITE

When citing sources from the Internet, include as much publication information as possible (see guidelines on p. 1472). In some cases, as in the following example, a date of publication for the document "Charles Dickens in America" is not available. The entry provides the author, title of document, title of site, URL, and access date:

Perdue, David. "Charles Dickens in America." *The Charles Dickens Page*, charlesdickenspage.com/charles-dickens-in-america.html. Accessed 13 Apr. 2023.

## AN ENTIRE WEBSITE

*Lift Every Voice*. Library of America / Schomburg Center for Research in Black Culture, 2020, africanamericanpoetry.org/.

## AN ONLINE POSTING

Bedford English. "Stacey Cochran explores Reflective Writing in the classroom and as a writer: http://ow.ly/YkjVB." *Facebook*, 15 Feb. 2016, www.facebook.com /BedfordEnglish/posts/10153415001259607.

## *Parenthetical References*

A list of works cited is not an adequate indication of how you have used sources in your paper. You must also provide the precise location of quotations and other information by using parenthetical references within the text of the paper. You do this by citing the author's name (or the source's title if the work is anonymous or if no author is listed) and the page number:

Collins points out that "Nabokov was misunderstood by early reviewers of his work" (28).

or

Nabokov's first critics misinterpreted his stories (Collins 28).

Either way a reader will find the complete bibliographic entry in the list of works cited under Collins's name and know that the information cited in the paper appears on page 28. Notice that the end punctuation comes after the parentheses.

If you have listed more than one work by the same author, you would add a brief title to the parenthetical reference to distinguish between them. You could also include the full title in your text:

Nabokov's first critics misinterpreted his stories (Collins, "Early Reviews" 28).

or

Collins points out in "Early Reviews of Nabokov's Fiction" that Nabokov's early work was
    misinterpreted by reviewers (28).

For electronic sources, provide the author's name. If your online source has paragraph, chapter, or section numbers, include those in your parenthetical reference; if not, the author's name alone will suffice. The following example shows an in-text citation to William Faulkner's acceptance speech for the Nobel Prize for Literature, found at the Nobel website.

William Faulkner believed that it was his duty as a writer to "help man endure by lifting
    his heart" (Faulkner).

This reference would appear in the works cited list as follows:

Faulkner, William. "Banquet Speech: The Nobel Prize in Literature." *Nobelprize.org*, 10 Dec.
    1950, nobelprize.org/nobel_prizes/literature/laureates/1949/faulkner-speech.html.

There can be many variations on what is included in a parenthetical reference, depending on the nature of the entry in the list of works cited. But the general principle is simple enough: provide enough parenthetical information for a reader to find the work in "Works Cited." Examine the sample research paper for more examples of works cited and strategies for including parenthetical references. If you are puzzled by a given situation, refer to the *MLA Handbook*.

## A SAMPLE STUDENT RESEARCH PAPER

### *How William Faulkner's Narrator Cultivates a Rose for Emily*

The following research paper by Tony Groulx follows the format described in the *MLA Handbook, Ninth Edition* (2021). This format is discussed in the preceding section on documentation. Though the sample paper is short, it illustrates many of the techniques and strategies useful for writing an essay that includes secondary sources. (Faulkner's "A Rose for Emily" is reprinted on p. 47.)

Groulx 1

Tony Groulx

Professor Hugo

English 109-3

4 February 2023

How William Faulkner's Narrator Cultivates a Rose for Emily

William Faulkner's "A Rose for Emily" is an absorbing mystery story whose chilling ending contains a gruesome surprise. When we discover, along with the narrator and townspeople, what was left of Homer Barron's body, we may be surprised or not, depending on how carefully we have been reading the story and keeping track of details such as Emily Grierson's purchase of rat poison and Homer's disappearance. Probably most readers anticipate finding Homer's body at the end of the story because Faulkner carefully prepares the groundwork for the discovery as the townspeople force their way into that mysterious upstairs room where a "thin, acrid pall as of the tomb seemed to lie everywhere" (52). But very few readers, if any, are prepared for the story's final paragraph, when we realize that the strand of "iron-gray hair" (the last three words of the story) on the second pillow indicates that Emily has slept with Homer since she murdered him. This last paragraph produces the real horror in the story and an extraordinary revelation about Emily's character.

References to text of the story

Groulx 2

The final paragraph seems like the right place to begin a discussion of this story because the surprise ending not only creates a powerful emotional effect in us but also raises an important question about what we are to think of Emily. Is this isolated, eccentric woman simply mad? All the circumstantial evidence indicates that she is a murderer and necrophiliac, and yet Faulkner titles the story "A Rose for Emily," as if she is due some kind of tribute. The title somehow qualifies the gasp of horror that the story leads up to in the final paragraph. Why would anyone offer this woman a "rose"? What's behind the title?

> Faulkner was once directly asked the meaning of the title and replied:
> Oh it's simply the poor woman had had no life at all. Her father had
> kept her more or less locked up and then she had a lover who was
> about to quit her, she had to murder him. It was just "A Rose for
> Emily"—that's all. (qtd. in Gwynn and Blotner 87–88)

*Reference to secondary source (Gwynn and Blotner)*

This reply explains some of Emily's motivation for murdering Homer, but it doesn't actually address the purpose and meaning of the title. If Emily killed Homer out of a kind of emotional necessity — out of a fear of abandonment — how does that explain the fact that the title seems to suggest that the story is a way of paying respect to Emily? The question remains.

Whatever respect the story creates for Emily cannot be the result of her actions. Surely there can be no convincing excuse made for murder and necrophilia; there is nothing to praise about what she does. Instead, the tribute comes in the form of how her story is told rather than what we are told about her. To do this Faulkner uses a narrator who tells Emily's story in such a way as to maximize our sympathy for her. The grim information about Emily's "iron-gray hair" on the pillow is withheld until the very end and not only to produce a surprise but to permit the reader to develop a sympathetic understanding of her before we are shocked and disgusted by her necrophilia.

Significantly, the narrator begins the story with Emily's death rather than Homer's. Though a number of studies discuss the story's narrator (see, for example, Curry; Kempton; Sullivan; and Watkins), Terry Heller's is one of the most comprehensive in its focus on the narrator's effects on the readers' response to Emily. As Heller points out, before we learn of Emily's

*Reference to secondary sources (Curry; Kempton; Sullivan; Watkins) with signal phrase for Heller*

bizarre behavior we see her as a sympathetic — if antiquated — figure in a town whose life and concerns have passed her by; hence, "we are disposed to see Emily as victimized" (306). Her refusal to pay her taxes is an index to her isolation and eccentricity, but this incident also suggests a degree of dignity and power lacking in the town officials who fail to collect her taxes. Her encounters with the officials of Jefferson — whether in the form of the sneaking aldermen who try to cover up the smell around her house or the druggist who unsuccessfully tries to get her to conform to the law when she buys arsenic — place her in an admirable light because her willfulness is based on her personal strength. Moreover, it is relatively easy to side with Emily when the townspeople are described as taking pleasure in her being reduced to poverty as a result of her father's death because "now she too would know the old thrill and the old despair of a penny more or less" (Faulkner 49). The narrator's account of their pettiness, jealousy, and inability to make sense of Emily causes the reader to sympathize with Emily's eccentricities before we must judge her murderous behavior. We admire her for taking life on her own terms, and the narrator makes sure this response is in place prior to our realization that she also takes life.

We don't really know much about Emily because the narrator arranges the details of her life so that it's difficult to know what she's been up to. We learn, for example, about the smell around the house before she buys the poison and Homer disappears, so that the cause-and-effect relationship among these events is a bit slippery (for a detailed reconstruction of the chronology, see McGlynn; Nebecker), but the effect is to suspend judgment of Emily. By the time we realize what she has done, we are already inclined to see her as outside community values almost out of necessity. That's not to say that the murdering of Homer is justified by the narrator, but it is to say that her life maintains its private—though no longer secret—dignity. Despite the final revelation, Emily remains "dear, inescapable, impervious, tranquil, and perverse" (Faulkner 51).

The narrator's "rose" to Emily is his recognition that Emily is all these things—including "perverse." She evokes "a sort of respectful affection for a fallen monument" (Faulkner 47). She is, to be sure, "fallen," but she is also somehow central — a "monument" — to the life of the community. Faulkner does not offer a definitive reading of Emily, but he does have the narrator

---

**Reference to secondary source (Heller) with signal phrase ("As Heller points out . . .")**

**Reference to text of the story**

**Reference to secondary sources (McGlynn and Nebecker)**

**Reference to text of the story**

Groulx 4

pay tribute to her by attempting to provide a complex set of contexts for her actions—contexts that include a repressive father, resistance to a changing South and impinging North, the passage of time and its influence on the present, and relations between men and women as well as relations between generations. Robert Crosman discusses the narrator's efforts to understand Emily:

> The narrator is himself a "reader" of Emily's story, trying to put together from fragments a complete picture, trying to find the meaning of her life in its impact upon an audience, the citizens of Jefferson, of which he is a member. (212)

Reference to secondary source (Crosman)

The narrator refuses to dismiss Emily as simply mad or to treat her life as merely a grotesque, sensational horror story. Instead, his narrative method brings us into her life before we too hastily reject her, and in doing so it offers us a complex imaginative treatment of fierce determination and strength coupled with illusions and shocking eccentricities. The narrator's rose for Emily is paying her the tribute of placing that "long strand of iron-gray hair" (Faulkner 52) in the context of her entire life.

Works Cited

Crosman, Robert. "How Readers Make Meaning." *College Literature*, vol. 9, no. 3, 1982, pp. 207–15.

Curry, Renee R. "Gender and Authorial Limitation in Faulkner's 'A Rose for Emily.' " *Mississippi Quarterly*, vol. 47, no. 3, 1994, pp. 391–402. *Expanded Academic ASAP*, connection.ebscohost.com/c/literary-criticism /9502231814/gender-authorial-limitation-faulkners-rose-emily.

Faulkner, William. "A Rose for Emily." *The Compact Bedford Introduction to Literature*, edited by Michael Meyer and D. Quentin Miller, 13th ed., Bedford/St. Martin's, 2024, pp. 47–52.

Gwynn, Frederick, and Joseph Blotner, editors. *Faulkner in the University: Class Conferences at the University of Virginia, 1957–58*. U of Virginia P, 1959.

Heller, Terry. "The Telltale Hair: A Critical Study of William Faulkner's 'A Rose for Emily.' " *Arizona Quarterly*, vol. 28, no. 4, 1972, pp. 301–18.

Kempton, K. P. *The Short Story*. Harvard UP, 1954, pp. 104–06.

McGlynn, Paul D. "The Chronology of 'A Rose for Emily.' " *Studies in Short Fiction*, vol. 6, no. 4, 1969, pp. 461–62.

Nebecker, Helen E. "Chronology Revised." *Studies in Short Fiction*, vol. 8, no. 4, 1971, pp. 471–73.

Sullivan, Ruth. "The Narrator in 'A Rose for Emily.' " *Journal of Narrative Technique*, vol. 1, no. 3, 1971, pp. 159–78.

Watkins, F. C. "The Structure of 'A Rose for Emily.' " *Modern Language Notes*, vol. 69, no. 6, 1954, pp. 508–10.

# Glossary of Literary Terms

**Accent** The emphasis, or stress, given a syllable in pronunciation. We say "*syl*lable" not "syl*lable*," "*em*phasis" not "em*phasis*." Accents can also be used to emphasize a particular word in a sentence: *Is* she con*tent* with the *con*tents of the *yel*low *pack*age? See also METER.

**Act** A major division in the action of a play. The ends of acts are typically indicated by lowering the curtain or turning up the houselights. Playwrights frequently employ acts to accommodate changes in time, setting, characters onstage, or mood. In many full-length plays, acts are further divided into scenes, which often mark a point in the action when the location changes or when a new character enters. See also SCENE.

**Affect theory** A critical approach that deals with feelings, bodily sensations, and the emotional effects of art. **Affect theorists** look at how readers respond to works emotionally (as opposed to rationally) as well as the forces within a text that elicit shifts in sensation. Often, a reader's emotions may not align with their instinctual thoughts and values; affect theory aims to understand these responses and the way emotions are represented in a work.

**Allegory** A narration or description usually restricted to a single meaning because its events, actions, characters, settings, and objects represent specific abstractions or ideas. Although the elements in an allegory may be interesting in themselves, the emphasis tends to be on what they ultimately mean. Characters may be given names such as Hope, Pride, Youth, and Charity; they have few if any personal qualities beyond their abstract meanings. These personifications are not symbols because, for instance, the meaning of a character named Charity is precisely that virtue. See also SYMBOL.

**Alliteration** The repetition of the same consonant sounds in a sequence of words, usually at the beginning of a word or stressed syllable: "*descending dew drops*"; "*luscious lemons*." Alliteration is based on the sounds of letters, rather than the spelling of words; for example, "*keen*" and "*car*" alliterate, but "*car*" and "*cite*" do not. Used sparingly, alliteration can intensify ideas by emphasizing key words, but when used too self-consciously, it can be distracting, even ridiculous, rather than effective. See also ASSONANCE, CONSONANCE.

**Allusion** A brief reference to a person, place, thing, event, or idea in history or literature. Allusions conjure up biblical authority, scenes from Shakespeare's plays, historic figures, wars, great love stories, and anything else that might enrich an author's work. Allusions imply reading and cultural experiences shared by the writer and reader, functioning as a kind of shorthand whereby the recalling of something outside the work supplies an emotional or intellectual context, such as a poem about current racial struggles calling up the memory of Abraham Lincoln.

**Ambiguity** Allows for two or more simultaneous interpretations of a word, phrase, action, or situation, all of which can be supported by the context of a work. Deliberate ambiguity can contribute to the effectiveness and richness of a work, for example, in the open-ended conclusion to Hawthorne's "Young Goodman Brown." However, unintentional ambiguity obscures meaning and can confuse readers.

**Anagram** A word or phrase made from the letters of another word or phrase, as *heart* is an anagram of *earth*. Anagrams have often been considered merely an exercise of one's ingenuity, but sometimes writers use anagrams to conceal proper names or veiled messages, or to suggest important connections between words, as in *hated* and *death*.

**Anapestic meter** See FOOT.

**Antagonist** The character, force, or collection of forces in fiction or drama that opposes the protagonist and gives rise to the conflict of the story; an opponent of the protagonist, such as Claudius in Shakespeare's play *Hamlet*. See also CHARACTER, CONFLICT.

**Antihero** A protagonist who has the opposite of most of the traditional attributes of a hero. He or she may be bewildered, ineffectual, deluded, or merely pathetic. Often what antiheroes learn, if they learn anything at all, is that the world isolates them in an existence devoid of God and absolute values. The Hit Man in T. C. Boyle's story "The Hit Man" is an example of an antihero. See also CHARACTER.

**Apostrophe** An address, either to someone who is absent and therefore cannot hear the speaker or to something nonhuman that cannot comprehend. Apostrophe often provides a speaker the opportunity to think aloud.

**Approximate rhyme** See RHYME.

**Archetype** A term used to describe universal symbols that evoke deep and sometimes unconscious responses in a reader. In literature, characters, images, and themes that symbolically embody universal meanings and basic human experiences, regardless of when or where they live, are considered archetypes. Common literary archetypes include stories of quests, initiations, scapegoats, descents to the underworld, and ascents to heaven. See also MYTHOLOGICAL CRITICISM.

**Aside** In drama, a speech directed to the audience that supposedly is not audible to the other characters onstage at the time. When Hamlet first appears onstage, for example, his aside "A little more than kin, and less than kind!" gives the audience a strong sense of his alienation from King Claudius. See also SOLILOQUY.

**Assonance** The repetition of internal vowel sounds in nearby words that do not end the same, for example, "asl*ee*p under a tr*ee*," or "*ea*ch *e*vening." Similar endings result in rhyme, as in "asl*eep* in the d*eep*." Assonance is a strong means of emphasizing important words in a line. See also ALLITERATION, CONSONANCE.

**Ballad** Traditionally, a ballad is a song, transmitted orally from generation to generation, that tells a story and that eventually is written down. As such, ballads usually cannot be traced to a particular author or group of authors. Typically, ballads are dramatic, condensed, and impersonal narratives, such as "Lord Randal." A **literary ballad** is a narrative poem that is written in deliberate imitation of the language, form, and spirit of the traditional ballad, such as Keats's "La Belle Dame sans Merci." See also BALLAD STANZA, QUATRAIN.

**Ballad stanza** A four-line stanza, known as a quatrain, consisting of alternating eight- and six-syllable lines. Usually only the second and fourth lines rhyme (an *abcb* pattern). Coleridge adopted the ballad stanza in "The Rime of the Ancient Mariner":

All in a hot and copper sky
The bloody Sun, at noon,
Right up above the mast did stand,
No bigger than the Moon.

See also BALLAD, QUATRAIN.

**Biographical criticism** An approach to literature that suggests that knowledge of the author's life experiences can aid in the understanding of their work. While biographical information can sometimes complicate one's interpretation of a work, and some formalist critics (such as the New Critics) disparage the use of the author's biography as a tool for textual interpretation, learning about the life of the author can often enrich a reader's appreciation for that author's work. See also CULTURAL CRITICISM, FORMALIST CRITICISM, NEW CRITICISM.

**Blank verse** Unrhymed iambic pentameter. Blank verse is the English verse form closest to the natural rhythms of English speech and therefore is the most common pattern found in traditional English narrative and dramatic poetry from Shakespeare to the early twentieth century. Shakespeare's plays use blank verse extensively. See also IAMBIC PENTAMETER.

**Cacophony** Language that is discordant and difficult to pronounce, such as this line from John Updike's "Player Piano": "never my numb plunker fumbles." Cacophony ("bad sound") may be unintentional in the writer's sense of music, or it may be used consciously for deliberate dramatic effect. See also EUPHONY.

**Caesura** A pause within a line of poetry that contributes to the rhythm of the line. A caesura can occur anywhere within a line and need not be indicated by punctuation. In scanning a line, caesuras are indicated by a double vertical line (||). See also METER, RHYTHM, SCANSION.

**Canon** Those works generally considered by scholars, critics, and teachers to be the most important to read and study, which collectively constitute the "masterpieces" of literature. Since the 1960s, the traditional English and American literary canon, consisting mostly of works by white male writers, has been rapidly expanding to include many female writers, LGBTQ+ writers, and writers of varying ethnic backgrounds.

*Carpe diem* The Latin phrase meaning "seize the day." This is a very common literary theme, especially in lyric poetry, which emphasizes that life is short, time is fleeting, and that one should make the most of present pleasures. Robert Herrick's poem "To the Virgins, to Make Much of Time" employs the *carpe diem* theme.

**Catharsis** Meaning "purgation," *catharsis* describes the release of the emotions of pity and fear by the audience at the end of a tragedy. In his *Poetics*, Aristotle discusses the importance of catharsis. The audience faces the misfortunes of the protagonist, which elicit pity and compassion. Simultaneously, the audience also confronts the failure of the protagonist, thus receiving a frightening reminder of human limitations and frailties. Ultimately, however, both these negative emotions are purged, because the tragic protagonist's suffering is an affirmation of human values rather than a despairing denial of them. See also TRAGEDY.

**Character, characterization** A character is a person presented in a dramatic or narrative work, and characterization is the process by which a writer makes that character seem real to the reader. A **hero** or **heroine**, often called the protagonist, is the central character who engages the reader's interest and empathy. The antagonist is the character, force, or collection of forces that stands directly opposed to the protagonist and gives rise to the conflict of the story. A **static character** does not change throughout the work, and the reader's knowledge of that character does not grow, whereas a **dynamic character** undergoes some kind of change because of the action in the plot. **Flat characters** embody one or two qualities, ideas, or traits that can be readily described in a brief summary. They are not psychologically complex characters and therefore are readily accessible to readers. Some flat characters are recognized as **stock characters**; they embody stereotypes such as the "dumb blonde" or the "mean stepfather." They become types rather than individuals. **Round characters** are more complex than flat or stock characters, and often display the inconsistencies and internal conflicts found in most real people. They are more fully developed, and therefore are harder to summarize. Authors have two major methods of presenting characters: showing and telling. **Showing** allows the author to present a character talking and acting, and lets the reader infer what kind of person the character is. In **telling**, the author intervenes to describe and sometimes evaluate the character for the reader. Characters can be convincing whether they are presented by showing or by telling, as long as their actions are motivated. **Motivated action** by the characters occurs when the reader or audience is offered reasons for how the characters behave, what they say, and the decisions they make. **Plausible action** is action by a character in a story that seems reasonable, given the motivations presented. See also PLOT.

**Chorus** In Greek tragedies (especially those of Aeschylus and Sophocles), a group of people who serve mainly as commentators on the characters and events. They add to the audience's understanding of the play by expressing traditional moral, religious, and social attitudes. The role of the chorus in dramatic works evolved through the sixteenth century, and the chorus occasionally is still used by contemporary playwrights such as Paula Vogel in *How I Learned to Drive*. See also DRAMA.

**Cliché** An idea or expression that has become tired and trite from overuse, its freshness and clarity having worn off. Clichés often anesthetize readers and are usually a sign of weak or unimaginative writing. See also SENTIMENTALITY, STOCK RESPONSES.

**Climax** See PLOT.

**Closet drama** A play that is written to be read rather than performed onstage. In this kind of drama, literary art outweighs all other considerations. See also DRAMA.

**Colloquial** Refers to a type of informal diction that reflects casual, conversational language and often includes slang expressions. See also DICTION.

**Comedy** A work intended to interest, involve, and amuse the reader or audience, in which no terrible disaster occurs and that ends happily for the main characters. **High comedy** refers to verbal wit, such as puns, whereas **low comedy** is generally associated with physical action and is less intellectual. **Romantic comedy** involves a love affair that meets with various obstacles (like disapproving parents, mistaken identities, deceptions, or other sorts of misunderstandings) but overcomes them to end in a blissful union. Shakespeare's comedies, such as *A Midsummer Night's Dream*, are considered romantic comedies.

**Comic relief** A humorous scene or incident that alleviates tension in an otherwise serious work. In many instances these moments enhance the thematic significance of the story in addition to providing laughter. When Hamlet jokes with the gravediggers, we laugh, but something hauntingly serious about the humor also intensifies our more serious emotions.

**Conflict** The struggle within the plot between opposing forces. The protagonist engages in the conflict with the antagonist, which may take the form of a character, society, nature, or an aspect of the protagonist's personality. See also CHARACTER, PLOT.

**Connotation** Associations and implications that go beyond the literal meaning of a word, which derive from how the word has been commonly used and the associations people make with it. For example, the word *eagle* connotes ideas of liberty and freedom that have little to do with the word's literal meaning. See also DENOTATION.

**Consonance** A common type of near rhyme that consists of identical consonant sounds preceded by different vowel sounds: *home, same; worth, breath*. See also RHYME.

**Contextual symbol** See SYMBOL.

**Controlling metaphor** See METAPHOR.

**Convention** A characteristic of a literary genre (often unrealistic) that is understood and accepted by audiences because it has come, through usage and time, to be recognized as a familiar technique. For example, the division of a play into acts and scenes is a dramatic convention, as are SOLILOQUIES and ASIDES. FLASHBACKS and FORESHADOWING are examples of literary conventions.

**Conventional symbol** See SYMBOL.

**Cosmic irony** See IRONY.

**Couplet** Two consecutive lines of poetry that usually rhyme and have the same meter. A **heroic couplet** is a couplet written in rhymed iambic pentameter.

**Crisis** A turning point in the action of a story that has a powerful effect on the protagonist. Opposing forces come together decisively to lead to the climax of the plot. See also PLOT.

**Cultural criticism** An approach to literature that focuses on the historical as well as social, political, and economic contexts of a work. Popular culture — mass-produced and mass-consumed cultural artifacts ranging from advertising to popular fiction to television to rock music — is given equal emphasis with "high culture." **Cultural critics** use widely eclectic strategies such as new historicism, psychology, gender studies, and deconstructionism to analyze not only literary texts but everything from radio talk shows, comic strips, calendar art, and commercials, to travel guides and baseball cards. See also HISTORICAL CRITICISM, MARXIST CRITICISM.

**Dactylic meter** See FOOT.

**Deconstructionism** An approach to literature that suggests that literary works do not yield fixed, single meanings, because language can never say exactly what we intend it to mean. Deconstructionism seeks to destabilize meaning by examining the gaps and ambiguities of the language of a text. Deconstructionists pay close attention to language in order to discover and describe how a variety of possible readings are generated by the elements of a text. See also NEW CRITICISM.

**Denotation** The dictionary meaning of a word. See also CONNOTATION.

**Dénouement** A French term meaning "unraveling" or "unknotting," used to describe the resolution of the plot following the climax. See also PLOT, RESOLUTION.

**Dialect** A type of informal diction. Dialects are spoken by definable groups of people from a particular geographic region, economic group, or social class. Writers use dialect to contrast and express differences in educational, class, social, and regional backgrounds of their characters. See also DICTION.

**Dialogue** The verbal exchanges between characters. Dialogue makes the characters seem real to the reader or audience by revealing firsthand their thoughts, responses, and emotional states. See also DICTION.

**Diction** A writer's choice of words, phrases, sentence structures, and figurative language, which combine to help create meaning. **Formal diction** consists of a dignified, impersonal, and elevated use of language; it follows the rules of syntax exactly and is often characterized by complex words and lofty tone. **Middle diction** maintains correct language usage, but is less elevated than formal diction; it reflects the way most educated people speak. **Informal diction** represents the plain language of everyday use, and often includes idiomatic expressions, slang, contractions, and many simple, common words. **Poetic diction** refers to the way poets sometimes employ an elevated diction that deviates significantly from the common speech and writing of their time, choosing words for their supposedly inherent poetic qualities. Since the eighteenth century, however, poets have been incorporating all kinds of diction in their work and so there is no longer an automatic distinction between the language of a poet and the language of everyday speech. See also DIALECT.

**Didactic poetry** Poetry designed to teach an ethical, moral, or religious lesson. Michael Wigglesworth's Puritan poem *Day of Doom* is an example of didactic poetry.

**Doggerel**  A derogatory term used to describe poetry whose subject is trite and whose rhythm and sounds are monotonously heavy-handed.

**Drama**  Derived from the Greek word *dram*, meaning "to do" or "to perform," the term *drama* may refer to a single play, a group of plays ("Jacobean drama"), or to all plays ("world drama"). Drama is designed for performance in a theater; actors take on the roles of characters, perform indicated actions, and speak the dialogue written in the script. **Play** is a general term for a work of dramatic literature, and a **playwright** is a writer who makes plays.

**Dramatic irony**  See IRONY.

**Dramatic monologue**  A type of lyric poem in which a character (the speaker) addresses a distinct but silent audience imagined to be present in the poem in such a way as to reveal a dramatic situation and, often unintentionally, some aspect of his or her temperament or personality. See also LYRIC.

**Dynamic character**  See CHARACTER.

**Editorial omniscience**  See NARRATOR.

**Electra complex**  The name comes from the Greek legend of Electra, who avenged the death of her father, Agamemnon, by plotting the death of her mother. See also OEDIPUS COMPLEX, PSYCHOLOGICAL CRITICISM.

**Elegy**  A mournful, contemplative lyric poem written to commemorate someone who is dead, often ending in a consolation. Tennyson's *In Memoriam*, written on the death of Arthur Hallam, is an elegy. *Elegy* may also refer to a serious meditative poem produced to express the speaker's melancholy thoughts, such as Thomas Gray's "Elegy Written in a Country Churchyard." See also LYRIC.

**End rhyme**  See RHYME.

**End-stopped line**  A poetic line that has a pause at the end. End-stopped lines reflect normal speech patterns and are often marked by punctuation. The first line of Keats's "Endymion" is an example of an end-stopped line; the natural pause coincides with the end of the line, and is marked by a period:

A thing of beauty is a joy forever.

**English sonnet**  See SONNET.

**Enjambment**  In poetry, when one line ends without a pause and continues into the next line for its meaning. This is also called a **run-on line**. The transition between the first two lines of Wordsworth's poem "My Heart Leaps Up" demonstrates enjambment:

My heart leaps up when I behold
A rainbow in the sky:

**Envoy**  See SESTINA.

**Epic**  A long narrative poem, told in a formal, elevated style, that focuses on a serious subject and chronicles heroic deeds and events important to a culture or nation. Milton's *Paradise Lost*, which attempts to "justify the ways of God to man," is an epic. See also NARRATIVE POEM.

**Epic theater**  A style of drama that relies on keeping emotional distance between the audience and the play's characters. Epic theater was developed by playwright

Bertolt Brecht to call audience attention to social problems and is characterized by loosely connected, episodic scenes and the dramatization of societal issues.

**Epigram** A brief, pointed, and witty poem that usually makes a satiric or humorous point. Epigrams are most often written in couplets, but take no prescribed form.

**Epiphany** In fiction, when a character suddenly experiences a deep realization about himself or herself; a truth that is grasped in an ordinary rather than a melodramatic moment.

**Escape literature** See FORMULA FICTION.

**Euphony** *Euphony* ("good sound") refers to language that is smooth and musically pleasant to the ear. See also CACOPHONY.

**Exact rhyme** See RHYME.

**Explication** A detailed examination and explanation of a passage (or entirety) of literary work, explication involves close reading and is a useful approach for analyzing how a writer achieves a certain effect through their choice of language and literary elements and how these choices work in relation to one another and to the overall work. See also NEW CRITICISM.

**Exposition** A narrative device, often used at the beginning of a work, that provides necessary background information about the characters and their circumstances. Exposition explains what has gone on before, the relationships between characters, the development of a theme, and the introduction of a conflict. See also FLASHBACK.

**Expressionism** A form of theater centering on nonrealistic elements. Often characterized by flashbacks and other nonchronological blendings of past and present, expressionism is meant to distort reality and explore the inner emotions of the characters. See also EPIC THEATER, NATURALISM, SYMBOLIST DRAMA.

**Extended metaphor** See METAPHOR.

**Eye rhyme** See RHYME.

**Falling action** See PLOT.

**Falling meter** See METER.

**Farce** A form of humor based on exaggerated, improbable incongruities. Farce involves rapid shifts in action and emotion, as well as slapstick comedy and extravagant dialogue. Malvolio, in Shakespeare's *Twelfth Night*, is a farcical character.

**Feminine rhyme** See RHYME.

**Feminist criticism** An approach to literature that seeks to correct or supplement what may be regarded as a predominantly male critical perspective with a feminist consciousness. Feminist criticism places literature in a social context and uses a broad range of disciplines, including history, sociology, psychology, and linguistics, to provide a perspective sensitive to feminist issues. Feminist theories also attempt to understand representation from a woman's point of view and to explain women's writing strategies as specific to their social conditions. See also GAY AND LESBIAN CRITICISM, GENDER CRITICISM, LGBTQ+ CRITICISM, SOCIOLOGICAL CRITICISM.

**Figures of speech** Ways of using language that deviate from the literal, denotative meanings of words in order to suggest additional meanings or effects. Figures of speech say one thing in terms of something else, such as when an eager funeral director is described as a vulture. See also METAPHOR, SIMILE.

**First-person narrator** See NARRATOR.

**Fixed form** A poem that may be categorized by the pattern of its lines, meter, rhythm, or stanzas. A sonnet is a fixed form of poetry because by definition it must have fourteen lines. Other fixed forms include limerick, sestina, and villanelle. However, poems written in a fixed form may not always fit into categories precisely, because writers sometimes vary traditional forms to create innovative effects. See also OPEN FORM.

**Flashback** A narrated scene that marks a break in the narrative in order to inform the reader or audience member about events that took place before the opening scene of a work. See also EXPOSITION.

**Flat character** See CHARACTER.

**Foil** A character in a work whose behavior and values contrast with those of another character in order to highlight the distinctive temperament of that character (usually the protagonist). In Shakespeare's *Hamlet*, Laertes acts as a foil to Hamlet, because his willingness to act underscores Hamlet's inability to do so.

**Foot** The metrical unit by which a line of poetry is measured. A foot usually consists of one stressed and one or two unstressed syllables. An **iambic foot**, which consists of one unstressed syllable followed by one stressed syllable ("away"), is the most common metrical foot in English poetry. A **trochaic foot** consists of one stressed syllable followed by an unstressed syllable ("lovely"). An **anapestic foot** is two unstressed syllables followed by one stressed one ("understand"). A **dactylic foot** is one stressed syllable followed by two unstressed ones ("desperate"). A *spondee* is a foot consisting of two stressed syllables ("dead set"), but is not a sustained metrical foot and is used mainly for variety or emphasis. See also IAMBIC PENTAMETER, LINE, METER.

**Foreshadowing** The introduction early in a story of verbal and dramatic hints that suggest what is to come later.

**Form** The overall structure or shape of a work, which frequently follows an established design. Forms may refer to a literary type (narrative form, short story form) or to patterns of meter, lines, and rhymes (stanza form, verse form). See also FIXED FORM, OPEN FORM.

**Formal diction** See DICTION.

**Formalist criticism** An approach to literature that focuses on the formal elements of a work, such as its language, structure, and tone. Formalist critics offer intense examinations of the relationship between form and meaning in a work, emphasizing the subtle complexity in how a work is arranged. Formalists pay special attention to diction, irony, paradox, metaphor, and symbol, as well as larger elements such as plot, characterization, and narrative technique. Formalist critics read literature as an independent work of art rather than as a reflection of the author's state of mind or as a representation of a moment in history. Therefore, anything outside of the work, including historical influences and authorial intent, is generally not examined by formalist critics. See also NEW CRITICISM.

**Formula fiction** Often characterized as "escape literature," formula fiction follows a pattern of conventional reader expectations. Romance novels, westerns, pulp science fiction, and detective stories are all examples of formula fiction; while the details of individual stories vary, the basic ingredients of each kind of story are the same. Formula fiction offers happy endings (the hero "gets the girl," the detective cracks the case), entertains wide audiences, and sells tremendously well.

**Found poem** An unintentional poem discovered in a nonpoetic context, such as a conversation, news story, or advertisement. Found poems serve as reminders that everyday language often contains what can be considered poetry, or that poetry is definable as any text read as a poem.

**Free verse** Also called **open form** poetry, *free verse* refers to poems characterized by their nonconformity to established patterns of meter, rhyme, and stanza. Free verse uses elements such as speech patterns, grammar, emphasis, and breath pauses to decide line breaks, and usually does not rhyme. See OPEN FORM.

**Gay and lesbian criticism** An approach to literature that focuses on how gays and lesbians are represented in literature, how they read literature, and whether sexuality, as well as gender, is culturally constructed or innate. See also FEMINIST CRITICISM, GENDER CRITICISM, LGBTQ+ CRITICISM.

**Gender criticism** An approach to literature that explores how ideas about gender — what is masculine and feminine — can be regarded as socially constructed by particular cultures. Gender criticism expands categories and definitions of what is masculine, feminine, or nonbinary and tends to regard sexuality as more complex than merely masculine or feminine, heterosexual or homosexual. See also FEMINIST CRITICISM, GAY AND LESBIAN CRITICISM, LGBTQ+ CRITICISM.

**Genre** A French word meaning "kind" or "type." The major genres in literature are poetry, fiction, drama, and essays. Genre can also refer to more specific types of literature such as comedy, tragedy, epic poetry, or science fiction.

**Ghazal** A poetic form originating in Arabic poetry in the seventh and eighth centuries and popular across the Arabian Peninsula, Persia, India, and other parts of the Middle East, Asia, Africa, and Spain. Common themes in ghazals revolve around the complexities of love. Ghazals are written in couplets, ranging from five to fifteen total, with the final couplet containing a proper name, usually that of the poet. The rhyme scheme and meter of ghazals are traditionally complex, though this can be somewhat flexible, given the long evolution of the form.

**Haiku** A style of lyric poetry borrowed from the Japanese that typically presents an intense emotion or vivid image of nature, which, traditionally, is designed to lead to a spiritual insight. Haiku is traditionally a fixed poetic form, consisting of seventeen syllables organized into three unrhymed lines of five, seven, and five syllables. Today, however, many poets vary the syllabic count in their haiku. See also FIXED FORM.

**Hamartia** A term coined by Aristotle to describe "some error or frailty" that brings about misfortune for a tragic hero. The concept of *hamartia* is closely related to that of the tragic flaw: both lead to the downfall of the protagonist in a tragedy. *Hamartia* may be interpreted as an internal weakness in a character (like greed or passion or hubris); however, it may also refer to a mistake that a character makes that is based not on a personal failure, but on circumstances outside the protagonist's personality and control. See also TRAGEDY.

**Hero, heroine** See CHARACTER.

**Heroic couplet** See COUPLET.

**High comedy** See COMEDY.

**Historical criticism** An approach to literature that uses history as a means of understanding a literary work more clearly. Such criticism moves beyond both the facts of an author's personal life and the text itself in order to examine the social and intellectual currents in which the author composed the work. See also CULTURAL CRITICISM, MARXIST CRITICISM, NEW HISTORICISM.

**Hubris or hybris** Excessive pride or self-confidence that leads a protagonist to disregard a divine warning or to violate an important moral law. In tragedies, hubris is a very common form of *hamartia*. See also HAMARTIA, TRAGEDY.

**Hyperbole** A boldly exaggerated statement that adds emphasis without intending to be literally true, as in the statement "He ate everything in the house." Hyperbole (also called **overstatement**) may be used for serious, comic, or ironic effect. See also FIGURES OF SPEECH.

**Iambic meter** See FOOT.

**Iambic pentameter** A metrical pattern in poetry that consists of five **iambic feet** per line. (An **iamb**, or **iambic foot**, consists of one unstressed syllable followed by a stressed syllable.) See also FOOT, METER.

**Image** A word, phrase, or figure of speech (especially a SIMILE or a METAPHOR) that addresses the senses, suggesting mental pictures of sights, sounds, smells, tastes, feelings, or actions. Images offer sensory impressions to the reader and also convey emotions and moods through their verbal pictures. See also FIGURES OF SPEECH.

**Implied metaphor** See METAPHOR.

*In medias res* See PLOT.

**Informal diction** See DICTION.

**Internal rhyme** See RHYME.

**Irony** A literary device that uses contradictory statements or situations to reveal a reality different from what appears to be true. It is ironic for a firehouse to burn down or for a police station to be burglarized. **Verbal irony** is a figure of speech that occurs when a person says one thing but means the opposite. **Sarcasm** is a strong form of verbal irony that is calculated to hurt someone through, for example, false praise. **Dramatic irony** creates a discrepancy between what a character believes or says and what the reader or audience member knows to be true. **Tragic irony** is a form of dramatic irony found in tragedies such as *Oedipus the King*, in which Oedipus searches for the person responsible for the plague that ravishes his city and ironically ends up hunting himself. **Situational irony** exists when there is an incongruity between what is expected to happen and what actually happens due to forces beyond human comprehension or control. The suicide of the seemingly successful main character in Edwin Arlington Robinson's poem "Richard Cory" is an example of situational irony. **Cosmic irony** occurs when a writer uses God, destiny, or fate to dash the hopes and expectations of a character or of humankind in general. In cosmic irony, a discrepancy exists between what a character aspires to and what universal forces provide. Stephen Crane's poem "A Man Said to the Universe" is a good example of cosmic irony, because the universe acknowledges no obligation to the man's assertion of his own existence.

**Italian sonnet**  See SONNET.

**LGBTQ+ criticism**  A mode of literary criticism that seeks to explore LGBTQ+ sexualities and/or gender identities as they are represented in literature. See also GAY AND LESBIAN CRITICISM; GENDER CRITICISM.

**Limerick**  A light, humorous style of fixed form poetry. Its usual form consists of five lines with the rhyme scheme *aabba*; lines 1, 2, and 5 contain three feet, while lines 3 and 4 usually contain two feet. Limericks range in subject matter from the silly to the obscene, and since Edward Lear popularized them in the nineteenth century, children and adults have enjoyed these comic poems. See also FIXED FORM.

**Limited omniscient narrator**  See NARRATOR.

**Line**  A sequence of words printed as a separate entity on the page. In poetry, lines are usually measured by the number of feet they contain. The names for various line lengths are as follows:

| | |
|---|---|
| monometer: one foot | pentameter: five feet |
| dimeter: two feet | hexameter: six feet |
| trimeter: three feet | heptameter: seven feet |
| tetrameter: four feet | octameter: eight feet |

The number of feet in a line, coupled with the name of the foot, describes the metrical qualities of that line. See also END-STOPPED LINE, ENJAMBMENT, FOOT, METER.

**Literary ballad**  See BALLAD.

**Literary symbol**  See SYMBOL.

**Low comedy**  See COMEDY.

**Lyric**  A type of brief poem that expresses the personal emotions and thoughts of a single speaker. It is important to realize, however, that although the lyric is uttered in the first person, the speaker is not necessarily the poet. There are many varieties of lyric poetry, including the DRAMATIC MONOLOGUE, ELEGY, HAIKU, ODE, and SONNET forms.

**Marxist criticism**  An approach to literature that focuses on the ideological content of a work — its explicit and implicit assumptions and values about matters such as culture, race, class, and power. Marxist criticism, based largely on the writings of Karl Marx, typically aims at not only revealing and clarifying ideological issues but also correcting social injustices. Some Marxist critics use literature to describe the competing socioeconomic interests that too often advance capitalist interests such as money and power rather than socialist interests such as morality and justice. They argue that literature and literary criticism are essentially political because they either challenge or support economic oppression. Because of this strong emphasis on the political aspects of texts, Marxist criticism focuses more on the content and themes of literature than on its form. See also CULTURAL CRITICISM, HISTORICAL CRITICISM, SOCIOLOGICAL CRITICISM.

**Masculine rhyme**  See RHYME.

**Melodrama**  A term applied to any literary work that relies on implausible events and sensational action for its effect. The conflicts in melodramas typically arise out of plot rather than characterization; often a virtuous individual must somehow confront and overcome a wicked oppressor. Usually, a melodramatic story ends happily, with the protagonist defeating the antagonist at the last possible moment. Thus, melodramas entertain the reader or audience with exciting action while still conforming to a traditional sense of justice. See also SENTIMENTALITY.

**Metafiction**  The literary term used to describe a work that explores the nature, structure, logic, status, and function of storytelling.

**Metaphor**  A metaphor is a figure of speech that makes a comparison between two unlike things, without using the word *like* or *as*. Metaphors assert the identity of dissimilar things, as when Macbeth asserts that life *is* a "brief candle." Metaphors can be subtle and powerful, and can transform people, places, objects, and ideas into whatever the writer imagines them to be. An **implied metaphor** is a more subtle comparison; the terms being compared are not so specifically explained. For example, to describe a stubborn man unwilling to leave, one could say that he was "a mule standing his ground." This is a fairly explicit metaphor; the man is being compared to a mule. But to say that the man "brayed his refusal to leave" is to create an implied metaphor, because the subject (the man) is never overtly identified as a mule. Braying is associated with the mule, a notoriously stubborn creature, and so the comparison between the stubborn man and the mule is sustained. Implied metaphors can slip by inattentive readers who are not sensitive to such carefully chosen, highly concentrated language. An **extended metaphor** is a sustained comparison in which part or all of a poem consists of a series of related metaphors. Robert Francis's poem "Catch" relies on an extended metaphor that compares poetry to playing catch. A **controlling metaphor** runs through an entire work and determines the form or nature of that work. The controlling metaphor in Anne Bradstreet's poem "The Author to Her Book" likens her book to a child. **Synecdoche** is a kind of metaphor in which a part of something is used to signify the whole, as when a gossip is called a "wagging tongue," or when ten ships are called "ten sails." Sometimes, synecdoche refers to the whole being used to signify the part, as in the phrase "Boston won the baseball game." Clearly, the entire city of Boston did not participate in the game; the whole of

Boston is being used to signify the individuals who played and won the game. **Metonymy** is a type of metaphor in which something closely associated with a subject is substituted for it. In this way, we speak of the "silver screen" to mean motion pictures, "the crown" to stand for the monarch, "the White House" to stand for the activities of the president. See also FIGURES OF SPEECH, PERSONI-FICATION, SIMILE.

**Metatheater** A contemporary and experimental genre that calls attention to the conventions of theater itself over the actual plot. Common characteristics include breaking the fourth wall, or even including audiences in the play. Less heavy and philosophical than absurdism, metatheater is a playful way for writers to explore the relationship between authors and their creations, as well as players on a stage and those watching them. See also ASIDE, THEATER OF THE ABSURD.

**Meter** When a rhythmic pattern of stresses recurs in a poem, it is called *meter*. Metrical patterns are determined by the type and number of feet in a line of verse; combining the name of a line length with the name of a foot concisely describes the meter of the line. **Rising meter** refers to metrical feet that move from unstressed to stressed sounds, such as the **iambic foot** and the anapestic foot. **Falling meter** refers to metrical feet that move from stressed to unstressed sounds, such as the trochaic foot and the dactylic foot. See also ACCENT, FOOT, IAMBIC PENTAMETER, LINE.

**Metonymy** See METAPHOR.

**Middle diction** See DICTION.

**Motivated action** See CHARACTER.

**Mythological criticism** An approach to literature that seeks to identify what in a work creates deep universal responses in readers, by paying close attention to the hopes, fears, and expectations of entire cultures. Mythological critics (sometimes called *archetypal critics*) look for underlying, recurrent patterns in literature that reveal universal meanings and basic human experiences for readers regardless of when and where they live. These critics attempt to explain how archetypes (the characters, images, and themes that symbolically embody universal meanings and experiences) are embodied in literary works in order to make larger connections that explain a particular work's lasting appeal. Mythological critics may specialize in areas such as classical literature, philology, anthropology, psychology, and cultural history, but they all emphasize the assumptions and values of various cultures. See also ARCHETYPE.

**Naive narrator** See NARRATOR.

**Narrative poem** A poem that tells a story. A narrative poem may be short or long, and the story it relates may be simple or complex. See also BALLAD, EPIC.

**Narrator** The voice of the person telling the story, not to be confused with the author's voice. With a **first-person narrator**, the *I* in the story presents the point of view of only one character. The reader is restricted to the perceptions, thoughts, and feelings of that single character. For example, in ZZ Packer's "Drinking Coffee Elsewhere," Dina is the first-person narrator of the story. First-person narrators can play either a major or a minor role in the story they are telling. An **unreliable narrator** reveals an interpretation of events that is somehow different from the author's own interpretation of those events. Often, the unreliable narrator's perception of plot, characters, and setting becomes the actual subject of the story, as in "Drinking Coffee Elsewhere." Narrators can be unreliable for a number of reasons: they might lack full self-knowledge (like Packer's Dina), they might be inexperienced, they might even be insane (like the narrator of Charlotte Perkins Gilman's "The Yellow Wallpaper"). **Naive narrators** are usually characterized by youthful innocence, such as Mark Twain's Huck Finn or J. D. Salinger's Holden Caulfield. An **omniscient narrator** is an all-knowing narrator who is not a character in the story and who can move from place to place and pass back and forth through time, slipping into and out of characters as no human being possibly could in real life. Omniscient narrators can report the thoughts and feelings of the characters, as well as their words and actions. The narrator of Ursula K. Le Guin's story "The Ones Who Walk Away from Omelas" is an omniscient narrator. **Editorial omniscience** refers to an intrusion by the narrator in order to evaluate a character for a reader, as when the narrator of Le Guin's story asks the reader questions about the scene she describes. Narration that allows the characters' actions and thoughts to speak for themselves is called **neutral omniscience**. Most modern writers use neutral omniscience so that readers can reach their own conclusions. **Limited omniscience** occurs when an author restricts a narrator to the single perspective of either a major or minor character. The way people, places, and events appear to that character is the way they appear to the reader. Sometimes a limited omniscient narrator can see into more than one character, particularly in a work that focuses on two characters alternately from one chapter to the next. Short stories, however, are frequently limited to a single character's point of view. See also PERSONA, POINT OF VIEW, STREAM-OF-CONSCIOUSNESS TECHNIQUE.

**Naturalism** A literary movement that emphasizes the cruelty and indifference of the natural world. Naturalism's core philosophy is that humans are subject to the laws and rules of nature, with behavior determined by heredity, the environment, and instinctual desires rather than by reason. See also EXPRESSIONISM, REALISM, VERISIMILITUDE.

**Near rhyme** See RHYME.

**Neutral omniscience** See NARRATOR.

**New Criticism** An approach to literature made popular between the 1940s and the 1960s that evolved out of formalist criticism. New Critics suggest that detailed analysis of the language of a literary text can uncover important layers of meaning in that work. New Criticism consciously downplays the historical influences, authorial intentions, and social contexts that surround texts in order to focus on explication — extremely close textual analysis. Critics such as John Crowe Ransom, I. A. Richards, and Robert Penn Warren are commonly associated with New Criticism. See also EXPLICATION, FORMALIST CRITICISM.

**New historicism** An approach to literature that emphasizes the interaction between the historic context of the work and a modern reader's understanding and interpretation of the work. New historicists attempt to describe the culture of a period by reading many different kinds of texts and paying close attention to many different dimensions of a culture, including political, economic, social, and aesthetic concerns. They regard texts not simply as a reflection of the culture that produced them but also as contributing to that culture by playing an active role in the social and political conflicts of an age. New historicism acknowledges and then explores various versions of "history," sensitizing us to the fact that the history on which we choose to focus is colored by being reconstructed from our present circumstances. See also HISTORICAL CRITICISM.

**Objective point of view** See POINT OF VIEW.

**Octave** A poetic stanza of eight lines, usually forming one part of a Petrarchan sonnet. See also SONNET, STANZA.

**Ode** A relatively lengthy lyric poem that often expresses lofty emotions in a dignified style. Odes are characterized by a serious topic, such as truth, art, freedom, justice, or the meaning of life; their tone tends to be formal. There is no prescribed pattern that defines an ode; some odes repeat the same pattern in each stanza, while others introduce a new pattern in each stanza. See also LYRIC.

**Oedipus complex** A Freudian term derived from Sophocles' tragedy *Oedipus the King*. It describes a psychological complex that is predicated on a boy's unconscious rivalry with his father for his mother's love and his desire to eliminate his father in order to take his father's place with his mother. See also ELECTRA COMPLEX, PSYCHOLOGICAL CRITICISM.

**Off rhyme** See RHYME.

**Omniscient narrator** See NARRATOR.

**One-act play** A play that takes place in a single location and unfolds as one continuous action. The characters in a one-act play are presented economically and the action is sharply focused. See also DRAMA.

**Onomatopoeia** A term referring to the use of a word that resembles the sound it denotes. *Buzz, rattle, bang*, and *sizzle* all reflect onomatopoeia. Onomatopoeia can also consist of more than one word; writers sometimes create lines or whole passages in which the sound of the words helps to convey their meanings.

**Open form** Sometimes called **free verse**, open form poetry does not conform to established patterns of METER, RHYME, and STANZA. Such poetry derives its rhythmic qualities from the repetition of words, phrases, or grammatical structures, the arrangement of words on the printed page, or by some other means. The poet E. E. Cummings wrote open form poetry; his poems do not have measurable meters, but they do have rhythm. See also FIXED FORM.

**Organic form** Refers to works whose formal characteristics are not rigidly predetermined but follow the movement of thought or emotion being expressed. Such works are said to grow like living organisms, following their own individual patterns rather than external fixed rules that govern, for example, the form of a SONNET.

**Overstatement** See HYPERBOLE.

**Oxymoron** A condensed form of paradox in which two contradictory words are used together, as in "sweet sorrow" or "original copy." See also PARADOX.

**Paradox** A statement that initially appears to be contradictory but then, on closer inspection, turns out to make sense. For example, John Donne ends his sonnet

"Death, Be Not Proud" with the paradoxical statement "Death, thou shalt die." To solve the paradox, it is necessary to discover the sense that underlies the statement. Paradox is useful in poetry because it arrests a reader's attention by its seemingly stubborn refusal to make sense.

**Paraphrase** A prose restatement of the central ideas of a literary work, in one's own language.

**Parody** A humorous imitation of another, usually serious, work. It can take any fixed or open form, because parodists imitate the tone, language, and shape of the original in order to deflate the subject matter, making the original work seem absurd. Anthony Hecht's poem "Dover Bitch" is a famous parody of Matthew Arnold's well-known "Dover Beach." Parody may also be used as a form of literary criticism to expose the defects in a work. But sometimes parody becomes an affectionate acknowledgment that a well-known work has become both institutionalized in our culture and fair game for some fun. For example, Peter De Vries's "To His Importunate Mistress" gently mocks Andrew Marvell's "To His Coy Mistress."

**Persona** Literally, a persona is a mask. In literature, a persona is a speaker created by a writer to tell a story or to speak in a poem. A persona is not a character in a story or narrative, nor does a persona necessarily directly reflect the author's personal voice. A persona is a separate self, created by and distinct from the author, through which he or she speaks. See also NARRATOR.

**Personification** A form of metaphor in which human characteristics are attributed to nonhuman things. Personification offers the writer a way to give the world life and motion by assigning familiar human behaviors and emotions to animals, inanimate objects, and abstract ideas. For example, in Keats's "Ode on a Grecian Urn," the speaker refers to the urn as an "unravished bride of quietness," or in Langston Hughes's "The Weary Blues," the player makes "the piano moan." See also METAPHOR.

**Petrarchan sonnet** See SONNET.

**Picture poem** A type of open form poetry in which the poet arranges the lines of the poem so as to create a particular shape on the page. The shape of the poem embodies its subject; the poem becomes a picture of what the poem is describing. Michael McFee's "In Medias Res" is an example of a picture poem. See also OPEN FORM.

**Plagiarism** The act of passing off someone else's work as one's own by failing to properly cite another's words or ideas words. Plagiarism is considered theft and unethical, even if done unintentionally.

**Plausible action** See CHARACTER.

**Play** See DRAMA.

**Playwright** See DRAMA.

**Plot** An author's selection and arrangement of incidents in a story to shape the action and give the story a particular focus. Discussions of plot include not just what happens, but also how and why things happen the way they do. Stories that are written in a **pyramidal pattern** divide the plot into three essential parts. The first part is the **rising action**, in which complication creates some sort of conflict for the protagonist. The second part is the **climax**, the moment of greatest emotional tension in a narrative, usually marking a turning point in the plot at which the **rising action** reverses to become the falling action. The third part, the **falling action** (or RESOLUTION), is characterized by diminishing tensions and the resolution of the plot's conflicts and complications. *In medias res* is a term used to describe the common strategy of beginning a story in the middle of the action. In this type of plot, we enter the story on the verge of some important moment. See also CHARACTER, CRISIS, RESOLUTION, SUBPLOT.

**Poetic diction** See DICTION.

**Point of view** Refers to who tells us a story and how it is told. What we know and how we feel about the events in a work are shaped by the author's choice of point of view. The teller of the story, the narrator, inevitably affects our understanding of the characters' actions by filtering what is told through his or her own perspective. The various points of view that writers draw upon can be grouped into two broad categories: (1) the third-person narrator uses *he*, *she*, or *they* to tell the story and does not participate in the action; and (2) the first-person narrator uses *I* and is a major or minor participant in the action. In addition, a second-person narrator, *you*, is also possible, but is rarely used because of the awkwardness of thrusting the reader into the story, as in "You are minding your own business on a park bench when a drunk steps out and demands your lunch bag." An **objective point of view** employs a third-person narrator who does not see into the mind of any character. From this detached and impersonal perspective, the narrator reports action and dialogue without telling us directly what the characters think and feel. Since no analysis or interpretation is provided by the narrator, this point of view places a premium on dialogue, actions, and details to reveal character to the reader. See also NARRATOR, STREAM-OF-CONSCIOUSNESS TECHNIQUE.

**Problem play** Popularized by Henrik Ibsen, a problem play is a type of drama that presents a social issue in order to awaken the audience to it. These plays usually reject romantic plots in favor of holding up a mirror that reflects not simply what the audience wants to see but what the playwright sees in them. Often, a problem play will propose a solution to the problem that does not coincide with prevailing opinion. The term is also used to refer to certain Shakespeare plays that do not fit the categories of tragedy, comedy, or romance. See also DRAMA.

**Prologue** The opening speech or dialogue of a play, especially a classic Greek play, that usually gives the exposition necessary to follow the subsequent action. Today the term also refers to the introduction to any literary work. See also DRAMA, EXPOSITION.

**Prose poem** A kind of open form poetry that is printed as prose and represents the most clear opposite of fixed form poetry. Prose poems are densely compact and often make use of striking imagery and figures of speech. See also FIXED FORM, OPEN FORM.

**Prosody** The overall metrical structure of a poem. See also METER.

**Protagonist** The main character of a narrative; its central character who engages the reader's interest and empathy. See also ANTAGONIST, CHARACTER.

**Psychological criticism**  An approach to literature that draws upon psycho-analytic theories, especially those of Sigmund Freud or Jacques Lacan, to understand more fully the text, the writer, and/or the reader. The basis of this approach is the idea of the existence of a human unconscious — those impulses, desires, and feelings about which a person is unaware but which influence emotions and behavior. Critics use psychological approaches to explore the motivations of characters and the symbolic meanings of events, while biographers speculate about a writer's own motivations — conscious or unconscious — in a literary work. Psychological approaches are also used to describe and analyze the reader's personal responses to a text.

**Pun**  A play on words that relies on a word's having more than one meaning or sounding like another word. Shakespeare and other writers use puns exten-sively, for serious and comic purposes; in *Romeo and Juliet* (III.i.101), the dying Mercutio puns, "Ask for me tomorrow and you shall find me a grave man." Puns have serious literary uses, but since the eighteenth century, puns have been used almost purely for humorous effect. See also COMEDY.

**Pyramidal pattern**  See PLOT.

**Quatrain**  A four-line stanza. Quatrains are the most common stanzaic form in the English language; they can have various meters and rhyme schemes. See also METER, RHYME, STANZA.

**Reader-response criticism**  An approach to literature that focuses on the process of reading rather than the work itself, by attempting to describe what goes on in the reader's mind during the reading of a text. Hence, the consciousness of the reader — produced by reading the work — is the actual subject of reader-response criticism. These critics are not after a "correct" reading of the text or what the author presumably intended; instead, they are interested in the reader's individual experience with the text, perhaps in conjunction with the responses of other similar readers, referred to as an "interpretive community." Thus, there is no single definitive reading of a work, because readers create rather than discover absolute meanings in texts. However, this approach is not a rationale for mistaken or bizarre readings, but an exploration of the possibil-ities for a plurality of readings. This kind of strategy calls attention to how we read and what influences our readings, and what that reveals about ourselves.

**Realism**  A literary technique that attempts to create the appearance of life as it is actually experienced. Realism is characterized by characters speaking in ordinary language according to their time of publication, with topics revolv-ing around commonplace events, such as work, love, marriage, children, and death. Conflicts tend to reflect problems in our own lives or society. See also NATURALISM, VERISIMILITUDE.

**Recognition**  The moment in a story when previously unknown or withheld information is revealed to the protagonist, resulting in the discovery of the truth of their situation and, usually, a decisive change in course for that char-acter. In *Oedipus the King*, the moment of recognition comes when Oedipus finally realizes that he has killed his father and married his mother.

**Resolution**  The conclusion of a plot's conflicts and complications. The resolu-tion, also known as the **falling action**, follows the climax in the plot. See also DÉNOUEMENT, PLOT.

**Revenge tragedy** See TRAGEDY.

**Reversal** The point in a story when the protagonist's fortunes turn in an unexpected direction. See also PLOT.

**Rhyme** The repetition of identical or similar concluding syllables in different words, most often at the ends of lines. Rhyme is predominantly a function of sound rather than spelling; thus, words that end with the same vowel sounds rhyme, for instance, *day, prey, bouquet, weigh*, and words with the same consonant ending rhyme, for instance *vain, feign, rein, lane*. Words do not have to be spelled the same way or look alike to rhyme. In fact, words may look alike but not rhyme at all. This is called **eye rhyme**, as with *bough* and *cough*, or *brow* and *blow*. **End rhyme** is the most common form of rhyme in poetry; the rhyme comes at the end of the lines:

It runs through the reeds

And away it proceeds,

Through meadow and glade,

In sun and in shade.

The **rhyme scheme** of a poem describes the pattern of end rhymes. Rhyme schemes are mapped out by noting patterns of rhyme with small letters: the first rhyme sound is designated *a*, the second becomes *b*, the third *c*, and so on. Thus, the rhyme scheme of the stanza above is *aabb*. **Internal rhyme** places at least one of the rhymed words within the line, as in "Dividing and gliding and sliding" or "In mist or cloud, on mast or shroud." **Masculine rhyme** describes the rhyming of single-syllable words, such as *grade* or *shade*. Masculine rhyme also occurs when rhyming words of more than one syllable, when the same sound occurs in a final stressed syllable, as in *defend* and *contend, betray* and *away*. **Feminine rhyme** consists of a rhymed stressed syllable followed by one or more identical unstressed syllables, as in *butter, clutter; gratitude, attitude; quivering, shivering*. All the examples so far have illustrated **exact rhymes**, because they share the same stressed vowel sounds as well as sharing sounds that follow the vowel. In **near rhyme** (also called **off rhyme**, **slant rhyme**, and **approximate rhyme**), the sounds are almost but not exactly alike. A common form of near rhyme is consonance, which consists of identical consonant sounds preceded by different vowel sounds: *home, same; worth, breath*.

**Rhyme scheme** See RHYME.

**Rhythm** A term used to refer to the recurrence of stressed and unstressed sounds in poetry. Depending on how sounds are arranged, the rhythm of a poem may be fast or slow, choppy or smooth. Poets use rhythm to create pleasurable sound patterns and to reinforce meanings. Rhythm in prose arises from pattern repetitions of sounds and pauses that create looser rhythmic effects. See also METER.

**Rising action** See PLOT.

**Rising meter** See METER.

**Romantic comedy** See COMEDY.

**Round character** See CHARACTER.

**Run-on line** See ENJAMBMENT.

**Sarcasm** See IRONY.

**Satire** The literary art of ridiculing a folly or vice in order to expose or correct it. The object of satire is usually some human frailty; people, institutions, ideas, and things are all fair game for satirists. Satire evokes attitudes of amusement, contempt, scorn, or indignation toward its faulty subject in the hope of somehow improving it. See also IRONY, PARODY.

**Scansion** The process of measuring the stresses in a line of verse in order to determine the metrical pattern of the line. See also LINE, METER.

**Scene** In drama, a scene is a subdivision of an act. In modern plays, scenes usually consist of units of action in which there are no changes in the setting or breaks in the continuity of time. According to traditional conventions, a scene changes when the location of the action shifts or when a new character enters. See also ACT, CONVENTION, DRAMA.

**Script** The written text of a play, which includes the dialogue between characters, stage directions, and often other expository information. See also DRAMA, EXPOSITION, PROLOGUE, STAGE DIRECTIONS.

**Sentimentality** A pejorative term used to describe the effort by an author to induce emotional responses in the reader that exceed what the situation warrants. Sentimentality especially pertains to such emotions as pathos and sympathy; it cons readers into falling for the mass murderer who is devoted to stray cats, and it requires that readers do not examine such illogical responses. Clichés and stock responses are the key ingredients of sentimentality in literature. See also CLICHÉ, STOCK RESPONSES.

**Sestet** A stanza consisting of exactly six lines. See also STANZA.

**Sestina** A type of fixed form poetry consisting of thirty-nine lines of any length divided into six sestets and a three-line concluding stanza called an *envoy*. The six words at the end of the first sestet's lines must also appear at the ends of the other five sestets, in varying order. These six words must also appear in the envoy, where they often resonate important themes. An example of this highly demanding form of poetry is Algernon Charles Swinburne's "Sestina." See also SESTET.

**Setting** The physical and social context in which the action of a story occurs. The major elements of setting are the time, the place, and the social environment that frames the characters. Setting can be used to evoke a mood or atmosphere that will prepare the reader for what is to come, as in Nathaniel Hawthorne's short story "Young Goodman Brown." Sometimes, writers choose a particular setting because of traditional associations with that setting that are closely related to the action of a story. For example, stories filled with adventure or romance often take place in exotic locales.

**Shakespearean sonnet** See SONNET.

**Showing** See CHARACTER.

**Simile** A common figure of speech that makes an explicit comparison between two things by using words such as *like, as, than, appears,* and *seems:* "A sip of Mrs. Cook's coffee is like a punch in the stomach." The effectiveness of this simile is created by the differences between the two things compared. There would be no simile if the comparison were stated this way: "Mrs. Cook's coffee is as strong as the cafeteria's coffee." This is a literal translation because Mrs. Cook's coffee is compared with something like it — another kind of coffee. See also FIGURES OF SPEECH, METAPHOR.

**Situational irony** See IRONY.

**Slant rhyme** See RHYME.

**Sociological criticism** An approach to literature that examines social groups, relationships, and values as they are manifested in literature. Sociological approaches emphasize the nature and effect of the social forces that shape power relationships between groups or classes of people. Such readings treat literature as either a document reflecting social conditions or a product of those conditions. The former view brings into focus the social milieu; the latter emphasizes the work. Two important forms of sociological criticism are Marxist and feminist approaches. See also FEMINIST CRITICISM, MARXIST CRITICISM.

**Soliloquy** A dramatic convention by means of which a character, alone onstage, utters his or her thoughts aloud. Playwrights use soliloquies as a convenient way to inform the audience about a character's motivations and state of mind. Shakespeare's Hamlet delivers perhaps the best known of all soliloquies, which begins: "To be or not to be." See also ASIDE, CONVENTION.

**Sonnet** A fixed form of lyric poetry that consists of fourteen lines, usually written in iambic pentameter. There are two basic types of sonnets, the Italian and the English. The **Italian sonnet**, also known as the **Petrarchan sonnet**, is divided into an octave, which typically rhymes *abbaabba*, and a sestet, which may have varying rhyme schemes. Common rhyme patterns in the sestet are *cdecde*, *cdcdcd*, and *cdccdc*. Very often the octave presents a situation, attitude, or problem that the sestet comments upon or resolves, as in John Keats's "On First Looking into Chapman's Homer." The **English sonnet**, also known as the **Shakespearean sonnet**, is organized into three quatrains and a couplet, which typically rhyme *abab cdcd efef gg*. This rhyme scheme is more suited to English poetry because English has fewer rhyming words than Italian. English sonnets, because of their four-part organization, also have more flexibility with respect to where thematic breaks can occur. Frequently, however, the most pronounced break or turn comes with the concluding couplet, as in Shakespeare's "Shall I compare thee to a summer's day?" See also COUPLET, IAMBIC PENTAMETER, LINE, OCTAVE, QUATRAIN, SESTET, VOLTA.

**Speaker** The voice used by an author to tell a story or speak a poem. The speaker is often a created identity and should not automatically be equated with the author's self. See also NARRATOR, PERSONA, POINT OF VIEW.

**Spondee** See FOOT.

**Stage directions** A playwright's written instructions about how the actors are to move and behave in a play. They explain in which direction characters should move, what facial expressions they should assume, and so on. See also DRAMA, SCRIPT.

**Stanza** In poetry, *stanza* refers to a grouping of lines, set off by a space, that usually has a set pattern of meter and rhyme. See also LINE, METER, RHYME.

**Static character** See CHARACTER.

**Stock character** See CHARACTER.

**Stock responses** Predictable, conventional reactions to language, characters, symbols, or situations. The flag, motherhood, puppies, God, and peace are common objects used to elicit stock responses from unsophisticated audiences. See also CLICHÉ, SENTIMENTALITY.

**Stream-of-consciousness technique** The most intense use of a central consciousness in narration. The stream-of-consciousness technique takes a reader inside a character's mind to reveal perceptions, thoughts, and feelings on a conscious or unconscious level. This technique suggests the flow of thought as well as its content; hence, complete sentences may give way to fragments as the character's mind makes rapid associations free of conventional logic or transitions. James Joyce's novel *Ulysses* makes extensive use of this narrative technique. See also NARRATOR, POINT OF VIEW.

**Stress** The emphasis, or accent, given a syllable in pronunciation. See also ACCENT.

**Style** The distinctive and unique manner in which a writer arranges words to achieve particular effects. Style essentially combines the idea to be expressed with the individuality of the author. These arrangements include individual word choices as well as matters such as the length of sentences, their structure, tone, and use of irony. See also DICTION, IRONY, TONE.

**Subplot** The secondary action of a story, complete and interesting in its own right, that reinforces or contrasts with the main plot. There may be more than one subplot, and sometimes as many as three, four, or even more, running through a piece of fiction. Subplots are generally either analogous to the main plot, thereby enhancing our understanding of it, or extraneous to the main plot, to provide relief from it. See also PLOT.

**Suspense** The anxious anticipation of a reader or an audience as to the outcome of a story, especially concerning the character or characters with whom sympathetic attachments are formed. Suspense helps to secure and sustain the interest of the reader or audience throughout a work.

**Symbol** A person, object, image, word, or event that evokes a range of additional meaning beyond and usually more abstract than its literal significance. Symbols are educational devices for evoking complex ideas without having to resort to painstaking explanations that would make a story more like an essay than an experience. **Conventional symbols** have meanings that are widely recognized by a society or culture. Some conventional symbols recognizable in American culture are a soaring bird to represent freedom or sweat to represent hard work. Writers use conventional symbols to reinforce meanings. Kate Chopin, for example, emphasizes the spring setting in "The Story of an Hour" as a way of suggesting the renewed sense of life that Mrs. Mallard feels when she thinks herself free from her husband. A **literary** or **contextual symbol** can be a setting, character, action, object, name, or anything else in a work that maintains its literal significance while suggesting other meanings. Such symbols go beyond conventional symbols; they gain their symbolic meaning within the context of a specific story. For example, the white whale in Melville's

*Moby-Dick* takes on multiple symbolic meanings in the work, but these meanings do not automatically carry over into other stories about whales. The meanings suggested by Melville's whale are specific to that text; therefore, it becomes a contextual symbol. See also ALLEGORY.

**Symbolist drama**  A style that, in opposition to **realism**, emphasizes the inherent symbols of life and is meant to only be understood emotionally and intuitively. Symbolist drama is characterized by references to mythology and the use of a mix of realistic and nonrealistic symbols to create a world that isn't outwardly fantastical, but also isn't identical to ordinary life. See also EXPRESSIONISM.

**Synecdoche**  See METAPHOR.

**Syntax**  The ordering of words into meaningful verbal patterns such as phrases, clauses, and sentences. Poets often manipulate syntax, changing conventional word order, to place certain emphasis on particular words. Emily Dickinson, for instance, writes about being surprised by a snake in her poem "A narrow Fellow in the Grass" and includes this line: "His notice sudden is." In addition to creating the alliterative hissing *s*-sounds here, Dickinson also effectively manipulates the line's syntax so that the verb *is* appears unexpectedly at the end, making the snake's hissing presence all the more "sudden."

**Telling**  See CHARACTER.

**Tercet**  A three-line stanza. See also STANZA, TRIPLET.

*Terza rima*  An interlocking three-line rhyme scheme: *aba, bcb, cdc, ded,* and so on. Dante's *The Divine Comedy* and Frost's "Acquainted with the Night" are written in *terza rima.* See also RHYME, TERCET.

**Theater of the absurd**  A theatrical reaction to post-WWII morals and a response to the twentieth century's loss of faith in reason, religion, and life itself, absurdist plots and performances thrive on chaos, irrational forces outside of our control, and the meaningless of existence. *Absurdism* rejects most religion and philosophy as well as the belief that life is ordered, and traditional values help give purpose to life. All sense of rationality/rational conventions, common sense, and logic are put aside on an absurdist's stage in favor of the fragmented voices and motivations that show there is no illusion of reality after all to imitate.

**Theater of cruelty**  A style of drama intended to shock audiences; "cruelty" doesn't necessarily connote violence, but rather this shock factor. Developed by French playwright Antonin Artaud, theater of cruelty is closely related to theater of the absurd; its goal is not to represent life in a realistic way, but rather to leave the audiences with a change in perspective. In addition to the script, this effect is achieved through lighting, sound, and scenery. See also THEATER OF THE ABSURD.

**Theme**  The central meaning or dominant idea in a literary work. A theme provides a unifying point around which the plot, characters, setting, point of view, symbols, and other elements of a work are organized. It is important not to mistake the theme for the actual subject of the work; the theme refers to the abstract concept that is made concrete through the images, characterization, and action of the text. In nonfiction, however, the theme generally refers to the main topic of the discourse.

**Thesis**  The central idea of an essay. The thesis is a complete sentence (although sometimes it may require more than one sentence) that establishes the topic of the essay in clear, unambiguous language and suggests a concluding interpretation.

**Tone**  The author's implicit attitude toward the reader or the people, places, and events in a work as revealed by the elements of the author's style. Tone may be characterized as serious or ironic, sad or happy, private or public, angry or affectionate, bitter or nostalgic, or any other attitudes and feelings that human beings experience. See also STYLE.

**Tragedy**  A story that presents courageous individuals who confront powerful forces within or outside themselves with a dignity that reveals the breadth and depth of the human spirit in the face of failure, defeat, and even death. Tragedies recount an individual's downfall; they usually begin high and end low. Shakespeare is known for his tragedies, including *Macbeth, King Lear, Othello,* and *Hamlet*. The **revenge tragedy** is a well-established type of drama that can be traced back to Greek and Roman plays, particularly through the Roman playwright Seneca (ca. 3 B.C.–A.D. 63). Revenge tragedies basically consist of a murder that has to be avenged by a relative of the victim. Typically, the victim's ghost appears to demand revenge, and invariably madness of some sort is worked into subsequent events, which ultimately end in the deaths of the murderer, the avenger, and a number of other characters. Shakespeare's *Hamlet* subscribes to the basic ingredients of revenge tragedy, but it also transcends these conventions because Hamlet contemplates not merely revenge but suicide and the meaning of life itself. A **tragic flaw** is an error or defect in the tragic hero that leads to his downfall, such as greed, pride, or ambition. This flaw may be a result of bad character, bad judgment, an inherited weakness, or any other defect of character. **Tragic irony** is a form of dramatic irony found in tragedies such as *Oedipus the King*, in which Oedipus ironically ends up hunting himself. See also COMEDY, DRAMA.

**Tragic flaw**  See TRAGEDY.

**Tragic irony**  See IRONY, TRAGEDY.

**Tragicomedy**  A type of drama that combines certain elements of both tragedy and comedy. The play's plot tends to be serious, leading to a terrible catastrophe, until an unexpected turn in events leads to a reversal of circumstance, and the story ends happily. Tragicomedy often employs a romantic, fast-moving plot dealing with love, jealousy, disguises, treachery, intrigue, and surprises, all moving toward a melodramatic resolution. Shakespeare's *Merchant of Venice* is a tragicomedy. See also COMEDY, DRAMA, MELODRAMA, TRAGEDY.

**Triplet**  A tercet in which all three lines rhyme. See also TERCET.

**Trochaic meter**  See FOOT.

**Turn**  See VOLTA.

**Understatement**  The opposite of hyperbole, understatement (or *litotes*) refers to a figure of speech that says less than is intended. Understatement usually has an ironic effect, and sometimes may be used for comic purposes, as in Mark Twain's statement, "The reports of my death are greatly exaggerated." See also HYPERBOLE, IRONY.

**Unreliable narrator** See NARRATOR.

**Verbal irony** See IRONY.

**Verisimilitude** The details in a work of literature that add a sense of truth or reality to the work. Although readers understand that imaginative literature is by definition not real in the way that history or lived experience is real, authors of realistic works include elements that provide the illusion of reality so that readers may immerse themselves in it. See also NATURALISM, REALISM.

**Verse** A generic term used to describe poetic lines composed in a measured rhythmical pattern that are often, but not necessarily, rhymed. See also LINE, METER, RHYME, RHYTHM.

**Villanelle** A type of fixed form poetry consisting of nineteen lines of any length divided into six stanzas: five tercets and a concluding quatrain. The first and third lines of the initial tercet rhyme; these rhymes are repeated in each subsequent tercet (*aba*) and in the final two lines of the quatrain (*abaa*). Line 1 appears in its entirety as lines 6, 12, and 18, while line 3 reappears as lines 9, 15, and 19. Dylan Thomas's "Do Not Go Gentle into That Good Night" is a villanelle. See also FIXED FORM, QUATRAIN, RHYME, TERCET.

**Volta** The Italian word for *turn*, volta is often used to signify the "turn" in a work of poetry — this can be a shift in events, chronological time, thought, course of action, argument, etc. If unsure, look for words like "But" or "Yet" to locate where the turn may be. A volta usually occurs in between the octave and sestet of Petrarchan, or Italian, sonnets, and before the final couplet in Shakespearean, or English, sonnets.

**Well-made play** A realistic style of play that employs conventions including plenty of suspense created by meticulous plotting. Well-made plays are tightly and logically constructed, and lead to a logical resolution that is favorable to the protagonist. This dramatic structure was popularized in France by Eugène Scribe (1791–1861) and Victorien Sardou (1831–1908) and was adopted by Henrik Ibsen. See also CHARACTER, PLOT.

**World building** Often appearing in works of speculative fiction, world building is the process of constructing a new imaginary or fictional world. Going beyond establishing setting, it is a dedicated and conscious effort on the part of the author to develop a coherent and fleshed-out "world" that operates according to its own sets of conventions. This may involve creating fictional geographies, genealogies, histories, technologies, or even magical abilities.

*Acknowledgments (continued from p. vi)*

FICTION

Margaret Atwood, excerpt from "Alice Munro: An Appreciation (2008)," *Burning Questions: Essays and Occasional Pieces,* 2004 to 2021. Copyright © 2022 by O.W. Toad, Ltd. Used by permission of Doubleday, an imprint of the Knopf Doubleday Publishing Group, a division of Penguin Random House LLC and by permission of McClelland & Stewart, a division of Penguin Random House Canada Limited. All rights reserved.

James Baldwin. "Sonny's Blues," Copyright © 1957 and renewed 1985 by James Baldwin. Originally published in *The Partisan Review.* Collected in *Going to Meet the Man,* published by Vintage Books. Reprinted by arrangement with The James Baldwin Estate.

Ann Beattie. "Janus" from *Where You'll Find Me: And Other Stories* by Ann Beattie. Copyright © 1986 by Irony & Pity, Inc. Copyright © 1986 by Ann Beattie. Reprinted with the permission of Scribner, a division of Simon & Schuster, Inc., and by permission of the author. All rights reserved.

T. C. Boyle. "The Hit Man" from *The Human Fly and Other Stories.* Copyright © 2005 by T. Coraghessan Boyle. Used by permission of Viking Children's Books, an imprint of Penguin Young Readers Group, a division of Penguin Random House LLC. All rights reserved.

John Cheever. "The Enormous Radio" from *The Stories of John Cheever* by John Cheever. Copyright © collected in *The Stories of John Cheever.* Copyright © 1947, 1948, 1949, 1950, 1951, 1952, 1953, 1954, 1955, 1956, 1957, 1958, 1959, 1960, 1961, 1962, 1963, 1964, 1965, 1966, 1967, 1968, 1970, 1972, 1973, 1977, 1978, by John Cheever, used by permission of The Wylie Agency LLC.

Judith Ortiz Cofer. "Volar" from *The Year of Our Revolution* by Judith Ortiz Cofer is being reprinted with permission from the publisher (©1988 Arte Publico Press - University of Houston).

Edwidge Danticat. "The Missing Peace" from *Krik? Krak!* by Edwidge Danticat. Copyright © 1991, 1995 by Edwidge Danticat. Reprinted by permission of Soho Press, Inc. All rights reserved.

Peter Ho Davies. "Minotaur." Copyright © 2022 by Peter Ho Davies. Used with permission.

Philip K. Dick. "To Serve the Master" by Philip K. Dick. Copyright © 1987 Estate of Philip K. Dick, used by permission of The Wylie Agency LLC.

Andre Dubus. "Killings" from *The Winter Father.* Copyright © 1980 by Andre Dubus. Reprinted with the permission of The Permissions Company, LLC on behalf of David R Godine, Publisher, Inc., godine.com.

Ralph Ellison. "King of the Bingo Game" from *Flying Home: And Other Stories* by Ralph Ellison, edited by John F. Callahan, copyright © 1996 by Fanny Ellison. Used by permission of Random House, an imprint and division of Penguin Random House LLC. All rights reserved.

Mariana Enriquez. "Back When We Talked to the Dead" from The Dangers of Smoking in Bed: Stories by Mariana Enriquez, translated by Megan McDowell, translation copyright © 2021 by Penguin Random House LLC. Used by permission of Hogarth, an imprint of Random House, a division of Penguin Random House LLC. All rights reserved.

Louise Erdrich. "The Red Convertible" from *The Red Convertible* by Louise Erdrich. Copyright © 2009 by Louise Erdrich. Used by permission of HarperCollins Publishers.

William Faulkner. "A Rose for Emily" from *Faulkner in the University,* Introduction by Douglas Day, Gwynn, Frederick L., and Joseph L. Blotner, eds. Copyright © 1995 by the Rector and Visitors of the University of Virginia. Reprinted by permission of the University of Virginia Press.

William Faulkner. "A Rose for Emily" from *Collected Stories of William Faulkner* by William Faulkner. Copyright © 1930 and renewed 1958 by William Faulkner. Used by permission of Random House, an imprint and division of Penguin Random House LLC, and by permission of W. W. Norton & Company, Inc. All rights reserved.

Dagoberto Gilb. "Love in L.A." from *The Magic of Blood* by Dagoberto Gilb. Copyright © 1993. Story originally published in Buffalo. Reprinted by permission of the author.

Dagoberto Gilb. "On Distortions of Mexican American Culture," from "La Próxima Parada Is Next," *American Book Review* 32.3 (March/April 2011). Copyright © 2011 by Dagoberto Gilb. Reprinted by permission of the author.

Dagoberto Gilb. "On Physical Labor," from "Work Union" in *Gritos* by Dagoberto Gilb. Copyright © 2003 by Dagoberto Gilb. Originally appeared in *The Carpenter* (magazine of the United Brotherhood of Carpenters). Reprinted by permission of the author.

Dagoberto Gilb. "Shout" from *Woodcuts of Women* by Dagoberto Gilb. Copyright © 2001 by Dagoberto Gilb. Reprinted by permission of the author.

Dagoberto Gilb. "Uncle Rock" from *Before the End, After the Beginning* by Dagoberto Gilb. Copyright © 2011 by Dagoberto Gilb. Reprinted by permission of the author.

Joy Harjo, "The Reckoning" from THIS BRIDGE WE CALL HOME by Joy Harjo-Sapulpa. Copyright © 2022 by Joy Harjo, used by permission of The Wylie Agency LLC.

Shirley Jackson. "The Lottery" from *The Lottery* by Shirley Jackson. Copyright © 1948, 1949 by Shirley Jackson. Copyright renewed 1976, 1977 by Laurence Hyman, Barry Hyman, Mrs. Sarah Webster, and Mrs. Joanne Schnurer. Reprinted by permission of Farrar, Straus and Giroux, LLC. All rights reserved.

N.K. Jemisin. "Sinners, Saints, Dragons, and Haints, in the City Beneath the Still Waters" from *How Long 'til Black Future Month?* by N. K Jemisin, copyright © 2018. Reprinted by permission of Orbit, an imprint of Hachette Book Group, Inc.

Claire Katz. "Flannery O'Connor's Rage of Vision," in *American Literature,* vol. 46, no. 1, pp. 54-67. Copyright 1974, Duke University Press. All rights reserved. Republished by permission of the copyright holder, and the Publisher. www.dukepress.edu.

Jamaica Kincaid. "Girl" from *At the Bottom of the River* by Jamaica Kincaid. Copyright © 1983 by Jamaica Kincaid. Reprinted by permission of Farrar, Straus and Giroux, LLC. All rights reserved.

## POETRY

Billy Collins. "Building with Its Face Blown Off" from *The Trouble with Poetry: And Other Poems* by Billy Collins. Copyright © 2005 by Billy Collins. Used by permission of Random House, an imprint and division of Penguin Random House LLC. All rights reserved.

Billy Collins. "Litany" from *Nine Horses: Poems* by Billy Collins. Copyright © 2008 by Billy Collins. Used by permission of Random House, an imprint and division of Penguin Random House LLC. All rights reserved.

Billy Collins. "Nostalgia" from *Questions About Angels* by Billy Collins. Copyright © 1995. Reprinted by permission of the University of Pittsburgh Press.

Billy Collins. "Osso Buco" from *The Art of Drowning* by Billy Collins. Copyright © 1995. Reprinted by permission of the University of Pittsburgh Press.

Billy Collins. "Questions About Angels" from *Questions About Angels* by Billy Collins. Copyright © 1995. Reprinted by permission of the University of Pittsburgh Press.

Billy Collins. "Introduction to Poetry" from *The Apple That Astonished Paris*. Copyright © 1988, 1996 by Billy Collins. Reprinted with the permission of The Permissions Company, Inc., on behalf of the University of Arkansas Press, www.uapress.com.

Edmund Conti. "Pragmatist" from *Light Year '86*. Reprinted by permission of the author.

Gregory Corso. "I am 25" from *Gasoline & The Vestal Lady on Brattle*. Copyright © 1958 by Gregory Corso. Reprinted with the permission of The Permissions Company, LLC on behalf of City Lights Books, citylights.com.

Gregory Corso. "Marriage" from *The Happy Birthday of Death*. Copyright © 1960 by New Directions Publishing Corp. Reprinted by permission of New Directions Publishing Corp.

Sally Croft. "Home-Baked Bread" from *Light Year '86*. Reprinted by permission of Bruce Croft.

E. E. Cummings. "l(a". Copyright © 1958, 1986, 1991 by the Trustees for the E. E. Cummings Trust, from *Complete Poems: 1904–1962* by E. E. Cummings, edited by George J. Firmage. Used by permission of Liveright Publishing Corporation.

Kwame Dawes. "History Lesson at Eight a.m." was originally published in *Resisting the Anomie*, copyright © 1995 by Kwame Dawes. Reprinted by permission of Goose Lane Editions.

Kwame Dawes. "The Habits of Love" from *Back of Mount Peace* by Kwame Dawes. Copyright © 2010 by Kwame Dawes. Reprinted by permission of Peepal Tree Press.

Emily Dickinson. "Because I could not stop for Death," "From all the Jails the Boys and Girls," "'Heaven'—is what I cannot reach!", "I dwell in Possibility —," "I heard a Fly buzz—when I died", "I never saw a Moor," "I taste a liquor never brewed," "If I shouldn't be alive," "Much Madness is divinest Sense," "Success is Counted Sweetest," "Tell all the Truth but tell it Slant" and "There's a certain Slant of light" from *The Poems of Emily Dickinson*, edited by Thomas H. Johnson, Cambridge, Mass.: The Belknap Press of Harvard University Press. Copyright © 1951, 1955 by the President and Fellows of Harvard College. Copyright © renewed 1979, 1983 by the President and Fellows of Harvard College. Copyright © 1914, 1918, 1919, 1924, 1929, 1930, 1932, 1935, 1937, 1942, by Martha Dickinson Bianchi. Copyright © 1952, 1957, 1958, 1963, 1965, by Mary L. Hampson. Used by permission. All rights reserved.

Ani DiFranco, Not a Pretty Girl. Words and Music by Ani DiFranco. Copyright © 1995 Righteous Babe Music. All Rights Administered by Modern Works Music Publishing. All Rights Reserved. Used by Permission. Reprinted by Permission of Hal Leonard LLC.

Rita Dove. "Daystar" from *Collected Poems: 1974–2004* by Rita Dove. Copyright © 1986 by Rita Dove. Used by permission of W. W. Norton & Company, Inc.

Denise Duhamel. "Please Don't Sit Like a Frog, Sit Like a Queen" from *Ka-Ching!* Copyright © 2009 by Denise Duhamel. Reprinted by permission of the University of Pittsburgh Press.

Bob Dylan. "It's Alright Ma (I'm Only Bleeding)." Words and Music by Bob Dylan. Copyright © 1965 by Universal Tunes. Used by permission. All rights reserved.

Cornelius Eady. "The Supremes" from *The Gathering of My Name*. Copyright © 1991 by Cornelius Eady. Reprinted with the permission of The Permissions Company, LLC, on behalf of Carnegie Mellon University Press.

Martín Espada. "The Mexican Cabdriver's Poem for His Wife, Who Has Left Him" from *A Mayan Astronomer in Hell's Kitchen* by Martín Espada. Copyright © 2000 by Martín Espada. Used by permission of the author and W. W. Norton & Company, Inc.

Martín Espada. "Latin Night at the Pawnshop" from *Rebellion Is the Circle of a Lover's Hands / Rebelión es el giro de manos del amante* by Martín Espada. Copyright © 1990 by Martín Espada. Translation copyright © by Camilo Pérez-Bustillo and Martín Espada. First printed in 1990 by Curbstone Press. Reprinted with the permission of the author and Northwestern University Press.

J. Estanislao Lopez. "Meditation on Beauty," *The New Yorker*, March 26, 2018. Copyright © 2018. Reprinted by permission of the author.

Ruth Fainlight. "Crocuses" from *New & Collected Poems* by Ruth Fainlight (Bloodaxe Books, 2010). Copyright © 2010 by Ruth Fainlight. Reproduced with permission of Bloodaxe Books. www.bloodaxebooks.com.

Lawrence Ferlinghetti. "Constantly Risking Absurdity (#15)" from *A Coney Island of the Mind*. Copyright © 1958 by Lawrence Ferlinghetti. Reprinted by permission of New Directions Publishing Corp.

Karen Jackson Ford. "Hughes's Aesthetics of Simplicity" from "Do Right to Write Right: Langston Hughes's Aesthetics of Simplicity," *Twentieth Century Literature* 38.4 (Winter 1992), pp. 436–56. Copyright 1992, Hofstra University. All rights reserved. Republished by permission of the copyright holder, and the present publisher, Duke University Press, www.dukeupress.edu.

Ruth Forman. "Poetry Should Ride the Bus" from *We Are the Young Magicians* (Boston: Beacon Press, 1993). Copyright © 1993 by Ruth Forman. Reprinted with the permission of the author.

Kate Hanson Foster. "Elegy of Color," *Salamander* 46 (Spring/Summer 2018), p. 34. Copyright © 2018 by Kate Hanson Foster. Reprinted by permission of the author.

Robert Francis. "Catch" and "The Pitcher" from *The Orb Weaver* © 1960 by Robert Francis. Published by Wesleyan University Press. Used by permission.

Jennifer Franklin. "Memento Mori: Apple Orchard" Copyright © 2020 by Jennifer Franklin, published in *If Some God Shakes Your House* (Four Way Books 2023).

Robert Frost. "Acquainted with the Night," "Desert Places," "Design," "Neither Out Far nor In Deep," and "The Gift Outright" from *The Poetry of Robert Frost,* edited by Edward Connery Lathem. Copyright © 1928, 1969 by Henry Holt and Company. Copyright © 1956 by Robert Frost. Reprinted by permission of Henry Holt and Company. All rights reserved.

Tess Gallagher. "Choices" from *Midnight Lantern: New and Selected Poems.* Copyright © 2006 by Tess Gallagher. Reprinted with the permission of The Permissions Company, LLC on behalf of Graywolf Press, graywolfpress.org.

Mirza Asadullah Khan Ghalib. "Ghazal 4" from *Celebrating the Best of Urdu Poetry,* translated by Khushwant Singh and edited by Khushwant Singh and Kamna Prasad. Copyright © 2007 by Khushwant Singh and Kamna Prasad. Reprinted with permission from the publisher, Penguin Random House India.

Sandra M. Gilbert and Susan Gubar. "On Dickinson's White Dress" from *The Madwoman in the Attic.* Copyright © 1979 by Yale University Press. Reprinted by permission of Yale University Press.

Allen Ginsberg. "Sunflower Sutra" from *Collected Poems 1947–1980* by Allen Ginsberg. Copyright © 1955 by Allen Ginsberg. Reprinted by permission of HarperCollins Publishers.

Elisa Gonzalez. "In Quarantine, I Reflect on the Death of Ophelia," *The New Yorker,* May 25, 2020. Used with permission from the author.

Amanda Gorman. "In this Place (An American Lyric)." Copyright © 2017 by Amanda Gorman. Reprinted by permission of the author.

Woody Guthrie. "Pretty Boy Floyd" (lyrics). Words and Music by Woody Guthrie. © Copyright 1958 (renewed) by Woody Guthrie Publications, Inc.

R. S. Gwynn. "Shakespearean Sonnet." Originally appeared in *Formalist* 12.2 (2001). Copyright © 2001 by R. S. Gwynn. Reprinted by permission of the author.

Mark Halliday. "Graded Paper," *Michigan Quarterly Review.* Reprinted by permission of the author.

Joy Harjo. "Granddaughters" and "Singing Everything" (14 lines) from *An American Sunrise* by Joy Harjo, published by W. W. Norton & Company, Inc. Copyright © 2019 by Joy Harjo.

Robert Hayden. "Those Winter Sundays". Copyright © 1966 by Robert Hayden, from *Collected Poems of Robert Hayden* by Robert Hayden, edited by Frederick Glaysher. Used by permission of Liveright Publishing Corporation.

Seamus Heaney. "Digging" from *Opened Ground: Selected Poems 1966–1996* by Seamus Heaney. Copyright © 1998 by Seamus Heaney. Reprinted by permission of Farrar, Straus and Giroux, LLC, and Faber and Faber, Ltd. All rights reserved.

Judy Page Heitzman. "The Schoolroom on the Second Floor of the Knitting Mill." Copyright © 1991 by Judy Page Heitzman. Originally appeared in *The New Yorker,* December 2, 1992, p. 102. Reprinted by permission of the author.

David Hernandez. "All-American," *Southern Review* 48.4 (Autumn 2012). Copyright © 2012 by David Hernandez. Used by permission of the author.

William Heyen. "The Trains" from *The Host: Selected Poems 1965–1990* by William Heyen. Copyright © 1994 by Time Being Press. Reprinted by permission of the author.

Edward Hirsch, "Edward Hopper and the House by the Railroad (1925)" (40 lines) from *Wild Gratitude* by Edward Hirsch, copyright © 1981 by Edward Hirsch. Used by permission of Alfred A. Knopf, an imprint of the Knopf Doubleday Publishing Group, a division of Penguin Random House LLC. All rights reserved.

Jane Hirshfield. "This Morning, I Wanted Four Legs" from *The Beauty: Poems* by Jane Hirshfield, compilation copyright © 2015. Used by permission of Alfred A. Knopf, an imprint of the Knopf Doubleday Publishing Group, a division of Penguin Random House LLC. All rights reserved.

Andrew Hudgins. "The Ice-Cream Truck" from *Shut Up, You're Fine! Poems for Very, Very Bad Children* by Andrew Hudgins. Copyright © 2009 by Andrew Hudgins. Reprinted by permission of the author.

Langston Hughes. "Ballad of the Landlord" and "Harlem [2]" from *The Collected Poems of Langston Hughes* by Langston Hughes, edited by Arnold Rampersad with David Roessel, Associate Editor. Copyright © 1994 by the Estate of Langston Hughes. Used by permission of Alfred A. Knopf, an imprint of the Knopf Doubleday Publishing Group, a division of Penguin Random House LLC, and by permission of Harold Ober Associates Incorporated. All rights reserved.

Major Jackson. "Autumn Landscape" and "The Chase" from *Holding Company: Poems* by Major Jackson. Copyright © 2010 by Major Jackson. Used by permission of the author and W. W. Norton & Company, Inc.

Brionne Janae. "Alternative Facts," *Salamander* 46 (Spring/Summer 2018). Copyright © 2018. Reprinted by permission of the author.

Mark Jarman. "Unholy Sonnet" ["Breath like a house fly batters the shut mouth."] from *Bone Fires: New and Selected Poems.* Copyright © 1997 by Mark Jarman. Reprinted with the permission of The Permissions Company, Inc., on behalf of Sarabande Books, www.sarabandebooks.org.

Randall Jarrell. "The Death of the Ball Turret Gunner" from *The Complete Poems* by Randall Jarrell. Copyright © 1969, renewed 1997 by Mary von S. Jarrell. Reprinted by permission of Farrar, Straus and Giroux, LLC. All rights reserved.

Kelli Lyon Johnson. "Mapping an Identity," excerpted from *Julia Alvarez: Writing a New Place on the Map* by Kelli Lyon Johnson. Copyright © 2005 University of New Mexico Press. Reprinted by permission of the University of New Mexico Press.

Alice Jones. "The Foot" and "The Lungs" from *Anatomy* by Alice Jones (San Francisco: Bullnettle Press, 1997). Copyright © 1997 by Alice Jones. Reprinted by permission of the author.

June Jordan. "Poem About My Rights" from *Directed by Desire: The Collected Poems of June Jordan* (Port Townsend, WA: Copper Canyon Press, 2005). Copyright © 2005 by The June M. Jordan Literary Estate Trust. Used by permission. www.junejordan.com

Jane Kenyon. "The Socks" and "The Thimble" from *Collected Poems*. Copyright © 2005 by The Estate of Jane Kenyon. Reprinted with the permission of The Permissions Company, LLC on behalf of Graywolf Press, graywolfpress.org.

Suji Kwock Kim. "The Korean Community Garden in Queens" (56 lines) from *Notes from the Divided Country* by Suji Kwock Kim, pp. 71-72. Copyright © 2003. Published by Louisiana State University Press.

Galway Kinnell. "When One Has Lived a Long Time Alone" from *When One Has Lived a Long Time Alone*, copyright © 1990 by Galway Kinnell. Used by permission of Alfred A. Knopf, an imprint of the Knopf Doubleday Publishing Group, a division of Penguin Random House LLC. All rights reserved.

Carolyn Kizer. "After Bashō" from *Yin: New Poems*. Copyright © 1984 by Carolyn Kizer. Reprinted with the permission of The Permissions Company, Inc., on behalf of BOA Editions, Ltd., www.boaeditions.org.

Yusef Komunyakaa. "Facing It" from *Dien Cai Dau* © 1988 by Yusef Komunyakaa. Published by Wesleyan University Press. Used by permission.

Danusha Laméris. "Feeding the Worms" from *Bonfire Opera* by Danusha Laméris. Copyright © 2020. Reprinted by permission of the University of Pittsburgh Press.

Philip Larkin. "Sad Steps" from *The Complete Poems of Philip Larkin* by Philip Larkin, edited by Archie Burnett. Copyright © 2012 by the Estate of Philip Larkin. Reprinted by permission of Farrar, Straus and Giroux, LLC, and Faber and Faber, Ltd. All rights reserved.

Tato Laviera. "Latero Story" from *Benedición: The Complete Poetry of Tato Laviera* by Tato Laviera is being reprinted with permission from the publisher (©2014 Arte Publico Press - University of Houston).

Andrianne Lenker (Big Thief - band), "Not" Written by Adrianne Lenker. Courtesy of Domino Publishing Company Limited.

John Lennon and Paul McCartney. "I Am the Walrus." © 1967 Sony/ATV Music Publishing LLC. All rights administered by Sony/ATV Music Publishing LLC, 424 Church Street, Suite 1200, Nashville, Tennessee 37219. All rights reserved. Used by permission.

David Lenson. "On the Contemporary Use of Rhyme" from "The Battle Is Joined: Formalists Take on Defenders of Free Verse," *Chronicle of Higher Education* (February 24, 1988). Reprinted by permission of the author.

Denise Levertov. "A Poem at Christmas, 1972, during the Terror-Bombing of North Vietnam" from *The Freeing of the Dust*, copyright ©1975 by Denise Levertov. Reprinted by permission of New Directions Publishing Corp.

Ada Limón. "The End of Poetry" from *The Hurting Kind*. Originally in *The New Yorker* (May 4, 2020). Copyright © 2020, 2022 by Ada Limón. Reprinted with the permission of The Permissions Company, LLC on behalf of Milkweed Editions, www.milkweed.org.

Audre Lorde. "Learning to Write" and "Power" from *The Collected Poems of Audre Lorde* by Audre Lorde. Copyright © 1986 by Audre Lorde. Used by permission of W. W. Norton & Company, Inc.

Robert Lowell. "Skunk Hour" from *Collected Poems* by Robert Lowell. Copyright © 2003 by Harriet Lowell and Sheridan Lowell. Reprinted by permission of Farrar, Straus and Giroux, LLC. All rights reserved.

Katharyn Howd Machan. "Hazel Tells LaVerne" from *Light Year '85*. Copyright © 1977 by Katharyn Howd Machan. Reprinted by permission of the author.

Elaine Magarrell. "The Joy of Cooking" from *Sometime the Cow Kick Your Head: Light Year '88/9*. Reprinted by permission.

John Maloney. "Good!" from *Proposal* by John Maloney. Zoland Books, 1999. Copyright © 1999 by John Maloney. Reprinted by permission of the author.

Dionisio D. Martínez. "Flood: Years of Solitude" (7 lines) from *Bad Alchemy* (W. W. Norton and Company, Inc.) Copyright © 1995 by Dionisio D. Martinez. Used by permission of W. W. Norton & Company, Inc.

Julio Marzán. "The Translator at the Reception for Latin American Writers." Reprinted by permission of the author.

Julio Marzán. "Ethnic Poetry." Originally appeared in *Parnassus: Poetry in Review*. Reprinted by permission of the author.

Florence Cassen Mayers. "All-American Sestina," © 1996 Florence Cassen Mayers, as first published in the *Atlantic Monthly*. Reprinted with permission of the author.

David McCord. "Epitaph on a Waiter" from *Odds Without Ends*, copyright © 1954 by David T. W. McCord. Reprinted by permission of the estate of David T. W. McCord.

Michael McFee. "In Medias Res" from *Colander* by Michael McFee. Copyright © 1996 by Michael McFee. Reprinted by permission of Michael McFee.

Elaine Mitchell. "Form" from *Light 9* (Spring 1994). Reprinted by permission of the Literary Estate of Elaine Mitchell.

Janice Townley Moore. "To a Wasp" first appeared in *Light Year, Bits Press*. Reprinted by permission of the author.

Jim Moore, "How to Come Out of Lockdown," *The New Yorker*, April 4, 2022. Copyright © 2022 by Conde Nast Publications, Inc. Used with permission.

Robert Morgan. "Mountain Graveyard" from *Sigodlin*. Copyright © 1990 by Robert Morgan. Reprinted by permission of the author.

Joan Murray. "We Old Dudes," copyright © 2006 by Joan Murray. First appeared in the July/August 2006 issue of *Poetry* magazine. Reprinted by permission of the author.

Marilyn Nelson. "How I Discovered Poetry" from *The Fields of Praise: New and Selected Poems* by Marilyn Nelson. Copyright © 1997 by Marilyn Nelson. Reprinted by permission of Louisiana State University Press.

Howard Nemerov. "Because You Asked about the Line between Prose and Poetry" from *Sentences* by Howard Nemerov. Copyright © 1980. Reprinted by permission of the Estate of Howard Nemerov.

Pablo Neruda. "Drunk as drunk on turpentine" from *The Man Who Told His Love*, trans. Christoper Logue. Copyright © Christopher Logue.

John Frederick Nims. "Love Poem" (24 lines). First published in *Five Young American Poets*, Vol. 3, New Directions Publishers, pub. 1944. Used with permission of New Directions Publishing Corporation; permission conveyed through Copyright Clearance Center, Inc.

Naomi Shihab Nye. "To Manage" from *Voices in the Air* by Naomi Shihab Nye. Copyright © 2018 by Naomi Shihab Nye. Used by permission of HarperCollins Publishers.

Mary Oliver. "The Poet with His Face in His Hands" from *New and Selected Poems,* Volume Two by Mary Oliver. Published by Beacon Press, Boston. Copyright © 2005 by Mary Oliver with permission of Bill Reichblum. Reprinted by the permission of The Charlotte Sheedy Literary Agency as agent for the author.

Mary Oliver. "Wild Geese" From *Dream Work* copyright © 1986 by Mary Oliver. Used by permission of Grove/ Atlantic, Inc. Any third-party use of this material, outside of this publication, is prohibited.

Tillie Lerner Olsen, "I Want You Women up North to Know" first appears in *The Partisan* (March 1934). Based on a letter by Felipe Ibarro in New Masses, Jan. 9th, 1934. Copyright © 1934 by Tillie Olsen. Reprinted by permission of The Frances Goldin Literary Agency.

Lisa Parker. "Snapping Beans" from the collection *This Gone Place* by Lisa Parker. Originally appeared in Parnassus 23, no. 2 (1998). Reprinted by permission of the author.

Linda Pastan. "Jump Cabling" from *Light Year: The Quarterly of Light Verse.* Copyright ©1984 by Linda Pastan. Used by permission of Linda Pastan in care of the Jean V. Naggar Literary Agency, Inc. (permissions@jvnla.com)

Laurence Perrine. "The limerick's never averse." Copyright © Laurence Perrine. Reprinted by permission of Douglas Perrine.

Kevin Pierce. "Proof of Origin" from *Light 50* (Autumn 2005). Copyright © 2005 by Kevin Pierce. Reprinted with the permission of the author.

Robert Pinsky. "Icicles" from *The Want Bone* by Robert Pinsky. Copyright © 1990 by Robert Pinsky. Reprinted by permission of HarperCollins Publishers.

Sylvia Plath. "Pheasant" from *Winter Trees* by Sylvia Plath. Copyright © 1971 by Ted Hughes. Reprinted by permission of HarperCollins Publishers.

Adelia Prado. "Denouement" from *Alphabet in the Park: Selected Poems* © 1990 by Adelia Prado, translated by Ellen Watson. Published by Wesleyan University Press. Used by permission.

Claudia Rankine. "Stop and Frisk" from *Citizen: An American Lyric.* Copyright © 2014 by Claudia Rankine. Reprinted with the permission of The Permissions Company, LLC on behalf of Graywolf Press, graywolfpress.org.

Lois Red Elk. "All Thirst Quenched" from *Dragonfly Weather.* Copyright © 2013 by Lois Red Elk. Reprinted by permission of Lost Horse Press.

Marny Requa. "From an Interview with Julia Alvarez," excerpted from "The Politics of Fiction," *Frontera* 5 (1997). Reprinted with the permission of Marny Requa.

Alberto Ríos. "Seniors" from *Five Indiscretions.* Copyright © 1985 by Alberto Ríos. Reprinted by permission of the author.

Kay Ryan. "Dew" and "Learning" from *Elephant Rocks.* Copyright © 1996 by Kay Ryan. Used by permission of Grove/Atlantic, Inc. Any third-party use of this material, outside of this publication, is prohibited.

Sappho. "Prayer to my lady of Paphos" [Fragment #38] from *Sappho: A New Translation* by Mary Barnard. Copyright © 1958 by the Regents of the University of California, renewed © 1986 by Mary Barnard. Reproduced with permission of University of California Press.

Charles Simic. "House of Cards" from *That Little Something.* Copyright © 2008 by Charles Simic. Used by permission of HarperCollins Publishers.

Paul Simon, "Slip-Sliding Away" (lyrics) © 1977 Sony Music Publishing (US) LLC. All rights administered by Sony Music Publishing (US) LLC, 424 Church Street, Suite 1200, Nashville, TN 37219. All rights reserved. Used by permission.

Louis Simpson. "In the Suburbs" from *The Owner of the House: New Collected Poems, 1940–2001.* Copyright © 1963, 2001 by Louis Simpson. Reprinted with the permission of The Permissions Company, Inc., on behalf of BOA Editions Ltd., www.boaeditions.org.

Ernest Slyman. "Lightning Bugs" from *Sometime the Cow Kick Your Head: Light Year '88/9.* Reprinted by permission of the author.

Danez Smith. "not an elegy for Mike Brown." (24 lines.) Copyright © 2014 by Danez Smith. Reprinted from *Split This Rock's The Quarry: A Social Justice Poetry Database.*

Patricia Smith. "Hip-Hop Ghazal," *Poetry,* July/August 2007. Copyright © 2007 by Patricia Smith. Reprinted by permission of the author.

Patricia Smith. "What It's Like To Be a Black Girl (For Those of You Who Aren't)" from *Life According to Motown* by Patricia Smith. Copyright © 1991 by Patricia Smith.

Stevie Smith. "Not Waving but Drowning" from *All The Poems,* copyright © 1937, 1938, 1942, 1950, 1957, 1962, 1966, 1971, 1972 by Stevie Smith. Copyright © 2016 by the Estate of James MacGibbon. Copyright © 2015 by Will May. Reprinted by permission of New Directions Publishing Corp.

Tracy K. Smith. "Self-Portrait as the Letter Y" from *The Body's Question.* Copyright © 2003 by Tracy K. Smith. Reprinted with the permission of The Permissions Company, LLC on behalf of Graywolf Press, graywolfpress.org.

Gary Snyder. "A Dent in a Bucket" from *Danger on Peaks.* Copyright © 2004 by Gary Snyder. Reprinted with the permission of The Permissions Company, LLC on behalf of Counterpoint Press, counterpointpress.com.

David Solway. "Windsurfing." Reprinted by permission of the author.

Cathy Song. "Girl Powdering Her Neck" and "The Youngest Daughter" from *Picture Bride.* Copyright © 1983 by Yale University Press. Reprinted by permission of Yale University Press.

Edna St. Vincent Millay. "I will put Chaos into fourteen lines" from *Collected Poems.* Copyright 1954 and renewed © 1982 by Norma Millay Ellis. Reprinted with the permission of The Permissions Company, Inc., on behalf of Holly Peppe, Literary Executor, The Millay Society, www.millay.org.

Timothy Steele. "Waiting for the Storm" from *Sapphics and Uncertainties: Poems, 1970–1986.* Copyright © 1986, 1995 by Timothy Steele. Reprinted with the permission of The Permissions Company, Inc., on behalf of the University of Arkansas Press, www.uapress.com.

Jim Stevens. "Schizophrenia." Originally appeared in *Light: The Quarterly of Light Verse* (Spring 1992). Copyright © 1992 by Jim Stevens. Reprinted by permission.

John Stone. "American Gothic" from *Where Water Begins: New Poems and Prose* by John Stone. Copyright ©1998 by John Stone. Reprinted by permission of Louisiana State University Press. First published in the Georgia Journal.

Mark Strand. "Eating Poetry" from *Selected Poems of Mark Strand* by Mark Strand, copyright © 1979, 1980 by Mark Strand. Used by permission of Alfred A. Knopf, an imprint of the Knopf Doubleday Publishing Group, a division of Penguin Random House LLC. All rights reserved.

Wisława Szymborska, "Brueghel's Two Monkeys" and "Vermeer" from *View with A Grain Of Sand* by Wisława Szymborska. English Translation copyright © 1995 by HarperCollins Publishers. Used by permission of HarperCollins Publishers.

Dylan Thomas. "Do Not Go Gentle into That Good Night" and "The Hand That Signed the Paper" from *The Poems of Dylan Thomas*. Copyright © 1952 by Dylan Thomas. Reprinted by permission of New Directions Publishing Corp.

Jim Tilley. "The Big Questions" from *In Confidence* by Jim Tilley (Pasadena, CA: Red Hen Press, 2011). Copyright © 2011 by Jim Tilley. Reprinted by permission of Red Hen Press.

Jean Toomer. "Unsuspecting," from *the Jean Toomer Papers*, James Weldon Johnson Memorial Collection, Reinecke Rare Book & Manuscript Library, Yale University. © 2022 Yale University.

Natasha Trethewey. "Graveyard Blues" (14 lines) from *Native Guard* by Natasha Trethewey. Copyright © 2006 by Natasha Trethewey. Used by permission of HarperCollins Publishers.

John Updike. "Dog's Death" and "Player Piano" from *Collected Poems, 1953–1993* by John Updike. Copyright © 1993 by John Updike. Used by permission of Alfred A. Knopf, an imprint of the Knopf Doubleday Publishing Group, a division of Penguin Random House LLC. All rights reserved.

Tom Waits and Kathleen Brennan. "Alice." Copyright © 1992, 2002 Jalma Music (ASCAP). Used by permission. All rights reserved.

Richard Wakefield. "The Bell Rope" from *East of Early Winters: Poems* by Richard Wakefield (University of Evansville Press, 2006). Copyright © 2006 by Richard Wakefield. Reprinted with permission from the author.

Ronald Wallace. "Building an Outhouse" from *The Makings of Happiness* by Ronald Wallace. Copyright © 1991. Reprinted by permission of the University of Pittsburgh Press.

Gail White. "Dead Armadillos." Copyright © 2000 by Gail White. Reprinted by permission of the author.

Hank Williams. "I'm So Lonesome I Could Cry." © 1949 Sony/ATV Acuff Rose Music. All rights administered by Sony/ATV Music Publishing LLC, 424 Church Street, Suite 1200, Nashville, Tennessee 37219. All rights reserved. Used by permission.

William Carlos Williams. "Poem (As the cat)" from *The Collected Poems: Volume 1, 1909–1939*. Copyright © 1938 by New Directions Publishing Corp. Reprinted by permission of New Directions Publishing Corp.

## DRAMA

Elliott Ackerman, Excerpt(s) from *Places and Names: On War, Revolution, and Returning* by Elliot Ackerman, copyright © 2019 by Elliot Ackerman. Used by permission of Penguin Press, an imprint of Penguin Publishing Group, a division of Penguin Random House LLC. All rights reserved.

Aristotle. "On Tragic Character" from *Aristotle's Poetics*, translated by James Hutton. Copyright © 1982 by W. W. Norton & Company, Inc. Used by permission of W. W. Norton & Company, Inc.

David Auburn. *Proof.* Copyright © 2001 by David Auburn. All rights reserved. Reprinted by permission of Paradigm Talent Agency.

Leonard Feather and John Coltrane. "Leonard Feather Interviews John Coltrane" from *Melody Maker,* December 19, 1964. Reprinted in *Coltrane on Coltrane: The John Coltrane Interviews,* edited by Chris Devito. Chicago Review Press, 2010. pp. 223–224. Reproduced with permission of Lorraine Feather.

Quiara Alegría Hudes. "Atonality" from *My Broken Language: A Memoir* by Quiara Alegría Hudes, copyright © 2021 by Quiara Alegría Hudes. Used by permission of One World, an imprint of Random House, a division of Penguin Random House LLC. All rights reserved.

Quiara Alegría Hudes. *Water by the Spoonful.* Copyright © 2012, 2017 by Quiara Alegría Hudes. Published by Theatre Communications Group. Used by permission of Theatre Communications Group.

Lisa Jardine. "On Boy Actors in Female Roles" from *Still Harping on Daughters: Women and Drama in the Age of Shakespeare* by Lisa Jardine. Copyright © 1983. Reprinted by permission.

James R. Kincaid. "On the Value of Comedy in the Face of Tragedy," excerpted from "Who Is Relieved by Comic Relief?" in *Annoying the Victorians* (New York: Routledge, 1995). Reprinted by permission of the author.

Lynn Nottage. "Poof!" Published in *Crumbs from the Table of Joy and Other Plays.* Copyright © 1993, 2004 by Lynn Nottage. Published by Theatre Communications Group. Used by permission of Theatre Communications Group.

Suzan-Lori Parks, "(Again) Groundhog," "Barefoot and Pregnant in the Park," "Beginning Middle End," "Fine Animal," "Here Comes the Message," "Orange," "The Ends of the Earth," "This is Shit," "What Do You See," and "Veuve Clicquot" from *365 Days/365 Plays* by Suzan-Lori Parks. Copyright © 2006 by Suzan-Lori Parks. Published by Theatre Communications Group. Used by permission of Theatre Communications Group.

Muriel Rukeyser. "On Oedipus the King," excerpted from "Myth" in *The Collected Poems of Muriel Rukeyser.* Copyright © 2005 by Muriel Rukeyser. Reprinted by permission of ICM Partners.

David Savran. "An Interview with August Wilson" from *In Their Own Words: Contemporary American Playwrights* by David Savran. Copyright © 1988 by David Savran. Published by Theatre Communications Group. Used by permission of Theatre Communications Group.

William Shakespeare. *Othello* (notes and commentary by Gerald Eades Bentley), edited by Gerald Eades Bentley. Copyright © 1958, 1970 by Penguin Random House LLC. Used by permission of Penguin Books, an imprint of Penguin Publishing Group, a division of Penguin Random House LLC. All rights reserved.

Sophocles. *Oedipus the King,* translated by David Grene, from *Sophocles I.* Copyright © 1942 by the University of Chicago. Reprinted by permission of the University of Chicago Press. Permission conveyed through Copyright Clearance Center, Inc.

August Wilson. Entire play from *Fences.* Copyright © 1986 by August Wilson. Used by permission of New American Library, an imprint of Penguin Publishing Group, a division of Penguin Random House LLC. All rights reserved.

# Index of First Lines

# Index of Authors and Titles

# Index of Terms

Boldface numbers refer to the Glossary of Literary Terms